Dictionary *of* Biblical Interpretation

Dictionary _of_ Biblical Interpretation

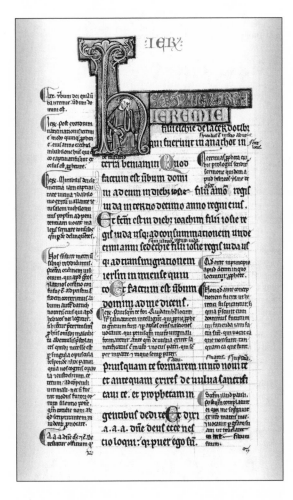

John H. Hayes, General Editor

A–J

Abingdon Press
Nashville

Dictionary of Biblical Interpretation

Copyright © 1999 by Abingdon Press

This book is printed on recycled, acid-free, elemental-chlorine free paper.

Library of Congress Cataloging-in-Publication Data

Dictionary of Biblical Interpretation / John H. Hayes, general editor
   p.   cm.
Includes bibliographical references.
ISBN 0-687-05531-8 (hardcover: alk. paper)
   1. Bible—Criticism, interpretation, etc.—History—Dictionaries. 2. Bible—Hermeneutics—Dictionaries. I. Hayes, John Haralson, 1934–
BS500.D5   1999   98-42795
220.6'03—dc21   CIP

Scripture quotations, unless otherwise indicated, are from the New Revised Standard Version Bible, copyright 1989, by the Division of Christian Education of the National Council of the Churches of Christ in the United States of America.

Scripture quotations noted as AT are the author's translation.

Manuscript on title page: The Bodleian Library, Oxford, MS. Digby 226, fol. 96v.

PUBLICATION STAFF

President and Publisher: Neil M. Alexander
Vice President and Editorial Director: Harriett Jane Olson
Director of Bible and Reference Resources: Jack A. Keller, Jr.
Senior Editor: Michael R. Russell
Production Editor: Joan M. Shoup
Editor: Deborah A. Appler
Assistant Editor: Emily Cheney
Production and Design Manager: Walter E. Wynne
Copy Processing Manager: Sylvia S. Street
Composition Specialist: Kathy M. Harding
Publishing Systems Analyst: Glenn R. Hinton
Prepress Manager: Billy W. Murphy
Prepress Systems Technicians: Thomas E. Mullins
                                                J. Calvin Buckner
Director of Production Processes: James E. Leath
Scheduling: Laurene M. Brazzell
Print Procurement Coordinator: Martha K. Taylor

99 00 01 02 03 04 05 06 07 — 10 9 8 7 6 5 4 3 2 1

MANUFACTURED IN THE UNITED STATES OF AMERICA

CONTRIBUTORS

Andrew K. M. Adam
Princeton Theological Seminary
Princeton, New Jersey

Kurt Aland (deceased)
Institut für Neutestamentliche Textforschung
Westfälische Wilhelms-Universität
Münster, Germany

Bertil Albrektson
Bibelkommissionen
Uppsala, Sweden

Dale C. Allison, Jr.
Pittsburgh Theological Seminary
Pittsburgh, Pennsylvania

John E. Alsup
Austin Presbyterian Theological Seminary
Austin, Texas

Marvin Anderson
Southern Baptist Theological Seminary
Louisville, Kentucky

Paul S. Ash
Emory University
Atlanta, Georgia

Ann W. Astell
Purdue University
West Lafayette, Indiana

Harold W. Attridge
The Divinity School
Yale University
New Haven, Connecticut

John H. Augustine
West New York, New Jersey

A. Graeme Auld
University of Edinburgh
Edinburgh, Scotland

David E. Aune
Loyola University Chicago
Chicago, Illinois

Randall Charles Bailey
Interdenominational Theological Center
Atlanta, Georgia

William R. Baird
Brite Divinity School
Texas Christian University
Fort Worth, Texas

Karen Baker-Fletcher
Claremont School of Theology
Claremont, California

Lewis V. Baldwin
Vanderbilt University
Nashville, Tennessee

Robert S. Barbour
Fincastle
Pitlochry, Scotland

Philip L. Barlow
Hanover College
Hanover, Indiana

John R. Bartlett
The Church of Ireland Theological College
Dublin, Ireland

Albert Baumgarten
Bar-Ilan University
Jerusalem, Israel

Timothy K. Beal
Eckerd College
St. Petersburg, Florida

Derek R. G. Beattie
The Queen's University of Belfast
Belfast, Northern Ireland

Roger T. Beckwith
Latimer House
Oxford, England

Christopher T. Begg
The Catholic University of America
Washington, DC

Ehud Ben Zvi
University of Alberta
Edmonton, Alberta
Canada

Jerry H. Bentley
University of Hawaii
Honolulu, Hawaii

Christoph Berger
Friedrich-Schiller-Universität Jena
Jena, Germany

Klaus Berger
Wissenschaftlich-Theologisches Seminar
Ruprecht-Karls-Universität Heidelberg
Heidelberg, Germany

Robert F. Berkey
Mt. Holyoke College
South Hadley, Massachusetts

Adele Berlin
University of Maryland
College Park, Maryland

David Berman
Trinity College
The University of Dublin
Dublin, Ireland

Lawrence V. Berman (deceased)
Stanford University
Stanford, California

Ernest Best
University of Glasgow
Glasgow, Scotland

Mark Edward Biddle
Baptist Theological Seminary at Richmond
Richmond, Virginia

C. Clifton Black
Perkins School of Theology
Southern Methodist University
Dallas, Texas

Richard J. Blackwell
Saint Louis University
St. Louis, Missouri

Sheldon H. Blank (deceased)
Hebrew Union College
Cincinnati, Ohio

Hendrikus Boers
Candler School of Theology
Emory University
Atlanta, Georgia

Robert G. Bratcher
Chapel Hill, North Carolina

Marc Brettler
Brandeis University
Waltham, Massachusetts

Pamela Bright
Concordia University
Montréal, Québec
Canada

Hans Bringeland
Norsk Loererakademi
Bergen-Sandviken, Norway

George J. Brooke
University of Manchester
Manchester, England

Bernadette Brooten
Brandeis University
Waltham, Massachusetts

William P. Brown
Union Theological Seminary and Presbyterian
    School of Christian Education
Richmond, Virginia

Walter Brueggemann
Columbia Theological Seminary
Decatur, Georgia

John M. Bullard
Wofford College
Spartanburg, South Carolina

Mark S. Burrows
Andover Newton Theological School
Newton Centre, Massachusetts

Martin J. Buss
Emory University
Atlanta, Georgia

John J. Carey
Agnes Scott College
Decatur, Georgia

David McLain Carr
Methodist Theological School in Ohio
Delaware, Ohio

P. Maurice Casey
University of Nottingham
Nottingham, England

Henry Chadwick
Magdalene College
University of Cambridge
Cambridge, England

James H. Charlesworth
Princeton Theological Seminary
Princeton, New Jersey

C. Conrad Cherry
Indiana University
Indianapolis, Indiana

Randall D. Chesnutt
Seaver College
Pepperdine University
Malibu, California

Brevard S. Childs
The Divinity School
Yale University
New Haven, Connecticut

Bruce Chilton
Bard College
Annandale-on-Hudson, New York

Duane L. Christensen
William Carey International University
Pasadena, California

Ronald E. Clements
King's College
University of London
London, England

James F. Coakley
Harvard University
Cambridge, Massachusetts

Ethel A. Coke
Austin, Texas

Marcia L. Colish
Oberlin College
Oberlin, Ohio

Billie Jean Collins
Emory University
Atlanta, Georgia

John J. Collins
The Divinity School
University of Chicago
Chicago, Illinois

Raymond F. Collins
The Catholic University of America
Washington, DC

John J. Contreni
Purdue University
West Lafayette, Indiana

John G. Cook
La Grange College
La Grange, Georgia

John W. Cook
The Henry Luce Foundation
New York, New York

Michael J. Cook
Hebrew Union College
Cincinnati, Ohio

S. Peter Cowe
University of California, Los Angeles
Los Angeles, California

Howard H. Cox
Moravian Theological Seminary
Bethlehem, Pennsylvania

Philip Culbertson
St. Johns Theological College
Auckland, New Zealand

Edwin M. Curley
University of Michigan
Ann Arbor, Michigan

Marcellino D'Ambrosio
University of Dallas
Irving, Texas

Mary Rose D'Angelo
University of Notre Dame
Notre Dame, Indiana

Philip R. Davies
University of Sheffield
Sheffield, England

John Day
University of Oxford
Oxford, England

John A. Dearman
Austin Presbyterian Theological Seminary
Austin, Texas

Ferdinand E. Deist
University of Stellenbosch
Stellenbosch, South Africa

John A. H. Dempster
Glenmavis
Airdrie Lanarhshire, Scotland

William G. Dever
University of Arizona
Tucson, Arizona

Simon J. DeVries
Methodist Theological School in Ohio
Delaware, Ohio

Alexander A. Di Lella
The Catholic University of America
Washington, DC

Devorah Dimant
University of Haifa
Haifa, Israel

John R. Donahue
Jesuit School of Theology at Berkeley
Graduate Theological Union
Berkeley, California

Thomas B. Dozeman
United Theological Seminary
Dayton, Ohio

Musa W. Dube Shomanah
University of Botswana
Gaborone, Botswana

James O. Duke
Brite Divinity School
Texas Christian University
Fort Worth, Texas

John H. Eaton
University of Birmingham
Birmingham, England

Robert S. Eccles
DePauw University
Greencastle, Indiana

Diana Edelman
James Madison University
Harrisonburg, Virginia

John A. Emerton
St. John's College
University of Cambridge
Cambridge, England

Peter C. Erb
Wilfrid Laurier University
Waterloo, Ontario
Canada

Tamara C. Eskenazi
Hebrew Union College
Los Angeles, California

Gillian R. Evans
University of Cambridge
Cambridge, England

Craig S. Farmer
Milligan College
Johnson City, Tennessee

William R. Farmer
University of Dallas
Irving, Texas

Cain Hope Felder
School of Divinity
Howard University
Washington, DC

Louis H. Feldman
Yeshiva University
Forest Hills, New York

Everett Ferguson
Abilene Christian University
Abilene, Texas

Janet F. Fishburn
The Theological School
Drew University
Madison, New Jersey

John T. Fitzgerald, Jr.
University of Miami
Coral Gables, Florida

Joseph A. Fitzmyer
Jesuit Community
Georgetown University
Washington, DC

Michael V. Fox
University of Wisconsin
Madison, Wisconsin

Albert H. Friedlander
Johann Wolfgang Goethe-Universität
Frankfurt am Main
Frankfurt am Main, Germany

Jerome Friedman
Kent State University
Bowling Green, Ohio

Maurice S. Friedman
San Diego State University
San Diego, California

Karlfried Froehlich
Princeton Theological Seminary
Princeton, New Jersey

Thomas Fudge
University of Canterbury
Christ Church, New Zealand

Reginald C. Fuller
London, England

Edward J. Furcha (deceased)
McGill University
Montreal, Quebec
Canada

Victor P. Furnish
Perkins School of Theology
Southern Methodist University
Dallas, Texas

Julie G. Galambush
College of William and Mary
Williamsburg, Virginia

Gershon Galil
University of Haifa
Haifa, Israel

Roy E. Gane
Seventh-Day Adventist Theological Seminary
Andrews College
Berrien Springs, Michigan

E. Clinton Gardner
Candler School of Theology
Emory University
Atlanta, Georgia

Beverly Roberts Gaventa
Princeton Theological Seminary
Princeton, New Jersey

B. A. Gerrish
Union Theological Seminary
Richmond, VA

Erhard Gerstenberger
Philipps-Universität Marburg
Marburg, Germany

John H. Giltner
Methodist Theological School in Ohio
Delaware, Ohio

M. E. Glasswell (deceased)
Essex, England

Robert Gnuse
Loyola University New Orleans
New Orleans, Louisiana

Frank H. Gorman, Jr.
Bethany College
Bethany, West Virginia

Moshe Goshen-Gottstein (deceased)
Hebrew University
Jerusalem, Israel

Alfred Gottschalk
Hebrew Union College
Cincinnati, Ohio

Michael D. Goulder
University of Birmingham
Birmingham, England

M. Patrick Graham
Pitts Theology Library
Emory University
Atlanta, Georgia

Robert M. Grant
The Divinity School
University of Chicago
Chicago, Illinois

Erich Grässer
Rheinischen Friedrich-Wilhelms
    Universität Bonn
Bonn, Germany

Fred Grater
Pitts Theology Library
Emory University
Atlanta, Georgia

Moshe Greenberg
Hebrew University
Jerusalem, Israel

Frederick Greenspahn
Center for Judaic Studies
University of Denver
Denver, Colorado

Leonard Greenspoon
Creighton University
Omaha, Nebraska

Edward L. Greenstein
Tel Aviv University
Ramat Aviv, Israel

Jacques M. Gres-Gayer
The Catholic University of America
Washington, DC

David M. Gunn
Texas Christian University
Fort Worth, Texas

W. C. Gwaltney, Jr.
Milligan College
Johnson City, Tennessee

Jo Ann Hackett
Harvard University
Cambridge, Massachusetts

Joachim Hahn
Evangelisches Stift
Eberhard-Karls-Universität Tübingen
Tübingen, Germany

Getatchew Haile
Hill Monastic Manuscript Library
St. John's University
Collegeville, Minnesota

Carolyn P. Hammond Bammel (deceased)
Girton College
University of Cambridge
Cambridge, England

Nancy A. Hardesty
Clemson University
Greenville, South Carolina

David Harnden-Warwick
Bellingham, Washington

Roy A. Harrisville
Luther Seminary
St. Paul, Minnesota

Alan J. Hauser
Appalachian State University
Boone, North Carolina

John H. Hayes
Candler School of Theology
Emory University
Atlanta, Georgia

Gary Herion
Hartwick College
Oneonta, New York

Siegfried Herrmann
Ruhr-Universität Bochum
Bochum, Germany

Susannah Heschel
Dartmouth College
Hanover, New Hampshire

Sten Hidal
Lunds Universitet
Lund, Sweden

Martha Himmelfarb
Princeton University
Princeton, New Jersey

Manfred Hoffmann
Candler School of Theology
Emory University
Atlanta, Georgia

Michael J. Hollerich
University of St. Thomas
St. Paul, Minnesota

Michael W. Holmes
Bethel College
St. Paul, Minnesota

Morna D. Hooker
University of Cambridge
Cambridge, England

Leslie J. Hoppe
Catholic Theological Union
Chicago, Illinois

Maurya P. Horgan
The HK Scriptorium, Inc.
Denver, Colorado

Friedrich W. Horn
Gerhard-Mercator-Universität-Gesamthochschule
Duisburg
Duisburg, Germany

Gottfried Hornig
Auf dem Aspei, Germany

Cornelius Houtman
Vrije Universiteit Amsterdam
Amsterdam, Netherlands

Herbert B. Huffmon
Drew University
Madison, New Jersey

Frank W. Hughes
Codrington College
St. John, Barbados

Jeremy R. A. Hughes
The Oriental Institute
Oxford, England

David G. Hunter
University of St. Thomas
St. Paul, Minnesota

John C. Hurd
Trinity College
University of Toronto
Toronto, Ontario
Canada

Ada Maria Isasi-Díaz
Drew University
Madison, New Jersey

Bernard S. Jackson
The University of Liverpool
Liverpool, England

Walter Jacob
Rodef Shalom Congregation
Pittsburgh, Pennsylvania

Louis Jacobs
New London Synagogue
London, England

Sara Japhet
Hebrew University
Jerusalem, Israel

David Lyle Jeffrey
University of Ottawa
Ottawa, Ontario
Canada

Joseph Jensen
Catholic Biblical Association
The Catholic University of America
Washington, DC

Robert Jewett
Garrett-Evangelical Theological Seminary
Evanston, Illinois

David Jobling
St. Andrews College
Saskatoon, Saskatchewan
Canada

David W. Johnson
First Presbyterian Church
Irving, Texas

Luke Timothy Johnson
Candler School of Theology
Emory University
Atlanta, Georgia

A. H. Jones
University College of St. Martin
Lancaster, England

Brian C. Jones
Eugene, Oregon

Scott J. Jones
Perkins School of Theology
Southern Methodist University
Dallas, Texas

Mark D. Jordan
University of Notre Dame
Notre Dame, Indiana

Donald H. Juel
Princeton Theological Seminary
Princeton, New Jersey

Otto Kaiser
Philipps-Universität Marburg
Marburg, Germany

Walter C. Kaiser, Jr.
Gordon-Conwell Theological Seminary
South Hamilton, Massachusetts

Charles Kannengiesser
Concordia University
Montréal, Québec
Canada

Arvid S. Kapelrud
University of Oslo
Oslo, Norway

Rimon Kasher
Bar-Ilan University
Ramat-Gan, Israel

K. A. Keefer
Baytown, Texas

S T Kimbrough, Jr.
General Board of Global Ministries
The United Methodist Church
New York, New York

Warren S. Kissinger
Library of Congress
Washington, DC

Walter Klaassen
Conrad Grebel College
Waterloo, Ontario
Canada

William Klassen
École Biblique
Jerusalem, Israel

Ralph W. Klein
Lutheran School of Theology
Chicago, Illinois

David E. Klemm
University of Iowa
Iowa City, Iowa

John S. Kloppenborg
University of St. Michaels College
Toronto, Ontario
Canada

Douglas A. Knight
The Divinity School
Vanderbilt University
Nashville, Tennessee

Bernd Kollmann
Georg-August-Universität Göttingen
Göttingen, Germany

Beate Köster
Institut für Neutestamentliche Textforschung
Westfälische Wilhelms-Universität
Münster, Germany

Steven J. Kraftchick
Candler School of Theology
Emory University
Atlanta, Georgia

Miles Krassen
Oberlin College
Oberlin, Ohio

Jeffrey Kah-Jin Kuan
Pacific School of Religion
Graduate Theological Union
Berkeley, California

Hans-Wolfgang Kuhn
Ludwig-Maximilians-Universität München
München, Germany

Marion L. Kuntz
Georgia State University
Atlanta, Georgia

Paul G. Kuntz
Emory University
Atlanta, Georgia

Richard Kyle
Tabor College
Hillsboro, Kansas

Robert D. Kysar
Candler School of Theology
Emory University
Atlanta, Georgia

Dietz Lange
Georg-August-Universität Göttingen
Göttingen, Germany

D. L. LeMahieu
Lake Forest College
Lake Forest, Illinois

Andrew Lenox-Conyngham
St. Catharine's College
University of Cambridge
Cambridge, England

Baruch A. Levine
New York University
New York, New York

Betty Jane Lillie
Mt. St. Marys Seminary
Cincinnati, Ohio

Tod Linafelt
Georgetown University
Washington, DC

Donald W. Livingston
Emory University
Atlanta, Georgia

James C. Livingston
College of William and Mary
Williamsburg, Virginia

Raphael Loewe (deceased)
University College
London, England

D. Eduard Lohse
Georg-August-Universität Göttingen
Göttingen, Germany

Burke O. Long
Bowdoin College
Brunswick, Maine

David E. Luscombe
University of Sheffield
Sheffield, England

Johan Lust
Katholieke Universiteit Leuven
Leuven, Belgium

Harvey K. McArthur
Hartford Seminary
Hartford, Connecticut

S. Dean McBride
Union Theological Seminary and Presbyterian
School of Christian Education
Richmond, Virginia

Lane C. McGaughey
Willamette University
Salem, Oregon

Paul McGlasson
Central Presbyterian Church
Stamford, Texas

Alister E. McGrath
Wycliffe Hall
University of Oxford
Oxford, England

Barbara J. MacHaffie
Marietta College
Marietta, Ohio

William McKane
St. Mary's College
St. Andrew's, Fife
Scotland

Cameron S. McKenzie
Providence College
Otterburne, Manitoba
Canada

Steven L. McKenzie
Rhodes College
Memphis, Tennessee

Donald K. McKim
Memphis Theological Seminary
Memphis, Tennessee

Edgar V. McKnight
Furman University
Greenville, South Carolina

Jennifer Berenson Maclean
Roanoke College
Roanoke, Virginia

Jonathan Magonet
Leo Baeck College
Sternberg Center for Judaism
London, England

Rudolf Makkreel
Emory University
Atlanta, Georgia

Sara R. Mandell
The University of South Florida
St. Petersburg, Florida

John H. Marks
Princeton University
Princeton, New Jersey

Rick R. Marrs
Pepperdine University
Malibu, California

Clarice J. Martin
Colgate University
Rochester, New York

James P. Martin
Vancouver School of Theology
Vancouver, British Columbia
Canada

J. Louis Martyn
Union Theological Seminary
New York, New York

E. Ann Matter
University of Pennsylvania
Philadelphia, Pennsylvania

Andrew D. H. Mayes
Trinity College
University of Dublin
Dublin, Ireland

William W. Meissner
Boston College
Chestnut Hill, Massachusetts

Otto Merk
Friedrich-Alexander-Universität Erlangen
Erlangen, Germany

J. Ramsey Michaels
Southwest Missouri State University
Springfield, Missouri

Gordon E. Michalson
New College of the University of South Florida
Sarasota, Florida

G. T. Milazzo
Greensboro, North Carolina

Gregory Mobley
Andover Newton Theological School
Newton Centre, Massachusetts

David P. Moessner
University of Dubuque Theological Seminary
Dubuque, Iowa

Johannes C. de Moor
Theologische Universiteit van de
Gereformeerde Kerken in Nederland
Kampen, The Netherlands

Carey A. Moore
Gettysburg College
Gettysburg, Pennsylvania

James Morey
Emory University
Atlanta, Georgia

Robert Morgan
University of Oxford
Oxford, England

Phil Mullins
Missouri Western State College
St. Joseph, Missouri

Frederick J. Murphy
College of the Holy Cross
Worcester, Massachusetts

Jerome Murphy-O'Connor
École Biblique
Archéologique Française
Jerusalem, Israel

Kathleen S. Nash
Le Moyne College
Syracuse, New York

Heinz-Dieter Neef
Eberhard-Karls-Universität Tübingen
Tübingen, Germany

Gordon D. Newby
Emory University
Atlanta, Georgia

Carol A. Newsom
Candler School of Theology
Emory University
Atlanta, GA

Jerome Neyrey
University of Notre Dame
Notre Dame, Indiana

Frederick W. Norris
Emmanuel School of Theology
Johnson City, Tennessee

Robert North
Pontificio Istituto Biblico
Rome, Italy

Julia M. O'Brien
Lancaster Theological Seminary
Lancaster, Pennsylvania

Gail R. O'Day
Candler School of Theology
Emory University
Atlanta, Georgia

Bernard O'Kelly
University of North Dakota
Grand Forks, North Dakota

John C. O'Neill
The University of Edinburgh
Edinburgh, Scotland

Thomas H. Olbricht
Pepperdine University
Malibu, California

Ben C. Ollenburger
Associated Mennonite Biblical Seminaries
Elkhart, Indiana

Eric F. Osborn
La Trobe University
Point Lonsdale, Victoria
Australia

Grant R. Osborne
Trinity Evangelical Divinity School
Deerfield, Illinois

Robert J. Owens, Jr.
Emmanuel School of Religion
Johnson City, Tennessee

Daniel L. Pals
University of Miami
Coral Gables, Florida

David B. Peabody
Nebraska Wesleyan University
Lincoln, Nebraska

Jordan S. Penkower
Bar-Ilan University
Jerusalem, Israel

Todd C. Penner
Emory University
Atlanta, Georgia

Richard I. Pervo
Seabury Western Theological Seminary
Evanston, Illinois

Vicki C. Phillips
West Virginia Wesleyan College
Buckhannon, West Virginia

Albert Pietersma
University of Toronto
Toronto, Ontario
Canada

William C. Placher
Wabash College
Crawfordsville, Indiana

W. Gunther Plaut
Holy Blossom Temple
Toronto, Ontario
Canada

William Poehlmann
St. Olaf College
Northfield, Minnesota

Max E. Polley
Davidson College
Davidson, North Carolina

J. R. Porter
University of Exeter
Exeter, England

Harry D. Potter
Barnards Inn Chambers
London, England

Mark A. Powell
Trinity Lutheran Seminary
Columbus, Ohio

John F. Priest (deceased)
Florida State University
Tallahassee, Florida

Paul R. Raabe
Concordia Seminary
St. Louis, Missouri

Heikki Räisänen
University of Helsinki
Helsinki, Finland

Jill Raitt
University of Missouri
Columbia, Missouri

Ilona N. Rashkow
State University of New York at Stony Brook
Stony Brook, New York

Roger D. Ray
University of Toledo
Toledo, Ohio

Marjorie E. Reeves
St. Anne's College
University of Oxford
Oxford, England

Bo Reicke (deceased)
University of Basel
Basel, Switzerland

Daniel J. Rettberg
Pitts Theology Library
Emory University
Atlanta, Georgia

Henning Graf Reventlow
Ruhr-Universität Bochum
Bochum, Germany

P. Lyndon Reynolds
Candler School of Theology
Emory University
Atlanta, Georgia

Dagfinn Rian
Norwegian University of Science and Technology
Dragvoll, Norway

Robert D. Richardson, Jr.
Middletown, CT

Harald Riesenfeld
Uppsala Universitet
Uppsala, Sweden

Helmer Ringgren
Uppsala Universitet
Uppsala, Sweden

Calvin J. Roetzel
Macalester College
St. Paul, Minnesota

Alexander Rofé
Hebrew University
Jerusalem, Israel

Max G. Rogers (deceased)
Southeastern Baptist Theological Seminary
Wake Forest, North Carolina

J. W. Rogerson
University of Sheffield
Sheffield, England

Wayne G. Rollins
Assumption College
Worcester, Massachusetts

Hans Rollmann
Memorial University of Newfoundland
St. Johns, Newfoundland
Canada

Jürgen Roloff
Friedrich-Alexander-Universität Erlangen
Erlangen, Germany

Stanley Ned Rosenbaum
Dickinson College
Carlisle, Pennsylvania

Wolfgang M. W. Roth
Garrett-Evangelical Theological Seminary
Evanston, Illinois

D. Geoffrey Rowell
Keble College
University of Oxford
Oxford, England

Leona Glidden Running
Andrews University
Berrien Springs, Michigan

Magne Saebø
Norway Lutheran School of Theology
Sandvika, Norway

Henry W. F. Saggs
University College
Cardiff, Wales

Robert B. Salters
St. Mary's College
University of St. Andrews
St. Andrews, Scotland

Norbert Samuelson
Arizona State University
Tempe, Arizona

Timothy J. Sandoval
Emory University
Atlanta, Georgia

John Sandys-Wunsch
Thorneloe College
Sudbury, Ontario
Canada

Richard S. Sarason
Hebrew Union College
Cincinnati, Ohio

Nahum Sarna
Brandeis University
Waltham, Massachusetts

Ernest W. Saunders (deceased)
Garrett-Evangelical Theological Seminary
Evanston, Illinois

John F. A. Sawyer
The University of Newcastle upon Tyne
Newcastle upon Tyne, England

Lawrence H. Schiffman
New York University
New York, New York

Donald G. Schley
Colorado Springs, Colorado

Thomas Schmeller
Institut für Katholische Theologie
Technische Universität Dresden
Dresden, Germany

Susan E. Schreiner
The Divinity School
University of Chicago
Chicago, Illinois

Glenn E. Schwerdtfeger
Maynard Drive United Methodist Church
Columbus, Ohio

J. Julius Scott, Jr.
Wheaton College
Wheaton, Illinois

J. J. Scullion (deceased)
Newman College
University of Melbourne
Melbourne, Australia

Fernando F. Segovia
The Divinity School
Vanderbilt University
Nashville, Tennessee

Bodo Seidel
Friedrich-Schiller-Universität Jena
Jena, Germany

Alan P. F. Sell
United Theological College
Aberystwyth, Dyfed
Wales

D. G. Selwyn
St. David's University College
University of Wales
Lampeter, Wales

Charles S. Shaw
Mount Zion United Methodist Church
Central, South Carolina

Gerald T. Sheppard
Emmanuel College
Victoria University
University of Toronto
Toronto, Ontario
Canada

Mary E. Shields
Drury College
Springfield, Missouri

Armin Siedlecki
Glaslyn, Saskatchewan
Canada

Michael A. Signer
University of Notre Dame
Notre Dame, Indiana

Uriel Simon
Bar-Ilan University
Jerusalem, Israel

Rudolf Smend
Georg-August-Universität Göttingen
Göttingen, Germany

Abraham Smith
Andover Newton Theological Seminary
Newton Centre, Massachusetts

Luther E. Smith
Candler School of Theology
Emory University
Atlanta, Georgia

Nigel Smith
Keble College
University of Oxford
Oxford, England

John Snarey
Candler School of Theology
Emory University
Atlanta, Georgia

Graydon F. Snyder
Chicago Theological Seminary
Chicago, Illinois

Marion L. Soards
Louisville Presbyterian Theological Seminary
Louisville, Kentucky

Richard N. Soulen
Virginia Union University
Richmond, Virginia

S. David Sperling
Hebrew Union College
New York, New York

Gary Stansell
St. Olaf College
Northfield, Minnesota

Graham N. Stanton
Fitzwilliam College
University of Cambridge
Cambridge, England

Naomi Steinberg
De Paul University
Chicago, Illinois

David C. Steinmetz
The Divinity School
Duke University
Durham, North Carolina

Ken Stone
Chicago Theological Seminary
Chicago, Illinois

Georg Strecker (deceased)
Georg-August-Universität Göttingen
Göttingen, Germany

G. M. Styler
Corpus Christi College
University of Cambridge
Cambridge, England

Theodore Stylianopoulos
Holy Cross Greek Orthodox School of Theology
Brookline, Massachusetts

R. S. Sugirtharajah
Selly Oaks Colleges
Birmingham, England

Charles H. Talbert
Baylor University
Waco, Texas

Walter F. Taylor
Trinity Lutheran Seminary
Columbus, Ohio

Winfried Thiel
Ruhr-Universität Bochum
Bochum, Germany

Frank S. Thielman
Beeson Divinity School
Samford University
Birmingham, Alabama

Thomas L. Thompson
Institute for Biblical Exegesis
University of Copenhagen
Copenhagen, Denmark

Burton H. Throckmorton, Jr.
Bangor Theological Seminary
Bangor, Maine

Jeffrey H. Tigay
University of Pennsylvania
Philadelphia, Pennsylvania

Hava Tirosh-Samuelson
Indiana University
Bloomington, Indiana

Elazar Touitou
Bar-Ilan University
Jerusalem, Israel

Emanuel Tov
Hebrew University
Jerusalem, Israel

W. Sibley Towner
Union Theological Seminary and Presbyterian
   School of Christian Education
Richmond, Virginia

Phyllis Trible
Wake Forest University Divinity School
Winston-Salem, North Carolina

Joseph W. Trigg
La Plata, Maryland

Peter L. Trudinger
Parkin-Wesley College
Adelaide, South Australia
Australia

James C. VanderKam
University of Notre Dame
Notre Dame, Indiana

Timo K. Veijola
University of Helsinki
Helsinki, Finland

Richard B. Vinson
Averett College
Danville, Virginia

Benedict T. Viviano
University of Fribourg
Fribourg, Switzerland

Arthur W. Wainwright
Candler School of Theology
Emory University
Atlanta, Georgia

Dewey D. Wallace, Jr.
George Washington University
Washington, DC

Mark I. Wallace
Swarthmore College
Swarthmore, Pennsylvania

Gerhard Wallis
Maring-Luther Universität Halle
Halle, Germany

Neal H. Walls
Candler School of Theology
Emory University
Atlanta, Georgia

Donald M. Walter
Davis and Elkins College
Elkins, West Virginia

Nikolaus Walter
Friedrich-Schiller-Universität Jena
Jena, Germany

Duane F. Watson
Malone College
Canton, Ohio

Francis Watson
King's College
University of London
London, England

Theodore R. Weber
Candler School of Theology
Emory University
Atlanta, Georgia

John W. Wevers
University of Toronto
Toronto, Ontario
Canada

Boyd Whaley
Mount Carmel United Methodist Church
Norcross, Georgia

L. Michael White
University of Texas
Austin, Texas

R. Norman Whybray (deceased)
University of Hull
Hull, England

Geoffrey Wigoder
Jerusalem, Israel

Thomas Willi
Ernst-Moritz-Arndt-Universität Greifswald
Greifswald, Germany

Ronald J. Williams (deceased)
University of Toronto
Toronto, Ontario
Canada

H. G. M. Williamson
Christ Church
University of Oxford
Oxford, England

John T. Willis
Abilene Christian University
Abilene, Texas

David Winston
Graduate Theological Union
Berkeley, California

Gail A. Yee
University of St. Thomas
St. Paul, Minnesota

Frances M. Young
University of Birmingham
Birmingham, England

Mark A. Zier
University of the Pacific
Stockton, California

ABBREVIATIONS

General

abr.	abridged	Heb.	Hebrew
AM	Anno Mundi	hon.	honorable
approx.	approximately	ill.	illustration
art(s).	article(s)	intro.	introduction
aug.	augmented	Ital.	Italian
b.	born	KS	*Kleine Schriften*
BCE	Before the Common Era	Lat.	Latin
Bd(e).	*Band(e)* (Ger.)	lit.	literally
bib.	biblical	LT	Latin translation
bk(s).	book(s)	LXX	Septuagint
CE	Common Era	masc.	masculine
c.	circa	MS(S)	manuscript(s)
cent(s).	century(ies)	MT	Masoretic Text
cf.	compare	n.	number
chap(s).	chapter(s)	n.d.	no date
comb.	combined	n.s.	new series
contr.	contributor	NT	New Testament
corr.	corrected	OG	Old Greek
d.	died	o.j.	*ohne Jahr*
dept.	department	OL	Old Latin
dir.	director	o.s.	old series
diss.	dissertation	OT	Old Testament
DH	deuteronomistic history	par.	paragraph
Dtr^1	first deuteronomistic redaction	pl.	plural
Dtr^2	second deuteronomistic redaction	posth.	posthumous
Dtr	deuteronomistic historian	prod.	producer
DtrG	*deuteronomistische Geschichte*	pt(s).	part(s)
DtrN	nomistic deuteronomist	pub.	published
DtrP	prophetic deuteronomist	R.	Rabbi
ed(s).	editor(s)/edition(s)	repr.	reprint
Eng.	English	repub.	republished
enl.	enlarged	rev. ed.	revised edition
esp.	especially	RGS	*Religionsgeschichtliche Schule*
est.	established	sec(s).	section(s)
ET	English translation	ser.	series
fem.	feminine	stud.	studies
fl.	flourished	supp.	supplement
frg(s).	fragment(s)	s.v.	*sub verbo*
FS	*Festschrift*	tr.	translator/translation
FT	French translation	trans.	transcribed
Ger.	German	u.a.	*unter anderem/und andere*
Gr.	Greek	v(v).	verse(s)
GS	*Gesammelte Schriften*	Vg.	Vulgate
GT	German translation	vol(s).	volume(s)
HB	Hebrew Bible		

Biblical Books (including the Apocrypha)

Gen	Nah	1–2–3–4 Kgdms	John
Exod	Hab	Add Esth	Acts
Lev	Zeph	Bar	Rom
Num	Hag	Bel	1–2 Cor
Deut	Zech	1–2 Esdr	Gal
Josh	Mal	4 Ezra	Eph
Judg	Ps(s)	Jdt	Phil
1–2 Sam	Job	Ep Jer	Col
1–2 Kgs	Prov	1–2–3–4 Macc	1–2 Thess
Isa	Ruth	Pr Azar	1–2 Tim
Jer	Cant	Pr Man	Titus
Ezek	Eccl	Sir	Phlm
Hos	Lam	Sus	Heb
Joel	Esth	Tob	Jas
Amos	Dan	Wis	1–2 Pet
Obad	Ezra	Matt	1–2–3 John
Jonah	Neh	Mark	Jude
Mic	1–2 Chr	Luke	Rev

Pseudepigraphical and Early Patristic Books

Adam and Eve	*Books of Adam and Eve*
Acts Pil.	*Acts of Pilate*
Apoc. Mos.	*Apocalypse of Moses*
Ap. Zeph.	*Apocalypse of Zephaniah*
As. Mos.	*Assumption of Moses*
Barn.	*Epistle of Barnabas*
Bib. Ant.	Ps.-Philo, *Biblical Antiquities*
1–2 Clem.	*1–2 Clement*
Did.	*Didache*
Diogn.	*Epistle to Diognets*
1–2–3 Enoch	*Ethiopic, Slavonic, Hebrew Enoch*
Ep. Arist.	*Epistle of Aristeas*
Gos. Eb.	*Gospel of the Ebionites*
Gos. Eg.	*Gospel of the Egyptians*
Gos. Heb.	*Gospel of the Hebrews*
Gos. Naass.	*Gospel of the Naassenes*
Gos. Pet.	*Gospel of Peter*
Gos. Thom.	*Gospel of Thomas*
Herm. Man.	*Hermas, Mandate(s)*
Herm. Sim.	*Hermas, Similitude(s)*
Herm. Vis.	*Hermas, Vision(s)*
Ign. Eph.	Ignatius, *Letter to the Ephesians*
Ign. Magn.	Ignatius, *Letter to the Magnesians*
Ign. Phld.	Ignatius, *Letter to the Philadelphians*
Ign. Pol.	Ignatius, *Letter to Polycarp*
Ign. Rom.	Ignatius, *Letter to the Romans*
Ign. Smyrn.	Ignatius, *Letter to the Smyrnaeans*
Ign. Trall.	Ignatius, *Letter to the Trallians*
Jos. Asen.	*Joseph and Aseneth*
Jub	*Jubilees*
Mart. Isa.	*Martyrdom of Isaiah*
Odes Sol.	*Odes of Solomon*
Pol. Phil.	Polycarp, *Letter to the Philippians*
Prot. Jas.	*Protevangelium of James*
Pss. Sol.	*Psalms of Solomon*
Shep. Herm.	*The Shepherd* (Hermas)
Sib. Or.	*Sibylline Oracles*
T. 12 Patr.	*Testaments of the Twelve Patriarchs*

T. Benj.	*Testament of Benjamin*
T. Dan	*Testament of Dan*
T. Iss.	*Testament of Issachar*
T. Jos	*Testament of Joseph*
T. Jud.	*Testament of Judah*
T. Levi	*Testament of Levi*
T. Mos.	*Testament of Moses*
T. Naph.	*Testament of Naphtali*
T. Reuben	*Testament of Reuben*
T. Sim.	*Testament of Simeon*
T. Zeb.	*Testament of Zebulun*

Dead Sea Scrolls and Related Texts

Sites

Ḥev	Naḥal Ḥever
Ḥev/Se	Naḥal Ḥever documents formerly attributed to Seiyal
Mas	Masada
Mird	Khirbet Mird
Mur	Murabbaʿat
Q	Qumran

Caves

Different caves at each site are denoted with sequential numbers, e.g., 1Q, 2Q.

Texts

1QapGen ar	*Genesis Apocryphon*
1QH^{a}	*Hodayot*^{a} or *Thanksgiving Hymns*^{a}
1QIsa^{a}	Isaiah^{a}
1QIsa^{b}	Isaiah^{b}
1QM	*Milḥamah* or *War Scroll*
1QpHab	*Pesher on Habakkuk*
1QpMi	*Pesher on Micah*
1QS	*Serekh ha-Yaḥad,* or *Rule of the Community* (formerly *Manual of Discipline*)
4QapocrJosh^{a}	*Apocryphon of Joshua*^{a}, formerly *Psalms of Joshua*
4QBeat	*Beatitudes*
4QCommGen A	*Commentary on Genesis A* (formerly *Patriarchal Blessings* or *Pesher Genesis*)
4QDeut^{j}	Deuteronomy^{j}
4QDeut^{n}	Deuteronomy^{n}
4QDeut^{q}	Deuteronomy^{q}
4QFlor (MidrEschat^{b})	*Florilegium,* also *Midrash on Eschatology*^{a}
4QHos^{a}	Hosea^{a}
4QJer^{b}	Jeremiah^{b}
4QJosh^{a}	Joshua^{a}
4QJosh^{b}	Joshua^{b}
4QJubilees^{a}	*Jubilees*^{a}
4QMess ar	Aramaic "Messianic" text
4QMMT^{a}	*Miqṣat Ma*ʿaseh ha-Torah^{a}
4QNum^{b}	Numbers^{b}
4QpaleoExod	Copy of Exodus in paleo-Hebrew script
4QpaleoExod^{jm}	Copy of Exodus in paleo-Hebrew script^{jm}
4QpaleoExod^{m}	Copy of Exodus in paleo-Hebrew script^{m}
4QPhyl	Phylacteries
4QPhyl G	Phylacteries G
4QpIsa^{a}	*Pesher on Isaiah*^{a}
4QpIsa^{b}	*Pesher on Isaiah*^{b}
4QpIsa^{c}	*Pesher on Isaiah*^{c}
4QpMic	*Pesher on Micah*
4QpNah	*Pesher on Nahum*
4QpPs^{a}	*Pesher on Psalms*^{a}
4QPrNab	*Prayer of Nabonidus*

4QPsDan[a] ar	Pseudo-Daniel[a] Aramaic
4QPsDan[b] ar	Pseudo-Daniel[b] Aramaic
4QPsDan[c] ar	Pseudo-Daniel[c] Aramaic
4QPssJosh	*Psalms of Joshua*
4QRP[c]	*Reworked Pentateuch[c]*
4QSam[a]	Samuel[a]
4QShirShabb[a]	*Songs of the Sabbath Sacrifice[a]*
4QTestim	*Testimonia*
4QtgLev	*Targum of Leviticus*
4QTLevi	*Testament of Levi*
5QDeut	Deuteronomy
5QpMal	*Pesher on Malachi*
8HevXiigr	Greek Scroll of the Minor Prophets from Naḥal Ḥever
11QMelch	*Melchizedek*
11QpaleoLev	Copy of Leviticus in paleo-Hebrew script
11QShirShabb	*Songs of the Sabbath Sacrifice*
11QT[a]	*Temple Scroll[a]*
11QT[b]	*Temple Scroll[b]*
11QtgJob	*Targum of Job*

Targumic Materials

Tg. Esth I, II	*First or Second Targum of Esther*
Frg. Tg.	*Fragmentary Targum*
Tg. Isa	*Targum of Isaiah*
Tg. Ket.	*Targum of the Writings*
Tg. Neb.	*Targum of the Prophets*
Tg. Neof.	*Targum Neofiti I*
Tg. Onq.	*Targum Onquelos*
T. Ps.-J.	*Targum Pseudo-Jonathan*
Sam. Tg.	*Samaritan Targum*
Yem. Tg.	*Yemenite Targum*
Tg. Yer. I	*Targum Yerušalmi I*
Tg. Yer. II	*Targum Yerušalmi II*

Orders and Tractates in Mishnaic and Related Literature

m.	Mishnah
b.	Babylonian Talmud
y.	Jerusalem Talmud
t.	Tosefta

ʾAbod. Zar.	*ʾAboda Zara*
ʾAbot	*ʾAbot*
ʾArak.	*ʾArakin*
B. Bat.	*Baba Batra*
Bek.	*Bekorot*
Ber.	*Berakot*
Beṣa	*Beṣa (= Yom Ṭob)*
Bik.	*Bikkurim*
B. Meṣ.	*Baba Meṣiʿa*
B. Qam.	*Baba Qamma*
Dem.	*Demai*
ʿErub.	*ʿErubin*
ʿEd.	*ʿEduyyot*
Giṭ.	*Giṭṭin*
Ḥag.	*Ḥagiga*
Ḥal.	*Ḥalla*
Hor.	*Horayot*
Ḥul.	*Ḥullin*
Kelim	*Kelim*

Ker.	Keritot
Ketub.	Ketubot
Kil.	Kilʾayim
Maʿaś.	Maʿaśerot
Mak.	Makkot
Makš.	Makširin (= Mašqin)
Meg.	Megilla
Meʿil.	Meʿila
Menaḥ.	Menahot
Mid.	Middot
Miqw.	Miqwaʾot
Moʿed	Moʿed
Moʿed Qaṭ.	Moʿed Qaṭan
Maʿaś. Š.	Maʿaśer Šeni
Našim	Našim
Nazir	Nazir
Ned.	Nedarim
Neg.	Negaʿim
Nez.	Neziqin
Nid.	Niddah
Ohol.	Oholot
ʿOr.	ʿOrla
Para	Para
Peʾa	Peʾa
Pesaḥ.	Pesahim
Qinnim	Qinnim
Qidd.	Qidduśin
Qod.	Qodašin
Roš Haš.	Roš Haššana
Sanh.	Sanhedrin
Šabb.	Šabbat
Šeb.	Šebiʿit
Šebu.	Šebuʿot
Šeqal.	Šeqalim
Soṭa	Soṭa
Sukk.	Sukka
Taʿan.	Taʿanit
Tamid	Tamid
Tem.	Temura
Ter.	Terumot
Ṭohar.	Ṭoharot
T. Yom	Ṭebul Yom
ʿUq.	ʿUqṣin
Yad.	Yadayim
Yebam.	Yebamot
Yoma	Yoma (= Kippurim)
Zabim	Zabim
Zebaḥ.	Zebahim
Zer.	Zeraʿim

Additional Rabbinic Works

ʾAbot R. Nat.	ʾAbot de Rabbi Nathan
ʾAg. Ber.	ʾAggadat Berešit
Bab.	Babylonian
Der. Er. Rab.	Derek Ereṣ Rabba
Der Er Zuṭ.	Derek Ereṣ Zuṭa
Gem.	Gemara
Mek.	Mekilta
MHG Shem.	Midrash HaGadol Shemot
Midr.	Midraš (cited with abbreviation for biblical book)

Pal.	Palestinian
Pesiq. R.	Pesiqta Rabbati
Pesiq. Rab Kah.	Pesiqta de Rab Kahana
Pirqe R. El.	Pirqe Rabbi Eliezer
Rab.	Rabbah (following abbreviation for biblical book)
Ṣem.	Ṣemaḥot
Sipra	Sipra
Sipre	Sipre
Sop.	Soperim
S. ʿOlam Rab.	Seder ʿOlam Rabbah
Tan. Shem.	Tanchuma Shemot
Talm.	Talmud
Yal.	Yalquṭ

Nag Hammadi Tractates

Acts Pet. 12 Apost	Acts of Peter and the Twelve Apostles
Allogenes	Allogenes
Ap. Jas.	Apocryphon of James
Ap. John	Apocryphon of John
Apoc. Adam	Apocalypse of Adam
1 Apoc. Jas.	First Apocalypse of James
2. Apoc. Jas.	Second Apocalypse of James
Apoc. Paul	Apocalypse of Paul
Apoc. Pet.	Apocalypse of Peter
Asclepius	Asclepius 21–29
Auth. Teach.	Authoritative Teaching
Dial. Sav.	Dialogue of the Savior
Disc. 8–9	Discourse on the Eighth and Ninth
Ep. Pet. Phil.	Letter of Peter to Philip
Eugnostos	Eugnostos the Blessed
Exeg. Soul	Exegesis on the Soul
Gos. Eg.	Gospel of the Egyptians
Gos. Mary	Gospel of Mary
Gos. Phil.	Gospel of Philip
Gos. Thom.	Gospel of Thomas
Gos. Truth	Gospel of Truth
Great Pow.	Concept of Our Great Power
Hyp. Arch.	Hypostasis of the Archons
Hypsiph.	Hypsiphrone
Interp. Know.	Interpretation of Knowledge
Marsanes	Marsanes
Melch.	Melchizedek
Norea	Thought of Norea
On Bap. A	On Baptism A
On Bap. B	On Baptism B
On Bap. C	On Baptism C
On Euch. A	On the Eucharist A
On Euch. B	On the Eucharist B
Orig. World	On the Origin of the World
Paraph. Shem	Paraphrase of Shem
Pr. Paul	Prayer of the Apostle Paul
Pr. Thanks.	Prayer of Thanksgiving
Sent. Sextus	Sentences of Sextus
Soph. Jes. Chr.	Sophia of Jesus Christ
Steles Seth	Three Steles of Seth
Teach. Silv.	Teachings of Silvanus
Testim. Truth	Testimony of Truth
Thom. Cont.	Book of Thomas the Contender
Thund.	Thunder, Perfect Mind
Treat. Res.	Treatise on Resurrection

Treat. Seth	*Second Treatise of the Great Seth*
Tri. Trac.	*Tripartite Tractate*
Trim. Prot.	*Trimorphic Protennoia*
Val. Exp.	*A Valentinian Exposition*
Zost.	*Zostrianos*

Institutions and Organizations

AAR	American Academy of Religion
ASOR	American Schools of Oriental Research
ATLA	American Theologicial Library Association
BFBS	British Foreign Bible Society
CBA	Catholic Biblical Association of America
CMS	Church Missionary Society
HUC	Hebrew Union College
IOSCS	International Organization for Septuagint and Cognate Studies
SBL	Society of Biblical Literature
SNTS	Society for New Testament Studies
SUNY	State University of New York
UBS	United Bible Society

Periodicals, Reference Works, and Serials

AA	*Archäologischer Anzeiger*
AAAbo	Acta Academiae Aboensis
AAAbo.H	Acta Academiae Aboensis. Ser. A. Humaniora
AAR.AS	AAR Academy Series
AAR.DS	AAR Dissertation Series
AAR.SR	AAR Studies in Religion
AARSBLA	American Academy of Religion/Society of Biblical Literature Abstracts
AARSBLVR	AAR/SBL Ventures in Religion
AAS	*Acta apostolicae sedis*
AASF	Annales Academiae Scientiarum Fennicae
AASOR	Annual of the American Schools of Oriental Research
AAWB	Abhandlungen der K. Akademie der Wissenschaften zu Berlin
AAWG.PH	Abhandlungen der K. Akademie der Wissenschaften zu Göttingen. Philologisch-historische Klasse
AAWLM.G	Abhandlungen der Geistes- und Sozialwissenschaftlichen Klasse, Akademie des Wissenschaft und der Literatur
AB	Anchor Bible
ABBL	J. G. Eichhorn (ed.), *Allgemeine Bibliothek der biblischen Litteratur* (10 vols., 1787–1801)
ABD	D. N. Freedman (ed.), *Anchor Bible Dictionary* (6 vols., 1992)
ABenR	*American Benedictine Review*
ABG	*Archiv für Begriffsgeschichte*
ABMA	Auctores Britannici medii aevi
ABQ	*American Baptist Quarterly*
ABR	*Australian Biblical Review*
ABRL	Anchor Bible Reference Library
ABRL	*Die Arbeiterbewegung in den Rheinlanden*
AbrN	*Abr-Nahrain*
ACCS.NT	Ancient Christian Commentary on Scripture. New Testament
ACEBT	Amsterdamse cahiers voor exegese en bijbelse theologie
ACJD	Abhandlungen zum christlich-jüdischen Dialog
ACNT	Augsburg Commentary on the New Testament
AcOr	*Acta orientalia*
ACW	Ancient Christian Writers
ADAJ	*Annual of the Department of Antiquities of Jordan*
ADB	*Allgemeine deutsche Biographie*
ADPV	Abhandlungen des Deutschen Palästina-Vereins
Aeg	*Aegyptus*

AES	*Archives européennes de sociologie*
AEWK	J. S. Ersch et al. (eds.), *Allgemeine Encyklopädie der Wissenschaften und Künste* (167 vols., 1818–1889)
AF	R. M. Grant (ed.), *Apostolic Fathers*
AFH	*Archivum Franciscanum historicum*
AfO	*Archiv fur Orientforschung*
AFP	*Archivum Fratrum Praedicatorum*
AGJU	Arbeiten zur Geschichte des antiken Judentums und des Urchristentums
AGL	C. G. Jöcher (ed.), *Allgemeines Gelehrten-Lexicon* (11 vols., 1750–1819, 1897)
AGLB	Aus der Geschichte der lateinischen Bibel
AGPh	*Archiv für Geschichte der Philosophie (und Soziologie)*
AGTL	Arbeiten zur Geschichte und Theologie des Luthertums
AGWG	Abhandlungen der (K.) Gesellschaft der Wissenschaften zu Göttingen
AGWG.PH	Abhandlungen der Gesellschaft der Wissenschaften zu Göttingen. Philologisch-historische Klasse
AHAW.PH	Abhandlungen der Heidelberger Akademie der Wissenschaften. Philologisch-historische Klasse
AHDLMA	*Archives d'histoire doctrinale et littéraire du moyen âge*
AHW	W. von Soden, *Akkadisches Handworterbuch*
AION	*Annali dell'Istituto Orientale di Napoli*
AISIG	*Annali dell'Istituto Storico Italo-Germanico in Trento*
AJA	*American Journal of Archaeology*
AJAS	*American Journal of Arabic Studies*
AJBA	*Australian Journal of Biblical Archaeology*
AJBI	Annual of the Japanese Biblical Institute
AJeA	American Jewish Archives
AJP	*American Journal of Philology*
AJS	*American Journal of Sociology*
AJSL	*American Journal of Semitic Languages and Literature*
AJSR	*Association for Jewish Studies Review*
AJT	*American Journal of Theology*
AJTh	*Asia Journal of Theology*
AKAWB	*Abhandlungen der königlichen Akademie der Wissenschaften zu Berlin*
AKG	Arbeiten zur Kirchengeschichte. Berlin
AKG	*Archiv für Kulturgeschichte*
AKM	Abhandlungen für die Kunde des Morgenlandes
AKML	Abhandlungen zur Kunst-, Musik- und Literaturwissenschaft
AKuG	*Archiv für Kulturgeschichte*
AKZ	*Allgemeine Kirchenzeitung*
AJut	Acta Jutlandica
AJut.T	Acta Jutlandica: Teologisk serie
ALBO	Analecta lovaniensia biblica et orientalia
ALGHJ	Arbeiten zur Literatur und Geschichte des hellenistischen Judentums
ALUOS	*Annual of Leeds University Oriental Society*
AnBib	Analecta biblica
AnBoll	Analecta Bollandiana
ANCL	*Ante-Nicene Christian Library*
ANEP	J. B. Pritchard (ed.), *Ancient Near East in Pictures*
ANESTP	J. B. Pritchard (ed.), *Ancient Near East Supplementary Texts and Pictures*
ANET	J. B. Pritchard (ed.), *Ancient Near Eastern Texts*
ANETS	Ancient Near Eastern Texts and Studies
ANF	The Ante-Nicene Fathers
AnGr	*Analecta Gregoriana*
AnOr	*Analecta orientalia*
ANQ	*Andover Newton Quarterly*
ANRW	*Aufstieg und Niedergang der römischen Welt*
AnSt	*Anatolian Studies*
ANTC	Abingdon New Testament Commentary
ANTF	Arbeiten zur neutestamentlichen Textforchung
ANTJ	Arbeiten zum Neuen Testament und Judentum
Anton	*Antonianum*
ANTZ	Arbeiten zur neutestamentlichen Theologie und Zeitgeschichte

AO	*Aula orientalis*
AOAT	Alter Orient und Altes Testament
AOS	American Oriental Series
AOSTS	American Oriental Society Translation Series
AOT	H. F. D. Sparks (ed.), *The Apocryphal OT* (1984)
AOx	*Athenae Oxonienses*
AP	*American Presbyterian*
APAT	E. Kautzsch (ed.), *Apokryphen und Pseudepigraphen des Alten Testaments* (2 vols., 1900)
APG	Abhandlungen zur Philosophie und ihrer Geschichte. Hg.v. B. Erdmann
APOT	R. H. Charles (ed.), *Apocrypha and Pseudepigrapha of the OT* (2 vols., 1913)
AR	D. D. Luckenbill (ed.), *Ancient Records of Assyria and Babylonia* (2 vols., 1926–27)
ARE	J. H. Breasted (ed.), *Ancient Records of Egypt* (5 vols., 1906–7)
ARG	*Archiv fur Reformationsgeschichte*
ARM	Archives royales de Mari
ArOr	*Archiv orientální*
ARSHLL	Acta Regiae Societatis Humaniorum Litterarum Ludensis
ARW	*Archiv fur Religionswissenschaft*
ARWAW	Abhandlungen der Rheinisch-Westfälischen Akademie der Wissenschaften
ASNU	Acta seminarii neotestamentici upsaliensis
ASORSVS	American Schools of Oriental Research Special Volume Series
ASS	*Acta sanctae sedis*
ASSR	*Archives des sciences sociales des religions*
AStE	*Annuario di studi ebraici*
ASTI	*Annual of the Swedish Theological Institute*
ASV	American Standard Version
AT	Arbeiten zur Theologie
ATA	Alttestamentliche Abhandlungen
ATANT	Abhandlungen zur Theologie des Alten und Neuen Testaments
ATAT	*Altorientalische Texte zum Alten Testament*
ATB	Auserlesene Theologische Bibliothek
ATD	Das Alte Testament Deutsch
ATDan	Acta theologica danica
ATLA.MS	American Theological Library Association Monograph Series
ATR	*Anglican Theological Review*
ATSAT	Arbeiten zu Text und Sprache im Alten Testament
Aug	*Augustinianum*
AusBR	*Australian Biblical Review*
AUSS	*Andrews University Seminary Studies*
AUU	Acta Universitatis Upsaliensis
AV	Authorized Version
AWEAT	Archiv für wissenschaftliche Erforschung des Alten Testaments
AWR	*Aus der Welt der Religion*
BA	*Biblical Archaeologist*
BAAR	*Bulletin of the American Academy of Religion*
BAC	Biblioteca de autores cristianos
BAG	Beiträge zur alten Geschichte
BAG(D)	W. Bauer, W. F. Arndt, F. W. Gingerich (2nd ed, and F. W. Danker), *Greek-English Lexicon of the New Testament*
BAH	Bibliothéque archéologique et historique
BAM	J. LeClerc (ed.), *Bibliothèque ancienne et moderne* (29 vols., 1714–30)
BAR	*Biblical Archaeologist Reader*
BARev	*Biblical Archaeology Review*
BASOR	*Bulletin of the American Schools of Oriental Research*
BASP	*Bulletin of the American Society of Papyrologists*
BAT	Botschaft des Alten Testaments
BB	*Biographia Britannica* (6 vols., 1747–63; 2nd ed., 5 vols., 1778–93)
BBB	Bonner biblische Beiträge
BBET	Beiträge zur biblischen Exegese und Theologie
BBGW	Basler Beiträge zur Geschichtswissenschaft

BBKL	*Biographisch-bibliographisches Kirchenlexikon*
BBLAK	Beiträge zur biblischen Landes- und Altertumskunde
BC	J. LeClerc (ed.), *Bibliothèque choisie* (28 vols., 1703–13)
BC	Biblischer Commentar über das Alte Testament
BCNH.T	Bibliothèque copte de Nag Hammadi. Section textes
BCPE	*Bulletin du Centre Protestant d'Études*
BCSR	*Bulletin of the Council on the Study of Religion*
BDB	F. Brown, S. R. Driver, and C. A. Briggs, *Hebrew and English Lexicon of the Old Testament*
BDBR	R. L. Greaves and R. Zaller (eds.), *Biographical Dictionary of British Radicals in the Seventeenth Century* (3 vols., 1982–84)
BDF	F. Blass, A. Debrunner, and R. W. Funk, *A Greek Grammar of the NT*
BDR	F. Blass, A. Debrunner, and F. Rehkopf, *Grammatik des neutestamentlichen Griechisch*
Bdt	Biliothèque de théologie
BEATAJ	Beiträge zur Erforschung des Alten Testaments und des antiken Judentum
BEHE	Biliothèque de l'École des Hautes Études
BeO	*Bibbia e oriente*
BER	*Biblisch-exegetisches Repertorium*
BETL	Bibliotheca ephemeridum theologicarum lovaniensium
BEvT	Beiträge zur evangelischen Theologie
BFCT	Beiträge zur Förderung christlicher Theologie
BFT	Biblical Foundations in Theology
BG	W. Schneemelcher at al. (eds.), *Bonner Gelehrte. Beiträge zur Geschichte der Wissenschaften in Bonn. Evangelische Theologie* (1968–)
BGBE	Beiträge zur Geschichte der biblischen Exegese
BGBH	Beiträge zur Geschichte der biblischen Hermeneutik
BGLRK	Beiträge zur Geschichte und Lehre der Reformierten Kirche
BGPTM	Beiträge zur Geschichte der Philosophie (und Theologie) des Mittelalters
BHEAT	Bulletin d'histoire et d' exegese de l'Ancien Testament
BHH	B. Reicke and L. Rost (eds.), *Biblisch-Historisches Handworterbuch* (4 vols., 1962–79)
BHK	R. Kittel, *Biblia hebraica*
BHPT	*Bibliotheca Historico-Philologico-Theologica*
BHR	*Bibliothèque d'humanisme et renaissance*
BHRTD	*Bibliothèque d'humanisme et renaissance. Travaux et Documents*
BHS	*Biblia hebraica stuttgartensia*
BHT	Beiträge zur historischen Theologie
BHWJ	Bericht der Hochschule für die Wissenschaft des Judentums
BI	J. J. Megivern (ed.), *Bible Interpretation* (Official Catholic Teachings, 1978)
Bib	*Biblica*
BibB	Biblische Beiträge
BibInt	*Biblical Interpretation*
BibLeb	*Bibel und Leben*
BibOr	Biblica et orientalia
BibRev	*Bible Review*
BibS	Biblische Studien
BibS(F)	Biblische Studien (Freiburg)
BibS(N)	Biblische Studien (Neukirchen)
BIES	*Bulletin of the Israel Exploration Society* (= Yediot)
BIFAO	*Bulletin de l'institut français d'archéologie orientale*
BIOSCS	Bulletin of the International Organization for Septuagint and Cognate Studies
BIRS	*Bibliographies and Indexes in Religious Studies*
BIS	Biblical Interpretation Series
BiSe	The Biblical Seminar
BiTr	*The Bible Translator*
BJDN	*Biographisches Jahrbuch und deutscher Nekrolog*
BJPES	*Bulletin of the Jewish Palestine Exploration Society*
BJRL	*Bulletin of the John Rylands University Library of Manchester*
BJS	Brown Judaic Studies
BJuS	Biblical and Judaic Studies
BK	*Bibel und Kirche*

BKAT	Biblischer Kommentar: Altes Testament
BLE	*Bulletin de littérature ecclésiastique*
BLit	*Bibel und Liturgie*
BN	*Biblische Notizen*
BNB	British National Bibliography
BNGKT	Beiträge zur neueren Geschichte der katholischen Theologie
BNTC	Black's New Testament Commentaries
BO	*Bibliotheca orientalis*
BOT	Boeken van het Oude Testament
BP	Bibliothéque de philosophie
BPCI	Biblical Perspectives on Current Issues
BPhC	Bibliothèque de philosophie contemporaine
BQ	*Baptist Quarterly*
BR	*Biblical Research*
BRL	*Biblisches Reallexikon*
BRQO	*Biblical Repository and Quarterly Observer*
BSac	Bibliotheca Sacra
BSLR	Beacon Series in Liberal Religion
BSMS	*Bulletin of the Society for Mesopotamian Studies*
BSNA	Biblical Scholarship in North America
BSO(A)S	*Bulletin of the School of Oriental (and African) Studies*
BT	*Babylonian Talmud*
BTA	Bible Through the Ages Series
BTAVO	Beihefte zum Tübinger Atlas des Vorderen Orients
BTB	*Biblical Theology Bulletin*
BThB	Bibliotek Theologie der Befreiung
BTS	*Bible et terre sainte*
BTT	Bible de tous les temps
BTZ	*Berliner Theologische Zeitschrift*
BU	Biblische Untersuchungen
BU	*Biographie universelle*
BUH	*Bibliotheque universelle et historique*
BurH	*Buried History*
BVC	*Bible et vie chrétienne*
BVSGW	Berichte über die Verhandlungen der Sächsischen Gesellschaft der Wissenschaften
BVSGW.PH	Berichte über die Verhandlungen der Sächsischen Gesellschaft der Wissenschaften. Philologisch-historische Klasse
BWANT	Beiträge zur Wissenschaft vom Alten (und Neuen) Testament
BWN	*Biografisch woordenboek van Nederland*
BWPGN	*Biografisch woordenboek van protestantsche godgeleerden in Nederland*
BZ	*Biblische Zeitschrift*
BZAW	Beihefte zur *ZAW*
BZNW	Beihefte zur *ZNW*
BZRGG	Beihefte zur *ZRGG*
BZSF	Biblische Zeit- und Streitfragen
CAD	*The Assyrian Dictionary of the Oriental Institute of the University of Chicago*
CAH	*Cambridge Ancient History*
CahThéol	Cahiers Théologiques
CAR	Cahiers de l'actualité religieuse
CAT	Commentaire de l'Ancien Testament
CATTA	V. Ferm (ed.), *Contemporary American Theology: Theological Autobiographies* (2 vols., 1932–33)
CB	Clarendon Bible
CB	*Cultura biblica*
CBA	Cronaca delle belle arti
CBC	Cambridge Bible Commentary
CBE	*Catholic Biblical Encyclopedia*
CBET	Contributions to Biblical Exegesis and Theology
CBQ	*Catholic Biblical Quarterly*
CBQMS	Catholic Biblical Quarterly—Monograph Series
CBSC	Cambridge Bible for School and Colleges

CBTEL	J. McClintock and J. Strong (eds.), *Cyclopedia of Biblical, Theological, and Ecclesiastical Literature* (12 vols., 1867–87)
CBW	*Cities of the Biblical World*
CC	*Christian Century*
CC	Corpus Christianorum
CCARJ	*Central Conference of American Rabbis. Journal*
CCath	Corpus Catholicorum
CCCM	Corpus Christianorum, Continuatio Mediaevalis
CCS	*The Communicator's Commentary Series*
CCSL	Corpus Christianorum. Series Latina
CD	*Das christliche Deutschland*
CE	P. G. Bietenholz and T. B. Deutscher (eds.), *Contemporaries of Erasmus: A Biographical Register of the Renaissance and Reformation* (3 vols., 1985–87)
CeB	The Century Bible
CF	Cogitatio fidei
CFr	Collectanea Friburgensia
CG	Coptic Gnostic Library
CGPNT	Catenae Graecorum Patrum in Novum Testamentum
CGTC	Cambridge Greek Testament Commentaries
CH	*Cahiers d'histoire*
CHB	P. R. Ackroyd et al. (eds.), *Cambridge History of the Bible* (3 vols., 1963–70)
ChH	*Church History*
CHR	*Catholic Historical Review*
ChW	*Christliche Welt*
CHZFBG	Calwer hefte zur Forderung biblischen Glaubens und christlichen Lebens
CIB	Centre: Informatique et Bible
CID	Comenius-Institut-Dokumentation
CIG	*Corpus inscriptionum graecarum*
CII	*Corpus inscriptionum iudaicarum*
CIL	*Corpus inscriptionum latinarum*
CIS	*Corpus inscriptionum semiticarum*
CJT	*Canadian Journal of Theology*
CJud	*Conservative Judaism*
CMCT	P. E. Hughes (ed.), *Creative Minds in Contemporary Theology* (1973^2)
CNT	Commentaire du Nouveau Testament
COHP	Contributions to Oriental History and Philology of the Columbia University
ConB	Coniectanea biblica
ConBNT	Coniectanea biblica, New Testament
ConBOT	Coniectanea biblica, Old Testament
Conc(D)	Concilium. Ensiedeln
ConJ	*Concordia Journal*
ConNT	Coniectanea neotestamentica
COr	Cahiers d'Orientalisme
COT	Commentaar op het Oude Testament
CP	*Classical Philology*
CPT	Cambridge Patristic Texts
CQ	*Church Quarterly*
CQR	*Church Quarterly Review*
CQS	Catholic and Quaker Studies
CR	Corpus reformatorum
CR	*Critical Review of Books in Religion*
CRAIBL	Comptes rendus de l'Académie des inscriptions et belles-lettres
CR:BS	*Currents in Research: Biblical Studies*
CRB	Cahiers de la Revue biblique
CRHPR	Cahiers de la Revue d'histoire et de philosophie religieuses
CRINT	Compendia rerum iudaicarum ad novum testamentum
CrSoc	*Cristianismo y sociedad*
CRSS	Classics in Religious Studies (series)
CS	J. G. Herder, *Christliche Schriften* (4 vols., 1794–98)
CSCO	Corpus scriptorum christianorum orientalium

CSCT	Columbia Studies in the Classical Tradition
CSEL	Corpus scriptorum ecclesiasticorum latinorum
CSRCT	Cambridge Studies in Religion and Criticial Thought
CSS	Cursus scripturae sacrae
CTA	A. Herdner, *Corpus des tablettes en cunéiformes alphabétiques*
CTJ	*Calvin Theological Journal*
CTM	*Concordia Theological Monthly*
CTom	*Ciencia Tomista*
CTP	Cadernos de teologia e pastoral
CTS	Contemporary Theology Series
CurTM	*Currents in Theology and Mission*
CW	*Catholic World*
CWS	Classics of Western Spirituality
DAB	*Dictionary of American Biography*
DACL	*Dictionnaire d'archéologie chrétienne et de liturgie*
DARB	H. W. Bowden, *Dictionary of American Religious Biography* (1993²)
DATDJ	R. Smend, *Deutsche Alttestamentler in drei Jahrhunderten* (1989)
DB	F. Vigouroux (ed.), *Dictionnaire de la Bible* (5 vols., 1891–1912)
DBAT	*Dielheimer Blätter zum Alten Testament*
DBF	*Dictionnaire de biographie française*
DB(H)	J. Hastings (ed.), *Dictionary of the Bible* (rev. F. C. Grant and H. H. Rowley, 1963)
DBJ	*Deutsches biographisches Jahrbuch*
DBSup	*Dictionnaire de la Bible, Supplément*
DCB	W. Smith and H. Wace (eds.), *Dictionary of Christian Biography* (4 vols., 1877–87)
DCH	*Dictionary of Classical Hebrew*
DDD	K. van der Torn et al. (eds), *Dictionary of Deities and Demons in the Bible* (1995)
DHGE	*Dictionnaire d'histoire et de géographie ecclésiastiques*
DISO	C.-F. Jean and J. Hoftijzer, *Dictionnaire des inscriptions sémitiques de l'ouest* (1965)
DJD	Discoveries in the Judaean Desert
DMA	J. R. Strayer (ed.), *Dictionary of the Middle Ages* (13 vols., 1982–89)
DMMRS	Duke Monographs in Medieval and Renaissance Studies
DMOA	Documenta et monumenta orientis antiqui
DNB	*Dictionary of National Biography*
DOTT	D.W. Thomas (ed.), *Documents from Old Testament Times* (1958)
DRu	*Deutsche Rundschau*
DS	Denzinger-Schönmetzer, *Enchiridion symbolorum*
DS	*Dictionaire de Spiritualité*
DSB	Daily Study Bible
DSD	*Dead Sea Discoveries*
DTC	A. Vacant et al. (eds.), *Dictionnaire de théologie catholique*
DtPfrBl	*Deutsches Pfarrerblatt* (15 vols., 1903–50)
DTT	*Dansk teologisk tidsskrift*
DUJ	*Durham University Journal*
DunRev	*Dunwoodie Review*
EAC	*Encyclopedia of the Early Church*
EAC	Études d'archéologie classique
EAJT	*East Asia Journel of Theology*
EBB	Elenchus bibliographicus biblicus
Ebib	Études bibliques
ECGNT	J. R. Kohlenberger III et al., *Exhaustive Concordance to the Greek New Testament* (1995)
EDB	L.F. Hartman (ed.), *Encyclopedic Dictionary of the Bible*
EdF	Erträge der Forschung
EEC	E. Ferguson (ed.), *Encyclopedia of Early Christianity* (1990)
EET	Einführung in die evangelische Theologie
EETS	Early English Text Society
EF	Enciclopedia filosofica
EGT	Expositor's Greek Testament
EgTh	*Église et theologie. Ottawa*
EHAT	Exegetisches Handbuch zum Alten Testament
EHPhR	Études d'histoire et de philosophie religieuses
EHS	Europäische Hochschulschriften
EHS.T	Europäische Hochschulschriften. Reihe 23. Theologie

EiT	*Explorations in Theology*
EJ	J. Klatzkin (ed.), *Encyclopaedia Judaica* (10 vols., 1928–34)
EKKNT	Evangelisch-katholischer Kommentar zum Neuen Testament
EKL	H. Brunotte and O. Weber (eds.), *Evangelisches Kirchenlexikon* (4 vols., 1956–62)
EM	*Emerita. Madrid*
EMMÖ	Erlanger Monographien aus Mission und Ökumene
EncBib	T. K. Cheyne and J. S. Black (eds.), *Encyclopaedia Biblica* (4 vols., 1899–1903)
EncBrit	*Encyclopedia Britannica*
EnchBib	*Enchiridion biblicum*
EncJud	C. Roth (ed.), *Encyclopaedia Judaica* (16 vols., 1971–72)
ENCPI	Edizione nazionale dei classici del pensiero italiano
EncRel	M. Eliade (ed.), *The Encyclopedia of Religion* (16 vols., 1987)
EPH	Études de philologie et d'histoire
EPhM	Études de philosophie médiévale
EpRe	*Epworth Review*
EPRO	Études préliminaires aux religions orientales dans l'empire Romain
EQ	*Evangelical Quarterly*
ERE	J. Hastings (ed.), *Encyclopaedia of Religion and Ethics* (13 vols., 1908–26)
ErIsr	Eretz-Israel: Archaeological, Historical, and Geographical Studies
ErJb	*Eranos Jahrbuch*
EstBib	*Estudios bíblicos*
EsTe	Estudos teologicos
ESW	*Ecumenical Studies in Worship*
ETH	Études de théologie historique
ETHS	Études de théologie et histoire de la spiritualité
ETL	*Ephemerides theologicae lovanienses*
ETR	*Études théologiques et religieuses*
ETS	Erfurter theologische Studien
EvErz	*Der evangelische Erzieher*
EvK	Evangelische Kommentare
EvTh	*Evangelische Theologie*
EWNT	H. Balz and G. Schneider (eds.), *Exegetisches Wörterbuch zum Neuen Testament* (3 vols., 1980–83)
ExpB	Expositor's Bible
ExpTim	*Expository Times*
EzAT	*Erläuterungen zum Alten Testament*
FAB	*Für Arbeit und Besinnung*
FAT	Forschungen zum Alten Testament
FB	Forschung zur Bibel
FBBS	Facet Books, Biblical Series
FC	Fathers of the Church
FFNT	Foundations and Facets: New Testament
FJCD	Forschungen zum jüdisch-christlichen Dialog
FKDG	Forschungen zur Kirchen- und Dogmengeschichte
FKGG	Forschungen zur Kirchen- und Geistesgeschichte
FMG	Forschungen zur mittelalterlichen Geschichte
FOTC	T. K. Cheyne, *Founders of Old Testament Criticism: Biographical, Descriptive, and Critical Studies* (1893)
FOTL	Forms of the Old Testament Literature
FRLANT	Forschungen zur Religion und Literatur des Alten und Neuen Testaments
FSThR	Forschungen zur systematischen Theologie und Religionsphilosophie
FThL	Forum Theologiae Linguisti
FThSt	Freiburger Theologische Studien
FuF	Forschungen und Fortschritte
FzB	Forschung zur Bibel
GAT	Grundrisse zum Alten Testament
GBS	Guides to Biblical Scholarship
GCP	Graecitas Christianorum Primaeva
GCS	Griechischen christlichen Schriftsteller
GCT	Gender, Culture, Theory
GDEL	*Grand Dictionnaire Encyclopedique Larousse*
GGA	Göttingische gelehrte Anzeige

GHKEAT	H.-J. Kraus, *Geschichte der historisch-kritischen Erforschung des Alten Testaments* (1988[4])
GKB	Gesenius-Kautzsch-Bergsträsser, *Hebräische Grammatik*
GKC	Gesenius' Hebrew Grammar (ed. E. Kautzsch, tr. A. E. Cowley)
GNB	Good News Bible (TEV)
GNS	Good News Studies
GNT	Grundrisse zum Neuen Testament
GOF.S	Göttinger Orientforschung. Reihe 1. Syriaca
GOTR	*Greek Orthodox Theological Review*
GRBS	*Greek, Roman, and Byzantine Studies*
Greg	*Gregorianum*
GRLH	Garland Reference Library of the Humanities
GS	*Germanische Studien*
GSWW	G. W. Meyer, *Geschichte der Schrifterklärung seit der Wiederherstellung der Wissenschaften* (5 vols., 1802–9)
GT.S	Gesellschaft und Theologie. Systematische Beiträge
GTA	Göttinger theologische Arbeiten
GTS	Gettysburg Theological Studies
GTW	Grundriss der theologischen Wissenschaft
HAR	*Hebrew Annual Review*
HB	*Historische Bibliothek*
HBC	J. L. Mays et al. (eds.), *Harper's Bible Commentary* (1988)
HBD	P. J. Achtemeier et al. (eds.), *Harper's Bible Dictionary*
HBI	Heritage of Biblical Israel
HBK	Herders Bibelkommentar
HB/OT	M. Saebø (ed.), *Hebrew Bible, Old Testament: The History of Its Interpretation* (1996–)
HBT	*Horizons in Biblical Theology*
HCNT	Handkommentar zum Neuen Testament
HCT	History of Christian Theology
HDB	J. Hastings (ed.), *Dictionary of the Bible* (5 vols., 1898–1904)
HDivB	*Harvard Divinity Bulletin*
HDR	Harvard Dissertations in Religion
Her	*Hermathena*
HeyJ	*Heythrop Journal*
HHMBI	D. K. McKim (ed.), *Historical Handbook of Major Biblical Interpreters* (1998)
HHS	Harvard Historical Studies
HibJ	*Hibbert Journal*
HJ	*Historisches Jahrbuch*
HJPAJC	E. Schürer, *History of the Jewish People in the Age of Jesus Christ* (3 vols., rev. G. Vermes et al., 1973–87)
HJTM	Harvard Judaic Texts and Monographs
HKAT	Handkommentar zum Alten Testament
HKNT	Handkommentar zum Neuen Testament
HMPEC	*Historical Magazine of the Protestant Episcopal Church*
HNT	Handbuch zum Neuen Testament
HNTC	Harper's New Testament Commentaries
HNTR	*History of New Testament Research*
HO	Handbuch der Orientalistik
HR	*History of Religions*
HRWG	*Handbuch religionswissenschaftlicher Grundbegriffe*
HS	*Hebrew Studies*
HS	Historische Studien
HSAT	Die Heilige Schrift des Alten Testaments (ed. H. Herkenne and F. Feldmann)
HSAT(K)	Die Heilige Schrift des Alten Testaments (ed. E. Kautzsch)
HSM	Harvard Semitic Monographs
HSS	Harvard Semitic Studies
HTC	Herder's Theological Commentary on the New Testament
HThK	Herders theologischer Kommentar zum Neuen Testament
HTIBS	Historic Texts and Interpreters in Biblical Scholarship
HTKNT	Herders theologischer Kommentar zum Neuen Testament
HTR	*Harvard Theological Review*

HTS	Harvard Theological Studies
HUCA	*Hebrew Union College Annual*
HUCM	Monographs of the Hebrew Union College
HUT	Hermeneutische Untersuchungen zur Theologie
HVLÅ	K. Humanistiska vetenskapssamfundete i Lund Åraberättelse
HWP	*Historisches Wörterbuch der Philosophie*
HZ	*Historische Zeitschrift*
IAHD	International Archives of the History of Ideas
IB	*Interpreter's Bible*
IBC	Interpretation: A Bible Commentary for Teaching and Preaching
IBS	*Irish Biblical Studies*
IBT	Interpreting Biblical Texts
ICC	International Critical Commentary
IDB	G. A. Buttrick (ed.), *Interpreter's Dictionary of the Bible* (4 vols., 1962)
IDBSup	K. Crim (ed.), *Interpreter's Dictionary of the Bible: Supplementary Volume* (1976)
IEJ	*Israel Exploration Journal*
IER	*Irish Ecclesiastical Record*
IHE	Indice histórico español
IHE	*Introduction à l'histoire de l'exégèse*
IMW	*Internationale Monatsschrift für Wissenschaft, Kunst, und Technik*
InnTS	Innsbrucker theologische Studien
Int	*Interpretation*
IOS	*Israel Oriental Studies*
IPAT	*Introduction aux pseudépigraphes grecs d'Ancien Testament*
IRM	*International Review of Missions*
IRT	Issues in Religion and Theology
ISBE	G. W. Bromiley et al. (eds.), *International Standard Bible Encyclopedia* (4 vols., 1979–88)
ISBL	Indiana Studies in Biblical Literature
ITC	International Theological Commentary
IThS	Innsbrucker theologische Studien
ITQ	*Irish Theological Quarterly*
IUO	*Istituto Universitario Orientale*
JA	*Journal asiatique*
JAAR	*Journal of the American Academy of Religion*
JAC	Jahrbuch für Antike und Christentum
JAF	*Journal of American Folklore*
JAL	Jewish Apocryphal Literature
JANES	*Journal of the Ancient Near Eastern Society*
JANESCU	*Journal of the Ancient Near Eastern Society of Columbia University*
JAOS	*Journal of the American Oriental Society*
JAS	*Journal of Asian Studies*
JB	A. Jones (ed.), *Jerusalem Bible*
JBC	R. E. Brown, et al. (eds.), *The Jerome Biblical Commentary*
JBL	*Journal of Biblical Literature*
JBLMS	Journal of Biblical Literature Monograph Series
JBR	*Journal of Bible and Religion*
JBS	Jerusalem Biblical Studies
JBS	*Journal of British Studies*
JBTh	*Jahrbuch für biblische Theologie*
JBW	*Jahrbücher der biblischen Wissenschaft*
JCBRF	*The Journal of the Christian Brethren Research Fellowship*
JC	Jus canonicum
JCS	*Journal of Cuneiform Studies*
JDS	Judean Desert Series
JDTh	*Jahrbücher für deutsche Theologie*
JE	I. Singer et al. (eds.), *The Jewish Encyclopedia* (12 vols., 1901–6)
JEA	*Journal of Egyptian Archaeology*
JEAT	*Jahrbuch. Evangelische Akademie Tutzingen*
JEH	*Journal of Ecclesiastical History*
JEOL	*Jaarbericht . . . ex oriente lux*
JES	*Journal of Ecumenical Studies*

JETS	*Journal of the Evangelical Theological Society*
JFHS	*Journal of the Friends' Historical Society*
JFSR	*Journal of Feminist Studies in Religion*
JGNKG	*Jahrbuch der Gesellschaft für Niedersächsische Kirchengeschichte*
JGPrÖ	*Jahrbuch für die Geschichte des Protestantismus in Österreich*
JHI	*Journal of the History of Ideas*
JHMTh	*Journal of the History of Modern Theology*
JHNES	Johns Hopkins Near Eastern Studies
JHS	*Journal of Hellenic Studies*
JHSCW	*Journal of the Historical Society of the Church in Wales*
JIBS	*Journal of Indian and Buddhist Studies*
JIPh	*Journal of Indian Philosophy*
JITC	*The Journal of the Interdenominational Theological Center*
JJS	*Journal of Jewish Studies*
JLB	*Jüdisches Literaturblatt*
JLR	*Journal of Law and Religion*
JLT	*Journal of Literature and Theology*
JMES	*Journal of Middle Eastern Studies*
JMRS	*Journal of Medieval and Renaissance Studies*
JMS	*Journal of Mithraic Studies*
JNES	*Journal of Near Eastern Studies*
JNSL	*Journal of Northwest Semitic Languages*
JP	*Journal of Philology*
JPH	*Journal of Presbyterian History*
JPh	*Journal of Philosophy*
JPOS	*Journal of Palestine Oriental Society*
JPSTC	Jewish Publication Society—The JPS Torah Commentary
JPSV	Jewish Publication Society Version
JPT	*Jahrbücher für protestantische Theologie*
JQR	*Jewish Quarterly Review*
JQRMS	Jewish Quarterly Review Monograph Series
JQRS	Jewish Quarterly Review Supplements
JR	*Journal of Religion*
JRAS	*Journal of the Royal Asiatic Society*
JRE	*Journal of Religious Ethics*
JRelS	*Journal of Religious Studies*
JRH	*Journal of Religious History*
JrnlRelAfr	*Journal of Religion in Africa*
JRS	*Journal of Roman Studies*
JRT	*Journal of Religious Thought*
JSHRZ	W. G. Kümmel at al. (eds.), Jüdische Schriften aus hellenistisch-römischer Zeit (1973–)
JSJ	*Journal for the Study of Judaism in the Persian, Hellenistic, and Roman Period*
JSJSup	Journal for the Study of Judaism in the Persian, Hellenistic and Roman Period, Supplement
JSJT	*Jerusalem Studies in Jewish Thought*
JSL	*Journal of Sacred Literature*
JSNT	*Journal for the Study of the New Testament*
JSNTSup	Journal for the Study of the New Testament. Supplement Series
JSOT	*Journal for the Study of the Old Testament*
JSOTSup	Journal for the Study of the Old Testament. Supplement Series
JSP	*Journal for the Study of the Pseudepigrapha*
JSPSup	Journal for the Study of the Pseudepigrapha. Supplement Series
JSS	*Journal of Semitic Studies*
JSSR	*Journal for the Scientific Study of Religion*
JSSSup	Journal of Semitic Studies. Supplement Series
JTC	*Journal for Theology and the Church*
JTL	*Journal für theologische Literatur*
JTS	*Journal of Theological Studies*
JTSA	*Journal of Theology for Southern Africa*
JudUm	Judentum und Umwelt

JuSS	Judaica Studies Series
JWCI	*Journal of the Warburg and Courtauld Institutes*
JZWL	*Jüdische Zeitschrift für Wissenschaft und Leben*
KantSt.E	Kantian Studies
KAO	Im Kampf um den Alten Orient
KAT	Kommentar zum Alten Testament
KB	L. Koehler and W. Baumgartner, *Lexicon in Veteris Testamenti libros*
KBANT	Kommentare und Beiträge zum Alten und Neuen Testament
KD	*Kerygma und Dogma*
KEH	Kurzgefasstes exegetisches Handbuch zum Alten Testament
KEHA	Kurzgefasstes exegetisches Handbuch zu des Apokryphen des Alten Testaments
KEK	Kritisch-exegetischer Kommentar über das Neue Testament (Meyer-Kommentar)
KHC	*Kurzer Hand-Commentar zum Alten Testament*
KJV	King James Version
KK	Kurzgefasster Kommentar zu den heiligen Schriften Alten und Neuen Testamentes
Klio.B	Klio. Leipzig. Beiheft
KlT	Kleine Texte für (theologische und philologische) Vorlesungen und Übungen
KS	*Kirjath-Sepher*
KT	Kaiser-Traktate/Kaiser-Taschenbücher
LAPO	Littèratures anciennes du Proche-Orient
LÄS	Leipziger ägyptologische Studien
LB	*Linguistica Biblica*
LBS	Library of Biblical Studies
LCC	Library of Christian Classics
LCL	Loeb Classical Library
LCT	Library of Constructive Theology
LD	Lectio divina
LEC	Library of Early Christianity
Leš	*Lešonénu*
LibRel	The Library of Religion
LJS	Lives of Jesus Series
LLAVT	E. Vogt, *Lexicon linguae aramaicae Veteris Testamenti* (1971)
LLP	Library of Living Philosophers
LouvSt	*Louvain Studies*
LPGL	G. W. H. Lampe (ed.), *Patristic Greek Lexicon* (1968)
LPT	Library of Protestant Thought
LQ	*Lutheran Quarterly*
LR	*Lutherische Rundschau*
LS	*Louvain Studies*
LSJ	Liddell-Scott-Jones, *Greek-English Lexicon*
LSSk.T	Det Laerde selskabs skrifter, Teologiske skrifter
LTK	J. Höfer and K. Rahner (eds.), *Lexicon für Theologie und Kirche* (2nd ed., 11 vols., 1957–67)
LTP	*Laval théologique et philosophique*
LUÅ	Lunds universitets årsskrift
LW	J. Pelikan and H. T. Lehman (eds.), *Luther's Works*
LW	*Lutheran World*
MBA	Y. Aharoni and M. Avi-Yonah. *Macmillan Bible Atlas* (1977)
MBM	Münchener Beiträge zur Mediävistik und Renaissance-Forschung
MBTh	Münsterische Beiträge zur Theologie
McCQ	*McCormick Quarterly*
MDOG	Mitteilungen der deutschen Orient-Gesellschaft
MennEnc	*Mennonite Encyclopedia*
MennQR	*Mennonite Quarterly Review*
MethH	*Methodist History*
MeyerK	H. A. W. Meyer, Kritisch-exegetischer Kommentar uber das Neue Testament
MFC	Message of the Fathers of the Church
MGH	*Monumenta Germaniae historica*
MGH.L	*Monumenta Germaniae historica. Leges*
MGH.PL	*Monumenta Germaniae historica. Poetae Latinae medii aevi*
MGWJ	*Monatsschrift für Geschichte und Wissenschaft des Judentums*
MM	J.H. Moulton and G. Milligan, *The Vocabulary of the Greek Testament*

MMHST	Münchner Monographien zur historischen und systematischen Theologie
MMT	The Making of Modern Theology
MNTC	Moffatt NT Commentary
MNDPV	Mitteilungen und Nachrichten des Deutschen Palästina-Vereins
MPAIBL	*Mémoires présentés à l'Académie des inscriptions et belles-lettres*
MPIL	Monographs of the Peshitta Institute Leiden
MPT	Manuels et précis de théologie
MQR	*Methodist Quarterly Review*
MRS	Mission de Ras Shamra
MRTS	Medieval and Renaissance Texts and Studies
MScRel	*Mélanges de science religieuse*
MSHH	J. P. Nicéron, *Mémoires pour servir à l'histoire des hommes illustres dans la République des Lettres, avec un catologue raisonné des leurs ouvrages* (43 vols. in 44, 1727–45)
MSME	Michigan Series on the Middle East
MSU	Mitteilungen des Septuaginta-Unternehmens
MThZ	*Münchener theologische Zeitschrift*
MTS	Marburger Theologische Studien
MUN	*Mémoires de l'Université de Neuchâtel*
Mus	*Muséon*
MUSJ	*Mélanges de l'université Saint-Joseph*
MVAG	Mitteilungen der vorderasiatisch-ägyptischen Gesellschaft
MW	*Muslim World*
NAB	New American Bible
NABPR.SS	National Association of Baptist Professors of Religion Special Studies Series
NAKG	*Nederlands(ch) archief voor kerkgeschiedenis*
NASB	New American Standard Bible
NBC	Nelson's Bible Commentary
NBG	*Nouvelle biographie (universelle) générale*
NBl	*New Blackfriars*
NBW	*Nationaal biografisch woordenboek*
NCB	New Clarendon Bible
NCBC	New Century Bible Commentary
NCCHS	R. D. Fuller et al. (eds.), *New Catholic Commentary on Holy Scripture* (1969)
NCE	M. R. P. McGuire et al. (eds.), *New Catholic Encyclopedia* (1967–)
NCeB	New Century Bible
NCRTW	N. Smart at al. (eds.), *Nineteenth Century Religious Thought in the West* (3 vols., 1985)
NDB	*Neue deutsche Biographie*
NDIEC	*New Documents Illustrating Early Christianity*
NEB	Die Neue Echter Bibel
NEB.AT	Neue Echter Bibel. Kommentar zum AT
NedThT	*Nederlands theologisch tijdschrift*
Neot	*Neotestamentica*
NFT	New Frontiers in Theology
NGWG	Nachrichten (von) der Gesellschaft der Wissenschaften (zu) in Göttingen
NHC	Nag Hammadi Codex
NHCT	D. W. Musser and J. L Price (eds.), *A New Handbook of Christian Theologians* (1996)
NHS	Nag Hammadi Studies
NIB	*New Interpreter's Bible*
NICNT	New International Commentary on the New Testament
NICOT	New International Commentary on the Old Testament
NIGTC	The New International Greek Testament Commentary
NIV	New International Version
NJB	H. Wansbrough (ed.), *New Jerusalem Bible* (1985)
NJBC	R. E. Brown et al. (eds.), *The New Jerome Biblical Commentary* (1990)
NKJV	New King James Version
NKZ	*Neue kirchliche Zeitschrift*
NNBW	*Nieuw nederlandsch biografisch woordenboek*
NND	*Neuer Nekrolog der Deutschen*
NNM	Numismatic Notes and Monographs

NorTT	*Norsk Teologisk Tidsskrift*
NovT	*Novum Testamentum*
NovTSup	Novum Testamentum, Supplements
NPNF	Nicene and Post-Nicene Fathers
NRSV	New Revised Standard Version
NRT	*La nouvelle revue théologique*
NS	Nietzsche-Studien
NSchol	*New Scholasticism*
NSHERK	S. M. Jackson (ed.), *New Schaff-Herzog Encyclopedia of Religious Knowledge* (12 vols., 1908–12)
NTA	*New Testament Abstracts*
NTAbh	Neutestamentliche Abhandlungen
NTD	Das Neue Testament Deutsch
NTF	Neutestamentliche Forschungen
NTG	Neue theologische Grundrisse
NTGu	New Testament Guides
NTHIP	W. G. Kümmel, *The NT: The History of the Investigation of Its Problems* (1970; ET 1972)
NThJ	*Neues theologisches Journal*
NThS	*Nieuwe theologische studien*
NTL	New Testament Literature
NTLi	New Testament Library
NTOA	Novum Testamentum et Orbis Antiquus
NTRG	New Testament Reading Guide
NTS	*New Testament Studies*
NTT	*Norsk teologisk tidsskrift*
NTTS	New Testament Tools and Studies
Numen	*Numen: International Review for the History of Religions*
NUSPEP	Northwestern University Studies in Phenomenology and Existential Philosophy
NZM	*Neue Zeitschrift für Missionswissenschaft*
NZST	*Neue Zeitschrift für systematische Theologie*
OAI	Orient ancien illustré
OBL	Orientalia et biblica lovaniensia
OBO	Orbis biblicus et orientalis
ÖBS	Österreichische biblische Studien
OBT	Overtures to Biblical Theology
OCA	Orientalia Christiana analecta
OCD	M. Cary et al. (eds.), *The Oxford Classical Dictionary* (1966)
ODCC	F. L. Cross and E. A Livingstone (eds.), *Oxford Dictionary of the Christian Church* (1997)
OEB	J. D. Michaelis (ed.), *Orientalische und exegetische Bibliothek* (24 vols. in 6, 1771–89)
OECS	Oxford Early Christian Studies
OECT	Oxford Early Christian Texts
ÖEH	Ökuminische Existenz heute
OIP	Oriental Institute Publications
OLA	Orientalia lovaniensia analecta
OLP	Orientalia lovaniensia periodica
OLZ	*Orientalische Literaturzeitung*
Or	*Orientalia* (Rome)
OrAnt	*Oriens antiquus*
OrChr	*Oriens christianus*
OrSyr	*L'orient syrien*
OSHT	Oxford Studies in Historical Theology
OstKSt	Ostkirchliche Studien
OTA	*Old Testament Abstracts*
ÖTBK	Ökumenischer Taschenbuch-kommentar
ÖTBK/NT	Ökumenischer Taschenbuch-kommentar, Neues Testament
OTCNC	J. W. Rogerson, *Old Testament Criticism in the Nineteenth Century: England and Germany* (1984)
OTE	*Old Testament Essays*
OTGu	Old Testament Guides

OTL	Old Testament Library
OTM	Oxford Theological Monographs
OTP	J. H. Charlesworth (ed.), *The Old Testament Pseudepigrapha* (2 vols., 1983)
OTRG	Old Testament Reading Guide
OTS	*Oudtestamentische Studiën*
OWS	Oxford-Warburg Studies
PAAJR	*Proceedings of the American Academy of Jewish Research*
PAPS	*Proceedings of the American Philosophical Society*
PatMS	Patristic Monograph Series
PBA	*Proceedings of the British Academy*
PBiS	Pamphlet Bible Series
PCB	M. Black and H. H. Rowley (eds.), *Peake's Commentary on the Bible* (1962)
PEFQS	*Palestine Exploration Fund, Quarterly Statement*
PEQ	*Palestine Exploration Quarterly*
PerspRelStud	*Perspectives in Religious Studies*
PerTeol	*Perspectiva theólogica*
PG	J. Migne, *Patrologia graeca*
PGM	K. Preisendanz (ed.), *Papyri graecae magicae*
PhAnt	Philosophia antiqua
PhEW	*Philosophy East and West*
PhRev	*Philosophical Review*
PIASH	*Proceedings of the Israel Academy of Sciences and Humanities*
PIBA	*Proceedings of the Irish Biblical Association*
PIOL	Publications de l'Institut Orientaliste de Louvain
PJ	*Palästina-Jahrbuch*
PL	J. Migne, *Patrologia latina*
PLO	Porta linguarum orientalium
PMLA	Publications of the Modern Language Association of America
PMS	Publications in Mediaeval Studies
PNTC	Pelican New Testament Commentaries
PO	Patrologia orientalis
POT	Princeton Oriental Texts
PrEc	*Presencia ecuménica*
PresR	*Presbyterian Review*
PrM	*Protestantische Monatshefte*
PRU	*Le palais royal d'Ugarit*
PSB	*Princeton Seminary Bulletin*
PSBA	*Proceedings of the Society of Biblical Archaeology*
PSTJ	*Perkins (School of Theology) Journal*
PTA	Papyrologische Texte und Abhandlungen
PThMS	Pittsburgh Theological Monograph Series
PTMS	Princeton Theological Monograph Series
PTS	Patristische Texte und Studien
PUM.H	Publications of the University of Manchester. Historical Series
PVTG	Pseudepigrapha Veteris Testamenti graece
PW	Pauly-Wissowa, *Real-Encyclopädie der classischen Altertumswissenschaft*
PWS	Pietist and Wesleyan Studies
PWSup	Supplement to PW
QD	Quaestiones disputatae
QDAP	*Quarterly of the Department of Antiquities in Palestine*
QFAGG	Quellen und Forschungen zur alten Geschichte und Geographie
QFRG	Quellen und Forschungen zur Reformationsgeschichte
QR	*Quarterly Review: A Scholarly Journal for Reflection on Ministry*
QR	Quellen der Religionsgeschichte
RA	*Revue d'assyriologie et d'archéologie orientale*
RAC	*Reallexikon für Antike und Christentum*
RACSup	Reallexikon für Antike und Christentum Supplements
RANE	Records of the Ancient Near East
RArch	*Revue archéologique*
RB	*Revue biblique*
RBén	*Revue bénédictine*
RBMA	*Repertorium biblicum medii aevi*

RBML	*Repertorium für biblische und morgenländische Literatur*
RCB	*Revista de cultura biblica*
RdQ	*Revue de Qumrán*
RE	A. Hauck (ed.), *Realencyklopädie für protestantische Theologie und Kirche* (24 vols., 1896–1913)
REA	*Revue des études augustiniennes*
REB	Revised English Bible
REB	*Revista eclesiástica brasileira*
RechBib	Recherches bibliques
REg	*Revue d'égyptologie*
REJ	*Revue des études juives*
RelLife	*Religion in Life*
RelS	*Religious Studies*
RelSoc	*Religion and Society*
RenQ	*Renaissance Quarterly*
RES	*Revue des études sémitiques*
ResQ	*Restoration Quarterly*
RevExp	*Review and Expositor*
RevistB	*Revista biblica*
RevQ	*Revue de Qumran*
RevScRel	*Revue des sciences religieuses*
RevSém	*Revue sémitique*
RevThom	*Revue thomiste*
RG	*Religion und Geisteskultur*
RGG	*Religion in Geschichte und Gegenwart*
RGS	E. Stange (ed.), *Die Religionswissenschaft der Gegenwart in Selbstdarstellungen* (5 vols., 1925–29)
RgV	Religionsgeschichtliche Volksbücher
RH	*Revue historique*
RHA	*Revue hittite et asianique*
RHE	*Revue d'histoire ecclésiastique*
RHPR	*Revue d'histoire et de philosophie religieuses*
RHR	*Revue de l'histoire des religions*
RiB	Revista interamericana de bibliografia
RICP	*Revue de l'Institut Catholique de Paris*
RIL.L	Rendiconti. Istituto lombardo di scienze e lettere. Classe di lettere e scienze morali e storiche
RivB	*Rivista biblica*
RLA	E. Ebeling et al. (eds.), *Reallexikon der Assyriologie* (1932–)
RLS	*Repertorium der lateinischen Sermones des Mittelalters*
RMM	B. Feldman and R. D. Richardson (eds.), *The Rise of Modern Mythology, 1680–1860* (1972)
RMT	Readings in Moral Theology
RNT	Regensburger Neues Testament
ROMM	*Revue de l'occident Musulman et da la mediterraneé*
RQ	*Römische Quartalschrift für christliche Altertumskunde und Kirchengeschichte*
RR	*Review of Religion*
RSO	*Revista degli studi orientali*
RSPT	*Revue des sciences philosophiques et théologiques*
RSR	*Recherches de science religieuse*
RSS	*Rome and the Study of Scripture* (1962[7])
RSSH	Recherches et synthèses. Section d'Histoire
RStR	*Religious Studies Review*
RSV	Revised Standard Version
RT	*Rabbinische Texte*
RTAM	*Recherches de théologie ancienne et médievale*
RTL	*Revue théologique de Louvain*
RTM	*Revista di teologia morale*
RTP	*Revue de théologie et de philosophie*
RUO	*Revue de l'Université d'Ottawa*
RV	Revised Version
SABS	Studies in American Biblical Scholarship

SacEr	*Sacris erudiri*
SacPag	Sacra Pagina
SANT	Studien zum Alten und Neuen Testament
SAOC	Studies in Ancient Oriental Civilization
SAQ	Sammlung ausgewahlter kirchen-und dogmengeschichtlicher Quellenschriften
SAT	Schriften des Alten Testaments in Auswahl
SB	Sources bibliques
SB(J)	Sainte bible traduite en français sous la direction de l'École Biblique de Jérusalem
SBA	Studies in Biblical Archaeology
SBAW	*Sitzungsberichte der bayerischen Akademie der Wissenschaften*
SBB	Stuttgarter biblische Beiträge
SBEC	Studies of the Bible and Early Christianity
SBFLA	*Studii biblici franciscani liber annuus*
SBJ	*La sainte bible de Jérusalem*
SBLABS	SBL Archaeology and Biblical Studies
SBLAS	SBL Aramaic Studies
SBLASP	SBL Abstracts and Seminar Papers
SBLBAC	SBL The Bible in American Culture
SBLBMI	SBL The Bible and Its Modern Interpreters
SBLBSNA	SBL Biblical Scholarship in North America
SBLDS	SBL Dissertation Series
SBLEJL	SBL Early Judaism and Its Literature
SBLMasS	SBL Masoretic Studies
SBLMS	SBL Monograph Series
SBLNTGF	SBL The New Testament in the Greek Fathers
SBLRBS	SBL Resources for Biblical Study
SBLSBS	SBL Sources for Biblical Study
SBLSCS	SBL Septuagint and Cognate Studies
SBLSP	SBL Seminar Papers
SBLSPSS	SBL Seminar Papers Series
SBLSS	SBL Semeia Studies
SBLTT	SBL Texts and Translations
SBLWAW	SBL Writings of the Ancient World
SBM	Stuttgarter biblische Monographien
SBONT	Sacred Books of the Old and New Testaments
SBOT	Sacred Books of the Old Testament
SBS	Stuttgarter Bibelstudien
SBT	Studies in Biblical Theology
SbWGF	*Sitzungsberichte der Wissenschaftlichen Gesellschaft*...Frankfurt a. M.
SC	Sources chrétiennes
ScEccl	*Sciences ecclésiastiques*
ScEs	*Science et esprit*
SCES	Sixteenth-century Essays and Studies
SCH	Studies in Church History
SCHNT	Studia ad corpus hellenisticum novi testamenti
SchwR	*Schweizer (1,1900–44, 1944: Schweizerische) Rundschau*
SCJ	*Sixteenth-century Journal*
SCM	Studies in the Christian Movement
SCR	*Studies in Comparative Religion*
ScrB	*Scripture Bulletin*
ScrHier	Scripta hierosolymitana
SCS	Studies of Church and State
SD	Studies and Documents
SDGSTh	Studien zur Dogmengeschichte und systematischen Theologie
SE	*Studia Evangelica I, II, III* (= TU 73 [1959]; 87 [1964]; 88 [1964]; etc.)
SEÅ	*Svensk exegetisk årsbok*
SEAJT	*South-east Asia Journal of Theology*
SecCent	*The Second Century*
Sef	*Sefarad*
Sem	*Semitica*
SemSup	Semeia Supplements
SFSHJ	South Florida Studies in the History of Judaism

SG	Sammlung Göschen
SGKIO	Studien zur Geschichte und Kultur des islamischen Orients
SGV	Sammlung gemeinverständlicher Vorträge und Schriften
SHANE	Studies in the History of the Ancient Near East
SHAW	Sitzungsberichte der heidelberger Akademie der Wissenschaften
SHAW.PH	Sitzungsberichte der heidelberger Akademie der Wissenschaften. Philosophisch-historische Klasse
SHCANE	Studies in the History and Culture of the Ancient Near East
SHCT	Studies in the History of Christian Thought
SHR	Studies in the History of Religions
SHT	Studies in Historical Theology
SHVL	Skrifter utgivna av (K.) Humanistika Vetenskapssamfundet i Lund
SIB	Studies of the Institute Pierre Bayle
SIGC	Studien zur interkulturellen Geschichte des Christentums
SJ	Studia judaica
SJCA	Studies in Judaism and Christianity in Antiquity
SJLA	Studies in Judaism in Late Antiquity
SJOT	*Scandinavian Journal of the Old Testament*
SJT	*Scottish Journal of Theology*
SKG.G	Schriften der Königsberger Gelehrten Gesellschaft. Geisteswissenschaftliche Klasse
SKI	Studien zu Kirche und Israel
SLH	Scriptores Latini Hiberniae
SLTGNT	Studies in the Lectionary Text of the Greek New Testament
SMC	Studies in Medieval Culture
SMHVL	Scripta minora. K. Humanistika Vetenskapssamfundet e Lund
SMRH	Studies in Medieval and Renaissance History
SMRT	Studies in Medieval and Reformation Thought
SMSR	*Studi e materiali di storia delle religioni*
SNT	Studien zum Neuen Testament
SNTSMS	Society for New Testament Studies Monograph Series
SNumen	Supplements to Numen
SO	Symbolae osloenses
SOR	Studies in Oriental Religions
SOTI	Studies in Old Testament Interpretation
SOTSMS	Society for Old Testament Study Monograph Series
SP	*Studies in Philology*
SP	Studies in Philosophy
SPap	*Studia papyrologica*
SPAW	Sitzungsberichte der preussischen Akademie der Wissenschaften
SPB	Studia postbiblica
SPCIC	*Studiorum Paulinorum Congressus Internationalis Catholicus* (2 vols., 1963)
SPhA	*Studia Philonica Annual*
SPIB	Scripta Pontificii Instituti Biblici
SPMed	Studia patristica Mediolanensia
SPSHS	Scholars Press Studies in the Humanities Series
SQAW	Schriften und Quellen der alten Welt
SR	*Studies in Religion/Sciences religieuses*
SRC	Studies in Religion and Culture
SSAW	Sitzungsberichte der Sächsischen Akademie der Wissenschaften zu Leipzig
SSAW.PH	Sitzungsberichte der Sächsischen Akademie der Wissenschaften zu Leipzig. Philosophisch-historische Klasse
SSEA	Schriften der Studiengemeinschaft der Evangelischen Akademien
SSL	Spicilegium sacrum Lovaniense
SSN	Studia semitica neerlandica
SSS	Semitic Study Series
SStLL	Studies in Semitic Language and Linguistics
ST	Studies in Theology
STÅ	*Svensk teologisk årsskrift*
StABH	Studies in American Biblical Hermeneutics
StB	Studia biblica
StD	Studies and Documents

StDel	Studia Delitzschiana
STDJ	Studies on the Texts of the Desert of Judah
StEv	*Studia Evangelica*
SThGG	Studien zur theologie und Geistesgeschichte des neunzehnten Jahrhunderts
STK	*Svensk teologisk kvartalskrift*
STL	Studia theologica Lundensia
StMed	*Studi medievali*
StPatr	*Studia patristica*
StPhilo	*Studia Philonica*
Str-B	[H.Strack and] P. Billerbeck, *Kommentar zum Neuen Testament*
StRos	*Studia Rosenthaliana*
STS	Sacrae theologiae summa
StTh	*Studia theologica*
STU	*Schweizerische theologische Umschau*
StudNeot	Studia neotestamentica
StudOr	Studia orientalia
StZ	*Stimmen der Zeit*
SubBi	Subsidia biblica
SUNT	Studien zur Umwelt des Neuen Testaments
SUVK	Videnskapsselskapets skrifter
SVBL	Svenskt biografiskt lexikon
SVEC	Studies on Voltaire and the Eighteenth Century
SVRG	Schriften des Vereins für Reformationsgeschichte
SVTP	Studia in Veteris Testamenti pseudepigrapha
SVTQ	*St. Vladimir's Theological Quarterly*
SWBA	Social World of Biblical Antiquity
SWR	Studies in Women and Religion
SymBU	Symbolae biblicae upsalienses
TANZ	Texte und Arbeiten zum neutestamentlichen Zeitalter
TAPA	*Transactions of the American Philological Association*
TARWPV	Theologische Arbeiten aus dem Rheinischen Wissenschaftlichen Prediger-Verein
TAVO	Tübinger Atlas des Vorderen Orients
TAzB	Texte und Arbeiten zur Bibel
TBC	Torch Bible Commentaries
TBei	*Theologische Beiträge*
TBl	*Theologische Blätter*
TBT	*The Bible Today*
TBü	Theologische Bücherei
TCGNT	B. M. Metzger, *A Textual Commentary on the Greek New Testament* (1975)
TD	Textus et documenta
TD	*Theology Digest*
TDNT	G. Kittel and G. Friedrich (eds.), *Theological Dictionary of the New Testament* (10 vols., 1964–76)
TDOT	G. J. Botterweck and H. Ringgren (eds.), *Theological Dictionary of the Old Testament*
TdT	H. J. Schultz (ed.), *Tendenzen der Theologie im 20. Jahrhundert* (1966)
TEAS	Twaynes English Authors Series
TED	Translations of Early Documents
TEH	Theologische Existenz heute
TeU	Tekst en uitleg
TEV	Today's English Version
TF	Theologische Forschung
TG	B. Moeller (ed.), *Theologie in Göttingen: Eine Vorlesungsreihe* (1987)
TGl	*Theologie und Glaube*
TH	Theologie historique
ThA	Theologische Arbeiten
ThBer	Theologische Berichte
ThBl	*Theologische Blätter*
THBW	Theologisch-homiletisches Bibelwerk
TheoDis	Theologische Dissertationen
THFen	Theologia Fennica
ThJb	*Theologisches Jahrbuch. Gütersloh*

ThJber	*Theologischer Jahresbericht. Leipzig*
ThJb(T)	*Theologische Jahrbücher. Tübingen*
THKNT	Theologischer Handkommentar zum Neuen Testament
ThL	Theologische Lehrbücher
ThÖ	Theologie der Ökumene
THR	Travaux d'humanisme et Renaissance
ThStud	Theologische Studien
ThT	*Theologisch tijdschrift*
ThTh	Themen der Theologie
ThV	*Theologische Versuche*
TJT	*Toronto Journal of Theology*
TLNT	C. Spicq, *Theological Lexicon of the New Testament* (3 vols., 1994)
TLZ	*Theologische Literaturzeitung*
TMLT	Toronto Medieval Latin Texts
TNTC	Tyndale New Testament Commentaries
TOT	A. W. Hastings and E. Hastings (eds.), *Theologians of Our Time* (1966)
TOTC	Tyndale Old Testament Commentaries
TP	*Theologie und Philosophie*
TPINTC	Trinty Press International New Testament Commentaries
TPMA	Textes philosophiques du moyen âge
TPNZJ	M. Greschat (ed.), *Theologen des Protestantismus im 19. und 20. Jahrhundert* (2 vols., 1978)
TPQ	*Theologisch-praktische Quartalschrift*
TQ	*Theologische Quartalschrift*
TR	*Theologická revue*
TRE	*Theologische Realenzyklopädie*
TRev	*Theologische Revue*
TRHS	*Transactions of the Royal Historical Society*
TRu	*Theologische Rundschau*
TS	Texts and Studies
TS	*Theological Studies*
TSAJ	Texte und Studien zum antiken Judentum
TSB	Theologische Studien. Basel
TSBA	*Transactions of the Society of Biblical Archaeology*
TSJTSA	Texts and Studies of the Jewish Theological Seminary of America
TSK	*Theologische Studien und Kritiken*
TSSI	J. C. L. Gibson, *Textbook of Syrian Semitic Inscriptions* (3 vols., 1971–82)
TSTS	Toronto Semitic Texts and Studies
TT	*Teologisk Tidsskrift*
TTK	*Tidsskrift for teologie og kirke*
TToday	*Theology Today*
TTS	Trierer theologische Studien
TTZ	*Trierer theologische Zeitschrift*
TU	Texte und Untersuchungen
TUAT	*Texte aus der Umwelt des Alten Testament*
TübTS	Tübinger theologische Studien
TUMSR	Trinity University Monograph Series in Religion
TW	*Theologie und Wirklichkeit*
TWAT	G. J. Botterweck and H. Ringgren (eds.), *Theologisches Wörterbuch zum Alten Testament*
TWNT	G. Kittel and G. Friedrich (eds.), *Theologisches Wörterbuch zum Neuen Testament*
TynBul	*Tyndale Bulletin*
TynNTL	Tyndale New Testament Lecture
TZ	Theologie en zielzorg
TZ	*Theologische Zeitschrift*
TZT	Texte zur Theologie
TZT	*Tübinger Zeitschrift für Theologie*
UBL	Ugaritisch-biblische Literatur
UBSGNT	United Bible Societies *Greek New Testament*
UBS.MS	United Bible Societies. Monograph Series
UCOP	University of Cambridge. Oriental Publication
UF	*Ugarit-Forschungen*

UNT	Untersuchungen zum Neuen Testament
UPATS	University of Pennsylvania Armenian Texts and Studies
USFSHJ	University of South Florida Studies in the History of Judaism
USQR	*Union Seminary Quarterly Review*
UTB	Uni-Taschenbücher
UTQ	*University of Toronto Quarterly*
UUÅ	Uppsala universitets årsskrift
VC	*Vigiliae christianae*
VCaro	*Verbum caro*
VCSup	Vigiliae christianae Supplements
VD	*Verbum domini*
VE	*Vida e espiritualidad*
VF	*Verkündigung und Forschung*
VIEGM	Veröffentlichungen des Instituts für Europäische Geschichte Mainz
VS	Verbum salutis
VSAT	Verbum Salutis, Ancien Testament
VT	*Vetus Testamentum*
VTG	*Vetus Testamentum Graecum*
VTSup	Vetus Testamentum, Supplements
VVAW	Verhandelingen van de koninklijke. Academie voor Wetenschappen, Letteren en Schone Kunsten van België
WA	M. Luther, Kritische Gesamtausgabe (= "Weimar" edition)
WB	Die Welt der Bibel
WBC	Word Biblical Commentary
WC	Westminster Commentaries
WdF	Wege der Forschung
WF	*Westfälische Zeitschrift*
WHJP	World History of the Jewish People
WiWei	*Wissenschaft und Weisheit*
WMANT	Wissenschaftliche Monographien zum Alten und Neuen Testament
WMS	Wolfenbütteler Mittelalter Studien
WO	*Die Welt des Orients*
WSA	Wolfenbütteler Studien zur Aufklärung
WSPL	Warwick Studies in Philosophy and Literature
WTJ	*Westminster Theological Journal*
WTS	Wijsgerige teksten en studies
WuD	*Wort und Dienst*
WUNT	Wissenschaftliche Untersuchungen zum Neuen Testament
WVDOG	Wissenschaftliche Veröffentlichungen der deutschen Orientgesellschaft
WW	*Word and World*
WZ(G)	*Wissenschaftliche Zeitschrift der Ernst-Moritz-Arndt-Universität Greifswald*
WZ(H)	*Wissenschaftliche Zeitschrift der Martin-Luther-Universität Halle-Wittenberg*
WZ(H).GS	*Wissenschaftliche Zeitschrift der Martin-Luther-Universität Halle-Wittenberg. Gesellschafts- und sprachwissenschaftliche Reihe*
WZ(J)	*Wissenschaftliche Zeitschrift der Friedrich-Schiller-Universität Jena*
WZKM	*Wiener Zeitschrift für die Kunde des Morgenlandes*
WZKSO	*Wiener Zeitschrift für die Kunde Süd- und Ostasiens und Archiv für indische Philosophie*
WZ(L)	*Wissenschaftliche Zeitschrift der Karl-Marx-Universität Leipzig*
YHP	Yale Historical Publications
YJS	Yale Judaica Series
YNER	Yale Near Eastern Researches
YOS	Yale Oriental Series
YOS.MS	Yale Oriental Series. Manuscript Series
YOS.R	Yale Oriental Series. Researches
YPR	Yale Publications in Religion
YSR	Yale Studies in Religion
ZA	*Zeitschrift für Assyriologie*
ZAH	*Zeitschrift für Althebraistik*
ZÄS	*Zeitschrift für ägyptische Sprache*
ZAW	*Zeitschrift für die alttestamentliche Wissenschaft*
ZBK	Zürcher Bibelkommentar

ZBNT	Zürcher Bibelkommentar/Neues Testament
ZDMG	*Zeitschrift der deutschen morgenländischen Gesellschaft*
ZDPV	*Zeitschrift des deutschen Pälastina-Vereins*
ZdZ	*Die Zeichen der Zeit*
ZEE	*Zeitschrift für evangelische Ethik*
ZfHB	*Zeitschrift für hebräische Bibliographie*
ZGJD	*Zeitschrift für die Geschichte der Juden in Deutschland*
ZGSHG	*Zeitschrift der Gesellschaft für Schleswig-Holsteinische Geschichte*
ZHT	*Zeitschrift für historische Theologie*
ZKG	*Zeitschrift für Kirchengeschichte*
ZKM	*Zeitschrift für die Kunde des Morgenlandes*
ZKT	*Zeitschrift für katholische Theologie*
ZKWL	*Zeitschrift für kirchliche Wissenschaft und kirchliches Leben*
ZLThK	*Zeitschrift für die (gesammte) lutherische Theologie und Kirche*
ZMR	*Zeitschrift für Missionskunde und Religionswissenschaft*
ZNThG	*Zeitschrift für neuere Theologiegeschichte*
ZNW	*Zeitschrift für die neutestamentliche Wissenschaft*
ZPrTh	*Zeitschrift für praktische Theologie*
ZRG	*Zeitschrift für Rechtsgeschichte*
ZRGG	*Zeitschrift für Religions- und Geistesgeschichte*
ZRIJ	*Zeitschrift für die religiösen Interessen des Judenthums*
ZS	*Zeitschrift für Semitistik*
ZST	*Zeitschrift für systematische Theologie*
ZTK	*Zeitschrift für Theologie und Kirche*
ZWT	*Zeitschrift für wissenschaftliche Theologie*

PREFACE

In 1646 the scientist-theologian John Wilkins (1614-72), a main organizer and first secretary of the Royal Society (chartered July 15, 1662), published *Ecclesiastes: Or, a Discourse Concerning the Gift of Preaching as It Falls Under the Rules of Art*. Much of the work was taken up by a bibliography that listed basic titles on various topics for the general minister. In the seventh edition (1693), pages 58-105 (double columns with only authors' names) listed the essential commentators on biblical books. The average cleric must have been overwhelmed by the extent of the bibliography. A similar list of works published since the seventeenth century would no doubt overwhelm Wilkins himself, were he a modern contemporary.

The *Dictionary of Biblical Interpretation* is intended as an aid and guide to the lengthy and complex history of biblical interpretation. Three types of articles appear in the work. (1) The history of the interpretation of all the canonical and deuterocanonical books as well of some other ancient non-biblical books is covered in one category of articles. In these essays emphasis has been placed on the last two centuries of interpretation. (2) The biographies and contributions of numerous interpreters are discussed in a second category of articles. In this area, no work can be exhaustive and differences of opinion would result in varying lists of entries. As the work goes to press, the editor could even suggest some modifications in the present entry list. The primary principles of selection were the importance of the person's contributions and the representative character of his or her work. A few living and still active persons born before 1930 have been included; here obviously the greatest uneasiness about selection exists. (3) A third category of articles includes review and discussion of various methods and movements that have influenced and informed the reading and study of Scripture.

In the initial stages of work on this project, the following served advisory roles in developing the entry list and suggesting possible contributors: Peter R. Ackroyd (Kings College, London), Michael Fishbane (University of Chicago), Robert M. Grant (University of Chicago), Robert Morgan (University of Oxford), G. H. M. Posthumus Meyjes (Leiden University), Lou H. Silbermann (Vanderbilt University), Rudolf Smend (Georg-August-Universität Göttingen), David A. Steinmetz (Duke University), Georg Strecker (Georg-August-Universität Göttingen), and Grover A. Zinn (Oberlin College).

Articles submitted in German were translated by William A. Brown, Phillip A. Callaway, Donald G. Schley, and Douglas W. Stott; those in French were translated by Henrietta Parker.

Several current and former MDiv and PhD students at Emory University assisted on the project in various ways: Julie Galambush, Paul Hooker, Glenn Schwerdtfeger, David Harnden-Warwick, and Logan Wright.

The staff of Pitts Theology Library, Candler School of Theology, Emory University and that of the Divinity Library, Vanderbilt University, have given assistance on many occasions.

Appreciation is extended to all of the above. A word of special thanks is due Michael Russell and his colleagues at Abingdon Press.

John H. Hayes

A

ABBO OF FLEURY (c. 945–1004)

Born near Orleans, France, A. became a monk at Fleury. He studied at Paris and Reims as well as at Fleury. From 985 to 987 A. taught in England at the school of Ramsey Abbey; during this period he was involved in the enterprise of Oswald, archbishop of York, to restore the quality of monastic life in England. In 988 A. became abbot of Fleury. His interests lay in grammar and logic, the foundation disciplines of medieval Bible study. A series of "grammatical questions" survives from A.'s time at Ramsey, involving primarily examples from the classical poets but including theological problems.

Works: *PL* 139; *Abbonis Floriacensis Opera Inedita* (A. van de Vyver, ed., 1966–).

Bibliography: H. Bradley, "On the Text of Abbo of Fleury's 'Quaestiones Grammaticales,' " *PBA* 10 (1921–23) 173-80.

G. R. Evans

ABBOT, Ezra (1819–84)

American NT textual critic and bibliographer, A. was born in Jackson, Maine, and educated at Phillips Academy and Bowdoin College, receiving the BA in 1840 and the MA in 1843. He taught briefly in Maine, but because of contacts with A. Norton, professor at Harvard Divinity School, A. was invited in 1847 to a high school post in Cambridge, Massachusetts. He prepared a catalog of the high school library, classified according to subject, that received widespread acclaim. During these years he assisted Norton in editing and preparing lists, bibliographies, and indexes. Appended to Norton's *Translation of the Gospels, with Notes* (1855) is A.'s table identifying the readings that differed from those of the KJV.

In 1856 A. became assistant librarian at Harvard and a member of the staff of the Boston Athenaeum. During the next sixteen years he produced bibliographies and articles on textual studies in Unitarian publications, especially in the *Christian Examiner,* and in other denominational journals. He also collaborated with H. B. Hackett (1808–1875) in preparing the American edition of Smith's *Dictionary of the Bible* (4 vols., 1867–70), to which he contributed over 400 initialed entries. In 1872 he was elected to the newly founded Bussey

professorship in NT TEXTUAL CRITICISM at Harvard Divinity School.

A. became a member of the American Oriental Society in 1852 and served as recording secretary in 1853. He was made a member of the American Academy of Arts and Sciences in 1861, and he was a charter member of the SOCIETY OF BIBLICAL LITERATURE, sitting on the governing council. A. also served with great distinction on the committee for the American Revised Version. He contributed a lengthy section to the prolegomena to L. TISCHENDORF's eighth critical edition of the Greek NT, which appeared the year of A.'s death.

According to J. Thayer and B. BACON, A. was the first American textual critic to be respected by European scholars as an equal. As a scholar A. was accurate, thorough, judicious, and candid. His contributions lay more in mining the sources and setting forth the details than in pioneering new methodologies.

Works: *The Authorship of the Fourth Gospel: External Evidences* (1880); *Critical Essays Selected from the Published Papers of E. A.* (ed. J. H. Thayer, 1888). See also the bibliography in Thayer's work.

Bibliography: B. W. Bacon, *DAB* 1 (1928) 10-11. J. H. Thayer, "Address," *Ezra Abbot* (1884) 28-73.

T. H. Olbricht

ABEL, Felix Marie (Louis Felix) (1878–1953)

A. was born Dec. 29, 1878, at St-Uze (Drôme) in southeastern France. After ordination as a Dominican priest (1902) of the Lyon province, he was assigned to the École Biblique, the French biblical and archaeological school in Jerusalem. There he taught advanced Greek grammar (esp. that of the Septuagint) and Greek epigraphy as well as the geography and history of Palestine; his publications reflect these research and teaching interests. He was epigrapher for L. VINCENT's many topographical volumes, and their names are linked as friends and collaborators. A. served as a consultor of the Pontifical Biblical Commission from 1940 until his death. Severely injured in an automobile accident Dec. 27, 1952, he did not recover and died Mar. 24, 1953.

Preeminently a philologist, A. synthesized his insights into a grammar of biblical Greek (1927), which included the grammar of the SEPTUAGINT, a subject rarely treated.

He viewed biblical Greek as a form of the Hellenistic *Koine,* which he illustrated by means of extracts from the papyri. His collaboration with Vincent included the latter's volumes on Bethlehem (1914), Jerusalem (1914, 1922, 1926), Hebron (1923), and Emmaus (1932). To better understand Palestine A. made himself the master of the Greek sources for the geography and history of the region. He first presented his geographical learning in the *Guide Bleu* guidebook to Syria, Palestine, Iraq, and the Transjordan (1932) and then in a still valuable geography of Palestine (1933, 1938). He next directed his attention to the biblical history of the Hellenistic period in a major commentary on the Greek text of 1 and 2 Maccabees (1949). A two-volume history of Palestine from the conquest of Alexander the Great to the Arab invasion (333 BCE–630 CE) followed in 1952. These works in some measure supplied a French equivalent of E. SCHÜRER's standard German treatment, but they carried the story further. A. was also responsible for the volumes on the Maccabees (1948) and on Joshua (1950) in the original fascicle edition of the *Bible de Jérusalem.* In the course of his career he published a further 150 articles on epigraphy and ARCHAEOLOGY.

Works: (with L. Vincent), *Bethléem: Le Sanctuaire de la Nativeté* (1914); (with L. Vincent), *Jérusalem Nouvelle* (1914–22, 1924); (with L. Vincent), *Hébron: Le Harem el-Kahlil* (1923); *Grammaire du grec biblique* (1927); (with L. Vincent), *Emmaüs: Sa basilique et son histoire* (1932); *Géographie de la Palestine* (2 vols., 1933, 1938); *Les Livres des Maccabées* (1949); *Histoire de la Palestine depuis la conquête d'Alexandre jusqu'à l'invasion arabe* (1952).

Bibliography: R. Dussaud, *Syria* 30 (1953) 374-75.

B. T. VIVIANO

ABELARD (ABAILARD), PETER (1079–1142)

A pupil of WILLIAM OF CHAMPEAUX and of Roscelin of Compiegne, A. showed early promise in the study of logic. He established himself as a master in theology after he had heard the lectures of ANSELM OF LAON, then an old man and one of the foremost masters of the day. A. found Anselm lacking in matter, and he stated publicly that he could do better himself. The next day he lectured on Ezekiel, notoriously one of the most difficult books for commentators to treat satisfactorily. He was condemned for his arrogance in presuming to lecture on the sacred page without a suitable period of study and preparation. However, his reputation was made among the students; and he continued to apply his knowledge of the principles of logic to the study of the Bible and to write treatises of speculative theology (*Theologia Christiana,* the *Dialogue* between a Christian, a philosopher, and a Jew) as well as commentaries. He taught principally at Paris, where he made himself unpopular

with the authorities by his manner and where his opinions came under cricitism.

In 1121 A. was tried as a heretic at Soissons for his teaching on the Trinity, was condemned, and was sent to live at the abbey of St. Denys. He proved a disturbing influence there and at St. Gildas in Brittany, where he became abbot in 1125. By the mid-1130s he was back in Paris, again drawing huge crowds to his lectures. His pupils included Arnold of Brescia and John of Salisbury, who gives a personal account of him. In 1141 A. was again tried, this time at Sens, and again condemned. Apparently broken by the experience, he died two years later at Cluny, where he took refuge.

Of his exegetical works, some sermons and the important experimental piece he called *Sic et Non,* in which a series of apparently conflicting quotations are placed side by side, survive. The problem of contradiction in Scripture and in the fathers had long been a preoccupation of medieval scholarship, which drew in its turn upon AUGUSTINE's *Harmony of the Gospels* and BEDE's *De Schematibus et Tropis.* It seems likely that A.'s intention was to provide material for school exercises. He offered no solutions for particular cases, but his preface puts forward a number of novel ideas, notably the perception that the meanings of words change over time and that it is sometimes necessary for the reader to allow for differences of usage. He also examined the ways in which texts become corrupted and made one or two daring suggestions about the possibility of error at an early stage of the Bible's composition and transmission.

Of A.'s commentaries, that on the *Hexaemeron* affords examples of his application of logical and scientific principles. The commentary on Romans exemplifies the developing method of pausing at intervals to consider at length a major general question raised by the text; e.g., A. looked at the reason why God became human. It was found in due course that this practice so interrupted the sequence of the commentary that it was more sensible to save consideration of such questions until later. In the work of masters of the mid-twelfth century we find such *Disputationes* (Simon of Tournai) already evolving toward their later medieval form, and A.'s method marks a significant stage in this process. He also perceived the value of the study of Hebrew and Greek, although he personally seems not to have progressed beyond the consideration of individual terms in their biblical context. In a letter to his erstwhile mistress Heloise, who had become abbess of the Paraclete, the house he had founded, he advised her and her nuns to try to learn some Hebrew and Greek to help them in their own studies.

Works: *PL* 178; *Commentaria in Epistolam Pauli ad Romanos* (CCCM 11, vol. 1, ed. E. M. Buytaert, 1969); *Sic et Non: A Critical Edition* (ed. B. B. Boyer and R. McKeon, 1977).

Bibliography: J. F. Benton, *DMA* 1 (1982) 16-20. **E. F. Kearney,** "Master P. A., Expositor of Sacred Scripture" (diss., Marquette University, 1980). **D. Luscombe,** *The School of P. A.: The Influence of A.'s Thought in the Early Scholastic Period* (1969); *P. A.'s Ethics: An Edition with Introduction* (1971), with full bibliography. **R. Peppermüller,** *TRE* 1 (1977) 7-17. **J. Sikes,** *Peter Abailard* (1932).

G. R. EVANS

ABRAHAM BAR HAYYA (1065/70?–1136?)

A Spanish Jewish polymath living in Barcelona, A. was the first philosopher to write in Hebrew. His biblical exegesis is to be found in two works: *Megillat ha-Megalleh* (The Scroll of the Revealer) and *Hegyon ha-Nefesh ha-Atzuvah* (Meditation of the Sad Soul). The former is an eschatological work adducing biblical and astrological proofs to determine the advent of the messianic era in 1383 CE—biblically through the interpretation of the book of Daniel and the correspondence of the seven days of creation with seven eras of world history. The latter work cites biblical passages to support his metaphysical and ethical viewpoints, especially concerning creation, good and evil, repentance, and the saintly life. Two of the four chapters are based on a verse-by-verse exposition of the prophetical portions read on the Day of Atonement (Isa 57:14–58:14; Jonah). A. used his exegetical skill to demonstrate that the Bible contains the metaphysical insights of Greek-Arabic philosophy and indeed is the source of all philosophies, Jewish and non-Jewish. His own system stems from the neo-Platonic tradition but also introduced many Aristotelian concepts into Jewish thought. The first chapters of Genesis, for example, contain the key to the philosophical view of creation (*tōhû* and *bōhû,* corresponding to form and matter), while the three terms for "soul" in Genesis 2 and 6 (living soul, breath of life, and spirit of life) represent the vegetable, the animal, and the rational souls of Greek philosophy.

A. mentioned (*Megillat ha-Megalleh,* 74) that his contemporaries objected to his deriving proofs for his philosophical theories through biblical exegesis on the grounds that others could base entirely different theories on the very same verses. His explanations were quoted by later Bible commentators, Jewish and non-Jewish (e.g., D. Kimhi, Bahya ben Asher, I. Abravanel, Pico della Mirandola) as well as by kabbalistic writers (see KABBALAH).

Works: *Megillat ha-Megalleh* (ed. A. Poznanski, 1924), Hebrew; *The Meditation of the Sad Soul* (ed. and tr. G. Wigoder, 1969).

Bibliography: L. D. Stitskin, *Judaism as a Philosophy: The Philosophy of A. b. H.* (1960).

G. WIGODER

ABRAVANEL (ABRABANEL), ISAAC BEN JUDAH (1437–1508)

A Jewish exegete and finance minister, A. was born in Lisbon and received a thorough education in both Judaism and (Latin) classical antiquity and Christian scholasticism; he knew no Greek or Arabic. He was treasurer to Alfonso V of Portugal but was suspected of complicity in the nobles' revolt against João II in 1483 and fled to Castile, where he entered the service of Ferdinand and Isabella. On the expulsion of the Jews in 1492, A. went to Naples, where he served Ferrante I and Alfonso II. The French invasion drove him to Corfu; but on French withdrawal he returned to Apulia, finally settling in Venice in 1503, where he helped to negotiate a commercial treaty with Portugal. He was buried in Padua.

A. began writing (in Hebrew) at an early age, but the chronology of his works reflects intervals between his leisureless periods of royal service. Besides commentaries on the Mishnaic *Ethics of the Fathers* and on the *Haggadah* (domestic celebration for Passover night) and a critique of MAIMONIDES' thirteen principles of Judaism, he commented on the prophetic (see PROPHECY AND PROPHETS, HB) order of the Jewish CANON (i.e., Joshua–Kings, Isaiah–Malachi) and on Daniel. His early (unfinished) commentary on Deuteronomy, begun while in his twenties, was completed in later life along with other commentaries that covered the entire Pentateuch.

A.'s work evinces (besides prolixity) two major characteristics in the philosophical sense: accidental and essential. "Accidental" refers to his wide Latin reading and derivative knowledge of both pagan and Christian classics. Despite denunciation of Christianity as a misconceived theological statement and historical failure, he was deeply influenced by AUGUSTINE and THOMAS AQUINAS and accepted from Christian Bible commentators whatever he could endorse. A.'s dependence on A. Tostado (Tostatus) of Avila (d. 1455) is much greater than acknowledged; from Tostado came the methodology that prefixed to each major section of text a series of questions that are then answered. "Essential" refers to features such as (a) adducing his own experience of political life and vicissitudes, above all the Jewish mass expulsions from Spain and Portugal (1497) with the consequent demoralization of the Jewish world; (b) holding a worldview that despite its renaissance-type intellectual equipment is medieval rather than humanistic in its political outlook and endorsement of theocracy; (c) being fascinated with messianism as the climax of providentially determined world history. These features inform all his scriptural writing, overshadowing a markedly scholarly attention to factual details and incompatabilities.

A.'s ideal constitution is republican, compounding aristocratic and democratic features and grafting biblical-rabbinic prototypes onto the governmental structure of

Venice. Deuteronomy 17:15 is construed—against the weight of Jewish tradition—not as prescribing, but as reluctantly admitting monarchy. The fourth world empire of Dan 2:40-43 is identified with pagan and Christian Rome, its iron and clay feet representing the Christian-Muslim political division. The little horn of Dan 7:8 is the papacy (*Ma'yenei Ha-yeshu'ah* viii, 5, middle. A.'s indictment of contemporary Christendom parallels that of Savonarola (1452–98). He held that all alleged eschatological enigmas in the HB and the TALMUD point to a messianic climax in 1503 (A. died in 1508), or at the latest 1573. Parts of A.'s works were translated into Latin and excited considerable Christian interest; his Isaiah commentary was placed on the index.

Works: *Mirkevet Ha-mishneh* (1551); *Ma'yenei Ha-yeshu'ah* (1860); *Mashmia' Yeshu'ah* (1871); *Joshua–Kings* (1954–55); *Isaiah–Malachi* (1956); *Pentateuch* (1963–64); *Yeshu'oth Meshiho* (1967).

Bibliography: S. Gaon, *The Influence of the Catholic Theologian A. Tostado on the Pentateuch Commentary of I. A.* (1993). M. Kellner, *Dogma in Medieval Jewish Thought from Maimonides to A.* (1986). J. S. Malherbe, "A.'s Theory of Prophecy: With Special Reference to His Commentary on Deuteronomy 18:9-22" (diss, University of Stellenbosch, 1993). B. Netanyahu, *Don Isaac Abravanel* (1968[2]). L. Rabinowitz, *Isaac Abravanel* (ed. J. B. Trend and H. Loewe, 1937) 77-92. A. J. Reines, *EncJud* 2 (1971) 103-10.

R. LOEWE

ACTS OF THE APOSTLES, BOOK OF THE

Although the name Luke occurs nowhere in the book, the early patristic tradition was unanimous in associating the book of Acts with the Third Gospel and in attributing both volumes to Luke. IRENAEUS wrote: "Luke the follower of Paul recorded in a book the gospel that was preached to him . . . this Luke was inseparable from Paul and was his fellow-worker in the gospel as he himself makes clear, not boasting of it, but compelled to do so by truth itself. For after Barnabas and John who was called Mark had parted from Paul and they had sailed to Cyprus, he says, 'We came to Troas'" (*Adv. Haer.* 3.1.1; see 3.14.1). Luke, mentioned in the NT as a companion of PAUL (Col 4:14; Phlm 24; 2 Tim 4:11), was understood to have been a native of Antioch, a physician by profession and one who in writing Acts "received his information with his own eyes, no longer by hearsay" (Eusebius *Hist. eccl.* 3.4). The Muratorian Canon (dated between the late 2nd and 4th cents.) declares: "Luke compiled . . . what things were done in his presence, as he plainly showed by omitting both the death of Peter and also the departure of Paul from the city [Rome], when he departed for Spain."

Two opinions already existed in the early church about the date when Luke wrote the work. One tradition, represented by the so-called *Anti-Marcionite Prologues* (late 2nd cent.?), placed the writing in Achaia sometime after Paul's death. The other, more widespread, tradition dated it just after Paul's release from his first imprisonment in Rome (so Eusebius).

The text of the book has been transmitted in two different recensions. That contained in the great uncial manuscripts (Sinaiticus, Vaticanus, and Alexandrinus), the so-called Egyptian or Alexandrian tradition, is shorter than the so-called Western tradition. The latter is not widely represented but appears in OL and in some Syriac manuscripts as well as in the bilingual (Latin and Greek) Codex Bezae, which contains the text of the Gospels and Acts (on the textual differences, see C. Barrett [1994–98] 1:2-29).

There is no evidence that the Gospel of Luke and the book of Acts circulated in the early church as a single work. Papyrus P[75] (Bodmer, 14-15), from the early third century, indicates that the two were detached from each another. In early canonical lists and in the great fourth- and fifth-century codices, Acts is variously placed: EUSEBIUS placed it after the four Gospels (*Hist. eccl.* 3.25) as did ATHANASIUS (Epistle 39), and Codex Alexandrinus. Other placements vary: after the Pauline epistles (Codex Sinaiticus and Mommsen Canon), after the book of Revelation (6th cent., Codex Claromontanus), and before the book of Revelation (Augustine *On Christian Doctrine* 2.8.13). CASSIODORUS noted that the Bible was generally in nine volumes, with Acts and Revelation constituting the ninth volume (*Institutiones* 1.11.3).

Very little quotation of and commentary on Acts from the first five centuries survives, much of it extant only in catenae—that is, in commentaries produced from the fifth century onward by stringing together chains of quotations from earlier writings to elucidate successive passages of Scripture (the texts on Acts are collected in J. Cramer [1838] and noted and supplemented by P. Stuehrenberg [1987], with bibliography). Substantial material has survived from EPHRAEM (ET by F. Conybeare in F. Foakes Jackson and K. Lake [1926] 3:373-453), who originally wrote in Syriac but whose fundamentally meditative expositions on Acts are preserved in Armenian. Of more substance is CHRYSOSTOM's *Homiliae in Acta* (ET in NPNF 1st ser. [1889] 11:1-328), fifty-five sermons preached in Constantinople c. 400 CE. As in earlier sermons at Antioch, Chrysostom complained that the book was little known in the church: "To many persons this Book is so little known, both it and its author, that they are not even aware that there is such a book in existence. For this reason especially I have taken this narrative for my subject, that I may draw to it such as do not know it, and not let such a treasure as this remain hidden out of sight. For indeed it may profit us no less than even the Gospels; so replete is it with Christian wisdom and sound doctrine, especially in what is said concerning the Holy Ghost. Then let us not hastily pass by it, but examine it closely. Thus, the predictions which in the Gospels Christ utters, here we may see these actually come to pass; and note in the very facts the bright evidence of Truth which shines in them, and the mighty change which is taking place in the disciples now that the Spirit has come upon them." (Chysostom's claim of ignorance about the book may, however, be only homiletical rhetoric.) He stressed the book's importance as a historical source about the life of the early church (see A. Wylie [1991]).

From the second half of the first millennium, four works are noteworthy. First, a Christian Latin poet, Arator, produced a poetic, hexametrical version of Acts (*De actibus apostolorum* or *Historia apostolica*; the exact title is disputed) first read publicly before Pope Vigilius on Apr. 6, 544, in the church of San Pietro in Vincoli at Rome. Although a metrical paraphrase, the poem also provided exegetical elaboration, often drawing out symbolic, sacramental meanings from the text. It was widely used as a curriculum text during the medieval period and was drawn on by various exegetes (for an ET see R. Schrader [1987]; for a major study, see R. Hillier [1993]). According to Hillier, BEDE quoted Arator directly on eleven occasions, and his "commentary is influenced on practically every page by Arator's mystical interpretations" (vii).

Second, in about 709 or shortly thereafter Bede hurriedly produced a commentary on Acts, which he followed about twenty years later with a *retractio* (*Expositio Actuum Apostolorum et Retractatio* [ed. M. L. W. Laistner, 1939] = CCSL 121 [1983]), both addressed to Bishop Acca. Bede's commentary followed the text, generally verse by verse, with ample quotations from the fathers. Between the two works he improved his Greek and sought to correct the first work in the second. He apparently had access to the so-called Laudian Acts manuscript, a Greek and OL parallel text with several distinctive readings, some of which appear in his *Retractatio*.

Third, the Syriac Nestorian bishop of Hedatta, Isho'dad of Merv (9th cent.), produced a succinct commentary on the entire Bible. The work on Acts, found in *Acts of the Apostles and Three Catholic Epistles* (ed. and tr. M. Gibson, Horae Semiticae 10, Commentaries of Isho'dad of Merv [1913] 4:1-35), preserves a number of quotations extracted from such Syriac writers as THEODORE OF MOPSUESTIA and Ephraem but also from a number of minor interpreters.

Fourth, among the extensive works of RABANUS MAURUS is his *Tractatus super Actus,* which exists only in manuscript and, like many of his works, has never been printed or subjected to detailed study. Bede and Rabanus were heavily drawn upon for the twelfth-century GLOSSA ORDINARIA. The Glossa was a multi-volume work; in its first printed edition (1480), Acts appeared between He-

brews and James. The thirteenth-century, single-volume "Parisian Bibles," although generally following the modern order of the biblical books, placed Acts, as a rule, between the Pauline and the catholic epistles.

Stuehrenberg notes over three dozen sources and commentaries on Acts in the High Middle Ages (1100–1350), but most of these are either fragmentary, unpublished, or unstudied (1987, 118-25; 1988, 111-58). In the Syriac church Dionysius bar Salibi (d. 1171) produced a commentary on the entire Bible composed primarily to summarize the work of previous exegetes (Syriac text and Latin translation of Acts in CSCO 53 and 60, vols. 18 and 20 of Scriptores Syri [ed. and tr. J. Sedlacek, 1909–10]). The *postillas* of HUGH OF ST. CHER and of NICHOLAS OF LYRA, covering the entire Bible, contain treatments of Acts (Stuehrenberg [1988] 124-34, 145-55). Nicholas drew on his acquaintance with Judaism to elucidate texts and showed a more than ordinary interest in the geographical references in the book as well as in the historical setting; however, he was not conversant with Greek and relied on the Latin text. Neither Hugh's nor Nicholas's work on Acts has been subjected to detailed analysis.

Both L. VALLA and ERASMUS subjected the Latin text of Acts to TEXTUAL CRITICISM. A portion of Valla's *Collatio Novi Testamenti* (not printed until 1970) concerns Acts, and folios 23-26 in his *In Latin am Novi Testamenti interpretationem,* published by Erasmus in 1505, are also on Acts. Erasmus included notes on Acts in the annotations to his *Novum instrumentum omne* (1516), the first published version of the Greek NT. The notes of both scholars were included in volume seven of the CRITICI SACRI (1660). Erasmus also published a paraphrase of Acts (1524), the last of his paraphrases on the NT. (His paraphrases were translated into English through the influence of Catherine Parr, the sixth wife of Henry VIII; and Edward VI ordered the translation to be placed in all church parishes.)

LUTHER did not write a commentary on Acts, but he applied his distinctive perspective in his preface to the book in the 1533 German edition of the Bible: "This book might well be called a commentary on the epistles of St. Paul. For what Paul teaches and insists upon with words and passages of scripture, St. Luke here points out and proves with instances and examples . . . namely, that no law, no work justifies men, but only faith in Christ" (35 [1960] 364). Some of the radical elements in the Reformation drew on the book of Acts in support of a theory of communitarianism or biblical communism in which property was to be held in common in imitation of the early church (see Acts 2:44-45; 4:32-37; G. Williams [1992³], index under communitarianism). Luther apparently sought to defuse this use, noting in his preface that "this practice did not last long and in time had to stop."

CALVIN published his commentary on Acts in two

installments, chapters 1–12 in 1552 and on the entire book in 1554 (first ET 1585; new ET, 2 vols., 1965–66). Here as elsewhere Calvin concentrated on the grammatical-historical dimensions of the text but with a homiletical and spiritualizing application. For him the book's theme fits the genre of sacred history, with a concern to show how God cared and still cares for the church and directed its life through the Spirit.

H. GROTIUS's commentary on Acts in his *Annotationes in Novum Testamentum* (1646) was the first commentary on the book to suspend theological and homiletical concerns and to focus strictly on philological and historical matters. Standing in the Erasmian/humanistic tradition, Grotius drew upon a broad range of classical and Hellenistic texts to elucidate the background and context of the biblical narratives. His work was highly influential in England, especially among persons associated with the so-called Great Tew Circle, whose members included Grotius's great English defender H. HAMMOND (see F. Beiser [1996] 84-133]). Hammond treated Acts in his *A Paraphrase and Annotations upon All the Books of the NT* (1653), a widely read but only mildly critical work that was nonetheless pioneering in English biblical criticism.

The Semiticist J. LIGHTFOOT produced two works on Acts, a commentary on chaps. 1–12 (1645) and *Horae hebraicae et Talmudicae in Acta Apostolorum* (date uncertain; ET in his *Works* 8 [1825] 353-501), drawing heavily upon both rabbinic/Talmudic and Hellenistic writings (especially Josephus) to elucidate the text's background. J. Pearson (1613–86) lectured on Acts at Cambridge, but the lectures plus his *Annales Paulini* were published posthumously (Latin in 1688; ET in 1851).

Within English DEISM, several radical thinkers raised issues that would later set the agenda for interpretation of the book. J. TOLAND and T. MORGAN argued that early church life was not characterized by theological harmony, as one finds in Acts, but by party strife (see W. Baird [1992] 1:39-41, 52-54). Morgan, who took a positive attitude toward Paul, argued that alongside the gentile, Pauline, anti-Jewish, anti-ceremonial, and universalistic form of Christianity stood a narrow, exclusivistic, legally oriented, Judaistic, Petrine version whose gospels were "as opposite and inconsistent as Light and Darkness, Truth and Falsehood" ([1969] 1:377; Morgan, of course, saw Paul as a forerunner of the deistic thinkers and Peter as representative of the traditional, clergy-controlled and ceremonially bound religious establishment of his day). These two parties in the early church eventually combined during the time of persecution to produce what became Roman Catholic Christianity. The implication of this position was the necessity to study NT documents in light of early church history.

In his *History and Character of St. Paul*, P. ANNET,

the most radical of the English Deists, raised the issue of the relationship between Paul's epistles and the narratives in Acts and the discrepancies he found between the two, e.g., Paul's association with the church in Jerusalem. Although generally trusting the book of Acts, Annet printed the three accounts of Paul's conversion in parallel columns to highlight their inconsistencies. Annet denied common authorship of the Gospel of Luke and Acts, denied that Luke wrote Acts, and suggested that the "we" sections in Acts may have been written by Silas (see Baird, 49-52).

In 1792 E. EVANSON, an Anglican turned Unitarian, declared Luke to be the only authentic Gospel and affirmed Luke–Acts (with some excisions) to be historically accurate. He considered most of the letters of Paul to be inauthentic. His work, like Annet's, raised the issue of the relationship of the Paul of the epistles to the Paul pictured in Acts.

The traditional view that Acts was written "to recount the achievements of the apostles, or the history of the early church" came under scrutiny with the dominance of the historical-critical approach to the Bible. "It was evident at once to the critical eye that the book fulfilled in a very imperfect way the historical purpose which had been ascribed to it by tradition. Instead of recording the acts of the apostles it confined itself almost exclusively to Peter and Paul, and even Peter received but scant attention. Moreover, the fragmentary nature of the account, the many omissions evident to any one acquainted with Paul's Epistles, the frequent repetitions, the extreme sketchiness of some parts and the minute detail of others, the marked emphasis upon certain matters, and the brief and casual reference to others of equal importance all seemed to demand some explanation. If the author was familiar with the period he was writing about, as had been commonly taken for granted, he must have had some other than a purely historical motive, or if not, then his knowledge of the period must have been very limited and fragmentary" (A. McGiffert [1922] 363-64).

In 1721 the German Lutheran theologian E. Heumann (1681–1764) published a short article that was a harbinger of matters to come ("Dissertation ed Theophilo, cui Lucas Historiam Sacram Inscripsit," *BHPT,* class 4 [1721] 483-505). He argued that Luke–Acts was written, not as a straightforward historical account, but as an apology for the Christian religion addressed to a pagan official, thus raising questions about the work's intended purpose and historical reliability.

In England N. LARDNER was aware of the rising historical issues in biblical interpretation. But in his *Credibility of the Gospel History* (14 vols., 1727–57) he merely collected the traditions testifying to the work's Lukan origins and to its historical value and reliability (see his *Works* 6 [1838] 388-98).

In his 1750 introduction to the NT (ET 1780), J. D.

MICHAELIS argued that Luke had more reasons for his work than merely "to write a church-history." Michaelis noted two: "to give an authentic relation of the effusion of the Holy Ghost, and the first miracles, by which the truth of the Christian religion was established" and "to impart those accounts, which evince the claim of the Gentiles to the church of Christ" (ET, 216). In his fourth edition (1788; ET, 4 vols., 1793–1801), Michaelis added another reason: "to record only those facts, which he had either seen himself, or heard from eye-witnesses," which explained Luke's silence about so much of early church history (ET, 3.1 [1802²] 331).

J. SEMLER, "directly dependent for the questions . . . as well as for many of the answers . . . on the writings of the English Deists" (W. Kümmel, [1970] 62), described the early church as possessing a "dissimilarity and disunity" in which "the aversion of the supporters of Peter for the followers of Paul is undeniable" (from preface to vol. 4, *Abhandlung von freier Untersuchung des Canon* [4 vols., 1771–75]; ET in W. Kümmel [1973²] 67).

The author of *A View of the Evidences of Christianity,* W. PALEY, wrote a work on Paul (*Horae Paulinae* [1790]) that typified mainline British scholarship of the time, based as it was on an anti-deistic methodology initially given widespread circulation by C. LESLIE. Carrying out a comparison of the Paul of the epistles with the Paul of Acts under the assumption that the epistles and the book were written independently of each other, Paley argued that, considering their "undesignedness," the number of coincidental agreements between the two versions indicates that they are based on events whose historicity cannot be doubted (on Paley, see J. Cadbury [1955] 123-27).

The idea that the early church was composed of diverse groups often in theological conflict was given wide circulation by W. DE WETTE. In his *Lehrbuch der christlichen Dogmatik in ihrer historischen Entwicklung* (1813), he argued that the NT books could be divided into three categories: "(1) Jewish Christian, to which belong the first three Gospels, the Book of Acts, the Letters of Peter, James, and Jude, and the Apocalypse. . . . (2) Alexandrian or Hellenistic, to which the Gospel and the Letters of John and the Letter to the Hebrews are to be reckoned. . . . (3) Pauline, including the Letters of Paul and, in part, the Book of Acts" (ET in Kümmel, 106-7).

F. C. BAUR, primarily a church historian, was the most influential and controversial NT scholar of the nineteenth century (see Baird, 258-69; W. Gasque [1975, 1989] 26-54; Kümmel, 127-43, with extracts from Baur's writings). Basic to his attempt to produce a history of early Christianity and to associate the NT writings with this history was his view that two parties, the Petrine (Jewish) and the Pauline (Hellenistic), were in open opposition, even conflict, in the early church

(first propounded in 1831). Various NT writings, he argued, reflect the interests and theologies of these parties. Other later NT writings (produced in the late 1st and early 2nd cents.) reflect attempts to reconcile these factions. Among the latter, "the Acts of the Apostles . . . is the apologetic attempt of a Paulinist to facilitate and bring about the *rapprochement* and union of the two opposing parties by representing Paul as Petrine as possible and, on the other hand, Peter as Pauline as possible" (1838; ET in Kümmel, 133). Because of its *tendenz* the book of Acts cannot be accepted as a reliable source for the history of the apostolic age or for the work and thought of Paul, which, Baur argued, must be based on the four genuine Pauline letters (Romans, Galatians, 1 and 2 Corinthians). Baur's positions were summarized and developed in his *Paul the Apostle of Jesus Christ: His Life, His Work, His Epistles and His Doctrine. A Contribution to the Critical History of Primitive Christianity* (1845; 1866² ed. E. Zeller; ET, 2 vols., 1876).

The followers and students of Baur, the so-called Tübingen School, further developed his main ideas on Acts—namely, that the work was tendentious and therefore generally unhistorical and that it was produced in the post-apostolic church of the second century (see Baird, 269-78; Gasque, 21-54). Among these were M. SCHNECKENBERGER, A. Schwegler (1819–57), and E. Zeller (1804–1908). Zeller's work, *The Contents and Origin of the Acts of the Apostles, Critically Investigated* (1854; ET, 2 vols., 1875–76), based on earlier articles, contained an examination of much of the book's content, only to reach negative conclusions with regard to its historicity. Zeller concluded that Acts originated in Rome about 110–130 CE, during a time of persecution, and was produced with an apologetic purpose: to demonstrate to the Romans that Christianity was not a politically dangerous religion but a religious development within Judaism.

The critics of the Tübingen School in Germany were numerous: H. MEYER, J. Neander (1789-1850), F. THOLUCK, and others (see Baird, 278-94; Gasque, 55-72). Several of the critics were church historians who challenged Baur's reconstruction of early church history. Some of Baur's followers were Hegelians, although Baur himself reached most of his conclusions before becoming acquainted with G. W. F. Hegel (1770–1831; see Kümmel, 427, no. 177); this allowed critics to argue that the presumed conflict and then consolidation of parties in the early church was based on the Hegelian concept of thesis-antithesis-synthesis. Critics also argued that just because a work was written for a special purpose did not automatically mean that its contents were primarily nonhistorical.

In contrast, some contemporary scholars felt that Baur and the Tübingen School had not gone far enough (see Gasque, 72-94). This element in scholarship reached its apogee in the so-called Radical Dutch School, which had early roots that drew on the work of E. Evanson. The most significant member of this circle was W. van Manen (1842–1905; for his views on Paul, see *EncBib* 3 [1902] 3603-38). The Tübingen approach was advocated in England by S. DAVIDSON in the second edition of his NT introduction (2 vols., 1868, 2:196-290) and by W. Cassels (1826–1907). In his widely read book *Supernatural Religion: An Inquiry into the Reality of Divine Revelation* (2 vols., 1874, pub. anonymously), Cassels argued for a natural explanation of church origins and that much of the NT, including Acts, was fictitious.

As a rule, British scholarship adhered to the more traditional interpretation of Acts. Two popular works widely circulated the views that Acts was historical and that Luke was its author: *The Voyage and Shipwreck of St. Paul* (1848), by J. Smith (1782–1867), drew on travel experience and literature to argue for the historicity of Acts 27:1–28:16; and *The Medical Language of St. Luke* (1882), by W. Hobart, examined the medical terminology in Luke–Acts to demonstrate that the work had to have been written by someone trained in medicine, i.e., by Luke the physician. However, two British scholars, J. B. LIGHTFOOT and W. RAMSAY, the staunchest and most effective proponents of the historical value of the NT writings and especially of Acts, undergirded their works with pragmatic realism and an appeal to archaeological (see ARCHAEOLOGY AND BIBLICAL STUDIES) and geographical evidence. This British line of scholarship has been continued by F. F. BRUCE (1951, 1990³), I. H. Marshall (1970, 1992), B. Winter (1993–97), and others.

In Germany, T. von ZAHN and A. von HARNACK strongly defended the historical value of Acts. The latter argued, in more scholarly fashion than did Hobart, that the writer of Luke–Acts was a physician (a view generally assumed to have been subsequently laid to rest by Cadbury in his dissertation [1919–20]).

By the early twentieth century radical approaches to Acts had almost disappeared from mainline scholarship, although one should note the work of J. O'Neill (1961, 1970²), who dates Acts to about 115–130 CE and views it as reflective of early Catholicism. The massive five-volume work edited by F. Foakes Jackson and K. LAKE (1920–33) sought to summarize and assess all Acts research but was weak on such issues as Lukan theology.

Throughout the nineteenth and early twentieth centuries, investigations also focused on two subsidiary elements in Acts research: the issue of possible sources and the two textual traditions that had circulated in the early church. Various theories were proposed about possible sources used by the author but produced no general consensus (see below). Renewed interest in this topic was stimulated by C. C. TORREY (1916), who proposed that Acts 1–15 was a translation of an Aramaic or Hebrew source made by the author of chaps. 16–28.

Explanations for the two textual traditions also led to no majority opinions. F. Blass (1843–1907) revised an old theory that the author of Acts had produced two editions of his own work. M. Boismard and A. Lamouille (1984) have explored the issues involved and decided in favor of the historical priority of the longer Western text (see J. Taylor [1990]).

The work of M. DIBELIUS (see Gasque, 201-50), partially anticipated by Cadbury, focused on the literary quality of the author, what Dibelius called style criticism (*Stilkritik*). He compared the work to ancient historiography, examining closely the role of the book's speeches; and this LITERARY analysis has produced a trajectory running through much recent scholarship (see R. Pervo [1987]; C. Talbert [1974]; R. Tannehill [1986–90], and others).

H. Conzelmann's 1954 monograph proved to be a major stimulus to the study of Lukan theology. He argued that Luke–Acts was written as a response to the delay of the parousia so as to emphasize the importance of the life of the church in the unfolding history of redemption.

Later interpretation of Acts takes as one of its principal points of departure the generally recognized fact that the book, together with the Gospel of Luke, forms the second part of an extensive historical monograph that was conceived as a unity (see L. T. Johnson [1992]; for a different conclusion see M. Parsons and R. Pervo [1993]). The unity of these two books is concealed, however, by the association of Luke with the three SYNOPTIC Gospels and its placement before John in the NT CANON. Because of stylistic, compositional, and thematic features that Luke and Acts share, there is little doubt in modern scholarship that a single person wrote them. All indications favor the view that from the beginning the author of Acts planned a two-part work and composed both parts in close temporal succession. Accordingly, the literary program set forth in Luke's prologue (Luke 1:1-4) refers to Acts, whose introductory sentence (Acts 1:1-2) can be understood as a recurring reference to the Gospel's prologue. Similar cross-referenced forewords are attested in multivolume works of Hellenistic antiquity (e.g., Josephus *Contra Apionem*). The double ascension story forms another skillfully created link between both parts. Luke 24:50-53 forms the conclusion to the earthly deeds of JESUS, the subject to which the first volume is dedicated; thus the continuing history plays no role in this initial work. In Acts 1:1-14, however, the ascension story forms the narrative core of a preface (Acts 1:1-8) that introduces the continuing history—the subject of the second part of the work, which also required a sequential presentation (Luke 1:3). A thematic arch is recognizable stretching from the beginning of the Gospel to the end of Acts. The rejection of the message of salvation by great parts of the Jewish people, anticipated in Luke 4:16-30, and the Gentiles' acceptance of it through the ministry of Paul are expressly confirmed as having been accomplished in the final scene of Acts (28:17-28).

The superscription *Praxeis [ton] apostolon,* "Deeds of the Apostles" (Irenaeus *Adv. Haer.* 3.133.; Clement of Alexandria *Strom.* 5.82.4), or *actus omnium apostolorum,* "Deeds of all Apostles" (Canon Muratori), is secondary and in no way fits the book's contents. The deeds of the apostles do not form the focus of the work, nor is Paul, the central figure of the book's second half, veiwed as an apostle. In order to appreciate the book's content, one must start with the statement of purpose in 1:8, which has been put into the mouth of the resurrected Jesus. Accordingly, the subject is the continuation of the salvation event that began with Jesus, who was led by the Holy Spirit. Under the guidance of this Spirit the witnesses spread the gospel over the entire earth, extending from Jerusalem into the way stations of Judea and Samaria to the ends of the earth—i.e., to Rome and beyond. The central theme is the Holy Spirit's diffusion of the church. Reports about individual apostles and witnesses, their deeds and words, should be understood solely in terms of their contribution to this subject. Thus Acts' failure to sketch out thoroughgoing biographical notices is understandable: Figures like Philip (6:5; 8:5-40; 21:8) and Barnabas (4:36; 9:27; 11:22, 30; 12:25; 13:1-15:39), found here and there in the history, disappear abruptly from the scene. Even Peter and Paul appear only in the course of the story when the macrotopic requires or tolerates them.

In searching for Acts' intended organization it seems best not to focus on the persons described. Certainly, Acts has frequently been divided into a Peter section (chaps. 1–12) and a Paul section (chaps. 13–28), but this division proves to be inadequate since Peter is by no means the focus of chaps. 1–12. Instead, he shares his protagonist role with many others (Stephen, 6:8–7:60; Philip, 8:4-40; Paul, 9:1-30). In contrast, the programmatic sentence in 1:8 suggests an organizaton based on geography: the spread of the gospel in Jerusalem (2:1–8:3), in Samaria and the coastal regions of Judaea (8:4–11:18), in the gentile world and "to the ends of the earth" (11:19–28:31). Of course, even this arrangement is unsatisfying because its third major section is much too long and thematically diverse. For this reason most of the more recent exegetes who maintain a geographical organization (E. Haenchen [1956; ET 1971]; G. Schneider [1980–82]; A. Weiser [1982–85]) indicate an additional break after the report about the apostolic council (15:35) and begin a fourth major section at 15:36, describing the path to Rome of the witness to Christ.

A satisfying organization can be attained only if the diverse thematic references found in the book's individual sections are considered along with the geographical aspects in 1:8. The summarizing remarks at the end of the book, which retrospectively describe the significance of the reported events for the development of the church, allude to the individual thematic references (5:42; 9:31; 15:35; 19:20). Accordingly, five major parts can be found after the preface (1:1-12, the instruction of the apostles by the risen Christ): Part 1 (2:1–5:42) depicts the early period of the church in Jerusalem. Part 2 (6:1–9:31) portrays the first stage of the church's diffusion, clearly beginning a new narrative context even though at 6:1 the stage at Jerusalem has not yet been abandoned. The persecution in Jerusalem results in the mission that spreads into Samaria and the coastal regions. The topic of part 3 (9:32–15:35) is the controversy surrounding the beginnings of the mission to the Gentiles. The climax and at the same time the compositional center of the book is the report about the apostolic council (15:1-35). From this point, the way is open for Paul's mission to Asia Minor and Greece in part 4 (15:36–19:20). The subject of part 5 (19:21–28:31) is introduced by Paul's solemn announcement that he intends to travel to Rome (19:21-22); thus Paul is the gospel's witness in Jerusalem and Rome.

Modern scholarship still widely questions authorship of Acts by Luke, a companion of Paul. This ancient identification seems to follow the general tendency to identify unknown figures with known ones. Its purpose was to derive Acts, which could not immediately be attributed to an apostolic author, from an apostolic circle. The only indications that might suggest that Paul's assistant was the author of Acts are the "we" sections (16:10-17; 20:5-15; 21:1-18; 27:1–28:16).

There are several counterarguments suggesting the improbability that Acts originated within Paul's closest circles: (1) From the specific motifs of Paul's theology (overcoming the law as a path to salvation, justification of the sinner by faith alone, the atoning death of Jesus as a salvation event), Luke–Acts has hardly appropriated anything. That is striking even if one takes into account the possibility of shifts in the theological emphasis of the more recent followers of Paul and if one recognizes additionally that Acts' chief interest was less Paul the theologian than Paul the missionary and founder of the church. (2) Acts does not include Paul in the circle of apostles (in spite of 14:4, 14). Instead, Luke–Acts limits apostleship to the circle of twelve established in the pre-Easter period (Luke 6:13; Acts 1:22). In doing so it contradicts the central perspective of Paul's own self-understanding, i.e., that he was an apostle of Jesus Christ (e.g., Gal 1:1). (3) Acts' history of Paul contradicts Paul's letters at important points. Acts has Paul traveling to Jerusalem twice between his call and the apostolic council (9:26-30; 11:30), whereas Paul emphasizes that he had been there only once (Gal 1:17-18). Acts reports the minimal requirements in regard to Jewish ritual law that the Jerusalem Christians at the apostolic council imposed on the gentile Christians (the so-called apostolic decree in 15:20, 29). Paul denies any such impositions (Gal 2:6). (4) Acts preserves hardly any biographical information, especially for Paul's early years, that would go beyond the legendary enhanced tradition about the great apostle that was alive in the Pauline communities (7:58–8:1; 9:1-19*a*; 22:3).

Scholars have often wanted to conclude that Acts came into being even in the lifetime of Paul, c. 60 CE (J. Munck [1967]), based on its open-ended conclusion, which neither reports the end of Paul's life nor mentions the persecution of Christians under Nero (62 CE). Since it is necessary to date the Gospel of Luke after 70 CE, the second part of the two-volume work must have come into existence at a significantly later period. The author of the Gospel of Luke writes as a Christian of the third generation. The conflicts and the theological difficulties of the incipient mission to the Gentiles are at some distance from him, even though his own background may have been in Jewish Christianity. The central question for him concerns the historical changes that he as a historian recognizes in the identity of the church. He expects the Roman Empire to grant Christians who behave as loyal citizens their own possibilities of development. Accordingly, the anti-Christian sanctions under Domitian, and particularly under Trajan, still lie in the future. Therefore, Acts was probably written around 90 CE.

Dependable references are lacking that would help to answer the question about the place where Acts was composed. Its origin in Palestine cannot even be considered because of its slight geographical knowledge of this area, although, in contrast, its statements about local conditions in Jerusalem are surprisingly exact. Its intense use of local Antiochian traditions might suggest Antioch as the place of composition; however, the arguments favoring Ephesus are even stronger: (1) the concern with the origin and history of the Ephesian community; (2) the distinctive veneration of Paul; and (3) the similarity of the presupposed communal conditions in Acts to those in the PASTORAL LETTERS, which likewise probably derive from Ephesian circles. However, one might just as seriously consider Rome, for there lies the narrative goal of Acts, whose final and most extensive section (19:21–28:31) reveals that Paul's arrival in Rome was an act carried out by God in the face of all forms of opposition. The parallels between Acts 28 and *1 Clem* 5:1-7 as well as Phil 1:12-17 regarding the situation prevailing within the Roman community are conspicuous (if a Roman origin is assumed).

In contrast to the Gospel of Luke, Acts is not dependent on extensive written sources for its composition. The numerous source hypotheses of older scholarship, which were concerned with the reconstruction of written *Vorlagen,* have proved to be failures. The widespread consensus maintains that Acts' author wanted to base his presentation on material that he as a historian judged to be more or less authentic. Nevertheless, this material was diverse in form, origin, structure, and content. Probably only a very small portion of it was available to him in written form. Two factors indicate that most of the material came from oral tradition. (1) Relatively convincing traces of written *Vorlagen* can be demonstrated for only five passages: (a) The presentation of the so-called first missionary trip (chaps. 13–14) probably had as its source a missonary report of the Antiochian community that preserved the important stations of the trip and briefly reviewed the course of the mission (13:1, 4-5, 13-14*a*, 43-45*a*, 49-52; 14:1-2, 4-7, 21-22*a*, 24-27). (b) A short itinerary (Dibelius) proves to be the basic framework for the presentation of Paul's great mission to the Aegean (the so-called second and third missionary journeys). Deriving from the circles of Paul's fellow travelers, this itinerary preserves a list of routes and way stations (16:6-8, 10*b*, 11-15; 17:1-4, 10-11*a*, 15*a*, 17, 34; 18:1-5*a*, 7-8, 11) that deals with travel routes, places visited, and special difficulties. (c) Lying behind the story about the collection trip was possibly an official protocol concerning this collection (20:2*b*-6, 14-16; 21:1-17). (d) Similarly, the story about the imprisoned Paul might depend on a prison report transmitted in the Pauline communities (21:27-36; 22:24-29; 23:12–24:23, 26-27; 25:1-12). (e) The source of the story about the sea voyage and the shipwreck possibly was the report of a traveling companion, perhaps the Macedonian Aristarchus (27:1-9*a*, 12-20, 27-30, 32, 38-44; 28:1, 11-13, 14*b*, 16*b*). (2) The multiform oral tradition preserved stories about notable events that occurred in the early years of the Jerusalem community (e.g., 4:46-47; 5:1-11; 6:1-6), legends about the founding of communities (8:4-13; 13:6-12), lists of names (1:13; 6:5), and legends about persons, principally concerning Peter (3:1-10; 9:36-42; 12:3-17) and Paul (9:1-19*a*) as well as legendary depictions of Paul's activities in individual communities (14:8-18; 16:16-24, 35-40; 19:1-7, 11-20).

The author of the Gospel of Luke and Acts was the first Christian to write a far-reaching piece of literature. This intention becomes clear in the prefaces to his two works, both of which, following a common practice in the Hellenistic period, are dedicated to an influential person. Even more so than the Gospel of Luke, Acts conforms to established norms in terms of composition and style (Thucydides, Polybius, Lucian, Josephus). That conformity, however, does not preclude his theological intention to present history as a medium for divine activity. In doing so he follows the OT's style of history writing. In contrast, the influence of Hellenistic and Roman biography and novel writing are of subordinate significance.

Like other ancient historians, Acts' author forgoes the use of all the facts and developments relevant to an extensive presentation of his subject—the initial history of Christianity. Instead, he restricts himself to central events and typical situations. Persons, places, and communities appear suddenly and disappear just as abruptly. Especially marked is his use of the "style of the dramatic episode" (Dibelius). He develops individual events (e.g., 10:1-48; 15:1-29; 17:16-21) in such a narrative fashion that these occurrences become transparent for prominent constellations (e.g., the confrontation between the gospel and gentile philosophy, 17:16-21) and typical developments (e.g., the transition to the gentile mission without the law, 15:1-29).

Of special weight are the numerous speeches, which, as is typical of ancient historians, are not the reproduction of speeches that were actually delivered but are, rather, a stylistic tool used to bring characters and situations to life (see M. Soards [1994]). The composition of these speeches proves that Acts was written by a thoughtful historian who attempted to reconstruct how the individual speakers might have dealt with historical circumstances and audiences. He also appropriates valuable old traditions to accomplish this: For Peter's speeches (2:14-36; 3:12-26; 4:9-12; 5:29-32; 10:23-43), he appeals to elements of an ancient Jewish-Christian christology; for Paul's orations (13:17-41; 14:15-17; 17:22-31), he depends on an old rudimentary model of the gentile missionary—*kerygma* (cf. 1 Thess 1:8-9).

Acts' language is an elevated *Koine* Greek, which is controlled to extremely varying degrees. Peter's speeches are written in a Hebraizing tone that attempts to echo the sound of the SEPTUAGINT, whereas the speech of Paul on the Areopagus (17:22-31) represents an attempt to imitate an elevated Greek style. On a middle level between these two extremes are those sections that report on deeds and miraculous occurrences involving the gospel's messengers. They employ a broadly informative and popular narrative tone (e.g., 12:6-17; 13:6-12; 19:24-40). Moreover, characteristic of Acts' style is the considerable change in the narratives' rhythm. Chapters 2–5 arouse a feeling of non-movement by constantly repeating similar material, whereas the forward-driving rhythm of chaps. 6–15, which is created by constantly changing scenes, reflects the dynamics of the early mission. In contrast, in 15:36–19:20 the narrator gives the impression of a continuing development by sketching out Paul's course. The concluding section (19:21–28:31) is conditioned by the connection of individual scenes that are parallel in content and in which a central, major motif is varied with growing intensification to make an impression on the reader. Paul's path from Jerusalem to Rome is depicted as the final break with Judaism.

The central concern of Acts, which has been hotly debated (see the surveys in Marshall [1998³]), is closely coupled with the identification of the book's intended readership. The opinion, based on the mundane literary form of Acts and on its purposefully positive depiction of Roman courts and authorities, that his reading audience consisted of non-Christian circles may lead to the assumption of an apologetic intention vis-à-vis the gentile public. Thus the intention of Acts has been thought to be either (based on an early dating) to defend Paul in his trial (A. Mattill [1970]) or, more generally, to argue that Christianity deserves the privileges of a *religio licita.*

However, it has become increasingly certain that Acts was primarily directed to Christian readers. Although a bit of truth can be found in the view that Acts' intention regarding its Christian readership was simply evangelization (Bruce [1990³]) or confirmation of the gospel (W. van Unnik [1973]), this does not do justice to the work's complex structure. In opposition to this view a greater number of scholars have seen Acts' primary intention as inner-Christian polemics or apologetics; however, no agreement has been reached as to the exact goal of such a purpose. According to some scholars (e.g., Talbert [1966]; G. Klein [1961]), Acts is defending the developing early catholic church against Gnosticism (see GNOSTIC INTERPRETATION). They cite (1) the obvious concern with demonstrating personally and institutionally secure tradition; (2) the leveling out of the profile of Paul's theology; and (3) the closeness to the pastoral letters, which overtly share the same intentions. Other scholars, following Conzelmann's influential interpretation, regard the overcoming of a crisis of faith caused by the delay of the parousia as Acts' main concern. They maintain that a sequel was annexed to the Gospel of Luke in order to demonstrate that the epoch of the church, which had dawned instead of the expected parousia, was a new period of salvation history anchored in the divine plan. In contrast, the theory that Acts was written to combat a radical Jewish Christianity (J. Jervell [1972]) makes a point of noting that Acts is concerned with proving Paul's devotion to the law and with legitimating the inclusion of the gentile Christians among the holy people of Israel.

In spite of their elements of truth, these attempts at interpretation have captured only partial aspects of Acts. One cannot be fair to Acts unless it is understood as an attempt to overcome the basic problem faced by the church in its third generation: securing its own identity. How can the church, which lived in transformed social, ethnic, and geographical circumstances, be certain of its legitimate connection with its historical Christian origins, which were totally different? Acts answers this question by presenting the deeds of the risen Christ as established in God's plan. It is the Spirit who guides the church on its way through history. In choosing narrative history as his mode of presentation, the writer of Acts acknowledges that God's salvation works through the medium of history, a view consciously based on the OT. From this salvation-historical perspective the relationship between the dominant gentile church in the third generation and Israel is of special significance. Therefore, the fulfillment of the promise to Israel is accented first in the Gospel and then in Acts 1–5. Created by the activity of Jesus, the church is the people of God gathered in the final days. Acts shows that the Gentiles whom Paul has won for the faith become members of this people, which thereby attains its eschatological fullness. The church is God's eschatological people made up of Jews and Gentiles. Moreover, the nature of God's people is not changed by the parallel development of opposition on the part of unfaithful Jews, a development that leads externally to their manifest separation from the eschatological people of salvation (Acts 28:17-28). While Jerusalem, the old place of the divine presence and of the gathering of God's people, turns into a place of hostile opposition, God grants the community new space for living and growing in the spaciousness of the inhabited world. God leads Paul, the missionary bearer of the gospel, from Jerusalem to Rome.

As previously noted, the text of Acts has been transmitted in two versions that diverge significantly: (1) the Egyptian text type represented by most of the textual witnesses, which prevailed canonically both in the East and in the West; and (2) the Western text, above all the text of Codex Bezae Cantabrigiensis (D), the OL, and part of the Syriac tradition. The second version, which is approximately 8.5 percent longer than the first, deviates significantly at points from the first in substance, e.g., 15:20, 29; 16:l0-11; and 28:29. The increasing criticism of Israel is especially obvious (see E. Epp [1966]). There is no doubt that this version must have already emerged in the second century CE; nevertheless, it is also clear that this version can be neither the original nor a variant from the hand of Luke. It must be considered a free reworking from a very early period, which was only possible for a writing that was not yet considered canonical and was not imbued with an aura of sacred awe.

Bibliography: W. Baird, *History of NT Research* (1992). C. K. Barrett, *Luke the Historian in Recent Study* (A. S. Peake Memorial Lecture 6, 1961); *A Critical and Exegetical Commentary on the Acts of the Apostles* (2 vols., ICC 30, 1994–98). W. Beider, *Die Apostelgeschichte in der Historie* (ThStud 61, 1960). F. C. Beiser, *The Sovereignty of Reason* (1996). M. E. Boismard and A. Lamouille, *Le text Occidental des Acts des Apôtres: Reconstitution et réhabilitation* (2 vols, Synthèse 17, 1984). F. Bovon, *De Vocatione Gentium: Histoire de l'interpretation d'Act. 10, 1-11, 18 dans les six premiers siècles* (BGBE 8, 1967); *Luke the Theologian: Thirty-three Years of Research (1950–83)* (1978; ET 1987); *L'oeuvre de Luc* (LD 130, 1987). F. F. Bruce, *The Acts of the Apostles: The Greek Text with Introduction and Commentary* (1951, 1990³); "The Acts of the Apostles: Historical Record or Theological Reconstruction?" *ANRW* II.25.3 (1985) 2569-2603. C. Burchard, *Der Dreizehnte Zeuge: Traditions- und kompositionsgeschichtliche Untersuchungen zu Lukas' Darstellung der Frühzeit des Paulus* (FRLANT 103, 1970). H. J. Cadbury, *The Style and Literary Method of Luke* (2 vols., HTS 6, 1919–20); *The Making of Luke–Acts* (1927); *The Book of Acts in History* (1955). H. Conzelmann, *Die Mitte der Zeit* (BHT 17, 1954; ET 1961); *Apostelgeschichte* (HNT 7, 1963; ET Hermeneia 1987). J. A. Cramer (ed.), *Catena in Acta SS. Apostolorum e Cod. Nov. Coll.* (CGPNT 3, 1838). M. Dibelius, *Aufsätze fur Apostelgeschichte* (ed. H. Greeven, FRLANT 60, 1951; ET 1956). M. Dömer, *Das Heil Gottes: Studien zur Theologie des lukanischen Doppelwerkes* (BBB 51, 1978). J. Dupont, *Les sources du livre des Actes* (1960; ET 1964); *The Salvation of the Gentiles: Esssays on the Acts of the Apostles* (1979). E. J. Epp, *The Theological Tendency of Codex Bezae Cantabrigiensis in Acts* (SNTSMS 3, 1966). P. F. Esler, *Community and Gospel in Luke–Acts* (SNTSMS 57, 1987). E. Evanson, *The Dissonance of the Four Generally Received Evangelists* (1792). J. A. Fitzmyer, *The Acts of the Apostles* (AB 31, 1998). H. Flender, *Heil und Geschichte in der Theologie des Lukas* (BEvT 41, 1965). F. J. Foakes Jackson and K. Lake (eds.), *The Beginnings of Christianity*, vol. 1, *The Acts of the Apostles* (5 vols., 1920–33, 1979). W. W. Gasque, *A History of the Criticism of the Acts of the Apostles* (BGBE 17, 1975; with addendum, 1989). B. R. Gaventa, "Towards a Theology of Acts: Reading and Rereading," *Int* 42 (1988) 146-57. E. Grässer, "Die Apostelgeschichte in der Forschung der Gegenwart," *TRU* 26 (1960)93-167; 41 (1976) 141-94, 259-90; 42 (1977) 1-68. E. Haenchen, *Acts of the Apostles: A Commentary* (1965¹⁴; ET 1971). H. Hammond, *A Paraphrase, and Annotations upon all the Books of the NT* (1653). A. von Harnack, *Luke the Physician* (1906; ET 1907); *The Acts of the Apostles* (1908; ET 1909). C. J. Hemer, *The Book of Acts in the Setting of Hellenistic History* (WUNT 49, 1989). M. Hengel, *Zur urchristlichen Geschichtsschreibung* (1979; ET 1980). R. Hillier, *Arator on the Acts of the Apostles: A Baptismal Commentary* (Oxford Early Christian Studies, 1993). J. Jervell, *Luke and the People of God: A New Look at Luke–Acts* (1972); *The Theology of the Acts of the Apostles* (NT Theology, 1996); *Die Apostelgeschichte* (KEK, 1998), with bibliography (9-47). L. T. Johnson, "Luke–Acts, Book of," *ABD* (1992) 4:403-20. L. E. Keck and J. L. Martyn (eds.), *Studies in Luke–Acts* (1966). G. Klein, *Die zwölf Apostel: Ursprung und Gehalt einer Idee* (FRLANT 77, 1961). W. L. Knox, *St. Paul and the Church of Jerusalem* (1925); *The Acts of the Apostles* (1948). J. Kremer (ed.), *Les Acts des Apôtres: Traditions, rédaction, théologie* (BETL 48, 1979). G. Krodel, *Acts* (ACNT, 1986). W. Kümmel, *NTHIP* (ET 1973²). J. C. Lentz, Jr., *Luke's Portrait of Paul* (SNTSMS 77, 1993). G. Lüdemann, *Early Christianity According to the Tradition in Acts: A Commentary* (1987; ET, ACNT, 1989). M. Luther, *Luther's Works* (ed. E. Bachman; v. 30, 1960). A. C. McGiffert, "The Historical Criticism of Acts in Germany," *The Beginnings of Christianity* (5 vols., ed. F. J. Foakes Jackson and K. Lake, 1922) 2:363-95. R. L. Maddox, *The Purpose of Luke–Acts* (FRLANT 126, 1982). I. H. Marshall, *Luke: Historian and*

Theologian (1970, 1988³); *The Acts of the Apostles* (NTGu, 1992). **I. H. Marshall and D. Peterson** (eds.), *Witness to the Gospel: The Theology of Acts* (1998), with bibliography (545-76). **A. J. Mattill, Jr.**, "Luke as a Historian in Criticism Since 1840" (diss., Vanderbilt, 1959); "The Purpose of Acts," *Apostolic History and Gospel* (ed. W. W. Gasque and R. P. Martin, 1970) 108-22; "The Jesus-Paul Parallels and the Purpose of Luke–Acts," *NovT* 17 (1975) 15-46; "The Date and Purpose of Acts," *CBQ* 40 (1978) 335-50. **A. J. Mattill, Jr. and M. B. Mattill**, *A Classified Bibliography of Literature on the Acts of the Apostles* (NTTS 7, 1966). **W. E. Mills**, *A Bibliography of the Periodical Literature on the Acts of the Apostles* (NovTSup 58, 1986). **T. Morgan**, *The Moral Philosopher* (repr. 1969). **J. Munck**, *The Acts of the Apostles* (AB 31, 1967). **J. C. O'Neill**, *The Theology of Acts in Its Historical Setting* (1961, 1970²). **M. C. Parsons and R. I. Pervo**, *Rethinking the Unity of Luke and Acts* (1993). **R. I. Pervo**, *Profit with Delight: The Literary Genre of the Acts of the Apostles* (1987); *Luke's Story of Paul* (1990). **R. Pesch**, *Die Apostelgeschichte* (EKKNT 5:1-2, 1986). **E. Plümacher**, *TRE* 3 (1978) 483-528; "Luke as Historian," *ABD* 4:398-402. **I. R. Reimer**, *Frauen in der Apostelgeschichte des Lukas* (1993; ET 1995). **J. Roloff**, *Die Apostelgeschichte* (NTD 5, 1981). **M. E. Rosenblatt**, *Paul the Accused: His Portrait in the Acts of the Apostles* (Zacchaeus Studies NT, 1995). **G. Schneider**, *Die Apostelgeschichte* (HTHK 5, 1-2, 1980–82). **R. J. Schrader** (ed.), *Arator's "On the Acts of the Apostles" (De Actibus Apostolorum)* (Classics in Religious Studies 6, 1987). **M. L. Soards**, *The Speeches in Acts: Their Content, Context, and Concerns* (1994). **P. F. Stuehrenberg**, "The Study of Acts Before the Reformation," *NovT* 29 (1987) 100-136; "Cornelius and the Jews: A Study of the Interpretation of Acts before the Reformation" (diss., University of Minnesota, 1988). **C. H. Talbert**, *Luke and the Gnostics* (1966); *Literary Patterns, Theological Themes, and the Genre of Luke–Acts* (SBLMS 20, 1974); (ed.) *Perspectives on Luke–Acts* (PerspRelStud Special Studies Series 5, 1978); (ed.) *Luke–Acts: New Perspectives from the SBL Seminar* (1984). **R. C. Tannehill**, *The Narrative Unity of Luke–Acts: A Literary Interpretation* (2 vols., 1986–90). **J. Taylor**, "The Making of Acts: A New Account," *RB* 97 (1990) 504-24. **C. C. Torrey**, *The Composition and Date of Acts* (HTS 1, 1916). **C. M. Tuckett** (ed.), *Luke's Literary Achievement: Collected Essays* (JSNTSup 116, 1995). **L. Valla**, *Collatio Novi Testamenti* (ed. A. Perosa, 1970). **W. C. van Unnik**, *Sparsa Collecta* (NovTSup 29-31, 1973). **A. Weiser**, *Die Apostelgeschichte* (ÖTK 5, 1-2, 1982–85). **U. Wilckens**, *Die Missionsrede der Apostelgeschichte* (WMANT 5, 1961, 1974³). **M. E. Wilcox**, *The Semitisms of Acts* (1965). **G. H. Williams**, *The Radical Reformation* (SCES 15, 1992³). **S. G. Wilson**, *The Gentiles and the Gentile Mission in Luke–Acts* (SNTSMS 23, 1973). **B. W. Winter et al.** (eds.), *The Book of Acts in Its First-century Setting* (6 vols., 1993–98). **B. Witherington** (ed.), *History, Literature, and Society in the Book of Acts* (1996); *The Acts of the Apostles: A Socio-rhetorical Commentary* (1997). **A. B. Wylie**, "The Exegesis of History in J. Chrysostom's *Homilies on Acts*," *Biblical Hermeneutics in Historical Perspective* (FS K. Froehlich, ed. M. S. Borrows and P. Rorem, 1991) 59-72.

J. H. HAYES and J. ROLOFF

AFROCENTRIC BIBLICAL INTERPRETATION

Afrocentricity is the concept that Africa and persons of African descent must be understood as making significant contributions to world civilization as proactive subjects within history, rather than being regarded as mere passive objects in the course of history. Afrocentrism requires reconceptualizing Africa as a center of value and a source of pride, without in any way demeaning other peoples and their historic contributions to human achievement. The term *Afrocentricity,* coined by M. K. Asante (1987), refers to an approach that reappraises ancient biblical traditions, their exegetical history in the West, and their allied hermeneutical implications (see HERMENEUTICS). An impressive number of scholarly volumes have appeared on this subject in the 1980s and 1990s; in various ways such books have attempted to clarify the ancient biblical views of race and of ancient Africa. Together they represent efforts in "corrective historiography," which demonstrates clearly that a new stage in biblical interpretation has arrived.

It is no longer enough to limit the discussion to "Black theology" or even to "African theology." Instead, Africa, its people, nations, and cultures must be acknowledged as having made direct primary contributions to the development of many early biblical traditions and as having played significant roles in biblical history. Rather than viewing ancient Africa in a negative way or minimizing its presence in and contributions to biblical narratives and thought, as has been all too often the case in Western scholarly guilds, the continent obtains a more favorable appropriation by those who wish more accurately to interpret the Bible and to appreciate the inherent racial and ethnic diversity or multiculturalism of the salvation history the Bible depicts.

Throughout the world it has become standard for Christians to think of almost all of the biblical characters from Noah, Abraham, Moses, the pharaohs, and even the Queen of Sheba, to Mary and Joseph, the parents of JESUS, and virtually all NT personalities as somehow typical Europeans. For example, most modern sacred Christian art portrays Mary, the mother of Jesus, as a European. Consequently, most people today believe that the mother of Jesus of Nazareth resembled the ordinary European of today. Such presumptions are only now being substantively challenged through Afrocentric modes of biblical interpretation, as studies devote more attention to ancient iconography and to the importance of Egyptian (see EGYPTOLOGY AND BIBLICAL STUDIES) and ETHIOPIAN civilizations in the shaping of the biblical world (see M. Bernal [1987, 1991]. Thus today there is a critical need to examine not only how this distorted view emerged in Western history but also how the Bible treats Africa in general and black people in particular.

Three basic factors must be placed at the forefront of any discussion of this kind. First, the MAPS of the ancient biblical lands must be considered. Countries in Africa

(Egypt, Cush, Put, and Punt) are mentioned again and again. The HB alone refers to Ethiopia over forty times and Egypt over one hundred times. Many ancient biblical and extra-biblical sources mention Egypt and Ethiopia together, almost interchangeably. Scarcely are such ancient African locations portrayed fully in biblical maps produced in Europe and especially in the United States. Usually Western biblical cartographers show as little as possible of the African continent, while by contrast they highlight areas to the north in Europe and Eurasia that are seldom, if ever, referred to in the Bible.

Second, the Bible provides extensive evidence that the earliest of its people must be located in Africa. The creation story (Gen 2:8-14) indicates that the first two rivers of Eden are closely associated with ancient Cush, whose Hebrew name the Greeks would later translate as "Aithiops" or Ethiopia, meaning literally "burnt face people." Genesis 2:11-12 connects the Pishon River with "Havilah," which according to Gen 10:7 is the direct descendent of Cush. The Gihon River, named in Gen 2:13 as the second river in Eden, is described as surrounding the whole land of Cush. Biblical scholars usually date this composite Jahwist (J) tradition in the tenth century BCE, suggesting that these verses are an early reference to the African river system known today as the Blue and the White Nile rivers. (The name *Nile* derives from the Latin *nilus,* but the Genesis story predates the Latin language.) Clearly, wherever else Eden extended, a substantial portion was within the continent of Africa.

Third, the ancient land of Canaan was an extension of the African land mass, and in biblical times African peoples frequently migrated from the continent proper through Canaan/Palestine to the east along the Fertile Crescent to the Tigris and Euphrates river valleys of ancient Mesopotamia. Thus, the term *Afro-Asiatic* is probably the most accurate way to identify the mixed stock of people who populated the ancient Near East. "Eurasians" and even Europeans (Greeks and Romans) begin to feature in later biblical narratives; but the fact remains that the earliest biblical people, by modern Western standards of racial types, would have to be classified as Blacks (meaning that they had African blood and some physical features similar to those of African Americans today).

The modern student of biblical history and interpretation has to keep in mind that the ancient authors of the Bible, together with the Greeks and the Romans, had no notion of color prejudice. As startling as it may seem to those schooled in modern European, South African, and North American modes of scriptural interpretation, the Bible actually reflects a world before color prejudice or racial discrimination (see F. Snowden, Jr. [1983]). The authors/redactors of the Bible had a rather favorable attitude about black people, and the Bible as a result often reflects the ancient greatness of African people and their civilizations. For example, Gen 10:8 identifies Nimrod, son of Cush, as "the mighty warrior"; Solomon marries the daughter of the pharaoh (1 Kgs 3:1, 7:8; 2 Chr 8:11); and the heroine of the Song of Songs is "black and beautiful" (Cant 1:5). Once one tackles the problem of how to define *Black,* it becomes quite easy to see that most of the early characters of the Bible would have to be so classified, even though the biblical authors had no notion of race in the modern sense of the term.

For more than a century, despite their exclusion from centers of theological education, leaders in the black church have undertaken studies of the Bible. Many of these efforts show clearly that Blacks long ago rejected the latter-day, post-biblical view that they were the progeny of the accursed Ham (there is no such curse in Gen 9:18-27). D. P. Seaton, a prominent leader in the African Methodist Episcopal Church, represents the thinking of Blacks who have identified a more wholesome interpretation of their role in biblical history. In a work written in 1895, Seaton displayed considerable knowledge about the Bible, the location of ancient religious sites, and the significance of many biblical characters, providing extensive descriptions of tombs, villages, and other ancient sites he visited during several field trips to Palestine. Regarding Ham and his descendants, Seaton observed: "Because these Hamites were an important people, attempts have been made to rob them of their proper place in the catalogue of the races. The Bible tells us plainly that the Phoenicians were descendants of Canaan, the son of Ham, and anyone who will take the time to read the Bible account of their lineage must concede the fact." What is particularly noteworthy about Seaton's study is his profound awareness of racism among the respected biblical scholars of his day.

In the last decades of the twentieth century, both in the United States and in Africa, there has been a resurgence of what may now be called Afrocentric approaches to the Bible (see, e.g., R. Bailey [1995]; C. Copher [1993]; C. H. Felder [1991]; M. A. Oduyoye [1995]; and A. Smith [1995]). Caution, however, is advised, for students of the Bible must avoid the tendency of taking the sons of Noah—Shem, Ham, and Japheth—as representing three different races (Whites, Blacks, and Asians). The traditional approach of European missionaries and others was to designate Ham as the father of Blacks, who were allegedly cursed in Gen 9:18-27 (see T. Peterson [1975]); but it is absurd to claim that Noah and his wife could produce offspring that would constitute three distinct racial types. In fact, "Ham" does not mean "black" in Hebrew; it means "hot" or "heated." Moreover, there is no curse of Ham in this passage, for the text explicitly says, "Let Canaan be cursed" (Gen 9:25). Any discussion on the subject of Blacks in the Bible should be held suspect if its author tries to argue that Blacks constitute the "Hamitic" line only.

Black women and men are fully a part of the Bible's salvation history (see Felder [1989, 1991]. Moses was an Afro-Asiatic, and according to Num 12:1 he married a Cushite or Ethiopian woman. The Queen of Sheba, a black African (1 Kgs 10:1-13; 2 Chr 9:1-12; also see Gen 10:6-9), is called "the queen of the South" in Matt 12:42. The NT mentions another black queen: Candace, queen of the Ethiopians, who ruled from her ancient Ethiopian capital at Meroe (Acts 8:26-40). For years persons of African descent have taken heart upon reading the celebrated passage in Ps 68:31: "Let princes come out of Egypt and let Ethiopia hasten to stretch forth her hand to God!" But today there is a much greater basis for Blacks to celebrate and otherwise take seriously their rich ancient heritage in the sacred Scriptures, for the real Black presence is by no means limited to isolated verses here and there.

Despite all the evidence indicating a manifest Black biblical presence, Eurocentric church officials and scholars in most of the prestigious academies and universities of Europe and the United States have tended to deny or otherwise to overlook or minimize the fact that black people are in any significant way part of biblical history. This standard academic and popular Western tendency has had grave consequences for persons of African descent. Thus modern biblical scholarship is just beginning to overcome centuries of tragic biases against Blacks and their biblical history, biases that continue to find expression in the view that Blacks are to be thought of as mere "hewers of wood and drawers of water" (see Felder [1991] 132).

In the period between 367 CE (the date of Athanasius's canonical lists) and the Enlightenment, Europeans recast the Bible into a religious saga of European-type people. What makes this racialist tendentiousness so difficult to counteract is that such reinterpretations of ancient ethnographic realities are accepted as fact by many scholars in the Western academic community. These scholars teach and influence others throughout the world, thereby effectively recasting biblical history in terms and images that are distinctly favorable to Whites while literally displacing Blacks. The result has been that even Blacks portray biblical characters within their churches as totally unlike themselves. For biblical characters to be viewed in black images is still seen as a terrible thing by many Blacks around the world.

One need not hesitate to suppose that Mary looked like the other Palestinian women of Nazareth of her day. It is more historically accurate to portray her physiognomy as that of an ancient Afro-Asiatic, who probably looked like a typical modern Yemenite, Trinidadian, or African American. Several factors challenge the traditional Western perception of the Madonna and child:

Matt 2:15, quoting from Hosea 11:1, reads "out of Egypt, I have called my son." The passage describes how Mary and Joseph fled to Egypt to hide the infant Jesus from King Herod. Imagine the divine family as white Europeans "hiding" in Africa! It is doubtful that they would remain unnoticed, for despite centuries of European scholarship that has diligently sought to portray Egypt as an extension of southern Europe, it has always been part of Africa.

Literally hundreds of shrines of the Black Madonna have existed in many parts of North Africa, Europe, and Russia. These are not weather-beaten misrepresentations of some original white Madonna; rather, they are uncanny reminders of the original ethnography of the people who inhabited ancient Palestine during Jesus' time and earlier. The "sweet little Jesus boy" of the Negro spiritual was, in point of fact, quite black. While that song intones "we didn't know it was you," it reminds most modern Christians that they still do not know what Jesus actually looked like.

The maps of biblical lands need to be reassessed in light of more recent studies that show the true attitudes about race in the ancient Greco-Roman ethos. At that time all of Africa was referred to as Ethiopia, while present-day Sudan was called Ethiopia proper. The greatness of the people from these areas was proverbial. Recall Ps 87:1-4, which asserts that not only were the Ethiopians among those who fully knew the God of ancient Israel but also that they may have been born in Israel ("This one was born there," [Ps 87:4b])! Similarly, Isa 11:11 includes Blacks among the righteous remnant, whereas Isa 18:1-4 celebrates those from "the land of whirring wings sending ambassadors by the Nile," a people "tall and smooth," "feared near and far."

Although Greeks and Romans are frequently mentioned in the Bible, Mary, Joseph, and Jesus were neither Greek nor Roman. So how did Jesus of Afro-Asiatic birth become whiter and whiter over the years? The answer is neither complicated nor profound: It is a simple matter of paint. Medieval and Renaissance artists skillfully employed the painter's brush, and gradually Jesus came to be depicted in images more familiar and favorable to persons of European descent. Thus there developed a brand-new manger scene and an infant Jesus for all the world, not least the Third World, to adore. Jesus' parents also were reimaged, as ancient darker and clearly more African icons were discarded or destroyed in favor of more "modern" ones. These artistic representations still remain in many cathedrals of Europe and North and South America as well as in a great new basilica on Africa's Ivory Coast. Clearly, Africa has for too long stretched out its hand to biblical characters remolded as non-Black.

In Jeremiah 13:23a the rhetorical question is raised, "Can the Ethiopian change his skin?" In the sixth century BCE, Jeremiah knew that it was unnecessary for any

Ethiopian to attempt to do so; that kind of thinking seems peculiar to our own modern age of pseudo-scientific theories of White supremacy and Negroid inferiority, a most "enlightened" by-product of what is known as the Western Enlightenment.

Many contemporary persons may think of a black Jesus as an oddity or as a scandalous distortion of reality. The claim may be tolerated as long as it is limited to the theological metaphors of black theologians like J. H. Cone or A. Boesak, but it is not taken seriously as ancient ethnography. Many Europeans and Euro-Americans insist that Jesus was Semitic and, as such, Middle Eastern. However, to call Jesus "Semitic" is not helpful inasmuch as this nineteenth-century term refers, not to a racial type, but to a family of languages including both Hebrew and Ethiopic. Moreover, about the same time the European academy coined the term *Semitic,* it also created the geographical designation *Middle East,* an expression that would have made no sense to Herodotus, to Strabo, or even to Thucydides, much less to biblical personalities. The point of creating a so-called Middle East was to avoid talking about Africa. It was a sign of academic racism, which sought to de-Africanize the sacred story of the Bible along with the whole sweep of Western civilization.

Whether one considers the "Table of Nations" that appears in Genesis 10 as a historical record, the fact remains that centuries before Jesus of Nazareth, those who compiled the list of the descendants of Noah appeared to have an ideological intent. They insisted that Canaan was a direct descendant of Ham—in fact his son, the very one who is conveniently cursed in Genesis 9 in order to discredit his right to his own land. Furthermore, when the Greeks rose up to conquer the land of Canaan after the exile, they infused Greek culture into the subjugated peoples of their empire. Greek culture became the standard of acceptance in the Greco-Roman world, leading both those in power and those dominated to be as Greek as possible and to flee north-ward for cultural roots. In contrast, when Jesus' parents fled Herod's domain in order to protect Jesus, they followed the established trail to Africa—not to Europe! Bernal (1987, 1991) suggests that the ancient model for the dawn of civilization, a model that was African centered, was later co-opted by a "white/pure" European model. Certainly historians should take seriously that the models for the origins of culture changed simultaneously with the rise of racism and antisemitism.

Subsequent Western civilization took a different path from that of the holy family—namely, one leading straight to Europe; it was aided by artists paid by the church and its universities, artists who sought to please those in power as opposed to rendering biblical characters in an accurate ethnographic fashion. Hollywood completed this revisionist imaging through movies like C. B. DeMille's *The Ten Commandments, The Robe, The Greatest Story Ever Told,* and *Ben Hur,* films in which Europeans magically populated the entire region of ancient Palestine, rendering its inhabitants White. Ancient Palestine has never been the same.

Bibliography: D. T. **Adamo,** *Africa and the Africans in the OT* (1998). **M. K. Asante,** *The Afrocentric Idea* (1987). **R. C. Bailey,** "They Are Nothing but Incestuous Bastards: The Polemical Use of Sex and Sexuality in Hebrew Canon Narratives," *Reading from This Place* (ed. F. F. Segovia and M. A. Tolbert, 1995) 1:121-38. **M. Bernal,** *Black Athena: The Afro-Asiatic Roots of Classical Civilization* (2 vols., 1987, 1991). **A. A. Boesak,** *Black Theology, Black Power* (1978). **C. B. Copher,** "3,000 Years of Biblical Interpretation with Reference to Black Peoples," *JITC* 30, 2 (1986) 225-46; "The Black Presence in the OT," *Stony the Road We Trod* (ed., C. H. Felder, 1991) 146-64; *Black Biblical Studies: An Anthology of C. B. Copher: Biblical and Theological Issues on the Black Presence in the Bible* (1993). **C. H. Felder,** *Troubling Biblical Waters: Race, Class, and Family* (1989); (ed.), *Stony the Road We Trod: African American Biblical Interpretation* (1991). **N. F. Gier,** "The Color of Sin/The Color of Skin," *JRT* 48, 1 (1991) 42-52. **C. J. Martin,** "A Chamberlain's Journey and the Challenge of Interpretation for Liberation," *Semeia* 47 (1989) 105-35. **M. A. Oduyoye,** *The Sons of the Gods and the Daughters of Men: An Afro-Asiatic Interpretation of Genesis 1–11* (1984); "Biblical Interpretation and the Social Location of the Interpreter: African Women's Reading of the Bible," *Reading from This Place* (ed. F. F. Segovia and M. A. Tolbert, 1995) 2:33-51. **T. Peterson,** "The Myth of Ham among White Antebellum Southerners" (diss. Stanford University, 1975). **A. Smith,** "A Second Step in African Biblical Interpretation: A Generic Reading Analysis of Acts 8:26-40," *Reading from this Place* (ed. F. F. Segovia and M. A. Tolbert, 1995) 1:213-28. **F. M. Snowden, Jr.,** *Blacks in Antiquity* (1970); *Before Color Prejudice: The Ancient View of Blacks* (1983). **L. A. Thompson,** *Romans and Blacks* (1989). **J. Vercoitter, J. Leclant, F. M. Snowden, Jr., and J. Desanges,** *The Image of the Black in Western Art,* vol. 1, *From the Pharaohs to the Fall of the Roman Empire* (1976).

C. H. FELDER

AGRICOLA, JOHANN (c. 1494–1566)

Born in Eisleben, A. was trained by the Franciscans in Braunschweig and schooled in the liberal arts at Leipzig before returning to Braunschweig as a teacher. In 1515/16 he began studying theology with LUTHER, became his close friend, and accompanied him to the Leipzig Disputation (1519). As professor (1520) and dean (1523) of the faculty of arts at Wittenberg, A. also lectured on the NT in the theological faculty and instructed the city youth in the Bible.

Probably for reasons of personal ambition he escaped the shadow of the Reformer by taking the job of school principal in his hometown (1525). He reformed the curriculum along humanistic lines, wrote catechisms, became a popular preacher, and on Saturdays held exegetical lectures for the clergy. Over the next ten years he published biblical commentaries, sermons, and a collection of hundreds of German proverbs.

In 1536 he returned to Wittenberg to resume his activities as a lecturer. Despite increasingly bitter controversies with the Reformers, he was appointed to the Wittenberg Consistory (1539). By 1540, however, his break with Luther was final. A. fled the city again, this time to accept the position of court preacher and general superintendent in Brandenburg. His prince took him along to the diets of Regensburg (1541) and Augsburg (1547/48), where he was instrumental in the Augsburg Interim. In the Philippist-Gnesiolutheran quarrels he sided with the strict Lutherans. He died in 1566 during the pestilence in Berlin.

Among A.'s forty-five publications the most notable exegetical works are his commentaries on Luke and Colossians. His antinomian interpretation of the relation between repentance and faith put him at odds with P. MELANCHTHON (1527) and finally with Luther (from 1537). While the Reformers taught that repentance arises from the coercion of the law, A. held that repentance must be preached in the name of Christ (Luke 24:47). Luther could reconcile the initial differences (Torgau [1527]), but A. published three sermons (1536) in which the law was subsumed under the new law of Christ. Luther suppressed A.'s teaching (*Theses Against the Antinomians*), insisting that the removal of the law weakens the gospel and invites libertinism.

Works: *In lucae euangelium adnotationes* (1529).

Bibliography: I. **Guenther,** *CE* 1 (1985) 15. **J. Rogge,** *J. A.s Lutherverständnis: Unter besonderer Berücksichtigung des Antinomismus* (1960); *TRE* 2 (1978), 110-18.

M. HOFFMANN

AGRICOLA, RUDOLPH (1444–85)

Born in Baflo, Frisia, on the day his father, an unordained parish pastor, was appointed abbot of Selwert, the nearby Benedictine monastery, A. (latinized for Huisman) received his primary education at St. Martin's in Groningen, a school influenced by the *Devotio moderna* of the Brethren of the Common Life. In 1456 the twelve year old matriculated in the university of Erfurt, where he completed his BA within three years. He took advanced courses at Cologne but moved on to Louvain to earn his MA (1465).

From 1468 to 1479 he sojourned in Italy. While reading law in Pavia he became an expert in eloquence, gaining a reputation as an accomplished orator. After moving to Ferrara to work as court organist for Duke Ercole I d'Este, he translated Greek literature into Latin and began his principal work, *De inventione dialectica.* Upon returning to his homeland, he was appointed town secretary (scribe and orator) of Groningen, a position that allowed him to cultivate humanist friendships, e.g., with Gansfort and Hegius. An invitation by the Palatinate chancellor von Dalberg brought him to Heidelberg (1484), where Elector Philip gave him a free hand in university activities. A. lectured on selected topics, participated in disputations, delivered speeches, and made a plea for the humanities in *De formando studio.* He died in Heidelberg on Oct. 27, 1485, after a trip with Dalberg to Rome.

A true Renaissance man, A. was a musician, painter, athlete, orator, translator, and humanist scholar. A friend of J. REUCHLIN and admired by ERASMUS and P. MELANCHTHON, he became a model for the new learning. Although during his lifetime he impressed more with his art of life than with his writings (*De inventione dialectica* and *De formando studio* were published posthumously), A.'s introduction of Italian rhetoric influenced decisively the beginnings of Northern humanism.

A. held that the reform of learning concurred with the renewal of spirituality. Returning to both the sources of antiquity and the Bible would improve intellectual and religious life. Thus he rejected the speculative, syllogistic method of dialecticians and scholastics alike and advocated reading historians, poets, and rhetoricians. However, he saw rhetoric from a dialectical perspective and continued to adhere to the dogmas of the Roman Catholic tradition. His coordination of dialectic and rhetoric was to engender a practical art of persuasion aimed at social utility. This ethical orientation of humanist rhetoric was for A. symbiotic with the practical piety of the *Devotio moderna.*

Works: *De inventione dialectica libri tres* (1528 ed.; 1976).

Bibliography: F. **Akkerman** (ed.), *Rodolphus Agricola Phrisius* (Brill's Studies in Intellectual History 6, 1988). C. G. **van Leijenhorst,** *CE,* 15-17. P. **Mack,** *Renaissance Argument: Valla and A. in the Traditions of Rhetoric and Dialectic* (1993). J. R. **McNally,** "An Appraisal of R. A.'s *De inventione dialectica*" (diss., Iowa, 1966). M. A. **Nauwelaerts,** *Rodolphus Agricola* (Helden van de geest 27, 1963). W. **Ong,** *Ramus, Method, and the Decay of Dialogue* (1958); *Ramus and Talon Inventory* (1958). L. W. **Spitz,** *The Religious Renaissance of the German Humanists* (1963) 20-40. H. E. J. M. **van der Velden,** *R. A., Roelof Huusman: een nederlandsch Humanist der vijftiende Eeuw* (1911). E. H. **Waterbolk,** *Een hond in het bad: Enige aspecten van de verhouding tussen Erasmus en Agricola* (1966).

M. HOFFMANN

AHAD HA'AM (ASHER HIRSCH GINZBERG)
(1856–1927)

Born to a Hasidic family in Skvira, Kiev province, Russia, A. received extensive training in classical Jewish texts; however, he educated himself in Western philosophy and literature. Earning a livelihood in business, he joined Zionist circles in Odessa, where he began publishing Hebrew essays stressing the need to prepare emigrants to Palestine by steeping them in Jewish ethics and culture. His outlook has been characterized as a somewhat paradoxical mixture of "intellectual positivism and practical idealism" (Y. Kaufmann [1928] 422). Adopting the pen name Aḥad Ha'am (One of the People), A. honed the Hebrew essay to an art form, making a lasting contribution to Hebrew language and letters. From 1896 to 1902 he edited the monthly *Hashiloaḥ* from his new residence in Berlin. Continuing his Zionist political activity, he moved to London in 1907. In 1922, suffering poor health, he settled in Palestine, where he edited his letters and memoirs during his final years. A.'s thought notably influenced the Israeli sociologist (see SOCIOLOGY AND HB/NT STUDIES) and Bible scholar Y. KAUFMANN.

Although A. did not write biblical commentary, he formulated much of his thinking within the framework of biblical ideas and institutions. He endeavored to trace the essence of Jewish peoplehood and values to ancient Israelite roots. The original biblical ideal of a just society, he wrote, was promulgated by the prophets (see PROPHECY AND PROPHETS, HB). Following the prophets' radical innovation, the priests sought to resolve conflicting social vectors and stabilize the nation ("Priest and Prophet"). The prophetic archetype is Moses, whose character embodies not so much a historical personage as a projection of the popular spirit ("Moses"). Impelled by a passion for justice, Moses sought not only to liberate his people but also to imbue them with ethical monotheism. A. held, nonetheless, that ethical monotheism did not take hold among the Judeans until after the exile, when they came to identify their national God as the Lord of all nature and history.

A. argued that the prophets did not withdraw from society to nourish their piety; they engaged with society in order to transform it. He maintained that in line with early biblical monism, in which there was no body/soul dichotomy, Judaism sought to elevate the physical through spiritual refinement ("Flesh and Spirit"). The individual finds meaning in developing the nation. The Bible's ethic is, A. claimed, social; reward and punishment are collective.

Works: *Ten Essays on Zionism and Judaism* (ed. L. Simon, 1922); *Ahad Ha-Am: Essays, Letters, Memoirs* (ed. L. Simon, 1946); *ʾiggĕrôt ʿaḥad hāʿām* (6 vols., 1956); *Kol kitbē ʿaḥad hāʿām bĕkereck ʾeḥād* (1956); *Selected Essays* (ed. L. Simon, 1912; repr. 1958).

Bibliography: A. Band, "Tadmîtô šel mōše(h) rabbēnû ʾesel ʿaḥad hāʿām. . . . " *World Congress of Jewish Studies* 8 (1983) pt. 3, 217-21. **N. Bentwich,** *A. H. and His Philosophy* (1927). **A. Gottschalk,** "A. H., the Bible, and the Bible Tradition" (diss., University of Southern California, 1965). **Y. Kaufmann,** "ʿiqqārē dē ʿ ôtā(y)w šel ʾaḥad hāʿām," *Hatekufah* 24 (1928) 421-39. **J. Kornberg** (ed.), *At the Crossroads: Essays on A. H.* (1983). **L. Simon,** *A. H., A. G.: A Biography* (1960). **S. J. Zipperstein,** *Elusive Prophet: A. H. and the Origins of Zionism* (1993).

E. L. GREENSTEIN

AHARONI, YOHANAN (1919–76)

Born in Frankfurt, Germany, in 1919, A. emigrated to Palestine in 1933. He was a member of Kibbutz Allonim from 1938 to 1947. He earned his PhD from the Hebrew University of Jerusalem in 1955 with a dissertation on the settlement of the Israelite tribes in upper Galilee (1957, Hebrew). He rose to the rank of associate professor at the Hebrew University (1966) but in 1968 left to found the Institute of Archaeology at Tel Aviv University and also to chair the department of ancient Near Eastern studies there (until his death on Feb. 10, 1976). A.'s field excavations began with Y. YADIN at Hazor (1955–58), and he worked with him again (1960–61) in the Judean desert caves. A. then directed numerous projects on his own: Ramat Rahel (1954–62), Arad (1962–67), Lachish (1966–68), and especially Tel Beersheva (1969–74).

A.'s career was unusual among Israeli archaeologists, combining ARCHAEOLOGY, historical geography, biblical studies, and epigraphy—no doubt partly due to the influence of his mentor, B. MAZAR. A.'s principal publications reflected this breadth of interests. He published many report volumes on archaeology (and epigraphy) as well as a synthetic textbook. His 1955 thesis on historical geography was followed by many articles and Hebrew studies on the subject as well as by two principal full-scale works in English (1967, 1968).

A. was a pioneer in many respects. One of his most significant contributions was the introduction of the now-popular regional approach, combining extensive surface survey with selective excavations (especially in his work in Galilee and later in the Negev). He will also be remembered for his founding of the Tel Aviv Institute and its journal *Tel Aviv*. This was a bold challenge to the Jerusalem establishment dominated by Yadin, but it proved extraordinarily stimulating to a younger generation of Israeli archaeologists. Despite the heated controversy surrounding A. because of his excavation methods and scholarly views, he remained personally a gentle, open-hearted man. He was deeply imbued with a love of the land of Israel and courageously dedicated to recovering its past.

Works: *The Settlement of the Israelite Tribes in Upper Galilee* (1957), Hebrew; *Excavations at Ramat Rahel, Seasons 1959 and 1960* (1962); *Seasons 1961 and 1962* (1964); *The Land of the Bible: A Historical Geography* (1967, rev. ed. 1979); (with M. Avi-Jonah), *The Macmillan Bible Atlas* (1968, rev. ed. 1993); *Beer-sheba I: Excavations at Tel Beer-Sheba, 1969–1971 Seasons* (1973); *Arad Inscriptions* (1975; ET 1981); *Lachish V: Investigations at Lachish. The Sanctuary and the Residency* (1975); *Archaeology of the Land of Israel* (1977); *The Archaeology of the Land of Israel: From the Prehistoric Beginnings to the End of the First Temple Period* (ed. M. Aharoni, tr. A. F. Rainey, 1982).

Bibliography: *ErIsr* 15 (1981). *IEJ* 26 (1976) 155-56. *Tel Aviv* 3, 1, and 4 (1976).

W. G. DEVER

AHLSTRÖM, GÖSTA WERNER (1918–92)

Born Aug. 27, 1918, in Sandviken in east central Sweden, A. was the son of a Methodist clergyman. By the time he was fifteen both of his parents had died and he was working full time; nevertheless, he earned his gymnasium certificate in 1943 through correspondence courses and went on to the University of Göteborg for a year. He then moved to the University of Uppsala, where he received his teol. kan. (1950), teol. lic. (1955), and teol. dr. (1959) from the faculty of theology; and his fil. kan. in history of religions, Semitic languages, and ASSYRIOLOGY (1961) from the faculty of humanities. At Uppsala he served as instructor in OT from 1954 to 1959, as *Docent* of OT from 1959 to 1964, and as professor *pro tempore* of OT in 1961. In 1957 he studied at Basel and Heidelberg on an international fellowship from the Olaus Petri Foundation.

While at Uppsala A. studied under the main representatives of the so-called Uppsala school of OT studies, I. ENGNELL, G. Widengren, and H. S. NYBERG, acquiring the usual interests and methods associated with this group of scholars: an emphasis on the consonantal MT as the best reflection of the underlying oral tradition that had undergone centuries of development before being committed to writing; an emphasis on Israelite cult, PROPHECY, and kingship and the need to place them in their larger, ancient Near Eastern contexts for proper understanding; and a use of traditio-historical methodology (see TRADITION HISTORY) for textual exegesis.

In 1962 A. accepted an invitation to be a visiting professor of OT at the University of Chicago divinity school; the following year he became a member of that faculty, teaching in both Bible and history of religions. In 1974 he received a joint appointment to the faculty of the department of Near Eastern languages and civilizations and in 1976 became full professor of OT and ancient Palestinian studies in both faculties.

A major turning point in A.'s career came in 1969–70

when he served as the annual professor at the Albright Institute of Archaeological Research in Jerusalem. He was introduced to Syro-Palestinian ARCHAEOLOGY and participated in the first of many excavations in Israel, Cyprus, and Tunisia. As a result, during the 1970s the focus of his research moved away from texts alone—their historical contexts and their subsequent development—to include artifactual data and a stronger emphasis on ancient Syro-Palestinian history, including the history of Israel and Judah. At a time when synchronic LITERARY studies were becoming the vogue in biblical studies and history was on the wane, he was one of the few scholars in America and Europe who kept a consistent focus on the historical reliability of details within the diachronic biblical texts, the social production of various biblical and extra-biblical texts, and the issues involved in using the Bible and artifactual remains recovered through excavation to write a history of ancient Syria-Palestine. When he died Jan. 17, 1992, he was awaiting the publication of his 905-page *magnum opus,* a history of ancient Syria-Palestine, which was the culmination both of two decades of interest and research in texts and artifacts and of his lifelong interest and training in history and religion. The volume, published posthumously, places the history of Israel and Judah in the wider context of ancient Syria-Palestine.

Works: *Psalm 89: Eine Liturgie aus dem Ritual des leidenden Königs* (1959); *Aspects of Syncretism in Israelite Religion* (1963); *Joel and the Temple Cult of Jerusalem* (1971); "Wine-Presses and Cup-Marks of the Jenin-Megiddo Survey," *BASOR* 231 (1978) 19-49; *Royal Administration and National Religion in Ancient Palestine* (SHANE, 1982); *An Archaeological Picture of Iron Age Religions in Ancient Palestine* (1984); "The Early Iron Age Settlers at Hirbet el-Msās (Tel Māśōś)," *ZDPV* 100 (1984) 35-52; *Who Were the Israelites?* (1986); *The History of Ancient Palestine* (1993); "Pharaoh Shoshenq's Campaign to Palestine," *History and Traditions of Early Israel: Studies Presented to E. Nielsen May 8th, 1993* (ed. A. Lemaire and B. Otzen, 1993) 1-16; "The Seal of Shema," *SJOT* 7 (1993) 208-15.

Bibliography: W. B. Barrick, "G. W. A. in Profile," *In the Shelter of Elyon* (ed. W. B. Barrick and J. R. Spencer, 1984) 27-30. **W. B. Barrick and J. R. Spencer,** "Parentheses in a Snowstorm: G. W. A. and the Study of Ancient Palestine," ibid., 43-65.

D. EDELMAN

AILRED OF RIEVAULX (c. 1109–67)

Born in England, A. was educated at the court of King David of Scotland. He was drawn to the monastic life and entered the Cistercian abbey of Rievaulx in Yorkshire c. 1133. In 1143 he was abbot of Revesby and from 1147 abbot of Rievaulx itself. He did not follow many able young men of his day by studying in the schools of northern France; his learning was chiefly biblical and patristic, with an especially profound debt to AUGUSTINE.

A.'s writings came out of the spiritual leadership he gave his monks and reflect Cistercian attitudes. He authored a treatise on friendship (*De Spirituali Amicitia*) that seeks to make Cicero Christian; *The Mirror of Love;* and *On the Soul,* a book that explores some of the problems raised and not fully settled by Augustine. His most important exegetical work is the treatise *Jesus as a Boy of Twelve,* in which he explored the story of JESUS talking with the elders according to its literal and spiritual senses. A. exemplifies twelfth-century monastic scholarship, which emphasized the reflective and prayerful side of *lectio divina.*

Works: *Opera Omnia* (CCCM 1, ed. A. Hoste and C. H. Talbot, 1971).

Bibliography: I. **Biffi,** "Bibbia e Liturgia nei sermoni liturgici di Aelredo di Rievaulx," *Bibbia e spiritualità* (ed. C. Vagaggini, 1967) 516-98. **A. Squire,** *Aelred of Rievaulx: A Study* (1969, rev. ed. 1981).

G. R. EVANS

AINSWORTH, HENRY (1571–1622)

An English Separatist educated at Caius College, Cambridge, A. removed to Amsterdam in 1593, where he was pastor to a congregation of exiles. Accomplished in Hebrew, he improved his knowledge through acquaintance with Dutch Jews. His translations of and commentaries on the Pentateuch (see PENTATEUCHAL CRITICISM) and other biblical books were literal renditions of Hebrew idiom and drew on comparisons with the SEPTUAGINT and "Chaldee" (Aramaic) versions as well as on rabbinic lore. His translation of the Psalms was one of the versions sung by the Puritans. A. thought that "the literal sense of the Hebrew should be the ground of all interpretation" but that the OT also contained "types and shadows" of what was to come in the NT. He interpreted the Song of Solomon as an allegory of the church as the bride of Christ and defended the Hebrew vowel points and the marginal variants of the Masoretes as part of the original text and of divine INSPIRATION. He controverted H. BROUGHTON's argument that the high priest's ephod could not be silk but had to be translated "wool" since the worms that made silk were ritually impure.

Works: *Certayne Questions Concerning 1. Silk, or Wool, in the High Priest's Ephod ... Handled between Mr. H. Broughton ... and Mr. H. A.* (1605); *Annotations Upon the Five Bookes of Moses, The Booke of Psalmes, and the Song of Songs, Or Canticles* (1627).

Bibliography: W. E. Axon, *DNB* 1 (1885) 191-94. T. **Liu,** *BDBR* 1 (1982) 3-4. **M. E. Moody,** "A Man of a Thousand: The Reputation and Character of H. A.," *Huntington Library Quarterly* 45 (1982) 200-214. **B. R. White,** *The English Separatist Tradition: From the Marian Martyrs to the Pilgrim Fathers* (1971).

D. D. WALLACE, JR.

AKIBA (c. 50–135 CE)

A. ben Joseph, born in the lowlands of Judea, was one of the most outstanding *tannaim* of his day. According to tradition, he was originally an unlearned man who disdained the rabbinic scholars (*b. Pesahim* 49b) and had to master language and learning from scratch (*'Abot R. Nat.* A 6:15). He studied at the academy in Lydda and founded his own academy at Bene-Berak. When the Jewish revolt against Rome erupted in 132 CE, he supported it enthusiastically and apparently recognized the Jewish leader Kosiba as a messianic redeemer, applying to him the reference to the "star out of Jacob" (Num 24:17)—thus the title Bar-Kochba (Son of the Star). A. was captured by the Romans, suffered torture, and died as a martyr.

In exegeting Scripture A. considered the entire Torah to have emanated from God and to contain no redundancies. Thus every word of the text, including particles and duplicated verbal forms, was significant and replete with meaning. Although A. is credited with reading significance into even the decorative marks on Hebrew letters (*b. Menah.* 29b), no examples of such reading have survived in rabbinic literature. He practiced the allegorical interpretation of some scriptural texts and spoke out in favor of the Song of Songs as a canonical book (*m. Yad.* 3:5; see CANON OF THE BIBLE), and his allegorical and mystical approach to the work (*t. Sanh.* 12:10; *b. Sanh.* 101a) became standard in many Jewish circles. A., his students, and his disciples played significant roles in the collection of early rabbinic traditions.

Bibliography: P. **Benoit,** "Rabbi Aquiba ben Joseph, sage et héros du Judaïsme," *RB* 54 (1947) 54-89. J. **Bornstein,** *EJ* 2 (1928) 7-22. L. **Finkelstein,** *A.: Scholar, Saint, and Martyr* (1936). H. **Freedman,** *EncJud* 2 (1971) 488-92. A. **Goldberg,** "Rede und Offenbarung in der Schriftauslegung Rabbi A.s," *Frankfurter Judaistische Beiträge* 8 (1980) 61-79. P. **von der Osten-Sacken,** *Rabbi A.: Texte und Interpretationen zum rabbinischen Judentum und NT* (ANTZ 1, 1987). G. G. **Porton,** "The Artificial Dispute: Ishmael and A.," *Christianity, Judaism, and Other Greco-Roman Cults* (SJLA 12, 4 vols., ed. J. Neusner, 1975) 4:18-29. S. **Safrai** (ed.), *The Literature of the Sages, First Part: Oral Tora, Halakha, Mishna, Tosefta, Talmud, External Tractates* (CRINT 2, 3a, 1987), see index. H. L. **Strack and G. Stemberger,** *Introduction to the Talmud and Midrash* (1991) 79-80. E. E. **Urbach,** "The Homiletical Interpretation of the Sages and the Exposition of Origen on Canticles, and Jewish-Christian Disputation," *Scripta* 22 (1971) 247-75.

J. H. HAYES

ALAN OF LILLE (d. 1202)

A. died a Cistercian monk in 1202, but his date of birth is uncertain. Evidence suggests that he may have been in his late eighties or nineties at his death. If so, he may have studied under P. ABELARD and GILBERT DE LA PORRÉE. A. taught in the schools of France for a lifetime and earned the title *doctor universalis* for the range of his learning. He was the author of a number of works in new genres of his age, of poetry as well as of commentaries and sermons. His writings display a knowledge of Scripture and the fathers, of the liberal arts, of the new logic and the new science, and of the *hermetica*. He probably lectured on the whole Bible. His "Elucidation of the Song of Songs" was saved by a prior of Cluny, and his pupils put together notes of his glosses on the songs of the HB and the NT; an allegory of the six wings of the cherubim in Isaiah 6 survives. Undoubtedly more is extant, but the problems of secure attribution are considerable.

A.'s most important contributions in exegesis were twofold. His manual *The Art of Preaching* preceded the series of handbooks on the method of delivering a university-style sermon that were produced from about 1230. He began with general advice and provided collections of material appropriate for use in considering certain topics (vices and virtues) and for addressing a variety of audiences (clergy, widows, princes). Biblical texts are arranged in these groups with patristic and some secular authorities. His own sermons show something of the way these commonplaces were used. The technique departs from the framework of the Augustinian or Gregorian homily, in which the biblical text was interpreted phrase by phrase, in favor of a topical treatment.

A. was the author of one of the first of the DICTIONARIES of theological terms that were among the novel aids to Bible study developed in the late twelfth and thirteenth centuries. Words occurring in the Bible are given in a rough alphabetical order, with texts to show the different meanings each may carry in context. A. regarded the "proper" sense as that which refers to the divine, whether or not it is figurative. ("Arm," for instance, properly means "Christ.") This is a development both of a technique used informally by GREGORY THE GREAT and by others among the fathers and of the work of the twelfth century on the theory of signification. A. was a pioneer among other pioneers in providing such aids to Bible study, even though his own work was not notably influential; he represents a significant shift in method in the late twelfth century from the *lectio divina* of monastic study of the Bible to study in the context of schools and universities, where the pace was brisk and textbooks were needed.

Works: *PL* 210; *Alain de Lille: Textes inédits avec une introduction sur sa vie et ses oeuvres* (M. T. d'Alverny, Études de philosophie medievale 52, 1965).

Bibliography: **G. R. Evans,** *Alan of Lille: The Frontiers of Theology in the Later Twelfth Century* (1983). **G. Silagi,** *TRE* 2 (1978) 155-60. **W. Wetherbee,** *DMA* 1 (1982) 119-20.

G. R. EVANS

ALAND, KURT (1915–94)

A. was born Mar. 28, 1915, in Berlin. Confirmation classes and the youth organization "Wartburgbund" influenced him deeply during the difficult times at the close of the Weimar Republic. After graduating in 1933 he studied Protestant theology, the classics, history, and ARCHAEOLOGY in Berlin. His studies received a decisive orientation through the church historian and text critic H. LIETZMANN, who became his teacher and led him to scientific work; Lietzmann made A. his personal assistant in 1937. In 1938 A. passed the first theological examination at the Bruderrat der Bekennenden Kirche, Berlin, and in 1939 he obtained a licentiate of theology. He habilitated and became superior assistant of the theological faculty in 1941; however, for political reasons he could not obtain a lectureship. In 1945 he became a *Dozent* in East Berlin and in 1946 an *ausserordentlicher* professor; from 1947 he was also on the faculty at Halle. Declared a public enemy, A. escaped from the German Democratic Republic in 1958 and the following year became a professor of church history and NT TEXTUAL CRITICISM in Münster, where he founded the Institute for NT Textual Research. He also built up a Bible museum (founded 1979) affiliated with the institute that offers exhibits on the history of the Bible from its manuscript beginnings to the present. A. was director of the institute until his retirement in 1983, when his wife, B. Aland, became director. He died Apr. 13, 1994, in Münster.

Although a productive scholar in church history, A.'s work in textual criticism of the NT established his worldwide reputation. By gathering films of all known manuscripts of the NT from around the world in his institute in Münster (more than 90 percent of the approx. 5,660 manuscripts), he created the basis for comprehensive research on the NT text and made Münster the international center for NT textual criticism. Beginning with the twenty-second edition (1956), he served as co-editor of Eberhard and Erwin Nestle's *Novum Testamentum graece*; in the course of time the "Nestle" became the "Nestle-Aland." He was also a member of the editorial committee of the *Greek New Testament* (*GNT*). Both editions (the *GNT* has reached its 4th edition, the Nestle-Aland its 27th) offer the same text, differing only in critical apparatus. According to an agreement between the Vatican and the United Bible Societies, these two editions are to be used for every TRANSLATION and every revision of traditional translations. A. wanted all readers of the NT in whatever translation to benefit from the results of NT textual research. This conviction energized his work.

A. also strove to compile an *Editio Critica Maior*

(*ECM*) of the Greek NT, an edition presenting all known variants in the Greek manuscript tradition of the first millennium in the early versions, and the Greek fathers. To this end he tried to record and penetrate the mass of Greek text manuscripts as completely as possible. The results of these investigations are published in *Text und Textwert der griechischen Handschriften des Neuen Testaments*. The first installment of the *ECM* appeared only after his death, in 1997. He also edited a *Synopsis Quattuor Evangeliotum* and took care that the Nestle-Aland was published in bilingual editions (e.g., Greek-Latin, Greek-English, Greek-German, Greek-Italian). He edited or initiated the publication of concordances, a dictionary (Bauer-Aland), and special editions like *Das Neue Testament auf Papyrus* and *Das Neue Testament in syrischer Überlieferung*. He also continued and revised the Itala series of the OL evidence of the Gospels of A. JÜLICHER and W. Matzkow. The series *Arbeiten zur neutestamentlichen Textforschung* testifies to the breadth of the continuing research carried on by the institute he founded.

Works: *Kirchengeschichtliche Entwürfe: Alte Kirche-Reformation und Luthertum—Pietismus und Erweckungsbewegung* (1960); (ed.), *P. J. Spener, Pia desideria* (1964³; textbook ed., with B. Köster, vol. 1, 1, 1996); (ed. with W. Müller), *I. H. von Wessenberg: Unveröffentlichte Manuskripte und Briefe* (1968, 1970, 1979, 1987); (ed.), *Die alten Übersetzungen des Neuen Testaments, die Kirchenväterzitate und Lektionare* (ANTT 5, 1972); (ed.), *Vollständige Konkordanz zum griechischen Neuen Testament* (vol. 2, 1978; vol. 1, ANTT 4, 1.2, 1983); *Neutestamentliche Entwürfe* (TBü 63, 1979); *A History of Christianity* (vol. 1, 1985; vol. 2, 1986); (ed.), *Die Korrespondenz H. M. Mühlenbergs* (4 vols., 1986, 1987, 1990, 1993; 5th in preparation; ET of the letters from 1740, 1747, 1993); *Die Reformatoren: Luther, Melanchthon, Zwingli, Calvin* (Gütersloher Taschenbücher 204, 1986⁴); *Text und Textwert der griechischen Handschriften des Neuen Testaments* (Katholische Briefe, ANTT 9-11, 1987; Paulinische Briefe, ANTT 16-19, 1991; Apostelgeschichte, ANTT 20-21, 1993; Markusevangelium, ANTT 26-27, 1998); (ed. with B. Aland), *Griechisch-deutsches Wörterbuch zu den Schriften des Neuen Testaments und der frühchristlichen Literatur von W. Bauer* (1988); (with B. Aland), *The Text of the NT: An Introduction to the Critical Editions and to the Theory and Practice of Modern Textual Criticism* (1989²); (ed.), *Luther Deutsch* (10 vols., 1991); (ed.), *The Greek NT* (1993⁴); *K. von Tischendorf (1815–1874): Neutestamentliche Textforschung damals und heute* (SSAW.PH 133, 2, 1993); (ed.), *Novum Testamentum graece* (Nestle-Aland, 1993²⁷); *Kurzgefasste Liste der griechischen Handschriften des Neuen Testaments* (ANTT 1, 1994²); (ed.), *Synopsis Quattuor Evangeliorum* (1996¹⁵); (ed.), *Novum Testamentum Graecum: Editio Critica Maior,* vol. 4, installment 1, *James* (1997).

Bibliography: M. Hengel, "Laudatio K. A.," *K. A. in memoriam* (1995) 17-34. H. Kunst, "K. A.: Eine Würdigung," *Text, Wort, Glaube: Studien zur Überlieferung, Interpretation, und Autorisierung biblischer Texte, K. A. gewidmet* (ed. M. Brecht, 1980) 1-15. E. Lohse, "Wahrheit des Evangeliums— zum Gedanken an K. A.," *K. A. in memoriam* (1995) 35-40.

B. KÖSTER

ALBRIGHT, WILLIAM FOXWELL (1891–1971)

Born May 24, 1891, A. was the son of Wesleyan Methodist missionaries in Chile. By age three (after he learned to read) he suffered typhoid fever, which probably caused his severe myopia. When he was five his family returned on furlough to his grandmother's farm in Iowa, where A.'s left hand was drawn into the pulley of a farm machine and crippled. Given these circumstances, after the family returned to Chile he was thrown onto the resources of his father's library of history and theology and assisted his parents in teaching his younger brothers and sisters in their home school.

The family returned to Iowa when he was twelve, and A. attended regular schools, graduating from Upper Iowa University in Fayette in 1912. Having taught himself Hebrew and Assyrian (see ASSYRIOLOGY AND BIBLICAL STUDIES), he submitted an article to a German scholarly journal, a proof of which he sent with his application to P. HAUPT, head of the Oriental Seminary at Johns Hopkins University, where A. would receive his PhD in 1916; his dissertation, "The Assyrian Deluge Epic," was never published.

After WWI A. went to Palestine, having won the Thayer Fellowship for study in Palestine at the young AMERICAN SCHOOL OF ORIENTAL RESEARCH in Jerusalem. He studied modern Hebrew and Arabic, soon became director of the school, and carried on explorations of the land, usually by walking or on horseback tours with his students, mostly clergy, there for a few months' study.

A. turned from exploration to excavation, beginning with Tel el-Ful north of Jerusalem, which he believed to have been Gibeah, King Saul's capital. His four seasons at Tell Beit Mirsim with M. Kyle became a model for archaeological work in the Holy Land for many decades; its stratigraphy, combined with pottery sequence-dating, put Palestinian ARCHAEOLOGY on solid footing. He made a valiant effort to put the Bible on a solid historical basis by showing how archaeological research validated much of the biblical narrative. Adopting a moderately critical position against J. WELLHAUSEN and other more radical critics, A. defended the essential historicity not only of the Mosaic period but also of the patriarchal period. He excavated at Beth-zur and Bethel with O. Sellers and J. Kelso, training such later famous scholars and archaeologists as G. E. WRIGHT, J. BRIGHT, N. GLUECK, and B. MAZAR.

A. returned to Johns Hopkins as successor to Haupt in the William Wallace Spence chair of Semitic languages and as chairman of the Oriental Seminary, a position he held until his mandatory retirement in 1958. From 1930 to 1968 he edited *BASOR*. This journal, begun by J. MONTGOMERY just as A. went to Palestine, became the main vehicle for his articles, first on explorations and excavations, then on ancient history, CHRONOLOGY, and linguistic studies. A. founded *JPOS* after helping to organize the Palestine Oriental Society in Jerusalem.

In the 1930s and 1940s he began publishing books, many of which were translated into other languages, and guiding his few but outstanding students to similar careers. He was one of the early decipherers and translators of the Ugaritic tablets (see UGARIT AND THE BIBLE), contributing numerous articles on their meaning and value, especially for the understanding of biblical Hebrew POETRY. A. was one of the first scholars to recognize the authenticity and early date of the DEAD SEA SCROLLS. He traveled widely, lecturing to nonspecialists as well as to scholarly audiences and receiving from universities in America and several foreign countries about thirty honorary degrees.

During the 1930s A. helped numerous German Jewish scholars find posts in the United States to escape the Hitler menace. In the 1940s many Catholic students, cut off from studies in Rome by the war, came to him. Among scholars he trained were D. N. FREEDMAN, F. M. CROSS, T. Lambdin, M. DAHOOD, W. Moran, R. BROWN, and J. FITZMYER.

In expeditions organized by W. Phillips, A. explored in Sinai and excavated in south Arabia. He spent a fall semester in Turkey in 1957; he made return visits to Israel in 1953, 1958, and in 1969 on a grand tour when he was made a "Worthy," or honorary citizen, of Jerusalem. Two months after his eightieth birthday he suffered strokes that culminated in his death on Sept. 19, 1971.

A. drew on his unparalleled knowledge of the languages and cultures of the Near East, utilizing primary sources from Egypt to Assyria and beyond. While there have since been refinements in detail and corrections at various points, his chronology still stands as a major contribution to scholarship on the ancient Near East. His studies in Egyptian syllabic orthography (see EGYPTOLOGY AND BIBLICAL STUDIES) were revolutionary in their day and are still important, and his studies in northwest Semitic and Proto-Sinaitic inscriptions were both seminal and substantial. His special expertise in epigraphy and orthography helped to establish those disciplines. In the field of biblical studies his main contributions were in the historical reconstruction of the experience of Israel from the beginning down to the postexilic period. Throughout he endeavored to correlate the latest archaeological findings with the biblical materials in making both a plausible and a factual reconstruction of Israelite history. For his insights and leadership A. is acknowledged as the "dean of biblical archaeology."

Works: *The Archaeology of Palestine and the Bible* (1932); *The Excavation of Tell Beit Mirsim* (AASOR, 1932, 1933, 1938, 1943); *The Vocalization of the Egyptian Syllable Orthography* (1934); *From the Stone Age to Christianity: Monotheism and the Historical Process* (1940); *Archaeology and the Religion of Israel* (1942); *The Archaeology of Palestine* (1949); *The Biblical Period from Abraham to Ezra* (1950, 1963); *Samuel and the Beginnings of the Prophetic Movement* (1961); *History, Archaeology and Christian Humanism* (1964); *The Proto-Sinaitic Inscriptions and Their Decipherment* (1966, 1969); *Yahweh and the Gods of Canaan: An Historical Analysis of Two Contrasting Faiths* (1968); (with C. S. Mann), *Matthew* (AB 26, 1971).

Bibliography: "Celebrating and Examining W. F. A.," *BA* 56, 1 (1993) 3-52 (with contributions by J. M. Sasson, N. A. Silbermann, W. Hallo, W. G. Dever, and B. O. Long). **D. N. Freedman** (ed.), *The Published Works of W. F. A.: A Comprehensive Bibliography* (1975), 1,100 titles. **S. E. Hardwick,** "Change and Constancy in W. F. A.'s Treatment of Early OT History and Religion, 1918–1958" (diss., New York University, 1966). **B. O. Long,** *Planting and Reaping A.: Politics, Ideology, and Interpreting the Bible* (1997). **A. Malamat** (ed.), *ErIsr* (W. F. A. vol. 9, 1969); **L. G. Running and D. N. Freedman,** *W. F. A.: A Twentieth-century Genius* (1975; centennial ed., 1991). **E. A. Speiser** (ed.), *BASOR* 122 (April 1951). **G. W. Van Beek** (ed.), *The Scholarship of W. F. A.: An Appraisal* (1989). **M. Weippert,** *TRE* 2 (1978) 193-95. **G. E. Wright** (ed.), *The Bible and the Ancient Near East: Essays in Honor of W. F. A.* (1961).

L. G. RUNNING

ALCUIN, ALBINIUS FLACCUS (c. 735–804)

A. was educated in the cathedral school at York, England, where he became master in 766. In 781 he met Emperor Charlemagne at Parma and became the emperor's adviser in religious matters and his tutor, providing him with a number of simple dialogues of elementary instruction in the liberal arts. Among his other pupils was RABANUS MAURUS, the encyclopedist. A.'s gifts as an educator were outstanding; he was able to present material in an easily digestible form for beginners. He carried the technique into his biblical commentary, for which other studies were a preparation, e.g., in his "Questions and Answers on Genesis." He also made collections of extracts from sources to help students without access to the full texts of the fathers, although he did so in a less scholarly manner than did BEDE and often by borrowing from other collections. In this way he made an important contribution to the process by which the biblical text acquired its medieval study apparatus, notably in establishing the practice of copying JEROME's prologue with each book. His own commentary, like those of his contemporaries, added almost nothing to what the fathers had said. The technique was to select and arrange extracts, and the value of an individual commentary lay in the skill and appropriateness with which this selection and arrangement were carried out.

A.'s most significant achievement as an exegete was the reform and standardization of the biblical text. He was not the only scholar of his day to see the need for correction of the corruptions that had crept in; Theodulf of Orleans also produced a revised version, but A.'s was the more influential revision, to judge from the number of surviving manuscripts. He presented it to Charlemagne on his coronation as emperor in 800. The difficulty was to collate versions, not all of which derived directly from the VULGATE (there are traces of the complex OL tradition). A. seems to have made use especially of English and Northumbrian manuscripts.

Works: *PL* 100-101.

Bibliography: **W. Edelstein,** *Eruditio und Sapientia* (1965). **F. L. Ganshof,** "La révision de la Bible par A.," *BHR* 9 (1947) 1-20. **W. Heil,** *TRE* 2 (1978) 266-76. **A. J. Kleinclausz,** *Alcuin* (Annals de l'universite de Lyon 3, 15, 1948). **L. K. Shook,** *DMA* 1 (1982) 142-43. **B. Smalley,** *The Study of the Bible in the Middle Ages* (1983³). **L. Wallach,** *A. and Charlemagne: Studies in Carolingian History and Literature* (1959, rev. ed. 1968).

G. R. EVANS

ALEXANDER, ARCHIBALD (1772–1851)

Born to Scotch-Irish parents near Lexington, Virginia, A. was strongly influenced by his heritage. An ordained Presbyterian minister, he served as professor of theology at Princeton Seminary (1812–48), an institution he helped to found in 1812 along with S. Miller and A. Green.

A.'s greatest contributions to the science of biblical interpretation lie in the institution he helped to begin and the students it produced. He was known as a gifted speaker, and his sermons and speeches were full of scriptural quotations and references. As a young man he had been exposed to revival preaching, and this influenced not only his decision to enter the ministry but also the pattern of his later teaching and writing. A firm Calvinist (see CALVIN), he adhered to the Westminster Standards as they were interpreted by such scholastics of the seventeenth century as F. Turretin; however, his experience with revivals made him appreciative of the issues of conversion, testimony, and evangelical piety. Thus his biblical interpretation was marked by Calvinist orthodoxy, with a strong emphasis on the testimony of miracles in the biblical period and in the inspired writings of the apostles (see INSPIRATION OF THE BIBLE). He was also an apologist, discussing religious experience and the evidence for the Bible's trustworthiness in his writings.

A.'s teaching and writing influenced many students who went on to important posts in teaching, educational administration, and Christian ministry. Among them were C. HODGE, W. GREEN, and A.'s sons James and Joseph ALEXANDER.

Works: *A Brief Outline of the Evidences of the Christian Religion* (1825); *The Canon of the Old and New Testaments Ascertained* (1826); *Evidences of the Authenticity, Inspiration, and Canonical Authority of the Holy Scriptures* (1836); *A Brief Compend of Bible Truth* (1846); *A History of the Israelitish Nation from Their Origin to the Dispersion at the Destruction of Jerusalem by the Romans* (1852).

Bibliography: **J. W. Alexander,** *The Life of A. A., DD, First Professor in the Theological Seminary at Princeton, New Jersey* (1854). **R. V. Huggins,** "A Note on A. A.'s Apologetic Motive in Positing 'Errors' in the Autographs," *WTJ* 57 (1995) 463-70. **L. Loetscher,** *Facing the Enlightenment and Pietism: A. A. and the Founding of Princeton Seminary* (1983). **D. McKim,** "A. A. and the Doctrine of Scripture," *JPH* 54 (Fall 1976) 355-75. **M. A. Noll,** *The Princeton Theology, 1812–1921: Scripture, Science, Theological Method from A. A. to B. B. Warfield* (1983) 59-104, with full bibliographical listings. **M. A. Taylor,** "The OT in the Old Princeton School" (diss., Yale University, 1988) 1-90.

J. A. DEARMAN

ALEXANDER, JOSEPH ADDISON (1809–60)

A Princeton Seminary professor and exegete, A. was born in Philadelphia, the third son of A. ALEXANDER, the first professor of the seminary. He showed early promise of outstanding linguistic skills, taking up the study of Latin soon after learning to read English. At age six he knew the Hebrew alphabet, and at ten he read the biblical Hebrew text fluently. He graduated from Princeton with highest honors at age seventeen. He then studied Hebrew and other Semitic languages for two years privately with a Jewish scholar from Philadelphia named Horwitz. From 1830 to 1833 A. served as adjunct professor of ancient languages and literature at Princeton while attending the seminary. He was eventually accredited with mastery of seven languages, but he could read and write fourteen others and had reading ability in yet five more. In 1833–34 he studied and traveled in Europe, especially Berlin, where he was impressed by E. HENGSTENBERG. He returned to teach at Princeton Theological Seminary as instructor (1834), associate professor (1838), and professor of oriental and biblical literature (1840–51); he held a chair in biblical and ecclesiastical history (1851–59); and he was professor of Hellenistic and NT literature from 1859 until his death. A. was in great demand as a preacher and published two volumes of sermons (1860).

A prolific writer, A. contributed numerous articles to

the *Biblical Repository,* which he edited for several years, and published commentaries on both OT and NT books. As an exegete his greatest contribution lay in translation and grammatical explanation, as is especially obvious in commentaries on Psalms, Mark, and Acts. He used works of European and British scholars and entered into dialogue with them, especially in his commentary on Isaiah, in which he defended the traditional position on the unity and christological interpretation of the book, on occasion faulting M. STUART for eroding the christological tendencies of various pericopes in Isaiah 40–66. Perhaps more than any other scholar, A. provided the exegetical foundations for "Princeton theology," and his commentaries on Isaiah, Psalms, and Mark were among the few American biblical studies respected by European scholars in the nineteenth century.

Works: *Isaiah* (2 vols., 1846–47); *The Psalms Translated and Explained* (3 vols. 1850); *Acts of the Apostles* (2 vols., 1857, 1860³); *The Gospel According to Mark* (1858); *The Gospel According to Matthew* (1861).

Bibliography: H. C. Alexander, *The Life of J. A. A.* (2 vols., 1870). **F. W. Loetscher,** *DAB* 1 (1928) 173. **J. H. Moorhead,** "J. A. A.: Common Sense, Romanticism, and Biblical Criticism at Princeton," *JPH* 53 (1975) 51-65. **M. A. Taylor,** "The OT in the Old Princeton School" (diss., Yale University, 1988) 166-307.

T. H. OLBRICHT

ALEXANDRIAN SCHOOL

This school is particularly associated with the practice of allegorical interpretation. The most notable practitioner, ORIGEN (c. 185–254), was later accused of excessive allegory, along with other faults, and condemned. Some of his followers went down with him. However, especially in the spirituality of the Eastern church, his methods and many of his exegetical proposals survived and were also influential in the medieval West through the medium of JEROME's commentaries.

Origen was by no means the first to employ allegory in exegesis. The method, derived from philosophical treatment of classical Greek texts like those of Homer, had been used extensively by the Alexandrian Jew PHILO. Early Alexandrian Christianity seems to have been GNOSTIC in tendency—both Valentinus and Basilides hailed from that center of Hellenistic syncretism—and Gnosticism used allegory to develop its systems from ancient sacred texts. Tradition has it that Origen was the third "head" of the catechetical school in Alexandria and that he and a number of named successors followed an educational and theological line pioneered by Pantaenus and CLEMENT OF ALEXANDRIA. The existence of this school as a continuous institution

has been questioned, but certainly there were successive teachers in several generations with a recognizably common intellectualism and approach to Scripture. Clement claimed to be seeking and teaching the way of the true gnostic, and the church subsequently recognized his orthodoxy by canonizing him. Ironically, though later condemned, Origen was in some ways closer to the mainstream than Clement was.

Origen's theory of scriptural interpretation was dependent on that of Philo, but it was developed in his own way and backed up by Scripture. Origen used the analogy of body, soul, and spirit, claiming that Scripture has three senses: the literal, the moral, and the spiritual. The threefold sense of Scripture was grounded in Prov 22:20-21: "Do thou record them threefold in counsel and knowledge, that thou mayest answer words of truth to those who question thee." The simple person, said Origen, may be edified by what we might call the flesh of Scripture, this name being given to the obvious interpretation; while the person who has made some progress may be edified by its soul; and the person who is perfect and, like those mentioned by the apostle in 1 Cor 2:6-7, able to receive God's wisdom in a mystery, may be edified by the spiritual law, which has "a shadow of the good things to come." Just as a person consists of body, soul, and spirit, so also in the same way does Scripture (*De Prin.* 4.2.4). Origen's practice of scriptural interpretation was not, however, so schematized as this theory suggests. He rarely set out each of the three meanings of any given text.

Although often undistinguished, two different things are meant by the "literal" meaning: the historical reference of a narrative and the actual practice of legal and ritual rulings. Origen tended to undermine the importance of both these "obvious" senses, on the one hand attributing literal interpretation to the Jews, who practice the law, and claiming that Christians are not meant to take legal texts literally but spiritually. On the other hand, he pointed out that such impossibilities as God's planting a tree like a farmer or walking in paradise in the cool of the day are to be taken as figurative expressions that indicate certain mysteries in the semblance of history and not actual events. His practice of contrasting the literal exegesis of the Jews with the "spiritual" exegesis of Christians is given NT backing. For example, Isaac's weaning suggests the necessity of leaving milk and moving on to solid food (see 1 Cor 3:2; Heb 5:12-14), while the story of Sarah and Hagar is interpreted in the light of Gal 4:21-24; a purely historical understanding is regarded as inadequate. The irony of all this is that contemporary Jews were practicing elaborate forms of exegetical deduction to turn the narratives of the law into *Halakhah,* none of which could ever be described in our terms as literal, while Origen was taking quite literally some narratives that we would regard as impossible, even speculating about where the refuse went in the ark!

When it comes to moral and spiritual meanings, the lack of correspondence between theory and practice becomes the more marked. There is never any question of *the* moral or *the* spiritual meaning; rather, Origen's fancy produces one or the other or a whole series of possible "deeper" meanings. Moral meanings seem to be those that speak of the soul's purification and acquisition of virtues; spiritual meanings are those that refer to heavenly or messianic realities. But often these things are inextricably interwoven as Origen reads out of Scripture his own theological vision. While deeply indebted to Philo and sharing many similar features, Origen's allegory is by comparison far less "philosophical" than some accounts have suggested. Where Philo focuses on the classical Hellenistic virtues and on the enlightenment of the soul as it discerns distinctly Platonic ideals, Origen's virtues include the Christian values of faith, hope, and love, willingness to follow Christ even to a martyr's death, and being merciful, while the spiritual realities are those of Christ, the church as Christ's bride, the enlightenment of God's Word in Christ, and the gifts of the Spirit.

This difference is because Origen's allegory draws on the church's tradition of seeing prophetic texts (see PROPHECY AND PROPHETS, HB) fulfilled in Christ and of tracing typological foreshadowings of Christ in the narratives and rituals of the old covenant. There was a time when scholars drew hard and fast distinctions between allegory and typology, but in the case of Origen such distinctions tend to break down. What we find is a deeply messianic interpretation of Scripture married to a philosophical system that embraces the Christian gospel in a coherent vision of the way things are. It is rooted in the intellectual world of Origen's time, while also being deeply Christian and scriptural in its fundamental character. Scripture informed Origen's intellect; and in his own understanding it was Scripture that was the vehicle of truth, not the alien philosophies that in effect gave him the rational categories through which to achieve a coherent vision.

Scripture also provided the relatively systematic set of symbols that actually makes Alexandrian allegory less arbitrary than has sometimes been suggested. Study of a later Alexandrian exegete, DIDYMUS THE BLIND, many of whose works have come to light comparatively recently, has shown that the allegorical understanding of Scripture was based on a consistent methodology and used consistent correspondences, finding a coherent set of references to heavenly realities throughout the Scriptures. Thus "Jerusalem" always refers to the church, the people of God, just as "Joshua" always means JESUS. The allegorical approach to interpretation is alien to modern assumptions about how texts should be interpreted, but it does not deserve some of the criticisms that have been advanced. It has a coherence of its own and acknowledges the importance of being aware of figurative uses of language and of the necessity for imaginative engagement with a text if it is to be appropriately read.

Bibliography: **J. N. B. Carleton Paget**, "The Christian Exegesis of the OT in the Alexandrian Tradition," *HB/OT* 1, 1 (ed. M. Saebø, 1996) 478-542. **H. Crouzel**, *Origène*, pt. 2: *L'Exégète* (1985). **J. D. Dawson**, "Ancient Alexandrian Interpretation of Scripture" (diss., Yale University, 1988). **R. P. C. Hanson**, *Allegory and Event: A Study of the Sources and Significance of Origen's Interpretation of Scripture* (1959). **J. H. Tigcheler**, *Didyme l'Aveugle et l'exégèse allégorique, étude semantique de quelques termes exegetiques importants de son commentaire sur Zacharie* (GCP 6, 1977). **J. W. Trigg**, *Biblical Interpretation* (MFC 9, 1988) 69-160. **M. F. Wiles**, "Origen as Biblical Scholar," *CHB* 1 (1970) 454-89.

F. M. YOUNG

ALT, GEORG ALBRECHT (1883–1956)

The son of a pastor, A. was born Sept. 20, 1883, in Stübach, northern Bavaria. From 1902 to 1906 he studied at the universities of Erlangen and Leipzig (theology and oriental philology). He was a member of the Munich preaching seminary from 1906 to 1908, when he made his first journey to Palestine. He attained the MA and completed his habilitation at the University of Greifswald in 1909, where he became a professor of OT in 1912, moving to the University of Basel in 1914. In 1921 he accepted a position at Halle/Saale, and in 1922 was called to Leipzig. The successor of R. KITTEL, A. was professor of OT in Leipzig until his death; however, he often lived in Palestine. From 1921 to 1935 he served as director of the Deutsches Evangelisches Institut für Altertumswissenschaft des Heiligen Landes zu Jerusalem. From 1919 to 1949 he was chairman of the DEUTSCHER VEREIN ZUR ERFORSCHUNG PALÄSTINAS. He died April 24, 1956, in Leipzig.

The focus of A.'s work lay in the attempt to study the early history of Israel against the background of Canaanite Palestine. One of the first scholars to do so, he consistently employed the geographico-historical method (*territorialgeschichtliche Methode*)—that is, he compared the connections between the historical geography and topography of Palestine with the witness of the HB and of the peoples bordering on Palestine. An extensive knowledge of both the region and its archaeological remains (see ARCHAEOLOGY AND BIBLICAL STUDIES), plus a study of the results of historical-critical scholarship, enabled A. to verify the biblical tradition to a considerable extent.

In two books (1925, 1939) A. described the penetration of individual Israelite tribes into the west- and east-Jordanian arable land as a gradual process comparable to the annual change of pasturage of seminomadic peoples ("transhumance"), which only occasionally led to warlike atercations ("the peaceful infiltration"). According to him, the conquest of Canaanite towns and cities recounted in the books of Joshua and Judges did not take place during the first phase of the conquest (*Landnahme*). This stage was instead confined to the occupation of the thinly populated mountains west of the Jordan. It was not until the next phase, which A. termed the *Landesausbau* (territorial expansion), that the tribes expanded their territorial possessions, conquering the towns while at the same time defending already acquired lands against the encroachments of the Philistines, who dwelled in the coastal regions to the west, and of the Ammonites, who had established themselves in the southern and eastern regions of east Jordan.

It would be a serious misunderstanding of A.'s position to imagine that he maintained that only a peaceful settlement had taken place or that he held the biblical accounts of a military conquest of the country to be the result of secondary literary developments of the HB traditions (in particular by means of etiological "sagas"). Instead, he painted a picture of a developmental occupation of the land and so included the sporadic warlike encounters within the scope of his theory.

A. argued that the entire defensive capabilities of the Israelite tribes were necessary for the resolution of local conflicts until the close of the period of the judges when these powers were consolidated and the new institution of the monarchy was inaugurated (1930, 1950). His numerous topographical studies, particularly of the lists of place-names in the book of Joshua, were accompanied and corrected by his accounts in the *Palästinajahrbuch* of his travels and studies in Palestine, which took place under the aegis of the Deutsches Palästina-Institut. A. pursued his research into the governmental structures of Judah and Israel in works dealing with the monarchy (dynastic in Judah, charismatic in Israel). He undertook further topographical and archaeological studies as well as examinations of the constitutional law of the city-states of Jerusalem and Samaria.

A.'s extensive and often subtly detailed studies of the historical geography and administrative structure of Roman and Christian-Byzantine Palestine have not received the attention they deserve. In this connection his main contributions were a monograph (1949); a number of studies on the *Limes Palaestinae* (*PJ* 1930–31; *ZDPV* 1940 and 1955); and the closely related writings entitled "Aus der 'Araba'" (*ZDPV* 1934–35), in which A. conducted an intensive dialogue with N. GLUECK's "Explorations in Eastern Palestine and the Negeb" (*BASOR* 55 [1934]; *AASOR* 14 [1934]; 15 [1935]) with particular emphasis on the dating of the fortresslike complexes on the elevated eastern flank of the Araba in the regions of ancient Edom and Moab. Glueck saw these fortresses as Nabataean caravanserais, whereas A. regarded them as Roman castles connected with the southern Limes

(cf. N. Glueck, *AASOR* 15, 141-42; response by A. in *ZDPV* 59 [1936] 166-67; 71 [1955] 88-89). A.'s "Beiträge zur historischen Geographie und Topographie des Negeb" (1929–38) dealt with Christian Palestine. In these studies he showed himself not only to be knowledgeable about the country and its archaeological problems but also to be an able epigrapher and interpreter of singular ancient sources.

In his famous religio-historical essay "Gott der Väter" (1929), A. proposed to have discovered a type of Israelite religion distinct from the worship of Yahweh, one that understood the patriarchs of Genesis as recipients of their own specific revelations. The discussions of this particular issue have not abated.

A.'s studies of the conquest led him, on the basis of the earliest Israelite legal traditions, to attempt to illuminate the origins of Israelite law. The distinction proposed in this work between casuistic (Canaanite) and apodictic (genuine Israelite) law has provided a standard for the further study of Israelite legal thought.

As Kittel's successor, A. became one of the co-editors of *Biblia Hebraica* (*BHK*); he served in this capacity together with O. EISSFELDT and P. KAHLE from 1929 onward and published the third edition of the work. The *BHK* was the predecessor of the contemporary *Biblia Hebraica Stuttgartensia* (*BHS*).

As an orientalist A. utilized both hieroglyphic and cuneiform sources to the extent that they were relevant to the history of Syro-Palestine. Notable essays in this connection include "Völker und Staaten Syriens im frühen Altertum" (1936) and "Der Rhythmus der Geschichte Syriens und Palästinas im Altertum" (1944). His topographical studies of the conquest were supported by references in the pharaonic lists of town names and in the Amarna letters.

The idea of a "school of A. and M. NOTH" oversimplifies the sophisticated and differentiated achievements of both scholars. Neither sought to form a school, nor did they always embrace the same ideas (see Noth, VTSup 7 [1960] 263).

Works: *Die Landnahme der Israeliten in Palästina* (1925); *Die Staatenbildung der Israeliten in Palästina* (1930); *Judas Nachbarn zur Zeit Nehemias* (1931); *Die Rolle Samarias bei der Entstehung des Judentums* (1934); *Galiläische Probleme* (1937–40); *Erwägungen über die Landnahme der Israeliten in Palästina* (1939); *Die Stätten des Wirkens Jesu in Galiläa, territorialgeschichtlich betrachtet* (1949); *Das Grossreich Davids* (1950); *Kleine Schriften zur Geschichte des Volkes Israel*, 1-2 (1953); 3 (1959); *Essays on OT History and Religion* (1966, 1989).

Bibliography: W. F. Albright, *JBL* 75 (1956) 169-73. **H. Bardtke,** "A. A.: Leben und Werk," *TLZ* 81 (1956) 513-22. **S. Herrmann,** *Tendenzen der Theologie im 20. Jh.* (ed. H. J. Schultz, 1966) 225-30; "Nachtrag zur Bibliographie A. A.," *TLZ* 81 (1956) 573-74. **K. H. Mann,** "Bibliographie A. A.:

Geschichte und Altes Testament," *Festschrift A. A.* (BHT 16, 1953) 211-23. **S. Morenz,** *ZÄS* (1956) I-III. **M. Noth,** "A. A. zum Gedächtnis," *ZDPV* 72 (1956) 1-8; *RGG3,* 1 (1957) 247-48. **S. Schauer, G. Bröker, and H. J. Kandler,** "Das literarische Werk von A. A.," *WZ(L)* 3 (1953/54) 173-78. **R. Smend,** *ZTK* 81 (1984) 286-321; repr. *DATDJ* (1989) 182-207. **M. Weippert,** *TRE* 2 (1978) 303-5. **W. Zimmerli,** *Göttingische Gelehrte Anzeigen* 209 (1955) 79-93.

S. HERRMANN

AMAMA, SIXTINUS (1593–1629)

The son of a leading political figure in Franeker, A. was born Oct. 13, 1593. In 1610 he enrolled in the local university, where he was under the special tutelage of J. DRUSIUS, who quickly saw A. as his potential successor. A. went to Leiden in 1614 to study Arabic with T. Erpenius and in 1615 to Oxford, where Drusius had long had close contacts, especially with T. Bodley (d. 1613). At Oxford A. enrolled in Exeter College, headed by J. Prideaux, where he also taught Hebrew. Returning home upon the death of Drusius (1616), A. assumed his post and taught at Franeker until his early death Dec. 9, 1629. His most famous student was J. COCCEIUS.

A. was a strong advocate of biblical language study and, like ERASMUS, saw this as one of the means of achieving moral reform in society, especially in university life. Through his influence the Friesian and other synods moved to require competence in biblical languages of all theological students. A. supplied new editions of the Martinez-BUXTORF Hebrew grammar and produced his own as well as a Hebrew wordbook.

Much of A.'s work took the form of attacks on what he called "barbarisms." Seven of these were denounced, especially in his massive 1625 work: (1) the emphasis on the INSPIRATION and value of the SEPTUAGINT and (2) the VULGATE; (3) the claim that the OT Hebrew text had been corrupted by heretics and Jews and was thus of reduced value (although he accepted the views of L. Cappel); (4) the view that the study of Hebrew and Greek was unnecessary; (5) the contention that the study of Scripture is not necessary for theology; (6) the contention that modern versions and editions of the Bible are adequate (he strongly criticized the contemporary Dutch translation); and (7) the view that Scripture should be interpreted in both a literal and a mystical sense. A.'s positions drew him into debate, especially with Roman Catholics, over his attack on the Vulgate (1620), which was answered caustically by the French polymath M. Mersenne (1588–1648) in his massive *Quaestiones celeberrimae in Genesim* (1623). Letters surviving in Mersenne's correspondence indicate that a cordial relationship was established between these two men of the "republic of letters" before A.'s death.

Works: *Dissertatiuncula, qua ostenditur praecipuos papismi errores ex ignorantia ebraismi et Vulgata versione partim or-*

tum, paetim incrementum. . . . (1618); *Censura vulgatae, atque a Tridentinis canonizatae, versionis quinque librorum Mosis* (1620); *Oratio de Ebrietate* (1621); *Anti-Barbarus biblicus in vi libros distributus* (1625); *Grammatica Ebraea a Martinio-Buxtorfiana* (1625); *Sermo Academicus ad locum Eccl. 12, 1* (1625); *De Hebreusche Grammatica ofte Taalkonst* (1627); *Ebreusch Woordboek* (1628).

Bibliography: *BWPGN* 1 (1907) 132-38. **F. S. Knipscheer,** *NNBW* 1 (1911) 105-7. **J. C. H. Lebram,** "Ein Streit um die Hebräische Bibel und die Septuaginta," *Leiden University in the Seventeenth Century: An Exchange of Learning* (ed. T. H. Lunsingh-Scheurleer and G. H. M. Posthumus Meyjes, 1975) 21-63. *MSHH* 34 (1736) 238-45. **J. E. Platt,** "S. A. (1593–1629): Franeker Professor and Citizen of the Republic of Letters," *Universiteit te Franeker 1585–1811: Bijdragen tot de geschiedenis van de Friese hogeschool* (Fryske Akademy 648, ed. G. T. Jensma et al., 1985) 236-48. **P. T. van Rooden,** *Theology, Biblical Scholarship, and Rabbinical Studies in the Seventeenth Century* (Studies in the History of Leiden University 6, 1989) 64-83.

J. H. HAYES

AMBROSE (c. 339–397)

Born in Trier, A. was educated in Rome and entered the imperial civil service. He was appointed governor of Aemilia Liguria (northern Italy), based in Milan, and in 374 was elected bishop of the city. A fluent reader of Greek, he could transmit to the West the most valuable insights of contemporary Greek Christian thought. Through his influence on the emperors of the West, especially Theodosius I (whom he compelled to undertake public penance after the Massacre of Thessalonica in 390), he greatly consolidated the position of the church in the state. He died in 397.

A.'s self-denying and energetic character captured the imagination of his own and of later generations. His personal, spiritual, and ecclesiastical life was rooted in the Bible. Unlike the Manichees, who rejected the HB, he emphasized the Bible's unity: "The NT was in the Old; in the Old it was running [*currebat*], through the Old it was announced" (*Expositio psalmi 118,* 4, 28; CSEL 62, 81). In his interpretation A. was strongly influenced by the allegorical exegesis of PHILO and of ORIGEN and by the more sober expositions of BASIL, although he often took an independent line. He defined *allegory* as "when one thing is done and another is indicated" (*De Abraham* 1.4.28; CSEL 32/1, 523). More specifically, three levels are to be found in Scripture: the natural, the mystical, and the moral (*Explanatio psalmi 36,* 1; CSEL 64, 70). The natural is the literal or historical interpretation. The mystical represents the culmination of exegesis; it is the mystical interpretation of the OT that points to Christ. The moral level deals with the practical conduct of life. A.'s preference was for moral—as also for OT—exegesis. The NT, being the fulfillment of the OT, did not require the same degree of allegorical treatment. He regarded PAUL's writings as self-explanatory (*Ep.* 7; 37 in *PL*), 1; CSEL 82/1, 43-44). Just as the OT comes before the NT and should, therefore, be read first (*Explanatio psalmi 1,* 33; CSEL 64, 28), so also moral matters come before mystical (*Expositio psalmi 118,* 1, 2; CSEL 62, 5).

A.'s attitude toward exegesis was part and parcel of his attitude toward his pastoral obligations. L. Pizzolato has emphasized the powerful link A. forged between exegetical activity and the spiritual life (1978, 29). An eyewitness account of A.'s exegetical method, based on the text "the letter killeth, but the spirit giveth life" (2 Cor 3:6), was provided by his greatest convert, AUGUSTINE (*Confessions* 6.4.6; CSEL 33, 119).

Works: *Exameron* (CSEL 32/1), *De paradiso* (CSEL 32/1), and *De Cain et Abel* (CSEL 32/1), all in ET by J. J. Savage, FC 42 (1961); *De Isaac vel anima* (CSEL 32/1), *De bono mortis* (CSEL 32/1), *De Iacob et vita beata* (CSEL 32/2), *De Ioseph* (CSEL 32/2), *De patriarchis* (CSEL 32/2), *De fuga saeculi* (CSEL 32/2), and *De interpellatione Iob et David* (CSEL 32/2), all in ET by M. P. McHugh, FC 65 (1972); *De Abraham* (CSEL 32/1); *Expositio evangelii secundum Lucam* (CSEL 32/4); *Expositio psalmi 118* (CSEL 62); *Explanatio psalmorum 12* (CSEL 64).

Bibliography: E. **Dassmann,** *TRE* 2 (1978) 362-86. **F. H. Dudden,** *The Life and Times of St. A.* (2 vols., 1935). **M. Grazia Mara,** *Patrology* 4 (1986) 144-80, esp. 153-65. **V. Hahn,** *Das wahre Gesetz; eine Untersuchung der Auffassung des A. von Mailand vom Verhältnis der beiden Testamente* (MBTh 33, 1969). **J. Huhn,** "Bedeutung und Gebrauch der Heiligen Schrift durch den Kirchenvater A.," *HJ* 77 (1958) 387-96. **J. B. Kellner,** *Der heilige A., Bischof von Mailand, als Erklärer des Alten Testamentes* (1893). **R. H. Malden,** "St. A. as an Interpreter of Holy Scripture," *JTS* 16 (1915) 509-22. **B. de Margerie,** *Introduction à l'histoire de l'exégèse* 2:99-143. **H. J. auf der Maur,** *Das Psalmenverständnis des A. von Mailand* (1977). **J. Pépin,** *Théologie cosmique et théologie chrétiénne (Ambroise, Exam. I, 1, 1-4)* (BPhC, 1964). **L. F. Pizzolato,** *La "Explanatio psalmorum XII": Studio letterario sulla esegesi dé sant'Ambrogio* (Archivio ambrosiano 17, 1965); "La Sacra Scrittura fondamento del methodo esegetico di sant'Ambrogio," *Ambrosius Episcopus* (SPMed 6, 1976) 1:393-426; *La dottrina esegetica di sant'Ambrogio* (Studia patristica Mediolanensia 9, 1978). **H. Savon,** *Saint A. devant l'exégèse de Philon le Juif* (2 vols. in 1, 1977); "Saint A. et saint Jérôme, lecteurs de Philoh," *ANRW* 2.21.1 (1984) 731-59.

A. LENOX-CONYNGHAM

AMERICAN PALESTINE EXPLORATION SOCIETY

The APES, inspired by the example of the British Palestine Exploration Fund, was established in 1870 at a meeting in New York City. The society immediately set about raising funds for the exploration and mapping of the Transjordan from the Dead Sea to northern Syria. Appealing to Americans' patriotic and religious sentiments, the society argued that its projects would enhance America's reputation as a center for scholarship and scientific investigation and would defend the Bible against the attacks of skeptics. The society sent its first expedition to Palestine in 1871 under Lt. E. Steever and a second team in 1875 under Col. J. Lane and Dr. S. Merrill. Although a number of reports and incomplete maps were forthcoming from these campaigns, both expeditions failed to produce what the society had expected, due in part to inadequate funding, inexperienced personnel, and the sheer immensity of the undertaking. The APES disbanded in 1884, leaving behind the issues of its *Statement* (1871–77) and a few bulletins as well as an interesting collection of over one hundred photographs of archaeological ruins in Palestine (see ARCHAEOLOGY AND BIBLICAL STUDIES).

Bibliography: W. J. **Moulton,** "The American Palestine Exploration Society," *AASOR* 8 (1928) 55-70.

M. P. GRAHAM

AMERICAN SCHOOLS OF ORIENTAL RESEARCH

ASOR was established in 1900 by funding from twenty-one American universities and assumed the task of enabling "qualified persons to prosecute Biblical, linguistic, archaeological, historical, and other kindred studies and researches under more favorable conditions than can be secured at a distance from the Holy Land." Originally the American School of Oriental Research in Jerusalem, the organization changed its name as it established additional research centers in Amman, Baghdad, Damascus, and Nicosia and sponsored excavations in Israel, Jordan, Iraq, Cyprus, Carthage, Syria, and Egypt. Currently, ASOR is supported by about 1,400 individual and institutional members and maintains centers for study in Jerusalem at The W. F. ALBRIGHT Institute of Archaeological Research, in Amman at the American Center of Oriental Research (est. 1968), and in Nicosia at the Cyprus American Archaeological Research Institute (est. 1978). ASOR's institutes at Baghdad and Damascus were closed because of political circumstances, but the Baghdad Committee for the Baghdad School and the Damascus Committee continue the organization's interests in those countries. In addition to monographic series, ASOR issues *ASOR Newsletter, Biblical Archaeologist, Bulletin of the American Schools of Oriental Research,* and *Journal of Cuneiform Studies.*

Bibliography: C. U. **Harris,** "The Role of CAARI on Cyprus," *BA* 52 (1989) 157-62. **P. J. King,** *American Archae-*

ology in the Mideast: A History of the American Schools of Oriental Research (1983).

M. P. GRAHAM

AMMON, CHRISTOPH FRIEDRICH VON
(1766–1850)

A. was professor at Erlangen and Göttingen between 1789 and 1813; he then became Saxon court preacher and held various administrative positions. He is representative of the moderate wing of the late eighteenth-century Enlightenment. I. KANT gave him his approach to religion; J. G. HERDER, his understanding of the PSYCHOLOGY of the biblical writers; and J. SEMLER, C. STÄUDLIN, and G. Less, his theological framework. A. was the third person in the eighteenth century (after G. Zachariae and W. Hufnagel) to attempt a modern biblical THEOLOGY.

For A., dogmatic theology had to present the basic Christian doctrines from a single viewpoint. He felt this had a certain utility for the instruction of society in general but did not do justice to all the variations in the individual perception of religion. In contrast to this feature of dogmatic theology, there is no single principle behind the books of the Bible; therefore, biblical theology can present what is said in the Bible so that the different stages in the apprehension of religion can be made clear.

Thus the most honorable concern for the prophets of the HB (see PROPHECY AND PROPHETS, HB) was to be teachers of morality concerned for the true worship of the one God; but they failed to rise above their national pride. The NT carries this teaching further, A. argued, in that JESUS set out purer moral truths that contain the notion of an encompassing love of humankind as a whole.

In his work A. tended to adhere to the old method of commenting on prooftexts, but he acknowledged that there was no unifying principle within the Bible that could be used for his arrangement. His erudition and exegetical skill were respected by his contemporaries as he was considered to be one of the greatest rationalist theologians of his era.

Works: *Entwurf einer reinen Biblischen Theologie* (2 vols., 1792); *Entwurf einer Christologie des Alten Testaments* (1794); *Ethic* (1795); *Biblische Theologie* (3 vols., 1801, 1802), a combination and 2nd ed. of the 1792 and 1794 vols.; *Dogmatic* (1803); *Fortbildung des Christentums zur Weltreligion* (1833).

Bibliography: R. C. Dentan, *Preface to OT Theology* (1963) 26. **H. J. Kraus,** *Die Biblische Theologie: Ihre Geschichte und Problematic* (1970) 40-51. **J. Sandys-Wunsch,** "A Tale of Two Critics," *Ascribe to the Lord: Biblical and Other Studies in Memory of P. C. Craigie* (ed. L. Eslinger and G. Taylor, 1988) 545-55. **J. D. Schmidt and J. Dietrich,** "Die theologischen

Wandlungen des C. F. v. A.: Ein Beitrag zur Frage des legitimen Gebrauches philosophischer Begriffe in der Christologie" (diss., Erlangen, 1953).

J. SANDYS-WUNSCH

AMOS, BOOK OF

R. Cripps calls Amos "perhaps *the* most important prophet in the OT." Although the book comes third in traditional orderings of the Minor Prophets (see PROPHECY AND PROPHETS, HB), Amos ranks first in the heart of most readers. There are many reasons for this: the beauty of his language—especially apparent in the Hebrew; his impassioned plea for social justice; and the man's courage, not to say temerity, in attacking the powerful politico-religious establishment of the northern kingdom of Israel. Here, however, is where unity concerning the interpretation of Amos ends; his very popularity and importance have generated an enormous amount of secondary literature with, predictably, many conflicting opinions.

J. Hayes lays out three stages of modern (c. 1880 onward) critical study of Amos concerned with the prophet, his religion, and finally, the text. A fourth area of inquiry, which we might call the SOCIOLOGY of Amos, may, thanks to N. Gottwald and others, be the next step. In any case, we are beginning to witness a rather remarkable reevaluation of Amos and his book, including his origin, status in society, place in and sense of history, language, and the unity of the book ascribed to him.

The traditional Christian view of Amos as a simple Judean shepherd goes back to AUGUSTINE, who marveled that such words as Amos's could come from a rustic. This immensely popular view, conjuring up images of David versus Goliath or JESUS and the Temple elders, had no trouble surmounting occasional challenges until the nineteenth century. It was an image that the Judeo-Christian tradition could appreciate.

LUTHER, for example, shared God's apparent delight in choosing the meek to challenge the mighty; he began his Amos commentary by comparing Amos's situation in Israel with his own vis-à-vis the pope. Following his example, commentators who reflect the first stirrings of modern (Protestant) scholarship at the end of the nineteenth century concerned themselves mainly with the person of the prophet, although Luther also maintained that the person was less important than his message.

Regarding the person of Amos, we know that the earliest Talmudic commentators (see H. Routtenberg [1971]) who mention Amos lived, like Augustine, nearly 1,000 years after the prophet—but only shortly after one who said that the meek would inherit the earth. Seeing Amos as one of the latter was natural for Christians; however, the scanty Jewish sources (*Tg. Onq., b. Ned.* 38a) suggest, rather, that Amos was a wealthy shepherd.

This would have contradicted Augustine's most dearly held notions. Indeed, there is almost nothing about Amos that commentators, Jewish and Christian, ancient and modern, have not contested.

1. Background. There is general agreement that Amos's career was very brief; no scholar assigns him more than a year's public ministry, sometime between 765 and 740 BCE (though few go as far as J. Morgenstern, who reduces it to a single day!). At least some of his remarks were delivered at the national shrine of Bethel, perhaps on the day of the fall festival.

The traditional view locates Amos's hometown in Judean Tekoa (1:1), where, according to EUSEBIUS's *Onomasticon,* his tomb was still extant in the third century. Contrarily, medieval Jewish commentary (D. Kimhi; see S. Berkowitz [1939]) casually identifies him as hailing from Asher in the north. CYRIL OF ALEXANDRIA (5th cent.) reported a northern origin, but few have taken this or any other northern suggestion seriously. The book gives us little help: neither a patronymic nor a designated place of origin like the ninth-century northern hero/prophet Elijah the Gileadite. Positing a northern origin for Amos would solve many problems, but the more obvious questions concerning his period and his profession(s) should be addressed first.

2. Chronology. Dates for Amos's prophetic activities have ranged from c. 780 to c. 740. Amos's placement in this forty-year period is significant because the signal event of that span—namely, the rise of Assyria under Tiglath-pileser III—can be pinpointed to 745 BCE. Was Amos knowledgeable of Assyria's new strength (R. Coote [1981])? Probably not. Consensus follows the book's superscription and places Amos between c. 767 and c. 753 BCE. But if Amos was not exactly contemporary to Tiglath-pileser, can it at least be suggested (with E. Hammerschaimb [1946]) that Assyria's rise was so imminent as to cast its shadow before it? (This presumes, for the moment, that the entire text of Amos was written before 745.) Here, too, the answer will probably be no.

Most scholars from 1880 onward accept the view that the northern kingdom, locus for Amos's activities, was enjoying almost unprecedented prosperity before the Assyrian invasion; but some (M. Haran [1968]; S. Cohen [1965]; J. Hayes [1989]) feel Israel was already in decline. Was Amos predicting ruin or merely describing in strong terms what others could already see?

Lost in this controversy concerning the international situation is any real sense of the sectional animosities in Israel. (Cf. the Judean reaction to help from the Samaritans in Ezra 4:1 or the reception of Philip's news by Nathaniel, John 1:46.) It is important to note that the fracture of Solomon's kingdom never mended. In fact, there had been a bloody encounter—scarcely noticed by Bible historians—won by the north in c. 792 BCE (following the chronology of E. Thiele) only twenty-five years before Amos's time. Perhaps these events had little

impact; but it is significant that the Judean king Amaziah, held hostage for a further ten years, returned home to find his son Uzziah king. Amaziah was murdered in c. 767, almost coincidental with the beginning of Amos's career.

3. Occupation. Amos's occupation is an area of great conjecture. Today he is enshrined "among the prophets," but there is a strong suspicion that this membership is posthumously conferred. For one thing, although he speaks prophetically, his words contain an explicit denial of having been a prophet (7:14). As H. ROWLEY (1947) pointed out, the crucial verse lacks a verb, leading E. Würthwein (1950) to posit that Amos underwent a sort of interruption or mid-career change in the nature of his prophecy from supporting the official cult to opposing it. But we do not really know whether he was a prophet at all. In 3:7 he seems to indicate that he is, indeed, one. And his capacity for predicting ruin is obvious from the oracles with which the book begins. J. Blenkinsopp (1983), however, states that 3:7 is the "most obvious Deuteronomistic interpolation" in the whole book; and the authenticity of many of the oracles is questioned.

Even if Amos were a prophet, he would likely have had another livelihood. In fact, he identifies himself as a "dresser" (?) of sycamore trees and a *bôqēr,* "herdsman" (7:14). Traditional identification sidesteps the fact that, although he says he was taken "from behind the flocks" (7:15), the usual word for "shepherd" is not used to describe his activities. Modern discoveries in cognate languages, especially Ugaritic (see UGARIT AND THE BIBLE), have convinced some scholars (A. Kapelrud [1956]; P. CRAIGIE [1982]) that Amos was an influential sheep owner/dealer (as the Jewish tradition had long remembered) with perhaps some connection to the cult.

This makes sense. As much as we admire his outburst, an Israelite festival was no New England town meeting at which anyone could speak at will. Besides, who would listen to a simple shepherd and, on top of that, a Judean? How could anyone, much less an uneducated outsider, have commanded an Israelite audience? The answer to these questions may lie in an examination of Amos's other occupation, which had nothing to do with religion. Scholars assume that harvesting sycamore fruits (7:14) is proof of humble origin; who but a poor man would tend figs barely fit for human consumption? H. OORT (1836–1927) caused some consternation one hundred years ago by pointing out that sycamores do not grow at the altitude of Judean Tekoa (2,800 ft. above sea level). In addition, if Amos owned groves of trees, how can he be considered humble? G. A. SMITH (1896–98), whose description of Judean Tekoa borders on the lyrical, responds that Amos must have been some sort of migrant worker; sycamores do grow in the Shephelah by Ein Gedi and in the north, the locus for Amos's preaching. But if he a migrant worker, how did he also care for his sheep?

4. Message. The content of Amos's preaching has been subject to much attention: It is widely believed that he was simply anti-ritual. An economic connection with the cult would not preclude this, but it makes more sense to suggest that Amos's objections were along the line of "the letter killeth but the spirit giveth life." An empty and unfelt religiosity, especially when yoked with exploitation of the disadvantaged, makes mockery of the faith as we now know and practice it. In Amos's time, however, the notion prevailed in the northern kingdom that the poor were poor because they deserved it. In such a theology, helping the downtrodden could actually be viewed as countermanding God's will. But Amos's indictment bears special scrutiny, both for what it says and for what it omits.

His excoriation of various Israelite malpractices reads like the particulars in a court case. He seems to have an insider's knowledge of the various ways in which certain classes of impecunious people were taken advantage of by the wealthier, more powerful elements in Israelite society. F. Dijkema's wartime study calls Amos a critic of "second stage capitalism."

J. Greenfield (1974) showed that Amos was intimately acquainted with the *marzeaḥ* (a term found only in Amos 6:7 and Jer 16:5), a sort of upper-class country club and burial society in which sybaritic and perhaps orgiastic religious rites were performed. These rites, of course, were not part of later orthodox Israelite Judaism, but we know from recent discoveries that Judeans and Israelites were, at the least, syncretistic. What was a part of the northern kingdom's cult, and a big part to judge from Judean denunciations of it, was the golden calf.

Amos nowhere criticizes the northern kingdom for its use of the calves, golden or otherwise, that Jeroboam ben Nebat set up throughout the country (see 2 Kgs 12:25-33). This was noticed as early as 1884 by W. R. SMITH, who said quietly that baals must not have been offensive to the northerners. But was not Amos a Judean? And in any case, why would the assumed Judean editors of Amos not have inserted this telling criticism of the northern kingdom, safely defunct after 720 BCE? The text holds the answer to these questions.

5. Text. The book of Amos did not escape the documentary dissectionists who sought to distinguish the different strands of tradition compiled by different editors or authors in different eras of the text's production. For example, W. Irwin (1933) divided the text into groups of apothegms. J. MORGENSTERN (1941) identified seventy-seven original verses, twenty-nine more added later by Amos, and the rest added by disciples. A. WEISER proposed two books, like Isaiah's but integrated rather than juxtaposed. Most scholars favor some sort of partition, assuming that the original text has been puffed up by additions representing the concerns of later Jews. J. WELLHAUSEN was particularly outraged by the ending of chapter 9, claiming that the prophet could not

have made a 180-degree shift virtually in mid-verse (9:8; but cf. 5:15).

Other sections that have come in for more than their share of scrutiny are the five "visions," the eight "oracles," and Amos's confrontation with the priest Amaziah in 7:10-17. (J. Watts [1956], however, noted that 4:13; 5:8; and 9:5-6 seem to be parts of a hymn that he assumed were inserted into the text later. But they could also be hymnic material that Amos quotes.) If one subtracts all the verses that have been called into question, the remainder would be only a small fragment of what we have now.

Wellhausen, H. GUNKEL, and A. ALT dominate much of twentieth-century writing on Amos. Following them, such scholars as H. W. WOLFF (1969) and R. Coote (1981) seem to vie with each other in proposing ever more layers of accretions, a kind of moss gathered by the text as it rolls through history. Although pre-modern commentators would have been scandalized by REDACTION CRITICISM (or by any of the modern schools), JEROME might have applauded M. BUBER's (1949) suggestion that the Judah oracle was inserted at some relatively late date to ensure that readers/listeners would know that the long oracle against Israel that follows it (2:9–3:2) was meant to criticize the northern kingdom exclusively.

Documentary or other reductionist hypotheses, however ingenious, are difficult to attach to a text that in its present state has only 146 verses. There is also some movement away from dissection and toward a more organic appreciation of Amos as a whole, e.g., S. Paul (1991). R. Smalley (1979) considers the book to be an organic whole pivoting on 5:9, but even so conservative a scholar as Y. KAUFMANN (1960) did not attempt to defend the authenticity of the entire text.

Buried in the avalanche of modern criticism is B. SPINOZA's suggestion that biblical texts ought to "wear down" through history, not grow. This may not hold, e.g., in the case of Isaiah; but certainly the smaller corpuses of the Minor Prophets, e.g., Obadiah, do not contain everything these men said.

Commentary is also interested in such broad subjects as the influences behind Amos. Wolff and his many disciples see a "wisdom" influence (depending in part on a certain vocabulary); others have seen "cultic" (G. Farr [1966]); "theophanic" (J. Crenshaw [1968]); "covenantal" (W. Brueggemann [1969]); "apodictic" (Würthwein [1950]); "psalmic" (A. Kapelrud [1956]); or "pre-Israelite prophetic" (N. Gottwald [1985]) influences. J. Mays (1969) compliments Amos on his versatility, and J. Barton (1980) cites his literary/intellectual merit.

6. Language. It might be that commentators are so concerned with the forest that they neglect its trees. There is a considerable number of strange or rare words and phrases in Amos; but since it is assumed that we do not have *ipsissima verba,* the exact words, there is relative neglect of those we do possess. Even if the words were not Amos's, are they the less carefully chosen? For example, in 1917 H. Schmidt noticed that Amos was not told to "return" to Judah but to "flee" there. Hayes correctly invokes J. BARR's *caveat* concerning overreliance on etymologies of single words; but there are so many lexical anomalies— loan words and strange forms and spellings—that one wonders who is responsible for the present state of the text and why the fastidious rabbis of later Judaism did not clean it up. To cite the most outstanding example, Amos twice spells the name "Isaac" differently from almost any other biblical book (*sin* for *tsade*). W. R. HARPER (1905) wrote that the "misspellings were all textual errors," but offered no clue as to how they were allowed to persist.

The prevailing view argues that Amos was a poor migratory shepherd from Judah who lived or worked in the north long enough to acquire detailed knowledge of its social and religious faults—and a local accent—and who, through a short public outburst at an important festival, manifested such charisma that he could command an audience of awestruck Israelites until the officiating priest could communicate with the king and secure some police (never mentioned or even alluded to in the text) to escort Amos politely off the premises. Furthermore, generations of admirers or disciples continually dredged up more of his words or, in some cases, invented words they felt their own times would like Amos to have said. This seems forced.

7. New Perspectives. The old view is currently being challenged from a number of perspectives. As early as 1915 Gunkel stated that copyists were not at liberty to change the texts that lay in front of them. If so, the presence of postexilic parts of Amos may be questioned. Furthermore, many modern writers now acknowledge that Amos was a person of some substance in his community, that his connection with Israelite flocks was on a high economic level, and that he may have even been an "inspector" of crown sycamores (S. Rosenbaum [1990]). If so, of which biblical kingdom was he a citizen?

In 1917 Schmidt mused that Amos's words would have a far different ring if spoken by an Israelite against his own king and country. It would appear that Amos's priestly adversary, Amaziah, thought so too, since he accused Amos of "treason" (*qešer*). A thorough study of this word in Scripture reveals it is always used to describe actions against one's own king or country. It is this suggestion that may finally point the way to a truer understanding of Amos. If Amos were a substantial and well-educated citizen of Israel (the northern kingdom), his book could show all the influences that Farr, Wolff, Brueggemann, et al. posit of it. The man himself might be assumed to have been influential enough to command an audience even during a national festival. Furthermore, his relatively mild treatment at the hands of the estab-

lishment, noticed by many scholars, would be better understood if Amos were not an indigent outsider, but a well-connected native; his intimate knowledge of the goings-on in a *marzeaḥ* also points in this direction. As much emotional appeal as the traditional view has, it may be too much to ask the present text to support it. To borrow Voltaire's *bon mot* concerning the Holy Roman Empire, it would appear that Amos was not simple, was not a shepherd, and was not even a Judean.

If Amos was an employee of the northern kingdom, then we may presume he was not, initially, a prophet. What is more important, he would not have been considered a prophet until some time after his outburst, e.g., until the fall of the house of Jereboam or even until the destruction of the northern kingdom. If so, his words might have been cherished for decades by only a few people without suffering much editorial change—the more so if he were a northerner whose words remained unknown in Jerusalem, where the famous "deuteronomists" were so hard at work.

Relative obscurity would also help to explain why he follows Hosea and Joel in the CANON, though perhaps he precedes both chronologically (see CHRONOLOGY, HB). If Amos's words came to light as late as the great Josianic reform (c. 625 BCE), it might not be remembered exactly when he had lived; everyone, however, would know of his refuge and eventual death in Judean Tekoa.

8. Importance. Luther wrote, "Neither the man nor the place [of his residence] are important." He concluded correctly that what is important is Amos's message, pieces of which have achieved lives independent of their context: "Let justice roll down as the waters and righteousness as a mighty stream" (5:24); "Seek me and live" (5:14). Even here, however, there is dispute about the audience for whom these words were intended. Jewish and Christian traditions want to read in Amos the first universalist (largely on the basis of 9:7), but several moderns read him as more narrowly nationalist.

It is the genius of Amos and a reason for his enduring popularity that he, an anguished patriot aghast at the evils in his own country, would write words that speak to any country whose leaders pervert the commandments of the Sinaitic covenant. We learn from Amos's visions that God protects a country only so long as that country remains righteous. In that light, much of Western history from Amos's time to ours may be read as a series of footnotes.

Bibliography: P. A. Ackroyd, "A Judgement Narrative Between Kings and Chronicles? An Approach to Amos 7:9-17," *Canon and Authority: Essays in OT* (ed. G. W. Coats and B. O. Long, 1977) 71-87. **F. I. Andersen and D. N. Freedman,** *Amos* (AB 24A, 1989). **A. G. Auld,** *Amos* (1986). **J. Barton,** *Amos's Oracles Against the Nations: A Study of Amos 1:3–2:5* (1980). **S. Berkowitz,** "Critical Edition of the Kimchi's Book of Amos" (diss., Cambridge, 1939). **J. A. Blenkinsopp,** *A History of Prophecy in Israel* (1983) 86-96. **W. Brueggemann,** "Amos's Intercessory Formula," *VT* 19 (1969) 385-99. **M. Buber,** *The Prophetic Faith* (1949). **S. Cohen,** "The Political Background of the Words of Amos," *HUCA* 36 (1965) 153-60. **R. B. Coote,** *Amos Among the Prophets* (1981). **J. F. Craghan,** "The Prophet Amos in Recent Literature," *BTB* 2 (1972) 242-61. **P. C. Craigie,** "Amos the *nōqed* in the Light of Ugaritic," *SR* 11 (1982) 29-33. **J. L. Crenshaw,** "Amos and the Theophanic Tradition," *ZAW* 80 (1968) 203-15. **R. S. Cripps,** *A Critical and Exegetical Commentary on the Book of Amos* (1929, 1955²). **E. Dassmann,** "Amos," *RAC* 3 (1985) 333-50. **G. Farr,** "The Language of Amos: Popular or Cultic?" *VT* 16 (1966) 312-24. **Y. Gitay,** "A Study of Amos's Art of Speech: A Rhetorical Analysis of Amos 3:1-15," *CBQ* 42 (1980) 293-309. **N. K. Gottwald,** *The HB, A Socio-literary Introduction* (1985) 353-58. **D. E. Gowan,** "The Book of Amos," *NIB* (1996) 7:337-431. **J. C. Greenfield,** "The *Mazeah* as a Social Institution," *Acta Antiqua* 22 (1974) 451-55. **E. Hammerschaimb,** *The Book of Amos: A Commentary* (1946, 1967³; ET 1970). **M. Haran,** "Observations on the Historical Background of Amos 1:2–2:6," *IEJ* 18 (1968) 201-12. **W. R. Harper,** *A Critical and Exegetical Commentary on Amos and Hosea* (ICC 23, 1905); **G. F. Hasel,** *Understanding the Book of Amos: Basic Issues in Current Interpretations* (1991). **J. H. Hayes,** *Amos—the Eighth-century Prophet: His Times and His Preaching* (1989). **W. A. Irwin,** "The Thinking of Amos," *AJSL* 49 (1933) 102-14. **A. S. Kapelrud,** *Central Ideas in Amos* (1956). **Y. Kaufmann,** *The Religion of Israel: From Its Beginnings to the Babylonian Exile* (1960) 363-68. **P. H. Kelley,** "Contemporary Study of Amos and Prophetism," *RevExp* 63 (1966) 375-85. **K. Koch,** *Amos: Untersucht mit den Methoden einer strukturalen Formgeschichte* (3 vols., 1976). **L. Koehler,** "Amos-Forschungen von 1917 bis 1932," *TRu* 4 (1932) 195-213. **M. Luther,** *Lectures on the Minor Prophets* (1975). **L. Markert,** "Amos/Amosbuch," *TRE* 2 (1978) 471-87. **J. L. Mays,** "Words About the Words of Amos: Recent Study of the Book of Amos," *Int* 13 (1959) 259-72; *Amos: A Commentary* (OTL, 1969). **L. Monloubou,** "Prophètes d'Israël: Amos," *DBSup* 8 (1969) 706-24. **J. Morgenstern,** *Amos Studies I* (1941); "The Address of Amos: Text and Commentary," *HUCA* 32 (1961) 295-350. **H. Oort,** "De Profeet Amos," *ThT* 14 (1880) 114-59; "Het vanderland van Amos," *ThT* 25 (1891) 121-25. **S. M. Paul,** *Amos: A Commentary on the Book of Amos* (1991). **C. Peifer,** "Amos the Prophet: The Man and His Book," *TBT* 19 (1981) 295-300. **M. E. Polley,** *Amos and the Davidic Empire: A Socio-historical Approach* (1989). **J. J. M. Roberts,** "Recent Trends in the Study of Amos," *ResQ* 13 (1970) 1-16. **S. N. Rosenbaum,** *Amos of Israel: A New Interpretation* (1990). **H. Routtenberg,** *Amos of Tekoa: A Study in Interpretation* (1971). **H. H. Rowley,** "Was Amos a *Nabi?*" *Festschrift für O. Eissfeldt* (ed. J. Fück, 1947) 191-98. **J. E. Sanderson,** "Amos," *Women's Bible Commentary* (ed. C. A. Newson and S. H. Ringe, 1992) 205-9. **H. Schmidt,** *Der Prophet Amos* (1917); "Die Herkunft des Propheten Amos," *K. Budde zum siebzigsten Geburtstag* (ed. K. Marti, BZAW 34, 1920) 158-71. **W. A. Smalley,** "Recursion Patterns and the Sectioning of Amos," *BiTr* 30 (1979) 118-27. **G. A. Smith,** *Book of the Twelve Prophets: Commonly Called the Minor* (2 vols., 1896–98). **W. R. Smith,** *The Prophets of Israel and Their Place in History to the Close of the Eighth Century* BC (1897). **H. R. Smythe,** "The Interpretation of Amos 4:13 in St. Athanasius and Didymus," *JTS* 1 (1950) 158-68. **J. A. Soggin,** *The Prophet Amos: A Translation and Commentary* (1987). **S. Terrien,** "Amos and Wisdom," *Israel's Prophetic Heritage* (ed. B. W. Anderson and W. Harrelson, 1962) 108-15. **A. van der Wal,** *Amos: A Classified Biography* (1988³). **J. D. W. Watts,** "An Old Hymn Preserved in the Book of Amos," *JNES* 15 (1956) 33-39; *Vision and Prophecy in Amos* (1958). **A. Weiser,** *Die Profetie des Amos* (BZAW 53, 1929). **J. Wellhausen,** *Die kleinen Propheten übersetzt und erklärt* (1892). **H. W. Wolff,** *Joel and Amos: A Commentary on the Books of the Prophets Joel and Amos* (1969; ET Hermeneia, 1977). **E. Würthwein,** "Amos-Studien," *ZAW* 62 (1950) 10-52 = *Wort und Existenz* (1970) 68-110.

S. N. ROSENBAUM

ANABAPTISTS

The name (from *anabaptizō*,—"to baptize again") designates one of the Reformation movements of the sixteenth century, a movement that denied the legitimacy of infant baptism over the baptism of believers. The Anabaptists first emerged within the Zwinglian reform (see ZWINGLI) in Zurich in 1525, made their appearance in the other German lands after 1526 and finally also in the Netherlands beginning in 1529. They were a major component of what has been called lay Protestantism in that the movement had a strong anti-clerical cast from its inception. Its gradual separation from Reformed and Lutheran Protestantism resulted from unbridgeable differences in biblical interpretation, giving rise to a different formulation of the faith-works polarity and of other ecclesiology.

Anabaptists joined the major Reformers in rejecting the medieval church's doctrine of authority and placing the sole AUTHORITY of the Scriptures in its stead. However, they differed not only from the Reformers but also from each other in the formulation of their views of scriptural authority.

It became customary to divide the movement into three fairly distinct groupings: Swiss, south German, and Dutch. The differences were not merely geographical and ethnic but resulted from fundamentally different formative influences, all of which are closely related to the interpretation of Scripture. Swiss Anabaptists emerged out of the Zwinglian Reformation, which was characterized by a strong humanist cast suggested by the humanist slogan *ad fontes!* South German Anabaptists bore the stamp of medieval mysticism and apocalyptic expectation (see APOCALYPTICISM). Dutch Anabaptism bore a significant resemblance to certain aspects of sacramentarianism and was in its early years a crusading apocalyptic movement. Following the destruction of the kingdom of Münster in 1535, Anabaptism constituted the Reformation in the Netherlands until the arrival of Calvinism (see CALVIN).

In its approach to biblical interpretation all of Anabaptism bore the marks of a lay movement. With the elimination of their educated leadership through persecution in both Roman Catholic and Protestant territories came a militant rejection by Anabaptists of the primary role of scholars in the interpretation of Scripture, especially in the early years, 1525–30. This was not so much anti-intellectualism, as has sometimes been asserted, but rather a strongly anti-clerical stance that denied the scholarly clergy the sole right to the interpretation of Scripture. This denial was a response to the abandonment after 1525 of the early Protestant flirtation with lay Bible reading and interpretation. Anabaptists concluded that because both Protestant and Roman Catholic clergy were involved in the exercise of coercive power in close cooperation with the secular authorities, their claim to reliable interpretation of Scripture was fatally compromised. They never denied the contribution of scholarship to the interpretation of Scripture per se, but the link of scholarship with coercive power put scholars under a permanent shadow in the tradition.

At many important points Anabaptists adopted the general Protestant principles of interpretation. For the most part they rejected the medieval fourfold interpretive scheme and with the great Reformers insisted on the literal meaning of the text as primary. It is possible, however, to find examples of allegorical interpretation in the writings of some Anabaptists, especially M. Hoffman (c. 1500–c. 1543) and P. MARPECK.

Anabaptists agreed with Protestants that the Scriptures are clear and not obscure, a principle that was directed against the insistence of the old church that only those especially trained and appointed can interpret Scripture and illuminate its obscurities. Part of that clarity lay in the principle of Scripture's interpreting itself: The clear passages clarify the more difficult parts, hence there is no real need to go beyond the confines of Scripture for interpretive aids. This principle too strengthened the claims of laypeople to competence in biblical interpretation.

Of great importance was the Anabaptist view of the relationship of the HB to the NT. Apart from some early south German authors, especially the more mystical H. DENCK and H. Hut (d. 1527), there was virtual unanimity that the HB is interpreted by the NT. Only what can be validated in the HB by "the doctrine of Christ and the Apostles" remains authoritative for the Christian. This strong separation of the testaments was not an echo of Marcionism (see MARCION), for the identity of God in both testaments was never in question. The separation arose in response to the Protestant use of the HB to validate the conception of a Christian society with a Christian government and especially to justify Christian resort to persecution and violence. The relationship of the testaments, as described most extensively by Marpeck in his *Testamentserläuterung,* was one of promise and fulfillment, of shadow and reality. The HB was not rejected, but it was relegated to second place as historically superseded by the NT. There are traces here of JOACHIM OF FIORE's successive ages of Father and Son, roughly identified with the HB and the NT.

Anabaptists also used the Apocrypha extensively as canonical Scripture because of its strong moral and ethical content, thus taking a position between the papal church and Protestantism on its importance. The early Anabaptist preference for the Zurich Froschauer Bible may be attributed in part to the fact that in it the apocryphal books were not separated from the rest of the CANON as they were in the LUTHER Bible.

Anabaptists seem to have adopted with some consistency what Zwingli called the "rule of Paul" (1 Cor 14:29), i.e., that any particular interpretation should be decided by the Christian congregation once the "experts" had spoken, thus asserting the role of the laity in the interpretation of Scripture. On the other hand, it is evident that the interpretations of earlier charismatic and later chosen leaders frequently dominated also in Anabaptist congregations.

Finally, one encounters in all parts of the tradition the view that only the one who obeys Scripture can reliably understand and interpret it. There could be no knowing of the truth without also doing it. The interpretation and understanding of Scripture was regarded as much more than an academic exercise; it was an existential matter.

Bibliography: "Anabaptists," *ODCC* (ed. F. L. Cross and E. A. Livingstone, 1997), esp. bibliography, 55-56. **H. S. Bender,** "Bible," *MennEnc* 1 (1955) 322-24. **W. Swartley** (ed.), *Essays on Biblical Interpretation: Anabaptist-Mennonite Perspectives* (Text-Reader Series 1, 1984). **W. Wiswedel,** "Bible: Inner and Outer Word," *MennEnc* 1 (1955) 324-28. **J. H. Yoder,** "The Hermeneutics of the Anabaptists," *Mennonite Quarterly Review* 42 (1967) 291-308.

W. KLAASSEN

ANDREW OF ST. VICTOR (d. 1175)

Most likely of Anglo-Norman heritage, A. seems to have arrived at the abbey of Augustinian canons at St. Victor in Paris in the 1130s. After the death of HUGH OF ST. VICTOR he began lecturing at the abbey but around 1149 was called to lead the new foundation of canons at Wigmore in Shropshire. The abbey and its abbot encountered difficulties, however, and by 1155 A. was again in Paris. Upon the entreaty of his brothers and the intervention of G. Foliot, Bishop of Hereford, he returned to Wigmore by 1163, where he remained as abbot until his death in 1175.

A. commented on the Hebrew CANON, except for Job,

Psalms, Song of Songs, and Ruth. In the spirit of Victorine exegesis enunciated by Hugh, A. devoted himself to the literal/historical meaning of the text, the foundation of any understanding of Scripture. What made him unique was his exclusive attention to the study of this dimension. His philological tools were no different from those of his contemporaries: His knowledge of the Hebrew language and of Greek was culled mainly from JEROME and other patristic writings. Yet he is described as a Christian Hebraist, a reputation stemming from his eagerness to seek out rabbis to hear their understanding of their own Scriptures and the degree to which he agreed with their interpretation, even when this stood counter to the weight of Christian interpretation. A. also gave the Jewish historian JOSEPHUS a privileged place among his sources. Although he rejected Jewish messianic claims, he was attacked in RICHARD OF ST. VICTOR's *De Emmanuele* for accepting the Jewish interpretation of Isa 7:14 ("Behold, a virgin shall conceive").

A.'s legacy took several forms: His pupil Herbert of Bosham, later secretary and biographer to T. Becket, surpassed his teacher's facility with Hebrew in his commentary on Jerome's Hebrew psalter. PETER COMESTOR frequently cited A.'s unique opinions, usually anonymously, in his *Historia Scholastica*. But perhaps most important for the mainstream of Christian exegesis, A. took great pains to demonstrate the narrative coherence of the text and to "polish" the Latin barbarisms of the VULGATE. Hundreds of his brief glosses found their way into the *Postillae* of HUGH OF ST. CHER and thence into the broader tradition. J. de Murro, a Franciscan master at Paris at the end of the thirteenth century, owned what is now the Vatican manuscript containing nearly all of A.'s commentaries and himself composed a commentary on Daniel citing A. that has been published among the *dubia* in the Parma 1868 edition of Aquinas's *Opera*.

A. never composed a treatise on HERMENEUTICS. His principles of exegesis were no different from those of his contemporaries; but he was much more thoroughgoing in his application of them, wrestling with minor descrepancies. The doggedness with which he pursued these questions can only be explained by his apparent conviction that the Scriptures were never nonsense even at a literal level but told a true story about real human beings that could be understood by analogy to his own experience.

Works: *Expositio super Heptateuchum* (CCCM 53, ed. C. Lohr and R. Berndt, 1986); *Expositio super Danielem* (CCCM 53F, ed. M. Zier, 1990); *Expostio in libris Salomonis* (CCCM 53B, ed. R. Berndt, 1991); *Expositio super Ezechielem* (CCCM 53E, ed. M. Signer, 1991); *Expositio in Regum* (CCCM 53A, ed. F. van Liere, 1996).

Bibliography: R. Berndt, *André de Saint-Victor (d. 1175): Exégète et théologien* (Bibliotheca Victorina 2, 1991). G. Ca-

landra, *De historica Andreae Victorini expositione in Ecclesiasten* (1948). **A. Penna,** "Andrea di S. Vittore: Il suo commento a Giona," *Bib* 36 (1955) 305-31. **B. Smalley,** *The Study of the Bible in the Middle Ages* (1983³).

M. A. ZIER

ANNET, PETER (1693–1769)

Little is known of A., and his writings are given little discussion in the history of biblical interpretation. His first publication (1739) lists him as a "minister of the gospel." He was also a sufferer for his cause—he stood twice in the pillory at age seventy, was imprisoned for a month, and was sentenced to a year's hard labor.

A strong advocate of free thought and natural religion, he argued in *Judging for Ourselves* (1739) that the foundations of one's beliefs should be scrutinized as much as one's actions. A. entered the debate over the resurrection of JESUS, responding to T. Sherlock's *Tryal of the Witnesses,* one of the most popular books of the eighteenth century, which was itself a response to T. WOOLSTON. A. argued that the Gospels are not credible witnesses to the resurrection, being full of interpolations and created sayings of uncertain date, contradictory, and by unknown authors. For him, the resurrection was a fraud; thus he anticipated H. S. REIMARUS.

His work on PAUL, translated into French by Baron d'Holbach (1770), set out to prove that Paul was a fanatic, an impostor, and a liar whose conversion experience was probably imagined in a delirium. Furthermore, one cannot be certain what in his epistles is genuinely Pauline.

A.'s *Free Enquirer,* which appeared in only nine weekly installments (Oct. 17 to Dec. 12, 1761) and for which he was condemned in 1763, contained attacks on Moses and ridicule of the Pentateuchal accounts of miraculous events (see PENTATEUCHAL CRITICISM). His most influential and best-written work was his life of David. VOLTAIRE acquired a copy in the year of its publication (D'Holbach published a French translation in 1768) and used it as the basis of his 1763 drama *Saül.* (Voltaire used most of A.'s works, referring to him as M Hut [or Huet] de Londres.) Building on P. BAYLE's article on David, A. presented perhaps the most secularized and caustic account of David's life ever written. ("Voltaire had found in A. a man truly after his own heart, a Bayle untrammeled," N. Torrey [1931] 193.) A. set out to examine the biblical material "with the same freedom, which is used in reading Tacitus, Rollin, or Rapin; and which we have a right to use toward all" (xii), thus disclaiming any special biblical HERMENEUTIC. In examining biblical history, he argued, one must recognize (1) "the broken unconnected manner in which the Jewish history is transmitted" and (2) "the partial representation of it, as being written by themselves" (xi). A. agreed with Bayle that the David narratives are composed in duplicate accounts—in the narratives of how he came to the court and the occasions he had to kill Saul. David's rise to power reflects the takeover of the kingdom by "a parcel of banditti" supported by the Levitic clergy around Samuel. David's reign is presented, not as divinely controlled history, but as the actions of a tyrant with little grace and tenderness.

Works: *Judging for Ourselves, or Free-thinking* (1739); *The Resurrection of Jesus Considered* (1744); *The Resurrection Defenders Stript of all Defence* (1745); *The Resurrection Reconsidered* (1745); *Supernaturals Examined* (c. 1748); *The History and Character of St. Paul, Examined* (c. 1748); *Social Bliss Considered: In Marriage and Divorce* (1749); *The Free Enquirer* (1761); *The History of the Man After God's Own Heart* (1761).

Bibliography: **H. G. Reventlow,** *The Authority of the Bible and the Rise of the Modern World* (1984) 369-74. **L. Stephen,** *History of English Thought in the Eighteenth Century* (1876, 1902³) 1:205-12; *DNB* 2 (1885) 9-10. **N. L. Torrey,** "Voltaire and A.: Radical Deism," *Voltaire and the English Deists* (1930) 175-98.

J. H. HAYES

ANSELM OF CANTERBURY (1033–1109)

Born in Aosta in northern Italy, A. was drawn to the abbey of Bec by the reputation of LANFRANC and became his pupil. He settled at Bec and in 1063 replaced Lanfranc as master of the school there. A. concentrated on developing the powers of the monks of Bec until they seemed to one chronicler to be all "like philosophers." After thirty years at Bec, the last fifteen as abbot, A. was made archbishop of Canterbury and was brought into conflict with two successive kings over his understanding of the rights of the church in England. He spent some time in exile, seeking advice and support from the pope, but while in England he kept a monastic community about him and discharged the duties of his office conscientiously.

A.'s writings do not include either of the traditional categories of exegesis—commentary and sermons—although reports of his talks to his own community and to communities he visited survive. He seems to have had a considerable reputation for his powers of conveying ideas to simple people with liveliness and clarity. He was a philosopher and theologian of a stature far beyond that of any of his contemporaries; during his years at Bec he acquired a profound knowledge of Scripture and of AUGUSTINE, as well as a grounding in the writings of other fathers available in the library there. It is likely that he had already received training in the liberal arts in Italy, and he certainly added to his knowledge under Lanfranc so that he was able to bring to bear well-developed skills in grammatical and logical

analysis. But he was able to make a more than mechanical use of these skills and sources; they served his own original thought.

A.'s first book, the *Monologion,* dealt with the divine nature. He was dissatisfied with its "chain of arguments" and sought a single argument that would prove not only that God exists but also that God is all that we believe about God; the result was the ontological argument of the *Proslogion.* While he was archbishop he finished a major work with which he had been engaged for some time, *Cur Deus Homo,* in which he sought to show by plain reasoning why God saved humankind as God did and in no other way. A.'s most important works for the history of exegesis are the little group of treatises on truth, freedom of choice, and the fall of Satan. He explained that these are intended for the use of those who are beginning the study of Scripture. Addressing two or three texts in each treatise, he showed the student how to weigh the manner in which the words are being used, employing Augustine's distinction between "common usage" (*usus loquendi*) and more exact usage but taking it much further technically. His aim was to give his students mastery of the working of language and of the special problems posed by biblical and theological language so that they would be able to tackle difficulties when they encountered them in their reading. The method was not taken up directly in succeeding generations, but the twelfth-century study of grammar and logic led to the framing of analogous procedures, proving A. to have been ahead of his time.

Works: *Opera Omnia* (6 vols., ed. F. S. Schmitt, 1938–68); *Memorials of St. A.* (ed. F. S. Schmitt and R. W. Southern, 1969).

Bibliography: *BB* 1 (1747) 161-69. **G. R. Evans,** *A. and Talking About God* (1978). **D. P. Henry,** *The Logic of St. A.* (1967). **L. Hödl,** *TRE* 2 (1978) 759-78. **J. Hopkins,** *A Companion to the Study of St. A.* (1972), with full bibliography. *DMA* 1 (1982) 311-15. **R. W. Southern,** *St. A. and His Biographer: A Study of Monastic Life and Thought, 1059–c. 1130* (1963). **C. Stephens,** *DNB* 2 (1885) 10-31.

G. R. EVANS

ANSELM OF HAVELBERG (c. 1100–1158)

A student of the brothers ANSELM OF LAON and Ralph, A. was attracted by the ideals of Norbert, founder of the Premonstratensian canons, and entered the order in its early period. In 1129 he was made bishop of Havelberg, taking office two years later when Lothar II had driven out the Wends. In 1135 he was sent as ambassador to Constantinople and in 1147 as papal legate in the crusade against the Wends. In the last decade of his life he fell in and out of favor as a result of his dabbling in politics. His *Dialogues* consists of three books on major problems of the day in the life of the church that he saw as threatening its unity and faithfulness to its head. Book 1 is a discourse on the history of the church, of importance for the development of ecclesiology in the twelfth century, in which he tried to bring out the nature of present dangers. The second and third books deal respectively with two aspects of the schism with the Greeks, the procession of the Holy Spirit, and the use of leavened or unleavened bread in the Eucharist. No scriptural commentary survives that can confidently be attributed to A., but he is of importance in the development of the use of the Bible in theological polemic.

Works: *Dialogi,* I (ed. G. Salet, 1966).

Bibliography: Salet's introduction and bibliography assemble conveniently what is known about A.

G. R. EVANS

ANSELM OF LAON (c. 1047–1117)

A.'s real name was Ansellus, but little is known about his life. The tradition that A. was educated at Bec under ANSELM OF CANTERBURY has no historical support. He may have studied in Paris under the exegete Manegold of Lautenbach or at Reims under Bruno of Chartreux. The evidence of his writings, reputation, and students shows that he taught at the cathedral school of Laon from about 1090; his brother Ralph collaborated in his teaching and writing. While continuing to teach, A. became dean in 1106 and archdeacon in 1115, dying at Laon in 1117.

A.'s reputation as an exegete drew students from all over Europe to Laon, where the first academic study of the Bible began. His school enjoyed a reputation second to none at the beginning of the twelfth century; and he numbered among his students WILLIAM OF CHAMPEAUX, GILBERT DE LA PORRÉE, William of St. Thierry, and the future bishops of Exeter and Lincoln as well as PETER ABELARD, whose denigration of A.'s teaching was an indirect cause of his own downfall. A.'s main contribution to biblical interpretation came in response to the needs of his students; it was characterized by a careful attention to the text of the Bible and a faithful adherence to patristic exegesis, especially that of AUGUSTINE. His primary interest in the biblical text was related to the practical subjects of the theological curriculum: moral experience, the sacraments, and such doctrinal subjects as creation, the fall, and redemption.

A. began the task of organizing the interpretation of the Scriptures systematically. As a biblical text was studied, theological questions (*quaestiones*) were discussed and answers (*sententiae*) given, usually based on the fathers. These *sententiae* were put into collections that after A.'s death were reworked and systematized, becoming the forerunners of PETER LOMBARD's *Sen-*

tences and of the great Summas of the thirteenth and fourteenth centuries. The other, and perhaps more important, work is the GLOSSA ORDINARIA. Manuscripts of the biblical texts had often carried glosses for teaching purposes, which appear to have served as notes for oral lectures and as commentaries for the benefit of future readers of the text. As manuscripts of the entire Bible or individual books were copied, an apparatus, which consisted of the prologues of JEROME and various glosses, was included; but it was not standardized and differed from copy to copy. The Glossa Ordinaria superseded these apparatuses and became the standard medieval commentary on the Bible; it was written in manuscripts both in the margins and between the lines of the biblical text. At one time it was thought that the marginal glosses were the work of WALAFRID STRABO and the interlineal glosses were by A. However, historical research has shown that A. instigated the standardized gloss and did the glossing on the psalter, the Pauline epistles, and the Gospel of John. Peter Lombard used the Glossa Ordinaria in his work, the *Sententiarum libri quatuor.* The corpus of A.'s works is not yet settled; the authorship of some of the sentence collections is particularly problematical.

Works: *PL* 162:1187-592 has texts under A.'s name, but their authorship is disputed. O. Lottin, O.S.B., *Psychologie et Morale aux XIIIe Siècles* 5 (1959) 9-183 gives a partial text of the sentences.

Bibliography: V. I. J. Flint, " 'The School of Laon': A Reconsideration," *RTAM* 43 (1976) 89-110. **B. Smalley,** "Glossa Ordinaria," *TRE* 13 (1984) 452-57; *The Study of the Bible in the Middle Ages* (1964) esp. 46-72. **E. A. Synam,** *DMA* 1 (1982) 315-16.

E. A. COKE

ANTIOCHENE SCHOOL

This school may be characterized as a reaction against ALEXANDRIAN allegory. Since most accounts of the Antiochene school's exegetical methods stress a concern with the literal and historical dimensions of the text, the Antiochenes sometimes appear as the precursors of modern historical exegesis, although this conclusion is somewhat misleading. Nevertheless, Eustathius of Antioch, Diodore of Tarsus and THEODORE OF MOPSUESTIA all criticize allegory; their general approach to exegesis was followed by CHRYSOSTOM and by THEODORET OF CYRRHUS. A treatise on biblical interpretation by one Adrianos also belongs to the Antiochene exegetical tradition.

Discussions of the Antiochene method have observed that its proponents all opposed *historia* to allegory. Most notorious is Theodore, who in the process challenged traditional prophetic (see PROPHECY AND PROPHETS, HB) and symbolic readings, refusing to allow that the Song of Songs was an allegory describing the marriage relationship of Christ and his bride the church, and interpreting the prophets and psalms in relation to the events of Israel's history rather than as cryptic oracles concerning the Messiah. Coupled with his christological views, which were taken to be Nestorian, these opinions contributed to his eventual condemnation.

Theodoret was more circumspect. He clearly knew the work of Theodore, but following Diodore he allowed for *theoria,* which might perhaps be translated "contemplative insight." Allegory was not permissible, but Scripture justified *theoria,* which included the traditional messianic interpretation of prophecies and psalms and the mystical understanding of the Song of Songs. Some scholars have characterized this approach as typological interpretation. Certainly Theodoret allowed longstanding traditions to inform his exegesis, while Theodore was less willing to do so. Theodore's insight into the eschatological dimension of the NT seems to have motivated his attacks on the messianic interpretations of the HB. He perceived successive stages in the creative purposes of God and viewed the gospel as a new stage. The problem with allegory was that the search for Christ everywhere in the HB undermined the newness of the gospel. The Bible became a flat cipher for eternal truths of a somewhat Platonic kind. But Theodore's criticism does not account for the school's general opposition to allegory.

Both methodological and doctrinal reasons informed the Antiochenes' critique. These exegetes followed the practices current in the schools of grammar and rhetoric, methods that were philological and classified as *to methodikon* and *to historikon.* The first method engaged in linguistic analysis, dealing with variant readings, punctuation, construal of sentences, style and diction, etymology, figures of speech, etc.; the second sought background information to elucidate sense and reference. The Antiochenes objected to the practice derived from the philosophical schools of claiming that whole texts had a *hyponoia,* or under sense—that is, that words were to be treated as ciphers and the "true sense" reached by cracking a code rather than by following the sequence (*akolouthia*) of the narrative or argument. Morals or doctrine were not to be deduced by allegory; rather, they were represented in the text, which provided models of how to behave and believe. The problem was that allegory took away what we might call the narrative logic of the text, what they called the *historia. Historia* derives from the Greek word meaning "to investigate," and research could turn up data of all sorts to provide explanatory notes, including variant versions of myths (see MYTHOLOGY AND BIBLICAL STUDIES). *Allegoria* was a recognized figure of speech, and the Antiochenes were perfectly ready to accept allegory as such if there was some indication in the text that it was present, just as

they were prepared to regard hyperbole as pointing to a sense larger than the immediate context and, therefore, as a textual signal pointing to a prophetic meaning (Adrianos's little treatise devotes four lines to allegory and sixteen to hyperbole!)

All the Antiochenes, then, were concerned with taking the narratives realistically, not with unpacking riddles referring to some heavenly reality. They elucidated the words and sentences of Scripture, conducted etymological and comparative studies to ascertain the "scriptural" sense of words, studied the concrete events and things referred to in the text, and examined the context and the sequences of thought. So they provided background notes, paraphrased the text to bring out its meaning, and summarized the text to highlight its *skopos* or intent. Indeed, such methods contributed to Theodore's controversial conclusions. Because in the SEPTUAGINT version of Psalm 22 the subject's "transgressions" are mentioned, Theodore concluded that none of the psalm referred to Christ or to his passion in spite of its use in the Gospel passion narratives; the principle of consistency of subject disallowed the traditional Christian approach to this key psalm. But the Antiochene approach was far from anticipating the historical-critical method of modern scholars. In spite of his recognition that Psalm 137 refers to the exile in Babylon, Theodore never questioned the Davidic authorship of the psalms; instead he claimed that David must have been prophesying.

Furthermore, Antiochene exegesis was avowedly dogmatic and moralistic. All of the Antiochenes found the christological dogmas under debate in their own time clearly represented in Scripture. Chrysostom did not hesitate to draw morals from whatever text he was commenting on. ORIGEN may have allegorized the feeding story in terms of spiritual feeding, but Chrysostom was hardly less anachronistic when he suggested that Christ looked up to heaven to prove he was of the Father and that he used the loaves and fish rather than creating food out of nothing to stop the mouths of dualist heretics like MARCION and Manichaeus. Indeed, what the Antiochenes really seem to have reacted against was a method of interpretation that spiritualized away the key narratives of the rule of faith: the creation, the fall, the incarnation, the restoration of paradise. The Origenist and christological controversies had an important bearing on this debate about HERMENEUTICS. The Antiochenes would have classed modern historical-critics with Origen as a destroyer of the *historia* of Adam and Eve.

The earliest anti-allegorical treatise emanating from this school, *On the Witch of Endor and Against Allegory,* written by Eustathius of Antioch (c. 300–377), proves that this kind of analysis of Antiochene method is along the right lines. This treatise is sometimes represented as a rejection of Origenist allegory since it deprives Scripture of its historical character. But an examination of the treatise soon proves that this representation is extremely misleading. It is true that Eustathius complained in an aside that Origen allegorized Moses' accounts of creation and paradise and even Gospel narratives; but his point was that it is scandalous to allegorize these while interpreting the story of the witch "by the letter." In fact, here Eustathius criticized Origen for his verbal and overly literal reading: It is too piecemeal. Origen made certain deductions about the resurrection on the basis of the statement that the witch summoned up Samuel from hades. Eustathius sought to prove that Samuel was not raised at all. Rather, the devil used the witch to play upon the mad mind of Saul and induce him to believe he saw Samuel. Only God can raise the dead, and Origen was misled by not taking account of the "narrative logic" of the text. The treatise is a series of rationalistic arguments to prove that Origen's literal reading is totally on the wrong lines. Other Scripture texts, the etymology of *engastrimythos* (one who has myths created in his or her inwards), and many other ploys are used. Eustathius is not defending literalism but, rather, a reading that takes context and thrust seriously. The story is not simply about the resurrection.

There was no genuine historical criticism of literature in the ancient world, and it is anachronistic to characterize the Antiochene reaction against allegory as arising from a concern with history. Typological, allegorical, messianic, and moral readings of texts remained the predominant approaches to exegesis throughout the Middle Ages despite the criticisms of excessive allegorical speculation.

Bibliography: G. W. Ashby, *Theodoret of Cyrrhus as Exegete of the OT* (1972). **R. Bultmann,** *Die Exegese des Theodor von Mopsuestia* (Habilitationsschrift, posthumously pub., 1984). **K. Froehlich,** *Biblical Interpretation in the Early Church* (1984). **R. Greer,** *Theodore of Mopsuestia: Exegete and Theologian* (1961). **L. R. A. van Rompay,** "Gennadius of Constantinople as a Representative of Antiochene Exegesis," *StPatr* 19 (1989) 400-405. **C. Schäublin,** *Untersuchungen zur Methode und Herkunft der Antiochenischen Exegese* (1974). **J. W. Trigg,** *Biblical Interpretation* (MFC 9, 1988) 161-220. **M. F. Wiles,** "Theodore of Mopsuestia as Representative of the Antiochene School," *CHB* 1 (1970) 489-510. **F. M. Young,** *Biblical Exegesis and the Formation of Christian Culture* (1997). **D. Z. Zaharopoulos,** *Theodore of Mopsuestia on the Bible: A Study of His OT Exegesis* (1989).

F. M. YOUNG

APOCALYPTICISM

Although a widely used word, *apocalypticism* remains without an equally widely agreed-upon definition. In biblical interpretation it can refer to (a) certain traditions of literary activity in ancient Judaism and Chris-

tianity; (b) the religious ideas and imagery that characterize this literature, chief among them judgment, the near end and/or transformation of the world, and a claim of access to secret knowledge about the world's destiny and/or structure; (c) social movements that initiated and responded to the apocalyptic message. Some scholars have attempted to clarify terminology by avoiding the substantive use of "apocalyptic" and by distinguishing apocalypse (genre), apocalyptic eschatology, and apocalypticism (Hanson). Attempts to restrict the word *apocalypticism* to a type of eschatology, to a symbolic universe, to historical movements, or to forms of communal behavior, however, have not yet succeeded; an understanding of apocalypticism as it has been used in scholarly literature requires looking at the interplay of literature, ideas, and movements.

Biblical interpretation has tended to place the flourishing of apocalyptic literature from the second century BCE through the second century CE. This period became the focus not only because it includes the two canonical (see CANON OF THE BIBLE) apocalypses (Daniel, c. 166 BCE; Revelation, c. 90–96 CE), but also because it is crucial to the understanding of the career of JESUS and of the emergence of early Christianity. The range of apocalypticism is far wider, however. Hanson placed "the dawn of apocalyptic" between the exile in the sixth century and the later fifth century, locating it in a movement represented by Isaiah 24–27; 34–35; 56–66; Malachi; Zephaniah 9–14; and possibly Joel. Most other scholars see this material as proto-apocalyptic and begin discussion of apocalyptic literature in the third century BCE with the *Book of the Watchers* (*1 Enoch* 1–36), perhaps the earliest example of the apocalypse genre.

1. Judaism in Antiquity. Scholarly attention to Jewish apocalypticism has generally waned with the literature resulting from the fall of the Temple in 70 CE (*4 Ezra, 2 Baruch, 3 Baruch, Apocalypse of Abraham*). It is certainly the case that Jewish apocalypticism underwent definitive changes after 135 CE, but it cannot be said to have disappeared. Apocalyptic eschatology perdured in rabbinic literature. Not only traditions of ascent and revelation but also works belonging to the apocalypse genre reemerged in the literature of Jewish mysticism. There is also the problematic evidence of Jewish apocalyptic works reworked by Christians, the date and original extent of which are very difficult to determine. A Falasha work called the *Apocalypse of Gorgorios* has been dated as late as the fourteenth century.

2. Early Christianity. Scholars once assumed that the delay of the parousia meant the disappearance or transformation of Christian apocalypticism. Montanism was frequently seen as a brief revival of Christian PROPHECY and apocalyptic fervor, but it is increasingly recognized that apocalypticism has remained a force throughout Christian history. Apocalypticism continued in antique Christianity under three guises: the continued production and use of apocalypses and related literature, the emergence of apocalyptic traditions of interpretation, and apocalyptic movements.

Montanism did indeed manifest the continuation of early Christian prophecy and apocalyptic expectation. The Donatists at some points also exhibited the traits of an apocalyptic movement. It is important, however, not to limit apocalypticism to movements that can be seen as sectarian. Early Christianity continued to produce and use apocalypses (e.g., *Shep. Herm., Apoc. Pet.*) and to rework Jewish apocalypses, testaments, and oracles (e.g., *Sib. Or., T. 12 Patr.*). Whereas once Gnosticism (see GNOSTIC INTERPRETATION) was seen entirely in terms of realized eschatology and was thus treated as the opposite pole of apocalypticism, apocalyptic aspects of Gnosticism are now more widely recognized, and a number of Gnostic works are now recognized as apocalypses (*2 Apoc. Jas., Gos. Mary, Hyp. Arch.*).

Perhaps the broadest stream of continued apocalyptic activity was interpretive. Hippolytus's *Commentary on Daniel* is among the earliest surviving biblical commentaries. Not only Daniel and Revelation but also 1 and 2 Thessalonians, 1 John, the SYNOPTIC apocalypses (Matt 24:1–26:1; Mark 13; Luke 21:5-36), the *Sibyllines* and the oracle of Hystaspes, Virgil's *Eclogue,* and many biblical texts that later interpretation would not view as apocalyptic were grist for the mill of early Christian apocalyptic interpretation. IRENAEUS already exhibited the major foci of Christian interpretation: the theory that the world's destined age is six days of a thousand years each (the cosmic week), the conviction of the thousand-year reign of the saints as the seventh day (chiliasm or millennialism), and the speculation on the antichrist (*Adv. Haer.* 5.28-36). Hippolytus defers the reign of the saints to a date two hundred years in the future, and Irenaeus argues against speculation on the name of the antichrist. But in Lactantius's *Divine Institutes* 7 (between 304 and 314) these elements combine as they would frequently in later Christian interpretation to argue for the nearness of consummation.

3. Apocalypticism in Medieval Christianity. After the formative centuries of Christianity interpretations of biblical apocalypses tended to be subsumed into a developing theory of symbolism of the church on earth. For example, the earliest Latin commentary on Revelation, that of Victorinus of Pettau (c. 300), was cleansed of its literal chiliasm by JEROME; it was this composite version that circulated widely and was the beginning of a vast tradition of ecclesiological interpretation of Revelation and Daniel. Scholars have recognized, nevertheless, that a literal sense of apocalyptic thought continued in both the Greek and the Latin Christian worlds. Much of this was based on already extant texts. In the Byzantine world this tradition was often reformulated to speak to particular instances of political oppression against Western Christian and Muslim expansion; examples include the *Apocalypse of Pseudo-Methodius,* found in Syriac and Greek versions, the Slavonic and Greek versions of the *Visions of Daniel,* the *Apocalypse of St. Andrew the Fool,* the *Cento of the Last Emperor,* and various legends of the antichrist and Gog and Magog.

Although the Latin-speaking world of Christendom had a very different political history from that of the Byzantine Empire, apocalyptic legends of the last emperor successfully fighting against the antichrist, adapted from Lactantius, *Pseudo-Methodius,* and the Byzantine texts, are also found in the West. The most famous of these is the letter *De ortu et tempore Antichristi,* written in the mid-tenth century by Adso of Montier-en-Der for Queen Gerberga of the West Franks. This text, which circulated widely under the name of such notable authorities as AUGUSTINE, ALCUIN, and ANSELM OF CANTERBURY, reflects the political situation of the tumultuous tenth century while describing the life of the antichrist in popular hagiographical form as an anti-saint's life.

The most influential tradition of medieval Latin apocalyptic writing began in twelfth-century Calabria with the Cistercian abbot JOACHIM OF FIORE. Joachim's three major works, the *Exposition on the Apocalypse,* the *Book of Concordance,* and the *Ten-Stringed Psaltery,* are long, difficult texts full of elaborate exegetical symbolism. These and his shorter works, like the "Letter to All the Faithful" and the "Letter to the Abbot of Valdona," reflect his impending sense of doom and deep pessimism for his own generation. Joachim did not see himself as an apocalyptic prophet but as an exegete of the prophecies God had already revealed in the biblical text. In applying biblical apocalyptic to his own historical period, Joachim distinguished between three periods of time (*tempora*), more properly conceived of as states (*status*). Each *status* was attributed to the action in history of one person of the Trinity. The *status* of the Holy Spirit was particularly associated in Joachim's thought with monastic Christianity, beginning with Benedictine monasticism, and heralded the coming of the antichrist and the end of the world.

Joachim's apocalyptic vision bore fruit in the later Middle Ages, especially in the thought of the Spiritual Franciscans, who saw themselves as the foes of antichrist in the last times. This very immediate and political apocalypticism was also a part of the continuing criticism of the ecclesiastical hierarchy, especially by figures rejected by that hierarchy as heretical, like Na Prous Boneta, a female mystic executed in 1325. The Dominican friar G. Savonarola continued this political current of apocalypticism to the eve of the sixteenth-century Reformation of the church. According to the categories of B. McGinn (1979, 1984), the Spiritual Franciscans, Na Prous Boneta, and Savonarola are all of the negative *a priori* mode of apocalyptic in which apocalyptic imagery inspires resistance to the ruling powers, who are seen as agents of evil.

Besides the Joachimite tradition, Christian apocalypticism is found throughout the Latin Middle Ages in mystical and spiritual writings, especially those by women. The related treatises of Hildegard of Bingen and Elisabeth of Schönau (12th cent.) present the mystics in a prophetic mode, passing on divine revelation in the language of the book of Revelation. These writings make use of the exegetical and symbolic apocalypticism common to Latin Christianity and may be seen as examples of McGinn's category of *a posteriori* apocalypticism, which tended to support rather than criticize the religious institutions from which it came.

Other medieval mystics, like Hadewijch of Antwerp (13th cent.) and Marguerite d'Oignt (14th cent.), are more difficult to fit on McGinn's scale of *a priori/ a posteriori* apocalypticism. Such authors nevertheless show the continuing importance of apocalyptic language and imagery in medieval visionary experience, especially among women—especially, that is, when the relationship of revelation to orthodoxy was inherently problematic to the ecclesiastical hierarchy.

4. Apocalypticism and Scholarly Biblical Criticism. Apocalypticism and the production of apocalyptic literature has never entirely disappeared from Western Christianity, but the rise of historical criticism provided a turning point at which scholarly interpretation and apocalyptic expectation diverged radically. While as major a thinker as J. EDWARDS continued to make apocalyptic predictions, the rationalist critique focused heavily on the problem of the fulfillment of prophecy and of the apocalyptic expectations of Jesus and his followers. In *A Discourse of the Grounds and Reasons of the Christian Religion* (1724) and *Scheme of Literal Prophecy Considered* (1727), A. COLLINS showed his awareness of *vaticinium ex eventu* and correctly placed the visions of Daniel in the reign of Antiochus IV Epiphanes. H. S. REIMARUS (*Wolfenbüttel Fragments* [pub. posthumously, 1774–78]) took over Collins's treatment of prophecy and the messianic expectations of Jesus and his disciples.

Thus apocalypticism entered the nineteenth-century scholarly world under the shadow of this critique and of the non-canonical status of much of the literature. Yet a few interpreters (F. Lücke, E. Reuss, A. Hilgenfeld) saw apocalypticism as the link between the two testaments, arising out of biblical prophecy, and sought to delineate its history. More widely influential was J. WELLHAUSEN's interpretation of apocalyptic writers as rigid borrowers and imitators who took over material from the prophets and from Persian religion in an unreflective and uncreative fashion. Wellhausen set the tone of scholarly attitudes toward apocalypticism. In some degree this tendency to denigrate apocalypticism was part of the general desire of Christian scholars to view the Judaism of the Second Temple as having degenerated from the true Israelite religion of the prophets; Jesus' preaching was seen as a restoration of this true Israelite religion.

At the turn of the twentieth century, R. CHARLES produced editions, translations, and descriptions of apocalyptic works that did not share Wellhausen's evaluation of this literature. Identifying the apocalyptic writers as heirs of the prophets and as the product of a branch of Phariseeism, he saw them as indigenous to Judaism and central to the interpretation of early Christianity. His work, though not without flaws, was tremendously influential, especially among English-speaking scholars.

Throughout the early part of the twentieth century, attention to apocalypticism was dominated by the questions of its origin and of its relation to Jesus and to early Christianity. Both of these questions polarized most interpreters.

Scholars of the HB were most concerned with the question of the origin of apocalypticism. The English scholars H. ROWLEY and D. Russell saw its origin in prophecy and gave it a positive evaluation, identifying its vision of history under God's direction as its characteristic and lasting contribution to theology. The tradition-historical studies (see TRADITION HISTORY) of H. GUNKEL, S. MOWINCKEL, A. BENTZEN, and the RELIGIONSGESCHICHTLICHE SCHULE in general made it possible to see apocalyptic use of mythic traditions, not as foreign influences, but as arising from sources deeply embedded in the life of Israel and of Judaism. German scholars continued to be heavily influenced by Wellhausen's view, in general distancing apocalypticism from prophecy and stressing foreign and, particularly, Persian influence.

The question of the relation of apocalypticism to early Christianity was equally disputed. In the early part of the twentieth century, English-speaking scholarship generally took for granted apocalypticism's significance for the NT. Although less widely accepted by German- and French-speaking scholars, this case was put forward in its most acute form by A. SCHWEITZER, whose critique of nineteenth-century readings of Jesus identified the message of Jesus as apocalyptic; his interpretation of PAUL presented him as an "apocalyptic mystic." But in succeeding years NT scholars tended to distance Jesus and early Christianity from apocalypticism. This tendency reached its peak with R. BULTMANN and those of his followers who sought to present both Jesus and Paul as demythologizing theologians.

By 1960 apocalypticism had begun to be an important and controversial concept for German theology and for NT interpretation. In this context E. KÄSEMANN made his claim that "apocalyptic . . . is the mother of all Christian theology." Between 1959 and 1969 a number of attempts to describe the social setting of apocalypticism appeared. These interpretations tended to depict apocalypticism as the product of a persecuted and prophetic minority (O. Plöger, P. Vielhauer). The study and first publications of the Qumran finds (see DEAD SEA SCROLLS) gave new impetus to the study of apocalypticism, providing not only a wide variety of new texts but also unsettling ideas about the character of Jewish apocalyptic expectation and drawing attention to the relationship between expectation and exegesis (N. Dahl [1964]; L. Hartmann [1966]).

5. Scholarship Since 1970. In 1970 K. Koch published a history of the investigations of apocalypticism that also called for more disciplined historical and literary study (see also J. Schmidt [1969]). Originally titled *Ratlos vor die Apocalyptik,* his study was published in English in 1972 as *The Rediscovery of Apocalyptic.* As the English title suggests, Koch articulated the concerns of a turning tide in scholarship. Since then a proliferation of scholarly study of apocalypses and apocalypticism have attempted both to free apocalypticism from the negative theological evaluations with which it had been burdened and to clarify the formal categories and the social and compositional context of apocalyptic literature.

P. Hanson (1962) traced the development of apocalyptic eschatology and the resurgence of mythic imagery in later prophetic literature. He proposed two apocalyptic movements in the period of the sixth to fifth centuries BCE that responded to the oppression at the hands first of the Persians and then of the Zadokites by creating a "counteruniverse" in which God's justice could create a new cosmic order. He described the second century in terms of multiple offshoots of an original apocalyptic resistance to the Seleucids.

Most scholars since Hanson have accepted his description of the origins of apocalyptic eschatology. The question of origin has receded in favor of interest in describing the genre of apocalypses and the relation of apocalypticism in Judaism and early Christianity to similar phenomena in the wider Hellenistic world. Apocalypticism is seen, not as deriving from wisdom, but as sharing a scribal and learned context with wisdom; concern with "foreign influence" has been supplanted by the recognition of apocalypticism as a tradition that is both indigenous to Judaism and shares elements with similar developments in other Hellenistic cultures (J. Smith [1975]).

With the description of the Enoch literature as the first true apocalypses, the third century BCE has become the starting point for most study of Jewish apocalypticism. The dominance of cosmology over eschatology in the Enoch material has drawn attention to the cosmological interests of the apocalypses (M. Stone [1976, 1980]; M. Himmelfarb [1983, 1988]). *First Enoch's* connection with priestly and official circles has helped to move scholars from explaining the apocalypses as the product of oppression and persecution toward seeing their eschatological concerns as products of more varied crises (Stone [1976, 1980]; J. Collins [1979, 1987]; A. Y. Collins [1984, 1988]). It is primarily the eschatological aspects of apocalypticism that engage scholars who use anthropological descriptions of millenarian sects to describe apocalypticism as the context of Jesus, Paul, and early Christianity (J. Gager [1975]; A. Segal [1980, 1986]; D. Flusser [1988]; W. Meeks [1983, 1986]).

The shift from genetic to generic description has been accompanied by more widespread collaboration and communication between Christian and Jewish scholars and among international scholars. The SOCIETY OF BIBLICAL LITERATURE Genres Group on apocalypses has articulated a definition of the genre and has studied apocalypses not only in Judaism and early Christianity but also in Greco-Roman, Persian, and Egyptian religions and in Gnosticism (J. Collins [1979]). The International Colloquium on Apocalypticism (Uppsala, 1979) likewise addressed itself to apocalypticism in the ancient Mediterranean and in the Near East, focusing on questions of phenomenology, genre, and social setting (D. Hellholm [1983]). The shifts described above and the definition of apocalypse as genre (articulated by the SBL Genres Group) have provided a basis for discussion, but consensus should not be overstated. The definition of the genre remains disputed, as do nearly all aspects of apocalypticism.

The question of the experiential aspect or compositional setting remains. There are explicit links between early Christian prophecy and at least those apocalypses that are not pseudonymous (Revelation, *Shep. Herm., Passion of Perpetua and Felicity* 11:1–13:8). Throughout the literature, vision narratives show connections with shamanistic practice and visionary literature elsewhere. Yet the scholarly, or at least conventional, character of the material is also made clear, in particular in the use of pseudonymity (J. Collins [1979, 1987). An analogy might be made with the practice of keeping a dream journal, in which interpretive tradition and experience inform each other. While investigations of Qumran's apocalyptic exegesis continue (M. Horgan [1979]), questions have been raised about the use of the Qumran texts to explain apocalypticism (see *JNES* 49 [1990] 101-94). A variety of cautions have been raised about the anthropological models of millennial movements to describe the movements that produced the Jewish and Christian apocalypses, Paul's mission, or the prophetic career of Jesus (J. Collins [1979, 1987]; Meeks in Hellholm [1983]). Especially in the case of Revelation attention has been given to the political context (E. Schüssler Fiorenza [1985]; A. Y. Collins [1984]), including that of sexual politics in the communities of Revelation (A. Y. Collins [1988]). At present the most urgent and fruitful area of investigation seems to be the investigation of literary and social functions not only of the apocalypse as a form but also of smaller apocalyptic forms and apocalyptic language (A. Y. Collins, Meeks, both in Hellholm).

The diverse and complex history of scholarly interpretation of apocalypticism in the nineteenth and twentieth centuries should not distract us from the recognition that apocalypticism has continued to be a viable mode of political discourse. Interpreters as diverse as H. Lindsey and A. Boesak find in it a medium to address their worlds.

Bibliography: P. J. Alexander, *The Byzantine Apocalyptic Tradition* (1985). A. Boesak, "Your Days Are Over: The Promises of God Confront the State," and "At the Apocalypse: The South African Church Claims Its Hope," *Sojourners* 17:8 (1988) 19-20, 28-35. W. Bousset, *Die Offenbarung Johannis* (1906). O. Capitani and J. Miethke, *L'attesa della fine dei tempi nel Medioevo* (AISIG 28, 1990). A. Y. Collins, *Crisis and Catharsis: The Power of the Apocalypse* (1984); "Early Christian Apocalypticism," *ANRW* II.25.6 (1988) 4665-711; *The Gospel and Women* (1988). J. J. Collins (ed.), *Apocalypse: The Morphology of a Genre* (Semeia 14, 1979); *The Apocalyptic Imagination: An Introduction to the Jewish Matrix of Christianity* (1987). J. J. Collins et al. (eds.), *The Encyclopedia of Apocalypticism* (3 vols., 1998). N. A. Dahl, "Eschatologie und Geschichte im Lichte der Qumran-texte," *Zeit und Geschichte: Dankesgabe an R. Bultmann zum 80. Geburtstag* (ed. E. Dinkler, 1964) 3-18 (ET in *The Crucified Messiah and Other Essays* [1974]). R. K. Emmerson and B. McGinn, *The Apocalypse in the Middle Ages* (1992). D. Flusser, "Jewish and Christian Apocalyptic," *Judaism and the Origins of Christianity* (1988) 229-465. J. Gager, *Kingdom and Community: The Social World of Early Christianity* (Prentice-Hall Studies in Religion, 1975). I. Gruenwald, *Apocalyptic and Merkavah Mysticism* (AGJU 14, 1980); *From Apocalypticism to Gnosticism: Studies in Apocalypticism, Merkavah Mysticism, and Gnosticism* (BEATAJ 14, 1988). P. D. Hanson, "Apocalypticism," *IDBSup* (1962) 28-34; *The Dawn of Apocalyptic* (1975); "Prologomena to the Study of Jewish Apocalyptic," *Magnalia Dei: The Mighty Acts of God* (ed. F. M. Cross, W. Lemke, and P. D. Miller, 1976) 389-413. L. Hartman, *Prophecy Interpreted: The Formation of Some Jewish Apocalyptic Texts and of the Eschatological Discourse Mark 13 par.* (ConBNT 1, 1966). D. L. Hellholm (ed.), *Apocalypticism in the Mediterranean World and the Near East: Proceedings of the International Colloquium on Apocalypticism, Uppsala, August 12-17, 1979* (1983). M. Himmelfarb, *Tours of Hell: An Apocalyptic Form in Jewish and Christian Literature* (1983); "Tours of Heaven," *Jewish Spirituality* 1 (ed. A. Green, 1988) 145-65. M. Horgan, *Pesharim: Qumran Interpretations of Biblical Books* (CBQMS 8, 1979); *JNES* 49 (1990) 101-94. E. Käsemann, "Die Anfänge christlicher Theologie," *ZTK* 57 (1960) 162-85; ET "The Beginning of Christian Theology," *Apocalypticism, Journal for Theology and Church* 6 (1969) 17-46. K. Koch, *Ratlos vor die Apocalyptik* (1970; ET *The Rediscovery of Apocalyptic* [1972]). H. Lindsey, *The Late Great Planet Earth* (1970). B. McGinn, *Apocalyptic Spirituality* (The Classics of Western Spirituality, 1979); "Early Apocalypticism: The Ongoing Debate," *The Apocalypse in English Renaissance Thought and Literature: Patterns, Antecedents, and Repercussions* (1984) 2-39. W. A. Meeks, *The First Urban Christians* (1983); *The Moral World of the First Christians* (LEC 6, 1986). F. J. Murphy, "Introduction to Apocalyptic Literature" *NIB* (1996) 7:1-16. E. A. Petroff, *Medieval Women's Visionary Literature* (1986). T. Pippin, *Death and Desire: The Rhetoric of Gender in the Apocalypse of John* (Literary Currents in Biblical Intepretation, 1992). O. Plöger, *Theocracy and Eschatology* (ET 1968). M. Reeves, *Joachim of Fiore and the Prophetic Future* (1977). J. M. Schmidt, *Die jüdische Apokalyptik: Die Geschichte ihrer Erforschung von den Anfängen bis zu den Textfunden von Qumran* (1969). A. F. Segal, "Heavenly Ascent in Hellenistic Judaism, Early Christianity, and Their Environment," *ANRW* II.23.2 (1980) 1333-94; *Rebecca's Children: Judaism and Christianity in the Roman World* (1986). J. Z. Smith, "Wisdom and Apocalyptic," *Religious Syncretism of Antiquity* (ed. B. Pearson, 1975) 131-56. M. Stone, "Lists of Things Revealed in Apocalyptic Literature," *Magnalia Dei: The Mighty Acts of God* (ed. F. M. Cross, W. Lemke, and P. D. Miller, 1976) 414-52; *Scriptures, Sects and Visons: A Profile of Judaism to the Jewish Revolt* (1980). P. Vielhauer, "Apocalypses and Related Subjects: Introduction," *NT Apocrypha* 2 (ed. E. Hennecke et al., 1964; ET 1965) 579-607.

M. R. D'ANGELO and E. A. MATTER

APOCRYPHA, NEW TESTAMENT

1. Definition and Scope of the Field. *a. Terminology.* The misleading terms *Pseudepigrapha* and *Apocrypha* stem in part from Protestant scholarship of the Reformation era. Because they set apart as "Apocrypha" books not included in the HB, Protestants characterized other writings dealing with Israelite persons and events as PSEUDEPIGRAPHA. Today it is widely recognized that pseudepigraphy and anonymity enjoyed something approaching privileged status in the ancient world and that a number of canonical texts are pseudepigraphs. Although *apocryphal* means "secret" and technically referred to materials not shared with outsiders (so Clement of Alexandria *Strom.* 1.15.69), the term soon acquired a pejorative sense in Christian writings from IRENAEUS, who seems to have used it as a synonym for "forged" (i.e., "pseudepigraphical," *Adv. Haer.* 1.20.1), onward, although the history and meaning of the term are not clear. "Apocryphal" was not routinely used to designate noncanonical writings until the time of AUGUSTINE (c. 400 CE; *C. Faust.* 11.2). The probably sixth-century *Decretum Gelasianum* condemns as "apocryphal" not only such works as the various apocryphal acts, gospels, and revelations but also the *Sentences of Sextus,* the *Testament of Job,* EUSEBIUS's *Ecclesiastical History,* the works of TERTULLIAN and of Lactantius, and the Synod of Ariminium.

b. Contemporary controversy. Debate about how the field should be characterized is encapsulated in the competing terms *NT* and *Christian* Apocrypha. The former, traditional label is vigorously defended by W.

Schneemelcher against E. Junod. Early Christian writings include the NT, the apostolic fathers, patristic literature of various types, and the Apocrypha. These divisions have resulted in a number of compartmentalized fields. In addition to the explicitly Christian material is the vast body of Jewish literature preserved (and thus edited and revised) by Christians, much of which is characterized as HB Pseudepigrapha. The latter are often quite similar in both content and function to works designated as NT Apocrypha. Contemporary scholars are prone to challenge the utility of these time-honored divisions. The insalubrious effects of compartmentalization constitute one ground for these scholars' objections. Other objections come from archaeological recoveries and revisionist histories of the formation of the Christian scriptural CANON.

For instance, the DEAD SEA SCROLLS have called attention to early Jewish literature not preserved by Christians, and the Nag Hammadi corpus has raised similar questions about Christian Apocrypha. Discussions of which Qumran and Nag Hammadi texts must be included in collected translations of HB and NT Pseudepigrapha and Apocrypha provide one readily accessible means for assessing this stress. The traditional structures have been somewhat modified, but their foundations are perilously fragile.

The distinction between canonical and non- or extra-canonical texts as a means for defining Christian Apocrypha is questionable for two related reasons. First, the canon is an ecclesiastical concept whereas historical analysis requires investigation of all the data. Second, the categories are anachronistic. The canonization of texts in the proper sense is, as one may observe on linguistic grounds (the term *canonical* is not applied to Scripture until c. 350 CE and not consistently then or for some time), a phenomenon of the fourth and later centuries, a project of the nascent imperial church, which possessed both the means and the motives for establishing norms, structure, and rules (H. Gamble [1985]; D. McDonald [1983]). Official recognition and support made a number of goals attainable, including unity and some uniformity. Governmental hopes for one God, one church, one faith, and one empire coincided with church aims. Canons in the proper sense emanated from councils that could promulgate and enforce them. This observation acknowledges that Christians had long regarded certain texts and collections of texts as authoritative (see AUTHORITY OF THE BIBLE), but facile description of this material as a "core canon" is historically incorrect. This perspective derives less from (selective) historical analysis than from the desire of (mainly Protestant) theologians to detach the creation of the canon from church history and assign it to the earliest possible date. The effect of this notion of an early core canon on the study of the Christian Apocrypha was substantial, for it led to the view that these writings were unworthy rivals to canonical texts. This understanding walked hand in hand with the now outmoded belief that canonical writings are all "early"—i.e., first century—whereas apocryphal texts are later imitations of their canonical prototypes. The label "NT Apocrypha" bears an explicit sense of inferiority. Another result of this characterization is the almost inevitable resort to a kind of uncritical FORM CRITICISM: NT Apocrypha must fit into the categories of gospels, acts, letters, or apocalypses.

With the partial exception of letters, defining these genres has been difficult. Gospels and acts share many features. Both are heroic narratives. If the acts lack birth stories, so do Mark and John, a deficiency more than supplied by "infancy gospels." All of the apocryphal acts remedy one defect of the canonical Acts: the death of the leading character, a feature that heightens their similarity to canonical Gospels. Non-canonical gospels, for their part, may, like *The Gospel of Thomas,* lack any narrative. Mark has no appearances of the risen Christ. A typical GNOSTIC gospel (e.g., the *Apocryphon of John*) contains nothing else. Appearances or revelations of the risen Christ also occur in the various acts. Definition of apocalypse as a genre has been equally problematic. Some even deny that there is such a *Gattung*. Revelations and revelatory addresses are, of course, also embedded within canonical texts (e.g., Mark 13; John 13–17).

Letters raise interesting issues. The history of the canonized pseudonymous Pauline letters (Colossians, Ephesians, 2 Thessalonians, 1–2 Timothy, and Titus) is precisely parallel to that of their "apocryphal" counterparts, like *Third Corinthians,* included in some Bibles, and *Laodiceans,* which found a place in Latin NTs until the advent of printed books. Segregation of such groups is one unhappy result of imposing ecclesiastical values on the discipline of history. The composition, revision, collection, and selection of and among gospels, acts, letters, and apocalypses continued for centuries. Anonymity and pseudonymity, with their implicit claims to authority, were enduring components of this process. Positive or negative judgments could be applied to the revelations to John and Peter (negative: *Stichometry of Nicephoros* [9th cent., possibly earlier]; positive: the catalogue found in the 6th-cent. Codex Claromontanus).

Division of the Christian Apocrypha into NT genres is maintained with considerable difficulty as a kind of convenience. Its importance for the field remains insofar as all definitions of Christian Apocrypha recognize some relationship to biblical texts, be it of form or of content. W. Schneemelcher (1991–92) upholds, with numerous qualifications, the traditional categories. All participants in the discussion agree that rivalry with texts that eventually became canonical applies to only some Apocrypha. Other works supplement texts that did or did not receive canonical status, while still others seem quite indifferent to or independent of such books.

The tendency for Apocrypha to bear the generic titles of canonical works is not evidence for mere imitation because it is uncertain when these titles began to be used. "Gospel" as a generic label is not attested until the middle of the second century, by which time a number of gospels had been composed. "Acts" is a designation not known until the final quarter of that same century. It is possible that the term was first applied to the *Acts of Paul* and thereupon to the canonical work. Moreover, these titles are often secondary, found in manuscripts but not in the works themselves.

Undoubtedly the generic approach to the definition of Christian Apocrypha is quite helpful for understanding the forms and genres of the NT. The Apocrypha show how literary types developed and provide important data for the history of the reception of works that would be canonized. Their existence contributes to the revision of F. OVERBECK's famous (1882) thesis about early Christian writings since they include types, styles, and viewpoints that Overbeck claimed were superseded when Christianity lost its pristine otherworldliness. Their primary character aids in the plotting of trajectories, for some of the apocryphal works attest to the survival of "pure" forms, like collections of sayings or of miracles, providing clues to the theological profile of these forms.

A final question relevant to definition is the issue of date. In theory the composition of Christian Apocrypha has no chronological limits. The adjective *ancient* must be an explicit or implicit component of the title. This raises the question of when the ancient world ends. A good case may be made for seeing that process as essentially complete in the ninth century. E. Junod (1983) argues for just such a chronological extension based on the continuing revision of earlier works and the production of new writings, especially those entitled "Later Acts of the Apostles" (de Santos Oro [1991–92]). His antagonist, Schneemelcher, holds fast to the fourth century as a breaking point, grounding his argument in both the transformation brought about by the growth of the imperial church in general and in particular in the replacement of apocryphal acts with hagiography. Both have a point. Yet Schneemelcher, like Overbeck, is prone to neglect the continued vitality of earlier genres. There are both ancient and medieval Christian Apocrypha. The former cannot properly be reconstructed and probably cannot fully be appreciated without attention to the latter.

The debate over definition involves not only extrication of the field from domination by dogmatic prejudices and non-historical models but also the issue of whether the Christian Apocrypha are to be an increasingly explored byway in NT studies or a firm part of church history. Given the contemporary distaste for secure boundaries among disciplines, it is likely that the future will belong to those who view Christian origins, including the NT and its background in the context of history (ecclesiastical and other). The emerging definition of Christian Apocrypha may well include works, usually pseudonymous or anonymous, that are set in biblical times, from the creation of Adam and Eve to the death of the apostle John; and/or have clear connections with characters, events, or, not least, the literature and forms of the Bible. It is nonetheless probable that primary attention will be devoted to the various narrative, revelatory, and epistolary works that have occupied the field for the last century and more.

2. Christian Apocrypha and Early Christian Writings. Many stories were told about JESUS, Peter, PAUL, James, Thomas, and others. For example, Galatians reveals that Paul is already contradicting rumors and reports about his conduct. The writer of Acts relates some of these in Paul's favor (see Galatians 1–2; 5:11; Acts 9:19*b*-31; 16:1-3). The Apocrypha, therefore, did not arise in response to such questions as, "What did Thomas do following the resurrection?" Names served as symbols for theological positions. Study of the Apocrypha helps to trace the development of traditions associated with such figures as Peter, James, Thomas, and Paul.

The Gospel of Thomas (Nag Ham. 2.2) gives that apostle the priority elsewhere held by Peter (*Gos. Thom.* 1; 13; Mark 8:27-30). This gospel is a collection of sayings devoid of narrative context. Study of them sheds light on how the canonical evangelists provide interpretation of various teachings through immediate and general contexts. A number of the parables in *Gos. Thom.* lack allegorizing details found in the SYNOPTIC tradition. Two noteworthy examples are the banquet (Matt 22:1-14; Luke 14:15-24; *Gos. Thom.* 64) and the workers in the vineyard (Mark 12:1-12, par.; *Gos. Thom.* 65–66). The most important contribution of this text, however, may be its restriction to a single type of tradition: Jesus as teacher of wisdom indispensable to life, wisdom that requires no story of birth, execution, or resurrection for authentication.

Many apocryphal works fill in gaps. In the *Protevangelium of James,* a gospel about Mary, the author skillfully uses various texts to weave a story that resolves some of the conflicts and inconsistencies in and between Matthew 1–2 and Luke 1–2 while defending the Virgin against slander. This text, which is more than an often charming tale, reveals that it was still possible, as late as the third quarter of the second century, to continue the practice of composing gospels. Had the author believed that Matthew and Luke enjoyed authoritative, even canonical, status, he or she would not have blended and corrected their texts.

The contents and date of the vision alleged by Paul in 2 Cor 12:2-4 have long been a thorn in the flesh. The Coptic *Apocalypse of Paul* (Nag Ham. 5.2, probably 2nd cent. CE) is a remedy to this deficit. The vision occurs in the narrative context of Gal 1:17-18. When interrogated in the heavenly court, the apostle replies that he will go down to the dead to take captivity captive. The wording comes from Ps 68:18, is cited in Eph 4:8, and is applied here, not to Christ, but to a Paul viewed more as a savior than as a herald. Colossians 4:16 refers to a letter dispatched to the Laodiceans. One solution to this lacuna was a brief letter to the church in Laodicea, composed at some time between 150 and 300 CE. The text is an apocryphon but not outrageously pseudonymous, for nearly every word comes from Pauline letters.

Acts says nothing about letters of Paul but does present a letter from the apostles and from other leaders at Jerusalem (15:23-29). The value of collective utterances by the apostolic college as a powerful instrument of authority and unity did not escape the attention of early Christians. The *Didache* received the same warrant. One of the more elaborate texts of this nature is the *Epistula Apostolorum* (Letter of the Apostles), which, among other things, includes an embedded gospel and subordinates Paul to the Jerusalem leaders. The *Acts of John* cleverly plays on traditions identifying the Fourth Evangelist as the son of Zebedee. This text also incorporates gospel traditions that show the apostle in his proper place (superior to Peter and the others) and gives the correct view of the passion, the meaning of which is explained to John by Christ in a cave on the Mount of Olives while he appears to be undergoing crucifixion below (87-105). (This docetic tradition occurs elsewhere, e.g., in *The Second Treatise of the Great Seth* [Nag Ham. 7.2].)

The *Acts of Paul,* which long enjoyed a good reputation in Roman Catholic circles and was still used as a historical source in the late Middle Ages, is a most interesting case. The author evidently knew the canonical Acts, for the work often seems to run parallel, reporting, for example, ministries in Philippi, Corinth, Ephesus, and Rome. Scholars dispute whether this book is a sequel to the eventually canonical book or an intended replacement of it. In this text, Paul contends against *Christian* opponents, writes a letter, has women colleagues, and operates as an independent missionary. Such events are familiar to readers of the epistles but are not reported in Acts. He also goes to Rome as a free man. There is an often antithetical relation to traditions found in 1–2 Timothy. Here, in short, is an apocryphon that complements, supplements, amplifies, and contradicts data found in the canonical writings.

3. History of Research. In one sense, critical investigation of Apocrypha begins with the selection and rejection of traditions by such early Christian authors as the canonical evangelists. By the late second century certain writings were stigmatized, but the data are inconsistent even within the corpus of such writers as ORIGEN. From the fourth century there were sustained efforts to condemn many apocryphal texts and to revise others. Historically this process cannot be separated from similar condemnations of the writings of various theologians or of gospel texts like the *Diatessaron.* Recognition of their pastoral value, however, enabled many apocryphal works to survive in more orthodox editions. The martyrdom sections of the various apocryphal acts, for example, are extant in numerous manuscripts because of liturgical use, while both infancy gospels and apocalypses, as well as other texts, continued to be handed on and reworked throughout the Middle Ages, not least in regions far from papal or patriarchal control. Shifts in techniques of book production have played leading roles in the fate of the Apocrypha. Among these were the transition to the Caroline minuscule style in the West and from uncial to minuscule in ninth-century Greece, both of which diminished the availability of these texts, and the rise of printed books in the fifteenth-century West, an event that coincided with the advent of humanist scholarship.

Early editions of the texts tended to be haphazard. The late seventeenth century saw the rise, particularly in France, of critical research on the NT and on nascent Christianity, exemplified by the NT introduction of R. SIMON and the hagiographical research of the Bollandists. In 1703 J. FABRICIUS of Hamburg published a three-volume *Codex Apocryphus Novi Testamenti,* a comprehensive collection of sufficient merit to warrant a recent reprint.

Deist (see DEISM) and Enlightenment criticism of Christian foundational texts called forth an English translation of Apocrypha. This project, which intended to show the sanity and reliability of canonical books by contrasting them with those rejected by the ancient church, comprises one of the two more vulgar manifestations of the discipline. Its *Doppelgänger* is the type of collection trumpeting interesting esoteric works that church authorities do not want you to read. The former approach, which characteristically extracts a few allegedly typical horror stories, long constituted the sole exposure of theological students to these texts. Why read something that describes Paul baptizing a lion?

With the nineteenth century came an explosion of data and methodological revolutions. Rediscovered manuscripts facilitated the preparation of critical editions. In this field the labors of C. von TISCHENDORF were scarcely less important than his work on the text of the NT. Following the revision of his edition of the apocryphal acts by R. Lipsius and M. Bonnet (1891–1903), the editorial process went on a long holiday. Theological and academic movements have also played their part. Among these are the model and method of F. C. BAUR (who took his departure from the Pseudo-Clementines); the RELIGIONSGESCHICHTLICHE SCHULE, which found much stimulus in various Christian Apocrypha; form criticism; and W. BAUER's provocative study of heresy.

E. Hennecke published his first edition of translated Apocrypha in 1904, followed shortly by a still valuable

Handbuch zu den Neutestamentlichen Apokryphen. Hennecke's translation quickly became the standard text. W. Schneemelcher assumed responsibility beginning with the third edition and has given the work an increasingly collaborative and international character. R. Wilson oversaw the complete translations of two editions of this work. American co-publication provided a strong stimulus to research. M. James, an able editor of apocryphal texts, produced an English translation in 1924, now succeeded by that of J. Elliott (1993). Two Italian editions exist, and French translations are now appearing.

New translations suggest renewed attention. H. Koester provoked an interest in the Christian Apocrypha among generations of Harvard students. Some of these have constituted an enduring seminar in the SOCIETY OF BIBLICAL LITERATURE. Many American scholars have turned toward the literary, social, and cultural dimensions of the Apocrypha. Christian Apocrypha are "in" for a number of reasons. Lacking the burdens and blessings of ecclesiastical oversight and mountains of monographs, the Apocrypha lie in wait for those attuned to new methods. Heightened appreciation for pluralism and the desire to honor minority voices also enhance their appeal.

Even more important are the projects of a group of Swiss and French scholars constituting the Association pour l'étude de la littérature apocryphe chrétienne, who have undertaken the production of new full-scale editions of the Apocrypha. Another international enterprise stems from scholars of the Netherlands and Hungary, who are producing essays on various apocryphal acts. The field thus includes scope for the most daring against-the-grain hypotheses and the most exacting philological labor. Numerous Byzantine manuscripts wait to be culled for embedded apocryphal texts, while the linguistic horizon is vast, including Latin, Coptic, Syriac, Georgian, Slavic, Arabic, ARMENIAN, Irish, and Ethiopic (see ETHIOPIAN BIBLICAL INTERPRETATION) materials. Modern translations are essential tools, but they can obscure the degree to which the extant Apocrypha are fragments, extracts, and greatly revised translations of original texts.

Bibliography: F. Bovon et al., *Les Actes apocryphes des apôtres* (1981). **J. H. Charlesworth,** *The NT Apocrypha and Pseudepigrapha: A Guide to Publications with Excursuses on Apocalypses* (1987). **J. K. Elliott** (ed.), *The Apocryphal Jesus: Legends of the Early Church* (1996); *The Apocryphal NT: A Collection of Apocryphal Christian Literature in an English Translation Based on M. R. James* (1994). **H. Y. Gamble,** *The NT Canon: Its Making and Meaning* (1985). **E. Junod,** "Apocryphes du NT ou Apocryphes chrétiens anciens?" *ETR* 58 (1983) 408-21. **K. L. King,** "The Gospel of Mary Magdeline," *Searching the Scriptures,* vol. 2, *A Feminist Commentary* (1994) 601-34. **J. R. Kohlenberger** (ed.), *The Parallel Apoc-*

rypha (1997). **B. Layton,** *The Gnostic Scriptures: A New Translation with Annotations and Introductions* (1987). **D. R. MacDonald,** *The Legend and the Apostle: The Battle for Paul in Story and Canon* (1983). **L. M. McDonald,** *The Formation of the Christian Biblical Canon* (1995). **F. Overbeck,** "Über die Anfänge der patristischen Literatur," *Historische Zeitschrift* 48 (1882) 412-72. **P. Perkins,** "The Gospel of Thomas," *Searching the Scriptures,* vol. 2, *A Feminist Commentary* (1994) 535-60. **A. de Santos Otero,** "Later Acts of the Apostles," *NT Apocrypha* (ed. W. Schueemelcher, rev. ed. R. M. Wilson, 1991–92) 2:426-83. **J. Schaberg,** "The Infancy of Mary of Nazareth," *Searching the Scriptures,* vol. 2, *A Feminist Commentary* (1994) 708-27. **W. Schneemelcher** (ed.), *NT Apocrypha* (rev. ed., tr. and ed. R. M. Wilson, 1991–92). **E. M. Schuller,** "The Apocrypha," *Women's Bible Commentary* (ed. C. A. Newsom and S. H. Ringe, 1992). **C. Tischendorf,** *Evangelia Apocrypha* (1853, 1876²).

R. I. PERVO

AQUILA (2nd cent. CE)

Born in Pontus in Asia Minor, A. lived during the reign of Hadrian (117–138). The TALMUD (*b. Meg.* 3a) knows a Bible translator Onqelos the proselyte, but he is probably the originator of the Aramaic translation only and not of the Greek (so M. Friedman [1897] and A. Silverstone [1931]) even though the names are basically identical. A. produced a Greek version (possibly two different eds.) of the Hebrew Scriptures that technically is a revision of an earlier translation but actually amounts to a new translation since he inserted so many new elements that the underlying base text can be discovered after only minute research. Fragments of his translation of most biblical books have been preserved. The SEPTUAGINT (LXX) translation of Ecclesiastes is usually ascribed to him, but K. Hyvärinen (1977) has demonstrated that it merely resembles A's work. Remnants of A.'s translations have also been preserved for some of the Apocrypha.

Fragments of A.'s translation of Kings, found in the Cairo Geniza, have been published by F. BURKITT. More A. fragments are among the fragments of the Hexapla, in which ORIGEN included A.'s text as the third column (see especially the fragments of Psalms published by G. Mercati [1958] and A. Schenker [1975, 1982]). Hundreds of readings from the Hexapla have been preserved in quotations by the church fathers and in certain manuscripts of the LXX. A.'s readings are recorded in the Göttingen and Cambridge editions of the LXX, in F. Field's edition of the Hexapla (1875), and in the concordance of A. by J. Reider and N. Turner (1966).

A.'s revision was not based directly on the OG translation but on an earlier revision, *kaige*-Th (previously named THEODOTION). This dependence, demonstrated by D. Barthélemy (1963), explains the background of the many readings that A., SYMMACHUS, and *kaige*-Th have in common. Ancient quotations from these sources are generally recorded as "the Three." Continuing the revision techniques developed by *kaige*-Th, A. produced the most literal translation in the biblical realm, matched only by the Syro-Hexapla. His special concern was to render all (even parts of) words consistently, preferably showing their etymological background (see Reider [1916] and Hyvärinen). According to *b. Qid* 59a, A. was a student of R. AKIBA, whose exegetical system and approach he followed. Because of his precision and the inclusion of Jewish exegesis, A.'s translation was much liked by Jews and used as late as the sixth century CE (decree by Justinian). The Hebrew text from which the translation was made was virtually identical to the MT.

Bibliography: D. **Barthélemy**, *Les devanciers d'Aquila* (VTSup 10, 1963). **F. C. Burkitt**, *Fragments of the Books of Kings According to the Translation of A.* (1897). **F. Field**, *Origenis Hexaplorum quae supersunt* (1875). **M. Friedmann**, *Onkelos und Akylas* (1897). **K. Hyvärinen**, *Die übersetzung von A.* (1977). **G. Mercati**, *Psalterii Hexapli reliquiae* 1 (1958). **A. Paul**, "La Bible grecque d'Aquila et l'idéologie du judaïsme ancien," *ANRW* II 20.1 (1987) 221-45. **J. Reider**, *Prolegomena to a Greek-Hebrew and Hebrew-Greek Index to A.* (1916). **J. Reider and N. Turner**, *An Index to A.* (VTSup 12, 1966). **A. Schenker**, *Hexaplarische Psalmenbruchstücke* (OBO 8, 1975); *Psalmen in den Hexapla* (1982). **A. E. Silverstone**, *A. and Onkelos* (1931).

E. TOV

ARCHAEOLOGY AND BIBLICAL STUDIES

1. Introduction. Where the term *archaeology* was once understood in a broad sense as referring to the study of the past in general, it is now commonly taken to describe the activity of those who excavate ancient sites. The best definition is perhaps that of the American archaeologist R. Braidwood: "The study of things men [and women] made and did in order that their whole way of life may be understood." The professional archaeologist, using a wide range of techniques, systematically studies the material remains of the past and thus contributes to the general historical task along with other scholars who study literary, inscriptional, artistic, or other recorded evidence. Archaeological evidence from the ancient states of Israel and Judah and from the ancient writings enshrined in our modern Bible are perhaps the two most important sources for the history of the people of ancient Israel and of the early Christian church; but evidence, both archaeological and literary, from the ancient surrounding nations—Egypt (see EGYPTOLOGY AND BIBLICAL STUDIES), Syria, Babylonia, Assyria (see ASSYRIOLOGY AND BIBLICAL STUDIES), and the Greco-Roman world—must not be ignored. Correct assessment of the relative value of evidence from these different sources is the concern of the historian. The study of artifactual and literary remains is, in theory, indivisible. Their separation in academic practice has led to much misunderstanding; the literary scholar has not always understood the limitations of the archaeological evidence, and the archaeologist has not always understood the complexities of the literary evidence. The relationship between the biblical student and the archaeologist has been further complicated by the fact that the two do not always share the same historical aims (let alone theological presuppositions).

2. Early and Medieval Travelers. It is hard to say when archaeological observation relating to biblical material began. For example, the ancient writer who noted the contemporary ruins of the ancient city of Ai (Josh 8:28) had an archaeologist's eye. So perhaps did Helena, mother of the emperor Constantine, who in 326 CE visited Palestine and founded basilicas at sites associated with Christ's life and death; and the Bordeaux pilgrim, who in 333 CE distinguished between modern Jericho and the earlier city of Jericho beside Elisha's fountain. From the Byzantine age to the time of the Crusades, most Western travelers to the Holy Land were pilgrims, interested in locating places associated with Christ or other famous biblical figures. Particularly important were the early fourth-century *Onomasticon* of EUSEBIUS (a gazetteer of biblical place-names soon translated into Latin by JEROME), the early fifth-century travelogue of the Spanish nun Egeria (a mine of carefully observed topographical information), and the sixth-century mosaic map of the Holy Land (see MAPS OF THE BIBLICAL WORLD) on the floor of a church in Madeba, east of the Dead Sea. These all reveal minds that were not simply pietistic; therefore, it will not do to deny the presence of academic observation before the Renaissance. In the late ninth century the Muslim scholar Ya'akubi identified the Dome of the Rock as the site of Solomon's Temple. A century later another Islamic scholar, Mukaddasi, traveled widely and wrote a description of the Muslim empire, including a section on Palestine and a description of the city of Jerusalem (985 CE). In the late twelfth century the Jewish rabbi Benjamin of Tudela in Spain explored and described Palestine (1167) and went on to visit Syria and Babylonia. These Islamic and Jewish scholars, however, were not known in the West and so did not influence Western scholarship until much later. The Crusades renewed Western interest in the geography and topography of the Holy Land, at least among the participants and pilgrims who followed in their wake. Important accounts were written by the English merchant-pilgrim Saewulf (1102); the Russian abbot Daniel (1106); Fetellus of Antioch (1130); the Germans John of Wurzburg (c.1160–70); and Theoderich (1172); the French Jacques de Vitry (1226–40); and NACHMANIDES, the Spanish rabbi Moshe ben Nachman (1267). Two hundred years later the German monk F. Fabri accompanied a large company of German pilgrims as chaplain and left a detailed account. Such pilgrims did not travel as archaeologists or antiquarians, but their writings frequently show that they were not unobservant or without concern for historical detail. The well-known *Travels of Sir J. Mandeville* (1322), however, seems to be the work of a writer of romance rather than of a seriously observant travel writer.

3. Renaissance and Enlightenment Study of the Near East. Western knowledge of and interest in the Holy Land and its antiquities revived with the Renaissance. Europeans began to venture farther east. In the sixteenth and seventeenth centuries Portuguese and Venetian merchants began to cross the Syrian desert from Aleppo to reach Baghdad and Basra (and thence eventually India). In 1575 a German, L. Rauwolff, visited Palestine in the course of wider travels and showed interest in its natural history; interest in archaeology and architecture was revealed by the Flemish J. Zuallart's illustrations (1586) and by the Dutch J. van Kootwyck's descriptions of the Holy Land (1596). In 1639 Quaresmius published a detailed study of the holy places, and in 1650–58 the Italian Pietro della Valle published an account of his wide-ranging travels in Egypt, Syria, and Mesopotamia, where he identified Ur correctly with Tell el-Mukayyar. One of the most observant of travelers was H. Maundrell, chaplain to the Levant Company's "factory" at Aleppo, who in 1697 traveled from Aleppo to Jerusalem, publishing an illustrated account in 1703. One of the first attempts to critically combine biblical and archaeological information in a scholarly work was that of A. RELAND, *Palaestina ex monumentis veteribus illustrata* (1714). Another important traveler was the Irish bishop R. Pococke (1704–65), whose well-illustrated *A Description of the East and Some Other Countries* (1745) is an important precursor of the work of J. Burckhardt (1784–1817). The Swedish botanist F. Hasselqvist published results of travel and research in the Levant (1749, 1751, 1752) in 1766; in 1762–67 C. Niebuhr pioneered the exploration of southern Arabia, publishing his account a decade later (1772–75).

None of this, except perhaps the work of Reland, belongs to the genre "biblical archaeology"—indeed, the practical science of archaeology had hardly begun—but all of it was important for the dramatic expansion of archaeological and biblical study in the nineteenth century. This expansion owed much to such political and economic factors as the quest for a land route from the eastern Mediterranean to India, the imperial designs of Napoleon (whose surveyors mapped Palestine), the arrival of the steamship and of the steam locomotive, the development of photography and of a cheaper printing technology, and the growth of public education. In an era when Protestant denominations set a high premium on biblical knowledge and Sunday schools flourished, there was increasing interest in biblical geography and in biblical peoples and their customs and a ready market for the hundreds of books published on Palestinian travel and life.

4. The Early Nineteenth Century. U. Seetzen, from Jever in Saxony, explored part of Transjordan and northern Arabia in 1805–10; he was followed by Burckhardt, who made his name by his rediscovery of Petra in 1812; both men had great powers of observation and kept accurate records. The most important scholar to explore Palestine was the American E. ROBINSON, professor of biblical literature at Union Theological College, New York. With E. Smith, a Protestant missionary and fluent Arabist, he traveled the length and breadth of Palestine in 1838–39 and in 1852 in order to locate places mentioned in the Bible. He based many of his identifications on the modern Arabic place names, which, he argued, preserved the Semitic names from biblical times. His results were published in *Biblical Researches in Palestine* (1841, 1856[2]). A. ALT later commented that "in Robinson's footnotes are forever buried the errors of many generations" (*JBL* 58 [1939] 374). "On May 4 and 5 he traveled north of Jerusalem and on the basis of Arabic place-names established nine identifications with biblical places: Anathoth, Geba, Rimmon, Michmash, Bethel, Ophrah, Beeroth, Gibeon and Mizpah. Of these only the identification of Beeroth has proved to be uncertain" (C. Geus [1986] 65). Robinson had his limitations—he did not recognize that the tels that dotted the Palestinian plains were not natural hillocks but the remains of city mounds—and he was occasionally wrong, but his work is the foundation of all biblical toponymy and remains an essential reference work for the biblical scholar and archaeologist.

Notable among other nineteenth-century scholarly travelers and explorers are the Frenchman L. de Laborde, who first drew and published pictures of Petra for the European world (1830, 1836); the German C. von TISCHENDORF, who searched the Near East for manuscripts and in 1844 found at St. Catherine's on Mt. Sinai a fifth-century codex of the Bible (Codex Sinaiticus); and the American naval lieutenant J. Lynch, who in 1848 explored the Jordan and surveyed the depths of the Dead Sea. Also notable are the artists D. Roberts (1838–39) and W. Bartlett (1841–44), whose works brought the first accurate, if somewhat romanticized, pictures of the Holy Land to their contemporaries.

5. The Beginnings of Archaeology. By 1850 the initial European exploration of Palestine and Transjordan had been achieved; there remained the accurate surveying and excavation of important biblical sites. An important step was taken with the foundation in 1865 of the PALESTINE EXPLORATION FUND, whose aim was the scientific investigation of "the Archaeology, Geography, Geology and Natural History of Palestine." Although at first heavily supported and subscribed to by church leaders, the fund kept to its scientific aims and flourishes still, especially through its journal, *PEQ.* In France, Germany, North America, Israel, and elsewhere, similar societies appeared: e.g., the French École Biblique was founded in Jerusalem in 1890 and its journal, the *RB,* in 1892. The German DEUTSCHER VEREIN ZUR ERFORSCH-UNG PALÄSTINAS was founded in 1877, with its *ZDPV.* The AMERICAN SCHOOLS OF ORIENTAL RESEARCH in Jerusalem was founded in 1900, followed shortly by its *BASOR*; in Israel, the Israel Exploration Society (formerly the Jewish Palestine Exploration Society) has produced the *IEJ* (1951).

The year 1865 saw also the completion of the survey of Jerusalem by the royal engineers of the British army under Capt. C. Wilson. The stimulus for this work was the concern of the Jerusalem Water Relief Society to provide clean water for Jerusalem. The Jerusalem survey was followed in 1871–77 by the full-scale survey of western Palestine led by C. CONDER and H. Kitchener; a similar survey of eastern Palestine was begun but was halted by the Turkish authorities in 1882 with only one small area (northeast of the Dead Sea) completed. An American attempt to survey Transjordan in the 1870s was also abandoned; G. Schumacher, however, was more successful in northern Transjordan (1884–1914). Until the military surveys of the mid-twentieth century, the best map of southern Transjordan was A. Musil's (1906). The Sinai region was surveyed by Capt. Wilson in 1868–69; southern Palestine was surveyed in 1913–14, again by British army personnel, while C. Woolley and T. Lawrence explored the archaeological sites of the region.

The first excavation in Palestine was F. de Saulcy's investigation of the "Tombs of the Kings" in 1863, which turned out to be the family tomb of Queen Helena of Adiabene, a first-century convert to Judaism; however, the excavation of this (and of any) Jewish tomb gave some offense to Jews in Jerusalem. Then in 1867–68 C. WARREN investigated the topography of ancient Jerusalem; he dug shafts and tunnels to explore the foundations of the Herodian platform of the Haram area, and he too met some opposition on religious grounds. (Sensitivity to the feelings of the present has not always been the first thought of those who explore the past, but it remains important.) Warren was the first to excavate at Jericho (1868), both at Tell es-Sultan and at the site on the Wadi Qelt later identified as the Hasmonean and Herodian palaces.

6. Egypt and Mesopotamia. A major contribution to biblical studies in the nineteenth century, both at the scholarly and at the popular level, was made by the growth of archaeological activity in Egypt and Mesopotamia. These activities cannot be reviewed in full here, but scholarly study of Egypt really began with Napoleon's expedition in 1799 and the resulting *Description de l'Égypte.* This led to Champollion's deciphering of the Egyptian hieroglyphs, to the explorations of Lepsius (1810–84), to the preservation of antiquities by men like Mariette (1821–81), and to the excavations of E. Naville (1844–1926) and W. F. PETRIE. Egypt was important for its own sake, but for many it was important also as the scene of the biblical book of Exodus. Much scholarly time has been given to identifying the "store cities," Pithom and Rameses, of Exod 1:11 and to dating the exodus and identifying the pharaoh of the exodus. The discovery of the archive of correspondence from Canaanite vassal kings in Palestine to the Egyptian pharaoh in the mid-fourteenth century BCE (the Amarna letters), with their reference to the military activity in Palestine of the "Habiru," who sounded suspiciously like the Hebrews, influenced scholarly debate on the date of the exodus from the 1890s to the 1960s, by which time it was generally accepted that neither the equation of Hebrew with Habiru nor the nature of the exodus story was as simple as previously thought.

In Mesopotamia the identification of Assyrian and Babylonian sites by explorers and excavators like C. Rich (1878–1921), E. Botta (1802–70), and A. Layard (1817–94), and the deciphering of their scripts and inscriptions by scholars like E. Hincks (1792–1866); H. Rawlinson (1810–95); and G. SMITH, who discovered a tablet giving an account of a flood remarkably similar to the account in Genesis 6–9, stirred even greater popular enthusiasm. In the twentieth century interest was maintained by L. Woolley's claim (1929) to have discovered evidence of the biblical flood at Ur; by the archival finds from the second millennium BCE at Mari, Nuzi (1925–31), and elsewhere; by H. WINCKLER's discovery (1911–13) of the Hittites' capital city at Boghaz Koy in north-central Turkey (see HITTITOLOGY AND BIBLICAL STUDIES); and by the discovery (1929) of an archive of tablets in cuneiform script and of a Northwest Semitic language (Ugaritic; see UGARIT AND THE BIBLE) at Ras Shamra on the Syrian coast. The discovery in 1974 of a huge archive of third-millennium texts from Tell Mardikh (ancient Ebla) in Syria raised new speculations about the authenticity of the biblical "patriarchal age"; but once the alleged reference to Sodom and Gomorrah in one of the texts was proved wrong, public excitement waned. Such discoveries raised both public and scholarly interest in biblical history, but they illuminated the Near Eastern background to the Bible rather than the Bible itself and are now the concern primarily of specialists in these fields.

7. Stratigraphy and Pottery. A new era in Palestinian archaeology began with Petrie's work at Tell el-Hesi in 1890. From his examination of this tell he discovered that tells were artificial, not natural, mounds, formed by the accumulated strata of building debris over long periods of time; and that each visible stratum of deposits contained its own distinctive types of pottery. Petrie produced a classified typology of the pottery taken from the different levels exposed on the mound. This gave a relative dating for the sequence of pottery that could then be used as an aid to dating similar levels elsewhere; the discovery of Egyptian inscriptions or royal scarabs in a stratified context made it possible to link the scheme with the accepted Egyptian chronology and so produced a basic chronology for Palestinian material. The cross-linkage of stratified pottery with Egyptian and Assyrian inscriptional evidence remains vital to the establishment of the CHRONOLOGY of biblical history to this day. Petrie, however, went on to correlate the strata excavated at Tell el-Hesi with the biblical evidence for the history of Lachish. This was a dangerous procedure, liable to distort his interpretation of the history of the site, for subsequent research has shown that Tell el-Hesi was not Lachish (see R. Doermann [1987] 132-34). Serious misinterpretation of the archaeological evidence resulted in later years from the mistaken identification (by F. Frank, followed by N. GLUECK) of Tell el-Kheleifeh with the Ezion-geber founded by Solomon (1 Kgs 9:26) and from the simplistic association of the destruction of the Late Bronze Age cities of western Palestine with the biblical stories of the Israelite conquest of Canaan. The direct association of biblical texts and archaeological evidence has always tempted scholars and needs very careful handling.

Petrie, however, had broken new ground, and his new techniques were influential. The trench method of excavation, with careful observation of stratigraphy and pottery sequences, had come to stay. His successors in the first three decades of the twentieth century applied his methods with greater or lesser skill but on the grand scale. R. Macalister at Gezer (1906–9) paid too little attention to stratigraphy and architecture, while G. Reisner and C. Fisher at Samaria (1908–10) were much more precise. Fisher, P. Guy, and G. Loud at Megiddo (1925–39) attempted to excavate the whole vast city layer by layer but found it too large even for a well-funded enterprise. On a much smaller scale, Glueck took the same approach at Tell el-Kheleifeh (1938–40), with the result that virtually nothing is left from which successors might check his results.

W. F. ALBRIGHT at Tell Beit Mirsim (1926–32), following the so-called Reisner-Fisher method, approached excavation by means of the locus, i.e., a small, easily defined area like a room or a wall or some other architectural structure. Related structures producing similar pottery were seen as belonging to a common stratum; indeed, for Albright prior knowledge of the pottery typology was all-important and determinative for interpretation of the site's history. (The problem with this approach is that a previously determined pottery typology may determine one's view of the stratification of a site, rather than vice versa. The stratum may become an artificial division rather than an observed one.) A consequence of this emphasis was that the interrelationships of the strata and structures were inadequately observed or recorded; Albright's publications show ground plans rather than stratified sections (P. Moorey [1981] 26-28). However, Albright greatly refined the Petrie-Bliss pottery chronology, constructing a new and generally accepted ceramic index for Palestine. His polymathic control of historical and linguistic as well as archaeological data established him as the leading interpreter of biblical history and archaeology in his generation. He valued equally the evidence of both biblical text and excavated artifacts and thus produced a synthesis that influenced a whole generation of American scholars.

8. Bible and Spade. Inevitably, however, as the twentieth century progressed it became more difficult for scholars to hold together the different tasks of biblical and archaeological research and interpretation. In the late nineteenth century many scholars had seen in archaeological discoveries a corrective to the hypotheses of the more radical biblical scholars like J. WELLHAUSEN; the discovery in Moab of the Mesha Stele (which mentions Israel's wars with Mesha of Moab); the discovery in Egypt of the Amarna letters (which mentioned Habiru [= Hebrews?], active in Palestine in the reigns of Amenophis III and IV) and of the Merneptah Stele (which mentioned Merneptah's defeat of a people called Israel in Palestine); and the discovery at Susa of the code of Hammurabi of Babylon (which contained close parallels to laws found in the Pentateuch) were all taken as supporting the veracity of the biblical story. S. DRIVER pointed out that the illustration of the biblical narrative was not the same thing as the confirmation of events described in the Bible (Moorey [1991] 44). Such German scholars as Alt and his pupil M. NOTH were well versed in the topography, geography, and archaeology of the land but were even better versed in analysis of the biblical text and wrote from that perspective. Noth, for example, saw archaeological discovery as illuminating the background to the biblical traditions rather than the traditions themselves, whose historical development required careful analysis. This approach differed widely from that of Albright and his pupils in America, who in general had a greater trust in the reliability of the outline of the biblical tradition and used their archaeological findings more positively to support the historical outline presented in the Bible (particularly in the cases of the patriarchal history and the Israelite conquest of Canaan). In Britain, with rare exceptions, biblical scholars and archaeologists kept to their separate trades. J. Crowfoot, J. GARSTANG, J. Starkey, R. Hamilton, and C. Johns were primarily archaeologists, though concerned with biblical history; K. KENYON studied modern history, assisted Crowfoot at Samaria, and became a protégé of M. Wheeler and a highly professional archaeologist who viewed biblical history from that perspective.

Kenyon developed what became known as the Wheeler-Kenyon technique, using the trench method but refining it by meticulously observing, recording, and checking the stratigraphy by preserving the balk and drawing its vertical section as a record of what has been dug. (Her techniques were adopted and adapted by many American archaeologists—including J. Callaway, who studied under her—but they were not immediately accepted by Israeli archaeologists, many of whom preferred methods that allowed for complete rather than partial excavation of a site and the exposure of architecture on a large scale.) Kenyon's excavation of Jericho (1952–59) by careful observation of stratigraphy corrected Garstang's dating of his so-called double wall from the Late Bronze Age to the Early Bronze Age and denied the existence of any but the smallest settlement at Jericho in the Late Bronze Age, thus undermining an influential view of the dating of the exodus and conquest of Canaan. More important in many ways, Kenyon revealed at Jericho flourishing Middle Bronze and Early Bronze cities and a history of the Neolithic period extending back to the tenth millennium BCE. In another major excavation (1961–67) at Jerusalem, she continued the century-old exploration of the topography and history of the city; this work continued in the 1970s and 1980s with dramatic success by the Israeli archaeologists N. Avigad, Y. Shiloh, B. MAZAR, and others. Kenyon was in no way a biblical scholar and in excavating had no biblical axe to grind. She was concerned to present what the archaeological evidence told her and took the biblical evidence mostly at face value, without critical analysis; if it fit, well and good. Israeli scholars, understandably, have tended to give greater credence to biblical traditions. "Quite naturally, every opportunity is taken to relate archaeological evidence to the biblical text" (Mazar [1988] 127). In this, as also in their approach to pottery analysis and stratification, they have been closer to the Albright tradition than to the British or German scholarly tradition. In particular, Israeli scholars (notably J. Aharoni) have contributed notably and for obvious reasons to our knowledge of the geography, topography, and toponymy of Israel. Major excavations have been those by Y. YADIN at Masada and Hazor, by Mazar and Shiloh at Jerusalem, by Netzer at Jericho, and by Biran at Tell Dan, to mention only a few.

Kenyon was independent of the Bible, yet not indifferent to it, and in her historical presuppositions was deeply influenced by its story. In many ways she belongs to the end of an era of biblical archaeology; her historical approach reveals the same limitations in scope as does that of her predecessors. For a century the Bible had influenced the choice of sites for excavation and the historical and cultural interests of the excavators. Concern to establish dates and to verify the biblical presentation of history led to the search for city walls

and palaces, temples and their cult vessels, inscriptions and coins, and evidence of destruction or cultural change at the end of the Late Bronze Age. This data was promptly related to the biblical account of the Israelite conquest of Canaan without further ado. This was not necessarily from motives of biblical fundamentalism (although this element was sometimes present) but rather from an uncritical acceptance of the familiar outline of the biblical story. In the twentieth century biblical scholarship has also moved on, and archaeologists have begun to learn from biblical scholars that the historical interpretation of biblical narratives is no simple matter and must be treated critically. Archaeologists are also under pressure from the explosion of information made possible by the development of new techniques and from new critiques of the Albright-Kenyon emphasis on the importance of pottery typology. H. Franken, in an important and undervalued book, *In Search of the Jericho Potters* (1974), argued that study of the techniques of manufacture might yield more evidence for the development of pottery than would the study of the changing shapes (the shape, after all, depended upon the technique used to create it).

9. New Concerns. Archaeology has also discovered other interests apart from the illustration of the political history to be found in biblical narratives. Social and anthropological interests, in fact, have been part of the archaeological agenda throughout its history; thus G. DALMAN, for example, director of the German Institute in Jerusalem (1902–14), studied daily life in rural Palestine and produced seven volumes of studies entitled *Arbeit und Sitte im Palastina* (*Work and Customs in Palestine,* 1928–42). Present archaeological concern is with understanding the settlement patterns and population distribution in ancient times, the ancient use of land and methods of agriculture, flora and fauna, hydrology, ancient technologies, and structures of ancient societies. Along with the excavation of a particular site goes the detailed survey of the surrounding land so that the site can be seen in a wider context; interest is no longer limited primarily to the biblical period but is extended to all periods from Paleolithic times to the present. The number of regional studies is growing rapidly; one might note the Shechem area survey (E. Campbell [1968]); work in the Negev by R. Cohen and W. Dever (1972, 1979); R. Gophna's survey of the central coastal plain (1977); R. Ibach's survey of the Hesban region (1976–78); M. Kochavi's survey of Judea, Samaria, and the Golan (1967–68); the work of E. Meyers and others in Galilee and the Golan (1978); and others. Work of this nature—e.g., I. Finkelstein's survey of Late Bronze/ Iron Age sites in the hill country of Israel—has had an effect on the interpretation of the biblical narratives of Israel's settlement in Canaan. The surveys of Transjordan, from those of Glueck in the 1930s to those of J. Miller, B. MacDonald, S. Mittmann, S. Hart, W.

Jobling, and others in the 1970s and 1980s, have brought new dimensions and added depth to our picture, drawn hitherto mainly from biblical sources, of the history and culture of the Iron Age kingdoms of the Ammonites, the Moabites, and the Edomites. The modern archaeologist has also learned to look for answers to questions about ancient populations and their political, economic, cultural, and religious organization and activities by beginning from observation of contemporary society as well as by drawing inferences from observed patterns of ancient settlements. The dangers of reading backward from the present are obvious; nevertheless, the questions raised are pertinent. Some recent historians have gone so far as to draw their picture of pre-monarchic and early monarchic Israel from archaeological evidence alone, putting to one side the late DEUTERONOMISTIC reconstruction of Israel's early history. The interests of classical historiography have been replaced by the concerns of archaeology, anthropology, and the social sciences (see SOCIAL-SCIENTIFIC CRITICISM). Not surprisingly, debates about method fill the journals.

10. Archaeology and Biblical Studies. One major debate concerns the value of archaeology for biblical studies. Clearly, archaeology has thrown light on Israel's material culture—buildings, architecture, city planning, city defenses, burial customs, religious cult, temples, synagogues, *miqvoth,* water supplies, clothing and jewelry, writing, trading, agriculture, domestic life, and so on. This evidence enables us to set Israel firmly in the wider context of the culture of the ancient Near East and to understand Israel as part of the wider world. On the other hand, few archaeological finds bear directly on the biblical narrative. The pool at el-Jib discovered by J. Pritchard may be the pool beside Gibeon of 2 Sam 2:13. The Siloam tunnel in Jerusalem with its inscription speaks eloquently of Hezekiah's preparation for an Assyrian siege in 701 BCE (although a Hellenistic date for this tunnel has recently been proposed). The tomb inscription of one Shebna in the village of Silwan across the Kedron Valley from Jerusalem may be from the tomb of the man criticized in Isa 22:6. The famous Moabite stone was erected in honor of King Mesha of Moab (cf. 2 Kings 3), but although it witnesses to Mesha's existence, it also raises questions for the historian of ancient Israel and Moab. From Assyria we have pictorial records of such events as the payment of tribute by King Jehu in 841 BCE and the capture of Lachish by Sennacherib in 701 BCE; and from Babylon, records relating to the imprisonment of King Jehoiachin of Judah and his sons. Most of these fortuitously refer to people known to us from biblical records; and they at least confirm that the Bible's historical records speak of real people and real events, even if they do not confirm the biblical reports in every detail.

Many interpreters, however, have tried to use archaeology to prove the "truth" of the Bible. The problem

here is that archaeology, while it might provide evidence for the site of Solomon's Temple, has nothing to say about the validity of such ideas as the kingdom of God or the meaning of the poem about the servant in Isaiah 53. Archaeological research has often offered more evidence than was desired, at least in some quarters. The Bible, for example, denies firmly that Yahweh has a female consort; yet recent evidence from Kuntillet 'Ajrud has suggested to many scholars that, at least in one place, a female consort of Yahweh, Asherah, was worshiped.

A major debate has focused around the term *biblical archaeology.* Albright approved the term, at least in a geographical sense: "Biblical archaeology covers all lands mentioned in the Bible." It was for him a wider term than "Palestinian archaeology"; it was archaeology that had any bearing on biblical studies (Albright [1966] 1). G. E. WRIGHT, one of his pupils, held a similar view; he identified biblical archaeology as "a special 'armchair' variety of general archaeology which studies the discoveries of excavators and gleans from them every fact which throws a direct, indirect, or even diffused light upon the Bible. Its central and absorbing interest is the understanding and exposition of the Scriptures. It is interested in floors, foundations and city walls; but also in epigraphic discoveries and in every indication of what people did with their minds as well as what they did with their hands" (1947, 7).

Dever objected strongly to the term because it suggests apologetic attempts to use archaeology to prove the Bible true. He preferred the descriptive regional designation "Syro-Palestinian archaeology." Biblical archaeology, he argued, did not describe what he and his colleagues did. They were professional archaeologists who happened to be exercising their skills in one part of the world rather than in another and to be using the same skills as all archaeologists everywhere. Archaeology exists as a discipline independently of the Bible, alongside other disciplines, like anthropology, philology, and philosophy. Dever reflected the fact that archaeology had established itself as a separate, independent academic discipline with its own scholarly agenda; it should no longer be regarded simply as the handmaid of history.

This leaves us with the question of how archaeology and biblical studies should relate. The answer must be that the reconstruction of all aspects of biblical history is an interdisciplinary affair in which linguists, philologists, paleographers, textual critics (see TEXTUAL CRITICISM), literary historians, archaeologists, and others all share. The archaeologist is no autonomous super-being; the archaeologist needs the help of other specialists— architects, radio-carbon dating technologists, paleobotanists, chemists, epigraphists, etc. Archaeology is a discipline that like all other academic disciplines thrives only in the company of others; biblical archaeology, insofar as it exists, refers to archaeology that is relevant to the field of biblical studies. In turn, the biblical scholar needs the expertise of the professional archaeologist to illuminate the biblical record. Difficulties and misunderstandings occur when an archaeologist chooses to interpret an excavated biblical site by uncritical use of the biblical text or when, conversely, a biblical scholar reconstructs history with the help of equally uncritical use of the archaeological evidence. The history of biblical interpretation contains many examples of both errors. It is to be hoped that in the future students of the text and students of the soil will develop mutual respect for one another's disciplines.

Bibliography: **Y. Aharoni,** *The Land of the Bible: From the Prehistoric Beginnings to the End of the First Temple Period* (1979²); *The Archaeology of the Land of Israel* (1982). **W. F. Albright,** *Archaeology and the Religion of Israel* (1942); *The Archaeology of Palestine* (1949 and rev. eds.); "The OT and the Archaeology of Palestine," and "The OT and the Archaeology of the Ancient East," *The OT and Modern Study: A Generation of Discovery and Research* (ed. H. H. Rowley, 1951) 1-47; *New Horizons in Biblical Research* (1966); *The Archaeology of Palestine and the Bible* (1973, 1974). **N. Avigad,** *Discovering Jerusalem* (1984). **J. Aviram** (ed.), *Biblical Archaeology Today: Proceedings of the International Congress of Biblical Archaeology, Jerusalem, April 1984* (1985). **J. R. Bartlett,** *Jericho* (CBW, 1982); *The Bible: Faith and Evidence, A Critical Enquiry into the Nature of Biblical History* (1990). **Y. Ben-Arieh,** *The Rediscovery of the Holy Land in the Nineteenth Century* (1979). **P. Bienkowski** (ed.), *Early Edom and Moab: The Beginning of the Iron Age in Southern Jordan* (1992). **J. A. Blakely,** "F. J. Bliss: Father of Palestinian Archaeology," *BA* 56 (1993) 110-15. **F. J. Bliss,** *The Development of Palestine Exploration* (1906). **J. H. Charlesworth and W. P. Weaver,** *What Has Archaeology to Do with Faith?* (1992). **R. B. Coote,** *Early Israel: A New Horizon* (1990). **R. B. Coote and K. W. Whitelam,** *The Emergence of Early Israel in Historical Perspective* (1987). **F. M. Cross,** "W. F. Albright's View of Biblical Archaeology and Its Methodology," *BA* 36 (1973) 2-5. **G. Daniel,** *A Hundred and Fifty Years of Archaeology* (1975). **W. J. Dever,** "Impact of the 'New Archaeology,' " *Benchmarks in Time and Culture* (ed. J. F. Drinkard et al., 1988) 337-52; *Recent Archaeological Discoveries and Biblical Research* (1989). **R. W. Doermann,** "Archaeology and Biblical Interpretation: Tell el-Hesi," *Archaeology and Biblical Interpretation* (ed. L. G. Perdue et al., 1987) 129-55. **J. F. Drinkard et al.** (eds.), *Benchmarks in Time and Culture: An Introduction to Biblical Archaeology Dedicated to J. A. Callaway* (1988). **J. Finegan,** *The Archaeology of the NT* (2 vols., 1969, 1981). **I. Finkelstein,** *The Archaeology of the Israelite Settlement* (1988); *Living on the Fringe: The Archaeology and History of the Negev, Sinai, and Neighbouring Regions in the Bronze and Iron Ages* (1995). **H. J. Franken,** "The Problem of Identification in Biblical Archaeology," *PEQ* 108 (1976) 3-11; "Archaeology of Palestine: Problems and Task," *The World of the Bible* (ed. A. S. Woude, 1986) 50-62. **H. J. Franken and C. A. Franken-Bettershill,** *A Primer of OT Archaeology* (1973). **H. J. Franken and J. Kalsbeek,** *In Search of the Jericho Potters: Ceramics from the Iron Age and from the Neolithicum* (1974). **W. H. C. Frend,** *An Archaeology of Early Christianity: A History* (1996). **V. Fritz,** *An Introduction to Biblical Archaeology* (1994). **L. T. Geraty and L. G. Herr,** *The Archaeology of Jordan and Other Studies: Presented to S. H. Horn* (1986). **C. J. de Geus,** "The Development of Palestinian Archaeology and Its Significance for Biblical Studies," *The World of the Bible* (1986) 63-74. **N. Glueck,** *The Other Side of the Jordan* (1940, 1970²). **C. P. Grant,** *The Syrian Desert* (1937). **H. V. Hilprecht,** *Explorations in Bible Lands During the Nineteenth Century* (1903). **D. C. Hopkins** (ed.), *Celebrating and Examining W. F. Albright, BA* 56 (1993). **T. G. H. James** (ed.), *Excavating in Egypt: The Egypt Exploration Society 1882–1982* (1982). **K. M. Kenyon,** *Archaeology in the Holy Land* (1979⁴); *The Bible and Recent Archaeology* (rev. by P. R. S. Moorey, 1987). **P. J. King,** *American Archaeology in the Mideast: A History of the ASOR* (1983). **O. S. LaBianca,** "Sociocultural Anthropology and Syro-Palestinian Archaeology," *Benchmarks in Time and Culture* (ed. J. F. Drinkard et al., 1988) 369-87. **R. A. S. Macalister,** *A Century of Excavation in Palestine* (1925). **B. MacDonald,** *The Wadi el Hasā Archaeological Survey, 1979–83, West-central Jordan* (1988). **A. Mazar,** "Israeli Archaeologists," *Benchmarks in Time and Culture* (ed. J. F. Drinkard et al., 1988) 109-28; *Archaeology and the Land of the Bible, 10,000–586 BCE* (1990). **J. M. Miller** (ed.), *Archaeological Survey of the Kerak Plateau* (1991). **P. R. S. Moorey,** *Excavation in Palestine* (1981); *A Century of Biblical Archaeology* (1991). **J. Murphy O'Connor,** *St. Paul's Corinth: Texts and Archaeology* (1983). **M. Noth,** *The OT World* (1940, 1964⁴; ET 1966); "Der Beitrag der Archäologie zur Geschichte Israels" (VTSup 7, 1960) 26-87. **L. G. Perdue et al.,** *Archaeology and Biblical Interpretation: Essays in Memory of D. G. Rose* (1987). **G. L. Peterman,** "Geographic Information Systems: Archaeology's Latest Tool," *BA* 55 (1992) 162-67. **G. D. Pratico,** *N. Glueck's 1938–40 Excavations at Tell el-Kheleifeh: A Reappraisal* (1993). **E. Robinson,** *Biblical Researches in Palestine, Mount Sinai, and Arabia Petraea in 1838* (1841); *Biblical Researches in Palestine and the Adjacent Regions: A Journal of Travel in the Years 1838 and 1852* (1856). **J. A. Sanders** (ed.), *Near Eastern Archaeology in the Twentieth Century: Essays in Honor of N. Glueck* (1970). **J. A. Sauer,** "Transjordan in the Bronze and Iron Ages: A Critique of Glueck's Synthesis," *BASOR* 263 (1986) 1-26. **N. Shepherd,** *The Zealous Intruders: The Western Rediscovery of Palestine* (1987). **N. A. Silbermann,** *Digging for God and Country: Exploration, Archaeology, and the Secret Struggle for the Holy Land 1799–1917* (1982). **D. W. Thomas** (ed.), *Archaeology and OT Study: Jubilee Volume of the Society for OT Study, 1917–67* (1967). **R. de Vaux,** *Archaeology and the Dead Sea Scrolls* (1973); "On Right and Wrong Uses of Archaeology," *Near Eastern Archaeology in the Twentieth Century* (ed. J. A. Sanders, 1970) 64-82. **C. M. Watson,** *Fifty Years of Work in the Holy Land* (1915). **J. Wilkinson,** *Jerusalem Pilgrims Before the Crusades* (1977); *Jerusalem as Jesus Knew It: Archaeology as Evidence* (1978). **G. E. Wright,** *Biblical Archaeology* (1957); "Biblical Archaeology Today," *New*

Directions in Biblical Archaeology (ed. D. N. Freedman and J. C. Greenfield, 1971) 167-86; "What Archaeology Can and Cannot Do," *BA* 34 (1971) 70-76.

J. R. BARTLETT

ARISTEAS, LETTER OF

Aristeas to Philocrates (the earliest application of the term *letter* to it is in a 4th-cent MS) purports to be an eyewitness account by Aristeas, a courtier of Ptolemy II Philadelphus (283–247 BCE), of the events connected with the Greek TRANSLATION of the Pentateuch. The work describes how Ptolemy Philadelphus commanded that the sacred writings of the Jews be translated into Greek, with the subsequent involvement of seventy-two elders working seventy-two days on the project. Scholars agree that the book is a literary fiction and that the author is in reality a Jew (undoubtedly Alexandrian) concerned to demonstrate the superiority of the Jewish faith (again and again the Greeks are filled with admiration and astonishment at things Jewish) and the possibility for mutual respect and peaceful coexistence between Jews and Greeks.

Within this larger apologetic framework the story of the translation, which probably rests on a popular tradition of Alexandrian Jewry, illustrates Pseudo-Aristeas's main theme and serves to consolidate the AUTHORITY of a revised version of the SEPTUAGINT, which had apparently appeared toward the end of the second century BCE. Although the royal connection with the translation enterprise is probably fictional, it is likely that the Ptolemaic court was pleased with the association and perhaps even encouraged it. Although there is little of the miraculous in Pseudo-Aristeas's account of the translation, this element becomes ever more prominent in successive accounts, from PHILO's insistence on the inspired character of the LXX (see INSPIRATION OF THE BIBLE) to Epiphanius's (c. 315–403) extension of the translation to all of Scripture, including the apocryphal books.

Interrupting the narrative of the translators' departure from Jerusalem is an important digression consisting of the high priest's rationale of the law (128-72). A critical question is raised by the Greek delegation: In view of the fact that creation is one, why is it that some things are regarded by Scripture as unclean? To this the high priest replies that the lawgiver has enclosed his people with unbreakable palisades and iron walls to prevent them from mingling with other nations and to keep them pure in body and spirit. They have justly been dubbed "men of God," whereas all others are men of food and raiment. Like ARISTOBULUS before him, Pseudo-Aristeas asserts that "nothing has been set down in Scripture heedlessly or in the spirit of myth" but rather to induce us to practice justice and be mindful of the divine sovereignty. All that is said, then, of food and of unclean

creeping things and of animals is directed toward justice (168-69). The dietary rules have as their purpose to promote holy contemplation and the perfecting of character, for the permitted animals are gentle and clean, whereas those forbidden are wild and carnivorous and with their strength oppress the rest and even do violence to humans. All this is a symbol that those for whom the legislation has been drawn up must practice righteousness and oppress no one.

This extensive allegorization employed by Pseudo-Aristeas may owe something to the influence of the Pythagoreans, since they too possessed dietary rules that they later justified philosophically (Aristotle *On the Pythagoreans* frgs. 5, 7, Ross). Although there is considerable similarity to Philo's allegorization of the dietary regulations, there is as yet nothing remotely resembling the Philonic "allegory of the soul." On the other hand, in insisting that these strange food laws have been legislated "with a view to truth and as a token of right reason" (161), Pseudo-Aristeas anticipates Philo's firm conviction that the Mosaic law is no arbitrary set of decrees handed down from on high but rather the truest reflection of the Logos.

Bibliography: **J. H. Charlesworth** (ed.), *OTP* 2:7-34. **M. Hadas,** *Aristeas to Philocrates* (1951). **S. Jellicoe,** *The Septuagint and Modern Study* (1968) 29-58; *Studies in the Septuagint: Origins, Recensions, and Interpretations: Selected Essays* (1974) 158-225. **H. G. Meecham,** *The Oldest Version of the Bible: Aristeas on Its Traditional Origin* (1932); *The Letter of Aristeas: A Linguistic Study with Special Reference to the Greek Bible* (1935). **A. Pelletier,** *Lettre d'Aristée à Philocrate* (SC 89, 1962). **E. Schürer,** *HJPAJC* (3 vols., ed. G. Vermes and F. Millar, 1973–87) 3:677-87.

D. WINSTON

ARISTOBULUS OF PANEAS (3rd to 2d cent. BCE)

In his *Interpretations of the Holy Laws* (c. 175 BCE), of which only five brief fragments survive in EUSEBIUS (*Praep. Evang.* 7:14, 8:10, 13:12; *Hist. eccl.* 7:32), A. inaugurated an interpretive approach to the Pentateuch (see PENTATEUCHAL CRITICISM) that dimly prefigures that of PHILO. His aim was to demonstrate that the Torah's teaching is in accord with philosophical truth. He asserted that Plato, Pythagoras, and Socrates as well as Hesiod, Homer, and Linus had borrowed from the books of Moses, which he indicated had been translated into Greek long before the SEPTUAGINT. To preserve the appropriate conception of God, Torah passages that attribute anthropomorphic characteristics to God must be interpreted allegorically. Thus the "hand of God" signifies divine power, and the "standing of God" refers to the existence and immutability of the world God created. The "voice of God" refers to "the construction of works," just as Moses had spoken of the whole creation of the world as works of God, for he says repeatedly, "And God said and it was so."

A. wanted the reader to understand the Torah "truly" (*physikos*), i.e., philosophically, not mythologically; but there is no evidence that he viewed the biblical text as an allegory in the Stoic and Philonic manner. He further asserted that if anything unreasonable remains in the text, the cause is not to be imputed to Moses but to himself, seeming thereby to indicate his awareness of using a relatively new exegetical method. He did not use terms later employed for allegory (*hyponoia*, "deeper sense"; *allegoria* or *tropikos*, "figuratively") but used instead *semainein*, "to signify" (used also by Philo), *apaggellein*, and *diasaphein*, "to make clear."

Bibliography: **J. H. Charlesworth** (ed.), *OTP* 2:831-42. **Y. Gutman**, *The Beginnings of Jewish-Hellenistic Literature* (1958) 1:186-229, 276-86 (Hebrew). **M. Hengel**, *Judaism and Hellenism: Studies in Their Encounter in Palestine During the Early Hellenistic Period* (2 vols., 1974) 1:164-69. **C. R. Holladay**, *Fragments from Hellenistic Jewish Authors*, vol. 3, *Aristobulus* (1995). **R. Radice**, *La Filosofia di A. e i suoi nessi* (1994). **E. Shürer**, *HJPAJC* (3 vols., ed. G. Vermes and F. Millar, 1973–87) 3:579-87. **N. Walter**, *Der Thoraausleger A.: Untersuchungen zu seinen Fragmentum und zu psuedepigraphischen* (TU 86, 1964); "Fragmente jüdisch-hellenisticher Exegeten: A., Demetrios, Aristeas," *JSHRZ* 3.2 (1975) 261-79. **D. Winston**, "A.: From Walter to Holladay," *Studia Philonica Annual* 8 (1996) 155-66.

D. WINSTON

ARIUS (c. 250–336)

Of Libyan descent, A. became famous in Alexandria when the local bishop, Alexander, excommunicated him as a heresiarch (c. 318). Only a few of his writings survive. He died, probably in Constantinople, on the eve of being readmitted into the Alexandrian church by imperial favor.

A.'s personal exegesis of Scripture is still a matter of controversy due to lack of evidence. The extant fragments of his *Thalia* testify to a strong logical rigor with a prevailing philosophical interpretation. They also demonstrate that A. combined abstract thought with a literal reading of biblical quotations. The Bible served as a proof text for establishing his christological argument.

Divine titles such as God, Word, Wisdom, and Son, inherited from canonical Scripture (see CANON OF THE BIBLE), received an Arian qualification in supporting the doctrine of the unique transcendency and absolute divinity of the Father. A. introduced notions of time and eternity based on classical metaphysics into trinitarian thought in order to categorize divine generation. Thus the Gospel narratives seemed to offer a physical and reduced image, in a platonic sense, of the essential inferiority and created nature of the Son, compared with the Father. A.'s commentaries on biblical texts are no longer available, but there is no doubt that his scholastic use of Scripture reflected a serious need for greater theological consistency in mainstream Origenist (see ORIGEN) traditions at the turn of the fourth century.

A.'s immediate supporters, like Asterius the Sophist (d. c. 341) and Eusebius of Nicomedia (d. c. 342), stressed the strictly polemical use of Scripture in favor of the Arian theory. A later generation of Neo-Arians, among them Eunomius (d. 394), condensed and systematized the typical collection of quotes used in their school of thought: "The words 'Your God and my God' (John 20:17), 'Greater than I' (John 14:28), 'created me the beginning of his ways' (Prov 8:22), 'he made him both Lord and Christ' (Acts 2:36), 'whom he sanctified and sent into the world' (John 10:36); [Christ's being] a slave, obedient; the text 'he gave all things into his hand' (John 3:35); that he was commanded, that he was sent, his inability to do or say anything of himself, or judge, or receive gifts, or take counsel . . . his ignorance, his subordination, his praying, his asking questions, his growth, his being perfected . . . his sleeping, being hungry, tired, his weeping, his experiencing agony, his submission" (R. Hanson [1989] 107).

Works: "Thalia," "Creed of A. and His Alexandrian Supporters," "Confession of Arius and Euzoius," *A.: Heresy and Tradition* (R. D. Williams, 1987) 100-103, 247-49, 255-56.

Bibliography: **R. P. C. Hanson**, *The Search for the Christian Doctrine of God: The Arian Controversy 318–381* (1989). **C. Kannengiesser**, *Holy Scripture and Hellenistic Hermeneutics in Alexandrian Christology: The Arian Crisis* (1982); "The Bible in the Arian Crisis," *The Bible in Greek Christian Antiquity* (BTA 1, ed. P. M. Blowers, 1997) 217-28; *A. and Athanasius: Two Alexandrian Theologians* (1991). **T. E. Pollard**, "The Exegesis of Scripture and the Arian Controversy," *BJRL* 41 (1959) 414-29. **R. D. Williams**, *A.: Heresy and Tradition* (1987).

C. KANNENGIESSER

ARMENIAN BIBLICAL INTERPRETATION

Organized Christianity existed at least in the southern districts of Armenia by the mid third century, as testified by EUSEBIUS (*Hist. eccl.* 6.xlvi.3); these early beginnings were later associated with the apostolate of Thaddeus and with the Abgar legend of Edessa. A subsequent missionary initiative, this time from Caesarea in Cappadocia, led to the acceptance of the new faith by King Trdat and his court in 314 (traditional date 301) in the aftermath of the Edict of Milan. According to the conversion account, the first bishop of Greater Armenia, Gregory the Illuminator (c. 240–332), was responsible for inaugurating theological education in the region by catechizing the sons of pagan priests to serve the church. In the absence of an indigenous written medium, the

Scriptures and liturgical texts were first studied in Greek and Syriac, depending on the geographical locale, and translated orally into Armenian, giving rise to what is regarded as an interpretative tradition akin to the TARGUMIM. However, in consequence of the region's transfer from Roman to Iranian suzerainty in 387, Syriac learning dominated for a time. This situation prompted attempts at constructing an Armenian alphabet and the establishment of an Armenian school at Edessa alongside that of the Syrians and the more illustrious school of the Persians, the latter of which proved an important conduit for ANTIOCHENE exegetical principles to reach the Armenian highlands.

Appreciating the difficulties of grounding the gospel in the less evangelized northern and eastern tracts of the country, the chorepiscopus Mashtots finalized an alphabet and immediately began translating the Bible with a group of disciples around 406. That the resulting product was intended as a polemical tool in the church's ongoing struggle with an indigenized syncretistic form of Zoroastrianism is evidenced by the technical terms for cultic paraphernalia: Armenian ecclesiastical terminology is applied to the licit Israelite ritual, in contrast to that of the Philistines, for example, which is distinguished by Mazdaean nomenclature. Another facet of the same hermeneutical process (see HERMENEUTICS) is the heightening of the anti-idolatry rhetoric in interpreting such books as Chronicles and the *Epistle of Jeremiah* (see P. Cowe [1990–91] 104-10).

Although it appears that the early TRANSLATION of the Gospels was based on a Syriac text with diatessaronic affinities, a number of HB books seem to derive mainly from the local Antiochene type of Greek text, supplemented by reference to the PESHITTA. This procedure parallels that of exegetes of the Antiochene school, who periodically appealed to the Syriac version to elucidate some aspect of the Greek. Some of the exegetes had studied in Antioch with Libanius (314–93), and there are indications that Armenians (though probably mainly from the western provinces) had done likewise.

Other features of Antiochene TEXTUAL analysis may also be discerned in the early Armenian translation. Maintaining a distinction between the literal reading and its underlying meaning, the commentators often began their task by paraphrasing the verse under consideration. Similarly, the translators permitted themselves great flexibility in matters of Greek morphology and syntax, selecting equivalents according to their appropriateness in a given context rather than reverting to a system of calques. Just as the exegetes sifted different versions of a passage to arrive at the most precise, so also some of the translators consulted parallel narratives (e.g., in Kings and Chronicles) in order to obtain a fuller comprehension of the events described. Representatives of the Antiochene school would typically apply their rhetorical training to clarifying figurative expressions in the biblical text. Congruently, the early Armenian version evinces a strong tendency to explicate metaphors in plainer terms. Finally, just as LUCIAN redacted the biblical *koine* to elevate it to a higher literary register, so also the early Armenian translators were careful to be fully idiomatic in structure and lexical choice; indeed, to that end they even employed formulae that may derive from oral epic (see Cowe [1992] 419-39).

The first commentaries to be made available in Armenian over the next few decades also exhibit Edessene and Antiochene connections. Most of CHRYSOSTOM's scriptural homilies were translated, including those on Psalms, Matthew, John, and the Pauline epistles (see PAUL). Further, a commentary on Isaiah in his name is extant in Armenian, of which only six homilies are extant in Greek; the Armenian version of the remainder, according to F. Dumortier (1988), was executed from a stenographic record. An even larger corpus exists under the name of EPHRAEM; however, as these are subjected to more rigorous scrutiny an increasing number have been judged pseudonymous. Apart from his treatment of the *Diatessaron,* which also survives in Syriac, there are commentaries on Acts and on the Pauline epistles as well as an inauthentic *Exposition of the Gospel.* The Edessene deacon is also ascribed published commentaries on HB books from Genesis to Chronicles (except Ruth) in addition to others preserved in manuscripts. However, T. Mathews (1991) has demonstrated that the first of these relies on material from the scholia of Jacob of Edessa (d. 708), subsequently reworked in the catena of Severus of Edessa from the mid ninth century. Also early are the commentary on the Octateuch by Eusebius of Emesa (d. c. 359), extant only in Armenian, and BASIL's nine homilies on the Hexaemeron, which were mediated by a Syriac recension significantly longer than the Greek original. Insofar as all the above works have been studied, the primary focus they display is the exposition of the literal and historical aspects of the scriptural text.

The condemnation of Nestorius, a prominent spokesman for Antiochene christology, at the Council of Ephesus in 431 roughly coincided with the deposition of the last Arsacid king of Armenia and with the last catholicos (chief bishop) from the line of Gregory the Illuminator. Hence for a time the church was governed by Syrians and by an Armenian cleric from the pro-Persian faction. It may be that the latter group is responsible for translating THEODORET's commentaries on the Psalms and on Ezekiel, ascribing them respectively to Epiphanius of Salamis (c. 315–403) and to Theodoret's opponent CYRIL OF ALEXANDRIA in order to elude censorship. Meanwhile, missives from Patriarch Proclus (d. c. 446) of Constantinople and from other hierarchs persuaded the faction surrounding the deposed catholicos Sahak and Mashtots to relinquish their ties with Antioch in favor of Constantinople and Alexandria. Biblical manuscripts brought from the former provided the base text for a revision of the earlier version in the second half of the 430s. The manuscripts' textual complexion in the HB was significantly Origenic (see ORIGEN), with several medieval manuscripts adducing hexaplaric signs, while that of the Gospels, which used to be assigned to the Caesarean text type, has been classified with the early *Koine* (J. Alexanian [1984] 382-83). In the case of some books (e.g., Chronicles) a new rendering was executed on different exegetical principles. The overall approach was much more literal, generally (though not systematically) translating verbatim through a pattern of stereotyped equivalents to the extent that sometimes Armenian idiom suffers in order to encode morphological data from the Greek text (Cowe [1992] 357-87, 431-32).

These theological trends are mirrored in translations of the next period, which probably include Cyril's commentaries on Genesis, Kings, and Hebrews; that of Hesychius of Jerusalem (5th cent.) on Job (extant only in Armenian); those of Hippolytus of Rome (c. 170–c. 236) on Song of Songs, Daniel, and John; and those of Origen and GREGORY OF NYSSA on Song of Songs. The greater allegorizing tendency these display was extended in the early sixth century by the rendering of a large portion of PHILO's works, including the *Quaestiones* on Genesis and Exodus (complete only in Armenian). The impact of the translations is first explicit in the works of the contemporary writer Eghishe (d. 480), who inaugurated the tradition of commentary, writing in Armenian with treatments of Genesis, Joshua, and Judges as well as homilies on NT themes. In these he appropriated such Chrysostomian traits as intensifying the emotional impact of the scene through elaborating addresses to the persons involved while indulging in Philonic number symbolism.

Eghishe illustrates the ALEXANDRIAN approach even more vividly in his treatment of the revolt of 451, which was led by Vardan Mamikonian against the Persian Shah Yazdgard II's campaign for the introduction of Sasanian Mazdaeism in Greater Armenia. The cataclysmic events precipitating this response were so reminiscent of the Maccabees that writers from the second half of the fifth century regularly accommodated battle scenes from those books to their descriptions of contemporary events. Moreover, just as Daniel employed *vaticinium post eventum* to offer a theodicy to despairing readers, so also the martyrs' heavenly rewards were predicted in Agathangelos's depiction of a vision by Gregory the Illuminator. The same author also developed the Danielic paradigm of relations between the prophet and Nebuchadnezzar, especially the latter's bestial transformation to inculcate humility, as an interpretative strategy to present the Armenians' incorporation in salvation history through King Trdat's metamorphosis into a swine and subsequent conversion at Gregory's hand. Eghishe's application of Daniel's *mise-en-scène* to the revolt of 451, however, is more symbolic than historical: Arguably, his purpose was to redefine martyrdom in terms of the spiritual athlete's lifelong struggle against demons, as an exhortation to Armenian monasticism.

The next Armenian commentator, Step'anos Siwnetsi (d. 735), also treated Daniel as well as Job and the four Gospels, according to citations in later compilations. Only his brief study of Ezekiel's vision is preserved intact; consequently, he is better known for his translations of scholia on Cyril's commentaries and a verse analysis of the Hexaemeron by the seventh-century scholar George Pisides, the latest Greek patristic commentary to be rendered into Armenian. Additionally, Step'anos instituted a uniquely Armenian genre, practiced until the seventeenth century, of commenting on the Eusebian canon tables or key to parallel passages in the Gospels, dwelling on their aesthetic, symbolic, and iconographic features. These were interpreted allegorically as a means for the mind to ascend to spiritual and intellectual heights, while historically they marked the transition from the first table, representing Moses' tabernacle, to the last, depicting the New Jerusalem (see V. Lazaryan [1995]). Grigoris Arsharuni, a contemporary of Step'anos, was also innovative in creating the first commentary on the Armenian lectionary.

Two other important events occurred around this time. In 726 a synod was called at Manazkert to condemn the aphthartodocetism propagated by extreme followers of Yovhannes Mayragometsi to the effect that Christ's flesh was not consubstantial with ours. They argued that his human passions—e.g., hunger, thirst, and fatigue—were somewhat of an outward semblance and denied that he had made any display of weakness. Consequently, they excised the pericope of the bloody sweat (Luke 22:43-44) as a Nestorian interpolation and exercised such influence for a time that the verses are lacking in most of the early Gospel books. The synod sanctioned the predication of incorruptibility to the incarnate flesh but defined it in a more orthodox fashion, so that the teaching became a distinctive characteristic of medieval Armenian christology. Meanwhile, c. 716–717 the first Greek catena was rendered into Armenean, containing comments on Leviticus by such authorities as Cyril, GREGORY OF NAZIANZUS, and Severus of Antioch (c. 465–538).

From the ninth century onward there is a gradual increase in the number of commentaries available in Armenian, both indigenous and translated, largely as a result of the development of monastic academies. Scriptural study lay at the heart of the academies' curriculum, necessitating the production of school texts such as synopses and more specialized *quaestiones* on difficult passages. The Syrian Orthodox (Jacobite) theologian Nana composed a commentary on John for the Armenian court, while Hamam Arevelc'i wrote on Proverbs. Moreover, the celebrated mystical poet Grigor

Narekac'i's first commission of 977 involved commenting on the Song of Songs, following Gregory of Nyssa's spiritual interpretation.

With the eleventh century began the golden age of Armenian commentary writing, which continued until the early fifteenth century. During this period most biblical books were encompassed, some even receiving multiple treatments (e.g., the Gospels, Psalms, Daniel, Ezekiel, and the Pauline epistles). Usually these commentaries were structured like catenae, yet often the compilers employed the form freely and creatively. Occasionally verse commentaries are found, as well as verse paraphrases (e.g., by Grigor Magistros [d. 1059] and Nerses Shnorhali [d. 1167]). Prolific commentators include Nerses Lambronac'i (1153–98), Vardan Arevelc'i (d. 1271), and Grigor Tat'ewac'i (d. 1409). In addition to producing several individual commentaries, the latter discussed biblical questions thoroughly in an encyclopedic ten-volume work (1397).

Tat'ewac'i's encounters with Dominican missionaries led to his writing a commentary on the psalter directed at refuting some of their doctrines, e.g., that of purgatory. However, by the seventeenth century some Armenian scholars had become Roman Catholic and began translating commentaries from Latin, e.g. those of NICHOLAS OF LYRA and C. LAPIDE. Mkhit'ar Sebastac'i (1676–1749) established a scholarly brotherhood in Venice under papal supremacy that has been active not only in printing the Bible but also in providing reference works like the 1731 dictionary of the Bible. Able ecclesiastics like Yakob Nalian, Armenian patriarch of Constantinople (1752–64), continued the indigenous tradition with a treatment of Ecclesiasticus. However, perhaps even more noteworthy is the achievement of Poghos Grigorian, who, although originally a tailor and ignorant of Armenian, was elected to the same patriarchate in 1815 and subsequently aspired to comment on several books of the HB. Also noteworthy is the Armenian Protestant movement, which has fostered a particularly Bible-based spirituality since its inception in 1849.

Armenian religious and intellectual life was severely disrupted at the beginning of the twentieth century by the genocide of Armenians under the Ottoman Empire (1915–23) and the incorporation of the independent Armenian Republic into the Soviet Union in 1920. Despite the relative dearth of formal commentary writing, biblical themes have continued to find literary expression and reinterpretation in such works as P. Sevak's (1924–71) classic epic Anlreli Zangakatun (*Ever Pealing Belfry* [1966]), in which Christ's sufferings are predicated on the Armenian people, and in the carefully crafted biblical symbolism of S. Parajanov's film *Color of Pomegranates* (1969). The promulgation of *glasnost* led to the publication of some medieval commentaries; and this task has been continued by the Ganjasar Institute of Erevan, founded by M. Aramyan, whose annual contains critical editions of older works as well as modern commentaries from a neo-patristic perspective.

Bibliography: A. Ajamian and M. E. Stone (eds.), *Text and Context: Studies in the Armenian NT* (UPATS 13, 1994). J. M. Alexanian, "The Armenian Gospel Text from the Fifth Through the Fourteenth Centuries," *Medieval Armenian Culture* (UPATS 6, ed. T. J. Samuelian and M. E. Stone, 1984) 381-94. C. Burchard (ed.), *Armenia and the Bible* (UPATS 12, 1993). S. P. Cowe, "Tendentious Translation and the Evangelical Imperative: Religious Polemic in the Early Armenian Church," *Revue des études arméniennes* 22 (1990–91) 97-114; *The Armenian Version of Daniel* (UPATS 9, 1992). F. Dumortier, *La patrie des premiers chrétiens* (1988). V. Lazaryan, *Xoranneri meknufyunner* [*Commentaries on the Canon Tables*] (Sargis Xacents, 1995). J.-P. Mahé, "Traduction et exégèse: Réflexions sur l'example arménien," *Mélanges A. Guillamont* (COr 20, ed. R. Coquin, 1988) 243-55. T. F. Mathews and A. K. Sanjian, *Armenian Gospel Iconography: The Tradition of the Glajor Gospel* (Dumbarton Oaks Studies 19, 1991). R. W. Thomson, *A Bibliography of Classical Armenian Literature to* AD *1500* (CC, 1995) 250-52.

S. P. COWE

ARMINIUS, JACOBUS (JAMES) (1560–1609)

A Dutch theologian, A. was born at Oudewater in south Holland near Utrecht. A's family pastor saw to his schooling in sciences and classical languages, and other friends arranged his matriculation at Marburg. While in Germany, at the age of fourteen A. learned that his family in Holland had been murdered by a Spanish army of the Inquisition. The next year he enrolled in the new university of Leiden, where he was an outstanding student for six years. He moved to Geneva in 1582 to study with T. BEZA, transferring later to Basel to work under J. Grynaeus (1540–1617). He returned to Geneva for theological study, then studied at the University of Padua. From 1588 to 1602 he served as preacher to the Reformed congregation at Amsterdam, where his exposition of Romans 7 and 9 and his words on election and reprobation caused him to be suspected of heresy. In 1602 he succeeded F. Junius (1545–1602) as professor of theology at Leiden and in 1603 accepted the university's first doctorate. He remained at Leiden until his death.

At Leiden A. delivered public lectures on predestination that stirred up controversy throughout the university, clearly defining his position in his *Disputations*. Even though the doctrine of predestination belonged to the basic teachings of the Reformed (Calvinist) Church, which were officially adopted by the new Dutch Republic in 1609, A., along with many other clergy, rejected it. He taught conditional predestination and stressed the importance of faith.

A. did not deny God's omnipotence or free grace, but he emphasized human free will and the truth of the doctrine of sin, thereby owing more to LUTHER than to either Beza or CALVIN. One year after his death his followers drew up the famous five *Remonstrantiae* in an attempt to justify Arminian theology. From these they took the name Remonstrants rather than Arminians, perhaps revealing their uncertainty that A. would wholly concur with their interpretations. At the Synod of Dort (1618–19) many of the Remonstrants were banished, deposed, and/or denied communion, and Arminianism was condemned. Nevertheless, the movement influenced many individuals, e.g., J. WESLEY and Methodism. Today it has thoroughly permeated Christian thought in many communions.

Works: *Complete Works and Life* (3 vols., 1842, repr. 1956); *The Creeds of Christendom,* vol. 3, *Canons* (3 vols., 1877) 550-97.

Bibliography: **C. Bangs,** *A.: A Study in the Dutch Reformation* (1971, 1985²); *The Encyclopedia of Religion* 1 (1987) 419-20. **R. L. Colie,** *Light and Enlightenment: A Study of the Cambridge Platonists and the Dutch Arminians* (1957). **A. W. Harrison,** *Arminianism* (1937). **G. J. Hoenderdaal,** "The Debate About A. Outside the Netherlands," *Leiden University in the Seventeenth Century* (ed. T. H. Lunsingh Scheurleer and G. H. M. Posthumus Meyjes, 1975) 137-59; *TRE* 4 (1979) 63-69. **J. Platt,** *Reformed Thought and Scholasticism: The Arguments for the Existence of God in Dutch Theology, 1575–1650* (SHCT 29, 1982). **H. A. Slaatte,** *The Arminian Arm of Theology* (1977).

J. M. BULLARD

ARNOLD, GOTTFRIED (1666–1714)

A German Lutheran Pietist historian, poet, theologian, and pastor, A. is best known for his study of the pre-Constantinian church (1696) and his general history of the Christian church (1699–1700), written from the point of view of those designated as heretics. Initially tied to the churchly PIETISM of P. J. SPENER, A. was attracted to a more radical rhetoric in the late 1690s and returned to established forms of Lutheranism (see LUTHER) after 1701, serving as a pastor and general superintendent until his death. While much of his prolific publication was directed to studies and editions of the early church, later spiritual masters, and devotional works, he compiled a *Kurzgefasste Kirchengeschichte des alten und neuen Testaments* (1697, repr. 1700) and *Das wahres Christenthum des altes Testament* (1707), and he wrote prefaces to a German edition of Wisdom (1705) and meditations on the psalms (1713). In all these works and in his numerous volumes of sermons, he followed general Pietist patterns in his interpretation of the Bible, although placing a slightly greater empha-

sis on the "spiritual" reading of the text than did Spener or A. FRANCKE (with a resultingly greater opposition to a scholastic, literal reading), and allowing more openness than they to the direct INSPIRATION of the Spirit in the work of interpretation, particularly during his more radical years.

Works: *Die erste Liebe* (1696); *Unpartheyischen Kirchen- und Ketzer-historie* (1699–1700); *Kurzgefasste Kirchengeschichte des alten und neuen Testaments* (1697, repr. 1700).

Bibliography: **P. C. Erb,** *Pietists, Protestants, and Mysticism: The Use of Late Medieval Spiritual Texts in the Work of G. A.* (PWS 2, 1989). **E. Seeberg,** *G. A.: Die Wissenschaft und die Mystik seiner Zeit* (1923). **Hans Schneider,** "Der radickale Pietismus im 17. Jahrhundert," *Der Pietismus vom siebzehnten bis zum frühen achtzehnten Jahrhundert* (ed. M. Brecht, 1993).

P. C. ERB

ARNOLD, MATTHEW (1822–88)

Long considered, with A. Tennyson and R. Browning, as preeminent among the Victorian poets, A. is acknowledged as one of the greatest English literary critics. However, his religious writings, which make up a third of his prose work and are largely devoted to the interpretation of the Bible, are little known today and undeservedly neglected. These works were often widely criticized when they appeared, but A.'s religious essays were influential in the period 1870–1920. They appealed especially to those who agreed with A. that traditional religious apologetic and biblical interpretation were "touched with the finger of death." A. initiated a program of "demythologizing" the Bible not unlike that undertaken by R. BULTMANN in the twentieth century. A. did not use the term *myth* (see MYTHOLOGY AND BIBLICAL STUDIES); rather, he spoke of *Aberglaube* or "extra-belief," by which he meant legend and eschatological PROPHECY—that by "which we hope, augur, imagine." *Aberglaube* is not to be removed; it is, rather, to be reinterpreted in what A. called "experimental," i.e., experiential or existential terms.

Religion was a constant preoccupation with A., and today many critics see religion as the real center of his life and literary work. He wrote a trenchant criticism of the then-prevalent Calvinist-Dissenter interpretation of the Pauline (see PAUL) writings (1870); *Literature and Dogma* (1873), his most influential religious book, in which he set forth his paradoxically radical yet conservative program of biblical reinterpretation; his response to the critics of *Literature and Dogma,* in which he revealed his knowledge of the work of the leading continental biblical scholars (1875); and *Last Essays on Church and Religion* (1877).

The influences on A.'s biblical interpretation were extraordinarily wide-ranging, but of particular importance were his father, T. ARNOLD, the famous educator, and the senior Arnold's close associates, the Oriel Noetics. They provided him with a deep historical sense and a sensitivity to the historicity of language and doctrine. Other important influences on A.'s biblical HERMENEUTICS were B. SPINOZA, S. T. COLERIDGE, J. H. NEWMAN, and the Cambridge Platonists. A.'s most important contribution to biblical interpretation is his insistence on the distinction yet interdependence of religion and culture. This is conveyed in his aphorism: "No man who knows nothing else, knows even his Bible." He was one of the founders of Anglican modernism.

Works: *St. Paul and Protestantism* (1870); *Literature and Dogma* (1873); *God and the Bible* (1875); *Last Essays on Church and Religion* (1877).

Bibliography: R. ApRoberts, *A. and God* (1983). **J. Drury,** *Critics of the Bible, 1724–1873* (1989) 152-92. **R. Garnett,** *DNB* Sup. 1 (1901) 70-75. **J. C. Livingston,** *M. A. and Christianity: His Religious Prose Writings* (1986).

J. C. LIVINGSTON

ARNOLD, THOMAS (1795–1842)

Born at East Cowes, Isle of Wight, June 13, 1795, A. was educated at Winchester School and Corpus Christi College, Oxford (1811–14), where he became an accomplished classical scholar. He was appointed a fellow of Oriel College in 1815 but left Oxford after ordination in 1818. After teaching for a period he was elected headmaster of Rugby School in 1828 and established a reputation as one of the foremost educators of his day. He returned to Oxford to become professor of modern history in 1841 but died the following year.

A.'s influence on biblical scholarship was indirect but nonetheless very considerable. During his days at Oxford the work of the pioneer German classical historian B. Niebuhr (1776–1831) caused an intellectual stir in England because of its new methods and critical approach to the history of ancient Rome. A., along with C. THIRLWALL and J. Hare (1795–1855), became a staunch advocate of Niebuhr's insights and recognized their applicability to a wide area of research in ancient history, not least that of the Bible. Through his friendship with the German diplomat C. von BUNSEN and through his encouragement of H. MILMAN and his former pupil A. STANLEY, A. taught the importance of new critical methods in the study of ancient history and fully recognized that these needed to be applied to the study of the biblical writings. It was also in large measure A.'s advocacy of giving full attention to German culture and scholarship that enabled the work of the German critics and historians, especially that of W. DE WETTE and H. EWALD, to be accepted in Great Britain.

Works: *Sermons* (6 vols., 1829–45; subsequently in various eds.), includes "An Essay on the Right Interpretation and Understanding of the Scriptures" (vol. 2, 1832); *Two Sermons on the Interpretation of Prophecy* (1839); *Sermons Chiefly on the Interpretation of Scripture* (1845).

Bibliography: **M. A. Christensen,** "T. A.'s Debt to German Theologians," *Modern Philology* 55 (1957) 14-20. **J. Drury,** *Critics of the Bible, 1724–1873* (1989) 122-36. **J. Rogerson,** *OTCNC* 188-92. **A. P. Stanley,** *The Life and Correspondence of T. A.* (2 vols., 1844, 1881). **T. Walrond,** *DNB* 2 (1885) 113-17. **E. L. Williamson,** *The Liberalism of T. A.: A Study of His Religious and Political Writings* (1964), esp. "A. and the Bible," 66-111.

R. E. CLEMENTS

ART, THE BIBLE AND

1. Biblical Themes in Jewish and Early Christian Art. In a Roman garrison town on the Euphrates River, the dry sands of the Syrian desert preserved convincing evidence that biblical themes were subjects of both Jewish and early Christian art. Dura-Europos (now Qalat es Salihiye), which was overrun by Sasanians in 257 CE, has been compared to Pompeii because, like that Roman city, it was destroyed suddenly. During the siege the city's defenders filled buildings near the walls and gate with earth to strengthen the fortifications. These sands preserved what was buried—even wood, leather, and papyrus. A few references to Dura-Europos appear in classical literature, but its exact location had been lost until a British officer discovered the site in 1921.

The frescos in the Dura-Europos synagogue were a revolutionary discovery: Contrary to previous opinion, images were being used in Jewish art during this period, at least in some regions. Inscriptions date the paintings to the time the synagogue was refurbished in 244–245 CE, but traces of figures from a generation earlier have been discovered under the surface drawings. Figurative paintings cover all four walls and include scenes of Moses, the exodus, Aaron, David, the ark of the covenant, Solomon, and Esther. No overriding theme or message is evident, yet the paintings appear to be a programmatic organization of scenes interpreting Scripture texts. Since the scenes surround the worship space, they would seem to relate to the liturgy of the synagogue. The walls of a smaller Christian church at Dura-Europos are painted with subjects from both the HB and the NT, including scenes of Adam and Eve, David and Goliath, the good shepherd, the healing of the paralytic, and a procession of figures to Christ's tomb.

2. The Origins of Christian Art. Imagery served the early Christian churches as a visual language of the community's faith. Constituted of complex art forms that signaled belief systems, signs of hope, and biblical texts, this imagery emerged as a kind of code used by believers. Styles and medias of execution were borrowed from the modes of artistic expression common to Roman culture and to indigenous forms from East and West; thus early Christian iconography was created out of the vernacular of the culture. For instance, bas-relief carving has similar stylistic characteristics on both Christian and non-Christian sarcophagi, showing early Christian art to be an aspect of Late Antique art. Furthermore, ambiguity about the identification of figures was a protection in times of persecution: A shepherd carrying a sheep over his shoulders could be either the good shepherd or Hermes. After Christianity became a permitted religion in 313, however, art flourished, and open portrayal of Christ, often shown as young and beardless, became common.

Artistic interpretations of Christian Scripture appeared prior to the time a fixed CANON was established and constituted the major subject matter of early Christian art, although portraits, symbols, and scenes from everyday life were also included. Since the Bible was not available as a printed book that one could own and read, the earliest experience of the sacred texts came into the life of Christian communities through their common liturgical experiences. The Scriptures were read aloud from lectionaries; the stories were told in sermons; and specific texts were repeated in prayers. Listening to the Scriptures established community experience of the Bible, and Christian art depicted those often-repeated, liturgically set references. The Bible was presented to worshipers, not author-by-author or book-by-book, but seasonally and episodically week-by-week in worship, the setting for best understanding its artistic interpretation in the early church. The liturgical location of biblical art suggests that from a very early stage it was programmatically arranged in settings prepared for burial, baptism, eucharistic feasts, and proclamation.

a. Burial settings. While Jewish funerary art remained principally symbolic, the earliest Christian works in both painting and sculpture presented scenes from Hebrew Scriptures learned in worship and appropriated in a sacred setting for burial. These themes of deliverance from death, rescue from the toils of life, and hope for resurrection included Noah in the ark, the sacrifice of Isaac, the crossing of the Red Sea, Moses striking the rock, Jonah and the whale, the Hebrew youths in the fiery furnace, and Daniel in the lion's den. Allusions to the Eucharist were common, and by the fourth century so also were stories from the NT that represent God's intervention in the natural order to rescue and deliver faithful believers: Christ's birth, the wedding at Cana, healing scenes, the resurrection of Lazarus, and so forth. An excellent example is the sarcophagus of J. Bassus (d. 359) in the museum of St. Peter's, Rome.

b. Baptismal settings. Biblical imagery for baptistery areas was highly selective and referred directly to the early church's practice of baptism as initiation into the community and as symbolic of dying and rising to new life in Christ. In the Dura-Europos house church the surviving frescoes in the baptismal room are a programmatic display of episodes from different books in the HB and the NT selected to enhance the experience of baptism. Water imagery, healing, salvation, and resurrection themes abound, including Peter and Christ walking on water, the paralytic at the pool of Bethesda, the woman at the well, the good shepherd, and a procession of figures to the tomb of Christ.

Baptismal rooms were separate spaces in early Christian architecture and were usually highly decorated. The best illustration, the mid–fifth-century Baptistery of the Orthodox, with its original mosaic decoration intact, stands at Ravenna, Italy. The complex iconographic biblical imagery that sheaths the greater part of the interior served the liturgy and the experience of baptism. In the interior a large medallion-shaped mosaic picture of Christ's baptism placed at the crown of the dome is surrounded by a procession of apostles above a wide band, with four empty thrones symbolizing Anastasis, and four tables holding Gospel books. Mosaic figures, bas-relief images, and symbolic references to biblical stories complete the composition.

c. Biblical cycles in settings for Eucharist and proclamation. Frescoes and mosaics were the preferred means of interpreting the Bible in early church art. The early fifth-century nave mosaics of Santa Maria Maggiore at Rome represent great leaders and military feats from the HB. Among them Abraham, Moses, and Aaron appear dressed in Roman fashion as victorious heroes. At the front of the nave, mosaics sheath the upper register of the triumphal arch in a series of scenes detailing the birth narrative that emphasize the figure of Mary. The biblical stories in the nativity cycle served the theology of the church, emphasizing the royalty of Mary and representing her declaration by the Council of Ephesus (431) as *Theotokos,* "Bearer of God." Extensive frescoes of biblical scenes taken from both the HB and the NT once covered the interior walls of San Paulo fuori le mura at Rome. Perhaps painted during the papacy of Leo I (440–461), they are known only through seventeenth- and eighteenth-century copies. Similar cycles appeared in old St. Peter's Church at Rome (dedicated 326).

d. Art of the apses. Among the largest compositions of the early Christian world were those created for the great apse structures (half domes) placed at the focal point of worship spaces in early basilicas. These concave surfaces were decorated primarily with paintings and mosaics of biblical figures. While their themes were always biblically based, they were created, not only to teach or to illustrate a biblical narrative, but also to provide a focal point for the liturgical celebrations of the church. The biblically related art of the apses served both preaching and liturgy in the ritual experience of believers.

The sixth-century church of San Vitale at Ravenna is one of the best examples of the interpretation of the Bible for a eucharistic setting. Rather than an iconography that illustrates a sequence of texts, HB and NT figures (Abraham and Sarah at the oak of Mamre; Cain and Melchizedek at an altar table; figures of Moses and Isaiah; the Gospel writers with their symbols; and Christ enthroned above the heavens, giving and receiving gifts) enhance the theme of sacrifice. This kind of programmatic presentation, using forms that made biblical themes visible as they enhanced worship, distinguished the Jewish and Christian biblical art of the Late Antique period. Ravenna, established as capital of the Western Empire (402), became an important Western outpost of early Byzantine art.

3. Byzantine Biblical Art. In 330 Constantine moved his capital from Rome to Constantinople, founded on the site of the Greek city of Byzantium. Greco-Roman art was brought into contact with Eastern and oriental cultures, and the art and architecture that resulted predominated in the Eastern Roman Empire until its fall. Its influence is also seen in the rest of the Mediterranean world, Russia, and the Balkans. Mosaics, wall paintings, and icons were the chief means of portraying biblical subjects.

In the worship life of the Byzantine traditions, art has enjoyed an exalted role unparalleled in the West and Far East. The imagery of sacred figures and narrative scenes has been held in equal esteem with Scripture. This art relates to and is itself a form of the Word, as can be seen in the Byzantine mosaics that cover the interior of such worship spaces as those in SS Comas and Damian at Rome (526–530); San Marco at Venice (1063–73); Cefalù Cathedral (1148); and the Church of Monreale (c. 1174), Sicily. Visually presenting the biblical texts, the mosaics also imply the living presence of the biblical message that can be spiritually perceived. The way the figures are presented, their relative size, and where various subjects are placed in the church were determined by strict rules. Subjects include the Pantocrator (Christ as judge, bearded and stern, divine and transcendent), the Virgin, apostles, saints, angels, the annunciation, scenes from the life and miracles of Christ, and the crucifixion. The mosaics' gold backgrounds and brilliantly colored tesserae catch the light, suggest movement, and give worshipers a sense of being in the presence of a glorious mystery.

When cost limited the use of mosaics, wall paintings became a substitute. Wall paintings were marked by greater freedom in both subject matter and presentation. In the thirteenth and fourteenth centuries they were characterized by greater narrative detail than mosaics. Storytelling was often emphasized more strongly than was doctrinal instruction.

Icons, smaller panels, followed even more strictly the rules governing mosaics and appear in many media, including paintings on wood, walls, and vellum; mosaics; carvings; and textiles, among others. The biblical subject matter of icons traditionally met the needs of corporate and private worship. An icon painted on wood may present a single holy figure (Christ), a pair (mother and child), a group (the transfiguration), or a central portrait of a saint surrounded by small scenes depicting episodes in his or her life. When the subject is a biblical figure or episode the icon is a visual form of biblical interpretation and represents the same truth as that of the printed and preached Scripture. Icons are visible manifestations of invisible mysteries and religious truth— not only images but also the real presence of the ones imaged, the ones who embody the religious truth. In Byzantine art the icon is the Word; therefore, the Bible in Byzantine tradition is found in scripted, spoken, and artistic form.

4. Art Within Scriptural Texts: Early Illuminated Manuscripts. Early texts of Hebrew and Christian Scriptures appeared in both roll and codex form. Illuminations, works of art interspersed within texts, were traditional in Greek, Roman, and Egyptian cultures prior to Jewish and Christian use. The fourth-century *Itala von Quedlinburg,* the oldest known illuminated Scripture, includes scenes from the books of Samuel and 1 Kings. The earliest Hebrew illuminated manuscript is the Moshe ben Asher Codex of the Prophets of 895 CE.

The masterpieces of this genre that appeared between the sixth and ninth centuries include the Cotton Genesis, the Rabula Codex, the Rossanensis Fragments, and the Vienna Genesis. The early Irish tradition produced extraordinary illuminated biblical texts, especially from the sixth to the ninth centuries, including the *St. Chad Gospels* and the *Book of Kells.* These artistic works were created not simply to illustrate selected themes of the Bible but to adorn sacred texts with images that emphasize theological priorities of the age, figurative compositions, and symbols that serve the life of contemplation and prayer.

Restoration of the theopolitical center of Europe at the beginning of the ninth century under Charlemagne brought renewed interest in learning, letters, and art; as a result Bible production increased in monastery scriptori. In contrast to Irish examples, narrative sequences were painted within the texts, e.g., rows of scenes from the lives of biblical heroes. In the ninth century the *Golden Psalter* and the *Bible of Charles the Bald* introduced classical styles of storytelling sequences and full-page illuminations that concentrate on the feats of heroes of the Christian tradition. More didactic than earlier illuminations, this Carolingian biblical art supported the religious and political hierarchy of society under Charlemagne and his successors.

5. Romanesque Biblical Art. The Roman Empire in the West suffered waves of invasion and fell to barbarians in 476. The papacy, churches, and monasteries preserved cultural heritage; but with poor roads and communications local differences increased, and Italian, French, and Spanish languages grew away from their Latin source. During the tenth century widespread apprehension that the world would end in the year 1000 was followed in the eleventh and twelfth centuries by renewed vigor in building and the arts. In Western Europe and Britain the art and architecture of this period were a mixture of northern barbaric, Mediterranean classical, and Byzantine elements and—unlike Byzantine art—had many local and national differences. The term *Romanesque* was coined by the nineteenth-century French archaeologist Gerville to describe a style of architecture he felt corresponded to the development of the Romance languages from Latin. Monasteries and churches, often built to accommodate thousands of pilgrims and to provide a suitable space for hearing Gregorian chants, had simplicity of plan, solidity, and grandeur of scale and effect.

Biblical subject matter appeared in the bas-relief sculpture of capitals in cloisters and on nave columns, presenting familiar biblical scenes along with mythological figures, strange creatures from bestiaries, and decorative patterns. The capitals of the porch and choir of St. Benoit sur Loire (late 11th cent.) include HB subjects that are types of Christ (the sacrifice of Isaac, Daniel in the lion's den, Jonah and the whale) as well as NT elements such as the annunciation, the flight into Egypt, the entombment of Christ, and the resurrection. Tympanum carvings over major entrance portals like those at Moissac, Conques, and Autun almost universally presented scenes of the last judgment. Other outstanding sculpture of biblical themes is found at Arles, St. Gilles-du-Gard, and Vézelay. One of the most unusual large compositions of biblical art of the period is in the Romanesque church at Zillis, Switzerland. Remarkably well-preserved painted wooden panels of the life of Christ from the annunciation to Holy Week make up the entire flat ceiling of the sanctuary. Although scenes of the crucifixion and resurrection are not included, the message of the overhead panorama emphasizes the power of Christ in the world.

In Romanesque art the supernatural, the visionary, and the mystical predominated in subject selection and interpretation: Christ in glory surrounded by the symbols of the four evangelists (Matthew, man; Mark, lion; Luke, ox; John, eagle), Christ as judge separating the elect from the damned. Although Romanesque styles present considerable variety, figures within a scene are generally shown relating to one another and reacting with intense emotion to the event, unlike Byzantine figures, who gaze serenely or sternly at the viewer. HB subjects were almost always selected and interpreted on the basis of their accepted relationship to the NT.

The eleventh to the mid-thirteenth centuries also saw an increase in the production of elaborately decorated,

often quite large Bibles. The beauty and rich detail of illuminated books like the *Lambeth Bible* and the *Winchester Bible* in England (both mid to late 12th cent.) include full-page compositions and inter-columnar decor. An initial letter at the beginning of Psalms in the *Winchester Bible* shows David killing a lion and a bear. The creation story painted in vertical strips of historiated roundels was an often-repeated convention. From Europe the *Erlanger Bible* and the *Souvigny Bible,* both dating to the last quarter of the twelfth century, include painted narratives of such biblical stories as the life of David. Serving ever-growing religious communities, these highly aesthetic works by master artists were created, not for mass viewing, but as gestures of offering and thanksgiving in the service of the liturgy at a time when both the message and the book itself were viewed as sacred.

Jews living under Islamic rule and in other areas where iconoclasm was strong did not approve of representational art, interpreting the commandment against graven images to apply to all creatures. However, in northern Europe RASHI did not object to frescoes in the home depicting such biblical scenes as the fight between David and Goliath. French tosafists even permitted three-dimensional representation of the human form provided it was incomplete.

6. Gothic Biblical Art. The Middle Ages reached its climax in the building of Gothic cathedrals, beginning with the abbey church of St. Denis near Paris, started in 1140. Both the Gothic style and cathedral building spread throughout Europe, with the thirteenth century being the great century of Gothic art and the fifteenth the ending of the period. Biblical scenes and figures were planned as part of the interior and exterior design of cathedrals. Sculptured HB and NT figures on the exterior portals of these vast structures portrayed in bold relief God's ordering and majestic power through creation and history.

Stained-glass windows replaced mosaics and frescoes and provided thousands of square meters of surface for vivid depiction of biblical figures and scenes. The brilliant glass surfaces allowed light to penetrate the sacred images and illuminate interior worship spaces. Stained-glass art not only taught the Scriptures to those who could not read but also provided a sacramental art that illuminated the faithful as they stood in the rays of light penetrating the sacred story. Thus, through the art in those settings worshipers could engage the Bible at different levels of human perception, experiencing its messages and stories physically and aesthetically as well as rationally.

Gothic art is majestic, serene, and sometimes lyrical, a mixture of realism and abstraction. Whereas much Romanesque art was created under the leadership of monasteries, the focus of religious life had since shifted to cathedrals and churches at the center of town and city life. Representation of HB stories and scenes from Jesus' earthly life and from Mary's life were closer to the everyday lives of the people than was the mystical and ecstatic art created for monasteries. Symbolism that identified biblical figures and the interpretation of HB figures as types of Christ was familiar to worshipers in the Middle Ages. The GLOSSA ORDINARIA, completed by the middle of the twelfth century, compiled traditional commentary on the Bible, including allegorical interpretations, and served as a guide for artists as well as for theologians. In a Gothic sculpture of Christ at the entrance of Notre Dâme d'Amiens called "Le Beau Dieu," Christ holds a Bible in one hand and lifts the other in blessing. Under his feet are creatures representing evil, which worshipers would recognize as the lion and adder that Ps 91:13 promises power to overcome. Like early Christian art, Gothic art was designed to accompany the liturgy and to support the theology of the priests who interpreted Scripture, with both HB and NT subjects usually having a christological reference or interpretation.

In the latter half of the twelfth and throughout the thirteenth and fourteenth centuries, Bible production continued to grow in Jewish and Christian traditions; and many Bibles included elaborate artistic interpretation. Among the best-known books from the Hebrew tradition are the early fourteenth-century *Schocken Bible* and the *Sarajevo Haggadah* with its sequence of paintings interpreting events from the creation through the exodus. During the Middle Ages, Christian texts were produced in scriptoria of monasteries; Hebrew Scriptures were made by lay artists who worked in newly emerging craft guilds. Jewish Haggadah and Christian books of hours rich with biblical art began to appear as early as the thirteenth century. These books were often owned by devout laypeople.

7. The Renaissance and Biblical Art. The Renaissance (14th to mid-16th cents.) had its beginning in Italy, where the classical tradition had never really died. Renewed interest in classical literature and art did not mean that the Bible ceased to have a significant role in arts and letters, however. In the production of biblical art, experiments continued in new visual formats, with new attention to scale and proportion. The work of Giotto (1266–1337) is a distinct change from late Byzantine style. His frescoes in the Arena Chapel at Padua interpret episodes from the lives of Mary and Jesus in a way that emphasizes human experience, natural environment, and depth of human feeling.

In frescoes showing scenes from the life of Peter, Masaccio (1401–28) was the first to achieve a three-dimensional realism and bring vibrant flesh-and-blood solidity to biblical figures by combining optical perspective and by modeling figures using natural light sources. He and such artists as Fra Angelico (1400–1455), P. della Francesca (1416–92), S. Botticelli (1444–1510),

Giorgione (c. 1478–1610), Titian (c. 1487–1576), and in sculpture, Donatello (c. 1385–1466) showed an interest in the people and events of the Bible for their own sakes more than for their symbolic or doctrinal significance. The Italian Renaissance reached its height in Leonardo's (1452–1519) *Last Supper* and in his devout and tender studies of the Madonna and child; in Raphael's (1483–1520) Madonnas; and in Michelangelo's (1475–1564) sculpture—the *Pietà, David,* and *Moses*—and in his paintings in the Sistine Chapel, the Genesis creation cycle on the ceiling (1508–12) and the great last judgment on the wall (1536–41). Renaissance artists did not deny the transcendent, but they affirmed life in this world and viewed the representation of the humanity of biblical characters as praising the Creator.

The art of northern Europe during this period differed significantly from the art of Italy. Since northern artists saw the whole visible world as reflecting the Creator, they gave careful attention to backgrounds and often set biblical figures and episodes in wide landscapes. Botanists can identify the plants in G. David's (Flanders, 1450–1523) serene *Rest on the Flight to Egypt.* J. Van Eyck's (Flanders, 1390–1440) *Annunciation* presents a meticulously detailed interior rich with symbolism, but the symbols are presented as a natural part of the setting. The floor tiles, for instance, show HB events as prefiguring Christ.

A. Dürer (Germany, 1471–1528), who was influenced by LUTHER, created a large body of biblical paintings, engravings, woodcuts, and etchings. Some of Dürer's paintings, e.g., the *Adoration of the Magi* and *Four Apostles,* are in the Italian style. He created several series on Jesus' passion as well as engravings of Jesus' life and parables. Many of Dürer's engravings, like *The Knight, Death, and the Devil* (which relates to Eph 6:11-17), show northern artists' penchant for the violent, the grotesque, and the mystical. Dürer created a striking series of woodcuts on the book of Revelation with many of the realistically portrayed apocalyptic scenes set in a contemporary German town.

M. Grünewald (Germany, c. 1470–1530), who had deep Protestant sympathies, is known for one work, the Isenheim altarpiece that stood in the chapel of a lazarhouse. The crucifixion, a scene of extreme agony, grief, and horror, includes Mary, John, and Mary Magdalene. Yet the presence of a lamb and a chalice suggests the words spoken at the altar every day, "Behold the Lamb of God who takes away the sins of the world" (John 1:29) and Isa 53:5-6, which was in part the inspiration for the work. The inmates of the lazar-house were invited to see Christ's identification with their suffering and to hope for eternal life. The altarpiece opens up to reveal an annunciation, a joyous nativity, and a mystical resurrection.

A unique composition of biblical art in fifteenth-century book production was the *Bible of the Poor*

(*Biblia Pauperum*), created primarily for persons who could not read. Full-page woodcuts of HB and NT scenes labeled with Scripture phrases were juxtaposed to show that Christ and episodes from the NT are the fulfillment of the prophecies and promises of the HB. One of the best examples is the Esztergom Blockbook of c. 1460. The invention of printing in the fifteenth century made available to a larger segment of society Bibles in which woodcuts and engravings provided vivid visual interpretations of Scripture. The first illustrated printed Bible, produced by G. Zainer of Augsburg in 1475, included six hand-colored woodcut prints. Dürer's engraved biblical illustrations, ranging from Adam and Eve to the apocalypse, are among the masterpieces of sixteenth-century art in northern Europe.

8. The Reformation and Biblical Art. With priority on proclamation of the written Word and rejection of the Roman Catholic Church, many leaders of the Protestant Reformation (16th cent.) verbally and physically attacked the arts and denied them a role in religion. Many works of art, including biblical art, were destroyed as iconoclasts in Europe and in England systematically attacked whatever embodied for them the power and teachings of Rome. Artists were discouraged from creating religious art and in Protestant countries rarely received patronage from the churches.

Luther, however, encouraged and even commissioned works of art with theological and biblical themes. He instructed artists on appropriate subject matter and preached and wrote theological works in support of the arts. The art produced, some of the most didactic in the history of Christian art, stressed Reformation doctrine. Luther inspired L. Cranach the elder (Germany, 1472–1553) to paint the NT subjects (the woman taken in adultery, Christ among the children) that he cited to illustrate the doctrine of justification by faith alone. Luther also collaborated on the engravings included in his translations of the Bible, e.g., the title page of the first edition printed by H. Luft at Wittenburg in 1534, which portrays a central image of the crucifixion surrounded by angels.

9. The Counter-Reformation and Biblical Art. In 1563 the Council of Trent, partly in response to Protestant iconoclasm, affirmed the legitimacy of images and instructed the bishops to teach that the people are instructed and confirmed in the faith by "the stories of the mysteries of our redemption portrayed in paintings." All art for churches had to have the approval of the bishop, and the term *decorum* was used to delineate what would be appropriate. Art produced for the Roman Catholic Church from the latter half of the sixteenth through the seventeenth centuries was used to teach Bible stories, to support the sacramental theology of the church, and to inspire the faithful.

Reflecting the influence of Trent, the title page of the 1592 first edition of the Sisto-Clementine VULGATE shows the pope beneath a crucifixion image receiving the Scriptures from a figure representing the church in a scene that incorporates HB and NT motifs. Beginning in the sixteenth century and extending through the eighteenth, spectacular biblical cycles of art in large and dramatic formats were placed at the *Sacri Monti,* pilgrimage sites mostly in the lower ranges of the Alps.

The works of J. Tintoretto (Italy, 1518–94) and El Greco (Spain, 1541–1614) show the influence of the Council of Trent. Between 1564 and 1587 Tintoretto painted an immense and intensely moving cycle of huge canvases of HB and NT scenes for the Scuola of San Rocco in Venice. Moving away from Italian Renaissance style, his paintings show great movement, even commotion and confusion, and make dramatic use of dark and light. In these works Jesus' disciples clearly come from the humble and poor of society. El Greco, influenced by the *Spiritual Exercises* of Ignatius of Loyola (1491–1556), expressed a devout spirituality in the elongated and sometimes distorted figures of his NT subjects.

10. Seventeenth- and Eighteenth-century Biblical Art. With the exception of the French artist N. Poussin (1594–1665), who painted biblical subjects in the classical style, Catholic artists of the Baroque period in general moved from rational, sequential telling of the biblical narrative to works created to induce immediate emotional reaction. Dramatic moments from Bible stories emphasized the sensations of religious experiences. M. Caravaggio's (Italy, 1573–1610) intense rendering of the blinding of St. Paul on the road to Damascus is an example. Caravaggio presented familiar subjects in a new way, with a simplicity that appealed to the hearts and minds of viewers. He was attacked for his realism in presenting biblical people as humble and poor, even as ragged and dirty.

Caravaggio influenced two great seventeenth-century interpreters of the Bible, G. La Tour (France, 1593–1652) and Rembrandt (Holland, 1606–69). Rediscovered in the twentieth century, La Tour's dark studies—notably *The Newborn Child* and *St. Joseph in the Carpenter Shop*—center on simply drawn, intimately lighted figures communicating in silence. Rembrandt, in the Reformed tradition, represented the biblical narrative in the life situations and faces of his contemporaries. He saw the stories of the Bible, not as past history, but as his own and everyone's story. For Rembrandt the HB was significant in its own right, not just as a prelude to the NT. His HB subjects include the sacrifice of Isaac, Joseph, and Saul and David; his NT subjects include Jesus preaching and healing, the return of the prodigal, the crucifixion, and resurrection appearances, especially the supper at Emmaus.

W. Blake (1757–1827), the English poet, artist, and visionary, produced watercolors and etchings of power and intensity, including illustrations for the book of Job and for other HB subjects. He also offered original and personal interpretations of biblical themes: *The Elohim Creating Adam, The Ancient of Days,* and *Albion Adoring Christ Crucified.*

In the New World, Puritan traditions rejected the role of the arts in religious life generally, presenting the Scriptures verbally rather than visually. Roman Catholic traditions, especially in the areas that are now the southwestern United States, transposed the Old World forms of Catholic art to the New, integrating them with the indigenous culture.

11. Nineteenth-century Biblical Art. Biblical art proliferated throughout Western civilization in the nineteenth century. In England the young painters who in 1848 formed the pre-Raphaelite group aimed to restore religious art by creating a new biblical iconography, painting subjects with high moral content and retrieving the best of medieval styles. Works like H. Hunt's (1827–1910) *The Light of the World* and E. Burne-Jones's (1833–98) mosaics of St. Paul's Cathedral within the walls at Rome illustrate the point. J. Tissot (1836–1902), a French artist living part time in Palestine, devoted the last fifteen years of his life to biblical illustration. His series on the life of Christ, featuring some 365 paintings, was exhibited in Paris in 1895 and in London in 1896; the entire series was published in 1899. By mid-century Jewish artists were creating paintings related to Jewish life, among them M. Oppenheim's (Germany, 1799–1882) *In the Sukkah* and S. Hart's (England, 1806–81) *Rejoicing in the Law.*

New attention to historical veracity was influencing the way the Bible appeared in the visual arts. Under the influence of the Christian education and missionary movements, biblical illustrations designed to fill didactic and evangelical roles abounded. Their impact was great and shaped perceptions that endure.

12. Twentieth-century Biblical Art. At the threshold of the twentieth century, religious art in the West took two parallel tracks: In the art of churches and synagogues, the didactic narrative mode continued both in the decoration of worship centers and in printed materials. In impressionism and postimpressionism, the most popular of the late nineteenth-century and early twentieth-century art movements, biblical subjects were rare (see, however, E. Manet's [1832–83] *Christ with the Angels* and P. Gauguin's [1848–1903] *Yellow Christ*). Then in the early twentieth century abstraction became a major preoccupation among leaders in the art world, and expressionists and their followers made explicit claims about the religious nature of some of their work. W. Kandinsky (1866–1944), a devout Russian Orthodox, set out his views in *Concerning the Spiritual in Art* (1912; ET 1947). P. Mondrian (Holland, 1872–1944), who had grown up in a Calvinist family (see CALVIN), applied theosophical teachings to the austere and elegant abstract compositions by which he is so well known. L. Feininger's (United States, 1871–1956) paintings of churches and cathedrals built out of prismatic planes are identifiable, but Y. Agam's (Israel, b. 1928) colorful three-dimensional abstraction *Rosh Ha-Shanah* can be identified only by its title. Although a deep religious impulse was a part of the work of individual artists, in highly abstract works subject matter is expelled and specific biblical referents are absent.

Artists who chose biblical subjects often did so as an expression of faith. G. Rouault (France, 1871–1958) was a Roman Catholic whose paintings of Christ and of Christ's passion were motived by his deep faith and by his response to human misery. E. Nolde (Germany, 1867–1956) wrote that his *Last Supper* and *Pentecost* grew out of "an irresistible impulse to express deep spirituality and ardent religious feelings." His *Entombment* expresses anguished grief; his *Christ Among the Children,* delight. M. Chagall (1887–1985), a Russian Jewish artist who lived most of his adult life in France, interpreted both HB and NT subjects in his own imaginative and colorful style in stained glass, painting, and etching. For synagogues he created windows depicting Jacob, Moses, and the twelve tribes of Israel and designed tapestries of the creation, the exodus, and entry into Jerusalem. In work for Christian churches he related creation and crucifixion and Torah and crucifixion. S. Dali's (1904–1989) Last Supper and crucifixion have a sense of the mystical and the surreal.

Few artists were receiving commissions from religious groups until well into the twentieth century. Rouault was almost seventy before one of his paintings was placed in a church. In 1939 he was commissioned by the church of Notre-Dâme-de-Toute-Grâce in Assy, France, to design a stained-glass window. This church also commissioned work from several other Christian artists and asked two Jews, Chagall and J. Lipchitz (Lithuania, 1891–1973) to design the baptismal font and murals. In Vence, France, H. Matisse (France, 1869–1954) was commissioned to design the Chapel of the Rosary. And in the 1940s St. Matthew's Church in Northampton, England, commissioned H. Moore (England, 1898–1986) to create his wonderfully strong and tender sculpture *Madonna and Child* and G. Sutherland (England, 1903–80) to paint a crucifixion. This kind of patronage, however, has been the exception. Yet in the United States in the last half of the century many churches, temples, and synagogues gave art a prominent place, often using the work of local or regional artists.

a. Where the message of the Bible meets the world. Significant art of the twentieth century lifts up the suffering and injustice that Scripture testifies God sees and from which God comes to bring deliverance through prophets and others. To name a few examples, in Berlin during the first half of the century K. Kollwitz (1867–1945) devoted her art to the victims of social injustice, inhumanity, and war—especially mothers and children. P. Picasso's (Spain, 1881–1973) *Guernica* (1937), expressing outrage at the nightmare of the Spanish Civil War, has become a protest against all war. The art that survived the Holocaust, including some by children in the Theresienstadt concentration camp, is a condemnation of hatred and inhumanity and a witness to the valiance of the human spirit. The spiritual power of the civil rights movement in the United States is evident in J. Lawrence's (United States, b. 1917) painting of African American pastors praying while helmeted soldiers look on.

b. Biblical art from non-European traditions. Art of the Bible has emerged in Latin America, Africa, Asia, Southeast Asia, Eastern Europe, and in the United States among non-European ethnic groups. Like many European artists of past centuries, each of these cultures has typically presented its images of the Bible in the settings, dress, physical characteristics, and styles of the culture in which they were created. Some of these works have become well known and have been given status among the arts of the world. Such is the case with the paintings and prints of Kitigawa of Japan, F. Wesley of India (*Forgiving Father* and *Blue Madonna*) and the Latin American paintings reproduced in the book *The Gospel in Art by the Peasants of Solentiname* (ed. P. Scharper and S. Scharper, 1984) In the United States much African American art has been exhibited and published, including A. Douglas's (1899–1979) illustrations for J. Weldon Johnson's *God's Trombones* and the wooden figures and relief carvings of biblical teachings by E. Pierce (1892–1984).

c. Popular art of the Bible. The narrative mode of biblical subject matter has predominated in popular works. Unfortunately, biblical stories in educational religious literature has often been illustrated with what is derisively called "bathrobe art." Yet many editors and illustrators have made a concerted effort to keep abreast of archaeological discoveries in order to present art that is accurate for the particular period in biblical history being illustrated. Some individuals have systematically introduced great biblical art of the past, while others who stress the need for Bible study have turned to the popular arts, such as the comic book, to educate the public concerning the Bible. Some of these publications are created, printed, and distributed by groups whose ancestors strenuously resisted the use of the visual arts in communicating and interpreting the Bible.

In the middle years of the twentieth century, interest in biblical art was stimulated by C. Maus's (1880–1970) books *Christ in the Fine Arts* (1938) and *The OT in the Fine Arts* (1954). The most popular Christian image of the time was W. Sallman's (United States, 1892–1968) *Head of Christ,* which in some quarters became a catalyst for discovering other images of Christ. In a more historically attentive form, the biblical narrative has been translated to modern cinema. With the expansion of cable and network television, major productions have been undertaken that tell stories from the Bible; and documentaries have included biblical art from many places and times. Thus the entire heritage of biblical art is more widely available than ever before through fine books and reproductions, access to museums, travel, and television.

13. Conclusion. At the end of the twentieth century, the ongoing emphasis on the historicity of Scripture continues to inspire the representation of biblical stories in a wide variety of media, e.g., electronic interactive media like the American Bible Society's NT series produced during the 1990s. Within the world of the visual arts at the end of the twentieth century, there is increased attention to form and materials, on the one hand, and to visual presentation of the plight of human beings in a pluralistic world, on the other hand. Art of the Hebrew and Christian Scriptures is hardly visible. When it is, more often than not it appears derivative and didactic rather than vital and revelatory. On the horizon, however, the emerging technologies are capturing the imagination of artists and teachers alike in ways that promise a bright future for the presentation of the Bible in a variety of artistic modes for the sake of future generations.

Bibliography: M. Aubert and S. Goubet, *Gothic Cathedrals of France and Their Treasures* (1958; ET 1959). J. Beckwith, *Early Christian and Byzantine Art* (1979²). B. Bernard, *The Bible and Its Painters* (1983). W. Bernt, *The Netherlandish Painters of the Seventeenth Century* (3 vols., 1970). A. Blount, *Art and Architecture in France, 1500–1700* (1982⁴). J. Brown, *The Golden Age of Painting in Spain* (1991). H. Chadwick and G. Evans (eds.), *Atlas of the Christian Church* (1987). J. Daniélou, *Primitive Christian Symbols* (1961; ET 1964). G. Duchet-Suchaux and M. Pastoureau, *The Bible and the Saints* (1994²; ET 1994). J. Dupont and C. Gnudi, *Gothic Painting* (1979). P. E. Dutton and H. L. Kessler, *The Poetry and Paintings in the First Bible of Charles the Bald* (1997). N. Grubb, *Revelations: Art of the Apocalypse* (1997). H. Heimann (notes on the plates) **and** M. Brion (intro.), *The Bible in Art* (1956). P. Holberton (commentary) **and** N. Usherwood (intro.), *The Bible in Twentieth-century Art* (1956). P. H. Jolly, *Made in God's Image? Eve and Adam in the Genesis Mosaics at San Marco, Venice* (1997). H. Landolt, *German Painting: The Late Middle Ages, 1350–1500* (2 vols. 1968). R. Muehlberger, *The Bible in Art,* vol. 1, *OT*; vol. 2, *NT* (1990). P. Murray and L. Murray, *The Art of the Renaissance* (1963); *The Oxford Companion to Christian Art and Architecture* (1996). G. Osten and H. Vey, *Painting and Sculpture in Germany and the Netherlands, 1500–1600* (1969). P. Scharper and S. Scharper (eds.), *The Gospel in Art by the Peasants of Solentiname* (1984). K. J. White, *Masterpieces of the Bible: Insights into Classical Art of Faith* (1997). S. Wright, *The Bible in Art* (1996). G. Zarnecki, *Art of the Medieval World* (1975).

J. W. COOK

ASIAN BIBLICAL INTERPRETATION

Asia is a vast continent characterized by tremendous racial, cultural, and religious diversity. As a part of their religio-cultural heritage, Asians had a long history of encounter with sacred texts—Hindu, Buddhist, Confucianist, Daoist, and Islamic—before the advent of Christianity on Asian soil. While Christianity arrived in many parts of Asia much earlier, it was not until the nineteenth century, at the heels of European colonization, that Christianity began to create some impact in Asian societies. As a result, the Bible began to be translated into the vernacular of the Asian people, and in the process it was read and interpreted by Asians in their own sociocultural contexts.

1. Wissenschaft. In biblical scholarship the dawn of historical-critical methodology marked a significant paradigm shift in the interpretation of the Bible. Clearly, since the methodology's introduction a significant number of Asian biblical scholars (mostly trained in the West) have adopted this *wissenschaftlich* approach, as evidenced in the works of several early scholars. T. Ishibashi (Japan), who was trained in Germany, published an introduction to the HB and a history of Israelite religion and culture in the 1920s. Z. Watanabe (Japan), who was trained in the United States, was interested in the intersection between the historical-critical study of the Bible and its function as the canonical text (see CANON OF THE BIBLE) for the faith community, leading him to the publication of his trilogy entitled *The Doctrine of the Scriptures* (1949–63). Likewise trained in the United States, K. Uchimura (Japan) approached the biblical texts from historical, grammatical, and philological perspectives but also sought to relate them to the context of the Bible as a whole and to the lives of readers. Joo-sam Yang (Korea), also trained in the United States and the first Korean appointed to teach in a seminary (1915), introduced historical-critical methodology to Korean scholars, arguing that in order to understand and interpret the Bible one needs to know the history of the Bible and its historical as well as literary contexts. His writings similarly reveal his acquaintance with the debate on Mosaic authorship of the Pentateuch (see PENTATEUCHAL CRITICISM), although he sidestepped the issue by focusing on the "holy instruction" of the text.

This *wissenschaftlich* approach to the Bible has continued among Asian scholars. An example is found in the 1972 work of C.-H. Kim (Korean American), who compares the structures of the available Christian letters of recommendation as well as the NT letters of commendation with familiar Hellenistic letters of recommendation.

A second example is the 1977 work of T. Ishida, a significant figure in the study of the United Monarchy in ancient Israel. Ishida investigates the issues of charismatic leadership and dynastic succession and, applying historical-critical analysis to the sources in Samuel and drawing on his knowledge of ancient Near Eastern literature, argues strongly that the Israelite monarchy was dynastic from the beginning. Citing Eli and Samuel as examples, he notes that hereditary leadership was already in place during the *šopeṭ*-regime. He further argues that the ideological conflict on the eve of the monarchy (1 Sam 8:7; 10:19; 12:12) was over monarchy versus theocracy, not over dynastic versus charismatic rule. Thus Ishida shows that A. ALT was wrong in suggesting that the Israelite monarchy was charismatic in its original conceptualization.

Ishida's interest in the period of the United Monarchy in ancient Israel is evident in the major role he played in organizing the International Symposium for Biblical Studies in 1979, the first international meeting for HB studies to be held in Japan, which focused on the Davidic-Solomonic period. More significant, the symposium was held under the patronage of Prince Takahito Mikasa, illustrating the support for *wissenschaftlich* research in biblical studies. The papers of this conference were published in 1982 and edited by Ishida, with contributions from four Japanese scholars: M. Sekine, K. Sacon, Ishida, and Y. Ikeda.

A third example of the *wissenschaftlich* approach is the commentary on Isaiah (ITC, 1990) by S. Widyapranawa, who taught at Duta Wacana Christian University in Yogyakarta, Indonesia. Although strongly theological in nature, the work is built on the results of the historical-critical method. In his comments on Isa 7:14-16, in reference to the *ʿalmâ* as a sign Yahweh gives to Ahaz, Widyapranawa notes: "Now since a sign in the biblical sign should be concrete and actual, it is not clear who this young woman is. She would have to be someone familiar to both Ahaz and Isaiah" (41-42).

C.-L. Seow (Singapore) is perhaps the most prominent Asian biblical scholar. A student of F. M. CROSS at Harvard, he wrote his dissertation on "Ark Processions in the Politics of the Monarchy" (1984), using the tools of comparative Semitics and historical criticism to show the connection of the ritual procession of the ark with the ancient Near Eastern myth of the divine warrior. His commentary on Ecclesiastes (AB 18C, 1997) brings together the tools of historical criticism, socio-anthropological approaches, comparative Semitics, and text linguistics. Through his detailed analysis Seow sees Qohelet as a sage who stood in the wisdom tradition, which derived its authority primarily from human observation and experience. He further suggests that while Qohelet used wisdom's methodologies and forms, "he also made his own distinctive contributions, often in agreement with most of the tradition but at times in criticism of it" (1997, 69).

As in the West, however, not all Asian scholars have been positively inclined toward the historical-critical method. For example, H. Byun, who received a ThD in

HB from Drew University in 1931, rejected higher criticism and held to the Mosaic authorship of the Pentateuch, insisting that the Bible is God's words spoken to the human beings who wrote them down. Another example is Jia Yu-ming (China), who was a seminary professor from 1915 to 1936 and an important biblical scholar within the conservative Chinese Christian circle until his death in 1964. Jia's hermeneutical methods (see HERMENEUTICS) include *scriptura ipsius interpres,* thematic interpretation, and emphasis on spirituality cultivation as the ultimate goal of biblical interpretation (1921). Spiritualization is the focal point of Jia's hermeneutics; however, for him this does not mean "freeplay," nor is spiritualization an inferior interpretational method to the historical-grammatical method.

2. Cultural Hermeneutics. Since the early period of biblical interpretation, Asian scholars have interpreted the Bible in the context of their own cultures and native religious traditions. The articulation of such hermeneutical work takes various forms, with some scholars speaking in terms of contextualization while others use Asian religious categories to understand the Christian tradition, especially JESUS Christ. Scholars have begun to refer to their hermeneutical approaches as "cross-textual," "dialogical," or "dialogical imagination," through which the realities of Asian cultures are brought into conversation with those of the biblical tradition.

A renowned theologian, C.-S. Song (Taiwan) studied HB at Edinburgh and theology at Union Theological Seminary in New York. Formerly president of Tainan Theological Seminary in Taiwan and associate director of the Faith and Order Commission of the World Council of Churches, he teaches at Pacific School of Religion and serves as the president of the World Alliance of Reformed Churches. In a 1976 article, Song raised his concern about the nature of history, especially what is termed "salvation history," and its relation to world history. He sees history first as a story in which a historian has put into continuity things and events that seem disjoined. Second, history consists not only of chronological data but also of the meaning of life and death. This meaning often disrupts the continuity of history—e.g., through revolution. He goes on to note that biblical history derives its meaning from God's redemptive acts, which are comparable to revolutions, describing the exodus as God's revolution *par excellence* and maintaining that the most drastic revolutionary act of God's redemption took place in the person of Jesus Christ on the cross. These to him are disruptions of historical continuity. From a contextual perspective Song goes on to argue that there have been two disruptions in "salvation history" since WWII: (1) The failure of Western missionaries to incorporate the masses of humanity in Asia into "salvation history" and (2) the resolute rejection of Christianity by China. He looks for a different meaning behind these disruptions, suggesting

that Asian Christians should engage in theological reflection concerning a direct relationship of Asia to God's redemption that bypasses Western Christianity. Thus he argues that Israel's history under God is but a model of how God would deal redemptively also with other nations.

Song's unceasing concern for the daily struggles and sufferings of Asians is revealed in his later works. In his 1990 book he poses the question of whether Jesus conceived of himself as a paschal lamb. Exegeting the Gospel account of the Last Supper and comparing it to the Passover narrative of Exodus 12–13, Song identifies a significant difference between the two accounts—namely, that God passed over the paschal lamb but remained with Jesus in his crucifixion. He suggests, therefore, that the event of the cross surpassed that of the Passover. Moreover, from a discussion of the various meanings of *hyper pollōn,* he contends that it should be understood as "in behalf of and representing all peoples." The conclusion Song draws from this study is that Jesus represents the crucified people and that he identifies with the struggles and sufferings of the Asian people.

The work of E. Singgih (Indonesia) also illustrates the importance of contextualization in Asian biblical scholarship. Taking its lead from Song's earlier article, Singgih's 1982 work begins by tracing the use of "contextualization" back to the Taiwanese theologian Shoki Coe (Ng Chiong-hui) in 1972. Singgih then argues that in order to take the contextualization program seriously, attention must be given to the reinterpretation of the biblical context, the reinterpretation of the systematic-dogmatic tradition, and the reinterpretation of the modern context (70). To illustrate, he discusses the works of two writers who have sought to interpret the good news in the religio-cultural context of the Jawanese people of Indonesia. Particularly significant is the work of J. Banawiratma (1977), who uses a dialogical method to discuss the two worldviews, that of the Jawanese society and that of the JOHANNINE Gospel.

V. Chakkarai (India), in his monograph on christology, (1926) used the Hindu concept of *avatār* (incarnation) to understand Jesus, proposing that Jesus is the dynamic and permanent incarnation of God.

Following his conversion to Christianity, Wu Lei-ch'uan (China), an educator and scholar of Chinese classics, attempted the union of Christian faith and Chinese culture as he sought to use Confucian categories in his interpretation of the Bible. In his 1936 work he used the ancient Chinese concept of *Tien-tzu* (Son of Heaven) to understand Jesus as Christ. Influenced by the understanding of the *Tien-tzu* as one who was at once the king who ruled the people, the prophet who taught them the heavenly will, and the priest who offered sacrifices on their behalf, Wu's conceptualization of Jesus is very political. For instance, he suggests that even as a twelve-year-old boy, Jesus had thoughts about serving as a political Christ when he said that he must be concerned about his Father's affairs (Luke 2:49), a statement Wu interpreted as foreshadowing both a political revolution to liberate the Jewish people from Roman hegemony and a social revolution to rebuild a moral society.

Asian scholars have begun to name their hermeneutical approaches. In a programmatic essay in 1989, K. Pui-lan (Hong Kong) advocates a dialogical approach. Using the term "dialogical imagination," she points out that "biblical interpretation in Asia . . . must create a two-way traffic between our own tradition and that of the Bible" (30) and that "it is dialogical, for it involves a constant conversation between different religious and cultural traditions" (31). She further notes that her hermeneutical model gives emphasis to plurality of meanings, multiplicity of narratives, and a multiaxial framework of analysis since such a model is rooted in the pluralisms and diversities of Asia. She insists that Asians "have to avoid superimposing a European framework on the development of Asian hermeneutics, which must remain rooted in its own specific cultural context." (1995, 39).

The 1990b essay by R. Sugirtharajah (Sri Lanka) uses a similar dialogical approach, which he defines as one that "acknowledges the validity of the varied and diverse religious experiences of all people and rules out any exclusive claim to truth by one religious tradition" (13). Working on texts associated with PAUL's conversion experience (Acts 9:1-9; 22:3-16; 26:9-18; Gal 1:11-17), Sugirtharajah seeks to show that Jesus was not introducing a new tradition but rather reiterating a forgotten aspect of the availability of God's mercy and grace to all. Paul's experience on the Damascus highway, therefore, is to be seen as a transformation as he began to retrieve the neglected elements of his own tradition in light of Jesus' words and actions.

A. Lee (Hong Kong) has used his "cross-textual hermeneutics" (1993a) in a number of articles. In his 1985 work, a response to the signing of the Sino-British Declaration in 1984, which set in motion the reversion of Hong Kong to China, Lee posed the question of the roles and functions the church could play during the time of transition. He compares the prophetic role of Nathan in the David-Bathsheba story with the role of the remonstrator in the Chinese tradition, particularly the role of Wei Cheng in the court of Emperor Tang Tai Tsung. In this role Wei Cheng had to remind the emperor of his responsibilities as a parent of his people, showing concern for them and working for their well-being. Nathan played a similar role when he called David to accountability for the murder of Uriah.

Lee's second work (1994) is a cross-textual analysis of the biblical creation narratives, especially that of Genesis 1–11, and of the Chinese creation myth of Nu Kua, one of the oldest Chinese stories of the origin of humanity. A female creator, Nu Kua, fashions human beings from the yellow earth, expertly sculpting the rich and noble but dripping mud from a rope to form the poor and lowly. In another version she re-creates the universe damaged by chaotic forces, including its social harmony and cosmic order. Thus this myth reveals both "anthrogonic" and "sociogonic" concerns. Lee observes that in the Chinese tradition Nu Kua is seen both as a human being who is becoming divine and as a divine being who is becoming human. Such a concept, he notes, presents a theological challenge to the Christian monotheistic faith; moreover, biblical creation stories are often reduced to a doctrine of creation. His concern, then, relates to how Asian Christians can begin to incorporate the worldview of Asian traditions into their theological formulation.

3. Liberation Perspectives. Since the introduction of LIBERATION THEOLOGY, liberation perspectives have found a home among many Asian biblical scholars. Such perspectives have a strong appeal for Asian scholars, first, because the socioeconomic situations in many parts of Asia are underdeveloped or developing. Many people live below the poverty level, and the exploitation of the poor is an everyday reality. In addition, many Asians live under oppressive governmental structures. Second, since liberation theology is contextual theology, it is a natural trajectory of the cultural hermeneutical interests of those who are already engaged in such interpretational approaches. Examples from Korea, India, and the Philippines illustrate the interest of Asian scholars in liberation perspectives.

In the 1970s Korea underwent a period of rapid economic and social change. Under the military regime Koreans also experienced political oppression and injustices. The impact on the poor and on laborers was tremendous since no one was allowed to criticize the government, leaving the people powerless to resist injustices. In this context minjung theology emerged as a theological voice of Korean Christians in their struggle for democracy and human rights.

In the construction and articulation of minjung theology, the Bible has been regarded as an important source along with the traditions and social biography of the *minjung* (the mass of the people). We find this, for example, in the writings of N.-D. Suh, a former professor of systematic theology at Yonsei University and a primary voice in the early conceptualization of minjung theology. According to Suh, the total witness of the Bible may be clarified and understood in terms of the two nuclear historical events—the exodus in the HB and the crucifixion-resurrection in the NT—that are paradigms of God's intervention in the political and socioeconomic histories of the people (1981).

Two biblical scholars have made significant contributions to the history of biblical interpretation from the perspective of minjung theology. First is B.-M. Ahn, a former professor of NT at Hanguk Theological Seminary. In his 1981 essay Ahn attempts a historical-critical study of the term *ochlos* and uses it to provide a biblical ground for minjung theology. He suggests that in Mark's Gospel the term *ochlos* is indicative of a social class that has been marginalized and abandoned—namely, the "sinners," the tax collectors, and the sick. They are the *minjung,* who are alienated, dispossessed, and powerless. It is this group with which Jesus sided and to whom he proclaimed the coming of God's kingdom.

The second is C. Moon, a former professor of HB at Presbyterian Theological Seminary in Seoul and presently on the faculty of San Francisco Theological Seminary. In his 1985 book Moon draws parallels between the social history of the Korean *minjung* and the Hebrews, describing a somewhat Albrightian model (see W. F. ALBRIGHT) of the exodus and the possession of the land of Canaan vis-à-vis a thirteenth-century exodus that took place during the reign of Rameses II. Moon goes on to describe the Hebrews as *habiru,* i.e., as "rebels standing in defiance of the prevailing social or power structure," and adds, "The *habiru,* therefore, were part of the *minjung* of their time, driven by their *han* (grudge or resentment) to act against what they felt to be injustices imposed on them by those in power" (4). It is clear that Moon's understanding of the ancient Hebrews is influenced by and reconstructed from the experiences of the *minjung* in Korean history. In another chapter on the prophets (see PROPHECY AND PROPHETS, HB), he suggests that the suffering and oppression in modern Korea are similar to that of ancient Israel during the eighth century BCE, particularly during the time of Amos and Micah. According to Moon, the central issue for Micah was the suffering of "my people," who were oppressed and robbed of their property by the ruling class of Judah. As a commoner, Micah stood on the side of the oppressed and acted as their advocate, living and identifying with *minjung.*

C. Abesamis (Philippines), who teaches NT at the Loyola School of Theology in the Philippines, uses the concept of "reign-kingdom of God" in a number of his writings. He declares unambiguously that his main exegetical instrument is "solidarity with the struggling poor of the Third World and viewing things through the eyes of the poor." He understands the reign-kingdom of God as "a new world experiencing a new history. . . . It involves a new earth where instead of poverty and oppression there is justice and liberation; where instead of hunger there is bread and rice; instead of sorrow, there is laughter; where the land belongs to the meek; where the compassionate will be repaid with compassion; where we have the direct experience of God; where we finally attain to the full status of the sons and daughters of God" (1993, 67). In an extensive study of the mission statements in Mark and the Q source (1987b), Abesamis

shows that both Mark and Q reveal that Jesus' mission centered around the proclamation of the reign-kingdom of God and justice and liberation for the poor and the oppressed. Clearly found in Q (Matt 11:2-6; Luke 7:18-23), the latter is implicitly present in Mark in such statements as "good news of the kingdom" (Mark 1:14-15).

In India liberation theology found expression in the form of Dalit theology beginning in the 1980s. The term *dalit* is used as a reference to oppressed peoples, especially the "untouchables," who belong at the bottom of the caste system. The first of two works representative of such hermeneutical interests is an article by A. Nirmal (1988), in which he locates the basis of Dalit theology in Deut 26:5-12. He suggests that in this ancient Israelite creedal statement concepts of being "few in number," of recognizing their "affliction," of achieving liberation through "terror," and of securing "a land flowing with milk and honey" have paradigmatic value for Dalit theology.

A second example of this hermeneutical interest is a work by D. Carr (1994), who argues that "Matthew provides the most comprehensive model for Dalit theology." Understanding the "lost sheep of the House of Israel" as the "despised Galileans, the exploited poor, the physically handicapped who were deemed cursed, the hated tax gatherers and the stigmatized women sexworkers," Carr sees strong parallels between Matthew's depiction and the situation of the Dalits, who are also "an oppressed, ostracised and stigmatised group," and argues that Matthew affirms God's bias toward them.

4. Feminist Hermeneutics. Scholars have rightly noted that feminism is an extension of liberationism. While liberationists are most concerned with injustices in the socioeconomic and political arenas, feminists add the issue of gender inequality in their critical engagement. In her 1995 book Kwok Pui-lan (Hong Kong), regarded as the foremost Asian feminist theologian, who is on the faculty at the Episcopal Divinity School, presents ten theses as the foundation of her FEMINIST approach to biblical interpretation. These include examining the politics of biblical AUTHORITY and the historical-critical method critically; taking seriously the story of women of color, particularly their multiple oppression in terms of class, gender, and race; and condemning antisemitism, oppression, and discrimination against any racial group. Her chapter "Woman, Dogs, and Crumbs: Constructing a Postcolonial Discourse," in which she deals with the story of the Syrophoenician woman (Matt 15:21-28; Mark 7:24-30), illustrates well her feminist concerns. She sees this story as one that "brings into sharp focus the complex issues of the relationship among different racial and ethnic groups, the interaction between men and women, cultural imperialism, and colonization" (72). Investigating the intersection of anti-

Judaism, sexism, and colonialism in the history of interpretation of this story, she offers sharp criticism of the use of the salvation-history model in this instance. Such a model stresses the unequal status of Jesus and the woman and, by interpreting the woman's remarks as signifying her faith and humility, portrays her as a paragon of Christian virtue. Moreover, the story has also been read as shifting the blessing of God's salvation from the Jews to the Gentiles, thus condoning anti-Judaism. Kwok further notes that when the gospel was spread to Asia the faith and humility of the Syro-Phoenician woman was used as a model for "heathens" in order to support colonialism and imperialism.

Another example of Asian feminist hermeneutics is the work of A. Gnanadason (India), who serves as the director of the subunit on women's issues in the World Council of Churches. Seeing women's struggles as a struggle for liberation, she calls for a reexamination of the issue of biblical authority and a reinterpretation of biblical texts from the perspective of women. An example of her work is her interpretation of the story of Jesus and the Samaritan woman in John 4:5-30 (1992) in which she suggests that the source of empowerment in the narrative is embedded not only in Jesus' dialogue with an outcast but also in his transformation of the woman into a missionary to the Samaritans. Gnanadason also notes that the woman's leaving her water jar behind symbolizes her break from a "life of oppression and sinfulness so as to internalize the liberating power of the living water" (120).

5. Post-colonial Interpretation. Kwok's work "Woman, Dogs, and Crumbs," mentioned above, is an example of the POST-COLONIAL interests that some Asian biblical scholars are beginning to exhibit. Another example is an essay (1997) by P. Chia, a Malaysian who teaches HB at the Alliance Bible Seminary in Hong Kong, that provides an alternative reading to Daniel 1 whereby representation, resistance, colonization, and neocolonialism are at work. By studying the narrator's plot and the characterizations of Nebuchadnezzar, Daniel, and others, Chia argues that what lies behind the stories is post-colonialism as an ideology (see IDEOLOGICAL CRITICISM). In articulating a representation of the colonized past and of the voices of the exile, the narrator reflects a colonized identity and a post-colonial ideology, mirrored through the characters in the stories. The renaming of Daniel and his friends in the Chaldean language is seen as an act of colonization by Nebuchadnezzar that is countered by Daniel's resistance to the royal food, an act of rejecting the king's claim of colonial power over life and death.

A second example is a paper by Lee presented at the 1997 SOCIETY OF BIBLICAL LITERATURE annual meeting in San Francisco. Using the context of post-colonial Hong Kong after its reversion to China, Lee attempts a rereading of Isaiah 56–66, beginning with a description

of the sociocultural context of Hong Kong, one he deems "highly hybridized" since it is culturally Chinese and pragmatically British (in economy and legal structures). Post-coloniality in such a context, Lee argues, must then be understood "in terms of the conscious effort to combat marginalization and to reaffirm the 'denied or allocated subjectivity' of Hong Kong against British colonizer before and the Chinese sovereign power at present." These efforts will include reappropriating traditions, retrieving repressed histories, and negotiating a different "in-between" identity. Turning his attention to the context of Trito-Isaiah, Lee notes that the community in Babylon was made up primarily of a younger generation who had begun to create a sense of identity as a people from Palestine living in a foreign land. The returnees from exile, then, must have been quite different from those left behind in Palestine in terms of their lifestyles, cultural orientations, sociopolitical identities, and religious practices. Just as in the situation in Hong Kong, where there are different voices and models for constructing the future of the city, so also there were dissenting movements and conflicting voices in the postexilic community of ancient Israel.

6. Conclusion. The abundance of works by Asian scholars in the last decades of the twentieth century has been made possible in part by the large number of Asian journals that provide avenues for publication. Most significant of these are the *Annual of the Japanese Biblical Institute,* the official organ of the Japan Biblical Institute founded by M. Sekine and others in 1950, which has published articles in English, French, and German since 1975; the *Asia Journal of Theology,* jointly published since 1987 by the Association for Theological Education in South East Asia, the North East Asia Association of Theological Schools, and the Board of Theological Education of the Senate of Serampore College (its predecessors are the *East Asia Journal of Theology* and the *South East Asia Journal of Theology*); *Bible Bhashyam,* published since 1975 by St. Thomas Apostolic Seminary in India; *Bina Darma,* which has published biblical, theological, and religious articles in the Indonesian language since 1983; *Boletin Eclesiastico de Filipinas,* published by the University of Santo Tomas in the Philippines; *Diwa: Studies in Philosophy and Theology,* published by Christ the King Mission Seminary in the Philippines; *Jeevadhara: A Journal of Christian Interpretation,* published in India since 1971; *Jian Dao: A Journal of Bible and Theology,* published by Alliance Bible Seminary, Hong Kong, since 1994; *Orientasi Baru,* published since 1986 in Indonesia; *The Theological Thought,* a journal that publishes articles on Bible and theology in the Korean language; and *Vidyajyoti,* a journal of theological reflection published by Catholic Press in India since 1938. Although a number of essays and books by Asian scholars are written in the scholars' native languages, there are sufficient works written in

English to make them accessible to the English-speaking world.

Bibliography: C. H. Abesamis, *Salvation, Historical and Total: Towards a Faith-life That Is Biblical, Historical, Indigenous* (The Integral Evangelism Series, 1978); *On Mark and the New World, the Good News: Letters from C. Abesamis* (1983); *Where Are We Going: Heaven or New World?* (Foundation Books, 1986); *The Mission of Jesus and Good News to the Poor: Biblico-pastoral Considerations for a Church in the Third World* (Nagliliyab 8, 1987a); "The Mission of Jesus and Good News to the Poor: Exegetico-Pastoral Considerations for a Church in the Third World," *AJTh* 1 (1987b) 429-60; *A Third Look at Jesus: A Catechetical Guidebook* (1988); "Some Paradigms in Re-reading the Bible in a Third World Setting," *Mission Studies* 7 (1990) 21-34; "The Contextual and Universal Dimensions of Christian Theology: A NT Perspective," *Bangalore Theological Forum* 24 (1992) 16-23; "A Third Look at Jesus and Salvation: A Bible Study on Mark 1:14-15," *Asian Christian Spirituality: Reclaiming Traditions* (ed. V. Fabella et al., 1992) 134-41; "Heart of the Matter: Re-discovering the Core-Message of the NT in the Third World," *Any Room for Christ in Asia?* (ed. L. Boff and V. Elizondo, 1993) 63-76. **B.-M. Ahn,** "Jesus and the *Minjung* in the Gospel of Mark," *Minjung Theology: People as the Subjects of History* (ed. The Commission on Theological Concerns of the Christian Conference of Asia, 1981) 138-52; "The Body of Jesus-event Tradition," *EAJT* 3 (1985) 293-310. **D. S. Amalorpavadass,** "The Bible in Self-renewal and Church-renewal for Service to Society," *Voices from the Margin: Interpreting the Bible in the Third World* (ed. R. S. Sugirtharajah, 1991) 316-29. **C. Amjad-Ali,** "The Equality of Women: Form or Substance (1 Cor 11:12-16)," ibid., 185-93. **K. Arayaprateep,** "The Covenant: An Effective Tool in Bible Study," *SEAJT* 18 (1977) 21-31; An Asian Group Work, "An Asian Feminist Perspective: The Exodus Story (Exod 1:8-22, 2:1-10)," *Voices from the Margin* (ed. R. S. Sugirtharajah, 1995 ²) 255-66. **T. C. Bacani, Jr.,** *God's Own People in the Scriptures* (1965); *The Bible for the Filipinos* (1989). **J. B. Banawiratma,** *Jesus Sang Guru: Pertemuan Kejawendengan Injil* (*Jesus the Teacher*) (1977). **R. Budiman,** "Contextual Witness and Exegesis," *Study Institute "Contextual Exegesis" di Ujung Pandang, 1980* (1981) 50-56. **N. C. Capulong,** "Land, Power, and People's Rights in the OT: From a Filipino Theological Perspective," *EAJT* 2 (1984) 233-50. **D. Carr,** "A Biblical Basis for Dalit Theology," *Indigenous People, Dalits: Dalit Issues in Today's Theological Debate* (ISPCK Contextual Theological Education Series 5, ed. J. Massey, 1994) 231-49. **V. Chakkarai,** *Jesus the Avatar* (Indian Series, 1926). **P. M. Chang,** "Jeremiah's Hope in Action: An Exposition of Jer 32:1-15," *EAJT* 2 (1984) 244-50. **S. H. Chao,** "Confucian Chinese and the Gospel: Methodological Considerations," *AJTh* 7 (1987) 17-40. **T. C. Chao,** "The Articulate Word and the Problem of Communications," *IRM* 36 (1947) 482-89. **P. P. Chia,** "Intersubjectivity, Intertextuality, Interconnectivity: On Biblical Hermeneutics and Hegemony," *Jian Dao* 5 (1996) 1-21; "On Naming the Subject: Postcolonial Reading of Daniel 1," *Jian Dao* 7 (1997) 17-36. **A. P. Corleto, Jr.,** "Creation and Fall in Genesis 1–3 and Philippine Creation Myths," *Diwa* 7 (1982–83) 1-17. **A. Gnanadason,** "Towards an Indian Feminist Theology," *We Dare to Dream: Doing Theology as Asian Women* (ed. V. Fabella and S. A. L. Park, 1989) 117-26; "Indian Women: New Voices, New Visions," *Third World Theologies in Dialogue: Essays in Memory of D. S. Amalorpavadass* (ed. J. R. Chandran, 1991) 143-51; "The Holy Spirit Liberates and Unites," *We Belong Together: Churches in Solidarity with Women* (ed. S. Cunningham, 1992) 116-21; "Dalit Women: The Dalit of the Dalit," *Indigenous People, Dalits: Dalit Issues in Today's Theological Debate* (ed. J. Massey, 1994) 168-76. **T. Ishida,** *The Royal Dynasties in Ancient Israel: A Study on the Formation and Development of Royal-dynastic Ideology* (BZAW 142, 1977); (ed.), *Studies in the Period of David and Solomon and Other Essays* (1982); "Adonijah the Son of Haggith and His Supporters: An Inquiry into Problems About History and Historiography," *The Future of Biblical Studies: The Hebrew Scriptures* (Semeia Studies, ed. R. E. Friedman and H. G. M. Williamson, 1987) 165-87; "The Role of Nathan the Prophet in the Episode of Solomon's Birth," *Near Eastern Studies: Dedicated to H.I.H. Prince Takahito Mikasa on the Occasion of His Seventy-fifth Birthday* (ed. M. Mori et al., 1991) 133-38; "The Succession Narrative and Esarhaddon's Apology: A Comparison," *Ah, Assyria . . . : Studies in Assyrian History and Ancient Near Eastern Historiography Presented to H. Tadmor* (ed. M. Cogan and I. Eph'al, 1991) 166-73. **Y. M. Jia,** *Shen-dao-Shueh* [*The Way of God*] (1921). **P. Kalluveettil,** "The Marginalizing Dialectics of the Bible," *Bible Bhashyam* 11 (1985) 201-14. **M. Katoppo,** *Compassionate and Free: An Asian Woman's Theology* (Risk Book Series 6, 1979). **H. Kayama,** "The Cornelius Story in the Japanese Cultural Context," *Text and Experience: Towards a Cultural Exegesis of the Bible* (BiSe 35, ed. D. L. Smith-Christopher, 1995) 180-94. **C.-H. Kim,** *Form and Structure of the Familiar Greek Letter of Recommendation* (1972); "Reading the Bible as Asian Americans," *NIB* (1994) 1:161-66. **E. K. Kim,** "Who Is Yahweh? Based on a Contextual Reading of Exod 3:14," *AJTh* 3 (1989) 108-17. **H. Kinukawa,** "The Story of the Hemorrhaging Woman (Mark 5:25-34) Read from a Japanese Feminist Context," *BibInt* 2 (1994) 283-93; *Women and Jesus in Mark: A Japanese Feminist Perspective* (The Bible and Liberation Series, 1994); "On John 7:53–8:11: A Well-Cherished but Much-Clouded Story," *Reading from This Place: Social Location and Biblical Interpretation in Global Perspective* 2 (ed. F. F. Segovia and M. A. Tolbert, 1995) 82-96. **G. Koonthanam,** "Yahweh the Defender of the Dalits: A Reflection on Isaiah 3:12-15," *Jeevadhara* 22 (1992) 112-23. **P.-L. Kwok,** "God Weeps with Our Pain," *EAJT* 2 (1984) 228-32; "Discovering the Bible in the Non-biblical World," *Semeia* 47 (1989) 25-42; *Discovering the Bible in the Non-biblical World* (The Bible and Liberation Series, 1995); "Chinese Christians and Their Bible," *BibInt* 4 (1996) 127-29. **S. Largunpai,** "The Book of Ecclesiastes and Thai Buddhism" *AJTh* 8 (1994) 155-62. **A. C. C. Lee,** "Doing Theology in Chinese Context: The David-Bathsheba Story and the Parable of Nathan," *EAJT* 3 (1985) 243-57; "The 'Critique of Foundations' in the Hebrew Wisdom Tradition," *AJTh* 4 (1990) 126-35; "Biblical Interpretation in Asian Perspective," *AJTh* 7 (1993a) 35-39; "Genesis 1 from the Perspective of a Chinese Creation Myth," *Understanding Poets and Prophets* (JSOTSup 152, ed. A. G. Auld, 1993b) 186-98; "The Chinese Creation Myth of Nu Kua and the Biblical Narrative in Genesis 1–11," *BibInt* 2 (1994) 312-24; "Death and the Perception of the Divine in Qohelet and Zhuang Zi," *Ching Feng* 38 (1995) 69-81; "Exile and Return in the Perspective of 1997," *Reading from This Place: Social Location and Biblical Interpretation in Global Perspective* 2 (ed. F. F. Segovia and M. A. Tolbert, 1995) 97-108; "Feminist Critique of the Bible and Female Principle in Culture," *AJTh* 10 (1996) 240-52. **K. Y. Liem,** "Enacting the Acts of God: One Important Aspect of Life and Proclamation of Jesus and Paul," *SEAJT* 14, 2 (1973) 21-33. **C. Lo,** "Chinese Biblical Interpretation in the Eyes of a Chinese Christian," *BibInt* 4 (1996) 124-26. **T. Manikkam,** "Towards an Indian Hermeneutics of the Bible," *Jeevadhara* 12 (1982) 94-104. **A. Mariaselvam,** *The Song of Songs and Ancient Tamil Love Poems: Poetry and Symbolism* (AnBib 118, 1988). **N. Minz,** "A Theological Interpretation of the Tribal Reality," *RelSoc* 34 (1987) 71-85. **C. H.-S. Moon,** "An OT Understanding of *Minjung*," *Minjung Theology: People as the Subjects of History* (ed. The Commission on Theological Concerns of the Christian Conference of Asia, 1981) 119-35; *A Korean Minjung Theology: An OT Perspective* (1985). **J. G. Muthuraj,** "NT and Methodology: An Overview," *AJTh* 10 (1996) 253-77. **D. P. Niles,** "Examples of Contextualization in the OT," *SEAJT* 21, 2 (1980) 19-33; "The Word of God and the People of Asia," *Understanding the Word: Essays in Honor of B. W. Anderson* (JSOTSup 37, ed. J. T. Butler et al., 1985) 281-313. **A. P. Nirmal,** "A Dialogue with Dalit Literature," *Towards a Dalit Theology* (ed. M. E. Prabhakar, 1988) 64-82. **C. Panackal,** "The Option of the Poor in the Letter of James," *Bible Bhashyam* 15 (1989) 141-53. **M. Pongudom,** "Creation of Man: Theological Reflections Based on Northern Thai Folktales," *EAJT* 3 (1985) 222-27. **D. N. Premnath,** "The OT Against Its Cultural Background and Its Implications for Theological Education," *AJTh* 2 (1988) 98-105; "The Concepts of Rta and Maat: A Study in Comparison," *BibInt* 2 (1994) 325-39. **R. J. Raja,** "The Gospels with an Indian Face," *Vidyajyoti* 55 (1991) 61-72, 121-41. **S. Rayan,** "Jesus and the Poor in the Fourth Gospel," *Bible Bhashyam* 4 (1978) 213-28. **G. Robinson,** "Jesus Christ, the Open Way and the Fellow-struggle: A Look into the Christologies in India," *AJTh* 3 (1989) 403-15. **K. K. Sacon and K. Matsunaga,** "Biblical Scholarship, Japanese," *ABD* 1:737-40. **S. J. Samartha,** *The Search for New Hermeneutic in Asian Christian Theology* (1987); *One Christ—Many Religions: Toward a Revised Christology* (1991); "Religion, Language, and Reality: Towards a Relational Hermeneutics," *BibInt* 2 (1994) 340-62. **C.-L. Seow,** *Myth, Drama, and the Politics of David's Dance* (HSM 44, 1989); *Ecclesiastes* (AB 18C, 1997). **E. G. Singgih,** *Dari Israel ke Asia: Masalah Hubungan di Antara Kontekstualisasi Teologia dengan Interpretasi Alkitabiah* [*From Israel to Asia: The Relationship Between Contextual Theology and Biblical Interpretation*] (1982); "Let Me Not Be Put to Shame: Towards an Indonesian Hermeneutics," *AJTh* 9 (1995) 71-85; "Contextualization and Inter-religious Relationship in Java: Past and Present," *AJTh* 11 (1997) 248-62. **G. M. Soares-Prabhu,** "Towards an Indian Interpretation of the Bible," *Bible Bhashyam* 6 (1980) 151-70; "The

Historical-Critical Method: Reflections on Its Relevance for the Studies of the Gospels in India Today," *Theologizing in India* (ed. M. Amaladoss et al., 1981) 314-49); "The Kingdom of God: Jesus' Vision of a New Society," *Indian Church in the Struggle* (ed. D. S. Amalorpavadass, 1981) 579-608; "The Prophet as Theologian: Biblical Prophetism as a Paradigm for Doing Theology Today," *AJTh* 2 (1988) 3-11; "Interpreting the Bible in India Today," *The Way* sup. 72 (1990) 70-80; "Class in the Bible: The Biblical Poor as a Social Class?" *Voices from the Margin: Interpreting the Bible in the Third World* (ed. R. S. Sugirtharajah, 1991) 147-71; "Jesus in Egypt: A Reflection on Matt 2:13-15, 19-21 in the Light of the OT," *Estudios Bablicos* 50 (1992) 225-49; "The Table Fellowship of Jesus: Its Significance for Dalit Christians in India Today," *Jeevadhara* 22 (1992) 140-59; "Anti-Greed and Anti-Pride: Mark 10:17-27 and 10:35-45 in the Light of Tribal Values," *Jeevadhara* 24 (1994) 130-50; "Two Mission Commands: An Interpretation of Matt 28:16-20 in the Light of a Buddhist Text," *BibInt* 2 (1994) 264-82; "The Bible as Magna Carta of Movements for Liberation and Human Rights," *The Bible as Cultural Heritage* (ed. W. Beuken et al., 1995) 85-96; "Laughing at Idols: The Dark Side of Biblical Monotheism (an Indian Reading of Isa 44:9-20)," *Reading from This Place: Social Location and Biblical Interpretation in Global Perspective* 2 (ed. F. F. Segovia and M. A. Tolbert, 1995) 109-31. **C. S. Song,** "From Israel to Asia: A Theological Leap," *Theology* 79 (1976) 90-96; *Jesus, the Crucified People* (1990); *Jesus and the Reign of God* (1993); *Jesus in the Power of the Spirit* (1994). **R. S. Sugirtharajah,** " 'For You Always Have the Poor with You': An Example of Hermeneutics of Suspicion," *AJTh* 4 (1990a) 102-7; *Studies* 7 (1990b) 9-20; "The Bible and Its Asian Readers," *BibInt* 1 (1993) 54-66; "Inter-faith Hermeneutics: An Example and Some Implications," *Mission, the Text and the Texts: Some Examples of Biblical Interpretation in Asia* (1993); "Introduction and Some Thoughts on Asian Biblical Hermeneutics," *BibInt* 2 (1994) 251-63; "From Orientalist to Post-colonial: Notes on Reading Practices," *AJTh* 10 (1996) 20-27; "Orientalism, Ethnonationalism, and Transnationalism: Shifting Identities and Biblical Interpretation," *Ethnicity and the Bible* (ed. M. Brett, 1996) 419-29; "Texts Are Always with You: Christians and Their Bibles," *Hindu-Christian Studies Bulletin* 9 (1996) 8-13. **N.-D. Suh,** "Historical References for a Theology of *Minjung*," *Minjung Theology: People as the Subjects of History* (ed. The Commission on Theological Concerns of the Christian Conference of Asia, 1981) 155-82. **M. T. Thangaraj,** *The Crucified Guru: An Experiment in Cross-cultural Christology* (1994). **I. Vempeny,** *Kṛṣna and Christ: In the Light of Some of the Fundamental Concepts and Themes of the Bhagavad Gita and the NT* (1988). **S. W. Wahono,** *Gambaran-gambaran Kontekstuil Hubungan Yahweh dan Bangsa Israel di dalam Perjanjian Lama* [*Descriptions of the Contextual Relationship Between Yahweh and the Israelites in the OT*] (1979). **S.-K. Wan,** "Allegorical Interpretation East and West: A Methodological Enquiry into Comparative Hermeneutics," *Text and Experience: Towards a Cultural Exegesis of the Bible* (ed. D. L. Smith-Christopher, 1995) 154-79. **Z. Watanabe,** *The Doctrine of Scriptures* (1949–63). **S. H. Widyapranawa,** *The Lord Is Savior: Faith in National Crisis. A Commentary on the Book of Isaiah*

1–39 (ITC, 1990). **A. Wire,** "Chinese Biblical Interpretation Since Mid-century," *BibInt* 4 (1996) 101-23. **L.-C. Wu,** *Chi-du-chiao yu chung-kuo wun-hwa* [*Christianity and Chinese Culture*] (1936). **K. K. Yeo,** "Amos (4:4-5) and Confucius: The Will (Ming) of God (Tien)," *AJTh* 4 (1990) 472-88; "The Rhetorical Herme-neutic of 1 Corinthians 8 and Chinese Ancestor Worship," *BibInt* 2 (1994) 294-311; "A Rhetorical Study of Acts 17:22-31: What Has Jerusalem to Do with Athens and Beijing?" *Jian Dao* 1 (1994) 75-107; "The 'Yin-Yang' of God (Exod 3:14) and Humanity (Gen 1:26-27)," *ZRGG* 46 (1994) 319-32; "Isa 5:2-7 and 27:2-6: Let's Hear the Whole Song of Rejection and Restoration," *Jian Dao* 3 (1995) 77-94; *Rhetorical Interaction in 1 Corinthians 8 and 10: A Formal Analysis with Preliminary Suggestions for a Chinese Cross-cultural Hermeneutic* (1995); "A Confucian Reading of Romans 7:14-25: *Nomos* (Law) and *Li* (Propriety)," *Jian Dao* 5 (1996) 127-41; "Christ-centered Multi-cultural Hermeneutics: The Examination of Gal 2:15-16, 3:1-20," *Jian Dao* 7 (1997) 57-76; *What Has Jerusalem to Do with Beijing? Biblical Inter-pretation from a Chinese Perspective* (1998). **J. Y. H. Yieh,** "Cultural Reading of the Bible: Some Chinese Christian Cases," *Text and Experience: Towards a Cultural Exegesis of the Bible* (BiSe 35, ed. D. L. Smith-Christopher, 1995) 122-53. **A. M. Zabala,** "Advent Reflections on Col 1:15-20 in the Philippines Setting," *AJTh* 3 (1989) 315-29.

J. KUAN

ASSYRIOLOGY AND BIBLICAL STUDIES

The word *Assyriology* came into use in the 1850s to denote the study of the civilization revealed by excavations in Mesopotamia (Iraq), mainly Assyria, during the preceding decade. The term ceased to be appropriate when the main area of research moved southward to Babylonia, but it continued in use. Since WWII the term *Sumerology* has gained general cur-rency for the subdivision of Assyriology specifically related to the Sumerian civilization of third-millennium southern Mesopotamia.

1. History of the Issues. The many overt references in the Bible to ancient Mesopotamian civilization and history, from the plain of Shinar and the Tower of Babel in Gen 11:2-9 to the accounts of the conquest and deportation of Israel and Judah by the Assyrians and Babylonians, have always made Mesopotamia of interest to readers of the Bible. Jewish communities maintained a memory of the sites of such biblical cities as Nineveh and Babylon and transmitted this information to Eastern Christians and Muslims. From medieval times onward, some devout Western Jewish and Christian pilgrims to the Holy Land extended their travels eastward to visit those sites. The first recorded instance was a Spanish Jew, Benjamin of Tudela, who in the twelfth century reached Mesopotamia and correctly identified the sites of both Nineveh and Babylon and climbed the ruins of a ziggurat at Borsippa, which he took to be the Tower of Babel.

Subsequently, French and English competition for the route to India joined with religious traditions to increase European interest in Mesopotamia. By the mid-eighteenth century overland travel by officials of the East India Company and their French counterparts had contributed to making the ruins of Mesopotamia and southwest Persia widely known in the educated world. Interest was further stimulated by Danish explorer C. Niebuhr's *Voyage en Arabie & en d'autres pays circon-voisins* (1776–80), in which he reproduced accurate copies of cuneiform inscriptions from the site of Perse-polis in southwest Persia. These aroused European in-terest in the cuneiform writing system, the Old Persian side of which was partially deciphered by G. Grotefend at Göttingen in 1802 (pub. 1805).

The first scientific investigations of the site of Baby-lon were by C. Rich, the East India Company's resident in Baghdad, who published two memoirs (1813, 1818), which gave a further stimulus to European interest in ancient Mesopotamia. The biblical context in which this was seen is attested in a poem by Byron, who linked Rich's discoveries to "Babel," "Where . . . Daniel tamed the lions in their den" (*Don Juan,* Canto V, LX-LXII).

In 1842 the French consul P. Botta began major excavations in Assyria, followed in 1845 by H. Layard; both men had quick success in finding major Assyrian antiquities. Although neither excavation was primarily motivated by a connection with biblical research, Layard's spectacular discoveries quickly made the bib-lical dimension apparent, and we find a pious American writing to tell him of "the importance which your solitary labors may have upon the right understanding of the Historical and Prophetical parts of the Holy Word." More cynically, a close friend advised him, "If you can . . . attach a Biblical importance to your discov-eries you will come the complete dodge over this world of fools and dreamers: you can get some religious fellow to inspire you with the necessary cant."

By the beginning of the 1850s H. Rawlinson was able to make out the sense of Layard's Assyrian inscriptions so that in 1854 he could relate Assyrian accounts of military action in Palestine by Shalmaneser V, Sargon, and Sennacherib to the narratives in 2 Kgs 18:9–19:36 (*Athenaeum* [1854] papers of Mar. 18 and Apr. 15). This initiated a period of publication of cuneiform material of biblical relevance.

By the 1860s the verbal infallibility of the Bible had become a matter of widespread controversy in the English-speaking world. One factor was the publication in 1859 of C. Darwin's *Origin of Species,* with a thesis incom-patible with a literal acceptance of the beginning of Genesis. The other factor was higher criticism. Although since the eighteenth century there had been increasingly penetrating critical analyses questioning the literary unity of the Pentateuch (see PENTATEUCHAL CRITICISM), the implications of this for the infallibility of the HB did not impinge generally on the English-speaking world until the ecclesiastical authorities attempted in 1863 to depose J. COLENSO, Bishop of Natal, for his *Pentateuch and the Book of Joshua Critically Examined,* a critical treatise published in 1862. In the consequent theological uproar many fundamentalists welcomed the young science of Assyriology, with its confirmation of some historical statements of the Bible, as an opportune weapon against higher criticism. G. SMITH, a banknote engraver who became a brilliant self-taught cuneiformist, explicitly avows his motivation: "Seeing the unsatisfactory state of our knowledge of those parts of Assyrian history which bore upon the history of the Bible, I felt anxious to do something towards settling a few of the questions involved." After being appointed in 1866 to work on cuneiform tablets in the Department of Oriental Antiquities in the British Museum, he particularly devoted his abilities to the search for texts relevant to the biblical narrative.

The strong initial link between the Bible and the young science of Assyriology was further shown by the name SOCIETY OF BIBLICAL ARCHAEOLOGY, given to a society founded in London in 1870 "to invesigate the archaeology, chronology, geography and history of Assyria . . . and other Biblical Lands." The society's *Transactions,* published from 1872 onward, were important for early research concerned with the bearing of Assyriology on the HB. In 1872 Smith found among the tablet fragments from Nineveh in the British Museum the Babylonian account of the deluge, which for him and for many of his contemporaries conclusively proved the literal truth of the early chapters of Genesis. After he had made his discovery public, the national enthusiasm in England for Assyriology as a weapon to prove the Bible was so great that the *Daily Telegraph* offered to pay Smith's expenses to go to Mesopotamia to seek further fragments of the deluge story.

Other scholars followed Smith's approach, emphasizing Assyriological material that appeared to have biblical significance. Enthusiasm for proving the historical truth of the Bible sometimes outran current understanding of the cuneiform material. Thus late Babylonian documents were wrongly taken to solve the problem of the otherwise unknown Darius the Mede in Dan 5:31 (W. Boscawen, *TSBA* 6 [1878] 29-30); specious cuneiform identifications were given of the kings with whom Abraham is said to have fought in Gen 14:9 (see A. Sayce [1894] 164-69); the flaming sword of Gen 3:24 was claimed to occur in the fight between Bel and the Dragon (H. Talbot, *TSBA* 5 [1876] 1-23); and Nimrod was identified with the Mesopotamian hero whose name we now know as Gilgamesh (F. Hommel, *PSBA* 8 [1895–96] 119-20). Some distinguished scholars published popular works that encouraged the view that Assyriology was virtually a branch of biblical ARCHAEOLOGY (see E. Schrader [1872] and Sayce [1894]; the latter work had an avowed apologetic purpose).

As the number of cuneiform texts available for study increased, giving insights into Babylonian civilization that had hitherto been known only through classical fragments and through the hostile eyes of biblical writers, a reaction set in against the view that the relevance of Assyriological material to the Bible was solely the extent to which it confirmed the historicity of narratives. This was particularly marked in Germany. The quantity and diversity of the cuneiform material becoming available and the sophistication of some of the religious concepts attested indicated a spiritual depth in ancient Babylonian civilization that demanded reexamination of the relationship between Babylonian and Israelite religion. The undeniable parallels came to be interpreted in terms of common origin. This view took several forms.

One view, associated with rejection of the conclusions of higher criticism, was that parts of the Pentateuch were translations from cuneiform (see Sayce [1908] 166), but this had little enduring influence. The development of most lasting significance was associated with H. GUNKEL, who in 1895 published *Schöpfung und Chaos in Urzeit und Endzeit.* As early as 1873 G. Smith had identified some fragments from the Babylonian myth of creation, *Enuma Elish.* In 1890 an improved edition became available (see Jensen [1890]) that attested to a Babylonian myth in which creation from chaos was consequent upon the defeat of a primeval monster by a god, and Gunkel showed that there were extensive traces of what he took as the same myth in the HB (see MYTHOLOGY AND BIBLICAL STUDIES). Later research has established that one element in Gunkel's hypothesis—his assumptions about the date of *Enuma Elish* and its place in Babylonian civilization—was invalid: Contrary to his assumption of great antiquity and general application, *Enuma Elish* has proved to be of no earlier origin than 1300 BCE and not a paradigmatic Babylonian myth. But this does not invalidate Gunkel's demonstration of the existence of biblical vestiges of creation myths; his work has spawned an enormous quantity of subsequent research about the nature of Israelite religion and its relationship to Babylonian religion.

New Assyriological material continued to appear, pointing to Babylonian chronological precedence in areas traditionally regarded as evidential for the revealed nature of Israelite traditions. Of particular importance was the discovery at Susa in 1901 of the stele of Hammurabi, containing a collection of laws *prima facie* similar to those of Moses, which even according to traditional biblical CHRONOLOGY they antedated by half a millennium: In some quarters the new find was taken as proof that the Mosaic laws were yet one more institution directly borrowed from Babylonia, although others rightly saw that resemblances were the result of both Mosaic and Babylonian laws resting on common Semitic custom (see Sayce [1908] 565).

The work of Gunkel was characterized by the strictest application of critical method and was limited to the application of a specific body of Assyriological data to research on Israelite literature and religion. Other scholars sought to apply Assyriological data more widely, with the basic thesis that since there were many parallels between Babylonian institutions and those of other parts of the ancient world, and since the Babylonian material in almost all instances demonstrably had chronological priority, the institutions of other parts of the ancient Near East, not least those of Israel, must have derived from Babylonian origins. As one scholar stated it, the Israelites, in touch with the advanced civilization of Mesopotamia, must "have found it extremely difficult to avoid high ideals of morality and religion" (C. Johns in A. Jeremias [1911] xvii). One facet of this approach became known as the BABEL UND BIBEL controversy after two lectures under that title given by Friedrich DELITZSCH. He overstated the Babylonian component in the HB and did so in a context that came into conflict with the orthodox view of revelation, arguing *inter alia* that the institution of the sabbath had been borrowed from the Babylonians, and treating Israelite monotheism as the result of an evolutionary process. The last vestige of the Babel und Bibel approach appeared in L. Woolley's (1936) attempt to derive the monotheism of Abraham from the worship of the moon god Sin, the patron deity of Ur and Haran, both associated in the Bible with Abraham.

The most extreme presentation of the significance of Babylonia, known as the Pan-Babylonian hypothesis (see PAN-BABYLONIANISM), held that all significant spiritual culture could be traced to origins in ancient Mesopotamia. This came to be applied not only to the HB but also to the central doctrines of the NT, so that the dying god Marduk (Bel) was seen as a precursor of JESUS Christ (see H. Radau [1908]; H. Zimmern [1910]).

New cuneiform texts and an improved understanding of older ones gradually made it clear that some of the Pan-Babylonian deductions about the relevance of Assyriological material to the Bible had been at the least naive and uncritical and in some cases (as in the supposed Babylonian origin of the sabbath) wrong. In consequence, Pan-Babylonianism gave way to a more sober evaluation of the relationship between Assyriological material and the Bible.

The tendentious use of Assyriological data to support a particular view of the Bible may still be found, but in the mainstream of HB research Assyriological material is mainly applied in one of two ways: by application to problems in individual biblical passages and in the investigation of the relevance of any new corpus of material to the HB.

2. Application to Problems in Individual Passages.
a. Data bearing upon chronology, history, or geography. i. Chronology. Assyrian material provides datings correct to one year for much of the monarchical period:

Synchronisms in biblical or cuneiform sources brought in relation to the data in Kings and Chronicles have given a comparable accuracy to biblical chronology at many points from the ninth century onward.

ii. History. Assyrian royal inscriptions from Shalmaneser III (858–824 BCE) onward contain much material of direct relevance to the Israelite and Judean kingdoms. Facile conclusions about inaccuracies in the biblical narrative are sometimes corrected by fuller understanding of the Assyriological data; thus claims by Sargon II (721–705 BCE) to have taken Samaria, contrary to the implication of 2 Kgs 17:3-6, have been shown to be false on the basis of Sargon's own earliest inscription. Letters by Assyrian administrators to the kings also contain material bearing on Israelite and Judean history, including a report by an officer of seeing a shrine in Samaria after its capture (unpublished text). Royal inscriptions of the neo-Babylonian kings yield data relevant to Judah. Thus an inscription of Nabonidus mentions the settling of military colonists, who included troops from the Levant, at oases in Arabia. Since those oases, although within Arab areas, had Jewish populations a millennium later, the colonists settled by Nabonidus must have been predominantly Jews (see C. Gadd [1958] 79-87). Neo-Babylonian economic records bearing on biblical history include ration documents found at Babylon listing provisions for Jehoiachin, king of Judah (see H. Saggs [1967] 45).

iii. Historical Geography. Assyriological material has provided a firm historical and geographical setting for many once obscure biblical place-names or tribal names. Thus Beth-Eden of Amos 1:5 was Bit-Adini in north Mesopotamia, annexed by Shalmaneser III; Togarmah, associated with Gomer and Ashkenaz in Gen 10:3, was Til-Garimmu in Asia Minor, a region important in the migrations of the Cimmerians (Gomer, cuneiform Gimirraia) and Scythians (Ashkenaz, cuneiform Asguzaia); Meshech and Tubal of Ezek 38:3 are the kingdoms of Mushki and Tabal in Asia Minor. Assyrian sources revealed the hitherto unrecognized place-name Kue as a source of Solomon's horses, concealed in MT *miqweh* of 1 Kgs 10:28.

b. Data bearing on Hebrew terminology. The existence of readily recognizable Akkadian cognates for many well-understood Hebrew words has led to a search for Akkadian cognates to elucidate problematic terms. An example is the suggestion that *qôl* in 1 Kgs 19:12 may be the equivalent of Akkadian *qūlu* (numinous silence) rather than meaning "voice." But the method may lead to dubious results if the use of comparative Semitic philology is not combined with an analysis of the literary, social, and historical contexts of the terms in both areas. Thus, although Hebrew *šabbāt* as a word is correctly equated with Akkadian *šapattu*, as an institution it neither derived from nor corresponded to the Babylonian *šapattu*. One proposed etymology for Hebrew *bĕrît* (covenant) links it to Akkadian *birīt* (between) on the grounds that a covenant is made "between" two parties; but this ignores the fact that only a small minority of the many occurrences of Akkadian *birīt* are in the context of covenant making and that the Akkadian word never became a noun with the sense of "covenant."

c. Data bearing on elements in Israelite institutions.

A. ALT's recognition of "The God of the Fathers" as an element in patriarchal religion led to a search for comparable terminology in cuneiform texts; relevant terminological parallels were shown to be present in Old Assyrian documents from Cappadocia (see *CAD,* I/J, 95a), although the significance of these for parallel concepts has been less clearly established.

Hypotheses concerning Israelite sacral kingship have made considerable use of cuneiform material. A key passage is the ritual for an Assyrian enthronement in which a priest made the cry, "*Aššur šar*" (Ashur is king!); on the basis of this the Hebrew phrase *Yahweh mālak* has been interpreted as "Yahweh has become king," which is taken as part of the evidence for an Israelite enthronement festival of Yahweh (or the human king as representative) on the Mesopotamian model (contra, see A. Johnson [1967²] 65, n. 1).

Other arguments on the sacral (or even divine) nature of the Israelite king have been based on analogy with data relating to deified kings of the III Ur Dynasty (c. 2100 BCE), but the relevance of this is highly questionable since the divine kingship attested for III Ur did not continue subsequently even in the same area and so cannot be taken as an essential element of all ancient Near Eastern kingship that may be extrapolated to Israel.

d. Data bearing on the uniqueness of Israelite religion.

This use of Assyriological data goes back to Deutero-Isaiah, who contrasted the Israelite concept of God as "the one who sits enthroned on the vaulted roof of the earth" with what he presented as the Babylonian idea of god as an image cut from a tree. But prophetic condemnations show the synchronic existence among Israelites of lower strata of religious belief alongside ethical monotheism; the Akkadian texts likewise attest a very wide range of levels of religious belief, some rising to an exalted concept of deity like that reflected in the text that says of a god, "He wears the heavens on his head like a turban." To place the highest development in Israel alongside the crudest in Babylonia, as Deutero-Isaiah did, is methodologically flawed (see Saggs [1978] 14-16).

There has been a productive comparison between Israelite and Mesopotamian religious thought in relation to ideas of divine activity in history, with some scholars seeking to establish a case for a fundamental distinction between an Israelite concept of God continuously acting in history and the Mesopotamians' seeing every aspect of human society as decreed in the beginning by the gods (see W. Lambert [1972]). This view has been challenged (see B. Albrektson [1967]; Saggs [1978] 69-92).

e. Data bearing on foreign influences on Israelite religion. i. Mythological elements possibly of Mesopotamian origin.

Research in this area has shown the continuing influence of the work of Gunkel. One important development making much use of Assyriological data was the hypothesis of a widespread pattern of cult myths throughout the ancient Near East, best attested in Babylonia but with abundant vestiges within the biblical texts, including PROPHECY (e.g., parts of Nahum, Joel, and Habakkuk), taken by some scholars as deriving from prophets acting within a cultic framework. Not only evident fragments of creation myths but also many references to destruction or combat have been interpreted within this context. The discovery of the Ugaritic mythological texts (see UGARIT AND THE BIBLE) introduced a new factor, destroying the basis for the older view that all ancient mythological material in the Bible must be ultimately of Mesopotamian origin. The search for this type of parallel tends to come from HB scholars rather than from Assyriologists, some of whom have pointed out the flimsy nature of some examples claimed (see Lambert [1965]; Saggs [1978] 192, n. 52).

ii. Pagan practices traceable to foreign influences during the monarchy.

The Prophets and historical books attest to pagan practices that were not part of accepted Mosaic Yahwism. For the proper understanding of the historical development of Israelite religion, it is necessary to distinguish between those aspects of paganism that had potentially affected Israel from the beginning as elements in the ancient religion of Palestine and those that had come in during the monarchy under foreign influences. Examination of contemporary Assyrian and Babylonian cults facilitates this distinction. There were sun cults, which the Bible regarded as recent foreign introductions (2 Kgs 23:11-12), and the details given enable these to be identified as being of Mesopotamian origin. Other cults clearly identifiable as being of late Mesopotamian origin include that of the Queen of Heaven, condemned in Jer 7:18 and 44:17-19, 25, and those mentioned in Ezek 8:14-17 (see Saggs [1960]).

3. Investigation of the Relevance of New Corpora of Assyriological Material.

The accidents of excavation constantly produce new cuneiform texts, any of which may prove to have biblical relevance; but some groups prove, or are claimed to have a setting that gives them wider relevance to the HB. Notable examples are the El Amarna tablets, cuneiform texts from Ugarit (only peripherally Assyriological), and the tablets from the Nuzi area, Mari, and most recently Ebla. Investigation of the biblical relevance of such corpora commonly follows a pattern. There is an initial brief period of exaggerated claims, followed by refutation of the wilder overstatements, and subsequently a long period of detailed research from which a general consensus about relevance to the biblical data emerges. Examples of these trends follow.

The El Amarna texts, known from 1887, did not become fully available to HB scholars until 1915 (see J. A. Knudtzon [1915]). These documents, mainly letters from rulers in Syria and Palestine, including Jerusalem, to their Egyptian suzerain in the first half of the fourteenth century BCE proved to say much about people known as Ḫabiru. Initially these references were widely regarded as directly related to the Hebrew conquest of Canaan under Joshua, which fit with the chronology apparently indicated by 1 Kgs 6:1. Further research over a long period disproved the identification of Hebrews with Ḫabiru as a people but left open the possibility that "Hebrew" as an ethnicon may have derived from the term *ḥabiru* (widespread in other cuneiform texts), which described a social class. In general the texts illustrate a political breakdown in Palestine that facilitated the subsequent Israelite settlement.

In the case of the Ugaritic material in alphabetic cuneiform from north Syria, the relevance of much of the mythology to biblical traditions about Canaanite religion was at once correctly seen. But earliest researchers mistakenly saw an even closer link to the Bible by geographical identifications that were subsequently proved to be untenable (see C. Virolleaud [1936] 16-18, 30).

Some of the most wide-reaching results of the application of Assyriology to HB research relate to the social background of particular major corpora of tablets. One of the most productive corpora in this respect has been the material from Nuzi in eastern Assyria, where about 4,000 tablets were found in excavations between 1925 and 1931, with further tablets being discovered at related sites in the same area. This material, dating from just after the middle of the second millennium, was written in Akkadian but had a strong Hurrian linguistic substratum; and the contents contained indications of many social practices that were not standard in south Mesopotamia or in Assyria. This indicated that ethnically the people were largely Hurrian; and it was known that the main Hurrian center was in Upper Mesopotamia, one of the regions that Genesis associates with the patriarchs. The social customs attested in the Nuzi documents, therefore, were applied to explain certain enigmatic features of the patriarchal narratives. A form of marriage in which a prospective son-in-law might give his services in lieu of a bride-price appeared to provide a parallel with the manner in which Jacob acquired his brides, Leah and Rachel (Genesis 29). Hurrian sale documents in which an apparently uneven bargain was made were taken as parallels to Esau's sale of his birthright for a mess of pottage (Gen 25:29-34). Data from Nuzi were also used to explain Rachel's theft of her father's household images called *těrāpîm* (Gen

31:19, 34), which in Genesis 31:30, 32 are referred to as Laban's *ʾelōhîm,* "gods." In the Nuzi material one adoption tablet mentions the right of an adoptee who was heir to take his adopted father's gods (*ilāni*). It was argued that this indicated that possession of the household gods was synonymous with rights of inheritance; the conclusion was drawn that Rachel's purpose in the theft was to establish a right to inherit from her father, an explanation given added strength by the complaint by Laban's daughters that their father had acted unjustly in relation to their inheritance (Gen 31:14-16).

Nuzi material was applied to the three narratives in Genesis in which, apparently to protect himself, a patriarch passed his wife off as his sister. The Nuzi texts show that Hurrian society had fratriarchal elements and that a brother enjoyed rights over a sister that he could transfer to another man. The other man thereby received the woman "for sistership" and could either marry her himself or marry her to a third man in return for the bride-price. In Hurrian society it was thus possible for a man to be married to a woman who in legal terms was his sister. E. SPEISER saw the biblical narratives as retaining a tradition of a Hurrian wife-sister relationship that was no longer fully understood. Nuzi parallels were also proposed for instances in the patriarchal narratives of adoption and of measures to protect the rights of a married woman.

More recently there has been a reaction, with some of the supposed parallels between patriarchal and Hurrian social customs being challenged as either irrelevant in that the basis of the parallel was not unique to the Hurrian context and period, questionable, or even invalid (see M. Selman [1980] 99-104). Thus significant differences of detail have been shown between the Hurrian form of marriage in which a son-in-law gave his services in lieu of a bride-price and the manner in which Jacob acquired Leah and Rachel as his wives. The argument rests upon the weight given to the differences of detail. In the matter of Rachel's theft of the *těrāpîm,* it has been shown that ownership of the household gods was relevant to inheritance only if they were legally transmitted as a bequest. Here again, it is possible that there was a connection but that later Israelite tradition, ignorant of Hurrian practice, omitted significant details. In the case of the supposed wife-sister marriage, it has been argued that the Nuzi evidence was misstated and, in the form presented by Speiser, never existed. The supposed parallel to Esau's sale of his birthright rested on a single Nuzi text in which what was being sold was a piece of land that had been inherited, not future inheritance rights. The bearing of Hurrian customary law on patriarchal practice in relation to adoption and marriage has also been challenged. This reaction weakens the earlier claims that much of the attested patriarchal social custom could be firmly placed within the context of Hurrian customary law but leaves open the possibility that the patriarchal narratives do contain vestiges of Hurrian practices.

Mari, the ancient city at the site of modern Tell Hariri, was excavated from 1933 onward and yielded over 20,000 cuneiform tablets, predominantly from around 1800 BCE and written in the Old Babylonian language. The initial biblical interest of the texts derived from their being dated to the period in which Abraham is traditionally placed and their discovery within the region along which Abraham must have moved in his migration from Ur, if that tradition is historical. One specific detail that appeared to have a potential biblical relevance was the frequent mention of a tribe called the Banu-iamina, who were obviously of war-like habits and troublesome to the authorities. The original excavator (not primarily a philologist) linked this tribe directly with the Israelite tribe of Benjamin, taking its presence in the Mari area as representing a stage in the Israelite migration from south Mesopotamia to Palestine. Subsequent research has shown that the postulated connection cannot be maintained.

Another detail that was invested with a direct biblical connection was the repeated occurence of the term *dawidum* in relation to warfare; the initial interpretation was that this was a term denoting "leader" or the like and that this title was the origin of the name of King David. This connection was destroyed when it was proved that *dawidum* was an earlier form of the well-known word *dabdu,* meaning "defeat," and that "to kill the *dawidum"* was an idiom meaning to inflict a defeat. A possible direct link with Abraham was seen in the mention of a city, Nahur, in the same region near Haran as the city associated with Abraham's brother Nahor (Gen 24:10). The occurrence of the name Yasmah-il has been offered as proof that the equivalent biblical Ishmael (*yiš*mā 'ē 'l*) came from the same social and historical setting. But this is inconclusive since names of the type Preterite + il also occur in south Mesopotamia in Old Akkadian, and the elements of the specific name are very common. Some scholars have seen the Hebrew tetragrammaton YHWH in the names Yawi-ila and Yawi-Adad in Mari texts, but there is no consensus on this. One significant parallel in ritual is evidence from Mari of the killing of animals in covenant making, which may be compared with the rite recorded in Gen 15:9-18 at the time of Abraham's covenant with Yahweh.

Apart from individual claimed parallels, there are two broad areas in which many scholars see the Mari material as being of major biblical relevance. First, the Mari texts give considerable information about the way of life of nomads at the time at which Abraham is convention-ally dated and in the area in which, in part, the Bible places him. This provides a setting in which the patri-archal narratives, if historical, could be placed; it does not in itself prove either that they are historical or that they were based on events datable to the time of the Mari documents.

The second broad biblical relevance claimed for the Mari material relates to prophecy. At least twelve letters from Mari refer to the giving of a message by a god through a male or female ecstatic, sometimes in con-nection with the cult but not always so. This, together with some similar evidence from Assyria and from Byblos at about 1100 BCE, makes it clear that ecstatic prophecy in the ancient Near East was not exclusively an Israelite phenomenon, although its attestation in Mari is much rarer than in Israel.

The most recent major corpus of cuneiform material with potential biblical importance comes from Tell Mardikh in north Syria, the site of the third-millennium city of Ebla. This site, excavated since 1964, up to 1978 yielded tablet fragments constituting approaching 3,000 cuneiform texts (see A. Archi [1984]). The texts are written largely in Sumerian logograms but with some words syllabically in a hitherto unknown west Semitic language that has been wrongly described as proto-Hebrew. There was the usual pattern of initial extrava-gant claims, in this case of the finding of the names of patriarchs (thus dated to the third millennium) and related place-names, including the five cities of Gen 14:2; a creation story similar to the first verses of Genesis; a flood story; and the name Ya, representing Yahweh (see C. Wilson [1977] 36-7, 48, 78). Publication and critical editing of the Ebla material is in progress, and the stage reached in investigation of its relevance to the Bible is refutation of the earliest excesses (see R. Biggs [1982]). The supposed patriarchal personal and place-names have proved to be largely phantoms, the supposed creation story is a piece of a hymn; no scien-tific evidence has yet been presented to support the claim of a flood story; and the reading Ya is doubtful, and if it is a correct reading there is no reason to link it to Yahweh (see H. Müller [1981]).

Bibliography: B. **Albrektson,** *History and the Gods: An Essay on the Idea of Historical Events as Divine Manifestations in the Ancient Near East and in Israel* (1967). A. **Archi,** "A Recent Book on Ebla," *Studi Eblaiti* 7 (1984) 23-43. R. D. **Biggs,** "The Ebla Tablets: A 1981 Persepctive," *BSMS* 2 (1982) 9-24. E. A. **Budge,** *The Rise and Progress of Assyriology* (1925). F. **Eller-Meier,** *Prophetie in Mari und Israel* (1968). I. **Engnell,** *Studies in Divine Kingship in the Ancient Near East* (1967[2]). C. J. **Gadd,** "The Harran Inscriptions of Nabonidus," *AnSt* 8 (1958) 35-92. H. **Gunkel,** *Schöpfung und Chaos in Urzeit und Endzeit: Eine religionsgeschichtliche Untersuch-ung über Gen 1 und ApJoh 12* (1895). P. **Jensen,** *Assyrische-babylonische Mythen und Epen* (1890). A. **Jeremias,** *The OT in the Light of the Ancient East: Manual of Biblical Archaeol-ogy* (1904[2]; ET, 2 vols., 1911); *Die Panbabylonisten, der alte Orient und die aegyptische Religion* (1907). A. R. **Johnson,** *Sacral Kingship in Ancient Israel* (1967[2]). J. A. **Knudtzon,** *Die El-Amarna-Tafeln* (1915). W. G. **Lambert,** "A New Look at the Babylonian Background of Genesis," *JTS* 16 (1965) 287-

300; "Destiny and Divine Intervention in Babylon and Israel," *The Witness of Tradition* (ed. G. Beck et al., 1972) 65-72. **P. Matthiae,** *Ebla, An Empire Rediscovered* (1981). **H.-P. Müller,** "Keilschriftliche Parallelen zum biblischen Hiob-buch: Möglichkeit und Grenze des Vergleichs," *Or* 47 (1978) 360-75; "Gab es in Ebla einen Gottesnamen Ja?" *ZA* 70 (1981) 70-92. **C. J. Mullo Weir,** "Nuzi," *Archaeology and OT Study* (ed. D. Winton Thomas, 1967) 73-86. **H. Radau,** *Bel, the Christ of Ancient Times* (1908). **H. C. Rawlinson,** *Abriss der babylonisch-assyrischen Geschichte* (1854). **H. W. F. Saggs,** "The Branch to the Nose [Ezek 8:17]," *JTS* 11 (1960) 318-29; "Babylon," *Archaeology and OT Study* (ed. D. Winton Thomas, 1967) 38-56; *Assyriology and the Study of the OT* (1969); *The Encounter with the Divine in Mesopotamia and Israel* (1978). **A. H. Sayce,** *The "Higher Criticism" and the Verdict of the Monuments* (1894, 1908[7], 1915[8]). **E. Schrader,** *The Cuneiform Inscriptions and the OT* (1872; ET of 2nd German ed., 2 vols., 1885–88). **M. J. Selman,** "Comparative Customs and the Patriarchal Age," *Essays on the Patriarchal Narratives* (ed. A. R. Millard and D. J. Wiseman, 1980) 93-138. **G. Smith,** *Assyrian Discoveries: An Account of Explorations and Discoveries on the Site of Nineveh, During 1873 and 1874* (1875). **E. A. Speiser,** "The Wife-sister Motif in the Patriarchal Narratives," *Oriental and Biblical Studies* (ed. J. J. Finkelstein and M. Greenberg, 1967) 62-88. **H. Tadmor,** "Azri-yau of Yaudi," *Studies in the Bible* (ed. C. Rabin, SH 8, 1961). **T. L. Thompson,** *The Historicity of the Patriarchal Narratives: The Quest for the Historical Abraham* (BZAW 133, 1974). **C. Virolleaud,** *La Légende de Keret* (MRS 2, 1936). **C. Wilson,** *Ebla Tablets: Secrets of a Forgotten City* (1977). **C. L. Wooley,** *Abraham: Recent Discoveries and Hebrew Origins* (1936). **H. Zimmern,** *Zum Streit um die "Christusmythe": Das babylonische Material in seinen Hauptpunkten dargestellt* (1910).

H. W. F. SAGGS

ASTRUC, JEAN (1684–1766)

Born at Suave, Languedoc, Mar. 19, 1684, A. was the son of a former Huguenot pastor who had con-verted to Catholicism following the Edict of Nantes (1685) and by whom he was taught the Bible and Hebrew. By age nineteen A. had earned BA, MA, and MD degrees. He rapidly won a wide reputation in medi-cine, teaching at Montpellier and Toulouse (1707–29), eventually becoming professor and dean of the medi-cal faculty at the College Royal in Paris (1730) as well as a consulting physician to the court of Louis XV (from 1720).

Acknowledging earlier suggestions by J. LE CLERC, R. SIMON, C. Fleury, and le François that Moses had used documents in composing Genesis, A. in 1753 reluctantly published his anonymous *Conjectures,* which set out to deconstruct the present text, to reproduce the original sources, to explain the present confusion and duplica-tions in the text, and to vindicate Moses from careless workmanship. His volume consisted of a preface (1-2), preliminary remarks (3-24), Genesis 1–Exodus 2 ar-ranged according to the reproduced sources (25-280), his conjectures (281-495), and an index (496-524). He distinguished four primary and eight minor sources (*memoirs*), some very fragmentary, which Moses inher-ited from his ancestors or procured from neighboring nations. The two major sources were distinguished pri-marily on the basis of their use of divine names, either Jehovah (YHWH) or Elohim; the other two significant sources contained further duplicate material and narra-tives about non-Hebrews. A. conjectured that Moses arranged these documents in parallel columns similar to a Gospel harmony so that accounts of the same event or period were placed side by side. Later copyists working prior to the time of Ezra destroyed the Mosaic presentation and in transcription integrated the columns, thus producing the present difficulties in the text. A. also suggested possible authors for some of the material: Joseph for his story, Levi for the Dinah story (Genesis 34), Amram and Levi for Exodus 1–2, and so forth.

An abridged version of A.'s volume was published in German (1782) and in English (*Scriptural Interpreter* 6 [1836] 218-26; 7 [1837] 23-31, 80-94). Unlike H. WIT-TER's earlier but more limited work, A.'s work stimu-lated and influenced the documentary analysis of the Pentateuch (see PENTATEUCHAL CRITICISM).

Works: *Conjectures sur les mémoires originaux dont il parait que Moise s'est servi pour composer la Genèse, avec des remarques qui appuient ou éclaireissent ces conjectures* (1753); *Dissertations sur l'immatériaité, l'immortalité et la liberté l'âme* (1755).

Bibliography: **A. Lods,** "A. et la critique biblique de son temps," *RHPR* 4 (1924) 109-39, 210-27. **A. Lods and P. Alphandéry,** *J. A. et la critique biblique au XVIIIe siècle* (1924). **A. C. Lorry,** "Vie d'Astruc," *Mémoires pour servir à l'histoire de la faculté de médecine de Montpellier* (J. Astruc, 1767). **E. O'Doherty,** "The *Conjectures* of J. A., 1753," *CBQ* 15 (1953) 300-304. **H. Osgood,** *Presbyterian and Reformed Review* 3 (1892) 83-102. **J. de Savignac,** "L'oeuvre et la personnalité de J. A.," *La Nouvelle Clio* 5 (1953) 138-47. **R. de Vaux,** "A propos du second centenaire d'Astruc: Réflexions sur l'état actuel de la critique du Pentateuque" (VTSup 1, 1953) 182-98.

J. H. HAYES

ATHANASIUS (c. 296–373)

A.'s attitude toward Scripture entailed a paradigmatic shift in the history of biblical interpretation. Too often acclaimed as the political and stubborn defender of the Nicene Creed, he revealed his true personality as an interpreter of holy writ. A. was thoroughly a biblical theologian. The turmoil of the so-called Arian crisis (see ARIUS), the rallying of the monastic movement in Egyp-tian Christianity, pastoral urgencies in Alexandria after a decade of persecution, and the beginning of the Constantinian era were reason enough for his exegesis of Scripture to be militant, dogmatic as well as mystical. Modern scholars have sometimes failed to appreciate how creative A. could be on both of these interpretive levels.

Elected to the see of Alexandria in August 328 when not yet thirty years old, A. wrote the first of his *Festal Letters* during the months to follow. A genuine piece of allegory in keeping with ORIGEN's letter and spirit, it celebrates Easter in a paraphrasis of the Song of Songs and is filled with references to biblical mysticism. As a proven pastor and a recognized intellectual leader, A. could still express his admiration for Origen in a manner uncharacteristic of a fourth-century bishop in his *Letter on the Decrees of Nicaea* (c. 350). A.'s mystical exegesis of Scripture is best illustrated in the *Festal Letters,* in the exquisite *Letter to Marcellinus on How to Read the Psalms,* and in the famous *Life of Antony.*

From the time of his second exile (339–346), A. had deliberately changed the style and motivation of his biblical exegesis. Scripture had become for him like a mirror reflecting the actual significance of God's incarnation. Only in Scripture did A. find the right words to describe what was happening in the church of his time, as well as in his own Christian experience. His exegesis had shifted toward a new kind of hermeneutic, from a highly spiritualized anthropology to the actual institutions of church communities as he knew them. Through a narrative paraphrase of HB stories and a bold appropriation of biblical statements, he could give an account of his own struggle in favor of ALEXANDRIAN orthodoxy. In the first decade of his episcopal ministry, when writing *On the Incarnation* (c. 335), he had opposed Arianism by making the incarnation of the divine Logos the sole and decisive point of departure for any Christian theory on the divine Trinity. In *Contra Arianos* 1-2 (c. 339), he conceived the whole system of his Trinitarian doctrine by which he intended to protect the faithful from Arianism through a set of dogmatic interpretations of such disputed scriptural quotations as Phil 2:5-7 and Prov 8:22-23. He would never modify further his HERMENEUTICS; Scripture as a whole voiced for him the truth of what was at stake in the debates between Christian factions.

Works: *Festal Letters* (329–373); *On the Incarnation of the Word* (c. 335); *Orations Against the Arians* 1-2 (c. 339); *Circular Letter to the Bishops of Egypt and Libya* (356); *Life of Antony* (c. 360); *Letter to Marcellinus* (date unknown).

Bibliography: D. **Arnold,** *The Early Episcopal Career of A. of Alexandria, AD 328–AD 335* (1990). **J. J. Brogan,** *HHMBI,* 17-22. **H. von Campenhausen,** *The Greek Fathers of the Church* (1959). **R. P. C. Hanson,** *The Search for the Christian Doctrine of God: The Arian Controversy, 318–381*

(1988); *IHE,* 1:137-64. **C. Kannengiesser,** "Les citations bibliques du traité athanasien sur l'Incarnation du Verbe et les Testimonia," *La Bible et les Pères* (1970); "Le recours au Livre de Jérémie chez A. d'Alexandrie," *Epektasis* (FS J. Daniélou, 1972); "A. of Alexandria and the Holy Spirit Between Nicaea I and Constantinople I," *ITQ* 48 (1981) 166-80; (ed. with P. Bright), *Early Christian Spirituality* (1986); "A. of Alexandria and the Ascetic Movement of His Time," *Asceticism* (1995) 479-92; "A. von Alexandrien als Exeget," *Stimuli* (FS E. Dassmann, 1996) 336-43. **P. Merendino,** *Paschale Sacramentum* (1965). **J. Quasten,** *Patrology* 3 (1983) 20-79. **W. Schneemelcher,** "Der Schriftgebrauch in den Apologien des A.," *Text-Wort-Glaube* (1980). **H. J. Sieben,** "A. über den Psalter: Analyse seines Briefes an Marcellinus," *Theologie und Philosophie* 48 (1973) 157-73. **G. C. Stead,** "St. A. on the Psalms," *VC* 39 (1985) 65-78.

C. KANNENGIESSER

ATHENAGORAS (2nd cent.)

A Christian apologist in the second half of the second century CE, A. addressed his *Plea,* written in defense of Christianity, to the emperors Marcus Aurelius and Commodus when they visited Athens in 177. In *Plea* he refuted accusations of atheism, cannibalism, and Oedipean incest, stressing the pure morality of the Christians and the rational convenience of their faith. In *On the Resurrection* he argued in favor of an afterlife: Given God's omnipotence, it is possible; given the duality of the human being, it is necessary. The body, destroyed by death, needs to be restored in the final resurrection of the dead for a judgment of the united and complete human being.

Both apologies present a similar lexical index and way of arguing. Objections against the authenticity of *On the Resurrection* have not been convincing. Scripture is sparsely used in both, addressed as they are to pagan audiences. Allusions to or quotations from the HB refer to Genesis 1 (*Plea* 13:2; *Res.* 12:6); 6:1-5 (*Plea* 24:5-6); Exod 20:12, 14 (*Res.* 23:3-4); Isa 22:13 (*Plea* 12:2; *Res.* 19:3); 43:10-11 (*Plea* 9:2); 44:6 (*Plea* 9:2); 66:1 (*Plea* 9:2); Psalm 103 (*Plea* 13:2); Prov 8:22 (*Plea* 10:4); 21:1 (*Plea* 18:2); Bar 3:36 (*Plea* 9:2); Add Enoch 6:1-2; 7:2-3; 9:9 (*Plea* 24:5-6). References to the Gospels occur even more rarely. Pauline literature is privileged with thirteen direct or indirect quotations in both apologies (for a full analysis, see B. Pouderon [1989]).

Works: *Opera: Ad optimos libros MSS* (Corpus apologetarum Christianorum Secundi 7, 1969).

Bibliography: L. W. **Barnard,** *A.: A Study in Second-century Christian Apologetic* (1972). **R. M. Grant,** *Greek Apologists of the Second Century* (1989) 100-111. **B. Pouderon,** *Athénagore d'Athènes Philosophe Chrétien* (1989). **W. Schoedel,** *A.: Legatio and De Resurrectione* (1972).

C. KANNENGIESSER

AUERBACH, ERICH (1892–1957)

A distinguished Romance philologist forced out of Nazi Germany in 1935, A. wrote *Mimesis: The Representation of Reality in Western Literature* (1946; ET 1953; since published in Spanish, Italian, and Hebrew) while in Turkey. He compared the epic of Abraham's conative sacrifice of Isaac with Homer's account of Odysseus's scar and concluded that the Hebrew narrator's relation to the truth of his story was far more passionate and definite than Homer's. He noted that in the HB "the sublime, tragic, and problematic take shape precisely in the domestic and commonplace" and that the "sublime and the everyday are not only actually unseparated but basically inseparable." He further compared Petronius's description of Fortunata with Mark's account of Peter's betrayal and concluded that the biblical author, by depicting the shabby act of a common person, is writing directly for every one. A.'s greatest debtors were the biblical realists (e.g., O. Piper), who took A.'s point seriously and concluded that the AUTHORITY OF THE BIBLE emerged primarily from its realism, the way it captured the imagination and the failings of common people and provided a source of hope for them. Both the evil and the good, the demonic and the divine emerge through the literary style of the Bible.

Works: For a list of A.'s works, see **K. Gronau,** *Literarische Form und gesellschaftliche Entwicklung* (1979) 191.

Bibliography: **F. Gogarten,** "Das abendländische Geschichtsdenken: Bermerkungen zu dem Buch von E. A. *Mimesis,*" *ZTK* 51 (1954) 270-360. **G. Green,** *Literary Criticism and the Structure of History: E. A. and L. Spitzer* (1982) 11-82.

W. KLASSEN

AUGUSTINE OF HIPPO (354–430)

During his Manichee decade (373–383), A. was a combative critic of Catholic orthodoxy, especially attacking the OT as incompatible in ethics with the NT and as containing no real prophecies; asserting the presence of drastic interpolations in the NT, e.g., the birth narratives of Matthew and Luke, pointing to the incompatible genealogies; and rejecting as impossible the actuality of the crucifixion. Manichees claimed to offer reasoned argument where the church only invited one to trust AUTHORITY and forbade questions.

The problem of authority was far from central to A.'s conversion at Milan (386) yet was entailed by it. Baptized in 387, he now gave his allegiance to the faith of the community for which Scripture was a God-given book. A series of anti-Manichee tracts vindicated the OT and the integrity of the NT and analyzed (*de utilitate credendi*) the question of authority. The OT prophesied Christ (see PROPHECY AND PROPHETS, HB); levitical sacrifices were types of his redemption, while the Hebrew prophets foretold the incarnation, the conversion of the Gentiles, the overthrow of idolatry, the persecutions of the faithful, and the last things. "The meaning of the NT lies hidden in the OT, that of the OT is revealed by the NT." The principal difficulties for this thesis lay in moral issues of the OT: the physical anthropomorphisms of OT language about God (jealousy, God of battles, divine wrath, the concern of religion with prosperity in this world, the ethnic ceremonies of circumcision and sabbath and food laws, instances of mendacity by OT heroes). Against Manichee catalogues of antitheses between the testaments, A. closed the gaps: Both testaments tell the same story; although they use different signs and sacraments, they have a single Author.

A. did not distinguish allegory and typology as modern writers do. His use of allegory did not deny the "history," although he granted that texts apparently incomprehensible or absurd are pointers to the necessity of spiritual interpretation. At Milan AMBROSE had taught him (through 2 Corinthians 3) that literal interpretation is pernicious; allegory, life-giving; later (*On the Spirit and the Letter,* 412) A. reinterpreted the Pauline text (see PAUL) in an anti-Pelagian sense (see PELAGIUS) to mean that law kills if the life-giving inner grace of the Spirit is absent. But even the creation story of Genesis 1–3 has a valid literal interpretation: The *Literal Exposition of Genesis* does not take these chapters as a matter-of-fact piece of creation science but insists that they are not a complicated way of talking about the eternity of the world and the immortality of the soul, as a Platonist might have hoped A. would say. Being inspired, Moses described the act and process of creation as an expression of God's will and goodness, implying that because it was created out of nothing this world is contingent and precarious, "tending to go to nothingness" were it not sustained by the Creator.

Allegory or spiritual interpretation for A. was far more than an exegetical device; it was a metaphysical principle, coherent with God's way of using symbols and external signs, which are necessary for fallen humanity. Bible and sacraments are alike in being God-given means of grace, but they are relative to our condition. "Even the NT is revelation only through a mirror and in an enigmatic form," for in this life we are pilgrims on the road and need mediating signs, which are all that words can be.

How can allegory avoid being merely arbitrary? Obscure texts should be interpreted by those that are clear. In some passages A. stressed the perspicuity of Scripture as the source in which everything essential to salvation can be found and as the very ground for the church's rule of faith. But other texts concede that not everything essential to a complete grasp of God's truth is self-evident to every reader and that control over the validity of exegesis is given by the traditional "rule of faith" of the Roman Catholic Church. A. often emphasized that the text of the Bible may have several different interpretations, all valid provided that they do not conflict with the rule of faith; he wrote critically (especially in the *Confessions*) of interpreters who imagine that their own exegesis is the only correct one.

Nevertheless, he sought to find rules and principles by which hermeneutical work (see HERMENEUTICS) could find objectivity. In this he was influenced by the "Book of Rules" (*liber regularum*) by the Donatist schismatic TYCONIUS, whose principles were mainly broad theological axioms: that as the Lord is head of his body, the church, there is some interchange between what is said of him and what is said of his people; that, nevertheless, the church is "two-sided" (A. preferred to say "mixed," of good and bad); that one must distinguish promises (Spirit, grace) from law and special or particular from general and universal; that Scripture sometimes uses part for whole or whole for part, especially with numbers, and sometimes narrates events in the reverse order (i.e., the "flashbacks"). A. himself observed other common features of biblical writers: their use of the past tense when foretelling the future; their frequent use of the third person when speaking autobiographically; the use of the generic *homo* (human being of either sex or humankind), which was translated *vir* (male) in the Latin Bible; and, of special theological interest, their speaking of signs as being the thing signified. In several places, but especially in *De doctrina christiana* (a work much concerned with principles of scriptural interpretation), he insisted that the study of Scripture should not be undertaken merely to satisfy "curiosity" but for the sake of Scripture's primary end, the love of God and one's neighbor.

Nevertheless, the Bible is not a self-contained and self-explanatory collection of writings. A. regretted that some Christians of his time read no book other than Scripture and even conversed with one another in the strange "translationese" of the OL Bible (an anticipation of Quaker English). A good interpreter needed to know the original languages. A. laboriously learned Greek but left Hebrew to his contemporary JEROME; he was relieved from the necessity of studying it by his belief that the Greek translators of the SEPTUAGINT were inspired, each translator (according to the legend) having worked independently and produced the same version. This belief went with the view of biblical INSPIRATION toward which A. increasingly moved as he grew older, that God inspired not only the substance and thought but also, at least in places, the very words. Hence A.'s exegesis of, e.g., the psalms often takes each word separately. Proper names, numbers, titles, and indeed the very order of the psalms are clues to their significance.

Yet the eternal words of Scripture were not, for him, "revelation." They remain mere words unless divine grace brings inward illumination. "Even the words of Jesus himself are problematic (*proverbia*), understood only by the Spirit's revealing." The NT discloses the meaning of the OT, but this does not mean that the text brings us a direct vision of all truth. The meaning of the Bible is disclosed to the person who reads it with love and humility (*amore revelatur*), for God is love, and it is by love that God is known. Because that relationship is a process of growth, A. could see Scripture both as an instrument of God's self-revelation in which both the OT and the NT tell the same essential story and as a means of progressive education toward salvation. Therefore, the expositor's exegesis can never be final but is always open to deeper understanding, subject to the broad, overriding principles that the Bible is the church's book, and that the church's faith in God through Christ in the Holy Spirit is the controlling criterion of interpretation.

By the same principle, apocryphal texts (popular among the Manichees) may not be read in the church lectionary. A.'s OT CANON included 1–2 Esdras, Tobit, Judith, Esther, Ecclesiasticus, Wisdom, and Maccabees; his NT canon included 2 Peter and Hebrews (of whose authorship and authority the West, but not the East, had doubts). He held apocryphal texts to be permitted reading for well-established believers but granted that "none is obliged to believe Joachim the name of Mary's father."

A. expressly denied that Scripture is the sole medium through which God speaks to humanity; God's Word may also be heard through the created order. But Scripture above all else represented for him, together with the universal consent of the church, the principal authority central to belief in a divinely given salvation for an ignorant, lost, neurotic humanity.

Works: *On the Psalms; Unfinished Commentary on Genesis; Exposition on the Sermon on the Mount; Exposition of 84 Propositions Concerning the Epistle to the Romans; Exposition of the Epistle to the Galatians; Unfinished Exposition of the Epistle to the Romans; The Agreement of the Gospel Writers; Literal Commentary on Genesis; Tractates on the Gospel and First Epistle of John; The Spirit and the Letter; Tractates on the Gospel According to John,* available in CCSL 13-57 and PL 32-47; ET in NPNF 1-8 (1887–92) and Fathers of the Church (1947–).

Bibliography: **A.-M. la Bonnardière,** *A. and the Bible* (BTT 3, 1986; ET 1997). **P. Brown,** *A. of Hippo: A Biography* (1967). **M. Comeau,** *A., exégète du quartième évangile* (1930). **B. Delarocche,** *Saint A. lecteur et interprète de Saint Paul dans le "De peccatorum meritis et remissione"* (1996). **U. Duchrow,** *Sprachverständnis und biblisches Hören bei A.* (HUT 5, 1965). **M. Fiedrowicz,** *Psalmos vox totius Christi: Studien zu A. "Enarrationes in Psalmos"* (1997). **V. Goldschmidt,** "Exégèse et Axiomatique chez St. A.," *Hommage à Martial Guérolt* (ed. L. J. Beck et al., 1964) 14-42. **C. Harrison,** *Beauty and Revelation in the Thought of Saint A.* (1992). **B. D. Jackson,**

"The Theory of Signs in St. A.'s *De doctrina christiana*," *REA* 15 (1969) 9-49. **C. Kannengiesser,** *HHMBI,* 22-38. **R. Lorenz,** "Die Wissenschaftslehre A.s," *ZKG* 67 (1955–56) 29-60, 213-51. **R. A. Markus,** "Saint A. on History, Prophecy, and Inspiration," *Augustinus* 12 (1967) 271-80. **C. P. Mayer,** *Die Zeichen in der geistigen Entwicklung und in der Theologie des jungen A.* (2 vols., 1969, 1974). **A. D. R. Polman,** *The Word of God According to St. A.* (1955; ET 1961). **M. Pontet,** *L'exégèse de St. A. prédicateur* (Theologie 7, 1944). **H. Sasse,** "Sacra Scriptura: Bemerkungen zur Inspirationslehre A.," *F. Dornseiff zum 65. Geburtstag* (FS, ed. H. Kusch, 1953) 258-73. **H. J. Sieben,** "Die res der Bibel," *REA* 21 (1975) 72-90. **G. Strauss,** *Schriftgebrauch, Schriftauslegung, und Schriftbeweis bei A.* (BGBH 1, 1959). **B. B. Warfield,** *Calvin and A.* (1907). **W. Wieland,** *Offenbarung bei A.* (TubTS 12, 1978). **D. F. Wright,** "A.: His Exegesis and Hermeneutics," *HB/OT: The History of Its Interpretation* (1, 1, ed. M. Saebø, 1996) 701-30.

H. CHADWICK

AUTHORITY OF THE BIBLE

Throughout history the Bible has influenced the development of Christian art (see ART AND BIBLICAL INTERPRETATION), literature (see WESTERN LITERATURE, THE BIBLE AND), morality, and especially theology. Christians have affirmed the authority of the Bible in church life, but different theologians, denominations, and schools of thought have exhibited great diversity in understanding the nature of this authority.

1. History of Biblical Authority. JESUS and the early church used Hebrew Scriptures and the SEPTUAGINT as their authoritative literature, even though the canonical form (see CANON OF THE BIBLE) had not yet arisen. In their interpretation some texts were more authoritative than others, and frequently passages were not understood literally. This approach set the standard for later Christians (see R. Grant and D. Tracy [1984] 8-16).

In the patristic church the writings of the NT received gradual acceptance until their fourth-century canonization. The faith of the church was the norm for canonization, but once created the canon assumed the greater authority. However, church fathers perceived that using scriptural passages as a theological authority without this "rule of faith" could lead to heresy. The apostolic faith remained the basic authority behind the Bible. Theologians differed in hermeneutical approaches (see HERMENEUTICS). The ALEXANDRIAN SCHOOL (see CLEMENT; ORIGEN) allegorized texts to avoid crude anthropomorphisms and to obtain Christian insights; the ANTIOCHENES (see THEODORE OF MOPSUESTIA; CHRYSOSTOM) were more literal in an attempt to find meaning without allegorical excesses. Theologians, especially Origen, Chrysostom, and AUGUSTINE, often spoke of divine "accommodation" or "condescension" in God's revelation to finite human beings (see J. Rogers and D. McKim [1979] 11-34).

In the Middle Ages the approach to the Bible was influenced by the rise of scholastic methods. Interpreters used the fourfold way to obtain meaning: literal, allegorical, tropological (moral), and anagogical (eschatological) senses. Only a few, like the Victorines (see HUGH OF ST. VICTOR, RICHARD OF ST. VICTOR, ANDREW OF ST. VICTOR) and NICHOLAS OF LYRA, who followed Jewish scholars like RASHI, pursued the literal-historical interpretative approach that later influenced the Reformers (see J. McNeil, *IB* 1:119-22).

With the Reformation the Protestant insistence on *sola scriptura* was an attempt to replace tradition, philosophy, and ecclesiastical structures with the Bible as the primary theological authority. Since both LUTHER and CALVIN held Christ to be the authority behind the Scriptures, they could assess critically the text and the culturally bound ideas found therein. For each the Scriptures spoke to the heart as much as to the mind and were validated by the inner testimony of the Spirit. Calvin was the more systematic theologian of the two, and his biblical commentaries were oriented more exegetically. Although he did not criticize the text as freely as Luther did, he nonetheless spoke of divine accommodation (see J. Reid [1957] 29-72; E. Kraeling [1955] 9-32).

Roman Catholic polemics against Protestant theology undermined the authority of the Bible in favor of ecclesiastical authority. Theologians produced models of INSPIRATION and authority that limited the extent of biblical authority; hence they were called minimalists (L. Lessius, F. Suarez, J. Bonfrère, R. Simon, J. Jahn, D. Haneberg [1550–1870]). The Bible was authoritative only because God provided negative assistance to avoid errors or because the church subsequently granted authority to these works (see J. Burtchaell [1969] 44-56). However, many defended a maximalist view that attributed a high view of inspiration or even dictation to the text (M. Cano, D. Bañez, C. Billuart [1550–1750]). The Council of Trent (1545–63) provided ideas not too dissimilar to Protestant definitions when it described Scripture as the *norma normans non normatus,* the "norm that governs but is not governed," so that Scripture was perceived as foundational for tradition.

With the rise of empirical sciences, DEISM, and rationalism, the authority of the Bible was challenged. The age of orthodoxy (1600–1750) saw the Bible as a compendium of theological statements, a view buttressed by increasingly defensive appeals to its authority by both Lutheran (J. Gerhard, J. Quenstedt) and Reformed (P. Vermigli, T. Beza, F. Turretin [1847; ET 1981]) theologians. The "material principle" (justification by faith or the gospel) became subordinate to the "formal principle" (Bible). In particular, Turretin (1632–87) used scholastic-Aristotelian methods to articulate the doctrine of Scripture (see Kraeling, 33-42; Rogers and McKim, 147-99).

The nineteenth century saw the rise of biblical criticism. The roots of this movement lay in seventeenth-century English Deism and in the eighteenth-century German Enlightenment (see H. G. Reventlow [ET 1985] 1-414). Combined with the philosophical idealism of G. W. F. Hegel (1770–1831) and the Romantic theology of F. SCHLEIERMACHER, the greater majority of theologians moved from orthodoxy to liberalism. Authority was posited in the human dimension, in the religious experience, or in the intellectual quest for understanding. Inspiration was attributed to the persons who created the Scriptures rather than to the biblical text (see W. Sanday's Bampton Lectures [1894]) and was defined as religious genius. NT methods were pioneered by the Tübingen school, and J. WELL-HAUSEN outlined the evolution of Hebrew Scriptures.

Critical thought influenced theology greatly, and the late nineteenth century witnessed the rise of liberal theologians like A. von HARNACK, A. RITSCHL, and E. TROELTSCH. Only a few theologians adhered either to confessional movements or to traditional orthodoxy. The most notable examples of the latter position were the Reformed Princeton theologians (see A. ALEXANDER, C. HODGE; A. A. HODGE; B. B. WARFIELD), who combined the scholastic theology of Turretin with the eighteenth-century Scottish commonsense realism of T. Reid (1710–96) as mediated through J. Witherspoon (1723–94) in America (see M. Noll [1983]). Their view of the Bible as inerrant became the point of dispute in the modernist-fundamentalist debates among twentieth-century Protestants (see Rogers and McKim, 235-361).

Although at first only conservative Protestants were threatened by critical thought, the same controversy also came to Roman Catholic circles, in which debate over the nature of inspiration arose in the nineteenth century. Advocates of "content inspiration" (Ger., *Realinspiration;* Lat., *res et sententiae*) proposed that only certain portions of Scripture were inspired, while other sections reflected a limited biblical worldview (J. Franzelin; F. Lenormant; C. Pesch; J. Newman [1967]). Most proponents of this view were Jesuits, and their position was criticized by Dominican theologians who advocated a more strict "verbal inspiration" (H. Denzinger, M.-J. Lagrange). The former position predominated until the encyclical PROVIDENTISSIMUS DEUS (1893) of Leo XIII; then the latter view was ascendant until the modernist controversy (1907–20) cast suspicion upon both positions. Encyclicals like *Pascendi Domenici Gregis* (1907) by Pius X and SPIRITUS PARACLITUS (1920) by Benedict XV condemned all views of inspiration that lacked the notion of inerrancy. This trend was reversed, however, when in 1943 Pius XII issued the encyclical DIVINO AFFLANTE SPIRITU, which accepted critical biblical methods. Roman Catholic biblical scholarship began anew, and the document "Verbum Dei" by Vatican II furthered this impetus (see B. Vawter [1972] 70-71, 143-50; Burtchaell, 58-163).

Among Protestants in the twentieth century a wide range of opinions has been presented on biblical authority and inspiration. K. BARTH, E. Brunner, and other Neo-orthodox theologians proclaimed the Bible as the medium through which the authoritative Word of God might address people. Related biblical studies used the model of salvation history to describe the Bible, and the authority behind the text lay in the events to which it testified (see G. von RAD; G. E. WRIGHT; J. BRIGHT [1967]; O. CULLMANN). Existential theology maintained that the text was authoritative when it addressed the situation of the reader or listener (see R. BULTMANN). Such trends in theology as process thought, theology of hope, LIBERATION THEOLOGY, FEMINIST theology, various POST-MODERN and deconstructionist theologies (see STRUCTURALISM AND DECONSTRUCTION), and others have moved in a more liberal direction; but they still attend to the biblical text as a primary theological resource. Concern with the hermeneutical approach to the Bible typifies the quest of these more contemporary theologies.

2. Models of Biblical Authority. The following typology may reflect in a general fashion the ways in which biblical authority has been understood.

a. Inspiration. The most frequently affirmed model is to declare the Bible authoritative by virtue of its inspiration or authorship by God (2 Tim 3:16; 2 Peter 1:20-21). Since the divine-human relationship in the process of inspiration is not explained by the text, great debate has arisen over its exact nature.

A modern conservative view declares the very words to be inspired or dictated by God (verbal inspiration) and the text to be inspired in all parts (full or plenary inspiration). The text is without error in matters of faith and human knowledge, though inerrancy is sometimes limited only to the original texts or autographs. Early advocates appeared in the age of orthodoxy (Gerhard, Quenstedt, Turretin), but the concept of inerrancy was developed most fully among the nineteenth-century Princeton theologians. For them Scripture was absolute truth, and texts were treated as propositional revelation for the articulation of theology and morals. Contemporary advocates stress biblical accuracy in matters of science and history and sternly criticize Christians who adhere to a position other than this (R. Pache, T. Engelder, E. Young, F. Schaeffer, J. Packer, J. Montgomery, J. Gerstner, G. Archer). Others who are less dogmatically inclined admit authentic Christian theology can be done without such a strict definition of inerrancy (E. Carnell; C. Henry [1976]; D. Fuller; C. Pinnock [1984]; J. R. Michaels).

Many evangelicals (see EVANGELICAL BIBLICAL INTERPRETATION) affirm a more flexible definition that views Scripture as inspired and infallible in regard to theology and morals but not inerrant in matters of history and science. Culturally and historically conditioned literature was produced by human authors through whom God communicated by accommodation. This view appears to reflect the position of Augustine, Luther, and Calvin more sensitively. Modern proponents have included European Reformed theologians (H. Bavinck; A. Kuyper G. Berkouwer [1975]; J. Orr [1910]) and Roman Catholics who advocated verbal inspiration (M.-J. Lagrange; A. Bea; G. Lohfink; O. Loretz [1964; ET 1968]; D. Harrington; J. Scullion [1970]). Contemporary evangelical Protestants defending this view, however, often find themselves on the defensive in denominational controversies (D. Beegle [1973]; S. Davis [1977]; R. Alley [1970]; D. Hubbard; P. Jewett; Rogers; McKim; see R. Johnston [1979] 15-47).

Some theologians perceive only the ideas or content to be inspired, considering the words to be the product of people culturally conditioned. The Word of God, mixed with erring human words, speaks authoritatively because it arises from theological, intellectual, and deep experiential dimensions (J. Semler, W. R. Smith, Franzelin, Newman). J. H. NEWMAN, for example, said that Scripture has authority in matters of faith, but the rest of the text, the *obiter dicta,* is not binding and could contain error (1967, 102-53).

Inspiration might be associated with the experience of the biblical spokespersons but not the writings, since the writings were produced by different people. Inspiration may refer to the divine/human encounter or to the religious genius of a sensitive individual, to the communion of a person with the divine force either externally or internally. This genius has authority today when it exhibits the power to create a religious community and relive the experiences of the original prophets (see PROPHECY AND PROPHETS, HB). Levels of inspiration exist according to the degree of divine truth expressed. Under the impulse of Romanticism this notion was born, and it was followed by later German idealists and by the confessional Erlangen School (see J. G. HERDER, J. J. GRIESBACH). More recent articulation was offered by SANDAY, H. FOSDICK, and especially C. H. DODD (1929, 27-28, 264-70).

The modern scholarly perception that the biblical text was the result of a long process of oral tradition, precipitation into writing, written redaction, and finally canonization has led to a view of inspiration attributing the charism to the entire community of faith that produced Scripture. Roman Catholics like P. BENOIT (1965), K. Rahner (1961), D. MCCARTHY, and especially J. MCKENZIE have defined this as social inspiration. Their more organic view understands the relation of Scripture and tradition, although the discussion about inspired community may lead to theological rationales for ecclesiastical authority (Rahner). Protestants like J. Barr use similar imagery, but the emphasis lies on individuals within the community who participated in the developmental process of creating Scripture. Since such individuals often stand in tension with their religious communities (Job, Paul), the charism or inspiration should not be attributed to the entire community (McKenzie [1962]).

b. Salvation history. Among late twentieth-century biblical theologians the Bible is viewed as the record of salvific events initiated by God for the chosen people, a record of divine irruptions into human history (exodus of Israel, resurrection of Jesus) whereby God delivered, constituted, and preserved the holy people. The community of faith was created by those events and looks to them for self-understanding. Traditions develop around those primal events, and theological interpretation turns to them as the norm for faith. The Bible's authority is derived from the events to which it testifies (von Rad; Wright [1952] 11-128; Cullman; Bright; P. Minear).

Several scholars have been reluctant to point to the events as the source of authority since events are inascertainable things, and all we have are interpretations of the events. An event is meaningless until interpreted by faith within the religious community, be it Israel or the ancient church. Von Rad and Bultmann considered Scripture to be faith interpretations of events with little or no historicity. Not only is the original history unrecoverable, it is unimportant, since the interpretations alone have meaning and authority for us.

W. Pannenberg (ET 1968, 90-152), J. Moltmann (ET 1967, 15-238); T. Rendtorff, U. Wilckens, and others moved the locus of authority from the text to the arena of history itself, turning to the present social and historical realities as the sources for theology. God does more than offer revelation in history; rather, history is revelation, the continuing arena of divine self-disclosure. Thus history becomes the primary category in theologizing rather than mere reports of divine events.

c. Existentialism. Existential models move the locus of authority from the text or the category of history to the individual who hears and responds to the Word of God. When a person is confronted by the preached word, the past becomes alive again in the context of faith.

This scholarly hermeneutic was advocated by Neoorthodox theologians (Barth, Brunner, F. Gogarten) and the Heideggerian existentialists of Bultmann's school. For Barth (ET 1928, 522-44) the Bible contains the Word of God, but it becomes such only when listeners are confronted by the *viva vox,* preaching and teaching. Bultmann declared the message to be authoritative when it confronts an individual to condemn inauthentic existence and to elicit response—the acceptance of freedom and responsibility (see Pannenberg, 153-62).

A less radical mode of interpretation views the text as authoritative when it describes situations parallel to our own. Since believers face many of the same problems as did their biblical counterparts, their elicited response may be a guideline for the modern age when properly translated from that cultural context. The rationale behind the biblical text is applied to the modern situation in a fashion appropriate to human need. Preaching should relive authentically the experience of the text in order to find the common spiritual bond between ancient and modern people. When the text addresses religious needs in similar situations, it speaks with authority.

Scholars sympathetic to artistic and literary dimensions perceive scriptural images, not in logical, ideational, or positivistic categories, but as poetic and symbolic images that inspire. Non-rational symbols communicate transcendent truth more effectively than propositions and evoke a full range of intellectual and emotive response: doctrine, liturgy, preaching, teaching, and art. Biblical authority lies in the power of its symbols to evoke a full religious response (F. Farrar [1886]; L. S. Thornton [1950]; G. Moran; H. Frei; L. Alonso-Schökel [1965] 91-105, 296-99, 376-85).

d. Christocentric models. A norm from part of the biblical text may provide the *norma normans* to interpret the rest of the text, and Christians often appeal to Christ or to the proclamation of the gospel as such a norm. There are different ways to view Christ as the center of the process. The Christ-event, the death and resurrection of Jesus, might constitute the gospel and serve as the locus of authority (Luther's justification principle). Nineteenth-century scholars sought to rediscover the real teachings of the historical Jesus in order to build an authentic Christianity on this foundation. In response, twentieth-century Christians would view the Christ of faith, the living Lord of the church, as the source of authority.

Luther is singled out as the exemplar of this approach, for he described the Bible as the cradle wherein lay the Christ child, and his theological and exegetical point of departure was the expression "what drives Christ home." In the same tradition Barth described Christ as the "immediate Word of God," while the Bible was a "derived" Word of God, and tradition and the preached message (*viva vox*) were the Word in a dependent sense (also P. Forsyth; Gogarten; H. Cunliffe-Jones [1948]; J. Reid; Dodd; G. Tavard).

E. KÄSEMANN (1964, 63-107, 169-95) took this principle to its logical conclusion when he spoke of the "canon within the canon" of Romans, Galatians, and 1–2 Corinthians. These works contain the gospel in its purest form; divergent views in the remaining books are subordinate. Hence the "primitive Catholicism" of the later epistles remains inferior to the charismatic and egalitarian theology of Paul.

e. Limitation. Various theologians limit the authority of the Bible in order to grant other theological sources greater respect. Roman Catholic minimalists elevated the importance of tradition by declaring that God merely provided negative assistance to biblical authors to prevent error (Jahn) or that God merely approved the creation of the texts subsequent to their writing (Bonfrére, Sixtus, Haneberg). Liberal Protestants subordinated biblical authority to religious feeling as a source for theology (Schleiermacher, Herder, J. D. Michaelis, Griesbach); biblical authority lay only in its experiential dimension. Later nineteenth-century Protestants tempered biblical authority with German idealism. Finally, twentieth-century theologians often emphasize that biblical authority must be balanced with philosophy, the humanities, social sciences (see SOCIAL-SCIENTIFIC CRITICISM), and current human need in the theological process.

3. Conclusion. Modern critical historical consciousness has led theologians to view biblical authority in a broader context. The biblical text was created by a developmental process: oral tradition, precipitation into writing, REDACTION, textual transmission, and canonization. Scripture was produced by an ongoing process of tradition making and theologizing, and the process did not end with the creation of the canon.

Recognition of this dynamic process may lead to several new observations: (1) The relationship between Scripture and tradition is closer than has been admitted by Protestants and more fluid and dynamic than admitted by Roman Catholics. (2) Inspiration as a charism should be applied properly to the entire process of creating the text. (3) Inspiration, however, is not the cause for authority but a chief characteristic of an authoritative text; nor is inspiration limited to just canonical writings. (4) The gospel or the "rule of faith" or "the tradition" is the guiding theological and interpretative norm underlying the Scriptures, which in turn are the norm for later Christian traditions. (5) To declare Christ, the resurrection, or the gospel testimony as the ultimate authority is theologically ideal; but ultimately these notions are too abstract to be a *theologoumena* to undergird any concrete discussion of biblical authority. (6) Finally, the canon has authority because it contains the spiritual experiences of the earliest communities of faith and has inspired generations of Christians past and present. The Scriptures contain the paradigms of the divine process still operative today (see Achtemeier [1980] 114-47; Gnuse [1985] 102-24).

Bibliography. **W. J. Abraham,** *The Divine Inspiration of Holy Scripture* (1981). **P. Achtemeier,** *The Inspiration of Scripture: Problems and Proposals* (1980). **R. S. Alley,** *Revolt Against the Faithful: A Biblical Case for Inspiration as Encounter* (1970). **L. Alonso-Schökel,** *The Inspired Word: Scripture in the Light of Language and Literature* (1965). **J. Barr,** *The Bible in the Modern World* (1973); *The Scope and Authority of the Bible* (1980); *Holy Scripture: Canon, Authority, Criticism* (1983). **K. Barth,** *The Word of God and the Word of Man* (1924; ET 1928); *Church Dogmatics* 1, 1-2 (1932; ET 1936). **D. L. Bartlett,** *The Shape of Scriptural Authority* (1983). **J. Barton,** *People of the Book? The Authority of the Bible in*

Christianity (1988). **D. M. Beegle,** *The Inspiration of Scripture* (1963); *Scripture, Tradition, and Infallibility* (1973). **P. Benoit,** *Aspects of Biblical Inspiration* (1965). **G. Berkouwer,** *Holy Scripture* (1975). **P. A. Bird,** "The Authority of the Bible," *NIB* (1994) 1:33-64. **J. Bright,** *The Authority of the OT* (1967). **E. Brunner,** *Revelation and Reason: The Christian Doctrine of Faith and Knowldge* (1941; ET 1946). **J. T. Burtchaell,** *Catholic Theories of Biblical Inspiration Since 1810: A Review and Critique* (1969). **R. Bryant,** *The Bible's Authority Today* (1968). **H. von Campenhausen,** *The Formation of the Christian Bible* (1972). **Y. Congar,** *La Tradition et les traditiones* (1960). **H. Cunliffe-Jones,** *The Authority of the Biblical Revelation* (1948). **S. Davis,** *The Debate About the Bible: Inerrancy versus Infallibility* (1977). **C. H. Dodd,** *The Authority of the Bible* (1929). **F. W. Farrar,** *History of Interpretation* (Bampton Lectures, 1886). **R. Gnuse,** *The Authority of the Bible: Theories of Inspiration, Revelation, and the Canon of Scripture* (1985). **R. Grant and D. Tracy,** *A Short History of the Interpretation of the Bible* (1984). **R. Grant, J. T. McNeil, and S. Terrien,** "History of the Interpretation of the Bible," *IB* (1952) 1:106-41. **F. Greenspahn** (ed.), *Scripture in the Jewish and Christian Traditions: Authority, Interpretation, Relevance* (1982). **C. F. Henry,** *God, Revelation and Authority,* 2 (1976). **A. G. Herbert,** *The Authority of the OT* (1947). **A. A. Hodge and B. B. Warfield,** *Inspiration* (1881). **R. Johnston,** *Evangelicals at an Impasse: Biblical Authority in Practice* (1979). **E. Käsemann,** *Essays on NT Themes* (1964). **D. Kelsey,** *The Uses of Scripture in Recent Theology* (1975). **E. G. H. Kraeling,** *The OT Since the Reformation* (1955). **O. Loretz,** *The Truth of the Bible* (1964; ET 1968). **J. McKenzie,** "The Social Character of Inspiration," *CBQ* 24 (1962) 115-24. **D. K. McKim** (ed.), *The Authoritative Word:*

Essays on the Nature of Scripture (1983). **J. Moltmann,** *Theology of Hope: On the Ground and the Implications of a Christian Eschatology* (1964; ET 1967). **J. H. Newman,** *On the Inspiration of Scripture* (ed. J. D. Holmes and R. Murray, 1967). **M. A. Noll,** *The Princeton Theology 1812–1921: Scripture, Science, Theological Method from A. Alexander to B. B. Warfield* (1983). **J. C. O'Neill,** *The Bible's Authority: A Portrait Gallery of Thinkers from Lessing to Bultmann* (1991). **J. Orr,** *Revelation and Inspiration* (1910). **W. Pannenberg,** *Revelation as History* (1961; ET 1968). **C. Pinnock,** *The Scripture Principle* (1984). **K. Rahner,** *Inspiration in the Bible* (1961, 1964[2]). **K. Rahner and J. Ratzinger,** *Revelation and Tradition* (1966). **J. K. S. Reid,** *The Authority of Scripture: A Study of the Reformation and Post-Reformation Understanding of the Bible* (1957). **H. G. Reventlow,** *The Authority of the Bible and the Rise of the Modern World* (1980; ET 1985). **A. Richardson,** *The Bible in the Age of Science* (1961). **A. Richardson and W. Schweitzer** (eds.), *Biblical Authority for Today* (1951). **J. B. Rogers** (ed.), *Biblical Authority* (1977). **J. B. Rogers and D. K. McKim,** *The Authority and Interpretation of the Bible* (1979). **W. Sanday,** *Inspiration* (Bampton Lectures, 1894[2]). **J. Scullion,** *The Theology of Inspiration* (1970). **N. Snaith,** *The Inspiration and Authority of the Bible* (1956). **P. Synave and P. Benoit,** *Prophecy and Inspiration* (1961). **L. S. Thornton,** *The Form of the Servant* (3 vols., 1950). **F. Turretin,** *The Doctrine of Scripture* (1847; ed. and tr. J. Beardslee, 1981). **B. Vawter,** *Biblical Inspiration* (1972). **B. B. Warfield,** *The Inspiration and Authority of the Bible* (1948). **G. E. Wright,** *God Who Acts* (SBT 8, 1952). **R. Youngblood** (ed.), *Evangelicals and Inerrancy* (1984).

R. GNUSE

B

BABEL UND BIBEL

Friedrich DELITZSCH, the most famous Assyriologist of his time (see ASSYRIOLOGY AND BIBLICAL STUDIES), initiated what became the "Babel und Bibel" controversy with his famous lecture by that title delivered before the Deutsche Orient-Gesellschaft and the German kaiser in 1902. The importance of the issue lay in the radical challenge the emerging discoveries in Babylonia presented to traditional study of the Bible.

Yet at first the thrust of Delitzsch's work was to show how Babylonian materials aided the interpretation and illustration of the Bible, especially the HB. Subsequently he argued that Babylonia was culturally dominant over Israel and also culturally—including religiously—superior. But Delitzsch not only extolled Babylonia, he also presented negative evaluations of Israel's religion. Thus the "Babel-Bibel" controversy differs from that over PAN-BABYLONIANISM as represented by such figures as H. WINCKLER, A. JEREMIAS, and, in a different way, P. JENSEN, in that its focus is not an extreme cultural diffusionism from Babylonia but an affirmation of Babylonian dominance and superiority and a derogatory evaluation of the HB.

Delitzsch found in Babylonia not only polytheism but also monotheism, which he viewed as a forerunner of Israel's religion; he found the peculiar Israelite divine name, Yahweh, attested in personal names from the time of Hammurabi; and above all, he found Babylonian religion and practice to be morally superior to that of Israel. (Delitzsch viewed Israel's religion as having many naive and even heathen features.) His three published *Babel und Bibel* lectures (delivered 1902–1904; published 1902–1905) and his related writings, especially his *Babel und Bibel: Ein Rückblick und Ausblick* (1904), forcefully demonstrated that biblical scholars had to come to terms with Babylonian civilization; they also stirred an immediate and immense controversy. Delitzsch was attacked by conservative clergy for his denigration of the HB, attacked by other Assyriologists over his interpretation of various Babylonian texts, and attacked by HB scholars for his somewhat naive reading of the Bible and for his failure to recognize the influence of other Near Eastern cultures, especially that of Egypt, on Israel.

Whereas Delitzsch correctly pointed to the importance of Babylonia's influence on Israel and was at least partially correct in many of his observations, he erred in emphasis and evaluation. His later general rejection of the HB in favor of German national traditions in *Die Grosse Täuschung* (1920–21) went well beyond his "Babel und Bibel" lectures, although the seeds had clearly been sown there. The early lectures were something other than "comparatively harmless."

Bibliography: W. **Baumgartner,** "Babylonien: III. Babel und Bibel," *RGG*[2] (1927) 1:714-18. **F. Delitzsch,** *Babel and Bible* (Lectures 1-3, tr. T. J. McCormack, W. H. Carruth, and L. G. Robinson, 1906), with criticisms and responses. **J. Ebach,** "Babel und Bibel oder: Das 'Heidnische' im Alten Testament," in *Die Restauration der Götter: Antike Religion und Neo-Paganismus* (ed. R. Faber and R. Schlesier, 1986) 26-44. **J. J. Finkelstein,** "Bible and Babel: A Comparative Study of the Hebrew and Babylonian Religious Spirit," *Commentary* 26 (1958) 431-44. **H. B. Huffmon,** *"Babel und Bibel:* The Encounter Between Babylon and the Bible," *Backgrounds for the Bible* (ed. M. P. O'Connor and D. N. Freedman, 1987) 125-36. **K. Johanning,** *Der Bibel-Babel-Streit: Eine forschungsgeschichtliche Studie* (1988). **H.-J. Kraus,** *GHKEAT* (1982[3]) 305-14. **W. G. Lambert,** "Babylonien und Israel," *TRE* 5 (1980) 67-79. **R. G. Lehmann,** *Friedrich Delitzsch und der Babel-Bibel-Streit* (OBO 133, 1994). **H. Weidmann,** *Die Patriarchen und ihre Religion* (FRLANT 94, 1968) 65-88.

H. B. HUFFMON

BACH, JOHANN SEBASTIAN (1685–1750)

Born in Eisenach, Germany, March 21, 1685, B. was the son, brother, and father of accomplished musicians. While his sons P. E. and J. C. Bach were more famous than their father during their lifetimes, B. is regarded today as one of the greatest composers in history. He served churches and royal patrons throughout his career; from 1723 until his death on July 28, 1750, he was music director at St. Thomas and St. Nicholas churches in Leipzig and at the Pauliner-Kirche of the city's university, as well as choir director at the Thomasschüle.

To speak of B.'s interpretation of the Bible assumes two foci: how he appropriated the biblical material for his own faith and how he communicated the biblical text in his art. In B.'s case there is abundant evidence for understanding both. His marginal comments and the underlined text and commentary in his Calov Bible make clear that Bach considered both the origin of church music (see MUSIC, THE BIBLE AND) and of his office as music director to belong to the chronicler's account of David's organization of the Temple. A. CALOV's exegesis, which B. followed, is markedly christological in interpreting the HB, using both allegory and historical links. For example, the twelve precious stones in Aaron's breastpiece (Exod 28:17-20), which B. numbered with the finest hand, are interpreted as qualities of Christ's character. B. also noted how David's line led to the birth of Christ. Calov quoted M. LUTHER profusely; the commentary on Ecclesiastes is nearly all from Luther, and B. marked more of it by far than any other book. This material is didactic, urging the reader to do his work diligently and faithfully, placing everything in God's hands, regardless of what others might do or think.

In his Bible B. referred to one musical composition, writing in the margin at Exod 15:20: "NB. First section for two choirs to be performed to the honor of God." This suggests Motet No. 1 "Sing to the Lord a new song. . . . They shall praise his name in a round dance" (*Reihen*). Miriam's round dance is illustrated musically in the first chorus, set for two choirs. (Since B. wrote the date 1733 in each of the three volumes of his Calov Bible, the new chronology, which dates Motet No. 1 in 1727, may need review.) In his sacred cantatas and passions B. created musical settings for biblical quotations and reflective poetry of his own time that, replete with biblical imagery, allowed the worshiper to identify subjectively and respond with affective faith. The heart of his biblical interpretation is his sacred choral music, which lifts up the suffering of JESUS on the cross and its efficacy for salvation.

The ingenious way B. communicated the biblical text can be seen in the Sanctus of the B Minor Mass, where the musical structure is a veritable image of the six-winged seraphim of Isaiah's vision (Isaiah 6; B. changed the wording of the Latin liturgy to make it conform to the biblical text in Luther's translation). The number six permeates the piece: six voice parts, the pervasive units of six notes, the use of sixths in the harmonic structure and in each of the two lines of the text stated repetitiously in units of six measures. The first section particularly sustains an antiphonal character with two sets of three voices calling and responding. Throughout, the music soars in waves like wings that rise and fall and sometimes glide. One stands in awe and asks: Did B. design the whole of 168 measures as an integration of symbols: 6 (wings) x 2 (antiphonal voices) x 14 (Bach)? Or could such a construction be mere coincidence?

Bibliography: H. Besch, *J. S. B.: Frömmigkeit und Glaube* (1950). **E. Chafe,** *Tonal Allegory in the Vocal Music of J. S. B.* (1991). **H. H. Cox,** *The Calov Bible of J. S. Bach* (1985). **C. Heunisch,** *Haupt-Schlüssel über die hohe Offenbahrung S. Johannis* (1684, repr. 1981). **R. A. Leaver,** *J. S. B. and Scripture* (1985). **W. Mellers,** *Bach and the Dance of God* (1981). **P. S. Minear,** *Death Set to Music* (1987). **J. Pelikan,** *Bach Among the Theologians* (1986). **M. Petzoldt** (ed.), *Bach als Ausleger der Bibel* (1985). **W. Scheide,** *J. S. B. as a Biblical Interpreter* (1952). **P. Spitta,** *Johann Sebastian Bach* (2 vols., 1874–80; ET 1899, repr. 1951). **G. Stiller,** *J. S. B. and Liturgical Life in Leipzig* (1984). **H. Werthemann,** *Die Bedeutung der alttestamentlichen Historien in J. S. B.s Kantaten* (1960).

H. H. COX

BACON, BENJAMIN WISNER (1860–1932)

Born in Litchfield, Connecticut, Jan. 15, 1860, B. was educated at private schools in Connecticut, Germany, Switzerland, and at Yale University and its divinity school. He was ordained in the Congregational ministry at Old Lyme, Connecticut, and later served in Oswego, New York. While he was at Old Lyme, W. R. Harper of Yale invited him to participate in his OT graduate seminars, and upon the transfer of G. Stevens to the chair of systematic theology, B. applied for candidacy to the vacant NT post. After a year of probation he succeeded to tenure as Yale's Buckingham Professor of NT Criticism and Interpretation in 1897, occupying that chair until retirement in 1928. During his career he authored more than 250 books, monographs, essays, articles, and reviews. He died in New Haven, Connecticut, Feb. 1, 1932.

B. was an American pioneer in what was later termed FORM CRITICISM and REDACTION CRITICISM. He set himself the task of determining the differences between the NT authors concerning the beliefs and practices of the communities for which they wrote, naming this attempt "aetiological criticism." The biblical authors' incorporation of the Christianity characteristic of the regions for which they wrote B. termed the "theory of pragmatic values."

Contending that Christian oral tradition was first embodied in ritual, B. wrote that the NT materials were agglutinated about the two foci of baptism and the Last Supper, the first symbolizing life in the Spirit; the second justification, or dying to live. This polarization he traced to PAUL and his predecessors. Mark thus represented Greek, Gentile, antinomian, ultra-Pauline Christianity. Matthew's "Five Books of Christian Torah," portraying JESUS as a second Moses, reflected a Jewish-Christian, Syrian reaction to Mark's minimizing of the historical Jesus. The evangelist Luke, whose Gospel was in many respects identical to Matthew's and from the same locale, nevertheless described Jesus' exaltation as occurring in spite of, rather than because of, the cross; and in Acts, Luke adopted a double standard, assigning to Paul the viewpoint of the apostle's opponents.

The Fourth or "Ephesian" Gospel represented the synthesis of concerns reflected in the Synoptics (see SYNOPTIC PROBLEM) and Paul and created a "sponsor" in the person of the "beloved disciple" for the sake of accommodation to a church committed to Peter's primacy.

In this combination of the Markan-Pauline "gospel about" with the Matthaean-Lukan "Gospel of" Jesus, B. believed he had located the foundation of Christianity as a new world religion. To Mark's Gospel of "what the eye saw," and to Matthew's and Luke's Gospels of "what the ear heard," the Fourth Evangelist had added "what had entered into the heart of man" to conceive the whole divine epiphany.

Since B. regarded Paul's gospel as in essence Petrine, described the sources of Mark together with Matthew and Luke as portraying Jesus according to the Petrine model of the Isaian servant, and regarded the Fourth Gospel as a development of the Pauline gospel in the heart of the gentile church, his "aetiological criticism" resulted in tracing the bulk of the Jesus tradition to Peter.

Behind B.'s method lay the influence of F. C. BAUR, although B. insisted that Baur's conception of a dogmatic conflict at the core of earliest Christianity required correcting, since reconciliation of the conflict had already begun in the lifetime of Paul. But the contention that each stage of gospel tradition formed a necessary condition for what followed or that the divine "Spirit" achieved consciousness in a rapprochement between the "gospel of" and the "gospel about" Jesus—a synthesis inherent in the original "Petrine" idea, which thus constituted Christianity as the "ultimate world religion"— had, not merely Baur, but G. W. F. Hegel (1770–1831) as its author.

There were striking similarities between B.'s method and European form-critical research. His link with Europe, however, was casual due to the disruption of scientific cooperation during WWI. In addition, B. remained a source critic to the end, contending that oral tradition played no vital role in the period immediately antecedent to Gospel composition. These factors rendered B. both an anachronism and a pioneer, the first American redaction critic and father of the socio-historical school of criticism concentrated at Chicago under his celebrated pupil, S. J. CASE.

Works: *The Beginnings of Gospel Story* (1909); *The Fourth Gospel in Research and Debate* (1918); *Is Mark a Roman Gospel?* (HTS 7, 1919); *Studies in Matthew* (1930); "Enter the Higher Criticism," *Contemporary American Theology: Theological Autobiographies* (2 vols., ed. V. Ferm, 1932) 1:1-50.

Bibliography: "Publications of B. W. B.," *Studies in Early Christianity* (ed. S. J. Case, 1928) 443-57. **R. H. Bainton,** *Yale and the Ministry* (1957). **R. H. Gabriel,** *Religion and Learning at Yale* (1958). **R. A. Harrisville,** *B. W. B.: Pioneer in American Biblical Criticism* (SABS 2, 1976).

R. A. HARRISVILLE

BACON, FRANCIS (1561–1626)

An English statesman, philosopher, and advocate of empirical science, B. held many political positions, including lord chancellor (1618), but ended his public career in disgrace. A Protestant biblical orientation was an important element in his attack on the authority of the Greeks, especially Aristotle. It also helped to shape his argument for a new natural science: He contended that according to the creation story humanity should have dominion over nature. In his fantasy *The New Atlantis,* he portrayed the pursuit of science as analogical to the worship of God in Solomon's Temple and, therefore, an act of praise. However, B. wanted to separate the knowledge of nature, which he considered God's book of creation to be drawn from observation and experiment, from religious faith, which is based on God's other book, the Bible. He was convinced that these two modes of knowledge harmonized since both came from God. B. applied to scriptural interpretation some of the methods used to study nature: Such study should be inductive, leading to an edifying "positive divinity" of biblical exegesis and avoiding the disputatiousness of Aristotelian scholasticism. Moreover, it should be morally practical, seeking the improvement of the human condition, as did natural science. This interpretive approach paralleled the traditional literal and moral levels of meaning in the Bible; B. allowed that there might be an allegorical level also, in which the new covenant of redemption was prefigured in HB.

Works: *The Advancement of Learning,* (1605); *Novum Organum* (1620); *The New Atlantis* (1627).

Bibliography: J. C. Briggs, *F. B. and the Rhetoric of Nature* (1989). **B. Farrington,** *The Philosophy of F. B.* (1964). **T. Fowler and S. R. Gardiner,** *DNB* 2 (1885) 328-60. **C. Whitney,** *F. B. and Modernity* (1986). **B. H. G. Wormald,** *Francis Bacon* (1993).

D. D. WALLACE, JR.

BACON, ROGER (c. 1213–c. 1292)

Only the general course of B.'s life is known; his birth and death dates are uncertain. A native of Ilchester, Somerset, he studied at Oxford and before 1239 received a degree in arts from either Oxford or the University of Paris. At Paris he served as regent master of the arts faculty and lectured on Aristotle. Probably in the 1250s he became a Franciscan and taught at the studium of the order at Paris. His interests and learning in the arts and sciences were prodigious. Although he apparently wrote no exegetical study on the Scriptures, he expressed his opinion on various matters concerning biblical study, especially in part three of his *Opus maius,* which, like his *Opus minus* and *Opus tertium,* was produced in 1266–68 at the request of Pope Clement IV. Most of this work was concerned with the reform of education and society.

B. argued that God had revealed the truths of philosophy to the Hebrew patriarchs and prophets (see PROPHECY AND PROPHETS, HB) and that Latin learning had come ultimately from other languages. He stressed the need for a knowledge of Hebrew and Greek for biblical study and wrote grammars on both. His *De signis* is a treatise on signification in language relevant to biblical study.

Works: *Opus maius* (ed. S. Jebb, 1733; 3 vols., ed. J. H. Bridges, 1879–1900, repr. 1964); *The Greek Grammar of R. B. and a Fragment of His Hebrew Grammar* (ed. E. Nolan and S. A. Hirsch, 1902); *Opus minus, Opus tertium. . . .* (ed. J. S. Brewer, 1959); "Opus maius: De signis," *Traditio* 34 (ed. K. M. Fredborg et al., 1978) 75-136.

Bibliography: *BB²* 1 (1778) 416-40. **E. Charles,** *R. B., sa vie, ses ouvrages, ses doctrines d'après des textes inédits* (1861). **T. Crowley,** *R. B.: The Problem of the Soul in His Philosophical Commentaries* (1950). **S. C. Easton,** *R. B. and His Search for a Universal Science* (1952). **J. M. G. Hackett,** *DMA* 2 (1983) 35-42. **A. G. Little,** "The Franciscan School at Oxford in the Thirteenth Century," *Archivum franciscanum historicum* 19 (1926) 803-74; "Roger Bacon," *Franciscan Papers, List and Documents* (1943) 72-97. **B. Smalley,** *The Study of the Bible in the Middle Ages* (1984³), esp. 329-33.

J. H. HAYES

BAECK, LEO (1873–1956)

B.'s secure place in history as the leader of the German Jewish community during its most difficult time sometimes obscures his importance as a scholar who opened new areas within Jewish and Christian scholarship related to the biblical and post-biblical period, particularly in the areas of mysticism and NT studies. However, these contributions must be viewed within the context of a life that has come to be seen as paradigmatic of the German Jew in the twentieth century.

B. was born in Lissa, Posen, the border area between Poland and Germany, and was trained for the rabbinate first by his father, the local rabbi. He later studied in Breslau, where he studied (along progressive lines) with J. Freudenthal, and in Berlin, with W. DILTHEY. His PhD on B. SPINOZA gives an indication of his broad vision. He served communities in Oppeln (1897–1907), Düsseldorf (1907–12), and Berlin (from 1912), where he taught at the Hochschule für die Wissenschaft des Judentums. B's first major work, still in print, was *The Essence of Judaism* (1905; ET 1936), a confrontation with A. von HARNACK's *The Essence of Christianity* (1900; ET *What Is Christianity* [1901]). Sharing the then current quest for an "essence," B. confronted Harnack with a Jewish religion of tension and growth vs. the platonic claim of possessing what was fixed and final, which he saw in Harnack's Christian "consummated faith." Here, too, one finds B.'s first challenge of PAUL

and "his longing after absolute certainty of salvation." B.'s approach to Paul changed radically after WWII, when he discerned far more of the Jewish tradition in the apostle. In the same way his distinction between the "classical" religion of Israel with its sober ethical realism in contrast to "romantic" Christianity with its sentimental yearning toward an abstract salvation later gave way to an awareness that he had made one aspect of Christianity paradigmatic for the totality.

B. was a pioneer in the study of Christianity by Jewish scholars, along with C. MONTEFIORE in England, J. Klausner in Israel, and S. SANDMEL in the United States. The difference was that B.'s study of the Gospels, published in 1938, was immediately confiscated and destroyed by the Nazis; his insistence that the *Evangelium* was part of Jewish history, written by Jews speaking the language and building upon the thought patterns of the rabbis, was unacceptable. The idea remained important for later biblical scholarship, however, and the Jewish dimensions of Christianity came to be recognized and appreciated. One may still argue that B.'s comparison of Jewish and Christian mysticism was too harsh—the emphasis that ethics and reason brought Jews toward communion as contrasted with Christian yearning for a mystical union is an overstatement—but it is not irrelevant. B.'s positive view of the Pharisees has become something of a truism; but again, it opened the way to a more sensitive approach within NT studies. Contemporary German scholarship has rediscovered B. as a significant influence on biblical studies.

B. lived his teachings. He was the head of German Jewry, appointed head of the Reichsvertretung der Juden in Deutschland (in 1933), and battled with the Gestapo for time and space in order to save as much as possible: children's transports to Great Britain (he rushed back from London in August 1939 to remain with his people before the borders closed); emigration to Palestine; support of the suffering Jews trapped in Germany—until he entered the ghetto/concentration camp Theresienstadt. In the camp he was the great teacher and pastor whose lectures became a rallying point of spiritual resistance, and there he wrote his great final work, *This People Israel.* The first volume is an exposition of the Pentateuch (see PENTATEUCHAL CRITICISM) as sacred history in which Judaism is affirmed in a new way. He had moved from "essence" to "existence," even though his neo-Kantian (see KANT) and rabbinic ethical rigorism remained unchanged. B. survived, and a final period of creative teaching (at HUC-JIR in Cincinnati) completed his work as the great Jewish teacher of the twentieth century.

Works: *Spinozas erste Einwirkungen auf Deutschland* (1895); *The Essence of Judaism* (1905; ET 1936); *The Pharisees and Other Essays* (1927, 1934²; ET 1947, repr. 1966 with introduction by K. Stendahl); "Judaism," *Religions of the World, Their*

Nature and Their History (1931); *Das Evangelium als Urkunde des jüdischen Glaubensgeschichte* (1938); *This People Israel: The Meaning of Jewish Existence* (2 vols., 1955–57; ET 1965); *Judaism and Christianity* (1958); *Paulus, die Pharisäer, und das Neue Testament* (1961).

Bibliography: **L. Baker,** *Days of Sorrow and Pain: L. B. and the Berlin Jews* (1979). **F. Bamberger,** *Yearbook of the L. B. Institute* 2 (1957) 1-44; 11 (1966) 3-27. **A. H. Friedlander,** *L. B.: Teacher of Theresienstadt* (1968, 1992); *EncBrit2* (1974) 580-81. **W. Homolka,** *L. B. and German Protestantism* (1992). **T. Wiener,** *Studies in Bibliography and Booklore* 1, 3 (1954).

A. H. FRIEDLANDER

BAENTSCH, BRUNO JOHANNES LEOPOLD
(1859–1908)

Born Mar. 25, 1859, in Halle/S., B. studied theology and Near Eastern languages at Halle with E. RIEHM, C. Schlottmann, and J. WELLHAUSEN. On completing his theological exams he served as pastor (1886–93) in Rotenbug and Erfurt. He received his PhD in Halle (1883) and his lic. theol. in Jena (1892), completed his habilitation (1893), and became a *Dozent* in OT studies. He went to Jena as *ausserordentlicher* professor in 1899, carrying sole responsibility in OT on account of the illness of professor C. Siegfried. With Siegfried's death in 1901, B. succeeded him as full professor. He was an esteemed teacher, the focus of his work lying more in the classroom than in literary production. Still, he contributed to the comprehensive commentary series SAT and to the *RGG*. He died in Jena Oct. 27, 1908.

B. advocated and defended the historical views of Wellhausen's school (1896) and in his study of the emergence and development of the covenant and holiness codes practiced the LITERARY-critical method after the manner of Wellhausen. B.'s chief work, a commentary on Exodus–Leviticus–Numbers (1903), rested on a thoroughgoing literary critique and explored historical, religio-historical, and cultural-historical questions; but it was quite sparse in the exegesis of individual details. The introduction is particularly successful, giving a concise overview of the component parts of the respective books. At the end of his career, influenced by the discovery of ancient Babylonian materials and the incisive works of H. WINCKLER and A. JEREMIAS, B. adopted elements of astral-mythological interpretation (1906; see MYTHOLOGY AND BIBLICAL STUDIES 1800 TO 1980).

Works: *Die Wüste: Ihre Namen und ihre bildliche Anwendung in den alttestamentlichen Schriften* 1 (1883); *Das Bundesbuch Ex XX 22–XXIII* (1892); *Die moderne Bibelkritik und die Autorität des Gotteswortes* (1892); *Das Heiligkeitsgesetz Lev XVII–XXVI* (1893); *Geschichtsconstruktion oder Wissenschaft?* (1896); *Exodus–Leviticus–Numeri* (HK I, 2, 1903); *Altorientalischer und israelitischer Monotheismus* (1906); *David und sein Zeitalter* (1907);

"Haggai" and "Sacharja," *Das Judentum* (M. Haller, SAT II, 3, 1914) 71–106.

Bibliography: **F. Bennewitz,** *BJDN* 13 (1908) 273-80. **H. Gunkel,** *RGG²* 1 (1927) 733-74. **B. Sauer,** *NDB* 1 (1953) 523-54. **W. Staerk,** *RE³* 23 (1913) 152-54.

W. THIEL

BAETHGEN, FRIEDRICH WILHELM ADOLF
(1849–1905)

Born Jan. 16, 1849, in Lachem, B. studied theology and Semitics in Göttingen, Kiel, and Berlin. In 1877 he became lic. theol. in Kiel and in 1878 received his PhD in Leipzig. He completed his habilitation the same year and was promoted to *Dozent* in OT at Kiel. In 1884 he was named an *ausserordentlicher* professor there; in 1888 he accepted a similar position in Halle. He became full professor in Greifswald in 1889 and was at the same time Konsistorial-Rat and a member of the Pommeranian Konsistorium. As full professor and Prussian Konsistorial-Rat he moved to Berlin in 1895. Retiring early, he died Sept. 5, 1905, in Rohrbach.

Although B. was influenced by J. WELLHAUSEN's school, his interests lay in Semitic languages, history of religions (SEE RELIGIONSGESCHICHTLICHE SCHULE), and the poetic texts of the HB (see POETRY, HB). Among his editions and translations of Syriac and Arabic texts, the fragments of earlier Syriac and Arabic historical works contained in the *Chronicle of Elias of Nisibis* (1880b) stand out. B.'s reconstruction of the Greek *Urtext* (1885), which formed the basis of the Syriac fragments of the Gospels published by W. Cureton, was important in NT TEXTUAL CRITICISM.

Through a religio-historical comparison of the Semitic pantheon with the unique Israelite faith in God (1888), B. disputed A. KUENEN's thesis that Hebrew religion had originally been polytheistic and was first transformed into monotheism by the preaching of the prophets (see PROPHECY AND PROPHETS, HB). The books of Job, Song of Songs, and Lamentations were brought to a wide readership through his new translations with brief commentary. But B.'s main accomplishment was his Psalms commentary (1892, 1897², 1904³), in which he especially analyzed early Christian psalms exegesis. The fourth edition of the commentary was completely recast by H. GUNKEL in 1926.

Works: *Untersuchungen über die Psalmen nach der Peschita* 1 (1878); (ed.) *Sindban oder die sieben weisen Meister* (1879); *Anmut und Würde in der alttestamentlichen Poesie* (1880a); (ed.) *Syrische Grammatik des Mar Elias von Tirhan* (1880b); (ed.) *Fragmente syrischer und arabischer Historiker* (1884, repr. 1966); *Evangelienfragmente: De griechische Text des Cureton'schen Syrers wiederhergestellt* (1885); *Beiträge zur semitischen Religionsgeschichte* (1888); *Die Psalmen* (HKAT

2.2, 1892, 1897², 1904³); (ed.) *Handwörterbuch des Biblischen Altertums* (E. C. A. Riehm, 2 vols., 1893–94²); "Das Buch Hiob, Das Hohelied, Die Klagelieder," *HSAT(K)* (1894, 1896²) 817-54, 854-60, 864-71; *Hiob: Deutsch mit kurzen Anmerkungen für Ungelehrte* (1898).

Bibliography: H. Gunkel, *RGG* 1 (1909) 897-98. M. Noth, *NDB* 1 (1953) 530-31.

W. THIEL

BARCLAY, WILLIAM (1907–78)

B. received his MA and BD at Glasgow (1932), studied at Marburg (1932–33), and served as pastor of Trinity Church of Scotland, Renfrew, from 1933 to 1946. He was lecturer, senior lecturer, and professor of divinity and biblical criticism at the University of Glasgow from 1947 to 1974, receiving a DD (hon.) at Edinburgh. B. was from a conservative evangelical tradition, and the Bible remained central to his faith throughout his life, although his original theological position gradually widened. His work was initially acceptable to many conservative readers, but he lost some of their support when he later strongly attacked fundamentalist views.

With the exception of *Educational Ideals in the Ancient World* (1959), B. did not publish for the academy but for the general public, schooling himself to write simply and clearly. To his biblical exposition he brought a deep understanding of the Greek language and an extensive knowledge of the ancient world, more particularly of the Hellenistic than the Jewish. He also drew on all forms of modern literature to illustrate what he wrote. His central aim was to lead his readers to understand the biblical text in its original sense and to make it relevant to their lives. The popularity of his books, which have been translated into many languages, testifies to his success. In Scotland he was a highly successful broadcaster. On critical matters concerning date, authorship, and so on, he adhered to a generally conservative position and was largely untouched by the modern debate about the historical reliability of the SYNOPTIC Gospels, whose picture of JESUS he accepted. Although he had studied under R. BULTMANN, he had little sympathy for many of his views and seemed unaware of the modern hermeneutical debate (see HERMENEUTICS). He published a translation of the NT, aiming to make it intelligible to the ordinary reader, obviating the need of a commentary to explain it. After completing his *Daily Study Bible* he turned from writing directly on the Bible to writing on more general topics, e.g., ethics and prayer. For many years he was a regular contributor to the *British Weekly* and *ExpTim*.

Works: *Daily Study Bible* (various dates and editions); *The Mind of St. Paul* (1958); *Educational Ideals in the Ancient World* (1959); *The Mind of Jesus* (1960); *NT Words* (1964a); *The Plain Man Looks at the Lord's Prayer* (1964b); *The Plain Man's Guide to Ethics: Thoughts on the Ten Commandments* (1973); *The Gospels and Acts* (2 vols., 1976); *Testament of Faith* (1975), autobiographical; *Ever Yours: A Selection of Letters* (1985).

Bibliography: R. D. Kernohan (ed.), *W. B.: The Plain Uncommon Man* (1980). J. Martin, *W. B.: A Personal Memoir* (1984). C. L. Rawlins, *W. B.: The Authorized Biography* (1984).

E. BEST

BARNABAS, EPISTLE OF

Regarded as authentic Scripture in early Alexandria (see ALEXANDRIAN SCHOOL), B. is primarily an exegetical exercise refuting the claims of Christians who say that "the covenant is both theirs [the Jews'] and ours." B. declares succinctly, "It is ours" (4:6-7). Since God's covenant was only with Christians, only Christians like the author can understand the HB.

The author's method is thoroughly allegorical, even though he avoids the vocabulary of Greek allegorical exegesis. He argues that the prophets (see PROPHECY AND PROPHETS, HB) prove that God does not need animal sacrifices or fasting and that Christ is the true scapegoat and the true heifer offered for sins. The true circumcision is that of the heart (7–9). At this point B. gives a numerological interpretation of the 318 servants circumcised by Abraham. Their number contains a concealed reference to the name of JESUS (IH = 18) and to the cross (T = 300). "No one has heard a more excellent lesson from me," the author tells his readers, "but I know that you are worthy" (9:7-9).

B. relies on contemporary animal lore to show that the dietary laws have a hidden meaning. When Moses forbids the eating of various animals, fish, and birds he is speaking spiritually, not literally. Abstaining from pork, for example, dissociates one from being like the pig, an animal that cries out only when hungry and, while eating, does not recognize its master. Some animals, like the hyena and the weasel, are forbidden because of their peculiar sexual habits. More imaginatively, B. suggests that eating cloven-hoofed animals places one as both living in this world and looking forward to the age to come (10). The author continues this allegory, claiming that the prophets spoke about both baptism and the cross (11–12). He then discusses God's covenant with Christians (13), insisting that Moses broke the first version of the DECALOGUE on stone because the Jews are unworthy (14). Finally he argues that both the sabbath and the temple are spiritual, not literal. In fact, the literal Temple has been destroyed by the enemy in war, though "now the servants of the enemy will build it up again" (15–16). Possibly this is a reference to the building of Hadrian's temple of Zeus in Jerusalem. Chapters 18–20 present an unrelated version of the "ways of life and death," apparently Jewish in origin.

B. pushes to the extreme the exegesis present in the letters of PAUL. For example, the author insists on the importance of "types" (models of prefigurations) in the HB, where everything has a hidden meaning available, not to Jews, but to Christians. Presumably, like Hebrews, the document originated in Alexandria, where it was first used and was often regarded as having been written by Paul's companion (TERTULLIAN thought that the apostle Barnabas wrote Hebrews). CLEMENT OF ALEXANDRIA frequently quoted from B., although at one point he corrected the author's fantasies about animals by Aristotle's more accurate notions; and ORIGEN was embarrassed by B.'s statement that "the apostles were sinners above all others." In the early fourth century EUSEBIUS regarded B. as "spurious," though the biblical Codex Sinaiticus still included it among the books of the NT.

Bibliography: L. W. Barnard, *Studies in the Apostolic Fathers and Their Background* (1966) 41-135. R. Kraft, *Barnabas and the Didache* (Apostolic Fathers 3, 1965). J. Muilenburg, *The Literary Relations of the Epistle of Barnabas and the Teaching of the Twelve Apostles* (1929). J. Quasten, *Patrology* (1950) 1:85-92.

R. M. GRANT

BARNES, WILLIAM EMERY (1859–1939)

Born May 26, 1859, B. began his education at Cambridge University in 1877 and was ordained to a curacy at St. John's Church, Lambeth. In 1885 he returned to Cambridge as a lecturer in Hebrew and spent most of his career there, serving as Hulsean Professor of Divinity from 1901 to 1934. He retired in 1934 to Canterbury as warden of the Central Society of Sacred Study for the diocese of Canterbury.

B.'s early career focused on Syriac studies. His publications in this area included critical editions of the PESHITTA of Psalms (1904) and the Syriac Pentateuch (1914). Perhaps his most enduring legacy in the field of biblical studies was his role in founding the renowned *Journal of Theological Studies,* which he edited jointly from its inception in 1899 until 1903. But he is probably best remembered for the volumes he contributed to The Cambridge Bible for Schools and Colleges. His brief commentaries in this series combined the insights of his linguistic expertise with the reflections of his pious spirit.

Works: Four vols. in the Cambridge Bible for Schools and Colleges: *The Book of Chronicles* (1899), *The Two Books of the Kings* (1908), *Haggai and Zechariah* (1917), *Malachi* (1917); (ed.) *A Companion to Biblical Studies* (1916); *The Psalms* (Westminster Commentaries, 1931); *Gospel Criticism and Form Criticism* (1936).

Bibliography: J. F. Bethune-Baker, *DNB* 1931–40 (1949) 42-44.

S. L. MCKENZIE

BARR, JAMES (1924–)

Born Mar. 20, 1924, in Glasgow, Scotland, B. is the son of the Rev. Prof. Allan Barr, professor of NT at the Joint Congregational and United Free Church College in Edinburgh, Scotland, and the grandson of the Rev. James Barr, a Labour MP (1924–31 and 1935–45). He served during WWII as a pilot in the Fleet Air Arm of the Royal Navy (1942–45). Following the war, he studied at Edinburgh University, completing the MA with first-class honors in classics in 1948 and the BD with distinction in OT in 1951. He also received the MA from Manchester University in 1969 and the MA and DD in, respectively, 1976 and 1981 from Oxford University. Over the course of his long academic career, he has also been awarded numerous honorary doctorates.

In 1950 B. married Latin scholar Jane J. S. Hepburn. After his ordination in 1951 he served as minister of the Church of Scotland in Tiberias, Israel (1951–53), during which time he acquired fluency in both modern Hebrew and Arabic. His first academic appointment was as professor of NT at Presbyterian College, Montreal (1953–55), following which he took his first OT position as professor of OT literature and theology at Edinburgh University (1955–61). He then moved to the United States to teach OT at Princeton Theological Seminary until 1965. During 1965–76 he was professor of Semitic languages and literatures at Manchester University. His longest tenure occurred at Oxford University, first as Oriel Professor of the Interpretation of Holy Scripture (1976–78), and then as Regius Professor of Hebrew (1978–89; emeritus beginning in 1989). Following a year as the Anne Potter Wilson Distinguished Visiting Professor of HB at Vanderbilt University in 1989–90, he was appointed professor of HB in 1990 and, beginning in 1994, Distinguished Professor of HB at Vanderbilt University, retiring in 1998. Through the years B. has also held visiting professorships at universities throughout the world and has delivered numerous major lecture series. He is a fellow of the British Academy, the American Academy of Arts and Sciences, and the American Philosophical Society; and he is affiliated with various other learned societies. He served as president of the Society for OT Study (1973) and of the British Association for Jewish Studies (1978).

B.'s reputation as one of the most influential biblical scholars and Semitists of the second half of the twentieth century rests on both the range of his interests and the incisive character of his contributions. His first book, *The Semantics of Biblical Language* (1961), addresses the linguistic and theological problems associated with transferring a religious tradition from one language into another. B. scrutinizes several features of biblical scholarship widely accepted at that time and demonstrates fundamental flaws underlying each: the notion that there was a basic difference between the Hebrew way of thinking and the Greek way of thinking; the practice of associating the history of a given word with the history of a theological concept; the use made of etymologies; and the philosophical and linguistic underpinnings of much work in biblical theology. Drawing on principles from the fields of semantics and linguistics, he argues that one cannot simply assume—as he shows many scholars have done—that the linguistic structure of a language reveals the thought structures of the people speaking that language. He is especially critical of G. KITTEL's *Theological Dictionary of the NT,* a widely used multi-volume project underway beginning in the 1930s, which B. finds to be all too often guilty of what he calls an "illegitimate totality transfer," i.e. the whole range of meanings that a word could have in its various semantic contexts is thought to be present in each individual case. According to B., it is much more appropriate to look for theology, not in a word, but in a sentence or combination of words, a principle that most subsequent scholarly efforts to produce a "theological dictionary" have tried to follow.

B. published another landmark study on a related problem, *Comparative Philology and the Text of the OT* (1968). Here he criticizes the widely attested tendency to attribute new meanings to difficult Hebrew words by comparing them to words in other Semitic languages, such as Arabic or Ugaritic (see UGARIT AND THE BIBLE). His careful argument had the effect of making philologists cautious about such speculations, and in a real sense his study put comparative Semitic philology on a new and firmer footing. B. edited the *Journal of Semitic Studies* during 1965–76 and also served (1974–80) as the editor of the *Oxford Hebrew Dictionary* project. In addition to his numerous studies of specific Hebrew and Greek words and his work on the history of the Hebrew text and its translation into Greek, he has produced a technical and detailed analysis of spelling variations in the HB.

While B.'s contributions to the study of biblical language are of direct interest primarily to specialists, his analyses of the role and AUTHORITY OF THE BIBLE in contemporary life have had a much wider impact. *The Bible in the Modern World* (1973) deals with the problem of cultural relativism and the radical questioning of traditional views of the Bible. In a subtle argument that attends to both biblical studies and theology, he seeks to show how a modern understanding of Scripture can be theologically and hermeneutically sound (see HERMENEUTICS) when it regards the processes of revelation, tradition, and interpretation in comparable ways for both the biblical and the modern periods. In other studies he has focused on the problem of the authority of Scripture

and especially the phenomenon of fundamentalism, which he describes not simply as a stance toward the Bible but as a particular type of religion and ideology with its own historical roots, its basic principles, and its reasons for such beliefs as biblical inerrancy and literalism. Recognizing that fundamentalism poses serious ecumenical problems among believers, he aims to develop a perspective on the Bible that is hostile neither to Christian diversity nor to critical biblical scholarship.

Several of his works deal directly with theological issues connected to the HB. He is intensely critical of the "biblical theology movement" on both linguistic and theological grounds and helped in the 1960s to bring about its demise. In *The Garden of Eden and the Hope of Immortality* (1992) he addresses questions of life, death, the soul, and the underworld, emphasizing that parts of the HB imply the naturalness of death and that the ideas of resurrection and immortality are complementary, not in conflict. *Biblical Faith and Natural Theology* (1993), based on the 1991 Gifford lectures at Edinburgh University, examines the complex problem of natural theology. He finds that the Bible, at least in certain of its texts and assumptions, supports the notion that God is knowable to humans through their humanity in a created world. In spite of his criticisms of biblical theology earlier in his career, B. has thus continued to be involved in biblical theology ever since.

Works: *The Semantics of Biblical Language* (1961); *Biblical Words for Time* (1962, rev. 1969); *Old and New in Interpretation* (1966); *Comparative Philology and the Text of the OT* (1968; expanded ed. 1987); *The Bible in the Modern World* (1973); *Fundamentalism* (1977); *The Typology of Literalism in Ancient Biblical Translations* (1979); *The Scope and Authority of the Bible* (1980); *Holy Scripture: Canon, Authority, Criticism* (1983); *Beyond Fundamentalism* (1984); *The Variable Spellings of the HB* (1989); *The Garden of Eden and the Hope of Immortality* (1992); *Biblical Faith and Natural Theology* (1993).

Bibliography: **S. E. Balentine and J. Barton,** "The Rev. Prof. J. B., MA, BD, DD, D.Theol., FBA," *Language, Theology, and the Bible: Essays in Honour of J. B.* (FS, ed. S. E. Balentine and J. Barton, 1994) 1-4. **S. E. Balentine,** "J. B.'s Quest for Sound and Adequate Biblical Interpretation," ibid., 5-15. **J. Barton,** "J. B. as Critic and Theologian," ibid., 16-26. **D. Penchansky,** *HHMBI,* 423-27. **P. R. Wells,** *J. B. and the Bible* (1980).

D. A. KNIGHT

BARTH, KARL (1886–1968)

A leading figure in twentieth-century Protestant theology, B. holds a prominent place in biblical interpretation that is assured both by the general influence of his theology of the Word of God and by the specific contributions to biblical exegesis he made throughout his career. Born in Basel, Switzerland, May 10, 1886, he was educated in Germany at the universities of Berlin, Tübingen, and Marburg, studying with W. HERRMANN and A. von HARNACK, among others. He served as pastor at the village church of Safenwil in the Aargau region of Switzerland (1911–21), during which time he became friends with E. Thurneysen. The breakdown of liberal Protestant culture during WWI urged B. toward a new appreciation for the theology of the Reformers and a fresh attempt to hear the biblical message in all its immediacy. His reflections from this period were published in the form of a commentary on Romans (*Der Römerbrief* [1919]), which soon thrust him into the world of academic theology.

During a series of academic appointments in theology at Göttingen and Münster (1921–30), then at Bonn (1930–35), B. experimented with various approaches to the problems of theology (*Theology and Church* [1928; ET 1962], *Theological Existence Today* [1933; ET 1933]) and biblical exegesis (*The Epistle to the Philippians* [1933; ET 1962], *The Resurrection of the Dead* [1924; ET 1933]). B.'s leadership in the Confessing Church's opposition to Nazism during the "church struggle"—especially his refusal to take the oath of loyalty to the Führer—led to his expulsion from Germany and took him to Basel, where he gained international acclaim as professor of theology (1935–62). After his retirement he continued to offer seminars and to write until his death on Dec. 10, 1968. The primary theological work of B.'s last thirty-five years is a multi-volume, though unfinished, rearticulation of Christian language entitled *Church Dogmatics.* Even as they appeared these volumes attained the stature of theological classics.

B.'s entire theological production can be characterized as a vast attempt to interpret the Scriptures. He tried to reorient theology to the Word of God attested in the Bible rather than to the "given" aspects of personal religious experience, historical situation, scientific "fact," or cultural life. Nevertheless, this general orientation to the Bible is difficult to measure, nor is it possible to determine with precision the impact his theology as a whole has had on the study of the Bible. Moreover, B. distinguished sharply the role of theology, with its orientation to the message of the contemporary church, and biblical interpretation, with its orientation to the biblical basis for the church's message. Therefore, side by side with his vast theological output is an equally vast exegetical output, united perhaps in spirit, but very different in task and procedure. His mature biblical exegesis, like his mature theology, can be found in *Church Dogmatics;* his bibilical exegesis is physically distinguished from the theological material, appearing in innumerable small-print excurses, which together constitute a commentary on a large portion of the Bible.

The most prominent characteristic of B.'s exegesis of the Bible is its enormous variety; nevertheless, a comprehensive unity is provided by his conception that the Bible functions as a witness to the Word of God. This implies, first, a limitation; in exegesis one is to realize that the Bible is an entirely human linguistic production—a text. B. spent much time in his biblical exegesis attending to the textuality of the Bible, mapping its linguistic, literary, and theological coordinates, always with reference to the canonical form (see CANON OF THE BIBLE) of the text (rather than a historically reconstructed form). Second, the Bible as witness does participate in the Word of God. The textual content attests a real object, precisely because this object has the power to speak through the text as its voice. The mode of this participation is analogical depiction, in which the human language of the biblical text comes to attest its divine object. We know this divine object only in its textual rendering, and yet only the knowledge of this object provides the condition for the possibility of true exegesis of the text. It is this problematic relation between text and object that constituted the driving force of all biblical exegesis for B.

B.'s biblical interpretation, like his theology generally, exhibits a christological focus. Biblical texts are to be brought into relation to the person of JESUS Christ, or rather are to be seen in this, their true light. Christocentric exegesis is as characteristic of B.'s exegesis of the NT as of the OT; whatever historical relation the NT writings may be thought to bear to the historical figure of Jesus is irrelevant to the problem of finding in them a real witness to Jesus Christ. Both OT and NT texts are read christologically in two different ways: On the one hand, Jesus Christ provides the conceptual center of the various theological values (positive and negative) of a text or texts and is thus the logical subject of biblical "predicates"; on the other hand, Jesus Christ becomes the effective agent of biblical occurrences and is thus the narrated subject of biblical stories.

It is the function of the Bible in the reading of it that provides the center of gravity of B.'s biblical interpretation, and not particular methods or procedures of exegesis. Nevertheless, two methodological approaches stand out in his interpretation: conceptual analysis and narrative exegesis. Nearly every excursus containing biblical exegesis in *Church Dogmatics* has as its aim the identification and analysis of a "biblical concept." These concepts are usually isomorphic with related concepts in church proclamation and technical theology; thus, by approaching the biblical text through conceptual analysis, B. enacted his conviction that biblical language, church mission, and the discipline of theology are, while not identical, nevertheless mutually addressable. Biblical concepts serve to organize biblical usage—the utterance meaning of individual texts and collections of texts—for the purposes of Christian witness, while at the same time preserving the biblical text in its own integrity.

The second methodological approach, narrative exegesis, is a collection of approaches rather than a single method. At least five elements of B.'s exegesis can be characterized as "narrative" in character: his use of the historical category of saga (as opposed to myth); his use of the literary category of story (as opposed to history); the pervasive presence of a narrative of revelation (expectation, presence, recollection); the internal and external history of God; and the narrative substructure of the Bible as a whole (from creation to incarnation to consummation). These elements do not seem to constitute a foundational narrative HERMENEUTIC; rather, they serve as techniques that B. frequently employed in the explication of the biblical text.

The immediate impact of B.'s interpretation of the Bible was not great. Apart from a vague sense that his theology as a whole helped to motivate a generation back to the Scriptures, little evidence can be found of a real impact on the normative tradition of biblical study in the first half of the twentieth century. His contribution cannot adequately be measured from within the conceptual framework of the historical-critical method, nor, indeed, is there much real congruity with the newer aesthetic approaches. But while B.'s work lacks a systematic hermeneutic commensurable with other hermeneutical systems, there remains the biblical exegesis itself, harnessed to the task of the explication of the *intellectus fidei* in the community of faith.

Works: *The Epistle to the Romans* (1919; ET 1933); *Church Dogmatics* (5 vols. in 14, 1932–59; ET 1936–62); *A Shorter Commentary on Romans* (1956; ET 1959).

Bibliography: O. **Bächli,** *Das Alte Testament in der Kirchlichen Dogmatik von K. B.* (1987). **C. A. Baxter,** "Barth a Truly Biblical Theologian?" *TynBul* 38 (1987) 3-27. **E. Busch,** *Karl Barth* (1976). **D. Ford,** *Barth and God's Story: Biblical Narrative and the Theological Method of K. B. in the Church Dogmatics* (SIGC 27, 1981). **G. Hunsinger,** "Beyond Literalism and Expressivism: K. B.'s Hermeneutical Realism," *Modern Theology* 3 (1987) 209-23. **W. G. Jeanround,** "K. B.'s Hermeneutic," *Reckoning with Barth* (ed. N. Biggar, 1988). **W. S. Johnson,** *HHMBI,* 433-39. **E. Jüngel,** *TRE* 5 (1979) 251-68. **W. Kreck,** *TPNZJ* (1978) 382-99. **J. C. O'Neill,** *The Bible's Authority: A Portrait Gallery of Thinkers from Lessing to Bultmann* (1991) 266-83. **R. Smend,** "Nachkritische Schriftauslegung," *Parrhesia* (ed. E. Busch et al., 1966) 215-37; "K. B. als Ausleger der Heiligen Schrift," *Theologie als Christologie* (ed. H. Köckert, 1988) 9-37.

P. McGLASSON

BARTON, GEORGE AARON (1859–1942)

An archaeologist and biblical scholar, B. was born at East Farnham, Quebec. He attended Oakwood Seminary, a Friends boarding school at Poughkeepsie, New York,

and in 1879 became a minister of the Society of Friends. He received the BA from Haverford in 1882 and in 1889 entered Harvard, receiving in 1891 the university's first PhD in Semitics with a thesis titled "The Semitic Ishtar Cult." That same year he was appointed professor of biblical literature and Semitic languages at Bryn Mawr. In 1902–03 he served as the third director of the recently formed AMERICAN SCHOOLS OF ORIENTAL RESEARCH in Jerusalem and in 1921 became the first director of the Baghdad School. (He made a bequest to ASOR that supports resident scholars in Jerusalem.) B. was professor of Semitic languages and the history of religion at the University of Pennsylvania from 1922 until his retirement in 1932 and professor of NT religion and language at the divinity school of the Protestant Episcopal Church in Philadelphia from 1921 until 1937.

B.'s HB works were linguistic, exegetical, archaeological, and historical. As a linguist he was an expert in Sumerian and Akkadian cuneiform epigraphy. His main exegetical publication, *Ecclesiastes* (ICC), cited current studies, mostly German and British. He highlighted "Semitic philosophy" and identified several sections as the glosses of a later editor. While he drew heavily on rabbinic sources, it is surprising that he gave little attention to other Near Eastern materials.

In his works on the HB and ARCHAEOLOGY, B. argued for progressive revelation from the divine side and evolution from the human. He sought to trace the evolution of the religion of Israel in its Middle and Near Eastern settings in similarities, not contrasts, as was characteristic of the W. F. ALBRIGHT school and of such scholars as W. EICHRODT. He viewed Israel's beginnings as focusing on spirit-filled objects in specific locations and believed that Moses, for the most part, introduced the worship of Yahweh, borrowed from the Kenites, to Israel. Later religious developments were influenced by the change from nomadic life to a settled agricultural society. In the later prophets (see PROPHECY AND PROPHETS, HB) the monotheistic-ethical dimensions of Israel's religion became obvious. B., in essence, followed the religio-historical developmental mapping of J. WELLHAUSEN and his successors. In his work on archaeology, which went through seven editions from 1916 to 1937, B. obviously kept abreast of new finds and syntheses; but he did not modify his historical-evolutionary perspectives.

In NT studies B. focused on JESUS and situated him in the context of the evolutionary development of the history of Israel's religion. Jesus in early manhood affirmed a messianic role and continued the prophetic emphasis on ethical monotheism, standing in the tradition of the great mystics. He was God's instrument for launching a moral and spiritual universe designated "the kingdom of God."

Works: *A Sketch of Semitic Origins, Social and Religious* (1902); *The Book of Ecclesiastes* (ICC, 1909); *Archaeology and the Bible* (1916); *The Religions of the World* (1917); *The Religion of Israel* (1928); *Jesus of Nazareth: A Biography* (1932); *Christ and Evolution* (1934); *Semitic and Hamitic Origins, Social and Religious* (1934).

Bibliography: "Prof. G. A. B.: An Appreciation," *Bryn Mawr Alumnae Quarterly* (ed. M. Jastrow, Jr., et al., 1919). *BASOR* (1942). **B. A. Brooks,** *A Classified Bibliography of the Writings of G. A. B.* (*BASOR*, 1947). **P. J. King,** *American Archaeology in the Mideast* (1983).

T. H. OLBRICHT

BARUCH, BOOK OF

This book of the HB Apocrypha claims to have been written by Baruch, the companion and secretary of the prophet Jeremiah (Jer 32:12, 16; 36:4), in the fifth year of the Babylonian exile (1:1-2). The opening verses specify that the book was first read to the exiles in Babylon and then sent to Jerusalem, where it served as part of the Temple liturgy (1:3-4, 14). In modern times, the book is often designated 1 Baruch to distinguish it from other works attributed to the same author (2 Baruch, or the Syriac Apocalypse of Baruch; 3 Baruch, or the Greek Apocalypse of Baruch; and 4 Baruch, or *Paraleipomena Jeremiou*). It is extant in Greek and in a number of ancient versions based on the Greek: Latin, Syriac, Coptic, Armenian, Ethiopic (see ETHIOPIAN BIBLICAL INTERPRETATION), and Arabic. In some manuscripts and versions, including the VULGATE, the *Letter of Jeremiah* is attached to the book of Baruch as if it were a part of the same work.

Following an introduction explaining the ostensible circumstances of writing (1:1-14) are three sections so disparate in form, style, use of divine names, and point of view as to suggest independent origin. The first part (1:15–3:8), entirely in prose, reports a series of confessions and prayers by the exiled community. In language strongly reminiscent of Deuteronomy 28, Jeremiah, and especially Dan 9:4-19, the exiles acknowledge that their misfortune is God's just punishment for their sins. Nevertheless, they appeal for forgiveness and express confidence that God will restore them to their homeland and renew the covenant with them. The second part (3:9–4:4), which begins with an abrupt shift to poetic form (see POETRY, HB), is a poem in praise of wisdom. Here the affinities are with Israel's wisdom tradition rather than with the prophetic writings (see PROPHECY AND PROPHETS, HB). Israel is "dead" in captivity because of having forsaken "the fountain of Wisdom." The people must therefore find life by returning to God, the only source of wisdom. The third section (4:5–5:9), also poetic, is a psalm of comfort and hope punctuated with the refrain "take courage" (4:5, 21, 27, 30). The poet

represents Jerusalem as a widow lamenting the loss of her children, but also assuring the children that they will be brought back to her. Then four strophes are addressed to Jerusalem herself; like her sons, Jerusalem is to "take courage" in view of the certain return of her children and punishment of her oppressors. The language of the third section is heavily indebted to Isaiah 40–55. There are also strong affinities with *Psalms of Solomon* 11.

The fictional character of the book's claims about authorship and setting is evident not only from the disparity among the various sections but also from the improbability that Baruch was ever among the exiles in Babylon (see Jer 43:1-7), inaccuracies in the description of that historical period, and affinities with Jewish writings of a much later date. The compositional history of the work is complex and has been variously reconstructed. The three separate compositions dealing with the exile and return may have been compiled by the unknown redactor who added the introduction in 1:1-14. The date and place of origin of both the component parts and the final composition are unknown. Assigning a date after 70 CE to the finished work, as some have done, is necessary only if the ostensible setting described in 1:2 reflects an actual devastation of Jerusalem and deportation of its inhabitants in the author's own time. If the exilic setting is an expression for the oppression of Jews generally rather than a cipher for specific oppressors and calamities, then a much earlier date is possible. On the whole, a date in the second century BCE during the Hasmonean period seems most likely. The Greek of the prose portion shows clear signs of having been translated from Hebrew; it is less certain but likely that the poetic sections were also originally composed in Hebrew.

Baruch has been used far more widely in Christianity than in Judaism. It was not included in the Hebrew CANON but is found in most manuscripts of the SEPTUAGINT. Late in the fourth century JEROME indicated that the Jews did not use or even possess a Hebrew text of Baruch. The *Apostolic Constitutions* (late 4th cent.) and a sixth-century text attributed to EPHRAEM THE SYRIAN may imply scattered liturgical use of Baruch by Jews, but the evidence is problematic in both instances.

In early Christian circles, on the other hand, Baruch was used widely and quoted as Scripture. The reference in 3:36-37 to the earthly appearance and existence of wisdom (or God; the subject is not specified and must be deduced from context) was a special favorite because of its christological potential. Quotations of this and other passages appear in ATHENAGORAS, IRENAEUS, CLEMENT OF ALEXANDRIA, Hippolytus, ORIGEN, Commodian, and Cyprian. Often these quotes are attributed to Jeremiah—a practice facilitated by the placement of the book of Baruch as an appendix to Jeremiah in the Greek manuscript tradition. The book is included in several canonical lists by the Greek fathers (Athanasius,

Cyril of Jerusalem, Epiphanius, Nicephorus), but never by the Latin fathers; the latter presumably shared Jerome's conviction that Baruch and the other books in the Septuagint, but not in the HB, are non-canonical. The book nevertheless made its way into the Vulgate, was included in the canon drawn up by the Council of Trent in 1546, and was ratified by the First Vatican Council in 1870. However, LUTHER and other Reformers denied the canonicity of Baruch and the rest of the Apocrypha; thus Protestant Bibles either exclude these writings or distinguish them from the OT canon by categorizing them separately as "Apocrypha."

Bibliography: J. A. Goldstein, "The Apocryphal Book of Baruch," *PAAJR* 46-47 (1979–80) 179-99. **A. H. J. Gunneweg,** *Der Brief der Jeremias* (JSHRZ 3.2, 1975) 165-81. **J. J. Kneucker,** *Das Buch Baruch, Geschichte und Kritik: Übersetzung und Erklärung* (1879). **R. A. Martin,** *Syntactical and Critical Concordance to the Greek Text of Baruch and the Epistle of Jeremiah* (1979). **B. Metzger,** *An Introduction to the Apocrypha* (1957) 89-94. **C. A. Moore,** *Daniel, Esther, and Jeremiah: The Additions* (AB 44, 1977) 255-316; "Toward the Dating of the Book of Baruch," *CBQ* 36 (1974) 312-20. **G. W. E. Nickelsburg,** *Jewish Literature Between the Bible and the Mishnah* (1981) 109-14. **E. Schürer,** *HJPAJC* 3, 2 (1987) 733-43. **H. St. J. Thackeray,** *The Septuagint and Jewish Worship: A Study of Origins* (1923) 80-111. **E. Tov,** *The Book of Baruch Also called I Baruch (Greek and Hebrew)* (SBLTT 8, Pseudepigrapha Series 6, 1975); *The Septuagint Translation of Jeremiah and Baruch* (HSM 8, 1976). **J. Ziegler,** *Jeremiah, Baruch, Threni, Epistula Ieremiae* (Septuaginta, Vetus Testamentum Graecum 15, 1957) 450-67.

R. D. CHESNUTT

BARUCH, BOOK OF 2 (SYRIAC APOCALYPSE OF)

Lost for nearly 1,200 years, the manuscript known as the Syriac Apocalypse of Baruch was rediscovered in the late nineteenth century by A. Ceriani (1871, 113-80). Until that time, only about nine and one half chapters survived in the Syriac Bible. This manuscript, found in a library in Milan, is the only source for the Syriac of chapters 1–77. The manuscript survives under the title "Epistle of Baruch," or something similar (*APOT* 2.470; *AOT* 835). Ceriani first published the text in Latin translation (1876–83) and later published the Syriac.

R. CHARLES (1896) argued that the Syriac was a translation from Greek. However, the presence of a number of unintelligible phrases or expressions in the Syriac, which become intelligible when translated, not into Greek, but into Hebrew, suggest that Hebrew and not Greek was the original language. Charles dated the Greek to sometime between 120 and 130 CE (*APOT* 2.473). L. Brockington noted that the title of the Syriac manuscript found by Ceriani claims to be a translation from the Greek. This was affirmed in 1897 by the

discovery of the Oxyrhynchus fragments (*AOT* 836). F. Zimmerman (1939, 151-56) and J. Collins (1984, 170) follow Charles's analysis, while A. Klijn (1976, 107-11) argues that the close parallels between 2 Baruch and other Jewish texts suggest that either Hebrew or Aramaic was the original language (*OTP* 616). He does not exclude the possibility that a different textual tradition might be represented by the Greek.

Charles identified seven distinct redactional strata (*APOT* 474), each the work of a different author (1896, liiiff). The earliest strata derive from three fragmentary apocalypses that date before 70 CE. The remaining strata were written after 70 CE. This distinction between earlier and later strata is reflected in distinctive eschatologies: an earlier, optimistic one that looks to the restoration of the Temple; and a later, pessimistic one that looks toward final judgment. This stratification implies redaction by a single editor. Final redaction of the Hebrew may have taken place between 110 and 120 CE (*APOT* 2.474-76); translation into Greek occurred sometime between 120 and 130 CE (*APOT* 2.473).

V. Ryssel, P.-M. Bogaert (1969; *AOT* 836-37), and Collins have all found this analysis wanting. Collins points to the description of the fast in 2 Bar 5:7: "And we sat there and fasted until evening." Unlike the remaining six fasts, this fast does not last seven days; it lasts only until evening. Thus, Collins concludes, this passage does not indicate a new section. Rather, 2 Baruch 5 must be viewed within the larger context of chaps. 1–8, which collectively form the opening section of the text. (G. Nickelsburg [1981] extends the introduction through chap. 9.) As such, this section provides the context for the rest of the book by describing the fall of Jerusalem to the Babylonians. Such narrative introductions are not unusual in apocalypses; as examples, Collins cites the *Apocalypse of Abraham and Daniel* 1–6. Collins finds Charles's hypothesis that there are two distinct eschatological perspectives in this text unfounded (1984, 171); no single layer or stratum of the text can be identified with the degree of certainty required by Charles's analysis. Here as in 4 Ezra, Collins argues, diverse eschatological perspectives have been woven together into a single fabric. In the present shape of the text they appear without contradiction (172).

Bogaert suggests that B. might have been authored by R. Joseph ben Hananiah during the Domitian persecution (1969, 287-95), whereas B. Violet (1924) associates B. with AKIBA's circle. Klijn dates the work to early in the first or second decade of the second century CE, basing his conclusion on the text itself and on its strong relationship to 4 Ezra, PSEUDO-PHILO, and the Epistle of BARNABAS. Focusing on three passages, 2 Bar 32:2-4; 67:1; and 68:5, he argues that 2 Bar 32:2-4 clearly mentions the first and the second destruction of the Temple, which would indicate that the author lived after the second destruction of the Temple in 70 CE.

Second Baruch 67:1, quoted in Barnabas 11:9, refers to Zion's present suffering. Read in the light of the reference to the second restoration of the Temple in 2 Baruch 68:5, which occurred c. 130 CE under Hadrian, this passage places the time of authorship in the early second century CE (*OTP* 116-17). In contrast, Nickelsburg finds precise dating of this text impossible and suggests a date of composition shortly after 70 CE, as did C. C. TORREY (1945). P. VOLZ (1903, 1934) suggested 90 CE.

The relationship between 2 Baruch and other texts is much debated. Charles, Klijn, and Ryssel have noted strong similarities between it and 4 Ezra. Klijn also notes strong parallels to Pseudo-Philo and the *Letter to Barnabas*. However, Nickelsburg finds the relationship between 2 Baruch and 4 Ezra to be tenuous (1981, 287).

Bibliography: **P.-M. Bogaert,** *L'Apocalpse de Baruch: Introduction, traduction du syriac et commentaire* (SC 144, 145, 1969); "Le nom de Baruch dans la littérature pseudépigrapha: L'apocalypse syriaque et le livre Deutéronomique," *La Littérature juive entre Tenach et Michna* (ed. W. C. van Unnik, 1974) 56-62; "Le personnage de Baruch et l'histoire du livre de Jeremie: Aux origines du livre de Baruch," *BIOSCS* 7 (1974) 19-21. **L. H. Brockington,** "The Syriac Apocalypse of Baruch," *AOT* 835-95. **A. M. Ceriani,** *Monumenta sacra et profana* 5.2 (1871) 113-80; *Translatio Syria Pescitto Veteris Testamenti ex codice Ambrosiano sec. fere vi, photolithographice edita* (1876–83) 257a-267a. **R. H. Charles,** "2 Baruch, or the Syriac Apocalypse of Baruch," *APOT* 2.470-526; *The Apocalypse of Baruch* (1896, 1918²). **J. J. Collins,** *The Apocalyptic Imagination* (1984) 170-80. **S. Dedering,** "Apocalypse of Baruch," *The OT in Syriac,* 4:3 (1973). **L. Gry,** "La Date de la fin des temps, selon les revélations ou les calcula du Pseudo-Philo et de Baruch (Apocalypse syrique)," *RB* 48 (1939) 337-56. **R. Kabisch,** "Die Quellen der Apokalypse Baruchs," *JPT* (1891) 125-67. **A. F. J. Klijn,** "2 (Syriac Apocalypse of) Baruch," *OTP* 1.615-52; "The Sources and the Redaction of the Syriac Apocalypse of Baruch," *JSJ* 1 (1970) 65-76; "Die syrische Baruch-Apokalypse," *JSHRZ* 5.2 (1976) 103-84. **M. Kmosko,** "Liber Apocalypseos Baruch Filii Neriae" and "Epistola Baruch Filii Neriae," *Patrologia Syriaca* I, II, 1056, 1207-37. **F. J. Murphy,** *The Structure and Meaning of Second Baruch* (SBLDS 78, 1985). **G. W. E. Nickelsburg,** "Narrative Traditions in the Paralipomena of Jeremiah and 2 Baruch," *CBQ* 35 (1973) 60-8; *Jewish Literature Between the Bible and the Mishnah* (1981) 281-87. **V. Ryssel,** "Die syrische Baruchapokalypse," *APAT* 2.404-46. **G. B. Sayler,** "Covenant in Crisis: Have the Promises Failed? A Literary Analysis of 2 Baruch in Comparison with Related Documents" (diss., University of Iowa, 1982); "2 Baruch: A Story of Grief and Consolation" (SBLSP 1982) 485-500. **E. Schürer,** *HJPAJC* 3 (1986) 750-56. **C. C. Torrey,** *The Apocryphal Literature: A Brief Introduction* (1945). **B. Violet,** "Die Apokalypsen des Esra und des Baruch in deutscher Gestalt," *Die Griechischen Christlichen Schriftsteller der ersten drei Jahrhunderten* (1924) 203-36, 334-63. **P. Volz,** *Jüdische Eschatologie von Daniel bis Akiba* (1903, 1934²). **F. Zimmerman,** "Textual Observations on the Apocalypse of Baruch," *JTS* 40 (1939) 151-6.

G. T. MILAZZO

BARUCH, BOOK OF 3 (GREEK APOCALYPSE OF)

Third Baruch survives in Greek and Slavonic. The Slavonic text was found in a fifteenth-century Serbian manuscript. The longer of two fifteenth-century Greek texts was discovered in 1896 by E. Butler (*AOT* 897; *APOT* 2.527) and published by M. James in 1897. Until the latter discovery only the Slavonic version of this apocalypse (see APOCALYPTICISM) was known to exist. The shorter Greek text was found by J.-C. Picard among papers from the monastery of Hagia. The Slavonic was published in 1886 by S. Novakovic (*APOT* 2.527); W. Morfill published an English translation in 1898, and N. Tikhonravov published the text of a second fifteenth-century Slavonic text in 1894. Since that time another Greek text and additional Slavonic manuscripts have been discovered. There are at least twelve known Slavonic manuscripts. The differences between the Greek and the Slavonic versions of this apocalypse are extensive, as are the differences among the various Slavonic texts. The Greek texts, however, bear close similarity to one another (*AOT* 898).

In his *De principiis* (2.3.6) ORIGEN refers to a "book of Baruch the prophet." This book, Origen recounted, offered a revelation that had as its centerpiece Baruch's journey through each of the seven heavens. None of the surviving manuscripts describes this exact journey, although the longer Greek text details a journey through five heavens. H. Hughes argues that this text, though incomplete, serves as the source for Origen's apocalypse (*APOT* 2.527). Tikhonravov's text details Baruch's journey through only two heavens.

Among more recent scholars, H. Gaylord argued that the Slavonic text is a translation of the Greek. He also held that there is no convincing argument that the Greek is a translation from any other language (*OTP* 1.655). Even though Semiticisms exist in the text, causing some scholars to argue for the existence of an original Semitic text, the presence of Semiticisms is not unknown in later *Koiné* Greek. This position is shared by J. Collins (1979).

According to D. Russell (1964, 65-66), this text was originally written in Greek during the second century CE. He contends that sections of the text show obvious Christian influence (3 Baruch 4:9-15; 11:1-15), although this opinion is not shared by all scholars. R. CHARLES, e.g., argued that the author of this text was influenced by "Hellenic-oriental syncretism" (*APOT* 2.529). James (1899) was convinced that the author was familiar with the Pauline epistles (see PAUL) and with Christian apocryphal writings (see APOCRYPHA, NT), among which he gave prominence to the Paraleipomena of Jeremiah (c.

136 CE; see BARUCH 4). This became the basis for James's dating of the text between 140 and 200 CE (*AOT* 898). James ruled out the possibility that the distinctively Christian passages are the work of a later redactor, thus arguing for Christian authorship. Hughes was most critical of James's claim that the author of this apocalypse had knowledge of the Pauline epistles, while L. Ginzberg (1902) argued that the author was a Jewish GNOSTIC.

Hughes maintained that the framework of this apocalypse is distinctively Jewish—including the story of the vine in chap. 4, which according to Ginzberg was the only element that showed Christian influence (*APOT* 2.528; *AOT* 898). Among other characteristics Hughes considered distinctively Jewish are the text's angelology and cosmic revelations. However, the hand of a Christian redactor is also clearly present: Hughes pointed to the apparent transformation of the story of the vine, where a narrative that originally equated the vine with the forbidden tree in Genesis now ties the image of the vine to the life-giving force of the Eucharist (*APOT* 2.528). The Christian redactor's influence is most evident in chaps. 11–17.

This redaction of the text reflects an appeal to the gentile church to be patient in its attempt to convert the Ebionites and the Jews. In effect, Hughes argued that this redaction reflects the plight of those Jews who attempted to be both Jewish and Christian and in the end failed to be either (*APOT* 2.529-30). He maintained that the text received its current form sometime around 136 CE. A. Argyle pressed Hughes's analysis a step further: While this text is clearly a part of the Baruch literature, its author was a Christian: "Whatever Jewish material he may have used he certainly re-phrased and very thoroughly recast" (*AOT* 900). Argyle restricted parallels to the Baruch tradition to the narrative setting in which this apocalypse takes shape. Such parallels arise "naturally" within that context and therefore do not necessarily reflect an appropriation of actual texts.

Following Picard (1970, 77-8; also 1967, 61-96) and U. Fischer (1978, 75), Collins argues that this text originated in Hellenistic diaspora. This conclusion is drawn on the basis of allusions to Greek and Egyptian MYTHOLOGY found in the text. Collins also notes the close affinities this text has to Egyptian Judaism. In addition, G. Nickelsburg (1981) supports the theory that this is a Jewish, if not Jewish Gnostic text, that shows clear Christian interpolation. The place of origin was probably Egypt; like Collins, Nickelsburg notes strong parallels with Egyptian and Greek mythology and also with the SEPTUAGINT Deuteronomy. He dates this text toward the end of the first century or early in the second century CE. Because the relationship between the Slavonic texts and the Greek manuscripts is unresolved, Picard did not include any of the Slavonic texts in his inquiry. Argyle, following Ginzberg, argued that there

is indirect evidence for a Latin version of the apocalypse that circulated in Spain in the seventh century.

Parallels with other apocalyptic texts, especially with the *Testament of Abraham,* 2 ENOCH, 2 BARUCH, *Apocalypse of Abraham,* and 4 Ezra, have been noted by many scholars.

Bibliography: **A. W. Argyle,** "The Greek Apocalypse of Baruch," *AOT* 897-914. **J. J. Collins,** "The Jewish Apocalypses," *Apocalypse: The Morphology of a Genre* (ed. J. J. Collins, *Semeia* 14, 1979) 41-2, 55. **A.-M. Denis and Y. Janssens,** *Concordance de l'Apocalypse grecque de Baruch* (PIOL 1, 1970); *Introduction aux pseudepigraphes greces d'Ancien Testament* (1970) 79-84. **U. Fischer,** *Eschatologie und Jenseitserwartung im Hellenistischen Diasporajudentum* (BZNW 44, 1978). **H. E. Gaylord,** "3 (Greek Apocalypse of) Baruch," *OTP* 1.653-80. **L. Ginzberg,** "Greek Apocalypse of Baruch," *JE* (1902) 2:549-551. **W. Hage,** "Die griechische Baruch-Apokalypse," *JSHRZ* 5.1 (1979) 17-44. **H. M. Hughes,** "3 Enoch and the Apocalypse of Baruch," *APOT* 2.527-41. **M. R. James,** "The Apocalypse of Baruch," *Apocrypha Anecdota* 2 (CTS 5.1. 1899) li-lxxi, 83-94. **E. Kautzsch,** *APAT* 2.446-57. **W. Lüdtke,** "Beiträge zu slavischen Apocryphen: 2 Apokalypse des Baruch," *ZAW* 31 (1911) 219-22. **G. W. E. Nickelsburg,** *Jewish Literature Between the Bible and the Mishnah* (1981) 299-303. **J.-C. Picard** (ed.), *Apocalypsis Baruchi Graece* (PVTG 2, 1967) 61-96; "Observations sur l'Apocalypse grecque de Baruch I: Cadre historique fictif et efficacite symbolique," *Sem* 20 (1970) 77-103. **D. S. Russell,** *The Method and Message of Jewish Apocalyptic* (1964). **V. Ryssel,** "Die greichische Baruchapokalypse," *APAT* 2.446-57. **E. Schürer,** *HJPAJC* 3 (1986) 789-92. **E. Turdeanu,** "Apocryphes bogomiles et apocryphes pseudo-bogomils," *RHR* 133 (1950) 177-181; "Les apocryphes slaves et roumains: Leur apport à la connaissance des apocryphes grecs," *Studi bizantini e neoellenici* 8 (1953) 47-52; "L'Apocalypse de Baruch en slave," *Revue des études slaves* 48 (1969) 23-48.

G. T. MILAZZO

BARUCH, BOOK OF 4

The Greek versions of this work bear the name *Paraleipomena Jeremiou,* "Things Omitted from Jeremiah"; the Ethiopic version (see ETHIOPIAN BIBLICAL INTERPRETATION) designates the work as "The Rest of the Words of Baruch." The writing exists in various forms of differing length in Greek, Ethiopic, Armenian, Slavonic, and Romanian. The Greek text was first published by A. Ceriani (*Monumenta Sacra et Profana* 5, 1 [1868] 9-18) and the Ethiopic by A. DILLMANN (*Chrestomathia Aethiopica* [1866] 1-15). Modern ETs can be found in J. Charlesworth (ed.), *OT Pseudepigrapha* (1985) 418-25 (by S. Robinson); H. Sparks (ed.), *The Apocryphal OT* (1984) 813-33 (by R. Thornhill); and Kraft-Purintum (along with an eclectic Greek text).

Three human characters carry the story line of the

book: the prophet Jeremiah, his scribe Baruch, and Abimelech the Ethiopian (= Ebed-melech, who rescued Jeremiah from his incarceration in a cistern; Jer 38:1-13). The plot centers on the fall of Jerusalem and the return from exile as well as the end of Jeremiah's life by stoning. According to 4 Baruch, after Jerusalem was "surrendered" to the Babylonians and the city burned by divine messengers, Jeremiah was carried captive to Babylon (contra the account in Jeremiah 43, where Jeremiah is forcibly taken to Egypt by his fellow Judeans, and the account of his stoning in Egypt in *The Lives of the Prophets* 2). During the period of exile—some sixty-six years—Jeremiah's servant Abimelech had slept under a tree in the vicinity of Jerusalem, having napped after picking figs. When Abimelech finally awakened his figs were still fresh, which was understood as a sign that the exiles were to return. The document has Jeremiah leading the exiles home from Babylon; the foundation of the city of Samaria is traced to those returnees who were denied access to the Jerusalem community because they refused to divorce their Babylonian spouses.

In its present form the document is clearly Christian, since Jeremiah, in his final proclamation, announces the coming of the Messiah, JESUS. Most recent scholars, however, argue that the original document was of Jewish origin, probably written in Hebrew, which was subjected to Christian redaction and interpolation. G. Nickelsburg (1973) has argued that lying behind this work and 2 BARUCH is a no longer extant narrative that served as a source for both. Such a Jewish document could be read as an exhortation to Jews to prepare for a return to Jerusalem by divesting themselves of foreign influences. At any rate, it belongs to the rather extensive non-biblical literature associated with Jeremiah and his works around the fall of Jerusalem (see 2 Macc 2:1-8).

Fourth Baruch comes from the Roman period, as references to the property of Agrippa indicate. Most interpreters relate it to the destruction of the Jewish community in the Bar-Kochba war (132–135 CE) and see the reference to Abimelech's sixty-six-year sleep as pointing to c. 136 CE—that is, sixty-six years after the Romans' first destruction of Jerusalem in 70 CE.

Bibliography: P. **Bogaert,** *Apocalypse de Baruch* (SC 144, 1969) 1:177-221. **J. H. Charlesworth,** *The Pseudepigrapha and Modern Research* (SCS 7, 1976) 88-91. **G. Delling,** *Judische Lehre und Frommigkeit in den Paralipomena Jeremiae* (BZAW 100, 1967), with bibliography. **A.-M. Denis,** *Introduction aux pseudipigraphes grecs d'Ancien Testament* (SVTP 1, 1970) 70-78. **J. R. Harris,** *The Rest of the Words of Baruch* (1889). **K. Kohler,** "The Pre-Talmudic Haggada: B. The Second Baruch or Rather the Jeremiah Apocalypse," *JQR* 5 (1893) 407-19. **R. A. Kraft and A.-E. Purintum,** *Paraleipomena Jeremiou* (SBLTT 1, Pseudepigrapha Series 1, 1972), with annotated bibliography, 7-10. **G. W. E. Nickelsburg,** "Narrative Tradition in the Paraleipomena of Jeremiah and 2 Baruch," *CBQ* 35 (1973) 60-68. **S. E. Robinson,** *OTP* (1985) 2:413-25. **M. E. Stone,** "Baruch, Rest of the Words of," *EncJud* 4 (1971) 276-77; "Some Observations on the Armenian Version of the Paraliepomena of Jeremiah," *CBQ* 35 (1973) 47-59.

J. H. HAYES

BASIL OF CAESAREA (c. 329–379)

A rhetor, priest, and bishop, B. was born of wealthy parents who owned land in Cappadocia and Pontus. He received his early education from his father, a noted teacher of rhetoric, his mother, Emmelia, and his grandmother, Macrina. After his father's death he was educated in Caesarea (c. 345–347) and Constantinople (c. 348–350), where he studied rhetoric and philosophy, probably under the famous rhetorician Libanius. He joined his friend GREGORY OF NAZIANZUS in Athens and continued his studies with Proehaeresius and Himerius (c. 350–355), then returned to Caesarea and taught rhetoric there for about two years.

B.'s interests, however, turned more and more to religion, and he embarked on a journey to Egypt and other lands to visit renowned ascetics and monasteries. Upon returning he joined his mother and sister Macrina in semi-monastic life at the family estate in Annesi in Pontus; but he remained active in the life of the church, establishing monasteries throughout the region. He was ordained a priest (c. 364), and after the death of EUSEBIUS, metropolitan of Caesarea in Cappadocia (c. 370), was elected bishop of Caesarea, with responsibilities for most of Cappadocia. He was effective as a bishop, both in encouraging benevolences and in promoting doctrinal and political unity in the East and between the East and the West. Generally orthodox in his views, he allied himself with ATHANASIUS, Gregory of Nazianzus, and his brother GREGORY OF NYSSA in opposing the Sabellians, the Arians (see ARIUS), and the Anomians.

As a young man B., perhaps through the influence of Gregory Thaumaturgus on his family, became interested in ORIGEN and with Gregory of Nazianzus compiled an anthology of his writings, the *Philocalia*. Although B. learned much from Origen, he sometimes reacted against his biblical interpretation, leaning more toward the ANTIOCHENE SCHOOL. In the last homily on the Hexaemeron he stated, "And I hearing grass, think grass; and hearing plant, and a fish, a wild beast, and a domestic animal, and all things as the Scripture reveal, I take them as they are stated."

B.'s exegetical skills are preserved in his sermons, of which forty-nine are extant: nine on the Hexaemeron, seventeen on the psalms, and twenty-four on miscellaneous subjects. In these sermons B., with his Jewish and Christian predecessors, developed discourse unaccounted for in Greco-Roman rhetoric since the structure and invention often proceeded from the features of a privileged text, that is, the Scriptures. In his exposition he drew upon the Scriptures, comparisons and contrasts with Greek philosophers, and common experiences.

Works: *PG* 29-32 (repr. 1959–61, with new introductions by J. Gribomont); *Exegetic Homilies* (FOTC 46, A. C. Way, 1963); *Homélies sur l'Hexaéméron* (SC 26, ed. S. Giet, 1968).

Bibliography: **P. J. Fedwick** (ed.), *Basil of Caesarea: Christian, Humanist, Ascetic* (2 vols., 1981). **W.-D. Hauschild,** *TRE* 5 (1979) 301-13. **T. H. Olbricht,** "A Rhetorical Analysis of Representative Homilies of Basil the Great" (diss., University of Iowa, 1959). **J. Quasten,** *Patrology* 3 (1960) 204-36. **P. Roussean,** *Basil of Caesarea* (The Transformation of the Classical Heritage 20, 1994). **W. A. Tieck,** "Basil of Caesarea and the Bible" (diss., Columbia University, 1953);

T. H. OLBRICHT

BAUDISSIN, WOLF WILHELM FRIEDRICH, GRAF VON (1847–1926)

Born in Kiel Sept. 26, 1847, to a family of academics (in literature and geography) and military leaders, B. completed his secondary education at the Lyceum in Freiburg i. Br. (1866) and studied theology and Near Eastern studies at Erlangen (1866–67), Berlin, Leipzig, and Kiel, where he stood his theological exams in 1871. B.'s principal influences were Franz DELITZSCH (at Erlangen and Leipzig); C. DILLMANN (Berlin, 1871–72), from whom he learned Ethiopic and Syriac; J. Wetzstein (Berlin), the most noteworthy Arabist of his day; and A. Weber (Berlin), who taught him Sanskrit. This training (which enabled him to read every Semitic language), along with a wide-ranging knowledge of geography, ARCHAEOLOGY, and profane history prepared B. for a broad career as an eclectic historian of religions. He completed his dissertation at Leipzig (1874, under Delitzsch) and two years later, his habilitation. His first appointment was as professor of OT at Strasbourg in 1876, where he became professor *ordinarius* in 1880. In the same year B. received his ThD from Giessen and the following year (1881) was called to Marburg, where he remained until 1900, when he was called to Berlin.

Although an able scholar of Hebrew grammar, text, source criticism, and exegesis, and like the Wellhausian school a student of Religionsgeschichte (see RELIGIONS-GESCHICHTLICHESCHULE), B. departed radically from the GRAF-WELLHAUSEN hypothesis. With Dillmann and Delitzsch (as well as R. KITTEL), he held that the priestly texts of the Pentateuch (see PENTATEUCHAL CRITICISM), while late in their present form, contained earlier materials—materials so old they could not be dated. The writing of the priestly corpus he dated to the waning years of the seventh century BCE (rather than the exilic or postexilic era), though he accepted that P had only become "law" for the entire community under Ezra. B.

also objected to the *religionsgeschlichtlich* theory on which the new documentary hypothesis had been built—namely, that a "higher" monotheism had evolved from fetishism, animism, totemism, and polytheism. For B. monotheism was the contribution to world religion of the Semitic peoples alone, for whom two major religious themes had been determinative: God as Lord and God as Life. The concept of God as Lord had been brought to Israel from the desert; that of God as Life came from the settled Semitic peoples of the Syro-Palestinian coast—the Phoenicians and Canaanites. B. did not share the contemporary view that the prophets (see PROPHECY AND PROPHETS, HB) had been the founders of Israelite religion; rather, they had expanded the national cult to a universal religion and had drawn into Israelite faith the Canaanite concept of deity as the giver of life, coupled with the corollary belief in the resurrection of life through the deity.

B.'s basic approach to his subject matter was similarly at odds with his age—that is, he eschewed the presentation of a theoretical reconstruction of his subject matter in favor of a thorough examination of the material and the concomitant methodological problems. Both his major early work (1889) and that of his middle years (1901) possessed this quality. A generation earlier the work of Graf had been ignored for its opposition to the views prevailing during the mid-nineteenth century. B.'s suffered the same fate, although many of his views, notably those on the antiquity of the priestly material, were subsequently vindicated. Because of the eclectic nature of his scholarship and his lifelong position outside the contemporary critical consensus, B.'s work is little known to twentieth-century scholars save through the writing of O. EISSFELDT.

Works: *Libri Iobi: quae supersunt ex apographo codicis Musei Britannici nunc primum, editit atquae illustravit* (1870); *Eulogius und Alvar: ein Abschnitt spanischer Kirchengeschichte aus der Zeit der Maurenherrschaft* (1872); *Jahve et Moloch, sive, De ratione inter Deum Israelitarum et Molochum intercedente* (1874); *Studien zur semitischen Religionsgeschichte* (1876, 1911); *Theologische Wissenschaft und Pfarramtliche Praxis* (1884); *Die Geschichte des alttestamentlichen Priesterthums untersucht* (1889); *Die alttestamentliche Spruchdichtung: Rede gehalten beim Antritt des Rectorats der Universität Marburg am 15. Oktober 1893* (1893); *August Dillmann* (1895); *Einleitung in die Bücher des Alten Testamentes* (1901); "Vorwort" to Curtiss, *Ursemitische Religion im Volksleben des heutigen Orients* (1903) v-xii; *Adonis und Esmun: Eine Untersuchung zur Geschichte des Glaubens an Auferstehungsgötter und an Heilgötter* (1911); *Tammuz bei den Harranern* (1912); *Zur Geschichte der alttestamentlichen Religion in ihrer universalen Bedeutung* (1914); *Das Angesicht Gottes schauen, nach biblischer und babylonischer Auffassung. Im Anhang: Gott schauen in der alttestamentlichen Religion* (1915); *Kyrios als Gottesname in Judentum und seine Stelle in der Religionsgeschichte* (1929).

Bibliography: **W. W. G. Baudissin,** *Briefwechsel zwischen Franz Delitzsch und W. W. G. B., 1866–1890* (ARWAW 43, 1973). **O. Eissfeldt,** "Vom Lebenswerk eines Religionshistoriker's," *KS* 1 (1962) 115-42; "Franz Delitzsch und W. G. B.," *KS* I (1962) 234-38.

D. G. SCHLEY

BAUER, BRUNO (1809–82)

B. was born Sept. 6, 1809, at Eisenberg near Weimar. He studied at the University of Berlin, where he was acquainted with both D. F. STRAUSS and J. VATKE and became an ardent follower of G. W. F. Hegel (1770–1831). After Hegel's death, B.'s dissertation was directed by P. Marheineke. In 1836 B. founded the *Zeitschrift für spekulative Theologie* (1836–38), to which all the young Hegelians contributed except Strauss, whose *Leben Jesu* (1835) B. had reviewed critically in the *Jahrbücher für wissenschaftliche Kritik* (1835–36). He served as a *Dozent* at Berlin (1834–39), where the young K. Marx was in his class on Isaiah. In 1839 he moved to Bonn, but was dismissed from his teaching post, and his *venia docendi* was rescinded in March 1841. Returning to Rixdorf, near Berlin, he continued to write on a wide variety of topics. He was a major contributor to Herrmann Wagener's *Staats- und Gesellschaft-Lexikon* (23 vols., 1859–67), in which his biographical sketch of J. SEMLER first appeared (repr. in his volume on Quakerism). He died at Rixdorf Apr. 15, 1882.

B. began his career as a conservative, right-wing Hegelian. His first major publication (1838) was an OT THEOLOGY in which he brushed aside most of the views of historical criticism and set about to outline "the presentation of the self-consciousness of the absolute Spirit in its free, historically mediated development" as depicted in the OT (1:xciii). He then offered a severe critique of the conservative E. HENGSTENBERG (1839) before turning to the NT Gospels, where he saw himself as continuing the work of Strauss or building "on the site which Strauss had levelled" (A. Schweitzer [1910] 140), although regarding Strauss's concept of mythical formation (see MYTHOLOGY AND BIBLICAL STUDIES) of NT material, B. argued for conscious invention by the NT writers. In two anonymously published pamphlets (1841 and 1842), perhaps contributed to by Marx but written as if by an anti-Hegelian Pietist (see PIETISM), B. argued that Hegel was actually an atheist and that the logical conclusion should be drawn that history is not the evolving self-consciousness of the divine Spirit but of humanity and the ego's drive to self-consciousness. In incisive analysis of the Gospel materials, he argued that the Gospel of John (1840b) was simply a work of literary theological reflection and that even though Mark's Gospel was the earliest, it too was theological, not historical, and offered no support for a picture of JESUS as Messiah (1841–42). In his analysis of Acts (1850) and the Pauline epistles (1850–52; see PAUL), he came to the conclusion that none of the texts were genuine or trustworthy. By 1852 he firmly denied the existence of both the historical Jesus and the early church and placed the Gospels and other NT writings in the second century. Later in life he offered a theory of the movement's origin, arguing that Christianity was a creation precipitated by the Roman state that drew upon the philosophy of Seneca and combined Greco-Roman spiritual currents with a stream of Jewish ideas going back to PHILO and JOSEPHUS. This new movement produced the imaginary figure Jesus as a purely literary creation, probably in the reign of Trajan (98–117).

Except for the radical school of Dutch NT studies (A. Pierson [1831–96], A. Loman [1823–97], and others; see van den Bergh van Eysinga) and extreme radicals like A. DREWS, few have followed the radical criticism of B. Nonetheless, his attention to the theological creativity of the early church and the NT writers forced scholarship to take this matter seriously. Many of his writings fostered the anti-Judaism of his day; however, his work on Quaker influence on German thought is not without its interesting aspects. Many of his works have recently been reprinted, and renewed interest is being shown not only in his biblical studies but also in his significant leadership among the young Hegelians and his contribution to Marx's thought.

Works: *Kritik der Geschichte der Offenbarung,* Teil I, *Die Religion des Alten Testamentes in der geschichtlichen Entwicklung ihrer Prinzipien dargestellt* (2 vols., 1838); *Herr Dr. Hengstenberg: Kritische Briefe über den Gegensatz des Gesetzes und des Evangeliums* (1839); *Die evangelische Landskirche Preussens und die Wissenschaft* (1840a); *Kritik der evangelischen Geschichte des Johannes* (1840b); *Kritik der evangelischen Geschichte der Synoptiker* (3 vols., 1841–42); *The Trumpet of the Last Judgment Against Hegel the Atheist and Antichrist: An Ultimatum* (1841; ET 1988); *Hegels Lehre von der Religion und Kunst von dem Standpunkt des Glaubens aus beurteilt* (1842); *Geschichte der Politik, Cultur, und Aufklärung des achtzehnten Jahrhunderts* (4 pts., 1843–45); *Die Judenfrage* (1843); *Die bürgerliche Revolution in Deutschland: Seit dem Anfang der deutsch-katholischen Bewegung bis zur Gegenwart* (1849); *Die Apostelgeschichte: Eine Ausgleichung des Paulinismus und des Judenthums innerhalb der christlichen Kirche* (1850); *Kritik der paulinischen Briefe* (3 pts., 1850–52); *Kritik der Evangelien und Geschichte ihres Ursprungs* (4 vols., 1851–52, 2d ed. of 1841–42); *Philo, Strauss, Renan und das Urchristentum* (1874); *Christus und die Cäsaren: Der Ursprung des Christentums aus dem römischen Griechentum* (1877); *Einfluss des englischen Quäkertums auf die deutsche Kultur und auf das englisch-russische Projekt einer Weltkirche* (1878); *Das Urevangelium und die Geger der Schrift: Christus und die Cäsaren* (1880); *Das Entdeckte Christentum: Eine Erinnerung an das 18. Jh. und ein Beitrag zur Krisis der 19.* (1927).

Bibliography: E. **Barnikol,** *RGG³* 1 (1957) 922-24; *B. B.: Studien und Materialien, aus dem Nachlass ausgewählt und zusammengestellt von P. Reimer und H.-M. Sass* (1972). E. **Bauer,** *B. B. und seine Gegner* (1842). G. A. van den Bergh van Eysinga, *Radical Views About the NT* (1912). W. W. **Gasque,** *A History of the Criticism of the Acts of the Apostles* (1975) 73-78. O. F. **Gruppe,** *B. B. und die akademische Lehrfreiheit* (1842). J. H. **Hayes and** F. C. **Prussner,** *OT Theology: Its History and Development* (1985) 103-5. M. **Kegel,** *B. B. und seine Theorien über die Entstehung des Christentums* (APG 6, 1908). G. **Lämmermann,** *Kritische Theologie und Theologiekritik: Die Genese der Religions- und Selbstbewusstseinstheorie B. B.s* (BEvT 84, 1979). J. **Mehlhausen,** *Dialektik, Selbstbewusstsein und Offenbarung: Die Grundlagen der spekulativen Orthodoxie B. B.s in ihrem Zussamenhang mit der Geschichte der theologischen Hegelschule* (1965). J. C. **O'Neill,** *The Bible's Authority: A Portrait Gallery of Thinkers from Lessing to Bultmann* (1991) 150-66. L. **Salvatorelli,** "From Locke to Reitzenstein: The Historical Investigation of the Origins of Christianity," *HTR* 22 (1929) 263-367. W. **Schmidt and** J. **Haussleiter,** *RE³* 2 (1897) 444-47. A. **Schweitzer,** *The Quest of the Historical Jesus* (1910) 137-60. L. S. **Stepelevich** (ed.), *The Young Hegelians: An Anthology* (1983) 175-205. W. **Wrede,** *The Messianic Secret* (1901; ET 1971) 281-83.

J. H. HAYES

BAUER, GEORG LORENZ (1755–1806)

B. was born Aug. 14, 1755, in Hiltpoltstein near Nuremberg, the son of a pastor. He studied theology and oriental languages at the University of Altdorf (1772–75), where he received his master's degree in 1775. From 1776 until he accepted a professorship of oriental languages in the philosophy department at Altdorf in 1789, he worked in Nuremberg as a pastor and preacher and later as a teacher and assistant headmaster (1786–89) at the Sebaldus school. Starting in 1793, he also lectured on exegesis of both the HB and the NT in the philosophy department because the theological faculty did not accept him due to his rationalistic leanings. In 1804 he was appointed to a position at the University of Heidelberg, which he accepted in 1805 after dispelling opposition to his rationalism. He died Jan. 12, 1806, in Heidelberg.

B.'s literary activity, which began in 1780, revealed from the start his interest in exegesis, theology, oriental languages, and the history of religions. Particularly important is his *Sammlung und Erklärung der parabolischen Erzählungen unseres Herrn* (1782). In this work the investigation of myths (see MYTHOLOGY AND BIBLICAL STUDIES TO 1800) becomes just as significant for PARABLE research as does the insight that—in total rejection of allegory—every parable has only one *tertium comparationis*. B. dealt with the basic issues of later parable studies in this work, thereby demonstrating his link with C. Heyne and J. G. EICHHORN and emphasizing his own historical-critical beginning.

Historical-critical research, according to B., demands a separate treatment of the two testaments. He maintained that a less dogmatic exegesis of documents might bear fruit for the developing discipline of biblical theology by explaining individual biblical authors and epochs in terms of their contemporary conditions, which in turn could be explained by references to profane myths and revelations. After such separate treatment the connection of the two testaments in terms of their gradual growth would be underscored and the HB seen as the basis for the NT. However, the methods required, although revealing the structural interconnectedness of the HB and the NT, exclude the possibility of combining both testaments into one biblical theology.

If B. could write in his *Theologie des alten Testaments* (1796) that "this attempt, which, as far as he [the author] knows, is the first that contains the presentation of the religious theory of the ancient Hebrews as a whole or the biblical theology of the OT," then something similar is true for his *Biblische Theologie des Neuen Testaments* (1800–1802). In the latter work the sayings of the first three Gospels—under the rubric "the teachings of Jesus"— are separated from those of the Gospel of John and the individual apostles for the first time. For B. such a historical-critical construction fulfills the objective of biblical theology because it includes the consistently applied historical-critical method as well as the distinction between the temporal/particular and the universally/ eternally valid aspects of biblical theology.

B. demonstrated, through significant methodological differences from the program of his colleague J. P. GABLER at Altdorf (who clearly gave precedence to interpretation in his biblical theology), that he was not, as is often maintained, Gabler's disciple. The discussions carried on by the two Altdorf scholars, who recognized the unalterable interconnection of reconstruction and interpretation and the need for an effective method to accomplish their goal, laid the groundwork for the developing discipline of biblical theology. Moreover, since B.'s time the term and method designated as "historical-critical" has been firmly anchored in biblical studies.

Works: *Entwurf einer Einleitung in die Schriften des alten Testaments, zum Gebrauch seiner Vorlesungen* (1794, 1806²; *Theologie des alten Testaments* (1796; partial ET 1838); *Hermeneutica sacra veteris Testamenti* (1797); *Dicta classica Veteris Testamenti, notis . . . illustrata* (2 pts., 1798–99); *Entwurf einer Hermeneutik des Alten und Neuen Testaments* (1799); *Biblische Theologie des Neuen Testaments* (4 vols., 1800–1802); *Beylagen zur Theologie des Alten Testaments* (1801); *Hebräische Mythologie des Alten und Neuen Testaments mit Parallelen aus der Mythologie anderer Völker, vornehmlich der Griechen und Römer* (2 vols., 1802); *Biblische Moral des Alten*

Testaments (1803); *Biblische Moral des Neuen Testaments* (2 vols., 1804–5); *Kurzgefasstes Lehrbuch der hebräischen Alterthümer des Alten und Neuen Testaments* (ed. E. F. K. Rosenmüller, 1835[2]).

Bibliography: W. **Baird,** *History of NT Research* (1992) 1:187-94. G. **Hasel,** *NT Theology: Basic Issues in the Current Debate* (1978). H.-J. **Kraus,** *Die Biblische Theologie: Ihre Geschichte und Problematik* (1970) 87-91. W. G. **Kümmel,** *NTHIP,* 104-7, 111-13. K. **Leder,** *Universität Altdorf: Zur Theologie der Aufklärung in Franken. Die Theologische Fakultät in Altdorf* (Schriftenreihe der Altnürnberger Landschaft 14, 1965). O. **Merk,** *Biblische Theologie des Neuen Testaments in ihrer Anfangszeit: Ihre methodischen Probleme bei J. P. Gabler und G. L. B. und deren Nachwirkungen* (MTS 9, 1972); *LTK³* (1993) 2:87. J. G. H. **Müller,** *Schattenrisse der jetztlebenden Altdorfischen Professoren nebst einer kurzen Nachricht von ihrem Leben und ihren Schriften* (1790). G. **Strathmann,** *NDB* 1 (1953) 637-38. G. A. **Will,** *Nürnbergisches Gelehrtenlexikon* (continuation of C. K. Nopitsch, vol. 5, 1805).

O. MERK

BAUER, WALTER (1877–1960)

B. was born in Königsberg, East Prussia, Aug. 8, 1877. He studied in Marburg, Berlin, and Strasbourg, where his teachers included A. von HARNACK, H. HOLTZMANN, A. JÜLICHER, and J. WEISS. He taught at Marburg as *Privatdozent* in NT (1903–13), went to Breslau in 1913 as *ausserordentlicher* professor, then to Göttingen in 1916, where from 1919 until he attained emeritus status in 1945 he taught as a full professor. He died there Nov. 17, 1960.

B. was closely connected to the liberal wing of Lutheran theology. His works are marked by strict historical-critical objectivity and range from patristics and lexicographical studies to NT exegesis, CANONICAL studies, and interpretative scholarly historical investigations.

In his Marburg dissertation, "Mündige und Unmündige beim Apostel Paulus" (1902 = *Aufsätze,* 122-54]), he discussed the Pauline (see PAUL) expression *teleios,* thereby anticipating a basic element of later lexicographical investigation. In his habilitation dissertation, "Der Apostolos der Syrer" (1903), he investigated the emergence and history of the Syrian NT CANON. The findings of this investigation were later developed into an independent work on church history (1934, 1964[2]).

In the essay "Der Palmesel" (*Aufsätze,* 109-21) B. determined—based on his own philological analyses—that JESUS had not entered Jerusalem on the colt of a donkey. Instead, the word *polos* refers to a horse. This essay remains of special scholarly significance because it demonstrated in exemplary fashion the relevance of Hellenistic linguistic parallels for NT exegesis.

B.'s essays on Matt 5:44; 19:12 (*Aufsätze,* 235-62) and Rom 13:1-7 (*Aufsätze,* 263-84) constitute an initial step in his exegetical-historical method. The latter study showed that reflection on the demand "Let everyone be subject to the governing authorities" is often occasioned by current conflicts and that interpretation of this demand is determined in most cases by the actual political situation. Following the tradition of the RELIGIONSGESCHICHTLICHE SCHULE, B. drew not only on religious texts from the Hellenistic environment but also on those from the oriental world. In his famous essay "Jesus, der Galilaer" (*Aufsätze,* 91-108), he proved that Jesus' place of origin was characterized by numerous syncretistic influences.

Most noteworthy is B.'s commentary on the Gospel of John (1912, 1925[2], 1933[3]), even if it was forced into the background by R. BULTMANN's commentary on John. In his presentation B. did not succumb to the temptation to carry out a speculative LITERARY analysis. He agreed with Bultmann that one must also include the Mandean writings on the religio-historical background of John (from the 2nd ed. on) and paid thorough attention both to historical and to philological details.

B.'s best-known work, the *Griechisch-Deutsche Wörterbuch zu den Schriften des Neuen Testaments und der übrigen urchristlichen Literatur,* belongs in this context. Although E. Preuschen founded the LEXICON project (1910), B. had been responsible since the second edition of 1928 for bringing it to international prominence as a standard work. The goal of the lexicon was to use Hellenistic Greek (*Koine*), including the Greek of the SEPTUAGINT, for understanding the NT, contemporary, and subsequent literature. The philological references from hitherto unused Greek sources reveal a plethora of commonalities that link the language of the NT and post-NT early Christian environment with the literature of the gentile and Jewish-Hellenistic worlds. Because the dictionary comprehensively took into consideration the secondary literature for individual words and exegetical problems, it has become a first-rate tool for exegesis. In spite of the meritorious translation of the lexicon into English (1979[2]), B.'s name should not be overlooked when citations are made in future English editions.

B.'s provocative work on church history, *Rechtgläubigkeit und Ketzerei im ältesten Christentum* (1934, 1964[2]), has exerted a significant influence on scholarship. In it he reexamined the view, which had largely been passed on uncritically, that at the beginning of church history heresies were "apostasy" from correct doctrine. In other words, heresies were secondary both temporally and materially to the orthodoxy of the established church. Based on testimony from diverse ecclesiastical provinces (especially Syria, Egypt, and Asia Minor), B. drew the conclusion that groups later characterized as heretical were often superior to the "orthodox" in terms of origin and number. Accordingly, the orthodoxy of the established church was a result of the expansion of the Roman church, whose victory over the heretics should be attributed to the support of the state authorities of that time.

In contrast to fundamentalist and biblicist attempts at exegesis, B.'s critical objectivity revealed the NT context and expressed the close connection of the NT and its initial readers to particular situations. By working out the "humanity" of the text, B. pointed out the goal of NT exegesis: One should inquire into the subject of the Christian faith as proclaimed in the NT, but this should not be done without considering its relationship to particular historical situations.

Works: *Das Johannesevangelium* (HNT 6, 1912, 1925[2], 1933[3]); *Griechisch-Deutsche Wörterbuch zu den Schriften des Neuen Testaments und der übrigen urchristlichen Literatur* (1925, 1928[2], 1937[3], 1949[4], 1958[5], 1988[6]; ET, *A Greek-English Lexicon of the NT and Other Early Christian Literature* [1957, 1979[2]]); *Rechtgläubigkeit und Ketzerei im ältesten Christentum* (BHT 10, 1934, 1964[2]; ET 1971, 1979[2]); *Aufsätze und Kleine Schriften* (ed. by G. Strecker, 1967).

Bibliography: **H.-D. Betz,** "Orthodoxy and Heresy in Primitive Christianity," *Int* 19 (1965) 315-16. **E. Fascher,** "W. B. als Kommentator," *NTS* 9 (1962–63) 23-38. **F. Gingrich,** "The Contributions of Prof. W. B. to NT Lexicography," *NTS* 9 (1962–63) 3-10. **W. Schneemelcher,** "W. B. als Kirchenhistoriker," *NTS* 9 (1962–63) 11-22. **G. Strecker,** "W. B.: Exeget, Philologe, und Historiker. Zum 100. Geburtstag am 8.8.1977," *NovT* 20 (1978) 75-80; *TRE* 5 (1979) 317-19. **G. Strecker and R. A. Kraft,** "The Reception of the Book," *Orthodoxy and Heresy in Earliest Christianity* (1971) 286-316.

G. STRECKER

BAUMGARTEN, SIEGMUND JACOB (1706–57)

Born March 14, 1706, B. received his early education from his clergyman father before studying at Halle. As professor at Halle from 1734 he influenced many eminent theologians of the eighteenth century, e.g., J. D. MICHAELIS, A. BÜSHING, J. SEMLER, G. ZACHARIAE, J. Noesselt, F. Lüdke, G. Less, and the philosopher J. Eberhard. Part of his influence may well have been his own kind and generous character, as recorded in Semler's *Lebensbeschreibung.* B.'s importance lies in his effort to make theology a scientific (*wissenschaftliche*) discipline and to develop a HERMENEUTIC that would respond to the needs of the new era. In the latter part of his career he also made a significant contribution to history, especially church history.

From C. Wolff (1679–1754), B. derived the notion that science involves not only the demonstration of certainties but also their relationship to one another in a rational structure. In his theology he tried to integrate individual certainties into a system, differing from Wolff in preserving the Pietist notion (see PIETISM) of religion

as the union of the soul with God (thus avoiding a reduction of religion to pure morality). Like Wolff he retained a generally positive and optimistic attitude toward philosophy; human reason was a sure source for some knowledge of God, and any revealed knowledge of God could not contradict reason, though it might go beyond it.

In his approach to interpreting the Bible, B. offered an apparently incongruous combination of the traditional and the new approach that was to emerge after him. He distinguished between revelation and INSPIRATION: Revelation is God's self-revelation, whether in the natural world, in human thought, or in Scripture. Inspiration is the work of God in providing Scripture; thus, in one sense revelation is larger in scope than Scripture. On the other hand, while everything in Scripture is inspired, it is not necessarily revelation. In this sense, then, revelation is less than the totality of Scripture.

B.'s sense of the historical made him aware of the force of R. SIMON's arguments that the Pentateuch (see PENTATEUCHAL CRITICISM) was based on documents older than Moses; he was also able to appreciate the problems involved in biblical CHRONOLOGY and inaccurate citation of texts within the Bible itself. Further, he distinguished between what texts may have meant historically and their present significance. Nevertheless, he asserted with equal force that there is no mixture of divine and human sayings in Scripture. This dichotomy in his thought was evident to his contemporaries and lessened his influence. B. consequently represents an incomplete transition from the essentially static approach to Scripture of the orthodox and Pietists to an approach based on historical investigation, with a consequent evaluation of documents in terms of their period of origin.

Works: *Evangelische Glaubenslehre* (3 vols., ed. J. S. Semler, 1759); *Ausfürlichervortrag der biblischen Hermaneutic* (ed. J. C. Bertram, 1768).

Bibliography: **H. Frei,** *The Eclipse of Biblical Narrative* (1974) 88-91. **E. Hirsch,** *Geschichte der neuern evangelischen Theologie* (1964[3]) 2:370-88. **M. Schloemann,** *S. J. B.* (FKD 26, 1972); "Wegbereiter wider Willen," *Historischer Kritik und biblischer Kanon* (ed. H. G. Reventlow et al., 1988) 149-155. **J. S. Semler,** *Lebensbeschreibung von ihm selbst abgefasst* (2 vols., 1781–82).

J. SANDYS-WUNSCH

BAUMGARTNER, WALTER (1887–1970)

A Swiss scholar of classical and Near Eastern philology, B. was born in Winterthur Nov. 24, 1887. He studied at the universities of Zurich, Marburg, and Giessen, completing his PhD at Zurich in 1912 with a dissertation on the problem of eschatology in Amos and

Hosea. In 1916 he became lecturer in Hebrew at Marburg, and in 1920, *Privatdozent* for OT. In 1929 he was appointed professor at the university of Giessen and in 1947 at the university of Basel. He retired in 1958 and died Jan. 31, 1970, in Basel.

B. was a modest man of much learning in Near Eastern languages and literature and in the history of religions (see RELIGIONSGESCHICHTLICHE SCHULE). One of his hobbies was the study of fairy tales. He strove to understand the Bible as a product of its contemporary historical and linguistic environment, a phenomenon of its own time and place. His Basel colleagues honored him on his seventieth birthday with a special issue of *TZ* (November-December 1957); and on his eightieth birthday his world peers presented him with a Festschrift, *Hebräische Wortforschung* (VTSup 16, 1967). His most important contribution to biblical scholarship was his work on the Koehler-Baumgartner (*KB*) LEXICON to the HB.

Works: "Kennen Amos und Hosea eine Heilseschatologie?" (diss., Zurich, 1913); *Jeremiah's Poems of Lament* (1916; ET 1987); *Das Buch Daniel* (1926); *Israelitische und altorientalische Weisheit* (1933); *Biblisch-aramäisches Wörterbuch* (1953); *Supplement zum KB* (1956); *Zum Alten Testament und seiner Umwelt* (1959), bibliography of B.'s works from 1913 to 1959, 1-26; *KB*, (1967³; ET 1994).

Bibliography: R. Degen, (review of *KB*) OLZ 66 (1971) 259-73. TRu 35.2 (1971) 93.

J. H. MARKS

BAUR, FERDINAND CHRISTIAN (1792–1860)

Born at Schmiden on June 21, 1792, B. grew up at Blaubeuren (in Württemberg), where his father was pastor. Having received his primary education from his father, he entered the lower seminary in Blaubeuren in 1805 and the Stift (or Theological Foundation) at the University of Tübingen in 1809. There he studied the idealist philosophy of F. von Schelling (1775–1854), who had been a contemporary of G. W. F. Hegel (1770–1831) at Tübingen two decades earlier. After serving as pastor at Rosswaag and Mülhaufen, in 1817 B. returned to teach at Blaubeuren, where one of his students would be D. F. STRAUSS. B. published his first work, *Symbolik und Mythologie, oder die Naturreligion des Alterthums* (3 vols.), in 1824–25. In 1826, a year after Strauss entered the Stift, B. was appointed professor of theology at Tübingen, where he taught and served as university preacher until his death on Dec. 2, 1860.

B.'s *Symbolik und Mythologie,* although written before he encountered Hegel's philosophy of history, reflects some of the historical concerns of his later work. He argued that the progress of human consciousness of God is analogous to the progressive revelation of God in human history. Whereas Christianity began enmeshed in Judaism (conceived as an institutional "church") and the religions of antiquity, its subsequent history, especially in the achievement of Protestantism, was to supersede these previous limitations of dogmatic legalism. The influence of F. SCHLEIERMACHER's *Der christliche Glaube* (1821–22) is evident here alongside that of Schelling's *Philosophische Untersuchungen über das Wesen der menschlichen Freiheit* (1809). The latter's notion of progress in religion is based on distinguishing three stages in the history of Christianity: the "Petrine" (Catholic), the "Pauline" (Protestant), and the "Johannine" (the future spiritual church).

B.'s approach to the development of early Christianity was influenced by the work of the Roman historian B. Niebuhr (1776–1831) on ancient source criticism and by that of J. SEMLER on the nature of the CANON. In particular the latter, like the English Deist T. MORGAN (see DEISM), had already posited two opposing lines of development in the early church, which Semler had associated with the names of Peter (the Eastern or Jewish) and PAUL (the Western or Hellenistic).

The basic lines of B.'s approach were worked out during his first decade at Tübingen before the full influence of Hegel. Whereas he initially assumed the book of Acts to be fundamentally reliable, by 1835 his view had changed. In 1831 he published his lectures on 1 Corinthians, entitled "Die Christuspartei in der korinthischen Gemeinde." Taking his cue from the factionalism reported in 1 Cor 1:11-13, B. indentified several lines of opposition between Pauline and Petrine Christianity, which he then correlated with the opponents noted in Philippians, Galatians, and 2 Corinthians. One such line he derived from 2 Cor 5:16 to indicate Paul's own sense of conversion from a "fleshly" Judaic outlook. A second he derived from the Pseudo-Clementines, noting that this later partisan document was built upon the legend of Peter's opposition to Simon Magus but was used as a covert attack on Paul. Finally, he identified the later tradition regarding Peter at Rome as a fabrication with similarly partisan tendencies.

In 1835 B. took up the authenticity of the pastorals (see PASTORAL LETTERS) in *Die sogenannten Pastoralbriefe,* basing his arguments on the work of J. G. EICHHORN as well as on parts of Acts. He argued that the pastorals betrayed an anti-GNOSTIC tendency, while Acts reflected an irenic tendency to smooth over the conflicts between Peter and Paul. Both tendencies were quite foreign to Paul's own day. Out of this work he developed his historical-critical approach to the NT, associated with the idea of *Tendenzkritik,* which would lead him also into the history of Christian dogma.

The effects of Hegel's thought and the future direction of the Tübingen school can be seen in B.'s *Paulus, der Apostel Jesu Christi* (1845) and his *Kritische Untersuchungen über die kanonischen Evangelien* (1847). The latter applied tendency criticism to the Gospels to seek an underlying historical core. B. saw Paul standing between the earlier Palestinian tradition and the later Hellenistic tradition of John. While B. agreed with Strauss in opposing the harmonizing tendencies of earlier life of JESUS research, teacher and student here began to diverge sharply. In his *Das Christentum und die christliche Kirche der drei ersten Jahrhunderte* (1853), B. summarized his conclusions on the dating and development of the NT writings. He viewed Matthew as most Jewish and earliest of the Gospels, John as latest. Four of Paul's letters he regarded as genuine: 1–2 Corinthians, Romans, and Galatians. The rest of the letters, Acts, and the catholic epistles he dated to the "catholicizing" tendencies of the second century, in which the opposition between early Jewish and gentile Christianity was harmonized.

B.'s later work concentrated mostly on church history and the development of Christian dogma, while research on the NT and earliest Christianity was left to his students and disciples, notably his son-in-law E. Zeller (1814–1908), C. Weizsäcker (1822–99), F. Schwegler (1819–57), A. HILGENFELD (1823–1907), and (in his early career) A. RITSCHL. A son, F. F. Baur (1825–99), edited and published some of B.'s works and lecture notes after his death.

Works: *Symbolik und Mythologie, oder die Naturreligion des Alterthums* (3 vols., 1824–25); "Die Christuspartei in der korinthischen Gemeinde, der Gegensatz des petrinischen und paulinischen Christenthums in der ältesten Kirche, der Apostle Petrus in Rom," *Tübinger Zeitschrift für Theologie* 4 (1831) 61-206; *Die sogenannten Pastoralbriefe des Apostels Paulus aufs neue kritisch untersucht* (1835); *Die Lehre von der Versöhnung* (1838); "Über den Ursprung des Episcopats in der christlichen Kirche," *Tübinger Zeitschrift für Theologie* 3 (1838) 1-185; *Die christliche Lehre von der Dreieinigkeit* (1841–43); "Über die Composition und den Charakter des johanneischen Evangeliums," *Theologischer Jahrbücher* (ed. F. C. Baur and E. Zeller, 1844) 1-191, 397-475, 615-700; *Paulus, der Apostel Jesu Christi: Sein Leben und Wirken, seine Briefe und seine Lehre. Ein Beitrag zu einer kritischen Geschichte des Urchristenthums* (1845; ET *Paul, the Apostle of Jesus Christ* (2 vols., ed. E. Zeller, 1873–75, 1876²); *Kritische Untersuchungen über die kanonischen Evangelien, ihr Verhältnis zu einander, ihren Charakter und Ursprung* (1847); "Die Einleitung in das Neue Testament als theologische Wissenschaft: Ihr Begriff und ihre Aufgabe, ihr Entwicklungsgang und ihr innerer Organismus," *Theologische Jahrbücher* 9 (1850) 463-566; 10 (1851) 70-94, 222-53, 291-329; *Geschichte der christliche Kirche* (5 vols., 1853–62), vol. 1, *Das Christentum und die christliche Kirche der drei ersten Jahrhunderte* (1853; ET *The Church History of the First Three Centuries*, 2 vols., 1878–79); *Lehrbuch der christlichen Dogmengeschichte* (1847, 1858²); *Die Tübinger Schule und ihre Stellung zur Gegenwart* (1859, 1860²); *Vorlesungen über die christliche Dogmengeschichte* (4 vols., ed. F.

F. Baur, 1865–67). For a full listing of B.'s works see H. Schmidt and J. Haussleiter, *RE*³ 2 (1897) 467-70; G. Fraedrich, 377-82, and K. Scholder (ed.), *F. C. B.: Ausgewählte Werke in Einzelausgaben* (5 vols., 1963–67).

Bibliography: E. **Barnikol,** *Das ideengeschichtliche Erbe Hegels bei und seit Strauss und Baur im 19. Jahrhundert* (1961). **G. Fraedrich,** *F. C. B., der Begründer der Tübinger Schule, als Theologe, Schriftsteller und Charakter* (1909). **K. Geiger,** *Spekulation und Kritik: Die Geschichtstheologie F. C. B.s* (1964). **P. C. Hodgson,** *The Formation of Historical Theology: A Study of F. C. B.* (1966); (ed.), *F. C. B. on the Writing of Church History* (1968). **W. G. Kümmel,** *NTHIP,* 127-43; **R. Morgan,** *NCRTW,* 1:261-89; *Biblical Interpretation* (1988) 62-76. **J. C. O'Neill,** *The Bible's Authority: A Portrait Gallery of Thinkers from Lessing to Bultmann* (1991) 117-25. **K. Scholder,** *TRE* 5 (1980) 352-59.

L. M. WHITE

BAYLE, PIERRE (1647–1706)

The son of a Protestant pastor, B. was born at Carla-le-Compte (Carla-Bayle) near Pamiers on Nov. 18, 1647, attended college at Puy-Laurens (1666–69), studied under the Jesuits at Toulouse for a time, and temporarily became Catholic. After reverting to Protestantism he moved to Geneva (1670) and then Paris (1674) before being appointed professor of philosophy at the University of Sedan through the influence of M. Jurieu (1675); he later held a similar position at Rotterdam (1681–93). After the appearance of the great comet of 1680, B. published a work challenging the view that comets presage catastrophes and that atheism naturally leads to immorality. Throughout his career he was a strong advocate of tolerance even for atheists and opposed military actions undertaken in the name of religion. From 1684 to 1687 he edited the influential periodical *Nouvelles de la république des lettres*. Growing tensions with Jurieu reached a climax in B.'s advocacy of conciliation between Protestants and the French government as opposed to Jurieu's advocacy of holy-war militancy. Under the latter's influence, B. was deprived of his professorship (1693) and thereafter devoted himself to his dictionary (see DICTIONARIES AND ENCYCLOPEDIAS), having published *Projets et fragments d'un Dictionnaire critique* in 1692.

B.'s place in the history of biblical studies rests on the articles written on various biblical topics and personages (mostly HB) in his famous dictionary, which became one of the most widely owned books of the eighteenth century. His articles, with their extensive annotations, allowed B. opportunity to give expression to his entertaining style, cleverness, moral commitments, skeptical and ironically critical sentiments, and relativizing tendencies, while writing on an almost unlimited number of subjects. Of all the articles in the first edition of the dictionary, the one on David raised the greatest opposition, and B. was censured by the consistory of the Walloon Church in Rotterdam and ordered to rewrite the article along stipulated lines. He did so and published both the revised and the earlier version in the second edition of the dictionary. The article, with its opening reference to "the man after God's own heart," contained many traditional and complimentary statements about David, which are then totally countered in the footnote annotations. Following the biblical text with almost painful scrupulosity, B. told a tale of David that is filled with adulteries, murders, massacres, treacheries, and injustices. In contrast to previous treatments of the biblical past, B.'s articles represented the first "profanation of sacred history." In addition to painting a picture of an unillustrious David, the article noted disjunctures and repetitions in the narrative: "If such a narrative as this should be found in Thucydides, or in Livy, all the Critics would unanimously conclude, that the transcribers had transposed the Pages, forgot something in one Place, repeated something in another, or inserted some preposterous Additions in the Author's Work. But no such Suspicions ought to be entertained of the Bible." The point, of course, was to raise just such suspicions.

The furor created by the article on David lasted throughout the eighteenth century and provided a perennial topic for popular discussion of the Bible's morality, the role of the Bible in modern culture, and the nature and origin of biblical literature. The Jesuit Merlin wrote an apology for David and an attack on B. (1737); in Britain similar tomes were produced by P. Delaney (3 vols., 1740–42) and S. Chandler (2 vols., 1766). P. ANNET picked up and extended B.'s picture in his *The History of the Man After God's Own Heart* (published anonymously, 1762), which appeared in French (in 1768, probably translated by Baron d'Holbach) and provided fuel and inspiration for VOLTAIRE's drama *Saül*.

B.'s threat to traditional views can be seen in the fact that the 1734–41 ET of his work added "reflections on such passages of Mr. Bayle as seem to favour *scepticism* and the *Manichee* system."

Works: *Pensées diverses sur la comète* (1681; 2 vols., ed. A. Prat, 1939); *Critique général de l'histoire du Calvinisme* (1682); *Dictionnaire historique et critique* (2 vols., 1696; 6 vols., 1702; 16 vols., ed. Beuchot, 1820–24; ET 4 vols., 1710; 5 vols., 1734–37; expanded 10 vols., 1734–41); *Philosophical Commentary: A Modern Translation and Critical Interpretation* (1987); *Oeuvres diverses de P. B.* (4 vols., 1727–31, 1737²); *Selections from Bayle's Dictionary* (ed. E. A. Beller, 1952); *P. B.: Historical and Critical Dictionary, Selections* (tr. and ed. R. H. Popkin, 1965).

Bibliography: A. Cazès, *P. B., sa vie, ses idées son influence, son oeuvre* (1905). E. Labrousee, *Pierre Bayle, 1647–1706* (1963, 1985²). F. J. M. Laplanche, *L'Écriture, le sacré et l'historie* (SIB 12, 1986) 601-8, 663-73. S. O'Cathasaigh, "Skepticism and Belief in Bayle's *Nouvelles lettres critiques*," *JHI* 45 (1984) 421-33. R. H. Popkin, "Skepticism and the Counter-Reformation in France," *ARG* 51 (1960) 58-86. R. G. Possen, *The Biblical Articles in P. B.'s Dictionnaire historique et critique: Their Structure and Function* (1974). W. Rex, "P. B.: The Theology and Politics of the Article on David," *BHR* 24 (1962) 168-89; 25 (1963) 366-403; *Essays on P. B. and Religious Controversy* (1965). H. Robinson, *The Great Comet of 1680: An Episode in the History of Rationalism* (1916); "Bayle's Profanation of Sacred History," *Essays in Intellectual History Dedicated to J. H. Robinson* (ed. J. Shotwell, 1929) 147-62; *Bayle the Sceptic* (1931). C. Serrurier, *P. B. en Hollande: Étude historique et critique* (1912).

J. H. HAYES

BEARE, FRANCIS WRIGHT (1902–86)

Born in Toronto on Aug. 16, 1902, B. graduated from the University of Toronto with an honors BA in classics (1925) and lectured in classics at Queens University. After two years of study in Paris he became lecturer in Greek at McMaster University (then situated in Toronto) in 1928. Simultaneously he read divinity at Knox College, graduating a year later.

In 1931 he was invited to the French Institute of Oriental Archaeology in Cairo, where for two years he assisted in the publication of Greek papyri. He then joined Presbyterian College, Montreal, as lecturer (later professor) of church history and history of religions. He was a founding member of the Canadian Society of Biblical Studies (1933) and later its president (1942). His first NT appointment was as visiting lecturer at Union Seminary in New York (1944–45). During that year he completed his commentary on 1 Peter, on the strength of which the University of Chicago awarded him a PhD (for its importance in NT scholarship, see Elliott [1976]). In 1946 he accepted the chair of NT studies at Trinity College, Toronto, where he taught until his retirement in 1968. While there he wrote four more commentaries and numerous articles. A member of the RSV committee, he also served as president of the SOCIETY OF BIBLICAL LITERATURE (1969). In his retirement he completed a commentary on Matthew and received honorary doctorates from Trinity College (1980) and, a week before his death (May 14, 1986), from Knox College.

B. came to NT studies through classics. When he made the NT his specialty he was not dependent on any particular master or school. He viewed the NT as a collection of documents from the late classical period, approaching it as a text critic (see TEXTUAL CRITICISM, NT) and historian. His greatest strength as an interpreter was his common sense, coupled with a generous sense of humor. Though not a classifier of forms, he found the conclusions of FORM CRITICISM congenial. Like the majority of NT scholars of his day, he resolved inconsistencies in the text by source criticism. Thus he considered Philippians composite, with 3:2–4:1 and 4:10-20 as interpolations. He was disinclined to accept Colossians as PAUL's, and he denied the authenticity of Ephesians.

Works: *The First Epistle of Peter* (1947, 1958², 1970³); "The Epistle to the Ephesians," *IB* 10 (1953) 595-749; "The Epistle to the Colossians," *IB* 11 (1955) 131-241; *The Epistle to the Philippians* (BNTC, 1959, 1969², 1988³; *St. Paul and His Letters* (1962); *The Earliest Records of Jesus* (1962, 1964²); *The Gospel According to Matthew* (1982).

Bibliography: J. H. Elliott, "The Rehabilitation of an Exegetical Step-Child: 1 Peter in Recent Research," *JBL* 95 (1976) 243-54. **J. S. Moir,** *A History of Biblical Studies in Canada: A Sense of Proportion* (1982), see index. **P. Richardson and J. C. Hurd** (eds.), *From Jesus to Paul: Studies in Honour of F. W. B.* (1984), with appreciations, xxv-xxx, and full bibliography, xix-xxiv. **I. S. Wishart,** "F. W. B., 1902–1986: A Tribute from a Former Student," *TJT* 3 (1987) 126-29.
J. C. HURD

BECK, JOHANN TOBIAS (1804–78)

Born in Balingen in 1804, B. studied at Tübingen, then held pastorates in Waldtann and Bad Mergentheim. From 1843 he was professor of systematic theology at Tübingen. B.'s thought was shaped by Württemburg PIETISM (J. Bengel), a Romantic naturalism (Schelling), and a profound moral concern. He stood against his age but with exemplary pastoral and moral strengths.

B.'s HERMENEUTICS developed in biblical interpretation that opposed both the prevailing Hegelianism and orthodox confessionalism and included three major principles. First, all Christian doctrine must be drawn from the Bible alone. The Bible reveals the redemptive-historical activity of the Spirit of God as being an organic whole. Interpretive method must, therefore, be genetic, not speculative or reflective, unfolding the life of faith (*Einleitung* [1870] 33).

Second, the moral in human nature is the basis of any correct scientific understanding of Christianity (*Glaubenslehre* [1886–87] 1:1). Theology's task is not to nourish an abstract science or to serve utilitarian concerns, but to be the mediator of eternal life from God (1:108). B. interpreted PAUL's justification language to mean "make righteous."

Third, the biblical kingdom of God guaranteed in JESUS Christ is real, an organic, dynamic, supersensible reality actually encompassing both heaven and earth. Hidden in the present yet visible in moral Christian life, it is destined to be wholly revealed in a final consummation (1886–87, 2:676).

Works: *Einleitung in das System der christlichen Lehre* (1838; 1870²; *Die christlichen Lehrwissenschaft nach den biblischen Urkunden,* 1 (1847; 1875²; *Erklärung des Briefes Pauli an die Römer* (1884); *Vorlesungen über christliche Glaubenslehre* (1886–87).

Bibliography: K. Barth, *Protestant Theology in the Nineteenth Century* (ET 1972). **T. Harjupaa,** "Beckian Biblicism and Finland: A Study in Historical Perspective," *Lutheran Quarterly* 20 (1976): 290-330. **A. Schlatter,** *B.'s theologische Arbeit* (1904). **A. Sturhahn,** *Zur systematischen Theologie J. T. B.s* (1903).
J. P. MARTIN

BEDE (c. 673–735)

The most important and prolific writer of Anglo-Saxon England, B. spent all but his early childhood in the Northumbrian twin monastery of St. Peter and St. Paul with houses at Wearmouth and Jarrow. He was a teacher and scholar who today is best known for his majestic historical work, the *Historia ecclesiastica gentis Anglorum.* In this book, finished in 731, he relates that he had given his "entire lifework to the study of Scripture." He was referring to a corpus of nearly twenty volumes, the only Latin commentaries ever written in England by an Anglo-Saxon. Soon after his death these writings began to circulate on the continent, where they became the bedrock of B.'s immense medieval fame. ALCUIN, P. ABELARD, and Dante were only three of the major authors who took for granted that B. was one of the Latin church fathers.

Almost entirely verse-by-verse exegesis, B.'s commentaries embrace a wide range of the biblical literature in both testaments. Perhaps his most important contribution to the Latin exegetical tradition was the first full prose commentary on the Acts of the Apostles, to which he later added a separate book of learned retractions. He read the text in both Latin and Greek; it was the only biblical book of which he had a manuscript in the original language. B. was a champion of JEROME's Bible, mainly because it included a translation of the HB from the Hebrew. The oldest full copy of the VULGATE, now known as the *Codex Amiatinus,* was written at Monkwearmouth-Jarrow during the age of B.

All of B.'s exegesis is suffused with a nearly programmatic purpose: to bring the new English church into the mainstream of Roman and patristic Christianity. To this end his typical method was to excerpt and adapt the writings of the fathers, especially AUGUSTINE and GREGORY THE GREAT. His commentaries are not, however, merely derivative; he used nothing without first understanding it, wrote many excerpts that are clearer than the original, and assimilated everything to his own instructional goal. For the rest, his exegesis owed a great debt to the liberal arts, above all to grammar and its theory of figures. In a small book written for other exegetes, the *De schematibus et tropis,* he gave to the Middle Ages a *locus classicus* for the theory of the fourfold senses of Scripture. The great expanse of B.'s exegesis is allegorical, but he seems most at home when expounding the literal and moral senses. His commentaries are pastoral in purpose and eclectic in method. Their enduring authority sprang from his exemplary scholarship and from a welcoming display of Roman spirituality.

Works: Critical editions of all but three of B.'s exegetical works appear in CCSL: Acts (121); Catholic Epistles (121); Ezra and Nehemiah (119A); Genesis (118A); Habbakkuk (119B); Luke (120); Mark (120); Proverbs (119B); 1 Samuel (119); Song of Songs (119B); Tabernacle [Exodus] (119A); Temple [Kings and Chronicles] (119A); Thirty Questions [Kings] (119); Tobit (119B). Revelation and Eight Questions [Psalms] are in *PL* 93; the *collectaneum* on the Pauline epistles has never been printed; all three of these will eventually appear in CCSL. The *De schematibus et tropis* is in CCSL (123A); for a translation by G. H. Tannenhaus, see J. Miller et al. (eds.), *Readings in Medieval Rhetoric* (1973). On the Catholic epistles, see *Bede the Venerable: Commentary on the Seven Catholic Epistles* (tr. D. Hurst, Cistercian Studies Series 82, 1985).

Bibliography: G. H. Brown, *B. the Venerable* (1987). **M. T. A. Carroll,** *The Venerable B.: His Spiritual Teachings* (Catholic University of America Studies in Medieval History, n.s. 9, 1946). **R. D. Ray,** "What Do We Know About B.'s Commentaries?" *RTM* 49 (1982) 5-20.

R. D. RAY

BEGRICH, JOACHIM (1900–45)

Born at Predel, Saxony, June 13, 1900, B. studied oriental languages and theology at Leipzig and Halle with H. GUNKEL (1919–23), who entrusted him with the completion of his *Introduction to the Psalms.* B.'s own teaching career took him from Halle (assistant, 1926), to Marburg (*Privatdozent,* 1928), to Leipzig (*ausserordentlicher* professor, 1930). In the 1930s B. was a leader in the Confessing Church's resistance to the Nazis. He was killed in military service on April 26, 1945.

As Gunkel's pupil, B. distinguished himself as a form critic (see FORM CRITICISM) with monographs on the psalm of Hezekiah (1926) and Deutero-Isaiah (1938), including discussion of genre questions, and he authored articles on biblical literary forms: the "expression of confidence" in the Israelite and Babylonian individual lament (1928), the priestly "oracle of salvation" (1934), and "torah" (1936). In his 1929 monograph on the CHRONOLOGY of the kings of Israel and Judah, and in articles on the Syro-Ephraimite war (1929) and the titles of David's functionaries (1940), he dealt with historical/

chronological questions. He devoted attention to text criticism (see TEXTUAL CRITICISM), editing the third edition of R. KITTEL's *Biblia Hebraica* (1937), and wrote on metrical questions, on biblical concepts (e.g., covenant), and on the place of the HB in Protestantism. Two of B.'s monographs and a collection of ten of his articles were reprinted in the 1960s.

Works: *Der Psalm des Hiskia* (1926); *Die Chronologie der Könige von Israel und Juda* (1929, repr. 1966); *Studien zu Deuterojesaja* (TBü 20, 1938, repr. 1969); *Gesammelte Studien zum Alten Testament* (TBü 21, 1964).

Bibliography: H. Bardtke, "In memoram J. B.," *TLZ* 75 (1950) 441-46.

C. T. BEGG

BEKHOR SHOR, JOSEPH BEN ISAAC OF ORLEANS (12th cent.)

Few biographical details about B. are known: He lived in northern France; he was a reputed Talmudist (see TALMUD), a student of the celebrated Rabbenou Tam; and he was a biblical exegete of renown. Of all his exegetical work only the commentary on the Pentateuch (see PENTATEUCHAL CRITICISM) has come down to us in its entirety, and even this was not published until 1956–60 in a complete, but not critical, edition.

B. is a faithful representative of the Jewish exegetical school in medieval France. It is easy to discern in his commentary the influence of his great predecessors RASHI and especially SAMUEL BEN MEIR (Rashbam). With respect for the tradition, B. attempted to present a literal exegesis of the text. He engaged in sharp controversy with Christian exegesis, especially on some basic dogmatic subjects but also on some detailed points. For this reason his commentary was much more "engaged" than that of his predecessors, probably because of the deterioration that marked the atmosphere of relations between Jews and Christians beginning about the middle of the twelfth century. The rationalist approach to the text—so dear in this twelfth-century renaissance—led B. to explain the details of some biblical narratives by the customs in use in the society of his own time, which he defined as *derekh haolam.* "It is from custom that the woman prefers the one who works with sheep and goats" (on Gen 25:28, to explain the preference of Rebecca). "It is the custom of the great to make a feast when they have hope of a high distinction" (on Gen 27:4). The miracles ought to be understood rationally because, "generally speaking God performs miracles according to the laws of nature" (on Exod 15:25; see also on Gen 19:17, 26; 41:7). His explanation of the diversity of human languages (on Gen 11:7) and his treatment of narrative doublets (on Exod 16:13; Num 20:8-12; Deut 32:51; 33:8) were original and already heralded modern criticism. Contrary to Rashi and Rash-bam, B. was almost never concerned with the philological problems of the text; rarely did he even propose a French translation of Hebrew words. His attitude toward the midrashic commentaries (see MIDRASH) was inconsistent. His exegesis occasionally contains explanations based on *gematria* (arithmetical values of the letters of the alphabet).

B. probably knew Latin. In any case, he was well versed in christological exegesis, with which he often argued, sometimes bitterly (on Gen 24:2), sometimes calmly (on the Trinity and the Incarnation; Gen 1:26; 18:1-2). He went out of his way to reject exegesis that allegorized the sense of the commandments of the law (on Num 12:7-8).

Works: *Commentaire sur le Pentateuque, Edition définitive* (1957–1960).

Bibliography: EncJud (1972) 4:410-11. **S. Kamin,** "The Polemic Against Allegory in the Commentary of Rabbi J. B. S.," *Jerusalem Studies in Jewish Thought* 3 (1983–84) 367-92. **Y. Nevo,** "The Exegetical Method of Rabbi J. B. S." (diss., Leiden, 1987). **N. Porges,** *J. B S.* (1908). **S. A. Poznanski,** *Kommentar au Ezechiel und das XII Kleinen Propheten von Eliezer aus Beaugency* (1913) LV-LXXXV (Hebrew). **G. Walter,** *J. B. S.: Der letzte nord-franzoesische Bibelexeget* (1890).

E. TOUITOU

BELLARMINE, ROBERTO FRANCESCO ROMOLO (1542–1621)

Born at Montepulciano, Tuscany, on October 4, 1542, B. attended the local Jesuit college and entered the Society of Jesus, where he was formally trained in Aristotelian philosophy and Thomistic theology in preparation for ordination (1570). He taught at the University of Louvain (1569–76) and at the Jesuit Collegio Romano (1576–88), during which time his studies in Scripture, church history, and patristics led to his *De controversiis* (1586–93), his monumental attack on the Protestant Reformers. He served as an editor of the Clementine edition of the Bible (1592). In 1599 he was named a cardinal, spending his remaining years in the Vatican Curia and as theological adviser to various popes, especially Paul V (1605–21). He participated as a judge at Bruno's trial (1600) and in the condemnation (1616) of Copernicanism, in which he was also assigned the task of admonishing Galileo to accept that judgment. B. died in Rome on Sept. 17, 1621. He was canonized in 1930 and declared a Doctor of the Church in 1931.

B. was a qualified literalist in his approach to the Bible, preferring the literal over a metaphorical reading wherever possible. As part of his Counter-Reformation stance, he insisted that the authority to determine the meaning of Scripture is not located in the individual but in the church, i.e., in the pope and church councils. He used the Tridentine doctrine of tradition extensively in his appeal to the church fathers as a means to establish the true meaning of the Bible. In his famous *Letter to Foscarini* (April 12, 1615) he argued that if heliocentricism were proven to be true, then the Bible would need to be reinterpreted accordingly. Yet in the same letter he also argued that even if a detail in the Bible, because of its subject matter, is not a matter of faith, it still remains a matter of faith because of the authority of the speaker (see AUTHORITY OF THE BIBLE).

Works: *Disputationes de controversiis christianae fidei adversus hujus temporis haereticos* (3 vols., 1586–93); *In omnes Psalmos dilucida exposito* (1611); *De scriptoribus ecclesiasticis* (1615).

Bibliography: **X.-M. Le Bachelet,** *Bellarmin avant son cardinalat, 1542–1598* (1911); *Bellarmin et le Bible Sixto-Clémentine* (1911). **U. Baldini and G. V. Coyne,** *The Louvain Lectures (Lectiones Lovanienses) of Bellarmine and the Autograph Copy of His 1616 Declaration to Galileo* (1984). **R. J. Blackwell,** *Galileo, Bellarmine, and the Bible* (1991). **J. Brodrick,** *The Life and Work of R. F. Cardinal Bellarmine, S.J.* (1928; rev. ed., *R. B.: Saint and Scholar,* 1961).

R. J. BLACKWELL

BEN-ASHER, AARON BEN MOSES (10th cent.)

A tenth-century Masorete (fl. c. 930), B. was the last and most important of five generations of Masoretes. He was mostly known for his Masoretic *Dikdukei ha-Te'amim,* rules concerning vocalization and accentuation, and for the list of *ḥillufim* (variants) between B. and BEN-NAPHTALI, mostly minor variants in accentuation, especially *ga'ayot.*

In 1958 the famous codex attributed to B. that had been in Aleppo (Syria) since at least the fifteenth century arrived in Israel. During the last half of this century, several studies have demonstrated the importance of this manuscript. The ancient tradition that MAIMONIDES (*Hilkhot Sefer Torah* 8:4) relied on the Aleppo Codex when it was in Egypt after being transferred there from Jerusalem was proven to be true, both with respect to the layout of the Song of Moses (Deuteronomy 32; M. Goshen-Gottstein [1960]), and the PENTATEUCHAL open and closed sections (J. Penkower [1981]). What is more, it was proven that from among the accurate Tiberian manuscripts (= the accurate Bible manuscripts of the 10th–11th century from the region of Eretz Israel-Egypt with Tiberian Masorah and vocalization) the text of the Aleppo Codex most accurately reflects the text of the Masoretic notes in the accurate Tiberian manuscripts (M. Breuer [1976]; M. Cohen [1973]). In addition, the system of vocalization and accentuation in the Aleppo Codex and in manuscripts close to its system has been the subject of detailed study, which has proven that from among the accurate Tiberian manuscripts the Aleppo Codex most faithfully reflects the tradition of B. (I. Yeivin [1968]). In short, one may rely on the eleventh-century dedicatory notice (concerning the date, see Glatzer [1988]) added to the codex (no longer extant; see J. Ofer [1988] for the latest edition of this dedication), which attributed the vocalization, accentuation, and Masorah of the codex to B. (the scribe being Solomon ben Buya' a).

The importance of B.'s Aleppo Codex, established by the above-mentioned studies, makes all the more sorely felt the loss of the portions that are no longer extant: the Pentateuch, except for Deut 27:17 to end; the Five Scrolls (partial), Esther, Daniel, Ezra; and sporadic pages from other books. Recently, part of this loss has been alleviated: (a) Penkower has discovered a sixteenth-century witness (= a 1490 printed Pentateuch with later handwritten glosses by Yishai ben 'Amram 'Amadi) to the Pentateuchal text (Exodus–Deuteronomy) in the Aleppo Codex (consonantal text; open and closed sections; songs layout). His study (1992) reinforces the conclusion that Maimonides relied on the Aleppo Codex. He further shows that the Pentateuchal text in the Aleppo Codex is the most accurate among the accurate Tiberian manuscripts (similar to Breuer's results concerning the Prophets), and that the Yemenite manuscripts reflect the Aleppo Codex in the Pentateuch (as hypothesized by Breuer; so too regarding open and closed sections and layout of the songs, with the exception of three cases based on a misinterpretation of Maimonides' *Mishneh Torah*). (b) Ofer (1988) has published a study based on M. CASSUTO's recently discovered notes concerning the Aleppo Codex, written in Aleppo in 1943. These notes deal mostly with selected cases of vocalization and accentuation in Genesis and with the Masoretic material at the beginning of the codex. Cassuto also copied there a nineteenth-century list of Pentateuchal texual variants in the codex. Ofer has presented a similar list found in a seventeenth-century responsum by R. Samuel Vital (see Penkower [1992]). (c) Ofer (1992) has published a study on the printed Bible belonging to R. Shalom Shakhna Yellin, with handwritten glosses by his son-in-law M. KIMHI based on the Aleppo Codex. These notes deal with selected cases of vocalization, accentuation, and text throughout the Bible. Also dealt with are open and closed sections in the Bible. (d) R. Zer (1987) published J. Sapir's *Me'orot Natan* (1855; rediscovered by Goshen-Gottstein in 1962), selected readings in the Pentateuch and the Haftarot of the Aleppo Codex (mostly cases of vocalization and accentuation).

During the Middle Ages there was an accepted ideal among Jewish scholars that "we follow the biblical tradition of B," e.g., Maimonides, *Hilkhot Sefer Torah* 8:4 (concerning the layout of the songs and the open and closed sections of the Pentateuch; so, too, regarding the consonantal text of the Pentateuch); D. KIMHI, introduction to *Sefer Ha-Shorashim* (concerning vocalization and accentuation); and in the seventeenth century, R. Menaḥem di Lonzano, '*Or Torah,* in *Shtei Yadot* (1618) f. 3b; R. Yedidyah Norẓi, *Minḥat Shai* (completed 1626, printed 1742–44), on Gen 1:4. However, in practice not all the manuscripts followed B. (as actualized in the Aleppo Codex) in the consonantal text (especially in the cases of plene-defective spelling), or in all the details of vocalization and accentuation, including *ga'ayot.* Thus some of the manuscripts exhibited different sub-systems (e.g., some tend to mark most of the "light *ga'ayot,*" whereas B.—as seen in the Aleppo Codex— does not mark them, except under special circumstances); others exhibited mixed systems. Most of these variants, it should be stressed, are minor in character. With the printing of the 1525 RABBINIC BIBLE, edited by JACOB BEN ḤAYYIM on the basis of accurate Spanish manuscripts (though with some influence from other sources; especially out of character was his marking "light *ga'ayot*" in the Pentateuch and Prophets, following Pratensis's 1517 rabbinic Bible, based here upon Ashkenazi sources), which came to be accepted as the *textus receptus,* the previous situation of heterogeneous sources tended toward standardization.

In the twentieth century scholars have attempted to return to the standard of the B. text. P. KAHLE especially began the momentum with the printing of MS Leningrad B19a (with its *massorah parva*) as the basis of the *Biblia Hebraica* (Stuttgart, 1937). A more accurate transcription of that manuscript (without Masorah) was published by A. Dotan (Tel-Aviv 1973, 1976). With the arrival of the Aleppo Codex in Israel, work began on preparing an edition on the basis of this ultimate B. manuscript. Thus Goshen-Gottstein chose that manuscript as the basis of the text, *massorah magna* and *massorah parva,* of the Hebrew University Bible. To date, the book of Isaiah has appeared (ed. M. Goshen-Gottstein, 3 fascicles: 1975, 1981, 1993 = one vol., Jerusalem 1995), as has the book of Jeremiah (ed. S. Talmon, Jerusalem, 1997); the book of Ezekiel (ed. S. Talmon) is in preparation. In addition, Goshen-Gottstein saw through the press a photo edition of the Aleppo Codex (Jersualem, 1976). M. Breuer published a Bible edition on the basis of the Aleppo Codex and manuscripts close to it (3 vols., Jerusalem, 1977, 1979, 1982 = 1 vol., 1989, 1993³), though the details of vocalization and accentuation, including *ga'ayot,* do not always conform to the Aleppo Codex (see his remarks at the end of vol. 3). Cohen of Bar-Ilan University is preparing a new edition of the rabbinic Bible with the Bible text, *massorah magna* and *massorah parva,* based on the Aleppo Codex. Four volumes have appeared to date: Joshua and Judges (1992; see the introduction for the editorial policy regarding the material missing in Aleppo Codex); 1 and

2 Samuel (1993); 1 and 2 Kings (1995); Isaiah (1996); Genesis (vol. 1 to 25:18, 1997). Genesis (vol. 2) is in press.

Bibliography: Diqduqe Ha-Teamim: S. Baer and H. L. Strack, *Die Dikduke Ha-Teamim des Aharon ben Moscheh ben Ascher* (1879; photo ed., 1970). **A. Dotan,** *The Diqduqé Hatte'amim of Aharon ben Mose ben Ašer....* (1967), Hebrew. **The Hillufim: A. Ben-David,** "The *Hillufim* between Ben-Asher and Ben-Naphtali in the Light of an Examination of Early Sources," *Beit Miqra* 3 (1958) 1-19 (Hebrew). **L. Lipshütz,** "*Kitab al-Khilaf,* the Book of the *Hillufim*," *Textus* 4 (1964) 1-29. **M. ben Uzziel,** "*Kitab al-Khilaf*" (ed. L. Lipshütz), *Textus* 2 (1962) 3-57 (Hebrew-Arabic). **The Aleppo Codex: I. Ben-Zvi,** "The Codex of Ben-Asher," *Textus* 1 (1960) 1-16. **M. Breuer,** *The Aleppo Codex and the Accepted Text of the Bible* (1976, Hebrew). **M. Cohen,** "Orthographic Systems in Ancient Massorah Codices and Their Import for the History of the Traditional HB Text" (diss., Hebrew University, 1973), Hebrew; "Systems of Light Ga'ayot in Medieval Biblical Manuscripts and Their Importance for the History of the Tiberian Systems of Notation," *Textus* 10 (1982) 44-83; "Sub-Systems of 'Extra-Massoretic' Tiberian Accentuation and Their Distribution in Medieval Biblical Manuscripts," *Leshoneinu* 51 (1987) 188-206 (Hebrew); "The Victory of the Ben-Asher Text: Theory and Reality," *Tarbiz* 53 (1984) 255-72 (Hebrew). **M. Glatzer,** "The Aleppo Codex: Codicological and Paleographical Aspects," *Sefunot* 19 (1988) 167-276 (Hebrew). **M. H. Goshen-Gottstein,** "The Authenticity of the Aleppo Codex," *Textus* 1 (1960) 17-58; [on *Me'orot Natan*] *Textus* 2 (1962) 53-59. **J. Ofer,** "M. D. Cassuto's Notes on the Aleppo Codex," *Sefunot* 19 (1988) 277-344 (Hebrew); "The Aleppo Codex and the Bible of R. Shalom Shakhna Yellin," *Rabbi M. Breuer Festschrift* (1992) 295-353 (Hebrew). **J. S. Penkower,** "Maimonides and the Aleppo Codex," *Textus* 9 (1981) 39-128; "Jacob ben Hayyium and the Rise of the Biblia Rabbinica" (diss., Hebrew University, 1982), Hebrew, with extensive summary in English and detailed bibliography of previous literature); *New Evidence for the Pentateuch Text in the Aleppo Codex* (1992), Hebrew. **I. Yeivin,** *The Aleppo Codex of the Bible: A Study of Its Vocalization and Accentuation* (1968), Hebrew. **R. Zer,** "*Me'orot Natan* by R. Jacob Sapir (MS JTS L729)," *Leshoneinu* 50 (1986) 151-213. **Moses Ben-Asher and the Cairo Codex:** **M. Cohen,** "Was Moshe Ben Asher Really the Scribe of the Cairo Codex of the Prophets?" *Alei Sefer* 10 (1982) 5-12 (Hebrew). **A. Dotan,** *Diqduqé* etc. (1967) 70-71; *Sefarad* 46 (1986) 162-68. **M. Glatzer,** *Sefunot* 19 (1988) 250-59. **L. Lipschütz,** *Textus* 4 (1964) 6-7. **J. S. Penkower,** "A Pentateuch Fragment from the Tenth Century Attributed to Moses Ben-Asher (MS Firkowicz B188)," *Tarbiz* 60 (1991) 355-70 (Hebrew; includes bibliography concerning the Cairo Codex).

J. S. PENKOWER

BEN-NAPHTALI, MOSES BEN DAVID (10th cent.)

A tenth-century Masorete, B. was a contemporary of A. BEN-ASHER. Several manuscripts preserve a list of biblical *hillufim* (variants) between these two Masoretes, mainly concerning minor variants in accentuation, especially *ga'ayot*. The list also contains examples where Ben Asher and B. agree with each other (versus another opinion). The compiler of the list was Mishael ben Uzziel (10th–11th cents.); a critical edition was published by L. Lipshütz. From this list we can deduce that B. and Ben-Asher do not represent two rival schools regarding the biblical text but rather the contrary. (1) Concerning the consonantal text, the list notes only eight variants between them. In other words, they agree on the consonantal text of the Bible aside from a handful of variants. This agreed-upon text, which we find in the accurate Tiberian manuscripts (e.g., A = Aleppo Codex; S = Sassoon 507; S1 = Sassoon 1053; L = Leningrad [St. Petersburg] B19a; C3 = Cairo 3-second hand; with a certain amount of internal variants among them), differs from other contemporary manuscripts (e.g., C3-first hand; L18 = Leningrad Firk. A, 59; N = JTS 232), which contain many textual variants, especially in plene-defective readings. The most perfect actualization of this consonantal text from the standpoint of Ben-Asher is A. (2) Most of the variants in the list deal with minor issues of accentuation, especially *ga'ayot*. Even in these issues B. and Ben-Asher do not represent two different systems; rather, they agree concerning the basic vocalization and accentuation system but disagree in several specific cases throughout the Bible. This agreed-upon Tiberian vocalization and accentuation system, which can be found in several accurate Tiberian manuscripts (e.g., A, S1, L), differs from other contemporary systems, e.g., the Eretz Israel system, and the Eretz Israel-Tiberian system. The most perfect actualization of this Tiberian vocalization and accentuation system from the standpoint of Ben-Asher is A. (3) At the beginning of the *hillufim* list—before the listing of the specific variants between B. and Ben-Asher as well as of *passim* in the list—a number of systematic variants between B. and Ben-Asher are noted; e.g., "*bin-Nun*"-first letter of second word without *dagesh* (Ben-Asher), with *dagesh* (B.); "*bysr'l*"/"*lysr'l*"-first letter with *shewa,* second letter with *hiriq* (Ben-Asher); first letter with *hiriq,* second letter with no vocalization (B.).

Based on the systematic and the specific variants of the list as well as the agreements, one may try to identify Tiberian manuscripts that agree with B. and Ben-Asher in matters of vocalization and accentuation (as noted in the *hillufim* list). The Aleppo Codex (A) has been shown to conform in the highest degree to Ben-Asher in the *hillufim* list. (C3-second hand also shows a high conformity; however, in other matters it does not agree with Ben-Asher's system as found in the Aleppo Codex.) On the other hand, no manuscript has been identified that conforms in a similar degree to B. in the *hillufim* list. Nevertheless, several manuscripts have been identified that show signs of B.'s systematic variants and a proclivity toward his specific variants (S, 46 percent; C3-first hand, 50 percent; S1, c. approx. 60 percent; C, 64 percent). It should be stressed that conformity to one of the opinions in the B./Ben-Asher ḥillufim list does not necessarily guarantee that a manuscript is following B. or Ben-Asher. That conclusion can only be granted once we study the rest of the biblical text, i.e., consonants, vocalization, and accentuation, and compare it to the Aleppo Codex, the perfect actualization of Ben-Asher's work.

Bibliography: A. Ben-David, "On What Did Ben-Asher and Ben-Naphtali Differ?" *Tarbiz* 26 (1957) 384-409 (Hebrew); "The *Ḥillufim* Between Ben-Asher and Ben-Naphtali in the Light of an Examination of Early Sources," *Beit Miqra* 3 (1958) 1-19 (Hebrew). **M. Cohen,** "The Victory of the Ben-Asher Text: Theory and Reality," *Tarbiz* 53 (1984) 255-72 (Hebrew). **L. Lipshütz,** *"Kitab al-Khilaf,* The Book of the *Ḥillufim,"* *Textus* 4 (1964) 1-29. **J. S. Penkower,** "A Tenth-century Pentateuchal Manuscript from Jerusalem (MS C3), corrected by M. ben Uzziel," *Tarbiz* 58 (1988) 49-74 (Hebrew with English abstract). **M. ben Uzziel,** *"Kitab al-Khilaf,"* *Textus* 2 (ed. L. Lipshütz, 1962) 3-57 (Hebrew-Arabic). **I. Yeivin,** *The Aleppo Codex of the Bible: A Study of Its Vocalization and Accentuation* (1968) Hebrew.

J. S. PENKOWER

BENGEL, JOHANN ALBRECHT (1687–1752)

Born near Stuttgart, B. was the son of a pastor. After theological studies at Tübingen he was ordained (1706) and served a parish for a year. From 1713 to 1741 he worked as teacher and leader of a theological prepatory school at Denkendorf. During the latter part of his career he held important ecclesiastical posts in Württemberg.

A prolific writer, B. published studies on classical philology as well as the Bible. His two most important works are his Greek NT and his *Gnomon.* When he was a student at Tübingen, he came across a copy of the Oxford edition of the Greek NT, reported to contain 30,000 variants. Concerned about the reliability of the text, he devoted himself to lower criticism. His edition of the text of the NT (*Novum Testamentum Graecum*) was published in 1734. Except for the text of Revelation (which he revised), he merely reprinted the received text; however, at the bottom of the page he listed an extensive number of variants, classified according to their quality.

In the *Apparatus criticus* B. presented his critical principles. He classified the manuscripts into two geographical groupings: Asiatic and African. His famous critical principle is *proclivi scriptioni praestat ardua* (to the easier reading, the harder is preferred). His critical work was conservative, e.g., he accepted as genuine 1 John 5:7.

Published in 1742, B's *Gnomon* (pointer) *of the NT*

is a multi-volume collection of notes on the NT. He accepted the Scriptures as inspired and infallible; in his exegetical work he attended primarily to grammatical and historical details, although he believed that interpretation should be enlightened by the Spirit. He recognized the traditional apostolic authorship of virtually all of the NT books.

B. had a special interest in biblical CHRONOLOGY and the Apocalypse (see APOCALYPTICISM). In *Ordo temporum* (1741) he used biblical temporal and prophetic references to reconstruct the chronology of world history—a total of 7,777 and 7/9 years. In his commentary on Revelation, using similar methods, he concluded that the return of Christ and the beginning of the millennium would occur on June 18, 1836.

Works: *Novum Testamentum Graecum* (1734); *Ordo temporum* (1741); *Gnomon of the New Testament* (1742; ET, 1866); *Erklärte Offenbarung Johannis* (ed. W. Hoffmann, 1834).

Bibliography: K. Aland, *Pietismus und Bibel* (1970). **W. Baird,** *History of NT Research* 1 (1992) 69-80. **M. Brecht,** *Orthodoxie und Pietismus* (ed. M. Greschat, 1982) 317-29; "J. A. B.s Theologie der Schrift," *ZTK* 64 (1967) 99-120; *TRE* 5 (1980) 583-89. **J. C. F. Burk,** *A Memoir of the Life and Writings of J. A. B.* (1837). **W. Hehl,** *J. A. B.: Leben und Werk* (1987). **E. Ludwig,** *Schriftverständnis und Schriftauslegung bei J. A. B.* (1952). **G. Mälzer,** *J. A. B.: Leben und Werk* (1970). **J. Weborg,** *HHMBI,* 289-94.

W. R. BAIRD

BENOIT, PIERRE MAURICE (1906–87)

Born in Nancy, Lorraine, France, Aug. 3, 1906, B. entered the Dominican order in 1924, receiving the name Pierre. He was ordained in 1930 after studies at the Saulchoir (Kain, Tournai, Belgium). In 1933 he was assigned to teach NT Greek and exegesis at the École Biblique, the French biblical and archaeological school (see ARCHAEOLOGY AND BIBLICAL STUDIES) in Jerusalem. His principal teacher was M.-J. LAGRANGE, founder of the school. B. remained at the École, serving as director from 1965 to 1972, and died there on Apr. 23, 1987.

B.'s was one of the first positive Roman Catholic receptions of FORM CRITICISM (1946). His essays on the INSPIRATION of Scripture helped to promote a distinction between inspiration and inerrancy, and this in turn encouraged critical work. His essays on HERMENEUTICS increased theological attention to the SEPTUAGINT and to the plurality of senses in the Bible. In his study of the SYNOPTIC Gospels he differed from Lagrange in maintaining that the Gospels do not give immediate access to the earthly JESUS; they give access to Jesus only through the mediation of the early Christian community, which selectively preserved and shaped the tradition about Jesus.

B. is probably best known for his work on the original Jerusalem Bible (1956) as NT editor and as commentator on Matthew, Philippians, Philemon, Colossians, and Ephesians. These biblical books were also the object of his teaching at the École. His last major project was a commentary on Colossians.

B. edited the *RB* (1953–68), adding the archaeological chronicle as a regular feature of the journal. After the death of his colleague R. de VAUX (1971), he became the general editor of the unpublished DEAD SEA SCROLL fragments from Qumran (succeeded by J. Strugnell of Harvard in 1986). He did not have a gift as epigrapher and failed as catalyst and organizer, but he brought good sense to oppose sensational views.

B. was an active participant in the Society of NT Studies from its beginning and served as its president (1962–63), the first Roman Catholic to hold the post. He was a member of the Pontifical Biblical Commission from 1972 until his death.

Works: *Exégèse et Théologie* (1961, 1968, 1982; the first two are partially available in ET: *Jesus and the Gospel,* 1973); *The Passion and Resurrection of Jesus Christ* (1966; ET 1970); *Aspects of Biblical Inspiration* (1965); (with P. Synave), *Prophecy and Inspiration* (1961); "French Archaeologists," *Benchmarks in Time and Culture: An Introduction to Palestinian Archaeology* (ed. J. F. Drinkard et al., 1988) 63-86.

Bibliography: **G. P. Fogarty,** *The Vatican and the American Hierarchy from 1870 to 1965* (1982). **H. Shanks,** "BAR Interviews P. B.: The Religious Message of the Bible," *BARev* 12, 2 (April 1986) 58-66.

B. T. VIVIANO

BENTLEY, RICHARD (1662–1742)

One of the foremost classical scholars, B. was born Jan. 27, 1662, at Oulton in Yorkshire. He entered St. John's College, Cambridge, at age fourteen and in 1682 became tutor to the son of E. STILLINGFLEET. In 1692 he delivered the first Boyle lectures on "A Confutation of Atheism" and was soon appointed royal librarian. From 1700 to 1738 he had a disputed and controversial career as master of Trinity College, Cambridge, and vice-chancellor of the university. He died July 14, 1742.

One of B.'s early projects was what he called "a sort of Hexapla" of the HB (never published and now in the British Museum). The Hexapla amounted to a LEXICON of all the words in the HB and the interpretations of the words in Aramaic, Syriac, VULGATE, Latin, SEPTUAGINT, and in AQUILA, SYMMACHUS, and THEODOTION. B. also supported the textual work of J. MILL, who edited a Greek NT with variant readings (1707), agreeing with Mill that there were at least 30,000 NT variant readings.

In 1720 he issued his proposal for printing an edition of the NT. This proposal followed several

years of work collating Greek and Latin manuscripts, with the end of reconstructing JEROME's Vulgate and comparing it with the oldest Greek sources. So confident was B. of his work that he aimed at producing the very Greek text of the time of the Council of Nicea (325 CE) with "not twenty words, nor even particles, difference." B.'s enthusiasm for starting projects, however, surpassed his interest in seeing them through, and his NT was never produced, although two of his assistants in the collating—J. WETTSTEIN and J. Walker—were important text critics (see TEXTUAL CRITICISM) in their own right.

B.'s most significant contribution to scholarship was his demonstration of the use of higher criticism, employed to disprove the authenticity of the so-called epistles of Phalaris. Although suspicion had been earlier raised about these presumed sixth-century BCE documents (by Politian in the 15th century, ERASMUS in 1521, and Leibniz in 1663), B. subjected the texts to a full literary-historical analysis that used the arsenal of arguments and approaches that would later be employed in higher biblical criticism. Using internal and external evidence, he demonstrated that anachronisms of various kinds, linguistic style, literary form, vocabulary, thought, and lack of external attestation suggest that the letters should be dated to a period a thousand years later than had been presumed. The thoroughness of his documentary criticism far exceeded that of any previous critic, including L. VALLA. The importance of B.'s work led C. von BUNSEN to declare that "historical philology, through the heritage and glory of German scholars, was the discovery of R. B." (*Ägyptens Stelle in der Weltgeschichte* I [1845] n.22).

Works: *The Folly and Unreasonableness of Atheism* (Boyle Lectures, 1692); *A Dissertation upon the Epistles of Phalaris. . . .* (first published in W. Wotton's *Reflections upon Ancient and Modern Learning* [1697]; enlarged ed. published separately, 1699); *Remarks upon a Late Discourse on Freethinking* [of A. Collins] (1713); *Dr. Bentley's Proposal for Printing a New Edition of the Greek Testament, and St. Hierom's Latin Version* (1721); *The Works of R. B.* (3 vols., ed. A. Dyce, 1836–38); *Bentleii Critica Sacra: Notes on the Greek and Latin Text of the NT, extracted from the Bentley Manuscripts in Trinity College Library* (ed. A. A. Ellis, 1862).

Bibliography: *BB*[2] 2 (1780) 224-47. **C. O. Brink,** *English Classical Scholarship: Historical Reflections on B., Porson, and Housman* (1986) 1-83. **A. Fox,** *J. Mill and R. B.: A Study of the Textual Criticism of the NT, 1675–1729* (1954). **R. C. Jebb,** *Life of Bentley* (1882); *DNB* 4 (1885) 306-14. **J. H. Monk,** *Life of R. Bentley, DD* (1830; 2 vols., 1833[2]). **J. E. Sandys,** *A History of Classical Scholarship* (3 vols., 1908) 2:400-410. **R. J. White,** *Dr. B.: A Study in Academic Scarlet* (1965).

G. E. SCHWERDTFEGER

BENTZEN, AAGE (1894–1953)

A professor at the University of Copenhagen, B. was born in Ordrup, Denmark, Dec. 13, 1894, and died in Copenhagen June 4, 1953. He studied theology, OT exegesis, and Semitic languages at the University of Copenhagen with F. BUHL, J. PEDERSEN, and J. Jacobsen, each of whom "exercised an influence that lasted all B.'s life" (E. Hammershaimb [1953]). Both Buhl and Jacobsen taught J. WELLHAUSEN's theories, which B. held to as the best solution to the vexing question of PENTATEUCHAL authorship.

From Pedersen, B. learned a psychological and sociological approach to the HB (see PSYCHOLOGY AND BIBLICAL STUDIES; SOCIOLOGY AND HB STUDIES) that led him to soften some of the edges of Wellhausen's theories and to fill in his structure with broader material. Pedersen's epoch-making work *Israel* (1920) and S. MOWINCKEL's *Psalmenstudien* (vol. 1, 1921) became decisive for B.'s work.

After finishing his cand. theol. examination in Copenhagen, B. went to Germany and England for further studies (1921–22). G. HÖLSCHER cemented his view on LITERARY criticism, and P. KAHLE influenced his opinions on the MT. On his journey to Palestine in 1924 in connection with the Deutsches evangelisches Institut für Altertumswissenschaft des Heiligen Landes, he acquired solid knowledge of the geography of the Holy Land and a keen interest in the ARCHAEOLOGY of ancient Israel.

In 1923 B. won a vacant position as lecturer in OT at Copenhagen. He published mainly minor articles but continued to work on a history of ancient Israel, which was published in 1930, the year after he was appointed full professor in OT at the University of Copenhagen, a chair he held until his death in 1953.

An industrious scholar, B's interest in ancient cultic life, stimulated by Pedersen and Mowinckel, led to his early study of the origin of the sabbath. At a time when the prophets were the dominating theme among scholars, B. wanted to demonstrate the great influence of the Temple cult in Israel-Judah. In his 1931 *Studier over det Zadokidiske Praesteskabs Historie* (Studies in the History of the Zadokite Priesthood) he explored this cult under the leadership of the Zadokite priests. He believed that the rural priests also played a greater role than was usually supposed, and he stressed their significance in his book *Die josianische Reform und ihre Voraussetzungen* (1926), pointing out that the reform in 622 BCE was strongly supported by the country priests, who were a driving force in its success.

The new outlook in the study of the psalms, introduced by Mowinckel's *Psalmenstudien,* fascinated B. In 1931 he lectured on the psalms and the following year published these lectures. In 1939 he followed with a 690-page commentary on the psalms in which he promoted Mowinckel's ideas while at the same time trying to go his own way. The University of Basel conferred

on him the degree of doctor of theology in 1950. He was subsequently elected president of the International Organization of OT Scholars, whose 1953 congress in Copenhagen he was preparing to lead at the time of his sudden death.

B. did not mark out new trails, but with his great knowledge and sound judgment he had an ability to mediate the ideas of others. With the addition of his own contributions, he brought a balanced judgment that served to make new ideas known and accepted.

Works: *Den israelitiske Sabbats Oprindelse og Historie indtil Jerusalems Erobring Aar 70 e.Kr.* (1923); *Die josianische Reform und ihre Voraussetzungen* (1926); *Israels Historie* (Haases Haandbøger 18-19, 1930); *Studier over det Zadokidiske Praesteskabs Historie* (Festskrift Københavns Universitet, 1931); *Forelaesninger over Indledning til de gammeltestamentlige Salmer* (1932); *Daniel* (HAT 1937, 1952²); *Fortolkning til de gammeltestamentlige Salmer* (1939); *Indledning til det gamle Testamente* (2 vols., 1941; ET 1948, 1952²); *Praedikerens Bog, fortolket* (1942); *Jesaja, fortolket* (2 vols., 1943); *Det sakrale Kongedømme* (Festskrift Københavns Universitet, 1945); *Messias—Moses redivivus—Menschensohn* (1948; ET, *King and Messiah,* 1955, 1970²).

Bibliography: E. Hammershaimb, "In Memorian Prof. A. B.," VTSup 1 (1953) vii-ix. S. Mowinckel, *NTT* 54 (1953) 111-12; *Dansk Kirkeliv* 30 (1953) 80-82. H. H. Rowley, "Foreword," *King and Messiah* (A. Bentzen, 1955, 1970²) 5-6.

A. S. KAPELRUD

BENZINGER, IMMANUEL GUSTAV ADOLF (1865–1935)

Born Feb. 21, 1865, B. was the son of a rector in Stuttgart. He was especially influenced by the Leipzig Semiticist and oriental researcher A. Socin, who awakened his interest in the ARCHAEOLOGY of Syria and Palestine. From 1898 to 1901 he was a *Privatdozent* in OT in Berlin. From 1901 to 1912 he lived in Jerusalem and explored Palestine and Syria in yearly trips. He was professor of Semitic languages in Toronto (1912–14), then professor of OT language and literature and the history of religions at Meadville Theological School, Pennsylvania (1915–18). From 1921 until his death in 1935 he taught at the University of Lettlands in Riga.

At the outset, B. was influenced by the method and historical view of J. WELLHAUSEN and his school; however, his knowledge of the Near East forced him to question the adequacy of such an approach. Convinced that ancient Israel had to be understood within the context of a common ancient Near Eastern culture and worldview, he turned to the Pan-Babylonian school (see PAN-BABYLONIANISM), most notably represented by H. WINCKLER.

B. is most noted for his research in archaeology in Palestine and for his interpretation of the historical books of the HB. His work *Hebräische Archäologie,* a comprehensive presentation of the social relations, customs, and institutions of the Israelites drawn from both written sources and the increasing data from archaeological finds, became a standard work on the archaeology of Palestine in the first half of the twentieth century. The various editions of Baedeker's *Palästina und Syrien,* which B. undertook and to which his yearly trips added new information, are still significant for research in Palestine, since they discuss many finds that have subsequently disappeared.

In his commentary B. saw the books of the Chronicles as devotional literature, maintaining that the author/redactor totally recast the old history according to the views of his time to provide for his contemporaries a devotional work. Among his sources, which are no longer preserved, were both midrashic works (see MIDRASH) and historically reliable sources, among which was a Jewish historical work from the time after 444 BCE.

According to B.'s commentary, the origin of the books of Kings is traceable to two deuteronomic redactions (see DEUTERONOMISTIC HISTORY), the first dated between 621 and 597 BCE (R^1), and the second from the exilic or postexilic period (R^2). Their sources essentially consisted of edited annals in addition to fragments from royal and prophetic biographies. This explanation B. later gave up (in *Jahvist und Elohist*), replacing it with a radical source theory: the assumption that the sources of the Pentateuch (see PENTATEUCHAL CRITICISM) continued into the historical books. The Jahwist (J) and the Elohist (E) represent two comprehensive historical works whose portrayals reach into late monarchical times: the work of J to 2 Kgs 17:3-4, taking its final form under Hezekiah (end of 8th cent. BCE); the work of E to 2 Kings 22–23, concluding before Josiah's death (609 BCE). B.'s theory marked the most far-reaching extension of Pentateuch source criticism into the historical books; it has not been developed in further research.

Works: *Palästina und Syrien* (ed. K. Baedeker, GTW, 1890³–1910⁷; ET 1912); *Hebräische Archäologie* (1894, 1907², 1927³); (ed.), *ZDPV* 20 (1897)–25 (1902); *Die Bücher der Könige* (KHC 9, 1899); *Die Bücher der Chronik* (KHC 20, 1901); *Geschichte Israels bis auf die griechische Zeit* (1904, 1908², 1924³); *Bilderatlas zur Bibelkunde* (with L. J. Frohnmeyer, 1905, 1912²); *Wie wurden die Juden das Volk des Gesetzes?* (1908); *Jahvist und Elohist in den Königsbüchern* (BWANT 27 n.f. 2, 1921); FS: *Studia Theologica I edidit Ordo Theologorum Universitatis Latviensis* (1935).

Bibliography: H. Gunkel, *RGG*² 1 (1927) 900.

W. THIEL

BERENGAR OF TOURS (c. 999–1088)

B. studied under Fulbert of Chartres. He taught at Tours and in 1040 became archdeacon of Angers. Like LANFRANC OF BEC he lectured on both the liberal arts and the Bible. He became famous for his unorthodox teaching about the Eucharist and the controversy that followed with Lanfranc and others. But to see B. principally as a heresiarch is to leave out of account his solid work of biblical commentary, which contributed to the accumulation of material that was to form the GLOSSA ORDINARIA. He was a professional teacher whose pupils came to him from far afield and were free to move on to another master if they were not satisfied. It was a system that encouraged both excellence and competitiveness. B. did not work in isolation; his friend Drogo of Paris in particular was a fellow author of glosses on PAUL's epistles. The fragments of B.'s work that survive make clear his ability to apply the principles of grammar and logic to the resolution of textual difficulties as well as to draw upon the fathers in the traditional way.

Works: B.'s arguments are reproduced and answered in Lanfranc's *De Corpore et Sanguine Domini* (*PL* 150).

Bibliography: M. T. Gibson, *Lanfranc of Bec* (1978). J. de Montclos, *Lanfranc et Bérenger: La controverse eucharistique du XIe Siècle* (1971); *TRE* 5 (1979) 598-601. B. Smalley, "La Glossa Ordinaria," *RTAM* 9 (1937) 372-99. R. Somerville, *DMA* 2 (1983) 188. R. W. Southern, "Lanfranc of Bec and Berengar of Tours," *Studies in Medieval History Presented to F. M. Powicke* (ed. R. W. Hunt et al., 1948) 27-48.

G. R. EVANS

BERGSTRÄSSER, GOTTHELF (1886–1933)

Trained in classical philology and Semitic languages at the University of Leipzig, B. taught at the University of Constantinople in 1914, using the opportunity to study modern Arabic and Aramaic dialects in Syria-Palestine as well as to research local medieval Arabic manuscripts. Most of his work was in TEXTUAL CRITICISM and exegesis of the Quran (see QURANIC AND ISLAMIC INTERPRETATION), Islamic law, and ancient history of science; but he also published important portions of a planned revision of H. GESENIUS's *Hebräische Grammatik.*

Works: *Die bisher veröffentlichten arabischen Hippokrates- und Galen-Übersetzungen, Sprach- und literargeschichtliche Untersuchungen* (1912); *Hunain Ibn Ishaq und seine Schule* (1913, 1996); *Pseudogaleni in Hippocratis de septimanis commentarius ab Hunaino q. f. arabice versum* (1914); *Neuaramäische Märchen und andere Texte aus Ma'lula* (1915, 1966); *Sprachatlas von Syrien und Palästina* (1915); *Neue meteorologische Fragmente des Theophrast, arabisch und deutsch* (1918); *W. Gesenius' Hebräische Grammatik,* vol. 1, *Einleitung, Schrift- und Lautlehre* (1918); vol 2, *Verbum* (1929); *Hebräische Lesestücke aus dem Alten Testament* (1920); *Glossar des neuaramäischen Dialekts von Ma'lula* (AKM 15, 4, 1921); *Zum* *arabischen Dialekt von Damaskus* (1924, 1968); *Einführung in die semitischen Sprachen: Sprachproben und grammatische Skizzen* (1928; ET 1995); *G. B.'s Grundzüge des islamischen Rechts* (Lehrbücher des Seminars für orientalische Sprachen zu Berlin 35, ed. J. Schacht, 1935).

Bibliography: H. **Gottschalk,** *Islam* 24 (1937) 185-91. **M. Meyerhof,** *Isis* 25 (1936) 60-62. **M. Plessner,** *EncJud* 4 (1971) 622.

R. J. OWENS, JR.

BERNARD OF CLAIRVAUX (1090–1153)

Generally regarded as the greatest monastic figure of the High Middle Ages, B. was born in 1090, the third of seven children. At age twenty-one he embraced the strict rule of the Cistercians with such ardor that he quickly inspired all of his brothers, as well as other relatives, to follow him into the monastery. Chosen as abbot for a new foundation at Clairvaux, he was ordained in 1115. From Clairvaux he directed the founding of sixty-eight new monasteries as his charismatic influence gradually spread throughout Europe.

An eloquent speaker and a fiery, often impetuous opponent of any perceived threat to the church, B. launched energetic polemics against the laxity of the Cluniacs; the teachings of PETER ABELARD, GILBERT DE LA PORRÉE, and Arnold of Brescia; the heresies of the Albigensians; and the schism caused by Anacletus II and his party. Commissioned by the Cistercian pope, Eugenius III, he preached the Second Crusade in 1146–47. The failure of that crusade shadowed his final years; he died on Aug. 20, 1153. Canonized by Alexander III in 1174, B. was proclaimed a Doctor of the Church by Pius VIII in 1830.

As a biblical interpreter B. is justly famous for his *Sermones super Cantica Canticorum.* He probably addressed preliminary versions of these eighty-six sermons on the Song of Songs to the monks of Clairvaux; the *Sermones* preserve the intimate tone and setting of such talks. However, as J. Le Clercq (1979) has shown, the *Sermones* are not simple transcriptions of the spoken word but rather carefully written and revised compositions prepared for a wider reading audience. B. clearly intended the sermon series to give a summary expression of the whole of Cistercian life and asceticism.

Following ORIGEN and the allegorical tradition he helped to establish, B. interpreted the Song of Songs as referring literally to the marriage between King Solomon and the daughter of Pharaoh; allegorically, to the mystical union either between Christ and his spouse, the church, or between the Word and the individual soul; and morally, to the practical way of life that stems from spiritual union with Christ. Unlike Origen, however, B. attached great importance to the lush imagery of the literal text and related it to the personal, affective experience of his auditors.

Psycho-historical scholars like Le Clerc maintain that B. stressed the imagery for pastoral reasons. Unlike the older orders, which drew extensively upon oblates for their members, the Cistercians attracted adults, who often came to religious life after having known and experienced erotic love. B., therefore, used the literal meaning of the Song as a psychologically significant starting point, first awakening the desire of his monks and then, via allegoresis, transferring that desire to the person of Christ. Once the allegorical meaning has been established, the allegory becomes, in metaphorical terms, a tenor for the vehicle of literal meaning. For B., the letter of the Song is indispensable because it captures the human affections and thus colors and conveys its ultimate meaning as a book about the love of God, both God's love for us and our love for God.

Although they deal only with material from the first three chapters of the Song of Songs, B.'s *Sermones* have proved extremely influential over the centuries among both biblical commentators and ordinary readers. Esteemed as a devotional classic, the work continues to be widely read.

Works: "De gratia et libero arbitrio," *Opera* (ed. J. Le Clerc, C. H. Talbot, and H. M. Rochais, 1957–74) 3:165-203; "De gradibus humilitatis et superbiae," *Opera* 3:13-59; "Liber de diligendo Deo," *Opera* 3:119-54; "Sermones super Cantica Canticorum," *Opera* 1–2; *On the Song of Songs* (tr. K. Walsh and I. Edmonds, 1971–80).

Bibliography: A. W. **Astell,** *The Song of Songs in the Middle Ages* (1990). K. **Elm** (ed.), *Bernhard von Clairvaux: Rezeption und Wirkung im Mittelalter und in der Neuzeit* (Wolfenbutteler Mittelalter-Studien 6, 1994). G. R. **Evans,** *The Mind of St. Bernard of Clairvaux* (1983). E. **Gilson,** *The Mystical Theology of Saint Bernard* (1955). J. **Le Clercq,** *The Love of Learning and the Desire for God* (1961); *Monks and Love in Twelfth-Century France: Psycho-historical Essays* (1979). E. A. **Matter,** *The Voice of My Beloved: The Song of Songs in Western Medieval Christianity* (1990). F. **Ohly,** *Hohelied-Studien: Grundzüge einer Geschichte der Hoheliedauslegung des Abendlandes bis um 1200* (1958). D. E. **Tamburello,** *HHMBI,* 91-95.

A. W. ASTELL

BERTHEAU, ERNEST (1812–88)

B. was born Nov. 23, 1812, in Hamburg into a family of Huguenot heritage. He died May 17, 1888, in Göttingen. He began studying theology and oriental languages in 1832, first in Berlin, then in Göttingen, where he spent the rest of his life. In 1842 he became an *ausserordentlicher* professor and in 1843 a full professor. Although his chair was in the philosophy faculty, he was closely connected to his theological colleagues.

With scholarly work marked by diligence, erudition,

and caution, B. gave his best in the four volumes he contributed to the KEH. Although he had no interest in daring theses, he took notice of K. GRAF's hypothesis, and in his last major work, the new edition of the commentary on the book of Judges (1883), he cautiously made use of the views of J. WELLHAUSEN. From 1870 on he worked continually on the revision of the "Lutherbibel" and participated in scholarly exchanges with other members of the revision commission.

In the 1840s B. had reconstructed from the middle books of the Pentateuch (Exodus–Numbers; see PENTATEUCHAL CRITICISM) a large collection of laws of Mosaic origin. He noted that they had developed out of seven single laws, with each of the seven being developed into seven series of ten to make a total of 490 rules. His preoccupation with numbers is also seen in the first of two combined essays under the title *Zur Geschichte der Israeliten,* in which he investigated the weights, coins, and measurements of the Hebrews in comparison with those of other ancient Near Eastern and European peoples. The second essay offered an interesting outline of the history of ancient Israel in relation to its neighbors based on contemporary scholarly positions, which already in B.'s lifetime were completely out-of-date.

Works: *Die sieben Gruppen mosaischer Gesetze in den drei mittleren Büchern des Pentateuchs* (1840); *Zur Geschichte der Israeliten* (1842); *Das Buch der Richter und Ruth* (KEH 6, 1845, 1883²); *Die Sprüche Salomo's* (KEH 7, 1847); *Die Bücher der Chronik* (KEH 15, 1854; ET 1857); "Die alttestamentliche Weissagung von Israels Reichsherrlichkeit in seinem Lande," *JDTh* 4 (1859) 314-75, 595-684; 5 (1860) 486-542; *Die Bücher Esra, Nechemia, und Ester* (KEH 17, 1862); "Besprechung von K. H. Graf, Die geschichtlichen Bücher des Alten Testaments," *JDTh* 11 (1866) 150-60.

Bibliography: C. **Bertheau,** *RE*³ 2 (1897) 645-48; *ADB* 46 (1902) 441-43.

R. SMEND

BERTHOLET, ALFRED (1868–1951)

Born in Basel Nov. 9, 1868, B. was educated at Basel, Strasbourg, and Berlin, studying under A. von HARNACK, B. DUHM, and T. NÖLDEKE. After earning his doctorate in 1895 with the dissertation "Die Stellung der Israeliten und der Juden zu den Fremden," he pastored the German-Dutch congregation at Livorno and taught at various levels at Basel. In 1913 he went to Tübingen and the following year succeeded R. SMEND at Göttingen, where he was the first professor of OT on the theological faculty. (His predecessors at Göttingen, J. Wellhausen and Smend, had been members of the philosophical faculty.) In 1928 he succeeded H. GRESSMANN at Berlin. Retiring in 1939 after a long illness, he spent the war years in Bavaria then returned to Basel in 1945, where

he remained active until his death on Aug. 24, 1951, in Munsterlingen.

B. wrote widely on the HB, intertestamental Judaism, and the NT. His work includes several commentaries on the HB books and a highly regarded appendix on the APOCRYPHA and PSEUDEPIGRAPHA. Although his scholarly work took place in the twentieth century, he was fundamentally a man of the nineteenth in that he sought to answer questions about Hebrew religion from general developmental theories of religion instead of from the emerging corpus of ancient Near Eastern religious texts. In this regard he must be considered the last great nineteenth-century scholar of Hebrew religion.

Works: *Das Verfassungsentwurf der Hesekiel in seiner religionsgeschichtlichen Bedeutung* (1896, 1922²); *Das Buch Hesekiel* (KHK 12, 1897); *Das Buch Ruth* (KHK 17, 1898); *Deuteronium* (KHK 5, 1899); *Die israelitischen Vorstellung vom Zustand nach dem Tode* (SGV 16, 1899, 1914²); *Leviticus* (KHK 3, 1901); *Die Bücher Ezra und Nehemiah* (KHK 19, 1902); *Buddhismus und Christentum* (SGV 28, 1902, 1909²); *Der Buddhismus und seine Bedeutung für unser Geistesleben* (1904); *The Transmigration of Souls* (1904; ET 1909); "Apokryphen und Pseudepigraphen," *Geschichte der althebräischen Litteratur* (K. Budde, Litteraturen des Ostens in Einzeldarstellungen 7, 1, 1906) 337-422; *Daniel und die griechische Gefahr* (RgV 2, 17, 1907); *Die jüdische Religion von der Zeit Esras bis zum Zeitalter Christi* (1911); *Religion und Krieg* (RgV 5, 20, 1915); *A History of Hebrew Civilization* (1919; ET 1926); *Der Beitrag des Alten Testaments zur Allgemeinen Religionsgeschichte* (SGV 106, 1923); *Das Die gegenwärtige Gestalt des Islams* (SGV 118, 1926); *Dynamistische im Alten Testaments* (SGV 121, 1926); *Die Religion des AT* (Religionsgeschichtlichen Lesebuch 2, 17, 1932); *Hesekiel* (HAT 1, 13, 1936). Full bibliography compiled by V. Tamann-Bertholet in *FS A. B.* (ed. W. Baumgartner et al., 1950) 564-78.

Bibliography: O. **Eissfeldt,** "A. B. zum 70. Geburtstag (9 Nov., 1938)," *KS* 2 (1963) 147-49. L. **Rost,** "A. B. in memoriam," *TLZ* 77 (1952) 114-18. G. **Stephenson,** *LTK* 2 (1933) 292-93.

D. G. SCHLEY

BEWER, JULIUS AUGUST (1877–1953)

Born in Ratingen, Germany, B. came at an early age to New York City, where he earned a BD degree at Union Theological Seminary (1898) and a PhD at Columbia University (1900). During 1899–1901 he returned to Europe to study at the universities of Basel, Halle, and Berlin. The University of Göttingen honored him in 1922 with a D. Theol., and on publication of his now classic *Literature of the OT* he was named honorary member of the university. From 1902 to 1904 he was professor of OT languages and literature at Oberlin Theological Seminary, then from 1904 to 1945 he held posts at Union Theological Seminary and Columbia University in biblical philology, OT exegesis, history, and theology, and finally as Davenport Professor of Hebrew and Cognate Languages at Union. From 1945 to 1947 he was visiting professor at New Brunswick Theological Seminary in New Jersey.

B. is known for his role in transmitting German historical-critical and form-historical research to the American theological scene and for his efforts in the resumption of relationships between German and American biblical scholars after WWI.

Works: *The NT Canon in the Syriac Church* (1900); *A Critical and Exegetical Commentary on Obadiah and Joel* (1911); *Jonah* (1912); *The Text of Ezra* (1921); *The Literature of the OT in Its Historical Development* (1922); "Ezechiel," *Biblia Hebraica* (ed. G. Kittel, 1932); in *Harper's Annotated Bible Series: The Twelve Minor Prophets,* 1949); *Isaiah* (1950); *Jeremiah* (1951–52); *Ezekiel* (1954); *Daniel* (1955).

Bibliography: *Directory of American Scholars* 2 (1951) 70-71. **K. Galling,** *RGG*[3] 1 (1957) 1112. *Who Was Who in America* 3 (1951–60) 73.

J. M. Bullard

BEZA, THEODORE (1519–1605)
Born June 24, 1519, in Vézaley, France, at age nine B. began studies with the humanist M. Wolmar, from whom he learned to write elegant Latin and Greek and to look favorably on the nascent French Reformation. In 1548 he went to Geneva and served as professor of Greek at Lausanne Academy (1549–58) and as first rector (1559–63) and professor of theology (1559–99) at Geneva Academy. He joined the Genevan clergy and on CALVIN's death in 1564 was elected moderator of the Venerable Company of Pastors, a post he held until 1580. His writings include completion of Marot's translation of the psalms into French verse and theological and polemical works in defense of Genevan theology. B.'s place in the history of biblical studies was assured by his translations, annotations, and Greek editions of the NT. He died Oct. 13, 1605.

B.'s humanist studies and concern for correct grammar and language prepared him to do excellent exegetical work that was incorporated into the English Geneva Bible of 1560, and on which later editions drew even more heavily. B.'s theological agenda, however, made him a narrow interpreter of the excellent texts he had in his hands (*Cantabrigiensis* or *Codex Bezae* and *Claromontanus*). For example, although in 1562 he received the NT manuscript now known as *Codex Bezae* and kept it until he sent it to Cambridge University in 1581, he did not make extended use of its variant readings, preferring established and more conservative readings. Nevertheless, his corrections of previous texts

outweighed his tendentious annotations and made of his Greek NT the best edition available at the time (1565, 1582[3]). The Geneva Bible of 1588, a revision by a committee of the Genevan pastors led by B. and C. Bertram, influenced subsequent Protestant Bibles.

Works: *Traduction en verse français des psaumes omis par Marot* (1563); *Methodica apostolicarum epistolarum brevis explicatio* (1565); *Lex Dei moralis, ceremonialis et politica ex libris Mosis excerpta et in certas classes distributa* (1577); *Jobus commentario et paraphrasi illlustratus* (1583; ET 1583); *Canticum canticorum latinis versibus expressum* (1584; ET 1587); *Ecclesiastes Salomonis paraphrasi illustratus* (1588); *Sermons sur l'histoire de la résurrection de Nostre Seigneur Jésus Christi* (1593); *Adnotationes majores in Novum D. N. Jesu Christi Testamentum in duas distributae partes* (1594).

Bibliography: **M. Delval,** *La doctrina du salut dans l'oeuvre homilétique de T. B.* (1983); "La prédication d'un réformateur au xvie siècle: l'activité homilétique de T. B.," *Mélanges de Sciences religieuses,* 41-42 (1984) 61-86. **J. L. Farthing,** *HHMBI,* 153-57. **J.-B. Fellay,** "T. B. exégète: Texte, traduction et commentaire de l'Épître aux Romains dans les 'Annotations in Novum Testamentum' " (diss., Geneva, 1984). **P. Fraenkel,** *De l'Écriture à la Dispute: La cas de l'Académie de Genève sous T. B.* (1977). **P. F. Geisendorf,** *T. B.* (1967[2]). **E. A. Gosselin,** *The King's Progress to Jerusalem: Some Interpretations of David During the Reformation Period and Their Patristic and Medieval Backgrounds* (1976), esp. 90-118. **B. Heurtebize,** *Dictionaire de la Bible* 1 (1895) 1772-73. **W. Kickel,** *Vernunft und Offenbarung bei T. B.* (BGLRK 25, 1967). **J. Raitt,** *TRE* 5 (1980) 765-74; "B., Guide for the Faithful Life (Lectures on Job, Sermons on Song of Songs, 1587)," *SJT* 39 (1986) 83-107. **B. Roussel,** "Commentar et traduire," *BTT* 5 (1989) 431-43.

J. Raitt

BICKERMAN, ELIAS JOSEPH (1897–1981)
Born in Kishinev in the Ukraine, July 1, 1897, B. studied first in St. Petersburg with M. Rostovtzeff, then escaped to Berlin and studied under U. Wilcken, completing a doctorate in 1926 (*Das Edikt des Kaisers Caracalla in P. Giss. 40*). The rise of Nazism forced his departure to France (1933) and the United States (1943), where his principal positions were at Columbia University (1952–67) and, after retirement there, at the Jewish Theological Seminary. B.'s father was not a practicing Jew, hence B. did not receive a thorough grounding in traditional Jewish sources. When dealing with rabbinic texts he acknowledged the help of such friends as B. Cohen, H. GINSBERG, S. Lieberman, and M. SMITH (1988, ix). B. died in Israel Aug. 31, 1981.

B.'s training was as a historian of the Hellenistic-Roman period, specializing in documents and their interpretation. He characterized himself as a "digger in texts." Building on this core, he made significant contributions to biblical studies, although he presented himself as a classicist whose examination of Seleucid institutions brought him to the Maccabees, and of Roman provincial legal practice to the trial of JESUS. Nevertheless, his contributions to biblical studies span his career, from an article on the messianic secret in Mark in 1923 (1976–86, 3:34-52) to the posthumous *The Jews in the Greek Age* (1988). His objective was to understand the Jewish and Christian past as part of universal history, and he saw his classical training as enabling him to approach that goal (1988, ix).

B. wrote important studies of the HB (1967), of the SEPTUAGINT (1976–86, 1:137-275), and of early Christianity (1976–86, 3:1-195). Nevertheless, the main focus of his enterprise was Hellenistic Judaism. His analyses of the documents in JOSEPHUS relating to the Seleucid era (1976–86, 2:24-104)—supporting their authenticity by comparison to what can be learned from papyri and inscriptions, and then using these sources to discern royal policy concerning the Jews—remain the point of departure for all subsequent endeavors. His revolutionary thesis concerning the role of Jewish reformers as initiators of the decrees of Antiochus IV (1937; ET 1979) has been taken up and expanded by others (e.g., M. Hengel, *Judaism and Hellenism* [1974]). Having elaborated the ideology of these reformers as cosmopolitan universalists using royal fiat to eliminate the distinctive characteristics of Jewish life, B. maintained that the Hellenization of Jerusalem in the period preceding Antiochus IV was sufficiently extensive to produce such individuals (1988).

His disdain for the cosmopolitan reformers was nearly total: Had they prevailed, Judaism would likely have disappeared. Nevertheless, B. saw Maccabean Hellenism not as the failure of the dynasty but as its ultimate success (1962, 153-82): The Maccabees employed the Torah as the standard by which elements from the outside were accepted or rejected. By these means, B. concluded, the Jews became one of only two cultures to successfully encounter the Hellenistic world (the other being the Romans, who conquered the Greeks militarily). This achievement, he argued, assured the survival of Judaism by preserving it as a living entity able to absorb the best from the surrounding world. Further, this characteristic remained true of Jews of the post-Maccabean era, including the Pharisees (1976–86, 2:256-358).

B.'s work struck Israeli historians like Klausner as insufficiently nationalistic. He was accused of naive cosmopolitanism, and his conclusions were subjected to sharp attack by A. Tcherikover (B. Bar-Kochva [1982] 3). However, respect for B.'s learning and the keenness of his insight was nearly universal. His most far-reaching assertions, e.g., those concerning responsibility for the persecutions of Antiochus IV or the nature of Macca-bean Hellenism, provoked the extensive debate he hoped they would engender.

Works: *The God of the Maccabees: Studies in the Meaning and Origin of the Maccabean Revolt* (1937; ET SJLA 38, 1979); *Institutions des Séleucides* (BAH 26, 1938); *The Maccabees: An Account of Their History from the Beginnings to the Fall of the House of the Hasmoneans* (Schocken Library 6, 1947); *From Ezra to the Last of the Maccabees: Foundations of Post-biblical Judaism* (Schocken Paperbacks 36, 1962); *Four Strange Books of the Bible: Jonah, Daniel, Koheleth, Esther* (1967); *Chronology of the Ancient World* (1968, 1980[2]); *Studies in Jewish and Christian History* (AGJU 9, 3 vols., 1976–86); *Religions and Politics in the Hellenistic and Roman Periods* (Biblioteca di Athenaeum 5, ed. E. Gabba and M. Smith, 1985; bib. xiii-xxxvii); *The Jews in the Greek Age* (1988).

Bibliography: *Ancient Studies in Memory of E. J. B.* = *Journal of the Ancient Near Eastern Society of Columbia University* 16-17 (1984–85). **B. Bar-Kochva,** "E. B.'s Research of the Second Temple Period," *Cathedra* 23 (1982) 3-10 (Hebrew). **A. I. Baumgarten,** "Bibliographical Note," *The Jews in the Greek Age* (E. Bickerman, 1988) 309-11. **J. and J. Bikerman,** *Two Bikermans: Autobiographies by Joseph and Jacob J. Bikerman* (1975). **G. D. Cohen,** "Foreword," *The Jews in the Greek Age* (E. Bickerman, 1988) vii-viii. **A. Momigliano,** "The Absence of the Third Bickerman," *Essays on Ancient and Modern Judaism* (1994) 217-21. **M. Smith,** *Studies in Jewish and Christian History, Part Three* (E. J. Bickerman, 1986) xi-xiii.

A. BAUMGARTEN

BIEL, GABRIEL (c. 1420–95)

Educated at Heidelberg, Erfurt, and Cologne, B. was a leading representative of the *via moderna* in Germany. Initially a cathedral preacher at Mainz, he was subsequently appointed to the newly founded theological faculty at Tübingen in 1484, becoming rector of the university in 1485 and again in 1489.

B.'s biblical interpretation rests largely upon a traditional appeal to the fourfold sense of Scripture (see QUADRIGA), by which the doctrinal and moral content of a biblical passage may be determined. He regarded the AUTHORITY of Scripture to be derivative rather than inherent, resting upon a prior decision of the church. Traditional rather than innovative and primarily a systematic theologian rather than a biblical interpreter, B. is nevertheless an important figure in the field of late medieval biblical interpretation, as is evident in his influence on the noted Tübingen exegete W. Steinbach. It is generally thought that B. may have exercised a formative influence on the development of LUTHER, whose *Dictata super Psalterium* (1513–15) shows affinity with B.'s ideas and methods.

Works: *Commentary on the Four Books of the Sentences* (c. 1486–88); *Exposition of the Canon of the Mass* (1488).

Bibliography: H. Feld, *M. Luthers und W. Steinbachs Vorlesungen über den Hebräerbrief: Eine Studie zur Geschichte der neutestamentlichen Exegese und Theologie* (1971); *Die Anfänge der modernen biblischen Hermeneutik in der spätmittelalterlichen Theologie* (1977). **L. Grane,** *Contra Gabrielem: Luthers Auseinandersetzung mit G. B. in der Disputatio contra scholasticam theologiam 1517* (1962). **H. A. Oberman,** *The Harvest of Medieval Theology: G. B. and Late Medieval Nominalism* (1963).

A. E. McGrath

BILLERBECK, PAUL (1853–1932)

Born in Prussia, Apr. 4, 1853, B. studied theology at Griefswald and Leipzig, was ordained to the pastorate in 1879, and spent his entire career in various pastoral positions in the region of modern-day Poland. He retired to Frankfurt in 1915 and remained there until his death Dec. 23, 1932. During his retirement years he produced the massive work *Kommentar zum Neuen Testament aus Talmud und Midrasch.*

All of B.'s articles except his last two, published posthumously in *ZNW,* appeared in the journal *Nathanael: Zeitschrift für die Arbeit der evangelischen Kirche an Israel.* Founded in 1883 by H. L. Strack (1848–1922), professor of OT at the University of Berlin, the journal published articles on ancient Judaism, particularly rabbinic thought. B.'s articles drew the attention of Strack, who provided him with rabbinic texts and encouraged him to write a replacement for J. Weber's systematic study of Jewish theology based on rabbinic texts. B., however, was more interested in collecting and translating rabbinic parallels to the NT and in 1906 produced a prototype of an envisioned larger project. He believed the NT could best be understood against the backdrop of rabbinic thought and that a collection of rabbinic parallels would be most appropriate. Although Strack's name is attached to the series, he in fact had little to do with the actual collecting and editing of the texts; he died in 1922 and thus saw only volume one. In the introduction to the fourth volume he stated that the project was his own; however, Strack helped to plan, procure sources, and secure financing for this prodigious achievement.

The first volume of the *Kommentar* (1922) dealt solely with the Gospel of Matthew. In the next two volumes (1924, 1926) B. continued verse by verse parallels to the remaining books of the NT from texts primarily associated with rabbinic Judaism, although the writings of Josephus, the Apocrypha, and the HB pseudepigraphical works (see PSEUDEPIGRAPHA) were also used to an extent. The fourth volume, published in two separate books, dealt with various Jewish themes and concepts of interest for NT study. The earlier volumes stand as the most thorough collection of rabbinic texts relating to the NT, and the essays remain very useful simply for the sheer bulk of material collated. The work has been criticized by more recent scholars (e.g., E. P. Sanders [1977]), and has its particular faults in method and content; nonetheless, it is a valuable contribution in both its breadth and its depth.

Works: "Abrahams Leben und Bedeutung für das Reich Gottes nach Auffassung der älteren Haggada," *Nathanael* 15 (1899) 43-57, 118-57, 161-79; 16 (1900) 33-57, 65-80; "Hat die alte Synagoge einen präexistenten Messias gekannt?" *Nathanael* 19 (1903) 1-31, 97-125; 20 (1904) 1-61, 65-92; 21 (1905) 89-150; "Rabbi Aqiba: Leben und Wirken eines Meisters in Israel," *Nathanael* 32 (1916) 81-94, 97-122; 33 (1917) 81-143; " 'Das Gleichnis vom Pharisäer und Zöllner (Lukas 18)': Erläutert aus der rabbinischen Literatur," *Nathanael* 33 (1917) 26-39; *Kommentar zum Neuen Testament aus Talmud und Midrasch* (6 vols.; vols. 1–4, 1922–28; vol. 5, *Rabbinischer Index,* 1956; vol. 6, *Verzeichnis der Schriftgelehrten, Geographisches Register,* 1963); "Ein Tempelgottesdienst in Jesu Tagen," *ZNW* 55 (1964) 2-17; "Ein Synagogengottesdienst in Jesu Tagen," *ZNW* 55 (1964) 143-61.

Bibliography: J. D. G. Dunn, "They Set Us in New Paths. VI. NT: The Great Untranslated," *ExpTim* 100 (1989) 203-7. **J. Jeremias,** *TRE* 6 (1980) 640-42. **D. J. Rettberg,** "P. B. as Student of Rabbinic Literature: A Description and Analysis of His Interpretive Methodology" (diss., Dropsie College, 1986). **E. P. Sanders,** *Paul and Palestinian Judaism: A Comparison of Patterns of Religion* (1977).

T. C. Penner

BIRKELAND, HARRIS (1904–61)

B. graduated from the theological faculty of the University of Oslo in 1929 (PhD 1933). He served as research fellow in OT (1930–33); associate professor in OT (1933–46); associate professor, Semitic languages, in the faculty of humanities (1946–47); and full professor, Semitic languages (1948–61). He studied and researched in Germany, Great Britain, Denmark, Sweden, and in such Arabic countries as Lebanon, Egypt, and Tunisia. A pupil of S. MOWINCKEL, B. engaged in psalms studies; but he went his own way, prompting Mowinckel to reconsider the views put forward in his *Psalmenstudien 1* (1921). Contrary to Mowinckel's view that the evildoers in the psalms of lamentation are sorcerers trying to impose spells on the praying person, B. argued in his 1933 volume that the suffering and praying person in these psalms is the king, as representative of the people. The enemies are national enemies threatening war or occupation. The sicknesses and sufferings in these laments are expressions of the mental and physical miseries felt by the praying person. B. followed up the studies of H. S. NYBERG in stressing the significance of oral tradition in the formation of the OT prophetical books (1938). In a series of shorter works and essays,

B. wrote about the principles of an OT theology, clearly inspired by the works of K. BARTH and O. EISSFELDT. B.'s main contributions, however, were his studies in Hebrew and other Semitic languages in which he made a considerable effort to introduce the phonological and structuralist methods of the so-called Prague school (1940). He also wrote a treatise on the language of JESUS (1954), arguing that the native language of Jesus was a late version of Hebrew and not, as commonly held, Aramaic. Norwegian students of theology still know him as the author of their introduction to biblical Hebrew (1950).

Works: *'Anî und 'ānāw in den Psalmen* (1933); "Die Feinde des Individuums in der israelitischen Psalmenliteratur" (diss. 1933); *Zum hebräischen Traditionswesen: Die Komposition der prophetischen Bücher des Alten Testaments* (1938); *Akzent und Vokalismus im Althebräischen* (1940); *Laerebok i hebraisk grammatikk* (1950); *Jeremia. Profet og dikter* (1950); *The Language of Jesus* (1954); *The Evildoers in the Book of Psalms* (1955).

Bibliography: L. Amundsen, *Universitetet i Oslo 1911–1961* (1961) 1:47-48, 473. A. S. Kapelrud, "Minnetale över professor H. B.," *Det Norske Videnskaps-Akademi i Oslo, Årbok* (1962) 29-34; "Scandinavian Research in the Psalms After Mowinckel," *ASTI* 4 (1965) 74-90. D. A. Knight, *Rediscovering the Traditions of Israel* (1975) 239-43. A. Melvinger, "Förteckning över H. B.s tryckta skrifter," *Det Norske Videnskaps-Akademi i Oslo, Årbok* (1962) 34-39. H. H. Rowley (ed.), *The OT and Modern Study* (1951) 129-30, 201-3.

D. RIAN

BLANK, SHELDON HASS (1896–1989)

Born in Mt. Carmel, Illinois, B. was a rabbi and Bible scholar, receiving BA and MA degrees from the University of Cincinnati, ordination as a rabbi in 1923 at Hebrew Union College, Cincinnati, and the PhD from the University of Jena, Germany, in 1925. He also studied at Hebrew University and the AMERICAN SCHOOLS OF ORIENTAL RESEARCH in Jerusalem. From 1926, for more than sixty years he was a meticulous and impassioned teacher of Bible at Hebrew Union College, eventually serving as Nelson Glueck Professor of Bible (see N. GLUECK). He guided and influenced generations of both rabbinical and Christian doctoral students to a deeper understanding of the prophetic faith and literature. For over six decades editor of the *Hebrew Union College Annual,* he served as president of the midwest section of the Society of Biblical Literature and Exegesis and in 1952 as national president of the SOCIETY OF BIBLICAL LITERATURE.

B. published extensively on questions of biblical text and of social and political history. His distinctive contribution was his explication of biblical characters, primarily prophets (see PROPHECY AND PROPHETS, HB); he

explored their religious experience and religious ideas, providing deep insight into their concepts, values, and mission. He was true to principles of biblical exegesis yet approached the text in the spirit of free inquiry and interpreted in the context of modernity. Identifying with the prophets in their zeal for ethical living and social justice, he lived according to their principles, thereby inspiring colleagues and students alike.

Works: "The LXX Renderings of OT Terms for Law," *HUCA* 7 (1930) 259-83; "Studies in Post-Exilic Universalism," *HUCA* 11 (1936) 159-91; "The Death of Zechariah in Rabbinic Literature," *HUCA* 12-13 (1937–38) 327-46; "Studies in Deutero-Isaiah," *HUCA* 15 (1940) 1-46; "The Confessions of Jeremiah and the Meaning of Prayer," *HUCA* 21 (1948) 331-54; "The Current Misinterpretation of Isaiah's *She'ar Yashub*," *JBL* 67 (1948) 211-15; "The Curse, Blasphemy, the Spell and the Oath," *HUCA* 32, 1 (1950–51) 73-95; "Men Against God, The Promethean Element in Biblical Prayer," *JBL* 72 (1953) 1-13; "Immanuel and Which Isaiah?" *JNES* 13 (1952) 83-86; "Traces of Prophetic Agony in Isaiah," *HUCA* 27 (1956) 81-92; *Prophetic Faith in Isaiah* (1958; repr. 1967); "Some Observations Concerning Biblical Prayer," *HUCA* 32 (1961) 75-90; *Jeremiah, Man and Prophet* (1961); *Understanding the Prophets* (1969); "Irony by Way of Attribution," *Semitics* 1 (1970) 1-6; "Prolegomenon," *The Song of Songs and Coheleth,* (ed. C. D. Ginsburg, LBS, reissued 1970) IX-XLIV; "The Prophet as Paradigm," *Essays in OT Ethics (J. P. Hyatt, in Memoriam)* (1974) 113-30; *Prophetic Thought: Essays and Addresses* (1977).

Bibliography: *Dictionary Catalog of the Klau Library* 4 (1964) 465-70.

A. GOTTSCHALK

BLEEK, FRIEDRICH (1793–1859)

Born July 4, 1793, in the small town of Ahrensbök, near Lübeck in Holstein, B. came from a family of modest means. At the Lübeck gymnasium (1809–12) he learned Hebrew, having already studied Greek and Latin. He then studied at Kiel (1812–14) and at Berlin (1814–17) under W. DE WETTE, F. SCHLEIERMACHER, and A. Neander. He taught at Berlin in various capacities (1818–29), although under some state suspicion since he was a student of de Wette, who had been dismissed from the Berlin faculty in 1819. In 1829, after declining offers elsewhere, he succeeded F. Lücke at the recently established university in Bonn, where he remained until his death on Feb. 27, 1859.

B. taught and wrote on both testaments. His lectures were noted for their clarity, and several series of these were published posthumously. On theological matters and the developing biblical criticism, he was a moderate who, in line with developments in the faculty at Bonn, tended to become more conservative with time. His early writings show an interest in the SIBYLLINE ORACLES (1819), the book of Daniel (1822a), and speaking in tongues (1829, 1830), and this interest in apocalyptic thought (see APOCALYPTICISM) continued throughout his career (1852, 1862c). His work on the Pentateuch (1822b, 1831) sought to support the Mosaic origin of PENTATEUCHAL traditions, whose developments he understood in terms of the supplementary hypothesis. As a student of Schleiermacher he had high respect for the Gospel of John and defended it against the Tübingen school (1846). His most significant publication was his three-volume work on Hebrews (1828–40).

B. became best known through his widely read OT and NT introductions, edited after his death. His OT introduction was reworked in six editions, the fourth by J. WELLHAUSEN; the NT introduction went through four editions, the fourth edited by W. Mangold. T. CHEYNE wrote of him as a "truly Christian scholar . . . though as a critic I cannot think that he was sufficiently keen" (1893, 148).

Works: "Ueber die Entstehung und Zusammensetzung der uns in 8 Büchern erhaltenen Sammlung Sibyllinischer Orakel," *TZ* 1 (1819) 120-246; "Ueber Verfasser und Zweck des Buches Daniel: Revision der in neuerer Zeit darüber geführten Untersuchungen," *TZ* 3 (1822a) 1717-294; "Einige aphoristische Beiträge zu den Untersuchungen über den Pentateuch," *Biblisch-Exegetisches Repertorium* 1 (1822b) 1-79; *Der Brief an die Hebraer erläutert durch Einleitung, Uebersetzung, und fortlaufenden Commentar* (3 vols., 1828–40); "Ueber die Gabe des glössais laleïn in der ersten Christlichen Kirche," *TSK* 2 (1829) 3-79; "Noch ein paar Worte über die Gabe des glössais laleïn," *TSK* 3 (1830a) 45-64; "Erörterungen in Beziehung auf die Briefe Pauli an die Corinther," *TSK* 3 (1830b) 614-31; "Beiträge zu den Forschungen über den Pentateuch," *TSK* 4 (1831) 488-524; *Beiträge zur Evangelien-Kritik* (Beiträge zur Einleitung und Auslegung der Heiligen Schrift, 1846); "Ueber das Zeitalter von Sacharja Kap. 9–14, nebst gelegentlichen Beiträgen zur Auslegung dieser Aussprüche," *TSK* 25 (1852) 247-332; *Introduction to the OT* (ed. with Kamphausen, 1860, 1865²; ET 1875); (ed.) *Introduction to the NT* (1862a; ET 2 vols., 1869–70); *Synoptische Erklärung der drei ersten Evangelien* (ed. H. Holtzmann, 1862b); *Dr. F. B.'s Lectures on the Apocalypse* (ed. T. Hossbach, 1862c; ET 1875); *Vorlesungen über die Briefe an die Kolosser, den Philemon, und die Ephesier* (ed. F. Nitzsch, 1865).

Bibliography: T. K. Cheyne, *Founders of OT Criticism: Biographical, Descriptive, and Critical Studies* (1893) 142-48. E. Levesque, *DB* 1 (1895) 1820. R. Smend, *Bonner Gelehrte: Beiträge zur Geschichte der Wissenschaften in Bonn. Evangelische Theologie* (1968) = Smend, *DATDJ* (1989).

J. W. ROGERSON

BLEEKER, LOUIS HENDRIK KAREL (1868–1943)

Professor of OT on the theological faculty at Groningen University (1907–41), B. wrote his doctoral dissertation on Jeremiah's foreign nations oracles with J. VALETON at Utrecht and shared Valenton's theological orientation (ethical-supernatural) and devotion to critical scholarship combined with respect for the Bible. B. was perhaps best known for effectively demolishing the tendentious treatment of the first two chapters of Genesis by the leading Calvinist dogmatician (see CALVIN), H. Bavinck, whose *Gereformeerde Dogmatiek* (1906²) had argued that these two chapters were from the same author, with differences that can be explained as mere shifts in emphasis. B. countered in a pamphlet (1908), arguing that Bavinck had committed exegetical nonsense in ascribing to these chapters intentions that the original writers could never have entertained. He showed that it was Bavinck's view of revelation rather than the text itself that determined his exegesis. This article and others of B.'s writings had the effect of showing how a belief in an inspired Bible encouraged and demanded nothing else than a critical methodology in the study of Scripture.

Works: *De zonde der gezindheid in het Oude Testament* (1907); *Genesis 1 en Genesis 2* (1908); *Over inhoud en oorsprong van Israels heilsverwachting* (1921); *Hermeneutik van het Oude Testament* (1948).

Bibliography: W. J. Aalders, *NThS* 22 (1929) 129-32. T. C. Vriezen et al. (eds.), "Bibliography of L. H. K. B. . . . " *Jaarbericht van het Voorasiatisch-Egyptisch Genootschap Ex Oriente Lux* 10 (1948) 231-36.

S. J. DEVRIES

BLOUNT, CHARLES (1654–93)

Born April 27, 1654, B. was from an upper-class English family. His father, H. Blount, apparently encouraged and assisted B.'s anti-religious work. B. committed suicide in Aug. 1693.

In 1679 B. issued *Anima Mundi,* written, like nearly all his works, in a disguised, indirect way; prima facie the work of a fideistic Christian mistrustful of reason and philosophy, in reality it is a powerful denial of personal immortality and divine providence. In 1678 B. had sent a letter with a copy of his book to T. HOBBES, who was apparently the major intellectual influence on B, and when Hobbes died in 1679 B. produced a broadsheet (1679b), taken mostly from *Leviathan,* which contains many of Hobbes's most outspoken criticisms of the Bible and religion. B. was a master at using the writings of others to attack Christianity. Thus his translation of *The Two First Books of Philostratus* (1680a) is chiefly aimed at discrediting the miracles of JESUS, although its manifest subject is the pagan miracle-worker Apollonius. Similarly, his overt criticism of pagan priestcraft (1680b) disguised his covert attack on the Christian priesthood. He drew even more directly on a manuscript of E. HERBERT for his *Religio Laici* (1683a) and on B. SPINOZA's *Tractatus Theologico-Politicus* for his *Miracles* (1683b). The intent of B.'s works was to undermine Christian claims to revelation and miracles.

Probably B.'s most influential employment of this oblique, insinuative strategy in the area of biblical interpretation is in *The Oracles of Reason* (1693), a free-thinking miscellany written mostly by him and his friend and editor, C. Gildon. To this work B. contributed a vindication of T. BURNET's *Archaelogiae Philosophicae* (1692), to which he added an English translation of the seventh and eighth chapters and the appendix. He demonstrated that equally or even more heterodox statements on Genesis had been made by other writers, quoted effectively from T. BROWNE's *Religio Medici* and *Vulgar Errors,* cast naturalistic doubts on the deluge and original sin, and argued that Moses could not have written the Pentateuch (see PENTATEUCHAL CRITICISM).

Works: *Anima Mundi, or the Opinions of the Ancients concerning Man's Soul after this Life* (1679a); *Last Sayings and Dying Legacy of Mr. T. Hobbes* (1679b); *The Two First Books of Philostratus Concerning the Life of Apollonius Tyaneus . . . with Philological Notes upon Each Chapter* (1680a); *Great Is Diana of the Ephesians* (1680b); *Religio Laici* (1683a); *Miracles No Violations of the Laws of Nature* (1683b); *The Oracles of Reason* (1693); *Miscellaneous Works* (1695).

Bibliography: *BB*[2] 2 (1780) 380-86. **D. Berman,** "A Disputed Deistic Classic," *The Library* 7 (1985) 58-59. **H. R. Hutcheson,** "Lord Herbert and the Deists," *JPh* 43 (1946) 219-21. **J. Redwood,** "C. B. (1654–93), Deism, and English Freethought," *JHI* 35 (1974) 490-98. **H. G. Reventlow,** *The Authority of the Bible and the Rise of the Modern World* (1984) 290-94. **L. Stephen,** *DNB* 5 (1886) 243-45.

D. BERMAN

BOCHART, SAMUEL (1599–1667)

Born on May 10, 1599, in Rouen, B. died on May 16, 1667, in Caen. The son of a learned Huguenot pastor, he studied philosophy in Sedan, then theology and biblical studies in Saumur with J. Caméron and L. CAPPEL. He later lived in Oxford as well as in Leiden, where he pursued oriental studies under T. Erpenius. From 1625 on he was pastor in the Reformed Church in Caen.

Among his treatises two voluminous books stand out, the result of decades of preparation: the *Geographia sacra* and the *Hierozoicon*. The first part of the *Geographia,* titled "Phaleg" (see Gen 10:25), deals with the peoples listed in Genesis 10 and where they lived when, according to Genesis 11, they were dispersed over the earth. The second part, titled "Chanaan," deals with the Phoenicians, their colonies, and their language. The *Hierozoicon* systematically discusses all kinds of animals mentioned in the Bible. Both works immediately evoked much admiration due to the abundance of material brought together from Jewish, classical, and Arabic literature. They remained standard works in the seventeenth and eighteenth centuries, as evidenced by their many editions and by the fact that J. D. MICHAELIS added *post Bochartum* to the title of his *Spicilegium geographiae Hebraeorum exterae* (1769, 1780) and in the preface named B.'s book as a "liber aeternitate dignus." However, R. SIMON (*Histoire critique,* 481 = 3, 20) warned against uncritically using these extensive but often too speculative works. Developing scientific knowledge and advances in biblical criticism support this warning, but they have not left B.'s material without worth.

Works: *Geographiae sacrae Pars Prior Phaleg seu de Dispersione gentium et terrarum divisione facta in aedificatione turris Babel, Pars altera Chanaan sue de Coloniis et Sermone Phoenicum* (1648 and several later eds.); *Hierozoicon Sive bipartitum opus de Animalibus Sacrae Scripturae* (1663; latest ed. with notes by E. F. C. Rosenmüller, 3 vols., 1793–96); *Opera omnia* (3 vols., 1692 and several later eds.; with a biography of B. by St. Morinus).

Bibliography: **E. and E. Haag,** *La France protestante* 2 (1847) 319-23. **C. Hippeau,** *NBG* 6 (1855) 304-7. **F. J. M. Laplanche,** *L'Écriture, le sacré et l'histoire* (SIB 12, 1986), esp. 250-54. **E. Levesque,** *DB* 1:1823-24. **F. Martin,** *Bio-Bibliographie Normande* 1-3 (1901–3) 376-413. *MSHH* 27 (1734) 201-15. **E. Reuss,** *Revue de théologie et de philosophie chrétienne* 8 (1854) 120-56. **R. Simon,** *Histoire critique de Vieux Testament* (1685). **E. H. Smith,** *S. B.: Recherches sur la vie et les ouvrages de cet auteur illustre* (1833).

R. SMEND

BOER, PIETER ARIE HENDRIK DE (1910–)

B. was professor of OT in the theological faculty at Leiden (1938–78). During WWII, when the university was shut down by German occupation, he was prevented from teaching and was active in the Dutch resistance. Although he occupied the chair of A. KUENEN and W. KOSTERS, he was more strongly in the tradition of B. EERDMANS, his immediate predecessor. He has shown little inclination for criticism but has had a strong interest in textual, philological, and RELIGIONSGESCHICHTLICHE aspects of exegetical study. He is best known for his skills in organizing and administering forums and projects like the International Organization for the Study of the OT, the journals *Oudtestamentische Studien* and *Vetus Testamentum,* and the Leiden PESHITTA project that focus on the work of various scholars.

Works: *De voorbede in het Oude Testament* (*OTS* 3, 1943); "Research into the Text of I Samuel 18–31," *OTS* 6 (1949) 1-100; "De godsdienst van het Jodendom," *Het oudste Christendom en de antieke Culture* (ed. J. H. Waszink et al., 1951) 1:433-536; "Second-Isaiah's Message," *OTS* 11 (1956) 1-126; *De zoon van God in het Oude Testament* (1957); *Fatherhood and Motherhood in Israelite and Judean Piety* (1974).

S. J. DEVRIES

BOHLEN, PETER VON (1796–1840)

Few biblical and oriental scholars had a more unusual life prior to beginning their studies than B. Born Mar. 13, 1796, in Wüppels, an area today flanked by Wilhelmshaven and Bremerhaven, he was orphaned at thirteen and apprenticed to a tailor. A year later he entered French military service when Napoleon ordered orphans in the region aged fourteen to twenty into the army. In May 1814, with the tide running against the French, he took refuge in Hamburg and worked at an inn. In the army he had learned French, and in Hamburg he learned English from visitors to the inn. He began secondary education in Hamburg at the age of twenty, and in 1821, aged twenty-five, he entered the University of Halle, where his principal teacher was H. GESENIUS. In October 1822 he proceeded to Bonn to study Arabic under G. Freytag and in 1824 began Sanskrit. He was appointed *ausserordentlicher* professor at Königsberg in 1826 and full professor in oriental languages in 1828. At Königsburg he taught Sanskrit, Persian, Hebrew, Arabic, Syriac, and HB. In 1837 he became seriously ill on a journey to England and spent the last year of his life in Halle, where he died on Feb. 5, 1840.

B. published only one book on the HB, a commentary on Genesis in 1835; but this was one of the few critical German works translated into English before 1860 (the translation appeared in 1855), and it gave English readers access to a position that anticipated J. WELLHAUSEN's 1878 view of the history of Israelite religion. B. argued that Genesis had been written in the eighth century by an author who had used various sources. Although he did not advocate a documentary source theory, he found evidence of more primitive "Elohim" passages and sophisticated, national "Jehovah" passages. He attacked the credibility of many of the historical narratives in the Pentateuch (see PENTATEUCHAL CRITICISM). His view of Israelite religion was that the levitical ordinances had not been given by Moses but had developed gradually from the time of Samuel, usually when weak kings could not control the priesthood. They were not made known to the people until the reign of Josiah and were not enforced until after the exile.

The Genesis commentary was published the same year as J. VATKE's *Biblical Theology* and D. F. STRAUSS's *Life of Jesus,* both of which overshadowed B.'s book. He remains, however, an important witness to German critical work of the 1830s and a reminder that English readers had access to this work in translation two decades before Wellhausen.

Works: *Die Genesis Historisch-Kritisch erläutert* (1835; ET of parts in *Introduction to the Book of Genesis, with a Commentary on the Opening Portion* [ed. J. Heywood, 1855]).

Bibliography: *Autobiographie des ordentlichen Professors der orientalischen Sprachen und Literatur Dr. P. von Bohlen* (ed. J. Voigt, 1841). **J. W. Rogerson,** *OTCNC,* 175-77.

J. W. ROGERSON

BÖHME, JAKOB (1575–1629)

Born near Görlitz, B. was a shoemaker who during the first decade of the seventeenth century saw a vision of the divine nature. He published an account of the vision in *Morgenröthe* (1612). Consequent persecution from the local Lutheran clergy forced him into silence until 1619, when until his death he produced a vast quantity of writing that refined and elaborated his original vision.

B.'s mystical "theosophy" owes some allegiance to the spiritualist and occult tradition of the sixteenth century, in particular PARACELSUS, *Theologia Germanica,* C. SCHWENCKFELD, and V. Weigel, but the complexity and consistency of his writings produce an originality that transcends eclecticism. The influence of his work, which was initially regarded as prophetic, was immense and continues today. Many different interpretations of B. have been offered. In N. Frye's memorable formulation, B.'s writings are a picnic to which each reader takes his or her own food.

For B., God is an abyss out of which come three principles. The first is God's wrath, or hellishness, and the second, the light and angelical world. These two constitute the "eternal nature" on a spiritual plane. The third principle is the external world, the "out-spoken visible Word" into which the first and second worlds emanate. In the spiritual world the first principle is subsumed into the second through the dynamic power of the "fire-flash," thereby assuring the ultimate predominance of love and angelic life.

B.'s thought is closely related to the text of the Bible. In particular, *Mysterium Magnum* is an exposition on Genesis in terms of B.'s mystical system, with regard to both personal and cosmic dimensions. Alchemical terms permit reference to both realms simultaneously; nature is humanized, and the human is refined through spiritual alchemy. Lucifer's rebellion is represented as a psychological aberration within the first two principles, while the fall of humankind is represented as a physiological and alchemical allegory that takes place initially inside an androgynous Adam. B.'s texts make extensive use of numerical patterning and of word mysticism: every speech-act represents the "speaking forth" of divine principles. His denial of a limited atonement has been as attractive to many as his cosmological insights.

Works: *The Works of J. B.* (ed. G. Ward and T. Langcake, 4 vols., 1764–81).

Bibliography: **S. A. Konopacki,** *The Descent into Words: J. B.'s Transcendental Linguistics* (1979). **A. Koyré,** *La Philosophie de J. B.* (1929). **J. G. Turner,** *One Flesh: Paradisal Marriage and Sexual Relations in the Age of Milton* (1987).

N. SMITH

BOLINGBROKE, HENRY ST. JOHN, VISCOUNT
(1678–1751)

Born Sept. 16, 1678, B. entered parliament in 1701. He held several positions under Queen Anne and was instrumental in negotiating the Peace of Utrecht (1713). Brilliant but unstable, B. had a reputation for profligacy and disloyalty. After Anne's death he fled to France and helped James Stuart, the Old Pretender, in his unsuccessful attempt to seize the English throne (1715). Pardoned by George I, B. returned to England, and although banned from parliament, became a leading organizer of the Tory opposition. He died Dec. 12, 1751.

Although he was an eloquent writer, B.'s arguments often lack consistency. A Deist (see DEISM), he based his theology on natural religion and was extremely critical of the HB, questioning its AUTHORITY, historical accuracy, theology, and morality. JESUS' teaching, he said, was based on natural law, the fundamental principle of which is universal benevolence. The original gospel was concisely and plainly stated but was distorted by later accretions. "The gospel gave birth to Christian theology, and the gospel suffers for the sins of her licentious offspring" (*Philosophical Works,* 2:303). B. regarded PAUL as a distorter of true Christianity and was scathing about the Apocalypse, denying its traditional authorship and dismissing it as the work of a fanatic.

Works: *Philosophical Works* (5 vols., 1754–77, repr. 1977); *Works* (4 vols., 1841, repr. 1969).

Bibliography: **H. T. Dickinson,** *Bolingbroke* (1970). **B. S. Hammond,** *Pope and B.: A Study of Friendship and Influence* (1984). **J. P. Hart,** *Viscount B., Tory Humanist* (1965). **S. W. Jackson,** *Man of Mercury: An Appreciation of the Mind of H. St. John, Viscount B.* (1965). **I. Kramnick,** *B. and His Circle* (Harvard Political Studies, 1968). **G. V. Lechler,** *Geschichte des englischen Deismus* (1841, repr. 1965) 396-408. **W. M. Merrill,** *From Statesman to Philosopher: A Study in B.'s Deism* (1949). **L. Stephen,** *DNB* 50 (1897) 129-44. **S. Varey,** *H. St.*

John, Viscount B. (TEAS 362, 1984). **W. Warburton,** *A View of B.'s Philosophy, in Four Letters to a Friend* (1754–55, 1977).

A. W. WAINWRIGHT

BOMBERG, DANIEL (1483–1553)

A successful Christian businessman from Antwerp, B. was the most important and prolific publisher of Hebrew books in Venice in the sixteenth century. Between 1515 and 1548 he printed over 200 titles with the help of several learned Jews, including some converts.

B. printed the first RABBINIC BIBLE (folio) and the quarto Bible, both edited by F. Pratensis. The first part of these two works—the Pentateuch, the five scrolls, and the Haftarot—were completed on the same day, Dec. 10, 1516, in folio and in quarto. These first two books from the press are extremely rare. One copy of the folio edition is preserved in the Bodleian Library, split between two volumes; and another copy, preserved in the second I. Mehlman collection (a microfilm copy is in the National and University Library, Jerusalem), was recently acquired by the D. Sofer Collection (London). One copy of the quarto edition is preserved in the Trinity College (Cambridge) library. Eight years after he had invested in publishing the first rabbinic Bible, expressing his pride in it in the colophon, B. turned to another editor, JACOB BEN ḤAYYIM, to publish a new edition, also in four folio volumes. The text of that second edition achieved the status of the *textus receptus* of the Bible.

B. generally concentrated on printing books for his typical buyers, mostly Jews—the complete Babylonian TALMUD (in at least three printings), the Jerusalem Talmud, liturgy, Bible and commentaries, and halakhic works—but printed few works in the realm of KABBALAH and grammar. Among the several categories of titles that B. published, the Bible and its commentaries achieved second place, with over forty titles. In addition to the rabbinic Bible (1517, 1525, 1548), which was very expensive, he also printed smaller-sized editions of the whole Bible and of several of its parts (Pentateuch; Psalms; Job and Daniel; Proverbs, Song of Songs, and Ecclesiastes), which were more affordable. In addition he printed some PENTATEUCHAL commentaries in separate editions: RASHI; two supercommentaries to Rashi— R. Israel Isserlein, R. Elijah Mizraḥi; R. Baḥya [ben Asher]; R. Levi Ben Gershon (see GERSONIDES); two kabbalistic commentaries—R. Menaḥhem Recanati, R. Abraham Saba. He also printed the Bible concordance *Meir Nativ* by R. Isaac Natan.

B.'s editions set the standard for several of the basic works of Judaism, including the rabbinic Bible, the Babylonian Talmud, and the *Mishneh Torah* of MAIMONIDES. They helped standardize these texts and their cross-referencing. To this day these works are printed in a layout similar to the one first adopted by B.

Bibliography: Z. **Baruchson,** "The Private Libraries of North Italian Jews at the Close of the Renaissance" (diss., Bar-Ilan University, 1985, Hebrew) 58-67 (the economic factor in B.'s undertaking), 78-82 (categories of B.'s books), 111-15 (types of books sold in B.'s shop in 1543), 135-43 (prices of B.'s books in 1543) = S. Baruchson, *Books and Readers* (1993, Hebrew, 31-33, 38-41, 2-54, 63, 217-20). **H. van Bomberghen,** *Généalogie de la famille van Bomberghen* (1914; rare: copy in British Museum Library). **W. Brulez,** "Lettres commerciales de Daniel et Antoine van Bombergen á Antonio Grimani (1532–43)," *Bulletin de L'Institut Historique Belge de Rome* 31 (1958) 169-205; L'Exportation des Pays-Bays vers L'Italie par voie de terre au milieu de XVIe siècle," *Annales-Économies-Sociétés-Civilisations* 14 (1959) 461-91. **A. Freimann,** "D. B. und seine hebräischen Druckerei in Venedig," *ZfHB* 10 (1906) 32-36, 79-88 (list of books B. printed). **A. M. Haberman,** *The Printer D. B. and the List of the Books Published by His Press* (1978, Hebrew). **M. J. Heller,** *Printing the Talmud* (1992) 135-82 (requires revision on pp. 135-37 regarding beginnings of B.'s press). **J. S. Hirsch,** "D. B. and His Work Reconsidered," *Yad LaQorei* 18 (1979, Hebrew) 105-8 (economic factor in B.'s undertaking). **M. Marx,** *Geschichte des hebräischen Buchdruckes in Venedig,* vol. 1, *Die Anfage-Bomberg* (1937, typescript, 2 vols., one devoted to the list of books; part of his larger work *Geschichte und Annalen des hebräischen Buchdruckes in Italien im Sechszehnten Jahrhundert,* in several vols.). **F. Van Ortoy,** "Les van Bomberghen d'Anvers," *De Gulden Passer* 2 (1924) 131-44. **J. S. Penkower,** "Bomberg's First Bible Edition and the Beginning of His Printing Press," *Kiryat Sefer* 58 (1983) 586-604 (Hebrew; n. 1 lists the previous bibliography). **I. Ron,** *The Bomberg Talmud: A Bibliographical Guide* (in preparation). **A. Rosenthal,** "D. B. and His Talmud Editions," *Gli Ebrei e Venezia, secoli XIV–XVIII* (ed. G. Cozzi, 1987) 375-416.

J. S. PENKOWER

BONAVENTURE (c. 1217–74)

B. was born c. 1217 at Bagnorea in Tuscany. In 1235, after initial studies at the local Franciscan convent, he entered the university of Paris and graduated as a master of arts. In 1243 he entered the faculty of theology and joined the Franciscan order. His curriculum toward becoming master of theology included study of the entire Bible and of PETER LOMBARD's *Sentences.* Assisting his master in disputations and in giving cursory readings, B. served as regent master of the Franciscan Studium in Paris from 1254 until he was appointed superior general of the Franciscans in 1257. He died in 1274 while participating in the Council of Lyons.

B.'s ability to recall and to use biblical quotations was extraordinary. His chief exegetical work was his commentary on Luke (1255–56), which fills vol. 7 of his *Opera Omnia.* He also wrote commentaries on Ecclesiastes and John (vol. 6; but the commentary on Wisdom in this volume is inauthentic). His commentary on Lom-

bard's *Sentences* (1254–56) is among the greatest theological syntheses of the period.

B. inherited a symbolism of books from HUGH OF ST. VICTOR. Nature and Scripture are comparable books of revelation. The Wisdom of God is a "book written within and without" (Ezek 2:9): The outer book is the created world, while the inner book is God's revelation within the soul. But sin has vitiated our ability to perceive the inner book and thus correctly to interpret the outer book, hence our need for Scripture (*Brev.* 2.11).

B. outlined his distinctive views on exegesis in the prologues to the commentary on Luke and to his theological compendium, the *Breviloquium* (1256–57). The ability to understand Scripture is a grace akin to the INSPIRATION of its authors. The teacher should humbly accept this calling and not dare to claim it. The student should be humble and obedient. Scripture mirrors the whole of creation, and yet it declares only what suffices for salvation. B. emphasized the methodological differences between Scripture and the secular sciences—e.g., there is no division into speculative and practical parts as there is in philosophy. Scripture has breadth, depth, length, and height (Eph 3:18). The breadth consists in topical divisions (the two testaments and the subdivision of each testament into legal, historical, sapiential, and prophetic books); length in the historical progression from the creation of the world to its end; height in the hierarchies and in the orders of being united in Christ, who is our ladder to God; and depth in diversity of senses (literal, allegorical, tropological, and anagogical). The story of the world is like a beautiful song, but reason without revelation (as in the case of Aristotle) cannot discover the beginning or the end of the song and therefore cannot understand what it means.

Works: *Opera Omnia* (10 vols., 1882–1902); *Opera Theologica Selecta* (5 vols., 1934–64); *Le Christ maôtre* (ed., tr., and commentary by G. Madec of the sermon "Unus est magister noster Christus," 1990); *Semones Dominicales* (ed. J. G. Bougerol, 1977; ET, *Rooted in Faith: Homilies to a Contemporary World* [1974]); *Breviloquium* (ET by J. de Vinck, 1963); *Collations on the Six Days* (ET by J. de Vinck, 1970).

Bibliography: J. G. **Bougerol** et al. (eds.), *S. Bonaventura, 1274–1974* (5 vols., 1973). **J. G. Bougerol,** *Introduction to the Works of B.* (1964). **W. Detloff,** *TRE* 7 (1981) 48-55. **H. Mercker,** "Schriftauslegung als Weltauslegung: Untersuchung zur Stellung der Schrift in der Theologie Bonaventuras," *Veröffentlichungen des Grabmann-Institutes* NF 15 (1971). **J. F. Quinn,** "Chronology of St. B. (1217–57)," *Franciscan Studies* 32 (1972) 168-86; *DMA* 2 (1983) 313-19. **J. Ratzinger,** *The Theology of History in St. B.* (1971; ET 1989). **H. G. Reventlow,** "Weltverstehen aus der Bibel heraus: Bonaventura," *EBA* 2 (1994) 212-30. **G. A. Zinn,** "Book and Word: The Victorine Background of B.'s Use of Symbols," *S. Bonaventura, 1274–1974* 2 (1973) 143-69.

P. L. REYNOLDS

BONHOEFFER, DIETRICH (1906–45)

B. began his theological studies in Tübingen (1923), but his academic career centered in Berlin, where he earned his lic. theol. (1927) and, after a year as vicar in Barcelona, his habilitation in systematic theology (1930). Already in 1933 he opposed the Nazi regime and sided with its Jewish victims. He became director of the Finkenwalde seminary of the Confessing Church (1934–37). Involved by 1938 in a plot against Hitler, he used his ecumenical contacts abroad as secret agent for the conspirators. In April 1943 he was arrested and two years later was hanged in Flossenburg.

Biblical interpretation informs all of B.'s work but particularly his Bible studies, sermons, devotions, meditations, and lectures. As witness to God, who in JESUS Christ loves the world, the Bible is the final AUTHORITY for all questions of life. Its message addresses humans by both revealing and transcending their limits. Humanity is accepted, judged, and renewed through the incarnation, crucifixion, and resurrection of Jesus Christ. This christocentric interpretation applies beyond human existence to nature and history. Thus the present time must be justified by Christ through the community of the church and the ethics of discipleship: In the church "Christ exists as congregation" for the world; in discipleship Christians "are Christ for others," realizing the worldwide kingdom of Christ.

For B., the Bible is a book of the church, read from Christ to Christ. While using the historical method within limits, B.'s exegesis responds to God's revelation in history as it preserves the tension between the biblical claim and modernity, but it transcends any dualism through a christology made real in community and an ethic in which revelation and the world coincide. B.'s HERMENEUTIC finally ventures toward post-criticism. He envisions a "non-religious interpretation of biblical terms" in a "world come of age." Analogous to the reciprocal relation between the HB and the NT, penultimate life in a world seemingly without God is to be interpreted in view of the ultimate, God. This nonreligious interpretation moves from the boundaries of life to its center, Christ. The end of religious Christianity is God's judgment, but at the same time it is God's renewal of the world in Christ.

Works: *D. B., Gesammelte Werke* (1958–74); *D. B. Werke* (1986–); *A Testament To Freedom, The Essential Writings of D. B.* (1990); *D. B. Works* (1996–).

Bibliography: E. **Bethge,** *D. B.: Man of Vision, Man of Courage* (1970). J. **Burtness,** *Shaping the Future: The Ethics of D. B.* (1985). G. **Ebeling,** "Die nicht-religiöse Interpretation biblischer Begriffe," *Wort und Glaube* I (1960) 90-160. E. **Feil,** *The Theology of D. B.* (1985). J. **de Gruchy,** *D. B.: Witness to Jesus Christ* (MMT, 1988). G. **Krause,** *TRE* 7 (1980) 55-66. M. **Kuske,** *The OT as a Book of Christ: An Appraisal of B.'s*

Interpretation (1976). H. **Ott,** *TPNZJ,* 367-81. P. **Ricoeur,** "L'interpretation non religieuse du Christianism chez B.," *Cahiers du Centre protestant de l'Ouest* (1966) 3-20. G. **Sauter,** "Zur Herkunft und Absicht der Formel 'Nichtreligiöse Interpretation biblischer Begriffe' bei D. B.," *EvTh* 25 (1965) 283-97.

M. HOFFMANN

BONSIRVEN, JOSEPH PAUL (1880–1958)

A French Jesuit NT exegete, B. was born at Lavaur in 1880 and educated at the Sulpician seminary in Paris and l'École Biblique under M.-J. LAGRANGE. In 1909 he received his lic. in sacred Scripture from the Pontifical Biblical Commission, but in 1910 his doctoral thesis on rabbinic eschatology was not accepted, and he was forbidden to teach sacred Scripture. During WWI, while a prisoner of war, he was appointed to teach dogmatic theology and Scripture to imprisoned seminarians. After the war he joined the Society of Jesus and later taught theology at Enghien, Belgium. In 1928 he returned to teaching NT exegesis at the Pontifical Biblical Institute in Rome (1948–53). He died in Toulouse.

B. is known above all for his studies on Judaism of the first century CE, although the Qumran discoveries (see DEAD SEA SCROLLS) have tended to diminish the scientific importance of his work.

Works: *Le Judaïsm palestinien au temps de J-C* (2 vols., 1934–35); *Exégèse rabbinique et exégèse paulinienne* (1939); *Saint Paul épître aus hebreux* (VS 12, 1943²); *L'Apocalypse de Saint Jean* (VS 16, 1951); *Théologie du NT* (1951); *Épîtres de Saint Jean* (VS 9, 1954²); *Textes rabbiniques des premiers siècles chrétiens pour servir à l'intelligence du NT* (1955); *La Règne de Dieu* (1957).

Bibliography: *GDEL* 2 (1982) 1352. S. **Lyonnet,** *Biblica* 39 (1958) 262-68. S. B. **Morrow,** *NCE* 2 (1967) 679.

J. M. BULLARD

BORNKAMM, GÜNTHER (1905–90)

Born at Görlitz in Silesia on Oct. 8, 1905, B. was educated in philosophy and theology at Marburg, Tübingen, Berlin, and Breslau. He taught at the universities of Königsberg and Heidelberg and at the theological college in Bethel, and from 1939 to 1945 he was pastor at Münster and Dortmund. He became a professor at Göttingen in 1946 and at Heidelberg in 1949, where he remained until his retirement in 1972. He died in 1990.

B.'s programmatic approach to the NT is rooted in the thinking of his Marburg *Doktorvater,* R. BULTMANN. Bultmann was intensely interested in both form-critical analysis of the NT and in reshaping Christian theology according to the pattern that he saw FORM CRITICISM inevitably dictating. According to Bultmann, form criticism had made impossible the writing of a "life of

JESUS" based on the facts of Jesus' career and had demonstrated that the Gospel tradition was throughout a product of post-resurrection faith. Analysis of the Gospels revealed no fact of simple history that could compel belief. Belief must come, said Bultmann, at God's initiative and from a decision made in response to the gospel message.

B. developed these ideas in two directions. First, he went beyond Bultmann's efforts to analyze the history of the individual forms within the Gospel tradition and made the first attempts in Germany at what later became known as REDACTION CRITICISM. "The Stilling of the Storm in Matthew" (1948) maintained that Matthew was not only a custodian of church traditions about Jesus but also their "earliest exegete." Since Matthew used the Markan tradition as a source, it is possible to detect Matthew's interests by observing the changes he made in the Markan story; Matthew changed what in Mark was a simple miracle story into an illustration of the cost of following Jesus. In 1956 B. published a more extensive redaction-critical study, "End-expectation and Church in Matthew's Gospel," to show how Matthew's eschatology and ecclesiology were tied together throughout the Gospel and how they afford insight into the Gospel's original, Jewish-Christian life setting. These two studies helped to propel NT scholarship out of a narrow focus on the pieces of the Gospel tradition and into a concern with the life setting of the Gospels themselves.

Second, with the 1956 publication of *Jesus von Nazareth,* B. moved beyond Bultmann's belief that historical data about Jesus' life are not significant for Christian faith. He accepted Bultmann's thesis that writing a "life of Jesus" is impossible, but he also believed that by rigorously applying various criteria of authenticity the SYNOPTIC tradition would yield historical information about Jesus. The book represents a blending of these two convictions. B. maintained that this compromise has significance for Christian faith: It demonstrates that the Gospels call us both to encounter Jesus' preaching of God's kingdom and to realize that the significance of Jesus' preaching cannot be reduced to the mere fact that it happened. B. was joined in the "new quest for the historical Jesus" by other students and followers of Bultmann, most notably E. KÄSEMANN and E. FUCHS. B.'s preeminence is shown, however, in his invitation to write the article on Jesus in the 1974 edition of the *Encyclopedia Britannica* and the translation of *Jesus von Nazareth* into eleven languages.

Works: "Die Sturmstillung im Matthaus-Evangelium," *WuD* NF 1 (1948) 49-54; *Mythos und Evangelium* (1950); *Das Ende des Gesetzes: Paulusstudien* (1952); "Enderwartung und Kirche in Matthausevangelium," *The Background of the NT and Its Eschatology* (ed. W. D. Davies and D. Daube, 1956) 122-260; *Jesus of Nazareth* (1956, 1959³; ET 1963); *Studien zu Antike und Urchristentum* (1959); *Überlieferung und Auslegung im Matthäusevangelium* (1960); *Paulus* (1969).

Bibliography: D. Lührman (ed.), *Festschrift für G. B. 75 Geburtstag* (1980). **R. Morgan,** *HHMBI,* 439-44. **J. M. Robinson,** *A New Quest of the Historical Jesus* (1983) 12-19. *Wer is Wer? Das Deutsche Who's Who* (1989) 142.

F. S. THIELMAN

BOSTRÖM, GUSTAV (1901–73)

B. studied in Lund, Sweden, with S. Herner, who was well acquainted with German scholarship and who provided a good foundation in Semitic languages. B. also received instruction from J. PEDERSEN in Copenhagen, who introduced him to comparative study. Graduating in 1928, B. taught in Lund for some years and was ordained in the Church of Sweden in 1934. With no university chairs vacant, he taught in a school in Stockholm from 1939.

B.'s fame rests on one book, the *Proverbiastudien.* In his inaugural dissertation he had dealt with Israelite wisdom literature, especially paronomasia in the book of Proverbs. The dissertation, typical for its time, concentrates on TEXTUAL CRITICISM and metrical subtleties. Rhyme, alliteration, and assonance in Hebrew POETRY are compared with corresponding features in Arabic poetry. B. displayed a fine perception of the peculiarity of wisdom poetry.

His intimate knowledge of this type of literature helped B. in his second and more widely known book on Proverbs (1935), in which he argued for a new approach to the sayings about the foreign woman (Prov 2:16-19; 5; 6:20-25; 7). He maintained that the woman in question is a devotee of the cult of the goddess of love, Ishtar, and that her promiscuity is a cultic act. Thus the wisdom teacher warns against participation in the fertility cult of a foreign religion, hence against idolatry, not against adultery in the usual sense. B. found support for this interpretation, particularly in Prov 2:18 ("for her house sinks down to death, and her paths to the shades"). This book showed B. to be well versed in the study of comparative religion, both Semitic and Greek. One chapter is headed "Hieros gamos," and another deals with some texts in Ben Sira. B. also searched the Mandaean texts for comparative material. Unfortunately, he had no opportunity to continue with his biblical research after 1934.

Works: *Paronomasi i den äldre hebreiske maschalliteraturen med Särskild hänsyn till proverbia* (1928); *Proverbiastudien, die Weisheit und das fremde Weiss in Spr. 1–9* (1935).

S. HIDAL

BOUSSET, WILHELM (1865–1920)

Born in Lübeck, B. was a leader of the RELIGIONS-GESCHICHTLICHE SCHULE (RGS). He studied in Erlangen (1884), Leipzig (1885), and Göttingen (1886–90, under A. RITSCHL), taught NT at Göttingen (1896–1916), and became professor at Giessen in 1916, where P. Wernle,

W. HEITMÜLLER, and H. GRESSMANN were his students. He was founding editor of the *Theologische Rundschau* (1897) and founding co-editor, on the invitation of H. GUNKEL, of *Forschungen zur Religion und Literatur des Alten und Neuen Testaments* (1903). He died March 8, 1920.

B.'s engagement in *Religionsgeschichte* began with *Jesu Predigt in ihrem Gegensatz zum Judentum,* written in response to J. WEISS's *Die Predigt Jesu vom Reiche Gottes* (both 1892). According to B., although Jewish APOCALYPTICISM was the setting for JESUS' thought, as Weiss maintained, Jesus' teaching only externally took the form of Jewish expectation of a near end. B. was persuaded that Jesus stood apart from his environment but that Christianity had to be interpreted as developing at the popular level of spontaneous religious practice. The world of apocalyptic thought revealed to Gunkel (*Schöpfung und Chaos* [1895]) and to B. (*Der Antichrist* [1895]) the moods, sufferings, and hopes of the broad masses of the people; and B. came to recognize contemporary Judaism as the background against which Jesus' teaching was possible.

Up to this point B.'s interest had been limited to the Jewish environment of early Christianity. By *Religion des Judentums* (1903) he had become aware of Iranian influence on the concept of the antichrist. The work of the classical philologist F. Boll opened his eyes to the pagan Hellenistic world with its fusion of Greek and oriental concepts.

In agreement with the proposals of W. WREDE (*Aufgabe und Methode der sogenannten Neutestament-lichen Theologie* [1897]), B. removed a double barrier in the interpretation of the NT in his best-known work, *Kyrios Christos* (1913): the barriers between NT theology and early church doctrine and between the religion of early Christianity and that of its environment. In this "history of the faith in Christ from the beginnings to IRENAEUS," B. recognized Jewish apocalypticism as the religious setting that prepared the way for the preaching of the gospel and provided Jesus' disciples with a ready solution to the riddle they faced because of his death, allowing them to save their hopes by elevating them even higher in recognizing Jesus as the Son of man who would soon return.

Drawing on the religious conceptions in the work of R. REITZENSTEIN and his own study of Gnosticism, *Hauptprobleme der Gnosis* (1907; see GNOSTIC INTERPRETATION), B. presented early Christianity in the Hellenistic world as developing into a cult of Christ. The influence of Judaism was being surpassed by that of pagan Hellenism. The gentile church used the title *kyrios* (Lord) to give expression to its convictions about Christ. The title originated from Syria and Egypt and was used for deities at the center of the cult. The young Christian religion gathered around the cult of the *kyrios* Jesus, whom they proclaimed over all other *kyrioi.* Hope for the parousia was replaced by faith in the *kyrios* always present. B. nevertheless remained convinced that the initial impulse of Jesus remained influential; even though the historical figure was being overshadowed, he never disappeared.

According to B., the Hellenistic churches of Antioch, Damascus, and Tarsus provided the setting for the conversion of PAUL, whose development as a Christian took place in an already existing Hellenistic church that had originated without him. In it Christianity had become a religion of redemption similar to the mystery cults. In the Fourth Gospel salvation came to be understood as a deification through the vision of God in Christ, a development culminating in the view of Irenaeus that God became human so that human beings could become divine.

Works: *Jesu Predigt in ihrem Gegensatz zum Judentum* (1892); *Der Antichrist in der Überlieferung des Judentums, des Neuen Testaments und der alten Kirche* (1895); *Die Offenbarung Johannis* (1896); *Der Apostel Paulus* (1898); *Die Religion des Judentums im neutestamentlichen Zeitalter* (1903; since the 3rd ed., *Die Religion des Judentums im späthellenistischen Zeitalter* [1926, 1986]); *Die jüdische Apokalyptik, ihre religionsgeschichtliche Herkunft und ihre Bedeutung für das Neue Testament* (1903); *Das Wesen der Religion dargestellt an ihrer Geschichte* (1903); *Jesus* (1904); *Was wissen wir von Jesus?* (1904); *Hauptprobleme der Gnosis* (1907); *Die Bedeutung Jesu für den Glauben* (1910); *Kyrios Christos: Geschichte des Christusglaubens* (1913; ET 1970); *Jüdisch-Christlicher Schulbetrieb in Alexandrien und Rom* (1915); *Religionsgeschichtliche Studien: Aufsätze zur Religionsgeschichte des hellenistischen Zeitalters* (NovTSup 50, ed A. F. Verheule, 1979).

Bibliography: H. Kahlert, *Der Held und seine Gemeinde: Untersuchungen zum Verhältnis von Stifterpersönlichkeit und Verehrergemeinschaft in der Theologie des freien Protestantismus* (1984). **O. Merk,** *Giessner Gelehrte in der ersten Hälfte des 20. Jahrhunderts* (ed. H. G. Gundel et al., 1982) 105-20. **J. M. Schmidt,** *TRE* 7 (1981) 97-101. **A. F. Verheule,** *W. B.: Leben und Werk* (1973).

H. BOERS

BOYLE, ROBERT (1627–91)

A British scientist, B. defended biblical revelation, which he thought could be harmonized with new scientific discoveries. He promoted wider dissemination of the Bible, encouraging and financing translations. In a frequently reprinted treatise on biblical interpretation, B. defended the style and coherence of the Bible against those who found it obscure, unmethodical, contradictory, and repetitious. He maintained that these charges, aimed especially at the HB, arose from insufficient recognition of the figurative character of Hebrew as an "Eastern" language. He was aware that the Bible was "a Collection of Composures of very differing sorts, and written at very different times," intended originally for those to whom it was first addressed, but clear enough in its main points. In his will B. provided for the influential Boyle lectures, many of which defended biblical faith and revelation.

Works: *Some Considerations Touching the Style of the Holy Scriptures* (1661); *Works of the Honourable R. B.* (5 vols., ed. with biography by T. Birch, 1744).

Bibliography: A. M. **Clerke,** *DNB* 6 (1886) 118-23. **M. Hunter** (ed.), *R. B. Reconsidered* (1994). **J. R. Jacobs,** *R. B. and the English Revolution: A Study in Social and Intellectual Change* (1977). **M. C. Jacobs,** *The Newtonians and the English Revolution, 1689–1720* (1976) 143-200. **R. E. W. Maddison,** "R. B. and the Irish Bible," *BJRL* 41 (1958–59) 81-101; *The Life of the Honourable R. B., F.R.S.* (1969). **L. T. More,** *The Life and Works of the Honourable R. B.* (1944). **H. D. Rack,** *TRE* 7 (1980) 101-4.

D. D. WALLACE, JR.

BRAUN, HERBERT (1903–91)

Born in Warlubien, West Prussia, B. studied theology (1922–26) in Königsberg, Rostock, and Tübingen (under A. Schlatter). Major influences were LUTHER, KANT, KIERKEGAARD, and K. BARTH. His dissertation was entitled *Gerichtsgedanke und Rechtfertigungslehre bei Paulus.* After serving as house tutor at Samland (1926/27) and assistant to E. von DOBSCHÜTZ in Halle (1928–30), he became a pastor in East Prussia (1930) and was imprisoned for resisting the Nazis (1937). After the war he was pastor in Magdeburg (1946–47), professor at the Kirchliche Hochschule in Berlin (1947–52), professor in Mainz (1952–71), and remained active in teaching after his retirement. He completed the commentary on Hebrews for the HNT in 1984 when he was eighty-one.

B.'s work had two major foci: (1) the relationship of the NT to its pagan and Jewish Hellenistic environment found in his volumes reviewing ten years of Qumran research (1966) and in such articles as "Plutarchs Kritik am Aberglauben im Lichte des Neuen Testaments" (1948) and (2) the question of meaning in the interpretation of texts. His major emphasis was on subject matter, interpreting the NT and other Hellenistic texts in a program of demythologizing under the influence of the work of R. BULTMANN.

The two foci were combined in *Spätjüdisch-häretischer und frühchristlicher Radikalismus* (1957), a comparison between Qumran (see DEAD SEA SCROLLS) and the Synoptics (see SYNOPTIC PROBLEM). As the title suggests, B. held that JESUS and Qumran shared a certain radicalized understanding of the demand of the Torah. In the teaching of Jesus the radicalized demand of the Torah was the framework for God's unconditional acceptance of the human

being in a coordination of the unqualified imperative "you shall" with the gracious invitation "you may." B. found this emphasis missing in Qumran.

In "Der Sinn der neutestamentliche Christologie," B. compared, not the titles of Jesus and other Hellenistic cult figures, but how the titles were used, e.g., *kyrios* (Lord) for Jesus and for Herakles. He came to the conclusion that the decisive difference between the religion of the NT and the religions of Hellenistic antiquity was that the NT proclaimed God's unreserved acceptance of human beings irrespective of merit while cults such as Herakles' inspired adherents to ideals exemplified by heroic figures from antiquity. In "Die Problematik einer Theologie des Neuen Testaments" (1961) these deliberations were expanded to include, in addition to christology, issues concerning soteriology, the law, APOCALYPTICISM, and the sacraments, with emphasis always on meanings.

Works: "Plutarchs Kritik am Aberglauben im Lichte des Neuen Testaments," *Der Anfang* 9 (1948) 1-26 = his *GS zum Neuen Testament und seiner Umwelt* (1962) 120-35 (ET "Plutarch's Critique of Superstition in the Light of the NT," Claremont Graduate School, Occasional Paper 5, 1972); *Spätjüdisch-häretischer und frühchristlicher Radikalismus* (BHT 24, 2 vols., 1957); "Der Sinn der neutestamentlichen Christologie," *ZTK* 54 (1957) 341-77 = *GS,* 86-99 (ET, "The Meaning of the Christology of the NT," *JTC* [1968] 89-127); "Die Problematik einer Theologie des Neuen Testaments," *ZTK* 58 (1961) 3-18 = *GS,* 325-41 (ET, "The Problem of a Theology of the NT," *JTC* 1 [1965] 169-83); *Qumran und das Neue Testament* (2 vols, 1966); *Jesus of Nazareth: The Man and His Time* (1969; ET 1979); *An die Hebräer* (HNT 14, 1984).

Bibliography: W. **Schottroff,** "H. B.: Eine theologische Biographie," *Die Auslegung Gottes durch Jesus: Festgabe für H. B. zu seinem 80. Geburtstag am 4. Mai 1983* (1983) 263-306.

H. BOERS

BRIGGS, CHARLES AUGUSTUS (1841–1913)

Born in New York City, Jan. 15, 1841, B. entered the University of Virginia at age sixteen, experienced a conversion in his second year, and decided to prepare for the ministry. After brief service in New York's Seventh Regiment during the Civil War, he entered Union Theological Seminary, but was forced to withdraw his senior year and run the family business for a time. He spent 1866–69 at the University of Berlin studying primarily with I. DORNER. Ordained in 1870, he served the First Presbyterian Church in Roselle, New Jersey, before becoming provisional professor at Union Seminary (1874), then professor of Hebrew and cognate languages as well as librarian. In 1876 he was appointed Davenport Professor of Hebrew.

B. helped to establish the journal *Presbyterian Review*, a joint venture between Union and Princeton seminaries published from 1880 to 1889. In Nov. 1890 he was transferred to the newly established Edward Robinson chair of biblical theology, and his inaugural lecture, informed by German critical scholarship, created a furor. The Briggs trial, inaugurated in the Presbyterian Church in 1891, became a celebrated case of orthodoxy versus "modernism." B. was accused of (1) giving too much prominence to reason in religion and salvation; (2) overemphasizing the role of the church, apart from Scripture, as a source of enlightenment; (3) admitting that errors may have existed in the original text of Scripture; (4) teaching that HB predictions have been reversed in history and that many messianic predictions have not and cannot be fulfilled; (5) denying Mosaic authorship of the Pentateuch (see PENTATEUCHAL CRITICISM); (6) denying that Isaiah wrote the last half of the book of Isaiah; (7) teaching that the processes of redemption extend to the world to come; and (8) teaching that sanctification is not complete at death. After much turmoil and debate B. was condemned in 1893 by the general assembly and suspended from the Presbyterian ministry. He retained his position at Union, which broke with the Presbyterian Church, and was ordained an Episcopal priest in 1899. In his later years B. worked for Christian unity between Protestants and Catholics, met with Pope Pius X in 1905, became involved with the Catholic modernist movement, and eventually became a critic of the Roman Catholic hierarchy after the church's condemnation of modernism in 1906.

Although in many ways a conservative, B. saw the necessity of applying critical and modern approaches to biblical study. He understood his work as defending the integrity of Scripture against excessive rationalism and the unity of Scripture within its amazing variety. A highly competent, well-educated, and wide-ranging scholar, B. and his trial contributed more to the introduction and dissemination of critical biblical scholarship in the United States than any other factor. He was general editor for the *International Critical Commentary* and the *International Theological Library*, to which he contributed the commentary on Psalms, and with S. Driver and F. Brown prepared a revised *Hebrew and English Lexicon of the OT*. B. also contributed introductory and exegetical works on biblical study that are still of value.

Works: *Biblical Study: Its Principles, Methods and History* (1883); *The Authority of Holy Scripture: An Inaugural Address* (1891); *The Bible, the Church, and the Reason* (1892); *The Messiah of the Gospels* (1894); *The Messiah of the Apostles* (1895); *General Introduction to the Study of Holy Scripture* (1899², repr. 1985); *Psalms* (ICC, 2 vols., 1906–7); (with F. von Hügel), *The Papal Commission and the Pentateuch* (1906); *History of the Study of Theology* (2 vols., 1916).

Bibliography: D. G. Dawe, *The Ecumenical Vision of C. A. B.* (1985). **C. R. Jeschke,** "The Briggs Case: The Focus of a Study in Nineteenth-Century Presbyterian History" (diss., University of Chicago, 1966). **M. S. Massa,** " 'Mediating Modernism': C. B., Catholic Modernism, and an Ecumenical 'Plot,' " *HTR* 81 (1988) 413-30; *C. A. B. and the Crisis of Historical Criticism* (1990); *C. A. B., Union Theological Seminary, and Twentieth-century American Protestantism* (1994). **T. H. Olbricht,** *HHMBI,* 294-98. **M. G. Rogers,** "C. A. B.: Conservative Heretic" (diss., Columbia University, 1964); "C. A. B.: Heresy at Union," *American Religious Heretics* (ed. G. H. Shriver, 1966) 89-147. **H. P. Smith,** *AJT* 17 (1913) 497-508.

M. G. ROGERS

BRIGHT, JOHN (1908–95)

B. was born Sept. 25, 1908, in Chattanooga, Tennessee. His mother was the daughter of a Presbyterian pastor whose family had produced a long line of Presbyterian clergy going back into the eighteenth century. B. received his BA from Presbyterian College (1928) and his BD (1931) and his ThM (1933) from Union Theological Seminary in Virginia. In 1935 he was ordained in the PCUS, serving as assistant pastor of First Presbyterian Church of Durham, North Carolina (1936–37), then as pastor of the Catonsville Presbyterian Church until 1940, when he received his PhD under W. F. ALBRIGHT at Johns Hopkins with a dissertation on the reign of King David. In the same year B. was appointed Cyrus H. McCormick Professor of Hebrew and OT Interpretation at Union, where he remained until his retirement in 1975, except for service as a chaplain during WWII (1943–46). He died March 26, 1995.

The first distinguished American historian of ancient Israel (preceded only by C. Kent, *A History of the Hebrew People* [2 vols., 1896–97]), B. was arguably the most influential scholar of the Albright school. His work had a distinctly American commonsense flavor similar to that of W. James. B.'s work evinced a strong commitment to the historical integrity of the HB, which he defended first in his 1956 monograph, arguing that the oral traditions on which Israel's pre-monarchic history was based were more historical than M. NOTH and the majority of German scholars generally allowed. In particular B. maintained (1956) that etiological stories should not be treated as historicizing inventions appended to rituals and practices whose true origins had been lost in the distant past. Rather, such stories, analogous to the account of the first Thanksgiving in America, could more reasonably be seen as actual historical explanations handed down from generation to generation. For this reason and because of the strong faith element implicit in his *History,* B. has been quietly characterized by some more recent critics as a "tradition-fundamentalist," a judgment that circumvents the serious issues he raised regarding the historical evaluation of Israel's early traditions and that overlooks the critical complexity of his views. Theologically insightful, his other works defended the value and importance of the HB.

Works: *The Kingdom of God: The Biblical Concept and Its Meaning for the Church* (1953); *Early Israel in Recent History Writing: A Study in Methods* (SBT 19, 1956); *A History of Israel* (1959, 1972[2], 1981[3]); *Jeremiah* (AB, 1965); *The Authority of the OT* (1967); *Covenant and Promise: The Prophetic Understanding of the Future in Pre-Exilic Israel* (1976).

D. G. SCHLEY

BRIGHTMAN, THOMAS (1562–1607)

An English biblical scholar, B. was born in Nottingham in 1562 and educated at Queen's College, Cambridge, where he became a fellow in 1584. He was rector of Hawnes in Bedfordshire from 1592 until his death on Aug. 24, 1607. An avid student of the Bible, he made a practice of reading the whole of the Greek NT every two weeks. His writings on apocalyptic subjects, published posthumously, won considerable popularity. The book of Revelation, in his opinion, prophesied two millennia, the first from 300 to 1300, and the second beginning with the renewal of true Christianity under WYCLIF and others. For B. Calvinistic churches were "godly Philadelphia" and all others fell far short.

Works: *Apocalypsis Apocalypseos* (1609; ET *A Revelation of the Revelation* [1615]); *Commentarius in Canticum Canticorum: Explicatio . . . Danielis a vers. 36 cap. 11 ad finem cap. 12* (1614); *Workes* (1644).

Bibliography: P. **Christianson,** *Reformers and Babylon: English Apocalyptic Visions from the Reformation to the Eve of the Civil War* (1978). **C. H.** and **T. Cooper,** *Athenae Cantabrigienses* 2 (1861) 458-59. **K. R. Firth,** *The Apocalyptic Tradition in Reformation Britain, 1530–1645* (1979). **T. Fuller,** *The Church History of Britain* 3 (new ed. 1837) 233-35. **J. Mew,** *DNB* 6 (1886) 339. **P. Toon,** *Puritans, the Millennium, and the Future of Israel: Puritan Eschatology 1600 to 1660* (1970).

A. W. WAINWRIGHT

BROCKELMANN, CARL (1868–1956)

The preeminent oriental philologist of his generation, B. earned his PhD in 1891 under T. NÖLDEKE at Strasbourg. He held professorships at Berlin (1900 and 1922); Erlangen (1900–1903); Königsberg (1903–10); Halle (1910–22); and Breslau (1922–35). In retirement he taught again at Halle (1947–54).

His greatest contribution was the comprehensive ap-

plication of the principles of modern Indo-European linguistics to the Semitic languages. His two most important publications were a magisterial comparative grammar of the Semitic languages and an exhaustive study of Arabic literature.

Works: *Lexicon Syriacum* (1895, 1928[2]); *Syrische Grammatik* (PLO 5, 1899 and 5 rev. eds.); *Geschichte der arabischen Literatur* (2 vols., 1898–1902; rev. ed., 1943–49; *Supplement,* 3 vols., 1937–42); *Arabische Grammatik* (PLO 4, 6th rev. ed., 1904); *Semitische Sprachwissenschaft* (SG, 1906, 1916[2]); "Die syrische und die christlich-arabische Literatur," *Die Literaturen des Orients in Einzeldarstellungen* 7, 2 (1907) 1-74; *Grundriss der vergleichenden Grammatik der Semitischen Sprachen* (2 vols., 1908–13); *Kurzgefasste vergleichende Grammatik der Semitischen Sprachen* (PLO 1908); *Mitteltürkischen Wortschatz nach Maḥmud al-Kashgaris Divan lugat at-turk* (1928); *Ugaritische Syntax* (1941); *Geschichte der islamischen Völker und Staaten* (1939, 1943[2]); ET, *History of the Islamic Peoples* [1947]); *Osttürkische Grammatik der islamischen Literatursprachen Mittelasiens* (1954); *Hebräische Syntax* (1956).

Bibliography: J. W. **Fück,** *FuF* 30 (1956) 255-56. **H. L. Gottschalk,** *AfO* 18 (1957–58) 226-27. **O. Speis,** *Verzeichnis der Schriften von C. B.* (1938). **B. Spuler,** *Islam* 33 (1957) 157-61.

R. J. OWENS, JR.

BROUGHTON, HUGH (1549–1612)

A biblical and rabbinic scholar educated at Cambridge, B. learned Hebrew from A. Chevallier. He insisted that rabbinic rather than classical Greek tradition was basic to the interpretation of the HB. In 1588 B. published *A Concent of Scripture,* in which he sought to reconcile all discrepancies of biblical CHRONOLOGY and PROPHECY. He called for a new Bible translation in 1597 and translated Daniel, Job, Ecclesiastes, and Lamentations, all with annotations to resolve difficulties in the Hebrew; he also translated Revelation. B. was omitted from the translators of the AV, perhaps because of his notorious quarrelsomeness. When it was published in 1611, he vehemently declared that he would rather be torn to pieces by wild horses than approve it. After his death J. LIGHTFOOT collected his writings and prefaced them with a biography.

Works: *The Works of the Great Albionean Divine, Renowned in Many Nations for Rare Skill in Salem's and Athens's Tongues and Familiar Acquaintance with All Rabbinical Learning* (1662).

Bibliography: K. **Firth,** *The Apocalyptic Tradition in Reformation Britain, 1530–1645* (1979) 153-63. **A. Gordon,** *DNB* 6 (1886) 459-62.

D. D. WALLACE, JR.

BROWN, FRANCIS (1849–1916)

An HB scholar and president of Union Theological Seminary, B. was born in Hanover, New Hampshire, and graduated from Dartmouth (1870) and Union Theological Seminary (1877). After two years in Berlin he became an instructor at Union and in 1890 professor of Hebrew and cognate languages. He was reported to be the first to teach Akkadian in America. (S. Curtiss may have taught it earlier at Chicago.) He served as editor-in-chief of the *Hebrew and English Lexicon of the OT* (see LEXICONS, HB), and according to G. MOORE, "the brunt of the prodigious toil fell on Brown." Although two major efforts are currently underway to revise the *Lexicon*, the work is still perceived as foundational. B. became president of Union in 1908. He was a charter member of the SOCIETY OF BIBLICAL LITERATURE (1880) and served as president (1895–96).

B. became enmeshed in the controversies over higher criticism surrounding C. BRIGGS, in which he stood by Briggs and approved the severing of Union from the Presbyterian Church. He remained a Presbyterian and was a leader among those who approved the GRAF-WELLHAUSEN documentary hypothesis and the stance that biblical revelation is located in religious ideas, not in historical details. Despite his liberal identity, B.'s posture was mediating. His chief contribution to scholarship was Semitic lexicography.

Works: *Assyriology: Its Use and Abuse in OT Study* (1885); *Hebrew and English Lexicon of the OT* (1907).

Bibliography: L. A. **Loetscher,** *The Broadening Church* (1954). A. C. **McGiffert,** *DAB* 3 (1929) 115-16. *Memorial Service in Honor of the Rev. F. B.* (1916). R. T. **Parsons,** "A Commentary by Dr. F. B. on the Book of Amos" (MA thesis, Baylor University, 1983). H. P. **Smith,** "F. B.: An Appreciation," *AJSL* 33 (1916–17) 75-88.

T. H. OLBRICHT

BROWN, RAYMOND E. (1928–98)

Born in New York City, May 22, 1928, B. completed preparatory studies for the Roman Catholic priesthood at St. Charles College, Cantonsville, Maryland (1945–46); the Catholic University of America, Washington, DC (BA 1948; MA 1949); Gregorian University, Rome (1949–50); and St. Mary's Seminary, Baltimore (STB 1951; STL 1953). He was ordained in 1953. After receiving the STD from St. Mary's in 1955, he studied Semitic languages at Johns Hopkins University, receiving the PhD in 1958. He held the SSB (1959) and the SSL (1963) from the Pontifical Biblical Commission. He died Aug. 8, 1998.

B. was Auburn Distinguished Professor Emeritus of Biblical Studies at Union Theological Seminary in New York City, where he taught for twenty years until his retirement in June 1990. He initially held a joint professorship between the Jesuit seminary, Woodstock, and Union (1971–74). He taught Scripture studies at St. Mary's (1959–71); was adjunct professor of religion at Columbia University, New York City (1979–90); visiting professor of NT at the Pontifical Biblical Institute in Rome (1973 and 1988); annual professor at the Albright School of Archaeology in Jerusalem (1978); and was several times scholar-in-residence at the North American College in Rome. He was the first person to have served as president of all three of the following societies: the Catholic Biblical Association of America, (1971–72); the SOCIETY OF BIBLICAL LITERATURE, (1976–77); and Studiorum Novi Testamenti Societas (1986–87).

B. wrote nearly forty books (his articles number in the hundreds), which may be divided into six categories. First, much of his work was devoted to exegetical treatment of books or key portions of books of the Bible. Among the significant volumes in this category is his two-volume work *The Death of the Messiah* (1994). Second, B. produced a series of focused works that examine topics in the realm of NT theology, such as *An Introduction to NT Christology* (1994). A third category of writings that take a variety of forms may be described as creative, summary works in critical biblical studies. Perhaps best known is *The New Jerome Biblical Commentary* (1990), done in conjunction with J. FITZMYER and R. Murphy as both an editor and a major contributor. Fourth, some contributions manifested B.'s commitment to ecumenical biblical studies, important examples of which include *Peter in the NT* (1973) and *Mary in the NT* (1978), each a collaborative assessment of the respective topics by Protestant and Roman Catholic scholars, sponsored by the United States Lutheran-Roman Catholic Dialogue and conducted by a task force of NT scholars from these denominations. Fifth, B.'s work frequently focused on the reconstruction of early Christian history. One well-known work is *The Community of the Beloved Disciple* (1979), in which he examined "the life, loves, and hates of an individual church in NT times." A sixth category may be described as writings advancing biblical studies, relating them to the life of the church, and educating clergy and laity alike in biblical studies and theological reflection. Above all others is his magisterial work, *An Introduction to the NT* (1997).

Works: *The Sensus Plenior of Sacred Scripture* (1955); *Gospel and Epistles of John* (NTRG 13, 1960, 1965, 1982); *Daniel* (1962); *The Parables of the Gospels* (1963); *Deuteronomy* (OTRG 10, 1965); *NT Essays* (1965, 1968, 1982); *The Gospel According to John* (AB 29, 1966; 29A, 1970); *Jesus, God and Man* (1967, 1972); *The Jerome Biblical Commentary* (1968); *The Semitic Background of the Term "Mystery" in the New Testament* (Facet Books/Biblical Series 21, 1968); *Biblical Tendencies Today: An Introduction to the Post-Bultmannians*

(1969); *Priest and Bishop: Biblical Reflections* (1970); *Peter in the NT* (1973); *The Virginal Conception and Bodily Resurrection of Jesus* (1973); *Biblical Reflections on Crises Facing the Church* (1975); *The Birth of the Messiah* (1977); *An Adult Christ at Christmas* (1978); *Mary in the NT* (1978); *The Community of the Beloved Disciple* (1979); *The Critical Meaning of the Bible* (1981); *The Epistles of John* (AB 30, 1982); *Antioch and Rome* (1983); *Recent Discoveries and the Biblical World* (1983); *The Churches of the Apostles Left Behind* (1984); *Biblical Exegesis and Church Doctrine* (1985); *A Crucified Christ in Holy Week* (1986); *A Coming Christ in Advent* (1988); *The Gospel and Epistles of John: A Concise Commentary* (1988); *The New Jerome Biblical Commentary* (1990); *Responses to 101 Questions on the Bible* (1990); *A Risen Christ in Eastertime* (1991); *The New Jerome Bible Handbook* (1992); *The Death of the Messiah* (1994); *Faith and Future: Studies in Christian Eschatology* (1994); *An Introduction to NT Christology* (1994); *A Once and Coming Spirit at Pentecost* (1994); *An Introduction to the NT* (ABRL, 1997).

Bibliography: M. L. **Soards,** *HHMBI,* 562-70.

M. L. SOARDS

BROWNE, THOMAS (1605–82)

Doctor of medicine and man of letters, educated at Oxford and Leiden, B. found the Bible, not a battlefield, but a playground. Much of what he wrote raised no murmur, e.g., he discoursed on the flowers and fish of Scripture, and he demonstrated that JESUS reclined rather than sat at supper. Poised between two worlds, the old one of authority and the new one of inquiry, as a scientist he was tempted to find naturalistic explanations for miracles, but as a Christian he conquered this temptation "on his knees." He could not, however, curb a persistent tendency to notice inconsistencies and improbabilities in the minutiae of the Bible. Still, he could at times reconcile both reason and revelation: On the relationship of diameter to circumference (2 Chr 4:2) one should "adhere unto Archimedes who speaketh exactly rather than the Sacred text which speaketh largely." He might protest that he did not question the metamorphosis of Lot's wife into a pillar of salt, "although some conceive that expression metaphorical." He might declare that the Bible is "a most singular book" and aver that its seeming inconsistencies merely reflect human limitation. Whatever his protestations, the chink in the armor of scriptural infallibility was revealed and the questioning intellect aroused. Conscious as he was of human fallibility, he always kept his skepticism circumspect. Just as he rejoiced in the natural world, so also he rejoiced in the Bible: "It is one of the hardest books I have met with; I wish there had been more of it."

Works: *Religio Medici* (1642); *Pseudoxia Epidemica: Enquiries into Vulgar Errors* (1646); *Hydriotaphia: Urn Burial* (1658); *The Garden of Cyrus* (1658); *Brampton Urns* (1667); *Certain Miscellany Tracts* (1683), incl. "Observations upon Several Plants Mentioned in Scripture" and "On the Fishes Eaten by Our Saviour After His Resurrection," *A Letter to a Friend upon the Occasion of the Death of His Intimate Friend* (Early English Books 173, 1690); *Christian Morals* (1716); *The Works of Sir T. B.* (G. L. Keynes, new ed., 1964); *Religio Medici and Other Writings* (M. R. Ridley, 1965).

Bibliography: J. **Bennett,** *Sir T. B.* (1962). M. **Bottrall,** *Every Man a Phoenix* (1958). G. K. **Chalmers,** "Sir T. B.: True Scientist," *Osiris* 2 (1936) 28-79. *Dictionary of National Biography,* vol. 7, 64-72. W. P. **Dunn,** *Sir T. B.: A Study in Religious Philosophy* (1950). E. M. **Forster,** "The Celestial Omnibus," *Collected Short Stories* (1947). E. **Gosse,** *Sir T. B.* (1905). P. **Green,** *Sir T. B.* (1959). E. S. **Merton,** *Science and Imagination in Sir T. B.* (1949). L. **Nathanson,** *The Strategy of Truth: A Study of Sir T. B.* (1968). C. A. **Patrides,** *The Major Works of Sir T. B.* (1977); *Approaches to Sir T. B.* (1982). R. P. **Pande,** *Sir T. B.* (1964). H. D. **Potter,** "Unburying Dr. B.," *The Expository Times,* vol. 100 (7) (1989) 258-63. A. B. **Shaw,** *Sir T. B. of Norwich* (1982). B. **Willey,** *The Seventeenth Century Background: Studies in the Age of Thought in Relation to Poetry and Religion* (1934) 49-75.

H. D. POTTER

BRUCE, ALEXANDER BALMAIN (1831–99)

B. was educated at the University and New College (the Free Church College) in Edinburgh. Ordained in 1859, he served as a parish preacher until 1875, when he was appointed to the chair of apologetics and NT exegesis in the Free Church College in Glasgow, where he remained until his death. In ecclesiastical matters he was much influenced by T. Chalmers and the leaders of the Free Church; in scholarly pursuits he learned from German sources (B. Weiss, O. Pfleiderer, and others); but he always remained his own master and reacted strongly against the historical skepticism of D. F. STRAUSS. Throughout his life he remained convinced that to see the historical JESUS truly and to show him as scholarship enables us to see him was both possible and an urgently necessary apologetic task.

B.'s influence in his own day derived quite as much from his work as an apologist as it did from his work as a biblical scholar. He was intensely sympathetic to those who found intellectual and other difficulties in Christianity. He was both a loyal churchman and a vigorous critic of traditional Scottish Calvinism (see CALVIN). In his theology and his biblical scholarship alike, it was his understanding of the mind of Jesus as revealed especially in the SYNOPTIC Gospels that lay at the base of his work. His first substantial book, *The Training of the Twelve* (1871), tackled a theme not often dealt with before or since and has stood the test of time better than much of his later work; but *The Kingdom of*

God, or Christ's Teaching According to the Synoptical Gospels (1889) expressed many views that a century later can still be considered well founded. His most substantial theological work, *The Humiliation of Christ* (1876), which espoused kenotic christology, also anticipated twentieth-century emphases; he was an early advocate of the view that patripassianism is not wholly a heresy. He wrote extensively on the Gospels, PAUL, and Hebrews; but perhaps his most enduring monument in biblical scholarship is his commentary on the Synoptics in the *Expositor's Greek Testament*.

Works: *The Training of the Twelve* (1871); *The Humiliation of Christ* (1876); *The Chief End of Revelation* (1881); *The Parabolic Teaching of Christ* (1882, 1899[8]); *The Miraculous Element in the Gospels* (1886); *The Kingdom of God, or Christ's Teaching According to the Synoptical Gospels* (1889); *Apologetics, or Christianity Defensively Stated* (1892); *St. Paul's Conception of Christianity* (1894); *With Open Face, or Jesus Mirrored in Matthew, Mark, and Luke* (1896); "The Synoptic Gospels," *The Expositor's Greek Testament* (ed. W. R. Nicoll, 1897); *The Providential Order of the World* (Gifford Lectures, 1897); *The Moral Order of the World in Ancient and Modern Thought* (Gifford Lectures, 1899); *The Epistle to the Hebrews* (1899); "Jesus," *EncBib* 2:2435-54.

Bibliography: W. M. Macgregor, *Persons and Ideals* (1939) chap. 1. **A. P. F. Sell,** *Defending and Declaring the Faith: Some Scottish Examples, 1860–1920* (1987) 89-116.

R. S. BARBOUR

BRUCE, FREDERICK FYVIE (1910–90)

B. was born in Elgin, Scotland, Oct. 12, 1910. As a student of the classics at the University of Aberdeen, he was touched by the lingering influence of W. RAMSAY and the tutelage of A. Souter. He later studied at the universities of Cambridge and Vienna and taught classics at Edinburgh and Leeds. At Leeds he took the certificate in Hebrew and became an accomplished Semitist. In 1947 B. established the department of biblical history and literature at the University of Sheffield. He was appointed John Rylands Professor of Biblical Criticism and Exegesis at the University of Manchester, England, in 1959. He died Sept. 11, 1990.

B. was a remarkably productive scholar; the number of his books exceeds fifty. In addition he wrote thousands of articles, essays, and reviews, some of which were published unsigned. He edited such periodicals as *Evangelical Quarterly* (1957–71) and *The Palestine Exploration Quarterly* (1957–71); and he was series editor for *The New International Commentary on the NT,* among others. He was also editor or associate editor of numerous collected writings, such as *The New Bible Dictionary* and *The International Bible Commentary.*

Although best known as a NT exegete, B.'s interests

and writings also included the HB, Jewish and classical studies, general history, Christian doctrine, patristics, apologetics, and ARCHAEOLOGY. He was both a technical scholar and a popularizer and user of the findings of scientific biblical studies for the benefit of students and laypersons. He usually identified with a conservative theological stance, but he considered this a result of his studies rather than the framework for them.

B.'s interpretative method was complex, centering on his commitment to listen faithfully to the text without presuppositions. Major features of his method include (1) knowledge of the texts and data of the Bible, its backgrounds, and cognate fields, which served as the foundation for his work; (2) careful, technical work with the text—he sought to apply to the Bible principles and methods used in the investigation of other ancient documents, which he believed permitted a dispassionate examination, unhindered by theological prejudice; (3) the assumption that the historical framework of the NT includes the HB, intertestamental Judaism, the Greco-Roman world, and early Christian history. (His three volumes, which combine to cover these areas, provide the matrix for his work on specific biblical texts. Archaeology, especially the study of the DEAD SEA SCROLLS, was also a tool with which he approached the NT; his classicist's eyes gave him a positive view of the historical value of the Bible); (4) a broad *Heilsgeschichtliche* approach to NT theology and interpretation, finding of particular importance studying the way the HB was used in the NT; and (5) scientific biblical criticism, which B. embraced and practiced as a method. However, he did not accept all the conclusions of contemporary critics. He rejected what he saw as an unnecessary antisupernatural bias that colored the results of much work in this field.

Works: *The Speeches in the Acts of the Apostles* (1942; see also "The Speeches in Acts: Thirty Years After," *Reconciliation and Hope: NT Essays presented to L. L. Morris* [1974] 53-68); *The NT Documents: Are They Reliable?* (1943; 1960[5]; see also "Are the NT Documents Still Reliable?" *Christianity Today* [Oct. 20, 1978] 28-33); *The Books and the Parchments: Some Chapters on the Transmission of the Bible* (1950, rev. ed., 1971); *The Book of the Acts* (NICNT, 1954; 1960; rev. ed., 1988) *Second Thoughts on the Dead Sea Scrolls* (1956; 1966[3]); *The Spreading Flame: The Rise and Progress of Christianity from Its First Beginnings to the Conversion of the English* (1958); *Biblical Exegesis in the Qumran Texts* (1959); *The English Bible: A History of Translations* (1961; 3rd rev. ed., 1978); *Israel and the Nations: From the Exodus to the Fall of the Second Temple* (1963); *The Letter of Paul the Apostle to the Romans* (TNTC, 1963, 1985[2]); *The Epistle to the Hebrews* (NICNT, 1965, rev. 1990); *The NT Development of OT Themes* (1968; British title: *This Is That: The NT Development of Some OT Themes*); *NT History* (1969); *The Epistles of John* (1970); *The Message of the NT* (1972); "Salvation History in the NT,"

Man and His Salvation: Studies in Memory of S. G. F. Brandon (1973) 77-90; "The NT and Classical Studies," *NTS* 22 (1975–76) 229-42; *Tradition Old and New* (1976); *Paul, the Apostle of the Heart Set Free* (1977); *The Time Is Fulfilled: Five Aspects of the Fulfillment of the OT in the New* (1978); "Exegesis and Hermeneutics, Biblical," *Encyclopedia Britannica* 4 (1980¹⁵) 2-3; *1 and 2 Thessalonians* (WBC 45, 1982); *The Epistle to the Galatians* (NIGTC, 1982); *The Gospel of John* (1983); *Philippians* (NIBC, 1983, 1989²); *The Epistles to the Colssians, Philemon, and to the Ephesians* (NICNT, 1984, rev. 1988); *The Canon of Scripture* (1988); *A Mind for What Matters* (1990).

Bibliography: "A Select Bibliography of the Writings of F. F. B.," *Apostolic History and the Gospel: Biblical and Historical Essays Presented to F. F. B. on His 60th Birthday* (1970) 21-34. "A Select Bibliography of the Writings of Prof. F. F. B., 1970–79," *Pauline Studies: Essays Presented to Prof. F. F. B. on His 70th Birthday* (1980) xxi-xxxvi. **L. and W. Gasque,** "F. F. B.: An Appreciation," *Ashland Theological Journal* 23 (1991) 1-8. **W. Ward Gasque,** "A Supplementary Bibliography of the Writings of F. F. B.," *JCBRF* (November 1971) 21-47; *HHMBI,* 444-49. **I. Howard Marshall,** "F. F. B., 1910–90," *1991 Lectures and Memoirs: Proceedings of the British Academy* 80 (1993) 245-60.

J. J. SCOTT, JR.

BUBER, MARTIN (1878–1965)

Born in Vienna Feb. 8, 1878, B. was reared by his grandparents in Lemberg (Galicia), where he received a traditional Jewish education. He subsequently studied at the universities of Vienna, Leipzig, Zurich, and Berlin. Although he had abandoned religious observance in his teens, he maintained a strong interest in the HB and in the life and literature of HASIDISM. In 1898, he joined the Zionist movement founded by his close friend T. Herzl (1860–1904) but eventually broke with the movement, which he held should advocate the renewal and promotion of Jewish culture rather than political goals. In 1901 he became editor of the Jewish journal *Die Welt,* and in 1916 he founded the journal *Der Jude,* which he edited until 1924. B. became professor of Jewish theology at Frankfurt in 1923 and in 1926 started the interreligious journal *Die Kreatur.* In 1933, with the rise of Hitler, he was dismissed from his teaching position but remained in Germany until 1938, when he emigrated to Palestine, becoming professor of social philosophy at the Hebrew University in Jerusalem. He taught at the university until his retirement in 1951; he died in Jerusalem June 13, 1965.

Although B. wrote widely on diverse topics, much of his work was devoted to biblical interpretation. His book *I and Thou* (1923; ET 1937, 1970) has been one of the most influential philosophical and theological works of the twentieth century. With F. Rosenzweig (1886–1929) he translated the HB into German (1925–61). "We

proceed from the insight," B. wrote, "that the [Hebrew] Bible stems from living recitation and is destined to living recitation, that speech is its true existence, writing only the form of its preservation." He and Rosenzweig expressed the importance of the oral as opposed to the written, of sound as opposed to sight, by dividing their translation of the Hebrew original into "cola," or breathing units. They rejected the calcified theological terminology of "spirit" in favor of the still-living metaphor of *Braus Gottes,* "rush of spirit" or "rushing wind." That primordial rushing that goes from God, commented B., is neither nature nor spirit but the two in one, prior to any division, so that it takes on its natural form in "wind," its psychological, or soul-form, in "spirit." In the Bible *rûaḥ* (spirit) everywhere means a happening. *Qādôš* (holiness), similarly, does not mean a state of being but a process: that of hallowing and of becoming hallowed. Moses stands before the thornbush not on holy ground but on the ground of hallowing. The sabbath is a festival of hallowing, and the people of Israel are called by God to become a people of hallowing (not a holy people). Holiness is a task in which the person's hallowing and God's hallowing meet.

B. held that the HB wants to be read as one book so that none of its parts remain closed within themselves; rather, each part remains open to the others. It wants to be present to its reader as a whole in such intensity that in reading or reciting a certain passage other passages connected with it, especially those identical, close, or related in speech, are brought to mind. Thus all the passages will illuminate one another in such a manner that they come together into a *theologoumenon*—a conception that is not expressly taught but one that is immanent in the words, emerging from their relations and correspondences. The repetition of the same or similar-sounding words or of words and phrases with the same or similar root that occur within a passage, a book, or a group of books shows the linguistic relationship between the prophets (see PROPHECY AND PROPHETS, HB) and the Pentateuch (see PENTATEUCHAL CRITICISM), between the psalms and the Pentateuch, and between the psalms and the prophets.

In his work on Moses (1946) B. held steadfast to the narrow line between the traditionalist's insistence on the literal truth of the biblical narrative and the modern critic's tendency to regard this narrative as having merely literary or symbolic significance. He called his treatment of biblical history tradition criticism (as distinct from source criticism), which seeks to penetrate beneath the layers of different redactions of tradition to a central unity already present in the first layer and developed, restored, or distorted in the later ones. The Bible is neither devotional literature nor symbolic theology; it is the historical account of God's relation to human beings as seen through human eyes. "Miracle," to B., is neither an objective event that suspends the laws of nature and history nor a subjective act of the imagination; rather, it is an event experienced by an individual or a group of people as an abiding astonishment that no knowledge of causes can weaken, as a wonder at something that intervenes fatefully in the life of this individual and this group. Thus it is an event of dialogue, an event of the *between*. B. insisted that the atypical and the unique have a central place in the history of the spirit just because it is history, not timeless truth. The "firm letter" ought not be broken down by any general hypothesis based on the comparative history of culture so long as what is said in that text is historically possible.

In his book on prophetic faith (1949) B. resumed the thesis of *The Kingship of God* (1932) that there can be no division between the "religious" and the "social," that Israel cannot become the people of Yahweh without just faith between human beings. The prophets of Israel are partners in God's revelation. Contrary to popular understanding, they rarely foretell an inevitable future but speak to an actual and definite situation in the present. Even the message of disaster is meant to awaken people's power of decision so that they may turn back to the covenant—the fulfillment of the kingship of God. The correspondence of human and divine turning is not that a person's turning brings about God's, but that God responds to the person's turning back, even as God responds to the person's turning away. Thus the name Yahweh, disclosed at the revelation to Moses in the thornbush, is unfolded in the "righteousness" of Amos, the "lovingkindness" of Hosea, and the "holiness" of Isaiah. The messianic prophecy also conceals a demand and an alternative. It is not prediction but a conditional offer. The Messiah of Isaiah is not a divine figure who takes the place of humanity's turning or brings about a redemption that human beings have merely to accept and enter into. The belief in the coming of a messianic leader is the belief that at last humans shall with their whole being speak the word that answers God's word. Through the nucleus of Israel that does not betray the covenant and the election (Isaiah's "holy remnant"), the living connection between God and the people is upheld, and from their midst will arise "the perfected one." Through God's word and life Israel will turn to God and serve as the beginning of God's kingdom.

When Isaiah's hope for the true king is disappointed, the hope of his successor, the anonymous prophet known as Deutero-Isaiah, turns to the prophet, the *nabi*, and here out of the depths of history and the suffering of the "servant," the messianic task is continued. Deutero-Isaiah's "suffering servant of the Lord" voluntarily takes on himself all the griefs and sicknesses of the people's iniquities in order to bring them back to Yahweh. In suffering for the sake of God, the servant comes to recognize that God suffers with him and that he is working together with God for the redemption of the world. The servant completes the work of the judges and the prophets, the work of making real God's kingship over the people. It is laid on him to inaugurate God's new order of peace and justice for the human world. Through God's word and life, Israel will turn to God and become God's people, which, redeemed and cleansed, will serve as the beginning of God's kingdom.

Works: *Kingship of God* (1932; ET 1967, 1990³); (with F. Rosenzweig), *Scripture and Translation* (1936; ET 1994); *Moses: The Revelation and the Covenant* (1946; ET 1946, repr. with intro. by M. Fishbane, 1988); *The Prophetic Faith* (1949; ET 1949); *Right and Wrong: An Interpretation of Some Psalms* (1952); *A Believing Humanism: My Testament, 1902–65* (1965; ET 1967); *On the Bible: Eighteen Studies* (ed. N. N. Glatzer, 1968).

Bibliography: **H.-C. Askani,** *Das Problem der Übersetzung, dargestellt an F. Rosenzweig: Die Methoden und Prinzipien der Rosenzweigschen und Buber-Rosenzweigschen Übersetzung* (HUT 35, 1997). **M. Cohn and R. Buber,** *M. B.: A Bibliography of His Writings, 1897–1978* (1980). **M. Fishbane,** *The Garments of Torah: Essays in Biblical Hermeneutics* (ISBL, 1989). **M. S. Friedman,** *M. B.'s Life and Work* (3 vols., 1981–84), esp. 2:50-75, 3:33-46. **S. Kepnes,** *The Text as Thou: M. B.'s Dialogical Hermeneutics and Narrative Theology* (1992). **W. Moonan,** *M. B. and His Critics: An Annotated Bibliography of Writings in English Thought Through 1978* (GRLH 161, 1981). **P. A. Schilpp and M. S. Friedman** (eds.), *The Philosophy of M. B.* (LLP 12, 1967). **P. Vermes,** *B. on God and the Perfect Man* (BJS 13, 1980); *Buber* (Jewish Thinkers, 1988). **U. Vetter,** *Im Dialog mit der Bibel: Grundlinien der Schriftauslegung M. B.s* (1993).

M. S. FRIEDMAN

BUCER, MARTIN (1491–1551)

A member of the Dominican order from 1506, B. was educated in a scholarly and monastic context sympathetic to ERASMUS. His move to Heidelberg (1517) led to an encounter with LUTHER at the Heidelberg Disputation (1518), and he began to preach Lutheran doctrines publicly in 1523. For most of his career he was concerned with directing the Reformation at Strasbourg. He appears to have exercised considerable influence over CALVIN (who spent 1538–41 in Strasbourg). In 1549 he settled in England, dying at Cambridge on Feb. 28, 1551.

Despite his early sympathy for Lutheranism, it is Erasmus who appears to have been the greatest influence on B.'s biblical exegesis. Unlike ZWINGLI, B. was critical of allegorical methods of biblical interpretation (especially in the case of the HB), which he regarded as little more than *eisegesis*. This emphasis on the literal sense of the HB is reflected in the fact that some of his HB commentaries (like the Psalms commentary of 1529) drew heavily on medieval rabbinical sources. The tension between the testaments, so characteristic of Luther's biblical interpretation, is largely absent from B.'s. In many ways, he anticipated (and almost certainly helped to shape) Calvin's understanding of the two testaments.

B.'s appeal to the tropological sense of Scripture was thoroughly Erasmian: Where Luther regarded this sense of Scripture as designating the work of God within the believer, B. understood it to refer to moral action demanded of the believer. Although both Luther and Erasmus regarded the tropological sense of Scripture as fundamental, they did so for very different reasons. B. understood the gospel in an Erasmian sense as *lex Christi,* which specifies human moral action. Through the action of the Holy Spirit the believer is enabled, in the first place, to interpret Scripture and, in the second, to fulfill its moral imperatives.

Works: *Deutsche Schriften* (ed. R. Stupperich, 1960–); *Operan latina* (ed. C. Augustijn, P. Fraenkel, and M. Lienhard, 1982–).

Bibliography: M. U. Chrisman, *CE* 1 (1985) 209-12. M. Grieschat, *M. B.: Ein Reformator und seine Zeit* (1990). R. G. Hobbs, "M. B. on Psalm 22," *Études de l'exégèse au XVI siècle* (ed. O. Fatio and P. Fraenkel, 1978) 144-63; "Pellican à Capito sur le danger des lectures rabbiniques," *Horizons européens de la Réforme en Alsace* (ed. M. de Kroon and M. Lienhard, 1980) 81-93; "How Firm a Foundation: M. B.'s Historical Exegesis of the Psalms," *CH* 53 (1984) 477-91. J. Müller, *M. B. Hermeneutik* (QFZR 32, 1965). R. Stupperich, *TRE* 7 (1980) 258-70. A. W. Ward, *DNB* (1886) 172-77. D. F. Wright, *HHMBI,* 157-64.

A. E. McGRATH

BUDDE, KARL (1850–1935)

Born Apr. 13, 1850, in Bensberg near Cologne, B. died Jan. 29, 1935, in Marburg. He studied theology at Bonn, Berlin, and Utrecht. In 1873 he received a doctoral degree at Bonn and in the same year completed his inaugural dissertation in HB. In 1878 he became the supervisor of a training college for clergy and in 1879 an *ausserordentlicher* professor; in 1889 he went to Strasbourg as successor to E. REUSS. In 1900 he was appointed to a position at Marburg, where, along with W. HERRMANN and A. JÜLICHER, he was one of the most important members of Marburg's theological faculty. He continued to give lectures even beyond 1921, when he attained emeritus status.

B. was won to study of the HB by A. KAMPHAUSEN and had close contact with A. KUENEN, but the greatest influence on him was J. WELLHAUSEN, who nevertheless considered B.'s works sometimes too fastidious. B. char-

acterized his own scholarship as follows: "I could bear down to the core of a passage that was pointed out or selected and make the most out of my discoveries by means of deductions and combinations. I was able thereby to open new vistas, and that gave me the greatest conceivable satisfaction" ("Erinnerungen eines Achtzigjährigen" [1930] 925).

His talent for shedding light on the meaning and formation of texts through persistent attention to philological detail made B. a born exegete. In contrast to his monograph-sized, detailed collections of ancient Israelite literature and religion, his numerous commentaries and other textual analyses have retained their value, if not through the sometimes overdrawn and complicated solutions they propose, then through the observations that underlie these solutions, observations that can be used to reach other conclusions. This assessment holds true for his analysis of the primevel history, in which he continued the work of C. DILLMANN and Wellhausen and reconstructed a J^1 in contradistinction to a J^2 and a J^3. Following the Grafian hypothesis (see K. GRAF), B. held that the *Grundschrift* (P) is the most recent source. He traced the sources J and E into the books of Samuel and defended the originality of the Elihu speeches in his commentary on Job, earning him the scorn of B. DUHM.

In his final years B. turned especially to the prophets (see PROPHECY AND PROPHETS, HB); his name is associated with the thesis of Isaiah's *Denkschrift* from the Syro-Ephraimite war. He was happy to support the critically proven results of his age and defended them not only against conservative attacks but also against more radical claims; he fended off J. MEINHOLD's theses concerning the sabbath and the DECALOGUE. Regarding Deuteronomy, he opposed G. HÖLSCHER and others, maintaining the view of W. DE WETTE and Wellhausen. He did not allow himself to be drawn from LITERARY criticism to the study of literary genre (*Gattungen*); nevertheless, H. GUNKEL recognized that B. had accomplished pioneering work in this area by discovering the lament and its meter (1882).

Works: *Beiträge zur Kritik des Buches Hiob* (1876); "Das hebräische Klagelied," *ZAW* 2 (1882) 1-52; *Die Biblische Urgeschichte (Gen 1–12, 5) untersucht* (1883); *Die Bücher Richter und Samuel, ihre Quellen und ihr Aufbau* (1890); "The Folksong of Israel in the Mouth of the Prophets," *The New World* 2 (March 1893) 28-51; *The Books of Samuel* (SBOT 8, 1894); "The Nomadic Ideal in the OT," *The New World* 4 (Dec., 1895) 724ff; *Hollenberg Hebräisches Schulbuch Bearbeitet* (1895[8]– 1935[16]); *Das Buch Hiob übersetzt und erklärt* (HK II,1, 1896, 1913[2]); *Das Buch der Richter erklärt* (KHC 7, 1897; *Das Hohelied erklärt, Die Klagelieder erklärt* (KHC 17, 1898); *Religion of Israel to the Exile* (American Lectures on the History of Religions, IV Series, 1898–99); "The So-Called 'Ebed-Yahweh-Songs' and the Meaning of the Term 'Servant of Yahweh' in Isaiah chaps. 40–55," *AJT* 3 (1899) 499-540; "Canon, A., OT," *EncBib* 1 (1899) 647-74; "Die ursprüngliche Bedeutung der Lade Jahwe's," *ZAW* 21 (1901) 193-97; "The OT and the Excavations," *AJT* 6 (1902) 685-708; *Die Bücher Samuel erklärt* (KHC 8, 1902); *Das Alte Testament und die Ausgrabungen* (1903); "On the Relations of OT Science to the Allied Departments and to Science in General," *AJT* 9 (1905) 76-90; *Geschichte der Althebräischen Litteratur* (1906, 1909²); *Das prophetische Schrifttum* (RgV 2/5, 1906, 1922²); "Das Buch Jesaia Kap. 40–66," *HSAT(K)* I (1909³) 609-71; (1922⁴) 653-720; *L. Richters Volkskunst* (1909, 1910²); "Das Hohelied," "Der Prediger," *HSAT(K)* II (1910³) 356-71, 384-403; (1923⁴) 390-407, 421-42; "Das Rätsel von Micha 1," *ZAW* 37 (1917/18) 77-108; *Das Lied Mose's: Deut 32 erläutert und übersetzt* (1920); "Eine folgenschwere Redaktion des Zwölfpropheten-buchs," *ZAW* 40 (1922) 218-29; *Der Segen Moses: Deut 33 erläutert und übersetzt* (1922); *A. L. Richter, Maler und Radierer, Verzeichnis seines gesamten graphischen Werkes von J. F. Hoff, von Grund aus neu gearbeitet* (1922); "Über die Schranken, die Jesajas prophetischer Botschaft zu setzen sind," *ZAW* 41 (1923) 154-203; *Das Alte Deutsche Weihnachtslied: Eine Auswahl* (ed. K. Budde and A. Mendelssohn, 1924); "Zu Text und Auslegung des Buches Amos," *JBL* 43 (1924) 46-121; 45 (1926) 63-122; "Der Abschnitt Hos 1–3 und seine grund-legende religionsgeschichtliche Bedeutung," *TSK* 96, 97 (1925) 1-89; "Das Deuteronomium und die Reform König Josias," *ZAW* 44 (1926) 177-224; "Zu Text und Auslegung des Buches Hosea," 1.2. *JBL* 45 (1926) 280-97; 3. *JPOS* 14 (1934) 1-41; 4. *JBL* 53 (1934) 118-33; "The Sabbath and the Week, Their Origin and Their Nature," *JTS* 30 (1928) 1-15; *Jesaja's Erle-ben: Eine gemeinverständliche Auslegung der Denkschrift des Propheten (Kap. 6, 1–9, 6)* (1928); "Erinnerungen eines Ach-zigjährigen," *Die Taube* 44 (1930) 923-27; 45 (1931) 940-41; "Zum Eingang des Buches Ezechiel," *JBL* 50 (1931) 20-41; "Zu Jesaja 1–5," *ZAW* 49 (1931) 16-40, 182-211; 50 (1932) 38-72; *Die Biblische Paradiesesgeschichte erklärt* (BZAW 60, 1932); "Das Immanuelzeichen und die Ahaz-Begegnung Jesaja 7," *JBL* 52 (1933) 22-54.

Bibliography: *Beiträge zur alttestamentlichen Wissenschaft: K. B. zum 70. Geburtstag gewidmet* (BZAW 34, ed. K. Marti, 1920); **H. J. Cadbury,** *JBL* 55 (1936) ii-iii. **O. Eissfeldt,** "Ergänzungen zu: K. B.s Schrifttum," *ZAW* 53 (1935) 286-89; *FuF* 11 (1935) 91-92 = *KS* 2 (1963) 98-100. **W. Hoffmann,** "K. B. und L. Richter," *ChW* 49 (1935) 310-12; *K. B.'s Schrifttum bis zu seinem 80. Geburtstage* (BZAW 54, 1930). **T. H. Robinson,** *ExpTim* 46 (1934–35) 298-301. **R. Smend,** "K. B. (1850–1935)," *Language, Theology and the Bible: Essays in Honor of J. Barr* (1994) 351-69.

R. SMEND

BUHL, FRANTS PEDER WILLIAM MEYER
(1850–1932)

Born in Copenhagen, Sept. 6, 1850, B. died in HillERöd, Denmark, Sept. 24, 1932. As a young student he took up special studies in Hebrew and Arabic and after his cand. theol. examination in 1874 went to Vienna and Leipzig for further studies, publishing his doctoral thesis in Arabic studies in 1878. He became interested in J.WELLHAUSEN's *Geschichte Israels* (1878), and although as a follower of Franz DELITZSCH he was originally skeptical of Wellhausen's work, he later in-troduced it to Scandinavian scholars and the general public. In 1880 he was appointed *Docent* in OT at the University of Copenhagen, in 1882 became full profes-sor, and in 1890 was called to succeed Delitzsch in Leipzig (1890). During his time there he published new works incessantly. His work on H. GESENIUS's LEXICON is famous; the twelfth edition was published in 1895, and he constantly revised the work. His revisions, gathering etymological material from other Semitic languages as well as from Egyptian, with numerous references, became the standard in the field. From the twelfth edition on the work was as much his as Ge-senius's.

Using Wellhausen's theories he also wrote a history of Israel in Danish (1893), which was constantly reedited and used in all Scandinavian universities. Every edition included new material, keeping pace with progress in OT studies. In addition, he also wrote a book on the messianic promises in the OT (1894) and an introduction to OT study, in which he explained Wellhausen's ideas in a way easy to grasp for the untrained reader. In 1894 he completed his commentary on the book of Isaiah, in which he proved convincingly that chaps. 40–66 were not part of the words of the first Isaiah. B. took a prominent role in the debate over the Wellhausenian approach that raged throughout Scandinavia (especially in 1885 and again in 1894–95).

When the chair in Semitic philology at the University of Copenhagen became vacant, he was called to that position (1898). The following year he published *Die socialen Verhältnisse der Israeliten* and in 1900 a com-prehensive commentary on the psalms (rev. 1918). He discussed the date of the book of Daniel, wrote articles for lexicons and encyclopedias (see DICTIONARIES AND ENCYCLOPEDIAS), and edited the Psalms and the book of Esther in R. KITTEL's *Biblia Hebraica*. In 1910 he published a Danish translation of the OT in clear and modern language and in 1920 a translation of the apoc-ryphal books.

Works: *Sproglige og historiske Bidrag til den arabiske Grammatik* (1878); *Fortolkning til Jesaja* (1889–94, 1914²); *Kanon und Text des Alten Testaments* (1891; ET 1985); *Geschichte der Edomiter* (1893); *Geographie des Alten Palästinas* (1896); *De messianske Forjaettelser i Det gamle Testamente* (1896); *Den hebraiske Syntax* (1897); *Die so-cialen Verhältnisse der Israeliten* (1899); *Psalmerne, over-satte og fortolkede* (1900, 1918²); *Muhammeds Liv* (1903;

GT, *Das Leben Muhammed* [1930]); *Muhammedanismen som Verdensreligion* (1914); *Hebraeerbrevet fortolket* (1923); *Muhammeds religiöse Forkyndelse efter Quranen* (1924).

Bibliography: J. Pedersen, *Det Kongelige danske Videnskabsselskab* (Oversigt, 1932–33) 87-111; *Dansk biografisk Leksikon* 4 (1934) 340-41; 3 (1979³) 61-64.

A. S. KAPELRUD

BULLINGER, JOHANN HEINRICH (1504–75)

On entering the *bursa montis* at Cologne in July 1519, B. began to be heavily influenced by humanism. The controversy surrounding LUTHER's reforming treatises of 1520 moved B. to turn to a detailed study of the NT, as a result of which he publicly declared himself in sympathy with the Reformation. While a lecturer at Kappel (1523–28), he wrote Latin commentaries on most of the NT. During this period he became increasingly familiar with ZWINGLI, spending five months working with him at Zurich in 1527; after Zwingli's death in 1531 B. succeeded him as *Antistes* (superintendent of clergy) at Zurich.

B.'s biblical interpretation shows obvious points of affinity with those of Zwingli. His most significant contribution to sixteenth-century biblical interpretation is his development of the concept of a covenant between God and humanity as a hermeneutical principle (see HERMENEUTICS), first clearly stated in his *Von dem Touff* (1525), which represents a substantial advance on Zwingli's views. The OT and the NT are viewed as differing primarily in terms of their chronological location (see CHRONOLOGY) and their outward signification: The former preceded the coming of Christ and is signified by circumcision; the latter follows him and is signified by baptism. Both testaments, however, bear witness to the same covenant. The soteriological and hermeneutical unity of the testaments rests on this covenantal continuity. Whereas Luther sharply distinguished between law and gospel, B. insisted on their inherent continuity: The divine norms for individual, church, and society found in the OT are not annulled or significantly altered in the NT, which is to be regarded as the confirmation, clarification, and fulfillment of the OT. In stressing the sufficiency of the OT, B. argued that there was nothing "new" about the NT; it merely republished the OT covenant with greater clarity and conviction, not least on account of the coming of Christ.

Works: *The Authority and Certitude of Holy Scripture* (1538); *Decades* (1557); commentaries on Matthew (1542), John (1543), and Isaiah (1567).

Bibliography: J. W. Baker, *H. B. and the Covenant* (1980). F. Banke, *Der junge Bullinger, 1504–21* (1942). F. Büsser, *TRE* 7 (1980) 375-87; "Bullinger as Calvin's Model in Biblical Exposition: An Examination of Calvin's Preface to the *Epistle to the Romans,*" *In Honor of J. Calvin (1509–1564)* (ed. E. J. Furcha, 1987) 64-95. S. Hausammann, *Römerbriefauslegung zwischen Humanismus und Reformation* (SDGSTh 27, 1970). R. L. Petersen, *HHMBI,* 164-71.

A. E. McGRATH

BULTMANN, RUDOLF KARL (1884–1976)

The outstanding NT theologian of his age, B. wrote his dissertation on *Der Stil der paulinischen Predigt und kynisch-stoische Diatribe* (Göttingen, 1919; repr. 1985) and Habilitationsschrift on *Die Exegese des Theodor von Mopsuestia* (1912, pub. 1984) at Marburg and returned there as professor (1921–51). His first major work, *Die Geschichte der synoptischen Tradition* (1921, 1931²; ET *The History of the Synoptic Tradition* [1963, rev. 1968]) advanced both the form critical (see FORM CRITICISM) and the comparative work of his teachers (H. Gunkel, J. Weiss) and the history of traditions method of his precursors (W. Wrede, J. Wellhausen) and established his reputation for historical skepticism.

B.'s subsequent NT scholarship also developed the history-of-religions research of W. HEITMÜLLER, W. BOUSSET, and R. REITZENSTEIN (see RELIGIONSGESCHICHTLICHE SCHULE), leading to some notable articles and word studies (including twenty-seven in G. KITTEL's *TDNT*) and to his Meyer-Kommentar, *Das Evangelium des Johannes* (1941, 1986¹²; ET *The Gospel of John* [1971]). Its critical hypotheses, especially that of a pre-Christian GNOSTIC redeemer myth, seem dated, but the commentary remains the twentieth century's outstanding monument of theological interpretation, integrated with the best NT scholarship of its day. The patristic and Reformation tradition of commentators articulating their contemporary theology in and through their exposition of the biblical text is here boldly revived under the changed conditions of modern historical consciousness. This work was followed in 1948–53 by *Die Theologie des Neuen Testaments* (ET *Theology of the NT* [1952–55]), containing a now classic Lutheran and existentialist interpretation of Pauline theology first outlined in an *RGG²* article on PAUL (1930; ET in *Existence and Faith* [1960]).

Behind these syntheses of B.'s literary, historical, philosophical, and theological maturity stands a Lutheran preacher whose thinking was decisively shaped by the neo-Kantian and incipiently existentialist theology of his Marburg teacher W. HERRMANN and enriched by his study of F. SCHLEIERMACHER, R. Otto, and E. TROELTSCH. But in 1921 he was sufficiently impressed by the second edition of K. BARTH's *Römerbrief* to become associated with dialectical theology in its break with historicism and psychologism, its discovery of S. KIERKEGAARD, and its renewal of LUTHER's kerygmatic theology. However, far from abandoning his liberal past, B. combined its anthropological slant with his neo-Reformation emphasis on the Word of God by attending to the human existence that is addressed: God can be spoken of only by talk of human existence, and the person of Christ is known only through the saving event. His *Jesus* (1926; ET *Jesus and the Word* [1934]) is neither a christology nor a life of JESUS, but an attempt to mediate an encounter. This approach is justified by appeal to W. DILTHEY's theory of history, a theory that also underlies B.'s later Gifford lectures, *History and Eschatology: The Presence of Eternity* (1957).

Whereas Barth moved on from the contentless event of the Word of God to develop a christology, B. remained true both to their initial rejection of "Jesus according to the flesh" and to their Ritschlian rejection of metaphysics (see RITSCHL), identifying himself with the Fourth Evangelist, for whom (he claimed) Jesus reveals only that he is the revealer. Paul and John are the only true theologians in the NT because they alone speak of God by speaking of human existence, and of Christ by speaking of the salvation he brings. Since the human side of the salvation event can be explicated only by describing faith's self-understanding and perception of the situation prior to faith, B.'s theological interpretation must be existential interpretation, unfolding human existence. From 1927 the phenomenological analysis of his friend M. Heidegger's *Being and Time* provided him with a language to articulate this interpretation.

Such a markedly anthropological orientation kept B. closer to Gogarten than to Barth, whose residual biblicism he had from the outset criticized by insisting on the necessity of *Sachkritik,* i.e., theological criticism of the NT. His own criticism of the NT writings, in which he judged their mode of expression inadequate to their theological subject matter, became notorious through his essay "Neues Testament und Mythologie" (1941; ET in *Kerygma and Myth* [1953; rev. tr. S. Ogden, 1984]), which led to the "demythologizing" controversy. However essential it is for theological interpretation to make critical judgments about the truth of the gospel, and however timely B.'s criticism of myth (see MYTHOLOGY AND BIBLICAL STUDIES) was during the Nazi regime, his particular restatement of the gospel without myth was at once criticized for rejecting the cosmic scope of the biblical witness and reducing its horizon to the individual's openness to the future. This loss of doctrinal content and historical perspective shared the social weakness that led to the rapid demise of existentialism. Most of B.'s liberal successors have abandoned Herrmann's theory of history in favor of a historical realism that gives more support to social ethics; some have recovered the cosmic and temporal dimensions of NT eschatology.

A related weakness in B.'s theology of the proclaimed Word was that it dissolved Jesus into the *kerygma* and so devalued the narrative dimensions of the Gospels, doing less than justice to their witness to the earthly Jesus. B. remains a model of critical biblical scholarship, but his true successors include conservative and Roman Catholic theologians who value the theological and ecclesial dimensions of his HERMENEUTICS. For them the next step may lie in rethinking his legacy in terms of a literary paradigm rather than his own historical one.

Works: *Stil der paulinischen Predigt und kynisch-stoische Diatribe* (1919); *Die Exegese des Theodor von Mopsuestia* (1912; pub. 1984); *The History of the Synoptic Tradition* (1921, 1931²; ET 1963, rev. 1968); *Jesus and the Word* (1926; ET 1934); *Glaube und Verstehen* (4 vols., 1933–65); *The Gospel of John* (1941, 1986¹²; ET 1971); *Kerygma and Myth* (1941; ET 1953, rev. tr. S. Ogden, 1984); *Theology of the NT* (1948–53; ET 1952–55); *Primitive Christianity in Its Contemporary Setting* (1949; ET 1956); *Essays Philosophical and Theological* (1955); *This World and the Beyond* (1956; ET 1960); *History and Eschatology: The Presence of Eternity* (1957); *Jesus Christ and Mythology* (1958); *Existence and Faith* (1960); *Exegetica* (ed. E. Dinkler, 1967); *The Johannine Epistles* (1967; ET Hermeneia, 1973); *Faith and Understanding* 1 (1969); *The Second Letter to the Corinthians* (ed. E. Dinkler, 1976; ET 1985); *Theologische Enzyklopädie* (ed. E. Jüngel and K. W. Müller, 1984); *NT and Mythology and Other Basic Writings* (ed. S. Ogden, 1984).

Bibliography: G. Bornkamm, "Die Theologie R. B.s in der neueren Diskussion: Zum Problem der Entmythologisierung und Hermeneutic," *TRu* 29 (1963) 33-141. **M. Boutin,** *Relationalität als Verstehensprinzip bei R. B.* (1974). **C. E. Braaten and R. A. Harrisville** (eds.), *Kerygma and History: A Symposium on the Theology of R. B.* (1962). **N. A. Dahl,** "R. B.'s Theology of the NT," *The Crucified Messiah and Other Essays* (1974) 90-128. **M. Evang,** *R. B. in seiner Frühzeit* (1988). **D. Fergusson,** *Bultmann* (1992); *HHMBI,* 449-56. **B. Jaspert** (ed.), *R. B. Werk und Wirkung* (1984). **R. A. Johnson,** *The Origins of Demythologizing* (1974); *R. B.: Interpreting Faith for the Modern Era* (1987). **G. Jones,** *Bultmann: Towards a Critical Theology* (1990). **E. C. Hobbs** (ed.), *Bultmann: Retrospect and Prospect* (1985). **J. F. Kay,** *Christus Praesens: A Reconsideration of R. B.'s Christology* (1994). **C. W. Kegley** (ed.), *The Theology of R. B.* (1966). **J. Macquarrie,** *An Existentialist Theology: A Comparison of Heidegger and Bultmann* (1968). **A. Malet,** *The Thought of Bultmann* (1962). **S. Ogden,** *Christ Without Myth* (1962). **J. Painter,** *Theology as Hermeneutics: R. B.'s Interpretation of the History of Jesus* (1987). **W. Schmithals,** *An Introduction to the Theology of R. B.* (1968). **J. M. Smith,** *The Composition and Order of the Fourth Gospel: Bultmann's Literary Theory* (1965). **A. C. Thiselton,** *The Two Horizons: NT Hermeneutics and Philosophical Description* (1980).

R. MORGAN

BUNSEN, CHRISTIAN CARL JOSIAS VON
(1791–1860)

Although he never held an academic position, B. became a prolific scholar of considerable influence in

Germany and Britain in the middle of the nineteenth century. Born Aug. 25, 1791, in Korbach, he studied theology, classics, and history at Marburg and Göttingen and oriental languages in Copenhagen and Paris. From 1818 to 1838 he worked at the Prussian embassy in Rome, eventually becoming ambassador. He owed his initial appointment to the historian B. Niebuhr, who inspired B.'s lifelong interest in history. From 1838 to 1841 he was ambassador in Rome and from 1842 to 1854 ambassador in London. He died in Bonn in Nov. 1860.

B.'s most important book on the HB was *God in History* (3 vols., 1857–58). Although a critical work, it took a positive view of the historical facts underlying the earliest books of the HB. The opening chapters of Genesis hinted at the original human race that was created about 20,000 BCE in the region of China. The flood occurred between 11,000 and 10,000. Abraham arrived in Canaan in the twenty-ninth century, while the Hebrews went to sojourn in Egypt in 2650. The exodus occurred in 1320 BCE, and the achievement of Moses was that he introduced to the human race the idea of an eternal, unbreakable covenant between God and humankind. The prophets deepened and elaborated the Mosaic faith, teaching that religion is a matter of the spirit, that all outward forms of religion are temporary, and that God will unite all humankind in a kingdom ruled by God.

On the authorship of biblical books B. held that the Pentateuch (see PENTATEUCHAL CRITICISM) was the work of an eighth-century author who supplemented an earlier work from the tenth century. The psalms were written in three periods from the time of David to the postexilic period. Isaiah 24–27, 35, and 40–66 were written by Baruch in the sixth century. B.'s view of PROPHECY was that it should be interpreted historically. At the end of his life, B. began to write a *Bibelwerk für die Gemeinde,* a massive multi-volume project that would make available to general readers all the philological, historical, and exegetical tools they would need for critical study of the Bible, which B. believed would show God at work in human history.

B. represented a positive critical position that firmly opposed the negative criticism of W. DE WETTE, J. VATKE, and others. In Britain, his work encouraged liberal Anglicans to take critical scholarship seriously as a positive way of discovering God's revelation in history.

Works: *Gott in der Geschichte oder der Fortschnitt des Glaubens an eine sittliche Weltordnung* (3 vols., 1857–58; ET *God in History* [3 vols., 1868–70]); *Vollständiges Bibelwerk für die Gemeinde* (completed by A. Kamphausen, 9 vols., 1858–70).

Bibliography: F. Bunsen, *A Memoir of Baron B.* (1868; GT, with many eds.; ed. by F. Nippold, 1868–71). **E. Geldbach** (ed.), *Der gelehrte Diplomat: Zum Wirken C. C. J. v. B.* (1980); *TRE* 7 (1980) 415-16. **J. W. Rogerson,** *OTCNC* 121-29.

J. W. ROGERSON

BURKITT, FRANCIS CRAWFORD (1864–1935)

One of Harrow's most brilliant students, B. studied mathematics at Trinity College, Cambridge, then theology, and was R. Kennett's first pupil in Hebrew. After graduation he studied Syriac, Arabic, and other languages. In 1892 A. S. LEWIS and M. D. Gibson brought back from the Convent of St. Catharine, Mt. Sinai, photographs of a palimpsest, the underwriting of which Lewis identified as an early Syriac version of the four Gospels. R. Bensly and B. pronounced it allied to the version discovered by W. Cureton among manuscripts brought to the British Museum in 1842–47 and published in 1858. B. and his wife accompanied Lewis, Gibson, Prof. and Mrs. Bensly, and R. HARRIS to St. Catharine's convent for further study (1893). The transcription, mostly B.'s work, was published in 1894. B. went on to publish the Curetonian version of the Gospels (1904) with readings from the Sinai palimpsest and early Syriac patristic evidence to show that this version represented the early text of the four separate Gospels that displaced TATIAN's *Diatessaron* (harmony of the Gospels); this early text was in turn later displaced by the PESHITTA (or Syriac Vulgate). B. designed the Syriac type still in use by Cambridge University Press. His work on text and versions culminated in an important article in *Encyclopaedia Biblica.*

In 1906 he delivered ten popular lectures on Gospel history and its transmission, which became his inaugural course as Norrisian Professor of Divinity at Cambridge. The Norrisian chair (after 1934 Norris-Hulse chair) was the only divinity chair open to laity of the Church of England, and B. held it until his death. These lectures were his most influential work. He argued, following J. WELLHAUSEN and K. LACHMANN, that Mark was the earliest Gospel; that only one tattered copy with a truncated ending in mid-sentence (16:8) survived; that it gave a reliable account of JESUS' movements and teaching—teaching that did not reflect the interests of the early church in general; that it showed Jesus' break with the synagogue and his deliberate effort to secure the permanence of the Christian society by being *Pastor pastorum;* that the other Gospels were more or less individual enterprises; and that "the Gospels we have would never have become the official charters of the Church but for the theological necessity of insisting on the true human nature of our Lord." He later strongly opposed the work of the form critics (see FORM CRITICISM).

In 1906 his reading of A. SCHWEITZER's *Von Reimarus zu Wrede* led him back to J. WEISS's *Predigt Jesu vom Reiche Gottes,* and he immediately recognized the truth of Weiss's contention that the kernel of Jesus' preaching was messianic and eschatological and that he expected God to deliver God's people in the near future. Feeling strongly the intellectual error of those who denied Weiss's position, B. arranged for Schweitzer's book as well as his subsequent books to be translated into Eng-

BURNET, THOMAS

lish by W. Montgomery. B. established an NT seminar in Cambridge that continues to attract specialists in many other fields as well as interested clergy (A. Ramsey, C. H. Dodd, C. F. D. Moule, M. Hooker).

Works: *The OL and the Itala* (Texts and Studies 7, 2, 1901); "Texts and Versions," *EnchBib* 4 (1903) 4977-5031; *Evangelion de-Mepharreshe: The Curetonian Version of the Four Gospels, with the Readings of the Sinai Palimpsest and the Early Syriac Patristic Evidence Edited, Collected, and Arranged by F. C. B.* (2 vols., 1904); *The Gospel History and Its Transmission* (1906, 1911³); "The Eschatological Idea in the Gospels," *Cambridge Biblical Essays* (ed. H. B. Swete, 1909) 193-213; "A New MS of the Odes of Solomon," *JTS* 13 (1912) 372-85; *Jewish and Christian Apocalypses* (Schweich Lectures, 1914); "J. Weiss: In Memoriam," *HTR* 8 (1915) 291-97; *Christian Beginnings: Three Lectures* (1914); *The Religion of the Manichees* (Donellan Lectures, 1925); "The Debt of Christianity to Judaism," *The Legacy of Israel* (ed. E. R. Bevan and C. Singer, 1927) 69-96; *Palestine in General History* (Schweich Lectures, 1929); *Church and Gnosis: A Study of Christian Thought and Speculation in the Second Century* (Morse Lectures, 1932).

Bibliography: **J. F. Bethune-Baker et al.,** *JTS* 36 (1935) 225-54 (includes bibliography, 337-46); *PBA* 22 (1936) 445-84; *DNB 1931–40* (1949) 124-25. **K. Lake,** *JBL* 55 (1936) 17-19.

J. C. O'NEILL

BURNET, THOMAS (1635?–1715)

An English theologian and scientist, B. was born at Croft, Yorkshire, educated at Clare Hall and Christ's College, Cambridge, and became a fellow of the latter in 1657. A pupil of J. TILLOTSON and a friend of R. Cudworth, he was elected master of Charterhouse, London, in 1685. He died Sept. 27, 1715.

B.'s most famous writing is *Telluris Theoria Sacra* (1681), which he published in English as *The Sacred Theory of the Earth* (1684). Writing in a fine literary style, he combined scientific speculation with biblical exegesis and differed from other physico-theologians, like Ray and Derham, in stressing the earth's present imperfections. He argued that when God created the earth its axis was not tilted in relation to the sun and life was in a perpetual springtime. Foreknowledge of human disobedience led God to arrange for the earth's crust to crack, its waters to flood the earth, and its axis to tilt. In the last days the earth will be consumed by fire, after which Christ will inaugurate the millennium and restore the earth to its untilted condition. Following the last judgment the earth will probably be changed into a fixed star.

Many of B.'s views were unorthodox. He suggested that each continent may have had a Noah's ark and that other planets may have had floods. The six-day creation story is "a narration suited to the capacity of the people,

and not to the strict and physical nature of things." Moses must be so interpreted as not "to be repugnant to clear and uncontested Science" (*Sacred Theory* [1965] 408). In a posthumous writing B. argued against the doctrine of eternal punishment.

Works: *The Sacred Theory of the Earth* (1965, repr. of 1690–91 ed.); *Archaeologicae Philosophicae; sive Doctrina Antiqua de Rerum Originibus* (1692); *De Statu Mortuorum et Resurgentium* (1720); *De Fide et Officiis Christianorum* (1772).

Bibliography: *BB²* 3 (1784) 16-20. **J. E. Force,** "Whiston, the Burnet Controversy, and Newtonian Biblical Interpretation," *William Whiston* (1985) 32-62. **L. Stephen,** *DNB* 7 (1886) 408-10. **B. Willey,** "Introduction," *Sacred Theory* (1965); "The Wisdom of God in the Creation," *The Eighteenth Century Background: Studies on the Idea of Nature in the Thought of the Period* (1940) 27-42.

A. W. WAINWRIGHT

BURNEY, CHARLES FOX (1868–1925)

Born Nov. 4, 1868, B. attended Oxford, where he received his BA (1890). He became deacon and lecturer in Hebrew at Oxford in 1893. In 1894 he received the MA and was ordained a priest. In 1914 B. was appointed Oriel Professor of the Interpretation of Holy Scripture, a post he occupied for the remainder of his career, becoming a friend and colleague of his mentor, S. DRIVER.

B. was a skilled exegete whose use of comparative literary and linguistic data from other ancient Near Eastern cultures in explicating the biblical text put him ahead of his time. He was also an insightful text critic (see TEXTUAL CRITICISM) who recognized the significance of the SEPTUAGINT as an independent witness to the text of the HB. Despite its age his *Notes* on the text of Kings contains still-valuable observations. His two works on the NT emphasize the importance of the Aramaic background of the Gospels. B.'s scholarship reflects his lifelong interests in Israelite history and Christian education and in using the results of historical criticism to instruct the church.

Works: *Notes on the Hebrew Text of the Books of Kings* (1903); *Israel's Hope of Immortality* (1909); *Israel's Settlement in Canaan* (Schweich Lectures 1917, 1918, 1985); *The Book of Judges* (1918); *The Gospel in the OT* (1921); *The Aramaic Origin of the Fourth Gospel* (1922); *The Poetry of Our Lord* (1925).

Bibliography: **W. F. Albright,** "Prolegomenon" *The Book of Judges and Notes on the Hebrew Text of the Book of Kings* (C. F. Burney, 1970) 1-38.

S. L. MCKENZIE

BURROWS, MILLAR (1889–1980)

Born in Ohio, educated at Cornell (AB 1912), Union Seminary (BD 1915), and Yale (PhD 1925), B. was ordained a Presbyterian minister and served rural Texas churches. He taught at Tusculum College, Brown University, and finally at Yale as Winkley Professor of Biblical Theology (1934–58). In addition, he taught at the American University of Beirut (1930–31), served two terms as director of the AMERICAN SCHOOLS OF ORIENTAL RESEARCH (ASOR) in Jerusalem (1931–32), and was chairman of the Standard Bible Committee (RSV) (1954–61).

During his second term as ASOR director the DEAD SEA SCROLLS came to light, and B. speedily edited and published the first texts (1950–51). His English translation and cautious interpretation of the scrolls (1955, 1958) set high standards and were a sensible alternative to extreme and sensational views circulating at the time. B. was a theologian whose prodigious mastery of the Bible and related disciplines rested on the firm conviction that human history exhibits "the activity of one eternal living God working out his own sovereign purpose for the good of his creatures." He championed scientific, critical study of the Bible at a time when Barthianism (see BARTH) appeared to threaten its integrity.

Works: *Literary Relations of Ezekiel* (1925); *Proverbs and Didactic Poems* (1927); *Founders of Great Religions* (1931); *Bible Religion* (1938); *Basis of Israelite Marriage* (AOS 15, 1938); *What Mean These Stones? The Significance of Archaeology for Biblical Studies* (1941); *Outline of Biblical Theology* (1946); *Palestine Is Our Business* (1949); (ed.) *The Dead Sea Scrolls of St. Mark's Monastery* (1950–51); *The Dead Sea Scrolls* (1955); *More Light on the Dead Sea Scrolls* (1958); *Diligently Compared* (1964); *Jesus in the First Three Gospels* (1977),

Bibliography: M. H. Pope, *BA* 44 (1981) 116-21.

J. M. BULLARD

BURTON, ERNEST DE WITT (1856–1925)

Born Feb. 4, 1856, in Granville, Ohio, B. graduated from Denison in 1876 and Rochester Theological Seminary in 1882. He began his teaching career at Newton Theological Institution as associate professor of NT interpretation. Ten years later he was called by President W. R. HARPER to head the department of NT literature and interpretation at the University of Chicago. In addition to teaching he was director of libraries beginning in 1910 and was elected president of the university in 1923, serving until his death in 1925.

B.'s commentary on Galatians in the ICC, with its valuable set of detached notes, stands as a monument to his scholarship. His struggle to understand the *crux interpretum* of 3:13 and "the curse of the law" remains a substantial contribution to an understanding of the apostle's mind. But his most notable contribution grew out of his conviction that the churches and the general public should be enlightened by the results of scholarly study of the Bible. To that end he wrote articles in *Biblical World* and the *American Journal of Theology,* collaborated with others in the series Constructive Bible Studies and Historical and Linguistic Studies in Literature Related to the NT, and with E. J. GOODSPEED prepared harmonies of the Gospels on the Greek and English texts. He learned from Harper concern for an educated laity and shared that concern with his colleagues S. MATHEWS and T. Soares and his student and colleague Goodspeed.

Works: *Syntax of the Moods and Tenses in NT Greek* (1893); *Some Principles of Literary Criticism and their Application to the Synoptic Problem* (Decennial Publications, 1904); *A Critical and Exegetical Commentary on the Epistle to the Galatians* (ICC, 1920); (with S. Mathews and T. G. Soares), *A Source Book for the Study of the Teaching of Jesus in Its Historical Relationships* (University of Chicago Publications in Religious Education, 1923); (with S. Mathews), *The Life of Christ* (University of Chicago Publications in Religious Education, 1927).

Bibliography: E. D. Burton, *Christianity in the Modern World: Papers and Addresses* (ed. H. R. Willoughby, 1927) 185-90 (with bibliography). E. J. Goodspeed, "President Burton," *University Record* 11 (1925) 169-73.

E. W. SAUNDERS

BUSHNELL, HORACE (1802–76)

A pivotal American figure in the transition from early nineteenth-century Calvinist "orthodoxy" to the "evangelical liberalism" that flourished by the century's end, B. was born in Litchfield, Connecticut, and completed theological study at Yale Divinity School. In 1833 he became pastor of North Church (Congregationalist) in Hartford, Connecticut. Illness forced him to resign this post in 1859, but until his death in 1876 he continued to preach, lecture, and write.

Controversial for his day, B. undertook a daring reconception of the aim, method, and spirit of theological inquiry that ushered evangelical Protestantism into the post-Kantian era (see I. KANT) of theology. His critique of revivalism and his plea for Christian nurture laid the groundwork for the modern religious education movement; and his insistence on the priority of religious experience over dogma, the symbolic character of religious language, and the necessity of recasting doctrine (e.g., revelation, original sin, the Trinity, and christology) into terms intelligible to the modern mind influenced generations of later liberals. His advocacy of a "comprehensive Christianity" contributed to the rise of ecumenism.

The social gospel movement considered him among its pioneers.

B.'s views of the AUTHORITY, interpretation, and use of the Bible played a key role in the development of critical biblical scholarship. By shifting theology from Enlightenment rational supernaturalism to post-Enlightenment Romanticism and idealism, he helped to free biblical study from dogmatic constraints and fostered new openness to the methods and results of modern biblical criticism.

Of most direct impact on biblical scholars was his theory of language. Stimulated by S. T. COLERIDGE's *Aids to Reflection* and the work of Yale's J. Gibbs, B. marshalled a large force of Romantic language theorists against the reigning empiricist-rationalist views derived from J. LOCKE. His chief premise was that all religious language is non-literal, figurative, metaphoric, or symbolic (terms often used interchangeably). Revelation is "God's gift to the imagination"; the Bible is a "grand poem of salvation"; Christ is "God's last metaphor." The task of interpretation is to discern the spiritual-moral truths of religious experience expressed in Scripture's diverse, time-bound symbols.

B.'s vision of the strategy best suited to the hermeneutical task—an aesthetic engagement with texts—was eclipsed by the historical-genetic paradigm. However, his approach reveals concerns with linguistic forms and effects familiar to those interested in LITERARY-critical biblical interpretation.

Works: *God in Christ: Three Discourses Delivered at New Haven, Cambridge, and Andover, with a Preliminary Dissertation on Language* (1849); *Christ in Theology, Being the Answer of the Author Before the Hartford Central Association of Ministers* (1851); *Nature and the Supernatural, as Together Constituting the One System of God* (1858); *Christian Nurture* (1861, repr. 1979); *Christ and His Salvation: In Sermons Variously Related Thereto* (1864; rev. ed., *Sermons on Christ and His Salvation,* 1877); *Work and Play: Or Literary Varieties* (1864); *Moral Uses of Dark Things* (1868); *Sermons on Living Subjects* (1872); *The Vicarious Sacrifice, Grounded in Principles Interpreted by Human Analogies* (2 vols., 1877); *Building Eras in Religion* (Literary Varieties 3, 1881).

Bibliography: J. W. **Brown,** *The Rise of Biblical Criticism in America, 1800–70: The New England Scholars* (1969) 171-79. C. **Cherry,** *Nature and the Religious Imagination: From Edwards to B.* (1980). M. B. **Cheyney,** *The Life and Letters of H. B.* (1880, repr. 1969). D. A. **Crosby,** *H. B.'s Theory of Language, in the Context of Other Nineteenth-Century Theories of Language* (Studies in Philosophy 22, 1975). B. M. **Cross,** *H. B.: Minister to a Changing America* (1958). J. O. **Duke,** *H. B.: On the Vitality of Biblical Language* (BSNA 9, 1984); R. L. **Edwards,** *Of Singular Genius, of Singular Grace: A*

Biography of H. B. (1992). E. **Geldbach,** *TRE* 7 (1980) 429-30. W. A. **Johnson,** *Nature and the Supernatural in the Theology of H. B.* (STL 125, 1963). D. L. **Smith,** *Symbolism and Growth: The Religious Thought of H. B.* (AAR.DS 36, 1981). H. S. **Smith** (ed.), *H. B.: Twelve Selections* (LPT, 1965).

J. O. DUKE

BUTLER, JOSEPH (1692–1752)

Born into a Presbyterian family, B. joined the Anglican faith, attended Oriel College, preached at Rolls chapel, and served as Anglican bishop of Bristol (1738) and Durham (1750). His chief work, the *Analogy of Religion* (1736), responded to the Deists' critique (see DEISM) of revealed religion. The Bible fulfills a threefold role in his argument: First, it is the function of both law and gospel to confirm the truths of natural religion. Second, certain truths imparted by biblical revelation are inaccessible to reason, although not contrary to it. Third, in response to Deist attacks on the evidence for Christianity, directed especially against arguments from the fulfillment of PROPHECY (A. Collins) and from miracles (T. Woolston), B. argued that accounts of miracles are rendered credible by their being embedded in straightforward historical narratives. The prophets may not have consciously borne witness to Christ, but we should allow for a double meaning intended by the divine rather than the human author. However, B.'s refusal to engage in detailed exegetical discussion meant that he evaded many of the challenges posed by Deist biblical criticism.

Works: *Analogy of Religion Natural and Revealed to the Constitution and Course of Nature* (1736).

Bibliography: G. **Gassmann,** *TRE* 7 (1981) 496-97. E. C. **Mossner,** *Bishop Butler and the Age of Reason* (1936). H. G. **Reventlow,** *The Authority of the Bible and the Rise of the Modern World* (1979; ET 1984) 345-50. L. **Stephen,** *English Thought in the Eighteenth Century* (1876) 1:279-308; *DNB* (1886) 67-72.

D. F. WATSON

BUTTENWEISER, MOSES (1862–1939)

Of German descent, B. was born Apr. 5, 1862, in Beerfelden, Hessen-Darmstadt. He entered the University of Würzburg in 1881, attended the University of Leipzig (1889–95), and received the PhD from Heidelberg (1896) with a dissertation on the Elisha apocalypse, published a year later. In 1897 after a brief stay in Canada, B. sought and obtained appointment as professor of biblical exegesis at Hebrew Union College in Cincinnati, Ohio, a Reformed Jewish rabbinical seminary founded in 1875.

B. was an enthusiastic teacher, and as such he was a significant contributor to the shaping of Reform Judaism in America during the first half of the twentieth century.

He developed much of his published work in classroom situations. His publications centered on the prophets (see PROPHECY AND PROPHETS, HB), Psalms, and Job. His interest in the prophets informed his views on contemporary social issues, concerns reflected in his membership in the Foreign Policy Association and the Peace League and in his classroom lectures. He retired in 1935 and died Mar. 11, 1939.

His book on Psalms is characterized by two special features: (1) B. arranged the vast majority of the psalms, plus sections of individual psalms, in chronological order, arguing not only that this was possible but also that many of the psalms could be assigned to special historical contexts, and that for some periods, the postexilic, for example, the psalms were among the most reliable historical sources. He dated the psalms from the pre-monarchical to the Hellenistic periods. (2) He argued that the "precative perfect" (like the so-called prophetic perfect) is frequently employed in the psalter so that a verb tense, which normally according to its form should describe an event belonging to times past, in context actually expresses a future hope or a fervent prayer, as in the opening verse of Psalm 85.

In his work on Job, a striking feature of his treatment of the text is the freedom with which he shifts the position of sections and verses and parts of verses, arranging the matter in a more logically convincing order. Readers are justified in asking how much subjectivity has gone into the treatment and whether twentieth-century scholars can indeed so radically reconstruct a text from antiquity. But they must admit that B.'s reconstruction of the Job dialogue is dramatic and appealing.

Works: *Die hebräische Elias-apokalypse und ihre Stellung in der apokalyptischen Literatur des rabbinischen Schrifttums und der Kirche*(1897); *Outline of the neo-Hebraic Apokalyptic Literature* (1901); *The Prophets of Israel from the Eighth to the Fifth Century: Their Faith and their Message* (1914); "Where did Deutero-Isaiah Live?" *JBL* 38 (1919) 94-112; *The Book of Job* (1922); "The Date and Character of Ezekiel's Prophecies," *HUCA* 7 (1930) 1-18; "The Importance of the Tenses for the Interpretation of the Psalms," *HUCA Jubilee Volume* (1935) 89-111; *The Psalms Chronologically Treated, with a New Translation* (1939; repr. with a prolegomenon by N. M. Sarna, 1969).

Bibliography: J. Bamberger, *EncJud* 4 (1971) 1540-41. M. N. Eisendrath, "In Memoriam: M. B.," *Hebrew Union College Monthly* (Apr. 1939) 1-12. S. H. Goldenson et al., "M. B. on His Twenty-fifth Anniversary as Teacher at Hebrew Union College," *Hebrew Union College Monthly* (May 1922) 185-209. M. A. Meyer and S. H. Blank, *Hebrew Union College—Jewish Institute at One Hundred Years* (1976) 24-310.

S. H. BLANK

BUXTORF, JOHANNES (1564–1629)

Born Dec. 25, 1564, in Camen, Westphalia, where his father was pastor, B. studied at the Latin school in Hamm, where he was introduced to the study of Hebrew, at the Gymnasium Illustre at Herbron with C. Olevian (1536–87) and J. Piscator (1546–1625), and at the University of Basel, where he graduated MA in 1590. At Basel, B. worked with J. Grynaeus, who recognized his talents and persuaded him to take a position there in Hebrew upon graduation, a post he occupied until his death, Sept. 13, 1629. The post in Hebrew at Basel was held by Buxtorfs for over a century (1590–1732); the elder was succeeded by his son Johannes (1599–1664), his grandson Jakob (1645–1704), and the latter's nephew Johannes (1663–1732).

B. was the most significant Christian Hebrew scholar between J. REUCHLIN and S. MÜNSTER in the first half of the sixteenth century and H. GESENIUS in the nineteenth century. B.'s competence lay in biblical, rabbinic, and medieval Hebrew, Aramaic, and Syriac. He sought to introduce Christians to the entire gamut of Hebrew language studies, from the biblical to the contemporary. His work involved a combination of humanistic and theological interests. The humanistic dimension is reflected in his widespread correspondence with Protestant scholars and Jewish intellectuals and his desire to make Hebrew one of the international languages of learning, like Greek and Latin. His *Synagoga judaica* described many aspects of Jewish faith and practice and displayed a less biased attitude toward Judaism than was characteristic of Christians at the time. He supplied a number of basic tools for learning and instruction in Hebrew, both biblical and medieval, pointed and unpointed (and even Yiddish); in Aramaic, both biblical and the later targumic and Talmudic; and in Syriac.

B. wanted to bring to Christians the work of Jewish interpreters—the Masorah, TARGUMIM, the TALMUD, and rabbinic commentaries. In his edition of the RABBINIC BIBLE, he hoped to make available in a form affordable to students the biblical text, the Masoretic notes on the text (Masorah), the major Aramaic translations (Targumim), and the best rabbinical commentators. Except for several of his own essays and minor corrections in the Targumim and Masorah, the material in this Bible was derived from the 1524–25, 1546–48, and 1568 editions of the D. BOMBERG or Venice printings. B. had already published a guide to Hebrew abbreviations with a bibliography of Jewish works on the Bible and planned studies on the biblical text, the Masorah, and the Jewish commentators as well as a complementary LEXICON. Because the Targumim and Jewish commentaries were published without translation, however, the work proved useful only to Christian scholars.

B. took a very conservative attitude toward the text of the OT, which was under severe attack from Catholics, who argued that it had been corrupted in transmission and was thus no secure basis on which to establish the Christian faith. In addition, Catholic polemicists had followed E. LEVITA, who in his *Masoret ha-Masoret* (1538) had argued that the Hebrew vowel points and accents were late additions to the text, having been added after its stabilization, and were thus human accretions to the text. Orthodox Protestant theologians, in spite of the fact that LUTHER, CALVIN, and most of the Reformers had taken a contrary view or ignored the issue, sought to defend the antiquity of the Masoretic pointing. B. argued for the antiquity and divine inspiration of the pointing, first in *Thesaurus grammaticus* (1609) and then more fully in his *Tiberias* (1620), a work dealing with the Masorah as a whole and the only supplement he ever published to his rabbinic Bible. B.'s defense of the vowel points was attacked by a fellow Protestant, L. CAPPEL (1624).

The younger B., a competent Hebrew scholar, succeeded his father at Basel in 1629; and the task of completing his father's work, issuing new editions, and defending the Hebrew text and Masoretic pointing fell to him. In 1622 he published *Lexicon chaldaicum et syriacum* and later completed and saw through the press his father's large concordance (1632) and great lexicon (1639). He did not attempt a refutation of Cappel until 1648. By then the case for the purity of the biblical text and vowel points had been further complicated by the knowledge of the Samaritan Pentateuch, a pre-Masoretic, unpointed Hebrew text written in archaic pre-Masoretic script. J. MORIN, a Calvinist convert to Catholicism, had built a strong case against the purity of the Hebrew text based on the SEPTUAGINT and Samaritan texts (1631). The younger B. defended his and the orthodox theologians' position in his *Tractatus de punctorum vocalium et accentuum in libris Veteris Testamenti hebraicis, origine, antiquitate et authoritate, oppositus Arcano punctationis revelato Ludovici Cappelli* (1648) and *Anticritica, seu vindiciae veritatis hebraicae adversus Ludovici Cappelli criticam quam vocat sacram* (1653). Although most scholarship was convinced by the publications of Cappel and his supporters, the position of the Buxtorfs that the Hebrew text of the OT had been transmitted without error or alteration and that the vowel points constituted part of the divine revelation retained its place in orthodox circles, especially in Germany and Switzerland, for some years to come.

Works: *Epitome radicum hebraicum* (1600); *Manuale hebraicum et chaldaicum* (1602; rev. Johann the younger, 1658; ET 1812); *Institutio epistolaris hebraica* (1603, 1610[2]; rev. Johann the younger, 1629[3]); *Juden Schul* (1603; LT as *Synagoga judaica*, 1604; ET 1656 and in J. P. Stehelin, *Rabbinical Literature* [2 vols., 1748] 2:225-363; repr. of 1680[4] Latin version, 1989); *Praeceptiones grammaticae de lingua hebraeae* (1605; 1613 as *Epitome grammaticae hebraea;* ET 1656, 1750); *Epitome radicum hebraicum et chaldaicum* (1607); *Lexicon radicum hebraicum et chaldaicum cum brevi lexico rabbinico philosophico* (1607); *Thesaurus grammaticus linguae sanctae hebraeae* (1609, 1615[2], 1620[3]; rev. Johann the younger, 1663[4]); *De abbreviaturis hebraicus liber novus et copiosus* (1613); *Grammaticae chaldaicae et syriacae libri tres* (1615); *Biblia hebraica cum paraphasi chaldaica et commentariis rabbinorum* (4 vols., 1618–19); *Tiberias, sive commentarius masorethicus* (1620; rev. Joahnn the younger, 1665; partial ET, C. Barksdale, *Masora: A Collection out of the Learned Master Johannes Buxtorfius's Commentarius Masorethicus* [1665]); *Concordantiae bibliorum hebraicae* (ed. Johann the younger, 1632); *Lexicon chaldaicum, talmudicum et rabbinicum* (ed. Johann the younger, 1639; repr. 1977).

Bibliography: C. Bertheau, *NSHERK* 2 (1908) 324-25. **S. G. Burnett,** "The Christian Hebraism of J. B. (1564–1629)" (diss., University of Wisconsin-Madison, 1990); *From Christian Hebraism to Jewish Studies: J. B. (1564–1629) and Hebrew Learning in the Seventeenth Century* (SHCT 68, 1996). **K. Buxtorf-Falkeisen,** *J. B. Vater . . . erkannt aus seinem Briefwechsel* (1860). **E. Kautzsch,** *J. B. der Ältere Rectorats-Rede* (1879). **H. Marsh,** *A Course of Lectures, Containing a Description and Systematic Arrangement of the Several Branches of Divinity* (pt. 2, Lectures VII-XII, 1810) 64-126. **R. Muller,** "The Debate over the Vowel Points and the Crisis in Orthodox Hermeneutics," *JMRS* 10 (1980) 53-72. *MSHH* 31 (1735) 206-25. **B. Pick,** "The Vowel-Points Controversy in the XVI. and XVII. Centuries," *Hebraicia* (= *AJSL*) 8 (1891–92) 150-73. **J. Prijs,** *Die Basler hebräischen Drucke (1492–1866)* (ed. B. Prijs, 1964). **P. T. van Rooden,** *Theology, Biblical Scholarship, and Rabbinical Studies in the Seventeenth Century: Constantijn L'Empereur (1591–1648), Professor of Hebrew and Theology at Leiden* (Studies in the History of Leiden University 6, 1989). **G. Schnedermann,** *Die Controverse des Ludovicus Cappellus mit den Buxtorfen über das Alter der hebräischen Punctuation* (1878).

J. H. HAYES

C

CADBURY, HENRY JOEL (1883–1974)

Born into a Quaker family in Philadelphia, Pennsylvania, Dec. 1, 1883, C. was educated in Quaker secondary schools, graduated from Haverford College with honors in Greek and philosophy (BA 1903), and from Harvard University (MA 1904; PhD 1914). He taught at Haverford (1910–19), Bryn Mawr College (1926–34), and was Hollis Professor of Divinity at Harvard (1934–54). C. was chairman of the American Friends Service Committee for twenty-two years, on behalf of whom and its British counterpart he accepted the Nobel Peace Prize in 1947. He published and lectured widely on Quaker history and thought and spoke on behalf of pacifism, remaining active until his death, Oct. 7, 1974.

C. was well trained in classical studies. His early publications laid out the interests and methodology that were to characterize his later publications in NT studies—lexically oriented textual studies, the style and character of the NT writings, especially Luke–Acts, and the figure of the historical JESUS. He was a major contributor to the massive five-volume *Beginnings of Christianity* (ed. F. J. Foakes Jackson and K. LAKE [1920–33]), which remains an indispensable work for NT study. In his dissertation (pub. 1920) he explored the individuality of Luke as a Hellenistic author and the sources he used, arguing against the widely held view that the appearance of medical terms in Luke–Acts demonstrated that Luke was a physician, which led to the widely circulated quip that C. received his doctor's degree by depriving Luke of his.

In a 1923 article C. became the first scholar in the English-speaking world to publish a description of the form-critical studies of R. BULTMANN and M. DIBELIUS, whose methodology he employed throughout his career, although he generally avoided the expression FORM CRITICISM. He explored not only the content but also the manner of Jesus' teachings, and he warned against imposing modern perceptions on Jesus' ministry or interpreting his teaching in terms of such limiting themes or concepts as the kingdom of God. Jesus' teachings, according to C., defy simple translation into a modern idiom or pattern of behavior.

Works: "The Basis of Early Christian Anti-Militarism," *JBL* 37 (1918) 66-94; "Luke—Translator or Author?" *AJT* 24 (1920) 436-55; *National Ideals in the OT* (1920); *The Style and Literary Method of Luke* (HTS 6, 1920); "Between Jesus and the Gospels," *HTR* 16 (1923) 81-92; *The Making of Luke–Acts* (1927; with an intro. by P. Anderson, 1999); *The Perils of Modernizing Jesus* (1937); *Jesus, What Manner of Man* (Shaffer Lectures, 1947); *The Book of Acts in History* (1955); "Acts and Eschatology," *The Background of the NT and Its Eschatology* (FS C. H. Dodd, ed. W. D. Davies and D. Daube, 1956) 300-321; *Jesus and Judaism* (1961); *The Eclipse of the Historical Jesus* (Pendle Hill Pamphlet 133, 1964); "Four Features of Lucan Style," *Studies in Luke–Acts* (FS P. Schubert, ed. L. E. Keck and J. L. Martyn, 1966) 87-102; *Behind the Gospels* (1968).

Bibliography: M. H. **Bacon,** *Let This Life Speak: The Legacy of H. J. C.* (1987), with bibliography, 235-44. W. **Cotter,** "A Letter from H. J. C. to A. von Harnack," *HTR* 78 (1985) 219-22. W. W. **Gasque,** *A History of the Criticism of the Acts of the Apostles* (1975, 1989) 169-83, 186-91. **B. R. Gaventa,** "The Peril of Modernizing H. J. C.," *SBLSP* (1987) 64-79 (with bibliography of C.'s work on Luke–Acts, 78-79). **S. G. Hall,** "The Contribution of H. J. C. to the Study of the Historical Jesus" (diss., Boston University, 1961). **M. H. Jones,** "H. J. C.: A Biographical Sketch," *Then and Now: Quaker Essays* (ed. A. Brinton, 1960) 11-70. **G. W. MacRae,** *Profiles from the Beloved Community* (ed. G. H. Williams et al., 1976) 13-21. **A. N. Wilder,** "In Memoriam: H. J. C., 1883–1974," *NTS* 21 (1975) 313-17.

J. H. HAYES

CAIRD, GEORGE BRADFORD (1917–84)

Born in London July 19, 1917, C. received a BA in classics from Cambridge (1936–39) and an MA and PhD in theology from Oxford (1939–43, 1944). H. ROBINSON and C. H. DODD were influential in shaping C.'s understanding of the unity and AUTHORITY in the biblical revelation of God's saving actions. In 1966 he earned the DD from Oxford and became Dean Ireland's Professor (NT) at Oxford in 1977, a position he held until his death on Easter eve 1984. He held earlier professorships at St. Stephens College, Edmonton (OT, 1946–50), and McGill University, Montreal (NT, 1950–59); and principalships at United Theological College, Montreal (1955–59), and Mansfield College, Oxford (1970–77).

Central to C.'s many books, articles, and sermons is the conviction that the CANON of Scripture draws its coherence from the presence of God in the historical events and the lives of persons attested to in the different forms and perspectives of the various biblical writers. He held that the writings of the Bible are intrinsically theological and that theological meaning and historical persons and events form an inseparable unity. This theological and historical unity must be equally and integrally the subject and object of critical linguistic and historical scrutiny.

C.'s approach, however, should in no way be confused with a literalist view. One of his enduring contributions will undoubtedly be the illuminating distinction between mythical ("beginnings" of world language) and eschatological ("end" of world language) modes of discourse and the role of metaphor in both, developed and illustrated in *The Language and Imagery of the Bible* (1980). To C., eschatological language was a way of speaking primarily about the ultimacy of God's actions in the imminent historical crisis. JESUS and the NT writers as a whole moved in the prophetic tradition of this use of eschatological imagery and should not be construed as naive or disillusioned adherents of an apocalyptic perspective (see APOCALYPTICISM). C.'s work, marked as it is by a forcefulness of wit and clarity of thought, is a fitting expression of his conviction that with proper exercise of God-given critical faculties the *cantus firmus* of the polyphonic pitches of the biblical voices can be heard loud and clear.

Works: *The Truth of the Gospel: A Primer of Christianity* 3 (1950); *The Shorter Oxford Bible* (with G. W. Briggs and N. Micklem, 1951); "Introduction and Exegesis to I and II Samuel," *IB* 2 (1952) 855-1175; *The Gospel of St. Luke* (1963); *Jesus and God* (with D. E. Jenkins, 1965); *The Revelation of St. John the Divine* (1966, 1984[2]); *Our Dialogue with Rome: The Second Vatican Council and After* (1967); "The Study of the Gospels: I. Source Criticism; II. Form Criticism; III. Redaction Criticism," *ExpTim* 87 (1975–76) 99-104 137-41, 168-72; *Paul's Letters from Prison: Ephesians, Philippians, Colossians, Philemon* (NCB, 1976); *War and the Christian* (1979); *The Language and Imagery of the Bible* (1980); *NT Theology* (comp. and ed. L. D. Hurst, 1994).

Bibliography: **J. Barr,** *PBA* 71 (1985) 492-521. **H. Chadwick,** *The Glory of Christ in the NT: Studies in Christology in Memory of G. B. C.* (ed. L. D. Hurst and N. T. Wright, 1987) xvii-xxii (complete bibliography, xxiii-xxvii). **L. D. Hurts,** *HHMBI,* 456-62.

D. P. MOESSNER

CAJETAN, TOMMASO DE VIO (1469–1534)

C. was born in Gaeta Feb. 20, 1469, in the kingdom of Naples. He entered the Dominican order in 1484. From 1488 until his ordination in 1491 he studied in Bologna, then at Padua. A gifted and influential scholar, he taught Thomistic theology at the Dominican convent at the University of Padua (1493–97), at Pavia (1497–99), at Milan (1499–1501), and at Rome (1501–08). He was Master-general of the Dominican order from 1508 to 1518. In 1517 he was named cardinal and in 1518 was made papal legate to Germany to examine LUTHER on charges of error and heresy. C. spent the last years of his life studying Scripture and producing commentaries. He died Aug. 10, 1534, while working on an expositon of the OT prophets (see PROPHECY AND PROPHETS, HB).

While all of C.'s theological treatises made use of Scripture, his approach to biblical interpretation is best illustrated by his commentaries, beginning with Psalms. Contrary to the practice of Catholic exegetes at the time, he insisted on using the Hebrew text for his exposition rather than the VULGATE. Since he did not know Hebrew he enlisted the help of a Christian and a Jewish scholar, who aided him in producing a word-for-word translation of the psalter. C. believed familiarity with the original languages of the texts was indispensable for a thorough interpretation of Scripture; he viewed the Vulgate as a fallible and often flawed translation. He based his NT expositions on the Greek text, carefully comparing his own translation with that of ERASMUS (pub. 1516). C.'s focus on the original languages may have contributed to his view of the APOCRYPHA as outside the biblical CANON. He is one of only a few Roman Catholic theologians to advocate a shorter canon (as found in Judaism and Protestantism).

Another basic principle of C.'s approach to the Bible was his adherence to the literal sense of the text, rejecting the medieval tradition of spiritual exegesis and other "transferred" applications. Furthermore, his commentaries make notably few references to the early church fathers, which prompted several Roman Catholic contemporaries, notably A. Catarini, to denounce C. as a heretic. Even Luther was said to have remarked after hearing of C.'s commentaries that the cardinal seemed to have turned Lutheran in his old age. C.'s work was, however, firmly entrenched in Roman Catholic theology, and many of his expositions were designed to give support to papal authority and church teaching. He did not view the Scriptures as the sole foundation of Christian theology (the Protestant position) but believed that the Bible was Scripture precisely because its sanctity was guaranteed by the church and its teachings. His literal exegesis should be seen as an attempt to confirm Roman Catholic teaching rather than an attempt to reform the church's teaching by reexamining the text.

Works: *Jentacula novi testamenti* (1525); *Liber Psalmorum ad verbum ex hebreo versorum* (1527); *Commentaria in Matthaeum* (1527); *Commentaria in Marcum* (1527); *Commentaria in Lucam* (1528); *Commentaria in Joannem* (1528); *Commentaria in Sancti Pauli epistolam ad Romanos* (1528); *Commentaria in Sancti Pauli epistolam I ad Corinthios* (1528); *Commentaria in Sancti Pauli epistolam II ad Corinthios* (1528); *Commentaria in Sancti*

Pauli epistolam ad Galatas (1529); *Commentaria in Sancti Pauli epistolam ad Ephesios* (1529); *Commentaria in Sancti Pauli epistolam ad Philipenses* (1529); *Commentaria in Sancti Pauli epistolam ad Colossenses* (1529); *Commentaria in Sancti Pauli epistolam I ad Thessalonicenses* (1529); *Commentaria in Sancti Pauli epistolam II ad Thessalonicenses* (1529); *Commentaria in Sancti Pauli epistolam I ad Thimotheum* (1529); *Commentaria in Sancti Pauli epistolam II ad Thimotheum* (1529); *Commentaria in Sancti Pauli epistolam ad Titum* (1529); *Commentaria in Sancti Pauli epistolam ad Philomenem* (1529); *Commentaria in epistolam ad Hebreos* (1529); *Commentaria in epistiolam Sancti Jacobi* (1529); *Commentaria in Acta Apostolorum* (1529); *Commentaria in epistolam I Sancti Petri* (1529); *Commentaria in epistolam II Sancti Petri* (1529); *Commentaria in epistolam I Sancti Joannis* (1529); *Commentaria in epistolas II et III Sancti Joannis* (1529); *Commentaria in epistolam Sancti Judae* (1529); *Commentaria in Genesim* (1530-31); *Commentaria in Exodum* (1530- 31); *Commentaria in Leviticum* (1530-31); *Commentaria in Numerum* (1530-31); *Commentaria in Deuteronomium* (1530-31); *Commentaria in librum Josuae* (1531); *Commentaria in Judices* (1531); *Commentaria in librum Ruth* (1531); *Commentaria in I Reg.* (1531); *Commentaria in II Reg.* (1531); *Commentaria in III Reg.* (1531); *Commentaria in IV Reg.* (1531); *Commentaria in I Paralip.* (1532); *Commentaria in II Paralip.* (1532); *Commentaria in librum Hezrae* (1532); *Commentaria in librum Nehemiae* (1532); *Commentaria in librum Job* (1533); *Commentaria in Parabolas Salomonis* (1534); *Commentaria in Ecclesiastem* (1534); *Commentaria in Isaiam* (1534, unfinished).

Bibliography: D. **Aguzzi-Barbagli,** *CE* 1 (1985) 239-42. **J. Beumer,** "Suffizienz und Insuffiezienz der Hl. Schrift nach Kardinal T. de V. C.," *Gregorianum* 45 (1964) 816-24. **T. A. Collins,** "Cardinal C.'s Fundamental Biblical Principles," *CBQ* 17 (1955) 363-78. **M. J. Congar,** "Bio-Bibliography de C.," *Revue Thomiste* 17 (1934–35) 1-49. **J. F. Groner,** *Kardinal C.: Eine Gestalt aus der Reformationszeit* (1951). **G. Hennig,** *C. und Luther* (1960). **U. Horst,** "Der Streit um die Heilige Schrift zwischen Kardinal C. und Ambrosius Catharinus," *Wahrheit und Verkündigung* (1967) 551-77. **E. Iserloh and B. Hallersleben,** *TRE* 7 (1981) 538-46. **R. C. Jenkins,** *Pre-Tridentine Doctrine: A Review of the Commentary on the Scriptures of T. de V. . . . C.* (1891). **M. O'Connell,** "Cardinal C.: Intellectual and Activist," *NSchol* 50 (1976) 310-22. **J. A. Weisheipl,** *NCE* 2 (1967) 1053-55. **J. M. Vosté,** "Cardinalis Cajetanus in Vetus Testamentu, praecipue in Hexameron," *Angelicum* 12 (1935) 305-32. **J. Wicks,** "Thomism Between Renaissance and Reformation: The Case of C.," *ARG* 68 (1977) 9-32; *C. Responds: A Reader in Reformation Controversy* (1978); *OER* (1996) 233-34.

A. SIEDLECKI

CALMET, DOM AUGUSTIN (1672–1757)

Born Feb. 26, 1672, in Ménil-la-Horgne, France, C. studied humanities at the local Benedictine college and rhetoric at the Jesuit university in Pout-à-Mousson. He entered the Benedictine order in 1689 while continuing the study of philosophy, theology, and Scripture as well as Hebrew with M. Fabre, a Lutheran clergyman in Münster. From 1698 to 1704 he worked on his commentary on the Bible, assisted by eight to ten religious associates. From 1706 to 1716 he lived at the abby of Blanc-Manteaux in Paris, where he received further assistance with his commentary after visiting libraries in Lorraine, Normandy, and Flanders, and began work on several other volumes. After returning to Lorraine he served as temporary abbot of Saint Leopold in Nancy (1718–23), eventually becoming abbot of Senones (1728), where he finished his career after refusing elevation by Pope Benedict XIII. He died Oct. 25, 1757.

C. produced an immense amount of writing. His biblical commentary of twenty-two volumes and almost 20,000 pages is filled with literal exegesis of the text, quotations from ancient and patristic sources, and dissertations on numerous topics and issues in biblical studies. The first major Roman Catholic commentary in French, the work was translated into Latin and Spanish and frequently reprinted, being partially incorporated into *La Sainte Bible* (1748–50), edited by L.-E. Rondet (1715–85). Never translated into English, although some of its dissertations have been (1727), the work could be described as late as 1854 as "one of the best which has ever been written . . . in which immense learning, good sense, sound judgment, and deep piety, are invariably displayed" (J. Darling, *Cyclopaedia Bibliographica*, 548). The commentary broke no new ground and generally confronted issues from a fideistic posture, although occasionally offering rationalist interpretations. VOLTAIRE, who was acquainted with C. after 1736, visited him at Senones in 1754 and relied heavily on the commentary as a major resource as well as an indirect jesting partner.

Of greater influence was C.'s dictionary of 1720–21. Translated into Latin, German, and English, the work went through numerous editions in various forms (a condensed ET was published in 1847) and did for the genre of biblical DICTIONARIES what P. BAYLE's work did for encyclopedias in general.

Works: *Commentaire littéral sur tous les livres de l'Ancien et du Nouveau Testament* (26 vols., 1707–16; various subsequent eds.); *Histoire de l'Ancien et du Nouveau Testament* (2 vols., 1718); *Dictionnaire historique, critique, chronologique, géographie et littéral de la Bible* (2 vols., 1720–21; various subsequent eds. and supplements; ET 3 vols., 1732, 5 vols., 1847[9]); *Nouvelles dissertations sur plusieurs questions important et curieuses* (3 vols., 1720; partial ET as *Antiquities, Sacred and Profane: Or a Collection of Critical Dissertations on the Old and NT* [tr. and annotated by N. Tindal, 1727]); *The Phantom World: The History and Philosophy of Spirits, Apparitions, etc.* (1746; ET 2 vol. in 1, 1850); *Bibliothèque Lorraine* (1751, repr. 1971), autobiography 209-17, bibliography 213-15.

Bibliography: **A. Ages,** "Voltaire's Critical Notes in the OT Portion of *La Bible enfin expliquée*" (diss., Ohio State University, 1963); "C. and the Rabbis," *JQR* (1965) 340-49; *Voltaire, C., and the OT* (1966). **G. Bobenrieter,** "Dom C. á Münster," *Annuaire de la Société d'Histoire du Val et de la ville de Münster* 29 (1975) 767-90; 30 (1976) 7-25; 31 (1977) 27-64; 32 (1978) 58-86; 33 (1979) 10-23. **A. Digot,** *Notice biographique et littérature sur D. C.* (1860). **D. A. Fangé,** *La vie du T. R. P. Dom Augustin Calmet, abbé de Senones* (1762). **J. Le Clerc,** "A. C., *Dictionnaire de la Bible*," *BAM* 19 (1723) 105-352. **P. Marsauche,** "Études sur le '*Commentaire littéral*' et les '*Dissertationes*' de D. A. C." (thesis, Nanterre, 1983); "Présentation de D. A. C. (1672-1757): *Dissertation sur les Passessions du Démon*," *BTT* 6 (1989) 233-53. **R. Taveneaux,** "Un théologien du 'juste milieu': D. A. C.," *Le Jansénisme en Lorraine* (1960) 523-35.

J. H. HAYES

CALOV, ABRAHAM (1612–86)

Born at Morungen, Brunswick, C. studied at Königsberg and Rostock and served as professor at Königsberg, rector at Danzig, and professor of theology at Wittenberg (from 1650), where he also served as general superintendent. A Lutheran scholastic, he defended the principles of *sola scriptura,* verbal INSPIRATION, and inerrancy, particularly against Roman Catholics and Socinians. His massive twelve-volume systematic theology is a monument of Lutheran orthodoxy. He vehemently opposed the work of his contemporary G. Calixtus (1586–1656) and the so-called syncretistic school of Helmstadt in their efforts to achieve Christian unity.

C.s' interpretation of the Bible is set forth in a three-volume commentary, a major portion of which consists of quotations from LUTHER. His hermeneutical method (see HERMENEUTICS) allowed only the literal interpretation of the text, but he used allegory at times in his markedly christological interpretation of the HB (e.g., Exod 28:20). Thus the Bible is God's history. The creation of the world took place in 4000 BCE; the activity of the Trinity is assumed by the plural form of Elohim. But, as C. noted on the title page, he was particularly interested in demonstrating "the evangelical truth, which alone can save." He referred to the whole HB as prophetical literature, and his prefaces to the Pentateuch (see PENTATEUCHAL CRITICISM) and the Prophets (see PROPHECY AND PROPHETS, HB) emphasize the witness borne to Christ. As examples of his approach, Christ is prefigured in the ram Abraham substituted for Isaac, the Ten Commandments are spoken by "the eternal Son of God" in conjunction with the Father and the Holy Spirit, and numerous psalms testify of Christ. C. utilized Hebrew and Greek in explaining significant biblical terms. He drew liberally from parallel passages and from the church fathers for his exposition.

Works: *Systema locorum theologicorum* (12 vols., 1655–77); *Biblia illustrata* (4 vols., 1672–76); *Die Heilige Bibel* (3 vols., 1681–82).

Bibliography: **R. Bäumer,** *LTK*[2], 2:886. **E. L. T. Henke,** *G. Calixtus und seine Zeit* 2 (1853–56). **J. Kunze,** *NSHERK* 2 (1952) 352-53. **F. Lau,** *RGG*[3], 1:1587. **F. A. G. Tholuck,** *Der Geist den lutherischen Theologen Wittenbergs* (1852).

H. H. COX

CALVIN, JOHN (1509–64)

C. was, with LUTHER, the premier Protestant theologian and biblical interpreter of the sixteenth century. His life was dedicated to understanding the Bible as the Word of God and to interpreting Scripture. He wrote commentaries on nearly every biblical book and lectured and preached daily in Geneva. In addition to his exegetical works, he was concerned with scriptural exposition throughout his many other writings, particularly his *Institutes of the Christian Religion* (various eds., 1536–60). He believed God has given the church "the gift of interpretation [1 Cor 12:10] which sheds light upon the word" (*Inst.* 4.17.25) through the ministries of preaching and teaching by true and faithful teachers.

C.'s training as a Christian Renaissance humanist in the universities of Orléans, Bourges, and Paris helped set his ultimate approach to biblical interpretation, affecting his methods of biblical exegesis and his approach to scriptural texts as historical documents. After his conversion to the evangelical Protestant faith, he drew on his classical studies to help him understand the Bible. Scripture, in turn, tested the insights he brought from his scholarship.

Christian humanists emphasized the sources of the Christian faith, particularly the Bible and early church theologians. They wished to discover what Christ intended Christianity to be. Although respecting Aristotelian logic, they did not permit it to take precedence over scriptural teachings. Rooted in the rhetorical tradition of Christian humanism, C. valued Cicero's ideal of linking "wisdom" and "eloquence," which led him to stress the simplicity of truth, its "practical" dimensions, and the problem of making it effective and powerful in human lives.

Initially directed by his father to study law, he was exposed to new methods of legal research being developed by humanist scholars, which stressed understanding law through examining history, philosophy, rhetoric, and institutions. This "modern" school of legal study sought the intent of ancient law codes in their original historical contexts as opposed to relying on accumulated commentaries in legal textbooks. C. carried over these emphases to his exegesis of Scripture. All this led him to a contextual rather than an atomistic approach to the Bible. In approaching texts he sought full understanding of biblical backgrounds, culture, and languages. He came to Scripture texts directly rather than through the glosses of medieval commentators and theologians.

Concern for context meant C. sought the divine intention in Scripture. His legal studies indicated that authorial intention was more significant than etymological word studies. C. called this latter approach "syllable-snatching" (*Inst.* 4.17.14; 4.17.23). Why a text is given, its reason or purpose, provides a key to interpretation. C.'s studies of rhetoric convinced him that such rhetorical forms as metonymies, synecdoches, and figures of speech must be clearly recognized and comprehended if a right interpretation of Scripture is to be gained.

Another important insight C. developed and stressed was "accommodation" (Lat. *accommodare*), used by Latin rhetoricians and jurists for the process of adapting, adjusting, and fitting language to the capacity (Lat. *captus*)—the context, makeup, situation, character, intelligence, and emotional state—of one's hearers. This was a means of helping in the persuasion process. Accommodation was used by such early theologians as ORIGEN, CHRYSOSTOM, and AUGUSTINE, who were all trained as rhetoricians. They saw it in the Christian context as God's strategy in presenting the truth of the Christian gospel through Scripture. To Calvin Scripture was the Word of God, divine revelation or divine wisdom that has come to the church by means of human writers and through human words. God has thus "accommodated" God's self to human capacities through the use of human language in order to communicate the divine message of salvation. Although scriptural language is less than eloquent, written by simple and uneducated authors, it is not a barrier to God's self-revelation. Indeed, Scripture is the very means of that revelation. C. stressed Scripture's content and function rather than its limitations of form.

God has accommodated to human limits and weaknesses in Scripture, and also supremely in JESUS Christ. In Christ, God's accommodation is complete, but it is only through Scripture that we learn of Jesus Christ. Scripture as the accommodated knowledge of God is given by God as a loving parent to convey the knowledge of Christ, condescending to human ways to lead people to salvation. C. approved of Augustine's image: "We can safely follow Scripture, which proceeds at the pace of a mother stooping to her child, so to speak, so as not to leave us behind in our weakness" (*Institutes* 3.21.4; Augustine *On Genesis* 5.3.6). Thus C. believed Scripture is best interpreted in relation to its purpose, which is to portray Jesus Christ and the salvation found in him. C. did not force a christological interpretation on every biblical text, but he summarized the purpose of all biblical interpretation when he wrote: "This is what we should in short seek in the whole of Scripture: truly to know Jesus Christ" (preface to Olivétan's NT).

C.'s classical training and familiarity with early Christian writings served him well when exegeting Scripture. He used humanist scholars like G. Budé and ERASMUS as well as early church theologians to assist on matters of text, philology, and interpretation. Most frequently, C. turned to Augustine for theological interpretations and Chrysostom for exegetical insights. He did not sanction Augustine's allegorical interpretations; instead, he appreciated Chrysostom's fidelity to "the plain meaning of the words" and a text's historical context (*Praefatio in Christostomi Homilias*).

Exegetically, C. had two guiding principles. *Brevitas* indicated his concern to find the "pertinence" and "relevance" of a passage in as short a compass as possible. *Facilitas* indicated his concern for "simplicity" or "what is easily understood." He quickly sought Scripture's natural and obvious meaning. Believing the commentator's "almost only task" is "to unfold the mind of the writer whom he has undertaken to expound" (*Commentary on Romans*, dedication to S. Grynaeus), he wished to expound the plain, genuine, natural, or literal sense of Scripture. This involved him in extensive study of the backgrounds, circumstances, language, and contexts of every text.

Works: *Institutes of the Christian Religion* (ed. J. T. McNeill; tr. F. L. Battles et al., LCC 20-21, 1960). *Ioannis Calvini opera quae superstunt omnia* (ed. G. Baum, E. Cunitz, E. Reuss, P. Lobstein, and A. Erichson, 1863–1900); *Supplementa Calviniana* (ed. E. Mulhaupt et al.); *Calvin: Commentaries* (tr. and ed. with intro. by J. Haroutunian, with L. P. Smith, LCC 23, 1958).

Bibliography: R. Gamble, *"Brevitas et facilitas:* Toward an Understanding of C.'s Hermeneutics," *WTJ* 47 (1985) 1-17; "Exposition and Method in C.," *WTJ* 49 (1987) 153-65; "C. as Theologian and Exegete: Is There Anything New?" *Calvin Theological Journal 23 (1988) 178-94.* **A. Ganoczy and S. Scheld,** *Die Hermeneutik C.s: Geistesgeschichtliche Voraussetzungen und Grundzüge* (1983). **H.-J. Kraus,** "C.'s Exegetical Principles," *Int* 31 (1977) 8-18. **E. A. McKee,** "Some Reflections on Relating C.'s Exegesis and Theology," *Biblical Hermeneutics in Historical Perspective* (ed. M. S. Burrows and P. Rorem, 1991) 215-26. **D. K. McKim,** "C.'s View of Scripture," *Readings in C.'s Theology* (ed. D. K. McKim, 1983) 43-68. **R. A. Muller,** "The Hermeneutics of Promise and Fulfillment in C.'s Exegesis of the OT Prophecies of the Kingdom," *The Bible in the Sixteenth Century* (ed. D. C. Steinmetz, DMMRS 11, 1990) 68-82. **J. Murray,** *C. on Scripture and Divine Sovereignty* (1979). **T. H. L. Parker,** *C.'s NT Commentaries* (1971); *C.'s OT Commentaries* (1986). **D. L. Puckett,** *J. C.'s Exegesis of the OT* (Columbia Series in Reformed Theology, 1995). **J. B. Rogers and D. K. McKim,** *The Authority and Interpretation of the Bible: An Historical Approach* (1979) 89-116. **D. Steinmetz,** *C. in Context* (1995). **T. F. Torrance,** *The Hermeneutics of J. C.* (1988).

D. K. MCKIM

CAMPBELL, ALEXANDER (1788–1866)

A religious leader and educator, C. was born in northern Ireland. After studying at the University of Glasgow, he came to the United States in 1809. He founded and edited *The Christian Baptist* (1823–30) as well as *The Millennial Harbinger* (1830–66) and was founding president of Bethany College (1841). He brought together several indigenous primitivist American religious groups that eventually developed into the Disciples of Christ, the Church of Christ, and the Christian Church.

Because of a desire to restore the ancient gospel and the NT church, C. focused on the NT, editing and supplying critical notes to an edition of the NT later designated the *The Living Oracles*. The American Bible Union published his translation of Acts with notes. C. gave special attention to the Pauline epistles (see PAUL), including Hebrews, because of his belief in a three-tiered dispensationalism, with the Christian being the latest and most authoritative. Although familiar with developing German criticism, he used Scottish and English scholarship extensively, relying on the grammatical-historical methods of M. STUART.

Works: *The Christian Baptist* (1823–30); *The Millennial Harbinger* (1830–66); *The Christian System* (1839); *The Living Oracles* (1826); *The Acts of the Apostles, Translated from the Greek, on the Basis of the Common English Version, with Notes* (1858).

Bibliography: M. E. Boring, "The Formation of a Tradition: A. C. and the NT," *Disciples Theological Digest* 2 (1987) 5-62. T. H. Olbricht, "A. C. in the Context of American Biblical Studies, 1810–74," *Restoration Quarterly* 33 (1991) 13-28. R. Richardson, *Memoirs of A. C.* (1897). H. K. Rowe, *DAB* 3 (1926) 446-48. C. K. Thomas, *A. C. and His New Version* (1958).

T. H. OLBRICHT

CANON OF THE BIBLE

Canon is a Greek word meaning a "rule"; but since the fourth century CE it has been used by Christians to denote the correct list of the Holy Scriptures and, by consequence, the collection of books so listed. Prior to the fourth century the canon was just as real; however, it was simply denoted by the various titles of the Holy Scriptures, a practice inherited from the Jews, who, though they made use of lists, had no proper word for *list* and so described lists by their contents.

The Holy Scriptures were esteemed as holy because they were believed to possess divine AUTHORITY owing to the special operation of the Spirit of God in their composition; their authors were characteristically thought of as "prophets" (see PROPHECY AND PROPHETS). In the early synagogue and church the Scriptures were considered not just the oldest books of the Jewish or Christian religion or the most reliable records of HB or NT revelation; they also partook of the nature of revelation and were therefore what 2 Tim 3:16 calls "inspired" (see INSPIRATION OF THE BIBLE). The belief in inspired Scriptures developed out of ideas expressed in the HB and is common to intertestamental, NT, and patristic writers. It explains what those who recognized the books and assembled the canons of the two testaments believed they were doing: acknowledging and assembling the revelatory literature of the Jewish and Christian religions.

1. The HB Canon. The HB is known as the OT to Christians, but it was first and remains the Bible of the Jews. It has, therefore, a distinct though related history in comparison to the NT. Because of its antiquity and its influence on the NT, the HB is best considered first and apart from the NT.

Discussion of the HB canon began, at latest, toward the end of the second century BCE when the schism between Jews and Samaritans became complete and the Samaritans promulgated their distinctive edition of the Pentateuch (see PENTATEUCHAL CRITICISM), repudiating all other scriptures. By this time, as we know from the prologue to Ecclesiasticus (c. 130 BCE) and other evidence, Jews recognized two other bodies of scriptures, the Prophets and the "other ancestral books" (later to be called the "Psalms" or the Hagiographa). Many of the books of this threefold canon are quoted as Scripture in the NT, and the authority of JESUS and his apostles commended the Jewish Scriptures to the infant church.

At this period scrolls and codices were not capacious enough to hold more than a few canonical books each, and the main way of identifying the canonical books was probably through memorized or written lists. The traditional Jewish list of the Prophets and Hagiographa is recorded in the Babylonian TALMUD (*B. Bat.* 14b), the list of the books of the "Law," or Pentateuch, being too well known to need recording. The earliest recorded Christian list of the HB books is that of MELITO in the latter half of the second century, and this list already shows Christians reorganizing the books in more divisions than three, according to literary character and chronological sequence (see CHRONOLOGY, HB). A great variety of Christian lists followed in the course of the patristic period. In some of these, other Jewish books that Christians used as edifying reading began to be included, and the same is true of Christian biblical manuscripts. In the fourth century, when manuscripts big enough to embrace the whole SEPTUAGINT started to appear, additional books were often included without anything to distinguish them as such. The opposite tendency also sometimes showed itself. MARCION, in the mid-second century, pushed his anti-legalism to the point of rejecting the entire HB; and in the late fourth century THEODORE OF MOPSUESTIA indulged in subjective biblical criticism by rejecting various HB books.

At the same time most of the more learned of the fathers attempted to maintain the Jewish and primitive Christian tradition about the identity of the HB books: notably ORIGEN, Cyril of Jerusalem (c. 315–387), ATHANASIUS, Epiphanius (c. 315–403), GREGORY OF NAZIANZUS, and JEROME. The contrast between Jerome and AUGUSTINE is instructive. Jerome, with his Jewish learning, was determined to distinguish the additional writings from the books of the HB. Augustine, knowing only Greek and Latin, could lay down the principle that Christ's HB canon should be ours; but he was seldom prepared to apply it against the authority of the additional books.

These two traditions continued throughout the Middle Ages and to this day coexist in the Eastern Orthodox Church (see ORTHODOX INTERPRETATION), which respects the additional books but distinguishes them from the books of the HB. In the West, however, matters came to a head during the sixteenth-century Reformation. The Reformers followed Jerome, and they retained the additional books, if at all, only as an edifying appendix to the HB (see below). In contrast, the Council of Trent declared the additional books to share the inspiration and authority of the other canonical books. Hence the distinct standpoints of the Protestant and Roman Catholic churches today.

In 1719 F. Lee (1661–1719) propounded the theory that the additional books of the fourth- and fifth-century Septuagint manuscripts go back to a larger canon peculiar to the Greek-speaking Jews of Alexandria who produced the Septuagint. In 1842 the Roman Catholic orientalist F. Movers (1806–56) proposed that this larger canon was at one time accepted by the Jews of Palestine as well. He also drew attention to the rabbinical disputes about Ezekiel, Proverbs, Ecclesiastes, the Song of Songs, and Esther as showing that the HB canon was still open when the Christian church inherited it; and he claimed that it was never subsequently closed until Trent closed it in the Roman Catholic form. In 1871 the Jewish scholar H. GRAETZ proposed that it was the "Council" of Jabneh (Jamnia), c. 90 CE, that led to the closing of the Jewish canon.

Contrary to this trend, C. Horneman (1751–1830) in 1776 demonstrated that PHILO OF ALEXANDRIA made no use of the additional books of the Septuagint. Subsequently, in 1849 M. STUART argued that the sacred archive of Scriptures in the Temple and the rivalry between the Pharisees, Sadducees, and Essenes must have been substantial obstacles to any change in the Jewish canon from about the second century BCE onward.

In 1892 H. RYLE put forward the afterward standard view that the three divisions of the HB were canonized during three different eras: the Pentateuch in the fifth century BCE (taken with them into schism, in the same century, by the Samaritans), the Prophets in the third century BCE, and the Hagiographa about 90 CE. In more recent years, A. Sundberg (1964) has refuted the Alexandrian canon hypothesis; J. Lewis and S. Leiman (1974) have refuted the Jamnia hypothesis; J. Purvis (1968), on the basis of the Qumran discoveries (see DEAD SEA SCROLLS), has shown that the Samaritan schism and canon are probably to be dated, not before, but well after the year of the canonization of the Prophets; and R. Beckwith (1988) has shown that the rabbinical disputes about Ezekiel and the other four books are based on arguments that the rabbis regularly use in discussing books already canonical. Thus the authority of the Jewish canon is being reaffirmed, and the date when it was closed is being pushed back again into pre-Christian times.

2. Appendixes to the HB Canon. The earliest evidence of an appendix to the HB canon is in the recently published Qumran letter 4QMMT, which refers its readers to the three divisions of the canon "and the annals of each generation" (perhaps alluding to the book of *Jubilees*). The second piece of evidence is in Philo, who says that the Therapeutae took nothing with them into their shrines except the books in the three divisions of the canon "and the other books whereby knowledge and piety are increased and completed" (*De Vita Contemplativa* 25). The Therapeutae were a quasi-Essene sect, and these other books are probably the revered sectarian books incorporating the "inspired interpretation" of the Scriptures that the Essenes, as at Qumran, claimed to possess. Books like *Enoch,* JUBILEES, and the *Temple Scroll* (pseudonymous apocalypses and prophecies that were cherished at Qumran and that claimed a sort of inspiration) would be the main books of this kind.

The third piece of evidence is 2 Esdras (4 Ezra) 14:44-48, which speaks of the twenty-four canonical books being openly published (twenty-four being the rabbinic numeration of the biblical books) and the other seventy inspired books being preserved in privileged circles. These seventy would be pseudonymous apocalypses (see APOCALYPTICISM) and prophecies of the same sort as before but with an admixture of Pharisaic or semi-Pharisaic examples, like 2 Esdras itself.

Books of this kind circulated freely in the early Christian church and were used, sometimes with interpolation and adaption, for Christian apologetic purposes. Even in the Epistle of Jude reference is made to two of them. They were known, nevertheless, to be outside the canon; and from the time of Origen onward (mid-third cent.) Christian opinion increasingly turned against them. Jerome, however, proposed a new appendix to the HB, consisting of the additional books of the Septuagint manuscripts; in Protestant Bibles, following Jerome's teaching, they often are appended under the title of APOCRYPHA.

3. The NT Canon. Alongside the inspired body of HB Scriptures inherited from the Jews that had been commended to the first Christians by Jesus and his apostles, the church from a very early period revered the records of Christ's teaching and work and the letters of the apostles. As eyewitnesses grew fewer and the uncertainties of oral transmission became more evident (see John 21:22-23), the importance of written records must have increased. In the early second century PAPIAS's (c. 60–130) passion for the "living and abiding voice" was all the more intense because that voice was in process of disappearing. The written records that remained, though increasingly revered, were until the mid-second century often called by names like "the Lord" and "the Apostles" rather than by the name of Scripture. However, since the incarnate Word, the apostles, and the NT prophets were organs of revelation no less exalted than Moses and the HB prophets (indeed, rather the reverse), it was natural that before long the idea of NT Scriptures developed. The earliest evidence is in the NT itself (1 Tim 5:18; 2 Pet 3:15-16), followed in the early second century by IGNATIUS, the *Epistle of* BARNABAS, and *2 Clement,* and by the writings of the GNOSTIC theologian Basilides. Since the *lingua franca* of the early church was Greek, and the Septuagint version was the form of the HB it knew best, the idea of a new body of Scriptures in Greek, not in Hebrew or Aramaic, was one it could accept without difficulty, though, according to Papias, Matthew, at least, is based on a Semitic original.

By about 180 CE, the writings of IRENAEUS, TERTULLIAN, and CLEMENT OF ALEXANDRIA, together with the list in the Muratorian Fragment, show the nucleus of the NT standing alongside the HB as Scripture in the Eastern and Western churches. It includes the four Gospels, Acts, the Pauline epistles, 1 Peter, and 1 John. Seven books, however (the so-called *antilegomena,* "books spoken against"), were still in doubt; these were Hebrews, James, 2 Peter, 2 and 3 John, Jude, and Revelation. Moreover, some apocryphal books, notably the *Shepherd of Hermas* and the *Apocalypse of Peter* (2nd-cent. works making prophetic claims), were contending for inclusion. Hebrews, Jude, and Revelation were attested early, and James fairly early, though not without opposition; but the grounds of the opposition are known or easy to infer. Hebrews is anonymous and was only universally accepted when the (probably mistaken) belief that it was by PAUL became generally accepted. Jude quotes Jewish apocalypses, though perhaps only as an *argumentum ad hominem* to readers who valued them or were troubled by heretics who did. The book of Revelation was appealed to by the Montanists (and other millennialists). James bore the name of one of the Judaizers (probably wrongly) regarded as their great patron. Second Peter and 2 and 3 John, on the other hand, seem to have been little known; but they were probably cherished in secluded corners of the church, since a book does not spring at once from being canonical nowhere to being canonical everywhere. In the fourth century Athanasius listed the NT canon as including all seven *antilegomena* and no apocrypha, and by the end of the century, partly owing to the influence of Jerome and Augustine, this belief had become universal in the Greek and Latin churches. Only the Syrian churches went on using a short canon, and because of the Nestorian and Monophysite schisms of the fifth century the Syrian churches continued for centuries to put the *antilegomena* on a lower level.

To the mind of faith the bringing together of the canon must be attributed to the providence of God, though in the case of the NT we have much more evidence of the secondary causes that contributed to the process than in the case of the HB. Thus authentic records about Jesus were essential for the church (see Luke 1:1-4). For a book to have its origin in the apostles or their circles was recognized by the fathers as an important criterion of authenticity, and consistency with received teaching (written and oral) was recognized as another. Some of the NT books had been read to congregations since the beginning (1 Thess 5:27, etc.), and in the case of the "prophecy" of John had probably been read to them as Scripture (Rev 1:3). The stimulus of rival canons like that of Marcion may have accelerated the process of forming the orthodox canon; but it would not (any more than the Samaritan canon in the case of the HB) have been the original cause.

Modern study of the NT canon may be said to have begun with LUTHER, who redirected attention to the ancient doubts about the *antilegomena.* As a result some of these books were for a time put on a lower level of authority in various Lutheran circles. In the first half of the eighteenth century, massive collections of ancient testimonies to the authenticity of the NT books were assembled by J. Jones (1726) and N. LARDNER (1727–57), a process that was continued in the following century by B. F. WESTCOTT (1855) and T. ZAHN (1888–92). J. G. EICHHORN (1804–12) attributed the formation of the NT canon to the stimulus of Marcion; A. von HARNACK (1889) attributed it to that of Gnosticism more generally; and H. von Campenhausen (1968) attributed it to that of Montanism. A. JÜLICHER (1894) attributed it to the reading of the NT books in the congregations, although it should be borne in mind that the books must already have had authority of some sort to qualify them to be read; and the parallel of the HB canon reminds us that some of its books were never read in the Jewish synagogue at all. In the case of both testaments various secondary causes, not just one, probably contributed to the providential outcome.

Bibliography: D. E. Aune, "On the Origins of the 'Council of Javneh' Myth," *JBL* 110 (1991) 491-93. **R. T. Beckwith,** *The OT Canon of the NT Church and Its Background in Early Judaism* (1985); "Formation of the HB," *Mikra: Text, Transla-*

tion, Reading, and Interpretation of the HB in Ancient Judaism and Early Christianity (ed. M. J. Mulder; CRINT 2, 1, 1988) 39-86. **F. F. Bruce,** *The Canon of Scripture* (1988). **H. F. von Campenhausen,** *The Formation of the Christian Bible* (1968; ET 1972). **J. G. Eichhorn,** *Einleitung in das Neue Testament* (2 vols., 1804–12). **E. E. Ellis,** "The OT Canon in the Early Church," *Mikra* (1985) 653-90. **H. H. Graetz,** *Kohelet oder der salomonische Prediger* (1871) 147–73. **A. von Harnack,** *Das Neue Testament um das Jahr 200: T. Zahn's Geschichte des neutestamentlichen Kanons* (1889). **J. Jones,** *A New and Full Method for Settling the Canonical Authority of the NT* (2 vols., 1726). **A. Julicher,** *Introduction to the NT* (1894; ET 1904). **N. Lardner,** *The Credibility of the Gospel History* (12 vols., 1727–57). **F. Lee,** "Prolegomena," *Vetus Testamentum Graece juxta LXX interpretes* (J. Grabe, 1720). **S. Z. Leiman** (ed.), *The Canon and Masorah of the HB: An Introductory Reader* (1974); *The Canonization of Hebrew Scripture: The Talmudic and Midrashic Evidence* (1976). **J. P. Lewis,** "What Do We Mean by Jabneh?" *JBR* 32 (1964) 125-32 = Leiman (1974) 254-61. **B. M. Metzger,** *The Canon of the NT* (1987). **F. K. Movers,** *Loci quidam historiae canonis Veteris Testamenti illustrati* (1842). **J. D. Purvis,** *The Samaritan Pentateuch and the Origin of the Samaritan Sect* (HSM 2, 1968). **H. E. Ryle,** *The Canon of the OT: An Essay on the Gradual Growth and Formation of the Hebrew Canon of Scripture* (1892, 1895²). **M. Stuart,** *Critical History and Defence of the OT Canon* (1849). **A. C. Sundberg, Jr.,** *The OT of the Early Church* (HTS 20, 1964). **B. F. Westcott,** *A General Survey of the History of the Canon of the NT* (1855, 1866²). **T. Zahn,** *Geschichte des neutestamentlichen Kanons* (2 vols., 1888–92).

R. T. BECKWITH

CANONICAL CRITICISM

A definition of this term and the approach to interpretation implied by it are complicated by a lack of scholarly consensus. Related terms include "canonical criticism" (see J. Sanders [1984]), "composition-critical approach" (*Kompositionsgeschichte,* R. Rendtorff [b. 1925]), "canon-contextual analysis" (G. Sheppard, b. 1946), or more loosely, "a canonical approach" and "assessing the role of canon in understanding the OT" (see B. Childs). What all of these approaches share is an effort to describe how ancient traditions are to be interpreted when they form part of a "scripture" within a religion.

The term *canon* is equivocal, signifying either the "norm, standard, or ideal" or "list, catalogue, or fixed measure." It was first used by the church father ATHANASIUS as a synonym for the Bible around 350 CE. Only in much later periods did Jews use the term to refer to the HB. In pre-modern introductions to Scripture, Christians traditionally treated the issues of text and canon before moving on to considerations of specific books of the Bible. In the modern period this order was reversed because canonical issues seemed to belong to the latest stages of the TRADITION HISTORY of the Bible. Therefore,

they were considered less significant for modern historical interpretation of either the Bible or the ancient traditions contained in it.

Despite its late usage, the term *canon* has recently proved helpful, especially for certain HB scholars, as a way to call attention to a basic feature of Scripture often overlooked in modern historical-critical exegesis: the special semantic implications of a "scripture" within Judaism and Christianity. Historical criticism in the modern period usually sought to recover the original versions of biblical traditions. Even if a pre-biblical tradition was once an oral unit of PROPHECY it would not be canonical in the sense of being Scripture, nor does the absence of claims of INSPIRATION necessarily preclude a tradition from becoming a normative and revelatory part of Scripture. What is clear is that the logic of the scriptural context is not that of modern historical writing. For instance, Scripture is riddled with historical anachronisms, and the context often warrants an interpretation that must exceed or even contravene an original author's intent. While some conflicting traditions have been harmonized, others remain remarkably unharmonized—like those found in the juxtaposition of opposing or differing claims.

In sum, historical-critical inquiry into the nature of "scripture" has led many scholars to the conclusion that a semantic transformation occurred whenever pre-biblical traditions were incorporated into the larger canonical context of Scripture. The unity of the Bible lies neither in a common historical property or "center" to these pre-biblical traditions nor in construals of development in the history of ancient religious ideas like those found in modern schemes of "salvation history." Instead, the later editors of the Bible assigned diverse ancient traditions to particular larger contexts based on a variety of religious or non-religious factors. This insight is not a theological judgment by biblical scholars but simply a historical claim about the nature of the form and function of a scripture within religion. Such comparative religionists as W. C. Smith (b. 1916) have strongly supported this canonical approach within religions generally. Perhaps the best way to show the internal debates among advocates of a canonical approach is to consider the positions of its first two major architects—SANDERS and CHILDS—then to consider other subsequent developments.

1. Canonical Process and Canonical Hermeneutics: James A. Sanders. The term "canonical criticism" was coined by Sanders and popularized in his book *Torah and Canon* (1972). He emphasized that his proposal calls for a special stance on the Bible—that it is an integrative "extension of biblical criticism" rather than merely another technique for analyzing the Bible. In contrast to Childs, Sanders considers as "canonical" any normative use of a tradition from the time of the Israelite prophets to contemporary Christian preaching; the canonization of the HB and the NT are only milestones in that larger canonical process.

In light of this long process of canonical interpretation leading to the formation of the Bible, Sanders has sought to find some continuity in what he calls "canonical hermeneutics." He has attempted to discern some constant factors that explain the difference between true and false prophecy in ancient Israel, assuming that these factors constitute a theological norm for contemporary Christian preaching. While canonical HERMENEUTICS necessarily change over time, true canonical hermeneutics must maintain interpretation in support of "monotheistic pluralism" and in opposition to various subtle types of polytheism. Scripture itself unevenly illustrates adherence to this principle. Still the HB and especially the NT repeatedly show, for Sanders, how the same canonical tradition proved to be adaptable to new situations with quite different "true" implications for each generation of believers.

Sanders proposes that "comparative Midrash" should be the study of how authoritative traditions are interpreted according to canonical hermeneutics. In this way he focuses on "the shape in the hermeneutics of the biblical authors." For example, he argues that the different authors of Ezek 33:24 and Isa 51:2-3 referred to the same normative tradition with opposite conclusions. Nonetheless, both are correct because they each applied properly the same canonical hermeneutics to different social contexts. By locating the key to proper interpretation in the canonical hermeneutics employed by the various interpreters, Sanders can view the Bible as a relatively open collection of normative traditions. He is, thus, understandably less concerned than Childs, Rendtorff, or Sheppard with the final form of HB books.

Nonetheless, Sanders has also offered some contextual descriptions of how books constitute whole, canonically significant collections in the HB. In this regard, Childs praises Sanders's theological assessment of the form and function of the Pentateuch (see PENTATEUCHAL CRITICISM). Sanders assesses the effect of separating Deuteronomy from the rest of the DEUTERONOMISTIC HISTORY (Joshua–2 Kings). The resulting Mosaic collection of five books (Genesis to Deuteronomy) became the crucial norm of the Torah for later Judaism. By this arrangement the events of the conquest and the monarchy are qualitatively distinguished from the definitive locus of Mosaic revelation and are made subordinate to its expression of God's covenant with Israel—past, present, and future.

2. The Canonical Context: Brevard S. Childs. In *Biblical Theology in Crisis* (1970), Childs began to explore what he called "the canonical context," especially the relationship between the HB and the NT. He defined canon as "the rule that delineates the area in which the church hears the Word of God." Later he introduced nomenclature of "the canonical shape" in a reexamination of Isaiah, the psalms, the crossing of the sea, and Daniel. In a programmatic article in 1972, "The

OT as Scripture of the Church," he set out his view of the interconnections between books in the Pentateuch. The same orientation appears in his commentary on Exodus (1974), in his introductions to the OT (1979) and the NT (1984), and in his *Biblical Theology of the Old and New Testaments* (1992). Childs has come to reject Sanders's terminology of "canon(ical) criticism" for his own work because it implies either an extension of historical criticism or another method of conventional historical analysis. His "canonical approach" has been consistently aimed at a description of what he considers to be the significance of the canonical context for the interpretation of Scripture.

In contrast to Sanders, Childs established his academic reputation as a traditio-historian and form critic (see FORM CRITICISM) who resists identifying the term *canon* with every authoritative tradition in the pre-biblical period or with the process of tradition history. Rejecting the possibility of detecting canonical hermeneutics in the process of the history of pre-biblical traditions, Childs argues only that the later formation and canonization of Scripture reflected "a hermeneutical activity which continued to shape the material theologically in order to render it accessible to future generations of believers" (1985, 6). The resulting canonical context of Scripture subordinated the intent of earlier authors and editors to this larger purpose. Modern redaction critics usually focus on minor additions and miss the full effect of this resultant text, which now has its own quite autonomous context. Childs has spoken occasionally of "the canonical intent" to express just this distinction between the sense made explicit by the canonical context and historical reconstructions of editorial intents, or *Tendenzen*.

A distinctive feature of Childs's description of the canonical approach is what he calls the "shape" of a biblical section, book, or collection of books. He argues that this description should not be confused with a purely LITERARY, RHETORICAL, or structuralist assessment (see STRUCTURALISM AND DECONSTRUCTION), on the one hand, or as part of an exercise in REDACTION CRITICISM, on the other hand. Instead, "shape" corresponds to a larger impression of the form and function of a text, preliminary to a close, philological interpretation of its full context and content. Thus, Childs states, "The canonical shaping serves not so much to establish a given meaning to a particular passage as to chart the boundaries within which the exegetical task is to be carried out" (1979, 83). This dimension may or may not reflect such specific editorial activity as "canon conscious redactions" (see below). It consists essentially of a description of how the form of Scripture lends itself to its theological function as Scripture within the believing community.

A Christian concern with the overarching form of biblical books as a key to their role as Scripture is certainly not a new one in the history of interpretation. In pre-modern periods, one frequently can find appeals to the "scope" of a text that helped to establish the *usus loquendi* or normative, literal sense in church interpretation. "Scope" included attention especially to how a text properly coheres within its context and within the aim of the Scripture as a whole. As is the case with Childs's shape, the signs of a text's scope often depended on appeals to the beginnings and endings of books, titles, and evidence of transitions that seemed to establish its essential purpose by marking out the boundaries, limits, and possibilities for the full interplay of biblical interpretation. The shape of a text points to its coherence as Scripture and to its relation to the subject matter of Scripture as a whole. Childs tends to highlight those elements in the shaping of a book that indicates elements of continuity.

Because he concentrates on these positive boundaries of a text, Childs shows less interest in the role of contextual ambiguity, extra-textual reference, undecidibility, or the survival of systemic dissonance inherited from the traditio-historical process. One might also argue that what should be acknowledged as different and thoroughly modern about Childs's shape is that he takes up the old concern with scope, but frames it specifically in response to the atomization of Scripture by various modern historical-critical methods. While the polemical tone of his work may seem at times to devalue historical criticism entirely, Childs actually relies on the results of modern criticism to state with new precision how different pre-biblical traditions conjoin in the shaping of biblical books within Scripture. In any case, at the heart of Childs's approach lies a way to claim POST-MODERN continuity with the old Roman Catholic and Protestant search for the true literal sense of Christian Scripture.

Consequently, when Childs describes the shape of the final text of a biblical book, he is fully aware that he concentrates on a recognition of the specific literary boundary or textual arena in which proper theological interpretation takes place. For example, the historicized psalm titles link certain prayers to events in the life of David as described in 1–2 Samuel, so that the resulting presentation of both the public and the private life of David contributes to a biblical anthropology. Psalm 1 identifies the prayers as a commentary on the Torah; and the royal psalms, rendered as messianic in the context of the psalter, recommend the reading of these biblical prayers as sources of prophetic promise, as asserted elsewhere (2 Sam 23:1-2 and 1 Chr 25:1-8).

As another example, in Isaiah 1–39, Isaiah 1 provides an introduction to the entire book; the song in chapter 12 concludes the first section by looking to a time when God's "wrath will turn" to "comfort" (12:1); and finally, the placement of the narrative in Isaiah 39 anticipates the very Babylonian exile presumed in Isaiah 40–66, when words of comfort are offered by the prophet to Israel. Conversely, Isaiah 40–66 announces "latter things" (e.g., 42:9, etc.) of promise that have credibility on the basis of fulfillment of "former things" familiar in Isaiah 1–39.

In another instance of canonical shaping, the association of Solomon with Proverbs, Qoheleth, and Song of Songs designates a corpus of biblical wisdom literature in distinction from the Torah and the Prophets. Although not all the traditions in these books are wisdom literature in terms of ancient Near Eastern genre designations, they are now to be read sapientially within Scripture as a guide to knowledge and skills shared with the rest of the world. Furthermore, the ending of Qoheleth asserts a complementarity between the Torah of Moses and the wisdom of Solomon without entirely resolving how future readers would reconcile the differences between divinely given wisdom and Torah.

Childs has, likewise, sought to detect similar features in the NT. For example, the editorial addition "The Gospel According to Luke" reflects an alteration in how the original memoir is to be read as one of the Gospels. By separating Acts from Luke with the Gospel of John, the effect is made even more emphatic. Luke is to be read as a Gospel alongside the other three even if it were not originally intended as such. The four Gospels, despite many glaring differences, are biblically interpreted together as witnesses to the one gospel of JESUS Christ. So, too, the Pauline epistles form a single collection, wedding so-called genuine Pauline letters written before the Gospels with later Pauline pastorals (see PASTORAL LETTERS) that reflect a later synthesis of Gospel traditions.

What the canon of Scripture resists is any assumption of great interpretive significance based on a sharp distinction between either the historical and the biblical PAUL or the historical and the biblical Jesus Christ. The historical significance of Paul and Jesus for faith finds its normative and sufficient expression through the testimonies of Scripture. Any attempt to make truth claims in the language of Christian faith based on pre-biblical or purely historical inquiry risks setting aside the very logic that underlies the formation of both Scripture and the church. Because canon and community are dialectically related and formative of each other, the religious community finds in Scripture a mirror of its own identity and confession. Without the self-reflection illuminated by competent biblical interpretation, the specific dimensions of Christianity may become blurred or will be lost entirely.

3. Attempts at Refinements and Collaboration. Students of Childs have sought to advance the same perspective in a variety of ways. For example, Sheppard has proposed that one may identify certain "canon conscious redactions" that assert a context between books and traditions not originally intended to be read together. Increasingly, contributions to a canonical approach have pursued interdisciplinary areas outside conventional biblical studies, including the history of interpretation within church and synagogue, literary criticism, comparative religions, and historical theology. Because these investigations must take seriously the post-biblical history of religion, a renewed concern has developed to recognize the hermeneutical differences between Jewish interpretation of Hebrew Scripture and the semantic differences in the Christian adaptation of the same as OT. At a minimum, a canonical approach redefines the role of biblical studies within the encyclopedic horizon of both religion in the university and theology in the seminary.

Among numerous related studies, only some representative ones can be mentioned here. Rendtorff's introduction to the OT (1985) is a good example of a highly independent contribution that builds directly on canon contextual considerations, especially those of Childs. Its major contribution in this respect lies in its close attention to detail and its argument for marked repetitions and transitions not pursued by Childs. Often this evidence involves the recurrence of unusual phrases, formulae, or key word connections. Similarly, J. Blenkinsopp (b. 1927) offers a fresh examination of the relationship between prophecy and Torah within the formation of Scripture (1977).

Because these assessments accept, depend on, and respond to modern historical criticism, they all stand in opposition to fundamentalism and its modern brand of right-wing historicism. Many approaches not labeled as canonical may well belong to this approach, broadly conceived. For example, R. BROWN acknowledges in similar ways that the context of Scripture has changed our perception of the literal sense, although he allows the Roman Catholic teaching *magisterium* to determine what of that sense belongs to the binding "canonical sense" of Scripture (1981). J. Neusner (b. 1932) likewise has explored the nature of canonical authority in Judaism, concentrating particularly on the implications of the oral Torah for canonical Jewish interpretation (1983). The spontaneity and independence of these contributions suggest that they belong to a major theme in current debates regarding the nature of Scripture and the contours of Jewish and Christian interpretation.

Bibliography: **J. Barr,** *Holy Scripture: Canon, Authority, Criticism* (1983). **J. Barton,** *Reading the OT: Method in Biblical Study* (1984, rev. ed. 1996) 77-103. **J. Blenkinsopp,** *Prophecy and Canon: A Contribution to the Study of Jewish Origins* (SJCA 3, 1977). **R. Brown,** *The Critical Meaning of the Bible* (1981). **B. S. Childs,** *Biblical Theology in Crisis* (1970); "The OT as Scripture of the Church," *CTM* 43 (1972) 709-22; "The *Sensus Literalis* of Scripture: An Ancient and Modern Problem," *Beiträge zur Alttestamentlichen Theologie* (FS W. Zimmerli, ed. H. Donner et al., 1976) 80-95; *Introduction to the OT as Scripture* (1979); *The NT as Canon: An Introduction* (1984); *OT Theology in a Canonical Context* (1985); *Biblical Theology of the Old and New Testaments* (1992). **J. Neusner,** *Midrash in Context* (1983). **R. Rendtorff,** *The OT: An Introduction* (1983; ET 1985). **J. A. Sanders,** *Torah and Canon* (1972); *Canon and Community: A Guide to Canonical Criticism* (GBS, 1984); *From Sacred Story to Sacred Text: Canon as Paradigm* (1987). **G. T. Sheppard,** "Canon Criticism: The Proposal of B. Childs and an Assessment for Evangelical Hermeneutics," *Studia biblica et theologica* 4, 2 (1974) 3-17; *Wisdom as a Hermeneutical Construct* (BZAW 151, 1980); "Canonization: Hearing the Voice of the Same God Through Historically Dissimilar Traditions," *Int* 36 (1982) 21-33; "Canon," *EncRel* 3, 62-69.

G. T. SHEPPARD

CAPPEL, LOUIS (1585–1658)

C. was born Oct. 15, 1585, at St. Elier near Sedan to a prominent French family that included several notable statesmen and scholars. After his father's death (1586) he was educated for a time by Roman Catholics before studying theology at Sedan, where he came into contact with the thought of the liberal, well-educated, Scottish-born theologian J. Cameron (c. 1579–1625). The Reformed Church of Bordeaux provided funds for C. to study for four years outside France. Two years (1610–12) were spent at Oxford, and some time was spent at Leiden. When he returned to France in 1613, he was appointed professor of Hebrew at the Academy of Saumur. Except for a few years in the early 1620s when war forced him to take refuge with his brother at Sedan, C. spent his career at Saumur, becoming professor of theology in 1626. He died there June 18, 1658; his son Jacques at age eighteen succeeded him as professor of Hebrew.

C.'s pioneering work in biblical criticism was produced during a time of extreme religious polemic and must be viewed in that light. In defense of the principle of *sola scriptura,* orthodox Protestant theologians had committed their position to a doctrine of scriptural infallibility that stressed the priority of the MT and the antiquity of the Masoretic vocalization and accentuation. New textual material in the form of the Samaritan Pentateuch (see PENTATEUCHAL CRITICISM)—written in archaic Hebrew characters and with significant textual variations from the MT—had been introduced into the textual debate by P. della Valle (1586–1652), who brought a copy to Europe from Damascus in 1616. At the Academy of Saumur a more liberal theology that challenged the Reformed doctrine of predestination was formulated by Cameron, M. Amyraut (1596–1664), and J. de la Place (1596–1655) and was met by widespread inter-Protestant polemic.

C.'s first major work was his *Arcanum punctationis,* which he sent to the elder J. BUXTORF, a staunch defender of the antiquity and pre-Christian origin of the Hebrew vowel points. Although C. had set out to work along Buxtorf's line, the latter recommended that C. not publish the work since the two men's conclusions differed radically; but Buxtorf never wrote a refutation of the book's argument that the Hebrew vowel pointing derived from the fifth century CE or later, a view held by most of the Reformers and expounded in detail by the Jewish scholar E. LEVITA in 1538. In 1624 T. Erpenius (1584–1624) published C.'s work anonymously in Leiden, contributing a preface. The work caused a furor among Protestants, who understood C.'s position to be an advocacy of the human origin of Scripture or at least of the Hebrew vocalization.

C.'s further work continued to raise conflict. In 1643 he published a volume that challenged F. Gomarus's (1563–1641) *Davidis Lyra* (1637), in which Gomarus had argued that Greek poetry derived from Hebrew and had outlined a theory of Hebrew verse structure (see POETRY, HB). When the younger J. Buxtorf (1599–1664) sought to refute him, C. responded with his *Vindiciae Arcani punctationis,* which was not, however, published until 1689 (in *Commentarii et nota*).

C.'s most significant work, which began a new era in biblical study, was his *Critica Sacra,* completed in 1634, but for which he could initially find no publisher because of Protestant opposition to the work. The treatise was eventually published in a slightly altered version in Paris through the assistance of J. MORIN, a Roman Catholic oriental scholar who had converted from the Reformed Church (as had C.'s oldest son, Jean) and had published works critical of the MT. *Critica Sacra* is composed of six books in which C. discussed the MT along the following lines: (1) internal variants among parallel texts in the HB; (2) variations between the HB text and NT citations; (3) variant readings reflected in the Masoretic *qeri* and *kethib;* (4) variations between the SEPTUAGINT and the MT; (5) variations among the MT, the TARGUMIM, ancient Greek versions, the VULGATE, and non-biblical Jewish writings; and (6) the use and utility of TEXTUAL CRITICISM. In his *Commentarii et nota,* several of C.'s exegetical studies show his textual criticism and his employment of a philological-annotative rather than theological commentary on the text.

C.'s work was epoch making, shifting the issues of textual criticism from the arena of theology to that of philology. The work of this Protestant, based partially on Jewish scholarship and supported by the Catholic Morin, represents one of the first examples of interconfessional scholarship. C. demonstrated that the Hebrew text of the HB had suffered corruption, how the versions and other evidence could be used to restore readings, and how on occasion the interpreter must resort to conjectural emendations. Although opposed by many of his fellow Protestants, who saw his work as advocating a human dimension to the biblical writings and who, against him, affirmed the INSPIRATION of the Hebrew vowel points in the Second Helvetic Consensus of 1675,

C. greatly influenced subsequent scholarship. In spite of his critical work he held a reasonably conservative attitude toward the Bible, arguing that although the Hebrew vocalization and accentuation of the text were late in developing, they were based on reliable tradition and that the content of the Bible contained the saving doctrine of the faith.

Works: *De sanctissimo Dei nomine Tetragrammato Jehovah, ac genuina ejus pronunciatione.... (1614); Arcanum punctationis.... (1624); Historia apostolica illustrata ex actis apostolorum et epistolis paulinis.... (1634); Ad novam Davidis lyram animadversiones cum gemina diatriba.... (1643); Le pivot de la Foy et Religion ou preuve de la Divinité contre les Athées et prophanes.... (1643; ET 1660); Diatriba de veris et antiquis Ebraeorum litteris opposita D. Ioh. Buxtorfii ab eodem argumento dissertationi (1645); Critica Sacra, sive de variis quae in sacris Veteris Testamenti libris occurrunt lectionibus Libri VI (1650); De Critica nuper a se edita ad reverendum et Doctissimum virum dom (1651); Chronologia sacra a condito Mundo ad eundem reconditum per Dominum Jesum Christum, atque inde ad ultimam Judaeorum per Romanos captivitatem deducta (1655); Commentarii et nota criticae in Vetus Testamentum.... Editionem procuravit Jacobus Cappellus (1689), with bibliography of C.'s works.*

Bibliography: B. G. Armstrong, *Calvinism and the Amyraut Heresy: Protestant Scholasticism and Humanism in Seventeenth-century France* (1969). **I. Baroway,** "The Lyre of David," *English Literary History* 8 (1941) 119-42. **S. G. Burnett,** "The Christian Hebraism of J. Buxtorf (1564–1629)" (diss., University of Wisconsin-Madison, 1990). **J. L. Kugel,** *The Idea of Biblical Poetry: Parallelism and Its History* (1981). **F. J. M. Laplanche,** *L'Écriture, le sacrè et l'histoire: Erudits et politiques protestants devant la Bible en France au XVIIe siècle* (SIB 12, 1986). **R. A. Muller,** "The Debate over the Vowel Points and the Crisis of Orthodox Hermeneutics," *JMRS* 10 (1980) 53-72; *MSHH* 22 (1733) 385-410. **B. Pick,** "The Vowel-Points Controversy in the XVI. and XVII. Centuries," *Hebraica* (= *AJSL*) 8 (1891–92) 150-73. **J.-P. Pittion,** "Intellectual Life in the Académie of Saumur (1633–1685)" (diss., University of Dublin, 1969). **J. F. Robinson,** "The Doctrine of Holy Scripture in the Seventeenth-century Reformed Theology" (diss., University of Strassbourg, 1971). **G. H. B. Schnedermann,** *Die Controverse des Ludovicus Cappellus mit den Buxtorfen über das Alter der hebräischen Punctation* (1879). **P. T. van Rooden,** *Theology, Biblical Scholarship and Rabbinical Studies in the Seventeenth Century* (Studies in the History of Leiden University 6, 1989). **F. P. van Stam,** *The Controversy over the Theology of Saumur, 1635–1650* (SIB 19, 1988).

J. H. HAYES

CARPZOV, JOHANN GOTTLOB (1679–1767)

Born Sept. 26, 1679, in Dresden, C. died Apr. 7, 1767, in Lübeck. He came from a learned Saxony family that had produced many orthodox Lutheran theologians. His father, Samuel Benedict (1647–1707), was court preacher in Dresden; his uncle Johann Benedict (1639–99) was an orientalist and theologian in Leipzig, and an opponent of the Pietists (see PIETISM) and of R. SIMON, against whose *Histoire critique* he wrote an inaugural address in 1684.

C. studied theology at Wittenberg, Leipzig, and Altdorf (1696–1701). In 1704 he became a deacon in the Kreuzkirche in Dresden, in 1714 archdeacon at the Thomaskirche in Leipzig, and in 1730 superintendent in Lübeck, where he sought to maintain the purity of the Lutheran Church from Roman Catholic, Reformed, and Pietistic elements, appealing to Lev 20:26 for justification. In 1713 he became *ausserordentlicher* professor at the university in Leipzig, and in 1724 he obtained a ThD with a disputation against W. WHISTON's "pseudo-criticism." This and other academic disputations are included in both his major works: the *Introductio* (on the individual books of the HB) and the *Critica sacra* (on text and translation), and also in the extensive annotations (predominantly concerning *realia*) to the Latin edition of T. Goodwin's (1587–1643) *Moses and Aaron: Civil and Ecclesiastical Rites Used by the Ancient Hebrews* (1685).

C.'s theological and personal mentor was the superintendent of Dresden, V. Löscher (1673–1749), the last great representative of Lutheran orthodoxy and an opponent of Pietism. The younger Buxtorf (Johannes B., 1599–1664) was a scholarly model for C. Like Buxtorf, who had written his *Anticritica* (1653) against the *Critica sacra* of L. CAPPEL (1650), C.'s major pursuit as a biblical scholar was "anticriticism." Without having any understanding of their justification or even necessity, he regarded all attacks against the full integrity and authenticity of the biblical text as dangerous for the Christian faith and repulsed them with a profusion of learned material. A major part of his works consists in polemics.

The decisive criterion in the *Critica sacra* was its differentiation from profane criticism. To treat both in the same way, as did J. LE CLERC, C. considered fatal. In his eyes the *Critica sacra* has to reckon from the very first and without any reservation with the INSPIRATION OF THE BIBLE, even extending to the vowel pointing in the HB. There can be no real contradictions in the text. Apparent contradictions can be eliminated, and wherever this appears too difficult one can assume that divine providence must have had a particular intent. Biblical information concerning the authorship of individual books must never be called into question.

Those in the eighteenth century who needed arguments against biblical criticism liked to consult C., hence his books were widely disseminated.

Works: *Introductio ad libros canonicos bibliorum Veteris Testamenti, omnes praecognita critica et historica ac autoritatis vindicias exponens* (3 vols., 1714–21, 1731[2], 1741[3]); *Critica sacra Veteris Testamenti* (1728, 1748[2]; ET of pt. 3, *A Defence of the HB in Answer to the Charge of Corruption Brought against it by Mr. Whiston* [1729]); *Apparatus historico criticus antiquitatum sacri Codicis et gentis Hebraeae, uberrimis annotationibus in Thomae Goodwini Mosen et Aaronem* (1748).

Bibliography: *AGL* 2 (1787) 133-36. **C. Siegfried,** *ADB* 4 (1876) 23-25. **R. Smend,** "Spätorthodoxe Antikritik: Zum Werk des J. G. C.," *Historische Kritik und biblischer Kanon in der deutschen Aufklärung* (Wolfenbütteler Forschungen 41, ed. H. G. Reventlow et al., 1988) 127-37; *Epochen der Bibelkritik* (1991) 33-42. **T. Wotschke,** "Briefe des Lübecker Superintendenten J. G. C.," *ZGSHG* 25 (1926) 414-49.

R. SMEND

CARTWRIGHT, THOMAS (1535–1603)

An English Puritan advocate of Presbyterianism, C. was educated at Cambridge and became Lady Margaret Professor of Divinity there in 1569; but he was deprived of the position the next year for his criticism of episcopacy. Thereafter he spent many years in the Low Countries, eventually returning to England, where he suffered several brief imprisonments for nonconformity.

In writing on polity he argued that while biblical warrant for every ceremony of the church is not necessary, generally the Word of God ought to direct church practice. Well known as a scholar of biblical languages, in 1583 he was encouraged by high government officials to write a refutation of the 1582 Roman Catholic Douay-Rheims English translation of the NT; he labored long at this, but in 1586 Archbishop Whitgift forbade its publication. Part of it was published in Scotland in 1602; but the whole was not published until 1618, after C.'s death. The work was a verse-by-verse refutation of both the translation and the annotations, completed through Revelation 15. His biblical scholarship was further evident in posthumous publications: Latin commentaries on Ecclesiastes and Proverbs, English commentaries on Colossians and Revelation, and a huge harmony of the Gospels aimed at reconciling all discrepancies. In a letter on biblical study, he called Deuteronomy "the fountain of the rest of scripture" and described the books of Daniel and Revelation as difficult to interpret.

Works: *Metaphrasis in Librum Solomonis, qui inscribitur Ecclesiastes* (1604); *A Commentary Upon the Epistle to the Colossians* (1612); *Commentarii succincti et dilucidi in Proverbia Solomonis* (1617); *A Confutation of the Rhemists Translation, Glosses and Annotations on the NT* (1618); *A Plaine Explanation of the Whole Revelation of Saint John* (1622); *Harmonia Evangelica* (1627).

Bibliography: **P. Lake,** *Anglicans and Puritans? Presbyterian and English Conformist Thought from Whitgift to Hooker*

(1988) 13-66. **J. B. Mullinger,** *DNB* 9 (1887) 226-30. **A. F. S. S. Pearson,** *T. C. and Elizabethan Puritanism* (1925).

D. D. WALLACE, JR.

CASAUBON, ISAAC (1559–1614)

A classical scholar and theologian, C. was born at Geneva, Feb. 18, 1559. At an early age he moved to France, where his father was pastor to a Huguenot congregation. In 1578 he returned to Geneva to complete his studies and became professor of Greek there. He held a similar position at Montpellier (1596–99), after which he moved to Paris, in 1605 becoming sublibrarian to Henry IV. Although under strong pressure to become Catholic, he remained Protestant. In 1610, after Henry IV's assassination, he moved to England, where he was befriended by L. Andrewes. James I had a high opinion of C.'s scholarship and gave him a prebend at Canterbury. He died July 1, 1614.

C. was a man of great learning who produced works, including critical editions and commentaries, on such Greek and Latin authors as Apuleius, Aristotle, Athenaeus, Diogenes Laertius, Persius, Polyaenus, Polybius, Strabo, Suetonius, Theocritus, and Theophrastus. C.'s notes on the NT were reprinted in CRITICI SACRI; however, his treatise on ecclesiastical freedom was suppressed on Henry IV's command. At the instigation of James I he engaged in controversy and wrote his *Exercitations* against Baronius, in which he argued that the Hermetic writings were, not ancient Egyptian works, but products of the Christian era.

C. exchanged correspondence with J. SCALIGER, H. GROTIUS, and J. ARMINIUS and shared with Grotius a desire to bring about a union between Protestants and Catholics. He was acknowledged as one of the greatest scholars of his day, and Scaliger called him "the most learned man in Europe" (M. Pattison [1892²] 64). His journal, *Ephemerides,* provides evidence of his industry and piety.

Works: *In Novi Testamenti Libros Notae* (1587); *De Satyrica Graecorum Poesi et Romanorum Satyra* (1605); *De Libertate Ecclesiastica* (1607); *De Rebus Sacris et Ecclesiasticis Exercitationes XVI: Ad Cardinalis Baronii Prolegomena in Annales.* . . . (1614); *Epistolae* (1709); *Ephemerides* (1850).

Bibliography: **T. J. van Almeloveen,** "Casauboni Vita," *Epistolae* (I. Casaubon, 1709). *BB²* 3 (1784) 301-6. **A. T. Grafton,** "Protestant Versus Prophet: I. C. on Hermes Trismegistus," *Journal of the Warburg and Courtauld Institutes* 46 (1983) 78-94. **J. Le Clerc,** *BC* 19 (1709) 208-40. *MSHH* 18 (1732) 118-47. **L. J. Nazelle,** *I. C., sa vie et son temps (1559–1614)* (1897, repr. 1970). **C. Nisard,** *Le triumvirat littéraire au XVIe siècle: J. Lipse, J. Scaliger, et I. C.* (1852, rep. 1970). **J. H. Overton,** *DNB* 9 (1887) 257-61. **M. Pattison,** *Isaac Casaubon* (1892²). **F. A. Yates,** *G. Bruno and the Hermetic Tradition* (1964) 398-403.

A. W. WAINWRIGHT

CASE, SHIRLEY JACKSON (1872–1947)

An NT scholar and early church historian, C. was born in Hatfield Point, New Brunswick, and received the BA (1893) and the MA (1896) from Acadia University. After receiving the BD (1904) and the PhD (1906) from Yale Divinity School, he was assistant professor of NT at the University of Chicago Divinity School (1908), professor of the history of early Christianity (1917), chair of church history (1923), and dean of the divinity school (1933–38). As president of the American Society of Church History (from 1924), he began regular publication of the journal *Church History.* He was president of the SOCIETY OF BIBLICAL LITERATURE and editor of the *Journal of Religion* (from 1927). In 1940 he became professor of religion at Florida Southern College and was dean of the Florida School of Religion in Lakeland until his death.

C.'s arrival at the University of Chicago marked the beginning of a shift in biblical studies, especially NT, from linguistic and philological perspectives to historical approaches. He may be regarded as the chief instigator of the famous Chicago socio-historical school, a center of attention until the early 1930s. For C., NT study "as socially conceived begins with emphasis upon the actual experience of the people who compose the Christian societies in NT" (1923, 32). Focusing on religious ideas, he intended to establish neither their uniqueness nor their honorable or disreputable origins but to judge "their functional significance in the life of the people by whom they had been espoused." He welcomed the rise of FORM CRITICISM, especially when it scrutinized social settings without concentrating on literary forms, as did such Germans as H. GUNKEL and R. BULTMANN.

C. denounced fundamentalists for a simplistic understanding of JESUS due to their refusal to attend to social contexts in Gospel materials. But he also rejected Bultmann's view that we can know almost nothing of Jesus' personality and inner life. C. believed in a continuity between the historical Jesus and the Christ of faith. Along with most other North American NT scholars prior to 1943 he chafed over the growing influence of K. BARTH and continental biblical THEOLOGY, believing that socio-historical analysis was the route to the Christ of faith.

Works: *The Historicity of Jesus* (1912); *The Evolution of Early Christianity* (1914); *The Social Origins of Christianity* (1923); *Jesus: A New Biography* (1927); *Experience with the Supernatural in Early Christianity* (1929); *The Social Triumph of the Ancient Church* (1933); *Makers of Early Christianity: From Jesus to Charlemagne* (1934); *The Christian Philosophy of History* (1943); "Education in Liberalism," *CATTA* 1:105-25 (autobiography with bibliography).

Bibliography: **C. H. Arnold,** *Near the Edge of the Battle* (1966). *DAB Supp* 4 (1974) 151-53. **W. J. Hynes,** "S. J. C.

and the Chicago School" (diss., University of Chicago, 1981). **L. B. Jennings,** *The Bibliography and Biography of S. J. C.* (1949).

T. H. OLBRICHT

CASPARI, WILHELM KARL ALFRED (1876–1947)

Born Nov. 3, 1876, the son of a clergyman, C. studied theology in Leipzig, Tübingen, and Erlangen. After his theological exams (1899) he served in the Evangelische Landeskirche in Bayern and was active as a vicar in Reichenhall and Augsburg. In 1903 he graduated from Erlangen with a PhD; after 1904 he worked as *Repetent* in theology at Erlangen while also teaching religion and Hebrew at the gymnasium. He earned the lic. theol. and the permission to teach in Erlangen in 1907, becoming *Privatdozent* in OT. In 1915 he was called to Breslau as *ausserordentlicher* professor and in 1922 as full professor at Kiel. He died Feb. 3, 1947.

C. was an original scholar who cannot be classified within any specific approach. He had reservations about LITERARY-critical work on the HB. Like other contributors to the KAT, he sought to join historical-critical exegesis and religio-historical work with a theologically conservative outlook. Adopting the form-critical method (see FORM CRITICISM) of H. GUNKEL and H. GRESSMANN, he used it in a deliberate manner. He often began his series of publications with works that were religion-historical (e.g., his 1903 work) and conceptual-historical (e.g., his study of *kbd*). The first HB scholar to investigate the concept and word *peace* (1910), he made the results of his scholarly studies accessible in popular form to a wide circle of readers (1916).

In dealing with historical questions the uniqueness of C.'s investigations consisted in joining historical themes with sociological and economic considerations. On the origin and crisis of the Israelite kingdom (1909), he depicted the conflicts between oligarchically composed local associations during the pre-monarchical period and the newly arisen central authority, with its demands and levies. He regarded the Absalom rebellion as an attempt of the local oligarchy to regain a position of power through a weak king and Sheba's revolt as an attempt to return to pre-monarchical conditions.

A disagreement with M. WEBER on the origin of Yahwistic religion led C. to write on God's community at Sinai (1922), affirming the sociological approach of Weber, but arguing against his results: Neither house nor tribe nor military confederation constituted the beginning of Yahwistic religion or preceded it; rather, it was the work of Moses at Sinai. In his commentary on Samuel, C. sought to retrace the origin of the books: the original individual stories and their parenetical and pedagogical transformation and compilation into a series up until the final form in the exilic and postexilic periods. However, the complexity of his depiction limits the commentary's usefulness.

C. called into question the existence of a prophet Deutero-Isaiah (1934). He explained the texts in Isaiah 40–55 as individual songs and divine sayings of diverse poets and visionaries with the purpose of encouraging Jews wanting to return from exile. This interpretation signaled an exaggeration of form-critical presuppositions and underestimated the uniqueness of Deutero-Isaiah.

Overall, C.'s work suffers from difficult and unclear diction, which often forces the reader to guess at what is meant. His influence has remained limited.

Works: *Die Religion der assyrisch-babylonischen Busspsalmen* (BFCT 7.4, 1903); *Die Bedeutungen der Wortsippe KBD im Hebräischen* (1908); *Die Bundeslade unter David* (1908); *Echtheit, Hauptbegriff, und Gedankengang der Messianischen Weissagung Jes. 9,1-6* (BFCT 12.4, 1908); *Aufkommen und Krise des israelitischen Königtums unter David* (1909); *Die Pharisäer bis an die Schwelle des Neuen Testaments* (1909); *Vorstellung und Wort "Friede" im Alten Testament* (BFCT 14.4, 1910); *Die israelitischen Propheten* (1914); *Der biblische Friedensgedanke nach dem Alten Testament* (1916); *Thronbesteigung und Thronfolge der israelitischen Könige* (1917); *Die Gottesgemeinde vom Sinai und das nachmalige Volk Israel* (BFCT 27.1, 1922); *Die Samuelbücher* (KAT 7, 1926); *Lieder und Gottessprüche der Rückwanderer (Jesaja 40–55)* (BZAW 65, 1934).

Bibliography: *EKL* 4 (1961) 365. **O. Rühle,** *RGG*[2] 1 (1927) 1468.

W. THIEL

CASSIODORUS, FLAVIUS MAGNUS AURELIUS (c. 485/90–c. 580)

C. was born into a Roman family that had continued in government service after Italy had come under Ostrogothic control. C. himself held various posts, including that of praetorian prefect—a sort of prime minister—under Athalaric. Sometime between 537 and 540 he retired from public life, prepared his letters, the *Varia,* for publication, and began a treatise on the soul, *De Anima,* which drew heavily but not exclusively on AUGUSTINE.

C. spent some time in Byzantium; the dates and circumstances are uncertain, but by 562 he was back in Italy. In Byzantium he became acquainted with the *Instituta regularia divinae legis* of Junilius Africanus and brought a copy back to Italy with him, thus introducing the basic handbook of ANTIOCHENE exegesis into the West. At the same time he was at work on a Psalms commentary, *Expositio Psalmorum.*

As Christian scholar and savant C. settled on his family estate to direct a monastic enterprise, Vivarium, modeled loosely on the Nestorian theological school at Nisibis and dedicated to a scholarly as well as a monastic way of life. He built a considerable library, oversaw the translation of some key Greek texts into Latin (including Josephus, Chrysostom's homilies on Hebrews, and *Historia ecclesiastica tripartita* taken from Socrates, Sozomen, and Theodoret), and continued his own writing. He completed his last major work, *De orthographia*, when he was ninety-three.

C.'s *Expositio Psalmorum* was intended to be a shorter and more orderly treatment of Psalms than Augustine's *Enarrationes in Psalmos*. C. made heavy but not slavish use of Augustine, also drawing on JEROME and less heavily on other patristic commentators. C. considered David the human author of every psalm but thought most of the psalter was either spoken by Christ or related directly to him. Psalms, then, was a compendium of Christian doctrine and spiritual teaching; but it also contained much secular learning and could serve as a resource for the liberal arts.

Three other of C.'s works had to do with biblical studies. His *Institutiones,* an introduction to sacred and secular learning written to guide the studies of the monks at Vivarium, provides an indispensable view of the state of learning during the sixth century. The very late *Complexiones in Epistulas* provides brief and rather stereotyped commentary on all of the NT materials except the Gospels. Finally, C. had obtained an anonymous copy of PELAGIUS's Pauline commentaries (see PAUL). Recognizing the Pelagian bent of the work, although he did not deduce that the author was Pelagius himself, C. revised the Romans section, inserting other authors, notably Augustine, into the Pelagian text, then assigned his students to complete the task of expurgation. This work was mistakenly attibuted to Primasius of Hadrumertum during the sixteenth century.

The *Expositio Psalmorum* was the most widely used of C.'s biblical works. It was the only patristic commentary on the entire psalter aside from Augustine's and circulated throughout Europe until it was superseded by the GLOSSA ORDINARIA. C.'s scholarly handbook, the *Institutiones,* was very quickly separated into its biblical and liberal-arts components, which for the most part were circulated separately. The influence of the *Complexiones* was apparently minimal; it survives in only one manuscript from the sixth century. The Pelagius revision was known to Zmaragdus under the name of Pelagius, to Sedulius Scottus as the work of ISIDORE, and to Claudius of Turin and Haymo of Auxerre anonymously.

Works: *Complexiones in Epistolas* (*PL* 70, 1309-1422); *Opera Omnia* (*PL* 69-70); *Cassiodori Senatoris Institutiones* (ed. R. A. B. Mynors, 1937); *Historia ecclesiastica tripartita* (CSEL 71, ed. W. Jacob and R. Hanslik, 1952); *Expositio Psalmorum* (CCSL 97-98, ed. M. Adriaen, 1958); *Institutiones: An Introduction to Divine and Human Readings* (ed. and intro. L. W. Jones, 1966); *De Anima* (CCSL 96, ed. J. W. Halporn, 1973); *Variae* (CCSL 96, ed. A. J. Fridh, 1973); *Cassiodorus: Explanation of the Psalms* (ACW 51-53, ed. P. G. Walsh, 1990). The

Pelagius revision may be found as *Primasii Commentaria in Epistolas S. Pauli* (*PL* 68, 417-794).

Bibliography: **G. Bardy,** "Cassiodore et la fin du monde ancienne," *Année theologique* 6 (1945) 383-425. **M. J. Cappuyns,** "Cassiodore," *DHGE* 11 (1949) 1349-408. **U. Hahner,** *Cassiodors Psalmenkommentar: Sprachliche Untersuchungen* (Münchener Beiträge zur Mediävistik und Renaissance-Forschung 13, 1973). **D. W. Johnson,** "Purging the Poison: The Revision of Pelagius' Pauline Commentaries by Cassiodorus and His Students" (diss., Princeton Theological Seminary, 1989). **M. L. W. Laistner,** *Thought and Letters in Western Europe,* AD 500–900 (1957). **J. J. O'Donnell,** *Cassiodorus* (1979). **R. Schlieben,** "Cassiodors Psalmenexegese: Eine Analyse ihrer Methoden als Beitrag zur Untersuchung der Geschichte der Bibelauslegung der Kirchenväter und der Verbindung christlicher Theologie mit antiker Schulwissenschaft" (diss., Tübingen, 1970); *Christliche Theologie und Philologie in der Spätantike: Die schulwissenschaftliche Methoden der Psalmenexegese Cassiodors* (Arbeiten zur Kirchengeschichte 46, 1974). **A. van de Vyver,** "Cassiodore et son oeuvre," *Speculum* 6 (1931) 244-92.

D. W. JOHNSON

CASSUTO, UMBERTO MOSES DAVID (1883–1951)

An Italian historian and a biblical and Semitic scholar, C. was born in Florence and educated simultaneously at the University of Florence and at the rabbinical seminary under the formative influence of S. Margulies. Ordained a rabbi, he taught at the seminary and served as secretary and assistant rabbi of the Jewish community.

At Margulies' death in 1922, C. succeeded him in the rabbinate and as director of the seminary. In 1925 he became professor of Hebrew language and literature at the University of Florence, leaving the field of Italian-Jewish history to concentrate on biblical studies. He was appointed to the University of Rome in 1933 and while there catalogued the Hebrew manuscripts of the Vatican Library.

In 1939 he left Fascist Italy and accepted a position at the Hebrew University, Jerusalem, where he continued publishing on biblical, Ugaritic (see UGARIT AND THE BIBLE), and oriental topics. Although he was conservative, even reactionary toward documentary criticism of the Pentateuch (see PENTATEUCHAL CRITICISM), his commentaries are filled with philological and aesthetic insights into the text. He served as editor-in-chief of the Hebrew biblical encyclopedia *Enziklopedyah Mikra'it* (see DICTIONARIES AND ENCYCLOPEDIAS).

Works: *La questione della Genesi* (1934); *Documentary Hypothesis and the Composition of the Pentateuch* (1941; ET 1961); *A Commentary on the Book of Genesis* (2 vols., 1944–49; ET 1961–64); *A Commentary on the Book of Exodus* (1951;

ET 1967); *The Goddess Anath* (1951; ET 1970); *Biblical and Oriental Studies* (2 vols., 1973–75).

Bibliography: I. Abrahams, *EncJud* 5 (1971) 234-36. *EI* 3 (1954). **The Hebrew University** (ed.), *Le Zikhro shel M. D. Cassuto*. . . . (1952).

D. G. HUNTER

CASTELL, EDMUND (1606–85)

Born into a well-to-do family at Tadlow by East Hatley, Cambridgeshire, C. attended Emmanuel College, Cambridge, where he acquired the BA (1625), MA (1628), BD (1635), and DD (1661) and served as professor of Arabic from 1667. He worked on Walton's London Polyglott (see POLYGLOTS), being responsible for the Samaritan, Syriac, Arabic, and Ethiopic versions (see ETHIOPIAN INTERPRETATION). In 1651 he began work on his *Lexicon Heptaglotton* of Hebrew, Aramaic (Chaldean), Syriac, Samaritan, Ethiopic, Arabic, and Persian, conceived as a sequel and supportive work to the Polyglott, and in 1661 moved to St. John's College because of its better library. Published in two folio volumes in 1669, the LEXICON cost C. dearly in personal funds and labor. Although it marked a milestone in Semitic scholarship, it sold slowly in England; and C. never recouped his investment. At his death over 500 copies remained unsold. The Syriac material in the volume was published separately by J. D. MICHAELIS (2 vols., 1778), as was the Hebrew (2 vols., 1790–92).

Other than the lexicon, to which such scholars as J. LIGHTFOOT contributed, C. wrote little else. His last years were spent serving churches in Essex and Bedfordshire.

Works: *Lexicon Heptaglotten, Hebraicum, Chaldaicum, Syriacum, Samaritanum, Aethiopicum, Arabicum, conjunctim, et Persicum separatim* (2 vols., 1669).

Bibliography: *BB*² 3 (1784) 310-11. **S. Lane-Poole,** *DNB* 9 (1887) 271-72.

J. H. HAYES

CASTELLIO, SEBASTIAN (1515–63)

Of humble parentage, C. (Châtillon, Chateillon, or Castalio) was born in St.-Martin-du-Fresne, Savoy, and studied at the Collége de la Trinité in Lyon, early on showing proficiency in Greek and Hebrew. In 1540 in Strasbourg he was converted to Protestantism by CALVIN, who subsequently invited him to Geneva as a teacher. C.'s strongly humanistic tendencies brought him into conflict with Calvin over the doctrines of election, predestination, and Christ's descent into hell, as well as over C.'s translation of the Bible and his view of the non-canonicity of the Song of Songs. About 1544, after

being denied ordination, he fled to Basel, where he worked with the publisher J. Oporin until appointed a professor of Greek at the university in 1553.

After the burning of M. SERVETUS (Oct. 27, 1553) at Geneva, C. became involved in a bitter controversy with Calvin and T. BEZA, arguing that heresy should not be treated as a criminal offense. He maintained that absolute certainty in religion could not be expected and that uncertainties and differences over biblical interpretation should be tolerated, since the Bible is occasionally obscure and opaque. His stand against intolerance in religious matters has earned him much respect over the years.

C. produced several biblical works, the most important being his translation of the Bible (1551) in a Latin aiming at classical eloquence. This edition, dedicated to Edward VI of England, was highly popular and frequently reprinted. Most of its notations were reproduced in the CRITICI SACRI (1660). A French version of his Latin Bible was written in the popular vernacular of the day. In addition he published editions of various classical authors (Herodotus, Diodorus, Homer, Thucydides) as well as editions of *Theologica Germanica* and *Imitatio Christi* and a Latin verse version of the SIBYLLINE ORACLES.

Works: *Psalterium reliquaque sacrarum literarum carmina et precationes* (1547); *Biblia Veteris et Novi Testamenti ex versione Sebast. Castalionis, cum ejusdem annotationibus* (1551; FT 1555); *De haereticis an sint persequendi* (1554; ET, ed. and tr. with additional material by R. H. Bainton, 1935); *Defensio suarum translationum Bibliorum et maxime Novi Faederis* (1562); *Dialoqi IV de praedistinatione, electione, libero arbitrio, ac fide* (1578).

Bibliography: R. A. Bainton et al., *Castellioniana* (1951). M. Bossard, "Le vocabulaire de la Bible française de Castellion (1555)," *Études de Lettres* (Lausanne) 2, 2 (1959) 61-86. F. Bouisson, *Sébastien Castellion, sa vie et son oeuvre (1515–1563): Étude sur les origines du protestantisme libéral français* (2 vols., 1892). H. R. Guggisberg, *Sebastian Castellio im Urteil seiner Nachwelt vom Späthumanismus bis zur Aufklärung* (BBGW 57, 1956); *TRE* 7 (1981) 663-65. E. Keller, "Castellios Übertragung der Bibel ins Französische," *Romanische Forschungen* 71 (1959) 383-403. H. Liebing, "Die Schriftauslegung Sebastian Castellios," *Humanismus-Reformation- Konfession* (ed. W. Biernert and W. Hage, 1986) 11-124. R. H. Popkin, *The History of Scepticism from Erasmus to Spinoza* (1979²) 8-14.

J. H. HAYES

CAUSSE, ANTONIN (1877–1947)

An important twentieth-century French Protestant OT scholar, C. integrated the study of Israelite religion with the canons of French sociological method (see SOCIOLOGY AND HB STUDIES), particularly as developed by E. Durkheim and L. Lévy-Bruhl. Born May 1, 1877, in the south of France near Montauban, he graduated from the Protestant seminary there in 1900 with the Bachelier en Théologie degree. In seminary he was greatly influenced by A. Westphal and C. Bruston, who shaped his interest in biblical studies and the historical-critical method.

C. studied in Germany at Halle and Berlin under A. von HARNACK, H. GUNKEL, and H. GRESSMANN. Gunkel and Gressmann greatly influenced his view of the Pentateuch (see PENTATEUCHAL CRITICISM), the psalms, and eschatology. In 1902 he accepted a parish at Segonzac Charente but continued his studies and completed the Licencié en Théologie degree and received a doctorate in OT from the University of Geneva under the eminent OT scholar, L. Gautier. His doctoral thesis (1913) explored the relationship of Yahwism to the religions of the orient and precipitated an invitation to join the Faculté de Théologie of the University of Strasbourg, where he taught OT until his death in 1947.

At Strasbourg C. founded the *RHPR,* became its editor, and began a lifelong pattern of publishing series of articles that later appeared in book form. His writings cover a broad spectrum of subjects: Pentateuch, prophets (see PROPHECY AND PROPHETS, HB), Hebrew POETRY, Wisdom, apocalyptic (see APOCALYPTICISM), eschatology, intertestamental history and literature, history of religions (see RELIGIONSGESCHICHTLICHE SCHULE), and mystery religions. His focus was primarily sociological; he was one of the first OT scholars to attempt a sociological analysis of Israelite religion. He was neither a disciple of nor heavily dependent on the German sociologist M. WEBER, independently of whom C. suggested some broad outlines of the social history of Israelite religion in a volume on the poor in Israel (1922). Two additional works in 1924 and 1929 continued these explorations and culminated in 1937 with the most important volume of his scholarly career, which ranks with J. PEDERSEN's *Israel,* Weber's *Ancient Judaism,* and the works of A. LODS in importance for OT sociological studies.

C. was the first competent OT scholar to develop a broad synthesis of Israel's social evolution, drawing on the works of Durkheim, Lévy-Bruhl, Pedersen, Weber, and J. FRAZER. He integrated sociological and psychological method (see PSYCHOLOGY AND BIBLICAL STUDIES) and data with an evolutionary explanation of Israel's life, thought, and literature and a vast knowledge of comparative religion and scholarship. In his 1937 work he traced Israel's development from clans and tribes to a religious community whose cohesive center is torah. However, his investigation of external and internal forces and their effect on the development of Israel's life, thought, and societal structure was viewed by many as hampered by a rather mechanical understanding of the transition from primitive or pre-logical mentality to logical mentality, with the rise of the monarchy in Israel supposedly paralleling a similar transition in fifth-

century BCE Greece. Unquestionably C. did not depart enough from a deterministic, linear view; it is clear that ancient Israel often broke the pattern of pre-logical thinking even prior to the monarchy. Nonetheless, his effort to engage sociological science with the process of historical synthesis gives his work lasting significance.

C.'s research did not have a major influence on OT studies because of factors related to the social location of knowledge and lacunae in his own sources. He bypassed a number of primary directions that OT studies followed: A. ALT's 1929 work on the patriarchs, M. NOTH's 1930 work on the tribal league, W. EICHRODT's development of the idea of covenant in his 1933 OT THEOLOGY, and Gunkel's form-critical studies (see FORM CRITICISM, HB), which broke with J. WELLHAUSEN's approach and carried OT scholarship in new directions.

Interestingly, however, much of the work of some of the above-mentioned scholars, considered germinal to historical critical method, has now eroded in influence. In that light, perhaps, it will be possible to discover C. from a new perspective and to realize that, although his sociological analysis may suffer from occasional arbitrary conceptualization, the historical synthesis he presented is of primary importance and has now come of age. His analysis of the historical background and the development of Israelite life, thought, and society does not seek to establish historicity based on analogy or utilization of central ideas, e.g., *Heilsgeschichte.* Instead, C. "was a precursor of what might be called 'the intellectual history of the OT'; in other words, a historical view from which one seeks not merely the establishment of the origin of historical phenomena, but the careful scrutiny of such phenomena within given periods of time and contexts in the light of both internal and external forces that may have precipitated them or influenced their development" (S T Kimbrough [1978] 139). It is from this perspective that his works should be read.

Works: *Les Prophètes d'Israël et les Religions de l'Orient: Essai sur les origines du monothéisme universaliste* (1913); *Les pauvres d'Israël* (1922); *Israël et la vision de l'humanité* (1924); *Les dispersés d'Israël* (1929); *Du groupe ethnique à la communaté religieuse: Le problem sociologique de la réligion d'Israël* (1937).

Bibliography: S T **Kimbrough, Jr.,** *Israelite Religion in Sociological Perspective: The Work of A. C.* (SOR 4, 1978).

S T KIMBROUGH, JR.

CELSUS (late 2nd cent.)

An eclectic Greek philosopher, C. wrote *True Doctrine,* attacking Christianity, answered in *Contra Celsum* by ORIGEN (c. 248), who preserved most of C.'s work in direct quotes in his eight-book reply. Often satirical and sometimes witty, C. attacked the HB, especially Genesis and its account of creation and early history, the Gospels' depiction of JESUS, and many of the basic beliefs of early Christians. For C. the idea that God created so much on one day and so much more on another (*Con. Cel.* 6:60) was absurd. He accused the Jews of being backward, uneducated people, Egyptian in origin (3:5), who had woven together incredible, insipid, and often borrowed stories and myths (see MYTHOLOGY AND BIBLICAL STUDIES) and had twisted the story of Deucalion in their account of the flood (4:36). Arguing that Jesus was a charlatan sorcerer who had learned magic in Egypt and given himself the title Son of God (1:38), C. challenged the doctrine of the incarnation (4:2) and the idea of the virgin birth; offered his own explanation of Jesus' parentage (1:28-32), baptism (1:41) and resurrection (2:55); and argued that Christianity was an apostasy from Judaism, a novelty without claim to antiquity (2:4; 5:33), and a possible threat to Roman government (8:2, 17, 73, 75).

Works: *Origène: Contre Celse* (M. Barret, SC 132, 136, 147, 150, 227, 1967–76); *Origen: Contra Celsum* (H. Chadwick, 1980); *Celsus, On the True Doctrine: A Discourse Against the Christians* (R. J. Hoffman, 1986).

Bibliography: C. Andersen, *Logos und Nomos: Die Polemik des Kelsos wider das Christentum* (1955). **M. Borret,** "Celsus: A Pagan Perspective on Scripture," *The Bible in Greek Christian Antiquity* (BTA 1, ed. P. M. Blowers, 1997) 259-88. **G. Burke,** "Celsus and Late Second-century Christianity" (diss., University of Iowa, 1981); "Celsus and the OT," *VT* 36 (1986) 241-45. **E. V. Gallagher,** *Divine Man or Magician? Celsus and Origen on Jesus* (SBLDS 64, 1982). **R. M. Grant,** *Greek Apologists of the Second Century* (1988) 133-39, 227-28. **R. J. Hauck,** *The More Divine Proof: Prophecy and Inspiration in Celsus and Origen* (AARAS 69, 1989). **K. Pichler,** *Streit um das Christentum: Der Angriff des Kelsos und die Antwort des Origenes* (1980). **W. Völker,** *Das Bild vom nichtgnostischen Christentum bei Celsus* (1928). **R. L. Wilken,** *The Christians as the Romans Saw Them* (1984) 94-125.

J. H. HAYES

CERFAUX, LUCIEN (1883–1968)

Born in Presles, Belgium, June 14, 1883, C. entered seminary to prepare for Roman Catholic priesthood. He obtained doctorates in both philosophy (1903–6) and theology (1906–10) in Rome's Gregorian University and was ordained priest Aug. 9, 1908. After study in Rome's Pontifical Biblical Institute (1910–11), he was named professor of sacred Scripture in the seminary at Tournai, where L. de Grandmaison (1868–1927) was a major influence. C. was appointed instructor at the Catholic University of Louvain (1928), professor (1930), and professor emeritus (1954). Thereafter he offered courses at the Lateran University in Rome and gave occasional lectures on the NT in Brussels until his death, Aug. 11, 1968.

C. was founding editor of *Studia Hellenistica,* served on the editorial board of *Ephemerides Theologicae Lovanienses* (1934–64), and with J. COPPENS established *Colloquium Biblicum Lovaniense.* In 1941 he was named consultor to the Pontifical Biblical Commission and used the position to promote historical-critical methods of exegesis. His influence on Roman Catholic NT scholarship was important following WWII. During Vatican Council II, C. served as a theological expert (*peritus*).

Before 1936 C. studied the NT environment; unlike many of his Roman Catholic contemporaries, he was convinced the NT must be interpreted within its authentic historical context. The works of W. BOUSSET and W. von BAUDISSIN prompted him to write several important articles on the significance of *Kyrios* as a christological title. C. studied the influence on Judaism of the mystery religions, Essenism, and various Near Eastern baptist sects. This period of interest in the history-of-religions approach (see RELIGIONSGESCHICHTLICHE SCHULE) concluded with a major study on Gnosis, which appeared in *DBSup* 3 (1936). His work on Gnosticism (see GNOSTIC INTERPRETATION) was continued by his student J. Dupont (b. 1915).

After 1936 C.'s principal interest and his greatest contribution to NT scholarship was his work on the writings of PAUL and on the Acts of the Apostles. A trilogy of works in French, translated into various languages and published over a twenty-year period, focused on the church (1942), Christ (1951), and the Christian in the theology of Paul (1962). His careful TEXTUAL analysis and comparison of the Pauline material in order to present Paul's own thought was at the time somewhat revolutionary within Roman Catholic circles.

C. also published one of the first Roman Catholic works showing the importance of oral tradition for the development of the Gospels (1946). His last major work, published posthumously (1968), also espoused a form-critical approach to the Gospels (see FORM CRITICISM).

Works: "Gnose (préchretienne et néotestamentaire)," *DBSup* 3 (1936) 659-701; *La théologie de l'Église suivant saint Paul* (Unam Sanctam 10, 1942); *La voix vivante de l'Évangile au debut de l'Église* (1946); *Une lecture de l'Épître aux Romains* (1947); "Kyrios," *DBSup* 5 (1950) 200-228; *Le Christ dans la théologie de saint Paul* (LD 6, 1951); *Le chrétien dans la théologie paulinienne* (LD 33, 1962); *Receuil Lucien Cerfaux* (BETL 6, 1954; 7, 1954; 71, repr. with Cerfaux's full bibliography, 1985); *Jésus aux origines de la tradition* (1968).

Bibliography: R. F. Collins, *LouvSt* 5 (1974–75) 298-305. **J. Coppens,** "La carrière et l'oeuvre scientifiques de Msgr. L.

C.," *L'évangile de Luc* (ed. F. Neirynck, BETL 32, 1973) 23-59.
A. Descamps, "Msgr. L. C.: Ébauche d'un portrait," *L'évangile de Luc* (ed. F. Neirynck, BETL 32, 1973) 9-21.

R. F. COLLINS

CHARLES, ROBERT HENRY (1855–1931)

Born Aug. 6, 1855, in Cookstown, Ireland, C. studied at Queen's College, Belfast (BA 1877; MA 1880), and at Trinity College, Dublin. He was ordained deacon (1883) and priest (1884) then served three curacies in London (1883–89). He spent a year in Germany, where he began studies of intertestamental literature especially. He returned to England and settled in Oxford, incorporating at Exeter College in 1891 and becoming a fellow of Merton College in 1910. His service to the church continued, however: In 1913 he was appointed a canon of Westminster and in 1919 he became archdeacon, both positions requiring that he preach. Severely injured in an accident in 1929, he died Jan. 30, 1931.

While in Germany after leaving his last curacy, C. studied A. DILLMANN's work on 1 ENOCH and began acquiring the daunting philological tools that were to be his trademark for the remainder of his career. His formal education had given him a knowledge of the classical languages and of Hebrew, but he later learned Aramaic and Armenian and became a master of Ethiopic (see ETHIOPIAN BIBLICAL INTERPRETATION). He noted that existing editions of apocalyptic (see APOCALYPTICISM) or pseudepigraphic (see PSEUDEPIGRAPHA) texts did not reflect the full range of manuscript traditions and demonstrated his linguistic brilliance in his editions of the Ethiopic book of JUBILEES (1895), Ethiopic or *1 Enoch* (1906), and the Greek TESTAMENTS OF THE TWELVE PATRIARCHS (1908). All remain valuable tools of study, having thirty to fifty detailed textual notes per page. C. worked with translations or translations of translations that often required him to reconstruct lost models; and in this endeavor he could be most impressive, although his work is frequently marred by what today seems too great an eagerness to emend existing texts or posit interpolations and sources. His most visible monument is the 1913 Oxford *Apocrypha and Pseudepigrapha of the OT.* As general editor of this two-volume work, he wrote the general introduction, supplied translations of *Jubilees,* the *Martyrdom of Isaiah, 1 Enoch,* the *Testaments of the Twelve Patriarchs,* the *Assumption of Moses,* 2 BARUCH, and the *Fragments of a Zadokite Work,* and he apparently wrote the notes for the translation of 2 ENOCH. C.'s editions and translations of pseudepigraphic texts became standards reference works, and he was recognized as the greatest authority of his day.

C.'s life work centered on what he considered apocalyptic texts. Although he is better known for his labors with non-canonical books (see CANON OF THE BIBLE), he wrote extended and detailed commentaries on Daniel and Revelation and synthesized his findings about the apocalypses in his Jowett lectures (1899, 1913[2]). He traced the roots and early developments of eschatological expectations and related beliefs in the HB and then described their flowering in the apocalypses written between 200 BCE and 100 CE. He attributed great importance to the work of the Hasidim (from whom he traced the Pharisees; see HASIDISM) in the evolution of teachings regarding a messianic kingdom and the resurrection of the dead. C. concluded that there had been two forms of pre-Christian Pharisaism: apocalyptic, from which Christianity would spring; and legalistic, from which talmudic Judaism (see TALMUD) would be born. Few follow him on this point today, but all agree that his work of collecting, describing, and analyzing apocalyptic texts greatly advanced work in a field that had been too long neglected.

Works: *The Book of Enoch* (1893); *Mashafa Kufālē or the Ethiopic Version of the Hebrew Book of Jubilees* (1895); *The Apocalypse of Baruch* (1896); *The Assumption of Moses* (1897); *A Critical History of the Doctrine of a Future Life, in Israel, Judaism, and Christianity* (Jowett Lectures, 1899, 1913[2]); *The Ascension of Isaiah* (1900); *The Book of Jubilees or the Little Genesis* (1902); *The Ethiopic Version of the Book of Enoch* (1906); *The Greek Versions of the Testaments of the Twelve Patriarchs* (1908); *The Book of Enoch or 1 Enoch* (1912); *Fragments of a Zadokite Work* (1912); (ed.) *The Apocrypha and Pseudepigrapha of the OT in English* (2 vols., 1913); *Religious Development Between the Old and the New Testaments* (1914); *The Chronicle of John, Bishop of Nikiu* (1916); *A Critical and Exegetical Commentary on the Revelation of St. John* (2 vols., ICC, 1920); *Lectures on the Apocalypse* (Schweich Lectures, 1922); *The Decalogue* (Warburton Lectures, 1923); *A Critical and Exegetical Commentary on the Book of Daniel* (1929); *Courage, Truth, Purity* (1931).

Bibliography: F. C. **Burkitt,** *PBA* 17 (1931) 437-45. **T. W. Manson,** *DNB Supp.* 5 (1949) 169-70. **C. F. D'Arcy,** "A Brief Memoir," *Courage, Truth, Purity* (R. H. Charles, 1931) xiii-xxxv.

J. C. VANDERKAM

CHAUCER, GEOFFREY (c. 1340–1400)

Generally recognized as one of the four or five most eminent poets of the English language, C. is, with Dante (1265–1321) and J. MILTON, one of the most eminently Christian poets in world literature. Born about 1340, he was a contemporary of J. WYCLIF and for a significant period both were in the patronage of John of Gaunt, the Duke of Lancaster, regent protector of Richard II during the latter's minority. C. thus had his principal *societas* at court and numbered among his acquaintances supporters of Wyclif's reforming ideas and ranking members of the university and theological communities. By the time of his death, Oct. 25, 1400, he had established himself for more than thirty years as the court laureate and was regarded by his peers as a poet of wise moral and spiritual counsel.

C.'s major poetry shows unusually pervasive indebtedness to the Bible. He was richly familiar with a wide range of biblical commentary: the major incorporated glosses like those found in the margins of medieval Bibles, e.g., the GLOSSA ORDINARIA and the various *postillae* of NICHOLAS OF LYRA; the exegesis of many patristic authors, e.g., AUGUSTINE, GREGORY THE GREAT, and JEROME; and the work of commentators, usually in the Augustinian tradition, closer to his own time, e.g., BONAVENTURE, T. Bradwardine (1295–1349), R. Holcot (d. 1349), and BERNARD OF CLAIRVAUX. The maturity of his scriptural knowledge is perhaps most richly displayed in *The Canterbury Tales*. The framework for this long work is a group pilgrimage undertaken as an act of penitence in which representatives of society at large travel from London, their "worldly city," toward Canterbury, figuratively the journey from Babylon to Jerusalem, in which obtuseness to the Spirit and literal-mindedness in approaching the precepts of Scripture are progressively challenged by more consistent applications of biblical truth. The tale pilgrim C. gives "himself" in the poem is a densely woven fabric of citations from Proverbs structured around a "Lady Wisdom's" instruction of her intemperate husband concerning how evil in the world is to be dealt with by the Christian. Various other units (e.g., Wife of Bath's Prologue, Miller's Tale, Friar's Tale, Summoner's Tale, Pardoner's Tale) pivot on a central biblical text; and the whole concludes with a treatise "sermon" on repentence. The principal text is Jer 6:6, but the sermon is interwoven with scores of passages from both testaments. The parson who "preaches" it is an exemplary interpreter of Scripture, a "poor priest" who serves the Word straightforwardly (and whom some of his fellow travelers suspect of being a Lollard).

All of C.'s major works make use of apt biblical allusion: *The Book of the Duchess, The House of Fame, The Parliament of Fowls,* and *Troilus and Criseyde.* John 8:32 is the evident text to which the reader is directed in his poem "Truth." But it is *The Canterbury Tales* that most extensively declares his love of Scripture and commitment to its guidance for himself and the nation for which he wrote his poetry as a counsel of wisdom.

Works: *The Complete Works of G. C.* (ed. F. N. Robinson and L. D. Benson, 1988).

Bibliography: L. Besserman, *Chaucer and the Bible: Critical Review of Research* (GRLH 839, 1988). **D. L. Jeffrey** (ed.), *Chaucer and Scriptural Tradition* (1984).

D. L. JEFFREY

CHEYNE, THOMAS KELLY (1841–1915)

Born Sept. 18, 1841, C. was educated at Worcester College, Oxford, and at Göttingen under H. EWALD. He was ordained in 1864 and became vice-principal of St. Edmund Hall, remaining there until 1868 when he gained a Semitic fellowship at Balliol College, a position he held until 1882. Rector of Tendring in Essex (1880–85), he became in 1884 a member of the HB revision company that produced the RV. He was Oriel Professor of the Interpretation of Holy Scripture at Oxford and canon of Rochester Cathedral (1885–1908). C. suffered from bad health all his life and from 1883 had sight in only one eye. He died Feb. 16, 1915.

C. was one of the early mediators of the critical approach to the HB in Britain, along with S. DRIVER and W. R. SMITH. His studies in Germany clearly had a decisive effect on his approach to biblical criticism; and Ewald in particular influenced him, especially in C.'s early work on Isaiah (1870). The book of Isaiah remained one of the dominant interests of his life; and he published additional studies in 1880–81, 1895, and 1912.

Another special interest was the psalms, on which C. published works in 1888 and 1891, the latter originally delivered as the Bampton lectures in Oxford in 1889. In this work he consigned the entire psalter to the postexilic period with the exception of Psalm 18. Perhaps C.'s most valuable book today is his 1893 work with its interesting comments on earlier and contemporary HB scholars as well as the light it sheds on his own outlook. Another of his more valuable studies was his book on HB wisdom literature (1887).

C. edited with J. Black the four volumes of the *Encyclopaedia Biblica* (1899–1903) to which he contributed many articles. In general a fine piece of work, it exhibits, however, the beginnings of the wild and bizarre notions that were to dominate C.'s work after 1900. Expanding the notion of the German scholar H. WINCKLER that Mizraim in the HB is often the name of a north Arabian kingdom of Muṣri rather than Egypt, as had previously been supposed, C. came to the view that Mizraim in the HB regularly denotes this postulated north Arabian kingdom. He believed that it was from this kingdom that the Israelites were delivered in the exodus. Near Muṣri, in the Negeb, there dwelt the Ishmaelite tribe of the Jerahmeelites, who (C. claimed) also worshiped a god called Jerahmeel. In the MT the Jerahmeelites are mentioned only a few times; C., however, produced vast numbers of textual emendations in order to find allusions to them all through the HB. He saw Jerahmeel and the neighboring kingdoms as the seat of hostility to the Jews. He claimed that they were the object of complaint in many of the psalms and also believed that the bulk of the exiles went to north Arabia rather than to Babylon.

Works: *Notes and Criticisms on the Hebrew Text of Isaiah* (1868); *The Book of Isaiah Chronologically Arranged* (1870); *The Prophecies of Isaiah* (2 vols., 1880–81, 1884³); *The Book of Psalms* (1884); *Job and Solomon* (1887); *The Origin and Religious Contents of the Psalter* (1891); *Founders of OT Criticism* (1893); *Introduction to the Book of Isaiah* (1895); *Jewish Religious Life After the Exile* (1898); (ed. with J. S. Black), *Encyclopaedia Biblica* (4 vols., 1899–1903); *Critica Biblica* (1903); *Traditions and Beliefs of Ancient Israel* (1907); *The Decline and Fall of the Kingdom of Judah* (1908); *The Two Religions of Israel* (1911); *The Mines of Isaiah Re-explored* (1912); *The Reconciliation of Races and Religions* (1914).

Bibliography: **R. H. Charles,** *PBA* (1915–16) 545-51. **G. A. Cooke,** *The Expositor,* 8th ser. (1915) 445-51. **W. R. Nicoll,** *The Expositor,* 3rd ser. (1889) 59-61. **A. S. Peake,** *ExpTim* 6 (1894–95) 439-44; *DNB Supp.* 3 (1927) 119-20. Information about C.'s personal life is sometimes included in the introductions to his own books.

J. DAY

CHILDS, BREVARD (1923–)

C. stands among the leading pioneers in OT studies and theology in the second half of the twentieth century. Reared in Southern Presbyterian churches, he earned his AB and MA degrees at the University of Michigan before completing an MDiv at Princeton Theological Seminary, with some of his course work taken at Yeshiva University in New York City. He pursued his ThD at the University of Basel under W. EICHRODT and W. BAUMGARTNER and with his future wife, Ann, attended K. BARTH's lectures in theology. C. took his first teaching position in 1954 at Mission House Seminary before accepting a position in 1958 at Yale Divinity School, where he has remained for the rest of his distinguished career. In 1981 he became the Holmes Professor of OT Criticism and Interpretation, with cross-appointments to the graduate school, to the undergraduate department of religious studies, and to the department of Near Eastern languages and civilizations.

A major part of C.'s Basel dissertation on myth (see MYTHOLOGY AND BIBLICAL STUDIES) and the opening chapters of Genesis was privately circulated in 1955 and became the basis for his first book, *Myth and Reality in the OT* (1960). This publication takes up a theme found in most of his other work—namely, the problem raised by modern historical criticism regarding the relation of "history" to a revelation of reality as mediated through the testimonies of Jewish and Christian Scripture. C. has since published nine more books, ranging from a full commentary on Exodus, to several highly technical traditio-historical studies (see TRADITION HISTORY), to treatments on the subject of biblical THEOLOGY and substantial introductions to the OT and NT. In the course of these highly detailed studies he has made a

number of major shifts in his proposals so that unresolved issues in later efforts cannot be answered by uncritical appeals to his earlier strategies.

In the 1960s C. became known for his skills in FORM CRITICISM and traditio-historical studies as well as his critique of failings in the older biblical theology movement. His *Isaiah and the Assyrian Crisis* illustrates his ability to offer fresh insights into the historical worth of ancient traditions that challenged both a conservative effort to accept uncritically the more realistic narratives and a liberal tendency to dismiss as historically useless any tradition with historically dubious motifs. His later efforts to describe the shape of biblical books can be understood properly only against the background of his persistent interest in these modern historical questions.

In the 1970s C. began to describe what he called the "shape" of whole biblical books or their "canonical context." While initially he described this analysis as CANONICAL CRITICISM, picking up terminology coined by J. SANDERS, he soon rejected this label because it suggested another criticism added to other older modern criticisms. He has preferred to describe his own proposal as a "canonical approach," a perspective on a particular text rather than a new methodology. Therefore, the "shape" of a biblical book is a set of observations describing the interplay between synchronic and diachronic dimensions of older ancient traditions when they function together in the new context of a single biblical book. This shape is the "canonical context" insofar as it focuses on the form and function of a scripture, even when the traditions used in it were originally pre-biblical or pre-canonical in that sense (see CANON OF THE BIBLE). It is "canonical" because it seeks to describe what Jews and Christians have classically seen to be the normative arena or boundary in which older traditions were received and heard as testimonies to God's revelation.

Yet, this perception of "shape" admittedly entails an engagement with a modern or POST-MODERN view of differences unforeseen in earlier periods. Its strength lies in its ability to explore the continuity as well as discontinuity we share with pre-modern visions of the same text of Scripture far more perceptively than could older modern approaches that treated reconstructions of ancient traditions as though they were all originally biblical texts. Consequently, C.'s "canonical approach" also invites a revision in how we interpret the history of interpretation and reopens the most elementary questions about what we regard a scripture to be and how we might conjoin in a fresh, not merely traditional, way communities of faith across the centuries who found in the same text the Bread of Life sufficient to the needs of their own time and circumstance.

Works: *Isaiah and the Assyrian Crisis* (SBT 3, 1967); *Biblical Theology in Crisis* (1970); *The Book of Exodus: A Critical Theological Commentary* (OTL, 1974); "The *Sensus Literalis* of Scripture: An Ancient and Modern Problem," *Beiträge zur alttestamentlichen Theologie* (FS W. Zimmerli, ed. H. Donner et al., 1976) 80-93; *Introduction to the OT as Scripture* (1979); *The NT as Canon: An Introduction* (1984); *Biblical Theology of the Old and New Testaments: Theological Reflection on the Christian Bible* (1992).

Bibliography: P. R. Noble, *The Canonical Approach: A Critical Reconstruction of the Hermeneutics of B. S. C.* (Biblical Interpretation Series 16, 1995). **G. T. Sheppard,** "Canon[ical] Criticism: The Proposal of B. C. and an Assessment for Evangelical Hermeneutics," *Studia Biblica et Theologica* 4, 2 (1974) 3-17; *HHMBI*, 575-84.

G. T. SHEPPARD

CHILLINGWORTH, WILLIAM (1602–44)

C. was educated at Trinity College, Oxford. His search for religious certainty and for a universal church that could heal the religious divisions of Europe led to his conversion to Catholicism. After spending time at Douai, he rejoined the Church of England in 1634.

In *The Religion of Protestants, a Safe Way to Salvation* (1638), C. argued that "the Bible only is the religion of Protestants" (335), appealing to universal tradition and to the early church to prove Scripture's AUTHORITY. He understood Scripture to be clear in necessary matters. Controversies between Christians show much of Scripture to be unclear, but the doctrines involved are "not decidable by that means which God hath provided, and so not necessary to be decided" (34). This large group of "nonfundamental" (37) doctrines was a strong argument for tolerance in an age marked by wars of religion. C. also emphasized the role of reason. No assent could be given to anything without evidence. Reason will discover the divine authority of Scripture and thus the truth of Christianity, including "many things above reason, but nothing against it" (336). C. stands as a significant link in the tradition of rational theology in England from R. HOOKER through J. LOCKE and J. TILLOTSON to the Deists (see DEISM).

Works: *The Religion of Protestants, a Safe Way to Salvation* (1664³); *The Works of W. C.* (1838).

Bibliography: *BB*² 3 (1784) 508-18; **M. Creighton,** *DNB* 10 (1887) 252-57. *MSHH* 3 (1727) 331-38. **R. R. Orr,** *Reason and Authority: The Thought of W. C.* (1967). **D. A. Pailin,** *TRE* 7 (1981) 745-47. **H. Trevor-Roper,** *Catholics, Anglicans, and Puritans: Seventeenth-century Essays* (1987).

S. J. JONES

CHRONICLES, BOOKS OF

The feature of Chronicles that has most determined the course of its study is that in certain ways it is a "doublet"—a description of the history of Israel that has already been told, mainly in the books of Samuel–Kings. Although repetition does occur elsewhere in the Bible, it is never as extensive as here; and it is with this idiosyncrasy that the interpretation of the book has had to struggle from its very beginning.

The earliest attempt to address the problem is to be found in the book's title in the SEPTUAGINT: *Paraleipomenon*—"[the book of the things] that remained." The assumption is that the information contained in Chronicles relates to matters omitted from the other historical books for unspecified reasons; presumably this information was to be considered as valid as that provided in the parallels and based on the same or similar sources. This view of Chronicles, while affirming its AUTHORITY, presents it essentially as a supplement to the other historical books and thereby plays down its significance. Whether consciously or not, this attitude greatly influenced the understanding of the literary nature of Chronicles and established its secondary position in the annals of scholarly activity. The echoes of this approach are heard in the nineteenth century, from J. G. EICHHORN (1780–83) onward (see D. Mathias [1977]), in various learned attempts to define the books' goals and indicate the sources.

1. Early Jewish Interpretation. In early Jewish exegesis Chronicles occupied a marginal position (E. Ben Zvi [1988]). Although its Aramaic TARGUM is attributed to "Rav Yoseph," a sage of the third century, it did not receive its final form before the eighth century (R. Le Déut and J. Robert [1971] 24-25). No midrashic composition (see MIDRASH) was ever written for Chronicles; the compilation of homiletic interpretations, mostly of the genealogical material, found in *Yalkut Shimoni* (secs. 1072-85), illustrate how little interest the book evoked. The attitude of the sages was that "the book of Chronicles was given for study only" (*Lev. Rab.* 1:3)—that is, not to be "read" (T. Willi [1972] 16). From the outset the book, and especially its genealogies, was reserved for the setting of the learned (*b. Pesah.* 62b) and not for liturgical or popular use.

Only a few medieval Jewish commentaries are known. A short commentary by an anonymous pupil of SAADIA Gaon dates from the tenth century, and a more comprehensive commentary, from the literal school of northern French exegesis, probably written in Narbonne around the middle of the twelfth century, was published in the RABBINIC BIBLE under the name of RASHI. The latter, while showing some midrashic inclination, contains many insightful remarks regarding the chronicler's goals and literary methods. The commentary by D. KIMHI (Redak, 1160-1235) was probably his first exegetical work, which he claims to have written because "a scholar from Gerona, a pupil of my lord father, asked me to interpret the book." In his prologue, Kimhi explains the need for such a commentary: "I have not seen that any of the exegetes has endeavored to interpret it, but here in Narbonne I have found a number of commentaries on this book; the names of their authors are unknown to me." Also noteworthy of mention are a midrashic commentary by R. Samuel ben Nissim Masnut (thirteenth cent.) and the commentary of GERSONIDES (R. Levi ben Gershon, 1288–1344), published in some of the editions of the rabbinic Bible. An unpublished commentary by R. Benjamin of Rome (1295–1335) exists in several manuscripts. There are a few late medieval and Renaissance commentaries, among them the "Mezudoth": "Mezudath David" and "Mezudath Zion." This commentary, written in the seventeenth century by D. and Y. Altschuler, although in fact but an epigone of Kimhi, is published in all editions of the rabbinic Bible. From more modern times one should mention the commentary of "HaGRA"—acronym for Hagaon Eliahu from Vilna (1720–97)—found in the appendix of several editions of the rabbinic Bible.

2. Early Christian Interpretation. Chronicles hardly fared better in the Christian scholarly milieu. Although highly recommended by JEROME, who stated that anyone claiming to know Scripture without having a knowledge of Chronicles ridicules himself (*ep.* 53.8; *PL* 22:548; A. Saltman [1978] 11), the book in fact received little attention. Of the church fathers only THEODORET OF CYRRHUS (5th cent.) devoted to it a worthwhile commentary (see the critical edition by N. Marcos and J. Busto Saiz [1984]), although later Western medieval circles took more note. The "general Christian consensus" (Saltman, 17) is represented by three influential works: Pseudo-Jerome's *Questiones Hebraicae in Paralipomenon* (the authenticity of which was already denied by NICHOLAS OF LYRA, but which was brought to the attention of a wider public by J. Martianay in the late seventeenth cent.) and the more original work of RABANUS MAURUS were both written in the ninth century (Maurus around 830; Pseudo-Jerome, who is sometimes identified as a converted Jew, somewhat earlier), and both works were incorporated into the twelfth century GLOSSA ORDINARIA. Also noteworthy is the somewhat later commentary of S. LANGTON, archbishop of Canterbury, written around 1200 and recently published by Saltman (1978). Two works of his older contemporaries, R. Niger and PETER THE CHANTER, are still unpublished (Saltman, 15, 22). From the thirteenth and fourteenth centuries are the *Postillae* of HUGH OF ST. CHER (d. 1264), whose commentary on Chronicles is, according to Saltman, "an abridgement of Langton's" but nevertheless "shows some technical advance" (45-46). A more original and influential commentary was that of Nicholas of Lyra (1270–1349), best known for its heavy reliance on Jewish sources, especially Rashi; Nicholas's work was published in 1471–72. For subsequent developments until the dawn of modern criticism see the references in E. Curtis (1910, 49-50) and J. Goettsberger (1974, 22-23).

3. Nineteenth-century Interpretation. The first comprehensive treatment of Chronicles in modern biblical scholarship was W. DE WETTE's "Historical-critical study of the book of Chronicles" published in 1806 as the first part of his *Beiträge zur Einleitung in das Alte Testament.* De Wette's study and the questions he posed determined the course of research for a long time, and their influence is felt forcefully even today. The central question he raised concerned the historical reliability of Chronicles. Although the issue of historical reliability is of relevance to any historical source and in time has indeed been applied to the entire biblical evidence, it was first and most vigorously broached regarding Chronicles, the "doublet" of earlier historiography. In principle, although not explicitly, de Wette followed B. SPINOZA in assigning to Chronicles little or no value (Spinoza [1670] 146, in the Elwes translation). Behind de Wette's treatise lay, not an interest in Chronicles, but rather the opposite: a wish to deny as forcibly as possible the book's reliability.

The subject with which de Wette was concerned was the composition of the Pentateuch (see PENTATEUCHAL CRITICISM): Was it composed by Moses, as claimed by tradition, or by a later, anonymous author? De Wette's standard method was the juxtaposition of literary and historical facts according to the following logic: If indeed composed by Moses, the Pentateuch would have made some impression on historical reality, and its impact would be discerned in the descriptions of the period following the conquest of Canaan. Such traces, however, are almost completely absent from Joshua–Kings; on the other hand, they are abundantly manifest in Chronicles. Accepting the historicity of Chronicles would mean, then, that the Pentateuch was indeed composed by Moses. De Wette directed his efforts toward disproving the chronicler's evidence by systematically comparing it with Samuel–Kings. His results can be subsumed under two categories: the chronicler's lack of literary qualification, his work being characterized by "imprecision," "negligence," and "compilatory manner," and his ideological motives ("tendencies"), which made history ancillary to certain political and religious goals. Among these de Wette mentioned "Levitism," the significance of the cult, love for Judah and hatred of Israel, and a fondness for miracles. De Wette's conclusions are stated categorically: Chronicles is worthless as historiography.

De Wette's forceful and unequivocal statement gave rise to an energetic discussion regarding the value and reliability of Chronicles. The scholarly world of the day divided into two camps over the issue: the critical school, which followed de Wette and went at times to even further extremes (C. Gramberg [1823]); and the conservative school, which endeavored to defend the book as a reliable witness for the early history of Israel (represented most strongly by C. Keil [1833]). This debate reached its climax in the work of J. WELLHAUSEN (1878); in the meantime its effects were clearly seen in the vascillating use of Chronicles as a supplementary source in "histories of Israel" and works on related subjects throughout the nineteenth century (see M. P. Graham [1990]).

The discussion of historical reliability was closely accompanied by the problem of sources. Although essentially an independent aspect of the historical-critical inquiry, this subject had been consistently discussed in the context of reliability (see, at great length, D. Mathias [1977]). In its most neutral form the question was, How much of Chronicles was composed by its author, and to what degree did he employ earlier sources? What kind of sources did he use, and in what way? And more specifically, what is the relationship between the chronicler's actual source material and the allusions to sources that one finds abundantly in his presentation?

This subject, however, when applied to the question of reliability, took an apologetic turn; for even if one grants that the chronicler himself was a late, careless, and tendentious author, one may, by regarding the bulk of his material as derived from ancient, authoritative sources, still preserve in the final analysis the book's value and authority. The eager discussion of sources thus became one more facet of the more burning issue of reliability. From the outset the general evaluation of the chronicler's use of sources was positive: He followed substantially the course of events as outlined in Samuel–Kings, of which his presentation is quite often an almost literal repetition. Regarding this common material, it has often been asked if the chronicler used Samuel–Kings in their present canonical form or whether he had at his disposal an earlier or later recension. While J. Eichhorn and his followers assumed a common source for both Samuel–Kings and Chronicles (*Einleitung,* [1787²] 2:450-550; this view was restated by Hänel-Rothstein in 1927 and recently reintroduced by B. Halpern [1981]), de Wette and his school insisted on the canonical form of Samuel–Kings as the chronicler's source for the common material. This latter attitude, more than the former, raised a further question regarding the non-parallel material: Did the chronicler rely on earlier sources, or is this additional material his own free composition?

While the most extreme views in this respect were expressed (e.g., C. Gramberg; C. C. Torrey [1896]), the reliance on some kind of source for the non-parallel material—in particular for the genealogical preface—was generally accepted; the conclusions drawn were, however, by no means unequivocal. Attention was then focused on further aspects of the problem: How many sources were used? Of what nature and origin? How reliable were they? The phenomenon of the chronicler's allusions to sources was brought heavily into play: Were

his authorities indeed prophetical writings as he claims? Do the general titles he cites refer to the canonical books of Samuel–Kings or to any other book or books of similar nature and origin?

In the course of the nineteenth-century debate on this issue, every conceivable answer was brought forward, from the claim that the citation of sources was fully and completely reliable, the chronicler having indeed made use of the books—prophetic or historical—that he mentioned, to the equally extreme conclusion that he used at most one rather dubious source, "the Midrash of the book of Kings" (2 Chr 24:27), as unreliable as Chronicles itself, and that allusions to sources were merely a literary device devised to promote the chronicler's authority.

The critical study of Chronicles was occupied to a lesser degree with the question of authorship. The traditional view expressed by the statement that "Ezra wrote his book and the genealogy of Chronicles up to him," and the Talmudic note (see TALMUD) that the book was completed by Nehemiah the son of Hachaliah (*b. B. Bat.* 15a), is itself ambiguous. Pseudo-Rashi presents this view in his prologue as "Ezra wrote this genealogical book with the sanction of Haggai, Zechariah and Malachi" (Saltman, 51), ignoring the identification of Ezra with Malachi (*b. Meg.* 15a; *Tg. Jonathan* Malachi 1:1). Kimhi, by contrast, identified the book as "the Chronicles of the kings of Judah" mentioned in the book of Kings and attributed to Ezra only its later inclusion in the CANON (Kimhi, prologue). Among Christian exegetes Ezra figures as either the author of Chronicles (John of Salisbury [c. 1115–80]; R. Niger) or its editor, the author himself being anonymous (Langton and others; see Saltman, 23). Spinoza relegated the book to the period of the Maccabees (146). The more conservative views of the eighteenth and nineteenth centuries preserve the attribution of Chronicles to Ezra without making too strong a connection between the two books and, in particular, without allowing the discussion of Chronicles to have any great influence on the study of Ezra–Nehemiah.

A significant turning point came with the 1832 work of L. Zunz, who came to the study of Chronicles from an altogether different angle. His interest lay with post-biblical Jewish literature, and his book *Die Gottesdienstlichen Vorträge der Juden* portrays the history of Jewish midrashic literature down to the fourteenth century. Following his basic assumption of continuity in Jewish spiritual creativity, Zunz sought the beginnings of Midrash in the Bible itself and found them in Chronicles. Here again his study was facilitated by the nature of the book as "repetition," which enabled him to uncover the midrashic elements of chronistic exegesis.

According to Zunz, Ezra is referred to in the third person in the book that bears his name and so, contrary to the traditional view, could not have been its author.

However, Zunz had no objection to the opinion, likewise traditional, that one and the same author wrote both Ezra–Nehemiah and Chronicles. He further emphasized the similarity between these books by pointing to their linguistic affinities, common stylistic features, methods of composition, and certain characteristic views, all of which proved, according to him, the thesis of common authorship. On the basis of these assumptions Zunz's conclusion was almost self-evident: It was not Ezra who wrote both books but "the chronicler," a later writer whose literary idiosyncrasies were most evident in the book of Chronicles. This view (reached independently also by F. Movers [1834]) was eventually adopted almost unanimously and had far-reaching consequences, not so much for Chronicles as for the books of Ezra–Nehemiah (S. Japhet [1985] 88-92).

The way taken by nineteenth-century research arrives via K. GRAF (1866) at Wellhausen. Graf's point of departure for the study of Chronicles and his conclusions regarding the general reliability of the book resemble those of de Wette, but since he dealt with the details his approach was more cautious and less dogmatic. Wellhausen was therefore correct in presenting himself as a follower of de Wette, although his actual work is influenced in equal measure by that of Graf.

For Wellhausen, as for de Wette, the discussion's point of departure lay, not in an interest in Chronicles itself, but in the problem of historical reliability in relationship to the composition of the Pentateuch. The central question for Wellhausen was, not this composition as a whole, but the formation of the priestly document; employing de Wette's method, he sought the traces of priestly material in the historical narrative and concluded that these are absent from the former prophets, while they are abundantly manifest in Chronicles. Consequently, he went on to disprove the authenticity of the chronicler's history, pronouncing it a tendentious "Judaizing of the past," a result of priestly theology and interests, including the idealization of David and Solomon in the spirit of the time; the centrality of the cult and its personnel; the concept of "the twelve tribes" as "all Israel"; and the "historical pragmatism" expressed by a developed doctrine of retribution. Although Wellhausen did not categorically deny the chronicler's use of additional materials, he considered the discussion of this matter greatly overworked and limited these sources to one major work, "the Midrash of the book of Kings," of the same historical and spiritual provenance as Chronicles. In all, Wellhausen showed scant interest in questions pertaining to the book and mentions its relationship to Ezra–Nehemiah only in passing.

4. Twentieth-century Interpretation. The development of research in the twentieth century follows two major lines. One is the continuation of former research, as befits a living scholarly tradition. This is evident not so much in the answers reached as in the handling of the same questions: historical reliability, sources, and authorship; and in the use of the same terminology: priestly history, historical pragmatism, Levitism, *Tendenz,* and so on. The other approach is innovative, i.e., the study of Chronicles in the light of interests that are entirely or relatively new. These in turn have their impact on the way in which the already established questions are addressed.

The question of historical reliability was inherited by scholars whose main interest was neither in literary problems nor in the history of religious institutions but in the reconstruction of the early history of Israel; to this end these scholars endeavored to enlist as many sources as possible (see H. WINCKLER). Although in principle there seemed to be a consensus regarding the tendentious nature of Chronicles, increasingly an attempt was made to salvage from this category as much information as possible and to ascribe an ever greater measure of historical reliability to the book. Here several factors come into play: On the one hand is the unwavering recognition that the intentions and motives of the chronicler make every additional detail the object of suspicion from the outset. On the other hand, the broadening of historical horizons; the accumulation of archaeological evidence (see ARCHAEOLOGY AND BIBLICAL STUDIES)—material as well as epigraphic—from throughout the ancient Near East; the reluctance to ascribe historical material to the "creative imagination" of an author or to his supposed sources; and the better understanding of the chronicler's literary method all imply that there must be some nucleus of fact within the guise of even the most tendentious descriptions.

The beginning of a conscious change of attitudes within the critical school is to be seen in Winckler (1892), followed by W. F. ALBRIGHT (1921, 1955) and his pupils, especially J. BRIGHT. The rehabilitation of Chronicles and the almost unhesitating reference to it as a historical source reach a zenith in the work of some Israeli scholars, initiated by B. MAZAR and followed by Y. AHARONI, H. Reviv (1989), and others. A more moderate approach to the same issue is shown also by such European scholars as K. GALLING and W. RUDOLPH. Between the two extremes—complete denial and full acceptance—all possible variations have found expression. In more recent times, however, an increasing reaction questioning the reliability of Chronicles is gradually setting in. The works of P. Welten (1979), C. NORTH (1974), and R. Klein (see Japhet [1985] 98-99) remind us that the issue has not reached its final resolution.

Regarding the questions of authorship and date, several new contributions have been made. The most prevalent views for the date of the chronicler have ranged between the late Persian period (early 4th cent. BCE) and the early Hellenistic (3rd cent. BCE), depending on the scholar's convictions concerning the supposed historical and theological background of the chronicler's work, the evidence of the genealogical and cultic material, the book's relationship to Ezra–Nehemiah, specific details of chronological consequence (see CHRONOLOGY, HB), and the scholar's general view of the development of biblical literature. In this category the "earliest" position is that of Albright (1921), who regarded Ezra as the author of Chronicles.

An altogether different approach, resembling in a way (probably unconsciously) the early Jewish views, has been the dating of Chronicles as far back as the restoration period in the second half of the sixth century BCE. For example, according to A. WELCH (1939), who regards Chronicles as having undergone a thorough priestly editing, "the annotator . . . belonged to the generation which followed the Return from Exile" (155), while the original author "belonged to the community which had never been in Exile" (157). The original composition of the book thus is actually contemporary with Ezekiel's vision of the future and the DEUTERONO-MISTIC historiography. A different reasoning is followed by those who seek the actual historical circumstances that served as the political background in the chronicler's assumed eschatological aspirations. These are found in the hopes attached to the figure of Zerubbabel during the early period of the restoration (D. N. Freedman [1961]; F. M. Cross [1975]; J. Newsome [1975]). As the book contains sections that are certainly later (the genealogy of Jehoiachin, 1 Chr 3:17-24; the list of priestly divisions, 1 Chronicles 24, and so on), the inevitable literary corollary would be a conception of the book's composition either as abounding in editorial or secondary material (Welch) or as resulting from complex literary evolution (Cross, see below).

One aspect of the problem of authorship is the chronicler's relationship to Ezra–Nehemiah. This problem, which seemed to have been completely settled at the beginning of the twentieth century, has been reopened for discussion (Japhet [1968]). This reevaluation has been motivated mainly by two factors: a greater awareness of the linguistic-stylistic developments of late biblical Hebrew, in particular as a result of the discovery of the Qumran scrolls and the study of the Samaritan Pentateuch and rabbinic Hebrew; and second, a growing appreciation of the theological views and literary method of Chronicles and Ezra–Nehemiah, factors that highlight the respective peculiarities and unique character of each composition. Although the traditional view of common authorship has not been abandoned (see among others R. Polzin [1976] and the commentaries of D. Clines [1984] and A. Gunneweg [1985; 1987] on Ezra–Nehemiah), it seems that more and more scholars distinguish between Chronicles and Ezra–Nehemiah, either as separate works by one author (Willi, 180; Welten, 4) or, more often, as compositions completely independent of each other in authorship and provenance.

While the similarities between the two have been explained as owing to the general background of the Persian period, their peculiar features—linguistic, historical, and theological—have been emphasized anew (M. Segal [1942/43]; Japhet [1968]; H. Williamson [1977]; R. Braun [1979, 1986]; T. Eskenazi [1986, 1988]; etc.).

The most important aspect of the study of Chronicles in the twentieth century, however, is a change in the general approach to the book. No longer merely a "supplement" to earlier historiography, an "ancillary source" for the reconstruction of the history of Israel, or a corollary of the critical study of the Pentateuch, Chronicles has been studied for its own sake as an integral part of biblical literature in which it claims a position in its own right. The catalyst for this change was probably an increasing interest in biblical THEOLOGY, in the framework of which the theology of Chronicles was studied, not as an instrument to prove the book's *Tendenz,* but on its own theological merits and for its special position within the religion of Israel. While it is difficult to assess the influence of J. Swart (1911), this new direction is indicated in Hänel's introduction to his commentary (1927) and receives decisive expression in G. von RAD's 1930 monograph.

Von Rad's attitude toward Chronicles should be understood in the framework of his general approach to biblical theology. Regarding as his task the demonstration of the HB's relevance for present-day Christianity, he undertook to explain the relationship between the HB and the NT in terms of internal development and put great emphasis on demonstrating the continuity of the theological process. The novelty of his position may be understood by comparing it to that of Wellhausen, for whom, from the vantage point of Christianity, the book of Chronicles might as well not have been included in Scripture and was a product of "Judaizing of the past" rather than of authentic Israelite spirit. For von Rad, by contrast, no book of the HB is without value for Christianity. Moreover, the "chronistic work" (Chronicles + Ezra–Nehemiah) occupies a very special position within biblical literature, reaching to the end of the HB period. To exclude its theological testimony would be paramount to severing the line of continuity at a crucial point. Von Rad made an impressive attempt to portray the theology of the chronicler as an integral part of biblical theology, emphasizing the influence of deuteronomic rather than priestly predecessors, focusing his theology in the figure of David, and summing up the book as "the Law of David," an intermediate stage between the "Law of Moses" and "the Law of Jesus" (1930, 136). Von Rad's monograph pointed the way to an intensive preoccupation with the chronicler's theology—with special attention given to the problem of eschatology—and formed a point of departure for all subsequent theological studies of the book. Individual theological facets as well as comprehensive themes have been intensively studied (A. Noordtzij [1940]; J. Botterweck [1956]; A. Brunet [1959]; Freedman; W. Stinespring [1961]; North [1963]; P. Ackroyd [1967, 1973]; R. Braun [1971, 1973]; R. Mosis [1973]; J. Newsome [1975]; Japhet [1977, 1978]; Williamson [1977]; and so on). Even studies oriented in the direction of other interests found the need to take into consideration the unfolding of the book's religious thought.

Another line of development was introduced with the inception and flourishing of FORM CRITICISM, the fruits of which for the study of Chronicles may be seen in three major directions: (a) The least energetically pursued has been the search for new genres within the literature of Chronicles. The most influential attempt was made by von Rad, who classified the specific addresses of Chronicles as "Levitical sermons" ("Levitische Predigt," 1934). Although this concept and its assumed *Sitz im Leben* have prompted justifiable criticism (Mathias [1984]; R. Mason [1984]), von Rad's statements nevertheless drew attention to the formal peculiarity of the chronistic speeches—in addition to their significance as expressions of the chronicler's theology (O. Plöger [1957]). Another genre, not restricted to Chronicles, but abundantly evidenced there, was identified as the "installation genre" (D. McCarthy [1971]).

(b) A more significant contribution has been made by the study of Chronicles in the framework of TRADITION HISTORY, forcefully presented by M. NOTH (1943; ET 1987). Noth attempted to unfold the historical development of biblical traditions in their entirety and dealt respectively with the Pentateuch (1948) and the deuteronomistic and the chronistic compositions, thus putting Chronicles on an equal footing with earlier historiography. Noth's methodological presupposition led him to regard even the literary format of biblical compositions as evidence of a "tradition-history" process; he analyzed in the historical works three literary stages: sources, the authentic work of the author (deuteronomistic or chronistic), and later accretions. Conceiving of the historical compositions as strongly bound to actual political situations, Noth connected them to particular political impulses—in the case of Chronicles, to the polemic against the Samaritans. The concept of a "chronistic work" encompassing also Ezra–Nehemiah is of primary importance as the anti-Samaritan attitude attested in Ezra–Nehemiah is at most only implied in Chronicles (see Willi, 190-94; Japhet [1977] 278-85; Braun [1977]), although often read into the text.

For the understanding of the literary composition of Chronicles, Noth's influence cannot be overestimated. His LITERARY analysis, which resulted in the labeling of many sections in Chronicles (and Ezra–Nehemiah) as "post-chronistic," seemed to present a useful solution to one of the most perplexing features of Chronicles—its heterogeneity. Noth's scheme was immediately adopted

by several influential scholars, and its effects are seen not only in the studies that explicitly follow his lead (the commentaries of W. Rudolph [1955] and J. Myers [1965]; the monographs of Willi and Mosis and others) but also elsewhere. Galling's hypothesis of two chroniclers and the reconstruction of the chronicler's work in three stages by F. M. CROSS probably owe their motivating force to Noth's work.

(c) Another effect of form criticism may be observed in the increased awareness of the overall nature of the book. The Hebrew name for Chronicles—*Dibrê-hayyāmîm*—as well as the Latin title, clearly reflect an understanding of the book as "history" and its author as a "historiographer" (see Langton on 2 Chr 10:2; Kimhi, prologue). For a long time this view was hardly questioned. Of the nineteenth-century scholars only Zunz deviated from this general consensus and related the book to the midrashic activity of the people of the Great Assembly. Without clear literary definitions it was linked to Midrash by W. BARNES (1896). The question of the book's literary form was consciously resumed in the research of the twentieth century and is evident in a wide range of studies. Willi conceives of Chronicles as an *Auslegung,* an exegesis of written Scriptures characterized by midrashic features (53-66). In his general approach he follows Zunz's presuppositions, but his study—greatly influenced by Movers—is much more detailed, accounting for all the minute differences between Chronicles and earlier material. Taking another tack, Goulder proffers the idea that the Chronistic work as a whole was composed for liturgical purposes as a series of sermons, to be read aloud as lections along with the weekly Torah portions (202-24). Brunet described the chronicler's method as "procédé rabbinique" (1953, 491), while Welten defines the book of Chronicles as a "free, parabolic writing of history" similar to the book of Judith (206), which might be understood as a "historical Midrash." Again, differently, Chronicles features prominently in M. Fishbane's (1985) general survey of INNER-BIBLICAL exegesis. Without analyzing the book's literary genre, but rather appreciating the chronicler's activity as evidenced from his work, the chronicler has been presented as a theologian—his work being almost a theological essay for the benefit of his contemporaries (Ackroyd [1977] 24: "The first OT theologian"; Mosis, 14-16)—or a preacher (Mason). At the same time, the definition of Chronicles as historiography has been reexamined and reasserted not only by those who adhere to its reliability (see J. Liver, 1956), but also by scholars who are fully aware of the theological message of the work (see R. Duke [1990]). They regard the chronicler as basically a historian and the literary nature of his work first and foremost as historiography (Noth, 166, 172; E. Bickerman [1962] 22-29; Japhet [1977] 426-31).

Interest in Chronicles has not been limited to these

"mainstream" topics; other aspects and specific subjects, some directly relevant to the parallel nature of the book, have engaged scholarly attention. A first fruit of this interest is the handbooks, which present the parallel texts with or without the evidence of the ancient versions, and further helpful material (see among others P. Vannutelli [1931–34]; A. Bendavid [1967]; J. Kegler-Augustin [1984]). More germane to the actual content are studies in the realms of text and language. The parallel character of Chronicles made it a natural point of departure for all studies of textual transmission. The existence of two and sometimes more versions of the same text within the MT serves as the best illustration of the problem of textual transmission and stabilization. Kimhi, in his commentary on 1 Chr 1:6-7, already indicates the chronistic evidence for the interchangeability of letters that are orthographically or phonetically similar. Chronicles features prominently in all studies of this nature, e.g., those of Friedrich DELITZSCH, G. Gerleman (1948), and M. Rehm (1937), with the work of the latter devoted more specifically to the textual transmission of Chronicles and Samuel–Kings. In the same general category may be included studies devoted more specifically to the ancient versions, the particular attraction of which, in the case of Chronicles, lies in the multiplicity of textual witnesses and the more general conclusions regarding translation and transmission that may be drawn. Thus note should be taken of some of the works on the Targum (K. Kohler and M. Rosenberg [1870]; Le Déaut and Robert), the PESHITTA (S. Fraenkel [1879]; Barnes), the comprehensive work on the Septuagint (L. Allen [1974]), and the study of the VULGATE (B. Neteler [1899]; R. Weber [1945]).

The discovery of the DEAD SEA SCROLLS has evoked new interest in this field. The categorical classification of orthographic, linguistic, stylistic, or theological variants has always been a matter of controversy (see W. Lemke [1965]). This question has been further complicated by the evidence of the scrolls, and in particular of 4QSam[a]. The concept of "variant" and the complicated process of textual transmission should be reexamined in view of the accumulating material. Early interest in the language of Chronicles focused mainly on its vocabulary, which served as an indication of the linguistic similiarity between Chronicles, Ezra–Nehemiah, and the priestly source. Lists to that effect were promulgated by S. DRIVER (*Introduction to the Literature of the OT* [1891] 535-40) and Curtis (28-36; see their reexamination by Williamson [1977] 37-59). A pioneering study, more linguistically oriented, is that of A. Kropat (1909). The growing interest in post-biblical Hebrew, encouraged by the discovery of the Qumran material, inspired as well a greater attention to late biblical Hebrew, of which Chronicles is the largest biblical corpus. The book's language, although no doubt reflecting the stylistic idiosyncrasies of its author, could

no longer be regarded as merely an individual stylistic expression; it has been gradually recognized as the important representative of a general linguistic stratum. However, although great progress has been achieved in this field (e.g., E. Kutscher [1959]; Japhet [1966/67]; Bendavid [1971]; A. Hurvitz [1972]; W. Watson [1972]; Polzin; M. Throntviet [1982]), it seems that a more systematic description of late biblical Hebrew is now indicated. Many pertinent questions must be addressed, e.g., the extent of Aramaic influence on Hebrew and the survival of the latter as a living language in the postexilic period, the simultaneous influence of other Semitic and non-Semitic languages, the actual transition from biblical to rabbinic Hebrew, and so on. The responses to these questions, taking into full consideration the chronistic material, will contribute to a clearer picture of this stage in the development of the Hebrew language.

Among the more specific subjects of interest in Chronicles two may be mentioned: (a) The genealogies of Chronicles were the focus of interest for the ancients, as is seen in both Jewish and Christian evidence (Willi, 14-26). In modern scholarship two conflicting approaches to this material can be detected. One is a very explicit lack of interest, to the extent of denying this material authenticity and historical value (Noth, Welch, Rudolph, Willi, et al.). The other is a certain fascination, prompting repeated attempts to decipher this material's genealogical code, to learn its geographical-historical-ethnological background, and to clarify its sociological significance (see SOCIOLOGY AND HB STUDIES). The genealogy of Judah in particular (see Wellhausen's 1870 dissertation; Noth's discussion [1934]; and recently Williamson [1979]; and G. Galil [1983]) and the socio-historical and literary aspects of the lists are repeatedly the subject of new studies (e.g., G. Richter [1914]; M. Johnson [1969]; R. Wilson [1975]; Liver [1968]; M. Razin [1977])—which have by no means exhausted the material's potential.

(b) The topic of PROPHECY has attracted growing attention in recent decades, as is in fact illustrated by the recent study of Mathias describing the attitudes of nineteenth-century scholars to this subject (112-302). Although often described as a "priestly history," in contrast to the deuteronomistic "prophetic history," Chronicles in fact assigns to prophets an important role. Many prophets who are not mentioned in earlier biblical material are here introduced; they appear before and address the king and people; they are alluded to as having recorded the history of their period; their fate is sometimes described; they are presented as communicating God's commandments to the people; and the title "prophets" is also given to the singers.

What, then, was the chronicler's familiarity with the phenomenon of prophecy? Was it a living institution of his day, or was he working with traditional and literary material? How authentic is his evidence concerning the names, deeds, words, and lives of the prophets? What social and religious functions does the chronicler attribute to them? Are figures like David and Solomon regarded as prophets? How is the chronicler's attitude here related to other biblical and post-biblical views? Some of these questions have been dealt with to some degree in studies dedicated to this subject (see, e.g., Newsome; Petersen, 55-96; Japhet [1977]; Willi, 215-44; R. Micheel [1983]; I. Seeligmann [1978]; J. Weinberg [1978]; Y. Amit [1982/83]), but it seems that here, too, a fuller portrayal of the subject is still a *desideratum*.

Concluding this review, which is by no means exhaustive, it seems fitting to draw the reader's attention to the tide of commentaries on Chronicles that have appeared in recent years in different languages, standards, and scopes, and from so many points of view, seeming to meet any existing or expected need.

Bibliography: **P. R. Ackroyd,** *The Chronicler in His Age* (1990). **W. F. Albright,** "The Date and Personality of the Chronicler," *JBL* 40 (1921) 104-24; "The Judicial Reform of Jehoshaphat," *A. Marx Jubilee Volume* (ed. S. Lieberman, 1950) 61-82. **L. C. Allen,** *The Greek Chronicles* (VTSup 25, 27, 1974). **Y. Amit,** "The Role of Prophecy and the Prophets in the Teachings of Chronicles," *Beth Mikra* 28 (1982/83) 113-33 (Hebrew). **W. E. Barnes,** "The Midrashic Element in Chronicles," *Expositor* 5th ser., 4 (1896) 426-39; *An Apparatus Criticus to Chronicles in the Peshitta Version* (1897). **A. Bea,** "Neuere Arbeiten zum Problem der biblischen Chronikbüchern," *Bib* 22 (1941) 46-58. **A. Bendavid,** *Biblical Hebrew and Mishnaic Hebrew* (1967); *Parallels in the Bible* (1972). **E. Ben Zvi,** "The Authority of 1–2 Chronicles in the Late Second Temple Period," *JSP* 3 (1988) 59-88. **E. J. Bickermann,** *From Ezra to the Last of the Maccabees* (1962). **J. Botterweck,** "Zur Eigenart der chronistischen David-geschichte," *TQ* 136 (1956) 402-35. **R. L. Braun,** "Solomonic Apologetic in Chronicles," *JBL* 92 (1973) 503-16; "Solomon, the Chosen Temple Builder: The Significance of 1 Chronicles 22, 28, and 29 for the Theology of Chronicles," *JBL* 95 (1976) 581-90; "A Reconsideration of the Chronicler's Attitude Toward the North," *JBL* 96 (1977) 59-62; "Chronicles, Ezra and Nehemiah: Theology and Literary History," VTSup 30 (1979) 52-64; *1 Chronicles* (WBC, 1986). **A.-M. Brunet,** "Le Chroniste et ses Sources," *RB* 60 (1953) 483-508; 61 (1954) 349-86; "La Théologie du Chroniste Théocratie et Messianism," BETL 12 (1959) 384-97. **A. Caquot,** "Peut-on parler de messianisme dans l'oeuvre du Chroniste?" *RTP* 16 (1966) 110-20. **D. J. A. Clines,** *Ezra, Nehemiah, Esther: Based on the RSV* (NCB, 1984). **F. M. Cross,** "A Reconstruction of the Judean Restoration," *JBL* 94 (1975) 4-18. **E. L. Curtis and A. A. Madsen,** *A Critical and Exegetical Commentary on the Books of Chronicles* (ICC, 1910). **F. Delitzsch,** *Die Lese- und Schreibfehler im Alten Testament* (1920). **W. M. L. De Wette,** *Kritischer Versuch über die Glaubwürdigkeit der Bücher der Chronik, mit Hinsicht auf die Geschichte der Mosaischen und Gesetzgebung: Ein Nachtrag zu den Vaterschen Untersuchungen über den Pentateuch (1806).* **R. K. Duke,** *The Persuasive Appeal*

of the Chronicler (JSOTSup 88, 1990). **J. G. Eichhorn,** *Einleitung in das Alte Testament* (3 vols., 1780–83). **T. C. Eskenazi,** "The Chronicler and the Composition of 1 Esdras," *CBQ* 48 (1986) 39-61; *In an Age of Prose: A Literary Approach to Ezra–Nehemiah* (SBLMS 36, 1988). **M. Fishbane,** *Biblical Interpretation in Ancient Israel* (1985). **S. Fraenkel,** "Die syrische Uebersetzung zu den Büchern der Chronik," *JPT* 5 (1879) 508-36, 720-59. **D. N. Freedman,** "The Chronicler's Purpose," *CBQ* 23 (1961) 436-42. **G. Galil,** "The Genealogy of the Tribe of Judah" (diss., Jerusalem, 1983), Hebrew. **K. Galling,** *Die Bücher der Chronik, Esra, Nehemia* (ATD, 1954). **G. Gerleman,** *Synoptic Studies in the OT* (1948). **J. Goettsberger,** *Die Bücher der Chronik oder Paralipomenon* (1939). **M. D. Goulder,** *Midrash and Lection in Matthew* (1974) 202-24. **K. H. Graf,** "Das Buch der Chronik als Geschichtsquelle," *Die Gesichtlichen Bücher des Alten Testments* (1866) 114-247. **M. P. Graham,** *The Utilization of 1 and 2 Chronicles in the Reconstruction of Israelite History in the Nineteenth Century* (SBLDS 116, 1990); (ed.), *The Chronicler as Historian* (JSOTSup 238, 1997). **C. P. W. Gramberg,** *Die Chronik nach ihrem geschichtlichen Charakter und ihrer Glaubwürdigkeit neu geprüft* (1823). **A. H. J. Gunneweg,** *Esra* (KAT 19, 1, 1985); *Nehemia* (KAT 19, 2, 1987). **B. Halpern,** "Sacred History and Ideology: Chronicles' Thematic Structure—Indications of an Earlier Source," *The Creation of Sacred Literature: Composition and Redaction of the Biblical Text* (ed. R. E. Friedman, 1981). **A. Hurvitz,** *The Transition Period in Biblical Hebrew* (1972), Hebrew. **S. Japhet,** "Interchanges of Verbal Roots in Parallel Texts in Chronicles," *Lesonenu* 31 (1966/67) 165-79, 261-79 (Hebrew); "The Supposed Common Authorship of Chronicles and Ezra–Nehemiah, Investigated Anew," *VT* 18 (1968) 330-71; *The Ideology of the Book of Chronicles and Its Place in Biblical Thought* (1977; ET BEATAJ 9, 1989); "Conquest and Settlement in Chronicles," *JBL* 98 (1979) 205-18; "The Historical Reliability of Chronicles: The History of the Problem and Its Place in Biblical Research," *JSOT* 33 (1985) 83-107; **E. Jenni,** "Aus der Literatur zur chronistischen Geschichtsschreibung," *TRu* 45 (1980) 97-108. **M. D. Johnson,** *The Purpose of the Biblical Genealogies* (SNTSMS, 1969) 37-76. **W. Johnstone,** *1 and 2 Chronicles* (JSOTSup 253–54, 1997). **I. Kalimi,** *Zur Geschichtsscheibung des Chronisten* (BZAW 226, 1995). **J. Kegler and M. Augustin,** *Synopse zum chronistischen Geschichtswerk* (BEATAJ 1, 1984). **C. F. Keil,** *Apologetische Versuch über Bücher der Chronik und über die Integrität des Buches Esra* (1833). **R. W. Klein,** "Abijah's Campaign Against the North (2 Chronicles 13): What Were the Chronicler's Sources?" *ZAW* 95 (1983) 210-17. **K. Koch,** "Das Verhältnis von Exegese und Verkünigung anhand eines Chroniktextes," *TLZ* 90 (1965) 659-70. **K. Kohler and M. Rosenberg,** "Das Targum zur Chronik," *JZWL* 8 (1870) 72-80, 135-63, 263-78. **A. Kropat,** *Die syntax des Autors der Chronik* (BZAW 16, 1909). **E. Y. Kutscher,** *The Language and Linguistic Background of the Isaian Scroll* (1959; ET 1974). **A. L. Laffey,** "1 and 2 Chronicles," *Women's Bible Commentary* (eds. S. Ringe and C. Newsom, 1992) 110-15. **R. Le Déaut and J. Robert,** *Targum des Chroniques* (AnBib 51, 1971). **W. E. Lemke,** "The Synoptic Problem in the Chronicler's History," *HTR* 58 (1965) 349-63. **J. Liver,** "History and Historiography in the Book of Chronicles," *FS A. Biram* (1946), Hebrew; *Chapters in the History of the Priests and the Levites* (1968, Hebrew). **D. J. McCarthy,** "An Installation Genre?" *JBL* 90 (1971) 31-42. **S. L. McKenzie,** *The Chronicler's Use of the Deuteronomistic History* (HSM 33, 1985). **N. F. Marcos,** *Scribes and Translators: Septuagint and OL in the Book of Kings* (1994). **R. Mason,** "Some Echoes of the Preaching in the Second Temple?" *ZAW* 96 (1984) 221-35. **D. Mathias,** "Die Geschichte der Chronikforschung im 19. Jahrhundert" (diss., Leipzig, 1977); " 'Levitische Predigt' und Deuteronomismus," *ZAW* 96 (1984) 23-49. **R. Micheel,** *Die Seher- und Prophetenüberlieferungen in der Chronik* (BBET 18, 1983). **R. Mosis,** *Untersuchungen zur Theologie des chronistischen Geschichtswerkes* (1973). **F. K. Movers,** *Kritische Untersuchungen über die biblische Chronik* (1834). **J. M. Myers,** *Chronicles* (AB, 1965). **B. Neteler,** *Die Bücher der Chronik der Vulgata und des Hebräischen Textes* (1899). **J. D. Newsome,** "Toward a New Understanding of the Chronicler and His Purposes," *JBL* 94 (1975) 201-17. **A. Noordtzij,** "Les intentions du Chroniste," *RB* 49 (1940) 161-68. **R. North,** "Theology of the Chronicler," *JBL* 82 (1963) 369-81; "Does Archaeology Prove Chronicles Sources?" *A Light Unto My Path* (ed. H. Bream, 1974) 375-401. **M. Noth,** "Die Ansiedlung des Stammes Juda auf den Boden Palästinas," *PJ* 40 (1921) 104-24; *Überlieferungsgeschichtliche Studien* (1943; ET 1981, 1987). **K. Peltonen,** *History Debated: The Historical Reliability of Chronicles in Pre-Critical and Critical Research* (2 vols., Publications of the Finnish Exegetical Society 64, 1996). **D. Petersen,** *Late Israelite Prophecy: Studies in Deutero-prophetic Literature and Chronicles* (SBLMS 23, 1976). **O. Plöger,** "Reden und Gebete im deuteronomistischen und chronistischen Geschichtswerk," *FS für G. Dehn* (ed. W. Schneemelcher, 1957) 35-49. **R. Polzin,** *Late Biblical Hebrew: Toward an Historical Typology of Biblical Hebrew Prose* (1976). **G. von Rad,** *Das Geschichtsbild des chronistischen Werkes* (BWANT 4, 3, 1930); "The Levitical Sermon in I and II Chronicles," *FS O. Procksch* (1934) 113-24; ET *The Problem of the Hexateuch and Other Essays* (1966) 267-80. **L. Randellini,** "Il Libro delle Cronache del decennio 1950–60," *RivB* 10 (1962) 136-56. **M. Razin,** *Census Lists and Genealogies and Their Historical Implications for the Times of Saul and David* (1977). **M. Rehm,** *Textkritische Untersuchungen zu den Parallelstellen der Samuel–Königsbücher und der Chronik* (ATA 13, 3, 1937). **H. Reviv,** *The Elders in Ancient Israel: A Study of a Biblical Institution* (1989). **G. Richter,** "Untersuchungen zu den Geschlechtsregistern der Chronik," *ZAW* 34 (1914) 107-41; 49 (1931) 260-70; 50 (1932) 130-41. **J. W. Rothstein and J. Hänel,** *Das erste der Chronik* (KAT, 1927). **W. Rudolph,** *Chronikbücher* (HAT, 1955). **A. Saltman,** *S. Langton: Commentary on the Book of Chronicles* (1978). **I. L. Seeligmann,** "Der Auffassung von der Prophetie in der deuteronomistischen und chronistischen Geschichtsschreibung," VTSup 29 (1978) 254-84; "The Beginnings of Midrash in the Books of Chronicles," *Tarbiz* 49 (1979/80) 14-32 (Hebrew). **M. H. Segal,** "The Books of Ezra and Nehemiah," *Tarbiz* 14 (1942/43) 81-88 (Hebrew). **B. Spinoza,** *Theologico-Political Treatise* (1670). **W. F. Stinespring,** "Eschatology in Chronicles," *JBL* 80 (1961) 209-19. **J. Swart,** "De Theologie van Kronieken" (diss., Groningen, 1911). **M. A. Throntviet,** "Linguistic Analysis and the Question of Authorship in Chronicles, Ezra, and Nehemiah," *VT* 32 (1982) 201-16; *When Kings Speak: Royal Speech and Royal Prayer in Chronicles* (SBLDS 93, 1987). **C. C. Torrey,** *The Composition and Historical Value of Ezra–Nehemiah* (BZAW 2, 1896). **P. Vannutelli,** *Libri Synoptici Veteris Testamenti* (1931–34). **W. G. E. Watson,** "Archaic Elements in the Language of Chronicles," *Bib* 53 (1972) 191-207. **R. Weber,** *Les ancienne versions latines du deuxième livre des Paralipomènes* (1945). **J. P. Weinberg,** "Die 'ausserkanonischen Prophezieungen' in den Chronikbüchern," *Acta Antiqua* 26 (1978) 387-404. **A. C. Welch,** *The Work of the Chronicler* (1939). **J. Wellhausen,** *De gentibus et familiis Judaeis quae 1. Chr 2.4. enumerantur* (1870); *Prolegomena to the History of Israel* (1878; ET 1885). **P. Welten,** "Lade-Tempel-Jerusalem: Zur Theologie der Chronikbücher," *Textgemäss: Aufsätze und Beiträge zur Hermeneutik des Alten Testaments* (ed. A. H. J. Gunneweg and O. Kaiser, 1979) 169-83. **G. Wilda,** "Das Königsbild des chronistischen Geschichtswerk" (diss., Bonn, 1959). **T. Willi,** *Die Chronik als Auslegung* (FRLANT 106, 1972) **H. G. M. Williamson,** "The Accension of Solomon in the Books of Chronicles," *VT* 26 (1976) 351-61; "Eschatology in Chronicles," *TynBul* 28 (1977) 115-54; *Israel in the Books of Chronicles* (1977); "The Origins of the Twenty-four Priestly Courses: A Study of 1 Chronicles xxiii-xxvii," VTSup 30 (1979) 251-68; "Sources and Redaction in the Chronicler's Genealogy of Judah," *JBL* 98 (1979) 351-59; *1 and 2 Chronicles* (NCBC, 1982). **R. R. Wilson,** "The OT Genealogies in Recent Research," *JBL* 94 (1975) 169-89. **H. Winckler,** "Bemerkungen zur Chronik als Geschichtsquelle," *Alttestamentliche Untersuchungen* (1892) 157-67. **S. Zalewski,** *Solomon's Ascension to the Throne: Studies in the Books of Kings and Chronicles* (1981), Hebrew. **L. Zunz,** *Die Gottesdienstlichen Vorträge der Juden* (1832).

S. JAPHET

CHRONOLOGY, HEBREW BIBLE

1. Introduction. The HB possesses a continuous chronology stretching from creation to the Babylonian exile, presented in a series of chronological markers that are interspersed throughout Genesis to Kings. For example, the book of Genesis contains genealogical information about Israel's ancestors, including the age at which each ancestor fathered his successor, making it relatively simple to construct a chronology of the early history of the world. Chronological markers outside Genesis are essentially regnal rather than genealogical in that they state the number of years a king or judge held office or specify periods in which Israel enjoyed peace under a judge's rule or was subject to foreign oppression. It should be noted that overall chronological totals are not stated, except where genealogical or regnal information is either missing or is deliberately bypassed (e.g., Exod 12:40; 1 Kgs 6:1).

Further chronological data may be found in the prophetic and other historical books. Jeremiah predicted that Babylonian dominion after the battle of Carchemish would last for seventy years (Jer 25:11; 29:10), and this was reinterpreted by later biblical authors to mean that seventy years would elapse between the destruction of the Temple and its restoration (Zech 1:12), or that the Babylonian exile was to last seventy years (2 Chr 36:21), or that seventy weeks of years would pass before the liberation of Jerusalem (Daniel 9). The notion that the Babylonian exile had lasted seventy years, although factually inaccurate, was important to later chronographers, who used it to synchronize biblical chronology with the chronology of other nations—the date of Cyrus's accession was known from Greek sources—while Daniel's PROPHECY concerning seventy weeks of years appeared to offer zealous eschatologists a way of calculating the (imminent) end of the world.

The interpretation of biblical chronology from ancient times to the present divides roughly into two main periods stretching from the second century BCE and earlier to the seventeenth century CE and from the seventeenth century to the present. Within the first period we may distinguish between Jewish, Samaritan, and Christian exegesis, while the second period may be subdivided into earlier and later periods: Modern study of biblical chronology dates essentially from the last quarter of the nineteenth century.

2. From the Second Century BCE to the Seventeenth Century CE. a. Jewish chronological interpretation. The earliest stage of Jewish chronological interpretation is represented by the chronological data of the Bible itself. A measure of the extent of this early interpretational activity may be seen in the fact that Masoretic, Samaritan, and Greek forms of the HB contain essentially three distinct sets of chronological data. In the chronology presented by the MT there are 1,946 or 1,948 years from creation to the birth of Abraham (there is a two-year discrepancy over the birth of Arpachshad), whereas the Samaritan Pentateuch gives 2,247/9 years for this period, and the Greek SEPTUAGINT (LXX) 3,312/4 years; the LXX also has an extra ancestor, Kenan II, in its postdiluvian chronology. Similarly, in Judges to Kings the MT and the LXX often specify differing time lengths and synchronisms. Further evidence of ongoing chronological (re)interpretation during the biblical period may also be discerned in the many internal chronological discrepancies that are particularly characteristic of Kings.

Similar discrepancies are found in the book of JUBILEES, written in about the second century BCE, which is our most important non-biblical evidence of early Jewish chronological interpretation, and which evidently has its own history of revision and reinterpretation. *Jubilees* is characterized by a distinctive jubilee chronology in which dates are specified in years, weeks of years, and jubilees (weeks of weeks of years) from the world's creation. In this scheme of chronology the history of the

world from creation to the settlement in Canaan occupies a total of fifty jubilees, or 2,450 years, while the interval from creation to the birth of Abraham is 1,876 years. It is of interest to note that *Jubilees,* like the LXX, also includes Kenan II in its postdiluvian chronology, while its antediluvian chronology is in broad agreement with the chronology of the Samaritan Pentateuch. *Jubilees* is significant for its clear evidence of chronological schematization, which may be viewed as a mythical expression of the belief that human history is ordered according to a divine plan. This belief is also prominent in later interpretations of biblical chronology and was arguably the central concern of the original biblical chronologists.

Hellenistic Jewish chronography of the second century BCE is represented by the fragmentary works of Demetrius and Eupolemus. The former anticipates later rabbinic exegesis in his concern for resolving apparent discrepancies in the biblical text and shows similar interest in working out and supplementing the details of biblical chronology, although unlike rabbinic interpreters Demetrius worked from the LXX text. By contrast, Eupolemus's chronology diverges from all existing biblical traditions and provides further evidence for a multiplicity of chronological traditions in this period. Various conflicting chronological schemes are also reflected in the works of JOSEPHUS two centuries later, but his main significance in the history of chronological interpretation lies in his apologetic use of biblical chronology. Countering Apion's attacks on Jewish culture, Josephus argued from biblical chronology that Jewish culture was significantly older than (and therefore superior to) Greek culture (*Con. Ap.;* the same apologetic motivation also underlies his *Jewish Antiquities*).

Later rabbinic interpreters apparently felt little need to demonstrate the antiquity of Jewish culture, and the chronology of the MT used by rabbinic exegetes is significantly shorter than the LXX chronology or the chronologies of Josephus and Eupolemus. *Seder Olam Rabbah,* traditionally ascribed to R. Jose ben Halafta (2nd cent. CE), is the most important rabbinic tractate devoted to the interpretation of biblical chronology, beginning with creation and continuing to the end of the biblical period and beyond. This shows a marked interest in the finer details of biblical chronology. Detailed calculations of the chronology of the flood or of Israel's time in the wilderness (Moses broke the tablets of the law on 17 *Tammuz,* etc.) are presented along with various harmonistic explanations of apparent contradictions in (MT) biblical chronology. The discrepancy between the chronology of Judges and the books of Samuel (giving 450 years from the settlement to the death of Eli) and the 480-year period referred to in 1 Kgs 6:1 is resolved by the claim that years of oppression were (usually) contained within other chronological periods and could therefore be disregarded in chronological calculations (*S. Olam Rab.* 12). This explanation was later adopted by EUSEBIUS (see A. Mosshammer [1979]) and has been repeated in various guises by a significant number of modern scholars.

Seder Olam Rabbah concludes with a summary of Jewish chronology from the foundation of the Second Temple to its destruction (*S. Olam Rab.* 30); this information was later incorporated into the Jewish era of the world, in which the year 1 Anno Mundi (AM) corresponded to 3761 BCE. This represents a strikingly low date for the creation of the world, which is partly explained by the fact that the chronology given in *Seder Olam Rabba* underestimates the true historical duration of the Second Temple period by almost two centuries, allowing only fifty-two years for the entire duration of the Persian Empire. It should be noted that this underestimate was clearly based on schematic considerations: Fifty-two, like seven and twelve, is a schematic chronological number (there are fifty-two weeks in a year), and the interval between the destruction of the First Temple and the destruction of the Second Temple (in 70 CE) is calculated to arrive at a round total of 490 years corresponding to the seventy weeks of years in Daniel 9 (cf. *S. Olam Rab.* 28). It may also be noted that the chronology of *Seder Olam Rabba* puts the destruction of the Second Temple in 3828 AM and that an early belief (attested in Pseudo-Philo *Biblical Antiquities* 28:8) was that the world would have a duration of four millennia. (According to other rabbinic calculations the world was to exist for six millennia, but the Messiah would appear after four millennia: *b. Abod. Zar.* 9a.) Jose ben Halafta (d. c. 160 CE) may therefore have believed that world history had entered its closing stages, though he may also have wished to counter any immediate expectations of a new era, like those that surfaced during the second Jewish revolt.

b. Samaritan chronological interpretation. The most important document of Samaritan chronological exegesis (apart from the Samaritan Pentateuch) is the Tolidah chronicle, which sets out the basic principles of Samaritan chronological calculations and summarizes Samaritan chronology from Adam to Uzzi (a contemporary of Eli). In its present form the chronicle dates from medieval times (it was copied by Jacob ben Ishmael in 747 AH = 1346/7 CE), but it undoubtedly contains earlier traditions. The year 747 AH is calculated to be the fourth year of the fifth week of the sixty-first jubilee from the settlement of Canaan and is also equated with the year 5778 from creation.

c. Christian chronological interpretation. Our earliest evidence for Christian interpretation of biblical chronology is to be found in the NT. According to Acts 13:19-21 PAUL apparently calculated a period of 450 years from the settlement to the time of Samuel—which is in broad agreement with the chronology of Judges and Samuel but conflicts with the 480-year period mentioned in 1 Kgs 6:1—and forty years for the reign of Saul (cf. 1 Sam 13:1). In Gal 3:17 Paul states that the Mosaic law was introduced 430 years after God's promise to Abraham, which agrees with LXX and Samaritan chronology but conflicts with (any natural interpretation of) chronological data in the MT. The MT of Exod 12:40-41 states that the Israelites lived for 430 years in Egypt before the exodus, whereas according to the LXX and the Samaritan Pentateuch they spent 430 years in Canaan and Egypt. However, one cannot infer that Paul was necessarily following LXX (or Samaritan) chronology at this point, since rabbinic exegesis adopted the same interpretation for the MT of Exod 12:40-41 (*S. Olam Rab.* 1).

Early Christian interpretation of biblical chronology after the NT period was largely shaped by the belief that the history of the (present) world was to last for six millennia, corresponding to the six days of the world's creation, and that this would be followed by a seventh sabbatical millennium, corresponding to the day on which God rested after creating the world (cf. the eschatological millennium referred to in Rev 20:2). This analogy between the creation of the world and its subsequent history resulted in Christ's birth's being dated in the sixth millennium of world history: Just as Adam had been created on the sixth day of creation and was the climax of God's creation, so also Christ (the second Adam) was born in the sixth millennium of the world and was the climax of previous world history. Since this belief also agreed rather closely with the chronological data of the LXX, the earliest Christian fathers agreed that the birth of Christ could be dated more or less exactly in the middle of the sixth millennium. THEOPHILOS OF ANTIOCH, writing in or soon after 180 CE, calculated a total of 5,698 years from Adam to the death of Marcus Aurelius in that year (*Ad Autolycum* 3.28), while CLEMENT OF ALEXANDRIA (b. c. 150 CE) calculated an interval of 5,784 years from Adam to the death of Emperor Commodus in 192 CE (*Strom.* 1.2). JULIUS AFRICANUS (c. 164–240), author of an influential world chronicle synthesizing biblical and non-biblical history (of which only fragments have survived), calculated a period of exactly 5,500 years to the birth of Christ. He also calculated a total of 3,000 years (half of 6,000 years) to the death of Peleg, whose name means "division."

Several basic motivations may be seen to underlie early Christian interest in chronology. One of these was apologetic: Christian writers sought to reject the accusation that Christianity was a recent superstition by claiming that Christianity was the legitimate continuation of Jewish religion and by using biblical chronology to prove that Moses and the prophets antedated Greek writers and philosophers by several centuries. At the same time they also wished to refute claims that the earth was hundreds of thousands of years old or that it had always existed, since these conflicted with their belief that history manifested a divine purpose that could be traced from creation to the end of the present era. This belief, which was probably the most fundamental reason for Christian interest in chronology, had one further consequence. If one could calculate how long ago the world had been created, and if it was agreed that the present era was to last for six millennia, one could presumably also calculate the date at which the present era would come to an end. In fact, Christian writers were usually careful to avoid offering explicit calculations (which might contravene such NT passages as Mark 13:32 and Acts 1:7), but they were generally also careful to allow a considerable interval between their own time and the year 6000, thereby discouraging any expectations of an immediate eschaton.

This attitude is also reflected in various Christian interpretations of Daniel's seventy week prophecy. Eusebius mentions a discussion of this prophecy by a certain Judas, who had inferred that the world would end shortly after 203 CE (*Hist. eccl.* 6.7); but other Christian writers related the prophecy to the ministry of Christ, and Hilary, writing in about 397 CE, interpreted it non-messianically as referring to the period from the second year of Darius to the purification of the Temple under Judas Maccabaeus. Eschatological expectations were also deemphasized by AUGUSTINE, who developed the traditional doctrine of six ages of world history while dissociating it from its 6,000-year scheme. An alternative approach, adopted by J. Malalas (6th cent.), retained this scheme but associated 6000 AM with the death of Christ, which thereby inaugurated the seventh, sabbatical millennium.

The most important Christian chronographer after Julius Africanus was Eusebius (c. 260–340 CE), who produced a synchronistic chronicle of world history to his own time in which the events of different nations were arranged in parallel columns and dated in years from the birth of Abraham. In the first book of the *Chronicle* Eusebius presented a general discussion of the chronologies of each nation—the section on Hebrew chronology discusses chronological differences between the LXX, the Samaritan Pentateuch, and the MT and offers a number of arguments to support the authenticity of LXX chronology (though it is worth noting that Eusebius, and Africanus previously, disregarded Kenan II in his calculations). But Eusebius also argued for a shorter chronology than had previously been accepted, dating the birth of Christ to 5199 AM (one year short of a schematic total of 5,200 years). Eusebius's *Chronicle* was translated into Latin and extended to 378 CE by JEROME, and this chronology subsequently gained general acceptance in the West. On the other hand, Eastern Christianity continued to maintain the earlier, longer chronology—the Byzantine world era began in Sept. 5509 BCE.

Western Christianity appears initially to have taken little notice of the fact that the Eusebian chronology transmitted by Jerome and later Western chroniclers conflicted with the chronological figures given in Jerome's VULGATE translation of the Hebrew biblical text, presumably because these figures did not support the traditional belief in a 6,000-year era of the world. This resulted in a popular expectation that the world would end around 800 CE. However, BEDE, writing in the early part of the eighth century, calculated from the Vg that there were in fact only 3,952 years from creation to the birth of Christ (for which he was accused of heresy). This chronology was subsequently accepted by the Western church, particularly after the expected end of the world had failed to materialize, and Bede's date for the creation of the world remained the accepted date for over eight centuries in the West. J. SCALIGER (1540–1609), commonly regarded as the founder of modern scientific study of chronology, hardly differed from Bede in his date for creation; by his reckoning, there were 3,948 years from creation to the birth of Christ (which he dated to 2 BCE).

3. From the Seventeenth Century to the Present. During the sixteenth and early seventeenth centuries, attitudes toward biblical chronology were not substantially different from the attitudes of patristic and medieval scholars. Biblical chronology provided a framework for the study of ancient history where it was useful to be able to express dates preceding the Christian era in years from creation. (The modern practice of counting years before the Christian era was not adopted until the end of the 17th cent.) J. USSHER (1581–1656) stands firmly in the tradition of Eusebius in combining historical scholarship with the mythical belief that history is governed by a divine purpose: According to Ussher's chronology, Christ was born in 4 BCE, exactly 4,000 years after the creation of the world and 1,000 years after the completion of Solomon's Temple in 3000 AM. Ussher also succeeded in reconciling numerous apparent contradictions in the chronology of Kings by inferring the existence of co-regencies or interregna, and his chronology was subsequently incorporated into the margins of English Bibles.

Doubts about the accuracy of biblical chronology began to be expressed during the latter part of the seventeenth century. In his *La Sainte Chronologie* (1632) J. d'Auzoles tabulated seventy-nine different opinions about the date of creation. T. BURNET, writing in 1681, restated the idea that the millennium would occur after 6,000 years of world history while arguing that the church fathers had been mistaken in basing their calculations on the LXX text. However, in *Archaeologiae Philosophicae* (1692), Burnet discarded the biblical date for creation and adopted an allegorical interpretation of the Bible that led to his being removed from theological office.

Two main factors contributed to a loss of confidence

in biblical chronology. It was noted that the historical traditions of the Egyptians (see EGYPTOLOGY) or the Chinese spanned a longer period of time than biblical chronology allowed. Moreover, scientific theories were developed during the eighteenth and nineteenth centuries that required considerably more than the 6,000 or so years of biblical chronology. Various harmonistic proposals were put forward for reconciling biblical and scientific or historical chronology. One possibility, advanced in 1655 by I. de la PEYRÈRE, was that Adam was not in fact the first man; there were pre-Adamic men and women. Another view, which dates back to patristic times, was that the six days of Genesis 1 were not to be interpreted as literal days. G. Buffon (1749; ET 1831), writing in the second half of the eighteenth century, calculated a period of 74,832 years for the cooling of the earth from its original incandescent state and suggested that the six days of Genesis 1 should be regarded as six epochs. An alternative possibility, which also goes back to patristic times, was suggested by T. Chalmers in 1804; he accepted the geological antiquity of the earth but argued that the first verse of Genesis described an initial creation of heaven and earth that preceded the six days of Genesis 1 by an indefinite interval of time.

Belief in the historical accuracy of early biblical chronology was finally eroded in the second half of the nineteenth century. The geological antiquity of the earth could be accommodated reasonably satisfactorily by the day/age and gap theories, both of which accepted the biblical date for the creation of man. However, biological theories requiring long periods of time for human evolution could not be accommodated in this way; and since evolution was obviously incompatible with a literal interpretation of Genesis, there was evidently little point in advancing new harmonizations to reconcile it with biblical chronology. It may be noted that modern "creationists" who maintain a literal interpretation of Genesis 1 have themselves abandoned a literal interpretation of biblical chronology by inferring gaps amounting to several thousand years in the biblical genealogies.

The realization that early biblical chronology was incompatible with geological and evolutionary chronology was followed by the discovery that later biblical chronology was apparently incompatible with historical chronology also. This realization followed from the discovery and decipherment of ancient Near Eastern historical texts in the eighteenth and nineteenth centuries. In particular, Mesopotamian chronographic texts provided a chronological framework that could be securely related to classical chronology through the Ptolemaic canon, and that was partially corroborated by astronomical evidence. Since Mesopotamian historical texts also contain a number of references to biblical persons and events, it was possible to compare the chronological data of Kings with ancient Near Eastern

chronology and thereby discover that biblical chronology was significantly longer than the chronological framework derived from ancient Near Eastern texts: There is a surplus of over twenty years in Israelite chronology from the death of Ahab to the fall of Samaria and a surplus of over forty years in Judean chronology for the same period.

This apparent discrepancy between the chronology of Kings and ancient Near Eastern historical chronology has since become the central issue in modern critical study of HB chronology. Four main approaches to the problem have emerged. The first approach, which has close links with pre-critical scholarship, asserts that this discrepancy is in fact only apparent and that it is possible to harmonize the chronology of Kings with ancient Near Eastern chronology and also to remove internal contradictions in the chronology of (the MT of) Kings by hypothesizing overlaps—e.g., coregencies within biblical chronology. This approach has been championed most notably by E. Thiele (1951); but it has in fact been adopted to some degree by the majority of modern biblical chronologists, including J. BEGRICH (1929) and A. Jepsen (1929). Its crucial weakness is that the inferred coregencies are not mentioned in the Bible and are indeed excluded by the usual wording of the text ("Such and such a king slept with his fathers and X his son/brother became king in his place").

An alternative approach, adopted by W. F. ALBRIGHT (1945), recognizes that the chronology of Kings is historically inaccurate and seeks to explain this inaccuracy by postulating a large number of corruptions in the biblical text, which is then emended to produce a chronology that is compatible with ancient Near Eastern chronology. Albright's chronology was criticized by Thiele for its hypothetical nature—the chronological emendations proposed have virtually no textual support—but Albright's methodology is in fact no more hypothetical than is the harmonistic approach adopted by Thiele. It should be said, however, that ancient Near Eastern chronographic literature offers no real parallel for the degree of textual corruption suggested by Albright.

A third approach to the chronology of Kings is to suppose that its inaccuracies may be explained as the result of miscalculations by its author, by one of his predecessors, or by later editors and scribes. This approach is sometimes combined with the harmonistic approach described above. Thus Thiele accounted for inconsistencies he was unable to harmonize by posting a well-intentioned but misguided editor who corrected what he thought were discrepancies; the problem—according to Thiele—was that this editor failed to recognize the existence of chronological overlaps between the reigns of Azariah and Jotham and between the reigns of Menahem and Pekah. The validity of this proposal (and of similar proposals put forward by Begrich and others) is of course dependent on the existence of the chronological overlaps postited by the harmonistic approach. This is not the case with all theories of the chronological miscalculation type. K. Andersen's (1969) reconstruction of Israelite and Judean chronology posits a large number of chronological "corrections" and miscalculations by successive scribes but traces the miscalculations back to redactional alterations to the account of Hezekiah's reign.

A fourth approach to the chronology of Kings was suggested by J. WELLHAUSEN (1875), who noted that Judean regnal years from Solomon's fourth year (when the Temple was founded) to the Babylonian exile add up to exactly 430, and that 430 years from the Temple to the exile plus fifty years to the end of the exile are balanced by an identical period of 480 years from the exodus to the foundation of the Temple (1 Kgs 6:1). The chronology of Kings was thereby shown to be fundamentally schematic, and discrepancies in this chronology could be explained as a natural consequence of this fact. Twentieth-century scholarship has generally rejected this explanation; but it was adopted by S. MOWINCKEL (1932) and has recently been restated by J. Hughes (1990), who has argued that the schematism noted by Wellhausen is part of a wider chronological schematism stretching from creation to the foundation of the Second Temple and attributable to the priestly school. Behind this schematism there would appear to be evidence of an earlier, DEUTERONOMISTIC scheme comprising 1,000 years from the settlement in Canaan to the Babylonian exile, which in turn overlays an original pre-schematic chronology.

It should be noted that reconstructions of these priestly and deuteronomistic chronologies are based in part on textual evidence from the Samaritan Pentateuch and the LXX (and on indirect texual evidence in Josephus). The presumption that the chronological figures of the MT are invariably superior to those of the versions has been questioned by a number of scholars, most notably J. Shenkel (1968) and J. Miller (1967; see also the work of A. Jepsen and R. Klein [1974] on priestly chronology). On the other hand, a number of modern scholars have also detected large-scale schematic patterns within Masoretic chronology in its present form; e.g., A. Murtonen (1954) has proposed that the MT's chronology was constructed so that the Maccabean rededication of the Temple coincided with the year 4000 from creation.

4. Conclusion. If recent proposals concerning the schematic nature of biblical chronology are correct, there would appear to be a close resemblance between the concerns of the original authors of biblical chronology and those of many of their later interpreters, who used biblical chronological data to construct highly schematic chronologies that mirrored their own beliefs concerning a divine plan in human history. It may also

be argued that the distinction between the original authors and later interpreters is in this instance an artificial distinction since it is clear that biblical chronology is the product of a long history of reinterpretation.

Archaeologists (see ARCHAEOLOGY AND BIBLICAL STUDIES) have recently debated issues pertaining to biblical chronology. I. Finkelstein (1996a; 1996b) and D. Ussishkin (1997) are among those who argue on the basis of archaeological evidence that many of the materials dated to the tenth century should be dated to the ninth century, making Ahab the probable builder of many things attributed to Solomon. The majority of archaeologists or biblical historians, including W. Dever (1998; see also H. Shanks [1997]), L. Stager, and A. Mazar, however, do not accept this view. Biblical scholars who have raised fundamental questions about history writing, particularly as it affects our understanding of the chronology of the ancient Near East, are T. Thompson (1974, 1992, 1994), P. Davies (1995a, 1995b), and N. Lemche (1988, 1994, 1996). These three, often labeled "biblical minimalists," argue that ancient Israel and the biblical text may be ideological concepts constructed by postexilic rulers of the Levant (the Persian Empire) to maintain control over the people in the land (see esp. Davies [1995]). They note the lack of material evidence corroborating the existence of the strong united monarchy they believe should exist were the monarchy really as great as the Bible suggests. The recent discovery of the Tel Dan inscription that mentions the *byt dwd,* has been translated as the "house of David," causing many scholars to consider this inscription to be proof of David's existence. Yet Thompson, Lemche, and Davies argue on the basis of the consonantal and grammatical form of this phrase that *bet dwd* can be translated other ways, including "house of love" or "house of uncle," proving little concerning David's existence (see Lemche and Thompson [1994]).

Issues of HB chronology are at the forefront of biblical studies primarily because of the volatile issues raised above. Should archaeological evidence date finds attributed to the tenth century to the ninth, the chronology and understanding of ancient Israel will take a new direction. This, however, will be revealed only over time.

Bibliography: W. F. Albright, "The Chronology of the Divided Monarchy of Israel," *BASOR* 100 (1945) 16-22. **K. T. Andersen,** "Die Chronologie der Könige von Israel und Juda," *StTh* 23 (1969) 69-114. **J. Barr,** "Why the World Was Created in 4004 BC: Archbishop Ussher and Biblical Chronology," *BJRL* 67 (1984) 575-608. **J. Begrich,** *Die Chronologie der Könige von Israel und Juda und die Quellen des Rahmes der Königs-bücher* (BHT 3, 1929). **E. J. Bickerman,** *Chronology of the Ancient World* (1968, 1980²). **A.-D. van den Brincken,** *Studien zur Lateinischen Weltchronistik bis in das Zeitalter Ottos von*

Freisling (1957); "Weltären," *Archiv für Kulturgeschichte* 39 (1957) 133-49. **G. Buffon,** *A Natural History of the Globe, of Man, of Beasts, Birds, Fishes, Reptiles, Insects, and Plants* (1749; ET 1831). **V. Coucke,** "Chronologie Biblique," *DBSup* 1 (1928) 1244-79. **P. Davies,** *In Search of "Ancient Israel"* (JSOT-Sup 148, 1995a); *Whose Bible Is It Anyway?* (JSOTSup 204, 1995b). **W. Dever,** "Archaeology, Ideology, and the Quest for an 'Ancient' or 'Biblical' Israel," *Near Eastern Archaeology* 61 (1998) 39-51. **J. Finegan,** *Handbook of Biblical Chronology* (1964, 1998²). **I. Finkelstein,** "The Archaeology of the United Monarchy: An Alternative View," *Levant* 28 (1996a) 177-87; "The Stratigraphy and Chronology of Megiddo and Beth-Shean in the Twelfth–Eleventh Centuries BCE," *Tel Aviv* 23 (1996b) 170-84. **F. K. Ginzel,** *Handbuch der mathematischen und technischen Chronologie* (1906). **V. Grumel,** *La Chronologie* (Traité d'Études Byzantines 1, 1958). **F. C. Haber,** *The Age of the World: Moses to Darwin* (1959). **W. Hales,** *A New Analysis of Chronology in Which an Attempt Is Made to Explain the History and Antiquities of the Primitive Nations of the World and the Prophecies Relating to Them* (3 vols. in 4, 1809–12), vol. 1 surveys dozens of previously proposed chronologies. **J. H. Hayes and P. K. Hooker,** *A New Chronology for the Kings of Israel and Judah* (1988). **J. Hughes,** *Secrets of the Times: The Chronology of the HB* (JSOTSup 66, 1990). **A. Jepsen,** "Zur Chronologie des Priesterkodex," *ZAW* 47 (1929) 251-255; "Zur Chronologie der Könige von Israel und Juda," *Untersuchungen zur israelitisch-jüdischen Chronologie* (BZAW 88, 1964) 1-47. **A. Kamphausen,** *Die Chronologie der hebräischen Könige: eine geschichtlich Untersuchung* (1883). **R. W. Klein,** "Archaic Chronologies and the Textual History of the OT," *HTR* 67 (1974) 255-63. **F. X. Kugler,** *Von Moses bis Paulus: Forschungen zur Geschichte Israels* (1922). **N. P. Lemche,** *Ancient Israel: A New History of Israelite Society* (Biblical Seminar, 1988). **N. P. Lemeche and T. Thompson,** "Did Biran Kill David? The Bible in Light of Archaeology," *JSOT* 64 (1994) 3-22; "Early Israel Revisited," *Currents in Research in Biblical Studies* 4 (1996) 9-36. **J. Lewy,** *Die Chronologie der Könige von Israel und Juda* (1927). **E. Mahler,** *Handbuch der jüdischen Chronologie* (Gundriss der Gesamtwissenschaft des Judentums, 1916). **A. Malamat,** "The Last Kings of Judah and the Fall of Jerusalem: A Historical-Chronological Study," *IEJ* 18 (1968) 137-56; "The Twilight of Judah: In the Egyptian-Babylonian Maelstrom," *VTSup* 28 (1975) 123-45. **J. M. Miller,** "Another Look at the Chronology of the Early Divided Monarchy," *JBL* 86 (1967) 276-88. **A. A. Mosshammer,** *The Chronicle of Eusebius and Greek Chronographic Tradition* (1979). **S. Mowinckel,** "Die Chronologie der israelitischen und jüdischen Könige," *AcOr* 10 (1932) 161-277. **A. Murtonen,** "On the Chronology of the OT," *StTh* 8 (1954) 133-37. **V. Pavlovsky and E. Vogt,** "Die Jahre der Könige von Juda und Israel," *Bib* 45 (1964) 321-47. **F. Rühl,** "Chronologie der Könige von Israel und Juda," *Deutsche Zeitschrift für Geschichtswissenschaft* 12 (1894/95) 44-76, 171. **C. Schedl,** "Textkritische Bemerkungen zu den Synchronismen der Könige von Israel und Juda," *VT* 12 (1962) 88-119. **H. Shanks,** "Face to Face: Biblical Minimalists Meet their Challengers," *BAR* (July/August 1997) 26-42. **J. D. Shenkel,** *Chronology and Recensional Development in the Greek Text of Kings* (HSM 1, 1968). **K. Scholder,** *The Birth of Modern Critical Theology: Origins and Problems of Biblical Criticism in the Seventeenth Century* (1966; ET 1990). **H. Tadmor,** "The Chronology of the First Temple Period: A Presentation and Evaluation of the Sources," *The World History of the Jewish People* 4, 1 (1979) 44-60, 318-320. **E. R. Thiele,** *The Mysterious Numbers of the Hebrew Kings: A Reconstruction of the Chronology of the Kingdoms of Israel and Judah* (1951, 1983³); "Coregencies and Overlapping Reigns Among the Hebrew Kings," *JBL* 93 (1974) 174-200. **T. L. Thompson,** *The History of the Patriarchal Narratives: The Quest for the Historical Abraham* (BZAW 133, 1974); *Early History of the Israelite People: From the Written Archaeological Sources* (Studies in the History of the Ancient Near East 4, 1992). **D. Ussishkin,** "The View From Megiddo, Jezreel, and Lachish," (AAR/SBL Lecture, 1997). **M. Vogelstein,** *Biblical Chronology I: The Chronology of Hezekiah and His Successors* (1944). **B. Z. Wacholder,** "Biblical Chronology in the Hellenistic World Chronicles," *HTR* 61 (1968) 451-81; *Eupolemus: A Study of Judaeo-Greek Literature* (HUCM 3, 1974). **J. Wellhausen,** "Die Zeitrechnung des Buchs der Könige seit der Theilung des Reiches," *JDTh* 20 (1875) 607-40; "Review of G. Smith, *The Assyrian Eponym Canon*," *TLZ* 1 (1876) 539-41. **W. R. Witfall,** "The Chronology of the Divided Monarchy of Israel," *ZAW* 80 (1968) 319-37.

J. R. A. HUGHES

CHRONOLOGY, NEW TESTAMENT

Ideological interests and the settings in which scholarship occurred have influenced the quest for chronological objectivity in the past two centuries. The differences in chronology within the Bible and between such evidence and the other available data from the ancient world ensured that unanimity could not be achieved and that objectivity remains a distant goal.

1. The Patristic Orientation in NT Chronology. In the patristic period apologetic and liturgical considerations motivated the interest in chronology and led to correlations of biblical data with extra-biblical data. TATIAN and CLEMENT OF ALEXANDRIA sought to prove the superior antiquity of Christianity over its pagan competitors, while TERTULLIAN argued for the fulfillment of Christian PROPHECY in response to Jewish criticisms. To calculate the proper dates for Easter celebrations, Hippolytus of Rome created a Passover schedule that incorporated astronomical calculations of full moons. Disagreements over the length of JESUS' ministry related to the number of Passovers he celebrated and in turn affected the date of Easter.

These apologetic and liturgical factors led to correlations with the various dating systems used in the Greco-Roman world. JULIUS AFRICANUS was apparently the first Christian writer to create a comprehensive chronology from Adam to Christ, correlating several decisive dates with the Greek Olympiad system of four-year cycles. The fragments of his work, available in EUSEBIUS and other patristic writers, indicate that he calculated the birth of Jesus in the second year of the 194th Olympiad (3–2 BCE) and placed the crucifixion in the first year of the 202nd Olympiad (29–30 CE). Hippolytus followed this scheme quite closely, as did Eusebius, who also correlated the dates of Jesus' birth and death with the reigns of Roman emperors. In JEROME's Latin version of the Eusebius chronology, the birth of Christ is placed in 3–2 BCE (according to modern dating), the opening of his public ministry in 28 CE, and his death in 31. It was not until the work of Dionysius Exiguus in 525 CE that calendric calculations began to be made *ab incarnatione Domini* (from the incarnation of the Lord), leading to the Christian designation AD (*anno Domini,* "in the year of the Lord," replaced in recent scholarship by CE, "Common Era," to recognize the integrity of other religions), which allowed a calculation from a single date in history. By the eighteenth century even the reckoning of dates before Jesus' life were calculated backward from this event, using the BC (before Christ) that appears so self-evident today and renders the patristic dating systems obscure to moderns. However, the patristic correlations with Olympiadic and regnal years as well as with astronomical data provided a measure of public accountability that later chronologies sometimes lacked.

2. Inner-biblical Chronologies in the Service of Religious Controversy. The works by J. SCALIGER, D. Petavius (1583–1652), and J. USSHER provide the foundation of modern biblical chronologies and reveal a significant shift in the cultural setting of biblical chronology. In addition to interacting with Greco-Roman and Jewish traditions, these studies show a primary reliance on evidence within the Bible itself and an interest in using biblical, church, historical, and astronomical details in the service of current religious controversies. The Christian calendar is ordinarily presupposed; other dating systems, including those in biblical references, were recalculated to fit the standard BC and AD nomenclature. The French Calvinist Scaliger created a chronology in 1583 opposed to Pope Gregory's reform of the Julian calendar the preceding year. The definitive Roman Catholic reply came in the work of Petavius, whose chronology (1627) was followed by a series of other works dating events in world history and polemicizing against Protestant scholarship. Ussher's influential studies (1650, 1654) stand in this polemical tradition, expressing the Puritan critique of Roman Catholicism. Despite his scholarly acumen and extensive knowledge of classical sources, Ussher relied primarily on the reconciliation and addition of biblical references, resulting in his famous calculation of the creation in 4004 BCE and the crucifixion of Christ in 33 CE, etc., printed in the margins of many editions of the KJV after 1701. Although Ussher died before completing his extension into later church history of a chronological

system based on prophetic biblical materials, his polemical scholarship opened up lines of inquiry for Protestant chronologists down to the present day.

Proposals about the chronology of biblical events continued. Using chronological erudition in the struggle against "popery," "Jews," and "skeptics," W. Hales (1809–12) divided world history into ten periods, ending with the nineteenth century, when the millennium was anticipated on the basis of clues in the book of Revelation. Coordinating evidence from Roman history with details in the NT, he placed the birth of Jesus in 5 BCE, the beginning of his ministry in 27 CE, his crucifixion in 31, PAUL's conversion in 35, and the Jerusalem council in 49. P. Akers (1856) attempted to correct Ussher's chronology as used in the Clarke commentaries, while retaining the Daniel cycles of weeks. He placed the birth of Christ in 7 BCE and the crucifixion in 28 CE. H. Browne (1904) provided a mystical correlation of biblical chronology in sabbatical sequences of 490 years (mentioned in Acts 13:19-21) in order to confirm the reliability of Scripture and counter the skepticism of contemporary theologians. He placed Jesus' birth in 5 BCE and the crucifixion in 29 CE, with each date allegedly having precise numerical relationships to other events of biblical history and prophecy.

A reliance on biblical details as innately superior to secular evidence surfaced in P. Mauro's *The Chronology of the Bible* (1922), which popularized M. Anstey's extensive investigations of chronology (1913). Mauro contended that the Bible contains "a *complete chronological scheme,* insomuch that it is not necessary to seek from other sources information concerning Bible events." Anstey and Mauro calculated the dates of Christ on the basis of the reference of seventy series of seven years in Dan 9:24-27, resulting in his birth in 5 BCE, baptism in 26 CE and crucifixion in 30. The futuristic interest remained alive in Anstey's work, which concluded with a projection of the beginning of the "seventh millennium" and the return of Christ in 1958. J. Stewart also defended the weeks system (1935), but relied on a coordination with historical and astronomical data to conclude that Jesus was born in 8 BCE and was crucified in 24 CE. A consequence of this chronological scheme was to remove the time compression in Pauline chronology, allowing his conversion to occur in 27 and the apostolic conference to take place in 51 or 52, the latter being quite plausible. But the apologetic program remained predominant in the attempt to prove "the reliability and trustworthiness of the Scripture." Others maintained the weeks system by coordinating it with other details, as in the case of H. Hoehner (1977). While maintaining the accuracy of all of the biblical details, he established the chronology of Jesus' ministry as beginning in 29 CE and continuing through the three Passovers mentioned in John's Gospel to the crucifixion on Apr. 3, 33. This chronology was coordinated with sixty-nine of the seventy weeks of years in Daniel's prophecy, each containing 360 days. The seventieth week, when Israel is "back in her homeland with her Messiah," is "yet to be fulfilled," a position that reveals an apocalyptic interest (see APOCALYPTICISM) shared with the Puritan chronologists of the seventeenth century.

3. Historical-critical Chronologies Coordinated with Secular History Under the Assumption of Biblical Accuracy. The conservative strand of historical-critical scholarship in the past two centuries has abandoned a primary reliance on the dating scheme in Daniel and on the futuristic construal of the book of Revelation. The international scholarly community represented in universities has replaced sectarian controversy and attempted to discover accurate correlations between chronological references in the NT and extra-biblical data from the ancient world. However, the commitment to the AUTHORITY of Scripture in the conservative strand of historical-critical scholarship demanded that secular evidence be adjusted or set aside, if necessary, to resolve contradictions with biblical references. The contradictions are clearly visible in H. Clinton's *Fasti Romani* (1845–50), which sets forth the evidence from the NT as well as from Greco-Roman and Jewish historians in parallel tables from 15–578 CE. His sober conclusion posed a serious challenge to conservative scholars and was widely echoed in critical scholarship: "We cannot name the year of the Nativity, or of the Baptism, or of the Passion, with absolute precision; but we can fix the limits of the uncertainty and mark the probable dates." While identifying certain conflicts within the evidence as "irreconcilable," Clinton retained an uncritical view of Gospel parallels and concluded that Jesus was probably born in 5 BCE and that the crucifixion occurred in 29 CE. T. Lewin (1865) attempted to remove conflicts by creating a summary narrative from 70 BCE to 70 CE, placing Jesus' birth in 6 BCE and the crucifixion in 33 CE after a four-year ministry. The attempt to reconcile conflicts in Paul's journeys led Lewin to place his conversion in 37 CE, the famine relief visit to Jerusalem in 44, the arrest at the time of the last Jerusalem journey in 58, a release from Roman imprisonment in 63, and Paul's execution in 65.

Many investigations of the chronology of Jesus responded to the rise of critical skepticism in the early decades of the nineteenth century. K. Wieseler (1843) offered a "scientific chronological system" based on coordinating all of the Gospel evidence to show that Jesus was born in 4 BCE, that his ministry began in 27 CE, and that he was crucified on Apr. 7, 30. W. CASPARI's (1868) chronology of Christ denied that conflicts in the historical evidence were irreconcilable and that "the authenticity of the gospels" should be questioned. Standing in the historical-critical tradition that assumed the priority of Mark and the separation between the Synoptics (see SYNOPTIC PROBLEM) and John, he accepted the birth narratives in Matthew and Luke as historical and placed the beginning of Jesus' ministry in 28 CE and the crucifixion on Apr. 7, 30. H. Sevin's (1874[2]) effort to place Jesus' ministry in 33–34 CE was less successful.

Roman Catholic responses to the critical challenge (J. van Bebber [1898]; C. Mommert [1909]; and J. Zellinger [1907]) agreed with Caspari and Wieseler on the date of the crucifixion but disagreed on the date of Jesus' birth and the length of his ministry. The 30 CE date of the crucifixion appealed to conservative Roman Catholic scholars because it allowed a coordination with other traditional data, including the reference to John's ministry as beginning in the fifteenth year of Tiberius (Luke 3:1), as one can see in the later work of U. Holzmeister (1933) and E. Ruckstuhl (1963; ET 1965). A similar orientation surfaced in M. Power's (1902) investigation of the Jewish calendar, resulting in Apr. 27, 31, for the date of the crucifixion. G. Ogg (1940) made a stronger case for a crucifixion date in 33 CE.

In Pauline chronology, conservative efforts to reconcile details from Acts with the facts of imperial history and the evidence in the Pauline letters led to awkward compromises. The apostolic conference of Galatians 2 was identified either with the second Jerusalem journey of Acts 11 or with the third Jerusalem journey of Acts 15. Lewin opted for the former, as did W. RAMSAY (1906, 1920[4], 1920[14]), whose studies of the itineraries of the missionary journeys were widely respected. Ramsay placed the Acts 11 journey in 45 CE, combining the famine visit of Acts 11:28-30 with the conference concerning circumcision reported in Gal 2:1-10, and then placed the Acts 15 report of the apostolic conference in 50 CE. This scheme was echoed by D. Plooij (1918), J. Gunther (1972), and many others. Since Paul indicates in Gal 1:18 and 2:1 that seventeen years elapsed between his conversion and the apostolic conference, this early placement of the conference at the point of Acts 11 necessitated drastic reductions of the seventeen years to as little as thirteen years and the elimination of such data as Paul's escape from Aretas (Acts 9:23-25; 2 Cor 11:32-33), which must have occurred when Aretas IV controlled Damascus between 37 and 39 CE.

The majority of conservative Pauline chronologists identified the Galatians 2 report of the apostolic conference with Acts 15, even though this failed to resolve the sharp contradiction between Acts 11 and Paul's claim in Galatians 1–2 that he made no other Jerusalem journeys between the conference and his conversion. W. Conybeare and J. Howson (1892) incorporated the Aretas datum in their scheme, which placed Paul's conversion in 36 CE, the famine visit in 45, and the apostolic conference in 50. Along with many scholars seeking to preserve the PASTORAL LETTERS as genuine Pauline letters, they argued that Paul was released from Roman imprisonment in 63 CE and was executed several years later. C. Turner (1901), following this scheme with slight modifications, placed the apostolic conference in 49 CE and the conversion in 35, while opting for an early arrest of Paul in Jerusalem in 56 and Paul's execution in 64–65. Despite the conservative matrix of his conclusions, Turner provided an indispensible resource for later chronologies. More recent expressions of this approach may be found in the studies of B. REICKE (1968) and in the definitive work of G. Ogg (1968). This type of chronology places less pressure on the seventeen-year span that lies between the apostolic conference and Paul's conversion, requiring in most instances a reduction to fourteen years.

J. Finegan (1964) provides a twentieth century version of the comprehensive nineteenth-century treatments of chronological evidence by Clinton and Lewin. His compendium offers a complete orientation to the problems of ancient chronological systems and a discussion of each piece of NT evidence that reconciles the evidence in the classical sources. Although his conclusions are sometimes tentative, he never questions the authenticity of biblical evidence. He favors a date of Apr. 7, 30, for the crucifixion of Jesus and follows the identification of Galatians 2 with Acts 15 in the scheme of Pauline chronology, placing the conversion in 33/34, the apostolic conference in 48/49, the Roman imprisonment from 58 to 60, and Paul's execution in 64.

Some of the articles in the volume of chronology essays in Finegan's honor (J. Vardaman and E. Yamauchi [1989]) continue this tradition, e.g., D. Moody follows a system of Pauline chronology similar to Finegan's. E. Yamauchi and K. Ferrari-D'Occhieppo assume the accuracy of the story of the magi's visit to the infant Jesus, dating their arrival on Nov. 12, 7 BCE, on the basis that Saturn and Jupiter appeared to be stationary in the zodiac. E. Martin attempts to coordinate all the chronological references in the Gospels with Jesus' birth occurring in 3–2 BCE and a public ministry beginning in 28 CE. Vardaman assumes the accuracy of Acts 11:30 that Paul's second visit to Jerusalem occurred before the death of Herod Agrippa I, which correlates with an innovative dating of Jesus' birth in 12 BCE and the crucifixion in 21 CE, based on a disputed passage from JOSEPHUS. P. Maier's essay appears to be somewhat less bound by the need to accept all of the chronological details in the Gospels, placing the birth in 5 BCE and following C. Humphreys and W. Waddington's astronomical evidence of a lunar eclipse to set the date of the crucifixion on Apr. 3, 33. Other recent works in this tradition are by C. Hemer (1989), K. Doig (1991), and R. Riesner (1994), the latter of whom places the crucifixion in 30, the Antioch collection in 44–45, the apostolic conference in 48, and Paul's arrival in Rome in 60.

4. Historical-critical Chronologies Based on Non-Apologetic Coordination with Secular History. The marks of the consistent advocates of the historical-

critical method in NT chronology are an unwillingness to allow a privilege of biblical over extra-biblical evidence and a tendency to establish ranges of probability when precise dates cannot reliably be established. This orientation surfaced in Clinton's *Fasti Romani,* as noted above, and was sustained by works like L. Ideler's *Handbuch der mathematischen und technischen Chronologie* (1826; 1883[2]), which discussed all of the ancient dating systems on the same level as the Christian system. Wieseler's chronological investigations interacted with such materials while retaining the traditional matrix of the birth narratives and a fusion of evidence between John and the Synoptics in determining the chronology of Jesus.

A. Hausrath (1863–79) offered the first comprehensive presentation of the critical perspective, a full development of which may be found in the work of O. Holtzmann (1895), who eliminated as legendary some of the data surrounding Jesus' birth, including the details concerning the wise men and the star of Bethlehem. After sorting out the contradictions between Matthew and Luke, Holtzmann set a rather broad date range for Jesus' birth "during the rule of Herod the First," and for the beginning of Jesus' ministry some time after 28 CE. The crucifixion was placed on Apr. 7, 30, although the alternative date of Apr. 3, 33, could not be eliminated on the basis of Gospel evidence alone. After weighing the correlations between evidence in Acts and in Roman history, Holtzmann placed the execution of James the son of Zebedee in 44 CE, the apostolic conference in 48 or 49, Paul's Corinthian ministry in 52 or 53, and the Roman imprisonment from 61 to 63, after which "Paul disappears from history," a position that eliminated the data from the Pastoral Epistles concerning Paul's alleged second trial in Rome.

A. VON HARNACK (1897), C. Clemen (1893), and G. Hoennicke (1903) manifested a similar spirit. Hoennicke used broad date ranges to convey the element of uncertainty in the correlation of evidence. Thus Paul was converted sometime between 33 and 35; the apostolic conference occurred sometime between 50 and 52; and the accession of Festus as procurator, on which the final imprisonments of Paul in Caesarea and Rome must be dated, occurred sometime between 59 and 61. The underlying cause of such uncertainty as well as of the fluctuations in dating key events in Pauline chronology was the contradictions between Acts and the rest of the data, which the traditional combination of Galatians 2 = Acts 15, followed by Holtzmann, von Harnack, and Hoennicke, proved unable to resolve.

E. Schwartz (1963, repr. of 1907 original) and E. MEYER (1923), seeking to remove these contradictions, argued that Acts 11 and 15 were doublets of the same Jerusalem journey for the apostolic conference that occurred in 43 or 44 CE. However, this argument required a drastic reduction of the seventeen-year span of Galatians 1–2 and prevented Paul's conversion from occurring before the implausibly early date of 27–28 for Jesus' crucifixion. K. LAKE (1920–33) adjusted the dates of the Schwartz/Meyer framework but could not eliminate the pressure on the ascertainable data. S. Dockx's (1977) and A. Suhl's (1975) more recent chronologies continue in this critical tradition.

In recent years the most consistent proponents of the critical method in Pauline chronology have decided either to eliminate the book of Acts or to give absolute priority to the Pauline letters over the book of Acts, which appeared to be the source of the irreducible contradictions. D. Riddle (1940), H. Hutson (1946), J. Hurd (1967), and C. Buck and G. Taylor (1969) proposed developmental schemes as the basis of Pauline chronology, with unconvincing results. The more widely accepted alternative was developed by J. KNOX (1950, 1987[2]), who granted priority to the primary evidence in the letters and then sought an elimination of the extraneous Jerusalem journeys in Acts. G. Volkmaar (1887) and E. Barnikol (1929, 1938) had taken preliminary steps in this direction. By identifying the apostolic conference of Galatians 2 with the fourth Jerusalem journey of Acts 18:22, while eliminating the second and third Jerusalem journeys, Knox was able to remove the pressure within Pauline chronology. G. Lüdemann (1980) closely followed Knox's dating of Paul's conversion in 34 or 35, the Corinthian ministry in 45, the apostolic conference in 51, and Festus's succession in 55. Revising Knox's scheme, Jewett placed the conversion in 34, the Corinthian ministry in 50–51, the apostolic conference in 51, Festus's succession in 59, and Paul's death at the end of a two-year Roman imprisonment in 62. (For further discussion and adaption of Knox's approach, see B. Corley [1983] and N. Hyldahl [1986]).

The critical discussion over the chronology of Jesus has a less evolutionary development. D. Chwolson (1908) sought to resolve the contradictions between Johannine and synoptic chronologies of Jesus' death by theorizing a corruption of an original Aramaic reference to the "first day of unleavened bread" (Matt 26:17). F. Westberg's investigations (1910, 1911) also identified misunderstandings on the part of the Gospel writers. Several critical scholars agree with Westberg's placement of the crucifixion on Apr. 3, 33, but there has been no interest in his placement of Jesus' birth as early as 12 BCE. R. Eisler's proposal (1928) that Jesus' ministry be placed in 19–21 CE on the basis of details in Josephus has also attracted no following. A. Jaubert's (1957) resolution of the conflicts in the Gospel reports of the last week of Jesus' ministry, involving an arrest on a Tuesday night followed by multiple trials until the crucifixion on a Friday, has evoked wide interest; but the precise chronological implications remain unclear. W. Reinbold (1994) provides an authoritative, critical sifting of the evidence of the crucifixion, concluding that it occured on a Friday before the beginning of the Passover, on a year when the 14th of Nisan fell on a sabbath.

This survey suggests that a rigorous use of historical-critical method requires that the evidence about Jesus' unexceptional upbringing as the son of Joseph in Nazareth (Luke 4:22) and the absence of a miraculous birth narrative in the Gospel of Mark be allowed to cancel the chronological details derived from later accounts involving a star of Bethlehem, the magi from the East, and Herod's slaughter of the infants. How to decide between the alternative dates for the crucifixion, whether 30 or 33 CE, remains the most significant problem.

Bibliography: **P. Akers,** *Introduction to Biblical Chronology* (1856). **M. Anstey,** *The Romance of Bible Chronology* (1913). **E. Barnikol,** *Die drei Jerusalem Reisen des Paulus* (1929); *Apostolische und Neutestamentliche Dogmengeschichte* (1938). **J. van Bebber** *Zur Chronologie des Lebens Jesu* (1898). **H. Browne,** *Ordo Saeclorum* (1904). **C. H. Buck and G. Taylor,** *Saint Paul* (1969). **C. E. Caspari,** *A Chronological and Geographical Introduction to the Life of Christ* (1868; ET 1876). **D. Chwolsen,** *Das letzte Passamahl Christi* (1908). **C. Clemen,** *Die Chronologie des Paulinischen Briefe* (1893). **W. J. Conybeare and J. S. Howson,** *The Life and Epistles of St. Paul* (1892). **B. C. Corley, ed.,** *Colloquy on NT Studies* (1983). **S. Dockx,** *Chronologies néotestamentaires et vie de l'Église primitive* (1977). **K. F. Doig,** *NT Chronology* (1991). **R. Eisler,** *The Messiah Jesus and John the Baptist* (1928; ET 1931). **J. Finegan,** *Handbook of Biblical Chronology* (1964, 1998[2]). **J. J. Gunther,** *Paul: Messenger and Exile* (1972). **W. Hales,** *A New Analysis of Chronology and Geography, History and Prophecy* (3 vols. in 4, 1809–12, 1830[2]). **A. von Harnack,** *Die Chronologie der altchristlichen Litteratur* (2 vols., 1897). **A. Hausrath,** *History of NT Times* (4 vols., 1863–79; ET 1895). **C. J. Hemer,** *The Book of Acts in the Setting of Hellenistic History* (WUNT 49, 1989). **H. W. Hoehner,** *Chronological Aspects of the Life of Christ* (1977). **G. Hoennicke,** *Die Chronologie des Lebens des Apostels Paulus* (1903). **U. Holzmeister,** *Chronologie Vitae Christi* (1933). **O. Holtzmann,** *Neutestamentliche Zeitgeschichte* (1895). **J. C. Hurd, Jr.** (ed.), *Christian History and Interpretation: Studies Presented to J. Knox* (1967). **H. H. Hutson,** *NT Life and Literature* (1946). **N. Hyldahl,** *Die Paulinische Chronologie* (ATDan, 1986). **A. Jaubert,** *The Date of the Last Supper* (1957; ET 1965). **R. Jewett,** *A Chronology of Paul's Life* (1979). **J. Knox,** *Chapters in a Life of Paul* (1950, 1987[2]). **K. Lake,** "The Chronology of Acts," *Beginnings of Christianity* (vol. 5, 1920–33). **T. Lewin,** *Fasti Sacri* (1865). **G. Lüdemann,** *Paul, Apostle to the Gentiles: Studies in Chronology* (1980; ET 1984). **E. Meyer,** *Ursprung und Anfänge des Christentums* (1923). **C. Mommert,** *Zur Chronologie des Lebens Jesu* (1909). **G. Ogg,** *The Chronology of the Life of Paul* (1968); *The Chronology of the Public Ministry of Jesus* (1940). **D. Petavius,** *Opus de doctrina temporum* (1627). **D. Plooij,** *De Chronologie van het Leven van*

Paulus (1918). **M. Power,** *Anglo-Jewish Calendar for Every Day in the Gospels* (1902)**. W. M. Ramsay,** *Pauline and Other Studies in Early Christian History* (1906); *The Bearing of Recent Discoveries on the Trustworthiness of the NT* (1920[4]); *St. Paul the Traveller and the Roman Citizen* (1920[14])**. B. Reicke,** *The NT Era* (1968). **W. Reinbold,** *Der älteste Bericht über den Tod Jesu: Literarische Analyse und historische Kritik der Passionsdarstellungen der Evangelien* (1994). **D. W. Riddle,** *Paul: Man of Conflict* (1940). **R. Riesner,** *Die Frühzeit des Apostels Paulus: Studien zur Chronologie, Missionsstrategie, und Theologie* (1994). **E. Ruckstuhl,** *Chronology of the Last Days of Jesus* (1963; ET 1965). **E. Schwartz,** "Zur Chronologie des Paulus" (1907; repr. in his *Gesammelte Schriften* [1963]). **H. Seven,** *Chronologie des Lebens Jesu* (1874[2])**. J. Stewart,** *When Did Our Lord Actually Live?* (1935). **A. Suhl,** *Paulus und seine Briefe: Ein Beitrag zur paulinischen Chronologie* (SNT 11, 1975). **C. H. Turner,** "Chronology of the NT," *DB(H)* 1 (1901) 403-25. **J. Ussher,** *Annales Veteris Testamenti* (1650); *Annalium Pars Posterior* (1654). **J. Vardaman and E. M. Yamauchi** (eds.), *Chronos, Kairos, Christos: Nativity and Chronological Studies Presented to J. Finegan* (1989). **G. Volkmaar,** *Paulus* (1887). **F. Westberg,** *Die Biblische Chronologie* (1910); *Zur Neutestamentlichen Chronologie* (1911). **K. G. Wieseler,** *A Chronological Synopsis of the Four Gospels* (1843; ET 1877); *Chronologie des apostolischen Zeitalters* (1848); *Beiträge zur richtigen Würdigen der Evangelien und der evangelischen Geschichte* (1869). **J. B. Zellinger,** *Die Dauer der öffentlichen Wirksamkeit Jesu* (1907).

R. JEWETT

CHRYSOSTOM, JOHN (c. 347–407)

The greatest preacher of the patristic era, C. was born and raised at Antioch. He received an excellent rhetorical education under Libanius, the famous pagan sophist. Trained for a career in law, he chose instead to join the clergy. After his baptism by the bishop Meletius (c. 367), he began to study Scripture under Diodore, the future bishop of Tarsus and a leading teacher of the exegetical method of Antioch. From him Chrysostom learned the characteristically ANTIOCHENE emphasis on historical and grammatical exegesis.

C.'s clerical career was interrupted for six years while he attempted to live the ascetic life in the nearby Syrian countryside. By 378, however, he had returned to the city and to clerical ministry. He was ordained deacon in 381 and presbyter in 386.

The next twelve years were a time of prolific literary activity. As presbyter, C. preached often; most of his works are sermons on the Bible. At Antioch he delivered homilies on Genesis, Isaiah, Psalms, Matthew, John, and most of the Pauline corpus (see PAUL). Also noteworthy is a series of seven sermons, *In Praise of St. Paul.*

In 398 C. was forced to accept consecration as bishop of Constantinople. His inability to deal tactfully with the imperial court, combined with the hostile activity of Theophilus, bishop of the rival see of Alexandria, led to his deposition and exile. He died Sept. 14, 407, at Comana, an obscure village of Pontus in Asia Minor.

C.'s biblical preaching bears the clear stamp of his rhetorical education and his exegetical formation. His language and style are pure and elegant; hence the epithet *Chrysostomos* (golden-mouthed). His sermons abound with images and *topoi* from the rhetorical handbooks, and he frequently addressed his hearers directly or constructed imaginary dialogues. He wrote that the audience expected a rhetorical show in no way different from secular oratory.

C.'s interpretation of the Bible was strongly literal. He was most interested in the practical application of the text to the lives of his congregation and frequently addressed the pressing social and religious issues of his day: competition with the synagogue, the persistence of paganism, and the ever-present specter of poverty. For C., the Bible offered patterns of the moral life for the imitation of the Christian community.

Works: *In principium Actorum* (*PG* 51, 65-112); *Homiliae in Genesim* (*PG* 53, 21-54, 580); *Sermones in Genesim* (*PG* 54, 581-630); *Expositiones in psalmos* (*PG* 55, 39-498); *De prophetiarum obscuritate* (*PG* 56, 163-92); *In Matthaeum homiliae* (*PG* 57, 13-58, 794); *In Acta apostolorum homiliae* (*PG* 60, 13-384); *Ioannis Chrysostomi interpretatio omnium epistularum Paulinarum* (ed. F. Field, 1845–62), contains critical ed. of homilies on Paul; *In illud: Vidi dominum* (Isa 6:1) (SC 277, ed. J. Dumortier, 1981); *De laudibus sancti Pauli apostoli* (SC 300, ed. A. Piédagnel, 1982); *In Isaiam 1:1–8:10* (SC 304, ed. J. Dumortier, 1983); *Commentarius in Iob* (SC 346 and 348, ed. H. Sorlin, 1988).

Bibliography: **C. Baur,** *S. Jean Chrysostome et ses oeuvres dans l'histoire littéraire* (1907; ET, *J. C. and His Time* [1959–60]). **R. Brändle,** *Matt 25:31-46 im Werke des J. Chrysostomos* (BGBE 22, 1979). **F. H. Chase,** *Chrysostom: A Study in the History of Biblical Interpretation* (1887). **B. Goodall,** *The Homilies of St. J. C. on the Letters of St. Paul to Titus and Philemon* (1979). **P. Gorday,** *Principles of Patristic Exegesis: Romans 9–11 in Origen, J. C., and Augustine* (1983). **S. Haidacher,** *Die Lehre des heiligen J. Chrysostomus über die Schriftinspiration* (1897). **J. N. D. Kelly,** *Golden Mouth: The Story of J. C., Ascetic, Preacher, Bishop* (1995). **R. A. Krupp,** *Saint J. C.: A Scripture Index* (1984). **M. M. Mitchell,** *HHMBI,* 28-34. **B. Nassif,** "Antiochene *theoria* in J. C.'s Exegesis" (diss., Fordham University, 1990). **J. Quasten,** *Patrology* (1960) 3:424-82. **J. A. Sawhill,** *The Use of Athletic Metaphors in the Biblical Homilies of St. J. C.* (1928). **C. Schäublin,** *Untersuchungen zu Methode und Herkunft der antiochenischen Exegese* (Theophaneia 23, 1974). **R. L. Wilken,** *J. C. and the Jews: Rhetoric and Reality in the Late Fourth Century* (1983).

D. G. HUNTER

CHUBB, THOMAS (1679–1747)

An English Deist (see DEISM), C. was a self-educated glovemaker from Salisbury who first came into prominence with a tract entitled *The Supremacy of the Father Asserted* (1715), published through the influence of W. WHISTON because of its Arian theology (see ARIUS). C. subsequently published about two tracts per year for the rest of his life. In *The True Gospel of Jesus Christ Asserted* (1738), his most significant work, he sharply distinguished between JESUS' preaching and that of the apostles. If Jesus preached the gospel during his earthly ministry, the true gospel cannot concern itself with matters of historical fact (e.g., Jesus' atoning death and resurrection), as the apostles claimed, since those alleged events had not yet occurred. C. separated the gospel Jesus preached from the opinions of the evangelists, e.g., the gospel is not dependent on the truth or falsehood of the JOHANNINE belief in the incarnation. C.'s purpose in these distinctions was to make it possible to identify Jesus' "true gospel" with the fundamental ethical and religious truths of natural religion. C. also extended his criticism to the HB, which he believed grossly misrepresents God's character.

Works: *The True Gospel of Jesus Christ Asserted* (1738); *Posthumous Works* (2 vols., 1748).

Bibliography: *BB*[2] 3 (1784) 521-32. **T. L. Bushell,** *The Saga of Salisbury: T. C.* (1967). **H. G. Reventlow,** *The Authority of the Bible and the Rise of the Modern World* (ET 1984) 384-95. **L. Stephen,** *DNB* 10 (1887) 297-98.

D. F. WATSON

CLARK, KENNETH WILLIS (1898–1979)

Born in New York City, educated at Yale, Colgate Rochester Divinity School, and the University of Chicago, where he came under the influence of E. GOODSPEED, C. taught NT studies and early Christian literature at Duke University for thirty-six years until his retirement in 1967. He gained early recognition as a leading specialist in the TEXTUAL CRITICISM and codicology of biblical and patristic manuscripts. Giving editorial leadership to the International Greek NT Project from its inception in 1948, he served as director of microfilming expeditions to the Greek and Armenian patriarchal libraries in Jerusalem (1949–50) and St. Catherine's Monastery in Sinai (1950) while annual professor at the AMERICAN SCHOOLS OF ORIENTAL RESEARCH in Jerusalem. He was secretary of the SOCIETY OF BIBLICAL LITERATURE (1946–50) and president (1965).

Inspired by the pioneering work of Goodspeed and his associates, C. devoted his lifetime research, travel, and publication to the collection, classification, and textual analysis of continuous text and liturgical manuscripts of the NT. The Clark Collection of Greek manuscripts at Duke honors his memory. He emphasized the importance of a complete codicological description of a manuscript and recognized the relationship of textual criticism to issues in historical theology and the whole range of critical studies of the NT.

Works: *A Descriptive Catalog of Greek NT Manuscripts in America* (1937); *Checklist of Manuscripts in St. Catherine's Monastery, Mt. Sinai* (1952); *Checklist of Manuscripts in the Libraries of the Greek and Armenian Patriarchates in Jerusalem* (1953); "The Effect of Recent Textual Criticism Upon NT Studies," *The Background of the NT and Its Eschatology* (ed. W. D. Davies and D. Daube, 1956) 27-51; "The Textual Criticism of the NT," *PCB* 663-70; *The Gentile Bias and Other Essays* (ed. J. L. Sharp III, NovTSup 54, 1980).

Bibliography: **B. L. Daniels and M. J. Suggs** (eds.), *Studies in the History and Text of the NT in Honor of K. W. C., PhD* (1967), bibliography, ix-xi. **H. W. Huston,** "An Appreciation of K. W. C.," *Duke Divinity School Review* 32, 2 (1967) 99-123.

E. W. SAUNDERS

CLARKE, ADAM (c. 1762–1832)

Born at Moybeg, County Londonderry, Ireland, C. became a follower of J. WESLEY in 1778 and was ordained to the Methodist ministry in 1782. Through Wesley's influence he was educated at Kingswood School near Bristol, England, then at the University of Aberdeen, Scotland (MA 1807). As a biblical and theological scholar, he was disciplined and assiduous, steeping himself in Greek and Latin classics, the early church fathers, Hebrew, Syrian, Arabic, Persian, Sanskrit, and other languages and literatures, plus natural and even occult sciences. His popularity and renown as a scholar led to his elevation on three occasions to the presidency of British Methodism (1806, 1814, 1822). After a lifelong career in service to Methodism, he died of cholera in London in 1832.

C. is best remembered for his commentary on Scripture in eight volumes, which exerted enormous influence on nineteenth-century biblical scholarship, was frequently reprinted, and remains in print today. It was designed to be useful by combining the critical or scientific with the popular and practical. Its theological standpoint is orthodox evangelical, but it exhibits remarkably original interpretations that continue to startle. For example, he maintained that the term *nahash* in Genesis 3 meant, not "serpent," but "devil," "ape," "baboon," or "orangutan," drawing on comparative philology with special reference to Arabic. It is highly significant that even though the NT identifies serpent with devil in its use of the Genesis passage, C. rejected on methodological grounds any appeal to the NT use of the OT in matters of philology, since the OT used by the NT writers was the LXX (see SEPTUAGINT) instead of the original Hebrew. Moreover, his orthodoxy was strained by his claim that Judas Iscariot was saved and that while the person JESUS Christ was divine, he was denied eternal sonship.

C. rejected CALVIN's teaching on predestination, preferring the more moderate position of John TAYLOR's influential *Scripture Doctrine of Original Sin* (1740). C.'s commentary exhibits an amazing openness and exegetical freedom. He emended the text where necessary; and although accepting the Mosaic authorship of the Pentateuch (see PENTATEUCHAL CRITICISM), he allowed the possibility that there had been interpolation into the text—most probably by Ezra. C. maintained, however, that Ezra was acting under divine INSPIRATION, and therefore the additions were of equal AUTHORITY with the text.

Works: *A Commentary on the Whole Books of Scripture in Eight Volumes* (1810–26); *Miscellaneous Works of A. C.* (13 vols., 1834).

Bibliography: **W. G. Blaikie,** *DNB* 10 (1877) 413-12. **J. B. B. Clarke** (ed.), *An Account of the Infancy, Religious and Literary Life of A. C., LLD, FAS* (3 vols., 1833). **J. Rogerson,** *OTCNC*, 180-82.

J. M. BULLARD

CLARKSON, LAURENCE (1615–67)

From Preston, Lancashire, England, C. spent his career as a sectarian and itinerant preacher (and sometime magus) in London, East Anglia, and the Home Counties. He is most famous as a Ranter but was later an important, and for a time factional, Muggletonian. Few radical Puritan persuasions in the mid-seventeenth century did not have C. as an adherent for at least a brief time. He claimed that he and his Ranter followers practiced free love in the name of spiritual liberty, taking his justification from Eccl 5:18-19. At a later period he developed a mystical pantheism and a disbelief in scriptural truth and constancy: "I judged all was a lie, and that there was no devil at all, nor indeed no God but only nature, for when I have perused the Scriptures I have found so much contradiction as then I conceived, that I had no faith in it at all, no more than a history."

Bibliography: **C. Hill,** *The World Turned Upside Down* (1972). **C. Hill, W. Lamont, and B. Reay,** *The World of the Muggletonians* (1983). **A. L. Morton,** *The World of the Ranters* (1970). **N. Smith** (ed.), *A Collection of Ranter Writings from the Seventeenth Century* (1983). **N. Smith,** *Perfection Proclaimed: Language and Literature in English Radical Religion, 1640–60* (1989).

N. SMITH

CLEMENT OF ALEXANDRIA (c. 150–213)

Titus Flavius Clemens traveled widely in pursuit of knowledge, until in Alexandria (see ALEXANDRIAN SCHOOL) he found Pantaenus, who, as C. described it, drew from the flowers of the apostolic and prophetic meadow, thus engendering a purity of knowledge in the souls of his hearers (*Strom.* 1.1.11). The meadow was the Scripture, which C. regarded as the ultimate source of truth, although he acknowledged that philosophy had been given to the Greeks, as the law to the Jews, to prepare them for Christ. In Alexandria (175–202) he taught in the catechetical school until the persecution of Septimius Severus. His three main works lead from paganism to Christian knowledge: *Protreptikus* urges pagans to turn to Christianity, *Paedagogus* is concerned with right action and spiritual welfare, and *Stromateis* presents true philosophy.

C. was the first writer to cite the NT (5,000 times) along with the HB (3,200 times) and to use these terms for writings and not just for the covenants (*Strom.* 5.13.85). His exegesis was governed by the two principles of symbolism and logic. Numbers, objects, and names have symbolic meaning; and symbolism is appropriate for the concealment of ultimate truth (*Strom.* 5.4.21). C. gave four reasons for its use: Truth must not be profaned by evil men (*Strom.* 5.4.19); truth should be handed on by interpreters who will keep it from corruption (*Strom.* 5.9.56); veiled truth makes a more powerful impression on recipients; and symbols can say many things at once (ibid.). Symbolism includes allegory, which means that nothing is superfluous; repetitions and omissions are always significant. C.'s use of allegory was partly derived from PHILO, whom he modified as he borrowed (see C. Mondésert [1944] 163–86). His massive, inexact, and unacknowledged use of Philo offers a difficult puzzle, for which a probable solution is that he used a tradition of exegesis that came through Philo and that some of his borrowings were expanded and corrected by well-meaning scribes.

Logic governed C.'s use of Scripture. In debate with Gnostics (see GNOSTIC INTERPRETATION) he demonstrated his position by direct citation from the Gospels (especially Matthew) or the epistles (especially Corinthians). Fundamental is his search for the connection or sequence (*akolouthia*) of Scripture by means of true dialectic (*Strom.* 1.28). The cause of all error is the inability to distinguish between universal and particular (*Strom.* 6.10.82), but through dialectic true knowledge is built on the foundation of faith. Considering philosophy essential, C. provided a small handbook of basic logic (*Strom.* 8). He maintained that the rule of the church and the central articles of faith indicate first principles from which Scripture may be consistently understood.

C.'s exegesis may be seen at work in other ways in his shorter works. The *Eclogae Propheticae* show the connection of Scripture by means of brief notes, while the *Hypotyposes* bring vividness to particular passages.

Works: *Clemens Alexandrinus* (GCS 12, 15, 17, 39, ed. O. Stählin, 1905–36; 12, 1972³; 15, 1960²; 17, 1970²; ET, *Clement of Alexandria* [ANCL 4, 12, 22, 24, ed. W. Wilson, 1882–84]); *Clement of Alexandria, Stromateis* 3, 7 (ET [LCC, 1954], with notes by H. Chadwick).

Bibliography: W. Bousset, *Jüdisch-Christlicher Schulbe-trieb in Alexandrien und Rom* (FRLANT 23, 1915). J. N. B. Carleton Paget, "Clement and the OT," *HB/OT* 1, 1 (1996) 484-99. A. Méhat, *Étude sur les Stromates de Clément d'Alexandrie* (1966); *TRE* 8 (1981) 101-13. C. Mondésert, *Clément d'Alexandrie: Introduction à l'étude de sa pensée religieuse à partir de l'Écriture* (1944). E. F. Osborn, *The Philosophy of Clement of Alexandria* (TS, NS 3, 1957); "The Bible and Christian Morality in C. of A.," *The Bible in Greek Christian Antiquity* (BTA 1, ed. P. M. Blowers, 1997) 112-30; *The Emergence of Christian Theology* (1993). A. B. Wylie, *HHMBI,* 35-39.

E. F. OSBORN

CLEMENT OF ROME (fl. c. 96 CE)

C. wrote a letter to the Corinthian church in the name of the Roman church c. 96 CE, which was carried by ambassadors sent to restore order and peace. He referred to the Corinthians' situation as fulfilling some prophecies of Isaiah and as resembling situations described in Genesis, Numbers, and 1 Samuel (3-4). Examples, either good or bad, are typical of C.'s exegesis; in this regard he followed the rhetoricians of his time. In proving the resurrection to come he began with the examples of day and night, seeds and crops, and even the phoenix, before quoting an unidentifiable bit of Scripture, Ps 3:5, and Job 19:26 (24). He had already alluded to the words of Christ as found in Acts (2) and quoted sayings from the SERMON ON THE MOUNT (13; see also 47); and later he alluded to verses from Romans (35), Hebrews (36), and 1 Corinthians (37-38). For his proof of the divine origin of apostolic succession he relied on tradition, not Scripture (42, 44). Toward the end of his letter, however, he provided direct quotations from the letter written by "the blessed apostle Paul" to the Corinthians (47-49) and then mixed HB quotations with examples both pagan and Jewish (55). The final prayer begins with biblical phrases, but as it comes to the point—obedience to rulers in state and church—it uses a different vocabulary (59-61).

In C.'s view the Scriptures, the sayings of Christ, and the letters of PAUL applied directly to the life of the church and to Christians in a later time. When dealing with the ministry as a dissuasive to disorder he not only referred to Christian tradition but also spoke of "the blessed Moses" who prevented disorder in Israel by proclaiming God's choice of Aaron as priest (43). The Corinthians must hold fast to examples proving that the righteous are persecuted only by the wicked (45), and

thus they must not expel their leaders. He insisted that they "have a good understanding of the sacred scriptures" and need only to be reminded of them (53; cf. 62).

Chapter 55 gives an excellent example of his method. After commending the self-exile of troublemakers, he proceeded to supply the examples of "the gentiles," vaguely mentioning the self-sacrifice of kings and rulers, the voluntary exile of others, and the self-sale of Christians to raise funds for feeding others. Many women, he wrote, have received power through God's grace; and he specifically mentions two who delivered themselves to danger: "the blessed Judith" and "Esther, perfect in faith." Since neither heroine was popular in Hellenistic Judaism, C. may well have chosen the examples personally.

In conclusion, he admonished his readers to "respect so many and such great examples" (63). More than that, they must not disobey "the words that have been spoken by God through us" or "what we have written through the Holy Spirit" (59, 63), implying that he shared in the INSPIRATION of the biblical writers and, having "looked into the depths of the divine knowledge" (40), could therefore interpret biblical meanings with authority.

Bibliography: R. M. Grant and H. H. Graham, *First and Second Clement* (AF 1, 1965). D. A. Hagner, *The Use of the Old and New Testaments in Clement of Rome* (1973). T. J. Herron, "The Most Probable Date of the First Epistle of Clement to the Corinthians," *Studia Patristica* 21 (1989) 106-21. J. Quasten, *Patrology* (1960) 1:42-63.

R. M. GRANT

CLERMONT-GANNEAU, CHARLES SIMON (1846–1923)

Born in Paris, C. attended the École des langues orientales vivantes, where he studied modern languages and ancient Semitic epigraphy and met E. RENAN, who later would publicize his archaeological successes. C. served as an interpreter, as a teacher at the École pratique des hautes études (1874), and as a diplomat; but in 1890 Renan had the College of France establish the chair of Semitic epigraphy and antiquities for him, a position he held until his death.

C.'s contributions to scholarship were primarily in the fields of ARCHAEOLOGY and epigraphy; he is best known for his work on the Moabite Stone, discovered at Dhiban in 1869. The text of the stone celebrates the triumph of Mesha, king of Moab, against Israel; the events are described from an Israelite perspective in 2 Kgs 3:4-27. When the Prussians failed to acquire the monument, C. intervened and secured an impression of it. After the Bedouin had shattered the stone he recovered many of the fragments, reconstructed most of the text, and issued a translation. Later he discovered the Greek inscription in Jerusalem that prohibited Gentiles from entering the court of Herod's Temple and inscriptions marking the boundary of Gezer.

C. also made substantial contributions in topographical identification. An advocate of using medieval Arabic writings and interviews with modern Arabic inhabitants as sources for the identification of ancient sites, he was thus led to identify Gezer with the modern Tell el-Jazar and was proven correct when he discovered boundary inscriptions near the tell. (However, the same principles led him to other identifications that have been contradicted by later scholarly opinion.) Similarly, he believed that Arabic offered scholars a useful tool for insights into biblical Hebrew and that interviews with contemporary Arabs of Palestine could shed light on biblical practices and references.

C. became famous as the exposer of archaeological frauds and published a book on the topic. In 1872 he revealed that the Moabite pottery the Germans had been purchasing in Jerusalem was in fact nothing but Moabite crockery, manufactured and inscribed for sale to Europeans. On another occasion he offered evidence that some supposedly ancient manuscripts of Deuteronomy were forgeries written on discarded synagogue scrolls.

C. presided over the editing of the *Corpus inscriptionum semiticarum* after the death of de Vogué, published many ancient inscriptions, and founded the journal *Syria*.

Works: *La Stèle de Dhiban* (1870); *La Palestine inconnue* (1876); *Les Fraudes archéologiques en Palestine* (1885); *Études d'archéologie orientale* (2 vols., 1888–96); *Recherches d'archéologie orientale* (8 vols., 1888–1907); *Recueil d'archéologie orientale* (8 vols., 1888–1923); *Archaeological Researches in Palestine During the Years 1873–74* (2 vols., 1896–99); *Album d'antiquités orientales* (1897).

Bibliography: S. A. Cook, *PEFQS* (1923) 137-39. A. Dearman (ed.), *Studies in the Mesha Inscription and Moab* (Archaeology and Biblical Studies 2, 1989). R. Dussaud, "Les Travaux et les Découvertes archéologiques de C. C.-G. (1846–1923)," *Syria* 4 (1923) 140-73. J. Feller, *DBF* 8 (1959) 1504-6. H. Ingholt, "Bibliographie de C. C.-G.," *RArch* 18 (1923) 139-58. E. Pottier, *Syria* 4 (1923) 83-84.

M. P. GRAHAM

COCCEIUS, JOHANNES (1603–69)

Born in Bremen, a professor at Franeker and Leiden, C. was a creative theologian who worked as a Hebraist and developed a "federal theology," a forerunner to modern biblical THEOLOGY. In addition to his *Summa doctrina de foedere et testamento Dei* (1648, 1691[6]), he wrote commentaries on virtually every book of the Bible, basing his theology squarely on philology. C. was one of the first Christian scholars thoroughly at home in rabbinics. He combined a salvation history approach

with a detailed knowledge of Hebrew; in 1669 he published a Hebrew LEXICON. He drew on the concept of the covenant to construct a biblical theology in which both old and new covenants were fully expressed. Like P. MARPECK in the sixteenth century, C.'s serious engagement with history allowed him to consider revelation by historical periods and even to summarize it in such a way that violence was done to neither the HB nor the NT. At the same time he availed himself of typology and freely found Christians and Christianity in the HB. His Christian reading of the HB gave rise to the quip, "While Grotius finds Christ nowhere, C. finds Christ everywhere." In the twentieth century he has been given credit for making the kingdom of God central to biblical themes.

Works: *Opera Omnia* (ed. J. H. Cocceius; 8 vols., 1673–75).

Bibliography: H. Faulenbach, *TRE* 8 (1981) 132-40. J. H. Hayes and F. C. Prussner, *OT Theology: Its History and Development* (1985) 19-32. A. L. Katchen, *Christian Hebraists and Dutch Rabbis* (1984) 75-85. C. S. McCoy, "J. C.: Federal Theologian," *SJT* 16 (1963) 352-70. *MSHH* 8 (1729) 193-217. G. Schrenk, *Gottesreich und Bund im älteren Protestantismus, vornehmlich bei J. C.* (1923).

W. KLASSEN

COELLN, DANIEL GEORG KONRAD (CONRAD) VON (1788–1833)

Born on Dec. 21, 1788, in Oerlinghausen, in what was at that time the principality Lippe-Detmold, C. was the son of a pastor. Following initial private instruction he attended gymnasium in Detmold and then studied theology and oriental languages at Marburg. After passing the consistory's theological examination in 1809 he studied further in Tübingen and Göttingen. Encouraged to pursue an academic career by his Marburg teachers A. Arnoldi (1750–1835) and W. Münscher (1766–1814), he received his PhD on Oct. 30, 1811, with the inaugural dissertation "De Joelis prophetae aetate dissertatio inauguralis"; and after a subsequent trial lecture before the philosophical faculty in Marburg he was habilitated. As a *Docent* he lectured on theological encyclopedia and methodology, introduction to the HB, and exegesis of the HB and the NT, and he taught Hebrew and Arabic. In 1816 he was transferred as *ausserordentlicher* professor to the theological faculty and promoted to ThD *honoris causa* by his faculty on Oct. 31, 1817; henceforth, he also taught history of the Christian religion. Beginning in 1816 he was, as curate, the representative of the first Reformed pastor of the University Church in Marburg. Almost simultaneously in 1818 he received offers from the philosophical faculty in Heidelberg and the Protestant theological faculty in Breslau; deciding on Breslau, he was installed there on May 17, 1818.

His pedagogical obligations, concerned primarily with the historical disciplines of theology, were combined with numerous duties with the Silesian Protestant ecclesiastical administration. He died unexpectedly from a stroke during his term as dean on Feb. 17, 1833, in Breslau.

This Reformed theologian was an emphatic defender of dogmatically unfettered academic freedom in Protestant theological faculties. A moderate rationalist, he considered rationalism to be one method of that particular historical understanding governing theological scholarship. This attitude was consistent with his strict rejection of PIETISM and any form of mysticism (*Beiträge zur Erläuterung und Berichtigung der Begriffe Pietismus, Mysticismus, und Fanatismus* [1830]). His writings on church history (particularly on the Reformation and on the history of Philipps University in Marburg), on HB and NT exegesis (particularly on the prophets Isaiah, Joel, Zephaniah, and on the use of the HB in Paul), and on Hebrew studies were as well received as were his articles in collections and reference works and his scholarly reviews.

C.'s enduring significance lies in his (partly) posthumous works—namely, his exemplary reworking of Münscher's (now retitled) *Lehrbuch der christlichen Dogmengeschichte* (2 vols., 1832–34) and above all the two-volume biblical THEOLOGY edited from the author's materials by D. Schulz (1779–1854). In the latter work the fundamental methodological concerns of G. BAUER and J. P. GABLER are considered together as regards the discipline "biblical theology." Both reconstruction, in the sense of Bauer, and interpretation, in the sense of Gabler, are brought to bear with clear delimitation between the testaments and differentiation among the various biblical authors and epochs. This led C. to distinguish between both specifically temporal elements, on the one hand, and enduring, atemporal elements, on the other hand, and to identify both mythic-symbolic and mythic-unsymbolic forms of expression in each biblical author. The work made enormous strides toward establishing biblical theology within the intellectual history of the early nineteenth century. As clearly limited as this work was—with the still vague reference to the concept of symbol and the simultaneous employment of advances in myth research (see MYTHOLOGY AND BIBLICAL STUDIES) made since the mid-eighteenth century—its thoroughness and insight made it nonetheless the most significant contribution to biblical theology between the founders of this discipline and F. C. BAUR's *Vorlesungen über neutestamentliche Theologie* (1864). Baur's work clearly shows the influence of C.'s *Biblical Theology*, and together they verify the beginning of the history of dogma within the NT.

Works: "Selbstbiographie mit Schriftenverzeichnis," *Grundlage zu einer Hessischen Gelehrten-Schriftsteller und Künstler-* *Geschichte, vom Jahre 1806 bis zum Jahre 1830* (ed. K. W. Justi, 1831) 64-72; *Biblische Theologie, mit einer Nachricht über des Verfassers Leben und Wirken,* vol. 1, *Die biblische Theologie des alten Testaments;* vol. 2, *Die biblische Theologie des neuen Testaments* (ed. D. Schulz, 1836), includes bibliography.

Bibliography: G. Frank, *RE*[3] 4 (1898) 208-10. F. Gundlach (ed.), *Catalogus Professorum Academiae Marburgensis: Die akademischen Lehrer der Philipps-Universität Marburg* (Veröffentlichungen der Historischen Kommission für Hessen und Waldeck 15, 1927). J. H. Hayes and F. Prussner, *OT Theology: Its History and Development* (1985) 94-97. H.-J. Kraus, *Die Biblische Theologie: Ihre Geschichte und Problematik* (1970) 60-69. O. Merk, *Biblische Theologie des Neuen Testaments in ihrer Anfangszeit: Ihre methodischen Probleme bei J. P. Gabler und G. L. Bauer und deren Nachwirkungen* (Marburger Theologische Studien 9, 1972). F. Passow, *AKZ* 12 (1833) no. 71, 569-74 = *Intelligenzblatt der Allgemeinen Literatur Zeitung* (1833) no. 27, 217-22. K. Rosenkranz, *Kritik der Schleiermacherschen Glaubenslehre* (1836), esp. 100-104.

O. MERK

COLENSO, JOHN WILLIAM (1814–83)

Born in St. Austell, Jan. 24, 1814, C. studied theology at St. John's, Cambridge (1832–39), tutored there (1839–45), and ministered in Forncett (1846–53). He arrived in South Africa in May 1855 to become bishop of the Church of England in the province of Natal. Between 1855 and 1862 he published a Zulu translation of the NT and some HB books (printed on his own press), a commentary on Romans, and part one of his seven-volume Hexateuch study. The Zulu people called him *Sobantu* (father of the people), an honorary title he lived up to during his tireless struggle (1865–83) to maintain peace and justice in Natal. Found guilty on charges of deviant doctrine regarding Scripture, christology, and soteriology, he was defrocked by the church (1863) but restored by the privy council. He died June 20, 1883.

Questions from his Zulu language assistant led him to make a careful study of the Hexateuch—initially carried out independently of European scholarship. His research earned him A. KUENEN's and J. WELLHAUSEN's appreciation for being the first to prove the historical unreliability of what was called at the time the "E source," thereby casting doubt on its (accepted) chronological priority. Through his profound influence on Kuenen, his insight that the legal material of the Pentateuch (see PENTATEUCHAL CRITICISM) could not be divorced from its narrative surroundings more than paved the way for the theory of a late dating for the P source. His views on the use of archaeological and biblical material in HB historiography remain valid: He rejected ARCHAEOLOGY's "truth proving" function and propagated the idea that the biblical documents reflected the times in which they originated rather than the times they professed to tell about. His suggestion of a "deuteronomic" edition of Genesis–2 Kings, especially Joshua–2 Kings, is perhaps even more relevant now than when he made it.

In translating the Bible, C. adopted a method that would today be called "dynamic equivalence." To avoid "Hebraistic" or "Graecist" Zulu he would translate the text literally and then ask his assistant to repeat that meaning in idiomatic Zulu, which was then used as the translation.

Although he was a deeply pious and earnest preacher, his major contribution was in the field of biblical HERMENEUTICS. Intrigued by the "immoral" material in the HB, he set out to answer such questions as how a Christian should react to the harsh prescribed punishments, the divinely commanded wars, or the talk about servants in terms of property or mere money. Regarding unhistorical material, he considered what its relevance is for Christians. He proposed that the Bible be read as literature relative to the cultures among which it originated and as such be critically filtered through the "sieve" of accepted Christian values. He also held that HB narratives be read as Hebrew fiction but at the same time as deposits of the thoughts of living people from living faith communities. Their convictions have become our traditions, and as such have lost their vitality. By reading these stories as products of particular cultures, while at the same time accepting the views expressed through them as statements of a (once) living faith, an encounter on the level of shared faith can take place. Through the work of the Holy Spirit, who alone can revitalize the old and re-create from it a living faith, such an encounter can guide and strengthen the reader's faith in the living Christ. C. thus took the problem of cultural relativism seriously without becoming a skeptic or subscribing to a dualistic view of Scripture, conclusions typical of many liberal theologians of the time. One might perhaps anachronistically term his reading strategy "proto-form historical," his hermeneutics "existential," and his view of Scripture "dialectical."

Works: *Ten Weeks in Natal* (1855); *The Epistle of St. Paul to the Romans Newly Translated and Explained from a Missionary Point of View* (1861); *Zulu-English Dictionary* (1861); *The Pentateuch and the Book of Joshua Critically Examined* (7 vols., 1862–79); *The Worship of Baalim in Israel* (1863); *Natal Sermons* (2 vols., 1866–68); *Lectures on the Pentateuch and the Moabite Stone* (1873); *Colenso Letters from Natal* (ed. W. Rees, 1958).

Bibliography: G. W. Cox, *DNB* 11 (1867) 290-93); *The Life of J. W. C., DD, Bishop of Natal* (2 vols., 1888). **F. E. Deist,** "J. W. C.: Biblical Scholar," *OTE* 2 (1984) 98-132, **J. Guy,** *The Heretic: A Study of the Life of J. W. C., 1814–83* (1983). **P. Hinchliff,** *J. W. C., Bishop of Natal* (1964). **G. W. Warwick,** "The Contribution of Bishop Colenso to Biblical Criticism" (MA thesis, University of Natal, 1966).

F. E. DEIST

COLERIDGE, SAMUEL TAYLOR (1772–1834)

Born Oct. 21, 1772, C. died July 25, 1834. He was educated at Christ's Hospital in London and at Jesus College, Cambridge. As a young man he supported republican causes and held Unitarian views. Important for C. was meeting W. Wordsworth (1770–1850) in 1795. They jointly published *Lyrical Ballads* and traveled together in Germany, where C. attended lectures on biblical criticism at Göttingen and became deeply imbued in German thought. He was instrumental in transmitting German philosophical ideas into England.

One of the most important English poets and thinkers of the nineteenth century, C.'s influence on both the Anglo-Catholic revival and the liberal, or broad church, movement within Anglicanism was enormous. Among the writers of the latter school he influenced were T. ARNOLD, J. Hare (1795–1855), F. Maurice, C. Kingsley (1819–75), and M. ARNOLD. C. represents better than any other literary figure in England the Romantic protest against rationalism and the deadening effect of what he called "mechanical philosophy."

For C., whose greatest poems were "Kubla Khan" and *The Rime of the Ancient Mariner,* great poetry is not a work of contrivance, but a fusion of mind and material into a spiritual unity through the faculty of imagination, a principle he derived from both Wordsworth and I. KANT. He believed the human mind is active and creative, "an Image of the Creator," and his religious writings reflect these early Romantic ideas.

The *Confessions,* published posthumously, is C.'s most important contribution to biblical interpretation and is directed against both orthodox literalists and skeptical rationalists. The book reflects his knowledge of current German biblical criticism, especially the work of J. G. EICHHORN and G. LESSING's edition of the Wolfenbüttel *Fragments* of H. S. REIMARUS. Using Lessing's developmental ideas, the *Confessions* seeks to show that the traditional literal view of Scripture and its INSPIRATION, what C. called "bibliolatry," is both untenable and unnecessary. Reading the Bible historically will reveal that it is not a homogeneous, inerrant unity, but a body of literature in varying stages of development. C. pointed out that one does not reject the work of Shakespeare *in toto* because it includes *Titus Andronicus.* He wrote that the Bible "finds me" only in its real humanity; its proof lies "in its fitness to our nature and our needs." The best and wisest of humankind have borne witness to its spiritual excellence and AUTHORITY. To say that "the Bible contains the religion revealed by God" is not the same as saying "whatever is contained in the Bible is religion and was revealed by God."

C. advanced the hermeneutical principle (see HERMENEUTICS) that the Bible becomes the living Word of God only when it is read in faith; thus it requires some interpretive "master key," which for him included all that constitutes the Christian tradition. His approach to the Bible and Christianity was experiential. He insisted that it is not enough to appeal to the honest doubter with speculative proofs; rather, one must call on such a person to "try it." The proof is found in the practice. As a good Romantic, he wrote: "Evidences of Christianity! I am weary of the word. Make a man feel the want . . . and you may safely trust it to its own evidence."

Works: *The Statesman's Manual: The Bible the Best Guide to Political Skill and Foresight* (1816); *Biographia Literaria* (2 vols., 1817); *Aids to Reflection* (1825); *The Constitution of the Church and State* (1829); *Confessions of an Inquiring Spirit* (1840, repr. 1956); *The Complete Works of S. T. C.* (ed. W. G. T. Shedd, 7 vols., 1853); *The Collected Works of S. T. C.* (ed. K. Coburn, Bollingen Series 75, 1969–).

Bibliography: J. D. Boulger, *C. as a Religious Thinker* (1961). **J. D. Campbell,** *S. T. C.: A Narrative of the Events of His Life* (1894). **E. K. Chambers,** *S. T. C.: A Biographical Study* (1938). **J. Coulson,** *TRE* 8 (1981) 149-54. **J. Drury,** *Critics of the Bible, 1724–1873* (1989) 105-21. **S. Prickett,** *Romanticism and Religion: The Tradition of C. and Wordsworth in the Victorian Church* (1976). **P. C. Rule,** "C.'s Reputation as a Religious Thinker: 1816–1972," *HTR* 67 (1974) 289-320. **E. S. Shaffer,** *"Kubla Khan" and the Fall of Jerusalem: The Mythological School in Biblical Criticism and Secular Literature, 1770–1880* (1975). **L. Stephen,** *DNB* 11 (1887) 302-17. **C. Welch,** *NCRTW* (1985) 2:1-28. **B. Willey,** *Samuel Taylor Coleridge* (1972).

J. C. LIVINGSTON

COLET, JOHN (1466/67–1519)

C. studied at Cambridge and Oxford, traveled in France and Italy, was ordained priest (1498), gave public lectures on PAUL's epistles, and formed a lasting friendship with ERASMUS. Named dean of St. Paul's Cathedral (by 1505), he refounded the cathedral school. T. More (1478–1535), W. Grocyn (1449?–1519), J. Fisher (1469–1535), T. Lupset, T. Linacre (1460–1524), C. Agrippa (1468–1535), and Henry VIII (1491–1547) were among C.'s admirers. He corresponded with M. Ficino, and Lollards traveled to hear him preach. Admired and loved by many who could not concur with one another, C.'s independence and dedication to the words of JESUS and Paul were manifest in his denouncing clerical abuses and preaching to King Henry that for a Christian no war is just. After C. died, Sept. 16, 1519, Erasmus vowed to keep alive the memory of "so peerless a preacher of Christian doctrine," "so constant a friend," and wrote a brief, affectionate biography.

Like his shorter expositions, C.'s Pauline commentaries are discursive and systematic, show intellectual toughness and often intricate thought, and owe relatively little directly to patristic, scholastic, or contemporary

authority, although C. incorporated passages from PICO DELLA MIRANDOLA and used Ficino for corroboration. C.'s principal references in elucidating, interpreting, or applying particular texts are other Pauline passages and the Gospel attributions to Jesus. The commentaries are strongly christocentric and soteriological, often homiletic, and frequently mystical. In this latter mode especially C. owes much to Pseudo-Dionysius. C. sometimes developed typological, anagogic, and allegorical interpretations. He gave attention to the historical circumstances in which Paul wrote and construed Paul's motives in adapting the manner and matter of his letters to his contemporary readers' needs and capacities: Paul appears as human, wise, and considerate, relying on human experience as well as on revelation.

Works: "Oratio ad Clerum in Convocatione," *Life of Dr. J. C.* (S. Knight, 1724, corr. 1823) 289-308 (Eng. version only in J. H. Lupton, *Life* [1909] 293-304). *De Sacramentis Ecclesiae* (ed. J. H. Lupton, 1867; ET 1867); *Super Opera Dionysi* (ed. J. H. Lupton, 1869); *Enarratio in Epistolam B. Pauli ad Romans* (ed. J. H. Lupton, 1873); *Enarratio in Epistolam S. Pauli ad Corinthios* (ed. J. H. Lupton, 1874); *Opuscula quaedam* (*Epistolae B. P. ad Rom. Expositio Literalis* ["Edmund's"], *In principium Geneseos* ["Radulphus"], *De compositione sancti corporis Christi mystici, Epistola Sancti Petri Apostoli* (ed. J. H. Lupton, 1876); "Catechyzon," "Statuta Paulinae Scholae," and "A ryght fruitefull monicion," *Life of J. C.* (J. H. Lupton, 1909) 271-92, 305-10; *Writings* (1966); *Commentary on First Corinthians* (ed. B. O'Kelly and C. A. L. Jarrott, 1985); "De Sacramentis," *John Colet* (J. Gleason, 1989) 270-333.

Bibliography: W. A. Clebsch, "J. C. and the Reformation," *ATR* 37 (1955) 167-77. **S. Dark,** *Five Deans* (1928) 15-53. **P. A. Duhamel,** "The Oxford Lectures of J. C.: An Essay in Defining the English Renaissance," *JHI* 14 (1953) 493-510. **Erasmus,** *The Lives of Jehan Vitrier . . . and J. C.* (ed. J. Lupton, 1883). **J. B. Gleason,** *John Colet* (1989). **S. Jayne,** *J.C. and Marsilio Ficino* (1963). **P. I. Kaufman,** "J. C. and Erasmus' *Enchiridion*," *ChH* 46 (1977) 296-312; "J. C.'s *Opus de sacramentis* and Clerical Anticlericalism . . . ," *JBS* 22 (1982) 1-22; *Augustinian Piety and Catholic Reform . . .* (1982). **S. Knight,** *The Life of Dr. J. C.* (1724, corr. 1823). **S. L. Lee,** *DNB* 11 (1987) 321-28. **J. H. Lupton,** *A Life of J. C., DD* (1887); *The Influence of Dean C. upon the Reformation of the English Church* (1893). **K. MacKenzie,** "J. C. of Oxford," *Dalhousie Review* 21 (1941) 15-28. **J. A. R. Marriott,** *The Life of J. C.* (1933). **C. Meyer,** "A Bibliography of J. C.," *Foundation for Reformation Research: Bulletin of the Library* 5 (1970) 23-28. **L. Miles,** *J. C. and the Platonic Tradition* (1961). **D. J. Parsons,** "J. C.'s Stature as an Exegete," *ATR* 40 (1958) 36-42. **E. F. Rice, Jr.,** "J. C. and the Annihilation of the Natural," *HTR* 45 (1952) 141-63. **F. Seebohm,** *The Oxford Reformers: J. C., Eramus, and T. More* (1867; 1887[3]). **E. L. Surtz,** "The Oxford Reformers and Scholasticism," *SP* 47

(1950) 547-56. **J. B. Trapp,** "J. C., His Manuscripts, and the Pseudo-Dionysius," *Classical Influences in European Cultures,* AD 1500–1700 (ed. R. R. Bolgar, 1976) 205-21; *CE* 1 (1985) 324-8; *Erasmus, C., and More . . . and Their Books* (Panizzi Lectures, 1990; 1991).

B. O'KELLY

COLLINS, ANTHONY (1676–1729)

Born in Middlesex, June 21, 1676, C. died Dec. 13, 1729. He was educated at Eton and King's College, Cambridge. In 1703–4 he became friends with J. LOCKE, whose philosophy influenced nearly all of C.'s works.

In his *Discourse* (1713) C. called attention to the different Scriptures "throughout the World," the differences even in the biblical CANON among Christians, the different readings, and the differences in interpretation of fundamental doctrines. He claimed that this exercise in comparative religion—a pioneer effort, deeply offensive to his contemporaries—was in the interests of free thought as well as of belief in the Bible and Anglicanism. But the many critics of his book recognized that his ulterior aim was to bring the Bible into disrepute by skeptically and slyly relativizing it.

His chief contribution to biblical criticism was on the messianic prophecies (see PROPHECY AND PROPHETS, HB) in his 1724 work, which elicited no fewer than thirty-five books or pamphlets in response within three years. C. argued that none of the HB prophecies concerning the Messiah could have been literally accomplished by JESUS as described in the NT, since most of them could be shown to be about events that occurred many years before his birth. Because there was no literal fulfillment of the messianic prophecies, and since the authenticity of the NT depends, he claimed, on this fulfillment, the conclusion would seem to be that the NT is not authentic.

C. continued his critique of the Bible in a 1726 work in which he attacked the authenticity of the prophecies in Daniel. He has not generally been given credit for dating the composition of the book of Daniel to the period of Antiochus Epiphanes on the basis of the writer's grasp of events up to that time.

Works: *An Essay Concerning the Use of Reason* (1707); *A Letter to Mr. Dodwell* (1707); *A Discourse of Free-thinking* (1713); *A Discourse of the Grounds and Reasons of the Christian Religion* (1724); *Letter to the Author of the Grounds* (1726); *Scheme of Literal Prophecy Considered* (1726); *Letter to Rogers* (1727).

Bibliography: *BB²* 4 (1789) 22-28. **D. Berman,** "A. C.: Aspects of His Thought and Writings," *Her* 119 (1975) 49-70; "Hume and Collins on Miracles," *Hume Studies* 6 (1980) 150-54; *A History of Atheism in Britain: From Hobbes to Russell* (1988) esp. 70-92. **J. Drury,** *Critics of the Bible, 1724–1873* (1989) 21-45. **H. Frei,** *The Eclipse of Biblical*

Narrative (1974) esp. 66-85. **J. O'Higgin,** *A. C.: The Man and His Works* (Archives internationales d'histoires des idées 35, 1970). **H. G. Reventlow,** *The Authority of the Bible and the Rise of the Modern World* (1984) 354-69. **J. M. Robertson,** *The Dynamics of Religion: An Essay in English Culture History* (1927²) esp. pt. 2, chap. 7. **L. Stephen,** *DNB* 11 (1887) 363-64.

D. BERMAN

COLOSSIANS, LETTER TO THE

1. The Early Church. The earliest interpretations of Colossians stem from MARCION and the Valentinian Gnostics (see GNOSTIC INTERPRETATION). Marcion characteristically omitted Col 1:15-16 from his text, although he did find support in 2:16-17, 21 for rejecting the Mosaic law. The Valentinians saw in 1:15-17 and 2:13-15 proof of the Savior's spiritual origin and his triumph over the rulers (Irenaeus *Haer.* 1.3.4; Clement of Alexandria *Exc. Theod.* 69-74.1). Reinterpreting many of the same verses, IRENAEUS and TERTULLIAN denied any fundamental opposition between God and the material world or between the Christian gospel and the Jewish law (e.g., *Adv. Marc.* 5.19). Unfortunately, ORIGEN's and CLEMENT OF ALEXANDRIA's works on Colossians are not extant, but from the mid-fourth to the mid-fifth centuries we possess works on Colossians by Ambrosiaster, CHRYSOSTOM, Severian of Gabala (fragments), PELAGIUS, THEODORE OF MOPSUESTIA, and THEODORET OF CYRRHUS. Chrysostom's homilies reflect his concerns as bishop of Constantinople; and he thus often strayed from the text to pursue tangential, pastoral topics. In contrast, Ambrosiaster and Theodore interpreted each verse in the light of the epistle's overall argument. Ambrosiaster's insistence that all humans are created free and that slavery results from sin is striking, as is Theodore's singularly contorted argument that "of his love" (1:13) indicates Christ's adoption. All these commentators used ANTIOCHENE exegetical methods; except when they allowed themselves to dabble in allegory (e.g., when Theodoret allegorized the "joints" of 2:20 as the apostles, prophets, and teachers), we are not well informed about ALEXANDRIAN exegesis of Colossians beyond the fact that Origen found in 2:16 justification for his typological reading of the HB (*De Prin.* 4.1.13).

A number of historical issues were contested by these early exegetes. Whether Archippus (Marcionite prologue) or Epaphras (Theodore) had first preached to the Colossians and whether PAUL was personally acquainted with them (Chrysostom, Severian, Theodoret; Marcionite prologue, Theodore) seem to have hinged on the variant readings of 1:7. The location of Paul's imprisonment was alternatively noted as Ephesus (Marcionite prologue) or Rome (Chrysostom). While the Marcionite prologue simply stated that the Colossian community was attacked by false prophets (see PROPHECY AND PROPHETS, NT), Chrysostom described the false teachings as the Jewish and Greek practices of approaching God through angels (so also Severian and Theodoret, who stated that this practice was still prevalent in Phrygia). Theodore identified the opponents as Jewish legalists who feared (but did not worship) angels. Ambrosiaster asserted that astrological beliefs and Jewish festivals lay behind 2:16-17 and 2:18-19 respectively.

The interpretation of 1:15-17 was highly disputed during the Arian (see ARIUS) and christological controversies. The primary issue dividing exegetes was whether the term *image* referred to Christ's divine or human nature. Origen interpreted it as proof of Christ's unity with God, despite his subordinate status (*De Prin.* 1.2.2-5). The Arian reading of "image" held that it demonstrated Christ's status as a created being. The orthodox response took two forms: Chrysostom adopted the more common understanding of "image" as a reference to Christ's invisible divine nature and its absolute equality with God. Theodore devoted one third of his commentary to 1:13-20, arguing that in 1:15 "image" applied to Christ's human nature and thus that this passage concerned redemption and not the creation of the world. Other points of debate included: whether "first-born" implies temporal priority (Severian) or preeminence (Theodore, Pelagius); whether baptism removes sin (Chrysostom, Severian) or mortality (Theodore); and whether according to 2:15 Christ stripped off the body (the Latin fathers) or the powers of evil (Chrysostom, Severian, Theodore, Theodoret). The reference to another Pauline letter in 4:16 initially provided scriptural validation of the *Epistle to the Laodiceans,* yet in order to discredit this pseudonymous work, exegetes through the eighteenth century commonly asserted that Paul was referring to a letter written by the Laodiceans, not by himself.

2. The Medieval Period. The conservative orientation of early medieval biblical scholarship can be credited with preserving some ancient commentaries and with producing new commentaries composed largely of paraphrases of the text and quotations from the fathers (*catena*). The most significant commentators on Colossians from 650–1000 were Theophylact and Euthymius Zigabenus, but commentaries were also composed by Oecumenius, Sedulius Scotus, RABANUS MAURUS, Photius, Atto of Vercelli, LANFRANC, and Hervaeus of Bourg-Dieu. Scholasticism brought a new interest in clarifying Paul's THEOLOGY. PETER LOMBARD and THOMAS AQUINAS, both of whom wrote commentaries or lectured on Colossians, noted the fathers' often divergent interpretations and weighed their relative authority. Earlier commentators, with their fourfold levels of exegesis, were concerned with moral theology; then Lombard, following contemporary LITERARY-critical methods, consistently sought a literal and historical interpretation on which to base dogmatic speculation. The earlier fascination with Col 1:15 had diminished considerably; comments on this verse are brief and betray little controversy over its precise meaning (only Aquinas mentions the Arians). Colossians 2:8, however, became the subject of intense debate. For Lombard this verse provided the opportunity to address the scholastic debate over the proper role of philosophy in theological speculation: In response to P. ABELARD's reduction of the Trinity to a philosophical problem, he echoed Paul's warning against deceptive philosophy (but see his comments on Rom 1:19-23; 11:33-36). According to Aquinas, however, Paul did not condemn philosophy in its entirety; the scholastic use of philosophy was vindicated by philosophy's proper application and subordination to Christ.

3. Sixteenth to Eighteenth Centuries. Renaissance and Reformation commentaries reflect the renewed interest in classical antiquity, the development of TEXTUAL CRITICISM, a commitment to Antiochene over Alexandrian exegesis, and a critical approach to the fathers. ERASMUS's annotations (1516; final ed. 1535) began by addressing the location of Colossae and refuting the popular opinion that the Colossians were inhabitants of Rhodes (where the Colossus stands). Erasmus's citation of classical authors (1:1), examination of textual variants (1:1, 7), appeal to philology (1:1; 2:18), and attention to idiomatic phrases (1:13) and figures of speech (1:23) demonstrate his humanistic approach to biblical interpretation. He engaged in patristic exegesis but rarely quoted the scholastics; of his contemporaries, he drew upon Lefèvre d'Etaples, the classical scholar and Pauline commentator (1512). Erasmus's comments on 1:15 were brief, although unlike his scholastic predecessors his christological opinions developed through the commentary's successive editions. While nearly one third of his commentary is devoted to 2:8-23, his notes on 2:8 are surprisingly brief and do not address the scholastic debate on philosophy.

Of the Protestant Reformers, the most important Colossian commentators were P. MELANCHTHON and CALVIN; LUTHER's interpretation of Colossians must be sought in occasional comments and in his sermons. In his scholia on Colossians (1527), Melanchthon used classical rhetorical categories to analyze the letter's structure and meaning. Contemporary theological and social issues also guided his exegesis. His lengthy comment on 2:8 was sparked by the debate between Luther and Erasmus on the freedom of the will. While maintaining the sovereignty of God (1:15; 3:3), Melanchthon, as both Reformer and humanist, vindicated humanistic scriptural interpretation and the philosophical analysis of reality and social morals. Philosophy errs when it goes beyond its divinely given propaedeutic function and formulates opinions about God's will or claims to impart virtue. In response to T. MÜNTZER's rebellion (1525), Melanchthon justified a conservative approach to social and religious change and a separation of ecclesiastical and spiritual authority in his extensive comment on 2:23. He argued that since secular laws are divinely given, civil officials do not require ecclesiastical guidance. Civil ordinances, unless enjoining sin, must always be obeyed; only those ecclesiastical traditions that blaspheme the gospel or endanger the weak may be disobeyed.

Although conversant with the fathers, Calvin wrote his commentary (1548) with different theological issues in mind (see his discussion on 1:15); and not surprisingly, in the context of the Protestant break with Rome, Colossians was often read by the Reformers as a polemic against medieval Catholicism. Calvin declared that Papists, ignoring the christology of 1:12, based the system of indulgences on the mistaken notion of the insufficiency of Christ's suffering (1:24). Following Luther, Calvin argued that the "worship of angels" (2:18) referred to papal religion—i.e., the worship of the saints—and that 2:23 was a graphic description of monasticism. According to Calvin, Paul condemned papal theology because it erroneously sought knowledge of things unseen and unrevealed (2:8, 18; commenting on 2:8, Luther had condemned scholasticism because it neglected an eschatological analysis of reality in favor of an Aristotelian one). With the exception of the Eucharist, Calvin condemned religious ceremonies as "shadows" abolished by Christ (2:14, 17).

In contrast, many commentaries of the seventeenth and eighteenth centuries lapse into an unimaginative orthodoxy. Some contain no more than footnotes (as by the proverbial J. Fell) or do little more than enumerate doctrines found within each verse (as by J. Fergusson and P. Bayne). The most substantial treatment of Colossians from this period was produced by J. Davenant, bishop of Salisbury, whose two-volume work went through several editions and was hailed as extraordinary through the nineteenth century. Davenant's exposition contained numerous polemics against papal teachings on apostolic succession (1:1), justification by works (1:12), and Christ (1:12); he was conversant with authors from the classical period up to his contemporaries, and he continued the RHETORICAL analysis begun by Melanchthon. Other influential commentators on Colossians from this period include H. GROTIUS, G. Estius (1542-1613), and J. BENGEL.

4. Nineteenth to Twentieth Centuries. Modern investigations of Colossians have concentrated on a limited number of issues, primarily its authenticity and the identification of the Colossian opponents; some attention has also been given to its use of traditional materials and its theological emphases.

a. Authenticity and dating. The Pauline authorship of Colossians had been accepted without question until 1839, when E. Mayerhoff argued that the letter contained lexical, stylistic, and theological differences from Paul, was dependent upon Ephesians, and could be traced to a conflict with Cerinthus. Although other nineteenth-century critics cast further doubt on the

authorship of Colossians (most notably F. C. Baur [1845], who placed it in the context of second-century Gnosticism, and H. HOLTZMANN, who thought the author of Ephesians had revised Colossians), its authenticity was still generally affirmed through the middle of the twentieth century (so M. Dibelius and H. Greeven [1953³]; P. O'Brien [1982]). Since the 1960s, however, an increasing defense of Colossians's pseudonymity (E. Lohse [1971]; W. Bujard [1973]; E. Schweizer [1982]) has occurred. Colossians lacks certain connective words and inferential particles characteristic of Paul (Lohse, 84-91); the length and complexity of the letter's sentences and its lack of logical argument (Bujard, 72-75, 129) are clear indications of non-Pauline authorship.

The dating of Colossians is primarily dependent on one's judgment of its authenticity. Those who hold it to be genuine have been guided by conventional theories of Paul's theological development and his place of imprisonment (4:3, 10, 18). A Roman or Caesarean (E. Lohmeyer [1930]) imprisonment would place Colossians's developed theology at the end of Paul's career (c. 57–61), although there are significant objections to both theories. Based on Paul's hints of trouble in Ephesus (c. 55; Rom 16:3-4; 2 Cor 1:8) and its proximity to Colossae, some scholars have suggested this location (G. Duncan [1930]). If Colossians is held to be pseudonymous, the presumed author's imprisonment contributes to the image of the suffering apostle perpetuated by his followers. In this case dating must be based on Ephesians's generally accepted dependence on Colossians (cf. E. Best [1997]); the composition of Ephesians (prior to c. 100; Ignatius *Pol.* 5.1; *Smyrn.* 1.1) would provide the latest date and Paul's death the earliest. In light of the destruction of Colossae c. 60 (Tacitus *Ann.* 14.27), the intended audience must be sought elsewhere, perhaps in southwest Asia Minor.

b. Identity and theology of Colossian opponents. The precise identification of the Colossian opponents has proved to be elusive. In addition to the difficulties of determining whether the language of the opponents has been adopted (e.g., whether "philosophy" or "mystery" was a self-designation) or of distinguishing polemic from independently formulated arguments, this project has been beset by recurring exegetical difficulties: (1) whether angels (2:18) were understood as malevolent or beneficial; (2) whether the *stoicheia* (2:8, 20; cf. Gal 4:3, 9) referred to these angels or to the four primal elements, the Jewish law, or religious regulations; (3) whether *thrēskeia tōn aggelōn* (2:18) consisted in worshiping angels or in the angelic worship of God; (4) whether *embateuō* (2:18) referred to initiation into a mystery cult or to entering heaven; (5) whether ritual and ascetic practices (2:16, 20-23) were necessary prerequisites for salvation or required acts of subservience. This constellation of disputed issues has further resulted in conflicting descriptions of the opponents' theology.

Most scholars concur that it was a synthesis of several religious traditions (including Gnosticism, Phrygian religious practices, Hellenistic philosophy, and Jewish apocalyptic and mysticism), although no consensus exists on the role Judaism played in their theology.

J. B. LIGHTFOOT 1879[3] understood the Colossian theology as a mixture of heterodox Jewish sabbath observance and dietary laws with a Gnostic interest in wisdom, cosmology, intermediary beings, and asceticism. DIBELIUS similarly argued (F. Francis and W. Meeks [1975] 61-121; followed by Lohse) that angels and the *stoicheia* were enslaving deities and that *embateuō* was a technical term for initiation into a mystery cult; he concluded that the opponents proclaimed a gnostic mystery religion that required preparatory ascetic practices and lacked any significant Jewish elements. G. BORNKAMM (Francis and Meeks, 123-45) understood the angels as positive forces who imposed ritual and ascetic practices; in contrast to Dibelius, he balanced pagan and Persian influences with the Jewish origin of these practices and cosmology. Recently parallels between the Colossian philosophy and *Hyp. Arch., Eugnostos, Soph. Jes. Chr., Ap. John,* and *Zost.* have been cited. Rejecting this widely held theory of Gnostic origins, Lyonnet explained the Colossian philosophy purely on the basis of the Essene interest in purity, wisdom, angelology, and the law found in the DEAD SEA SCROLLS (Francis and Meeks, 147-61).

A more convincing theory of Jewish origins argues for parallels with Jewish apocalyptic (see APOCALYPTICISM) and mystical literature: Francis (Francis and Meeks, 163-207) argued that *thrēskeia tōn aggelōn* should be understood as the angelic worship of God glimpsed during a mystical ascent; this foretaste of heaven assured the adherent of salvation. A third line of interpretation (most recently C. Arnold [1995]) draws significantly on archaeological evidence (see ARCHAEOLOGY AND BIBLICAL STUDIES) and argues that the Colossian theology was a synthesis of Judaism (of varying degrees) with local Phrygian religious expression, including asceticism, interest in intermediary beings, and folk belief. A final line of interpretation understands the Hellenistic philosophical schools as the key to the Colossian philosophy. Schweizer links the Colossian interest in ritual laws, asceticism, and the four primal elements (*stoicheia*) to Pythagoreanism. R. DeMaris (1994) argues for a blend of Middle Platonism with Jewish and Christian elements, while T. Martin (1996) identifies the opponents as Cynics. In view of such diverse results, further investigations should refine a reliable methodology for analyzing polemical literature and must contain a historically grounded explanation of the origin of the particular syncretism observed.

c. Use of traditional materials. On the basis of stylistic and linguistic criteria vv. 15-20 have been identified as a christological hymn that presents Christ as a preexistent being (v. 15) whose supremacy extends over both creation (vv. 16-17) and redemption (vv. 18-20). Numerous structural analyses have been proposed, and there is debate over the extent to which the original hymn has been altered and whether those alterations were done by the author of Colossians. The history-of-religions background (see RELIGIONSGESCHICHTLICHE SCHULE) of the hymn is variously identified as philosophically influenced Judaism, pre-Christian Gnosis, the Jewish Day of Atonement, rabbinic biblical interpretation, Hellenistic Jewish wisdom speculation, the heavenly *Anthropos,* and Jewish monotheistic confessions. Despite the failure to achieve consensus on these issues, most scholars acknowledge the presence of a pre-Pauline hymn in these verses; some, however, have suggested that they are better understood as the author's own composition from fragments of traditional materials (Dibelius and Greeven, 10-12; O'Brien, 36). Form-critical studies (see FORM CRITICISM) have also identified two other liturgical fragments: Col 1:12-14 and 2:13c-15 (some scholars include as much as vv. 9-15). Both portray the work of Christ as a victory over the forces of evil and may stem from a baptismal liturgy (see G. Cannon [1983] 37-49). Earlier exegetes followed the patristic understanding of the *cheirographon* (v. 14) as the pact made between humanity and the devil; more appropriate is the meaning "note of indebtedness," although its exact meaning and relationship to *dogma* are still debated. But again the lack of consensus on the extent, structure, and setting of these fragments has led some to reject their identification as traditional material.

The virtue and vice catalogues in 3:5-12 contain prohibitions and encouragement to a conventional morality. Discussion has centered on the precise form and source of this type of exhortation (Hellenistic, Jewish, or Iranian); whether the elements of the catalogues were chosen to fit the precise situation addressed, e.g., baptism in Colossians (Cannon, 51-94), remains an open question. Of recent interest are the household codes (*Haustafeln;* 3:18–4:1), which detail the duties and responsibilities of the members of the ancient household. The majority of research has again addressed the issues of form and source (Stoicism, Hellenistic Judaism, Aristotle); more pertinent to Colossians in particular is the observation that in the letter the household codes have been only marginally christianized (so also 1 Pet 2:18–3:7; cf. Eph 5:22–6:9) and that despite their restriction of women's behavior for the sake of the church's social acceptance (E. Johnson [1992]; see also C. Martin [1991]), they do contain a critique of the slave system (D. Balch [1981]; for a different view, see M. D'Angelo [1994]).

d. Theological emphases and Pauline response. Comparatively less emphasis has been given to analyzing the author's response to the Colossian teaching. His aim is clearly to ensure that the Colossians continue to obey the gospel as it had been delivered to them (1:23).

Previously hidden, this newly manifest gospel (2:2; 4:3), which consists in Christ's presence among the Gentiles (1:27), is now reaching the entire world (1:6, 23). The angelic beings with whom the Colossians have become obsessed are not relevant to Christian experience. Preeminent in all spheres (1:12-20; 3:11) and embodying the divine (2:9), Christ rescued them from oppression and offers forgiveness through baptism (1:12-14); their allegiance to him alone must be vigilantly maintained (1:23). Further analysis of the author's theological construction in response to the Colossian teaching is necessary. The polemical response to a syncretistic religious movement rooted in Judaism may later have been understood as an attack on Judaism (e.g., by Marcion). The author of Ephesians may have sought to reinterpret this seeming contradiction in the Pauline writings in his appropriation of Colossians and its traditional materials (J. Maclean [1995]). In addition, the role of moral instruction in community formation (W. Meeks [1993]) is a fruitful new line of approach.

Bibliography: **C. E. Arnold,** *The Colossian Syncretism: The Interface Between Christianity and Folk Belief at Colossae* (WUNT 77, 1995). **D. L. Balch,** *Let Wives Be Submissive: The Domestic Code in 1 Peter* (SLBMS 26, 1981). **F. C. Baur,** *Paulus, der Apostel Jesu Christi* (1845; ET 1873-75). **E. Best,** "Who Used Whom? The Relationship of Ephesians and Colossians," *NTS* 43 (1997) 72-96. **W. Bujard,** *Stilanalytische Untersuchungen zum Kolosserbrief als Beitrag zur Methodik von Sprachvergleichen* (SUNT 11, 1973). **J. Calvin,** *Commentarii in Pauli Epistolas* (ed. H. Feld, Ioannis Calvini Opera Exegetica 16, 1992). **G. E. Canon,** *The Use of Traditional Materials in Colossians* (1983). **L. Cope,** "On Rethinking the Philemon–Colossians Connection," *BR* 30 (1985) 45-50. **J. Chrysostom,** *Homilies on the Epistle of St. Paul the Apostle to the Colossians* (NPNF 1.13; 1983). **M. R. D'Angelo,** "Colossians," *Searching the Scriptures,* vol. 2, *A Feminist Commentary* (ed. E. Schüssler Fiorenza, 1994) 313-24. **J. Davenant,** *An Exposition of the Epistle of St. Paul to the Colossians* (1831-32). **M. Dibelius, and H. Greeven,** *An die Kolosser, Epheser, an Philemon,* erklärt von M. Dibelius (HNT 12, 1953[3]). **R. E. DeMaris,** *The Colossian Controversy: Wisdom in Dispute at Colossae* (JSNTSup 96, 1994). **G. S. Duncan,** *St. Paul's Ephesian Ministry* (1930). **F. O. Francis and W. A. Meeks (eds.),** *Conflict at Colossae: A Problem in the Interpretation of Early Christianity* (SBLSBS 4, 1975). **M. Goulder,** "Colossians and Barbelo," *NTS* 41 (1995) 601-19. **A. Hockel,** *Christus, Der Ertsgeborene: Zur Geschichte der Exegese von Kol 1,15* (1965). **E. E. Johnson,** "Colossians," *Women's Bible Commentary* (ed. C. A. Newsom and S. H. Ringe, 1992) 346-48. **J. B. Lightfoot,** *Saint Paul's Epistles to the Colossians and to Philemon* (1879[3]). **E. Lohmeyer,** *Die Briefe an die Philipper, an die Kolosser, und an Philemon* (1930). **E. Lohse,** *Colossians and Philemon* (Hermeneia, 1971). **J. K. B. Maclean,** "Ephesians and the Problem of Colossians: Interpretation of Text and Tradition in Eph 1:1-2:10" (diss., Harvard University, 1995). **C. J. Martin,** "The *Haustafeln*

(Household Code) in African American Biblical Interpretation: 'Free Slaves' and Subordinate Women," *Stony the Road We Trod: African American Biblical Interpretation* (ed. C. H. Felder, 1991) 206-31. **T. W. Martin,** *By Philosophy and Empty Deceit: Colossians as Response to a Cynic Critique* (JSNTSup 118, 1996). **E. T. Mayerhoff,** *Der Brief an die Colosser mit vornehmlicher Berücksichtigung der drei Pastoralbriefe* (1838). **W. A. Meeks,** " 'To Walk Worthily of the Lord': Moral Formation in the Pauline School Exemplified by the Letter to Colossians," *Hermes and Athena: Biblical Exegesis and Philosophical Theology* (ed. E. Stump and T. P. Flint, 1993) 71-74. **P. Melanchthon,** *Paul's Letter to the Colossians* (HTIBS, 1989). **P. T. O'Brien,** *Colossians, Philemon* (WBC 44, 1982). **A. Reeves** (ed.), *Erasmus' Annotations on the NT: Galatians to the Apocalypse* (SHCT 52, 1993). **J. A. Robinson,** *Pelagius's Expositions of Thirteen Epistles of St. Paul* (TS 9.2, 1926). **W. Schenk,** "Der Kolosserbrief in der neueren Forschung (1945–85)," *ANRW* II.25.4 (1987) 3327-64. **E. Schweizer,** *The Letter to the Colossians: A Commentary* (1982). **K. Staab,** *Pauluskommentare aus der griechischen Kirche* (NTAbh 15, 1933). **H. B. Swete,** *Theodori Episcopi Mopsuesteni in Epistolas b. Pauli Commentarii* (1880–82). **H. J. Vogels,** *Ambrosiastri Qui Dicitur Commentarius in Epistolas Paulinas* (CSEL 81, 1966–69). **M. F. Wiles,** *The Divine Apostle: The Interpretation of St Paul's Epistles in the Early Church* (1967). **N. T. Wright,** "Poetry and Theology in Colossians 1:15-20," *NTS* 36 (1990) 444-68.

J. B. MACLEAN

CONCORDANCES, HEBREW BIBLE

The first actual concordance (and not lexicon) to the HB in the MT was compiled according to the same format and purposes as earlier Latin ones (for a definition of concordance and for its early history, see CONCORDANCES, NT). As a service to Jewish scholars, R. Isaac, or Mordecai (the identity is unclear), Nathan of Arles, registered the various Hebrew roots found in Scripture alphabetically and listed under each its attestations, regardless of grammatical form or part of speech, according to the order of the VULGATE. He called the "concordance" *Mēˈîr* (or *Yāˈîr*) *nātîb,* "Illuminator of the Path" after the phrase in Job 41:24. Compiled hurriedly between 1437 and 1445, Nathan omitted proper nouns, function words, and Aramaic, and apologized for not rechecking the references. D. BOMBERG printed this concordance in Venice in 1523. Revised editions appeared in 1556 (Basel) and 1564 (Venice). Mario de Calasio, a Franciscan, produced a four-volume expanded edition including Aramaic words, Hebrew particles, and one attestation each of personal names in 1621 (Rome) based on a revision of Nathan's opus by A. Frobenius (1580, Basel). In it the Hebrew and Vulgate were printed in facing columns. An abridged version of Nathan's concordance, really a LEXICON, called *Šōreš yešaˈ,* was published in Frankfurt (1768) by R. Isaac ben Zebi Hirsch of Seldin. B. Baer expanded this work by adding the root *h-w-y* and the tetragrammaton as well as function words in 1861. For purposes of study it is important to separate roots into parts of speech and grammatical forms. This was first accomplished by E. LEVITA, an Italian Jewish Hebraist. His concordance, called *Sēper hazzikrônôt,* was produced in two handwritten copies (1521; 1536) but never printed.

The first serviceable modern concordance in biblical studies was produced by a professor of Hebrew at the University of Basel, J. BUXTORF, Sr., and his son, successor, and namesake. The *Concordantiae bibliorum hebraicae . . . accesserunt novae concordantiae chaldaicae* (1632) provided Latin glosses alongside Nathan's in Hebrew but barely treated function words. C. Nolde published a supplement of Hebrew particles in Copenhagen (1679). Notable among revised editions is the two-volume English version by John TAYLOR (London, 1954–57), which includes Nolde's additions. It contains no citations of text, however, only references to chapter and verse.

A linguistically sophisticated, though idiosyncratic, concordance was produced in Leipzig (1840) by a Jewish scholar, J. Fürst. *'ôṣar lĕšôn haqqōdeš (Thesaurus of Hebrew)* was a thorough revision of Buxtorf's concordance, including etymological analysis (based on Franz Delitzsch's theory that Hebrew roots were basically biconsonantal), proper names, and a compendium of Masoretic notes. This work attained wide use, especially in its photographically reduced edition of 1932 and various abridgements. The most standard concordance of the HB is that of S. MANDELKERN, published in Leipzig in 1896 and called *Hêkal haqqōdeš.* It furnishes a concise lexical article at the head of each root, includes all words and proper nouns, Hebrew and Aramaic, and presents forms in context. Mandelkern sought not only to assist Bible study but also to enhance research in Hebrew language. Despite painstaking care thousands of errors were discovered, published, and corrected in later revised editions (from 1925 by F. Margolin through the seventh edition by M. Goshen-Gottstein in 1967). Mandelkern's scriptural references follow the order of the HB. To make use of the new critical edition of the HB by R. KITTEL and P. KAHLE, based on the authoritative Leningrad manuscript, and to analyze verbs and nouns in their syntactic functions, G. Lisowky published *Konkordanz zum hebräischen Alten Testament* (1958) in Stuttgart. Written by hand, the concordance lists words alphabetically, not by root, and features an apparatus providing such useful information as the subjects of verbs and references of pronouns. S. Loewenstamm, J. Blau, M. Kaddari, and other Israeli scholars collaborated on a full concordance and lexicon of biblical Hebrew, *'ôṣar lĕšôn hammiqrā'* (1957–68), which is also arranged alphabetically and uses the Kittel-Kahle edition. Its lengthy citation of contexts is an important aid, but its three volumes only reach the letter *ṭet.*

The four-volume Hebrew concordance by A. Even-Shoshan (Jerusalem, 1977–80) also combines the features of a lexicon with a concordance (2nd. ed. modified for English readers, 1989). Not only does it separate words morphologically, but it is also sensitive to usage, such as the preceding preposition or connective *wāw.* Combining Hebrew and Aramaic as well as common and proper nouns, it does not furnish full references for widely occurring words but does preface listings with various idiomatic usages and synonyms.

Computers enable researchers to print words and forms in any number of ways. Y. Radday and colleagues have published an "analytical linguistic concordance" to Isaiah (1971) and Haggai, Zechariah, and Malachi (1973), as well as a "key-word-in-context" concordance to Judges (1977). The word in focus is printed in the middle of the page, with extended context on either side. *The Complete Practical Concordance to the Holy Scriptures,* by H. Wachsman (2 vols., 1989), presents all words, Hebrew and Aramaic mixed, alphabetically. In the 1990s a number of electronic editions of the biblical text provided word-search functions that approximate those of a concordance.

Concordances to the Vulgate version of the HB, for which the genre was first developed, are treated in the following article. A concordance to the SEPTUAGINT was produced by Conrad Kirch at Frankfurt (1607), to which Abraham Tromm added recensional readings at Amsterdam (1718). An excellent Oxford standard edition is that of E. HATCH and H. REDPATH in two volumes (1892–97), with a personal name supplement (1900).

Some concordances organize passages from Scripture according to theme. A Hebrew concordance by key words was published by J. Eisenstein (New York, 1925). A more complete reference in Hebrew and English is E. Katz, *A Classified Concordance to the Bible in Its Various Subjects in Four Volumes* (Jerusalem, 1979–80). The English reader may turn to "topical" concordances by C. Joy (1940) and D. Miller (1965).

Bibliography: A. Even-Shoshan, "Haqqônqôrdanṣîyôt ha-'ibrîyôt lammiqrā': sĕqîrâ bîblîyôgrā'pît," *Qônqôrdanṣîyâ hădāšâ lĕtôrâ nĕbî'îm ûkĕtûbîm* (1977) 1:15-35. **B. B. Kirschner,** "Qônqôrdanṣîyôt lammiqrā'," *EncBib* 7 (1976) 94-103. **A. Kleinhans,** "De prima editione catholica concordantiarum hebraico-latinarum sacrorum Bibliorum," *Bib* 5 (1924) 39-48. **S. Mandelkern,** "Pĕtîḥâ lĕqônqôrdanṣîyâ," *Hêkal haqqōdeš (1896)* ix-xiv. **H. A. Redpath,** "Concordances to the OT in Greek," *The Expositor,* 5th ser., 3 (1896) 69-77. **A. Tauber,** "Mî hû' mĕḥabbēr haqqônqôrdanṣîyâ hattanakît?" *Kiryath-Sepher* 2 (1925) 141-44. **H. H. Wellisch,** "HB Concordances, with a Bibliographical Study of S. Mandelkern," *Jewish Book Annual* 43 (1985–86) 56-91.

E. L. GREENSTEIN

CONCORDANCES, NEW TESTAMENT

A concordance is an alphabetically arranged index of words or subjects contained in a book, with citations of the passages in which they occur. Concordances exist for the works of many authors, both ancient and modern, including Homer, Seneca, JOSEPHUS, ANSELM OF CANTERBURY, Shakespeare, MILTON, and Yeats. The first concordances were produced in the Middle Ages and pertained to the Bible. From the beginning, two basic types have existed. The most common is the verbal concordance, which (a) lists in alphabetical order most or all of the words of the Bible and (b) under each word cites in canonical order (see CANON OF THE BIBLE) the passage where it is found. The second type is the topical concordance, which provides a listing of the biblical passages where various subjects or themes appear. Of the two types, the verbal concordance is both more comprehensive and more important for exegesis and will constitute the focus of this article.

1. The Earliest Biblical Concordances. Like other study aids and research tools (e.g., subject indexes and collections of biblical *distinctiones*), the concordance was the product of the revival of interest in original sources that occurred in the late twelfth and early thirteenth centuries. The first verbal concordances to the Scriptures were based on the VULGATE and were used primarily as practical aids to teaching and preaching. According to R. and M. Rouse, whose research informs the following treatment of the Latin *concordantiae,* the first three verbal concordances to the Bible were produced by the Dominicans. The first was compiled by the friars of St. Jacques at Paris, probably during 1230–35, when HUGH OF ST. CHER occupied one of the chairs of theology there. Adopting the new system of chapter divisions traditionally attributed to S. LANGTON, the St. Jacques Dominicans subdivided the chapters of the Bible into seven units, designating each by one of the first seven letters of the alphabet, A through G.

The major weakness of the St. Jacques concordance (*Concordantiae S. Jacobi*) was that it listed only the word and biblical references without giving the context in which the word occurred. The second verbal concordance was an attempt to correct this deficiency. Known as the English Concordance (*Concordantiae anglicanae*), it was produced, possibly also at the house of St. Jacques, under the direction of the English Dominican Richard of Stavensby. Its compilers not only provided a full sentence context for each reference but also introduced a number-code system to convey syntactical information. Unfortunately, the English Concordance proved more ambitious than successful, for its great length rendered it too difficult to copy and too cumbersome to use.

The third verbal concordance, sometimes falsely attributed to Conrad of Halberstadt (fl. 1321), was probably also a compilation of the St. Jacques Dominicans.

The compilers, who completed their work no later than 1286, successfully avoided the extremes of their two predecessors by providing simply the salient words of the context for each reference listed. In addition, they subdivided the shorter chapters into four units rather than seven. Partly because this concordance was available in sections (*peciae*), it circulated widely; and its success helped to establish the concordance as a standard reference tool.

2. Greek Concordances to the NT. The first person to compile a concordance to the Greek Bible may have been Euthalius of Rhodes, who, according to Sixtus of Siena (d. 1569), did so in 1300. The first extant concordance to the Greek NT was compiled by Xystus Betuleius (Sixtus Birken) and published in 1546. One weakness of this work was that references were cited only by book and chapter, with no further specification attempted. This defect was corrected in the Greek concordance published in 1594 by H. Estienne (Stephanus), who used the NT verse divisions that his father, Robert, had devised and employed in his fourth edition of the Greek NT (1551), his 1555 edition of the Latin Bible, and his concordance to the Vulgate (1555). For the versification of the OT in the latter two works the elder Estienne used the divisions made by I. Nathan, the compiler of the first concordance to the HB. Estienne's verse divisions became part of English Bibles chiefly through their adoption by the translators (esp. W. Whittingham) of the Geneva Bible (1560).

E. Schmid's concordance, published posthumously in 1638 and reprinted in 1717 with minor revisions, marked a major advance over its predecessors and became the standard work for some two centuries. Indeed, an abridged revision of his concordance was published in Greece as recently as 1977. For scholarly purposes, however, it was supplanted in the latter half of the nineteenth century by the concordance of K. Bruder (1842; 1913[7]; repr. 1975). The major deficiency of Schmid's concordance was that it, like the earlier Greek concordances, was based almost exclusively on the *textus receptus.* Ironically, Bruder's attempt to address this problem by noting the principal readings found in the editions of K. LACHMANN, S. Tregelles, and others (see esp. 1888[4]), only served to emphasize the pressing need for a new concordance based on a modern critical edition of the NT.

The first to offer a concordance on this basis were W. Moulton and A. Geden (1897), who adopted the Greek text of B. F. WESTCOTT and F. HORT (1881) as their standard and also made use of the texts of L. TISCHENDORF and the English revisers. Their concordance has been widely used by NT scholars throughout the twentieth century, and the usefulness of the work has been enhanced through the addition (1978[5]) of a supplement by H. Moulton that gives full citations for seven commonly used words only listed by chapter and verse in earlier editions. The Greek text adopted for this supplement is that of the United Bible Societies' third edition (= *GNT*[3] [1975; corr. ed., 1983]), which is equivalent in wording to the new fourth edition (*GNT*[4] [1993]) and differs from *GNT*[4] only in its critical apparatus. The text of *GNT*[3] and *GNT*[4] is also equivalent to that printed in the twenty-sixth and twenty-seventh editions of the *Novum Testamentum Graece* (= Nestle-Aland[26] [1979]; Nestle-Aland[27] [1993]). The internationally recognized critical text that is common to these four editions also forms the basis of the eighth edition (by B. Köster [1989 rev. 1994[3]]) of A. Schmoller's pocket concordance (1st ed. by O. Schmoller [1868]).

The premier concordance to the Greek NT is now the *Vollständige Konkordanz zum griechischen Neuen Testament* (= *VKGNT* [1975–83]), a massive work produced by the Institut für Neutestamentliche Textforschung at Münster, Germany. Prepared under the direction of K. Aland, it is based on the text common to *GNT*[3]/*GNT*[4] and Nestle-Aland[26]/Nestle-Aland[27], but it also incorporates all the different readings found in most of the major critical editions since Tischendorf (1841–69) and in the *textus receptus*. Volume one contains the concordance proper and is in two parts. Volume two contains vocabulary statistics, an alphabetical arrangement of the words of the NT and their grammatical forms, a survey of NT vocabulary frequencies arranged in descending order, and a reverse index of inflected forms. A less exhaustive version of this *magnum opus* is the *Concordance to the Novum Testamentum Graece* (= *CNTG* [1987[3]]), formerly entitled the *Computer-Konkordanz* (1977, 1980[2]). It lacks the textual variants and the index system of the complete concordance, omits some twenty-nine high-frequency words, and uses accents only when they are significant for meaning.

An attractive alternative to the *CNTG* is *The Exhaustive Concordance to the Greek NT* (= *ECGNT* [1995]) by J. Kohlenberger III, E. Goodrick, and J. Swanson. With the exception of twenty-six high-frequency words that it cites by reference only, this work provides an exhaustive index with contexts to the entire vocabulary of *GNT*[4]. In addition, it takes note of all variant readings between *GNT*[4] and the Greek text that underlies the NIV (as best as it can be reconstructed).

Important as a companion and supplement to the *VKGNT,* the *CNTG,* the *ECGNT,* and the concordance of Moulton-Geden is *NT Vocabulary* by F. Neirynck and F. van Segbroeck (1984). It gives lists of compounds and derivatives; deals with SYNOPTIC parallels and synonyms; includes readings from the first two editions of *GNT,* the *Synopsis* of H. Greeven (1981), and the variants printed in the margin of the edition of the NT by Westcott and Hort (1881), and in general corrects some of the deficiencies that Neirynck (1982) observed in the *VKGNT.*

3. Greek-English Concordances. An enormously successful bilingual concordance to the NT was pro-

duced in the nineteenth century under the direction of G. Wigram (1839). Adopting a plan suggested to him by W. Burgh, Wigram used Greek headings to organize his work but cited the passages in English rather than Greek. The Greek words used for the headings were based on Schmid's concordance, and the biblical citations were taken from the AV (KJV). Often reprinted with various enhancements, it inspired several later works, including J. Gall's bilingual analytical concordance (1863, repr., 1975) and the concise concordance prepared by C. Hudson under the direction of H. Hastings. In preparing his concordance Hudson made skillful use of Bruder's work, four critical editions of the Greek NT, and Codex Sinaiticus. Revised and completed after Hudson's death by E. ABBOT of Harvard, this work was widely used as a pocket concordance in the latter nineteenth century (1870, 1898[9]). In the twentieth century the most notable entirely new bilingual work was until recently that of J. Smith (1955, repr., 1983), who contributed a statistical Greek-English concordance based, unfortunately, on the *textus receptus* and the AV. In addition, J. Stegenga (1963) compiled a Greek-English concordance using the root-word-family method to call attention to cognate terms.

Since its publication, R. Winter's *Word Study Concordance* (1978) has enjoyed wide use because it contains a revised and enlarged edition of two versions of Wigram's concordance as well as references to BAG, the *TDNT,* and the Moulton-Geden concordance. It and all other Greek-English concordances now have been superseded by the *Greek-English Concordance to the NT* (= *GECNT*), which uses the NIV. The editors are Kohlenberger, Goodrick, and Swanson—the same as those for the *ECGNT.* The volume employs the numbering system devised by Goodrick and Kohlenberger, and for each entry it gives in the heading the Greek lexical form, a transliteration, the total number of occurrences of the word in the *GNT*[3]/*GNT*[4] and Nestle-Aland[26]/Nestle-Aland[27], Greek cognate information, special phrases, and a list of the way(s) in which the NIV has translated the word, with word counts for each. The concordance cites the passages with contexts. For laity and other general readers who know or are willing to learn the Greek alphabet, this should prove to be an extremely helpful work.

4. Concordances to the English Bible, NT. The first concordance to the NT in English was printed about 1535 by T. Gibson, to whom some have given credit for also compiling this work, whereas others have attributed its compilation chiefly to the printer J. Day, who produced the first English edition of J. Foxe's famous book of martyrs, *Acts and Monuments.* The first concordance to the entire English Bible was produced in 1550 by the musician J. Marbeck, who was imprisoned for his labors on the work and nearly executed. He was spared through the intercession of S. Gardiner, the bishop of Winchester, who had sharply rebuked Marbeck for his work on the concordance but did not wish to lose the services of the talented organist. A. Cruden's concordance, which first appeared in 1737, eclipsed all previous English concordances. It soon became a classic (1761[2], 1769[3]) and made the name of its author a household word among English-speaking Protestants. Indeed, in popular circles Cruden's concordance was viewed as the authoritative tool with which to study the AV, the version on which it was based.

The proliferation of modern biblical translations during the past century has been matched by a similar increase in the number of concordances to accompany the new versions. For example, concordances exist for at least the ASV, Douay-Rheims, GNB (TEV), JB, TLB, Moffatt, NAB, NASB, NEB, NIV, NKJV, NRSV, RV, and RSV. Some concordances are partial and thus limit their references to only the more important theological terms and more frequently used words, whereas others are more or less complete, with only the most common articles, conjunctions, prepositions, and pronouns not indexed. English-only concordances index the passages where words occur without attempting to indicate their various meanings or usages; examples of this type include J. Ellison's concordance of the RSV (1957, 1972[2]) and S. Hartdegen's concordance of the NAB (1977). The better concordances are multilingual and usually are designated as either "analytical" or "exhaustive," although editors and publishers are not consistent in their use of these terms. Analytical concordances typically subdivide each entry according to the Hebrew, Aramaic, Latin (for 2 Esdras), or Greek word that underlies the English translation. Exhaustive concordances ideally list the references for each English word in biblical order but use some kind of numbering system so that the ancient word underlying the modern translation can be determined by consulting the LEXICONS appended to the concordance proper. Analytical concordances exist for both the AV (R. Young [1879], and often reprinted) and the RSV (C. Morrison for the NT [1979] and R. E. Whitaker for the HB, NT, and Apocrypha [1988]). Exhaustive concordances exist for the AV (J. Strong [1894], often reprinted with various enhancements), the NASB (R. Thomas [1981]), and the NIV (Goodrick and Kohlenberger [1990]). For the NRSV the best concordance currently available is the unabridged edition by Kohlenberger (1991), which covers not only the HB, NT, and apocryphal/deuterocanonical books but also the NRSV footnotes. In addition, it contains a topical concordance prepared by V. Verbrugge. Unfortunately, it does not indicate the original biblical words underlying the NRSV. A new analytical concordance for the NRSV by R. Whitaker and Kohlenberger (1997) indicates the Greek terms underlying the NT portion of the NRSV as well as supplies other information helpful for exegesis. Whitaker and Kohlenberger plan to complete an analytical concordance for the entire NRSV before the year 2000.

5. Modern Concordances to the Vulgate. Two major concordances to the Vulgate produced in the nineteenth century were those of F. Dutripon (1838, 1880[8], repr. 1976) and E. Peultier, L. Étienne, and L. Gantois (1897, 1939[2]). The most recent and best modern concordance is that by B. Fischer (5 vols., 1977), which is based on the Stuttgart critical edition, edited by R. Weber (1969).

6. Miscellaneous. Other works pertinent for the study of the NT include (a) the two-volume *Analytical Concordance of the Greek NT* (1991), edited by P. Clapp, B. Friberg, and T. Friberg. Based on the text of *GNT*[3] and designed to be especially helpful for discourse analysis, the first volume indexes words in alphabetical order, subdivided according to inflected form; the second indexes words according to parts of speech (adjectives and adverbs, conjunctions, etc.); an important appendix lists alphabetically all the variant readings and their references (without contexts) that are printed in the critical apparatuses of *GNT*[3] and Nestle-Aland[26]; (b) concordances to Q by R. Edwards (1975) and J. Kloppenborg (1988); (c) the comparative Greek concordance of the synoptic Gospels compiled by E. Camillo dos Santos and edited by R. Lindsey and J. Burnham (1989); (d) the concordance to Codex Bezae by J. Yoder (1961); (e) the list of NT cognate terms compiled by X. Jacques (1969); (f) the statistical analysis of NT vocabulary by R. Morgenthaler (1958, 1982[3] with supp.); (g) *The Computer Bible* (1971–), a multi-volume series that provides enhanced concordances for individual books of the Bible as well as some non-canonical works like the Coptic *Gospel of Thomas* (1995). NT volumes typically contain word counts, frequency profiles, and both forward and reverse key-word-in-context concordances that are context-sorted; these features are designed to facilitate linguistic-grammatical and LITERARY-critical analyses of the text. Produced by Biblical Research Associates, the project is intended to make the concordance not simply a reference tool with which to study the Bible but also a primary document that is to be studied along with the biblical text; (h) the Centre: Informatique et Bible (CIB) at the Abbaye de Maredsous in Belgium is currently preparing a multi-lingual, multi-volume concordance to the Bible. It will be known as the *Concordantia polyglotta* and will provide an important index of all the primary biblical texts and selected Latin, French, and English translations; (i) among other works in preparation, the syntactical concordance of D. Carson, P. Miller, and J. Boyer merits mention; when published, it will serve as an important advanced reference grammar; (j) various electronic concordances are now available, often as part of a computer software package (Hughes and Patton [1991]). Electronic concordances enable users to manipulate texts in various ways and to conduct Boolean and other searches that are far more sophisticated and less time-consuming than those conducted with printed concordances. Of the programs currently available, those produced by the GRAMCORD Institute are particularly useful for syntactical and lexical searches and are available for DOS, Windows, and Macintosh; (k) for the Syriac NT, two concordances are available: the Aramaic Computer Project's *The Concordance to the Peshitta Version of the Aramaic NT* (1985) and G. Kiraz, *A Computer-Generated Concordance to the Syriac NT* (1993); (l) for the Sahidic (Coptic) NT there is L. Lefort and M. Wilmet's *Concordance du Nouveau Testament sahidique* (1950, 1957–59), with an index prepared by R. Draguet, *Index copte et greco-copte de la Concordance du NT sahidique* (1960); and (m) for the Greek words in the Bohairic (Coptic) NT, G. Bauer, *Kondkordanz der nichtflektierten griechischen Wörter im bohairischen NT* (1975), is available.

Concordances of some non-canonical early Christian works include (a) for the apostolic fathers: E. GOODSPEED, *Index Patristicus* (1907, repr. 1960) and H. Kraft, *Clavis Patrum Apostolicorum* (1963); collectively these cover the entire corpus, but eventually they will be superseded by the multi-volume series edited by A. Urbán, *Concordantia in Patres Apostolicos,* with concordances to the *Epistle to Diognetus* (1993), the *Didache* (1993), *1 Clement* (1996), and *Barnabas* (1996) currently available; (b) for JUSTIN MARTYR and other early apologists: the index of Goodspeed (1912, repr. 1969); (c) for TERTULLIAN: H. Quellet's concordances of *De corona militis* (1975), *De cultu feminarum* (1986), *De patientia* (1988), *De exhortatione castitatis* (1992), and *Ad uxorem* (1994); (d) for Minucius Felix's *Octavius:* the concordance of B. Kytzler and D. Najock, assisted by A. Nowosad (1990); (e) for Cyprian's treatises: P. Bouet et al., *Cyprien: Traités Concordance* (1986); a companion volume by the same editors is in preparation; (f) for CHRYSOSTOM: A.-M. Malingrey in collaboration with M.-L. Guillaumin has compiled two indexes—one on the letters to Olympias, the letter on exile, and his treatment of the providence of God (1978) and the other on his "On the Priesthood" (*De sacerdotio* [1988]); (g) for JEROME's letters: the index by J. Schwind (1994); (h) for AUGUSTINE: the concordance on the *Confessions,* compiled by R. Cooper et al. (1991), who are also preparing one for the *The City of God;* and (i) for the *Poimandres,* a work of considerable interest to students of early Christianity: the concordance of D. Georgi and J. Strugnell (1971).

Bibliography: **L. R. Bailey,** "What a Concordance Can Do for You," *BARev* 10, 6 (1984) 60-67. **H. E. Bindseil,** "Ueber die Concordanzen," *TSK* 43 (1870) 673-720. **F. W. Danker,** *A Century of Greco-Roman Philology* (1988) 29-41; *Multipurpose Tools for Bible Study: Revised and Expanded Edition* (1993) 1-21. **C. R. Gregory,** "Concordances," *NSHERK* 3 (1909) 205-10. **M. C. Hazard,** "Introduction," *The Compre-* hensive Concordance to the Scriptures (J. B. R. Walker, 1894) 8-25. **J. J. Hughes and P. C. Patton,** "Concordances to the Bible: A History and Perspective," *Analytical Concordance of the Greek NT* (1991) 1:xiii-xxxii. **E. Mangenot,** "Concordances de la Bible," *DB* 2 (1926) 892-905. **F. Neirynck,** *Evangelica* (BETL 60, 1982) 955-1002; "NT Vocabulary: Corrections and Supplement," *ETL* 62 (1986) 134-40. **J. Quétif and J. Echard,** *Scriptores Ordinis Praedicatorum recensiti, notisque historicis et criticis illustrati. . . .* (1719) 1:203-209, 466-67, 610-11, 632. **R. H. and M. A. Rouse,** "Biblical Distinctions in the Thirteenth Century," *AHDLMA* 41 (1974) 27-37; "The Verbal Concordance to the Scriptures," *AFP* 44 (1974) 5-30. **J. Schmid,** "Bibelkonkordanz," *LTK*[2] 2 (1958) 360-63. **J. Stegenga,** *The Greek-English Analytical Concordance of the Greek-English NT* (1963). **S. Tregelles,** *An Account of the Printed Text of the Greek NT* (1854).

J. T. FITZGERALD, JR.

CONDER, CLAUDE REIGNIER (1848–1910)

Born at Cheltenham Dec. 29, 1848, C. attended but did not graduate from University College, London, before enrolling in the Royal Military Academy at Woolwich, where he excelled in surveying and drafting. Commissioned as a lieutenant in the royal engineers Jan. 8, 1870, he was drafted in 1872 to work with the PALESTINE EXPLORATION FUND survey, inaugurated in 1871. Under his direction, with the assistance of H. Kitchener, the crew surveyed 4,700 square miles of Palestine west of the Jordan (1872–75); Kitchener completed the survey in 1877, extending the area to 6,000 square miles. C. and his party were attacked and almost killed by the inhabitants of Safed, a town northwest of the Sea of Galilee, in July 1875. MAPS of the survey, along with the memoirs of the participants, were published in 1880, providing accurate maps of the region for the first time in history. In 1881–82 C., on behalf of the fund, surveyed east of the Jordan (about 500 square miles). He retired from the military in 1904 and died Feb. 16, 1910.

The work of the fund included not only the mapping of the region but also the collection of information on topography, existing ruins, site identifications, and observations on local customs. The *Memoirs* and C.'s two accounts of the surveys (1878, 1883) contain invaluable information on the region. A natural linguist, C. became fluent in Arabic and even tried his hand at explaining ancient Hittite (see HITTITOLOGY AND BIBLICAL STUDIES).

Works: *Tent Work in Palestine: A Record of Discovery and Adventure* (1878); *Judas Maccabaeus and the Jewish War of Independence* (1879); (with R. P. Conder), *Handbook to the Bible* (1879); (with H. H. Kitchner et al.), *Memoirs of the Survey of Western Palestine* (4 vols., 1881–83); *Heth and Moab: Explorations in Syria* (1883); *Primer of Biblical Geography: Founded on the Latest Explorations* (1884); *Syrian Stone Lore*

(1886); *The Canaanites* (1887); *Altaic Hieroglyphos and Hittite Inscriptions* (1887); *Palestine* (1889); *The Survey of Eastern Palestine* (1889); *Tell Amarna Tablets* (1893); *The Bible and the East* (1896); *The Latin Kingdom of Jerusalem, 1099–1291 AD* (1897); *The Hittites and Their Language* (1898); *The Hebrew Tragedy* (1900); *The First Bible* (1902); *Critics and the Law* (1907); *The Rise of Man* (1908); *The City of Jerusalem* (1909).

Bibliography: E. Elath, *PEQ* 97 (1965) 21-41. J. Lewis, *Near East Archaeological Society Bulletin* 39-40 (1994–95) 41-47.

J. H. HAYES

COOK, STANLEY ARTHUR (1873–1949)

Educated at Gonville and Caius College, Cambridge, C. was lecturer there in Hebrew (1904–32) and in comparative religion (1912–20). In 1932 he became university lecturer in Aramaic and Regius Professor of Hebrew (1932–38) at Cambridge. A student of W. R. SMITH, C. manifested his indebtedness to Smith and his own scholarship in his editing of Smith's works. Through T. CHEYNE C. became a member of the *Encyclopaedia Biblica* editorial staff (1896–1903). He died Sept. 26, 1949.

C. contributed to biblical studies through his philological, archaeological (see ARCHAEOLOGY AND BIBLICAL STUDIES), and comparative religion studies: his 1898 study of Semitic epigraphy and Hebrew philology; his editing of the *Quarterly Statement of the Palestine Exploration Fund* (1902–32); his article on the Nash papyrus containing the DECALOGUE and the Shema (*PSBA* 25 [1903] 34-56); his volume on the laws of Moses and the code of Hammurabi (1903); his Schweich lectures on Israelite religion in the light of archaeological studies (1930); his contributions to the *Cambridge Ancient History*, of which he was a joint editor; and his work on Saul and David (1907), which followed his own independent line.

An important turning point in C.'s life came in 1910. While maintaining his earlier interests, he sought to restate the message of the Bible and Christianity in light of modern knowledge. Many articles and books from this period display a liberal theological approach.

Works: *A Glossary of the Aramaic Inscriptions* (1898); (contributed to), *A Catalogue of the Syriac Manuscripts Preserved in the Library of the University of Cambridge* (W. Wright, 1901); (ed), *Kinship and Marriage in Early Arabia* (W. R. Smith, 1903); *The Laws of Moses and the Code of Hammurabi* (1903); "A Pre-Massoretic Biblical Papyrus," *PSBA* 25 (1903) 34-56; (ed), *Painted Tombs in the Necropolis of Marissa (Marêshah)* (J. P. Peters and H. Thiersch, 1905); (ed. and contributed to), *Nestoriana* (F. Loofs, 1905); *Critical Notes on OT History* (1907); *The Religion of Ancient Palestine in the*

Second Millennium BC in the Light of Archaeology and the Inscriptions (1908); *The Foundations of Religion* (1914); *The Study of Religions* (1914); (contributed to), *The Cambridge Ancient History* (1923–27); (ed.), *The Religion of the Semites* (W. R. Smith, 1927); *The Religion of Ancient Palestine in the Light of Archaeology* (1930); *The OT: A Reinterpretation* (1936); *The "Truth" of the Bible* (1938); *The Rebirth of Christianity* (1942); *An Introduction to the Bible* (1945).

Bibliography: D. W. Thomas, *PBA* (1950) 261-76; (ed.), *Essays and Studies Presented to S. A. C.* (1950), full bibliography, 1-13; *DNB, 1941–50* (1959) 174-75.

J. DAY

COOPER, ANNA JULIA (1858–1964)

C. was a Christian feminist educator, an eminent speaker, and founding member of the nineteenth-century black women's club movement. Born in Raleigh, North Carolina, she attended St. Augustine's College during Reconstruction, Oberlin in 1884, and received a doctorate from the Sorbonne in 1925. She lived in Washington, D.C., most of her adulthood, dying at age 105. Her peers included M. Terrell, I. Wells-Barnett, and F. Watkins Harper.

C. interpreted Christian Scriptures as presenting principles of freedom, equality, and dignity for women and men of all races and as speaking to the oppressive social situation of black women and men as well as that of Whites. She believed "Christ gave ideals not formulae" and that the gospel was a "germ requiring millenia for its growth and ripening." C. held that the gospel is comprehended only as it unfolds within the "rich soil of civilization." Christ's message requires continuous interpretation. Misunderstanding is a part of the process, and no interpretation of the gospel is ever complete.

C. was critical of white social gospel interpreters of Scripture who overlooked racial equality. In a letter to L. Abbott, editor of the social gospel weekly *The Outlook*, C. commended his emphasis on Christ's compassion but was troubled by his exclusive attention to white poverty. She criticized Abbott and white clergy for neglecting the "weightier matters of the law" on the subject of race. C. recorded Scripture passages she found essential to Christ's message, including Matt 18:2-6, being humble and not causing little ones to stumble; Matt 22:37-39, the great commandments; Luke 10:25-37, the parable of the good Samaritan; Matt 25:31-45, care for the least ones (in her parable "Christ's Church" a poor stranger is refused admittance to a church because he is black); Acts 10:34-48 and Jas 2:3-10, God shows no partiality.

C. wrote several essays presenting Jesus as teaching unconditional love of women and men of all races. She believed the radical improvement of women's situations would come from "the gospel of Jesus Christ" and criticized all domination of the weak by the strong.

Principles of freedom and equality for all, she argued in *A Voice from the South,* are "mutely foreshadowed or directly enjoined in" the "simple tale" of Jesus' life. Hers was a concrete, historical interpretation of Jesus in contrast to more abstract White social-gospel concepts. For C., Jesus was "the Nazarene" and a living presence whose "quiet face" still is "ever seen a little way ahead" to touch the life of the lowly.

Works: "Christ's Church," *A. J. C. Papers* (Moorland-Spingarn Research Center, Howard University); *A Voice from the South* (ed. M. H. Washington, 1988).

Bibliography: **K. Baker-Fletcher,** *A Singing Something: Womanist Reflections on A. J. C.* (1994). **L. D. Hutchinson,** *A. J. C.: "A Voice from the South"* (1981).

K. Baker-Fletcher

COPHER, CHARLES B. (1913–)

C. was born in Troy, Missouri, March 3, 1913. He received his BA from Clark University, Atlanta (1938), BD from Gammon Theological Seminary, Atlanta (1939), BD from Oberlin University (1941), and PhD in OT from Boston University (1947), the fourth black person in the United States to receive the PhD in OT. At Gammon, C. studied with W. King, the third black person to receive the degree (twenty years prior to C.). At Boston, C. studied with R. Pfeiffer and E. Leslie. Joining the faculty of Gammon in 1947, C. became first dean of faculty at the Interdenominational Theological Center in Atlanta, the largest Black theological center in the country. He retired in 1978 after serving as first vice president for academic affairs.

C. is viewed as parent of modern-day scholarly study of Blacks in the Bible. His articles on the subject began to appear in the early 1970s during the Black consciousness movement in response to pressure for relevancy in addressing in curriculum the needs of non-Caucasians. His works in the early stages delved into findings of Archaeology, historiography, philology, and historical-critical investigation of the text. As a follower of J. Bright's reconstructions of OT history, C. combed ancient and secondary works for evidence of Black presence, giving credence to biblical chronological notations as well as to biblical genealogies as containing historically reliable data (1974).

In these early works he began with the history of the debate as to whether Blacks appear in the Bible and the biblical world at all. Starting with the "Table of Nations" in Genesis 10, he noted that the descendants of Ham were the Blacks/Africans in the text and that Cush should be understood as being on the continent of Africa. This understanding challenged theories that there were "black Caucasians," a way of arguing that the ancient Egyptians were not Africans/Blacks and that the Hamites were proto-Europeans (1975, 1984).

C. amassed references in classical texts, like those produced by E. Budge (1857–1934) and J. Pritchard (1909–), that mention the existence of "Negroes and Negro-types" in ancient records. He then traced their presence in the text and their influence on Israel. He paid close attention to names of people and locations, similar to M. Noth's method in *Personnamen.* Thus C. noted that since the Phinehas mentioned in the Aaronite (Exod 6:25) and Elide (1 Sam 1:3) priestly lines means "the Nubian or the black one," it should be taken as evidence of Africans in the Israelite priestly family lines. Similarly, he took the marriage between Joseph and Asenath, daughter of Potiphera, priest of On (Gen 41:45), to mean that Manasseh and Ephraim were of Egyptian parentage, thereby signaling them as the eponymous heads of this Afro-Asiatic group in Israel (1975, 1991, 1995).

Of major significance in C.'s work is the documenting of White supremacy in biblical interpretation. He traces the development of racialist HERMENEUTICS in biblical interpretation back to early rabbinic sources and their treatment of the curses of Cain (Genesis 4) and Ham/Canaan (Genesis 9; 1986b). He also points to the ways nineteenth- and twentieth-century notions of Blacks have influenced Eurocentric historical-critical treatments of Bible passages referring to the Cushites (1993b).

C. is credited with doing much of the basic work in the area of Blacks and the Bible. His work is both a starting point for present day AFROCENTRIC BIBLICAL INTERPRETATION and a major corrective to heretofore normative views of Caucasians and the Bible.

Works: *Men and the Book* (1962); "The Black Man in the Biblical World," *JITC* 1 (1974) 7-16; "Blacks and Jews in Historical Interaction: The Biblical/African Experience," *JITC* 3 (1975) 9-16; "Egypt and Ethiopia in the OT," *Journal of African Civilizations* 6 (1984) 163-78; "Biblical Characters, Events, Places, and Images Remembered and Celebrated in Black Worship," *JITC* 14 (1986a) 75-86; "Three Thousand Years of Biblical Interpretation with Reference to Black Peoples," *JITC* 13 (1986b) 225-46; *Journal of African Civilizations* 7 (1988) 179-86; *African American Religious Studies: An Interdisciplinary Anthology* (ed. G. S. Wilmore, 1989) 105-28; "The Black Presence in the OT," *Stony the Road We Trod: African American Biblical Interpretation* (ed. C. H. Felder, 1991) 146-64; *Black Biblical Studies: An Anthology* (1993a); (ed.) "Racial Myths and Biblical Scholarship," *Black Biblical Studies* 121-31; "Blacks/Negroes: Participants in the Development of Civilization in the Ancient World and Their Presence in the Bible," *JITC* 23 (1995) 3-47.

Bibliography: **E. A. W. Budge,** *The Literature of the Ancient Egyptians* (1914). **J. B. Pritchard,** *Ancient Near Eastern Texts in Relation to the OT* (1950).

R. C. Bailey

COPPE, ABIEZER (1616–72)

Born in Warwick, C. studied at Oxford but left without taking a degree. He became a noted Baptist preacher, later emerging as the most outspoken of the Ranter prophets in their brief heyday (1650–51). He did not so much interpret Scripture as become it, in the sense that his inspiration was such that his own behavior and writing took on the character of HB prophets (especially Ezekiel) and even the deity. Within an antinomian framework, in which swearing is a form of spiritual liberation, C. often inverted the usual interpretations of dense biblical references or radically allegorized them in line with his socially and sexually leveling message.

Works: *A Collection of Ranter Writings from the Seventeenth Century* (ed. N. Smith, (1983).

Bibliography: J. C. Davis, *Fear, Myth, and History: The Ranters and the Historians* (1986). **C. Hill,** *The World Turned Upside Down: Radical Ideas During the English Revolution* (1972). **A. L. Morton,** *The World of the Ranters* (1970). **N. Smith,** *Perfection Proclaimed: Language and Literature in English Radical Religion, 1640–60* (1989).

N. SMITH

COPPENS, JOZEF (1896–1981)

Born Oct. 12, 1896, in Dendermonde, Belgium, C. died May 23, 1981, in Leuven, Belgium. After his ordination to the priesthood in 1920 he was sent to the University of Leuven (Louvain) for advanced studies in theology. He received the PhD in 1923 and the "Magister" degree in 1925. In 1927 he succeeded A. van HOONACKER as professor of OT exegesis at Leuven. He retired in 1967.

C. was a prolific and brilliant author with a rich variety of interests. In the HB he directed attention to the fundamental moral values, the monotheistic notion of God, the belief in resurrection and life after death, and, most of all, messianism. On the hermeneutical level (see HERMENEUTICS) he distinguished between "literal meaning" (*sensus literalis*) and "full meaning" (*sensus plenior*), or the supernatural depth of the literal meaning. Later he developed the related theory of "rereadings" (*relectures*), focusing on the final text and the CANON and their reinterpretations of earlier traditions. In his search for parallels to HB literature, the finds of UGARIT and Qumran (see DEAD SEA SCROLLS) aroused his interest. As a good historian he composed excellent surveys of past biblical research and many biographies; fine examples are his "Histoire Critique" and his biography of his predecessor, van Hoonacker. He was also a good organizer and manager, directing the periodical *ETL*; he was founder of the Colloquium Biblicum Lovaniense (with L. Cerfaux).

The majority of C.'s scholarly contributions deal with messianism. The value of his work in this field is best recognized when compared with earlier presentations of the messianic argument and their apologetic connotations (P.-M. Beaude [1980] 169-72). In his view the prophecies no longer lead in a direct way to their fulfillment; each PROPHECY must be studied on its own. He did not avoid discussion of textual difficulties and fully applied the LITERARY-critical methods, exploring the final meaning of the text with the help of new hermeneutical principles (*sensus plenior, relectures*) against the background of the Bible as a whole. In general his historical surveys remain valuable introductions to past scholarship, and all his works are vast sources of bibliographic information.

Works: *Le chanoine Albin van Hoonacker* (1935); *L'histoire critique de l'Ancien Testament* (1938, 1942²; ET, *The OT and the Critics* [1942]); *La connaissance du bien et du mal et le péché du paradis: Contribution à l'interpretation de Gen. II–III* (ALBO 2, 3, 1948); *Le messianisme royal* (LD 54, 1969); *Le messianisme et sa relève prophétique* (BETL 38, 1974); *La relève apocalyptique du messianisme royal* (3 vols., BETL 50, 55, 61, 1979–83).

Bibliography: P.-M. Beaude, *L'accomplissement des Écritures* (CF 104, 1980). **J. Lust,** "Msgr. J. C., the OT Scholar," *ETL* 57:4 (1981) 241-65, also included in the vol. are contributions by J. Etienne, A. Houssiau, F. Neirynck, M. Sabbe, G. Thils, and G. Van Belle (C. bibliography). **A. Schoors,** "Het wetenschappelijk werk van Monseigneur C.," *De Mari à Qumrân: Hommage à Mgr. J. Coppens* 1 (FS ed. H. Cazelles, 1969) 9-28, 29-49.

J. LUST

CORINTHIANS, FIRST LETTER TO THE

1. The Early Period. *a. The original interpeters.* This letter is the only Pauline writing with an undisputed sequel. Originally it was part of a series of exchanges between PAUL and the Corinthians: (i) Paul's "previous" letter to Corinth (see 5:9-11); (ii) the Corinthians' written response to Paul (see 1 Cor 7:1); (iii) Paul's response to that letter and to oral news from Corinth (1 Corinthians); (iv) Paul's "severe" letter (now lost; see 2 Cor 2:3-4; 7:8); (v) 2 Corinthians 1–9; and (vi) 2 Corinthians 10–13 (probably separate and later).

Paul's converts in Corinth, as the recipients of the letter, were its first interpreters. As far as we can tell from the later letters, the Corinthians understood 1 Corinthians to Paul's satisfaction. In contrast to his claim in 5:9-11 that they had misinterpreted his "previous" letter (i), Paul does not complain in subsequent correspondence that they had misunderstood 1 Corinthians. Paul's discussion of the topics in chaps. 7–14 is convoluted, but he makes no further reference to these subjects. Some scholars have argued that 2 Cor 5:1-10 is a clarification of 1 Corinthians 15 in response to Corinthian misunderstanding, but it is more probable that Paul had simply learned new ways to express his eschatological beliefs. In fact there are only two topics that continue: the "incestuous" man whom Paul orders to be excommunicated (5:1-5) and the collection of money for the relief of the poor among the Jerusalem Christians (16:1-4). The case of the incestuous man may have been the occasion for the severe letter, and he may be the one who has (finally) been "punished by the majority" (2 Cor 1:23–2:11). The collection and general concerns about money are the subject of 2 Cor 8–9; 11:7-10; 12:13-18. On these topics Paul complains, not that they have misunderstood him, but that they have not carried out his wishes quickly enough.

b. Text history as interpretation. The letter was preserved privately by the Corinthian congregation and seems to have remained in relative obscurity until near the end of the first century. Then Paul's letters were collected and "published" as a corpus. In this new format the historical situation of Paul and the Corinthians was no longer the focus of interpretation; instead Christian readers applied the material to their own situations, personally and corporately. Some of their concerns can be identified by tracing the variations that occurred in the letter as it was copied and recopied.

Three examples illustrate this type of interpretation: (1) Paul expected that he and a portion of his converts would live to see the return of Christ (the parousia), at which time the whole community would receive spiritual bodies. Thus, he wrote, "We shall not all sleep, but we shall all be changed" (15:51). Later, as the hope of an immediate parousia faded, some copyists "corrected" the first half to read, "We shall all sleep." Similarly, when the church became conscious of itself as a mixed community (see Matt 13:24-30, 36-43, 47-50), other copyists altered the second half: "We shall not all be changed." Early manuscripts exist with either or both of these adaptations. (2) In 11:23-26 Paul gives us the earliest account of the Lord's Supper, a description of its celebration in Corinth at the time he founded the congregation. Numerous variant readings to the text indicate that Paul's account was made to conform to such later eucharistic practices as those found in Matt 26:26-29 and Luke 22:14-20. Conversely, some of Paul's words found their way into the canon of the mass. (3) Paul seems to have thought that sexual distinctions, which would be eliminated in the kingdom (Mark 12:25), were already to be discarded in his eschatological communities. Thus he allowed women to preach and lead prayer in the church's worship (11:5). It appears that a protesting note ("Let the women keep silence." [14:34-35]) was later added near or at the end of Paul's long discussion of worship (chaps. 11–14).

c. Patristic Interpretation. After their publication Paul's letters became increasingly well known. Second Peter recognizes Paul's letters as authoritative (2 Pet 3:16). CLEMENT OF ROME (*1 Cor.* 1.1; 24.13), IGNATIUS (*Trall.* 11.13; *Eph.* 15.17, 16.4, 18.12; *Magn.* 1.5, 10.10), Polycarp (d. c. 155; *Phil.* 2.14)), and JUSTIN MARTYR (*Apol.* 1.5) knew and used 1 Corinthians. In the second quarter of the second century the GNOSTIC Basilides cited 1 Cor 2:13 as Scripture, and MARCION included the letter in his brief CANON. IRENAEUS made over sixty quotations from 1 Corinthians (note his idea that Christ "recapitulates" Adam in *Adv. Haer.* 12.2; see 1 Cor 15:45); CLEMENT OF ALEXANDRIA, more than 130; and TERTULLIAN, more than 400.

The first full-scale commentary on 1 Corinthians was ORIGEN's, now, unfortunately, known only through fragmentary quotations. His commentaries established the ALEXANDRIAN SCHOOL of interpretation whereby the text was considered in three senses—literal, moral, and allegorical, the latter (in the style of Philo of Alexandria) being the most important. Although some of his theological ideas were later considered heretical, his exegetical work continued to be quoted in the catena, or "chain" commentaries, into the Middle Ages. From CHRYSOSTOM (P. Schaff [1956]) we have forty-four homilies with exegetical notes, some of his best. His work was the foundation of the ANTIOCHENE SCHOOL, which opposed allegory beyond that already found in Scripture (e.g., 1 Cor 10:1-10) and emphasized the literal grammatical meaning of the text. He was followed by THEODORE OF MOPSUESTIA (only fragments remain) and by THEODORET, whose commentary is philological and remarkably critical.

Among the Latin authors a complete commentary survives from Ambrosiaster (4th cent.), also Antiochene in approach. The heretic PELAGIUS wrote (before 410) brief, but learned notes on the letter, which the school of CASSIODORUS (6th cent.) in turn revised and passed on to the medieval church. In particular he and the orthodox wing of the church argued over 15:22 concerning Adam and the sin of humankind.

Both orthodox and heterodox Christians mined the letter in the debates of the patristic period. Valentinian Gnostics (2nd cent.) drew support for their "libertarian" sexual morality from 6:12-20, their secret wisdom from 2:6–3:4, and the psychic resurrection of the enlightened believer from chap. 15. Their opponents (e.g., Irenaeus *Adv. Haer.* 12.2) counterattacked by citing, e.g., the bodily nature of resurrection as Paul viewed it. In general, however, the orthodox appealed to church polity and discipline rather than to Pauline theology. In the controversies over asceticism, which eventuated in the monastic tradition of the church, Paul's treatment of sexual morality in 1 Corinthians 7, where he recommended both his own ascetic example and normal marriage relationships, was repeatedly cited (e.g., by Tatian and by Clement of Alexandria) as justification of whichever practice the author espoused.

2. Middle Ages. In the Byzantine east, Chrysostom influenced the commentaries of Oecumenius of Tricca (10th cent.), Theophylact (11th cent.), and Euthymius Zigabenus (12th cent.), although an interest in allegory was by no means lost among Greek interpreters, especially when dealing with the HB. In the West, Origen's three senses of Scripture were expanded to four with the addition of the "analogical" meaning. Generally it is the Latin "doctors of the church," AUGUSTINE, JEROME, AMBROSE, and GREGORY OF NYSSA, who are most quoted in such catenae as BEDE's and Atto's (d. 961). PETER LOMBARD compiled a long commentary on the Pauline letters, and there are a number of others. In general, commentary was a matter of collecting quotations from authorities of the past.

In addition, however, there was a "dialectical" tradition that was more actively concerned with the theological meaning of the text. The outstanding work is the commentary of THOMAS AQUINAS, who stuck closely to the literal meaning of the text, which he illumined with quotations from the fathers (including some Greek authors), theological reflection, and moral application. He was systematic, logical, and interested in the definition of words. This tradition was continued in T. CAJETAN, whose exegetical interests were unexpectedly modern, and in J. COLET (B. O'Kelly and C. Jarrott [1985]), who was more discursive, less systematic, and more aware of Paul as a historical person than was Thomas.

3. Renaissance-Reformation. Cajetan and Colet, while theological in their interests, were already part of the Renaissance revival of classical learning. Cajetan wrote to reclaim Scripture from the humanists, and Colet was a friend and supporter of ERASMUS, another commentator on the letter. With the Reformation the interpretation of Scripture underwent a profound change. The view that Scripture should be interpreted by and within tradition was rejected in favor of the conviction that Scripture is the sole judge of the church and Christian conduct. ZWINGLI, also indebted to humanism, commented on 1 Corinthians, using Erasmus's new Greek text. But the most influential Reformation exegete was CALVIN (1960), who wrote a commentary on 1 Corinthians and attempted in his *Institutes* to summarize biblical THEOLOGY. On the Roman Catholic side, Estius (d. 1613) continued the Antiochene tradition at Douai, and C. LAPIDE, a Jesuit, while learned, favored a mystical and allegorical exegesis.

4. Enlightenment. The rationalism of the eighteenth century caused a reaction to the traditional, "supernaturalist" reading of Scripture. The English Deist J. LOCKE (see DEISM) pointed out (1695) the extent to which 1 Corintians and the rest of Paul's letters were historically conditioned and thus occasional. M. TINDAL (1730) cited the texts in 1 Corinthians about Paul's expectation to live to see the parousia as evidence that, like all human documents, Scripture contained mistakes. T. MORGAN (1738–40), using the letter to affirm a radical opposition

between Peter and Paul, concluded that both could not have been infallibly inspired (see INSPIRATION OF THE BIBLE). Such observations were not based on a concern for history, however, but had theological and philosophical motives. J. BENGEL, who published a critical edition of the Greek text, also produced the notably pithy commentary, *Gnomon of the NT* (1742).

5. Modern Period. While the patristic and medieval commentators tended to attach traditional theological ideas to the text, and the Reformation authors sought Paul as an ally in their theological controversies, the nineteenth century introduced a disinterested, historical approach to the NT and the investigation of a wide range of literary, historical, theological, and exegetical problems. Although considerable attention continued to be devoted to Paul's theology, the modern period has increasingly appreciated the historical and psychological factors (see PSYCHOLOGY AND BIBLICAL STUDIES) that motivated Paul and has valued immensely the literary forms and structures through which he expressed himself. Instead of harmonizing the letters into a theological system, the modern interpreter tends increasingly (and rightly) to treat the letters individually.

a. Authenticity. Historical criticism addressed first the question of authorship. Although 1 Corinthians does not contain the characteristic Pauline doctrine of justification by faith, F. C. BAUR accepted the letter as genuine because of what it revealed about tensions in the early church. Using the letter as the key for understanding the evolution of early Christianity, he concluded that the groups Paul mentioned, "I am of Paul . . . I am of Cephas, I am of Christ" (1:12), corresponded to the thesis-antithesis-synthesis pattern of G. W. F. Hegel's (1770–1831) dialectical analysis of history: (i) Cephas (Peter), the proponent of original, Jewish Christianity; (ii) Paul, the innovating apostle to the Greeks; and (iii) the "Christ party," representing the resulting catholic Christianity as found, e.g., in the Fourth Gospel (1831). His model has had great influence on NT historians (see the strictures of J. Munck [1959] 69-86), although his time scale has been greatly compressed; John's Gospel is now usually dated about 100 CE, a century earlier than Baur's dating.

Baur's heirs, the so-called Tübingen school, made the criteria for genuineness increasingly more stringent, reaching its extreme expression in the "Dutch radical school," which rejected 1 Corinthians along with the rest of the canonical letters and believed that the Acts traditions about Paul were the only surviving traces of the early missionary hero. However, the mainstream of later scholarship, which is no less critical but has a fuller understanding of the historical evidence, has no doubts about the authenticity of this letter.

b. Integrity. In 1 Corinthians the abrupt changes of subject, the repetitions, and the apparent inconsistencies on some points made this letter a natural candidate for theories of editorial compilation. The first theory with lasting influence appeared in the 1910 commentary of

J. WEISS (see also C. Clemen [1894] 19-57). He took 2 Cor 6:14–7:1 as part of the letter to which Paul referred in 1 Cor 5:9-11. To this vigorous letter he also assigned 1 Cor 10:1-23 (which he believed to be at variance with chaps. 8–9), as well as 6:12-20 and 11:2-34 (which he took to have a similar tone). He next suggested that when Paul received the Corinthians' letter, mentioned in 7:1, he responded with 1 Corinthians 7–9; 10:24–11:1; 12:1–16:6; 16:15-19. Shortly thereafter, when "those of Chloe" arrived (1 Cor 1:11), he wrote 1:1–6:11 and 16:10-14 in some distress.

Although other arrangements have been suggested, a number of important scholars have followed Weiss, albeit with individual variations (see J. Hurd [1965, 1994]). Theories that involve smaller units or multiple interpolations are inherently improbable and have not found a following. Weiss's analysis does follow the subject matter of the letter in a reasonable fashion and provides a single letter for each occasion for writing. Nevertheless, it is probably better (as most scholars do) to take the letter as a unity and understand its disjointed nature as the result of the circumstances that occasioned it.

c. Cultural background. O. PFLEIDERER (1906–10), one of Baur's pupils, was the first to interpret Paul consistently against the religious background of his day. He understood Paul as the combination of Pharisaic and Hellenistic Judaism transformed by Christian faith. This approach informed the two commentaries on 1 Corinthians by C. HEINRICI (1881), who was the first to use Hellenistic parallels extensively to explain Paul's thought. In 1895 A. DEISSMANN began to publish his large collection of material illustrative of the NT drawn from the non-literary papyri, the first editions of which were just beginning to appear. R. REITZENSTEIN (1904, 1910) and W. BOUSSET (1895, 1913) as well as others presented deeper parallels between Paul and Greco-Roman religion and MYTHOLOGY and especially illuminated Paul's ideas about sacraments and food in 1 Corinthians. A. SCHWEITZER objected, as did P. BILLERBECK (1922–28), G. KITTEL (1926), and W. D. DAVIES (1948), who emphasized the rabbinic parallels.

d. The date of writing. Traditionally scholars have used Acts to provide the biographical background for Paul's letters. First Corinthians is assigned to Paul's stay in Ephesus (1 Cor 16:8-10 = Acts 19:22) following his founding visit to Corinth, a visit dated by the reference to the proconsul Gallio (Acts 18:12-17). J. KNOX (1950), however, has challenged the use of Acts to date Paul's travels and has instead reconstructed Paul's life primarily on the basis of his letters. A number of scholars (see G. Lüdemann [1980] 1-43) have adopted this procedure, and its influence on Pauline studies is growing. This approach allows the letters to find their natural place in relationship to each other. The early eschatology of 1 Corinthians (see Lüdemann, 201-61) may indicate an earlier dating for the letter than is usually supposed. Further, the later biography of Paul can be organized around the collection for the saints first described in 1 Cor 16:1-4 (see 2 Corinthians 8–9; Rom 15:25-32).

e. Epistolary conventions. Deissmann called attention to the importance of the non-literary papyri, especially the letters, for the study of Paul (1908, 1925). Building on Deissmann's view of letters as conversation, Hurd (1965) attempted to reconstruct the exchanges between Paul and the Corinthians prior to 1 Corinthians. From a more functional/structural point of view (see STRUCTURALISM AND DECONSTRUCTION) P. Schubert made a pioneering study (1939) of the initial thanksgiving sections of the letters. Then in 1971 the SOCIETY OF BIBLICAL LITERATURE, at R. FUNK's initiative, established a seminar to study Paul's writings specifically as letters. A letter (as Deissmann maintained) is part of an actual conversation between two parties. An epistle, on the other hand, is an essay in epistolary form intended for a general audience. A letter does not include information the author knows that readers know. By contrast, an epistle must include all the information needed by its readers. The seminar, however, went further by noting many structural and traditional aspects of Paul's letters. Schubert had shown how the thanksgiving section of 1 Corinthians (1:4-9) anticipates the major themes of the letter (ecstatic speech, knowledge, spiritual gifts, the parousia, and fellowship). The seminar discussed, among many other things, how Paul in 1 Corinthians followed the usual custom by beginning with a reminder to his readers of their past relationship, then by dealing with present concerns, and finally by anticipating their future contact. Notable, too, in 1 Corinthians are the large ABA' structures (chaps. 8, 9, 10; and 12, 13, 14), and a number of chiastic passages (e.g., 1:18-25; 9:19-23).

f. Rhetorical criticism. In contrast to the study of Paul's letters as "letters," other scholars have analyzed the extent to which Paul reflected the literary, philosophical, and rhetorical conventions of his day (see RHETORICAL CRITICISM). In 1910 R. BULTMANN wrote on "Paul's preaching and the Cynic-Stoic diatribe." More recently the ancient handbooks of rhetoric have been used to illuminate the structure of Paul's arguments. Although 1 Corinthians lacks the sustained theological argument of, e.g., Galatians (see H. Betz [1979]), M. Mitchell (1991), H. Probst (1991), A. Wire (1990), and B. Witherington (1995) have made fruitful use of this approach in the interpretation of the letter.

g. Social-scientific criticism. As early as 1880 C. Heinrici specifically examined the sociological background of 1 Corinthians (see SOCIOLOGY AND NT STUDIES and SOCIAL-SCIENTIFIC CRITICISM). In the 1930s a school of criticism flourished at Chicago that emphasized the sociological component of history. More recently through the work of G. Thiessen (1979), W. Meeks (1983), and others this emphasis has reemerged. First

Corinthians is an especially rich source of data of which we can ask questions like, "From what social levels did the Corinthian converts come?" "What kind of education did they have?" "What sort of organization did this house church have?" "What was the nature of family relationships?" and "What was the relationship between men and women?" There is a growing consensus, e.g., that Deissmann underestimated their social level and that the congregation included a number of tradesmen, small business owners, and perhaps some persons of greater economic means.

h. Feminist interpretation. Recent studies have also focused on the role of women in the Corinthian church (SEE FEMINIST INTERPRETATION), in particular, Paul's instructions about women's prayer and PROPHECY (11:2-16) and his command for women's silence in the church (14:33*b*-36). J. Bassler (1992) summarizes and evaluates several possible interpretations: (1) 11:2-16 is directed toward women's prophesying and praying at home, whereas 14:33*b*-36 is directed toward women's speaking in worship; (2) Paul approves of inspired speech but not of uninspired speaking; (3) Paul allows holy unmarried women to speak but not married women (see E. Schüssler Fiorenza [1983] 231); (4) the critical cirumstances at the Corinthian church led Paul to silence the women; (5) Paul is quoting the Corinthian position in 14:34-35 in order to correct the church members in 14:36; and (6) 14:34-35 originally was a marginal gloss that a scribe placed in the body of the letter (see also Wire [1990, 1994]).

Bibliography: F. Altermath, *Du corps psychique au corps spirituel: Interpretation de 1 Cor. 15,35-49* (BGBE 18, 1977). W. S. Babcock (ed.), *Paul and the Legacies of Paul* (1990). J. M. Bassler, "1 Corinthians," *The Women's Bible Commentary* (ed. C. A. Newsom and S. H. Ringe, 1992) 321-29. F. C. Baur, "Die Christuspartie in der korinthischen Gemeinde," *TZT* 4, 4 (1831) 61-136. J. A. Bengel, *Gnomon of the NT* (1742; ET 1860–62). J. H. Bentley, *Humanists and Holy Writ: NT Scholarship in the Renaissance* (1983). H. D. Betz, *Der Apostel Paulus und die sokratische Tradition* (BHT 45, 1972); *Galatians* (Hermeneia, 1979). P. Billerbeck, *Kommentar zum Neuen Testament aus Talmud und Midrash* (6 vols.; vols. 1–4, 1922–28). W. Bousset, *Der Antichrist in der Überlieferung des Judentums, des Neuen Testaments, und der alten Kirche* (1895); *Kryios Christos: Geschichte des Christos glabens* (1913; ET 1970). R. Bultmann, *Der Stil der paulinischen Predigt und die kynischstoische Diatribe* (1910). J. Calvin, *The First Epistle of Paul the Apostle to the Corinthians* (tr. J. W. Fraser, Calvin Commentaries, 1960). C. Clemen, *Die Einheitlichkeit der paulinischen Briefe* (1894). J. Colet, *J. Colet's Commentary on First Corinthians* (tr. B. O'Kelly and C. A. L. Jarrot, 1985). J. A. Cramer, *Catenae graecorum patrum* 5 (1844). W. D. Davies, *Paul and Rabbinic Judaism: Some Rabbinic Elements in Pauline Theology* (1948). A. Deissmann, *Light from the Ancient East* (1908; ET 1910); *Paul: A Study in Social and Religious History* (1925; ET 1926). W. G. Doty, *Letters in Primitive Christianity* (1973). P. Henry, *New Directions in NT Study* (1979). C. Heinrici, *Der erste Brief an die Korinther* (KEK 5⁶, 1881). J. C. Hurd, *The Origin of 1 Corinthians* (1965); "Good News and the Integrity of 1 Corinthians," *Gospel in Paul: Studies on Corinthians, Galatians, and Romans for R. N. Longenecker* (JSNT Sup 108, 1994). C. Jenkins, "Origen on 1 Corinthians," *JTS* 9 (1908) 231-47, 353-72, 500-514; 10 (1909) 29-51. G. Kittel, *Die Probleme des palästinischen Spätjudentums und das Urchristentum* (BWANT 3, 1926). J. Knox, *Chapters in a Life of Paul* (1950). W. G. Kümmel, *The NT: The History of the Investigation of Its Problems* (1958; ET 1972). J. Locke, *Vindications* (1695). G. Lüdemann, *Paul, the Apostle to the Gentiles* (FRLANT 123, 1980; ET 1984). W. A. Meeks, *The First Urban Christians: The Social World of the Apostle Paul* (1983). M. M. Mitchell, *Paul and the Rhetoric of Reconciliation: An Exegetical Investigation of the Language and Composition of 1 Corinthians* (1991). T. Morgan, *The Moral Philosopher* (3 vols., 1738–40, repr. 1969). J. Munck, *Paul and the Salvation of Mankind* (1959). S. Neill, *The Interpretation of the NT, 1861–1961* (1964). E. H. Pagels, *The Gnostic Paul* (1975). O. Pfleiderer, *Primitive Christianity* (1906–10). H. Probst, *Paulus und der Brief: Die Rhetorik des antiken Briefes als Form der paulinischen Korintherkorrespondenz (1 Kor 8–10)* (WUNT 2, 45, 1991). R. Reitzenstein, *Poimandres: Studien zur griechisch-ägyptischen und frühchristlicher Literatur* (1904); *Hellenistic Mystery-Religions: Their Basic Ideas and Significance* (1910; ET 1978). P. Schaff (ed.), *Saint Chrysostom: Homilies on the Epistles to the Corinthians* (NPNF 12, 1956). E. Schendel, *Herrschaft und Unterwerfung Christi: 1 Kor. 15,24-28 in Exegese und Theologie der Väter biz zum Ausgang des 4. Jahrhunderts* (BGBE 12, 1971). P. Schubert, *The Form and Function of the Pauline Thanksgiving* (BZNW 20, 1939). E. Schüssler Fiorenza, *In Memory of Her: A Feminist Theological Reconstruction of Christian Origins* (1983). J. H. Schütz, *Paul and the Anatomy of Apostolic Authority* (1975). A. Schweitzer, *Paul and His Interpreters* (1911; ET 1912). G. Sellin, "Hauptprobleme des ersten Korintherbriefes," *ANRW* II.25.4 (1987) 2940-3044. K. Staab, *Pauluskommentare aus der griechischen Kirche* (1933). G. Theissen, *The Social Setting of Pauline Christianity: Essays on Corinth* (1979; ET 1982). M. Tindal, *Christianity as Old as the Creation* (1730). L. Vischer, *Die Auslegungsgeschichte von I. Kor. 6,1-11* (BGBE 1, 1955). J. Weiss, *Der erste Korintherbrief* (KEK, 1910). J. L. White, *The Body of the Greek Letter* (SBLDS 2, 1972); *Light from Ancient Letters* (1986). A. N. Wilder, *Early Christian Rhetoric: The Language of the Gospel* (1971). M. F. Wiles, *The Divine Apostle* (1967). A. C. Wire, *The Corinthian Women Prophets: A Reconstruction Through Paul's Rhetoric* (1990); "1 Corinthians," *Searching the Scriptures: A Feminist Commentary* (ed. E. Schüssler Fiorenza, 1994) 2:153-95. B. Witherington, *Conflict and Community in Corinth: A Socio-Rhetorical Commentary on 1 and 2 Corinthians* (1995). G. Zuntz, *The Text of the Epistles* (Schweich Lectures, 1946, 1953).

J. C. HURD

CORINTHIANS, SECOND LETTER TO THE

1. The Early Period. *a. First to third centuries.*
There are no clear traces of the use or influence of
PAUL's so-called second letter to the Corinthians before
the middle of the second century. Alleged echoes in 1
Clement (c. 96) and in the letters of IGNATIUS (martyred
c. 107) remain questionable, even though acquaintance
with 1 Corinthians is sure in the case of *1 Clement* and
likely in the case of Ignatius. It is possible that 2 Cor
5:10 is quoted by Polycarp (d. c. 155) in Phil 6:2; but
the first certain use of 2 Corinthians is by MARCION (d.
c. 160), who included it in his CANON (see Tertullian
Adv. Marc. 5.11-12). In Paul's reference to "the god of
this world" (2 Cor 4:4) both Marcion and the Valentinian
Gnostics (see GNOSTIC INTERPRETATION) found support
for a distinction between the HB God (to whom they
attributed creation) and the God of JESUS Christ. This
understanding of the phrase was vigorously opposed by
IRENAEUS (c. 130–c. 200) and TERTULLIAN (c. 160–
c. 225), who argued for what they believed to be Paul's
true meaning (Irenaeus *Adv. Haer.* 3.7.12; 4.29.1; Tertullian *Adv. Marc.* 5.11, 17). So, too, their comments on
the apostle's account of his ascent to "the third heaven"
in 2 Cor 12:2-4 (Irenaeus *Adv. Haer.* 2.30.7-8; 5.5.1;
Tertullian *De praescr haeret* 24.56), a passage that was
of special interest to the theological opposition (e.g., the
Gnostic *Apoc. Paul* from Nag Hammadi, V, 2). Tertullian
also employed 2 Cor 3:6-18 in his arguments against
the teachings of Marcion (*Adv. Marc.* 5.11), contending
that what Paul says about the old and new covenants
requires belief in just one God. These same verses were
especially important to the ALEXANDRIAN exegete,
ORIGEN (c. 185–c. 254), who found in them—above all
in 3:6 ("the letter kills, the Spirit gives life")—support
for the allegorical method of biblical interpretation (*De
Prin.* 1.1.2; *Con. Cel.* 5.60; 6.70; 7.20).

b. Fourth and fifth centuries. During the fourth
century, passages from 2 Corinthians (esp. 2:15; 3:6,
14-18; 13:13) were regularly invoked (e.g., by Athanasius [c. 296–373] and Basil [c. 330–79]; see Haykin
[1994]) to argue for the full divinity of the Holy Spirit.
Also, following Origen, the practice of writing commentaries on individual books of the Bible had become more
common, and during the course of the fourth and fifth
centuries various expositions of 2 Corinthians were
produced. Unfortunately, only fragments remain of those
by CYRIL OF ALEXANDRIA (d. 444), a brilliant practitioner
of allegorical exegesis, and his fellow Alexandrian, DIDY-
MUS THE BLIND (c. 313–398). The same is true of the
commentaries by two exegetes of the opposing ANTI-
OCHENE SCHOOL of interpretation, THEODORE OF MOP-
SUESTIA (c. 350–428) and THEODORET OF CYRRHUS (c.
393–c. 466). However, the homilies on 2 Corinthians
composed in Antioch between 386 and 398 by CHRYSOS-
TOM (c. 347–407) do survive (P. Schaff [1956]). As
appropriate for sermons, Chrysostom's expositions were
directed primarily toward the moral and spiritual edification of his congregations. He commented only infrequently on the place of the letter within the historical
context of Paul's Corinthian ministry (e.g., *Homily*
1.12), yet wherever it seemed important to him he
offered his opinion on specific questions (e.g., Paul's
"thorn in the flesh," 2 Cor 12:7 [*Homily* 26.2] and his
anti-Marcionite reading of 2 Cor 4:4 [*Homily* 8.2]).

The surviving Latin commentaries by the so-called
Ambrosiaster (an unknown expositor of the late 4th
cent.) and PELAGIUS (written prior to 410) are also
notable. In Ambrosiaster's commentary on Paul's letters,
more than in most others of this period, close attention
is paid to the apostle's words and intentions. Pelagius's
expositions, including his comments on 2 Cor 3:6, show
him to be cautious about interpreting the texts allegorically.

2. Middle Ages. Neither 2 Corinthians as such nor
specific passages within it played a prominent role in
theology during the medieval period. Commentaries on
the letter, as on scriptural books generally, usually took
the form of homiletical glosses that were often little
more than collections of citations from the church fathers. The most notable and influential Greek commentaries on the Pauline letters were produced by
Oecumenius of Tricca (10th cent.), Theophylact (d.
1108), and Euthymius Zigabenus (early 12th cent.). All
three were influenced by Antiochene exegesis as represented especially in the homilies of Chrysostom. Of the
Latin expositions, those by PETER LOMBARD (c. 1100–
60), THOMAS AQUINAS (c. 1225–74), and the learned
Hebraist NICHOLAS OF LYRA (c. 1270–1340) deserve
special mention. Although Aquinas was not primarily an
exegete, his concern for the literal sense of Scripture,
as distinguished from its spiritual senses, was of signal
importance and exerted a profound influence on Nicholas.

3. Renaissance and Reformation. Along with the
other writings of the NT, 2 Corinthians was subjected
for the first time to careful TEXTUAL and philological
analysis by the Renaissance humanist ERASMUS (1469?–
1536). Not content simply to compile quotations from
the fathers, he was quite deliberate about investigating
the NT texts and discerning their original meaning. The
first edition of his Greek NT, accompanied by annotations, appeared in 1516; and Erasmus lived to see a fifth
edition published, with the annotations significantly expanded, in 1535. Although he wrote admiringly of
Origen, Erasmus did not resort to excessive allegorizing
but aimed at a strictly grammatical and literal reading
of Scripture.

Allegorical exegesis was emphatically rejected by
LUTHER and CALVIN. In particular, both Reformers took
issue with the Origenist reading of chap. 3. Luther, who
often preached on 2 Cor 3:4-11, found in the contrast
between "letter" and "spirit" (v. 6) a succinct summary

of the opposition between law and gospel, works and grace. While the letter can only say what one should and should not do, the gospel declares what Christ has done; and with this word the Holy Spirit penetrates to the heart with saving power. Calvin offered similar comments on this passage. In his commentary on 2 Cor 3:6, he specifically charged Origen and other allegorists with profoundly distorting the meaning of Paul's contrast between letter and spirit, with the result that "any mad idea, however absurd or monstrous, could be introduced under the pretext of an allegory" (1964, 43).

4. Seventeenth and Eighteenth Centuries. The textual and philological investigations of Paul's letters begun by Erasmus and others continued into the seventeenth and eighteenth centuries. These studies, coupled with the Reformers' conviction that Paul must be understood on his own terms, prompted interpreters to pay increasingly close attention to the argument in each letter and thus also to the occasion and purpose of each. On the continent these concerns are especially evident in the prefaces to the Pauline letters that H. GROTIUS included in his *Annotationes in Novum Testamentum* (1641–50). In England Grotius's work found an echo in that of H. HAMMOND and M. POOLE.

Regarding 2 Corinthians specifically, the annotations that J. Collinges (1623–90) contributed to Poole's *Annotations upon the Holy Bible* (1688) exhibit the author's interest in both the purpose of the letter ("partly Apologetical or Excusatory . . . partly Hortatory," and "Partly Minatory or Threatening") and its argumentative structure (each chapter is introduced with a synopsis of the argument). The same interests are even more apparent in J. LOCKE's remarkable *Paraphrase and Notes on the Epistles of St. Paul to the Galatians, 1 and 2 Corinthians, Romans, Ephesians* (1707).

In Europe this historical reading of Paul's letters is also seen in the work of such eighteenth-century scholars as J. BENGEL, J. WETTSTEIN, and S. BAUMGARTEN. Indeed, it is to one of Baumgarten's students, J. SEMLER, that credit must go for inaugurating a thoroughly historical-critical study (see H. Betz [1985] 3-7). While some earlier interpreters had noted that chaps. 10–13 were much more severe in tone than chaps. 1–9, the usual explanation was that in the last four chapters Paul has some small group of antagonists in view. Thus Collinges (1688), commenting on 2 Cor 10:1, had postulated "another (though possibly the lesser) Party who had much vilified him." But Semler departed from that kind of explanation, arguing that 2 Corinthians must be a composite of at least two originally distinct letters. The earlier, he held, was composed of chaps. 1–9, 13:11-13[14], and Romans 16, and the later of 10:1–13:10. He thought it possible, however, that Paul had not intended both of the collection chapters (8, 9) for Corinth, but that chap. 9 had been directed to churches elsewhere in Achaia. Although Semler's partitioning of 2 Corinthians was not widely accepted at the time, he had succeeded in placing the question of the letter's literary unity on the scholarly agenda, where it has remained a major item for more than two hundred years.

5. Nineteenth and Twentieth Centuries. Semler's views about 2 Corinthians prompted others to examine more closely both the argument of the letter and the course of Paul's Corinthian ministry and correspondence. As a result, while the significance of the letter for an understanding of Paul's thought has not gone unnoticed (see esp., R. BULTMANN [1976]), most of the important studies in the last two centuries have been devoted to LITERARY and historical matters.

a. Literary Integrity. Many, perhaps even a majority of, interpreters have come to agree with Semler's separation of chaps. 10–13 from the rest of 2 Corinthians (notable exceptions include P. Hughes [1962], N. Hyldahl [1973], C. Wolff [1989]; also F. Young and D. Ford [1987] 28-36). Yet in contrast to Semler, certain advocates of this partitioning found indications that the last four chapters had been written prior to some, if not all, of chaps. 1–9 and that they constituted at least part of the "tearful" letter to which Paul refers in 2 Cor 2:3-4 and 7:8 (first A. Hausrath [1870], J. Kennedy [1900]; later J. Weiss [1917], A. Plummer [1915], Bultmann). Although subsequent studies have shown that an association with the tearful letter is unlikely, the earlier dating of chaps. 10–13 is not thereby precluded and is often proposed (G. Bornkamm [1971], D. Georgi [1964, 1965], H. Betz [1985], G. Dautzenberg [1987]; otherwise, H. WINDISCH [1924], C. K. Barrett [1973], V. Furnish [1984], R. Martin [1986], M. Thrall [1994]).

Questions have also been raised about the literary integrity even of chaps. 1–9. There is general agreement that 6:14–7:1 to some extent interrupts the appeal of 6:11-13, which is in fact continued only in 7:2. A number of interpreters believe that Paul is responsible for the interruption (E. Allo [1956]; Barrett; Hughes; Thrall), while others have argued that 6:14–7:1 is a fragment from the letter to Corinth mentioned in 1 Cor 5:9 that has been inserted after 2 Cor 6:13 by some later redactor (A. Hilgenfeld [1875]; W. Schmithals [1973] 282-86). Still others, citing the style and content as well as the inappropriateness of the paragraph in this context, have argued that it is a later, non-Pauline interpolation (first proposed by K. Schrader [1935]; see also Bornkamm; Betz [1973] calls it anti-Pauline). A few have described the passage as non-Pauline material incorporated (with certain adaptations) by the apostle himself (Martin; Wolff; tentatively, N. Dahl [1977] 62-69).

Numerous scholars (following a suggestion by Weiss, 348-49) believe that 2:14–7:4 (excluding 6:14–7:1) is also separable from chaps. 1–9. The argument in general is that (a) the section interrupts a travel narrative that begins in 2:12-13 and is completed only in 7:5-16; and (b) in 2:14–7:4 Paul is concerned to legitimate his apostleship in the face of challenges to it, while in the remainder of chaps. 1–9 he writes as if his position with the Corinthians is relatively secure. Some scholars have suggested that this unit originally went with chaps. 10–13 as part of the tearful letter (Weiss, Bultmann). The more usual conclusion has been that it is (or belongs to) a letter written after 1 Corinthians and at some point before the tearful letter (Betz [1985]; Bornkamm; Georgi [1964, 1965]; Schmithals [1973]). Among those who remain unconvinced by the evidence adduced for 2:14–7:4 as a separate letter are Barrett, Dautzenberg, Furnish (1984), Martin, and Thrall.

Semler's suggestion that the two collection chapters (8, 9) might not have belonged to the same letter has found favor with many investigators, but specific proposals about their original locations vary. Weiss (353-55) identified chap. 8 as an independent letter written earlier than the tearful letter and kept chap. 9 with 1:1–2:13; 7:5-16. Others have proposed that chap. 9 was part of the tearful letter and thus earlier than chap. 8 (e.g., Bultmann). In the most extensive and important study of the matter so far, Betz (1985; followed by Carrez [1986]) has argued that the chapters represent two independent letters written at the same time (chap. 8 to the church in Corinth, chap. 9 to other Achaian churches), and later than any other part of 2 Corinthians. Thrall affirms the integrity of chaps. 1–8 but suggests that chap. 9 may have been dispatched a bit later.

Advocates of partition theories have usually dated 2 Corinthians in its present form to about the end of the first century, but relatively little attention has been given to what may have prompted and guided the redactor's work (see Furnish [1984], 38-41; F. Zeilinger [1992] 24-25; Thrall, 45-47). The two principal suggestions have been (a) a need to invoke Paul's authority in the fight against Gnosticism (Schmithals [1971] 239-74; elaborated by Jewett) and (b) a concern to enhance Paul's image and to give the redacted letters a testamentary character (Bornkamm, 179-90). D. Trobisch has advanced the highly original, but also highly speculative, theory that Paul himself edited Romans, his letters to Corinth (originally seven in number), and Galatians for the instruction of the Ephesian church and, in case of his death, to stand as his literary testament (1989, esp. 119-31; 1994, esp. 55-96).

b. Paul's Visits and Letters to Corinth. Until the nineteenth century it was usual to identify the tearful letter with 1 Corinthians, the painful visit (2 Cor 2:1) with Paul's first, evangelizing visit, and the wrongdoer mentioned in 2 Cor 2:5-11; 7:12 with the man Paul had earlier wanted to expel from the congregation (1 Cor 5:1-13). The difficulties with the first of these identifications were originally pointed out by F. BLEEK (1830), who postulated that the tearful letter had been written in the interim between the two canonical letters (see CANON OF THE BIBLE) and does not survive. Sub-

sequently, H. EWALD (1857) proposed that the painful visit had occurred during the same interim, that it had been unsuccessful because of Paul's difficulties with the wrongdoer, and that the lost tearful letter had been written in response to the whole unpleasant affair.

After more than 150 years of further research and discussion, most scholars concur that the tearful letter cannot be identified with 1 Corinthians and that an interim visit must be hypothesized (exceptions, P. Hughes [1962], N. Hyldahl [1973]). Thus the currently prevailing view is that references in 2 Cor 2:1, 3-4, 5-11; 7:8, 12 (and, to an impending third visit, in 12:14; 13:1- 2) presume two prior visits and at least three prior letters to Corinth: the first, evangelizing visit, the letter referred to in 1 Cor 5:9, 1 Corinthians itself, a subsequent painful visit, and a tearful letter written in the wake of the painful visit.

Moreover, consequent upon conclusions reached about the literary integrity of 2 Corinthians, various interpreters have hypothesized as many as three additional letters to Corinth: one sent in the interim between 1 Corinthians and the tearful letter (2:14–7:4, excluding 6:14–7:1) and two separate letters about the collection for Jerusalem (chaps. 8, 9). Betz, for example, has derived five separate letters from 2 Corinthians and arranged them in the following sequence: (1) 2:14–6:13 and 7:24; (2) 10:1–13:10, two "apologies" sent in response to challenges of Paul's apostolic legitimacy; (3) 1:1–2:13, 7:5-16, and 13:11-13, a "letter of reconciliation" sent following Titus's successful resolution of the crisis; (4) chapter 8; and (5) chapter 9, two "administrative letters" sent to the Corinthians and other Achaians, respectively, on behalf of the collection for Jerusalem (1985, 142-43; cf. Bornkamm, Georgi [1964, 1965]).

c. The opposition to Paul. No clear consensus has emerged about the opponents with whom Paul had to reckon during the period represented by 2 Corinthians (surveys of research: Georgi [1964] 1-9; J. Sumney [1990] 15-73). On the one hand, F. C. BAUR (1831) argued that in both 1 and 2 Corinthians Paul was contending with Judaizers, representatives of Peter who were intent on imposing certain requirements of the Mosaic law on gentile converts. This view was dominant throughout most of the nineteenth century and has been newly argued, with modifications, in the twentieth (D. Oostendorp [1967]; G. Lüdemann [1989]). On the other hand, with W. Lütgert's (1908) contention that it was the Spirit, not the law, that was at issue, the way was opened for identifying the opponents as GNOSTIC enthusiasts (Bultmann; Schmithals [1971]).

Advocates of both of these views have ordinarily believed that Paul was contending with essentially the same kind of opposition in 1 and 2 Corinthians. Others, however, have insisted that one must distinguish between the resident opposition evident in 1 Corinthians and an intrusion by outsiders, for which 2 Cor 11:4 provides evidence. Some have identified the intruders as Jewish-Christian emissaries sent out from, or who claimed to have been sent out from, the Jerusalem apostles (E. Käsemann [1942]; Barrett). Others have identified them as itinerant Christian propagandists with a Hellenistic-Jewish background, which does not, however, preclude their Palestinian connections (esp. Georgi [1964]). Most proponents of these two views have defined the main point of dispute as neither the law nor the Spirit but the legitimacy of Paul's apostleship.

d. Newer Areas of Research. In the last half of the twentieth century several special areas of research were developed that show promise of shedding new light on 2 Corinthians. Studies devoted to the genre and RHE-TORICAL characteristics of particular sections (Betz [1972, 1985] 129-40; J. Zmijewski [1978]; J. Fitzgerald [1990]; F. Hughes in D. Watson [1991]), or of the whole (G. Kennedy [1984] 86-96; Young and Ford, 27-59; F. Danker in Watson [1991]), are contributing not only to a better understanding of Paul's style but also to a better understanding of his dealings with the Corinthians and of his self-understanding as an apostle. The same can be said about investigations of the social setting of Paul's ministry in important urban centers like Corinth (e.g., W. Meeks [1983]) and of the particular Greco-Roman social conventions that influenced the apostle (e.g., P. Marshall [1987]).

Few of the scholars who have been responsible for new understandings of the compositional history, genre(s), rhetorical character, or social setting of 2 Corinthians have considered the possible consequences of their work for the interpretation of Paul's theology. Although several short theological studies of 2 Corinthians have taken account of recent developments in these areas (e.g., essays by D. Hay; S. Kraftchick; and B. Gaventa in Hay [1993]), a major theological reassessment of the letter(s) has yet to appear.

Bibliography: E.-B. Allo, *Saint Paul: Seconde Épître aux Corinthiens* (1956). **W. S. Babcock** (ed.), *Paul and the Legacies of Paul* (1990). **C. K. Barrett,** *A Commentary on the Second Epistle to the Corinthians* (HNTC, 1973). **J. M. Bassler,** "2 Corinthians," *The Women's Bible Commentary* (ed. C. A. Newsom and S. H. Ringe, 1992) 330-32. **F. C. Baur,** "Die Christus partei in der korinthischen Gemeinde" (1831; repr. in *Ausgewählte Werke in Einzelausgaben* 1 [1963], 1-164). **J. H. Bentley,** *Humanists and Holy Writ: NT Scholarship in the Renaissance* (1983). **H. D. Betz,** *Der Apostel Paulus und die sokratische Tradition* (BHT 45, 1972); "2 Cor 6:14–7:1: An Anti-Pauline Fragment?" *JBL* 92 (1973) 88-108; *2 Corinthians 8 and 9* (Hermenia, 1985). **R. Bieringer and J. Lambrecht,** *Studies on 2 Corinthians* (BETL, 1994). **F. Bleek,** "Erörterungen in Beziehung auf die Briefe Pauli an die Korinther," *TSK* 3 (1830) 614-32. **G. Bornkamm,** "Die Vorgeschichte des sogenannten Zweiten Korintherbriefes," *Geschichte und Glaube*

2 (1971) 162-94. **R. Bultmann,** *The Second Letter to the Corinthians* (ed. E. Dinkler 1976; ET 1985). **J. Calvin,** *The Second Epistle of Paul to the Corinthians* (1547; tr. T. A. Smail, 1964). **M. Carrez,** *La deuxième Épître de Saint Paul aux Corinthiens* (1986). **W. Chau,** *The Letter and the Spirit: A History of Interpretation from Origen to Luther* (1995). **N. Dahl,** *Studies in Paul: Theology for the Early Christian Mission* (1977). **E. Dassmann,** *Der Stachel im Fleisch* (1979). **G. Dautzenberg,** "Der zweite Korintherbrief als Briefsammlung: Zur Frage der literarischen Einheitlichkeit und des theologischen Gefüges von 2 Kor 1–8," *ANRW* II.25.4 (1987) 3045-66. **H. G. A. Ewald,** *Die Sendschreiben des Apostels Paulus* (1857). **J. T. Fitzgerald,** "Paul, the Ancient Epistolary Theorists, and 2 Corinthians 10–13," *Greeks, Romans, and Christians: Essays in Honor of A. J. Malherbe* (1990) 190-200. **V. P. Furnish,** *II Corinthians* (AB 32A, 1984); "2 Corinthians," *1 and 2 Corinthians* (ed. D. Hay, 1993), bibliography, 270-84. **D. Georgi,** *The Opponents of Paul in Second Corinthians: A Study of Religious Propaganda in Late Antiquity* (1964; ET 1986); *Remembering the Poor: The History of Paul's Collection for Jerusalem* (1965; ET 1992). **A. Hausrath,** *Der Vier-Capitel-Brief des Paulus an die Korinther* (1870). **D. Hay** (ed.), *Pauline Theology,* vol 2, *1 and 2 Corinthians* (1993). **M. A. G. Haykin,** *The Spirit of God: The Exegesis of 1 and 2 Corinthians in the Pneumatomachian Controversy of the Fourth Century* (1994). **A. Hilgenfeld,** *Historisch-kritische Einleitung in das Neue Testament* (1875). **P. E. Hughes,** *Paul's Second Epistle to the Corinthians* (NICNT, 1962). **N. Hyldahl,** "Die Frage nach der literarischen Einheit des Zweiten Korintherbriefes," *ZNW* 64 (1973) 289-306. **R. Jewett,** "The Redaction of I Corinthians and the Trajectory of the Pauline School," *JAAR* 44, supp. B (1978) 389-444. **E. Käsemann,** "Die Legitimität des Apostels," *ZNW* 41 (1942) 33-71. **G. Kennedy,** *NT Interpretation Through Rhetorical Criticism* (1984). **J. H. Kennedy,** *The Second and Third Epistles of St. Paul to the Corinthians* (1900). **A. Lindemann,** *Paulus im ältesten Christentum* (BHT 58, 1979). **G. Lüdemann,** *Opposition to Paul in Jewish Christianity* (1989). **W. Lütgert,** *Freiheitspredigt und Schwärmgeister in Korinth* (1908). **M. Luther,** *Luther's Works* (ed. J. Pelikan, 1955–76). **P. Marshall,** *Enmity in Corinth* (1987). **R. P. Martin,** *2 Corinthians* (WBC 40, 1986). **S. Matthews,** "2 Corinthians," *Searching the Scriptures: A Feminist Commentary* (ed. E. Schüssler Fiorenza, 1994) 196-217. **W. A. Meeks,** *The First Urban Christians: The Social World of the Apostle Paul* (1983). **J. Murphy-O'Connor,** *The Theology of the Second Letter to the Corinthians* (1991). **R. Noormann,** *Irenäus als Paulusinterpret: Zur Rezeption und Wirkung der paulinischen und deuteropaulinischen Briefe im Werk des Irenäus von Lyon* (WUNT 66, 1994). **D. W. Oostendorp,** *Another Jesus: A Gospel* (1967). **A. Plummer,** *A Critical and Exegetical Commentary on the Second Epistle of St. Paul to the Corinthians* (CGTC 8, 1915). **P. Schaff** (ed.), *Saint Chrysostom: Homilies on the Epistles to the Corinthians* (NPNF 12, 1956). **W. Schmithals,** *Paul and the Gnostics* (1965; ET 1972); *Gnosticism in Corinth* (1969³; ET 1971); "Die Korintherbriefe als Briefsammlung," *ZNW* 64 (1973) 263-88. **W. Schneemelcher,** "Paulus in der griechischen Kirche des zweiten Jahrhunderts," *ZKG* 75 (1964) 120.

K. Schrader, *Der Apostel Paulus* 4 (1835). **J. S. Semler,** *Paraphrasis II: Epistolae ad Corinthios* (1776). **B. Smalley,** *The Study of the Bible in the Middle Ages (1983³).* **L. Staab,** *Pauluskommentare aus der griechischen Kirche* (1933). **C. L. Stockhausen,** "Early Interpretations of II Corinthians 3: An Exegetical Perspective," *Studia Patristica* 19 (1989) 392-99. **J. Sumney,** *Identifying Paul's Opponents* (1990). **M. E. Thrall,** *A Critical and Exegetical Commentary on the Second Epistle to the Corinthians,* vol. 1, *Introduction and Commentary on II Corinthians I–VII* (1994). **D. Trobisch,** *Die Entstehung der Paulus-briefsammlung: Studien zu den Anfängen christlicher Publizistik* (NTOA 10, 1989); *Paul's Letter Collection: Tracing the Origins* (1994). **D. Watson** (ed.), *Persuasive Artistry: Studies in NT Rhetoric in Honor of G. A. Kennedy* (1991). **J. Weiss,** *The History of Primitive Christianity* (1917; ET 1937). **M. F. Wiles,** *The Divine Apostle* (1967). **H. Windisch,** *Der zweite Korintherbrief* (1924). **C. Wolff,** *Der zweite Brief des Paulus an die Korinther* (1989). **F. Young and D. Ford,** *Meaning and Truth in 2 Corinthians* (1987). **F. Zeilinger,** *Krieg und Friede in Korinth: Kommentar zum 2 Korintherbrief des Apostels Paulus,* vol. 1, *Der Kampfbrief; Der Versöhnungsbrief; Der Bettelbrief* (1992). **J. Zmijewski,** *Der Stil der paulinischen "Narrenrede"* (1978).

V. P. FURNISH

CORNILL, CARL HEINRICH (1854–1920)

Born in Heidelberg on Apr. 26, 1854, into a family of French Huguenot background, C. studied oriental languages and theology in Leipzig, Bonn, and Marburg. In 1875 he received a PhD from Leipzig and in 1878 graduated from Marburg with a degree in theology (lic. theol.). Beginning in 1877 he worked in Marburg as a tutor, in 1878 became a *Dozent,* and in 1886 an *ausserordentlicher* professor. He moved to Königsberg (1886), where he became a full professor in 1888, later teaching in Breslau (from 1898) and in Halle (from 1910). He died June 10, 1920, in Halle (Saale).

His love for the OT had been awakened when as a youth he was especially taken with the book of Jeremiah. As a student in Leipzig he was impressed by the theologian C. Luthardt. Among his significant teachers were J. Gildemeister in oriental languages and A. KAMPHAUSEN in OT at Bonn. P. de LAGARDE, with whom he regularly had stimulating exchanges, had an influence on his text-critical studies. In the early 1880s he became convinced of the views of J. WELLHAUSEN, which he henceforth popularized effectively in simplified form. With his students he was successful in his laconically written (therefore disliked by Wellhausen) introduction to the OT (1891) and reached a broad audience in his lecture series on Israelite prophecy (1894). The success of both works is witnessed by his repeated revisions: The former enjoyed seven editions, the latter, thirteen.

C. was a staunch defender of his own views against those who held other opinions. After E. SELLIN had published his considerably more conservative introduction to the OT (1910), C. submitted it to severe criticism (124 pages) under the title *Zur Einleitung in das Alte Testament,* which was answered by Sellin in a similar tone in a volume with the same title (1912). In juxtaposition, these two controversial writings present a good picture of OT scholarship at that time. It is symptomatic of the continuing history of OT studies, initially influenced in various ways by Wellhausen, that Sellin's introduction soon outstripped that of C. among German students and held its own a half century longer (final revision by L. Rost, 1959).

C.'s most valuable studies were devoted to the text of the books of Ezekiel and Jeremiah. In his 1878 dissertation he still relied heavily on the MT, but his 1880 study of Ezekiel, which Wellhausen was responsible for pushing onto center stage, put an end to that. For that reason and also because he believed that TEXTUAL CRITICISM had been underestimated in R. SMEND's commentary (1880), he published a critical edition of Ezekiel in 1886, along with a German translation and an extensive discussion of the ancient versions. He relied greatly on the SEPTUAGINT to establish the textual base. At that time he also announced similar editions of Isaiah and Jeremiah but was able to complete only Jeremiah. Even his edition of Jeremiah was executed in a different way. In 1895 the text was published in SBOT. Awaiting the publication of B. DUHM's commentary, C. held back his translation and commentary and restricted himself at first to reconstructing the poetical parts (1901). When Duhm's commentary appeared in 1901, it sent the exegesis of Jeremiah into new directions (as could only be expected). C., who had initially intended his work as a revision of K. GRAF's earlier commentary (1862), now largely based his commentary (1905) on that of Duhm. Because it was not as bold and consistent as Duhm's, it has almost fallen into an oblivion, a fate it does not deserve. Its text-critical observations, which had at the outset been C.'s chief goal, remain useful because the printed text of his translation makes clear the differences between the MT and the Septuagint.

Works: "Maṣḥafa Falâsfâ Tabîhân, das Buch der weisen Philosophen, nach dem Äthiopischen untersucht" (diss., Leipzig, 1875); "Das Glaubensbekenntnis des J. Baradaeus in äthiopischer Übersetzung," *ZDMG* 30 (1876) 417-66; "De psalmi sexagesimi octavi indole atque origine" (diss., Marburg, 1878); *Das Buch des Propheten Ezechiel* (1886); *Introduction to the Canonical Books of the OT* (GTW 2, 1, 1891, 1913⁷; ET 1907); *The Prophets of Israel* (1894, 1920¹³; ET 1895); *The Book of the Prophet Jeremiah* (SBOT 9, 1895); *Melanchthon als Psalmenklärer* (1897); *History of the People of Israel* (1898; ET 1898); *Die metrischen Stücke des Buches Jeremia rekonstruiert* (1901); *Das Buch Jeremia* (1905); *Music in the OT* (repr. from *The Monist,* 1909); *Zur Einleitung in das Alte Testament* (1912); *The Culture of Ancient Israel* (1914).

Bibliography: **K. von Rabenau,** *NDB* 3 (1957) 367-68.

R. SMEND

COTTON, JOHN (1584–1652)

A Puritan clergyman and commentator, C. was born in England in 1584 and entered Trinity College, Cambridge, in 1597, receiving the AB, MA, and BD and winning a fellowship at Emmanuel College (Cambridge) for proficiency in Hebrew. In 1612 he accepted an appointment at St. Botolph's, Boston, Lincolnshire. To avoid harassment for his beliefs, C. sailed for Massachusetts Bay colony in 1633, where he served as pastor of First Church in Boston until his death.

C. was the patriarch of American biblical commentators, publishing commentaries on Song of Songs, Ecclesiastes, 1 John, and parts of 1 Corinthians and Revelation, some written in America but all printed in England. His approach reflected the best in English scholarship, emphasizing philology and occasionally Ramist structure. The object of his commentaries, which first were sermon series, was not only understanding of the text but also transformation into concrete action and inner joy for life in the believing community. He was flexible in regard to conventional structures but always explained the text and indicated its "use." Obviously acquainted with classical commentators, but aspiring to a plain style, he eschewed the patristic citations common among non-Puritan, Anglican commentators.

Works: *Canticles* (1642); *Revelation 16* (1642); *Ecclesiastes* (1654); *Revelation 13* (1655); *First John* (1656); *First Corinthians 14* (1660).

Bibliography: J. T. Adams, *DAB* 4 (1030) 460-62. **T. D. Bozeman,** *To Live Ancient Lives: The Primitivist Dimension of Puritanism* (1988). *DAB* (1930) 460-62. E. Davidson, "J. C.'s Biblical Exegesis: Method and Purpose," *History of Early American Literature* 17 (1982) 119-293. **E. H. Emerson,** *John Cotton* (1965). **J. H. Tuttle,** *Bibliographical Essays; A Tribute to W. Eames* (1924). **L. Ziff,** *The Career of J. C.: Puritanism and the American Experience* (1962).

T. H. OLBRICHT

COVERDALE, MILES (c. 1488–1568)

A Yorkshire native and translator of the first complete Bible printed in English, C. studied at Cambridge as an Augustinian friar, coming under the influence of his prior and the Lutheran R. Barnes. He read for the arts before becoming bachelor of theology c. 1526. From 1528 he was in exile at Hamburg, assisting W. TYNDALE in translating the Pentateuch, and at Antwerp, where he completed his own Bible (1535). From 1535 to 1540, he was in England preparing the Great Bible (1539) under the patronage of Cromwell. In a further period of exile (1540–48) at Strasbourg he met CALVIN. From 1548 to 1553 he was active in the Edwardine reformation and became bishop of Exeter in 1551. Exiled again under Queen Mary I, he finally settled at Geneva as an elder under J. KNOX, where he may have contributed to the Geneva Bible. Returning to England (1559) with proto-Puritan tendencies, he officiated at Archbishop Parker's consecration but declined to resume his bishopric, although he remained active as a preacher and was briefly beneficed in London until 1566.

C.'s enduring contribution lies in his biblical translations, especially the beauty of language in his psalter, which was included in T. CRANMER's prayer books. Like Tyndale, he desired to make the whole Bible freely available to all; but unlike Tyndale, he refrained from exegetical and polemical annotations, though the 1535 Bible included chapter summaries, some variant readings, and cross-references. He retained LUTHER's rearrangement of the NT until 1539 and included the apocryphal books in an appendix to the OT. Lacking Tyndale's learning in Hebrew and Greek, he acknowledged his debt to "fyve sundry interpreters": Tyndale's version for the NT, Pentateuch, and Jonah; Luther's German Bible; the Swiss-German Zurich Bible, especially for Job–Maccabees; the VULGATE, especially in the Psalms; and the literal Latin OT of PAGNINUS (1528). For the Great Bible (first two editions, 1539–40) he revised T. Matthew's version (which had incorporated Tyndale's OT up to 2 Chronicles), using two main sources: S. MÜNSTER's annotated Hebrew-Latin Bible (1534/35) and ERASMUS (1527 edition), with further additions from the Vulgate.

Works: *Works* (2 vols., ed. for the Parker Society by G. Pearson, 1844–46), excludes his biblical translations; *The Bible* (Coverdale version, 1535; later eds., 1535–37; facsimile of Cologne 1535 ed., with intro. by S. L. Greenslade, 1975); *Latin-English NT* (Vg text, with tr. by Coverdale, 1538); *The Great Bible* (1539; 2nd ed. ["Cranmer's Bible"] 1540); *Latin-English Psalter* (Vg text with ET, 1540); *Concordance of the NT* (1535), compiled by Coverdale. Translations of Campensis's *Paraphrases on the Psalms and Ecclesiastes* (1535); Luther's *Exposition of Psalm 22 [23]* (1537); and *Exposition of the Magnificat* (1538); Erasmus's *Paraphrase upon the NT* 2 (1549), preface and tr. of Romans, 1–2 Corinthians, and Galatians.

Bibliography: F. F. Bruce, *History of the Bible in English* (1961, 1979[3]). **C. C. Butterworth,** *The Literary Lineage of the King James Bible, 1340–1611* (1941). **T. H. Darlow and H. F. Moule,** *Historical Catalogue of Printed Editions of the English Bible, 1525–1961* (rev. by A. S. Herbert, 1968). **S. L. Greenslade,** "English Versions of the Bible, 1525–1611," *CHB* 3 (1963); "Introduction," *The Coverdale Bible 1535* (1975). **H. Guppy,** "M. C. and the English Bible, 1488–1568," *BJRL* 19 (1935). **H. A. Havgaard,** *HHMBI,* 179-84. **C. Hughes,** "C.'s Alter Ego," *BJRL* 65 (1982) 100-24. **J. Isaacs,** "Sixteenth-century English Versions," *The Bible in Its Ancient and English Versions* (ed. H. W. Robinson, 1940) 146-95. **J. F. Mozley,** *C. and His Bibles* (1953). **A. W. Pollard,** *Records of the English Bible* (1911). **R. Stokes,** "The Printing of the Great English

Bible of 1539," *Proceedings of the American Library Association* 31 (1977) 108-19. **B. F. Westcott,** *A General View of the History of the English Bible* (rev. by W. A. Wright, 1905[3]). **A. P. Wikgren,** "Introduction," *The Coverdale Bible, 1535* (1974).

D. G. SELWYN

COWLEY, ARTHUR ERNEST (1861–1931)

Born near London in 1861, C. was educated at St. Paul's School and Trinity College, Oxford (AB 1883), where he showed marked interest in Semitic languages, preferring them to Latin and Greek. After Oxford he studied at Lausanne then returned to Oxford to teach French and German at Sherborne and Magdalen schools, which gave him access to the Semitic collections at Oxford. In 1892 the university sent him to examine the library at St. Catherine's Monastery on Mt. Sinai. He was appointed assistant librarian at Oxford's Bodleian Library in 1896, succeeding A. Neubauer in 1899 as head of the oriental department. Elected a fellow of Magdalen College, Oxford, in 1902, he was appointed to teach rabbinic Hebrew literature and came to be regarded as the world's leading non-Jewish authority on the subject. From 1919 to 1931 he was chief librarian of the Bodleian. He died in Oxford in 1931 and was posthumously knighted.

C. published important works on Hebrew and Aramaic literature and attempted to decipher Hittite hieroglyphic texts (see HITTITOLOGY AND BIBLICAL STUDIES) in the Schweich lectures of 1918. This attempt was not considered successful, but his command of Hebrew and Aramaic was so exhaustive that his work in these fields is deemed definitive. His English translation of H. GESENIUS's *Hebrew Grammar* (1898, 1910) placed students of the Hebrew language in his debt. He was known for painstaking accuracy and a strictly scientific outlook on problems of biblical criticism.

Works: *The Original Hebrew of a Portion of Ecclesiasticus* (with A. Neubauer, 1897); *Gesenius' Hebrew Grammar Translated from the German* (1898, 1910[2]); *Aramaic Papyri Discovered at Assuan* (with A. H. Sayce, 1906); *Catalogue of Hebrew Manuscripts in the Bodleian Library,* vol. 2 (1906); *The Samaritan Liturgy* (2 vols., 1909); "Judith," *APOT* (1914); *Jewish Documents of the Time of Ezra* (1919); *The Hittites* (Schweich Lectures, 1920); *Aramaic Papyri of the Fifth Century* BC (1923, repr. 1967); *Concise Cataloque of Hebrew Printed Books in the Bodleian Library* (1929).

Bibliography: **T. W. Allen,** *PBA* 19 (1933) 351-59. **G. R. Driver,** *DNB* Supp. 5 (1949) 194-95. **R. Loewe,** *EncJud* 5 (1972) 1025.

J. M. BULLARD

CRAIGIE, PETER CAMPBELL (1938–85)

A Scot best known for his work in OT and related studies, C. held an MA in Semitic languages and literature (Edinburgh, 1965), an MTh (Aberdeen, 1968), and a PhD (McMaster, 1970). He spent the bulk of his academic career at the University of Calgary (1974–85), where he served in both academic and administrative capacities. He died Sept. 26, 1985.

A highly regarded teacher and productive scholar, C.'s interests and energies focused on three areas: (1) the use and insights of Ugaritic materials (see UGARIT AND THE BIBLE) for biblical studies; (2) biblical commentaries; and (3) general and thematic works on the OT. His work was characterized by a careful, judicious use of the Ugaritic materials and a sensitive awareness of the theological implications of higher criticism for those from a conservative perspective. His expository work and study of traditional difficulties (for conservative readers) is marked by balance and thoroughness.

Works: *The Book of Deuteronomy* (NICOT, 1976); *The Problem of War in the OT* (1978); *Psalms 1–50* (WBC 19, 1982); *Ezekiel* (DSB, 1983); *Ugarit and the OT* (1983); *Twelve Prophets* (DSB, 1984–85); *The OT: Its Background, Growth and Content* (1986); (ed.), *Newsletter for Ugaritic Studies* (vols. 1–33, Apr. 1972–Apr. 1985; vols. 1-30 reissued in 3 vols. as *Ugaritic Studies* [1972–83]).

Bibliography: **L. Eslinger and G. Taylor** (eds.), *Ascribe to the Lord: Biblical and Other Essays in Memory of P. C. C.* (JSOTSup 6, 1988), bibliography 603-7. **S. G. Wilson,** "Obituary," *BAR* 12 (1986) 8-9.

R. R. MARRS

CRANMER, THOMAS (1489–1556)

Born at Aslockton, Nottinghamshire, C. was educated at Jesus College, Cambridge (BA 1511; MA 1514; BD 1521; DD 1526) and was a fellow there. While at Cambridge he tested the new Lutheran ideas by an intensive study of Scripture and the early fathers, in which he was influenced by the methods of ERASMUS and the humanists (as his surviving library and various commonplace collections show). While ambassador to Emperor Charles V in 1532, he forged links with the Lutheran A. Osiander at Nuremberg. On his return he was appointed to the see of Canterbury (1533). During the reign of Mary I he was sentenced for high treason (1553) and later for heresy (1555) and was put to death at Oxford in 1556.

While not himself active as a translator or commentator (although he possessed Hebrew and Greek Bibles and other tools of humanist scholarship), he supported T. Cromwell's efforts to secure the king's approval for an English Bible following the ban on vernacular versions in 1530. In 1534 he proposed that Convocation petition the king for an authorized TRANSLATION and in 1537 recommended J. Roger's revision of COVERDALE's Bible ("Thomas Matthew's Bible") to Cromwell for the royal license. In his preface to the second edition of Coverdale's *Great Bible* (also known as "Cranmer's Bible") he defended (against Chrysostom and Gregory of Nazianzus) the provision of a vernacular translation for all classes to read as a guide to life and for increase of virtue, while warning of the dangers of contentious interpretation by the unlearned, although in the reaction that followed Cromwell's fall C. accepted the restrictions on Bible reading (1543). In his writings he defended his position from Scripture ("as a most sure ground and an infallible truth"), reinforced by patristic quotations, and he attacked the notion of "unwritten verities" as an independent doctrinal source (later edited as *Confutation of Unwritten Verities,* 1556). His belief in the sufficiency of Scripture was stated in the fifth of the Forty-two Articles of Religion (1553) and exemplified in the prayer books (1549, 1552), which restored the continuous reading of Scripture in the offices of matins and evensong.

Works: "Preface," *The Great Bible* (1540^2); Commonplace Books (Collectiones ex S. Scriptur. et Patribus, British Library, MSS Royal, 7BXI, 7BXII, unpub.); *Confutation of Unwritten Verities* (ed. and tr. from previous work, RSTC 5996, 1556); *The Work of T. C.* (4 vols., ed. H. Jenkyns, 1833; 2 vols., ed. J. E. Cox, Parker Society, 1844, 1846; selections, ed. G. E. Duffield, 1964).

Bibliography: P. Ayris and D. G. Selwyn (eds.), *T. C.: Churchman and Scholar* (1993). G. W. Bromiley, *T. C.: Theologian* (1956); *M. Bucer and T. C.: Annotationes in octo priora capita evangelii secundum Mattaeum, Croydon 1549* (ed. H. Vogt, 1972). D. MacCulloch, *T. C.: A Life* (1996). A. Null, "T. C.'s Doctrine of Repentance" (diss., Cambridge, 1994). A. F. Pollard, *T. C. and the English Reformation, 1489–1556* (1904). J. Ridley, *Thomas Cranmer* (1962). D. G. Selwyn, *The Library of T. C.* (1996). H. R. Willoughby, *The First Authorised English Bible and the Cranmer Preface* (1942).

D. G. SELWYN

CREED, JOHN MARTIN (1889–1940)

Born in Leicester, England, Oct. 14, 1889, C. entered Gonville and Caius College, Cambridge, in 1908, becoming Bell Scholar in 1909. He was elected fellow of Caius in 1915, where he served as chaplain. From 1919 to 1926, he was fellow and dean of St. John's College, Cambridge, and from 1926 until his death he was Ely Professor of Divinity and canon of Ely Chapel. He served as editor of the *Journal of Theological Studies,* 1935 to 1940.

C.'s *Divinity of Jesus Christ* was a review of the christologies of F. SCHLEIERMACHER, G. W. F. Hegel (1770–1831), A. RITSCHL, and others and a move toward the neo-orthodoxy of K. BARTH and E. Brunner. C. stressed Christ as creator and revealer of God and struck a middle ground between conservative propositional revelation and liberal natural revelation.

C.'s biblical exegesis shows the transition from source criticism toward FORM CRITICISM and REDACTION CRITICISM. In the introduction to his commentary on Luke, he characterized the author as a copyist who had no definite controlling theological interests. Yet in the text of the commentary, C. constantly showed how Luke shaded Mark, softening the harsh language directed toward the disciples and JESUS' family. He acknowledged his debt to and disagreements with R. BULTMANN and K. SCHMIDT; his interpretations stay close to the conservative tradition of J. B. LIGHTFOOT, though not slavishly so.

Works: *The Gospel According to Luke* (1930); (ed.), *Religious Thought in the Eighteenth Century* (1934); *The Divinity of Christ: a Study in the History of Christian Doctrine Since Kant* (1938).

Bibliography: J. F. Bethune-Baker, *PBA* 26 (1940) 517-30. J. S. Boys Smith, *DNB, 1931–40* (1949) 202-3.

R. B. VINSON

CRELL (or KRELL), JOHANN (Latin CRELLIUS, JOHANNES) (1590–1633)

Born at Helmetzheim, near Nuremberg, in 1590, the son of a Lutheran clergyman, C. was educated at Altdorf, where he became a follower of F. SOCINUS. In 1613 he settled in Krakow, Poland, where he was rector of the academy from 1616 to 1621. Thereafter he served as a pastor in that city until his death on June 11, 1633.

A leading exponent of Socinian theology and the most important Socinian commentator on the Scriptures, C. entered into controversy with H. GROTIUS about the atonement. Together with J. Stegmann the elder, he produced a translation of the NT (1630). Among his works are paraphrases of Romans, Galatians, and Hebrews, and commentaries on Matthew 1–5, Romans, 1 Corinthians, Ephesians, Philippians, Colossians, 1 and 2 Thessalonians, and 1 Peter 1–2. On the basis of his lectures, commentaries later appeared on Galatians, 1 Timothy, Titus, and Philemon. He was also the author of important theological treatises. His works are included in the *Bibliotheca Fratrum Polonorum.*

Works: *Declaratio sententiae de causis mortis Christi* (1618); *De Deo et attributis ejus* (1630); *De uno Deo patre* (1631); *Vindiciae pro religionis libertate* (1637); *De Spiritu Sancto* (1640); *Opera omnia exegetica* (1656).

Bibliography: *ADB* 4 (1876) 586-87. *BU* 9 (1854) 463-64. J. von Hirtenberg, "Life," *The Polish Brethren* (ed. G. H. Williams, Harvard Theological Studies 30, 1980) 1:131-48.

A. W. WAINWRIGHT

CRITICI SACRI

This famous work was first published in London in 1660 in nine folio volumes under the title *Critici sacri, sive doctissimorum vivorum in Ss. Biblia annotationes et tractatus. Opus summâ curâ recognitum. Quid in hos opere practitum sit prafatio ad lectorem ostendit.* Compiled by J. Pearson (1613–86), A. Scattergood (1611–87), F. Gouldman (d. 1688), and R. Pearson (d. 1734), the work bears some similarity to medieval catenas on Scripture and was intended as a complementary work to the London POLYGLOT. Following the order of the biblical books, including the APOCRYPHA, the work contains the annotations and commentaries of numerous sixteenth- and seventeenth-century interpreters (predominantly Protestant but excluding the major Reformers) as well as several dozen dissertations on diverse topics and texts. The volumes were reissued in Frankfort in 1695 and in Amsterdam in 1698. Two supplementary volumes entitled *Thesaurus theologico-philologicus* were issued in 1701 and two additional volumes entitled *Thesaurus novus theologico-philologicus* in 1732 (in Amsterdam). The four additional volumes contained no new material on the Apocrypha. A detailed outline of the contents of the thirteen volumes is given in J. Darling, *Cyclopaedia Bibliographica* 1 (1854, 815-26). The material in the original edition was condensed and recast by M. POOLE in his *Synopsis criticorum* (5 vols., 1669–76), with additional commentators added to bring the number of interpreters quoted to about 150.

J. H. HAYES

CROSS-CULTURAL BIBLICAL INTERPRETATION

The Christian Bible is, among other things, a cultural text. Its textual features document theological and doctrinal elements and embody the spiritual and political aspirations of a people whose way of life, customs, and manners are very different from those of comtemporary readers. Thus reading these texts can be a difficult endeavor. Cross-cultural biblical interpretation seeks to overcome the remoteness and strangeness of the texts by employing the reader's cultural resources and social experiences to make links across the cultural divides, thus illuminating the biblical narratives. This approach to interpretation invites readers to use their own indigenous texts and concepts to make hermeneutical sense of biblical texts and concepts imported across time and space. In opening up biblical narratives, cross-cultural HERMENEUTICS, to use R. Schreiter's categories (1997, 29), draws on the three-dimensional aspects of a culture: ideational (worldviews, values, and rules), performantial (rituals and roles), and material (language, symbols, food, clothing, etc.). In other words, using indigenous beliefs and experiences, cross-cultural hermeneutics attempts to provide important analogies with ancient texts that readers from other cultures may not notice or be

aware of. What, in effect, such readings have done is to make culture an important locus for hermeneutics.

The emergence of indigenous ways of reading the Bible by the peoples of the third world has given the impression that cross-cultural hermeneutics is something recent and exotic, confined to cultures "out there" and absent from Western readings. Biblical interpretation, however, has always been culturally specific and has always been informed and colored by reigning cultural values, be they Western, Eastern, or Southern. Western scholars have not been free from such tendencies. For example, when H. S. REIMARUS (1694–1768) and D. F. STRAUSS (1808–74) extended the use of the critical methods developed in the linguistic and historical disciplines during the eighteenth century to investigation of biblical narratives; or when R. BULTMANN (1884–1976) mobilized M. Heidegger's (1889–1976) existential philosophy to interpret NT *kerygma;* or when current biblical scholars borrow critical methodologies and theories from contemporary LITERARY or social science studies (see SOCIAL-SCIENTIFIC CRITICISM), they, too, are engaged in cross-cultural hermeneutics in the sense that they are trying to relate ancient texts to their own contexts by employing the Western cultural codes of their time. Such practices, however, tend to be treated as value free and to be subsumed under the rubric of scientific exegesis. Yet even a brief perusal of the history of hermeneutics will reveal that there has never been an interpretation that has been without reference to or dependence on the particular cultural codes, thought patterns, and social location of the interpreter.

Surveying the field of cross-cultural biblical interpretation, one can identify at least three modes of cross-cultural reading: conceptual correspondences, narratival enrichments, and performantial parallels.

1. Conceptual Correspondences. The first mode is to seek textual or conceptual parallels between biblical texts and the traditions of one's own culture. Such an effort, unlike historical criticism, looks beyond the Judaic or Greco-Roman context of the biblical narratives and seeks for corresponding conceptual analogies in the readers' textual traditions. Indian Christian interpreters of an earlier generation were the pioneers in this mode. K. Banerjea (1813–85) demonstrated remarkable similarities between biblical and Vedic texts. He selected overlapping narrative segments that touched on the creation, the fall, and the flood from the great wealth of Vedic writings and juxtaposed them with passages from the Bible, emphasizing that the expectations of the Indian texts were fulfilled in Christianity. A. Appasamy (1891–1971) borrowed key ideas from *bhakti,* the Hindu devotional tradition, to make sense of JOHANNINE spirituality. By conscripting concepts like *moksa* (liberation), *antaryamin* (indweller), and *avatar* (incarnation) as a way of getting into the thought world of John, Appasamy invested these Hindu concepts with Christian meanings and also accentuated the role of JESUS. In China, Wu Lei-ch'uan (1870–1944) was engaged in a similar exercise, attempting to integrate Confucian concepts with biblical ones. He utilized the fundamental Confucian concept of highest virtue, *jen,* as well as those of *Tien-tzu* (Son of Heaven) and *Sheng Tien-tzu* (Holy Son of God) to elucidate the Holy Spirit and the role of Jesus (see J. Yieh [1995]). The Japanese theologian K. Kitamori's (1965) employment of *tsura* to explain the pain of God; the South African artist A. Mbatha's (1986) use of *ubunto* to appropriate the story of Joseph as that, not of an individual, but of a community (1986); and G. West's (1993) recovery of the African notions of *indlovukazi* (first wife), *inthandokazi* (favorite wife), and *isancinza* (helper to the wife) as interpretative keys to explain the matrilineal presence and power and to determine the role of Leah, Rachel, Bilhah, and Zilpah also fall within this mode.

In this same mode, insights from popular culture are summoned to critically illuminate biblical texts. O. Hendricks (1994), an African American, calls for the use of such cultural expressions as blues, soul, and jazz to formulate a guerrilla exegesis. Australian aboriginals' attempts to translate aboriginal dreaming stories in Christian terms, citing passages from both testaments to convey the essential moral message (see A. Pattel-Gray [1995]), and the reclamation of two pivotal Indian tribal values, anti-pride and anti-greed, that resonate with the Markan narrative (Mark 10:17-27, 35-45) as an alternative model for a world driven by greed and consumerism are further examples of the use of elements from popular culture (see G. Soares-Prabhu [1995]).

2. Narratival Enrichments. The second mode of cross-cultural reading is to place some of the popular folktales (see FOLKLORE), legends, riddles, plays, proverbs, and poems that are part of the common heritage of a people alongside biblical materials, thus drawing out their hermeneutical implications. C. Song, the Taiwanese theologian who pioneered the method of creatively juxtaposing myths (see MYTHOLOGY AND BIBLICAL STUDIES), stories, and legends with biblical narratives, often goes beyond the written word to the symbolic meaning. In *The Tears of Lady Meng* (1982), Song blends a well-known Chinese folktale with the biblical theme of Jesus' death and resurrection. P. Lee (1989) juxtaposes the book of Ruth and a Chinese drama of the Yuan period, "The Injustice Done to Ton Ngo." Both stories are about a daughter-in-law and her devotion to her mother-in-law, and both emerge out of a patriarchal society. Although the two stories differ in plot, the ethical and metaphysical perspectives shine through. S. Rayan, in his essay "Wrestling in the Night" (1989), juxtaposes in an imaginative way three texts, two ancient—the *Bhagavadgita* and the book of Job—and one modern—the posthumous writings of a young girl, eponymously entitled the *Poems of Gitanjali.* These three

works represent three religious traditions: Hindu, Jewish, and Islamic. In spite of the time span and the different religious orientations, the characters Arjuna, Job, and Gitanjali testify that sorrow and pain are universal. All three wrestle with death, pain, love, and God; and through sorrow and anguish each grows in faith and love. Africans too are engaged in retrieving their folktales. The "Parable of the Two Brothers," a popular story among the Sukuma people of Tanzania, has interesting parallels with the Lukan prodigal son. Both these stories have a father and two sons, and in both the younger son is received back into the family and rewarded. Although in their plots and in their thematic emphases they may differ, the additional insights that the Sukuma parable provides, such as values of community and unity, can enrich the biblical story.

3. Performantial Parallels. The third mode of cross-cultural reading is to utilize ritual and behavioral practices that are commonly available in a culture: The Johannine saying of Jesus, "Very truly, I tell you, unless you eat the flesh of the Son of Man and drink his blood, you have no life in you. Those who eat my flesh and drink my blood have eternal life, and I will raise them up on the last day, for my flesh is true food and my blood is true drink" (John 6:53-55), may sound awkward and cannibalistic to those who are reared with Western Enlightenment values. But read analogically to Malawian witchcraft talk, as A. Musopole (1993) has done, the saying takes on a different meaning: "Anyone who feeds on Jesus takes into themselves the very life-force of Jesus to re-enforce their own lives" (352). Such a reading can be understood metaphorically as a eucharistic saying or literally as witchcraft talk.

The African concept of the trickster, though it differs from context to context, is also a helpful channel through which to appraise the behavior of some biblical characters who, viewed from a Western moral perspective, may seem unreliable and deceitful. From an African trickster point of view, such actions are recognized as performed by people who lack power and live in hopeless situations. Trickery is something men and women often turn to in situations where they have no other recourse. Abraham's deceptive statements to Pharaoh and Abimelech (Gen 12:10-20; 20:1-18), the explanation given by Hebrew midwives for their unwillingness to discharge Pharaoh's order to kill all male children born to Israelites (Exod 1:15-19), and Delilah's attempts to woo and overcome Samson (Judges 16) are examples of the trickster role played in the Bible by individuals who are otherwise powerless (N. Steinberg [1988]).

In assessing cross-cultural hermeneutics, one finds both positive and negative features. Positively, cross-cultural hermeneutics has enabled Christian interpreters to gain credibility and cultivate deeper contact with their people, who otherwise would have regarded Christians as foreigners in their own country. A variety of culture-informed interpretations has offered counterreadings to those of Western interpretations, with their ethnocentric and rationalistic prejudices, and helped to reverse the missionary condemnation of indigenous cultures. The mobilization of cultural insights has served as an acknowledgment that religious truths were present in indigenous cultures even before the arrival and introduction of Christianity. It has also strengthened the notion that indigenous people are not passive receivers; rather, they are architects of their own hermeneutics. Creatively intermixing and synthesizing biblical faith with indigenous religion has enabled, for instance, Mayan identity in Guatemala to survive.

Negatively, in pressing for comparable cultural elements cross-cultural hermeneutics has tended to overemphasize the positive aspects of ancient cultures while overlooking their dehumanizing aspects. It is tempting to assume that indigenous people have access to privileged knowledge in unraveling the mysteries of ancient texts. However, to do so would be to reinscribe a hermeneutical hierarchy in which some have an unequal access and relation to texts. Cross-cultural hermeneutics became a celebratory event when indigenous people were assumed to lead a settled life and were thought of in terms of cultural wholes. But now, at a time when there is an intermixing of cultures both at popular and elitist levels and when local/global and vernacular/cosmopolitan divides are shrinking and people's lives are being rearranged by globalization, finding culture-specific analogues may be an increasingly difficult task. Alternatively, of course, the new multi-vision may throw up its own hitherto undiscovered parallels.

Bibliography: *Biblical Interpretation: A Journal of Contemporary Approaches* 2 (3) (1993), special issue on Asian hermeneutics. **M. Brett** (ed.), *Ethnicity and the Bible* (BIS 19, 1996). **C. H. Felder,** *Stony the Road We Trod: African-American Biblical Interpretation* (1991). **J. Healey and D. Sybertz,** *Towards an African Narrative Theology* (Faith and Culture Series, 1996). **O. O. Hendricks,** "Guerrilla Exegesis: A Post Modern Proposal for Insurgent African American Biblical Interpretation," *JITC* 22, 1 (1994) 92-109. **K. Kitamori,** *Theology of the Pain of God* (1965). **P. K. H. Lee,** "Two Stories of Loyalty," *Ching Feng* 32:1 (1989) 24-40. **A. Mbatha,** *In the Heart of the Tiger: Art of South Africa* (1986). **A. C. Musopole,** "Witchcraft Terminology, the Bible, and African Christian Theology: An Exercise in Hermeneutics," *JITC* 23, 4 (1993) 347-54. **A. Pattel-Gray,** "Dreaming: An Aboriginal Interpretation of the Bible," *Text and Experience* (ed. D. Smith-Christopher, 1995) 247-59. **S. Rayan,** "Wrestling in the Night," *The Future of Liberation Theology: Essays in Honor of G. Gutierrez* (ed. M. H. Ellis and O. Maduro, 1989) 450-69. **G. M. Soares-Prabhu,** "Anti-Greed and Anti-Pride: Mark 10.17-27 and 10.35-45 in the Light of Tribal Values," *Voices from the Margin* (ed. R. S. Sugirtharajah, 1995) 117-37. **R. Schreiter,** *The New Catholicity: Theology Between Global and Local* (Faith and

Culture Series, 1997). **F. F. Segovia and M. A. Tolbert** (eds.), *Reading from this Place,* vol. 2, *Social Location and Biblical Interpretation in Global Perspective* (1995). **D. Smith-Christopher** (ed.), *Text and Experience: Towards A Cultural Exegesis of the Bible* (BiSe 35, 1995). **C. S. Song,** *The Tears of Lady Meng: A Parable of People's Political Theology* (1982). **N. Steinberg,** "Israelite Tricksters: Their Analogues and Cross-Cultural Study," *Semeia,* 42 (1988) 1-13. **R. S. Sugirtharajah** (ed.), *Voices from the Margin: Interpreting the Bible in the Third World* (new ed., 1995). **G. O. West,** *Contextual Bible Study* (1993). **J. Y. H. Yieh,** "Cultural Reading of the Bible: Some Chinese Christian Cases," *Text and Experience* (ed. D. Smith-Christopher, 1995) 122-53.

R. S. Sugirtharajah

CROSS, FRANK MOORE, JR. (1921–)

Born July 13, 1921, in Ross, California, C. attended Maryville College in Tennessee (AB 1942); McCormick Theological Seminary (BD 1946); and Johns Hopkins University, where he studied under W. F. Albright (PhD in Semitic languages, 1950). He taught at Wellesley College (1950–51) and McCormick Theological Seminary (1951–57) before going to Harvard in 1957. He held the Hancock Chair of Hebrew and Other Oriental Languages at Harvard from 1958 until his retirement in 1992, when he became emeritus. During his tenure at Harvard he directed over one hundred dissertations.

C.'s many contributions to biblical studies can be arranged into six broad groupings: Northwest Semitic epigraphy; the orthography of the HB; biblical and Ugaritic poetry (see Ugarit and the Bible); the study of the Dead Sea Scrolls; Textual Criticism; and the history of Israel's religion within its ancient Near Eastern milieu. His influence has extended into a number of other areas as well: Archaeology (he directed or participated in excavations in Israel, Carthage, and off Sardinia); publications (he has served on a number of editorial boards and edited HSM, HSS, and Hermeneia); and professional organizations (he has been a fellow of the American Academy of Arts and Sciences and the Institute for Advanced Studies at the Hebrew University in Jerusalem and a member of the American Philosophical Society; he is affililiated with various other learned societies; and he has served as president of SBL, ASOR, and the Biblical Colloquium).

C. is known for an uncanny ability to classify and date alphabetic inscriptions—from the earliest Canaanite and Aramaic inscriptions, through the Samaria Papyri from the Wādi ed-Dāliyeh and the Dead Sea Scrolls—and for his skill at reconstructing texts based on extant fragments. This talent for epigraphic studies is notable in two publications co-written with D. N. Freedman. C. and Freedman examined early northwest Semitic inscriptions to chart the development of spelling practices evident in various scribal traditions (1952). Relying on those orthographic results as well as on text-critical methods, the parallelistic nature of Ugaritic and biblical POETRY, and an understanding of the religious vocabulary of the ancient Near East, they establish and interpreted the oldest passages in the Bible (1975a, 1997).

Much of C.'s scholarly career has been taken up with the study of the Qumran scrolls. One of the original members of the international committee appointed to prepare the manuscripts for publication, he is especially known for his work on the scrolls' paleography and dating and for his contributions on the transmission of the biblical text, based in part on the variant text types attested in the biblical scrolls. He has also explored the archaeology and history of Qumran, its religious symbolism and beliefs, and its identification as Essene.

The hallmark of C.'s essays on Israelite religion is his ability to draw often disparate elements into a synthesis. He employs philology (of biblical and extrabiblical texts), textual criticism, archaeology, onomastics, historical geography, paleography, anthropology, and an understanding of the natural world to forge proposed solutions to such diverse problems as the relationship between El and Yahweh, the purpose of the contracts contained in the Samaria Papyri, the mythic structure of Exodus 15, the structure and dating of the DEUTERONOMISTIC HISTORY, the description of Reuben as Jacob's firstborn, the identity of the Qumran community, and the nature of early Israel's kinship structure.

Works: (with D. N. Freedman), *Early Hebrew Orthography: A Study of the Epigraphic Evidence* (AOS 36, 1952); *The Ancient Library of Qumran* (1958, 1961[2], 1995[3]); "The Development of the Jewish Scripts," *The Bible and the Ancient Near East: Essays in Honor of W. F. Albright* (ed. G. E. Wright, 1961) 133-202; *Canaanite Myth and Hebrew Epic: Essays in the History of the Religion of Israel* (1973); "The Evolution of a Theory of Local Texts," *Qumran and the History of the Biblical Text* (ed. F. M. Cross and S. Talmon, 1975a) 306-20; (with D. N. Freedman), *Studies in Ancient Yahwistic Poetry* (1975b, new ed. 1997); *From Epic to Canon: History and Literature in Ancient Israel* (1998).

Bibliography: B. Halpern and J. D. Levenson (eds.), *Traditions in Transformation: Turning Points in Biblical Faith* (FS, 1981), includes bibliography through 1979. **P. D. Miller, Jr., P. D. Hanson, S. D. McBride** (eds.), *Ancient Israelite Religion: Essays in Honor of F. M. C.* (1987), includes bibliography through 1985. **H. Shanks** (ed.), *F. M. C.: Conversations with a Bible Scholar* (1994).

J. A. HACKETT

CULLMANN, OSCAR (1902–)

Born in Strasbourg Feb. 25, 1902, C. studied theology and classics at the university there. W. Baldensperger (*Der Prolog des vierten evangeliums* [1898]) was influ-

ential in C.'s relating early Christianity to "nonconformist" Judaism. Lectures by A. LOISY and M. GOGUEL and a dissertation on the Pseudo-Clementines (1930) climaxed studies at the University of Paris. C. became professor of NT and church history at Strasbourg (1930–38), Basel (1938–72), and simultaneously from 1948 professor of early Christianity at Paris (École des Hautes Études—Faculte des Lettres, Sorbonne, and Faculte Libre de Theologie Protestante).

Preeminent in contributions to biblical studies is C.'s conception of *Heilsgeschichte,* which encompasses the entire biblical revelation and is the norm of its coherence and meaning. He welcomed FORM CRITICISM as a more objective method of viewing the Gospels than the subjective tendencies of the liberal conception of JESUS. With this new tool C. struck upon what he conceived to be the essence of early Christian belief: "Jesus is Lord." This early confession encapsulated the inescapable historicalness of the Jesus of Nazareth who also transcends history and is worshiped as its Lord. This dialectic led C. to formulate the essential core of the NT writers'/communities' understanding of history in light of the Jesus events (*Christ and Time* [1946]). Endeavoring in this seminal work to steer a path free of philosophical and moral-theological presuppositions/systems in biblical exegesis, C. acknowledged the importance of current problematics, especially the eschatological as posed in the "consistent" eschatology of A. SCHWEITZER, the existential demythologizing of R. BULTMANN, and the theological exegesis of K. BARTH.

For C. the Christ event forms the center of God's revelation to the world through Israel in two basic ways: (1) Christ is the midpoint of history in that his life, death, and resurrection have already fulfilled God's purposes for creation in defeating evil and establishing the re-creation of all things in a way in which the future, "not yet," consummation of the world is decisively determined and assured. This "already/not yet" tension becomes characteristic of the present age in which Jesus is recognized in the church as Lord of the entire universe, including the invisible "principalities and powers" that exert control over nations and systems (see "Kingship of Christ," *Early Church* [1956a]). That this view of history is not an attempt to elucidate philosophical notions of time per se is evident in the second principle: (2) Universal history proceeds from its mythically perceived origins and ends by means of soteriological representation through the events of Israel narrowing to a remnant and eventually to the one, Jesus Christ, widening again through the apostles to the church and to the whole world.

In his *magnum opus* (1965) the relation between revelation and "events" or "history" is refined: Salvation is not an event or history per se, but history is an indispensible medium of God's saving presence/action for the world. Salvation history, then, entails particular events within history that are experienced, interpreted, and reinterpreted in light of later events and developing tradition(s), and that themselves interpret history as a whole, preeminently as all history is summed up in Jesus Christ. "Saving events" in this sense thus give rise to faith (and not vice-versa), and the Christ events are ultimately responsible for the Gospels and, indeed, the whole of the NT. C.'s version of *Heilsgeschichte* thus stresses the essential character of history for biblical revelation vis-à-vis other ancient religions, guards against primarily experiential HERMENEUTICS, and with its theocentricity ensures the fundamental and ongoing importance of Israel while highlighting the functions of Messiah with respect to the past, the present, and the future of God's saving history (1957a).

C.'s early interest in Jewish Christianity (1930) received a fruitful impulse from the publication of the Qumran scrolls (see DEAD SEA SCROLLS); for it now appeared that a line of development/influence could be drawn from a pre-Christian, Palestinian-based cultic-critical Judaism through such other baptist groups as John the Baptizer and on through early Christianity in the anti-Temple oriented Hellenists of Acts to JOHANNINE Christianity and beyond. With this "non-conformist," often esoterically and gnostically-oriented (see GNOSTIC INTERPRETATION) Judaism as a second major type of Palestinian Judaism, the "orthodox" (e.g., Tübingen school) view of the linear development of Christianity from Palestinian to a Jewish-Hellenistic to a gentile church had to be discarded. C. developed a triangular relation among the Hellenists, Johannine Christianity, and the book of Hebrews in consolidating his insight that much of earliest Christianity can only be understood properly as taking root from this non-conformist soil (1975).

C.'s *Peter* (1952) provided an important opening in Protestant-Catholic dialogue and led to his invitation to the Second Vatican Council. His *Unity Through Diversity* (1986) expresses his mature thinking about the ways and probabilities of church unity. It shows that a *Heilsgeschichte* approach illuminates the unity of the church universal in the singular events of the Christ precisely through the various *charismata* and diverging structures bestowed to and elicited from the church by the Holy Spirit since the very beginning.

Works: *Le problème littéraire et historique du roman pseudo-clémentin* (EHPhR 23, 1930); "Le caractère eschatologique du devoir missionnaire et de la conscience apostolique de S. Paul: Étude sur le *katechon(ōn)* de 2 Thess 2:6-7," *RHPR* 16 (1936a) 210-45; "The Meaning of the Lord's Supper in Primitive Christianity" (1936b); *The Earliest Christian Confessions* (1943; ET 1949); *Christ and Time: The Primitive Christian Conception of Time and History* (1946; ET 1952[2]); "Das wahre durch die ausgebliebene Parusie gestellte neutestamentliche Problem," *TZ* 3 (1947) 177-91; *Baptism in the NT* (1948;

ET, SBT 1, 1950); *Early Christian Worship* (1950; ET, SBT 10, 1953); *Peter—Disciple, Apostle, Martyr* (1952; ET 1958[2]); "Die Neuentdeckten Qumrantexte und das Judenchristentum der Pseudoklementinen," *Neutestamentliche Studien für R. Bultmann* (BZNW 21, 1954) 35-51; "The Significance of the Qumran Texts for Research into the Beginnings of Christianity," *JBL* 74 (1955) 133-41; *The Early Church: Studies in Early Christian History and Theology* (ed. A. J. B. Higgins, 1956a); *Immortality of the Soul or Resurrection of the Dead: The Witness of the NT* (1956b) = *Harvard Divinity School Bulletin* 21 (1955–56) 5-36; "R. Bultmann's Concept of Myth and the NT," *CTM* 27 (1956c) 13-24; *The State in the NT* (1956d; ET 1956); *The Christology of the NT* (1957a; ET 1963[2]); "Que signifie le sel dans la parabole de Jésus? Les évangélistes, premiers commentateurs du logion," *RHPR* 37 (1957b) 36-43; "Ebioniten, Ebioniterevangelium," *RGG[3]* 2 (1958a) 297-98; *Essays on the Lord's Supper* (ESW 1, 1958b) 5-23; "Geschichtsschreibung (im Neuen Testament)," *RGG[3]* (1958c) 1501-3; *A Message to Catholics and Protestants* (1958d; ET 1958); "A New Approach to the Interpretation of the Fourth Gospel," *ExpTim* 71 (1959) 8-11, 39-42; "Das Thomasevangelium und die Frage nach dem Alter der in ihm enthaltenen Tradition," *TLZ* 85 (1960) 321-34; "An Autobiographical Sketch by Prof. O. C.," *SJT* 14 (1961a) 228-33; "Ecumenical Collection and Community of Goods in the Primitive Church," *Pax Romana Journal* 6 (1961b) 7-9; "Out of Season Remarks on the 'Historical Jesus' of the Bultmann School," *USQR* 16 (1961c) 131-48; "Petrusevangelium, Petruskergyma," *RGG[3]* 5 (1961d) 260-61; "Die Bedeutung der Zelotenbewegung für das Neue Testament," *La foi et le culte de l'Église primitive* (1963a); "Infancy Gospels," *NT Apocrypha* (ed. E. Hennecke and W. Schneemelcher, 1963b) 1:363-417; *Salvation in History* (1965; ET 1967); *The NT: An Introduction for the General Reader* (1966a; ET 1968); *O. C.: Vorträge und Aufsätze (1925–62)* (ed. K. Froelich, 1966b) 292-302; *Vatican Council II: The New Direction* (Religious Perspectives 19, 1968); *Des sources de l'Évangile a la formation de la théologie chrétienne* (1969); *Jesus and the Revolutionaries* (1970; ET 1970); *The Johannine Circle* (1975; ET 1976); *Unity Through Diversity* (1986; ET 1987).

Bibliography: **T. M. Dorman,** *HHMBI,* 467-71. **J. Fangmeier,** "Heilsgeschichte? Einige Marginalien besonders zum Gespräch zwischen K. Barth und O. C.," *Geschichte und Zukunft* (ed. J. Fangmeier and M. Geiger, ThStud 87, 1967) 5-27. **E. Fascher,** "Christologie oder Theologie: Bermerkungen zu O. C.s Christologie der Neuen Testment," *TLZ* 87 (1962) 881-910. **J. Frisque,** *O. C.: Une théologie de l'histoire du salut* (CAR 11, 1960). **K. Froehlich,** "O. C.: A Portrait," *JES* 1 (1964) 22-41; "Die Mitte des Neuen Testaments: O. C. Beitrag zur Theologie der Gegenwart," *Oikonomia: O. C. zum 65. Geburtstag gewidmet* (ed. F. Christ, 1967) 203-19. **H.-G. Hermesmann,** *Zeit und Heil: O. C. Theologie der Heilsgeschichte* (Konfessionskundliche Schriftenreihe 43, 1979). **K.-H. Schlaudraff,** *"Heil als Geschichte"? Zur Cullmann-Rezeption und Cullmann-Kritik in der neutestamentlichen Wissenschaft* *des deutschsprachigen Protestantismus seit 1946* (1986). **K. G. Steck,** *Die Idee der Heilsgeschichte: Hofmann—Schlatter— Cullmann* (ThStud 56, 1959). **J. J. Vincent,** *TOT,* 112-22. **A. Vöglte,** *TdT,* 488-93. **D. H. Wallace,** *CMCT,* 163-202.

D. P. MOESSNER

CULTURAL STUDIES

1. Definition of Cultural Studies and Its Role in Biblical Studies. Cultural studies resists a rigid definition, but its proponents usually see it as a practice of both cultural critique and cultural intervention (b. hooks [1990] 124-25). As a practice of cultural critique it posits conjunctural (i.e., historically specific) analyses of all parts of culture to expose their operations of power in the production of identity and in the maintenance of hegemony. As a practice of intervention within culture, it participates in culture in several ways: through the democratization of culture, the creation of collectives to link scholars across disciplines and to connect intellectuals to grassroots organizations, and the production of more liberative forms of pedagogy.

In biblical studies, cultural studies likewise has a dual role. On the one hand, as a form of cultural critique it assesses the contributing role of contextualization (or social location) for biblical reading strategies, interpretation practices, and evaluation standards (F. Segovia [1995a] 370-378). On the other hand, it reclaims the residual or lost voices refracted through biblical texts (E. Schüssler Fiorenza [1984] 15), opens up spaces for so-called marginalized readings of these texts (J.-P. Ruiz [1995] 73-84; O. Hendricks [1994] 92-109), creates collectives or coalitions to offset insidious neutralizing practices of interpretation validity (Bible and Culture Collective [1995] 15-19), and decries pedagogical theories that support unilateral lines of authority (G. West [1993] 131-46).

2. Development of the Cultural Studies Paradigm. Cultural studies' democratization of culture places it within the broad parameters of post-modernism (see POST-MODERN BIBLICAL INTERPRETATION). Yet its intellectual roots lie deep in several theoretical fields: the mass market (commodification) theory of the Frankfurt school, the hegemony theory of A. Gramsci (1891–1937; specifically, on dominant groups' continuous use of civic formation to win the consent of resisting, dominated groups), L. Althusser's (1918–90) view of ideology as a dynamic complex of structural constraints (or systems of representation), M. Foucault's (1926–84) view of knowledge discourses as power, and pragmatism's pedagogical theory.

F. Segovia has given a persuasive history of the influence of the cultural studies paradigm in biblical studies (1995a, 2-7). Arguing that biblical criticism has evolved in three stages, he avers that the initial dominance of historical criticism (biblical criticism's first

stage, which began in the mid-19th cent.) gave way between the mid-1970s and the mid-1990s to two other types of biblical criticism—namely, biblical LITERARY criticism and biblical [socio]cultural criticism (stage two). Later in the 1990s (stage three) these approaches merged interests to set off an explosion of methodologies or "a situation of radical plurality"—that is, the emergence of the cultural studies paradigm in biblical studies (Segovia [1995a] 4-15, esp. 4).

3. Distinctions Within Cultural Studies. At least two significant formulations of cultural studies have emerged, the first, British; the second (typically known as cultural criticism), North American. In its British form cultural studies began with the British sociologists (see SOCIOLOGY AND HB/NT STUDIES) of culture, R. Williams (1921–88), R. Hoggart (b. 1918), and E. Thompson (b. 1924). Later it confronted the French "linguistic turn" under S. Hall's influence; and in the most recent decades, it has taken an interest in a variety of subaltern studies (à la Gramsci). In this formulation, proponents of cultural studies produced the Centre for Contemporary Cultural Studies, now known as the Department of Cultural Studies, cross-fertilized with FEMINIST work in the British Women's Studies Group, and published works in several important journals (e.g., *Screen* and *Culture, Media, Language*) for the investigation of power relations in a variety of literary and non-literary discursive practices.

In its North American form, C. West and b. hooks are representative. Writing apart and together, they demonstrate several emphases: the democratization of culture; the decolonization of representations; the critical retrieval of subjugated voices; and the construction of provisional forms of liberative pedagogy.

Both formulations have influenced biblical studies. For example, I. Mosala, influenced by S. Hall, exploits cultural studies to expose the biblical authors' possible collusion with hegemony. K. Cannon's critique of slavery's use of the so-called Hamite hypothesis (1995, 119-28) owes much to C. West's ruminations on Gramsci. And S. Reid's challenge to the African American scholar or preacher to read the biblical texts with the African American community (1994–95, 476-87) evokes b. hooks and C. West's charge to black intellectuals to remain connected to grassroots communities (b. hooks [1990] 130; West [1989] 231).

4. Cultural Studies' Relation to Other Methods of Biblical Interpretation. With Marxist theory, cultural studies shares an interest in ideology but not in the fashion of classical Marxists, who defined ideology as false consciousness, i.e., a narrow set of ideas or beliefs naturalized to promote dominant class interests. Cultural studies' proponents most often prefer to view ideology as a wide range of competing values of which many are neither economically based nor institutionally grounded.

Because of its multidisciplinary history and its keen

interest in relations of power, cultural studies bears striking parallels to many vibrant approaches under the banner of post-modernism. With post-structuralist theory (see STRUCTURALISM AND DECONSTRUCTION), it shares concerns about the state and production of knowledge and the complex notion of identity. With feminist studies, it enjoys a rich cross-fertilization. Both approaches have origins in radical politics; both also use collectives, resist passive absorption models of learning, and embrace the interface between theory and the ethnographic documentation of experiences (S. Franklin, C. Lury, and J. Stacey [1991] 1-19).

Segovia's history of biblical studies reveals the influence of historical criticism, literary criticism and [socio]cultural criticism on the cultural studies paradigm. Furthermore, both the critical and the interventionist interests of cultural studies are found in a number of current critical approaches to the Bible. Exploiting the cultural critique dimension, biblical IDEOLOGICAL CRITICISM questions the use of the Exodus-conquest narratives as sources of LIBERATION because these texts support the annihilation of Canaanite people and because the texts have been used against Native Americans in support of manifest destiny (R. Liburd [1994] 79). Likewise, feminist biblical criticism has exposed both the patriarchal character of the biblical texts and the androcentric interests of biblical studies (Schüssler Fiorenza [1984] 5). Taking on the interventionist dimension of cultural studies, ideological criticism advocates an ethics of accountability (T. Pippin [1996] 51-78). Feminist biblical criticism and the biblical criticism of other marginalized groups have sought to rewrite the histories of ancient biblical cultures and to recover the residual voices of the biblical texts (Schüssler Fiorenza [1984] 15; R. Bailey [1995] 25-36).

5. Examples of a Cultural Studies Approach to the Bible. Among the several examples of a cultural studies approach to biblical studies, three are particularly illustrative: the *Postmodern Bible* (1995), the two volumes of *Reading from This Place* (1994, 1995) and B. Blount's *Cultural Interpretation* (1995). Like other proponents of cultural studies, the authors of the *Postmodern Bible* worked collaboratively (in the Bible and Culture Collective) to offset the politics of exclusion. In the cultural studies tradition of criticism, they proffer solid critiques of contemporary biblical practices of interpretation, particularly on the questions of suppressed meaning, the formation of identities, and the use of the Bible to "ratify the status quo" (Bible Collective [1995] 4). *Reading from This Place* encourages multiple interpretations (thus a democratization of culture) through its exposure of strategies of reading the Bible with a wide variety of scholars within and beyond North America. In addition, its authors intervene in culture in proffering liberative yet provisional forms of pedagogy to teach the Bible. In *Cultural Interpretation* Blount's

goal is to reorient biblical interpretation through the genuine interchange of so-called peripheral and centrist interpretations. Moreover, his broadening of culture to include several biblical approaches becomes evident in his examination of several interpretive strategies (e.g., R. Bultmann's existentialist hermeneutics; the *campesinos'* biblical hermeneutics in *The Gospel in Solentiname* [4 vols., 1976–82]; the North American slaves' biblical hermeneutical strategy in the black spiritual; and the black preacher's biblical hermeneutics in sermons), even as he exposes the limitations of each. All of these examples of cultural studies prove the heuristic value and prominence of this recent paradigm in biblical studies.

6. Summary. In sum, with its dual goals of culture critique and culture intervention, cultural studies is a vital part of the academic landscape, the post-modernist focus on difference, and the current practices of biblical studies. Under the cultural studies paradigm, moreover, biblical studies moves outside the walls of a strict discipline to examine all discursive practices critically and, potentially, to create more liberative relations of power in society.

Bibliography: V. **Anderson,** *Beyond Ontological Blackness: An Essay on African American Religious and Cultural Criticism* (1995). **R. C. Bailey,** " 'Is That Any Name for a Nice Hebrew Boy?': The De-Africanization of an Israelite Hero," *The Recovery of the Black Presence: An Interdisciplinary Exploration* (ed. R. C. Bailey and J. Grant, 1995) 25-36. **The Bible and Culture Collective,** *The Postmodern Bible* (1995). **B. K. Blount,** *Cultural Interpretation: Reorienting NT Criticism* (1995). **K. Cannon,** "Slave Ideology and Biblical Interpretation," *The Recovery of the Black Presence* (1995) 119-28. **D. N. Fewell,** "Reading the Bible Ideologically: Feminist Criticism," *To Each Its Own Meaning* (ed. S. Haynes and S. McKenzie, 1993) 237-51. **S. Franklin, C. Lury, and J. Stacey** (eds.), *Off-Centre: Feminism and Culture Studies* (1991). **H. Giroux, D. Shumway, P. Smith, and J. Sosnoski,** "The Need for Cultural Studies: Resisting Intellectuals and Oppositional Public Spheres," *Dalhousie Review* (1984) 472-86. **S. Hall,** "Cultural Studies and Its Theoretical Legacies," *Cultural Studies* (ed. L. Grossberg, C. Nelson, and P. A. Treichler, 1992) 277-94. **O. Hendricks,** "Guerilla Exegesis: A Post-Modern Proposal for Insurgent African American Biblical Interpretation," *JITC* 22 (1994) 92-109. **b. hooks,** *Yearning: Race, Gender, and Cultural Politics* (1990); "Representing Whiteness in the Black Imagination," *Cultural Studies* (1992) 338-46. **V. Leitch,** *Cultural Criticism, Literary Theory, Poststructuralism* (1992). **R. Liburd,** " 'Like . . . a House upon the Sand': African American Biblical Hermeneutics in Perspective," *JITC* 22 (1994) 71-91. **I. Mosala,** *Biblical Hermeneutics and Black Theology in South Africa* (1989). **C. Nelson, P. A. Treichler, and L. Grossberg,** "An Introduction," *Cultural Studies* (1992) 1-22. **T. Pippin,** "Ideology, Ideological Criticism, and the Bible," *Currents in Research: Biblical Studies* 4 (1996) 51-78. **S.**

B. Reid, "Endangered Reading: The African-American Scholar Between Text and People," *Cross Currents* (1994–95) 476-87. **J.-P. Ruiz,** "New Ways of Reading the Bible in the Cultural Settings of the Third World," *The Bible as Cultural Heritage* (Concilium 1995, 1, ed. W. Beuken and S. Freyne, 1995) 73-84. **F. Segovia,** "Cultural Studies and Contemporary Biblical Criticism: Ideological Criticism as a Mode of Discourse," *Reading from This Place,* vol. 2, *Social Location and Biblical Interpretation in Global Perspective* (ed. F. Segovia and M. A. Tolbert, 1995a) 1-17; "The Significance of Social Location in Reading John's Story," *Interpretation* 49 (1995b) 370-78. **E. Schüssler Fiorenza,** *Bread Not Stone: The Challenge of Feminist Biblical Interpretation* (1984). **M. A. Tolbert,** "Reading for Liberation," *Reading from This Place,* vol 2, *Social Location and Biblical Interpretation in Global Perspective* (1995) 263-76. **C. West,** *The American Evasion of Philosophy: A Genealogy of Pragmatism* (1989); "The New Cultural Politics of Difference," *Out There: Marginalization and Contemporary Cultures* (ed. R. Ferguson, 1990) 19-36; "The Postmodern Crisis of the Black Intellectuals," *Cultural Studies* (1992) 689-705. **G. West,** "No Integrity Without Contextuality: The Presence of Particularity in Biblical Hermeneutics and Pedagogy," *Scriptura* 11 (1993) 131-46.

A. SMITH

CURTISS, SAMUEL IVES (1844–1904)

Born Feb. 5, 1844, C. graduated from Amherst (1867) and from Union Theological Seminary (1870). He completed his PhD at Leipzig (1876) and received his lic. theol. at Berlin (1878), writing a Latin monograph on the Aaronite priesthood. He became professor of biblical literature at Chicago Theological Seminary, later moving to the chair of OT literature and interpretation, which he held until his death. He was a clergy member of the congregational and (later) Presbyterian traditions, ordained in the presbytery of New York in 1874 and serving as pastor of the American Chapel at Leipzig (1874–78). He also served as president of the Chicago Missionary Society (1888–98, 1899–1903).

A student of Franz DELITZSCH, C. translated much of Delitzsch's work into English. C. was also a friend of W. BAUDISSIN, who wrote the preface to the German edition of C.'s work on primitive Semitic religion (1902). A critical scholar who departed from the reigning consensus of his day, C. argued for the antiquity of many aspects of the priestly traditions of the Pentateuch (see PENTATEUCHAL CRITICISM) in his work on the Aaronite priests, whom he linked to the Elohistic tradition. His view was similar to that of the elder R. SMEND, who regarded the Aaronites as the authentic ancestral priesthood of the northern kingdom, and to that of O. PROCKSCH, for whom the Elohistic source was "the North Israelite saga book." Like Baudissin, W. R. SMITH, and J. WELLHAUSEN, C. believed Israelite religion was a manifestation of a "primitive" Semitic religion that

could best be recovered by a careful investigation of the practices of modern Arabian bedouin. To that end, he made two long trips to the Near East (1898–99, 1900–2), the results of which are found in his final work.

Works: *The Name Machabee (historically and philologically examined)* (1876); *The Levitical Priests: A Contribution to the Criticism of the Pentateuch* (1877); *De Aaronitici sacerdotii atque Thorae elohisticae origine dissertatio historico-critica* (1878); *A Plea for a More Thorough Study of the Semitic Languages in America* (1878a); *Moses and Deuteronomy* (1878b); *Ingersoll and Moses: A Reply* (1880); *The Date of Our Gospels: In the Light of the Latest Criticism* (1881); *Delitzsch on the Pentateuch* (1884); *Lectures on the OT History of the People of Redemption* (1889); *Franz Delitzsch: A Memorial Tribute* (1891); *Primitive Semitic Religion Today: A Record of Researches, Discoveries, and Studies in Syria-Palestine and the Sinaitic Peninsula* (1902); *Ursemitische Religion im Volksleben des heutigen Orients: Forschungen und Funde aus Syrien und Palästina* (1903).

D. G. SCHLEY

CYRIL OF ALEXANDRIA (c. 375–444)

A bishop of Alexandria (412–44), C. died June 27, 444. He is best known as an architect of patristic christology. His works reveal a thorough mastery of Scripture, theology (notably that of ATHANASIUS), and grammar, along with competence in philosophy. C.'s possible role in civic conflicts and his masterful use of ecclesiastical politics have given him a sinister reputation that may be undeserved. After 428 he devoted his life to polemic against Nestorius (d. c. 451), bishop of Constantinople, whose condemnation he secured at the Council of Ephesus in 431. As a student of THEODORE OF MOPSUESTIA, Nestorius represented an ANTIOCHENE theological and exegetical tradition that C. may not have fully understood.

Before 428 C. had already written works interpreting most of the Bible. Much survives, including commentaries on Psalms, Isaiah, the Minor Prophets, and John, along with homilies on Luke in a Syriac translation. Two exegetical works on the Pentateuch (see PENTATEUCHAL CRITICISM) sought to demonstrate the superiority of Christianity to Judaism.

C. shared CLEMENT OF ALEXANDRIA's and ORIGEN's belief that the superiority of allegorical to literal interpretation corresponded to the superiority of the imperceptible to the perceptible world. Like them he held that a deep understanding of the Bible was a gift of the Spirit accessible only to certain persons whom he called the *nounechesteroi,* "the more sensible." C., however, lacks their speculative interests and exegetical daring. Unlike Origen he held that some passages of Scripture had a literal sense but lacked a spiritual sense, allowed that the literal sense can be figurative, and took pains to insist that figurative interpretations of historical events do not cast doubt on their having occurred. C.'s exegesis underlies his christology but not in the sense that ALEX-ANDRIAN allegorism led him to devalue the historic Christ along with the letter of Scripture. Rather, his understanding of Christ as the new Adam underlay his opposition to Nestorius (see R. Wilken [1971]).

Works: *PG* 66-77; *Commentary on the Gospel of St. Luke* (tr. R. Payne Smith, 2 vols., 1859); *Commentary on the Gospel of St. John* (2 vols., tr. P. E. Pusey and T. Randell, 1832, 1885).

Bibliography: Y.-M. Duval, *Le livre de Jonas dans la littératur chrétienne grecque et latine* (2 vols., 1973) 1:397-416. *IHE,* 1: 270-303. **A. Kerrigan,** *St. Cyril of Alexandria: Interpreter of the OT* (AnBib 2, 1952). **J. Quasten,** *Patrology (1960) 3:116-42.* **M.-J. Rondeau,** *Commentaires patristiques du Psautier* 1 (1962) 131-34. **M. F. Wiles,** *The Spiritual Gospel: The Interpretation of the Fourth Gospel in the Early Church* (1960). **R. L. Wilken,** *Judaism and the Early Christian Mind: A Study of Cyril of Alexandria's Exegesis and Theology* (1971). **F. M. Young,** *From Nicaea to Chalcedon* (1983) 124-33, 346-47, 382-83.

J. W. TRIGG

D

DAHL, NILS ALSTRUP (1911–)

Born into a pastor's family in 1911, D. grew up in western Norway. He attended the cathedral school in Bergen and studied theology at the University of Oslo; among his teachers were S. MOWINCKEL in OT and L. Brun (1870–1950) in NT. Graduate study took him abroad to Strasbourg, Tübingen, Leipzig, and Marburg, where he worked with R. BULTMANN. From 1936 to 1943 he served on the faculty at Oslo; he defended his thesis, *Das Volk Gottes,* during the Nazi occupation (1941). Under threat of arrest, he fled to Sweden in 1943 when the university was closed, returning as professor of NT in 1946. During his years in Norway he served as chair of the Norwegian Christian Movement, a member of the Norwegian Bible Society, dean of the faculty of theology, editor of *Norsk Kirkeblad,* and a member of the Theological Commission of the Lutheran World Federation (1957–70). Visiting professor at Yale Divinity School (1961–62), he returned to a joint appointment at the divinity school and Yale University from 1965 until his retirement.

D. has also worked within the context of the church. His Lutheran heritage is visible throughout his career, although most work done explicitly for the church—including a commentary on Matthew and Ephesians in Norwegian and numerous popular articles—was done in Norway. The ethos at American universities seemed to him to dictate less explicit attention to ecclesial matters.

Characteristically independent, D. belongs to no school. He has read with understanding and appreciation J. WELLHAUSEN, A. SCHWEITZER, and especially Bultmann; what he has taken from them are major questions.

D.'s preferred genre is the essay, and his work has appeared in a remarkable variety of periodicals and Festschriften. Typically, D. identifies a problem and through careful work offers an insight that opens onto whole new vistas. Included among his groundbreaking essays are "Anamnesis: Memory and Commemoration in Early Christianity" (his inaugural address at Oslo, 1946), "Two Notes on Romans 5" (1951), "The Crucified Messiah" (1960), "The Particularity of the Pauline Epistles" (1962), and "Trinitarian Baptismal Creeds and NT Christology" (1991).

D.'s concentration on essays has had drawbacks in that few scholars have glimpsed the breadth and coherence of his work. Some scholars appreciate his christological contributions, others his Pauline work (his 105-page unpublished "Paul's Letter to the Galatians: Epistolary Genre, Content, and Structure," is known only to the SBL Pauline Seminar). A smaller group has taken up the challenge of his text-critical work (see TEXTUAL CRITICISM) on the Pauline letters. His "Trinitarian Baptismal Creeds and NT Christology" (*Jesus the Christ* [1991] 165-80) moves into church history; "Contradictions in Scripture" (*Studies in Paul* [1977] 159-77) is a contribution to midrashic studies (see MIDRASH). His unpublished lectures in NT christology remain largely unmined. In D.'s case essay collections are not simply the gathering of leftovers; rather, they afford a glimpse of a coherent proposal about the setting of the NT and its major themes and offer ways of appreciating its theological impact.

A feature of D.'s work has been dissatisfaction with old syntheses. One target has been the heritage of idealism that tends to view the history of doctrine in disembodied fashion, working with grand themes. D. is more impressed by the particularity of the tradition and by the crucible in which theology was actually formed. Although appreciative of Schweitzer and Bultmann, he has been impressed more by their historical and exegetical insights than by "consistent eschatology" or "demythologizing." His "Eschatology and History in Light of the Qumran Scrolls" (*Jesus the Christ,* 49-64) shows the interplay of scriptural (HB) interpretation, social and historical circumstances, and theology that has taken shape in particular texts. Beyond dismantling old syntheses, he has taken major steps toward reimagining the history of the early church.

Although better known for his work in christology and ecclesiology, D. is also a NT theologian. His essays "The Neglected Factor in NT Theology" (*Jesus the Christ,* 153-64) and "Trinitarian Baptismal Creeds and NT Christology" have kindled interest in questions about God, while his earliest work shows an awareness of and concern for others who worship the same God and read the same Scriptures. His dissertation (1941) reveals a broad knowledge of Jewish tradition and deep religious sensitivities. By pressing Jewish-Christian questions he has made a deep impact on NT studies and on continuing Jewish-Christian conversation.

Works: *Das Volk Gottes: Eine Untersuchung zum Kirchenbewusstsein des Urchristentums* (1941, repr. 1963); "Anamnesis: Memory and Commemoration in Early Christianity" (1946;

ET in *Jesus in the Memory of the Early Church* [1976] 11-29); "Two Notes on Romans 5," *StTh* 5 (1951) 37-48; "The Crucified Messiah" (1960; ET in *Jesus the Christ* [1991] 27-48); "The Particularity of the Pauline Epistles as a Problem in the Ancient Church," *Neotestamentica et patristica* (1962) 261-71; "Eschatology and History in Light of the Qumran Scrolls" (1964; ET in *Jesus the Christ* [1991] 49-64); "Contradictions in Scripture" (1969; ET in *Studies in Paul* [1977] 159-77); "The Neglected Factor in NT Theology," *Reflections* 75 (1975) 5-8 = *Jesus the Christ* (1991) 153-64; *Jesus in the Memory of the Early Church* (1976); *Studies in Paul* (1977); "Ephesians," *HBC* (1988) 1212-19; "Trinitarian Baptismal Creeds and NT Christology," *Jesus the Christ* (1991) 165-80; "Jewish Messianic Ideas and the Crucifixion of Jesus," *The Messiah* (ed. J. Charlesworth, 1992) 382-403.

Bibliography: H. **Karstein**, *N. A. D.: A Bibliography of His Writings, 1935–91* (1991).

D. H. JUEL

DAHOOD, MITCHELL JOSEPH (1922–82)

A Jesuit priest, D. was trained at Weston College (ThD) and Johns Hopkins University (PhD), where he studied with W. F. ALBRIGHT. Following ordination, D. was assigned to Rome, where he spent his entire career at the Pontifical Biblical Institute. He died in Rome on Mar. 8, 1982.

D.'s scholarly output was both prolific and controversial. Developing a passion for northwest Semitic philology and lexicography, he mined the comparative data (especially Ugaritic) with unflagging zeal for new and (to his thinking) superior meanings of lexical terms and grammatical constructions within HB POETRY.

Positively, many of D.'s contributions are now standard fare in Semitic studies (e.g., double duty particles; omission of prepositions and pronominal suffixes required by sense; collection of abstract and concrete word pairs). Negatively, his work frequently manifests a lack of balance and methodological rigor in source analysis.

Best remembered for his Psalms commentaries (AB), D. was heavily criticized for his exhaustive use of Ugaritic materials (see UGARIT AND THE BIBLE) and disregard for the general audience for whom the AB was intended. With the discovery of the Ebla tablets, D. entered into reanalysis of the biblical text in the light of these discoveries with the same intensity and enthusiasm with which he had earlier greeted the Ugaritic materials.

Works: *Canaanite-Phoenician Influence in Qoheleth* (1952) = *Bib* 33 (1952) 30-52, 191-221; *Northwest Semitic Philology and Job* (1962; originally pub. in *The Bible and Current Catholic Thought* [ed. J. MacKenzie, 1962]); *Ugaritic Studies and the Bible* (repr. from *Greg* 43 [1962] 56-79; *Proverbs and Northwest Semitic Philology* (*SPIB* 113, 1963); *Ugaritic-Hebrew Philology: Marginal Notes on Recent Publications*

(1965); *Psalms* (AB 16, 17, 17a, 1966–70); *Ugaritic and the OT* (1968).

Bibliography: D. N. **Freedman**, *BA* 45 (1982) 185-87. **E. R. Martinez,** *Hebrew-Ugaritic Index II with an Eblaite Index to the Writings of M. J. D.* (1981). **B. Vawter and J. Swetnam,** *CBQ* 44 (1982) 470-71.

R. R. MARRS

DALMAN, GUSTAF HERMANN (1855–1941)

A German biblical scholar and Palestinologist, D. was born June 9, 1855, in Niesky, the son of J. Marx; in 1886 he took the family name of his mother, who had been a strong influence on him. He was educated at a theological seminary in Gnadenfeld and taught there from 1881 to 1887 as *Dozent* for OT and practical theology. In 1887 he became head of the "Institutum Judaicum" in Leipzig, which had been founded by Franz DELITZSCH in 1880. In 1891 he became *Privatdozent* and in 1895 *ausserordentlicher* professor of OT exegesis at Leipzig. After visiting Palestine in 1899 he became director of the German Evangelisches Institut für Altertumswissenschaft des Heiligen Landes (1902–16); and from 1917 to 1923 he was professor in the theological faculty in Greifswald, continuing to teach as emeritus professor until 1940. He died Aug. 19, 1941, in Herrnhut.

Through the influence of his mother he developed a strong interest in the mission to the Jews. This led him to begin translating the NT into Hebrew, and in 1892 he produced a new edition of Delitzsch's translation of the NT into Hebrew.

Following publication of the NT in Hebrew, D.'s studies may be divided into two broad periods. Up to the turn of the twentieth century his main scholarly interest was in Aramaic studies and in the words of JESUS. His works on Aramaic were good pioneering efforts; however, his two books on the original Aramaic of the words of Jesus were less successful.

The second period of D.'s scholarly work followed his visit to Palestine, after which he assumed the directorship of the German Palestine Institute. During this period he undertook vast researches into the customs and sites of Palestine, and many students attended the institute. Publication of the results of his research came for the most part during his time at Greifswald; however, in 1901 D. published a collection of Arabic songs and melodies in a book entitled *Palästinischer Diwan*. Only a scholar with his musical interest and extensive knowledge of Arabic would have been capable of successfully completing this kind of project.

D. was also interested in ARCHAEOLOGY, and as a result of his firsthand study of the imposing Nabatean remains at Petra he produced two books on the subject that are still of value. Earlier, on a related but more specific topic he had written *Die Via dolorosa in Jeru-*

salem (1906). He also wrote a useful topographical and geographical study of the life of Jesus (1919) and at a later period *Jerusalem und seine Gelände* (1930).

The *magnum opus* and crown of D.'s career was the publication of an eight-volume work entitled *Arbeit und Sitte in Palästina* (1928–42), a massive and detailed study of the customs of the Palestinian Arabs based on many years of close observation, which continues to be an extremely valuable source of information. The depth of the personal experience of Arabic life that underlies these volumes needs to be emphasized: During his many years of residence in Palestine D. learned how to bake and weave like the Arabs, put his hand to the plow, and personally cultivated wine and oil; he even wrote Arabic poems.

All this makes his work a first-rate study that still has value in illuminating the oriental background of the biblical narratives. D. worked among the Arabs rather than among the Jews of Palestine because it was here that the ancient lifestyle was better preserved. However, it should be noted that D. did not naively think that one could simply equate the customs of the Palestinian Arabs with those of biblical times—he noted the differences as well as the similarities.

Works: *Grammatik des jüdisch palästinischen Aramäisch* (1892, 1905²); *Aramäische Dialektproben* (1896, 1927²); *Aramäisch-neuhebräisches Handwörterbuch zu Targum, Talmud, und Midrasch* (2 vols., 1897–1901, 1922², 1938³); *Die Worte Jesu, mit Berücksichtigung des nachkanonischen jüdischen Schrifttums und der aramäischen Sprache erörtert* (1898, 1930²; ET *The Words of Jesus* [1902]); *Palästinischer Diwan* (1901); *Die Via dolorosa in Jerusalem* (1906); *Petra und seine Felsheiligtümer* (1908); *Neue Petra-Forschungen und der heilige Felsen von Jerusalem* (1912); *Orte und Wege Jesu* (BFCT 23, 1-2, 1919, 1967⁴; ET *Sacred Sites and Ways,* 1935); *RGS* 4 (1928) 1-29 (autobiography with bibliography); *Jesus-Jeschua: Die drei Sprachen* (1922; ET 1929); *Arbeit und Sitte in Palästina* (8 vols., 1928–42); *Jerusalem und seine Gelände* (BFCT 2. reihe, 19, 1930).

Bibliography: **A. Alt,** *PJ* 37 (1941) 5-18. **K. H. Bernhardt,** *TRE* 8 (1981) 322-23. **H. W. Hertzberg,** "Die Stellung G. D.s in der Palästinawissenschaft," *WZ(G)* 4 (1954–55) 367-72. **J. Männchen,** *G. D. als Palästinawissenshaftler in Jerusalem und Greifswald, 1902–41* (ADPV 9:2, 1993). **K. H. Rengstorf,** "G. D.s Bedeutung für die Wissenschaft vom Judentum," *WZ(G)* 4 (1954–55) 373-77. **K. H. Rengstorf and W. Müller,** "Das Schrifttum G. D.," *WZ(G)* 4 (1954–55) 209-32.

J. DAY

DAMIAN, PETER (1007–72)

Born at Ravenna, D. studied at Faenza and Parma and in 1035 became a Benedictine monk at Fonte Avella, where he was prior from 1043. In 1057 he became cardinal bishop of Ostia. He died Feb. 22, 1072. Best known for his preaching and writing against clerical corruption and worldliness and against simony, D. was also active in monastic reform. A number of sermons survive as well as collections of authorities for use in exegesis. He wrote prolifically, including a considerable number of *opuscula* on topical and spiritual subjects, many of them exegetical in character. His principal commentaries to survive are those on the DECALOGUE and the *Expositio mystica* on the book of Genesis. He represents a tradition of monastic exegesis founded on AUGUSTINE and GREGORY THE GREAT, but his alertness to political affairs in his own day makes him a scholar of some significance in bringing together the active and the contemplative life.

Works: *PL* 144-45; *De Divina Omnipotentia e altri opuscula* (ed. P. Brezzi and B. Nardi, 1943); *Lateinische Hymnendichter des Mittelalters* 1 (ed. G. M. Dreves, 1905) 29-78.

Bibliography: J. A. Enders, *Petrus Damianus* (1910). **T. Wunsch,** *Spiritalis intellegentia: Zur allegorischen Bibelinterpretation des Petrus Damiani* (1992).

G. R. EVANS

DANIEL, BOOK OF

Modern critical scholarship has reached a near-consensus that the book of Daniel essentially attained its canonical form (see CANON OF THE BIBLE) in the years 167–164 BCE, during the reign of the Greco-Syrian king Antiochus IV Epiphanes (175–163 BCE). This means that Daniel is the last composition to have been written that is now included in the collection of works known as the HB.

1. Early Interpretation. The impact of the book of Daniel on early Judaism was felt almost immediately and is well attested in the first century BCE. This history of interpretation developed partly in the Egyptian diaspora and partly at home in the sectarian milieu of the Judean community. In Egypt the process remains visible in the shape taken by the book of Daniel in the LXX (see SEPTUAGINT). This Greek version of Daniel is thought to have been produced at Alexandria about 100 BCE. Although both Jews and early Christians eventually stopped making use of LXX-Dan in favor of a more literal Greek TRANSLATION of the book attributed to THEODOTION, which is possibly as old as the first century BCE, the presence in both of these versions of rather extensive additions to the canonical book (including the narratives of Susanna and of Bel and the Dragon and the two-part poem inserted between Dan 3:23 and 3:24 called The Prayer of Azariah and the Song of the Three Young Men) suggests that the cycle of legends about Daniel was larger and richer than the canonical version would admit.

The same can be said about the foreground of the book of Daniel in the milieu of Jewish sectarianism in Judea. At Qumran the book was essential to the self-understanding of the elect members of the sect who considered themselves to be "saints" (Dan 7:21-22; cf. the *War Scroll* [1QM] 3:5; 6:6). Fragments of the actual text of Daniel used there disclose only minor variations from the received MT and with a few exceptions support it and Theod-Dan against LXX-Dan. The Aramaic portion begins at 2:4*b* and ends at 7:28, exactly as in the Masoretic tradition. More significant for our purposes are the echoes of the book that ring throughout the literature of the sectarians at Qumran. The book of Daniel is reckoned by them among the prophets (cf. Matt 24:15), and is not considered a wisdom writing as it is in the HB. The hero, Daniel, is the inspiration for three Aramaic pseudo-Daniel stories found in Cave 4; further, chapter 4 is paralleled in significant ways by the important Aramaic *Prayer of Nabonidus* (4QPrNab), in which the last Babylonian king is cured of a serious disease by a Jewish exorcist, who then directs him to honor in writing the name of God Most High.

The evolution of the concept "son of man" from its origins in Daniel cannot be understood apart from its elaboration in the Jewish apocalypses *4 Ezra* (= 2 Esdras 3–14 of our Apocrypha) and ENOCH. Unlike his prototype in Dan 7:13, the cloud-riding son of man of *4 Ezra* 13 is clearly a heavenly figure who was created at the beginning of time and whose epiphany in the world of human beings is associated with the Day of Judgment. The same is true of the son of man in the *Parables of Enoch* (chaps. 37–71). In *1 Enoch* 46—which is a retelling or MIDRASH on the judgment scene of Daniel 7—and in chaps. 48 and 62, the son of man is himself the judge. From these extra-canonical sources it becomes easier to understand the picture drawn of the son of man in the so-called little apocalypses of the SYNOPTIC Gospels (Matthew 24–25; Mark 13; Luke 21:5-36; cf. Luke 17:22-37). Whether JESUS ever intended to identify himself with a coming eschatological judge, or whether that link with the elaborated "son of man" imagery of contemporary Jewish apocalyptic was made by the early church are subjects discussed by H. Tödt (1965), using insights already developed by R. BULTMANN, E. LOHMEYER, and others.

In addition to the uses to which the book of Daniel was put in the synoptic Gospels, a complete discussion of the earliest chapter in the history of Christian interpretation of the book—namely, the NT—would include extended examination of its many reutilizations and transformations in Revelation. In this brief treatment of the subject, suffice it to point out that the cloud-borne Son of man of Rev 1:7 is both Jesus and judge, whose clothing and appearance resemble those of God (Rev 1:12-16; cf. Rev. 14:14-16). The animal allegory of Revelation 13 builds on the prototype of Dan 7:1-8; the

final judgment scene in Rev 20:11-15 (cf. Rev 4:2-11) is also a refraction of Dan 7:13-14.

2. Patristic Interpretation. The book of Daniel continued to have a lasting effect on the thought of Christian writers after the first century CE. Although IRENAEUS (c. 130–200), bishop of Lyons, did not leave a commentary on it, he did help to set the basic lines of interpretation that were followed in subsequent centuries. The "stone not made by human hands" (Dan 2:34) is Jesus Christ and so is the "one like a son of man" who comes in the clouds (Dan 7:13). However, the appearance of the Christ in the clouds is deferred until the second advent, at which time the consummation of history would also result in the awarding of dominion to "the saints of the most high" (Dan 7:27)—that is, Christian believers and martyrs (see Rev 20:4-6). Irenaeus helped to establish the tradition of millenarian eschatology by suggesting that the span of time from the completion of creation until the consummation is in fact an exact equivalent to the six-day period of creation, reckoned on the formula one day = 1,000 years (i.e., a millennium). The seventh millennium, corresponding to God's day of sabbath rest in the beginning of time, would separate the consummation of history from the day of the final judgment of cosmic evil.

Patristic commentators on the book of Daniel included Hippolytus of Rome (170–236), ORIGEN, CHRYSOSTOM, JEROME, and THEODORET OF CYRRHUS. EPHRAEM, one of the Syriac-speaking church fathers of Eastern Christianity, contributed a commentary in the fourth century CE. Jerome's commentary is the most accessible to us through the reprint of the translation by G. Archer, Jr. (1958) and the excellent monograph on the work by J. Braverman (1978). As is well known, Jerome returned to the original Hebrew/Aramaic text of the HB for his work of translation into Latin (see VULGATE), and a concern for accuracy and for thorough attention to Jewish interpretation characterizes his commentary as well.

Using his discussion of Daniel 7 as an example of Jerome's work, we find him paying exquisite attention to the textual and historical details of the beasts and horns of vv. 1-8. Although he had precedent even in the NT, Jerome argued vigorously that the sequence of world empires represented by the four beasts is Babylon, Persia (the Persians were so bear-like in their spartan manner of life that "they used to use salt and nasturtium-cress in their relish," 74), the Macedonians (the four wings and four heads of the third beast, the leopard, are taken to refer to the so-called Diadochi, the four successors of Alexander among whom his empire was divided), and Rome. If the fourth beast is Rome, then the ten little horns of Dan 7:7-8 are clearly Roman rulers. However, since they appear simultaneously and not *seriatim,* they must be leaders who divide the empire among themselves; and because this event had not in fact happened, the seer must now be looking forward to the end times. Such an understanding enabled Jerome to assimilate the balance of the judgment scene, and indeed the entire chapter, to NT apocalyptic texts (see APOCALYPTICISM). The little horn is the antichrist (see 2 Thessalonians 2); the throne is that spoken of in Rev 4:2-11; the one like the son of man is the triumphant Christ of the eschaton called by John the lion of the tribe of Judah (Rev 5:5), who, though equal with God, had humbled himself by taking on the form of a servant (Phil 2:6-8). The saints are, of course, those who belong to Christ; and the kingdom they are given (Dan 7:18) is not an earthly one but is the heavenly abode of the saints. Their kingdom thus stands in stark contrast to that of the four earthly kingdoms of the beasts. This established, Jerome cries, "Away, then, with the fable about a millennium!" The establishment of the kingdom of the saints is for him the final event of history and is not part of a 1,000-year transitional period as it was for Irenaeus and Hippolytus.

Throughout his discussion of chapter 7 and the rest of the commentary, Jerome is at pains to rebut the critical views of PORPHYRY, the Neoplatonist philosopher of Tyre. Although Porphyry's work is lost, by assembling the references to him in Jerome's commentary it is possible to show that Porphyry understood the four beasts to refer respectively to the Babylonian, Medo-Persian, Alexandrian, and Seleucid empires. In other words, Porphyry's views were identical with those of many modern critical commentators. Furthermore, the stone of Dan 2:34 and the "one like a son of man" in Dan 7:13 were symbols of human figures—the Jews in their triumph at the eschaton in the first instance, and perhaps the triumph of the Maccabees over the forces of Antiochus IV Epiphanes in 164 BCE in the second. M. Casey (1976) has shown that Porphyry was not entirely original in this rather more realistic understanding of the book's historical scenario and that indeed much of the same position is taken in writers of the Eastern and Syriac-speaking church—Aphrahat (early 4th cent.), Ephraem, Polychronius (d. c. 430), and the glosses in the Syriac version of the HB.

3. Medieval Jewish and Christian Interpretation.

The medieval scholastics Albertus Magnus (c. 1200–1280) and NICHOLAS OF LYRA, a Franciscan professor at the University of Paris (d. c. 1340), each wrote important commentaries on the book of Daniel. Like other medieval writers, including the great THOMAS AQUINAS, these commentators' understanding of the book reflects their knowledge of Jewish interpretation. All the great Jewish commentators of the period interpreted the book, including SAADIA Gaon, RASHI, and A. IBN EZRA. The fullest and most accessible commentary is the sectarian exegesis of the KARAITE Jephet Ibn Ali (c. 1000). Scattered comments elsewhere in the rabbinic corpus reveal the basic lines of Jewish interpretation, particularly of

the crucial chapter 7. The ninth century CE Midrash *Pirqe de R. Eliezer*, perhaps drawing upon considerably older traditional material, uses the description of the divine court in Dan 7:10 to explicate the scene of the second day of creation (Gen 1:6-8): "The *hayyoth* [living ones, one of the four classes of ministering angels known in Jewish exegesis] stand in awe and dread, in fear and trembling, and from the perspiraton of their faces a river of fire arises and goes forth before him, as it is said, 'A fiery stream issued and came forth before him. . . . ' (Dan 7:10)." In other words, the fiery stream that illuminates the heavenly firmament is proved from Dan 7:10 to be angels' sweat.

More significant for our purposes is the clear identification made earlier in the rabbinic tradition of the son of man in Dan 7:13 with the Messiah. In a long list of sayings beginning, "The son of David will not come until," found in the Babylonian TALMUD, this tradition is preserved: "R. Alexandri said: 'R. Joshua opposed two verses: it is written, "And behold, one like the son of man came with the clouds of heaven" [Dan 7:13] whilst [elsewhere] it is written, "[Behold, thy king cometh unto thee . . .] lowly, and riding upon an ass!" [Zech 9:9]. If they are meritorious, [he will come] "with the clouds of heaven"; if not, "lowly and riding upon an ass" ' " (*b. Sanh.* 98a). This understanding of the son of man sees him as a future figure, a metaphor of a yet-to-come Messiah whose mode of epiphany is linked with the obedience of Israel and whose glory is thus bound up with Israel's own merited honor.

4. The Reformation.

Although LUTHER made considerable use of the book of Daniel, both in his polemic against papal authority and in pastoral settings, and wrote a lengthy preface to the book in his Bible translation of 1530, he did not publish a separate commentary on the work. The great commentary deriving from the Reformation is that of CALVIN, whose work appeared in 1561, only a year before the devastating wars of religion began. In his interpretation of the key phrases "one like a son of man" (Dan 7:13) and the "saints of the Most High" (Dan 7:18), Calvin avoids "subtle allegories" and forced expositions in favor of what he believes to be the plain meaning of the text. Of the expression "son of man," he says, "Without doubt, this is to be understood of Christ" (40). However, Calvin takes the simile seriously: The figure appearing in the clouds is *like* the Son of man. Although Christ had not yet assumed his incarnate form, he would in time do so. (Calvin quotes Tertullian here: "Then the Son of God put on a specimen of his humanity," and then adds, "This was a symbol, therefore, of Christ's future flesh, although that flesh did not yet exist" [41].) By referring to Christ both as Son of man and as one who "came to the Ancient of Days" (taken as a reference to Christ's ascension and the commencement of his heavenly reign), Daniel thus affirms both the humanity and the divinity of Christ and gives no comfort to those of Manichaean tendencies who would see in Dan 7:13-14 evidence that the human appearance of Christ was only an illusion.

If the son of man who receives the dominion from God in Dan 7:13-14 is the Christ, a burning question makes itself felt: To which of Christ's advents is the writer referring? Here Calvin takes a position that is, by his own admission, contrary to the consensus of previous Christian interpreters. This event is not the second advent of Christ and the last judgment but rather the first advent: "This vision ought not to be explained as the final advent of Christ, but of the intermediate state of the church. The saints began to reign under heaven, when Christ ushered in his kingdom by the proclamation of his gospel" (75). This position is reinforced not only by the equation of the "books" to the gospel but also by Calvin's acceptance of the by then commonplace idea that the fourth beast is Rome and is therefore contemporaneous with Jesus of the first century CE. The ten horns signify the collective leadership of the Roman republic, and the little horn in a general way signifies the dictatorship of the Caesars, which plucks up the former democracy. In Calvin's view, the rule of Christ certainly supplants that of the fourth beast, both visibly and invisibly, and the PROPHECY of destruction of v. 11 was fulfilled "from the time when foreigners obtained mastery" in Rome.

Given the violent hostilities of the time in which Calvin wrote on Daniel, one might have expected him to identify the event of Dan 7:9-14 with the second advent of Christ and to link the fourth beast, not with Rome, but with the Roman Catholic Church. The text could then have functioned admirably as solace to the embattled and endangered communities of the French and Swiss Reformation. But Calvin is led by his understanding of the plain meaning of the text away from such an extravagant extension of the prophecy out of the chronological horizon demanded by the animal allegory. Nevertheless, the text as he understands it does offer a basis for profound hope to the forces of righteousness in his own day. That hope lies in his identification of the "saints of the lofty ones" of vv. 18, 22-23, and 27, as "sons of God, or his elect people, or the church."

But if the son of man and the saints are equated in the text of Daniel 7, how can Calvin separate them into Christ and the church? To do so amounts to separating the dream (7:2-14) from its interpretation (7:17-27). Calvin is not troubled by this problem, for the principle of *pars pro toto* comes to his rescue. The two terms can simply be assimilated to each other; where Christ is, there is the church. The power exercised by the saints in v. 27 depends utterly upon the dominion being exercised by Christ at the Father's right hand (vv. 13-14). The covenant of adoption that the saints enjoy is founded on Christ, and the identity of the two depends

thus utterly on the sequence: first the incarnation and the exaltation of Christ, figuratively represented in 7:13; then the adoption of the saints and the dominion of the church in and through Christ, represented in vv. 18, 22, and 27.

This leads to a final observation about Calvin's interpretation of the most important chapter of Daniel. If the events referred to in chap. 7 center around the first advent of the Christ and if the exaltation of Christ is also the beginning of the dominion of his body the church, then we have in Calvin the basis for the high eschatological expectation that so often characterized Calvinists and the Reformed movement in later generations. Christ and the saints have dominion in the earth for a period of limited but unspecified duration, beginning with the first advent of Christ and the first proclamation of his gospel and ending with the parousia. Daniel 7 is thus a vision "of the intermediate state of the church. The saints began to reign under heaven, when Christ ushered in his kingdom by the promulgation of his gospel" (75)—and the implications of this exalted if hidden status of the church for its proper authority in the earth are profound. These are given concrete shape not only in Calvin's Geneva but also in Cromwell's Holy Commonwealth and in the colony of Massachusetts Bay.

5. Puritan Interpretations. In fact, it was among English and American Puritans of the seventeenth century that the book of Daniel enjoyed what was perhaps its greatest interpretive vogue. In it as well as in other biblical texts the Reformers of church and state found warrant for the radical social changes they sought—the egalitarian rule of the saints and the rejection of hierarchy in all of its forms, civil and religious. They even found there a basis for regicide (in the execution of King Charles I on Jan. 30, 1649) and for the establishment of the modern world's first "republic," the British Commonwealth led by the Lord Protector O. Cromwell.

When the increasingly normative millennialist reading of the end-time scenarios of Daniel 7–12 among English-speaking Reformed Christians was combined with a typological approach to the text of the Bible, a powerful dynamic for social and political action was unleashed. It worked this way. The rule of the saints (for whom the "one like a son of man" is a cipher, according to Dan 7:18) is, according to the transformation of the Danielic picture found in Rev 20:1-6, to occur on earth under Christ's aegis during the millennium before the last judgment and the end of the world as we know it. The "saints" of biblical expectation were related by analogy to the Reform movement in Protestantism; and the binding of the "dragon, that ancient serpent, who is the Devil and Satan" (Rev 20:2), which marks the beginning of the 1,000-year transitional period between this age and the next was seen as the type of the Protestant Reformation. Thus did it become abundantly clear to the radical Puritans, the Diggers, Ranters, Levellers, and Fifth-Monarchy men (those who claimed to be the vanguard of that eternal kingdom that will succeed the four world empires—the stone not made with human hands of Dan 2:34, 44-45, and the saints of the Most High of Dan 7:18, 27) that they were in fact those saints whose destiny it was to introduce the new order of the age (*novus ordo seclorum,* a motto that not accidentally can still be seen on the obverse of the Great Seal of the United States).

The names of authors and titles of works that contributed to this ferment are legion: T. Parker wrote *The Visions and Prophecies of Daniel Expounded* in 1646; J. Archer's book, *The Personal Reign of Christ upon Earth, etc.,* went through at least six editions down to 1661. M. Cary contributed *The Little Horn's Doom and Downfall: Or a Scripture-Prophesie of King James, and King Charles, and of this present Parliament unfolded, etc.* (1651). Perhaps the most interesting of the lot is the Fifth Monarchy man and sometime New Englander W. Aspinwall, who in 1654 urged the revolution on with his book, *An Explication and Application of the Seventh Chapter of Daniel . . . Wherein Is Briefly Shewed the State and Downfall of the Four Monarchies; But More Largely of the Roman Monarchy, and the Ten Horns or Kingdoms; and in Particular, the Beheading of Charles Stuart, Who Is Proved to Be the Little Horn by Many Characters, That Cannot be Applied to Any Before or After Him, etc.* The literature of the period has been helpfully surveyed in the studies of K. Firth (1979), B. Ball (1975), P. Rogers (1966), and P. Toon (1970). R. Bloch (1985) pushes farther into eighteenth-century American Puritan writing.

6. Eighteenth-Century Interpretation. With the restoration of the Stuart monarchy of Charles II in 1669 and the reestablishment of the Church of England, much of the apocalyptic fervor that had animated public life subsided, and with it much interest in the book of Daniel. Late in the seventeenth century H. MORE, one of the group of "Cambridge Platonists" who believed in the twin lights of human faith and human reason, wrote a relatively sober account of the book called *A Plain and Continued Exposition of the Several Prophecies or Divine Visions of the Prophet Daniel, etc.* (1681). Here was an effort to assess the significance of this book in a manner that backed away from the enthusiasm of millennialism and direct historical application.

Much of the interest in the ensuing decades turned to calendrical matters and to the book's relationship to the large sweep of human history rather than to its significance for understanding immediately contemporary history. I. NEWTON's 1733 work, *Observations Upon the Prophecies of Daniel and the Apocalypse of St. John,* is in this vein. For Newton, a great deal was at stake with the book of Daniel, for "to reject his prophecies, is to reject the Christian religion. For this religion is founded upon his prophecy concerning the MESSIAH" (155 in Whitla ed. [1922]). As scientist, astronomer, and mathematician, Newton was naturally inclined to calculate CHRONOLOGY. Beginning with the accepted notion that the legs that terminate in feet and toes composed of iron and clay represented Rome (Dan 2:33), he found it necessary to examine the many digits into which the Roman Empire broke in its latter days. By dint of close calculations Newton assigned the toes (and the ten horns of Dan 7:7) to kingdoms ranging from the Vandals in Spain and Africa at the beginning, through the Britons, the Huns, the Lombards, and the kingdom at Ravenna at the end. The eleventh horn of the fourth beast is the church of Rome, which in the eighth century uprooted the exarchate of Ravenna, the kingdom of the Lombards, and the senate and dukedom of Rome (= the three horns of Dan 7:8). The power of this eleventh horn to change the times and the laws is demonstrated through citations of papal decretals as well as of secular sources under the political power of the Roman see. Newton reckoned the dominion of that power (the time, two times, and half a time of Dan 7:25) to be 1,260 solar years, after which (v, 26) "the judgment is to sit, and they shall take away his dominion, *not at once but by degrees*" (215-16). This same Newton, who was confident that he could perceive in the book a true chronology of future history, was one of the early ones to raise a critical question about it. He made a distinction between the last six chapters, which he said "contained prophecies written at several times by Daniel himself" and the first six chapters, which are "a collection of historical papers written by other authors" (Whitla ed., 145).

7. Modern Critical Interpreters and Their Opponents. Since the flowering of historical criticism in the nineteenth century, controversial passages such as the seventy weeks of Dan 9:24-27 (a text J. Montgomery called "the dismal swamp of OT criticism" [1927, 400]) became the battlefields between those who expected to find the timetable for the culmination of world history cryptically hidden within them and those who sought, not historical and predictive values, but an overall theological appreciation of God's lordship over the future. Larger issues that have usually divided the more traditional commentators from the more critical ones have been these:

a. The unity of the book. Traditionalists generally contend that the narratives about Daniel in chaps. 1–6 are from the same hand or circle that gave us the vision accounts by Daniel in chaps. 7–12. Critical commentaries have often found the materials to differ too radically in both literary style and theological content to have come from the same hand, although one of the most eminent modern critical scholars, H. ROWLEY, argued that a single person wrote the entire book of Daniel. Other studies have said that it does not matter and that the two halves belong together because a program of "interim ethics" (chaps. 1–6) is appropriately coupled to the assurance of final victory and the vindication of the saints (chaps. 7–12).

b. Language. Nobody has yet explained to the general satisfaction why the book of Daniel, which begins in a clear late biblical Hebrew, suddenly in 2:4*b* switches to the *lingua franca* of the Middle East known as Official Aramaic and then reverts to Hebrew again in chaps. 8–12. Traditionalists and critical interpreters do not separate into their respective camps on this issue. H. GINSBERG's theory that the entire book, except for the "interpolated" prayer of 9:4*b*-19, was originally written in Aramaic and that parts of it were then translated into Hebrew in order to make it more accessible and perhaps more authoritative (see AUTHORITY OF THE BIBLE) to its devout Jewish readers has often been favored.

c. Author. Traditional interpreters take at face value the claim of the book that Daniel wrote down the dreams and visions of chaps. 7–12 (see Dan 7:1) and that he or some contemporary recorded the tales of chaps. 1–6. Modern critical interpreters tend to view the entire book as a pseudepigraphon (see PSEUDEPIGRAPHA), attributed by the circles that actually wrote it to the ancient worthy and wise man Dan'el, known even in the fourteenth century BCE Canaanite literature of UGARIT and mentioned twice in Ezekiel—once in the same breath with the ancient righteous Gentiles, Noah and Job (Ezek 14:14, 20), and once as a man of preeminent wisdom (28:3).

d. Date. Traditionalists take seriously the internal dates of the book, beginning with the conquest of Jerusalem by Nebuchadnezzar, king of Babylon (Dan 1:1), and ending with the third year of Cyrus, king of Persia (Dan 10:1). This span of years, sometimes reckoned as 597–536 BCE, suggests that Daniel worked for about sixty-one years entirely within the community of the Jewish exiles in Babylon. Adherence to the given dates renders the visions of four succeeding world empires in chaps. 2 and 7, only the first two or three of which could have existed during Daniel's own lifetime, impressively accurate predictions of the future; even more impressive is the detailed account of Near Eastern history contained in 11:2–12:3. It also builds confidence that the denouement of history, which forms part of the same prophetic sequence in such texts as Dan 2:34-35; 7:9-13; and 11:40–12:3, will also come about as foreseen. The problem of timing, involving the proper interpretation of such chronological references as the seventy weeks of Dan 9:24-27 and the "time, two times, and half a time" of Dan 7:25 (cf. 8:14; 9:27; 12:7, 11-12) hinges for traditional interpreters, as we have already seen, on identifying the fourth part of the colossus in Daniel 2 and the fourth beast in Daniel 7 with Rome. Inasmuch as Rome lingered for a long time and may even be said to be with us to this day in modern European nations, the gap between the fulfilled and the unfulfilled prophecies ("the great parenthesis" elaborated by H. Ironside [1943]) can by this means be closed. Daniel, who foresaw the rise of Rome even before the end of the HB period, can be understood to be predictive for our own future.

Critical interpreters, in contrast, view the question of the book's date very much in the same way as did the pagan Porphyry of ancient times, without, however, scorning the book because much of its "prophecy" is after the fact. On the contrary, to argue, as this scholarly tradition does, that the book reached its present form during the three years of oppression and persecution of the Jews by Antiochus IV Epiphanes (167–164 BCE) and that this Greco-Syrian tyrant is in fact the "little horn" of Dan 7:8, the "one who makes desolate" of 9:27, and the "king of the north" of 11:20-45 is to take the book seriously as an "incarnate Word of God." It shares the limitations all human beings have when it comes to predicting the events of the future; in fact, it erred in suggesting that the eschaton would occur "a time, two times, and half a time" (= three and a half years?) from the writing of the book. But it addressed the crucial issue that confronted the community of observant, faithful Jews who were determined to resist the onslaught of Hellenistic culture and religious opposition. It gave them the encouraging messages that tyranny cannot prevail because God loathes it; that God will vindicate all obedience and loyalty in God's kingdom, which is coming; and that the saints have work of courage and obedience to do in the interim.

It remains simply to identify some of the participants on either side of this debate from the end of the nineteenth through the twentieth centuries. At the extreme edge of the traditionalist stream of interpretation are the exponents of the ideology of "premillennial dispensationalism," who incorporate Daniel's chronology of the future into a unified synthetic scheme for calculating the rapid and near approach of the Day of Judgment. From the turn of the century work of R. Anderson (1895), the full-scale commentary of A. Gaebelein (1911), and the annotations in the C. SCOFIELD Reference Bible, first published in 1909, through the writings of Ironside, J. Walvoord (1971), J. Pentecost (1958), and the pages of Dallas Theological Seminary's periodical *Bibliotheca Sacra,* this ideological use of the book of Daniel is seen today in the popular form given it by H. Lindsey (1970).

The sectarian readings of Daniel by W. Miller and E. White, the founder and prophetess of Seventh-Day Adventism, have yielded to contemporary Adventist commentators whose work belongs more nearly in the mainstream of traditional conservative "messianic" interpretation—e.g., G. Price (1955) and G. Hasel (1976). They join the 150-year-old company of other commentators who have defended the book's "integrity" against critical approaches: C. KEIL, E. HENGSTENBERG, and T. Kliefoth (1868) in Germany; E. B. PUSEY and

C. Boutflower (1903) in Britain; M. STUART, R. Wilson (2 vols. 1917, 1938), and E. Young (1949) in the United States. (The entire traditionalist stream is discussed in detail by D. Beegle [1978].)

Even before Newton's time commentators occasionally had concluded that Daniel was written in the days of Antiochus IV Epiphanes and that the "prophecies" are *vaticinia ex eventu*, "prophecies after the fact." However, it remained for the nineteenth century to bring forth full-scale commentaries based on a historical-critical reading, including those of L. Bertholdt (1806), H. EWALD (1868), and G. Behrmann (1894) in Germany; and those of S. DRIVER (1900), F. FARRAR (1895), and A. Bevan (1892) in England. Early in the twentieth century R. CHARLES (1929) interested himself in Daniel as he interested himself in the non-canonical Jewish apocalyptic books; however, perhaps the fullest expression of the critical approach was Montgomery's work in the ICC series. Since that 1927 benchmark the critical tradition has been enriched by other works, including K. MARTI (1901), O. Plöger (1865), and A. BENTZEN (1952) in Germany; M. Delcor (1971) and A. Lacocque (1979) in France; Ginsberg (1948), Rowley (1950–51), N. Porteous (1965), and L. Hartman and A. Di Lella (1978) in England and America. Daniel's theological and hermeneutical issues (see HERMENEUTICS) have been explored by W. Towner and J. Gammie; J. Collins has given special attention both to the mythological traditions (see MYTHOLOGY AND BIBLICAL STUDIES) and to the literary genres employed by the book's authors. Collins's magisterial commentary on Daniel in the Hermeneia series (1993) will define the state of the art in Daniel studies for years to come.

Bibliography: R. **Anderson,** *Daniel in the Critics' Den* (1895). B. W. **Ball,** *A Great Expectation: Eschatological Thought in English Protestantism to 1660* (1975). G. K. **Beale,** *The Use of Daniel in Jewish Apocalyptic Literature and in the Revelation of St. John* (1984). D. M. **Beegle,** *Prophecy and Prediction* (1978). G. **Behrmann,** *Das Buch Daniel* (HKAT 3, 2, 1894). A. **Bentzen,** *Daniel* (HAT 1, 19, 1937, 1952²). K **Berger,** *Die griechische Daniel-Diegese: Eine Altkirchliche Apokalypse. Text, Übersetzung, und Kommentar* (SPB 27, 1976). L. **Bertholdt,** *Daniel* (1806). A. A. **Bevan,** *A Short Commentary on the Book of Daniel* (1892). R. **Bloch,** *Visionary Republic: Millennial Themes in American Thought, 1756–1800* (1985). R. **Bodenmann,** *Naissance d'une exégèse: Daniel dans l'église ancienne des trois premiers siècles* (BGBE, 1986). C. **Boutflower,** *In and Around the Book of Daniel* (1903). J. **Braverman,** *Jerome's Commentary on Daniel: A Study of Comparative Jewish and Christian Interpretations of the HB* (CBQMS 7, 1978). J. **Calvin,** *Commentaries on the Book of the Prophet Daniel* (2 vols., 1948). M. **Casey,** "Porphyry and the Origin of the Book of Daniel," *JTS* 27 (1976) 15-33; *Son of Man: The Interpretation and Influence of Daniel 7* (1979). R. H. **Charles,** *A Critical and Exegetical Commentary on the Book of Daniel* (1929). **J. J. Collins,** *The Apocalyptic Vision of the Book of Daniel* (HSM 16, 1977); *Daniel: With an Introduction to Apocalyptic Literature* (FOTL 20, 1984); *Daniel* (Hermeneia, 1993). **T. Craven,** "Daniel and Its Additions," *The Women's Bible Commentary* (ed. C. A. Newsom and S. H. Ringe, 1992) 191-94. **M. Delcor,** *Le livre de Daniel* (SB, 1971). **S. R. Driver,** *The Book of Daniel* (CBSC 23, 1900). **G. H. Ewald,** *Daniel* (1868). **F. W. Farrar,** *The Book of Daniel* (1895). **M. H. Farris,** "The Formative Interpretations of the Seventy Weeks of Daniel" (diss., University of Toronto, 1990). **D. N. Fewell,** *Circle of Sovereignty: Plotting Politics in the Book of Daniel* (1988). **K. R. Firth,** *The Apocalyptic Tradition in Reformation Britain, 1530–1645* (Oxford Historical Monographs, 1979). **F. Fraidl,** *Die Exegese der siebzig Wochen Daniels in der alten und mittleren Zeit* (1883). **A. C. Gaebelein,** *The Prophet Daniel: A Key to the Visions and Prophecies of the Book of Daniel* (1911). **J. G. Gammie,** *Daniel* (Knox Preaching Guides, 1983); "A Journey Through Danielic Spaces: The Book of Daniel in the Theology and Piety of the Christian Community," *Int* 39 (1985) 144-56. **H. L. Ginsberg,** *Studies in Daniel* (TSJTSA 14, 1948). **L. Hartman and A. Di Lella,** *The Book of Daniel: A New Translation with Notes and Commentary on Chapters 1–9* (AB 23, 1978). **G. F. Hasel,** "The Seventy Weeks of Daniel 9:24-27," *The Ministry,* supp. (May 1976). **E. W. Hengstenberg,** *Die Authentie des Daniel und die Integrität des Sacharjah* (1831). **H. A. Ironside,** *The Great Parenthesis* (1943). **Jerome,** *Jerome's Commentary on Daniel* (tr. Gleason Archer, Jr., 1958). **C. F. Keil,** *The Book of the Prophet Daniel* (1884). **T. Kliefoth,** *Das Buch Daniel* (1868). **K. Koch,** *Das Buch Daniel* (EdF 144, 1980). **A. Lacocque,** *The Book of Daniel* (1979). **H. Lindsey,** *The Late Great Planet Earth* (1970). **D. S. Margoliouth** (ed.), *Commentary on the Book of Daniel by Jephet Ibn Ali the Karaite* (1889). **K. Marti,** *Das Buch Daniel* (KHC, Anecdota Oxoniensia, 1901). **A. Mertens,** *Das Buch Daniel im Lichte der Texte vom Toten Meer* (SBM 12, 1971). **J. A. Montgomery,** *A Critical and Exegetical Commentary on the Book of Daniel* (ICC, 1927). **I. Newton,** *Observations Upon the Prophecies of Daniel and the Apocalypse of St. John* (1733). **J. D. Pentecost,** *Things to Come* (1958). **O. Plöger,** *Das Buch Daniel* (KAT 18, 1965). **N. Porteous,** *Daniel* (OTL, 1965). **G. M. Price,** *The Greatest of the Prophets* (1955). **E. B. Pusey,** *Daniel the Prophet* (1868²). **P. G. Rogers,** *The Fifth Monarchy Men* (1966). **H. H. Rowley,** "The Unity of the Book of Daniel," *HUCA* 33 (1950–51) 233-73; *The Servant of the Lord and Other Essays on the OT* (1965²) 249-80. **C. I. Scofield** (ed.), *Scofield Reference Bible* (1909; new ed., 1967). **D. L. Smith-Christopher,** "The Book of Daniel," *NIB* (1996) 7:17-152. **M. Stuart,** *A Commentary on the Book of Daniel* (1850). **H. E. Tödt,** *The Son of Man in the Synoptic Tradition* (NTL, 1965). **P. Toon** (ed.), *Puritans, the Millennium, and the Future of Israel* (1970). **W. S. Towner,** "Were the English Puritans 'The Saints of the Most High'? Issues in the Pre-critical Interpretation of Daniel 7," *Int* 37 (1983) 46-63; *Daniel* (Interpretation, 1984). **J. F. Walvoord,** *Daniel the Key to Prophetic Revelation* (1971). **W. Whitla,** *Sir I. Newton's Daniel and the Apocalypse* (1922). **R. D. Wilson,** *Studies in the Book of Daniel: A Discussion of the Historical*

Questions (2 vols., 1917, 1938). **E. J. Young,** *The Prophecy of Daniel: A Commentary* (1949). **M. A. Zier,** "The Latin Interpretation of Daniel in the Middle Ages: An Historical Survey" (diss., Toronto, 1981); "The Medieval Latin Interpretation of Daniel: Antecedents to Andrew of St. Victor," *RTAM* 58 (1991) 43-78.

W. S. TOWNER

DANIEL, BOOK OF (ADDITIONS TO)

The additions to the book of Daniel, which are considered apocryphal by Jews and Protestants but deuterocanonical by Roman Catholics and Orthodox Christians, comprise the Prayer of Azariah and the Hymn of the Three Jews and the stories of Susanna and of Bel and the Dragon. These stories, haggadic folk tales like those in Daniel 1–6, belong to a "Daniel cycle." Fragments found at Qumran indicate that several other stories of the cycle also circulated among the Jews in pre-Christian times (see J.-T. Milik [1981]), but these never became canonical.

1. Place in the Canon and Canonicity. In the LXX (see SEPTUAGINT) form of Daniel, extant in only three witnesses (Cod. 88, Syrohexaplar, Pap. 967), the Prayer of Azariah and the Hymn of the Three Jews are found in chap. 3 between vv. 23 and 24 of the MT; in the Greek, Syriac, and VULGATE editions these are given as 3:24-90. In Codex 88, Syrohexaplar, and Vulgate, the order of material is chaps. 1–12, Susanna, and Bel and the Dragon. In prehexaplaric Pap. 967, the order is chaps. 1–12, Bel and the Dragon, and Susanna; the Syriac edition has a similar order, but with Susanna appearing between Ruth and Esther. The text of so-called THEODOTION-Daniel is found in all the other Greek witnesses; in them the order is Susanna, chaps. 1–12 (including 3:24-90), Bel and the Dragon (see L. Hartman and A. Di Lella [1978] 26-28). Roman Catholic editions of the HB follow the same order as the Vulgate: chaps. 1–12 (including 3:24-90), Susanna (chap. 13), and Bel (14:1-22) and the Dragon (14:23-42). Protestant editions that contain the additions relegate them to an appendix.

Until recently, the scholarly consensus was that the Greek HB represented the list of books accepted as sacred only by the Jews of Egypt, where the LXX had been translated from the third to the first century BCE (Daniel in c. 100). It is now widely accepted that Theod-Dan also had its origin in pre-Christian times in Asia Minor, Palestine, or Syria-Mesopotamia, hence in that region during the first century BCE there were Jews who viewed the additions to Daniel as sacred. Near the end of the first century CE the rabbis of Pharisaic Judaism, who fixed the Jewish CANON, excluded the additions. But by the beginning of the fifth century when the Western church determined the limits of the Christian canon, it included the additons (see Hartman and Di Lella [1978] 78-84).

2. Contents and Literary Genre. *a. Prayer of Azariah and Hymn of the Three Jews.* In the fiery furnace Daniel's faithful companions Hananiah, Mishael, and Azariah sing and bless the Lord. Azariah in his prayer praises divine justice, confessing that God has been righteous in visiting disaster on the Israelites because of their sins. He begs for forgiveness and deliverance from their pitiful state. A narrative then tells of the stoking of the furnace, the burning up of the Chaldeans nearby, and the descent of the angel to drive out the flames, thereby protecting the loyal Jews. Finally, the three Jews sing their hymn to the Lord, urging all creatures, great and small, to join in the chorus of praise. Not part of the original story in chap. 3, the Prayer and Hymn are a pastiche of earlier biblical verses, as is the intrusive prayer in Daniel 9. The Prayer contains many expressions and motifs found in Psalms 44, 74, 79, and 80. The Hymn, echoing ideas and phrases of Psalm 148, follows the structure of Psalm 136 in that the refrain "praise and exalt him above all forever" occurs in the second colon of thirty-eight successive bicola of the Hymn (see the NAB).

b. Susanna. Susanna, transmitted better in Theod-Dan than in the LXX (but see Milik [1981]), is a charming detective story that has been included in some modern anthologies. Its point is that fidelity to the law of conjugal chastity will win out in the end, thus foiling the schemes of the wicked (Deut 28:1-14). Susanna (the word means "lily") is the pious and lovely wife of Joakim, a prosperous Jew in Babylon. Two Jewish elders, seeing her on her daily walk in the garden, begin to lust after her. One warm day Susanna decides to take her bath in the garden. While her maids go to fetch soap and oil, the two lechers, hiding nearby, come forward and threaten to accuse her of adultery with a young man unless she consents to have intercourse with them. She refuses their advances and cries out for help. Making good their threat, the elders testify that Susanna had lain with a young man. Though innocent, she is condemned to death. When she is led to execution, God inspires a young man named Daniel to rebuke the people for condemning Susanna without thorough examination of the witnesses. In the clever cross-examination Daniel shows that the witnesses have perjured themselves. The assembly thanks God for intervening and then inflicts on the two elders the death penalty they had plotted against Susanna.

The story has had a profound impact on literature, being the basis of some twenty-eight German dramas from the fifteenth to the twentieth century and of sixteen French, ten Italian, six Dutch, four Spanish, and three English dramas (see P. Casey [1976] 203-4, 235-40). Shakespeare refers to the story in *The Merchant of Venice* (IV.i.223) when Shylock, about to receive his due (the pound of Antonio's flesh), says in praise of the young judge Balthazar (Portia in disguise), "A Daniel come to judgment. Yea a Daniel." Scenes from Susanna are depicted in catacomb frescoes from the third and fourth centuries and in many other works of art through the ages (see Milik [1981] 357).

c. Bel. Like Susanna, Bel is a well-crafted and entertaining detective story; its purpose is to mock paganism and the worship of lifeless idols that cannot see or hear, eat or smell, (Deut 4:28; Wis 13:1–15:17). In the reign of Cyrus the Persian, Daniel, the king's favorite, refuses to worship the Babylonian idol named Bel (Isa 46:1; Jer 50:2). Daniel says he worships only the living God who made heaven and earth. The king protests that Bel is a living god, for he eats and drinks so much every day. Daniel laughs, much to the king's annoyance. The king orders the priests to find out who consumes all the provisions. The priests tell the king to provide the usual food and wine for Bel; after everybody leaves the temple, he is to seal the door with his ring. If Bel does not consume everything, the priests agree to die; otherwise Daniel is to die. With only the king present, Daniel has ashes scattered over the floor of the temple, which is then sealed. During the night, the priests, their wives, and their children enter the temple through a secret door and eat and drink everything. The next morning Daniel and the king find the seals unbroken and the table empty. The king exclaims, "Great are you, O Bel; there is no trickery in you!" Daniel laughs again, then asks the king to examine the floor, where there are footprints of the priests and their families. Enraged, the king puts them all to death and hands Bel over to Daniel, who destroys it and the temple.

d. The Dragon. This story, which is not as well constructed as the other two, also has as its purpose to ridicule the paganism of the Gentiles and their abhorrent idolatry (Isa 44:9-20). Daniel is ordered to worship a great dragon, whom the king describes as a living god. Daniel refuses and then receives permission from the king to kill the dragon without sword or club. Making cakes of pitch, fat, and hair, Daniel feeds them to the dragon, and it bursts asunder. Daniel exclaims, "This is what you worshiped!" The angry Babylonians accuse the king of becoming a Jew and demand that Daniel be handed over to them. They throw Daniel into a lions' den for six days. Each day the lions had been fed two carcasses and two sheep, but now they receive nothing so as to find Daniel the more appetizing. But the lions do not touch him. An angel transports to the den a prophet, Habakkuk, who had prepared a substantial meal. He tells Daniel to eat what God has sent; Daniel praises God and eats. On the seventh day, the king comes to the den to mourn, only to discover that Daniel is alive and well. Amazed, the king confesses that the God of Daniel alone is God; he then removes Daniel and casts his enemies into the den, where they are quickly devoured. This story is clearly a variant of the one in Daniel 6.

3. Original Language and Date. Although there has been considerable dispute in the past, most scholars today agree that, like the rest of Daniel, the additions were composed originally in either Hebrew or Aramaic. Since the additions have the same vocabulary, style, and syntax as the Greek of the rest of the book, it is reasonable to conclude that the Semitic originals were written in the second century BCE and then translated into Greek about the time of the Greek translation of Daniel, c. 100 BCE (see C. Moore [1977] 25-29).

Bibliography: **W. H. Bennett,** "Prayer of Azariah and Song of the Three Children," *APOT* 1:625-37. **P. F. Casey,** *The Susanna Theme in German Literature: Variations of the Biblical Drama* (AKML 214, 1976). **J. J. Collins,** *Daniel: A Commentary on the Book of Daniel* (Hermeneia, 1993). **T. Craven,** "Daniel and Its Additions," *Women's Bible Commentary* (ed. C. A. Newsom and S. H. Ringe, 1992) 191-94. **T. W. Davies,** "Bel and the Dragon," *APOT* 1:652-64. **M. Delcor,** *Le livre de Daniel* (SB, 1971). **H. Engel,** *Die Susanna Erzählung: Einleitung, Übersetzung, und Kommentar zum Septuaginta-Text und zur Theodotion-Bearbeitung* (OBO 61, 1985). **A. A. Di Lella,** *Daniel: A Book for Troubling Times* (1997). **L. F. Hartman and A. A. Di Lella,** *The Book of Daniel* (AB 23, 1978); "Daniel," *NJBC* (1990) 406-20. **M. Heltzer,** "The Story of Susanna and the Self-government of the Jewish Community in Achaemenid Babylonia," *Annali* 41 (1981) 35-39. **D. M. Kay,** "Susanna," *APOT* 1:638-51. **K. Koch,** *Deuterokanonische Zusätze zum Danielbuch: Entstehung und Textgeschichte* (AOAT 38, 1987). **A. LaCoque,** *Feminine Unconventional: Four Subversive Figures in Israel's Tradition* (1990). **R. A. F. MacKenzie,** "The Meaning of the Susanna Story," *CJT* 3 (1957) 211-18. **J.-T. Milik,** "Daniel et Susanne à Qumrân?" *De la Tôrah au Messie ... Mélanges H. Cazelles* (ed. M. Carrez et al., 1981) 337-59; " 'Prière de Nabonide' et autre écrits d'un cycle de Daniel: Fragments araméens de Qumran 4," *RB* 63 (1956) 407-15. **C. A. Moore,** *Daniel, Esther, and Jeremiah: The Additions* (AB 44, 1977). *The OT in Syriac According to the Peshitta Version,* 3, 4: *Dodekapropheton—Daniel-Bel-Draco* (1980). **G. Rinaldi,** *Daniele* (La Sacra Biblia, 4th rev. ed., 1962). **D. L. Smith-Christopher,** "The Additions to Daniel," *NIB* (1996) 7:153-94. **J. Ziegler,** *Susanna, Daniel, Bel et Draco* (Septuaginta 16, 2, 1954).

A. A. DI LELLA

DATHE, JOHANN AUGUST (1731–91)

Born July 4, 1731, in Weissenfels, D. died Mar. 17, 1791, in Leipzig. He began theological and oriental studies in Wittenberg in 1751, moved to Leipzig in 1754 to study philology with J. ERNESTI, and completed his MA in 1756. He went on to study with J. D. MICHAELIS in Göttingen and became *Dozent* in Leipzig in 1757, associate in oriental languages in 1762, and in the same year full professor of Hebrew. In 1769 he completed his ThD.

The strength of D.'s work in biblical scholarship lay in TEXTUAL CRITICISM and TRANSLATION. The learned insights in his numerous studies of the HB show him to be a master of "antiquarian" studies. Simultaneously, however, his exegetical works sought to maintain connection with dogmatics. In his Latin translation of the HB he "forces the ancient prophets to speak 'ciceronically' " (L. Diestel [1869]); hence D., who rarely ventured beyond the realm of "lower criticism," is a representative of hermeneutical inquiry (see HERMENEUTICS) that hardly attempted to proceed to literary-critical investigations (see LITERARY THEORY/LITERARY CRITICISM) within the text itself. Only in his explanation of the fall did he reach for historical interpretation and employ the concept of myth (see MYTHOLOGY AND BIBLICAL STUDIES). He produced significant research into the PESHITTA, the Syriac translation of the Bible.

Works: *De Origene interpretationis librorum sive grammaticae autore* (1756); *Dissertatio in religuiis Aquilae in interpretatione Hoseae* (1757); *Prolusio de difficultate rei criticae in VT caute disjudicanda* (1761); *De Anarcho philosopho eudaimonico* (1762); *Psalterium syriacum* (1768); *Prophetae minores* (1773, 1790³); *Bearbeitung der Philologia sacra von Glassius* (1776); *Sal. Glassii Philologia sacra his temporibus accomodata* (1776); *Prophetae majores* (1779, 1785²); *Pentateuchus ex recensione textus Hebraici* (1781, 1791²); *Libri historici VT* (1784); *Psalmi* (1787, 1794²); *Jobus, proverbia Salomonis Ecclesiaste et canticum canticorum* (1789); *Opuscula ad crisin et interpretationem VT spectantia* (ed. E. F. K. Rosenmüller, 1796).

Bibliography: *ADB* (1876) 4:764-66. **L. Diestel**, *Geschichte des AT in der christlichen Kirche* (1869) 646. **J. G. Meusel**, *Lexikon der vom Jahr 1750 bis 1800 verstorbenen teutschen Schriftsteller* 2 (1803) 286-87 (with bibliography). **G. W. Meyer**, *Geschichte der Schrifterklärung seit Wiederherstellung der Wissenschaften* 5 (1809) 466, 715.

B. SEIDEL

DAUBE, DAVID (1909–)

Born in Freiburg, Germany, D. graduated JD with distinction from the University of Göttingen in 1932, where he came under the influence of the foremost Roman lawyer of that generation, O. Lenel. Circumstances in Germany brought him to Cambridge as a refugee, where he was received by the Romanist W. Buckland (obtaining his Cambridge PhD in 1936) and participated in C. H. DODD's NT seminar. He was a fellow of Gonville and Caius College, Cambridge (1946–51) and professor of jurisprudence at Aberdeen (1951–55) before being called to Oxford as Regius Professor of Civil Law and fellow of All Souls College. He left Oxford in 1969 to become professor-in-residence at the law school of the University of California at Berkeley and director of the Robbins Hebraic and Roman Law Collection. Since 1966 he has also been a permanent visiting professor at the University of Konstanz. He is a doctor of civil law at the University of Oxford.

D.'s scholarship is characterized by a deep knowledge of the content, form, and methodologies of both European and Jewish literature. His first major book, *Studies in Biblical Law* (1947), opened a new era for study by its sensitive treatment of the relationship between laws and narratives and its judicious use of comparative material. *The NT and Rabbinic Judaism* (1956) has proved even more influential, not only by pointing to the Jewish background of many nuances of the NT text but also by its methodological sensitivity to the way such comparison should be made in the context of the development of traditions within both Judaism and the early Christian community. In these early books he applied FORM CRITICISM to the linguistic characteristics of biblical norms and the manner of their utterance. In *Forms of Roman Legislation* (1956) he applied similar principles to the Roman legal texts, again with judicious use of biblical and other comparisons.

D.'s interests in legal history have never been purely antiquarian. He has frequently pursued ancient manifestations of political and philosophical issues that still exercise us today, notably his studies of suicide, civil disobedience, and the position of women. He has made powerful contributions toward sensitizing the study of ancient law to many of the issues that dominate the general intellectual scene—particularly in the areas of literature and linguistics. Through his writing and the research training he has provided, he has considerably influenced scholarship on Roman law, Jewish law, and NT studies. His sixty-fifth birthday was celebrated by the publication of three separate Festschriften, one in each of these areas. In 1992 the Robbins Collection commenced the publication of the *Collected Works of D. D.* with a volume on Talmudic law (see TALMUD) edited by C. Carmichael.

Works: *Shakespeare on Aliens Learning English* (1942); *Studies in Biblical Law* (1947, repr. 1969); *Forms of Roman Legislation* (1956); *The NT and Rabbinic Judaism* (1956, repr. in 1973); *The Exodus Pattern in the Bible* (1963); *The Sudden in the Scriptures* (1964); *Collaboration with Tyranny in Rabbinic Law* (1965); *He That Cometh* (1966); *Roman Law, Linguistic, Social, and Philosophical Aspects* (1969); *Gewaltlöser Frauenwiderstand in Altertum* (1971); *Legal Problems in Medical Advance* (1971); *Civil Disobedience in Antiquity* (1972); *Ancient Hebrew Fables* (1973); *Medical and Genetic Ethics* (1976); *The Duty of Procreation* (1977); *Jewish Law* (1981).

Bibliography: **W. D. Davies**, "Foreword," *Donum Gentilicium: NT Studies in Honour of D. D.* (ed. C. K. Barrett, E. Bammel, and W. D. Davies, 1978) v-vi. **B. S. Jackson**, "Introduction," *Studies in Jewish Legal History in Honour of D. D.*

(ed. B. S. Jackson, 1974) 2-5. **W. A. J. Watson,** "Introduction," *Daube Noster* (1974) vii-ix.

B. S. JACKSON

DAVIDSON, ANDREW BRUCE (1831–1902)

Born near Aberdeen, D. was educated at Marischal University (MA 1849) and at New College, Edinburgh (BD 1856). He studied under H. EWALD at Göttingen, then succeeded J. Duncan as professor of Hebrew and oriental languages (later OT exegesis) at New College, Edinburgh, from 1863 to his death.

D. was one of the revisers of the KJV (1870–84), producing the English RV in 1885. He devoted his life's work to research into the language, historical exegesis, and theology of the OT. He felt that the Bible—even as the Word of God—must be initially approached as any other book, believing it to be a record of human religious experience, not a compendium of doctrine. His method was founded on the scientific study of grammar, which he held to be the foundation of analysis, exegesis, and biblical THEOLOGY. He felt that in Britain the work often proceeded from the wrong end and insisted that OT books must be read on their own terms and in their own context without the hindsight of later revelation. Yet he argued with equal force that the OT could never be fully understood apart from the NT, that it is necessary to see Scripture as a whole. His favorite study was OT PROPHECY, but his never-finished commentary on Job, one-third published in 1862, was highly regarded by such scholars as G. A. SMITH. D.'s influence may be seen in his pupils W. R. SMITH, G. A. Smith, and J. SKINNER, while generations of Bible students learned their Hebrew from his famous *Hebrew Grammar.*

Works: *Commentary on the Book of Job* (1862); *An Introductory Hebrew Grammar* (1874 and many subsequent eds.); *Epistle to the Hebrews* (1882); *The Book of Job* (CBC, 1884); *Ezekiel* (1892); *Hebrew Syntax* (1896); *Nahum, Habakkuk, Zephaniah* (CBC, 1896); *Biblical and Literary Essays* (1902); *OT Prophecy* (1902); *Theology of the OT* (ed. S. D. F. Salmond, 1904); full bibliography in *ExpTim* 15 (1904) 453.

Bibliography: **S. R. Driver,** *DNB, 1901–11* (1912) 471-72. **A. T. Innes,** "Introduction," *The Called of God* (A. B. Davidson, 1902) 3-58. **R. A. Riesen,** *Criticism and Faith in Late Victorian Scotland* (1958) 252-376. **J. Rogerson,** *OTCNC,* 275. **J. Strahan,** *A. B. Davidson* (1917).

J. M. BULLARD

DAVIDSON, SAMUEL (1806–98)

D. was born into a Presbyterian family at Kellswater, Ireland, in 1806, and his early schooling was in Ballymena and Belfast. He trained to enter the ministry but was not licensed to preach until 1833. A professor of biblical interpretation at Belfast College (1835–41), he was awarded the DD by Aberdeen University in 1838. Upon leaving the Presbyterian ministry in 1841, he transferred his allegiance to the Independent (Congregational) Church and was appointed to a professorship at Lancashire Independent College, Manchester, in 1842. In 1857 he was compelled to resign amid a storm of controversy. The most specific charge against him was that he denied the Mosaic authorship of the Pentateuch (see PENTATEUCHAL CRITICISM), although he was also accused of undermining biblical AUTHORITY more generally. After a period as a writer he was appointed a Scripture examiner at London University in 1862. In London he associated himself with the Unitarian Church, where he found a more open spirit. He died Apr. 1, 1898.

D.'s dismissal in 1857, occasioned by his embracing newer methods of biblical criticism learned from German scholars (esp. H. Hupfeld and K. Keil), focused attention on him as a biblical scholar and reflected a major ecclesiastical upheaval. D. rightly saw this critical approach as a major tool of biblical interpretation, and it remained his dominant interest throughout his life. In 1844 he made the first of several visits to Germany (particularly Halle), where he established links with Hupfeld and was awarded a DD from the University of Halle in 1848.

D.'s major concern was the far-reaching implications for biblical interpretation of the newly emerging research into the Bible's LITERARY origin, authorship, and textual transmission. His major writings were literary and textual "introductions" to the Bible. In 1852 he published a revision of his first work, now entitled *A Treatise on Biblical Criticism* (2 vols.). However, it was not this work but the appearance in 1856 of his "Introduction to the Sacred Scriptures" in volume 2 of the tenth edition of T. HORNE's *Introduction to the Scriptures* that was the immediate cause of his enforced resignation in 1857.

Probably his most characteristic achievement was a large three-volume work, *An Introduction to the OT, Critical, Historical, and Theological* (1862–63). A major service to the development of Hebrew studies in Great Britain was his translation of J. Fürst's Hebrew and Chaldee LEXICON (1865, 1871). D. endeavored to encourage a critical approach to NT studies by publishing *An Introduction to the NT* and an English translation of the NT from the critical text of C. von TISCHENDORF (1875). He made a consistent effort to keep abreast of biblical scholarship in Germany and desired to mediate, if not to innovate, in the science of biblical criticism. After his death in 1898 his daughter edited for publication his autobiography and diary, which also contains a detailed account by J. Picton of the controversy surrounding

D.'s dismissal in 1857 and a brief bibliography listing his major works.

Works: *Lectures in Biblical Criticism* (1839); *Sacred Hermeneutics Developed and Applied, Including a History of Biblical Interpretation from the Earliest of the Fathers to the Reformation* (1843); *An Introduction to the NT* (3 vols., 1848–51; 2 vols. 1868); *The Text of the OT Considered, with a Treatise on Sacred Interpretation and Brief Introduction to the OT Books and the Apocrypha* (1856); *An Introduction to the OT* (2 vols. 1862–63); *The Canon of the Bible* (1877); *The Book of Job* (1878); *The Doctrine of the Last Things Contained in the NT* (1882); *The Autobiography and Diary of S. D.* (ed. A. J. Davidson, 1899).

Bibliography: Anon., *Dr. D.: His Heresies, Contradictions, and Plagiarisms* (1857). **R. Bayne,** *DNB* Supp. 2 (1901) 115-16. **T. Nicholas,** *Dr. D.'s Removal from the Professorship of Biblical Literature in the Lancashire Independent College, Manchester, on Account of Alleged Error in Doctrine* (1860). **J. Rogerson,** *OTCNC* 170-73, 197-208.

R. E. CLEMENTS

DAVIES, W. D. (1911–)

Born in Glanaman, South Wales, D. studied classical Greek under H. Tillyard and K. Freeman and comparative Semitic philology under T. ROBINSON and H. ROWLEY at the University of Wales. He went from there to Memorial College, Wales, for a ministerial degree (BD) and then, after serving as a Congregational clergyman in the early 1940s, did research in Paulinism at Cambridge. There he studied under the dominating influences in his academic life, C. H. DODD and D. DAUBE. He came to the United States in 1950 and thereafter taught at Duke (1950–55, 1966–82), Princeton (1955–59), Union Theological Seminary in New York (1959–66), and Texas Christian University (1982–85).

The product of D.'s research at Cambridge was *Paul and Rabbinic Judaism,* one of the twentieth century's most influential studies of PAUL. The book, which has now passed through four editions, takes issue especially with those who have explained the apostle as a diaspora Jew who failed to understand the best of Judaism. According to D., Paul's thought is best explicated against the background of Palestinian Judaism. The apostle's theology was largely the outcome of his conviction that the Messiah had come and that a new exodus had taken place. The demonstration of this, which displaces justification by faith from the center of Pauline theology, involves countering the once-popular dichotomy of Hellenism and Judaism and showing how Paul's arguments are often clarified by rabbinic and intertestamental materials.

D.'s second major book was *The Setting of the Sermon on the Mount* (1964), an abbreviated version of which has been translated into several languages. Here, too, the main strategy is to look at Christian texts in the light of Jewish texts. D. maintains that the SERMON ON THE MOUNT and much else in Matthew were partly a response to emergent rabbinic Judaism. When, after the disaster of 70 CE, the descendants of the Pharisees sought to reconsolidate Judaism, they put forth certain ideas and enacted certain measures; these ideas (e.g., the importance of Hos 6:6) and measures (e.g., the benediction against heretics) supply the context by which we may reconstruct the original meaning and function of Matthew 5–7.

The Gospel and the Land, D.'s third major book, turned to a topic much neglected by NT scholars. While the land of Israel is fundamental for much Jewish thought, it is seemingly at the margins of the early church. This book seeks to understand this fact and explores how Christianity "Christified" holy space: It deterritorialized theology as the risen JESUS increasingly drew to himself the theological functions of the land.

Works: *Paul and Rabbinic Judaism: Some Rabbinic Elements in Pauline Theology* (1948; 50th anniversary ed., with preface by R. B. Hays and E. P. Sanders, 1998); *Christian Origins and Judaism: A Collection of NT Studies* (1962); *The Setting of the Sermon on the Mount* (1964); *The Gospel and the Land* (1974); *Jewish and Pauline Studies: Collected Essays of W. D. D.* (1984); "My Odyssey in NT Interpretation," *Bible Review* 5 (1989) 10-18.

Bibliography: G. Aulen, *Jesus in Contemporary Research* (1976) 32-53. **D. R. A. Hare,** *HHMBI,* 471-76. **E. P. Sanders,** *Paul and Palestinian Judaism* (1977) 7-12, 511-15.

D. C. ALLISON, JR.

DEAD SEA SCROLLS

1. Introduction. The term *Dead Sea Scrolls* refers to scrolls and fragments discovered mostly between 1947 and 1960 at seven sites near the Dead Sea: eleven caves near Qumran, two caves in Wadi Murabba'at, the caves of Naḥal Ḥever, Naḥal Mishmar, and Naḥal Ṣe'elim, and at Khirbet Mird and Masada. Often the term is used to refer only to the writings from the caves near Qumran. These writings are referred to by cave number, site, and abbreviated title: e.g., 1QS = cave number 1, Qumran, *Serek ha-Yaḥad (Rule of the Community).*

From the Qumran caves there are remains of over 750 documents dating from the third century BCE to the first century CE, in Hebrew, Aramaic, and Greek, mostly written on skin. About a quarter of these documents are texts of biblical books, all of which were extant at Qumran except Esther. To some extent it is anachronistic to speak of the interpretation of the Bible in the Dead Sea Scrolls since generally the form of the text for each book was not then definitively fixed nor was the CANON authoritatively delimited.

2. Interpretation in the Scrolls from Qumran. *a. Biblical witnesses.* Assessing the variety of texts found at Qumran for each biblical book is the task of the text critic (see TEXTUAL CRITICISM); among the surviving witnesses there are many orthographic variants and some differences explicable as scribal errors. However, part of the textual variety, including the marginal markings and paragraphing in some manuscripts and the various ways of writing the Tetragrammaton (YHWH), must be explained in terms of the interpretive practices of scribes in the Second Temple period. Some texts contain clarifications: e.g., 4QpaleoExod^m often agrees with the Samaritan Pentateuch (see PENTATEUCHAL CRITICISM) in its clarifying expansions, especially in the plague narrative (Exod 7:8–11:10). Some clarifications involve the harmonization of two versions of material: e.g., the DECALOGUE (Deut 5:1-21) in 4QPhyl G is written with allusions to the parallel version in Exodus 20, as well as to Deut 4:12-13 and 11:19. Some variants may represent a particular theological opinion: whereas MT Isa 52:14 reads *mišhat,* "marred," 1QIsa^a 44:12 reads *mšhty,* possibly to be understood as "I anointed," thus implying a different evaluation of the servant figure. None of these variations need be characteristically Essene, although E. Tov (1988) has argued for the possibility of grouping the biblical manuscripts according to non-interpretive scribal practices as either Qumran or non-Qumran.

b. Biblical paraphrases. Several kinds of paraphrastic texts feature among the scrolls. Reworked forms of the Pentateuch, 4Q158 and 4Q364-367 contain some expansions and clarifications not unlike some parts of the Samaritan Pentateuch. The so-called *Temple Scroll,* 11QT^a, contains a reorganized form of the Pentateuch from Exodus 34 to Deuteronomy 23, with various cultic laws neatly harmonized, sometimes in ways that provide new interpretations of those laws; the whole is presented as a divine speech to Moses and so claims to be authoritative (see AUTHORITY OF THE BIBLE). Also to be construed as authoritative because it is cited alongside biblical texts in 4QTestim is the so-called *Psalms of Joshua* (4Q378-379), an expansively rewritten form of parts of Joshua, perhaps intended to be a farewell speech of Joshua modeled on Deuteronomy.

There are also rewritten forms of biblical books that follow the outline of particular books more closely. The Aramaic *Genesis Apocryphon* (1QapGen) contains non-legal narrative additions, e.g., prayers, dreams and their interpretations, a description of Sarah's beauty. There are also several fragmentary manuscripts of JUBILEES and of works like *Jubilees* (4Q225-227), a tradition taken as authoritative in the laws of the *Damascus Document* (CD 16:3-4). (*Jubilees* is a rewritten form of Genesis 1–Exodus 15; it contains cultic and other legal alterations of the Genesis narratives so that the patriarchs in particular conform to a certain interpretation of the law.)

Also in this category of interpretation fall the Aramaic paraphrastic scriptural translations, which are more like the later TARGUMIM than is 1QapGen. Although these are close to the Hebrew as we know it in the MT, some of the translation is less literal, more interpretive: e.g., in its translation of Lev 16:12, 4QtgLev specifies the kind of incense, apparently using Exod 30:34, part of a chapter also linked with the Day of Atonement (Exod 30:7-10).

c. Biblical commentaries. The commentaries from Qumran range from the continuous to the thematic. Strictly speaking, the continuous commentaries interpret a biblical book or passage section by section. Most of the commentaries are interpretations of books or pericopes that were considered prophetic, including Psalms. After the quotation of the text comes the interpretation, usually introduced with a formula including the word *pesher* (hence many of these commentaries are known as *pesherim*). Sometimes it seems as if the biblical text cited has been deliberately altered to facilitate the interpretation. An often quoted example is the reading of *whby,* "lovers of," in Ps 37:20 (4QpPs^a 3:5a), whereas the MT, supported by all the versions, reads *yby,* "enemies of." In 1QpHab 11:2-8 the interpreter plays on the ambiguity of *mw dyhm* in his version of Hab 2:15 by making comments about both "festivals" and "stumbling"; he may also have known the reading *mw ryhm,* "their shame/nakedness" (as in the MT), since in the commentary there is allusion to the "uncovering" of the Teacher of Righteousness.

The commentary is linked to the biblical passage in a variety of ways. Commonly, biblical words or phrases are borrowed directly and applied to a new context, sometimes with some consideration of their original context, usually more atomistically. Sometimes the ambiguity of the biblical text is exploited. Often interpretative techniques are used, such as letter substitution or juxtaposition: the presence of God in the "temple," *hykl* (Hab 2:20), is suitably understood in the commentary as "he will destroy," *yklh* (1QpHab 13:3).

The more thematic commentaries (e.g., 4Q174, 4QpIsa^c, 11QMelch), treat in sequence a selection of passages, often including in the interpretation secondary supportive biblical texts linked together by catchword analogy, not unlike some of the later rabbinic Midrashim (see MIDRASH). However, although in 4Q174 the section on Psalms 1–2 is introduced with the formulaic "Midrash of," because of their overarching eschatological concern these commentaries should not be seen as the direct forebears of rabbinic Midrashim, nor should their exegetical techniques be designated with unqualified rabbinic terminology.

The term *pšr* occurs in other texts. Notably in 1QDM (1Q22) the verb is used for the interpretations that are given to the Levites and the priests alone. *Pesher*-like interpretation, involving atomistic identification of elements in biblical texts, occurs in other texts too, especially in some sections of CD. *Commentary on Genesis A* (4Q252) is an important example of early Jewish commentary. It treats selected passages of Genesis 6–49, giving its comments sometimes through paraphrase, sometimes as *pesher,* and sometimes through the juxtaposition of various legal texts within the rewritten form of Genesis.

d. Other biblical interpretation. Many of the scrolls explicitly use biblical texts to support the writer's paraenetic or homiletical point. Isaiah 40:3 is used in 1QS 8:14 to justify the community's study of the law. For specific matters of legal interpretation, the biblical text is also cited explicitly, together with comment on it: Such legal interpretation involves either linguistic precision (as in the use of Deut 5:12 in CD 10:14-15), analogical extension or correlation (as in the extension of sabbath rules through the use of Isa 58:13 in CD 10:17-20), or topical specification (as in the use of Exod 12:47 in 11QT^a 17:6-9 to refer to those age twenty years or older; see Fishbane [1988] 368-71).

There are also many texts in which interpretation of the Bible is implicit in allusions to biblical passages. These allusory interpretations occur most often in poetic and liturgical texts, some of which seem to be pastiches of biblical material. These uses are not arbitrary; e.g., in one of the poems, 1QH 12:11-12, the author, reflecting on his own experiences and those of his community, uses phrases from Hab 2:15 that are interpreted similarly of the Teacher of Righteousness and of the wicked priest in 1QpHab 11:2-15.

e. New "biblical" texts. Alongside the many manuscripts that reflect implicit or explicit exegesis of biblical passages, there are also some texts containing non-sectarian compositions that are generally similar to some biblical texts. Several previously unknown non-canonical psalms have come to light (e.g., in 4Q372, 381) as well as other new liturgical texts containing prayers and blessings, which include allusions to biblical texts and also imitate their genres (e.g., 4Q499, 502, 503). Likewise, it may be possible to associate several texts with the developing Daniel corpus (4QPsDan ar^{a-c}), 4QPsDan A^a). The *Temple Scroll* may be claiming for itself an authority equal to that of the Pentateuch.

3. The Dead Sea Scrolls and the Modern Interpretation of the Bible. *a. Textual criticism.* All the biblical texts found in Wadi Murabba'at, Naḥal Ḥever (pre-135 CE), and at Masada (pre-74 CE) are proto-Masoretic. They differ from the MT in orthography and content only in very minor ways. MurXII, basically very close to the MT anyway, even contains nine corrections to MT (eight supralinear additions and one erasure). These biblical manuscripts have provided evidence for the stabilization of the Hebrew text in the first century CE. Manuscripts like 8ḤevXIIgr have also provided infor-

mation that improves our understanding of the transmission of the LXX (see SEPTUAGINT).

The same is not the case with the biblical texts from Qumran. The variety of texts for most biblical books among the finds as a whole and even within individual caves is bewildering and has not yet been satisfactorily explained. Some scholars have tried to group the texts in three families based on the MT (e.g., 1QIsa^b), the Samaritan Pentateuch (e.g., 4QpaleoExod^m), and the Hebrew behind the LXX (e.g., 4QJer^b); other scholars have noted how text-types associated with particular religious groups have been preserved. Each biblical manuscript needs to be studied in its own right.

b. Judaism of the Second Temple period. The Dead Sea Scrolls have radically altered the way scholars reconstruct the history of the Second Temple period. The evidence of the scrolls impinges on the way biblical scholars perceive the composition of some of the biblical books and the transmission of them all. They have also provided information about one or more Jewish groups of the first centuries BCE and CE, Jews who share some characteristics with features of the early Christian churches. The discovery and publication of the scrolls have also been part of the stimulus toward increased research into all forms of Jewish literature, commonly known as APOCRYPHA and PSEUDEPIGRAPHA (e.g., eleven manuscripts of ENOCH material have been found in cave 4), which together reflect the diversity of Palestinian and disapora Judaism out of which both Judaism and Christianity emerged.

c. Jewish biblical interpretation. Much of the interpretative methodology and even some of the content of the Targumim and of the halakhic and haggadic traditions in the Mishnah and the later Midrashim is anticipated in the Dead Sea Scrolls, even though these later Jewish texts are based on a fixed form of the biblical text and an agreed canon. Moreover, the rabbinic canon of interpretative method, linked in the first instance with HILLEL the elder, shares much in common with the techniques discernible in the Qumran scrolls, although the later rabbis appear to restrict what earlier may have been far more varied; yet even they gradually acknowledge an increasing number of exegetical techniques.

d. The use of the HB in the NT. The scrolls have affected the modern interpretation of every NT book. They illuminate in particular how the early Christian writers used the HB; e.g., the *pesherim* improve the understanding of the prophetic proof-texting of Matthew 1–2; 4QBeat shows how makarisms were used to teach Wisdom; Isaiah 61 is used in a similar way in both 11QMelch and Luke 4:17-21; Paul's use of Deut 21:23 in Gal 3:13 seems to reflect the same text of Deuteronomy 21 as is cited in 11QT^a 64:11-13; the combination of 2 Samuel 7 and Psalm 2 in Heb 1:5 can also be found in 4Q174; 4Q385 Frg. 5 illuminates the use of Ezekiel 1 and 10 in Rev 4:1-8.

e. Early Christianity and the Essenes. Several texts that are generally associated with the Essenes because of the parallels to them in classical sources (especially in Philo and in Josephus) show certain similarities of organization and belief with early Christian communities as these are reflected in the various NT writings. For example, the office of *mĕbaqqēr* (e.g., 1QS 6:12, 20) is like that of the early Christian *episkopos* (1 Tim 3:1-7; Titus 1:7-9); the sharing of property by full members (1QS 6:21-23) is echoed in Acts 4:32–5:11; the mutual disciplining of members (1QS 5:26–6:1) is similarly outlined in Matt 18:15-17. These similarities should not necessarily be interpreted as showing the direct dependence of early Christian groups on the Essenes; rather, they reflect the general ambience of religious groups within Judaism in the first century CE.

Bibliography: M. **Bernstein,** "4Q252: From Re-Written Bible to Biblical Commentary," *JJS* 45 (1994) 1-27. **O. Betz,** *Offenbarung und Schriftforschung in der Qumransekte* (WUNT 6, 1960). **G. J. Brooke,** *Exegesis at Qumran* (JSOTSup 29, 1985). **W. H. Brownlee,** *The Meaning of the Qumrân Scrolls for the Bible* (1964); "The Background of Biblical Interpretation at Qumrân," *Qumrân: Sapiété, sa théologie et son milieu* (ed. M. Delcor, BETL 46, 1978). **F. F. Bruce,** *Biblical Exegesis in the Qumran Texts* (Exegetica 3, 1, 1959). **F. M. Cross and S. Talmon** (eds.), *Qumran and the History of the Biblical Text* (1975). **M. Fishbane,** "Use, Authority, and Interpretation of Mikra at Qumran," *Mikra* (ed. M. J. Mulder, CRINT 2, 1, 1988) 339-77. **J. A. Fitzmyer,** *The Dead Sea Scrolls: Major Publications and Tools for Study* (SBLSBS 8a, 1977). **H. Gabrion,** "L'interprétation de l'écriture dans la littérature de Qumrân," *ANRW* II.19.1 (1979) 749-848. **F. García Martínez,** (ed.), *The Dead Sea Scrolls Translated: The Qumran Texts in English* (1996²). **M. P. Horgan,** *Pesharim: Qumran Interpretations of Biblical Books* (CBQMS 8, 1979). **B. Nitzan,** *Biblical Influence in Qumran Prayer and Religious Poetry* (1989), Hebrew. **L. H. Schiffman,** *Reclaiming the Dead Sea Scrolls* (1994). **E. Tov,** "Hebrew Biblical Manuscripts from the Judaean Desert: Their Contribution to Textual Criticism," *JJS* 39 (1988) 5-37; *Textual Criticism of the HB* (1992). **J. C. Vanderkam,** *The Dead Sea Scrolls Today* (1994).

G. J. BROOKE

DECALOGUE

Although not the oldest known legal code, Yahweh's covenantal requirements of the Israelites, the Decalogue (from the Greek *deka logoi,* "ten words"), found in Exod 34:28 and Deut 10:4, has become the best known in human culture. Applications to the most varied circumstances appear in the HB prophets (see M. Weiss, "The Decalogue in Prophetic Literature," in B. Segal [1990] 67-81), in the sayings of JESUS, in the writings of PAUL, and in other early Christian and rabbinic sources (see W. Rordorf [1984]; G. Stemberger [1989]; F. Vokes [1968]; and D. Flusser, "The Ten Commandments and the NT," in Segal, 219-46).

The Decalogue's tenfold pattern has become a cultural archetype. It has been vigorously expounded by Jewish, Catholic, and Protestant thinkers throughout the centuries; and there have been endless imitations, offered as substitutes or parallels, and numerous critiques.

Although the stones on which the Ten Commandments were said to have been written, perhaps on both sides, before being deposited in the ark of the covenant have disappeared along with the ark, manuscript copies like the Nash Papyrus at Cambridge are among the oldest surviving biblical fragments. Some pious Jews believed the Decalogue to be the earliest model of alphabetic writing (the "ten words" teaching writing as well as righteousness).

Variations exist between the wording of the commandments in Exod 20:2-17 (172 words) and Deut 5:6-21 (189 words) and between the MT and ancient versions (Samaritan and Greek). Even the order of some of the commandments vary: Where the MT has murder, adultery, and theft, some traditions have adultery, theft, murder (Greek Exodus; see Luke 18:20; Rom 13:9) or adultery, murder, theft (Nash Papyrus, Greek Deuteronomy, and Philo; see M. Greenberg, "The Decalogue Tradition Critically Examined," in Segal, 83-119).

Three main systems of numbering the commandments exist. (Even the MT has been pointed for two different cantillations and thus two different divisions of the commandments; see M. Breuer, "Dividing the Decalogue into Verses and Commandments," in Segal, 291-330.) In one system, now used by most Protestants and found in PHILO (*On the Decalogue* 50-51) and JOSEPHUS (*Ant.* 3.91-92), the order is (1) no other gods, (2) prohibition of images, (3) taking God's name in vain, (4) sabbath, (5) honoring parents, (6) killing, (7) adultery, (8) theft, (9) false witness, and (10) covetousness. The second system, used by Roman Catholics and Lutherans and already found in AUGUSTINE, combines (1) and (2) above and divides (10) into two commandments. The third, the traditional Jewish system, considers Exod 20:2 (Deut 5:6) as the first commandment ("I am YHWH ... out of the house of bondage") and Exod 20:3-6 (Deut 5:7-10) as the second commandment. Early rabbinical sources, however, suggest that there was no absolute system of dividing the commandments in antiquity.

The division of the commandments into two tablets, with 1 to 5 on the first and 6 to 10 on the second (see first and third enumerations above), was already present in early tradition. The first five, all of which contain a reference to God, were considered to be concerned with proper worship of God; and the second five, none of which refers to God, with proper social and interpersonal relations (see G. Sarfatti, "The Tablets of the Law as a Symbol of Judaism," in Segal, 383-418).

Roman Catholic tradition has generally divided the commandments into 1-3 and 4-10. This already appears in Augustine (*PL* 3.620, 644), who associated the first three commandments with loving God and the final seven with love of neighbor. He was followed by RA-BANUS, (*PL* 108.95-97, 863-64), PETER LOMBARD (*Sentences* 3.33.1-2; *PL* 192.830-31), and many others.

In Judaism there is also a tradition that the five laws on one tablet parallel those on the other:

> How were the Ten Commandments arranged? Five on one tablet and five on the other. On the one tablet was written: "I am the Lord thy God." And opposite it on the other tablet was written: "Thou shalt not murder. . . ." On the one tablet was written: "Thou shalt have no other god." And opposite it on the other tablet was written: "Thou shalt not commit adultery. . . ." On the one tablet was written "Thou shalt not take." And opposite it on the other tablet was written: "Thou shalt not steal. . . ." On the one tablet was written: "Remember the sabbath day to keep it holy." And opposite it on the other tablet was written: "Thou shalt not bear false witness. . . ." On the one tablet was written: "Honor thy father," etc. And opposite it on the other tablet was written: "Thou shalt not covet thy neighbor's wife" (*Mek. Qod.* 8).

The Decalogue was recited together with the Shema in the daily sacrificial service in the Temple (*m. Tam.* 5:1) during the Second Temple period but was prohibited by the rabbis outside of the Temple and after its destruction for fear that this practice would give the impression that only the Decalogue, and not the other laws, was given to Moses at Sinai (*b. Ber.* 12a; see E. Urbach, "The Role of the Ten Commandments in Jewish Worship," in Segal, 161-89).

The Jewish philosopher-exegete Philo considered the Ten Commandments to represent the essence of biblical law or its fundamental principles. For him the Decalogue embodied the whole of the Torah, and the other laws in the HB represented various manifestations or detailed elaborations. He expounded this position in his *On the Decalogue* (*De decalogo*), the first work to present a detailed exposition of the Decalogue, and in his *About the Particular Laws* (*De specialibus legibus*). It appears that he alone in antiquity regarded the Decalogue as a unique summation of the Torah (see Y. Amir, "The Decalogue According to Philo," in Segal, 121-60).

The NT quotes Jesus as referring positively to the Decalogue's stipulations (Matt 19:16-30; Mark 10:17-31; Luke 18:18-30). A Matthean saying of Jesus affirms the commandments and condemns those who break them in act, in word, or even in thought (Matt 5:17-32). Jesus also appears to have reduced them to two basic principles: love of God and love of neighbor (Matt 22:34-40; Mark 12:28-31; Luke 10:25-28, quoting Deut 6:5 and Lev 19:18, neither in the Decalogue). Paul sums up the law in one principle: "Love your neighbor as yourself" (Rom 13:8-10; Gal 5:14), referring only to what would have been the second table of stipulations.

The author of the epistle of James speaks of fulfilling the "royal law," which is stated as "You shall love your neighbor as yourself." What is meant by the "royal law" is uncertain, but the text continues to speak of adultery and murder as if the author were stating a central principle summarizing the second half of the Decalogue. The writer declares that "whoever keeps the whole law but fails in one point has become guilty of all of it" (Jas 2:10). This text appears to grant priority to a simple principle but then places all the laws on the same footing.

The idea that transgression of one commandment leads to or is equivalent to breaking all commandments also occurs in rabbinic literature. The *Mek. Shim.* on Exod 20:14 declares: "When a person breaks one of them, he will end up by breaking them all" (quoted by Flusser in Segal, 225; see 4 Macc 5:19-21; Philo *Legatio ad Gaium* 115-17).

The practice of summarizing the commandments in a single principle was also known among the rabbis. R. AKIBA declared "You shall love your neighbor as yourself" to be the "great general rule of the Torah" (*Sipra Qod.* 2). HILLEL, in responding to a pagan's request for a summary of the law, declared: "What is hateful to you, do not do to anyone else—that is the whole Torah, and all the rest is commentary—go and learn it" (*b. Šabb.* 31a). Hillel's statement presents the negative form of what is called Jesus' Golden Rule (Matt 7:12; Luke 6:31), which, however, is not presented in the NT as a synopsis of the commandments.

Rabbinic tradition also holds the view that the biblical characters summarized or reduced the commandments of the HB: "David came and reduced them to ten [Psalm 15]. . . . Isaiah came and reduced them to six [Isa 33:15]. . . . Micah came and reduced them to three [Mic 6:8]. . . . Habakkuk came and reduced them to one" [Hab 2:8] (*b. Mak.* 24a).

Although in general early Christians believed that the cultic and purity laws of the HB were superseded in the Christian era, the Decalogue, with the exception of the sabbath law, was considered obligatory. Paul had written that "when Gentiles who have not the law do by nature what the law requires, they are a law to themselves" (Rom 2:14). Thus the Decalogue came to be viewed as a manifestation of this natural law.

The second-century Valentinian Gnostic Ptolemy, in his *Letter to Flora* (preserved in Epiphanias's *Panarion* 33), argued, on the basis of his exegesis of sayings of Jesus, that only the Decalogue was given by the absolute God: "God's law in its pure form, unentangled with the inferior, is the Decalogue. . . . Although they present the legislation in a pure form they need completion by the Savior since they did not possess perfection" (33.5.3). The other laws were attributed to Moses and the elders and were abolished by Christ. Ptolemy considered laws that require vengeance and retribution to be unjust.

Some Christians even allegorized the Ten Commandments. For example, CLEMENT OF ALEXANDRIA in his *Stromata* (6.133-48) considered the prohibition against murder to refer to the destruction of true knowledge. In his more elementary *Paedagogos* (3.89), however, he stated that they needed no allegorization.

In the early medieval period rabbinic authorities developed the theory that there were 613 commandments in the HB: "Three hundred and sixty-five of them are negative commandments, like the number of days of the solar year, and two hundred and forty-eight are positive commandments, corresponding to the parts of the human body" (*b. Mak.* 23b). Homiletically it was argued that each part of the body requested its use to keep the commandments and each day asked that it not be used to transgress a commandment. The 613 commandments were traced to the numerical value of the word *Torah* (TWRH = 400 + 6 + 200 + 5 = 611), given by Moses, plus the first two commandments in the Decalogue, spoken by God directly.

SAADIA, apparently independently of Philo, developed in his liturgical poem *Azharot* the idea that all 613 commandments are embodied in the Decalogue. He assumed that the entire body of laws had been spun out of the Ten Commandments. Although earlier rabbis had hesitated to emphasize the laws of the Decalogue over the other commandments, later, more philosophically oriented medieval Jewish thinkers generally were less hesitant to follow this idea.

In the eleventh century, in the *Bereshit Rabbati,* produced by or in circles associated with R. Moses ha-Darshan, the number of commandments was associated with the number of consonantal letters in the Exodus pericope enumerating the Decalogue: "The Tablets encompassed the 613 commandments, corresponding to the 613 letters from *'ānōkî* [I; the first word of the Decalogue] to *rē'eka* [your neighbor; the last word of the Decalogue], no more, no less" (quoted by Sarfatti in Segal, 389). Although MAIMONIDES expounded the 613 commandments, he clearly argued against any privileged status of one law over another—that is, against considering some laws, e.g., the Decalogue, as essential and others as peripheral.

Medieval Christian thinkers tended to expound the Ten Commandments as manifestations of natural law. THOMAS AQUINAS divided the "old law" into *moralia, ceremonialia,* and *judicialia,* identifying the Decalogue as the former—moral rules that reason could discover to be necessary and timeless. The remaining regulations are either ritual-ceremonial or civic, with the latter being local, specific to a particular culture, and belonging to specific circumstances of time. In his *Summa Theologiae* (Ia2ae, Question 100), Thomas formulated his position to refute arguments that the Decalogue merely represented a collection of taboos or tribal customs and was relative rather than absolute (see 29:56-111 in the Blackfriars ed.).

Most medieval Christian theologians discussed the Decalogue, frequently offering very spiritualized and broad applications. L. Smith has surveyed several treatments in her dissertation (1986; in addition, see the discussions by R. Rolle in R. Allen [1988] and by Gregory Palmas [1296–1359] in S. Mouselimas [1980]).

In the fourteenth and fifteenth centuries the Decalogue came to play an important role in lay handbooks of spiritual guidance and in confessional works. Examples of such handbooks are the *Lay Folk's Catechism* attributed to J. Thoresby (d. 1373), archbishop of York; *Les fleurs des commandments* (c. 1490); and J. GERSON's *ABC des simple sens.* The Reformers placed the Decalogue in most of their catechisms, and some popular booklets associated the commandments with particular biblical narratives, illustrating them with woodcuts.

In the sixteenth century diverse attitudes toward the Decalogue and the laws of the HB developed. LUTHER primarily saw the law as making sin manifest and driving the conscience toward grace. This emphasis can be seen in his commentary on Gal 3:19 and 4:3. In his *How Christians Should Regard Moses* (1525), he argued that the "law of Moses . . . is no longer binding of us because it was given only to the people of Israel . . . even The Ten Commandments do not pertain to us" (*Luther's Works* 35 [1960] 164-65). In his preface to the Pentateuch he wrote, "When Christ comes the law ceases. . . . The Ten Commandments also cease, not in the sense that they are no longer to be kept or fulfilled, but in the sense that the office of Moses [to produce a sense of sin and to drive one to God's mercy] in them ceases" (ibid., 244).

CALVIN was much more positive toward the laws of the HB and toward the Decalogue than Luther was. His classical discussion of the topic is found in his *Institutes of the Christian Religion* (bk. 2, chaps. 7–8). In chapter 7 he outlined what came to be designated the threefold use of the law, which was also expounded by P. MELANCHTHON in the 1535 edition of his *Loci communes,* by J. BULLINGER in his *Decades* (ET 1577), and by numerous Anglican divines. This theory argues that the law has a civil use, applying to all, Christian and non-Christian alike; a pedagogical use, leading sinners to recognize their hopelessly sinful state and to throw themselves upon God's mercy; and a didactic use, teaching even those saved by Christ's sacrifice and forgiveness restraint from vice and from yielding to never-ending temptation. In Calvin the third was the principal use since through it even the Christian gains a surer knowledge of the Lord's will and is exhorted and aroused to obedience (*Institutes* 2.7.12).

The mainline Protestant Reformers found themselves combating radical elements at the periphery of their movement: libertines and segments of the ANABAPTISTS who held that Hebrew law and even the Decalogue were no longer binding. For a time this antinomian movement's most articulate spokesperson was J. AGRICOLA (1527–40). Antinomianism was taken up by many of the spiritualist groups within the radical Reformation.

Four additional factors should be noted about Calvin's important interpretation: (1) His lucid exposition of the Decalogue and of HB moral law as a specially granted restatement of natural law, or as the law engraved upon the heart, prepared the way for later humanists and for Deists (see DEISM) to stress the priority of natural law and religion over any form of revelatory law and religion and even to deny the necessity of the latter. (2) He stressed that the first tablet of the Decalogue contained commandments one to four, expressing duties toward God; and the second tablet, commandments six to ten, duties toward other humans. Thus the command to honor parents belonged to the second tablet. (3) In his exposition of the laws in Exodus–Deuteronomy, he related all of them to one or the other of the Ten Commandments. His commentary on these books took the form of a Mosaic harmony (1563; ET, 4 vols., 1852–55; for a summary, see T. Parker [1986] 122-75). (4) He argued that a moral commandment always implied and required its opposite counterpart (*Institutes* 2.8.8-9). "The commandment, 'You shall not kill' . . . contains . . . the requirement that we give our neighbor's life all the help we can."

Even prior to the rise of historical criticism, a wide diversity in the interpretations of the individual commandments existed. The following represent some of the most disputed.

The prohibition against images was understood in Judaism as prohibiting any representation of God or of any god, but not artistic decoration in general. Protestants protested against artistic practices in Roman Catholic and Orthodox iconography, with Calvinism and the radical Reformation being more iconoclastic than Lutheranism. Discussing this commandment, Calvin wrote: "Whatever visible forms of God man devises are diametrically opposed to his nature . . . as soon as idols appear, true religion is corrupted and adulterated" (*Institutes* 2.8.17; see 1.11.2, 12).

The prohibition against vain use of the divine name was generally understood in Judaism as referring to swearing falsely, frivolously, or superfluously (Philo *On the Decalogue* 84-91; *b. Ber.* 33a). Many Anabaptists, on the basis of Jesus' statement, "Do not swear at all" (Matt 5:34; see Jas 5:12), refused to swear oaths in any forms. G. Fox (1624–91) and others followed this practice.

The sabbath command with different motivational clauses (cf. Exod 20:11 with Deut 5:15) was understood in Judaism as commanding a day of rest (further elaborated in the Mishnaic tractate *Šabbat*) but also six days of work. The day is not declared a day of worship in the HB. Early Christians celebrated the first day of the week (Sunday) as the Lord's day and a time of assembly (Acts 20:7; 1 Cor 16:2). Sunday as a day of rest was enjoined in 306 at the Council of Elvira, and in 321 it was promulgated by Constantine and subsequently regulated in the church. The sabbath commandment was understood by Augustine as an adumbration of spiritual and heavenly rest (see, e.g., his *Letters* 55.9.17 in FC 12.274). Calvin saw the sabbath as foreshadowing spiritual rest. Its ceremonial aspects were abolished: "To overthrow superstition, the day sacred to the Jews was set aside" (*Institutes* 2.8.33). A strict "sabbathianism" in observing Sunday was advocated by neither Calvin nor Luther but was primarily an English and American Puritan phenomenon (see N. Bound, *True Doctrine of the Sabbath* [1595] and James I, *Books of Sports* [1618]). S. McGee (1976) has argued that two opposed interpretations of the laws of the Decalogue, e.g., the sabbath commandment, marked the two sides of the English civil war.

The commandment enjoining honor to parents, considered part of the first tablet in Judaism, was related to parental creativity, which parallels that of the divine. R. Simeon ben Yohai noted: "The three of them—God, one's father and one's mother—are partners in every person" (quoted by Greenberg in Segal, 104). Philo wrote of parents standing between the mortal and the immortal: "Parents copy His nature by begetting particular persons" and "the act of generation assimilates them to God, the generator of the All" (*On the Decalogue* 51, 107). Christian tradition, which associated this command with the second tablet, tended to extend its coverage to all in authority, priest, bishop, and pope (Roman Catholic) as well as princely ruler (stressed by Lutherans), or magistrates (especially favorite authorities for Calvin and the Reformed). Anabaptist and other radical Reformers, like PARACELSUS, took the narrowest meaning in the interest of generally rejecting civil and ecclesiastical government and expressing a hope for the emergence of a kingdom of God on the moral basis of Christ's teachings in the SERMON ON THE MOUNT.

The commandment against killing has historically been related to the category of premeditated murder, excluding execution of criminals condemned by trial in courts of law, killing in self-defense or by accident, and killing by soldiers in times of war. Calvin read into it the positive—"concern oneself with the safety of all"—and extended it—"all violence, injury, and any harmful thing at all that may injure our neighbor's body are forbidden to us" (*Institutes* 2.8.39). Pacifists, like Paracelsus, have argued for as broad an application of the prohibition as possible, including opposition to capital punishment.

The prohibition of adultery was generally understood in antiquity as prohibiting sex with a married or betrothed female. Philo devoted a long discussion to the damage done to society from the violation of this commandment (*On the Decalogue* 121-31). Although RASHI, commenting on this text, declared that "adultery is only with another man's wife," other Jewish interpreters, like A. IBN EZRA, extended the prohibition to include other forms of sexual activity. The medieval church interpreted the command to include all forms of *luxuria* (see Matt 5:27-28). Calvin concluded that "any union apart from marriage is accursed in his sight" (*Institute* 2.8.41). The Reformers generally argued that each man ought to take one wife and that none are to remain virgins as a vocation, the latter in contrast to Roman Catholicism.

The prohibition against stealing was understood by early Jewish rabbis as prohibiting kidnapping, the theft of persons, a conclusion arrived at on the basis of context: "And what is the context here? It is persons. Consequently, this commandment, too, deals with persons" (*b. Sanh.* 86a). This view has been adopted by some modern scholars (A. Alt, *KS* 1 [1953] 330-40; A. Phillips [1970] 130). The more general interpretation sees this command as prohibiting taking property by stealth and thus as defending the right of private property.

Although the commandment against false witness originally applied to preserving the integrity of the judicial process, it was quickly applied to lying in general.

Perhaps the most controversial of all the commandments is the one concerning covetousness (Exod 20:17 and Deut 5:21 are divided into two commandments in the Roman Catholic and Lutheran traditions, perhaps because of the "and" at the beginning of Deut. 5:22 and the introduction of a new verb, "desire/crave"). The main issue concerns whether the commandment forbids internal envious desire or whether it prohibits calculation and taking steps to acquire the object of one's desire—"anything that is your neighbor's" (for the issues see A. Rofé, "The Tenth Commandment in the Light of Four Deuteronomic Laws," in Segal, 45-65). Numerous rabbinical statements as well as Maimonides reflect the latter position. In discussing prohibitions 265 and 266 he wrote that "developing stratagems" and "devising a scheme" were prohibited. Levi ben Gershon concluded that "one does not violate the prohibition if one does not actually do something in order to obtain the coveted object" (quoted by Greenberg in Segal, 107). Philo (*On the Decalogue* 142-53) understood the prohibition as forbidding appetite and desire in general, seeing the idea as one of the issues behind the dietary laws. Christian tradition, relying on Jesus' teaching in the Sermon on the Mount, has applied this commandment to internal dispositions. Following Augustine, Calvin argued that "God commands us to keep the possessions of others untouched and safe, not only from injury or the wish to defraud, but even from the slightest covetousness that may trouble our hearts" (*Institutes* 2.8.50). In the eighteenth and nineteenth centuries some Jewish and Christian interpreters advocated the older rabbinic

position (see A. Rofé in Segal, 46-50), but many continued to argue that it concerns "a state of mind" (M. Weinfeld [1995] 9) and "aims to prevent the flagrantly evil acts enumerated in the preceding Commandments, by mastering those impulses which drive people to commit such acts" (Greenberg in Segal, 109; see B. Jackson [1971]).

The rise of the historical-critical approach to the Bible produced far-ranging changes in the treatment of the Decalogue. In 1772 the young J. Goethe (1749–1832) proposed that the original Decalogue was not to be found in Exod 20:2-17 or in Deut 5:6-21 but rather in Exod 34:14-26. His arguments were based on the fact that reference to the ten words occurs in Exod 34:28 but not in Exodus 20 and that the cultic interests of Exod 34:14-26 probably more correctly indicate the concerns of the early Israelites than do the other two texts. A similar view was advanced independently by F. HITZIG in 1838 and since then has been advocated by many scholars, especially under the influence of J. WELLHAUSEN. Those supporting the latter position also argued that the traditional Decalogue presupposes a settled, agricultural life-style, not the nomadic desert conditions of Mosaic times, and that its high ethical ideals were probably produced under the influence of the prophets (see PROPHECY AND PROPHETS, HB).

Historical-critical scholarship has given primary attention to three interrelated issues: the date and origin of the Decalogue, its original form and content, and its use and influence in ancient Israel. Four arguments were addressed that supposedly indicated that the MT form of the Decalogue was not original: (1) the mixture of positive and negative commands; (2) the presence of motive clauses in some commandments but not in others; (3) the different motivations for observing the sabbath (cf. Exod 20:11, with its cosmic, creation rationale, with Deut 5:14-15 and its humanitarian and salvation-history rationales); and (4) the shift from direct divine speech in the first two commands to indirect speech in the remainder. Assuming a uniformity in style and brevity in expression (the Decalogue is called "ten words" not "ten commandments"), scholars have made various attempts to reconstruct an original form generally containing all negative statements (see H. Rowley [1952]; E. Nielsen [1968]; W. Harrelson [1980, rev. ed. 1997]). Most of these reconstructions are highly similar (see Weinfeld, 5-7, for a combination of negative and positive commands).

Proposed datings for the reconstructed Decalogue range from the Mosaic period to very late in First Temple times or even in the Second Temple period. In his *History of Israel* (1938) T. ROBINSON, arguing for an early date, wrote: "The moral code in Exodus xx is timeless, and its provisions are valid for any condition of organized human society. There is, then, nothing in the code itself to prevent its having been promulgated by Moses, especially if the first few commandments are reduced to a simpler form" (96). Interpreters who assign an early date generally argue that the other laws were influenced by those in the Decalogue. Those advocating a late date tend to view the Decalogue as the summation rather than as the source of other biblical laws. Most scholars today view both versions of the Decalogue as late, probably postexilic, and as having been placed in their present position during the editing process. Some interpreters have argued that the laws of Deuteronomy 12–26 are structured to follow and elaborate on the stipulations of the Decalogue.

New impetus to the study of the Decalogue's origin was made by S. MOWINCKEL, who argued in his 1927 work that it originated and was used in worship services. Drawing on the so-called entry liturgies in Psalms 15 and 24 and on allusions to the Decalogue in Psalms 50 and 81, he suggested that it was used as part of a covenant renewal service in the annual fall festival of Sukkot (Tabernacles). Other scholars have also associated the Decalogue with worship; e.g., Weinfeld associates it with the spring festival of Shavuot (Weeks/Pentecost; see Weinfeld, 34-44 and J. Stamm and M. Andrews [1967] 22-75).

The form of the commandments in the Decalogue, apodictic without any accompanying consequence stipulation, was explored by A. ALT in a 1934 article (79-132). He distinguished this form of law from casuistic law, the latter characterized by its conditional style and accompanying stipulation of consequence ("if . . . then. . . . "). Alt argued that the apodictic laws, and thus the Decalogue, were genuine Israelite law, not adopted from the Canaanites, and were primarily at home in the sphere of worship rather than in the judicial arena.

The study of ancient Near Eastern treaties, especially Hittite treaties (see HITTITOLOGY AND BIBLICAL STUDIES), first widely developed in the 1950s by G. MENDENHALL, led to new arguments about the Decalogue. These treaties (see M. Barré, *ABD* 6:653-56) contained preambles, stipulations, references to divine witnesses, and curses (sometimes blessings also) pronounced on the violator. Mendenhall argued that the Decalogue represents the stipulations of the treaty/covenant between God and Israel. And since the Hittite treaties dated from the fifteenth to the fourteenth centuries, then the biblical treaty form and the Decalogue could date from the era of Moses. More recent investigations have raised questions about the comparison of the Decalogue to treaty stipulations and have concluded that ancient Near Eastern treaty material influenced biblical texts the most in the eighth and seventh centuries BCE.

The distinctive nature and simplistic character of apodictic law advocated by Alt and the connection of the Decalogue with treaty stipulations and/or worship was challenged by Gerstenberger, who connected "the prohibitive form" with the life of the clan and the family. Today no single position about the Decalogue has complete support. C. Carmichael (1985) has even argued that laws in the HB, including those in the Decalogue, are primarily the product of deductions drawn from biblical narratives.

Several characteristics of the Ten Commandments have given them an appeal beyond the confines of synagogue and church: " 'categorical imperatives' universally applicable, timeless, not dependent on any circumstances whatever . . . couched in the second person singular . . . addressed personally to each individual. . . . " (Weinfeld, 8, 10). Commandments five to ten resonate with universally recognized virtues. The Enlightenment rationalist I. KANT developed his own categorical imperative, one form of which was "so act that the rule of your act can be law universal." The utilitarians J. Bentham (1748–1832) and J. S. Mill (1806–73) hypothesized that the right act is that done for the greatest pleasure and the least pain. Harrelson has shown that the Decalogue can be related to the issue of human rights. G. Anscombe (1958) has explored the fact that secular thought has inherited in its deontology a sense of the "ought" ("thou shalt . . . thou shalt not") in its statement of duties but has rejected the theological context of revelation and tradition presupposed by the Decalogue. She questions whether methods of modern ethics can derive the "ought" from other than a divine command. If not, something like the Decalogue seems irreplaceable.

Bibliography: **R. S. Allen** (ed. and tr.), *R. Rolle: The English Writings* (ClWS, 1988) 86-89, 143-51. **A. Alt**, *Essays on OT History and Religion* (1966). **G. E. M. Anscombe**, "Modern Moral Philosophy," *Philosophy* 33 (1958) 1-19. **J. Blenkinsopp**, *Wisdom and Law in the OT: The Ordering of Life in Israel and Early Judaism* (Oxford Bible Series, 1983). **G. Bourgeault**, *Décalogue et morale chrétienne* (Recherches 2, 1971). **R. Brooks**, *The Spirit of the Ten Commandments: Shattering the Myth of Rabbinic Legalism* (1990). **E. Brunner**, *The Divine Imperative: A Study in Christian Ethics* (1937). **M. Buber**, *Moses* (1946). **C. M. Carmichael**, *Law and Narrative in the Bible: The Evidence of the Deuteronomic Laws and the Decalogue* (1985). **P. Delhaye**, *Le Décalogue et sa place dans la morale chrétienne* (1963²). **E. Dublanchy**, "Decalogue," *DTC* 4 (1911) 161-76. **S. Goldman**, *The Ten Commandments* (1963²). **R. M. Grant**, "The Decalogue in Early Christianity," *HTR* 40 (1967) 1-17. **W. Harrelson**, *The Ten Commandments and Human Rights* (1980, rev. ed., 1997). **D. Hartman**, *A Living Covenant: The Innovative Spirit in Traditional Judaism* (1985). **B. Jackson**, "Liability for Mere Intention in Early Jewish Law," *HUCA* 42 (1971) 197-225. **M. M. Kaplan**, *The Ten Commandments Today* (n.d.). **S. McGee**, *The Godly Man in Stuart England: Anglicans, Puritans, and the Two Tablets, 1620–70* (1976). **M. Maimonides**, *The Commandments: "Sefer Ha-Mitvoth" of Maimonides* (1967). **C. H. Moehlman**, *The Story of the Ten Commandments: A Study of the Hebrew Decalogue in Its Ancient and Modern Application* (1928). **S.**

Mouselimas, "Saint Gregory Palamas' *The Decalogue of the Law According to Christ, That Is, the New Covenant*," *GOTR* 25 (1980) 297-305. **S. Mowinckel,** *Le Décalogue* (EHPhR 16, 27). **E. Nielsen,** *The Ten Commandments in New Perspective: A Traditio-historical Approach* (SBT 2, 7, 1968). **T. H. L. Parker,** *Calvin's OT Commentaries* (1986). **J. Pelikan,** *Spirit Versus Structure: Luther and the Institutions of the Church* (1968). **L. Perlitt et al.,** *TRE* 8 (1981) 408-30. **A. C. J. Phillips,** *Ancient Israel's Criminal Law: A New Approach to the Decalogue* (1970). **J. Plaskow,** *Standing Again at Sinai: Judaism from a Feminist Perspective* (1990). **E. M. Poteat,** *Mandate to Humanity: An Inquiry into the History and Meaning of the Ten Commandments and Their Relation to Contemporary Culture* (1953). **H. A. Roetlisberger,** "The Decalogue in Catechetical Teaching of the Church" (diss., University of Edinburgh, 1962). **W. Rordorf,** "Beobachtungen zum Gebrauch des Dekalogs in der vorkonstatinisches Kirche," *The NT Age: Essays in Honor of B. Reicke* (1984) 437-92. **H. H. Rowley,** "Moses and the Decalogue," *BJRL* 32 (1952) 81-118 = his *Men of God: Studies in OT History and Prophecy* (1963) 1-36. **R. J. Rushdoony,** *The Institutes of Biblical Law: A Chalcedon Study* (1973). **W. H. Schmidt,** *Die Zehn Gebote im Rahmen alttestamentlicher Ethik* (EdF 281, 1993), with bibliography, 151-72. **M. S. Seale,** *Qur'an and Bible: Studies in Interpretation and Dialogue* (1978). **B. Z. Segal** (ed.), *The Ten Commandments in History and Tradition* (ET 1990). **L. J. Smith,** "Academic Commentaries on the Ten Commandments (c. 1150–c. 1279)" (diss., Oxford University, 1986). **J. J. Stamm and M. E. Andrews,** *The Ten Commandments in Recent Research* (SBT 2, 2, 1967). **D. C. Steinmetz,** "The Reformation and the Ten Commandments," *Int* 43 (1989) 256-66. **G. Stemberger,** "Der Dekalog im frühen Judentum," *JBTh* 4 (1989) 91-103. **A. R. Vidler,** *Christ's Strange Work* (1944). **F. E. Vokes,** "The Ten Commandments in the NT and in First-century Judaism," *StEv* 5 (TU 103, ed. F. L. Cross, 1968) 146-54. **M. Weinfeld,** *Social Justice in Ancient Israel and in the Ancient Near East* (1995). **I. Wise,** "The Law," *The Hebrew Review* 1 (1886) 12-31. **J. Witte, Jr. and T. C. Arthur,** "The Three Uses of the Law: A Protestant Source of the Purposes of Criminal Punishment?" *JLR* 19 (1993–94) 433-65. **D. Wright,** "The Ethical Use of the OT in Luther and Calvin: A Comparison," *SJT* 36 (1983) 463-85.

P. G. KUNTZ

DE DIEU, LOUIS (1590–1642)

Born at Vliessingen, Apr. 7, 1590, the son of a Reformed clergyman, D. was placed at an early age under the care of an uncle, D. Colonius, regent of the Walloon College at Leiden. After showing proficiency in theological studies, D. served churches in Middleburg (1615), Vliessingen (1617), and finally at Leiden (from 1619). He died Dec. 22, 1642.

An outstanding orientalist, D. enjoyed a significant reputation in his day and contributed to the establishment of linguistic-philological study in the Netherlands. In addition to the publication of several grammatical studies (on Hebrew, Syriac, Aramaic, and Persian), he published the Syriac version of Revelation (missing from the *Peshitta*) and prepared and saw through the press E. POCOCKE's Syriac edition of some of the catholic epistles. He translated into Latin the histories of Christ and Peter from the Persian translation of the Portuguese. These histories, prepared by the Jesuit Spanish missionary H. Xavier at the request of Akbar, the Mogul emperor of India (1542–1602), combined eccentric-syncretistic versions of these figures, drawing upon biblical and apocryphal texts (see APOCRYPHA, NT). D.'s *animadversiones* (or annotations) on the HB and the NT offered not only philological notes on the texts but also a comparison of the various ancient and Latin translations critiquing the latter, especially T. BEZA's translation of the NT, using the former to examine the nature of the text and as a means of elucidating it.

Works: *Compendium grammaticae Hebraicae* (1626); *Apocalypsis S. Johannis ex manuscripto exemplair e bibliotheca . . . Jos. Scaligeri deprompto, edita charactere Syro et Ebraeo, cum versione Latina, Graeco textu et notis* (1627); *Grammatica trilinguis, Hebraica, Syriaca, et Chaldaica* (1628); *Animadversiones, sive commentarius in quatuor Evangelia, in quo collatis, Syri imprimis, Arabis, Evangelii Hebraei, Vulgati, Erasmi et Beza versionibus, difficilia loca illustrantur et variae lectiones conferuntur* (1631); *Animadversiones in Acta Apostoloum. . . .* (1634); *Historia Christi Persice conscripta . . . Historia S. Petri, Persice conscripta* (1639); *Rudimenta linquae Persicae* (1639); *Animadversiones ad loca quaedam difficiliora Veteris Testamenti* (1646); *Animadversiones in epistolam ad Romanos. . . .* (1646); *Critica sacra, sive animadversiones in loca quaedam difficiliora Veteris et Novi Testamenti* (ed. Leydecker, 1693).

Bibliography: H. J. de Jonge, "The Study of the NT," *Leiden University in the Seventeenth Century* (ed. T. H. Lunsingh Scheurleer and G. H. M. Posthumus Meyjes, 1975) 64-109, esp. 72-75; *De bestudering van het Nieuwe Testament aan de Noordnerderlandse universiteiten en het Remonstrants Seminaire van 1575 tot 1700* (1980) see index. **J. Le Clerc,** "L. de Dieu, *Critica sacra*," *BUH* 25 (1693) 281-301. **G. W. Meyer,** *Geschichte der Schrifterklärung* 3 (1804) 414-16. *MSHH* 15 (1731) 88-95. **G. H. M. Posthumus Meyjes,** *Geschiedenis van het Waalse College te Leiden (1606–99)* (1975) 78-97.

J. H. HAYES

DEISM

l. General Character of the Movement. Deism is a European movement with elusive origins and indistinct contours (E. Troeltsch [1925] 429). Its adherents were convinced that a "natural religion" preceded all revelatory religions. This natural religion consisted of a minimal confession (that God exists and must be worshiped) and exclusively moral commandments sufficing to render access to eternal salvation if followed. These principles continued the inheritance of the Stoics of antiquity, already renewed by the Renaissance humanists, and were complemented by an element of spiritualism expressed in criticism of cultic institutions ("ceremonies," priesthood). Specific revelation was rejected only by the most radical French representatives of Deism, e.g., VOLTAIRE, P. d'Holbach (1723–89), and D. Diderot (1713–84). Above all, English Deists defended a dogmatically minimalized, morally conceived Christianity that is identical with natural religion (J. Locke: the confession "that Jesus be the Messiah" suffices). The idea of tolerance—though, significantly, excluding Roman Catholics—was also widespread among Deists, as it had been among the earlier humanists.

2. History. The term *Deists* was originally the self-appellation of a group with whose representatives the Geneva Reformed theologian P. Viret (1511–71) became acquainted in southern France in 1561–63. However, Viret gave an unclear picture of their doctrines (see G. Gawlick [1841] VIII-X). Things became clearer in the work of E. HERBERT, Lord of Cherbury, generally considered the "father of Deism." In his principal work, *De Veritate,* first published in 1624, he developed a eudaemonistic-moral theory of religion on the basis of the Stoic doctrine of ideas inborn within all human beings (*ideae innatae* or *notitiae communes*), ideas whose content as regards religion is the existence of God, the obligation to worship or honor God by means of moral action, and the prospect of reward and punishment in the beyond.

Deists of the "golden age" of Deism in England were bequeathed a modern theory of cognition (with an empirical foundation) by J. LOCKE, who stood in proximity to the Latitudinarians and designated reason as the source of religious knowledge. While C. BLOUNT adhered to the ideas of Herbert, Locke's pupils included J. TOLAND, A. COLLINS, and M. TINDAL. A popularized form of Deism was espoused by T. CHUBB and H. BOLINGBROKE. This golden age of English Deism lasted until about 1740. Its demise was significantly hastened by the skepticism of D. HUME, which destroyed the grounding of natural religion within reason.

While Deism in France developed more and more into atheistic materialism, the Deist position in Germany was represented once more in classical form by H. S. REIMARUS, whose *Schutzschrift* summarized all the arguments of his predecessors and developed them further with his own views. In the United States, Deism had a final, influential adherent in T. PAINE.

3. Understanding of the Bible. The English Deists' biblical criticism was prompted above all by the theology of the Anglican state church of the Restoration period, which grounded ecclesiastical and civil order on passages in the Bible, especially the HB. In contrast, the Deists—who generally supported the Whigs politically—

tried to diminish the significance of the Bible. Initial steps in this direction can already be found in Herbert's assertion that "correct reason" must decide where in the holy Scriptures one finds the Word of God and where merely human words (*Religio Laici,* in *De Veritate* [1645] 134; cf. *Dialogue* [1768] 7 ff., 104). One also encounters moral criticism of the HB in Herbert.

An indirect criticism of biblical miracles is found in Blount's commentary and translation of the first two books of the work of Philostratos on the miracle worker from antiquity, Appollonius of Tyana (1680). In contrast, most other Deists agreed with the apologetic attitude in Toland's *Christianity not Mysterious* (1696) in which, on the basis of Locke's concept of reason, he claimed that the Gospels contain nothing contradictory to reason. All doctrines and commandments of the NT agree with reason, Toland maintained; one encounters nothing there that exceeds reason or that is mysterious. Neither can miracles contradict reason, although they are recognized as extraordinary events. On the other hand, sacrifices, ceremonies, and other mysteries have penetrated the depraved Christianity of the present only in the course of church history and in opposition to the simple message of JESUS. Elsewhere (*Origines Judaicae* [1709]) Toland considered the original Mosaic religion to be a pure primitive religion; sacrifices and ceremonies entered only later and as God's punishment (Ezek 20:24-25).

The contribution of A. Collins is important above all in the debate over prophecies (see PROPHECY AND PROPHETS, HB). H. GROTIUS had already shown that those HB passages understood by the NT as prophecies pointing toward Christ (e.g., Isa 7:14) actually refer to contemporary persons and events. W. WHISTON (1722) then maintained that the present HB text had been falsified by rabbis in order to expurgate prophecies that earlier had been unequivocal. Collins (*Discourse* [1724]; cf. *Scheme*) rejected this thesis and asserted that the wording of the HB prophecies does refer to contemporary events and that only an allegorical understanding can rescue the NT proofs.

A debate over miracles followed the one over prophecies. It was prompted by the apologete T. WOOLSTON, who denied the miracle stories in the Gospels and declared them rationally impossible, at the same time rescuing them in a mystical-allegorical sense. P. ANNET argued against the actuality of the central miracle of resurrection; for him, historical faith and true religion were absolute antitheses.

In his main work (1730) Tindal affirmed that natural religion (which is commensurate with reason, ethically oriented, and accessible to all) suffices; Christian revelation is merely its renewal. The Bible's significance derives only from the divine commandments it contains. It is difficult, however, to understand, and its figures are morally repugnant, particularly in the HB. Even Jesus' commandments can be validated solely by their agreement with the laws of nature.

In contrast, Chubb considered it self-evident that the "laws of Christ" are the foundation of life for Christians. His distinction between the teachings of Jesus and theological statements about Jesus is important. The latter are exemplified by what we find in John and PAUL, particularly concerning the Son of God, the Trinity, and Christ's representative suffering and death, which are unworthy of any moral conception of God.

T. MORGAN rejected the HB, both of the ceremonial law and of the moral law of Moses, and criticized the morality of its leading figures (1738–40). Yahweh was merely a local national God, and natural explanations can be offered for miracles described in the text. Whereas Morgan rejected the HB as a witness of historical religion, he declared Christianity to be identical with natural religion.

The English Deists did not create any encompassing system of interpretation. Usually proceeding from the thesis that true Christianity is identical with natural religion, they criticized the current proofs of historical religion, the cult, and morally repugnant elements in the Bible. They generally wanted to rescue a purified (morally interpreted) NT. Reimarus, who published a Deist system of religion with his "foremost truths," summarized all the arguments criticizing the Bible (1972). He demanded much more consistently than the English Deists a purely historical interpretation of the HB (rejecting mystical understandings of Scripture), distinguished the teachings of Jesus from those of the Gospel writers, rejected prophecies and miracles, and criticized Paul for his doctrine of sin and justification. On the basis of biblical criticism he rejected any biblically grounded Christianity for the sake of a religion of reason.

Bibliography: P. **Annet,** *The Resurrection of Jesus Considered* (1744³). C. **Blount,** *The Two First Books of Philostratus, Concerning the Life of Appolonius Tyanaeus* (1680). P. **Byrne,** *Natural Religion and the Nature of Religion: The Legacy of Deism* (Routledge Religions Studies, 1989). T. **Chubb,** *A Collection of Tracts on Various Subjects* (1730); *The True Gospel of Jesus Christ Asserted* (1738); *Posthumous Works* (2 vols., 1748). A. **Collins,** *A Discourse of Free-Thinking* (1713, repr. 1965); *A Discourse of the Grounds and Reasons of the Christian Religion* (1724); *The Scheme of Literal Prophecy Considered* (1727). E. **Feil,** "Die Deisten als Gegner der Trinität: Zur ursprünglichen und speziellen Verwendung des Begriffs 'Deistae' für die Sozinianer," *ABG* 33 (1992) 115-124. M. **Fontius,** "Deismus," *Philosophisches Wörterbuch*¹¹ 1 (1975) 253-56. G. **Gawlick,** "Vorwort," *Geschichte des englischen Deismus* (G. W. Lechler, 1841; repr. 1965) V-XXXIX; "Deismus," *HWP* 2 (1972) 44-47; "Der Deismus als Grundzug der Religionsphilosophie der Aufklärung," *H. S. Reimarus (1694–1768), ein "bekannter Un-*

bekannter" der Aufklärung in Hamburg (1973) 15-43. C. **Gestrich,** "Deismus," *TRE* 8 (1981) 392-406. E. **Herbert,** *De Veritate. Ed. Tertia. De Causis Errorum. De Religione Laici. Parerga.* (1645, repr. 1966); *De Religione Gentilium errorumque apud eos causis* (1663, repr. 1967); *A Dialogue Between a Tutor and His Pupil* (1768, repr. 1971). E. **Hirsch,** *000Geschichte der neueren evangelischen Theologie* 1 (1975⁵). G. W. **Lechler,** *Geschichte des englischen Deismus* (1841, repr. 1965). J. **Leland,** *A View of the Principal Deistical Writers* (3 vols., 1755–57, repr. 1978). F. E. **Manuel,** "Deism," *Encyclopaedia Britannica* (1974) 5:561-63. G. **Mensching, I. T. Ramsey, M. Schmidt,** "Deismus," *RGG*³ 2 (1958) 57-69. T. **Morgan,** *The Moral Philosopher* (3 vols., 1738–40, repr. 1969). C. **Motzo Dentice di Accadia,** *Preilluminismo e deismo in Inghilterra* (1970). J. **Orr,** *English Deism: Its Roots and Fruits* (1934). W. **Philipp,** *Das Werden der Aufklärung in theologiegeschichtlicher Sicht* (FSThR 3, 1957). J. **Redwood,** *Reason, Ridicule, and Religion: The Age of Enlightenment in England, l660–1750* (1976). H. S. **Reimarus,** *Die vornehmsten Wahrheiten der natürlichen Religion* (2 vols., 1766³, repr. 1985); *Apologie oder Schutzschrift für die vernünftigen Verehrer Gottes* (1972). H. G. **Reventlow,** "Das Arsenal der Bibelkritik des Reimarus: Die Auslegung der Bibel . . . bei den englischen Deisten," *Hermann Samuel Reimarus* (1973) 44-65; *The Authority of the Bible and the Rise of the Modern World* (1980; ET 1984). M. **Sina,** *L'avvento della ragione: "Reason" e "above Reason" dal razionalismo teologico inglese al deismo* (Scienze filosofiche 14, 1976). R. N. **Stromberg,** *Religious Liberalism in Eighteenth-century England* (1954). R. E. **Sullivan,** *J. Toland and the Deist Controversy* (HHS 101, 1982). M. **Tindal,** *Christianity as Old as the Creation* (1730, repr. 1967). J. **Toland,** *Christianity Not Mysterious* (1696, repr. 1964); *Dissertationes Duae, Adeisidaemon et Oriqines Judaicae* (1709, repr. 1970). N. L. **Torrey,** *Voltaire and the English Deists* (1930). E. **Troeltsch,** "Deismus," *RE*³ (1898) 4:532-59 = *Gesammelte Schriften* 4 (1925) 429-87. J. **Tulloch,** *Rational Theology and Christian Philosophy in England in the Seventeenth Century* (2 vols., 1874², repr. 1966). P. **Viret,** *Instruction chrestienne en la doctrine de la loy et l'evangile* (1564). W. **Whiston,** *An Essay Towards Restoring the True Text of the OT* (1722).

H. G. REVENTLOW

DEISSMANN, ADOLF (1866–1937)

Born in 1866 in Langenscheid (Nassau), Germany, D. studied at the universities of Tübingen and Berlin and at the Lutheran seminaries of Herborn and Marburg. In 1892 he was appointed *Privatdozent* at Marburg (in NT), later as pastor and instructor in the theological seminar at Herborn. In 1897 he became professor of NT at Heidelberg, and from 1908 to his death in 1937 he served with distinction as professor of NT at the University of Berlin.

D. was deeply concerned with the mystical element in early Christianity. However, he made many of his most important contributions in biblical philology and

SOCIOLOGY. As a biblical interpreter he made popular three influential opinions: (1) Beginning with his *Bibelstudien* (1895), he determined on the basis of inscriptions and papyri from Egypt (see EGYPTOLOGY AND BIBLICAL STUDIES) the meaning of countless NT words and phrases, demonstrating that the NT is "a monument of late colloquial Greek," the common language (*koine*) of the common people. Thus, he showed that the prodigal son did not vaguely "gather together" his share of his father's substance: He "realized" it, converted it to cash. PAUL had not heard that some of the Thessalonians were "walking disorderly," but that they were "playing truant," not going to work, in expectation of the eschaton. D. may have exaggerated the popular character of *koine* Greek, neglecting the more scholarly modes of expression common in Jewish literature of the time.

(2) Also by means of comparison with extant papyri letters, D. distinguished between genuine letters (private, warm, personal, spontaneous, unliterary, occasional) and epistles (public, cold, impersonal, conventional, artful, written for posterity). He classified Paul's letters as being of the first type, while he assigned the pastorals (see PASTORAL LETTERS), Hebrews, James, 1 and 2 Peter, and Jude to the second type, which he likened to the epistles of Epicurus, Seneca, and Pliny. In this D. was influenced by nineteenth-century Romanticism. Current LITERARY THEORY maintains that all intelligible human behavior has a conventional dimension; thus all letters are literature in the broad sense. Certainly Paul's letters, while not dogmatic essays, were intended for repeated public use in the assembled churches in order to teach, to lead, and to establish Christian norms.

(3) By comparing the NT books with the non-literary texts of the same period, D. concluded that the social structure of primitive Christianity points unequivocally to the lower and middle classes. But the papyri show us the life and culture of several small provincial towns in Egypt, in some respects remote from the great centers of Hellenistic culture Paul visited. Thus, although D.'s influence on his own generation was enormous and his contributions were correctives to previous scholarly attitudes, which, for example, compared NT writings to those of Plato and Demosthenes to the disadvantage of the NT, his positions have had to be subsequently modified.

Works: *Die neutestamentliche Formel "in Christo Jesu" untersucht* (1892); *Bibelstudien: Beiträge zumeist aus den Papyri und Inschriften zur Geschichte und des Urchristentums* (1895; ET 1901); *Neue Bibelstudien: Sprachgeschichtliche Beiträge* (1897; combined ET by A. Grieve, *Bible Studies* [1901, 1923³]); *Die sprachliche Erforschung der griechischen Bibel* (1898); *Die Hellenisierung des semitischen Monotheismus* (1903); *Evangelium und Urchristentum: Das NT im Lichte der historischen Forschung* (1905); *Die Septuaginta-Papyri und andere altchristliche Texte* (1905); *Licht vom Osten: Das NT*

und die neuentdeckten Texte der hellenistisch-römischen Welt (1908, 1923⁴; ET, *Light from the Ancient East* [1910, 1926³]); *The Philology of the Greek Bible: Its Present and Future* (1908); *Die Urgeschichte des Christentums im Lichte der Sprachforschung* (1910); *Paulus: Ein kultur- und religionsgeschichtliche Skizze* (1911, 1925²; ET, *Paul: A Study in Social and Religious History* [1912, 1926²]); *Der Lehrstuhl für Religionsgeschichte* (1914); *The Religion of Jesus and the Faith of Paul* (1923); *De Profundis: Ein Dienst am Wort* (1925); *Vom Mysterium Christi* (1931); (with C. G. K. Bell), *Una Sancta* (1937).

Bibliography: **D. E. Aune,** *The NT in Its Literary Environment* (1987). **W. G. Doty,** *Letters in Primitive Christianity* (Guides to Biblical Scholarship, 1973). **K.-G. Eckart,** "A. D., Licht vom Osten," *450 Jahre Evangleische Theologie in Berlin* (ed. G. Beiser and C. Gestrick, 1989) 381-85. **G. Harder,** *Kirche in der Zeit* 22 (1967); *Zum Gedenken an A. D.* (1967). **W. F. Howard,** *The Romance of NT Scholarship* (1949). **W. G. Kümmel,** *NTHIP* (1972) 218-21, 471. **H. Lietzmann,** *ZNW* 35 (1936) 299-306. **S. Neill,** *The Interpretation of the NT* (1964) 149. *RGS* 1 (1925) 43-78 (autobiographical with bibliography). **S. K. Stowers,** *Letter Writing in Greco-Roman Antiquity* (1986) 17-20. **H. Strathmann,** *NDB* 3 (1957) 571-72.

J. M. BULLARD

DELITZSCH, FRANZ JULIUS (1813–90)

A native of Leipzig, born Feb. 23, 1813, D. had a difficult youth. A Jewish friend of the family, L. Hirsch (or F. J. Hirsch) became his patron. D. attended the University of Leipzig, studying philology and philosophy. After a period in which he lost religious faith, he underwent a reconversion experience. He became the leader of a devotional circle that met regularly (1835–42) and remained very pious throughout his life. He received the PhD in 1835 and became a *Dozent* at Leipzig with his work *De Habacuci prophetae vita* (1842). After teaching for a time at Leipzig, he taught at Rostock (1846–50), where he succeeded J. HOFMANN, and at Erlangen (1850–67), where he was Hofmann's colleague, before returning to Leipzig. At Erlangen he became a widely known conservative biblical scholar, primarily through his commentary work, attracting many students even from the English-speaking world.

Prior to becoming *Dozent* D. had become highly interested in Jewish studies and Christian missionary work among Jews and had worked in the city library cataloguing Jewish manuscripts. He received good instruction in Semitic languages from J. Fürst (editor of a well-known Hebrew concordance [1840]), from H. Fleischer (one of the best Arabic scholars of the time), and from converted Jewish missionaries. A staunch Lutheran, D. edited the *ZLThK* (1863–78) and founded and edited *Saat auf Hoffnung* (from 1863), a missionary periodical. He published numerous articles in the latter journal and elsewhere on Jewish studies and on the relationship and value of rabbinic and Talmudic materials (see TALMUD) for understanding the NT and saw himself as continuing the work of J. LIGHTFOOT. In 1870 he published a Hebrew translation of Romans, followed by his revision of a Hebrew translation of the NT (1877, 1891[11]), which is still in print. Although D. was interested in and supportive of Christian missionary work among Jews and founded what came to be called in his memory the Institutum Judaicum Delitzschianum for training missionaries, he nonetheless was a defender of Jewish rights at a time when anti-Judaism was increasing in strength in Germany. He published several works near the end of his life against anti-Judaic agitation.

D. was known for hospitality and friendliness toward students, especially English-speaking student circles in Leipzig, and his willingness to contribute editorial advice and editing labors on various projects for publishers and authors. A great lover of flowers and colors, he wrote several articles on these topics. With S. Baer he edited an edition of the HB, except for the books of Exodus–Deuteronomy (1861–97). He died Mar. 4, 1890, only a few days after reading the proofs for his last work. He did not live to see his son Friedrich DELITZSCH lead a caustic attack on the value of the HB.

D. initially took a negative attitude toward the historical-critical approach to the Bible developing in his day. Beginning in 1843, he and C. KEIL, a staunch traditionalist in the line of E. HENGSTENBERG, produced a series of Bible commentaries that primarily used and defended a traditional approach to the Scriptures. The Keil-Delitzsch HB commentary series, to which D. contributed Job, Psalms, Proverbs, Ecclesiastes and Song of Songs, and Isaiah, appeared in ET in twenty-seven volumes (including Keil's two-volume introduction) and remains in print. In his early work D. was willing to engage in very modified source analysis but argued that Moses wrote Exodus 19–24 and delivered the other laws orally during the wilderness wanderings, and that during the first generation in the land Joshua and Eleazar put the PENTATEUCHAL materials into final form. According to S. CURTISS (560), D. was forced to rethink his positions beginning in the summer of 1876, especially under the influence of A. Kayser's *Das vorexilische Buch der Urgeschichte und seine Erweiterungen* (1874). In a series of articles in the ZKWL for 1880 and 1882 and in the *Hebrew Student* for 1882, D. discussed various HB issues and acknowledged his move toward a more critical position in line with the work of J. WELLHAUSEN. One sees in D. the struggle between what he called the "old theology and the new" in which he sought to hold together traditional supernatural orientations and critical perspectives. In his apologetic statement of the issues he concluded, "Even if in many biblical questions I have to oppose the traditional opinion, certainly my opposition remains on this side of the gulf, on the side of the

theology of the Cross, of grace, of miracles, in harmony with the good confession of our Lutheran Church. By this banner let us stand; folding ourselves in it, let us die" (1889, 55).

Works: *Zur Geschichte jüdischen Poesie vom Abschluss der heiligen Schriften Alten Bundes bis auf die neueste Zeit* (1836); *Jesurun sive Prolegomenôn in Concordantias Veteris Testamenti* (1838); *Wissenschaft, Kunst, Judenthum, Schilderungen und Kritiken* (1838); *Philemon oder das Buch von der Freundschaft in Christo* (1842); *Wer sind die Mystiker?* (1842); *Der Prophet Habakuk* (1843); *Das Sacrament des wahren Leibes und Blutes Jesu Christi* (1844); *Die biblisch-prophetische Theologie, ihre Fortbildung durch C. A. Crusius und ihre neueste Entwicklung seit der Christologie Hengstenbergs* (1845); *Symbolae ad psalmos illustrando isagogicae* (1846); *Vier Bücher von der Kirche* (1847); *Vom Hause Gottes oder der Kirche* (1849); *Das Hohelied untersucht und ausgelegt* (1851); *Die Genesis ausgelegt* (1852, 1853[2], 1860[3], 1872[4]); *A System of Biblical Psychology* (1855, 1861[2]; ET 1879[2]); *Commentary on the Epistle to the Hebrews* (1857; ET 2 vols., 1868–70); *Handschriftliche Funde* (2 pts., 1861–62); *Jesus and Hillel* (1865, 1867[2], 1879[3]; ET in the following); *Biblical Commentary on the Prophecies of Isaiah* (1866, 1869[2], 1879[3], 1889[4]; ETs 1873, 1890[2] = 2 vols., with an introduction by S. R. Driver and additions and corrections by the author, 1969); *Jewish Artisan Life in the Time of Our Lord* (1868, 1878[3]; ETs 1877, 1883[2]); *System der christlichen Apologetik* (1868); *Studien zur Entstehungsgeschichte der Polyglottenbibel des Cardinals Ximenes* (1871); *Komplutensische Varianten zu dem alttestamentlichen Texte* (1878); *OT History of Redemption* (ET from manuscript notes by S. I. Curtiss, 1881); *The Hebrew NT of the British Foreign Bible Society: A Contribution to Hebrew Philology* (1883); *Fortgesetzte Studien zur Entstehungsgeschichte der komplutensischen Polyglotte* (1886); *A New Commentary on Genesis* (1887; ET 2 vols., 1889); *Ernste Fragen und die Gebildeten jüdischer Religion* (1888, 1890[2]); *Iris: Studies in Color and Talks About Flowers* (1888; ET 1890); *Messianic Prophecies* (1889); "The Deep Gulf Between the Old Theology and the New," *The Expositor*, 3rd ser., 9 (1889) 42-55; *Sind die Juden wirklich das auserwählte Volk?* (1889); *Messianic Prophecies in Historical Succession* (1890; ET 1891).

Bibliography: W. **Baudissin,** *The Expositor,* 4th ser., 1 (1890) 465-72. T. K. **Cheyne,** *FOTC,* 155-71. S. I. **Curtiss,** "D. on the Origin and Composition of the Pentateuch," *Presbyterian Review* 3 (1882) 553-88; *F. D.: A Memorial Tribute* (1891), contains ET of D.'s short autobiographical sketch (82-85) and a bibliography (85-96). S. R. **Driver,** *ExpTim* 1 (1889–90) 197-201. O. **Eissfeldt and R. H. Rengstorff** (eds.), *Briefwechsel zwischen F. D. und W. W., Graf Baudissin, 1866–90* (ARWAW 43, 1973). D. **Kaufmann,** "F. D. (1812–90): A Palm-branch from Judah on His Newly-covered Grave," *JQR* 2 (1890) 386-99. H.-J. **Kraus,** *GHKEAT,* 230-41. E. **Plümacher,** *TRE* 8 (1981) 431-33. J. **Rogerson,** *OTCNC,*

111-20. **S. D. F. Salmond,** *The Expositor,* 3rd ser., 3 (1886) 456-71; *ExpTim* 1 (1889–90) 201-3. **S. Wagner,** *F. D.: Leben und Werk* (BEvT 80, 1978), with bibliography of and about D. (446-98).

J. H. HAYES

DELITZSCH, FRIEDRICH (1850–1922)

The son of Franz DELITZSCH, D. was born in Erlangen Sept. 3, 1850, and received his initial schooling there. At the University of Berlin he studied Semitic languages and was attracted to the emerging field of ASSYRIOLOGY by E. Schrader. He concentrated on Semitic philology but briefly engaged in Indo-European–Semitic comparison in his inaugural dissertation (1873). To Assyrian (Akkadian) studies he contributed a grammar (1889, 1906[2]), a collection of introductory cuneiform readings (1876, 1912[5]), and a dictionary (1896), together with many textual studies. He died Dec. 19, 1922.

D.'s first academic position was at Leipzig (1878), where he published in Assyriology and in HB studies, following his interests in philology, in Assyriological contributions to the study of the HB, and in biblical geography and ethnography. He also saw through the press the fifth edition of his father's commentary on Psalms (1894), for which he thoroughly reworked the philological notes (he was an accomplished Hebraist). He became professor at the University of Breslau (1893) and then at the University of Berlin (1899–1920), where, in addition, he served as curator of the Western Asiatic collection of the Royal Museum (1899–1919). He contributed to Sumerian studies with a grammar and a glossary (1914), having overcome his earlier skepticism about Sumerian as a language. His last scholarly publication was devoted to the analysis of scribal errors in the HB text (1920), a study undertaken preparatory to a Hebrew dictionary. He and his students (among them P. Haupt of Johns Hopkins) dominated the field of Assyriology until WWI.

D.'s greatest impact on biblical studies, however, was his opening the BABEL UND BIBEL controversy (1902–4), which culminated for him in his diatribe against the HB (1920–21). In his "Babel und Bibel" lectures as published and initially revised, he drew on Babylonian discoveries as an aid in interpreting the HB—in many ways illuminating biblical references and ideas—and offered a cultural comparison between Babylonia and the Bible, the clear advantage for him lying with Babylonia, which represented a greater civilization than did ancient Israel and also embodied a more appealing religious outlook. Arguing that Palestine was part of an area dominated by Babylonian culture, D. traced many biblical ideas and institutions to a Babylonian source. He also argued that the Israelite counterpart was at times inferior, e.g., he saw the recently discovered law collection of Hammurabi as superior to biblical law in various

respects. In Israel's sense of election he saw chauvinism. The name of Israel's god, Yahweh, and monotheism itself he traced to Babylonian sources, while allowing that the Babylonian conception of divinity, although sophisticated, was dominantly polytheistic. He increasingly attacked the HB as unworthy of being generally authoritative (see AUTHORITY OF THE BIBLE) for the Christian community—a religion no more admirable than that of Babylonia. The concluding lecture affirmed that the religion of JESUS is a "truly new religion" that, freed from the "human additions foreign to the person and life of Jesus," is called to win the world.

D.'s denigration of the HB reached an intensified climax in his final work, *Die grosse Täuschung* (The Great Deception), his title for the HB. (The first part of this work was essentially complete in 1914 but was not published until 1920; a new edition of part one was printed with the second part in 1921.) D. viewed his "history-of-religions investigations" from 1902 to 1921 as having proceeded in a "thoroughly straightforward fashion," yet he now concluded that the Hebrews were but "robbing and murdering nomads" responsible for a book full of errors and exaggerations. He argued that the HB should be excluded from the church and replaced by something like W. Schwaner's *Germanen-Bibel.*

Works: *Wo lag das Paradies?* (1881); *Hebrew Language Viewed in the Light of Assyrian Research* (1883); *Prolegomena eines neuen hebräisch-aramäischen Wörterbuch zum Alten Testament* (1886); *Babel und Bibel* (3 lectures, 1902–5); *Babel und Bibel: Ein Rückblick und Ausblick* (1904); *Babel and Bible* (Lectures 1-3, tr. T. J. McCormack, W. H. Carruth, and L. G. Robinson, 1906), with criticisms and responses; *Die Lese- und Schreibfehler im Alten Testament* (1920); *Die Grosse Täuschung* (rev. pt. 1 and pt. 2, 1921).

Bibliography: **J. Barr,** *EncRel* 4 (1987) 276-77. **K.-H. Bernhardt,** *TRE* 8 (1981) 433-34. **H. B. Huffmon,** "*Babel und Bibel:* The Encounter Between Babylon and the Bible," *Backgrounds for the Bible* (ed. M. P. O'Connor and D. N. Freedman, 1987) 125-36. **K. Johanning,** *Der Bibel-Babel-Streit: Eine forschungsgeschichtliche Studie* (1988). **R. G. Lehmann,** "F. D. als Hebraist," *Zeitschrift für Althebraistik* 3 (1990) 24-39; *F. D. und der Babel-Bibel-Streit* (OBO 133, 1994). **F. Weissbach,** *RLA* 2 (1938) 198.

H. B. HUFFMON

DENCK, HANS (c. 1500–1527)

A humanist scholar and teacher, D. left a literary legacy contained in fewer than two hundred pages in W. Fellmann's critical edition. Most of D.'s writings appeared as short tracts, except for a translation of and commentary on the book of Micah, which he co-authored with L. Haetzer. Nonetheless, D. used Scripture more than patristic sources to bolster his own thought. He referred to the Wisdom of Solomon and to Ecclesiasticus as if they were canonical, although he did not mention the other apocryphal books. References to some biblical books occur frequently; D. seems to have had a "canon within the canon." Most often cited from the HB are Genesis (25x), Deuteronomy (28x), Psalms (72x), Isaiah (63x), and Jeremiah (41x); from the NT references to Matthew (112x), John (72x), and Romans (66x). D. rarely quoted a biblical text in full and not often verbatim, citing chapter but not verse. He undoubtedly attached a certain AUTHORITY to Scripture, although he was clearly not a literalist. His mature theological position has been aptly described as "evangelical spiritualism."

Works: *H. D. Schriften*, pt. 1 (ed. G. Baring, 1955); *H. D. Schriften*, pt. 2 (ed. W. Fellmann, 1956); pt. 3 (1960); *Selected Writings of H. D.* (ed. and tr. E. J. Furcha, 1989); *The Spiritual Legacy of H. D.* (ed. and tr. C. Baumann, 1991).

Bibliography: J. J. Kiwiet, "The Theology of H. D.," *MennQR* 32 (1958) 3-27. G. G. Roehrich, *Essay on the Life, the Writings, and the Doctrine of the Anabaptist H. D.* (1983). O. Vittali, "Die Theologie des Wiedertäufers H. D." (PhD diss., Freiburg, 1932).

E. J. FURCHA

DENNEY, JAMES (1856–1917)

After study at Glasgow University in classics and philosophy (under E. Caird), D. attended theological seminary and was ordained in 1886. Commentaries and theological studies published during his first pastorate earned him appointment in 1897 as professor of systematic theology at Glasgow Free Church College (his alma mater), where he later held the chair of NT exegesis and theology and became principal in 1915.

D. participated actively in Free Church administration, wrote on theological education, and contributed extensively to ecclesiastical journals, magazines, DICTIONARIES AND ENCYCLOPEDIAS. The central theme of his theology, exhibited both in his Pauline commentaries (see PAUL) and in theological studies was the doctrine of atonement. For him the sacrifice of Christ for humanity was the center and *sine qua non* of authentic Christianity. Theologically, D. could appreciate the thought of A. RITSCHL and accept moderate biblical criticism, but he sternly rejected critical doubts concerning JESUS and the historicity of the Gospels.

Works: *Thessalonians* (1892); *II Corinthians* (1894); *Studies in Theology* (1894); *The Death of Christ* (1902); *The Atonement and the Modern Mind* (1903); *Jesus and the Gospel* (1908); *The Christian Doctrine of Reconciliation* (1917).

Bibliography: I. H. Marshall, *CMCT,* 203-38 (with bibliography). S. J. Mikolaski, "The Theology of Principal J. D.,"

EQ 35 (1963) 89-96, 144-48, 209-22. A. S. Peake, *DNB* 24 (1927) 153-54. A. P. F. Sell, "J. D., 1856–1917: A Preachable Theology," *Defending and Declaring the Faith* (1987) 195-220. B. G. Worrall, "Substitutionary Atonement in the Theology of J. D.," *SJT* 28 (1975) 341-57.

D. L. PALS

DEUTERONOMISTIC HISTORY

The deuteronomistic history (DH), comprising Deuteronomy, Joshua, Judges, 1–2 Samuel, and 1–2 Kings, as a literary entity is hypothesized on the basis of the methods of LITERARY and historical criticism. The classic theory of its delineation is credited to M. NOTH, although he was anticipated by A. KUENEN, J. WELLHAUSEN, and others who had recognized deuteronomistic influence in the composition of these books. Noth's work, however, separated these books from Genesis–Numbers, showing them to be an independent composition unconnected with the older Pentateuchal documents. Composed during the exile, according to Noth, the DH provided the first continuous history of Israel from the eve of its entry into the land until its exile from it, using a variety of older independent traditions.

1. The Unity of the DH. The unity of the work was clear to Noth (*Deuteronomistic History* [1943, ET 1981]) on four grounds. First, he considered the language (though not described with the detail later provided by M. Weinfeld [1972] and H.-D Hoffmann [1980]) to be easily recognizable and consistent. Second, Noth noted that speeches or narratives in deuteronomistic style appear at critical points in the history (Joshua 1; 12; 23; Judg 2:11-23; 1 Samuel 12; 1 Kgs 8:14-64; 2 Kgs 17:7-41), where they functioned to review the history, drawing from it the consequences of the people's obedience or disobedience to the divine demands. Third, a consistent CHRONOLOGY creates a unifying framework: For the monarchic period the chronologies of the kings of the two states of Israel and Judah interlink to provide a total single chronology of the period; for the pre-monarchic and early monarchic periods, the summary statement that 480 years separate the exodus from Egypt and the fourth year of the reign of Solomon (1 Kgs 6:1) could be reconciled with the detailed chronological information provided earlier, mainly through the omission of the concluding statement of 1 Sam 4:18 as a post-deuteronomistic addition. Fourth, Noth saw the work as having a theological consistency: There is a marked lack of positive interest in the cult, the relationship between Yahweh and Israel depending on obedience to covenant law rather than on sacrifice and other cultic practice.

The last point is related to Noth's description of the purpose of the work: to account for the course of the history of Israel and the definite end to which it came with the destruction of Jerusalem. Even when the opportunity presented itself (as in the reflections on the destruction of Israel [2 Kings 17] and Judah [2 Kings 24]), the deuteronomist did not make use of it to sketch out a future for the people beyond the disaster that had overtaken them. The history of Israel had come to an end in conformity with the curse attached to the covenant law.

A. Jepsen (1953) considered his independent study of the books of Kings generally to conform with Noth's results. Arguing that these books were based on two sources that were combined and supplemented by a priestly redactor after the destruction of Jerusalem, Jepsen held that a further prophetic (*nebiistic*) stage of REDACTION, which took place during the exile, represented the work of Noth's deuteronomistic historian. At this stage the quantity of the work was almost doubled through the inclusion of the Isaiah legends, oral traditions about the prophets (see PROPHECY AND PROPHETS, HB), and other materials relating to the pre-monarchic and early monarchic periods, together with the familiar deuteronomistic themes of election, divine law, and apostasy.

Noth's work found wide agreement, but difficulties were perceived in relation to inconsistencies in the history. A major problem was the deuteronomistic attitude to the monarchy, for Noth's explanation of the conflicts apparent in 1 Samuel 8–12 (the deuteronomist, though anti-monarchic, was faithful to his sources and was satisfied simply to "correct" their pro-monarchic expression by adding his own views) did not fit with other evidence, especially from Kings, that the historian was not bound in this way to his source material. In order to resolve this problem and so to preserve Noth's view of the unity of the history, H. Boecker (1969) argued for a different evaluation of the deuteronomistic attitude toward the monarchy. Accepting as deuteronomistic those parts of 1 Samuel 8–12 proposed as such by Noth, Boecker held that they cannot be classified as anti-monarchic: Criticisms exist, but they are leveled not against the monarchy as such, but rather against particular aspects of it. So the problem inherent in Noth's study was resolved by the argument that Noth was right in assigning certain texts to the deuteronomist but wrong in his assessment of what those texts said about the monarchy. This revision, moreover, eased the tension in Noth's presentation between the deuteronomist's apparent anti-monarchism in 1 Samuel 8–12 and his approval of David in Kings.

Hoffmann's comprehensive study considers the main problem to lie in the view that the deuteronomist used written sources: This suggests that the work is the outcome of a redactional history, and that in turn weakens the case for its unity. Hoffmann, therefore, has adopted a traditio-historical view (see TRADITION HISTORY), which he understands to mean that the deuteronomist had little to do with written sources but was an original, creative author, making use of mainly oral tradition. Arguing that the intention of the deuteronomist was to write a history of Israel as a history of cultic reforms and reformers, Hoffmann proposes that for the monarchic period the deuteronomist has provided what is effectively a cult history: The many detailed accounts of cultic reforms carried out by both Israelite and Judean kings culminate in the account of Josiah's reform, in which the deuteronomist's exilic and early postexilic contemporaries are given a model of faithfulness to the law. Cultic reform is also the principle of organization for the pre-monarchic time: The accounts here are fewer, however, being found only for Saul, Gideon, Joshua, and Moses. The reform of Moses (Deut 9:7-29) presents an ideal program and model for all future cult reformers in the DH and prefigures the reform of Josiah.

The deuteronomist is understood by Hoffmann to be the author of the descriptions of these cultic reforms: The vocabulary, both general cultic terminology long recognized as deuteronomistic and also specific cultic terminology in the detailed accounts of reforms, does not reflect historically verifiable events but is part of the literary presentation, its detail being the deuteronomistic way of giving historical verisimilitude to his account.

Neither these proposals to maintain the unity of the DH nor those that attempt to apply modern literary criticism with the same purpose (R. Polzin [1980]; J. van Seters [1983]) can be regarded as successful. The DH has been marked out in the first instance by the methods of historical-critical analysis, and it is appropriate that those methods should be followed through consistently in order to comprehend the origin of that work. Thus the internal breaks and points of unevenness remain significant indicators of the work's origin and history of construction. Boecker's proposals undervalue the strong anti-monarchism of some deuteronomistic passages in 1 Samuel 8–12, especially chap. 12. Hoffmann's view of cult reform as the deuteronomist's principal theme leaves too many gaps and inconsistencies: Cult reforms are ascribed to Jehoshaphat (1 Kgs 22:46) that are already credited to his predecessor (1 Kgs 15:12); there is a lack of symmetry in the reform stories, and it is particularly striking that none is provided for David. In addition to this lack of balance, the point and purpose of the work in this description remain difficult to comprehend: It is inconceivable that an exilic or early postexilic deuteronomist would write for his contemporaries a work that insisted that no matter how good the individual might be (Josiah), the end of the nation could only be destruction.

2. Editions of the DH. That the deuteronomistic historian had a wholly negative view of Israel's history, regarding it as finally closed, has been a point of major contention in Noth's thesis, in reaction to which two divergent views of the work have been developed (see H. Weippert [1985]). The first may be traced to H. W. WOLFF (1982) and the second to G. VON RAD. Wolff argued that it was unlikely that the deuteronomist would have composed such an extensive history only to show Israel's guilt. Moreover, he preferred to think in terms of a deuteronomistic circle as the setting for deuteronomistic redaction; and to a second deuteronomistic hand in this circle he assigned such passages as Deut 4:29-31 and 30:1-10, where the theme of return after judgment is prominent.

The shift of responsibility for the DH away from an individual author to a school or circle provided the possibility of distinguishing between layers of deuteronomistic editorial work, within which context it would then be possible to understand its having both negative and positive purposes. The most significant contributions to this development have come from R. Smend, W. Dietrich (1972), and T. Veijola.

Smend (1971) has argued that deuteronomistic texts in Joshua 1, 13, and 23 and Judges 2 are not unified compositions but incorporate later supplements to a basic deuteronomistic text. These supplements, forming a single, secondary layer, are concerned with obedience to the law and make Israel's success in its conquest of the land conditional on such obedience. Thus a distinction is drawn between the deuteronomistic historian (Dtr), for whom Israel's conquest of the land was complete and successful, and a later "nomistic" deuteronomistic editor (DtrN), for whom that conquest has been successful only "to this day" (Josh 23:9b).

Dietrich's detailed study of Kings attempted to distinguish a prophetic stage of redaction of the DH preceding the work of DtrN. Noting the regular formal pattern of prophecy and fulfillment, he argued that such prophetic passages are all additions to their contexts, that their form is found with the classical prophets, especially Jeremiah, and that their language has been influenced by both the prophets and the DH. The general intention of the redactor responsible for them (DtrP) is to unite prophecy with the deuteronomistic movement, showing history as the arena in which the prophetic word works itself out. The work of the deuteronomistic historian (Dtr), which reaches its conclusion in 2 Kgs 25:21, was carried out shortly after the fall of Jerusalem; DtrN added the conclusion in 2 Kgs 25:22-30, shortly after the release of King Jehoiachin; DtrP precedes DtrN and should be dated to the early part of the exilic period.

Veijola (1975) traced all three layers back into the books of Samuel: DtrH is favorably disposed toward the monarchy and has a positive view of David as the servant of Yahweh; DtrP has subordinated the king to the prophet and presented the king as a source of guilt; DtrN holds up David as an ideal but only on the basis of his obedience to the commandments, while seeing the monarchy in general as an evil institution (1977). Smend later (1978) brought these studies together into a modified synthesis that, although unable to assign every verse to its appropriate layer, attempted a full

account of the development of the DH: Dtr offered a continuous account, based on different sources, beginning in Deut 1:1 and ending with 2 Kgs 25:30; DtrP introduced prophetic stories into the presentation of the monarchic period, the history of which ran its course according to the scheme prophecy-fulfillment; DtrN introduced an emphasis on the law throughout the work. All three belong closely together, the additions of the later redactors making use of the language of the work being edited; the task of distinguishing them is, therefore, difficult. In time, also, they are not far separated: Dtr, whose account ends with the release of Jehoiachin, cannot be dated before 560 BCE; and the two stages of redaction were completed by the early postexilic period.

The approach initiated by von Rad involved understanding more radical change in the course of the development of the DH. Von Rad acknowledged that the deuteronomist wished to explain why the saving history had ended in catastrophe but argued that for the deuteronomist the judgment of the law was not the only power active in history; equally effectual was the promise of salvation in the Nathan prophecy (see also D. McCarthy [1965]). The work contains a messianic motif: The description of David and the measuring of his successors by means of his standard show that the deuteronomist "had a picture of the perfect anointed unremittingly present to his mind" (von Rad [1962] 345).

This tension between judgment and promise has been exploited by F. M. CROSS [1973], who has argued that there are two themes in the DH. The first is the sin of Jeroboam and his successors, which reaches its climax in the account of the fall of the northern kingdom and in the meditation on that event in 2 Kgs 17:1-23. The second is the promise of grace to David and his house, which reaches its climax in the account of Josiah's reform in 2 Kings 22–23, where Josiah is said to have extirpated the cult of Jeroboam and attempted to restore the kingdom of David. By contrasting these two themes the deuteronomist created a work that functioned to propagate Josiah's reform: Josiah is the new David, and in him is to be found true faithfulness to Yahweh, as a result of which the restoration of the Davidic kingdom is taking place. The DH ended with the account of Josiah's reform and so was a preexilic composition. Its extension to bring the work up to the destruction of Jerusalem and the exile is the work of a second deuteronomistic editor, who has turned the history as a whole into an explanation of that catastrophe; this later editor's work can be found in Deuteronomy, Joshua, 1–2 Samuel, and 1–2 Kings.

Cross's thematic argument was given literary-critical support by D. Nelson (1981) in his study of the regnal formulas that frame the references to each king in Israel and Judah. The formulas normally display considerable variety, but in the case of the last four kings of Judah they are terse and fixed. Here they are the work of a later hand extending the work at a secondary stage. Nelson also marked out those parts of Kings that are with all probability to be assigned to the later editor: 1 Kgs 8:44-51; 9:6-9; 2 Kgs 17:7-20, 34*b*-40; 21:3*b*-15, all of which prepare for the destruction of Jerusalem and the exile.

Although there are points of contact between this approach and that of Smend, particularly in the anti-monarchic characterization of the later editor and in the passages assigned to him, Cross's approach is distinct in its conception of the significance of the change introduced by editorial work on the original DH. While according to Smend the editors introduced new emphases into a work whose basic nature remained relatively stable, Cross maintained that the original DH was fundamentally transformed by the later editor: The original work was designed as a paean of praise in support of the reforms of Josiah; the edited version is intended to explain the failure of the Davidic dynasty and the destruction of Jerusalem.

3. Further Study of the DH. Any attempt to synthesize the approaches of Cross and Smend (see A. Mayes [1983]) will not only yield a complex picture of the DH very different from that of Noth but will also inevitably raise fundamental questions about the DH. There is considerable uncertainty about the criteria by which redactional layers might be distinguished and so also about the functions of any of these redactions. Moreover, it is now clear that it cannot be assumed that a given stage of redaction is to be found through the whole or the majority of the DH. Those books that have traditionally been seen as parts of the DH have undergone processes of redactional development that cannot easily be traced through more than limited parts of that history, thus raising the question of the validity of referring to any such single literary entity as the DH (E. Knauf [1996]).

Major contributions to uncovering the redactional history of limited parts of the DH have come from a number of directions. First, Weippert (1972) has sought to achieve results for the books of Kings through a study of the judgment formulas. Three groups of these formulae are distinguished, relating to progressively more extensive or later sections of Kings, thus providing an outline of the history of the development of these books. This account of the history of Kings has been critically examined by A. Lemaire (1986) and I. Provan (1988). The latter in particular has pointed to different understandings in Kings of what is meant by worship at the high places as a means of distinguishing a preexilic edition, culminating in the account of the reign of Hezekiah from an exilic editing, to which only isolated additions were subsequently made. Similarly, W. Richter (1964) has sought to determine the history of the book of Judges by a study of the frameworks that brought the independent stories into a collection, and of introductory passages that brought deliverers and judges together into

a comprehensive account of the period of the judges. G. Seitz (1971) has argued for two significant stages in the growth of Deuteronomy marked by two series of super-scriptions, the latter of which belongs to the stage that incorporated the work into the DH (see also Mayes [1979]).

Second, N. Lohfink's study (1981) of the *kerygmata* of the DH has isolated a distinctive form of expression in Deuteronomy 1–Joshua 22, through which the deuteronomist describes the conquest as Yahweh's dispossession of the older inhabitants of the land in favor of Israel. It suggests that Deuteronomy 1–Joshua 22 existed independently, perhaps in the historical context of Josiah's military intervention in the north and his taking of the land from the Assyrians (see ASSYRIOLOGY AND BIBLICAL STUDIES). A deuteronomistic edition of Kings probably belonged to the same time, but only in the exile was any combination effected to yield the whole work extending from Deuteronomy to 2 Kings. Smend's DtrN is found by Lohfink also in Deuteronomy, but it is only a partial commentary since it does not appear in 1–2 Samuel and 1–2 Kings.

Third, a conjunction of literary-critical approaches with developing interest in the social, political, and religious milieu of the deuteronomist and in the question of the ideological function of the material in that milieu (P. Dutcher-Walls [1991]; R. Albertz [1996]) has led to a better-founded appreciation of certain stages in the development of the DH. Thus the analysis of the deuteronomic law by G. Braulik (1993) and Lohfink (1993) has shown that Deuteronomy 12–16 is the first major section of the law to which Deut 16:18–18:22 has been abruptly related at a secondary stage, while the social laws of Deuteronomy 19–25 differ from both in showing the least evidence of deuteronomic language and no concern with centralization. These sections reflect stages of growth that are integrally related to changing functions in a society in a process of rapid and fundamental transformation. The emphasis of the first section, the older cultic law of the lawbook, on cultic unity and purity has been expanded in the later sections to include a concern for the constitution and everyday life of the people in its relationship with Yahweh. The cultic law functioned to legitimate the reform of Josiah, but the more comprehensive law code, with its concern for the whole life of the people, relates to the needs of the exilic and early postexilic community. This development is open to being related to the history of the DH. Insofar as older stages of the DH may be related to Josiah's reform, they reflect its concern with the monarchy and with cultic unity and purity; later exilic stages, however, introduced such theological commentary as 2 Kgs 17:7-23, 34*b*-41, in which the welfare of Israel rests on the people as a whole and not solely on the king (see Mayes [1996]).

The relationship of the DH to the Tetrateuch also

remains problematic. The issues here are exacerbated by the turmoil in PENTATEUCHAL CRITICISM (see R. Whybray [1987, 1995]). Wellhausen and Noth (Pentateuchal traditions) distinguished between the continuous strands J and E, which were later combined by a redactor and set within the framework of an originally independent P document. P extended only to the death of Moses; so the original conclusion of the J and E sources, relating the conquest of the land, was dropped in favor of the P framework. This work was then connected with the DH by transferring the priestly account of the death of Moses to the end of Deuteronomy.

Questions have been raised especially by H. Schmid (1976), R. Rendtorff (1977), M. Rose (1981), and Van Seters in relation to the existence of continuous J and E sources, the date of the J and E material, and its relationship to the DH. Rendtorff in particular finds that the links between the larger units of the Pentateuch go back to no earlier than an editorial layer to be identified as deuteronomic (see also Mayes [1983]). This may be taken to suggest that it was only at some stage(s) in the development of the DH that the Tetrateuch received a deuteronomistic editing (Smend [1978]), if not indeed its formative organization based on older independent traditions (Rendtorff, Rose).

Bibliography: R. Albertz, "Le milieu des Deutéronomistes," *Israel construit son histoire: L'historiographie deutéronomiste à la lumière des récherches recentes* (Le Monde de la Bible 34, ed. A. de Pury, T. Romer, J.-D. Macchi, 1996) 377-407. H. J. Boecker, *Die Beurteilung der Anfänge des Königtums in den deuteronomistischen Abschnitten des 1. Samuelbuches: Ein Beitrag zum Problem des "Deuteronomistischen Geschichtswerks"* (WMANT 31, 1969). G. Braulik, "The Sequence of the Laws in Deuteronomy 12–26 and in the Decalogue," *A Song of Power and the Power of Song: Essays on the Book of Deuteronomy* (Sources for Biblical and Theological Study 3, ed. D. L. Christensen, 1993) 313-35. A. F. Campbell, "M. Noth and the Deuteronomistic History," *The History of Israel's Traditions: The Heritage of M. Noth* (ed. S. L. McKenzie, M. P. Graham, JSOTSup 182, 1994) 31-62. F. M. Cross, *Canaanite Myth and Hebrew Epic: Essays in the History of the Religion of Israel* (1973). W. Dietrich, *Prophetie und Geschichte: Eine redaktionsgeschichtliche Untersuchung zum deuteronomistischen Geschichtswerk* (FRLANT 108, 1972). P. Dutcher-Walls, "The Social Location of the Deuteronomists: A Sociological Study of Factional Politics in Late Pre-Exilic Judah," *JSOT* 52 (1991) 77-94. H.-D. Hoffmann, *Reform und Reformen: Untersuchungen zu einem Grundthema der deuteronomistischen Geschichtsschreibung* (ATANT 66, 1980). A. Jepsen, *Die Quellen des Königbuches* (1953). E. A. Knauf, "L'Historiographie Deutéronomiste (DtrG) existet'elle?" *Israel construit son histoire (1996)* 409-18. G. Knoppers and J. G. McConville (eds.), *Recent Studies on the Deuteronomistic History* (Sources for Biblical and Theological Study 8, 1998). A. Lemaire, "Vers l'histoire de la rédaction des livres des Rois," *ZAW* 98 (1986) 221-36. N. Lohfink,

"Kerygmata des deuteronomistischen Geschichtswerks," *Die Botschaft und die Boten* (FS H. W. Wolff. ed. J. Jeremias and L. Perlitt, 1981) 87-100; "Distribution of the Functions of Power: The Laws Concerning Public Offices in Deuteronomy 16:18–18:22," *A Song of Power and the Power of Song* ed. D. L. Christensen, 1993) 336-52. D. J. McCarthy, "II Samuel 7 and the Structure of the Deuteronomistic History," *JBL* 84 (1965) 131-38. A. D. H. Mayes, *Deuteronomy* (NCBC, 1979); *The Story of Israel Between Settlement and Exile: A Redactional Study of the Deuteronomistic History* (1983); "De l'ideologie deutéronomiste à la Theologie de l'Ancien Testament," *Israel construit son histoire (1996)* 477-508. R. D. Nelson, *The Double Redaction of the Deuteronomistic History* (JSOTSup 18, 1981). M. Noth, *Überlieferungsgeschichtliche Studien* (1943; ET, *The Deuteronomistic History* [JSOTSup 15, 1981, 1986²]) *Überlieferungsgeschichte des Pentateuch* (1948; ET, *A History of Pentateuchal Traditions [1972]*). M. A. O'Brien, *The Deuteronomistic History Hypothesis: A Reassessment* (OBO 92, 1989). R. Polzin, *Moses and the Deuteronomist: Deuteronomy, Joshua, Judges* (A Literary Study of the DH, pt. 1, 1980). I. W. Provan, *Hezekiah and the Books of Kings: A Contribution to the Debate About the Composition of the Deuteronomistic History* (BZAW 172, 1988). G. von Rad, *Theologie des Alten Testaments* (vol. 1, 1957; vol. 2, 1960; ET, *OT Theology* [vol. 1, 1962; vol. 2, 1965]). A. N. Radjawane, "Das deuteronomistische Geschichtswerk," *TRu* 38 (1973–74) 177-216. R. Rendtorff, *Das überlieferungsgeschichtliche Problem des Pentateuch* (BZAW 147, 1977). W. Richter, *Die Bearbeitungen des 'Retterbuches' in der deuteronomischen Epoche* (BBB 21, 1964). M. Rose, *Deuteronomist und Jahwist: Untersuchungen zu den Berührungspunkten beider Literaturwerke* (ATANT 67, 1981). H. H. Schmid, *Der sogenannte Jahwist: Beobachtungen und Fragen zur Pentateuchforschung* (1976). G. Seitz, *Redaktionsgeschichtliche Studien zum Deuteronomium* (BWANT 5, 93, 1971). R. Smend, "Das Gesetz und die Völker: Ein Beitrag zur deuteronomistischen Redaktionsgeschichte," *Probleme biblischer Theologie* (G. von Rad zum 70. Geburtstag, ed. H. W. Wolff, 1971) 494-509; *Die Entstehung des Alten Testaments* (1978). J. Van Seters, *Abraham in History and Tradition* (1975); *In Search of History* (1983). G. Vanoni, "Beobachtungen zur deuteronomistischen Terminologie in 2 Kon 23, 25–25, 30," *Das Deuteronomium: Entstehung, Gestalt und Botschaft* (BETL 68, ed. N. Lohfink, 1985) 357-62. T. Veijola, *Die ewige Dynastie: David und die Entstehung seiner Dynastie nach der deuteronomistischen Darstellung* (1975); *Das Königtum in der Beurteilung der deuteronomistischen Historiographie: Eine redaktionsgeschichtliche Untersuchung* (1977). M. Weinfeld, *Deuteronomy and the Deuteronomic School* (1972). H. Weippert, "Die 'deuteronomistischen' Beurteilungen der Könige von Israel und Juda und das Problem der Redaktion der Königsbücher," *Bib* 53 (1972) 301-39; "Das deuteronomistische Geschichtswerk," *TRu* 50 (1985) 213-49. J. Wellhausen, *Die Composition des Hexateuchs und der historischen Bücher des Alten Testaments* (1889², 1899³). R. N. Whybray, *The Making of the Pentateuch: A Methodological Study* (JSOTSup 53, 1987); *Introduction to the Pentateuch* (1995). H. W. Wolff, "The Kerygma of the Deuteronomistic

Historical Work," *The Vitality of OT Traditions* (ed. W. Brueggemann and H. W. Wolff, 1982[2]) 83-100.

A. D. H. MAYES

DEUTERONOMY

The fifth book of the Christian OT, in Jewish and Samaritan scriptures it is the last of the traditional books of Moses, which together comprise pentateuchal *Torah* (*hamissâ hômse tôrâ* [the five fifths of Torah], e.g., *b. Hag.* 14a). In addition to its many individual texts of liturgical, homiletical, and creedal import, two broad features of content account for the book's unusual significance in the history of biblical interpretation. First, the central portion of the book (4:14–28:68) consists of an ordered exposition of divinely authorized law, addressed by Moses to an Israelite plenary that is about to occupy a national homeland in Canaan. Second, this core legislation is promulgated in a framework of poignant theological and prophetical reflection (see PROPHECY AND PROPHETS, HB), also in the first-person voice of Moses, on his own vocation and on Israel's as the perennial people of God. In short, the deuteronomic conjugation of covenantal theory and practice substantiates a normative sense of Torah as the constitutional legacy of Moses (Deut 29:10-15 [Hebrews 9–14]; Deut 31:9-13; 33:4-5).

1. Textual and Hermeneutical Foundations. Some of the key issues pursued in modern historical-critical study of Deuteronomy—pertaining especially to the character and coherence of the book's contents and their relationships to other scriptural traditions—were intimated early on by the several communities of its ancient guardians and interpreters. The crux of the matter is how these communities variously identified and appropriated the AUTHORITY of "this Torah" (e.g., Deut 1:5; 4:8) or, with specific reference to its written form, "this book of the Torah" (e.g., Deut 30:10; 31:26; cf. 17:18-20; Josh 1:7-8).

a. The Essene community of Qumran. Apart from inner-scriptural testimony (2 Kings 22–23; Nehemiah 8–10), the scrolls of Hasmonean and Herodian date, recovered from caves in the vicinity of Khirbet Qumran (see DEAD SEA SCROLLS), provide the earliest data to confirm the role of Deuteronomy in shaping Judaic piety and theological politics. More than thirty manuscripts of the book, or excerpted portions thereof, have been identified among the fragmentary finds (cf. F. García Martínez [1994]). This number is well above extant witnesses to any other book of the Pentateuch or Prophets and is possibly exceeded only by Qumran exemplars of the Psalms. The textual horizon of these manuscripts is considerably wider than the tradition stabilized in the MT of Deuteronomy, displaying features that had previously been identified as Samaritan and septuagintal in type (e.g., 4QDeut[q] and 5QDeut; see E. Ulrich [1992]).

Some of these manuscripts, such as 4QDeut[j] and 4Q Deut[n], can be classified as deutero-scriptural because they exhibit extracts from and rearrangements or paraphrases of the biblical text. Like the Nash Papyrus (comparable in date and textual character but of Egyptian provenance), they were apparently written for liturgical or scholarly use (J. Duncan [1992]; S. White [1990]; also DJD 14:7-142). Similarly, the manuscript known as 4Q *Testamonia* links together Deut 5:28-29; 18:18-19; Num 24:15-17; Deut 33:8-11; Josh 6:26—apparently as scriptural proof texts for prophetical-priestly leadership, whether individual or collective, in the succession of Moses. Other Qumran documents attest early forms of *Tefillin* (phylacteries) and *Mezuzot* (doorpost scroll) whose catena of passages include Deut 5:1–6:3 and 10:12-20 as well as the classical (rabbinic) pericopes of 6:4-9 and 11:13-21 (see Y. Yadin [1969]; J. Milik in DJD 6:34-85).

The difficulty in establishing sharp divides between biblical, deutero-scriptural, and derivative sectarian works among the Qumran finds is posed especially by documents that rewrite or imitate Pentateuchal literature. Some of these compositions have been called pseudo-deuteronomies: They take the form of testamentary addresses of Moses and are comparable to the already known *Testament* [*Assumption*] *of Moses,* which expansively recasts Deuteronomy 31–34 (J. Strugnell in DJD 19:131-36; D. Harrington [1973]). Even more dramatic is the comprehensive reworking of Pentateuchal legislation in the *Temple Scroll.* This work includes deuteronomic laws drafted in the form of divine rather than Mosaic first-person speech, as though the text were a primal record of Sinaitic revelation—the pristine "Torah of YHWH" (Ezra 7:10; Jer 8:8)—on which Moses based his exposition of Torah (Exod 34:11-27; Deut 5:22-31; Y. Yadin [1983] 1:390-97).

Nevertheless, in works that expressly describe communal piety and polity, the Essenes claim to be strict constructionists of the Torah of Moses. They identify themselves as a remnant of faithful disciples who have covenanted to engage in diligent study and observance of this law's prescriptions (e.g., CD 15.2–16.6; 1QS 5.8-10; 8.15-26). To judge by the literary remains, however, this commitment was not expressed in the production of commentaries on either Deuteronomy or other juridical-cultic corpora in the Pentateuch. Nor is literalistic exegesis of Pentateuchal laws a significant feature even in the sectarian "Rules"—though certainly these works make liberal use of deuteronomic idioms, and they often cite and allude to specific texts (e.g., Deut 9:5 in CD 8.1-15; Deut 17:17 in CD 5.2; Deut 10:16 and 30:6 in 1QS 5.4-5). It seems that the Qumran community appropriated the Mosaic Torah less as a fixed text to be interpreted through exposition than as a revealed vision of divine providence. One way of honoring the fullness of that vision was to expand its literary manifestations; another was to implement it as a discipline for daily life, under the guidance of leaders who were supposed to exercise the inspired authority of Moses (e.g., CD 1.11-12; 3.12-17; 6.2-11; 1QpHab 8.1-3; cf. Deut 34:9). As the principal witness in Scripture to Moses' inheritable vocation and to his own recomposition of the revealed Torah, Deuteronomy supplied both the hermeneutical warrant (see HERMENEUTICS) and the literary template for these complementary ways in which the Essene community was faithful to Torah as a living tradition (see 1QDM).

b. Samaritan Pentateuch (Sam. Pent.). The Pentateuch alone comprises Samaritan scripture, which is called "holy Torah." Each of its five parts may be referred to as "this Holy Book"; individual parts are designated by number, Deuteronomy being the fifth book (*sēper hāḥamîšî*). Such circumspect terminology respects the Torah's coherent, even unitary character while safeguarding the authority of the whole as peerless revelation received through Moses.

Consistent with this viewpoint is the textual profile of the Sam. Pent., now well illuminated by the Qumran scrolls (E. Tov [1989]; B. Waltke [1992]). The profile is also a principal reason for dating the Sam. Pent.'s discrete transmission only from the later Hasmonean or early Herodian period (F. M. Cross [1966]; J. Purvis [1968]). The text-base exhibits inner-Pentateuchal harmonizations, often identical to those attested in Qumran manuscripts (e.g., 4QpaleoExod^m and 4QNum^b). Typical are instances in which the first version of an event is filled out with variants from the Mosaic review of the same event in Deuteronomy: e.g., Exod 18:21-27 is reshaped in accord with Deut 1:9-18, and Deut 1:27-33 is interpolated following Num 13:33. In such fashion Scripture is made to interpret Scripture not only exegetically but also textually.

Some readings in the Sam. Pent. extend this general harmonizing proclivity in a peculiarly Samaritan direction. At the end of Deut 11:30, for example, the Sam. Pent. specifies the location of the oak of Moreh as "in front of Shechem," an identification based on Gen 12:6 (cf. *Sipre Deut.* 56, with the charge that this gloss in the Sam. Pent. is needless sectarian falsification of Torah). Much more elaborate—and comparable to reworked texts in 11QTemple—is the construction of a novel tenth commandment in Sam. Pent. versions of the DECALOGUE by interpolating after Exod 20:17 and Deut 5:21 a pastiche of readings adapted from Deut 11:29 + 27:2-7 + 11:30. The effect, no doubt intended, is to conjoin stipulations for a sanctuary on Mt. Gerizim, as Israel's mandatory and sole legitimate cult-place, to the zenith of Sinaitic revelation. Similarly, the Mosaic prescriptions in Deut 12:5, 14, 21 (etc.) were grammatically adjusted to read "the place that YHWH your God *has chosen*" [MT: "will choose"], since sacrificial worship at the "place" of Shechem had already been authorized and initiated at the time of God's appearance there to Abraham (Gen 12:6-7).

What was at stake in such contextual modifications of the Sam. Pent., and may have contributed to their introduction, is illustrated in JOSEPHUS's account of a dispute between the Samaritan and the Jewish communities in Alexandria during the reign of Ptolemy Philometor (c. 150 BCE). The matter in deadly contention was whether Scripture provided Mt. Gerizim or Zion/Jerusalem to be the site divinely chosen for an Israelite temple; according to Josephus, Ptolemy passed judgment in favor of the Jewish argument and executed the Samaritan opponents (*Ant. Jud.* 13.74-79; cf. 13.275-83). Whatever the truth of this account, the Samaritan case does not lack Pentateuchal support (Gen 33:18-20; Deut 11:29-30; 27:1-13) and is considerably stronger without the additional witnesses of Jewish scriptures to the inspired work of David and Solomon (e.g., 2 Samuel 6–7; 1 Kings 6–8). There is reason enough here for the restricted, or attenuated, Mosaic CANON of the Samaritans.

Early Samaritan hermeneutical traditions, to the extent that they can be recovered (R. Bóid [1988]; A. Tal [1989]), seem to bear closer resemblance to those of the Qumran community than to either the formal development of pharisaic-rabbinic *halakah* (authoritative guidance) or to the fundamentalism of the later KARAITES. That is, the Mosaic Torah was appropriated by the Samaritan community as reliable testimony to the revelation that became full and preeminent at Sinai (Exod 34:1-27; Deut 10:1-5; 31:24-26). Some internal reshaping of the text of the Torah made it more perspicuous, at least in an early stage of its transmission. Samaritan religious practices, however, did not have to be legitimated through rigorous exegesis of this text (as in Karaism), nor did the Samaritans acknowledge a supplemental oral Torah per se. Rather, their traditional praxis was sufficiently warranted by pedagogical lore whose transmission they traced back to Moses. This hermeneutical perspective is, once again, shaped by interpretation of Deuteronomy (31:22, 28-29; 32:1-3, 44-47).

c. Pharisaic-rabbinic scriptures. Designations of Deuteronomy used in classical Jewish sources suggest a somewhat ambiguous understanding of its character. The book is most often identified by its incipit, i.e., the initial phrase of the editorial preface in 1:1-5: *ʾelleh haddebārîm* (These [are] the words), which is commonly shortened to *Debārîm,* "Words." According to the traditional view, the whole Pentateuch consists of Moses' words; hence the more discrete sense of the appellation in 1:1 must be Moses' "words of reprimand" (*dibrê tôkāḥôt*)—recognized to be a prophetical genre—which are recorded in the following chapters (Deuteronomy 1–3; also 29–32) as a prologue to his testamentary review of covenantal law (see *Sipre Deut.* 1; Rashi). However, other authorities took "words" in 1:1 to refer to legal stipulations of the Torah proper, a topic reintroduced in Deut 4:44–5:1 and followed first by Moses' recall of the foundational divine words of the Decalogue and then by his amplification of them (so, e.g., Nachmanides [Ramban]). These alternatives intimate the pivotal position that Deuteronomy occupies between the earlier books of the Pentateuch and the Prophets.

The issue of the book's relationship to earlier Pentateuchal traditions is posed more sharply by the Hebrew appellation *Mishneh Torah* (e.g., *b. Meg.* 31b; cf. *Sipre Deut.* 160). The sense can be construed either as "repetition of Torah," thus identifying the book as a general reprise of Pentateuchal legislation in its narrative setting; or as "supplemental Torah," identifying the deuteronomic polity as Moses' secondary elaboration of the Decalogue (Deut 4:1-2, 13-14; 5:28–6:2). These distinctive nuances are not insignificant: The first was emphasized in Jewish tradition and the latter by many Christian interpreters, who sometimes used it to relativize the authority of Mosaic legislation (see sec. 2 below). The Greek equivalent of *Mishneh Torah* is [*to*] *deuteronomion* (e.g., *T. Mos.* 1.8; Philo *Leg. All.* 3.174; see Eusebius *Hist. eccl.* 6.25.1-2), which yields, via Latin, the name "Deuteronomy." This Greek designation, apparently favoring the second nuance, was introduced into the SEPTUAGINT of Deut 17:18 as an interpretative title for the book of Mosaic Torah, most likely reflecting the Greek rendition of a similar expression in Josh 8:32 [LXX 9:5]: *to deuteronomion nomon Mouse*, "Deuteronomy, Moses' law."

Even apart from the Greek translation, however, the ambiguity of *Mishneh Torah* points to the hermeneutical significance of Deuteronomy in the extended, three-part scriptures of rabbinic Judaism. In a conventional sense, the book completes the principal codification of law authorized at Sinai/Horeb (cf. Deut 1:3, 5; 5:1–6:3). In a less conventional sense, it creates collective scriptural Torah by drawing earlier parts of the Pentateuch into its own unique self-identification as "[the book of] the Torah [of Moses]" (Deut 31:9-11, 24-26; see Neh 8:1-3). Moreover, this self-identification forms the referential link between the Pentateuch and the following collections of the *Nebi'im* (both former and latter prophets), whose initial and concluding exhortations (Josh 1:1-9; Mal 4:4-6 [Heb 3:22-24]) reaffirm in deuteronomic idiom the efficacy of Mosaic Torah (see also, e.g., Josh 23:6; 1 Kgs 2:3; 2 Kgs 14:6; 23:25). The third scriptural division, the *Ketubim* (various writings), was also understood to give manifold witness to the continuing relevance of Torah in Israel's communal life (e.g., Neh 13:1-3; Psalm 1; 19; Dan 6:5; 9:11-14; cf. Eccl 12:13-14). Beyond these canonical corpora, the putative distillations of oral Torah into *Mishnah* (Instruction) and *Talmud* (Teaching) were deemed to be rabbinical permutations of the fuller Sinaitic revelation as transmitted and interpreted by Moses and his successors (Deut 17:8-11; 33:10; 34:9; *m.* '*Abot* 1; *Sipre Deut.* 351; *Pesiq. R.* 5).

The preeminent holiness, textual immutability, and insuperable authority of Pentateuchal Torah are fundamentals of rabbinic Judaism (e.g., *m. Meg.* 3.1; *b. Erub.* 13a; see Josephus *Apion* 2.184-89). No less basic, however, is the hermeneutical strategy that opens this scriptural inner sanctum outward, extending its sanctifying power into the history of God's faithful people (W. Green [1987]; D. Kraemer [1991]). Accordingly, not Deuteronomy alone, but the rest of Scripture—Prophets and Writings—together with the complementary *Halakot* of oral Torah and even the rabbinical traditions that continue to interpret them, become in effect *Mishneh Torah*—repetition or, better, amplification of the divine words spoken to Israel's generations through the voice of Moses (see *b. Qidd.* 49a).

d. Christian Scriptures. The ordering of books in the Christian Bible, emergent in the late second century CE, effectively prescribed a sequential, salvation-historical reading of the conjoined Jewish and apostolic Scriptures of the early church (e.g., Eusebius *Hist. eccl.* 4.26.12-14). This arrangement, which finally yielded Genesis to Malachi (with the Law and the Prophets absorbing the more fluid collection of the Writings) and Matthew to Revelation, reflects the narrative design that developed from early apostolic preaching (e.g., Acts 3:11-26; 13:13-41) into the more comprehensive periodization of history attested in the patristic rule of faith (e.g., Irenaeus *Proof;* see P. Blowers [1997]; R. Greer [1986] 126-54; R. Soulen [1996] 25-56). In this scheme the primal epoch of creation and fall has its endtime counterpart in the events of redemption and consummation. What stretches between primal and endtime epochs is preparation for the gospel—i.e., the scriptural history of Abraham's lineage through Isaac, Jacob, and the people Israel, separated from other nations but living among them as chosen witnesses to God's interim covenants and sublime promises that would come to universal fulfillment through the redemptive work of Christ (Luke 1:68-79).

In such canonical hermeneutics, Deuteronomy marks the transition or, better, forms a bond between the Pentateuchal and the prophetical segments of the extended protoevangelical narrative. The linkage is conceptual as well as serial. Although the nomistic character and contents of the deuteronomic Torah could scarcely be ignored, the work in its early Christian appropriation figures less as a corpus of perdurable divine legislation than as a farsighted testament, composed of oracular "words" (Deut 1:1 [Gr. *hoi logoi*]; 31:1, 28; 32:44-47; see J. Blenkinsopp [1977] 80-95; J. Barton [1986]). Here Moses, the principal instrument of divine guidance in Israel's constitutive experiences of exodus and covenant-making (e.g., Exod 3:7-12; 14:31; 34:10; Num 12:6-8; Deut 34:10-12), models the spiritual acuity of those who, in his succession (Deut 18:15-22), will also be empowered to impart knowledge of God's providential sovereignty, to warn of impending judgment, and to preach repentance that can lead to renewal of life (Deut 4:25-40; 31:16–32:47; cf. 2 Kgs 17:13; Neh 1:5-11; 9:26-31; Dan 9:3-19; Mal 4:4-6; Matt 3:1-3; 11:11-15; Acts 3:17-26; 7:35-53). The words of Deuteronomy thus inaugurate the testimony of Moses and the prophets; they shape a legacy that prefigures the efficacy of the gospel and articulates a desperate human need for it (Luke 16:29-31; 24:27, 44; John 1:45; 5:39-47; Acts 26:22; 28:23; 1 Pet 1:10-12; see also, e.g., *Barn.* 6.8-10; *1 Clem.* 43.1-6; Irenaeus *Proof* 28-30, 95-96; *Adv. Haer.* 3.12.11-5; and Tertullian *Apology* 18.5; 19.1-4).

Characteristic, but still flexible, features of this hermeneutical profile are widely exhibited in NT sources. Portraits of JESUS' life and teaching in the Gospels identify, with varying degrees of clarity, prototypes in the intertwined careers of Moses and of early Israel (R. France [1989]; D. Hay [1990]; W. Meeks [1967]; D. Moessner [1983]). Among striking instances of this is the episode of Jesus' trial in the desert following his baptism, in which he employs Mosaic admonitions, summarizing the lessons of Israel's sojourn in the wilderness, to thwart Satan's wiles (cf. Matt 4:1-10 and Luke 4:1-12 with Deut 8:3; 6:13, 16). Both continuity of roles and supplantation are apparent in the SYNOPTIC transfiguration accounts (Matt 17:1-13; Mark 9:2-13; Luke 9:28-36) and so too in reports of Jesus' authoritative teaching about what the law and the prophets demand (e.g., cf. Matt 5:17-20; 19:1-22; 22:34-40 with Deut 5:1-21; 6:4-5; 24:1-4; see Luke 16:16-17). Vocational supersession as well as metaphysical precession is explicit in the JOHANNINE prologue, which juxtaposes promulgation of the law through Moses with manifestation of God's "grace and truth" in the work of Christ (John 1:17; Heb 3:1-6; 8). Similarly, displacement of the Mosaic law by the gift of God's righteousness, received through faith in Christ, is integral to the salvation-history sketched in the Pauline epistles (e.g., Rom 3:21-26; 10:1-4; 2 Cor 3:7–4:6; Phil 3:7-11; cf. Eph 2:11-22). This is stated most vituperatively in PAUL's address to the Galatian Christians: He declares diligent observance of Torah (Gr. *nomos*)—which is the practical discipline of faith extolled as life-sustaining in deuteronomic discourse—to be a "yoke of slavery" (Gal 5:1), implicating any Gentiles who are persuaded to accept it in the covenantal curses from which Christ has already freed the spiritual heirs of Abraham (cf. Gal 3:6–4:7 with Deut 4:1-4; 11:26-28; 21:23; 27:26; 28:58-59). The argument is more extensive and artful in Paul's epistle to the Romans, a difference suited to the particular audience and issues treated. Here deuteronomic texts are prominent among those Paul cites and creatively reworks to construct a grand economy of salvation whose just denouement requires parity between faithful, Torah-observant Jews and believing Gentiles (cf. Rom 1:18-25;

3:29-30; 10:5-10, 19; 12:19; 15:8-12 with Deut 4:15-20; 6:4; 30:11-14; 32:4-6, 21, 35, 43; see R. Hays [1989] 34-83, 163-64).

2. Interpretation of Deuteronomy in Traditional Jewish and Christian Sources (1st–15th cents.). Commentary linked consecutively to the biblical text did not become a primary medium for interpretive study of Deuteronomy until the Middle Ages. By then the mainstreams of classical Judaic and Christian interpretations of the book's resources were well established—shaped during the centuries of Hellenistic antiquity through liturgical performance, preaching, and communal praxis as well as through scholarly apologetics and polemics, both extramural and internecine. The devastating blows to Jerusalem's Temple cultus and Jewish national aspirations struck by Rome in response to the revolts of 66–70 and 132–135 CE were critical factors in the divergence of these interpretive mainstreams.

a. Formation of rabbinic and patristic orthodoxies (1st–5th cents.). The appropriate role of Mosaic Torah in sustaining the communal faith and the discrete political identity of Israel in the midst of other nations was not Paul's preoccupation alone, of course, nor was it a new one in his era. Deuteronomy directly addressed some of the chief theological and cultural issues, especially in 4:1-40. The agenda for Israel's survival as the unique people of God, which is eloquently sketched in this preamble to the legislative corpus, was developed in both visionary and institutional forms from the exile through the extended Judean restoration of the later sixth and fifth centuries BCE (e.g., Ezra 3:2; 7:11-26; Neh 10:28-31 [Heb 29–32]; Neh 13:1-3; Isa 51:4-8; 61:1-11; Jer 31:31-37). Moreover, the semi-autonomous polity of the Judean commonwealth, based on scriptural Torah and consolidated by Ezra and Nehemiah under Persian auspices, was apparently privileged as ancestral law in the wake of Alexander's conquest of the Near East (late 4th cent. BCE; see Josephus *Ant. Jud.* 11.329–39). The polity seems to have retained this benign status through the first century and a half of Ptolemaic and Seleucid hegemony in Syro-Palestine, until it was undermined and forcefully abrogated during the reign of Antiochus IV Epiphanes (175–164 BCE; see 1 Maccabees 1; 2 Maccabees 1–7; 4 Macc 3:20–4:26).

The latter crisis, with the successful Maccabean-led response to it and the often fractious politics of Hasmonean rule that ensued, is the starting point for Josephus's review of the centuries of Judean civil strife and international conflict that culminated during his own lifetime in Rome's destruction of the commonwealth (*Bel. Jud.* 1.17-30). Already in this account of the Jewish War (or First Revolt of 66–70 CE), but more expressly in his later works that define and defend the centrality of Torah in Jewish life, Josephus's theopolitical perspective is deuteronomic, again as epitomized by the paradigm of Deut 4:1-40 (see also Josh 1:1-9; 2 Kgs 17:7-20).

Since its constitution in the time of Moses, Josephus maintained, the Jewish state prospered, or decreased and failed, according to the strict measure of its fidelity to God's will, articulated in the laws promulgated through Moses (e.g., *Ant. Jud.* 1.14; 4.176-93; *Apion* 1.42-43; 2.45-47, 145-89). Judea's recent defeat by Rome is no exception, attributable to the latter's superior might and culture; rather, the Roman legions prevailed because they were implementing God's judgment on the divisive policies and deviant practices of Judea's tyrannical leadership (*Bel. Jud.* 1.9-12; 5.375-419; 6.38-41, 99-110; 7.358-60; cf. *Ant. Jud.* 20.215-18; see *'Abot R. Nat.* A 4).

Josephus's overview of Israel's Mosaic "constitution" (Gr. *politeia*) takes the form of a broad paraphrase of Deuteronomy 12–26, into which he interpolated some supplementary ordinances from earlier Pentateuchal corpora (*Ant. Jud.* 4.196-301). He emphasized the fairness and practicability of this ancestral legislation, occasionally adding juridical details that are not found in the biblical text but that are most often congruent with Pharisaic and later rabbinic interpretation (e.g., *Ant. Jud.* 4.219, 248, 254; see 13.297-98).

The influence of Deut 4:1-40 may also be discerned in the erudite reworking of the Greek Pentateuch authored by PHILO, a leader of the Jewish community resident in Alexandria, Egypt, who flourished in the earlier first century CE (i.e., before the war between the Jewish state and Rome). Using terminology and philosophical concepts familiar to his Hellenized audience, Philo extolled at length the virtues of Moses and of Mosaic legislation. He argued that not only is Israel's polity both more ancient than and superior to the ancestral laws of other nations but also that it manifested from the outset the sublime ideals of reason, piety, equity, and amity celebrated in Platonic thought and pursued toward the ultimate goal of the intellect's freedom in the spiritual regimen of Stoicism (e.g., *Vita Mos.* 1.156, 162; 2.12, 25-44, 50-51; *Virt.*; *Liber* 41-47; cf. Deut 4:5-8). According to Philo's influential analysis, the Decalogue is a legislative précis consisting of divinely articulated general laws (*Heres* 167-68; *Spec. Leg.* 4.132); these ten stipulations serve as the main heads under which all other Pentateuchal ordinances may be arranged and interpreted as either oracular pronouncements of Moses or his own authoritative specifications of divine will (*Vita Mos.* 2.187-91; cf. Deut 4:12-14; 5:22–6:3). This scheme for relating the specifics of Mosaic legislation to the moral precepts of the Decalogue facilitated Philo's claim that there is no real disparity between the universal natural order of divine law, idealized by Hellenistic culture, and such sacral rites as Passover that are peculiar features of Israel's experience, shaping its unique vocation as God's priesthood among the world's nations (e.g., *Spec. Leg.* 2.150-67; see *Op. Mun.* 1.1-3). Conversely, although Philo made extensive use of allegory to exposit the universal significance of particular laws (e.g., Deut 23:1-2 [Heb 2-3] in *Spec. Leg.* 1.326-32), he insisted that the literal, practicable sense of Mosaic legislation should not be denigrated or exegetically abrogated (*Mig. Ab.* 89-93).

Philo's work, which brilliantly illuminates an intersection between first-century Judaism and Hellenistic culture, had formative influence on the development of the ALEXANDRIAN SCHOOL of early Christian biblical scholarship. The principal architects of rabbinic Judaism, on the other hand, were the generations of Jewish scholars active at Jabneh and at other sites in Roman Palestine, who are known collectively as *Tannaim* (teachers, transmitters [of tradition]). Their labors extended from the beginning of the first century CE through the early third, when the Mishnah and the chief collections of Tannaitic Pentateuchal MIDRASH, including *Sipre* to the book of Deuteronomy, were stabilized in written forms. The achievement these works attest is the reconstitution of a coherent Jewish identity, one still resolute as to the insuperable authority, efficacy, and integrity of revealed traditions of Torah ("Torah from Heaven," *m. Sanh.* 10.1) and able to withstand at least interim loss of the Temple service as a means of divine grace and blessing (*'Abot R. Nat.* A 4, 14, 38).

The Mishnah documents the jurisprudential consolidation of rabbinic Judaism as an integrated system of faith and praxis. The key integrating factor is a rigorous discipline of piety that, in continuity with the themes of Pentateuchal legislation, interrelates sacral obligations—including those of the defunct Temple cultus—with civil duties and ethical responsibilities. One who resists the entrapments of worldly culture and follows this discipline (accepting "the yoke of Torah," *m. 'Abot* 3.5; see *'Abot R. Nat.* A 20) serves God with the whole self in all aspects of personal and communal life; hence the Mishnah aptly begins with instruction about twice-daily recitation of the *Shema'*, whose keynote in Deut 6:4-9 epitomizes this covenantal commitment of those who comprise Israel (*m. Ber.* 1-2).

The relationship between the Pentateuchal traditions of law and the Mishnah's tractates is complex. The Mishnah frequently cites scriptural sources, often as proof texts for particular arguments; and it sometimes links expository remarks to segments of text (e.g., the serial comments on Deut 26:13-15 in *m. Ma'aś. S.* 5.10-14, replicated in *Sipre Deut.* 303; see also *m. Soṭ.* 8 on Deut 20:2-9). On the whole, however, the work presents a complex reconfiguration of traditional Judaic polity, for the most part loosely arranged around scriptural loci, rather than an exegetical extension of Pentateuchal laws. For example, the tractate *Makkot* (Stripes), which derives its name from the practice of flogging regulated in Deut 25:1-3, treats various aspects of judicial due process and punishment, matters that are associated with the implementation of a number of

Pentateuchal provisions (including Deut 19:1-13, 15-21). The archaic institution known as levirate marriage, sketched in Deut 25:5-10, is presupposed in tractate *Yebamot* (Brothers' Widows), which is largely concerned with contingencies and exemptions in application of the scriptural precedent (see, similarly, *m. Pe'a* on Deut 24:19-21 and *m. Seb.* 10.3-7 on Deut 15:2). Note is sometimes taken of scholarly differences in interpretation of biblical regulations; a classic example is the dispute between the schools of Shammai and HILLEL over the grounds for divorce allowed by Deut 24:1 (*m. Git.* 9.10; see also 8.9).

Midrash *Sipre* to Deuteronomy provides a lucid expositional complement to the associative concatenations of the Mishnah's legal reasoning. *Sipre* is also an anthology of Tannaitic scholarship, composed in this case of selected interpretations and rulings of various rabbinical authorities and schools, attached segmentally to rubrics of the scriptural text (see R. Hammer [1986]; J. Neusner [1987]; S. Fraade [1991]). The legislative corpus of Deuteronomy 12:2–26:15 receives fullest treatment (secs. [*pisqa'ot*] 60-303). Although some comments of antiquarian and homiletical character are included here (e.g., in secs. 148, 152, 275) most are concerned to give succinct definition to such matters as the logical sense, strict applicability, and continuing relevance of the scriptural ordinances as received and interpreted by the scribes and by their Tannaitic successors (e.g., secs. 153-54, 248, 285; see *m. Yad.* 4.3). Interconnections with the regulations and expository remarks of the Mishnah are both common and illustrative of the exegetical foundations of rabbinic orthopraxis (e.g., cf. *m. Hag.* 1.1-5 with sec. 143 on Deut 16:16-17, and *m. Sanh.* 2.4 with sec. 159 on Deut 17:17; cf. secs. 127-43 on Deut 16:1-17, providing a virtual textbook on method). Moreover, the value of *Sipre* as a complement to Mishnaic jurisprudence is greatly enhanced by sections of exposition devoted to portions of Deuteronomy that frame the central polity (specifically secs. 1-59 treating Deut 1:1-29; 3:23-29; 6:4-9; 7:12; 11:10–12:1; and secs. 304-57 on Deut 31:14; 32:1-52; 33:1-29; and 34:1-12). Sensitivity to theological and hermeneutical issues is sharply attested here, articulated often in view of Israel's threatened status among the world's nations and sometimes in apparent defense against the competing claims on scriptural traditions made by Samaritans and Christians (e.g., secs. 31, 56, 311-12, 336). Prevalent themes are that God has neither abandoned the sole legitimate lineage of Abraham, which extends through Jacob and his physical offspring, nor negated the efficacy of the Torah. In sum, the whole Torah, promulgated through Moses, remains Israel's unique and unifying inheritance, witnessing still to its favor with God (eloquently expounded in secs. 342-46 on Deut 33:2-5).

Tannaitic insistence that faithful observance of Torah continued to define the existence of Abraham's true heirs is one of the two major poles with reference to which patristic Christianity sought to establish an identity for the church as "the Israel of God" (Gal 6:16). The second pole is represented by otherwise diverse parties, eventually marginalized as heretical, who shared a view that the cultural idiosyncrasies of scriptural Torah made it largely irrelevant or even antithetical to the universal spiritual redemption effected through Christ. Negotiating a middle course that respected the revelatory import of Pentateuchal legislation while transcending many of its ostensible demands required both vigorous and flexible argumentation. Philo's agile hermeneutics had shown the way.

Themes that developed into characteristic patristic views on the significance of the Mosaic law are adumbrated in the *Epistle of* BARNABAS, probably composed in the late first or early second century CE. By then, destruction of the Temple in Jerusalem and further loss of Judean civil autonomy after the failed First Revolt had decisively altered the terms of the early apostolic debate regarding the extent to which observance of Torah was incumbent on either Jewish or gentile Christians (e.g., Acts 10:1–11:26; 15:1-29; cf. Jas 1:19–4:12). Most substantively, the traditional sacrificial cultus—revealed at Sinai and implemented under Moses' direction (e.g., Exodus 40; Numbers 7–8)—had been physically abrogated, thus rendering key portions of the Torah no longer institutionally practicable. According to *Barnabas,* however, this did not negate Mosaic law; it confirmed that what the old cultus had imperfectly materialized was now spiritually realized through Christ's expiation of sins, a remission that transformed the church's membership into a new temple of God's indwelling presence (*Barn.* 4:11; 5:1-7; 8:1-3; 16:1-10; cf. 1 Cor 6:19; 2 Cor 6:14-18; Eph 2:19-22; Hebrews 7–11; 1 Pet 2:4-5). Accordingly, Christ repristinated Moses' work as mediator: Moses restored the covenant to conform with God's original intention, removing from it the heavy "yoke of necessity" imposed because of Israel's apostasy in the golden calf affair (*Barn.* 2:4-10; 4:6-8; 6:19; 14:1-6); and he unveiled the law's spiritual significance, which had become obfuscated by Jewish literalism (e.g., *Barn.* 10 on the dietary laws of Leviticus 11 and Deut 14:3-21). Freed from the incrustations of traditional Jewish praxis, the Decalogue especially undergirds the moral "law of Christ" (Gal 6:2), which guides the consecrated community along the "way of light" (*Barnabas* 15; 19; see also *Didache* 1–2).

The costly second Judean revolt of 132–135 CE, whose messianic nativism had significant Tannaitic support, sharpened the divide already evident in *Barnabas* between a Christian "we" and a Jewish "they" (e.g., *Barn.* 3:6; 8:7; 10:12; 13:1; see Justin *First Apology* 32; Eusebius *Hist. eccl.* 4.5-6; 4.8.4). From the later second through the fifth centuries, this polarization is exhibited in patristic apologetic and adversative writings that defend, often stridently, the church's claim to be the chosen legatee of ancient Israel's Scriptures and covenantal identity (Eusebius *Praep. Evang.* 14.52; Augustine *Adv. Jud.* 3; 12; *Trinity* 1.13; *Answer to Maximinus* 2.10.1; 2.23.1-3). Two approaches to the significance of Pentateuchal law, distinguished in part by the interpretive uses they make of Deuteronomy, are represented in these sources. One of these approaches is identified with prominent Alexandrian scholars.

Alexandrian Christianity, which may have been the provenance of *Barnabas,* developed a catechetical curriculum indebted to Philo that integrated scriptural testimony to divine sovereignty with popular currents of Hellenistic learning. An eclectic Stoicism is the intellectual medium used by CLEMENT OF ALEXANDRIA to commend the ethical sublimity of biblical law in his *Paidagogos* and *Stromateis,* written at the close of the second century. The Word brought near to Israel in Mosaic legislation and in the new law manifest in Christ, the incarnate Word, are understood in these treatises to be complementary, successive stages in a divine pedagogy of saving knowledge (e.g., *Paid.* 1.9, 53-61; cf. Deut 30:11-14; John 1:14-18). As Philo had argued, Moses was a preeminent paradigm of wisdom and virtue; Moses' instructions to Israel, therefore, continue to provide a foundational education for Christian initiates in humanitarian values, preparing them for the advanced course in the soul's spiritual ascent taught by Christ (*Strom.* 1.23-26; 2.78-96; 2.105). ORIGEN, who studied under Clement, made extensive use of allegory and typology to discern the figurative import of Pentateuchal traditions, while disparaging Jewish literalism as parochial (e.g., *Con. Cel.* 1.47; 2.78; 4.49-53; 5.42-50; *De Prin.* 4.3.2.). In Origen's view, Deuteronomy—the "second law" that succeeds the cultic provisions of the Sinaitic covenant—is the type of Christ's moral law, just as Joshua, who succeeded Moses in the leadership of God's people, prefigures his namesake Jesus (*De Prin.* 4.3.12-13; cf. Num 13:16; Deut 31:7-23; 34:9). In the earlier fifth century this position was elaborated by CYRIL OF ALEXANDRIA in his *Glaphyra,* extant portions of which include typological exposition of selected texts in Deuteronomy 21–31. For example, the strange expiatory ritual featuring an unworked heifer in 21:1-9 became intelligible to Cyril as a type of Christ's sacrificial atonement (*Glaph. in Deut.* 643-50).

A second strategy, shaped more by Pauline than by Philonic considerations, emphasized, not the metaphysical harmony of law and gospel, as did Alexandrian hermeneutics, but ostensible discord between them as well as perceived tensions within the Pentateuch. Justin's *Dialogue with Trypho,* set soon after the Second Revolt, exhibits the ambivalence toward Mosaic revelation that characterizes this approach. Although the polity revealed at Horeb specifically for the Jews is declared obsolete, some of the former legislation is

acknowledged to remain "good, holy, and just" because it correlates with the new covenant universalized through Christ (e.g., *Dial.* 11, 45, 67). A number of works composed in the later second and third centuries attempt to differentiate between two or more categories of Pentateuchal legislation: Laws instituted by Moses or elaborated by his successors are deemed to be of questionable authority (see Deut 17:8-13; Matt 15:2; *m. Yad.* 4.2; *y. Sanh.* 11.3-4); only the Decalogue receives full approbation as efficacious instruction for the moral life of Christians (Ptolemaeus, *Letter to Flora; Pseudo-Clementine Homilies* 2.38-40; 3.41-51; *Didascalia Apostolorum* 1.6; 6.15-17; and, somewhat later in date, the *Apostolic Constitutions*). IRENAEUS, in his *Adversus Haereses,* develops an influential and relatively moderate form of this position. Especially on the basis of Deuteronomy 4–6, he distinguishes between the sufficient revelation to Israel of God's "natural precepts," encoded as the Decalogue, and two categories of supplemental legislation (Heb. *haḥuqqîm wehammišpāṭîm* [NRSV: the statutes and ordinances, e.g., Deut 4:1, 14, 45; 6:1] rendered in Latin by *caerimonias et iudicia* [the ceremonial and judicial laws]). The latter types were imposed through Moses as interim restraints on Israelite sinfulness; after Christ, they retain only figurative import (*Adv. Haer.* 4.15-17). This broad distinction, used to affirm Christian fidelity to the universal moral law as revealed to ancient Israel and to relativize Pentateuchal support for Jewish particularism, became a mainstay of patristic apologetics (see Tertullian *Adv. Iud.* 2-3; *Apology* 21.1-3; Chrysostom *Adv. Iud.* 1.5; 6.6; *Homilies on the Statues* 12; Augustine *Spirit and Letter* 36; *Adversus Faustum Manichaeum* 4.1-2; 6.2; 10:2-3; 16.10; 32.8-15).

b. Medieval developments (6th–15th cents.). By and large, interpretation of Deuteronomy during the Middle Ages conformed to the respective mainstreams of rabbinic and patristic orthodoxy. Important developments may be observed even so, especially in ways that traditional views of Moses' legacy were defended and, as became necessary after the turn of the millennium, adjusted to new intellectual circumstances.

AUGUSTINE's four-part *De doctrina christiana,* completed in 427, defined the curriculum for Christian biblical scholarship and teaching that prevailed through the Middle Ages and beyond. (The later medieval handbooks of Cassiodorus Senator, Isidore of Seville, and Hugh of St. Victor are in large measure revised editions of Augustine's work.) According to Augustine, Scripture must be understood and effectively exposited in order to fulfill its innate purpose, which is instruction in how to love God and neighbor. By giving careful attention to matters of historical context and to the diction of texts in their original languages, interpreters seek to understand what the inspired authors of Scripture (see INSPIRATION OF THE BIBLE) intended to convey. If the "letter" of the text does not yield a sense in accord with the rule of charity, then the interpretation is either false or incomplete; recognition of semantic figurations and use of allegorical method may facilitate discernment of the text's true spiritual sense, which is the only one that can teach Christian morality and nurture faith worth propagating. In short, sound exposition of Scripture is the essential handmaid of practical theology.

This influential agenda helps to account for the unsystematic, disjunctive character of most medieval Christian commentaries on Deuteronomy (and some other biblical books as well): Such works are typically composed of sparse explanatory notes, mostly gleaned from earlier sources, recorded to assist expository study, teaching, and preaching by identifying spiritual tropes that a literal reading of the text might miss (see the commentaries ascribed to Bede [c. 700] and Rabanus Maurus [c. 850]). The earliest extant commentary on Deuteronomy of this type (known as catena) is attributed to Procopius of Gaza (c. 520); it consists in the main of paraphrased extracts from Alexandrian and other Greek patristic sources. Introductory notes, apparently influenced by Philo and Origen, sketch an overview of the book's significance: Read literally, Deuteronomy is a record of the covenantal legislation promulgated by Moses in Moab, supplementing the covenant already enacted at Horeb (citing Deut 29:1); read figuratively, the Mosaic polity points to the natural law of the cosmic "city of God" (citing Ps 87:3). Although most of the expository notes pertain to types and tropes (e.g., the two wives in Deut 21:15-16 connote the Jewish synagogue and the gentile church; Joshua is a figure of Jesus, who is the prophet like Moses announced in 18:15-19), "this Deuteronomy" in 17:18 (LXX) is identified—as JEROME, among others, had done (*PL* 25, 17B; commenting on the date in Ezek 1:1)—with the book found in the Jerusalem Temple during Josiah's reign and read aloud to the assembled people (2 Kgs 22:8; 23:21). Deuteronomy 32:1-43 receives the fullest treatment, testifying to the importance of this prophetic canticle in Christian as well as in Jewish liturgy and preaching (see Josephus *Ant. Jud.* 4.303-4; *Sipre Deut.* 306-33; *Roš. Haš.* 31a).

Talmudic amplification of the Torah, in the form of commentary on the tractates of the Mishnah, was substantially complete by the end of the sixth century. The definitive Babylonian version (denoted by *b.* before the title of the tractate) includes at least oblique response to hermeneutical moves characteristic of patristic theology. Above all, the rabbinical sages insist that the whole Torah of Moses suffices to sustain Israel's sacral vocation, countering presumptions of Christians and others that new revelation has superseded it or that any of its components are "not from Heaven" or lack full, permanent, divine authorization (see *b. Sanh.* 99a; *b. Šabb.* 104a). Several deuteronomic texts provide the scriptural

foundations for prosecution of this case. First, Deut 33:1-5 establishes that Torah was neither revealed to the Gentiles nor meant for secondary appropriation by them; its 613 prescriptions and prohibitions (the numerical value of Torah plus two, which are the initial stipulations of the Decalogue addressed to the Israelite assembly at Sinai in divine first-person voice [Exod 20:2-6; Deut 5:6-10]) remain the legitimate possession of Jacob/Israel alone (*b. Sanh.* 59a-b; cf. *b. Mak.* 23b-24a; *b. 'Abod. Zar.* 2b-3b; and compare *Sipre Deut.* 322, 343). Second, Deut 4:1-40 and Lev 18:2-5 frame reconsideration (see Sirach 24; Philo; Josephus) of how this covenantal legacy of law comports with general wisdom or rationalistic knowledge ostensibly shared among the world's cultured nations. On the basis of these texts the sages identify a significant difference between the Mosaic statutes [*ḥuqqîm*] and ordinances [*mišpāṭîm*], one that resembles the distinction represented by the Latin renderings "ceremonials" [*caerimonias*] and "judicials" [*iudicia*]. The ordinances are precepts that Jews, certainly, but also enlightened Gentiles should recognize to be prudent and just (Deut 4:5-8): They include rules for judicial due process and proscriptions of idolatry, blasphemy, murder, theft, and sexual immorality—all matters covered, according to rabbinical exegesis of Gen 2:16-17, by the so-called Noahic or Adamic laws (see *b. Sanh.* 56a-b; *Deut. Rab.* 2.25). The statutes, on the other hand, are sacral rites and regulations, such as the injunction against wearing garments woven of both wool and linen (Deut 22:11), that may be opaque to conventional reason and whose faithful observance honors God's rule but offends the minions of Satan (*b. Yoma* 67b). Torah's discrete, coherent purpose of sustaining Israel's relationship with God is thus violated by any attempt to extract from its corpora universal, natural precepts of morality or to set aside laws supposed to have only temporary or parochial import. Third, the Great Court instituted in accord with Deut 17:8-13 (see 1:9-18; Exod 18:13-26; Num 11:16-25) assumes the mantle of Moses in jurisprudential affairs (*b. Sanh.* 86b-89a). Because this court's decisions, based on Mosaic precedents, are deemed at once to be rulings intended by God (Deut 1:17; 15:1-2), it is unnecessary as well as illegitimate to revise the Torah by adding to or subtracting from its provisions (Deut 4:2). In sum, constitutional Torah encompasses its own authoritative interpretation (see *b. Sanh.* 87a; *b. Qidd.* 49b).

Other currents of Jewish interpretation of Deuteronomy, flowing from late antiquity through the Middle Ages, are represented in the major Aramaic TARGUMIM, *Onqelos* (*Tg. Onq.*) and the freer, more expansive Palestinian versions, especially *Neofiti* (*Tg. Neof.*) and *Pseudo-Jonathan* (*Tg. Ps.-J.*). The contemporizing style of these Targumim features paraphrase and adaptation (e.g., *Shekinah* replaces the indwelling divine name in Deut 12:5, etc.) but not allegory; figurative readings are few and usually intertextual (see INTERTEXTUALITY) in character (e.g., the toponyms "Laban" and "Di-zahab" in Deut 1:1 are understood etymologically, in the senses "white" and "of gold" respectively, to connote the manna and golden-calf episodes [so already *Sipre Deut.* 1]; "Lebanon" in Deut 11:24 is read as an epithet of the Jerusalem Temple [*Tg. Neof.; Tg. Ps.-J.*]).

Although apparently redacted in the eighth or ninth century, *Midraš Debarim Rabbah* (*Deut. Rab.*, tr. J. Rabbinowitz) is another repository of older Palestinian-Jewish traditions, some taken over from *Sipre* and other Tannaitic sources. The work is composed of twenty-seven homilies linked to consecutive lectionary pericopes of Deuteronomy in the triennial cycle of sabbath readings. Exposition is diffuse, associative, and anecdotal, often incorporating elements of FOLKLORE (e.g., Moses' encounter with Og [*Deut. Rab.* 1.24-25, on Deut 3:1-2; cf. *Tg. Neof.; Tg. Ps.-J.*]; the origin and import of the declaration in Deut 6:4 [*Deut. Rab.* 2.35; cf. *Sipre Deut.* 31]; and the extended account of Moses' death [*Deut. Rab.* 11.10; cf. *Sipre Deut.* 357; *Midraš Peṭirat Mošeh*]).

The broad turn that occurred in biblical scholarship during the eleventh and twelfth centuries toward closer, philologically informed engagement with the literal text affected exegetical style more than substance in the interpretation of Deuteronomy. The scholar known as RASHI made exemplary use of the method commonly called *peshat* to produce a spare, fluent, lucid exposition of the Pentateuch; but while the work eschews homiletical embellishments (of the kinds attested, e.g., in *Deut. Rab.*), it is vigilant in its defense of classical rabbinic interpretive traditions (giving frequent approbation to readings of *Sipre Deut.* and *Tg. Onq.*). A. IBN EZRA, another early master of philological method, stated explicitly in the introduction to his Pentateuch commentary (see PENTATEUCHAL CRITICISM) that he intended to uphold rabbinical orthodoxy, especially in matters of Mosaic law (*halakah*), against the extremes represented by the reductive, anti-traditionalist scripturalism of Karaite "distorters," on the one hand, and the illogical fantasies of Christian allegorists and of some Jewish homileticians on the other. He claimed scrupulous reason as his ally, and he did not refrain from identifying key Pentateuchal anachronisms—a number of them in Deuteronomy (esp. 1:2; 3:11; 34:6)—that would eventually be used to argue the case against Mosaic authorship (see 3*a* below). A century later the new style of exegetical study and discourse, still used in resolute advocacy of traditional Judaism, was brilliantly displayed in the work of NACHMANIDES. He often expressly called into question the interpretive views of Rashi and Ibn Ezra, sometimes even when they had ostensible support in classical sources, and argued for his own positions on grounds of their greater fidelity to contextual plain sense (see, e.g., his remarks on Deut 1:12, 25; 5:15; 6:2-3; 8:4;

29:29[28]). Yet Nachmanides was not a philosophical rationalist. More than occasionally he alluded to a spiritual sense—the mystical "way of truth" (Kabbalah)—which transcends but does not negate the rational contours of *peshat* (e.g., on Deut 4:21; 5:26; 32:20).

Duality of textual "letter" and "spirit" remained fundamental to Christian interpretation of the Pentateuch during this period and the rest of the Middle Ages, but renewed attention was given to Augustine's emphases on literary context and philology (which had anticipated key aspects of *peshat*) as necessary guides in the pursuit of right spiritual understanding (B. Smalley [1952]; K. Froehlich [1977]). The earlier twelfth-century works of RUPERT OF DEUTZ and of HUGH OF ST. VICTOR, different though they are, exhibit a shift away from disjointed tropology in favor of broad salvation-historical designs that highlight thematic continuities of Scripture. Still, the older eclectic style of the catena continued in the GLOSSA ORDINARIA, which prevailed as a Christian expository resource from the eleventh through the thirteenth centuries (finally to be superseded in the 14th cent. by Nicholas of Lyra's *Postilla litteralis*). Annotations to Deuteronomy in the *Glossa* are quite mixed in character. Jerome, Augustine, ISIDORE OF SEVILLE, and RABANUS MAURUS are often cited, but most comments are unattributed. A few display rudimentary knowledge of Hebrew (e.g., the note on Deut 16:1, naming Nisan as the month in which the exodus occurred). Many more identify figurative readings: for example, the eleven-day journey from Horeb to Kadesh-barnea symbolizes the move from the Mosaic law to the proclamation of the gospel in the preaching of the original apostles, minus Judas, of course (1:2); manna is a trope for Christ's body (8:3); the three cities of refuge to be appointed in the promised homeland signify faith, hope, and charity (19:2).

The line between classical Jewish and Christian approaches to Mosaic law was redrawn in the monumental syntheses constructed by MAIMONIDES and by THOMAS AQUINAS. There is a close intellectual bond between these scholars. Influenced by the resurgence of Aristotelian philosophy as cultivated initially in Islam, each wanted to discern and describe comprehensively, to codify, how normative faith and religious praxis are grounded in the ultimate rationality of scriptural revelation.

The centerpiece of Maimonides' vast project is entitled, not coincidentally, *Mishneh Torah*—borrowing the descriptive Hebrew name for the book of Deuteronomy (see 1*c* above). In an earlier work, *The Book of the Commandments,* Maimonides first explained his criteria and then offered a schematic enumeration of the 613 perennial precepts of Pentateuchal Torah (i.e., 248 prescriptions and 365 prohibitions that Israel is covenantally obliged to observe in perpetuity). *Mishneh Torah* completes this codification (I. Twersky [1980]). Following the precedent of Deuteronomy (e.g., 1:5; 4:1; 29:1 [28:69]) Maimonides redrafted and exposited the authoritative extensions of the Mosaic Torah crystallized in classical rabbinic sources. His work not only reconfigured the provisions of the TALMUD in order to make them more intelligible and accessible to Jewish practitioners but also bound them closely to their Pentateuchal loci, thereby countering the charges of the Karaites and others that rabbinical traditions had violated divine law by presumptuously adding to it. In both *Mishneh Torah* (esp. *Me'ilah* 8.8; *Melakim* 11-12) and his later, far more controversial *Guide of the Perplexed* (esp. 2.25, 39; 3.26-35, 51), Maimonides argued that the whole Torah was given to Israel to provide this people alone with a sufficient, practicable, and purposeful revelation of God's will, as complete and perdurable as the divine orders of creation. Each of the Torah's provisions has utility, though the reasons for some of them are not meant to be readily discerned lest human arrogance deem them too easy or idle: the ordinances [*mišpāṭîm*] establish rules of justice and guard against unhealthy and immoral acts; the statutes [*ḥuqqîm*] shield Israel from idolatrous practices and opinions and prescribe the spiritual discipline that leads to communion with God.

Thomas Aquinas entered the Dominican order in 1243, a decade after the Dominicans had staged a public burning of Maimonides' *Guide*. Yet Thomas not only read this synthesis of biblical and philosophical theology, which many Jews as well as Christians considered dangerous (H. Ben-Sasson [1971]), but also acknowledged the value of its scholarship in his own masterwork (e.g., *Summa Theologiae* [*ST*] Ia2ae 101.1, 102.6.8). Nevertheless, the difference of emphasis separating these approaches to Mosaic law is intractable. According to Maimonides' analysis, the divinely legislated particularity of Israel's sacral identity, revealed through the Torah, remains cogent when articulated within an Aristotelian framework of universal wisdom. Conversely, Thomas's scholasticism understood the rational coherence of the "old law" to be an axiomatic witness, together with the rest of Scripture, to the all-encompassing scope of God's providence (see esp. *ST* Ia. I.6, citing Deut 4:6 as proof text).

Thomas's overview of the old law, although anticipated in important respects by Philo and Irenaeus, adverts directly to the hermeneutical agenda of Augustine (*ST* 1a2ae 98-105; cf. *On Charity*, art. 7). The central claim is that Scripture's moral legislation, epitomized in the Decalogue, reveals what sin had obscured: the natural, universal duties of humankind to love God and the neighbor as oneself (*ST* 1a2ae 100.3-5, 11). The Jewish people were chosen to receive this mandate in order to predispose them to reject idolatry and to encourage "a certain preeminence in sanctity" because Christ was to be descended from them (*ST* 1a2ae 98.2-6). Moreover, scholarly reason is able to discern how the principal

categories of Mosaic law—the ceremonial statutes and the judicial ordinances—apply precepts of the moral law to the circumstances of ancient Israel's historical existence. Ceremonials were given to teach right worship of God in preparation for the advent of Christ, who is prefigured by them: For example, the literal sense of Deut 12:2-28 prescribes the unification of Israel's worship by restricting sacrifical service to one divinely chosen sanctuary; the spiritual sense signifies the unity of the church in Christ (*ST* 1a2ae 102.4). The literal sense alone suffices to show how the ordinances are designed to promote justice in human society. Although these rules have also been superseded by Christ's "new law" of grace, civil government may choose to reinstitute them on the grounds of their rational merit (*ST* 1a2ae 103-4; see, e.g., the use of Deut 17:6 and 19:15 as judicial exempla in *ST* 2a2ae 70.2). Thomas's form of the distinction between statutes and ordinances is momentous: It portends renewed conflict between ecclesial and civil claims to exercise the authority of Scripture.

3. From the Reformation to the Present Day. The taxonomy and the theological significance of biblical law received considerable attention during the Middle Ages; the particular character and purpose of the book of Deuteronomy did not. That began to change in the sixteenth century. Some German Reformers and, more successfully, CALVIN and his heirs, who developed the Protestant Reformed tradition, appropriated Deuteronomy as a model for reconstruction of civil society. Their experiments with theocractic government touched off a much wider debate that extended through the seventeenth and eighteenth centuries and whose results include works foundational to modern political theory. The debate also encouraged the development of a critical historiography of scriptural literature, setting the agenda of nineteenth- and twentieth-century biblical scholarship.

a. Deuteronomic law in early Protestant exegesis, Reformed politics, and rationalist critiques (16th–18th cents.). W. TYNDALE's English TRANSLATION of the Hebrew Pentateuch (1530) is an exuberant witness to the confluence of Renaissance scholarship and evangelical zeal that reshaped Western Christendom during the sixteenth century. Tyndale stated in prefatory remarks that he intended his work to nurture renewal of personal faith among English laity but also to provide a mandate for both social reform and ecclesial revolution. He spurned allegorical interpretation because it veils the literal, practical import of Mosaic laws for the maintenance of the "common weal." Moses himself should be honored, not as "a figure of Christ," but as "an example unto all princes and to all that are in authority, how to rule unto God's pleasure and unto their neighbors' profit" (Mombert ed., 161 [archaic spelling modified here and below]). Deuteronomy receives particular approbation:

"This is a book worthy to be read in day and night and never to be out of hands. For it is the most excellent of all the books of Moses. It is easy also and light . . . a preaching of faith and love: deducing the love to God out of faith, and the love of a man's neighbor out of the love of God" (Mombert, 517). Tyndale's sparse marginal notes to Deuteronomy usually offer benign explanations of words (e.g., the sense of "unclean" in 12:15), but rhetorical jabs at papal authority and clericalism of the kind that Henry VIII considered so treacherous as to earn Tyndale a sentence of death (carried out in 1536) are also liberally represented. At Deut 5:15, for example, he remarks that "God shows a cause why we ought to keep his commandments—the pope does not" (Mombert, 543; see also comments at 1:43; 6:18-19; 19:15; 23:18).

While working abroad on his translation of the Pentateuch, Tyndale observed social turmoil in Europe, instigated by Reformers like A. von KARLSTADT, M. BUCER, and H. ZWINGLI, who invoked biblical legislation, especially the Decalogue and Deuteronomy, to authorize anti-Roman Catholic iconoclasm and broad political change. In sermons delivered in July of 1524, T. MÜNTZER exhorted Saxon princes to use the sword to implement Deut 7:5-6, just as Judah's reforming kings Hezekiah and Josiah had effectively done (2 Kgs 18:4; 23:4-8). In one arena of the so-called Peasants' Revolt of 1524–25, Swabian serfs demanded that overlords grant them a measure of autonomy and economic relief, citing the "godly law" of Scripture (esp. Deut 12:8-12; 15:1-18; 26:12-15) to overturn the complicity of Roman imperial and canon law with oppressive feudalism (P. Blickle [1981]).

LUTHER remained substantially Thomistic in his approach to Mosaic law, although this is sometimes concealed by his strident rhetoric in countering the arguments of Karlstadt and others. His 1523 treatise, *On Secular Authority,* argues that "true Christians," those who are ruled by love of God and neighbor inscribed in their hearts, should need neither human government nor external codes to restrain them (citing Matthew 5; 1 Tim 1:9). But liberated Christians also acknowledge—in accord with scriptural witnesses (esp. Romans 13; 1 Pet 2:13-17)—that civil rulers are divinely authorized to govern and to use the sword when necessary "to punish the wicked and protect the just" (H. Höpfl [1991] 7; *LW* 45, 87). Luther's response to the "enthusiasts" who "desire to govern people according to the letter of the law of Moses" was sharply stated in a sermon delivered in 1526 (*How Christians Should Regard Moses*; see also his treatise written in the same year, *Against the Heavenly Prophets*): "Moses is dead. His rule ended when Christ came." Even the Decalogue, Luther added, is not pristine "moral law"; its precepts pertain only to those specifically addressed, the ancestors of the Jews whom God delivered from Egypt (Exod 20:1; Deut 5:6). "We

will regard Moses as a teacher, but we will not regard him as our lawgiver—unless he agrees with both the NT and the natural law" (*LW* 35, 165). For Luther, to be sure, Moses as teacher looms large: "If I were emperor, I would take from Moses a model for [my] statutes; not that Moses should be binding on me, but that I should be free to follow him in ruling as he rules" (*LW* 35, 166). More important than Moses' juridical acumen, however, is his testimony to what humanity could not learn through natural revelation alone: "the promises and pledges of God about Christ" (such as the prognosis of Moses' messianic counterpart in Deut 18:15-16 [*LW* 35, 168-69, 173; cf. *LW* 9, 176-90]).

In his *Lectures on Deuteronomy* (1525), Luther offered a quite positive assessment of Moses' work not only as harbinger of the gospel but also as practical lawgiver and effective teacher. He understood the book to consist of testamentary discourses, summarizing "the total Law and wisdom of the people of Israel," which Moses delivered over the course of perhaps as many as ten days (*LW* 9, 14, 60). The central portion of the book publishes Moses' authoritative exposition of the Decalogue: The three precepts of the "first table" (Deut 5:6-15 according to Luther's count and partition), concerned with right worship and godliness in civil affairs, are elaborated in Deuteronomy 6–18; the seven commandments of the "second table" (Deut 5:16-21) are more loosely treated in chapters 19–26 (*LW* 9, 63, 67, 193). Luther's exegetical style here is episodic and homiletical; though generally engaging the "literal" sense of the text, his exposition also includes considerable allegorizing (e.g., the single sanctuary is a trope for the unity of apostolic faith [*LW* 9, 126]; the proscription of women bearing arms or wearing male clothing in Deut 22:5 teaches that faith should not be perverted by works [*LW* 9, 224]).

Calvin's approach to Pentateuchal legislation resembles Luther's in some respects but is more consistently Thomistic (e.g., in using the traditional categories: moral, ceremonial, judicial) and also much bolder in advocating the law's import for contemporary Christian life. Editions of his *Institutes,* published between 1536 and 1559, are consonant in treating law and gospel as integral dispensations of divine grace. While these dispensations are historically conditioned, differing in their covenantal or administrative emphases, they are equally devoted to reconciliation between God and humankind; precepts of the Mosaic law, even those that are no longer obligatory, thus continue to provide the faithful with useful, practicable knowledge of God's sovereign will (*Institutes* 1.6.2; 2.7.3-15; 4.20.15-16). Similarly, while Calvin declared it foolish for any Christian commonwealth to constitute itself formally on the restrictive basis of the Pentateuchal revelation of divine or natural law, which had been promulgated specifically for ancient Israel, he nonetheless insisted that Moses' legislation authorizes civil government that is competent to defend "a public form of religion" as well as to secure social justice and judicial equity (*Institutes* 4.20.2-30; see Höpfl, 49-82).

It is not surprising, then, that Calvin—unlike Luther, but in line with Maimonides and Thomas Aquinas— wanted to systematize the scattered and ostensibly repetitious corpora of Mosaic law. The hermeneutical model he adapted in attempting to do so is the familiar one, which understands Mosaic legislation to amplify individual precepts of the Decalogue (see Philo; also Rashi on Exod 24:12, citing Saadia Gaon). This results in the contrived expository arrangement in Calvin's *Harmony*, which catalogs in decalogic order the nomistic traditions serialized in the books of Exodus through Deuteronomy. For example, under the rubric of the commandment prohibiting homicide, Calvin treated Deut 21:1-9 and 12:15-16, 20-25 as ceremonial supplements; many other deuteronomic rulings are included among those identified as judicial applications of the same prohibition (treated in this order: Deut 17:6; 19:15; 22:8; 24:7; 21:22-23; 25:1-3; 24:16; 20:10-18; 23:15-16; 22:6-7, 4; 19:1-13; cf. Philo *Spec. Leg.* 3.83-203).

Calvin's investment in this scheme is much more energetically displayed in his 200 *Sermons sur le Deutéronome,* preached on consecutive weekdays (from Mar. 20, 1555, through July 15, 1556) at the former cathedral of St. Peter in Geneva. The published transcriptions are introduced in a preface contributed by some of Calvin's fellow Genevan clergy, which hails Deuteronomy as the grand summation of Pentateuchal law and a bastion for defense of true piety against the idolatries of Roman Catholicism. Polemic is also well represented in the sermons. While it is most often directed against the "papists," whose errors include turning the Lord's Supper into the Mass, also targeted are Jews and "Turks," who rightly abhor the veneration of images but who do not acknowledge Jesus to be "the law's soul" and "the living image of God, his Father" (Sermon 45 on Deut 6:1-4 [delivered July 19, 1555]; *J. Calvin's Sermons on the Ten Commandments,* 289-307; cf. *Institutes* 2.6.4; 4.18-19). Calvin's sermons on Deuteronomy 5 in this series exposit the Decalogue as the epitome of moral law. Because these moral provisions remain in full force for Christians, Moses' ceremonial and judicial applications of them should be received as authoritative guidance in such matters as relief from burdensome debts (Deut 15:1-11), a democratically constituted and accountable magistracy (16:18-20), neighborly assistance (22:1-4), restraints on usury and collateral (23:19-20; 24:10-13), fair wages (24:14-15), and honest business practices (25:13-16). Calvin made forceful sermonic use of these texts to indict egregious economic exploitation, especially of Protestant refugees from France, by Geneva's entrenched mercantile elite. Moreover, the timing of these

sermons was politically cogent: In the election of February 1555 Calvin's allies regained majority on the Small Council of the Genevan Republic, leading to close collaboration in civil reforms with the consistory, an ecclesial court modeled by Calvin in large part on Deut 17:8-13 (on these issues and the era, see *J. Calvin's Sermons,* 13-29, and now esp. M. Valeri [1997]).

The shift during the middle decades of the sixteenth century toward deuteronomic theocracy in Calvin's Geneva was not unproblematic, of course, as the trial and execution of M. SERVETUS for heresy in 1553 may attest (Deut 13:6-11). Yet the Reform party claimed as principal motive, not imposition of theological orthodoxy on a diverse populace, but devotion to the political enfranchisement and economic ideals enacted into law for ancient Israel by God's preeminent prophet, Moses. Moreover, this commitment to a civil polity designed to implement what were supposed to be the timeless moral precepts of the Decalogue became a hallmark of Calvinist Reformed and Federal traditions generally (D. Steinmetz [1989]; D. Weir [1990], esp. 3-33). If Luther's Reformation reclaimed the gospel of God's egalitarian grace in Christ, Calvin's renewed the revolutionary social mandate of the Mosaic law. The mandate was exported when many who had found refuge in Geneva returned to their homelands—some to the Netherlands; some who came to be known as Huguenots to France; and others, the Marian exiles soon to be called Puritans and Presbyterians, to Elizabethan England and Scotland. Interpretation of Deuteronomy played an important role in the series of intellectual and often violent political struggles that ensued from the 1560s through the end of the eighteenth century.

The first century of conflict pitted the authority of Scripture—as warrant for a society constituted in accord with biblical notions of covenantal law, equity, and morality—against absolutist monarchical rule by divine right and its elitist corollaries, ecclesial prelacy and magisterial discretionary justice. Major impetus for this engagement in the English-speaking world came from the Marian exiles, among them M. COVERDALE and his colleagues, whose Geneva Bible (1560) brought to completion Tyndale's annotated translation of the Hebrew and Greek Scriptures. The dedicatory epistle to Queen Elizabeth, dated Feb. 10, 1559, commends as examples of effective governance Josiah and other Judean rulers who reestablished "true religion" based upon God's Word (see also the 1556 "Confession of Faith" of Geneva's English congregation in A. Cochrane [1966] 127-30; and the 1558 tract of C. Goodman, one of the congregation's pastors, invoking Deuteronomy 13 and 17:14-20 against Queen Mary as a pagan Jezebel [E. Morgan [1965] 1-14]). Introductory notes to Deuteronomy identify the book as a discrete "second law," composed of "a commentarie or exposition of the ten commandments" in which Moses prescribes all that is necessary for faithful service of God and for the preservation of God's people (i.e., Moses' ceremonial and judicial laws). This understanding of Israelite polity provided a platform for the largely unsuccessful efforts of T. CARTWRIGHT and other Puritans during Elizabeth's reign (1558–1603) to rid the established church of practices not specifically sanctioned by their literal reading of Scripture (such as prelacy and its accoutrements of vestment, fixed liturgy, and social privilege) but also to institute deuteronomic laws as normative guidance for civil courts, particularly in capital cases (G. Haskins [1960] 145; D. McGinn [1949] 110-47). English Puritans and Presbyterians labored in concert to attain and expand these goals through the agency of Parliament, assisted by the Westminster Assembly, during the reign of Charles I (1625–46) and the eleven-year Interregnum, or Commonwealth, that followed his execution in January 1649.

In the same era English Puritans who established the Massachusetts Bay Colony made much less conflicted progress toward implementation of a civil polity inspired by Deuteronomy. With a view toward safeguarding the colony's freemen against arbitrary treatment by professional magistrates, pastor J. COTTON, at the request of the General Court, presented for consideration in 1636 a draft of "fundamental laws" based on Moses' "judicials," which he deemed to be still authoritative not only for Jews but also for the "new Israel" of Puritan Christians bound together in covenant with God (W. Ford [1902]; Morgan, 160-77; Haskins, 119-27). At least some of Cotton's proposals were adapted into the Massachusetts "Body of Liberties," enacted in 1641, which identifies foundational rights of citizenship (Morgan, 177-203). In article 94, for example, scriptural precedents are noted in the margins for crimes punishable by death (e.g., Deut 19:16, 18-19 in a case of false witness). In some other instances, articles paraphrase biblical laws without citing them (e.g., art. 43 limits punitive flogging to forty stripes [Deut 25:1-3]; art. 47 requires "two or three witness or that which is equivalent thereunto" to sustain a capital charge [Deut 19:15]; art. 90 prescribes that finders return lost property to rightful owners [Deut 22:1-3]). This populist document, expanded into the code of 1648 entitled "The Lawes and Liberties of Massachusetts," marks a substantial departure from English common law as well as from European traditions of Roman jurisprudence (Haskins, 136-47).

Anglican royalists were not alone in resisting what they perceived to be the inflexible biblical particularism of the Calvinist political agenda. In colonial Rhode Island, R. Williams (c. 1603–83) questioned the theological cogency of the Massachusetts model of governance. He maintained that Christian congregations are neither continuous with nor counterparts of ancient Israel, constrained by its sacral obligations; nor should a God whose beneficent sovereignty is universal be claimed as party to an exclusive civil covenant that compromises the integrity of individual consciences in matters of faith (*The Bloudy Tenent of Persecution* [1644]; see Morgan, 203-33). In response to the aggressive biblicism of Dutch Calvinists, who did much to encourage popular support of the House of Orange in the struggle against Spanish imperialism, jurist H. GROTIUS argued that Roman law continued to provide a sound, irenic, and internationally acceptable foundation for civil polity and public morality, whereas both the Decalogue and deuteronomic legislation had been addressed only to historical Israel (e.g., *De jure* [1645] 1.1.16, citing Deut 6:4 as proof text). Similarly, T. HOBBES mounted an elaborate defense of monarchy as "the most commodius government" in his *Philosophical Rudiments* (= *De Cive* [1642]), a position sharply restated during the Interregnum in *Leviathan* (1651). Human rights and the civil orders legitimately instituted to protect them are, he argued, grounded in natural law, of which Pentateuchal law is a historically conditioned manifestation. Although Hobbes denied that either the entire Pentateuch or Deuteronomy as a whole could be the authoritative work of Moses (citing Deut 34:6 and other anachronisms), he identified Deuteronomy 11–27 as an archaic Mosaic code establishing God's kingship over Israel, which was entrusted for interpretation to an aristocracy of clergy and elders (Deut 31:9-10, 26). He considered this document to be the book of the Law found again by the priest Hilkiah in Josiah's reign that gave rise to the reforms and renewal of covenant described in 2 Kings 22–23 (*Rudiments* 16.11-17; *Leviathan* chap. 33).

The historicizing approach to biblical traditions, adumbrated in the writings of Hobbes, is more programmatically exhibited in B. SPINOZA's *Tractatus theologico-politicus* (pub. anonymously in 1670). Like Grotius's *De jure* earlier in the century, Spinoza's treatise is a plea for reason and tolerance in matters of both politics and religion—crafted here as a Cartesian response to the theocratic pretensions of Dutch Reformed clergy in their continuing efforts to suppress especially what the Synod of Dort (1618–19) had defined as the heterodoxy of the Remonstrant party (representing a more liberal Calvinist as well as Anabaptist theopolitical position). In his provocative analysis of the Pentateuch's nomistic traditions, Spinoza drew on the heritage of late medieval Jewish scholarship. He declared "useless and absurd" the attempt of Maimonides to salvage the revelatory authority of Mosaic-rabbinic jurisprudence for Jewish orthopraxis by accommodating primitive ceremonial precepts, as well as the Torah's ethical norms that Spinoza considered accessible to Gentiles and Jews alike through reason, to Aristotelian philosophy (*Treatise* [tr. Elwes] 79-80, 116-18, 190). On the other hand, Spinoza developed the evidence cryptically noted by Ibn Ezra in order to refute the "irrational" claim that Moses was the sole author of the Pentateuch (*Treatise* 120-27). It is important to observe, however, that Spinoza did not engage in wholesale deconstruction of Pentateuchal legislation. In his view the original Sinai/Horeb covenant instituted a democratic theocracy that almost immediately became a limited monarchy: Elected by the Israelite assembly to serve as its king and to exercise divine authority, Moses promulgated the civil polity preserved in Deuteronomy 6–28 (cf. Deut 5:22-33; *Treatise* 219-21). Spinoza directed particular attention to what he considered the eminently wise system of checks and balances in this Mosaic constitution: It enfranchises common citizens to be military leaders and judges, and it separates the function of levitical interpretation of the law from royal administration of it (*Treatise* 226-28, 235). Yet this rational polity of Moses was subverted through priestly control of Jewish government during the Second Commonwealth—a usurpation which, in effect, prefigured the hegemony sought by orthodox Calvinist clergy in Spinoza's own day (*Treatise* 236-56).

The influential writings of J. LOCKE in the final decades of the seventeenth century championing democracy and expansive religious tolerance should be counted in significant part as the secular harvest not only of his own Puritan heritage but also of Spinoza's reassessment of Mosaic traditions (L. Feuer [1958] 254-58). While Locke vigorously opposed royal absolutism, he also eschewed as frivolous traditional efforts to distinguish between Moses' moral, ceremonial, and judicial prescriptions for the purpose of identifying some still binding on Christians or any contemporary civil order. Locke argued that a society's positive laws should be humane, protecting natural rights, and grounded in reason rather than in privileged and privileging revelation; just laws obligate only those who consent to the government that enacts and enforces them (see esp. *Letter Concerning Toleration* [1689]).

Much political and religious thought of the eighteenth century participated in the renewed conflict between the ostensible demands of revelation and of reason (see Philo). One noteworthy attempt at compromise was M. MENDELSSOHN's *Jerusalem* (1783), which addressed the issues posed by Spinoza's critique of Maimonides. Mendelssohn insisted that Judaism, at least since the destruction of the Temple, is a superbly rational, non-dogmatic faith rather than a theo-political commonwealth. This means that Jews are free to embrace enlightened modernity by participating with Gentiles in the quest for scientific knowledge, humanistic culture, and social well-being. Yet their separate religious identity as Jews remains contingent on adherence to the orthopractical traditions of Torah revealed to their ancestors through Moses; Jewish piety is viable in an age of reason.

Political themes of deuteronomism resounded strongly in Congregationalist and Presbyterian preaching during the era of the American Revolution and constitutional formation (C. Cherry [1971] 67-92; E. Sandoz [1991] 835-62). For example, S. Langdon's (1723–97) 1788 sermon on Deut 4:5-8 compared the emergent American states to the confederated tribes of Israel, and Moses' legislative wisdom to the work of the Constitutional Convention. Deuteronomy, he averred in the tradition of Tyndale, is a "pattern to the world in all ages" (Cherry, 93-105; Sandoz, 941-67). To be sure, such theo-political sentiments were not shared by all American patriots. In *The Age of Reason* (1794–95) T. PAINE delivered what even many of his fellow Deists (see DEISM) thought to be an intemperate attack on biblical authority and values. According to Paine, the Pentateuch is "an attempted history of the life of Moses . . . written by some very ignorant and stupid pretenders . . . several hundred years after the death of Moses. . . . "; the literary character of Deuteronomy, with its interchange between the voices of a narrator and Moses, shows that the latter is not the book's author. This saves Deists, Paine declared, from the embarrassment of supposing that the moral justice of God is represented in Deuteronomy's brutal, xenophobic traditions.

b. Development of the critical-historical agenda (19th–20th cents.). The religio-historical interests of Reformed biblical THEOLOGY and of Enlightenment scholarship converge in the work of W. DE WETTE during the early decades of the nineteenth century (J. Rogerson [1992]). Three issues pertinent to an informed critical interpretation of Deuteronomy are identified in de Wette's dissertation (pub. 1805) and subsequently elaborated in editions of his *Beiträge* and *Lehrbuch*. First, Deuteronomy exhibits a literary and thematic profile that distinguishes it from the preceding books of the Pentateuch, which in de Wette's view were composed earlier. Second, this profile links Deuteronomy closely with Joshua and, to a lesser extent, with subsequent books of the former prophets. Third, deuteronomic legislation is characterized by a concern to unify ancient Israel's cultus and national life. This supports the position (reported, e.g., by Procopius of Gaza and revived by Hobbes, among others) that Deuteronomy preserves within its narrative framework the book of the law implemented in the seventh-century Judaean reforms of King Josiah.

During the second half of the nineteenth century, studies of such European scholars as E. RIEHM (1854) and A. KUENEN (1861–65) made considerable progress in developing de Wette's three-part agenda. Riehm argued that the book of the Law (Deuteronomy 5–26; 28) rediscovered in Josiah's time represented reform policies initiated by Hezekiah in the late eighth century BCE, but the document itself he supposed to have been written during and in reaction to the reign of Manasseh, which followed. A more complex compositional history of Deuteronomy, interconnected with other components of the Pentateuch and with the former prophets, emerged from Kuenen's astute, thoroughgoing analysis of stylistic features and themes. Although on formal grounds Kuenen differentiated between the legislative corpus of Deuteronomy 12–26 and the hortatory introduction to it in chapters 5–11, he considered both to be the work of an early deuteronomist (designated D[1]). This author, who was possibly the priest Hilkiah (2 Kgs 22:3-10), used identifiable sources—a prophetic narrative of Israel's early history (a composite of the tetrateuchal documents J and E), as well as sundry archaic laws preserved in Exodus 20–23—to design the reform program sponsored by Josiah (*Hexateuch* 24-32, 107-17, 214-20). According to Kuenen, another deuteronomist (D[2]) later prefixed chapters 1–4 in order to sketch a historical setting and a rationale for the promulgation of the Torah ascribed to Moses. He discerned the work of this same author in Deuteronomy 27–34 and continuing through the book of Joshua, although he also identified even later elements of hexateuchal redaction, which include priestly strata associated with Ezra's postexilic reforms (*Hexateuch* 117-38, 165-73, 221-25).

Rhetorical features of Deuteronomy were also highlighted by other notable studies in this period. E. REUSS (1879) supported a Josianic dating of Deuteronomy, citing affinities of idiom and theological theme with the book of Jeremiah (e.g., Jer 11:1-13; 15:1). In his view the central corpus of Deuteronomy 5–26 is composed largely of religious instruction rather than of positive law per se; it originated as an expository reworking of Exodus 21–23 designed to promote priestly interests in theocratic centralization. In a similar vein A. KLOSTERMANN (1893) associated the book's contents with what he considered to be a long tradition of covenantal preaching (cf. Exod 24:7; Deut 33:9), here specifically formulated to win popular support for Josiah's policies. Outside the critical mainstream as regards the book's date of composition is the provocative study (1872) of P. Kleinert (1837–1920), who called attention to the coordinated series of editorial headings in Deut 1:1-5; 4:44-49; 29:1 [28:69]; and 33:1. This device suggested to him a classified collection of Mosaic traditions, perhaps compiled by the prophet Samuel as a testamentary archive to remind tribal Israel of its distinctive covenantal identity and to warn of the dangers posed by Canaanite practices, including monarchical excesses (cf. 1 Samuel 8 with Deut 17:14-20).

The challenge at least implicit in earlier critical scholarship to traditional views of the authority and primacy of revealed Torah in the history of ancient Israelite religion was expressed forcefully in J. WELLHAUSEN's *Prolegomena* (1885[2]; *Geschichte Israels* [1878]). Hobbes and Spinoza, but also de Wette and most of Wellhausen's critical predecessors, had left some room for the Mosaic origins of Israel's civil polity and official cultus. Wellhausen's analysis left little such room, if any. In his view, a free-form spirituality or family piety was the earliest stage of Israelite religion; its features are residual in the narratives of Genesis and Judges. On the other hand, much of the later stages of religious development, which presuppose not only the politics of statehood but also the social ideals shaped by eighth-century PROPHECY, is exhibited in the traditions of codified law and institutionalized worship that predominate in the books of Exodus through Joshua. The latest of these stages, as Kuenen, among others, had already recognized, is Judah's postexilic theocracy; it is expansively displayed in the priestly corpora that make Sinai the locus for the inauguration of the tabernacle cultus, with its elaborate system of sacrificial rites, a fixed liturgical calendar, and an exclusive Aaronid priesthood. This blatant retroversion takes for granted what Josiah accomplished, based on the book of the law—a document that had been drafted, in the guise of Mosaic authorship, to inspire him. Wellhausen did not doubt that the document in question is substantially attested in the self-conscious revisionism of Deuteronomy 12–26 (see esp. 12:8-12; 17:8–18:8).

Wellhausen's reconstruction, with Deuteronomy as its centerpiece, established the principal salient in a historical-critical and hermeneutical war that continued into the 1930s and has occasionally flared up since (W. Baumgartner [1929]; S. Loersch [1967]; H. Preuss [1982]; T. Römer [1994]). One of the early participants was W. R. SMITH, who defended a Josianic date for Deuteronomy at the cost of his own professorial and ecclesiastical status in the Free Church of Scotland (R. Smend [1995]). Even so, Smith sought to bring Wellhausen's religio-historical views into closer accord with Reformed theology, arguing that a doctrine of inspiration need not be restricted to autographs but should rather embrace the coherent growth of scriptural traditions (*OT in the Jewish Church;* see already R. Simon's response to Spinoza, two cents. earlier.) S. DRIVER's erudite, long-lived commentary to Deuteronomy, first published in 1895, places greater emphasis on origination as the locus of authority. After reviewing the critical case for why Moses could not have been the book's author, Driver gave considerable attention to how the deuteronomic legislation and other collections of Pentateuchal Torah may still be interpreted as "moral, ceremonial, and civil" developments of "a Mosaic nucleus" (1901[3], lv-lvii). The nucleus was not otherwise identified.

The quest to recover the compositional history of Deuteronomy became a conspicuous feature in German scholarship of this period. C. STEUERNAGEL (1894, 1896, 1900), W. STAERK (1894, 1924), A. PUUKKO (1910), and others tried to disentangle literary strata within Deuteronomy or to distinguish editions of the legislative corpus, especially on the basis of stylistic criteria like the use of second-person singular and plural forms of address to Israel (C. Begg [1979, 1994]). J. HEMPEL (1914) and later F. HORST (1930) argued that the book's oldest stratum was a Temple document of Solomonic date that grew through multiple stages of redaction and accretion, culminating in the edition of the exilic deuteronomist (Kuenen's D^2). D. HOFFMANN's commentary (1913, 1922) merits note in this context as an informed Jewish response to critical historiography. T. Oestreicher (1923) made an effort to sever the connection between Deuteronomy and Josiah's reforms, arguing that the book is much older than the seventh century and promotes religious purity, not a centralized cultus. Conversely, R. Kennett (1920) maintained that the centralizing legislation is a literary crystallization of Josiah's policies, with Deuteronomy being created in the late exilic or early restoration era (similarly G. Hölscher [1922], although he questioned some of the key reform measures attributed to Josiah).

An insightful line of argument recalling the position of Klostermann was developed during this period by A. WELCH (1924, 1932). He linked proto-Deuteronomy to northern levitical traditions of religious instruction, which he thought could also be identified in the so-called Elohist document as well as in the later anti-Baalistic preaching of Hosea and Jeremiah; this older tradition was reworked in the Josianic era. G. VON RAD took a similar approach in his form-critical studies (see FORM CRITICISM) on the origins and development of deuteronomic traditions (1929, 1938; see also 1948^2 and 1966; cf. H. Breit [1933]). The ceremony at Shechem, described in Deuteronomy 27, suggested to von Rad a recurrent event, a fall festival convened every seventh year to renew the covenant (see also 11:29; 31:9-13; Josh 8:30-35; 24:1-27). Such rites were supposed to include a historical retrospect and reproof, an exposition of covenantal law, an oath of allegiance, and an invocation of sanctions—features corresponding to the broad literary arrangement of Deuteronomy 7–28 ("The Form-critical Problem of the Hexateuch," 26-33). In his later work, von Rad identified levitical preaching as the primary medium through which these ancient liturgical traditions were shaped and transmitted and eventually recast in the Josianic era to promote cultic centralization (*Studies*, 60-73; cf. *Deuteronomy*, 23-27). Studies by F. Dumermuth (1950) and A. ALT (1953) offered additional support for the thesis that the core traditions of Deuteronomy antedate Josiah's reign and are of north Israelite provenance (see also Wright [1953] 323-26; F. McCurley [1974]; H. Ginsberg [1982]; M. Weinfeld [1985]).

M. NOTH's historical-critical views complemented the form-critical work of von Rad in significant respects, lending weight to the notion, widely held at the middle of the twentieth century (C. North [1951]), that Wellhausen's reconstruction of the history of Israelite religion had been undermined. According to Noth, Pentateuchal traditions of law are not the idealistic creations of a civil state or of a royal establishment; rather, they presuppose a sacral community "Israel," the people of God, whose identity was primarily shaped through the centralized cultus of a tribal confederation in the pre-monarchical period (depicted in Joshua and Judges). The ceremony described in 2 Kgs 23:1-3 chronicles an attempt by Josiah, in the interests of Judah's political consolidation, to revive the erstwhile covenantal identity of Israel as set forth in the scroll recovered from the Temple. In effect, the liturgical instruction of Deuteronomy 5–30 was co-opted, "quite against the actual sense of its contents," to become a civil code enforced by the state ("Laws," 41-49; cf. von Rad, *Theology*, 1:195-231). Developing Kuenen's view of D^2, Noth also argued that Josiah's co-opting of the Torah was subsequently canonized in the work of an exilic historiographer who set the *Temple Scroll* in the narrative frame of Deuteronomy 1–4 and 31; this textual conjunction produced the initial Mosaic segment of a political history of Israel that extended through the destruction of both the northern kingdom in the later eighth century and the Judean successor state in the early sixth (*Deuteronomistic History;* cf. *Pentateuchal Traditions,* 156-75; von Rad, *Studies,* 74-91).

Before the middle of the twentieth century surprisingly little use was made of recovered traditions of cuneiform law and international diplomacy in critical interpretation of either Deuteronomy or of other corpora of Pentateuchal legislation. (On the important work of Alt and his students, which had emphasized the discrete sacral character and Israelite origins of apodictic prescriptions as opposed to the common ancient Near Eastern currency of casuistic jurisprudence, see the review in W. Clark [1974] 103-16). In 1954 G. MENDENHALL charted a new course of comparative study by demonstrating the close resemblance in structure and contents between Hittite suzerainty treaties of the Late Bronze Age and both the Decalogue of Exod 20:1-17 (cf. Exod 19:3-6; 24:1-8) and the Shechem pact described in Josh 24:1-27. He suggested that the genuinely archaic protocol of international treaties had been adapted to define a covenant relationship between the nascent league of Israelite tribes and their divine overlord; he also identified the protocol as vestigial in Deuteronomy, accounting for some of the striking themes and structural features that von Rad had considered indicative of a liturgical provenance ("Covenant Forms," 57-75; see also K. Baltzer [1964^2; ET 1971] 1-38).

The line of inquiry initiated by Mendenhall and Baltzer—which was soon broadened to take into consideration Iron Age Assyrian and Aramean documents as well as Late Bronze Age sources—proved to be enormously productive, even in the short term (e.g., F. Fensham [1962]; G. E. Wright [1962]; D. McCarthy [1963]; W. Moran [1963]; D. Hillers [1964, 1969]; R.

Frankena [1965]; Weinfeld [1972] 59-157; Cross [1973] 265-73; cf. P. Riemann [1976]). To be sure, some scholars have continued to defend Wellhausen's view that the concept of a covenant between Israel and its God is an IDEOLOGICAL construction of the later monarchical period (L. Perlitt [1969]; E. Nicholson [1986]); some others have used the comparative data to claim support for the Mosaic antiquity of the received deuteronomic textual corpus (M. Kline [1963]; P. Craigie [1976] 20-32, 79-83; J. McConville [1984]; cf. the responses of S. McBride [1973] 287-89; [1987] 236-38; A. Mayes [1979] 32-34; R. Clements [1989] 20-22). No doubt critical interpretation of deuteronomic traditions will continue to profit from comparative studies that make cogent use of Near Eastern contextual evidence (H. Tadmor [1982]; R. Westbrook [1985]; Weinfeld [1991] 6-9; Mendenhall and G. Herion [1992] 1180-88; E. Otto [1994]).

In the last decades of the twentieth century, the three major critical premises that de Wette's work on Deuteronomy identified in the earlier nineteenth century have been subjected to thorough scholarly reconsideration. A concise review of several broad trends in these multifaceted labors must suffice (McBride [1981] 536-39; Preuss; E. Cortese [1990]; Römer [1994]).

European scholarship has devoted considerable attention to analysis of the rhetorical contours of Deuteronomy, focusing especially on the textual segments framing the core legislation in chapters 12–26 (e.g., N. Lohfink [1963]; J. Plöger [1967]; P. Buis [1969]; R. Merendino [1969]; S. Mittmann [1975]; G. Seitz [1971]; F. García López [1978]; G. Braulik [1978]; D. Knapp [1987]; R. Achenbach [1991]). Much of this work, like the efforts of Steuernagel and others at the beginning of the twentieth century, has sought to discern not only the book's detailed literary design but also its history of composition. Component strata are identified on the basis of reasonable stylistic criteria—again, such as the conspicuous variation in second-person singular and plural forms of address (C. Minette de Tillesse [1962]; H. Cazelles [1967])—and clusters of paraenetic themes. Although the ostensible results are diverse and often too diachronically speculative and complex to be persuasive, they are supposed to favor exilic and even later DEUTERONOMISTIC stages of redaction as decisive for the book's formation (e.g., Lohfink [1985] 55-75; Mayes [1981]; U. Rüterswörden [1987]; Braulik [1994] 151-64, 183-98). The general effects are an emphasis on theological and ideological dimensions of the developing traditions (rather than, e.g., their practical social and jurisprudential significance) and a weakening of the book's connections to the Josianic era (F. Crüsemann [1992; ET 1996] 204-12; Clements [1996]).

Other critical approaches have highlighted intertextual features that profile Deuteronomy in relationship to the coherent growth and crystallization of Pentateuchal tra-

ditions. While M. Noth and others had acknowledged the presence of scattered proto-deuteronomic materials or of an inchoate deuteronomic revision in parts of Exodus (esp. in 13:1-16; 19:3-9; and 32:7-14; see M. Caloz [1968]; C. Brekelmans [1966]), scholarship has entertained hypotheses regarding a more extensive deuteronomic or later deuteronomistic redaction of the Pentateuch (e.g., Perlitt [1969]; W. Fuss [1972]; W. Johnstone [1987]; E. Blum [1990]; cf. M. Rose [1981]; J. Van Seters [1991]; J. Blenkinsopp [1992] 186-94). A tighter focus on intertextual drafting and revision in juridical corpora has yielded provocative insights in the work of a number of other scholars (J. Milgrom [1976]; M. Fishbane [1985] 91-277, esp. 163-64, 195; Otto [1993, 1995]). To this category belongs the influential analysis of S. Kaufman (1978–79), which revived the traditional thesis (e.g., Philo, Luther, Calvin) that Deuteronomy 12–25 is a coherent, unified expansion of the Decalogue (Braulik [1985, 1991]; A. Rofé [1988]). Also of particular note is B. Levinson's 1997 study examining the hermeneutics involved in deuteronomic reworking of older laws, a recasting designed to promote centralizing reforms under the auspices of Mosaic authority.

Renewed attention to the sociopolitical implications of deuteronomic jurisprudence is another noteworthy trend—one that has generally favored preexilic circumstances as generative of the book's characteristic features (e.g., R. Wilson [1983]; L. Stulman [1990]; B. Halpern [1991]; N. Steinberg [1991]; C. Pressler [1993]; J. Tigay [1996] xx-xxvi; cf. the earlier studies of A. Causse [1933a, 1933b]). This trend, together with the others sketched above, may suggest that at the end of the twentieth century the right interpretive balance between diachronic analysis of deuteronomic traditions and recognition of the book's conceptual as well as structural coherence exists primarily in the eye of the critical beholder (cf. Mayes [1993]). If so, the interpretive situation invites further research and rigorous debate.

Bibliography: R. Achenbach, *Israel zwischen Verheissung und Gebot: Literarkritische Untersuchung zu Deuteronomium 5–11* (Europäische Hochschulschriften 23, 422, 1991). A. Alt, "Die Heimat des Deuteronomiums," *Kleine Schriften zur Geschichte des Volkes Israel* (1953) 2:250-75. Augustine, "Reply to Faustus the Manichaean [*Adversus Faustum Manichaeum*]," *St. Augustine: The Writings Against the Manichaeans and Against the Donatists* (NPNF, 1st ser. 4, 1887) 155-345; "In Answer to the Jews [*Adversus Judaeos*]," *Treatises on Marriage and Other Subjects* (FC 27, 1955) 387-414; "Answer to Maximinus the Arian" and "Answer to an Enemy of the Law and the Prophets," *Arianism and Other Heresies* (Works of St. Augustine 1, 18, 1990) 299-36, 339-56; *The Trinity* (Works of Saint Augustine 1, 5, 1991); "The Spirit and the Letter," *Answer to the Pelagians* (Works of St. Augustine 1, 23, 1996) 139-202; *Teaching Christianity [De Doctrina Christiana]* (Works of St. Augustine 1, 11, 1996). O. Bächli,

Israel und die Völker: Eine Studie zum Deuteronomium (ATANT 41, 1962). **K. Baltzer,** *Das Bundesformular* (1964²; ET, *The Covenant Formulary in OT, Jewish, and Early Christian Writings* [1971]). **J. Barton,** *Oracles of God: Perceptions of Ancient Prophecy in Israel After the Exile* (1986). **W. Baumgartner,** "Der Kampf um das Deuteronomium," *TRu* NF 1 (1929) 7-25. **Bede,** *Explanatio in V. Librum Moisis* (*PL* 91) 379-94. **C. Begg,** "The Significance of the *Numeruswechsel* in Deuteronomy: The 'Pre-history' of the Question," *ETL* 55 (1979) 116-24; "The Literary Criticism of Deut 4:1-40: Contributions to a Continuing Discussion," *ETL* 56 (1980) 10-55; "1994: A Significant Anniversary in the History of Deuteronomy Research," *Studies in Deuteronomy in Honour of C. J. Labuschagne* (VTSup 53, ed. F. García Martínez et al., 1994) 1-11. **H. H. Ben-Sasson,** "Maimonidean Controversy," *EncJud* (1971) 11:745-54. **A. Bertholet,** *Deuteronomium* (KHC 5, 1899). **J. Blenkinsopp,** *Prophecy and Canon: A Contribution to the Study of Jewish Origins* (SJCA 3, 1977); *The Pentateuch: An Introduction to the First Five Books of the Bible* (ABRL, 1992). **P. Blickle,** *The Revolution of 1525: The German Peasants' War from a New Perspective* (1981). **P. M. Blowers,** "The *Regula Fidei* and the Narrative Character of Early Christian Faith," *Pro Ecclesia* 6 (1997) 199-228. **E. Blum,** *Studien zur Komposition des Pentateuch* (BZAW 189, 1990). **R. Bóid (M. N. Saraf),** "Use, Authority and Exegesis of Mikra in the Samaritan Tradition," *Mikra: Text, Translation, Reading, and Interpretation of the HB in Ancient Judaism and Early Christianity* (ed. M. J. Mulder and H. Sysling, CRINT 2, 1, 1988) 595-633. **G. Braulik,** *Die Mittel deuteronomischer Rhetorick: Erhoben aus Deuteronomium 4,1-40* (AnBib 68, 1978); "Die Abfolge der Gesetze in Deuteronomium 12–26 und der Dekalog," *Das Deuteronomium: Entstehung, Gestalt, und Botschaft* (BETL 68, ed. N. Lohfink, 1985) 252-72 (ET, "The Sequence of the Laws in Deuteronomy 12–26 and in the Decalogue," *Song of Power and the Power of Song: Essays on the Book of Deuteronomy* [ed. D. L. Christensen, 1993] 313-35); *Die deuteronomischen Gesetze und der Dekalog: Studien zum Aufbau von Deuteronomium 12–26* (SBS 145, 1991); *The Theology of Deuteronomy: Collected Essays* (Bibal Collected Essays 2, 1994). **H. Breit,** *Die Predigt des Deuteronomisten* (1933). **C. Brekelmans,** "Die sogenannten deuteronomischen Elemente in Genesis bis Numeri: Ein Beitrag zur Vorgeschichte des Deuteronomiums," (VTSup 15, 1966) 90-96. **M. Bucer,** *De Regno Christi (1550)* (Martini Buceri Opera Latina 15, 1955). **J. Buchholz,** *Die Ältesten Israels im Deuteronomium* (GTA 36, 1988). **P. Buis,** *Le Deutéronome* (VSAT 4, 1969). **P. Buis and J. Leclercq,** *Le Deutéronome* (SB, 1963). **M. Caloz,** "Exode 13:3-16 et son rapport au Deutéronome," *RB* 75 (1968) 5-62. **J. Calvin,** *Mosis reliqui libri quatuor in formam harmoniae* (CR LII-LIII, 416, 1564; ET, *Commentaries on the Four Last Books of Moses, Arranged in the Form of a Harmony* [1852–55]); *Sermons sur le Deutéronome, 1555–56* (CR LIII, 571-LVII, 232; ET, *The Sermons of M. Iohn Calvin Upon the Fifth Booke of Moses Called Deuteronomie* [1583]); *Institutes of the Christian Religion* (LCC 20-21, 1960); *J. Calvin's Sermons on the Ten Commandments* (ed. and tr. B. W. Farley, 1980); *The Covenant Enforced: Sermons on Deuteronomy 27 and 28* (ed. J. B. Jordan, 1990). **C.**

M. Carmichael, *The Laws of Deuteronomy* (1974); *Law and Narrative in the Bible: The Evidence of the Deuteronomic Laws and the Decalogue* (1985). **A. Causse,** "L'ideal politique et social du Deutéronome: La fraternité d'Israël," *RHPR* 13 (1933a) 289-323; "La transformation de la notion d'alliance et la rationalisation de l'ancienne coutume dans la réforme deutéronomique," *RHPR* 13 (1933b) 1-29. **H. Cazelles,** "Passages in the Singular Within Discourse in the Plural of Dt 1–4," *CBQ* 29 (1967) 207-19. **C. Cherry** (ed.), *God's New Israel: Religious Inerpretations of American Destiny* (1971). **A. Cholewinski,** *Heiligkeitsgesetz und Deuteronomium: Eine vergleichende Studie* (AnBib 66, 1976). **D. L. Christensen,** *Deuteronomy 1–11* (WBC 6A, 1991); (ed.), *Song of Power and the Power of Song: Essays on the Book of Deuteronomy* (Sources for Biblical and Theological Study 3, 1993). **J. Chrysostom,** "The Homilies on the Statues," *St. Chrysostom* (NPNF 9, 1908) 315-514; *Discourses Against Judaizing Christians* [*Adv. Iud.*] (FC 68, 1979). **W. M. Clark,** "Law," *OT Form Criticism* (TUMSR 2, ed. J. H. Hayes, 1974) 99-139. **Clement of Alexandria,** *Christ the Educator* [*Paigogogos*] (FC 23, 1954); *Stromateis* (FC 85, 1991). **R. E. Clements,** "Deuteronomy and the Jerusalem Cult Tradition," *VT* 15 (1965) 300-312; *God's Chosen People: A Theological Interpretation of the Book of Deuteronomy* (1968); *Deuteronomy* (OTGu, 1989); "The Deuteronomic Law of Centralisation and the Catastrophe of 587 BC," *After the Exile: Essays in Honour of R. Mason* (ed. J. Barton and D. J. Reimer, 1996) 5-25. **A. C. Cochrane** (ed.), *Reformed Confessions of the Sixteenth Century* (1966). **R. H. Connolly,** "Introduction," and "Notes," *Didascalia Apostolorum: The Syriac Version Translated and Accompanied by the Verona Latin Fragments* (1929). **E. Cortese,** "Theories Concerning Dtr: A Possible Rapprochement," *Pentateuchal and Deuteromistic Studies: Papers Read at the XIIIth IOSOT Congress, Leuven, 1989* (BETL 94, ed. C. Brekelmans and J. Lust, 1990) 179-90. **P. C. Craigie,** *The Book of Deuteronomy* (NICOT, 1976). **F. M. Cross,** "Aspects of Samaritan and Jewish History in Late Persian and Hellenistic Times," *HTR* 59 (1966) 201-11; *Canaanite Myth and Hebrew Epic: Essays in the History of the Religion of Israel* (1973). **F. Crüsemann,** *Die Tora: Theologie und Sozialgeschichte des alttestamentlichen Gesetzes* (1992; ET, *The Torah: Theology and Social History of OT Law* [1996]). **Cyril of Alexandria,** *Glaphyrorum in Deuteronomium liber* (PG 69, 1864) 645-78. **U. Dahmen,** *Leviten und Priester im Deuteronomium: Literarkritische und redaktionsgeschichtliche Studien* (BBB 110, 1996). **D. Daniell,** "Introduction," *Tyndale's OT: Being the Pentateuch of 1530, Joshua to 2 Chronicles of 1537, and Jonah* (1992). **W. M. L. de Wette,** *Dissertatio critico-exegetica qua Deuteronomiumn a prioribus Pentateuchi libris diversum, alius cuiusdam recentioris auctoris opus esse monstratur* (1805); *Beiträge zur Einleitung in das Alte Testament* (2 vols., 1806–7); *Lehrbuch die historisch-kritischen Einleitung in der kanonischen und apocryphischen Bücher des AT* (1840⁵; ET, *A Critical and Historical Introduction to the Canonical Scriptures of the OT* [2 vols., 1843]). **P. Diepold,** *Israels Land* (BWANT 95, 1972). **C. Dogniez and M. Harl,** *Le Deutéronome* (La Bible d'Alexandrie 5, 1986). **S. R. Driver,** *A Critical and Exegetical Commentary on Deuteronomy* (ICC 5, 1895, 1896², 1901³). **F. Dumermuth,** "Zur deuteronomischen Kulttheologie und ihren Voraussetzungen," *ZAW* 70 (1950) 59-98. **J. A. Duncan,** "Considerations of 4QDtj in Light of the 'All Souls Deuteronomy' and Cave 4 Phylactery Texts," *The Madrid Qumran Congress* (STDJ 11, 1, ed. J. Trebolle Barrera and L. Vegas Montaner, 1992) 1:199-215. **Eusebius of Caesarea,** *Preparation for the Gospel* [*Praeparatio evangelica*] (2 vols., 1903; repr. 1981); *The Ecclesiastical History* (LCL, 2 vols., 1926). **F. C. Fensham,** "Malediction and Benediction in Ancient Near Eastern Vassal-treaties and the OT," *ZAW* 74 (1962) 1-9 (repr. in *A Song of Power and the Power of Song* [ed. D. L. Christensen, 1993] 247-55). **L. Feuer,** *Spinoza and the Rise of Liberalism* (1958). **S. Fisch** (ed.), *Midrash haggadol on the Pentateuch, Deuteronomy* (ET 1972). **M. A. Fishbane,** *Biblical Interpretation in Ancient Israel* (1985). **W. Ford,** "Cotton's 'Moses his Judicials,' " *Massachusetts Historical Society, Proceedings* (October 1902) 274-84. **S. D. Fraade,** *From Tradition to Commentary: Torah and Its Interpretation in the Midrash Sifre to Deuteronomy* (SUNY Studies in Judaica, 1991). **R. T. France,** *Matthew: Evangelist and Teacher* (1989). **R. Frankena,** "The Vassal-treaties of Esarhaddon and the Dating of Deuteronomy," *OTS* 14 (ed. P. A. H. de Boer, 1965) 122-54. **K. Froehlich,** " 'Always to Keep the Literal Sense of Holy Scripture Means to Kill One's Soul': The State of Biblical Hermeneutics at the Beginning of the Fifteenth Century," *Literary Uses of Typology from the Late Middle Ages to the Present* (ed. E. Miner, 1977) 20-48. **W. Fuss,** *Die deuteronomistische Pentateuchredaktion in Exodus 3–17* (BZAW 126, 1972). **F. García López,** *Analyse litteraire de Deuteronome, V–XI* (1978). **F. García Martínez,** "Les manuscrits du désert de Juda et le Deutéronome," *Studies in Deuteronomy in Honour of C. J. Labuschagne* (VTSup 53, ed. F. García Martínez et al., 1994) 63-82. **H. L. Ginsberg,** *The Israelian Heritage of Judaism* (TSJTSA 24, 1982). "Liber Deuteronomii," *Glossa Ordinaria* (*PL* 113) 446-506. **W. S. Green,** "Scripture in Rabbinic Judaism," *HBT* 9 (1987) 27-40. **R. A. Greer,** "The Christian Bible and Its Interpretation," *Early Biblical Interpretation* (J. L. Kugel and R. A. Greer, LEC, 1986) 107-203. **H. Grotius,** *De jure belli et pacis* (1645; ET, *The Rights of War and Peace* [Universal Classics Library, 1901]). **R. Hammer** (tr.), *Sifre: A Tannaitic Commentary on the Book of Deuteronomy* (YJS 24, 1986) = *Siphre ad Deuteronomium* (ed. L. Finkelstein, Corpus Tannaiticum 3, 3, 1939). **B. Halpern,** "Jerusalem and the Lineages in the Seventh Century BCE: Kinship and the Rise of Individual Moral Liability," *Law and Ideology in Monarchic Israel* (JSOTSup 124, ed. B. Halpern and D. Hobson, 1991) 11-107. **J. Hamilton,** *Social Justice and Deuteronomy: The Case of Deuteronomy 15* (SBLDS 136, 1992). **D. J. Harrington,** "Interpreting Israel's History: *The Testament of Moses* as a Rewriting of Deuteronomy 31–34," *Studies on "The Testament of Moses": Seminar Papers* (ed. G. W. E. Nickelsburg, SCS 4, 1973) 59-70. **G. L. Haskins,** *Law and Authority in Early Massachusetts: A Study in Tradition and Design* (1960). **D. M. Hay,** "Moses Through NT Spectacles," *Int* 44 (1990) 240-52. **R. B. Hays,** *Echoes of Scripture in the Letters of Paul* (1989). **J. Hempel,** *Die Schichten des Deuteronomiums: Ein Beitrag zur israelitischen Literatur- und Rechtsgeschichte* (Beiträge zur Kultur- und Universalgeschichte 33, 1914). **M. D. Herr,** "Midrash," *EncJud* (1971) 11:1507-14. **S.**

Herrmann, "Die Konstruktive Restauration: Das Deuteronomium als Mitte biblischer Theologie," *Probleme biblischer Theologie: G. von Rad zum 70. Geburtstag* (ed. H. W. Wolff, 1971) 155-70. **D. Hillers,** *Treaty-curses and the OT Prophets* (BibOr 16, 1964); *Covenant: The History of a Biblical Idea* (Seminars in the History of Ideas, 1969). **T. Hobbes,** *Leviathan* (1651) = *Leviathan: Or, The Matter, Form, and Power of a Commonwealth, Ecclesiastical and Civil* (English Works of T. Hobbes of Malmesbury 3, ed. W. Molesworth, 1839); *De Cive* (1642) = *Philosophical Rudiments Concerning Government and Society* (English Works of T. Hobbes of Malmesbury 2, ed. W. Molesworth, 1841). **D. Hoffman,** *Das Buch Deuteronomium* (2 vols., 1913, 1922). **G. Hölscher,** "Komposition und Ursprung des Deuteronomiums," *ZAW* 40 (1922) 161-225. **H. Höpfl,** *Luther and Calvin on Secular Authority* (Cambridge Texts in the History of Political Thought, 1991). **W. Horbury,** "OT Interpretation in the Writings of the Church Fathers," *Mikra: Text, Translation, Reading, and Interpretation of the HB in Ancient Judaism and Early Christianity* (CRINT 2, 1, ed. M. J. Mulder, 1988) 727-87. **F. Horst,** *Das Privilegrecht Jahwes* (FRLANT 28, 1930). **C. Houtman,** *Der Pentateuch: Die Geschichte seiner Erforschung neben einer Auswertung* (CBET 9, 1994) 279-342. **Hugh of St. Victor,** *De Scripturis et Scriptoribus Sacris* (*PL* 175) 9-28; *The Didascalicon of Hugh of St. Victor: A Medieval Guide to the Arts* (Records of Western Civilization, 1961, 1991²). **A. Ibn Ezra,** *Pêrûsê hattôra lerabbînû 'ibn ʿ ezra ʾ* 3 (ed. A. Wieser, 1977). **Irenaeus of Lyon,** *Against Heresies* [*Adversus haereses*], (*The Writings of Irenaeus* 1, ANCL 5, 1, 1874); *Proof of the Apostolic Preaching* (tr. J. P. Smith, ACW 16, 1952). **J. Janzen** "The Yoke That Gives Rest," *Int* 41 (1987) 256-68. **W. Johnstone,** "Reactivating the Chronicles Analogy in Pentateuchal Studies, with Special Reference to the Sinai Pericope in Exodus," *ZAW* 99 (1987) 16-37. **Josephus,** *Against Apion* [*Contra Apionem*] (*Josephus* 1, LCL, 1926) 161-411; *Jewish Antiquities* [*Antiquitates Judaicae*] (*Josephus* 4-9, LCL, 1926). **Justin Martyr,** *The Dialogue with Trypho* (Translations of Christian Literature, 1930). **A. von Karlstadt,** "On the Removal of Images and That There Should Be No Beggars Among Christians," *The Essential Carlstadt* (1522; ET, Classics of the Radical Reformation 8, 1995). **S. Kaufman,** "The Structure of the Deuteronomic Law," *Maarav* 1 (1978–79) 105-58. **M. Keller,** *Untersuchungen zur deuteronomisch-deuteronomistischen Namenstheologie* (BBB 105, 1996). **R. Kennett,** *Deuteronomy and the Decalogue* (1920). **P. Kleinert,** *Das Deuteronomium und der Deuteronomiker* (Untersuchungen zur alttestamentlichen Rechts- und Literaturgeschichte 1, 1872). **M. G. Kline,** *Treaty of the Great King: The Covenant Structure of Deuteronomy* (1963). **A. Klostermann,** "Das deuteronomische Gesetzbuch," *Der Pentateuch: Beiträge zur seinem Verständnis und seiner Entstehungsgeschichte* (1893, 1907²) 154-428. **D. Knapp,** *Deuteronomium 4: Literarische Analyse und theologische Interpretation* (GTA 35, 1987). **D. A. Knight,** "Deuteronomy and the Deuteronomists," *OT Interpretation: Past, Present, and Future* (ed. J. L. Mays et al., 1995) 61-79. **E. König,** *Das Deuteronomium* (KAT 3, 1917). **C. Kraemer,** "The Formation of Rabbinic Canon: Authority and Boundaries," *JBL* 110 (1991) 613-30. **A. Kuenen,** *Historische-kritische Onder-*

zoek naar het ontstaan en de verzameling van de Boeken den Ouden Verbonds 1.1 (1861, 1885²; ET, *An Historico-critical Inquiry into the Origin and Composition of the Hexateuch: Pentateuch and Book of Joshua* [1886]). **G. Langer,** *Von Gott Erwählt—Jerusalem: Die Rezeption von Dtn 12 im frühen Judentum* (ÖBS 8, 1989). **N. Leibowitz,** *Studies in Devarim (Deuteronomy)* (1982³). **J. D. Levenson,** "Who Inserted the Book of the Torah?" *HTR* 68 (1975) 203-33. **B. M. Levinson,** *Deuteronomy and the Hermeneutics of Legal Innovation* (1997). **B. Lindars,** "Torah in Deuteronomy," *Words and Meanings: Essays Presented to D. W. Thomas* (ed. P. R. Ackroyd and B. Lindars, 1968) 117-36. **J. Locke,** "A Letter Concerning Toleration [1689]," *The Works of J. Locke* (1823) 6:1-58. **S. Loersch,** *Das Deuteronomium und seine Deutungen: Ein forschungsgeschichtlicher Überblick* (SBS 22, 1967). **N. Lohfink,** *Das Hauptgebot: Eine Untersuchung literarischer Einleitungsfragen zu Dtn 5–11* (AnBib 20, 1963); "Deuteronomy," *IDBSup* (1976) 229-32; (ed.), *Das Deuteronomium: Entstehung, Gestalt, und Botschaft* (BETL 68, 1985); *Die Väter Israels im Deuteronomium: Mit einer Stellungnahme von T. Römer* (OBO 111, 1991); *Theology of the Pentateuch: Themes of the Priestly Narrative and Deuteronomy* (1994). **M. Luther,** "Preface to the OT [1523]," *Word and Sacrament* 1 (*LW*, 1960) 35:235-51 = WA, DB 8, 11-31; "Against the Heavenly Prophets in the Matter of Images and Sacraments [1525]," *Church and Ministry* 2 (*LW*, 1958) 40:73-223 = *Wider die himmlischen Propheten, von den Bildern und Sacrament* (WA 18) 62-125, 134-214; "How Christians Should Regard Moses [1525]," *Word and Sacrament* 1 (*LW*, 1960) 35:155-74 = *Eyn Unterrichtung wie sich die Christen ynn Mosen sollen schicken* (WA 16) 363-93; *Lectures on Deuteronomy* (tr. R. R. Caemmerer, *LW* 9, 1960) = *Deuteronomium Mosi cum annotationibus* (WA 14) 497-744. **S. D. McBride,** "The Yoke of the Kingdom: An Exposition of Deuteronomy 6:4-5," *Int* 27 (1973) 273-306; "Deuteronomium," *TRE* 8 (1981) 530-43; "Polity of the Covenant People: The Book of Deuteronomy," *Int* 41 (1987) 229-44 (repr. in *A Song of Power and the Power of Song* [ed. D. L. Christensen, 1993] 62-77). **D. J. McCarthy,** *Treaty and Covenant* (AnBib 21A, 1963, 1978²). **J. G. McConville,** *Law and Theology in Deuteronomy* (JSOTSup 33, 1984). **J. G. McConville and J. G. Millar,** *Time and Place in Deuteronomy* (JSOTSup 179, 1994). **F. R. McCurley,** "The Home of Deuteronomy Revisited: A Methodological Analysis of the Northern Theory," *A Light unto My Path: OT Studies in Honor of J. M. Myers* (GTS 4, ed. H. Bream et al., 1974) 295-317. **D. McGinn,** *The Admonition Controversy* (Rutgers Studies in English 5, 1949). **Maimonides,** *The Book of the Divine Commandments* (2 vols., tr. C. Chavel, 1940); *The Guide of the Perplexed* (tr. S. Pines, 1963). **J. Malfroy,** "Sagesse et loi dans le Deutéronome," *VT* 15 (1965) 49-65. **T. Mann,** *Deuteronomy* (Westminster Bible Companion, 1995). **A. D. H. Mayes,** *Deuteronomy* (NCB, 1979); "Deuteronomy 4 and the Literary Criticism of Deuteronomy," *JBL* 100 (1981) 23-51 (repr. in *A Song of Power and the Power of Song* [ed. D. L. Christensen, 1993] 195-224); "On Describing the Purpose of Deuteronomy," *JSOT* 58 (1993) 13-33. **W. A. Meeks,** *The Prophet-king: Moses Traditions and the Johannine Christology* (NovTSup 14, 1967). **M. Mendelssohn,** *Jerusalem oder über religiöse Macht und Judentum* (1783; ET,

Jerusalem, or On Religious Power and Judaism [1983]). **G. E. Mendenhall,** "Ancient Oriental and Biblical Law," *BA* 17 (1954) 26-46; "Covenant Forms in Israelite Tradition," *BA* 17 (1954) 50-76. **G. E. Mendenhall and G. A. Herion,** "Covenant," *ABD* (1992) 1:1179-202. **R. P. Merendino,** *Das Deuteronomische Gesetz: Eine literarkritische, gattungs- und überlieferungsgeschichtliche Untersuchung* (BBB 31, 1969). **J. Milgrom,** "Profane Slaughter and a Formulaic Key to the Composition of Deuteronomy," *HUCA* 47 (1976) 1-17. **P. D. Miller,** "The Gift of God: The Deuteronomic Theology of the Land," *Int* 23 (1969) 451-65; " 'Moses My Servant': The Deuteronomic Portrait of Moses," *Int* 41 (1987) 245-55; *Deuteronomy* (IBC, 1990). **C. Minette de Tillesse,** "Sections 'tu' et sections 'vous' dans le Deutéronome," *VT* 12 (1962) 29-87. **S. Mittmann,** *Deuteronomium 1,1-6, 3 literarkritisch und traditionsgeschichtlich Untersucht* (BZAW 139, 1975). **D. P. Moessner,** "Luke 9:1-50: Luke's Preview of the Journey of the Prophet Like Moses of Deuteronomy," *JBL* 102 (1983) 575-605. **J. I. Mombert (ed.),** *W. Tyndale's Five Books of Moses Called the Pentateuch* (1967). **W. L. Moran,** "The Ancient Near Eastern Background of the Love of God in Deuteronomy," *CBQ* 25 (1963) 77-87. **E. Morgan** (ed.), *Puritan Political Ideas, 1558–1794* (American Heritage Series, 1965). **T. Müntzer,** "Sermon Before the Princes [1524]," *Spiritual and Anabaptist Writers* (LCC 25, 1957) 47-70. **Nachmanides (Ramban),** *Pêrûšê hattôra lerabbînû mošē ben nahman,* 3 (ed. C. Chavel, 1965; ET, *Commentary on the Torah: Deuteronomy* [1976]). **J. Neusner,** *Sifre to Deuteronomy: An Introduction to the Rhetorical, Logical, and Topical Program* (BJS 124, 1987). **E. W. Nicholson,** *Deuteronomy and Tradition* (1967); *God and His People: Covenant and Theology in the OT* (1986). **C. R. North,** "Pentateuchal Criticism," *The OT and Modern Study* (ed. H. H. Rowley, 1951) 48-83. **M. Noth,** *Die Gesetze im Pentateuch: Ihre Voraussetzungen und ihr Sinn* (SKG.G 17, 2, 1940; ET, "The Laws in the Pentateuch: Their Assumptions and Meaning," *The Laws in the Pentateuch and Other Studies* [1966] 1-107); *Überlieferungsgeschichte des Pentateuch* (1948; ET, *A History of Pentateuchal Traditions* [1972]); *Überlieferungsgeschichtliche Studien* (1957²) 1:1-110 (ET, *The Deuteronomistic History* [JSOTSup 15, 1981, 1991²]). **T. Oestreicher,** *Das deuteronomische Grundgesetz* (BFCT 27, 4, 1923). **D. T. Olson,** *Deuteronomy and the Death of Moses: A Theological Reading* (OBT, 1994). **Origen,** *On First Principles* [*De Principiis*] (tr. G. W. Butterworth, 1936); *Contra Celsum* (tr. and ed. H. Chadwick, 1953). **E. Otto,** "Von Budesbuch zum Deuteronomium: Die deuteronomische Redaktion in Dtn 12–26," *Biblische Theologie und Gesellschaftlicher Wandel: FS für N. Lohfink* (ed. G. Braulik, W. Gross, and S. McEvenue, 1993) 260-78; "Aspects of Legal Reform and Reformulation in Ancient Cuneiform and Israelite Law," *Theory and Method in Biblical and Cuneiform Law: Revision, Interpolation, and Development* (ed. B. Levinson, JSOTSup 181, 1994) 160-96; "Gesetzesfortschreibung und Pentateuchredaktion," *ZAW* 107 (1995) 373-92. **T. Paine,** *The Age of Reason* (1794–95; Carol ed., 1995). **M. J. Paul,** "Hilkiah and the Law (2 Kings 22) in the 17th and 18th Centuries," *Das Deuteronomium* (BETL 68, ed. N. Lohfink, 1985) 9-12; *Het archimedisch punt van de Pentateuchkritiek: Een historisch en exegetisch onderzoek naar de verhouding van Deu-*

teronomium en de reformatie van konig Josia (2 Kon. 22–23) (1988). **L. Perlitt,** *Bundestheologie im Alten Testament* (WMANT 36, 1969); *Deuteronomium* (BKAT 5, 1990–); *Deuteronomium-Studien* (FAT 8, 1994). **Philo of Alexandria,** "On the Creation [*De Opificio Mundi*]," "Allegorical Interpretation of Genesis II., III. [*Legum Allegoria*]," *Philo* 1 (LCL, 1929); "On the Migration of Abraham [*De Migratione Abrahami*]," "Who Is the Heir of Divine Things [*Quis Rerum divinarum Heres*]," *Philo* 4 (LCL, 1932]; "Moses [*De Vita Mosis*]," "On the Decalogue [*De Decalogo*]," "On the Special Laws [*De Specialibus Legibus*]," "On the Virtues [*De Virtutibus*]," "On Rewards and Punishments [*De Praemiis et Poenis*]," *Philo* 6–8 (LCL, 1935–39); "Every Good Man is Free [*Quod Omnis Probus Liber Sit*]," *Philo* 9 (LCL, 1941). **J. G. Plöger,** *Literarkritische, formgeschichtliche, und stilkritische Untersuchungen zum Deuteronomium* (BBB 26, 1967). **R. Polzin,** *Moses and the Deuteronomist: Deuteronomy, Joshua, Judges* (A Literary Study of the Deuteronomic History 1, 1980). **C. J. Pressler,** *The View of Women Found in the Deuteronomic Family Laws* (BZAW 216, 1993). **H. D. Preuss,** *Deuteronomium* (ErFor 164, 1982). **Procopius of Gaza,** *Commentarii in Deuteronomium* (*PG* 1865) 87:893-992. **Ptolemy,** "Letter to Flora," *Biblical Interpretation in the Early Church* (tr. and ed. K. Froehlich, Sources of Early Christian Thought, 1984) 37-43. **J. D. Purvis,** *The Samaritan Pentateuch and the Origin of the Samaritan Sect* (HSM 2, 1968). **A. F. Puukko,** *Das Deutronomium: Eine literarkritische Untersuchung* (BWAT 5, 1910). **Rabanus Maurus,** *Enarrationis super Deuteronomium* (*PL* 108) 837-998. **J. Rabbinowitz** (tr.), *Midrash Rabbah: Deuteronomy* (1939; Heb. ed. S. Liebermann, *Midraš debarîm rabba* [1974³]). **G. von Rad,** *Das Gottsvolk im Deuteronomium* (BWANT 47, 1929); *Das formgeschichtliche Problem des Hexateuch* (BWANT 74, 1938; ET, "The Form-critical Problem of the Hexateuch," *The Problem of the Hexateuch and Other Essays* [1966] 1-78; *Deuteronomium-Studien* (FRLANT 58, 1948²; ET, *Studies in Deuteronomy* [SBT 1, 9, 1961]); *Theologie des Alten Testaments* 1 (1957, 1960²; ET, *OT Theology,* vol. 1, *The Theology of Israel's Historical Traditions* [1965]); "Deuteronomy," *IDB* (1962) 1:831-38; *Das fünfte Buch Mose: Deuteronomium* (ATD, 1964; ET, *Deuteronomy: A Commentary* [OTL, 1966]). **Rashi,** *Raš"y 'al hattôra* (ed. A. Berliner, 1905²; ET, *Pentateuch with Tg. Onkelos, Haphtaroth, and Prayers for Sabbath and Rashi's Commentary: Deuteronomy* [n.d.]). **J. Reider,** *The Holy Scriptures: Deuteronomy, with Commentary* (1937). **E. Reuss,** *L'histoire sainte et la loi* (1879). **E. Reuter,** *Kultzentralisation: Entstehung und Theologie von Dtn 12* (Athenaums Monografiens 87, 1993). **E. K. A. Riehm,** *Die Gesetzgebung Moisis im Lande Moab* (1854). **P. Riemann,** "Covenant, Mosaic," *IDBSup* (1976) 192-97. **A. Rofé,** "The Strata of the Law About the Centralization of Worship in Deuteronomy and the History of the Deuteronomic Movement," *Congress Volume, Uppsala, 1971* (VTSup 22, 1972) 221-26; "The Monotheistic Argumentation in Deuteronomy 4:32-40: Contents, Composition, and Text," *VT* 35 (1985) 434-45; "The Arrangement of the Laws in Deuteronomy," *ETL* 64 (1988) 265-87. **J. W. Rogerson,** *W. M. L. de Wette: Founder of Modern Biblical Criticism: An Intellectual Biography.* (JSOTSup 126, 1992). **T. Römer,** *Israels Väter: Untersuchungen zur Väterthema-*

tik im Deuteronomium und in der deuteronomistischen Tradition (OBO 99, 1990); "The Book of Deuteronomy," *The History of Israel's Traditions: The Heritage of M. Noth* (ed. S. L. McKenzie and M. P. Graham, JSOTSup 182, 1994) 178-212. **M. Rose,** *Der Ausschliesslichkeitsanspruch Jahwes: Deuteronomische Schultheologie und die Volksfrömmigkeit in der späten Königszeit* (BWANT 106, 1975); *Deuteronomist und Jahwist: Untersuchungen zu den Berührungspunkten beider Literaturwerke* (ATANT 67, 1981). **Rupert of Deutz,** "In Deuteronomium," *De Trinitate et Operibus Eius* (*PL* 167) 917-1000. **U. Rütersworden,** *Von der politischen Gemeinschaft zur Gemeinde: Studien zu Dt 16,18–18,22* (BBB 65, 1987). **J. A. Sanders,** "Deuteronomy," *The Books of the Bible* (ed. B. W. Anderson, 1989) 1:89-102. **E. Sandoz** (ed.), *Political Sermons of the American Founding Era: 1730–1805* (1991). **F. W. Schultz,** *Das Deuteronomium* (1859). **G. Seitz,** *Redaktionsgeschichtliche Studien zum Deuteronomium* (BWANT 93, 1971). **A. R. Siebens,** *L'origine du code deutéronomique* (1929). **R. Simon,** *Histoire critique du Vieux Testament* (1678; ET, *A Critical History of the OT* [1682]). **D. E. Skweres,** *Die Rückverweise im Buch Deuteronomium* (AnBib 79, 1979). **B. Smalley,** *The Study of the Bible in the Middle Ages* (1952). **R. Smend,** "W. R. Smith and J. Wellhausen," *W. R. Smith: Essays in Reassessment* (ed. W. Johnstone, JSOTSup 189, 1995) 226-42. **G. A. Smith,** *The Book of Deuteronomy* (1918). **W. R. Smith,** *The OT in the Jewish Church* (1881, 1892²). **R. K. Soulen,** *The God of Israel and Christian Theology* (1996). **B. de Spinoza,** *Tractatus theologico-politicus* (1670; ET R. H. M. Elwes, *A Theologico-political Treatise* [1951]). **W. Staerk,** *Das Deuteronomium: Sein Inhalt und seine literarische Form. Eine kritische Studie* (1894); *Das Problem des Deuteronomiums: Ein Beitrag zur neuesten Pentateuchkritik* (BFCT 29, 2, 1924). **N. Steinberg,** "The Deuteronomic Law Code and the Politics of State Centralization," *The Bible and the Politics of Exegesis: Essays in Honor of N. K. Gottwald on His Sixty-fifth Birthday* (ed. D. Jobling et al., 1991) 161-70. **D. Steinmetz,** "The Reformation and the Ten Commandments," *Int* 43 (1989) 256-66. **C. Steuernagel,** *Der Rahmen des Deuteronomiums: Literarcritische Untersuchungen über seine Zusammensetzung und Entstehung* (1894, 1923²); *Die Entstehung des deuteronomischen Gesetzes* (1896, 1901²); *Deuteronomium und Josau* (HKAT 1, 3, 1, 1900, 1923²). **L. Stulman,** "Encroachment in Deuteronomy: An Analysis of the Social World of the D Code" *JBL* 109 (1990) 613-32. **H. Tadmor,** "Treaty and Oath in the Ancient Near East: A Historian's Approach," *Humanizing America's Iconic Book* (SBLBSNA 6, ed. G. M. Tucker and D. A. Knight, 1982) 127-52. **A. Tal,** "Samaritan Literature," *The Samaritans* (ed. A. Crown, 1989) 413-67. **Tertullian,** *An Answer to the Jews [Adversus Iudaeos]* (*The Writings of Tertullian,* ANCL 18, ed. A. Roberts and J. Donaldson, 1870) 3:202-49; *Apology [De Spectaculis]* (LCL, 1931); *Apology* (LCL, 1953). **Thomas Aquinas,** *On Charity [De Caritate]* (1960); *Summa Theologiae,* vol. 29, *The Old Law* (Ia2ae, 98-105, 1969). **J. H. Tigay,** *Deuteronomy: The Traditional Hebrew Text with the New JPS Commentary* (JPS Torah Commentary, 1996); "The Significance of the End of Deuteronomy (Deut 34:10-12)," *Texts, Temples, and Traditions: A Tribute to M. Haran* (ed. M. Fox et al., 1996) 137-43. **E. Tov,** "Proto-Samaritan Texts and the Samaritan Pentateuch,"

The Samaritans (ed. A. Crown, 1989) 397-407. **I. Twersky,** *Introduction to the Code of Maimonides (Mishneh Torah)* (YJS 22, 1980). **E. Ulrich,** "Pluriformity in the Biblical Text, Text Groups, and Questions of Canon," *The Madrid Qumran Congress* (ed. J. Trebolle Barrera and L. Vegas Montaner, STDJ 11, 1, 1992) 1:23-41. **M. Valeri,** "Religion, Discipline, and the Economy in Calvin's Geneva," *SCJ* 28 (1997) 123-42. **J. Van Seters,** "Confessional Reformulation in the Exilic Period," *VT* 22 (1972) 448-59; "The Conquest of Sihon's Kingdom: A Literary Examination," *JBL* 91 (1972) 182-97; "The So-called Deuteronomistic Redaction of the Pentateuch," *Congress Volume, Leuven, 1989* (ed. J. Emerton, VTSup 43, 1991) 58-77. **J. Vermeylen,** *Le Dieu de la Promesse et le Dieu de l'Alliance: Le dialogue des grandes institutions théologiques de l'Ancien Testament* (LD 126, 1986). **M. Vervenne and J. Lust** (eds.), *Deuteronomy and Deuteronomic Literature: FS C. H. W. Brekelmans* (BETL 133, 1997). **B. K. Waltke,** "Samaritan Pentateuch," *ABD* (1992) 5:932-40. **M. Weinfeld,** *Deuteronomy and the Deuteronomic School* (1972); "The Emergence of the Deuteronomic Movement: The Historical Antecedents," *Das Deuteronomium: Entstehung, Gestalt, und Botschaft* (ed. N. Lohfink, BETL 68, 1985) 76-98; *Deuteronomy 1–11* (AB 5, 1991); "Deuteronomy, Book of," *ABD* (1992) 2:168-83. **D. Weir,** *The Origins of the Federal Theology in Sixteenth-century Reformation Thought* (1990). **A. C. Welch,** *The Code of Deuteronomy: A New Theory of Its Origin* (1924); *Deuteronomy: The Framework of the Code* (1932). **J. Wellhausen,** *(Prolegomena zur) Geschichte Israels* (1878, 1883²; ET, *Prolegomena to the History of Israel* [1885]); *Die Composition des Hexateuchs und der historischen Bücher des Alten Testaments* (1889², 1899³). **R. Westbrook,** "Biblical and Cuneiform Law Codes," *RB* 92 (1985) 247-64. **J. W. Wevers,** *Notes on the Greek Text of Deuteronomy* (SBLSCS 39, 1995). **S. A. White,** "The All Souls Deuteronomy and the Decalogue," *JBL* 109 (1990) 193-206. **J. N. M. Wijngaards,** *The Dramatization of Salvific History in the Deuteronomic Schools* (OTS 16, 1969). **R. Wilson,** "Israel's Judicial System in the Preexilic Period," *JQR* 74 (1983) 229-48. **G. E. Wright,** "The Book of Deuteronomy: Introduction and Exegesis," *IB* (1953) 2:309-537; "The Lawsuit of God: A Formcritical Study of Deuteronomy 32," *Israel's Prophetic Heritage* (ed. B. W. Anderson and W. Harrelson, 1962) 26-67. **Y. Yadin,** *Tefillin from Qumran (XQPhyl 1-4)* (1969); *The Temple Scroll* (3 vols., 1983). **K. Zobel,** *Prophetie und Deuteronomium: Die Rezeption prophetischer Theologie durch das Deuteronomium* (BZAW 199, 1992).

S. D. MCBRIDE

DEUTSCHER VEREIN ZUR ERFORSCHUNG PALÄSTINAS

The DVEP was established in 1877 by H. GUTHE, E. KAUTZSCH, A. Socin, and other scholars from German-speaking lands who were reluctant to let the French, British, and American societies and explorers dominate research in Palestine. The goal of the DVEP was to promote research into the history of Palestine and adjacent territories, particularly in the disciplines of geography and ARCHAEOLOGY; and to this end it began publishing the *ZDPV,* which has been issued since 1878, except for the hiatus between 1945 and 1953, when it was replaced by one volume of *BBLAK* (1951). An additional periodical, *MNDPV* (1895–1912), and a monographic series, ADPV (1969–), have also been produced by DVEP. The society's antiquity collection, publications repository, and archives were destroyed by air attacks on Leipzig in 1943, and so in 1952 the organization was reconstituted in Bonn and set about rebuilding its library and publishing *ZDPV* in cooperation with the Deutsches evangelisches Institut für Altertumswissenschaft des Heiligen Landes.

Bibliography: E. **Kautzsch,** "Vorwort," *ZDPV* 1 (1878) 1-9.

M. P. GRAHAM

DE WETTE, WILHELM MARTIN LEBERECHT
(1780–1849)

D. was a complex person, a rationalist, a mystic, and an aesthete whose life was partly tragic; but he made some of the most decisive contributions to historical biblical criticism in the nineteenth century. Born Jan. 12, 1780, in Ulla near Weimar, the son of a Lutheran pastor of remote Dutch origins (whence the "de"), he attended the gymnasium in Weimar, where the superintendent, J. G. HERDER, made a lasting impression on him. He entered the University of Jena in 1799 and soon lost his faith under the impact of Kantian philosophy (see I. KANT) and such rationalist teachers as H. Paulus; but after attending Schelling's lectures on the philosophy of art, he sought desperately to reconcile rationalism and the aesthetic. In 1804 he gained his doctorate with a dissertation that argued that Deuteronomy had a different author from the rest of the Pentateuch (see PENTATEUCHAL CRITICISM) and was probably written in the seventh century. He began to enlarge this work into a book covering the whole of the Pentateuch and was devastated when the third volume of J. VATER's *Commentary on the Pentateuch* of 1805 seemed to forestall some of his results. He worked feverishly on the books of Chronicles, expanding points from his doctoral thesis and in 1806 published the first volume of his *Beiträge.* This epoch-making work dismissed the picture of the history of Israelite religion found in Chronicles and opened the way for a new and radical account of Israel's religious history, which was ultimately given classical expression by J. WELLHAUSEN in 1878. According to D., Moses was not the founder of a complex cultic religion with its priestly personnel. Instead, the cult had developed gradually in Israel from simple and spontaneous beginnings. In its final form the Pentateuch was no earlier than the seventh century BCE.

From 1807 to 1810 D. was professor in Heidelberg,

where he began a lifelong friendship with the philosopher J. Fries and where he began work on a new translation of the Bible in collaboration with C. Augusti. In 1810, on the recommendation of F. SCHLEIERMACHER, he moved to the newly founded University of Berlin. There, between 1810 and 1819, he published his Psalms commentary and textbooks on HB introduction, ARCHAEOLOGY, and church dogmatics. In Berlin he made a new and deep study of Fries's philosophy and reached his mature theological position when he accepted that the life of Christ was an expression of an ideal and necessarily true principle within historical contingencies. He now began to write on ethics from his newfound christological vantage point.

In 1819 D. was dismissed from Berlin on account of a letter of sympathy he wrote to the mother of K. Sand, the assassin of the diplomat A. Kotzebue. He settled in Weimar, where he worked on a semi-autobiographical novel, *Theodor* (ET 1841), and on a critical edition of LUTHER's letters. In 1822 he accepted a call to Basel. The salary was small in comparison to that in Berlin, but he had little choice but to accept. His second wife (his first died in childbirth in 1806 after less than a year of marriage) disliked Basel and separated from him. Although D. hoped to get back to Germany, he remained in Basel until his death June 16, 1849, making an outstanding contribution to the university. He reorganized the theological syllabus and teaching, founded a scholarly journal, and sucessfully encouraged the citizens of Basel to make financial support for the university a top priority. In Basel D. moved in the direction of ethics, dogmatics, and the NT and produced a complete set of commentaries on the NT that presented the results of recent criticism. At the same time he produced revised editions of his Psalms commentary, his TRANSLATION of the Bible, and his OT *Einleitung*.

His most important work was the *Beiträge* of 1806–7. His general theological position owed too much to Fries's philosophy with its association of religion with aesthetics to gain a wide following, although in the twentieth century R. Otto's *The Idea of the Holy* restated Fries's position. D. remained a rationalist in that he valued the rational above the historical; but his rationalism was aesthetic, emphasizing art (see ART AND BIBLICAL INTERPRETATION), music (see MUSIC, THE BIBLE AND), POETRY, and drama as paths to a kingdom of ultimate values that received concrete expression in the life of JESUS. In a sense D. was a man of the late eighteenth century; but in his stress on the importance of literature and aesthetics in biblical studies and in theology, he anticipated some of the concerns of the late twentieth century.

Works: *Beiträge zur Einleitung in das Alte Testament* (1806–7); *Kommentar über die Psalmen* (1811 and subsequent eds.); *Lehrbuch der Christlichen Dogmatik* (1813–16); *Lehrbuch der*

historisch-kritischen Einleitung in die Bibel Alten und Neuen Testaments (1817–26; ET, of 5th Ger. ed. by T. Parker, 2 vols., 1843); *Christliche Sittenlehre* (1819–23); *Kurzgefasstes exegetisches Handbuch zum Neuen Testament* (1836–48).

Bibliography: **R. Otto,** *The Philosophy of Religion, Based on Kant and Fries* (1970) 151-215. **S. B. Puknat,** "D. W. in New England," *PAPS* 102 (1958) 376-95. **J. W. Rogerson,** *OTCNC,* 28-49; *W. M. L. d. W., Founder of Modern Biblical Criticism: An Intellectual Biography* (JSOTSup 126, 1992); *HHMBI,* 298-302. **R. Smend,** *W. M. L. d. W.s Arbeit am Alten und am Neuen Testament* (1958). **E. Staehelin,** *Dewettiana* (1956). **A. Wiegand,** *W. M. L. d. W., 1780–1849: Eine Säkularschrift* (1879).

J. W. ROGERSON

DHORME, EDOUARD PAUL (1881–1966)

Described as the "best French semitist of his generation" (A. PARROT); Hebraist; Assyriologist (see ASSYRIOLOGY AND BIBLICAL STUDIES); archaeologist (see ARCHAEOLOGY AND BIBLICAL STUDIES); historian, especially of religions; exegete; and Bible translator, D. was born Jan. 15, 1881, at Fleurbe (Pas-de-Calais), France. He died in Paris Jan. 19, 1966. After schooling at Armentières (Nord) he entered the Dominican novitiate and in 1899 was sent to Jerusalem to study. Ordained May 24, 1904, he taught Hebrew and Assyro-Babylonian language and literature at the École Biblique in Jerusalem until 1929, except from 1914 to 1918 when he served in the Eastern Expeditionary Corps, excavating and preserving the sarcophagi of the necropolis of Alexander the Great at Eleontis in Thrace. He also served as editor of the *RB* (1922–31) and as director of the École Biblique (1923–29).

In 1929 D. left the École Biblique to lecture at Louvain. He never returned. In 1931 he left the Dominican order and the church and married a daughter of E. Ben-Yehuda. He claimed to be a rationalist, but observers noticed no change in his moderate, objective biblical criticism. He was a professor at the École Pratique des Hautes Etudes (1933–51), in the Faculté des Lettres of the Sorbonne (1937–45), and in the College de France (1946–51). He was a dynamic teacher with an encyclopedic range of knowledge.

D.'s most historic achievement occurred in 1930 when he, along with H. Bauer and C. Virolleaud, deciphered Ugaritic, the language of texts recently discovered at Ras-Shamra (see UGARIT AND THE BIBLE). Another major achievement was a TRANSLATION of the HB into French.

Work: *Choix de textes religieux assyro-babyloniens* (1907); *La religion assyro-babylonienne* (1910); *Les livres de Samuel* (1910); *Les pays bibliques et l'Assyrie* (1911); *L'emploi métaphorique des noms de parties du corps en hébreu et en akkadien* (1923); *Le livre de Job* (1926; ET 1967); *Langues et* *écritures sémitiques* (1930); *La poésie biblique* (1931); *La littérature babylonienne et assyrienne* (1937); *La religion des Hébreux nomades* (1937); *Les religions de Babylonie et d'Assyrie* (1945); *Recueil E. D.: études bibliques et orientales* (1951), a collection of his articles; *La Bible: l'Ancien Testament* (Bibliothèque de la Pléiade, 2 vols., 1967); *St. Paul* (1956–59).

Bibliography: A. Guillaumont, *BHR* 169 (1966) 123-32. J. Nougayrol, *AfO* 22 (1968/69) 208-10. A. Parrot, *RA* 55 (1961, a special issue on his eightieth birthday; *Le Monde* (January 1966) 30-31; *CRAIBL* (Feb. 18, 1966) 90-94; *Syria* 43 (1966) 155-57; *RA* 60 (1966) i-iv.

B. T. VIVIANO

DIBELIUS, MARTIN (1883–1947)

D. was born in Dresden, Sept. 14, 1883, and died in Heidelberg, Nov. 11, 1947. After studying in Neuchâtel, Leipzig, Tübingen, and Berlin, he received his PhD in Tübingen in 1905, his ThD in Berlin in 1908, and completed his inaugural dissertation in Berlin in 1911 as NT scholar ("Das Selbstzeugnis des Paulus von seiner Bekehrung und Sendung," unpub.). His theological and scholarly direction was decisively influenced by A. von HARNACK. In 1915 D. became professor of NT in Heidelberg and remained there until his death. As a young man he acquired an interest in social problems from his father, and after 1918 he engaged in political activity on the side of democratic values as well as working intensively in the ecumenical movement.

Three main, variously overlapping areas of interest undergirded D.'s scholarly work:

1. Religious History of Primitive Christianity. H. GUNKEL won D. over to the history-of-religion methodology (see RELIGIONSGESCHICHTLICHE SCHULE), which D. first employed in his two dissertations and in the HNT commentaries. In his later contributions he was even more concerned than in his early works both with determining the specific types of various history-of-religion relationships and with working out the uniqueness of the primitive Christian religion and its message. He discussed the fundamental methodological and theological problems of history-of-religion research in his little-known Montpellier lectures (1930).

2. Form and Development of Primitive Christian Writings. Similarly influenced by Gunkel, D. turned his attention early to stylistic and transmission questions concerning the Gospels. This interest in stylistic problems was aided by his own aesthetic gifts and by his familiarity with German literature; his interest in sociological questions (see SOCIOLOGY AND NT STUDIES) regarding early Christian literature was influenced by A. DEISSMANN, E. TROELTSCH, and M. WEBER. These interests generated the idea of a form history (see FORM CRITICISM) of the Gospels or for a form-historically conceived history of primitive Christian literature. The fundamental assertions of his book (1919) were already present in his inaugural lecture in Berlin, "Der literarische Charakter der Evangelienliteratur" (1910, unpub.), and in his book on John the Baptist (1911): The Gospels originated from orally transmitted individual units from whose form one can deduce their original function and situation. The historical foundation of the new theological sensibility that emerged after WWI rested on both the reliability of central Gospel traditions D. established as well as on the central role preaching occupied within his reconstruction of primitive Christianity. The premier exponent of this new sensibility was *kerygma* theology.

A compressed comprehensive presentation of the history of primitive Christian literature appeared in 1926; and although the projected thorough treatment was never finished, this program found its heir in the literary history of his pupil P. VIELHAUER. In the last decade of his life, D.'s LITERARY-critical work was concerned especially with Acts.

3. The Relationship of the Gospel or of Primitive Christianity with Its Environment. D.'s concern with serious problems of his own time posed the question of what contribution Christianity might make to their solution. He sought the answer in his research into the relationships between primitive Christianity and the world in which it found itself, with early Christian ethics being a particular interest. D.'s commentary on James (1921) not only determined the shape of the concept of paraenesis but also largely determined both the direction of subsequent research into James and the discussion of the origin and character of primitive Christian ethics. In the second edition of his commentary on the PASTORAL LETTERS (1931) he presented his related thesis of the "ideal of Christian citizenship," which he maintained was already extant in later primitive Christianity. His contributions to early Christian social ethics, which unfortunately appeared in rather obscure publications, received less attention since D. never wrote his long-planned comprehensive presentation of the development of primitive Christian ethics in the fashion, for example, of his pupil H.-D. Wendland.

F. OVERBECK's understanding of the development of primitive Christianity appears to have decisively influenced D.'s overall concept: After "non-worldly" beginnings, or beginnings "apart from the world," primitive Christianity experienced in various areas an increasing accommodation to and sense of responsibility for the world in which it found itself. Unlike Overbeck, however, D. saw in the enduring polarity between fundamental non-worldliness, on the one hand, and continuing demands for responses to and responsibility for the world, on the other hand, the fruitful essence of Christianity. His influence, which also began quite early outside German-speaking contries, may well be characterized more by fruitful impulses in the various exegetical areas of research than by the influence of a single, unified program.

Works: *Die Lade Jahves* (FRLANT 7, 1906); *Die Geisterwelt im Glauben des Paulus* (1909); *Die Briefe des Apostels Paulus* (HNT 3, 2): *An die Thessalonicher I, II. An Die Philipper* (1911, 1925[2], 1937[3]), *An die Kolosser, Epheser. An Philemon* (1912, 1927[2], 1953[3]), *An Timotheus I, II. An Titus* (1913, 1932[2], 1953[3]), *An Timotheus I, II. An Titus* (ed. by H. Conzelmann, 1913, 1931[2], 1955[3], 1966[4]; ET Hermeneia, 1976); *Die urchristliche Überlieferung von Johannes dem Täufer* (1911); *Die Formgeschichte des Evangeliums* (1919, 1933[2]; ET *From Tradition to Gospel* [1971]); *Der Brief des Jakobus* (KEK 15, 1921, 1956[2]; ET Hermeneia, 1975); *Der Hirt des Hermas* (HNT Ergänz. Bd. 4, 1923); *Geschichtliche und übergeschichtliche Religion im Christentum* (1925; *Evangelium und Welt* [1929[2]]); *Geschichte der urchristlichen Literatur I, II* (SG 934-35, 1926; ET, *Fresh Approach to the NT and Early Christian Literature* [1936, repr. 1971]); *Urchristentum und Kultur* (1927); "Le Nouveau Testament et l'histoire des religions," *ETR* 5 (1930) 211-26, 295-316; 6 (1931) 330-50; "Zur Formgeschichte des Neuen Testaments (ausserhalb der Evangelien)," *TRu* NF 3 (1931) 207-42; "Das soziale Motiv im Neuen Testament," *Kirche, Bekenntnis, und Sozialethos* (1934) 9-32; *Gospel Criticism and Christology* (1935); "The Message of the NT and the Orders of Human Society," *Christian Faith and Common Life* (ed. N. Ehrenström et al., 1938) 17-43; *Jesus* (SG 1130, 1939, 1947[2]); *Aufsätze zur Apostelgeschichte* (ed. H. Greeven, 1951); *Paulus* (ed. and completed by W. G. Kümmel, SG 1160, 1951); *Botschaft und Geschichte: Gesammelte Aufsätze* (ed. G. Bornkamm, 1953–56); *I. Zur Evangelienforschung* (1953), *II. Zum Urchristentum und zur hellenistischen Religionsgeschichte* (1956).

Bibliography: A. **Fridrichsen,** "Bibliographia Dibeliana atque Bultmanniana," ConNT (ed. A. Fridrichsen, 1944) 1-22. **H. Greeven,** *FAB* 2 (1948) 26-31. **W. G. Kümmel,** *RGS* 5 (1929) 1-37; "M. D. als Theologe," *TLZ* 74 (1949) 129-40 = his *Heilsgeschehen und Geschichte* (1965) 192-206; *TRE* 8 (1981) 726-29. **G. Theissen,** "Zum Stand der Diskussion in der neutestamentlichen Theologie: Überlegungen anlässlich des 100. Geburtstags von M. D. (1883–1947)," *Neue Stimme* 5 (1984) 20-24.

H. BRINGELAND

DICTIONARIES AND ENCYCLOPEDIAS

These reference works provide systematic, alphabetized information on various topics within canonical and extra-canonical books of the Bible (see CANON OF THE BIBLE) or pertaining to biblical studies, especially persons, events, books, geography, objects, theological terms, religious practices, history, SOCIOLOGY, CHRONOLOGY, MAPS, pictures, criticism, and ARCHAEOLOGY.

1. Early Dictionaries and Encyclopedias. Speusippus (d. 338 BCE) among the Greeks and Pliny (d. 79 CE) among the Romans compiled some of the earliest Western encyclopedic works. These collections were organized topically, with the earliest alphabetical encyclopedias appearing less than a thousand years ago.

Most dictionaries or encyclopedias were written in Latin prior to 1700 and were authored by a single scholar.

The earliest effort to compile biblical information other than lexical was EUSEBIUS's *Onomasticon,* although it was limited to Palestinian topography. JEROME published *De nominibus hebraicis* and *De viris illustribus,* both of which contained information about biblical persons. During the next thousand years, general theological encyclopedias appeared that also included references to biblical topics, for example, CASSIODORUS's *Institutiones divinarum et humanarum lectionum,* ISIDORE OF SEVILLE's *Etymologiarum sive originum libri viginti,* and Vincent of Beauvais's (d. 1264) *Speculum maius.* Numerous biblical wordbooks and LEXICONS were produced in the late Middle Ages and during the Renaissance and Reformation periods (see E. Mangenot [1899]).

The pioneering Bible dictionary of the modern genre was *Le Grand Dictionnaire de la Bible ou Explication littérale et historique de tous les mots propres du Vieux et du Nouveau Testaments* (1693) by French priest R. Simon. This work discussed people, animals, festivals, geography, fauna and flora, and weights and measures. It did not include articles on the books of the Bible or on approaches to biblical criticism.

2. Eighteenth and Nineteenth Centuries. Simon's beginnings were taken over by D. CALMET in *Dictionnaire historique, critique, chronologique, géographique et littérale de la Bible* (2 vols., 1719, also appearing in Latin), the work upon which, in a sense, all later Bible dictionaries are based. Another edition (with supplements) in four volumes was published in 1730. The title expresses well the subjects addressed. A few delimited Bible dictionaries appeared in English prior to Calmet (see W. M. Smith [1979]), for example, T. Wilson's *Complete Christian Dictionary* (1661, 1667[5]), and F. Shaw's *A Summary of the Bible; or the Principal Heads of Natural and Revealed Religion; Alphabetically Disposed in the Words of Scripture Only* (1730). The first major dictionary in English, however, was a translation and revision of Calmet by S. d'Oyley and J. Colson (1732), volume 1 of which contained a 300-page annotated bibliography of books on biblical studies. The most reprinted English translation was that of C. Taylor (1797, 1823[4]); a large section picturing ancient coins is still of use. An American translation under the editorship of E. ROBINSON was published in 1832 in which Robinson revised a few of the articles. Also in the tradition of Calmet, but original and updated, is the first comprehensive German Bible dictionary, by G. Winer, *Biblisches Real-Wörterbuch zum Handgebrauch für Studirende, Candidaten, Gymnasiallehrer und Prediger ausgearbeitet* (2 vols., 1820). This dictionary went through several editions, increasing in size, and was even published in German in New York in 1849.

Until after the middle of the nineteenth century most

dictionaries were single-scholar, entrepreneurial undertakings, designed to inform and entertain those interested in the Scriptures. While they may have represented the best in scholarly insight, they were not produced for a scholarly guild, since such a targeted audience considerably limited the market. Many times the entries were merely biblical citations or repeated biblical narratives with little comment. Wonders were reported from the long history of Christianity as well as from rabbinic and classical sources. The more important articles tended to be discursive and reflected theological controversies, especially of a Calvinist mold (see CALVIN). These dictionaries also often reflect a specific confessional stance.

One of the best known and most widely reprinted of these dictionaries was a two-volume work by J. Brown of Haddington, first published in 1768. By the sixth edition (1816) it was titled *The Whole Comprising Whatever Important Is Known Concerning the Antiquities of the Hebrew Nation and the Church of God* (American printings of an earlier edition, 1798, 1811). The first Bible dictionary to be printed in the United States was *The Dictionary of the Bible,* with no editor identification (1792). In 1816 W. Jones of Finsbury published a two-volume *The Biblical Cyclopaedia; or Dictionary of the Holy Scriptures.* Several editions of the very popular one-volume dictionary *A Biblical Cyclopedia or Dictionary* (1848) were printed until 1901.

About the middle of the nineteenth century the forward-looking dictionaries took a different turn by taking notice of the views of more radical biblical critics, although for the most part rejecting their conclusions. The style became more exact and succinct or, as expressed by the editors, more "scientific." Dictionaries began to appear that were multi-authored by both Europeans and Americans (Protestants) and were designed to bring the church abreast of current scholarship. Archaeological data was interjected, and critical conclusions in regard to the specific books of the Bible were discussed at length. More Bible dictionaries of all sorts were produced in the last half of the nineteenth century than before or since.

J. Kitto's *Cyclopoedia of Biblical Literature* (2 vols., published in both London and New York, 1845) was the first major Bible dictionary in English to solicit articles, in this case from forty authors, mostly British except for a few Americans and Germans, and eschewed the sometimes questionable narratives of previous works. A revised edition, prepared by W. Alexander, included articles on biblical scholars (3 vols., 1866). In 1860 W. Smith commenced publishing his widely sold *Dictionary of the Bible* (3 vols., 1860–64), authored by fifty-three English and American scholars. H. Hackett and E. ABBOT prepared an American edition (4 vols., 1868–70), revising and adding numerous articles. P. Fairborn also recruited a large number of authors for his *Imperial Bible Dictionary* (2 vols., 1865; 6 vols., 1885). The first German effort at a major multi-authored dictionary was a work edited by D. Schenkel, *Bibel-Lexikon* (5 vols., 1869). During the same period a Jewish scholar, J. Hamburger, published *Real-Encyclopädie für Bibel und Talmud* (5 vols., 1883–97), and J. Davis, a Princeton OT professor wrote the popular one-volume *A Dictionary of the Bible* (1898), which was revised by H. Gehman as the *WDB* (1944, 1970³). The scholarly dictionary of T. CHEYNE and J. Sutherland Black, *Encyclopaedia Biblica* (4 vols., 1899–1902) was the first expanded dictionary in English that significantly incorporated "higher," as it was then called, biblical criticism. The authors were drawn from international circles, including Americans.

3. Twentieth Century. Twentieth-century Bible dictionaries have changed little in form or approach from the principal dictionaries at the close of the nineteenth. The content is obviously different, especially as the result of new forms of biblical criticism, conservative/liberal rifts, archaeological finds, the biblical THEOLOGY movement, ecumenicity, and nationalism. The result is that dictionaries represent different positions on the theological spectrum and national vernaculars. At the same time ecumenical dictionaries have emerged that bracket both confessional and ethnic groupings. The production of major dictionaries slowed considerably as compared with the last half of the nineteenth century, but from the middle of the twentieth century many new dictionaries of a non-technical kind, especially conservative ones, have appeared.

a. British. At the beginning of the century, J. HASTINGS edited *A Dictionary of the Bible Dealing with Its Language, Literature, and Contents Including Biblical Theology* (5 vols., 1898–1904). Authors were international (but Protestants), and entries on books of the APOCRYPHA were included. Although abreast of critical matters, the conclusions tended to be more moderate than in the Cheyne volumes. A one-volume Hastings *Dictionary of the Bible* was published in 1909 (revised in 1963 under the editorship of F. Grant and H. Rowley). In 1966 the *Concise Dictionary of the Bible* (2 vols., London), reflecting moderate conclusions, came out under the editorship of S. Neill, J. Goodwin, and A. Dowle. Other projects have been completed jointly with American evangelicals under the editorship of J. Douglas, *The New Bible Dictionary* (1962), and *The Illustrated Bible Dictionary* (3 vols., 1980), which expanded the former and added numerous excellent illustrations.

b. American. The *International Standard Bible Encyclopedia* (5 vols., 1915) was the first predominately American Bible dictionary, even though the editor was J. ORR, a Scot. The authors were mostly conservative British and American, but interdenominational. Americans under the leadership of G. Bromiley undertook a major revision (1979–88), including articles by Jews and

Roman Catholics. The overall mood is still conservative; e.g., R. Harrison assigns the final form of the book of Daniel to no later than 450 BCE and announces the demise of the documentary hypothesis, while D. Guthrie defends Pauline authorship (see PAUL) of the PASTORAL LETTERS. When published it was the most expansive Bible dictionary in English, containing articles of recent interest, e.g., on RHETORICAL CRITICISM.

A moderately critical dictionary most influential among Americans and the English-speaking world has been the *IDB* (ed. G. A. Buttrick, 4 vols., 1962). The authors of these articles were Protestant, Jewish, and international. A 1976 supplement updated various entries and added such new topics as Nag Hammadi. As the editor, K. Crim, pointed out, Roman Catholics were now included as authors.

The first Roman Catholic biblical encyclopedia in the English language was the *Catholic Biblical Encyclopedia* (1950) by J. Steinmueller and K. Sullivan, respectively authors of the HB and the NT sections, which are separated. J. MCKENZIE, a Catholic, published *Dictionary of the Bible* in 1967. In 1975 M. TENNEY edited the first completely new evangelical dictionary in a half century, *The Zondervan Pictorial Encyclopedia of the Bible* (5 vols.), using a group of international scholars. The one-volume *Harper's Dictionary of the Bible* (ed. P. Achtemeier, 1985), printed jointly by the SOCIETY OF BIBLICAL LITERATURE and Harper and Row, is the first Bible dictionary to be published under the auspices of a biblical society. The dictionary was revised and published in 1997 as the *Harper Collins Dictionary of the Bible*.

A more recent multi-volumed work is the *ABD* (ed. D. N. Freedman, 6 vols., 1992), which represents the flowering of American biblical scholarship, especially on the HB. Its one thousand contributors are international and ecumenical; but Americans comprise more than twice those from elsewhere, with other key contributors from the United Kingdom and Israel. The distinctive features of the dictionary highlight cultural history, social institutions, archaeology, and texts that have surfaced in the last half of the twentieth half-century. The positions taken are often non-traditional, critical, and reflective of cutting-edge perspectives. The dictionary contains both surprising entries and absences. Several articles are helpful in assessing the history of biblical scholarship, while others are not. Bibliographies are lengthy and helpful; however, few illustrations and photos are included, and none in color.

c. European. Bible dictionaries have been published in many European languages: French, Dutch, German, Italian, Spanish, Dutch, Danish, Swedish, Norwegian, Finnish, and Polish. These tend to be either Protestant or Roman Catholic. F. Vigouroux' *Dictionnaire de la Bible* (5 vols., 1905–12; with supplements, vols. 1-11, 1928–   ) includes articles on biblical scholars; however,

since Vatican II this dictionary has become more reflective of the insights of international biblical scholarship. A significant dictionary with many illustrations is the Spanish work edited by S. Bartina and A. Diez-Macho, *Enciclopedia de la Biblia* (6 vols., 1963–65), which has also been translated into Italian as *Enciclopedia della Bibbia* (ed. A. Rolla, 6 vols., 1969–71). The major German dictionary is *BHH* (ed. B. Reicke and L. Rost, 4 vols., 1962–69), whose authors are mostly German and Swiss but include a few American and British scholars. Also noteworthy is *Reclams Bibellexikon* (ed. K. Koch, E. Otto, J. Roloff, and H. Schmoldt 1978, 1987) and *Bijbels Woordenboek,* edited by A. van den Born (1941, 1954–57²), a Dutch Catholic dictionary, which has been translated into many languages, including English, with substantial revisions (1963). I. ENGNELL produced the Scandinavian dictionary *Svenskt Bibliskt Uppslags Verk* (2 vols., 1962–63), with authors from many countries and confessions; and E. Dabrowskiego edited an important Polish Catholic work, *Podreczna Encyklopedia Biblijna* (2 vols., Poznan, 1959).

d. Others. A multi-volume HB dictionary published in Jerusalem with U. CASSUTO as the first editor is *Ensiqlopedyah mizra'it* (*Encyclopaedia Biblica* [1950–   ]) written in modern Hebrew by international Jewish authors under the auspices of the Jewish Agency of Palestine and the Museum of Jewish Antiquities at the Hebrew University.

Bibliography: *CBTEL* 2 (1869) 777-90. **G. E. and L. Gorman,** "Biblical Studies: Dictionaries," *Theological and Religious Reference Materials, General Resources, and Biblical Studies* (1984) 248-74. **E. Mangenot,** *Dictionnaire de la Bible* 2 (1899) 1411-28. **W. M. Smith,** *ISBE* 1 (1979) 492-98.

T. H. OLBRICHT

DIDYMUS THE BLIND (313–398)

An Egyptian monk who headed the catechetical school at Alexandria, D. lost his sight as a child but cultivated his memory to become one of the most respected scholars of his time. He was the foremost expositor of Scripture in the tradition of ORIGEN, whom he revered. He was influential, particularly on the West, via Rufinus, who studied with him for eight years, and JEROME, who frequently acknowledged his debt to D. and solicited his *Commentary on Zechariah.*

D. wrote dogmatic treatises and extensive commentary on Scripture. His commentaries covered most of the Bible as well as Origen's *Peri Archon.* Although celebrated as a champion of orthodoxy in the fourth and fifth centuries, he was condemned along with Origen in 553. As a result, D.'s exegetical works were lost until 1941, when five of his HB commentaries were discovered along with works by Origen at an ancient quarry at Tura near Cairo. These works have excited considerable interest in D., both in his own right and as a source of information related to other fields, like TEXTUAL CRITICISM.

It has been argued that D. refined Origen's HERMENEUTICS, but further clarity on Origen's methods would be needed to prove this. Like Origen, D. believed that Scripture was written in figurative language, *allegoria.* Its deeper sense, *anagoge,* could be uncovered by a process of spiritual interpretation involving consistent patterns of biblical symbolism. An example is his interpretation of Zech 14:16, which speaks of a time when the Gentiles will celebrate the Feast of Booths ("tents" in Greek). He interprets this spiritually to refer to the general resurrection by reading it in the light of 2 Pet 1:14 and 2 Cor 5:4, which refer to the body as a tent (SC 85, 1066-68).

Works: *De Sancto Spiritu, PG* 39:1033-85; *Sur Zacharie* (3 vols., ed. L. Doutreleau, SC 83, 84, 85, 1962); *Kommentar zum Ecclesiastes* (6 vols., ed. G. Binder et al., PTA, 1968–79); *Kommentar zu Hiob* (3 vols., ed. A. Heinrichs, PTA, 1968); *Psalmenkommentar* (5 vols., ed. L. Doutreleau, M. Grönewald et al., PTA, 1968–70); *Sur la Genese* (2 vols., ed. P. Nautin and L. Doutreleau, SC 233, 244, 1976–78).

Bibliography: G. Bardy, *Didyme l'Aveugle* (ETH 1, 1910). W. A. Bienert, *"Allegorie" und "Anagoge" bei Didymos dem Blinden* (1972). R. P. C. Hanson, *The Search for the Christian Doctrine of God: The Arian Controversy* (1988) 653-58, 755-56. K. Krämer, *TRE* 8 (1981) 741-46. T. W. Mackay, "Didymous the Blind on Psalm 28 (LXX): Text from Unpublished Leaves of the Tura Commentary," *StPatr* 20 (1989) 40-49. R. Merkelbach, "Konjekturen und Erläuterungen zum Psalmkommentar des Didymos," *VC* 20 (1966) 214-26. J. Quasten, *Patrology* 3 (1960) 85-100. M.-J. Rondeau, *Les commentaires patristiques du Psautier* 1 (1962) 116-21; 2 (1985) 223-74. P. Sellew, "Achilles or Christ? Porphyry and D. in Debate over Allegorical Interpretation," *HTR* 82 (1989) 70-100. J. H. Tigcheler, *Didyme l'Aveugle et l'exégèse allégorique: Étude sémantique de quelques termes exégètiques* (1977). F. M. Young, *From Nicaea to Chalcedon* (1983) 83-91, 341, 367-68.

J. W. TRIGG

DIESTEL, LUDWIG (1825–79)

Born at Königsberg Sept. 28, 1825, D. studied at Königsberg, Berlin, and Bonn under H. HÄVERNICK, E. HENGSTENBERG, and F. BLEEK. His own teaching career unfolded at Bonn (1851–62), Greifswald (1862–67), Jena (1867–72), and Tübingen (1872–79), where he died May 15, 1879.

In his OT studies D. concentrated on theological questions while not completely neglecting emerging critical and philological issues. His attention to the latter

is attested by his 1853 monograph on the age and unity of the "Blessings of Jacob" (Genesis 49), which he viewed as having been based on fragmentary sayings of the patriarch, supplemented by additions from the time of Samuel and Saul. D.'s major work is an 800-plus-page survey (1869) of the exegetical, theological, homiletical, practical, and artistic treatment of the OT from 100 CE to his own day. He also edited the fourth edition of A. KNOBEL's KEH commentary on Isaiah (1872) and authored extensive articles on such biblical concepts as divine holiness and righteousness.

Works: *Der Segen Jakobs in Genesis XLIX* (1853); *Die Geschichte des Alten Testaments in der christlichen Kirche* (1869).

Bibliography: E. Kautzsch, *RE*[3] 4 (1898) 647-50.

C. T. BEGG

DILLMANN, CHRISTIAN FRIEDRICH AUGUST (1823–94)

Born Apr. 25, 1823, in Würtemberg, Germany, D. died on July 4, 1894, in Berlin. He studied theology from 1840 to 1845 in Tübingen, where his main interest was oriental languages and his most important teacher by far was H. EWALD. After receiving his PhD, in 1846 D. left for two years in Paris, London, and Oxford to study and catalog ETHIOPIAN manuscripts in the British Museum and in the Bodleian Library. In 1848 he became a *Repetent* at the theological seminary in Tübingen, in 1851 a *Docent,* and in 1853 *ausserordentlicher* professor. In 1854 he was *ausserordentlicher* professor and in 1860 full professor for oriental studies on the philosophical faculty in Kiel. In 1864 he became full professor on the theological faculty in Giessen and in 1869 full professor in Berlin as the successor of E. HENGSTENBERG. After D.'s death his library went to Johns Hopkins University in Baltimore.

D.'s literary production was confined mainly to two areas: Ethiopian language, literature, and history and HB commentaries. Considered the founder of modern Ethiopian studies, he was well equipped for this role even early on. In the summer of 1855 a publisher asked him to write an Ethiopian grammar, and in April 1857 the work was finished. It was dedicated to Ewald as the "Master of Semitic Linguistics." In his further years in Kiel D. worked on the monumental *Lexicon linguae Aethiopicae* (1865), a work that in spite of weaknesses has never been eclipsed and certainly never replaced. It was followed immediately by a textbook for academic instruction, the *Chrestomathia Aethiopica.* D.'s point of departure for his Ethiopian studies was 1 ENOCH, which he published in 1851 in Ethiopian and in 1853 in a translation with a commentary. Also in 1853 he began to publish the complete edition of the Ethiopian Bible, although it remained unfinished. At the end of his life D. wanted to return to Ethiopian studies, which were less controversial than HB scholarship at that time; he was, however, no longer able to fulfill this wish.

In comparison to his Ethiopian studies D.'s accomplishments as a commentator, though great, were not pioneering. As a representative figure of the right wing of liberal exegesis, he summarized the results of this exegesis substantively, precisely, and reliably to such a degree that his commentaries could be used by those who did not necessarily agree with his scholarly direction. They enjoyed the reputation of virtual exegetical classics. In his first year in Berlin (1869) his commentary on Job marked the beginning of a series that was concluded by a commentary on Isaiah (1890); the latter had the misfortune of appearing shortly before B. DUHM's commentary, which immediately overshadowed it. In between D. treated the entire Hexateuch, succeeding A. KNOBEL, to whom these volumes (including Isaiah) had originally been commissioned.

D.'s commentary work falls in the years 1875–86 (Genesis 6th ed., 1892). It was a period during which ancient oriental sources, particularly important for the understanding of Genesis, were disclosed, above all the Babylonian flood story. D. employed these sources without their influencing his views in any fundamental way; however, he had to take a position regarding the upheaval in hexateuchal criticism brought about at precisely this time by J. WELLHAUSEN. In any case, in 1876/77 as co-editor of the *JDTh* he personally saw to it that Wellhausen's "Composition des Hexateuchs" appeared. A decade later he appended the results of his own reflections under the title "Über die Composition des Hexateuch," to the end of his commentary on Numbers, Deuteronomy, and Joshua (591-690) and thus declared it unquestionably a response to Wellhausen—a learned and careful but nonetheless somewhat laborious apologetic response. In contrast to Franz DELITZSCH shortly thereafter (*Neuer commentar über die Genesis* [1887]), D. was really unable to turn his thinking around and thus considered himself to be a *uatechon*, a "brakeman," who felt obligated to arrest the "journey into destruction"—which is how the latest phase of PENTATEUCHAL CRITICISM appeared to him (W. Baudissin [1898] 667-68). He stood in the position of the "recent source hypothesis" by distributing the material essentially to the sources A (Priestly Code), B (Elohist), C (Yahwist), and D (Deuteronomist); however, he rejected K. GRAF's hypothesis and replaced it with the temporal succession B (9th cent.), A (around 800), C (8th cent.), and D (7th cent.).

The *Handbuch der Alttestamentlichen Theologie*, posthumously published by R. KITTEL on the basis of lecture notes, proceeds in a systematic way essentially according to the traditional scheme (1. Doctrine of God; 2. Doctrine of Man; 3. Path of Salvation or Doctrine of the Kingdom of God), although it does seek both within this scheme and by means of a preliminary historical section to bring historical elements into play. The theological goal is to follow the "gradual and stepwise disclosure and fulfillment" of the "divine resolution" that culminates in "Christianity and thus to establish on historical grounds the proof of the consistency and necessity, and thus the inner truth of Christianity" (9). The book presents many of Ewald's ideas more precisely and clearly than Ewald himself was able to do.

Works: *Liber Henoch, Aethiopice* (1851); *Das Buch Henoch: Übersetzt und erklärt* (1853); *Das christliche Adambuch des Morgenlandes: Aus dem Äthiopischen mit Bermerkungen übersetzt* (1853); *Octateuchus Aethiopicus* (2 vols., 1853–55); *Grammatik der äthiopischen Sprache* (1857; ed. C. Bezold, 1899[2]; ET 1907); *Liber Jubilaeorum Aethiopice* (1859); *Veteris Testamenti Aethiopici libri Regum* (2 vols., 1861–71); *Lexicon linguae Aethiopicae cum indice Latino* (1865); *Chrestomathia Aethiopica* (1866); *Hiob* (KEH 2, 1869[3], 1891[4]); *Die Genesis* (KEH 11, 1875[3], 1882[4], 1886[5], 1892[6]); *Der Verfall des Islâm* (Berliner Rektoratsrede, 1876); *Ascensio Isaiae: Aethiopice et Latine* (1877); "Über die Anfänge des Axumitischen Reiches," *AAWB* (1878) 177-238; *Die Bücher Exodus und Leviticus* (KEH 12, 1880[2]); "Über die Herkunft der urgeschichtlichen Sagen der Hebräer," *SPAW* (1882) 427-40; *Die Bücher Numeri, Deuteronomium, und Josua* (KEH 13, 1886[2]); *Der Prophet Jesaja* (KEH 5, 1890[5]); "Über den neugefundenen griechischen Text des Henoch-Buches," *SPAW* (1892) 1039-54, 1079-92; *Veteris Testamenti Aethiopici libri apocryphi* (1894); *Handbuch der Alttestamentlichen Theologie* (ed. R. Kittel, 1895).

Bibliography: W. W. Graf Baudissin, *August Dillman* (1895); *RE[3]* 4 (1898) 662-69. R. Kittel, *ADB* 47 (1903) 699-702. E. Littmann, *Ein Jahrhundert Orientalistik* (1955) 1-10.

R. SMEND

DILTHEY, WILHELM (1833–1911)

Born in Biebrich, Germany, D. was educated at the universities of Heidelberg and Berlin. As a student of theology he examined early formulations of the Christian worldview in IRENAEUS, CLEMENT OF ALEXANDRIA, and ORIGEN in an effort to determine how dogma is revised in light of new religious experiences. This approach to the history of religion reflects the influence of F. SCHLEIERMACHER. In 1860 D. received a prize from the Schleiermacher-Stiftung for his treatise "Schleiermacher's Hermeneutical System in Relation to Earlier Protestant Hermeneutics," in which he discussed the hermeneutical writings of M. FLACIUS, S. Glassius (1593–1656), J. D. MICHAELIS, J. SEMLER, J. ERNESTI, C. KEIL, and F. Ast (1778–1841), among others, as well as the influences exerted by I. KANT, J. G. Fichte (1762–1814), and F. Schlegel (1772–1829) on the formation of Schleiermacher's hermeneutical system. The last part of the treatise deals with the relation between general HERMENEUTICS and the special hermeneutics of the NT, ending with chapters on grammatical and psychological interpretation (see PSYCHOLOGY AND BIBLICAL STUDIES).

In 1861 D. transferred to philosophy to work with F. A. Trendelenburg (1802–72). D.'s philosophical contribution to hermeneutics lies in his efforts to expand the scope of interpretation beyond religious and literary texts to include all human objectifications. The historical deposits and effects of human actions are as much texts to be interpreted as are written texts. His life project was to write a critique of historical reason, which would ground the human sciences as Kant had grounded the natural sciences. D. stressed the need for descriptive and comparative methods to refine understanding in the human sciences and limited the use of hypothetical explanations characteristic of the natural sciences. Philosophy is a human science that tries to understand the nature of science in general, but to the extent that it reflects on the meaning of life it is also like poetry and religion in articulating a worldview. Whereas religious worldviews tend to have their source in "a lived experience of the invisible," poetic worldviews focus more on the visible relations given in life itself. The philosophical worldview is an effort to give a metaphysical or totalistic conceptual order to the experience of life. Such attempts can only be partially successful, however, and shift back and forth between either a pluralistic type of naturalism as exemplified by Epicurus and D. HUME, a dualistic idealism of freedom as exemplified by Plato and I. KANT, or a monistic type of objective idealism as exemplified by Heraclitus and G. W. F. Hegel (1770–1831).

The main task of D.'s hermeneutics was to explicate not only the ideal conceptual presuppositions but also the real life conditions of human existence. Only by so enriching the scope of the hermeneutical circle can one escape the vicious cycles of the history of metaphysical types. D.'s own interpretive approach was to articulate what is typical in human experience on the basis of pre-theoretical involvements in life. The hermeneutical circle between parts and wholes brings out the paradox that one must already have a preliminary understanding of the whole before one can adequately interpret the meaning of the parts. The human sciences can provide the general structures that mediate in this process and serve to make the circle productive. Such structures are located in the shared features of the human psychic nexus; in the external organization of the institutions into which human beings are born (e.g., church and state); and in the even more pervasive cultural systems, ranging from artistic to economic, in which they choose to work together. Among the many thinkers that D. influenced are M. BUBER, G. Simmel, E. Husserl, E. Cassirer, G. Lukács, J. Ortega y Gasset, M. Heidegger, and H.-G. Gadamer.

Works: *Schleiermacher's Hermeneutical System in Relation to Earlier Protestant Hermeneutics* (1860; ET 1996); *Leben Schleiermachers* (2 vols., 1870); *Introduction to the Human Sciences* (1883; ET 1989); *Idea for a Descriptive and Analytical Psychology* (1894; ET 1977); *The Rise of Hermeneutics* (1900; ET 1996); *The Understanding of Other Persons and Their Life-Expressions* (1900; ET 1977); *The Formation of the Historical World in the Human Sciences* (1910); *The Problem of Religion* (1911); *Types of World View and Their Development in Metaphysical Systems* (1911; ET 1957). D.'s works are collected in his *Gesammelte Schriften* (21 vols., 1914–96) and appear in ET as *Selected Works* (6 vols.; vol. 1, *Introduction to the Human Sciences* [1989]; vol. 4, *Hermeneutics and the Study of History* [1996]; vol. 5, *Poetry and Experience* [1985]).

Bibliography: O. **Bollnow,** *D.: Eine Einführung in seine Philosophie* (1955). M. **Ermarth,** *D.'s Critique of Historical Reason* (1978). M. **Jung,** *D.: Zur Einführung* (1996). R. **Makkreel,** *D.: Philosopher of the Human Studies* (1975). G. **Misch,** *Lebensphilosophie und Phänomenologie: Eine Auseinandersetzung mit der Diltheyschen Richtung mit Heidegger und Husserl* (1930). J. **Owensby,** *D. and the Narrative of History* (1994). F. **Rodi,** *Morphologie und Hermeneutik: Zur Methode von D.s Aesthetik* (1969).

R. MAKKREEL

DIONYSIUS OF ALEXANDRIA (d. c. 264)

A bishop of Alexandria, D. was a distinguished and well-educated citizen of that city who studied with ORIGEN and succeeded a fellow student as bishop. He interpreted biblical passages in relation to events of his own time, as EUSEBIUS notes in his *Church History.* According to D., the emperor Gallus fulfilled Rev 13:5 because of his "mouth speaking great things and blasphemy." There was given him "authority and forty-two months." Macrianus and Valerian were predicted in Ezek 13:3 and Isa 66:3-4 as well as in Exod 20:5 (7.10). Indeed, in D.'s view "the human race upon earth is constantly diminishing and consuming away . . . its total disappearance draws nearer and nearer" (7.21). When the emperor Gallienus succeeded Valerian, however, the events recalled Isa 42:9 with 43:19: "Behold, the former things are come to pass, and new things which shall now spring forth" (7.23). Obviously in this sketch of history D. provided an apocalyptic interpretation (see APOCALYPTICISM) and placed a high value on revelation.

Presumably it was at a later date that he gave a different picture. As bishop in charge of country districts as well as of metropolitan Alexandria, D. decided to attack the notion that "the kingdom of Christ will be on earth." He therefore brought together "the presbyters and teachers" in the villages to discuss the topic for three days. His opponents relied on a literal interpretation of the Revelation of John; but since D. knew others who rejected the book entirely, he was able to present his own position as mediating. He praised its author as "holy and inspired" but argued on philological grounds that the Revelation was not written by the author of the Gospel and of 1 John. Many examples (not all of them correct) showed differences in ideas, vocabulary, and syntax. The Gospel and the epistle "are not only written in faultless Greek but also show the greatest literary skill in their diction, reasonings, and constructions." Revelation, on the other hand, is written in bad Greek. Still not content with these arguments, he examined the whole book to show that it could not be taken literally: Its meaning is hidden, more marvelous, deeper, and too high for human understanding. (Presumably, then, he regarded the Gospel and the first epistle as clear and straightforward, especially in view of John 18:36: "My kingdom is not of this world.") He tells us that the leader of the opposition found the discussion completely convincing (7.24-25).

D. went well beyond Origen's acceptance of Revelation and used exegesis in the service of a political theology. He had his reward when the emperor Gallienus restored confiscated church properties to the bishops (7.13). It was the emperor who, as in later theology, ruled the world and Christ who guided him. Christ would not, in the foreseeable future, reign directly. The AUTHORITY of Revelation had to be diminished in opposition to millenarians.

Bibliography: C. L. Feltoe, *The Letters and Other Remains of Dionysius of Alexandria* (1904). **J. Quasten,** *Patrology* (1950) 2:101-9.

R. M. GRANT

DIVINO AFFLANTE SPIRITU

The encyclical letter of Pope Pius XII on the promotion of biblical studies, issued on Sept. 30, 1943, to commemorate the fiftieth anniversary of *Providentissimus Deus,* was mainly occasioned by a brochure written by an Italian priest (D. Ruotolo, using the penname D. Cohenel) and sent anonymously to all Italian bishops and superiors of religious congregations (1941). The brochure inveighed against the "critico-scientific system" of interpreting Scripture, advocating rather a "meditative" or "spiritual" type of exegesis. The Pontifical Biblical Commission sent a corrective letter to the same addressees (*AAS* 33 [1941] 465-72; *RSS,* 138-47 [522-33]), but Pius XII followed that up with this encyclical addressed to the universal church. In it, though he never named the method, he advocated the proper use of the historical-critical method of interpreting Scripture in order to ascertain the literal sense of the inspired biblical text (see INSPIRATION OF THE BIBLE).

Following two introductory paragraphs the encyclical is divided into two parts, the first historical, the second doctrinal. In the first part Pius XII recalled the work of Leo XIII (his encyclical *Providentissimus Deus,* his approval of the founding of the École Biblique in Jerusalem [1890], his apostolic letter *Vigilantiae* instituting the Biblical Commission [1902]) and that of Leo's successors (Pius X and Pius XI), significantly passing over Benedict XV and *Spiritus Paraclitus.* In the second part Pius XII built on the Leonine directives, acknowledging the impact of nineteenth-century historical, archaeological (see ARCHAEOLOGY AND BIBLICAL STUDIES), and TEXTUAL discoveries and stressing the need for recourse to the original languages of the biblical text. He insisted on the interpretation of the Bible according to its literal sense, "that the mind of the author may be made abundantly clear"; and he clarified in what sense the Tridentine decree about the authenticity of the VULGATE is to be understood: juridically authentic for church use but not critically authentic. Hence vernacular translations of the Bible were to be produced.

In speaking of the "spiritual sense" of Scripture, Pius XII used only its traditional meaning, the christological sense of the OT. Besides the literal sense, the interpreter must explain this spiritual sense, "provided it is clearly intended by God." The "allegorical or figurative sense" of patristic interpreters, which was recommended by Leo XIII, is not mentioned, however. While yielding that "figurative senses" of Scripture might be useful in preaching, Pius XII insisted that such senses are "extrinsic to it and accidental" and "especially in these days, not free from danger." Moreover, he clarified that "there are but few texts whose sense has been defined by the authority of the Church," and fewer still "about which the teaching of the Holy Fathers is unanimous." The encyclical's main emphasis falls on interpretation according to "literary forms," espousing an idea that Benedict XV had condemned.

Bibliography: "Litterae encyclicae *Divino afflante Spiritu. . . .* " *AAS* 35 (1943) 297-325; *RSS,* 80-107; *BI,* 316-42. **J. Levie,** *The Bible: Word of God in Words of Men* (1962) 133-90.

J. A. FITZMYER

DOBSCHÜTZ, ERNST VON (1870–1934)

Born at Halle/Saale, Germany, D. was professor of NT exegesis in Jena, Strasbourg, Breslau, and finally at Halle from 1913 to 1934. In 1914 he was a visiting professor at Harvard, where he published his famous book on the influence of the Bible. Primarily a text critic (see TEXTUAL CRITICISM) and exegete of the NT, his main interests, influenced by his teachers M. KÄHLER and A. von HARNACK, were the history, iconography, and theology of earliest Christianity. Perhaps his chief contribution to biblical interpretation was his concern for maintaining the AUTHORITY OF THE BIBLE as a historical source for theology rather than as an authoritative proof for doctrines imposed on it. D. championed historical-critical understanding as superior to all that preceded it as a means of controlling theological appropriation. He regarded ORIGEN as the greatest biblical scholar of the ancient church, if not of all times. Yet he rejected the fanciful treatment of supposedly historical material as "the greatest damage ever done to religion" and denounced the treatment of manifestly allegorical material (e.g., Ezekiel 37) as historical fact. He conceived the essence of Christianity as a life of love, offering the kingdom of God to all peoples.

Works: *Christian Life in the Primitive Church* (1904); *Thessalonicher-Briefe* (1909); *Eschatology of the Gospels* (1910); "Bible in the Church," *ERE* 2 (1910) 579-615; *Influence of the Bible on Civilization* (1914); *Der Apostel Paulus* (1926–28); *Vom Auslegen des NT* (1927); *Der Apostolicum in Biblisch-theologischer Bedeuchtung* (1932); *Die Bibel im Leben d. Völker* (1934; rev. A. Adam, 1952).

Bibliography: A. Adam, *NDB* 4 (1936) 7-8. **E. Klostermann,** "In memoriam E. v. D.," *TSK* 106 (1934–35) 1-8 (with bibliography). *RGS* 4 (1928) 31-62 (bibliography 59-62).

J. M. BULLARD

DODD, CHARLES HAROLD (1884–1973)

D. was brought up in Wrexham, North Wales, in a devout Congregationalist family. He had a brilliant career as a student at Oxford, at University and Magdalen Colleges, with interludes of teaching in Leeds and studying in Berlin. While at Oxford he trained at Mansfield College for the Congregationalist ministry and returned there as a member of the staff in 1915 after three years of preaching and pastoral work in Warwick. He quickly gained an international reputation as a scholar, in 1930 moving to Manchester to the Rylands Chair of Biblical Criticism and Exegesis and in 1935 to Cambridge as Norris-Hulse Professor of Divinity. Besides lecturing and teaching, he was chair of the seminar formerly led by F. BURKITT, which enabled him to share and discuss with other senior scholars (notably W. Knox) their ideas and research. After his retirement in 1949 he directed the main work on the NEB and continued writing and speaking for more than twenty years.

D. employed his great skills as linguist, historian, theologian, and critic in the study of NT writings and their background in thought, language, cultures, and religions of the ancient world, including the Jewish and (most characteristically) Hellenistic. Besides an unswerving pursuit of truth through rigorous critical study, he used his talent as an expositor to interpret Scripture and express it clearly in modern language to a wide audience.

In *The Authority of the Bible* (1928) he examined the compatibiity of Christian belief with critical study. God's truth and purpose are communicated through fallible prophets (see PROPHECY AND PROPHETS) in definitive (but still fallible) writings to worshiping communities. The events and writings are inside human history and must be studied by the appropriate critical techniques; nevertheless, in their inner core the truth of God is there to be apprehended—above all, at the very center, in the person and event of JESUS Christ.

Much of D.'s earlier work was on PAUL, e.g., *The Meaning of Paul for Today* (1920). His commentary on Romans (1932) remains a classic, marked by careful scholarship, sympathetic (but never uncritical) insight into Paul's thought, concentration on essentials, and lively clarity that carries the reader through many intricacies. Psychological interests (see PSYCHOLOGY AND BIBLICAL STUDIES) are reflected here as they are in his article "The Mind of Paul" (repr. in *NT Studies* [1953]). *The Bible and the Greeks* (1935) gives a technical account of his word studies.

One of D.'s most influential books was *The Parables of the Kingdom* (1935), a critical study of the central teaching of Jesus that drew chiefly on the PARABLES. After stripping away the reinterpretations made not only in later exegesis but also during the period of oral transmission, he searched for the meaning originally intended by Jesus—a study carried further by J. JEREMIAS. D. stressed the indications in the parables (and elsewhere in the Gospel traditions) that for Jesus the Kingdom (i.e., rule of God) was now present in his coming and in his ministry of preaching and healing, a claim denoted as "realized eschatology." He saw Jesus' predictions of the coming of the Son of man as having been fulfilled in the resurrection and its sequel; any passages that point to a "second coming" at the end of the world he ascribed to early misunderstanding or reinterpretations. Other scholars have judged parts of his exegesis to be one-sided, but D.'s stress on the note of fulfillment is of lasting importance. The search for a firm historical basis in accordance with critical principles and with the methods of FORM CRITICISM was carried further in *History and the Gospel* (1938).

In *The Apostolic Preaching and Its Developments* (1936) D. reconstructed the primitive preaching and beliefs from references and allusions in Paul—important because they supply firm historical evidence, in contrast to what may well be anachronistic material in Acts. He popularized the label *kerygma* to denote the content of what was preached: the fulfillment of God's saving promises in Jesus' coming, death, resurrection, and exaltation and the gift of the Spirit to the church, together with the prediction of Jesus' return as Judge and Savior and a call to repentence and faith. This *kerygma*, he showed, underlies the THEOLOGY of the more developed NT writings and was in due course expressed in the baptismal creeds. The *kerygma* was further illuminated in *According to the Scriptures* (1952), which also developed the line of study pioneered by J. HARRIS into biblical exegesis in the early church. After making a careful analysis of the HB quotations (*testimonia*) used by various NT writers, often (it seems) independently of one another, D. exposed the basic articles of faith that the *testimonia* illustrate and urged that these beliefs must therefore have been held at a very early date.

D.'s greatest work is generally agreed to be *The Interpretation of the Fourth Gospel* (1953). The leading JOHANNINE themes are sifted and compared in respect to both language and content with an almost overwhelming wealth of religious writings, both Jewish and Hellenistic, including Gnostic and Mandaean as well as the Hermetic literature. It was to this last group especially that he had devoted years of study, and his work in this area (found also in *The Bible and the Greeks*) is perhaps the most weighty of his many contributions to scholarship. He did not overlook John's strong links with the primitive Christian traditions and strongly defended the essential unity and integrity of the Fourth Gospel. In a companion volume, *Historical Tradition in the Fourth Gospel* (1963), he set out a detailed but fascinating examination of representative passages in comparison with parallels in the Synoptics (see SYNOPTIC PROBLEM) and argued that John was not dependent on the latter for his material but was in touch with an early stream of Palestinian tradition. In his final book, *The Founder of Christianity* (1970), he presented his picture of Jesus' life and teaching in a way accessible to the average reader but always faithful to the methods of biblical criticism.

Not only was D. an outstanding scholar, teacher, and preacher, but he was also a man who won the admiration, respect, and affection of all who knew him. He combined magisterial knowledge with modest and tolerant gentleness, a lively wit with deep seriousness, a loyalty to the truth with pastoral warmth and Christian zeal, and much practical common sense with just a touch of otherworldly eccentricity.

Bibliography: F. F. Bruce, *CMCT,* 239-69. W. D. Davies and D. Daube (eds.), *The Background of the NT and Its Eschatology: Studies in Honour of C. H. D.* (1954). F. W. Dillistone, *C. H. D.: Interpreter of the NT* (1977). E. W. Heaton, *DNB* Supp. 9 (1986) 243-44. G. Strecker, *TRE* 9 (1981) 15-18.

G. M. STYLER

DODDRIDGE, PHILIP (1702–51)

An English hymn writer and commentator, D. was born in London June 26, 1702. In 1723 he became a dissenting clergyman at Kibworth, Leicestershire, and also in 1725 at Market Harborough, where in 1729 he started a dissenting academy. Later in 1729 he became pastor at Castle Hill, Northampton, and moved his academy there. One of the leading Dissenters in England, he was a tolerant man who tried to heal the rifts within nonconformity. He died Oct. 26, 1751.

D. was an outstanding writer of hymns, several of which continue to be used in the twentieth century. Most of his hymns are explicitly based on biblical texts, and some of them lay emphasis on the social implications of the message. He also won popularity through his *Family Expositor,* a commentary on the NT that includes his own translation, a paraphrase, notes, and a devotional meditation on each section. The work reflects his concern to strike a balance between intellectual and devotional disciplines and his emphasis on the religious life of the family.

Works: *The Family Expositor* (6 vols., 1739–56); *Hymns Founded on Various Texts in the Holy Scriptures* (1755); *Works* (10 vols., 1802–5).

Bibliography: J. Belknap, *Memoirs of the Lives, Characters, and Writings of Those Two Eminent and Useful Ministers of Jesus Christ, Dr. I. Watts and Dr. P. D.* (1793). M. Deacon, *P. D. of Northampton, 1702–51* (1980). A. Gordon, *DNB* 15 (1888) 158-64. G. F. Nuttall (ed.), *Philip Doddridge* (1951). J. Orton, *Memoirs of the Life, Character, and Writings of the Late P. D., DD, of Northampton* (1766).

A. W. WAINWRIGHT

DÖDERLEIN, JOHANN CHRISTOPH (1745–92)

Born Jan. 20, 1745, in Windsheim (northwest of Nuremberg), D. studied in Altdorf, where soon after publication of his first work, *Curarum exegeticarum et criticum in quaedam Vetus Testamenti oracula specimen* (1770), he was appointed professor of theology (1772). Ten years later he accepted a position at Jena, where he stayed until his death, Dec. 2, 1792. Among his important works are his 1778 translation of Proverbs and his popular work on Christian theology (1780), which went through at least six editions and is generally regarded as representative of the transition to the modern critical method that was underway in German theological scholarship.

D.'s work on Isaiah has earned him an enduring place in the history of biblical interpretation, although the assertion that he was the first to propose the Deutero-Isaiah hypothesis (in his 1775 work on Isaiah) is no longer tenable. Statements concerning a Second Isaiah are not found until the 1789 edition of the commentary. J. KOPPE, in his 1780 translation of R. LOWTH's 1778 Isaiah commentary, is more properly credited with first identifying a Deutero-Isaiah, while it was especially through J. G. EICHHORN's 1783 introduction that the notion was widely disseminated and taken up by a number of scholars.

D.'s role in the momentous shift in Isaiah and prophetic studies (see PROPHECY AND PROPHETS, HB), however, was far from minimal. As early as the 1775 edition of his work, he offered interpretations that played an important role in the eventual formation of the Deutero-Isaiah hypothesis, including the suggestion that chapters 40–66 concern the liberation from exile and that these oracles were addressed by the prophet to his contemporaries. Although D. was speaking of the eighth-century BCE prophet, the implications of these historical interpretations for more radical positions were by no means lost to many of his contemporaries, as the so-called *Jesajastreit,* which his work precipitated, evidences. Two years before the appearance of Eichhorn's introduction, in the *Auserlesene Theologische Bibliothek*—a journal he founded and edited from 1780 until his death—D. had already investigated the likelihood that Isaiah 40–66 was written during the Babylonian exile. Eichhorn remarked that others had previously suggested an exilic provenance for Isaiah 40–66 but noted only Koppe by name, conspicuously omitting D., his Jena rival.

Works: *Esaias ex recensione textus hebrai ad fidem codd. quorundam mss. et versionum antiquarum latine vertit notasque varii argumenti subiecit* (1775, 1789); *Sprüche Salomos, neu übersetzt mit kurzen erläuternden Anmerkungen* (1778); *Institutio theologi christiani in capitibus religionis theoreticis, nostris temporibus accomodata* (1780); "Fortsetzung der Anzeige von Lowth, Michaelis, Dathe, und Koppe über den Esaias," *ATB* 1, 11 (1781) 805-42.

Bibliography: **K. Hagenbach,** *NSHERK* 3 (1909) 465. **K. Leder,** *Universität Altdorf: Zur Theologie der Aufklärung in Franken. Die theologische Fakultät in Altdorf, 1750–1809* (1965) 170-73. **M. Mulzer,** "D. und Deuterojesaja," *BN* 66 (1993) 15-23. **R. Smend,** "Lowth in Deutschland," *Epochen der Bibelkritik* (1991) 43-62.

T. J. SANDOVAL

DODS, MARCUS (1834–1909)

Born Apr. 11, 1834, in Belford, Northumberland, D. was educated at the University of Edinburgh and New College, Edinburgh. He was pastor of the Renfield Free Church, Glasgow (1864–89), chair of NT criticism and exegesis, New College (1889–1909), and principal (1907). He died Apr. 26, 1909.

Primarily a biblical expositor, D.'s liberal views on INSPIRATION caused concern. The Glasgow Presbytery queried his published sermon, "Revelation and Inspiration" (1877), but the General Assembly of 1878 took no action against him. In 1890 D. and A. B. BRUCE were charged with holding defective views on inspiration, but whereas W. R. SMITH had been deposed from his Aberdeen chair only nine years earlier, both D. and Bruce retained their positions. D. both helped many to square personal faith with modern knowledge and prompted B. B. WARFIELD's sardonic rejoicing that D. "would preserve to us a supernatural Redeemer, even if he draws back from too supernatural a Bible."

Works: *The Parables of Our Lord* (2 vols., 1883–85); *The Gospel of St. John* (EGT, 1897); *The Bible: Its Nature and Origin* (1905); *Early and Late Letters* (ed. M. Dods [son], 1910–11).

Bibliography: **W. F. Gray,** *DNB* 2nd Supp. 1 (1912) 510-12. **H. F. Henderson,** *The Religious Controversies of Scotland* (1905) 231-70. **P. C. Simpson,** *The Life of Principal Rainy* (2 vols., 1909). **H. Watt,** *New College Edinburgh: A Centenary History* (1946).

A. P. F. SELL

DONNE, JOHN (c. 1572–1631)

Born into a prominent Roman Catholic family, D. was educated at Oxford, Cambridge, and Lincoln's Inn, where he endured the prejudices of the times against his religious heritage. In 1615, at the age of forty-three, he was ordained in the Anglican Church and served as dean of St. Paul's from 1621 until his death in 1631. D.'s retreat from Roman Catholicism involved a period of profound religious questioning during which he turned to the writings of the church fathers, particularly those of AUGUSTINE, whose spiritual development he saw as resembling his own and whose writings were an influence on D. second only to PAUL's epistles and the psalms.

The volume *Poems* (1633, 1635, with extensive revisions and additions) contains virtually all of the poetry ascribed to D. During his lifetime only two of his poems and six of his sermons were published. Most of his secular lyrics were written before 1600 and have romantic love as their theme; some reflect frustration and cynicism with love, while others exalt passion, describing it as a perfect union between two souls. His secular lyrics gave way to more theologically oriented poems that have come to be known as the *Divine Poems*. They seek to make vivid and personal the impact of divine love in the way that his earlier love poems exulted in sexual love. Some of these poems describe immediate personal fears, e.g., "Hymne to God my God, in my sicknesse," while many of them examine difficult paradoxes and complex theological concepts. The poet analyzes these intellectually and emotionally, through both direct biblical allusions and broader religious symbols.

D.'s later prose works, including his sermons, reflect his particular interest in Job, Psalms, and Proverbs, through direct appropriation of these texts, broader allusions to their themes, and imitation of their styles. His *Essays in Divinity* (composed 1611–1614) often allude to Genesis and Exodus in their depiction of D.'s struggle to understand his faith. Reminiscent of Job's description of his trials, D.'s *Devotions upon Emergent Occasions* (1624) provides a detailed account of his near-fatal illness in 1623, often rendered in allegorical terms. His 160 published sermons, delivered between 1615 and 1630, are intense and dramatic in style yet subtle and intellectually challenging in their careful analysis of scriptural texts. He reminded his audience of their duties as Christians in the process of a detailed examination of biblical words, phrases, images, or ideas. Although he sought religious truth by way of poetic analogy, metaphor, and symbol rather than by philosophical speculation, intellectual analysis was never far from his writings.

Works: *Poetical Works* (2 vols., ed. H. J. C. Grierson, 1912); *The Divine Poems* (ed. H. Gardner, 1952); *The Sermons* (10 vols., ed. G. R. Potter and E. M. Simpson, 1953–62); *Selections* (CWS, ed. and intro. J. E. Booty, 1990).

Bibliography: **J. Carey,** *J. D.: Life, Mind, and Art* (1981). **B. Lewalski,** *D.'s "Anniversaries" and the Poetry of Praise: The Creation of a Symbolic Mode* (1973); *Protestant Poetics and the Seventeenth-century Religious Lyric* (1979). **L. L. Martz,** *The Poetry of Meditation* (1954). **J. M. Mueller,** *D.'s Prebend Sermons* (1971). **D. Quinn,** "D.'s Christian Eloquence," *Journal of English Literary History* 27 (1960) 276-97; "J. D.'s Principles of Biblical Exegesis," *Journal of English and German Philology* 61 (1962) 313-29. **C. Summers and T.-L. Pebworth** (eds.), *The Eagle and the Dove: Reassessing J. D.* (1986).

J. H. AUGUSTINE

DORNER, ISAAK AUGUST (1809–84)

Born June 2, 1809, at Neuhausen ob Eck in Württemberg, D. was educated at the University of Tübingen (1827–32), where he was a student of F. C. BAUR. He later returned to Tübingen as *Repetent* in THEOLOGY (1834) and became *ausserordentlicher* professor in 1837. He was named professor of theology at Kiel in 1839, was called to Königsberg in 1843, to Bonn in 1847, to Göttingen in 1853, and to Berlin in 1862. His influence was extensive over both the Lutheran Church in Prussia and over students from throughout the world who studied with him. He spent his last years in Wittenberg and died July 8, 1884, in Wiesbaden.

At the urging of a former teacher, C. Schmid (1794–1852), an untiring opponent of Baur, D. began work on his history of christology, the first part of which appeared in 1835, the same year his colleague D. F. STRAUSS published his *Leben Jesu*. D.'s work, completed in 1839, was an indirect response to Strauss, stressing the role of the historical Christ throughout the history of the Christian church. The impact of this work led to his call to Kiel, where he published a work (1841) in which he considered the relationship of the two components of the Protestant church, insisting that justification by faith and the supreme AUTHORITY of Scripture (the material and formal principles of the Reformation) were in fact two inseparable components of Christian doctrine.

The nucleus of D.'s faith centered around the divine/human person of the Christ, supernatural in origin, the complete revelation, and the redeemer from sin and death. D. strongly adhered to the Reformation principle of the Holy Spirit speaking through Scripture as a criterion of its INSPIRATION. Faith was produced by the personal experience of God's presence. Only faith embodied both the assurance of the reality it experienced and the knowledge it apprehended. Scripture was a medium of God's presence, a witness to God's revelation in history but not itself the revelation. Only God was the content of revelation; only God could provide absolute assurance to the individual through faith. Like CALVIN D. considered the language and form of Scripture to be the human contribution that God had condescended to use. To the practitioners of scholastic theology, who made Scripture the exclusive work of the deity, D. insisted that God had inspired men, not books.

Works: *History of the Development of the Doctrine of the Person of Christ* (5 vols., 1835–39; ET 1861–63); *Das Princip unserer Kirche nach dem innern Verhältnis seiner zwei Seiten betrachten* (1841); *History of Protestant Theology* (2 vols., 1867; ET 1871); *A System of Christian Doctrine* (4 vols., 1879–81; ET 1880–82); *A System of Christian Ethics* (ed. A. J. Dorner [son], 1885; ET 1887).

Bibliography: **I. Bobertag,** *Isaak August Dorner* (1906). **A. J. Dorner,** *ADB* 48 (1904) 37-47. **O. Kirn,** *RE³* 4 (1898) 802-7. **P. Kleinert,** *Zum Gedächtniss I. A. D.s* (1884). **J. Rothermundt,** *TRE* 9 (1981) 155-58. **P. Schaff,** *Germany: Its Universities, Theology, and Religion* (1857) 376-80. **N. Smyth,** *D. on the Future State* (1883).

M. G. ROGERS

DREWS, ARTHUR CHRISTIAN HEINRICH (1865–1935)

A devotee of the monistic-vitalistic philosophy of E. von Hartmann (1842–1906), D. taught at the technical high school in Karlsruhe. He expounded an identification of the world and God in a form of monism and viewed religion based on reason as the human consciousness of being supra-historical.

Combining an anti-historical approach and a revulsion for contemporary liberal lives of JESUS, D. denied Jesus' historical existence. His work provided a compendium of materials drawn from various sources and relied upon earlier and contemporary explanations of the "non-existence" of a historical Jesus as well as elements from more traditional NT scholarship. From the French C.-F. Dupuis (1742–1809) and C. Volney (1757–1820) he borrowed the idea of Jesus as a solar-mythical figure; from the Dutch radicals, the idea that HB texts and Jewish ideas were "historicized" in the Jesus figure; from the American W. Smith (1850–1934) and the Briton J. Robertson (1856–1933), ideas about a pre-Christian "Christianity" and cult centered on the figure of Joshua; from the RELIGIONSGESCHICHTLICHE SCHULE, ideas about comparative MYTHOLOGY; from B. BAUER, the idea of Jesus as a literary creation; and from the German pastor A. Kalthoff (1850–1906), the idea of Christianity as a myth-creating mystery cult. According to D. nothing in the Gospels, neither the actions nor the words of Jesus, could be shown to rest on historical fact. "In the long run the contents of the Gospels may be traced to the prophet Isaiah, whose 'predictions,' sayings, penitential appeals, and promises reappear in the Gospels in the form of narrative. Hence Isaiah, not Jesus, would be the powerful personality to whom Christianity would owe its existence. . . . It is more probable that Jesus and Isaiah are one and the same person than that the Jesus of liberal theology brought Christianity into existence" (1910, 296).

The so-called Jesus-myth movement was at its height in the first two decades of the twentieth century. (P.-L. Couchoud and his followers later kept the movement alive.) D.'s attack on the historicity of Jesus struck a nerve as did no other and roused a widespread popular reaction. His work was significant in that it illustrated the limits to which research could venture in attempting to reconstruct the origins of Christianity and the role of Jesus in those origins. At the same time it elicited responses and refinement of method by numerous major scholars and posed to theology the issue of whether a historical Jesus was necessary to the Christian faith.

Works: *Die Religion als Selbst-Bewusstsein Gottes; eine philosophische Untersuchung über das Wesen der Religion* (1906); *The Christ Myth* (1909; ET 1910); *Petuslegende: Ein Beitrag zur Mythologie des Christentums* (1910); *The Witnesses to the Historicity of Jesus* (1910; ET 1910); *Freie Religion* (1921); *Das Markusevangelium als Zeugnis gegen die Geschichtlichkeit Jesu* (1921); *Die Entstehung des Christentums aus dem Gnostizismus* (1924); *Die Bestreitung der Geschichtlichkeit Jesu* (1926); *Hat Jesus gelebt?* (1928).

Bibliography: S. J. Case, "The Historicity of Jesus: An Estimate of the Negative Argument," *AJT* 15 (1911) 20-42; "Is Jesus a Historical Character? Evidence for an Affirmative Opinion," *AJT* 15 (1911) 205-27. F. C. Conybeare, *Historical Christ: Or an Investigation of the Views of J. M. Robertson, A. D., and W. B. Smith* (1914). B. A. Gerrish, "Jesus Myth and History: Troeltsch's Stand in the Christ-myth Debate," *JR* 55 (1975) 13-35 = *The Old Protestantism and the New* (1982) 230-47. A. McGrath, *The Making of Modern German Chris-*

tology (1986) 69-93. **D. C. Mackintosh,** "Is Belief in the Historicity of Jesus Indispensable to Christian Faith?" *AJT* 15 (1911) 362-72. **L. Salvatorelli,** "From Locke to Reitzenstein: The Historical Investigation of the Origins of Christianity," *HTR* 22 (1929) 263-389. **T. J. Thorburn,** *Jesus the Christ: Historical or Mythical? A Reply to Prof. D.'s Christus-mythe* (1912). **E. Troeltsch,** "The Significance of the Historical Existence of Jesus for Faith" (1911; ET in E. Troeltsch, *Writings on Theology and Religion* [1977] 182-207). **B. B. Warfield,** "Christless Christianity," *HTR* 5 (1912) 423-73. **J. Weiss,** *Jesus von Nazareth: Mythus oder Geschichte? Eine auseinandersetzung mit Kalthoff, D., Jansen* (1910).

J. H. HAYES

DRIVER, GODFREY ROLLES (1892–1975)

Born in Oxford, Aug. 20, 1892, D. was the son of S. DRIVER, Regius Professor of Hebrew and Canon of Christ Church, Oxford. After schooling at Winchester College he went to Oxford University as a scholar of New College. He had inherited an interest in Hebrew and was awarded a university Hebrew scholarship and a SEPTUAGINT prize. In 1915 he joined the army; and military service took him to the Near East, where he made his first acquaintance with Palestine. In 1919 he returned to Oxford as a fellow and tutor in classics at Magdalen College, but his research was in Semitic languages. He was appointed lecturer in comparative Semitic philology in 1927 and became professor of Semitic philology in 1938. WWII again involved him in national service, this time as a civilian, and he once more lived in Palestine. Both before and after his retirement in 1962 D. worked on the translation of the OT for the NEB (1970), and he became the convener of the OT panel in 1957 and joint director (with C. H. Dodd) in 1965. He was awarded the Burkitt Medal for Biblical Studies in 1953; he was the president of the Society for OT Study in 1938 and of the International Organization for the Study of the OT, 1953–59. An issue of the *JSS* was dedicated to him in 1962, and a volume was published in his honor in 1963. He died Apr. 22, 1975.

D. was a generous, good-natured person with a lively mind and sense of humor. As a teacher he was inspiring, always ready to help former pupils and others who sought his advice, which was usually sent on postcards packed with information but barely legible. A member of the Church of England with decidedly low church views, he worshiped regularly in his college chapel and parish church. Since he felt no vocation to be ordained, he remained a layman, although that made it impossible for him to become the Regius Professor of Hebrew, who at that time had to be a canon of Christ Church, Oxford.

D.'s academic career began at a time when it was still possible for a scholar to acquire expertise in a number of Semitic languages. Thus, in 1925 his first three books covered three different languages: colloquial Arabic,

Babylonian letters, and a Syriac text. Later books concerned Assyrian and Babylonian laws (see ASSYRIOLOGY AND BIBLICAL STUDIES), Aramaic papyri, the origin of the alphabet, and Ugaritic poetic texts (with transliteration, translation, and a glossary; see UGARIT AND THE BIBLE). His work centered, however, on Hebrew. He took an interest in the DEAD SEA SCROLLS as soon as information about them became available. At first he argued (for reasons that seemed strong at the time) for a later date than that favored by most scholars, but he realized that he had been mistaken and in 1965 argued for an origin of the major sectarian texts among the Zealots during the Jewish revolt of 66–70 CE. His theory has not stood the test of time; but his book contains much valuable information, and some of his criticism of widely accepted theories retain their force.

It was not, however, in the Qumran scrolls that D.'s principal contribution to Hebrew studies lay but in his investigation of the light shed on biblical Hebrew by a comparison with other Semitic languages. He used comparative evidence in his study of the Hebrew verbal system in 1936 and published a large number of articles on lexicographical, philological, and textual questions in the HB; many of his suggestions have found their way into the NEB. He planned to write a Hebrew dictionary in collaboration with his former pupil D. Thomas; but although they amassed a large collection of slips containing philological information, the project was never completed. D. believed, doubtless correctly, that ancient Hebrew must have contained a much larger vocabulary than is presented in the standard LEXICONS and that some lost meanings are preserved in cognates in other Semitic languages. An obscure Hebrew word might, for example, be explained by comparison with an Akkadian or Arabic word with the same consonants. In many instances his enthusiasm undoubtedly carried him too far, and many of his theories are unconvincing. On the other hand, many suggestions are persuasive; and there are places where he has drawn attention to genuine problems that need solution, even though his own proposals are not accepted.

Works: *A Grammar of the Colloquial Arabic of Syria and Palestine* (1925); *Letters of the First Babylonian Dynasty* (1925); (with L. Hodgson), *Nestorius: The Bazaar of Heracleides* (1925); (with J. C. Miles), *The Assyrian Laws* (1935); *Problems of the Hebrew Verbal System* (1936); *Semitic Writing: From Pictograph to Alphabet* (1948); *The Hebrew Scrolls* (1951); (with J. C. Miles), *The Babylonian Laws* (2 vols., 1952–55); *Aramaic Documents of the Fifth Century BC* (1954); *Canaanite Myths and Legends* (1956); *The Judean Scrolls* (1965).

Bibliography: J. Barr, *DNB 1971–80* (1986) 252-53. J. A. Emerton, *PBA* 63 (1977) 345-62. **D. W. Thomas and W. D. McHardy** (eds.), *Hebrew and Semitic Studies Presented to G. R. D.* (1963). *VT* 30 (1980) 185-91.

J. A. EMERTON

DRIVER, SAMUEL ROLLES (1846–1914)

Born in Southampton Oct. 2, 1846, D. went to Oxford as a scholar of New College, where he became a fellow in 1870 and a tutor in classics in 1875. He was already interested in Hebrew and won university scholarships in Hebrew and prizes in the SEPTUAGINT and in Syriac. As early as 1871 he published an edition of a medieval Jewish commentary on Jeremiah and Ezekiel, following it with other publications on Hebrew. When E. B. PUSEY died in 1882, the regius professorship of Hebrew and the associated canonry at Christ Church fell vacant. The prime minister, W. Gladstone, offered this crown appointment to D., who had been made deacon in 1881 and was ordained priest in December 1882 just in time to take up his new post in January 1883. D. was one of the founding fellows of the British Academy in 1902. He died Feb. 26, 1914.

D.'s most important early work was his treatise on the Hebrew tenses (1874). He analyzed biblical usage in a way that is still useful, although the theory by which he sought to explain it can no longer be accepted. Between 1875 and 1884 he was a member of the committee working on the OT for the RV. The majority of the committee members were too conservative to accept many needed changes, but the revisions favored by D. and other younger members are often found in the marginal notes (see G. Gray in the *Contemporary Review* for April 1914). D.'s work on TEXTUAL CRITICISM is seen at its best in his study of the Hebrew text of the books of Samuel (1890), which offers a training in sound methodology and still retains its value.

The burning question in OT studies at the time was, however, that of higher criticism. D. worked carefully through the evidence before committing himself, but in an article in the *Contemporary Review* for February 1890 (215-31) he gave reasons for accepting critical views that were presented in detail in his OT introduction (1891). This book did much to win acceptance of critical scholarship not only because D. argued lucidly and convincingly but also because he did so in a reverent spirit, maintaining that such opinions are compatible with belief in divine INSPIRATION OF THE BIBLE. Such an approach is found in his later commentaries on various books of the OT. Special mention may be made of his influential commentary on Genesis (1904) and of two volumes in the ICC series, of which he was one of the editors from 1895: Deuteronomy (1895) and Job (1921, completed by G. Gray after D.'s death).

In lexicography D.'s major contribution consists of his many entries in the *Oxford Hebrew Lexicon* (completed in 1907), which he prepared with F. BROWN and C. BRIGGS (see LEXICONS, HB). D. was the greatest British OT scholar of his time, not because his ideas were unusually original but because he had sound judgment, presented his arguments with lucidity and moderation, and treated the Bible with reverence.

Works: *A Commentary on Jeremiah and Ezekiel by Mosheh ben Shesheth* (1871); *A Treatise on the Use of the Tenses in Hebrew* (1874, 1892³); (with A. Neubauer), *The 53rd Chapter of Isaiah According to the Jewish Interpreters* (1877); *A Commentary on the Book of Proverbs, Attributed to A. Ibn Ezra* (1880); *Isaiah: His Life and Times and the Writings Which Bear His Name* (1888); *Notes on the Hebrew Text of the Books of Samuel* (1890, 1913²); *An Introduction to the Literature of the OT* (1891, 1913⁹); (with H. A. White), *The Book of Leviticus . . . Critical Edition of the Hebrew Text* (1894); *A Critical and Exegetical Commentary on Deuteronomy* (ICC, 1895); *The Books of Joel and Amos* (1897); (with H. A. White), *The Book of Leviticus . . . A New English Translation . . . with Explanatory Notes* (1898); *The Parallel Psalter* (1898); *The Book of Daniel* (1900); *The Book of Genesis* (1904); *Deuteronomium et Liber Josuae* (1905); *The Book of Job* (1906); *The Book of the Prophet Jeremiah* (1906); *The Minor Prophets (Nahum . . . Malachi)* (1906); (with F. Brown and C. A. Briggs), *A Hebrew and English Lexicon of the OT* (1907); *The Book of Exodus* (1911); *The Ideals of the Prophets* (ed. G. A. Cooke, 1917), contains a complete bibliography of D.'s publications; (with G. B. Gray), *A Critical and Exegetical Commentary on the Book of Job* (ICC, 1921).

Bibliography: G. A. Cooke, "D. and Wellhausen," *HTR* 9 (1914) 249-57. *DNB, 1912–21* (1927) 162-63. **G. B. Gray,** *Contemporary Review* 105 (1914) 483-90. **J. W. Rogerson,** *TRE* 9 (1981) 190-92. **W. Sanday,** *The Life-Work of S. R. D.* (1914).

J. A. EMERTON

DRUSIUS, JOHANNES CLEMENS (1550–1616)

Born in Oudenarde in Flanders, June 28, 1550, D. was educated at Ghent and Louvain. His father, deprived of his estate in 1567, took refuge in England, where D. pursued his studies, becoming professor of oriental languages (Hebrew, Aramaic, and Syriac) at Oxford (1572–76). He returned to Louvain, studied law for a time, and became professor of oriental languages at Leiden (1577–84). Unable to tolerate the dogmatics there, D. joined the new university in Franeker as professor of Hebrew (1585–1616), where he taught for the remainder of his life, dying Feb. 12, 1616.

A learned Semitic scholar, D. was at home in rabbinic literature, both ancient and medieval. He saw himself as primarily a philologist: "What I deal with pertains mostly to grammar. I do not claim for myself any deeper knowledge. I do know this: 'I am neither a prophet nor the son of a prophet' " (quoted in Katchen [1984] 33). In 1600 he was commissioned by the states general to annotate difficult texts in the HB but was criticized for tardiness in the project. Many of his writings were incorporated into CRITICI SACRI, the great compilation of biblical scholarship produced in London (1660).

Works: *Parallela sacra, seu comparatio locorum Vet. Test. cum iis, quae in Novo citantur* (1588); *Proverbiorum sacrorum classes duae* (1590); *Ecclesiasticus, Graece et Latine* (1600); *Liber Hasmonaeorum. . . .* (1600); *Opuscula quae ad grammaticam spectant* (1609); *Annotationum in totum Jesu Christi Testamentum, sive praeteritorum libri decem* (1612); *Veterum interpretum Graecorum in totum Vetus Testamentum fragmenta* (1622); *Libri decem Annotationum in totum Jesu Christi Testamentum* (1632).

Bibliography: C. Bertheau, *NSHERK* 4 (1909) 404. **A. Curiander,** *Vitae operumque Johannis Drusii* (1616). **A. L. Katchen,** *Christian Hebraists and Dutch Rabbis* (1984), esp. 31-37. **J. C. H. Lebram,** "Hebräische Studien zwischen Ideal und Wirklichkeit und der Universität Leiden in den Jahren 1575–1619," *NAKG* 56 (1975–76) 317-57, esp. 330-41. *MSHH* 22 (1733) 57-76. **P. T. van Rooden,** *Theology, Biblical Scholarship, and Rabbinical Studies in the Seventeenth Century* (Studies in the History of Leiden University 6, 1989).

J. H. HAYES

DUHM, BERNHARD LAUARDUS (1847–1928)

Born in Bingum in Ostfriesland, Oct. 10, 1847, D. studied theology in Göttingen, where A. RITSCHL and P. LAGARDE were two of his teachers and where he became friends with J. WELLHAUSEN. Especially influential was the OT scholar H. EWALD, who introduced him to the Semitic languages and with whom D. shared a strong preference for the prophets. D. became a *Repetent* at the theological Stift in Göttingen (1871), graduated lic. theol. and habilitated as a *Privatdozent* (1873), and taught as *ausserordentlicher* professor of OT after 1877. In 1885 he became the theological honorary doctor at the University of Basel, in 1888/89 accepting a call as full professor of OT and of general history of religion. Noted as a fascinating personality and an inspirational academic teacher, he remained in Basel until his death, highly esteemed by his fellow citizens and by the university, whose rector he became in 1896.

An academic "lone wolf," D. did not feel obligated to follow the Wellhausen school or the developing RELIGIONSGESCHICHTLICHE SCHULE in Göttingen or the FORM and TRADITION criticism begun by H. GUNKEL and H. GRESSMANN. He remained an individualist who lived by his own intuition. His special merit lies in the areas of text reconstruction and LITERARY criticism and in interpretation of prophetic and poetic literature.

D. felt an essential connection with the prophets and was one of the first scholars to emphasize their poetic and aesthetic qualities. The prophets pervaded his entire life's work, which was greatly to influence further research. He judged the remaining OT literature against them, thereby reaching unfair appraisals. The elementary, the original, the individual, the ecstatic, and the visionary particularly interested him, while the institutional seemed to him a hardening of vital religious life. Thus he had no appreciation for the significance of worship and priesthood in Israel. The development of the Yahwistic faith into cult, book, and legal religion appeared to him as a fall from the heights of the ethical religion of the prophets.

D. presented a consistent definition of the phenomenon of PROPHECY. The writing prophets he praised as great religious and ethical personalities who broke through the nature orientation of the older Israelite religion and proclaimed a new ethical religion. Of special importance was his claim that the prophetic epoch did not arise out of a Mosaic-legal age and that the prophets did not refer to a codified law. He accepted a late post-prophetic dating for the priestly writing, which E. REUSS, A. KUENEN, and K. GRAF anticipated and Wellhausen soon championed.

D.'s Isaiah commentary was not only his most effective work, but it also became a gem of commentary literature. His first goal was to reproduce the original text on the basis of the Hebrew meter. As a result he made ingenious but very plausible conjectures, some of which have been confirmed by the Isaiah scroll from Qumran. He also made some incorrect speculations. Behind his consistent TEXTUAL CRITICISM stood a recognition of the character of the prophet as author and poet. More important for D. was the appraisal of the prophets as religious personalities, whose message he brought to light by applying CULTURAL and religion-historical criticism. This kind of appraisal in his Isaiah commentary represented for many readers a new discovery of prophetism. In the first half of Isaiah D. evaluated the especially controversial (even in the 20th cent.) salvation oracles as almost completely authentic. Within Isaiah 40–55 he isolated the Servant Songs as unique, separated them from Deutero-Isaiah, and dated them in the postexilic period. He regarded the Suffering Servant as a postexilic figure, a prophetic disciple and teacher of the Torah who died of leprosy. Isaiah 50–66 was, according to him, a further, originally independent book, which he assigned to a postexilic prophet Trito-Isaiah. Scholars widely accepted this thesis, although the relationship of Deutero-Isaiah to the Servant Songs, the identity of the Suffering Servant, and the unity of Trito-Isaiah remain controversial.

Less influential was D.'s commentary on Jeremiah, although it represented a landmark in the research on this difficult prophetic book. He sought to solve the problem of the relationship between poetry and prose in the book by assigning the sayings with the *qinah* meter of funeral songs (3 + 2) to the prophet, characterizing him as the lyricist among the prophets. D. assigned 280 verses to Jeremiah's poetry and some 220 verses to a biographical work about Jeremiah by Baruch, which was successively worked into the developing book. However, he traced the major part of the book (some 850 verses) to an abundance of additions that transformed the traditions of Jeremiah and Baruch into a pedagogical and devotional work advocating nomism and the doctrine of retribution. Here as elsewhere he dispensed with these "epigonen" in the original prophetic poetry and arrived at sharp verdicts concerning their literary capabilities and theology.

Textual and literary-critical conclusions distinguish his commentary on Job. With great precision D. distinguished between the popular book and the speeches and pointed out the secondary character of the Elihu-speeches (chaps. 32–37) and other subsequently added texts.

D. abandoned his gift of intuition in his approach to the psalms. The piety of the psalmist was foreign to him; the roots of the psalms in Israel's worhip and in conventional speech forms remained closed to him. His dating of most psalms in Maccabean-Hasmonean times was immediately and strongly questioned and has since been rejected.

Works: *Pauli apostoli de Judaeorum religione iudicia exposita et dijudicata* (1873); *Die Theologie der Propheten als Grundlage für die innere Entwicklungsgeschichte der israelitischen Religion* (1875); *Über Ziel und Methode der theologischen Wissenschaft* (1889); *Das Buch Jesaia* (HK 3.1, 1892, 1968[5]); *Kosmologie und Religion* (1892); *Das Geheimnis in der Religion* (SGV 1, 1896, 1927[2]); *Das Buch Hiob* (KHC 16, 1897, 1901[2]); *Das Buch Hiob übersetzt* (1897); *Die Entstehung des Alten Testaments* (SGV 6, 1897, 1909[2]); *Die Psalmen* (KHC 14, 1899, 1922[2]); *Die Psalmen übersetzt* (1899, 1907[2]); *Das Buch Jeremia* (KHC 11, 1901); *Das Buch Jeremia übersetzt* (1903, 1907[2]); *Die Gottgeweihten in der Alttestamentlichen Religion* (1905); *Das Buch Habakuk* (1906); *Das kommende Reich Gottes* (1910; ET *The Ever-coming Kingdom of God* [1911]); *Die Zwölf Propheten: In den Versmassen der Urschrift übersetzt* (1910; ET *The Twelve Prophets* [1912]); *Anmerkungen zu den Zwölf Propheten* (1911) = ZAW 31 (1911) 1-43, 81-110, 161-204; *Israels Propheten* (1916, 1922[2]).

Bibliography: W. Baumgartner, *Das Buch Jesaia* (B. L. Duhm, 1968[5]) V-XIII. A. Bertholet, DBJ 10 (1928) 45-52. R. E. Clements, *One Hundred Years of OT Study* (1976) 52-56. J. Ebach, TRE 9 (1981) 214-15. H. Gunkel, RGG[2] 1 (1927) 2043-44. W. Hübner, "Die Prophetenforschung des Alten Testaments seit der Mitte des 18. Jahrhunderts" (diss., Heidelberg, 1957). H.-J. Kraus, GHKEAT 275-83. E. Kutsch, RGG[3] 2 (1958) 281-82. E. von Matter, "Die Auffassung der alttestamentlichen Prophetie von Eichhorn bis Volz" (diss., Halle, 1943). H. G. Reventlow, "Die Prophetie in Urteil B. D.," ZTK 85 (1988) 259-74. R. Smend, "Über einige ältere Autoren des Verlages Vandenhoeck und Ruprecht," *Zweihundertfünfzig Jahre Vandenhoeck und Ruprecht in Göttingen* (1985) 15-40, esp. 30-34; DATDJ 114-28. E. Speiss, "B. D.: Religionshistoriker und Exeget in Basel," SchwR 28 (1928) 750-55. W. Thiel, ZdZ 32 (1978) 352-56.

W. THIEL

DUNS SCOTUS (c. 1266–1308)

Considered one of the most distinguished thinkers of the late Middle Ages, this Scot as a young man entered the Franciscan Order and studied first at Oxford and later at Paris. In 1297 he was back in Oxford as a teacher of theology, and in 1301 or 1302 he returned to Paris to begin a doctorate in theology. Within two years those who had supported the papacy against the French king were banished, but D. was able to return and complete his doctorate in 1305, after which he was sent to Cologne to teach. He died there in 1308.

His main output in the short career allowed him includes two commentaries on PETER LOMBARD's *Sentences* and a series of treatises on logic and on Aristotelian physics and metaphysics, building on R. GROSSTESTE's mathematical and scientific approach as well as upon BONAVENTURE's Augustinianism (see AUGUSTINE). He became for the Franciscans the scholar to whom reference seemed as proper as appeal to THOMAS AQUINAS did for the Dominicans. D.'s chief difference from Aquinas seems to have lain in the primacy he gave to will and love against reason and intellect. He held that our theology as distinct from God's, which embraces all things knowable, treats only of those things "that are contained in Scripture or that can be derived from these." His importance for the history of exegesis, however, lies in the influence of the system of thought he imparted to the Franciscans and more widely in the later Middle Ages rather than in his own work on the Bible.

Works: *Opera Omnia* (ed. C. Balic et al., 1950–).

Bibliography: **J. V. Brown,** *DMA* 4 (1984) 308-11. **W. Dettleff,** *TRE* 9 (1981) 218-31. **E. Gilson,** *Jean Duns Scotus* (1952). **L. Honnefelder,** *TRE* 9 (1981) 232-40. **J. M. Rigg,** *DNB* 16 (1888) 216-20.

G. R. EVANS

DU PIN, LOUIS ELLIES (1657–1719)

A Gallican theologian and historian, more a popularizer and compiler than an original thinker, and famous for his vast *Nouvelle bibliothèque des auteurs ecclésiastiques* (1686), D. devoted an important part of his work to biblical topics: a general introduction, twice revised (*Prolégomènes sur la Bible* [1799]); a commentary on the Pentateuch (*Dissertations historiques* [1711]) and on the book of Revelation (*Analyse de l'Apocalypse* [1712]); Latin editions of the Pentateuch and of the psalter; and even a French version of the psalms. Because of its success and influence, D.'s biblical output is important for two major reasons: as representative of the place of the Bible in the Gallican church at the turn of the eighteenth century and as an endeavor to present a modern approach to the sacred books.

In claiming access to the Bible for all believers, D.

simply repeated the same arguments as had A. Arnauld (1612–94) and P. Quesnel (1634–1719), who saw a "moral" (i.e., spiritual) approach to Scripture as the basis for Christian growth. This position was condemned as "Jansenist" by the papal bull *Unigenitus* (1713); however, in his scientific approach to the Bible, D. appears more as a "Molinist." Like R. SIMON and the Jesuits L. Lessius (1554–1623) and J. Bonfrère (1573–1642), he proposed a theory of limited INSPIRATION that admitted human participation in the process of revelation. On the authorship of the Pentateuch, however, he refused to accept entirely Simon's theory of later compilation by "public scribes."

Despite the Council of Trent's recommendation of the VULGATE, D. was more in favor of an edition of the Bible based on Hebrew and Greek. His own editions of the Pentateuch and the psalter show that he advocated revising the Vulgate Sixto-Clementine on the basis of the original sources. In his translation of the psalter, he considered the Vulgate only as a source of verification when there was a reason to think that the transmission of the original was corrupt.

If D.'s approach to the Bible aimed at being spiritual, the didactic method he followed was very typical of his age. He wanted to answer his readers' curiosity (a term that is not derogatory) and tell them "everything they wanted to know about the Bible." In this desire to foster a clear "intelligence of Holy Scripture," the Gallican historian, perhaps unwittingly, relied too much on a scientific perception of the Bible. This "literal" procedure anticipated A. CALMET's *Commentaires,* offering a text presented with all available information but divested of its faith-communicating purpose. His work already mirrors the conflicts between faith and reason that were to develop in the decades following his death.

Works: "Dissertation préliminaire sur les auteurs de la Bible," *Nouvelle bibliothèque des Auteurs ecclésiastiques* (1686) 1:16-34 (rev. 1693, *Nouvelle Bibliothèque,* 2d ed., 19-72; ET in *A New History of Ecclesiastical Writers* [1722[3]] 1:2-30; aug. and rev. as *Prolégomènes sur la Bible* [1700]; ET *A Complete History of the Canon and Writers of the Books of the OT and NT, by Way of Dissertation* [2 vols., 1699–1700]); *Liber Psalmorum cum notis, quibus eorum sensus litteralis exponitur* (1691); *Le Livre des Psaumes, traduit selon l'Hébreu, avec des courtes notes* (1691); *Notae in Pentateuchum, sue Pentateuchus Mosis cum notis, quibus sensus litteralis exponitur* (1701); *Dissertations historiques, chronologiques, géographiques et critiques sur la Bible* (1711); *Analyse de l'Apocalypse, contenant une nouvelle explication simple et littérale de ce livre, avec des dissertations sur les millénaires* (1712).

Bibliography: **J. T. Burtchaell,** *Catholic Theories of Biblical Inspiration Since 1810* (1969) 44-49. **J. Gres-Gayer,** "Un théologien gallican témoin de son temps: L. E. Du Pin (1657–1719)," *Revue d'histoire de l'Église de France* 188 (1986)

67-121; "Un théologien gallican et l'Ecriture Sainte: le 'Projet biblique de L. E. Du Pin," BTT 6 (1989) 255-75; *Théologie et pouvoir en Sorbonne: La Faculté de théologie de Paris et la bulle Unigenitus* (1990). **J. M. Janssens,** *Herméneutique sacrée* (1851) 27. **A. Monod,** *De Pascal à Chateaubriand: Les défen-* *seurs français du christianisme* (1916). *MSHH* 2 (1727) 25-48; 10, 2 (1730) 80-81. **J. Turmel,** *Histoire de la théologie positive* (1906) 2:31. **B. Vawter,** *Biblical Inspiration* (1972).

J. M. Gres-Gayer

E

ECCLESIASTES, BOOK OF (see QOHELET)

ECCLESIASTICUS, BOOK OF (or WISDOM OF JESUS BEN SIRA)

In one sense the history of the interpretation of Ecclesiasticus, or the Wisdom of Jesus Ben Sira, begins within the work itself. From the prologue we learn that Ben Sira's grandson translated the book from Hebrew into Greek. The grandson also offers his opinion that Ben Sira wrote his teaching so that "those who love learning should make even greater progress in living according to the law." In addition, the reader learns that the grandson translated and published the book for the sake of "those living abroad who wished to gain learning." Whatever the original purpose of the book, Ecclesiasticus proved to be immensely popular and influential in both Judaism and Christianity.

The first question in the history of the interpretation of Ecclesiasticus is that of the book's status within Christianity and Judaism. That Ben Sira was highly regarded in the early church is suggested by its possible influence on the book of James and by the fact that it is quoted in the *Didache* (c. 130–160). Moreover, it is quoted as Scripture by CLEMENT OF ALEXANDRIA, ORIGEN, and Cyprian. Only JEROME denied it the status of canonical Scripture by designating it as one of the "ecclesiastical" books, in contrast to the canonical books. Nevertheless, AUGUSTINE accepted it as canonical, along with the other books of the LXX (see SEPTUAGINT); and the Councils of Hippo (393) and Carthage (397 and 418) included it in the CANON of the church.

During the Reformation LUTHER revived Jerome's opinion that, although Ben Sira was an edifying book, it did not have inspired, canonical status. Luther thus removed Ben Sira along with those other books not found in the Hebrew Scriptures and placed them together in a distinct section between the OT and NT (1534). Consequently, in contrast to Roman Catholicism and the Eastern Orthodox Church, Protestantism has either followed the practice of placing these books (designated Apocrypha) in a separate section or excluding them altogether. Not surprisingly, Protestant scholars have not given Ben Sira the same attention devoted to the books they consider to be canonical.

Judaism in the time of the *tannaim* and the *amoraim* reveals a degree of ambivalence toward the book. Numerous quotations in rabbinic literature and the TALMUD demonstrate not only a familiarity with it but also a high regard for its teachings. Indeed, many of the rabbinic quotations of Ben Sira begin with the expression "it is written," which is usually reserved for canonical works. In addition, the fact that the manuscripts found at Qumran (see DEAD SEA SCROLLS) and Masada are written in the stichometric style normally used for sacred texts may indicate that certain Jewish groups had given a special status to the book.

In light of the number and nature of the quotations from Ben Sira, it is surprising to discover that no less an authority than Rabbi AKIBA (d. 135 CE) banned its reading and declared that those who read such "outside books" would have no share in the world to come. Attempts to reconcile Akiba's ban of Ben Sira with the high respect for the book within Judaism were made within the Talmud (see *J. Sanh.* 28a). An anonymous commentary found in the Cairo Geniza suggested that the ban resulted from the public's confusion of Ben Sira with similar works. Others have suggested that the ban applied primarily to public, liturgical reading or to the serious study of the book. S. Leiman (1976) has argued that the ban on Ben Sira was a measure directed against sects within Judaism that had granted it virtual canonical status. Once the canon was firmly established and the threat to normative Judaism had passed, the ban was relaxed or disregarded.

It is doubtful that normative Judaism ever considered Ben Sira to be a part of its canon. It is described by the rabbis as a book that "does not defile the hands," i.e., that is not inspired (see INSPIRATION OF THE BIBLE) or canonical. Since there is no evidence that the so-called Council of Jamnia seriously considered the status of Ben Sira, it is safe to conclude that, although highly respected, the book was not considered to be inspired or to have the status of a canonical book. Indeed, the grandson of Ben Sira appears to refer to a more or less fixed, three-part canon at the time he translated the book into Greek (c. 120–117 BCE).

A second important area of research on Ben Sira has been the investigation of its TEXTUAL history. The ban on reading Ben Sira, the fixing of the canon, and the emergence of the Talmud all contributed to the loss of the Hebrew text of the book, perhaps shortly after the time of Jerome, although it survived in both Greek and Syriac translations. The Greek manuscripts as well as the Syriac suggest that at an early date two different

Hebrew *Vorlagen* had emerged. The Syriac version also shows evidence of a Christian revision before the middle of the fifth century (M. Winder [1977]; D. Nelson [1988]).

The textual situation changed dramatically between 1896 and 1900 with the discovery and publication of parts of four distinct Hebrew manuscripts, designated A, B, C, and D, that were found in the Geniza of the Ezra Synagogue in Cairo and dated to the tenth–twelfth centuries. In 1931 a fifth manuscript (E) was found in the Adler Collection of the Jewish Theological Seminary of America. Between 1958 and 1960 a few more leaves of manuscripts B and C were identified and published. Finally, in 1982 a fragment of manuscript C and a new leaf of another manuscript were identified in the Geniza materials of the Taylor-Schlechter Additional Series Collection at Cambridge. Although initially identified as part of manuscript D, it is now clear that the newly discovered leaf represents a previously unknown manuscript (F). Thus the Geniza material ultimately yielded fragments of six distinct Hebrew manuscripts.

Almost immediately after the initial discoveries of the Geniza manuscripts, their authenticity was challenged. In 1899 both D. Margoliouth and G. Bickell argued that the Geniza fragments were translations from the Persian and/or Syriac. Later these scholars would be joined by others, including C. C. TORREY (1950), E. GOODSPEED (1939), and H. GINSBERG (1955), who believed that the Geniza manuscripts were translations from the Greek and/or Syriac. In each case the main objections to authenticity were the presence of both late Hebrew and poor idiomatic Hebrew in the manuscripts.

Although the challenges to the authenticity of the Geniza manuscripts were effectively and repeatedly refuted by various scholars, the decisive defense of their essential authenticity came only with additional manuscript discoveries. In 1956 two short fragments of a Hebrew manuscript of Ben Sira dating to the early first century BCE were found at Qumran (2Q 18). This discovery played a crucial role in establishing the authenticity of the Geniza manuscripts, since the text of the Qumran fragments is almost identical to manuscript A. Moreover, like manuscripts B and E, the Qumran manuscript is arranged stichometrically.

A scroll containing Sir 51:13-20, 30*b* was also found (11QPs^a) at Qumran, and in 1964 a Hebrew scroll dating to the first century BCE and containing Sir 39:27–44:17 was found at Masada (M). This scroll was crucial in demonstrating the general faithfulness of the Greek translation. No less important is the fact that the scroll proves the essential authenticity of the Geniza fragments, although it also demonstrates that a number of corruptions have entered the text of the Geniza manuscripts (Y. Yadin [1965]). Similarly, the earlier discovery of a scroll containing Sir 51:13-20, 30*b* at Qumran (11QPs^a) also demonstrated both essential authenticity and the presence of corruptions in the Geniza fragments.

Although the authenticity of the Geniza fragments has been established, scholarship is still attempting to establish the textual history of the book. For example, A. Di Lella (1988) argues that many of the examples of poor or late Hebrew in the Geniza manuscripts indicate that the translator had to work from the Syriac at places where his *Vorlage* was corrupt or missing. In contrast, H. Rüger (1970) maintains that the readings in the Geniza fragments can all be explained in light of later developments of language, exegetical tendencies, and style. A third option is offered by T. Middendorp, (1973) who contends that the differences are due to oral transmission. Undoubtedly, scholarship will continue to attempt to define the nature and the relationships of the various Hebrew texts. Also important are similar efforts to establish the nature and development of other versions, including the Greek rescensions (J. Ziegler [1965]) and the Syriac (Winder; Nelson).

Beyond textual investigations, much scholarly work on the book in the past century can be viewed as an attempt to understand the person and perspective of Ben Sira within his historical context. In particular, the book's place within Judaism and, vis-à-vis, Hellenism has been the focus of many studies. A number of earlier scholars located the book within the party of the Sadducees because of the author's praise of the priesthood and the conspicuous lack of references to Ezra (R. Moulton [1896]; W. Oesterley [1912]). Later investigations showed that it was historically impossible for Ben Sira to have been a Sadducee, although his thought has affinities with a conservative, nationalistic party that was replaced by the Hasmoneans (M. Hengel [1974]).

Ben Sira's place within the wisdom tradition of Israel has been an important subject of study (H. Kieweler [1992]). His equation of wisdom and Torah is a significant development within the wisdom tradition in Judaism. Some scholars have concluded that for Ben Sira the Torah has actually replaced the older wisdom point of view that norms of conduct were to be derived from observation and experience (Hengel). G. von RAD (1972) took exception to this conclusion, however, and argued that a careful examination of the relevant texts shows that Ben Sira sought to legitimate and interpret Torah from the wisdom tradition.

In addition to an interest in Ben Sira's place within Judaism, the question of his attitude toward Hellenism has been the focus of a number of major studies. In 1906 R. SMEND characterized the book as a "declaration of war" against Hellenism. A number of subsequent studies found that a marked anti-Hellenistic *Tendenz* pervades and shapes the whole work. On the other hand, recent investigations have discerned a more complex and ambivalent attitude toward Hellenism; indeed, on a number of points Ben Sira is influenced by Hellenistic ideas and attitudes. Not only does he reveal a cautious attitude toward the Ptolemies, but he also borrows ideas and quotations from Greek literature and thought (T. Middendorp [1973]; J. Marböck [1971]; L. Prokter [1990]). Recent work also raises the possibility that Ben Sira's presentation of Lady Wisdom/Sophia is influenced by Hellenistic hymns to Isis (E. Schuller [1992]). In any case, a number of studies have shown that many of Ben Sira's concerns with such subjects as freedom of the will and the importance of human action and wisdom are a response to Hellenism in general and to Stoic and Epicurean philosophies in particular (G. Maier [1971]; R. Pautrel [1963]; Marböck [1975]). Undoubtedly, the investigation of Ben Sira's relation to the wisdom tradition and to Hellenism will continue to be fertile ground for research in the years to come.

Bibliography: **E. N. Adler,** "Some Missing Chapters of Ben Sira (7:20–12:1)," *JQR* 12 (1899–1900) 466-80. **W. Baumgartner,** "Die literarischen Gattungen in der Weisheit des Jesus Sirach," *ZAW* 34 (1914) 161-98. **P. C. Beentjes,** "Recent Publications on the Wisdom of Jesus ben Sira (Ecclesiasticus)," *BTFT* 43 (1982) 188-98; *The Book of Ben Sira in Hebrew: A Text Edition of All Extant Hebrew Manuscripts and a Synopsis of All Parallel Hebrew Ben Sira Texts* (VTSup 68, 1997). **G. Bickell,** "Der hebräische Sirachtext eine Rückübersetzung," *WZKM* 13 (1889) 251-56. **T. A. Burkhill,** "Ecclesiasticus," *IDB* 2 (1962) 13-21. **A. E. Cowley and A. Neubauer,** *Facsimiles of the Fragments Hitherto Recovered of the Book of Ecclesiasticus in Hebrew* (1897). **J. L. Crenshaw,** "Wisdom," *OT Form Criticism* (ed. J. H. Hayes, 1974) 225-64; "The Book of Sirach," *NIB* (1997) 5:601-867. **A. A. Di Lella,** "Recently Identified Leaves of Sirach in Hebrew," *Bib* 45 (1964) 153-67; *The Hebrew Text of Sirach: A Text Critical Study* (Studies in Classical Literature 1, 1966); "The Newly Discovered Sixth Manuscript of Ben Sira from the Cairo Geniza," *Bib* 69 (1988) 226-38. **M. Gilbert,** "The Book of Ben Sira: Implications for Jewish and Christian Traditions," *Jewish Civilization in the Hellenistic-Roman Period* (ed. S. Talmon, 1971). **H. L. Ginsberg,** "The Original Hebrew of Ben Sira 12:10-14," *JBL* 74 (1955) 93-95. **L. Ginzburg,** "Randglossen zum hebräischen Ben Sira," *Orientalische Studien T. Nöldeke gewidmet* (ed. C. Bezold, 1906) 609-25. **E. J. Goodspeed,** *The Story of the Apocrypha* (1939). **D. J. Harrington,** "Sirach Research Since 1965: Progress and Questions," *Pursuing the Text: Studies in Honor of B. Z. Wacholder on the Occasion of His Seventieth Birthday* (JSOTSup 184, ed. J. Kampen and J. C. Reeves, 1994) 164-76. **J. D. Harvey,** "Toward a Degree of Order in Ben Sira's Book," *ZAW* 105 (1993) 52-62. **J. Haspecker,** *Gottesfurcht bei Jesus Sirach: Ihre religiöse Struktur und ihre literarische und doktrinäre Bedeutung* (AnBib 30, 1967). **M. Hengel,** *Judaism and Hellenism: Studies in Their Encounter in Palestine During the Early Hellenistic Period* (2 vols., 1974). **M. A. Jolley,** *The Function of Torah in Sirach* (1993). **O. Kaiser,** "Die Begründung der Sittlichkeit im Buch Jesus Sirach," *ZKT* 55 (1958) 51-63. **C. Kearns,** "Ecclesiasticus, or the Wisdom of Jesus the Son of Sirach," *A New Catholic Commentary on Holy Scripture* (ed. R. C. Fuller et al., 1969) 541-62. **H. V. Kieweler,** *Ben Sira zwischen Judentum und Hellenismus: Eine Auseinandersetzung mit T. Middendorp* (BEATAJ 30, 1992). **T. R. Lee,** *Studies in the Form of Sirach 44–50* (SBLDS 75, 1986). **S. Z. Leiman,** *The Canonization of Hebrew Scripture: The Talmudic and Midrashic Evidence* (1976). **H. McKeating,** "Ben Sira's Attitude to Women," *ExpTim* 85 (1973–74) 85-87. **G. Maier,** *Mensch und frier Wille: Nach den jüdischen Religionsparteien zwischen Ben Sira und Pauls* (WUNT 12, 1971). **J. Marböck,** *Weisheit im Wandel: Untersuchungen zur Weisheitstheologie bei Ben Sira* (BBB 37, 1971); "Sirachliteratur seit 1966: Ein Überblick," *TRev* 71 (1975) 177-84. **D. S. Margoliouth,** *The Origin of the "Original Hebrew" of Ecclesiasticus* (1899). **J. D. Martin,** "Ben Sira: A Child of His Time," *A Word in Season: Essays in Honour of W. McKane* (ed. J. D. Martin and P. R. Davies, JSOTSup 42, 1986) 141-61. **D. Michaelis,** "Das Buch Jesus Sirach als Typischer Ausdruck für das Gottesverhältnis des nachalttestamentlichen Menschen," *TLZ* 83 (1958) 601-08. **T. Middendorp,** *Die Stellung Jesus ben Siras zwischen Judentum und Hellenismus* (1973). **R. G. Moulton,** *Ecclesiasticus: The Modern Reader's Bible* (1896). **D. N. Nelson,** *The Syriac Version of the Wisdom of Ben Sira Compared to the Greek and Hebrew Materials* (SBLDS 107, 1988). **W. O. E. Oesterley,** *The Wisdom of Jesus the Son of Sirach or Ecclesiasticus* (1912). **S. M. Olyan,** "Ben Sira's Relationship to the Priesthood," *HTR* 80 (1987) 261-86. **R. Pautrel,** "Ben Sira et le Stoicisme," *RSR* 51 (1963) 535-49. **E. Pax,** "Dialog und Selbstgespräch bei Sirach 27, 3-10," *SBFLA* 20 (1970) 247-63. **L. J. Prokter,** "His Yesterday and Yours Today (Sir 38:22)," *J. Sem* 2 (1990) 44-56. **G. von Rad,** *Wisdom in Israel* (1972). **H. P Rüger,** *Text und Textform in hebräischen Sirach: Untersuchungen zur Textgeschichte und Textkritik der hebräischen Sirachfragmente aus der Kairo Geniza* (BZAW 112, 1970). **J. A. Sanders,** *The Psalms Scroll of Qumran Cave 11 (11QPs^a)* (DJD 4, 1965). **S. Schlechter and C. Taylor,** *The Wisdom of Ben Sira: Portions of the Book Ecclesiasti from Hebrew Manuscripts in the Cairo Genizah Collection Presented to the University of Cambridge by the Editors* (1899). **E. M. Schuller,** "The Aprocrypha," *The Women's Bible Commentary* (1992) 235-43. **E. Schürer,** *HJPAJC* 3, 1 (1986) 198-212. **P. W. Skehan,** "Ecclesiasticus," *IDBS,* 250-55. **P. W. Skehan and A. A. Di Lella,** *The Wisdom of Ben Sira* (AB 39, 1987). **R. Smend,** *Die Weisheit des Jesus Sirach* (1906). **C. C. Torrey,** "The Hebrew of the Geniza Sirach," *Alexander Marx Jubilee Volume* (1950) 585-602. **W. C. Trenchard,** *Ben Sira's View of Women: A Literary Analysis* (BJS 38, 1982). **D. S. Williams,** "The Date of Ecclesiasticus," *VT* 44 (1994) 536-66. **M. M. Winter,** "The Origins of Ben Sira in Syriac," *VT* 27 (1977) 237-53, 494-507. **O. Wischmeyer,** *Kultur des Buches Jesus Sirach* (1994). **Y. Yadin,** *The Ben Sira Scroll from Masada* (1965). **J. Ziegler,** *Sapientia Iesu Filii Sirach* (Septuaginta 12, 2, 1965).

C. S. SHAW

EDERSHEIM, ALFRED (1825–89)

Born in Vienna to a wealthy Jewish family that adopted English as the household language, E. received both a secular and a Jewish early education. While teaching languages in Pest, he was converted to Christianity by a Scottish chaplain, J. Duncan, with whom he then went to Britain. After study in Edinburgh and Berlin he served a mission in Europe, held Presbyterian pastorates in Scotland, took Anglican orders, and served in Dorsetshire until 1882. When ill health forced him out of active ministry, he retired, eventually to Oxford, where he continued to write while serving at intervals as select preacher to the university and as Grinfield lecturer on the SEPTUAGINT.

E. translated several German theological works and wrote numerous pieces of popular religious exposition. But his distinct and abiding contribution to biblical study lay in the immense store of knowledge he held concerning the language, history, literature, and lore of Judaism. The variety and precision of his Hebraic learning first came to notice in works he wrote on the history of postexilic Judaism and on the Jewish Temple. It was put on fullest display, however, in the two impressive volumes of his most ambitious and popular work, *The Life and Times of Jesus the Messiah* (1883). Although not without its deficiencies, E.'s grasp of the Jewish world in JESUS' day—its habits, rituals, ideas, and institutions—was impressive and influential. As scholarship it rivaled the best German work of the time, while its eloquence and rhetorical style appealed greatly to ordinary readers. On the crucial matter of sources, however, E.'s uncritical approach to the Gospel texts relegated him to the past rather than to the future of biblical criticism.

Works: *History of the Jewish Nation After the Destruction of Jerusalem Under Titus* (1856); *The Temple: Its Ministry and Services as They Were at the Time of Jesus Christ* (1874); *Bible History* [OT] (7 vols., 1876–87); *Jewish Social Life in the Time of Christ* (1876); *The Life and Times of Jesus the Messiah* (2 vols., 1883).

Bibliography: **S. R. Driver,** *DNB* Supp. 2 (1901) 175-76; *DNB* Supp. 22 (1921) 600-601. **D. L. Pals,** *The Victorian "Lives" of Jesus* (TUMSR 7, 1982) 104-8.

D. L. PALS

EDWARDS, JONATHAN (1703–58)

Born Oct. 5, 1703, in East Windsor, Connecticut, E. did his college (BA, 1720) and post-graduate (1721–22) work at Yale. He served in a New York City Presbyterian church and was tutor at Yale College before becoming pastor of the Congregational Church in Northampton, Massachusetts (1726). While scrupulously preforming his ministerial duties he developed the habit of studying thirteen hours a day, a regimen that produced numerous treatises, written sermons, and notebooks. During those Northampton years New England was swept by the revivals of the Great Awakening. Although he was critical of some of the excesses of the revivals, E. defended them as a whole and engaged in revivalist preaching.

Led by the revivalist milieu to a heightened sense of the church as a community of the regenerate, he admitted to the Lord's Supper only those persons who could profess their regeneration. Disagreements with his congregation over his demanding requirements led to his dismissal from the Northampton church in 1750. From 1751 to 1758, he ministered to the settlers and the Housatonic Indians in Stockbridge, Massachusetts, where he completed four major theological treatises. In 1758 he became president of the College of New Jersey (later Princeton) but died March 22, 1758, from a smallpox inoculation only a few months after assuming office.

E.'s thought constitutes a transition between the pre-critical and the critical, the pre-modern and the modern worlds of theological and biblical scholarship. Standing squarely within the tradition of Reformed theology, he was influenced by his wide reading in American and British Puritan literature. His views of Scripture were shaped especially by M. POOLE, M. HENRY, P. DODDRIDGE, J. OWEN, T. Manton (1620–77), and T. Sherlock (1678–1761). But he was fascinated by Enlightenment writers as well and incorporated into his thinking the ideas of such figures as I. NEWTON and J. LOCKE. Believing that all departments of knowledge are mutually supportive, he was as comfortable drawing analogies out of the Bible as he was reflecting upon the epistemological implications of Newton's *Optics.*

E. gave more time to the study of Scripture than to any other writing, and that study was directed toward several ends. In his sermons he instructed his congregation in the moral lessons of the Bible, comforted the afflicted with biblical promises, and roused his hearers to their need for conversion. In his private notebooks he meditated on the connections between the testaments, the analogies between nature and Scripture, and the meaning of PROPHECY. In even the most philosophical of his treatises, he appealed to the AUTHORITY of Scripture for proof of his arguments. And in several projected works, he planned to convince a large eighteenth-century audience of the unity and authority of Scripture.

To implement these uses of Scripture, E. employed a number of exegetical approaches. Persuaded that OT history predicted NT events, he was prone to read the entire OT in the light of the NT. Convinced that in Christ God had established a correspondence between nature and supernature, he reflected systematically upon the images of supernature in nature and history. Satisfied that God had spoken uniformly throughout time, he set about to demonstrate the fundamental doctrinal unity of scriptural and ecclesiastical history. Pervading all of these approaches was his view of Scripture as a collection of "symbolical representations" of "spiritual truths," a view that anticipated POST-MODERN attitudes while still representing a transition between the pre-critical and the critical worldviews.

Works: *The Works of J. E.* (ed. J. E. Smith, 1957–).

Bibliography: **C. Cherry,** "Symbols of Spiritual Truth: J. E. as Biblical Interpreter," *Int* 39 (1985) 263-71. **K. D. Pfisterer,** *The Prism of Scripture: Studies on History and Historicity in the Work of J. E.* (1975). **S. J. Stein,** "The Spirit and the Word: J. E. and Scriptural Exegesis," *J. E. and the American Experience* (ed. N. O. Hatch and H. S. Stout, 1988) 118-30. **D. A. Sweeney,** *HHMBI,* 309-312.

C. C. CHERRY

EERDMANS, BERNARDUS DIRK (1868–1948)

Professor of OT in the theological faculty at the University of Leiden (1898–1938), E. set aside his teaching responsibilities from 1914 to 1927 while active in politics. Receiving his doctorate at Leiden in 1891, the year of A. KUENEN's death, he became a radical critic of Kuenen, who was one of his teachers, along with C. Tiele, one of the founders of the RELIGIONSGESCHICHTLICHE SCHULE. Having studied at Strasbourg, Leipzig, and Heidelberg, E. felt himself on familiar ground with contemporary German criticism, but his study at Oxford gave him what was to become a strong following in England. In Holland he established himself early on as a modernist who went beyond modernism and as a biblical critic willing to question the validity of the Kuenen-WELLHAUSEN theories of biblical criticism. An outspoken leader of the *Rechtsmodernisme* movement, E. made advantageous use of his appointment as editor of the journal of scholarly liberalism, *Theologisch Tijdschrift,* to censure the overconfident naturalism of the Dutch modernists, calling for a more responsible attitude to spiritual issues (see Agnotos, "Reactie of vooruitgant?" *ThT* 34 [1909] 1-16, 146-80). Although it cannot be said that E.'s theology directly determined his biblical criticism, he studiously endeavored to avoid a fault that he attributed to the majority of his fellow modernists, that of giving blind assent to liberal criticism without accepting responsibility for mastering its methods and assumptions.

While E. was defending the new tack taken by *ThT* under his editorship, he was also presenting to the scholarly world his revolutionary four-volume critique of Kuenen-Wellhausen hexateuchal criticism, *Alttestamentliche Studien.* The first, third, and fourth volumes were on Genesis, Exodus, and Leviticus; the second, on Israel's pre-history. It was unfortunate that the German scholars for whom this series was intended aimed their attacks mainly against the Genesis volume (see W. Eichrodt, *Die Quellen der Genesis* [BZAW 31, 1916]), which was the most vulnerable. The essential claim of the series as a whole was that the documentary hypothesis must give way to a fragmentary-supplementary scheme in which J, E, and P are seen as redactors and supplementers rather than as composers. E. rejected the evolutionary model of religious and literary development in favor of a concept based on *Religionsgeschichte*

insights. The earliest compositional levels are those that preserve the divine name *elohim,* a plural form that preserves evidence of primitive polytheism among the Israelites; wherever the Tetragrammaton appears, it reflects interference by late monotheistic editors.

From the perspective of current scholarship it is evident that E. was too heavily influenced by a construct superimposed on the biblical data, yet he must be credited with establishing that Israel's religious life and literary activity were far more varied than the Kuenen-Wellhausen theory would allow. The cessation of his writing activity at the beginning of WWI was due to his frustration at finding so little acceptance among the Germans. The British were more favorable, however, and in Holland two generations of OT scholars have taken from him a stance of deep caution concerning the documentary theory. From 1925 until his death E. resumed writing in this field, producing two important surveys of the religion of Israel, LITERARY analyses of Numbers, Deuteronomy, Job, and Psalms, and a variety of significant studies on related subjects.

Works: "Melekdienst en vereering van hemellichamen in Israëls Assyriche periode" (diss., 1891); *Alttestamentliche Studien,* vol. 1, *Die Komposition der Genesis* (1908); vol. 2, *Die Vorgeschichte Israels* (1908); vol. 3, *Das buch Exodus* (1910); vol. 4, *Das Buch Leviticus* (1912); "Primitive Religious Thought in the OT," *Expositor* 6 (1913) 385-405; "Deuteronomy," *OT Essays* (1927) 77-85; *Studies in Job* (1939); "The Hebrew Book of Psalms," *OTS* 4 (1947); *The Religion of Israel* (1947).

Bibliography: **P. A. H. de Boer,** *Leids Universiteitsblad* (May 21, 1948); "Lijst van geschriften B. D. E.," *JEOL* 6 (1939) 4-8, 761; "Lijst van de voornaamste geschriften van Prof. B. D. E.," *OTS* 2 (1942) 1-9. **S. J. De Vries,** *Bible and Theology in the Netherlands* (1968) 107-21. **O. Eissfeldt,** "Zwei Leidnischer Darstellungen der israelitischen Religionsgeschichte," *ZDMG* 10 (1931) 172-95.

S. J. DEVRIES

EGYPTOLOGY AND BIBLICAL STUDIES

Interest in Egypt and its relationship to Israelite and early Christian history and to biblical literature and thought has been present throughout the history of church and synagogue. At times interest has been so intense that it could be classified as Egyptomania.

Several factors have contributed to this abiding concern. (1) Throughout the Bible Egypt plays a role: as a place of refuge for the patriarchs Abraham and Jacob; as a place where Joseph exercised power; as the land of oppression from which the Hebrews escaped in the exodus; as a major political power throughout much of Israelite/Judean history; as the place where the Torah was translated from Hebrew into Greek (see ARISTEAS and SEPTUAGINT); and as the place of refuge for the holy family according to Matt 2:13-23. (2) Two biblical texts imply a possibly strong Egyptian influence on Moses: According to Exod 2:1-10 Moses was raised at the Egyptian royal court as the son of Pharaoh's daughter, and Acts 7:22 states that "Moses was instructed in all the wisdom of the Egyptians." PHILO in his *Life of Moses* (1.21-24) reported that as a youth Moses was taught not only by the Egyptians but also by teachers from neighboring countries and Greece, noting especially "the philosophy conveyed in symbols, as displayed in the so-called holy inscriptions." (3) Numerous classical and Hellenistic sources provided readers with descriptions of Egyptian life and thought, stimulating discussion throughout the centuries. (4) Unlike firsthand knowledge of the Mesopotamian and Hittite civilizations (see HITTITOLOGY AND BIBLICAL STUDIES), which was practically lost until modern times, some firsthand knowledge of Egypt was available throughout the centuries, since Egypt was a part of the Mediterranean world and travelers from other countries were able to view its monumental antiquities.

1. Earliest Accounts. The earliest known non-biblical account of the Israelites in Egypt and of the exodus is found in the *Aegyptiaca* by Hecataeus of Abdera (c. 300 BCE), fragmentarily preserved in Diodorus's *Bibliotheca Historica* (40.3; *GLA* 1.20-35), which reports that during a plague the Egyptians expelled all aliens, some of whom colonized Greece (see Diodorus 1.28.1-29.5, 1.55.5; and M. Bernal [1987], who takes as factually historical what is obviously of legendary quality), while others under the leadership of Moses settled in Palestine and established their religion there. (Most scholars assume that this legend, and perhaps the biblical narrative of the exodus, is based on an old Egyptian tale of the expulsion of the Hyksos from Egypt in the 16th cent. BCE) Many of the features of Hecataeus's source reappear in the writings of later Greek and Latin authors: Manetho (3rd cent. BCE; preserved in JOSEPHUS's *Contra Apionem* 1.73-91, 93-105, 228-52; *GLA* 1.62-86), Lysimachus (unknown date; preserved in *Contra Apionem* 1.304-11; *GLA* 1.382-86), Charemon (1st cent. CE; preserved in *Contra Apionem* 1.288-92; *GLA* 1.417-21), Apion (1st cent. CE; preserved throughout *Contra Apionem; GLA* 1.389-415); Strabo (late 1st–early 2nd cent. CE; *Geographica* 16. 2.34-46; *GLA* 1.294-311), and Tacitus (c. 56–120 CE; *Historiae* 5.1-13; *GLA* 2.17-63). Some of the accounts of Jewish history provide elements not found in Hecateus's version: The Hebrews and Moses were Egyptian; Moses was an Egyptian priest; the people were expelled from Egypt because they were leprous, lame, and blind.

2. The Classical Period. Discussions of other aspects of Egyptian life and thought appeared in various classical authors (see E. Iversen [1961] 38-56). Particularly significant are descriptions and statements about Egyptian writing, especially the hieroglyphics (Clement of Alexandria, *Stromata* 5.4.20-21; Tacitus, *Annals* 11.14; Diodorus, *Bibliotheca Historica* 3.4.1-3; Plutarch, *Moralia* 12E-F), which were presented as a special way of representing thought allegorically through symbols. Plotinus (c. 205–70 CE) concluded that hieroglyphic images were endowed with symbolic qualities and thus could reveal knowledge of the very essence of things that could be grasped by intuitive inspiration and illumination (*Enneades* 5.8.6). The so-called *Corpus Hermeticum,* a collection of Greek texts probably produced in Alexandria in the first to third centuries CE, purports to present many elements of ancient Egyptian learning, although extant forms of the texts show Hellenic, Jewish, and Christian influence. The "author," Hermes Trismegistus (the thrice-great Hermes), was associated with the Egyptian god Thoth.

Obelisks transported to Europe by Roman monarchs were reminders of a past civilization on the Nile; the one now adorning the courtyard of St. Peter's in the Vatican was still standing at the beginning of the Renaissance. ART in the church of St. Mark in Venice depicts the Egyptian pyramids as the granaries of Joseph.

3. The Renaissance. The Renaissance phase of Egyptomania was triggered by the recovery of two documents. In 1419 a copy of a two-volume work by Horapollo (otherwise unknown) was discovered on the island of Andros (for a modern translation, see G. Boas [1950]). In its introduction the work claims to have been written originally in Egyptian by Horapollo of Nilopoles and translated into Greek by Philippos. The widely circulated work was printed in 1505, and a Latin version appeared in 1515. The second work was a collection of the *Corpus Hermeticum,* brought to Italy in 1460 and presented to C. de Medici, the duke of Florence. The Florentine Platonic philosopher M. Ficino (1433–99) interrupted his translation of Plato's works to produce a Latin version, published in 1471. (By 1500 eight editions of the work had appeared.) Ficino believed that these texts predicted the birth of Christ and the origins of Christianity (see F. Yates [1964] 14-17).

Horapollo's work, with its argument that hieroglyphic writing conveyed its meaning through allegorical symbols, was appealing to Platonic philosophers. The *Corpus Hermeticum* was taken as the work of Hermes Trismegistus, considered to be a contemporary if not a predecessor of Moses. Renaissance scholars searching for the *prisca philosophia/theologia* believed that in addition to the Greek and Roman classics they now had another access to non-biblical thought that revealed a universal religious perspective commensurate with Christianity. Scholars interested in the magical, the occult, and the esoteric, e.g., G. Bruno (1548–1600), an ex-Dominican monk burned at the stake by the Inquisition, welcomed the recovery of Egyptian thought, arguing that Christianity was a corruption of mystical Egyptian Hermeticism. The concern with Egyptian history and culture subsequently influenced art, archechtiture, and eventually even MUSIC throughout the sixteenth and subsequent centuries as well as such secret societies as the Freemasons and the Rosicrucians (see M. Jacobs [1981]).

The symbolic reading of the hieroglyphics reached its apogee in the work of the Jesuit A. Kircher (1601–90), whose *Lingua aegyptiaca restituta* (1664) was assumed by many scholars to be the final word on the mystery of these writings. Kircher argued for a view of the universe in which the divine dynamic, evident in all things, was revealed through symbolism. Divine truth can thus be revealed through all phenomena and was first grasped by the ancient Egyptians.

Although I. CASAUBON had published an essay challenging the antiquity of the *Corpus Hermeticum* (1614), this work continued to be used to substantiate the existence of an early, primitive, pre-biblical monotheistic faith. This was the view advocated by the Cambridge Platonist R. Cudworth (1617–88) in his monumental attack on atheism, *The True Intellectual System of the Universe* (1678).

A different approach to the issues was taken by J. Marsham (1602–85), J. SPENCER, and others. Marsham, like many of his contemporaries, such as I. de la PEYRÈRE, was concerned with CHRONOLOGY and the question of priority in religious matters. In his *Canan chronicus aegyptiacus, hebraicus, graecus* (1672), he argued for the priority of Egyptian history over Israelite history even though he had several Egyptian dynasties ruling simultaneously. Spencer, who W. R. SMITH said "laid the foundations of the science of comparative religion," in his *De legibus Hebraeorum ritualibus et earum rationibus* (1685) traced many Israelite practices and beliefs back to an Egyptian origin (see J. Assmann [1997] 55-79). His work thus relativized claims that Israelite law and rituals were the product of divine revelation since many of these appeared to be simply borrowings from other cultures. Dutch theologian H. WITSIUS, in his *Aegyptiaca* (1696), along with many others, attacked Spencer's arguments, maintaining that it was the Egyptians who borrowed rather than the Israelites. Deists J. TOLAND, M. TINDAL, and C. MIDDLETON (see DEISM) utilized Spencer's position to challenge all claims of a revealed religion in support of natural religion.

4. Eighteenth Century. A new stage in the scholarly approach to Egyptian hieroglyphics developed in the eighteenth century. In his *The Divine Legation of Moses* (3 vols., 1741), W. WARBURTON argued that the hieroglyphics do not represent a symbolic system but are instead an actual written language, views already anticipated by the English philosopher F. BACON (1561–1626) and J. Wilkins (1614–72), the first secretary of the Royal Society. Efforts to decipher the Egyptian language reached a new level with the discovery of the Rosetta Stone, with its bilingual inscription (hieroglyphic, de-

motic, and Greek), by Napoleon's troops in Egypt in 1799. The scientists and artists accompanying the French troops, operating under the guidance of the recently founded Institut d' Égypte, subsequently published over 7,000 pages in *Discription de l'Égypte*. The decipherment of Egyptian by J. Champollion (1790–1832) made it possible to read the ancient hieroglyphics and thus Egyptian literature on its own terms.

5. Nineteenth and Early Twentieth Centuries. With the development of Egyptology and the exploration of Egypt in the nineteenth and early twentieth centuries, study of the relationship between ancient Israel and Egypt was more scientifically focused. Periodic discoveries at the end of the nineteenth century opened new vistas on Israelite history and literature. From 1887 onward the discovery at el-Amarna in Egypt of numerous letters written in Akkadian cuneiform created excitement. Addressed both from the Egyptian court and from Syro-Palestinian vassal kings, these letters referred to conditions in Late Bronze Age Palestine and mentioned groups of troublemakers called the *habiru*, whom many scholars identified with the Hebrews because of the similarity in their spelling. In 1896 at Thebes W. F. PETRIE discovered the Merneptah stela, an inscription of the Egyptian king that contains the first non-biblical reference to "Israel" (see M. Hasel [1994]), suggesting that there was such an entity in Palestine about 1200 BCE.

The recovery from el-Amarna of texts from the reign of the heretical king Akhenaten, "the first monotheist," led Chicago Egyptologist J. Breasted (1894) to argue that biblical monotheism was borrowed from Egypt, a view partially adopted by W. F. ALBRIGHT. More extravagant claims were made by A. Yahuda (1929; ET 1932), who traced an enormous amount of biblical terminology and many biblical concepts to Egypt, and by S. FREUD, who in *Moses and Monotheism* (1939) accepted the view that Moses was an Egyptian.

6. Mid and Late Twentieth Century. Scholarship of the mid to late twentieth century has generally concluded that the culture and world of ancient Egypt did have a deep impact on the Israelites and the HB but has not engaged in the excessive claims of some earlier interpretations. Epigraphical finds from ancient Egypt, discovered during the late nineteenth and early twentieth centuries, have shown that during the latter half of the second millennium BCE (1450–1140) Egypt maintained suzerainty over all of Palestine. These texts attest to the presence of Egyptian governors, soldiers, messengers, priests, and other officials in Palestine during the Late Bronze Age (G. Ahlström [1993] 217-81; D. Redford [1992]). It is also known that during this period of suzerainty it was Egyptian practice to educate the future leaders of Palestinian cities in Egypt, thus inculcating in them respect for Egypt and its culture (W. Ward [1992] 404). In addition, there is good reason to believe that during the late seventh century BCE, at least by the time of King Josiah of Judah, Egypt once again asserted its authority over Palestine (J. Miller and J. Hayes [1987] 383-85).

Archaeological discoveries (see ARCHAEOLOGY AND BIBLICAL STUDIES) in both Egypt and Palestine provide ample evidence attesting to strong political and cultural connections between them during the period from c. 1450 to 600 BCE, the time of Israel's emergence, development, and exile from the land of Canaan. From strata dated to the latter half of the Late Bronze period (c. 1400–1200 BCE) many Egyptian and Egyptian-related finds have been unearthed (A. Mazar [1990] 232-91; Ahlström, 217-81). These finds include Egyptian-style residences and forts at Gaza, Beth-Shean, Tell Halif, and elsewhere (E. Oren [1992] 117-20); temples (Lachish, Ashkelon, Gaza, and Jerusalem); Egyptian-type graves, grave goods, and pottery; remains of inscriptions written in hieratic (a cursive form of hieroglyphs); and large quantities of Egyptian scarabs (beetle-shaped amulets made of stone, metal, or glass), magical amulets, and other items. These finds attest to both the physical presence of Egyptians living in Palestine and to a healthy importation of material goods.

This strong Egyptian cultural influence on Palestine continued into the Iron Age (c. 1200–550 BCE), although direct Egyptian political influence and presence disappear after c. 1150 BCE. Temples and buildings in Iron Age Palestine often used Egyptian standards of measurement (e.g., the famous six-chamber gates unearthed at Gezer, Megiddo, and Hazor; D. Milson [1986]); Egyptian scarabs and amulets were still in use, although made locally, and Egyptian artistic motifs still appeared. According to the archaeological evidence Egyptian presence and contacts were lowest during the tenth century BCE, the time of David and Solomon. However, a clear resuscitation of Egyptian cultural forms occurred c. 900–850 BCE with the appearance of Egyptian motifs in graves (E. Bloch-Smith [1992]), the use of hieratic numerals in Hebrew inscriptions (A. Lemaire [1977] 278), and Egyptian motifs on various types of luxury items. Therefore, one can and should expect that Egypt also left its cultural imprint on the writings in the HB, a product of Israelite culture of the Iron Age and later.

Egyptian influences on the HB postulated or identified by scholars of the mid to late twentieth century can be categorized roughly into three groups: linguistic influences, literary influences, and institutional influences.

a. Linguistic influences. Numerous works, including those by M. Görg [1985, 1997], T. Lambdin [1953], and R. Williams [1969, 1971, 1975, 1981], among others, have identified many Egyptian loan words and idioms in the HB. A few clear examples are the Hebrew words for "ink" (*dĕyô*) and "scribal kit" (*qeset*), the word "pharaoh," and the word for "magicians" (*hartummim*). Two Egyptian words for measures have made their way into Hebrew: *ephah* and *hin.* In total about forty Egyp-

tian words appear in the HB (so Redford [1992] 385). Moreover, other scholars have postulated that certain idioms in the HB, like "hearing heart" (1 Kgs 3:9) and Solomon's referral to himself as an "innocent little child" (1 Kgs 3:7), derive from Egypt.

b. Literary influences. Scholars have also proposed that several genres of literature found in the HB originated in Egypt, but none of these views is indisputable. Psalm 104, for instance, has been compared to the "Hymn to the Aten"; at one time scholarship held that the psalmist was directly inspired by this hymn. However, after the death of Akhenaten there was a concerted effort in Egypt to eradicate all traces of his reign, and to date only one example of the "Hymn to the Aten" has been found. Since it would hardly have been known to the psalmist, dependence has been challenged (see C. Uehlinger [1990]). G. von RAD argued that the writer of the book of Job drew on Egyptian onomastic literature (lists of names) for his presentation of the divine speeches (Job 38–41; 1966, 281-91). This view has been seriously challenged by M. Fox (1986), who in an earlier writing connected the poetry in the Song of Songs with Egyptian love poetry (1985).

The similarity between the Egyptian *Teachings of Amenemope,* and Prov 22:17–24:22 is another example. Scholars have long recognized that Israelite scribes adopted the Egyptian wisdom book genre in their production of Proverbs, and many have argued that this section was directly borrowed from the *Teachings of Amenemope,* since the two works are so similar in content and both mention "thirty sayings" (Prov 22:20). Others scholars have contended, however, that the similarities in content are negligible, only what would be typical of any wisdom writing (e.g., J. Ruffle [1977]). These scholars also note that the appearance of the word "thirty" in Proverbs is derived from an emendation of the biblical text. Hence there is considerable debate over the relationship between these two writings and the exact nature of the borrowing.

A final example concerns the issue of the Egyptian *Königsnovelle* and its relation to Hebrew literature. First A. Herrmann (1938) and later S. Herrmann (1953) argued that certain sections of Hebrew narrative literature (e.g., 1 Kgs 3:4-15; 5–8; 2 Samuel 7) were based on the Egyptian *Königsnovelle,* or royal romance. T. Ishida has cogently argued, however, that the similarities are minimal and that these texts owe more to Mesopotamian than to Egyptian influences (1977, 81-92; also Redford [1992] 374-77). Although there seems to be no doubt that the wisdom book genre derived from Egypt, there is little consensus beyond this; and the claims for other borrowings are problematic.

c. Institutional influences. Many scholars have claimed that several Israelite institutions drew on Egypt for inspiration. Von Rad argued for the Egyptian derivation of the Israelite coronation ritual detailed in 2 Kgs

11:12 (1967, 222-31). R. de VAUX traced the practice of anointing to Egypt (1972, 119-33). More pervasive among scholars is the contention that the court of David and Solomon not only was based on Egyptian models but also comprised Egyptian scribes and officials. Many scholars believe that the name of the scribe of David and Solomon, Sheva/Shisha (2 Sam 20:25; 1 Kgs 4:3), is a corruption or transcription of the Egyptian word for the office of scribe. These scholars have also contended that the office of "recorder" is modeled after that of the Egyptian *whmw* (J. Begrich 1940–41]; de Vaux [1972]; A. Cody [1965]; T. Mettinger [1971]). Redford (1972) argued that Solomon obtained the model for his twelve-fold division of the kingdom (1 Kgs 4:7-19) from Egypt.

None of the positions noted above has gone unchallenged. Despite his assertions regarding the organization of Solomon's kingdom, Redford has been a strong opponent of the majority of these alleged institutional influences (1972; 1992, 369-74). He has challenged the notion that Egyptian models underlie the monarchy and has persuasively opposed the arguments advanced for the connection of David and Solomon's royal court to Egypt. K. Kitchen (1988) has likewise offered strong proof against the Egyptian connection, and recently S. Weeks has followed their lead (1994, 115-31). Hence it is more likely that "Canaanite" or Syro-Palestinian models provided the basis on which David and Solomon built their kingship.

There is no doubt that Egypt has had a deep impact on the world of ancient Israel and the writings of the HB; however, the impact has often been overstated. This is especially the case with the alleged institutional influences of Egypt on Israel and the Bible. The most apparent influences appear in the writing, artwork, and architecture of Israel and the vocabulary and literary forms of the HB.

Bibliography: G. W. Ahlström, *The History of Ancient Palestine from the Palaeolithic Period to Alexander's Conquest* (JSOTSup 146, 1993). J. Assmann, *Moses the Egyptian: The Memory of Egypt in Western Monotheism* (1997). P. Auffret, *Hymnes d'Egypte et d'Israel: Études de structures Littéraires* (OBO 34, 1981). M. L. Barre, "The Extrabiblical Literature," *Listening: Journal of Religion and Culture* 19 (1984) 53-72. J. Begrich, "Sōfēr und Mazkīr," *ZAW* 58 (1940–41) 1-29. M. Bernal, *Black Athena: The Afroasiatic Roots of Classical Civilization* (1987). E. Bloch-Smith, *Judahite Burial Practices and Beliefs About the Dead* (JSOTSup 123, 1992). G. Boas, *The Hieroglyphics of Horapollo* (tr. G. Boas, Bollingen Series 23, 1950). F. G. Bratton, *A History of Egyptian Archaeology* (1967). J. H. Breasted, *De Hymnis in Solem sub Rege Amenophide IV. Redactis* (1894); *The Development of Religion and Thought in Ancient Egypt* (Morse Lectures, 1912). A. Cody, "Le titre Égyptien et le nom propre du scribe de David," *RB* 72 (1965) 381-93. J. D. Currid, *Ancient Egypt and the OT* (1997). K. H. Dannenfeldt, "Egypt and Egyptian Antiquities

in the Renaissance," *Studies in the Renaissance* 6 (1959) 7-27. L. Dieckmann, *Hieroglyphics: The History of a Literary Symbol* (1970). A. Faivre, "Hermetism," *Encyclopedia of Religion* 6 (1987) 293-302. M. V. Fox, *The Song of Songs and the Ancient Egyptian Love Songs* (1985); "Egyptian Onomastica and Biblical Wisdom," *VT* 36 (1986) 302-10. J. G. Gager, *Moses in Greco-Roman Paganism* (SBLMS 16, 1972). M. Görg, "Methodological Remarks on Comparative Studies of Egyptian and Biblical Words and Phrases," *Pharaonic Egypt: The Bible and Christianity* (ed. S. Israellit-Groll, 1985) 57-64; *Die Beziehungen zwischen dem alten Israel und Ägypten von den Anfangen bis zu Exil* (Erträge der Forschung 290, 1997). M. G. Hasel, "Israel in the Merneptah Stela," *BASOR* 296 (1994) 45-61. A. Herrmann, *Die ägyptische Königsnovelle* (LÄS 10, 1938). S. Herrmann, "Die Königsnovelle in Ägypten und in Israel: Ein Beitrag zur Gattungsgeschichte in den Geschichtsbüchern des Alten Testaments," *WZ(L)* 3 (1953) 51-62; "Operationen Pharao Schoschenks I. am östlichen Ephraim," *ZDPV* 80 (1964) 55-79; "2 Samuel VII in the Light of the Egyptian Königsnovelle—Reconsidered," *Pharaonic Egypt: The Bible and Christianity* (ed. S. Israelit-Groll, 1985) 119-28. J. K. Hoffmeier, *Israel in Egypt: The Evidence for the Authenticity of the Exodus Tradition* (1997). T. Ishida, *The Royal Dynasties in Ancient Israel: A Study on the Formation and Development of Royal-Dynastic Ideology* (BZAW 142, 1977). E. Iversen, *The Myth of Egypt and Its Hieroglyphs in European Tradition* (1961). M. C. Jacobs, *The Radical Enlightenment: Pantheists, Freemasons, and Republicans* (Early Modern Europe Today 3, 1981). K. A. Kitchen, "Egypt and Israel During the First Millennium BC," *Congress Volume 1986* (ed. J. Emerton, 1988) 107-23. T. O. Lambdin, "Egyptian Loan Words in the OT," *JAOS* 73 (1953) 145-55. A. Lemaire, *Inscriptions Hébraïques*, vol. 1, *Les Ostraca* (LAPO 9, 1977). A. Mazar, *Archaeology of the Land of the Bible* (ABRL, 1990). I. Merkel and A. G. Debus (eds.), *Hermeticism and the Renaissance: Intellectual History and the Occult in Early Modern Europe* (Folger Institute Symposia, 1988). T. N. D. Mettinger, *Solomonic State Officials: A Study of the Civil Government Officials of the Israelite Monarchy* (ConBOT 5, 1971). J. M. Miller and J. H. Hayes, *A History of Ancient Israel and Judah* (1986). D. Milson, "The Design of the Royal Gates at Megiddo, Hazor, and Gezer," *ZDPV* 102 (1986) 87-92. E. D. Oren, "Palaces and Patrician Houses in the Middle and Late Bronze Ages," *The Architecture of Ancient Israel: From the Prehistoric to the Persian Periods* (ed. A. Kempinski and R. Reich, 1992) 105-20. G. von Rad, *The Problem of the Hexateuch and Other Essays* (2 vols., TBü 8, 48, 1958; ET, 1966). D. B. Redford, "Studies in Relations Between Palestine and Egypt During the First Millennium BC, I: The Taxation System of Solomon," *Studies on the Ancient Palestinian World* (TSTS, ed. J. W. Wevers and D. B. Redford, 1972) 141-56; "Studies in Relations Between Palestine and Egypt During the First Millennium BC, II," *JAOS* 93 (1973) 3-17; "The Relations Between Egypt and Israel from El-Amarna to the Babylonian Conquest," *Biblical Archaeology Today* (1985) 192-205; *Egypt and Canaan in the New Kingdom* (Beersheba 4, 1990); *Egypt, Canaan, and Israel in Ancient*

Times (1992). **P. Rossi,** *The Dark Abyss of Time: The History of the Earth and the History of Nations from Hooke to Vico* (1984). **J. Ruffle,** *"The Teaching of Amenemope* and Its Connection with the Book of Proverbs," *TynBul* 28 (1977) 29-68. **R. B. Y. Scott,** "Weights and Measures of the Bible," *BA 22 (1959) 22-40.* **N. Shupak,** "The 'Sitz im Leben' of the Book of Proverbs in the Light of a Comparison of Biblical and Egyptian Wisdom Literature," *RB* 94 (1987) 98-119; "Some Idioms Connected with the Conception of 'Heart' in Egypt and the Bible," *Pharaonic Egypt: The Bible and Christianity* (ed. S. Israelit-Groll, 1985) 202-12; "Stylistic and Terminological Traits Common to Biblical and Egyptian Literature," *WO* 14 (1983) 216-30; *Where Can Wisdom Be Found? The Sage's Language in the Bible and Ancient Egyptian Literature* (OBO 130, 1993). **D. Syndram,** *Ägypten-Faszinationen: Untersuchungen zum Ägyptenbild im europäischen Klassizismus bis 1800* (1990). **T. L. Thompson,** *Early History of the Israelite People: From the Written and Archaeological Sources* (SHANE 4, 1992). **R. de Vaux,** "Le Roi d'Israël, vasal de Yahvé," *Melanges E. Tisserant* (ed. P. Hennequin et al., 1964) 119-33; "Titres et fonctionnaires Égyptiens à la cour de David et de Salomon," *RB* 48 (1972) 394-402. **C. Uehlinger,** "Leviathan und die Schiffe in Psalm 104, 25-26," *Bib* 71 (1990) 499-526. **W. A. Ward,** "Egyptian Relations with Canaan," *ABD* 2 (1992) 399-408. **S. Weeks,** *Early Israelite Wisdom* (Oxford Theological Monographs, 1994). **R. J. Williams,** "Some Egyptianisms in the OT," *Studies in Honor of J. A. Wilson* (ed. E. Kadish et al., SAOC 35, 1969) 93-98; *"Egypt and Israel," The Legacy of Egypt* (ed. J. R. Harris, 1971) 257-90; *"A People Come Out of Egypt,"* VTSup 28 (1975) 231-52; *"The Sages of Ancient Egypt in the Light of Recent Scholarship,"* JAOS 101 (1981) 1-19. **J. A. Wilson,** *Signs and Wonders upon Pharaoh: A History of American Egyptology* (1964). **A. S. Yahuda,** *The Language of the Pentateuch in Its Relation to Egyptian* (1929; ET 1932). **F. Yates,** *G. Bruno and the Hermetic Tradition* (1964). **Y. H. Yerushalmi,** *Freud's Moses: Judaism Terminable and Interminable* (1991).

P. S. ASH

EHRLICH, ARNOLD BOGUMIL (1848–1919)

E. received a traditional Jewish education in his native Wlodawa, Russian Poland. Possessed of an astonishing memory and drive to learn, he studied classical languages as well as Hebrew sources. At seventeen he broke with his family and completed a high school education in Berlin, continuing his studies at Leipzig, where Franz DELITZSCH assigned him to polish his Hebrew translation of the NT. In 1876 he migrated to New York, where he gave classes and private lessons in Hebrew and published a chrestomathy of rabbinic literature (1883). He learned Arabic and Syriac, applying them, together with his profound control of Hebrew, to three volumes of a philological commentary on the Bible, *Mikrâ Ki-Pheschutô* (1899–1901), written in classical Hebrew style, seeking to revolutionize Jewish understanding of Scripture by injecting a critical spirit.

Dissatisfied with the reception of his efforts, he never wrote the final volume. He composed a German translation and commentary on Psalms (1905) and went on to publish in German a somewhat different seven-volume commentary on the entire HB (1908–14). Although he was widely recognized as the most resourceful Hebrew philologist of his day, he found no academic position. Among his private students were R. Gottheil and J. BEWER.

Like the leading contemporary German scholars, E. regarded biblical narrative prior to the so-called divided kingdoms largely as legend. He assumed a complex literary history behind the received text of the Pentateuch (see PENTATEUCHAL CRITICISM), dating its redaction to the exilic period; but he did not hold by the particulars of the documentary hypothesis (*M. K.* 1:263-64). He maintained that higher critical judgments should rest upon a prior linguistic and RHETORICAL analysis (*Die Psalmen*) and further adopted the Romantic idea that one could recover the spirit of ancient Israel through its use of language (*M. K.* on Deut 23:1).

Accordingly, E. attempted to clarify every uncommon or subtly nuanced Hebrew usage. For example, he incorporated into his commentary an excursus on prepositional *l* as an indicator of secondary position (*M. K.* on Gen 2:3; see 1:6) and another on the functions of the prefix-particle *wa* (*M. K.* on Gen 3:18). Although he knew little Akkadian, he drew routinely on Arabic as well as on his encyclopedic knowledge of Hebrew to explain obscure or misunderstood words. For example, *ḥārā(h) 'ap̄*, in contrast to the idiom *'erek 'appāyim*, "long of nose," i.e., "patient," E. interpreted not as "to be angry," but as "to shrink the nose," i.e., "to be impatient," adducing an Arabic etymon in support (*M. K.* 1:83-84). When philological analysis failed he turned increasingly to emending the received text.

A maverick, though brilliant, E. cited little current scholarship; most Christians, he felt, had a tin ear for Hebrew idiom. He put no store in traditional Jewish exegesis per se but used post-biblical Hebrew as a key to understanding the classical tongue and referred to rabbinic literature for its potential conservation of earlier notions and practices (e.g., *M. K.* 1:140-41, n. 1). His influence on the New Jewish Version of the Bible is strong.

Works: *Mikrâ Ki-Pheschutô* (3 vols., 1899–1901; repr. 1969); *Die Psalmen* (1905); *Randglosen zur hebräischen Bibel: Textkritisches, sprachliches, und sachliches* (7 vols., 1908–14; repr. 1968).

Bibliography: **R. J. H. Gottheil,** *The Life of G. Gottheil: Memoir of a Priest in Israel* (1936) 75-79. **B. Z. Halper,** " 'arnôld b. 'ehrlîk měb 'ēr hammiqrā '," *Miqlaṭ* 2 (1920) 417-26. **M. Haran,** "Ḥaqîrat hammiqrā ' bě ' ibrît mērē ' sît hatteqûpa(h) hallē ' ûmît 'ad zěmanēnû," *Bitzaron* 22 (1950), esp. 193-96. **J.**

Kabakoff, "New Light on A. B. E.," *AJeA* 36 (1984) 202-24. **H. M. Orlinsky,** "Prolegomenon," *Mikrâ Ki-Pheschutô* (A. B. E., 3 vols., repr. 1969) ix-xxxiii. **S. D. Sperling,** *Students of the Covenant* (1992) 45-47. **R. M. Stern,** "A. B. E.: A Personal Recollection," *AJeA* 23 (1971) 73-85.

E. L. GREENSTEIN

EICHHORN, JOHANN GOTTFRIED (1752–1827)

E. was one of the last of the "encyclopedic" scholars whose learning extended far beyond his strictly professional field. In biblical scholarship he was the architect of modern "introductions" to the Bible as well as an important contributor to the development of biblical criticism. Born Oct. 16, 1752, in Dörrenzimmern, northeast of Heilbronn, he entered the University of Göttingen in 1770, where his teachers were the orientalist J. D. MICHAELIS and the classicist C. Heyne. In 1775, at the age of twenty-two, he became professor of oriental languages at Jena, returning to Göttingen in 1788, where he remained until his death June 25, 1827.

In Göttingen he lectured not only on the OT, the NT, and Semitic languages but also on the history of literature and culture as well as world history. His historical interests resulted in a number of massive works that are testimony to his learning and industry. As a biblical scholar he was a neologist—that is, he accepted that the Bible contained a divine revelation, but he reserved the right of reason to interpret the revelation in the light of modern knowledge. This is most clearly seen in his view of the "mythical" nature (see MYTHOLOGY AND BIBLICAL STUDIES) of some biblical narratives. He argued that the early narratives of Genesis, for example, came from a time when the human race was in its infancy. Therefore, interpretation of the narratives had to go further than merely grammatical exegesis; it was necessary to see through the naive and childlike language of the narratives to the reality that lay behind them. In the case of Genesis 2–3 the reality was that the original ancestors of the human race had lived in a garden from which they had fled in terror when a thunderstorm occurred. The references to a talking serpent and cherubim with flaming swords came from the naive oriental conceptualizing of earliest humankind. The same method was applied to the NT, with the difference that E. believed that the first three Gospels were based on an original "primitive" gospel written in Hebrew/Aramaic and that naive conceptualizing in terms of the miraculous in the Gospels was not necessarily present in the original gospel.

His OT introduction of 1780–83 set standards for this genre that have been operative ever since. Although he believed Moses to have been the author of the Pentateuch (see PENTATEUCHAL CRITICISM)—a necessary consequence of his view of Genesis 2–3 as authentic history once it was demythologized—he held that Moses had

used documents, especially for Genesis 1–12. His division of these chapters into a Jehovah source, with a mainly geographical interest, and an Elohist source, with a mainly chronological interest (see CHRONOLOGY, HB), drew upon the work of J. ASTRUC and agreed substantially with the results of the documentary hypothesis developed nearly a century later. Also in the introduction, E., like several other scholars of the period, began to place the composition of Isaiah 40–66 in the time of the Babylonian exile. He also questioned the authenticity of several chapters within Isaiah 1–39 and the unity of Daniel and Zechariah.

As a complement to the foregoing work E. published between 1804 and 1827 an NT introduction that discussed the origin of the Gospels; denied the authenticity of 2 Peter; was uncertain about 1 Peter, James, and Jude; and showed that the PASTORAL LETTERS differed in their religious language from letters undoubtedly by PAUL. From 1777 to 1803 E. edited two successive journals in which he displayed a comprehensive knowledge of research in biblical studies throughout Europe. Although his contribution to the progress of biblical criticism was less decisive than that of W. DE WETTE, the achievements of the nineteenth century would not have been possible without his work.

Works: *Introduction to the Study of the OT* (3 vols., 1780–83, 1803³, 1823–24⁴; ET 1888); *Einleitung in die apokryphischen Schriften des AT* (J. G. Eichhorns kritische Schriften 4, 1795); *Einleitung in das Neue Testament* (2 vols., 1804–12); *Die hebraischen Propheten* (1816–19).

Bibliography: **E. Bertheau** (C. Bertheau), *RE³* 5 (1898) 234-37. **O. Kaiser,** "Eichhorn und Kant," *Von der Gegenwartsbedeutung des ATs: Gesammelte Studien zur Hermeneutik und zur Redaktionsgeschichte* (1984) 61-70. **J. W. Rogerson,** *Myth in OT Interpretation* (1974) 3-6; *OTCNC* 17-24. **J. Sandys-Wunsch,** *HHMBI,* 312-16. **E. Sehmsdorf,** *Die Prophetenauslegung bei J. G. E.* (1971). **B. Seidel,** "J. G. E.: Konstruktionsmechanismen in den Anfängen einer historisch-kritischen Theoriebildung," *WZ(H)* 39 (1990) 73-81. **R. Smend,** "J. D. Michaelis und J. G. E.: Zwei Orientalisten am Rande der Theologie," *Theologie in Göttingen: Eine Vorlesungsreihe* (ed. B. Moeller, 1987) 58-81 = *DATDJ* 13-24. **H.-J. Zobel,** *TRE* 9 (1982) 369-71.

J. W. ROGERSON

EICHHORN, KARL ALBERT AUGUST LUDWIG (1856–1926)

Born Oct. 1, 1856, in Garlstorf near Lüneburg, into the family of a Lutheran pastor, E. received his university education in Leipzig (1875–76), Erlangen (1876–77), and Göttingen (1877–78). Like his close friend W. WREDE after him, he was greatly disappointed by the scholarship of the Lutheran theologians at Leipzig. Although he studied with such notable exegetes and historians as E. SCHÜRER, W. BAUDISSIN, and P. de LAGARDE, E. remained a loner who shared his teacher Reuter's suspicion of all "historical studies, which [he] was unable to test himself." He served pastorates with his ailing father and attended—like his friend Wrede—the elite Lutheran seminary of Loccum (1879–81); he left the parish in 1884 to prepare himself for the lic. theol. and an academic teaching career. While in Göttingen (1884–86) he greatly influenced Wrede and later from Halle other members of the RELIGIONSGESCHICHTLICHE SCHULE, of which he has been declared the head. At Halle he received the lic. theol. (1886) with a dissertation on ATHANASIUS and taught subsequently as *Extraordinarius* for church history (1888–1901). Ill health caused a transfer to Kiel (1901–13) and his later retirement. He died Aug. 3, 1926.

E.'s influence on the so-called *Religionsgeschichtliche Schule,* especially on Wrede and H. GUNKEL, cannot be overestimated, although much of it took place in personal conversations and letters. This influence was exerted in three directions: (1) the contextual study of religious phenomena and ideas, as opposed to the literary enumeration of the contemporary source critics; (2) the tradition-historical approach in Gospel research; and (3) the significance of Mandaean writings for the understanding of the JOHANNINE literature.

His NT methodology aimed at uncovering the TRADITION HISTORY of an idea, a motif, or a practice and at presenting the history of its transformation as exhaustively as the data permitted. The history-of-religions method denoted for E. a twofold approach: (1) the precise investigation of the conceptual shifts in meaning of a motif or idea in response to overall changes of history and to the theological needs of the early Christian community and (2) a thorough investigation of the larger religious, intellectual, and social horizon in which motifs and ideas flourished.

E. rejected LITERARY criticism's immediate transference of narrative and sayings into history and stressed instead the theological and dogmatic meanings with which original events and thoughts became imbued. He became a further witness to the diminished attention paid to source-critical research, although such studies continued to serve tradition-historical inquiry in detecting shifts of meaning and breaks in thought. E.'s exegetical contribution, as found in his monograph on NT accounts of the Lord's Supper, lay in demonstrating that the accounts were intelligible only within a cultic sacramental setting and as part of a larger process of dogmatic reflection by the Christian community on the significance of JESUS' suffering, death, and resurrection. The sacramental background of the cultic meal E. specified as a "syncretistic oriental Gnosticism" (see GNOSTIC INTERPRETATION).

Works: *Athanasii de vita ascetica testimonia collecta* (1886); "Die Rechtfertigungslehre der Apologie," *TSK* 60 (1887) 415-

91; *Das Abendmahl im Neuen Testament* (Hefte zur Christlichen Welt 36, 1898); "Aphorismen zur Dogmengeschichte," *ZTK* 18 (1st ser., 1909) 154-56.

Bibliography: E. Barnikol, "A. E. (1856–1926): Sein 'Lebenslauf,' seine Thesen 1886, seine Abendmahlsthese 1898, und seine Leidensbriefe an seinen Schüler E. Franz (1913–19) nebst seinen Bekenntnissen über Heilige Geschichte und Evangelium, über Orthodoxie und Liberalismus," *Wissenschaftliche Zeitschrift der Martin-Luther Universität Halle-Wittenberg* (Ges.-Sprachw. 9, 1960) 141-52. H. Gressmann, *A. E. und die Religionsgeschichtliche Schule* (1914). W. Klatt, "Ein Brief von H. Gunkel über A. E. an H. Gressmann," *ZTK* 66 (1969) 1-6. G. Lüdemann, "Die Religionsgeschichtliche Schule," *Theologie in Göttingen: Eine Vorlesungsreihe* (ed. B. Moeller, 1987). G. Lüdemann and M. Schröder, *Die Religionsgeschichtliche Schule in Göttingen: Eine Dokumentation* (1987). J. C. O'Neill, *The Bible's Authority* (1991) 78-94. H. Renz and F. W. Graf, *Troeltsch Studien: Untersuchungen zur Biographie und Werkgeschichte* (1982). H. Rollmann, "Theologie und Religionsgeschichte: Zeitgenössische Stimmen zur Diskussion um die religionsgeschichtliche Methode und die Einführung religionsgeschichtlicher Lehrstühle in den theologischen Fakultäten um die Jahrhundertwende," *ZTK* 80 (1983) 69-84. E. Troeltsch, "Die 'Kleine Göttinger Fakultät' von 1890," *Die Christliche Welt* 34 (1920) 281-83.

H. ROLLMANN

EICHRODT, WALTHER (1890–1978)

Born Aug. 1, 1890, in Gernsbach, Baden, E. studied in Bethel, Greifswald, and Heidelberg, completing his first dissertation in 1914 under Beer on the source problems of Genesis. He continued his study at Erlangen as *Repetent* and then *Privatdozent* from 1915 to 1922 and finished his second dissertation under O. PROCKSCH in 1918 on the subject of the hope of eternal peace. He was called to Basel in 1922, becoming full professor in 1934 with responsibilities for OT and history of religions. He served as rector of the university in 1953, retiring in 1961. He died May 20, 1978.

Although E.'s major scholarly contribution lay in his multivolume OT THEOLOGY, he produced a variety of commentaries and smaller works. Especially influential in the English-speaking world has been the translation of his Ezekiel commentary and the book *Man in the OT.* His monumental theology began to appear in 1933, preceded in 1929 by a programmatic essay. He envisioned his new approach as a means of overcoming the impasse into which the discipline had entered. On one hand, he rejected the proof-texting method of traditional orthodoxy. On the other hand, he opposed the historicist approach, which turned the theological content of the OT into a history of religion. Because E. defined the real content of the OT as the eruption of the kingship of God into the world, his major concern was to develop a method that would do justice to this history of revelation while avoiding the methodological pitfalls of the right and the left.

Toward this end E. set forth his cross-sectional method, by which he sought to combine historical and systematic principles in order to obtain a comprehensive picture of OT belief. By tracing the historical development through its changing conditions, he sought to describe an organic structural unity in its growth. By taking a cross-sectional slice of OT thought, he tried to uncover the peculiar dynamics of Israel's religious life through systematic examination with objective classification and rational arrangement.

E. envisioned OT theology as a historical discipline that, if rid of the narrowness of scientific historicism, could demonstrate the uniqueness of Israel's life. His attempt to establish a close coherence between Israel's expression of faith and the facts of Israelite history was later to distinguish his OT theology sharply from that of G. von RAD. E. offered two further controls by which to gain a clear profile of Israel's faith. First, he set each topic within a broad context of the history of religion, describing in detail the continuity and discontinuity. Second, he sought to show an essential coherence with the NT in terms of structural unity. Generally, this later move has been regarded as less successful than the former and as sporadic in execution.

Another essential feature of E.'s OT theology was the pronounced emphasis on covenant. Particularly in vol. 1, covenant provided the category under which he organized all of his material. Because of much criticism and misunderstanding, E. was continually forced to defend his use of covenant (see the preface to the 5th ed.). He argued that the term was a convenient symbol to describe a living process controlling the formation of the national faith at its deepest level and not just a particular tradition or motif. Nevertheless, many critics have continued to feel that he was not consistent in his application of the term. It seemed to work far better as an organizing principle when related to law, cult, and leadership than to cosmology, wisdom, and morality.

E. structured his theology into three major parts: God and People, God and World, God and Man. In the first part he set forth the paradigm of Yahweh's entering into a historic relationship with the covenant people by manifesting God's nature and will. E. outlined the history of Israel as a struggle to realize the full implications of the covenant as it continued to shape and transform Israel's understanding of its institutions in the light of the divine will. Particularly impressive was his attempt to show how threats to the cult from inherited elements of Canaanite MYTHOLOGY were held in check and slowly rendered inoperative. His chapter on the priesthood was also a major attempt to give a positive interpretation to the office rather than seeing it as a foil to prophetism (see PROPHECY AND PROPHETS, HB). In the second part E. offered a detailed treatment of cosmology, anthropology, and providence. In the third part he addressed the subject of ethics and the nature of sin and forgiveness. E.'s talent in systematizing this disparate material remains impressive, but his categories often appear more closely linked to post-Kantian philosophy (see I. KANT) than to uniquely biblical concepts of covenant.

The lasting contribution of E.'s theology derives from several factors. First, he succeeded brilliantly in establishing the legitimacy of the discipline of OT theology after it had been shattered by nineteenth-century historical criticism. Second, he made good use of the tools of LITERARY-critical research to reconstruct Israel's world of faith, which had its own integrity and uniqueness even when fully anchored in ancient Near Eastern culture. Third, he wrestled with the problems of theological unity and coherence within a faith that had undergone great change and development.

Criticism of E.'s theology has arisen from various quarters on several persistent issues. Some scholars questioned whether it was any longer possible to defend the close coherence of faith and history in light of modern tradition-historical research (see TRADITION HISTORY) like that of A. ALT and M. NOTH. Others contested the highly systematic form of E.'s theology as a form of philosophical abstraction, distant from Israel's actual traditions. Finally, criticism fell on his tendency to deprecate the postexilic period as one largely of decay and to trace a historical line of development of Israel's faith so that it naturally unfolded into Christianity.

Works: *Die Quellen der Genesis von neuem untersucht* (BZAW 31, 1916); *Die Hoffnung des ewigen Friedens im Alten Israel* (BFCT 25, 3, 1920); "Hat die alttestamentliche Theologie noch selbständige Bedeutung innerhalb der alttestamentlichen Wissenschaft?" *ZAW* 47 (1929) 83-91; *Theologie des Alten Testament* (3 vols., 1933–39; ET 1961–67); *Das Menschenverständnis des Alten Testaments* (1944; ET, *Man in the OT* [SBT 4, 1951]); "Religionsgeschichte Israels," *Historia Mundi* 2 (1953) 377-448; *Der Prophet Hesekiel: Kap. 1–18* (ATD 22, 1, 1959); *Der Heilige in Israel: Jesaja 1–12* (BAT 17, 1, 1960); *Der Prophet Hesekiel: Kap. 19–48* (ATD 22, 2, 1966; ET, *Ezekiel: A Commentary* [1970]); *Der Herr der Geschichte: Jesaja 13–23 und 28–39* (BAT 17, 2, 1967).

Bibliography: **F. Baumgärtel,** *Verheissung* (1952) 95-102. **F. F. Bruce,** "The Theology and Interpretation of the OT," *Tradition and Interpretation* (ed. G. W. Anderson, 1979) 385-416. **N. K. Gottwald,** "W. E.: Theology of the OT," *Contemporary OT Theologians* (ed. R. B. Laurin, 1970) 25-62. **E. A. Martens,** *HHMBI,* 482-87. **N. W. Porteous,** "OT Theology," *The OT and Modern Study* (ed. H. H. Rowley, 1951) 311-45. **M. Saebø,** *TRE* 9 (1982) 371-73. **D. G. Spriggs,** *Two OT Theologies: A Comparative Evaluation of the Contributions of Eichrodt and von Rad to Our Understanding of the Nature of OT Theology* (SBT II, 30, 1974). **W. Zimmerli,** "Biblische Theologie I," *TRE* 6 (1980) 426-55.

B. S. CHILDS

EISSFELDT, OTTO WILHELM HERMANN LEOPOLD (1887–1973)

Born in Nordheim, Hanover, Sept. 1, 1887, E. began his study of theology at Göttingen in 1905, enrolled in Berlin in 1906, and then returned to Göttingen the following year. Among his teachers in Göttingen were R. SMEND and J. WELLHAUSEN in OT, E. SCHÜRER, W. HEITMÜLLER, and the historian of religions W. BOUSSET in NT. In Berlin E. studied OT under W. BAUDISSIN, NT under H. von Soden (1881–1945), ASSYRIOLOGY under Friedrich DELITZSCH and H. WINCKLER, and classical philology under U. von Wilamowitz-Möllendorf (1848–1931). He also crossed paths with H. GUNKEL for the first time and was personally influenced by the Semiticist E. Littmann (1865–1958).

An academic career was first opened to him in the student quarters, the "Johanneum" in Berlin, where after the completion of his exams the office of *Inspektorat* offered him the opportunity to develop his academic interests and collect his first experiences in university teaching. He received his lic. theol. in 1911 and wrote his habilitation in 1913 (*Der maschal im Alten Testament* [BZAW 24, 1913]). Afterward, he served as *Privatdozent* until 1918, when he became a titular professor at the University of Berlin. At the same time he served as associate pastor at the early service of the Jerusalem and New Churches in Berlin and completed his PhD in Göttingen in 1916 ("Erstlinge und Zehnte im Alten Testament: Ein Beitrag zur Geschichte des altisraelitischen Kultes").

E. published his *Hexateuch-Synopse* in 1922; it still serves as a standard work on the subject. In the same year he was offered the position of professor *ordinarius* for OT and the history of Semitic religion on the faculty of theology at the University of Halle, where he remained until his retirement. In 1929 and 1946 he was elected *Rector magnificus der Alma mater hallensis*. He died Apr. 23, 1973, in Halle.

During his time at Halle E. experienced many fruitful years of achievement. The first edition of his OT introduction appeared in 1934 (768 pp.), to be followed by two major revisions (1956, 970 pp.; 1964, 1,145 pp.), an unchanged edition (1976), and English (1965) and Italian (1970) translations. His introduction presents a conclusive and comprehensive treatment of the results and methods of LITERARY-critical research, without at the same time neglecting either the genre- or the form-critical school of H. Gunkel (see FORM CRITICISM), or the TRADITION-historical school of A. ALT, G. von RAD, M. NOTH, and others. The continuously increasing number of pages in his introduction give clear indication of the massive amounts of old and new material taken up and worked into the successive editions of the work. The section on "additional literature and notes" in the third edition (1964; ET [1965] 722-85) prove that E.'s pursuit of his subject matter continued unabated. He may be viewed, in fact, as the last great representative of the classical literary-critical school.

At approximately the midpoint of E.'s life (1929–30), a heretofore unknown variety of cuneiform emerged from the excavations of tablets at Ras Shamra: UGARIT, which presented a new task for Semitic studies. Through his friendship with the Halle Semiticist H. Bauer (d. 1937), who had deciphered the new script independently of E. DHORME in Paris, E. was from the first drawn into the research and interpretation of these tablets because he had already shown himself to be an outstanding scholar of Near Eastern religions, and these texts were essentially religious in their content. He enriched this study through a wealth of monographs, essays, and LEXICON articles. His suggestions for ordering the tablets in "Bestand und Benennung der Ras-Schamra Texte" (*ZDMG* 96 [1942] 505-39 = *KS* 2 [1963] 330-55) received wide attention. His contributions also influenced research and interpretation of the DEAD SEA SCROLLS from Qumran (first discovered in 1947).

Through his cooperation with other scholars E. also demonstrated competence as both an organizer of academic study and a major authority on Near Eastern religions. E.'s time in Halle saw him serving as editor or co-editor of various publications, including Baudissin's *Kyrios als Gottesname im Judentum und seine Stellung in der Religionsgeschichte* (6 vols., 1929; 3rd rev. ed from 1937); *Theologische Studien und Kritiken* (1934/35–47); the commentary series *Handbuch zum Alten Testament* (1934–68); *Alter Orient* (1936–45); *Biblica Hebraica Kittel* (after R. Kittel's death in 1929, 1937[4], 1951, 1952–66[8-14]); *Hallische Monographien* (1948–51); P. Thomsen, *Die Palästina-Literatur* (1960–72); *Zeitschrift für die alttestamentliche Wissenschaft* (1948–65); *Orientalische Literaturzeitung* (1953–61); and J. Aistleitner, *Wörterbuch der ugaritischen Sprache* (1963, 1965[2], 1974[3], 1976[4]). His last contributions appeared in the year of his death (see *KS* 6:1-14).

Works: *Kleine Schriften* (ed. R. Sellheim and F. Maass, 6 vols., 1962–73).

Bibliography: R. Smend, *Understanding Poets and Prophets: Essays in Honour of G. W. Anderson* (JSOTSup 152, ed. A. G. Auld, 1993) 318-35.

G. WALLIS

ELECTRONIC HERMENEUTICS

Despite the enormous variety of approaches within biblical studies, almost all work, critical and uncritical, has been grounded in tacit suppositions about text and interpretation that have been second nature in the culture of print. However, at the end of the twentieth century the culture of print is rapidly changing as innovations in digital technology merge with other electronic technologies and enter the cultural mainstream. "Electronic hermeneutics" refers to a stance toward interpretative issues that is specially attuned to this emerging sea change. It studies the manner in which earlier cultural understandings of text and meaning are now rapidly being transformed by increasing reliance on the computer as a vehicle for creating, manipulating, disseminating, and preserving cultural lore. Electronic HERMENEUTICS is thus an emerging perspective concerned with basic issues central to the cultural appropriation of a sacred text like the Bible in a digital media environment. It includes (but is not limited to) study of such matters as how to transmediate a heretofore printed sacred text in the emerging media environment and how persons socialized by digital media will likely respond to both printed and digital sacred texts.

Electronic hermeneutics attends to ways in which increasing reliance on digital communication tools is reshaping cultures of the late twentieth century. It recognizes the epistemological naiveté that the long era of print has induced and hopes to chart the changing epistemic assumptions and orientations of persons shaped by digital media. In religious studies, theology, and biblical studies, electronic hermeneutics aims to apply a deeper understanding of the interpretative dynamics of digital culture to all issues relevant to appreciating special cultural artifacts like the Bible.

It was only in the early 1980s that personal computers became affordable tools useful for writing and for data manipulation; a few years later networking and more sophisticated hardware and software became commonplace. In the 1990s new digital phenomena like the World Wide Web emerged. The culture of the late twentieth century saw an epochal shift in communications technology comparable to what European culture experienced with the development of the printing press in the middle of the fifteenth century. Important earlier communications technologies, including print and electronic broadcast media, are now supplemented by and linked to digital technology. As a result, the proliferation of communication artifacts in contemporary culture is staggering. The rising culture is a networked domain in which media are often integrated and interactive. Although not everyone is fully affected by all aspects of these changes, it is clear that the mental habits of the increasing numbers of people using digital tools differ decisively from those of even the late book culture of mid century.

Computers are tools that can be linked together (or networked at the local or global level) and that capitalize on the large, efficient storage and quick random access of the electronic medium. Information nodes can be associated or linked by the user (hypertext or hypermedia); thus the user is able to jump almost instantaneously from one chosen locus for making meaning to another.

The digital environment is self-consciously interactive in ways that a print environment is not. Since anything digitized (e.g., image, alphabetic symbols, and sound) can be rapidly brought together (integrated), the digital communication world is increasingly a multimedia environment. Practical experience with digital tools challenges many of the presuppositions that are foundational in a world of printed books. Electronic text is not only multisensate, it is almost infinitely malleable. It always offers new permutations, and to different readers/users it can offer different possibilities. Not only habits of thought about text but also those about authors and authority shift in digital media. It is not so simple in a digital environment to determine what it means to be an author; collaboration and the recycling and reconstitution of digital artifacts are more basic functions with digital tools than with industrial print. In the communicative excess of this milieu, authority (i.e., when a text is regarded as offering the definitive case), too, becomes more diversified and diffuse.

It is worth noting that the digital technologies available in high technology societies change rapidly. Most of the preceding discussion has focused on hypertextual and hypermedia applications, but certainly the type of simulations commonly dubbed "virtual reality" are digital technologies that promise to be more disjunctive with the world of printed texts than are current hypertext/hypermedia applications. It seems likely that the improvement and increased prominence of virtual reality technologies will force digital culture thoroughly to rethink basic philosophical ideas about signs and their role in the cosmos. Electronic hermeneutics at its broadest thus becomes SEMIOTICS.

Within biblical studies, or even in the broader domains of religious and theological studies, little attention has, until very recently, been devoted to the significance of the cultural shift toward digital technology. Now a few scholars have begun to question how this technology reshapes consciousness and how approaches to sacred texts may reflect new attitudes (see T. Boomershine [1993]; P. Mullins [1990, 1996a, 1996b, 1997]; R. Fowler [1993]). Clearly, the endeavors of electronic hermeneutics are at an early stage.

As digital tools developed, textual scholars were among the first to make practical use of them. In the 1980s the uses of computer technology were discussed and demonstrated at American Academy of Religion/SOCIETY OF BIBLICAL LITERATURE annual meetings and a column "Offline" was added to *Religious Studies News* (published by AAR/SBL). However, most of the early interest expressed through these professional venues was intensely practical and even anti-theoretical. More recent columns (now online at http://scholar.cc.emory.edu/scripts/schol/schol-tools.html), while still practical in orientation, do raise (or review literature that raises) broader questions (see, e.g., "Off-line 47," *RSN* 8, 4 [Nov. 1994] 32-37).

Some of the impetus for thinking carefully about new digital communication tools and their impact on sacred texts and religious sensibility has come from scholarship that has probed issues concerned with earlier epochal shifts in communication technology: from orality to literacy; from manuscript culture to print culture; and from print culture to pre-digital electronic culture. W. Ong's work on orality and literacy as well as the cultural impact of the press (1971, 1977, and 1982) has already been important for scholars in biblical and religious studies (e.g., W. Kelber [1983] and J. Dewey [1995]) as well as for those in many other fields. Ong does not really explore the dynamics of digital culture, but his approach is suggestive. He makes good use of other important scholarly work (e.g., E. Havelock [1963] and A. Lord [1960]) in showing how writing reshapes human consciousness; he also helpfully unpacks and synthesizes elements of M. McLuhan (1962, 1964). Other scholars who have chronicled the shift to print and have studied literacy (e.g., E. Eisenstein [1979]; I. Illich [1993]; J. Goody [1968, 1987]; H. Graff [1987]; B. Stock [1990]) have helped to contextualize interpretative studies.

Within the broader field of religious studies, the comparative studies of sacred text promoted by W. C. Smith (1993), his students, and a few others (e.g., W. Graham [1987]; M. Levering [1989]; F. Denny and R. Taylor [1985]) are an interesting attempt to absorb broader scholarship on orality and literacy into historical and comparative religious studies. Most biblical scholars have not paid much attention to such work or even to earlier criticisms of biblical studies as not being truly historical (Smith [1971]). Although they have not yet considered the shift to digital culture, these comparative studies situate sacred texts in changing historical communities and recognize the ways in which changing technologies, especially communication technologies, affect belief and practice.

Since the mid-1980s literary scholars and theoreticians have devoted more attention than scholars in other fields to the shift to digital culture. Discussion about the dynamics of electronic reading and writing emerged as computers came to be used to teach writing in colleges and as electronic discussion groups made regular exchange possible; a few philosophers (e.g., M. Heim [1987]) also probed such phenomena as electronic writing. In the late 1980s and early 1990s, partly in conjunction with technical scholarship in computer science and technical developments generally, interest shifted to hypertext and ultimately hypermedia. J. Bolter (1991), G. Landow (1992), R. Lanham (1993), M. Tuman (1992b, 1996), and others (see also separate essays in collections by Landow [1994]; P. Delany and Landow [1991]; Tuman [1992a]; and C. Ess [1996]) examined the ways in which networking and the interactivity of digital media were recasting many of print culture's associations for text and textual meaning. Some scholars (Landow [1992]; Bolter [1991]; S. Gaggi [1997]) have also begun to explore the connection between deconstruction as a current literary and philosophical perspective and the change in communication technology. Some semioticians, cultural critics (see CULTURAL STUDIES), and philosophers of technology have begun to study the future of the book (G. Nunberg [1996]) and to consider the impact of such new digital technology as virtual reality (M. Heim [1993]). In the mid-1990s, as the World Wide Web became a widely accessible network of staggering scope, discussion about the dynamics of digital culture has expanded; much of this exploration now occurs in the fledgling institutions (e.g., electronic journals) emerging in digital culture, institutions that are sometimes as volatile as the electronic culture they analyze.

Bibliography: **J. D. Bolter,** *Writing Space: The Computer, Hypertext, and the History of Writing* (1991). **T. E. Boomershine,** "Biblical Megatrends: Towards a Paradigm for the Interpretation of the Bible in Electronic Media," *The Bible in the Twenty-first Century* (ed. H. C. Kee, 1993) 209-30. **P. Delany and G. Landow** (eds.), *Hypermedia and Literary Studies* (1991). **F. M. Denny and R. L. Taylor** (eds.), *The Holy Book in Comparative Perspective* (1985). **J. Dewey** (ed.), *Semeia* 65: *Orality and Textuality in Early Christian Literature* (1995). **E. Eisenstein,** *The Printing Press as an Agent of Change: Communications and Cultural Transformations in Early-Modern Europe* (1979). **C. Ess** (ed.), *Philosophical Perspectives in Computer-mediated Communication* (1996). **R. M. Fowler,** "The Fate of the Notion of Canon in the Electronic Age," *Foundations and Facets Forum,* 9:1-2, 151-72. **S. Gaggi,** *From Text to Hypertext: Decentering the Subject in Fiction, Film, the Visual Arts, and Electronic Media* (1997). **J. Goody** (ed.), *Literacy in Traditional Societies* (1968); *The Interface Between the Written and the Oral* (1987). **H. J Graff,** *The Legacies of Literacy: Continuities and Contradictions in Western Culture and Society (1987).* **W. A. Graham,** *Beyond the Written Word: Oral Aspects of Scripture in the History of Religion* (1987). **E. Havelock,** *Preface to Plato* (1963); *The Muse Learns to Write* (1986). **M. Heim,** *Electric Language: A Philosophical Study of Word Processing* (1987); *The Metaphysics of Virtual Reality* (1993). **I. Illich,** *In the Vineyard of the Text: A Commentary to Hugh's "Didascalicon"* (1993). **W. Kelber,** *The Oral and the Written Gospel: The Hermeneutics of Speaking and Writing in the Synoptic Tradition* (1983). **G. Landow,** *Hypertext: The Convergence of Contemporary Critical Theory and Technology* (1992). **R. A. Lanham,** *The Electonic Word: Democracy, Technology, and the Arts* (1993). **M. Levering** (ed.) *Rethinking Scripture: Essays from a Comparative Perspective* (1989). **A. Lord,** *The Singer of Tales* (1960). **M. McLuhan,** *The Gutenberg Galaxy: The Making of Typographic Man* (1962); *Understanding Media: The Extensions of Man* (1964). **P. Mullins,** "Sacred Text in an Electronic Era," *BTB* 20, 3 (1990) 99-106; "Imagining the Bible in Electronic Culture," *Religion and*

Education 23, 1 (1996a) 38-45; "Sacred Text in the Sea of Texts: The Bible in North American Electronic Culture," *Philosophical Perspectives in Computer-Mediated Communication* (ed. C. Ess 1996b) 271-302; "Media Ecology and the New Literacy: Notes on an Electronic Hermeneutic," *From One Medium to Another: Basic Issues for Communicating the Bible in New Media* (ed. R. Hodgson and P. A. Soukup, 1997) 301-36. **G. Nunberg** (ed.), *The Future of the Book* (1996). **W. J. Ong**, *Rhetoric, Romance, and Technology: Studies in the Interaction of Expression and Culture* (1971); *Interfaces of the Word: Studies in the Evolution of Consciousness and Culture* (1977); *Orality and Literacy: The Technologizing of the Word* (New Accents, 1982). **W. C. Smith**, "The Study of Relgion and the Study of the Bible," *JAAR* 39 (1971) 131-40; *What Is Scripture? A Comparative Approach* (1993). **B. Stock**, *Listening for the Text: On the Uses of the Past* ((1990). **M. Tuman** (ed.), *Literacy Online: The Promise and Peril of Reading and Writing with Computers* (1992a). **M. Tuman**, *Word Perfect: Literacy in the Computer Age* (1992b); "Literacy Online," *Annual Review of Applied Linguistics* 16 (1996) 26-45.

P. MULLINS

ELIEZER OF BEAUGENCY (12th cent.)

E. was born in northern France during the last half of the twelfth century. References suggest that he wrote commentaries on the entire HB, but only those on Isaiah, Ezekiel, the twelve prophets (see PROPHECY AND PROPHETS, HB), and selections on Job have been preserved. His writings indicate contact with the major scholars of the northern French school of biblical commentators: Solomon ben Isaac of Troyes (see RASHI), J. KARA, Joseph of Orléans, and SAMUEL BEN MEIR (RASHBAM). Some scholars believe that E. was a student of Rashbam, but this has not been established conclusively. E. was far more independent of the classical rabbinic writings of TALMUD and MIDRASH than were his contemporaries. With the exception of a few quotations from Menahem Ibn Saruq and Dunash ibn Labrat, there is little focus on the morphological dimensions of Hebrew grammar in his writings. The commentaries provide evidence of extensive glosses of Old French on the HB and indicate knowledge of the VULGATE and some of the classical christological interpretations of the HB. Like his contemporaries Samuel ben Meir and Joseph of Orléans, he offered refutations of these interpretations.

E.'s commentaries systematically attempt to develop a set of generalized rules for the interpretation of the HB. This approach forced him to concentrate on the meaning of difficult biblical words or passages within their own context. For example, he acknowledges that the word *hasmal* in Ezek 1:4 cannot be fully explained because "we are not thoroughly conversant with the language of the Bible in a majority of cases, and we can have only a general notion." E.'s commentaries focus on the historical events alluded to by the prophets and usually attempt to set them within the lifetime of the prophet.

Works: *Isaiah* (ed. J. Nutt, 1879); *Ezekiel and Twelve Prophets* (ed. S. Poznanski, 1909–13); *Hosea* (ed. S. Poznanski, (1902); *Job* (selections), *Mavo leFerush Yehezkiel uTre ʾAsar* (ed. S. Poznanski, 1913) 219-25.

Bibliography: **R. A. Harris**, "The Literary Hermeneutic of R. Eliezer of Beaugency" (diss., Jewish Theological Seminary, 1997). **S. Poznanski**, *Mavo leFerush Yehezkiel uTre ʾAsar* (1913) cxxv-clxvi.

M. A. SIGNER

ELIJAH BEN SOLOMON ZALMAN OF VILNA (1720–97)

A Jewish scholar known acronymically as Hagraʾ (Ha-Gaʾon Rabbi ʾEliyyahu), and popularly as "the Vilna Gaon," E. was born into a family distinguished for rabbinic scholarship in Selets (Grodno) and was an infant prodigy. Although he never occupied an official position, the honorific title *Gaʾon* (Pride, i.e., Eminence), disused rabbinically since the eleventh century, testifies to his reputation for intellectual power and leadership. After a period of traveling he settled in Vilna, where his acumen, intellectual energy, spiritual stature, asceticism, and modesty secured him (from private and communal funds) a livelihood, leaving him free for study. His linguistic range comprised only Hebrew and Aramaic, Judeo-German (and presumably some Russian), but he taught himself geography, mathematics, and astronomy. He annotated rabbinic texts marginally for personal use and taught select disciples; nothing he wrote was published before his death. Opposed—despite his interest in Hebrew grammar—to contemporary Jewish enlightenment (*Haskalah*) and—despite his interest in the *Zohar* and Kabbalism (see KABBALAH)—to revivalism (HASIDISM), E.'s intellectual universe remained Talmudic scholasticism (see TALMUD). Mentioning the rainbow, for example, he criticized (without naming) A. IBN EZRA and NACHMANIDES for adopting its physical explanation through the refraction of light. His biblical commentaries evince powerful logical construction; he also discovered parallels both textual and conceptual on which he based exegesis that sometimes transcended his talmudic and medieval sources. Thus he found that Job's reference in 3:14-19 embraced all classes comprised by (degenerate) humanity—government (king, counselors), judiciary, proletariat (working class, social parasites, the oppressed), etc. Prompted by the *Zohar*, he found in Jonah an allegory for the soul: The ship signifies embodiment; Nineveh, the world; Tarshish, its material blandishments; the fish, death; Jonah's second call, reincarnation. The spared inhabitants of Nineveh are penitent Israel; the cattle (4:11), remaining humanity.

Works: ʾAddereth ʾEliyyahu (1804), on Pentateuch; *Proverbs* (1814); *Job* (1874); *Esther* (1876); *Habbakuk* (1898); *Miqraʾth Gedoloth* (1860), remainder (parts only).

Bibliography: **H. H. Ben-Sasson,** *Zion* 31 (1966) 39-86, 197-216 (Hebrew). **M. Z. Kaddari,** *EncJud* 6 (1971) 651-58. **B. Landau,** *Ha-gaʾon he-ḥasid mi-Wilna* (1965).

R. LOEWE

ELLIGER, KARL (1901–77)

Born in Rüstringhausen-Welhelmshaven, March 7, 1901, E. died in Tübingen, Oct. 31, 1977. In spite of his wide range of interests in the history, geography, and ARCHAE-OLOGY of ancient Palestine as well as in philology and TEXTUAL CRITICISM from the Amarna tablets to the Qumran scrolls (see DEAD SEA SCROLLS), E. maintained throughout a central focus and interest in the exegesis of the OT and its theological significance (see THEOLOGY, OT). In his early education in Münster he concentrated on the book of Isaiah both in his licentiate (1927) and in his habilitation (1929); both dissertations were published (1928, 1933). He worked as a religion teacher until he moved to Leipzig in 1934 as *Dozent* and assistant to A. ALT. The following year he took a temporary post at Kiel and in 1937 received a call to teach OT in Tübingen, where he remained, holding the chair in OT from 1948 until his retirement in 1968. His work in Tübingen was interrupted during WWII by military service and imprisonment.

OT scholarship is indebted to him for three major accomplishments: (a) the wide-ranging breadth of his exegetical work, which is particularly rich in his uncompleted commentary on Deutero-Isaiah (1970–78); (b) the creation of the Biblical-Archaeological Institute in 1960, which has unfortunately remained the only institute of its type in Germany; and (c) the editing of the monumental edition of the *BHS* (1977) on which he spent the last twenty-five years of his life.

Works: *Die Einheit des Tritojesaja (Jesaja 56–66)* (BWANT 3, 9, 1928); *Deuterojesaja in seinem Verhältnis zu Tritojesaja* (BWANT 4, 11, 1933); *Das Buch der zwölf Kleinen Propheten,* vol. 2, *Die Propheten Nahum, Habakuk, Zephanja, Haggai, Sachaija, Maleachi* (ATD 25, 1950, 1956³); *Studien zum Habakuk-Kommentar vom Toten Meer* (BHT 15, 1953); *Leviticus* (HAT 1, 4, 1966); *Kleine Schriften zum Alten Testament* (TBü 32, 1966); *Deuterojesja,* vol. 1, *Teilband Jesaja 40, 1-45, 7* (BKAT 11, 1, 1978).

Bibliography: **D. Kellermann,** "Bibliographie K. E. für die Jahr 1966ff.," *Wort und Geschichte: Festschrift für K. E. zum 70. Geburtstage* (AOAT 18, ed. H. Gese and H. P. Rüger, 1973) 209-11. **D. Kellermann and E. Sehmsdorf,** "Bibliographie K. E.," *Kleine Schriften* (K. Elliger, 1966) 260-65. **S. Mittmann,** "K. E. zum Gedächtnis," *ZDPV* 94 (1978) 86-88.

T. L. THOMPSON

ENGNELL, IVAN (1906–64)

E. received his linguistic and theological training under T. Andrae in comparative religion, S. Dedering in Arabic, S. Linder in OT exegesis, H. S. NYBERG in Semitic philology, and G. Widengren in comparative religion and ASSYRIOLOGY, all of Uppsala, where he received the ThD May 31, 1943, for his work on divine kingship. In 1945 he published the first volume of his tradition-historical introduction to the OT (in Swedish); volume 2 was never published. He established a theological institute in Stockholm in 1958. His *magnum opus* was the *Svenskt Bibliskt Uppslagsverk,* to which he contributed numerous articles (see *Studies in Divine Kingship* [1943, 1967²] 255-61). He died Jan. 10, 1964.

E.'s major contribution to HB studies was his TRADI-TION-historical method. First the biblical literature is analyzed to determine various forms of tradition (collections, complexes, and individual units) lying behind the final form of biblical books. This study focuses on oral tradition, which, after being developed and modified, attained fixed form in circles or schools of traditionists who preserved it long before it was written down. Comparison with similar ancient Near Eastern literature will help to reconstruct the form and status of this material, but Israel's own contribution to and modification of inherited traditions must be considered, and thus there can never be certainty about the content of these traditions during the fluid stage of transmission. The second and related task is to interpret the smaller units within their larger contexts.

E. based his method on his conclusion that the texts of HB books reached their final form during the oral stage. The circles or schools that preserved them functioned primarily in the cult and viewed themselves as custodians of sacred traditions. Thus they held a conservative attitude toward these traditions, which suggests that they preserved them fundamentally intact so that they are authentic and reliable. These traditions were written down late (in the exilic and postexilic periods), when confidence in the spoken word waned; but the oral traditionists did their work so well that it is virtually impossible to determine what is primary and what is secondary and to recover a speaker's *ipsissima verba.* Accordingly, the TEXTUAL critic attempts to recover the final form of the biblical text.

E. rejected the Wellhausenian reconstruction (see J. WELLHAUSEN) of Israelite religion from a lower to a higher plane. Using the tradition-historical method, he proposed his own view of the development of Israelite religion, which falls into four stages: (1) There was a pre-Israelite tribal desert religion built around the worship of a sky god or high god named El or El-shadday. (2) Moses had a personal encounter with this El of the fathers, a giver of fertility and an ethical god who "activated" him under the name of Yahweh, bound him to a tribal amphictyony, and organized a sophisticated cult. (3) Mosaic religion came into contact with Canaanite religion, and Yahweh became a national deity, assuming the characteristics of the Canaanite high god, El Elyon. Israel adopted the ideas and forms of Canaanite sacral kingship, so that the king became the focal point of the cult, with his most important role occurring in the annual festival. As "the servant of the Lord," he fought the powers of evil in a cultic sham battle, suffered and died at their hands, and descended into Sheol to expiate the sins of the people. Later, as "savior" and "messiah," he rose from the dead, defeated Israel's enemies, took the throne, experienced a sacral marriage, and created fertility for the future. (4) With the classical prophets (see PROPHECY AND PROPHETS, HB), eschatological messianism replaced royal messianism. Accordingly, messianism is the theme that holds the HB together.

E.'s dynamic personality, impassioned rhetorical style, and radical position brought sharp opposition. S. MOWINCKEL argued that if the stages of a tradition could not be reconstructed, the approach could hardly be called "history of tradition." Mowinckel was much more optimistic about the possibility of recovering these stages than was E. G. Widengren challenged E.'s insistence on oral transmission as the primary means of preserving traditions in the early period of Israel's history. Evidence from the ancient Near East and the HB indicates that prophetic oracles, historical narratives, etc. were written down quite early. C. NORTH observed that if HB traditions reached a fixed form in the oral tradition stage, then the LITERARY source-critical method could be applied to them as readily as to written sources. Although many scholars have severely criticized his ideas, E.'s works are still significant in HB research.

Works: *Studies in Divine Kingship in the Ancient Near East* (1943, 1967²); *Gamla Testamentet: En traditionshistorisk inledning* 1 (1945); (ed. and major contributor), *Svenskt Bibliskt Uppslagsverk* (1948, 1962–63²); *The Call of Isaiah: An Exegetical and Comparative Study* (UUÅ, 1949); "Methodological Aspects of OT Study," *VTSup* 7 (1960) 13-30; *Critical Essays on the OT* (ET, *A Rigid Scrutiny* [1969]).

Bibliography: D. A. Knight, "I. E.: The Center of the Debate," *Rediscovering the Traditions of Israel* (SBLDS 9, 1973) 260-95. **H. Ringgren,** "Mowinckel and the Uppsala School," *SJOT* 2 (1988) 36-41. **H. S. Nyberg,** "Die schwedischen Beiträge zur alttestamentlichen Forschung in diesem Jahrhundert," VTSup 22 (1972) 1-10. **J. T. Willis,** "I. E.'s Contributions to OT Scholarship," *TZ* 26 (1970) 385-94.

J. T. WILLIS

ENOCH, FIRST BOOK OF

Part of the Jewish PSEUDEPIGRAPHA, *1 Enoch,* also called the *Ethiopian Book of Enoch,* is falsely attributed to the Enoch of Gen 5:24. Modern scholarship recog-

nizes *1 Enoch* as an anthology of five separate works: the *Book of the Watchers* (chaps. 1–36), the *Parables* or *Similitudes of Enoch* (chaps. 37–71), the *Astronomical Book* (chaps. 72–82), the *Book of Dreams* (chaps. 83–90), and the *Epistle of Enoch* (chaps. 91–105). It concludes with a short appendix about the birth of Noah (chaps. 106–107) and an exhortation (chap. 108). The *Astronomical Book* and the *Book of the Watchers* date to the third century BCE. The *Book of Dreams* comes from the time of the Maccabean revolt; the *Epistle,* from some time in the second century BCE; and the *Parables,* probably from the first half of the first century CE. Aramaic fragments of all of the major units of *1 Enoch* except the *Parables* were found at Qumran (see DEAD SEA SCROLLS). The Aramaic works were translated into Greek at an early date, although the provenance of the translations is unclear.

This Enochic literature, and especially the *Book of the Watchers*, exercised considerable influence on literature of the late Second Temple period. The later sections of *1 Enoch* involve interpretation and development of themes found in the earlier ones (on the *Book of Dreams* and the *Epistle,* see J. VanderKam [1984] 141-78; G. Nickelsburg [1981a] 190-94, 150-51; on the *Parables,* Nickelsburg [1981a] 214-21). The writer of JUBILEES seems to have known the *Astronomical Book,* the *Book of the Watchers,* and the *Book of Dreams,* and *Jubilees* also reflects traditions about Enoch beyond those found in these works (VanderKam [1984] 179-88). The ascent to heaven in 2 ENOCH reinterprets the *Book of the Watchers'* account of Enoch's ascent (*1 Enoch* 14) and journey to the ends of the earth (*1 Enoch* 17–36) in relation to its schema of seven heavens; other parts of *2 Enoch* appear to be modeled on the *Epistle of Enoch* and the account of Noah's birth (Nickelsburg [1981a] 185-88; M. Himmelfarb [1993] 38-41). While the *Testament of Levi* in its present form is a Christian work, part of the TESTAMENTS OF THE TWELVE PATRIARCHS dating from the second century CE, it is appropriate to consider it with these Jewish pseudepigrapha because it clearly draws on the Aramaic Levi document, which is partially preserved at Qumran and in the Cairo Geniza. The ascent to heaven in the *Testament of Levi* 2–7 reworks the ascent in *1 Enoch* 14 (but not the journey to the ends of the earth) to fit a schema of seven heavens (Nickelsburg [1981c] 588-90; Himmelfarb [1993] 30-33). (For lists of references to Enochic traditions and Enochic books in early Jewish literature, see R. CHARLES [1912] lxx-lxxix, and F. Martin, cvi-cxi. These should be used with caution; Charles especially displayed the parallelomania that was so often a feature of scholarship at the turn of the century.)

There is very little in classical rabbinic literature to suggest knowledge of *1 Enoch* or its traditions; the references to Enoch are few, and some are not altogether positive. The relative silence may be polemical. On the other hand, 3 ENOCH, a *hekhalot* text from perhaps the end of the talmudic period (see TALMUD), makes Enoch the hero of the greatest success story in human history: Upon his ascent to heaven, he is transformed into the angel Metatron, God's vice-regent. Thus *3 Enoch* represents a clear continuation of the traditions about Enoch's ascent found in *1* and *2 Enoch,* although the precise nature of the relationship between *3 Enoch* and these ealier works remains to be clarified (Himmelfarb [1978]).

Christian literature in the first four centuries contains a number of quotations of Enochic texts, often regarded as authoritative. The letter of Jude (vv. 14-15) in the NT, for example, quotes the *Book of the Watchers* (see *1 Enoch* 1:9) as a prophecy of Enoch. Not all of the quotations, however, can be matched to extant Enochic works. In addition to quotations there are many allusions to traditions drawn from the Enochic corpus, particularly the story of the descent of the angels and its aftermath. Among the early Christian authors and works that seem to know parts of *1 Enoch* are the *Epistle of* BARNABAS, JUSTIN MARTYR, IRENAEUS, TERTULLIAN, CLEMENT OF ALEXANDRIA, ORIGEN, Priscillian, AUGUSTINE, and JEROME. (For more inclusive lists, see E. Schürer [1986] 3:1.261-63; and the extensive discussions in H. Lawlor [1897]; VanderKam [1996]; W. Adler [1978]). Enochic literature appears to have been particularly popular among Christians in Egypt, with clear evidence of interest in North Africa and Syria-Palestine as well (Nicklesburg [1990]; VanderKam [1996]).

Despite the existence of some Latin fragments, there is very little evidence that *1 Enoch* as a whole was ever translated into Latin; the Latin authors who quote it may also have known Greek. It does not appear to have had wide circulation in the West, and it certainly did not have a long career there (Lawlor, 223-25). In the Greek-speaking East it lived on in the work of the ninth-century Byzantine chronographer G. Syncellus, who did not know the work directly but rather through excerpts transmitted in compilations of texts relevant to antediluvian history (Adler [1989], esp. Gen 6:1-4). The channels through which the book reached Ethiopia (see ETHIOPIAN BIBLICAL INTERPRETATION) are poorly understood, but the Ethiopic version of the work was so highly valued that it was transmitted with the HB. It is only in Ethiopic translation that the complete contents of the anthology have been preserved.

The West rediscovered *1 Enoch* only in the late eighteenth century, when the English traveler J. Bruce brought back three manuscripts from Ethiopia. The first modern translation was the English version by R. Laurence in 1821. Laurence also edited the first edition, which appeared in 1838.

The newly discovered work provoked considerable discussion, including debate about whether it was Jewish or Christian. The *Parables,* of particular interest because

of its description of a heavenly Son of man, was sometimes considered a separate, Christian source in an otherwise Jewish work. There was, however, no consensus on the number of sources making up the larger work, on their boundaries, or on whether the original language was Hebrew or Aramaic. Dates proposed for various parts of the book ranged from the period of the Maccabean revolt to the second century CE. (For an annotated listing of nineteenth-century work on *1 Enoch,* see Charles [1912] xxx-lviii.)

At the end of the nineteenth century Charles (1893) proposed dividing the book into the five units recognized today. By the beginning of the twentieth century two great critical editions had appeared, one by the German scholar J. Fleming (1902), the other by Charles (1906). Charles's edition has not been fully replaced even today; the only major edition since Charles's, that of M. Knibb (1978), transcribes a single manuscript, although it provides an extensive critical apparatus. M. Black's translation and commentary (1985) is a thorough revision of Charles's 1912 translation; Black's work is the first to take full account of the evidence of the Aramaic fragments from Qumran.

Charles's edition marks the culmination of the pioneering stage of study of *1 Enoch.* Between Charles and the Qumran discoveries Enochic studies slowed down sharply as part of the general decline of interest in the Pseudepigrapha. Nonetheless, a few contributions from that period are particularly worthy of note. G. Dix (1926), drawing on Charles's division of the book into five sections, argued that this structure represented conscious imitation of the Pentateuch (see PENTATEUCHAL CRITICISM). H. Ludin Jansen (1939) related the traditions of *1 Enoch* to ancient Mesopotamian parallels. E. Sjöberg (1946) argued that the Son of man in the *Parables* is to be understood as a heavenly being, active only at the eschaton yet sharing many of the characteristics of the ancient Near Eastern *Urmensch.*

The discovery at Qumran of Aramaic fragments of all of the works contained in *1 Enoch,* except the *Parables,* and their publication by J. Milik (1976) has given a new impetus to Enochic studies. The question of the original language of the works represented in these fragments has been resolved in favor of Aramaic. Moreover, the impact of the fragments on the question of date has been particularly dramatic: The third-century date of the *Astronomical Book* and the third- or early second-century date for the *Book of the Watchers,* determined on the basis of paleography, make them the two earliest apocalypses (see APOCALYPTICISM), earlier than Daniel, which can be dated to 167–164 BCE and had previously been considered the earliest. On the basis of its absence at Qumran, Milik suggested a rather late Christian date for the *Parables.* He also took the presence at Qumran of another Enochic work, the *Book of the Giants* adopted by the Manicheans, as evidence for an Enochic pentateuch; this claim has been disputed (J. Greenfield and M. Stone [1977]; D. Suter [1981]).

The new dates for the *Astronomical Book* and the *Book of the Watchers* have led to a new interest in those aspects of apocalyptic literature more or less ignored in Daniel but so well represented in these earliest Enochic works: astronomical secrets, cosmology, the heavenly throne room, and the seer's journey to view them (M. Stone [1976, 1978]; Nickelsburg [1981c]; Himmelfarb [1993]). This in turn has contributed to interest in the question of the definition of the genre of the apocalypses by making it clear that apocalypses are not defined by apocalyptic eschatology alone (Stone [1976]; J. Collins [1979, 1983]). By placing two apocalypses with comparatively little interest in eschatology at the beginning of the development of the genre, the new dates also have important implications for the origins of apocalyptic literature and the question of the contributions of PROPHECY and wisdom (Stone [1976] 439-44; VanderKam [1984] 52-75). Considerable attention has been focused on the Babylonian connections of the early Enoch traditions (Grelot [1958a, 1958b]; VanderKam [1984]). VanderKam has suggested that mantic wisdom in the form of Mesopotamian divination is an important source for the Enochic traditions and for apocalyptic literature more generally. The relations among the various Enochic works are complex, and the place of the Qumran community in the creation and transmission of this material requires further clarification (Nickelsburg [1983]; Suter [1979]).

Bibliography: **W. Adler,** "Enoch in Early Christian Literature," *SBLSP* (1978) 271-76; *Time Immemorial: Archaic History and Its Sources in Christian Chronography from Julius Africanus to George Syncellus* (1989). **M. Black,** in consultation with J. C. VanderKam, *The Book of Enoch or 1 Enoch: A New English Edition* (1985), appendix by O. Neugebauer. **R. H. Charles,** *The Book of Enoch* (1893); *The Book of Enoch or 1 Enoch* (1912). **J. J. Collins** (ed.), *Apocalypse: The Morphology of a Genre* (Semeia 14, 1979). **J. J. Collins,** *The Apocalyptic Imagination: An Introduction to the Jewish Matrix of Christianity* (1984). **G. H. Dix,** "The Enochic Pentateuch," *JTS* 27 (1926) 29-42. **J. Flemming,** *Das Buch Henoch* (1902). **J. C. Greenfield and M. E. Stone,** "The Enochic Pentateuch and the Date of the Similitudes," *HTR* 70 (1977) 51-65. **P. Grelot,** "La géographie mythique d'Hénoch et ses sources orientales," *RB* 65 (1958a) 33-69; "La légende d'Hénoch dans les apocryphes et dans la Bible," *RSR* 46 (1958b) 181-210. **P. D. Hanson,** "Rebellion in Heaven, Azazel, and Euhemeristic Heroes in Enoch 6–11," *JBL* 96 (1977) 195-233. **M. Himmelfarb,** "A Report on Enoch in Rabbinic Literature," *SBLSP* (1978) 259-70; *Ascent to Heaven in Jewish and Christian Apocalypses* (1993). **H. L. Jansen,** *Die Henochgestalt: Eine vergleichende religionsgeschichtliche Untersuchung* (1939). **M. A. Knibb,** *The Ethiopic Book of Enoch* (1978). **R. Laurence,** *The Book of Enoch the Prophet* (Secret Doctrine Reference Series, 1821); *Libri Enoch Versio Aethiopica* (1838). **H. J. Lawlor,** "Early Citations from the Book of Enoch," *JP* 25 (1897) 164-225. **F. Martin,** *Le livre d'Hénoch* (1906). **J. T. Milik,** *The Books of Enoch* (1976). **G. W. E. Nickelsburg,** "Apocalyptic and Myth in 1 Enoch 6–11," *JBL* 96 (1977) 383-405; *Jewish Literature Between the Bible and the Mishnah* (1981a); "The Books of Enoch in Recent Research," *RStR* 7 (1981b) 210-17; "Enoch, Levi, and Peter: Recipients of Revelation in Upper Galilee," *JBL* 100 (1981c) 575-600; "Social Aspects of Palestinian Jewish Apocalypticism," *Apocalypticism in the Mediterranean World and the Near East* (ed. D. Hellholm, 1983); "Two Enochic Manuscripts: Unstudied Evidence for Egyptian Christianity," *Of Scribes and Scrolls* (ed. H. J. Attridge et al., 1990). **E. Schürer,** *A History of the Jewish People in the Time of Jesus Christ,* vol. 3.1 (rev. and ed. G. Vermes et al., 1986). **E. Sjöberg,** *Der Menschensohn im äthiopischen Henochbuch* (1946). **M. E. Stone,** "Lists of Revealed Things in the Apocalyptic Literature," *Magnalia Dei* (ed. F. M. Cross et al., 1976) 414-52; "The Book of Enoch and Judaism in the Third Century BCE," *CBQ* 40 (1978) 479-92. **D. W. Suter,** "Fallen Angel, Fallen Priest: The Problem of Family Purity in 1 Enoch 6–16," *HUCA* 50 (1979) 115-35; "Weighed in the Balance: The Similitudes of Enoch in Recent Discussion," *RStR* 7 (1981) 217-21. **J. C. VanderKam,** *Enoch and the Growth of an Apocalyptic Tradition* (CBQMS 16, 1984); "1 Enoch, Enochic Motifs, and Enoch in Early Christian Literature," *The Jewish Apocalyptic Heritage in Early Christianity* (CRINT 3.4, ed. J. C. VanderKam and W. Adler, 1996) 32-100.

M. HIMMELFARB

ENOCH, SECOND BOOK OF

Slavonic or *2 Enoch* draws on traditions about the antediluvian patriarch of Gen 5:24 related to those found in sections of *1 Enoch,* recasting them in the light of its own cosmology and ethical concerns (G. Nickelsburg [1981] 185; M. Himmelfarb [1993] 37-41, 83-87). The work first came to the attention of scholars outside Russia at the end of the nineteenth century. The two English editions of R. CHARLES (1896; 1913) distinguish a long form and a short form of the work, offering a single manuscript for each. Both Charles and G. Bonwetsch (1896), the first German translator, considered the short version a condensation of the long, although Charles also argued that the long version contained many interpolations. In Charles's view the author of the work was an Egyptian Jew who wrote in Greek while the Temple was still standing; some parts of the work, however, were originally written in Hebrew. Charles based his claims on parallels to the thought of Jewish writers in Egypt and native Egyptian elements; he dated the work by its reference to animal sacrifice. There are no clear ancient testimonies to the work, and the earliest manuscripts are late medieval. No Greek (or Hebrew) fragments survive.

In 1918 a strong challenge to Charles's views appeared in the unlikely forum of an astronomy journal. A. Maunder (1918) argued that the astronomy and calendrical system of the fourth heaven required a much later date than Charles proposed, the end of the fifth century at the earliest, as well as a Christian author. Taking seriously the absence of any clear traces of the supposed Greek original, she suggested that *2 Enoch* was composed in Slavonic by the dualist Bogomil between the twelfth and the fifteenth centuries. While Charles and later others (e.g., A. Rubinstein [1962]; E. Turdeanu [1981]) argued convincingly against the claim of Bogomil features, Maunder's astronomical arguments were accepted by the historian of ancient astronomy J. Fotheringham and by K. LAKE.

The next era in the study of *2 Enoch* began several decades later with the 1952 French translation of A. Vaillant, who claimed the short version as the translation of the original Greek. (He was anticipated in his preference for the short version by N. Schmidt, who had argued for its priority in 1921, although on quite different grounds.) The long manuscripts form two groups representing different stages of recension, which took place in Slavonic. Vaillant argued that *2 Enoch* was a "Jewish-Christian" work, by which he meant a work written by an early Christian but containing Jewish traditions. The arguments Vaillant offered in favor of this view are not very compelling and were criticized even by Rubinstein, who concurred with the conclusion of Christian authorship. Unlike Charles and Bonwetsch, Vaillant treated the Melchizedek section at the end of *2 Enoch* as an integral part of the work.

All subsequent scholarship on *2 Enoch* has drawn on Vaillant's textual work. In his study of the Aramaic fragments of *1 Enoch* from Qumran, J. Milik (1976) accepts Vaillant's view of the short version as more original but dates *2 Enoch* to the ninth or tenth century on the basis of astronomical considerations and other arguments, which have not been widely accepted.

The two most recent translators of *2 Enoch* differ considerably in their approach to the textual problems. A. Pennington (1984) translates the short version from Vaillant's edition. F. Andersen (1983), on the other hand, argues that the textual situation is so complex that no conclusions are possible at this stage of study. He distinguishes four recensions: very long, long, short, and very short. His translation offers a synoptic presentation of a very long manuscript and a short manuscript. Both manuscripts include a form of the Melchizedek story.

Despite almost a century of scholarship that has called into question many of Charles's basic assumptions, most scholars continue to maintain his view that *2 Enoch* is the work of an Egyptian Jew writing in Greek before the destruction of the Temple. This view may be correct, but it has not been adequately grounded. Progress in the study of the date and provenance of the work is linked to further progress on its central textual problems, but there is reason for optimism: Since the fall of the Soviet Union and the emergence of a new group of scholars of ancient Judaism and Christianity well-versed in Slavonic and familiar with the history of the Russian church, *2 Enoch* may receive the attention it deserves.

Bibliography: **F. I. Andersen,** *"2* (*Slavonic Apocalypse of*) *Enoch,"* *OTP* 1:91-221. **G. N. Bonwetsch,** *Das slavische Henochbuch* (Abhandlungen der königlichen Gesellschaft der Wissenschaften zu Göttingen, Philologisch-historische Klasse, NF 1, 3, 1896); *Die Bücher der Geheimnisse Henochs: Das sogenannte slavische Henochbuch* (*TU* 44.2, 1922). **R. H. Charles,** "The Date and Place of Writing of the *Slavonic Enoch,"* *JTS* 22 (1921) 161-63. **R. H. Charles** (ed.) **and W. R. Morfill** (tr.), *The Book of the Secrets of Enoch* (1896). **R. H. Charles** (ed.) **and N. Forbes** (tr.), *"2 Enoch or the Book of the Secrets of Enoch,"* *APOT* 2:425-69. **U. Fischer,** *Eschatologie und Jenseitserwartung im hellenistischen Diasporajudentum* (BZNW 44, 1978) 37-70. **J. K. Fotheringham,** "The Date and Place of Writing of the Slavonic Enoch," *JTS* 20 (1919) 252; "The Easter Calendar and the Slavonic Enoch," *JTS* 23 (1922) 49-56. **M. Himmelfarb,** *Ascent to Heaven in Jewish and Christian Apocalypses* (1993) 37-41, 83-87. **K. Lake,** "The Date of the Slavonic Enoch," review of *Die Bücher der Geheimnisse Henochs* by G. N. Bonwetsch, *HTR* 16 (1923) 397-98. **A. S. D. Maunder,** "The Date and Place of Writing of the *Slavonic Book of Enoch,"* *The Observatory* 41 (1918) 309-16. **J. T. Milik,** *The Books of Enoch* (1976) 107-16. **G. W. E. Nickelsburg,** *Jewish Literature Between the Bible and the Mishnah* (1981) 185-88. **A. Pennington,** *AOT,* 321-62. **M. Philonenko,** "La cosmogonie du 'Livre des secrets d'Hénoch,' " *Religions en Égypte hellénistique et romaine* (1969) 109-16. **S. Pines,** "Eschatology and the Concept of Time in the *Slavonic Book of Enoch,"* *Types of Redemption* (Numen Sup. 18, ed. R. J. Z. Werblowsky and C. J. Bleeker, 1970) 72-87. **A. Rubinstein,** "Observations on the *Slavonic Book of Enoch,"* *JJS* 13 (1962) 1-21. **N. Schmidt,** "The Two Recensions of *Slavonic Enoch,"* *JAOS* 41 (1921) 307-12. **E. Turdeanu,** *Apocryphes slaves et roumains de l'Ancien Testament* (1981) 37-43, 404-35. **A. Vaillant** (ed. and tr.)**,** *Le livre des secrets d'Hénoch* (Textes publiés par l'Institut d'Études slaves 4, 1952).

M. HIMMELFARB

ENOCH, THIRD BOOK OF

The earliest evidence for interest in *3 Enoch* comes from the twelfth and thirteenth centuries when the German Hasidim studied and copied it along with other *hekhalot* texts. There are extensive quotations from *3 Enoch* in the work of Eleazar of Worms (c. 1165–c. 1230), one of the great exponents of German HASIDISM.

The modern study of *3 Enoch* begins with H. GRAETZ (1859), although Graetz did not know the book itself but only works dependent on it. Graetz understood Enoch/Metatron speculation to be closely linked to the

Shiʿur Qomah literature, descriptions of the size of God's limbs and their names, because of the appearance of Metatron in the *Shiʿur Qomah*. For Graetz the anthropomorphism of the *Shiʿur Qomah* was a "monstrosity" (115). He preferred to see it not as an internal development of rabbinic thought but as the result of the influence of certain strands of Islam (108, 115-18), pointing out that the idea of the transformation of Enoch into Metatron is in conflict with the much more negative view of Enoch in classical rabbinic literature. He saw the positive picture of Enoch as another result of Islamic influence, since Enoch was highly regarded in the Quran (107-8; see QURANIC AND ISLAMIC INTERPRETATION). The influence of Islam, along with the *terminus ante quem* provided by quotations in KARAITE polemical works, led Graetz to a date in the early ninth century for these mystical texts (113).

The first extended treatment of *3 Enoch* itself was H. Odeberg's critical edition and English translation with introduction and notes (1928). It was Odeberg who gave the work the title *3 Enoch;* in the manuscripts it is usually called *Sefer Hekhalot.* In opposition to his predecessors, Odeberg placed the work in the second half of the third century and argued that, while the rabbis would not have looked on the composition with favor, the compilers of the work viewed themselves as rabbinic Jews. Odeberg saw the transformation of Enoch as a development of a theme found in the early Jewish apocalypses (see APOCALYPTICISM) and related the figure of Metatron to apocalyptic and GNOSTIC traditions.

G. Scholem, the great student of Jewish mysticism, was highly critical of Odeberg's choice of manuscript base for his edition but praised Odeberg's rejection of a date in the gaonic period (1929–30, 1930). Scholem dated *3 Enoch* later than did Odeberg, to the fifth or sixth century, since he saw it as one of the latest of the *hekhalot* texts. Although he recognized striking parallels to contemporary Gnostic literature and magical texts for *3 Enoch* as for other *hekhalot* texts, he also saw continuity with early Jewish apocalyptic traditions. Like Odeberg, he understood the transformation of Enoch into Metatron as a development of these traditions. Scholem also insisted on the "halakhic character" of the *hekhalot* literatuare, despite certain conflicts with the outlook of the classical rabbinic works (1954, 1965, 1974).

Perhaps the most thorough examination of *3 Enoch* since Scholem is that of P. Alexander (1977, 1983). Alexander concurs with Scholem on a fifth- or sixth-century date and suggests a Babylonian provenance. In terms not unlike Odeberg's he locates the work on the fringes of rabbinic Judaism.

It has long been noted that because of its use of Enoch traditions *3 Enoch* is closer than the other *hekhalot* texts to the early Jewish apocalypses. Recent work on the *hekhalot* literature has shown that the work is unusual in other respects as well. In his articles (e.g., 1983) and his synoptic edition of the *hekhalot* texts (with M. Schlüter and H. von Mutius, 1981) P. Schäfer has called into question old assumptions about the limits and identity of individual *hekhalot* works by showing the fluidity of the forms they take in the manuscripts. *Third Enoch* stands out as a relatively well-defined redactional entity. Further, Schäfer (1992) and D. Halperin (1988) have challenged Scholem's view that heavenly ascent is the dominant theme of the *hekhalot* literature, emphasizing the central importance of the adjuration of angels for the revelation of magical secrets as well. Almost alone of the *hekhalot* texts, *3 Enoch* fits Scholem's model: It is an account of heavenly ascent, but it lacks adjurations completely (Schäfer [1992] 123-38, 147-48). Schäfer notes, however, that a Geniza fragment contains astrological material (1992, 137-38, 147-48; for the fragment, Schäfer [1984] 137). This fragment, which appears to come from an earlier stage of the text, raises interesting questions about the process by which *3 Enoch* reached its present form in which magical elements are absent. The process of the work's development, its place among the *hekhalot* texts, and its relation to earlier traditions will continue to occupy scholars.

Bibliography: P. Alexander, "The Historical Setting of the Hebrew Book of Enoch," *JJS* 28 (1977) 156-80; "3 (*Hebrew Apocalypse of*) Enoch," *OTP,* 1:223-315. H. Graetz, "Die mystische Literatur in der gaonäishcen Epoche," *MGWJ* 8 (1859) 67-78, 103-18, 140-53. J. Greenfield, "Prolegomenon," *3 Enoch or the Hebrew Book of Enoch* (H. Odeberg, repr. 1973). D. Halperin, *The Faces of the Chariot: Early Jewish Responses to Ezekiel's Vision* (TSAJ 16, 1988). H. Odeberg, *3 Enoch or the Hebrew Book of Enoch* (1928). P. Schäfer, "Tradition and Redaction in Hekhalot Literature," *JSJ* 14 (1983) 172-81; *The Hidden and Manifest God: Some Major Themes in Early Jewish Mysticism* (1992). P. Schäfer (ed.), *Geniza-Fragmente zur Hekhalot-Literatur* (TSAJ 6, 1984). P. Schäfer (ed., in collaboration with M. Schlüter and H. G. von Mutius), *Synopse zur Hekhalot Literatur* (TSAJ 2, 1981). G. Scholem, review of *3 Enoch or the Hebrew Book of Enoch* by H. Odeberg, *Kirjath Sepher* 6 (1929-30) 62-64; review of *3 Enoch or the Hebrew Book of Enoch* by H. Odeberg, *CLZ* 33 (1930) 193-97; *Major Trends in Jewish Mysticism* (1954³); *Jewish Gnosticism, Merkabah Mysticism, and Talmudic Tradition* (1965²); *Kabbalah* (1974).

M. HIMMELFARB

EPHESIANS, LETTER TO THE

1. Early and Medieval. Second-century Gnostics (see GNOSTIC INTERPRETATION), especially Valentinians, adopted Ephesians as a favorite text. They considered the PAUL of Ephesians the first Gnostic because of his language about *gnosis, pleroma,* the heavenly *anthropos,* and the latter's partner, the *ekklesia.* The anti-Gnostic bishop IRENAEUS used Ephesians against them as had

IGNATIUS before him. Irenaeus emphasized the oneness motifs of the letter: one God, who is both Creator and Redeemer; one Christ; and one church, the unity of which was guaranteed by apostolic tradition and succession.

The next period of major study occurred during the Arian dispute (see ARIUS). Marius Victorinus wrote a commentary on Ephesians shortly after 360 in which he answered objections to Christ's divinity. Ambrosiaster and JEROME also wrote commentaries. Jerome was among the first to register surprise that Paul, who knew the Ephesians so well, could write as though he did not know them. In his early fifth-century commentary, THEODORE OF MOPSUESTIA also wondered whether the Ephesians were the proper addressees of the letter.

THOMAS AQUINAS gave lectures on Ephesians either between 1261 and 1263, or in 1266. The theme of ecclesiological unity in Ephesians contributed to the construction of his doctrinal system.

2. Renaissance and Reformation. In 1519 ERASMUS identified stylistic peculiarities in Ephesians that separated it from other letters of Paul, although he ultimately decided on the basis of spiritual content that Paul wrote it. LUTHER penned many scattered comments and preached a number of sermons on Ephesians (see E. Ellwein [1973] 11-174). He thought the letter was theologically one of Paul's most important letters. CALVIN wrote a detailed commentary and forty-eight sermons on Ephesians and cited Ephesians 277 times in his *Institutes of the Christian Religion.*

3. Rise of Historical Scholarship. The earliest historical questions focused on the letter's recipients. In 1598 BEZA wrote that the letter was written for the Ephesians but that it was also a circular letter for other churches in Asia Minor. J. USSHER moved one step further (1654), maintaining that Paul had left a space after the words *tois ousin* in 1:1 so that each church could insert its own name when reading the letter. Grotius, going back to the opinion of MARCION, decided that the letter was written to both Laodicea and Ephesus (1646), while J. MILL thought that the Laodiceans alone were the original recipients (1710).

The first person to maintain in print that someone other than Paul was the author was E. EVANSON, for whom the contradiction between the address and the content was too great to reconcile (1792). The first European to take that step was Usteri, for whom the relationship with Colossians was crucial (1824). The earliest major work to investigate thoroughly the authenticity of Ephesians was that of W. DE WETTE (1843). His reasons have remained fundamental to those who identify an author other than Paul: (1) the literary dependence on Colossians; (2) the complex and overloaded Greek style; and (3) the large number of phrases atypical of Paul's time (e.g., 2:20 and 3:5)

F. C. BAUR and his followers understood Ephesians as an example of an attempt by followers of Pauline Christianity to effect a synthesis with the followers of Petrine Christianity (1845). The combination of Gnostic ideas and an approach typical of early Catholicism caused Baur to place Ephesians in the second century. H. HOLTZMANN also argued for non-Pauline authorship (1872), identifying an original, shortened letter to the Colossians written by Paul that in the second century was used as the model for a pseudonymous letter to the Ephesians. This letter, in turn, became the basis of an expanded Colossians.

4. Twentieth-Century Interpretation. *a. History of religions and place in the early church.* H. Schlier (1971) and E. KÄSEMANN, both students of R. BULTMANN, first applied to Ephesians insights from newly discovered manuscripts, especially from Gnostic texts that seemed to evidence a pre-Christian Gnosticism. Schlier detected a meditation on the mystery of the church's unity with Christ (1930). The Gnostic myth (see MYTHOLOGY AND BIBLICAL STUDIES) is applied to Christ, the heavenly Man. As the Man, Christ is simultaneously in heaven (as the head) and on earth (as the body). Other concepts like knowledge, the worldview, *pleroma,* the church as the wisdom of God, and the marital tie between Christ and the church all confirmed for Schlier the Gnostic background, hence he argued for non-Pauline authorship.

In his commentary, first published in 1957, Schlier continued to hold that Gnosticism had strongly influenced the letter, especially in its cosmology and ecclesiology. In the intervening decades, however, he had decided that Paul did in fact write the letter, and he traced the roots of the Ephesian THEOLOGY to the undisputed letters, explaining that the latter deal with the *kerygma,* while Ephesians develops the *sophia,* or wisdom, of Paul's thought (1 Cor 2:6ff.) Thus he styled the letter a wisdom speech written by Paul while a prisoner in Rome.

Käsemann distinguished between the body of Christ as represented in the undisputed letters of Paul and in Ephesians–Colossians (1933). In the undisputed letters the cosmic aspect of the body of Christ is not a primary motif and is modified by the concept of the body as organism. In contrast, in Ephesians–Colossians the body of Christ is much more central, and the background of its usage is Gnostic. In Colossians the dominant perspective is that of image and members because the emphasis is on the relationship of the individual Christian to Christ, while in Ephesians the chief schema is that of body and head because the meaning of the church is most important. Similarly to Schlier, Käsemann viewed Christ as the heavenly Man and the eschatology as Gnostic.

Käsemann also had definite views of the place of Ephesians within early Christianity. The emphasis on the church in Ephesians led him to identify it, pejoratively, as early Roman Catholic. He also linked the letter with Acts because of their common use of church tradition, which he saw as another sign of the centrality of the church. In tandem with the weight placed on the church were the new importance in Ephesians of the apostles and the clear movement toward bishops despite the absence of explicit references to them.

The themes of church order and Gnosticism have continued in scholarly discussion. For F. Mussner (1982) the ecclesiological developments in Ephesians are a natural development of the early confession of the church and are unrelated to any supposed Gnostic influence. K. Fischer (1973) has also moved in a direction quite different from Käsemann. Since bishops are not mentioned in 4:7-16, even though the letter was written at a time when the role of bishop was elsewhere being adopted, Fischer concludes that Ephesians was a post-Pauline utopian attempt both to rescue the charismatic organization of Paul's missionary congregations and to unify the church. Thus Ephesians is the opposite of early Catholic. H. Merklein, however, agrees with Käsemann on the early Roman Catholic label, although for him that designation is positive and establishes the legitimacy of the development from the undisputed letters through Ephesians to the PASTORAL LETTERS.

Gnosticism has been the key to other studies. According to E. Schweizer (1963), Ephesians attempts to combat a type of cosmic christology that viewed Christ as a macro-*anthropos*. P. Pokorny (1965) pushes further the theme of opposition to Gnosticism, seeing in Ephesians a homily against the Gnostic danger and dating it to the 80s or 90s. He significantly softens that position in his commentary (1992), stating that Ephesians was not written as a direct defense against Gnosticism. R. Martin (1968), who also sees Ephesians as anti-Gnostic, argues that the author, the same Luke as the author of Acts, wrote to combat antinomian tendencies in the gentile church. For E. Best (1993), the author of Ephesians was refuting no heresy, including Gnosticism. The use of any Gnostic terminology resulted from the fact that such terms were familiar to the letter's recipients. A. Lindemann (1975) does not understand Ephesians as anti-Gnostic at all. For him the past, present, and future have been collapsed together in such a way that the church is a timeless entity that does not exist within history. The idea that Christians are already resurrected (2:5-6) indicates an ethics based on a past salvation event rather than on the future. The proper background for both ideas is Gnostic. Not only is the language similar to Gnosticism, it is thoroughly Gnostic.

Less widely debated has been the apparent influence on Ephesians of the type of Jewish apocalyptic thinking (see APOCALYPTICISM) and formulation evident in the DEAD SEA SCROLLS. Election, predestination, mystery, conflicting spirits of light and darkness, spiritual warfare, the community as a holy house or temple, and the revealing of the divine plan of salvation are all paralleled at Qumran. The Greek of Ephesians shows strong Semitic coloring quite close to the Hebrew of the Dead Sea Scrolls, especially the hymns. K. KUHN (1968) has argued that both the author of Ephesians and the Dead Sea community drew on a common tradition.

b. Authorship and purpose. Many scholars have continued to argue for Pauline authorship. T. Abbott (1897) introduced the argument that a development in Paul's theology, in part spurred by the delay of the parousia, accounts for the differences in Ephesians. E. Percy (1946) wrote a most thorough defense of Pauline authorship, dealing one-by-one with the peculiarities of thought and style and illustrating how each is rooted in Paul's earlier writings. G. Schille (1957) suggested another line of approach based on FORM CRITICISM, explaining the unusual writing style by isolating Paul's heavy quotation of pre-Pauline hymnic and paraenetic material. M. Barth (1974) built on his predecessors, placing heavy weight on the liturgical background, especially as it related to the Qumran literature, but consistently discounted theories of Gnostic influence. A. van Roon (1974) has also surveyed the literature and defended Paul as author; for him the content of Ephesians is typically Pauline and, indeed, quite close to Romans. He places Paul in Caesarea, thus accounting for Semitic influences by the bilingual milieu, but identifies no traces of Gnosticism. The relationship between Ephesians and Colossians is explained by a common draft completed in different ways by different scribes.

Other scholars have developed a variety of positions on pseudonymous authorship. E. GOODSPEED (1933) proposed that Paul's letters were soon forgotten. Near the end of the first century the former slave Onesimus received a copy of Luke–Acts; he then gathered Pauline letters and decided to publish them. To update the letters he wrote Ephesians as an introduction to the collection, using Colossians as his basic source. The theory (except for Onesimus as the author) has continued to exert a great deal of influence, as is seen in the work of C. Mitton (1951). Identifying a more gradual process of letter collection, Mitton views the publication of Acts as the final factor that caused the author to summarize Paul's message. F. W. BEARE (1953) found no evidence that Paul was ever forgotten, although he did think that the purpose of Ephesians was to commend Paul's teaching to a later generation.

Other directions have been set by N. DAHL, who understood Ephesians as an appeal to gentile Christians to be united with their Jewish(-Christian) predecessors and contemporaries. He styled Ephesians as a letter of reminder and congratulation in which baptism is the basic teaching and serves as the foundation for both unity and ethical action. The letter is further meant to establish a relationship between the Asian recipients and the author, who in his earlier writings Dahl held to be the historical Paul; his later work, however, identified a post-Pauline author. At the same time Dahl saw a quiet polemic against heresy, particularly in the author's statements about ministry and marriage, although he refused to identify the heresy as Gnostic, here agreeing with G. Johnston (1962), who found the supposed Gnostic material to be amply paralleled outside Gnostic texts.

Providing another theory of authorship, J. Kirby (1968) argued that an elder of the church in Ephesus was asked to furnish a collector of Paul's letters with a copy of Paul's correspondence with Ephesus. Since such a letter did not exist, the elder composed one based on his memory of Paul's preaching but structured around the Pentecost liturgy followed by the early church. J. Gnilka (1971) rejects Kirby's theory and views Ephesians as a reworking of Colossians and the authors of both books as heavily dependent on pre-existent traditions.

R. Schnackenburg's commentary (1991) summarizes the non-Pauline authorship position. The deciding factor for him is the distinctive theology of Ephesians in which Paul's theology of the cross has become a theology of the resurrection, exaltation, and heavenly enthronement of JESUS Christ. That view inevitably moved toward a position in which the church is at the center of human existence. Determinative for P. Pokorny in opting for pseudonymous authorship was the great care exercised by the author in preserving and applying the tradition of Paul to a new situation in which the peculiar features and unity of the church were being threatened.

W. Taylor (1985), building on Dahl, calls Ephesians a congratulatory communication written in letter format. He argues that the genre of Ephesians is epideictic, a type of literature usually devoted to praising a person, an object, or an event and is particularly concerned to show nascent Gnosticism as the opponent against whom the letter was written sometime between 75 and 90. V. Furnish (1992) disputes Taylor's classification of Ephesians as epideictic but agrees with him and others that Ephesians is pseudonymous (see also J. Sampley [1993]). Especially important for Furnish are two arguments for authorship by Paul: The non-Pauline vocabulary and style are partly due to the author's use of traditions; Paul's imprisonment and his more fully developed thought explain the differences between Ephesians and the undisputed letters. According to Furnish, the first argument provides another reason to question authorship by Paul since nowhere in the undisputed letters does Paul make similar wholesale use of traditional material. The second argument falls because scholars who argue for Pauline authorship for Ephesians usually place it during the same imprisonment mentioned in Philippians. The latter epistle, however, exhibits neither the marked stylistic peculiarities nor the same kind of "developed" theology as Ephesians.

Sampley posits identity formation as the chief purpose of the letter. That formation begins in baptism and instructs the readers concerning who they are and how they are to live the Christian life. A. Lincoln has a parallel understanding, although without the more exclusive emphasis on baptism. Chapters 1–3 remind gentile Christians of their privileges and status as believers in Christ and members of the church; chaps. 4–6 appeal to them to demonstrate that identity in their lives. Lincoln understands Ephesians, therefore, as a combination of the epideictic (chaps. 1–3) and deliberative (chaps. 4–6) rhetorical genres. In his commentary (1990) he moves from his earlier position that Paul wrote Ephesians to the assertion that the author belonged to a Pauline "school." The usual arguments and the dependence of Ephesians on Colossians and other Pauline letters convinced Lincoln that Paul did not write Ephesians. He explains various concerns of the letter (e.g., lack of unity and communal identity) by referring to the serious shift caused by Paul's death. He thinks that the letter may have been written for the churches of Hierapolis and Laodicea in the Lycus Valley.

Scholars who have studied the household code in Eph 5:2–6:9 have also rejected Pauline authorship. C. Martin (1991), who classifies Ephesians as a deutero-Pauline letter, argues for a study of the household code that advocates black women's as well as black men's liberation. S. Tanzer (1994) thinks that a disciple of Paul wrote Ephesians and another writer later added 5:22–6:9 to teach Christians how to fulfill their calling (4:1). Tanzer notices that the household code interrupts the instructions in chaps. 4–6 about how Christians can put into practice the equality of the Jews and Gentiles in the church that chaps. 1–3 claim Christ has accomplished. Both Martin's and Tanzer's studies draw from E. Schüssler Fiorenza's hermeneutics of suspicion. Schüssler Fiorenza (1983) argues that the author's concern for the unity of the church might account for the instructions about the proper social behavior of women.

Bibliography: **T. K. Abbott,** *A Critical and Exegetical Commentary on the Epistles to the Ephesians and to the Colossians* (ICC, 1897). **C. E. Arnold,** *Ephesians: Power and Magic: The Concept of Power in Ephesians in Light of Its Historical Setting* (SNTSMS 63, 1993). **M. Barth,** *Ephesians* (AB 34 and 34a, 1974), **F. C. Baur,** *Paulus der Apostel Jesus Christi* (1845). **F. W. Beare,** "The Epistle to the Ephesians: Introduction and Exegesis," *IB* (1953) 10:597-749. **E. Best,** *Ephesians* (NTGu, 1993); "Recipients and Title of the Letter to the Ephesians: Why and When the Designation 'Ephesians'?" *ANRW* 2.25.4 (1987) 3247-79. **N. A. Dahl,** "Adresse und Proömium des Epheserbriefes," *TZ* 7 (1951) 241-64; "Anamnesis," *StTh* 1 (1947 [1948]) 69-95; *IDBSup* (1962) 268-69; "Gentiles, Christians, and Israelites in the Epistle to the Ephesians," *HTR* 1-3 (1986) 31-39; "Interpreting Ephesians Then and Now," *CurTM* 5 (1978) 133-43; *TD* 25 (1977) 305-15. **E. Ellwein** (ed.), *D. Martin Luthers Epistel-Auslegung,* vol. 3: *Die Briefe an die Epheser, Philipper, und Kolosser* (1973). **K. M. Fischer,** *Tendenz und Absicht des Epheserbriefes* (FRLANT

111, 1973). **V. P. Furnish,** *ABD* (1992) 2:535-42. **M. A. Getty,** *Ephesians, Philippians, Colossians* (Read and Pray Series, 1980). **J. Gnilka,** *Der Epheserbrief* (HTKNT, 1971). **E. J. Goodspeed,** *The Meaning of Ephesians* (1933); *The Key to Ephesians* (1956). **G. Johnston,** *IDB* (1962) 2:108-14. **E. Käsemann,** "Epheserbrief," *RGG³* 2:517-20; "Ephesians and Acts," *Studies in Luke–Acts* (ed. L. E. Keck and J. L. Martyn, 1966) 288-97; "Das Interpretationsproblem des Epheser-briefes," *Exegetische Versuche und Besinnungen* (1965²) 2:253-61; *Leib und Leib Christi: Eine Untersuchung zur paulinischen Begrifflichkeft* (BHT 9, 1933); "Paul and Early Catholicism," *NT Questions of Today* (NTLi, 1969) 236-51; "The Theological Problem Presented by the Motif of the Body of Christ," *Per-spectives on Paul* (1971) 102-21. **J. C. Kirby,** *Ephesians: Baptism and Pentecost* (1968). **W. W. Klein,** *The Book of Ephesians: An Annotated Bibliography* (Books of the Bible 8, 1996). **K. G. Kuhn,** "The Epistle to the Ephesians in the Light of the Qumran Texts," *Paul and Qumran* (ed. J. Murphy-O'Connor, 1968) 115-31. **A. T. Lincoln,** *Ephesians* (WBC 42, 1990); "The Theology of Ephesians," *The Theology of the Later Pauline Letters* (NT Theology, A. T. Lincoln and A. J. M. Wedderburn, 1993) 75-166. **A. Lindemann,** *Die Aufhebung der Zeit: Geschichtsverständnis und Eschatologie im Epheserbrief* (SNT 12; 1975). **C. J. Martin,** "The *Haustafeln* (Household Code) in African American Biblical Interpretation: 'Free Slaves' and 'Subordinate Women,' " *Stony the Road We Trod: African American Biblical Interpretation* (ed. C. H. Felder, 1991). **R. P. Martin,** "An Epistle in Search of a Life-Setting," *ExpTim* 79 (1968) 296-302. **H. Merklein,** *Christus und die Kirche: Die theologische Grundstruktur des Epheserbriefes nach Eph. 2.11-18* (SBS 66, 1973); "Der Epheserbrief in der neueren exegetis-chen Diskussion," *ANRW* 2.25.4 (1987) 3156-246; *Das kirchliche Amt nach dem Epheserbrief* (SANT 33, 1973). **C. L. Mitton,** *Ephesians* (NCB, 1976); *The Epistle to the Ephesians* (1951). **F. Mussner,** *Der Brief an die Epheser* (ÖTBK/NT 10, 1982); *Chris-tus, das All und die Kirche* (TTS 5, 1968²); "Contributions made by Qumran to the Understanding of the Epistle to the Ephesians," *Paul and Qumran* (ed. J. Murphy-O'Connor, 1968) 159-78. **E. Pagels,** *The Gnostic Paul: Gnostic Exegesis of the Pauline Letters* (1975) 115-33. **E. Percy,** *Die Probleme der Kolosser- und Ephe-serbriefe* (1946). **P. Pokorny,** *Der Brief des Paulus an die Epheser* (THKNT 10, 2, 1992); *Der Epheserbrief und die Gnosis: Die Bedeutunq des Haupt-Glieder-Gedankens in der entstehenden Kirche* (1965). **P. Perkins,** *Ephesians,* (ANTC, 1997). **J. H. P. Reumann,** *Colossians* (ACNT, 1985). **L. M. Russell,** *Imitators of God: A Study Book on Ephesians* (1984). **J. P. Sampley,** *The Deutero-Pauline Letters* (Proclamation Commentaries, ed. Ger-hard Krodel, 1993) 1-23. **G. Schille,** "Der Autor des Epheserbrief-es," *TLZ* 82 (1957) 325-34. **H. Schlier,** *Der Brief an die Epheser: Ein Kommentar* (1971⁷). **R. Schnackenburg,** *Ephesians: A Com-mentary* (1991). **E. Schüssler Fiorenza,** *In Memory of Her: A Feminist Theological Reconstruction of Christian Origins* (1983). **E. Schweizer,** "Die Kirche als Leib Christi in den paulinischen Antilegomena," *Neotestamentica* (1963) 293-316. **C. L. Stock-hausen,** *Letters in the Pauline Tradition* (1989). **S. J. Tanzer,** *Searching the Scriptures,* vol. 2, *A Feminist Commentary* (ed. E.

Schüssler Fiorenza, 1994) 323-48. **W. F. Taylor, Jr.,** *Ephesians* (ACNT, 1985). **A. van Roon,** *The Authenticity of Ephesians* (1974).

W. F. TAYLOR

EPHRAEM THE SYRIAN (306–73)

Born in Nisibis in northern Mesopotamia, then still a part of the Roman Empire, E. was educated there and was influenced by its bishop, Jacob, and by his successor, Vologeses. During Vologeses' episcopate (346–61), E. was ordained a deacon and commissioned to teach at the theological school. When Nisibis was surrendered to the Persians in 363, E. moved westward to Edessa (now Urfa) in southern Turkey, where he continued teaching on the Bible and preaching against the heretics of his time, espe-cially the followers of ARIUS and Bar-Daisan.

E. left a vast amount of hymns, gathered in a number of collections (*De Virginate, De Ecclesia,* etc.) The hymns are important as expositions of the early Syriac theology with its profound biblical foundation, little influenced by Greek theology. E. is the first Christian theologian who expressed his thoughts mainly in poetical form.

According to tradition, E. commented on the whole Bible. A great number of his commentaries are found in the first printed edition of his works (1737–46, the so-called *Editio Romana*); their authenticity, however, is doubtful. Certainly genuine are the commentaries on Genesis and Exodus, in which E. showed himself to be a moderate adherent of the ANTIOCHENE SCHOOL of exegesis, with its stress on the *sensus litteralis.* Allegorical interpretations are almost totally rejected (with some exceptions in Genesis 49); some typology is admitted. A number of haggadic traditions (especially in the Genesis commentary, with an accumulation at the Cain/Abel episode in Genesis 4) show a certain affinity to Jewish Midrashes (see MIDRASH), but it is difficult to discern a definite dependence on Jewish exegetical traditions. No knowledge of Hebrew is indicated. In his hymns, E. drew on still more haggadic traditions.

E. had a very far-reaching influence on the Syriac church and its interpretation of the Bible, "the harp of the Holy Spirit." In the West he was virtually unknown until the eighteenth century.

Works: *Works* (ed. and GT E. Beck, CSCO, Scriptores Syri, 1955–); *Hymns* (CWS, tr. and intro. K. E. McVey, 1989); *Hymns on Paradise* (tr. S. Brock, 1990; Genesis); *St. Ephraem's Commentary on Tatian's "Diatessaron": An English Transla-tion of Chester Beatty Syriac MS 709* (JSSsup 2, tr. C. McCarthy, 1993); *Selected Prose Works* (ed. K. E. McVey, tr. E. G. Mathews, Jr. and J. P. Amar, 1994); *The Armenian Commentary on the Book of Genesis Attributed to Ephraem the Syrian* (2 vols., CSCO 572–73, tr. E. G. Mathews, Jr., 1998).

Bibliography: S. H. **Griffith,** *Faith Adoring the Mystery: Reading the Bible with St. Ephraem the Syrian* (P. Marquette

Lecture, 1997). **S. Hidal,** *Interpretatio Syriaca: Die Kommentare des heiligen Ephräm des Syrers zu Genesis und Exodus mit besonderer Berücksichtigung ihrer auslegungsgeschichtlichen Stellung* (ConBOT 6, 1974). **T. Kronholm,** *Motifs from Genesis 1–11 in the Genuine Hymns of Ephrem the Syrian, with Particular Reference to the Influence of Jewish Exegetical Tradition* (ConBOT 11, 1978). **R. Murray,** *TRE* 9 (1982) 755-62 (includes bibliography).

S. HIDAL

ERASMUS, DESIDERIUS (1466/69–1536)

Born in Rotterdam, E. received his primary education at Gouda, and then at Deventer, where he was influenced by the Brethern of the Common Life. In 1487 he was sent to the Augustinian canon regulars at Steyn. One year after his ordination to the priesthood (1492), he became secretary to the bishop of Cambrai. Subsequently he studied theology at the Collège de Montaigu in Paris (1495–99). A seven-month stay in England (1499–1500) engendered his friendship with J. COLET, whose NT exegesis strengthened his desire to devote his life to biblical studies.

Between 1500 and 1516 E. moved frequently, sojourning from 1506 to 1509 in Italy, where he obtained his doctorate in theology from the university of Turin. His third stay in England (1509–14) dampened his enthusiasm for English academic life, and from 1514 to 1516 he settled in Basel. Appointed counselor to Emperor Charles V and released from his monastic vows, E. lived on the support of influential patrons, working as a freelance biblical humanist.

E.'s 1517–21 stay in Louvain became frustrating when Roman Catholic theologians (B. Latomus, E. Lee, L. de Stuniga) attacked his work on the NT and associated him with LUTHER. Trying to maintain the integrity of *studia humanitatis* and to keep his peace of mind, he returned to Basel. Yet even there he was not spared controversy. The Protestant U. von Hutten accused him of having left Luther in the lurch (1523). Prompted by his patrons, E. wrote *De libero arbitrio* (1524) to come to terms with his adversary; but Luther's uncompromising rebuttal in *De servo arbitrio* (1525) made the break final. When critics associated E. with ZWINGLI's and J. OECOLAMPADIUS's teaching on the Lord's Supper, E. affirmed his loyalty to the Roman Catholic tradition. Religious disturbances in Basel (1529) forced him to escape to nearby Freiburg, where, troubled by further controversies with M. BUCER, Luther, and Roman Catholics (A. Pio), he pleaded for the concord of the church (1533). After returning to Basel in 1535 to supervise the printing of a work on ORIGEN, E. died on July 12, 1536.

For E., erudition enhanced by piety could renew theology and restore both church and society (*restitutio Christianismi*). Returning to the sources of classical antiquity and Scripture (*ad fontes*), he refused to separate ancient wisdom from biblical faith. Even so, he believed that human knowledge is ancillary to divine revelation. While theology depends on its handmaidens (language, grammar, and rhetoric), it remains the queen of sciences. To demonstrate the significance of philology for study of the Bible, E. edited L. VALLA's *Adnotationes* (1505) and published his own Latin translation of the Greek NT sources (*Novum Instrumentum* [1516]), together with *Annotationes* and introductory writings, the *Paraclesis, Apologia,* and *Methodus.* The latter was expanded for the second edition of the NT (*Novum Testamentum* [1518]) and entitled *Ratio verae theologiae.* It contains hermeneutical principles (see HERMENEUTICS) and exegetical rules based in part on AUGUSTINE's *De doctrina christiana.* E.'s own exegesis is found in his *Paraphrases* on all the NT books (1517–24) and in his *Commentaries* on selected psalms (1515–36). The monumental *Ecclesiastes* (1535) finally marshalled his views on biblical interpretation and preaching, relating rhetoric to theology in a hermeneutic that draws on Quintilian (fl. 1st cent. CE), Cicero (106–43 BCE), and Augustine.

E.'s rhetorical theology relies on the Bible specifically but also on the wider cultural context of language. Since human speech expresses thought, prompts motion, and displays style, at its best it can teach the truth, move to moral action, and please by its beauty (*docere, movere, delectare*). *Bonae litterae* possess the power of persuasion to transform readers into what they say (*studia in mores transeunt*), drawing them into a formation process to render them literate and humane. Beyond nature and culture, however, language is symbolic of a religious presence as God accommodates to human speech (*sacrae litterae*). This is already true for the allegorical foreshadowing of Christ in HB literature; but it is in the NT where divinity has taken the form of the written word, which is now embodied in the divine mediator. Christ, therefore, is the hermeneutical principle of Scripture, the unique *scopus* of all reality. The AUTHORITY of its author, God, and Christ's allegorical presence endow the sacred text with the highest power of persuasion and transformation. Restoring the NT to its original purity, then, represents the premier task of the humanist theologian.

Although the supreme text, the Bible is still subject to the dualism of all things. Spirit and letter remain mutually exclusive (*littera occidens, spiritus vivificans*). To bridge this gap, E. adopted the fourfold, or QUADRIGA, method of interpretation (literal, allegorical, tropological, and anagogical), qualifying it, however, by the rules of rhetoric so as to free it from the dialectic of scholastic dogmatism. The two middle links, tropology and allegory, enable a metaphorical transition, revealing a meaning that reconciles external appearance and inner significance. Especially allegory is mediatory because it reconciles history and mystery.

E. refused to abandon the letter (*littera*), for it declares its hidden content (*res*). Still, tropology and allegory liberate the confined word to reveal its broader and deeper meaning. Similarly to the rule of TYCHONIUS, E. took the allegorical meaning to point to Christ, to the church, and to Christians. The tropological method uncovers moral instruction, aiming at ethical utility for individuals, church, and society. The anagogical sense adumbrates the last things of God and, therefore, makes us speechless in the face of mystery. So, keeping the historical sense intact as the irremovable starting point of interpretation, E. emphasized the middle—the allegorical and tropological *transitus* toward the spirit—while leaving the end point—anagogical consummation—veiled in the mystery of God's Spirit.

Allegory is an expression of accommodation because the transition from the literal to the spiritual is impossible unless God adapts to human speech. Since author and recipient of the revelation are essentially dissimilar, accommodation is required according to the principle *similia similibus*. This is why Scripture abounds with allegories, similitudes, metaphors, and parables. By virtue of divine accommodation, then, allegory functions as a medium between contraries, revealing similarities, attracting affection, and enabling the transformation from flesh to spirit. And it is Christ, the supreme allegory, in whom this persuasive power of reconciliation has become incarnate.

Allegorical interpretation must be oriented in the perfect circle of the *philosophia Christi,* however. Because the harmony of Christ's teaching is inseparable from his way of life, allegory includes a specifically Christian ethic; but inasmuch as this ethic perfects rather than eliminates natural morality, the allegorical method puts tropology to use. Just as the Spirit does not destroy nature, history, and culture, so also Christ perfects the natural virtues in faith, love, and hope. While the literal meaning of the word can be ignored if absurd, its ethical import is always present, even if the allegorical sense is lacking.

To understand Christ's teaching and to arrange theological *topoi* around the *scopus Christi,* E. employed the rhetorical method of comparison (*collatio*). Both an exegetical and systematic procedure, *collatio* functions to organize subject matter according to similarity. Having first clarified the particular circumstances in a text by ascertaining the coincidence of a variety of persons, things, times, and places, the interpreter looks for commonalities with other contexts in order to bring about agreement. The judgment about visible things (*iudicium*) serves to identify the particular situation of a text, whereas the discernment of invisible things (*consilium*) helps to integrate the text into its appropriate place in the overall order, which is characterized by the unity of truth (*consensus*) and love (*concordia*). The text does not release its real meaning until the interpretation is harmonious with natural equity, ethical utility, and above all the *scopus Christi.*

Finding the suitable place of a text in the overall order (*commoditas*) requires that the interpreter be exegetically moderate and ethically modest. One must look for the advantage of others—a behavior patterned after Christ's innocence, simplicity, and humility. Rhetorical theology, therefore, teaches the means of LITERARY analysis and instills a humanist disposition of prudence, decorum, and moderation. Caution, discretion, and decency enable the theologian to find proper means, fitting ways, and common denominators to accommodate to a variety of conditions, whether it is adapting the interpretation to the nature of the text, adjusting the literary genre to the subject matter, fitting the instruction to the student, or observing propriety in one's relation to others.

Works: *Desiderii Erasmi Roterodami Opera omnia, Lugduni Batavorum* (ed. J. Le Clerc, 1703–6; repr., 1961–62); *Opera omnia Desiderii Erasmi Roterodami* (ed. J. H. Waszink et al., 1969–); *Ausgewählte Werke* (ed. H. Holborn, 1933; repr. 1964); *Collected Works of Erasmus* (1974–); *Erasmus von Rotterdam: Ausgewählte Schriften* (ed. W. Welzig, 1967–80).

Bibliography: C. **Augustijn,** *TRE* 10 (1982) 1-18; *E.: His Life, Works, and Influence* (Erasmus Studies 10, 1991). **J. H. Bentley,** *Humanists and Holy Writ: NT Scholarship in the Renaissance* (1983). **A. Bludau,** *Die beiden ersten Erasmus-Ausgaben des Neuen Testaments und ihre Gegner* (1902). **J. Chomarat,** *Grammaire et rhétorique chez Erasme* (1981). **M. Hoffmann,** *Erkenntnis und Verwirklichung der wahren Theologie nach E. von Rotterdam* (BHT 44, 1972); *Rhetoric and Theology: The Hermeneutic of E.* (Erasmus Studies 13, 1994). **H. Holeczek,** *Humanistische Bibelphilologie als Reformproblem bei E. von Rotterdam, T. More, und W. Tyndale* (1975). **F. Krüger,** *Humanistische Evangelienauslegung: D. E. von Rotterdam als Ausleger der Evangelien in seinen Paraphrasen* (1986). **M. O'Rourke Boyle,** *E. on Language and Method in Theology* (Erasmus Studies 2, 1977). **J. B. Payne,** "Toward the Hermeneutics of E.," *Scrinium Erasmianum* 2 (ed. J. Coppens, 1969) 13-49. **A. Rabil,** *E. and the NT: The Mind of a Christian Humanist* (1972). **E. Rummel,** *E.'s Annotations on the NT* (1986). **W. Schwarz,** *Principles and Problems of Biblical Translation: Some Reformation Controversies and Their Background* (1955). **G. B. Winkler,** *E. und die Einleitungsschriften zum NT: Formale Strukturen und theologischer Sinn* (1974). **P. Walter,** *Theologie aus dem Geist der Rhetorik: Zur Schriftauslegung des E. von Rotterdam* (1991).

M. HOFFMANN

ERIUGENA (JOHN SCOTTUS) (c. 810–c. 877)

E. was among the Irish (*scotti*) scholars who came to Europe in the eighth and ninth centuries to ply their skills as grammarians, poets, and biblical exegetes in the cathedrals, monasteries, and courts of the Carolingians. In the preface to his translation of the Pseudo-Dionysian corpus, he called himself Eriugena (of Ireland by birth), perhaps emulating Virgil's "Graiugena" (*Aeneid* 3.550). E. enjoyed the patronage of King Charles the Bald (840–877) and associated with scholars and students in Compiègne, Laon, Reims, and Soissons. He commented on Priscian's (fl. c. 500–530) grammar and on Martianus Capella's (5th cent.) *Marriage of Philology and Mercury;* and his treatise *On Divine Predestination* contributed to the theological controversy swirling around that contentious topic. As a court poet, he wrote verse that praised the accomplishments of his patrons and celebrated Easter and Christmas, but he made his most significant contributions to medieval learning and biblical exegesis as an interpreter of Greek texts and of the Bible.

E.'s translations of the works of Pseudo-Dionysius the Areopagite (c. 500), Maximus the Confessor (c. 580–662), GREGORY OF NYSSA, and Epiphanius of Salamis (c. 315–403) opened the world of Byzantine Greek scholarship to the Latin West. The Neoplatonism E. encountered in these texts combined with his deep Augustinianism (see AUGUSTINE) to enrich his biblical exegesis. He worked at biblical interpretation from early in his teaching career, when he glossed biblical vocabulary, to his last days, when he left the unfinished *Commentary on the Gospel of John.* In between he composed a homily on the prologue of John's Gospel, the *Voice of the Mystic Eagle*; a commentary on Matthew, surviving in the so-called *Opus imperfectum in Matthaeum*; and his theological and philosophical masterpiece, the hexameral *Periphyseon* (On Natures). In the latter work he wrote that "true authority does not conflict with right reason, nor right reason with true authority, since both flow from the same source, the Wisdom of God" (bk. 1, 511b). That source was the Bible.

In an age of encyclopedic biblical scholarship when many interpreters combined the words of earlier exegetes (often in very creative ways) in their own commentaries, E. went beyond an "exegesis of exegesis" (S. Cantelli [1980] 298) to interpret the Bible directly. He personified Scripture as an artist (*artifex scriptura*), the textual equivalent of the Creator (É. Jeauneau [1996]). The key to understanding Scripture as artist lay in using the tools of reason God provided in the liberal arts, especially the arts of grammar and dialectic, to interpret the artistry and thereby unlock Scripture's multiple meanings. E.'s exceptional literary skill and his lively intelligence combined with his deep spirituality to animate the Augustinian, Neoplatonic, and liberal arts traditions he mastered. The combination enabled him to interpret the Bible in strikingly bold and original ways. In the commentary on John he defined two types of allegory in a new way; and among the many exegetical insights of *Periphyseon,* his discussions of contempla-

tion, contradiction, human dignity, and the division of the sexes are pioneering.

E. appreciated the hard work and danger inherent in biblical interpretation and to characterize the perils he faced often used the image of a sailor whose small boat contended with dangerous seas and rocky shoals. In the homily on John, his comparison of the apostle Peter to the evangelist John, E.'s namesake, suggests that the Irish exegete faced those perils with confidence (*Jean Scot: Homélie sur le prologue de Jean* [1969] I-V). Peter represented faith and action, while John stood for wisdom and contemplation. Both apostles ran to Christ's tomb, which is "the divine scriptures in which, protected by the mass of its letters just as the tomb was protected by stone, the mystery of Christ's humanity and divinity are contained. John got to the tomb before Peter because contemplation penetrates quicker and with greater sharpness than action the secrets of the divine letters." E.'s learned, personal exegesis contrasted sharply with the compilatory editorial exegesis of the ninth century.

Works: *Iohannis Scotti Eriugenae Periphyseon (De Divisione Naturae)* (SLH 7, 9, 11, 13 [bks. 1–3 ed. I. P. Sheldon-Williams; bk. 4 ed. É. Jeauneau] 1968–95); *Jean Scot: Homélie sur le prologue de Jean* (SC 151, ed. É. Jeauneau, 1969); *Jean Scot: Commentaire sur l'Évangile de Jean* (SC 180, ed. É. Jeauneau, 1972); *Glossae Divinae Historiae: The Biblical Glosses of J. S. E.* (ed. J. J. Contreni and P. P. O Néill, 1997).

Bibliography: S. Cantelli, "L'esegesi al tempo di Ludovico il Pio e Carlo il Calvo," *Giovanni Scoto nel suo tempo: L'Organizzazione del sapere in età carolingia* (ed. C. Leonardi and E. Menestò, 1980) 261-336. J. J. Contreni, "Carolingian Biblical Culture," *Iohannes Scottus Eriugena: The Bible and Hermeneutics* (ed. G. Van Riel, C. Steel, and J. McEvoy, 1996) 1-23; "Carolingian Biblical Studies," *Carolingian Learning, Masters, and Manuscripts* (ed. J. J. Contreni, 1992) chap. 5. É. Jeauneau, "Artifex Scriptura," *Iohannes Scottus Eriugena: The Bible and Hermeneutics* (ed. G. Van Riel, C. Steel, and J. McEvoy, 1996) 351-365. G. A. Piemonte, "Recherches sur les 'Tractatus in Matheum' attribués à Jean Scot," *Iohannes Scottus Eriugena: The Bible and Hermeneutics* (ed. G. Van Riel, C. Steel, J. McEvoy, 1996), 321-350.

J. J. CONTRENI

ERNESTI, JOHANN AUGUST (1707–81)

E. played an important part in the emergence of the historical-critical method in eighteenth-century Germany, although his own position remained one of traditional orthodoxy. He was born Aug. 4, 1707, in Tennstädt, Thüringia, and following his education in Schulpforte he entered the University of Wittenberg in 1726, where the influence of C. Wolff's (1679–1754) philosophy was strong. In 1728 he moved to Leipzig and on completing his studies became a schoolmaster.

In 1731 he was appointed co-rector of St. Thomas's school in Leipzig, becoming rector in 1734, a post he held for twenty-eight years alongside positions as *ausserordentlicher* (1742) and then full professor (1756) at the university. Believing that music had little to contribute to education, during his time at St. Thomas's school he came into conflict with J. BACH, who won this initial battle. An uneasy truce followed; however, in his review of the school year 1750–51, E. failed to mention Bach's death in 1750. E. died in Leipzig, Sept. 11, 1781.

E. was a distinguished classical scholar who published many editions of Greek and Latin texts. His contribution to biblical scholarship resulted from a combination of his skills as a classicist, the philosophy of Wolff, and the humanistic spirit of the age. E. believed that God had communicated a series of necessary truths, which the biblical authors had recorded in human language. The primary task of theology, therefore, is the elucidation of these truths by means of grammatical and historical exegesis of the Bible. In this task no special spiritual illumination is needed; exegesis is a purely scientific enterprise that provides the data from which doctrine can be fomulated. This position is set out in E.'s most important work, the *Institutio interpretis novi testamenti* (1761).

E.'s approach implied that a purely scientific exegesis would result in an acceptable Christian (Lutheran) interpretation. His opinions about the authorship of NT books were unshakably orthodox; he accepted the facts recounted in the NT as unassailable, to be resolved by harmonization where they seemed to be in conflict. The effect of his position, however, was to help to establish NT study as a separate philological and scientific discipline within theology, with the implied consequence that ultimately research, unfettered by dogma, might radically question traditional Christian orthodoxy.

Works: *Institutio interpretis novi testamenti* (1761; ET, *Elements of Interpretation* [1824–33]).

Bibliography: K. Blaschke and F. Lau, *NDB* (1957) 4:604-5. H. Frei, *The Eclipse of Biblical Narrative* (1974) 247-60. E. Hirsch, *Geschichte der neueren evangelischen Theologie* (1964³) 4:10-14. W. G. Kümmel, *The NT: The History of the Investigation of Its Problems* (1972) 60-61.

J. W. ROGERSON

ESDRAS, FIRST BOOK OF

The Greek book of 1 Esdras depicts the history of Israel during a pivotal period, tracing the major events from a high point of prosperity in Judah under King Josiah (d. 609 BCE) to a nadir of destruction and exile (587/86), followed by return and restoration in the Persian period under Zerubbabel and Ezra (538–458). The first book in the Apocrypha, in the SEPTUAGINT 1 Esdras appears as Esdras *a,* to be distinguished from Esdras *b* (i.e., the canonical Ezra–Nehemiah), which follows it. In the VULGATE it is designated as 3 Esdras (or 3 Ezra). Although the most ancient Greek manuscripts include 1 Esdras, the book nevertheless has been excluded from the Christian CANON (the only book consistently attested to in the Septuagint to suffer such a fate) and from the HB. Since the Council of Trent (1546) many Roman Catholic Bibles append it after the NT as a supplement.

The earliest extant copies of 1 Esdras are in Greek. Most modern scholars concur, however, that the book goes back to a Hebrew or an Aramaic original. The translation comes from the second century BCE and is independent of (and in many cases superior to) that of Ezra–Nehemiah in the Septuagint. The estimated date of the original remains controversial. Some scholars date some form of the original as early as the fifth century BCE (F. M. Cross [1975]) or the third (C. C. Torrey [1910]), but most place it in mid second century BCE because its vocabulary largely corresponds to that of other second-century compositions, such as Ben Sira, Judith, and 1–2 Maccabees (J. Myers [1974] 6).

With very few (yet often telling) exceptions, 1 Esdras overlaps portions of the canonical books of 1–2 Chronicles and Ezra–Nehemiah, which explains why the dominant interpretive debates have concentrated on its scope and relations to these two books. In particular, scholars disagree as to whether 1 Esdras is a fragment of the original work of the chronicler or a later compilation from the canonical books. The following charts the relations:

1 Esdr 1:1-22 = 2 Chr 35:1-19
(Josiah's Passover in Jerusalem)
1 Esdr 1:23-24 = without canonical parallel
(summary of Josiah's deeds and the nation's sins)
1 Esdr 1:25-58 = 2 Chr 35:20–36:21
(decline and fall of Judah and Jerusalem to the Babylonians)
1 Esdr 2:1-5*a* = 2 Chr 36:22-23 = Esra 1:1-3*a*
(Cyrus's edict calling for return to Judah and rebuilding the Temple. End of Chronicles)
1 Esdr 2:5*b*-15 = Ezra 1:3*b*-11
(Cyrus's decree continues; the return to Judah during Cyrus's time)
1 Esdr 2:16-30 = Ezra 4:7-24
(hostile neighbors interrupt the building of the house of God)
1 Esdr 3:1–5:6 = without canonical parallel
(story of the three guardsmen)
1 Esdr 5:7-73 = Ezra 2:1–4:5
(return and rebuilding under Jeshua and Zerubbabel)
1 Esdr 6:1–9:36 = Ezra 5:1–10:44
(completion of the Temple, the story of Ezra, and the separation from foreign wives)
1 Esdr 9:37-55 = Neh 7:72–8:13*a*
(Ezra's mission and the reading of the law in Jerusalem, followed by a celebration)

First Esdras contains the story of the three guardsmen (1 Esdr 3:1–5:6) and the summary of King Josiah's deeds (1 Esdr 1:23-24), which have no parallels in the canonical books. Another key difference from the canonical books involves when and where the reading of the law occurs. In Ezra–Nehemiah, this event takes place after Nehemiah rebuilds the wall (Nehemiah 8). In 1 Esdras, which lacks the story of Nehemiah, the reading directly follows the expulsion of the foreign wives (leading some scholars to conclude that this represents the original version of the story). This and other details, some of them seemingly minor, significantly shape the material, offering a distinctive account of ancient Israel's history.

First Esdras begins and ends with grand celebrations in Jerusalem. The opening scene, set in seventh-century Jerusalem, focuses on Passover during King Josiah's reign, a high-water mark on which the narrator lavishes many details (1:1-24). After Josiah's sudden death, however, the nation plunges into apostasy and suffers divine punishment: The Babylonians destroy Jerusalem and exile or kill its people (587/86), leaving the land desolate for a seventy-year sabbatical (1:25-58).

The rest, and longest, part of 1 Esdras depicts the three stages of Jewish restoration. In the first stage (2:1-25) the Jews respond to Cyrus's edict and go up to rebuild the Temple in Jerusalem. Their efforts, however, come to a halt when Judah's neighbors harass the returnees. In the second stage (3:1–7:15) more Jews return and this time successfully rebuild the Temple under the leadership of Zerubbabel, a descendant of David. According to the story of the three guardsmen (3:1–5:3 and unique to 1 Esdras), Zerubbabel rises to prominence in King Darius's court. He wins the admiration of the Persian king with an eloquent exposition on the power of women and the even greater power of truth. As a result, Zerubbabel receives unstinting support for the reconstruction of the Temple and for communal life in Judah. He leads a major return, culminating in the completion of the Temple, full restoration of worship, and a grand celebration of Passover by all. In the third and final stage (8:1–9:55) Ezra the priest brings further support for the Temple and implements the law during Artaxerxes' reign. Under his guidance the community separates from foreign influences (in particular from foreign wives). The final scene of 1 Esdras is the climactic public reading of the law in Jerusalem followed by yet another grand celebration (cf. 1 Esdr 1:1-22).

1. Ancient Interpretations. The Jewish historian JOSEPHUS provides the main witness for 1 Esdras in antiquity. His reliance on it for a rendition of the return from exile (*Antiquities* 11) indicates that the book circulated and was granted importance in the first century CE. Other ancient Jewish sources do not refer to 1 Esdras, although some Talmudic teachings (see TALMUD)

about truth recall Zerubbabel's speech on truth in 1 Esdr 4:33-40 (e.g., ʾAbot 1:18 and Šabb. 55a).

The early church fathers widely used and quoted 1 Esdras but rarely commented on it. CLEMENT OF ALEXANDRIA wrote that Zerubbabel, "having by his wisdom overcome his opponents, and having obtained leave from Darius for the rebuilding of Jerusalem, returned with Esdras to his native land" (*Strom.* 1:21). We find references to the book in JUSTIN MARTYR, EUSEBIUS, ATHANASIUS, CHRYSOSTOM, and others (see J. Myers [1974] 17). ORIGEN not only cited 1 Esdras but also may have used this book, rather than canonical Ezra–Nehemiah, in his Hexapla. Several Latin fathers also used 1 Esdras; e.g., AUGUSTINE saw Zerubbabel's praise of truth as a possible PROPHECY about Christ (*City of God* 28.36). JEROME, however, rejected the work as apocryphal (see his *Preface to Ezra and Nehemiah*). Largely as a result of Jerome's objections, 1 Esdras was eventually taken out of the Vulgate and relegated to non-canonical status—the only book fully attested to in the various LXX manuscripts to be excluded. Although it appears in some fifteenth-century Latin Bibles, it was regarded as apocryphal by the sixteenth century and was ignored by LUTHER, who wrote: "The third book of Esdras I threw into the Elbe." Luther also mentioned in his preface to BARUCH, "The same two books of Ezra we simply did not want to translate because they contain nothing that one cannot find much better in Aesop or still more inferior books; moreover . . . Jerome himself says that Lyra did not desire to exposit; it is not found in Greek" (cited by Myers, 18).

2. Modern Interpretations. Lack of canonical status may explain the long neglect of 1 Esdras. It gained attention during the nineteenth century with the rise of source criticism, when its nature, scope, and relation to the canonical books became a subject of controversy. Already H. GROTIUS (17th cent.) and J. D. MICHAELIS (18th cent.) had suggested that 1 Esdras preserves a more reliable account than MT Ezra–Nehemiah, but it was H. Howorth (19th cent.) and later TORREY who brought 1 Esdras into the limelight.

As advocates of what has been called the fragment hypothesis, these and other scholars maintained that 1 Esdras is a fragment from the original work of the chronicler. Initially connected to the books of Chronicles, it preserves the original form of 2 Chronicles' account of the return and restoration. The canonical Ezra–Nehemiah, according to this view, is a later rearrangement of Ezra–Nehemiah. Arguments in support of this position include the use of 1 Esdras by JOSEPHUS and the absence of comparable early witnesses to Ezra–Nehemiah. This hypothesis uses the separate traditions about Ezra and Nehemiah in the postexilic era (Ben Sira and 2 Maccabees mention only Nehemiah, not Ezra, and Josephus keeps them apart) to support the contention that the linking of the two men in Ezra–Nehemiah is later than 1 Esdras. J. D. Michaelis, A. Treuenfels, Howorth, J. Marquart, Torrey, G. HÖLSCHER, and most recently K.-F. Pohlmann, among others, have been supporters of the fragment hypothesis.

Torrey claimed that 1 Esdras is "simply a piece taken without change out of the middle of a faithful Greek translation of the Chronicler's History of Israel" (18). According to him, the original version of the chronicler's history was written in the mid-third century BCE and included the following: 1 and 2 Chronicles; Ezra 1; 1 Esdr 4:47-56; 4:62–5:6; Ezra 2:1–8:36; Neh 7:70–8:18; Ezra 9:1–10:44; Neh 9:1–10:40; 1:1–7:69; 11:1–13:31 (30). A redactor later added the story of the three guardsmen and transposed certain chapters of the Ezra narrative. Further revisions had emerged by the first century BCE, out of which 1 Esdras grew. The canonical Ezra–Nehemiah only came into being in the second century CE. First Esdras, however, remains as "the one surviving fragment of the old Greek version of the Chronicler's history" (34). Torrey's thorough analysis and his reconstruction of a Semitic original underlying 1 Esdras have been influential.

Pohlmann, an articulate proponent of the fragment hypothesis, also claims that 1 Esdras is an older and better translation than LXX Esdras *b* (Ezra–Nehemiah). In addition, he argues that the original sequence of Ezra history, as far as it can be ascertained, corresponds to the account preserved in 2 Chronicles–1 Esdras. Pohlmann examines the beginning and end of 1 Esdras, the interpolation of the story of the three guardsmen, the Ezra narrative in 1 Esdras and its relation to Ezra–Nehemiah, and especially the evidence of Josephus. He concludes that all of these data support the fragment hypothesis.

A contrasting view, generally labeled the compilation hypothesis, maintains that 1 Esdras presupposes the canonical books of 1–2 Chronicles and Ezra–Nehemiah and was compiled from them. The most important evidence for the compilation hypothesis appears in studies by P. Bayer (1911) and B. Walde (1913), whose detailed textual analysis of variants supports the dependence of 1 Esdras on 1–2 Chronicles and Ezra–Nehemiah. Advocates of this position claim that 1 Esdras has been preserved largely as its author had intended (although some, like W. Rudolph, modify the ending somewhat). They maintain that the omission of Nehemiah is deliberate and that Josephus's reliance on 1 Esdras is understandable in light of his own apologetic reasons. Neither feature requires the priority of 1 Esdras over Ezra–Nehemiah. The LXX, which consistently presents 1 Esdras as a distinct composition, and the subsequent ancient lists and records lend further support to this theory. Advocates of the compilation hypothesis include L. Bertholdt, Bayer, Walde, Rudolph, and H. Williamson.

Williamson (1977) provides the most thorough contemporary expression of the compilation hypothesis by

criticizing Pohlmann's version of the fragment hypothesis. He claims that 1 Esdr 1:23-24, which Pohlmann largely ignores, indicates a new beginning, not merely a continuation of 2 Chronicles, hence that 1 Esdras is a distinct compilation (Williamson, 18). He, like Pohlmann, recognizes it as an ancient and independent translation of an alternative reading or a misunderstanding of the Hebrew text (13); but he questions the plausibility of two different contemporary translations of the same work, both done in Egypt, as implied by Pohlmann's theory (15). Whereas Pohlmann argues that Josephus did not know Ezra–Nehemiah in its present form (114-26), Williamson turns the matter around. He points out that Josephus's account of Ezra breaks off just where 1 Esdras does, which suggests that Josephus's *Vorlage* ended as did the present version of 1 Esdras and implies, therefore, that the latter is a complete composition and not a fragment.

Although forms of the fragment and compilation hypotheses continue to be held (see Pohlmann [1980]; G. Garbini [1988]; Myers; R. Klein [1989]), new interpretations have been proposed. Cross models his interpretation of 1 Esdras on approaches to the two recensions of Jeremiah, identifying one as Palestinian (i.e., Ezra–Nehemiah) and one as Alexandrian (i.e., 1 Esdras). Basing his findings on those of Klein, he argues for a more pristine *Vorlage* for 1 Esdras. Cross envisions three different editions of Chronicles: The first included 1 Chronicles 10–2 Chronicles 34, plus a *Vorlage* of 1 Esdras 1:1–5:65 (= 2 Chr 34:1–Ezra 3:13, composed shortly after 520 BCE). The second included 1 Chronicles 10–2 Chronicles 36:23, plus the *Vorlage* of 1 Esdras (composed around 450 BCE). The third and final edition included 1 Chronicles 1–9, plus 10:1–2 Chr 36:23, plus Hebrew Ezra–Nehemiah (composed around 400 BCE). Cross concurs with D. N. Freedman (1961, 437-38) that the books of Chronicles, hence 1 Esdras, focus on "City and ruler, temple and priest—these appear to be the fixed points around which the Chronicler constructs his history and his theology." First Esdras (as part of the larger work of the chronicler) was designed to support the restoration of the kingdom under Zerubbabel (Cross [1975] 13), but the third revision suppressed material concerning Zerubbabel in light of the changed political climate.

T. Eskenazi suggests that 1 Esdras is a compilation from the canonical Ezra–Nehemiah but claims that it was composed as a distinct and complete work by the school of the chronicler, representing the chronicler's ideology. Much as 1–2 Chronicles uses Samuel and 1–2 Kings for a retelling of the story of the preexilic era, 1 Esdras, with the same point of view, uses Ezra–Nehemiah for the later era in Israel's history. She argues that omissions and additions to 1 Esdras shape the book to conform to the central emphases of 2 Chronicles: direct retribution (wherein persons and generations are responsible for their own fates); insistence on the decisive role of the prophets; and a more lenient attitude toward non-Jews than is found in Ezra–Nehemiah. But the most telling signs are the elevation of David's house and the Temple: Whereas Ezra–Nehemiah ignores Zerubbabel's Davidic origin, 1 Esdras spells it out, exalting Zerubbabel with the story of the three guardsmen and the rearrangement of the chapters and making him uniquely responsible for the successful restoration. Eskenazi also links the ending of 1 Esdras and 2 Chronicles: Both books end, seemingly in mid-sentence, with a key word that sums up the important communal task: "going up" for 2 Chronicles and "gathering together" for 1 Esdras. These and other details convince Eskenazi that 1 Esdras does have a thematic and ideological relationship to the books of Chronicles as the fragment hypothesis maintains; but, as the compilation hypothesis maintains, it is nevertheless a distinct composition, not a fragment of Chronicles.

Other contemporary contributions to the interpretation of 1 Esdras include Myers's linguistic analysis, which establishes a second-century BCE date for the Greek translation, and his suggestion that the book may be an apologia for Jews who assisted Antiochus III. Myers relates the book's heightened emphasis on divine presence with the existence of competing temples (e.g., at Leontopolis), which may have necessitated special pleading on behalf of Jerusalem. A. Gardner (1986) links its purpose and date to the Maccabean era, reading it as a specific response to priestly abuses; and Garbini reasserts the priority of 1 Esdras over Ezra–Nehemiah, claiming that this independent second-century BCE composition reflects reforms directed toward removing the rigid separation between clergy and laity and implementing a new popular liturgy.

Bibliography: D. Bohler, *Die heilige Stadt in Esdras und Esra-Nehemia: Zwei Konzeptionen der Wiederherstellung Israels* (OBO 158, 1997). **S. A. Cook,** "I Esdras," *APOT* (1913) 1:1-20. **F. M. Cross,** "A Reconstruction of the Judean Restoration," *JBL* 94 (1975) 4-18. **T. C. Eskenazi,** "The Chronicler and the Composition of 1 Esdras," *CBQ* 48 (1986) 39-61. *In an Age of Prose: A Literary Approach to Ezra–Nehemiah* (1988). **D. N. Freedman,** "The Chronicler's Purpose," *CBQ* 23 (1961) 436-42. **G. Garbini,** *History and Ideology in Ancient Israel* (1988). **A. E. Gardner,** "The Purpose of 1 Esdras," *JJS* 37 (1986) 18-27. **R. Hanhart,** *Text und Textgeschichte des 1. Esrabuches* (Mitteilungen des Septuaginta 12, 1974). **R. W. Klein,** "Studies in the Greek Texts of the Chronicler" (diss., Harvard University, 1966); "1 Esdras," *The Books of the Bible* (ed. B. W. Anderson, 1989) 2:13-19. **T. Muraoka,** *A Greek-Hebrew/Aramaic Index to 1 Esdras* (Septuagint and Cognate Studies 16, 1984). **J. M. Myers,** *I and II Esdras* (AB 42, 1974). **K.-F. Pohlmann,** *Studien zum dritten Esra* (FRLANT 104, 1970); *Historische und legendarische Erzählungen: 3. Esrabuch* (FRLANT 104, 1980). **C. C. Torrey,** *Ezra Studies* (Library of Biblical Studies, 1910). **B. Walde,** *Die Esdras-bucher der Septuaginta: Ihr gegenseitiges Verhältnis* (BibS(F) 18, 4, 1913). **J. C. Vanderkam,** *The Jewish Apocalyptic Heritage in Early Christianity* (1996). **H. G. M. Williamson,** *Israel in the Books of Chronicles* (1977).

T. C. ESKENAZI

ESDRAS, SECOND BOOK OF

Second Esdras is the name given in the English APOCRYPHA to an expanded version of an apocalypse (see APOCALYPTICISM) identified in Latin manuscripts as 4 Ezra. That apocalypse is found in chaps. 3–14 of 2 Esdras. Fourth Ezra is part of a fairly extensive body of Ezrianic traditions, the breadth and importance of which are reflected in the wealth of extant manuscripts. Of the eleven Latin codices that survive, perhaps the oldest and most important is Codex Sangermanensis. Written about 822 CE, this codex lacks some sixty-nine verses of chap. 7. In 1875 R. Bensly published a fragment that restored these missing verses, 4 Ezra 7:36-105, which appear to deny the value of prayer for the unrighteous dead. B. Metzger (1957) and L. Gry (1938) also believed that this codex was the source of "the vast majority of extant manuscripts" of the book. An ARMENIAN text was published in 1805 by Zohrab (or Zohrabian) and later by Hovsepheantz; it was translated into English in 1901 by Issaverdens. Ezrianic material distinct from the more "mainline" Ezrianic traditions survives in Arabic; Ethiopic (see ETHIOPIAN BIBLICAL INTERPRETATION); Syriac; Coptic/Sahidic; Georgian; and, in fragmentary form, Greek. Important editions of the Ethiopic and related texts were published by A. DILLMANN in 1894 and by J. HALÉVY in 1902.

With respect to the question of the text's original language, three languages are proposed: Greek, Aramaic, and Hebrew. While Metzger argued that all extant manuscripts derive from the Greek, he left open the possibility that the Greek may itself derive from a Semitic text. With the possible exception of the Armenian texts, differences between the various versions of 4 Ezra can be explained "by presupposing corruptions in or misunderstanding of a Greek text underlying them" (*OTP* 1:520) A. HILGENFELD used the Latin version to reconstruct the original Greek. Supporters of this position included G. Volkmar (1863), O. Fritzsche (1851), F. Rosenthal (1885), and H. Thackeray.

In 1633 J. MORIN postulated that either Hebrew or Aramaic was the original language of 4 Ezra (Gry, 1:xxi). Accordingly, J. WELLHAUSEN argued that the work's vocabulary, grammar, syntax and use of formulas were more consistent with Semitic usage than with Greek (Gry, 1:xxii) and argued in favor of Hebrew (234, note 3). Later, however, he reversed himself and endorsed Aramaic as the original language (1911, 1:xxiii-lxxx). Likewise, Gry, C. C. TORREY, and J. Bloch argued that the original language was Aramaic.

The presence of "notable Hebraisms" has led others—including G. Box (1912), A. Kaminka (1932), F. Zimmerman (1960–61), and G. Nickelsburg (1981)—to speculate that the original language was Hebrew. J. Schreiner (1981, 295) offers a practical perspective: "Textual problems dissolve against the backdrop of Hebrew, but not against the backdrop of Aramaic."

In light of 3:1 and the reference to the thirtieth year after the destruction of the city, most scholars argued that 4 Ezra could not have been written before c. 100 CE. Moreover, by the end of the Bar-Kokhba revolt, Christian and Jewish circles totally separated, making it unlikely that the original Hebrew dates much after 120 CE. Nickelsburg places the date of authorship in the second century CE.

How the present text came into existence remains an open issue. Most scholars fall into one of two groups: those who see it as a collection of independent sources woven together by a redactor and those who see it as essentially the work of a single hand. Those who ascribe to the first position include Box, Metzger (*OTP* 1:517), M. Knibb (1979, 76), W. OESTERLEY, and R. KABISCH. Scholars who hold the second opinion include B. Violet (1910–24), Gry, D. Russell (1964), H. GUNKEL (1900), J. Collins, J. Keulers (1922), W. SANDAY, and M. Stone (at least in later works). These scholars do not rule out the possibility that more than one source was used by the author; rather, they all argue in some shape or form that, however many independent traditions might be reflected in the text's present form, the book as it now stands is the work of one hand, although chaps. 3–10 or 14 may have existed as an independent work.

A number of scholars, including Violet, Collins, Box, and R. CHARLES (*APOT* 2:476-77), have noted many similarities between 4 Ezra and 2 BARUCH. These parallels have led some of them, notably E. Ewald (1863) and M. James (1895), to speculate that these texts had a common author. For Charles, these points of convergence are matched by nearly as many points of divergence. Box regarded 4 Ezra and 2 Baruch as "twin" works that are at once related yet distinct. They are related in that they have been subject to a mingling of rabbinic and apocalyptic material, and distinct because each is the product of a different rabbinic school. They, therefore, do not share common authorship (*APOT* 2.542; Box, lxii-lxvi, esp. lxv). Box noted other, less direct parallels between 4 Ezra and the PSALMS OF SOLOMON (Box, lxxiii). In addition, parallels to 1 ENOCH, the *Testament of Napthali*, and the *Testament of Levi* have been noted.

Bibliography: **R. L. Bensly,** *The Missing Fragment of the Latin Translation of the Fourth Book of Ezra* (1875); *The Fourth Book of Ezra: The Latin Version Edited from the* MSS (1895). **J. Bloch,** "Was there a Greek Version of the Apocalypse of Ezra?" *JQR* 46 (1956) 309-20; "The Ezra Apocalypse: Was It Written in Hebrew, Greek, or Aramaic?" *JQR* 48 (1957) 279-94; "Some Christological Interpolations in the Ezra-Apocalypse," *HTR* 51 (1958) 87-94. **G. H. Box,** *The Ezra Apocalypse* (1912); "4 Ezra" *APOT* 2.542-624. **R. J. Coggins and M. A. Knibb,** *The First and Second Books of Esdras* (1979) 76-305. **J. J. Collins,** "The Jewish Apocalypses," *Apocalypse: The Morphology of a Genre* (ed. J. J. Collins, Semeia 14, 1979) 33-34, 53; *The Apocalyptic Imagination* (1984) 156-69. **A.-M. Denis,** "Les fragments grecs de l'Apocalypse 4 Esdras," *Introduction aux Pseudepigraphes Grecs d'Ancien Testament* (SVTP 1, 1970) 194-200. **E. G. A. Ewald,** *Das vierte Ezrabuch nach seinem Zeitalter, seinem arabischen Ubersetzungen, und einer neuen Wiederherstellung* (Abhandlungen der Königlischen Gesellschaft der Wissenschaften zu Göttingen 11 1863). **O. F. Fritzsche,** *Kurzgefasstes exegetisches Handbuch zu den Apokryphen des Alten Testaments* (1851). **J. Gildemeister,** *Esdrae liber quartus arabice e codice Vaticano* (1877). **L. Gry,** *Les dires prophetiques d'Esdras* (2 vols 1938). **H. Gunkel,** "Das 4. Buch Ezra," *APAT* 2.331-401. **R. Hanhart,** *2 Esdras* (1993). **A. Hilgenfeld,** *Messias Judaeorum* (1869) 36-113. **M. R. James,** *2 Esdras* (TS 3, 1895). **R. Kabisch,** *Das vierte Buch Ezra und seine Quellen untersucht* (1889). **A. Kaminka,** "Beiträge zur Erklärung der Esra-Apokalypse und zur Rekonstruktion ihres hebraischen Urtextes," *MGWJ* 76 (1932) 121-38, 206-12, 494-511; 77 (1933) 339-55. **J. Keulers,** "Die Eschatologische Lehre des vierten Esrabuches," *Biblische Studien* 20 (1922) 1-204. **B. W. Longnecker,** *2 Esdras* (Guides to Apocrypha and Pseudepigrapha, 1995). **B. M. Metzger,** "The 'Lost' Section of II Esdras (= IV Ezra)," *JBL* 76 (1957) 153-57; "The Fourth Book of Ezra" *OTP* 1.516-59. **G. T. Milazzo,** *The Protest and the Silence: Suffering, Death, and Biblical Theology* (1992). **G. W. E. Nickelsburg,** *Jewish Literature Between the Torah and the Bible* (1981) 287-94. **W. O. E. Oesterley,** "The Ezra Apocalypse (2 [4] Esdras)," *The Books of the Apocrypha: Their Origin, Teaching, and Contents* (1914) 509-33; *II Esdras (The Ezra Apocalypse), with Introduction and Notes* (1933). **F. Rosenthal,** *Vier apokryphische Bücher aus der Zeit und Schule R. Akiba's: "Assumptio Mosis," "Das vierte Buch Esra," "Die Apokalypse Baruch," "Das Buch Tobi "* (1885). **R. Rubinkiewicz,** "Un fragment grec du IVe livre d'Esdras (chapitres xi et xii)," *Muséon* 89 (1976) 75-87. **D. S. Russell,** *The Method and Message of Jewish Apocalyptic* (1964) 62-64. **J. Schreiner,** "Das 4. Buch Ezra," *JSHRZ* 5.4 (1981) 291-412. **E. Schürer,** *HJPAJC* (1986) 3:294-306. **M. E. Stone,** "Some Features of the Armenian Version of IV Ezra," *Muséon* 79 (1966) 387-400; "Some Remarks on the Textual Criticism of IV Ezra" *HTR* 60 (1967) 107-15; "Apocryphal Notes" *IOS* (1971) 1:123-31; *The Armenian Version of IV Ezra* (1979); *Features of the Eschatology of IV Ezra* (1989); *Fourth Ezra* (Hermeneia, 1990). **B. Violet,** *Die Esra-Apokalypse* (2 vols., GCS, 1910–24). **G. Volkmar,** *Second Esdras* (Handbuch der Einleitung in die Apokryphen 2, 1863). **J. Wellhausen,** *Skizzen und Vorarbeiten* (1899) 215-49. **F. Zimmerman,** "Underlying Documents of IV Ezra," *JQR* 51 (1960–61) 107-34.

G. T. MILAZZO

ESTHER, BOOK OF (AND ADDITIONS)

1. Introduction. No other biblical book has occasioned as much strong feeling and scholarly debate over its historicity, canonical status, textual integrity, and theological and moral stature as has the book of Esther. Excluded by some Jews from their CANON of the first century CE (and possibly from that of the second or even the third), Esther was gradually accepted as canonical by both Jews and Christians, only to be virtually ignored by the latter even as Jews increasingly venerated the *Megilla* (Scroll), as they called it. Judaism developed a rich talmudic and midrashic tradition about the book that was totally ignored by Christians, while the latter in turn were divided, first into Eastern and Western camps, and then later into sharply contrasting Protestant and Roman Catholic perspectives. All this becomes more understandable when one realizes that in the MT of Esther God is not mentioned (yet the Persian king is referred to 190 times in 167 verses!); nor are such key Jewish concepts as prayer, Temple, *kaśrû,* Jerusalem, or covenant (fasting is the only religious practice mentioned!). Moreover, the Greek version has two radically different texts (the Septuagint, or B-text; and the A-text), neither of which closely corresponds to the MT, plus six Additions (ADDS), which appreciably affect the book's purpose, dramatic appeal, appearance of authenticity, and religious and moral character. Jews and Protestants have regarded the ADDS as uncanonical and "apocryphal," while Roman Catholics, since the decrees of the Council of Trent in 1546, have called them "deuterocanonical."

Esther's ADDS (107 verses) differ from one another—and from the canonical sections—in purpose, content, and style. They consist of ADDS A: Mordecai's dream (vv. 1-11) and a conspiracy uncovered by him (vv. 12-17); B: the royal edict composed by Haman for the destruction of the Jews (vv. 1-7); C: the prayers of Mordecai (vv. 1-11) and Esther (vv. 12-30); D: Esther's dramatic unannounced audience with the king (vv. 1-16); E: the royal edict dictated by Mordecai (vv. 1-24); and F: an explanation of Mordecai's dream (vv. 1-10) and the book's colophon (v. 11).

2. Early Jewish Interpretations. Although the earliest form of the Esther story may go back to the fourth century BCE, its Hebrew text probably took its final form in the early or middle Hellenistic period (331–168 BCE). Nonetheless, Esther was one of the last books of the HB to be canonized. The Essene community at Qumran (c. 150 BCE–68 CE) did not regard it as canonical, for not even a fragment of it has been found there (see J. Milik [1992]), nor was Purim part of their liturgical calendar. At least two rabbis in the third century (*b. Meg.* 7a) and two in the third/fourth (*b. Sanh.* 2) also regarded the book as noncanonical, and it is not found in the second-century Jewish Greek translations of AQUILA, SYMMACHUS, or THEODOTION. The Jewish historian

JOSEPHUS evidently accepted Esther's canonicity, however, for he paraphrased it and ADDS B-E in his *Antiquities of the Jews* (c. 94 CE) and added to it haggadic (narrative or non-legal) materials, including some of his own.

Some of the book's haggadic and halakhic (legal) materials, although not written down in the TALMUD until the early sixth century, must have originated in the second and first centuries BCE. *Megilla,* a tractate of the Mishna, contains halakhic discussions of such problems as when, how, and where Esther may be read and Purim celebrated. To it was added the *Gemara,* the oral discussions of the Mishna's *Halakoth* by the Amorin. Meanwhile, the book's growing *Haggadoth* (oral explanations and legends) were assembled into the MIDRASH (commentary) and added to the Talmud. An often quoted passage, especially by modern Christian critics, is in *b. Meg.* 7b, where Jews celebrating Purim were allowed to drink wine until unable to distinguish between "Blessed is Mordecai" and "Cursed is Haman!" Esther has two TARGUMIM (Aramaic translations) that are also Midrashes: 1 Targum (7th cent.) containing the biblical text as well as halakhic and haggadic materials, including portions of *Megilla;* and 2 Targum (9th cent.), which is twice as long and contains more of the same.

3. The Early Christian Era. Esther was not quoted by JESUS or alluded to by any NT writer. Even though included in the canonical lists of a few Eastern church fathers (notably, Origen, Epiphanius [c. 315–403], Cyril of Jerusalem [c. 315–386], the Laodicene Canons [343–381], the Apostolic Canons [380], the Synod of Trullo [692], John of Damascus [c. 675–c. 745]) and of most Western fathers, ranging from Hilary (c. 315–c. 367) to ISIDORE OF SEVILLE as well as the councils of Hippo (393) and Carthage (397), it was rarely alluded to, let alone quoted.

CLEMENT OF ROME alluded to Esther and Judith as examples of brave and godly women in *1 Clem.* 55, as did CLEMENT OF ALEXANDRIA in *Strom.* 4:19, ATHANASIUS of Alexandria in his *Fourth Festal Letter,* and the author of the *Constitutions of the Holy Apostles* 5. iii, 20 (c. 380). Esther was always read in either the Greek or the Latin, and it was her prayer that was most frequently mentioned, being quoted by ORIGEN (*peri euches* 13.2) and JEROME (*apologeticum ad Pammachius*). But AUGUSTINE also made much of the miraculous transformation of the king's attitude in ADD D 8 (*de Civitate Dei* 18.36 and *de Gratia Christi et de peccato originali* 1.24) and even mentioned Mordecai's dream (*de divinis scripturis* 130). Paulinus Nolanus (c. 353–431) commented on Haman's end and Esther's beauty (*Carmina* 26.95; 28.27). All this notwithstanding, the fathers virtually ignored the book.

4. The Medieval Period. *a. Jewish.* Of special note is the twelfth-century exegetical Midrash *Esther Rabbah,* consisting of *Esther Rabbah* 1, an amoraic Midrash

in mishnaic Hebrew with material from tannaitic literature, the Jerusalem Talmud and other earlier sources (but
not the Targums!) and dating to the sixth century; and
Esther Rabbah 2, which, along with other older homilies, also contained ADDS A and C as translated from
the LXX (see SEPTUAGINT) by Josippon (10th cent.) and
dated to the eleventh century. Many later medieval
midrashes drew upon this work.

A radically different type of scholarship that rejected
traditional rabbinic exegesis and, like Arabic scholarship, emphasized a literalistic interpretation of Scripture
was that of RASHI (1040–1105), who emphasized lexical
and grammatical analysis. The greatest of all Arabic-
Jewish exegetes, A. IBN EZRA (1092–1167), also wrote
a commentary on Esther. This literalistic approach to
Scripture was productive, but short-lived, for the thirteenth century witnessed the rise of KABBALAH, a type
of esoteric mysticism that emphasized anew allegorical
and midrashic interpretations.

b. Christian. The year 836 marked the appearance of
the first full-length commentary on Esther, RABANUS
MAURUS's *Expositio in librum Esther.* Confining his
exegesis to the canonical sections, he nonetheless continued the medieval practice of offering allegorical interpretations, e.g., the "linen and purple cords" in Esth
1:6 represent "mortification of the flesh" and "the blood
of the martyrs," respectively.

Devotional and homilectical concerns prevailed over
exegetical ones (e.g., the commentaries of WALAFRID
STRABO [c. 808–849] and HUGH OF ST. VICTOR [1096–
1141]). While regarding the book as essentially historical, R. Tuitiensis (1135) mentioned Mordecai's dream
and prayer and continued allegorical interpretations of
the text; e.g., Mordecai's witness of Haman's downfall
foreshadowed Christ's witness of his own victory over
Satan, a view espoused in the twentieth century by the
Barthian scholar W. VISCHER (1937). The major contribution to the critical study of Esther was NICHOLAS
OF LYRA's (c. 1270–1349) *Postillae perpetuae,* which
included the exegetical work of Rashi and Ibn Ezra.

**5. The Renaissance-Reformation Period. *a. Jew-
ish.*** Virtually unaffected by the intellectual revolution
then going on among Christian scholars, Jewish commentators continued their midrashic approach to Scripture.

b. Christian. With the West's discovery of classical
languages and literature, plus the Protestants' insistence
on Scripture as the sole AUTHORITY for doctrines, the
second half of the sixteenth century witnessed a strong
emphasis on the study of the Bible in its original
Hebrew and Greek, although most Roman Catholic
scholars still used the VULGATE. Thus Roman Catholics
continued to study the ADDS while Protestants increasingly ignored them.

Following the earlier interpretations of the fathers,
many Roman Catholics continued the allegorical approach (especially the idea that Queen Esther was a type
of the Virgin Mary); but others showed a strong interest
in textual and historical matters, notably, J. Menochius
(1630), who also utilized Jewish and Protestant scholarship. J. de la Haye's *Biblia Maxima* (1660) was a
compendium of Roman Catholic study for the previous
150 years.

Protestants, too, regarded Esther as essentially historical but employed allegory less, preferring to emphasize
the book's literal, historical, and grammatical aspects.
Neither CALVIN nor LUTHER wrote a commentary on the
book. The latter's attitude toward it is still sometimes
quoted with approval: "I am so hostile to this book [2
Maccabees] and to Esther that I could wish that they
did not exist at all; for they judaize too greatly and have
much pagan impropriety" (*Table Talks,* 24).

S. MÜNSTER's Latin translation of Esther (1546) was
based on the Hebrew text. Critical studies were also
made by scholars like H. GROTIUS (1644), who cited
such classical sources as Herodotus's *History of the
Persian Wars* and Josephus, while S. PAGNINUS (1556),
the *Westminster Assembly's Annotations* (1657), and
others continued along more devotional or homiletical
lines. M. POOLE's *Synopsis criticorum aliorumque Sacrae Scripturae interpretum* (1669) included the critical
insights of both Protestant and Roman Catholic scholarship for the past century and a half.

6. The Post-Reformation Period. The next 150
years was a period of retrenchment and theological
narrowness for both churches during which little scholarly progress was made on Esther by either Roman
Catholics or Protestants. Although B. SPINOZA's *Tractatus theologico-politicus* (1670) demonstrated a genuinely critical spirit, it exerted little influence on his own
compatriots, let alone on Christians.

**7. The Modern Period. *a. Die Aufklärung, or the
Enlightenment.*** Under the influence of German rationalists and English Deists (see DEISM), biblical books
were scrutinized with a most critical eye. "Lower criticism" was advanced by J. H. MICHAELIS (*Biblia hebraica*
[1720]), B. KENNICOTT (*Vetus Testamentum Hebraicum*
[1776–80]), and G. de ROSSI (*Variae lectiones Veteris
Testamenti* [1784–88]), all of whom collated variants of
the Hebrew text, although most of the manuscripts were
unfortunately of a late medieval date.

Considerable progress was also made in the area of
higher criticism, i.e., the who, what, where, when, and
why of a biblical book. When J. D. MICHAELIS (*Esther*
[1783]) conceded that one could be "a perfect [*vollkom-
mener*] Lutheran" and yet have doubts about the historicity of the book, J. SEMLER had already made an all-out
attack on its historicity, characterizing the book as "a
Jewish romance" or novel, a view to which a majority
of scholars still subscribe.

The sustained attack on the book's historicity and its
"unacceptable moral tone" by scholars like J. G. EICH-

HORN (1780) and A. Niemeyer (1782), who first made the often repeated observation that Queen Vashti was the only decent person in Esther, elicited conservative responses on the part of J. Vos (1775) and others. Increasingly, Christian scholars were divided into two camps: those contesting Esther's historicity and those defending it, the latter position more often taken by Roman Catholics.

b. The nineteenth century. i. Jewish. Jewish scholars began addressing some of the same problems as Christians, sometimes in the same journals, e.g., J. Bloch, *Hellenistische Bestandtheile im biblischen Schriftthum, eine kritische Untersuchung über Abfassung, Charakter, und Tendenzen des Buches Esther* (1877) and "Der historische Hintergund und die Abfassungszeit des Buch Esther" (*MGWJ* [1886]); B. Hause, "Noch einmal das Buch Esther" (*JBL* 8 [1879] no. 42); and J. J. de Villiers "Modern Criticism and the Megilla" (*JC* [Feb., 1893]).

ii. Christian. Conservative treatments of Esther appeared in Jahn, *Einleitung in die osttlichen Bücher des Alten Bundes* 2 (1803); J. Scholz, *Einleitung in Die heiligen Schriften des Alten und Neuen Testaments* 1 (1845); C. KEIL's very scholarly and ultra-conservative *Lehrbuch die historisch-kritischen Einleitung in die kanonischen Schriften des Alte Testament* (1873); A. Scholz's scholarly but allegory-laden *Commentar über das Buch Esther mit seinen Zusätzen* (1892); and E. Kaulen, *Einleitung in die Heilige Schrift* (1890).

Liberal treatments included W. DE WETTE, *Lehrbuch des historischen-kritischen Einleitung* (1817); H. EWALD, *Geschichte des Volkes Israel bis Christus* (1843); T. NÖLDEKE, *Die Alttestamentliche Literatur* (1868); E. REUSS, *Geschichte der heiligen Schriften* (1890); T. CHEYNE, *Founders of OT Criticism* (1893); E. KAUTZSCH, *HSAT(K)* (1896); and E. SCHÜRER, *Geschichte des jüdischen Volkes im Zeitalter Jesu Christi* (1898–1901). V. RYSSEL's commentary in E. BERTHEAU's KEH (1887) was the best of the liberal treatments.

As part of his efforts to reconstruct the *Urtext* of the LXX, P. LAGARDE (*Librorum Veteris Testamenti Canonicorum* [1883]) "proved" that Esther's A-text was part of the Lucianic recension of the LXX, a view that universally prevailed among scholars until the discovery of the DEAD SEA SCROLLS, when various apocryphal and pseudepigraphical works (see PSEUDEPIGRAPHA) now appeared in Semitic form. Earlier, Lagarde had edited *Targum Rishon* and *Targum Sheni* for Hagiographa Chaldaice (1873).

Protestants, too, exhaustively treated the ADDS and regarded them as composed in Greek (so O. Fritzsche, KEHA [1851]; J. Fuller in H. Wace's *Apocrypha of the Speaker's Commentary,* 1 [1888], with special emphasis on the Talmudic and targumic materials; and Ryssel, *APAT* [1900] 1.193-212).

The nineteenth century's (and the twentieth's) decipherment of various cuneiform scripts and languages, as well as the excavation of various archaeological sites (see ARCHAEOLOGY AND BIBLICAL STUDIES) and their artifacts, contributed much toward illuminating the book's Achaemenid setting but little toward confirming its historicity. During this same period scholars began looking for Purim's origins in pagan sources, in some Greek, Babylonian, or, especially, Persian festival—but without conspicuous success.

The critical work of the nineteenth century was actually best summarized in three works appearing in 1908: P. HAUPT, *Critical Notes on Esther,* and L. Paton, "A Text-critical Apparatus to the Book of Esther" (both in the *Harper Memorial,* 2), and Paton's *A Critical and Exegetical Commentary on the Book of Esther* (ICC), the latter being the most comprehensive and detailed discussion in English thus far of the book's history of interpretation and its problems of higher and lower criticism.

c. The twentieth century. Especially after the works of Paton, Haupt, and H. GUNKEL (*Esther* [1916]), the literary aspects of Esther became the primary concern of scholars, with some even arguing that the Joseph narrative in Genesis (A. Meinhold, *ZAW* 88 [1976] 72-93) or the Moses story in Exodus 1–12 (G. Gerleman [1970–73]) provided the paradigm for Esther's plot and all its details of "fact."

While the dominant theory among liberal scholars at the turn of the century was that Esther was "pure" fiction, in the twentieth century (especially second half), the "combination theory" has gained ascendancy—that is, the book is a combination of fiction and "fact," the combining of a harem tale about Vashti, a Mordecai story, and an Esther/Hadassah story, the latter two stories being independent tales with a possible core of historicity to each. Thus Esther is a historical novel in which literary considerations determine the plot and details of fact (so H. Bardtke [1963], C. Moore [1971, 1992], S. Berg [1979], and D. Clines [1984]). The book provides a lifestyle for Jews of the diaspora (W. L. Humphreys [1973]).

i. Jewish. In some respects, Jewish scholarship on Esther is more impressive than either Roman Catholic or Protestant studies, if only because of its marked increase in both quantity and scope. Some Jewish scholars were still concerned with the centuries-long Judaic approaches to Esther; e.g., L. Ginzberg (1939); H. Freedman and M. Simon (1939); J. Brown (1976); and B. Grossfeld (1983). But apart from J. Hoschander's *The Book of Esther in the Light of History* (1923), which was concerned with establishing the full historicity of the book, Jewish scholars became primarily interested in problems of higher criticism, especially those concerning the historical origins and theological meaning of Purim: N. Doniach (1933), S. Ben-Chorin (1938), J. LEWY (1939), T. GASTER (1950), S. Besser (1969), J. Lebram (1972), R. Herst (1973), and A. Cohen (1974). Their consensus is that although God is not mentioned in Esther and Purim may well be of pagan origin, the book has a genuinely religious meaning, veiled though it may be.

But Jewish scholars had other concerns as well; e. g., A. Yahuda, "The Meaning of the Name Esther" (*JRAS* [1946] 174-78); S. TALMON, " 'Wisdom' in the Book of Esther" (*VT* 13 [1963] 419-55), which viewed Esther as a historicized wisdom tale; E. BICKERMAN, *Four Strange Books of the Bible* (1967); S. Zeitlin, "The Books of Esther and Judith: A Parallel" in M. Enslin's *The Book of Judith* (1972); and R. GORDIS (1974, 1976, 1981), who hypothesized that the book was written by a gentile chronicler. S. Berg's study (1979) is, to date, the best RHETORICAL analysis of Esther and clearly shows that the MT in its present form is an integrated and literary whole whose themes are those of power, loyalty to God and Israel, the inviolability of the Jewish people, and reversal.

In contrast to previous centuries, Jewish articles featured the Greek text, including its ADDS; e.g., Bickerman, "The Colophon of the Greek Book of Esther" (*JBL* 63 [1944] 339-62) and "Notes on the Greek Book of Esther" (*PAAJR* 20 [1950] 101-33); and E. Tov, "The Lucianic Text of the Canonical and the Apocryphal Sections of Esther" (*Textus* 10 [1982] 1-25), which argued that Esther's A-Text is a recension of the LXX corrected toward a Hebrew (or Aramaic) text quite different from the MT.

ii. Christian. Commentaries continuing the liberal tradition included those of A. Streane (1907); B. Anderson (1954); G. Knight (1955); H. Ringgren (1958), and H. Bardtke (1963), the most scientific and complete German commentary on Esther in the last two hundred years; Moore (1971); G. Gerleman (1970–73); W. Fuerst (1975); and J. Cragham (OTM, 1982). Roman Catholic commentaries, often more conservative and frequently containing the ADDS, included those of J. Schildenberger, *Das Buch Esther* (HSAT 4.3 [1941]); L. Soubigou, *Esther traduit et commenté* (1952); A. Barucq, *Judith-Esther* (1959); and B. Girbau, *La Biblia* (1960).

Separate and detailed studies of the ADDS were made by J. Gregg (1913, 665-84), and F. Roiron (*RSR* [1916]), the latter arguing that ADDS B and E are the actual Greek edicts of Haman and Mordecai respectively; and R. PFEIFFER, *History of NT Times* (1949). But thanks to the catalytic study of the problem by C. C. TORREY (1944), scholars, while granting a Greek origin for ADDS B and E, have increasingly argued for a Hebrew or Aramaic *Vorlage* for such interpolations as ADDS A, C, D, and F (so E. Ehrlich, *ZRGG* 7 [1955] 69-74; Moore [1973]; R. Martin, *JBL* 94 [1975] 65-72).

In contrast to the previous one hundred years, scholars increasingly maintained that the A-text is a separate and independent translation of another Semitic text, not a recension of the LXX (so Torrey [1944]; Moore, *ZAW* 79 [1967] 351-58; and Clines, [1984]). In a foreshad-

owing of Vatican II, L. Soubigou (*Esther* [1952] 581-82, 597) noted that Roman Catholic scholars must accept as doctrinally true the ADDS's inspirational character, but not that they were part of the original book.

Now, however, the legitimate, centuries-old distinctions between Jewish scholarship on Esther and that of Christians (including Catholic versus Protestant) are no longer useful. It is now much more the academic or methodological perspective rather than the theological or religious orientation that determines the nature and character of any particular study of Esther. Redactive and LITERARY criticism (e.g., C. Dorothy [1989]; M. Fox [1991]; L. Day [1995]; K. Craig [1995]), feminist scholarship (such as A. LaCoque [1990]; K. Darr [1991]; W. Phipps [1992]; S. White [1992]; A. Bellis [1994]), and computer-generated studies (J. Miles [1985] and K. Jobes [1996]) dominate the field of Esther studies—for now.

Bibliography: B. W. Anderson, "The Book of Esther," *IB* (1954) 3:823-74. H. Bardtke, *Das Buch Esther* (KAT 17, 5, 1963); *Luther und das Buch Esther* (1964). A. O. Bellis, *Helpmates, Harlots, and Heroes: Women's Stories in the HB* (1994). S. Ben-Chorin, *Kritik des Estherbuches* (1938). S. B. Berg, *The Book of Esther: Motifs, Themes and Structure* (SBLDS 44, 1979). S. Besser, "Esther and Purim—Chance and Play" *CCARJ* 16 (1969) 36-42. J. M. Brown, *Rabbinic Interpretations of the Characters and Plot of the Book of Esther: As Reflected in Midrash Esther Rabbah* (1976). D. J. A. Clines, *The Esther Scroll: The Story of the Story* (1984). A. Cohen, " 'Hu Ha-goral': The Religious Significance of Esther," *Judaism* 23 (1974) 87-94. K. M. Craig, Jr., *Reading Esther: A Case for the Literary Carnivalesque* (Literary Currents in Biblical Interpretation, 1995). K. P. Darr, *Far More Precious Than Jewels: Perspectives on Biblical Women* (1991). L. Day, *Three Faces of a Queen: Characterization in the Books of Esther* (JSOTSup 186, 1995). W. Dommershausen, *Die Estherrolle* (SBM 6, 1968). N. Doniach, *Purim or the Feast of Esther: An Historical Study* (1933). C. V. Dorothy, *The Books of Esther: Structure, Genre, and Textual Integrity* (JSOTSup 187, 1989). J. G. Eichhorn, *Einleitung ins Alte Testament* (3 vols., 1780–83). M. V. Fox, *The Redaction of the Books of Esther* (SBLMS 40, 1991). H. Freedman and M. Simon, *Midrash Rabbah* 9 (1939) 1-124. W. J. Fuerst, *The Books of Ruth, Esther, Ecclesiastes, the Song of Songs, Lamentations* (CBC, 1975). T. Gaster, *Purim and Hanukkah in Custom and Tradition* (1950). G. Gerleman, *Esther* (BKAT 21, 1970–73). L. Ginzberg, *The Legends of the Jews* 4 (1913) 365-448; 6 (1928) 451-81; 7 (1939). R. Gordis, *Megillat Esther: The Masoretic Hebrew Text with Introduction, New Translation and Commentary* (1974); "Studies in the Esther Narrative," *JBL* 95 (1976) 43-58; "Religion, Wisdom and History in the Book of Esther—A New Solution to an Ancient Crux," *JBL* 100 (1981) 359-88. J. A. F. Gregg, "The Additions to Esther," *APOT* 1 (1913) 665-71. H. Grossfeld, *The First Targum to Esther* (1983). R. Herst, "The Purim Connection," *USQR* 28 (1973) 139-45. W. L.

Humphreys, *JBL* 92 (1973) 211-23. **K. H. Jobes,** *The Alpha-Text of Esther: Its Character and Relationship to the Masoretic Text* (SBLDS 153, 1995). **G. F. Knight,** *Esther, Song of Songs, Lamentations: Introduction and Commentary* (TBC, 1955). **A. LaCoque,** *The Feminine Unconventional: Four Subversive Figures in Israel* (1990). **J. Lebram,** "Purimfest und Estherbuch," *VT* 22 (1972) 208-22. **J. D. Levenson,** *Esther* (OTL, 1997). **J. Lewy,** "Old Assyrian *puru'um* and *purum*," *RHA* 5 (1939) 117-24; "The Feast of the 14th Day of Adar," *HUCA* 14 (1939) 127-51. **J. R. Miles,** *Retroversion and Text Criticism: The Predicability of Syntax in an Ancient Translation from Greek to Ethiopic* (SBLSCS 17, 1985). **J. T. Milik,** "Les Modeles Araméens du Livre d'Esther dans La Grotte 4 de Qumran," *RdQ* 15 (1992) 321-99. **C. A. Moore,** *Esther* (AB 7B, 1971); *JBL* 92 (1973) 382-93; *Daniel, Esther, and Jeremiah: The Additions* (AB 44, 1977); *ABD* (1992) 2:626-43. **A. Niemayer,** *Charakteristick der Bibel* (1782). **L. B. Paton,** *A Critical and Exegetical Commentary on the Book of Esther* (ICC, 1908). **W. E. Phipps,** *Assertive Biblical Women* (Contributions in Women's Studies 128, 1992). **H. Ringgren,** *Das Buch Esther* (ATD 16, 1958). **M. Simon,** "Megillah: Translated into English with Notes, Glossary, and Indices," *Babylonian Talmud* (1938). **A. W. Streane,** *The Book of Esther, With Intro and Notes* (CBSC, 1907). **C. C. Torrey,** "The Older Book of Esther," *HTR* 37 (1944) 1-40. **W. Vischer,** *Esther* (TEH 48, 1937). **S. A. White,** "Esther: A Feminine Model for Jewish Diaspora," *Gender and Difference in Ancient Israel* (ed. P. Day, 1989) 161-77; *Women's Bible Commentary* (eds. C. A. Newsom and S. H. Ringe, 1992) 124-29.

C. A. MOORE

ETHIOPIAN BIBLICAL INTERPRETATION

1. The Coming of Christianity to Ethopia. According to local tradition, Christianity was brought to Ethiopia, on the Horn of Africa, by the eunuch of Candace, queen of the Ethiopians. The Ethiopian eunuch was baptized by the apostle Philip when the two met at Gaza while the eunuch was returning to his homeland after worshiping in Jerusalem (Acts 8:26-39). According to tradition, at his return this "great authority" preached Christianity; but the country remained without priestly authority until about 330 CE, at which time Frumentius, a young man from Tyre, Syria (in today's Lebanon), was ordained as its first bishop by ATHANASIUS of Alexandria (c. 296–373). Since the eunuch was a Jew, the HB must have been known in Ethiopia, and the language was undoubtedly the Greek of the SEPTUAGINT. Moreover, Ethiopian tradition firmly maintains that the prevailing religion of the country before Christianity was Judaism.

The question remaining with this story is the exact location of biblical Ethiopia, the eunuch's homeland. Biblical Ethiopia is the Greek equivalent of Cush, which refers to several places, including regions outside Africa. If a traveler returning from Jerusalem passed through Gaza as the eunuch did, he or she was most probably going to Africa, either to Meroe (Sudan) or to Aksum (Ethiopia or Abyssinia) or to somewhere in Punt. Regardless, there are valid reasons for assuming that Christianity came to Ethiopia during the first century of the religion's existence, since the country's capital, Aksum, and its seaport, Adulis on the Red Sea, were so close to the Middle East, were continuously visited by Christian and Jewish merchants. But Christianity became the official religion of the royal house—hence of the kingdom—when Frumentius was able to convert to Christianity the young king Ezana.

Rufinus, the famous church historian of the fourth and fifth centuries, states that a ship carrying a certain philosopher, Meropius, was attacked at an Ethiopian seaport, possibly Adulis. The others on the ship were killed except for Meropius's two students, Frumentius and Aedesius, who were later taken to the palace, where they were employed in the service of the king, Frumentius as guardian of the law, or secretary of Aksum, and Aedesius as steward of the palace. This situation gave the two Syrian Christians, especially Frumentius, the opportunity to spread Christianity in the country, beginning with the palace household, and to organize the Christian merchants in the city into a community with an oratory, which served also as a school. When Aedesius and Frumentius were finally given their freedom, the former returned to Tyre, while the latter went to Alexandria (see ALEXANDRIAN SCHOOL) to ask the Alexandrian church to support the incipient church in Ethiopia by sending them bishops and priests. The reigning patriarch, Athanasius, ordained Frumentius as the first bishop of Ethiopia, saying, "We will find no one who is better than he" (see G. Haile [1979] 318). In Aksum, Frumentius was received as Abbà (i.e., Father) Salàmà the Illuminator. With the advent of its episcopacy, the church of Ethiopia became a branch of the Coptic Church of Alexandria, receiving from them its metropolitans (and Christian literature). It became autocephalic only in the middle of the twentieth century, with the authority to ordain its patriarch locally. The church, however, remains a faithful member of the group of oriental churches that are "Monophysites," or those who reject the formula of faith—Dyophysism—adopted by the council of Chalcedon in 451 CE.

The local tradition that Christianity was sown on a Jewish field should not be dismissed as incredible. Anyone with even a superficial knowledge of Ethiopian Christianity can see clearly the church's Jewish character, including the observance of the sabbath (from Friday evening to Saturday evening), the HB dietary rules, and the practice of circumcision at the age prescribed in the Bible.

2. The Ethiopic Version of the Bible. The preceding story may throw some light on the background of the Ethiopic Bible. A church founded by a Syrian "Apostle of Ethiopia" who was ordained bishop in Egypt would inevitably look to Antioch and Alexandria for its Christian literature, including the Bible. In addition, the foreign language with which Ethiopians of the time, especially the expatriate members of the small Christian community of Aksum, were best acquainted was Greek, which was also the language of the church of Alexandria. Therefore, the Ethiopic HB was most likely translated from the Septuagint, a Greek version accepted as the standard form of the HB by the churches of the East, including Alexandria and Antioch. That the Ethiopian HB was translated from the Septuagint has been corroborated with compelling internal evidence; consequently, the Ethiopian church also accepts as canonical (see CANON OF THE BIBLE) those books of the Septuagint that are otherwise considered APOCRYPHA. Likewise, the NT was translated from the Greek in the Lucianic recension. In addition the books of JUBILEES (as part of the books of Moses) and ENOCH (as part of the books of the prophets) as well as the *Testament of Our Lord,* the *Didascalia of the Apostles,* and the *Synodicon* (decrees of the apostles and of the councils to the 4th cent.) are authoritative sources in the Ethiopian Orthodox Church. The church teaches that its canonical Scriptures are eighty-one. It has also received, although not as canonical, other PSEUDEPIGRAPHA from the sister churches of Antioch and Alexandria. All these are quoted in the *Maṣeḥaf bet,* "Biblical or exegetical school," to explain ambiguous passages of the Bible and to interpret their spiritual message.

Other books that are quoted extensively are homilies and treatises by church fathers of the universal church, who flourished before 451 CE, or by those who rejected the formula of faith of the Council of Chalcedon held in that year. Among these are Athenasius of Alexandria, CYRIL OF ALEXANDRIA, J. CHRYSOSTOM, and Epiphanius of Cyprus. Commentaries on Hebrews, the three Gospels of Mark, Luke, and John, and the Ten Commandments (see DECALOGUE), all ascribed to Chrysostom, are preserved in Ethiopia entirely in their Geʿez versions, whereas other patristic texts are represented only by catenae. The authors of the commentaries on the scriptural readings for passion week are yet to be identified.

3. Biblical Interpretation. Biblical interpretation in the Ethiopian church aims at a direct translation of the texts from Geʿez, the church's language, into Amharic, the vernacular, which is understood by most of the students. It also aims at an explanation of grammatical problems manifested in the Geʿez of the texts; an explanation of ambiguous passages inherited through the Septuagint; and an explanation of the texts' spiritual and symbolic messages. In the *Maṣeḥaf bet,* the Bible is known only in Ethiopic or Geʿez, which ceased to be spoken over 1,000 years ago. Students have to learn Geʿez in traditional schools because the literature is preserved in this language, and the church uses it to administer its services, despite complaints from the faithful, who do not understand what the clergy say when speaking this language. It is the responsibility of the biblical teacher to ensure that students comprehend the particular Geʿez text. To facilitate this understanding, a direct word-for-word translation is first made from Geʿez into Amharic, especially if the Geʿez sentences are complicated. This process, called *ṭerē tergum,* is not as easy as it appears. The Geʿez Bible is rich in ambiguities that derive from various sources, including a misunderstanding of the *Vorlage* that sometimes occurs during the translation from the Greek. Moreover, ineffective attempts made by some scholars to revise the text, apparently using an Arabic version (or even a Hebrew original in the case of the HB), causes ambiguities, as does a failure to understand the fifth-century Geʿez in which the Bible is preserved. An example of the latter case would be the present/future and subjunctive forms of some verbs, which are spelled the same in writing but are pronounced differently. There are many cases in which the correct pronunciation has not been preserved in the oral transmission of the Bible. The explanation biblical scholars put forth for the many grammatical "mistakes" is that books do not always observe grammatical rules. Ambiguous points that stem from a misunderstanding of the *Vorlage* are elucidated without consulting the original text.

The traditional school did not produce many scholars who knew the languages of the Bible. In addition, schooling for students from families whose vernacular was not Amharic, the language of instruction, probably took longer than for those whose native tongue was Amharic. Amharic was not (and still is not) taught in traditional schools. It is learned by listening to the instruction and by interaction with Amharic speakers.

Looked at from the point of view of Western biblical scholars, the symbolic interpretation of the Bible in Ethiopia may seem excessive. Objects and numbers frequently have other meanings besides their literal sense. The symbolic interpretation of why there are four Gospels, for example, would fill pages. The historical reason for four is not considered. Almost every story in the HB is interpreted to be a PROPHECY of some incident in the life of Christ or in the history of the Christian church. The Bible is not looked at critically; every word in it is accepted as divinely inspired. The attempt, therefore, is not to question why there are discrepancies, when one meets them, but to find excuses for them even if the excuses may not sound reasonable. Sometimes the proper signification of words may be distorted to preserve the spiritual message in accordance with tradition and church teaching. For example, because Mary was chosen by God before the world to be the virgin mother of the Son, the teachers do not accept that she was betrothed to Joseph. Instead, the verb "to be betrothed to" is said to have the meaning "to be guarded by," thus the Blessed Virgin was given to Joseph, "the old man," to be guarded by him for the long-expected virgin birth. The church was equally reluctant to accept the biblical story that the spirit of the prophet Samuel was raised by the power of a witch. The official position or interpretation is that the witch claimed to have done what was actually done by the holy Trinity.

In the *Maṣeḥaf bet* a Scripture text is divided into small sections to be taught at sessions or "lecture periods." These sections are independent of the chapters (which, in any case, are different from the chapters known in the West). The teacher sits on a chair, and the students gather around on the floor to all sides. One of the students starts to read the section assigned for the day, stopping when asked by the teacher to do so; only a few words are read at a time. Only this student holds a book (a manuscript written by hand on parchment); the other students and the teacher do not. The student's reading of a line or a word is followed by the teacher's simple translation (*ṭerē tergum*) and interpretations (*tergwāmē* or *andemm*), which are done from memory (with closed eyes for concentration); the students are expected to memorize what is recited. It takes two to three hours to complete the section of the day, during which there is no discussion and questions are not encouraged. The issue at hand, as far as the teacher is concerned, is the oral transmission of knowledge to the next generation of teachers. The role the teacher plays is not much different from the one adopted by a village storyteller in some societies. Writing is discouraged; it is considered teaching the paper or the parchment.

Concentration for such a long session is aided by the interesting stories the teacher tells to illustrate points. These stories come from native and foreign cultures or were created by the earlier teachers who shaped the *andemm* (exegetical) tradition. For example, the teacher tells the following story to show how the Scripture warns those who envy their neighbors: "There was a man who dreaded death. He prayed to God daily that he might not die. God appeared to him one day and told him to take a jar of water from the spring of life and be baptized with it. Then he revealed to him the spring of life. The man rejoiced greatly at the prospect of not dying. He immediately brought a jar and drew water from the spring. Now a new and evil worry possessed his mind: What if another person who did not pray as much as he did were to touch the water after he had been baptized? He too would live forever for free! So he decided to take the water to a deserted place where no other person would come and be baptized there. While traveling with the jar of water on his shoulder, he stumbled and fell. The jar broke, and the water poured out on one side of his body. Years later at the time of his death, only the side of his body that was not touched by the water died; the other half lived forever—somewhere in this world!" The stories that derive from native cultures promise to be important

sources of Ethiopian social and political history, although they have not yet been exploited by modern historians.

The session (on the same section of Scripture) is repeated two more times, with one of the students reading the text and the teacher translating it into Amharic, explaining the grammatical oddities of the Geʿez and interpreting the text, all in exactly the same language of the previous session. (During my study of the NT, I heard my teacher only once recite a story at the second or third session with a sentence that differed slightly at one particular point.) The second section of the Bible starts at the fourth session, the third at the seventh, and so on.

4. Schools and Disciplines. There are four *Maṣeḥaf bets:* (a) for the HB, (b) for the NT, (c) for the fathers, and (d) for the canon laws (which are actually the ecclesiastical and civil laws embodied in the *Fetḥa Nagast,* "Code of Kings," the *Didascalia of the Apostles,* and the *Synodicon*). A teacher in any of these disciplines, especially the NT, is expected to know and teach the *andemm* of the Psalms of David and the Praises of Mary, *Weddāsē Māryām,* hymns from Syria divided into the days of the week, together with the *Anqaṣa Berhān* (Gate of Light), and hymns for Sundays composed by Yāarēd, a local scholar of the sixth century, in praise of the Blessed Virgin. The interpretation of the liturgy, which includes fourteen anaphoras, is taught by the teacher of the NT or of the fathers. Occasionally there arises a scholar who can teach all four disciplines, who is called a four-eyed teacher. Understandably, the church has more teachers of the NT than of any of the other disciplines; however, it is in the nature of Christian education that the teacher of one discipline draw heavily on materials from the other three fields. It is interesting to note that NT teachers know the HB basically through what the *andemm* of the NT provides them—which is legendary or apocryphal in some places—not from a firsthand acquaintance with the HB books themselves, since they do not own them.

As stated above, teaching *andemm* transmits the received knowledge to the next generation. Introduced with the word *andemm,* a long list of possible and impossible interpretations received from previous teachers is recited to the students as possible and impossible explanations. However, one occasionally finds teachers who augment the received knowledge with personal observations from personal readings of the Geʿez literature, including the lives of saints and the *Apophthegmata patrum.* The monasteries of the Egyptian deserts and the monastery of Deir Sultan in Jerusalem, all of which had a reasonably large community of Ethiopian monks at one time or another, were channels through which one acquired new or additional interpretations of a text. The word *andemm* means "or"—that is, if a given interpretation is unlikely, unsatisfactory, uncertain, or insufficient, there is also another one. That other one is told immediately after the word *andemm*. This allows the teacher to incorporate new or additional interpretations without totally negating or discarding what has preceded. However, this unauthorized foreign contact risks the adoption as orthodox of some of the writings of other churches that otherwise would be considered heretical. A case in point is the monastic work of Isaac of Nineveh, much admired in Ethiopia, which was composed by a Nestorian, a heretic for the Ethiopian Orthodox *Tawāhedo* "Monophysite" church. For the church of Ethiopia, Iso'dad of Merv ought also to be a heretic, but his biblical interpretations have become part of its tradition.

5. Origin of Biblical Interpretations. One question that has preoccupied E. Ullendorff (1968) and R. Cowley, authorities on the Ethiopian biblical tradition, is the source of this exegetical tradition. A glance into this genre of literature, as preserved in modern manuscripts—the tradition was not written down until the late twentieth century—and in the books printed in this century suggests that the *andemm* is a combination of foreign and local contributions. In order to give a definite answer to the questions, "With which exegetical tradition(s) does the traditional biblical (and patristic) Amharic commentary material of the Ethiopian Orthodox Church stand in essential continuity?" and "What are the processes that have made this tradition what it is?" Cowley (1988), who lived for many years in Ethiopia among teachers of traditional education and who copied many commentary manuscripts, thoroughly compared the Ethiopian tradition with those of the sister churches, as preserved in Syriac and Coptic-Arabic, and with Jewish tradition. The conclusion of this meticulous study is that the "Ethiopian materials are mostly translations or adaptations from Arabic. The exegetical content of the Amharic commentary is largely dependent on sources external to the corpus, but the shaping and the ordering of the material is not, and must be attributed to the Ethiopian scholars who are recorded as having formed and developed the tradition." Ethiopia's access to foreign commentaries (including those of Iso' dad of Merv and the other Syrian scholars) is through the Ge'ez version of Ibn at-tayyib's commentaries and the Ge'ez adaptation of the Coptic-Arabic catenae. But it must be emphasized that these foreign commentaries provide little more than the skeleton of the exegetical tradition, which is fleshed out extensively from local sources. The commentary on Chrysostom's commentary or homilies on Hebrews illustrates this point.

Today one can find commentary manuscripts on any book of the Bible in European libraries, especially in the Vatican Library, the Bibliothèque Nationale, Paris, and the British Library, London. In the United States the Hill Monastic Manuscript Library, Saint John's University, Collegeville, Minnesota, possesses many important microfilms of such manuscripts. Commentaries on some biblical books have also been printed in Ethiopia at different times, including the NT books, Chrysostom's homilies on Hebrews, Psalms, the books of Solomon, and Ezekiel. An English translation by Cowley of one version of the commentary on Revelation, or "Interpretation of the Apocalypse of St. John," was published in 1983 by Cambridge University Press. K. Pedersen's PhD dissertation on the commentary on the psalms deserves publication.

Bibliography: R. Beylot, *Commentaire éthiopien sur les bénédictions de Moïse et de Jacob* (CSCO 410, 411, script. aeth. 73, 74, 1979). R. W. Cowley, "The Biblical Canon of the Ethiopian Orthodox Church Today," *OstKSt* 23 (1974) 318-23; "NT Introduction in the Andemta Commentary," *OstKSt* 26 (1977) 144-92; "Patristic Introduction in the Ethiopian Andemta Commentary Tradition," *OstKSt* 29 (1980) 39-49; *The Traditional Interpretation of the Apocalypse of St John in the Ethiopian Orthodox Church* (1983); *Ethiopian Biblical Interpretation: A Study in Exegetical Tradition and Hermeneutics* (1988). G. Haile, "The Homily in Honour of St. Frumentius, Bishop of Axum," *AnBoll* 97 (1979) 309-18. E. Hammerschmidt, "Kultsymbolik der koptischen und der äthiopischen Kirche," *Symbolik des orthodoxen und orientalischen Christentums* (ed. F. Herrmann, Symbolik der Religionen 10, 1962, 1966) 212-33. F. Heyer, "The Teaching of Tergum in the Ethiopian Church," *Proceedings of the Third International Conference of Ethiopian Studies, Addis Ababa, 1966* 2 (1970) 140-50. I. Kalewold, *Traditional Ethiopian Church Education* (1970). K. S. Pedersen, "Traditional Ethiopian Exegesis of the Book of Psalms" (diss., Hebrew University, 1989). Rufinus, *Historia Ecclesiastica* (*PL* 21) 478-80. T. Tamrat, *Church and State in Ethiopia* (1972) 1270-1527. E. Ullendorff, *Ethiopia and the Bible* (1968).

G. HAILE

EUSEBIUS OF CAESAREA (c. 260–c. 339)

E. is of unknown parentage. His patronymic, Pamphili, indicates his service in the household of the presbyter Pamphilus, curator of the library in Caesarea assembled by ORIGEN of Alexandria. Here E. learned the Origenist theology and the philological skills that shaped his life's work. He first won renown as the author of such apologetic and historical works as his *Chronicle* (first edition before 300, second after 325), a synchronization of sacred history and world history from Abraham to the twentieth year of Constantine's reign, and his *Church History* (four editions, extending perhaps from before 300 to after 325), an invaluable source of information about the Bible in the early church. Soon after persecution ended in 313 he was made bishop of Caesarea. He became an influential advocate of Christianity's reconciliation with the Roman Empire under Constantine, for whom he later wrote a panegyric (335) and a posthumous biography (begun in 337, left unfinished at E.'s death two years later).

E. was a zealous exponent of the tradition of learned exegesis inaugurated by Origen, as the defense of Origen and his exegetical method in *Church History* shows. As Pamphilus's collaborator at Caesarea E. corrected LXX manuscripts (see SEPTUAGINT) on the basis of Origen's Hexapla. Possibly as a result, Constantine later asked E. to provide fifty copies of the Scriptures for liturgical use in Constantinople. His exegetical monographs and commentaries show that he was more influenced by ALEXANDRIAN philology than by Alexandrian allegory. The two-part work called *Gospel Questions and Solutions* (c. 320) treats contradictions in the Gospel accounts of JESUS' genealogy and of the resurrection. The *Onomasticon* (perhaps before 300, perhaps after 325) is an annotated list of biblical place names and their contemporary locations. The work commonly known as the *Eusebian Sections and Canons* is a primitive Gospel parallel. In it E. assigned numbers to the various sections of the Gospels and collated them according to whether they appeared in one, two, three, or four Gospels, making a total of ten categories or canons.

Sometime after 325 he wrote two full-length biblical commentaries, on the psalter and on Isaiah, the former massively but incompletely preserved among medieval catenae, the later rediscovered almost complete in modern times. The Isaiah commentary is the oldest extant Christian line-by-line commentary on Isaiah. It blends traditional Christian PROPHECY fulfillment with extensive literal and historical interpretation, all designed to show the veracity of biblical prophecy in the history both of Israel and of the Christian church. Moral and spiritual allegory is not prominent. Although E. occasionally drew on Jewish exegetical expertise, the commentary is based on Origen's Tetrapla (Aquila, Symmachus, Origen's corrected LXX, and Theodotion, all of which he used, though the LXX was usually preferred). E. could not read Hebrew, despite his frequent allusions to "the Hebrew reading."

The psalter and the prophetic books also figure heavily in such apologetic works as the *Prophetic Eclogues* and *The Demonstration of the Gospel,* which consists of lengthy glosses on selected biblical texts with messianic and christological import. The *Eclogues* is organized by biblical book and the *Demonstration* by apologetic thesis. They are the culmination of the proof-texting method so popular in early Christianity's anti-Jewish apologetics.

Works: *Prophetic Eclogues: Eusebii Caesarensis Eclogae Propheticae* (ed. T. Gaisford, 1842; repr., *PG* 22:1021-1262); *Church History: Eusebius Werke,* vol. 2, pts. 1-3 (ed. E. Schwartz, GCS 9, 1903–1909); *Onomasticon: Eusebius Werke,* vol. 3, pt. 1, *Das Onomastikon der biblischen Ortsnamen* (ed. E. Klostermann, GCS 11, pt. 1, 1904); *Chronicle: Eusebius Werke,* vol. 5, *Die Chronik aus dem Armenischen übersetzt mit textkritischen Kommentar* (ed. J. Karst, GCS 20, 1911); *Eusebius Werke,* vol. 7, *Die Chronik des Hieronymus* (ed. R. Helm, GCS 47, 1956[2]); *The Demonstration of the Gospel: Eusebius Werke,* vol. 6, *Die Demonstratio Evangelica* (ed. I. Heikel, GCS 23, 1913); *OrChr* NS 12, 14 (ed. G. Beyer, 1922–24) 30-70; 3rd series 1 (1927) 80-97, 284-92; 3rd series 2 (1927) 57-69 (Syriac text); *Eusebian Sections and Canons: PG* 22:1275-92; *Gospel Questions and Solutions: PG* 22:879-1006 (Greek fragments); *Commentary on Isaiah: Eusebius Werke,* vol. 9, *Der Jesajakommentar* (ed. J. Ziegler, GCS, 1975); *Commentary on Psalms, PG* 23, 24:9-76; *Life of Constantine, Eusebius Werke,* vol. 1, pt. 1, *Über das Leben des Kaiser Konstantins* (ed. F. Winkelmann, GCS, 1975[2]).

Bibliography: **H.W. Attridge and G. Hata** (eds.), *Eusebius, Christianity, and Judaism* (SPB 42, 1992). **T. D. Barnes,** *Constantine and Eusebius* (1981). **R. M. Grant,** *Eusebius as Church Historian* (1980). **M. J. Hollerich,** *Eusebius of Caesarea's Commentary on Isaiah: Christian Exegesis in the Age of Constantine* (1998). **E. des Places,** *Eusèbe de Césarée commentateur: Platonisme et écriture sainte* (1982). **M.-J. Rondeau,** *Les commentaires patristiques du psautier (IIIe–Ve siècles),* vol. 1, *Les travaux des pères grecques et latins sur le psautier* (OCA 219, 1982) 64-75. **E. Schwartz,** "Eusebios von Caesarea," *PW* 6:1370-439. **J. Sirinelli,** *Les vues historiques d'Eusèbe de Césarée durant la période prénicéenne* (1961). **D. S. Wallace-Hadrill,** *Eusebius of Caesarea* (1960).

M. J. HOLLERICH

EVANGELICAL BIBLICAL INTERPRETATION

Evangelical has a broad range of meaning in the Christian world. However, in this context the term refers to the conservative Christian movement originating in the twentieth century that has rejected the higher critical conclusions concerning biblical texts and the radical skepticism inherited from the Enlightenment and has sought to retain the Reformation doctrines. Contrary to popular opinion, the movement is not monolithic; rather, it represents a wide diversity of traditions and religious groups, from high church to low church and from extreme conservatives to moderates.

The Evangelical movement emerged from the foment of the conservative-liberal controversies of the nineteenth century. In Germany that century saw the complete triumph of higher-critical concerns. First the Tübingen school of tendency criticism in the first half of the century and then the history-of-religions school (see RELIGIONSGESCHICHTLICHE SCHULE) at the end of the century cast more and more doubt on the veracity of the Bible. F. C. BAUR originated the Tübingen school when he rewrote the history of the early church along Hegelian lines, arguing that the Jewish Christianity of the early decades of the first century (the thesis) was opposed by the Hellenistic Jewish Christianity of the

Pauline school in the middle decades (the antithesis) and was taken over by Hellenistic Christianity in the early part of the second century (the synthesis). One of Baur's students, D. F. STRAUSS, applied this model to the life of JESUS, arguing that Jesus was turned into a mythical or supernatural figure by the early church. The history-of-religions school took a more Darwinian approach, arguing that all religions have their origins in their predecessors and that Christianity moved from a Jewish religion to a Jewish-Hellenistic and finally to a Hellenistic religion during the NT period. Many adherents—e.g., O. PFLEIDERER, E. HATCH, W. BOUSSET, and R. REITZENSTEIN—centered on Iranian and Hellenistic origins of Christianity.

These movements were opposed by a large number of conservative scholars. In Germany T. von ZAHN wrote important works on NT introduction and the CANON, and A. SCHLATTER wrote on the Jewish (not Hellenistic) origins of PAUL's thought and on NT THEOLOGY. In England the "Cambridge trio" of J. B. LIGHTFOOT, B. F. WESTCOTT, and F. HORT championed a conservative approach to the NT while remaining proponents of critical methodology. In fact, Westcott is generally credited with introducing higher critical study of the Gospels into England, and Lightfoot's magisterial *Apostolic Fathers* stemmed the tide of Baur's theories in England.

In the United States the liberal-conservative battle took place from 1870 to 1920. Until that time the American church was predominantly conservative, but in the universities and seminaries a counter movement began to grow, mainly influenced by German higher criticism. When conservative professors retired they were often replaced by younger critical scholars, many of whom had been educated in Europe. In addition, such popular preachers as H. Beecher and L. Abbott combined a pietistic morality with critical views on the Bible, championing a new understanding of biblical AUTHORITY and its relation to theology. A good example of this approach would be the Evangelical Alliance, founded in 1846. J. McCosh (1811–94), president of Princeton, used this forum to reconcile Scripture with Darwinism in 1873. For the next few decades higher criticism increasingly dominated the alliance, which became the Federal Council of Churches in 1908.

Conservatives responded in diverse ways. Some, like the evangelist D. Moody (1837–99), believed that the best approach was that of Gamaliel in Acts 5:38-39: "Keep away from these men and let them alone; because if this plan or this undertaking is of human origin, it will fail; but if it is of God, you will not be able to overthrow them." Therefore, he centered upon revivalism and refused to take part in the debates. Others believed in apologetic response; e.g., B. B. WARFIELD, who produced a succession of articles on biblical infallibility, later collected into *The Inspiration and Authority of the Bible* (1948). A series of Bible conferences from 1876 to 1910 stressed apologetics to answer the higher critics and biblical PROPHECY to warn of the growing "apostasy" (2 Thess 2:3) seen in the liberal group. In 1895 the Niagara Conference developed a five-point program that became the basis of a movement: the inerrancy of Scripture, the virgin birth, the deity of Jesus Christ, a substitutionary theory of atonement, and the physical resurrection and second coming of Jesus. Coalescence around these points led to the most famous work of this period, the twelve-volume *The Fundamentals* (1910–15), written by conservative scholars from a broad array of denominations to defend the five points as well as cardinal tenets like traditional views of authorship and date of biblical books, the attribution of the *Logia Jesu* to Jesus, and similar issues. This series of books led to the use of the term *fundamentalists* for those adhering to the principles advocated therein.

As higher criticism came to dominate an increasing number of universities and seminaries, fundamentalists began to found their own schools, with the Bible the core of the educational experience. Thus began the Bible institute movement, whose goal was to develop church leaders and teachers rather than to train young people in a broad-based arts-centered education. Contemporary Christian education drew little theory from its secular counterpart but centered on pragmatics and theology. The purpose was not so much to retreat from the world as it was to return to the Bible-centered education of the Reformation period. Nevertheless, the rift between fundamentalists and others became greater and greater.

Two events made this rift complete. First, the so-called monkey trial of J. Scopes in 1925 heaped ridicule on fundamentalism. Scopes, charged with teaching evolution in a Dayton, Tennessee, public school in defiance of state law, was defended by the famous trial lawyer C. Darrow; W. J. Bryan, four-time candidate for the presidency, assisted the prosecution. Darrow publicly humiliated Bryan and belittled fundamentalist beliefs; the movement is still considered backward and anti-intellectual. Second, in 1929 the last bastion of conservative theology, Princeton, came under the control of the *modernists* (the term often used for higher critics). As a result, J. G. MACHEN and R. Wilson resigned from Princeton and moved to Philadelphia, establishing Westminster Theological Seminary. The separation was absolute; there was no interaction between the two camps.

As a result, fundamentalism retreated into itself and refused to dialogue with the broader intellectual world. Moreover, for the next two decades its adherents split into a series of sectarian groups that failed even to interact with one another: Presbyterians and ANABAPTISTS, dispensationalists and Reformed moved farther apart. The ensuing years saw numerous disputes over issues that had not previously divided the conservative movement; e.g., paedobaptism, predestination, and chiliasm. Although conservatives came from virtually every

Protestant tradition, until the 1930s there had been a remarkable unity in the movement. However, the various groups ceased to dialogue with each other once they lost their "common enemy"; differences began to take center stage. Denominations started to demand adherence on peripheral as well as cardinal issues, and denominational splits began to multiply.

A new theory of biblical interpretation also became dominant in the fundamentalist movement. C. HODGE and Warfield had drawn on the philosophy of F. BACON and later T. Reid (1710–96) in developing their views on the authority and interpretation of the Bible. This philosophy, known from its association with Reid and other Scot thinkers as "Scottish common sense realism," held that objective knowledge could be derived through the senses; Hodge and Warfield, therefore, proposed that the Bible could be understood simply by reading it. Because many fundamentalists believed that critical tools were unnecessary, even dangerous, an inductive approach to Bible study resulted. A person would simply sit down with the Bible (preferably the KJV) and study it, looking for key terms and themes. Biblical truth was thus accessible to the average person, and little special training was needed. Inductive study moved synthetically from the whole to the parts, searching for major themes. Theology was determined by proof-texting, or searching for key verses to anchor a doctrine; it was believed that one or two verses were sufficient to anchor a doctrine biblically. In this sense one of the more influential books was R. A. Torrey's *What the Bible Teaches* (1898), which sought to prove doctrines "scientifically" (in 500 pages) by anchoring them to specific texts. HERMENEUTICS was identified, not with critical study of the biblical texts, but with personal interaction with them.

Thus, the 1930s and early 1940s were characterized by withdrawal from the public arena and internalization within specific traditions. Not only did fundamentalists as a whole refuse to speak to the broad world of scholarship, those from divergent traditions—Reformed, Anabaptist, Arminian, dispensational, and Pentecostal—did not communicate with one another. However, while splits resulted for the most part in a proliferation of small, disenfranchised denominations, the movement itself did not taper off. Statistics show that fundamentalism actually grew in number during the 1930s and 1940s due to an evangelistic fervor and a revivalist spirit.

In the early 1940s a new attitude emerged within some segments of fundamentalism and was quickly seen as a separate camp within the conservative movement; it began to be identified as "evangelicalism." In September 1941 the fundamentalists formed the American Council of Christian Churches, and in October of that same year the National Association of Evangelicals was formed at Moody Bible Institute. Interestingly, the two groups held many of the same doctrinal beliefs, but they differed in attitudes toward outsiders. Seven characteristics distinguished evangelicalism: (1) a commitment to dialogue with the world of scholarship; (2) a rejection of radical separation, i.e., the refusal to interact with anyone not following the fundamentalist creed; (3) openness on non-cardinal issues, e.g., modes of baptism, Calvinism/Arminianism, eschatological differences; (4) cooperative evangelism, e.g., the involvement of mainline denomination pastors in Billy Graham crusades; (5) a more eclectic education, as seen in the formation of Fuller Seminary in 1947; (6) eclectic political allegiance, involving the refusal to demand a flag-waving conservatism; (7) social concern, seen in the emergence of missionary agencies, like World Vision, that center on relief and care for the poor.

Several vital organizations and publications appeared during this period, including the magazine *Christianity Today* (1945), which became a forum for a more open discussion of theological and social issues; the Tyndale Fellowship, founded at the Cambridge in 1944; and the Evangelical Theological Society, founded in the United States in 1949. The purpose of the latter two was to bring academic scholarship back into the mainstream of the evangelical world. Evangelical scholars began to interact with the broader world of scholarship, although this was not always easy. For instance, G. Ladd of Fuller Seminary was refused membership in the Gospels section of the SOCIETY OF BIBLICAL LITERATURE in the early 1950s because of his conservative writings. Progress was slow; nevertheless, such formidable scholars as F. F. BRUCE (the only person in history named president of both NT and OT international societies), R. Harrison, E. Ellis, and L. Morris led the way. By the 1970s a resurgent evangelical scholarship began to claim its place in the world of scholarship; I. Marshall, R. Longenecker, R. Martin, G. Wenham, and others were recognized in the broader fraternity of scholars. Still, a certain amount of disdain often greeted conservative scholars, because they were suspected of fundamentalist and obscurantist positions by mainstream academics.

At the same time, debates on hermeneutics and the authority of Scripture began to cause divisions within evangelical churches. Many evangelical scholars had strong doubts about the doctrine of inerrancy, and forums like the International Council of Biblical Inerrancy on Scripture (1978) and on hermeneutics (1982) failed to resolve the issue. The Evangelical Theological Society debated higher-critical conclusions regarding REDACTION CRITICISM from 1976 to 1982, finally accepting the validity of a nuanced approach. Wide diversity became apparent on such issues as the role of women in the church, the unity of Isaiah, and Pauline authorship of the pastorals (see PASTORAL LETTERS). In short, evangelicalism had become a divided movement.

Still, the movement continued to grow, both in number and in academic prestige. In the 1980s Tyndale

Fellowship sponsored a six-volume Gospel Perspectives series in which a number of evangelical Gospel scholars demonstrated the historical veracity of the Gospels. By the 1990s evangelicals were not only members of academic societies but also chaired major seminars within them. The new era of tolerance as well as the quality of the work produced by scholars like G. Fee, H. Williamson, D. Carson, and N. T. Wright has brought evangelical scholarship back into the mainstream as an equal partner.

Biblical interpretation among evangelicals centers on several issues. Foremost, of course, is the authority and centrality of Scripture for doctrinal formulation. Although debate over inerrancy (the belief that the Bible is without error in scientific or historical detail as well as in doctrinal matters) remains, there is universal agreement regarding infallibility (the belief that the Bible is the Word of God and completely authoritative and true on doctrinal issues). Evangelicals recognize not just the author of biblical books but also the Author behind those books; therefore, the Bible contains a timeless message, binding upon the church at all times. This is a key difference between conservative and non-conservative interpretation. For the latter the Bible is a set of open-ended symbols to be interpreted on the basis of the current context. For the former the current context must be challenged and, if necessary, changed by biblical truth. The POST-MODERN rejection of absolute truth is not shared by evangelicals, who believe that there is one source of final truth: the Bible.

This does not mean that evangelicals take a naive approach to biblical interpretation. While some do employ an atomistic, proof-texting technique in Bible study, the majority reject simplistic methods for sophisticated approaches grounded in the world of scholarship. According to the predominant view, the text is not considered to be autonomous from the author; rather, it is seen from an intentionalist perspective. The author/text/reader dilemma is resolved by centering on the text: The author produces a text with a set of intended messages, and the reader studies that text in order to discover those intended messages. While readers cannot get back to the author, they can search for signs embedded in the text that guide them to the intended messages. The author, of course, is not present to guide the reader; and the pre-understanding of the reader (the product of church tradition and reading community) certainly has some controlling influence on the interpretation. But does this automatically generate the interpretation? Or can readers go beyond such forces to discover the intended meaning of a biblical text? Certainly polyvalence or multiple meanings attributed by different readers is a necessary result, but can one go behind these to discover the probable meaning of a text? Evangelicals believe not only that the probable meaning can be discovered but also that it must be

discovered due to the very nature of the biblical text as the Word of God. For example, 1 Pet 3:21 ("And baptism . . . now saves you . . . as an appeal to God for a good conscience") is at the heart of the debate over baptism as a salvific force. While scholars are divided over the interpretation of this verse, evangelicals believe that it can be understood as originally intended. The predominant evangelical interpretation is that "good conscience" is a subjective genitive ("out of a good conscience") rather than an objective genitive ("for a good conscience"); and so baptism "saves," not in the sense of baptismal regeneration, but in the sense that it "appeals" to the God who has already saved the person.

Two major interpretive approaches have been suggested. The first is associated with E. Hirsch (1967), who argues for separating what the text meant (the single intended meaning that must be the goal of all interpretation) and what it means (the many possible significances of that single meaning in various contexts). The scholars who follow Hirsch believe that it is possible to get behind the latter in order to discover the former. As M. Silva says, "The moment we look at a text we contextualize it, but a self-awareness of that fact opens up the possibility of modifying our point of reference in the light of contradictory data" (1983, 148). Such scholars recognize the importance of the reader in the act of interpretation, but they believe that it is possible for readers to study and determine the original meaning of a text.

The second approach is A. Thiselton's "action theory," based on the work of J. Austin (1911–60) and J. Searle. Thiselton begins with the "transformative power" of the Bible to draw readers into its world of meaning and to transform their understanding. Biblical truth functions at both static (propositional truths) and dynamic (life-changing mechanisms) levels. The Bible is not just "a handbook of information and description"; it entails "a whole range of dynamic speech-acts" that are based on "the truth of certain states of affairs in God's relation to the world" (1980, 437).

The means by which this is accomplished is the classic grammatical-historical method supplemented by modern hermeneutical theory. First, we learn to work with our pre-understanding positively. Awareness of our own worldview and theological underpinnings keeps us from turning presupposition into prejudice. The best way to do this is to respect and learn from opposing theories about the meaning of the text—i.e., to allow these theories to challenge our understandings and drive us to a reexamination of the text from a new perspective. In one sense we study the text from the vantage point of our own system, and in another sense we bracket our traditional understanding in an openness to new possibilities. The resulting tension forces us to be more honest with the text; e.g., when studying a difficult passage, like Romans 9–11, on sovereignty and justification, both Arminians (see ARMINIUS) and Calvinists (see CALVIN) need to open themselves to each other's interpretation and look at the text in a new way.

Exegetical methodology combines grammar, semantics, background, and biblical theology to ascertain those embedded clues to the original, intended meaning of the text. Grammar and semantics help readers to go behind their community-driven interpretation to consider the ancient meaning of the words. Here the recent school of discourse analysis is critical for seeing the message as a whole and not as an atomistic series of isolated parts. The larger context within which a pericope is encased becomes essential to its fuller meaning. In John 7:37-39, for example, there are several difficult aspects, including whether "the one who believes in me" in v. 38*a* belongs with v. 38 or v. 37 and whether "out of his innermost being" refers to the believer or to Christ. Grammatically, the answer to the first issue is that it belongs to v. 37 ("let the one who believes in me drink"); and due to the strong christology of the context in chap. 7, it is more likely that Christ is the source of the Holy Spirit in vv. 38-39. Primarily, evangelicals are concerned to seek John's original meaning and not just one interesting possibility among many.

Background is another essential component guiding the reader back to a text-driven interpretation. Within the extensive debate over sociological analysis (see SOCIOLOGY AND HB/NT STUDIES) evangelicals prefer social description (seeking the background behind the text itself) to sociological interpretation (speculating about the social dynamics that led to the production of the text). In other words, they seek to deepen understanding of the text rather than to use current sociological theory to revise our understanding of the history behind the text. Seeing the conquest of Canaan as a "peasant revolt" or the early church as a "millenarian sect" is viewed as reductionistic and revisionist. However, to study the ancient military and topographic details behind Joshua and Judges is seen as extremely helpful; and to look at the influence of sociological factors behind Paul's tent-making as a key to his mission strategy is regarded as an important contribution. The key is that the text guides the employment of the critical tools.

Biblical theology is also crucial to discovering the author's intention. Most biblical books are theological at the core, so evangelical interpretation looks at the developing theological threads that together weave the tapestry of the text. These threads are discovered by studying the developing text and seeing how the theological emphases emerge context by context. The theology of a book is found not just in the parts but more in what the parts contribute to the whole. According to Thiselton's speech-act theory, one must consider the locutionary aspect (the theological message), the illocutionary force (how the text involves the reader in its

message), and the perlocutionary purpose (what the text asks the reader to do with its message). All of this constitutes the biblical theology of a text.

Finally, there is systematic theology. Evangelicals for the most part accept K. STENDAHL's classic distinction between biblical theology as descriptive and systematic theology as normative. However, they rework the relation between the two, arguing for a direct movement from exegesis (the historical meaning of individual texts) to biblical theology (the theology of the early church derived from collating passages into the theological message of a book or an author) and systematic theology (the contextualization of biblical theology into church dogma for today). Mainly, evangelicals believe that the task is not finished until interpreters have discovered and applied God's truths derived from Scripture to develop a systematic theology for the modern church. Two principles guide this pursuit: (1) A systematic theology is possible as we collate biblical passages into "covering laws" for doctrinal statements; and (2) the theological task is mandatory for the church. In other words, it is not enough to determine the meaning of a passage; one must also determine what the passage contributes to the theology and life of the church.

Bibliography: D. A. Black and D. S. Dockery (eds.), *NT Criticism and Interpretation* (1991). G. Bray, *Biblical Interpretation Past and Present* (1996); D. A. Carson and J. D. Woodbridge (eds.), *Scripture and Truth* (1983). N. F. Furniss, *The Fundamentalist Controversy, 1918–1931* (YHP 59, 1954). N. Hatch and M. Noll (eds.), *The Bible in America: Essays in Cultural History* (1982). E. D. Hirsch, *Validity in Interpretation* (1967). W. C. Kaiser and M. Silva, *An Introduction to Biblical Hermeneutics: The Search for Meaning* (1994). W. W. Klein, C. I. Blomberg, and R. L. Hubbard, *Introduction to Biblical Interpretation* (1993). G. B. Marsden, *Fundamentalism and American Culture: The Shaping of Twentieth-Century Evangelicalism, 1870–1925* (1980). G. R. Osborne, *The Hermeneutical Spiral: A Comprehensive Introduction to Biblical Interpretation* (1991); "Evangelical Interpretation of Scripture," *The Bible in the Churches: How Various Christians Interpret the Scriptures* (ed. K. Hagen, 1994). E. D. Radmacher and R. Preus, *Hermeneutics, Inerrancy, and the Bible* (1984). J. Rogers and D. McKim, *The Authority and Interpretation of the Bible: An Historical Approach* (1979). M. Silva, *Biblical Words and Their Meaning: An Introduction to Lexical Semantics* (1983). A. C. Thiselton, *The Two Horizons: NT Hermeneutics and Philosophical Description* (1980); *New Horizons in Hermeneutics: The Theory and Practice of Transforming Biblical Reading* (1992). D. F. Wells and J. D. Woodbridge, *The Evangelicals* (1975). J. D. Woodbridge, *Biblical Authority: A Critique of the Rogers-McKim Proposal* (1982).

G. R. OSBORNE

EVANS, CHRISTOPHER FRANCIS (1909–)

E. attended King Edward's School in Birmingham, England, and took his degree in classics and theology from Corpus Christi College, Cambridge. Ordained as an Anglican minister, he studied at Lincoln Theological College, where he was tutor (1938–44). For the next four years he served as chaplain and divinity lecturer at Lincoln Training College, and then he went to Corpus Christi College, Oxford, as fellow, chaplain, and lecturer in divinity (1948–58). After serving as Lightfoot Professor of Divinity, University of Durham, and canon of Durham Cathedral (1959–62), he accepted a position as professor of NT studies at King's College, London (1962–77). He was elected emeritus fellow at Corpus Christi, Oxford, in 1977.

E. has written fine articles and monographs on various topics in NT history and theology. His four lectures on Mark, published as *The Beginning of the Gospel* (1968), were an early redaction-critical interpretation (see REDACTION CRITICISM). He interpreted Mark's JESUS as a charismatically powerful figure bent on destroying the kingdom of evil and baptizing his hearers in the Spirit's power. E. also argued effectively against the views that Mark's Gospel presents the gospel of Jesus in an uninterpreted form and that Mark proves the early *kerygma* to be simple and uncomplicated. In E.'s view, Mark's christology, for example, turns out to be a blending of three fairly disparate notions of Messiah, Son of God, and Son of man and holds together futuristic apocalyptic metaphors (see APOCALYPTICISM) with pictures of salvation coming via Jesus' model of patient obedience.

E.'s *Resurrection and the NT* (1970) is an excellent study of the whole issue of the resurrection. He showed how the older views of an unbroken line extending from Jewish ideas of resurrection to Jesus' predictions to the church's interpretations are hard to maintain. He surveyed the backgrounds of resurrection, made redaction-critical studies of the NT resurrection texts, and concluded with a theological essay on the nature of Christian faith in the resurrection. In both his studies on the texts and his synthesis of their ideas, E. endeavored to hold together the "now" and the "not yet" found within the Gospel sayings attributed to Jesus.

Works: *The Beginning of the Gospel: Four Lectures on St. Mark's Gospel* (1968); (with P. R. Ackroyd, eds.), *CHB* 1 (1970); "The NT in the Making," ibid. 232–83; *Resurrection and the NT* (SBT 2nd ser. 12, 1970); *Essays* (EiT 2, 1977); *Parable and Dogma* (1977); *Saint Luke* (TPINTC, 1990).

Bibliography: **M. D. Hooker** (ed.), *What About the NT? Essays in Honor of C. F. E.* (FS, 1975).

R. B. VINSON

EVANSON, EDWARD (1731–1805)

Born at Warrington, Lancashire, on Apr. 23, 1731, E. was educated from the age of seven by an uncle who served as rector at Mitcham, Surrey, and ran a small school. E.'s progress in classical studies led to his enrollment at Emmanuel College, Cambridge, at age fourteen (BA 1749, MA 1753). After service with his uncle and ordination, he became vicar at South Mimms (1768) and then at Tewkesbury (1769). He exchanged the former for the post at Longdon in Worcestershire (1770), in the meantime having been awarded the perpetual curacy at Tredington, Worcestershire, by Bishop W. WARBURTON.

Having become convinced of variances between the teachings and the practices of the church and the Bible, E. began to make alterations in the liturgy and creed. His Easter sermon in 1771, in which he declared, "Jesus Christ was truly and literally a man, of the same nature, and having the same kind of soul and body, with which the first Adam was created," stirred controversy and eventually led to his prosecution. In spite of widespread support in his congregations, E. was placed on trial; the case was dismissed on a technicality, but appealed. In 1778 he resigned his church posts and returned to school work at Mitcham. During the remainder of his life, he resided in several places, living on income from teaching, a lifetime annuity established by a friend, and wealth acquired through marriage (1786). He continued to hold informal worship services, serving the Eucharist (which he considered the only sacrament) on social occasions attended by Christians, and expounding the authentic NT Scriptures before his "Christo philanthropists." He died in Colford in Devonshire on Sept. 25, 1805.

E.'s sincere and strongly held opinions about the NT and church practices and beliefs involved him in constant debate and made him one of the most radical biblical scholars of his day. He argued that the NT prophecies (see PROPHECY AND PROPHETS, NT) predict the rise of trinitarian apostasy (1777). In a controversy with J. PRIESTLEY he denied that the NT sanctioned the observance of Sunday (1792a). His most controversial work was on the authenticity of the NT writings (1792b). Claiming to work on the basis of "internal marks of authenticity or spuriousness" (viii), he argued for the genuineness of Luke–Acts (which had suffered from some additions and interpolations), written, according to E., by Paul's traveling companion (Silas/Silvanus = Luke). The interpolations in Luke–Acts were considered to be the "the first two chapters of Luke's Gospel which follow the short introductory preface or dedication to Theophilus: the account of the baptism, temptation and transformation of Jesus: the story of the herd of swine, the conversation respecting paradise, with the thief on the cross, besides some passages in the Lord's prayer . . . the miracle of diseases and lunatics being cured by the handkerchiefs or aprons brought from Paul's body" (1807a, vii).

E. considered the rest of the Gospels to be forgeries from the second century written to support developing church positions, but similar to the apocryphal writings (see APOCRYPHA, NT) referred to by the church fathers. Luke and Matthew (whose author knew nothing of the topography of Palestine or Jewish customs) were used by the author of Mark, who was the first to attempt a harmony between Matthew and Luke. John was written as a spiritual Gospel but had no connection with the apostle. Utilizing the evidence of Acts and early church tradition, E. argued that the epistles of Romans, Ephesians, Colossians, Hebrews, James, Peter, John, Jude, and the letters to the seven churches in Revelation were non-apostolic and datable to the second century. An annotated version of the NT, based on his conclusions and using the translation and notes of Archbishop Newcome, was published in 1807, containing, freed from interpolations, Luke–Acts, 1–2 Corinthians, Galatians, Philippians, 1–2 Thessalonians, 1–2 Timothy, Titus, Philemon, and the Revelation of John.

Works: *A Letter to Dr. Hurd, Bishop of Worcester, Wherein the Importance of the Prophecies of the NT and the Nature of the Grand Apostasy Predicted in Them are Particularly and Impartially Considered* (1777); *Arguments Against and for the Sabbatical Observance of Sunday* (1792a); *The Dissonance of the Four Generally Received Evangelists, and the Evidence of Their Authenticity Examined* (1792b, 1805[2]); *A Letter to Dr. Priestley's Young Man* (1794); *Second Thoughts on the Trinity* (1805); *A NT; or the New Covenant according to Luke, Paul, and John; Published in Conformity to the Plan of the Late E. E.* (1807a); *Sermons* (2 vols., with a "Life" by G. Rogers, 1807b).

Bibliography: *DNB* 18 (1889) 78-79. **T. Falconer,** *Certain Principles in Evanson's "Dissonance. . . . " examined in Eight Discourses* (Bampton Lectures 1810, 1811); *Gentleman's Magazine* 75 (1805) 1233-36. **N. Havard,** *Origin and Progress of the Prosecution in Twekesbury* (1778); *Monthly Magazine* 20 (1805) 477-83.

J. H. HAYES

EWALD, GEORG HEINRICH AUGUST (1803–75)

One of the greatest biblical scholars of the nineteenth century, E. was a man of amazing learning and deeply held religious and political beliefs, and a formidable opponent of all who disagreed with him. He was born Nov. 16, 1803, in Göttingen and studied at the university there, gaining his doctorate in 1823 at the age of nineteen. His principal teachers were J. G. EICHHORN and T. Tychsen (1758–1834). After a brief spell in Wolfenbüttel he taught in Göttingen from 1824, becoming full professor in 1831. In this early period he published grammars of Hebrew (1827) and Arabic (1831–33) as well as a work on Sanskrit poetry. He also began to publish on the HB; in his first publication, when he was nineteen, he opposed both the fragmentary and the documentary hypotheses of the composition of the Pentateuch (see PENTATEUCHAL CRITICISM).

One of the "Göttingen Seven," in 1837 he was dismissed from his post for refusing to accept the suspension of the constitution of Hanover by E. August. He moved to Tübingen, where his stay of ten years, until 1848, saw the production of some of his greatest work. This included *Commentary on the Prophets of the OT* (1840–41) and his *History of Israel,* which began to appear in 1843. He returned to Göttingen in 1848, the year of the revolution, and taught at the university until he was again dismissed in 1867–68 because of his opposition to the Prussian takeover of Hanover. Active in politics, he was a member of one of the regional assemblies; he died in Göttingen, May 4, 1875.

E., along with some other German Protestant scholars of his day, believed that the critical method presented no threat to biblical studies but, rather, that it was a necessary tool to enable the message of the Bible to be properly understood. Historical criticism made it possible to reconstruct the process of history through which God had been made known to humankind. Thus E. was deeply opposed, on the one hand, to W. DE WETTE's "negative" criticism, with its skepticism about what could be known of the times of the patriarchs and Moses, and, on the other hand, to F. C. BAUR and the Tübingen school of NT scholarship, with its view that many Gospel traditions were myths (see MYTHOLOGY AND BIBLICAL STUDIES) based on the HB. E. followed such scholars as B. Niebuhr (1776–1831) and O. Müller (1790–1870), who saw in the legends and myths of Rome and Greece the reflections of authentic happenings; and in his monumental history of Israel he presented a critical but positive account of the earliest history of the Israelites.

Although he did not think that it was possible to recover the historical Abraham or the other patriarchs, he believed that the stories about them could be used to reconstruct the history of the tribal groups that constituted Israel. Abraham and the patriarchs were presented as "ideal types" in the literature; however, a positive assessment could be made of the work of Moses, who had given the Israelites a type of monotheism, laws, and cultic observances. The prophets (see PROPHECY AND PROPHETS) were also important; through them, God had given the most important truths to humanity, and this fact alone underlined the significance of the Bible.

E.'s historical conclusions were based on complex theories of the composition of the books of the HB, which assumed that the Pentateuch, for example, had passed through the hands of five authors, each of whom had supplemented and in some cases modified the material. In his work on the NT, E. supported the then less than fashionable view that Mark was a source used by Matthew and Luke. E. was a highly individualistic scholar, confident of his own results and dismissive of those of his opponents. Although he founded no "school," he taught such later giants as J. WELLHAUSEN.

From 1848 to 1865 E. wrote and published twelve volumes of "Bible Yearbooks" that remain an invaluable guide to the scholarship of the period as well as to his own opinions. In these he opposed the Hegelians (as he called D. Strauss and the Tübingen school), the "negative critics," and such conservative scholars as E. HENGSTENBERG. He also reviewed much literature from British scholarship, most of which he regarded as superficial and as dominated by England's high church party.

British scholars became interested in E. in the latter part of the nineteenth century. A. STANLEY's *History of the Jewish Church* (1863–65) introduced E.'s history to British readers, and translations were made of it (1867–86) as well as of E.'s works on the prophets (1875–81) and on Job (1882), to name but a few. His work suited the British liberals of the late nineteenth century with its positive criticism and its convictions that biblical history showed God at work in the world, revealing to humankind the highest truths by which to live. From 1860 to 1880 the "negative" criticism of de Wette triumphed in Germany in the work of Wellhausen. During the same period in Britain it was E. who was honored in liberal circles.

Works: *Die Komposition der Genesis kritisch untersucht* (1823); *Kritische Grammatik der hebraischen Sprache* (1827; ET 1870); *Grammatica critica linguae arabicae* (1831–33; *Die Propheten des alten Bundes* (3 vols., 1840–41, 1867–68[2]; ET, *Commentary on the Prophets of the OT* [5 vols., 1875–81]); *Geschichte des Volkes Israel bis Christus* (7 vols., 1843–55 and later eds.; ET, *History of Israel* [8 vols., 1867–86]); *Jahrbücher der biblischen Wissenschaft* (12 vols., 1848–65); *Buch Hiob* (1854[2]; ET, *Commentary on the Book of Job* [1882]).

Bibliography: C. Bertheau, *RE*[3] 5 (1898) 682-87. **J. S. Black,** *EncBrit* 8 (1889) 773-74. **T. K. Cheyne,** *FOTC,* 66-118. **T. Witton Davies,** *Heinrich Ewald* (1903). **A. Dillmann,** *ADB* 6 (1877) 438-42. **J. Ebach,** *TRE* 10 (1982) 694-96. **J. C. O'Neill,** *The Bible's Authority* (1991) 135-49. **L. Perlitt,** "H. E.: Der Gelehrte in der Politik," *Theologie in Göttingen: Eine Vorlesungsreihe* (ed. B. Moeller, 1987) 157-212 = L. Perlitt, *Allein mit dem Wort: Theologische Studien* (1995) 263-312. **J. W. Rogerson,** *OTCNC* 91-103. **R. Smend,** "H. E.s Biblische Theologie: Hinweis auf ein vergessenes Buch," *TW* (FS W. Trillhaus, ed. H. W. Schütte and F. Wintzer, 1974) 176-91 = R. Smend, *Epochen der Bbielkritik: Gesammelte Studien* (1991) 3:155-67. **J. Wellhausen,** *Grundrisse zum Alten Testament* (TBü 27, ed. R. Smend, 1965) 120-38.

J. W. ROGERSON

EXODUS, BOOK OF

The forty chapters of the book of Exodus report on the liberation of the Israelites from slavery in Egypt, their trek to Sinai, and the revelation of the law that took place there.

1. The HB. The events portrayed in the book are partially reinterpreted and theologically deepened in the remainder of the HB. The speeches and sermons of individual men of God refer to the exodus traditions (Moses in Deut 29:1-5; Joshua in Josh 24:5-7, with the answer of the people in 24:16-17; Samuel in 1 Sam 10:18; Nehemiah in Neh 9:9-21). Altogether, Deuteronomy borrows from Exodus numerous traditional materials (e.g., texts from the book of the covenant, Exod 21:22–23:33; cf. Exod 21:1-11 with Deut 15:12-18, etc.) Among the preexilic prophets, Hosea saw in the period of desert wanderings the bridal period of the people with their God (in this, Jeremiah is dependent on Hosea: Jer 2:2; Hos 2:15; 11:1-2). At the same time Hosea announced the judgment of God as a return to Egypt (Hos 8:13; 9:3, 6; 11:5). According to Amos, Israel could derive no special status from the exodus, since even the Philistines had been called out of Kaphtor and the Aramaeans out of Kir (Amos 3:1-2; 9:7). Ezekiel viewed the early history of Israel in the desert as a history of sin, insofar as Israel held fast to the idols of Egypt and broke the law (Ezek 20:6-26). Exilic and postexilic salvation PROPHECY looked forward to a new exodus out of the exile: The old exodus would be completed when Israel was led home in healing (Ezek 20:32-38). Deutero-Isaiah calls the people to forget the early history of Israel in order to understand the time to come (Isa 43:16-21; cf. Jer 23:7-8). Many exodus events are mentioned in the psalms (see Pss 78:12-53; 105:23-45; 106:7-33; 114; 136:10-16); e.g., the wonder at the Red Sea and the revelation at Sinai are described in cosmic terms as well as with the application of mythic elements (e.g., Ps 77:17-21), and Israel is allegorically and poetically transfigured as the vine Yahweh brought out of Egypt (Ps 80:9).

2. Extra-canonical Writings of the HB and Contemporary Literature. In Hellenistic-Roman Judaism the memory of the exodus acquired a central significance (see 1 Macc 4:9). The conflict between Yahweh and Nebuchadnezzar/Holofernes in Judith has the same structure of events as that between Yahweh and Pharaoh in Exodus. The hymn in Judith 16 was inspired by the Song of Miriam in Exodus 15. Exodus also lends to the book of Judith the terminological means of its theological exposition.

A presentation of the oppression of Israel in Egypt until the exodus is found in the book of JUBILEES (chaps. 46–49), where the Mosaic traditions in Exodus 3–14 are depicted as the struggle between Satan (Mastema) and the angel of God. *Jubilees* presents itself as a revelation of the angel of God to Moses on Sinai (*Jubilees* 1), during which Moses received the contents of the books of Genesis through Leviticus.

The dream-visions of the Ethiopian book of ENOCH interpret the exodus from Egypt as the flight of sheep from wolves (*1 Enoch* 89:10-27) and Moses as the sheep who leads the flock into the promised land (*1 Enoch* 89:28-40). The tragedian Ezekiel attempted to edit dramatically the material of Exodus 1–15 in his drama "Exagoge" and in this way created a counterpart to profane Greek tragedy. In the Wisdom of Solomon the THEOLOGY of Exodus and wisdom theology are united in an imposing symbiosis. In an artful literary composition the wisdom of Israel is celebrated as having already proved itself superior to the wisdom of Egypt, the land of wisdom, during the exodus (Wisd Sol 11:2-19, 21).

The exodus events were turned completely around by several non-Jewish historians (Manetho [3rd cent. BCE], Chaeremon [1st cent. CE], Lysimachos [c. 361–281 BCE], Apion [1st cent. CE], Tacitus [b. 55 CE]), according to whom the exodus was a case of the flight of lepers who had earlier oppressed the Egyptians with the help of the Hyksos. In contrast, the Jewish historian Artapanus (fl. 2nd cent. BCE), describing the life of Moses with considerable haggadic expansions and in a novelistic style, maintained that Moses had provided the Egyptians with a variety of cultural institutions.

JOSEPHUS offered an exhaustive version of the exodus traditions (*Ant. Jud.* 2.9–3.15), though one that has been embellished with various legends. Moses appears as, among other things, the victorious leader of the army of the Egyptians against the Ethiopians (*Ant. Jud.* 2.10). The miraculous nature of the event at the Red Sea is weakened (2.16.5), while the story of the golden calf (Exodus 32) is consciously left out. PHILO of Alexandria composed two books on the life of Moses (*Vita Mos.* 1 and 2) and an Exodus commentary (*Quaestiones in Exodum*). Understanding the exodus as a philosophical allegory, he depicted the Sinai event as a supra-dimensional mystery: The wanderings of the Israelites in the Sinai desert became a transposition into a divine locale, a growing of the soul out of and beyond the world of materiality, the senses, and suffering.

3. The NT. Christological, ecclesiological, sacramental, paraenetic, and anti-Jewish polemical interpretations of various exodus traditions are found in the NT.

a. Christological interpretations. The way of the child JESUS leads to Egypt and back, according to Matthew. As was once true of Israel, so also it is now true of Jesus: "Out of Egypt I have called my son" (Hos 11:1 in Matt 3:15). The story of "the massacre of the innocents" in Bethlehem (Matt 2:16-18) corresponds to the return of Moses from Midian (Exod 4:19-20). Even at the end of Matthew features of the exodus tradition become clear: The Last Supper of Jesus with his disciples is a passover meal (Matt 26:17; cf. Exod 12:14-20).

The entire NT tradition sees in Jesus the passover lamb (John 19:36; 1 Cor 5:7; cf. Exod 12:36). Hebrews 12:18-24 compares the revelation on Sinai in its entirety with the revelation manifested in Jesus Christ.

b. Ecclesiological interpretation. What is ascribed to the Israelites in Exod 19:16 now applies to the Christians, who, according to 1 Pet 2:9, are now "the royal priesthood and the holy people."

c. Sacramental and paraenetic modes. Paul uses a haggadic MIDRASH on the exodus and wilderness wanderings to demonstrate to the Corinthians that one's salvation is never ultimately secured. In this treatment he sets the march through the sea in parallel with baptism, manna with the communion bread, and Christ with the rock of Exod 17:6. Hebrews 3:7-19 juxtaposes the behavior of the Christians with that of the Israelites in the wilderness. Hebrews 11:23-29 lists as paradigmatic for faith the behavior of the midwives (Exod 2:2), of Moses (Exod 2:11-15; 12:11, 22-23), and of the people during the crossing of the sea (Exod 14:22, 27).

d. Anti-Jewish polemic. In the sermon of Stephen parts of the exodus story (particularly Exodus 1–3; 32) are taken up in order to show that the Israelites are "stiff-necked" and that they have broken the law (Acts 7:51-53). Moses is depicted as a "type" of Christ, who is rejected by the people even though God has sent him as a liberator (Acts 7:35). At numerous other places in the NT individual verses from Exodus are cited or expounded (e.g., in the "antitheses" of the SERMON ON THE MOUNT; cf. Matt 5:21 with Exod 20:13; Matt 5:27 with Exod 20:14; in Jesus' discourse on the resurrection, Matt 22:32; cf. Exod 3:6; in the Pauline epistles, cf. Rom 9:15 with Exod 33:19, etc.). In addition, one finds legendary expansions stemming from contemporary literature (e.g., 2 Tim 3:8, legends of Jannes and Jambres).

4. The Early Church. During this period, Exodus was usually expounded in PENTATEUCHAL commentaries or in sermons. Important contributions in the third to the sixth centuries were composed by ORIGEN (*Selecta et Homiliae in Exodus*), Diodore of Tarsus (*Fragmenta in Exodus*), JEROME (*Liber Exodi*), AUGUSTINE (*Quaestiones et locutiones in Exodum*), CYRIL OF ALEXANDRIA (*Glaphyri in Exodum*), THEODORET OF CYRRHUS (*Quaestiones in Exodum*), Procopius of Gaza (*Commentarii in Exodum*), GREGORY THE GREAT (*Expositio sup. Exodum*), and ISIDORE OF SEVILLE (*Quaestiones in Exodum*). In these works the modes of interpretation applied in NT times are carried farther. The typological interpretation of people, events, and instructions from Exodus took on considerable significance, and these features expressed the events of the Christian truth and *Heilsgeschichte* (salvation history).

a. Christological interpretations. Several features were taken to signify the incarnation of God: Exod 3:14-15, with the designation of the God who is unchanging and unchangeable, "the God of Abraham,

Isaac and Jacob" (Augustine *Sermo* 6.84-87); the transformation of Moses' staff into a serpent (Exod 4:3; Augustine *Sermo* 6.104-108), and the miracle of the manna (Exodus 16; Origen *Homily* on Exod 7:5). According to other interpretations, the manna and quails point to the coming of Christ for the last judgment (Hilary *Tract. myst.* 1.40).

The christological interpretation of Exodus 12 achieved great significance: The description of the paschal lamb (v. 5) became a *locus classicus* for the sinlessness of Christ, the virgin birth, and the single year of his effective ministry. In the dating of the paschal feast to the 14th of Nisan (vv. 3, 6) the church fathers found a prophecy of the crucifixion. That the paschal lamb was slaughtered in the evening (v. 6) announced Christ's crucifixion at the end of the world (for exhaustive interpretations of Exodus 12 see Zeno of Verona [*Tractate on Exodus* 12] and Gaudentius of Brescia [*Tractate on Exodus* 12]).

Moses was frequently compared with Christ, e.g., the threatening situations at their respective births and the correspondence between Pharaoh and Herod (e.g., Hilary *Tract. myst.* 1.28). Moreover events from the life of Moses were interpreted christologically: Moses' slaying of the Egyptian signified Christ, who slays the devil (Hilary *Tract. myst.* 1.29; Cyril of Alexandria *Glaphyr. on Exod* 1:7; Augustine *Cont. Faust.* 22.90).

b. Ecclesiological and sacramental interpretations. Jerome interpreted the wandering of the people of Israel through the desert as the wandering of the church through history (*Epist.* 78), in which the church was not destroyed in spite of persecution. Receiving the law on Sinai foreshadowed the reception of the Holy Spirit at Pentecost (Exodus 19, cf. Acts 2; Jerome *Epist.* 78). Some argued that the bush that burned without being consumed (Exodus 3) referred to the constant renewal of the church after times of persecution (Jerome *Epist.* 78; Theodoret of Cyrrhus *Graec. affect. curatio*, 9.27).

The sacramental interpretation of the exodus received its firm place in the catechism partially because baptism was administered at Easter, the Christian Passover. According to the prescriptions laid down by PAUL (1 Corinthians 10), the wonder of the manna was transformed into the model of the Eucharist—that is, of the spiritual feeding of the church during its own exodus here on earth (repeatedly attested by Cyprian, Ambrose, Augustine, J. Chrysostom, and Theodoret of Cyrrhus). Just as the blood of the Passover lamb was smeared on the doorposts and lintels, so also should Christians receive the *sacramentum passionis* with the mouth unto salvation. Exodus 15:1-19 won liturgical significance as the first of the "cantica" only after the time of the early church.

c. Paraenetic interpretations. Paraenetic (homiletic) texts from Exodus, above all the DECALOGUE (Exod 20:1-21), were frequently used and had a long, effective history, although details and events from other Exodus pericopes were interpreted paraenetically as well. Paraenetic texts are exhoratory texts used as homiletical vehicles to impart values and wisdom for the contemporary audience; thus, e.g., the manna stories become precursors to the Eucharist and a preparation for Christian martyrdom (see B. Childs [1974] 297). Additionally, exegetes, beginning with Augustine (and through the late Middle Ages), suggested that since the Israelites were told to request objects of silver and gold from the Egyptians (Exod 3:22; similarly, Exod 11:2; 12:35), Christians were required to make use of the ancient arts (and secular literature and philosophy) and further that a synthesis between ancient philosophy and Christian theology was possible. Exodus 3:22 served as a *locus classicus* for this interpretation.

d. Monastic and spiritual-mystical interpretations. From quite early times the liberation of the Israelites was interpreted as an example for the call to the monastic life (J. Cassian [c. 360–after 430]). The ever-recurring wish to return to Egypt (Exod 16:3, etc.) recalled the monk who, pulled by the old passions, returned to the old proclivities (Cassian *Conl.* 21.28). The elders (Exod 18:21) recalled the senior monk who was installed over ten monks (Cassian *Inst.* 4.7), and the fasting of Moses (Exod 34:28) was seen in connection with monastic asceticism (Cassian *Conl.* 21.28).

GREGORY OF NYSSA, in his *Life of Moses* (*De vita Moysis*), took the path already trod by Philo when he interpreted the exodus as a progression toward God. He tied this theme together with a rich variety of individual typological interpretations and explained the details of the exodus as symbols of a timeless philosophical truth and as prefigurations of Christ. The monastic writers often depicted the events of the exodus as symbols of the path of the soul, especially Cassian (*Conl.* 3.7; 5.14-16), Philoxenus of Mabbug (*Hom.* 9), and John Climacus (*Lib. ad. Past.* 15).

e. Anti-Jewish interpretations. Although the church fathers frequently appropriated rabbinic traditions (e.g., Origen's *Hom.* 5:5 on Exodus 14, and the haggadic perspective that each of the twelve tribes had made its own way through the Red Sea; cf. *DevR* 11:10), in other instances their interpretations ignited strife between Jewish and Christian theologians. The exegesis of Exodus 12 and 32 makes clear that something substantial was at stake; e.g., after the church fathers aligned the paschal lamb with Christ, they stressed that the Jewish Passover had no further value (e.g., Aphrahat [early 4th cent.], Chrysostom, Zeno of Verona [d c. 375]). The smelting of the golden calf (Exodus 32) marked, according to some church fathers, the dissolution of the Sinaitic covenant (Ephraem the Syrian *Comm. in Diatessaron* 20.35; Augustine, *Sermo* 88.21, 24); and the ceremonial law was treated as a divine penalty for this sin (Justin, *Dial.* 20.3). Rabbinic exegesis developed a converse tendency to defend the Israelites and to ameliorate their guilt. According to one extreme perspective, God had to share in the guilt, since God gave the people so much gold when they left Egypt (*b. Ber.* 32a).

5. Rabbinic Interpretations. In the rabbinic literature the individual aspects of the exodus events and the revelation on Mt. Sinai were frequently treated in halakhic and haggadic texts. Important interpretations outside the TALMUD and Mishnah are found in the *Mekhilta* of Rabbi ISHMAEL (*Mek.*) and in the *Mekhilta* of Rabbi Shim'on ben Yohai (*Mek. R. Shim.*). From a later time (though with earlier components) stem the *Exodus Rabba*, with an exegetical Midrash on Exodus 1–10 (*Exod. Rab.* 1) and a homiletical Midrash on Exodus 12–40 (*Exod. Rab.* 2), the homily-Midrash *Tanchuma Shemot* (*Tan. Shem*), the *Pirqe* of Rabbi ELIEZER (*Pirqe R. El.*), with the Mosiac history down to the revelation after the sin with the golden calf (*Pirqe R. El.* 40-48), as well as the collection found in the *Midrash HaGadol* (*MHG. Shem.*) and other works.

Besides the reference to individual verses as *dicta probantia* of halakhic reflections, several legends have been woven into haggadic texts (a typical example: *b. Sot.* 11a-12b on Exod 1:18–2:7), including the stories of Jannes and Jambres, the wise men of Pharaoh's court, and the report of an initial abortive exodus of the tribe of Ephraim under the leadership of Jagons thirty years before the actual exodus (*Shem. R.* 2:11; *Pirqe R. El.* 48, etc.). Individual episodes, moreover, were given novel interpretations, e.g., the sojourn of Moses in Midian (Exodus 2) became his time of testing; the burning bush (Exodus 3) symbolized Israel's need and God's compassion (*Tan. Shem.* 14; *MHG. Shem.* 3:2).

The exodus, the revelation at Sinai, and the acceptance of the obligations that grew out of those experiences remained of central significance for Judaism. According to the Babylonian Talmud, every Jew in every age was obligated to imagine that he or she personally had come up out of Egypt (*Pes.* 10:5; *b. Pes.* 116b). The relevant events were brought together and interpreted in the Passover *Haggadah,* where the hope in the eschatological liberation of Israel stood next to the remembrance of the deliverance from Egypt (*b. Ber.* 12b; *Exod. Rab.* 3:12; *Shir. R.* 2:8).

6. The Quran. The Quran (see QURANIC AND ISLAMIC INTERPRETATION) allots extensive space to the events reported in Exodus; reports of this kind are found above all in Suras 2:49-75; 4:153-54; 7:103-71; 10:75-92; 11:96-99; 17:101-3; 20:9-98; 23:45-49; 26:10-68; 27:7-14; 28:3-51; 40:23-47; 43:46-56; 44:17-33; 51:38-40; 79:15-26. The exodus traditions are here presented exhaustively, with partial repetitions and considerable divergences (cf. the report of the golden calf in Suras 7 and 20). Thus Moses, as a typical representative of God, begins with the task of converting unbelievers (Pharaoh and his people). The Israelites comprise a minority who are finally saved along with Moses, while the great mass

of the people (Egyptians) fall victim to divine judgment (e.g., Sura 51:38-40; 79:15-26). In addition to HB traditions, rabbinic traditions are enumerated (twelve streams from the rock [Sura 7:160]; the elevation of Sinai over the people [Sura 4:154]).

7. The Middle Ages (Christian Interpretations). *a. The early Middle Ages.* Among the learned Irish of the seventh century, scholars strove to explain the wonders of the exodus reports rationally: The dry seabed (Exod 14:16, 22) was explained through freezing; the miracle of the manna (Exod 16:14-15) through clouds, which could hold manna seeds just as they could contain hail (Pseudo-Augustine *De mirabilibus Sacrae Scripturae*). The commentaries of the Carolingian period show little originality and largely take over exegetical traditions from the early church. BEDE, besides his commentaries *Comm. in Exodum* and *Quaestiones super Exodum*, composed *De tabernaculo et vasis eius ac vestibus sacerdotum* on Exod 24:12–30:21, in which he delineated the origin, midpoint, and goal of the church and the ideal forms of the Christian life. WALAFRID STRABO (*Glossa ordinaria lib. Exod.*) borrowed numerous interpretations from Josephus to explain strange phenomena and geographical details. RABANUS MAURUS (*Comm. in Exodum*) ascribed to the book of Exodus the central place in the Pentateuch since nearly all the sacraments of the church are prefigured there.

b. The High and Late Middle Ages. In the eleventh century P. DAMIAN wrote an investigation *De decalogo et decem Aegypti plagis* in addition to his Exodus commentaries (*Collectanea in librum Exodi; Testimonia Exodi*). From the twelfth century a number of Exodus commentaries by theologians of the various orders are extant, particularly from the Benedictines, Bruno of Segni (*Expositio in Exodum*), RUPERT OF DEUTZ (*In Exodum*), Georgius Brituliensis (*Explanatio Exodi*), Richard of Préaux (*Comm. in Exodum*), and from the Augustian canon, ANDREW OF ST. VICTOR (*Expositio historica super Exodum*). Relevant meditations on partial pericopes, individual cult objects, and legal provisions in the book come from these and other authors. In many individual cases the exegetes followed the typological-allegorical, the *heilsgeschichtlich*-ecclesiological, and the moral interpretations of the earlier exegetical tradition but at the same time often provided some characteristic, novel interpretations.

Bruno of Segni considered the instructions of Exodus primarily as instructions for the contemporary church, particularly with respect to bishops and priests. Thus the purple in the curtain (Exod 26:31) recalled the obligation of the pope to practice justice. The secret of Jesus Christ and the stations of his passion were also brought forth to the reader (e.g., in Exod 29:10-14). Rupert of Deutz emphasized the christocentric character of Exodus as well, while Andrew of St. Victor's love of interpreting the Scriptures in vernacular language and interest in philological questions stamped his commentary with rational explanations.

During this period the ascetic-mystic perception became of particular concern and gripped, e.g., Richard of Préaux, especially in texts dealing with the theophany on Mt. Sinai. The natural phenomena that accompanied the theophany (Exod 19:16) made plain the path leading from the fear of God to the person's conversion, although even at its conclusion the fear of God remained (Exod 20:18-19). RICHARD OF ST. VICTOR (*Expositio difficultatum suborientium in expositione tabernaculi foederis*) chose the form of the ark of the covenant as the starting point for a consideration of the six stages of contemplation, with the two cherubim symbolizing the two highest steps. For Georgius Brituliensis, the fire and the thornbush designated the whole person with whom God became one, the fleshly essence becoming thereby spiritual. The tent shrine played an important role in this mystical mode of interpretation (Exodus 26) and from the time of Gregory I was seen as a model of the *ecclesia universalis*. Petrus of Celle (*De tabernaculi Moysi*) carried out a mystical and moral interpretation. In contrast, Adam of Dryburgh (*De tripartitu tabernaculo*) attempted to illustrate and concretize the tent's individual components by creating great cycles in which the saints of the Bible and early church history as well as personalities of contemporary history corresponded to its parts.

In the fourteenth century, partially under the influence of Jewish exegesis, the first commentaries began to appear in which a determination of the literal and/or historical sense of the text was the central consideration. This was particularly the case with the commentary of NICHOLAS OF LYRA (*Postillae perpetuae in Exodum*), which was heavily dependent on RASHI. Even M. Eckhart had laid special emphasis on an interpretation of individual verses through comparative biblical citations in his commentary (*Expositio libri Exodi*). For the interpretation of individual laws he drew on MAIMONIDES, while for allegorical interpretations he generally referred to other authors.

8. Medieval Jewish Exegesis. In the Babylonian talmudic schools of the ninth and tenth centuries, interpretations by SAADIA IBN JOSEPH (Tafsir) and by Samuel of Chofni, among others, were added to the Torah commentaries. Numerous commentaries were composed in the High and Late Middle Ages, including works by R. Abraham IBN EZRA, who wrote a long and a short commentary on Exodus; R. Shelomo ben Isaac (Rashi, 12th cent.); R. Hisquia bar Manoach (13th cent.); R. Moses ben Nachman (see NACHMANIDES); and R. Nissim Gerondii (14th cent.). These commentaries focused primarily on the literary sense and were concerned with a synoptic presentation in light of later biblical-exegetical traditions. Thus, on the basis of Exod 20:5-9, Ibn Ezra assumed that before Moses the Israelites had generally

worshiped other gods. He interpreted the forty years of wandering in the wilderness as a time for a free and independent generation able to liberate Canaan to arise (in opposition to the Christian explanation of the wilderness wanderings as the penalty for the sins of the people).

9. The Reformation Era. In his "Sermons on the Second Book of Moses" (composed 1524–27; *WA* 16), LUTHER maintained that Exodus was an example of how God held faithfully to God's promise, how the grace and goodness of God were still valid for distressed, afflicted, and frightened Christians, and how God's wrath was directed toward stiff-necked, unrepentant people. There are sermons on every chapter, including allegorical interpretations of chaps. 1–4, 12, 14–15, 17, 23, and 25–30. Yet Luther avoided the overdrawn allegorizing of others; e.g., the explanation of the burning bush (Exodus 3) as Mary the mother of God. For him the bush represented Christ, while in chap. 1 he saw not only Israel under Pharaoh but also Christians living in affliction under the pope. Yet in chap. 12 he maintained the traditional allegorical interpretations and considered Christ to be the paschal lamb; the waters of Marah (Exod 15:22-26) to refer to the law of God; and the wandering in the wilderness to signify the melancholy of life.

CALVIN gave a strictly historical interpretation of the exodus traditions (*Comm. in quatuor reliquos Mosis libros in formam harmoniae digestus* [1563]), avoiding the allegorical wherever possible. The burning bush (Exodus 3) was for him, as in Jewish exegesis, an image of oppressed Israel, who nonetheless suffered no damage, since God was with them. The Passover (Exodus 12) prefigured the death of Jesus. The manna (Exodus 16) represented Christ's flesh, on which the Christian soul fed in hope of eternal life. The ark of the covenant (Exodus 25) was the focal point for the collection of the legal and historical records of Israel and thus the locus for the formation of the HB.

An interpretation of Exodus 1–24 by ZWINGLI survives (*Annotationes zu Exodus* [1527]). He placed a historic-grammatical approach in the foreground of his exegesis (under the influence of Josephus and D. Kimhi, among many others), which nonetheless gave ample space to typological references to Christ; e.g., Christ the paschal lamb (Exodus 12) and the container in which the manna was kept (Exod 16:33-4), which reflected the humanity of Christ in which lay the deity—the actual bread of life.

10. Early Period of Biblical Criticism. In the early history of criticism, from the sixteenth to the beginning of the nineteenth centuries, numerous Exodus commentaries were composed, overwhelmingly in Pentateuchal or biblical commentaries, with the main issues being the philological clarification of difficult passages. Ancient translations, Christian and Jewish exegesis of earlier centuries, ancient authors, and other sources were assembled in a rich mass and compared and evaluated in order to interpret individual verses. Of particular note were the commentaries, usually written in Latin, listed here by author and year of publication: A. Tostado (1528); C. PELLICAN (1532); D. Carthusianus (1534); J. Brenz (1539); R. Stephanus (1541); L. Lippomann (1550); N. des Gallars (1560); C. Spangenberg (1563); J. Ferus (1571); L. Osiander (1573); H. Oleaster (1586); B. Pereira (1601); L. Ystella (1609); E. Sa (1610); J. DRUSIUS (1617); J. de Mariana (1620); L. Marius (1621); J. Bonfrère (1625); H. AINSWORTH (Eng. [1627]); C. à LAPIDE (1630); J. Menochius (1630); A. Rivet (1633); T. CAJETAN (1639); C. Jansen (1639); H. GROTIUS (1644); J. Piscator (1646); L. de Dieu (1648); J. Tirinus (1656); A. Varenius (1659); J. Trappe (Eng., 1662); G. Estius (1667); J. Osiander (1676); M. Polo (1678); C. Frassen (1705); J. Clericus (1733); C. Starke (1763); C. Houbigant (1777); W. Hezel (1780); A. CALMET (1789); E. ROSENMÜLLER (1828).

11. Modern Exegesis in the Nineteenth and Twentieth Centuries. *a. Historical-critical exegesis.* Modern historical-critical research began in the first half of the nineteenth century. Previously an inestimable number of monographs, commentaries, and individual contributions had been concerned with questions pertaining to the book's interpretation. Historical, LITERARY-critical, TRADITION-historical, and religion-historical lines of inquiry stood in the foreground of these works. Among these commentaries are those of G. Bush (Eng., 1841); M. Kalisch (Eng., 1855); A. KNOBEL (KEH, Ger., 1857); C. KEIL (BC, Ger., 1861); J. Murphy (Eng., 1868); J. Lange (THBW, Ger., 1874); A. DILLMANN (KEH², Ger., 1880); G. Chadwick (Eng., 1890); S. Hirsch (Ger., 1893); B. BACON (Eng., 1894); R. MOULTON (Eng., 1896); H. Strack (KK, Ger., 1894); A. Dillmann/ V. RYSSEL (KEH³, Ger., 1897); F. von Hummelauer (CSS, Lat. 1897); J. Macgregor (Eng., 1898); H. Holzinger (KHC, Ger., 1900); (HSAT[K], Ger., 1909); B. BAENTSCH (HK, Ger., 1903); W. Benneth (CeB, Eng., 1906); A. McNeile (WC, Eng., 1908); B. EERDMANS (Ger., 1910); J. WEISS (Ger., 1911); S. DRIVER (Eng., 1911); J. Conell (NBC, Eng., 1912); G. Harford (PCB, Eng., 1919); H. GRESSMANN (SAT, Ger., 1921); H. Grimmelsmann (Eng., 1927); F. Böhl (TeU, Dutch, 1928); P. HEINISCH (HSAT, Ger., 1934); J. H. Hertz (Ger., 1937); B. Beer and K. GALLING (HAT, Ger., 1939); E. Kalt (HBK, Ger., 1948); U. CASSUTO (Heb., 1951; ET 1967); W. Gispen (Dutch, 1951); J. Rylaarsdam (IntB, Eng., 1952); H. Frey (BAT, Ger., 1953); H. Schneider (EB, Ger., 1955); A. Clamer (Fr., 1956); H. Junker (EB, Ger., 1958); M. NOTH (ATD, Ger., 1959); R. Murphy (PBiS, Eng., 1960–62); G. Auzou (Fr., 1961); D. Stalker (PCB, Eng., 1962); B. Napier (LCB, Eng., 1965); G. te Stroete (BOT, Dutch, 1966); G. Davies (TBC, Eng., 1967); B. Couroyer (SB, Fr., 1968); M. Greenberg (HB I, Eng.,

1969); F. FENSHAM (Dutch, 1970); J. P. HYATT (NCeB, Eng., 1971); R. Clements (CBC, Eng., 1972); E. Munk (Fr., 1972); R. Cole (TOTC, Eng., 1973); F. Michaeli (CAT, Fr., 1974); B. Childs (OTL, Eng., 1974); W. Schmidt (BK, Ger., 1974); G. Knight (Eng., 1976); W. Fields (Eng., 1976); N. Leibowitz (Heb./Eng., 1976); B. Boschi (Ital., 1978); E. Zenger (Ger., 1978); F. Huey (Eng., 1980); H. Ellison (Eng., 1982); L. Meyer (Eng., 1983); N. SARNA (Eng., 1986, 1991).

i. Literary-critical approaches. The history of modern interpretation of the exodus traditions begins in the middle of the eighteenth century with the literary-critical study of the Pentateuch. In 1753 Exod 6:3 gave J. ASTRUC the key to PENTATEUCHAL CRITICISM: On the basis of this text he separated the texts in Genesis and Exodus according to their respective uses of the divine names Yahweh and Elohim. In the course of the nineteenth century, literary-critical lines of investigation stood in the forefront of Pentateuchal research, and with regard to Exodus these reached their high point toward the end of the century. Important in addition to the numerous treatments of the entire Pentateuch were A. JÜLICHER's 1880 dissertation, "Die Quellen von Ex I–VII"; his "Die Quellen von Ex VII, 8–XXIV, 11 in *JpT* 8 (1882) 79-127, 272-315; and B. Bacon's *The Triple Tradition of the Exodus* (1894). The priestly pericopes in Exodus were separated with relative ease, especially in Exod 6:2-12; 7:1-7, 12, 16; and in 25:1–31:17 and chaps. 35–40. However, the literary-critical isolation of the J and E materials was developed with much greater difficulty in Exodus than in Genesis (according to the various theories as well as the further identification of sources and differentiations within J and E), since after Exodus 3 the divine name criterion could no longer be applied reliably. Generally, sufficient arguments are now lacking to ascribe a particular pericope to any source with certainty. For example, it can now be established on the basis of a synthesis of forty-eight analyses of Exodus 32 in the period between 1857 and 1978 that five scholars ascribed Exod 32:1-6 to J and nineteen to E; six scholars found parts of both J and E, while eighteen were unable to prefer any assignment to one of these sources. More recent research rejects an indentification of texts with one of the older sources (J or E) and places high value on differentiating between earlier and later passages. In this process, literary layers have also been discovered that belong in the realm of the proto-deuteronomic (Exod 4:21-23; 19:3b-9; 24:3-8, 18-21; 32:7-14).

ii. Tradition-historical approaches. The results of investigations starting from a tradition-historical perspective began to have a decisive influence on the historical interpretation of the book of Exodus no later than the work of G. von RAD (*Das formgeschichtliche Problem des Hexateuchs* [1938] = *The Problem of Hexateuch* [1966]). J. WELLHAUSEN (*Die Composition des Hexateuch* [1899²]) had already recognized the isolation of the Sinai tradition, and Galling had elaborated the exodus tradition as the primary tradition, in contrast to the Sinai tradition (*Die Erwählungstradition Israels* [1928]). Von Rad referred to the absence of the Sinai tradition in the confession in Deut 26:5-10 and localized the exodus and Sinai traditions at two distinct cultic sites in Israel. Even Noth regarded the exodus and Sinai as two variant themes that in the history of the traditions had gone their own separate ways before being bound together in the Pentateuch (*Überlieferungsgeschichte des Pentateuch* [1948] = *A History of Pentateuchal Traditions* [1972]). Others rejected this separation of the two traditions (J. Bright, *A History of Israel* [1960]), and assured results were not forthcoming in spite of numerous further studies in the following years. In all probability different groups of the Israelites' ancestors had taken part in either the exodus or Sinai events, although this hypothesis can at present be neither proved nor refuted. It is at the same time unclear in which relationship Yahweh and Moses originally stood to the exodus and Sinai traditions, although Moses plays the most important role in the Sinai tradition as the recipient of the revelation of Yahweh (see H. Gese [1974]).

Since literary-critical and tradition-historical investigations ceased to take into account the book's present unity, certain approaches have established new emphases in research, including stylistic-structural and linguistic studies conducted on the basis of a "canonical approach" (see CANONICAL CRITICISM) and "stylistic criticism." Here the composition of the book's various parts is emphatically considered in terms of each part's final literary form (see Childs, *Exodus* [1974, 1979]). Stimulated by these perspectives, R. Moberly has interpreted Exodus 32–34 as a "coherent and clearly defined unit" (*At the Mount of God* [JSOTSup 22, 1983]).

iii. Religion-historical approaches. The study of ancient and modern Near Eastern cultures and religions resulted in new sources of knowledge for the derivation of numerous exodus traditions. In the nineteenth century the study of Canaanite religion resulted in a new understanding of calf images (the golden calf, Exodus 32). A complete consensus had existed as late as the first decades of the nineteenth century that these images derived from the Egyptian gods Apis and Mnevis. However, the investigations in the following decades led to the conclusion that they derived from the territory of Canaan, where the originally nomadic Israelites had found a new homeland.

With research into Babylonian culture and religion at the end of the nineteenth century, the obvious relationship between the book of the covenant (Exod 20:22–23:33) and the code of Hammurabi was recognized. The connections as well as the peculiarities of Israelite religion in relation to its environment became clear through further religion-historical studies.

iv. Historical approaches. It had been recognized already in the nineteenth century that the events of the exodus, the deliverance at the Red Sea, the revelation on the mountain of God, and the wandering in the wilderness had been rewoven into the genre of *Sage* and illuminated by the light of *Heilsgeschichte*. This transformation led to numerous uncertainties in the clarification of the historical circumstances of the book. Nevertheless, there were repeated attempts to tie the exodus events to historical developments drawn from other sources. The thesis that the exodus of the Israelites could be connected to the expulsion of the Hyksos was represented until about 1900 (see Steindorff, *RE³* 1:211) and had been maintained as early as Josephus (*Cont. Ap.* I. 14.25). In the course of the twentieth century, historical research could discover no traces in Egyptian texts of the migration to and emigration from Egypt of the people who would become the Israelites. It was still accepted, however, that the events behind Exodus 1 occurred in the first half of the thirteenth century BCE. With the Israelites it was a question of Semitic nomads who had settled in the eastern delta and who had fallen into forced labor there. The "Pharaoh of the Liberation" was, presumably, Rameses II (1290–1224); the "Pharaoh of the Exodus" was Merneptah (1224–1204) or even Seti II (1200–1194).

Attempts to localize the geographical sites named in Exodus are connected with lines of historical inquiry concerning the exodus from Egypt and the wilderness wanderings. Such attempts go back to the time of the early church (e.g., the pilgrimages of the nun Etheria in the 4th cent., *Peregrinatio Etheriae*, and of the pilgrim of Placenza in the 6th cent., *Antonini Placentini Itinerarium*). Exact knowledge of these geographical relationships was not acquired, however, until the numerous expeditions of the nineteenth century, which occasioned many provisional localizations. Nevertheless, none of the places of the exodus events has been unequivocally identified, despite intensive efforts. The same is true of the "mountain of God" in the wilderness: While most scholars identify this site with the massive range in the southern part of the Sinai peninsula, others seek it, with good reason, in the district southeast of the Gulf of Aqaba.

b. Systematic-theological and philosophical exegesis. No special role was ascribed to the exodus traditions (apart from the ethical interpretation of the Decalogue) in the systematic theology of the twentieth century. K. BARTH saw the exodus as the history of God's covenant of grace and the realization and completion of God's love (*Church Dogmatics*, 2:2, 673ff.). With W. VISCHER (*Das Christuszeugnis des ATs* [1936²]) the traditional allegorical interpretations of the historical church reemerged: The child Moses in his little ark of reeds prefigures the child in the stall in Bethlehem; the Passover is set aside and fulfilled by the consecration of the

Last Supper of Jesus; the trek through the Red Sea symbolizes Christian baptism, etc. D. BONHOEFFER ("Opposition and Surrender," Letter of June 27, 1944) emphasized that the exodus represents historical salvation this side of the boundary of death, in contrast to the salvation myths of the ancient Near East.

New impulses came into theology through the Marxist philosopher E. Bloch (*The Principle of Hope* [1959; ET 1986]), who interpreted Israel's exodus in the sense of emancipation, rebellion, change, transformation, and expectation. The exodus became a symbol for the program of a permanent exodus of socio-historical hope. Bloch was criticized from various sides, above all for tracing the salvation events back to a revolutionary people's movement and not to the initiative of Yahweh (see H. Kraus [1972]). Conversely, J. Moltmann took up Bloch's suggestion in his *Theology of Hope* (1964; ET 1967) and thereby gave strong impulse to a stream of thought that became important in Latin American LIBERATION THEOLOGIES, where present experiences and hopes are placed in parallel with the biblical events of the exodus (see *TRE* 10 [1982] 746-47). For Latin American interpreters G. Pixley and C. Boff (1991), the liberation of the Hebrew people has significance for the entire oppressed world. Accordingly, C. Moon (1991) aligns the history of Korean *minjung* with the history of the Hebrews in Exodus, while J.-M. Ela (1991) suggests an African reading of this text requiring the interpreter to enter into solidarity with the marginalized.

Liberation theologies based on the exodus, however, have been challenged due to the rise of POST-COLONIAL and FEMINIST interpretations of the Bible. While recognizing the potential for liberation inherent in the exodus, I. Mosala (1989; 1993) and R. Weems (1992) notice that this same liberating message has been used to exploit and dominate other groups. For this reason they suggest that interpreters take into account issues of gender, class, and racial struggles when reading Exodus in order to expose possible underlying ideologies (see IDEOLOGICAL CRITICISM). This is further demonstrated by Palestinian scholar N. Atteek (1991), who argues that liberation for the Hebrew people creates hostility for the Egyptians and the Canaanites as the Hebrew God displaces these indigenous people; this "liberating" story is used by some to justify the displacement of the indigenous Palestinians in modern Israel. Similarly, Native American scholar R. Warrier (1991) parallels the displaced Native Americans with the Canaanites and argues that the exodus fails to be a liberating model for all people.

Meanwhile, feminist interpreters have noticed the prominent roles played by women in the exodus story (An Asian Group Work [1991]; D. Setel [1992]). Were it not for women (Miriam, the midwives, Moses' mother, Pharoah's daughter), the exodus would not have happened. In addition, feminists (see N. Steinberg [1993]) are beginning to examine biblical law (e.g. the book of the covenant [Exodus 21–23]), searching for clues that may shed light on the status and role of women in ancient Israel.

Bibliography: C. S. Anderson, "Divine Governance, Miracles, and Laws of Nature in the Early Middle Ages: The *De mirabilibus Sacrae Scripturae*" (diss., UCLA, 1982). **G. W. Ashby,** *Go Out and Meet God: A Commentary on the Book of Exodus* (ITC, 1998). **An Asian Group Work,** "An Asian Feminist Perspective: The Exodus Story (Ex. 1:8-22; 2:1-10)," *Voices from the Margin* (ed. R. S. Sugirtharajah, 1991) 255-66. **N. S. Ateek,** "A Palestinian Perspective: Biblical Perspectives on the Land," ibid., 267-76. **W. Brueggemann,** "The Book of Exodus," *NIB* (1994) 1:675-982. **J. Daniélou,** *RAC* 7 (1969) 22-44. **D. Daube,** *The Exodus Pattern in the Bible* (All Souls Studies 2, 1963). **J. J. Davis,** *Moses and the Gods of Egypt: Studies in the Book of Exodus* (1986²). **H. Donner,** *Pilgerfahrt ins Heilige Land* (1979). **T. B. Dozeman,** *God at War: A Study of Power in the Exodus Tradition* (1996). **J.-M. Ela,** "A Black African Perspective: An African Reading of Exodus," *Voices from the Margin* (ed., R. S. Sugirtharajah, 1991) 244-54. **T. Fretheim,** *Exodus* (IBC, 1995). **A. H. Friedlander,** "Die Exodus-Tradition: Geschichte und Heilsgeschichte aus jüdischer Sicht," *Exodus und Kreuz im ökumenischen Dialog zwischen Juden und Christen* (Aachener Beiträge 8, 1978) 30-44. **H. Gese,** *Vom Sinai zum Zion* (BEvT 64, 1974). **N. K. Gottwald and R. A. Horsley** (eds.), *The Bible and Liberation: Political and Social Hermeneutics* (1993). **R. Gradwohl,** *Bibelauslegungen aus jüdischen Quellen* (1986). **J. Hahn,** *Das "Goldene Kalb"* (EHS.T 154, 1981). **S. Herrmann et al.,** "Exodusmotiv," *TRE* 10 (1982) 732-47. **J. G. Janzen,** *Exodus* (1997). **R. B. Kenney,** "Ante-Nicene Greek and Latin Patristic Uses of the Biblical Manna Motif" (diss., Yale University, 1968). **K. Kiesow,** *Exodustexte im Jesajabuch: Literarkritische und motivgeschichtliche Analysen* (OBO 24, 1979). **H. J. Kraus,** "Das Thema 'Exodus': Kritische Anmerkungen zur Usurpation eines biblischen Begriffs," *Biblisch-theologische Aufsätze* (1972) 102-19. **W. Langewellpott,** "Untersuchungen zur Geschichte der lateinischen Exodusauslegung" (diss., Zürich, 1979). **G. Larsson,** *Bound for Freedom: The Book of Exodus in Jewish and Christian Traditions* (1999). **N. Leibowitz,** *Studies in Shemot in the Context of Ancient and Modern Jewish Bible Commentary* (2 vols., 1976). **F. Maschkowski,** "Raschis Einfluss auf Nikolaus von Lyra in der Auslegung des Exodus," *ZAW* 11 (1891) 268-90. **C. H. S. Moon,**" A Korean Minjung Perspective: The Hebrews and the Exodus," *Voices from the Margin* (ed. R. S. Sugirtharajah, 1991) 228-44. **I. J. Mosala,** *Biblical Hermeneutics and Black Theology in South Africa* (1989); "Biblical Hermeneutics and Black Theology in South Africa: The Use of the Bible," *The Bible and Liberation* (ed. N. K. Gottwald, 1993). **E. W. Nicholson,** *Exodus and Sinai in History and Tradition* (Growing Points in Theology, 1973). **R. E. Nixon,** *The Exodus in the NT* (TynNTL, 1962). **R. J. Owens,** *The Genesis and Exodus Citations of Afrahat the Persian Sage* (MPIL 3, 1983). **R. Paret,** *Der Koran: Übersetzung, Kommentar, und Konkordanz* (2 vols., 1980–81²). **G. V. Pixley,** *On Exodus: A*

Liberation Perspective (1983; ET 1987); **G. V. Pixley and C. Boff,** "A Latin American Perspective: The Option for the Poor in the OT," *Voices from the Margin* (ed. R. S. Sugirtharajah, 1991) 215-27. **H. P. Schlosser,** "Quellengeschichtliche Studie zur Interpretation des Leben-Mose Zyklus bei den Vätern des 4. Jahrhunderts" (diss., Freiburg i. Br., 1972). **H. Schmid,** *Die Gestalt des Mose* (EdF 237, 1986). **R. Schmidt,** *Exodus und Passa* (OBO 7, 1982²). **W. H. Schmidt,** *Exodus, Sinai, und Mose* (EdF 191, 1983). **D. Setel,** "Exodus" *Women's Bible Commentary* (ed. C. A. Newsom and S. H. Ringe, 1992) 26-35. **N. Steinberg,** "The Deuteronomic Law Code and the Politics of State Centralization," *The Bible and Liberation* (N. K. Gottwald, 1993). **A. Stock,** *The Way in the Wilderness: Exodus, Wilderness, and Moses Themes in OT and NT* (1968). **S. S. Stuart,** "The Exodus Tradition in Late Jewish and Early Christian Literature" (diss., Vanderbilt University, 1973). **P. Trible,** "Bringing Miriam Out of the Shadows," *BR* 5 (1989) 14-25. **R. S. Sugirtharajah** (ed.), *Voices From the Margin: Interpreting the Bible in the Third World* (1991). **R. A. Warrior,** "A Native American Perspective: Canaanites, Cowboys, and Indians," ibid., 277-88. **R. J. Weems,** "The Hebrew Women are Not Like the Egyptian Women," *Semeia* 59 (1992) 25-34. **P. Weimar and E. Zenger,** *Exodus: Geschichten und Geschichte der Befreiung Israels* (SBS 75, 1975, 1979²).

J. HAHN

EZEKIEL, BOOK OF

1. Early Rabbinic Interpretation. In early rabbinic interpretation controversy over Ezekiel centered on three topics: (1) The vision of chaps. 1, 8, and 10 is referred to already in Ben Sira 49:8 as a vision of the divine "chariot" (Heb., *merkābâ*, a term not used by Ezekiel himself). Some considered the study of chap. 1 a source of joyful enlightenment (*b. Hag.* 14b), but others held it to be extremely dangerous (cf. *b. Hag* 13a, in which fire devours a child who is studying chap. 1). (2) Ezekiel intensely condemned Israel and Jerusalem, especially in chap. 16. (3) The vision of chaps. 40–48 contains laws contradicting laws in the Torah (e.g., Ezek 44:22; Lev 21:14). Only after extensive argument was the book accepted as canonical (see *b. Šabb.* 13b; see also CANON OF THE BIBLE), and some authorities continued to prohibit the public reading of chaps. 1 and 16 (*Meg.* 4:10). Chapter 1 is, however, the prescribed *haftarah* for the first day of Shavuot (cf. *t. Meg.* 4:34).

Already in the Tannaitic period speculation on the *merkābâ* had grown into a complex tradition of mystical practice and writing (see, e.g., *t. Hag.* 211-12), which included early *hekhalot* literature (reports of, and instructions for achieving, visions of the heavenly palaces) and various apocalypses that included visions of the *merkābâ* (e.g., Daniel 7–8; 10; *Apocalypse of Abraham; 1 Enoch;* see APOCALYPTICISM). The Qumran *Songs of the Sabbath Sacrifice* are part of this *hekhalot* tradition. The "living creatures" of Ezekiel's vision formed the basis for the development of angelology in this period,

and angelic hymns were prominent in both *hekhalot* and apocalyptic literature. Ezekiel's vision of the dry bones in chap. 37 was interpreted as evidence for the resurrection of the body (see, e.g., the depictions of Ezekiel in the third-century BCE frescoes from Dura-Europos, and *b. Meg.* 31a).

2. Early Christian Interpretation. a. NT. Although never quoted directly in the NT, Ezekiel is the source for the image of the Davidic Messiah as "the good shepherd" (Ezekiel 34; Matt 18:12-14; John 10:11-18, etc.; cf. Heb 13:20; Ezek 37:24), and the book of Revelation contains extensive reworking of Ezekiel's visions and prophecies (see PROPHECY AND PROPHETS, HB) in terms of the events of the Roman period. Like early Jewish apocalypses, Revelation includes a vision of the divine throne/chariot patterned after Ezekiel 1 and adds the hymns of angel choruses (Rev 4:1-8). Other images in Revelation derived from Ezekiel include the eating of the scroll (Ezek 2:8-9; Rev 5:1, 10:1-4, 8-11), condemnation of the "whore" (Ezekiel 16, 23; Rev 17:1-6, 15-18), the battle with Gog (Ezekiel 38–39; Revelation 19–20), and the vision of the new temple (Ezekiel 40–48; Revelation 11, 21–22).

b. Early fathers. ORIGEN's twenty-five-book commentary on Ezekiel was the most influential of the early Christian commentaries but survives only in a few fragments. Fourteen of his homilies on Ezekiel are preserved in JEROME's translation. Major commentaries by both Jerome and THEODORET as well as several homilies by GREGORY THE GREAT are extant, together with comments on isolated passages by JUSTIN, Cyprian, CLEMENT OF ROME, AMBROSE, TERTULLIAN, and others. The book figures in patristic writings primarily in typological readings of the HB. Origen, for example, depicts Ezekiel as a type of Christ, who in his thirtieth year saw the heavens opened while standing by a river; Ezekiel's struggles with false prophets represent the church's struggle against the heretics; and the corruption of the woman Jerusalem in chap. 16 represents the soul's corruption by sin. Ezekiel 9:4-6 is read by various fathers as prefiguring the salvation of the Christians, whose foreheads are marked (in baptism) with the cross. Chapter 1 is interpreted in this period as a vision of Christ seated on the throne. The four living beings are the four Gospels (Irenaeus) or the evangelists themselves (Hippolytus), with the lion representing Matthew; the man, Mark; the ox, Luke; and the eagle, John. Interpretation of chap. 1 figures in patristic debate on the substance of God, with some fathers maintaining that Ezekiel saw only Christ and not God (since God is invisible), others arguing that Christ and God were represented by the *hašmal* and fire (1:27) respectively (and are therefore two substances), and so on. Ezekiel 37 is widely cited as a prophecy of the resurrection of the body and Ezekiel 14 as proof that salvation depends on individual repentance.

3. Medieval Interpretation. *a. Jewish.* Within Jewish circles speculation on Ezekiel's chariot vision contributed to the flowering of the mystical tradition, including the development of Kabbalism (see KABBALLAH) and HASIDISM in the twelfth century and following. The commentaries of RASHI, ELIEZER OF BEAUGENCY, and D. KIMHI represent the range of approaches taken toward Ezekiel in Jewish biblical scholarship of the period. Rashi took a relatively traditionalist stance in his comments, deferring to the early rabbis as authoritative and refusing to comment on the "forbidden" verses (1:27; 8:2). He did, however, consistently temper midrashic tradition (see MIDRASH) by his preference for the *pĕšat,* the literal sense of the text, and frequently elucidated passages in terms of the historical events of the prophet's own time. Eliezer's interpretation is relatively independent of the rabbinic tradition and is primarily based on semantic and rhetorical rather than theological criteria. Kimhi's work reflects this same relative freedom from rabbinic tradition but includes both literalist and speculative philosophical interpretation. A brilliant philologist, Kimhi was also a follower of MAIMONIDES, whose *Guide of the Perplexed* used philosophical categories to expound the chariot for the already advanced (but still perplexed) student. Kimhi wrote a philological commentary for the lay reader, following it with an esoteric treatise interpreting the chariot as a revelation to human intelligence of the divine intelligence guiding the spheres.

b. Christian. Many medieval Christian works on Ezekiel, including a series of popular and controversial lectures by ABELARD, have been lost. Although most of the extant commentaries expand on the allegorical interpretations of Gregory the Great, the Victorines represent the movement within Christian exegesis toward a literal reading. HUGH OF ST. VICTOR explicitly criticized Gregory's failure to address the literal meaning of Ezekiel's visions, and RICHARD OF ST. VICTOR, after paying due respect to Gregory, explicated the visions according to the "plain" sense, describing in detail the animals and chariot of chap. 1 and giving diagrams of Ezekiel's temple. ANDREW OF ST. VICTOR, informed by the work of Jewish scholars, focused on the book's meaning for Ezekiel and his first audience. In his comments on 1:1, for example, he ignored the traditional debate over how Ezekiel could "see" God and read the verse simply as the book's introduction: Ezekiel "saw visions of God"—namely, God's intentions as expressed in the book.

4. Reformation and Enlightenment Interpretation. As typological interpretations declined two strands in the interpretation of Ezekiel predominated: the increasingly important historical study of the text and an almost independent tradition of mystical interpretation. The book was not especially important in the work of the Reformers. In the preface to his translation LUTHER commented briefly on Ezekiel's visions as prophecies of the reign of Christ but referred the reader to the work of NICHOLAS OF LYRA for details. CALVIN began a substantial commentary but died before its completion. In the dialogue with Jerome and Theodoret, Calvin rejected typological interpretations (the notion that the mark on the forehead in Ezek 9:4 is a cross, he considered a "figment") in favor of "the simple and genuine"—that is, historical and moral sense. The 1605 commentary of Prado and Villalpando ("The Champollion of the Temple") was acclaimed for both its philological excellence and its detailed (if anachronistic) illustrations of the temple. In the eighteenth century, analysis of the prophet's poetic style was added to historical concerns. Although written after the supposed golden age of Hebrew poetry, the book's style was praised by both J. G. EICHHORN and R. LOWTH (though J. D. Michaelis considered it inferior). The tradition of mystical speculation on Ezekiel spread to Christian circles during this period, taking such diverse forms as J. REUCHLIN's Christian Kabbalist exposition of the chariot (1517) and W. Blake's engravings of, and reported "conversation" with, the prophet (1790).

5. Nineteenth- and Twentieth-century Interpretations. In the early nineteenth century interpretators focused on refining text-critical and historical analysis of Ezekiel. Although a few eighteenth-century writers had already challenged the book's unity (most notably an anonymous critic who in 1798 claimed Daniel as the author of fourteen chapters of Ezekiel), these challenges had little initial impact (see the responses of E. Rosenmüller [1826] and H. Hävernick [1843]). Only gradually did doubts regarding Ezekiel's unity and authenticity take hold. H. EWALD in 1841 claimed several stages in the book's writing, all at the hand of Ezekiel. F. HITZIG (1847) contributed primarily to the book's TEXTUAL CRITICISM (favoring, as had Ewald, the text of the LXX over the MT) but also pronounced several verses to be glosses. As late as 1880 R. SMEND, while sharing Ewald's view of Ezekiel's essential literary origins, believed the book to have been written as a unit and to be so finely structured that "it must be accepted or rejected as a whole." In 1886 C. CORNILL systematically reconstructed a Hebrew text based largely on the LXX (see SEPTUAGINT), a work that remained the standard for textual criticism of Ezekiel well into the twentieth century. Cornill, while radical in his textual criticism, considered Ezekiel the author (although writing in several stages) of the entire book. The studies of C. KEIL (1868) and especially of A. DAVIDSON (1892) are noteworthy in this period for their attention both to the book's historical background and to the distinctive features of its literary style. In addition to scholarly treatments Ezekiel figured prominently in African American spirituals and preaching, in which the prophet's message of hope to an exiled and dispersed people was reinterpreted in light of the

African American experience (see AFROCENTRIC INTER-PRETATION).

By the turn of the century scholarly doubts regarding the book's unity were giving way to the assumption of disunity. In 1900 R. Kraetzschmar argued on the basis of the book's many repetitions that Ezekiel contained a combination of two parallel recensions of an original text. J. Herrmann (1908, 1924) claimed to find strata of both early and late work by Ezekiel plus material added by a redactor. Only in 1924, however, did the full impact of REDACTION CRITICISM hit Ezekiel studies with the publication of G. HÖLSCHER's argument that fewer than 144 of the book's 1,273 verses contained the actual words of the impassioned prophet. The rest was the work of a plodding and prosaic fifth-century redactor. Ezekiel had long been criticized by such scholars as H. GESENIUS, W. DE WETTE, and F. Hitzig for his "narrow" and "shallow" legalism and was considered a precursor of the "decline" toward rabbinic Judaism. Rather than decrying Ezekiel as "legalistic," Hölscher declared Ezekiel's legal material and most of the book's other prose material inauthentic. He could thus extol Ezekiel the free-spirited poet while condemning the author of the bulk of the book as "the stiff, priestly writer and pathfinder of a legalistic and ritualistic Judaism." Hölscher's radical conclusions gave new impetus to redaction criticism of the book, and for the next twenty years research focused on the "problem of Ezekiel"—namely, questions regarding the date, unity, and place of the book's composition. Numerous studies traced Ezekiel's (the prophet's and the book's) migrations through various countries and over several centuries. In *Pseudo-Ezekiel* (1930) C. C. TORREY claimed the book to be a pseudepigraph (see PSEUDEPIGRAPHA) from Jerusalem of the second or third century that originally purported to have been written under Manasseh but was subsequently rewritten in Judah with a Babylonian setting. V. Herntrich (1932) posited that Ezekiel wrote chaps. 1–24 in Jerusalem (and therefore had the knowledge of events in the city these chapters imply), but that a later exilic editor had added a Babylonian framework to the original prophecies. A. BERTHOLET (1936) and W. A. Irwin (1943) each argued that Ezekiel had begun his career in Jerusalem but finished it in Babylonia, after which his collected prophecies had been further edited. In addition Irwin isolated a small core (parts of 251 verses) as containing Ezekiel's original prophecies, brief poetic utterances that had been interpreted and misinterpreted over several centuries of redaction.

In the early 1950s both C. Howie (1950) and G. FOHRER (1952) rejected attempts to reconstruct a date, place, and author other than those claimed within the book itself. Fohrer argued primarily on the basis of rhythmic analysis that Ezekiel wrote and edited most of the book. H. ROWLEY, in an excellent review of the state of the discipline (1953), also concluded with a relatively traditional assessment of the text. Nonetheless, in the same year Irwin claimed widespread agreement that the book is a composite construction and that Ezekiel delivered some or all of his oracles in Jerusalem. W. EICHRODT's 1965 commentary illustrates the difficulties of finding a middle way between naive acceptance and radical reconstruction of the text. Purporting to trust what the book says about itself, Eichrodt envisioned Ezekiel as a writing prophet who did much "collecting" and arranging of his own writings. Eichrodt then isolated a series of authentic oracles saved and added, not by the prophet, but by his disciples, and finally posited a redactor who also contributed "extensive additions."

The work of W. ZIMMERLI moves toward reconciliation of redaction criticism with the compelling sense of the book's unity that had prevailed into the twentieth century. His massive commentary (1969) provides a definitive critical apparatus and a form-critical analysis (see FORM CRITICISM) and puts forth a new theory on the redaction history of the book, arguing that an original "core" of prophetic material underwent a process of *Nachinterpretation,* ongoing commentary within an Ezekielien school, each generation of which reread both the core and the earlier interpretations in light of its own situation. Zimmerli thus claimed that even the secondary and tertiary additions and revisions, which he saw throughout, "point back" to the prophet.

While Zimmerli's work represents a significant moderation of the redaction-critical extremes of the first half of the century, the commentary of M. Greenberg (1983, 1997) marks a decisive break with redaction criticism of Ezekiel. Rejecting attempts to judge an ancient text according to modern notions of unity and consistency, he proposes a "holistic" method for reading the book, combining the tools of textual criticism, historical reconstruction, observations of ancient and medieval commentators, and close LITERARY analysis with the goal of explicating the inner logic and implications of the text on its own terms. Without denying the presence of glosses and later editorial work, his commentary reopens the synchronic study of Ezekiel in its full complexity, and along with a widespread interest in "final form" modes of criticism in the final decades of the twentieth century, has produced a profusion of studies that focus on the book's unity and explore its literary technique. E. Davis's 1989 monograph, *Swallowing the Scroll,* explores the possibility that Ezekiel was the first writing prophet, claiming that many of the book's idiosyncrasies are consistent with the prophet's effort to forge a new literary idiom. Such commentators as R. Hals (1988) and D. Block (1997) as well as scholars undertaking more specialized research assume the book's substantial unity and the probability that much of the material and its compilation derive from a historical Ezekiel. FEMINIST critics have published widely on the previously unexplored dynamics and implications of the sexual violence depicted in chaps. 16 and 23 (see K. Darr [1992] and J. Galambush [1992]). D. Halperin's *Seeking Ezekiel* (1993) attempts a PSYCHOANALYTIC INTERPRETATION of the historical Ezekiel based on the bizarre persona depicted in the text. After several decades of intensive work isolating, dating, and analyzing the book's various layers, scholars have returned to the earlier consensus regarding Ezekiel's essential unity and set about to explicate its distinctive literary features.

Bibliography: M. Aberbach, "Ezekiel in the Aggadah," *EncJud* 6 (1971) 1095. D. I. Abrabanel, *Peruš ʿal neviʾîm ʾaharonim* (1957). L. C. Allen, *Ezekiel 20–48* (WBC 29, 1990); *Ezekiel 1–19* (WBC 28, 1994). Andrew of St. Victor, *Expositionem in Ezechielem* (CCCM 53E, ed. M. A. Signor, 1991). P. Auvray, "Ezéchiel," *DBSup* 8 (1972) 759-91. A. Bertholet and K. Galling, *Hesekiel* (HAT, 1936). D. I. Block, *The Book of Ezekiel: Chapters 1–24* (NICOT, 1997). E. Broome, "Ezekiel's Abnormal Personality," *JBL* 65 (1946) 277-92. J. Calvin, *Commentaries on the First Twenty Chapters of Ezekiel* (1565; see the ET of T. Meyers [1848] for a review of literature [2:403-7] and of then current research [1:v-xxxii]). J. G. Carpzov, *Introductio ad libros canonicos bibliorum Veteris Testamenti omnes* (1721) 3:225-27. G. A. Cooke, *A Critical and Exegetical Commentary on the Book of Ezekiel* (ICC, 1936). C. H. Cornill, *Das Buch des Propheten Ezechiel* (1886). J. Daniélou, *Études d'exégèse judéo-chrétienne* (1966). J. Darling, *Cyclopaedia Bibliographica* 2 (1859) 670-82. K. P. Darr, "Ezekiel," *Women's Bible Commentary* (ed. C. A. Newsom and S. H. Ringe, 1992) 183-90. E. Dassmann, "Hesekiel," *RAC* 14 (1988) 1132-191. A. B. Davidson, *The Book of the Prophet Ezekiel* (CBSC, 1892). E. F. Davis, *Swallowing the Scroll: Textuality and the Dynamics of Discourse in Ezekiel's Prophecy* (JSOTSup 78, 1989). W. Eichrodt, *Der Prophet Hesekiel* (ATD 22, 2 vols., 1959–66; ET, OTL [1970]). Eliezer of Beaugency, *Kommentar zu Ezechiel und den XII Kleinen Propheten* (ed. S. Poznanski, 1909). H. Ewald, *Die Propheten des Alten Bundes erklärt* (1841). G. Fohrer, *Die Hauptprobleme des Buches Ezechiel* (BZAW 72, 1952). K. S. Freedy and D. B. Redford, "The Dates in Ezekiel in Relation to Biblical, Babylonian, and Egyptian Sources," *JAOS* 90 (1970) 462-85. J. Galambush, *Jerusalem in the Book of Ezekiel: The City as Yahweh's Wife* (SBLDS 130, 1992). H. Gese, *Der Verfassungsentwurf des Ezechiel (Kap. 40–48) traditionsgeschichtlich untersucht* (BHT 25, 1957). M. Greenburg, *EncJud* 6 (1971) 1078-95; *Ezekiel, 1–20* (AB 22, 1983); *Ezekiel 21–37* (AB 22A, 1997). Gregory I, Pope, *Sancti Gregorii Magni Homiliae in Hiezechihelem Prophetam* (CCSL 142, ed. M. Adriaen, 1971). D. J. Halperin, *The Faces of the Chariot* (1988); "Origen, Ezekiel's Merkabah, and the Ascension of Moses," *CH* 50 (1981) 261-75. R. Hals, *Ezekiel* (FOTL, 1988); *Seeking Ezekiel: Text and Psychology* (1993). J. B. Harford, *Studies in the Book of Ezekiel* (1935). V. Herntrich, *Ezechielprobleme* (BZAW 61, 1932). J. Herrmann, *Ezechiel* (KAT 11, 1908, 1924²). F. Hitzig, *Der Prophet Ezechiel* (1847). G. Hölscher, *Hesekiel: Der Dichter und das Buch* (BZAW 39, 1924). C. G. Howie, *The Date and Composition of Ezekiel* (JBLMS 4, 1950). A. Hurvitz, *A Linguistic Study of the Relationship Between the Priestly Source and the Book of Ezekiel: A New Approach to an Old Problem* (CRB 20, 1982). W. A. Irwin, *The Problem of Ezekiel: An Inductive Study* (1943); "Ezekiel Research Since 1943," *VT* 3 (1953) 54-66. Jerome, *Commentarii in Ezechielem* (CCSL 75, ed. M. Adriaen and F. Glorie, 1964). K. F. Keil, *Biblischer Commentar über den Propheten Ezechiel* (1868; ET 1896); *Introduction* (1882) 1:353-63 (review of literature). D. Kimhi, commentary in *Mikra'ot Gedolot*. C. Kuhl, "Zur Geschichte der Hesekiel-Forschung," *TRu* NF 5 (1933) 92-118; "Neuere Hesekiel-literatur," *TRu* NF 20 (1952) 1-26; "Zum Stand der Hesekiel-Forschung," *TRu* NF 24 (1956–57) 1-53. E. Kutsch, *Die chronologischen Daten des Ezechielbuches* (OBO 62, 1985). B. Lang, *Ezekiel, Der Prophet und das Buch* (Enträge der Forschung 153, 1981), esp. his review of recent research, 1-18. J. D. Levenson, *Theology of the Program of Restoration of Ezekiel 40–48* (HSM 10, 1976). J. Lust (ed.), *Ezekiel and His Book: Textual and Literary Criticism and Their Interrelation* (BETL 74, 1986). C. MacKay, "Ezekiel in the NT," *CQR* 162 (1961) 4-16. W. Neuss, *Der Entwicklung der theologischen Auffassung des Buches Ezechiel zur Zeit der Frühscholastik* (1911); *Das Buch Ezechiel in Theologie und Kunst bis zum Ende des 12. Jahrhunderts* (1912). Origen, *Homiliae in Ezechielem* (GCS 33, ed. W. A. Baehrens, 1925); *In Ezechielem Homiliae* (SC 352, ed. M. Borret, 1989). E. Philippe, "Ezéchiel," *DB* 2 (1926) 2149-62. H. Prado and J. B. Villalpando, *In Ezechielem* (3 vols., 1596). Rashi, commentary in *Mikra'ot Gedolot*. C. C. Rowland, "The Influence of the First Chapter of Ezekiel on Jewish and Early Christian Literature" (diss., Cambridge University, 1974). H. H. Rowley, "The Book of Ezekiel in Modern Study," *BJRL* 36 (1953–54) 146-90 = his *Men of God* (1963) 169-210. J.-P. Ruiz, *Ezekiel in the Apocalypse: The Transformation of Prophetic Language in Revelation 16, 17–19, 10* (1989). G. Scholem, *Jewish Gnosticism, Mysticisim, and Talmudic Tradition* (1965). S. Spiegel, "Ezekiel or Pseudo-Ezekiel?" *HTR* 24 (1931) 245-321; "Toward Certainty in Ezekiel," *JBL* 44 (1935) 145-71. S. Talmon and M. Fishbane, "The Structuring of Biblical Books: Studies in the Book of Ezekiel," *ASTI* 10 (1976) 129-53. F. Van Dijk-Hemmes, "The Metaphorization of Woman in Prophetic Speech: An Analysis of Ezekiel 23," *VT* 43 (1993) 162-70. W. A. Van Gemeren, "The Exegesis of Ezekiel's 'Chariot' Chapters in Twelfth-century Hebrew Commentaries" (diss., University of Wisconsin, 1974). A. Vanhoye, "L'utilisation du livre d'Ézéchiel dans l'Apocalypse," *Bib* 43 (1962) 436-76. R. Wischnitzer-Bernstein, "The Conception of the Resurrection in the Ezekiel Panel of the Dura Synagogue," *JBL* 60 (1941) 43-55. W. Zimmerli, *Ezekiel 1, 2* (BKAT 13, 1969; ET, Hermeneia [2 vols., 1979–83]), with review of literature in 1:3-8; and update, 2:xi-xviii.

J. G. GALAMBUSH

EZRA AND NEHEMIAH, BOOKS OF

1. Relationship to Other Texts. There is considerable controversy concerning the distinction between composition and interpretation with regard to the books of Ezra and Nehemiah because of the apocryphal work known as 1 ESDRAS (Ger., 3 Esra). First Esdras includes a Greek translation of 2 Chronicles 35–36; Esdra; and Neh 8:1-12. Included in Esdras, however, is an account not found in the canonical books (see CANON OF THE BIBLE) of a contest of wisdom between three guardsmen at the court of Darius that resulted in Zerubbabel's mission to Jerusalem. Other minor additions and differences in order and CHRONOLOGY exist in 1 Esdras.

On the one hand, some scholars have argued that this work represents a translation of the original ending of the chronicler's history and that the present books developed only subsequently (opinions about this process differ; see, e.g., C. C. Torrey [1910]; S. Mowinckel [1964–65] 1-28; K. Pohlmann [1970]; F. M. Cross [1975]). If this were the case, of course, 1 Esdras could tell us nothing about the early interpretation of Ezra and Nehemiah. Many scholars, however, reject this view and regard 1 ESDRAS as possibly a fragment of a work compiled from various sources for purposes of its own (R. Hanhart [1973]; W. In der Smitten [1973]; H. Williamson [1977], 12-36, and [1983]; A. van der Kooij [1991]). The centrality of the Temple and its restoration in 1 Esdras have long been noted, and A. Gardner (1986) has linked this theme with the purpose of giving comfort and succor to the faithful during the Maccabean crisis. If this is true, it indicates that from an early date a major theme in Ezra and Nehemiah was interpreted paradigmatically—if not indeed typologically—in terms of the restoration of the people of God and their sanctuary in times of trouble.

It is worth noting that in later centuries 1 Esdras was frequently preferred as a source for the restoration period to the SEPTUAGINT version of the canonical books of Ezra and Nehemiah. It was used by JOSEPHUS as the basis for his account (*Ant. Jud.* 11.1-158), perhaps because of its superior Greek style, while in the early centuries of the Christian church there are undoubtedly more surviving references to it than to Ezra and Nehemiah (see J. Myers [1974] 17-18; M. Goodman in G. Vermes et al. [1987] 714).

Apart from the disputed evidence of 1 Esdras, early Jewish interpretation of Ezra and Nehemiah focused largely on the use of their central characters in subsequent apocryphal tradition. The use of Ezra's name in the pseudonymous *Apocalypse of Ezra* (2 ESDRAS 3–14 = 4 Ezra) shows a comparable development to that noted in connection with 1 Esdras. The work represents an attempt to come to terms with the fall of Jerusalem and the destruction of the Temple in 70 CE. Although a number of visions provide assurance that Israel's distress will soon be brought to an end, the climax appears with the miraculous restoration of the Scriptures to Ezra. This illustrates that Ezra's outstanding qualities as a scribe (as recorded, e.g., in Ezra 7:10) had already made a deep impression and had become a source for fruitful reflection; hopes for a restoration of the Temple could take second place to the study of Scripture as a focus for Jewish life (for this and other later, mainly Christian, pseudepigraphical literature related to Ezra, see J. Charlesworth, 516-604).

Not surprisingly, in the case of Nehemiah it was his restoration of the walls of Jerusalem that made the greatest impression, initially as part of the restoration started by Zerubbabel and Jeshua (Sir 49:11-13). The lack of chronological distinction in this passage is not new with Ben Sira, however (U. Kellermann [1967] 114) but continues a line of historical interpretation whose origins are to be found already in the biblical text (Williamson [1985] xlviii-xlix). There is thus no good reason to suppose that Ben Sira knew the Nehemiah source in isolation or that his surprising omission of a reference to Ezra is due to anything other than reasons of selection in view of his overall purpose. It is of further interest to note that in a letter cited in 2 Macc 1:10–2:18, which doubtless rests on earlier material, Nehemiah is credited with both the restoration of the Temple and the collection of books "about the kings and prophets, and the writings of David, and the letters of kings about votive offerings" (2 Macc 2:13). However, this apparent "takeover" by Nehemiah of other major elements in the restoration, attributed in the biblical text to Zerubbabel and Jeshua (Temple restoration) and to Ezra (scribal activity), is due more to claims for legitimacy among the rival priestly groupings under the Hasmoneans than to biblical interpretation proper.

2. Early Jewish and Christian Interpretation. In Jewish writings of the subsequent centuries, any appreciation based on an approach to these books as a whole, such as we have noticed above to a limited extent, becomes lost from sight among occasional references to the exploits of the various leading characters. It is true that in the TALMUD a number of legal rulings are said to derive from the time of the return from Babylon, as are the founding of the Great Assembly and the age of the Soferim, and that this attests an appreciation of the age of Ezra and Nehemiah as one of major restoration; but there is little in this that can be explicitly associated with the literature. Similarly, the several references to Ezra's restoring the forgotten law (*b. Suk.* 20*a*) or to his changing the style of writing (*b. Sanh.* 21-22) may owe as much to later tradition as to biblical interpretation. More noteworthy are discussions over chronology (e.g., of Neh 1:1 and 2:1 and the identification of the Persian kings in *b. Roš Haš.* 3-4), the identification of Nehemiah with Shealtiel, which shows continuing flexibility in the role and date of Nehemiah (*b. Sanh.* 38*a*), the identification of Ezra with Malachi based on comparable conditions prevailing in their days (*b. Meg.* 15*a*), and especially discussions of authorship. In the well-known passage *b. B. Bat.* 15*a* we are told, "Ezra wrote the book that bears his name and the genealogies of the Book of Chronicles up to his own time"; this was believed to include Nehemiah and is supported by the opinion expressed by R. Jeremiah b. Abba in *b. Sanh.* 93*b* that although the book of Nehemiah was narrated by Nehemiah it was called by Ezra's name because of the way in which Nehemiah claimed credit for himself. Not until the medieval period do we find a return to more extended consideration of Ezra and Nehemiah with the commentaries of RASHI and A. IBN EZRA, followed by those mentioned in G. Bartolocci's *Bibliotheca Magna Rabbinica* 4—by R. Simeon ben Joiakim, by Joseph ben David Ibn Yahya (1538), and by Isaac ben Solomon Jabez (end of 16th cent.).

Apart from a few occasional references there is little evidence regarding the interpretation of Ezra and Nehemiah in the Christian tradition of the earliest centuries. Working on the basis of 1 Esdras, Pseudo-Cyril of Alexandria (5th cent.) spoke of the "new Zerubbabel, who is JESUS Christ," and from the few lines of ISIDORE OF SEVILLE (7th cent.) that survive it seems likely that he pursued a similar approach. Unless this silence is severely misleading, the work of the Venerable BEDE (8th cent.) stands out as a remarkable and unique achievement for its time, for his commentary on these books stretches to some 150 printed pages and is generally described as an *Expositio Allegorica*. In his preface Bede referred to JEROME's opinion that the deeds of Ezra and Nehemiah prefigured those of Christ and foreshadowed things that should be done to the church. It is not uncommon to find such characterizations of the work as that of M. Laistner: "The work is figurative in the spiritual mode, that is, it sees in the restoration of Jerusalem a figure of the return to grace of the repentant sinner" (1957, 120). It should be emphasized, however, that this is true only of Bede's HERMENEUTIC. The commentary itself gives full (if inevitably sometimes misguided) attention to the tasks of biblical scholarship. Josephus, for instance, is cited not only for extra-biblical background material but also in an attempt to solve the problems of Ezra 4. The chronological difficulties at Ezra 6:14 are appreciated, the identification of the months at Neh 1:1 and 2:1 are discussed (though without finding the problems that have troubled more recent commentators), the topography of Jerusalem is given due attention at Nehemiah 3, and so on. It would thus be a distortion to imply that Bede was concerned only with allegorical interpretation.

3. From the Sixteenth Century to the Modern Era. After Bede we have no information until the sixteenth century. No exposition of these works from the leaders of the Reformation is known, but it seems probable from occasional references in other works that they would have regarded the accounts primarily as examples for Christian living. Of their place in the history of salvation, however, CALVIN was evidently not particularly impressed: "Then Ezra and Nehemiah fol-lowed them, the authority of whom was great among the people; but we do not read that they were endued with the Prophetic gift" (Preface to Haggai; see PROPHECY AND PROPHETS, HB).

Despite this, the sixteenth and seventeenth centuries saw the publication of many commentaries, both Roman Catholic and Protestant, and among them for the first time some explicitly intended for a lay readership. For instance, J. Pilkington left a "Godlie Exposition" on the first five chapters of Nehemiah at his death in 1575 (his commentary on Ezra, to which he referred at Neh 2:20, was lost). He regarded the two books as separate compositions by the authors whose names they bear (an opinion that has only recently been revived independently by J. VanderKam [1992] and D. Kraemer [1993]). His exposition is highly discursive and generally edifying in nature, Nehemiah being "a worthie paterne for all courtiers to follow" (6). Since he claimed to write especially for "the unlearned" (12), we learn little about his attitude to more erudite matters, although a clue is furnished in his introduction to Nehemiah 3. After explaining that it would not be profitable for his readers were he to go through all the names mentioned, he added in parentheses, "though the learned may with pleasure picke out good lessons of them by Allegorical interpretation of the places, etc." (45).

Quite different in tone is the learned commentary of C. LAPIDE (= van den Steen [1645]), in which for the first time a thorough knowledge of classical sources with their many references to the wider history of the Persian Empire and its kings is brought to bear on the interpretation of these books. Lapide was also well read in earlier Christian interpreters and was confident enough to take issue with them when he saw fit; e.g., he disagreed with Bede over the identification of "the Province" at Ezra 2:1, arguing that it refers to Babylon (just as "the city" could refer to Rome in his own day) and not to Judah, as the allegorical method had led Bede to suppose. Furthermore, Lapide was not afraid to compare the ancient versions with the MT in an elementary form of TEXTUAL CRITICISM. It is not surprising, therefore, to find that Lapide's commentary is largely a scholarly attempt to do justice to the plain meaning of a historical text, dealing at some length, for instance, with the questions of the identity of the various Persian kings. Only occasionally does his hermeneutic come through. In contrast with Calvin, he insisted that Ezra was a prophet (because he wrote Scripture), and elsewhere he referred to both Ezra and Nehemiah as types of Christ. On the few occasions where he adopted this approach in the text, he used the formula *allegorice* (allegorically) and *tropologice* (metaphorically) to apply the passage to Christ and the behavior of Christian believers respectively. Only at Neh 8:11 ("the joy of the LORD is your strength"), however, do his remarks become properly homiletical.

It is often suggested that the modern era of critical biblical scholarship is best represented first by J. G. EICHHORN's introduction (1803³). With regard to Ezra and Nehemiah, however, there is no fundamental advance here over the much earlier introduction of J. CARPZOV (1741³), both writers being concerned largely with such basic issues as authorship (about which they add little to the discussions already noted except for a somewhat fuller use of internal evidence) and authenticity. And when a significant step forward was achieved a few decades later, it had the ironic effect of diverting attention away from Ezra and Nehemiah and onto the books of Chronicles, books that from the time of W. DE WETTE, at the start of the nineteenth century, to J. WELLHAUSEN, near its close, were the real focus of attention in the great debates about the composition of the Pentateuch (see PENTATEUCHAL CRITICISM) as representing postexilic historical writing.

L. Zunz (1832) for the first time set out a full case for the common authorship of Chronicles, Ezra, and Nehemiah based on four principal arguments—namely, the overlap between the end of 2 Chronicles and the beginning of Ezra, the testimony of 1 Esdras, the similarity of Hebrew style, and the common religious outlook of the books in question. Although this argument was not accepted by everyone (see, e.g., the introduction to C. KEIL's commentary on Chronicles [1870]); nevertheless, at the end of the century C. C. TORREY could reasonably begin his important monograph of 1896 with the words, "It is at present generally agreed that Chronicles–Ezra–Nehemiah originally formed one book, which was put in its final form by the author of the book of Chronicles, commonly called 'the Chronicler.' " Indeed, this assumption remained virtually unchallenged until the late twentieth century. It is thus not surprising that throughout most of the nineteenth century, and with the partial exception of commentaries like those of E. BERTHEAU (1862) and Keil (1870), interest in Ezra and Nehemiah focused on their historical testimony regarding the restoration rather than on more specifically literary or theological concerns; for an outstanding example, see E. MEYER (1896), whereas by contrast K. GRAF (1866), writing explicitly on the historical books of the HB, gave no sustained attention to Ezra and Nehemiah. It should be noted that in 1890 A. Van HOONACKER first advanced the theory that he continued to elaborate during the next thirty years and that is still a major unresolved issue in the history of the period: that Ezra's mission should be dated to the reign of Artaxerxes II, later, therefore, than the mission of Nehemiah. For summaries that reach opposite conclusions, see H. ROWLEY (1965²) and Williamson (1987, 55-69).

4. Modern Research. The next major turning point in the interpretation of these books came with Torrey's monograph of 1896, which he followed with a series of essays collected in 1910. Since this marks the start of the modern period of research, the discussion will be clearer if a purely chronological survey is abandoned in order to treat the major sections of the books: Ezra 1–6, the Ezra memoir, and the Nehemiah memoir.

a. Ezra 1–6. Since the overwhelming majority of scholars since Zunz have accepted the argument that the editor of Ezra 1–6 was the chronicler, attention has been focused mainly on the question of the authenticity of the documents incorporated into this narrative. In the same year that Torrey expressed considerable skepticism in this regard, Meyer set out a more conservative line of approach, at least with regard to the Aramaic documents in chaps. 4–6, that has been further refined in the intervening decades and now commands a considerable degree of consensus (cf. L. Grabbe [1991] and [1992] 32-36). This is to compare the texts with indubitably authentic documents of the Achaemenid period with regard to their language, their political and historical verisimilitude, and their LITERARY shape or genre. The latter half of the twentieth century has seen not only the publication of still additional texts but also a considerable advance in the form-critical analysis (see FORM CRITICISM) of the whole corpus of letters written in Imperial Aramaic (see P. Alexander [1978]; P. Dion [1979]; J. Fitzmyer [1979]; and J. White [1982]). Similarly, the authenticity of the inventory of Temple vessels in 1:9-11 is generally accepted. Much greater doubt remains, however, over the Hebrew version of Cyrus's edict in 1:2-4 (though see E. Bickerman [1946]), while no agreement has been reached concerning the precise historical setting of the long list in Ezra 2 of those who returned from Babylon. An attractive theory that has gained a good deal of support is that of K. GALLING (1951), who suggested that it was drawn up as part of the Jewish response to Tattenai's inquiry (5:3-4, 10) about who was engaged in the rebuilding of the Temple.

The chronicler, then, is believed to have drawn on an Aramaic source (4:6–6:12) and some other material to construct his account of the early return and restoration. Doubts persist over whether chap. 3 is a parallel account to that in chaps. 5–6 or whether the two passages should be taken sequentially. The author's purpose is to be seen as part of a larger concern to present the postexilic Jewish theocracy as the legitimate heir of the preexilic monarchy (e.g., W. Rudolph [1949]; O. Plöger [1959]).

The last half of the twentieth century, however, has seen a strong challenge to the view that Ezra and Nehemiah are to be regarded as part of the chronicler's work (see S. Japhet [1968]; Williamson [1977] 5-70; for a more nuanced position, Cross [1975]), and many of those currently writing in this field have embraced this new (rather, revitalized older) approach. Not many have yet worked through its implications for Ezra 1–6 (though see R. Braun [1979]; B. Halpern [1990]), but Williamson (1983) has proposed that these chapters were written after the combining of the accounts concerning Ezra and Nehemiah as the last major stage in the composition of the books as a whole. Taking a high view of the authenticity of all the alleged documents in Ezra 1–6, he argues that a much later editor worked directly from the firsthand sources, which were preserved in the Temple archives. The only information he had at his disposal was in these sources, together with what he could glean from such other biblical books as Haggai and Zechariah. This accounts for the large gaps in his information (e.g., regarding the return journey) as well as for some of the apparent historical confusion. Writing in the early Hellenistic period, his purpose would have been to defend the legitimacy of the Jerusalem Temple against its newly established Samaritan rival on Mt. Gerizim.

b. The Ezra memoir. With regard to the material about Ezra, attention has chiefly been focused on the relationship between the literature and the historical Ezra. Four main views may be distinguished, with the first and most radical that of Torrey. Until the end of the nineteenth century, the Ezra material was generally taken at face value; but in his monograph and subsequent publications Torrey subjected it to the most searching criticism. Because of its Hebrew style he concluded that it could not be distinguished from the editorial hand of the remainder of Chronicles, Ezra, and Nehemiah. He concluded, therefore, that there was no Ezra source; Ezra was no more than a figure of the chronicler's imagination. In the modern period, Grabbe (1994), in particular, remains skeptical about the history of Ezra.

Although much discussed, Torrey's views were not followed by many scholars in their entirety (but see G. Hölscher, *HSAT(K)*). However, one aspect of his analysis has continued to attract widespread support. He argued that the Ezra material was originally written in the order Ezra 7–8; Nehemiah 8; Ezra 9–10; Nehemiah 9–10, and that its present order was the result of mistakes by later copyists. (This view, of course, is unacceptable to those who hold that 1 Esdras, which places Nehemiah 8 after Ezra 10, represents the original ending of the chronicler's work.) Torrey was obliged to speak of later copyists' errors because in his opinion the chapters had been written from scratch by the editor of the books as a whole. Those who, by contrast, accept that the editor was here reworking an independent source have been able to transfer Torrey's reconstruction to that source and to investigate the potentially more fruitful suggestion that the editor rearranged them into their present order for purposes of his own.

A second approach was developed independently by M. NOTH (1943) and A. Kapelrud (1944). Literary and historical considerations led Noth to believe that the edict of Artaxerxes in Ezra 7:12-26 and the list in 8:1-14 of those who accompanied Ezra on his journey to Jerusalem were both sources that were available to the chronicler, as, of course, was the Nehemiah memoir. On the basis of this material the chronicler himself wrote the whole of the Ezra account. This suggestion explained why the style so closely resembles the chronicler's, why Nehemiah 8 appears where it does (the chronicler wrote it for that setting for theological reasons), and why part of the account is in the first person (inconsistent imitation of Nehemiah).

Kapelrud, meanwhile, undertook a study of the Hebrew style of the Ezra narrative. Like Torrey he concluded that it must be attributed to the hand of the chronicler, but at the same time he allowed the probability that some earlier tradition underlay the account. Kapelrud was not as specific as Noth about this, however, and his stylistic analysis is also open to criticisms of method. It is not surprising, therefore, that Noth's form of this theory has had the most influence, especially on the more recent major studies of Kellermann (1967) and W. In der Smitten (1973). The attraction of this approach is that it enables scholars to discount the possibility of an Ezra source while nevertheless holding on to the historicity of Ezra himself.

The third approach to the Ezra material is that of S. MOWINCKEL. As with the Nehemiah memoir, Mowinckel had published a monograph on Ezra as early as 1916, but since it was in Norwegian it was inaccessible to most scholars (though see F. Ahlemann [1942–43]). He returned to these books at the end of his life, however, publishing three monographs in German (1964–65) that are of great importance for all aspects of the interpretation of Ezra and Nehemiah. Regarding Ezra, his opinion was more conservative than that of Noth; but paradoxically it was far from traditional. Finding some editorial comments in the Ezra material, Mowinckel argued that this editor is the chronicler; therefore, he must have been working on an already existing text—an Ezra source. Mowinckel could find no reason, however, to attribute this to Ezra. It was, he thought, the work of an admirer who had been a young man during Ezra's activity and who years later wrote an idealized version of the events for purposes of edification. Since history was not its main aim, allowances should be made for all manner of legendary embellishment. Needless to say, Mowinckel had no difficulty in citing other examples of narratives that use the first-person singular but that are not autobiographical.

Fourth, there have always been scholars who have held to a more traditional approach (e.g., H. Schaeder [1930]; Rudolph [1949]; K. Koch [1974]; Williamson [1985]; J. Blenkinsopp [1988]; K. Hoglund [1992]). That is to say, they accept that the material about Ezra was originally written by Ezra in the first person throughout in order to give an account of his work to the Persian king. It was later reworked by an editor (whether the chronicler or another), who among other things cast some of it in the third person. However, since Torrey's time all but the most conservative (e.g., F. Kidner [1979]; F. Fensham [1982]) have agreed that Nehemiah 8 (and perhaps 9–10) was once an integral part of the Ezra material in Ezra 7–10. Furthermore, if the view that Ezra and Nehemiah were not part of the chronicler's work is correct, then a major plank in the arguments of those who deny the existence of an Ezra source is removed.

Alongside these literary concerns, historical and theological disagreements have continued with regard to Ezra's mission. Some scholars held that Ezra's mission should be dated to the seventh year of Artaxerxes I or II while others argued that he came in either the twenty-seventh or the thirty-seventh year of Artaxerxes I, thus viewing his reforms as building more closely on the work of Nehemiah (see Rudolph [1949]; V. Pavlovsky [1957]; J. Bright [1959] 375-86; for a searching criticism of this view, see J. Emerton [1966]). Also noteworthy is the suggestion of Schaeder (1930) that Ezra was the "secretary of state for Jewish affairs" at the Achaemenid court prior to his mission and Koch's more speculative view (1974) that he came with high hopes of reestablishing the community of the full twelve tribes of Israel around the holy center of the Jerusalem Temple— a view that implies that he failed in his mission rather more disastrously than later interpretation might have led us to expect. (For a fuller exposition and discussion of these views, see Williamson [1987] 69-76.) Finally, one should not overlook the continuing discussions of the identity of the book of the law that Ezra brought with him, whether it was the Pentateuch in its finished form or one of its major constitutive sources, such as P or D, or some other quite separate document since lost to us. (For full surveys of research, see Kellermann [1968] and C. Houtman [1981].) Alongside this, attention has turned to a consideration of the interpretation of the law evident in this material and its formative influence in the development of later Jewish hermeneutics (D. Clines [1981]; M. Fishbane [1985]; Williamson [1988] 25-38).

c. The Nehemiah memoir. In contrast to the Ezra material, the authenticity of the Nehemiah memoir has been widely accepted. Discussion has centered, rather, on the question of its genre and purpose. It was Mowinckel (1916, Norwegian; GT 1923), who first pointed out that the term "Nehemiah memoir" is inappropriate as a technical literary classification; he suggested instead that the work might be more appropriately compared with a number of ancient Near Eastern royal inscriptions in which various kings commemorate their achievements. G. von RAD (1964) later endeavored to refine this thesis by comparing the memoir instead to various tomb and temple inscriptions from Egypt that date from roughly the same period as Nehemiah and that recall in first-person narrative the duties of senior officials faithfully performed, often in spheres of public life closely resembling those of Nehemiah (see Blenkinsopp [1987]).

An alternative approach takes the distinctive "remember" formula as its starting point and finds the closest parallels to the Nehemiah memoir in the common votive or dedicatory inscriptions known in several Aramaic dialects from later times. Problems for this view that have never been faced, however, are the disparity in length between these brief inscriptions and the Nehemiah memoir and the fact that Nehemiah never asked God to remember his greatest achievement, the building of the wall.

Another suggestion is that Nehemiah needed to write in order to justify himself to the Persian king. Based more on the contents of the text than on formal analogies with other sources, this view suggests that accusations had been leveled against Nehemiah by some of his opponents. The main problem here, however, is that the document appears to be addressed directly to God rather than to the king. In a major study of the whole topic, Kellermann (1967) has sought to avoid this objection by comparing the Nehemiah memoir with the type of psalm known as "the prayer of the accused." The differences between the two bodies of material he explains on the basis of the particular circumstances in which Nehemiah was placed.

As an alternative to this whole approach, Williamson (1985, xxiv-xxviii) has suggested that the Nehemiah memoir developed in two distinct stages, the first a report to the king on Nehemiah's first year in office and the second a later reworking of this report in votive style in order to claim credit for his achievements as a whole. (It is observed that most of the accounts of Nehemiah's accomplishments are paralleled by third-person narratives elsewhere in the book that ascribe the same reforms to the community at large under priestly leadership.) On this view it will not be surprising that attempts to compare the Nehemiah memoir as a whole with other unified texts have never proved fully convincing.

5. New Approaches. It will be apparent from this survey of work on Ezra and Nehemiah during the twentieth century that most attention was directed to specific literary and historical issues rather than to the interpretation of the books as a whole and that such consideration as there has been of this latter topic has been subsumed under the umbrella of the books of Chronicles. There are several indications, however, that this is likely to change (see the useful survey of T. Eskenazi [1993]): first, the challenge already mentioned to the common authorship of Chronicles, Ezra, and Nehemiah; second, the rise of the CANONICAL approach (B. Childs [1979]; J. Shaver [1992]), which believes that interpretation should start from the study of the books as we now have them and the mutual influence of the text and the believing community on their formation and understanding; third, more sophisticated application of insights from the social services as well as ARCHAEOLOGY (see, e.g., Tolletson and Williamson [1992]; J. Weinberg [1992]; Hoglund [1992]; and the many essays in P. Davies [1991] and T. Eskenazi and K. Richards [1994]); and finally, the general rise in HB scholarship of a more genuinely literary approach that seeks to understand the books in their present shape regardless of the processes that led to their formation (A. Gunneweg [1981]; see also his important commentary [1985]; Eskenazi). Work in all these fields as it affects Ezra and Nehemiah is only beginning, but there is every prospect that the coming years will see in consequence a genuine advance in the literary and theological interpretations of these books.

Bibliography: **P. R. Ackroyd,** *I and II Chronicles, Ezra, Nehemiah* (TBC, 1973); *The Chronicler in His Age* (1991). **F. Ahlemann,** "Zur Esra-Quelle," *ZAW* 59 (1942–43) 77-98. **P. S. Alexander,** "Remarks on Aramaic Epistolography in the Persian Period," *JSS* 23 (1978) 155-70. **L. W. Batten,** *A Critical and Exegetical Commentary on the Books of Ezra and Nehemiah* (ICC, 1913). **Bede,** *Bedae Venerabilis Opera, Pars II/2A* (ed. D. Hurst, CCSL, 1969) 235-392. **E. Bertheau,** *Die Bücher Esra, Nehemia, und Ester* (KEH, 1862). **A. Bertholet,** *Die Bücher Esra und Nehemia* (KEH, 1902). **J. A. Bewer,** *Der Text des Buches Ezra* (1922). **E. J. Bickermann,** "The Edict of Cyrus in Ezra 1," *JBL* 65 (1946) 249-75. **J. Blenkinsopp,** "The Mission of Udjahorresnet and Those of Ezra and Nehemiah," *JBL* 106 (1987) 409-21; *Ezra–Nehemiah* (OTL, 1988). **R. A. Bowman,** "Introduction and Exegesis to the Book of Ezra and Nehemiah," *IB* (1954) 3:551-819. **R. L. Braun,** "Chronicles, Ezra, and Nehemiah," *VTSup* 30 (1979) 52-64. **J. Bright,** *A History of Israel* (1959). **L. H. Brockington,** *Ezra, Nehemiah, and Esther* (NCBC, 1969). **J. G. Carpzov,** *Introductio ad Libros Historicos Veteris Testamenti* (1741³). **J. H. Charlesworth** (ed.), *OTP* 1. **B. S. Childs,** *Introduction to the OT as Scripture* (1979). **D. J. A. Clines,** "Nehemiah 10 as an Example of Early Jewish Biblical Exegesis," *JSOT* 21 (1981) 111-17; *Ezra, Nehemiah, and Esther* (NCBC, 1984). **R. J. Coggins,** *The Books of Ezra and Nehemiah* (CBC, 1976). **F. M. Cross,** "A Reconstruction of the Judean Restoration," *JBL* 94 (1975) 4-18. **P. R. Davies** (ed.), *Second Temple Studies,* vol. 1, *Persian Period* (1991). **P.-E. Dion,** "Les types épistolaires hébréo-araméens jusqu'au temps de Bar-Kokhbah," *RB* 86 (1979) 544-79. **J. G. Eichorn,** *Einleitung in das Alte Testament* II (1803³). **J. A. Emerton,** "Did Ezra Go to Jerusalem in 428 BC?" *JTS* NS 17 (1966) 1-19. **T. C. Eskenazi,** "The Structure of Ezra-Nehemiah and the Integrity of the Book," *JBL* 107 (1988) 641-56; *In an Age of Prose: A Literary Approach to Ezra-Nehemiah* (SBLMS 36, 1988); "Current Perspectives on Ezra-Nehemiah and the Persian Period," *CR:BS* 1 (1993) 59-86. **T. C. Eskenazi and K. H. Richards** (eds.), *Second Temple Studies,* vol. 2, *Temple and Community in the Persian Period* (1994). **F. C. Fensham,** *The Books of Ezra and Nehemiah* (NICOT, 1982). **M. Fishbane,** *Biblical Interpretation in Ancient Israel* (1985). **J. A. Fitzmyer,** "Aramaic Epistolography," *A Wandering Aramean: Collected Aramaic Essays* (1979) 183-204. **K. Galling,** "The 'Gōlā-list' According to Ezra 2–Nehemiah 7," *JBL* 70 (1951) 149-58; *Die Bücher der Chronik, Esra, Nehemia* (ATD, 1954); *Studien zur Geschichte Israels im persischen Zeitalter* (1964). **A. E. Gardner,** "The Purpose and Date of 1 Esdras," *JJS* 37 (1986) 18-27. **L. L. Grabbe,** "Reconstructing History from the Book of Ezra," *Second Temple Studies,* vol. 1, *Persian Period* (ed. P. R. Davies, 1991) 98-106; *Judaism from Cyrus to Hadrian* (1992); "What Was Ezra's Mission?" *Second Temple Studies,* vol. 2, *Temple and Community in the Persian Period* (ed. T. C. Eskenazi and K. H. Richards, 1994) 286-99. **K. H. Graf,** *Die geschichtlichen Bücher des Alten Testaments: Zwei historisch-kritische Untersuchungen* (1866). **A. H. J. Gunneweg,** "Zur interpretation der Bücher Esra-Nehemia," VTSup 32 (1981) 146-61; *Esra* (KAT, 1985); *Nehemia* (KAT, 1987). **B. Halpern,** "A Historiographic Commentary on Ezra 1–6," *The HB and Its Interpreters* (W. H. Propp et al., BJuS 1, 1990) 81-142. **R. Hanhart,** "Zu Text und Textgeschichte des ersten Esrabuches," *Proceedings of the Sixth World Congress of Jewish Studies* (ed. A. Shinan, 1973) 1:201-12. **K. G. Hoglund,** *Achaemenid Administration in Syria-Palestine and the Missions of Ezra and Nehemiah* (SBLDS 125, 1992). **G. Hölscher,** "Die Bücher Esra und Nehemia," *HSAT(K)* 1:449-92. **C. Houtman,** "Ezra and the Law," *OTS* 21 (1981) 91-115. **W. T. In der Smitten,** *Esra: Quellen, Überlieferung, und Geschichte* (SSN 15, 1973). **S. Japhet,** "The Supposed Common Authorship of Chronicles and Ezra-Nehemiah Investigated Anew," *VT* 18 (1968) 330-71; "Sheshbazzar and Zerubbabel," *ZAW* 94 (1982) 66-98; 95 (1983) 218-29; "'History' and 'Literature' in the Persian Period," *Ah, Assyria: Studies in Assyrian History and Ancient Near Eastern Historiography Presented to H. Tadmor* (ed. M. Cogan and I. Eph'al, 1991) 174-88; "The Temple in the Restoration Period: Reality and Ideology," *USQR* 44 (1991) 195-251. **A. S. Kapelrud,** *The Question of Authorship in the Ezra-Narrative: A Lexical Investigation* (1944). **U. Kellermann,** *Nehemia: Quellen, Überlieferung, und Geschichte* (BZAW 102, 1967); "Erwägungen zum Problem der Esradatierung," *ZAW* 80 (1968) 55-87; "Erwägungen zum Esragesetz," *ZAW* 80 (1968) 373-85. **C. F. Keil,** *Biblischer Commentar über die nachexilischen Geschichtsbücher: Chronik, Esra, Nehemiah, und Esther* (1870). **F. D. Kidner,** *Ezra and Nehemiah* (TOTC, 1979). **R. W. Klein,** "Ezra and Nehemiah in Recent Studies," *Magnalia Dei: The Mighty Acts of God* (ed. F. M. Cross et al., 1976) 361-76. **K. Koch,** "Ezra and the Origins of Judaism," *JSS* 19 (1974) 173-97. **A. van der Kooij,** "On the Ending of the Book of 1 Esdras," *VII Congress of the IOSCS* (ed. C. E. Cox) 37-49; "Zur Frage des Anfangs des 1. Esrabuches," *ZAW* 103 (1991) 239-52. **D. Kraemer,** "On the Relationship of the Books of Ezra and Nehemiah," *JSOT* 59 (1993) 73-92. **M. L. W. Laistner,** *Thought and Letters in Western Europe* (AD 500–900) (1957). **C. à Lapide,** *Commentaria in Scripturam Sacram* 4 (1645, 1877) 200-261. **F. Michaeli,** *Les livres des Chroniques, d'Esdras et de Néhémie* (CAT, 1967). **E. Meyer,** *Die Entstehung des Judenthums* (1986). **S. Mowinckel,** *Ezra den Skriftlaerde* (1916); *Statholderen Nehemia* (1916); "Die vorderasiatischen Königs- und Fürsteninschriften," *Eucharisterion: H. Gunkel zum*

60. Geburtstage (FRLANT 36, 1923) 278-322; *Studien zu dem Buche Ezra–Nehemia I-III* (1964–65). **J. M. Myers,** *I and II Esdras* (AB, 1974). **A. Noordtzij,** *Ezra–Nehemia* (1951). **M. Noth,** *Überlieferungsgeschichtliche Studien* (1943; ET, The Chronicler's History [1987]). **V. Pavlovsky,** "Die Chronologie der Tätigkeit Esdras: Versuch einer neuen Lösung," *Bib* 38 (1957) 275-305, 428-56. **J. Pilkington,** *A Godlie Exposition upon Certaine Chapters of Nehemiah* (1585). **O. Plöger,** *Theokratie und Eschatologie* (WMANT 2, 1959; ET, *Theocracy and Eschatology* [1968]). **K.-F. Pohlmann,** *Studien zum dritten Esra* (FRLANT 104, 1970). **G. von Rad,** "Die Nehemia-Denkschrift," *ZAW* 76 (1964) 176-87. **H. H. Rowley,** "The Chronological Order of Ezra and Nehemiah," *The Servant of the Lord and Other Essays on the OT* (1965²) 137-68. **H. E. Ryle,** *The Books of Ezra and Nehemiah* (CBSC, 1893). **W. Rudolph,** *Esra und Nehemia* (HAT, 1949). **H. H. Schaeder,** *Esra der Schreiber* (1930). **R. J. Saley,** "The Date of Nehemiah Reconsidered," *Biblical and Near Eastern Studies: Essays in Honor of W. S. Lasor* (ed. G. A. Tuttle, 1978) 151-65. **H. Schneider,** *Die Bücher Esra und Nehemia* (HSAT, 1959). **J. R. Shaver,** "Ezra and Nehemiah: On the Theological Significance of Making Them Contemporaries," *Priests, Prophets and Scribes: Essays on the Formation and Heritage of Second Temple Judaism in Honour of J. Blenkinsopp* (ed. E. Ulrich et al., 1992) 76-86. **D. C. Siegfried,** *Esra, Nehemia, und Esther* (HKAT, 1901). **K. D. Tolletson and H. G. M. Williamson,** "Nehemiah as Cultural Revitalization: An Anthropological Perspective," *JSOT* 56 (1992) 41-68. **C. C. Torrey,** *The Composition and Historical Value of Ezra–Nehemiah* (BZAW 2, 1896); *Ezra Studies* (1910). **A. Van Hoonacker,** "Néhémie et Esdras, une nouvelle hypothèse sure la chronologie de l'époque do la restauration," *Le Muséon* 9 (1890) 151-84, 317-51, 389-401. **J. C. VanderKam,** "Ezra–Nehemiah or Ezra and Nehemiah?" *Priests, Prophets, and Scribes: Essays on the Formation and Heritage of Second Temple Judaism in Honour of J. Blenkinsopp* (ed. E. Ulrich et al., 1992) 55-75. **R. de Vaux,** "The Decrees of Cyrus and Darius on the Rebuilding of the Temple," *The Bible and the Ancient Near East* (1971) 63-96. **G. Vermes, F. Millar, and M. Goodman,** *HJPAJC* (E. Schürer 3, 2, 1987). **J. P. Weinberg,** *The Citizen-Temple Community* (1992). **J. L. White** (ed.), *Studies in Ancient Letter Writing* (*Semeia* 22, 1982). **H. G. M. Williamson,** *Israel in the Books of Chronicles* (1977); "The Composition of Ezra i-vi," *JTS* NS 34 (1983) 1-30; *Ezra, Nehemiah* (WBC, 1985); *Ezra and Nehemiah* (OTGu, 1987); "History," *It Is Written: Scripture Citing Scripture. Essays in Honour of B. Lindars, SSF* (ed. D. A. Carson and H. G. M. Williamson, 1988) 25-38. **L. Zunz,** *Die gottesdienstlichen Vorträge der Juden* (1832).

H. G. M. WILLIAMSON

F

FABER STAPULENSIS (c. 1455–1536)

F., also known as Jacques Lefèvre, was born in Etaples, Picardy, and completed his liberal arts education at the Collège du Cardinal Lemoine in Paris (BA 1479; MA 1480). While teaching at Lemoine, he studied Greek and began to occupy himself with Aristotle, translating the entire Aristotelian corpus and commenting on it in a humanist rather than a scholastic manner. He also published the work of Dionysius the Areopagite (1499) and the *Hermetica* (1505).

After journeys to Italy (1500, 1507), F. followed the invitation of his patron Briçonnet to live in the abbey Saint-Germain des Près. He turned to the study of Scripture, publishing in 1509 the *Quincuplex Psalterium* (used by Luther and Zwingli) and three years later his *Commentarii in Pauli epistolas* (which occasioned a dispute with Erasmus over the exegesis of Heb 2:7).

Attacks by Paris theologians caused F. in 1521 to join Briçonnet, then bishop of Meaux. Appointed vicar general in spiritual matters, F. was assigned to help reform the diocese. His *Commentarii initiarii in quatuor evangelia* appeared in 1522 and *Commentarii in epistolas catholicas* in 1525, followed by *Épîtres et Evangiles pour le cinquante et deux dimanches de l'an.* After a short retreat to Strasbourg (1525) he was called by Francis I to serve as court librarian and tutor of the royal children. F.'s translation of the Bible into French (1530) influenced Olivetan's, which in turn was revised by CALVIN for use in Geneva. In 1530 F. moved to the court of Marguerite of Navarre, where he lived until his death.

F.'s biblical exegesis combined humanist TEXTUAL CRITICISM with a christocentric interpretation. While his theology incorporated classical wisdom (Aristotle more than Plato), borrowed from the mysticism of Dionysius and Cusanus, and was tinged with the *Devotio moderna,* he taught an "evangelical" salvation by grace. He believed that God's Word illumines Christians as they enter a formation process toward Christlikeness (*Christiformitas*) under the inspiration of the Holy Spirit. This inward turn both overcomes all religious externalities and engenders harmony in all theological controversies. In interpreting the OT he argued that its literal sense is made known by the Holy Spirit, first revealed at the time of Christ and the apostles.

Works: *The Prefatory Epistles of J. Lefèvre d'Etaples and Related Texts* (ed. E. Rice, 1972); *Quincuplex psalterium* (1972); *Commentarii in Pauli epistolas* (1976).

Bibliography: **G. Bedouelle,** *Lefèvre d'Etaples et l'intelligence des écritures* (Leavaux d'humanisme et Renaissance 152, 1976); *Le Quincuplex Psalterium de Lefèvre d'Etaples: Un guide de lecture* (Leavaux d'humanisme et Renaissance 171, 1979); *TRE* 10 (1982) 781-83. **R. Cameron,** "The Attack on the Biblical Work of Lefèvre d'Etaples, 1514–21," *CH* 38 (1969) 9-24. **J. Dagens,** "Humanisme et Evangélisme chez Lefèvre d'Etaples," *Courants religieux et humanisme à la fin du XVe et au début du XVIe siècle* (1959) 121-34. **H. Feld,** "Der Humanistenstreit um Hebräer 2,7 (Psalm 8,6)," *ARG* 61 (1970) 5-33. **K. H. Graf,** *Essai sur la vie et les écrits de J. Lefèvre d'Etaples* (1970). **H. Heller,** "The Evangelicism of Lefèvre d'Etaples, 1525," *Studies in the Renaissance* 16 (1969) 42-77; *Contemporaries of Erasmus* II (ed. P. G. Bietenholz, 1986) 315-18. **P. E. Hughes,** *Lefèvre: Pioneer of Ecclesiastic Renewal in France* (1984). **H. J. de Jonge,** "The Relationship of Erasmus' Translation of the NT to That of the Pauline Epistles by J. Lefèvre d'Etaples," *Erasmus in English* 15 (1987–88) 2-7. **P. D. W. Krey,** *HHMBI,* 204-8. **A. Laune,** "Lefèvre d'Etaples et la traduction française de la Bible," *RHR* 32 (1895) 56-72. **J. B. Payne,** "Erasmus and Lefèvre as Interpreters of Paul," *ARG* 65 (1974) 54-83. **J. S. Preus,** *From Shadow to Promise: OT Interpretation from Augustine to the Young Luther* (1969) 137-42. **E. F. Rice,** "J. Lefèvre d'Etaples and the Medieval Christian Mystics," *Florilegium historiale: Essays Presented to W. K. Ferguson* (ed. J. G. Rowe and W. H. Stockdale, 1971) 89-124.

M. HOFFMANN

FABRICIUS, JOHANN ALBERT (1668–1736)

Born at Leipzig on Nov. 11, 1668, F. studied theology, philology, philosophy, and medicine at the university there. Beginning in 1693, he served for five years as assistant and librarian to J. Mayer, an important pastor in the city of Hamburg, before becoming professor of rhetoric and philosophy in the local gymnasium (1699), a post he held until his death on Apr. 3, 1736. Owner of a library of over 32,000 volumes, F. was still described over a century after his death as "the most learned, most voluminous, and most useful of bibliographers." Neciron in *MSHH* lists 128 volumes in his bibliography. His own contributions to theology, *Hydrotheologie* (1730) and *Pyrotheologie* (1732) on the goodness of God in creating water and fire, as well as his history of LUTHER and the Reformation (*Centifolium Lutheranum* 2 [1728–30]) were insignificant contributions to scholarship.

F.'s significance lies in his bibliographical volumes and collections of source material. He compiled Latin, Greek, ecclesiastical, and other bibliographies that are still useful. His most enduring and consequential work was bringing together the apocryphal materials (see APOCRYPHA, NT) related to the NT (1703) and the pseudepigraphal materials (see PSEUDEPIGRAPHA) related to the HB (1713). These long remained standard works and made readily available handy collections of texts that were used in diverse ways during the Enlightenment, especially by such radicals as VOLTAIRE, to raise questions about the Scriptures.

Works: *Bibliotheca latina* (1697; 3 vols., ed. J. A. Ernesti, 1773–74); *Codex apocryphus Novi Testamenti, collectus, castigatus, testimoniisque, censuris et animadversionibus illustratus* (2 vols., 1703; enlarged ed. 1719); *Bibliotheca graeca* (14 vols., 1705–28; 12 vols., ed. G. C. Harless, 1790–1809); *Bibliographia antiquaria* (1713; 2 vols., 1760); *Codex pseudepigraphus Veteris Testamenti* (1713; enlarged ed., 2 vols., 1722–23); *Bibliotheca ecclesiastica* (1718); *Bibliotheca latina mediae et infimae* (5 vols., 1734–36; 6 vols., completed by J. D. Mansi, 1754).

Bibliography: *MSHH* 32 (1735) 31-45; 40 (1739) 107-62. **H. S. Reimarus,** *De vita et scriptis J. A. F.* (1737).

J. H. HAYES

FAGIUS, PAUL (1504–49)

Born in Rheinzabern in the Palatinate in 1522, F. moved to Strasbourg to study with the noted Hebraist C. PELLICAN. There he met M. BUCER, with whom he established a lifelong friendship, and became an important participant in this early center of reform. In 1527 he accepted the post of schoolmaster in Isny in Swabia, became a pastor there ten years later, and with local support established a small press in 1541. He was able to induce the foremost Jewish Hebrew scholar of the century, E. LEVITA, to work with him in the publication of scriptural materials. He later taught Hebrew at Strasbourg, Marburg, Constance, and Heidelberg. He died in England in 1549 shortly after arriving there with Bucer.

F.'s scriptural studies were among the finest expressions of serious Christian use of Jewish sources. Like other Christian Hebraists he was convinced that early Christianity had borrowed a great deal from contemporary pharisaic Judaism. Rejecting the strict Lutheran dichotomy of law and gospel, F. attempted to reconstruct this influence. His primary task, he believed, was to demonstrate to Christian scholars the linguistic and philological depth to biblical Hebrew; consequently his publications demonstrate an extremely high level of achievement in Hebrew and Aramaic. In one instance he translated the first four chapters of Genesis, then devoted 155 pages to explaining a large variety of

rabbinic materials in order to demonstrate the richness and variability of the Hebrew text.

His other publications were equally meticulous studies of Jewish thought and practice understood from a Christian perspective. To explain the true nature of the Eucharist, he published and commented upon the entire order of Jewish table blessings, which he believed important to understanding the Lord's Supper. He also published rabbinic opinion concerning the concepts of grace and other pharisaic ideas that he believed might shed light on early Christian thought.

Works: *Sententiae Vere Elegentes Piae. . . .* (1541); *Tobias Hebraice. . . .* (1541); *Precationes Hebraicae quibus in Solemnioribus Festis Judaei. . . .* (1542); *Exegesis sive expositiones Dictionum Hebraicorum literalis et simplex in quatour capita Geneseos pro studiosis morales Ben Syrae, Vetustissimi authoris Hebraei* (1542).

Bibliography: **R. Bayne,** *DNB* 18 (1889) 120. **J. Friedman,** *The Most Ancient Testimony: Sixteenth Century Christian Hebraica in the Age of Renaissance Nostalgia* (1983). **R. Raubenheimer,** *P. F. aus Rheinzabern: Sein Leben und Wirken als Reformator und Belehrter* (1957).

J. FRIEDMAN

FAIRBAIRN, ANDREW MARTIN (1838–1912)

After study at Edinburgh University, F. took his first academic degree in 1860 from the Theological College of the Evangelical Union and then assumed a pastorate. He embraced Congregationalism in 1877, became principal of Airedale Theological College in Bradford, England, and worked energetically in ecclesiastical affairs. In 1886 he became the first principal of Mansfield College, Oxford, founded as a center for Congregational theological training. In later life he preached, wrote, traveled widely, and advanced reforms in Free Church theological education.

F.'s chief interests were theology, philosophy of religion, and apologetics. His sympathy with newer intellectual developments, especially in Germany, won many admirers among theological students—in part because his commitment to historic supernaturalist orthodoxy remained equally strong. Though chiefly theological, his *Studies in the Life of Christ* (1880) rode well the current of popular historical interest in JESUS set in motion by F. FARRAR. More significant was *The Place of Christ in Modern Theology* (1893), a creative restatement of traditional views in the light of new developments in philosophy and biblical study. F.'s reforms of theological education and sympathetic view of German historical criticism were pivotal in guiding British nonconformity toward moderate and, after 1900, even liberal views on the Bible and its interpretation.

Works: *Studies in the Philosophy of Religion and History* (1876); *The City of God* (1882); *Catholicism, Roman and Anglican* (1899); *The Philosophy of the Christian Religion* (1902); *Studies in Religion and Theology: The Church in Idea and History* (1910).

Bibliography: W. B. Selbie, *Life of A. M. F.* (1914); *DNB* 24 (1927) 179-80. **A. P. F. Sell,** "An Englishman, an Irishman, and a Scotsman," *SJT* 38 (1985) 41-83.

D. L. PALS

FARMER, HUGH (1714–87)

A liberal dissenting clergy of north Welsh ancestry, F. was born near Shrewsbury. About 1730 he came under the tutelage of P. DODDRIDGE and was one of his best pupils. After completing his academic work, F. served dissenting congregations, eventually pastoring a large congregation at Walthamstow as well as being a regular preacher at Salters Hall and a respected member of society. His liberal leanings can be seen in his advice to fellow clergy that they sell their commentaries and buy H. GROTIUS. He died Feb. 6, 1787. Unfortunately, the executors of his estate, following the requirements of his will, burned his papers, which included revisions for his treatise on miracles and a work on Balaam.

His first major publication (1761) was a study of JESUS' temptations, which he argued were actually a prophetic vision symbolizing the nature of the difficulties Jesus would confront in carrying out his office and ministry. After a volume on miracles (1771; GT 1777) in which he denied the miraculous, except in cases of direct divine intervention, he published two controversial volumes on the demoniacs of the NT (1775 [GT by J. Semler, 1776]; 1778 [GT by Semler, 1783]). In these works he argued a number of important theses: (1) Demonic possession is not to be related to the work of Satan, since demons in the ancient world were understood as the spirits of deceased persons (see his 1783 work). (2) Modern reason clearly realizes that there is not sufficient evidence to warrant belief in demonic possession. (3) Demoniacs were actually persons suffering from such illnesses as madness and epilepsy. (4) Jesus and the early apostles understood the true nature of what was called demonic possession but accommodated themselves to popular belief, not considering it their divine mission to instruct the people in the true nature of matters: "It is customary with all sorts of persons, with the sacred writers in particular, and our Saviour himself, to speak on many subjects in the languages of the vulgar, though known and admitted to have been originally grounded on a false philosophy." (5) Persons understood by their contemporaries as demonically possessed were cured by Jesus, and such persons often showed a greater tendency than the general population to acknowledge Jesus as Messiah.

F.'s work is significant, giving expression to the belief that the NT Gospels have not always presented the course of Jesus' ministry in its true form, and thus the texts must be reinterpreted (or to use later terminology, "demythologized") to disclose their true meaning. In addition, the idea that even Jesus and the writers of the NT accommodated themselves to popular but misconceived ideas and practices meant that the biblical materials must be sifted to distinguish the essential and truthful from the accidental and vulgarly distorted.

Works: *An Inquiry into the Nature and Design of Christ's Temptation in the Wilderness, Matt 4:1-11* (1761, 1765[2], 1776[3], 1805[4]; ed. J. Joyce, 1822[5]); *A Dissertation on Miracles Designed to Shew that They are Arguments of an Interposition, and Absolute Proofs of the Mission and Doctrine of a Prophet* (1771, 1804[2]; ed. J. Joyce, 1810[3]); *An Examination of Mr. LeMoine's Treatise on Miracles* (1772); *An Essay on the Demoniacs of the NT* (1775, 1779[2], 1805[3]; ed. J. Joyce, 1818[4]); *Letters to the Rev. Dr. Worthington, in Answer to His Late Publication, Entitled "An impartial Inquiry into the Case of the Gospel Demoniacs"* (1778); *The General Prevalence of the Worship of Human Spirits in the Ancient and Heathen Nations Asserted and Proved* (1783).

Bibliography: *BB[2]* 5 (1793) 664-82. **M. Dodson,** *Memoirs of the Life and Writings of the Rev. H. F.: To Which Is Added, a Piece of His, Never Before Published. Also, Several Original Letters, and an Extract from His Essay on the Case of Balaam* (1805). **A. Gordon,** *DNB* 18 (1889) 211-13.

J. H. HAYES

FARMER, WILLIAM REUBEN (1921–)

F. was born Feb. 1, 1921, in Needles, California. He earned his AB (1942) in psychology and religion from Occidental College in Los Angeles as well as a BA (1949) and an MA (1956) in philosophy of religion and Christian ethics from Cambridge University. His BD (1950) and ThD (1952) were conferred by the Union Theological Seminary in New York.

F.'s influential teachers at Union included R. NIEBUHR, P. TILLICH, and J. KNOX, who served as chair of F.'s dissertation committee. No doubt each of these former teachers also encouraged F. in his commitments to social justice that have so characterized his life outside the classroom as well as within it. F.'s longtime colleague at Perkins School of Theology, A. Outler, also became a formative influence somewhat later in life.

F.'s academic appointments have included positions at Emory University (visiting instructor, 1950–52), De-Pauw University (visiting instructor, 1952–1954), Drew University (assistant professor, 1955–59), and the Perkins School of Theology of Southern Methodist University (associate professor, 1959–64; professor, 1964–91; professor emeritus, 1991–). Since 1991 he has continued research, writing, editorial work, and some teaching at the University of Dallas, a Roman Catholic institution (research professor, 1991 to present). In 1990 F. was also appointed general editor for the *International Catholic Bible Commentary,* a one-volume ecumenical international resource for the church of the twenty-first century (1998).

In 1968 Cambridge University conferred on F. a third degree, the BD, in recognition of his epochal book *The Synoptic Problem: A Critical Analysis.* In the opening chapters he traced the historical development of the scholarly consensus that the two-document hypothesis was "one of the assured results of nineteenth century gospel criticism." He then led his readers through a systematic, multi-step, logical argument that came to three fundamental conclusions: (1) Matthew was most likely the earliest Gospel; (2) Luke made use of Matthew and other sources in composing the second Gospel; and (3) Mark wrote third on the basis of a conflation of Matthew and Luke. He concluded this book with an illustrative, redaction-historical analysis (see REDACTION CRITICISM) of Mark 1–13 on the two Gospel hypothesis. Other scholars responded quickly and sometimes emotionally to this book, but its publication marked the dawn of a new era. Discussion of the SYNOPTIC PROBLEM had been reopened.

F.'s interest in the synoptic problem also took his research into the area of NT TEXTUAL CRITICISM with an analysis of the last twelve verses of Mark (1974) in which he challenged a second scholarly consensus—namely, that the manuscript tradition and considerations of Markan literary style clearly argued for the inauthenticity of these verses. His continuing work in the history of nineteenth-century Gospel criticism (1964, 1994, 1995a) was sparked by a question he formulated while researching *The Synoptic Problem:* "What did lead scholars to the consensus on Markan priority, when the scientific arguments were neither sound nor convincing?"

Although F. is best known for reopening the discussion of the synoptic problem (1964, 1969) and his advocacy of the two Gospel (Neo-Griesbach, Owen-Griesbach; see J. J. GRIESBACH) source theory of the Synoptics (1982, 1990a, 1994), his research interests and publications range widely (E. P. Sanders [1987]). He began his career working as an archaeologist in Israel and Jordan (1955–57). With that background, he wrote his first book, *Maccabees, Zealots, and Josephus* (1956), which also marked a new era. Specifically, he convincingly demonstrated for the first time the historical connections and relationships between the Maccabees and their revolt against the Seleucids and Josephus's fourth philosophical sect (the Zealots) and the revolt against Rome.

The works of C. H. DODD and J. JEREMIAS on the PARABLES provided the foundation for F.'s work on the life of JESUS (1967, 1982). In his 1967 contribution to the Knox Festschrift, F. began to extend their work by contributing a modest but carefully constructed chronological framework of the life of Jesus into which he placed the earliest forms of the parables in a developmental sequence. With these in place he had the beginnings of a reasonable and credible reconstruction of both the message and the life of Jesus.

F. has also published revisionary studies of patristic testimonies relating to the Gospels (1983a, 1990a) and has made contributions in the areas of composition criticism (1982), CANONICAL CRITICISM (1982, 1998), ecumenism (1983b, 1990b, 1998), and christology (1995b). His interest in the history of the development of the biblical CANON (1982, 1983b, 1998) was a logical outgrowth of his interest in patristic evidence relating to the Gospels, but his conclusion that the canon is essentially a "martyrs" canon is both original and independent of this other work. As W. Willis (1987) has pointed out, what is most radical about the work of this leading twentieth-century advocate of the two Gospel hypothesis is his "irenic view of Christian origins," a feature that stands in stark contrast to similar work done by a leading nineteenth-century advocate of essentially the same hypothesis, F. C. BAUR.

Works: "The Economic Basis of the Qumran Community," *TZ* (1955) 295-308; *Maccabees, Zealots, and Josephus: An Inquiry into Jewish Nationalism in the Greco-Roman Period* (1956); *The Synoptic Problem: A Critical Analysis* (1964); (ed. with C. F. D. Moule, R. R. Niebuhr), *Christian History and Interpretation: Studies Presented to John Knox* (1967); *Synopticon: The Verbal Agreement Between the Greek Texts of Matthew, Mark and Luke Contextually Exhibited* (1969); *The Last Twelve Verses of Mark* (SNTSMS 25, 1974); *Jesus and the Gospel: Tradition, Scripture, and Canon* (1982); (ed.), *New Synoptic Studies: The Cambridge Gospel Conference and Beyond* (1983a); (with D. M. Farkasfalvy), *The Formation of the NT Canon: An Ecumenical Approach* (Theological Inquiries, 1983b); *The Interrelations of the Gospels: A Symposium Led by M.-É. Boismard, W. R. F., and F. Neirynck, Jerusalem 1984* (BETL 95, ed. D. L. Dungan, 1990a); (with R. A. Kereszty), *Peter and Paul in the Church of Rome: The Ecumenical Potential of a Forgotten Perspective* (Theological Inquiries, 1990b); *The Gospel of Jesus: The Pastoral Relevance of the Synoptic Problem* (1994); (ed. with H. G. Reventlow), *Biblical Studies and the Shifting of Paradigms, 1850–1914* (JSOTSup 192, 1995a); (ed.), *Crisis in Christology: Essays in Quest of Resolution* (1995b); (gen. ed.), *International Catholic Bible Commentary: A One-volume Ecumenical International Resource for the Church of the Twenty-first Century* (1998).

Bibliography: **T. R. W. Longstaff and P. A. Thomas** (eds.), *The Synoptic Problem: A Bibliography, 1716–1988* (New Gospel Studies 4, 1988). **E. P. Sanders** (ed.), *Jesus, the Gospels, and the Church: Essays in Honor of W. R. F.* (1987). **W. Willis,** "An Irenic View of Christian Origins," ibid., 265-86.

D. B. PEABODY

FARRAR, FREDERIC WILLIAM (1831–1903)

A theologian, popular novelist, essayist, religious historian, Bible expositor, and devotional writer, F. was the son of Anglican missionaries to India. He took a BA from the University of London, entered Trinity College, Cambridge, where he joined the celebrated Apostles' Club, took another BA, and later received both an MA and a DD. For fifteen years a house master at Harrow College, he became headmaster of Marlborough in 1871. In 1876 he became a canon of Westminster and preached with success both at the abbey and in his parish church. Made dean of Canterbury in 1895, he served in that post until his death.

F. was a prolific writer possessed of imagination, wide interests, and an engaging prose style. He published works on philology, Greek grammar, current social issues, theology, church history, and Roman antiquity. His greatest skill, however, lay in the realm of popular religious literature, especially biblical exposition, where he published scores of magazine articles and books, the most famous of which was *The Life of Christ* (1874)—called by some the best-selling biography of the entire Victorian era. In it F. combined basic trust in the Gospel texts with colorful descriptions of the Palestinian landscape, vivid historical detail, and dramatic narrative to furnish a portrait of Christ that was fresh, yet reassuring to orthodoxy. It was often imitated.

F.'s theological convictions were evangelical and quite broadminded. *Eternal Hope* (1877) brought him into controversy for questioning the doctrine of eternal punishment. His *History of* [Biblical] *Interpretation* (1885), still an informative work, reiterated his belief that the modern reign of historical knowledge and scientific fact has only enhanced the Scriptures by liberating their true evangelical message from the alien conceptual schemes imposed on them by earlier hands.

Works: *An Essay on the Christian Doctrine of Atonement* (1858); *Seekers After God* (1868); *The Witness of History to Christ* (1871); *The Life of Christ* (1874); *Eternal Hope* (1877); *The Life and Work of St. Paul* (1879); *The Gospel According to St. Luke* (1880); *The Early Days of Christianity* (1882); *History of Interpretation* (1885); *Solomon: His Life and Times* (1888); *The Minor Prophets* (1890); *The Lord's Prayer: Sermons in Westminster Abbey* (1893); *The Life of Christ as Represented in Art* (1894); *The Life of Lives: Further Studies in the Life of Christ* (1900).

Bibliography: R. Bayne, *DNB* 23 (1912) 9-12. I. Ellis, "Dean F. and the Quest for the Historical Jesus," *Theology* 78 (1975) 108-15. R. Farrar, *The Life of F. W. F.* (1904). D. L. Pals, *The Victorian "Lives" of Jesus* (TUMSR 7, 1892) 77-85, 93-94.

D. L. PALS

FARRER, AUSTIN MARSDEN (1904–68)

F. combined the insights of a philosopher and a literary critic with a high-church devotion and a mastery of the English language that make his work intoxicating to read. His imagination, however, soared where few have been willing to follow; thus his approach has been creative and seminal rather than directly influential.

F. wrote two books on the Apocalypse. In his 1949 work he saw the book as six series of sevens—letters, seals, trumpets, beasts, vials, and last things—each culminating in sabbath worship, with the whole looking forward to the ultimate sabbath. Further, the six sevens are also seen as reflecting a liturgical sequence of a year and a half: from the seven lamps used at the Feast of Dedication in chap. 1 through the lamb of Passover and the throne of Pentecost in chap. 4 to the trumpets of New Year, and so round to a second Passover, with the Lord's coming in chap. 22. Nor is this all, for there are reflections of epicycles of feasts as well as the pattern of a day of worship in the Temple; and there is also a march around six sides of the four-square city, whose gates are the twelve apostles and the twelve tribes and the twelve jewels of the high priest's robe. Much of this extravagance is pruned away in his 1964 commentary; in particular the liturgical sequence is now taken to be primary, with a structure limited to a single year. This remains an interesting and perhaps correct option, for chap. 1 is much more reminiscent of Easter than of Dedication, and an annual cycle is more plausible than one of a year and a half. Unfortunately, F. overlaid his scheme with supposed zodiacal echoes that are less than convincing.

The most widely read of his biblical writings is probably his article on Q. For a century Q had been almost universally assumed to be a lost source of Matthew and Luke, but F. challenged this position. His more convincing points were: A lost source is in principle a worse hypothesis than Luke's use of Matthew; Q is an amorphous document without proper ancient parallel and with no specific flavor; it consists of those non-Markan parts of Matthew that might have appealed to Luke; if Luke did not know Matthew, we have a number of insoluble minor agreements; claims that Luke sometimes preserves the earlier form are based on weak criteria; Luke's order follows Mark, with the clearest Galilean incidents from Matthew inserted. Unfortunately, the effect of the argument was spoiled by F.'s claim of a massive hexateuchal structure running through both Gospels.

A similar search for structure dominates F.'s two books on Mark (1951, 1954). He saw cycles and paracycles, a pattern of twelve Israelites healed and a Gentile, alongside twelve apostles called and Levi, a riddle of numbers behind the loaves and thousands (to which he attempted several solutions), and many other possibilities. The bold outlines he drew are not often found in more recent works on Mark; but some of the details survive. More important, F.'s influence is felt in the awareness that ancient texts should be treated as unities. They cannot be understood if taken as heavily interpolated, as R. CHARLES understood the Apocalypse, or as beads on a string, as form critics (see FORM CRITICISM) understood Mark. Courage, imagination, and empathy will be needed if the curtain is to be pierced between Mark's mind (or the seer's) and our own.

Works: *The Glass of Vision* (Bampton Lectures, 1948); *A Rebirth of Images: The Making of St. John's Apocalypse* (1949); *A Study in St. Mark* (1951); "Loaves and Thousands," *JTS* NS 4 (1953) 1-14; *St. Matthew and St. Mark* (Edward Cadbury Lectures, 1954; 1966²); "On Dispensing with Q," *Studies on the Gospel* (1955) 55-88; *The Revelation of St. John the Divine: Commentary on the English Text* (1964); *Saving Belief: A Discussion of Essentials* (1964, 1994); *The Triple Victory: Christ's Temptation According to St. Matthew* (1965).

Bibliography: P. Curtis, *A Hawk Among Sparrows: A Biography of A. F.* (1985; esp. M. Goulder, "F. the Biblical Scholar," 192-212).

M. D. GOULDER

FEINE, PAUL (1859–1933)

Having trained in classical philology at Jena, F. became a gymnasium teacher in Göttingen in 1889 and at once turned to NT studies, gaining his licenciate there in 1893 and becoming a *Dozent.* He was appointed professor in the small Protestant faculty at Vienna in 1894, moved to Breslau as a sharply contrasting successor to W. WREDE in 1897, and to the very large Halle faculty in 1910. Hostile to both radical criticism and to the new RELIGIONS-GESCHICHTLICHE trend, he saw his main task as opposing F. C. BAUR's "historical-critical school," as represented and given a stronger exegetical base by C. Holsten. After initial research on Jewish Christianity and the sources of Luke, from 1899 on he wrote mainly on PAUL, attempting to demonstrate continuity between the apostle and JESUS (1902). Finding the current textbooks too radical, he provided alternatives in his two most widely used works, an NT THEOLOGY (1910, 1922⁴) and an introduction to the NT (1913; rev. ed. 1923³) developed by J. Behm in 1936 and taken over by W. KÜMMEL in 1963. Also substantial are his works on NT religion (1921); on Paul (1927, which includes a long and tendentious history of interpretation from Usteri to K. Barth); and on Jesus (1930). However, his work was without lasting significance.

Works: *Eine vorkanonische Überlieferung des Lukas in Evangelium und Apostelgeschichte* (1891); *Der Jakobusbrief nach Lehranschauungen und Entstehungsverhältnissen untersucht* (1893); *Das gesetzesfreie Evangelium des Paulus nach seinem Werdegang dargestellt* (1899); *Jesus Christus und Paulus* (1902);

Der Römerbrief: Eine exegetische Studie (1903); *St. Paul as a Theologian* (1906; ET 1908); *Theologie des Neuen Testaments* (1910, 1919³); *Einleitung in das Neue Testament* (1913); *Die Abfassung des Philipperbriefes in Ephesus: Mit einer Anlage über Röm. 16,3-20 als Epheserbrief* (1916); *die Religion des Neuen Testaments* (1921); *Die Gestalt des apostolischen Glaubensbekenntnisses in der Zeit des Neuen Testaments* (1925); *Der Apostel Paulus: Das Ringen um das geschichtliche Verständnis des Paulus* (Beiträge zur Förderung christilicher Theologie 2, 1927); *Jesus* (Evangelisch-theologische Bibliothek, 1930).

Bibliography: *RGS* 5 (1929) 39-84 (autobiographical with bibliography, 80-84).

R. MORGAN

FELL, JOHN (1625–86)

An English bishop and biblical, patristic, and classical scholar, F. was born in Berkshire (now Oxfordshire) June 23, 1625. Educated at Christ Church, Oxford, he served during the civil war as an ensign in the king's army. After the restoration of the monarchy in 1660 he was made dean of Christ Church, where he initiated important building programs. In 1675 he became bishop of Oxford, a position he held jointly with the deanship until his death July 10, 1686. The epigram, "I do not like thee, Doctor Fell," was written by his pupil T. Brown.

F. edited several classical and patristic texts and was distinguished for his edition of Cyprian. His main contribution to biblical scholarship was his edition of the Greek NT, which attempted to systematize the findings of textual scholars in the previous 150 years and was based on the Elzevir 1633 edition. F. claimed to have listed variants from more than a hundred versions and manuscripts, though he did not always make clear which witnesses provided evidence for a reading. He supported J. MILL in his preparation of a more comprehensive edition of the Greek NT and was also one of the prime movers in starting the Oxford University Press.

Works: *The Life of the Most learned, Revered and Pious Dr. H. Hammond* (1661); *Novi Testamenti libri omnes* (1675); *Athenagoras* (1682); *Sancti C. Cypriani Opera* (1682); *Clemens Alexandrinus* (1683).

Bibliography: *BB*³ (1750) 1912-14. **A. Fox,** *J. Mill and R. Bentley: A Study of the Textual Criticism of the NT, 1675–1729* (Avlarian Series 3, 1954). **B. M. Metzger,** *The Text of the NT* (1964) 107. **G. G. Perry,** *DNB* 18 (1889) 293-95. **A. à Wood,** *Athenae Oxonienses* 4 (new ed. 1820) 193-201, 869-70.

A. W. WAINWRIGHT

FEMINIST INTERPRETATION.

Feminist biblical interpretation involves readings and critiques of the Bible informed by feminist theory and criticism, which are the conceptual means and analytic tools developed to envision and implement the goals of feminism, a movement committed to women's self-determination and to fashioning humane alternatives to prevailing male-dominated political and social structures. Assisting such social change is the reassessment of male-centered knowledge; the transformation of such knowledge to include women; and, where necessary, the generation of new knowledge.

Feminist biblical interpretation is as diverse as the theories and analytic tools it uses to study the Bible. Adding to its complexity and depth are the many stances from which feminist interpretation proceeds, for the Bible is read from differing theological positions, religious perspectives, and ideological interests (for examples see E. Schüssler Fiorenza [1993] and A. Brenner and C. Fontaine [1997]). Feminists differ in assessing how religions contribute to women's oppression and empowerment. For example, Jewish and Christian feminists stand in tension with their traditions, neither completely dismissing nor completely endorsing the Bible and their communities' use of it, but subjecting it to criticism and reformulation. Other feminists subject to criticism the cultural impact of the Bible on women of specific cultures (A. Bach [1990; 1997]; J. C. Exum [1993, 1996]). For many feminists in developing nations, cultural critique and theological reformulation are simultaneous goals of LIBERATION theology and POST-COLONIAL INTERPRETATION (P-L. Kwok [1995]; M. Oduyoye [1992]).

Amid the diversity stands a core feminist conviction: Women are "by nature" neither inferior to nor derivative of men; nor do men "by nature" embody a normative humanity to which women are subordinated. Rather, women's humanity, with its attendant rights and responsibilities, including the authority to interpret sacred texts, must be acknowledged and respected by civil and religious communities. Feminist biblical interpretation presupposes women's authority to interpret Scripture, an authority systematically denied to women from early Christianity until recently. The duration of women's absence from the production of knowledge should not be eclipsed by the current acceptance and substantial development of feminist interpretation since the 1960s.

Focusing primarily on feminist interpretation of the Christian Bible and predominantly, on Christian feminist work in the United States, this article discusses: first, women's efforts to gain authority to interpret the Bible; second, issues in feminist HERMENEUTICS; and third, feminist biblical studies.

1. Gaining Authority to Interpret the Bible. *a. Historical overview.* Feminist biblical interpretation took root in the seventeenth century in Europe and in the United States and can be assigned to women's struggle not only to preach and teach the Bible but also to rid the world of slavery. The women involved did not use

the word *feminist* to describe themselves; that term gained widespread use only in the 1960s. But because they resisted the patriarchal assumption that women by nature are subordinate to men and hence must defer to men's judgments, they may be regarded as feminist precursors. (For the development of feminist consciousness, see G. Lerner [1993]; D. Riley [1988].)

i. Seventeenth and eighteenth centuries. Under the impact of the Protestant Reformation and its insistence that individual believers can interpret Scripture for themselves, several Protestant and sectarian Christian women of the seventeenth and eighteenth centuries claimed the authority to preach and to teach (e.g., Lady Eleanor Davis and Mrs. Attaway [1630s]; Anne Hutchinson [1591–1643]; Susanna Wesley [1670–1742]; for others see R. Tucker and W. Leifeld [1987] 171-244). These women justified their authority to interpret as being faithful to God's call for them to proclaim the truth of Scripture as they discerned it. For this stance many endured persecution and some suffered torture and death. For example, Mary Dyer (seventeenth century), angered by the Puritans' excommunication of Anne Hutchinson, spoke out on her behalf and was excommunicated and banished from this group. Nevertheless, Dyer returned to Boston to follow her call to preach and was executed by the Puritans in 1660. Shortly thereafter, Margaret Fell Fox's *Women's Speaking Justified* (1667) became a primary resource for the numerous biblical passages from Genesis to Revelation to which seventeenth-century women appealed for vindication. In addition, the Great Awakening of the eighteenth century, with its emphasis on individual conversion and salvation, opened doors for women to become active members in religious communities as they voted, led prayers, offered testimonies, and preached.

ii. Nineteenth century. The defense of women's preaching as faithfulness to God's call continued in the works of P. Palmer (1859), C. Booth (1860), and A. Smith (1893). Early in the nineteenth century, on the basis of their equality with men in both civil and spiritual life, women began to contest men's interpretation of certain biblical texts as justifying women's subordination. M. Stewart (1830s) was the first woman in the United States to advance issues of social justice and gender equality before an audience of both men and women (see K. Baker-Fletcher in L. Russell and J. S. Clarkson [1996] 316). S. Grimké's *Letters on the Equality of the Sexes* (1838) is a signal text that anticipated arguments on equality later advanced by feminist biblical scholars.

A. Brown Blackwell (1825–1921), the first woman ordained in any Christian denomination, composed a thorough exegesis of 1 Cor 14:34-35 and 1 Tim 2:11-12 as the culminating project of her theological program at Oberlin. Although Oberlin refused to matriculate her in the theological course of study, the school published her essay (1849). She argued that the texts in question applied solely to the historical context in which they were written and were not intended to silence women in the church for all times. F. Willard (1888), founder of the Women's Christian Temperance Union, the largest nineteenth-century women's organization, also defended women's equality, making women's suffrage more palatable by creatively linking it with prohibition. Willard argued that the home, the sacred responsibility of women, could only be protected from moral depravity by combining the vote of men and women to defeat the liquor industry (S. Lindley [1996] 104).

At the close of the century E. C. STANTON, in her increasingly well-known *The Woman's Bible* (1898), emphasized the control men exercised over the Bible and its interpretation. She produced *The Woman's Bible* to provoke women into examining Scripture for themselves and to illustrate how interpreters employed this text to subjugate women. Two others who championed the rights of women and slaves in the United States based on their understanding of the Christian Bible are S. TRUTH (1779–1883) and A. COOPER (1858–1964). Truth, considered one of the founders of black feminism, relied on intuition and on her personal relationship with God as she interpreted biblical texts. She argued that Jesus came into the world by the power of God and a woman; therefore, women have been and will be called to leadership roles in both the religious and the secular worlds. Cooper, who earned a PhD from the Sorbonne in 1925, promoted Truth's views on women, drawing on the historical Jesus as the model for social justice and equality among the sexes, races, and classes.

Women and men began not only to question the status of women but also to examine the nature and gender of God. One who emphasized the androgynous nature of God and established a new Christian movement was M. Baker Eddy (1821–1910). Basing her theology on Jesus' healing miracles, Eddy established the Church of Christ, Scientist in 1884, a church devoted to healing through the power of prayer and meditation without the use of traditional medicine. This movement quickly spread throughout the United States, helped along by her book *Science and Health* (1875, 1883²), which stressed that all reality is spiritual; sin, disease, and death are illusions that can be healed through mental discipline alone (Lindley [1996] 268-70). Christian Science opened doors for many women as they became leaders, healers, and missionaries, earning economic liberation. The addition of the Mother God in conjunction with a woman founder provided strong role models for women. Ironically, Eddy supported traditional gender roles and expelled potential women rivals from the movement, filling the executive offices with men.

iii. Twentieth century. Near the beginning of the century, K. Bushnell published a book of Bible studies (1905) that schooled women in textual and historical criticism of the Bible. Bushnell argued that the churches' resistance to women's equality and freedom in Christ was a fundamental scandal because it undermined central theological claims about soteriology. Like *The Woman's Bible,* however, her work was largely forgotten.

In Germany, H. JAHNOW expanded her role in teaching women the Bible to include working with H. GUNKEL, the pioneer of HB FORM CRITICISM. Jahnow's seminal study on Israelite laments (1923) remains relevant to HB studies. This and other works earned her the respect of the academy and an honorary doctorate in 1926, the highest degree then available for women in Germany. Until her death in the concentration camp at Theresienstadt, Jahnow was an outspoken proponent of women's rights and appealed to the academy and to the world to take women's scholarship seriously.

With the winning of suffrage in the United States in 1919, active political campaigning by women on a national scale ceased. Little has been written about women's preaching and teaching from the 1920s onward. Women were trained as professional biblical scholars in small numbers; most found teaching positions at women's colleges (D. Bass [1982]). Meanwhile, efforts in the church to expand women's responsibilities and leadership roles in denominations and polities continued with slow, incremental success (G. Harkness [1972]). Beginning in the late 1950s, theological schools and seminaries began to admit women in increasing numbers; the pace of admissions accelerated during the mid-1970s and early 1980s, a development that can be linked to the women's liberation movement, which began in the late 1960s.

M. Crook, a professor of biblical studies at Smith College, wrote the first book by a female professional biblical scholar in support of feminist concerns (1964). She concluded that religion "is man-formulated, man-approved, and man-directed." Shortly thereafter, K. Stendahl (1966) published the first book by a male professional biblical scholar on the issues of women's changing roles and biblical AUTHORITY. These two books and M. Daly's *The Church and the Second Sex* (1968), with its explicit reliance on feminist theory (see S. de Beauvoir [1952; ET 1989]), placed core feminist issues on the scholarly theological table. These issues include the historical and theological issue of women in patriarchal religions, the hermeneutical dimension of biblical authority, and the role of feminist theory as a theoretical resource for religious studies.

Feminist biblical studies emerged as an academic discipline in the 1980s. Again, historical reviews and assessments are few. However, it is clear that schools and departments responded (sometimes reluctantly) to women students' pressure for the hiring of feminist scholars as well as to (sometimes begrudging) acknowledgment of the quality of feminist scholarship and interpretation.

b. Exegetical arguments for women's authority to interpret the Bible. Traditional Christian exegesis maintained that women are subordinate to and derivative of men in the order of creation and that a woman's purpose is fulfilled in her relationship to her husband, unless she is called to the religious life. This understanding arose from reading the second creation story (Gen 2:4*b*–3:24) and PAUL's affirmation of men's headship over women (1 Cor 11:2-9). "Eve's curse" (Gen 3:16) was also invoked to legitimate men's rule over women in the fallen world; and 1 Tim 2:11-14 furthered the connection between Eve's actions and men's hegemony: "I permit no woman to teach or to have authority over a man; she is to keep silent. For Adam was formed first, then Eve; and Adam was not deceived, but the woman was deceived." Women's speaking or teaching was also prohibited on the basis of 1 Cor 14:34-35. Finally, texts that enjoined women to obey their husbands (Eph 5:22-24; Col 3:18-19; 1 Pet 3:1-6) were taken to mean that women's authority must be surrendered to their husbands and so to men in general.

Women proposed various interpretative strategies to respond to these readings. One was to reinterpret the passages adduced. A second was to adduce countertexts that legitimated women's exercise of authority. A third was to demonstrate inconsistencies and biases in men's translation, thereby differentiating what Scripture said from what men said.

i. Reinterpreting key passages. Against the argument from the order of creation it was asserted that the Bible is not a divine revelation of the natural order but a collection of ancient myths about the creation of the cosmos and humanity's place within it. To continue to treat the accounts of the origins of humanity uncritically in light of later knowledge is foolish (Stanton [1898]; Bushnell [1905]; R. R. Ruether [1979]). Instead, the myths need to be critically interpreted (V. R. Mollenkott [1977]). Moreover, some argued, the creation of woman from Adam's rib is a patriarchal inversion and subversion of women's power to give birth (Daly [1966] and Ruether [1979]).

Women also countered that "Adam," even in the second creation story, was not a male human being, but a sexually undifferentiated human being (Grimké [1838]; P. Trible [1978]). The subsequent creation of Adam and Eve did not render Eve subordinate or secondary (Grimké [1838]; Willard [1888]; Bushnell [1905]; Trible [1978]), nor did calling her "helper" (Trible [1978]).

Finally, in terms of Christian theology, even if woman was subordinated in the fall, the salvific activity of JESUS restored men and women in the Christian community to their original relationship of equality before God (L. Russell [1976]); to argue otherwise is to argue that Jesus' saving work was limited in scope (Bushnell [1905]; L. Scanzoni [1974]; N. Hardesty [1974]; P. Gundry [1987]).

In order to counter the explicit prohibitions of women's speaking, women interpreters contextualized Paul's remarks to the particular situation at Corinth. Because Paul accepted women praying and prophesying in Corinth, his prohibitions cannot be absolute. Some interpreters accounted for this inconsistency by alleging that 14:31-32 is an interpolation or that it is an instance of Paul's citing his adversaries (Bushnell [1905]). A similar strategy was applied to 1 Tim 2:15's prohibition of women teaching.

ii. Appealing to countertexts. Interpreters argued that the second creation story's account of the woman's creation is countered with the first (Gen 1:26-27), in which the human being is described as both "male and female" and created in the image of God. In opposition to the use of 1 Cor 11:8-9 as establishing the priority of the second creation account, women adduced 1 Cor 11:11-12 ("Though woman cannot do without man, neither can man do without woman in the Lord; woman may come from man, but man is born of woman") as implying mutuality. Similarly, women countered the scriptural demand that wives obey their husbands (Eph 5:22; Col 3:18) with the passage that reminded men of their responsibilities to or mutuality with their wives (Eph 5:23; Col 3:19). Against 1 Cor 11:3-9, which grants headship to man, women opposed Gal 3:28: "There are no more distinctions between Jew and Greek, slave and free, male and female, but all of you are one in Christ Jesus."

Finally, women produced texts that approve of women's speaking; e.g., John 20:21, in which Jesus sends Mary to announce his resurrection to the absent male disciples, and Matt 28:5-11, in which an angel as well as Jesus sends the women to carry news of the resurrection to the male disciples. Also, warrant is drawn from Peter's first speech after Pentecost (Acts 2:14-36), in which he cites the promises made in Joel 2:28-29: "I will pour out my spirit on all mankind. Their sons and daughters shall prophesy . . . even on my slaves, men and women, in those days I will pour out my spirit." Women also appealed to women in the HB who maintained positions of leadership and authority; e.g., Miriam, a prophet; Deborah, a prophet and judge; and Huldah, a prophet who authorized a newly discovered text as Scripture (see A. O. Bellis [1994]; L. Bronner [1994]).

iii. Demonstrating biases in men's translation. Grimké (1838) enumerated possible alternative translations and noted that an all-male clergy had a vested interest in women's subordination. Willard (1888) adduced numerous examples of biased translations, among them the issue of Phoebe as *diakonos* (deacon or deaconess) or as *prostatis* (elder or president). She suggested that male clergy tended to play down Phoebe's leadership by calling her deaconess rather than deacon, a title suggesting significant church leadership. About a decade later Bushnell analyzed the problem as "sex bias," rooted simply in privileged control of the text:

"Supposing women only had translated the Bible, from age to age, is there a likelihood that men would have rested content with the outcome? Therefore, our brothers have no good reason to complain if, while conceding that men had done the best they could alone, we assert that they did not do the best that could have been done" ([1905] 372). In addition, M. Royden (1924) and L. Starr (1926) demonstrated the existence of "sex bias" in men's translations of biblical passages concerning women's leadership positions.

iv. Conclusion. By the 1970s the cumulative effect of these interpretive strategies made evident that direct appeal to the Bible's stance on women's subordination was little more than proof-texting justified on grounds other than simply that "the Bible said so." Further, the distinction between the Bible as "man's word" and as "God's Word" indicated that gender as well as historical context is a factor in contextualization and interpretation.

2. Feminist Biblical Hermeneutics. Feminist biblical hermeneutics explicates feminists' self-understanding in relation to biblical interpretation. Since much contemporary hermeneutical theory asserts that consciousness and text are mutually constituted through the process of interpretation, a key problem for feminist interpretation is whether feminists can find anything of value or, to put it theologically, anything revelatory in the Bible once its patriarchal and androcentric character is confronted. (C. Osiek [1985] offers a useful typology of feminist positions on this point.) A second key problem concerns the scope of feminist hermeneutics: Because no text comes unmediated, feminists cannot focus on the Bible as if it were a free-floating object but must contend with traditions of interpretation and their historical effects.

a. Evaluating the patriarchal Bible as Scripture. Even when translated without the distortions of sex bias, the Bible remains at least a product of the ancient patriarchal culture in which it originated and of the patriarchal cultures that transmitted it. A fundamental question is whether the Bible is anything more than an oppressive, patriarchal text; if it is not, feminist interest calls for its summary rejection. Among feminists who have rejected the Bible as an authority are Stanton (1895), M. J. Gage (1900), Daly (1966), and D. Hampson (1990).

For other feminists, awareness that women claim the Bible as a significant religious authority and source of empowerment cautions against dismissing it as simply and solely patriarchal. Women's testimony to the power of the Bible cannot be attributed simply to false consciousness; doing so gives too much power to patriarchal tradition and insufficiently respects women's subjectivity. Respecting the dual effect of the Bible as friend and enemy (M. A. Tolbert [1983]) requires a critical approach to the text.

To use terms proposed by Osiek (1984), loyalists affirm the essential validity and goodness of the biblical tradition as the Word of God; when correctly interpreted the Bible affirms women's full humanity (L. Scanzoni and N. Hardesty [1984]; P. Gundry [1987]; V. Mollenkott [1977]; A. Mickelsen [1986]). Revisionists distinguish the contingent patriarchal dimension of biblical texts from the enduring theological values expressed therein (P. Trible [1978, 1984]). Liberationists affirm God's concern for justice and liberation from oppression, locating that affirmation in biblical authority (Ruether [1979]; Russell [1976]) or in the community working for liberation (E. Schüssler Fiorenza [1984]).

b. Dealing with tradition. Feminists bring a variety of concerns to their reading of the Bible. Historically, its teachings about women's status and relationships with men have been of great concern; but other issues have demanded attention as well.

i. Discovering women in the Bible. As women affirmed the intrinsic value of their experience in opposition to its androcentric marginalization, they sought themselves "in" the text, as historical figures and as literary images. Rather than ponder David and Saul, women wondered about Michal and Bathsheba; rather than ask if Paul silenced women, they inquired after Chloe, Junia, Syntyche, and Euodia (F. Gillman [1992]). Women asked why Sarah dismissed Hagar; why Martha is not praised; and why, if women learned about the resurrection first, they are excluded from ordination.

Contrary to male-dominated readings, feminists noted imagery from women's experience with pregnancy, mothering, and nurture; domestic work and marriage as metaphors for the relationship between the deity and humanity. God's wisdom is personified as a woman in Proverbs, and women's delight in sexuality is affirmed by the Song of Songs.

ii. Inclusive language. Having discovered women in every layer of biblical tradition, from female judges to women missionaries, and having found female imagery for God and the kingdom of God, feminists insisted that liturgies and translations acknowledge women's presence and cease to render them invisible by exclusive use of androcentric language (N. Morton [1985]; A. M. Bennett [1989]) and by excluding texts about women from the lectionary (M. Procter-Smith [1990]). Feminists also described the pain of invisibility and the fragmentation that comes with reading themselves into male-defined language (Morton [1985]; Bennett [1989]). They proposed that female imagery of God, like "Bakerwoman God," "Mother God," and "Sophia," be used in prayers, hymns, liturgy, and theology (B. Bowe [1992]; M. Winter [1990]).

iii. The maleness of Jesus. As feminists clarified the value of female identity and self, they wrestled with the significance of Jesus' maleness. C. Christ (1987) argued that women needed to envision the divine as female, and Ruether asked, "Can a male saviour save women?"

(1979). The response to the statue Christa, which depicts a crucified woman, has shown how charged is the issue of Jesus' maleness, on the one hand, and women's suffering under men's domination, on the other. Christian feminists also examined Jesus' relationship to women as a warrant for changing gender roles in contemporary churches.

iv. Sexual violence. Feminists worked to free women's sexuality from men's control and from its association with sin, forged in the portrayal of Eve's transgression. Acutely conscious, for example, that rapists and batterers would assert that the women provoked or asked for the violence, women angrily read Adam's blaming Eve as his refusing responsibility. Feminists grieved over the concubine raped and dismembered (Judges 19) and for the sacrifice of Jephthah's daughter (Judg 11:34-40), and they pondered why women's bodies are repeatedly violated in biblical texts (see Gal 4:21-31; Rev 2:18-29, 17:15-18; also D. Fewell and D. Gunn [1993]).

Feminists working in rape crisis centers and shelters for battered women listened to Christian women explain their shame at failing to endure suffering that would rescue their husbands and tell how teachings about obedience to husbands and fathers (Eph 5:21-23; Col 3:18-19; 1 Pet 3:1-3) left them with no sense of a right to reject sexual abuse and with intense guilt over their anger and sinfulness (S. Thistlethwaite [1985]). Feminists wrestle with reinterpreting such texts and search for biblical perspectives that can assist women to heal from the trauma of sexual abuse.

c. Social location and biblical hermeneutics. Feminist theory affirms differences among women and complicates its analysis of women's experience by wrestling with elements of particularity. Women's social location, the community and heritage from which a given feminist emerges and finds support, and issues of race, class, sexual preference, and gender become subject to hermeneutical reflection. Thus feminist biblical hermeneutics from a white, Western, middle-class perspective might focus on gender oppression and issues of subordination to men but not wrestle with other forms of oppression, like poverty and racism. Feminist biblical hermeneutics has become aware of the need to pay greater attention to articulating the role of factors of social location in its self-understanding so that its self-description does not marginalize important members of its constituency. Attending to social location honors the diversity of women's experience and enriches the store of reading strategies for and insights into biblical texts. For example, R. N. Brock (1993) draws on the Japanese American tradition of honoring mature insight to formulate a hermeneutics of wisdom for understanding women's relationship to the CANON. This relationship is ambiguous and paradoxical because the Bible serves as a source for both freedom and oppression. A hermeneutics of wisdom takes seriously the need to incorporate Asian cultural experience and history into the reading of texts, the need to reject innocence as a biblical virtue, since it often reinforces victimization, and the need to retain the multilayered dimensions of those interpreting the Bible (Brock [1993] 64-5). MUJERISTA biblical scholars approach the Bible with the lens of liberation (see Schüssler Fiorenza [1993] for this and other feminist/womanist biblical approaches).

An outgrowth of feminist biblical hermeneutics is WOMANIST INTERPRETATION (from a term coined by A. Walker [1983] xi-xii). According to K. Baker Fletcher, "contemporary womanists challenge interlocking systems of oppression: racism, classism, homophobia, and ecological abuses" (in Russell and Clarkson [1996] 316). J. Grant (1989) emphasizes the survival strategies involved in womanist thought, while D. Williams (1993) declares womanists to be those who name their own experience. Womanists believe that mainline feminism has failed to acknowledge the complexities women of color face as members of at least two socially oppressed groups. For example, Williams argues that black women broaden the scope of patriarchy and consider white women to be participants in both patriarchy and black women's oppression. Even though both groups of women are exploited, there are different levels of exploitation; thus the unique experience of slavery and/or racism affects a womanist interpretation of biblical texts. Also, white feminism often silences the voices of women of color (including those in biblical texts) providing the need for womanist interpretations of the Bible. R. Weems (1991) proposes an investigation into all silenced voices in the text. This principle opens a doorway for analyzing women's complicity in women's oppression, class oppression, and ethnographic composition.

d. The scope of feminist biblical hermeneutics. Schüssler Fiorenza differentiates feminist biblical hermeneutics into a fourfold model of interrelated aspects. The need for a complex model arises from the many uses to which the Bible is put and from the conviction that women must become fully responsible for interpretation.

Because women have been excluded from the production of knowledge, feminists assume that the knowledge they inherit serves male-dominated interests and cannot be accepted as "critical" or "objective" knowledge. Critical analysis calls for a hermeneutics of suspicion toward tradition and traditional interpretations of biblical texts and for unmasking patriarchal assumptions that render women invisible, marginal, or incidental to the text or issue under discussion. The next interpretative task is to engage in a hermeneutics of remembrance that reconstructs women's historical agency in foundational Christian tradition. This requires critical methods for interpreting inclusive language and for considering canonical and extra-canonical sources. The aim of this (re)interpretation is both to contest the patriarchal view of Christian origins as transmitted solely by men by constructing an alternative historical account and to empower women by restoring to them a past. Because the Bible is used as a source for theology, ethics, and policy formation, feminists also engage in a hermeneutics of proclamation that relates the reconstructed traditions to contemporary community life. Last, a hermeneutics of imagination is called for in recognition that not all knowledge is cognitive, by which contemporary women express empowering traditions in ritual, prayer, and creative means such as hymns, banners, and art.

Schüssler Fiorenza's model indicates the necessary breadth of feminist biblical hermeneutics and suggests a means for integrating critical biblical studies with other theological disciplines.

3. Feminist Biblical Studies. Feminist biblical studies developed rapidly over the 1980s and 1990s and has become increasingly sophisticated in its recasting of critical biblical studies and in its methods. Resistance to feminist biblical studies is rooted partly in the continuing sexism of academic institutions and theological education and partly in the centrality the notion of objectivity has had in critical biblical studies. Mainstream biblical scholarship has prided itself on its objectivity in the study of the Bible and has grounded that objectivity in methodology. Since feminist theory and criticism are invested in social change and the transformation of knowledge, their validity as critical disciplines is suspect. Feminist biblical scholars have argued strenuously that the vaunted ideal of objectivity masks male-dominated investments in interpreting the Bible as a patriarchal text. Feminist historical criticism and LITERARY criticism demonstrate the ideological investment of male-dominated biblical scholarship by contesting key assumptions regarding methods and by offering alternative historical reconstructions and literary analyses.

a. Feminist historical criticism. This form of criticism reconstructs biblical history as women's history by investigating the historical experience of women in biblical times and the role of women in shaping tradition.

i. Feminist historical criticism of the NT. The NT provides ample evidence of women's agency in early Christianity. There are many texts that name women or in which women act. This may seem to be an obvious point, but traditional historical criticism pays little attention to their presence. Even a cursory listing of women whom Paul commends demonstrates that women contributed to the spread of early Christianity. Phoebe, "a deacon of the church at Cenchreae" (Rom 16:1); Mary, "who has worked very hard" (16:6); Junia, "outstanding among the apostles" (Rom 16:7); Prisca, a deacon and a "benefactor of many" (16:1-2); Chloe, a leader (1 Cor 1:10); Mary (Rom 16:6); Tryphaena and Tryphosa (Rom 16:12); and Euodia and Syntyche (Phil 4:2-3) are all lauded for their leadership on behalf of the church.

Given such textual evidence from Paul's letters and adding to it evidence from the narratives in the Gospels and Acts and the many extra-canonical traditions with reports about female Christian disciples, the decision to leave women's history unexplored reveals the selectivity with which "objective" historical criticism proceeds. Schüssler Fiorenza argues that historical reconstruction cannot evade selectivity because paradigms and frameworks govern historical reasoning. Her intent is not to establish feminist historical criticism as more objective than androcentric historical criticism but to demonstrate that every criticism and reconstruction serves interests. Such demonstration offers the possibility of regrounding the critical element of biblical studies in public discourse through evaluation of theological warrants, hermeneutical and historical paradigms, and political concerns.

ii. Examples of feminist historical reconstruction of Christian origins. Feminist interpreters have examined Jesus' relationships with women in order to counter the sexism they experience and to provide a higher authority than Paul, whose proscriptions were adduced against women's teaching with authority. Many concluded that Jesus liberated women from their secondary and degraded status in Judaism by treating them as equals and by ignoring ritual purity concerns (C. Parvey [1974]; L. Swidler [1971]; E. Tetlow [1980]). Yet the reconstruction suggesting that emergent Christianity liberated women from an oppressive Judaism was seriously flawed by anti-Semitic depictions of the Judaism of Jesus' time (J. Plaskow [1990]; Schüssler Fiorenza [1993]; K. von Kellenbach [1994]). Critical response to this reconstruction has generated more complete historical knowledge of Jewish, Christian, and pagan women in antiquity and alternative models for understanding the appeal of early Christianity to women.

Through epigraphical and archaeological means B. Brooten (1982, 1985) has established that Jewish women exercised leadership and patronage in synagogues. R. Kraemer (1988, 1992) has assembled primary sources for the study of women and religion in antiquity and offered a SOCIAL-SCIENTIFIC account of the relative appeal of religions to women in ancient times, while L. Schottroff (1995) has investigated the social and material history of women. Schüssler Fiorenza (1983) has offered a theological reconstruction of Christian origins as a renewal movement within Judaism that proffered men and women "a discipleship of equals," a non-patriarchal vision imperfectly embodied and ultimately suppressed by the second century. By means of rhetorical criticism A. Wire (1990) has reconstructed the theology of the women prophets at Corinth whom Paul opposed. A.-J. Levine (1994) has demonstrated that feminists require a clearer understanding of early Christianity and Judaism. Misconceptions have led many Christian feminists to declare Jesus a feminist based on the belief that he overrode the "oppressive purity laws" of the day. Levine argues that it is unclear that the purity laws were in effect or were being followed during the first century. Moreover, if they were followed, it is uncertain that these laws were deemed oppressive by those practicing them.

iii. Women and the HB. Several issues have dominated feminist historical studies of the HB: e.g., the contributions of women in the various historical layers (patriarchal times through postexilic Israel); the status of women in ancient Israelite society and cult; and the problems related to sexuality that led many women to explore fertility cults, goddess worship, and intermarriage with the indigenous population.

In the 1970s and early 1980s the study of the status of women in the HB, especially in the patriarchal narratives and law codes, frequently served to demonstrate the feminist claim that the Bible's patriarchal society was oppressive to women. The stories of violence against women (Genesis 34; Judges 11; 19; 1 Kings 13; 2 Kings 9) displayed men's disregard for women's humanity. The patriarchal narratives showed that the tradition regarded women as significant solely because they produce sons for the patriarch. Study of the teachings about women in the ancient cult, which underscored their exclusion from key cultic practices such as the priesthood, were often preparatory for the study of the NT's interpretation of religious leadership.

Since the mid 1980s some critical works have emerged that contest the portrait of the HB as oppressively patriarchal. C. Meyers (1988) has used social-scientific models of preindustrial agrarian societies and HB texts to argue that women in premonarchical Israel were regarded with respect and had, if not leadership authority, significant power in their families because of their economic contributions to the household. A. Brenner (1985) has argued for a necessary distinction between the literary representation of women in the text and the social roles women may have actually played. P. Bird (1997) has recognized the need to recast the categories for studying women's religious experience, since categories cast in terms of leadership or cultic practice rendered women invisible (see P. Day [1989] for a reconceptualization of the gender roles in the HB).

b. Feminist literary criticism. Feminist literary criticism challenges the claim to objectivity in critical biblical studies. Those espousing objectivity assume that the reader of the text neither distorts nor informs it; the text is understood to surrender information in response to disciplined critical analysis. Feminist literary critics question the neutral role of the reader in even the most preliminary reading of the text and offer critical tools for studying the construction of meaning. Two major trends have developed: NARRATIVE CRITICISM and READER-RESPONSE CRITICISM. Narrative criticism examines the construction, representation, characterization, and image of women in the text to uncover how rhetoric

may function ideologically. Feminist interest in the construction of meaning and in reader response has been complemented by trends in poststructuralist literary theory.

M. Bal (1988) has drawn on SEMIOTICS and STRUCTURALISM to apply a feminist narratological approach to the book of Judges. She notes an ideological and political coherence that is reflected in the manner women are treated in the text. Traditional interpretations of Judges are gender biased; they center around the judges themselves, focusing on political and military situations (the realm of men) instead of on the private sphere (the realm of women). Bal considers such interpretations to be examples of a political coherence that "functions as closure; it allows critics to escape the painful experience of awareness of the deep-seated relationship between social institutions and violence against women" (1988, 237). This political coherence, she argues, has allowed many interpreters to insist that Judges 17–21, chapters containing stories of extreme violence toward hundreds of women, are an appendix to the book. Bal disagrees and provides a "counter coherence" that concentrates on the marginalized, who live predominantly in the private sphere where, in Judges, women are murdered (Jephthah's daughter, Samson's first wife, the Levite's concubine), whereas men are murdered by women in the public sphere (Sisera, Abimelech, and Samson).

T. Pippin (1992) applies rhetorical and gender criticism to the book of Revelation as she examines the literary portrayals of the four feminine figures in this apocalypse (see APOCALYPTICISM). Apocalyptic literature, she argues, serves a cathartic function by helping the reader to expunge unwanted feelings. In Revelation women become the victims and scapegoats for male catharsis as men throw all of the evils and problems of the world onto the bodies of women. For example, two desires are acting simultaneously in the text: the desire for wealth and power, represented in the bodies of the whore of Babylon and the prophet called Jezebel; and the desire for God's world, represented in the bodies of the woman clothed in the sun and the bride of Christ. These desires generate an ambiguous and dualistic portrayal of women and their bodies. In order to choose good over bad it is necessary to annihilate the "bad" women; therefore, both the whore and Jezebel are violently destroyed. In contrast, the "good" women are controlled (the bride) or sent away for safe keeping (the woman clothed in the sun). Pippin concludes that the apocalypse is not a safe place for women.

R. Weems (1995) explores the sexual and sexist metaphors employed by Hosea, Jeremiah, and Ezekiel to ascertain their capacity to condone sexist human power. She is motivated by such questions as why the prophets chose to humiliate women and their bodies to demonstrate God's love for the people and why there is such a fascination with naked, mangled female bodies.

Weems builds on gender and on literary, sociological, and IDEOLOGICAL CRITICISM to explore these sexual metaphors.

Bal, Pippin, and Weems exemplify three of the feminist literary approaches that biblical scholars apply to biblical texts. Other feminist literary critics choose to focus on the images of women in the texts; however, there are limitations to such an approach. First, looking for images of good women promotes selectivity. For example, regarding the Gospel of Mark, arguments that women exemplify true discipleship systematically overlook the evil woman Herodias. Selective focus on the goodness of women, which is valuable in countering alienation and misogyny or sexist dismissal of women, can itself contribute to the stereotype that women are by nature more moral and more religious than men. Second, the images, especially of bad women but even of good women, were produced by men and should be subjected to critique. For example, E. Fuchs's (1985) study of the characterization of women as deceptive excellently demonstrates how narrative treatment of women can confirm—e.g., by not giving their motives—the patriarchal ideology about women being deceitful. Similarly, the image of Wisdom in Proverbs is problematic. Both Lady Wisdom (good) and Lady Folly (bad) call out in the city for the young men. From all outward appearances both women are the same, serving only to confuse young men and reinforcing the belief that women are not to be trusted. Because of midleading images in the Gospel of Luke, T. Seim (1994), J. Schaberg (1987), and B. Reid (1996) have all leveled significant challenges to reading Luke as a book that empowers women.

A new trend in literary criticism and reader-response criticism is cultural criticism (see CULTURAL STUDIES). Bach (1997) and Exum (1996) apply this critical method to issues of gender as they compare biblical texts with their representations in art and film. Both argue that readers are often influenced by these cultural representations of biblical women and bring these pre- (and sometimes mis-) conceptions to their readings of biblical texts.

J. Fetterly (1978) argues that the very process of reading androcentric literature causes women to define themselves in terms opposed to their identity as women. Biblical texts systematically mislead women by asking them to identify with the hero rather than with the heroine. Women read a narrative about Samson, for example, and identify with Samson, not Delilah; or they read about and identify with David, not Bathsheba. Fetterly's analysis clarifies how it is possible to ignore the female characters in the Bible and proposes that feminists intentionally read against the grain, distancing themselves from the male point of view by focusing on marginalized voices. This tack permits rereading biblical narratives not only by observing the marginalizing of

female characters but also by reconstructing the voice of the silenced or marginalized reader. Bach (1997) does this with Michal and Abigail.

Feminists insist that reading is interested rather than neutral. This insistence leads to readings grounded in and exploratory of the variety of social locations from which women read. Analyses of and from social locations do not dispense with gender as a category but chart or theorize its interactions with other factors in women's experience, e.g., class or status; race, ethnicity, or culture; geo-political concerns; and sexual preference.

4. Future Directions. In its first two decades feminist biblical interpretation succeeded in establishing the importance of feminist theory and criticism. This accomplishment required contesting traditional gender roles, especially the assumption that women are not authoritative interpreters of the Bible. In the future other dimensions of gender will need to be studied, with an emphasis on the interrelation of gender, religion, and sexuality.

Because of the effort to draw attention to women's absence from biblical interpretation, feminists have stressed women's experience and readings. As greater numbers of women have taken up biblical studies, tensions among women have revealed fundamental questions: How is the diversity of feminist standpoints to be negotiated? Must feminist theory have a "dream of a common language," and if so, how would consent to that dream be secured? What is the relationship between feminist cultural criticism and feminist theological hermeneutics? What is the relationship between academic feminist scholars and feminists outside of academia? All of these questions and more will be food for thought in years to come.

Bibliography: **A. Bach,** *Ad Feminam* (USQR 43, 1989); (ed.), *The Pleasure of Her Text: Feminist Readings of Biblical and Historical Texts* (1990); *Women, Seduction, and Betrayal in Biblical Narrative* (1997). **K. Baker-Fletcher,** *A Singing Something: Womanist Reflections on Anna Julia Cooper* (1994). **M. Bal,** *Murder and Difference: Gender, Genre, and Scholarship on Sisera's Death* (ISBL, 1988). **D. C. Bass,** "Women's Studies and Biblical Studies: An Historical Perspective," *JSOT* 22 (1982) 6-12. **A. M. Bennett,** *From Woman-Pain to Woman-Vision: Writings in Feminist Theology by A. McGrew Bennett* (ed. M. E. Hunt, 1989). **P. Bird,** *Missing Persons and Mistaken Identities: Women and Gender in Ancient Israel* (OBT, 1997). **M. Booth,** *Female Ministry: Or, Woman's Right to Preach the Gospel* (1860, 1975). **S. de Beauvoir,** *The Second Sex* (1952; ET 1989). **B. Bowe** (ed.), *Silent Voices, Sacred Lives: Women's Readings for the Liturgical Year* (1992). **A. Brenner,** *The Israelite Woman: Social Role and Literary Type in Biblical Narrative* (1985); (ed.), *The Feminist Companion to the HB* (10 vols., 1993–96). **A. Brenner and C. Fontaine** (eds.), *A Feminist Companion to Reading the Bible: Approaches, Methods, and Stategies* (Feminist Companion to the Bible 1-11, 1997).

R. N. Brock, "Dusting the Floor: A Hermeneutics of Wisdom," *Searching the Scriptures: A Feminist Commentary* (ed. E. Schüssler Fiorenza, 1993) 1:64-75. **L. L. Bronner,** *From Eve to Esther: Rabbinic Reconstructions of Biblical Women* (1994). **B. J. Brooten,** " 'Junia . . . Outstanding Among the Apostles' (Rom 16:7)," *Women Priests: A Catholic Commentary on the Vatican Declaration* (ed. L. Swidler and A. Swidler, 1977) 141-44; *Women Leaders in the Ancient Synagogue* (BJS 36, 1982); "Early Christian Women and Their Cultural Context: Issues of Method in Historical Reconstruction," *Feminist Perspectives on Biblical Scholarship* (ed. A. Y. Collins, BSNA 10, 1985) 65-91; *Love Between Women: Early Christian Responses to Female Homoeroticism* (Chicago Series on Sexuality, History, and Society, 1996). **A. L. Brown,** "Exegesis of I Corinthians XIV, 34, 35 and I Timothy II, 11, 12," *Oberlin Quarterly* (1849). **K. C. Bushnell,** *God's Word to Women: One Hundred Bible Studies on Women's Place in the Divine Economy* (1905; repr., ed. R. B. Munson, 1976). **K. G. Cannon,** "The Emergence of Black Feminist Consciousness," *Feminist Interpretation of the Bible* (ed. L. M. Russell, 1985); *Black Womanist Ethics* (1988); *Katie's Canon: Womanism and the Soul of the Black Community* (1995). **E. A. Castelli,** "Les Belles Infidèles/ Fidelity or Feminism? The Meanings of Feminist Biblical Translation," *JFSR* 6 (1990) 25-39. **C. Christ,** *The Laughter of Aphrodite: Reflections on a Journey to the Goddess* (1987). **A. Y. Collins,** (ed.), *Feminist Perspectives on Biblical Scholarship* (BSNA 10, 1985). **K. E. Corley,** *Private Women, Public Meals: Social Conflict in the Synoptic Tradition* (1993). **M. B. Crook,** *Women and Religion* (1964). **M. Daly,** *The Church and the Second Sex* (1966). **M. R. D'Angelo,** "Women Partners in the NT," *JFSR* 6 (1990) 65-86. **P. L. Day** (ed.), *Gender and Difference in Ancient Israel* (1989). **V. B. Demarest,** *God, Woman, and Ministry* (1978). **P. Demers,** *Women as Interpreters of the Bible* (1992). **S. E. Dowd,** "H. B. Montgomery's Centenary Translation of the NT: Characteristics and Influences," *PerspRelStud* 19 (1992) 133-50. **J. C. Exum,** *Fragmented Women: Feminist (Sub)versions of Biblical Narratives* (1993); *Plotted, Shot, and Painted: Cultural Representations of Biblical Women* (JSOTSup 125; Gender, Culture, Theory 3, 1996). **M. A. Farley,** "Feminist Consciousness and the Interpretation of Scripture," *Feminist Interpretation of the Bible* (ed. L. M. Russell, 1985). **J. Fetterley,** *The Resisting Reader: A Feminist Approach to American Fiction* (1978). **D. N. Fewell and D. M. Gunn,** *Gender, Power, and Promise: The Subject of the Bible's First Story* (1993). **M. A. F. Fox,** *Women's Speaking Justified* (1667). **E. Fuchs,** "Who Is Hiding the Truth? Deceptive Women and Biblical Androcentrism," *Feminist Perspectives on Biblical Scholarship* (ed. A. Y. Collins, BSNA 10, 1985) 137-44. **M. J. Gage,** *Woman, Church, State* (1900, 1972). **F. M. Gillman,** *Women Who Knew Paul* (Zacchaeus Studies NT, 1992). **J. Grant,** *White Woman's Christ and Black Women's Jesus: Feminist Christology and Womanist Response* (1989); (ed.), *Perspectives on Womanist Theology* (1995). **S. M. Grimké,** *Letters on the Equality of the Sexes* (1838). **P. Gundry,** *Neither Slave nor Free: Helping Women Answer the Call to Church Leadership* (1987). **D. D. Hampson,** *Theology and Feminism* (Signposts in Theology, 1990). **G. E. Harkness,** *Women in Church and Society: A Histori-* *cal and Theological Inquiry* (1972). **S. Heine,** *Women and Early Christianity: A Reappraisal* (tr. J. Bowden, 1988; Ger., *Frauen der frühen Christenheit* [1987]). **T. Ilan,** *Jewish Women in Greco-Roman Palestine: An Inquiry into Image and Status* (TSAJ 44, 1995). **A. M. Isasi-Díaz and Y. Tarango,** *Hispanic Women* (Prophetic Voice in the Church, 1988). **H. Jahnow,** *Das Hebraische Leichenlied im Rahmen der Völkerdichtung* (BZAW 36, 1923). **R. Kraemer,** *Maenads, Martyrs, Matrons, Monastics: A Source-book on Women's Religions in the Greco-Roman World* (1988); *Her Share of the Blessings: Women's Religions Among Pagans, Jews, and Christians in the Greco-Roman World* (1992). **C. C. Kroeger and J. K. Beck,** *Women, Abuse, and the Bible: How Scripture Can Be Used to Hurt or to Heal* (1996). **R. C. Kroeger and C. C. Kroeger,** *I Suffer Not a Woman to Speak: Rethinking 1 Tim 2:11-15 in Light of Ancient Evidence* (1992). **P. Kwok,** "Racism and Ethnocentrism in Feminist Biblical Interpretation," *Searching the Scriptures: A Feminist Introduction* (ed. E. Schüssler Fiorenza, 1993) 1:101-166; *Discovering the Bible in the Non-Biblical World* (Bible and Liberation Series, 1995). **A. L. Laffey,** *An Introduction to the OT: A Feminist Perspective* (1988). **G. Lerna,** *The Creation of Feminist Consciousness from the Middle Ages to 1870* (Women and History 2, 1993). **A.-J. Levine** (ed.), *"Women Like This": New Perspectives on Jewish Women in the Greco-Roman World* (Early Judaism and Its Literature 1, 1991); "Second Temple Judaism, Jesus, and Women," *BibInt* 2 (1994) 8-33. **S. H. Lindley,** *"You Have Stept Out of Your Place: A History of Women and Religion in America* (1996). **C. L. Meyers,** *Discovering Eve: Ancient Israelite Women in Context* (1988). **A. Mickelsen** (ed.), *Women, Authority, and the Bible* (1986). **V. R. Mollenkott,** *Women, Men, and the Bible* (1988). **E. Moltmann-Wendel,** *The Women Around Jesus: Reflections on Authentic Personhood* (1982). **L. A. Moody** (ed.), *Women Encounter God: Theology Across the Boundaries of Difference* (1996). **N. Morton,** *The Journey Is Home* (1985). **W. Munro,** "Women Disciples in Mark?" *CBQ* 44 (1982) 225-41. **C. A. Newsom and S. H. Ringe** (eds.), *The Women's Bible Commentary* (1992, 1998[2]). **J. Nunnally-Fox,** *Foremothers: Women of the Bible* (1981). **M. A. Oduyoye and M. R. A. Kanyoro** (eds.), *The Will to Arise: Women, Tradition, and the Church in Africa* (1992). **A. Ogden Bellis,** *Helpmates, Harlots, Heroes: Women's Stories in the HB* (1994). **C. Osiek,** *Beyond Anger: On Being a Feminist in the Church* (1984); "The Feminist and the Bible: Hermeneutical Alternatives" *Feminist Perspectives on Biblical Scholarship* (ed. A. Y. Collins, BSNA 10, 1985); "Reading the Bible as Women," *NIB* (1994) 1:181-87. **P. Palmer,** *Promise of the Father, or a Neglected Speciality of the Last Days* (1859, 1981). **C. Parvey,** "The Theology and Leadership of Women in the NT," *Religion and Sexism* (ed. R. R. Ruether, 1974) 117-49. **M. D. Pellauer,** *Toward a Tradition of Feminist Theology: The Religious Social Thought of E. C. Stanton, S. B. Anthony, and A. H. Shaw* (Chicago Studies in the History of American Religion 15, 1991). **M. Peskowitz,** *Spinning Fantasies: Rabbis, Gender, and History* (Contraversions 9, 1997). **T. Pippin,** *Death and Desire: The Rhetoric of Gender in the Apocalypse of John* (1992). **J. Plaskow,** *Standing Again at Sinai: Judaism from a Feminist Perspective* (1990); "Anti-Judaism in Feminist Christian Interpretation," *Searching* the Scriptures: A Feminist Commentary (ed. E. Schüssler Fiorenza, 1993) 117-29. **M. Procter-Smith,** *In Her Own Rite: Constructing Feminist Liturgical Tradition* (1990). **B. E. Reid,** *Choosing the Better Part? Women in the Gospel of Luke* (1996). **I. Richter Reimer,** *Women in the Acts of the Apostles: A Feminist Liberation Perspective* (1995). **D. Riley,** *Am I That Name? Feminism and the Category of "Women" in History* (Language, Discourse, Society, 1988). **S. H. Ringe,** "A Gentile Woman's Story," *Feminist Interpretation of the Bible* (ed. L. M. Russell, 1985). **R. R. Ruether and E. McLaughlin** (eds.), *Women of Spirit: Female Leadership in the Jewish and Christian Traditions* (1979). **A. M. Royden,** *The Church and Woman* (The Living Church, 1924). **L. M. Russell** (ed.), *The Liberating Word: A Guide to Non-Sexist Interpretation of the Bible* (1976); (ed.), *Feminist Interpretation of the Bible* (1985). **L. M. Russell and J. S. Clarkson,** *Dictionary of Feminist Theologies* (1996). **L. D. Scanzoni and N. A. Hardesty,** *All We're Meant to Be: Biblical Feminism for Today* (1974; rev. ed., 1992³). **A. J. Schmidt,** *Veiled and Silenced: How Culture Shaped Sexist Theology* (1989). **J. Schaberg,** *The Illegitimacy of Jesus: A Feminist Theological Interpretation of the Infancy Narratives* (1987). **S. M. Schneiders,** *Women and the Word: The Gender of God in the NT and the Spirituality of Women* (Madeleva Lecture in Spirituality, 1986). **L. Schottroff,** *Let the Oppressed Go Free: Feminist Perspectives on the NT* (1993); *Lydia's Impatient Sisters: A Feminist Social History of Early Christianity* (1995). **E. Schüssler Fiorenza,** *In Memory of Her: A Feminist Theological Reconstruction of Christian Origins* (1983); *Bread Not Stone: The Challenge of Feminist Biblical Interpretation* (1984); *But She Said: Feminist Practices of Biblical Interpretation* (1992); (ed.), *Searching the Scriptures: A Feminist Commentary* (2 vols, 1993-94). **T. K. Seim,** *The Double Message: Patterns of Gender in Luke–Acts* (Studies of the NT and Its World, 1994). **M. J. Selvidge,** *Notorious Voices: Feminist Biblical Interpretation, 1550–1920* (1996). **A. Smith,** *An Autobiography: The Story of the Lord's Dealings with Mrs. A. Smith, the Colored Evangelist* (1893, 1988). **E. Stagg and F. Stagg,** *Woman in the World of Jesus* (1978). **L. A. Starr,** *The Bible Status of Women* (1926). **E. C. Stanton,** *The Woman's Bible* (2 vols., 1895-98). **K. Stendahl,** *The Bible and the Role of Women: A Case Study in Hermeneutics* (Facet Books Biblical Series 15, 1966). **C. de Swarte Gifford,** "American Women and the Bible: The Nature of Woman as a Hermeneutical Issue," *Feminist Perspectives on Biblical Scholarship* (ed. A. Y. Collins, BSNA 10, 1985) 11-33. **L. J. Swidler,** "Jesus Was a Feminist," SEAJT 13 (1971) 102-10; *Biblical Affirmations of Woman* (1979). **E. M. Tetlow,** *Women and Ministry in the NT* (1980). **S. B. Thistlethwaite,** "Every Two Minutes: Battered Women and Feminist Interpretation" *Feminist Interpretation of the Bible* (ed. L. M. Russell, 1985). **M. A. Tolbert** (ed.), *The Bible and Feminist Hermeneutics* (Semeia 28, 1983). **E. M. Townes** (ed.), *Embracing the Spirit: Womanist Perspectives on Hope, Salvation, and Transformation* (1997). **P. Trible,** *God and the Rhetoric of Sexuality* (OBT 13, 1978); *Texts of Terror: Literary-Feminist Readings of Biblical Narratives* (1984). **R. A. Tucker and W. L. Liefeld,** *Daughters of the Church: Women and Ministry from NT Times to the Present* (1987). **K. von Kellenbach,** *Anti-Judaism in Feminist Religious*

Writings (AAR Cultural Criticism Series 1, 1994). **A. Walker,** *In Search of Our Mothers' Gardens: Womanist Prose* (1983). **R. J. Weems,** *Just a Sister Away: A Womanist Vision of Women's Relationships in the Bible* (1988); "Reading Her Way Through the Struggle: African American Women and the Bible," *Stony the Road We Trod* (ed. C. H. Felder, 1991) 57-77; *Battered Love: Marriage, Sex, and Violence in the Hebrew Prophets* (OBT, 1995). **J. R. Wegner,** *Chattel or Person: The Status of Women in the Mishnah* (1988). **F. E. Willard,** *Woman in the Pulpit* (1888). **D. S. Williams,** *Sisters in the Wilderness: The Challenges of Womanist God Talk* (1993). **M. T. Winter,** *WomanWord: A Feminist Lectionary and Psalter* (Women of the NT, 1990). **A. C. Wire,** *The Corinthian Women Prophets: A Reconstruction Through Paul's Rhetoric* (1990).

V. C. Phillips

FENSHAM, FRANK CHARLES (1925–89)

Born at Koppies Oct. 13, 1925, in the Orange Free State in the Republic of South Africa (RSA), F. graduated from the University of Pretoria and was appointed lecturer of Semitic languages at the University of Stellenbosch in 1951. He was awarded a DD degree in NT by Pretoria and a PhD under W. F. Albright. He retired in 1985 and died July 26, 1989.

F. grew up and was trained in a fundamentalist tradition, but he became a critically inclined conservative and attracted many undergraduate students through whom he exercised a strong influence on the view of Scripture in the Dutch Reformed Church. Since at least twelve of his twenty-six doctoral students became lecturers at various South African universities, he profoundly influenced Semitic studies and OT theology in the Republic of South Africa as well. He served as chairperson of the South African Academy of Science and Arts and was awarded the nation's Totius prize for his contribution to biblical studies.

In line with the Albright tradition, his scholarly work, for which he received international recognition, consisted mainly of (positivist) comparative studies in Canaanite and Israelite cultures, notably their legal practice and religions. These two fields of interest alone resulted in twenty-three scholarly articles on Ugarit and fifty on ancient treaties and the (OT) covenant concept. He contributed to various Festschriften (e.g. for Albright, Beinart, Schaeffer, Van Selms, Volterra), international congresses, and series of commentaries.

Works: *Die Brief aan die Hebreërs* (1962, 1981²); "Malediction and Benediction in Ancient Near Eastern Vassal Treaties and the OT," *ZAW* 74 (1962) 1-9; "Widow, Orphan, and the Poor in Ancient Near Eastern Legal and Wisdom Literature," *JNES* 21 (1962) 129-39; "Clauses of Protection in Hittite Vassal-Treaties and the OT," *VT* 13 (1963) 133-43; "The Treaty Between Israel and the Gibeonites," *BA* 27 (1964) 557-62; "Psalm 21: A Covenant Song?" *ZAW* 77 (1965) 193-202; *'n Ondersoek na die geskiedenis van die interpretasie van die*

Hebreeuse poësie (1966); "Covenant, Promise, and Expectations in the Bible," *TZ* 23 (1967) 305-22; "The Obliterations of the Family as Motif in the Near Eastern Literature," *AION* 19 (1969) 191-99; "The Son of a Handmaid in Northwest Semitic," *VT* 19 (1969) 312-21; *Exodus* (POT, 1970, 1977[2]; "Father and Son Terminology for Treaty and Covenant," *Near Eastern Studies in Honor of W. F. Albright* (ed. H. Goedicke, 1971) 121-35; "The First Ugaritic Texts in Ugaritica V and the OT," *VT* 22 (1972) 296-303; "The Rôle of the Lord in the Covenant Code," *VT* 26 (1976) 262-74; "Transgression and Penalty in the Book of the Covenant," *JNSL* 5 (1977) 23-41; "Liability in the Case of Negligence in the OT Covenant Code and Ancient Legal Traditions," *Essays in Honor of B. Beinart* 1 (1978) 283-94; "A Few Observations on the Polarisation Between Yahweh and Baal in 1 Kings 17–19," *ZAW* 92 (1980) 227-36; *The Books of Ezra and Nehemia* (NICOT, 1982); "The Marriage Metaphor in Hosea for the Covenant Relationship Between the Lord and His People," *JNSL* 12 (1984) 71-78.

Bibliography: W. Claassen, "A Tribute to F. C. F.," *Text and Context: OT and Semitic Studies for F. C. F.* (ed. W. Claassen, 1988) 1-4; "Bibliography F. C. F.," *Text and Context* 301-10. **F. E. Deist,** "F. C. F.: A Theological Evaluation," *OT Essays,* NS 2, 3 (1989) 1-12.

F. E. DEIST

FISHER, SAMUEL (1605–65)

A Presbyterian and Baptist but best known as a Quaker, F. was the son of a Northampton hatter and was educated at Trinity College and New Inn Hall, Oxford, England. A Puritan lecturer at Kent in the 1630s, he accepted Presbyterian ordination in 1643 but later became a Baptist minister in Ashford, Kent. He published a defense of baptism by dipping as opposed to sprinkling, but his contribution to scriptural interpretation came after he became a Quaker in the mid-1650s.

F.'s *Rusticus ad Academicos* (1660) was a reply to the views of several more orthodox Puritan divines, notably R. Baxter (1615–91) and J. OWEN. In 1659 Owen had argued that the written or printed Bible contained the power and AUTHORITY of the supernatural Word. Quakers believed in the equivalence, if not also the superiority, of the personally known inner light to scriptural authority. F. maintained that all human language was natural, that Scripture was irretrievably textually corrupt, and that the divine was an entity who could only be reflected in earthly forms, internal (the inner light) or external (the Bible).

F. wrote in a humorous, ebullient style derived from the Marprelate Tracts. This could be seen as a detraction from the main purpose of scriptural criticism, but dramatic satirical portrayal and endless word play helped him to demonstrate the slippery and tenuous arguments of his opponents. Thus he made Owen appear more extreme than even the Quakers and trapped by his habits of argumentative circularity: "Though [Owen] who says elsewhere, the *Scripture,* is *without need of other helps or advantages, or revelation by the Spirit, or Light within . . . living, absolute, full of power and efficacy to save souls,* and yet rides *the Rounds* so here, as to say that *without the Spirit the word* (and that's more than the *Qua:* dare say, howbeit he means thereby but the *Scripture*) is a *dead letter, of no efficacy to the good of souls*" (*An Additionall Appendix* [1660, 20]).

F. was well informed, using the commentaries of B. Arias Montano (1527–98). The similarity of his views on scriptural corruption and uncertainty to those of B. SPINOZA has been noted, and it has recently been argued that F. was translated into Hebrew by the young Spinoza himself (R. Popkin, 1982, 1985).

Works: *Christianismus Redivivus* (1655); *The Scorned Quakers True and Honest Account* (1656, repr. 1978); *An Additionall Appendix to "Rusticus Ad Academicos"* (1660); *Rusticus ad Academicos* (1660); *The Testimony of Truth Exalted* (1679).

Bibliography: A. C. Bickley, *DNB* 19 (1889) 70-72. **D. Freiday,** *The Bible: Its Criticism, Interpretation, and Use in Sixteenth and Seventeenth Century England* (CQS 4, 1979) 97-102. **C. Hill,** *The World Turned Upside Down: Radical Ideas During the English Revolution* (1972) 208-15. **J. F. McGregor and B. Reay** (eds.), *Radical Religion in Early Modern England* (1984). **R. Popkin,** "Spinoza's Relationship with the Quakers in Amsterdam," *Quaker History* 73 (1982) 14-20; "S. F. and Spinoza," *Philosophia* 15 (1985) 219-36. **N. Smith,** *Perfection Proclaimed: Language and Literature in English Radical Religion, 1640–60* (1989).

N. SMITH

FITZMYER, JOSEPH A. (1920–   )

Born Nov. 4, 1920, in Philadelphia, Pennsylvania, F. entered the Society of Jesus on July 30, 1938 (Maryland Province, Novitiate of St. Isaac Jogues, Wernersville, Pennsylvania), and was ordained priest on Aug. 15, 1951. He studied at Loyola University of Chicago (BA 1943; MA 1945), Facultés St-Albert de Louvain, Belgium (STL 1952), Johns Hopkins University, Baltimore (PhD, 1956), and the Pontifical Biblical Institute, Rome (SSL 1957).

F.'s teaching career began in 1945 at Gonzaga High School, Washington, D.C., and in subsequent years he taught at Woodstock College, Johns Hopkins, Yale Divinity School, Loyola House of Studies (Manila), University of Chicago, Fordham, Weston Jesuit School of Theology, Oxford, Boston College, and The Catholic University of America. After retiring from Catholic University he was named professor emeritus (1986) and professorial lecturer in biblical studies (1990–   ).

F.'s service to the professional societies in biblical studies and theology has promoted scholarly publishing and ecumenical dialogue. He holds membership in the following groups: CBA (president, 1969–70), SOCIETY OF BIBLICAL LITERATURE (president, 1978–79), SNTS (president, 1992–93), and the American Theological Society. He has been associate editor and editor of *CBQ* and *JBL,* consulting editor for *JNES,* and a member of the board of editorial consultants for *TS.* He served on ecumenical study commissions of the Lutheran World Federation, the World Alliance of Reformed Churches, and the Vatican Secretariate for Promoting Christian Unity. From 1984 to 1995 he was a member of the Pontifical Biblical Commission, and he serves on the board of trustees of The Dead Sea Scrolls Foundation, Israel/USA.

In addition to his general service to the academic community, F. has excelled as a scholar in several disciplines. His bibliography as of 1998 comprised over 780 items, including more than thirty-five books. His primary area of research has been NT studies; he is the only scholar to have produced AB commentaries on three major NT books (Luke, Acts, Romans). A second area of F.'s activity has been study of the DEAD SEA SCROLLS. In 1957–58, while a fellow at the AMERICAN SCHOOLS OF ORIENTAL RESEARCH in Jerusalem, he began work on the scrolls, assisting in the early stages of the production of a concordance to the non-biblical texts. Since then he has published widely on the scrolls and has provided bibliographical tools for research on the subject. A third field in which F. has an international reputation is Aramaic studies. He has published analyses and commentaries on numerous Aramaic texts and has used Aramaic to elucidate various aspects of early Christian life and thought. He is presently co-director of a long-term project to produce a comprehensive Aramaic LEXICON.

F. has been an interpreter of the Roman Catholic Church's teachings to the academic and lay communities and likewise an interpreter of Bible to the hierarchy of the church. Many of his writings have addressed a general reading audience in an effort to make understandable both traditional Roman Catholic beliefs and new scholarly investigations.

Works: *The Genesis Apocryphon of Qumran Cave 1: A Commentary* (BibOr 18, 1966; 1971[2]); *Pauline Theology: A Brief Sketch* (1967, 1989[2]); *The Aramaic Inscriptions of Sefire* (BibOr 19, 1967; rev. ed., BibOr 19A, 1995); (ed. with R. E. Brown and R. E. Murphy), *The Jerome Biblical Commentary* (1967); *Essays on the Semitic Background of the NT* (1971); *The Dead Sea Scrolls: Major Publications and Tools for Study* (SBLSBS 8, 1975; with addendum, 1977; rev. ed., SBLSBS 20, 1990); (with D. J. Harrington), *A Manual of Palestinian Aramaic Texts (Second Century BC–Second Century AD)* (BibOr 34, 1978); *A Wandering Aramean: Collected Aramaic Essays* (SBLMS 25, 1979); *An Introductory Bibliography for the Study of Scripture* (SubBi 3, 1981[2], 1990[3]); *To Advance the Gospel: NT Studies*

(1981); *The Gospel According to Luke* (2 vols., AB 28, 28A, 1981–85); *Scripture and Christology: A Statement of the Biblical Commission* (tr. and commentary, 1986); *Luke the Theologian: Aspects of His Teaching* (1989); (ed. with R. E. Brown and R. E. Murphy), *The New Jerome Biblical Commentary* (1990); *Responses to 101 Questions on the Dead Sea Scrolls* (1992); (with S. A. Kaufman), *An Aramaic Bibliography,* pt. 1, *Old, Official, and Biblical Aramaic* (Publications of the Comprehensive Aramaic Lexicon Project 2, 1992); *Romans* (AB 33, 1993); *Scripture, the Soul of Theology* (1994); *Spiritual Exercises Based on Paul's Epistle to the Romans* (1995); *The Biblical Commissions' Document "The Interpretation of the Bible in the Church": Text and Commentary* (SubBi 18, 1995); *The Semitic Background of the NT* (comb. repr. of *Essays on the Semitic Background of the NT* and *A Wandering Aramean,* 1997); *The Acts of the Apostles* (AB 31, 1998).

Bibliography: *CBQ* 48, 3 (FS, 1986). **M. P. Horgan and P. J. Kobelski** (eds.), *To Touch the Text: Biblical and Related Studies in Honor of J. A. F., S.J.* (FS, 1989).

M. P. HORGAN

FLACIUS ILLYRICUS, MATTHIAS (1520–75)

F. was born Mar. 3, 1520, in Albona (modern-day Labin, Croatia). His Croatian name was latinized to *Flacius,* while *Illyricus* expressed his devotion to his homeland, the old Roman province of Illyria. He studied in Venice and then, on the advice of his uncle Baldo Lupetino, went to Wittenberg (1541), where he became a friend of LUTHER, who guided him through a serious spiritual crisis. F. served as professor of Hebrew at Wittenberg (1544–48) but was forced to leave because of the invading imperial troops in the Schmalkald War. A leader in the struggle against the interims imposed by Charles V after his victory over the Protestant forces, for the remainder of his life F. was involved in controversy with P. MELANCHTHON and other Lutherans and was almost constantly on the move, although he did serve for a time as NT professor at the new university at Jena (1557–62). He was the driving force behind the Centuriators of Magdeburg, whose multivolume history of the church, published as *Historia Ecclesiae Christi* (1559–74), was rigidly anti-Catholic but helped to develop the discipline of ecclesiastical history. He died in Frankfurt a. M., Mar. 10, 1575.

While at Regensburg (1562–66) F. did much of the work on his *Clavis scripturae sacrae* ("Key to the Holy Scriptures"), probably the most influential book on biblical HERMENEUTICS over the next century (see O. Olson [1981] 15). The first part of the work (1,344 columns) is a monumental theological LEXICON following a Latin alphabetical order, perhaps the first such work of its kind. Some essays are as much as twenty columns long. The second part consists of discussions on how to understand Scripture, style, parts of speech, etc. Combating both Roman Catholics and fellow Protestants whom he felt had surrendered many of Luther's insights, F. carried out what has been called a policy of "dehellenization" of biblical interpretation. He advocated close adherence to the text and offered suggestions for how a reader should approach and understand it. In his controversy with C. von SCHWENCKFELD (1553–58), who exegeted from the perspective of outer and inner meanings of the text, F. stressed Article V of the Augsburg Confession, that God is not present within the believer apart from external means, thus identifying the Word of God with the Bible and arguing that no real contradiction could exist in Scripture. Entering the budding debate over the antiquity of the Hebrew vowel points, he wrote a section on the subject in part two of the *Clavis,* in which he traced their use back to Adam.

Works: *Clavis scripturae sacrae seu de sermone sacrarum literarum* (1567), portions repr. in *De Ratione Cognoscendi Sacras Literas: Über den Erkenntnisgrund der Heiligen Schrift* (ed. L. Geldsetzer, 1968); *Glossa compendiaria in Novum Testamentum* (1570).

Bibliography: **J. Baur,** "Flacius: Radikale Theologie," *ZTK* 72 (1975) 365-80. **L. Haikola,** *Gesetz und Evangelium bei M. F. I.* (1952); *NTHIP,* 27-30. **G. Kawerau,** *NSHERK* 4 (1909) 321-23. **R. Keller,** *Der Schlüssel zur Schrift: Die Lehre von Word Gottes M. F. I.* (AGTL NF 5, 1984). **R. Kolb,** *HHMBI,* 190-95. **J. L. Kugel,** *The Idea of Biblical Poetry* (1981) 228-32. **M. Mirkovic,** *Matija Vlačić Ilirik* (1960). **G. Moldaenke,** *Schriftverständnis und Schriftdeutung im Zietalter der Reformation,* vol. 1, *Matthias Flacius Illyricus* (1936); *MSHH* 24 (1733) 1-25. **O. K. Olson,** *Shapers of Religious Traditions in Germany, Switzerland, and Poland, 1560–1600* (ed. J. Raitt, 1981) 1-17. **W. Preger,** *M. F. I. und seine Zeit* (2 vols., 1859–61, repr. 1964). **B. Roussel,** *BTT* 5 (1989) 258-62.

F. GRATER

FOHRER, GEORG (1915–)

Born Sept. 6, 1915 in Krefeld-Uerdingen in Germany's Ruhr region, F. studied theology and comparative religious studies in Marburg and Bonn (1934–38). He received a PhD in 1939 in religious studies ("Der heilige Weg: Eine religionswissenschaftliche Untersuchung") and a ThD five years later in 1944 (*Die symbolischen Handlungen der alttestamentlichen Propheten* [ATANT 25, 1953, 1968[2]]). After WWII he became an *ausserordentlicher* professor in Marburg in 1946 and was made full professor in 1950. He taught OT in Marburg until 1954, then moved to Vienna (1954–62) and Erlangen-Nurmberg (1962–79). He was general editor of the *Zeitschrift für alttestamentliche Wissenschaft* and its supplementary volumes, *BZAW* (1960–81), and of the *Züricher Bibelkommentare* (1972–82); and he was

co-editor of the *Theologische Realenzyklopädie* (1968–74). After converting to Judaism he moved to Jerusalem in 1979.

F.'s engagement of the biblical text is comprehensive and touches on all types of biblical literature. In his reworking of E. SELLIN's *Einleitung in das Alte Testament,* regarding the composition of the Pentateuch (see PENTATEUCHAL CRITICISM) F. has posited the existence of an early nomadic, or N, source written in response to the pro-monarchic Yahwist. This source, he argued, preserved some pre-monarchic traditions that emphasized a more decentralized view of government and of religion (*Introduction to the OT* [1965[10]] 173-79; ET 1968). In an influential article ("Altes Testament: Amphiktyonie und 'Bund'?" *TLZ* 91 [1966] 801-16, 893-904) F. was one of the first scholars to call into question the idea of an amphictyony, prominently advanced by M. NOTH, as the organizational structure of pre-monarchic Israel. He argued in the same article against an overestimation of the notion of covenant as the theological basis of early Israelite society, suggesting that the term *covenant* is used only infrequently in pre-deuteronomistic texts. Similarly, he was an early critic of G. von RAD's theory that certain short credos, especially Deut 26:5-9, constitute the roots of the historical traditions of the Hexateuch, proposing instead that these texts represent later summaries of the traditions ("Tradition und Interpretation im Alten Testament," *ZAW* 73 [1961] 1-30).

F.'s writings are also concerned with theological questions pertaining to the HB. He generally favors an anthropological theology to interpret the religious writings of ancient Israel. This is evident in his reading of Hebrew PROPHECY, where his contributions to biblical studies are perhaps most significant. Among the five basic impulses he identifies as constitutive for the religious development of Israelite religion (Mosaic Yahwism, monarchy, prophecy, deuteronomistic theology, and eschatology), he considers prophecy the most important, for it marks both the transition from early to high religion and the link between national and world religion. F. sees prophecy as relatively independent of Israel's historical traditions, even though many prophets employed traditional themes in their proclamations. He proposes that the prophetic writings were based on the individual uniqueness of the prophetic figure and his concrete historical and political context. Rooted in the existential experience of the prophet, the writings have a universal relevance for all human beings regardless of specific circumstances. F. views the basic message of prophecy as a call for repentance and return to God, which in itself constitutes the salvation of humanity. Thus the prophetic proclamation is not primarily an announcement of punishment, which may be followed by a divine restoration, but rather a call to embrace the divine salvation implicitly present in humanity's return to God's justice. F.'s theology of prophecy, therefore, is primarily concerned with the human condition rather than with the divine punishment. This view as well as his attempt to link individual experience with universal ideas gives expression to F.'s persistent concern with a balanced approach to the HB based on theological as well as comparative religious principles.

Works: *Das Buch Hiob* (1948); *Glaube und Welt im Alten Testament* (1948); *Die Hauptprobleme des Buches Ezechiel* (BZAW 72, 1952); *Ezechiel* (HAT 1, 13, 1955); *Elia* (ATANT 31, 1957, 1968[2]); *Messiasfrage und Bibelverständnis* (1957); *Das Buch Jesaja: Kapitel 1–23* (ZBK, 1960, 1966[2]); "Remarks on Modern Interpretations of the Prophets," *JBL* 80 (1961) 309-19; *Das Buch Jesaja: Kapitel 24–39* (ZBK, 1962, 1967[2]); *Das Buch Hiob* (KAT XVI, 1963, 1989[2]); *Studien zum Buche Hiob* (1963, BZAW 159, 1983[2]); *Das Buch Jesaja: Kapitel 40–66* (ZBK, 1964, 1986[2]); *Überlieferung und Geschichte des Exodus* (BZAW 91, 1964); *Studien zur alttestamentlichen Prophetie (1949–65)* (BZAW 99, 1967); *Das Alte Testament,* Teil 1 (1969, 1980[3]); *History of Israelite Religion* (1969; ET 1972); *Studien zur alttestamentlichen Theologie und Geschichte (1949–66)* (BZAW 115, 1969); *Das Alte Testament,* Teil 2, 3 (1970, 1980[3]); (with W. H. Hoffmann et al.), *Hebrew and Aramaic Dictionary of the OT* (1971, 1989[2]; ET 1973); *Theologische Grundstrukturen des Alten Testaments* (1972); (with H. W. Hoffmann et al.), *Exegese des Alten Tesaments* (1973, 1989[5]); *Die Propheten des Alten Testaments* (7 vols. 1974–77); *Geschichte Israels: Von den Anfängen bis zur Gegenwart* (1977, 1990[5]); *Glaube und Leben im Judentum* (1979, 1991[3]); *Studien zu alttestamentlichen Texten und Themen (1966–72)* (BZAW 155, 1981); *Vom Werden und Verstehen des Alten Testaments* (1986); *Erzähler und Propheten im Alten Testament: Geschichte der israelitischen und frühjüdischen Literatur* (1988); *Studien zum Alten Testament (1966–88)* (BZAW 196, 1991), includes full bibliography to 1991; *Psalmen* (1993).

Bibliography: J. A. Emerton (ed.), *Prophecy: Essays Presented to G. F. on his Sixty-fifth Birthday* (BZAW 150, 1980). J. Gray, *Aberdeen University Review* 43, 2, 142 (1969) 194-95. L. Markert and G. Wanke, "Die Propheteninterpretation: Anfragen und Überlegungen," *Kerygma und Dogma* 22 (1976) 191-220. H. Sebass, "Über den Beitrag des Alten Testaments zu einer theologischen Anthropologie," *Kerygma und Dogma* 22 (1976) 41-63.

A. SIEDLECKI

FOLKLORE IN HEBREW BIBLE INTERPRETATION.

1. Defining Folklore. The single term *folklore* refers to the primary material, the lore, and the formal task of studying these materials. While there is no standard definition of folklore, most definitions emphasize the concepts of oral and traditional, contrasting oral with written and traditional with novel. Such a discipline has much to offer biblical interpreters, since much of the Bible has roots in oral performance. Furthermore, parts of the Bible appear to represent traditions that were handed down over generations before appearing in written form.

The concept of tradition requires additional comment. One aspect of the term *traditional* is "communal" authorship. In cases where lore has been handed down and shaped by many persons in a culture over time, the concept of an individual creative author is insignificant. Such a chain of tradition has so many links that in the end the material reveals more about the ethos of the group than it does about any individual. As a discipline folklore emphasizes the relationship between lore and the group that produced and bore it.

A common assumption about the term *traditional* is that it means "old." Folklore can, but need not, be as old as the hills, since folklore continues to be created. By definition all communication in a group into which writing has not been introduced is folklore. Yet even among literate groups folklore persists as an alternative, often informal, mode of communication. This latter type of folklore, observed in such genres as greetings, gossip, jokes, and urban legends, is traditional in that it draws on a standard repertoire of conventions; at the same time variations on these conventions are coined every day. Ancient Israel was a culture in transition from primary orality to some degree of literacy in which oral and written styles coexisted and overlapped. This means that one cannot assume that a given passage with a high degree of orality (a subjective assessment) is earlier than a parallel treatment with a high degree of literary features.

The hallmark of folklore is patterned repetition. Because oral communication is ephemeral, its composers repeat themselves on multiple levels to make their points, relying on conventions mutually intelligible to performer and audience (see W. Ong [1982] 31). This holds true for the Bible; words, phrases, and ideas are repeated or, better, "seconded" (J. Kugel [1981]). Typical episodes ("traditional episodes" in D. Irvin [1978] 9-13; "type-scenes" in R. Alter [1981] 47-62, though he considers them as a literary rather than an oral-traditional phenomenon), and stock characters like the hero (R. Hendel [1987] 133-165), the trickster (S. Niditch [1987]), the wise woman, the "strange" woman (C. Camp [1985]), and the wild man (G. Mobley [1997]) are used. On the thematic level such key themes as creation or exodus are repeated and reinterpreted in new contexts (Niditch [1985]; D. Ben-Amos [1992] 823). One of the most basic levels of patterning in folklore is that of rhythmic speech, although there is no consensus among biblical scholars regarding the metrical quality of ancient Hebrew verse (see M. O'Connor [1980]; J. Kugel [1981]).

Despite its reliance on the formulaic, there is originality in folklore in the choice and arrangement of traditional materials and in the way that each performance is a unique interaction between composer and audience. Furthermore, these redundant patterns are more than mere repetition; conventions are commonly subverted in contrasting, surprising ways.

2. The Relevance of Folklore to the HB. Folklore, as a discipline that observes, describes, and analyzes repetitive patterns in traditional discourse, has implications for HB study. First, many parts of the Bible, if not transcriptions of oral performance, have roots in oral performance. Examples include oracles delivered by prophets (see PROPHECY AND PROPHETS, HB), victory songs chanted by musicians, psalms offered by worshipers, proverbs uttered by teachers, and teachings spoken by priests. Second, "folkloristic" motifs can be detected throughout the Bible's prose and poetic sections (see POETRY, HB) and can be compared with folkloric material outside the Bible.

Third, folklore provides tools for reconstructing the oral traditions of Israel (Ben-Amos [1992] 819). Through analogy with extra-biblical folklore light is shed on Israelite popular traditions alluded to in the Bible but not given full treatment, e.g., the story of the primeval battle between God and the dragon of chaos. This is important both for understanding the social world out of which the Bible emerged and for giving fuller shape to material the Bible preserves incidentally. Folklore, then, provides tools for digging out Israelite popular traditions submerged in the Bible.

At the same time the limits of folklore must be recognized. Contemporary folklore research is based on field work with living informants and on the collection of many variants of a given type of story, song, or proverbial saying. Biblical researchers do not have access to native informants; however, in some cases it is possible that traditions preserved in late Second Temple, rabbinic, early Christian, and even medieval literature preserve lore stemming from the biblical period (Ben-Amos [1992] 819-20). It is clear that Second Temple and rabbinic texts contain details and elaborations of oriental mythological themes that preserve oral traditions from the First Temple period. This is particularly evident in the creation stories and their recurring themes.

In certain cases the Bible itself preserves variants of a given type of traditional tale, like the three stories in Genesis in which a patriarch pretends his wife is his sister (Gen 12:10-20; 20:1-18; 26:6-11). For the most part the paucity of extant native variants inevitably leads biblical folklorists to other cultural fields in search of parallel material, in some cases so far afield that they risk going off the deep end (see below regarding J. Frazer). The comparative method is fundamental to folklore research but must be used with care (see S. Talmon [1993]).

The very application of methods designed for use with oral tradition to a literary corpus may seem inappropriate. This, however, is not just a problem for biblical folklore specialists; all research into the folklore of past cultures must rely on texts. How does one isolate oral tradition in written text? Many schemes, like Olrik's laws, purport to offer trait lists of oral tradition (A. Olrik [1965]; for a more recent list, see Ong, 36-57). Often these observations about the characteristics of oral narrative are based on a certain cultural corpus, in Olrik's case European folktales, and cannot be assumed to be universal. Furthermore, much of the data Olrik considered was written material with putative oral roots, like the Bible. This does not mean that there are not recognizable differences between oral and written discourse. Nevertheless, there is no sure methodological filter capable of empirically isolating the oral residue in written materials.

Then why even use the methods of folklore in biblical study? Because the Bible, although literature, is a certain kind of literature: traditional literature (Niditch [1987] xiii-xiv). Reliance on literary methods, largely devised for the interpretation of contemporary prose and poetic forms, has its own potential for distorting material rooted in oral performance or composed in the oral style and shaped by many tradents rather than by a single author. The tools of folklore must be utilized along with the tools of LITERARY analysis in order to adequately account for the Bible's oral and written qualities.

3. The Use of Folklore in Biblical Studies. The collection of folklore materials—e.g., myths, legends, and tales—and their juxtaposition with similar biblical materials has had a dramatic effect. This comparative task has underscored the similarities between ancient Israel and other cultures, serving as an antidote to dogmatic tendencies that overemphasize the uniqueness of the Bible. At the same time the comparative task illuminates what is distinctive and unique about the Bible by exposing how the lore is integrated into this specific cultural context (Niditch [1993] 11).

The pioneer in comparative folklore of the HB was H. GUNKEL (1862–1932), who initially sought to expose Israelite popular tradition through comparisons with ancient Near Eastern myths deciphered from cuneiform (1895). Eventually he expanded his analyses to the larger world of folktales drawn from ancient and contemporary sources (1917). In the three editions of his Genesis commentary, Gunkel systematically described and traced the development of the basic genres (*Gattungen*) in Israelite oral tradition. According to him, these conventional forms developed from brief poetic units, each functioning in a different performance arena, or "setting in life" (*Sitz im Leben*). A class of storytellers wove these into larger, coherent narratives that later became the basis for the literary sources already detected by J. WELLHAUSEN and others.

Gunkel's assumptions about the character of oral tradition were shaped by the anthropology of his day. He imagined that oral traditions were by definition brief, poetic, and reflective of a kind of childlike mentality. On the one hand, his emphasis on oral tradition provided a foil to theories about the development of biblical literature that emphasized the documentary quality of formative biblical traditions. The multiform quality of biblical material may be evidence of the variation characteristic of oral tradition rather than of the existence of distinct literary documents secondarily spliced together by later editors. On the other hand, Gunkel's insistence that the oral repertoire consisted of brief isolated units facilitated an atomization of biblical materials akin to that produced by the subsequent excesses of some source critics. Subsequent research into oral tradition has made clear that traditional materials can be quite extensive and complex (A. Lord [1960]).

Nevertheless, Gunkel's work with folklore remains valuable. Although he was not alone in this, his analysis of biblical texts in light of Near Eastern myth took biblical studies across a threshold from which it has never returned. His basic method of adducing parallels from myth and folklore as a means of highlighting the popular motifs embedded in biblical narratives is sound, although this exercise in itself is a half-measure that must be accompanied by a thoroughgoing analysis of how a given motif functions in its host culture. Gunkel, however, did not neglect what we now call the ethnographic task. His FORM CRITICISM of Genesis and the psalms can be seen as early attempts to observe and describe Israel's own traditional forms.

Frazer's *Folk-lore* (1918), appearing in the same period, arranged colorful stories and obscure customs from the Bible alongside a wide-ranging collection of textual artifacts—legends, myths, and travelers' accounts of the "savage" races—in an attempt, in the fashion of a Victorian museum, to illustrate the stages of humanity's social evolution. Beyond his outdated assumptions about the "primitive" nature of the ancients, the mere adducing of anecdotal and impressionistic parallels with no attention to geographic and chronological settings (see CHRONOLOGY, HB) often obscures what is distinctive about the original subject. Despite its lack of discrimination, Frazer's compendium has been used as a "quarry" of suggested parallels (see J. Rogerson [1978] 73).

In the vein of catalogues of lore, T. Gaster's (1969) revision of Frazer is a better quarry to mine. Although he intended to revise Frazer, his work advanced far beyond Frazer's because as a Semiticist Gaster was able to see in texts patterns related to Israel and its neighboring cultures. This kind of work, which adduces parallels from folklore and MYTHOLOGY in selected passages throughout the Bible, is out of step with recent ethnographic approaches that attempt to detect native genres and elements rather than universal ones. Never-

theless, Gaster's work remains the best single comparative reference for biblical folklore. Even with its occasional forced parallel, the overall impact dramatically shows that the Bible cannot be adequately interpreted in isolation from comparative folklore and myth.

Beyond the confines of biblical scholarship the major reference works for cross-cultural folklore analysis are A. Aarne and S. Thompson's *Types of the Folktale* (1964) and S. Thompson's *Motif-Index of Folk Literature* (1955–58). Aarne and Thompson are part of the historical-geographic school, whose approach is to assemble all the variants of a type or feature of a tale. By tracing each variant, the movements of folklore through time and place become exposed. However, given the paucity of extant variants and the myriad complications of dating biblical materials and detecting their original provenance, it is virtually impossible to genetically trace the family tree of biblical folklore. These indexes, however, are useful in a more general way. They have provided folklorists with a common analytic language and, despite their largely European scope, have sketched a reliable portrait of the shape of common tales and their constituent parts. The *Motif-Index* is of more direct help to biblical scholars than is *Types of the Folktale* because the Bible contains few (if any) intact folktales (perhaps Jotham's fable of the trees in Judg 9:8-15) but abounds in folkloristic motifs. Gaster provides a cross-reference to Thompson's *Motif-Index*.

There are comparative approaches that focus on the form of materials rather than on their content. Loosely described as types of STRUCTURALISM, these involve a secondary translation of linguistic materials into abstract codes that reveal the form, or structure, underneath the surface details. The two most influential forms of structuralism in folklore have been those of C. Lévi-Strauss (1968) and V. Propp (1958). Eschewing surface details of content, Levi-Strauss isolated elements in Native American myths that expressed binary oppositions representative of "the primary conflicts of human existence" (W. Doty [1986] 200). Myths function to resolve these dilemmas by introducing third, anomalous terms that mediate the conflict. Lévi-Strauss's work has not been influential among biblical folklorists beyond the level of drawing attention to these binary oppositions (see E. Leach's attempt [1969] and Rogerson's critique [1974] 109-12, 124).

More influential has been the work of Propp, whose study of Russian fairy tales was written in 1928 but not widely known in Europe and the United States until the early 1960s. Propp charted the linear sequence of events ("functions") in these fairy tales, all of which, according to him, contain a limited number of functions that occur in an unvarying order, although every possible function is not present in each tale. Propp's abstract scheme of traditional plot sequence demonstrates how the fairy tales worked out problems of human development, beginning with the hero leaving home, then confronting various dangers, and ultimately marrying. Some biblical scholars have closely followed Propp's scheme, employing his terms for these plot functions (J. Sasson [1989]); others have used his work as a model for examining on a synchronic level the sequence of actions in biblical narratives (H. Jason [1979]; D. Patte [1980]; R. Culley [1976a] 69-115).

Since the 1960s folklorists have paid increasing attention to ethnic studies, the analysis of materials within specific cultural contexts, eschewing CROSS-CULTURAL analytic concepts of genre in favor of native terms. Closely aligned with this is an emphasis on performance context. Ben-Amos observes that the imposition of European categories, like folktale, myth, or legend, on biblical materials is anachronistic (1976, 217). He charts a promising new direction for biblical folklorists that begins with an analysis of the HB's own terms for poetic (e.g., šîr, mizmôr, qînâ, dĕbar YHWH, ḥāzôn, maśśā᾽), prose (ma῾ăśëh, niplā᾽ôt), and conversational (māšāl, ḥîdâ) genres and suggests performance contexts for each (1992, 823-26). The contemporary emphasis on performance continues and updates Gunkel's attempt to define the life settings of oral traditions in Genesis and the psalms.

Other scholars have used comparative material and various modern folklore theories to refine the picture of Israel's ethnic repertoire. These range from studies of traditional formulas in the psalms (Culley [1967]), to the genre of proverbs (C. Fontaine [1982]), to the shape of the Israelite heroic biography (R. Hendel [1987]), and to the ethos of Israelite folklore as seen in its attraction to the theme of the underdog (Niditch [1987]).

4. From Oral Tradition to Oral Register. The most important work in oral tradition has been that of A. Lord. Based on fieldwork with south Slavic folk singers, Lord suggests that oral epic is composed by persons immersed in all the conventions of a tradition: formulaic phrases, larger motifs, and even larger typical narrative patterns. In each performance the composer extemporaneously creates a unique version of the song, although the constituent elements of the performance are traditional.

This oral-formulaic theory has been employed by biblical scholars to understand the conventional language with its myriad variations in the HB (see the articles in Culley [1976b]). Most of this work has been done in poetic genres, although some has been done with prose genres (Culley [1976a]; D. Gunn [1974]). Biblical scholars have been slow to extend this theory beyond poetic genres. Part of this hesitancy, perhaps, lies in too great a reliance on the metrical element in Lord's theory, which was formulated on the basis of a genre with a high degree of metrical organization. It is as if one based a general theory of oral tradition on the performances of square-dance callers. There are countless other oral modes without the rhythm of poetry and the accompaniment of music. Other of Lord's general

principles—the immersion in a traditional repertoire, the variations produced by the creative arrangement of these conventions in performance—need not be tied to the metrical principle. Charting their course from contemporary specialists in oral tradition (see J. Foley [1992]), biblical folklorists need to advance more readily into non-poetic genres.

A recent development in oral tradition is the emergence of the concept of *register* (see Foley, 287-89; Niditch [1996]). In vocal music the term refers to a portion of the entire range of a voice. A person can sing in different registers, articulating from the chest or from the head, as in falsetto. The concept of an oral register recognizes a variety of speech styles available to speakers depending on the social situation. For instance, in informal settings one uses one voice; in formal settings, another. Each register has its own repertoire of conventions. This concept bridges the great divide between oral and written modes of communication, both of which are available simultaneously to speakers and cultures.

What are the implications of this for biblical study? From the beginnings with Gunkel, biblical scholars, laboring under the contradiction of analyzing the written with tools designed for the oral, have struggled to isolate the oral substratum in written texts. The concept of register fundamentally recognizes transitional modes between these falsely drawn oppositions. In the Bible, for instance, most of the prose narratives in the primary history (Genesis–Kings), draw on the oral register whether their origins are in oral tradition or in written documents. The biblical authors had heard more stories than they had read; and even when they wrote, their materials reflect the kinds of traditional characterizations, formulaic language, and patterned repetition of oral tradition, of folklore. Furthermore, many of the written portions of the Bible in Jewish tradition, often referred to as *Miqra'* (Proclamation), were formulated for the express purpose of public reading.

This does not mean that it is all folklore; nor does it mean that all parts and genres of the Bible draw equally from the oral register. It does mean that the tools of folklore, alongside those of literary criticism, can and must be applied to the kind of writings contained in the Bible, which emerged from a culture in gradual transition from primary orality to some degree of popular literacy (see A. Demsky [1988] 15-20). Folklore analysis, then, has implications for biblical writings beyond those with clear performance contexts and beyond those genres—e.g., myths, legends, and folktales—commonly thought of as "folkloristic."

Bibliography: **A. Aarne and S. Thompson,** *The Types of the Folktale: A Classification and Bibliography* (1964). **R. Alter,** *The Art of Biblical Narrative* (1981). **D. Ben-Amos** (ed.), "Analytical Categories and Ethnic Genres," *Folklore Genres* (1976) 215-42; "Folklore in the Ancient Near East," *ABD*

(1992) 2:818-28. **C. Camp,** *Wisdom and the Feminine in the Book of Proverbs* (JSOT Bible and Literature 11, 1985). **R. C. Culley,** *Oral Formulaic Language in the Biblical Psalms* (1967); *Studies in the Structure of Hebrew Narrative* (*Semeia* Sup., 1976a); (ed.), "Oral Tradition and the OT: Some Recent Discussion," *Semeia* 5 (1976b) 1-33; "Exploring New Directions," *The HB and Its Modern Interpreters* (ed. D. Knight and G. Tucker, 1985) 167-200. **A. Demsky,** "Writing in Ancient Israel and Early Judaism: The Biblical Period," *Mikra* (ed. J. Mulder, 1988) 1-38. **W. Doty,** *Mythography: The Study of Myths and Rituals* (1986). **J. M. Foley,** "Word-Power, Performance, and Tradition," *JAF* 105 (1992) 275-301. **C. Fontaine,** *Traditional Sayings in the OT* (1982). **J. G. Frazer,** *Folk-lore in the OT* (1918). **T. H. Gaster,** *Myth, Legend, and Custom in the OT* (1969). **H. Gunkel,** *Schöpfung und Chaos in Urzeit und Endzeit* (1895); *Das Märchen im Alten Testament* (1917, 1921; ET *The Folktale in the OT* [1987]). **D. Gunn,** "Narrative Patterns and Oral Tradition in Judges and Samuel," *VT* 24 (1974) 286-317. **R. Hendel,** *The Epic of the Patriarch* (HSM 42, 1987). **D. Irvin,** *Mytharion: The Comparison of Tales from the OT and the Ancient Near East* (AOAT 32, 1978). **H. Jason,** "The Story of David and Goliath: A Folk Epic?" *Bib* 60 (1979) 36-70. **P. Kirkpatrick,** *The OT and Folklore Study* (JSOTSup 62, 1988). **D. Knight,** *Rediscovering the Traditions of Israel* (SBLDS 9, 1975). **J. Kugel,** *The Idea of Biblical Poetry: Parallelism and Its History* (1981). **C. Lévi-Strauss,** "The Structural Study of Myth," *Myth: A Symposium* (ed. T. Sebeok, 1968) 81-106. **E. Leach,** *Genesis as Myth and Other Essays* (1969). **A. Lord,** *The Singer of Tales* (1960). **G. Mobley,** "The Wild Man in the Bible and Ancient Near East," *JBL* 116 (1997) 217-33. **S. Niditch,** *Chaos to Cosmos: Studies in Biblical Patterns of Creation* (SPSHS 6, 1985); *Underdogs and Tricksters* (New Voices in Biblical Studies, 1987); (ed.), *Text and Tradition: The HB and Folklore* (Semeia Studies, 1990); *Folklore and the HB* (Guide to Biblical Scholarship OT Series, 1993); *Oral Word and Written Word: Ancient Israelite Literature* (1996). **M. O'Connor,** *Hebrew Verse Structure* (1980). **A. Olrik,** "Epic Laws of Folk Narrative," *The Study of Folklore* (ed. A. Dundes, 1965) 129-41. **W. J. Ong,** *Orality and Literacy: The Technologizing of the Word* (1982). **D. Patte** (ed.), "Genesis 2 and 3: Kaleidoscope Structural Readings," *Semeia* 18 (1980) 1-164. **V. Propp,** *The Morphology of the Folktale* (1928; ET tr. L. Scott, Bibliographical and Special Series of the American Folklore Society 9, 1958). **J. W. Rogerson,** *Myth in OT Interpretation* (BZAW 134, 1974); *Anthropology and the OT* (Growing Points in Theology, 1978). **J. M. Sasson,** *Ruth* (1989[2]). **S. Talmon,** "The Comparative Method in Biblical Interpretation: Principles and Problems," *Congress Volume* (ed. W. Zimmerli et al., 1977) 320-56. **S. Thompson,** *Motif-Index of Folk Literature* (1932–36; rev. and enl. ed., 6 vols., 1955–58).

G. MOBLEY

FORM CRITICISM, HEBREW BIBLE.

The term *form criticism* designates, not just one procedure, but several different ones that deal in one manner or another with patterns—usually thought of as dynamic, oriented toward a function. The variations reflect, in part, divergent conceptions of form. Procedures designated thus include (1) the study of kinds of speech (genre analysis, *Gattungsforschung*), which has been carried out throughout the history of biblical interpretation; (2) the tracing of the history of a type of speech (genre history, *Gattungsgeschichte* or *Formengeschichte*), of which there are only a relatively few examples, two of them provided by H. GUNKEL; (3) the reconstruction of the history of a tradition on the basis of formal considerations, largely in the belief that the simplest forms are early (history on the basis of form, often *Formgeschichte*), attempted to some extent by Gunkel and even more by many of his followers; and (4) the examination of the structure of a particular text (form-oriented criticism), as executed by W. Richter (*Formkritik*) and (with attention to genres) by many ancient and modern exegetes, including recent contributors to the series The Forms of OT Literature.

Classical Greek theory distinguished between rhetorical and poetic genres, although it did not draw an altogether sharp line between them, and discussed levels of style in terms of phenomena belonging to both. Insofar as one follows this distinction, RHETORICAL and poetic (or "literary") study become subdivisions of formal analysis. One can also contrast a portrayal of general patterns (theory, including attention to genres) with the examination of the structure of a specific text; the former plays a greater or lesser role in the various operations that go under the name form criticism.

Genres were described by Gunkel in 1924 as involving (a) characteristic thoughts and feelings, (b) typical lexical and syntactic features ("form" in a narrow sense), and (c) a traditional connection with human (especially social) life (*Sitz im Leben*). It thus became characteristic of work inspired by Gunkel to give attention to all three of these aspects, which are comparable to the semantic, syntactic, and pragmatic dimensions of linguistics. Classical rhetoric had already considered all three, the second at least insofar as it enters into questions of style. An acquaintance with this tradition contributed to the production of multifaceted analyses in early (including medieval) interpretations of the Bible.

The beginning of biblical form criticism lies within the CANON itself, although the process was there often only implicit. Those who collected the biblical materials gathered them largely according to types of speech and social location. For instance, the third division of the Hebrew canon contains almost exclusively literature belonging to the realm of wisdom and of singers, with three of its books devoted entirely to proverbs, psalms, and love poetry; little of this kind of literature appears in any of the other books. Major types of biblical speech were represented by prototypical figures: Moses for laws, Solomon for wisdom, David for psalms of lament.

Israelites had names for genres, although they were fluid in meaning, as are classificatory terms in most language systems.

Early post-biblical interpreters frequently analyzed biblical materials according to their literary types. For instance, rabbinic tradition formulated rules for the halakhic exegesis of laws, which differed from standards applicable to the aggadic interpretation of other literature, like narratives. PHILO described biblical genres as complementary to one another, with a central focus on precepts, which he regarded as persuasive (rather than dogmatic) and as personal, with direct address (e.g., *Decal.,* 36-39). Stories of world origins, as he knew from comparative data, contain symbolic elements. According to ORIGEN (as well as others), the primary aim of biblical literature is not the narration of ancient history, but "discipline and usefulness" (Homily 2 on Exodus). The anonymous *Teaching of the Twelve Apostles* (3rd cent.) regarded as unnecessary the use of non-Christian literature on the grounds that the Bible already gives examples of the various types.

The use of rhetorical categories in early Christian interpretation became especially common after the state establishment of Christianity early in the fourth century. A description of speech by type according to its purpose (e.g., to exhort or praise), partially following Greco-Roman patterns of exegesis, was widespread. Psalms were classified (into prayers, hymns, etc.) and characterized according to their major thrust, e.g., by ATHANASIUS (d. 373) and GREGORY OF NYSSA. Of these, Athanasius regarded the representation of different feelings in the psalms as a mirror that can either support or therapeutically correct one's own emotions and as a guide for expressing appropriate feelings in words (*Letter to Marcellinus*). Some commentators, including CYRIL OF ALEXANDRIA, paid attention to characteristic forms of PROPHECY. AMBROSE and CHRYSOSTOM, among others, analyzed the roles of several major genres.

An especially thorough overview was presented by Hadrian (d. c. 440) in the first work to be called an "introduction" to the Scriptures. He distinguished between "prophetic" (strictly revelational) and "historical" or "inquiring" types of speech; each of these was divided according to its orientation toward the past, the present, or the future, as Aristotle had already divided secular rhetorical genres. The books normally called prophetic were described by a hybrid term meaning "prose-poetry." A fourfold classification was outlined by JULIUS AFRICANUS (c. 550): history, prophecy (manifesting the concealed), proverbs, and "simple" teaching (descriptive of ordinary life, e.g., Qohelet). CASSIODORUS described psalms both as a division of sacred literature, for the characterization of which he drew on AUGUSTINE's *De doctrina Christiana,* and as a special type that can be further subdivided. He paid attention to their role in worship and to the aptness of their content and style in relation to their use.

Jewish medieval interpreters, especially the greatest philosophical thinkers, analyzed the kinds of speech found in the Bible. SAADIA Gaon placed them into three major classes: commandments, announcements of consequences, and narratives, each with a positive and a negative aspect. He viewed the commandments as central and the others as effective ways to support them. In the psalms he recognized eighteen forms of speech, differentiated by such criteria as speaker and temporal orientation and connected with a variety of roles in worship. In his view they were not so much actual prayers as divinely revealed models for prayer. Two centuries later MAIMONIDES made use of a philosophical framework derived from Aristotle that analyzes the essences (inherent central nature) of objects. For him the psalms were in their essential nature really human prayers, inspired, but not in a specific sense revealed by God (*Guide,* II, 46). To a number of genres (such as creation accounts and prophetic autobiographies) he attributed an at least partially symbolic nature.

Many KARAITE and rabbinic exegetes from the tenth century on, including Yefet ben 'Ali and D. KIMHI, characterized biblical texts according to their kind of speech act or thrust, e.g., to explain, reprove, or comfort; this thrust was called *kawwanah* (Heb., intention) by ABRAVANEL (c. 1500). Some commentators—often the same ones, including Saadia and SAMUEL BEN MEIR (RASHBAM)—noted relations of parts of a text to one another, as well as stylistic features.

Medieval Christian interpretation of the Bible was in many ways similar to the Jewish. A widespread outlook regarded biblical patterns as archetypal models for life; it reflected a traditional perspective according to which an origin expresses a standard. (A Platonic understanding of forms as transhistorical models provided a philosophical version of this perspective, appealing especially to the intellectually and socially elite.) Indeed, from pre-Christian Hellenistic Judaism on, biblical patterns were often thought to be both older and better than those of Greece, with the latter not infrequently believed to have been derived from the former. This view, expressed especially in relation to non-Christian literature, implied a fairly positive attitude toward that literature and did not object to recognizing its at least partial continuity with the Bible. Biblical literature, in harmony with this orientation, was analyzed in terms of established rhetorical or poetic categories. For instance, ABELARD (in part like Augustine in his "literal" interpretation) gave a metaphoric view of the details of the creation story, with express reference to Plato's view of myth (see MYTHOLOGY AND BIBLICAL STUDIES).

Female interpreters (see FEMINIST INTERPRETATION), having on the whole received less formal classical rhetorical training than men, relied in good part on mystical illumination, but did not ignore literary forms (e.g., Angela of Foligno, 13th cent.). Such interpretation continued beyond the Middle Ages (e.g., by Teresa of Avila, 16th cent.).

A prominent feature of medieval Christian exegesis was a system of analysis that appeared also (perhaps first) in introductions to non-Christian Greco-Roman works; drawing on a mixed philosophical background, the analysis specified a work's circumstance, literary form (poetic or rhetorical genre, etc.), type of content ("kind of philosophy"), aim, and value for the reader. That system was widespread in eleventh- and twelfth-century commentaries like those by RUPERT, HUGH OF ST. VICTOR, PETER LOMBARD, and Gerhoch. In the thirteenth century the scheme was reformulated in terms of the four causes of Aristotle's conception of form (efficient cause: author; material cause: contents; formal cause: the patterning of a text, including its organization; final cause: goal). Analyses of this sort were applied systematically to the entire text of biblical books by THOMAS AQUINAS and BONAVENTURE and included reflections about the interrelationships between different aspects and phenomena; e.g., Aquinas observed that the symbolic mode of Jeremiah's words was appropriate to his office as a prophet. This kind of systematic "scholastic" exegesis continued into the fourteenth century.

The popularity of Aristotelianism reflected a partial movement away from an aristocratic structuring of society, a development exhibited in the spirit of emerging universities; a major step in the same direction was taken by a philosophical way of thinking that was called "modern" since it consciously broke to a considerable extent with the traditions of the past. This new way recognized only particulars as primary realities and was thus closely related to the rise of individualism, which occurred in late medieval semi-independent cities. For this kind of thought (formulated profoundly by William of Ockham [d. 1349]), form represents, not a general reality reflected by, or present in, an object, but a particular shape. In many spheres of thought, practice, and experience, the new perspective gradually gained ground until it became close to being dominant in the nineteenth century as part of what was known as a historical orientation.

Structural observations continued within the less particularist streams of tradition during the period from the sixteenth to the eighteenth centuries. For instance, stylistic and classificatory comments were made during the sixteenth century by ERASMUS, T. CAJETAN, LUTHER, P. MELANCHTHON, ZWINGLI, CALVIN, J. BULLINGER, T. CRANMER, and others. The Lutheran M. FLACIUS ILLYRICUS presented a thorough analysis of biblical patterns. Although he sought to be less humanistic than Melanchthon, he was deeply influenced by Aristotle. He believed that genres, determined especially by content but also by style, each have a special impact on life, so

that a consideration of them clarifies the aim of biblical literature. Biblical genres, as he described them, form a rich set of structures, including both divine address and speech directed toward God. Thereafter, often in association with Aristotelian ideas, classifications of biblical materials continued to appear, as in treatments by C. LAPIDE (1625), A. FRANCKE (1693), and J. Turretin.

Three major tendencies moving away from a consideration of general forms marked the period from the sixteenth to the eighteenth centuries: a strong interest in factual history, increased attention to differences between the styles of individual authors (partially present already in Jerome), and a removal of content from rhetorical analysis. The last of these reflected in part a skepticism about coherence in reality, e.g., about the question of an appropriateness of forms of expression in relation to thought.

Another tendency related to these was the placing of a dividing line between biblical forms and those of classical or other non-Christian traditions. It showed itself in directions that state that one should not combine in the same poem contents derived from both of these sources and in analyses that suggest that sacred rhetoric has special rules. One of the factors contributing to this differentiation was a sharpened contrast between faith and reason characteristic of particularism; another was a sense for the variety of traditions, which is an integral part of that outlook. A third, more special one was an avoidance of ornate forms in middle-class public speaking, causing the style of biblical speech, like that of the prophets, to seem out of the ordinary. R. LOWTH in 1753 effectively addressed these and related issues in what is probably still the finest overall study of biblical poetry. He solved the problem of style by characterizing prophecy—together with parallelism, which had previously been considered a rhetorical feature—as poetic. In regard to differences in poetic standards, he argued that the biblical forms were more basic and less special or artificial than the Greco-Roman. In its careful treatment of biblical structures together with their purposes, this work represents in important ways the culmination of a classical approach, while showing sensitivity to the newer movement toward a historical outlook.

M. MENDELSSOHN (in a January 1757 letter to G. Lessing) pointed in this new direction by rejecting the idea of separate classes in literature. Nevertheless, he recognized three kinds of poetry—song, elegy, and ode (the last kind, reflective)—in the psalms. J. G. HERDER, who interacted with him, provided sensitively drawn pictures of biblical literature in *The Spirit of Hebrew Poetry* (1782–83) and other studies. He continued to employ classifications but did so quite loosely and sometimes in an unusual manner; for instance, he classed the psalms according to their complexity (1787). A sign of the change in outlook is that J. G. EICHHORN (1780–83) viewed genres as external forms (*Einkleidung,* "clothing").

W. DE WETTE rejected Mendelssohn's typology since de Wette believed that Hebrew poetry is "formless and special." Radicalizing an older view that each genre requires a special HERMENEUTICS, he said that "every writing requires its own hermeneutic" (*Beiträge* 2 [1807] 25). He ordered the psalms by "content," however; the resulting classification was very similar to the one later set forth within a different theoretical framework by Gunkel. Somewhat like de Wette, F. BLEEK (in his 1860 introduction) regarded older psalms as personal in character and later ones as imitations.

One consequence of the emerging historical orientation was a sequencing of genres according to their antiquity. Thus myth was treated as the oldest form of expression by the classicist C. Heyne near the end of the eighteenth century and, following him, by Eichhorn, J. P. GABLER, G. BAUER, and J. Jahn (Catholic). This perspective modified the one according to which revelation took place during an original period, now envisioning progress, at least intellectually, beyond that time.

The liberal critical approach, nevertheless, far from dominated all publications. Conservative works or those oriented toward a general public continued to present LITERARY and full-scale rhetorical analyses, usually with extensive typologies. They included analyses by A. Gügler, J. Wenrich, C. Plantier, G. Gilfillan, I. Taylor, C. Ehrt, T. NÖLDEKE (1869), J. Fürst, and D. Cassel; the majority of these authors, the last two of whom were Jewish, were not specifically biblical scholars. In a partial contrast, specialists in the field attended more closely to external forms not directly related to content, like meter.

As particularism reached a high point during the nineteenth century, its problematic side also became apparent. Intellectually it threatened all rationality. Socially it created a free-for-all in which the strong defeated the weak. Some thinkers, notably Nietzsche, largely affirmed these consequences. Many, however, found them intellectually and ethically unacceptable and resurrected a partial interest in commonness, which supported an integrative role in society for the socioeconomic lower class.

The new social orientation was important to a "school" that pursued a RELIGIONSGESCHICHTLICHE approach, meaning by "religion" a general category of human experience. For the content of its investigation this school gave close attention to the social structures that embody popular life. Its members, including Gunkel (who politically held some sympathy for socialism), made efforts in lectures and writings to propagate the results of their investigations to a broad audience.

Sensitive to the social dimension, Gunkel reversed the position of the psalms held by de Wette and Bleek; he regarded standardized features not as secondary developments but as temporally primary generic patterns that are adapted in individual psalms. For other traditions

Gunkel also envisioned highly predictable structures that closely relate to recurring events in the life of a group where they have their "seat in life" (*Sitz im Leben*). Still, Gunkel was ambivalent about individuality. He appreciated the "living" character of patterned popular, largely oral, culture; but he valued, at least equally, the individualized personal expressions available in the written documents (e.g., in his commentary on Psalms [1926]).

Gunkel's interest in generality reached far beyond the Israelite or even the Near Eastern sphere. By frequently citing evidence from all parts of the world, he made clear that he was concerned with human structures and not merely with isolated and accidental phenomena. This general orientation was not shared by all of the many scholars inspired by him; it was, however, well represented by H. JAHNOW in her study of the dirge (1923).

Gunkel considered linguistic form to be an easily recognizable feature, but he listed content first among the determiners of a generic structure. Accordingly, he could take over de Wette's content-oriented classification of psalms. Thus the word *form* in the term *form criticism*, as it was applied by other scholars to his procedure, refers, not primarily to external phenomena, but to a structure or pattern. Crucial for Gunkel was the connection of genres with life; that interest gave his work a sociological cast (see SOCIOLOGY AND HB STUDIES). Mood, a psychological category (see PSYCHOLOGY AND BIBLICAL STUDIES), was also significant for him—placed next to thought as a part of content.

Gunkel's generic and structural orientation fits in well with the revolt against individualism and historicism widely current in the culture. For him as for others, however, the question was not one of choosing between the different visions but one of finding appropriate ways to combine them. In regard to the historical dimension he made the debatable assumption that the early stage of genres as well as of particular texts exhibited simple and "pure" forms, while later ones combined those into complex structures.

Quite a few scholars took this historical view very seriously and attempted to reconstruct on its basis a prehistory for a text, often thought to be oral. Many, especially in NT studies, focused exclusively on small units. Somewhat differently, G. von RAD argued that the ritual "credo" of Deut 26:4-9 formed one of the two basic structures out of which the Hexateuch as a whole emerged (1938). (More holistically, G. Mendenhall [1954] derived the structure of the Pentateuch and many other features of biblical literature from Hittite and other treaty forms.) Gradually, however, it became clear that the assumption that early forms are simple or pure is largely unfounded. Thus the enterprise of writing history on the basis of formal consideration (form criticism in sense 3 above) came under a cloud; the procedure used (formal analysis) was not well matched to this aim (history).

A significant consequence of a concern with genres was the realization that many of them were complementary to one another, operating simultaneously in the service of varied human needs. Indeed, it became apparent that, although biblical literature was given its shape over a period of perhaps one thousand years—much of it after the first fall of Jerusalem—the genres exhibited in it were virtually all copresent in the culture even before the exile. Although few scholars denied that genres changed to some extent over the centuries, there was a widespread willingness to acknowledge that many biblical psalms, proverbs, ritual laws, etc., were preexilic in a form at least closely approximating that in which they now appear. Similarly, in structural-functional sociology and anthropology a largely synchronic view could displace a primarily diachronic one.

The shift in perspective was far from universal, of course. The historian A. ALT (1934) viewed the several kinds of Israelite law as competing structures derived from different traditions. With a widened knowledge of ancient culture and a more functional view, H. Cazelles argued that they represent complementary genres with a range comparable to that of both Hittite and modern laws and instructions (1946).

When structural and historical perspectives, each with its own procedure, were combined systematically, a history of a genre or of a group of related genres resulted. Gunkel furnished such histories for PROPHECY (1917) and psalms (1933, with J. Begrich). The same topics were treated again, with at least some attention to history, by S. MOWINCKEL (psalms [1951; ET 1962]); C. WESTERMANN (psalms [1954, ET 1981]; judgmental prophecy [1960, ET 1967]; words of salvation [1987]); and J.-N. Aletti and J. Trublet (psalms [1983]). P. Hanson, among others, traced the emergence of apocalyptic forms (1975; see APOCALYPTICISM). Partial histories of the genres of wisdom included one by H. Schmid (1966). A. Rofé examined prophetic stories from a developmental perspective (1982; ET 1988); S. Niditch, symbolic visions (1983); J. Van Seters, historiography (1983); and D. Damrosch, narrative forms more generally (1987).

A step partially diverging from Gunkel was to envision a genre, not as a structure lying behind and utilized in a text, but as the dynamic pattern of the text seen as an actually or potentially general one. It was possible to follow this line only if a genre was permitted to have a considerable amount of variability, for clearly the individual texts that are examples of the genre are not completely stereotyped.

Thus Mowinckel considered most of the biblical psalms as being cultic, i.e., used on organized ritual occasions (1916). In this he was followed at least partially by many others. H. G. Reventlow took the cultic approach perhaps farther than anyone else, especially by viewing Jeremiah's confessions largely in non-personal terms. In most cultures, to be sure, the line between organized ritual and other expressions of religion is very fluid, if it can be drawn at all. Perhaps to some extent aware of that (his father was an important Africanist), Westermann rejected a specifically cultic view and related the psalms to the basic operations of praise and lament (1954). W. Brueggemann reformulated their patterns in sociopsychological terms (orientation, disorientation, and new orientation [1984]).

Westermann's analysis of genres grouped its features into substructures, e.g., within a lament there are first-person, second-person (often God-directed), and third-person (enemy, etc.) elements. This kind of patterning resembles that characteristic of STRUCTURALISM. P. Beauchamp, a representative of that movement, provided a view of the systematic interweaving and contrasting of elements of this sort as they occur in different genres, so that a system of genres becomes visible (1971). Somewhat similarly, the cult-oriented tradition represented by Mowinckel stood close to the work of what can loosely be called the MYTH AND RITUAL SCHOOL, which emphasized, as its name implies, both structure and type of context. Structuralism and a "patternism" appearing within the myth and ritual school represent, of course, anti-particularist perspectives.

One line of endeavor has related the structures of biblical literature to linguistics. W. Richter (1971), who moved in this direction, distinguished between form and genre. In his view form represents the organization of a particular text; he treated separately its "external," syntactic-stylistic, and "inner" meaning aspects. A genre, according to Richter, is to be identified on the basis of the external features of texts. Unlike most twentieth-century linguistic theorists, he holds that one should operate inductively, proceeding from the particular to the general. His is thus a thoroughly particularist viewpoint, which, as noted, typically separates the external from the internal. K. Koch (1974) has also sought to relate genre criticism to linguistics. He refers to a version of the latter known as text linguistics or discourse analysis, which, as is not well known, has absorbed insights from biblical studies. C. Hardmeier (1978) provides a detailed reformulation of form criticism in terms of a theory of linguistic action. He has been reinforced by linguistics in the view that verbal features are not strictly correlated with content or situation. A reflective analysis of biblical genres within the framework of a general communication theory that explores the human meaning of the literary structures has been furnished by a group of scholars in a work edited by F. Deist and W. Vorster (1986).

The works just mentioned entered increasingly into the realm of theoretical discussions of language that, especially since about 1920, had focused on the variety of speech "functions" (expressed especially by the first, second, or third person, according to K. Bühler), language "games" (constituting "forms of life," L. Wittgenstein), or speech "acts" (performances, J. Austin). A theological wing of this discussion had begun, also about 1920, with a distinction between personal ("I" and "you") and impersonal speech. Following this tradition, a number of biblical scholars and theologians emphasized the personal thrust of much of biblical speech. Thus A. Heschel showed the directedness of divine speech toward humanity (1936; ET 1962); W. ZIMMERLI discussed divine self-presentations (1963); and C. Westermann argued that many biblical expressions are not assertion but direct address (1984, 202). It was also noted that psalms are often directed toward God. A number of theologies of the HB (including von Rad's, with his focus on *Heilsgeschichte* [1957; ET 1962]) were based largely on attempts to identify in the text generic patterns like those outlined above. Rather than focus on particular ideas or directives, the theologian focused on generic forms and structures to understand how these forms functioned in the faith community.

A recognition of different types of speech with divergent functions allowed those who believe in the divine verbal inspiration of the Bible to distinguish between biblical truth and historical or scientific accuracy. Such an orientation has been discussed intensively by Roman Catholics since the turn of the twentieth century (M.-J. LAGRANGE [1896]), resurrecting and extending medieval and earlier reflections. It was given official approval by the encyclical *Divino afflante Spiritu* (1943), which encouraged the study of genres. Similar considerations have moved a number of traditional Protestants to reject a highly literal (better: historicist) interpretation of biblical narratives, although not many of them have gone so far as C. Pinnock (1984). Analyses along these lines should not be understood as being primarily negative, for their main interest is in apprehending on the basis of literary types the purposes of the texts (e.g., W. Kaiser [1981] 95), in a manner not unlike that of earlier exegesis.

Interpreters who are more questioning of biblical AUTHORITY, including non-theologians, also found in literary analysis a way to reveal the character and significance of the Bible and to do so in relation to a broad public. C. BRIGGS, who presented an overview of the literary forms (types and styles) of the Bible with the aim that "the ordinary reader can enjoy it" without being a professional (1883, 216), believed that a new critical period was dawning, for which literature rather than history would be the central focus (1899, 247). This judgment proved to be largely correct. Not only biblical specialists but also others provided an extensive and notable succession of literary, often generic, studies. Representing a variety of religious orientations, they included M. ARNOLD, W. R. HARPER, R. MOULTON, C. Kent, J. Gardiner, H. Fowler, L. Wild, J. MUILENBURG, A. Culler, M. BUBER, F. Rosenzweig, E. GOODSPEED, S. Freehof, Z. Adar, E. Good,

J. Ackerman, and L. Ryken. Many of them were deeply involved in social issues, including women's rights. A number of the studies did not concentrate on providing technical information for the academic specialist and consequently have been partially forgotten in academia. Repeatedly, however, they raised profound theoretical issues about the relation of the content and manner of biblical expression to human life.

Twentieth-century applications of rhetorical criticism have included a number of analyses based on a narrow conception of rhetoric, with a focus primarily on external form as it had been advocated by members of the particularist tradition since the fifteenth century. Other studies partially revived a more comprehensive classical approach, attending closely to content. A full-scale revival of the rhetorics of Aristotle and Menander (c. 300 CE) would have resembled much of twentieth-century form criticism, since genres identified within the latter were to a large extent treated by the former.

Interaction with FOLKLORE studies has been fruitful and was important, e.g., for Gunkel. An analysis that can serve as a model for form criticism was furnished by C. Fontaine (1982); she integrates a folklore perspective informed by Gunkel's approach in attending simultaneously to content and use without following his more questionable assumptions.

The acquisition of a post-historical perspective—one that includes, but is not limited to, historical criticism—has not been an easy one for biblical scholarship. Older ways of thinking have repeatedly been resurrected without much change and added to the historical, even though they are not strictly compatible. Specifically, Gunkel and many others following him relied in good part on Aristotelian essentialism, i.e., the notion that there is only one correct typology for objects. In doing so they failed to take part in an intellectual development that in a certain way both synthesizes and transcends the previous approaches. Most important, for a point of view often called relationism—closely connected with pragmatism, following C. Peirce—both particularity and generality are fundamental, playing roles in real relations; an object is not separated from a subject (M. Buss [1991]). Characteristic of this view is an acceptance of probability connections (partial indeterminacy) and of a variety of orders (with relativity to a standpoint). Within this outlook, form can be treated as a complex of relations.

A number of attempts have been made to reformulate the form-critical task along such lines. A probabilistic multidimensional approach was applied by M. Buss to Hosea (1969). In a theoretical article R. Knierim opposes a "monolithic conception of genre" (1973, 467), as, in fact, some scholars did before him. G. Fohrer, in his OT introduction (1965; ET 1968, 28), rejects the equating of a life setting with an "institution"; other scholars followed suit by arguing for a loose connection between texts and situations insofar as these are externally describable. The question then arises whether particularism should prevail after all—or perhaps skeptical relativism. One can answer in the negative by pointing to a rationale that places phenomena at least partially into intrinsic relations (as opposed to those, including J. Barton [1984, 32], who see genres only as conventions). An exploration of such relations requires the continued and expanded investigation of psychological and sociological, as well as logical, questions.

About 1970 a group of scholars gathered to produce an overview of the forms of OT literature. G. Tucker (1971) presented a model for their procedure based in good part on the joint discussions. Notable is that the procedure discusses particular texts in the light of applicable genres and that it provides an outline ("structure") and identifies a context ("setting") and thrust ("intention") for each unit, both large and small. This procedure implies a basically synchronic understanding of the task of form criticism. It may also reflect some skepticism about the feasibility of describing separately the many genres of biblical literature; nevertheless, an essentialist tendency appears in the series in that its form of presentation typically implies that a text's structure and especially its genre are correctly identifiable in only one way. A consequence of this text-centered, synchronic, and partially Aristotelian approach is that the analysis resembles medieval, especially scholastic, exegesis—a fact that is largely to its credit. It does not simply represent a return to earlier exegesis, however, for a critical-historical perspective shines through at various points.

A basic issue remains current, mentioned when R. Murphy, a member of the group just discussed, calls the psalms a "school of prayer" (1983, 113). Do biblical forms constitute models for the expressions and beliefs of all time? Insofar as forms are not just particular they potentially apply to the present, but are there not divergences between past and present that require changes in speech and behavior? In answer one can say that a relational analysis, with a recognition of the roles of forms in their contexts, provides a basis for an application of the principle of analogy, which joins sameness with difference.

Bibliography: **J.-N. Aletti and J. Trublet,** *Approche poétique et théologique des psaumes: analyses et méthodes* (1983). **L. Alonso Schökel,** *Estudios de poética hebrea* (1963), with a history of formal study; *The Inspired Word* (1966; ET 1967). **A. Alt,** *Die Ursprünge des israelitischen Rechts* (1934). **I. Baldermann,** *Einführung in die Bibel* (1988). **H. Barth and O. Steck,** *Exegese des Alten Testaments* (1978⁸). **J. Barton,** *Reading the OT: Method in Biblical Study* (1974, rev. 1996). **P. Beauchamp,** "L'analyse structurale et l'exégèse biblique" (VTSup 22, 1971) 113-28. **W. Brueggemann,** *The Message of the Psalms: A Theological Commentary* (1984). **C. Briggs,**

Biblical Study (1883); *General Introduction to the Study of Holy Scripture* (1899). **M. J. Buss,** *The Prophetic Word of Hosea: A Morphological Study* (1969); *Biblical Form Criticism in Its Context* (JSOTSup 274, 1999). **H. H. Cazelles,** *Études sur le code de l'alliance* (1946). **D. Damrosch,** *The Narrative Covenant: Transformations of Genre in the Growth of Biblical Literature* (1987). **J. Daniélou,** "Les genres littéraires d'après les Pères de l'Église," *Los generos literarios de la Sagrada Escritura* (Congreso de Ciencias Eclesiásticas, 1957) 275-83. **F. E. Deist and W. S. Vorster** (eds.), *Words from Afar* (1986), including a useful bibliography. **J. G. Eichhorn,** *Introduction to the Study of the OT* (1780–83; ET 1888). **G. Fohrer,** *Introduction to the OT* (1965; ET 1968). **C. Fontaine,** *Traditional Sayings in the OT* (Bible and Literature Series 5, 1982). **A. Francke,** *Manuductio ad lectionem Scripturae Sacrae* (1693). **H. Gunkel,** *Die Propheten* (1917); "Der Micha-Schluss," *ZS* 2 (1924) 145-78 (ET in *What Remains of the OT and Other Essays* [1928] 115-49); *Die Psalmen* (HZAT 24, 1926); (with J. Begrich), *Einleitung in die Psalmen: Die Gattungen der religiosen Lyrik Israels* (GHAT 2, 1933). **H. Hahn,** *OT in Modern Research* (1954). **P. Hanson,** *The Dawn of Apocalyptic* (1975). **C. Hardmeier,** *Texttheorie und biblische Exegese* (1978). **W. R. Harper** (ed.), *The Biblical World* 1 (1893) 243-47. **J. H. Hayes** (ed.), *OT Form Criticism* (1974). **J. G. Herder,** *The Spirit of Hebrew Poetry* (1782–83; ET 1833). **A. Heschel,** *The Prophets* (1936; ET 1962). **H. Jahnow,** *Das Hebräische Leichenlied im Rahmen der Völkerdichtung* (BZAW 36, 1923). **W. Kaiser, Jr.,** *Toward an Exegetical Theology* (1981). **R. Knierim,** "OT Form Criticism Reconsidered," *Int* 27 (1973) 435-68. **K. Koch,** *Was ist Formgeschichte?* (1974³; ET of 2nd ed., *The Growth of the Biblical Tradition* [1969]). **M.-J. Lagrange,** "L'inspiration et les exigences de la critique," *RB* (1896) 496-518. **C. A. Lapide,** *Duodecim minores prophetas* (1625). **G. E. Mendenhall,** "Ancient Oriental and Biblical Law," *BA* 17 (1954) 24-46; "Covenant Forms in Israelite Tradition," ibid., 49-76. **S. Mowinckel,** *The Psalms in Israel's Worship* (1951; ET 1962). **H.-P. Müller,** "Formgeschichte/Formenkritik, I. Altes Testament," *TRE* 11 (1983) 271-85. **R. Murphy,** *Wisdom Literature and Psalms* (IBT, 1983). **S. Niditch,** *The Symbolic Vision in Biblical Tradition* (HSM 30, 1983). **T. Nöldeke,** *Untersuchungen zur Kritik des Alten Testaments* (1869). **G. Osborne,** "Genre Criticism—Sensus Literalis," *Trinity Journal* 4, 2 (1983) 1-27. **C. Pinnock,** *The Scripture Principle* (1984). **G. von Rad,** *The Problem of the Hexateuch and Other Essays* (1938; ET 1966); *OT Theology* (1957; ET 1962). **W. Richter,** *Exegese als Literaturwissenschaft* (1971). **A. Robert,** "Littéraires (genres)," *DBSup* 5 (1957) 405-21. **R. B. Robinson,** *Roman Catholic Exegesis Since "Divino Afflante Spiritu"* (1988). **A Rofé,** *The Prophetic Stories: The Narratives About the Prophets in the HB, Their Literary Types and History* (1982; ET 1988). **H. H. Schmid,** *Wesen und Geschichte der Weisheit: Eine Untersuchung zur altorientalischen und israelitischen Weisheitsliteratur* (1966). **G. M. Tucker,** *Form Criticism of the OT* (Guides to Biblical Scholarship, 1971). **J. Van Seters,** *In Search of History: Historiography in the Ancient World and Origins of Biblical History* (1983). **C. Westermann,** *Praise and Lament In the Psalms* (1954; ET 1981);

Basic Forms of Prophetic Speech (BBET 31, 1960; ET 1967); *The Parables of Jesus in the Light of the OT* (1984; ET 1990). **W. Zimmerli**, *I Am Yahweh* (1963; ET 1982).

M. J. BUSS

FORM CRITICISM, NEW TESTAMENT

1. Definition. Form criticism (in German usually *Form-* or *Gattungsgeschichte*) is understood in both a broad and a narrow sense.

a. The broader and older meaning. NT form criticism relates above all to the transmission of the Gospels, less so of the epistles. Its goal is the reconstruction of the oral stages of tradition lying behind the fixed written products accessible to us now. This procedure is called form criticism because in the initial attempt to solve the SYNOPTIC question it came to be oriented toward the pure forms of oral transmission. It was assumed that only in the course of the traditions' further transmission and reduction to written form, with subsequent editorial changes, were they robbed of their purity. With the reconstruction of the presumed pure form of a text, one theoretically had access to its oldest form, a situation that often tempted scholars to take this reconstruction to be the words of JESUS himself (*ipsissima vox*).

The standard assumptions in this undertaking were hypotheses drawn from biblical FOLKLORE studies, according to which a basic entity in the course of time becomes increasingly enriched (like an onion covered with layers of skin) and is linked with other entities. The question of form in older form criticism thus stood in the service of the question of the pre-Easter "historical" Jesus. Wherever this mode of inquiry was employed outside the Gospels, it focused on the fragments of songs and confessional formulas that had been part of the early presentation of the *kerygma* (this was particularly the case, on the heels of H. Conzelmann, with K. Wengst). Here, too, interest was directed completely to the "fragments of the very oldest" transmission stages (even if in this case only to those of the immediately post-Easter period). Accordingly, form criticism became the embodiment of critical-methodical NT research in general, since "critical" was employed precisely in the sense of a separation of the older, genuine material from the younger, subsequent accretions.

b. The more recent, narrower meaning. More recent form criticism is oriented toward modern LITERARY criticism (linguistics) and to questions concerning textual types and genres. This cooperation between exegesis and linguistics is heralded by such scholars as R.-A. de Beaugrande and W. Dressler (*Introduction to Text Linguistics* [1981]), and H. Kalverkämper (*Orientierung zur Textlinguistik* [1981]). The point of departure for the classification of forms and genres is no longer the larger classical genres (epic, drama, lyric poetry). Text classification is now determined on the basis of those domi-

nant elements (and thus not simply the ones prevailing overall) that lie fairly close to the textual surface or that betray the composition of a text by means of connective or organizational signals. Thus characteristics of linguistic form in the narrower sense of the term determine the subdivisions into textual types and genres. Accordingly, it has been discovered (de Beaugrande-Dressler) that for descriptive texts, attributes and description of conditions are important; for narrative texts, the portrayal of temporal sequence according to the model of cause, ground, purpose, and possibility; and for argumentative texts, conflict (opposition), value judgments, and the statement of reasons. Using these beginnings as a point of departure, K. Berger employed the tripartite division of ancient rhetoric into symbuleutic (admonishing), epidictic (descriptive), and dikanic (judgmental) textual types and attempted to transfer into this framework the various results of previous form and genre research (including HB research). Given this orientation toward rhetoric, the intended effect on the reader is particularly important for the determination of genre. This intended effect stands in close relationship to the means of forming and molding the textual surface, hence the question of origin (and prehistory) of the material contained in a text is, not what stands in the foreground, but rather the problem of its function. By "function" we mean the persuasive power of a text for the addressee, its actual effect, and the contextual connection to certain situations in primitive Christian history.

Discussions in the last decades of the twentieth century have uncovered at least some problems within the older model of form criticism. The most important are the postulate that the pure form stood at the beginning of a development (since even the reverse is easily possible and documented—namely, that through the editorial process oral variety is reduced to its basic framework); the optimism concerning the unbroken continuity between the oral and written forms of a text; and the deprecation of the present written text (which in form criticism led particularly to a neglect of the literature of the epistles). The frequently extreme and somewhat subjective employment of literary criticism for the purpose of separating sources has also become questionable since literary criticism is often precipitously engaged whenever the interpreter, simply because of the influence of modern logic and world views, insists on questioning the unity of a text.

2. Form Criticism and "Situation in Life" (*Sitz im Leben*). NT research took over the concept of the "situation in life" from HB scholars, most notably H. GUNKEL. This concept refers to the institutionally recurring recitation of certain texts in the life of a community. The problem in older form criticism was that almost exclusively such life situations could only be imagined as cultic occasions (precisely in the sense of a recitation of holy texts). This left as Christian cultic occasions only baptism, Eucharist, and sermon; texts in question were accordingly assigned to one of these three. Thus, for example, 1 Peter was understood as the rendering of a baptismal service rather than as a letter addressed to the exiles of the Dispersion (1 Pet 1:1).

The less that was known about the religious services of the early Christians, the greater the attempt to fill out that knowledge with the postulated life situations in a kind of circular logic. One can say, therefore, that, aside from the questionable literary-critical delimitation of the song and confessional fragments, this mode of inquiry has not proved reliable.

More recent form criticism, on the other hand, inquires much more comprehensively into the function of a genre in "typical situations of early Christian history," a procedure that includes rather than excludes situations within religious services. It can be demonstrated, for example, that certain genres of miracle stories served to resolve problems within early Christian communities that had to do with the topic of "full authority" (e.g., deprecation of the Jewish purity commandments) or that PARABLES served as argumentative vehicles to suggest or encourage certain behavior (e.g., the acceptance of those who joined the community at a later period, Matt 20:1-16). Thus one can conclude that a text was read anew and with different intentions in different phases of the history of early Christianity.

3. The Relationship Between Oral Character and Written Character. Older form criticism developed out of a religiously motivated and almost complete veneration of the oral character of materials in tandem with a strong resistance to any kind of "literature." This holds true—in spite of different points of departure—for J. HERDER as well as for F. OVERBECK. Herder concluded that only an oral character is appropriate for the gospel, since written character is an attribute of "law." Therefore, his efforts, like those of later form criticism, are already directed toward the reconstruction of the oral, original gospel. For Overbeck the early Christian tradition is anything but literature; this verdict influenced scholars right up to M. DIBELIUS, who was unable to attribute any of the more rigidly defined or literary forms to early Christianity with its intense eschatological expectations. Overbeck arrived at his thesis of Christianity as a proto-literature essentially on the basis of his hypothesis of the world-negating, eschatological character of the earliest Christian faith. Consequently, form criticism also became the arena in which the systematic problem of the relationship between church and world was treated.

More recent form criticism, on the other hand, no longer possesses the optimism to assume—apart from isolated sayings and formulas—that one can reconstruct the form of that initial oral character at all. Instead, its substitute is the offer to paraphrase or circumscribe the content of the older stages of tradition much more

broadly and cautiously by listing motifs. (For example, the tradition lying behind Mark 14:1-10, Luke 7:36-50, and John 12:1-9 cannot be described as an original or proto-text but rather almost certainly in the sense of a "motif field": When Jesus sits at the table and is anointed by a woman, the other participants at the meal are incensed. Jesus concludes the scene according to the form of the *chria* with a brief word justifying the woman's objectionable behavior.) Only in individual instances do concretely indentifiable words belong to this common corpus of tradition.

This means, however, that the written text in question has gained in value in comparison to every oral preliminary stage. On the one hand, the possibility of reconstructing that oral stage has been reduced since the criteria that J. JEREMIAS and E. KÄSEMANN proposed in the 1950s and 1960s have disappeared—namely, the identifying characteristics of later, communal constructions: allegorization, traceable roots in Judaism or in typical interests of the Christian community, and additions or accretions to the purer forms. On the other hand, ideological prejudices against written forms and literary characteristics have been at least partly, if not yet completely, overcome. Thus it is no longer assumed unconditionally that eschatological expectation precludes expressing oneself in forms also common to literature. The immediate manifestation of this change of perspective was the discussion concerning the nature of a "gospel."

4. Form-critical Discussion of the Genre "Gospel." For Overbeck the Gospels belong to proto-literature because "alongside the book itself there is no room for the life of the author" (*Overbeckiana* 2 [ed. M. Tetz, 1962] 90). Dibelius and R. BULTMANN integrated this concept of "unliterary lesser literature" from Overbeck. For Dibelius the substantive contrast between gospel and world has consequences in the realm of form criticism: The history of primitive Christian forms is the history of an increasing secularization and simultaneously a paganization. The struggle between gospel and world is directly manifested in the history of forms (hence "form history"—*Formgeschichte*), for the pure and simple forms of the initial Christian preaching still stand completely under the auspices of near eschatological expectation. Dibelius's concept, however, stands or falls with the historically related question of whether anything like genuinely Christian or pagan forms exists at all. Hence in the end this project proves to be in a certain sense apologetic, since it attempts to demonstrate both formally and substantively the particularity and uniqueness of the gospel.

Bultmann's hypothetical assumption of the existence of a complete genre similarly originates from systematic premises. For the genre "aretalogy"—allegedly presupposed by the Gospels—there exists not one single independent example from antiquity in the sense of the listing of the miraculous deeds of a human hero (see K. Berger, "Hellenistische Gattungen im Neuen Testament," *ANRW* II, 25.2 [1982] 1218-31). In the subsequent exegetical scholarship influenced by Bultmann, this genre is needed not only for reconstructing the (hypothetical) *semeia* (sign) source in the Gospel of John but also to support the assumption of pre-Markan miracle story collections. This systematic agenda suggests that these genres became orthodox Christian only after being linked with the theology of the cross, because "the cross" criticizes naive faith in miracles. According to Bultmann, only in this way could the unique genre "gospel" originate at all. Bultmann asserts that this genre is unique (and not, e.g., to be confused with the genre "biography") because the miraculous intervention of God in the world is suspended by reference to the cross. As with Dibelius, the basic position here is apologetic and concentrated around the concept of gospel. Dibelius's eschatological expectation (and delay of the parousia) corresponds to Bultmann's theology of the cross; both are also well-known parts of the moveable scenery of theological discussion in subsequent German scholarship.

In more recent form criticism the discussion centers intensively on the relationship between gospel and the biography of antiquity. A. Dihle (1983) has categorically denied any connection between Christian gospel and ancient biography, whereas the connection was in principle not excluded in Anglo-Saxon research (C. Talbert [1977]; R. Tannehill [1981]) and was affirmed by Berger (1984). In this view the Gospels are more strongly bound to a mythologically oriented type of biography (it must be pointed out that the genre biography does not exist; one should speak rather of variously organized arrangements of biographical material). The *Lives of the Ten Speakers* by Plutarch is an example of such—in part weakly structured—collections.

5. Form-critical Research of Epistolary Literature. A. DEISSMANN's old differentiation between the more literary epistles (Hebrews in the NT) and the private letter of antiquity, to which the Pauline letters (see PAUL) stood particularly close, was based on social-romantic premises similar to those underlying the older form criticism of the Gospels. The alleged folkloric-popular elements of the Pauline letters, their artlessness—allegations based on the papyrus letters found in Egypt—corresponded all too precisely to the thesis of the Gospels as proto-literature. This thesis was an attempt to keep early Christianity far from the world of literature. This form-critically established path—in the older sense of "form-critical" with the sociological implications related to the "folk" in the early communities—proved untraversable. Paul's acquaintance with the rules of ancient rhetoric has been amply demonstrated (see F. Siegert [1984]; M. Bünker [1984]; the works of A. J. Malherbe; J. Schoon-Janssen [1990]).

If one not only views the NT letters as the repositories of fixed fragments (from hymns and confessions; see Wengst [1972]) but also takes their literary form as an object of form criticism, then the works of Bultmann (1910) and H. Thyen (1955) appear to be genuine contributions to the form criticism of letters, similarly the investigations of S. Stowers (1981) and T. Schmeller (1987) concerning the diatribe. It is not just a matter of "style" but a case of the relationship between the oral and written characters and precisely of the contributions to the form of specific sections. Furthermore, the form of the "diatribe" has a specific function that concerns pastoral care and presupposes a certain hierarchy of authority between the sender and the recipient. Research, especially in the United States, has contributed a series of works concerning NT epistolary formulas dealing with the epistolary thanksgiving and the self-recommendation as well as the genre of the epistolary recommendation. Concerning the epistolary prescript and postscript, the work of S. Schnider and W. Stender (1987) should be mentioned (see also Berger [1974]; and D. Lührmann [1980], who has compared the analogies of "household codes" to the ancient *oikonomikos*). The so-called hymns in the epistolary literature might have analogies in the ancient *enkomion*. From this perspective it is possible to explain affinities to the biographical elements within the Gospels through form criticism. For future research it would be of particular importance to identify additional typically epistolary forms in comparison with other letters of antiquity in order to describe and evaluate them for theological statements.

6. Future Tasks of Form Criticism. *a.* From a history-of-religion perspective the relationship between gospel and biography should be determined on the basis of the entire range of biographical material from antiquity. Similarly, as has already been done with the pronouncement stories, the historical-critical comparative material concerning individual genres should be made available and discussed in a comprehensive fashion. Of prime importance is an ordering of the NT material within the literature of early Judaism and the first three Christian centuries. The question of the reception and utilization of Hellenistic forms by the early rabbinate is also important.

b. The separation of form criticism and the history of textual transmission (tradition criticism) must be taken seriously. Instead of the relatively fruitless and endless discussion of the SYNOPTIC and JOHANNINE questions using source hypotheses, it would be preferable to see a discussion that reckons not only with fixed sources but also with a common oral tradition, thus freeing the way for a history of theology (also with regard to a relationship with the epistolary literature of the NT).

c. Clarification is needed concerning such basic methodological questions as the relationship between form and *Sitz im Leben* (understood in the more comprehensive sense) and between form and content. Clarification is also needed concerning the structure of Christian worship services in the first century CE. The individual stations of primitive Christian daily life are still unknown. Concerning the methodological clarification of TRADITION HISTORY, the phenomenon of semantic fields will have to be investigated more intensively, both theoretically and practically. Also, the methodological questions of the origin and delimitation of genres needs to be discussed (e.g., are miracle stories a genre?).

d. The ideological background of the history of form criticism needs to be investigated critically as well. This includes the critical relativization of the importance of the Easter faith for traditional form criticism. Scholars also need to examine whether the pronounced inclination of Protestant theology against the aesthetic examination of forms and against rhetoric (which is considered demagogic and worldly) does not mirror the phenomenon already discernible in the church fathers that whoever makes the most sovereign and comprehensive use of rhetoric in preaching is considered theoretically least worthy of trust.

7. Theological-substantive Meaning of Form Criticism. In older form criticism this question had multiple theological implications: (1) Scholars focused on determining the oldest material concerning Jesus, thereby presupposing a contrast between Jesus and the Christian community and between Jesus and Judaism. (2) Apologetically, the uniqueness of primitive Christian literature was to be demonstrated as lying as far as possible from literature as such and closer to the "lower classes" and in general as "simple" or "naive." Apologetic agendas of the older RELIGIONSGESCHICHTLICHE SCHULE were also perpetuated. (3) Form criticism was only partly critical since the notion persisted that one did have access to at least hypothetically reliable material concerning Jesus as well as to early confessions (as witnesses to the earliest orthodoxy).

Such apologetic agendas are missing within recent form criticism, as are the questionable attempts to separate Jesus from Judaism and from everything connected with "church," including the attempts to turn such distinctions within texts into form-critical arguments. Rather, form criticism has come to be concerned with determining the substantive value of the individual forms and genres: What is substantively being indicated by the fact that a certain genre is employed at all (e.g., biographical genres for portraying Jesus)? Or what does it mean when early Christianity takes up the genre tradition of household codes (or of the *oikonomikos,* etc.)? In other words, what substantive statement is made concerning the whole of a text by the genre itself? Form criticism not only enormously facilitates history-of-religion comparisons (by at least comparing analogous entities) but also draws attention to the substantive and rhetorical implications of the form in question. The

reception of more recent form criticism is admittedly influenced by the traditional prejudice against rhetoric by Kantian influenced theology (see KANT).

Bibliography: P. Benoit, "Reflexions sur la 'Formgeschichtliche Methode,' " *RB* 53 (1956) 481-512. **K. Berger,** *ZNW* 65 (1974) 190-231; *Exegese des Neuen Testaments* (UTB 658, 1977, 1991[3]); *Formgeschichte des Neuen Testaments* (1984); *Einführung in die Formgeschichte* (UTB 1444, 1987); "Form und Gattungsgeschichte," *HRWG* 2 (1990) 430-45; *Studien und Texte zur Formgeschichte* (TANZ 7, 1992). **G. Bornkamm,** "Evangelien, formgeschichtlich," *RGG³* 2 (1958) 749-53; "Formen und Gattungen," *RGG³* 2 (1958) 999-1005. **R. Bultmann,** *The History of the Synoptic Tradition* (1921, 1979[9]; ET 1963, 1968[2]); *Der Stil der paulinischen Predigt und die kynisch-stoische Diatribe* (FRLANT 13, 1910). **M. Bünker,** *Briefformular und rhetorische Disposition im 1. Korintherbrief* (1984). **A. Deissmann,** *Light from the Ancient East* (1910, 1923[4]; ET 1910, 1926[3]). **M. Dibelius,** *From Tradition to Gospel* (1919, 1971[6]; ET 1934); "Zur Formgeschichte der Evangelien," *TRu* NF 1 (1929) 185-216. **A. Dihle,** "Die Evangelien und die biographische Tradition der Antike," *ZTK* 80 (1983) 33-49. **W. G. Doty,** "The Discipline and Literature of NT Form Criticism," *ATR* 51 (1969) 257-321. **E. Fascher,** *Die formgeschichtliche Methode* (BZNW 2, 1924). **B. Gerhardsson,** *Memory and Manuscript: Oral and Written Transmission in Rabbinic Judaism and Early Christianity* (ASNU 22, 1961, 1964[2]). **F. C. Grant,** *The Gospels: Their Origin and Their Growth* (1957). **K. Grobel,** *Formgeschichte und synoptische Quellenanalyse* (FRLANT 53, 1937). **E. Güttgemanns,** *Candid Questions Concerning Gospel Form Criticism* (BEvT 54, 1971[2]; ET 1979). **G. Iber,** "Zur Formgeschichte der Evangelien," *TRu* NF 24 (1957–58) 283-338. **A. Jolles,** *Einfach Formen: Legende, Sage, Mythe, Rätsel, Spruch, Kasus, Memorabile, Märchen, Witz* (1930, 1958[2]). **E. Kamlah,** *Die Form der katalogischen Paränese im NT* (WUNT 7, 1964). **H. Köster,** "Formgeschichte/Formenkritik II: Neues Testament," *TRE* 11 (1983) 286-99. **G. Lohfink,** *The Bible: Now I Get It! A Form Criticism Handbook* (1973, 1974[2]; ET 1979). **D. Lührmann,** *NTS* 27 (1980) 63-97. **E. V. McKnight,** *What Is Form Criticism?* (Guides to Biblical Scholarship, 1969). **G. W. E. Nickelsburg,** "The Genre and Function of the Marcan Passion Narrative," *HTR* 73 (1980) 153-84. **E. Norden,** *Agnostos Theos: Untersuchungen zur Formgeschichte religiöser Rede* (1913, 1956[4]). **F. Overbeck,** *Über die Anfänge der patristischen Literatur* (1882, repr. 1970). **H. Riesenfeld,** *The Gospel Tradition and Its Beginnings: A Study in the Limits of "Formgeschichte"* (1957). **J. M. Robinson and H. Koester,** *Trajectories Through Early Christianity* (1971). **T. Schmeller,** *Paulus und die "Diatribe": Eine vergleichende Stilinterpretation* (1987). **W. Schmithals,** "Kritik der Formkritik," *ZTK* 77 (1980) 149-85. **S. Schnider and W. Stender,** *Studien zum neutestamentlichen Brieffformular* (1987). **J. Schoon-Janssen,** *Umstrittene Apologien in Paulusbriefen* (1990). **F. Siegert,** *Argumentation bei Paulus* (1985). **S. Stowers,** *The Diatribe and Paul's Letter to the Romans* (1981). **P. Stuhlmacher** (ed.), *Das Evangelium und* *die Evangelien* (WUNT 28, 1983, 1991). **C. H. Talbert,** *What Is a Gospel? The Genre of the Canonical Gospels* (1977). **R. C. Tannehill,** (ed.), *Pronouncement Stories* (*Semeia* 20, 1981). **G. Theissen,** *Urchristliche Wundergeschichten* (SNT 8, 1974). **H. Thyen,** *Der Stil der jüdisch-hellenistischen Homilie* (FRLANT 65, 1955). **K. Wengst,** *Christologische Formeln und Lieder des Urchristentums* (1972, 1973²). **A. N. Wilder,** *The Language of the Gospel: Early Christian Rhetoric* (1964). **W. Wrede,** *The Messianic Secret* (1901; ET 1971).

K. BERGER

FORSYTH, PETER TAYLOR (1848–1921)

Born May 12, 1848, in Aberdeen, Scotland, F. was educated at the University of Aberdeen, Göttingen, and New College, London. He served as a private tutor (1874–76) and held five pastorates (1876–1901). Subsequently he was principal of Hackney College, London (1901–21), and served as chairman of the Congregational Union of England and Wales (1905). He died Nov. 11, 1921.

F. drove to the heart of the gospel as few others have done. He declared that "the moral is the real" and (against theological sentimentality) emphasized the holiness of God's love and the priority of objective grace over subjective illumination. Sin is tragic, and redemption is wrought in history. God's power, authority, and love are not simply displayed, but are active and victorious in the cross. Christian freedom is by, in, and for—but never from—the gospel.

Works: *The Cruciality of the Cross* (1909); *The Person and Place of Jesus Christ* (1909, 1948); *The Work of Christ* (1910); *Faith, Freedom, and the Future* (1912); *The Principle of Authority in Relation to Certainty, Sanctity, and Society* (1913); *The Justification of God* (1916).

Bibliography: **J. F. Andrews** (daughter), "Memoir," *The Work of Christ* (1938²). **R. Benedetto,** *P. T. F. Bibliography and Index* (BIRS 27, 1993). **W. L. Bradley,** *P. T. F.: The Man and His Work* (1952). **R. M. Brown,** *P. T. F.: Prophet for Today* (1952). **G. O. Griffith,** *The Theology of P. T. F.* (1948). **T. Hart** (ed.), *Justice the True and Only Mercy: Essays on the Life and Theology of P. T. F.* (1995). **A. M. Hunter,** *P. T. F.: Per Crucem ad Lucem* (1974). **D. G. Miller et al.,** *P. T. F.: The Man, The Preacher's Theologian, Prophet for the Twentieth Century* (1981). **S. J. Mikolaski,** *CMCT,* 307-39 (with bibliography).

A. P. F. SELL

FOSDICK, HARRY EMERSON (1878–1969)

A native of Buffalo, New York, F. was educated at Colgate University (AB 1900), Union Theological Seminary (BD 1904), and Columbia University (MA 1908). From 1915 to 1946 he served on the faculty of Union Theological Seminary as professor of practical theology while ministering to New York's First Presbyterian

Church, then to Park Avenue Baptist, which moved in 1931 to John D. Rockefeller's magnificent Riverside Church in Morningside Heights, a deliberately interdenominational, inter-racial, international Protestant church. Under F.'s leadership New York City's Riverside Church became a world-famous center of religious instruction and social service. In 1922 he became one of the first to make use of radio in disseminating religious views. He retired from Union and Riverside in 1946, living in Bronxville, New York, until his death in 1969.

As a seminarian F. was greatly influenced by W. Clarke and by the writings of W. Rauschenbusch. He thus stressed the reality of the presence of God in humanity and the world, providing the basis for social action in addition to beliefs in the divinity of Christ, human immortality, and a generally optimistic view of cultural progress. His sermons and writings became the most effective expression of moderate United States Protestant liberalism in the first half of the twentieth century. He opposed fundamentalist rigidity in biblical interpretation, setting forth his positive views on the subject in two justly famous and powerfully influential works: *The Modern Use of the Bible,* using the theme of abiding experiences in changing categories, and *A Guide to Understanding the Bible,* considered one of the finest surveys in English of the results of nineteenth-century critical scholarship. His method reveals a mind gentle and patient yet forceful and clearly persuasive. He composed for the dedication of Riverside Church a hymn that rapidly became one of the most popular American hymns of the twentieth century: "God of Grace and God of Glory."

Works: In addition to many devotional books and collections of sermons: *Christianity and Progress* (1922); *The Modern Use of the Bible* (1924); *A Pilgrimage to Palestine* (1927); *A Guide to Understanding the Bible* (1938); *The Man from Nazareth, as His Contemporaries Saw Him* (Schaffer Lectures at Yale, 1949); *The Living of These Days: An Autobiography* (1956).

Bibliography: **H. W. Bowden,** *DARB* 163-64. **H. E. Ernst,** *American Protestant Liberalism as Exemplified in the Life and Thought of H. E. F.* (diss., St. Mary's Seminary and University [1988]). **R. M. Miller,** *H. E. F.: Preacher, Pastor, Prophet* (1985); *National Cyclopedia of American Biography,* vol. E, 266-67; vol. 55, 13-14 (1974).

J. M. BULLARD

FRANCK, SEBASTIAN (c. 1499–c. 1542).

After studying at Ingolstadt and Heidelberg, F. began his professional career as a priest. He left the priesthood to marry and for a while had his own publishing business, working first at Nuremberg, then from 1533 to 1539 at Ulm. He died in Basel.

F. produced a staggering number of books, beginning with a free translation of Althamer's *Diallage* (1528), in which he challenged certain ideas of Hans DENCK on how contradictions in the Scriptures are to be resolved. In the same year he wrote a tract on drunkenness, followed by three works (1534a; 1538b; 1539) devoted to his spiritualistic understanding of the Scriptures. Through F's work, people now had available massive historical treatments about the world and the church (1531a; 1531b; 1534b; 1538a). In addition F. translated ERASMUS's *In Praise of Folly* (1534), wrote three books critical of the times in which he lived, and a *Battle Manual Leading to Peace* (1539). W. DILTHEY said that F's ideas anticipate modern times in hundreds of streams. As biblical interpreter, F. is the classical spiritualist who sees everything external as a concession to human weakness. For him historical progress meant to get into the spirit and away from any material or bodily things. The Scriptures represent an eternal allegory containing nothing historical, but only the eternally typical; in Jungian terms, "archetypical" (see JUNG). More consistently spiritualistic than C. von SCHWENCKFELD and indeed less rooted in the church, he nevertheless made an enormous contribution to Western spirituality and liberal thought.

Works: *Chronica* (1531a); *Türkenchronik* (1531b); *Paradoxa* (1534a); *Weltbüch* (1534b); *Germaniae Chronicon* (1538a), *Die güldin Arch* (1538b); *Das verbütschierte Buch* (1539) .

Bibliography: H. R. Guggisberg, *CE* 2 (1986) 53-54. **W. Klassen,** *Covenant and Community: The Life, Writings and Hermeneutics of P. Marpeck* (1968) 149-56. **A. Séguenny,** *TRE* 11 (1983) 307-12. **H. Ziegler,** *S.F.'s Paradoxa* (1909).

W. KLASSEN

FRANCKE, AUGUST HERMANN (1663–1727)

The most significant Pietist follower (see PIETISM) of P. SPENER, F., born Mar. 22, 1663, was reared in an orthodox Lutheran family. After studying at Erfurt and Kiel he went to Hamburg for Hebrew instruction. Following brief periods of study in Gotha (completing an intensive study of the Bible), Leipzig (finishing his *Dissertatio philologica de grammatica hebraeica* in 1685), Lüneburg (in 1687), and Dresden (where he spent time with P. J. Spener), he returned to Gotha and then proceeded to Leipzig as lecturer on the Bible. While at Leipzig he founded the *collegium philobiblicum*, a Bible study club in which Scripture was studied from a devotional perspective. In 1690 he was called as a pastor to Erfurt, and two years later he moved to the newly established University of Halle as professor of Greek and Hebrew and pastor at nearby Glaucha. He remained in this dual appointment until his death on June 8, 1727.

At Halle F. developed numerous welfare, educational, and pastoral institutions that influenced practice throughout Germany and Europe and even in North America. Among the innovations he helped to introduce was the substitution of the vernacular (German) for Latin as the lecture language at the university and a program for the printing and dissemination of Bibles that gave training to hundreds of impoverished students. In his teaching and writing, F. worked in line with Spenerian principles (see SPENER), although he placed particular emphasis on the importance of repentence (*Busskampf*). He completed his most significant works on biblical interpretation during his years at Halle: the *Manuductio ad lectionem Scripturae Sacrae* (1693), *Observationes biblicae* (1695), an edition of the Greek NT (1702), the *Praelectiones hermeneuticae* (1717), introductions to the psalms, the prophets (see PROPHECY AND PROPHETS, HB), and preaching, numerous sermon collections, and catechetical and other treatises.

Works: *Dissertatio philologica de grammatica hebraica* (1685); *Praelectionum publicarum auspicia* (1692); *Manductio ad lectionem Scripturae Sacrae* (1693); *Observationes biblicae* (1695); *Praelectiones hermeneuticae* (1717); *Methodus studii theologici* (1723).

Bibliography: E. Beyreuter, *A. H. F., 1663–1727, und die Anfänge der Ökunenischen Bewegung* (1958, 1961²). **F. de Boor,** *TRE* 11 (1983) 312-20. **M. Brecht,** "A. H. F. und der Hallische Pietismus," *Der Pietismus vom siebzehnten bis zum frühen achtzehnten Jahrhundert* (ed. M. Brecht, 1993), 440-540; *MSHH*, 14 (1731) 100-113. **E. Peschke,** "Zur Hermenutik A. H. F.s," *TLZ* 89 (1964) 97-110; *Bekehrung und Reform: Ansatz und Wurzeln der Theologie A. H. F.* (1977).

P. C. ERB

FRAZER, JAMES GEORGE (1854–1941)

Born in Scotland Jan. 1, 1854, F. was educated at Glasgow University and Trinity College, Cambridge, where he took a first in classics, and in 1879 was elected to a fellowship he retained for the rest of his life. Although he held a chair of social anthropology at Liverpool from 1907 to 1922, he largely remained in his rooms in Cambridge, amassing FOLKLORE material from all over the world to form the basis of his numerous publications.

F. was impelled toward the study of anthropology by his friend, the famous OT scholar, W. R. SMITH. F.'s major work, *The Golden Bough,* in which his comparative technique was fully developed, was a formative influence on the MYTH AND RITUAL SCHOOL, both by its methodology and by its theories of the function of ritual, the sacral role of the king, and the significance of the dying and rising god. More directly concerned with the Bible was his *Folk-lore in the OT,* which sought to illuminate various OT stories and customs from a wide range of early and primitive societies. In recent years F.'s general approach has been largely abandoned, but the immense amount of material he collected and surveyed remains a valuable quarry for biblical students.

Works: *The Golden Bough* (12 vols., 1907–15); *Totemism and Exogamy* (4 vols., 1910); *Folk-lore in the OT* (3 vols., 1918); *The Fear of the Dead in Primitive Religion* (3 vols., 1933–36, 1966).

Bibliography: R. Ackermann, *J. G. F.: His Life and Work* (1987). **E. O. James,** *DNB* 1941–50 (1959) 272-78. **B. K. Malinowski,** "Sir J. F.: A Biographical Appreciation," *A Scientific Theory of Culture and Other Essays* (1944) 177-221.

J. R. PORTER

FREEDMAN, DAVID NOEL (1922–)

Born and reared in a secular Jewish family in New York City, F. attended City College (1935–38), the University of California, Los Angeles (AB, 1939), Princeton Theological Seminary (ThB, 1944), and Johns Hopkins University (PhD, 1948). He was an ordained Presbyterian minister from 1944 until his retirement in 1984. He has held faculty positions and endowed chairs at Western Theological Seminary in Pittsburgh/Pittsburgh Theological Seminary (1948–64), San Francisco Theological Seminary (1964–71), the University of Michigan (1971–92), and the University of California, San Diego (1985–). He was also a professor at Graduate Theological Union (1964–71) and a visiting professor at numerous institutions.

Through his outstanding and indefatigable work as editor, author, teacher, and speaker, F. has greatly influenced virtually every area of biblical scholarship during the second half of the twentieth century. Author of numerous books and countless articles, he has also edited dozens of works, most notably the prestigious *Anchor Bible* projects as general editor of the multivolume commentary series and reference library and editor-in-chief of the six-volume dictionary.

A student of W. F. ALBRIGHT, F. follows his distinguished teacher's example in the breadth of his learning and the wide range of fields under his control. He has done significant work in almost every area related to biblical studies: Hebrew, Phoenician, and Aramaic orthography and grammar; TEXTUAL CRITICISM; Hebrew POETRY; the "primary history"; the formation and structure of the Hebrew CANON; Hebrew lexicography; Israelite history, ARCHAEOLOGY, and CHRONOLOGY; prophetic literature (see PROPHECY AND PROPHETS, HB); biblical THEOLOGY; and Qumran studies (see DEAD SEA SCROLLS).

Together with F. M. CROSS, F. has identified early Hebrew poems—which he dates from the twelfth to the ninth centuries—and from these he has recovered significant information regarding the early history of Israel

(1975a, 1997[2]). He and Cross have also done groundbreaking work in Hebrew orthography regarding the introduction and use of vowel letters (1952). F. has devoted much attention to the nature and conventions of Hebrew poetry by observing line lengths, the infrequency of prose particles, the intricacies of acrostics, and the structural symmetries of whole poems. He argues for seeing an overall symmetry in the arrangement of the books of the Hebrew canon, with the first nine books—what he calls the "primary history"—serving as the canonical core and foundation. The commentaries on Hosea (1980a) and Amos (1989) that he coauthored with F. Andersen are considered standards in the field. In the area of biblical theology he has written on the nature of biblical religion, divine names, the covenant theme, and divine repentence, among other topics.

Works: (with F. M. Cross, Jr.), *Early Hebrew Orthography: A Study of the Epigraphic Evidence* (AOS 36, 1952); (with F. M. Cross, Jr.), *Studies in Ancient Yahwistic Poetry* (SBLDS 21, 1975a; 1997[2]); (with L. G. Running), *W. F. Albright: A Twentieth-Century Genius* (1975b); (with F. I. Andersen), *Hosea* (AB 24, 1980a); *Pottery, Poetry, and Prophecy: Studies in Early Hebrew Poetry* (1980a); (with K. A. Mathews), *The Paleo-Hebrew Leviticus Scroll (11 QpaleoLev)* (1985); (with F. I. Andersen), *Amos* (AB 24A, 1989); *The Unity of the HB* (1991); (with A. D. Forbes and F. I. Andersen), *Studies in Hebrew and Aramaic Orthography* (BJuS 2, 1992); (with S. Mandell), *The Relationship Between Herodotus' History and Primary History* (SFSHJ 60, 1993); *Divine Commitment and Human Obligation: Selected Writings of D. N. F.,* vol. 1, *History and Religion;* vol. 2, *Poetry and Orthography* (ed. J. R. Huddlestun, 1997).

Bibliography: A. B. Beck et al. (eds.), *Fortunate the Eyes That See: Essays in Honor of D. N. F. in Celebration of His Seventieth Birthday* (1995). *BibRev* 9 (1993) 28-39; 10 (1994) 34-41, 63. **C. L. Meyers and M. O'Connor** (eds.) *The Word of the Lord Shall Go Forth: Essays in Honor of D. N. F. in Celebration of His Sixtieth Birthday* (ASORSVS 1, 1983).

P. R. RAABE

FREI, HANS WILHELM (1922–88)

Born in Breslau, Germany, Apr. 29, 1922, of Jewish background, F. fled Germany with his family, first to Britain and then to the United States, where he did his undergraduate work at North Carolina State University. A meeting with H. R. NIEBUHR, his most influential teacher, led to seminary and graduate work at Yale. F. was ordained an Episcopal priest in 1952. He taught at Wabash College (1950–53) and the Episcopal Seminary of the Southwest (1953–56), returning to Yale in 1957, where he was a powerfully influential teacher until his death, Sept. 12, 1988.

In *The Eclipse of Biblical Narrative* (1974) F. surveyed the history of biblical interpretation in the eighteenth and nineteenth centuries. Before that time, in his opinion, the Bible had defined the world for most Christian scholars, setting out a story from creation to the last judgment; and Christians made sense of their lives by fitting them into that framework. By the eighteenth century, however, the world of their own experience primarily defined reality for many Christians. If the biblical narratives were true (and it was the task of apologetics to argue that they were), they had to be connected with that experiential world, either as conveying moral lessons about how we should live our lives or as including more or less historically accurate reports of past events. Either way, their status as narratives was lost. F. argued that the meaning of the stories as stories is to be understood by the interaction of character and incident they present. If one begins by asking, for the sake of apologetics, if these texts are true, then one inevitably turns from narrative structure to moral lesson or fragments of historical raw material and distorts the texts' meaning. The question of truth should arise only as a more general question of whether the world as limned by these narratives seems to describe the world in which people find themselves—a matter where argument will be complex and indirect and grace may play as much a role as does reasoned analysis.

K. BARTH's reading of Scripture, especially in the later volumes of *Church Dogmatics,* struck F. as a good example of the kind of biblical interpretation he wanted to recover; and in *The Identity of Jesus Christ* (1975) he tried his own hand at showing how such a reading might shape a christology. He had begun his work at a time when Bultmannians (see R. BULTMANN), who tended to focus on interpreting individual biblical pericopes, dominated the field of biblical THEOLOGY. A number of trends, from LITERARY approaches to REDACTION CRITICISM, have more recently drawn attention to the narratives and other larger structures of the Bible. F. proposed such an approach early on, and his work remains the best account of its theological implications. He has sometimes been cited as a founder of "narrative theology," but the association always made him nervous. Believing that the particular character of the biblical text generates particular rules appropriate for its interpretation, he had little in common with those who begin their interpretations with the narratives of their own lives or general theories about the narrative quality of human experience. He most directly influenced what his Yale colleague G. Lindbeck christened "post-liberal theology."

Works: "The Doctrine of Revelation in the Thought of K. Barth, 1909–22: The Nature of Barth's Break with Liberalism" (diss. Yale, 1956); *The Eclipse of Biblical Narrative: A Study in Eighteenth- and Nineteenth-Century Hermeneutics* (1974); *The Identity of Jesus Christ: The Hermeneutical Bases of Dogmatic Theology* (1975); *Types of Christian Theology* (ed. G. Hunsinger and W. C. Placher, 1992); *Theology and Narrative: Selected Essays* (ed. G. Hunsinger and W. C. Placher, 1993).

Bibliography: C. L. **Campbell,** *NHCT* (1996) 151-57; *Preaching Jesus: New Directions for Homiletics in H. F.'s Postliberal Theology* (1997). **D. E. Demson,** *H. F. and K. Barth: Different Ways of Reading Scripture* (1997). **G. Green** (ed.), *Scriptural Authority and Narrative Interpretation* (FS, 1987). **G. Loughlin,** *Telling God's Story: Bible, Church, and Narrative Theology* (1996).

W. C. PLACHER

FREUD, SIGMUND (1856–1939)

Born in Freiberg, Moravia, on May 6, 1856, F. moved with his family to Vienna as a child. He graduated from the medical school of the University of Vienna in 1881, continued in research and clinical training for several years, became *Privatdozent* at the university in 1885, and entered private practice in 1886. Although he traveled widely, Vienna remained his home until he and his family were forced by the Nazis to flee Austria in 1938. He then settled in England, dying in London on Sept. 23, 1939.

F. came to view himself as an atheist and agnostic—a true son of the natural science of his day. He wrote to his friend and colleague of many years, the Swiss Lutheran pastor O. Pfister, "Why have the religiously devout not discovered psychoanalysis, why did one have to wait for a totally godless Jew?" He also claimed that he knew no Hebrew and that his family was not particularly religious. However, it seems that F. studied the Bible and learned Hebrew as a child and that his father was a member of the Haskalah as well as a lifelong student of the Bible and the TALMUD. Evidence of this connection and training is found in an inscription—written in Hebrew—in a Bible Jacob Freud sent his son Sigmund on the latter's thirty-fifth birthday:

My dear son,

It was in the seventh year of your age that the spirit of God began to move you to learning. I would say that the spirit of God speaks to you: "Read in My book; there will be opened to you sources of knowledge and of the intellect. It is the Book of Books; it is the well that wise men have dug and from which lawgivers have drawn the waters of their knowledge."

F. was reared, then, in a family whose interest in the Bible was both pious and scholarly. His subsequent life demonstrates his ambivalence toward both his father and his religion; but he would have known the Bible well, having read and studied much of it in Hebrew. Indeed, among the books found in F.'s library after his death was a Bible in Hebrew and German; it contained extensive notes in F.'s handwriting. Nonetheless, he treated Scripture not as a repository of religious truth but as one of the great books of WESTERN LITERATURE, using it as he did other literary sources to illustrate, to draw comparisons, to make points. Most numerous are his references to the Pentateuch; but he also alluded to the psalms, to historical books, and, less often, to other books in the HB. He seldom referred to the NT.

F.'s own contribution to biblical lore came in his late work *Moses and Monotheism* (1939). The Moses legend had fascinated him from childhood and led in adulthood to a powerful identification with the figure of Moses, who would lead his people into the promised land—for F., psychoanalysis. In *Totem and Taboo* (1912–13) he had theorized that the murder of the father in the primal horde lay at the root of primal guilt that had to be expiated through worship of the father-god. In the work on Moses, he refashioned the PENTATEUCHAL material and reinterpreted it to fit his own earlier hypothesis about the origins of religion. F. was familiar with higher biblical criticism, especially the work of J. WELLHAUSEN and W. R. SMITH, and drew on the work of E. SELLIN, who had suggested that Moses was murdered; but his reading was his own. He advanced the claim that Moses was an Egyptian who transposed the worship of the one god (Aten) to the Israelites. In the manner of the primal horde, the murder of Moses and the following guilt and undoing of the original crime were the foundation for Israelite religious beliefs.

F.'s imaginative interpretation regarding Moses has had little influence on biblical studies. However, his theories in general and thoughts on religion in particular have made a powerful impression on subsequent understanding of both religion and the Bible (see PSYCHOANALYTIC INTERPRETATION).

Works: *The Standard Edition of the Complete Psychological Works of S. F.* (24 vols., 1966–74).

Bibliography: J. Assmann, "S. F.: The Return of the Repressed," *Moses the Egyptian: The Memory of Egypt in Western Monotheism* (1997). E. Jones, *The Life and Work of S. F.* (3 vols., 1953, 1963). P. Gay, *A Godless Jew: F., Atheism, and the Making of Psychoanalysis* (1987); *F.: A Life for Our Times* (1988). D. L. Pals, "Religion and Personality: S. F.," *Seven Theories of Religion* (1996) 54-87. J. S. Preus, "Psychogenic Theory: S. F.," *Explaining Religion: Criticism and Theory from Bodin to Freud* (1987) 178-204.

W. W. MEISSNER

FRIDRICHSEN, ANTON JOHNSON (1888–1953)

Born at Meraker, Norway, Jan. 4, 1888, F. died at Uppsala, Sweden, Nov. 16, 1953. He received his theology degree from the University of Kristiania (now Oslo) in 1911, for two years studied classical languages at German universities, and from 1915 to 1927 taught NT at the University of Kristiania. Already renowned for numerous philological contributions to the study of the NT and for his doctoral dissertation on the miracles in early Christianity, presented at the University of Strasbourg (1925), F. was appointed in 1928 to the NT chair at Uppsala and became rooted in Sweden for the rest of his life (although he engaged in relief work for Norway during WWII).

At Uppsala he fascinated undergraduates by his teaching and attracted a remarkable number of postgraduate students who wrote theses, continued their scholarly work, and found positions in Sweden or at foreign universities. Thus he made Uppsala a center for personal relations with colleagues in central Europe, Great Britain, and the United States. On the yearly Exegetical Day, which he arranged, participants from all over Sweden could meet with well-known scholars from other parts of the world. The Swedish Exegetical Yearbook, which he established in 1936, and other more exclusive series have since provided wider access to Scandinavian work in the biblical field.

Stimulated by his academic position and by Swedish church life, F. turned more consistently to problems of biblical THEOLOGY. He was one of the first scholars in his generation to emphasize the central position in the Gospels of the self-consciousness of JESUS as it is expressed primarily in the symbolism of the Son of man and his followers. In similar perspectives he studied the apostolate and the concept of the church in primitive Christianity. An English translation of a selection of F.'s exegetical writings appeared in 1994.

Works: *Hagios-Qadosh: Ein Beitrag zu den Voruntersuchungen zur christlichen Begriffsgeschichte* (1916); *Le problème du miracle* (1925; ET *The Problem of Miracle in Positive Christianity* [1972]); *Johannes-evangeliet* (1939); *The Apostle and His Message* (1947); *Markusevangeliet* (1952); (ed. and contributor), *The Root of the Vine: Essays in Biblical Theology* (1953); *Exegetical Writings: A Selection* (WUNT 76, 1994).

Bibliography: W. Bauer, "Zur Erinnerung an A. F.," *ZNW* 45 (1954) 123-29. *Coniectanea Neotestamentica XI in honorem A. F. sexagenarii* (1947). B. Gerhardsson, *F., Odeburg, Aulén Nygren: Fyra teologer* (1994) 9-83; "A. F. R. Bultmann, Form Criticism and Hermeneutics," *Geschichte—Tradition—Reflexion* (FS M. Hengel, ed. H. Cancik et al., 1996) 657-75. R. A. Harrisville, "Introduction," *The Problem of Miracle* (A. J. Fridrichsen, 1972) 10-23. H. Riesenfeld, *Svenskt Biografiskt Lexikon* 16 (1964–66) 513-14. A. Smith, *A. F.'s kristendomsforstaelse* (1976). K. Stendahl, "Foreword," *The Problem of Miracle* (A. J. Fridrichsen, 1972) 5-9. *Uppsala Universitets "Matrikel," 1937–50* (1963) bibliography, 158-62.

H. RIESENFELD

FRIES, SAMUEL ANDREAS (1867–1914)

By introducing historical-critical exegesis into Sweden F. played an important role in Swedish *Rezeptionsgeschichte* of the J. WELLHAUSEN school. His enormous energy and many publications made a great impact on his contemporaries, even though he never obtained an academic chair and his life was short. He studied in Uppsala, where he became a member of a circle of young liberal theologians. After his ordination in the Church of Sweden, he worked as a curate for some years, applying in vain for three chairs at Swedish universities. His good friend N. Söderblom—then professor at Uppsala—tried to help; but finally F. became vicar in a newly established parish in Stockholm.

In his dissertation (1895) F. denied that Deuteronomy contains any decree on the centralization of the cult. He did not deny the centralization of the cult after the exile but held that this development was neither intended nor demanded by the deuteronomists (see DEUTERONOMISTIC HISTORY), thus distancing himself from Wellhausen and his school.

In other matters he was a decided adherent of the new German approach to the HB (as well as in other branches of theology—his good friend F. Fehr had introduced A. Ritschl's theology into Sweden). This can be seen in his history of Israel (1894), which was a turning point in biblical scholarship in Sweden. He was attacked vehemently from the conservative wing for disputing the truth of the Bible. A contributory cause was his lack of discretion in choice of words; he was often misunderstood by his opponents. However, he defended himself and "the critical cause" vigorously; in his opinion the church had nothing to fear from an unconditional investigation into the biblical texts. Through numerous articles he informed his contemporaries about developments in biblical scholarship and was one of the first to recognize the importance of the Amarna letters for the study of the HB.

Gradually F. turned his interest toward the NT. In a number of publications he dealt with the JOHANNINE tradition, trying to shed new light on the biblical text from a RELIGIONSGESCHICHTLICHE viewpoint. He was convinced that the Fourth Gospel contains some authentic information about JESUS and that the Gospel originally was written in Hebrew or Aramaic. This proto-Johannine Gospel was then interpolated from the gospel according to the Hebrews, mainly with episodes from Jesus' ministry in Galilee. F. maintained that finally Cerinthus in Alexandria translated the whole Gospel into Greek, making his own interpolations.

Works: *Israels historia till studerandes tjenst* (1894); *Den israelitiska kultens centralisation* (1895); *Ist Israel jemals in Ägypten gewesen?* (1897); *Gamla och nya testamentets religion: En historisk skildring* (1912).

Bibliography: *S. A. F., 1867–1914: Minnesskrift utgiven av Uppsala exegetiska sällskap* (1942). **S. Hidal,** *Bibeltro och bibelkritik* (1979) 86-96.

S. HIDAL

FUCHS, ERNST (1903–83)

Born June 11, 1903, in Heilbronn am Neckar, Württemberg, F. died Jan. 15, 1983, in Langenau bei Ulm. He was nurtured in the Swabian culture of Esslingen and Cannstatt and attended minor seminaries in Schoental and Urach (1918–22). His student years at Tübingen (1922–24, 1925–27) and Marburg (1924–25, 1927–29) during the heyday of dialectical theology were indelibly stamped by the theology of K. BARTH, the philosophy of M. Heidegger, and the NT studies of R. BULTMANN, under whom he received his doctorate at Marburg in 1929.

F.'s career combined acclaim and censure, insight and enigma as did no other German NT theologian in the mid-twentieth century. A Social Democrat, he was expelled in 1933 by the National Socialists from his post as *Privatdozent* at Bonn and from his Winzerhausen pulpit by the Gestapo in 1938. As a passionate interpreter of Bultmann's program of "demythologization," F. became a center of theological controversy within the *Landeskirche* of Württemberg. Although honored by Marburg (ThD, 1947), he was denied a post at the University of Giessen and became a *Dozent* in NT at Tübingen in 1949, where he formed a productive friendship with church historian G. Ebeling. F.'s enigmatic style and propensity for vitriolic retort worked against him, however, and following an ecclesiastical trial he was removed from membership in the still pietistic (see PIETISM) state church of Württemberg. Without hope of promotion, he left Tübingen in 1954 to assume a position at the Kirchliche Hochschule in Berlin. Exoneration came in 1961 when he was called to Bultmann's chair at the University of Marburg. He retired in 1970. Although he was repeatedly censured by the church hierarchy, as an NT theologian his impact on a whole generation of theological students on both sides of then divided Germany was highly significant.

Considered cocreator with Ebeling of the "new hermeneutic" (see HERMENEUTICS) and an original contributor to the "new quest of the historical Jesus," F.'s achievement lay in bringing the insights of Barth, Bultmann, and Heidegger into fruitful conjunction. He sought to bridge Barth's Calvinist emphasis (see CALVIN) on the revealed Word of God with Bultmann's Lutheran emphasis on the nature of human existence before God by employing a phenomenology of language derived in part from Heidegger's later position, arguing that both human existence and the being of God are ultimately linguistic—made available in language—and that theology is thus properly "faith's doctrine of language"

(*Sprachlehre des Glaubens*). Theology's task is essentially hermeneutical, i.e., theology translates Scripture into contemporary terms and contemporary existence into scriptural terms. F.'s doctrine of language helped to inspire a "new quest" of the historical JESUS because it could now be said that Jesus' words and deeds constituted that "language event" (*Sprachereignisse*) in which faith first entered into language, thereby becoming available as an existential possibility within language, the "house of being" (Heidegger). Conversely, the reality of God's love is verbalized in Jesus' words and deeds recorded in the Gospels and is thus preserved as language gain (*Sprachgewinn*). In the freedom of proclamation God's presence in the gospel as the "Yes of love" happens again—that is, comes to be as language, opening up the future to authentic existence (faith, hope, and love).

Beginning in the 1960s, the Fuchs-Ebeling project, avidly promoted by leading biblical scholars in the United States, greatly influenced liberal biblical studies and theology for over a decade.

Works: *Hermeneutik* (1954; 1958[2], with *Ergänzungsheft;* 1970[4]); *Gesammelte Aufsätze,* vol. 1, *Zum hermeneutischen Problem in der Theologie* (1959); vol. 2, *Zur Frage nach dem historischen Jesus* (1960); vol. 3, *Glaube und Erfahrung* (1965); *Studies of the Historical Jesus* (SBT 42, 1964, selected essays from *Gesammelte Aufsätze* vols. 1 and 2); *Marburger Hermeneutik* (1968); *Jesus, Wort und Tat* (1971); *Wagnis des Glaubens* (1979).

Bibliography: **P. J. Achemeier,** *Introduction to the New Hermeneutic* (1969). **J. Fangmeier,** *E. F.: Versuch einer Orientierung* (ThStud 80, 1964). **J. M. Robinson and J. B. Cobb** (eds.), *The New Hermeneutic* (New Frontiers in Theology 2, 1964). **R. N. Soulen,** "E. F.: NT Theologian," *JAAR* 39 (1971) 467-87.

R. N. SOULEN

FUNK, ROBERT W. (1926–   )

F. was born July 18, 1926 in Evansville, Indiana. He was educated at Butler University (AB 1947; BD 1950, MA 1951) and Vanderbilt University (PhD 1953), where he studied with the German NT scholar K. Grobel and the Philonic scholar S. SANDMEL. He has served on the faculties at Texas Christian University (1953–56), Harvard Divinity School (1956–57), Emory University (1958–59), Drew University (1959–66), Vanderbilt Divinity School (1966–69), and the University of Montana (1969–86).

F. was instrumental in transforming the SOCIETY OF BIBLICAL LITERATURE from a small circle of scholars from the northeastern region of the United States into a large inclusive, international learned society during his tenures as executive secretary (1968–73) and president (1974–75). At the same time he and his colleague from Drew and Vanderbilt universities, R. Hart, established the department of religious studies at the University of Montana and, in collaboration with others, transformed

the National Association of Biblical Instructors, an offshoot of the SBL, into the American Academy of Religion. In the face of escalating costs for academic monographs and periodicals, F. founded Scholars Press in 1974 to serve as the publishing venue for learned societies in religious and classical studies. After retiring from teaching he founded and is the director of Polebridge Press and the Westar Institute in Santa Rosa, California, which sponsors the Jesus Seminar.

For five decades F. has been a productive scholar, outstanding teacher, and innovative leader in the expansion of religious studies as a discipline in American higher education. His scholarly contributions have shaped current developments in at least six areas of American NT scholarship.

1. NT Greek Grammar. Trained in classical Greek at Butler, F. wrote his Vanderbilt dissertation on PAUL's use of the Greek article. His first major scholarly work was the translation and thorough revision of the ninth-tenth editions of F. Blass and A. Debrunner's *Grammatik des neutestamentlichen Griechisch* in 1961. N. DAHL (Yale Divinity School) has written that B-D-F, as the English edition has come to be known, "is one of those rare cases in which a translation is definitely better than the original." In the process of this massive work, F. was confronted with two questions about the status of the field: Should not the language of the NT be treated as a dynamic idiom that deserves its own definition rather than as a corruption of the Attic dialect, and should not insights from modern linguistics and second-language pedagogy be used for the analysis and teaching of NT Greek? In order to address these questions, he produced his own three-volume grammar (1973), a work that has defined the study of NT Greek as an NT sub-field with its own integrity rather than simply as an exegetical tool or appendage to classical Greek.

2. Hermeneutics. F. also engaged theoretical questions about the nature and function of religious discourse in general. This resulted in a programmatic work (1966a) in which he argues that the crisis of contemporary Christianity is related to the decay of traditional theological language and the archaic worldview it sponsors. The impetus for this project was his effort to mediate the work of G. Ebeling, E. FUCHS, and other German theologians to an America audience through a series of consultations at Drew University in the early 1960s, editing the *Journal for Theology and the Church* from 1964 to 1974, translating and interpreting the work of R. BULTMANN, and helping to establish the Hermeneia commentary series.

3. Parables. F.'s work on HERMENEUTICS was based on two probes into the way a new tradition (primitive Christianity) is attendant upon a new language for its birth, the new language of parable (Jesus) and personal letter (Paul). Beginning with a series of studies on the good Samaritan, F. argued that the PARABLES OF JESUS should be read as absolute metaphors of God's presence, not as allegories (Middle Ages) or as moral illustrations (see A. JÜLICHER). The language of parable is the language of invitation: In light of contemporary work on the phenomenology of language, he showed that for Jesus God's empire is not simply another idea in the history of religions but a new destination that is glimpsed through the parables. He followed these initial studies with two volumes (1975a, 1982), in which he juxtaposed the major parables of Jesus with later textual voices for which those parables were precursors in order to ask about the authentic heirs of the JESUS tradition, in distinction from putative Christianity.

4. Letters. In the face of disputes over the authenticity and integrity of the Pauline corpus, F. analyzed common letters from the Greco-Roman era to demonstrate that Paul's letters follow a highly conventional form. He then used this typical pattern as a criterion for settling disputes over the authorship and editing of the letters. His essay in the J. KNOX Festschrift (1967a), in particular, made an important contribution to the understanding of Paul's travel plans and their connection to his apostolic vocation.

5. The Bible in the American Tradition. American biblical scholarship has, by and large, been dependent on European antecedents. Beginning with a colloquium he organized at Vanderbilt in 1968 on the distinctiveness of the "Chicago School of Theology," however, F. has encouraged work on the ways in which the uniqueness of the American experience has altered European theological currents after they have crossed the Atlantic. The colloquium was followed by his 1974 SBL presidential address, "The Watershed of the American Biblical Tradition," and a monograph series he organized on the role of the Bible in North America as a part of the SBL's centennial celebration in the 1980s.

6. Historical Jesus. Since the Enlightenment scholars have recognized that the Christ of faith had eclipsed the Jesus of history by the time the Gospels were composed. This set in motion a scholarly project known as the "quest for the historical Jesus" to recover the unscripted figure of Jesus behind the theological portraits of the evangelists. Most nonspecialists have been unaware of this research project and its implications for the Christian tradition. F. founded the Jesus Seminar in 1985 to collate and communicate the scholarly results of the quest to the literate public. The seminar consists of about one hundred Gospel scholars who have surveyed the results of critical work since the Enlightenment on all the sayings and deeds attributed to Jesus in the first three centuries. The aim was to indicate clearly and concisely which sayings and deeds scholars believe can be historically verified as stemming from Jesus, in distinction from materials that originated in the experience of the early church. The results of the seminar's investigations have been published in two volumes (1993, 1998). Its work has been controversial, both because it accepts the historical-critical method and because it challenges biblical scholars to indicate how their work affects religious faith. F.'s larger purpose in founding the Jesus Seminar was to elevate the historical Jesus from a religious icon to a culturally significant figure for the modern world.

Works: "The Syntax of the Greek Article: Its Importance for Critical Pauline Problems" (diss. Vanderbilt, 1953); (tr. and rev.), *A Greek Grammar of the Greek NT and Other Early Christian Literature* (F. Blass and A. Debrunner, 1961); "Creating an Opening: Biblical Criticism and the Theological Curriculum," *Int* 18 (1964a) 387-406; "Colloquium on Hermeneutics," *TToday* 21 (1964b) 287-306; "The Hermeneutical Problem and Historical Criticism," *The New Hermeneutic* (ed. J. M. Robinson and J. B. Cobb, 1964c) 164-97; *Language, Hermeneutic, and Word of God: The Problem of Language in the NT and in Contemporary Theology* (1966a); "Saying and Seeing: Phenomenology of Language and the NT," *JBR* 34 (1966b) 197-213; "The Apostolic Parousia: Form and Significance," *Christian History and Interpretation: Studies Presented to J. Knox* (ed. W. R. Farmer, C. F. D. Moule, R. R. Niebuhr, 1967a) 249-68; "The Form and Structure of II and III John," *JBL* 86 (1967b) 424-30; "Apocalyptic as a Historical and Theological Problem in Current NT Scholarship," *JTC* 6 (1969) 175-91; "Beyond Criticism in Quest of Literacy: The Parable of the Leaven," *Int* 25 (1971) 149-70; *A Beginning-Intermediate Grammar of Hellenistic Greek* (3 vols., 1972); "The Good Samaritan as Metaphor," *Semeia* 2 (1974a) 74-81; "The Narrative Parables," *St. Andrews Review* (1974b) 299-323; "Structure in the Narrative Parables of Jesus," *Semeia* 2 (1974c) 51-73; *Jesus as Precursor* (1975a); "The Significance of Discourse Structure for the Study of the NT," *No Famine in the Land: Studies in Honor of J. L. McKenzie* (ed. J. W. Flanagan and A. W. Robinson, 1975b) 209-21; "The Watershed of the American Biblical Tradition: The Chicago School, First Phase, 1892–1920," *JBL* 95 (1976) 4-22; "The Narrative Parables: The Birth of a Language Tradition," *God's Christ and His People: Studies in Honour of N. A. Dahl* (ed. J. Jervell et al., 1977) 43-50; "The Form of the NT Healing Miracle Story," *Semeia* 12 (1978) 57-96; "On Dandelions: The Problem of Language," *JAAR Thematic Studies* 48, 2 (1981a) 79-87; "Parable, Paradox, Power: The Prodigal Samaritan," *JAAR Thematic Studies* 48, 1 (1981b) 83-97; *Parables and Presence: Forms of the NT Tradition* (1982); "From Parable to Gospel: Domesticating the Tradition," *Forum* 1, 3 (1985a) 3-24; "The Issue of Jesus," *Forum* 1, 1 (1985b) 7-12; *New Gospel Parallels* (Foundations and Facets. NT, 2 vols., 1985c); "Gospel of Mark: Parables and Aphorisms," *Forum* 4, 3 (1988) 124-43; (with B. B. Scott and J. R. Butts), *The Parables of Jesus: Red Letter Edition* (Jesus Seminar Series, 1988a); *The Poetics of Biblical Narrative* (Foundations and Facets. Literary Facets, 1988b); "Unraveling the Jesus Tradition: Criteria and Criticism," *Forum* 5, 2 (1989) 31-62; (with M. H. Smith), *The Gospel of Mark: Red Letter Edition* (Jesus Seminar Series, 1991); (with R. W. Hoover), *The Five Gospels: The Search for the Authentic Words of Jesus* (1993); *Honest to Jesus: Jesus for a New Millennium* (1996); *The Acts of Jesus: What Did Jesus Really Do?* (1998).

L. C. McGAUGHEY

G

GABLER, JOHANN PHILIPP (1753–1826)

Born in Frankfurt a. M., G. studied philosophy, history, and theology in Jena under J. G. EICHHORN and J. J. GRIESBACH (1772–78), concluding with a dissertation on Heb 3:3-6. At Göttingen (1780–83) he came under the influence of C. Heyne (1712–91). G. became professor of philosophy at the Archigymnasium in Dortmund (1783–85) and was professor of theology in Altdorf (1758–1804) and Jena (from 1804).

G. is known as the father of biblical THEOLOGY as an independent discipline, for which he laid the groundwork in Altdorf on March 30, 1787, in his programmatic inaugural address, "De justo discrimine theologiae biblicae et dogmaticae regundisque recte utriusque finibus." Perhaps overwhelmed by the size of the task, he never carried out his program, instead deferring to more experienced scholars. Neither did he produce any major works, although his literary output was considerable (his contribution to Eichhorn's *Urgeschichte* [1790–93] alone ran several hundred pages). The greater part of his literary activity went into editing and contributing to three journals: *Neuestes theologisches Journal* (1798–1800), *Journal für theologische Literatur* (1801–03), and *Journal für auserlesene theologische Literatur* (1805–11). G.'s primary focus in these works was to further refine his program for a biblical theology, his closest approximation being the transcript of his 1816 lectures, *Biblische Theologie,* by his student E. Netto.

G.'s purpose was not to establish a biblical theology unrelated to dogmatic theology, but to provide a sound, unchanging basis for dogmatic theology that, by its nature, is subject to constant flux due to its relationship to many other disciplines and to the shifting temporal and local situations, denominations, or schools of thought in which theologians philosophize on divine matters. To provide such an abiding basis, biblical theology had to be independent of dogmatic theology.

G. identified two steps in the production of a biblical theology. The first is biblical theology in a broader sense, or "true" biblical theology. Its task is to collect and order systematically all concepts concerning the divine in the Bible, including those that could be inferred by the comparison of more than one passage. This process involves distinguishing between OT and NT and individual authors and their forms of speech, whether historical, didactic, or poetic. He divided the task further into two steps, both of which should proceed histori-

cally. The first is exegetical in the best sense of the term, the second systematic. In the exegetical step attention should be given to (a) differentiation in the meanings of words and sentences; (b) different ways of expressing the same meanings; and (c) noting whether the apostle (apparently PAUL) used his own words or those of another, whether he merely presented a thesis or intended to prove it, and, if the latter, whether he did so from the nature of the teaching itself or from the OT. The systematic step is to systematize all the teachings by distinguishing individual opinions and general conceptions but in such a way that the individual features remain intact.

G.'s second main step in a biblical theology is the narrower sense or "pure" biblical theology. After the views of the biblical authors "have been gathered meticulously, ordered properly, traced back carefully to general concepts, and compared accurately with each other" (1831, 191), it becomes possible to investigate which conceptions relate to the unchanging form of Christian teaching and which were intended only for a particular time. G. emphasized that all of this had to be carried out "through purely exegetical observations" (1831, 192). His rejection of I. KANT's methodology for biblical interpretation, specifically as it was carried out by C. von AMMON in his *Entwurf einer reinen biblischen Theologie* (1792), underscores that he did not intend the imposition of universal ideas on the biblical materials but rather an abstraction of those ideas from the biblical materials. The conceptions of such a "pure" biblical theology can then function as the basis for a dogmatic theology.

G. considered the ways a scholar could distinguish between what was contingent and what applied for all times, most notably in the essay "Über den Unterschied zwischen Auslegung und Erklärung" (1800). In the sense of a true biblical theology (*Auslegung*) the task is "to step completely out of our time . . . and to place [oneself] in the spirit and character of that time" (*Neuestes theologisches Journal* 19 [1801] 314-15). In the sense of a "pure" biblical theology (*Erklärung*) the interpreter then has to move from a literal interpretation (*Worterklärung*) to an interpretation of its meaning (*Sacherklärung*).

Subsequent generations of biblical scholars ignored G.'s distinctions. The only real exception is the RE-LIGIONSGESCHICHTLICHE SCHULE, in which the distinct tasks of a true biblical theology and a dogmatic theology in G.'s sense were carried out with outstanding sensitivity and clarity, but unfortunately without attention to the intermediate step of a distinctively pure biblical theology.

Works: *Dissertatio exegetica in illustrem locum Heb 3, 3-6* (1778); (ed.) *Urgeschichte* (J. G. Eichhorn, 1790–1793[2]); "Über die Unterschied zwischen Auslegung und Erklärung," *NThJ* 17 (1800; repr. in *Dr. J. P. G.'s kleinere theologische Schriften* [2 vols., ed. T. A. and J. G. Gabler, 1831] 201-14); *Einleitung ins Neue Testament* (2 vols., 1815); *Biblishe Theologie* (transcr. E. F. C. A. H. Netto, 1816; partial GT in Merk [1972], 114-34); *Dogmatik* (2 vols., 1816); "De justo discrimine theologiae biblicae et dogmaticae regundisque recte utriusque finibus," *Kleinere theologische Schriften* (1831) 179-98; GT in Merk (1972) 273-84; ET in Sandys-Wunsch and Eldridge (1980) 134-44.

Bibliography: H. **Boers,** *What Is NT Theology?* (Guides to Biblical Scholarship, 1979) 23-38. O. **Merk,** *Biblische Theologie des Neuen Testaments in ihrer Anfangszeit* (1972) 29-140, 273-84; *TRE* 12 (1983) 1-3. R. **Morgan,** "Gabler's Bicentenary," *ExpTim* 98 (1986–87) 164-68. M. **Saebø,** "J. P. G.s Bedeutung für die biblische Theologie," *ZAW* 99 (1987) 1-16. J. **Sandys-Wunsch and L. Eldridge,** "J. P. G. and the Distinction Between Biblical and Dogmatic Theology: Translation, Commentary, and Discussion of His Originality," *SJT* 33 (1980) 133-58. W. **Schröter,** *Erinnerungen an Dr. J. P. G.* (1827). R. **Smend,** "J. P. G.s Begründung der biblischen Theologie," *EvTh* 22 (1962) 345-57.

H. BOERS

GALATIANS, LETTER TO THE

The epistle of PAUL to the Galatians has come down to us as part of the corpus of Pauline letters. These letters belong to a class of Jewish and Christian epistles, sacred books written by prophets (see PROPHECY AND PROPHETS) or apostles with AUTHORITY from God, the archetype being the epistle Jeremiah wrote to the exiles in Babylon (Jeremiah 29), which was assumed by tradition to have been dictated to Baruch (Bar 6:1; see Jer 36:4). Epistles were treasured in religious communities as holy documents to be read in worship and studied for further meaning. (So Jeremiah's reference to seventy years [Jer 29:10] became a key apocalyptic text) that was interpreted and reinterpreted in later writings.)

1. Galatians as Evidence of Paul's Gospel. The epistle to the Galatians first became a scholarly problem when MARCION published a version he claimed was freed from the Jewish-Christian additions that had obscured Paul's original message about a God of mercy who was superior to the Jewish God of judgment. TERTULLIAN attacked Marcion's hypothesis on the grounds that even Marcion's shorter version showed a Paul who believed in the one God, the Creator, who was both merciful and just. Perhaps as a result of Marcion's two-part CANON, consisting of the Gospel (a shorter version of Luke) and the apostolic corpus (shorter versions of Galatians, 1–2 Corinthians, Romans, 1–2 Thessalonians, Laodiceans [Ephesians], Colossians, Philippians, Philemon), the corpus of Paul's letters began to attain full canonical status in all provinces of the church. The main problem about Galatians as part of the canon was its reference to the rebuke Paul administered to Peter in Antioch. The Eastern church interpreted Peter's silence under Paul's rebuke as a sign of the tacit agreement of both apostles in holding the same gospel; the Western church interpreted Peter's silence as his morally praiseworthy submission to a well-earned censure (see F. Overbeck [1877]). The Western tradition was continued by LUTHER, who drew comfort in his own struggle against the papacy, with its cry "the church, the church," from the fact that Paul withstood false apostles and that he even reproved Peter when the article of justification was at issue—though Peter's lapse was only temporary, since Peter defended this article at Jerusalem (Acts 15).

In the eighteenth century Dutch and English scholars began to deploy Galatians as evidence that "the Jewish and Gentile Christianity, or Peter's Religion and Paul's, were as opposite and inconsistent as Light and Darkness, Truth and Falsehood" (T. Morgan [1737]). J. SEMLER took over this theory, opposing Paul's inner spiritual religion to Peter's Jewish external religion on the basis of his reading of 1 Corinthians and Galatians. Semler believed that the early church was divided between Paul's disciples and the admirers of Peter and the Palestinians. The latter fabricated a history of Peter in Rome to match the history of Paul in Rome, remnants of which are extant in the Pseudo-Clementine literature (Semler [1779] 5, 6). F. C. BAUR took over and elaborated this theory (1831). According to Baur's hypothesis about the deep split in the early church, many other letters in the Pauline corpus reflected catholic Christianity and could not, therefore, be regarded as genuine. Baur summed up the critical consensus of his day by dividing the Pauline corpus into three parts: the four genuine epistles (Galatians, 1–2 Corinthians, and Romans), the questionably genuine (1–2 Thessalonians, Ephesians, Colossians, Philemon, and Philippians), and the inauthentic (1–2 Timothy and Titus). Baur regarded the Acts of the Apostles, with its attempt to make the histories of Peter and Paul run parallel to each other and to make the two men agree in doctrine, as tendentious.

In 1850 B. BAUER published two books, one on Acts and the other on Galatians, to show that both Acts and Galatians belonged to the same stage in the history of the church and that they were equally tendentious. He argued that Galatians presupposed the split between Judaism and Christianity that had not occurred during Paul's lifetime and that the epistle was clumsily derived from Romans and the Corinthian epistles. He thought

Romans, 1 Corinthians, and perhaps 2 Corinthians were written before Acts; Galatians, in full knowledge of Acts; then 1 Thessalonians, Ephesians, Colossians, Philippians, 1–2 Timothy, and Titus. He held all of the Pauline corpus to be pseudonymous.

C. WEISSE (1855) took up Bauer's challenge, which was otherwise ignored for thirty years, and proposed that 1 Corinthians, 1 Thessalonians, and Philemon were genuine and that 2 Corinthians was compiled from three genuine letters. Romans and Philippians were compiled from more than one genuine letter, but they were also interpolated with other material. Galatians and Colossians were each based on a genuine letter but interpolated by the same hand. Weisse distinguished the work of Paul from the work of the interpolator by the criterion of style, "the defraction a beam of thought undergoes when it passes through the prism of a personality." Thus he omitted from the genuine Galatians such remarks as the asides that the other gospel is not really different (1:7) and "if really in vain" (3:4b) as well as such a notoriously complicated passage as 3:16b-20, 21b. (J. O'Neill [1972, 1982] has argued that Weisse's approach should be taken seriously. If the text of Galatians as part of the NT canon was glossed [e.g. 3:1 + "that you not obey the truth," *textus receptus;* "crucified" + "among you," *textus receptus*], it is more likely that it was glossed before the Pauline corpus became part of the canon and more likely that it was glossed before Galatians became part of the Pauline corpus; Galatians was always a sacred writing and, therefore, likely to be glossed.)

This whole approach flourished in the Netherlands from about 1879 to 1890, culminating in a commentary by J. Cramer (1890). The revival of Bauer's theory (by R. Steck [1888] and J. Friedrich [1891]) that the entire epistle was spurious probably helped to discredit the school; Steck converted W. van Manen (1842–1905) from an earlier belief that Galatians was interpolated. R. Lipsius noted the suggested excisions of the school in his commentary (1891, 1892[2]).

Since the time of the Reformation exegetes have tried to identify the center of Paul's thought. Luther said Paul taught the law and works for the "old man" and taught passive righteousness, the righteousness received from heaven, and the promise of forgiveness of sins for the "new man." Luther was answered by those who cited Gal 5:6—Paul taught faith working through love (H. Schlier [1949]). Many scholars couple Paul's defense of his apostolic office with his defense of the gospel as the double theme of the epistle (e.g., J. B. Lightfoot [1865]). Others see the center in Gal 4:4-6: God sent the Son, born under the law, to redeem those under the law, in order that we might receive adoption and the gift of the Spirit. H. Betz (1979) has argued that the center is liberty: Paul presents his defense of the gospel as a defense of the Spirit. H. Räisänen (1983) maintains that

Paul's thought in Galatians is full of unresolved contradictions concerning the law.

2. Style and Arrangement of Galatians. The style and arrangement of Galatians are on the small scale disjointed, although on the large scale clear, consisting of three parts: after greetings and introduction (1:1-10), first a defense of the apostle and his gospel (1:11–2:21); second a theological part (3:1–4:31); and third a hortatory part (5:1–6:18). Betz (1974–75, 1979) contends that the epistle belongs to the genre of apologetic autobiography in an epistolary framework and that every division in the apologetic autobiography is governed by the conventions of rhetoric (epistolary prescript 1:1-5; exordium 1:6-11; narratio 1:12–2:14; propositio 2:15-21; probatio 3:1–4:31; exhortatio 5:1-6:10; epistolary postscript = conclusio 6:11-18). P. Kern (1994) argues that there is little evidence that Paul reflects the advice of the handbooks on rhetoric and notes that the church fathers did not think Paul's writing was like Greco-Roman oratory.

3. Date of Galatians and Its Recipients. The contention that Galatians borrowed from Romans was one of Bauer's main arguments against its authenticity. C. Clemen (1894), who wrote a decisive refutation of Bauer and Steck, regarded the dating of Galatians after Romans as the grain of truth in his opponents' case. Marcion probably placed Galatians first in his canon, and CHRYSOSTOM said Galatians seemed to him prior to Romans ("Preface to Romans"). L. CAPPEL was probably the first to suggest the order 1–2 Thessalonians, Galatians, 1 Corinthians (*Historia apostolica illustrata* [1634]). He dated Galatians to 51 CE, the twelfth year of Claudius. Most scholars date the writing of the book soon after (see Gal 1:6, "so quickly") Paul's visit to the Galatians, mentioned in Acts 18:23, and settle on anything from 51 CE to 58 CE; e.g., J. MILL (*Novum Testamentum* [1707]), J. G. EICHHORN (*Einleitung in das Neue Testament* [2 vols., 1804–12]). J. D. MICHAELIS (*Introductory Lectures to the Sacred Books of the NT* [1761]) put the writing of Galatians before Paul left Thessalonica on his second journey (Acts 17:10) and dated it to 49 CE on the grounds that it was written while all those who had accompanied him in Galatia were still with him.

The discrepancy between Acts, which says Paul made three visits to Jerusalem before his last visit to that city (Acts 9; 11; 15), and Galatians, which says Paul made only two visits to Jerusalem up to the date of writing the epistle, did not much trouble scholars, who put the discrepancy down to Acts' hearsay information. However, the suggestion that the Galatians had been evangelized by Paul and Barnabas on their first missionary journey when they fled Iconium to the Lycaonian cities of Lystra and Derbe and the surrounding parts (Acts 16:6) opened up other possibilities. The opinion that the Galatians were inhabitants of Lycaonia seems to have been offered first by J. Schmidt (1748, 1754), who argued that as Derbe and Lystra were part of the Roman province of Galatia, the Christians there could have been addressed as "Galatians." H. Paulus (1831) and T. von ZAHN (1905), among others, followed this same line, which became popular in the English-speaking world through the writings of W. RAMSAY, professor of humanities at Aberdeen (1890, 1899), and which has been revived by J. Dunn (1993). The issues are fully treated in *Encyclopaedia Biblica* (1899–1903). J. KOPPE (1778) argued the earlier date for the Galatian mission without the supposition that the citizens of Derbe and Lystra were addressed as "Galatians." He based his case on the grounds that the visit to Galatia mentioned in Acts 16:6 was to strengthen the brethren (Acts 15:36, 41), not to found new churches. If the Galatians had been evangelized on Paul's first missionary journey it becomes possible to suppose that the events recorded in Gal 2:1-10 were not the same as the events recorded in Acts 15 but took place before that meeting. This view was assumed in the CHRONOLOGY of the seventh-century *Chronicon Paschale* and was adopted by CALVIN. The most common of the possible identifications of Gal 2:1-10 (if not with Acts 15) is with the visit to Jerusalem recorded in Acts 11:30 (F. F. Bruce [1982]; R. Longenecker [1990]).

4. Paul's Opponents. The Marcionite prologue to Galatians said that the Galatians were tempted by false apostles to turn to the law and circumcision, and this is the usual view to this day. These false apostles are usually thought of as incomers, though some think they were local; and they are most often regarded as Jewish Christians (Dunn [1993]), although J. MUNCK (1954) thought they were Gentiles and N. Walter (1986) has revived the possibility that they were simply Jews engaged in a countermission. W. Lütgert (1919) argued that Paul was fighting on two fronts: (1) Heathen influence of a pneumatic kind had begun to penetrate the Galatian churches, and the representatives of this party accused Paul of still being a half-Jew. (2) Jews began to persecute the churches, and Jewish Christians in defense preached circumcision for all gentile Christians. This theory was taken over and adapted by J. Ropes (1929). W. Schmithals (1965) has argued that Paul's opponents combined the characteristics of both of Lütgert's imagined parties and were Jewish Christian Gnostics (see GNOSTIC INTERPRETATION).

Bibliography: **B. Bauer,** *Die Apostelgeschichte, eine Ausgleichung des Paulinismus und des Judenthums innerhalb der christlichen Kirche* (1850); *Kritik der paulinischen Briefe,* pt. 1, *Der Ursprung des Galaterbriefs* (1850, repr. 1972). **F. C. Baur,** *Tübinger Zeitschrift für Theologie* 4 (1831) 61-206; repr. in *Ausgewählte Werke in Einzelausgabe* (ed. K. Scholder, vol. 1, *Historisch-kritische Untersuchungen zum Neuen Testament* [1963]). **H. D. Betz,** "The Literary Composition and Function of Paul's Letter to the Galatians," *NTS* 21 (1974–75) 353-79; *Galatians: A Commentary on Paul's Letter to the Churches in Galatia* (Hermeneia, 1979). **F. F. Bruce,** *The Epistle to the Galatians: A Commentary on the Greek Text* (1982). **E. D. Burton,** *The Epistle to the Galatians* (ICC, 1921). **C. Clemen,** *Die Einheitlichkeit der paulinischen Briefe an der Hand der bisher mit bezug auf sie aufgestellten Interpolations- und Compilationshypothesen geprüft* (1894). **J. Cramer,** *De Brief van Paulus aan de Galatiërs in zijn oorsprokelijken Vorm hersteld, en verklaard* (1890). **J. D. G. Dunn,** *The Epistle to the Galatians* (BNTC, 1993). **J. Friedrich,** *Die Unechtheit des Galaterbriefes: Ein Beitrag zu einer kritischen Geschichte des Urchristentums* (1891). **P. H. Kern,** "Rhetoric, Scholarship, and Galatians: Assessing an Approach to Paul's Epistle" (diss., University of Sheffield, 1994). **J. B. Koppe,** *Novum Testamentum Graece perpetua annotatione illustratum* (1778[3]; rev. and ed. T. C. Tychsen, 1823). **J. B. Lightfoot,** *Saint Paul's Epistle to the Galatians: A Revised Text with Introduction, Notes, and Dissertations* (1865). **R. A. Lipsius,** *Briefe an die Galater, Römer, Philipper* (HCNT II.ii, 1891, 1892[2]). **R. N. Longenecker,** *Galatians* (WBC 41, 1990). **W. Lütgert,** *Gesetz und Geist: Eine Untersuchung zur Vorgeschichte des Galaterbriefes* (BFCT 22, 6, 1919d). **J. L. Martyn,** *Galatians* (AB 33A, 1997). **F. J. Matera,** *Galatians* (Sacra Pagina 9, 1992). **T. D. Morgan,** *The Moral Philosopher: In a Dialogue Between Philalethes, a Christian Deist, and Theophanes, a Christian Jew* (1737). **J. Munck,** *Paulus und die Heilsgeschichte* (1954; ET *Paul and the Salvation of Mankind* 1959). **J. C. O'Neill,** *The Recovery of Paul's Letter to the Galatians* (1972); "Glosses and Interpolations in the Letters of St. Paul," *StEv* 7 (TU 126, 1982) 379-86; "The Holy Spirit and the Human Spirit in Galatians: Gal 5:17," *ETL* 71 (1995) 107-120. **F. Overbeck,** *Über die Auffassung des Streits des Paulus mit Petrus in Antiochien (Gal. 2,11ff.) bei den Kirchenvätern* (Programm zur Rectoratsfeier der Universität Basel, 1877; repr., 1968). **H. E. G. Paulus,** *Des Apostels Lehr-briefe an die Galater und Romer Christen* (1831). **Heikki Räisänen,** *Paul and the Law* (WUNT 29, 1983). **W. M. Ramsay,** *Historical Geography of Asia Minor* (1890, repr. 1962); *A Historical Commentary on St. Paul's Epistle to the Galatians* (1899, repr. 1965). **J. H. Ropes,** *The Singular Problem of the Epistle to the Galatians* (HTS 14, 1929) 28-42. **H. Schlier,** *Der Brief an die Galater* (Meyer, 1949, 1965[4]). **J. J. Schmidt,** *Prolusio de Galatis, ad quos Paulus literas misit* (1748); *Prolusionem suam de Galatis—ab objectionibus doctissimorum virorum vindicare conatur* (1754). **W. Schmithals,** *Paul and the Gnostics* (1965; ET 1972). **J. S. Semler,** *Paraphrasis epistolae ad Galatas cum Prolegomenis, Notis, et varietate Lectionis Latinae* (1779). **R. Steck,** *Der Galaterbrief nach seiner Echtheit untersucht nebst kritischen Bemerkungen zu den paulinischen Hauptbriefen* (1888). **A. Suhl,** "Der Galaterbrief—Situation und Argumentation," *ANRW* II. 25.4 (1987) 3067-3134. **N. Walter,** "Paulus und die Gegner des Christusevangeliums in Galatien," *L'Apôtre Paul: personnalité, style et conception du ministère* (ed. A. Vanhoye, 1986) 351-56. **C. H. Weisse,** *Philosophische Dogmatik oder Philosophie des Christenthums* (3 vols., 1855–62); *Beiträge zur Kritik der paulinischen Briefe an die Galater, Römer, Philipper, und*

Kolosser (ed. E. Sulze, 1867). **S. K. Williams,** *Galatians,* (ANTC, 1997). **T. Zahn,** *Der Brief des Paulus an der Galater* (1905, 1922³)

J. C. O'NEILL

GALE, THEOPHILUS (1628–78)

An English dissenter, G. was educated at Magdalen College, Oxford, but was ejected from his university fellowship at the Restoration (1660). Thereafter he traveled in Europe for several years, returning to conduct a dissenting academy at Newington Green, near London. He was reputed to be an "exact philologist," and his enormous *The Court of the Gentiles* contains extensive discussion of Hebrew words and cognates and suppositious derivatives. According to his platonic theory of language, the original names given by Adam at God's direction disclose the inherent natures of things. Etymology proves that all language comes from Hebrew (especially through the Phoenecians) and that therefore all literature, philosophy, and learning derives from Hebrew prototypes, which are based on God's original revelation to the Jews, thus accounting for their truths. All error, in contrast, is the result of sinful corruptings of the primeval deposit. G.'s viewpoint was a strongly Calvinistic (see CALVIN) and biblically centered variation of the widespread Renaissance doctrine of an ancient wisdom, or *prisca theologia,* and was similar to the views of some of the Cambridge Platonists. At his death he left unfinished a LEXICON of NT Greek. His will bequeathed a large collection of Hebraica to Harvard College.

Works: *The Court of the Gentiles* (4 vols., 1669–78).

Bibliography: J. W. Ashley Smith, *The Birth of Modern Education* (1954) 41-46. **N. Fiering,** *Moral Philosophy at Seventeenth-Century Harvard* (1981) 279-94. **A. Gordon,** *DNB* 20 (1889) 377-78. **D. D. Wallace, Jr.,** *Puritans and Predestination* (Studies in Religion [Chapel Hill], 1982) 178-80.

D. D. WALLACE, JR.

GALILEI, GALILEO (1564–1642)

Born at Pisa Feb. 15, 1564, G. received his early education at the monastery of Vallombrosa. Later he studied medicine and mathematics at the University of Pisa (1581–84), but he left without a degree. He held the chair of mathematics at Pisa (1589–92) and later at the University of Padua (1592–1610), having become persuaded of the truth of Copernicanism sometime before 1600. In 1609 he improved on the recently invented telescope and began systematic observations of the heavens; these findings, published in his *Sidereus nuncius* (1610), made him internationally famous. In 1610 he returned permanently to Florence under the patronage of the grand duke.

G.'s telescopic observations raised the question of how the new discoveries related to the geocentric language of the Bible. Thus the classic confrontation between science and religion was born, reaching its climax with the church's condemnation (Mar. 5, 1616) of Copernicanism as "false and completely contrary to the Scriptures" and with G. being admonished by Cardinal R. BELLARMINE to accept that judgment under threat of injunction. G. turned to other scientific work until 1624 when, with the election of the more tolerant Pope Urban VIII, he felt free to undertake the writing of his *Dialogue Concerning the Two Chief World Systems.* However, when it was published in 1632 the question was immediately raised as to whether it violated the decree and the injunction of 1616. G.'s trial ended June 22, 1633, with his being judged "vehemently suspected of heresy" and with his forced abjuration. He lived under house arrest, continuing his scientific work despite blindness (1637) until his death at Arcetri, Jan. 8, 1642.

G.'s views on the Bible and science were formulated between 1613 and 1616. His friend B. Castelli informed him that the scriptural orthodoxy of his scientific views had been questioned at the court of the grand duke. G.'s reply took the form of his *Letter to Castelli* (Dec. 21, 1613), later expanded into his *Letter to the Grand Duchess Christina* (1615, not published until 1636), in which he argued that, since God is the author of both nature and revelation, science and the Bible cannot be in contradiction, provided that each is properly understood. This proviso applies especially to the Bible, which, in carrying out its purpose of providing all people with the means of salvation, often accommodates its language to the crass understanding of the common person and to the mode of speech of the times in which it was written. As a result the surface meaning of Scripture is often not its true meaning. The most frequently debated passages concerning heliocentricism were Josh 10:13 and Ps 19:4-6. Also, the Bible contains much material not pertaining to salvation and, therefore, not strictly matters of faith. For G. scriptural remarks about the motion of the heavens are in that category; thus his famous quotation from Cardinal Baronius: "The Bible teaches us how to go to heaven, not how the heavens go."

Thus, if a scientific truth has been conclusively proven, G. argued, then we must follow the Augustinian advice to interpret the Scriptures accordingly. But in cases where a theory is not conclusively proven (the state of Copernicanism at that time), G.'s advice is less clear. He usually advocated abstention from fixing the true meaning of the Bible in such cases lest later scientific proof go contrary to that interpretation, thus compromising the Scriptures. And in matters beyond natural science the issue of conflict, of course, never arises. G.'s views did not convince the Holy Office in 1616 but were destined to be accepted by the Roman Catholic Church by the end of the nineteenth century.

Works: *Sidereus nuncius* (1610); *Il saggiatore* (1623); *Dialogo sopra i due massimi sistemi del mondo, Tolemaico e Copernicano* (1632); *Discorsi e demonstrazioni mathematiche intorno à due nuove scienze* (1638).

Bibliography: R. J. Blackwell, *G., Bellarmine, and the Bible* (1991). **S. Drake**, *G. at Work: His Scientific Biography* (1978). **A. Fantoli**, *G.: For Copernicanism and for the Church* (1994, 1996²). **L. Geymonat**, *Galileo Galilei* (Studi Galileiani 3,1957, 1969²). **J. J. Langford**, *G., Science, and the Church* (1966). **E. McMullin** (ed.), *G.: Man of Science* (1967). **G. Morpurgo-Tagliabue**, *I processi di G. e l'epistemologia* (1963). **S. M. Pagano** (ed.), *I documenti del processo di G. G.* (1984). **O. Pedersen**, "*G.* and the Council of Trent: The *G.* Affair Revisited," *Journal of the History of Astronomy* (1983) 1-29. **P. Redondi**, *G. eretico* (1983). **G. de Santillana**, *The Crime of G.* (1955). **W. A. Wallace**, *G. and His Sources* (1984).

R. J. BLACKWELL

GALLING, KURT (1900–87)

Born June 8, 1900, in Wilhelmshaven, G. died July 12, 1987, in Tübingen. G. developed four of the cardinal virtues of his generation: breadth of knowledge, detailed observation, originality of perspective, and integrity. He was educated at Jena and Berlin in ancient history, ancient Near Eastern studies, and OT, with his doctoral dissertation in Jena in 1923 (published in 1925) and his habilitation in Berlin in 1925 (published in 1928), which, strongly influenced by his teacher H. GRESSMANN, has only in the 1980s and 1990s had its full impact. After lecturing on OT in Berlin he went in 1928 to Halle, where he worked in the administration of the university library through the Hitler years until 1946. During this long hiatus in his scholarly career, G.'s writing turned in the direction of biblical ARCHAEOLOGY, a burgeoning new field that his own work helped to define for European scholarship, especially through his very influential *BRL*, which with great originality systematically defined the archaeological remains of Palestine independently of biblical traditions.

In 1946 G. received his first chair in OT in Mainz, where he began the immense task of editing the third edition of *RGG* (6 vols., 1957–65). He was called to Göttingen in 1955 to teach OT and history of Palestine and in 1961 accepted the newly established chair in biblical archaeology at the University of Tübingen, where, until his retirement in 1968, he developed the finest research library in the field in Germany. The research of his latter years concentrated on studies of the Persian period. Beginning in the late sixties, he drew many students and younger colleagues to his home for the free and open discussions of "Diptychon." This circle of scholars, through the many substantial publications of its members, has profoundly changed contemporary historical research related to the OT and biblical archaeology.

Works: *Der Altar in den Kulturen des alten Orients* (1925); *Die Erwählungstraditionen Israels* (BZAW 48, 1928); *Die israelitische Staatsverfassung in ihrer vorderorientalischen Umwelt* (AO 28, 3, 4, 1929); *Biblisches Reallexikon* (HAT 1, 1, 1937); *Syrien in der Politik der Achaemeniden bis zum Aufstand des Megabyzos 448 v. Chr.* (AO 36, 3, 4, 1937); "Der Prediger," *Die Fünf Megilloth* (HAT I 18, 1940, 1969²); *Textbuch zur Geschichte Israels* (1950, 1968²); *Die Bücher der Chronik: Esra, Nehemia* (ATD 12, 1954); *Studien zur Geschichte Israels im persischen Zeitalter* (1964).

Bibliography: M. **Weippert**, *ZDPV* 104 (1988) 190-94. **P. Welten**, "Bibliographie K. G.," *Archäologie und Altes Testament: Festschrift für K. G.* (ed. A. Kuschke and E. Kutsch, 1970) 333-47.

T. L. THOMPSON

GARDINER, FREDERIC (1822–89)

Born in Gardiner, Maine, G. graduated from Bowdoin College in 1842. Ordained a priest in the Protestant Episcopal Church, he served several churches in Maine before beginning his teaching career. In 1865 he was appointed professor of Scripture interpretation at the Protestant Episcopal Theological Seminary in Gambier, Ohio. He taught OT literature at Berkeley Divinity School (Connecticut) from 1868 to 1882 and NT literature and interpretation from 1883 until his death. He is remembered for his principal role in the conception and organization of the Society of Biblical Literature and Exegesis (see SOCIETY OF BIBLICAL LITERATURE), as it was known in its first half century. Together with C. BRIGGS and P. Schaff he took part in the preliminary meeting in 1880 and called together the organizational meeting in June of that year, drafting the constitution and bylaws, and serving as its first secretary and journal editor (1880–83) and its second president (1887–89). He and his colleagues were cautiously, but favorably, disposed to the higher criticism of German scholars, which made its entrance into American biblical scholarship in the late nineteenth century.

Works: *The Last of the Epistles: A Commentary upon the Epistle of St. Jude* (1856); *The Principles of Textual Criticism* (1876); "Leviticus," *A Commentary on the Holy Scriptures* (ed. J. P. Lange, American Lange Series 2, 1876); "II Samuel" and "Ezekiel," *An OT Commentary for English Readers* (ed. C. J. Ellicott, 1883) 2:444-511; (1883) 5:203-353.

Bibliography: "Memorial: F. G.," *JBL* 9 (1890) vi. **E. W. Saunders**, *Searching the Scriptures* (1982) 3-9.

E. W. SAUNDERS

GARSTANG, JOHN (1876–1956)

Born in Blackburn, Lancashire, May 5, 1876, G. was a mathematical scholar of Jesus College, Oxford, as an undergraduate. His interest in ARCHAEOLOGY was aroused by the ruins of the Roman camp at Ribchester, which he excavated while still an undergraduate. He also excavated such other Roman sites in Britain as Melandra Castle.

When twenty-three he joined W. F. PETRIE in Egypt and took part in his excavations at Abydos. In 1902 he became reader in Egyptian archaeology at Liverpool University and in 1907 professor of the methods and practice of archaeology at Liverpool, a newly created post that he held until 1941.

From 1909 to 1914 he excavated Meroë, the capital of ancient Ethiopia, revealing evidence of Roman occupation. He was director of the British School of Archaeology in Jerusalem (1919–26) and director of antiquities under the Palestine government (1920–26). He excavated at Ashkelon in 1920–21 and identified the site of Hazor (*Tell el-Qedaḥ*) in 1926, where he made the first excavations. But it is his work at Jericho that is most famous in biblical archaeology. His excavations there, under the patronage of C. Marston, were undertaken from 1930 to 1936, when he was forced to leave Palestine because of the political situation. His work first revealed the antiquity of the site, something that has been further underlined by the excavations of K. KENYON. G. discovered a double wall that he believed to date from the Late Bronze Age and to have fallen to Joshua, c. 1400 BCE. This fit with the fifteenth-century date for the exodus and the equation of the Habiru of the el-Amarna letters with the invading Hebrews, opinions then popular. Kenyon's subsequent excavations, however, overturned this conclusion: It emerged that Late Bronze Age remains were few and that the double wall dated much earlier—from the Early Bronze Age—when there was certainly no wall as is depicted in Joshua.

After leaving Palestine G., following his interest in the Hittites (see HITTITOLOGY AND BIBLICAL STUDIES), undertook important excavations in Turkey at Mersîn (1937–47). In addition, he founded the British Institute of Archaeology at Ankara, serving as its director (1947–48) and president (1948–56). Throughout his career he was interested in and published on the Hittites; his posthumously published geography of the Hittite Empire (1959) has served as a standard work on the topic.

Works: *The Land of the Hittites* (1910); *The Hittite Empire* (1929); *Joshua–Judges* (Foundations of Biblical History, 1931); *The Heritage of Solomon* (1934); (with J. B. E. Garstang), *The Story of Jericho* (1940; 1948²); *The Geography of the Hittite Empire* (1959).

Bibliography: *Anatolian Studies* 6 (1956) 27-34. **P. Bienkowski,** *Jericho in the Late Bronze Age* (1986), information gathered from G.'s unpublished papers on Jericho. **O. R. Gurney,** *DNB* 1951–60 (1971) 395-96.

J. DAY

GASTER, MOSES (1856–1939)

Born in Bucharest in 1856, G. studied at the University of Breslau and at the Jewish Theological Seminary of Breslau. He was ordained and received the PhD in 1881. From 1881 to 1885 he lectured on the history of Romanian literature and comparative MYTHOLOGY at the University of Bucharest. During this period he published a popular history of Romanian literature and began a chrestomathy of Romanian literature, which was published in 1891. His activities on behalf of Jews in Romania led to his expulsion by the government; even though the expulsion was overturned, he moved to England, where he was naturalized in 1893, and never again lived in his native country. He died Mar. 5, 1939.

In 1886 G. delivered the Ilchester lectures on Greco-Slavic literature at Oxford, an appointment he received again in 1891. He became the chief rabbi of the Sephardi Jews in England in 1887 and maintained this post until his failing eyesight forced him out in 1918. Appointed director of the Judith Lady Montefiore College at Ramsgate in 1890, he resigned in 1896 amid serious differences with the board regarding management of the school. He continued his role as a Jewish activist in England, being founder and president of the English Zionist Federation and serving as vice president of four congresses held in Basel and London between 1898 and 1900. He was instrumental in the development of the Balfour declaration of Nov. 1917.

A versatile scholar, G. published works on Jewish liturgy, comparative mythology, and lost and obscure Hebrew language texts and was an advocate for the authenticity of the Samaritan religious community. He collected an outstanding selection of manuscripts, most of which were sold to the British Museum. G. delivered the Schweich lectures in 1925 on the Samaritans, arguing that the sect represented an authentic Hebrew tradition, with roots reaching back to preexilic Israel. Although his conclusions have not found wide acceptance, his arguments must be considered by any student of the Samaritans.

Works: *Literatura Populara Romana* (1883); *Jewish Sources and Parallels to the Early English Metrical Romances of King Arthur and Merlin* (1888); *Chrestomatie Romana* (1891); *The Sword of Moses* (1896); *The Chronicles of Jerahmeel* (1899); *Hebrew Illuminated Bibles of the Ninth and Tenth Centuries* (1901); *Rumanian Bird and Beast Stories* (1915); *The Exempla of the Rabbis* (1924); *The Samaritans* (Schweich Lectures, 1925); *Studies and Texts in Folklore, Magic, Medieval Romance, Hebrew Apocrypha, and Samaritan Archaeology* (3 vols., 1925–28); *The Tittled Bible* (1929); *Samaritan Eschatology* (1932); *Ma'aseh Book* (1934; ET 1981).

Bibliography: **A. M. Hyamson,** *DNB Sup. 5* (1949) 309-10. **C. Roth,** *EncJud* 7 (1971) 332-34. **B. Schindler** (ed.), *Occident and Orient: Gaster Anniversary Volume* (1936); *Gaster Centenary Publication* (1958).

B. WHALEY

GASTER, THEODOR HERZL (1906–1992)

Son of the distinguished Jewish scholar M. GASTER, G. was born in London, July 21, 1906, and educated at the University of London and later at Columbia University. Between 1944 and 1972 he held professorships of religion at Dropsie College, Fairleigh Dickinson University, and Barnard College. He died Feb. 2, 1992.

Following his father, G. made his main contributions to biblical studies in the fields of FOLKLORE and MYTHOLOGY, especially with reference to the ancient Near East, as in his edition of the Ugaritic mythological texts, *Thespis* (see UGARIT AND THE BIBLE). He continued and defended the comparative method of J. FRAZER, whose work on biblical folklore he extended and updated in a major study, *Myth, Legend, and Custom in the OT* (1969). He interpreted Jewish annual festivals along similar lines.

Works: *Thespis, Ritual, Myth, and Drama in the Ancient Near East* (1950); *Festivals of the Jewish Year* (1953); *The Dead Sea Scrolls* (1956); *Myth, Legend, and Custom in the OT: A Comparative Study with Chapters from Sir J. Frazer* (1969).

Bibliography: R. H. Hires and H. M. Stahmer, "T. H. G., 1906–92, A Biographical Sketch and a Bibliographical History of Identified Published Writings," *UF* 27 (1995) 59-114; *UF* 28 (1996) 277-85.

J. R. PORTER

GAY/LESBIAN INTERPRETATION

The phrase "gay/lesbian biblical interpretation" can be understood in both a narrow and a broad sense. A narrow use of the phrase would refer to biblical interpretation carried out by individuals identified as lesbian or gay. More broadly, the phrase might refer to a mode of biblical interpretation that deals with issues thought to be of special interest to lesbians, gay men, and bisexuals, irrespective of the sexual identity or sexual practices of the individual interpreter. Such issues could include not only the specific topic of same-sex sexual relations but also questions about the wider framework of social assumptions and practices within which same-sex sexual relations are given certain meanings. By way of comparison, some scholars working in the humanities and the human sciences use the phrase "lesbian and gay studies" to refer to an academic interrogation of the process whereby sexual meanings (e.g., the assumption of heterosexuality as a norm and homosexuality as a deviation) are produced and reproduced in culture and society. In a similar manner a gay/lesbian biblical interpretation in the broad sense might focus on sexual meanings in relation to both the production and the reception of the biblical text but in a manner that makes problematic certain normative assumptions about heterosexuality and homosexuality.

Several developments within society in general and the realm of biblical interpretation in particular make it possible today to raise the question of a gay/lesbian biblical interpretation. By the late 1960s the impact of the sexual revolution, feminism, and lesbian and gay political movements began to be felt in churches and synagogues. Lesbians, gay men, and their supporters increasingly called for a gay-affirmative transformation of Jewish and Christian attitudes toward sexuality, sometimes using emergent LIBERATION THEOLOGIES as models for articulating such a call. As a result scholars and religious leaders began to reexamine both the traditional religious condemnations of same-sex sexual relations and the biblical texts usually cited to justify those condemnations. At the same time an increasing interest among biblical scholars in the social world of the biblical texts opened the door for new questions about the social and cultural organization of gender and sexuality in the ancient world. Finally, a growing interest in interdisciplinary biblical interpretation has taken place simultaneously with the appearance of lesbian and gay studies across the humanities and the human sciences, allowing for the possibility that lesbian and gay studies will come to have an influence on biblical scholarship similar to the influence of LITERARY THEORY, cultural anthropology, and SOCIOLOGY.

Several trends in biblical interpretation have emerged as a result of these factors. First, a number of studies have tried to argue that supposed biblical condemnations of same-sex sexual contact have been overstated or misunderstood altogether. Levitical condemnations of sex between men, for example, are reinterpreted by some readers as condemnations of the cultic prostitution that was long thought to have been practiced among Israel's neighbors. Similarly, Pauline statements are reinterpreted by some readers as condemnations of cross-generational sexual activity known to have been practiced among Greeks and Romans or as condemnations of same-sex sexual activity between heterosexual persons. A number of relationships between biblical characters of the same sex (such as Jonathan and David, Ruth and Naomi, and Jesus and the beloved disciple) have also been reinterpreted as having some sort of erotic dimension.

Flaws in at least some of these interpretations have become increasingly apparent, however. For example, the appeal to ancient cultic prostitution as the real object of biblical condemnation has become less convincing as scholars have increasingly come to question the widespread existence of such cultic practices. The appeal to Greco-Roman pederasty as an explanation for Pauline statements cannot adequately account for PAUL's apparent condemnation of female homoeroticism (Rom 1:26), since most of our evidence for ancient cross-generational sexual activity concerns males rather than females. To suggest that Paul intended to condemn heterosexuals who participate in homosexual activity but not homosexuals themselves is to import into Paul's world a distinction between "heterosexuals" and "homosexuals" that does not cohere with the ancient evidence. Perhaps most important, studies that argue that the biblical texts do not themselves condemn same-sex sexual activity frequently avoid the crucial question of whether the biblical texts, shaped as they are by the assumptions of another time and place, can really provide an adequate foundation for contemporary sexual ethics.

On the other hand, through their attempts to question the assumption that the Bible clearly condemns same-sex eroticism, scholars have demonstrated both the relative scarcity of such condemnations and the difficulties involved in understanding some of the texts in question. For example, two texts that have often been cited as condemnations of homosexuality, the story of Sodom in Genesis 19 and the story of the Levite and his concubine in Judges 19, are now widely interpreted as focusing on rape, violence, inhospitality, and divine retribution, even when it is acknowledged that the threat of some form of same-sex contact also plays a role in these stories. The process whereby the story of Sodom in particular came to be read as primarily a story about the evils of same-sex eroticism has been shown to be extremely complex (see, e.g., M. Jordan [1997]).

Moreover, while the argument that the biblical texts do not oppose same-sex sexual contact has not been entirely convincing to most interpreters, attempts to make the argument have led to an increasing interest in the social and cultural assumptions that structure biblical attitudes toward homoeroticism. Thus a second trend in biblical interpretation accepts elements of the traditional view that certain biblical texts look negatively upon same-sex sexual relations; but it insists upon the need to understand that negative assessment in the context of ancient sexual and gender codes. FEMINIST research into the gender notions and gender-related social structures presupposed by the biblical texts has been an important influence in this regard. Biblical condemnations of same-sex sexual contact are now widely interpreted in terms of their relation to a sharp and hierarchical differentiation between culturally defined male and female gender roles.

So, for example, sex between men may have been viewed with horror by the authors of the levitical codes (Lev 18:22; 20:13) in part because such activity was thought to involve the symbolic emasculation of one of the male partners. This emasculation was no doubt considered shameful in a society structured by rigid gender categories and hierarchy. Insofar as sexual contact between men was thought to blur the symbolic boundaries between men and women, the inclusion of a condemnation of male homoeroticism in the priestly sections of Leviticus also fits in well with a general tendency of that portion of biblical literature to emphasize the categories and distinctions according to which the world was thought to be ordered. A concern about both procreation and the potentially defiling nature of bodily emissions may underlie the levitical condemnations of male same-sex sexual contact, while the emphasis on procreation in the HB may help to account for the complete absence therein of any reference to female homoeroticism. Since male seed seems to have been considered the crucial substance for conception in the ancient world, sexual activities that did not involve male ejaculation may have been less troubling to some observers than those sexual activities that did.

Paul, on the other hand, like some of his Jewish contemporaries (e.g., PHILO, Pseudo-Phocylides), does apparently condemn both male and female same-sex sexual contact. At least in Paul's case, however, such condemnation does not seem to have resulted from a concern about procreation and may have resulted instead from assumptions about proper gender roles. Indeed, Brooten's recent work on female homoeroticism (1996) suggests that such sexual contact may have been troubling for Paul not only because of its blurring of gender boundaries but also because of the perception that by assuming a man's sexual role a woman was usurping a man's social position or, at least, rebelling against a woman's subordinate social position. While such an interpretation is not accepted by all of Paul's readers, it does seem both to confirm that biblical norms about sexuality are related in complex but significant ways to ancient gender beliefs and to question any simplistic assumptions about the relevance or applicability of such norms to contemporary disputes over sexual ethics.

While a great deal of light has been shed on biblical attitudes toward sexual practice, much less work has been done on the production of readings of biblical texts from explicitly lesbian, gay, or bisexual reading locations. This is somewhat surprising given, on the one hand, the greatly increased emphasis among biblical scholars on reading strategies, READER RESPONSE, and social location and, on the other hand, the growing influence of lesbian and gay studies and "queer theory" in the humanities and the human sciences. The relative scarcity of such readings of biblical texts may be due in part to professional and ecclesial factors that discourage biblical scholars from self-identifying as lesbian, gay, or bisexual or from working on gay-related projects. Most of the available examples of such readings tend to be theologically oriented (see, e.g., G. Comstock [1993]) and give only minimal attention to the important work being done outside the fields of religious and theological studies. Nevertheless, it seems likely that lesbian and gay readings of a whole range of biblical and related texts will constitute the next significant development in gay/lesbian biblical interpretation.

Bibliography: D. **Boyarin,** "Are There Any Jews in the History of Sexuality?" *Journal of the History of Sexuality* 5, 3

(1995) 333-55. **R. L. Brawley** (ed.), *Biblical Ethics and Homosexuality* (1996). **B. J. Brooten,** *Love Between Women: Early Christian Responses to Female Homoeroticism* (Chicago Series on Sexuality, History, and Society, 1996). **G. D. Comstock,** *Gay Theology Without Apology* (1993). **L. W. Countryman,** *Dirt, Greed and Sex: Sexual Ethics in the New Testament and Their Implications for Today* (1988). **D. Good,** "Reading Strategies for Biblical Passages on Same-Sex Relations," *Theology and Sexuality* 7 (September 1997) 70-82. **M. D. Jordan,** *The Invention of Sodomy in Christian Theology* (Chicago Series on Sexuality, History, and Society, 1997). **D. B. Martin,** "Heterosexism and the Interpretation of Romans 1:18-32," *Biblical Interpretation* 3, 3 (1995) 332-55. **S. M. Olyan,** " 'And with a Male You Shall Not Lie the Lying Down of a Woman': On the Meaning and Significance of Lev 18:22 and 20:13," *Journal of the History of Sexuality* 5, 2 (1994) 179-206. **R. Scroggs,** *The NT and Homosexuality: Contextual Background for Contemporary Debate* (1983). **K. Stone,** "The Hermeneutics of Abomination: On Gay Men, Canaanites, and Biblical Interpretation," *BTB* 27, 2 (1997) 36-41; *Sex, Honor and Power in the Deuteronomistic History* (JSOTSup 234, 1996).

K. STONE

GEDDES, ALEXANDER (1737–1802)

Born in Banffshire, Scotland, G. offered himself for the Roman Catholic priesthood. From 1758 he studied classics and theology at Scots College, Paris, and Hebrew at the Sorbonne, where he was strongly influenced by the Enlightenment. After ordination (1764) he was assigned to pastoral work in Scotland, but he also found time for academic work. In 1781 he was awarded the LLD at Aberdeen but was dismissed by his bishop for his liberal views and unconventional habits.

In London, under the patronage of Lord Petre, a wealthy Catholic, G. again took up biblical studies. He began preparations for translating the Bible from the original languages and, inspired by the work of B. KENNICOTT and A. Holmes, studied and collated manuscripts. A visit to Germany in 1783 made him aware of the critical work done there. His *Prospectus* (1786) won general approval and made his name known throughout Europe; however, his Bible translation (vol. 1, 1792), which included his first steps in LITERARY and historical criticism, aroused vigorous opposition in Britain from both churches and universities. Volume 2 (1797) and *Critical Remarks* (1800) only confirmed his critics in their views. His loyal patron, Lord Petre, died in 1801, and G., weighed down by grief, opposition, and ill health, died the following year. Before his death he very probably burned a quantity of his writings prepared for the press.

G. insisted on the need for freedom of research without constraint from church authority or dogmatic presuppositions. The Bible must be examined as any other literature; and reason, in the shape of critical principles, must be applied to all the records. The main barrier to progress, he felt, was the prevailing doctrine of the absolute and universal INSPIRATION of the Scriptures, which excluded the possibility of error of any kind. Following J. SEMLER, G. rejected allegorical interpretation, so prevalent in earlier centuries when a plausible literal meaning could not be found in the text. Signs of error and fallibility of judgment were, he thought, so abundant as to be beyond all doubt. With J. G. EICHHORN, G. refused to allow that principles applicable to secular literature should not be applied to the Scriptures on the grounds that they were sacred. Hebrew historians gathered their materials like any other historians, with the same chances of error.

G. maintained that miracle stories in the Bible must be examined as rigorously as in other literature and proposed a number of "natural" explanations for events he could not take literally, like the plagues of Egypt and the crossing of the Red Sea. Likewise, "immoral" events, like the slaughter of the Midianites (Numbers 31), he considered to be mistakenly ascribed by the author or editor to a command from God. The dramatic setting for the giving of the law was contrived by Moses to impress the people, making them more ready to observe its precepts.

But "natural" explanations did not satisfy him. With Eichhorn he was now asking, "Why might not the Hebrews have their mythology as well as other nations?" (*Bible* 1, x). Genesis 1 seemed to him a beautiful mythos dressed as history and adapted to its readers or hearers (see MYTHOLOGY). The story of the fall was "an excellent *mythologue* to account for the origin of human evil."

Where Eichhorn's belief in the Mosaic authorship proved an obstacle, G. was able to investigate matters further. He had long been convinced that, in view of the many signs of multiple authorship and later composition, Moses could not have composed the entire Pentateuch (see PENTATEUCHAL CRITICISM). Eichhorn's theory of originally separate and continuous documents incorporated into Genesis and distinguishable by their use of the divine names, G. likewise rejected. He could find only fragments of various origins in which the marks of difference predominated. Moreover, unlike Eichhorn, he identified other fragments in the succeeding biblical books that would have been put together by a collector or editor probably in the time of Solomon or even as late as Hezekiah. The use of particular names of God in the so-called J and E sections could be due to other causes, e.g., circumstances of origin or later editing. G. found similar marks of composite authorship in Joshua, thus anticipating the work of F. BLEEK. Although death prevented him from pursuing his analysis, it was developed by J. VATER as the fragment hypothesis.

Works: *Prospectus of a New Translation* (1786); *The Holy Bible, or the Books Accounted Sacred by Jews and Christians. . . .*

vol. 1, *Genesis–Joshua* (1792); vol. 2, *Judges–Ruth* (1797); *Critical Remarks on the Hebrew Scriptures: Corresponding with a New Translation of the Bible* (1800).

Bibliography: S. **Bullough,** "British Interpreters: Dr. A. G.," *ScrB* 14 (1984) 26-30. **T. K. Cheyne,** *FOTC* 4-12. **T. Cooper,** *DNB* 21 (1890) 98-101 (useful details and book list; inexact dates 1780–83). **R. C. Fuller,** *A. G., 1737–1802, A Pioneer of Biblical Criticism* (1984). **J. G. MacGregor,** *The Bible in the Making* (1961) 259-62. **J. W. Rogerson,** *OTCNC* 154-56. **E. S. Shaffer,** *"Kubla Khan" and the Fall of Jerusalem: The Mythological School in Biblical Criticism and Secular Literature, 1770–1880* (1975) 26-28. **J. S. Vater,** *Commentar über den Pentateuch* (vols. 1 and 2, 1802; vol. 3, 1805).

R. C. FULLER

GEIGER, ABRAHAM (1810–74)

A rabbi, theologian, and leader of Reform Judaism, G. was a main figure in *Wissenschaft des Judentums.* Born in Frankfurt a. M., he was influenced by local scholars like M. Creizenach and W. Heidenheim. With the latter, G. studied Hebrew grammar and Masorah studies, but he considered J. G. HERDER and J. G. EICHHORN his "early guides through the realm of the Bible" (M. Wiener [1962] 142). Although his doctoral degree was from Marburg, G. studied classics and oriental languages at Heidelberg and philosophy and history at Bonn; and he was influenced to a certain extent by the Tübingen school. He held rabbinical positions in Wiesbaden (1832–38), Breslau (1838/40–63), Frankfurt (1863–69), and Berlin (1870–74) and made important contributions to the development of reform theology and liturgy.

G. taught at the Hochschule für die Wissensschaft des Judentums in Berlin, for the first time including biblical criticism as an integral part of the curriculum of a rabbinical school. He was convinced that critical studies on Judaism would show that the Jews shaped Judaism and not vice versa and that, therefore, these studies would contribute to the dismissal of the traditional position that Judaism consists of a revelation independent of time. Accordingly, his research was motivated by both his passion for critical studies and his theological goals.

Urschrift und Übersetzungen der Bibel in ihrer Abhängigkeit von der innern Entwicklung des Judentums (1857) is G.'s main scholarly contribution to biblical studies. Building on S. LUZZATO's claim that sometimes the Aramaic translators—and the *naqdanim* as well— intentionally changed the received Hebrew text if the text as it stood could have led a "simple" reader to an improper reading, G. reconstructed a picture of different and competing Hebrew readings for numerous biblical verses. These readings are understood as intentional departures from an original text (closer to the MT than

to any other version) brought about by a variety of points of view on social, political, theological or halakhic issues. Also important for biblical studies is G.'s *Das Judentum und seine Geschichte,* a popular work with clear theological overtones (e.g., accepting the spiritual stream of Judaism in contrast to the dead letter of the law [81], considering [evolving] tradition "the daughter of Revelation and of equal rank with her" [86], and claiming that sacrifices were tolerated only in the biblical period [67]). In this work G. argued that the basic idea of Judaism (ethical monotheism) was not the result of an evolutionary process, but of revelation. He also claimed that the idea of Judaism was developed with almost nothing being adopted from other peoples in the biblical period and that the violent rejection of foreign peoples in some texts of the Bible is to be understood as a necessity in defending the existence of the religious idea.

Works: *Urschrift und Übersetzungen der Bibel in ihrer Abhängigkeit von der innern Entwicklung des Judentums* (1857, 1928[2]); *Das Judentum und seine Geschichte* (1864, 1865[2], 1910[3]; ET, *Judaism and Its History* [1866, 1911, 1985]); *A. G.'s Nachgelassene Schriften* (ed. L. Geiger, 5 vols., 1875–78, 1980), esp. 4:1-279.

Bibliography: S. **Heschel,** "A. G. on the Origins of Christianity" (diss. University of Pennsylvania, 1989, 1993); *A. G. and the Jewish Jesus* (1998). **Y. Klausner,** Introduction to Hebrew tr. of *Urschrift und Übersetzungen der Bibel* (1949). **M. A. Meyer,** *Response to Modernity: A History of the Reform Movement in Judaism* (Studies in Jewish History, 1988), esp. 89-99. **J. Petuchowski** (ed.), *New Perspectives on A. G.* (1975), esp. 11-29. **M. Wiener** (ed.), *A. G. and Liberal Judaism: The Challenge of the Nineteenth Century* (1962).

E. BEN ZVI

GEIKIE, JOHN CUNNINGHAM (1824–1906)

A widely read Bible expositor, devotional writer, and religious historian, G. received a theological education in Canada and was ordained in the Presbyterian church. He did mission work until his return to Britain, where he was later ordained in the Church of England and held several vicarates.

G. was a lucid and prolific writer who enjoyed a wide readership. Interested in the ARCHAEOLOGY of Palestine, he visited the Near East and filled his works with historical details of the biblical world. His *Life and Words of Christ* (1877) used these materials extensively and became a popular success. The same interests appear in *Hours with the Bible, or the Scriptures in the Light of Modern Discovery and Knowledge* (1881–84), a ten-volume work. G. eagerly embraced historical knowledge, but he rejected most of historical criticism, holding fast to orthodox views on the person of Christ and the reliability of the Scriptures.

Works: *Life and Words of Christ* (1877); *Hours with the Bible, or the Scriptures in the Light of Modern Discovery and Knowledge* (10 vols., 1881–84); *OT Characters* (enl. ed., 1884); *The Holy Land and the Bible* (2 vols., 1887); *Landmarks of OT History* (1894).

Bibliography: W. F. Gray, *DNB* 23 (1912) 92-93. D. L. Pals, *The Victorian "Lives" of Jesus* (TUMSR 7, 1982) 94-98.

D. L. PALS

GELL, ROBERT (1595–1665)

A scholar of biblical translation who was accused of being a Familist, G. was born at Pamphisford, Cambridgeshire, educated at Christ's College, Cambridge, and possibly was chaplain to the archbishop of Canterbury before becoming rector of St. Mary Aldermanbury in London. G.'s criticism of B. Walton's 1657 POLYGLOT Bible, his suggestions for alternative translations, and his further comments on scriptural meaning (many of which were published after his death by R. Bacon) are an important but almost entirely neglected avenue of seventeenth-century theology. His preference for allegorical readings won him the hostility of more orthodox Puritans, and his concern for an absolutely literal rendering of obscure metaphors in the Bible brought charges of incomprehensibility. His range of reference was remarkably rich, and he was the acknowledged intellectual authority in an as yet still largely unknown network of nonconformist "perfectionists."

Works: *Stella Nova* (1649); *Angelokratia theou, or, A Sermon Touching God's Government of the World by Angels* (1650); *Noah's Flood Returning* (1655); *An Essay Toward the Amendment of the Last English-Translation of the Bible* (1657); *Gell's Remaines* (ed. R. Bacon, 1676).

Bibliography: G. F. Nuttall, *J. Nayler: A Fresh Approach* (JFHS 26, 1954); "The Last of J. Nayler, R. Rich, and the Church of the First-Born," *Friends' Quarterly* 60 (1985) 527-34.

N. SMITH

GENESIS, BOOK OF

1. Poetry, Drama, Novels. The earliest interpretations of Genesis are found in the biblical CANON itself. Thus Psalms 33 and 136 are poetic retellings of the story of creation; Job 40:15 begins a long paean that serves as a poetic homily on Gen 1:21; and Isa 54:9-10 evokes the image of the rainbow covenant (Gen 8:21-22). This tradition had its successors in Jewish as well as Christian liturgies and has inspired poetry across the centuries, of which J. MILTON's *Paradise Lost* (1667) has become the most widely read. In the twentieth century biblical poetry was spurred by A. Klein and flowered

in Hebrew writing. It has had echoes in medieval miracle plays and such modern dramas as Beer-Hoffmann's *Jacob,* reaching its apex in T. Mann's Jacob-and-Joseph cycle, which has been called "the most profound treatment of this biblical theme in literature" (S. Liptzin, *EncJud* 11 [1971] 883).

While all of these are interpretations of Genesis themes and evoke them vividly, they develop them independently in their own modes. This is the function of fiction, poetry, and liturgy; but this very function also removes them from our specific focus, which is the elucidation of the sacred text, its history and setting.

2. Translations. This exclusion applies also to the translations of Genesis that have appeared over the past two millennia and more. To be sure, every TRANSLATION is a form of commentary; and more often than not it has been through the medium of translation that the text has had its greatest impact. But intelligibility rather than interpretation is the primary purpose of most translations. Thus the SEPTUAGINT holds comment to a minimum, as does the Aramaic version of *Tg. Onkelos,* although the latter eschews all anthropomorphisms and uses euphemisms when a sense of propriety calls for them. The Palestinian TARGUMIM indulge frequently in homiletical expansions of the text and for this purpose freely employ midrashic materials (see MIDRASH). *Tg. Jonathan,* for instance, explains the plural verb form describing God's activity in Gen 1:26 (*wayyōʾmer ʾelōhîm naʾăseh ʾādām,* literally, "And God said 'Let *us* make *ʾādām*'") by expanding it into: "God said *to the angels who ministered to him,* 'Let us make *ʾādām.'* " In rendering the next verse it adds that God created *ʾādām* with 248 members and 365 nerves, then overlaid them with skin, which God filled with flesh and blood. *Tg. Yerushalmi* also takes liberties with the biblical text and enlarges Gen 1:27 philosophically by saying that it was the Word of God that created *ʾādām.*

Other translations, especially the VULGATE, the Douay, the KJV, and the LUTHER Bibles, have by their very impact on language shaped the understanding of the text. A small example: Genesis 3 leaves the nature of the fruit that Adam and Eve ate unspecified, and the rabbis speculated that it might have been the grape. But because the Latin *malum* can mean either "apple" or "evil," the notion arose that the fatal fruit had been an apple.

3. Quran. Islam, although using many Genesis tales and images, did not incorporate the Torah as such into its faith structure and, therefore, did not claim to interpret the biblical text, as did Jewish and Christian traditions. Rather, the biblical text was reshaped in the Quran (see QURANIC AND ISLAMIC INTERPRETATION) and supplanted by it, thereby removing it from our purview of biblical interpretations.

4. Early Interpretations. Along with the written text went an oral tradition that preceded the written collections found in Mishnah, TALMUD, and the many midrashic compendia. While there were relatively few occasions for halakhic starting points in Genesis (among the exceptions were Gen 1:28 [see *m., Yeb.* 6:6] and 32:33) the book engendered an enormous amount of aggadic comment.

a. ʾAggadah. This *ʾaggādâ* is distinguished by a unique approach to the Torah text that stretches the basic principles of HERMENEUTICS by a free-flowing, imaginative approach to religious questions in the widest sense. It makes its points by treating God at the same time in the most respectful and yet familiar way; it takes the text seriously but not literally; and it freely invents divine and human discourses and actions—all for the purpose of finding deeper meaning in the Word of God. This led later on to the habit of exploring the text in four different ways: through *pěšaṭ*, plain meaning; *remez,* allusive meaning; *děraš*, homily; and *ṣōd*, hidden meaning. The first letters of these four methods spell *pardeṣ,* which in the oral tradition stood for the garden containing the tree of knowledge from which Adam and Eve were removed and to which human beings no longer have access. If there was a way back it could only be, this tradition held, through a thorough and many-sided knowledge of the biblical text. It is possible that this fourfold interpretation was assimilated from medieval Christianity through the *Zohar,* the fountainhead of Jewish mysticism. (For a large sampling of this vast material see L. Ginzberg [1921–38].) A few examples must suffice.

On Gen 3:9, in asking, "Where are you?" did God not know where Adam was? God asked in order to open the way to repentance (*Tanchuma, Tazriʾa* 1:9). On Adam's answer, "I was afraid because I was naked" (Gen 3:10), not physical, but religious nakedness is meant. Adam was afraid because by his transgression he was stripped of the one commandment (*mitzvah*) he had received. A human being without a *mitzvah* is truly naked (*Pirqe R. El.* 14). What was the real sin of Sodom and Gomorrah? The cities were so rich that their streets were paved with gold, but instead of sharing their wealth with others the inhabitants closed the access roads to keep unwanted strangers away (ibid., 25). On the deception of Isaac, when the blind patriarch said, "The voice is the voice of Jacob, yet the hands are the hands of Esau" (Gen 27:22), he spoke prophetically. "The voice of Jacob" means learning and truth; "the hands of Esau" denotes force and violence. As long as the voice of Jacob is heard in the houses of prayer and learning, the hands of Esau will not prevail (*Bereshit Rabbah* 65:20). Of Joseph facing the entreaties of Potiphar's wife: The text says "he refused" (Gen 39:8). The rarely used *shalshelet* sign is placed over the word to indicate delay, for the woman insisted again and again and Joseph refused again and again (ibid., 98:20). Jewish preaching until today has leaned heavily on such ancient *ʾaggādâ.*

b. Philo. The first individual writer to comment broadly on Genesis was PHILO Judaeus of Alexandria, who saw the text through the lens of *remez.* For him the sacred Word hinted at allegorical and philosophical rather than "plain" meanings, and it is this deeper understanding that reveals the real intent of Scripture. In Philo's view abstractions are the highest level of reality and must therefore be discovered in the text. Thus the story of primal humanity is a symbol of the moral development of the soul; the ancestors are the impersonations of the active law of virtue; and Joseph is a study in how the wise must live. Philo calls the serpent in the garden of Eden the symbol of pleasure. It is said to have uttered a human voice because pleasure employs innumerable champions and defenders who take care to advocate its interests and who dare to assert that it should exercise power over everything.

c. Ishmael and Akiba. While Philo's direct influence on Jewish tradition was small, in part because he wrote in Greek, his basic concept had its parallel in the rabbinic mainstream. Two rabbis of the second century who exerted great influence on the interpretation of the biblical text argued (not unlike Philo) the basic question: How was one to approach God's Word—through its plain meaning or through extended understanding? R. ISHMAEL (the principal purveyor of hermeneutical principles) held that Torah "speaks in human language"— that is, plainly. R. AKIBA, on the other hand, taught that Torah was unlike any other book and had to be read with attention to every stroke and letter (see *b. Ber.* 31b; for an example of Akiba's attention to the smallest detail, see *b. Men.* 29b on the meaning of the untranslatable ʾet). In subsequent Jewish tradition both Ishmael's and Akiba's approaches found their place in the ʾaggādâ, which often blurred their disagreement, for it became the nature of this tradition not to claim that one had arrived at the only authoritative understanding of the divine Word. It was different with the determination of what constituted *hǎlākhâ,* but it was always clear that this was the result of a human decision, arrived at by majority vote or consensus.

5. Medieval Jewish Commentaries. *a. Saadia.* Systematic comment on Genesis (as on Torah in general) begins with the Babylonian scholar and communal leader SAADIA ibn Joseph, who wrote a word-by-word commentary on the Torah as well as philosophical considerations on its major themes, especially creation (defending the notion of *creatio ex nihilo*). He was also the first to treat of biblical *hapax legomena,* and his contribution to the understanding of difficult words was considerable. Saadia's commentary was made possible by the work of the Masoretes, who arrived at a standard text.

b. Rashi. The most celebrated Jewish commentator of all time was the French scholar Solomon ben Isaac, commonly known as RASHI. To him, the text was to be understood by way of *pěšaṭ,* by which he meant "common sense approved by tradition." Thus on Gen 3:8 he wrote: "I am concerned only with the literal meaning of Torah and with such *ʾăggādōt* which explain the biblical passages in a suitable manner." A full three quarters of his explanations incorporate midrashic explanations, and the rest rely on his far-reaching mastery of all Jewish sources as well as on his keen linguistic sense. He paid close attention to the Masoretic accents, often followed *Onkelos*, occasionally explained him (Gen 49:24; 43:15), and sometimes rejected him (15:11). The terseness of his style, his lucidity, and his unquestioned authority made his commentary in turn the subject of intensive study among Jews and even some Christian scholars, especially NICHOLAS OF LYRA. Two examples: Genesis 2:2 relates that God created Adam from the dust of the earth, which according to Rashi God took from the four corners of the earth so that human beings might be at rest everywhere. Genesis 32:8 says that on meeting Esau, Jacob was beset by both fright and anxiety. Comments Rashi (based on *Bereshit Rabbah* 76:2): "Fright—that he might be killed [by Esau]; anxiety—that he might be led to kill the others."

c. Abraham ibn Ezra. Next in importance to Rashi ranks A. IBN EZRA, who was not inclined to follow Rashi's basic reliance on the use of Midrash for the purpose of explaining the plain meaning of the text. Of independent mind, he was the first to cast doubts on Mosaic authorship of the Torah, although he merely hinted at it. Thus Gen 12:6 ("The Canaanites were then in the land"—clearly a post-Mosaic phrase) drew his observation that "the informed will understand."

d. Others. Of the many successors to Rashi and ibn Ezra few exerted a greater influence than M. ben Nachman ("Ramban" or NACHMANIDES). His wider perspective of the book's spiritual context has had continued appeal and brought him increased attention in the twentieth century. He was also convinced that the text contained hidden meanings, and thus he became an important link in the spread of medieval mysticism.

D. KIMHI ("Radak") brought to the text his great knowledge of grammar and syntax; and I. ABRAVANEL was the first to approach the text, not so much on a word-by-word basis, but by raising questions that he thought needed answers. O. ben Jacob SFORNO achieved wide popularity by his trenchant observations; in commenting on the Babel story he called attention to "the real crime" of the builders: They tried to impose one religion on humankind. God prevented this and by dispersing the nations kept alive a variety of idolatries, for God knew that out of this adversity would eventually come a recognition of the supreme ruler.

e. Hasidism. The hasidic movement (see HASIDISM) arose in the middle of the eighteenth century in Eastern Europe. Among its characteristics was renewed attention to the spiritual life of the individual, and frequently the interpretation of the biblical text served as a vehicle for

this purpose. Two examples: God's command to Abraham in Gen 12:1, *lek-lĕkā* (lit., "get on with it!" [so Nachmanides]) was interpreted to mean "Go to yourself," i.e., God asks Abraham to discover his own spiritual core (see *ʿIṭṭûrēy Tôrâ* 1:83). Similarly, the words *wayyiggaš yĕhûdâ* (Gen 44:18) are usually rendered, "Then Judah drew near." The hasidic teacher asks, "To whom did Judah draw near?" and answers, "To himself, for only when Judah became himself at his best was he able to speak as he did" (ibid., 1:389).

f. In the wake of emancipation. Three commentaries of the emancipation and post-emancipation era signify the tensions in which Jews found themselves. (1) M. MENDELSSOHN's German rendering of the Torah text was a work of revolutionary impact, which was to be counterbalanced by the *Bîʿur*, a Hebrew commentary that aimed to preserve traditional views. (2) This latter task was undertaken with greater success by S. Hirsch in his thoroughly orthodox commentary, which was written in German and laid the spiritual foundation for the emergence of Jewish neo-orthodoxy. Hirsch looked to the text for contemporary relevance and was at all times a homiletician *par excellence*. Two examples: Why, in Gen 10:9 is Nimrod's name linked to that of God? Because he oppressed people in God's name. Nimrod was the prototype of all tyrants who pretend that their crown is "by God's grace," and thus their power politics and hypocrisy are characterized by the expression "like Nimrod." Hirsch interpreted *lek lĕkā* (Gen 12:1) as "go by yourself." "This is one journey which must be made alone. One must become a stranger in the world to view it clearly." (3) Meʿir Loeb ben Yehiʿel Michael (MALBIM) was the last great link to medieval tradition in the midst of emancipation. He followed Abravanel's method of asking questions arising from the text and ibn Ezra's close attention to words and meanings. Thus, on the story of the tower of Babel he commented on the words "All the earth had . . . the same words" (Gen 11:1). This expression, *dĕbārîm ʾăḥadîm*, could also mean "few words," i.e., that humans had a small vocabulary. Since both the learned and the unlearned spoke "the same words" there was no technical or philosophic jargon to separate people from each other.

6. Modern Jewish Commentaries. One of the greatest single contributions to the study of Genesis was made by B. JACOB, a German rabbi whose massive commentary was published during the early days of the Nazi regime and must be considered a masterpiece of careful scholarship and wide erudition. Jacob gave special attention to the weaknesses of the documentary hypothesis and insisted on the basic unity of the book (though he did not see Moses as its author).

His intellectual successor, U. CASSUTO, also upheld the unitary nature of the Genesis text and expanded on Jacob's explication of the numbers system, which he showed underlies all of Genesis. Most important, he gave special attention to the literary structure of the book, to its nuances of language, and to its relationship to Ugaritic sources (see UGARIT AND THE BIBLE).

The most popular Jewish commentary of the twentieth century came out of England. Edited by J. Hertz (1929–36), it tried to fortify traditional values through a vigorous rejection of all higher criticism. While it does mention non-Jewish writers, it does so only when they praise the ethical and literary values of Genesis. This apologia attempted to combat the rise of anti-Semitic sentiment and at the same time give the Jewish reader a renewed sense of pride and worth.

Y. KAUFMANN (1937-57), in his large history of Israel's faith, disputed some of the basic tenets of the then regnant critical school without rejecting its methods outright. He denied that Israel's monotheism was the result of a gradual development away from the pagan worldview, seeing it rather as a sudden spiritual eruption. He saw Moses rather than Abraham as the progenitor of the new faith.

A generation later W. Plaut's [Bereshit] Genesis (1974) set out to enlarge the insights of Jewish tradition with those from Christian, Muslim, and secular sources as well as to take full cognizance of the findings of LITERARY, archaeological (see ARCHAEOLOGY AND BIBLICAL STUDIES), cognate, and linguistic inquiries. It distinguishes between three levels of commentary: The first, historical-antiquarian, accepts the basic insights of critical scholarship and explains the text as it was understood in its own day; the second, traditional, shows how the text was interpreted across the millennia by exegesis or eisegesis; and the third level is represented by considerations of what the text might mean in our day, regardless of what it meant yesterday. (Later editions of Plaut's Genesis commentary appeared as part of The Torah: A Modern Commentary [1981, 1995[10]].)

7. Between Jew and Christian. On the whole the rich work of Jewish commentary rarely reached students outside the Jewish realm, just as Jews paid little attention to Christian savants. Even after the advent of emancipation Jewish and Christian Bible scholars often remained largely ignorant of each other. Thus, in the Christian camp The Interpreter's Bible and The Jerome Biblical Commentary, to name but two, contain few references to the two millennia of Jewish scholarship. Both these works, oriented toward the Protestant and Roman Catholic communities respectively, support critical scholarship but generally do not look across the demarcations of faith communities to widen their appreciation of the text. This is so in part because each tradition has been concerned with firming up its own foundations and, therefore, has been inhospitable to independent inquiry that might weaken it.

8. Christian Interpretations. a. Foundations. There is a fundamental difference in the approach Jewish and Christian interpreters have taken when dealing with Genesis. Both saw God's work rehearsed in its pages,

but its goal was viewed differently. To the former the book was essentially a prolegomenon to the creation of God's chosen people: God had created the world and crowned it with the human species, which, however, disappointed God, who subsequently turned to Abraham and made him the progenitor of Israel to whom the Torah would be entrusted and thereby the task of tiqqûn 'ōlām, the perfection of the world. To Christians, in contrast, Genesis is a double prolegomenon: to history in general (including Israel) and thence to Christ. Thus the focus shifted; the forward thrust of the book was not salvation through Sinai but through the Savior.

Christian commentary has tended to view Genesis (like all of the HB) as pointing toward JESUS and his mission. Words and passages have been seen to hint at his coming and at the theology of the developing ecclesia. Thus the sweeping rûaḥ in Gen 1:2 has been understood not as "wind" but as "Spirit," a hint at the Holy Spirit of the Trinity. The expulsion from Eden became a special focus of Christian teaching. While in normative Judaism the myth (see MYTHOLOGY AND BIBLICAL STUDIES) found no resonance whatsoever, it became central to Christian teaching: "By the offense of one, judgment came upon all men to condemnation" (Rom 5:12, 18; see also 2 Esdras 7:18). This basic human flaw was to be redeemed through Jesus Christ. In this fashion Genesis became a theological starting point for the church.

It is interesting to note that ORIGEN (d. c. 254) fell into disfavor in part because he was thought to be too close to the Jewish view and that his allegorizing followed Philo more than the emerging Christian consensus, which was firmed up by JEROME (d. 420), who was also well acquainted with rabbinic sources. AUGUSTINE (d. 430) influenced subsequent commentary on Genesis, not only through the application of hermeneutical rules, but by his emphasis on the Christian view necessary to employ them properly. For instance, he understood Jacob's supplanting of Esau to hint at Jesus, whose ministry helped the Gentiles to supplant the Jews; hence Jacob's acts were not deception but divine mystery. Thereafter, all Christian commentary on Genesis remained Christ-centered.

The same is true even for some moderns who have fully accepted the results of modern scholarship and have themselves contributed greatly to it. A prime example is G. von RAD. In his commentary he comments on F. Rosenzweig's discussion of the redactional process. Rosenzweig had called the final arranger of the text "R," to stand for rabbēnû, "our teacher" or "master" (see M. Buber and Rosenzweig [1939] 322). Von Rad responded, "From the standpoint of Judaism that is consistent. But for us, in respect to hermeneutics, the redactor is not our master. . . . We receive the OT from the hands of Jesus Christ, and therefore all exegesis of the OT depends on whom one thinks Jesus Christ to be" (1956, 41). To him and many others Genesis is essentially

Heilsgeschichte in the Christian perspective. Much of what will appear below under the heading of "higher criticism" qualifies as Christian interpretation as well.

b. Literalism. A literal reading of Genesis by the church resulted in the seventeenth-century trial of GALILEO, who was forced to recant his teaching that the earth revolves around the sun and is therefore not the center of the universe. The latter part of the nineteenth century saw the bitter controversy over Darwinism in which the "biblicists" were headed by S. Wilberforce and the "rationalists" by T. Huxley. In the United States the conflict was played out in the Scopes trial of 1925. For the time being it ended the hold on public education the literal understanding of the creation process had previously exercised. But in the latter part of the century the conflict once more came to the fore. American and Canadian "creationists" have claimed that the biblical account in Genesis 1–2 is as scientific as the theory of evolution and, therefore, deserves equal treatment in schools and textbooks and is to be presented to the student as a viable alternative.

This battle has been waged by Protestant fundamentalists, who see "secular" approaches to the creation of the world as a threat to their faith. The Roman Catholic Church, on the other hand, not unlike Jewish tradition, has taken a more relaxed "analogous" view of the biblical creation stories. "They relate in simple and figurative language . . . the fundamental truths presupposed for the economy of salvation, as well as the popular description of the origin of the human race and of the Chosen People" (*JBC*, 8).

9. Higher Criticism. a. Beginnings. It needs to be stated again that the study of the Bible has come primarily from scholars belonging to one or another faith community. The majority have been academics teaching in seminaries or university departments of theology whose function it was to strengthen their religion by enlarging the scope of its intellectual underpinnings. In works on Genesis one finds, therefore, scholarly agendas that are sometimes clear and at other times unspoken. When an independent writer like SPINOZA (d. 1677) set out to explore the text "in a spirit of entire freedom and without prejudice" (*Tractatus theologico-politicus* [1670] chaps. 7–10) the Amsterdam Jewish community punished him with the ban. Generally, however, scholars have made their contributions from within the bounds of their own communities. In addition, one must keep in mind that the study of Genesis—because of its material a crucial book—has frequently borne the stamp of particular perceptions of history.

This is demonstrable in the case of the founders of PENTATEUCHAL CRITICISM—K. GRAF and J. WELLHAUSEN—who attempted to reconstruct the development of the Genesis document. Building on the work of their predecessors, they separated three main literary streams and assigned them to the J, E, and P documents, dated them,

judged their historical value, and viewed them from the perspective of Israel's spiritual development. Graf and Wellhausen began with the assumption that history started from primitive beginnings and slowly, but inexorably, moved in an upward fashion. Applying this view to Genesis (and to biblical history in general), they saw its concepts of God and ethics grow from simple and crude perceptions to more exalted levels, pointing ultimately to the advent of Christianity.

They proceeded to deny Genesis an intrinsic historical value. The tales, they said, were largely etiological. One could not gather from them "any historical knowledge of the Patriarchs, but only about the time when the narratives which concern them took shape in the people of Israel" (Wellhausen, *Prolegomena to the History of Israel* [1883] 331).

b. Gunkel. The debate over historicity was shifted to another arena with H. GUNKEL's pathbreaking commentary in 1901. He concentrated on what became known as form-critical analysis (see FORM CRITICISM) and viewed the book as a repository of sagas, which he described as ancient forms of poetic stories dealing with events and personalities of the distant past. They were at first passed along by oral transmission and contained much etiological material. Genesis, he wrote, dealt primarily with individual sagas, and he proceeded to set them into their proper framework. His incisive exploration had a profound influence on biblical scholarship, which now focused on the literary character of the text.

Unfortunately Gunkel was also infected with a sense of personal animus against Judaism, which colored his writings. The biblical figure of Jacob was the special target of his disdain; he described him as the archetypical Jew, whose deception delighted his "happy heirs." A similar animus was exhibited by Friedrich DELITZSCH, who tried to show that Genesis was unoriginal in that most of its tales were borrowed from the Babylonians (*Babel und Bibel* [1902–1905; ET 1906]; see BABEL UND BIBEL). Because of such judgments many Jewish scholars viewed higher biblical criticism as "a form of subtle anti-Judaism, if not anti-Semitism . . . often present in much of the 'critical' literature" (H. Hummel, *EncJud* 4 [1971] 907).

c. Radicals and conservatives. The understanding of the literary and theological nature of Genesis was developed in a new direction by a cadre of German scholars. Building on Gunkel, von Rad attempted to show that biblical saga was not merely poetic fantasy but the sum total of living historical recollection. "No stage in this work's long period of growth is really obsolete, something of each phase has been conserved and passed on as enduring" (1956, 31, 27). Primeval history was seen as a period of alienation from God, with Abraham the key to the *Heilsgeschichte* and Israel's journey the key to the world's history. This view has been contested by C. WESTERMANN (1966–82) in his extensive commentary. He does not see chaps. 1–11 as subservient to salvational history but as providing a perspective of their own—a universal canvas that attempts to describe the world as it was and does not at all focus on Israel. Its overriding theme, as that of all of Genesis, is the praise of God's majesty.

While von Rad related the Genesis sagas to traditions of the exodus, M. NOTH (1950) saw them stemming from the league of tribes, each of which had specific traditions concerning its own ancestors prior to settlement in Canaan. Thus the sagas were largely etiological; therefore, nothing could be said about the time and place of the patriarchs. Noth's views, built on his highly conjectural theory of an Israelite amphictyony, attracted a great deal of critical attention; and some of his successors expanded it radically.

G. Mendenhall (1962) conjectured that the whole idea of Israel's peoplehood came after the league of tribes had been instituted and that the conjoint Genesis and Exodus traditions reflect nothing of the tribes' true history. According to Mendenhall, there was no "patriarchal history," since Israel did not have ancestors different from those of the Canaanites. J. Van Seters (1975) went one step further and saw the entire Abraham saga to be a late, perhaps postexilic, theological invention.

Alongside this radical school has been a more conservative wing that sharply criticized the views of Noth as "nihilistic" and instead asserted that much of Genesis was indeed rooted in historical events (see J. Bright [1956] 52, 54). "As a whole the picture in Genesis is historical, and there is no reason to doubt the general accuracy of the biographical details and sketches of personality which bring the Patriarchs to life with a vividness unknown to a single extrabiblical character in the whole literature of the Ancient Near East" (W. F. Albright [1963] 5). Others taking a somewhat similar point of view were R. de VAUX, who adduced supporting evidence from the research of N. GLUECK and the occurrence of Genesis names in Mari and Nuzi sources. To these have been added the Ebla finds, but their meaning has been the subject of much debate, especially since many of the extant texts remain unpublished.

The moderate wing includes I. ENGNELL, whose Uppsala school has stressed the long line of oral traditions that were said to have been committed to writing only at a late date. E. SPEISER saw the accepted J/E/P schools themselves to have derived from a common tradition (which he calls T). To him Abraham is the father of biblical monotheism, and the history of the biblical process is the story of the monotheistic ideal (1964, XLIX). The motive power of this process was spiritual rather than economic or political, and this gave it its particular character. In his assessment of Abraham's role he departed from the view proposed by Y. KAUFMANN, who ascribed this distinction to Moses.

d. New Vistas. The writings of B. CHILDS (1979) have made an important new contribution to our understanding of Genesis. In his analysis of chaps. 1–11 he strikes a middle ground between von Rad and Westermann in that he emphasizes the unifying theme of *tōlĕdōt,* which makes Genesis into a perceptual whole, while at the same time giving the primeval stories a distinct place of their own. "The Genesis material is unique because of an understanding of reality which has subordinated common mythopoetic tradition to a theology of absolute divine sovereignty" (1979, 158). Childs also takes up Kaufmann's view and stresses the role of Moses in the formation of the tradition, a role earlier critical commentators had played down. Last but not least, he sees oral and literary traditions, on the one hand, and cultic traditions, on the other hand, as shaping each other in a process of dynamic tension and in an attempt to separate modern perceptions from the text as it is, stresses the importance of looking at it through the eyes of ancient Jewish comment as well. N. SARNA (1989) and *Olam ha-Tanakh* combine close attention to traditional Jewish interpretation with insights derived from cognate languages and cultures as well as recent archaeological studies that have shed new light on prominent places mentioned in Genesis, like Shechem and Ber Sheba.

Another stage of interpretation may be termed literary and has been pioneered by E. AUERBACH, Z. Adar (1967), and R. Alter (1981). It goes beyond Gunkel in its attention to the nuances of Hebrew words and phrases and of key terms and images and thus reveals a new dimension of comprehension. Its interest lies less in how the text came into being than in what it says in its present form. Finally, FEMINIST criticism has entered the field and has explored aspects of understanding and thereby significantly added to the exploration of the biblical text (see P. Trible [1978] and the surveys by A. Brenner [1993] and P. Bird [1994]).

In fact, there has been a turning away from the preoccupation with historiography and documentary analysis and to a concern with the completed surface of the text (Sarna, XVIII). "Literary criticism has often been paralyzed by a too minute distinction of sources which pulverizes the texts and makes them unintelligible" (de Vaux [1951] 23). The holistic approach developing in many disciplines must also find its way into the appreciation of the text, and nowhere is this more urgent than in our view of Genesis. Although there are elements of etiology, the text overwhelmingly conveys a sense of authenticity. Genesis primarily retells; it does not originate (E. Speiser [1957] 201-16; similarly de Vaux [1951] 24). We must be cautious not to superimpose our own modern ideas on an ancient text that arose in a mind-set very different from our own. And finally, the long-standing separation between Jewish and Christian scholarship is being bridged by such scholars as Childs and Plaut, and the enlarged view thus made possible will contribute to further fruitful exploration of the book.

Bibliography: Z. **Adar,** *Sefer bĕrešît, mābhō˒ lĕ˒ālām hammiqrā ˒î* (1967). W. F. **Albright,** *The Biblical Period from Abraham to Ezra* (1963³). R. **Alter,** *The Art of Biblical Narrative* (1981); *Genesis/Translation and Commentary* (1996). G. T. **Armstrong,** *Die Genesis in der alten Kirche* (BGBH 4, 1962). K. **Armstrong,** *In the Beginning: A New Interpretation of Genesis* (1996). E. **Auerbach,** *Mimesis* (1953; ET 1954). B. W. **Bacon,** *The Genesis of Genesis: A Study of the Documentary Sources of the First Book of Moses in Accordance with the Results of Critical Science Illustrating the Presence of Bibles Within the Bible* (1892). P. **Bird,** *Feminism and the Bible: A Critical and Constructive Encounter* (1994). A. **Brenner,** *A Feminist Companion to Genesis* (1993). J. **Bright,** *Early Israel in Recent Biblical Writing* (SBT 19, 1956). M. **Buber and F. Rosenzweig,** *Die Schrift und ihre Verdeutschung* (1939). U. **Cassuto,** *A Commentary on the Book of Genesis* (2 vols., 1944–49; ET 1961–64). B. S. **Childs,** *Introduction to the OT as Scripture* (1979). O. **Eissfeldt,** *Die Genesis der Genesis: Vom Werdegang des ersten Buches der Bibel* (1958, 1961²). J. M. **Evans,** *Paradise Lost and the Genesis Tradition* (1968). T. W. **Flanxman,** *Genesis and the "Jewish Antiquities" of Flavius Josephus* (BibOr 35, 1979). J. P. **Fokkelman,** *Narrative Art in Genesis* (SSN 17, 1975). T. **Fretheim,** "Genesis," *NIB* (1994) 1:319-675. J. **Gable,** *The Bible as Literature: An Introduction* (1986). L. **Ginzberg,** *The Legends of the Jews* (7 vols., 1921–38). W. H. **Green,** *The Unity of the Book of Genesis* (1895). A. J. **Greenberg** (ed.), *˒Ittûrēy Tōrâ* (5 vols., 1965–). H. **Gunkel,** *Genesis* (HKAT I, 1, 1901, 1910³; ET 1997). B. **Halpern,** *The First Historians: The HB and History* (1988). R. P. C. **Hanson,** *Allegory and Event: A Study of the Sources and Significance of Origen's Interpretation of Scripture* (1959). M. **Harl,** *Les Bibles d'Alexandrie,* vol. 1, *La Genèse* (1986). J. H. **Hertz** (ed.), *The Pentateuch and Haftorahs: Hebrew Text, English Translation, and Commentary* (1929–36). P. **Humbert,** "Die neuere Genesis-forschung," *TRu* 6 (1934) 147-60, 207-28. "Israel, History of," *ABD* 3:526-76. Y. **Kaufmann,** *The Religion of Israel: From Its Beginnings to the Babylonian Exile* (8 vols., 1937–57; abridged ET 1960). N. **Leibowitz,** *Studies in the Book of Genesis: In the Context of Ancient and Modern Jewish Bible Commentary* (1972). N. **Lemche,** *Ancient Israel: A New History of Israelite Society* (Biblical Seminar 5, 1988). A. **Levene,** *Early Syrian Fathers on Genesis* (1951). E. G. **Mendenhall,** "The Hebrew Conquest of Palestine," *BA* 25 (1962) 66-87. S. **Niditch,** "Genesis," *Women's Bible Commentary* (ed. C. A. Newsom and S. H. Ringe, 1992) 10-25; *Oral World and Written Word: Ancient Israelite Literature* (Library of Ancient Israel, 1996). M. **Noth,** *The History of Israel* (1950; ET 1960²). W. G. **Plaut,** *[Bereshit] Genesis* (1974); *Torah: A Modern Commentary* (1981, 1995¹⁰). G. **von Rad,** *Genesis* (ATD, 1956; ET 1961). I. N. **Rashkow,** *The Phallacy of Genesis: A Feminist-psychoanalytic Approach* (Literary Currents in Biblical Interpretation, 1993). D. **Redford,** *Egypt, Israel, and Canaan in Ancient Times* (1992). G. A. **Rendsburg,** *The Redaction of Genesis* (1986). F. E. **Robbins,** *The Hexaemeral Literature: A Study of the Greek and Latin Commentaries on Genesis* (1912). G. A. **Robbins** (ed.), *Genesis 1–3 in the History of Exegesis: Intrigue in the Garden* (SWR 27, 1988). N. M. **Sarna,** *Genesis: The Traditional Hebrew with the New JPS Translation* (JPSTC, 1989). J. **Skinner,** *Genesis* (ICC, 1910). E. A. **Speiser,** "The Biblical Idea of History in Its Common Near Eastern Setting," *IEJ* 7 (1957) 201-16; *Genesis* (AB 1, 1964). T. **Thompson,** *The Origin Tradition of Ancient Israel* (JSOTSup 55, 1987). P. **Trible,** "A Love Story Gone Awry," *God and the Rhetoric of Sexuality* (1978) 72-143. J. **Van Seters,** *Abraham in History and Tradition* (1975); *In Search of History: Historiography in the Ancient World and the Origins of Biblical History* (1983). R. **de Vaux,** *Genèse* (1951); "Method in the Study of Early Hebrew History," *The Bible in Modern Scholarship* (ed. J. P. Hyatt, 1965) 15-29. C. **Westermann,** *Genesis* (BKAT 1, 3 vols., 1966–82; ET 1984–86). J. **Wilcoxen,** "Narrative," *OT Form Criticism* (TUMSR 2, ed. J. H. Hayes, 1974) 57-98. A. **Williams,** *The Common Expositor: An Account of the Commentaries on Genesis, 1527–1633* (1948).

W. G. PLAUT

GEORGE, JOHANN FRIEDRICH LUDWIG

(1811–73)

G. was born and studied in Berlin. He became a follower of F. SCHLEIERMACHER before losing his Christian faith and becoming a disciple of G. W. F. Hegel (1770–1831). He wrote two important books on biblical studies but was prevented from academic advancement by the movement toward orthodoxy in Prussia from 1820. After various teaching posts, he became professor of philosophy in Greifswald in 1856, remaining there until his death in 1873.

G.'s book on Jewish festivals (1835) was significant in that it demonstrated that the legal and cultic parts of Exodus, Leviticus, and Numbers needed to be treated separately from their narrative sections and that some of this material was later than the book of Deuteronomy and thus to be dated to the exile. Thus G. completed what had been begun by W. DE WETTE, solving the problems caused by de Wette's insistence that the books of Genesis–Numbers were earlier than Deuteronomy. He presented a three-stage development of Israelite religion: a period of freedom from priestly control; the centralization of Josiah's reforms; and after the exile a priestly dominated religion at the single sanctuary. All that was needed for J. WELLHAUSEN's position was for G.'s view of Israelite religion to be integrated with the new documentary hypothesis; G. had worked with a fragmentary hypothesis. His book on myth and saga (1837; see MYTHOLOGY AND BIBLICAL STUDIES) was an attempt to distinguish between these two types of narrative in regard to their origin and significance. Basically, myth originates from philosophical insights into reality and is of value if interpreted correctly, while saga tries to account for historical causality. Saga can be replaced by more correct knowledge of historical facts and causes and does not have the abiding value of myth. G.'s writings were distinguished by originality and clarity; had he written twenty years earlier or forty years later they would have made the impact upon scholarship that their quality deserved.

Works: *Die älteren jüdischen Feste mit einer Kritik der Gesetzgebung des Pentateuch* (1835); *Mythus und Sage: Versuch einer wissenschaftlichen Entwicklung dieser Begriffe und ihres Verhältnisses zum christlichen Glauben* (1837).

Bibliography: *ADB* 8 (1878) 710-12. **M. Lenz,** *Geschichte der Königlichen Friedrich-Wilhelms-Universität zu Berlin* 2, 1 (1910) 484. **J. W. Rogerson,** *Myth In OT Interpretation* (BZAW 134, 1974) 24-27; *OTCNC* (1984) 63-68.

J. W. ROGERSON

GERSON, JEAN (1363–1429)

Born Dec. 14, 1363, G. was educated at the College of Navarre (Paris), where he attained his *licentia* (1381) and *magister* (1382) in arts before completing his *baccalaureus formatus* (1390–92) and attaining the lic. theol. (1392) and DTh (c. 1394). In 1395 he received papal appointment as chancellor of Notre Dame and of the University of Paris. He made significant contributions at the Council of Constance (1414–18); at its conclusion, to escape political enemies, he went to Austria and then eventually took up residence at the Celestine priory at Lyons (1419). Although he retained his appointment as university chancellor until his death, G. never returned to Paris. He died July 12, 1429.

G.'s works are well preserved and were published in several complete editions during the later fifteenth century (Cologne [1483–84] and Strasbourg [1488; repr. 1489, 1494]). In the midst of violent conflicts in church and state, his writings, which represent a wide range of interests, supported his commitment to bring about reconciliation and reform through the renewal of a spirit of prayer and sacrifice. The influence of these writings during the later fifteenth and early sixteenth centuries was considerable, leading one historian to call this period "the century of G." (E. Delaruelle).

G. is important in biblical interpretation for two reasons: (1) because of his several extended biblical commentaries (*G* 8:163-534; 8:565-639; 9:245-373), sermons (*G* 5, *L'oeuvre oratoire*), university lectures based on Markan texts (*G* 3. nos. 88a-90, 92-97, 99-100, 102-3, 104-5), and various treatises specifically devoted to exegetical principles and problems (*G* 3:333-40; 10:232-53; 10:55-59); and (2) because of his role in reforming the university curriculum to highlight the proper use of Scripture for theological study (*G* 2:26-28; 3:224-49).

In his biblical interpretation G. often cited AUGUSTINE, NICHOLAS OF LYRA (d. 1349), and his own teacher H. Totting of Oyta (d. 1396) as *auctoritates* when discussing specific exegetical principles or questions (e.g., *G* 3:334-35; 10:241). He applied these authorities in distinctive fashion, however, particularly when addressing problems raised in ecclesial controversies, in order to clarify the much disputed question of his day: i.e., the true *sensus litteralis* of Scripture. In several treatises written during the Council of Constance, G. affirmed the central significance of Scripture as itself the *regula fidei* (*G* 10:55), while also insisting that it not be received *nude et in solidum* (*G* 10:57). Against such a "bare" reading, "de-contextualized" from the church's tradition, he argued that Scripture must be interpreted on the basis of the "meaning handed on by the holy fathers." This defense of the normative (but not constitutive) role played by the early church fathers (*ecclesia primitiva;* *G* 10:58; also *G* 3:139) represented Oyta's third hermeneutical principle (see HERMENEUTICS) set forth in the prologue to his *Sentences* commentary, the first two being the wider biblical context and the *modus loquendi,* or common rhetorical conventions (*G* 3:334; see Augustine *De doctrina christiana* 3.2-4, 26-28).

In defending the primary authority of the patristic *usus loquendi,* G. argued that when confronted with "various heresies," often occasioned by ambiguities in the biblical text, the "holy doctors" had "drawn forth" the true literal sense of Scripture (*G* 3:335). Such authoritative guidance was necessary to interpret ambiguous or controversial texts correctly because biblical texts—unlike secular literature—have their own peculiar logic and grammar and could not be properly understood in terms of common rhetorical conventions only or by the methods of the "speculative sciences" (*G* 10:241). Thus the historical church, governed and directed in its exegesis by the Holy Spirit (*G* 3:335), played an indispensable role in determining a text's authentic meaning.

Finally, G. insisted that the reader's moral character influenced the proper retrieval of this "sense" (e.g., *G* 9:237; 10:56; see also the similar pronouncement in "De canonicis scripturis," *Canons and Decrees of the Council of Trent* [ed. H. J. Schroeder, 1941] 18-19, 298). This conviction led him to conclude that the theological enterprise depended not only on the intellect (*eruditio solius intellectus*) but also on the "erudition of the heart"; consequently he insisted that "the spirit of catholic judgment" might well reside with the ignorant but moral layperson rather than with the learned but immoral scholar (*G* 9:237-38). The proper interpretation of biblical texts and the retrieval of the literal sense thus depended on two factors: the "sense" of the early church's interpretation and the moral integrity of the reader.

Works: *Opera Omnia* (4 vols., ed. L. E. du Pin, 1706); *Oeuvres complètes* (10 vols., ed. P. Glorieux, 1960–73; references to texts taken from this edition are noted as *G* and are followed by volume and page numbers).

Bibliography: **D. C. Brown,** *Pastor and Laity in the Theology of J. G.* (1986). **C. Burger,** *Aedificatio, Fructus, Utilitas: J. G. als Professor der Theologie und Kanzler der Universität Paris* (BHT 70, 1986); *TRE* 12 (1984) 532-38. **M. S. Burrows,** "G. After Constance: *Via Media et Regia* as a Revision of the Ockhamist Covenant," *CH* 59 (1990) 467-81; *J. G. and 'De Consolatione Theologiae' for a Disordered Age* (BHT 78, 1991); "J. G. on the 'Traditional Sense' of Scripture as an Argument for an Ecclesial Hermeneutic," *Biblical Hermeneutics in Historical Perspective: Studies in Honor of K. Froehlich on His Sixtieth Birthday* (ed. M. Burrows and P. Rorem, 1991) 152-72; *HHMBI*, 99-106. **A. Combes,** *Essai sur la critique de Ruysbroeck par G.* (3 vols. in 4, ETHS 4-6, 1945–72); *La théologie mystique de G.: Profil de son évolution* (2 vols., 1963–64). **W. Dress,** *Die Theologie G.'s: Eine Untersuchung zur Verbindung von Nominalismus und Mystik im Spätmittelalter* (1931). **K. Froehlich,** " 'Always to Keep the Literal Sense in Holy Scripture Means to Kill One's Soul': The State of Biblical Hermeneutics at the Beginning of the Fifteenth Century," *Literary Uses of Typology from the Late Middle Ages to the Present* (ed. E. Miner, 1977) 20-48. **F. Hahn,** "Die Hermeneutik G.," *ZTK* 51 (1954) 34-50. **M. Hurley,** " 'Scriptura sola': Wyclif and His Critics," *Traditio* 16 (1960) 275-352. **L. Mourin,** *J. G.: Prédicateur français* (Recueil de travaux de Gand 113, 1952). **H. Oberman,** *The Harvest of Medieval Theology: G. Biel and Late Medieval Nominalism* (1963). **S. Ozment,** *Homo Spiritualis: A Comparative Study of the Anthropology of J. Tauler, J. G., and M. Luther (1509–16) in the Context of Their Theological Thought* (SMRT 6, 1969). **L. Pascoe,** *J. G.: Principles of Church Reform* (SMRT 7, 1973). **G. H. M. Posthumus Meyjes,** *J. G.: Zijn Kerkpolitiek en Ecclesiologie* (SMRT 26, 1963). **J. Schwab,** *J. G.: Professor der Theologie und Kanzler der Universität Paris* (2 vols., 1858).

M. S. Burrows

GERSONIDES (1288–1344)

A French philosopher, mathematician, astronomer, Talmudist (see TALMUD), and biblical scholar referred to in Hebrew literature by the acronym RaLBaG (Rabbi Levi Ben Gershon), G. was also known as Magister Leo Hebraeus and Leon de Bagnols. Little is known of his life, which began at Bagnols-sur-Cèze and ended in Perpignan, although it is thought that he came from a scholarly background and that he lived in both Orange and Avignon. Remarks in his writings indicate that life, even in Provence, was not easy for Jews and that he had his share of disruption and suffering.

G. was a genius, writing authoritatively and prolifically on many topics, and is said to have earned his living practicing medicine. He is known mainly for his philosophical writings, of which *Sepher Milhamot Adonai* (The Book of the Wars of the Lord) is the major work. In six sections of this treatise he discussed the immortality of the soul, PROPHECY and divination, God's prescience, providence, the heavenly bodies, the creation of the world, and miracles. He also wrote commentaries on the HB. Surviving are those on the Pentateuch (see PENTATEUCHAL CRITICISM), the former prophets, Job (one of the first books to be printed in Hebrew [1477]), Daniel, Nehemiah, Chronicles, Proverbs, Song of Songs, Ecclesiastes, Esther, and Ruth. In these commentaries G. often alluded to and quoted from his *Sepher Milhamot Adonai*, almost assuming that the reader has some knowledge of the views expressed there. This is especially true in his commentary on Job, which he treated as a philosophical book; but as a philosopher G. was inclined to "find" philosophy in all of Scripture, and his commentaries may be described as philosophical exegesis.

G.'s initial approach to commentary was to divide the relevant text into what he discerned to be its natural parts. Thus it is clear that he divided Ecclesiastes into nine sections (1:1-2; 1:3-11; 1:12–4:12; 4:13-16; 4:17–6:12; 7:1-22; 7:23–9:6; 9:7–11:8; 11:9–12:14) and that some of these sections coincide with later interpretations of the text. This is an important characteristic of his commentaries and sets him apart somewhat from other commentators of his day. SAMUEL BEN MEIR (Rashbam, c. 1080–1174) had shown a decided interest in extended units but not so obviously as did G. In commenting on a particular pericope G. selected a few words within that section for explanation, either because they were difficult and not easily understood or because he was particularly interested in them. His explanations were brief but usually helpful. He then launched into the exegesis of phrases and sentences, often paraphrasing the biblical text under discussion and alluding to Talmudic and other biblical passages. He occasionally resorted to Arabic, Aramaic, or French to help clarify a particular point.

G. was particularly interested in the logical connection of verses, and he emphasized the context as a necessary element in interpretation. This concentration on context, while also considered important by his predecessors Rashbam and J. KARA, was more clearly drawn in G.'s exegesis. His interest in midrashic exegesis (see MIDRASH) was minimal, although, unlike Rashbam and Kara, he did not feel obligated to fight the battle against it. Finally, his view of the purpose of Scripture was underlined as he deduced from the pericope the lessons to be learned, referring to these as *Toaliyyot* (advantages) gained from the study of the passage.

Works: *The Commentary of Levi ben Gerson (Gersonides) on the Book of Job* (ed. and tr. A. L. Lassen, 1945); *Commentary by Levi ben Gershon on the Five Megillot* (ed. J. Marcaria, 1560) Hebrew; *The Wars of the Lord* (1560; ET 1977).

Bibliography: I. **Broydé,** *JE* 8 (1904) 26-32. L. **Jacobs,**
Jewish Biblical Exegesis (Chain of Tradition Series 4, 1973)
89-99. C. **Touati and B. R. Goldstein,** *EncJud* 11 (1971)
92-98.

R. B. SALTERS

GESENIUS, HEINRICH FRIEDRICH WILHELM
(1786–1842)

Born Feb. 3, 1786, in Nordhausen, G. studied at the
University of Helmstedt under the rationalist Henke and
the classical historian Bedrow. In 1806 he became *Repetent* in the theological faculty in Göttingen, where he
lectured on Greek and Latin and in 1806 gained his
doctorate. However, in 1808 G. began to teach Hebrew,
Arabic, and OT because the powerful C. Heyne objected
to the advancement of a classics scholar not from his
own school. G. was appointed *ausserordentlicher* professor in Halle in 1810 and the same year was appointed
to the fourth chair in theology. Often as many as 200
students attended his lectures. In 1813 he formed a
group for biblical interpretation whose members included such future scholars as P. von BOHLEN, H. HUP-
FELD, E. Rödiger (1801–74), J. TUCH, J. VATKE, and E.
ROBINSON. G. remained in Halle until his death, Oct. 23,
1842.

G. was best known as a lexicographer and grammarian of Hebrew. As early as 1807 he began work on his
Hebrew-German LEXICON and sent the first volume to
J. VATER in Halle in 1808. Volume 1 was published in
1810, vol. 2 in 1812, and G.'s Hebrew grammar in 1813.
Both the lexicon and the grammar went through many
editions and were made available to English readers.
The lexicon was translated for American use by J. Gibb
(1824) and for British use by C. Leo (1825). From 1829
the *Thesaurus philologicus criticus* began to appear (it
was completed in 1853 by Rödiger), and a Latin translation of the lexicon supplemented with material from
the *Thesaurus* appeared in 1833. This Latin version was
translated by Robinson in 1836, and after several revisions it became the basis for the Anglo-American lexicon of F. BROWN, G. DRIVER, and C. BRIGGS. In
Germany, the lexicon was constantly revised in the
nineteenth and twentieth centuries and is currently being
revised again under the editorship of R. Meyer and H.
Donner. The grammar, too, was constantly revised, and
in the form given it by E. KAUTZSCH (1909) was translated into English by A. COWLEY (1910). G.'s 1814 work
decisively challenged the position of such scholars as
C. Houbigant (1686–1783) and A. GEDDES, who relied
on the Samaritan Pentateuch (SEE PENTATEUCHAL CRITI-
CISM) to make radical emendations in the MT.

On matters of authorship of HB books and the history
of Israelite religion, G. followed the views of W. DE
WETTE, with whom he had a strong friendship. His other
most important books on the HB were the *History of*

Hebrew Language and Script (1815) and the Isaiah
commentary of 1820–21, which was a philological and
historical rather than a theological work (for ET of the
commentary on Isaiah 15–16, see *BRQO* 7 [1836] 107-
61).

G.'s lectures were too negative and dismissive of the
crudely supernatural for traditionally orthodox students,
and in 1830 a public accusation of his being a rationalist
provoked the "Hallischer Streit." But if students looked
to other teachers for theological direction, from G. they
learned the nature and importance of scientific philological and historical study of the Bible.

Works: *Hebräisch-deutsches Handwörterbuch über die Schriften des Alten Testments* (1810–12; ETs of 1823 ed. by J. W.
Gibbs [1824] and C. Leo [1825]; LT of 3rd. ed., *Lexicon
manuale Hebraeicum et Chaldaicum in veteris testamenti libros*
[1833]; ET by E. Robinson [1836]; ET of 28th ed. [1909] rev.
by E. Kautzsch by A. E. Cowley [1910]); *De Pentateucho
Samaritano, ejusque indole et auctoritate* (1814); *Geschichte
der hebräischen Sprache und Schrift* (1815); *Thesaurus philologicus criticus linguae Hebraeae et Chaldaeae Veteris Testamenti* (1829–53); *Philologisch-kritischer und historischer
Commentar über den Jesaia* (2 vols., 1820–21).

Bibliography: Anon. (Robert or Rudolf Haym), *G.: Eine
Erinnerung für seine Freunde* (1842). T. K. **Cheyne,** *FOTC*,
53-65. J. **Hahn,** *TRE* 13 (1984) 39-40. E. F. **Miller,** *The
Influence of G. on Hebrew Lexicography* (COHP 11, 1927). **G.
M. Redslob,** *ADB* 9 (1879) 89-93. J. W. **Rogerson,** *OTCNC*
50-57. R. **Smend,** *Deutsche Altestamentlicher in drei Jahrhunderten* (1989) 53-70.

J. W. ROGERSON

GIESELER, JOHANN CARL LUDWIG (1792–1854)

Born March 3, 1792, G. received his PhD in 1817
and was employed as a secondary school teacher the
same year. After receiving his ThD in 1819 he became
a full professor of theology at Bonn and in 1831 full
professor of church history, history of dogmatics, and
dogmatics at Göttingen. In addition to numerous obligations in commissions, foundations, and university
committees, his life work was characterized by various
specialized studies of church history that benefited
the partly posthumously published *Lehrbuch der
Kirchengeschichte* (3 vols. in 8 pts., 1824–35; 5 vols.
in 10 pts., 1844–57, vols. 4-5 ed. E. Redepenning). This
work was published in varying ETs and is noteworthy
for understanding history only from the perspective of
source analysis. Other scholars considered G. to be a
rationalist, although Redepenning disputed this
(*Lehrbuch* 5 [1857] XLIII-LV). G. died July 8, 1854.

G. made a unique contribution to NT exegesis with
his first work (1818); postulating an oral original gospel
established his reputation in the scholarly world. He

attacked primarily the hypothesis proposed by the followers of J. G. EICHHORN of a written Syro-Chaldean (Aramaic) original gospel. Although J. G. HERDER and J. Eckermann had offered preliminary studies that supported his views, G. considered his book to be the first "proof of the historical probability of this hypothesis" (1818, 92).

G. argued that the oral original gospel was first composed in Hebrew and originated "among the apostles through repetition of the same stories," (93). The complete homogeneity of the apostles had enabled them by mutual support to render JESUS' words in "their undiminished spiritual power" (99). This homogeneity explained the extensive similarity of organization in the various Gospels and the occurrence of singular expressions in all of them. The low educational level of the apostles, their faith in the appearance of the Paraclete, and their certainty of the eschatological age precluded an early rendering of the gospel in written form. PAUL did not presuppose the existence of any collections or fragments of Jesus' sayings.

G. maintained that the oral translation of the Hebrew original gospel began within the Jerusalem church for the benefit of its Hellenist members. When this process was continued in the Antioch community and was influenced by a gentile Christian choice of material, however, the community in Jerusalem completed its translation and carried it into the mission field as a more fixed form that agreed with the Hebrew wording. From that point on the gospel existed not only in two languages but also in separate collections whose elements expressed different perspectives.

The fixing of the Gospels in written form originated from private interests and was understandable only in the Greek world with its tendency toward multiple written languages. This rendering in written form did not, however, affect the oral transmission of the gospel. G. dated the composition of the SYNOPTIC Gospels to the middle of the first century. He followed the older church traditions in asserting that Matthew was originally written in Hebrew for Jews and that Mark was a follower of Peter and repeated his proclamation. Whereas Matthew and Mark represent the Jewish-Christian perspective, Luke, as a follower of Paul, composed the gentile Christian Gospel. G. clearly saw the various presuppositions and goals of the Gospels, although his repeated references to private interests somewhat one-sidedly described how the texts were fixed in written form. He held that the Gospel of John also refers to the generally disseminated cycle of narratives—the original gospel—in a form appropriate for more educated Christians. G.'s hypothesis was widely accepted in his own time because, in contrast to the hypothesis of a written original gospel or of collections of shorter sayings or fragments, he recognized the authors of the synoptic Gospels as independent writers and editors of the oral original gospel.

Works: *Historisch-kritscher Versuch über die Entstehung und die frühesten Schicksale der schriftlichen Evangelier* (1818).

Bibliography: W. **Baird,** *History of NT Research,* vol. 1, *From Deism to Tübingen* (1992). **N. Bonwetsch,** *RRE*³ 6 (1899) 663-64. **E. R. Redepenning,** "G.'s Leben und Wirken," *Lehrbuch der Kirchengeschichte* 5 (J. Gieseler, 1857) xliii-lvi (ET in *JSL* NS 7 [1856]).

F. W. HORN

GIKATILLA, ISAAC IBN (10th cent.)

A Hebrew poet and grammarian from the southern Spanish town of Lucena during the latter half of the tenth century, G. was probably not related to Moses ibn GIKATILLA. G. was one of the three students of Menaḥem ibn Saruq who joined in defending their master against Dunash ben Labraṭ's criticisms of 150 entries in Menaḥem's LEXICON of biblical Hebrew. Many of these entries relate to the interpretation of specific words in the Bible; however, some may have been construed as supporting KARAITE rather than normative rabbinic practices and beliefs. Although Menaḥem's defenders wrote collectively, Dunash's student Yehudi ibn Sheshet's rejoinder refers to G. as "the greatest among you." Another one of the three, Judah ibn Daud, is often identified with the prominent Spanish grammarian Judah (Abu Zakariya Yaḥya ibn Daud) Ḥayyuj. Jonah ben Ganaḥ, another major Spanish Hebraist, claimed G. as a teacher.

The students defended Menaḥem on about one-third of the points Dunash had raised, but their approach was not substantially different from that of either Menaḥem or Dunash. Although they supported the biblical basis of free will, most of their responses relate to specific words or grammatical structures. Menaḥem's students, whose response is dedicated to their teacher's patron, Ḥisdai ibn Shaprut, opposed the use of evidence from Arabic or Aramaic to elucidate biblical texts, arguing that this method treats the languages as if they were identical. Such an approach was later rejected by Judah Ḥayyuj, who would draw heavily on linguistic insights gleaned from other Semitic languages.

G. also wrote several *azharot,* liturgical poems for the holiday of Shavuot that describe the 613 commandments Judaism derives from the Pentateuch. His poetic style reflects the influence of Saadia Ibn Joseph.

Bibliography: S. G. Stern, *Liber Responsionum* (1870). **M. Zulay,** "Azharot of R. Isaac ibn Gikatilla," *Tarbiz* 20 (1949) 161-76 (Hebrew).

F. GREENSPAHN

GIKATILLA, MOSES HAKOHEM BEN SAMUEL IBN
(11th cent.)

G. was born in Cordoba, Spain, in the eleventh century. His name, which is spelled in various ways, appears to be a diminutive form of the Spanish word *chico*, meaning "small." Probably not related to Isaac ibn GIKATILLA, he lived most of his life in Sargossa, where he apparently studied with the eminent Hebrew grammarian J. ben Janaḥ.

G. was a highly regarded poet, described by M. ibn Ezra as "the greatest in two languages" (Hebrew and Arabic); however, only a handful of his poems, which deal with both secular and religious themes, have survived. He was also the first to render important Arabic texts into Hebrew, translating the two treatises on irregular verbs by J. Ḥayyuj, with occasional expansions of his own. G.'s linguistic skills were held in high esteem. A. IBN EZRA called him "the greatest of grammarians," and A. ibn Daud listed him alongside Ḥayyuj and ibn Janaḥ. Although virtually none of his works is entirely extant, much has been reconstructed from other authors' comments and citations. He is known to have written a grammatical treatise entitled *Kitāb al-Tadkīr wa al-Ta ʾnit* (Book of Masculine and Feminine), which enumerates Hebrew words with unusual forms, particularly feminines and plurals. He wrote commentaries on most of the books in the HB. An Arabic translation of Job has also been discovered.

In addition to its philological content, G.'s work has a rationalistic orientation; e.g., rather than using the prevalent allegorical approach, his commentary on the Song of Songs is said to have focused on the *pešaṭ* (straightforward interpretation). He offered naturalistic explanations of biblical miracles, most notably ascribing the Bible's statement that Joshua had made the sun stand still to the persistence of its light even after it had set.

G. generally sought historical contexts for prophetic writings rather than interpreting them eschatologically; e.g., the allusions to Jehoshaphat in the last chapter of Joel led him to infer that the prophet (see PROPHECY AND PROPHETS, HB) had lived during that king's reign. On the basis of similar methods he identified the king mentioned in Zech 9:9 as Nehemiah and implied the non-Davidic authorship of several psalms (e.g., 42, 47, and 137), which he recognized as having been written during or even after the Babylonian exile. He also distinguished the prophecies in the first half of Isaiah, which he generally ascribed to the period of Hezekiah, from those in chaps. 40 and following, which he applied to the exilic and Second Temple periods. Cited by ibn Ezra, this observation has led most modern scholars to distinguish between the authors of the book's two parts.

Bibliography: N. Allony, "Fragments of the Book on Masculine and Feminine Gender (*Kitāb al-Tadkīr wa al-Taʾnit*) by R. Moses ibn Gikatilla," *Sinai* 24 (1948) 34-67 (Hebrew). W. Bacher, "Arabische Uebersetzung und arabischer Kommentar zum Buche Hiob von Mose ibn Chiquitilla," *Festschrift zu ehren Dr. A. Harkavy* (ed. Baron D. v. Günzburg and I. Markon, 1908) 1:221-72. H. Brody, "Poems of Moshe Hacohen Ibn Chiquitilla," *Studies of the Research Institute for Hebrew Poetry* (1936) 3:65-90. J. Ḥayyuj, *Two Treatises on Verbs Containing Feeble and Double Letters, Translated into Hebrew from the Original Arabic by R. Moses Gikatilla. . . .* (ed. and trans. J. W. Nutt, 1870). S. Poznanski, *Mose B. Samuel Hakkohen ibn Chiquitilla nebst den Fragmenten seiner Schriften* (1895); "Aus Mose ibn Chiquitilla's arabischem Psalmenkommentar," *ZA* 16 (1912) 38-60.

F. GREENSPAHN

GILBERT DE LA PORRÉE (GILBERT OF POITIERS)
(c. 1076–1154)

G. was born c. 1076 and died Sept. 4, 1154. He studied in northern France, probably under Bernard of Chartres, and taught there until he became bishop of Poitiers in 1142. He became a highly controversial figure because of his teaching on the Trinity and was tried for his opinions at Reims in 1148 by BERNARD OF CLAIRVAUX and other leading churchmen of the day who were concerned that he was misleading the faithful. Opposition arose because of his lectures on the theological tractates of Boethius, in which he found technical terms and concepts of logic and language theory that brought to bear on Christian theology with a rigor not to be found in AUGUSTINE. As a foremost exponent of speculative grammar and logic in his own day, G. strove for still greater technical exactitude in the use of terms, and it was in this way that he fell afoul of the authorities. It is hard to say whether his teaching was in fact unorthodox; one commentator says that his gloss was more obscure than the text, and it seems more likely that he was misunderstood. His pioneering work in this area left its mark on his scriptural commentaries, which remain unedited for the most part; but his principal importance lies in the impact of his more controversial work, which won disciples and made enemies, thus stirring many scholars to work along similar lines.

Works: *The Commentaries on Boethius* (Pontifical Institute of Medieval Studies 13, ed. N. M. Häring, 1966); Commentary on First Corinthians (Studi e testi 117, ed. A. M. Landgraf, 1945).

Bibliography: H. C. van Elswijk, *Gilbert Porreta: Sa vie, son oeuvre, sa pensée* (SSL 33, 1966). N. Haring, *TRE* 13 (1984) 266-68. J. R. Strayer, *DMA* 5 (1985) 528.

G. R. EVANS

GINSBERG, HAROLD LOUIS (1903–1990)

An American Jewish scholar recognized as one of the outstanding biblicists of the century, G. was born in Montreal, Canada, and studied Semitics at the University of London. Upon completing his doctorate he moved to mandatory Palestine, where he worked closely with B. MAZAR (then Maisler), the founder of Israeli ARCHAEOLOGY. During the early 1930s in Palestine G. concentrated on ancient Semitic, especially on the Ugaritic tablets (see UGARIT AND THE BIBLE) that had just been unearthed. His 1936 Hebrew translation and commentary pioneered study of the Ugaritic language and demonstrated the cultural continuity between the literature of ancient Syria and the HB. He was one of the first to employ the Ugaritic texts as a tool in TEXTUAL CRITICISM of the HB and as an aid in recovering some of the forgotten grammatical and lexical features of classical Hebrew.

Although the writings of G.'s Palestine period contain numerous biblical references, it was only on coming to Conservative Judaism's Jewish Theological Seminary in New York in 1936 that he began to make the Bible the center of his scholarly interests. Nonetheless, he continued his research in Northwest Semitic and over the years made significant contributions to the study of the grammar, LEXICON, and dialectology of Ugaritic, Aramaic, and Phoenician. His English translations of the Ugaritic epics remain unsurpassed.

G.'s text-critical work on the Bible, like that of many scholars of his generation, is characterized by abundant emendations. If current scholarship is more deferential toward the Masoretic texts, it nonetheless concedes that G.'s emendations always demonstrate the depth of his penetration of biblical diction. His publications, most of a philological orientation, contribute to an understanding of biblical history and culture. He employed his analysis of biblical diction to reconstruct INNER-BIBLICAL literary development and IDEOLOGICAL influences, and the common sense of his observations is always striking. Thus he accounted for the Aramaisms in Job by the convincing observation that the book's protagonists are "Easterners"; and as we (and Job's author) know from Gen 29:1 and 31:37, Easterners speak Aramaic. G.'s numerous articles and monographs are essential for the proper understanding of Isaiah, Hosea, Daniel, Job, and Ecclesiastes. Although other scholars had argued that the extant Hebrew sections of Daniel and all of Ecclesiastes had been translated from Aramaic originals, it was G. who proved the case.

For many years G. was an advocate of the theories of Y. KAUFMANN, who had attempted to confute classical source criticism by assigning chronological priority (see CHRONOLOGY, HB) to the P(riestly) source over the D(euteronomic). In his later years G.'s concentration on the Pentateuch (see PENTATEUCHAL CRITICISM) caused him to move much closer to the classical position of J. WELLHAUSEN. In *The Israelian Heritage of Judaism* (1982) he provocatively reconstructed the history of the ancient Israelite calendar and its festivals. The results of much of his research are available to a larger public

because he served as an editor and translator of the Torah (1962) and the Prophets (1978) for the revised Jewish Publication Society Bible translation (NJV). He was also Bible editor of *Encyclopaedia Judaica* (1971), to which he contributed several original, detailed articles.

Works: *Kitve Ugarit* (1936); *The Legend of King Keret: A Canaanite Epic of the Bronze Age* (ASORSup 2-3, 1946); *Studies in Daniel* (1948); *Studies in Koheleth* (TSJTSA 17, 1950); *Koheleth: A New Commentary* (1961) Hebrew; "Hosea, Book of," *EncJud* 8 (1972) 1010-24; "Isaiah: First Isaiah," *EncJud* 9 (1972) 49-60; "Job," *EncJud* 10 (1972) 111-21; *The Israelian Heritage of Judaism* (TSJTSA 24, 1982).

Bibliography: **M. Held,** *Conservative Judaism* 30 (1976) 3-9. **J. Tigay,** "Classified Bibliography of H. L. G.'s Writings," *EI* 14 (1978) xiii-xxvii (Hebrew).

S. D. SPERLING

GINSBURG, CHRISTIAN DAVID (1831–1914)

Born of Jewish parents in Warsaw (Dec. 25, 1831), G. acquired a good foundation in Jewish learning at the rabbinic school in Warsaw. At about age sixteen he converted to Christianity, adding "Christian" to his name. Shortly thereafter he immigrated to England (his mother's native land), where he spent the remainder of his life. Through two marriages into prominent families (his first wife died in 1867), G. had the means to carry on his literary work without ever receiving an academic appointment. In 1870 he became a member of the board of revisers for the OT, which published its revision of the KJV in 1885. G. was a strong supporter of liberal causes and minority trends, which perhaps partially explains his interests in groups like the Essenes and the KARAITES. He died Mar. 7, 1914.

G.'s first literary goal was to produce commentaries on the five *Megilloth*, but he published works on only the Song of Songs (1857) and Qohelet (1861). Each volume contained his own translation and superb (and still valuable) history of the previous exegesis of the respective biblical book. In his work on these commentaries G. became absorbed in the field of Hebrew Masorah, which was to occupy him for the remainder of his life. To make available material on the Masorah in English, he translated and published the introduction by JACOB BEN HAYYIM to D. BOMBERG's RABBINIC BIBLE (1865) and E. LEVITA's study of the Masorah (1867). G.'s work on the Masorah was part of his larger goal of publishing a new edition of the HB. In 1894 the Trinitarian Bible Society for the Circulation of Protestant or Uncorrupted Versions of the Word of God issued G.'s edition of the Biblia Hebraica in two volumes with the English title *The Massoretico-Critical Text of the*

HB. This work was a reprint of Bomberg's second rabbinic Bible with G.'s critical apparatus primarily based on previously published HBs; his introduction, published in 1897, remains one of his most substantial contributions to biblical study. For his massive effort to publish the Masorah itself, of which four volumes appeared (1880–1905), he raised money, sold subscriptions, and served as the publisher (the printer was in Vienna).

In his last years G. was occupied with a new four-volume edition of the Hebrew biblical text under the sponsorship of the British and Foreign Bible Society. Texts for individual books were issued as the work progressed: The Torah appeared in 1908; the latter prophets and the former prophets (in two volumes), in 1911. G. died before the publication of the Writings (1926); the project was completed by his associates R. Kilgour, H. Holmes, and A. Geden. The text for this edition was substantially that of the 1525 rabbinic Bible (with isolated, minor changes). For the critical apparatus G. and his associates used over seventy Hebrew manuscripts dating from the fifteenth century or earlier. Overshadowed by R. KITTEL's *Biblia Hebraica* (1906), G.'s edition did not receive prolonged popularity. However, his annotated edition of a Hebrew NT (1885, using the translation of J. F. Salkinson) was widely used; the twelfth edition was released in 1910.

Works: *The Song of Songs* (1857); *Coheleth (Commonly Called the Book of Ecclesiastes)* (1861); both reissued in one volume with a prolegomenon by S. H. Blank (1970); *The Karaites: Their History and Literature* (1862); *The Kabbalah: Its Doctrines, Development, and Literature* (1863); *The Essenes: Their History and Doctrines* (1864); *Jacob ben Chajim ibn Adonijah's Introduction to the Rabbinic Bible, Hebrew and English; with Explanatory Notes* (1865); *The Massoreth Ha-Massoreth of E. Levita, Being an Exposition of the Masoretic Notes on the HB, with an English Translation and Critical and Explanatory Notes* (1867), both reissued with a prolegomenon by N. H. Snaith (1968); *The Moabite Stone: A Facsimile of the Original Inscription with an English Translation and a Historical and Critical Commentary* (1870, 1871²); *The Massorah Compiled from Manuscripts Alphabetically and Lexically Arranged* (4 vols., 1880–1905), reissued with prolegomenon, analytical table of contents, and lists of identified sources and parallels by A. Dothan (1975); *The Third Book of Moses, Called Leviticus* (1882); *Essays on the Massorah* (c. 1895); (with A. Edersheim), *L'Israélite de la naissance à la mort* (1896); *Introduction to the Massoretico-Critical Edition of the HB* (1897), reissued with a prolegomenon by H. M. Orlinsky (1966); *A Series of XV Facsimiles of MSS of the Hebrew* (1897); *A Series of XVIII Facsimilies. . . .* (1898).

Bibliography: L. Blau, "Dr. G.'s Edition of the HB," *JQR* 12 (1900) 217-54. A. E. Cowley and B. W. Ginsburg, *DNB 1912–21* (1927) 215-16. A. S. Geden and R. Kilgour, *Intro-duction to the Ginsburg Edition of the Hebrew OT* (Bible House Paper No. XIII of the British and Foreign Bible Society, 1928). C. Roth, *EncJud* 7 (1972) 582.

J. H. HAYES

GLOSSA ORDINARIA

Since the fourteenth century the term *Glossa Ordinaria* has designated the reference edition of the VULGATE with exegetical explanations; this edition was in universal use among medieval academics and monastics from the twelfth century to the Reformation and in Roman Catholic circles even beyond. The earlier designation was "the Gloss" (*glos[s]a*) or "the glossed Bible" (*biblia glossata*). Although covering the whole Bible, HB and NT, the Gloss was rarely present in its entirety in a medieval library before the advent of printing. Copies were acquired by biblical book or groups of books, often following the nine subdivisions of biblical manuscripts in CASSIODORUS's library (*Institutiones* I.11.3): Genesis to Ruth, six books of Kings, the Major and Minor Prophets, the psalter, the Solomonic books, lives of great men and women (Job, Tobit, Esther, Judith, Maccabees, Ezra–Nehemiah), the four Gospels, PAUL and the catholic epistles, and Acts and Revelation.

The scribes adopted a peculiar format for the biblical Gloss that distinguished its manuscripts from other commentaries, which were usually written as a continuous text. Most pages show a window of several lines of the Vulgate in large letters surrounded by comments written on half-spaced lines in the margins (marginal gloss) and between the Vulgate text (interlinear gloss). The comments consist essentially of excerpts from the Western fathers (Ambrose, Augustine, Jerome, Hilary [4th cent.], Gregory the Great, Cassiodorus, Isidore, and Bede) but also some from Carolingian exegetes and compilers (Rabanus Maurus, Alcuin, Walafrid Strabo, Paschasius Radbertus, Remigius [d. c. 533], and Haymo of Auxerre [d. c. 855]) and a few quotations from later authors (Lanfranc of Bec, Berengar, and Gilbert of Auxerre [d. 1134]). Identification of these sources, if given at all, was usually by name alone, rarely by name and work.

Prologues, short summaries (*argumenta*), and introductory glosses (*prothemata*) appear at the beginning of most biblical books as they do in other Bibles of the time. The main source for them was JEROME. The early manuscripts did not clearly distinguish between the marginal and the interlinear gloss; a particular interpretation may appear in either. Interlinear glosses, however, tended to give short explanations of single words or phrases. The more extensive marginal glosses provided coherent comments on a particular verse, often classified according to standard senses: *allegorice, mystice, moraliter.* The complicated arrangement of textual elements on each page undoubtedly fostered a rapid standardization of the content. In the normative Paris *Glossa ordinaria* of the thirteenth century, both marginal and interlinear glosses show a remarkable degree of stability, with little variation. Text and format of the glossed Bible, which in principle was open to addition, subtraction, and replacement of its materials, had become fixed.

The *Glossa ordinaria* had no single author. Based on the exegetical work of the Carolingian age and its glossed Bibles, it emerged in the early to mid-twelfth century as the composite effort of a number of redactors. Such French cathedral schools with good libraries as Laon, Auxerre, and Paris seem to have been at the center of the activity, while monastic scriptoria like St. Victor in Paris and Clairvaux probably played a crucial role in the dissemination of the text. Medieval sources connect some names with the production of the Gloss: ANSELM OF LAON for the psalter, the Pauline epistles, and perhaps the Gospel of John; his brother Ralph (d. 1131/33) for Matthew and perhaps the Minor Prophets; Gilbert of Auxerre ("the Universal") for Lamentations, Ezekiel, and Revelation. The attribution of the Gloss to WALAFRID STRABO as its main author, which dominated scholarship into the twentieth century, was an invention of the German abbot of Sponheim, J. Trithemius (d. 1516), in the service of patriotic interests among early German humanists.

The success of the enterprise was phenomenal. By the end of the twelfth century manuscripts of the Gloss were owned by libraries in all parts of Europe. PETER LOMBARD is credited with a revision of the Gloss on the Psalms and the Pauline epistles, which circulated independently as *magna glosatura* but did not replace the standard form (*parva glosatura*) in the manuscripts. It is estimated that more than 2,500 copies of the various parts of the Gloss, most of them written in the twelfth and thirteenth centuries, survive today. The first complete printed edition was published anonymously in four large folio volumes by A. Rusch of Strasbourg in 1480/81. All subsequent editions of the fifteenth and sixteenth centuries derived their text from Rusch but were enriched by the addition of NICHOLAS OF LYRA's *Postill*. The earliest evidence for the use of the Gloss as a scholarly tool comes from Paris masters lecturing in the late twelfth century: GILBERT DE LA PORRÉE, PETER COMESTOR, PETER THE CHANTER, S. LANGTON, and especially Peter Lombard. By the beginning of the thirteenth century its place in the scholastic interpretation of the Bible was firmly established. The influence of the Gloss is visible not only in biblical commentaries, theological treatises, disputations, and sermons of the period, which treat it as an authoritative source, but also in works of secular literature and works of art. Humanistic philology and the Reformation's call to the biblical sources discredited its authority, however. The revisions in the great editions of Paris 1590, Douai/Antwerp 1617, and Antwerp 1634 were an attempt to revive the Gloss as an updated tool for the Catholic understanding of Scripture

and tradition; but the attempt remained an episode. The partial printing in vols. 113–14 of Migne's *Patrologia Latina* (1852) is seriously flawed; its editorial principles are based on the fiction of Strabo's authorship.

Bibliography: K. Froelich and M. T. Gibson (eds.), *Biblia Latina cum Glossa Ordinaria: Facsimile Reprint of the Editio Princeps, A. Rusch, Strassburg 1480/81* (4 vols., 1992). M. T. Gibson, "The Twelfth Century Glossed Bible," *StPatr* 23 (ed. E. A. Livingstone, 1990) 232-44; "The Place of the Glossa Ordinaria in Medieval Exegesis," *Ad Literam: Authoritative Texts and Their Medieval Readers* (ed. K. Emery and M. D. Jordan, 1992) 5-27. C. F. R. de Hamel, *Glossed Books of the Bible and the Origins of the Paris Book Trade* (1984). E. A. Matter, "The Church Fathers and the Glossa Ordinaria," *The Reception of the Church Fathers in the West* (2 vols., ed. I. Backus, 1997) 83-111. M. A. Signer, "The *Glossa Ordinaria* and the Transmission of Medieval Anti-Judaism," *A Distinct Voice: Medieval Studies in Honor of L. E. Boyle, O.P.* (ed. J. Brown and W. P. Stoneman, 1997) 591-605. B. Smalley, "Gilbertus Universalis, Bishop of London (1128-34) and the Problem of the 'Glossa Ordinaria,' " *RTAM* 7 (1935) 235-62; *The Study of the Bible in the Middle Ages* (1941, 1983³); *TRE* 13 (1984) 452-57. M. A. Zier, "Peter Lombard and the *Glossa Ordinaria* on the Bible," *A Distinct Voice: Medieval Studies in Honor of L. E. Boyle, O.P.* (ed. J. Brown and W. P. Stoneman, 1997) 629-41.

K. FROEHLICH

GLUECK, NELSON (1900–71)

Born in Cincinnati, Ohio, June 4, 1900, G. graduated from the University of Cincinnati in 1920. He received his rabbinical degree from Hebrew Union College in Cincinnati in 1923 and was ordained as a Reform rabbi the same year. His PhD was granted from the University of Jena (Germany) in 1927. In 1928–29 he became a fellow of the AMERICAN SCHOOLS OF ORIENTAL RESEARCH in Jerusalem under the tutelage of W. F. ALBRIGHT, joining him on the staff for excavations at Tell Beit Mirsim in 1930 and 1932. Having accepted a position at Hebrew Union College in 1929, G. held joint appointments in Cincinnati and Jerusalem until 1947. At Hebrew Union he rose from instructor to professor of Bible and biblical ARCHAEOLOGY (1936–47). On repeated leaves in Jerusalem, he was appointed director of ASOR, alternating with Albright (1932–33, 1936–40, 1942–47). He maintained the strictest scholarly neutrality amid the Palestinian political cross-currents, always representing the best interests of ASOR. Imbued with a passionate love for the land of the Bible, he was the first American rabbi-archaeologist in Palestine; indeed, for nearly fifty years he was the only Jewish scholar prominent in the largely Protestant biblical archaeology movement in America. In 1947 he became president of the then merging Cincinnati Hebrew Union College-Jewish Institute of Religion (New York City), a post he held almost until his death, Feb. 12, 1971.

From 1963 onward G. spent part of each year in residence at the Hebrew Union College Biblical and Archaeological School (now renamed the Nelson Glueck School of Biblical Archaeology). G. had founded this school to complement ASOR, since 1948 cut off in Arab east Jerusalem. Characteristic of his ecumenical spirit, he sponsored Christian post-doctoral fellows from the very beginning. He resumed field archaeology from this base in 1964, when he joined G. E. WRIGHT as adviser to launch the Hebrew Union College-Harvard Semitic Museum excavations at Gezer (1964–74; directed successively by Wright, W. Dever, and J. Seger).

G.'s own field work consisted primarily of large-scale surface surveys throughout Transjordan and the Jordan Valley (1937–47), followed by intensive surveys in the Negev of Israel. His in-depth excavations were limited to work at Tell el-Kheleifeh near Eilat (1936–38), which he identified (mistakenly) as Solomon's copper refinery at Ezion-geber, and at the remote Nabataean Temple of Khirbet et-Tannur in Edom (1937).

G.'s lasting contribution to the archaeology of Palestine was his mapping of former *terra incognita,* especially in Transjordan. More recent surveys have partially rectified the picture he drew of a "gap in occupation" in the Middle-Late Bronze Age (2000–1200 BCE), particularly in central and northern Jordan. But considering the time and the circumstances of his surveys, they constituted a remarkable achievement. Had he not devoted most of his energies to education and administration after 1947, his early successes in archaeology would no doubt have been multiplied many times over.

Works: "Das Wort Ḥesed im altestamentlicher Sprachgebrauche als menschliche und göttliche gemeinschaftgemässe Verhaltungsweise" (diss. 1927; ET, *"Ḥesed in the Bible,"* 1967); *Explorations in Eastern Palestine* (AASOR 14, 15, 18/19, 25/28, 1934–51); *The Other Side of the Jordan* (1940); *The River Jordan* (1946); *Rivers in the Desert: A History of the Negeb* (1959); *Deities and Dolphins: the Story of the Nabateans* (1965).

Bibliography: W. F. Albright, "N. G. in Memoriam," *BASOR* 202 (1971) 2-6; *EI* 12 (1975; the Glueck vol.). **J. A. Sanders** (ed.), *Near Eastern Archaeology in the Twentieth Century: Essays in Honor of N. G.* (1970).

W. G. DEVER

GNOSTIC INTERPRETATION

Discussing "Gnostic interpretation" is complicated by problems of definition. Many prominent second-century Christians, e.g., CLEMENT OF ALEXANDRIA, used the term *gnostic* of themselves and their teaching, thus claiming

to have true "knowledge of" or "acquaintance with" ultimate reality. Clement and other critics, following 1 Tim 6:20, distinguished their position from that of "gnosis falsely so called." Individuals and groups who fell under that rubric and were so described by the heresiologists IRENAEUS, TERTULLIAN, Hippolytus (c. 170–c. 236), and Epiphanius (c.315–403) are of concern here. New material on these Gnostics has emerged from modern discoveries, particularly the library of Coptic translations, of many original Gnostic works found at Nag Hammadi in upper Egypt in 1945–46.

It is useful to distinguish more mythologically oriented (and more superficially Christian) Gnostic works from more clearly Christian ones. Many of the former, which share literary and conceptual features, are now frequently labeled "Sethian." They probably constituted the earlier phase of the Gnostic phenomenon, the source of and inspiration for the latter type of Gnosticism. Particularly prominent among Christian Gnostic works are the writings of the sophisticated second-century ALEXANDRIAN teacher Valentinus and the members of his school.

A paradigmatic Sethian text is the *Apocryphon of John,* preserved in three copies in the Nag Hammadi collection as well as in the Berlin Gnostic Codex, discovered in the nineteenth century. Part of its system is also attested by Irenaeus (*Adv. Haer.* 1.29) as an example of what he calls "Barbeloite" Gnosis. The text, of which two distinct recensions survive, is a complex mélange of speculation and exegesis. An important constituent is a reading of the account of creation found in Genesis 1–4, a reading typical of the Sethian Gnostic appropriation of Jewish Scripture. The overall approach, both to Genesis and to other subsidiary texts, combines several interpretative devices. Allegory plays a relatively minor role, but some elements of the Genesis story are taken to refer to spiritual entities. More significant is narrative expansion, in which characters are provided motivations that fit the presupposed myth (see MYTHOLOGY AND BIBLICAL STUDIES) of origins. A dramatic tale thereby unfolds in which spiritual forces struggle against psychic and material realms. Finally, the biblical text is often treated with a wooden literalism that subverts its received meaning. Thus, if the God of Scripture is proclaimed to be jealous (Isa 45:5, cited in *Ap. John* [NHC II, 1] 13.8-12), then God is indeed so and is obviously not a god to be worshiped.

The subversive reading of Genesis (*Ap. John* [NHC II, 1] 13.17-25, 14) proceeds within the framework of questions posed by John and answers given by the Savior in a post-resurrection appearance. John's questions are prompted by the Savior's revelation of (1) a rupture in the transcendent world, (2) the fall of divine Wisdom, and (3) Wisdom's generation of a psychic creator, Ialtabaoth. Explaining that the spirit's movement (Gen 1:2) is the disordered motion of forgetfulness and shame experienced by fallen Wisdom, the Savior reveals the process of creation. After the fallen spirit returned on high, Ialtabaoth learned about the heavenly world and through the appearance of an image discovered the spiritual entities "Humanity" and "Child of Humanity" (or "Son of man"). This knowledge prompted Ialtabaoth, in the words of Gen 1:26, to call his assistants to fashion a copy of the image in order to obtain its power. (An excursus attributed to a *Book of Zoroaster* lists the forces that contributed to the fashioning of Adam's soul.) The protoplast, who had been formed literally "according to the image and likeness," lay inert, like the Golem of Jewish *haggada,* until finally Ialtabaoth, as Gen 2:7 indicates, breathed into him. As usual, however, appearance is not reality: Ialtabaoth's attempt to capture the divine spirit is but a device by which the divine mother, Wisdom, can recover the portion of her spirit left in creation.

As the Savior's account continues, the wicked archons try to imprison Adam; but he is given a spiritual assistant, *Zoe* (or "Life"), who teaches him about his origin and destiny. This episode heightens the dramatic conflict and offers an allegorical reading of Eve's creation, a more literal version of which appears later. Embodied and ensconced in a garden, Adam is restrained by the command not to eat of the tree of life, since the physical life of the creator's minions is inimical to Adam's true spiritual self. The negative evaluation of the tree of life contrasts with the positive evaluation of the tree of knowledge. It is obvious to the Gnostic exegete that the powers who prevent consumption of knowledge cannot be beneficent. In some versions of this reading of Genesis, the serpent, because he induces Adam and Eve to eat of the tree of knowledge, is evaluated positively. The *Ap. John,* however, restricts his role and attributes the inducement to taste of knowledge to the Savior, identified with the spiritual principle who is Adam's helpmeet.

Again in the question and answer format, the Savior turns to the creation of Eve. The anti-traditional character of the reading becomes clear, for the Savior tells John (*Ap. John* [NHC II, 1] 22, 21-27): "It is not as you have heard that Moses wrote." The "deep sleep" into which Adam was cast before Eve's extraction was not physical, but spiritual; the operation was not a beneficent attempt to give Adam a helper, but an assault by the rulers of creation on the revealing spirit within Adam. The oppositions established thus far continue through brief accounts of Cain, Abel, and Seth and through the admonition that the inimical rulers of creation continue "to this day" to use sexual desire to try to restrain the "virginal spirit" that ever strives to attain its heavenly home.

Interpretation of the creation narrative of Genesis, with its complex and subversive rereading, is characteristic of several other Sethian works from Nag Hammadi, including *Hypostasis of the Archons* (NHC II, 4)

and *On the Origin of the World* (NHC II, 5) and of testimonies in the heresiologists. In fact, most of the texts that merit the label Gnostic display elements of the reading of Genesis as the record of attempts by the rulers of creation to keep control of spirit.

Allegorical interpretation is more evident in the *Exegesis on the Soul* (NHC II, 6). This elaborate exegetical treatise tells the story of the virginal soul that fell into a body and lost her virginity at the hands of robbers. She was saved from adultery and prostitution and restored to her primordial condition by the mercy of the Father, who sent to the rescue her true husband, who is also her brother. This tale of the soul's fall and restoration is told through a series of citations from Homer and from both the HB and the NT, including Genesis, Isaiah, Jeremiah, Hosea, Ezekiel, Psalms, Matthew, John, Acts, 1 Corinthians, and Ephesians.

The combination of biblical and classical texts interpreted as ciphers for anthropological and cosmogonic theories is found in an even more extravagant form in the *Book of Baruch.* Attributed to a Justin, *Baruch* is described in Hippolytus (*Ref.* 5.26.1-5.27.5) and in the literature of the Naassenes discussed in Hippolytus (*Ref.* 5.6.3-5.11.1).

A concern to use texts from throughout the Scriptures is characteristic of clearly Christian Gnostics, particularly the Valentinians. This school left not only several significant examples of practical interpretation but also a theoretical hermeneutical statement (see HERMENEUTICS). This programmatic reflection appears in a letter, preserved in Epiphanius (*Pan.* 33.3.1-33.7.20) by Ptolemy, a major disciple of Valentinus active in the third quarter of the second century. The recipient, Flora, had apparently questioned Valentinian interpretations of the Torah. Ptolemy explained that the law comes neither directly from the perfect God nor from a principle of evil. Some portions derive from the Demiurge—the creator—some from Moses, and some from the elders of Israel. The second and third elements are clearly not binding on sophisticated Gnostic Christians. The portion attributed to the Demiurge is mixed. Some parts, e.g., the DECALOGUE, are pure but imperfect; these the Savior perfected. Some parts, e.g., the law of retribution, are mixed with injustice; these, too, have been abrogated. Finally, some parts, e.g., the regulation of ritual, are symbolic; they now refer to the spiritual plane. Ptolemy's letter shows Valentinian theologians wrestling with issues of the relationship between new and old that troubled much of the second-century church. The HB is preserved as a source of revelation but with severe qualifications. Each restricting move is warranted by elements of the NT.

Several examples of practical Valentinian exegesis survive. The most intriguing is the *Gospel of Truth* (NHC II, 3), a meditative homily sometimes attributed to Valentinus. It cites no scriptural texts but throughout weaves obvious allusions, particularly to the NT. Biblical imagery is read at the same time on both cosmogonic and psychological levels, as the homilist evokes the experience of "awakening" that is at the heart of Gnostic piety.

Disciples of Ptolemy were responsible for the Gnosticism encountered by Irenaeus, and the first eight chapters of his *Adversus Haereses* (c. 185) recount their theological system. Scripture regularly serves as a warrant. Biblical language, e.g., the reference to "aeons of aeons" (Eph 3:21; *Adv. Haer.* 1.3.1), sometimes points directly to spiritual realities; other references, such as the one to "iota" (Matt 5:18, *Adv. Haer.* 1.3.2), require interpretation by *gematria* or other forms of symbolic exegesis. This handling of Scripture represents a more scholastic and artificial appropriation than the poetic creativity of the *Gospel of Truth* and probably reflects debates between Valentinian and orthodox readers of biblical texts.

An approach to scriptural interpretation similar to that of Ptolemy appears in the fragments of another Valentinian disciple, Heracleon, active in the late second century. His commentary on John, the first extended interpretation of a book of the NT, uncovered in the Fourth Gospel a symbolic statement of Valentinian cosmogony and anthropology. ORIGEN took the work seriously enough to refute it in his own commentary on John, in the process citing Heracleon extensively and thus preserving this major example of Christian Gnostic exegesis.

In sum, Gnostic interpretation of both the OT and the NT generally operated with exegetical methods similar to those widely deployed in the first centuries CE. Such methods served particular religious interests. The God of creation and all that is God's handiwork are rejected in favor of a transcendent world of spirit, the contours of which can be symbolically perceived in the biblical texts.

Bibliography: H. W. Attridge, "The Gospel of Truth as an Exoteric Text," *Nag Hammadi Gnosticism and Early Christianity* (ed. C. W. Hedrick and R. Hodgson, 1986) 239-56. **D. Dawson,** *Allegorical Readers and Cultural Revision in Ancient Alexandria* (1992). **W. Foerster and R. M. Wilson** (eds.), *Gnosis: A Selection of Gnostic Texts* (2 vols., 1972–74). **J. Frickel,** *Hellenistische Erlösung in christlicher Deutung: Die gnostische Naassenerschrift. Quellenkritische Studien-Strukturanalyse-Schichtenscheidung-Rekonstruktion der Anthropos-Lehrschrift* (NHS 19, 1984). **E. Haenchen,** "Das Buch Baruch: Ein Beitrag zum Problem der christlichen Gnosis," *ZTK* 50 (1953) 1123-58. **C. W. Hedrick** (ed.), *The Nag Hammadi Codices XI, XII, XIII* (NHS 28, 1990). **H. Jonas,** *The Gnostic Religion* (1963). **B. Layton,** *The Gnostic Scriptures* (1987). **C. Markschies,** *Valentinus Gnosticus? Untersuchungen zur valentinianischen Gnosis mit einem Kommentar zu den Fragmenten Valentins* (WUNT 65, 1992). **E. H. Pagels,** *The Johannine*

Gospel in Gnostic Exegesis: Heracleon's Commentary on John (1973); *The Gnostic Paul: Gnostic Exegesis of the Pauline Letters* (1975); *The Gnostic Gospels* (1979); "Exegesis and Exposition of the Genesis Creation Accounts in Selected Texts from Nag Hammadi," *Nag Hammadi Gnosticism and Early Christianity* (1986) 257-85. **B. A. Pearson,** "Jewish Sources in Gnostic Literature," *Jewish Writings of the Second Temple Period* (ed. M. Stone, CRINT, 1984) 443-81. **J. M. Robinson** (ed.), *The Nag Hammadi Library in English* (1988[2]). **K. Rudolph,** *Gnosis: The Nature and History of Gnosticism* (1983). **M. Scopello,** *L'Exégèse de l'Ame: Introduction, traduction, commentaire* (NHS 25, 1985). **J.-M. Sevrin,** *L'exégèse de l'Ame* (BCNH.T 9, 1983).

H. W. ATTRIDGE

GOGUEL, MAURICE (1880–1955)

G. was born Mar. 20, 1880, and died Mar. 31, 1955. His academic career was closely bound up with the Protestant faculty of theology in Paris, where he was successively student, teacher, and dean. From A. Sabatier (1839–1901) he imbibed the principles of liberal Protestantism, to which he remained faithful, reinforced by the influence of W. HERRMANN, under whom he studied in Germany. After an initial foray into theology he devoted his life to NT studies, adopting a resolutely historical approach, since he believed that the study of Christianity required solid historical foundations. From 1927 on he also taught at the Sorbonne.

The only eminent representative in France of the historical-critical approach to biblical interpretation, G. published copiously. A historian, he did not offer commentaries or a "theology of the NT." His first major enterprise was an NT introduction (5 vols., though not quite complete); his life's work was summed up in a trilogy: *La Vie de Jésus* (1932); *La Naissance du christiannisme* (1946); and *L'Eglise primitive* (1947), the latter distilled in *Les premiers temps de l'Eglise* (1949). His critical positions remained remarkably consistent: He did not rally to the history-of-religions school (see RELIGIONSGESCHICHTLICHE SCHULE) because he thought it undermined the distinctiveness of early Christianity, and he rebuffed FORM CRITICISM as theologically motivated and over-skeptical. More positively, he constantly urged the need for a psychological appreciation (see PSYCHOLOGY AND BIBLICAL STUDIES) of the persons and ideas in the NT, since the primary datum embodied in the documents is "religious experience," variously expressed through language and symbols. He tended, therefore, to regard those elements in early Christianity that are collective, formulated, and contingent (e.g., dogma and institutions) to have been derived from what is individual, spontaneous, and absolute. In analyzing documents he felt it necessary to keep separate the "history of the facts" and the "history of the ideas and the feelings" (the latter being the "interpretation" of the facts). G. came to the notice of a wider public in 1925 with his able rebuttal of the Christ-myth school headed by P. Couchoud.

Although taking a fairly radical view of the Acts narrative, G. provided a sequential account of Christian origins, including a finely nuanced treatment of detail. He believed that the main outline of the life and teaching of JESUS was recoverable from the SYNOPTICS but that the Fourth Gospel was a "mystical" interpretation. Belief in the resurrection was based on the "visions" of those who had been Christ's disciples, and this belief created a "new religious object." Among the varieties of early Christianity, the two main types were those of Jerusalem (apostolic, dynastic, and non-charismatic) and of Antioch (prophetic and "christocratic"). PAUL belonged to the latter tradition, and his epistles reflect an early stage in which religious experience is translated into "formulas." Later the two types fused to form "precatholicism." Sociological factors (see SOCIOLOGY AND NT STUDIES) played their part in the formation of early Christian organization, doctrine, and ethics, resulting in the birth of a new religion. G.'s solid achievements in the field of Christian origins brought him international recognition, as testified by the translation of his work into a number of languages.

Works: *L'Apôtre Paul et Jésus-Christ* (1904); *W. Herrmann et le problème religieux actuel* (1905); *L'Évangile de Marc et ses rapports avec ceux de Matthieu et de Luc* (1909); *L'Eucharistie des origines à Justin Martyr* (1910); *Introduction au NT* (5 vols., 1922–26); *Jésus de Nazareth, mythe ou histoire?* (1925; ET 1926); *Au seuil de l'Évangile: J. Baptiste* (1928); *La Vie de Jésus* (1932, rev. ed. 1950); *La foi à la résurrection dans le christianisme primitif* (1933); "Témoignage d'un historien," *Protestanisme français* (ed. M. Boegner and A. Siegfried, 1945) 318-52. *La Naissance du christianisme* (1946, rev. ed. 1955); *L'Église primitiv* (1947); *Les premiers temps de l'Église* (1949).

Bibliography: M. **Carrez,** *TRE* 13 (1984) 567-70. **O. Cullmann,** *Vorträge und Aufsätze, 1925–62* (1966) 667-74. **A. H. Jones,** *Independence and Exegesis* (BGBE 26, 1983), chaps. 4 and 5. **F. Michaeli,** "Vies parallèles: A. Lods et M. G.," *ETR* 52 (1977) 385-401. **M. Simon,** "Les origines chrétiennes d'après l'oeuvre de M. G.," *RH* (1949) 221-31.

A. H. JONES

GOODENOUGH, ERWIN RAMSDELL (1893–1965)

Born in Brooklyn, New York, Oct. 24, 1893, G. was reared a devout Methodist and trained for the ministry. Through work at Hamilton College, Drew Theological Seminary, Garrett Bible Institute, Harvard University, and Oxford University (PhD 1923) he was drawn into the wider intellectual world. He moved from his initial PIETISM and religious orthodoxy to absorption in histori-

cal study of religion, but he always respected the capacity of religion to foster human values. He taught at Yale from 1923 to 1962 and served as editor of *JBL* from 1934 to 1942. He died Mar. 20, 1965.

Convinced by research on the theology of JUSTIN MARTYR that Hellenistic elements in early Christianity derived, not directly from the pagan religious world, but from Hellenized Judaism, which had absorbed these elements, G. proposed to investigate the origins of earliest Christianity, giving particular attention to its Hellenistic elements. The works of PHILO OF ALEXANDRIA were a primary source for his understanding of Hellenistic Judaism, and he found echoes of this Hellenism in the NT. He believed also that certain elements of primitive Christian art derived from still earlier Hellenistic Jewish iconography, a view rejected by those who held that Judaism always and universally rejected image making. However, the discovery of the frescoes in the synagogue at Dura-Europos convinced him that his theory was correct. He argued that well before the common era a Hellenized form of Judaism began to emerge that flowered in the writings of Philo, who was its most prominent expositor. Through allegory and symbolism this Judaism absorbed many elements of Hellenistic religion without abandoning its scriptural base.

G.'s major research ultimately concentrated on Jewish symbolism in the Greco-Roman world. His analysis of thousands of amulets, tomb inscriptions, and other artifacts bearing both Jewish and pagan symbols convinced him that these reflected a widespread popular Judaism of the times. Each symbol—the grape, the cup, the sun, and many others—wherever found in Hellenistic religion always retained the same meaning, thus furnishing a *lingua franca* shared by pagans and Jews alike.

Works: "The Theology of Justin Martyr" (diss., Oxford, 1923); *The Jurisprudence of the Jewish Courts in Egypt* (1929); *By Light, Light: The Mystic Gospel of Hellenistic Judaism* (1935, 1969); *Toward a Mature Faith* (1935, 1961); *The Politics of Philo Judaeus: Practice and Theory* (1938); *An Introduction to Philo Judaeus* (1940, 1962); *Jewish Symbols in the Greco-Roman Period* (13 vols., 1953–65); *G. on the Beginnings of Christianity* (BJS 212, ed. A. T. Kraabel, with a memoir by M. Smith, 1990).

Bibliography: R. S. **Eccles,** *E. R. G.: A Personal Pilgrimage* (1985). E. B. **Mattes,** *Myth for Moderns: E. R. G. and Religious Studies in America, 1938–55* (ATLA Monograph Ser., 1997). **J. Neusner** (ed.), *Religions in Antiquity: Essays in Memory of E. R. G.* (1968).

R. S. ECCLES

GOODSPEED, EDGAR JOHNSON (1871–1962)

Born Oct. 23, 1871, in Quincy, Illinois, son of a Baptist clergyman, G. was educated at Denison (AB 1890), Yale, and the University of Chicago (DB 1897;

PhD 1898), with two years of study abroad. Formative influences were W. R. HARPER in linguistic studies in Semitic languages and E. BURTON in linguistic and exegetical studies that gave the foundation for G.'s teaching career in biblical and patristic Greek. Beginning as instructor at Chicago in 1902, he assumed chairmanship of the department of NT and early Christian literature from 1923 until his retirement in 1937. During his career at Chicago he published more than sixty books, sixteen collaborative works, and over 190 articles. He died Jan. 13, 1962.

What J. MOFFAT accomplished for the British with his TRANSLATION of the NT from the original Greek (1913), G. did for the American public with his translation into everyday English of the NT (1923) and the Apocrypha (1938). He valued the integrity of oral and written common speech and the dynamic character of living language. Praised and blamed, his translation was widely received and influenced several generations of college students and other readers.

G. is best known professionally for his ingenious hypothesis that the letter to the Ephesians was originally a covering letter to the first collection and publication of the Pauline corpus (see PAUL) made at Ephesus about 90 CE. This hypothesis assumed fullest formulation in *The Meaning of Ephesians* (1933) and was elaborated in *The Key to Ephesians* (1956). Although it evoked limited acceptance, the argument nonetheless invited new interest in the formation of the NT.

G. figured prominently in the debates of the 1920s and 1930s over the original language of the Gospels. Combating the Aramaic hypothesis of C. C. TORREY, he categorically dismissed the likelihood of written Aramaic sources behind the Gospels, Acts, and the Apocalypse and minimized Semitic influences on these Greek documents. The outcome of the debate was a new recognition of the vigorous interaction of Semitic and Hellenistic cultures in the first century and of the importance of that interaction for understanding the literature.

In his retirement years G. presented the results of his studies in two books: *Paul* (1947) and *A Life of Jesus* (1950), both written from a liberal theological standpoint and making little use of FORM CRITICISM or reference to Jewish backgrounds. However, by skillful interpretation of the results of biblical research for the educated public, G. refused to permit the discipline to become arcane and esoteric, setting a model for a scholarship that accepts responsibility for the enlightenment of society as a whole.

Works: *Index Patristicus* (1907); *Index Apologeticus* (1912); *The NT: An American Translation* (1923); *An Introduction to the NT* (1937); *The Apocrypha: An American Translation* (1938); (with J. M. P. Smith), *The Complete Bible: An American Translation* (1939); *A History of Early Christian Literature*

(1942); *As I Remember* (1953).

Bibliography: **G. W. Barker,** "A Critical Evaluation of the Lexical and Linguistic Data Advanced by E. J. G. . . . in a Proposed Solution to the Problem . . . of Ephesians" (diss., Harvard, 1962). **J. H. Cobb and L. B. Jennings,** *A Biography and Bibliography of E. J. G.* (1948). **J. I. Cook,** "A Critical Evaluation of the Contributions of E. J. G. as a NT Scholar" (diss., Princeton, 1964); *E. J. G.: Articulate Scholar* (Biblical Scholarship 4, 1981); *HHMBI,* 584-88. **B. M. Metzger,** *RGG*[3] 2 (1958) 1693. **D. W. Riddle,** "E. J. Goodspeed," *University of Chicago Magazine* (March 1962). **H. R. Willoughby,** "Gutenberg Award," *Divinity School News* (1958).

E. W. SAUNDERS

GOPPELT, LEONHARD (1911–73)

Born Nov. 6, 1911, and reared in Munich, Germany, G. majored in philosophy and the natural sciences before turning to theology at the University of Erlangen, where he earned his doctorate with a dissertation on the NT use of the HB (1939) and a habilitation on Christianity and Judaism in the first and second centuries (1942, 1954). In 1947–48 he represented J. JEREMIAS in Göttingen during the latter's convalescence then taught at Hamburg's Kirchliche Hochschule (1948–52). He became professor of NT on the newly formed Protestant theological faculties at two universities: Hamburg (1952–67) and Munich (1967), until his sudden death Dec. 21, 1973.

G. was a man both of the church and of the university, and he maintained a critical posture toward both groups. In the university these were the years of the R. BULTMANN school. However, G. sought neither to join a following nor to acquire one around himself; his posture was one of dialogue and critical debate with all positions represented in the spectrum of NT interpretation. Although commonly grouped with Jeremias, W. KÜMMEL, and the conservative right, G. was in more active conversation with Bultmannians, as amply evidenced by the footnotes in his publications. These partners in conversation were posing the right questions, he maintained, but for the most part were giving the wrong answers.

G. was exceedingly interested in charting a course for the future of NT studies. The chief literary result was his NT theology. He saw great promise in the works of *Heilsgeschichte* scholars like T. von ZAHN, A. SCHLATTER, J. SCHNIEWIND, O. CULLMANN, and G. von RAD; he viewed his conversation with them as a door open to the opportunity to ponder and describe the reality of God at work in history. He sought dialogue toward an understanding that would honor the intention of the NT writers, using the principles of critique, analogy, and correlation (see E. TROELTSCH). While this orientation obligated him to maintain dialogue with all the classical disciplines of theological education, he was most purposeful in addressing HB studies. He was convinced that the ongoing dialogue on the relationship between the testaments was crucial, particularly because of the manner in which this discussion forced the issue of God and history.

Both as scholar and as churchman G. was a critic of easy identification of the church and Christian mission with culture and *Zeitgeist*. He could be equally determined, however, in his opposition to the empty slogans of popular ecclesiastical conservatism; he was not pleased with the "anti-modern theology" voices of the 1960s in Germany and regularly appealed for balanced reason in critical debates.

Works: *Types: The Typological Interpretation of the OT in the New* (BFCT 2, Reihe 43, 1939; ET 1982); *Jesus, Paul and Judaism: An Introduction to NT Theology* (1954; ET 1964); *Apostolic and Post-Apostolic Times* (1962, 1966²; ET 1970); *Christologie und Ethik: Aufsätze zum Neuen Testament* (1968); *Theology of the NT* (2 vols., ed. J. Roloff, 1975–76; ET 1981–82 [full bibliography, 2:307-14]); *A Commentary on I Peter* (ed. F. Hahn, 1978; ET 1993).

Bibliography: M. **Murrmann-Kahl,** *Strukturprobleme moderner Exegese: Eine Analyse von R. Bultmanns und L. G.s "Theologie des Neuen Testaments"* (1995). **J. Roloff** (ed.), *Die Predigt als Kommunikation* (FS, 1972).

J. E. ALSUP

GORDIS, ROBERT (1908–92)

An American Jewish biblicist, G. was born in New York City, graduated from the College of the City of New York (CCNY), and pursued graduate studies at Dropsie College in Philadelphia, the first free-standing, non-sectarian, non-theological graduate school for Hebrew and cognate learning in the United States. His primary teacher at Dropsie was the renowned textual critic (see TEXTUAL CRITICISM), M. MARGOLIS. G. was awarded the PhD in 1929 for his dissertation on the Masoretic traditions of *qere* and *ketib* (pub. 1937).

With prospects for academic employment at the start of the Great Depression bleak, G. entered the rabbinic program of Conservative Judaism's Jewish Theological Seminary in New York City. Ordained in 1932, he served a temple in Rockaway Park, New York, until his retirement in 1968. However, he did not desert academic life. In 1937 he was invited as an annual lecturer to the faculty of Jewish Theological Seminary, where he became a professor of Bible in 1940. For many years he divided his time among communal concerns, seminary teaching, and the pulpit. As a rabbinic leader of Conservative Judaism, he articulated a centrist position, mitigating his movement's conflicting internal tendencies to Reform and Orthodoxy. He served as editor of the periodical *Judaism* and as president of the Rabbini-

cal Assembly of America, and he founded the first private parochial school under Conservative Jewish auspices. He also taught at Columbia and Temple universities and in 1960 became the first Jewish scholar to teach Bible at New York's Union Theological Seminary.

G. wrote on a wide variety of subjects: ideological, theological, and academic. In biblical studies, he mostly devoted himself to wisdom literature, paying particular attention to Masoretic problems, to the form and style of biblical poetry, and to general literary technique. Gifted with a superior writing style, he wrote several book-length studies in which his strengths lay primarily in his appreciation of the larger literary and conceptual concerns of the writers and readers of the Bible. Thoroughly conversant with rabbinic literature, he made important observations on biblical lexicography in the light of the Middle Hebrew dialects employed in Mishnah, TALMUD, and MIDRASH. In like manner his work demonstrates a fine appreciation of medieval Jewish Bible scholarship and its potential to shed light on the biblical text.

Works: *The Biblical Text in the Making* (1937, augmented 1971); *Koheleth: The Man and His World* (1951); *Book of God and Man: A Study of Job* (1965); *Poets, Prophets, and Sages: Essays in Biblical Interpretation* (1971); *Faith and Reason: Essays in Judaism* (1973); *The Song of Songs and Lamentations* (1974); *The Word and the Book: Studies in Biblical Language and Literature* (1976); *The Book of Job* (Phoenix Ed., 1978); *The Dynamics of Judaism: A Study of Jewish Law* (1990).

Bibliography: S. **Daniel Breslauer,** *The Ecumenical Perspective and the Modernization of Jewish Religion* (BJS 5, 1978). **J. Robinson,** *EncJud* 7 (1971) 790.

S. D. SPERLING

GORDON, CYRUS HERZL (1908–)

Born in Philadelphia, G. was educated at the University of Pennsylvania. He worked as a field archaeologist (see ARCHAEOLOGY AND BIBLICAL STUDIES) in Jerusalem and Baghdad (1931–35), then taught Semitics at Johns Hopkins University (1935–38); Bible at Smith College (1938–41) and at Princeton (1939–42); ancient Near Eastern languages at Dropsie College (1946–56); Mediterranean studies at Brandeis University (1956–73); and biblical and Semitic studies at New York University (1973 until retirement, 1990).

G. pioneered Ugaritic grammatical studies (see UGARIT AND THE BIBLE) with *Ugaritic Grammar* (1940), *Ugaritic Handbook* (1947), *Ugaritic Literature* (1949), and *Ugaritic Manual* (1955; rev. as *Ugaritic Textbook* [AnOr 38, 1965]). He also made major contributions in Helleno-Semitics, the comparison of Hellenistic civilizations with ancient Near Eastern cultures. To this subject he contributed *Before the Bible* (1962; rev. as *The*

Common Background of Greek and Hebrew Civilizations [1965]) and *Homer and the Bible* (1967). In 1966 he published *Ugarit and Minoan Crete* and *Evidence for the Minoan Language.*

Works: *The Living Past* (1941); *Lands of the Cross and Crescent* (1948); *Smith College Tablets* (1952); *Introduction to the OT Times* (1953; rev. as *The World of the OT* [1958]); *Hammurapi's Code: Quaint or Forward Looking* (1957); *Adventures in the Nearest East* (1957); *New Horizons in OT Literature* (1960); *Ancient Near East* (1965); *Mediterranean Literature* (1967); *Forgotten Scripts* (1968); *The Pennsylvania Tradition of Semitics: A Century of Near Eastern and Biblical Studies at the University of Pennsylvania* (1986); *Eblaitica: Essays on the Ebla Archives and Eblaite Language* 1 (1987).

Bibliography: *A Student Tribute Presented to C. G.* (1962), with annotated bibliography. **D. C. Hopkins,** "C. H. G.: A Synthesis of Cultures," *BA* 59 (1996) 2-55. **M. Lubetski et al.** (eds.), *Boundaries of the Ancient Near Eastern World: A Tribute to C. H. G.* (JSOTSup 273, 1998). **G. Rendsburg** (ed.), *The Bible World: Essays in Honor of C. H. G.* (1980).

W. C. KAISER, JR.

GORE, CHARLES (1853–1932)

Born Jan. 23, 1853, G. was educated at Harrow and Balliol College, Oxford, and served as a fellow of Trinity College, Oxford; as vice principal of Cuddesdon Theological College; and as the first principal-librarian of Pusey House (1884–93). In 1894 he accepted a canonry at Westminster Abbey. Bishop of Worcester, Birmingham, and Oxford, G. is considered to have been the most influential Anglican clergyman in Britain at the turn of the twentieth century. He died Jan. 17, 1932.

G. participated in meetings of the "Holy Party," a group of liberal Anglo-Catholics who together published *Lux Mundi* (1889). The authors included the theologians H. Holland (1847–1918), J. Illingworth (1848–1915), A. Moore (1848–90), R. Moberly (1845–1903), and G. The book set forth the guiding principles of a new liberal Anglo-Catholicism, one that would remain loyal to the traditions of high Anglicanism while being open to biblical criticism as well as evolutionary and idealistic categories of theological interpretation. Because of his position and reputation G.'s *Lux Mundi* essay "The Holy Spirit and Inspiration" caused the greatest shock and offense to conservative Anglicans. Accepting the idea of development, G. acknowledged that the work of the Holy Spirit was gradual and that it could be expected that there would be degrees of INSPIRATION in the HB. He claimed that the history of the patriarchs was "idealized," that Genesis contained myth (see MYTHOLOGY AND BIBLICAL STUDIES), and that the stories in Jonah and Daniel were not

historical. Furthermore, these critical facts could not be dismissed by quoting Christ's own words against them. G. concluded that the humanity of JESUS entailed real limitations; Jesus was mistaken in some of his judgments and limited in knowledge. Here and in his later works (1891, 1895), he introduced his version of the kenotic theory of Christ's divine "self-emptying," whereby, in taking on human nature, God was emptied of omniscience and omnipotence. This appeared to G.'s critics to challenge not only the veracity of Scripture but also Christ's divine authority as a teacher.

G., however, placed limits on NT criticism, claiming that it did not face the same historical problems as the HB and that in the NT there is a "coincidence of idea and fact." His critical ideas soon became an entrenched orthodoxy, and as bishop he became the intrepid opponent of more liberal biblical critics, e.g., of the NT scholar W. SANDAY. The new generation of biblical scholars felt that G. was all too ready to prescribe the limits of criticism.

Works: *The Ministry of the Christian Church* (1888); (ed.) *Lux Mundi: Series of Studies in the Religion of the Incarnation* (1889); *The Incarnation of the Son of God* (Bampton Lectures, 1891); *Dissertations on Subjects Concerned with the Incarnation* (1895); *Body of Christ* (1901); *The Question of Divorce* (1911); *The Religion of the Church* (1916); *Belief in God* (1921); *Belief in Christ* (1922); *The Holy Spirit and the Church* (1924); *The Anglo-Catholic Movement Today* (1925); *Jesus of Nazareth* (1929).

Bibliography: **C. Brown,** *CMCT,* 341-76. **A. Dunelm** [A.T.P. Williams], *DNB, 1931–40* (1949) 349-53. **J. Carpenter,** *G.: A Study in Liberal Catholic Thought* (1960). **G. Crosse,** *Charles Gore* (1932). **W. R. Inge,** "Bishop G. and the Church of England," *Edinburgh Review* 207 (1908) 79-104 = his *Outspoken Essays* (1919) 1:106-36. **A. Manchester,** *E. S. Talbot and C. G.* (1935). **G. L. Prestige,** *The Life of C. G.: A Great Englishman* (1935). **B. M. G. Reardon,** *TRE* 13 (1984) 586-88. **G. Wainwright** (ed.), *Keeping the Faith: Essays to Mark the Centenary of "Lux Mundi"* (1988).

J. C. LIVINGSTON

GOSHEN-GOTTSTEIN, MOSHE HENRY (1925–91)

G. was born in Berlin Sept. 6, 1925, and immigrated to Israel (then Palestine) in 1939. In 1942 at the age of seventeen he enrolled in the Hebrew University of Jerusalem, studying Arabic, Semitic languages, Bible, and sociology. His PhD dissertation was written on Arabic-influenced Hebrew ("Medieval Hebrew Syntax and Vocabulary as Influenced by Arabic" [1951]). He joined the staff of the Hebrew University (1950), teaching Semitic languages and biblical philology in its department of linguistics. In 1970 he founded the department of ancient Semitic languages, in which he taught until his retirement, and also began teaching the same subjects at Bar-Ilan University, Ramat-Gan. From 1960 on he was visiting professor at several universities outside Israel, including Harvard, Brandeis, New York University, Jewish Theological Seminary, and Yeshiva University. He died Sept. 14, 1991, in Jerusalem.

Among G.'s most significant achievements were the Hebrew University Bible Project (= HUBP; founded in 1955, together with S. Talmon and C. Rabin; later, E. Tov joined the editorial board) and the Institute for Jewish Bible Study at Bar-Ilan University (founded in 1972, together with U. Simon). These projects and others (e.g., the Institute of [Hebrew] Lexicography and the Arabic Dictionary Project) reflect not only his initiative and talents as an organizer but also the range of his fields of knowledge and scientific interest.

Through the HUBP G. wished to present a new critical edition of the Bible based on all available textual evidence, from Qumran findings (see DEAD SEA SCROLLS), the SEPTUAGINT, and other early translations, through rabbinic literature, to medieval Hebrew manuscripts. This edition represents his overall perception of the history of the biblical text. First, the text should not be treated from one narrow standpoint (Qumran, the sages; Middle Ages). Rather, it should be painstakingly investigated, beginning with the earliest findings and continuing right up to the final canonization of the MT (see CANON OF THE BIBLE). Second, G. rejected the theories of an *Urtext* and an *Urrezenzion,* preferring instead to assume that there were several textual traditions (or text types); he was particularly critical of the "local traditions" theory of F. M. CROSS and his school. G.'s work on a new edition of the biblical text led him, on the one hand, to reconsider certain basic Qumran problems like the status and nature of the *Psalms Scroll* (11QPsᵃ) and, on the other hand, to a comprehensive and penetrating discussion of the history of the MT.

G.'s deep empathy for the MT inspired him to trace its history and final canonization, among other things leading him to some brilliant discoveries regarding the Aleppo Codex and its relationship to MAIMONIDES' halakhic rulings. In the context of his interest in direct contact with primary sources, G. laid the theoretical foundations for a critical edition of the PESHITTA (1954, 1961) and (with H. Shirun) published a critical edition of the Syro-palestinian version of the Pentateuch (see PENTATEUCHAL CRITICISM) and the Prophets (1973). He also published a deluxe facsimile edition of the Aleppo Codex (1976) and an important introduction to a facsimile edition of the Venice *Miqra'ot Gedolot* (1972). The book of Isaiah, which he undertook to publish as his responsibility in the HUBP, appeared in several parts: introduction (1965); 1:1–22:4 (1975); 22:5–44:28 (1981); and the remainder after his death (1993, 1995).

The Institute for Jewish Bible Study represents an other aspect of G.'s scientific and intellectual interests: Jewish Bible exegesis through the generations. On behalf of the institute he published (with M. Perez) Judah ibn Balaam's commentary on Isaiah (the commentary on Ezekiel is forthcoming); as well as two volumes of fragments of lost TARGUMIM that reveal multifaceted aspects, translational as well as exegetical, of ancient Jewish Aramaic translations of the Bible.

In 1980 G. launched a series of studies intended to establish a new field of academic endeavor, "Jewish Bible theology" distinct from both *Religionswissenschaft* and Christian theology. It is concerned with questions about the status of law in biblical theology as well as with the theological status of the people of Israel and the land of Israel—questions not frequently tackled by Christian theology. His great work, *Biblical Theology: Prolegomena to a Biblical Theology,* still in manuscript, is awaiting publication and will surely influence the evolution of the study of biblical THEOLOGY.

Works: *Text and Language in Bible and Qumran* (1960); *The Book of Isaiah: Sample Edition with Introduction* (HUPB, 1965); "Prolegomena to a Critical Edition of the Peshitta," *Scripta Hierosolymitana* 8 (1961) 26-67; "The Rise of the Tiberian Bible Text," *Biblical and Other Studies* (ed. A. Altmann, 1963) 79-122; "The *Psalms Scroll (11QPsᵃ*): A Problem of Canon and Text," *Textus* 5 (1966) 22-33; "Hebrew Biblical Manuscripts: Their History and Their Place in the HUPB Edition," *Bib* 48 (1967) 243-290; "The 'Third Targum' on Esther and MS Neofiti 1," *Bib* 56 (1975) 301-329; "The Language of Targum Onkelos and the Model of Literary Diglosia in Aramaic," *JNES* 37 (1978) 169-179; "Tanakh Theology: The Religion of the OT and the Place of Jewish Biblical Theology," *Ancient Israelite Religion* (FS F. M. Cross, ed., P. D. Miller, Jr., et al., 1987) 617-44.

Bibliography: S. Assif and R. Hass, "Bibliography of M. G.-G.," *Studies in Bible and Exegesis,* vol. 3, *M. G.-G.: In Memoriam* (ed. M. Bar-Asher et al., 1993), full bibliography, 11-25. **S. Talmon,** "In Memory of M. G.-G.," *Jewish Studies* 32 (1992) 61-67 (Heb.).

R. KASHER

GOTTWALD, NORMAN KAROL (1926–)

Born in Chicago, Oct. 27, 1926, G. received his BA and ThB degrees from Eastern Baptist Seminary (1949), his MDiv from Union Theological Seminary in New York (1951), and his PhD in biblical literature from Columbia University (1953). His dissertation was on the book of Lamentations (published in revised form in 1954). He taught at Columbia University (1953–55); Andover Newton Theological School (1955–65); American Baptist Seminary of the West (1966–73); Graduate Theological Union, Berkeley (1966–82); and New York Theological Seminary (1980–94).

G.'s contributions to contemporary biblical scholarship may be seen most clearly in his blending of the best of "established" scholarship with promising new approaches. He has worked diligently in new methodological areas that present considerable promise for both challenging and enriching biblical studies, seen most notably in his expansive 1979 volume. In this work he built on G. MENDENHALL's conquest theory and argued that the origin of Israel was to be seen primarily as a retribalization of indigenous peoples living within Canaan, motivated by socioeconomic factors toward the achievement of an egalitarian society. He showed convincingly that a careful, in-depth study of the social world of ancient Israel could challenge existing theories of the origin of Israel—e.g., W. F. ALBRIGHT's conquest theory, and A. ALT and M. NOTH's settlement theory—while at the same time adding a great deal to our knowledge about the matrix in which ancient Israel arose. Since the 1980s his work has had a major impact on biblical scholarship. Following his lead, scholars now see SOCIAL-SCIENTIFIC exploration into the world of ancient Israel as a necessary area of biblical research. G. has had an impact in an even broader sense, in LIBERATION exegesis and Third World theology and on the work of many junior scholars as they began to enter serious dialogue with adjacent disciplines and methodologies.

G., however, has not focused only on new areas of research; he has also rigorously maintained a positive and productive dialogue with the dominant paradigms in biblical scholarship, asking how his work on the social world of ancient Israel could influence and be influenced by the more traditional perspectives within the discipline. A careful reading of his *Tribes* reveals the thoroughness with which he interacted with the then prevailing assumptions in the field, e.g., the presumed uniqueness of Israelite religion, which was at that time part of biblical theology's agenda; and the amphictyonic model for understanding the interconnectedness of premonarchic Israel.

G. has been strongly interested in the LITERARY analysis of biblical literature. His groundbreaking 1985 volume nicely wove together interest in the literary character of biblical books, growing interest in social sciences methods, and continuing interest in more traditional methods of study within the discipline. The work decisively indicated that henceforth introductions to the HB would have to take seriously emerging new methodologies.

G.'s interest in HERMENEUTICS is clear. For example, his 1993 book looks beyond the world of the biblical scholar and explores ways the findings of biblical scholarship may have an impact on contemporary theology and social ethics. His hermeneutic has been attentive to the voice of his students; and this attentiveness has enabled him to mesh his insight that the scriptural texts cannot be understood without attention to their social, political, and economic matrices with the need of his students to address the social, political, and economic realities of their parishioners.

Works: *Studies in the Book of Lamentations* (SBT 14, 1954, 1962²); *A Light to the Nations: An Introduction to the OT* (1959); *All the Kingdoms of the Earth: Israelite Prophecy and International Relations in the Ancient Near East* (1964); *The Church Unbound: A Human Church for a Human World* (1967); *The Tribes of Yahweh: A Sociology of the Religion of Liberated Israel, 1250–1050* BCE (1979); (ed.), *The Bible and Liberation: Political and Social Hermeneutics* (1983, 1993²); *The HB: A Socio-Literary Introduction* (1985); *The HB in Its Social World and in Ours* (Semeia Studies, 1993).

Bibliography: F. R. Brandfon, "N. G. on the Tribes of Yahweh," *JSOT* 21 (1981) 101-10. C. E. Carter and C. L. Meyers (eds.), *Community, Identity, and Ideology: Social Science Approaches to the HB* (1996). D. Jobling et al. (eds.), *The Bible and the Politics of Exegesis* (FS N. G., 1991), with full bibliography of G.'s works (291-95). N. P. Lemche, *Early Israel: Anthropological and Historical Studies in the Israelite Society Before the Monarchy* (VTSup, 1985). A. D. H. Mayes, *The OT in Sociological Perspective* (1989), esp. chaps. 4–5. J. M. Sasson, "On Choosing Models for Recreating Israelite Premonarchic History," *JSOT* 21 (1981) 3-24.

A. J. HAUSER

GRAETZ, HEINRICH (1817–91)

G. was the most widely read and influential of the Jewish historians who emerged in the wake of the *Wissenschaft* movement in nineteenth-century European Jewish life. He was born at Xions in the eastern part of Germany, Oct. 31, 1817, a time when the first stirrings of new intellectual ferment in Jewish life were being felt following partial emancipation of European Jews at the close of the Napoleonic era. After an orthodox school education G. entered the University of Breslau (1842) and proceeded to Jena, where he received a doctorate in 1845 for his thesis "Gnosticismus und Judenthum." In 1854 he joined the teaching faculty at the Jewish seminary in Breslau, remaining until his death Sept. 7, 1891.

From an initially strong sympathy with conservative orthodox learning, G. saw the need to embrace contemporary intellectual issues and to engage in a wide range of debate over fundamental questions of the religious, philosophical, and cultural situation of Jews and Judaism. This led to his advocacy of a measure of reform and renewal in the belief that it was vital for Jews to engage in the intellectual life of the age. He brought together a rich grasp of traditional Hebrew learning with nineteenth-century historicism and Romantic idealism.

G. wrote extensively on biblical topics, with three volumes of his history of the Jews devoted to the biblical period. His partial adoption of a historical-critical approach, combined with a willingness to embrace extensive text-critical emendation in the study of the Prophets and the Writings, served to introduce and encourage modern critical research into biblical literature within Jewish circles. Adopting a mediating role between the more conservative and liberal wings of Jewish scholarship, he commanded great respect, becoming the most influential figure in critical Jewish biblical research before Y. KAUFMANN.

G.'s history of the Jews, published in 1853–75, was his *magnum opus*. The work incorporated many of his ideas concerning the importance of a historically critical attitude to the biblical literature, the centrality of history for an understanding of the Jewish "idea" or "spirit," and the impossibility of defining Judaism in terms of formal principles or dogma. It was translated into several languages, including English, and was also abbreviated to appear in a more popular form. Volume 4 was the first to appear, with volumes 1 and 2, which cover the biblical period, emerging last after G. had visited the biblical lands. Volume 3 was significant for its evaluation of the rise of the early Christian church from within Judaism; he saw the church as the product of a group of heretical Jewish sectaries. Although willing to engage fully in techniques of TEXTUAL and LITERARY analysis, until then almost exclusively the province of Christian scholarship, G. was able to engage in a strong polemical debate with contemporary Christian scholars. His recognition of the need for a fully critical historical methodology was allied to warm poetic sensitivity (as shown in his 1846 essays).

G. wrote extensively in the *Monatschrift* of the Jewish seminary in Breslau and published commentaries on Ecclesiastes and Song of Songs (1871). His commentary on the psalms (2 vols., 1882–83) marked a major step in the adoption of modern text-critical approaches. All these studies were characterized by an extensive and skillful use of textual emendation based on a study of the ancient versions but also including a wide range of his own conjectures. Although G. did not carry this approach forward to a study of the Torah, he planned a critical, annotated edition of the entire HB; the volumes on Isaiah and Jeremiah appeared shortly before his death. G. went so far as to advocate the critical division of biblical books on the basis of their presumed sources, recognizing the case for identifying a Second Isaiah, a proto- and deutero-Hosea, and a division of Zechariah among three separate prophets.

Works: *Gnosticismus und Judenthum* (1846); "Die Konstruktion der jüdischen Geschichte," *ZRIJ* 3 (1846) 81-97, 121-32, 361-68, 413-21 = *The Structure of Jewish History and Other Essays* (1975) 63-124; *Geschichte der Juden von den ältesten Zeiten bis zur Gegenwart* (11 vols., 1853–75; repub. and tr. in various eds.; ET *History of the Jews*, 6 vols., 1891–98); *Kohelet* (1871); *Shir-Ha-Shirim, oder das salomonische Hohelied*

(1871); *Kritischer Kommentar zu den Psalmen* (2 vols., 1882–83).

Bibliography: I. **Abrahams,** "H. G., the Jewish Historian," *JQR* 4 (1892) 165-203 (bibliography, 194-203). **P. Bloch,** *H. G.: A Memoir* (1898), = ET of G.'s *History* 6 (1949) 1-86. **R. E. Clements,** "H. G. as Biblical Historian and Religious Apologist," *Interpreting the HB: Essays in Honour of E. I. J. Rosenthal* (ed. J. A. Emerton and S. C. Reif, 1982) 35-55. **S. Ettinger,** *EncJud* 7 (1971) 845-50. **M. Graetz,** *TRE* 14 (1985) 112-15. **L. Kochan,** *The Jew and His History* (1977) 69-87. **M. A. Meyer** (ed.), *Ideas of Jewish History* (1974) 217-44. **E. I. J. Rosenthal,** "H. Cohen and H. G.," *S. W. Baron Jubilee Volume* (1974) 2:725-43.

R. E. CLEMENTS

GRAF, KARL HEINRICH (1815–69)

Born Feb. 28, 1815, in Mühlhausen, Alsace, G. pursued theological and oriental studies in Strasbourg (1833–36), where his most influential teachers were E. REUSS and J. Bruch (1792–1874). G. earned the bachelor of theology degree (1836), received a stipend in Geneva (1837–38), was a private tutor in Paris (1839–43), and was promoted to lic. theol. in Strasbourg in 1842. For the rest of his life he taught in Saxony, Germany: from 1843 to 1847 in Kleinzschoer near Leipzig (where he also studied with H. Fleischer and received his PhD in 1847) and from 1847 to 1868 at the famous state school St. Afra in Meissen (from 1852 as professor). He died July 16, 1869, in Meissen.

G.'s life, thought, and work are most clearly reflected in his correspondence with E. Reuss from 1837 to 1869. In turn Reuss spoke of G. as being spiritually the most closely related to him of all his students (*Briefwechsel* [1904] 619). Reuss failed in his efforts to secure a university position for G., perhaps because of G.'s lack of facility and style in writing and speaking, perhaps because of his liberal theology.

As an HB scholar G. wrote individual works on ancient Israelite history and a commentary on Jeremiah. The commentary largely paraphrases the text, offers voluminous citations from earlier exegetes, and understands the book of Jeremiah as a "larger whole originating from an earlier entity by means of additions and expansions" by the hand of the prophet himself (1862, XXXV). G. attributed no value whatsoever to the divergent text of the SEPTUAGINT.

G. is best known for his studies of the historical books, whose results—known as the Graf hypothesis—brought about a virtual revolution in PENTATEUCHAL CRITICISM and subsequently in the entirety of OT scholarship. His *Die geschichtlichen Bücher* (1866) unites two different studies, the first concerned with the Pentateuch and the former prophets; the second, with Chronicles as a historical source.

Both take up and modify older theses—not always successfully. The second addresses W. DE WETTE's thesis from his "Historischen-kritischen Untersuchung über die bücher der Chronik" in the first volume of his *Beiträge* (1806); the first discusses the supplementary hypothesis, according to which the Pentateuch originated through repeated reworkings of an original foundation document—the *Grundschrift* (later called the Priestly source, or P).

G. showed that the priestly ritual legislation of P is later than Deuteronomy, which he dated to the seventh century; and he thus arrived at a successive supplementation of the *Grundschrift*, first by the "Yahwist" narrative, then by the deuteronomic material, and finally in the postexilic period through the priestly laws. In this process he did not recognize that the priestly laws cannot be separated from the *Grundschrift* and thus, assuming the correctness of the newly postulated dating, that the latter also belongs in the postexilic period. After having been made aware of this inconsistency by A. KUENEN and E. RIEHM, in his final year of life (1869) he dated the entire *Grundschrift* to the postexilic period. He understood only vaguely what this would mean for future understanding of biblical Israel. After his death, Kuenen and—with extraordinary effect—J. WELLHAUSEN made scholarship realize the significance of these ideas.

Works: "De librorum Samuelis et Regnum compositione, scriptoribus, fide historica, imprimus de rerum a Samuele gestrun auctoritate" (diss. theol., Argentor, 1842); *Moslicheddin Sadi's Rosengarten: Aus dem Persischen übersetzt mit Anmerkungen und Zugaben* (1846, 1920); "Richard Simon," *Beiträge zu den theologischen Wissenschaften* 1 (1847) 158-242; *Moslicheddin Sadi's Lustgarten (Bostan): Aus dem Persischen übersetzt* (2 vols., 1850); "Die Moral des persischen Dichters Sadi," *Beiträge zu den theologischen Wissenschaften* 3 (1851) 141-94; "Jacobus Faber Stapulensis: Ein Beitrag zur Geschichte der Reformation in Frankreich," *ZHTh* 22 (1852) 3-86, 165-237; *Der Segen Moses* (1857); *Le Boustân de Sa'dî: Texte persan avec un commentaire persan* (1858); *De templo Silonensi* (1861); *Der Prophet Jeremia erklärt* (1862); *Die geschichtlichen Bücher des Alten Testaments* (1866); *Der Stamm Simeon: Ein Beitrag zur Geschichte der Israeliten* (1866); "Zur Geschichte des Stammes Levi," *AWEAT* 1, 1.2 (1867–68) 68-106, 208-36; "Die s.g. Grundschrift des Pentateuchs," *AWEAT* 1, 4 (1869) 466-77.

Bibliography: G. **Beer,** *RE³* 23 (1913) 588-92. C. **Macholz,** "Ein Altestamentler an einer sächsischen Fürstenschule," *Lese-Zeichen für A. Findeiss* (Beihefte zu den Dielheimer Blättern zum AT 3, ed. C. Burchard and G. Theissen, 1984) 51-73. E. **Reuss,** *Briefwechsel mit seinem Schüler und Freunde K. H. G.* (ed. K. Budde and H. J. Holtzmann, 1904).

R. SMEND

GRAMBERG, CARL PETER WILHELM
(1797–1830)

Born Sept. 22, 1797, at Seefeld near Oldenburg, the son of a clergyman, G. entered the university of Halle in 1816, where his principal biblical teacher was H. GESENIUS. His desire to gain an academic post was never fulfilled; instead, he taught school, first in Oldenburg, then from Easter 1822 in Züllichau (now Sulechow in Poland). He died in Oldenburg Mar. 29, 1830, leaving among his unpublished papers two further parts of his *magnum opus* (1830) as well as a commentary on the Pentateuch (see PENTATEUCHAL CRITICISM). Death at age thirty-two prevented G. from becoming an established OT scholar; yet in a short life troubled by poor health, he published four books and many contributions to newspapers and journals.

The aim of the *Kritische Geschichte* (1830) was to work out thoroughly the basic position advanced by W. DE WETTE in his 1806–7 *Beiträge* and in his OT introduction. In these works de Wette had sketched a revolutionary view of the history of Israelite religion, but he had left much room for elaboration of his ideas. The plan of the *Kritische Geschichte* was straightforward: It assumed that Israelite religious history could be divided into seven periods and that the OT books could be assigned to these periods and be regarded as reflecting their respective ideas. The periods were (1) from David to Hezekiah, with Genesis, Exodus, and Judges; (2) shortly before the exile when Samuel and Ruth were compiled from older oral and written sources; (3) from Uzziah to Josiah, with most of Isaiah 1–35, Hosea, Joel, Amos, Micah, Nahum, Zephaniah; (4) beginning of the exile, with Leviticus, Numbers, Jeremiah, Ezekiel, Habakkuk, Obadiah, and some psalms; (5) end of the exile, with Deuteronomy, Joshua, Pseudo-Isaiah (chaps. 36–66), Proverbs, Job, Jonah; (6) Persian period, with Ezra, Nehemiah, the last three Minor Prophets, Ecclesiastes; (7) the death of Antiochus IV, with Esther, Daniel, and Chronicles, the latter being an arbitrary rewriting of Samuel and Kings without any additional authentic sources. G. then described the following subjects in relation to each of the periods: sanctuaries, sacrifices, priesthood, festivals, ceremonies (e.g., vows, prayer, and marriage), idolatries, leaders of the theocracy, prophets, and messianic hopes. The result was an exhaustive, if tedious, account of Israelite religious history in all of its manifestations from the standpoint that a centralized and then priestly-levitical type of religion had taken over from an originally diversified religion with many sanctuaries and no centralized priestly power. Chronicles was a falsified account of Israelite religion that claimed that David had instituted the levitical arrangements of the Temple. Moses had been responsible for only simple ordinances like the DECALOGUE, for the ark of the covenant, and for the tabernacle.

Although G. largely followed de Wette, he saw the

difficulty in the latter's position that Josiah's lawbook was substantially the book of Deuteronomy while Deuteronomy was later than Leviticus and Numbers. This meant that the levitical ordinances of Leviticus and Numbers were earlier than the seventh century and hardly a postexilic development. G. solved the problem by arguing that Josiah's lawbook was part of Exodus and by dating Leviticus and Numbers to the early exile and Deuteronomy to the late exilic period. The idea that parts of Exodus, Leviticus, and Numbers might be later than Deuteronomy had not, apparently, occurred to de Wette or to G.; but it was the latter who drew attention to the problem of maintaining that Deuteronomy was the youngest part of the Pentateuch. He thereby opened up the way for J. GEORGE to suggest in 1835 that parts of Exodus, Leviticus, and Numbers were indeed later than Deuteronomy, thus presenting in almost complete form the position advocated by J. WELLHAUSEN in 1878. The resurgence of orthodoxy, led by E. HENGSTENBERG, from 1830 and the "positive" criticism of H. EWALD overshadowed G.'s views as well as those of de Wette and George until their rediscovery in the late 1860s.

Works: *Die Chronik nach ihren geschichtlichen Charakter und ihrer Glaubwürdigkeit neu geprüft* (1823); *Das Buch der Sprüche Salamos* (1828); *Libri Geneseos secundum fontes rite dignoscendos adumbratio nova; in usum praelectionum* (1828); *Kritische Geschichte der Religionsideen des alten Testaments,* vol. 1, *Heirarchie und Cultus;* vol. 2, *Theocratie und Prophetismus* (1830).

Bibliography: *ADB* 9 (1879) 577-78. *AEWK* 1, 78 (1864) 328. **J. H. Hayes and F. C. Prussner,** *OT Theology: Its History and Development* (1985) 92-94. *NND* 1 (1830) 270. **J. W. Rogerson,** *OTCNC* 57-63.

J. W. ROGERSON

GRANT, FREDERICK CLIFTON (1891–1974)

Born in Beloit, Wisconsin, Feb. 2, 1891, G. attended Lawrence College (1907–9), Nashotah House (1909–11), and General Theological Seminary (BD 1913). Upon graduation he was ordained in the Protestant Episcopal Church and served in various church positions while continuing graduate school. He received the STM (1916) and ThD (1924) from Western Theological Seminary; his dissertation was published in 1926. G. served as dean of Bexley Hall at Kenyon College (1924–26); as professor of systematic theology at Berkeley Divinity School, Connecticut (1926–27); as president of Seabury-Western Theological Seminary (1927–38); and as professor of biblical theology at Union Theological Seminary, New York (1938–59).

Pastoral, ecumenical, and ecclesiastical concerns influenced his life's work, and he wrote extensively for a wide, popular audience. He edited the *Anglican Theological Review* (1924–55) and served on the RSV translation committee. His general contributions to biblical studies are exemplified in his editorship (with H. Rowley) of the new edition of J. HASTINGS's *Dictionary of the Bible* (1963) and of the seven-volume *Commentary on the RSV,* to which he contributed vols. 6–7 (1962). He died July 11, 1974.

G.'s work had three primary foci: (1) He explored the eschatological nature of the preaching of JESUS and the faith of the early church. One of his first published papers was "The Permanent Value of the Primitive Christian Eschatology" (*Biblical World* 49 [1917] 157-68). He acknowledged the influence on NT study of J. WEISS, A. SCHWEITZER, and R. CHARLES, but he described their school as more properly apocalyptic (see APOCALYPTICISM) than eschatological. G. was careful to distinguish eschatology from the apocalyptic speculation that had arisen in first-century Jewish thought (*IB* [1951] 7:639-40). He viewed all Hebrew PROPHECY and religion as eschatological, i.e., as concerned with "last things," with the purposes of God, who as ruler of history judges, brings to an end, and restores. In his 1940 work he presented Jesus' preaching as focused on spiritual, not political, revolution.

(2) He enthusiastically welcomed the developing field of NT FORM CRITICISM. His 1934 work on the method provided a translation of writings of R. BULTMANN. He also translated M. DIBELIUS's *The Message of Jesus Christ* (1937) and was co-translator of J. Weiss's *History of Primitive Christianity* (2 vols., 1937). G.'s book on the growth of the Gospels (1933) and its major revision (1957a) illustrate how he adopted and used a moderate form-critical approach. This approach can also be seen in his volume on Mark (1943) and his commentary on the Gospel in the *IB* (1951).

(3) He studied the general sociocultural-religious background of the NT. This area of G.'s interest was reflected in his doctoral dissertation (1926). He not only taught courses in Greek and Roman religions, but he also published collections of annotated texts in translation (1953, 1957b) in the Library of Religion series. In spite of his emphasis on the Greco-Roman backgrounds, G. stressed the priority of the HB for understanding the NT, with rabbinic Judaism next in significance (1959); he did not give the DEAD SEA SCROLLS any special prominence.

Works: *The Economic Background of the Gospels* (1926); *New Horizons of the Christian Faith* (Hale Lectures, 1928); *The Growth of the Gospels* (1933); *Form Criticism: A New Method of NT Research* (1934a); *Frontiers of Christian Thinking* (1934b); *The Gospel of the Kingdom* (1940); *The Earliest Gospel* (1943); *The Practice of Religion* (1946); *An Introduction to NT Thought* (1950a); *Christ's Victory and Ours* (1950b); *Hellenistic Religions: The Age of Syncretism* (LibRel 2, 1953); *The Gospels: Their Origin and Growth* (1957a); *Ancient Roman*

Religion (LibRel 8, 1957b); *Ancient Judaism and the NT* (1959); *Roman Hellenism and the NT* (1962).

Bibliography: S. E. Johnson (ed.), *The Joy of Study: Papers on NT and Related Subjects Presented to Honor F. C. G.* (1951), with foreword by S. Johnson (v-x) and list of G.'s publications (149-63). **S. E. Johnson,** *ATR* 57 (1975) 3-13, with supplement to G.'s bibliography (14-15).

B. H. THROCKMORTON, JR.

GRAY, GEORGE BUCHANAN (1865–1922)

Born in Blandford, Dorset, the son of a Congregational clergyman, G. was educated at the universities of London and Oxford, completing his studies at Marburg (where K. Budde then held a chair). After graduating in Semitic languages at Oxford he became tutor at Mansfield College, Oxford, where in 1900 he was appointed professor of Hebrew and the exegesis of the OT, a post he held until his sudden death.

G.'s special interest was the Hebrew language. His first book was *Studies in Hebrew Proper Names* (1896), in which he argued that different types of personal names tended to be employed at different periods in ancient Israel, a conclusion he believed would aid the critical examination of the OT source documents, with a view to determining their antiquity. In this aim he acknowledged his adherence to the approach of J. WELL-HAUSEN, who had been at Marburg (1885–92) and who, perhaps more significantly, greatly influenced G.'s teacher and mentor at Oxford, S. DRIVER. G.'s OT introduction (1913), although very similar in approach to Driver's (1891, 1913[9]), is a far more elegant and persuasive exposition of the "critical approach" as it was then called.

For the ICC, edited by Driver, G. contributed Numbers (1903) and, on the death of A. DAVIDSON, Isaiah 1–39 (1912). G. was never an uncritical follower of Wellhausen; while he confessed as his main task the recovery of the original words of the prophet (see PROPHECY AND PROPHETS, HB), he wished to "approach with sympathy the work of, perhaps, many nameless writers that now forms so large a part of [the book of Isaiah]." In this commentary he also found himself grappling with the problems of Hebrew POETRY, particularly that of meter. His *Forms of Hebrew Poetry* (1915) is the outcome of further research and lecturing; while it offers no striking new theory, it represents a carefully nuanced and sensitive description of parallelism, rhythm, and meter, the latter remaining for him an unresolved problem.

At Driver's request, G. took over the ICC Job commentary (1921), which, apart from the philological notes, is substantially G.'s own. His last major work, published posthumously (1925), was on Hebrew sacrifice. Here he amended W. R. SMITH's thesis that the

essence of Semitic sacrifice is communion by proposing instead the notion of gift to the deity. G.'s work is characterized by clarity of thought and style, flexibility, and lack of dogmatism, qualities that made him a first-class expositor as well as a fresh and original scholar.

Works: *Studies in Hebrew Proper Names* (1896); *A Critical and Exegetical Commentary on Numbers* (ICC, 1903); *A Critical and Exegetical Commentary on the Book of Isaiah i–xxxix* (ICC, 1912); *A Critical Introduction to the OT* (1913); *The Forms of Hebrew Poetry* (1915); (with S. R. Driver), *A Critical and Exegetical Commentary on the Book of Job* (ICC, 1921); *Sacrifice in the OT: Its Theory and Practice* (1925), including a complete bibliography, ix-xi.

Bibliography: G. R. Driver, *DNB, 1922–1930* (1937) 356-58.

P. R. DAVIES

GREEN, WILLIAM HENRY (1825–1900)

Born in Groveville, New Jersey, Jan. 27, 1825, G. graduated BA with honors from Lafayette College at age fifteen (1840), taught mathematics for a time, and attended Princeton Seminary, graduating in 1846. He taught Hebrew at Princeton (1846–49), served as pastor of Central Presbyterian Church in Philadelphia (1849–51), and returned to replace J. ALEXANDER as professor of oriental and OT literature at Princeton, where he taught until his death Feb. 10, 1900.

A staunch Presbyterian, strongly influenced by Scottish realism and Reformed confessionalism, G. was a leading scholar of the traditionalist wing of the church in its opposition to higher critical theories in biblical studies. At the celebration of his fiftieth anniversary at Princeton, he was described as "the Nestor of the conservative OT School." He was not opposed to higher criticism, however, only to what he considered its anti-supernaturalistic bias. He was a careful reviewer, presenting his own views only after detailed consideration of the issues in question and a fair representation of his opponents. He had a thorough command of Semitics, classical languages and literature, and several European languages, all of which made him conversant with a wide range of scholarship.

G. believed the OT had an "organic structure" based on the covenant law of Moses addressed to Israel. This teaching found application in the historical books, individual appropriation among poetic books (see POETRY, HB), and enforcement among the writing prophets (see PROPHECY AND PROPHETS, HB). He also interpreted the OT as preparation for Christ not strictly from messianic prophecies but also on the Reformed model of Christ as the final prophet, priest, and king.

Because of the debates over the dating of PENTATEUCHAL sources, G.'s emphasis on covenantal law as foundational for the rest of the OT required that he defend the chronological priority of the law (see CHRONOLOGY, HB). This he did in numerous publications, arguing against the multiple-source hypothesis for the Pentateuch and for the prophets' dependence on the covenant law for their critique of Israel and Judah. In his Pentateuchal studies G. anticipated some elements of the LITERARY and RHETORICAL analysis being done nearly a century later but saw any surrender of Mosaic authorship of the Pentateuch and full INSPIRATION of the Scriptures as surrender of the faith.

Works: *A Grammar of the Hebrew Language* (1861); *The Pentateuch Vindicated from the Aspersions of Bishop Colenso* (1863); *The Argument of the Book of Job Unfolded* (1874); *Moses and the Prophets* (1883); *The Hebrew Feasts in Their Relation to Recent Critical Hypotheses Concerning the Pentateuch* (Newton Lectures, 1885); "The Pentateuchal Question," *Hebraica* (= *AJSL*) 5 (1888–89) 137-69; 6 (1889–90) 109-38, 161-211; 7 (1890–91) 1-38, 104-42; 8 (1891–92) 15-64, 174-243; *The Unity of the Book of Genesis* (1895); *The Higher Criticism of the Pentateuch* (1896, repr. 1978); *General Introduction to the OT* (2 vols., 1898–99).

Bibliography: **H. H. Bendes,** *DAB* 7 (1931) 560-61; *Celebration of the Fiftieth Anniversary of the Appointment of Prof. W. H. G. as an Instructor in Princeton Theological Seminary, May 5, 1896* (1896). **J. D. Davis,** *The Life and Work of W. H. G.* (1900). **M. A. Taylor,** "The OT in the Old Princeton School" (diss., Yale, 1988) 308-480.

J. A. DEARMAN

GREENBERG, MOSHE (1928–   )

G. was born in Philadelphia, July 10, 1928. Reared in a Hebrew-speaking, Zionist home, he studied Bible and Hebrew literature from his youth. At the University of Pennsylvania, where he received his PhD in 1954, he studied Bible and ASSYRIOLOGY with E. SPEISER; simultaneously he studied post-biblical Judaica at the Jewish Theological Seminary of America. Strongly influenced by the comparative biblical-Assyriological approach of Speiser and by the studies of the Israeli scholar Y. KAUFMANN in biblical thought and religion, G.'s explication of the Bible is characterized by the critical integration of ancient Near Eastern and Jewish materials.

G. taught Bible and Judaica at the University of Pennsylvania (1964–70) and at the Hebrew University of Jerusalem (1970–96). The first Jewish biblical scholar appointed to a position in a secular university after WWII, he has had an important influence on the development of biblical scholarship, particularly, but not limited to, Jewish biblical scholarship. He has devoted most of his attention to the phenomenology of biblical religion and law, the theory and practice of interpreting biblical texts, and the role of the Bible in Jewish thought.

In the area of prayer G. has traced the development of biblical petition and praise from their roots in the concept that the deity literally needs to be informed of the worshiper's plight and propitiated by flattery, to the concept of prayer as "a vehicle of humility, an expression of un-selfsufficiency, which in biblical thought is the proper stance of humans before God" (1995, 75-108). In *Biblical Prose Prayer* (1983) he showed that the prose prayers embedded in biblical narratives reflect the piety of commoners and reasoned that the frequency of spontaneous prayer must have sustained a constant sense of God's presence, strengthening the egalitarian tendency of Israelite religion that led to the establishment of the synagogue. The fact that prayer was conceived as analogous to a social transaction between persons fostered an emphasis on sincerity and may lie at the root of the classical-prophetic view of worship as a gesture whose acceptance depends on adherence to the values of God.

In his "Reflections on Job's Theology" (1995, 327-33) G. observes that Job's experience of God's inexplicable enmity could not wipe out his knowledge of God's benignity, gained from his earlier experience; hence Job became confused instead of simply rejecting God. Accordingly, the fact that the Bible retains Job as well as the Torah, the Prophets (see PROPHECY AND PROPHETS, HB), and Proverbs reflects the capacity of the religious sensibility to affirm both experiences.

In the area of biblical law G. argues that "the law [is] the expression of underlying postulates or values of culture" and that differences between biblical and ancient Near Eastern laws were reflections, not of different stages of social development, but of different underlying legal and religious principles (1995, 25-41). Analyzing economic, social, political, and religious laws in the Torah, he shows that their thrust was to disperse authority and prestige throughout society and to prevent the monopolization of prestige and power by narrow elite groups (1995, 51-61).

In his commentaries on Exodus (1969) and Ezekiel (1983, 1997), G. develops his "holistic" method of exegesis. While building on the source-critical achievements of earlier scholarship, the holistic method redirects attention from the text's "hypothetically reconstructed elements" to the biblical books as integral wholes, the products of thoughtful and artistic design that convey messages of their own. This approach recalls scholarly attention to the "received text [which] is the only historically attested datum; it alone has had demonstrable effects; it alone is the undoubted product of Israelite creativity." In this connection he argues that since midrashic (see MIDRASH) and later pre-critical Jewish exegesis operated on the assumption of unitary authorship, they have many insights to offer the holistic commentator.

G.'s research on Jewish thought includes important

studies of (1) the intellectual achievements of medieval Jewish exegesis (1988 lecture, unpublished); (2) rabbinic reflections on defying illegal orders (1995, 395-403); and (3) attitudes toward members of other religions (1995, 369-93; 1996). In the latter 1996 essay he argues that a Scripture-based religion can and must avoid fundamentalism by being selective and critical in its reliance on tradition and by reprioritizing values. In "Jewish Conceptions of the Human Factor in Biblical Prophecy" (1995, 405-19), he shows that from the TAL-MUD to the Renaissance, classical Jewish exegetes and thinkers who never doubted the divine INSPIRATION and authorship of the Torah and other prophetic writings nevertheless acknowledged the LITERARY evidence of human shaping of the text.

Works: *The Ḥab/piru* (1955); *The Religion of Israel* (1960; abridged ET of Y. Kaufmann, *Tôledôt hā-'Emûnâ ha-Yisre'ēlît,* vols. 1–7); *Introduction to Hebrew* (1965); *Understanding Exodus* (1969); "Decalogue," "Ḥerem," and "Sabbath," *EncJud* (1972) 5:1435-46, 8:345-50, 14:557-62; "Prophecy in Hebrew Scripture," *Dictionary of the History of Ideas* (ed. P. P. Wiener, 1973) 3:657-64; "Biblical Judaism (20th–24th cents. BCE)" *Encyclopaedia Britannica: Macropaedia* (1974[15]) 10:303-310; *Ezekiel 1–20* (AB 22, 1983a) *Biblical Prose Prayer as a Window to the Popular Religion of Ancient Israel* (Taubman Lectures in Jewish Studies 6, 1983b); *Studies in the Bible and Jewish Thought* (JPS Scholar of Distinction Series, 1995); "A Problematic Heritage: The Attitude Toward the Gentile in the Jewish Tradition—An Israel Perspective," *Conservative Judaism* 48, 2 (Winter, 1996) 23-35; *Ezekiel 21–37* (AB 22A, 1997).

Bibliography: "M. G.: An Appreciation" and "Bibliography of the Writings of M. G.," *Tehilla le-Moshe: Biblical and Judaic Studies in Honor of M. G.* (ed. M. Cogan, B. L. Eichler, and J. H. Tigay, 1997) ix-xxxviii. *Perāsê Yisrā'el 5754* (1994) 5-7 (Hebrew). **S. D. Sperling** (ed.), *Students of the Covenant: A History of Jewish Biblical Scholarship in North America* (1992).

J. H. TIGAY

GREGORY THE GREAT (c. 540–604)

A monk, diplomat, and administrator, G. became one of the most influential popes of the late Roman and early medieval world through his teaching on the nature and exercise of the office and through his exegesis. By far the greater part of his writings (apart from letters) are exegetical. Homilies on the Gospels given to his monastic community in the daily *collatio* survive; on Job, Ezekiel, Song of Songs, and 1 Kings, he delivered and wrote substantial commentaries. His preaching concerns dominate his exegesis, and often there is a topical reference. In the homilies on Ezekiel he spoke of the invaders at the gates of Rome, and in the *Moralia in Job* he emphasized what is to be learned from the text about living a good Christian life. Those to whom he preached and with whom he expounded the texts pressed him to collect his sermons and talks in a book.

Preaching and exegesis were for G. the natural vehicle of theological inquiry, as they were in some measure for AUGUSTINE. But G. wrote no treatises of the Augustinian sort to complement his studies of the text. Only the *Dialogues* approach the genre, and they seek to meet a popular demand for edifying tales of holy lives rather than systematically to consider theological questions. In the *Dialogues* G. allowed himself one full inquiry into the state of the soul after death and related questions on which Augustine had failed to arrive at a settled view. But in general he was not of a speculative bent, and he drew from Augustine and other fathers only a digest of a theology with which they were consciously wrestling. G. succeeded in presenting what he derived in a clear and simple way for the general reader, and his achievement in doing so must not be underestimated; Augustine is not easy to summarize. G. was a synthesizer of rare caliber but not on the whole an originator of fresh speculation.

His most important contribution to the history of exegesis is his transmission of the system of fourfold interpretation (see QUADRIGA), which he drew from the ORIGEN tradition and in part from Augustine (although Augustine did not formulate it as did G.). He was so widely read and so popular in the Middle Ages that his system became universal in the West for a thousand years. In it he distinguished the historical or literal sense, the allegorical, the moral or tropological, and the anagogical, which points forward prophetically in history and to the life to come. G. saw the literal sense as the foundation upon which all the other senses stand like the superstructure of a building. The "building" was done by comparing parallel passages, by pointing out ways in which an OT figure might be seen as a "type" of an NT figure, by eliciting points of doctrine, and by free digression into topics that suggested themselves. The thread of the text and the internal coherence of everything that was said with sound doctrine held everything together. This method lent itself admirably to the needs of earlier medieval exegesis, predominantly carried out within monastic communities, where the abbot would expound the text and the monks would ask questions or the individual would read slowly and reflectively for himself.

Works: *PL* 75–78; CCSL 140, 140A, 142, 143, 143A, 143B, 144.

Bibliography: **P. Batiffol,** *Gregory the Great* (1928; ET 1929). **F. H. Dudden,** *Gregory the Great* (2 vols., 1905). **G. R. Evans,** *The Thought of Gregory the Great* (1985). **S. C. Kessler,** *Gregor der Grosse als Exeget: Eine theologische Interpretation der Ezechielhomilien* (InnTS 43, 1995). **R. A.**

Markus, *Gregory the Great and His World* (1997); *TRE* 14 (1985) 135-45. **C. J. Pfeifer,** *DMA* 5 (1985) 668-69.

G. R. EVANS

GREGORY OF NAZIANZUS (329–390)

The son of the bishop of Nazianzus, G. studied in Athens and then entered monastic life. Called "the Theologian" by Eastern orthodoxy, he wrote forty-four orations, 17,000 poetic verses, 245 letters, and probably at least one commentary on Ezekiel (which has been lost). Unlike CHRYSOSTOM, his sermons were not exegetical homilies. Nevertheless, concern for Scripture dominates his *Theological Orations,* in which over 750 biblical allusions and citations mark five declamations.

In G.'s view God's nature is not open to our examination and is not revealed by the divine names; it is indescribable and incomprehensible. Thus no theology can be based on definitions and demonstrative syllogisms; all theologies are approximations best put forward by poets who offer better images. Indeed, all language, including that of Scripture, is conventional, not natural.

G. accepted part of ORIGEN's description of Scripture: The Bible speaks of real things in a real way, real things in a fictional way, unreal things in a real way, and unreal things in a fictional way. In G.'s case, however, this understanding did not lead to wildly allegorical interpretation. He was educated through the study of grammar and rhetoric; on that basis he is best described as a philosophical rhetorician. He well understood Plato's *Phaedrus* and Aristotle's *Rhetoric* as descriptive of logical procedures, particularly the handling of probability questions like those that concern theology. Yet he knew that much could be learned by close attention to the grammar, syntax, and actual wording of the Bible. Verb tenses vary, with present sometimes standing for future and past for present. The meanings of words like "cannot" or "until" must be determined contextually from a large number of cases, from both scriptural and everyday language. In other words, philology matters.

When read in this way, G. maintained, the Bible is perspicacious, although it must be understood within the context of the developing Christian tradition. Pagans who do not belong to the community must not be made judges of Christian truth. Only the community knows its own language.

Although deeply rooted in his fourth-century context, G. offered much advice about scriptural interpretation that appears to be modern and to fit our contemporary perspectives, particularly the insights of historical grammatical study and READER-RESPONSE theory. It is regrettable that his contribution to biblical HERMENEUTICS has not been more widely claimed.

Works: *PG* 35-38; SC 149, 208, 247, 250, 284, 309, 318.

Bibliography: **F. W. Norris,** "Gregory of Nazianzus: Constructing and Constructed by Scripture," *The Bible in Greek Christian Antiquity* (BTA 1, 1997); *Faith Gives Fullness to Reasoning: The Five Theological Orations of Gregory Nazianzen* (VCSup 13, 1991). **J. Quasten,** *Patrology* (1983) 3:236-54. **M. A. Siotou,** *Hoi Treis Hierarchai hos hermeneutai tēs Hagias Graphēs* (1963). **F. Trisoglio,** "Filone Alessandrino e l'esegesi cristiana: Contributo alla conoscenza dell'influsso esercitato da Filone sui IV secolo, specificatamenta in Gregorio di Nazianzo," *ANRW* II.21.1 (1984) 488-730. **H. Weiss,** *Die grossen Kappadozier: Basilius, Gregor von Nazianz und Gregor von Nyssa als Exegeten* (1872).

F. W. NORRIS

GREGORY OF NYSSA (c. 335–395)

Born between 335 and 340 in Cappadocia, G received much of his education from his sister Macrina and his brother BASIL. G. was appointed bishop of Nyssa in 372 by Basil, who was then metropolitan of Caesarea. When Basil died in 379 G. became his literary and theological heir. He played a leading role in the second ecumenical council at Constantinople in 381.

The ALEXANDRIAN tradition, especially ORIGEN, was a major early theological influence on G. He was well informed on Platonic philosophy (his theology has been described as a Christianized Platonism), but he also employed Aristotelian and Stoic ideas. Instead of showing how Christianity agreed with previous systems of thought, he thoroughly synthesized philosophy into Christian presuppositions and rejected what would not fit. He influenced later Greek Orthodox spirituality and theology, notably Pseudo-Dionysius (c. 500) and Maximus the Confessor (c. 580–662), but was less well known in the West, although he influenced ERIUGENA and later J. WESLEY.

Fundamental to G.'s theology was the distinction between the Creator and the creature. He was one of the formulators and spokesmen for the orthodox doctrine of the Trinity. But perhaps his most original and significant contribution to Christian thought was the idea of the infinity of God. The corollary for Christian spirituality was the perpetual progress in perfection, for philosophical theology supports the practice of asceticism and right conduct. Moral virtue requires the exercise of human free will, assisted by the grace of the Holy Spirit.

G. was concerned to give a scriptural grounding to his theology and spirituality. The Holy Spirit inspired the Scriptures and must guide their interpretation (1 Cor 2:10 was an important text). His biblical interpretation was influenced by PHILO and Origen, and expositions of biblical books formed a large part of his literary output: *In hexaemeron, De opificio hominis, Vita Moysis, In inscriptiones psalmorum, In sextum psalmum, In Ecclesiasten, In Canticum canticorum, De oratione dominica, De beatitudinibus.*

While G. gave very careful interpretation of doctrinal texts and frequently employed traditional moral and typological interpretations, his nonliteral interpretations have drawn the greatest interest. He used the term *historia* for the literal or historical sense of the text. For its spiritual sense he used the terms *allegoria, dianoia* (understanding, the deeper sense), or most often *theoria* (contemplation or spiritual insight). Following Origen, he claimed the authority of PAUL in support of this twofold sense of Scripture, citing Rom 7:14; 1 Cor 9:9-10; 10:11; 13:12; 2 Cor 3:6, 16; Gal 4:22-24.

For G. certain features of the text pointed to an allegorical meaning: theological impropriety (e.g., physical descriptions of God); physical or logical impossibility (e.g., duplicating the circumstances of biblical heroes); useless or unnecessary information (e.g., food laws); and immorality in the letter of the text (e.g., killing of the firstborn of the Egyptians). On the positive side he looked for what was edifying and when confronted with several interpretations accepted any that conformed to Christian doctrine and contributed to virtue.

Works: *PG* 3–4; NPNF 2, 5 (ET, W. Moore and H. A. Wilson, 1893); *The Lord's Prayer, the Beautitudes* (ET, H. C. Graef, ACW 18, 1954); *Gregorii Nysseni Opera* (ed. W. Jaeger et al., 1960–); *Gregory of Nyssa: The Life of Moses* (ET, A. J. Malherbe and E. O. Ferguson, CWS, 1978); *Gregory of Nyssa, Homilies on Ecclesiastes: An English Version with Supporting Studies* (ed. S. G. Hall, 1993); *Gregory of Nyssa's Treatise on the Inscriptions of the Psalms: Introduction, Translation, and Notes* (OECS, tr. R. E. Heine, 1995).

Bibliography: M. Alexandre, "La théorie de l'exégèse dans le *De Hominis Opificio* et *l'In Hexaemeron*," *Écriture et culture philosophique dans la pensée de Grégoire de Nysse* (ed. M. Harl, 1971) 87-110. **M. Altenburger and F. Mann** (eds.), *Bibliographie zu Gregor von Nyssa: Editionen-Übersetzungen-Literatur* (1988). **D. L. Balás,** *TRE* 14 (1985) 173-81; "Gregory of Nyssa (331/40–c. 395)," *Encyclopedia of Early Christianity* 1 (1997). **M. Canévet,** *Grégoire de Nysse et l'herméneutique biblique* (1983). **J. Daniélou,** "La typologie biblique de Grégoire de Nysse," *Studi in onore di A. Pincherle: Studi e materiali di storia delle religioni* (1967) 185-96; "La *theoria* chez Grégoire de Nysse," *StPatr* 11, 2 (= TU 108, 1972) 103-45. **H. R. Drobner,** *Bibelindex zu den Werken Gregors von Nyssa* (1988). **F. Dünzl,** *Braut und Bräutigam: Die Auslegung des Canticum durch Gregor von Nyssa* (1993). **E. Ferguson,** "Some Aspects of Gregory of Nyssa's Interpretation of Scripture Exemplified in his *Homilies on Ecclesiastes*," *StPatr* 27 (1993) 29-33. **G.-I. Gargano,** *La tebria di Gregorio di Nissa sul Cantico dei Cantici* (OCA 216, 1981). **R. E. Heine,** "Gregory of Nyssa's Apology for Allegory," *VC* 38 (1984) 360-70. **J. Meyendorff,** *DMA* 5 (1985) 666-67. **M. J. Rondeau,** "D'ou vient la technique exégètique utilisée par Grégoire de Nysse dans son traité *Sur les titres des Psaumes?*" *Mélanges d'histoire*

des religions offerts à H.-C. Puech (ed. A. Bareau, 1974) 263-87.

E. FERGUSON

GRESSMANN, HUGO ERNST FRIEDERICH WILHELM (1877–1927)

Born Mar. 21, 1877, in Mölln (Lauenburg), G. studied theology and Semitic languages in Griefswald, Göttingen, Marburg, and Kiel. His teachers included W. BOUSSET, A. EICHHORN, R. SMEND, J. WELLHAUSEN, and M. LIDZBARSKI. He received his doctorate at Göttingen (1900) and the lic. theol. at Kiel (1902), completing his habilitation in 1902 to become *Privatdozent* in OT. In 1906 he spent eight months as G. DALMAN's coworker in Jerusalem and on his expedition to Petra, acquiring an interest in the ARCHAEOLOGY of Palestine. In 1907 he accepted a call to Berlin as an *ausserordentlicher* professor and in 1920 became a full professor. After the death of H. Strack (1848–1922) he took over leadership of the Institutum Judaicum Berolinense, whose character he completely transformed, creating a scholarly institute for research on post-biblical Judaism. He died April 6, 1927, in Chicago while on a lecture tour.

G. united scholarship and a phenomenal capacity for work with rare literary productivity. Besides his many monographs and essays he produced innumerable articles, reports, and reviews. He was amazingly well read and surveyed the literature not only of the orient but also of classical antiquity and general FOLKLORE. He made use of the newest discoveries and information from archaeology and oriental studies in interpreting the OT, and he did not shy away from daring hypotheses.

Through his studies (particularly with Wellhausen) G. was familiar with LITERARY-critical work on the OT. He did not dispute the method's authority, and he counted himself with those who were breaking new ground with it. However, he understood the method to address the end product of a developmental process. Inspired especially by Eichhorn, G. belonged to the RELIGIONSGESCHICHTLICHE SCHULE, concerned with the influence of extra-biblical concepts and traditions on the formation of biblical texts. With H. GUNKEL, G. founded FORM CRITICISM and TRADITION HISTORY approaches to the HB. Gunkel demonstrated these methods in Genesis and the psalms; G. employed them on the earliest historical traditions and the classical prophets (see PROPHECY AND PROPHETS, HB) of Israel (Amos, Hosea) in his SAT commentaries as well as in his book on Moses (1913).

Brilliant displays of style criticism and historical interpretation are represented in many of G.'s articles, among them: "Das salmonische Urteil," *DRu* 130 (1907) 212-28; "Sage und Geschichte in den Patriarchenerzählungen," *ZAW* 30 (1910) 1-24; "Die literarische Analyse Deuterojesajas," *ZAW* 34 (1914) 254-97; and "Ursprung und Entwicklung der Joseph-Sage," *Euchariste-*

rion H. Gunkel dargebracht I (ed. H. Schmidt, 1923) 1-55.

G. was an authority on ancient oriental literature, culture, and religion. He created the *Altorientalischen Texten und Bildern zum Alten Testament,* which was long an indispensable standard work and later served as a model for *ANET* and *ANEP.* For the *Texte* G. secured the collaboration of renowned scholars; however, the collection and annotation of the material for the *Bilder* he undertook alone. This monumental work has not yet been surpassed in the German language.

G. distanced himself from the literary-critical school in his investigation of OT eschatology. This subject belongs to his earliest interests (*Ursprung* [1905]), and at the end of his life he returned to it in a rather different way (*Messias,* published posthumously). He did not regard the expectation of the future and the messianic hope as products of the exilic and postexilic periods but as something already established in the popular faith of early Israel, influenced by concepts from Israel's neighboring environment and discovered and transformed by the classical prophets.

G. extended his religious-historical investigations to the NT (*Weihnachts-Evangelium* [1914]; *Vom reichen Mann* [1918]). He also devoted time to research on the Hellenistic-Roman period, which he regarded as an epoch of great syncretism and as a formative time for developing the essential presuppositions in the formation of both Judaism and Christianity.

Works: *Ueber die in Jes. c. 56–66 vorausgesetzten zeitgeschichtlichen Verhältnisse* (1898); *Musik und Musikinstrumente im Alten Testament* (1903); *Studien zu Eusebs Theophanie* (TU NF 8 H.3, 1903); *Der Ursprung der israelitisch-jüdischen Eschatologie* (FRLANT 6, 1905, repr. 1980); *Die Ausgrabungen in Palästina und das Alte Testament* (1908); (with A. Ungnad and H. Ranke), *Altorientalische Texte und Bilder zum Alten Testament* (2 vols., 1909, 1926²); *Palästinas Erdgeruch in der israelitischen Religion* (1909); *Die älteste Geschichtsschreibung und Prophetie Israels (Von Samuel bis Amos und Hosea)* (SAT 2.1, 1910, 1921²); (with A. Ungnad), *Das Gilgamesch-Epos* (FRLANT 14, 1911); *Mose und seine Zeit* (FRLANT 18 NF 1, 1913); *A. Eichhorn und die religionsgeschichtliche Schule* (1914); *Die Anfänge Israels (Von 2 Mosis bis Richter und Ruth)* (SAT 1.2, 1914, 1922²); *Das Weihnachts-Evangelium auf Ursprung und Geschichte untersucht* (1914); *Vom reichen Mann und armen Lazarus* (1918); *Die Lade Jahves und das Allerheiligste des Salomonischen Tempels* (BWANT 26 NF 1, 1920); *Tod und Auferstehung des Osiris nach Festbräuchen und Umzügen* (AO 23.3, 1923); *Die Aufgaben der alttestamentlichen Forschung* (1924) = ZAW 42 NF 1 (1924) 1-33; *Die Aufgaben der Wissenschaft des nachbiblischen Judentums* (1925) = ZAW 43 NF 2 (1925) 1-32; *Die hellenistische Gestirnreligion* (AO Beih. 5, 1925); *Israels Spruchweisheit im Zusammenhang der Weltliteratur* (1925); (with E. Ebeling, H. Ranke, N. Rhodokanakis), *Altorientalische Texte zum Alten Testament* (1926²); *Altorientalische Bilder zum Alten Testament* (1927²); *The Tower of Babel* (1928); *Der Messias* (FRLANT 43 NF 26, 1929); *Die orientalischen Religionen im hellenistischrömischen Zeitalter* (1930).

Bibliography: K. Galling, *RGG³* 2 (1958) 1856; *NDB* 7 (1966) 50-51. H. Gressmann, G. A. Kohut, S. S. Wise, and J. A. Bewer, "Gressmann Memorial Number," *Jewish Institute Quarterly* 3, 4 (1927) 2-10. H. Gunkel, *RGG²* 2 (1927) 1454. W. Horst, A. Titius, T. H. Robinson, E. Sellin, and J. Hempel, *H. G.: Gedächtnisworte* (1927) = ZAW 45 NF 4 (1927) i-xxiv. J. Obermann, "Preface," *The Tower of Babel* (H. Gressmann, 1928) iii-xvi. M. Rade, *ChW* 41 (1927) 458-59. H. Schmidt, "H. G. in Memoriam," *TBl* 6 (1927) 157-62. W. Thiel, "Zum 100. Geburtstag H. G.," *Standpunkt* 5 (1977) 302-3. R. Wonneberger, *TRE* 14 (1985) 212-13.

W. THIEL

GRIESBACH, JOHANN JAKOB (1745–1812)

Born Jan. 4, 1745, in Butzbach/Hesse, Germany, G. studied theology, philology, and philosophy in Tübingen, Halle, and Leipzig. In 1769–70, with the purpose of continuing J. SEMLER'S TEXTUAL CRITICISM research, he studied sources that might contribute to a reliable text of the NT in libraries in Germany, Holland, England, and France. His academic activity began in Halle in 1771. In Jena from 1775 until his death, Mar. 24, 1812, he taught NT, church history, and dogmatics. He believed that genuine Christianity and genuine philosophy are not mutually contradictory; rather, a whole series of theological truths is already accessible to reason. Nonetheless, a conservative position oriented toward orthodoxy is discernible in his work.

A primary focus of G.'s work was NT text-critical research. He developed a theory for determining a reliable NT text after extensive research in early textual history, with special attention to the different variant readings and to hitherto neglected citations from the church fathers and other translations. His theory subdivided the NT manuscripts along the lines of J. BENGEL into an older and younger group. In addition, he followed Semler by subdividing the older manuscript group into yet two more groups so that all told he differentiated three "recensions": a "Western" and an "Alexandrian" as the older, and a "Constantinopolitan" or "Byzantine" as the younger, emerging from the first two. This theory led to three critical editions of the NT, all of which also offered a textual-critical apparatus and selected variants; these proved valuable editions for many years. Of particular significance was G.'s consistent development and employment of certain text-critical principles for selecting textual variants. He was the first German scholar who dared to publish an edition of the NT that departed from the *textus receptus.*

G.'s text-critical works were both the high point of

previous efforts and the beginning of a new era in this research. In section one of the first edition (1774–75) the first three Gospels were ordered synoptically for the first time. Not only did G. coin the designation *synoptic,* but he consciously laid out the foundations of focused research on the SYNOPTIC PROBLEM. Concerning the explanation of the agreements and differences between the synoptic Gospels, he represented the hypothesis (in his *Commentatio* [1789–90]) that Mark is not merely a partial excerpt from Matthew (a position overwhelmingly supported during G.'s time by those following Augustine) but is also drawn from Luke, which as a rule Mark followed whenever it deviated from Matthew. Mark's goal was the composition of a Gospel of limited parameters. This hypothesis—presented earlier by H. Owen (1764) and A. Büsching (1766; see B. Reicke [1976] 341)—found general acceptance through G.'s presentation. Although it was defended above all by W. DE WETTE, it had little effect on similar positions within the Tübingen school, even though representatives and successors of the latter (e.g., D. F. Strauss) used G. in their own defense. As a counterpoint to the two-source theory, G.'s hypothesis has repeatedly been discussed and supported—with more prominent mention of Owen and as the "two Gospel hypothesis" (see B. Orchard [1980]).

G. regularly taught courses in NT HERMENEUTICS, though he did not publish in this field. His lecture notes, first edited by J. Steiner (1815), reveal a comprehensive attempt to determine and analyze the practical task of exegesis and interpretation. The goal of hermeneutics is a consistent and well-documented interpretation directed toward intensive comprehension, one that does justice to the NT in its uniqueness as the only "source of knowledge of the Christian religion" and one that provides "insight into the genuine original teachings of Christ." G. replaced dogmatically oriented interpretation with a determination of the grammatical-historically accessible concerns of the NT without ignoring its dogmatically relevant passages. Significantly, the point of departure for his hermeneutics was an analysis of the structure of speech: He distinguished words, sentences, and speech and attributed to them meaning, understanding, and sense. He emphasized the appropriate rendering of the meaning and sense found in the text as part of the hermeneutical task.

G.'s exegetical-theological treatises exemplify the employment of these hermeneutical guidelines. That each of these treatises—especially the explanation of the suffering and resurrection stories of Christ—was presented in his lectures on hermeneutics underscores their practical orientation. Compared to G.'s other publications and activities, aside from his lectures, his biblical-theological works are relatively few. Yet these lectures show that G. helped to introduce a process of careful analysis of the NT in its existing form through which a more intensive inquiry into its theological significance can be made.

Works: *Libri historici Novi Testamenti Graece: Pars prior, sistens synopsin Evangeliorum Matthaei, Marci et Lucae. Textum ad fidem codicum, versionum et patrum emendavit et lectionis varietatem adiecit Io. Iac. Griesbach* (1774); *Pars posterior, sistens Evangelium Ioannis et Acta Apostolorum. Textum....* (1775); *Novum Testamentum Graece: Textum....* 2 (1775); 1 (1777); *Synopsis Evangeliorum Matthaei, Marci et Lucae: Textum Graecum ad fidem....* (1776, 1809³); *Anleitung zum Studium der populären Dogmatik....* (1779, 1789⁴); *Symbolae criticae ad supplendas et corrigendas variarum NT lectionum collectiones* (2 pts., 1785–93); *Commentatio qua Marci Evangelium totum e Matthaei et Lucae commentariis decerptum esse monstratur* (1789–90); *Novum Testamentum Graece: Textum ad fidem....* (2 vols., 1796–1806); *Novum Testamentum Graece: Ex recensione Jo. Jac. Griesbachii cum selecta lectionum varietate* (2 vols., 1803–7); *Vorlesungen über die Hermeneutik des NT mit Anwendung auf die Leidens- und Auferstehungsgeschichte Christi* (ed. C. S. Steiner, 1815); *Io. Iacobi Griesbachii Opuscula academica* (2 vols., ed. J. P. Gabler, 1824–25).

Bibliography: *Catalogus bibliothecae J. J. G....* (1814). **B. R. Abeken,** *Johann Jakob Griesbach.* (1829). **J. W. Augusti,** "Über J. J. G.s Verdienste," *Akademische Vorlesung* (Breslau, 1812). **O. L. Cope,** *Matthew: A Scribe Trained for the Kingdom of Heaven* (CBQMS 5, 1976). **G. Delling,** "J. J. G.: Seine Zeit, sein Leben, sein Werk," *TZ* 33 (1977) 81-99 (includes complete bibliography). **W. R. Farmer,** *The Synoptic Problem: A Critical Analysis* (1964, 1977²); "Modern Developments of G.'s Hypothesis," *NTS* 23 (1976–77) 275-95. **K. Heussi,** *Geschichte der Theologischen Fakultät Jena* (1954). **F. A. Koethe,** *Gedächtnisrede auf J. J. G.... nebst einer Skizze seines Lebenslaufs* (1812). **T. R. W. Longstaff,** *Evidence of Conflation in Mark? A Study in the Synoptic Problem* (1977). **B. M. Metzger,** *TRE* 14 (1985) 253-56. **B. Orchard,** "The Two-Gospel-Hypothesis," *Downside Review* 98 (1980) 267-79. **B. Orchard and T. R. W. Longstaff** (eds.), *J. J. G.: Synoptic and Textcritical Studies, 1776–1976* (SNTSMS 34, 1978). **D. B. Peabody,** *HHMBI,* 319-25. **B. Reicke,** "G. und die synoptische Frage," *TZ* 32 (1976) 341-59. **E. Reuss,** *RE³* 7 (1924) 170-72. **H. H. Stoldt,** *History and Criticism of the Marcan Hypothesis* (1977; ET 1980). **C. M. Tuckett,** *The Revival of the Griesback Hypothesis: An Analysis and Appraisal* (SNTSMS 43, 1983). **J. Wach,** *Das Verstehen* 2 (1929).

C. BERGER

GROSSETESTE, ROBERT (c. 1175–1253)

After teaching in the Franciscan house at Oxford (1224–35), G. became bishop of Lincoln (1235–53). As Oxford master he was up-to-the-minute in his interest in the newly available scientific works of Aristotle and in his study of Greek, philosophy, and mathematics. As bishop he was a controversial figure who made himself unpopular in England and Rome by his efforts to end certain corrupt practices in the church.

His principal importance as a scholar lies in his work on optics and astronomy, in his effort to translate some Greek Christian literature (St. John of Damascus, Pseudo-Dionysius, Ignatius of Antioch), and above all in his recognition of the importance of the study of Greek. In all this he was followed by R. BACON, who admired and approved of his work. G. is also the author of biblical commentaries—on Genesis, the first hundred psalms, Romans, and Galatians in particular—and of mixed collections of "sayings" (*Dicta*) of some relevance to Bible study. One of very few scholars of his day to possess a knowledge of Greek language and literature, he was not able to take its application very far; but he pioneered an approach that was to influence J. WYCLIF greatly, and he asked fundamental questions about method and practice in exegesis. The tentative realization of the implications of his new learning can be seen in his *Hexaemeron,* where the biblical text is used as a starting point for scientific inquiry into matters arising out of the account of the creation of the world. The mention of light leads into optics, and so on.

Works: *Episcopi quondam Lincolniensis Epistolae* (ed. H. R. Luard, 1861); *Hexäemeron* (ABMA 6, ed. R. Dales, 1982).

Bibliography: D. A. Callus (ed.), *Robert Grosseteste* (1955). **A. C. Crombie,** *R. G. and the Origins of Experimental Science* (1953). **J. McEvoy,** *TRE* 14 (1985) 271-74. **S. P. Marrone,** *DMA* 6 (1985) 1-2. **R. W. Southern,** *R. G.: The Growth of an English Mind in Medieval Europe* (1986). **S. H. Thomson,** *The Writings of R. G.* (1940).

G. R. EVANS

GROTIUS, HUGO (1583–1645)

Born at Delft, Apr. 10, 1583, G. was a prodigy. He entered the University of Leiden at age eleven, where he studied law, mathematics, theology, and classical philology with J. SCALIGER. He began practicing law at the Hague in 1599. This so-called founder of international law published his first work in this field (*Mare liberum*) in 1609. Appointed permanent pensioner of Rotterdam (1613), he entered the states-general. On a mission to England (1615), he met I. CASAUBON and began his lifelong interest in the union of Roman Catholics and Protestants.

An outspoken Arminian (see ARMINIUS), G. frequently became embroiled in religious disputes. After the Synod of Dort (Nov. 13, 1618–May 25, 1619), he was tried and condemned to perpetual imprisonment in the fortress of Loevestein; while there he wrote several works, including a Dutch verse version of *De Veritate religionis christianae.* With his wife's help he escaped in a box of books (Mar. 21, 1621) and fled to France, where he was enthusiastically welcomed. There he composed several works, including *De jure belli et pacis* (1624; ET 3 vols., 1853). In 1634 he was appointed councilor to Queen Christina of Sweden and her ambassador to the court of France. In Paris G. had contact with E. HERBERT of Cherbury, T. HOBBES, and I. de la PEYRÈRE. G. encouraged Herbert to publish his *De Veritate* and wrote a work against Peyrère's theory of pre-Adamic humans (*Dissertatio altera de origine gentium americanarum adversus obtrectatorem* [1643]). G. died at Rostock, Aug. 28, 1645, on his way from Stockholm to Holland.

G. wrote works in drama, classics, ecclesiastical law, church history, international jurisprudence, and other areas; but his most widely disseminated work was an apology on the truth of the Christian religion (1627). Its six volumes treat the existence and attributes of God (1); the excellence of the doctrines and ethics of Christianity (2); the authenticity of the NT books (3); and objections against Christianity on the part of pagans, Muslims, and Jews (4–6). Translated into a multitude of languages, including Arabic, Persian, Chinese, and Malay, the work established apologetics as a science and contributed to the tendency to establish the truth of Christianity on the basis of "evidences."

In biblical-exegetical studies G. published annotations on the entire Bible, begun while imprisoned at Loevestein and completed just before his death: *Annotationes in libros evangeliorum et varia loca S. Scripturae* (1641), *A. in Epist. ad Philemonem* (1642), *A. in Vetus Testamentum* (1644), and *A. in NT* (1644). The OT notes were reedited as late as 1775–76 (3 vols., with Vogel's and J. Döderlein's additions) and the NT as late as 1827–29 (7 vols., ed. Gröning). Unlike earlier traditional commentaries his notes reflect the developing tendency to focus on philological and historical issues (as in classical studies) rather than on overtly theological matters, partially in the interest of promoting theological consensus and ecclesiastical unification. They are filled with quotations and illustrative material drawn from patristic sources, classical writers, and Jewish exegetical traditions. G. offered philological explanations of terms, drawing on his knowledge of Hebrew and Aramaic; collated textual variants; attempted to locate the writings within a historical context; and offered explanations of the historical referents in the text. He held a low view of INSPIRATION, seeing no need to posit revelation to the writers of historical texts. On the other hand, he saw the HB prophets (see PROPHECY AND PROPHETS, HB) as genuinely inspired, with their predictions often having a double reference, one more contemporary and the other pointing toward Christ. G. viewed the miracles as proof of the truth of the gospel and generally took the biblical books as being written by those whose names they bear or by very trustworthy men. His exegesis shows a strong interest in morality, ethics, and the law.

Works: *Opera omnia theologica* (3 vols. in 4, containing his annotations on the OT [vol. 1]; the Gospels and Acts [vol. 2/1]; and the epistles and Revelation [vol. 2/2], 1679); *The Truth of the Christian Religion . . . Corrected and Illustrated with Notes by Mr. Le Clerc* (ET 1719).

Bibliography: A. **Corsano,** *U. Grozio: L'umanista—il teologo—il giurista* (1948). M. **De Burigny,** *The Life of the Truly Eminent and Learned H. G.* (1752; ET 1754). A. H. **Haentjens,** *Hugo de Groot als godsdienstig denker* (1946). I. **Husik,** "The Law of Nature, H. G., and the Bible," *HUCA* 2 (1925) 381-419. H. J. **de Jonge,** "The Study of the NT," *Leiden University in the Seventeenth Century* (ed. T. H. Lunsingh Scheurleer and G. H. M. Posthumus Meyjes, 1975) 65-109; *De bestudering van het Nieuwe Testament aan de Noordnederlandse universiteiten en het Remonstrants Seminarie van 1575 tot 1700* (1980); "Grotius as an Interpreter of the Bible, particularly the NT," *H. G.: A Great European, 1583–1645* (1983) 59-65; "H. G.: Exégète du Nouveau Testament," *The World of H. G. (1583–1645)* (1984) 97-115. W. S. M. **Knight,** *The Life and Works of H. G.* (1925). A. **Kuenen,** "H. G. als Ausleger des Alten Testaments," *Gesammelte Abhandlungen zur biblischen Wissenschaft* (1894) 161-85. *MSHH* 19 (1732) 315-83. H. J. M. **Nellen and E. Rabbie** (eds.), *H. G.: Theologian* (FS G. M. H. Posthumus Meyjes, SHCT 55, 1994), with bibliography of Grotius studies, 1840–1993, 219-45. H. G. **Reventlow,** "Humanistic Exegesis: The Famous H. G.," *Creative Biblical Exegesis: Christian and Jewish Hermeneutics Through the Centuries* (JSOTSup 59, 1988) 175-91 = *BTT* 6 (1989) 141-54. A. W. **Rosenberg,** "H. G. as Hebraist," *StRos* 12 (1978) 62-90. J. **Schlüter,** *Die Theologie des H. G.* (1919). W. C. **van Unnik,** "H. G. als uitlegger van het Nieuwe Testament," *NAKG* 25 (1932) 1-48.

J. H. HAYES

GUIBERT OF NOGENT (1053–1124)

After receiving a thorough grounding in grammar from a schoolmaster secured by his ambitious mother, G. eventually became abbot of Nogent. While a monk at Fly he was encouraged in his studies by ANSELM OF CANTERBURY, who visited there. Commentaries probably by G. on Genesis and on various Major and Minor Prophets (see PROPHECY AND PROPHETS, HB) are extant. His principal contribution to the history of exegesis is the *Moralia* on the book of Genesis, in which he attempted to do for Genesis what GREGORY THE GREAT had done for Job. He is also the author of a preaching manual that antedates by a century the development of the *ars praedicandi*. In it he showed himself much indebted to Gregory the Great and to AUGUSTINE, whose homilies were usually preferred to original sermons in G.'s day; but G. encouraged would-be preachers to feel free to preach for themselves, with special emphasis on the moral sense, practical advice drawn from Scripture for those striving to live a good Christian life.

Works: *PL* 156.

Bibliography: J. F. **Benton,** *Self and Society in Medieval France* (1970).

G. R. EVANS

GUIGNEBERT, CHARLES ALFRED HONORE (1867–1939)

A historian, G. was without religious beliefs or affiliation. In 1906 he was appointed to teach early Christianity at the Sorbonne because, in the wake of the separation of church and state and the departure of both Roman Catholic and Protestant biblical scholars, it was felt that the tradition of E. RENAN should be kept alive. G. made it clear that he would steer an independent course between the extremes of Catholicism and anti-Christian rationalism. For more than thirty years he ranged widely over church history; but Christian origins remained his focus, and he regularly conducted classes of NT exegesis. He died two years after retirement.

Much of G.'s published work is semi-popular writing since he believed educated French public opinion needed to be weaned away from viewing Christian origins as a battleground. More solid were volumes on TERTULLIAN (1901) and the figure of Peter (1909a). G. allowed himself to be drawn into the religious debates concerning Roman Catholic modernism (1909b), the evolution of dogma (1910), and the religiosity of the French (1922b). His final trilogy appeared in the multi-volume series *L'évolution de l'humanité* (gen. ed. H. Berr). From these and from his unpublished lectures on NT exegesis the following features of his biblical interpretation emerge: (1) an assiduous agnosticism where he felt the original meaning was hopelessly obscure; (2) a concentration of interest on passages important for later Christian orthodoxy; (3) the pressing of evidence in favor of positions of the RELIGIONSGESCHICHTLICHE SCHULE, of which he and A. LOISY were the leading representatives in France; and (4) patient and careful debate with other exegetes, whatever their confessional allegiance. He stressed the discontinuity between successive stages of doctrinal development (e.g., in christology) and adopted a strong anti-confessional stance in the belief that theology was the mortal enemy of history. Although skeptical about acquiring much information concerning JESUS of Nazareth from the Gospels, he never joined the Christ-myth school. He is sometimes called a rationalist, which may be taken to mean that he wished secular historiographical criteria to be applied to NT documents so that they might yield information about how a religion is born.

Works: *Tertullien* (1901); *Manuel d'histoire ancienne du christianisme: Les origines* (1906); *La Primauté de Pierre et la venue de Pierre à Rome* (1909a); *Modernisme et tradition catholique* *en France* (1909b); *L'Evolution des dogmes* (1910); *Le Problème de Jésus* (1914); *Le Christianisme antique* (1921a); *La Vie cachée de Jésus* (1921b); *Le Christianisme médiéval et moderne* (1922a); *Le Problème religieux dans la France d'aujourd'hui* (1922b); *Jésus* (1933; ET 1959); *Le Monde juif vers le temps de Jésus* (1935); *Le Christ* (posthumous, 1943).

Bibliography: **M. Brunot,** "C. G. (1867–1939): Sa Vie et Son Oeuvre," *Annales de l'université de Paris* (1939) 365-80 (supplemented by further information in *RH* [1940] 181-82). **P. L. Couchoud,** *Le Dieu Jésus* (1951) pt. 2. **A. H. Jones,** *Independence and Exegesis* (1983) chaps. 3 and 5.

A. H. JONES

GUNKEL, JOHANNES HEINRICH HERMANN
(1862–1932)

G. was born May 23, 1862, in Springe and grew up in Lüneburg. He studied theology in Göttingen (1881–85), and he also attended lectures of A. von HARNACK and B. STADE in Giessen. In Oct. 1888 he was granted "venia legendi" for biblical theology and exegesis for two years, the degree of *Habilitation,* and a stipend. He lectured in Halle (1890–94), becoming professor *extraordinarius* first there and then in Berlin (1894). During this period he publised *Schöpfung und Chaos* (1895) and the first edition of *Genesis* (1901). He was called as professor *ordinarius* to Giessen (1907–20) and to Halle (1920–27). These were years of intensive work on the psalms and editorship of the second edition of *RGG,* to which he contributed 151 articles. He retired in 1927 because of ill health. At Christmas 1931 he handed over to his former student and collaborator J. BEGRICH his manuscript of *Einleitung in die Psalmen,* which Begrich saw through the press in 1933. G. died Mar. 11, 1932.

G.'s contributions to study of the HB and to biblical interpretation can be grouped under five themes:

1. The Bible and the Ancient Near East. G. was the first HB scholar to make systematic use of literary discoveries in the ancient Near East, especially in Mesopotamia. In *Schöpfung und Chaos* he asked: Is Genesis 1 of Babylonian origin? If so, to what extent? He discussed all biblical references outside Genesis to the primeval dragon and the tradition of the primeval sea and concluded that the religio-historical sequence was (a) the original Marduk myth, (b) a poetic recension of the Yahweh myth, and (c) Genesis 1. With regard to Genesis 1, G. maintained that the Babylonian myth came to Israel, lost much of its mythological character and almost all of its polytheism, and became fully Judaized. Genesis 1 should be regarded as the reworking of ancient Israelite tradition that had taken over the Babylonian material early in its development. G. was also well aware of the Canaanite background and observed that many Genesis stories associated with specific

sacred places could be considered of Canaanite origin. He was not looking for analogy in parallel ancient Near Eastern texts but for genealogy, i.e., for discerning the history of an idea, symbol, or image from Mesopotamia or elsewhere through early Israel to the biblical text.

2. Literary Forms, Oral Tradition, and the Bible. The introduction to the third edition of *Genesis* (1910) shows G. to be a child of the romantic movement in German literature. He believed his own approach to the genre of folk-story (see FOLKLORE) was confirmed by A. Olrik's influential essay "Epic Laws of Folk Narrative" (Danish 1908; GT 1909; ET in *The Study of Folklore* [ed. A. Dundes, 1965] 129-41). But it was G. alone who worked out his theory in the history of literature, literary forms, and story as applied to the Bible. He described Genesis as "eine Sammlung von Sagen" (a collection of stories). The German word *Sage* means folk-story, popular story, or simply story, with no prejudice as to whether the narrative conveys actual happenings. G. understood the editors more as collectors than as redactors, as more concerned to gather material than to shape it. *Sage* belongs to oral tradition, deals with personal and family affairs, derives from tradition molded by imagination, moves in the realm of the incredible, and is poetic in nature. He distinguished many types of story, from the brief, carefully honed narrative of Abram, Sarai, and Pharaoh (Gen 12:10-20) to the *novelle,* or short story, about Joseph (Genesis 37–50). One of his chief aims was to grasp the religious meaning of the HB by means of the *Sagen.*

3. The Bible as Israelite Literature. G. considered aesthetic appreciation of biblical narratives an essential element of exegesis and saw no conflict between aesthetics and serious critical scholarship, writing in the foreword to the first edition of *Genesis* (1901) that "a treatment of the OT in which philology, archaeology, or 'criticism' alone predominates is inadequate." One of G.'s guiding principles was that it is impossible to grasp completely the content of the Hebrew text if one has not recognized its type or form. He described a literary type (*Gattung*) as exhibiting a common store of ideas and attitudes, a clear and constant form of speech, and a setting in life (*Sitz im Leben*) from which alone the content and form can be understood ("Die Israelitische Literatur" [1925] 57 [109]; H. Rollmann [1981] 284). He distinguished various forms of early literature—*Märchen* (tale), *Sage* (story), *Legende* (elaborated story about a well-known figure), *Mythos* (prophetic speech)—and sought to relate these to the sociological-cultural life of ancient Israel (see SOCIOLOGY AND HB STUDIES; CULTURAL STUDIES).

4. The Bible and the History of Religions. G.'s approach to the history of religion was not part of the general history-of-religions movement; it belonged to theology, not to comparative religion. Prominent members of the his circle were A. EICHHORN, W. WREDE, W.

BOUSSET, and H. GRESSMANN. G. held two axioms regarding the history of religions. The first was that revolutionary and influential ideas in the history of the human race—religious ideas being foremost among these—predominate only after extended struggle. They achieve clarity in outstanding personalities, who are not in themselves the decisive element but who are carried forward by anonymous historical movements. The second axiom was that revelation is not opposed to history and does not exist outside the course of history; it takes place within the history of the human spirit. The special contribution of JESUS and Christianity lies in the unique use Christianity made of the idea of resurrection. Christ in his resurrection brings life to light, and people share the experience with Christ when they unite mystically with him.

5. Psalms in the Bible.
G.'s contribution to the study and classification of the types (*Gattungen*) of psalms was substantial. He was not the first to work in this area, but he was the first to classify and describe in detail all the types of psalms of the Bible. Israel's psalms have their origin in the life of the people, collectively and individually. The people sang when Yahweh gave them victory (Exod 15:1, 21), when the ark was moved (Num 10:35), when they walked to God's house (Pss 24:7-10; 42:4-5; 95:1-7*a;* 100), and when God responded to a person's longing (1 Sam 2:1*b*-10). The basic cry at worship was brief and keen: "Hallelujah" (Praise Yah[weh]). Psalms brought together under one type belong to a particular situation in the cult, share a common store of ideas and attitudes, and have a common form of speech; the content and the form are inseparable.

G. classified psalms as hymns, songs of enthronement of Yahweh, communal laments, royal psalms, individual laments, individual songs of thanksgiving, and lesser types. Among the latter are pronouncements of curse and blessing, pilgrim songs, victory songs, Israel's thanksgiving songs, legends, and the Torah. The psalms arose from the cult. When collections of psalms were made, giving rise to the psalter, public worship took possession of them; and the psalms were used as hymns in the Temple. Thus the circle from cult to cult was closed.

Works: *Die Wirkung des Heiligen Geistes* (1888; ET *The Influence of the Holy Spirit* [1979]); *Schöpfung und Chaos in Urzeit und Endzeit: Eine religionsgeschichtliche Untersuchung über Gen 1 und Apoc Joh 12* (1895); *Genesis* (1901, 1910[3]; unaltered to 1977[9]; ET 1997); *Zum religionsgeschichtliche Verständnis des Neuen Testaments* (1903) = "The Religio-Historical Interpretation of the NT," *The Monist* 13 (1903) 398-455; *Ausgewählte Psalmen* (1904, 1917[4]); "Die Israelitische Literatur," *Kultur der Gegenwart* (1906; repr. 1925, 1963[3]); *Reden und Aussätze* (1913); *The Folktale in the OT* (1917; ET 1987); *The Psalms* (*RGG*[2]; ET 1967); *Die Psalmen übersetzt und erklärt* (1929); *Introduction to Psalms* (1933, 1985[4]; ET 1998).

Bibliography: W. **Baumgartner,** "Zum 100. Geburtstag von H. G.," VTSup 9 (1963; repr. in 6th [1964] and subsequent eds. of *Genesis,* CV-CXXII). **M. J. Boss,** *HHMBI,* 487-91. F. Bovon, "H. G.: 'Historian de la Religion et exégète des Genres Littéraires,' " *Éxégèsis: Problèmes de méthode et exercises de lecture (Genèse 22 et Luc 15)* (ed. F. Boyon and G. Rouillet, 1975) 86-101. **P. Gibert,** *Une théorie de la légende: H. G. et les légendes de la Bible* (1979). **W. Klatt,** *Hermann Gunkel* (FRLANT 100, 1969), complete bibliography 272-74. **H. Rollmann,** "Zwei Briefe H. G.s an A. Jülicher zur religionsgeschichtlichen und formgeschichtlichen Methode," *ZTK* 78 (1981) 276-88. **H. Schmidt** (ed.), *Euxaristhrion* (FRLANT 36, 1923) 214-25 (complete bibliography). **R. Smend,** *DATDJ* (1989) 160-72.

J. J. SCULLION

GUTHE, HERMANN (1849–1936)

Born in Westerlinde, Germany, G. completed his doctorate at Leipzig in 1877 with the thesis *De foederis notione Jeremiana commentatio theologica.* Appointed professor at Leipzig in 1884, he remained there until his retirement in 1921. G. helped establish the DEUTSCHER VEREIN ZUR ERFORSCHUNG PALÄSTINAS, serving the society in many capacities (corresponding secretary, treasurer, librarian, editor, and president). He edited the *Zeitschrift des Deutschen Palaestina-Vereins* (1878–96) and the *Mittheilungen und Nachrichten des Deutschen Palaestina-Vereins* (1897–1906) and served as president of the society (1911–25). It was in the latter capacity that he sought to change the group's focus from historical and literary endeavors to archaeological ones.

In 1881 on the first of three trips to Palestine, G. excavated at Ophel in Jerusalem. He was the first German excavator in Palestine and in the course of his work located the southeast corner of the Temple mount and traced the course of the wall from the southeast corner to the Siloam Pool, work that would prove useful for F. Bliss (1859–1937) and later excavators. In addition, G. copied the Siloam inscription, which had been discovered the year before; his edition became the standard source for the critical study of the work since the original was damaged when it was excised and removed to Istanbul. In 1904 he visited the German excavation at Megiddo and later went to Madeba, where he copied the famous mosaic map. He toured a number of other sites in Palestine in 1912, making plans for a systematic program of excavation, the implementation of which was thwarted by WWI. In addition to his contributions as an excavator and epigraphist, G. built support for the Deutsche Verein in Jerusalem, established an archaeological museum there, and exposed as fraudulent the claims that M. Shapira's (c. 1830–84) manuscript of Deuteronomy was the autograph.

G.'s travels and researches into Palestinian ARCHAEOLOGY, topography, and geography strongly influenced his history of Israel, which was one of the earliest important histories to be written from J. WELLHAUSEN's perspective. An abbreviated English version of G.'s views on this topic is available in his article "Israel" in *EncBib* (1899). It reflects the author's late dating of P, his view of Christianity's superiority to Judaism, and his conviction that modern Palestinian culture is important for understanding circumstances of biblical times. In addition to this and to his other contributions to *EncBib*, G. wrote forty-eight articles dealing primarily with archaeological, geographical, and historical topics for Hauck and Herzog's *Realencyklopädie für protestantische Theologie und Kirche* (1896–1913³), which was translated into English and became *The New Schaff-Herzog Encyclopedia of Religious Knowledge*. He also published *Palästina in Bild und Wort* (1883), based on C. Wilson's *Picturesque Palestine, Sinai, and Egypt*; a Bible dictionary (1903); and an atlas (1911). The latter two works were particularly important mediators of the results of archaeological explorations to the wider community of scholars in Germany. In addition, his atlas was one of the first to be based on a critical reading of the biblical text and carefully distinguished site identifications that were certain from those that were not.

Works: *De foederis notione Jeremiana commentatio theologica* (1877); *Ausgrabungen bei Jerusalem* (1883); (with G. M. Ebers), *Palästina in Bild und Wort* (1883–84); *Das Zukunftsbild des Jesaia* (1885); *Geschichte des Volkes Israel* (GTW, 1. Reihe, 2. Th., 3. Bd., 1899); *Kurzes Bibelwörterbuch* (1903); *Die Mosaikkarte von Madeba* (1906); *Palästina* (1908); *Jesaia* (RV, 2. Reihe, 10. Heft, 1907); *Bibelatlas* (1911, 1926²).

Bibliography: A. Alt, *ZDPV* 59 (1936) 177-80. **M. Avi-Yonah,** *EncJud* 7 (1971) 985-86. **A. Kuschke,** *RGG*² (1958) 1918. **M. Noth,** "H. G. zum 80. Geburtstag," *ZDPV* 52 (1929) 97-98. **P. Thomsen,** "Professor Dr. theol. et phil. H. G. zum 10. Mai, 1919," *ZDPV* 42 (1919) 117-31.

M. P. GRAHAM

GUYON, JEANNE-MARIE BOUVIER DE LA MOTTE
(1648–1717)

A French mystic, G. was born Apr. 18, 1648, at Montargis. In 1668 she claimed to experience absorption into God and four years later signed a covenant declaring her spiritual marriage to the child JESUS. After the death of her husband in 1676 she devoted herself to the spiritual life. Her teachings aroused opposition from church leaders, who accused her of Quietism and reacted against her claim to be "clothed with the Apostolic state" (*Autobiography,* 2.62). In 1688 G. was forced to remain for several months in a convent. After lengthy discussions with J.-B. Bossuet (1627–1704), she was imprisoned in 1695 and eventually sent to the Bastille. Released in 1702, she died at Blois, June 9, 1717. She exercised a strong influence on F. Fénelon (1651–1715), who defended her in controversy with Bossuet, and had disciples not only from France but also from other countries, including Protestants as well as Catholics.

G. wrote works on prayer and a devotional commentary on the Bible. Her *Moyen court et très facile de faire oraison* (*A Short and Easy Method of Prayer;* 1685) won great popularity. Her Quietist tendencies are seen in her account of her method of writing biblical commentary: "Before writing I did not know what I was going to write; while writing I saw that I was writing things I had never known, and during the time of manifestation light was given me that I had in me treasures of knowledge and understanding that I did not know myself to possess" (*Autobiography,* 2.90). Her commentary, published in various parts between 1688 and 1714, makes frequent use of typology and gives expression to her understanding of the spiritual life. The Protestant P. Poiret (1646–1719) arranged for the publication of a large number of her writings.

Works: *Moyen court et très facile de faire oraison* (1685; ET, *A Short and Easy Method of Prayer* [1812]); *Les torrents spirituels* (1704; ET 1926); *La vie de Madame J. M. B. de la Mothe Guion, écrite par elle-même* (3 vols., 1720; new ed., 3 vols., 1791); *Lettres chrétiennes* (5 vols., 1767–68); *La sainte Bible ou le Vieux et le Nouveau Testament, avec des explications et réflexions qui regardent la vie intérieure* (20 vols., 1790); *Autobiography of Madame Guyon* (2 vols., 1897).

Bibliography: E. Aegerter, *Madame Guyon, une aventurière mystique* (c. 1940). **M. de la Bedoyere,** *The Archbishop and the Lady* (1956). **H. Delacroix,** *Les grands mystiques chrétiens* (1908). **M.-L. Gondal,** *Madame Guyon (1648–1717): un nouveau visage* (1989). **H Heppe,** *Geschichte der quietistischen Mystik in der katholischen Kirche* (1875, repr. 1978). **E. Jungclaussen,** *Suche Gott in Dir: Der Weg des inneren Schweigens nach einer vergessen Meisterin, J.-M. G.* (1987²). **R. A. Knox,** *Enthusiasm* (1950) 319-52. **F. Mallet-Joris,** *Jeanne Guyon* (1978).

A. W. WAINWRIGHT

H

HABAKKUK, BOOK OF

Habakkuk occupies the eighth place in the Book of the Twelve (Hebrew canon) or the Minor Prophets (Christian canon) and is comprised of three brief chapters, the first two of which consist of prophetic speeches and the last of a prayer. The prophet (see PROPHECY AND PROPHETS, HB) is not mentioned elsewhere in the HB, but in the story of Bel and the Dragon in the deutero-canonical Additions to Daniel he is reported to have been carried by an angel to Babylon, where he gave food to Daniel in the lion pit (Dan 14:33-39). Before the modern era Habakkuk was mined for its eschatological or christological value as well as for its teaching on faith and obedience to God. These interests continued into the Reformation period but with the additional concern for the book's historical background. In the nineteenth century scholarly attention began to focus on the literary unity and arrangement of the book, the relation of the prophet and his book to the cult, the most appropriate form-critical categories (see FORM CRITICISM, HB) to describe the work and its parts, the origin of chap. 3, and the historical setting and theological message of the book.

Evidence of early Jewish interpretation of Habakkuk may be found in the Greek versions, the TARGUM of *Jonathan,* and the Habakkuk pesher from the DEAD SEA SCROLLS found at Qumran (1QpHab lacks the final chapter). The pesher from Qumran interprets the text with reference to the Teacher of Righteousness, the Wicked Priest, the Prophet of Lies, and other matters of immediate concern to the author and the community at Qumran. Habakkuk 2:4b is understood to mean that God will deliver from "the house of judgment [= damnation?]" all in Judah who obey the law because of their patient suffering and their steadfast faith in the Teacher of Right" (i.e., their faith in the one who teaches the law correctly; W. Brownlee [1979] 125). In Jewish discussions of eschatology and the delay of the end, Hab 2:3-4 played a critical role, warning against unbridled expectations and assuring that the end was imminent.

While early Jewish interpreters regularly used Hab 2:3 for eschatological reflection, their Christian counterparts favored Hab 2:4. PAUL, for example, cited the verse twice (Rom 1:17; Gal 3:11) as a prooftext for his doctrine of justification by faith, contrasting with typical Jewish use of the verse to exhort audiences to faithful obedience to God. Nevertheless, Heb 10:35-38 cites Hab 2:3-4 in the course of an exhortation to Christians to endure persecution and hardship for the sake of their hope, a point underscored by the memorable discourse on faith in Hebrews 11. Finally, Acts 13:41 reports that Paul concluded his sermon at the synagogue in Antioch of Pisidia with a citation of Hab 1:5, warning his Jewish audience not to repeat the example of their ancestors by refusing to accept God's most recent activity in JESUS. A. Strobel's 1961 historical and philological study examined the motifs and traditions at work in the idea of the delay of the parousia in light of the late Jewish and primitive Christian history of Hab 2:2ff.

Among later Christian writers the christological interpretation of Habakkuk was dominant: Hab 2:3 and chap. 3 were related to the parousia and eschaton, and Hab 2:4 to faith in Jesus Christ. CYRIL OF ALEXANDRIA's commentary on Habakkuk (*PG* 71.871-72), for example, finds the historical fulfillment of the promise that the prophet's vision would be accomplished (Hab 2:3) in Cyrus's victory over Babylon, but its spiritual fulfillment in Christ. Similarly, the condemnation of the arrogant man in Hab 2:5 should be related historically to Nebuchadnezzar but spiritually to Satan (*PG* 71.873-74). AUGUSTINE (*City of God* 18:32) also provides an example of christological interpretation of Habakkuk, suggesting that the prayer of Habakkuk 3 was the prophet's address to Christ and that the statement of the LXX text (see SEPTUAGINT) of Hab 3:2, "in the midst of two living ones, thou shalt be known," was a reference to the position of Christ between the OT and the NT, or his crucifixion between two robbers (Mark 15:27), or his place between Moses and Elijah in the transfiguration scene (Mark 9:2-8). Moreover, the deuterocanonical story (Dan 14:33-39) about an angel transporting Habakkuk with food to Daniel in the lions' den was accepted by JEROME (*Commentariorum in Abacuc prophetam* [CCSL 76A] 580) and others as evidence that the prophet was a contemporary of Daniel and finds expression in early Christian iconography, which typically depicts the prophet bearing a gift of food, usually loaves and/or fish.

In the Reformation period LUTHER rejected Jerome's use of "Daniel, Bel, and the Dragon" for the dating and interpretation of Habakkuk since the former was not in the Hebrew CANON. Luther concluded that Habakkuk prophesied to Judah and Benjamin before the Babylonian captivity that God would punish them by the power of Babylon (Habakkuk 1), which would in turn be destroyed (Habakkuk 2); he interpreted Habakkuk 3 as a prayer for the godly who went into Babylonian exile. Since the destruction of Babylon was not completed until after the exile, Luther suggested that the prophet's activity extended from the preexilic to the postexilic period, although he allowed for the possibility that the prophet spoke of future events as though they were past or presently occurring ("described as past or as now present things that were still in the future," *LW* 19:119). Luther believed that Hab 2:4 meant that godly people were saved from destruction and lived because they waited on the Lord; in a more christological vein he maintained that Habakkuk intended to strengthen and comfort his people so that they would not despair of Christ's coming.

CALVIN (*Commentaries on the Twelve Minor Prophets,* vol. 4) opposed the traditional christological interpretation of Habakkuk, proposing instead that the book be understood against the background of the prophet's own day. He claimed that, while certainty is impossible, the prophet probably prophesied under Manasseh or another king before Zedekiah, condemning the sin of Judah and warning of destruction by Babylon. Habakkuk 3 consists of a prayer that the prophet dictated for his people to use in their devotions in exile. In spite of his strictures against traditional christological interpretation of the book, however, Calvin approved of the use of Hab 1:5 in Acts 13:41 and that of Hab 2:4 by Paul.

Although E. ROSENMÜLLER (1827) had suggested that Habakkuk 2 was from a time later than the prophet Habakkuk, it was with J. von Gumpach (1860) that the source-critical study of Habakkuk began in earnest in the nineteenth century. Noting the similarities between Hab 1:6-11 and Jeremiah 4–6, von Gumpach concluded that Hab 1:1-14 was a separate oracle that referred to the Scythian invasion. Most of the rest of the book was, he thought, a later oracle concerning Judah's deliverance. (Only M. de Goeje [1861] would follow closely this analysis of two separate oracles.) Almost thirty years passed, however, before further progress was made in solving the problems that von Gumpach had identified.

The most notable nineteenth-century source-critical study of the book was issued by B. STADE (1884), who argued that only Hab 1:2–2:8 derived from the prophet. He maintained that Hab 2:9-11 and 2:15-17 described a Palestinian enemy and not the Chaldean invader of 1:6; that Hab 2:12-14, 18-20 were also later additions to the book; and that Hab 3:2-19 was probably a postexilic psalm. Another influential contribution from this period was F. Giesebrecht's proposal (1890) that Hab 1:5-11, which mentions the Chaldeans, interrupts Habakkuk's complaint and so in its present context is apparently misplaced. He proposed that the verses be restored to their original place before Hab 1:1, where

they had been set during the exile as an introduction to the book. In addition, Giesebrecht regarded Hab 2:12-17, 20, and chap. 3 as secondary expansions. Although J. WELLHAUSEN (1892) and W. NOWACK (1922) agreed with Giesebrecht's conclusions about Habakkuk 2–3, they dated the book as a whole to the preexilic period. Moreover, Wellhausen (1898[3]) later argued that chap. 3 was the community's prayer for God to act again as at the exodus and that the proper close for the poem has been lost, since vv. 17-19 cannot be genuine.

In response to the fragmenting effects of source analysis on the interpretation of Habakkuk, K. BUDDE (1893) maintained that Habakkuk 1–2 was a literary unity. Since Hab 1:5-11 interrupted the continuous complaint of 1:2-4, 12-17, however, the former should be read as God's answer to the prophet's complaint and relocated after 2:4, before the woe sayings that begin in 2:5. Therefore, the foreign oppressor, Assyria, would be conquered by another, Chaldea. This view was accepted by C. CORNILL (*Einleitung in das AT* [1898]) and G. A. SMITH (*The Book of the Twelve Prophets* [1896–98]), although Smith regarded the first oppressor as Egypt. O. Happel (1900) also viewed Habakkuk as a literary unity and believed that it portrayed the eschatological messianic age in terms of the Seleucid persecutions of the Jews. W. Betteridge (1903) followed Budde's suggestion that the Chaldeans were the punishers of Assyria but accepted the canonical ordering of the text and dated Habakkuk to c. 700 BCE.

In 1894 W. Rothstein proposed an interpretation that would find final acceptance in some form among a number of later scholars. He believed that the core of Habakkuk was an older prophecy referring to the godless in Judah that was reworked later to refer to Babylon. M. Lauterburg's proposal (1896) that the reference to "Chaldeans" in 1:6 was a scribal correction or insertion and that 1:5-11 originally referred to the Persians led him to assign an exilic or postexilic date to the book and signaled the importance that the reference to the Chaldeans in 1:6 would play for subsequent research. K. MARTI (1904), instead of reckoning with later supplementations as Rothstein had, believed that the book was composed from various independent fragments of tradition from the preexilic, exilic, and postexilic periods. Only the "Chaldea-oracle" (1:5-10, 14-15) could be traced back with confidence to the prophet.

B. DUHM (1906) responded to the extreme views of Marti and other source critics by suggesting that "Chaldeans" (Hab 1:6) be emended to "Kittim" and that the latter be interpreted with reference to the Greeks and the book thus dated to the reign of Alexander the Great (333–331 BCE). Independent of Duhm's influence, C. C. TORREY (1935) reached similar conclusions, adding that "wine" in 2:5 be emended to "Javan" (Gr.); he believed that the entire work was a "meditation" on the conquests of Alexander the Great. While Duhm and Torrey won few converts to their view, they demonstrated the critical role of Hab 1:6 for assessing the historical setting of the entire book.

In 1911 two other works appeared that produced distinctive source-critical interpretations. Continuing the work of his 1909 Oxford dissertation, G. Stonehouse dated Habakkuk to the time of the Chaldean invasion of Syria-Palestine in 604/3 but held that chap. 3 was the prophet's reworking of an earlier composition. P. Riessler, on the other hand, proposed that Habakkuk was little more than a collection of various pre- and postexilic prophecies.

Form-critical and cult-functional analyses of Habakkuk became dominant in the twentieth century. H. GUNKEL (1895) had described the mythical function (see MYTHOLOGY AND BIBLICAL STUDIES 1800–1980) of the themes in Habakkuk 3, comparing the chapter with the Babylonian creation stories and associating it with religious ritual. Among the first to suggest that there was a liturgical redaction of Habakkuk was F. Kelly (1902); and in 1911, H. Thackeray, working from the Barberini Greek version of Habakkuk 3, found a liturgical function for this part of Habakkuk. On the basis of the late dating of Habakkuk and its literary unity, S. MOWINCKEL (1923), as well as E. Balla (1928), E. SELLIN (1929[2], 1930[3]), P. HUMBERT (1944), and others came to regard the book as a cult-prophetic liturgy. Mowinckel regarded it as the prophetical part of an actual Temple liturgy and eventually (1953) came to associate it with the autumnal new year's festival. W. CASPARI (1914) suggested that the entire book was liturgical; F. Stephens (1924) pointed out parallels between Habakkuk 3 and the Babylonian creation stories; and U. CASSUTO (1935–37) saw a Ugaritic origin for the mythical elements in chap. 3 (see also W. Irwin [1942]). P. Humbert (1944) concluded that the book was composed for a day of repentance and condemned the actions of Jehoiakim's supporters (1:2-4, 13; 2:4-5). Finally, J. JEREMIAS (1970) argued that Habakkuk was a cult prophet whose various sermons were edited in the late exilic period for an anti-Babylonian liturgy.

Scholars continue to debate the book's literary unity, historical setting, genre, and manner of origin as well as its and the prophet's relation to the cult and the nature of the commentary on the book found at Qumran. Many writers view the book as a literary unity (e.g., the rhetorical investigation of the book by D. Bratcher [1984]; an exploration of the form-critical aspects of the book by M. Sweeney [1991]; and commentaries by M. Roberts [1991] and R. Haak [1991]); and while they differ over the identification of its genre, they tend to agree that it has little direct connection with the cult. Sweeney calls the book a "prophetic affirmation of divine sovereignty and justice" and believes that it was intended to persuade Judah in the late seventh century that God's elevation of the Neo-Babylonian empire to power contradicts neither God's nature nor the divine promises to the people. Roberts also dates Habakkuk's speeches—which he sees as oral compositions—to this period, although he assigns Hab 1:11-17 and 2:6-19 to the period after 597 BCE. Either the prophet, whose relation to the cult is unclear, or a later editor arranged these oral compositions into a connected meditation about theodicy, in some instances redirecting them (e.g., woe speeches originally uttered against a Judean oppressor like Jehoiakim now address Babylon). Although Haak also doubts the cultic or legal setting of the book, he believes that it was from the first a written—rather than oral—composition. The prophet supported the deposed king Jehoahaz and was pro-Babylonian; but since his early declarations in Babylon's favor had not been fulfilled, he wrote these to confirm them. He did not survive Babylon's assault on Jerusalem; and his prophecies were carried to Babylon, where they were revised with an anti-Babylonian slant. The genre of the book is that of a complaint.

Finally, investigations of Habakkuk 3 typically seek its origin in an archaic hymn (T. Hiebert [1986]; Roberts [1991]). The most elaborate and imaginative expression of this view is in Hiebert's 1984 Harvard dissertation (1986), which concludes that the chapter was a single literary unit in the form of a victory song for Yahweh and was structured according to the mythological scheme found in the Baal cycle at UGARIT and the Accadian *Enuma Elish*. The chapter derived from the pre-monarchic period, had a cultic setting, and was associated with the southern sanctuary at Kuntillet 'Ajrud. In the postexilic period the chapter was attached to Habakkuk and was reinterpreted—perhaps by those who edited Isaiah and Zechariah—with reference to God's future actions as a cosmic divine warrior.

Bibliography: E. Balla, "Habakuk," *RGG*[2] (1928) 1556-557. A. J. Baumgartner, *Le prophète Habakuk: Introduction, critique et exégèse, avec examen spécial des commentaires rabbiniques du Talmud et de la tradition* (1885). W. R. Betteridge, "The Interpretation of the Prophecy of Habakkuk," *AJT* 7 (1903) 647-61. D. R. Bratcher, "The Theological Message of Habakkuk: A Literary-Rhetorical Analysis" (diss., Union Theological Seminary, Richmond, 1984). W. H. Brownlee, *The Midrash Pesher of Habakkuk* (SBLMS 24, 1979). K. Budde, "Die Bücher Habakkuk und Sephanja," *TSK* 66 (1893) 383-93; "Habakkuk," *EncBib* (1901) 1921-28. W. Caspari, *Die israelitischen Propheten* (1914). U. Cassuto, "Il capitolo 3 di Habaquq e i testi di Ras Shamra," *AStE* (1935–37) 7-22. S. Coleman, "The Dialogue of Habakkuk in Rabbinic Doctrine," *Abr-nahrain* 5 (1964–65) 57-85. E. Cothenet, "Habacuc," *DBSup* 8 (1972) 791-811. B. Duhm, *Das Buch Habakuk* (1906). K. Elliger, *Studien zum Habakuk-Kommentar vom Toten Meer* (BHT 15, 1953). M. Eszenyei Széles, *Wrath and*

Mercy: A Commentary on the Books of Habakkuk and Zephaniah (1987). **J. A. Fitzmyer,** "Habakkuk 2:3-4 and the NT," *De la Tôrah au Messie* (ed. M. Carrez et al., 1981) 447-55 = his *To Advance the Gospel* (1981) 236-46. **F. Giesebrecht,** *Beiträge zur Jesaiakritik: Nebst einer Studie über prophetische Schriftstellerei* (1890). **M. J. de Goeje,** "Beoordeling van: *Der Prophet Habakuk* von J. de Gumpach," *Nieuwe Jaarboeken voor wetenshappelijke Theologie* 4 (1861) 304-19. **D. E. Gowan,** "The Triumph of Faith," *Habakkuk* (1976). **J. von Gumpach,** *Der Prophet Habakuk* (1860). **H. Gunkel,** *Schöpfung und Chaos in Urzeit und Endzeit* (1895). **R. D. Haak,** *Habakkuk* (VTSup 44, 1991). **O. Happel,** *Das Buch des Propheten Habackuk* (1900). **T. Hiebert,** *God of My Victory: The Ancient Hymn in Habakkuk 3* (HSM 38, 1986); "Habakkuk," *NIB* (1996) 7:619-55. **P. Humbert,** *Problèmes du livre d'Habacuc* (MUN 18, 1944). **W. A. Irwin,** "The Psalm of Habakkuk," *JNES* 1 (1942) 10-40; "The Mythological Background of Habakkuk, Chapter 3," JNES 15 (1956) 47-50. **J. Jeremias,** *Kultprophetie und Gerichtsverkündigung in der späten Königszeit Israels* (WMANT 35, 1970). **P. Jöcken,** *Das Buch Habakuk: Darstellung der Geschichte seiner kritischen Erforschung mit einer eigenen Beurteilung* (BBB 48, 1977). **F. T. Kelly,** "The Strophic Structure of Habakkuk," *AJSL* 18 (1902) 94-119. **M. Lauterburg,** "Habakuk," *Theologische Zeitschrift aus der Schweiz* 13 (1896) 74-102. **K. Marti,** *Das Dodekapropheton* (KHC, 1904). **S. Mowinckel,** *Psalmenstudien III* (1923); "Zum Psalm des Habakuk," *TZ* 9 (1953) 1-23. **W. Nowack,** *Die kleinen Propheten* (HKAT, 1922³). **P. Riessler,** *Die kleinen Propheten oder das Zwölfprophetenbuch* (1911). **J. J. M. Roberts,** *Nahum, Habakkuk, and Zephaniah: A Commentary* (OTL, 1991). **E. F. K. Rosenmüller,** *Scholia in VT, Pars VII* (1827²). **J. W. Rothstein,** "Über Habakkuk Kap. 1 und 2," *TSK* 67 (1894) 51-85. **J. A. Sanders,** "Habakkuk in Qumran, Paul, and the OT," *JR* 38 (1959) 232-44. **J. E. Sanderson,** *The Woman's Bible Commentary* (ed. C. A. Newsom and S. H. Ringe, 1992) 222-24. **E. Sellin,** *Das Zwölfprophetenbuch* (KAT 12, 1929², 1930³). **B. Stade,** "Miscellen. 3. Habakuk," *ZAW* 4 (1884) 154-59. **W. Staerk,** "Zu Habakuk 1,5-11: Geschichte oder Mythos?" *ZAW* 51 (1933) 1-29. **F. J. Stephens,** "The Babylonian Dragon Myth in Habakkuk 3," *JBL* 43 (1924) 290-93. **G. G. V. Stonehouse,** *The Book of Habakkuk* (1911). **A. Strobel,** *Untersuchungen zum eschatologischen Verzögerungsproblem auf Grund der spätjüdisch-urchristlichen Geschichte von Habakuk 2,2ff.* (SNT 2, 1961); "Habakuk," *RAC* 13 (1986) 203-26. **M. A. Sweeney,** "Structure, Genre, and Intent in the Book of Habakkuk," *VT* 41 (1991) 63-83. **H. S. J. Thackeray,** "Primitive Lectionary Notes in the Psalm of Habakkuk," *JTS* 12 (1911) 191-213. **C. C. Torrey,** "The Prophecy of Habakkuk," *Jewish Studies in Memory of G. A. Kohut* (1935) 565-82. **A. van der Wal,** *Nahum, Habakkuk: A Classified Bibliography* (Applicatio 6, 1988). **J. Wellhausen,** *Skizzen und Vorarbeiten* 5 (1892); *Die kleinen Propheten* (1898³). **J. Ziegler,** "Ochs und Esel in der Krippe: Biblisch-patristische Erwägungen zu Jes 1, 3 und Hab 3, 2 (LXX)," *MThZ* 3 (1952) 385-402.

M. P. Graham

HAGGAI, BOOK OF

1. Early Jewish and Christian Interpretation. Haggai is the first of three postexilic books in the Book of the Twelve, or the Minor Prophets. Early interpreters of this book appear to focus on the person of Haggai rather than on the content of the book. Ancient traditions (Pseudepiphanus, Dorotheus, Epiphanus) portray him coming to Israel as a youth from Babylon and at his death being buried with priestly honors near the priests. Pseudepiphanus believed that Haggai saw the Solomonic Temple, and Hesychius added that the prophet was of the tribe of Levi. The LXX (see SEPTUAGINT), Itala, VULGATE, and PESHITTA support these traditions by carrying the name of Haggai in the superscription to several psalms. A few rabbis believed that Haggai and Malachi were the same person, the former called *ml'k yhwh* and the latter called *ml'ky.* JEROME, however, went the farthest by citing the tradition that Haggai, Malachi, and John the Baptist were not real people but angels appearing in human form.

2. Medieval and Reformation Periods. Medieval Jewish exegetes connected Haggai with the Great Synagogue, either as a member (Rashi, I. Abravanel; J. G. Carpzov held a similar view in the 18th cent.) or as the one who assisted in handing down the tradition to the members (*Aboth 1:1,* Krakau [1662]; A. Hallevi ben David; D. Gans). In the medieval-Reformation period there was also discussion of the specific Darius (I or II) during whose reign Haggai prophesied. J. SCALIGER, J. Tarnovius (1586–1629), J. Piscator (1546–1625), and A. Strauchius (1632–82) argued for Darius II, while the majority proposed Darius I (Calvin, L. Cappel, D. Petavius; so too already Josephus, Jerome, Theodore of Mopsuestsia, and Theodoret). This debate raged as late as the seventeenth century, when H. WITSIUS set out the grounds for both sides without coming to a firm decision.

3. Enlightenment. In accordance with their disdain for material dealing with cult and priestly matters, scholars of the Enlightenment were almost uniformly negative in their assessment of Haggai. J. G. EICHHORN, for example, held that the style was affected and that the writer made the kind of mistakes to be expected of someone playing with a dead language. L. Bertholdt (1774–1822), J. Jahn (1750–1816), W. DE WETTE, and C. KEIL also spoke negatively of Haggai's style. In addition, Eichhorn believed that only summaries of Haggai's oracles are extant in the present book. Bertholdt disagreed, maintaining that the oracles are too well-rounded to be mere summaries. He proposed instead that there remains at least a historical kernel to the oracles, which were reworked when put in written form. It was de Wette, however, who made the strongest negative assessment, writing that Haggai—without enthusiasm—reprimanded, exhorted, and promised in accordance with vulgar conceptions of retaliation and chauvinism, and that he displayed an unprophetical zeal for the establishment of the ancient cult (see A. Köhler [1860] 26).

During the Enlightenment scholars for the first time challenged the traditional view that Haggai came from Babylon. In contrast to Franz DELITZSCH, who held to the traditional view, H. EWALD (1868) and Keil (1888) both maintained that Haggai was born in the land of Israel and thus was never one of the exiles.

4. Critical Scholarship. With the development of historical criticism there was a shift in the scholarly attitude toward Haggai. Köhler (1835–97), who wrote the first major commentary on Haggai (1860), rehabilitated the prophet, differentiating between the older prophets' poetical style and Haggai's rhetorical mode. He pointed out that very little can be known about the person of the prophet, although he believed that Haggai did not return from Babylon as a youth. In addition, he held a positive view of Haggai's work and argued against de Wette that the prophet's oracles must have had some spirit and power because they accomplished his goal: His hearers agreed with him.

Since Köhler's time, the major critical issues in Haggai studies have been LITERARY and redactional in nature (see REDACTION CRITICISM). Literary critical study has focused particularly on the problems of 2:10-19. Köhler was one of the first to note that vv. 15-19 do not seem logically to follow 2:10-14. Later E. SELLIN (1900–1901) argued that 1:15a was the date formula for a lost oracle. J. Rothstein (1908) put the two ideas together, theorizing that 2:15-19 was the lost oracle. He has been followed with some adaptations by the majority of scholars (e.g., H. Mitchell [1912]; F. Horst [1938]; K. Elliger [1967]). It is only more recently that Rothstein's hypothesis has been questioned by K. Koch (1967). While Koch's proposal of a shared threefold structure between the oracles in 1:2-8; 2:3-7; and 2:10-19 is gaining ground (see B. Childs [1979], D. Petersen [1984]), many scholars still hold the older view (H. W. Wolff [1988]; R. Mason [1977b]; C. Stuhlmueller [1988]).

Redactional discussions have revolved around the narrated discourse in Haggai, with W. Beuken (1967; see also P. Ackroyd [1951, 1952a]) doing the definitive work. On the basis of style, vocabulary, and theological perspective, Beuken isolated a systematic chronistic redaction. However, Mason has challenged Beuken's view, positing instead a redaction closer to the time of the oracles themselves. O. Plöger (1968) and P. Hanson (1975) have dealt with this question differently, distinguishing between "theocratic" and "apocalyptic" groups at work in early postexilic times and maintaining that the theocratic group, which was concerned with re-establishing a priestly power base, edited Haggai. This view, which contrasts the theocratic group adversely with the apocalyptic group, returns to a more negative view of the book, albeit from a new perspective.

Another related issue in recent scholarship is the amount and character of the redaction the book received. Whereas Beuken and Wolff view the original text as a group of short oracles that were bound together by an editor, O. Steck (1971), A. van der Woude (1988), and H. G. Reventlow (1993) see the original text as a group of longer discourses from the hand of the prophet set within a narrative editorial framework. M. Floyd (1995) has taken the debate a step further, arguing that the narrative introductions to Haggai's speeches are not to be seen as the work of a redactor(s). Rather, he argues that the narrative framework is integral to the work as a whole, acting to blur the boundaries between the narrator's and the prophet's voices.

C. Meyers and E. Meyers (1987) argue that "Haggai and the first eight chapters of the canonical book of Zechariah belong together as a composite work" (xliv; see also Klostermann [1896]). D. Petersen (1984) offers a form-critical study (see FORM CRITICISM) using Lohfink's rubric *historische Kurzgeschichte* to classify the book as "brief apologetic historical narrative" (35). J. Tollington's study (1993) discusses the ways in which Haggai continues in and modifies the tradition of classical prophecy. Among her more provocative conclusions are that Haggai's use of Amos "suggests . . . that the practice of direct 'borrowing' or quoting was beginning to be developed" at the time of Haggai (215) and that previous works were beginning to be seen in much the same way that Scripture is viewed today (202). Finally, W. March's commentary in the *NIB* (1996) is a well-balanced and accessible scholarly and theological work, useful for those in academia and those in the parish alike. As these works reveal, the study of Haggai is branching out in different directions; there is a much more positive view of the prophet and his work than that held by pre-critical scholars.

Bibliography: **P. R. Ackroyd,** "Studies in the Book of Haggai," *JJS* 2 (1951) 163-76; "Studies in the Book of Haggai," *JJS* 3 (1952a) 1-13; "The Book of Haggai and Zechariah 1–8," *JJS* 3 (1952b) 151-56; "Some Interpretive Glosses in the Book of Haggai," *JJS* 7 (1956) 163-67; "Two OT Historical Problems of the Early Persian Period," *JNES* 17 (1958) 13-27; "Haggai," *PCB* (ed. M. Black, 1962) 643-45; *Exile and Restoration: A Study of Hebrew Thought of the Sixth Century BC* (OTL, 1968) 153-70. **R. Bach,** "Haggai, Haggaibuch," *RGG³,* 24-26. **J. G. Baldwin,** *Haggai, Zechariah, Malachi* (TOTC, 1972). **J. Begrich,** "Die Priesterliche Tora," *Werden und Wesen des Alten Testaments* (BZAW 66, 1936) 63-68. **L. Bertholdt,** *Historisch-kritische Einleitung in sammtliche kanonische und apokryphische Schriften des alten und neuen Testaments* (6 vols., 1812–19). **W. A. M. Beuken,** *Haggai–Secharja 1–8* (SSNID, 1967). **K.-M. Beyse,** *Serubbabel und die Königserwartungen der Propeten Haggai und Sacharja: Ein historische und traditionsgeschictliche Untersuchung* (AT 1, 48, 1972). **E. J. Bickerman,** "En Marge de L'Écriture," *RB* 88 (1981) 19-41. **J.**

Blenkinsopp, *A History of Prophecy in Israel* (1983). **P. F. Bloomhardt,** "The Poems of Haggai," *HUCA* 5 (1928) 153-95. **K. Budde,** "Zum Text der Drei Letzten Kleinen Propheten," *ZAW* 26 (1906) 1-28 (7-17). **T. Chary,** *Aggée–Zacharie–Malachie* (SB, 1969); "Le Culte Chez les Prophètes Aggée et Zacharie," *Les Prophétes et le Culte a Partir de l'exil* (BdT 3, 1955) 119-59. **B. S. Childs,** *Introduction to the OT as Scripture* (1979). **R. J. Coggins,** *Haggai, Zechariah, Malachi* (OTGu, 1987). **A. Deissler,** "Aggée," *DBS* 8, 701-6; *Zwölf Propheten III: Zefanjia, Haggai, Sacharja, Maleachi* (Die Neue Echter Bibel 21, 1988). **B. Duhm,** "Anmerkungen zu den zwölf Propheten," *ZAW* 31 (1911) 1-43, 81-110, 161-204. **J. G. Eichhorn,** *Die Hebraischen Prophten* (3 vols., 1816–19). **K. Elliger,** *Das Buch der zwölf kleinen Propheten,* vol. 2, *Die Propheten Nahum, Habakuk, Zephanja, Haggai, Sacharja, Maleachi* (ATD 25, 1967⁶). **H. Ewald,** *Die Propheten des Alten Bundes* (1868²). **M. H. Floyd,** "The Nature of the Narrative and the Evidence of Redaction in Haggai," *VT* 45 (1995) 470-90. **D. N. Freedman,** "The Chronicler's Purpose," *CBQ* 23 (1961) 436-42. **A. Gelston,** "The Foundations of the Second Temple," *VT* 16 (1966) 232-35. **P. D. Hanson,** *The Dawn of Apocalyptic* (1975) 140ff., 173-78, 240-62. **F. Hesse,** *Verbannung und Heimkehr* (FS W. Rudolph, 1961) 109-34. **D. R. Hildebrand,** "Temple Ritual: A Paradigm for Moral Holiness in Haggai II 10-19," *VT* 39 (1989) 154-68. **F. Horst,** *Die zwölf kleinen Propheten* (HAT 1, 4, 1938). **F. James,** "Thoughts on Haggai and Zechariah," *JBL* 53 (1934) 229-35. **D. R. Jones,** *Haggai, Zechariah, and Malachi: Introduction and Commentary* (TBC, 1962). **C. F. Keil,** *Biblischer Commentar über die zwölf kleinen Propheten* (BCAT 3, 4, 1888³). **A. Klostermann,** *Geschichte des Volkes Israel bis zur Restauration unter Esra und Nehemiah* (1896). **K. Koch,** "Haggais unreines Volk," *ZAW* 79 (1967) 52-66. **A. Köhler,** "Die Weissagungen Haggai's," *Die nachexilischen Propheten* (1860). **W. E. March,** "Haggai," *NIB* (1996) 7:706-32. **R. A. Mason,** *The Books of Haggai, Zechariah, and Malachi* (CBC, 1977a); "The Purpose of the 'Editorial Framework' of the Book of Haggai," *VT* 27 (1977b) 413-21. **H. G. May,** " 'This People' and 'This Nation' in Haggai," *VT* 18 (1968) 190-97. **H. G. Mitchell,** *Haggai, Zechariah, Malachi, and Jonah* (ICC, 1912). **A. Moenikes,** "Messianismus im Alten Testament (vor-apokaliptische Zeit)," *ZRGG* 40 (1988) 289-306. **E. M. Meyers,** "The Use of Tora in Haggai 2:11 and the Role of the Prophet in the Restoration Community," *The Word of the Lord Shall Go Forth* (FS D. N. Freedman, 1983) 69-76. **F. S. North,** "Critical Analysis of the Book of Haggai," *ZAW* 68 (1956) 25-46. **D. L. Petersen,** "Zerubbabel and Jerusalem Temple Reconstruction," *CBQ* 36 (1974) 366-72; *Haggai and Zechariah 1–8* (OTL, 1984). **O. Plöger,** *Theocracy and Eschatology* (1968). **O. Procksch,** *Die kleinen prophetischen Schriften nach dem Exil* (EzAT 3, 1916). **P. L. Redditt,** *Haggai, Zechariah, Malachi* (NCBC, 1995). **H. G. Reventlow,** *Die Propheten Haggai, Sacharja, und Maleachi* (ATD, 1993). **J. W. Rothstein,** *Juden und Samaritaner: Die grundlegende Scheidung von Judentum und Heidentum. Eine kritische Studie zum Buche Haggai und zur jüdischen Geschichte im ersten nachexilischen Jahrhundert* (BWANT 3, 1908). **W. Rudolph,** *Haggai, Sacharja 1–8, Sacharja 9–14, Maleachi* (KAT 13, 4, 1976). **G. Sauer,** "Serubbabel in der Sicht Haggais und Secharjas," *Das ferne und nahe Wort* (FS L. Rost, BZAW 105, 1967) 199-207. **K.-D. Schunk,** "Die Attribute des eschatologischen Messias: Strukturlinien in der Ausprägung des alttestamentlichen Messiasbildes," *TLZ* 111 (1986) 642-51. **E. Sellin,** *Studien zur entstehungsgeschichte der jüdischen Gemeinde nach dem babylonischen Exil* (1900–1901). **K. Seybold,** "Die Königserwartung bei den Propheten Haggai und Sacharja," *Jud* 28 (1972) 69-78. **R. T. Siebeck,** "The Messianism of Aggaeus and Proto-Zacharias," *CBQ* 19 (1957) 312-28. **O. H. Steck,** "Zu Haggai 1:2-11," *ZAW* 83 (1971) 3:35-79. **C. Stuhlmueller,** "Haggai, Zechariah, Malachi," *JBC* (ed. J. A. Fitzmyer, R. E. Brown, and R. E. Murphy, 1968) 387-401; *Rebuilding with Hope: A Commentary on the Books of Haggai and Zechariah* (ITC, 1988). **J. E. Tollington,** *Tradition and Innovation in Haggai and Zechariah 1–8* (JSOTSup 150, 1993). **T. N. Townsend,** "Additional Comments on Haggai II, 10-19," *VT* 18 (1968) 559-60. **A. S. van der Woude,** "Serubbabel und die Messianischen Erwartungen des Propheten Sacharja," *ZAW* 100 (Supp., 1988) 138-56. **A. van Hoonacker,** *Les Douze Petits Prophètes* (ÉB, 1908). **J. Wellhausen,** *Die kleinen Propheten übersetzt und erklärt* (1898³ = 1963⁴). **J. W. Whedbee,** "A Question-Answer Schema in Haggai 1: The Form and Function of Haggai 1:9-11," *Biblical and Near Eastern Studies: Festschrift in Honor of W. S. LaSor* (ed. G. A. Tuttle, 1978) 184-94. **H. Witsius,** *Miscellanea Sacra* 4 (1692). **H. W. Wolff,** *Haggai: A Commentary* (tr. M. Kohl, 1988).

M. E. Shields

HAMMOND, HENRY (1605–60)

Born at Chertsey, Aug. 18, 1605, H. was educated at Eton and at Magdalen College, Oxford, of which he was elected a fellow in 1625. He became rector of Penshurst, Kent, in 1633 and was made archdeacon of Chichester in 1643. He was also appointed to the Westminster Assembly of Divines; but his nomination was revoked, probably because of his support for a royalist uprising. In 1645 he became a canon of Christ Church, Oxford, and in 1647 was a chaplain in attendance on Charles I when the king was in custody. After the capture of Oxford the forces of Parliament held H. prisoner in that city, and he was deprived of his canonry. He was later released and in 1651 supported Charles II in his unsuccessful attempt to regain power. Thereafter H. lived in seclusion and devoted himself to writing. At the restoration of the monarchy he was chosen to be bishop of Worcester but died April 25, 1660, before the choice could be implemented.

H. is known as "the father of English biblical criticism." His claim to that title rests on his paraphrases and notes on the NT (1653), the psalms (1659), and the first ten chapters of Proverbs (pub. 1683). These works contained the text of the AV, together with H.'s paraphrase of passages he believed to need explanation and detailed notes. Opposed to preachers and prophets who claimed to interpret the Scriptures through direct divine revelation, he outlined scholarly principles of interpretation and was strongly influenced by H. GROTIUS's work on the Scriptures. Like Grotius he gave a preterist interpretation of the book of Revelation and often preferred the text of Codex Alexandrinus to the *textus receptus*. An important feature of H.'s work is his contention that the book of Revelation and all the NT epistles except Philemon were directed against Gnosticism (see GNOSTIC INTERPRETATION), which he believed to have its origin in Simon Magus and to be a form of enthusiasm. He argued that the Gnostics, many of whom did not keep the Jewish law, allied themselves with Judaizing Christians in demanding that others should keep it. His work on the NT went through several editions in the seventeenth, eighteenth, and nineteenth centuries. It was frequently mentioned in M. POOLE's *Synopsis Criticorum* and had a considerable influence on subsequent commentators; it also led H. into controversy with the Puritan theologian J. OWEN. J. LE CLERC, who was highly critical of some of its interpretations, translated it into Latin.

H. assisted B. Walton (c. 1600–61) in the preparation of his POLYGLOT Bible. He also defended the genuineness of the seven Ignatian epistles. He was a powerful apologist for the episcopacy and the prayer book and defended the legitimacy of the Church of England's separation from Rome. A belief in the lordship of Christ, he claimed, was the fundamental Christian doctrine; and on it were built the superstructures of the traditional creeds. H. affirmed the ability of reason to make judgments about moral issues and natural objects, though not about divine revelation. He argued that the Christian religion was in accordance with reason and that its truth was attested by divine utterances about Christ during his earthly life and also by the operation of the Spirit through the NT and early patristic writers.

Works: *A Practical Catechism* (1644); *Of the Reasonableness of Christian Religion* (1650); *A Paraphrase and Annotations upon all the Books of the NT* (1653); *Of Fundamentals, Schisme, and Heresie* (1654); *A Paraphrase and Annotations upon the Books of the Psalms* (1659); *Works* (4 vols., 1674–84; repr. 1847–50 with Fell's biography); *A Paraphrase and Annotations on the Ten First Chapters of the Proverbs* (1683); *Novum Testamentum . . . cum Paraphrasi et Annotationibus* (2 vols., tr. with notes by J. Le Clerc, 1698–99).

Bibliography: *BB* 4 (1757) 2520-26. **J. Fell,** *The Life of the Most Learned, Reverend, and Pious Dr. H. H.* (1661). **T. Fuller,** *History of the Worthies of England* 3 (new ed. 1840, repr. 1965) 215-16. **J. B. Hibbits,** *Hammond as Pastor, Preacher, and Expositor of the Psalms* (1962). **R. Hooper,** *DNB* 24 (1890) 242-46. **J. Le Clerc,** *A Supplement to Dr. Hammond's Paraphrase and Annotations on the NT* (1699). **J. W. Packer,** *The Transformation of Anglicanism 1643–60 with Special Reference to H. H.*
(1969). **A. à Wood,** *Athenae Oxonienses* 3 (new ed. 1817) 493-99.

A. W. WAINWRIGHT

HARDT, HERMANN VON DER (1660–1746)

Born Sept. 15, 1660, in Melle (Osnabrück), H. pursued oriental and Hebrew studies at the University of Jena, studied the TALMUD in Hamburg, completed his masters degree in Jena (1683), and maintained contacts with A. FRANCKE and P. J. SPENER (member of the *collegium philobiblicum*). In 1690 he became full professor of oriental languages in Helmstedt and in 1702 provost of the Marienburg convent. He died Feb. 28, 1746, in Helmstedt.

H.'s primary focus was oriental philology. He produced Hebrew and Chaldean (Aramaic)-Syriac grammars that enjoyed great respect in his time, and his competence in Talmudic studies was both significant and respected. While many of his more fantastic theories, like the argument that all Semitic languages derived from Greek, elicited mockery, some of his proposals, e.g., that Jeremiah was not the author of the book of Lamentations and that the prophets (see PROPHECY AND PROPHETS, HB) wrote in verse, were later widely advocated. H. acquired a certain reputation as an exegete, although as a biblical scholar who turned away from scholarly PIETISM and toward rationalism he encountered resistance from the governing body of his university and was forced into retirement in 1727.

Works: *De fructu, quem ex libroum Judaicorum lectione percipiunt Christiani* (1683); *Autographa Lutheri aliorumque celebrium virorum. . . .* (3 vols., 1690–93); *Brevia atque solidas syriacae linguae fundamenta* (1693, 1701); *Elementa Chaldaica* (1693); *Ephemerides philologicae* (1693); *Brevia atque solida Hebraeae linguae fundamenta* (1694); *Magnum oecumenicum Constantiense concilium* (6 vols., 1697–1700; index vol. 7, 1742); *Hoseas illustratus Chaldaica Jonathanis . . . Raschi, Aben Esrae et Kimchi* (1702); *Tres primae Joelis elegiae sacrae* (1706); *Commentarii linguae Hebraeae et Graecia Apologia* (1727).

Bibliography: *ADB* 10 (1879) 595-96. **L. Diestel,** *Geschichte des AT in der christlichen Kirche* (1869). **F. Lamy,** *Hermann von der Hardt* (1891). **A. Tholuck,** *Akademisches Leben des 17. Jahrhunderts* 2 (1854) 49-61. **P. Tschackert,** *RE*[3] 7 (1889) 417-20.

B. SEIDEL

HARNACK, KARL GUSTAV ADOLF VON (1851–1930)

H. was born May 7, 1851, in Dorpat, where his father, Theodosius (1817–89), was professor of theology. Beginning his study at Dorpat, H. was strongly influenced by the work of A. RITSCHL, then at Göttingen, a student of F. C. BAUR, who would depart from the Tübingen school. In 1872 H. went to the university at Leipzig, where he wrote a dissertation and *Habilitationsschrift* on the history of Gnosticism (see GNOSTIC INTERPRETATION). He became a *Dozent* at Leipzig in 1874 and *ausserordentlicher* professor in 1876, and he commenced a seminar on church history that continued until his death. F. Loofs (1858–1928) and E. SCHÜRER participated in the seminar. In 1879 H. was made full professor at Giessen, where H. GUNKEL was his student; and in 1881 he became editor of *TLZ*, founded by Schürer, who had come to Giessen in 1878. With O. von Gebhardt (1844–1906), H. founded the series *Texte und Untersuchungen zur Geschichte der altchristlichen Literatur* in 1882. He published the first two volumes of his *Lehrbuch der Dogmengeschichte* in 1886 and took a chair at Marburg the same year. In 1888 as he completed the third volume of *Dogmengeschichte,* he took a chair at Berlin despite conservative resistance to his appointment.

Sixteen public lectures delivered in 1899–1900 with Kaiser Wilhelm in attendance were published as *Das Wesen des Christentums* (1900) and were widely circulated (ET, *What Is Christianity?*). H. became president of the Lutheran Social Congress (1903–11), director of the Prussian Staatsbibliothek (1905–21), and president of the new Kaiser Wilhelm Gesellschaft (1911). Because of his increased duties K. Holl (1866–1926), a former student, was added to the faculty at Berlin in 1906, A. DEISSMANN in 1908, and M. DIBELIUS as *Dozent* in 1910. Other students included both K. BARTH and D. BONHOEFFER; but those who carried on H.'s work most closely included A. JÜLICHER, E. von DOBSCHÜTZ, H. von Soden (1881–1945), and Holl, together with the other leading Ritschlians at Berlin, E. TROELTSCH and W. DILTHEY. In 1924 H. retired from his chair at Berlin, succeeded by H. LIETZMANN. He died June 10, 1930, in Heidelberg.

H.'s vast output, especially in studies of patristic literature and the development of dogma, was dependent on Ritschl's view of early Catholicism, conceived as a corrective to that of the Tübingen school. Following Ritschl, H. rejected the notion of a dialectical tension between Peter and PAUL since such particularizing of their message vitiates both. Catholicism involved the development of dogma through the effect of Greek thought on the soil of the gospel, but neither JESUS nor Paul was influenced by Greek thought. The essence of Christianity remained constant throughout the ages despite the development of dogma. In sharp contrast to the emerging RELIGIONSGESCHICHTLICHE SCHULE, H. argued that the message of Jesus, understood rightly by Paul, remained almost totally isolated from the social and institutional forms through which it found expression in history. The study of history, like the progress of history itself, thus becomes a process of sifting for those elements that preserve the true core, while viewing all else as temporal and impermanent. For H. even MARCION, as a seeker of the truth of the gospel, was a heroic figure; and the Protestant Reformation was a new beginning.

This perspective led H. to a reevaluation of the historical place of many of the NT books. Whereas he had earlier followed Baur's second-century dating of Acts, by the time of his *Beiträge zur Einleitung in das Neue Testament* (4 vols., 1906–11) he concluded that Acts was written by the physician Luke, the companion of Paul, well before 70 CE. His tendency was to date most of the NT writings, including the Gospels and SYNOPTIC sayings source (Q), early and generally all before 70 CE. The Synoptics, therefore, reflect the essence of Christianity as located in the teachings of Jesus about God and the worth of the human soul. In effect, 70 CE marks the beginning of church history and the syncretistic amalgamation with the Greco-Roman world. H.'s *Mission und Ausbreitung des Christentums* (1902, 1906[2], 1924[4]), the first social history of the early church, reflects this view of the preparation of the authentic gospel in the first-century environment and its gradual transformation with the spread of the church in the following centuries.

Works: *Patrum Apostolicorum Opera* (3 vols., 1875–77); *Lehre der zwölf Apostel nebst Untersuchungen zur älteren Geschichte der Kirchenverfassung und des Kirchenrechts* (1884); *History of Dogma* (3 vols., 1886–89, 1890[2], 1894[3], 1909[4]; ET 7 vols., 1894); "Geschichte der Lehre von der Seligkeit allein durch den Glauben in der alten Kirche," *ZTK* 1 (1891) 82-178; *Das apostolische Glaubensbekenntnis* (1892); *Geschichte der altchristlichen Literatur bis Eusebius* (3 vols., 1893–1903); *What Is Christianity?* (1900; ET 1901; reissued with intro. by R. Bultmann, 1950); *Die Aufgabe der theoligischen Facultäten und die allgemeine Religionsgeschichte: Rede zur Gedächtnisfeier des Stifters der Berliner Universität* (1901); *The Mission and Expansion of Christianity in the First Three Centuries* (2 vols., 1902, 1906[2], 1915[3], 1924[4]; ET 2 vols., 1908); *Militia Christi: The Christian Religion and the Military in the First Three Centuries* (1905; ET 1981); *Beiträge zur Einleitung in das Neue Testament* (4 vols., 1906–11), vol. 1, *Lukas der Arzt: Der Verfasser des dritten Evangeliums und der Apostelgeschichte* (1906; ET *Luke the Physician* [1907]); vol. 2, *Die Jesusworten* (1907; ET *The Sayings of Jesus* [1908]); vol. 3, *Die Apostelgeschichte* (1908; ET *The Acts of the Apostles* [1909]); vol. 4, *Neue Untersuchungen zur Apostelgeschichte und zur Abfassungszeit der synoptische Evangelien* (1911; ET *The Date of Acts and the Synoptic Gospels* [1911]); *The Constitution and Law of the Church in the First Two Centuries* (1910; ET 1910); *Marcion: The Gospel of the Alien God* (TU 44, 1921; TU 45, 1924[2]; ET 1990); *Briefsammlung des Apostels Paulus* (1926).

Bibliography: E. Bammel, "Die historische Jesus in der Theologie A. H.s," *JEAT* 12 (1963) 25-38. **W. Dobertin,** *A. H.: Theologie, Pädagoge, Wissenschaftspolitiker* (1985). **G. W.**

Glick, *The Reality of Christianity: A Study of A. H. as Historian and Theologian* (1967). **K. Holl,** *Briefwechsel mit A. H.* (ed. H. Karpp, 1966). **F. W. Kantzenbach,** *TRE* 14 (1985) 450-58. **W. G. Kümmel,** *NTHIP,* 178-84. **E. P. Meijering,** *Theologische Urteil über die Dogmengeschichte: Ritschl's Einfluss auf v. H.* (BZRGG 20, 1978); *Die Hellenisierung des Christentums in Urteil A. H.s* (1985). **J. C. O'Neill,** *The Bible's Authority: A Portrait Gallery of Thinkers from Lessing to Bultmann* (1991) 214-29. **W. Pauck,** *H. and Troeltsch: Two Historical Theologians* (1968). **H. M. Rumscheidt,** *HHMBI,* 491-95. **F. Smend,** *A. H.: Verzeichnis seiner Schriften* (1927, 1931²). **L. M. White,** "A. H. and the 'Expansion' of Early Christianity," *SecCent* 5 (1985–86) 97-127. **A. von Zahn-Harnack,** *Adolf von Harnack* (1936, 1951²).

L. M. WHITE

HARPER, WILLIAM RAINEY (1856–1906)

An OT scholar and founding president of the University of Chicago, H. was born in New Concord, Ohio. He received the BA from Muskingum College at fourteen, was admitted to the Yale PhD program in OT, and after receiving that degree at age eighteen accepted a teaching post at Denison University in 1876. Three years later he taught Semitic languages at Baptist Union Theological Seminary, Morgan Park, Illinois, where he also received the BD. He developed a correspondence course in Hebrew that enrolled over three thousand students. Very active in the Chautauqua movement, he served for some years as president of the college of liberal arts. He also published several books on Hebrew, Greek, and Latin and started two journals: *Hebrew Student* (1882) and *Hebraica* (1884; later named *American Journal of Semitic Languages*). Beginning in 1886 he taught OT at Yale Divinity School, where he became nationally known as a teacher, lecturer, and editor. As founding president of the University of Chicago (1892), he quickly created a major comprehensive research university. He continued teaching full time while serving as president, and because of his interests biblical studies flourished there. In 1905 he served as president of the SOCIETY OF BIBLICAL LITERATURE.

As a scholar H.'s greatest contribution lay in his promotion of the study of Hebrew. The materials he prepared were inductive and sound and were successful from the standpoint of both motivation and insight. Aside from his many handbooks and articles, he published a major commentary on Amos and Hosea in the ICC series (1905). As an exegete he was perspicuous yet meticulous in reference to previous scholarship, text variations, and the available historical and archaeological data (see ARCHAEOLOGY AND BIBLICAL STUDIES). He essentially embraced the documentary view of the Hexateuch and the reconstruction of OT history. H. was adamant in his insistence on a modern critical approach to the Scriptures and on the freedom of the Chicago faculty to teach whatever they judged right and true. The Chicago school emphasized empirical experience, history, and social backgrounds.

Works: *A Critical and Exegetical Commentary on Amos and Hosea* (ICC, 1905, 1929).

Bibliography: **F. Brown,** "President Harper and OT Studies," *AJSL* 22 (1905/6) 177-94; "Introduction," *OT and Semitic Studies in Memory of W. R. H.* (ed. R. F. Harper et al., 1908) 1:xi-xxxiv. **T. W. Goodspeed,** *W. R. H., First President of the University of Chicago* (1928). **J. G. de R. Hamilton,** *DAB* 8 (1932) 286-92. **F. W. Shepardson,** *The Biblical World* (Jan.-June 1906) 162-66. **R. J. Storr,** *Harper's University: The Beginnings. A History of the University of Chicago* (1966). **J. P. Wind,** *The Bible and the University: The Messianic Vision of W. R. H.* (1987).

T. H. OLBRICHT

HARRIS, JAMES RENDEL (1852–1941)

Born in Plymouth, England, Jan. 27, 1852, H. studied with F. HORT at Clare College, Cambridge, where he was elected fellow in 1875, and taught mathematics until 1882. Reared a Congregationalist, he later became a Quaker and taught at several schools, including Johns Hopkins University and Haverford College in the United States (1882–92). However, most of his career was spent at Cambridge (1893–1903), where he was lecturer in palaeography, and as the director of studies at Woodbroke (1903–18), a Quaker institute of learning in Selly Oak, Birmingham. He also served as curator of manuscripts at the John Rylands Library, Manchester (1918–25).

H. made enduring contributions to NT study through his work as a textual critic (see TEXTUAL CRITICISM) and as an editor of Syriac manuscripts. While visiting St. Catherine's Monastery on Mt. Sinai in 1889, he discovered a Syriac version of the *Apology of Aristides,* which remains the most important recension of the text. In 1909 he found the most important manuscript to date of the *Odes of Solomon;* his critical edition remains a standard, and his accompanying commentary was significant for its arguments supporting a late first-century BCE date. H. published the facsimile edition of the Jerusalem Codex of the *Didache,* and he edited a critical edition of the *Diatessaron.* He also proposed that the early church drew up collections of HB texts that it used as "testimonies" in advocating and defending its faith, a view later utilized by C. H. DODD.

Works: *Fragments of Philo Judaeus Newly Edited* (1886); *The Origin of the Leicester Codex* (1887); *The Teachings of the Apostles and Sibylline Books* (1887); *The Diatessaron of Tatian: A Preliminary Study* (1890); *The "Apology of Aristides" on Behalf of the Christians from a Syriac MS Preserved on Mount Sinai* (1891, 1893²); *Codex Bezae: A Study of the*

So-Called Western Text of the NT (1891); *The Codex Sangallensis (Delta): A Study in the Text of the OL Gospels* (1891); *The Origin of the Ferrar Group* (1893); *Stichometry* (1893); *The Four Gospels in Syriac Transcribed from the Sinaitic Palimpsest* (ed. R. L. Bensly, J. R. Harris, and F. C. Burkitt, with an intro. by A. S. Lewis, 1894); *The Annotators of the Codex Bezae* (1901); *An Early Christian Psalter* (1909); *The Odes and Psalms of Solomon Published from the Syriac Version* (1909, 1911²); (with A. Mingana), *The Odes and Psalms of Solomon Re-edited for the Governors of the John Rylands Library,* (2 vols., 1916, 1918); (with V. Burch), *Testimonies* (pt. 1, 1916; pt. 2, 1920); *The Origin of the Prologue to St. John's Gospel* (1917).

Bibliography: J. H. **Charlesworth,** "Odes of Solomon," *OTP* (1985) 1:725-27. C. A. **Phillips,** *ExpTim* 52 (1941) 349-52. H. G. **Wood,** (ed.), *Amicitiae Corolla: A Volume of Essays Presented to J. R. H. on the Occasion of His Eightieth Birthday* (1933); *DNB, 1941–50* (1959) 360-62.

R. B. VINSON

HASIDISM

1. History. In the history of Judaism the term *hasidism* refers to the ethos of the especially pious and saintly; but it has come to be primarily associated with members of a popular mystical movement called "Hasidism," which began in the eighteenth century. Adherents, the "Hasidim," recognize as their founder R. Israel ben Eliezer (c. 1700–60), a charismatic mystic, magician, and peripatetic healer known as the Ba'al Shem Tov (Master of the Good Name), who was employed as a Kabbalist (see KABBALAH) by the Jewish community in Miedzyboz, Poland (see M. Rosman [1996]). The new Hasidim gradually distinguished themselves from older, more ascetic and esoteric hasidim, who continued kabbalistic studies, mystical practices, and customs that had crystallized in the sixteenth century in Safed in Palestine. The distinguishing feature of the new Hasidim was their activist approach and concern for improving the spiritual and material well-being of ordinary Jews.

Initially limited to several provinces in the Ukraine and eastern Galicia, Hasidism spread throughout eastern Europe after the Ba'al Shem Tov's death. Eventually the majority of observant Jews in Poland, as well as substantial communities in Austro-Hungary, became affiliated with Hasidic leadership. Most religious opposition to the movement was concentrated in Lithuania and White Russia, where, nevertheless, important Hasidic communities were also established. By the third generation a unique form of religious-social organization began to emerge that was centered around individual charismatic leaders called "Rebbes" or *Zaddiqim* (Righteous Ones). The term *Hasidim* began to take on the meaning of followers of a particular Rebbe. Rebbes were often succeeded by sons, close relatives, or outstanding disci-

ples; thus dynasties of Hasidic Rebbes were created, which were often identified with the founder's place of residence. Many of these Hasidic courts continued to flourish in eastern Europe until WWII; most of the Hasidim were martyred during the Holocaust. However, after the war those who survived succeeded in reestablishing their courts in the United States, primarily in Brooklyn, and in the State of Israel, mainly in Jerusalem and B'nai Brak.

2. Leading Figures. All Hasidim consider themselves to be followers of the Ba'al Shem Tov and his teachings. The founder of Hasidism, however, presented most of his teachings orally. Only a few of his authentic writings are extant, the most important being a letter to his brother-in-law that describes several mystical experiences and meditative practices. Most of the teachings attributed to the Ba'al Shem Tov are found in the writings of his followers, especially four volumes of homilies composed by his close disciple, R. Jacob Joseph of Polonoye (1710–84; see S. Dresner [1960]). The earliest of these volumes, *Tole dot Ya'aqov Yosef,* marked the first publication of Hasidic teachings. Another important disciple, R. Dov Baer, the *Maggid* (Preacher) of Mezhirich (1704–72), was instrumental in training many of the Hasidic leaders who would spread Hasidism throughout eastern Europe. Dov Baer's teachings were posthumously published in several volumes edited by his disciples. The first of these was *Maggid Devarav le-Ya'aqov* (see R. Schatz Uffenheimer [1993]).

Beginning in the 1770s, a number of important *Zaddiqim* established Hasidic centers. R. Yehiel Mikhel, the *Maggid* of Zlotchov (1726–81), a disciple of the Ba'al Shem Tov, was highly influential in the Brody region of Galicia (see A. J. Heschel [1985]). R. Levi Isaac of Berditchev (1740–1809), a disciple of R. Dov Baer of Mezhirich and author of *Qedushat Levi,* was preeminent in the Ukraine (see Dresner [1994]). R. Shneur Zalman of Liadi (1745–1813) established Hasidism in Lithuania and White Russia and founded the Habad school of Hasidism, whose voluminous literature is preserved by the Lubavitcher Hasidim (see R. Elior [1993]). R. Elimelekh of Lizensk (d. 1787), author of *Noam Elimelekh,* a commentary on the Pentateuch (see PENTATEUCHAL CRITICISM), flourished in Galicia. His disciple, R. Jacob Isaac Horowitz, "the Seer of Lublin" (1745–1815), was spiritual master of most of the Rebbes who founded major Hasidic centers in Poland during the nineteenth century (see Elior [1988]). Among the hundreds of later Polish masters, R. Judah Aryeh Leib Alter of Gur (1847–1905) stands out for his inspired commentary on the Pentateuch, *Sefat Emet.*

Although most Hasidic schools ultimately derive from the teachings of R. Dov Baer of Mezhirich and his disciples, one major school traces its origins to the teachings of a great-grandson of the Ba'al Shem Tov, R. Nahman of Bratzlav (1772–1810; see A. Green [1979]). The principal collection of his teachings appeared in 1808. The Bratslaver Hasidim are unique in never having chosen a successor to their founder.

Hasidim associated with the Ba'al Shem Tov settled in Palestine in 1764. R. Menachem Mendel of Vitebsk and R. Abraham of Kalesk, both disciples of R. Dov Baer, established a community of Hasidim in the Tiberias in 1777.

3. Hasidic Literature and Its Principal Concerns. The literature of the Hasidim consists of several thousand volumes that can be subdivided into five main genres: homilies, usually arranged according to the weekly readings of the Pentateuch and Prophets (see PROPHECY AND PROPHETS, HB); homilies concerning the Holy Days and sacred calendar; advice concerning spiritual practice; theological tracts; and brief remarks and anecdotes drawn from the lives of Hasidic masters. Hasidic authors also composed commentaries on kabbalistic and rabbinic texts. A collection of wonder tales, the *Sippurey Ma'asiyot* of R. Nahman of Bratzlav, is a unique vehicle for Hasidic teaching.

While a certain number of these works are genuine literary efforts, for the most part Hasidic teachings were presented orally. Hasidic masters typically addressed their followers at the ritual third meal following the sabbath afternoon prayers. These often spontaneously improvised homilies were later recalled and committed to writing by the master's disciples. Typically, a Hasidic homily focuses on selected verses from the weekly Torah portion. The master's lesson is supported by a wide range of biblical verses and rabbinic comments, and reference is often made to the standard medieval commentaries, like those of RASHI and, especially, to the late thirteenth-century kabbalistic classic, *Sefer ha-Zohar.* However, the typical early Hasidic homily usually focused on a number of specific theological and practical spiritual issues that are often ingeniously connected to the verses under discussion.

Hasidic theology primarily inherited the religious worldview of the sixteenth century Safedian Kabbalist, R. Isaac Luria (see G. Scholem [1954] chap. 7). Lurianic Kabbalah views the process of creation as having involved a rupture and dislocation in the divine cosmic order. As a result, sparks of holiness fell from their supernal location into captivity in the outermost reaches of creation, where they enliven the forces of evil. All aspects of Jewish practice are intended to release these sparks and to bring about a perfected cosmic order. Since the Lurianic myth provided a basic framework for the Hasidic outlook, Hasidic biblical interpretation makes great use of Lurianic terminology and concepts. Biblical verses are frequently treated as symbolic references to hidden aspects of the process of divine and cosmic restitution.

The principal interest of Hasidic commentators, however, generally lies in elucidating issues dealing with an individual's direct relationship to God. Here Hasidism

was, perhaps, more influenced by ecstatic and magical elements in the Kabbalah of Luria's teacher, R. Moses Cordovero (see M. Idel [1995]). Cordoverian Kabbalah placed greater emphasis on divine immanence, which the Hasidim associated with Isa 6:3 and the Zoharic expression "there is no place where God is not to be found."

The spiritual values of sixteenth-century Safed in general and Cordoverian Kabbalah in particular were popularized in several works that greatly influenced the Hasidim. Two of the most important were R. Isaiah Horowitz's *Sheney Luhot ha-Berit* (see M. Krassen [1996]) and R. Elijah De Vidas's *Reishit Hokhmah* (see L. Fine [1984]).

At the center of Hasidic interest were the concept of *devequt,* adhesion to God; the nature and role of the spiritual exemplar, the *Zaddiq;* and the foundational virtues of humility and detachment from corporeality. *Devequt,* the ultimate religious value, could be achieved in all circumstances; but Hasidic conceptions of *devequt* were extremely varied. Common uses included contemplative practices involving concentration on the letters of the Tetragrammaton, complete faith in divine providence, and more mystical forms of direct apprehension of God, whether as immanent or as manifest in supernal worlds. Hasidic works contain some of the most extreme formulations of intimacy with God, including even expressions of *unio-mystica* (see Idel [1995]).

Hasidism remained loyal to the strict observance of all aspects of traditional Jewish life, including Torah study, prayer, and celebration of the sacred calendar. However, the Hasidim regarded all of these as divinely bestowed means of achieving *devequt*; religious observance for any other motivation was considered an expression of pride, the failure to efface oneself before the exclusive reality of the divine. Thus humility was viewed as the key to *devequt,* while pride, as an expression of independence from God, was often targeted as the fundamental flaw inherent in human nature.

One consequence of Hasidism's activist approach to ordinary Jews was the tendency to widen the parameters of religious and spiritual interest. This was accompanied by the rejection of some of the ascetic ideals of Safedian Kabbalah and their replacement with the controversial ideal of detachment from corporeality. This meant that permissible corporeal acts that may appear to be incompatible with ascetic ideals could be spiritualized through focusing the mind on God rather than on the pleasure of the act itself.

Detachment from corporeality was primarily an ideal that was attributed to the spiritual life of the Hasidic masters, the *Zaddiqim.* Ordinary people were not generally expected to measure up to so exalted a level of purity and attachment to God. More characteristically, ordinary Hasidim were given the opportunity to attach themselves through spiritual bonding and monetary support to the *Zaddiqim,* who were believed to have the power to elevate their followers' prayers and to act as channels through which divine abundance could be drawn down for the benefit of the Hasidim and all of creation. The attempt to give an account of this process and of the magical role played by the *Zaddiq* appears in many of the classic, early Hasidic texts. Because many Hasidim believed that their masters had the power to benefit them both spiritually and materially through their extraordinary intimacy with God, *Zaddiqim* became the focus of veneration. However, *Zaddiqim* also fulfilled the important role of spiritual guides. They were expected to direct the spiritual progress of their Hasidim, through their own customs and behavior modeling ways of serving God that their followers strove to emulate. Some *Zaddiqim,* notably R. Shneur Zalman of Liadi and his Habad successors, developed comprehensive programs for spiritual practice and transformation. In the twentieth century, the writings of M. BUBER and A. HESCHEL have made aspects of Hasidism known to both a wider Jewish audience and non-Jewish readers.

Bibliography: A. Y. Bromberg, *Rebbes of Ger: Sfas Emes and Imrei Emes* (1987). **M. Buber,** *For the Sake of Heaven* (1945). **S. H. Dresner,** *The Zaddik* (1960); *The World of a Hasidic Master: Levi Yitshak of Berditchev* (1994), Hebrew. **R. Elior,** *The Paradoxical Ascent to God: The Kabbalistic Theosophy of Habad Hasadism* (1993); "Between *Yesh* and *Ayin*: The Doctrine of the Zaddik in the Works of Jacob Isaac, the Seer of Lublin," *Jewish History: Essays in Honour of C. Abramsky* (ed. A. Rapoport-Albert and S. J. Zipperstein, 1988) 393-445. **L. Fine,** *Safed Spirituality: Rules of Mystical Piety, the Beginning of Wisdom* (1984). **A. Green,** *Tormented Master: A Life of Rabbi Nahman of Bratslav* (JuSS 9, 1979). **A. J. Heschel,** *The Circle of the Baal Shem Tov: Studies in Hasidism* (1985). **G. Hundert,** *Essential Papers on Hasidism: Origins to Present* (1991). **M. Idel,** *Hasidism: Between Ecstasy and Magic* (1995); *Kabbalah: New Perspectives* (1988). **L. Jacobs,** *Hasidic Prayer* (1972); *Seeker of Unity: The Life and Works of Aaron of Starosselje* (1966). **Isaiah Horowitz,** *The Generations of Adam* (ed. and tr. M. Krassen, 1996). **M. Piekarz,** *The Beginning of Hasidism* (1978), Hebrew. **M. J. Rosman,** *Founder of Hasidism: A Quest for the Historical Ba'al Shem Tov* (Contraversions 5, 1996). **B. Safran** (ed.), *Hasidism: Continuity or Innovation?* (HJTM 5, 1988). **R. Schatz Uffenheimer,** *Hasidism as Mysticism: Quietistic Elements in Eighteenth-century Hasidic Thought* (1993). **G. Scholem,** *Major Trends in Jewish Mysticism* (1954³). **J. Weiss,** *Studies in East European Jewish Mysticism* (1985).

M. KRASSEN

HASTINGS, JAMES (1852–1922)

Educated in Aberdeen, Scotland, at the grammar school, university, and Free Church Divinity College, H. combined the pastoral ministry with the notable editorial enterprises for which he is remembered. Confronted by the fear that new critical methods were undermining the historical basis of Christianity, he contended that, if properly understood, sound scholarship in the fields of biblical studies and comparative religion would be seen, in fact, to undergird the faith. The works he edited, notably the periodical *Expository Times* (founded 1889), the *Dictionary of the Bible* (4 vols. plus a supplement, 1898–1904), and the *Encyclopaedia of Religion and Ethics* (13 vols., 1908–26), so effectively mediated scholarly discoveries to both clergy and laity that his obituarists accorded to him much of the credit for the wide acceptance of the critical method.

Works: (ed.), *Dictionary of Christ and the Gospels* (2 vols., 1906–8); (ed.) *The Great Texts of the Bible* (21 vols., 1910–19); (ed.), *The Greater Men and Women of the Bible* (6 vols., 1913–16); (ed.), *Dictionary of the Apostolic Church* (2 vols., 1915–18); (ed.), *The Great Christian Doctrines* (3 vols., 1915–22); (ed.), *The Children's Great Texts of the Bible* (6 vols., 1920–21).

Bibliography: J. A. H. Demspter, " 'Incomparable Encyclopaedist': The Life and Work of Dr. J. H.," *ExpTim* 100 (1988–89) 4-8. *ExpTim* 34 (1932–33) 102-6.

J. A. H. DEMPSTER

HATCH, EDWIN (1835–89)

University administrator, preacher, poet, and hymnwriter, ("Breathe on Me, Breath of God"), H. was probably, after J. B. LIGHTFOOT, the most gifted English historian of early Christianity in the period after the Church of England came to accept critical biblical scholarship. He served as professor of classics (Toronto, 1859–66), vice-principal of St. Mary's Hall (Oxford, 1867), and reader in ecclesiastical history (Oxford, from 1884). His liberal Protestantism was not popular in Oxford, however; denied a chair, he combined his heavy administrative burdens with a parish charge at Purleigh from 1883 until his early death at a time when the mature fruits of his learning were beginning to be written up. His Bampton lectures (1881) are a landmark in the study of the origins of the Christian ministry and were translated into German by A. von HARNACK. His derivation of the episcopate from the financial administrators of Greek religious associations contradicted the Catholic theory of apostolic succession, which was important for high Anglican ecclesiology. C. GORE's reply initiated an English discussion that lasted almost a century. Other important books were published posthumously. H. contributed seventeen articles to the *Dictionary of Christian Antiquities* (ed. W. Smith and S. Cheetham, 1875–80) and eight (six on NT) in *Encyclopaedia Britannica* (9th ed. 1875–89).

Works: *The Organization of the Early Christian Churches* (Bampton Lectures, 1881); *The Growth of Church Institutions* (1887, 1895); *The Influence of Greek Ideas and Usages on the Christian Church* (Hibbert Lectures, 1888, 1890, 1907); *Essays in Biblical Greek* (1889); *A Concordance to the Septuagint and Other Greek Versions of the OT* (completed by H. A. Redpath, 1897; supplement, 1906; repr. 1998 with intro. by R. A. Kraft and E. Tov).

Bibliography: C. Gore, *The Church and the Ministry: A Review of the Rev. E. H.'s Bampton Lectures* (1886). S. C. Hatch (ed.), *Memorials of E. H.* (1890). N. F. Josaitis, *E. H. and Early Church Order* (RSSH 3, 1971). W. Sanday, "In Memoriam Dr. E. H.," *The Expositor,* 4th ser., 1 (1890) 93-111; *DNB* 25 (1891) 149-50.

R. MORGAN

HAUPT, PAUL (1858–1926)

Born at Görlitz, Silesia, Nov. 25, 1858, H. began study of Hebrew at a young age with a rabbi who was the father of a playmate. In 1878 he received a doctorate in Semitic languages from Leipzig, where he was influenced by and collaborated with Franz DELITZSCH on studies of Sumerian and Assyrian philology. After some time spent at the British Museum, H. was appointed *Privatdozent* for ASSYRIOLOGY at Göttingen (1880). A recognized authority on Sumerian at the age of twenty-four, he was promoted to professor in 1883. At Göttingen he came under the influence of P. de LAGARDE, who influenced his subsequent Hebrew scholarship. In 1885 H. was appointed professor of Semitic languages at Johns Hopkins University and held the post simultaneously with the Göttingen position for six years, but he spent the remainder of his academic career at Johns Hopkins.

Beginning in 1886 H.'s attention turned increasingly toward biblical studies; and from 1901 on he worked almost exclusively on the Bible, bringing to its text the same skill in comparative philology and etymology he had demonstrated with other Semitic literature. In addition, he developed a strong interest in biblical POETRY, particularly in metrical studies. One of his more important and ambitious projects was the planning and editing of *The Polychrome Bible,* designed to be a complete critical edition of the HB. Launched by H. in 1891, the volumes of text and commentary that appeared during the next decade included contributions by the leading critical scholars of the day. Different colors were used to designate the literary strata that scholars saw as comprising certain of the biblical books. Despite his many important publications on the literature and languages of the ancient Near East and the Bible, H.'s greatest and most enduring impact on these fields has come indirectly through the students he trained at Johns Hopkins, most notably W. F. ALBRIGHT.

Works: (ed.), "The Sacred Books of the OT," *The Polychrome Bible* (1893–1904); *Bibles Within the Bible* (1899); (tr.), *The Book of Canticles: A New Rhythmical Translation* (1902); (tr.), *The Book of Ecclesiastes* (1905, 1967); *Koheleth oder Weltschmertz in der Bibel* (1905); *Biblische Liebeslieder* (1907); (tr.), *The Book of Nahum* (1907); (tr.), *The Book of Esther* (1908); (tr.), *The Book of Micah* (1910).

Bibliography: W. F. Albright, "Prof. Haupt as Scholar and Teacher," and A. Ember, "Bibliography of P. H.," *Oriental Studies Presented to P. H.* (ed. C. Adler and A. Ember, 1926) xxi-lxx.

S. L. MCKENZIE

HÄVERNICK, HEINRICH ANDREAS CHRISTOPH (1811–45)

A confessional orthodox scholar whose untimely death prevented him from making original contributions to OT scholarship, H. was born Dec. 29, 1811, in Kröpelin, twelve miles west of Rostock. He entered the University of Leipzig in 1827 and moved to Halle a year later, where he was attracted to the conservative F. THOLUCK. When H. GESENIUS was publicly accused of rationalism, some of H.'s notes of Gesenius's lectures were apparently examined by the investigating commission; from then on H. was associated with the indictment against Gesenius. In 1830 he studied in Berlin under E. HENGSTENBERG, gaining his doctorate and licentiate there in 1831. From 1832 to 1834 he was professor at the École de théologie in Geneva. He became *Privatdozent* in 1834 and then *ausserordentlicher* professor in Rostock; however, his presence caused division in the theological faculty. In 1841 he became a full professor in Königsberg, but again he encountered opposition from some colleagues and students. He died in Neustrelitz July 19, 1845.

At first sight H. was simply a follower of Hengstenberg, defending the traditional views of the authorship of OT books. This was how he appeared to the English-speaking world as the result of the translation of two parts of his introduction: on the Pentateuch (1850; see PENTATEUCHAL CRITICISM) and on the CANON, languages, and versions (1852). However, he was an original and independent thinker. He found no trace of a belief in immortality in Job 19:25, and his view of the relation between the testaments is reminiscent of that of J. von HOFMANN. H. maintained that the testaments are connected as the result of an organic development in which God is revealed through a series of gracious actions in the context of a covenant relationship with God's people. H. insisted that OT THEOLOGY should be a historical description of these successive stages of God's dealings with the covenant community but died before working this idea out in practice.

Works: *Neue kritische Untersuchungen über das Buch Daniel* (1838); *Handbuch der historisch-kritischen Einleitung in das Alte Testament* (vols., 1–2, 1836–44; vol. 3, ed. C. F. Keil [1849]; ET *An Historico-critical Introduction to the OT* [1850]; *A General Historico-critical Introduction to the OT* [1852]); *Vorlesungen über die Theologie des Alten Testaments* (ed. H. Hahn, 1848, 1863).

Bibliography: J. H. Hayes and F. C. Prussner, *OT Theology* (1985) 109-10. **Redslob,** *ADB* 11 (1880) 118-19.

J. W. ROGERSON

HAWKINS, JOHN CEASAR (1837–1929)

Educated at Harrow and Oriel College, Oxford, H. served various cures but made his scholarly contribution at Oxford, where he was a regular participant in the ongoing seminar on the SYNOPTIC PROBLEM organized by W. SANDAY in 1894. H.'s careful, detailed work is evidenced in his essays in the volume Sanday edited (1911). His first article advances the theory that Luke used Mark as well as a source of JESUS' sayings in his Gospel, and "some kind of record, or early Gospel" (1911, 90). His second article attempts to describe the contents of the sayings source, Q, which he takes to have been used independently in Matthew and Luke.

Both of these positions were crucial for the consensus that emerged at Oxford, of which the best-known exponent is B. STREETER. But H.'s greatest monument is *Horae Synopticae,* "Synoptic Hours," the title chosen to show his emphasis on tabulating data rather than forwarding theories. The volume sets out dictional and stylistic characteristics of Matthew, Mark, and Luke (pt. 1), possible indications of their use of sources (pt. 2), and possible evidence concerning the composition of each Gospel (pt. 3). It is notable that Streeter, in the index of his classic *The Four Gospels* (1924), lists references to H. as "passim" in the section on "The Synoptic Problem."

Works: *Horae Synopticae: Contributions to the Study of the Synoptic Problem* (1899; rev. ed. 1909; repr. 1968); "Three Limitations to St. Luke's Use of St. Mark's Gospel," and "Probabilities as to the So-called Double Tradition of St. Matthew and St. Luke," *Studies in the Synoptic Problem by Members of the University of Oxford* (ed. W. Sanday, 1911) 27-138.

Bibliography: W. R. Farmer, *The Synoptic Problem: A Critical Analysis* (1964, 1976).

B. CHILTON

HEBREWS, LETTER TO THE

1. Authorship and Background. The Epistle to the Hebrews has always confronted interpreters with difficulties, the first of which is its authorship. ORIGEN recognized that its style differed from that of PAUL, although he deemed its thought as Pauline and in casual reference usually quoted the epistle as Paul's words. CLEMENT OF ALEXANDRIA claimed that Paul had written in Hebrew and then Luke had translated his words into Greek. According to JEROME, TERTULLIAN attributed the epistle to Barnabas, while others attributed it to Luke the Evangelist or to CLEMENT OF ROME.

Although Pauline authorship came to be assumed as the epistle established itself in the CANON of Scripture, LUTHER, reopened the question. Aware of the early discussion, he concluded that Paul could not be the author. He noticed that the refusal to permit repentance after baptism in Hebrews (6:4-6) differed from the acceptance of repentance after baptism in the Gospels and in Paul's epistles. Instead, he suggested that Apollos (Acts 18:24) was the author. The rejection of Pauline authorship led him and others to question the epistle's canonicity.

Modern critical scholarship has universally rejected Pauline authorship. Various candidates have been suggested as author, including Priscilla (A. von Harnack [1900]; R. Hoppin [1969]); but the most plausible suggestion is undeniably Apollos because his characterization in Acts 18:24 fits very well with the contents of Hebrews. Furthermore, he came from Alexandria, and many links have been traced with the works of PHILO, the Jewish philosopher and scriptural exegete who lived during the rise of Christianity (C. Spicq [1952]; H. Montefiore [1964]). No solution can be regarded as proven, and many feel drawn to Origen's conclusion that only God knows the author of Hebrews.

Modern critical scholarship has also been engaged in the search for the true origin and background of Hebrews. The traditional idea that it was addressed to Jews has been questioned on the grounds that the addressees are exhorted as lapsing Christians, that Heb 13:4 implies readers who did not share basic Jewish moral standards, and that the treatment of sacrifice and Temple ritual rests not on knowledge of contemporary practice but on theoretical assumptions based on the LXX (see SEPTUAGINT). Connections with the problems in the Pauline or deutero-Pauline epistles have also been made. T. MANSON (1949–50) suggested that the opening chapters imply a heresy similar to that at Colossae; and C. MONTEFIORE related various elements in the epistle with the problems in the Corinthian church. On the other hand, W. MANSON (1951) noted parallels with Stephen's speech in Acts and, therefore, connected the work with non-Pauline gentile missions.

The discovery among the DEAD SEA SCROLLS of 11Q Melchisedek has further complicated the question of background. Melchisedek is undeniably an important figure in the epistle. The etymological discussion can be paralleled in Philo; however, it is now claimed that the fragment from Qumran, which depicts Melchisedek as the eschatological agent who judges the world at the end, more adequately explains the speculations about the eternity of Melchisedek and JESUS's affiliation with Melchisedek's priesthood. If this position is further validated, then a closer relationship with Palestine and the Jewish mission might reassert itself. Meanwhile, the vexing question concerning the origins of Gnosticism (see GNOSTIC INTERPRETATION) and its possible presence in the background to the NT continues to affect the discussion of Hebrews. The perception that Gnosticism may have its roots in Judaism, and particularly the dualism of APOCALYPTICISM, compounds the question about the thoughtworld of this epistle.

2. Platonism and Eschatology. Platonism and eschatology are closely related to the complex exegetical difficulties in Hebrews. Origen, for instance, assumed that the epistle was about the relationship between the old and the new covenants. Although his homilies on Hebrews are unavailable, certain statements from Hebrews recur in his writings: "for the law made nothing perfect" (Heb 7:19); "they serve a copy and a shadow of the heavenly sanctuary" (Heb 8:5); "the law has a shadow of the good things to come and not the very image of the things" (Heb 10:1). Hebrews gave Origen scriptural warrant for his view that Christ is the key to the HB and justified his typological interpretation. Yet Origen also looked forward to a further fulfillment when what we see in shadow we shall see face to face; and for him the heavenly realities belong to a transcendent, rather platonically conceived realm. The same texts from Hebrews supported this double typology.

The "Platonism" of Hebrews has also figured in modern discussion, in particular its relationship with the epistle's eschatology. Those who assign to Hebrews an Alexandrian and Philonic background take Hebrews 8 and 10 as Platonic and speak of the eschatological perceptions of the earliest church as modified in these terms; the city of God is no longer future but transcendent. However, Hebrews 11–12 point forward, and the tension between "realized" and "future" eschatology is present in Hebrews as much as elsewhere in the NT. There is no unresolved conflict here and no need to call in Platonic influence, since apocalypticism already contained ideas about heaven that could explain the thought of the author (see A. Lincoln [1981]). Both Heb 8:5 and the rabbinic literature treat the Exodus text about Moses' revelation of the pattern of the tabernacle in a similar way. Therefore, Platonism is not necessarily helpful for explaining features of this epistle, although the question of Platonic influence remains intriguing, since verbal parallels with Philo cannot be denied.

3. Interpretation of the OT. Origen appreciated Hebrews's typological method of treating the HB and used it to justify his own procedures. Modern commentators, however, find it embarassing. Responsible critics carefully explain how the author uses the HB because the

method is foreign to modern readers. Critical studies have shown that the argument of Heb 10:5-10 depends on a scribal error that could have occured only in Greek and does not work if the Hebrew text is followed; that the argument of Heb 2:5-10 depends on a misunderstanding of the Hebrew of Psalm 8 if proper attention is paid to context; that unrelated texts are conflated by catchword; and that the arbitrary methods of typology and allegory recur throughout the epistle. Such features can be paralleled in scriptural interpretation in this period and sometimes seem to have been deliberate techniques of exegesis. Although a study of ancient interpretive methods can account for the HERMENEUTICS of Hebrews, this study has the effect of distancing the epistle from the modern reader. The hermeneutical style of Hebrews is a subject at the center of any modern interpretative endeavor but one that tends to rest purely at the descriptive and explanatory level (see S. Sowers [1965] and G. Hughes [1979], who have tried to go further).

4. Christology. The christology of Hebrews has been a perennial topic of interest. R. Greer (1973) has suggested that the christological controversies of the fourth and fifth centuries significantly affected the interpretation of the epistle. Origen used Heb 1:3 to explain that the Logos was the image of the invisible God. He cited other texts to prove the subordination of the Son to the Father (Heb 1:2; 2:9) and the accommodation of God's revelation to humanity (Heb 1:1; 5:13-14). "High priest" was a favorite title for Origen, because it expressed Christ's fundamentally mediatorial function. In the course of the Arian controversy (see ARIUS) other texts from Hebrews became significant in the discussion: Arians used Heb 1:4; 2:8-9; and 3:1-2 to support the creaturely nature of the Logos and his progress to superior status. Many other references to the weakness and temptation of the Son embarassed those who attempted to refute the Arian stance. On the other hand, Heb 1:3 was interpreted in terms of the *homoousion* and developing trinitarian definition, while Heb 13:8 affirmed the immutability of the Logos against the Arian view.

This discussion paved the way for THEODORE's radical distinction between texts referring to the humanity of Christ and those referring to the divine nature of the Logos. He took one or two texts to refer to the *prosopon* of union, but he exploited many to show that the man (Jesus) shared the same "anointing" as his brethren. The most notable feature of Theodore's exegesis is his espousal of the reading "apart from God" rather than "by the grace of God" in Heb 2:9. This reading was Origen's too; but Theodore, unlike Origen, exploited it to insist that Christ's suffering and death should be attributed to the physical body he had assumed and not to God.

The extent to which Hebrews became controversial in the subsequent Nestorian controversy can be seen in the way it figures in the anathemas drawn up by CYRIL and discussed in a series of controversial pamphlets produced by each side. Cyril anathematized those who suggested that the incarnate divine Word had not been made apostle and high priest for us but that someone else, a man born of a woman and different from the Word, had. The Antiochenes (see ANTIOCHENE SCHOOL) on their side insisted that God could not be the subject of many things in Hebrews, including the apostleship and high priesthood. They questioned how God could offer prayers and supplications with many tears and learn obedience through suffering. Since Scripture speaks of Christ's anointing with the Holy Spirit, it must be the physical body, not the Godhead, that is anointed in this way. Hebrews clarifies the weakness of the assumed nature. The unchangeable nature did not change into flesh and learn obedience by experience.

Consciously or unconsciously informed by this ancient debate, modern commentators have often spoken of the paradoxical nature of Hebrews's christology. From a modern historical perspective the terms of the patristic discussion appear anachronistic; yet critics continue to note that Hebrews has both the highest christology in the NT, except perhaps that of John's Gospel, and the most realistic portrayal of Christ's genuine human experiences of temptation, weakness, suffering, and death.

Modern discussion has focused on the background to Heb 1:3 in the figure of personified Wisdom found in Proverbs 8, Ecclesiastes 24, and especially Wis 7:25-26. It has also noted the way in which the scriptural quotation in Heb 1:8-9 implies that the Son is addressed as "God." Such comment tries to avoid anachronistic dogmatic interpretation, yet the questions it raises in relation to the humanness of Jesus perhaps distract from a proper perception of the integration of the author's thought. The "two natures" problem still lurks in the background. If the author simply regarded Jesus as the final embodiment of God's Word and Wisdom, which had been visible before in many and various ways, the apparent tension may be somewhat resolved. Wisdom may be described as the "image" of God; but then humans were created in the "image" of God. There is undoubtedly some "Adam-typology" in the thought of the epistle. The problems of interpreting Hebrews's christology may lie in the heritage of dogmatic interpretation rather than in the text itself.

5. Paraenesis. The dominant theme in the epistle's overall argument is the pioneering and exemplary character of the Jesus story. Some modern commentators have tried to distinguish the paraenetic passages from the exegetical and theological passages, but in fact they are closely integrated and reinforce one another. Modern critical discussion has taken the paraenesis seriously and deduced that the epistle may have originated as a homily, especially since there is no epistolary introduction. It has also deduced that the epistle was written to a Christian community that was in danger of giving up,

probably in the face of persecution. Some scholars have suggested on these grounds that Hebrews must be a second-generation document.

Patristic interest in the epistle also focused on the paraenesis. Origen found much material that related to his ideas of the spiritual journey and the parental discipline of God's fundamental purpose (esp. Hebrews 12). More serious were the Montanists' and Novatianists' appeals to Heb 6:4-6 to justify a hard line on post-baptismal sin. For the Antiochenes, however, the mercy of the faithful high priest who shared our weaknesses and conquered them became an important soteriological theme. Modern studies have also turned to the pilgrimage theme of the epistle, and it is perhaps here that the unity of its christology with every other aspect of its thrust is to be perceived.

Bibliography: **H. W. Attridge,** *The Epistle to the Hebrews* (Hermeneia 1989). **I. Backus et al.,** "Text, Translation and Exegesis of Heb. 9 (1516–99)," *JMRS* 14 (1984) 77-119. **F. F. Bruce,** *The Epistle to the Hebrews* (NICNT, 1964); " 'To the Hebrews': A Document of Roman Christianity?" *ANRW* II.25 (1987) 3496-3521. **J. Casey,** *Hebrews* (1980). **M. R. D'Angelo,** "Hebrews," *The Women's Bible Commentary* (ed. C. A. Newsom and S. H. Ringe, 1992) 364-67. **F. B. Craddock,** "Hebrews," *NIB* (1998) 12:1-173. **B. A. Demarest,** *A History of Interpretation of Hebrews 7, 1-10 from the Reformation to the Present* (BGBE 19, 1976). **H. Feld,** *M. Luthers und W. Steinbachs Vorlesungen über den Hebräerbrief: Eine Studie zur Geschichte der neutestamentlichen Exegese und Theologie* (1971); "Der Hebräerbrief: Literarische Form, religionsgeschichtlicher Hintergrunde, theologische Fragen," *ANRW* II.25.4 (ed. W. Haase, Principat 25, 4, 1987) 3522-3601. **R. A. Greer,** *The Captain of Our Salvation: A Study in the Patristic Exegesis of Hebrews* (BGBE 15, 1973). **K. Hagen,** *Hebrews Commenting from Erasmus to Bèze, 1516–1598* (BGBE 23, 1981). **K. G. A. von Harnack,** "Probabilia über die Addresse und den Verfasser der Hebräer-briefs," *ZNW* 1 (1900) 16-41. **R. Hoppin,** *Priscilla: Author of Epistle to the Hebrews and Other Essays* (1969). **F. L. Horton,** *The Melchizedek Tradition* (SNTSMS 30, 1976). **G. Hughes,** *Hebrews and Hermeneutics* (SNTSMS 36, 1979). **M. de Jonge and A. S. van der Woude,** "11Q Melchisedek and the NT," *NTS* 12 (1965–66) 318-26. **E. Käsemann,** *The Wandering People of God: An Investigation of the Letter to the Hebrews* (1938; ET 1984). **C. B. Kittredge,** *Searching the Scriptures: A Feminist Commentary* (ed. E. Schüssler Fiorenza, 1994) 428-52. **W. L. Lane,** *Hebrews 1–8* (WBC 47A, 1991); *Hebrews 9–13* (WBC 47B, 1991). **S. Lehne,** *The New Covenant in Hebrews* (JSNTSup 44, 1990). **A. T. Lincoln,** *Paradise Now and Not Yet: Studies in the Role of the Heavenly Dimension in Paul's Thought with Special Reference to His Eschatology* (SNTSMS 43, 1981). **T. G. Long,** *Hebrews* (Interpretation, 1997). **T. W. Manson,** "The Problem of the Epistle to the Hebrews," *BJRL* 32 (1949/50) 1-17 = *Studies in the Gospels and Epistles* (1962) 242-58. **W. Manson,** *The Epistle to the Hebrews* (The 1949 Baird Lecture, 1951). **H. W. Montefiore,**

A Commentary on the Epistle to the Hebrews (HNTC, 1964). **D. Peterson,** *Hebrews and Perfection* (SNTSMS 47, 1982). **V. C. Pfitzner,** *Hebrews* (ANTC, 1997). **S. G. Sowers,** *The Hermeneutics of Philo and Hebrews* (1965). **C. Spicq,** *L'Épitre aux Hébreux* (Études bibliques, 1952). **F. M. Young,** "Christological Ideas in the Greek Commentaries on the Epistle to the Hebrews," *JTS* 20 (1969) 150-62.

F. M. YOUNG

HEINISCH, PAUL (1878–1956)

Born at Leobschütz, Upper Silesia, Mar. 25, 1878, H. studied at Breslau and taught there as *Privatdozent* (1908–11) and again as guest professor (1919–23). He was professor at Strasbourg (1911–18); then in 1928 he accepted the chair of OT at the new University of Nijmegen, the Netherlands, which he held until 1945. As a German national he suffered much at the hands of both the Nazis and the Allied/Dutch side in the 1930s and 1940s. He died at Salzburg, Mar. 11, 1956.

H. was a leading figure in Roman Catholic biblical studies in the difficult period of the modernist crisis and its aftermath. His stance on the controverted critical questions of the day was a moderately conservative one; e.g., he viewed the Pentateuch (see PENTATEUCHAL CRITICISM) as originating via a prolongued process of amplification of a Mosaic core. H.'s early writings focused on Alexandrian Judaism (Philo; the book of Wisdom). Subsequently, he concentrated on the Pentateuch, also authoring surveys of Israelite history and OT THEOLOGY. His interest in promoting popular appreciation of the Bible within Catholicism was evidenced by his extended editorship of the series *Biblische Zeitfragen* to which he personally contributed several studies.

Works: *Der Einfluss Philos auf die älteste christliche Exegese* (ATA 1 and 2, 1908); *Die griechische Philosophie im Buche der Weisheit* (ATA 4, 1908); *Das Buch der Weisheit* (EHAT 24, 1912); *Das Buch der Ezechiel* (1923); *Das Buch der Genesis* (1930); *Das Buch der Exodus* (1934); *Das Buch der Leviticus* (1935); *Das Buch der Numeri* (1936); *Theologie des Alten Testaments* (1940; ET 1950); *Geschichte des Alten Testaments* (1950; ET 1955).

Bibliography: **J. van der Ploeg,** "In memoriam Prof. Dr. P. H.," *Studia catholica* 31 (1956) 81-86.

C. T. BEGG

HEINRICI, CARL FRIEDRICH GEORG (1844–1915)

Born Mar. 14, 1844, in Karkeln (East Prussia), H. studied in Halle (PhD 1866) and Berlin (lic. theol. 1868; inaugural diss. in NT exegesis, 1871). He accepted a position in Marburg in 1873 (1874 full professor), then in Leipzig in 1892 as the successor of T. ZAHN. He died Sept. 29, 1915.

In his exegetical works (Sermon on the Mount [1900–05]; two differently executed commentaries on Corinthians [1880–87, 1881–83, 1896–1900][3]) and in his work on the history of primitive Christianity, H. placed the NT decisively in the context of Hellenistic culture and religion, revealing relationships and analogies but also emphasizing differences. He saw primitive Christianity's religious singularity and capacity to assert itself within the context of world history as grounded in the HB, specifically the Israelite-prophetic legacy. According to H., the gentile Christian church developed through acceptance or rejection of influences from its Hellenistic environment. His "Hellenismus und Christentum" (1909) carries the motto "Distinguamus!" With this, H.'s approach to the religious-historical task clearly differentiated itself from that of the slightly older O. PFLEIDERER and the younger RELIGIONSGESCHICHTLICHE SCHULE, which more strongly emphasized the proximity of primitive Christianity to Hellenistic religiosity (mysteries, Gnosis; see the sharp criticism of H.'s posthumous work, *Die Hermes-Mystik und das Neue Testament* by R. REITZENSTEIN in *GGA* [1918] 241-42). H. located the particularity of Christianity in the "unity of religious certainties and the obligation to ethical behavior" (1911). His efforts to make Hellenistic religious and philosophical history fruitful for the understanding of the NT generated, toward the end of 1914, the plan for a "Wetstenius redivivus" or "Corpus Hellenisticum Novi Testamenti," which after his death was taken over by E. von DOBSCHÜTZ (Halle) and is being pursued in Halle, Utrecht, and Chicago.

Works: "Die Christengemeinden Korinths und die religiösen Genossenschaften der Griechen," *ZWT* 19 (1876) 465-526; *Das erste Sendschreiben des Apostels Paulus an die Korinther* (1880); *Der erste Brief an die Korinther* (KEK V[6], 1881; V[8], 1896); *Der zweite Brief an die Korinther* (KEK VI[6], 1883; VI[8], 1900); *Das zweite Sendschreiben des Apostels Paulus die Korinthier* (1887); "Hermeneutik, biblische," *RE*[3] 7 (1899) 718-50; *Die Bergpredigt, quellenkritische untersucht* (1900); *Das Urchristentum* (1902); "Kritik, biblische," *RE*[3] 11 (1902) 119-46; *Die Bergpredigt, Matt 5–7, Luk 6.20-49, begriffsgeschichtlich untersucht* (1905, 1989); *Der literarische Charakter der neutestamentlichen Schriften* (1908); *Hellenismus und Christentum* (BZSF 5, 8, 1909); *Die Hermes-Mystik und das Neue Testament* (ed. E. von Dobschütz, 1918); see "Leben und Werke," in *Die Hermes-Mystik* (XVIII-XXXII) for H.'s further bibliography.

Bibliography: **U. Berner,** *Die Bergpredigt: Rezeption und Auslegung im 20. Jahrhundert* (1983[2]) 73-74. **E. von Dobschütz,** "Zur Einführung," *Die Hermes-Mystik und das Neue Testament* (1918) VII-XVII. **A. Hauck,** "Worte zum Gedächtnis an G. H.," *BVSGW. PH* 67 (1915) 121-31. **W. G. Kümmel,** *NTHIP* 210-12, 245, 321-22, 463; *NDB* 8 (1969) 434-35.

N. WALTER

HEINSIUS, DANIEL (1580–1655)

An illustrious member of the Dutch Renaissance, H. was born at Ghent, June 9, 1580. He began university study at Franeker (1594) but soon transferred to Leiden, where he worked with J. SCALIGER and remained for the rest of his life, becoming professor of Latin (1602) and Greek (1605) and librarian (1607). He died at the Hague, Feb. 25, 1655.

Although a published classicist, H. was also an NT scholar, having been influenced by I. CASAUBON. His 1627 work was both a commentary (critique) on Nonnus's work on John and a commentary on the Gospel. Stressing the importance of septuagintal Greek (see SEPTUAGINT) for understanding the NT, he designated NT Greek as a *lingua hellenistica* with strong influence from Hebrew and Aramaic. He assisted in the publication of several Greek NTs at the Elzevier publishing house in Leiden (1624, 1633, 1641), which had a wide circulation and influence throughout the seventeenth and eighteenth centuries. H.'s 1639 work offered philological annotations to the NT, drawing upon a wide selection of HB, pagan, and Jewish materials while avoiding theological controversy. It evoked much criticism not only for an apparently unfounded charge of plagiaristic reliance on Scaliger, but also for its theory regarding the nature of NT Greek. H.'s colleague and successor C. Salmasius (1588–1653) strongly attacked this theory in his *De Hellenistica commentarius* (1643), but history has shown H.'s understanding to be correct.

Works: *Aristarchus sacer, sive ad Nonni in Johannem metaphrasin exercitationes* (1627); *Sacrarum exercitationum ad Novum Testamentum* (1639); *Operum historicorum collectio* (1673).

Bibliography: H. J. de Jonge, *D. H. and the Textus Receptus of the NT* (1971); "The Study of the NT," *Leiden University in the Seventeenth Century: An Exchange of Learning* (ed. T. H. Lunsingh Scheurleer and G. H. M. Posthumus Meyjes, 1975) 64-109, esp. 87-99. J. H. Meter, *De literaire theorieën van D. H.* (1975; ET 1984). S. Peppink, *D. H., een proefschrift aan de Leidsche Hoogeschool* (1935). P. T. van Rooden, *Theology, Biblical Scholarship, and Rabbinical Studies in the Seventeenth Century* (Studies in the History of Leiden University 6, 1989). P. R. Sellin, *D. H. and Stuart England* (1968). P. R. Sellin and J. J. McManmon, *On Plot and Tragedy by D. H.* (1971).

J. H. HAYES

HEITMÜLLER, WILHELM (1869–1926)

Born August 3, 1869, in Hannover, H. studied at Greifswald, Marburg, Leipzig, and Göttingen (1888–92). At Göttingen in 1902 he qualified as a university lecturer with a dissertation on the baptismal language in the NT. In 1903 he published a more extensive treatment of the subject in the prestigious FRLANT series edited by W. BOUSSET and H. GUNKEL. From 1902 to 1908, H. lectured at Göttingen, in 1908 received a professorship as successor to J. WEISS at Marburg, in 1920 went to Bonn, and in 1924 moved to Tübingen to succeed A. SCHLATTER. H. died Jan. 29, 1926.

H., Weiss, E. TROELTSCH, and P. Wernle are generally considered the first generation of the RELIGIONSGESCHICHTLICHE SCHULE (RGS), following Gunkel, Bousset, and W. WREDE. H. shared the RGS's concern to understand the NT in its religious environment and adopted its comparative methodology. His work *Im Namen Jesu* was both a linguistic study of the baptismal language in the NT and a comparison of the conception of baptism within the wider religious history of the period. Emphasizing the magical power of a deity's name in antiquity, he argued that the invocation of JESUS' name gave baptism a supernatural quality; that in baptism one was sealed, unified, and possessed by the deity; and that at the same time the demonic powers were driven out by the power of the name.

In *Taufe und Abendmahl bei Paulus* (1903) H. turned his attention to the Eucharist and baptism, arguing that both reflected the profound influence of the penchant for mysteries in antiquity. According to H., PAUL viewed the Eucharist as an act of devouring the deity, and both baptism and the Eucharist as sacramental activities resulting in real, mystical union with the Godhead. He also set these sacramental rituals in opposition to the Pauline notion of faith, which H. understood in the traditional Lutheran formulation as a personal and spiritual relationship with God. He maintained that the mystical rites of baptism and the Eucharist were Pauline concessions to the pagan world; moreover, the syncretistic ancient world was so enamored of mysteries that Paul's true religious expression of his gospel by faith could never have gained a foothold on its own. Thus, as was the case with the RGS as a whole, H. found in the development of Christianity an increasing paganization of religious expression the further one moved away from Jesus. He was adamant that the mystical aspects of baptism and the Eucharist did not go back to Jesus, whose message was more purely ethical and spiritual.

Among H.'s articles, perhaps the most significant is "Zum Problem Paulus und Jesus," in which he set forth some of the ideas Bousset would develop a year later in his *Kyrios Christos*. The most notable is the delineation of the stages in the development of early Christianity (Jesus-primitive community-Hellenistic community-Paul) and the influence of the Hellenistic environment on the developing conception of Jesus as Lord.

H. adopted the RGS interest in communicating the results of biblical and historical scholarship to the laity. He contributed to the commentary on John in the *Göttinger Bibelwerk,* served as NT editor and contributor to the first edition of *RGG,* and contributed a volume to the RGS series *Religionsgeschichtliche Volksbücher* summarizing for the laity his scholarship on baptism and the Eucharist. In his 1913 work he set forth an analysis of the sources for Jesus' life, an outline of important questions surrounding the life of Jesus, and a representation of Jesus' basic message and personality.

Works: *Im Namen Jesu: Eine sprach-u. religionsgeschichtliche Untersuchungen zum Neuen Testament, speziell zur altchristlichen Taufe* (1903); *Taufe und Abendmahl bei Paulus: Darstellung und religionsgeschichtliche Beleuchtung* (1903); "Das Johannes-Evangelium," *Die Schriften des Neuen Testaments neu übersetzt und für die Gegenwart erklärt* 2 (1907) 162-314; *Taufe und Abendmahl im Urchristentum* (1911); "Zum Problem Paulus und Jesus," *ZNW* 13 (1912) 320-37; *Jesus* (1913).

Bibliography: **R. Bultmann,** *Die Christliche Welt* 40 (1926) 209-13. **O. Eissfeldt,** "Die Religionsgeschichtliche Schule," *RGG*² 4 (1930) 1898-905. **G. Lüdemann and M. Schröder,** *Die Religionsgeschichtliche Schule in Göttingen* (1987).

T. C. PENNER

HEMPEL, JOHANNES (1891–1964)

Born at Bärstein, Saxony, July 30, 1891, H. studied at Leipzig with R. KITTEL (1910–14). Following service in WWI, he taught at Halle (1920–25), Greifswald (1925–28), Göttingen (1928–37), and Berlin (1937–45). He also edited *ZAW* (1927–59; with O. Eissfeldt from 1945 on) and after WWII did pastoral work (1945–58). He was named professor emeritus at Göttingen in 1958 and died there Dec. 8, 1964, an active scholar to the end.

H.'s initial work was a literary-critical analysis (see LITERARY THEORY/LITERARY CRITICISM) of Deuteronomy (1914). As a text critic (see TEXTUAL CRITICISM), he edited Deuteronomy for the third edition of Kittel's *Biblia Hebraica* (1937) and wrote extensively on the biblical text of the Qumran scrolls (see DEAD SEA SCROLLS). As an associate of H. GUNKEL, H. extended and systematized the former's form-critical approach (see FORM CRITICISM) to cover the entire range of HB materials (1934). Above all, however, he devoted himself to religio-psychological (see PSYCHOLOGY AND BIBLICAL STUDIES) and theological studies concerning the HB's piety and ethos and questions of myth (see MYTHOLOGY AND BIBLICAL STUDIES), history, and the biblical transmission process.

Works: *Die Schichten des Deuteronomiums* (Beiträge zur Kultur- und Universalgeschichte 33, 1914); *Gebet und Frömmigkeit im Alten Testament* (1922); *Gott und Mensch im Alten Testament* (BWANT 3, 1926, 1936²); *Die althebräischen Literatur und ihr hellenistisch-jüdisches Nachleben* (1934, 1968); *Das Ethos des Alten Testaments* (BZAW 67, 1938, 1964²);

Worte der Propheten neu übertragen (1949); *Glaube, Mythos, und Geschichte im Alten Testament* (1954); *Apoxysmata: Vorarbeiten zu einer Religionsgeschichte und Theologie des Alten Testaments. Geschichten und Geschichte in Alten Testament bis zur persischen Zeit* (1964).

Bibliography: "Bibliographie J. H.," *TLZ* 76 (1951) 502-6; 87 (1962) 395-98. **R. Smend,** "Die älteren Herausgeber der Zeitschrift für die alttestamentliche Wissenschaft," *ZAW* 100 Sup. (1988) 2-21, esp. 17-20. **W. Zimmerli,** *ZAW* 78 (1966) I-XI.

C. T. BEGG

HENGEL, MARTIN (1926-)

Born Dec. 14, 1926, in Aalen (Baden-Württemberg Land), H. studied theology at Heidelberg and Tübingen between 1947 and 1951. After working in the church and in a family business, he began PhD studies with the evangelical faculty at Tübingen in 1954 under O. Michel. He became convinced that, as he put it, the "sweet wine of Marburg" (i.e., R. Bultmann's hermeneutical program) had for too long distorted the relationship between the NT and its underlying sources, particularly its Jewish background. Taking the scholarship of J. JEREMIAS and E. BICKERMAN as his model, H. believed that the best way to respond to the perceived deficiencies of BULTMANN's overemphasis on HERMENEUTICS was to return to a rigorous study of the Jewish (Second Temple and rabbinic) and Greco-Roman materials that formed the intellectual and cultural environment from which Christianity arose. Thus he set out to undercut some of the older work of the German RELIGIONSGESCHICHTLICHE SCHULE, which in his view had misconstrued critical points in the development of Christian theology through its overemphasis on the importance of diaspora Judaism and neglect of Palestinian roots.

H.'s dissertation on the Zealots and the political upheaval in first-century Palestine was delayed by his return in 1957 to the family's textile operation, which he ran while he completed work on this study (submitted in 1959 and published in 1961). In 1964 he returned to full-time study, working on a *Habilitationschrift* that would forge his reputation as a preeminent scholar of Second Temple Judaism. This study arose out of the interest generated by his research on the Zealots: the nature of the political hopes of Judaism that provided the catalyst for three rebellions (in Judea and Egypt) against Rome. His thesis, submitted in 1966, was published in 1969, becoming in a very short time a classic in the modern study of Second Temple Judaism.

H. argued two fundamental points in this work. First, he contended that Hellenism, often associated with diaspora Judaism but seldom with Palestine, had in fact penetrated the inner recesses of Palestinian Judaism and that all forms of Judaism of the period—even those in conflict with Hellenism—were deeply affected by Greek language, culture, and thought. This position would lay the groundwork for his later research, largely carried out in a series of essays, which argued that the key developments in NT religious belief should not be relegated to late periods of Christian development outside Palestine but in fact should be situated at the very beginning of the Christian movement in Jerusalem. Second, he maintained that Jews both in the diaspora and in Palestine forged a unified religious identity in reaction to the onslaught of Hellenism, erecting strict boundaries centered on an absolutized Torah. For H. it was this solidification of Jewish identity focused on nation and religion that led to the political revolts against Rome and ultimately created the environment in which Christianity arose, providing, in his view, the catalyst for Christian dissent against the exclusivist tendencies of the Judaism of the period.

While some have faulted H. for pushing evidence too far (L. Feldman [1977]), scholars recognize the sheer weight of the data he brings to his case. Despite his interest in Second Temple Judaism, H.'s primary commitment has always been to the NT. By mapping out the backgrounds and interconnections of sources, he hopes to demonstrate that Judaism prepared the way for the Christian faith and to establish the reasons why Christianity diverged from Judaism. Thus he shares the fundamental conviction of the RELIGIONSGESCHICHTLICHE SCHULE—that the NT is firmly grounded in the religious and cultural ethos of the ancient world—and his work, although a variation on the earlier positions, nonetheless reaffirms them. To this end he has committed himself to uncovering any piece of data—no matter how tiny or fragmentary, whether Jewish or Greco-Roman—that might illuminate some feature of early Christian belief and practice. Christology has been a major focus; but he has also worked extensively on the cultural and intellectual background of PAUL, of JESUS' ministry, of the Gospel of John, of the mission of the Hellenists, and of other facets of early Christian history.

History-of-religion methodology has been foundational for his approach to the NT; but the Tübingen connection was never lost on H., who has remained at the university since 1968. Although it is not the major focus of his research, he has done work on the history of early Christian communities using F. C. BAUR's model of interaction and conflict among competing "schools." In an article written in 1987, H. made a case for the struggle between Paul and James in early Christian circles, arguing that resultant, rampant anti-Paulinism was reflected in the epistle of James. Although his research is not concentrated in this area, it is evident that the presupposition of a Paulinism in conflict with Judaizing forms of early Christianity offers a significant impulse for his stress on the relevance of Judaic backgrounds for NT interpretation.

Works: *The Zealots: Investigations into the Jewish Freedom Movement in the Period from Herod I Until 70* AD (1961; ET 1989); *The Charismatic Leader and His Followers* (1968; ET 1981); *Judaism and Hellenism: Studies in Their Encounter in Palestine During the Early Hellenistic Period* (1969; ET 1974); *Crucifixion in the Ancient World and the Folly of the Message of the Cross* (1977); *The Son of God: The Origin of Christology and the History of Jewish-Hellenistic Religion* (1977²; ET 1976); *Acts and the History of Earliest Christianity* (1979; ET 1980); *The Atonement: The Origins of the Doctrine in the NT* (1981); *Between Jesus and Paul: Studies in the Earliest History of Christianity* (1983); *Studies in the Gospel of Mark* (1985); "Der Jakobusbrief als antipaulinische Polemik," *Tradition and Interpretation in the NT* (1987) 248-78; *The "Hellenization" of Judaea in the First Century After Christ* (1989); *The Johannine Question* (1990, expanded German ed. 1993); *Studies in Early Christology* (1995); *Kleine Schriften* (ed. R. Deines et al., 1996); (with A. M. Schwemer), *Paul Between Damascus and Antioch* (1997).

Bibliography: **H. Cancik et al.** (eds.), *Geschichte—Tradition—Reflexion* (FS M. H., 3 vols., 1996), bibliography 3:695-722. **J. J. Collins,** "Judaism as *Praeparatio Evangelica* in the Work of M. H.," *RStR* 15 (1989) 226-28. **L. H. Feldman,** "Hengel's Judaism and Hellenism in Retrospect," *JBL* 96 (1977) 371-82; "How Much Hellenism in Jewish Palestine?" *HUCA* 57 (1986) 83-111. **L. L. Grabbe,** *Judaism from Cyrus to Hadrian,* vol. 1, *The Persian and Greek Periods* (1992) 148-53. **L. L. Grabbe and F. Miller,** "The Background to the Maccabean Revolution: Reflections on M. H.'s Judaism and Hellenism," *JJS* 29 (1978) 1-21.

T. C. PENNER

HENGSTENBERG, ERNST WILHELM (1802–69)

The leading member of the confessional orthodox group of scholars who bitterly opposed the development of biblical criticism in the nineteenth century, H. was born Oct. 20, 1802, in Fröndenberg near Unna. His father, a Reformed clergyman, was responsible for his early education. In 1819 he entered the University of Bonn, where he studied philosophy, especially that of I. KANT and S. FRIES, and oriental languages, especially Hebrew and Arabic (PhD 1823). His teacher, the orientalist G. Freytag (1788–1861), followed the encyclopedic, mildly rationalist line of E. ROSENMÜLLER. From 1823 to 1824 H. was tutor to J. STÄHELIN in Basel and lecturer at the Basel mission. During this period he began to move toward a confessional and conservative position, influenced by a study of the Augsburg Confession and the writings of LUTHER, P. MELANCHTHON, and CALVIN. He was also deeply impressed by a book by H. Steffens (1773–1845) that emphasized that the Bible is a revelation inaccessible to human reason that discloses the fact, cause, and cure of human sinfulness. In 1824 H. moved to Berlin, where he became *ausser-*

ordentlicher professor (1826) and full professor from 1828 until his death May 28, 1869. In 1827 he became editor of the *Evangelische Kirchen-Zeitung,* an organ dedicated to combating and destroying rationalism. He was to remain editor for forty-two years.

H. regarded rationalism, not simply as a fashion among academics, but as a poison that threatened the very existence of the church, undermining the biblical revelation, as interpreted by formularies like the Augsburg Confession, of human sinfulness and divine grace. Rationalism was "the born and sworn enemy of Christ and his church." In biblical studies H. set himself to refute the theories of critical scholars by scholarly demonstration. It was no use merely affirming traditional views; the arguments of critical scholars had to be met point by point. This he did in works on the unity and integrity of Daniel and Zechariah, on the genuineness of the Pentateuch (see PENTATEUCHAL CRITICISM), and above all in his *Beiträge zur Einleitung ins Alte Testament* (3 vols., 1831–39), a title chosen deliberately with W. DE WETTE's 1806–7 work in view. Against the position that had emerged through the work of J. VATER, de Wette, C. GRAMBERG, J. VATKE, and others that the OT had little or no trace of the Mosaic law before the reign of Josiah, H. sought to demonstrate the opposite and found many early allusions to the law, e.g., in the period of Judges, assuming that this book was a reliable witness to the period, something denied by the critics. His *Christology of the OT* defended the traditional OT prophecies (see PROPHECY AND PROPHETS, HB) of the coming Messiah and expounded its witness to the work of a suffering and atoning Messiah.

H. exercised great influence in Germany and in the English-speaking world. He prevented Vatke from obtaining a full professorship in Berlin. During the 1840s he was regularly consulted about faculty appointments, and from 1850 his influence was very considerable. At least twelve of his books were translated into English, probably a record in the nineteenth century, allowing the tide of critical scholarship to be checked among English readers. However, despite all his power and influence, he failed to prevent the triumph of criticism. Had he used his learning to oppose the undoubted excesses of some of the critics rather than the critical approach itself, he might have made a more lasting contribution to scholarship.

Works: *Beiträge zur Einleitung ins Alte Testament* (3 vols., 1831–39; ET of pts. 2–3, *Genuineness of the Pentateuch* [1847]; of pt. 1, *Genuineness of Daniel and Integrity of Zechariah* [1848]); *Christologie des Alten Testamentes und Commentar über die Messianischen Weissagungen der Propheten* (1829, 1856–57[2]; ET *Christology of the OT* [1854–58]).

Bibliography: J. Bachmann, *E. W. H.: Sein Leben und Wirken* (3 vols., 1876–92). J. Mehlhausen, *TRE* 15 (1986)

39-42. **S. H. Nafzger,** "Struggle Against Rationalism: A Study of E. W. H.'s Understanding of Criticism" (diss., Harvard, 1979). **J. W. Rogerson,** *OTCNC* 79-90. **J. C. Taylor,** "E. W. H. as OT Exegete" (diss., Yale, 1966).

J. W. ROGERSON

HENRY, MATTHEW (1662–1714)

Born Oct. 18, 1662, at Broad Oak, Flintshire (now Clwyd), H. was educated at Doolittle's academy, Islington, and Gray's Inn, London. In 1687 he was ordained a nonconformist minister in Chester, and in 1712 he moved to a congregation in Hackney. He died June 22, 1714.

H's. major work is his commentary, or "exposition," on the Bible, begun in 1704. At his death he had reached the end of Acts, and fourteen other nonconformists completed the work. He was familiar with a wide range of biblical scholarship and acknowledged his debt to other writers, including S. Patrick (1625–1707), M. POOLE, J. LIGHTFOOT, and D. WHITBY; but he aimed at writing an expository commentary without the technical discussions found in works of critical scholarship. Wishing to interpret the Bible in simple, clear language and to give it a practical application, he aimed to arrange his exposition in "a continued discourse, digested under proper heads" and to observe the connection of each chapter with what preceded it. The question he asked of the Scriptures was not just "What is this?" but "What is this to us?" He had a gift for memorable phrases, and his commentary won great popularity. It was highly esteemed by the Wesleys (see J. WESLEY), P. DODDRIDGE, and many others. Its popularity has lasted into the twentieth century, and it continues to be reprinted.

Works: *Exposition of All the Books of the Old and New Testament* (1706, 1725; subsequently in various forms); *The Works of the Late Rev. Mr. M. H.* (1726); *The Miscellaneous Writings of the Rev. M. H.* (1809).

Bibliography: W. L. Alexander, *JSL* 2 (1848) 222-23. A. Gordon, *DNB* 26 (1891) 123-24. H. O. Old, *HHMBI*, 195-98. S. Palmer, "Memoir," *Miscellaneous Writings* (1809, 1830[2]). W. Tong, *An Account of the Life and Death of Mr. M. H.* (1716). J. B. Williams, *Memoir of the Rev. M. H., the Commentator, an Immediate Descendant of the English Puritans* (1828).

A. W. WAINWRIGHT

HERBERT, EDWARD, LORD OF CHERBURY (1583–1648)

Born Mar. 3, 1583, in Eyton (Severn), H. studied at Oxford (1596–1600) and became known as a cosmopolitan man of humanist-eclectic education, traveling in France and Italy, serving as British envoy in Paris from 1616 to 1624, and becoming Lord of Cherbury in 1629.

An amateur philosopher, he exchanged ideas with such scholars as M. Mersenne and H. GROTIUS. H. died Aug. 20, 1648, at Montgomery Castle in Wales.

H.'s contribution to biblical studies is indirect. Owing to his theory of cognition (in his main work *De Veritate* [1624, 1645³]) and its application to religion, he is considered the "father" of English DEISM. He grounded his religious studies (in *De Religione Gentilium*) on the thesis of a monotheistic-ethical primal religion that was originally present everywhere and was only later falsified by priests with a superstitious polytheistic cult. The *notitiae communes circa religionem* consider virtue to be the chief element in worship and reckon with rewards and punishments in an afterlife. In *De Religione Laici* and *Dialogue* latent biblical criticism finds expression in the assertion that God's Word can only be attributed to those things in the Bible that correspond to "correct reason" and faith and that are not morally repugnant; everything else is attributable to human beings.

Works: *De Veritate prout distinguitur a revelatione, a verisimili, a possibili, et a falso* (1624, 1645³; ET with introduction by M. H. Carrè, 1937); *De Religione Laici* (1645³; ET by H. L. Hutcheson, 1944); *De Religione Gentilium errorumque apud eos causis* (l663; ET by J. A. Butler, 1995); *A Dialogue Between a Tutor and His Pupil* (1768, repr. 1971); *Autobiography* (ed. H. Walpole, 1764; ed. S. Lee, 1886, 1906²; ed. J. M. Shuttleworth, 1976).

Bibliography: R. D. Bedford, *The Defence of Truth: Herbert of Cherbury and the Seventeenth Century* (1979). D. Braun, *De verareligione: Zum Verhältnis von Natur und Gnade bei Herbert of Cherbury und T. Hobbes* (1974) 81-120. G. Gawlick, "Einleitung," *De Veritate* (1966, repr.) VII-XLVIII. G. V. Lechler, *Geschichte des englischen Deismus* (1841, repr. 1965) 26-29, 36-54. D. A. Pailin, "Herbert of Cherbury and the Deists," *ExpTim* 94 (1982–83) 196-200; *TRE* 15 (1986) 62-66; *Grundriss der Geschichte der Philosophie: Überweg: 17. Jahrhundert 3, 1* (ed. J.-P. Schobinger, 1988) 224-39. J. S. Preus, "The Deist Option: Herbert of Cherbury," *Explaining Religion: Criticism and Theory from Bodin to Freud* (1987) 23-39. H. G. Reventlow, *The Authority of the Bible and the Rise of the Modern World* (1980; ET 1984) 185-93. M. Rossi, *La vita, le opere, i tempi di Eduardo Herbert di Cherbury* (3 vols., 1947). M. Sina, *L'avvento della ragione: "Reason" e "above Reason" dal razionalismo teologico inglese al deismo* (1976) 147-66.

H. G. REVENTLOW

HERDER, JOHANN GOTTFRIED (1744–1803)

Although he was not primarily a biblical scholar and did not contribute any specific theory to the advancement of biblical criticism, H.'s influence was considerable and lasting. Born Aug. 25, 1744, in Mohrungen in East Prussia, H. studied at the University of Königsberg, where he was a pupil of I. KANT in the latter's pre-critical phase and began an important friendship with J. Hamann (1730–88). From 1764 to 1769 he taught at the cathedral school in Riga; during this period he was ordained and undertook pastoral duties. He left Riga in May 1769 on a sea journey to widen his knowledge. His travels lasted nearly two years, including a stay in Strasbourg, where he met J. von Goethe (1749–1832) and wrote a prize-winning treatise *On the Origin of Language* (1772; ET 1966). In 1771 he was appointed superintendent clergyman in Bückeburg and during his five years there wrote an important work on the Genesis creation story, notes on the NT, and a commentary on the book of Revelation. Through the influence of Goethe he moved in 1776 to Weimar to be general superintendent and stayed there until his death, Dec. 18, 1803. During the Weimar period he wrote *On the Spirit of Hebrew Poetry* (1782–83; ET 1833), *Letters on the Study of Theology* (1780, 1785²), and what is regarded as his masterpiece, *Reflections on the Philosophy of the History of Mankind* (1784–91; ET 1800).

H.'s writings cover many areas: theology, philosophy, history, poetry, literary criticism, psychology, and natural science. The interpretation of his thought has produced differing scholarly views. For example, in 1787 in *God: Some Conversations* (ET 1949) he confessed that he was a follower of B. SPINOZA; but this does not mean, as some have maintained, that he had become an atheist or a materialist. His use of Spinoza, which has been traced back to the early Riga period, was a type of pan-entheism, which saw God manifested in nature and culture and which enabled H. to oppose Kant's critical philosophy.

H.'s significance for biblical interpretation lies in his opposition to the rationalist approach of the late eighteenth century in favor of a poetic-historical approach. Like Hamann, he participated in the rising Romantic opposition to the Enlightenment. He regarded language, and thus literary compositions, as both God's gift to humankind and humankind's most distinctive cultural possession; and part of being human involved becoming acquainted with literature, especially that originating from the childhood period of the human race. It was at this point that he developed an interest in the Bible, including the belief that Hebrew was close to the original "picture" language of earliest humankind and that Hebrew poetry expressed intuitions of the divine perceived by early humanity in nature. Thus he was interested in Job and Song of Songs because of their poetry; like R. LOWTH, who influenced him, he wrote on the spirit of Hebrew poetry. In Genesis 1 H. believed that he had found the account of creation from which all known creation narratives in the ancient world derived. This account was not a record of how the universe had been made, but a divine communication based on earliest humanity's experience of a sunrise.

H. rejected the rationalist modernizing of the Bible, arguing that a knowledge of the Near East, ancient and modern, would enable modern interpreters to be confronted by an alien text in a way that would allow it to impinge on the modern world. Thus H. was not interested in retrieving scraps of history from a demythologized text. He was concerned, rather, with the history and the genres of the traditions that made up the Bible and with letting each speak in its own way. He thought it impossible and in any case pointless to reconstruct a history of Israel. He did, however, briefly undertake this task in *Reflections* and concluded that the later, postexilic religion of Israel had lost the poetic power of the earlier period.

H. emphasized that, as the fulfillment of the HB, the NT necessarily had a Hebrew and Near Eastern character. Indeed, in his explanatory notes on the NT (1775) he saw in the recently published teachings of Zoroaster a key to NT interpretation. His view of the Gospels was that they were not biographies of JESUS but presupposed the oral preaching of the gospel together with its rule of faith and were the attempt of four different writers to enable people to believe in Jesus. Mark was the most primitive Gospel. The center of the NT was Jesus' proclamation of the kingdom of God, a future order that would triumph over evil, as intimated in Revelation, and that would exemplify Jesus' message of the fatherhood of God and the brotherhood of humankind.

Many of H.'s critical positions are now known to be wrong, e.g., Genesis 1, far from being the original account of creation, is later than other accounts from the ancient Near East. In spite of this H. has been a source of inspiration to scholars seeking an alternative to rationalist biblical interpretation. In the nineteenth century a type of poetic, aesthetic criticism was maintained by W. DE WETTE and F. UMBREIT. H. EWALD's interest in types of TRADITION and their history was clearly anticipated by H.'s work, and H. GUNKEL was a confessed admirer of H.'s poetic and origin-of-traditions approach. The rediscovery of the ancient world through ASSYRIOLOGY and ARCHAEOLOGY from the 1870s enabled the Bible to be understood by interpreting it in terms of its own world; and the importance of language and texts as a clue to human identity is a theme of recent philosophical HERMENEUTICS. In short, although he lacked modern critical resources, H.'s insights were such that many of the questions he raised remain on the agenda for biblical interpretation.

Works: *H.s sämmtliche Werke* (33 vols., ed. B. Suphan, 1877–1913), vols. 6–7, *Älteste Urkunde des Menschengeschlects* (1774–76); vol. 7, *Erläuterungen zum Neuen Testament aus einer neueröfneten Morgenländischen Quelle* (1775); vols. 11–12, *Vom Geist der Ebräischen Poesie* (1782–83; ET *On the Spirit of Hebrew Poetry* [1833]); vol. 19, *Vom Erlöser der Menschen: Nach unsern drei ersten Evangelien* (1796); *Von Gottes Sohn, der Welt Heiland: Nach Johannes Evangelium* (1797); *Reflections on the Philosophy of the History of Mankind* (4 vols., 1784–91; ET abridged with intro. by F. E. Manuel, 1968).

Bibliography: I. **Berlin,** *Vico and H.* (1976). **C. Bultmann,** "Creation at the Beginning of History: J. G. H.'s Interpretation of Genesis 1," *JSOT* 68 (1995) 23-32. **M. Bunge,** "J. G. H.s Auslegung des Neuen Testaments," *Historische Kritik und biblischer Kanon in der deutschen Aufklärung* (Wolfenbütteler Forschungen 41, ed. H. G. Reventlow, et al., 1988) 249-62. **R. T. Clark,** *H.: His Life and Thought* (1955, 1969[2]). **H. Frei,** *The Eclipse of Biblical Narrative* (1974) 183-201. **D. Gutzen,** "Ästhetik und Kritik bei J. G. H.," *Historische Kritik* (1988) 263-85. **R. Haym,** *H. nach seinem Leben und seinen Werken dargestellt* (2 vols., 1880–85; repr. 1978). **E. Herms,** *TRE* 15 (1986) 70-95 (with extensive bibliography). **W. G. Kümmel,** *NTHIP,* esp. 79-83. **H.-J. Kraus,** "H.s alttestamentliche Forschungen," *Bückeburger Gespräche, 1971* (1973) 59-75; *RMM,* 224-40. **R. Smend,** "H. und die Bibel" and "Kommentierung," *J. G. H.: Schriften zum Alten Testament* (ed. R. Smend, 1993) 1311-483. **T. Willi,** *H.s Beitrag zum Verstehen des Alten Testaments* (1971).

J. W. ROGERSON

HERMENEUTICS

Hermeneutics denotes the theoretical and methodological process of understanding meanings in signs and symbols, whether written or spoken. Hermeneutics has vital importance for the task of interpreting the Bible because it is the discipline through which people reflect on the concepts, principles, and rules that are universally necessary for understanding and interpreting any meanings whatsoever. Biblical interpretation must be intelligible as a particular form of interpretation in general.

Hermeneutics as an explicit theoretical construction did not appear until the seventeenth century, when the Latin word *hermeneutica* was first used in this sense. Various scattered insights into interpretive processes, however, have an ancient history. The term *hermeneutics* derives from the Greek *hermeneuein,* which carries the senses of expression (uttering a thought or intention), explication (interpreting an utterance), and translation (mediating meanings from one language to another). The religious function of interpreting hidden messages was treated by Plato (*Statesman* 260 d 11; *Epinomis* 975 c 6). PHILO OF ALEXANDRIA discussed *hermeneuein* in connection with interpreting biblical allegory. ORIGEN presented the outlines of a hermeneutical theory with his doctrine of the three levels of biblical meaning: the literal level, associated with the body; the figurative level, associated with the soul; and the spiritual sense, which contains divine wisdom (*On Principles,* bk. 4). AUGUSTINE became immensely influential in the subsequent literature on hermeneutics by recommending that clear passages of Scripture be used to illuminate obscure ones and by focusing on the formal and material relations between sign (*signum*) and word (*verbum*) in both inner and outer speaking (*On Christian Doctrine*, bk. 3). LUTHER's practice of biblical interpretation was also important to hermeneutics because he advanced the claim that the literal word of Scripture provides its own spiritual significance when understood properly.

Modern hermeneutics is distinguished by three important characteristics. First, it begins with universal theories of interpretation that were developed independently of any received tradition of interpreting a particular body of texts, such as the Bible, classical literature, or civil laws. Second, it is linked to the emergence of philosophical critique as a power to dislodge the being of whatever appears as self-evidently given, including any objects considered to be sacred in themselves, e.g., the Bible, clergy, and eucharistic bread and wine. Third, it is conscious that objects of interpretation are always situated in complex historical contexts; various strata of presuppositions, beliefs, and interests both shape and are reflected in texts from the past.

F. SCHLEIERMACHER is frequently credited with having founded modern hermeneutics. Prior to Schleiermacher, however, several other scholars wrote normative and technical theories of interpretation, including J. Dannhauer (1603–66), J. Chladenius (1710–59), and G. Meier (1718–77). Schleiermacher did not publish a major work on hermeneutics; he left behind only his handwritten lecture notes on the subject (amply supplemented by student notes) and two addresses to the Berlin Academy of the Sciences from 1829. Nonetheless, the quantity of material and the quality of thought in these manuscripts, coupled with Schleiermacher's enormous influence on subsequent theories, secure his central place in the history of hermeneutics.

Schleiermacher was a systematic thinker *par excellence*. In his 1819 notes on hermeneutics as well as in his 1822 lectures on dialectic, he related hermeneutics both to dialectic and to rhetoric. He viewed the three as fundamental and interrelated philosophical arts (*Kunstlehren*) and held living dialogue to be the natural home and empirical starting point of each. Everything he said about interpretation was intended to illuminate the everyday processes by which people do in fact come to know others. The problem of understanding texts from the distant past always derives from the primary hermeneutical problem of understanding others. Most simply put, Schleiermacher claimed that hermeneutics is the art of understanding, rhetoric the art of speaking, and dialectic the art of thinking. Hermeneutics and rhetoric are, therefore, simply the reverse sides of each other. In any conversation with another person, one is either uttering words or listening to words uttered by the other. Hermeneutics and rhetoric primarily have to do with language in actual use. However, insofar as language is the exterior of thinking and thinking is the interior of language they both have an intrinsic reference to dialectic.

Dialectic is dependent on hermeneutics and rhetoric, according to Schleiermacher, because dialectic is both produced and understood through the principles and rules of rhetoric and hermeneutics, respectively. But hermeneutics and rhetoric are in the nature of the case subordinate to dialectic. Hermeneutics without dialectic is interpretive free association lacking ground in the author's thought; rhetoric without dialectic is unscrupulous persuasion for personal ends without regard to truth. Interest in dialectic arises whenever there is concern for truth in understanding or speaking; dialectic, thus, is the measure of both hermeneutic and rhetoric. More properly put, hermeneutics is thinking about the principle and rules for true understanding of the meaning of judgments articulated in particular linguistic signs. Rhetoric is thinking about the principle and rules for truthful and effective presentation of judgments in new discourse. Dialectic is thinking about the principle and rules of relating the forms of thinking with the material of being in true judgments.

Schleiermacher reversed the inherited tendency in hermeneutics to assume that understanding occurs on its own accord, so that hermeneutics assists in avoiding misunderstanding. He proposed instead that misunderstanding, rather than understanding, naturally takes place and that hermeneutics makes us aware of the scope and depth of our misunderstanding. To understand well is an infinite interactive task for finite humans, who always find themselves in the middle of an ongoing conversation without the means to elevate themselves above their limited perspectives. Schleiermacher believed that interpretation is a never-ending process that always inadequately approximates the ultimately unattainable truth of things.

Schleiermacher distinguished two kinds of interpretation: grammatical and technical/psychological. He further specified two methods of interpretation: comparative and divinatory. Methodical interpretation uses both methods in both kinds of interpretation. Comparison is the objective-analytic method of distinguishing the material element of discourse from the formal element in order to find the right concepts for understanding particular meanings. Divination, by contrast, is the subjective-intuitive method of directly apprehending individuals as living combinations of formal and material elements, universal concepts and particular meanings.

Grammatical interpretation is the art of finding the precise sense of a given statement from its language; it requires knowledge of the languages common to the author and the original audience. Grammatical interpretation uses the comparative method to determine the objective meaning of each word, sentence, and paragraph accessible to any competent user of the language; it uses the divinatory method to apprehend the subjective meaning of the text for the original audience. Technical/psychological interpretation is the art of finding the theme of the work grasped as its unity, i.e., the dynamic motive and leading thought that impels the author; it requires knowledge of the different ways humans think. Technical/psychological interpretation uses the comparative method to focus on the text as a work of art, concentrating on the author's distinctive style and means of composition within the established genre; it uses the divinatory method to understand the text as a creative event in the author's life. The aim of interpretive activity is to produce at least partial agreement among the results of these four possibilities. Schleiermacher stated quite clearly that the "true" meaning of a text is no more to be found through grammatical interpretation than through technical/pyschological interpretation, no more through the comparative method than through the divinatory method. The genre of the text determines in part what proportion of skills one brings to it. For example, maps require less psychological than grammatical skill; personal letters require more psychological than grammatical skill. Schleiermacher advised everyone to identify personal hermeneutical strengths and weaknesses and to work on the weaknesses to help transform misunderstanding into understanding.

Following Schleiermacher a new development had an impact on modern hermeneutics. Schleiermacher was fully aware that texts from the past are written from their own conceptual, linguistic, and social contexts. He was less attentive, however, to the fact that modern interpreters likewise understand these texts from their own historically situated presuppositions, beliefs, and interests. The problem of historicism thereby arises: If modern interpretations of historical texts are themselves historical, then how is historical knowledge possible?

W. DILTHEY is notable for directly addressing the problem of historicism. A philosopher who concentrated his efforts on providing an epistemological foundation for the human sciences, he attempted to conceive a critique of historical reason that would secure theoretical justification for the human sciences with the same rigor that I. KANT's critique of pure reason had done for the natural sciences. In his later writings (1900 and following), Dilthey sought this basis in hermeneutics, which he called the methodology of the interpretation of written records. In his famous essay "The Development of Hermeneutics" (1900), he focused on three ideas connected to hermeneutics so conceived. First, whereas the natural sciences study outer appearances through the senses, the human sciences study expressions of the "inner reality [*Erlebnis*] directly experienced in all its complexity." This inner reality is the immediate experience of a whole human being, which always includes a movement of reflexive self-awareness. In other words, when persons see or hear something in the world to which they feel an inner response, they are also immediately aware

of themselves as seeing, hearing, and feeling something. In Dilthey's conception the phenomenon of self-consciousness grows directly out of the experiences of life. According to his famous distinction, the natural sciences explain outer appearances with reference to causal laws; but the human sciences understand states of inner psychological reality by means of the initially diverse and strange words and gestures that express these states of self-awareness.

Second, the human sciences are possible because understanding is a universal rule-governed activity that reaches from linguistic expressions back to the inner reality that gives rise to them. Dilthey maintained that verbal expressions refer to historically conditioned systems of cultural meaning and to states of inner experience. The art of understanding explores both references and coordinates them into meaningful wholes. Historical understanding involves empathetically transposing oneself into the inner experiences of other human beings by means of and within their proper worlds of cultural and linguistic meanings.

Third, understanding of others is possible because of two central conditions of human life: (1) No matter how different people may be, they share a common human nature as historical and meaning-conferring beings; therefore, nothing human is altogether alien to another human being. (2) Everywhere and at all times people express their thoughts and experiences in structured, translatable languages that enable interpreters to reconstruct cultural settings radically different from their own.

Modern hermeneutics underwent a profound transformation through the thought of philosopher M. Heidegger (1889–1976). In his early lectures leading up to the publication of *Being and Time* in 1927, Heidegger revised the concept of hermeneutics inherited from Schleiermacher and Dilthey, rejecting the view of hermeneutics as a distinctive art or method of understanding whose explication can ground the human sciences. Rather than framing hermeneutics within epistemology, he referred it to fundamental ontological inquiry. Heidegger no longer considered understanding primarily to be a particular mode of knowing but rather a basic element of the human mode of being, *Dasein*. *Dasein* is the being whose structure is care, for it is characterized by concern for itself—concern about what it means to be the one it is. In its care-structure, *Dasein* exhibits a pre-understanding of the meaning of its own being as well as of the meaning of being at all. It is thus the opening or clearing in the whole of being, where the meaning of being is manifest for interpretation. In *Being and Time,* Heidegger constructed a hermeneutics of facticity in which he interpreted the basic elements of *Dasein's* care-structure in order to make explicit its pre-understanding of the meaning of being. He held that the goal of hermeneutics is philosophical self-understanding, conceived as a way of combating a pervasive forgetfulness of what it means to be human.

According to Heidegger, the essence of *Dasein* lies in its existing, in that its being differs fundamentally from that of a thing bearing properties. *Dasein* is a "who," not a "what"; its being is always one of possibilities rather than fixed actualities. *Dasein* is its possibilities to be, in that it is always deciding who it is in its everyday understanding of itself in the world. Moreover, *Dasein* is in each case "mine." Each person as *Dasein* is his or her own existence and must make the individual choice to be so. Because *Dasein* is in each case essentially its own possibility to be itself, it can either gain itself authentically by accepting responsibility for its own choices or lose itself inauthentically by allowing popular opinion or unexamined traditions to determine its choices.

In *Being and Time,* Heidegger analyzed the basic elements of *Dasein's* being as care. The first of these structural elements is *Befindlichkeit* (mood or state of mind). *Dasein* always finds itself "there," thrown into the world, delivered over to its being, not knowing from whence it comes or where it is going. Through its fundamental moods, especially that of anxiety, *Dasein* is disclosed to itself as thrown and is opened to the question of the meaning of its own being and of being anything at all. The second and equally original element is *Verstehen* (understanding). *Dasein* orients itself within the situation of its thrownness by projecting possibilities for things to be; in perceiving something, one thinks of it "as" something and thereby understands a possibility of its being. For example, one sees a stone and thinks of it as a tool for pounding or as a beautiful object for one's shelf. By projecting possibilities for the being of worldly things, *Dasein* also projects an understanding of its own being as the one for whose sake it understands. In its capacity to understand, *Dasein* reveals its capacity to transcend its given situations in the world. A third element is *Rede* (discourse). *Dasein's* capacity for language is similarly rooted in its care-structure in that mood and understanding come to light in language.

Interpretation, another basic structural element of *Dasein,* is the working out of the possibilities projected in understanding. In interpreting something that is already understood, *Dasein* makes explicit the content of what was projected. Understanding so interpreted is never merely a matter of perceiving or conceiving but an activity of figuring or imagining the possible relations between perceiving and conceiving. Understanding is a social practice of seeing what possibilities for thought and action a situation calls for. There is no presuppositionless understanding or naked perception of uninterpreted objects. *Dasein* is always making sense of what it has already understood by projecting onto it *Dasein's* own interests.

Heidegger's concept of *Dasein* and his ontological redirection of hermeneutics was immensely influential for subsequent thinkers. For example, R. BULTMANN, the NT scholar and theologian, made direct use of Heidegger in interpreting the meaning of faith as a possible mode of human being. Christian faith, according to Bultmann, is a decision the self as *Dasein* makes to entrust itself to the grace of God that breaks into the world through the *kerygma* of the NT. Basically *Dasein* can understand itself either (inauthetically) as having to secure its own existence in the world (unfaith) or (authentically) as trusting in an invisible and liberating power that comes to the self from outside in the word of the gospel (faith).

The enormous amount of attention given to hermeneutics since 1960 is in large degree due to the publication of *Truth and Method* in that year by the Heidelberg philosopher, H.-G. Gadamer (b. 1900). Whereas Heidegger largely ignored the methodological concerns of Schleiermacher and Dilthey, Gadamer's *magnum opus* returned to the question of legitimating the human sciences by articulating the method proper to them. Gadamer revisited that issue on the grounds of Heidegger's early work on the hermeneutics of existence as well as Heidegger's later thinking about language in relation to being. Gadamer questioned the demand that the human sciences produce in hermeneutics a method appropriate to their objects of study in order to justify themselves as sciences. He argued that the modern dogma that method is the privileged path to truth in fact instantiates a basic attitude of alienation from the objects of humanistic inquiry. This methodically imposed alienation covers up a more primordial belongingness to human meanings where the truth appropriate to the human sciences in fact appears. *Truth and Method* is a historical and systematic analysis of how methodologism obscures the essential dimension of participation in the human experiences of truth manifested in art, history, and language. Gadamer's philosophical hermeneutics extend and deepen Heidegger's insights into the role of pre-understanding in all three spheres.

The first part of *Truth and Method* is dedicated to aesthetic experience. Gadamer discovered an experience of truth in art that precedes and is obscured by the application of aesthetic methods of analysis. In experiencing a work of art one undergoes something similar to the experience of play in games. The participants in both are drawn into an event with its own subjectivity and life. Releasing oneself to the structured movement of play, one can say both "I play the game" and "the game plays itself through me." In playing a game a higher subjectivity than that of the players manifests itself. So too with art: We experience truth in art when the work draws us into its play of meaning and allows us to see something previously hidden about the everyday world in which we live.

The second part of *Truth and Method* focuses on historical consciousness. Both Schleiermacher and Dilthey, among others, were aware of the difficulties of achieving historical knowledge that does not rewrite the past in the modern historian's image. Their tendency was to work out interpretive methods that would reduce as much as possible the intruding influences of the historian, and thereby to allow the voices of history to speak without distortion. Gadamer acknowledged that it is not possible to impose a method that will eliminate subjective interference with the historical objects as they are in themselves. His concept of *wirkungsgeschichtliches Bewusstsein,* or consciousness that is open to the effects of history, shows that it is an illusion to think that historians can elevate themselves above the stream of historical effects. For example, someone who writes a history of the French Revolution cannot rise above the ongoing effects of the event; the historian belongs to that historical stream and participates in those effects. Any understanding of the historical world is itself historical. According to Gadamer, historians are better advised to recognize how their deeply rooted prejudices (pre-understandings, pre-judgments) are historically shaped and historically effective. By entering a back-and-forth movement of question and answer, which includes allowing the voices of the past to pose questions to the historians, they can come to understand in a self-critical way the truth of historical existence. The historian belongs to the effects of history in a much more profound way than history belongs to the historian as a neutral object of study.

In the third section of *Truth and Method,* Gadamer universalized the hermeneutical experience of belongingness to language. Language is not a separate sphere alongside art and history; it is the medium of our entire experience of the world. All understanding happens as an event within language—indeed, as an event of language. Understanding occurs in the back-and-forth movement of genuine dialogue, and what is understood is being. Language allows being to show itself, and being shows itself only in language. Language, however, is not the prison of understanding; it is the universal medium of the self's dialogical openness to the other. Gadamer's hermeneutics is an eloquent testimony to the finitude of all human interpretations and to the infinity of meaning in which we participate as linguistic beings. For Gadamer, we always understand more than we can say.

Gadamer's hermeneutics have had a widespread influence on biblical interpretation, especially through G. Ebeling (b. 1912) and his followers. Ebeling emphasized that the NT writers were highly aware of how understanding the gospel message can result in the gift of faith mediated through "word event." For both Ebeling and Gadamer, understanding a text from the past and applying its meaning to our present circumstances occur together and not as two separate events.

The French philosopher P. RICOEUR has been a major contributor to modern hermeneutical inquiry. Ricoeur works on the basis of the key insights into philosophical hermeneutics proposed by Heidegger and Gadamer: Human being is distinguished as a mode of being through understanding; the intentional object of the activity of understanding is being; and language is the universal medium through which humans understand being. At one level Ricoeur has been a key figure in mediating German philosophical hermeneutics to the much broader domains of Anglo-American analytic philosophy and cross-disciplinary methodological discussions. His highly complex philosophical program is nonetheless quite different from those of Heidegger and Gadamer. Ricoeur criticizes Heidegger's sudden reversal of hermeneutics from an essentially epistemological concern into an ontological one. He is interested in the meaning of human finite being and in the meaning of being itself, but he does not want to short-circuit the legitimate hermeneutical interest in understanding and interpreting as modes of thinking that intend knowing. He places ontology at the end, not the beginning of his program. Moroever, Ricoeur criticizes Gadamer's apparent dichotomy between inquiry into truth in the human sciences and method. He wants to recover Schleiermacher's methodological interest in articulating the principles, concepts, and rules of interpreting written texts truthfully. Ricoeur does not want to eschew method in favor of truth but to place method in service of truth.

Ricoeur's program began with the two-volume *Philosophy of the Will* (vol. 1, *Freedom and Nature* [1950]; ET 1966; vol. 2, *Finitude and Guilt* [1960]; ET 1965). The second volume has two independently published parts: *Fallible Man,* a phenomenological reflection on the essential structures of finite thinking, willing, and feeling; and *The Symbolism of Evil,* a hermeneutical study of human testimony of evil-doing in Greek myths and tragedies and in biblical texts. *Fallible Man* reveals the essential rift or split that runs through thinking, willing, and feeling; this rift constitutes the possibility of evil and presents a limit-point for philosophical reflection. *The Symbolism of Evil* follows the irrationality of the fall into the language of confession and posits hermeneutics as the methodology appropriate for the study of symbolic language. Subsequently, Ricoeur has written a series of studies in philosophical hermeneutics, including works on the functions of language (both literal and figurative), the nature and interpretation of texts, the conflicts among different kinds of interpretations, the relation between the temporality of human existence and the narrative form of texts, and the interpretation of human action and character on the basis of its text-like nature. He has also written hermeneutical reflections on various NT texts, including the PARABLES OF JESUS and the Gospel of Mark.

Bibliography: J. Bleicher, *Contemporary Hermeneutics: Hermeneutics as Method, Philosophy, and Critique* (1980). W. Dilthey, *Der Aufbau der Geschichtlichen Welt in den Geist-*

eswissenschaften (1958). **M. Ermarth,** *W. Dilthey: The Critique of Historical Reason* (1978). **H.-G. Gadamer,** *Truth and Method* (1960, 1975[4]; ET 1975, 1989[2]); *Philosophical Hermeneutics* (ed. and tr. D. E. Linge, 1976). **J. Grondin,** *Introduction to Philosophical Hermeneutics* (1994); *Sources of Hermeneutics* (1995). **M. Heidegger,** *Being and Time* (1927; ET J. Macquarrie and E. Robinson, 1962; ET J. Stambaugh, 1996); *Ontologie (Hermeneutik der Faktizität)* (ed. K. Bröcker-Oltmans, 1988). **W. Jeanrond,** *Theological Hermeneutics: Development and Significance* (1991). **D. Klemm,** *The Hermeneutical Theory of P. Ricoeur: A Constructive Analysis* (1983). **D. Klemm** (ed.), *Hermeneutical Inquiry* (AAR.SR 43-44, 2 vols., 1986). **D. Klemm and W. Schweiker** (eds.), *Meanings in Texts and Actions: Questioning P. Ricoeur* (SRC, 1993). **R. Makkreel,** *Dilthey: Philosopher of the Human Studies* (1975, 1992). **K. Müller-Vollmar** (ed.), *The Hermeneutics Reader* (1985). **O. Pöggeler,** *M. Heidegger's Path of Thinking* (Contemporary Studies in Philosophy and Human Sciences, 1987). **P. Ricoeur,** *Fallible Man* (1950; ET 1965); *Conflict of Interpretations: Essays in Hermeneutics* (ed. D. Ihde, 1974); *Interpretation Theory* (1976); *Essays on Biblical Interpretation* (ed. L. Mudge, 1980); *Time and Narrative* (3 vols., 1984, 1985, 1988); *Oneself as Another* (1992). **F. D. E. Schleiermacher,** *Hermeneutics: The Handwritten Manuscripts* (ed. H. Kimmerle, tr. J. Duke and J. Forstman, 1977); *Hermeneutik und Kritik* (ed. M. Frank, 1977). **J. Van Den Hengel,** *The Home of Meaning: The Hermeneutics of the Subject of P. Ricoeur* (1982). **G. Warnke,** *Gadamer: Hermeneutics, Tradition, and Reason* (1987). **J. Weinsheimer,** *Gadamer's Hermeneutics: A Reading of Truth and Method* (1985); *Philosophical Hermeneutics and Literary Theory* (1991).

D. E. KLEMM

HERRMANN, WILHELM (1846–1922)

Born in Melkow, Prussia, Dec. 6, 1846, H. studied at the University of Halle from 1864 to 1870 and became *Privatdozent* there in 1875. His academic work included a dissertation on GREGORY OF NYSSA, published in 1875, and the groundwork for a major study of I. KANT published in 1879. In 1889 H. accepted a position at Marburg and remained there until 1916. He died Jan. 2, 1922. He is significant to biblical studies, first, as a teacher and important influence on both R. BULTMANN and K. BARTH; and second, for his significant work on the life of JESUS (1886), which went through several revised editions and was translated into English as *The Communion of the Christian with God.*

H. stood within the tradition of F. D. E. SCHLEIERMACHER and can be viewed as attempting to reformulate Schleiermacher's assertions for a modern era. Influenced to a great extent by A. RITSCHL, he was interested in vindicating religion for a modern world. The foremost Ritschlian scholar of the time, his work is inundated with the themes of the experiential focus of faith and justification; the central role of divine love and human moral responsibility; the crucial function of Christ and the church; and last and probably most important, the correlation of faith and revelation.

One of the main foci of his work was an attempt to provide experiential certainty for the theological facts of the Christian faith. Whereas for Schleiermacher it was religious feeling that gave rise to the cognitive content of revelation, H., trying to overcome extreme subjectivism, suggested that faith was the basis for the cognitive content. He consequently made his well-known separation between the basis of faith represented by Jesus and the content of faith represented by Christ. He worked out this basic theological program in *The Communion of the Christian with God.* The book actually has little to do with presenting a life of Jesus but, rather, is a theological treatise in which H. aspired to illustrate the nature of Christian revelation, faith and experience. He concluded that the "inner life of Jesus" provides the basis for faith insofar as that inner life communes with the consciousness of a particular person. Jesus as human— one like us—provides the ground of union between God and humanity (it was here that M. Kähler had the most serious problem with H.'s position). In this semi-mystical view, when one trusts in God on the basis of experiencing the "inner life of Jesus," faith will produce in that person the content of belief through "thoughts of faith," which include all significant theological tenets, such as the divinity of Christ and the resurrection.

The objectivity of God's communion with the believer is apparent in the simple fact of the existence of the historical Jesus and the presence of the internal demands of moral law that reside in each human being, the latter being particularly important for defining the nature of the life in communion with God. Crucial for H.'s scheme is the understanding that historical-critical investigation of the Bible cannot overturn the insights of faith, since faith is based on the "inner life of Jesus." Thus, the radically different world of the modern era is not an obstacle to belief and faith in God because the Jesus of history is the basis, but not the content, of the Christian's faith; consequently, faith is protected from being ravaged by modern historical investigation of the NT.

Works: *Gregorii Nysseni sententiae de salute adipiscenda* (1875); *Die Religion im Verhältnis zum Welterkennen und zur Sittlichkeit* (1879); *The Communion of the Christian with God Described on the Basis of Luther's Statements* (1886, 1903[4]; ET J. S. Stanyon 1895, 1906[2]; ET ed. R. T. Voelkel, 1971).

Bibliography: **D. L. Deegan,** "W. H.: A Reassessment," *SJT* 19 (1966) 188-203. **P. Fischer-Appelt,** *Metaphysik im Horizont der Theologie W. H.* (1965). **S.-W. Lee,** *Das Wesen der Religion und ihr Verhältnis zu Wissenschaft und Sittlichkeit bei W. H.* (1995). **T. Mahlmann,** *TRE* 15 (1986) 165-72. **K.-H. Michel,** *Glaubensdokument contra Geschichtsbuch? Die Schrift-*

lehre W. H.s (1992). **C. Welch,** *Protestant Thought in the Nineteenth Century,* vol. 2, *1870–1914* (1985) 44–54.

T. C. PENNER

HESCHEL, ABRAHAM JOSHUA (1907–72)

The foremost Jewish theologian of the modern era, H. carried out original scholarship on biblical, rabbinic, and medieval Jewish sources and also developed an original interpretation of Jewish religious thought. Born in Warsaw in 1907, the son of a Hasidic Rebbe, as a young man he received a thorough education in classical Jewish texts. While studying for a doctorate in philosophy at the University of Berlin, which he completed in 1933, he also attended the Hochschule für die Wissenschaft des Judentums, Berlin's liberal seminary that trained its students in the techniques of modern Jewish scientific scholarship. During the Hitler years he sought an academic position outside Europe and just weeks before Germany's invasion of Poland was brought to the United States by the Hebrew Union College in Cincinnati. In 1945 he joined the faculty of Conservative Judaism's Jewish Theological Seminary in New York, where he taught until his death in 1972.

Although H. was conversant with the major figures of modern philosophy and theology, the most important influences on his thought were the teachings of HASIDISM, KABBALAH, and rabbinic theology. By bringing classical Jewish concepts into discussion with modern philosophy, he developed a theology that was deeply rooted in Judaism yet in lively debate with philosophical views of religion. His work has been widely read by Christian as well as by Jewish theologians, shaping, for example, J. Moltmann's influential discussion of divine suffering.

H.'s most important theological category, divine pathos, was first developed in his doctoral dissertation on prophetic consciousness and became central to all of his later theological writings. He argued that the central feature of prophetic religiosity was the teaching that God responds to human deeds, gaining strength or experiencing injury in response to the ways human beings treat one another. His formulation is drawn from classical kabbalistic and Hasidic understanding of *Zoreh Gavoha* (divine need), according to which God voluntarily went into exile with the Jewish people and required redemption along with them. Each mitzvah, when performed with the proper intention, can bring about a reunification within God. H. expanded the classical understanding, as A. Green points out, making God responsive not only to private acts of religious observance but also to public acts of social justice.

Making the marginal of society the center of their concern, the prophets, H. wrote, were "intent on intensifying responsibility"; their goal was to abolish indifference. Rather than preaching a God of wrath, as some have charged, the prophets presented God as profoundly emotional and resonant to humanity, whether in anger, love, or forgiveness; the prophetic God is characterized above all as compassionate. H.'s study of the prophets further argued that their subjective experience, and not simply the content of their message, was crucial to understanding the phenomenon of PROPHECY. He described "prophetic sympathy" as the ability to hold God and humanity in one thought and at one time, resulting in an intense, passionate concern for justice: "Prophecy is the voice that God has lent to the silent agony, a voice to the plundered poor, to the profaned riches of the world."

Tracing his theme of divine pathos in post-biblical literature, H. argued in his three-volume study of rabbinic theology, *Torah min HaShamayim*, that many categories of classical Kabbalah are anticipated in the TALMUD and MIDRASH. In his synthetic theological writings, including *God in Search of Man* and *Man Is Not Alone,* H. further developed the motif of divine pathos, arguing that God is in need of human beings; that the Bible is God's book about humanity rather than a humanly authored book about God; and that evil should be considered foremost, not as a question of theodicy, but of anthropodicy, i.e., God's continued faith in human beings.

Acting on his conviction that the prophets form models for Jewish behavior today, H. became deeply engaged in social and political issues. He is best known for his work in the civil rights movement and as a founder of an anti-Vietnam war organization, Clergy and Laity Concerned About Vietnam. He also served as Jewish representative to the Second Vatican Council during its deliberations on Catholic-Jewish relations.

Works: *God in Search of Man: A Philosophy of Judaism* (1955); *The Prophets* (2 vols., 1962); "Prophetic Inspiration After the Prophets: Maimonides and Other Medieval Authorities," *Torah Min HaShamayim* (vol. 1, 1962; vol. 2, 1965; vol. 3, 1990); *The Insecurity of Freedom: Essays on Human Existence* (1966).

Bibliography: **S. Heschel,** "Introduction," *Moral Grandeur and Spiritual Audacity: Essays of A. J. H.* (1996). **J. C. Merkle** (ed.), *A. J. H.: Exploring His Life and Thought* (1985); *The Genesis of Faith: The Depth Theology of A. J. H.* (1985). **D. J. Moore,** *The Human and the Holy: The Spirituality of A. J. H.* (1989). **L. Perlman,** *A. H.'s Idea of Revelation* (1989). **F. Rothschild,** "Introduction," *Between God and Man: An Interpretation of Judaism from the Writings of A. J. H.* (1959, 1965).

S. HESCHEL

HILGENFELD, ADOLF (1823–1907)

Born June 2, 1823, H. was one of the most prolific and noteworthy NT scholars of the nineteenth century, although he never achieved the fame of his contemporaries F. C. BAUR and D. F. STRAUSS. H. began studies at Berlin in 1841, where he was influenced by the Hegelian P. Marheineke (1780–1846) and Strauss's friend W. VATKE. H. also became acquainted with the newly published *Theologische Jahrbücher* of the Tübingen school and became an ardent proponent of the school. He went to Halle in 1843, completing his doctoral program in 1846; however, his liberal views made it very difficult for him to find a teaching post. He received a position at Jena in 1847 but was not made full professor until 1890. He died Jan. 12, 1907.

H.'s publications included work on the Synoptics (see SYNOPTIC PROBLEM), PAUL, John, Hebrews, the Jewish background to the NT, Gnosticism (see GNOSTIC INTERPRETATION), and various early Christian documents. He published a major work on the Clementine literature (1848); a commentary on John (1849); a major text on Jewish apocalyptic (1857), for the first time drawing attention to the role this literature played in preparing the way for Christianity; a work on the Passover controversy in the early church (1860); a major critical introduction to the NT (1875); and a history of heretics and heresy in the early church (1884). In 1858 he founded the journal *Zeitschrift für wissenschaftliche Theologie,* which became a major vehicle for studies on early Christianity and contined after his death until 1914.

H.'s work on Jewish apocalyptic (see APOCALYPTICISM) was formative for scholars who came after him and foreshadowed in a major way the later methodological developments of the RELIGIONSGESCHICHTLICHE SCHULE. In addition, he was, with A. VON HARNACK, among the first to promote the view that Gnosticism played a major role in the development of early Christianity. H. believed that Gnosticism was a non-Christian phenomenon orginating out of Samaritanism, that the Gnostic movement entered the Christian church via the Jewish-Christian anti-Paulinist groups, and that the Gospel of John was a product of this Christian Gnosticism. He thus established a path many later German scholars would follow.

Later in his career H. attempted to distance himself from the Tübingen school, maintaining that because he held to the authenticity of 1 Thessalonians, Philippians, Philemon, and the final chapters of Romans he could not include himself among the Tübingen *Tendenz* critics. In 1852 he attacked Baur's view on the priority of Mark and offered his own position that Mark was dependent on Matthew but independent of Luke. While these may be viewed as minor divergences from the Tübingen positions, neither H. nor Baur understood them to be such. Rather, they hit at the very heart of Baur's historical method. H. maintained that Baur first set out a basic historical framework and then went about fitting various documents into that mold, forcing them if need be. H., on the other hand, argued that one must give more attention to the particularities of early Christian literature, first appreciating a given document in its own right.

As evidenced in his specific studies, H. never shed the larger Tübingen theory of historical development and the importance placed on the ideational Paulinist and Jewish Christian movements in the early church. However, his main approach was to focus on specific documents in their contexts and to refrain from general historical speculation. In this way he contributed to the development of the historical-critical method of interpretation and was an important bridge between the biblical scholarship of the nineteenth century and that of the twentieth.

Works: *Die Clementinischen Recognitionen und Homilien nach ihrem Ursprung und Inhalt dargestellt* (1848); *Das Evangelium und die Briefe Iohannis: Nach ihrem Lehrbegriff dargestellt* (1849); *Die apostolischen Väter: Untersuchungen über Inhalt und Ursprung der unter ihrem Namen erhaltenen Schriften* (1853); *Die Evangelien nach ihrer Entstehung und geschichtlichen Bedeutung* (1854); *Die jüdische Apokalyptik in ihrer geschichtlichen Entwicklung: Ein Beitrag zur Vorgeschichte des Christentums nebst einem Anhange über das gnostische System des Basilides* (1857); (ed.), *Zeitschrift für wissenschaftliche Theologie* (1858–1914); *Der Paschastreit der alten Kirche* (1860); *Historisch-kritische Einleitung in das neue Testament* (1875); *Die Ketzergeschichte des Urchristentums: Urkundlich dargestellt* (1884); *Judentum und Judenchristentum: Eine Nachlese zu der Ketzergeschichte des Urchristentums* (1886).

Bibliography: **W. Baird,** *HNTR* (1992) 273-77. **R. H. Fuller,** "Baur Versus Hilgenfeld: A Forgotten Chapter in the Debate on the Synoptic Problem," *NTS* 24 (1978) 355-70. **H. Harris,** *The Tübingen School: A Historical and Theological Investigation of the School of F. C. Baur* (1975). **H. Pölcher,** "A. H. und das Ende der Tübinger Schule: Untersuchungen zur Geschichte der Religionswissenschaft im 19. Jahrhundert," vol. 1, "Hilgenfelds wissenschaftlicher Weg und seine Stellung in der zeitgenössischen Forschung"; vol. 2, "Hilgenfelds Beitrag zur Erforschung des Urchristentums"; vol. 3, "Briefe und andere ungedruckte Dokumente" (diss., Erlangen-Nürnberg, 1961). **H. Rollmann,** "From Baur to Wrede: The Quest for a Historical Method," *SR* 17 (1988) 443-54. **J. M. Schmidt,** *Die jüdische Apokalyptik: Die Geschichte ihrer Erforschung von den Anfängen bis zu den Textfunden von Qumran* (1969) 127-47.

T. C. PENNER

HILLEL (end of 1st cent. BCE–beginning of 1st cent. CE)

H. "the Elder," according to tradition, came to Palestine from Babylonia. Other less reliable traditions made him a member of the Davidic family line. Although many of the traditions preserved about him have legendary traits, he was undoubtedly the most outstanding rabbi of his day, noted for his more liberal and lenient interpretation of the *halakha* than that of his counterpart Shammai. His students and school were especially influential in later Judaism.

Tradition traced back to H. seven hermeneutical *middot* (measures, norms, or rules) for the interpretation of Scripture. These were used in extending a text's applicability, reconciling differences and contradictions, and clarifying obscurities. These principles were probably the product of deliberate reflection on methods already in existence for employing Scripture. They parallel hermeneutical principles (see HERMENEUTICS) of Hellenistic rhetoric, but whether there was direct influence or dependence between the two remains a debatable issue. The rules are found in *Tosephta Sanhedrin* 7:11; *Sipra* (on Leviticus), introduction 1:7; and *Abot de Rabbi Nathan* A 37:110.

The seven *middot* are as follows: (1) *Qal wa-ḥomer* (light and heavy or lesser and greater) relates to arguing *a minori ad maius*—that is, from a minor to a major premise. (2) *Gezerah shawah* (equal ordinance or similar injunction) involves drawing conclusions by analogy between texts that have some similarities like vocabulary. (3) *Binyan ab mi-katub eḥad* (building a family from one text) involves the drawing of inferences from a single verse or applying a specific stipulation to other conditions. (4) *Binyan ab mi-shnê ketubim* (building a family from two texts) involves drawing inferences and establishing regulations on the basis of two verses. (5) *Kelal u-ferat u-ferat u-kekal* (the general and the particular, the particular and the general) concerns the interpretation of texts in which general instances are followed by particular instances and vice versa, whereby the particular following a general constitutes a limitation and vice versa. (6) *Ke-yoṣe bô be-magom aḥer* (something similar to this in another place) is similar to the use of analogy but always allows deductions from one passage to elucidate another passage when the two texts share some similarity. (7) *Dabar ha-lamed me-inyano* (a matter of the argument from context) stipulates that a passage is to be read and understood in terms of its larger context.

These seven *middot* were expanded and elaborated upon in the thirteen *middot* attributed to Rabbi ISHMAEL and in the thirty-two attributed to the second-century CE teacher Eliezer ben Yose ha-Gelili (the latter actually probably deriving from Samuel ben Hophni [d. 1013]).

Bibliography: D. Daube, "Rabbinic Methods of Interpretation and Hellenistic Rhetoric," *HUCA* 22 (1949) 239-64. N. N. Glatzer, *Hillel the Elder* (1956); *EncJud* 8 (1971) 482-85. J. Neusner, *From Politics to Piety: The Emergence of Pharisaic Judaism* (1973) 13-44. E. Schürer, *HJPAJC* 2 (1979) 363-67. H. L. Strack and G. Stamberger, *Introduction to the Talmud and Midrash* (1991) 19-23. W. S. Towner, "Hermeneutical Systems of Hillel and the Tannaim: A Fresh Look," *HUCA* 53 (1982) 101-35. E. E. Urbach, *The Sages: Their Concepts and Beliefs* (1975) 576-93. S. Zeitlin, "Hillel and the Hermeneutic Rules," *JQR* NS 54 (1963–64) 161-73.

J. H. HAYES

HISPANIC AMERICAN BIBLICAL INTERPRETATION

An explicit and self-conscious focus on biblical interpretation on the part of Hispanic Americans or Latinos/as from the standpoint of their status as an ethnic minority group within the country accompanies the emergence of Hispanic American theology on the United States theological scene at the end of the 1980s and the beginning of the 1990s. With the rise of theological reflection on the reality and experience of Hispanic Americans comes a corresponding interest in biblical HERMENEUTICS, in the interpretation of the Bible from the point of view of and with regard to such a reality and experience. Two different sequential developments can be readily identified within this newly constituted reading tradition of the Bible.

At first such a turn to the Bible was profoundly theological in nature. The early voices in the movement, given their primary training in theological studies (broadly conceived, ranging from constructive theology, to social ethics, to church historiography, to pastoral theology), turned to the biblical texts for reflection, inspiration, and argumentation in the elaboration of their respective theological constructions. In this initial phase of the movement the hermeneutical element remained by and large subordinate to the primary theological aims of the discussion. In time this use of the Bible became a much more self-conscious critical activity and hence profoundly hermeneutical in character. Subsequent voices whose primary training was in biblical studies began to examine the use of the Bible on the part of their theological colleagues and to turn to the biblical texts in the light of both contemporary biblical criticism and the aims of the movement as a whole. In this second phase of the movement, the theological element remained for the most part secondary to the prevailing hermeneutical aims of the discussion.

Such a concern with biblical interpretation among Hispanic American theologians and critics in the late 1980s and early 1990s should be seen as neither unique nor fortuitous but rather as yet another sign of the times. Indeed, the emergence of this concern can be readily accounted for by a variety of developments, all ultimately interrelated and interdependent, in the social fabric of the country, the world of the academy at large, the field of theology in general, and the discipline of biblical studies in particular.

At the broadest level of American society, the social upheavals of the 1960s and 1970s set the stage through the various movements of emancipation unleashed in the country, among which both the Mexican American and the Puerto Rican communities—the long-standing Hispanic American communities in the country—featured prominently. Such movements clamored for an end to cultural prejudice, social discrimination, economic injustice, and political marginalization. In the process the larger society became highly conflicted, or to put it differently, long-standing conflicts were brought to the fore more sharply than ever before. As a result Hispanic Americans began to analyze critically as well as assertively their history in the country, their present fragile condition in society, and their dreams and visions for the future. Such was the beginning of the long process of conscientization, of self-understanding and self-reflection, on the part of the group as a minority.

From the viewpoint of the academy such social turmoil led to drastic changes in the conception of knowledge throughout the 1970s and 1980s. Across the disciplinary spectrum, in the human sciences as well as in the social sciences, the object of study was no longer regarded as universal and unidimensional and its analysis as objective and disinterested. On the contrary, analysis was now perceived as profoundly contextual and perspectival, while the object of study was approached as local and multidimensional. The pursuit of knowledge had thus become highly conflicted as well, as the various constitutive factors of human identity—including race and ethnicity—began to be seen not only as sharply diversifying the object of study but also as directly affecting the process of analysis. From such a theoretical point of view, issues of representation, power, and ideology became foremost in every discipline. As a result, the study of Hispanic Americans—in terms both of the group as a whole and the different segments within the group—became a valid exercise in its own right, whether in terms of history and literature or culture and society. What had begun as a social movement eventually turned into an intellectual movement as well, lending ever greater maturity and sophistication to the ongoing process of conscientization on the part of the group.

With regard to the field of theology, the study of Christianity as a religion, such social upheavals and academic transformations were clearly reflected in the swift processes of decentralization and globalization at work in the theological world as the traditional Western hold on theological reflection became increasingly fractured throughout the 1970s and 1980s. From a global point of view theological construction was now actively pursued in all corners of the world, beginning with Latin America and then rapidly spreading to the continents of Africa and Asia. From the viewpoint of the United States, a similar process ensued as theological construction was increasingly undertaken by ethnic and racial minority groups, commencing with African American

theology (see AFROCENTRIC INTERPRETATION) and ultimately witnessing the emergence of such other theologies as Hispanic American theology, Native American theology, and ASIAN American theology. As with every other discipline, theological studies also became highly conflicted, forced to take into consideration the local and multidimensional character of their object of study as well as the contextual and perspectival nature of the process of analysis. Inevitably, given their increasing numbers in the field, what had already become a social and intellectual movement was now also turning into a theological movement for Hispanic Americans.

Within the field of theology all of the different areas of study could not help being directly affected by such developments, and biblical criticism was no exception. The signs were clear. To begin with, the long-established critical paradigm in the discipline, historical criticism, was severely challenged, eventually being displaced by a number of other critical paradigms and thus yielding a situation of pronounced methodological and theoretical diversity. In the process, increasing importance was placed on the role of readers and on the reading process (see READER-RESPONSE CRITICISM) in the task of interpretation, ultimately leading to a view of all interpretation as both contextual and perspectival. Consequently, close attention to the social location and the IDEOLOGICAL stance of readers became imperative. The result was pronounced sociocultural diversity. The traditional conception of the discipline as a rigorously scientific exercise involving an empiricist worldview as well as universal and disinterested readers yielded to a radically different view of biblical interpretation as highly conflicted, both at the level of the text and the level of the reader. Quite naturally, the emerging theological movement among Hispanic Americans spawned a corresponding concern for biblical hermeneutics as Hispanic American theologians and critics sought to examine, from the viewpoint of their self-understanding and self-reflection as a minority group, their interpretation and use of the biblical texts. In the end the process of conscientization had come to embrace the world of biblical criticism as well, giving rise to a new and self-conscious reading tradition of the Bible.

In this turn toward the Bible and biblical criticism the two different developments within the movement noted above—the theological and the hermeneutical—can be distinguished in terms of their positions on five fundamental issues of interpretation, (1) perceived affinity with the text, (2) proposed locus of LIBERATION in the text, (3) point of entry into the text, (4) validity in interpretation, and (5) perceived agenda of liberation in the text.

The initial, primarily theological, approach shows a clear commitment to the hermeneutics of liberation in the interpretation and use of the Bible. For these early voices the biblical texts constituted an effective weapon in the struggle against prejudice, discrimination, injustice, and marginalization as well as a faithful ally in the struggle for liberation. All concerned adopted variations of a basic model of liberation hermeneutics involving both a formal analogy between the past and the present, between the relationship of the Bible and the relationship of the group to their respective sociohistorical and sociocultural contexts, and a basic correspondence between Hispanic Americans today and the people of God in the Bible. These variations were the result of different positions adopted with regard to the five key issues of interpretation listed above.

This first phase in the interpretation and use of the Bible by Hispanic Americans may be summarized as follows: (1) With respect to perceived affinity with ancient texts on the part of present-day readers who come from a very different sociocultural and sociohistorical context, the Bible was looked upon as neither distant nor strange; and the biblical texts were seen as easily accessible to Hispanic Americans. The life and struggle of the biblical people of God were seen as anticipating the life and struggle of Hispanic Americans today, making it possible for the latter to identify with the Bible and its message of liberation.

(2) In terms of the proposed locus of liberation within the text, two major positions emerged: the concept of a canon within the CANON, on the basis of which the rest of the Bible was to be judged, and the notion of a unified and consistent text. Either way, the Bible was looked upon as conveying a message of liberation—a God not at all removed or foreign but rather a God who was on the side of Hispanic Americans.

(3) Regarding the point of entry into the text, marginalization and oppression were seen as the key to the liberating message of the Bible, although oppression and marginalization were defined in different ways and thus resulted in different constructions of the God of liberation. At a fundamental level, however, it was the similar experience of oppression and marginalization that allowed Hispanic Americans to identify with the biblical people of God.

(4) In terms of validity in interpretation or correct and incorrect readings, despite different emphases there was a general call for a resistant biblical reading from the experience of oppression and marginalization aligned against reading strategies associated with power and privilege.

(5) With respect to the perceived agenda for liberation in the text, a common utopian and subversive vision of liberation prevailed. This vision, which encompassed different views of the new order, questioned the present world order while advancing an alternative.

The subsequent predominantly hermeneutical approach reveals a continued commitment to a hermeneutics of liberation in the interpretation and use of the Bible. Alongside such a commitment, however, these later voices begin to offer a much more guarded picture of the Bible as an effective weapon and faithful ally in the struggle against oppression and for liberation.

This second phase in the interpretation and use of the Bible on the part of Hispanic Americans may be depicted as follows: (1) In terms of perceived affinity with the text the consensus on correspondence between the people of God and Hispanic Americans gives way to a more guarded approach to the question of distance and kinship. The Bible emerges as a more distant and strange text, a text whose accessibility to Hispanic Americans becomes problematic. The reasons for such a move in favor of distancing differ: a view that the concept of a chosen people of God has xenophobic connotations and ramifications; the ever-present danger of enslaving the ancient text; a view of the text as a culturally and historically removed other.

(2) Regarding the proposed locus of liberation within the text, while the consensus on the Bible as a liberating text perdures, this message is now perceived as more ambiguous: The Bible begins to be seen as a source of both liberation and oppression. Thus, in effect, the God of the Bible emerges as a God who may actually work against the liberation of Hispanic Americans, while the message of liberation can fall victim to the captivity of present-day readers or can be understood in different ways by different readers.

(3) With respect to the point of entry into the text, the consensus of marginalization and oppression as key to the liberating message of the Bible still holds, with oppression and marginalization again being defined in different ways. However, the process of identification with the people of God on the part of Hispanic Americans is depicted as more difficult given such factors as the oppressive tactics of the people of God in the Bible, the differences among Hispanic Americans, and the problem of pointing to any one experience in particular as the key to the liberating message of the Bible.

(4) Regarding the question of validity in interpretation, the consensual call for a reading of resistance also continues, a reading similarly characterized as biblical and distinguished from reading strategies associated with power and privilege. At the same time such a reading becomes more complex insofar as it must remain attuned to the different voices present in the text, be made subject to constant self-revision, or deny the possibility of any one reading as the correct reading.

(5) In terms of the perceived agenda of liberation, the consensus regarding a highly utopian and subversive vision of liberation prevails. At the same time such a vision becomes more subtle: It is now a vision that must choose among competing biblical ideologies and, where one biblical ideology must prevail in place of another, a vision that calls for theological and hermeneutical dialogue, or a vision that emphasizes both the multiplicity of readers and visions and their mutual engagement.

As an explicit and self-conscious reading tradition of the Bible, Hispanic American hermeneutics has witnessed rapid development during its brief life span, from its initial moorings in the discourse of countermodernity, given its option for the classic patterns of the hermeneutics of liberation, to its recent engagement with the discourses of post-modernity (see POST-MODERN BIBLICAL INTERPRETATION) as reflected in its growing concern with issues of representation, power, and ideology in interpretation. In this it has followed the course of Hispanic American theology, becoming ever more diverse and sophisticated in the process. As additional voices continue to join its ranks, participate in its discussions, and seek to shape its discourse, such sophistication and diversity are bound to grow at an even more rapid pace, making of Hispanic American biblical interpretation an increasingly vibrant, complex, and powerful reading tradition of the Bible.

Bibliography: **A. J. Bañuelas,** "U.S. Hispanic Theology," *Missiology* (April 1992) 275-300. **V. Elizondo,** *Galilean Journey: The Mexican American Promise* (1983). **E. C. Fernández,** " 'Reading the Bible in Spanish': U.S. Catholic Hispanic Theologians' Contribution to Systematic Theology," *Apuntes* 14 (1994) 86-90. **F. García-Treto,** "The Lesson of the Gibeonites: A Proposal for Dialogic Attention as a Strategy for Reading the Bible," *Hispanic/Latino Theology: Challenge and Promise* (ed. A. M. Isasi-Díaz and F. F. Segovia, 1996) 73-85; "Crossing the Line: Three Scenes of Divine-Human Engagement in the HB," *Teaching the Bible: Discourses and Politics of Biblical Pedagogy* (ed. F. F. Segovia and M. A. Tolbert, 1998). **J. L. González,** *Mañana: Christian Theology from a Hispanic Perspective* (1990); "Reading from My Bicultural Place: Acts 6:1-7," *Reading from This Place,* vol. 1, *Social Location and Biblical Interpretation in the United States* (ed. F. F. Segovia and M. A. Tolbert, 1995) 139-48; "Metamodern Aliens in Postmodern Jerusalem," *Hispanic/Latino Theology: Challenge and Promise* (ed. A. M. Isasi-Díaz and F. F. Segovia, 1996) 340-50; *Santa Biblia: Through Hispanic Eyes* (1995). **A. M. Isasi-Díaz,** "La Palabra de Dios en nosotras: The Word of God in Us," *Searching the Scriptures,* vol. 1, *A Feminist Introduction* (ed. E. Schüssler Fiorenza, 1993) 86-100: " 'By the Rivers of Babylon': Exile as a Way of Life," *Reading from This Place,* vol. 1, *Social Location and Biblical Interpretation in the United States* (ed. F. F. Segovia and M. A. Tolbert, 1995) 149-63. **P. Jiménez** (ed.), *Lumbrera a nuestro camino* (1994); "In Search of a Hispanic Model of Biblical Interpretation," *Journal of Hispanic/Latino Theology* 3 (1995) 44-64. **H. J. Recinos,** *Hear the Cry! A Latino Pastor Challenges the Church* (1989). **J. D. Rodríguez,** "De 'apuntes' a 'esbozo': diez años de reflexión," *Apuntes* 10 (1990) 75-83. **C. G. Romero,** *Hispanic Devotional Piety: Tracing the Biblical Roots* (Faith and Culture Series, 1991); "Tradition and Symbol as Biblical Keys for a U.S. Hispanic Theology," *Hispanic Theology in the United States* (ed. A. F. Deck, 1992) 41-61; "Amos 5:21-24: Religion, Politics, and the Latino Experience," *Journal of Hispanic/Latino*

Theology 4 (1997) 21-41. **J.-P. Ruiz,** "Beginning to Read the Bible in Spanish: An Initial Assessment," *Journal of Hispanic/ Latino Theology* 1 (1994) 28-50; "Contexts in Conversation: First World and Third World Readings of Job," *Journal of Hispanic/Latino Theology* 2 (1995) 5-29; "Four Faces of Theology: Four Johannine Conversations," *Teaching the Bible: Discourses and Politics of Biblical Pedagogy* (ed. F. F. Segovia and M. A. Tolbert, 1998). **F. F. Segovia,** "A New Manifest Destiny: The Emerging Theological Voice of Hispanic Americans," *RStR* 17, 2 (April, 1991) 102-9; "Hispanic American Theology and the Bible: Effective Weapon and Faithful Ally," *We Are a People! Initiative in Hispanic American Theology* (ed. R. S. Goizueta, 1992) 21-50; "Reading the Bible as Hispanic Americans," *NIB* (1994) 1:167-73; "Toward a Hermeneutics of the Diaspora: A Hermeneutics of Otherness and Engagement," *Reading from This Place,* vol. 1, *Social Location and Biblical Interpretation in the United States* (ed. F. F. Segovia and M. A. Tolbert, 1995) 57-74; "Toward Intercultural Criticism: A Reading Strategy from the Diaspora," *Reading from This Place,* vol. 2, *Social Location and Biblical Interpretation in Global Perspective* (ed. F. F. Segovia and M. A. Tolbert, 1995) 303-30.

F. F. SEGOVIA

HITTITOLOGY AND BIBLICAL STUDIES

Until the nineteenth century known references to the Hittites were limited to the forty-seven occurrences of the term in the HB used in speaking of particular individuals like Ephron (Gen 23:10), Ahimelech (1 Sam 26:6), and Uriah (2 Sam 11:3); to describe an element of the pre-Israelite population of Canaan (Gen 15:20; Ezek 16:3); or to denote Syrian states to the north of Israel (2 Kgs 7:6; 2 Chr 1:17). With the decipherment of the Egyptian hieroglyphics (see EGYPTOLOGY AND BIBLICAL STUDIES) in 1822 by J. Champollion (1790–1832) and the subsequent decipherment of Mesopotamian cuneiform in the 1850s, non-biblical references to the Hittites became known. Egyptian texts referred to a country Ht in Syria; and Assyrian texts, to the "land of Hatti" west of the Euphrates. Among the el-Amarna texts from Egypt were two tablets (in the 1887 cache) written in an unknown language from a king of Arzawa, which came to be associated with the Hittites. In 1876 the British orientalist A. SAYCE had proposed that basalt blocks at Aleppo and Hama inscribed with hieroglyphic signs were probably Hittite. The finding of a cache of inscribed clay tablets near the village of Boghazköy in modern Turkey in 1893 would eventually lead to our modern knowledge of the Hittites. Excavations at this site were begun by the Germans in 1906; it proved to be Hattusha, the capital of the ancient Hittites. In 1915 the Czech Assyriologist (see ASSYRIOLOGY AND BIBLICAL STUDIES) F. Hrozny succeeded in deciphering the texts, which turned out to be written in the oldest known Indo-European language, a theory already advocated in 1902 by the Norwegian scholar J. Knudtzon (1915), famous for his work on the el-Amarna texts. Subsequent excavations and discovery and decipherment of additional texts have made Hittitology a significant component of ancient Near Eastern studies.

Hittite civilization flourished in Anatolia from about 1680 BCE until the destruction of its major cities at the end of the Late Bronze Age (c. 1180 BCE), due at least in part to the disturbances caused by the so-called Sea Peoples. The Hittites commanded an extensive realm by Near Eastern standards and were powerful enough to rival the Babylonians, Assyrians, and Egyptians for control of the valuable trade routes of Syria-Palestine. Under the first well-attested Hittite king, Hattusili I, the Hittite Old Kingdom established a military foothold over much of Anatolia. Hattusili I's grandson and successor, Mursili I, was able to add to the kingdom's prestige by marching south through Syria and Mesopotomia and sacking Babylon, bringing an end to that city's First Dynasty (c. 1595).

Many of the cities of northern Syria-Palestine, including Carchemish, UGARIT, Aleppo, and Emar were under Hittite hegemony at the end of the Late Bronze Age. The Egyptians and Hittites fought their great battle at Kadesh in 1285 BCE over the territories of Syria-Palestine, and the Egypto-Hittite peace treaty of 1256 BCE that ended hostilities ushered in a period of cooperation between the Hittite Empire (which extended as far south as Kadesh) and the Egyptian Empire that lasted more than sixty years. A royal marriage between Ramses II and a daughter of Hattusili III cemented the peace.

Although the Hittite civilization and language did not survive the catastrophe at the end of the Late Bronze Age, the former provincial Hittite capitals in Syria did. It is now generally accepted that much of the Hittite population of Anatolia, weary of famine, plague, and political upheaval, left the highlands of Anatolia for the relatively peaceful and still somewhat affluent regions of northern Syria, where some measure of Hittite culture could still be found. In some cases new Hittite centers were established at sites like Hama that formerly had no Hittite population. The archaeological evidence (see ARCHAEOLOGY AND BIBLICAL STUDIES) from this Syrian city suggests an Iron Age influx of immigrants from southern Anatolia who introduced into the area a new ceramic repertoire, Hittite architectural styles and burial customs, and the hieroglyphic Luwian script.

Some of the Hittites who moved south may have settled in Palestine and may represent the Hittites of biblical texts. Such trade items as ivory and jewelry, an epigraphic find at Aphek, a portion of a bulla, the Hittite style of the Hazor temple, private seals, and burial practices employing jar burials and cremation urns unearthed at various sites add archaeological support to a Hittite presence in Palestine (see A. Kempinski [1979]; I. Singer [1977, 1994]).

One of the first comparisons of HB and Hittite material is found in the 1910 work of P. Karge, who compared the cuneiform version of a treaty between Pharaoh Ramses II and the Hittite king Hattusili III and OT covenant material. Two decades after the publication of a number of Hittite international treaty texts by V. Korošec (*Hethitische Staatsverträge* [1931]), several scholars (see G. Mendenhall [1954], K. Baltzer [1960; ET 1971], K. Kitchen [1979], D. McCarthy [1963, 1978[2]]) drew parallels between the structure of Hittite vassal treaties and HB covenant texts. The Hittite treaties reflect a sixfold structure: (1) royal titulature, (2) historical introduction, (3) stipulations, (4) list of divine witnesses, (5) blessings and curses, and (6) references to recital of the treaty and deposit of copies. This structure was compared to elements in Exodus 19–24 and the outline of the book of Deuteronomy, and many scholars concluded that the similarities and the contemporaneity of the Hittites's texts with the Mosaic age established the Mosaic origin of an Israelite treaty with Yahweh. Some scholars have opposed this view (see E. Nicholson [1986]) with various arguments: The biblical parallels are produced by combining narratives and legal material and are more reports of covenant making than covenant documents per se; the biblical texts are composite from various periods; the eighth-century prophets (see PROPHECY AND PROPHETS, HB) indicate no knowledge of a theology based on a Yahweh-Israel covenant; and the Mosaic age would not indicate a time when the Hebrews were involved in international relations. Possibly the biblical parallels to international treaties were more influenced by neo-Assyrian than Hittite practices and texts (see the collection in S. Parpola and K. Watanaba [1988]).

Hittite historiographic texts have been compared with biblical historiographic material, especially the so-called Hittite royal apologies and the biblical material on David and Solomon (see H. Cancik [1976] and J. Van Seters's critique [1983]). The parallels here seem, however, to be more analogous due to the propagandistic nature of the material rather than to any Israelite reliance upon Hittite literature.

Numerous parallels between Israelite and Hittite legal practices exist, including such incidental matters as the use of a shoe in certain failures to fulfill personal responsibilities (see Deut 25:5-10; Ruth 4:7-10; H. Hoffner [1969] 42-44). Although such similarities provide reciprocal illumination, there is no need to assume direct dependency but simply parallel developments.

In the area of religious and ritual practices, parallels again exist. Like the Israelites, the Hittites believed in divine revelation through divination, direct oracles, and dreams. The Hittites shared with the Israelites a great concern for ritual purity and the avoidance of pollution. Special Hittite temple officials charged with guarding the sacredness of the sanctuary have been compared to OT Levites (see J. Milgrom [1970]). As in the OT, kings and priests were anointed.

A selection of Hittite texts appears in *ANET*: myths (120-28, 519), laws (188-97), treaties (199-206, 529-30), instructions (207-11), historiography (318-19), rituals (346-61, 497-98), and prayers (393-401).

Bibliography: E. **Akurgal,** *The Art of the Hittites* (1962). K. **Baltzer,** *The Covenant Formulary in OT, Jewish, and Early Christian Writings* (WMANT 4, 1960; ET 1971). G. M. **Beckman,** *Hittite Diplomatic Texts* (Writings from the Ancient World 7, 1996). K. **Bittel,** *Hattusha, the Capital of the Hittites* (1970). F. F. **Bruce,** *The Hittites and the OT* (1947). H. **Cancik,** *Mythische und historische Wahrheit: Interpretation zu Texten Grundzüge der hethitischen und alttestamentlichen Geschichtsschreibung* (1976). A. **Goetze,** *Kleinasien* (1956²). O. R. **Gurney,** *The Hittites* (1952, rev. ed. 1966); *CAH³* 2.1 (1973) 228-55, 659-83; *Some Aspects of Hittite Religion* (1977). H. G. **Güterbock,** "Hittite Religion," *Forgotten Religions Including Some Living Primitive Religions* (ed. V. Ferm, 1950) 83-109; "Hittite Mythology," *Mythologies of the Ancient World* (ed. S. N. Kramer, 1961) 139-79. J. D. **Hawkins,** "The Neo-Hittite States in Syria and Anatolia," *CAH³* 3, 1 (1982) 374-441. H. A. **Hoffner,** "Second Millennium Antecedents to the Hebrew 'ôb," *JBL* 86 (1967) 385-401; "Hittite *Tarpiš* and Hebrew *Terāphîm*," *JNES* 27 (1968) 61-68; "Some Contributions of Hittitology to OT Study," *TynBul* 20 (1969) 27-55; "Histories and Historians of the Ancient Near East: The Hittites," *Orientalia* 49 (1980) 283-332; "Propaganda and Political Justification in Hittite Historiography," *Unity and Diversity* (ed. H. Goedicke and J. J. M. Roberts, 1975) 49-62; "Hittite Religion," *EncRel* 6 (1987) 408-14; *Hittite Myths* (tr. H. A Hoffner, ed. G. M. Beckman, Writings from the Ancient World 2, 1990); "Hittites," *Peoples of the OT World* (ed. A. J. Hoerth et al., 1994) 127-55. P. **Karge,** *Geschichte des Bundesgedankens im Alten Testament* (1910). A. **Kempinski,** "Hittites in the Bible: What Does Archaeology Say?" *BAR* 5, 4 (1979) 21-45. K. A. **Kitchen,** *Ancient Orient and OT* (1966); "Egypt, Ugarit, Qatna, and Covenant," *UF* 11 (1979) 453-64. J. **Knudtzon,** *Die el-Amarna-Tafeln: Mit Einleitung und Erläuterungen* (1915). M. R. **Lehmann,** "Abraham's Purchase of Machpelah and Hittite Law," *BASOR* 129 (1953) 15-18. D. J. **McCarthy,** *Treaty and Covenant: A Study in Form in the Ancient Oriental Documents and in the OT* (AnBib 21, 1963, 1978²). G. **McMahon,** "Hittites in the OT," *ABD* 3 (1992) 231-33. A. **Malamat,** "Doctrines of Causality in Hittite and Biblical Historiography: A Parallel," *VT* 5 (1955) 1-12. G. E. **Mendenhall,** "Law and Covenant in Israel and the Ancient Near East," *BA* 17 (1954) 26-46, 49-76. J. **Milgrom,** "The Shared Custody of the Tabernacle and a Hittite Analogy," *JAOS* 90 (1970) 204-9. E. **Neufeld,** *The Hittite Laws* (1951). E. W. **Nicholson,** *God and His People: Covenant and Theology in the OT* (1986). S. **Parpola and K. Watanabe,** *Neo-Assyrian Treaties and Loyalty Oaths* (1988). I. **Singer,** "A Hittite Hieroglyphic Seal Impression from Tel Aphek," *Tel Aviv* 4 (1977) 178-90; "A Hittite Signet Ring from Tel Nami," *kinattūtu ša dārâti: Raphael Kutscher Memorial Volume* (Journal of the Institute of Archaeology of Tel Aviv University, 1993) 189-93. J. **Van Seters,** "Hittite Historiography," *In Search of History* (1983; repr. 1997) 100-26. H. M. **Wolf,** "The Apology of Hattušiliš Compared with Other Political Self-Justifications of the Ancient Near East" (diss., Brandeis University, 1967). D. P. **Wright,** *The Disposal of Impurity: Elimination Rites in the Bible and in Hittite and Mesopotamia Literature* (SBLDS 101, 1987).

B. J. COLLINS

HITZIG, FERDINAND (1807–75)

A purely historical critic of great learning, H. championed the critical method during the reaction against it in Germany from 1830 to 1860 and lived to see its triumph. He was born June 23, 1807, in Hauingen near Lörrach and studied in Heidelberg (1824–25) under the rationalist Paulus, then with H. GESENIUS in Halle (1825–27). Gaining his doctorate in Göttingen in 1829, he returned to Heidelberg to become a *Privatdozent,* and in 1833 accepted a post in Zurich, where he remained for twenty-eight years. In 1839 he supported an attempt to appoint D. F. STRAUSS to a chair in Zurich; as a consequence only when the influence of confessional orthodoxy began to wane did he receive a call to his old university of Heidelberg at Easter 1861. He remained in Heidelberg until his death, Jan. 22, 1875.

H. was an outstanding Hebraist and a formidable classicist. His knowledge was encyclopedic, and his aim in biblical interpretation was to understand the text in its historical setting. This setting was to be elucidated with all the help of critical scholarship, including the evidence of comparative religion. His most important HB works were his commentaries for the KEH series on Isaiah (1833), Psalms (1835–36), the Minor Prophets (1838), Jeremiah (1841), Ezekiel (1847), Ecclesiastes (1847), Daniel (1850), and Song of Songs (1855). In addition, in 1869 he published a two-volume history of Israel. The commentaries were characterized by exacting philological and grammatical comments and by H.'s belief that he could date with some precision the individual prophetic oracles (see PROPHECY AND PROPHETS, HB) and interpret them in their historical setting. It was probably this confidence that resulted in his work's becoming dated as criticism became more refined. Also, his conviction that the cuneiform texts from Assyria and Babylon were written in an Indo-European language is now only a curiosity. However, his unconventional approach and his almost perverse determination to oppose received critical ideas led him to argue, against the trend, that Mark's Gospel was an original work by PAUL's erstwhile companion John Mark; but he also argued that John Mark wrote the book of Revelation.

H. was an outstanding teacher whose lectures were full of wit but who insisted on the highest standards of knowledge. His tall figure was always welcome where students gathered to drink. He represented that type of German Protestant scholarship that believed that the unfettered quest for truth was a duty and an enterprise that could only harm Christian faith if it was not pursued totally.

Works: *Begriff der Kritik am Alten Testament* (1831); *Historischer und Kritischer Commentar zu den Psalmen* (1835–36); *Ueber Johann Markus und seine Schriften* (1843); *Geschichte des Volkes Israel* (1869); *Sprache und Sprachen Assyriens* (1870); *Zur Kritik Paulinischer Briefe* (1870).

Bibliography: "Zur Erinnerung an F. H.: Ein Lebens und Charakter-Skizze," *Dr. F. H.s Vorlesungen ueber Biblische Theologie und Messianische Weissagungen des Alten Testaments* (ed. J. J. Kneucher, 1880). **J. W. Rogerson,** *OTCNC,* 134-36.

J. W. ROGERSON

HOBBES, THOMAS (1588–1679)

An English philosopher, H. was born Apr. 5, 1588, and died Dec. 4, 1679. He was educated at Magdalen College, Oxford, and spent most of his life as a private tutor and retired scholar. Reputed a skeptic, his theological views, presumably sincere although unconventional, were an amalgam of Anglican support for episcopacy and royal supremacy, Calvinist determinism (see CALVIN), and sectarian heterodoxies about the soul. He devoted much time to biblical study, and his writings contain large sections of biblical exegesis. HB ideas about law and kingship were significant for his political views. His importance for biblical scholarship is based on his rejection of the Mosaic authorship of most of the Pentateuch (see PENTATEUCHAL CRITICISM); he called attention to passages that suggest a date long after Moses' time (e.g. Gen 12:6, Num 21:14, Deut 34:6) but affirmed that Moses wrote those portions specifically attributed to him in the text, e.g., Deuteronomy 11–27. H. thought that other biblical books, like Joshua, Judges, and 1–2 Samuel, were written long after the recorded events and that the completed HB was a product of the period after the exile. The book of Job is not so much a history as a treatise concerning the prosperity of the wicked. Questions of authorship and date are questions of fact to be settled by internal evidence.

H. was a perceptive exegete: He recognized the centrality of the kingdom of God as a biblical theme (although giving it a political meaning) and maintained the mortalist view that the Bible does not teach the immortality of the soul but the bodily resurrection, an approach that fit his materialism. He also maintained, in consonance with his political philosophy, that Scripture should not be interpreted otherwise than as allowed by the law of the state.

Works: *Leviathan* (1651, with many subsequent eds), see esp. pt. 3, chaps. 32–41.

Bibliography: N. T. Burns, *Christian Mortalism from Tyndale to Hobbes* (1972) 83-88. **L. Damrosch, Jr.,** "Hobbes as Reformation Theologian," *JHI* 40 (1979) 339-52. **W. B. Glover,** "God and T. H.," *CH* 29 (1960) 275-97. **F. C. Hood,** *The Divine Politics of T. H.* (1964). **M. Malherbe,** "Hobbes et la Bible," *Le Grand Siecle et la Bible* (BTT 6, ed. J.-R. Armogathe, 1989) 691-700. **A. P. Martinich,** *The Two Gods of Leviathan* (1992). **Gerard Reedy, S.J.,** *The Bible and Reason* (1985). **H. G. Reventlow,** *The Authority of the Bible and the Rise of the Modern World* (1984) 194-222. **R. Ross, H. W. Schneider, and T. Waldman** (eds.), *T. H. in His Time* (1974). **A. Schwan,** *TRE* 15 (1986) 404-12. **L. Stephen,** *DNB* 27 (1891) 37-45. **T. B. Strong,** "How to Write Scripture: Words, Authority, and Politics in T. H.," *Critical Inquiry* 20 (1993) 128-59.

D. D. WALLACE, JR.

HODGE, ARCHIBALD ALEXANDER (1823–1886)

A seminary educator and clergyman, son of C. HODGE, H. graduated from Princeton University in 1841 and from the seminary in 1847. He served in India as a missionary for three years and thereafter pastored churches in the United States. In 1864 he accepted a chair in systematic theology at Western Theological Seminary, then in 1877 was called to be associate to his father at Princeton, succeeding him at his death in 1878.

Although H. published no commentaries, he continually affirmed dependence upon the Bible for doctrinal AUTHORITY. He took pains, however, to compare the positions of various theologians in the standard classical framework of theology, anthropology, soteriology, and eschatology. He cited many scriptures, for example, in regard to INSPIRATION and to the divinity of Christ but did not often refer to the conclusions of the commentators. Therefore, whatever his scrutiny preceding the listing of texts, his citations may justly be labeled "prooftexting," as opposed to careful explication and exegesis.

Works: *Outlines of Theology* (1860); *The Atonement* (1868); *Commentary on the Confession of Faith* (1869).

Bibliography: Francis L. Patton, *A Discourse in Memory of A. A. H.* (1887). *DAB* 9 (1932) 97-98.

T. H. OLBRICHT

HODGE, CHARLES (1797–1878)

One of the most influential American theologians of the nineteenth century, H. was professor at Princeton Theological Seminary (his alma mater) from 1820 until his death, June 19, 1878. Born in Philadelphia, Dec. 28, 1797, he graduated from the College of New Jersey (later Princeton). He represented a strict Calvinistic confessionalism, what has been called the "old Princeton theology." The classical statement of this school is his three-volume work on systematic theology, heavily indebted to the Reformed scholasticism of Turretin and the philosophical movement inculcated at Princeton known as Scottish realism.

H. studied Hebrew with J. Banks (1819–20) and became instructor of biblical languages at Princeton Seminary. He studied in Paris, Halle, and Berlin (1826–28), primarily in oriental and modern languages, attended lectures of F. SCHLEIERMACHER, J. Neander, F. THOLUCK, H. GESENIUS, E. HENGSTENBERG, and H. EWALD, and established a lifelong friendship with Tholuck. H. developed considerable facility in Hebrew, Arabic, Aramaic, Greek, Latin, French, and German as well as familiarity with trends in European thought; but he remained confirmed in his theological views.

H.'s influence on biblical studies in America was manifold. He taught biblical languages and exegesis at the seminary and took the leadership in publishing an early scholarly organ, *The Biblical Repertory and Princeton Review*, which kept readers abreast of biblical and theological scholarship and enjoyed an international readership. Perhaps H.'s greatest contribution to biblical studies came through articles and reviews in this journal, which was a significant influence in the rise of American scholarship. Later he concentrated on teaching theology, leaving the teaching of languages and most exegesis courses to students-turned-colleagues, including his son A. A. HODGE; J. B. ALEXANDER, a language prodigy who taught biblical studies and church history; W. GREEN, a distinguished OT scholar; and B. B. WARFIELD, who carried on H.'s legacy of struggle against liberalism and Pelagianism (see PELAGIUS).

Throughout his career, however, H. continued to teach the exegesis of the Pauline epistles and published several commentaries on individual epistles (Romans [1835]; 1 and 2 Corinthians [1857]; Ephesians [1856]). The commentary on Romans went through at least eighteen editions, with one edition being translated into French. H.'s doctrinal concerns are the key to the nature of these commentaries. He believed PAUL was essentially a systematic thinker whose works could be analyzed for doctrinal content. In his exegesis of Rom 5:12-21 he argued vigorously for the federal headship of Adam and Christ: Because of Adam, the human race is subject to death; through union with Christ, believers are accepted by God since Christ's righteousness is imputed to them. All his life H. argued exegetically and theologically against what he feared was Pelagian or Arian influence (see ARIUS) among his contemporaries. He championed what he believed was a consistent Reformed theology carefully buttressed by exegetical argumentation.

Scholars have maintained that H. depended more on Turretin than on CALVIN, that he overemphasized the divine origin of Scripture to the exclusion of its humanity, and that under the philosophical influence of Scottish realism he underestimated the effect the subjectivity of the human observer has in assessing the phenomenal world. There is merit to each criticism; H., however, saw himself as a proponent of Chalcedonian and Reformed orthodoxy, which he sought to defend exegetically. Perhaps no other scholar of his time was as influential as he in the combined role of scholar, teacher, and churchman.

Works: *Essays and Reviews* (1857); *Systematic Theology* (3 vols., 1872–73); *What Is Darwinism?* (1874).

Bibliography: **A. A. Hodge,** *The Life of C. H.* (1880). **M. A. Noll,** *The Princeton Theology (1812–1921): Scripture, Science, Theological Method from A. Alexander to B. B. Warfield* (1983) 105-207, with full bibliography; *HHMBI,* 325-30. **T. H. Olbricht,** "C. H. as an American NT Interpreter," *JPH* 57 (1979) 117-33. **S. J. Stein,** "Stuart and Hodge on Romans 5:12-21: An Exegetical Controversy," *JPH* 47 (1969) 340-59. **M. A. Taylor,** "The OT in the Old Princeton School" (diss., Yale University, 1988) 91-165. **D. F. Wells** (ed.), *The Princeton Theology* (1989) 37-62.

J. A. DEARMAN

HODY, HUMPHREY (1659–1706)

Born Jan. 1, 1659, the son of the rector at Odcombe, Somersetshire, H. was educated at Wadham College, Oxford, where he was made a fellow in 1685 (BA 1679; MA 1682; BD 1689; DD 1692). He served as chaplain to E. STILLINGFLEET, as domestic chaplain to archibishops J. TILLOTSON and Tension, as regius professor of Greek at Oxford (1698), and as archdeacon of Oxford (1704).

H.'s contribution to biblical interpretation was in SEPTUAGINT studies. In 1684 he published a volume challenging the account of the origin of the Septuagint found in the *Letter of* ARISTEAS and demonstrating that the work was a late forgery. His 1704 volume in four books was a classical and epochal work in the history of HB text and versions: (1) a revision of his treatise on Aristeas, (2) an account of the origin of the Septuagint, (3) a history of the Hebrew and VULGATE texts, and (4) a discussion of other Greek versions.

Works: *Contra Historiam Aristeae de LXX interpretibus dissertatio* (1684, 1685[2]); *De Bibliorum textibus originalibus, versionibus Graecis, et Latina Vulgata: libri iv* (1704); *De Graecis illustribus, linguae Graecae, literarumque humaniorum instauratoribus* (ed. S. Jebb, 1742), with a life of H.

Bibliography: *BB* 4 (1757) 2622-24. **G. Goodwin,** *DNB* 27 (1891) 77-78. **C. Hayes,** *A Vindication of the History of the Septuagint from the Misrepresentation of the Learned Scaliger, DuPin, Dr. H., Dr. Prideaux and Other Modern Criticks* (1736). **J. Le Clerc,** "H. Hodii, *De Bibliorum textibus originalibus,*" *BC* (1706) 345-70.

J. H. HAYES

HOFFMANN, DAVID ZEVI (1843–1921)

A noted rabbi and scholar, H. was born in Verbo (Slovakia) and studied at various Yeshivot (Talmudic academies) in Hungary, also attending the Hildesheimer Seminary in Eisenstadt. He acquired his secular learning at the universities of Vienna, Berlin, and Tübingen; his commitment to secular learning marked him as a pioneer in the camp of German Orthodox Jewry. An exemplary Orthodox biblical scholar, he was famed in his own day as an outstanding Talmudic authority (see TALMUD) and as the author of authoritative Jewish legal *responsa.*

H. wrote commentaries in German on Leviticus (1905/6) and Deuteronomy (1913/22), later translated into Hebrew, in which he exhibited his great command of philology, exegesis, and TEXTUAL CRITICISM. At the same time he devoted considerable space to argumentation on higher criticism, along with enlightening references to traditional sources of Jewish exegesis and biblical interpretation—Talmudic literature and medieval Jewish biblical commentary. His commentaries provide a lucid, careful exegesis, deeply rooted in Jewish tradition but intensely aware of modern research; he often referred to the *Bi'ur,* the modernist Bible commentary produced by M. MENDELSSOHN and his circle. Even H.'s engagements with source-critical themes, which are poignantly objectionist, are in themselves instructive and stimulating. They represent one of the few efforts by a modern Orthodox Jewish biblical scholar to come to terms with critical research, especially relative to Torah literature, the most sacrosanct division of the Hebrew CANON. H. seems to have possessed, in addition to his great learning, a structuralist sense, a *Gestalt,* or coherent overview of Leviticus and Deuteronomy, with the result that his comments on specific passages and discrete units within these books are always relevant to the overall meaning and import of Torah literature. He was a major influence on B. Levine in his commentary on Leviticus in the Jewish Publication Society Torah Commentary (1989).

Works: *Mar Samuel* (1873); *Die erste Mischna und die Controversen der Tannaim* (1882); *Der Schulchan-Aruch und die Rabbinen uber das Verhältnis in die halachischen Midraschim* (1887); *Die Mischna-Ordnung Nisikin* (1893–97); *Midrash Tannaim zum Deuteronomium* (2 vols., 1900–09); *Die Wichtigsten Instanten gegen die Graf-Wellhausensche Hypothese* (2 vols., 1903–16); *Die Mechilta des R. Simon b. Jochai* (1905); *Das Buch Leviticus* (2 vols., 1905–06); *Das Buch Deuteronomium* (2 vols., 1913–22); *Midrash ha-gadol zum Buche Exodus* (2 vols., 1914–21); *Melammed Leho'il* (3 vols., 1926–32).

Bibliography: D. Ellenson, *EncRel* 6 (1987) 415. **L. Ginzberg,** *Students, Scholars, and Saints* (1928) 258-62. **M. D. Herr,** *EncJud* 8 (1971) 808-10. **B. A. Levine,** "The European Background," *Students of the Covenant: A History of Jewish Bible Scholarship in North America* (ed. S. D. Sperling, Confessional Perspectives, 1992) 15-32. **A. Marx,** *Essays in Jewish Bibliography* (1947) 185-22.

B. A. LEVINE

HOFMANN, JOHANN CHRISTIAN KONRAD VON (1810–77)

H. is often described as the originator of the idea of *Heilsgeschichte* (salvation history). However, this simple characterization does scant justice to the complex fusion of ideas that underlay his theology, and it reduces to a single dimension a man whose influence extended beyond biblical studies to political and ecclesiastical affairs.

H. was born Dec. 21, 1810, in Nuremberg, where he attended the gymnasium and absorbed the spirit of Romanticism and the idea that Christianity views history as a process in which God is involved. On entering the university at Erlangen in 1827, he encountered the renewal movement (*Erweckungsbewegung*), with its stress on personal experience of Christ and the role of the Bible in confirming that experience. In 1829 he went to Berlin, devoting himself to historical studies under L. von Ranke (1795–1886). He became a schoolmaster in Erlangen (1833) and a *Privatdozent* in history (1835). In 1838 he moved to theology, eventually holding a chair in Rostock (1842–45); he returned to Erlangen and was professor of theology there from 1845 until his death, Dec. 20, 1877.

Several points can be made about H.'s thought: (1) His interest in world history and his belief that history is a process through which God is revealed led him to hold that Christ is the center of history, not only in Israel's history but also in that of other nations; (2) the meaning of history cannot be discovered by examining the events themselves, but only through inner reflection that, in religious terms, involves personal experience of Christ; (3) history is not simply a human phenomenon, but a manifestation in the human world of the life of God; (4) the Bible is the supreme instance of the life of God manifesting itself in history, and for this reason it cannot be questioned by the methods of biblical criticism; (5) biblical studies are a theological science whose purpose is to aid the church in its proclamation of Christ as the center of history and of individual human experience. Directly or indirectly, H. took ideas from the pietist J. BECK (see PIETISM) and from G. W. F. Hegel (1770–1831) and F. Schelling (1775–1854); however, the resultant synthesis was his own.

H.'s two most important works were *Weissagung und Erfüllung im Alten und im Neuen Testamente* (1841–44) and *Der Schriftbeweis* (1852–55). In the former he traced the patterns of PROPHECY (*Weissagung*) and fulfillment (*Erfüllung*) from the OT to the NT. However, this was not a matter of expounding those parts of the OT that were regarded as prophecies of the coming of Christ. Rather, the whole history of Israel was prophetic, each segment preparing the ground for the following segment until Christ came. H. was particularly concerned to rescue the prophets from being seen merely as forecasters of the future. They spoke to the people of their times, but the Spirit that inspired them was the same Spirit that was moving history toward the coming of Christ.

Der Schriftbeweis was an ambitious attempt to combine theology and biblical studies by expounding the Bible from eight standpoints (*Lehrstücke*), not to construct a theological system, but to exemplify the conviction that Christianity is a present reality in which the believing community effects fellowship with God through JESUS Christ. The book deals with many theological subjects, e.g., the internal relationship of the persons of the Trinity as the basis for fellowship between God and humankind. It represents an approach to the OT that was possible only on the basis of mid-nineteenth-century neo-orthodox Lutheranism and the German idealistic philosophy of the period.

H. opposed the rise of biblical criticism, not from a narrow orthodox standpoint, but from a highly individualistic blend of piety and philosophy. It is to his credit that, although his position is totally outdated, he has been the subject of more scholarly works than any other biblical scholar of the nineteenth century.

Works: *Weissagung und Erfüllung im Alten und im Neuen Testamente: Ein theologischer Versuch* (1841–44); *Der Schriftbeweis: Ein theologischer Versuch* (1852–55, 1857–60²); *Biblische Hermeneutik* (1860; ET *Interpreting the Bible*, 1959).

Bibliography: F. **Mildenberger,** *TRE* 15 (1986) 477-79 (with extensive bibliography). **J. W. Rogerson,** *OTCNC* (1984) 104-11. **K. G. Steck,** *Die Idee der Heilsgeschichte: Hofmann, Schlatter, Cullmann* (ThStud 56, 1959). **P. Wapler,** *J. von Hofmann: Ein Beitrag zur Geschichte der theologische Grundproblem der kirchlichen und der politischen Bewegung in 19. Jahrhundert* (1914).

J. W. ROGERSON

HOLOCAUST, BIBLICAL INTERPRETATION AND THE

Whatever position one takes in the ongoing debate over the uniqueness of the Holocaust—defined here as the systematic attempt to exterminate European Jewry in the 1930s and early 1940s—there can be little doubt that it is an event of major consequence for the twentieth century. Nonetheless, although there have been innumerable volumes published on the implications of the Holocaust for historical, philosophical, ethical, and theological studies, there is a dearth of works that specifically consider either the theoretical or practical effects of the event on biblical interpretation. This is not to deny that since the 1940s there have been people reading the Bible differently because of the Holocaust; rather, it is to recognize that human situatedness in a post-Holocaust milieu has only begun to penetrate significantly into either academic or religious publications

concerned with biblical interpretation (T. Linafelt [1994]).

1. Jewish Interpretation. The place where one is most likely to find reference to the Bible in relation to the Holocaust is in Jewish theological responses to the event. While not primarily concerned with the effects of the Holocaust on how one reads the Bible, these works will typically mine the Bible for paradigms to explain the event and its significance for Jewish religious thought. One such biblical paradigm, used mainly by Orthodox thinkers, is the notion that the Holocaust is a punishment for the sins of the Jewish people (J. Teitelbaum [1959-61]). While biblically rooted, this model has been understandably rejected by most Jews (both Orthodox and otherwise) as well as by non-Jews (see esp. I. Greenberg [1977] 23). One can identify four other biblical models that have been employed in an attempt to explain the Holocaust (see S. Katz [1990] 749): (a) the binding of Isaac by Abraham; (b) the notion of a "Suffering Servant" from Isaiah; (c) the "hiding" of the face of God found in a number of psalms; and (d) the story of Job. Although all of these examples no doubt offer some comfort to survivors and their families and address certain aspects of the Holocaust, each ultimately fails to comprehend or explain it.

Another line of thinking holds that one should not read the Bible in hopes of explaining the Holocaust; rather, one should allow the event to impinge on the way one reads the Bible. An early example of this approach is R. Rubenstein's (1966) rejection of texts that depict God's working in history in favor of priestly texts concerning ethical and ritual matters. The most explicit (albeit brief) theoretical statement of this position is E. Fackenheim's *The Jewish Bible After the Holocaust* (1990; see Linafelt [1994]). Fackenheim argues that the Holocaust represents a rupture in history such that one cannot today read the Bible in the same way that it was read before the event. A. Neher's earlier book *The Exile of the Word* (1980) made a similar point with an exploration of the incommensurability of biblical patterns of silence with the silence of God at Auschwitz, but Fackenheim more directly engages the discipline of biblical studies.

Two writers who have done sustained interpretive work from this theoretical orientation are E. Wiesel and D. Blumenthal. Although the Bible tends to pervade all of Wiesel's work, his three volumes of collected "biblical portraits" (1976–91) offer the best entry into his agonistic relationship with the Bible. The portraits in these volumes are primarily composed of Wiesel's retelling of biblical stories and their midrashic complements. Still, the Holocaust continues to erupt into these retellings, thereby problematizing the tradition and forcing us to read the stories differently. Thus Job becomes "Our Contemporary," and the story of Cain and Abel becomes "The First Genocide" (Wiesel [1976]).

Blumenthal, in the central section of his book *Facing the Abusing God* (1993), demonstrates a post-Holocaust hermeneutic (see HERMENEUTICS) in the exegesis of four psalms. He provides a verse-by-verse commentary in four different voices (reminiscent of the Talmud or the rabbinic Bible): a philological commentary ("Words"), comments from the Hasidic tradition ("Sparks"), an emotional-spiritual commentary ("Affections"), and a counter-reading of the texts in light of the experience of abuse or the Holocaust ("Con-verses"). On each page the four voices surround the biblical text, not only vying for space and for the reader's attention but actively contradicting each other, thereby creating an interpretive approach that mirrors the fragmentary nature of post-Holocaust thought.

2. Christian Interpretation. Among Christian writers, the most significant interface between the Holocaust and biblical studies has resulted as a side effect of the renewed emphasis on Jewish-Christian relations. For many Christian thinkers, the Holocaust demands a re-thinking of latent anti-Judaism in traditional Christian theology as well as in the NT (e.g., P. van Buren [1980–88]; P. von der Osten-Sacken [1986]). Thus NT scholarship in the 1980s and 1990s tends to emphasize the Jewishness of JESUS in the Gospels (e.g., J. H. Charlesworth [1988]; P. Fredriksen [1988]; P. Meier [1991]) and God's continuing faithfulness to Israel in the thought of PAUL (e.g., L. Gaston [1987]; J. D. G. Dunn [1990]; N. Lohfink [1991]). Although these writers do not typically mention the Holocaust, it is no doubt a driving force behind the trend to underscore Jesus' ethnicity (see C. Williamson [1993] 48-106). However, they stress that a serious reconsideration of anti-Jewish tendencies in Christian thought would be necessary whether or not the Holocaust had taken place; the event has simply moved these issues to center stage. Still, the question of how Christians might read the Bible differently in light of the specific event of the Holocaust has scarcely been raised.

One way in which a more serious engagement between the Holocaust and Christian biblical interpretation might take place is by pursuing the hermeneutical implications of the widespread Jewish appropriation of the crucifixion image in works of art. Paintings such as M. Chagall's *White Crucifixion* and *The Martyr* and M. Hoffman's *Six Million and One* as well as sculptures such as G. Segal's *The Holocaust* in San Francisco's Lincoln Park, illustrate a trend in post-Holocaust Jewish art wherein the traditional Christian symbol of crucifixion is transformed into a Jewish symbol of suffering and persecution (Z. Amishai-Maisel [1982]; C. Quehl-Engel [1994]). What might it mean to reread the passion narratives of the NT through the hermeneutical lens of this artistic image? This is just one example of how a Christian post-Holocaust hermeneutic might be manifested. (A move in this direction may be seen in J. Marcus [1997].)

The 1990s witnessed increased public interest of Americans in the Holocaust, evidenced by massive turn-outs at the United States Holocaust Memorial Museum in Washington, DC and the reception of S. Spielberg's movie *Schindler's List*. If this interest continues into the twenty-first century, it may in fact seep into biblical scholarship and result in a more profound engagement between biblical and Holocaust studies.

Bibliography: Z. Amishai-Maisels, "The Jewish Jesus," *Journal of Jewish Art* 9 (1982) 85-104. **D. R. Blumenthal,** *Facing the Abusing God: A Theology of Protest* (1993). **J. H. Charlesworth,** *Jesus Within Judaism* (1988). **J. D. G. Dunn,** *Jesus, Paul, and the Law* (1990). **E. Fackenheim,** *The Jewish Bible After the Holocaust: A Re-reading* (1990). **P. Fredriksen,** *From Jesus to Christ* (1988). **L. Gaston,** *Paul and the Torah* (1987). **I. Greenberg,** "Cloud of Smoke, Pillar of Fire: Judaism, Christianity, and Modernity after the Holocaust," *Auschwitz: Beginning of a New Era?* (ed. E. Fleischner, 1977) 7-55. **S. T. Katz,** "Jewish Philosophical and Theological Responses to the Holocaust," *Encyclopdeia of the Holocaust* (4 vols., ed. I. Gutman, 1990) 2:748-51. **T. Linafelt,** review of E. Fackenheim's *The Jewish Bible After the Holocaust* in *Koinonia* 6, 2 (1994) 114-18; "Mad Midrash and the Negative Dialectics of Post-Holocaust Biblical Interpretation," *Bibel und Midrasch* (FAT 22, ed. G. Bodendorfer and M. Millard, 1998) 263-74. **N. Lohfink,** *The Covenant Never Revoked: Biblical Reflections on Christian-Jewish Dialogue* (1991). **J. Marcus,** *Jesus and the Holocaust* (1997). **J. P. Meier,** *A Marginal Jew: Rethinking the Historical Jesus* (ABRL, 1991). **A. Neher,** *The Exile of the Word: From the Silence of the Bible to the Silence of Auschwitz* (1981). **C. Quehl-Engel,** "Jewish Interpretative Art on Christian Anti-Judaism and the Holocaust: A Visual Hermeneutic for Christian Theology," *The Holocaust: Progress and Prognosis, 1934–94* (1994) 591-604. **R. L. Rubenstein,** *After Auschwitz: Radical Theology and Contemporary Judaism* (1966). **J. Teitelbaum,** *Va'Yoel Moshe* (3 vols., HEB, 1959–61). **P. M. van Buren,** *A Theology of the Jewish Christian Reality* (3 pts., 1980–88). **P. von der Osten-Sacken,** *Christian-Jewish Dialogue: Theological Foundations* (1986). **E. Wiesel,** *Messengers of God: Biblical Portraits and Legends* (1976); *Five Biblical Portraits* (1981); *Sages and Dreamers: Biblical, Talmudic, and Hasidic Portraits and Legends* (1991). **C. M. Williamson,** *A Guest in the House of Israel: Post-Holocaust Church Theology* (1993).

T. LINAFELT

HÖLSCHER, GUSTAV (1877–1955)

Born at Norden in northwest Germany, June 17, 1877, H. studied theology and Semitic languages at Erlangen, Leipzig, Berlin, Munich, Marburg, and Halle (1896–1905). He received his first teaching post at Halle (1905–20) and thereafter taught at Giessen (1920–21), Marburg (1921–29), and Bonn (1929–33). His anti-Nazi stance led to his suspension from Bonn and an initial boycott of his classes at Heidelberg, where he taught from 1935 to 1949. He died at Heidelberg, Sept. 16, 1955.

H.'s numerous writings, spanning a half-century from 1903 to 1952, reveal him as, above all, a LITERARY critic in the line of J. WELLHAUSEN. As such, he approached the books of the HB with a view to recovering the component strata/sources, evaluating their age and historical reliability, and finally utilizing them in reconstructing the course of Israel's religious development. His approach led him in several cases to quite distinctive results: J and E both extend into the books of Kings; Deuteronomy is postexilic, as is the bulk of Ezekiel; Deutero-Isaiah preached after 539, and so forth. H.'s research interests ranged over a variety of other sorts of questions as well: Palestinian topography and geography, the PSYCHOLOGY of PROPHECY, the meter of Semitic POETRY, and post-biblical Judaism (Josephus, the Sadducees).

Works: *Palästina in der persischen und hellinistischen Zeit: Eine historisch-geographische Untersuchung* (QFAGG 5, 1903); *Kanonisch und Apokryph* (1905); *Der Sadduzäismus* (1906); *Geschichte der Juden in Palästina seit dem Jahre 70 nach Christus* (1909); *Die Profeten: Untersuchungen zur Religionsgeschichte Israels* (1914); *Geschichte der israelitischen und jüdischen Religion* (1914); "Komposition und Ursprung des Deuteronomiums," *ZAW* 40 (1922) 161-255; *Hesekiel: Der Dichter und das Buch. Eine literarkritische Untersuchung* (BZAW 39, 1924); *Das Buch Hiob* (HAT 1, 17, 1937, 1952[2]); *Die Anfänge der hebräischen Geschichtsschreibung* (SHAW 3, 1942); *Drei Erdkarten* (1949); *Geschichtsschreibung in Israel: Untersuchungen zum Jahvisten und Elohisten* (ARSHLL 50, 1952).

Bibliography: G. C. Macholz, *NDB* 9 (1972) 334.

C. T. BEGG

HOLTZMANN, HEINRICH JULIUS (1832–1910)

Born in Karlsruhe, May 17, 1832, H. studied in Heidelberg (1850–51, 1852–54), where he was influenced by R. Rothe (1799–1867), and in Berlin (1851–52) under J. VATKE. After serving a church in Baden (1854–57), he turned to an academic career, acquiring his lic. theol. in 1858. On the basis of his *Kanon und Tradition: Ein Beitrag zur Dogmengeschichte und Symbolik* (1859) he was promoted to lecturer at Heidelberg. In 1861 he became *ausserordentlicher* professor and in 1865 full professor. From 1874 to 1904 he taught at Strasbourg. He died Aug. 4, 1910.

In his *Die synoptischen Evangelien, ihr Ursprung und geschichtlicher Charakter* (1863), he summarized scholarship to that time on the SYNOPTIC question. In contrast to the Tübingen school (F. C. Baur, J. J. Griesbach), he argued for the priority of the Gospel of Mark because of its primitive mode of narration and its language. Moreover, he demonstrated the necessity of a source common to Matthew and Luke in addition to A—the so-called basic document of Mark (proto-Mark)—consisting of a collection of sayings and speeches of JESUS, which in a comparatively original form is preserved in Luke. In addition, H. posited further oral and written sources for Matthew and Luke. As a result of his precise and detailed analysis of the linguistic characteristics of the sources and their literary connections, the two-source hypothesis has since stood on firm ground. On the basis of source A, whose existence he later rejected, H. developed a picture of the historical Jesus in terms of a "liberal psychological expression" (A. Schweitzer [1911, 1933[2]] 229) without regard for the central importance of Jesus' eschatological message of the kingdom of God for early Christianity (J. Weiss).

H. wrote numerous articles to clarify problems of NT introductory study (see the overview by W. Bauer, [1932] 313-15), preceding his *Lehrbuch der historisch-kritischen Einleitung in das Neue Testament* (1885, 1886[2], 1892[3]). In his *Lehrbuch der neutestamentlichen Theologie* (2 vols., ed. A. Jülicher and W. Bauer [1897, 1911[2]]), H. summarized scholarly discussion after BAUR. Without abandoning earlier approaches and not wanting to isolate the THEOLOGY of the NT from its environment, H. included the interests of the RELIGIONSGESCHICHTLICHE SCHULE and thus a section on "the religion and ethical thought-world of contemporary Judaism" (1897, 28-110; 1911, 27-159). In his presentation of the "preaching of Jesus" he followed his earlier formulated picture of Jesus. In his treatment of the theology of PAUL, whom he characterized as a "second religious founder," he perceived a "spiritual and intellectual synthesis of fundamental Jewish anchorage with a Greek thought structure."

At H.'s instigation the series Handkommentar zum Neuen Testament was produced to meet the needs of students and clergy by briefly summarizing the independent results of scientific exegesis. H. authored two of the four planned volumes (*Die synoptischen Evangelien: Die Apostelgeschichte* [1890, 1901[3]]; *Evangelium, Briefe, und Offenbarung des Johannes* [1891; rev. W. Bauer, 1908[3]]). He also wrote on philosophy of religion and on church history and turned to practical theology in numerous contributions seeking to set the Bible in a living relationship to contemporary religious and ethical viewpoints but in terms of a scientific academic exegesis. He even addressed the questions of HERMENEUTICS (*Das Problem der Geschichte der Auslegung* [1886]), and his contributions to the subject of art (e.g., "Zur Entwicklung des Christusbildes der Kunst," *JPT* 10 [1884] 71-136) brought him recognition as an "art authority in his own right" (O. Merk [1986] 521).

H. sought to bring the enduring elements of the positions of Baur and Rothe, who had so strongly influenced him, into liberal theology, whose genuine representative he was. He combined exegetical and systematic-theological thought, exerting great influence on NT scholarship toward the end of the nineteenth century.

Works: (with G. Weber), *Geschichte des Volkes Israel und der Entstehung des Christenthums,* vol. 2, *Judenthum und Christenthum im Zeitalter der apokryphischen und neutes-tamentlichen Literatur* (1867); *Kritik der Epheser- und Kolosserbriefe auf Grund einer Analyse ihres Verwandschaftsverhältnisses* (1872); *Über Fortschritte und Rückschritte der Theologie unseres Jahrhunderts und über ihre Stellung zur Gesamtheit der Wissenschaften* (1872); *Die Pastoralbriefe kritisch und exegetisch bearbeitet* (1880); *Luther als Prediger* (Predigt der Gegenwart, 1884); (with R. Zöppfel, ed.), *Lexikon für Theologie und Kirchenwesen* (1882, 1888², 1895³); *R. Rothe's Speculatives System* (1899); "Die Markus-Kontroverse in ihrer heutigen Gestalt," *ARW* 10 (1907) 18-40, 161-200; *Das messianische Bewusstsein Jesu* (1907).

Bibliography: H. Brassermann, "H. H. als praktischer Theologe," *PrM* 6 (1902) 172-84. W. Bauer, *H. J. H.: Ein Lebensbild* (AWR 9, 1932 = his *Aufsätze und Kleine Schriften* [ed. G. Strecker, 1967] 285-341). E. Dinkler, *RGG³* 3 (1959) 436-37; *NDB* 9 (1972) 560-61. E. von Dobschütz, *RE³* 23 (1913) 655-60. A. Faux, *DBSup* 4 (1949) 112-16. J. Hering, "De H. J. H. à A. Schweitzer," *Ehrfurcht vor dem Leben* (FS A. Schweitzer, ed. F. Buri, 1954) 21-29. A. Jülicher, "H. H. Bedeutung für die neutestamentliche Wissenschaft," *PrM* 6 (1902) 165-72. W. G. Kümmel, *NTHIP* (1972). O. Merk, *TRE* 15 (1986) 519-22. B. Reicke, "From Strauss to Holtzmann and Meijboom: Synoptic Theories Advanced During the Consolidation of Germany, 1830–1870," *NovT* 29 (1987) 1-21. O. Rühle, *Der theologische Verlag von J. C. B. Mohr (P. Siebeck): Rückblicke und Ausblicke* (1926). A. Schweitzer, *Geschichte der Paulinischen Forschung von der Reformation bis auf die Gegenwart* (1911, 1933²); *Geschichte der Leben-Jesu-Forschung* (UTB 1302, 1984⁹ = 1966⁷). J. Timmer, *J. Wellhausen and the Synoptic Gospels: A Study in Tradition Growth* (1970) 30-33.

G. STRECKER

HOOKE, SAMUEL HENRY (1874–1968)

Born at Cirencester, England, Jan. 21, 1874, H. entered academic life in his mid-thirties, taking degrees in theology and oriental languages at Jesus College, Oxford, then becoming associate professor of oriental languages at Victoria College, Toronto. He returned to London in 1926 with a Rockefeller fellowship in anthropology, devoting himself primarily to the study of ancient Near Eastern texts. In 1930 he was appointed to the Samuel Davidson chair of OT studies at London University. H. retired in 1942 but remained an active scholar almost until his death.

H.'s scholarly interests were wide-ranging: His earliest books concerned the NT and Christianity, as did one of his last works, *Alpha and Omega* (1961). His fame, however, was in HB scholarship as the founder of the MYTH AND RITUAL SCHOOL, although he was reluctant to accept the notion of a clearly defined "school." This approach was the result of two seminal collections of essays published in 1933 and 1935, which H. edited and contributed to; a further volume containing his final assessments appeared in 1958. These works, propounding the thesis that a pattern of myth and ritual in which the king had a central significance was common to all the ancient Near East and also characterized ancient Israel, presented a new understanding of OT religion and had a profound influence beyond the English-speaking world, particularly in Scandinavia. H. defined his purpose as building a bridge between the disciplines of anthropology, ARCHAEOLOGY, and biblical studies; and he continued to pursue this aim in such works as his 1935 Schweich lectures, a pioneering study of the then recently discovered Ugaritic texts (see UGARIT AND THE BIBLE). He also made important contributions to the discussion of the Pentateuch, especially Genesis. Biblical FOLKLORE was another of his interests: He was a president of the Folklore Society, and a number of his articles in the society's journal were collected in a volume published in 1956. In addition, his activity as a translator made several standard works of European scholarship available in English.

Works: *Christ and the Kingdom of God* (1919); (ed.), *Myth and Ritual: Essays on the Myth and Ritual of the Hebrews in Relation to the Culture Pattern of the Ancient East* (1933); (ed.), *The Labyrinth: Further Studies in the Relation Between Myth and Ritual in the Ancient World* (1935); *The Origins of Early Semitic Ritual* (1935 Schweich Lectures, 1938); *In the Beginning* (Clarendon Bible, OT, 6, 1947); *The Siege Perilous: Essays in Biblical Anthropology and Kindred Subjects* (1956); (ed.), *Myth, Ritual, and Kingship: Essays on the Theory and Practice of Kingship in the Ancient Near East and in Israel* (1958); *Alpha and Omega: A Study in the Pattern of Revelation* (LCT, 1961).

Bibliography: G. B. Caird, *DNB, 1961–70* (1981) 536-37. E. C. Graham, *Nothing Is Here for Tears: A Memoir of S. H. H.* (1969). W. R. Matthews, "S. H. H.: A Personal Appreciation," *Promise and Fulfillment: Essays Presented to Prof. S. H. H.* (ed. F. F. Bruce, 1963) 1-6. J. R. Porter, "Two Presidents of the Folklore Society: S. H. H. and E. O. James," *Folklore* 88 (1977) 131-45.

J. R. PORTER

HOOKER, RICHARD (1554–1600)

An apologist for the government and ceremonies of the Church of England, H. was educated at Corpus Christi, Oxford, and remained there as a tutor and fellow. His classic *Of the Laws of Ecclesiastical Polity* (5 vols., 1594–97) developed principles of biblical AUTHORITY and interpretation that were influential in shaping an Anglican ethos. He argued that Scripture both confirms the law of nature and reveals the mysteries of grace. He thought that the Bible was centered on redemption in Christ and should not be taken as a blueprint for details of polity and ceremony. Custom, so long as it did not contradict Scripture, might be followed in such matters, though the Bible does provide some general guiding principles, e.g., that all should be done decently and in order. H. also emphasized the importance of reason in biblical interpretation.

Bibliography: G. Gassmann, *TRE* 15 (1986) 581-83. **W. P. Haugaard,** *HHMBI,* 198-204. **W. S. Hill** (ed.), *Studies in R. H.: Essays Preliminary to an Edition of His Works* (1972). **P. Lake,** *Anglicans and Puritans? Presbyterianism and English Conformist Thought from Whitgift to Hooker* (1988) 145-238. **S. Lee,** *DNB* 27 (1891) 289-95. **A. S. McGrade** (ed.), *R. H. and the Construction of Christian Community* (MRTS 165, 1997)

D. D. WALLACE, JR.

HOONACKER, ALBIN VAN (1857–1933)

Born in Brugge (Bruges), Belgium, Nov. 10, 1857, H. was ordained to the priesthood in 1880. After ordination he was sent to the University of Leuven (Louvain) for advanced studies in theology, receiving his doctoral degree in 1886. From 1887 to 1889 he specialized in Semitic languages at Leuven, and in the latter year he was appointed to a new chair at the university to teach "Introduction à l'histoire critique de l'Ancien Testament." In 1901 he became a member of the newly established Pontifical Biblical Commission, which later severely criticized him (see F. Neirynck [1981]). H. became professor emeritus in 1927 and died in Brugge Nov. 1, 1933.

H.'s major fields of interest were (1) questions pertaining to the Hexateuch and the critical hypotheses of A. KUENEN, J. WELLHAUSEN, et al.; (2) the CHRONOLOGY of Ezra and Nehemiah; and (3) the prophetic literature (SEE PROPHECY AND PROPHETS, HB). Adopting the methods and some of the results of contemporary LITERARY criticism, he developed his own critical views, strongly advocating the relative antiquity of the priestly code and the more recent composition of Deuteronomy. His major criteria were laws concerning the unity of the cult and the organization of the levitical priesthood. According to H., the law of Deuteronomy 12 was not the innovation Wellhausen supposed it to be. Long before Deuteronomy the laws of Exodus 21–23 recognized only one legitimate public sanctuary. Deuteronomy brought an innovation in abolishing popular altars still tolerated by the priestly laws (*Le Sacerdoce* [1899], 14-15) for the ordinary slaughter of animals. H. had no well-defined convictions concerning the absolute dating of hexateuchal sources. In early publications he accepted the view that the law proclaimed by Josiah (2 Kings 23) was to be identified with the core of Deuteronomy. Later he was inclined to identify Josiah's book with the holiness code and the laws introduced by Ezra and Nehemiah with Deuteronomy (J. Lust [1985] 19-21). His finest source-critical studies are found in some of his shorter articles, especially ones on the first chapters of Genesis (1914) and on the miracle of Joshua (1916).

As for Ezra and Nehemiah (1923, 1924), he launched the hypothesis still held by many (G. Widengren [1977] 504-9; cf. H. Williamson [1985] XL-XLIV), that Ezra's expedition (Ezra 7–10) took place after, not before, Nehemiah's mission. The conviction that Nehemiah's handling of mixed marriages (Neh 13:23-28) must have preceded Ezra's more drastic and systematic treatment (Ezra 10) was the major basis of his theory (see Williamson [1985] XLIII). Less innovative and finding less support in today's literature is his detailed defense of the identification of Zerubbabel with Sheshbazzar, *Zerubbabel* being Sheshbazzar's Hebrew name.

In prophetic literature H. provided an excellent commentary on the twelve Minor Prophets (1908) and published several shorter articles of high philological interest. His commentary was subjected to a severe inquiry by the Pontifical Biblical Commission. The section on Jonah questioning its historical character appears to have been responsible for the threat of condemnation.

H.'s work was and remains significant for several reasons. Against the background of increasingly restrictive and oppressive interventions of Roman official opposition to "modern" exegesis, his scholarly honesty is exemplary. Similarly, in his disputes with the protagonists of the source-critical hypotheses, he always gave a clear and fair exposition of the views of his opponents before taking his own stand. Several of his theses and comments are still highly respected by scholars, especially the ones concerning the chronological order of Ezra and Nehemiah. Also his commentary on the Minor Prophets remains a valuable reference work. In light of the discussions concerning the priority of P over D, his detailed dialogues with Wellhausen and Kuenen merit renewed attention.

Works: "L'origine des quatre premiers chapitres du Deutéronome," *Le Muséon* 7 (1888) 464-82; 8 (1889) 67-85, 141-49; *Néhémie et Esdras: Nouvelle hypothèse sur la chronologie de l'époque de la Restauration Juive* (1890); *Le lieu du culte dans la législation rituelle des Hébreux* (1894); *Le Sacerdoce lévitique dans la loi et dans l'histoire des Hébreux* (1899); *Les douze petits prophètes traduits et commentés* (EBib, 1908); "The Literary Origin of the Narrative of the Fall," *The Expositor* 8 (1914) 481-98; *Une communauté judéo-araméenne à Eléphantine en Egypte aux VIe et Ve Siècles av. J.-C.* (Schweich

Lectures, 1914); " 'And the Sun Stood Still,' Joshua 10:13," *The Expositor* 12 (1916) 321-39; "La succession chonologique Néhémie-Esdras," *RB* 32 (1923) 481-94; 33 (1924) 33-64; *De compositione litteraria et de origine Mosaica Hexateuchi disquisition historico-critica* (posthumous ed. with intro, J. Coppens, VVAW 11, 11, 1949).

Bibliography: J. Coppens, *Le chanoine A. H.: Son enseignement, son oeuvre et sa méthode exégétiques* (1935); *DBSup* 4 (1941) 123-28. **J. Lust,** "A. H. and Deuteronomy," *Das Deuteronomium* (ed. N. Lohfink, 1985) 13-23, 363-67 (full bibliography of his writings). **F. Neirynck,** "A. H. et l'index," *ETL* 57 (1981) 293-97; *NBW* 11 (1985) 379-85. **G. Widengren,** "The Persian Period," *Israelite and Judaean History* (ed. J. H. Hayes and J. M. Miller, 1977) 489-538. **H. G. M. Williamson,** *Ezra, Nehemiah* (WBC 16, 1985).

J. LUST

HORNE, THOMAS HARTWELL (1780–1862)

Born in Chancery Lane, London, Oct. 29, 1780, H. studied at Christ's Hospital (1789–95), where he was tutored by S. T. COLERIDGE. He worked as a barrister's clerk, catalogued the British Museum's Harleian manuscripts, and from 1824 to 1860 was senior assistant librarian in the department of printed books at the museum. Although a Methodist, he was ordained in the Anglican Church and served several congregations in London. The grandfather of the OT scholar T. CHEYNE, H. died in London, Jan. 27, 1862.

H. sought to supplement his income by writing, and his introduction to the Bible (1818) established itself as the primary textbook on the topic in the English-speaking world. Unengaged in active teaching, H. was not routinely confronted with academic requirements. Thus, while his biblical scholarship was compendious, it demonstrated little originality; a mine of bibliographical aid, it was parochial in outlook, practically ignoring contemporary German scholarship. Although his introduction pointed out problems, contradictions, and difficulties in the text and interpretations, it offered solutions within the traditional frames of reference. The suggestion that derangements in the order of the text had occurred was about as radical as H. proposed. That his work filled a need, however, is indicated by its popularity. For the tenth edition of the work (4 vols., 1856) he was assisted by S. DAVIDSON. The eleventh and final edition had the assistance of J. Ayre and S. Tregelles (4 vols., 1860).

Works: *An Introduction to the Study of Bibliography; to Which Is Prefixed a Memoir on the Public Libraries of the Antients* (2 vols., 1814); *An Introduction to the Critical Study and Knowledge of the Holy Scriptures; with Maps and Facsimiles of Biblical Manuscripts* (3 vols., 1818; with supp. vol. 1821; 4 vols., 1821[2]; 5 vols., rev., corr., and enl. 1846[9]); *Deism Refuted; or Plain Reasons for Being a Christian* (1819, 1826[2]); *The Scripture Doctrine of the Trinity Briefly Stated and Defended, with a Defense of the Athanasian Creed* (1820, 1826[2]); *A Compendious Introduction to the Study of the Bible* (1827, 1862[10]); *Romanism Contradictory to the Bible* (1827); *Manual of Parochial Psalmody* (1829, 1861[41]); *Manual of Biblical Bibliography Compromising a Catalogue* (1839, vol. 5 of the 7th ed. of his *Introduction*); *A Summary of the Evidence for the Genuineness, Authenticity, Uncorrupted Preservation and Inspiration of the Holy Scriptures* (1856, vol. 1 of 10th ed. of his *Introduction*).

Bibliography: T. C. Cooper, *DNB* 27 (1891) 363-64. **S. Davidson,** *Facts, Statements, and Explanations Connected with the Publication of the Second Volume of the Tenth Edition of Horne's Introduction to the Study of the Holy Scriptures, Entitled "The Text of the OT Considered"* (1857); *Reminiscences, Personal and Bibliographical, of T. H. H., with Notes by His Daughter, S. A. Cheyne, and an introduction by the Rev. J. B. McCaul* (1862). **J. B. McCaul,** *The Rev. T. H. H.: A Sketch* (1862). **J. W. Rogerson,** *OTCNC,* 182-84.

J. H. HAYES

HORST, FRIEDRICH (1896–1962)

Born Feb. 8, 1896, in Hattingen (Ruhr), Germany, H. died June 12, 1962, in Mainz. He studied theology and pursued oriental studies in Tübingen and Bonn, where he received his PhD in 1922. Promoted to lic. theol. in 1923, he was seminary inspector from 1922 to 1935 then became *Dozent* in 1923 and *ausserordentlicher* professor for OT in 1930. As an active member of the Confessing Church, he was dismissed from his academic position in 1935 along with his teacher G. HÖLSCHER and K. BARTH. He assumed a pastorate in Steeg and continued to work for the Confessing Church. After the war, in which he lost both sons, he received a position at the University of Mainz in 1947 and became a revered teacher there. He retired early because of severe illness and was able to advance his final, most mature work, the commentary on Job, only through chapter 19.

As all his works, particularly his commentaries demonstrate, H. was an excellent exegete with particular mastery of FORM CRITICISM, but he was also a passionate theologian and pastor in whom the themes of his life and scholarship were inextricably interwoven. He repeatedly returned to certain questions, particularly legal ones, in which he pursued comparative studies extending far beyond the Bible and the ancient Near East. By casting pertinent HB statements in modern legal terminology he made them accessible to contemporary discussion. He was above all concerned that in HB law one encounters not only universal-natural or even positivistic legal thinking but also the living will of the God of Israel who mercifully grants life to human beings while simultaneously holding them fully accountable to the divine commandments.

H. sought to establish a fundamental document of divine legal demands in Deuteronomy by continuing the supplementary hypothesis advocated by Hölscher— namely, by reconstructing as a basis for Deuteronomy 12–18 a variously reworked "privilege law of Yahweh" in DECALOGUE form and of northern Israelite origin. In his later works on legal history (collected in *Gottes Recht,* further in *RGG³*) he addressed many important individual legal questions from various angles in addition to more fundamental questions.

Works: "Die Anfänge des Propheten Jeremia," *ZAW* 41 (1923) 94-123; "Die Kultusreform des Königs Josia," *ZDMG* 77 (1923) 220-38; *Das Privilegrecht Jahwes: Rechtsgeschichtliche Untersuchungen zum Deuteronomium* (FRLANT 45, 1930); "Nahum bis Maleachi," *Die zwölf kleinen Propheten: Hosea bis Micha* (HAT 1, 14, 1936, 1964³) 153-275; "Recht und Religion im Bereich des Alten Testaments," *EvTh* 16 (1956) 49-75; *Gottes Recht: Gesammelte Studien zum Recht im Alten Testament* (ed. H. W. Wolff, TBü 12, 1961); *Hiob* (BKAT 16, 1, 1968).

Bibliography: E. Kutsch, "Bibliographie F. H.," *Gottes Recht* (F. Horst, 1961) 315-20; "Nachtrag zur Bibliographie F. H.," *TLZ* 88 (1963) 317-18. **H. W. Wolf,** *EvTh* 22 (1962) 662-64.

R. SMEND

HORT, FENTON JOHN ANTHONY (1828–92)

Born Apr. 23, 1828, H. died Nov. 30, 1892. He studied at Trinity College, Cambridge (1850–51), where he was a fellow (1852–57), taking the BD in 1875. He became Hulsean professor in 1878 and Lady Margaret's in 1887, continuing in that position until his death. First a botanist, his scientific training led him to combine a recognition of "the human elements in the Bible" with a "providential ordering" of Scripture.

H.'s major contribution to biblical scholarship lay in TEXTUAL CRITICISM of the Greek NT, in particular the critical edition he edited with B. F. WESTCOTT in 1881 and for which he wrote the introduction and notes in the second volume. This text was the foundation of the RV of the English Bible on which he also worked. The principles of the edition are set out in volume 2: The documents are classified in groups having certain characteristics, called "Western," "neutral" (identified in relation to the Alexandrian type of text and seen as the most reliable), and "Syrian" (a later 4th-century revision of "mixed" antecedents, and mostly secondary). His aim was, by a genealogical method of seeing the documents in series in contrast to simply assessing individual readings, to trace families back to the earliest and most authentic form of the text, internal evidence playing a

supporting, though possibly conclusive, role. He succeeded in destroying the credibility of the *textus receptus,* but flaws in the applicaton of his method prevented his achieving his ultimate aim. His procedure was to move from internal evidence of readings, based on intrinsic and transcriptional probability, to internal evidence of documents, then of groups of manuscipts, where "community of reading implies community of origin." But this could not be fully carried out since the groupings were not easily fixed by agreement alone; the phenomenon of "mixture" was not overcome; and the "Western" type of text was not adequately dealt with in terms of age and variety or where it differs from the "neutral" text in the so-called non-Western interpolations.

Improvements in his method allied with use of more recently discovered evidence has either supported or modified his conclusions. For example, the Sinaitic Syriac palimpsest (see F. Burkitt's additional notes to the 1896 edition of Westcott and H.'s text) has helped the late dating of the "Syrian" text, but not Hort's distrust of all "non-Western interpolations," while papyrus evidence supports the early date of precursors of H.'s "neutral" text in Egypt. A debate continues as to whether internal evidence is more important than evaluating groups of manuscripts (so-called rigorous eclecticism). H.'s aim of a genealogy of the text has not been completely abandoned, facilitated by better editions of texts and versions, improved use of lectionaries and of the fathers, and clearer evaluation of the text types.

Works: "S. T. Coleridge," *Cambridge Essays* 5 (1856) 292-351; "On Μουογεὴς θεός in Scripture and tradition" and "On the 'Constantinopolitan' and Other Eastern Creeds of the Fourth Century," *Two Dissertations* (1876); (with B. F. Westcott), *The NT in the Original Greek: The Text Together with Introduction and Notes* (2 vols., 1881); *The Way, the Truth, and the Life* (1871 Hulsean Lectures, 1893); *Prolegomena to St. Paul's Epistles to the Romans and the Ephesians* (1895); *Six Lectures on the Ante-Nicene Fathers* (1895); *The First Epistle of St. Peter 1.1–2.17: The Greek Text* (1898); *Judaistic Christianity* (1898); *The Christian Ecclesia* (1900); *Clementine Recognitions* (1901); *Revelation* (1908); *James* (1909).

Bibliography: E. C. Colwell, *Studies in Methodology in Textual Criticism of the NT* (NTTS 9, 1969). **H. Exon,** *DNB* Sup. 2 (1901) 443-47. **M. E. Glasswell,** *TRE* 15 (1986) 584-86. **C. R. Gregory,** *RE³* 8 (1900) 368-70. **A. F. Hort,** *Life and Letters of F. J. A. H.* (2 vols., 1896). **G. A. Patrick,** *F. J. A. H.—Eminent Victorian* (1988). **E. G. Rupp,** *Hort and the Cambridge Tradition* (1970). **H. E. Ryle,** *DNB* Sup. 2 (1901) 443-47. **W. Sanday,** "Hort, Life and Letters," *AJT* 1 (1897) 95-117. **T. B. Strong,** "Dr. Hort's Life and Works," *JTS* 1 (1900) 370-86.

M. E. GLASSWELL

HOSEA, BOOK OF

1. The Early Church. Significant exegeses of the book of Hosea were composed by JEROME (d. 420). THEODORE OF MOPSUESTIA (d. 428), CYRIL OF ALEXANDRIA (d. 444), Julian of Aeclanum (d. 454), and THEODORET OF CYRRHUS (d. c. 466). The most important work from the early church is the commentary of Jerome, who, writing his interpretation c. 406 CE in old age and under physical distress, sought above all to explore the literal sense of Hosea's words. According to him there were already individual writings on the prophecies of Hosea before his day. He mentions first the commentary of Apollinaris Laodicenus (d. c. 390), then that ORIGEN (d. 254) had written a small book on Hosea: *peri tou pos onomasthe en to Osee Egraim.* Jerome also claimed to have read a *Tractatus longissimus* by Pierius (d. c. 309). EUSEBIUS OF CAESAREA (d. 341) also wrote about Hosea in the eighteenth book of his *Euaggelike apodeixis,* and DIDYMUS THE BLIND (d. 398) composed three books on Hosea at Jerome's request.

The commentary on the twelve Minor Prophets by Theodore of Mopsuestia remains the only one of his works preserved entirely in the Greek. Two features govern his exegesis: a historical-grammatical approach oriented to the literal sense of the biblical text and the typological interpretation of HB texts (only thus could the connection to the NT be established). Cyril of Alexandria defended the historicity of the events portrayed in the book but interpreted the text allegorically. Thus Jezreel, Hosea's first son, stood for JESUS Christ on account of his name, *spora theou,* (The Seed of God). Julian of Aeclanum proceeded from the text before him: Text-critical remarks (see TEXTUAL CRITICISM) are totally absent from his work, and he almost never drew a comparison with the Greek or the OL. Despite a basically historical-grammatical approach, the exegesis of Theodoret of Cyrrhus is frequently typological and allegorical.

2. The Middle Ages. Several important commentaries were written during this period. Theophylakt of Achrida (d. c. 1108) understood his exegesis of Hosea as a compendium of earlier exegeses. GUIBERT OF NOGENT (d. 1124) limited himself to a moral interpretation. RUPERT OF DEUTZ (d. c. 1130) sought to trace out the mystery of the kingdom of God and to inquire after the meaning hidden in the letters. ANDREW OF ST. VICTOR (d. 1175), who composed his commentary on Hosea around the middle of the twelfth century, based his exegesis on Jerome and attempted to understand Hosea from the prophet's own time. Around 1200 S. LANGTON (d. 1268) commented on Hosea according to the threefold sense of the text: literal, moral, and allegorical. Albertus Magnus (d. c. 1280) contributed an important commentary as well.

3. Luther and Calvin. LUTHER's principal concern in his exegesis of the book of Hosea was the "uncom-promising assertion of the literal sense" (G. Krause [1962] 115). Characteristically, he saw Hosea primarily as a preacher, as he saw all the prophets (see PROPHECY AND PROPHETS, HB); he stressed that Hosea was rooted in Israel's tradition of faith; he concluded that since Hosea preached over several decades individual parts of the book derived from different periods; he was extremely concerned with the clarification of questions of fact, e.g., Hos 5:1, Mizpah (*WA* 13, p. 22, 1. 15); Hos 4:13, names of plants (*WA* 13, p. 19, 1. 20). CALVIN, on the other hand, concentrated his efforts on philological questions and on the academically precise exegesis of individual words and sentences, occasionally making connections to the Christian church.

4. The Sixteenth Through the Eighteenth Centuries. Treatments written during the sixteenth century include J. Wigand, *In XII Prophetas Minores explicationes succinctae, ordinem rerum, textus sententiam, et doctrinas praecipuas strictissime indicantes* (1566); H. Mollerus, *Enarratio brevis et grammatica concionum Hoseae, excepta ex publicis praelectionibus . . . in schola Wittenbergensi* (Möller [1567]); and L. Osiander the Elder, *Biblia latina. . . .,* vol. 5, *Ezechiel, Daniel, Osse . . .* (1579). Of particular note in the seventeenth century are the works of S. Gesner, *Commentarius in oseam Prophetam. . . .* (1614); B. Krakevitz, *Commentarius in Hoseam. . . .* (1619); B. Meisner, *Hoseas novo commentario per textus analysin, ejusdem exegesin, dubiorum solutionem, et locorum communium annotationem. . . .* (1620); J. H. Ursinus, *Hoseas, commentario literali ex optimis interpretibus concinnato . . . Opus posthumum* (1677); and S. Schmidt, *In Prophetam Hoseam Commentarius. . . .* (1687). But above all stands the great work of E. POCOCKE, *A Commentary on the Prophecy of Hosea* (1685). Exegesis during the eighteenth century includes the work of H. von der HARDT, *Hoseas historiae et antiquitati redditus libris XXIX pro nativa interpretandi virtute cum dissertationibus in Raschium* (1712); J. W. Petersen, *Die Erklärung der zwölf kleinen Propheten. . . .* (1723); W. Lowth, *A Commentary upon the Larger and Lesser Prophets. . . .* (1739[4]); J. G. Schroeer, *Der Prophet Hosea. . . .* (1782); J. C. Volborth, *Erklärung des Propheten Hosea* (1787); C. G. Kuinoel, *Hosea oracula hebraice et latine perpetua annotatione. . . .* (1792); and E. G. Bockel, *Hoseas* (1807).

5. Important Commentaries Since 1800. The foundation for the modern historical-critical work on the book of Hosea was laid in the nineteenth century through a number of important commentaries, beginning with the interpretation of E. ROSENMÜLLER, *Scholia in Vetus Testamentum im Compendium Redacta* (ed. J. C. S. Lechner, Scholia in Prophetas Minores 6 [1836] 4-70) and carried on through the work of F. HITZIG/H. Steiner (1838), H. EWALD (1867), A. Wünsche (1868), T. CHEYNE (1884), C. KEIL (1888), and C. von ORELLI

(1908). All of these are primarily philological in nature and are concerned with the text. Wünsche's commentary *Der Prophet Hosea* (1868) surveyed the medieval rabbinic exegetes as well as the book's targumic translation (see S. Coleman [1960]; see also TARGUMIM). Keil concentrated on the clarification of questions of biblical ARCHAEOLOGY in addition to philology. With the appearance of J. WELLHAUSEN's commentary (1898), intense LITERARY-critical questions came into focus alongside philological ones. Noteworthy from the first half of the twentieth century are the commentaries of K. MARTI, *Das Dodekapropheton* (KHC, 1904); W. R. HARPER, *A Critical and Exegetical Commentary on Amos and Hosea* (ICC, 1905); A. EHRLICH, *Randglossen zur hebräischen Bibel: Textkritisches, sprachliches und sachliches,* vol. 5 (1912 = 1968); E. SELLIN, *Das Zwölfprophetenbuch* (KAT XII, 1922); J. LINDBLOM, *Hosea, literarisch untersucht* (1927); S. Brown, *The Book of Hosea* (WC, 1932); T. ROBINSON and F. Horst (1964); J. Lippl and J. Theis, *Die zwölf kleinen Propheten,* 1. Halfte, *Osee, Joel, Amos, Abdias, Jonas, Michaas* (HSAT VIII 3 I, 1937); and F. Nötscher, *Zwölfprophetenbuch oder kleine Propheten* (1954²). The most influential commentaries have been those of H. W. WOLFF (1965); W. RUDOLPH (1966); J. Mays, *Hosea: A Commentary* (OTL, 1969); F. Andersen and D. N. Freedman, *Hosea: A New Translation with Introduction and Commentary* (AB 24, 1980); A. Deissler, *Zwölf Propheten: Hosea–Joel–Amos* (Die Neue Echter Bibel, 1981); and J. JEREMIAS, *Der Prophet Hosea* (ATD 24, 1, 1983).

6. The Text. The text of Hosea is in many verses so badly preserved that the original sense can scarcely be determined with certainty (e.g., 9:13, 11:7). Consequently, commentaries deal exhaustively with text-critical issues, and the relationship of the MT to the SEPTUAGINT takes on particular significance. That the textual recensions diverge considerably from each other is variously interpreted by scholars. On the one hand, H. S. NYBERG (1935, 113-17) assumes that the Septuagint can make no essential contribution to the solution of the text-critical problems in Hosea. Conversely, G. Patterson (1890/91, 190-121) views the value of the Septuagint positively in this respect, explaining most of the discrepancies through the thesis that the Septuagint translator consciously sought to tailor his work to his audience. Indeed, Patterson's position is to be preferred to that of Nyberg, since the interpretative *Tendenz* of the Septuagint is clear where it completes, improves, smooths over, and interprets the text on theological-contentual and syntactical-stylistic grounds without altering its fundamental sense. Where the Septuagint diverges from the essence of the MT, however, one must reckon with an unclear and corrupt *Vorlage.*

7. The Transmission of Hosea's Words. A difficult, and until now largely unresolved, problem is the tracing of the transmission of Hosea's words. Since the beginning of the nineteenth century there has been agreement among scholars that the present book of Hosea was put together from two separate parts: chaps. 1–3 and chaps. 4–14 (Rosenmüller [1836] 8-9). H. GINSBERG (1971), however, following H. GRAETZ and Y. KAUFMANN, has argued for two Hoseas. The first (chaps. 1–3) belonged to the period of the Omride dynasty in the ninth century, with the second being the eighth-century prophet. This theory seems unlikely, however, and is intent on explaining the difference between chaps. 1–3 and chaps. 4–14.

a. Chapters 1–3. The third-person report of Hosea's marriage in chap. 1 and the first-person report of his marriage in chap. 3 show that Hosea 1–3 itself stems from different literary connections. Perhaps these two chapters contain two different reports of a single marriage of Hosea from two different hands. Chapter 3 may also be seen as the autobiographical resumption of the biographical narrative of chap. 1 (Robinson [1964] 15-16). Perhaps a prophetic disciple who wanted to present the beginning of Hosea's life as a prophet stands behind chap. 1 (H. Wolff [1965] xxix-xxxii). L. Ruppert (1982) regards the history of the transmission of chaps. 1–3 as far more complicated since he assumes a total of four phases of transmission: the core unit A, 2:4-7, 10-15; the composition B, 2:4-7, 8-9, 10-15, 16-17, 19; the composition C, 2:4-7, 8-9, 10-15, 16-17*ab*, 18*ab*, 19, 21-22; the composition D, 2:4-7, 8-9, 10-15, 16-17, 18*ab*, 19, 21-22, 23*ab*, 24.

Concerning the marriage of Hosea, the following positions can be roughly differentiated since 1800. (1) In the nineteenth century one often finds the interpretation of Hosea's marriage as a plain allegory on Yahweh's relationship to Israel (Hitzig/Steiner [1838] 8; Wünsche [1868] 9). (2) Hosea's marriage was actually carried out so that the prophet would experience in his own life the infidelity of his wife. He sees, therefore, in his own experience an *imitatio* of the experience God has with Israel and reinterprets it by saying that Yahweh has commanded him to marry a wife inclined to adultery (Ewald [1867] 192; Wellhausen [1898] 105-8). (3) Chapters 1–3 constitute a report of an actual marriage of Hosea, at Yahweh's command, to a woman given over to sacral prostitution (Robinson [1964] 17) who is, therefore, described as a whore. The real argument here is that Canaanite fertility cults in which virgins were ritually sacrificed to the deity had gained a hold in Israel (Wolff [1976] 14-16).

FEMINIST and WOMANIST biblical scholars wrestle with the book of Hosea, particularly with Gomer's marriage to Hosea, and question this metaphor's usefulness for the church and synagogue as a desirable image for God. Why, they ask, is so much violence and pornography present in Hosea 1–3 (see D. Setel [1985]; G. Yee [1992]; R. Weems [1989, 1995])? Moreover, the violence is perpetrated by Hosea (God) as a punishment for wayward Israel, who is embodied female. Feminists worry that this marriage metaphor, which many readers interpret as a powerful illustration of a loving and forgiving God, in reality becomes a model and justification for physically abusive relationships.

b. Chapters 4–14. The process by which these chapters came into their present form is just as difficult to explain as is the case with chaps. 1–3 since chaps. 4–14 consist of different units with diverse imagery. Wolff (1976, xxix-xxxii) believes that kerygmatic units can be recognized here. Jeremias's (1983) thesis that disciples of Hosea composed, shortened, and assembled in chaps. 4–11 the words of Hosea most important to them is not improbable. According to the investigation by Yee (1987), four redactional phases can be distinguished: Hosea (H), the collector (C), the first redactor (R^1), and a final redactor (R^2). What is clear about the formation process is that the final stage is to be ascribed to a Judean editor (Jeremias [1983] 18; G. Emmerson [1984] 156-64).

8. The Spiritual Provenance of Hosea. In the earlier, and in some cases more recent, commentaries the question of whether Hosea came from a priestly or a prophetic background was deliberately left open because of the uncertain textual basis (Wünsche [1868]; Rudolph [1966]). Nevertheless, Wolff (1956) and E. Zenger (1982, following Wolff) have dared to push past this point. Wolff concluded on the basis of 6:4-6; 9:7-9; 12:8-11, 13-15 that Hosea stood in closest alliance to the prophets and in decided opposition to Israel's monarchy and priesthood, but that because Hosea had taken up the announcement of God's justice, God's deeds, and God's covenant, he was still permitted to maintain connections to levitical circles. According to Zenger the book of Hosea documents the claim of Hosea and those handing on his words that he was the bearer of a particular prophetic office (*successio prophetica,* 11:4). This form of prophecy stood in fundamental political competition with the existing organs of state; therefore, the anti-Canaanite and anti-monarchical polemic of Hosea must be understood as criticism of state and cult.

9. The Salvation Traditions of Israel. In contrast to the rest of the eighth-century prophets, the book of Hosea relies extensively on the traditions of Israel. This fact is generally recognized among scholars, but the interpretation of individual texts is nonetheless extremely controversial.

Allusions to the Jacob traditions are found in 5:1-2 and 12:4-5. It is heavily disputed whether Jacob is understood here as a positive or a negative figure. Among those reaching a positive evaluation of the Jacob traditions are the commentaries of the last third of the nineteenth century and the Roman Catholic exegetical work in the first half as well as some few works in the late twentieth century. The negative interpretation of the figure of Jacob in Hosea 12 has been represented in the majority of commentaries in the wake of Wellhausen's work (H.-D. Neef [1987] 15-49).

In 12:14 the Moses tradition is taken up. The majority of exegetes assume that in 12:13-14 it is a question of an opposition between Jacob, who serves a woman, and Moses, who stands in service to God. A sizable group of scholars deny that 12:13-14 come from Hosea at all.

Features of the desert election tradition appear in 2:16-17; 9:10-17; 10:1-2, 11-13a; 11:1-7; 12:10; 13:4-8. Their derivation and function, however, are seen variously in the research: as a symbol of a nomadic ideal of Hosea; as part of the exodus and Sinai tradition; as an independent election tradition distinct from the exodus; or as an Ishmaelite tribal tradition. Texts ascribed to the desert election tradition share a description of the desert period as the time of intimate community between Yahweh and Israel (Neef, 58-119).

Highly controversial in the discussion is the covenant tradition in Hosea (2:20; 6:7; 8:1; 10:4; 12:2). Many scholars eliminate as non-Hoseanic passages that employ the term "covenant" (L. Perlitt [1969] 150-53; but see E. Nicholson [1986]).

In addition to these important traditions one finds connections to the DECALOGUE (4:2; 8:4-6; 12:10; 13:1-4), to the wisdom tradition (2:21; 4:1; 5:12; 8:7; 12:8), to Gilgal (4:15; 9:15; 12:11), to Gibeah (5:8; 9:9; 10:9), and to Admah and Zeboim (11:8).

10. The Portrayal of the Divine in Hosea and in Ugarit. Hosea sharply polemicizes against the Canaanite god Baal and his cult. The excavations at UGARIT since 1929 have given new impetus to study of the book since many of the practices and attitudes criticized in it are found in the Ugaritic texts. W. Kuhnigk (1974) seeks to clarify the often difficult text of Hosea with the help of Ugaritic. In contrast, D. Kinet (1977) is concerned with the comparison of Yahweh to Baal and reaches these conclusions: The work of Baal is determined by the seasonal cycle of nature, while Yahweh proves to be the absolute Lord over nature, life, and death; in contrast to Yahwism, Baalism lacks a historical dimension; in the Ugaritic texts no ethical order is bound up with the being or working of Baal, whereas the book of Hosea is completely caught up in Israel's moral failure as the people of God; the citizen of Ugarit knew that every death in the world of vegetation would be followed by rebirth, but Hosea struggled passionately against the religious complacency of his people; in Ugarit the numerous offerings find their justification in the certainty of the return of Baal, while in Hosea sacrifice can replace neither the obligations of Israel to Yahweh nor the ethical relationship as such; the Hoseanic understanding of Yahweh is determined by the intensive depiction of conflict between Yahweh and the people, while in the religion of Baal the only conflict is between the various gods (209-27).

11. Hosea's Relationship to the Monarchy.

Hosea comments on the monarchy several times in his preaching (1:4; 3:4; 7:3-7; 8:4; 10:3-4, 7, 15; 13:9-11), and his pronouncements are frequently resolved through a succession of bloody revolutions and regicides. Hosea does not, however, reject the monarchy in and of itself; rather, he criticizes the complete contempt for divine justice among the kings, who are representatives of Yahweh's people. The deep entanglement of Israel in guilt and divine wrath is seen, according to Hosea, in the demise of the monarchy.

Bibliography: **P. R. Ackroyd,** "Hosea and Jacob," *VT* 13 (1963) 245-59. **R. Bach,** "Die Erwählung Israels in der Wüste," (diss., Bonn, 1952). **C. Barth,** "Zur Bedeutung der Wüstentradition," *VTSup* 15 (1966) 137-51. **B. C. Birch,** *Hosea, Joel, Amos* (Westminster Bible Companion, 1997). **S. Bitter,** *Die Ehe des Propheten Hosea: Eine auslegungsgeschichtliche Studie* (GTA 3, 1975) 102-80. **P. G. Borbone,** "L'uccisione dei profeti (Osea 6:5)," *Henoch* 6 (1984) 271-92; "Il terzo incomodo: L'interpretazione del testo masoretico di Osea 3:1," *Henoch* 7 (1985) 151-60; "Riflessioni sulla critica del testo dell'antico testamento ebraico in riferimento al libro di Osea," *Henoch* 8 (1986) 281-309. **G. Bouwman,** *Des Julian von Aeclanum Kommentar zu den Propheten Osee, Joel, und Amos* (AnBib 9, 1958). **K. Budde,** "The Nomadic Ideal in the OT," *The New World* (December, 1895) 1-20. **M. Buss,** *The Prophetic Word of Hosea: A Morphological Study* (BZAW 111, 1969). **J. Calvin,** *Hoseas* (CR 70, 198-514; ET *Commentaries on the Twelve Minor Prophets* [4 vols. 1846-49, repr. 1950]). **A. Caquot,** "Osee et la Royaute," *RHPR* 41 (1961) 123-46. **U. Cassuto,** "The Prophet Hosea and the Books of the Pentateuch," *Biblical and Oriental Studies,* vol. 1, *Bible* (1973) 79-100. **H. Cazelles,** "The Problem of the Kings in Osee 8:4," *CBQ* 11 (1949) 14-25. **T. K. Cheyne,** *Hosea* (CBSC, 1884). **S. Coleman,** *Hosea Concepts in Midrash and Talmud* (1960). **Cyril of Alexandria,** *Cyrilli Alexandriae Archiepiscopi in Oseam Prophetam Commentarius* (PG 71, 1-328). **D. R. Daniels,** *Hosea and Salvation History: The Early Traditions of Israel in the Prophecy of Hosea* (BZAW 191, 1990). **F. Diedrich,** *Die Anspielungen auf die Jakob-Tradition in Hosea 12:1–13:3: Ein literaturwissenschaftlicher Beitrag zur Exegese früher Prophetentexte* (FzB 27, 1977). **G. I. Emmerson,** *Hosea: An Israelite Prophet in Judean Perspective* (JSOTSup 28, 1984). **H. Ewald,** *Die Propheten des Alten Bundes,* Bde. 1, 2 (1867²). **K. Galling,** *Die Erwählungstraditionen Israels* (BZAW 48, 1928). **A. Gelston,** "Kingship in the Book of Hosea," *OTS* 19 (1974) 71-85. **H. L. Ginsberg,** "Hosea, Book of," *EncJud* 8 (1971). **E. M. Good,** "The Composition of Hosea," *SEA* 31 (1966) 21-63; "Hosea and the Jacob Tradition," *VT* 16 (1966) 13-51. **Guibert von Nogent,** *Ad Tropologias in Prophetas Osee et Amos ac Lamentationes Jeremiae* (PL 156, 337-416). **Hieronymus** (Jerome), *Commentariorum in Osee Prophetam* (CCSL 76, 1-158). **F. Hitzig and H. Steiner,** *Die zwölf kleinen Propheten* (KEH, 1838 = 1881⁴). **F. L. Hossfeld,** *Der Dekalog: Seine späten Fassungen, die originale Komposition, und seine Vorstufen* (OBO 45, 1982). **E. Jacob,** "Der Prophet Hosea und die Geschichte," *EvTh* 24 (1964) 281-90. **C. Jeremias,** "Die Erzväter in der Verkündigung der Propheten," *Beiträge zur alttestamentlichen Theologie: Festschrift W. Zimmerli zum 70 Geburtstag* (1977) 206-22. **C. F. Keil,** *Biblischer Commentar über die zwölf kleinen Propheten* (1888³). **A. Kerrigan,** O.F.M., *St. Cyril of Alexandria, Interpreter of the OT* (AnBib 2, 1952). **D. Kinet,** *Ba'al und Jahwe: Ein Beitrag zur Theologie des Hoseabuches* (EHS.T 87, 1977). **M. Köckert,** "Prophetie und Geschichte im Hoseabuch," *ZTK* 85 (1988) 3-30. **G. Krause,** *Studien zu Luthers Auslegung der kleinen Propheten* (BHT 33, 1962). **W. Kuhnigk,** *Nordwestsemitische Studien zum Hoseabuch* (BibOr 27, 1974). **R. Kümpel,** "Die Berufung Israels: Ein Beitrag zur Theologie des Hosea," (diss., Bonn, 1973). **M. Luther,** *Hosea* (WA 13, 2-66; ET *Lectures on the Minor Prophets* [1975]). **T. Naumann,** *Hoseas Erben: Strukturen der Nachinterpretation im Buch Hosea* (BWANT 131, 1991). **H.-D. Neef,** "Der Septuaginta-Text und der Masoreten-Text des Hoseabuches im Vergleich," *Bib* 67 (1986) 195-220; *Die Heilstraditionen Israels in der Verkundigung des Propheten Hosea* (BZAW 169, 1987). **E. W. Nicholson,** *God and His People: Covenant and Theology in the OT* (1986). **M. Nissinen,** *Prophetie, Redaktion, und Fortschreibung im Hoseabuch: Studien zum Werdegang eines Prophetenbuches im Lichte von Hos 4 und 11* (AOAT 231, 1991). **H. S. Nyberg,** *Studien zum Hoseabuche* (1935). **C. von Orelli,** *Die zwölf kleinen Propheten* (KK, 1908³). **G. H. Patterson,** "The Septuagint Text of Hosea Compared with the MT," *Hebraica* (7 (1890/91) 190-221. **L. Perlitt,** *Bundestheologie im Alten Testament* (WMANT 36, 1969). **T. H. Robinson and F. Horst,** *Die zwölf kleinen Propheten* (HAT 14, 1964³). **E. F. C. Rosenmüller,** *Scholia* 6 (1836) 4-170. **H. H. Rowley,** "The Marriage of Hosea," *Men of God* (1963) 66-97. **W. Rudolph,** *Hosea: A Commentary* (KAT XIII, 1, 1966). **Rufinus,** *Commentarius in Prophetas Minores Tres Osee, Joel et Amos, Rufino Aquileiensi Presbytero, Commentarius in Oseam* (PL 21, 959-1034). **Rupert von Deutz,** *Ruperti Abbatis Tuitiensis Commentariorum in Duodecim Prophetas Minores. Libri XXXI. Prologus Ruperti in Osee Prophetam—In Osee Prophetam* (PL 168, 11-204). **L. Ruppert,** "Herkunft und Bedeutung der Jakob-Tradition bei Hosea," *Bib* 52 (1971) 488-504; "Beobachtungen zur Literar- und Kompositionskritik von Hosea 1–3," *Künder des Wortes: Festschrift J. Schreiner zum 60. Geburtstag* (1982) 163-82. **Theodore of Mopsuestia,** *Theodori Mopsuesteni Commentarius in XII Prophetas: Einleitung und Ausgabe von H. N. Sprenger* (Göttinger Orientforschungen V, 1, 1977). **Theodoret of Cyrrhus,** *Beati Theodoreti Episcopi Cyrensis Enarratio in Oseam Prophetam* (PG 81, 1551-632). **Theophylact,** *Theophylacti Expositio in Prophetam Oseam, Commentaris in Oseam* (PG 126, 565-820). **T. D. Setel,** "Prophets and Pornography: Female Sexual Imagery in Hosea," *Feminist Interpretation of the Bible* (ed. L. Russell, 1985) 86-95. **W. Thiel,** "Die Rede vom 'Bund' in den Prophetenbüchern," *ThV* IX (1977) 11-36. **L. Treitel,** *Die alexandrinische Uebersetzung des Buches Hosea, Heft* 1 (1887); "Die Septuaginta zu Hosea," *MGDJ* 41 (1897) 433-54. **H. Utzschneider,** *Hosea: Prophet vor dem Ende* (OBO 31, 1980).

K. Vollers, "Das Dodekapropheton der Alexandriner," *ZAW* 3 (1883) 219-72. J. Vollmer, *Geschichtliche Rückblicke und Motive in der Prophetie des Amos, Hosea, und Jesaja* (BZAW 119, 1971). T. C. Vriezen, "La Tradition de Jacob dans Osee XII," *OTS* 1 (1942) 64-78. R. J. Weems, "Gomer: Victim of Violence or Victim of Metaphor?" *Semeia* 47 (1989) 87-104; *Battered Love: Marriage, Sex, and Violence in the Hebrew Prophets* (OBT, 1995). J. Wellhausen, *Die kleinen Propheten* (1898, 1963[4]). I. Willi-Plein, *Vorformen der Schriftexegese innerhalb des Alten Testaments: Untersuchungen zum literarischem Werden der auf Amos, Hosea, und Micha zurückgehenden Bücher im hebräischen Zwölfprophetenbuch* (BZAW 123, 1971). H. W. Wolff, "Hoseas geistige Heimat," *TLZ* 81 (1956) 83-94 = *Gesammelte Studien zum Alten Testament* (TBü 22, 1973[2]) 232-50; *Hosea* (Hermeneia, 1965[2]; ET 1974). A. Wünsche, *Der Prophet Hosea übersetzt und erklärt mit Benutzung der Targumin, der jüdischem Ausleger Raschi, Aben Ezra, und D. Kimchi* (1868). G. A. Yee, *Composition and Tradition in the Book of Hosea: A Redaction Critical Investigation* (SBLDS 102, 1987); "Hosea," *Women's Bible Commentary* (ed. C. A. Newsom and S. H. Ringe, 1992) 195-204; "The Book of Hosea," *NIB* (1996) 7:195-298. E. Zenger, " 'Durch Menschen zog ich sie. . . . ' (Hos 11:4): Beobachtungen zum Verständnis des prophetischen Amtes im Hoseabuch," *Künder des Wortes: Festschrift J. Schreiner zum 60. Geburtstag* (1982) 183-201.

H.-D. NEEF

HOSKYNS, EDWYN CLEMENT (1884–1937)

Born in London, Aug. 9, 1884, H. was educated at Jesus College, Cambridge, and at Wells Theological College. Serving as dean of chapel, Corpus Christi College, Cambridge, and university lecturer from his return from military service (1919) to his premature death, June 28, 1937, he was the most inspiring British NT teacher of his generation. Through his lectures on the THEOLOGY and ethics of the NT, his preaching, and his books, he came to be seen as a pioneer in England of biblical theology. A student of A. von HARNACK, admirer of A. LOISY, and friend of A. SCHWEITZER, he found the early K. BARTH's passion and paradox congenial and translated *Der Römerbrief* into powerful English (*The Epistle to the Romans* [1933]). His debt to dialectical theology, however, was minimal; and he was critical of R. BULTMANN. More important German influences on his biblical theology were G. KITTEL and A. SCHLATTER.

A liberal catholic Anglican with a strong doctrine of the church and sacraments, H. insisted on the historical particularity of the incarnation and thought that biblical scholarship supported his beliefs. His essays "The Christ of the Synoptic Gospels," in *Essays Catholic and Critical* (ed. E. Selwyn, 1926), and "Jesus the Messiah," in *Mysterium Christi* (ed. G. Bell and A. Deissmann, 1930), were followed by *The Riddle of the NT* (1931), in which F. Davey (1904–73) collaborated. All these

publications claimed that the SYNOPTIC tradition and the emergence of Christianity were best explained by the hypothesis that a high christology, based on a creative interpretation of the OT, derived from JESUS himself. H. saw the riddle of the NT to lie in "the relation between Jesus of Nazareth and the primitive Christian church," but he answered it differently from liberal Protestantism and from Bultmann. Although he demonstrated the christological character of the earliest traditions, H. never really justified his conviction that they could be traced back to the historical Jesus. He did not press the question of the authenticity of each saying as W. WREDE, J. WELLHAUSEN, and Bultmann had done.

H.'s *magnum opus* on the Gospel of John (1940) was heavily edited by Davey. H. revised most of the incomplete introduction and the commentary down to 6:31, but the remainder is a draft written before 1931 and before his engagement with Barth's *Romans*. Unsatisfactory in many respects, it remains an English classic of theological interpretation. In 1981 more fragments of H.'s thought and teaching became available in a posthumous joint publication with Davey (d. 1973) intended as a sequal to *Riddle*. H. had written six of the seventeen chapters (2, 3, 6–9), and the remainder reflects his influence on his junior partner. Their view of biblical theology is ecclesial, historical, thematic, and shaped by the OT. It opens onto metaphysical questions but does not offer hermeneutical strategies (see HERMENEUTICS) for relating past and present. Although this rich work falls short of greatness, it continues to stimulate. In addition to several reviews, some lectures, slight articles, and a fifteen-page commentary on the JOHANNINE LETTERS in C. GORE's *New Commentary* (1928), published in H.'s lifetime, two volumes of sermons were posthumously published (1938, 1960).

Works: (with F. N. Davey), *The Riddle of the NT* (1931, 1947[3]); *Cambridge Sermons* (1938), with an appreciation by C. Smyth; *The Fourth Gospel* (ed. F. N. Davey, 1940); *We Are the Pharisees* (1960); (with F. N. Davey), *Crucifixion-Resurrection: The Pattern of the Theology and Ethics of the NT* (1981).

Bibliography: J. O. Cobham, "E. C. H.: The Sunderland Curate," *CQR* 158 (1957) 280-95. *DBN 1931–40* (1949) 448-49. C. F. Evans, "Crucifixion-Resurrection: Some Reflections on Sir E. H. as Theologian," *EpRe* 10, 1 (1983) 70-76; 10, 2 (1983) 79-86. R. H. Fuller, "Sir E. H. and the Contemporary Relevance of His Biblical Theology," *NTS* 30 (1985) 321-34. R. E. Parsons, *Sir E. H. as a Biblical Theologian* (1985). G. S. Wakefield, "Biographical Introduction," *Crucifixion-Resurrection: The Pattern of the Theology and Ethics of the NT* (E. H. Hoskyns and F. N. Davey, 1981) 27-81.

R. MORGAN

HOWARD, WILBERT FRANCIS (1880–1952)

H. took his undergraduate degree at Didsbury College, where he studied under J. Moulton (1863–1917), his MA at Manchester University, and his BA, BD, and DD degrees at the University of London. An ordained Methodist minister, he served a parish in Hundsworth before joining the faculty at Hundsworth College, Birmingham, in 1919. There he was tutor in NT language and literature and in 1943 was named principal, a post he held until 1951. He served on the translation committee for the NEB and was one of the principle organizers for the Studiorum Novi Testamenti Societas. He died on July 10, 1952.

After Moulton's death, H. took up the task of completing his *Grammar of NT Greek,* editing the second volume and contributing much of the material on accidence, including a helpful list of Semitisms. He began work on the third volume (*Syntax*) but died before it could be completed; it was edited and published in 1963 by N. Turner (b. 1916). H. was an outstanding grammarian of the pre-linguistics era, and his volume is extremely valuable.

H.'s other major contribution is in JOHANNINE studies. He was influenced by the form critics (see FORM CRITICISM) but still held mostly traditional points of view: The author of the Gospel also wrote the epistles, using the Synoptics or sources very like them. He held that the Gospel is a polemic against "Synagogue Judaism" and Gnosticism (see GNOSTIC INTERPRETATION). H. used PHILO, the Hermetic writings, and the *Odes of Solomon* to illuminate Johannine vocabulary. He tended to harmonize John and the synoptics; but where he could not, he generally viewed John as providing the better CHRONOLOGY for JESUS' life. He also argued that the Johannine eschatology was not as strictly "realized" as C. H. DODD claimed and posited a more balanced now-then tension. His summary of Johannine scholarship, revised after his death by C. Barrett (b. 1917), is still cited in bibliographies of modern commentaries on John.

Works: *A Grammar of NT Greek,* vol. 2 (1929); *The Fourth Gospel in Recent Criticism and Interpretation* (1931, rev. ed. by C. K. Barrett, 1955); *Christianity According to St. John* (1943); "The Gospel According to St. John: Introduction and Exegesis," *IB* (1952) 8:435-811.

Bibliography: W. F. Lofthouse et al., *W. F. H.: Appreciations of the Man* (1954).

R. B. VINSON

HUGH OF ST. CHER (d. 1263)

H. was born sometime in the 1190s in St. Cher, not far from Vienne in the south of France. He had become a doctor of canon law and a bachelor of theology even before he joined the Dominicans at Paris in 1225, where he studied under Roland of Cremona (d. 1259), the first Dominican to hold a chair in theology at the University of Paris. H. soon set upon a vocation that would make him one of the most prominent churchmen of his day. He first served in an administrative capacity as provincial general of the order for France from 1227 to 1229. Subsequently, he took up the posts of master of theology (1230–36) at the university and prior of the Dominican convent of St. Jacques (1233–36). After leaving these posts he resumed his duties for the next eight years as provincial general while continuing to maintain a lively interest in the scholarly activities of his order in Paris. He became vicar general in 1240 and attained his highest administrative post with his selection as the first Dominican cardinal (cardinal priest of Santa Sabina) on May 28, 1244. H. died in Orvieto on Mar. 19, 1263, and was buried at the Dominican convent in Lyons.

H. played a central role in the study of the Bible and theology in the thirteenth century. At St. Jacques he assembled a team to produce three works that would serve as essential starting points for the theologians and preachers of his day: a version of the VULGATE incorporating a vast series of linguistic notes "correcting" the contemporary version of the text; an expanded commentary on the Bible; and the first alphabetical CONCORDANCE to the Bible.

H.'s "corrected" Vulgate, the *Correctoria,* gives as full a sense of the literal meaning of the text as was possible for the thirteenth century, providing alternative readings culled from earlier (generally patristic) authors, together with occasional comments on the transmission of the Latin text. He began work on the *Correctoria* as early as 1227, although the latest versions of this work date from his years as cardinal (1244–63).

His set of commentaries, known as *Postillae,* uses as its starting point the GLOSSA ORDINARIA, itself largely a digest of patristic and Carolingian exegesis, and adds to it the fruits of biblical study from the middle of the twelfth century up to H.'s own time as well as comments reflecting contemporary issues. It seems that at least his postil on Revelation appeared in two editions—known by their incipits: *Aser pinguis* (mid 1230s) and *Vidit Jacob* (1240s)—that reflect the shift in the concern with the holding of multiple benefices, a practice roundly attacked by the mendicants until it was resolved in 1238. Possibly the postils on other books were also revised over time. Nevertheless, the earliest version of the *Postillae* on the entire Bible dates from H.'s years as master (1230–36).

Finally, his *Concordantia,* which first appeared between 1238 and 1240 and to which some 500 friars contributed, greatly facilitated the task of preaching, allowing a relative novice to find his way around in the Bible without having to commit the entire text to memory. An integral part of this work was a new reference system. Although the Bible had been given standard chapter divisions by S. LANGTON at the end of the twelfth century, H. was the first to introduce chapter subdivisions (a, b, c, d, e, f, g). The third edition of this work (c. 1280) in which shorter chapters were subdivided into only four parts, became the standard Latin biblical concordance for the balance of the Middle Ages. It would be most accurate to see H.'s role in this work as that of general editor, given that its scope was so vast and H.'s duties so considerable.

Works: *Postillae in universa Biblia juxta quadruplicem sensum litteralem, allegoricum, moralem, anagogicum* (1487 and later printings); *Concordantiae Bibliorum Sacrarum Vulgatae editionis* (1656); *Repertorium Biblicum medii aevi,* 3 (F. Stegmüller, 1947) nrs. 3604-784; *Repertorium commentariorum in Sententias Petri Lombardi* 1 (F. Stegmüller, 1947) no. 372.

Bibliography: H. A. Feiss, *Commentary on the Parable of the Prodigal Son by Hugh of St. Cher, OP (d. 1263)* (Peregrina Translations Series, 1996). **J. Fischer,** "Hugh of St. Cher and the Development of Medieval Theology," *Speculum* 31 (1956) 57-69. **T. Kaeppeli,** *Scriptores ordinis praedicatorum medii aevi* 2 (1975) 269-81. **R. E. Lerner,** "Poverty, Preaching, and Eschatology in the Commentaries of Hugh of Saint-Cher," *The Bible in the Medieval World: Essays in Memory of B. Smalley* (1985) 157-89. **S. Paulsell,** *HHMBI,* 112-16. **W. Principe,** *The Theology of the Hypostatic Union in the Early Thirteenth Century* 3 (Studies and Texts 19, 1970), with bibliography. **R. H. Rouse and M. A. Rouse,** "The Verbal Concordance to the Scriptures," *AFP* 44 (1974) 5-30; "La concordance verbale des Écritures," *Le Moyen Age et la Bible* (ed. P. Riché and G. Lobrichon, Bible de tous les temps 4, 1984) 115-22. **B. Smalley,** *The Study of the Bible in the Middle Ages* (1983³). **J.-P. Torrell,** *Théorie de la Prophétie et philosophie de la connaissance aux environs de 1230: La contribution d'Hughes de Saint-Cher* (SSL 40, 1977), with bibliography.

M. A. ZIER

HUGH OF ST. VICTOR (1096–1141)

Perhaps born to the noble family of Blankenburg in the Harz region (although some scholars claim the Low Countries as his birthplace), H. spent a short time at the house of Augustinian canons at Hammersleben before going to Paris. On his journey he may have traveled first to Marseilles, from whence he brought relics of St. Victor to the Paris abbey named after the saint, probably before 1118. St. Victor, a house of Augustinian canons regular, had an excellent library and an active intellectual life. H. taught there from about 1125 until his death.

H.'s principal reputation rests on his doctrinal work, *De sacramentis Christianae fidei,* intended as an introduction to the allegorical meaning of Scripture, as well as on his two mystical treatises on Noah's ark and his commentaries on the works of Dionysius the Aereopagite, which were used by theologians for centuries

to come. H. was a teacher *par excellence,* gaining a reputation as a second "AUGUSTINE"; and he composed a number of works introducing his students to various methods and aids for study. The first of these is his *Didascalicon: De studio legendi,* in which he outlined and integrated all forms of human knowledge as they serve the economy of salvation. The second half of this work focuses specifically on the Bible and outlines H.'s program for reading Scripture: first, reading history, from Genesis to Revelation, for which he provided maps and chronologies (see CHRONOLOGY), and then reading allegory, beginning with the NT and proceeding to the OT—a reading for which doctrine, as outlined in *De sacramentis,* is the necessary aid. Indeed, as H. presented the metaphor of a building for the senses of Scripture in the *Didascalicon,* doctrine is a "second foundation" of polished stones resting upon the subterranean foundation of history and supporting the walls of allegory. The final mode of reading Scripture is tropology, which seeks from the contemplation of the works of God to learn what our own actions should be.

H. also wrote a number of brief biblical commentaries: a series of literal *Notulae* to the Octateuch; sermons on portions of Ecclesiastes; and notes on the psalms, Lamentations, Joel, Obadiah, and perhaps Nahum. In all of these he focused on the literal/historical sense, precisely because this was the meaning of the text that the tradition had overlooked. As he wrote in *De Scripturis* (v. 13-15): "The outward form of God's word seems to you, perhaps, like dirt, so you trample it underfoot, like dirt, and despise what the letter tells you was done physically and visibly. But hear! that dirt which you trample opened the eyes of the blind. Read Scripture then, and first learn carefully what it tells you was done in the flesh." In probing the historical meaning H. distinguished among the letter, the sense, and the "sentence." The first refers to the construction of the words themselves; the second, to their meaning in context; the third, to the deeper meaning that can only be apprehended through interpretation.

H. set the program and approach that was to characterize the work of the Victorine school (see B. SMALLEY [1941, 1952J², 1983³]); indeed, it was in the works of his successors, ANDREW OF ST. VICTOR and RICHARD OF ST. VICTOR, that his vision and principles of biblical study came to flower. This vision meant a special emphasis on the literal-historical sense of the text, an interest fed both by the contact of the Victorines with French Jewish scholarship and its non-Christian reading of the OT and by the revival of interest in the metaphysical and scientific works of Aristotle, which stressed that the substance of things can be known only through manifestation to the senses. In spite of H.'s emphasis on a historical reading of the OT, he did not assign a theological value to that reading in and of itself since it points to a higher truth revealed in the Christ-event and in the NT (see S. Preus [1969]).

Works: *Opera* (*PL* 175-177); *Hugh of St. Victor on the Sacraments of the Christian Faith (De sacramentis)* (tr. R. J. Deferrari, 1951); *The "Didascalicon" of Hugh of St. Victor: A Medieval Guide to the Arts* (tr. J. Taylor, 1961); *Hugonis de Sancto Victore Opera Propaedeutica* (ed. R. Baron, 1966).

Bibliography: R. **Baron**, *Science et Sagesse chez Hugues de Saint-Victor* (1957); *Études sur Hugues de Saint-Victor* (1963); *DS* 7, 1 (1969) 901-39. J. **Châtillon**, *TRE* 15 (1986) 629-35. F. E. **Croydon**, "Notes on the Life of Hugh of St. Victor," *JTS* 40 (1939) 232-53. J. **Ehlers**, *Hugo von St. Victor* (1973). G. R. **Evans**, *Old Arts and New Theology: The Beginnings of Theology as an Academic Discipline* (1980); *The Language and Logic of the Bible: The Earlier Middle Ages* (1984). M. T. **Gibson**, "The Twelfth-Century Glossed Bible," *StPatr* 23 (1989) 232-44. H. **Hailperin**, *Rashi and the Christian Scholars* (1963). C. L. **Patton**, *HHMBI*, 106-12. S. **Preus**, *From Shadow to Promise: OT Interpretation from Augustine to the Young Luther* (1969) 24-37. P. **Sicard**, *Hugues de Saint-Victor et son École* (1991); *Diagrammes médiévaux et exégèse visuelle: Le Libellus de formatione arche de Hugues de Saint-Victor* (1993), esp. good bibliography. B. **Smalley**, *The Study of the Bible in the Middle Ages* (1941, 1952², 1983³). R. W. **Southern**, "Aspects of the European Tradition of Historical Writing: 2. Hugh of St. Victor and the Idea of Historical Development," *Transactions of the Royal Historical Society,* 5th ser., 21 (1971) 159-79. J. **Taylor**, *The Origin and Early Life of Hugh of St. Victor: An Evaluation of the Tradition* (1957). D. **Van den Eynde**, *Essai sur la succession et la date des écrits de Hugues de Saint-Victor* (1960). G. A. **Zinn, Jr.**, "Mandala Symbolism and Use in the Mysticism of Hugh of St. Victor," *HR* 12 (1973) 317-41; "*De gradibus ascensionum:* The Stages of Contemplative Ascent in Two Treatises on Noah's Ark by Hugh of St. Victor," *SMC* 5 (1975) 61-79; "The Influence of Hugh of St. Victor's *Chronicon* on the *Abbreviationes chronicorum* by Ralph of Diceto," *Speculum* 52 (1977) 38-61; *DMA* 6 (1985) 321-23.

M. A. ZIER

HUMBERT, PAUL (1885–1957)

H. was born at Neuchatel in 1885 and studied at Basel under B. DUHM, who profoundly influenced him. After obtaining a diploma from the École des Langues Orientales in Paris in 1912, H. served as OT professor in the theology faculty of the Free Church of the Canton of Vaud (1913–14) and the University of Neuchatel, where he taught for forty years. He died in Neuchatel in 1957.

H. admired and defended the views of J. RENAN, J. WELLHAUSEN, and H. GUNKEL, insisting that the task of scientific exegesis is simply and uniquely that of allowing the ancient texts to speak for themselves. He realized that this task requires a mind sensitive to the content of the texts, and he saw the NT as providing a "vaster vision" of the OT. He believed that scientific biblical work should always be free of dogmatic imperatives and ecclesiastical considerations; but as a devout Christian, he did not underestimate the church and its mission.

H. excelled in the study of Hebrew vocabulary. His philological research method utilized statistics and flexibility of judgment. He classified linguistic elements, distributing them carefully among discrete literary types (narrative, prophecy, lyric, wisdom) and seeking to reveal the history of the word, its origin, its passage into other domains, the evolution of its meaning, etc. He wrote many exegetical Hebrew word studies and important articles on Job, Ruth, Proverbs, the Israelite new year's liturgy, Samson, and the Ugaritic texts (see UGARIT AND THE BIBLE) as well as a commentary on Psalms 29–72 in *Bible du Centenaire.*

H. was also much occupied with the problem of OT prophetism (see PROPHECY AND PROPHETS, HB). He depicted Amos as the "most personal" of the prophets, the pitiless critic of the civilization and religion of his time. The prophets were to H. the "tragedies of the Bible," with their message of radical opposition between God and humanity and between faith and unfaith. The NT, however, shows the love of God and the idea of true sonship in the gospel, which forms a unity with the prophetic writings.

Works: "Osée, le prophete bedouin," *RHPR* 1 (1921) 97-118; *Recherches sur les sources égyptiennes de la littérature sapientiale d'Israél* (1929); *Art et leçon de l'histoire de Ruth* (1939); *Études sur le récit du paradis et de la chute dans la Genèse* (1940); *Problèmes du livre d'Habacuc* (1944); *La "terqu'a"; analyse d'un rite biblique* (1946); *Observations sur le vocabulaire arabe du Châhnâmeh* (1953); *Opuscules d'un Hébraïsant* (1958).

Bibliography: W. **Baumgartner**, "Preface," *Opuscules d'un Hébraïsant par P. H.* (1958).

J. M. BULLARD

HUME, DAVID (1711–76)

A Scottish philosopher and historian, H. was born in Edinburgh on May 7, 1711, to a devout Presbyterian family. Educated in Edinburgh, he early abandoned revealed religion, although he remained a theist. His skepticism contained a strain of piety and respect for custom and tradition that distinguished it from the iconoclasm of the French *philosophes.* At the age of twenty-eight he published *A Treatise of Human Nature,* a work that undertook the monumental task of establishing the framework for a universal science of human nature. Because of its skepticism the *Treatise* was not successful; and during the next two decades H. set about recasting its philosophy into more readable form and applying its doctrines to an increasing range of subjects, including ethics, politics, economics, aesthetics, religion, and history. In the last years of his life he wrote little. He died in Edinburgh, August 25, 1776.

The central principle of H.'s philosophy is the autonomy of custom. The Enlightenment had supposed that philosophy must emancipate itself from custom in order to evaluate it, but H. argued that philosophy purged of custom and tradition would be either empty or arbitrary and thus incapable of rational criticism. In this way he stood the Enlightenment on its head. With respect to religion, H.'s philosophy of custom could be developed in different directions. It has been used to support fideism and the idea of sacred tradition, but it has also been used (and was so employed by H.) to criticize religious traditions. In *The Natural History of Religion* (1757) he traced the logic of popular religious belief to self-debasing fear of the invisible powers that govern life. Popular religion is corrupting and impious because it conceives of the deity as acting in the interests of the believer through supernatural intervention in the form of miracles. True religion is belief in an intelligent author of the universe and a sentiment of awe and adoration on contemplating the order of nature. In *Dialogues Concerning Natural Religion,* published posthumously, H. argued that true religion is rooted in human nature but is incapable of rational proof. In "Of Miracles" (1748), he argued that no system of religion could be established merely on the testimony that miracles had occurred. The same argument applies to prophecies, which H. defined as a species of miracle. As a record of miracles and prophecies (the purport of which is to establish a religion) the Bible has no value; H. saw no other way to read it. Although steeped in the biblical tradition, he rarely mentions it in his writings.

Works: *A Treatise of Human Nature* (3 vols., 1739–40); "Of Miracles," *An Enquiry Concerning Human Understanding* (1748); *An Enquiry Concerning the Principles of Morals* (1751); *The History of England* (6 vols., 1754–62); *The Natural History of Religion* (1757); *Essays, Moral, Political, and Literary* (1777); *Dialogues Concerning Natural Religion* (1779); *Hume on Natural Religion* (ed. S. Tweyman, 1996).

Bibliography: P. Addinall, *Philosophy and Biblical Interpretation: A Study in Nineteenth-Century Conflict* (1991). **F. Beckwith,** *D. H.'s Argument Against Miracles* (1989). **J. E. Force,** "Hume and Johnson on Prophecy and Miracles: Historical Context," *JHI* 43 (1982) 463-76; "Hume and the Relation of Science to Religion Among Certain Members of the Royal Society," *JHI* 45 (1984) 517-36. **J. C. A. Gaskin,** *Hume's Philosophy of Religion* (1978). **J. A. Herdt,** *Religion and Faction in Hume's Moral Philosophy* (CSRCT 3, 1997). **D. W. Livingston,** *Hume's Philosophy of Common Life* (1984). **B. Logan,** *A Religion Without Talking: Religious Belief and Natural Belief in Hume's Philosophy of Religion* (1993). **E. C. Mossner,** "The Religion of D. H.," *JHI* 39 (1987) 579-98. **J. S. Preus,** "Religion Within the Limits of 'The Science of Man':

D. H.," *Explaining Religion: Criticism and Theory from Bodin to Freud* (1987) 84-103. **S. Tweyman,** *Skepticism and Belief in Hume's Dialogues Concerning Natural Religion* (1986); (ed.) *D. H.: Critical Assessments* (6 vols., 1995) vol. 5. **K. Yandell,** *Hume's "Inexplicable Mystery": His Views on Religion* (1990).

D. W. LIVINGSTON

HUPFELD, HERMANN CHRISTIAN KARL FRIEDRICH (1796–1866)

Born Mar. 31, 1796, in Marburg, Germany, H. died Apr. 24, 1866, in Halle. He began study in theology at Marburg in 1813, particularly under A. J. Arnoldi (1750–1835), and also pursued classical philology and oriental studies. In 1817 he passed the standard theology examination and completed his doctorate in philosophy; over the next few years he taught in secondary schools and pursued private studies. Initially he was plagued by doubts concerning the possibility of a theology based on revelation, doubts occasioned by historical-critical research. He reconciled revelation and critical research in the idea of a developmental process of religious ideas guided by the divine Spirit. Deciding to pursue an academic career in theology, he went to Halle in 1824, where he was supported by H. GESENIUS and J. Wegscheider (1771–1849). In 1825 he returned to Marburg as *ausserordentlicher* professor of theology, became a full professor of oriental languages in 1827; and in 1830, full professor of theology. He succeeded H. Gesenius in Halle in 1843.

H.'s position within biblical scholarship is described in his treatise on the concept and method of biblical introduction (1844), which simultaneously makes his methodological interest clear. It is characteristic that he replaced the traditional "introduction" with "biblical literary history" or "history of the holy Scriptures of the OT and NT." His intense concern with placing exegesis on a solid foundation is shown by the number of his learned smaller works concerning such auxiliary disciplines as grammar, Semitics, and textual history.

An especially influential monograph was *Die Quellen der Genesis* (1853), a cornerstone in the history of PENTATEUCHAL CRITICISM in its establishment of the "new documentary hypothesis": The "Yahwist" was no mere supplemental writer and editor of an Elohistic "basic text" (*Grundschrift*), but rather the author of an independent text; there was not just one Elohist, but two. Three (or, including Deuteronomy, four) sources were synthesized by an editor, who is to be distinguished from the sources.

H.'s commentary on the psalms was initially prompted by the commission to rework W. DE WETTE's commentary. However, a completely new work resulted, more comprehensive than De Wette's, particularly in linguistic matters and in the history of exegesis. Unlike his mentor and predecessor Gesenius, whom he highly revered as a philologist, H. himself did not neglect the task of theological interpretation, which he viewed as the most important goal of his work.

Works: "Animadversiones philologicae in Sophoclem" (diss. phil., Marburg, 1817); *Exercitationes Aethiopicae sive observationum criticarum ad emendandam rationem grammaticae semiticae specimen primum* (1825); *Über Begriff und Methode der sogenannten biblischen Einleitung* (1844); *De rei grammaticae apud Judaeos initiis antiquissimisque scriptoribus* (1846); "Die Stellung und Bedeutung des Buchs Hiob im Alten Testament nach seinem didaktischen und dramatischen Charakter," *DZCW* 1 (1850) 273-78, 284-92; *Commentatio de primitiva et vera festorum apud Hebraeos ratione ex legum Mosaicarum varietate eruenda* (3 Hefte, 1851–58); *Die Quellen der Genesis und die Art ihrer Zusammensetzung* (1853); *Die Psalmen* (4 vols., 1855–61); *Die heutige theosophische oder mythologische Theologie und Schrifterklärung* (1861); *Commentatio qua festorum memoriae apud rerum hebraicarum scriptores cum legibus Mosaicis collatae examinantur* (1865).

Bibliography: J. Annandale, "H. H.'s Contribution to OT Scholarship," *OTE* (Pretoria) 4 (1986) 177-89; *Grundlage zu einer Hessischen Gelehrten-Schriftsteller- und Künstler-Geschichte* (ed. K. W. Justi, 1831) 277-84; (ed. O. Gerland, 1863) 306-20, (autobiographical). A. Kamphausen, *ADB* 13 (1881) 423-26; *RE*38 (1900) 462-67. G. Ott, *NDB* 10 (1974) 72-73. E. Riehm, *Dr. H. H.: Lebens- und Charakterbild eines deutschen Professors* (1867).

R. SMEND

HUS, JAN (1372–1415)

Born to a peasant family in Husinec, H. studied at the university in Prague, earning a BA in 1393 and an MA three years later. Ordained to the priesthood in 1400, he became Charles University master and preacher at Bethlehem Chapel in Prague. He was influenced principally by AUGUSTINE, J. WYCLIF, and native Czech reform tradition. Although his theology and preaching were entirely orthodox, his calls for moral reform became increasingly strident, leading finally to his censure and excommunication. He received the king's support until he attacked the selling of papal indulgences; after an interdict was imposed on Prague in 1412, he withdrew voluntarily, in exile composing several important works on theology and reform. Appearing before the Council of Constance in 1414 with a guarantee of safe conduct, he was nevertheless arrested and imprisoned. His trial consisted of attempts to force him to recant and submit to ecclesiastical authority. When he refused to abjure he was degraded from the priesthood and his teachings were banned. He was burned at the stake along with his books on July 6, 1415, whereupon he became "Saint Jan Hus" to the Hussite revolution that followed.

H.'s career was guided by the rubric "search the Scriptures." In theology and reform he attempted to be consistent with biblical mandates, maintaining that Scripture was to be "read, heard and preached for the sake of eternal life" (*Super IV Sententiarum,* 14-20). Since Scripture contained a saving knowledge of Christ it must be believed. Although H. may have said that every word of Scripture is true (*Postilla,* 86), it is impossible to conclude that Scripture was his absolute source for all Christian doctrine (M. Spinka [1966] 326). Canon law and patristic and medieval authorities remained relevant: AUTHORITY for the Christian resided in the triad of Scripture, tradition, and reason, in that order. The doctrine of *sola Scriptura* is not a tenet that can accurately be applied to H. since his extant writings and sermons argue on the basis of the authority of both Scripture and tradition: "Read the Bible gladly, particularly the NT, and where you do not understand, refer at once to commentaries" (*Letters,* 170).

H.'s career at Bethlehem Chapel was a decade of biblical preaching. For him scriptural knowledge formed the beginning of regeneration (*Sebrane Spisy,* 1:302), thus his sermons were extended expositions of biblical texts. The first to introduce biblical exegesis into Czech preaching, he regarded Scripture as his center, although the Word of God did not find its limit in the text. The Hussite Reformation principle—the law of God—is applicable for him as a guiding religious motif. In this conviction the Bible is central but not exclusive. Believing that the benefits of hearing the Word were innumerable (*Postilla,* 28), H. preached in the vernacular and urged the production of Scripture in the common language (*Letters,* 106-7).

H. revised and improved existing texts of the Czech NT in 1406 and in 1413–14 undertook a revision of the entire second redaction of the Czech Bible (F. Bartoš [1941]). In addition, he wrote numerous commentaries on biblical texts. In terms of exegesis, he followed the medieval principles of exploring the literal (historical), allegorical, moral, and anagogical meanings, consistently using the entire Bible as a basis for exegesis (P. De Vooght [1960] 49).

At his last trial for heresy H. appealed to the Bible, refusing to abjure unless convicted by scriptural proof (Spinka [1966] 228). He subordinated scholastic reasoning to the Scriptures and approved private interpretation of the Bible, considering this more important than rote acceptance of tradition and the pronouncements of the official church. In these convictions he belongs more to the sixteenth century than to the Middle Ages.

Works: *Mistra Jana Husi Sebrané spisy české* (2 vols., ed. K. J. Erben, 1865–68); *M. J. H. Super IV Sententiarum* (3 vols., ed. V. Flajšhans, 1904–6); *Mistr J. H. Postilla* (ed. J. B. Jeschke, 1952); "On Simony," *Advocates of Reform from Wyclif to Erasmus* (ed. M. Spinka, 1953) 196-278; *Magistri J. H. Tractatus "De ecclesia"* (ed. S. H. Thomson, 1956); *Magistri*

Iohannis Hus Opera Omnia (25 vols., ed. A. Molnár, 1959–   );
The Letters of J. H. (ed. M. Spinka, 1972).

Bibliography: **F. M. Bartoś,** *Počátky české Bible* (1941).
P. De Vooght, L'Hérésie de Jean Huss (1960). **T. A. Fudge,**
*The Magnificent Ride: The First Reformation in Hussite Bohe-
mia* (1998); "'Ansellus dei' and the Bethlehem Chapel in
Prague," *Communio Viatorum* 35 (1993) 127-61. **Petr of
Mladoňovice,** *John Hus at the Council of Constance* (Records
of Civilization, Sources and Studies 73, ed. M. Spinka, 1965,
1997). **M. Spinka,** *J. H. and the Czech Reform* (1941); *J. H.'s
Concept of the Church* (1966); *J. H.: A Biography* (1968, 1983).
E. Werner, *J. H.: Welt und Umwelt eines Prager Frühreforma-
tors* (FMG 34, 1991). **J. K. Zeman,** *The Hussite Movement
and the Reformation in Bohemia, Moravia and Slovakia, 1350–
1650: A Bibliographical Study Guide* (1977).

T. FUDGE

HUTCHINSON, JOHN (1674–1737)

An informally educated English author, H. precipitated much controversy with his *Moses' Principia,* in
which he argued that all knowledge was to be found in
the HB, properly understood as symbolic and read
without the vowel points. He thought the confusion of
tongues at the Tower of Babel had led to ignorance as
the original divine language, in which there was a
correlation between words and the natures of things, had
been supplanted by many languages. But God's revealed
truth is still to be found in the HB, and its study in the
original Hebrew is the key to all knowledge. H. attacked
the study of nature by I. NEWTON as a mistaken approach. Contemporaries ridiculed his views; but he had
ardent supporters, including S. Johnson (1696–1772) in
the American colonies, who introduced H.'s ideas into
the curriculum of King's (later Columbia) College in
New York.

Works: *Moses' Principia* (2 pts., 1724–27).

Bibliography: **J. Ellis,** *The New England Mind in Transi-
tion: S. Johnson of Connecticut* (1973) 228-32. **L. Stephen,**
DNB 28 (1891) 342-43; *History of English Thought in the
Eighteenth Century* (1902, 1927) 1:330-33.

D. D. WALLACE, JR.

HVIDBERG, FLEMMING FRIIS (1897–1959)

H. studied in Copenhagen, Marburg, Oslo, London,
Oxford, and Cambridge. His dissertation on the Damascus document, published by S. SCHECHTER in 1910,
offered a translation, a thorough TEXTUAL analysis, and
an attempt to describe the theological position of the
document and to determine its provenance and religious
milieu—a difficult undertaking before the DEAD SEA
SCROLLS were discovered.

In 1938 H. published his famous book on weeping
and laughter in the HB, making extensive use of the
recently discovered texts from Ras Shamra (see UGARIT
AND THE BIBLE) to shed new light on the relation between
Israelite and Canaanite religion. Published in Danish,
the book did not receive due international attention until
it was translated in 1962. The influence of J. PEDERSEN
is unmistakable, but H. was an original scholar who in
his turn influenced many scholars in the "Uppsala circle." I. ENGNELL explicitly recognized his debt to H.

H.'s view of the history of Israelite religion was
summarized and popularized in two books in Danish in
the 1940s, edited together in 1943 under the title *Den
israelitiske Religions Historie.* Always very attentive to
the amount of Canaanite influence in Israelite religion,
H. insisted on the importance of syncretism in the
ancient world but did not neglect the distinctive marks
of Israel's religion.

H. was appointed professor at the University of Copenhagen in 1941. He engaged in the Danish Bible
translation project, providing the entire translation with
text-critical notes. He also became deeply involved in
political life and during the German occupation of Denmark published newspaper articles in which he pointed
to texts in the HB predicting the fall of the tyrant. In
1943 he was elected to the Danish diet and in 1950–53
served as minister of education. Eager to study the
Qumran texts when he left the government, H. went to
Palestine in January 1959, where he died unexpectedly.

Works: *Menigheden af den nye Pagt i Damascus: Noge
Studier over de af Salomo Schechter fundne og under Titlen
"Fragments of a Zadokite Work" udgivne Genizafragmenter
("Damascusskriftet")* (1928); *Graad og Latter i det gamle
Testamente: En Studie i kanaanaeisk-israelitisk Religion* (1938;
ET *Weeping and Laughter in the OT* [1962]); *Det Gamle
Testamente: Autoriseret Oversaettelse af 1931 med tekstkritisk
Noteapparat* (1942); *Den israelitiske Religions Historie* (1943).

Bibliography: **E. Hammershaimb,** *Dansk Biografisk Leksikon* 6 (1980) 629-30.

S. HIDAL

HYATT, JAMES PHILIP (1909–72)

H. received his BA at Baylor (1929), MA from Brown
(1930), and BD (1933) and PhD (1938) from Yale with
a dissertation on final vowels in Neo-Babylonian. He
taught at Wellesley College (1935–41) and Vanderbilt
University (1941–72), where he served as chairman of
the graduate department of religion (1944–64).

H.'s major contributions to HB studies were in AR-
CHAEOLOGY and linguistics, in the commentary on Exodus in the *NCB* and on Jeremiah in the *IB,* as well as
several articles on these biblical books. He also wrote
numerous encyclopedia articles (see DICTIONARIES AND

ENCYCLOPEDIAS) on HB subjects. His approach was "literary historical" in the tradition of J. WELLHAUSEN (see *The Heritage of Biblical Faith* [1964] 31-38, 47-85).

The most significant positions H. advocated are the following: The prophet Jeremiah was born in 626 BCE and received his call in 609 BCE; thus he had no connection with Josiah's reform. The "Foe from the North" in the book of Jeremiah is not the Scythians, but the Babylonians. The present book of Jeremiah was subjected to an extensive DEUTERONOMISTIC revision. Deuteronomy 6:20-25; 26:5-9 and Josh 24:2-13 are not early historical credos (contra G. von Rad), but late historical summaries. The Sinai tradition was handed down along with the traditions of the exodus, the wilderness wanderings, and the like, and not in isolation. The classical prophets rejected the Israelite cult radically and completely and not merely abuses of the cult.

Works: *The Treatment of Final Vowels in Early Neo-Babylonian* (YOS 23, 1941); *Prophetic Religion* (1947); "The Book of Jeremiah: Introduction and Exegesis," *IB* (1956) 5:777-1142; *Jeremiah: Prophet of Courage and Hope* (1958); *The Heritage of Biblical Faith: An Aid to Reading the Bible* (1964); *Exodus* (NCB, 1971).

Bibliography: **J. L. Crenshaw and J. T. Willis,** *Essays in OT Ethics (J. P. H., In Memoriam)* (1974) VII-XXXI.

J. T. WILLIS

HYLMÖ, GUNNAR (1878–1940)

Born in Malmö, Sweden, where he spent his life, H. was ordained in the Church of Sweden and for some years worked in a parish. After defending his doctoral dissertation on the composition of Micah in 1919, he became *Docent* in OT at the University of Lund and taught at a training college for teachers and at a grammar school. He was active when few professorial chairs in Sweden fell vacant, however, he was an unobtrusive person who liked teaching. His publications are in Swedish, and because of the language barrier are seldom referred to, one exception being by A. BENTZEN in his *Introduction.*

H. was a pioneer in FORM CRITICISM of the prophets (see PROPHECY AND PROPHETS, HB). His dissertation on Micah was primarily text-critical. Heavily dependent on W. Rothstein's and E. Sievers's metrical studies, H. suggested many corrections of the MT *metri causa.* He used this work as a basis for LITERARY criticism, separating the genuine prophetic sayings from later additions. His work on Micah was rather traditional, as was his study of Psalms 120–134. Although form-critical interest is more pronounced, the most important feature is still TEXTUAL CRITICISM.

Gradually H. began to take an interest in the form-critical study of the prophetical sermon. In a 1929 volume on style in the OT prophetical books, dependent on H. GRESSMANN and H. GUNKEL, he divided the prophetical sayings into distinctly prophetic, didactic, and lyrical forms. The distinctly prophetic sayings he divided into oracles or sayings concerning the future (which could be classified in several types), rebukes or reproaches, exhortations, and prophetic legal sayings or Torah. Didactic types are divided into historical reflections, prophetic contention, trial speeches, and proverbs. Lyrical types are divided into secular and religious poems (with many subdivisions). H. applied this scheme of classification to Isa 25:1–26:21 in a study also published in 1929.

H. wrote a much-used introductory university textbook on the OT (1938) in which he summarized work on prophetic literature and gave a comprehensive synopsis of contemporary exegetical scholarship. His position in isagogical matters was rather conservative. On legal sayings in the Pentateuch (see PENTATEUCHAL CRITICISM) he did not mention A. ALT's study *Die Ursprünge des israelitischen Rechts,* which perhaps had not reached him yet. Otherwise he was well versed in current scholarship.

Works: "Kompositionen av Mikas bok" (diss., 1919); *De s. k. vallfartssångerna* i Psaltaren (Psalmi CXX-CXXXIV) (1925); *Studier över stilen i de gammaltestamentliga profetböckerna. 1. De eg. profetiska diktarterna* (1929); *De s. k. profetiska liturgiernas rytm, stil och komposition. 1. Jes 25:1–26:21* (1929); *Gamla testamentets litteraturhistoria* (1938).

S. HIDAL

I

IBN EZRA, ABRAHAM BEN MEIR (1092/93–1167)

I. was an author of both Hebrew poetry and biblical exegesis. Until 1140 he lived in Spain as part of the intellectual circle of JUDAH HALEVI, and his writings focused on poetry. After 1140 he lived as a wandering scholar in Italy, northern France, England, and Provence, writing on biblical exegesis, Hebrew language, mathematics, and ethics and bringing the sophisticated linguistic developments of Spanish Jewish authors to the centers of Jewish biblical exegesis in Provence and northern France.

I. wrote commentaries on all books of the Bible, often producing two recensions of a commentary on the same book. The commentaries on the early prophets, Chronicles, Proverbs, Ezekiel, Ezra, and Nehemiah are no longer extant. His commentaries are distinguished by their cryptic style, by their focus on questions of grammar, and by a critical attitude toward the exegetical solutions offered by both rabbinic and KARAITE exegetes. The introduction to the commentary on the Pentateuch (see PENTATEUCHAL CRITICISM) outlines and critiques four approaches that his predecessors and contemporaries used. The first group, the Gaonim in Islamic countries, explicated the Pentateuch as a book of "Greek wisdom" that obscured the meaning of the biblical text. A second group, the Karaites, explained the biblical text based entirely upon their own reason and ignored the traditions of the sages or oral law. A third group, probably Christians, expounded the Pentateuch as a book of riddles and mysteries. The fourth group, rabbinic exegetes in Byzantine countries, simply repeated the MIDRASH traditions of the ancient rabbis without any regard to how they cohere with the biblical text. I.'s approach, offered as a fifth way, balances grammar, reason, and the rabbinic tradition. He considered that his judicious use of Talmudic (see TALMUD) or Midrashic traditions as the framework for presenting the insights of the most sophisticated linguistic scholarship available made his exegesis superior to all other methods.

The commentary on the book of Exodus contains a number of lengthy excursuses in which he reveals his own views on (a) the names of God (Exod 3:14-15); (b) the Jewish calendar (see Exod 12:2); (c) the two presentations of the Decalogue in the Pentateuch (Exod 20:1-21); (d) the derivation of later Jewish laws from biblical verses ('asmakhta; Exod 21:7-9); (e) the supe-

riority of angels to human beings (Exod 23:20, shorter recension); (f) fate (Exod 23:5); (g) the form and nature of the universe (Exod 25:40); and (h) the knowledge of God (Exod 33:21).

His commentary on the Song of Songs exists in two recensions. It is unique in the history of Jewish exegesis of this biblical book because it is divided into three sections: (1) I. promises to explain the lexical and grammatical difficulties of the book; (2) he includes the description of a parable in which a young girl falls in love with a shepherd; and (3) he provides an allegorical interpretation wherein the Song of Songs narrates the relationship between God and the people Israel from Abraham through the exile of Israel and its ultimate restoration to grandeur among the nations of the world. What is unique about his interpretation is that he viewed all three levels—grammatical, parable, allegory—as part of a unified exposition of the book. In his commentaries on Lamentations and Job, he also divided his comments into different levels.

The commentary on Psalms contains a lengthy discussion of the authorship of individual poetic units within the book. He ascribed the psalms to poetic-prophetic authors who were inspired by the Holy Spirit. Although he suggested that some of the psalms may have been written after the Babylonian exile, he hesitated to draw a firm conclusion. On several occasions in the commentary on Isaiah, he hinted that there may have been two different authors for chaps. 1–39 and chaps. 40–66, and the commentary on the Pentateuch points to certain chronological difficulties (see CHRONOLOGY, HB) that would contradict a unified authorship. His allusions to radical revisions of classical rabbinic theories of biblical authorship need to be understood in the light of his overall approach to the Bible, however. Recent scholarship suggests that although he raised these questions I. had great reverence for the rabbinic tradition and did not deviate from it in his conclusions.

Works: Editions. **Pentateuch:** Gen 47:7–49:12, *Essays on the Writings of Abraham ibn Ezra* (M. Friedlaender, 1877) 1-68; *Exodus* (short recension, ed. F. L. Fleisher, 1926). **Prophets:** L. Levy, *Reconstruction des Commentars Ibn Esras zu den ersten Propheten* (1903); *Isaiah* (ed. M. Friedlaender, 1873); *Jeremiah and Ezekiel* (sections), *MGWJ* (ed. S. Ochs, 60 [1916]) 41-58, 118-34, 193-212, 279-94, 437-52; *Twelve Prophets* (ed. U. Simon, 1989); *Song of Songs* (first recension, ed.

H. J. Matthews, 1874); *Esther* (ed. J. Zedner, 1850); Daniel (shorter recension), *Miscellany of Hebrew Literature* (ed. H. J. Matthews, 2 [1887]) 257-62.

Bibliography: W. **Bacher,** *Abraham ibn Esras Einleitung zu seinen Pentateuch-Commentar* (1876). M. **Friedlaender,** *Essays on the Writings of Abraham ibn Ezra* (1877). J. **Galliner,** *Abraham ibn Esras Hiobkommentar auf seine Quellen untersucht* (1901). H. **Grieve,** *Studien zum jüdischen Neuplatonismus: Die Religionsphilosophie des A. ibn Ezra* (1973); *TRE* 1 (1977) 389-92. L. **Prijs,** *Die grammatikalische Terminologie des Abraham ibn Esra* (1950). S. **Uriel,** *Four Approaches to the Book of Psalms: From Saadi Gaon to Abraham ibn Ezra* (SUNY Series in Judaica, 1991).

M. A. SIGNER

IBN JANAH, JONAH ABŪ AL-WALĪD MARWĀN
(c. 990–c. 1050)

The places and exact dates of I.'s birth and death and his father's name are unknown. His name as cited above is a composite form of the various names by which he or others referred to him. In his writings he calls himself (in Arabic) Abū al-Walīd, Marwān, or Ibn Janaḥ. Later Hebrew writers refer to him as R. Jonah or R. Marinus. Ibn Janaḥ (The Winged) is not a patronymic but a play on the Hebrew name Jonah (Dove). Scholars speculate that he was born in either Cordoba or neighboring Lucena, Spain. It is known that he left Cordoba as a young man after the death of his father. He received his formal education in Lucena, home of a large Jewish community, where his principal teachers were R. Isaac b. Levi ibn Mar Saul (early 11th cent.), and R. Isaac ibn GIKATILLA (end of 10th cent.). He later returned to Cordoba, but left the city in 1012 as a result of persecution, and after much wandering settled in Saragossa, where he spent the rest of his life.

By his own testimony, his chief subjects of study from his youth were language and Scripture. This included biblical Hebrew as well as the Hebrew of the Mishna and TALMUD, the Aramaic of the Talmud and the TARGUMIM, and Arabic, the language in which all of his extant works are written. He also studied medicine, which became his profession. He is reputed to have written a book of remedies, but it has not come down to us. The language of the Bible became his lifelong scholarly occupation, and the major influence on him was, in fact, not the work of his own teachers, but that of a scholar of the previous generation, Judah ben David Ḥayyuj (c. 945–c. 1000).

To Ḥayyuj is attributed the establishing of a triconsonantal base for the Hebrew weak verb; he also relied heavily on the methods and structures of Arabic grammarians. I. followed him on both of these counts. In his major work *Kitāb al-Tanqīh,* which Judah ibn Tibbon translated as *Sefer ha-Dikduk,* I. completed Ḥayyuj's work, confirming his theories, and in doing so

produced the first complete work on Hebrew philology extant in its entirety. The work is divided into two parts, the first a grammar (*Kitāb al-Luma* ʿ; Heb., *Sefer ha-Rikmah*), and the second, a dictionary (*Kitāb al Uṣūl;* Heb., *Sefer ha-Shorashim*). His other extant works, with one possible exception, also address grammatical and syntactical issues, often in a polemical context. They include the *Kitāb al-Mustalhaq* (Heb., *Sefer ha-Hassagah*), a work describing, analyzing, and expanding on Ḥayyuj's theories, and the *Kitāb* [sometimes *Risālat*] *al-taqrīb wa al-Tashīl* (Heb., *Iggeret ha-Keruv ve-ha-Yishur*), an explanation of difficult passages in Hayyuj, together with a discussion of basic grammar. His polemical works include the *Risālat al-Tanbīh* (Heb., *Sefer ha-Heʿarah*) and the *Kitāb al-Taswiya* (Heb., *Sefer ha-Tokhahat* or *Sefer ha-Hashvaʿah*), both replies to criticism of the *Kitāb al-Mustalhaq* and the *Kitāb al-Tashwīr* (Heb., *Sefer ha-Hakhlamah*). The one exception may be a commentary on the book of Chronicles, a fragment of which was published in the journal *Tarbiz* in 1989.

Bibliography: W. **Bacher,** *Leben und Werke des Abulwalîd Merwân ibn Ganâch (R. Jonah), und die Quellen seiner Schrifterklärung* (1885); (ed.), *Sepher Ha-shorashim Wurzelwörterbuch der hebräischen Sprache von Abulwalid Merwan Ibn Ganah (R. Jona): Aus dem Arabischen in's Hebräische übersetzt von Jehuda Ibn Tibbon* (1896), Hebrew. D. **Becker,** "Linguistic Rules and Definitions in Ibn Janah's Kitab al-Luma (Sefer ha-Riqmah) copied from the Arab grammarians," *JQR* 86 (1996) 257-98. G. **Busi,** "Materiali per una storia della filologia e dell' esegesi ebraica: Abû ʾl-Walîd Marwân ibn Ganâh," *IUO* 46 (1986) 167-95. M. S. **Demichelis,** "La racine hébraïque d'après le grammairien Abu ʾl-Walîd Marwân ibn Ganâh (XIe siecle)," *Henoch* 18 (1996) 177-95. J. **and** H. **Derenbourg,** *Opuscules et traités d'Abou ʾl-Walid ibn Merwan ibn Djanah de Cordoue* (1880). J. **Derenbourg** (ed.), *Ibn Jannah: Le Livre des parterres fleuris* (1886). A. **Neubauer** (ed.), *The Book of the Hebrew Roots* (1875, 1968). M. **Perani,** "I manoscritti ebraici della 'Genîzâ italiana': frammenti di una traduzione sconosciuta del 'Sefer ha-Sorasim' di Yona ibn Ganah," *Sefarad* 53 (1993) 103-42. M. **Perez,** "Serid mi-perush shel R. Yonah ibn Ganah le-Divre ha-yamim," *Tarbiz* 58 (1989) 283-88; " 'Derekh ketsarah': Midah parshanit ba-mishnat R. Yonah ibn Ganah," *ʾIyune Mikra u-farshanut* 3 (1993) 317-48. U. **Simon,** "Who Was the Proponent of Lexical Substitution Whom Ibn Ezra Denounced as a Prater and a Madman?" *Frank Talmage Memorial Volume* (ed. B. Walfish, 1993) 217-32. D. **Tene,** *EncJud* 8 (1971) 1181-86. M. **Wilensky** (ed.), *Ibn Janāh, Sefer ha-Rikmah* (1969).

D. J. RETTBERG

IDEOLOGICAL CRITICISM

When discussing ideological criticism, one must be clear about the definition of *ideology.* Although the term has acquired the pejorative connotation of "false consciousness," in contemporary theory it usually refers to a complex system of ideas, values, and perceptions held by a particular group that provides a framework for the group's members to understand their place in the social order. Ideology constructs a reality for people, making the bewildering and often brutal world intelligible and tolerable. Ideology motivates people to behave in specific ways and to accept their social position as natural, inevitable, and necessary.

Ideologies should not be identified with "reality," however. While they help to foster and sustain a distinctive worldview that structures and informs people's lives, ideologies also disguise or explain away features of society that may be unjust. For example, some ideologies help to explain why certain people in a society are accorded economic privileges. Other ideologies provide a rationalization for why a particular gender or race is allowed to perform specified actions while others cannot. In these and other ways, ideologies "resolve" inequalities, struggles, and contradictions that individuals or groups may experience in their everyday lives. (For further discussion, see Eagleton [1991].)

Ideological criticism investigates (1) the production of the text by a particular author in a specific, ideologically charged historical context, (2) the reproduction of ideology in the text itself, and (3) the consumption of the text by readers in different social locations who are themselves motivated and constrained by distinct ideologies. In its broadest sense, ideological criticism examines ideology at work in three variables of biblical interpretation: the author, the text, and the reader.

Investigations of gender or racial ideologies in the biblical text and in its interpretation can be understood as ideological criticism. In biblical circles, however, such studies are usually classified as FEMINIST criticism or African (Asian, Hispanic) American HERMENEUTICS, respectively. Influenced by Marxist or materialist theories, early proponents of ideological criticism more narrowly defined networks of economic class relations involved in the production of the biblical text. These critics investigated ways in which ideology "explained" unequal distribution of wealth, prestige, and control over the means of production (land, natural resources, etc.) in a given population. They analyzed ways in which the dominant class generated ideologies in order to reproduce and legitimate specified class relations. As some of the first to take seriously the material and economic conditions under which the biblical text was constructed, the works of N. K. Gottwald (1979, 1985, 1993) have been foundational for developing ideological criticism as a biblical method of interpretation. Social class and access to material resources cannot, however, be studied in isolation. Because socio-economic relations and opportunities have often been determined by one's gender or race, ideological critics have begun to make use of these categories in order to calculate their impact on class relations (see G. Yee [1995] 152-167; R. Carroll [1994]; D. Jobling [1991]; articles by I. Mosala and R. Weems in Jobling and T. Pippin [1992] 25-34.)

Ideological criticism, more narrowly defined, uses LITERARY-critical methods within a historical and social-scientific frame (see SOCIAL-SCIENTIFIC CRITICISM) in a comprehensive strategy for reading the biblical text. Ideological critics have a twofold task in their investigation: an extrinsic and an intrinsic analysis. Extrinsic analysis uses the historical and social sciences to help reconstruct or "unmask" the material and ideological conditions under which the text was produced. The primary focus of an extrinsic analysis is the mode of production dominant in the society that produced the text—i.e., the social relations (family, status, class, gender, etc.) and forces (e.g., technology, politics, law, education) that interconnect in a society's material production. In ancient Israel, for example, three dominant modes of production can be identified. The tribal period was characterized by a familial mode of production that valued kin group connections and had no outside agencies that taxed their resources. The monarchical and colonial periods had a tributary mode of production in which various social classes paid tribute or taxes to the state or to foreign powers, with the lower classes carrying the heaviest burden. Finally, Judaism under Roman hegemony operated under a slave mode of production. The ideological critic examines the social structures, relations, groups, and interests that profited under a particular mode of production and those that were deprived under it.

An extrinsic analysis of a biblical text is particularly concerned with the category of power. It tries to determine the types of social, political, and economic structures wielding power when the text was written; and it clarifies the kinds of power these structures exhibit, i.e., formal or informal, legal, cultic or religious. Extrinsic analysis investigates power groups according to gender, class, race, religion, region, etc., to see if any patterns of power emerge. It determines the control these groups exert over the means of production and sources of power; and it explores the antagonisms, clashes, and contradictions that exist wherever power operates.

Since ideologies themselves are forms of power that influence and direct social groups, an extrinsic analysis searches for the ways in which groups produce and manipulate ideology to legitimate or exert their place in society—that is, it examines whose interests are being served by ideologies. Further, extrinsic analysis identifies and locates a society's disempowered voices or interests and determines how these break down according to gender, race, and class. It tries to reconstruct alternative ideologies that may have resisted the dominant ones.

Just as each text has been written by a particular author, so also an extrinsic analysis scrutinizes the author's position in society and access to power, exploring the circumstances under which the author produced the text. It investigates the author's own ideology, comparing it with the ideologies of the time and noting the author's complicity with or challenge to the dominant ideology.

In an intrinsic analysis, the ideological critic takes up literary critical methods to examine how the text assimilates or "encodes" socioeconomic conditions to reproduce a particular ideology in its rhetoric. Feminist literary criticism, NARRATIVE CRITICISM, and STRUCTURALISM AND DECONSTRUCTION are some of the literary methods that have been useful for the method's intrinsic analysis. The ideological critic assumes that the text symbolically resolves real social contradictions by inventing and adopting "solutions" for them. For example, the *Malleus Malleficarum,* a medieval treatise by two Roman Catholic priests, explained a wide range of personal and social disorders, such as male sexual impotency and lust, harvest failures, miscarriages, and plagues, as the demonic acts of witches. Scapegoating of witches led to the widespread persecution and slaughter of lower-class women in particular during the Middle Ages. During the nineteenth century, however, tracts like *Godey's Lady's Book* flourished, which promoted what came to be called the "cult of true womanhood." Women were not regarded as evil or demonic, but rather as morally superior to men. Ruling the household as queen, women were mothers and keepers of hearth and home. They provided a refuge of peace and tranquility for their husbands, who struggled in the brutal jungle of the outside world. Nevertheless, women were still economically dependent on and respectfully submissive to their husbands and confined to the home. The ideology of the "cult of true womanhood," moreover, was primarily a middle to upper-class phenomenon. White slaveholders did not apply this ideology to black women, nor Boston Brahmins to their Irish immigrant maids.

Of course, with these examples or any other, different texts exist that present opposing dominant ideologies and offer their own solutions to social problems and conflicts. An intrinsic analysis, then, tries to discover the precise relationship of the specific text's ideology to the ideology(s) surrounding and affecting its production.

To determine a text's ideology, an intrinsic analysis takes special note of the "absences" in the text. In the words of Marxist literary critic P. Macherey, "In order to say anything, there are other things *which must not be said"* (1978, 85). In arguing for what it regards as the "truth," the text cannot indicate matters that will deny that "truth." By focusing on the text's gaps and absences, one can unmask the dominant ideologies and recover the voices of the silenced—perhaps women, the conquered, the foreign, and the poor. In attempting to resolve contradictory opinions and articulate the "truth," the text must conceal and repress these voices. An intrinsic analysis attempts to retrieve them.

Intrinsic analysis also entails a close reading of the text's rhetoric, the literary ways in which a text attempts to convince its readers to embrace a certain ideology. Because it is a means of persuasion, rhetoric is thus a form of power; it unites groups, moves them to action, reinforces attitudes and beliefs, and universalizes local standards and principles. The text reproduces ideology in a style pitched to a specific audience. It appropriates literary genres and devices—e.g., sermons, refrains, exhortations—that will particularly appeal to and persuade this audience. The text manipulates literary features, such as irony, plot, characterization, and point of view, to convey a certain ideology. This ideology is revealed in who speaks, who sees, and who acts in a text—and especially in who does not.

Extrinsic and intrinsic analysis can be viewed as a Janus-like operation, given the intricate relationship between ideology's production in a particular place and time and reproduction in a particular text. Used as a means of interpreting the biblical text, ideological criticism begins first with a preliminary intrinsic analysis, taking note of any ideological gaps, inconsistencies, and dissonant voices. It then works backward, so to speak, to determine the social location of production hinted at in the text. An extrinsic analysis then determines the nature of the material-ideological disputes the text's ideology tries to resolve. Finally, a more complete intrinsic analysis determines how the text encodes and reworks the ideological conditions of its production.

Because ideological criticism investigates both text and context inclusively, it helps to shed light on the economic, political, and historical circumstances of the text's production, often overlooked by literary-critical methods. Because it grapples with the text as an ideological reproduction of a specific sociohistorical context, ideological criticism uncovers a textual politics often overlooked by historical and social-scientific methods. Lacking a literary theory that investigates the workings of textual ideology, historical and social-scientific methods often naively regard the text as a "mirror" of the past or dismiss the text as useless for sociohistorical reconstruction. Ideological criticism, however, presumes that the text itself is a sociohistorical artifact.

For example, ideological criticism reveals that the text of Isaiah 40–55 is "a weapon of struggle to preserve the sociocultural identity and political future of a former Judahite ruling elite faced with dissolution in Babylonian society" two generations after it lost its power base in Judah (Gottwald in Jobling and Pippin [1992] 43). In Judges 17–20 the Deuteronomist (see DEUTERONOMISTIC HISTORY) deliberately portrays the Levites in a negative way to promote the centralization of worship under Josiah's reform policies (Yee [1995]). Several postexilic texts incorporate two pervasive myths, that of the empty land and of the Canaanite pollution of the land, to legitimate the resettlement claims of the Second Temple community (Carroll in Jobling and Pippin [1992] 79-93).

Ideological criticism is one of the more recent methods to be used by biblical scholars, and its impact on biblical interpretation remains to be seen. Its interdisciplinary utilization of historical, social-scientific, and literary methods makes ideological criticism a more inclusive method, offering exciting possibilities for biblical studies. Because of its focus on the biblical text as a site of struggle for competing ideologies during its production in antiquity, ideological criticism can help the exegete to become more aware of how the biblical text is currently being used to support opposing groups. Such an analysis can enable the exegete to become conscious of personal ideological blind spots and constraints to produce a more ethically responsible reading.

Bibliography: R. P. Carroll, "On Representation in the Bible: An *Ideologiekritik* Approach," *JNSL* 20 (1994) 1-15; "An Infinity of Traces: On Making an Inventory of Our Ideological Holdings. An Introduction to *Ideologiekritik* in Biblical Studies," *JNSL* 21 (1995) 25-43. **D. J. A. Clines,** *Interested Parties: The Ideology of Writers and Readers of the HB* (1995). **T. Eagleton,** *Ideology: An Introduction* (1991). **N. K. Gottwald,** *The Tribes of Yahweh: A Sociology of the Religion of Liberated Israel, 1250–1050* BCE (1979); *The HB: A Socio-Literary Introduction* (1985); *The HB in Its Social World and in Ours* (1993). **D. Jobling,** "Feminism and 'Mode of Production' in Ancient Israel: Search for a Method," *The Bible and the Politics of Exegesis* (ed. D. Jobling, P. Day, and G. T. Sheppard, 1991) 239-51. **D. Jobling and T. Pippin** (eds.), *Ideological Criticism of Biblical Texts* (*Semeia* 59, 1992); see especially articles by Carroll, Gottwald, Jobling, Mosala, and Weems; also includes a bibliography. **P. Macherey,** *A Theory of Literary Production* (tr. Geoffrey Wall, 1978). **I. J. Mosala,** *Biblical Hermeneutics and Black Theology in South Africa* (1989). **G. A. Yee,** "Ideological Criticism: Judges 17–21 and the Dismembered Body," *Judges and Method: New Approaches in Biblical Studies* (ed. G. A. Yee, 1995) 146-70.

G. A. YEE

IGNATIUS OF ANTIOCH (c. 35–c. 107)

Bishop of Antioch at the beginning of the second century, I. was arrested and sent under guard to Rome, where he expected to die in the arena. From Ephesus and Smyrna he wrote six letters to churches (Ephesus, Magnesia, Philadelphia, Rome, Smyrna, and Tralles) and one to his younger colleague Polycarp. He was alarmed by the possible existence of heresy in these churches and urged unity by adherence to a bishop and his presbyters, by emphasis on the Eucharist, and by proper understanding of the person and life of JESUS Christ.

In his first extant letter he entered upon the question of exegesis on the first point: "It is written, God resists the proud." He concluded that God resists those who resist the bishop (*Eph.* 5). He believed, however, that "the beloved prophets had a message pointing to Christ, but the Gospel is the perfection of incorruption" (*Philad.* 9; cf. 5). Christians must not accept Judaism or, for that matter, rely on proofs from the HB. I. had heard some people say, "If I do not find it in the archives [the HB] I do not believe [that it is] in the gospel." Rather than enter into an inconclusive exegetical debate, I. appealed to basic Christian belief: "For me the archives are Jesus Christ, the inviolable archives are his cross and death and his resurrection and faith through him" (*Philad.* 8).

Beyond formal exegesis lay his singular understanding of 1 Corinthians, to which he alluded when identifying his own life with that of the apostle PAUL. His identification seems not official but personal. He no longer lives (he had been condemned to die), but Paul lives in him. He attacked his opponents with Pauline phrases (e.g., *Eph.* 18). His critics at Tralles evidently understood heavenly things, such as "angelic locations and archontic conjunctions" (astrology mixed with early Gnostic ideas) and presumably read them into the Bible, but I. said he avoided harming them with what they could not receive, since they were infants—an allusion to 1 Cor 3:1-2. He did not quote Paul's words explicitly, however.

Similar allusions explain his use of the Gospels. Behind his ideas about the Eucharist lie expressions found in the Gospel of John. The Eucharist bread is the antidote for death and provides life forever in Jesus Christ (*Eph.* 20). The bread of God is the flesh of Jesus Christ (*Rom.* 7). Thus, too, the Spirit "knows whence it comes and whither it goes," as in John 3:8 (*Philad.* 7). And in *Eph.* 19 he was probably interpreting the infancy narrative of Matthew in the light of his own astrological or semi-Gnostic background, not taking over a ready-made Gnostic myth. He was a more imaginative and less pedestrian exegete than his older contemporary CLEMENT OF ROME and remained highly individual in spite of his devotion to unity in the church.

Bibliography: V. Corwin, *St. Ignatius and Christianity in Antioch* (YPR 1, 1960). **R. M. Grant,** *Ignatius of Antioch* (1966); "Scripture and Tradition in Ignatius of Antioch," *After the NT* (1967) 37-54. **H. Paulsen,** *Der Brief des Ignatius von Antiochia und der Brief des Polykarp von Smyrna* (HNT 18, 1985). **J. Quasten,** *Patrology* (1950) 1:63-76. **W. Schoedel,** *Ignatius of Antioch: A Commentary on the Letters of Ignatius of Antioch* (Hermeneia, 1985).

R. M. GRANT

ILGEN, KARL DAVID (1763–1834)

An outstanding schoolmaster, I. secured his place in the history of OT study by a small part of one of his numerous books. Born Feb. 26, 1763, in Sehna, between

Weimar and Naumburg, he entered the University of Leipzig in 1783, where he studied theology and philosophy. A book on Job published in 1788 established him as an orientalist, and in 1789 he became rector of the *Stadtgymnasium* in Liepzig. In 1794 he succeeded J. G. EICHHORN as professor of oriental languages in Jena and in 1799 gained a chair of theology. During the Jena period his work on the archives of the Jerusalem Temple was published (1798). He was unsuccessful as a university teacher. Tall and gaunt, he was considered unfriendly, rude and coarse, and a poor lecturer. In May 1802 he accepted a position as rector of a gymnasium in Pforta, where he remained until his retirement in 1831 following a distinguished rectorship. He died Sept. 17, 1834.

When I. published his book on the Jerusalem archives, two rival critical theories of the origin of the Pentateuch (see PENTATEUCHAL CRITICISM), the documentary theory and the fragmentary theory, were in their infancy. I. combined both theories into the view that underlying the Pentateuch and other historical books were seventeen fragments written by three authors that had been combined into one work by a redactor. Later scholarship condemned this theory as both arbitrary and unlikely; but in the course of his argument, I. was apparently the first scholar to propose that the story of Joseph (Genesis 37–50) consisted of two distinct sources, Elohim 1 and Elohim 2. His arguments included points that were later widely accepted. Thus Gen 37:28 was divided into two sources, in one of which Joseph was taken from the pit by Midianites and in the other of which Joseph was sold by his brothers to Ishmaelites for twenty shekels of silver. At Gen 39:1 the original text read that the Ishmaelites sold Joseph to an unnamed Egyptian, and the redactor added the reference to Potiphar so as to harmonize 39:1 with 37:36. In chaps. 42–43 I. pointed to the apparent absurdity that, although Simeon was left behind as a hostage in Egypt, his brothers returned, not to secure his release, but to buy more food.

I.'s importance in the history of scholarship is that he provided a number of arguments that were later used (e.g., by J. Wellhausen) for the three document hypothesis for the composition of Genesis–Numbers.

Works: *Job, antiquissimi carminis Hebraeici, natura et virtutes* (1788); *De notione tituli filii Dei Messaiae* (1794); *Die Urkunden des Jerusalemischen Tempelarchivs in ihrer Urgestalt als Beytrag zur Berichtigung der Geschichte der Religion und Politik* (1798); *Das Buch Tobias: Die Geschichte Tobi's nach drey verschiedenen Originalen dem Griechischen dem Lateinischen des Hieronymus und einem Syrischen* (1800).

Bibliography: *AEWK* II.6 (1839) 158-62. **H. Kämmel,** *ADB* 14 (1881) 19-23. **F. K. Kraft,** *Vita Ilgenii* (1837). **J. W. Rogerson,** *OTCNC* 20-21. **B. Seidel,** *K. D. I. und die Pen-*

tateuchforschung im Umkreis der sogenannten älteren Urkundenhypothese (BZAW 213, 1993).

J. W. ROGERSON

INNER-BIBLICAL INTERPRETATION, HEBREW BIBLE

Inner-biblical interpretation concerns how the authors of the HB and the NT cited and alluded to HB materials. The process of reuse, reinterpretation, and reapplication of previous texts from within the HB can be described most accurately as "innerbiblical exegesis" (M. Fishbane [1996]; but see L. Eslinger [1992] and B. Sommers [1996]). The end product of this exegetical tradition is a richly textured collection of documents incorporating residual literary traditions of the great ancient Near Eastern civilizations as well as the original literary traditions of ancient Israel.

Fishbane has undertaken the most thorough examination of inner-biblical exegesis (1979, 1985, 1989, 1996). Distinguishing between the textual tradition (*traditum*) and its transmission in a new interpretive context (*traditio*), he has established four basic categories in relation to the HB: scribal comments and corrections, also known as glosses (J. Weingreen [1957]); legal exegesis; aggadic exegesis; and mantological exegesis (1985). Fishbane works from the assumption that the Torah (Pentateuch) was historically and literarily antecedent to the other portions of the HB CANON.

1. Glosses. While no one doubts that complex oral traditions underlie the scribal heritage of the HB, the task of the biblical scholar is firmly rooted in the final form of the written text. This written witness is, however, the product of a lengthy process of transmission and redaction. Whether for the purposes of clarification, theological conformity, or legal uniformity, the *traditum* was revised and transmitted to new groups in new time by scribes (1 Chr 27:32), who inserted various taxonomic elements common to most anthological writings: superscriptions, colophons, titles, generic indicators, and closures. Glosses are most apparent in the poetic and wisdom traditions (Pss 3:1; 72:20; Prov 25:1; 31:1), but they also occur in other portions of the HB (Lev 6:2, 7; 7:37-38; Num 6:21; 1 Kgs 11:41; 1 Chr 9:1). Scribes annotated the text for purposes of clarification, e.g., using the particles *hû'* and *hî'* to mark the changes in place names (Gen 14:17; Josh 18:13; 1 Chr 11:14), and frequently contemporized anachronistic references (Gen 12:6; Josh 15:8-10; 1 Kgs 6:38; Esth 2:16; 3:7). Explanatory and parenthetical comments often intrude into the text, disturbing the flow of syntax (Isa 29:10; Ezek 3:12) and sometimes confusing what must originally have been quite clear to the original readers (Lev 19:19). Fishbane (1996) suggests that this intrusive form of annotation was employed when the scribes were faced with a fixed *traditum* (e.g., Deut 22:12; 2 Sam 7:10; 1

Kgs 5:22 [MT], where it appears that older terms were simply reworked with more contemporary language). As the textual traditions were developed and standardized, the scribes also undertook to "clarify" misleading orthographic features and variant grammatical forms (Weingreen [1957]).

2. Legal Exegesis. The giving of the law at Mt. Sinai was—according to the final narrative—a part of the constitutive act of ancient Israel; along with the various teachings given in the wilderness between Sinai and the entrance into the land, it forms the core of the HB. The history of the development of the legal corpus is complex and suffers from a lack of source material. Critical reconstructions of the text suggest a millennium or more of composition and transmission, during which the ongoing interpretation of the *traditum* flourished. As one explores the texture of the legal traditions, it is possible to discern a variety of exegetical methods as well as patterns of legal reflection, interpretation, and transformation, which Fishbane classifies as legal exegesis. This process of legal reflection and transformation served to clarify ambiguities in the *traditum,* as is seen in the case of the "Hebrew slave" (Exod 21:2; Lev 25:39-46; Deut 15:12-17). In later times there was also a concern to expand the parameters of the law in the interest of comprehensiveness. This can be seen in the laws for the atonement of sins committed in ignorance (Num 15:25-26; cf. Lev 4:20*b*); the laws for the making of vows (Num 6:2; 30:3); the laws concerning accidental death (Num 35:16); and the laws for returning other people's livestock (Deut 22:1-2; cf. Exod 23:4), where a variety of particles and conjunctions are employed to expand the parameters of legal application. Other frequent elements in legal exegesis are the harmonizing of contradictions (e.g., those found in the ordinances for seventh-year release: Neh 10:32; cf. Exod 23:11; Deut 15:1-2) and the unifying of legal traditions with the descriptions of the historical narratives (2 Sam 5:21; cf. Deut 7:25; 1 Chr 14:12; 1 Kgs 6:7; Deut 27:5-6). Finally, the reapplication of the law to a new situation often posed exegetical problems for the ancient interpreter that needed to be resolved (the law of the second Passover, 2 Chr 30:1-3, 15; cf. Num 9:1-14; the law on mixed marriages, Ezra 9:1-2; cf. Deut 7:1-6; 23:4-7).

3. Aggadic Exegesis. This third category is concerned with the reapplication of the *traditum* to facilitate theological and historical understanding. It is distinct from legal exegesis insofar as the sources employed represent the whole canon of the HB. The prophets (see PROPHECY AND PROPHETS, HB) are among the primary practitioners of aggadic exegesis, often reworking legal traditions for rhetorical purposes. Frequently the *traditio* employed by the prophetic writer is itself the end result of an aggadic reworking of an older *traditio.* This is the case with the holiness motif developed by the prophet Jeremiah (Jer 2:3; cf. Exod 19:4-6; Lev 22:14-16; Deut

7:6; Ezra 9:1-2). In Isaiah, the prophet interprets the language of the fast in order to highlight the socially oriented character of true religion (Isa 58:1-2; cf. Lev 16:31; 23:24). In both these cases aggadic exegesis, while reflecting an expanded interpretive *traditio,* does not abrogate the legal *traditum.*

In other situations there is a more conscious attempt at theological innovation. The punishment of children for the sins of parents (Exod 20:5) presented a theological dilemma to a later generation highlighted by the deuteronomist's unambiguous rejection of the principle (Deut 7:9-10; 24:16). The resulting contradiction became the nexus for Ezekiel's aggadic discussion of sin and punishment (Ezek 18:2-4, 18-32), in which the legal principle is invoked, affirmed, and then abandoned in favor of a more "gracious" divine attitude toward sin.

Aggadic exegesis also occurs in the presentation of the heroes of old in later texts. The patriarchs are frequently appealed to in this light (Abraham in 2 Kgs 13:23; Isa 51:2; 63:16; Jer 33:26; Ezek 33:24; Ps 47:9; Neh 9:7; and Jacob in Isa 43:1, 22; Jer 9:3-5; Ps 14:7). Related, but with its own emphasis, is the aggadic development of the verbal traditions of ancient Israel's faithful (Deut 31:4-6; Josh 1; cf. 1 Kgs 2:1-9, esp. 3-4).

4. Mantological Exegesis. The last of Fishbane's categories is mantological exegesis, by which he means the reformulation and reinterpretation of prophetic oracles so that they continually "make sense and project a conceivable future" (1996, 46). Whether the focus of the oracle was doom or blessing, the condition of expectation eventuated. However, when fulfillment was then deferred a reinterpretation of the prophetic *traditum* became necessary (see R. Carroll [1979]), thus the scribes sometimes emended toponyms by using the demonstrative pronouns *hū'* and *hî'* for purposes of clarification or specification (Isa 9:13-14). Such specification was also used, with or without the deictic particles, in dreams and visions and in their interpretations (Gen 41:26-30; Zech 4:2-6*a*, 10*b*-14; Dan 4:17-23; 5:25-27). More problematic than such clarifications was the interpretation of oracles that were once clear but later seemed obscure (Isa 16:13-14; Jer 25:9-12; Ezek 29:17-20; cf. 2 Chr 36:19-21; Lev 26:34-35; Daniel 9–12). Daniel's reinterpretation of Jeremiah 25, for example, is particularly significant for employing an angelic mediator to clarify the apparent misunderstanding of the Jeremiah traditum (see esp. Dan 9:20-27).

The term MIDRASH, though usually applied to later normative Jewish writings, is also appropriate to the framers of the biblical traditions (2 Chr 13:22; 24:27; Ezra 7:10). The two Chronicles passages are particularly important because they use the noun *midrāš* in the same sense as that found in later rabbinic texts. The postexilic roots of Midrash—the use of biblical phrases in later biblical works with meanings different from their original context—were identified by A. Robert (1934, 1944) and are scattered throughout the HB. Genesis (S. Sandmel [1961]), Deuteronomy (G. Vermes [1961]), Ezekiel (L. Zunz [1966]; J. Halperin [1976]; F. F. Bruce [1972]), Psalms (B. Childs [1971]; Bruce) and Chronicles (Zunz; Weingreen [1951–52]; T. Willi [1972]) have all been identified as books that reflect midrashic activity or, as appears to be the case in Chronicles, are Midrashes.

The case for Chronicles as Midrash found early support in the work of W. Barnes (1896). More recently, the term *Midrash* has given way to "exegesis" (Willi). In either case the focus is on the reworking of an authoritative text by secondary authors to produce changes in language, style, content and ideology (H. Williamson [1982]; S. Japhet [1977; ET 1989]). This happens in two complementary ways. Working from an authoritative *Vorlage*, the chronicler transposed, sometimes literally and sometimes in a drastically altered form, the existing textual material, which he then juxtaposed with his own original material (Japhet [1989]). His apparent principal sources were the former prophets, particularly Samuel–Kings (P. Vanutelli [1931–34]; A. Bendavid [1972]; S. McKenzie [1985]). Evidence from Qumran (see DEAD SEA SCROLLS) suggests that the *Vorlage* may already have contained some of the chronicler's emendations (W. Lemke [1965]). The possibility that 2 Kings 20 was reused in Isaiah 38 suggests that an even earlier practice of midrash-like activity on the part of the biblical authors (A. Konkel [1993]; Williamson [1994]) may have formed the precedent for the chronicler's work.

Bibliography: **P. R. Ackroyd,** "Some Interpretive Glosses in the Book of Haggai," *JJS* 7 (1956) 163-68; *Studies in the Religious Tradition of the OT* (1987). **G. Aichele and G. A. Phillips** (eds.), *Intertextuality and the Bible* (Semeia 69-70, 1995). **M. Amihai et al.** (eds.), *Narrative Research on the HB* (Semeia 46, 1989). **B. W. Anderson,** "Exodus Typology in Second Isaiah," *Israel's Prophetic Heritage* (ed. B. W. Anderson et al., 1962) 177-95. **G. W. Anderson** (ed.), *Tradition and Interpretation* (1979). **W. E. Barnes,** "The Midrashic Element in Chronicles," *Expositor* 5, 4 (1896) 426-39. **A. Bendavid,** *Parallels in the Bible* (1972). **F. F. Bruce,** "The Earliest OT Interpretation," *OTS* 17 (1972) 37-52. **A.-M. Brunet,** *Le Chroniste et ses sources* (1953). **R. P. Carroll,** *When Prophecy Failed* (1979). **D. A. Carson and H. G. M. Williamson** (eds.), *It Is Written: Scripture Citing Scripture* (1988). **B. S. Childs,** "Psalm Titles and Midrashic Exegesis," *JSS* 16 (1971) 137-50. **J. Day,** "A Case of Inner-Scriptural Interpretation: The Dependence of Isaiah xxvi.13-xxvii.11 on Hosea xiii.4–xiv.10 (Eng. 9) and Its Relevance to Some Theories of the Redaction of the Isaiah Apocalypse," *JTS* 31 (1980) 109-19. **S. Draisma** (ed.), *Intertextuality in Biblical Writings* (1989). **L. Eslinger,** "Inner-biblical Exegesis and Inner-biblical Allusion: The Question of Category," *VT* 42 (1992) 47-58. **M. Fishbane,** "Numbers 5:11-31: A Study of Law and Scribal Practices in Israel and the Ancient Near East," *HUCA* 45 (1974) 25-45; *Text and Texture*

(1979); *Biblical Interpretation in Ancient Israel* (1985); *The Garments of the Torah* (1989); "Inner-Biblical Exegesis," *HB/OT* 1, 1 (1996) 33-48. **G. B. Gray,** "The Parallel Passages in 'Joel' and Their Bearing on the Question of Date," *Expositor* 8 (1893) 209-25. **J. Halperin,** "The Exegetical Character of Ezek. X.9-17," *VT* 26 (1976) 129-41. **M. Herr,** *Continuum in the Chain of Transmission* (1979). **P. R. House** (ed.), *Beyond Form Criticism: Essays in OT Literary Criticism* (1992). **C. Houtman,** "Ezra and the Law," *OTS* 21 (1981) 91-115. **S. Japhet,** *The Ideology of the Book of Chronicles and Its Place in Biblical Thought* (1977; ET BEATAJ 9, 1989); *I and II Chronicles* (OTL, 1993). **K. Koch,** *The Growth of the Biblical Tradition* (1969). **A. H. Konkel,** "The Sources of the Story of Hezekiah in the Book of Isaiah," *VT* 43 (1993) 462-82. **B. Lategan and W. Vorster** (eds.), *Text and Reality: Aspects of Reference in Biblical Texts* (Semeia Studies, 1985). **W. E. Lemke,** "The Synoptic Problem of the Chronicler's History," *HTR* 58 (1965) 349-63. **T. Longman,** *Literary Approaches to Biblical Interpretation* (Foundations of Contemporary Interpretation 3, 1987). **S. L. McKenzie,** *The Chronicler's Use of the Deuteronomistic History* (HSM 33, 1985). **A. Robert,** "Les attaches littéraires bibliques de Prov I-IX," *RB* 42 (1934) 42-68, 172-204, 374-84; *Le genre littéraire du Cantique des cantiques* (1944). **S. Sandmel,** "The Haggada Within Scripture," *JBL* 80 (1961) 105-22. **N. Sarna,** "Psalm 89: A Study in Inner Biblical Exegesis," *Biblical and Other Studies* (ed. A. Altmann, 1963) 29-46. **I. L. Seeligmann,** "Voraussetzungen der Midraschexegese" (VTSup 1, 1953) 150-81. **P. A. Smith,** *Rhetoric and Redaction in Trito-Isaiah* (VTSup 62, 1995). **B. D. Sommers,** "Exegesis, Allusion, and Intertextuality in the HB: A Response to L. Eslinger," *VT* 46 (1996) 479-89. **M. Sternberg,** *The Poetics of Biblical Narrative* (1985). **S. Talmon,** *Literary Studies in the HB* (1993). **B. Uffenheimer and H. G. Reventlow** (eds.), *Creative Biblical Exegesis: Christian and Jewish Hermeneutics Through the Centuries* (JSOTSup 59, 1988). **P. Vanutelli,** *Libri Synoptici Veteris Testamenti* (1931–34). **G. Vermes,** *Scripture and Tradition Within Judaism* (SPB 4, 1961). **J. Weingreen,** "The Rabbinic Approach to the Study of the OT," *BJRL* 24 (1951–52) 166-90; "Rabbinic-Type Glosses in the OT," *JSS* 2 (1957) 149-62; *From Bible to Mishna: The Continuity of Tradition* (1976). **T. Willi,** *Die Chronik als Auslegung* (FRLANT 106, 1972). **H. G. M. Williamson,** *I and II Chronicles* (NCB, 1982); *The Book Called Isaiah: Deutero-Isaiah's Role in Compilation and Redaction* (1994). **C. Winquist** (ed.), *Text and Textuality* (Semeia 40, 1987). **L. Zunz,** *Die gottesdienstlichen Vorträge der Juden* (1966).

C. S. MCKENZIE

INNER-BIBLICAL INTERPRETATION, NEW TESTAMENT

Throughout the NT, citations, allusions, themes, and types drawn from the HB surface repeatedly, indicating that the NT debt to the HB, particularly in the SEPTUAGINT translation, was pervasive. This NT use of the HB has been a major area of interest in twentieth-century scholarship.

Numerous attempts have been made to understand the development and significance of NT inner-biblical interpretation. A primary impetus for twentieth-century scholarly investigation was the work of R. HARRIS (1916, 1920), who argued that the prevalence of HB citations and allusions in the NT can be accounted for by an early Christian indebtedness to testimony collections (cf. Fitzmyer [1974] 59-89). These alleged collections would have consisted of groupings of relevant testimony texts that witnessed to the fulfillment of HB prophecies (see PROPHECY AND PROPHETS, HB) in the ministry of JESUS and the church, used polemically by the early Christians in their contacts with Jews. While the existence of a specific unified collection of this sort remained hypothetical, C. H. DODD (1952) reinforced the key premise in Harris's work by arguing that NT writers relied on key HB passages for elucidation of their theological affirmations but that rather than selecting isolated prooftexts they focused on large blocks of prophetic materials (e.g., Isaiah, Jeremiah) and the psalms, which they referenced *en bloc* through isolated citations and allusions. Thus these large blocks of HB material rather than simply the cited text, form the "substructure" of NT theology. B. Lindars (1961) took Dodd's proposal one step further, arguing that one could study the NT use of the HB for shifts in application and modification, in order to determine internal NT doctrinal development from early apologetic use of a particular text to a more nuanced theological use of that same text in a later NT period. The interest reflected in the trajectory from Harris to Lindars concerns the basic issue of how the NT writers utilized HB texts to develop and sustain theological arguments.

From early on attention was also given to the mechanics of NT interpretation of the HB. For instance, questions of CANON and HERMENEUTICS were addressed already in O. Michel's early work on PAUL's use of the HB (1929). The interest in Paul's interpretative method was central from the beginning; and numerous studies set out to analyze his midrashic process, comparing it with both rabbinic and Second Temple Jewish writers (J. Bonsirven [1939]; E. Ellis [1957]), a process that was given further impulse after the discovery of the Qumran *pesher* texts (see DEAD SEA SCROLLS). These concerns have expanded into the study of Jewish hermeneutic practices in general, focusing on their relevance for understanding NT interpretation of Scripture (J. Doeve [1954]; L. Goppelt [1939; ET 1982]; R. Longenecker [1975]; M. McNamara [1978]; S. Sowers [1965]; B. Chilton [1994]; J. Barton [1986]; R. Bauckham [1990]), which has culminated in comparative studies of certain passages, contrasting NT and Jewish interpretations (C. Evans [1989]; M. Callaway [1986]). Scholarship has thus grown increasingly interested in learning what the cultural and social environment of

early Christianity can contribute to understanding the NT use of the HB.

From this interest in the mechanics of interpretation, a variety of issues has come to the fore. For instance, some scholars set about trying to uncover the text form of the HB used by early Christians (E. Freed [1965]; K. Stendahl [1967]). Others have made use of later Jewish lectionary cycles as a way of explaining the patterns and conjunctions of various HB references in the NT (A. Guilding [1960]; M. Goulder [1974]). Defining the term MIDRASH has also taken on increasing importance (R. Le Deaut [1971]; J. Neusner [1987]; A. G. Wright [1967]; G. Porten [1979]), as has its application to particular NT texts (M. Gertner [1962]; M. Miller [1971]; J. Derrett [1977–95]). In recent scholarship the debate has centered on what constitutes a quotation/citation as opposed to an allusion (E. Porter [1997]), as from the beginning scholars have categorized NT citations using a diverse—and often conflicting—set of criteria. There has been an increasing tendency to return to the direction of such scholars as Dodd and Lindars in attempting to understand the function and role HB citations perform in NT theological expression, providing some scholars with the basis for a coherent biblical theology (H. Hübner [1996]). This takes into account that inner-biblical interpretation is more than a mechanical act; it is an argumentative strategy to persuade readers (C. Stanley [1997]). Thus scholars differentiate between different types of uses, e.g., the messianic application in the Gospels (D. Juel [1988]) as contrasted to the ecclesiological utilization in Paul (D. Koch [1986]; R. Hays [1989]). Moreover, scholars have increasingly recognized that one cannot speak generally about the use of the HB in the NT but must refer to the function and use of the HB in specific writers and texts, thus spawning myriad studies focusing on individual NT writings/writers (R. Gundry [1975]; J. Marcus [1992]; A. Suhl [1965]; C. Evans and J. Sanders [1993]; T. Holtz [1968]; B. Schuchard [1992]; F.-M. Braun [1964]; A. Hanson [1974, 1991]; Koch; Hays; Stanley [1992]; J. Fekkes [1994]), specific SYNOPTIC narratives (W. Stegner [1989]; D. Moo [1983]), and the influence and interpretation of a particular HB text in its appropriation by a variety of NT writers (Hay; M. Hooker [1959]; J. Gnilka [1961]). The citation of HB texts has also been utilized in the investigation of the interrelationship of NT writings (S. New [1993]).

The study of inner-biblical interpretation in the NT must inevitably begin with a treatment of both the diversity of uses and the basic problem of identifying when that use takes place, which has been a perennial problem. There are three basic categories of NT use of the HB: citations, allusions, and echoes. The simplest to identify is direct citation, when a writer explicitly intends to reference a specific HB text (see lists in G. Archer and G. Chirichigno [1983]; Hübner [1997–]; B. McLean [1992]). The formula quotations, which include a short introductory citation formula, often followed by reference to the HB writer/"author"/text, are the most apparent examples of direct HB citation (Matt 1:23, 4:15-16; Mark 12:10-11*a*; Luke 20:42*b*-43; John 12:38-40, 19:24; Acts 2:16-21, 25-28; 8:32-33; Rom 9:25-29; Gal 4:27; Eph 4:8; Heb 2:6-8; 3:7-11; 10:5-7; Jas 4:6; 1 Pet 2:6-10; see Fitzmyer [1974] 3-58). Some direct citations of the HB simply appear without any introduction but in places where there is little doubt that both writer and readers knew that a quotation from the HB was intended (Gal 3:6, 11-12; Heb 10:37-38; 13:6; 1 Pet 3:10-12). Moreover, the NT writers often include a chain of citations (2 Cor 6:16-18; Rom 3:10-18; 15:9-12; 1 Pet 2:6-10) in which a variety of texts on a related theme are strung together, a phenomenon that initially led to the testimony book hypothesis. In addition, one finds both conflations of HB texts (Matt 2:6; Mark 1:2-3; Acts 7:7)—in which two HB texts are combined into one reference—and numerous modifications in the HB citation in order to conform the text to the writer's argument (see Rom 1:17, where Paul drops the personal pronoun in order to obtain a dual meaning in Hab 2:4). In many of these instances it is evident that the NT writers were not concerned with uncovering the original intent of the HB writer. Rather, texts were often used for what they would contribute to christological and ecclesiological exegesis in the church, without regard for their larger context and meaning in the HB. At the same time there are instances in which the larger context of the HB is apparently in view (the use of Leviticus 19 in James 2; see L. T. Johnson [1982]). Overall, there is no hard and fast rule about the relationship of HB citation in the NT to its larger HB context; one must analyze each instance in turn.

Direct citations are by far the least common aspect of HB use in the NT. Most prominent are allusions to HB texts, which are made throughout the NT; and it becomes particularly difficult to establish when these allusions were intended by an author, when they would have been understood by the readers (irrespective of authorial intent), and when they were unintentional, simply echoes of biblical language resulting from people so thoroughly immersed in the HB text and thought world that their own words were unconsciously shaped by and modeled on HB patterns. The Bible of the early church, it must be remembered, was the HB (2 Tim 3:16); and first-century Christians were taught to mine the Scriptures for their theological and moral formation. Hence the language of that formation is, from beginning to end, explicitly biblical. Consequently, it is difficult in many cases to separate allusion from echo and both of these from quotation (J. Paulien [1988]; Porter). Is the allusion just a direct citation without introduction that

the reader is expected to catch? Is the allusion more subtle, belying the author's indebtedness to the HB for theological expression? Or is the writer even aware of alluding to the HB? These are difficult questions, and the fact that at one time or another a HB text has been postulated to underlie almost every verse in the NT demonstrates the far-reaching implications of this debate. It is clear, however, that there are many intentional allusions in the NT (for some possible allusions see Exod 3:14 in John 18:5-6; Isa 49:1 in Gal 1:15; Isa 45:23 [LXX] in Phil 2:10-11 [Rom 14:11]; Job 13:16 [LXX] in Phil 1:19; Isa 40:6-8 in Jas 1:10-11; Gen 1:1-5 in John 1:1-5; Dan 9:27 in Mark 13:14; [cf. Hays]). Of course, many of the allusions that exist now are the end result of exegetical reflections and developments prior to the existence of the present text (see Phil 2:10-11, which is probably a Christian hymn fragment).

The NT evinces a variety of uses of the HB in its inner-biblical exegesis. There are straightforward citations often used as prophetic prooftexts (Matt 12:17-21), sometimes in a *pesher*-like mode, as one finds at Qumran (Acts 2:22-36; 15:13-18). Scripture is also used to bolster theological (Rom 4:6-8; Gal 3:10-14; Heb 10:15-17) and practical arguments (1 Cor 10:7; 2 Cor 6:16-18; 8:15; 9:9; Jas 2:8). Hebrews presents some fine examples of midrashic exegesis in which the exegetical reflection is still embedded in the sermon (Heb 3:7–4:13; 7:1-17). There is at least one explicit example of the use of allegorical interpretation, wherein a HB story is understood to contain a deeper, symbolic meaning corresponding to various components of a literal interpretation (Gal 4:21-31). The NT also has several instances of the ancient Jewish practice of rewriting the Bible, a convention in which the biblical story is retold with some modifications in light of the specific purposes of the writer (Acts 7; 13:16-22; Hebrews 11). Moreover, there are numerous examples of typological exegesis, in which typology is premised on the HB text, thus forming a paradigm or *exemplum* for either theological argument or moral exhortation. For instance, the exodus event provides a typology of the Corinthian community in 1 Cor 10:1-14; and Adam provides a type of Christ in Rom 5:12-21 (cf. 2 Cor 3:1-18 [S. Hafemann, 1995]; Hebrews 11 [P. Eisenbaum, 1997]; Jude 5-13). This common use of the HB as *paradeigma* reflects the strong emphasis placed on examples in Greco-Roman education and rhetoric. Also notable is the typological value of certain characters like Moses in Matthew (D. Allison [1993]) and the figure of the Son of man (Dan 7:13-14) throughout the Gospels. Furthermore, certain key events, themes, and institutions of the HB take on a typological or paradigmatic quality in the NT (creation, exodus/new exodus [Isaiah]; covenant/new covenant [Jeremiah]; priesthood, prophecy/prophets, kingly office, "anointed one"). Finally, one must consider one of the foundational uses of the HB by early Christian writers: the generation of NT narratives based on HB models (Stegner, Moessner, Aus, Daube, Derrett [cf. Dan 12:6-7 and Rev 10:5-7]). Here it becomes apparent that when early Christians told their stories they were often consciously modeling them on the prior narratives of the HB.

Bibliography: **D. C. Allison,** *The New Moses: A Matthean Typology* (1993). **G. L. Archer and G. C. Chirichigno,** *OT Quotations in the NT: A Complete Survey* (1983). **R. Aus,** *Barabbas and Esther and Other Studies in the Judaic Illumination of Earliest Christianity* (SFSHJ 54, 1992); *Samuel, Saul, and Jesus: Three Early Palestinian Jewish Christian Gospel Haggadoth* (SFSHJ 105, 1994). **J. Barton,** *Oracles of God* (1986). **R. Bauckham,** *Jude and the Relatives of Jesus in the Early Church* (1990). **J. Bonsirven,** *Exégèse Rabbinique et Exégèse Paulinienne* (Biblioteque de la theologie historique, 1939). **F.-M. Braun,** *Jean le Théologien: Les Grandes Traditions D'Israel L'Accord des Écritures D'Aprés le Quatrieme Évangile* (Ebib, 1964). **M. Callaway,** *Sing, O Barren One: A Study in Comparative Midrash* (SBLDS 91, 1986). **B. Chilton,** *Targumic Approaches to the Gospels* (1986); *Judaic Approaches to the Gospels* (USF International Studies in Formative Christianity and Judaism 2, 1994). **C. H. Dodd,** *According to the Scriptures* (1952). **D. Daube,** "A Reform in Acts and Its Models," *Jews, Greeks, and Christians: Religious Cultures in Late Antiquity* (ed. R. Hamerton-Kelly and R. Scroggs, SJLA 21, 1976) 151-63. **R. Le Deaut,** "Apropos a Definition of Midrash," *Int* 25 (1971) 259-82. **J. D. M. Derrett,** *Studies in the NT* (1977–95). **J. W. Doeve,** *Jewish Hermeneutics in the Synoptic Gospels and Acts* (1954). **P. M. Eisenbaum,** *The Jewish Heroes of Christian History* (SBLDS 156, 1997). **E. E. Ellis,** *Paul's Use of the OT* (1957); *The OT in Early Christianity* (1991). **C. A. Evans,** *To See and Not Perceive: Isaiah 6:9-10 in Early Jewish and Christian Interpretation* (JSOTSup 64, 1989). **C. A. Evans and J. A. Sanders,** *Luke and Scripture* (1993). **C. A. Evans and J. A. Sanders** (eds.), *Paul and the Scriptures of Israel* (JSNTSup 83, 1993); *The Gospels and the Scriptures of Israel* (JSNTSup 104, 1994); *Early Christian Interpretation of the Scriptures of Israel* (JSNTSup 148, 1997). **J. Fekkes,** *Isaiah and Prophetic Traditions in the Book of Revelation* (JSNTSup 93, 1994). **J. A. Fitzmyer,** "4QTestimonia and the NT," *Essays on the Semitic Background of the NT* (1974) 59-89; "The Use of Explicit OT Quotations in Qumran Literature and the NT," ibid., 3-58. **E. Freed,** *OT Quotations in the Gospel of John* (SNT 11, 1965). **M. Gertner,** "Midrashim in the NT," *JSS* 7 (1962) 267-92. **L. Goppelt,** *Typos: The Typological Interpretation of the OT in the New* (1939; ET 1982). **J. Gnilka,** *Die Verstockung Israels: Isaias 6,9-10 in der Theologie der Synoptiker* (1961). **M. D. Goulder,** *Midrash and Lection in Matthew* (1974). **A. Guilding,** *The Fourth Gospel and Jewish Worship* (1960). **R. H. Gundry,** *The Use of the OT in St. Matthew's Gospel* (SNT 18, 1975). **A. T. Hanson,** *Studies in Paul's Technique and Theology* (1974); *The Prophetic Gospel: A Study of John and the OT* (1991). **R. Harris and V.-Baruch,** *Testimonies* (2 vols., 1916, 1920). **S. J. Hafemann,** *Paul, Moses, and the History of Israel* (WUNT 81, 1995). **D. M. Hay,** *Glory at the Right Hand: Psalm 110 in Early Christianity* (SBLMS 18, 1973). **R. B. Hays,** *Echoes of Scripture in the Letters of Paul* (1989). **T. Holtz,** *Untersuchungen über die alttestamentlichen Zitate bei Lukas* (TU 104, 1968). **M. D. Hooker,** *Jesus and the Servant* (1959). **H. Hübner,** "NT Interpretation of the OT," *HB/OT* 1, 1 (1996) 332-72; *Vetus Testamentum in Novo* (1997–). **L. T. Johnson,** "The Use of Leviticus 19 in the Letter of James," *JBL* 101 (1982) 391-401. **D. H. Juel,** *Messianic Exegesis: Christological Interpretation of the OT in Early Christianity* (1988). **D.-A. Koch,** *Die Schrift als Zeuge des Evangeliums: Untersuchungen zur Verwendung und zum Verstandnis der Schrift bei Paulus* (BHT 69, 1986). **B. Lindars,** *NT Apologetic: The Doctrinal Significance of the OT Quotations* (1961). **R. N. Longenecker,** *Biblical Exegesis in the Apostolic Period* (1975). **B. H. McLean,** *Citations and Allusions to Jewish Scripture in Early Christian and Jewish Writings Through 180* CE (1992). **M. McNamara,** *The NT and the Palestinian Targum to the Pentateuch* (Aramaic Bible 27a, 1978). **J. Marcus,** *The Way of the Lord: Christological Exegesis of the OT in the Gospel of Mark* (1992). **O. Michel,** *Paulus und seine Bibel* (1929). **M. P. Miller,** "Targum, Midrash, and the Use of the OT in the NT," *JSJ* 2 (1971) 29-82. **D. P. Moessner,** *Lord of the Banquet* (1989). **D. J. Moo,** *The OT in the Gospel Passion Narratives* (1983). **J. Neusner,** *What Is Midrash?* (1987). **D. S. New,** *OT Quotations in the Synoptic Gospels and the Two-Document Hypothesis* (SBLSCS 37, 1993). **J. Paulien,** "Elusive Allusions: The Problematic Use of the OT in Revelations," *BR* 33 (1988) 37-53. **G. Porten,** "Midrash: Palestinian Jews and the HB in the Greco-Roman Period," *ANRW* II.19.2 (1979) 103-38. **S. E. Porter,** "The Use of the OT in the NT: A Brief Comment on Method and Terminology," *Early Christian Interpretation of the Scriptures of Israel* (ed. C. A. Evans et al., 1997) 79-96. **B. G. Schuchard,** *Scripture Within Scripture: The Interrelationship of Form and Function in the Explicit OT Citations in the Gospel of John* (SBLDS 133, 1992). **S. G. Sowers,** *The Hermeneutics of Philo and Hebrews* (1965). **C. D. Stanley,** *Paul and the Language of Scripture* (1992); "The Rhetoric of Quotations: An Essay on Method," *Early Christian Interpretation of the Scriptures of Israel* (ed. C. A. Evans et al., 1997) 44-58. **W. R. Stegner,** *Narrative Theology in Early Jewish Christianity* (1989). **K. Stendahl,** *The School of St. Matthew and Its Use of the OT* (1967). **A. Suhl,** *Die Funktion der alttestamentlichen Zitate und Anspielungen im Markusevangelium* (1965). **A. G. Wright,** *The Literary Genre Midrash* (1967).

T. C. PENNER

INSPIRATION OF THE BIBLE

Beginning in the nineteenth century there has been considerable interest in the inspiration of the Bible. The discussion of that topic is closely linked to the AUTHORITY OF THE BIBLE and hence is extensively covered in that entry. There remains, however, to set the question into its earliest historical context.

Johannes Leipoldt (1961) has traced the early history of the idea of inspiration, illuminating in a remarkable way the dominant role it plays among the Greeks and the virtual absence among the Hebrews. In oriental religions the gods are directly accountable for holy texts, either writing them or dictating them to scribes. In Egypt, Thot is both god of the scribes and scribe for the gods, and since 2000 BCE many writings were attributed to him, the autograph being considered reliable.

Among the Hebrews, Yahweh commanded Moses to serve as scribe (Exod 34:27-28), although in the Elohist narrative it was God who wrote the Torah on the tablets and then gave them to Moses (24:12). Even more directly, the tablets are described as written by the "finger of God" (31:18; 32:16), similar to the portrayal of the code of Hammurabi as coming from Shamesh, the sun god. Later such anthropomorphisms were rejected, and the angel of the Presence was seen as dictating (or writing down) the law to Moses (*Jub* 1:27; 2:1). Rabbinic belief in the pre-existence of the law before creation assumes the existence of a heavenly original, and it was asserted that the history as well as the law existed in tablets written in heaven (*Jub* 23:32; 31:32; 32:28; *T. Levi* 5:4). In Ethiopic Enoch after it is said that the angel Uriel did the writing (33:3) this is changed to Enoch's doing the writing himself (33:4).

Strictly speaking, inspiration emerged among the prophets of Israel (see PROPHECY AND PROPHETS, HB) when they seemed to lose their rationality and uttered syllables or words no one could understand. Yet this prophetic rapture did not carry revelation (1 Sam 10:10). Although the Spirit is described as descending upon a person to bring about a certain action and "the Word of the LORD," the difference between prophet and God was always maintained, and the prophet always had the right of refusal to carry the message. The experience of Jonah is perhaps meant to illustrate that.

Among the Greeks the idea of inspiration flourished, beginning at least as early as Euripides' *The Bacchae,* in which the poet sought to fathom the mental attitude of a man who prophesied after the total deity had passed into his body or when he was captured and forced to serve his god. But inspiration as madness, described as a "special gift from heaven and the source of the chiefest blessing from heaven," was most fully developed by Plato in the *Phaedrus* and *Ion.* Previously Democritus had written that "whatever a poet writes being driven by God and the holy spirit is certainly beautiful," and Hesiod conceived of divine inspiration when he wrote that the Muses of Mount Olympus "had breathed a Divine voice [or syllables?] into him" (*Theogony* 31). According to Plato, God takes away the minds of the poets and possesses them, and the priceless words are spoken in a state of unconsciousness. Yet Plato decried the invention of writing and described all writings as

dangerous (*Phaedrus*) because what is written is no longer under the protection of the author, and written words are simply not adequate to express the truth. The highest truths must be communicated orally and "written in the soul," which is the only true form of writing.

The most detailed discussions of this topic came in connection with the oracles. Cicero (106–43 BCE) observed that the SIBYLLINE books had a certain deliberate artistry that could hardly have come about in a state of ecstasy, but must have been constructed in a writer's workshop. The longest treatment this subject received was from Plutarch (46–120 CE), who was struck by the fact that the high priestess of Delphi no longer spoke in verses. He rejected the suggestion that perhaps she no longer spoke for Apollo and proposed instead that god does not provide the words, but only inspires the author with the subject. "God gives her only the images and concepts and kindles in her soul a light that she may know the future; in that consists her dependence upon God."

Solid evidence of the belief that holy writings depend on holy inspiration for authority is first found in the Greek-speaking segment of Judaism. The concept of the writer's union with God appears in many sources here, but not, for some reason, in ARISTEAS (2nd cent. before Christ), where one might expect it. Although Aristeas firmly believed in the miraculous origin of the Greek HB, he did not avail himself of a theory of inspiration to account for it. In rabbinical circles the theory of inspiration figures hardly at all, and one can be reasonably certain that it was virtually never discussed in the first century.

Certainly the NT writers had little interest in the issue. Yet JESUS would appear to follow HB patterns when he referred to David's speaking (not writing?) "in the Holy Spirit" (Mark 12:36) and thus indicated that the source of what David said was beyond himself. Likewise, he urged his disciples not to worry about what they shall say when they are arrested, "because it will be given you in that hour what you shall say, for you yourselves will not be speaking but the Holy Spirit" (Mark 13:11). It is almost as if we were back in Plato's world. PAUL, on the other hand, made it very clear that Christians are not out of control when the Spirit possesses them, "for the spirits of the prophets are subject to the prophets" (1 Cor 14:32). In his dealing with HB Scripture, Paul displayed a freedom in going beyond it, but also in viewing it as fully expressive, not only of God's purpose and will, but also of human individuality. So in citing one prophet he wrote, "As Isaiah even is bold enough to say. . . ." (Rom 10:20).

In this respect, Paul was not followed. Later Christian sources stressed the lifelessness of man (Epiphanius 48; *Odes of Solomon* 6:1; Justin Martyr), all assuming that the human writer is passive and under the complete control of God. A mediating position is taken in 2 Tim

3:16, which uses the rare word *theopneustos* to distinguish secular writings from those that have their origin in God. No theory of inspiration is here in view, but the stress is laid on the usefulness of Scripture, which has its origin in God (see E. Schweitzer [1968]). As throughout the NT, the Scriptures are not called *hagios* here, but rather *hiera;* only the gospel and people are called "holy" (Rom 1:2). Second Peter 1:20-21 speaks of "being carried along by the Spirit of God," and one has the clear impression that they had no choice. For the most part people, not writings, were considered inspired (G. Lampe [1962]).

In subsequent years all this changed, and many nonbiblical views came to dominate the discussions of inspiration. The authority of the Bible had at one time been assured by the way in which its message transformed lives, but as ages of uncertainty came through the demise of Christianity as a state religion or dominant culture and as views of inspiration changed, attempts were made to impose a theory of inspiration on the Scriptures. It is ironic that often those who proclaimed a "high view of Scripture" actually went outside of Scripture to find a view of inspiration.

There is little evidence that theories of inspiration have made any difference in how the biblical text has been interpreted over the generations. Rather, it has been the conviction that God was the inspiring power behind the events described and that at times God inspired writers to preserve for posterity their witness to the faith in these Scriptures. Since the discussions of inspiration came not from within the Scriptures themselves but as an answer to outside detractors, they served only a modest apologetic purpose. The risk that such an approach takes is that it detracts from an inductive study of the Scriptures and distorts the original function and purpose of the Scriptures, which is to witness to the reality of a covenanting God.

Bibliography: W. J. **Abraham,** *The Divine Inspiration of Holy Scripture* (1981). P. **Achtemeier,** *The Inspiration of Scripture* (BPCI, 1980). L. **Alonso-Schöckel,** *The Inspired Word* (1963). D. **Beegle,** *The Inspiration of Scripture* (1963). P. **Benoit,** *Aspects of Biblical Inspiration* (1965). J. T. **Burtchaell,** *Catholic Theories of Biblical Inspiration Since 1810: A Review and Critique* (1969). A. A. **Hodge and B. B. Warfield,** *Inspiration* (1881). G. W. H. **Lampe,** "Inspiration and Revelation," *IDB* 2 (1962) 713-18. J. **Leipoldt,** "Die Frühgeschichte der göttlichen Eingebung," *Von den Mysterien zur Kirche* (1961) 116-49. J. **McKenzie,** "The Social Character of Inspiration," *CBQ* 24 (1962) 115-24. J. H. **Newman,** *On the Inspiration of Scripture* (ed. J. D. Holmes and R. Murray, 1967). R. D. **Preus,** *The Inspiration of Scripture: A Study of the Theology of the Seventeenth Century Lutheran Dogmaticians* (1955). W. **Sanday,** *Inspiration* (1896). E. **Schweitzer,** *"theopneustos"* (*TDNT* 6, 1968) 453-55. J. **Scullion,** *The Theology of Inspiration* (1970). N. **Snaith,** *The Inspiration and Authority of the Bible* (1956). P. **Synave and P. Benoit,** *Prophecy and Inspiration* (1961). K. R. **Trembath,** *Evangelical Theories of Biblical Inspiration* (1988). P. M. **Van Bemmelen,** *Issues in Biblical Inspiration: Sanday and Warfield* (1987). B. **Vawter,** *Biblical Inspiration* (1972). B. B. **Warfield,** *The Inspiration and Authority of the Bible* (1948).

W. KLASSEN

INTERPRETATION OF THE BIBLE IN THE CHURCH

This document was issued by the Biblical Commission of the Roman Catholic Church on Nov. 18, 1993, to commemorate the centenary of Leo XIII's PROVIDENTISSIMUS DEUS and the fiftieth anniversary of Pius XII's DIVINO AFFLANTE SPIRITU.

Because the Bible was written twenty to thirty centuries ago in ancient languages, its interpretation encounters difficulties in light of modern progress in human sciences and recent discoveries and developments in historical and LITERARY CRITICISM. The Biblical Commission intended in its 1993 document to indicate the paths most appropriate for arriving at an interpretation of Scripture that is faithful to its character as the inspired Word of God (see INSPIRATION OF THE BIBLE) and to its role in the church and in the spiritual formation of the people of God. To attain such a goal, the commission discusses four topics: (1) various methods of biblical interpretation and approaches to the Bible; (2) certain hermeneutical questions (modern hermeneutical philosophies, the meaning of inspired Scripture, its senses [literal, spiritual, fuller]; see HERMENEUTICS); (3) characteristics of Roman Catholic interpretation of the Bible (relation of the OT to the NT; *relectures*; relation of Scripture to tradition, canon, and patristic exegesis; the roles of various members of the church in interpretation); and (4) the role that biblical interpretation must play in the life of the church (actualization of the Bible, its inculturation; use of the Bible in the liturgy, in *lectio divina,* pastoral ministry, ecumenism).

Of the four topics, the first is discussed at great length: The methods and approaches are described and assessed. The commission maintains that the "indispensable" method, "required" for the correct interpretation of the Bible is the historical-critical method, despite the criticism of it heard in some quarters today. It is judged to be a neutral method, which can, however, be used with presuppositions (rationalistic, existentialist, but also with Christian faith). This basic method has at times been used inadequately, with little concern for the meaning of the Bible as the Word of God; but it can be properly oriented. That basic method, moreover, can be improved and refined by elements of various approaches to the Bible, such as new modes of literary analysis (rhetorical, narrative, semiotic), by approaches based on tradition (canonical criticism, Jewish interpretation, the history of biblical interpretation [*Wirkungsgeschichte*]), by approaches using human sciences (sociology, anthropology, psychology), and by contextual approaches (liberationist, feminist). This basic method so modified becomes an interpretation quite different from a fundamentalist reading of the Bible. Also noteworthy in the document is its treatment of "actualization," i.e., the contemporary application of the literal sense of Scripture arrived at by the properly oriented historical-critical method of interpretation.

Bibliography: Commission Biblique Pontificale, *L'Interprétation de la Bible dans l'Église* (Libreria Editrice Vaticana, 1993; ET *The Interpretation of the Bible in the Church*; repr. *Origins* 23, 29, (Jan. 6, 1994) 497-524. **J. A. Fitzmyer,** *The Biblical Commission's Document, "The Interpretation of the Bible in the Church": Text and Commentary* (SubBi 18, Pontifical Biblical Institute, 1995; available in the United States from Loyola University Press).

J. A. FITZMYER

INTERTEXTUALITY

As a self-conscious literary-critical approach, intertextuality emerged in the late 1960s and early 1970s and has in significant ways informed the practice of criticism and contemporary understandings of literary history in North America and Europe. The root concerns of this approach are not new: the role of tradition in literature, the relationship of newly created literary works to the classics of a given "canon," and the role of literary and cultural systems of meaning in literary composition. Intertextual methods, however, offer alternatives to the stringent evolutionary and historically determined models with which these concerns have been conventionally addressed. Beginning in the late 1970s and early 1980s, biblical scholars have increasingly used the methods of intertextual studies to interpret biblical texts.

The progenitor of contemporary intertextual studies was T. S. Eliot's 1919 essay, "Tradition and the Individual Talent." Eliot wrote this essay against the backdrop of Romantic theories of poetic inspiration and genius of the poet, which claimed that the poet's originality is an expression of personality. Eliot challenged these conventional assumptions about genius and inspiration by reclaiming the centrality of literary tradition. His central thesis was that no poet or artist receives complete meaning in isolation, but must be set "among the dead": "We shall often find that not only the best, but the most individual parts of his work may be those in which the dead poets, his ancestors, assert their immortality most vigorously" (1950, 4).

Eliot replaced the evolutionary model of influence with a model of literary interrelationships. The poet incorporates the traditions of the past into a work so that it transforms past and present. POETRY is "a living whole of all the poetry written"; "what happens when a new work of art is created is something that happens simultaneously to all the works of art which preceded it" (1950, 49-50). Eliot conceived of literature as a "system of coequal, copresent texts" that hold "literature as history and literature as system" in balance (T. Morgan [1989] 242).

Eliot's most lasting contribution to intertextual studies is this emphasis on literature as a system of interrelated texts. Subsequent work in intertextuality is developing his observations in two distinct, but not wholly unrelated directions. The first stream of intertextuality focuses on literary interrelationships and patterns of literary borrowing within literature proper. The second stream broadens the understanding of "text" to include a variety of linguistic phenomena and thus studies the interrelationship of text and culture.

Scholars employ a wide variety of methodologies to study intertextual relations in literary texts. For example, H. Bloom (1973, 1975) draws on theories from modern philosophy and Freudian PSYCHOLOGY to identify and explain the dynamics and motivations of literary borrowing. Although Bloom attempts to distance himself from what he perceives as the classical and Christianizing tendency of Eliot, his study of "intra-poetic relationships" shares with Eliot similar conceptualizations of influence and the interaction of past and present in literary composition. Bloom maintains that every reading of a text is a misreading. A new poet creates a personal space by misreading the poetic precursors. Bloom describes this misreading in terms of a Freudian struggle between fathers and sons. His psychological orientation leads him to focus on authorial intention, a focus other intertextual studies often try to avoid.

A second methodology can be seen in the work of J. Hollander (1981), which belongs to the more general category of RHETORICAL CRITICISM. He identifies allusions to and echoes of earlier poets in the work of their successors and studies the way those textual echoes create new meanings. Echo is understood as a rhetorical trope that establishes links between texts chronologically removed from one another. Hollander's work proceeds by close readings of individual poetic texts and by design is more suggestive of intertextual possibilities than it is methodologically precise. Under the general category of rhetorical approaches to intertextuality, one can also place studies that investigate the way various rhetorical figures are used (e.g., citation), the effects produced by literary borrowing, and the reader's experience of literary borrowing.

A third methodology used to study intertextuality within literature proper is SEMIOTICS. Unlike semiotic studies that focus more broadly on text and culture (see below), the semiotic studies of M. Riffaterre (1978) and G. Genette (1982), for example, focus on the act of reading specific literary texts. Both assume that intertextuality is operative in all literature, and their studies attempt to identify what the reader must do in order to recognize and follow the intertextual signals in any given text. Riffaterre provides close readings of texts "to show how each literary text guides the reader toward its own intertexts" (Morgan, 262). Genette offers a taxonomy of intertextual signs and relations to enable the reader to follow the dynamics of intertextuality. (For a thorough discussion of Riffaterre and Genette, see Morgan, 262-71.)

When the definition of intertextuality broadens to include relationships between text and culture, structuralist (see STRUCTURALISM AND DECONSTRUCTION) and semiotic methods move to the forefront. Semiotics speaks of "text" differently from rhetorical and more traditional literary critics. "Text" includes any system of signs, not simply a literary text. In this broader understanding of text, all communication is seen as inherently "intertextual"—that is, any act of communication always occurs in the context of other signs. The semiotic approach to text and culture splits into two divergent philosophical camps. One approach, modeled on the linguistic theory of R. Jacobson and embodied in the structural anthropology of C. Lévi-Strauss, believes that one can identify the structures and basic elements that account for and explain the signifying practice of a "text." This approach operates with linguistic models and metaphors, but it shares with the methods discussed above a basic presupposition about the stability of texts and communication. The second semiotic approach to text and culture is critical of any sense of the stability of language and literature and uses semiotic models to point toward the increasing ambiguity and instability of communication. The key figures in this second approach are M. Bakhtin, R. Barthes, J. Kristeva, J. Culler, and J. Derrida. With these literary critics intertextuality becomes part of a broader deconstructionalist reading of literature (see Morgan, 256-61, 272-74).

In biblical studies the narrower use of intertextuality—that is, patterns of literary borrowing among literary texts proper and textual relationships between specific literary corpora—is most prevalent. Intertextuality in the broader sense has been absorbed into general deconstructionist biblical interpretation.

Intertextual biblical interpretation attempts to address the interaction between traditions and texts without recourse to answers of strict historical construction. It attempts to hold together literature as history and literature as system without dissolving the tension between these two understandings of literature. Historical criticism tends to explain the presence of an earlier tradition or text with the formula, "the use of. . . ." or "the influence of . . . on. . . ." This understanding of textual interrelationships dominated studies of the relationship between the Hebrew and Christian canons until the second half of the twentieth century (C. H. Dodd [1952];

B. Lindars [1961]; D. Carson and H. Williamson [1988]). This approach is grounded in an exclusively diachronic understanding of texts and an evolutionary model of influence. Its focus is primarily apologetic, and consequently its concerns revolve around authorial intention.

The work of M. Fishbane (1985, 1986) provides a compelling alternative to an evolutionary and apologetic model of textual interrelations. Fishbane makes explicit connections between his work and the categories proposed by Eliot (Fishbane [1986] 34-36), but his concern is not theoretical. He defines intertextual relations in terms of inner-biblical interpretation and exegesis within the Hebrew CANON, focusing on the textual-exegetical dimensions of the Jewish imagination and suggesting that it is the essence of biblical texts to be reinterpreted by successive generations. He brings together the imaginative and social dimensions of Jewish exegesis and transforms a strictly evolutionary model of influence into a model grounded in the ongoing and unending life of literary traditions. Like Eliot, Fishbane holds together literature as history and literature as system in a way that reflects the richness and complexity of inner-biblical interpretation. He also clearly articulates the difference between TRADITION HISTORY and inner-biblical exegesis. Tradition history moves backward from written sources to oral traditions. Inner-biblical exegesis starts with a received text and moves forward to subsequent interpretations based on it (1985, 7-13).

Fishbane excludes the Gospel writers and PAUL from the category of inner-biblical interpretation, maintaining that the christological dimension of their work stresses fulfillment and supersession rather than the reanimation of tradition (1985, 10). Yet because these writers were schooled in the same textual-exegetical imagination as the Jewish interpreters, the exegetical and interpretive methods that Fishbane indentifies within the Hebrew canon do seem to illuminate the play of traditions within the Christian canon (G. O'Day [1990]). His assessment of the handling of Hebrew traditions by the Gospel writers and Paul actually provides a telling critique of those interpreters cited above who reduce the relationship between the Hebrew and the Christian canons to prophecy/fulfillment and apologetic motives. Forcing scholars of the Christian canon to reassess their working exegetical assumptions, he restores a balance to scholarly understanding of the interplay of traditions.

Other biblical scholars have studied intertextual relations with more explicit reference to contemporary LITERARY THEORY, employing a wide variety of methodologies. S. Handelman (1982) grounds her study of the Moses tradition in biblical and rabbinic writings in the psycho-rhetorical categories of H. Bloom. R. Hays (1989) employs the rhetorical categories of J. Hollander to study "echoes of scripture" in Paul. D. Boyarin (1990) uses M. Riffaterre's semiotic categories in his reading of MIDRASH. These studies provide alternatives to the traditional evolutionary models of intertextual influence. Intertextual studies provide a bridge between strictly diachronic and strictly synchronic approaches to biblical texts, challenging traditional notions of influence and causality while at the same time affirming that every biblical text must be read as part of a larger literary context.

Bibliography: M. Bakhtin, *Problems of Dostoevsky's Poetics* (1973). H. Bloom, *The Anxiety of Influences* (1973); *The Map of Misreading* (1975). D. Boyarin, *Intertextuality and the Reading of Midrash* (1990). D. A. Carson and H. G. M. Williamson (eds.), *It is Written: Scripture Citing Scripture. Essays in Honor of Barnabas Lindars* (1988). J. Culler, *The Pursuit of Signs: Semiotics, Literature, Deconstruction* (1981). C. H. Dodd, *According to the Scriptures: the Substructure of NT Theology* (1952). S. Draisma (ed.), *Intertextuality in Biblical Writings: Essays in Honour of Bas van Iersel* (1989). T. S. Eliot, *Selected Essays 1917–1932* (1950). M. Fishbane, *Biblical Interpretation in Ancient Israel* (1985); "Inner Biblical Exegesis: Types and Strategies of Interpretation in Ancient Israel," *Midrash and Literature* (ed. G. H. Hartmann and S. Budick, 1986) 19-37. G. Genette, *Palimpsestes: La Literature au second degre* (1982). S. Handelman, *The Slayers of Moses: The Emergence of Rabbinic Interpretation in Modern Literary Theory* (1982). R. Hays, *Echoes of Scripture in the Letters of Paul* (1989). J. Hollander, *The Figure of Echo: A Mode of Allusion in Milton and After* (1981). B. Lindars, *NT Apologetic* (1961). T. Morgan, "The Space of Intertextuality," *Intertextuality and Contemporary American Fiction* (ed. P. O'Donnell and R. C. Davis, 1989) 239-79. G. O'Day, "Jeremiah 9:22-23 and 1 Corinthians 1:26-31: A Study in Intertextuality," *JBL* 109 (1990) 259-67. M. Riffaterre, *Semiotics of Poetry* (1978).

G. R. O'DAY

IRENAEUS OF LYONS (c. 130–c. 200)

I. came from Asia Minor, where he learned the earliest traditions of the gospel from Polycarp (EUSEBIUS *Hist. eccl.* 5.20.4-8), to Lyons, where he was made bishop after the persecution of 177 (Eusebius *Hist. eccl.* 5.5.8). He provides the first clear evidence of a Christian Bible, although his "NT" is not yet a document (*Adv. haer.* 4.9.1). His two main works indicate a central concern for right use of the Scripture, which nourished and determined his language (*Adv. haer.* 5.20.2): *The Demonstration of the Apostolic Preaching* establishes the truth of the Christian proclamation on the basis of its fulfillment of prophecies (see PROPHECY AND PROPHETS, HB), while his longer work, *Against Heresies,* sets out and effectively argues against the various positions of GNOSTIC sects. I. is commonly contrasted with the Alexandrians (see ALEXANDRIAN SCHOOL) because he gave less importance to the place of philosophy and worked more obviously within biblical categories; but he was vigorous in argument, a Hellenist in culture, and an allegorist in exegesis. His evolutionary view of history has attracted modern interest, especially from Teilhard de Chardin. His approach to the problem of evil has been contrasted with that of AUGUSTINE as a "rise" theory as opposed to a "fall" theory, but he united both by his emphasis on the divine grace that turns a catastrophe to good effect.

Against Heresies draws extensively on NT writings (1,819 verses), mainly the Gospels and Acts of the Apostles, then the sayings of the Lord and the epistles of Paul. It uses haggadic tradition, e.g. to claim that Lot's wife is still to be seen in salt (*Adv. haer.* 4.31.3).

I. worked with five principles of interpretation: (1) The rule of faith is the starting point behind which stands the one canon of truth, the content of the faith written on the heart by the Holy Spirit (*Adv. haer* 1.9.4; 1.22.1; 2.27.1; 3.2.1; 3.11.1; 3.12.6; 3.15.1; 4.35.4; *Demonstration* 3). (2) Logical coherence is the working test. The heretics have taken a mosaic and jumbled the pieces around to produce a fox instead of a king; they have made a new poem by juggling lines into a different order (*Adv. haer.* 1.8-9). (3) Scripture is understood as the fulfillment in Christ of what has been foretold. PAUL's method of distinguishing letter and Spirit gives the orientation of Romans 10; I. faithfully produced this method. The Scriptures are entirely spiritual (2.28.3). (4) The fulfillment is significant only because Christ sums up the purposes of God and crowns the long dispensation of saving history. *Anakephalaiosis,* or recapitulation, unites a range of concepts. It is the perfection and correction of what was begun in Adam, who never left God's hands until perfect in Christ, the universal Word. What was lost in Adam is regained in Christ, death is replaced by life, and the triumph of sin is undone by the victory of Christ. (5) I. saw the victory of Christ continued in the kingdom of the Son, who will reign for a thousand years on earth. All the wonders of chiliastic plenty will flood the earth. This vision of the future is more moderate in the later work, *Demonstration.*

Works: *Against Heresies* (ed. W. W. Harvey, 2 vols., 1857); and SC, vols. 100, 152-153, 210-211, 263-264, 293-294 (1964–82); *The Demonstration of the Apostolic Preaching* (tr. J. A. Robinson, 1920); *Proof of the Apostolic Preaching* (tr. J. P. Smith, 1952).

Bibliography: F. Battles, *Irenaeus* (1993). A. Benoit, *Saint Irénée, Introduction à l'étude de sa théologie* (1960). Y. M. Blanchard, *Aux sources du canon, le témoignage d'Irénée* (Cositatio fide 75, 1993). N. Brox, *Offenbarung, Gnosis, und gnostischer Mythos bei Irenäus von Lyon* (1966). H. von Campenhausen, *The Formation of the Christian Bible* (1972). J. Fantino, *La théologie de Irénée* (1994). M. Jourjon, "Irenaeus's Reading of the Bible," *The BIble in Greek Christian*

Antiquity (BTA 1, ed. P. M. Blowers, 1997) 105-11. **J. L. Kugel and R. A. Greer,** *Early Biblical Interpretation* (1986). **J. Lawson,** *The Biblical Theology of Saint Irenaeus* (1946, 1982). **D. Minns,** *Irenaeus* (Outstanding Christian Thinkers, 1994). **R. Noormann,** *Irenäus als Paulusinterpret* (WUNT 66, 1994). **R. A. Norris, Jr.,** *HHMBI*, 39-42.

E. F. OSBORN

ISAAC BEN SAMUEL AL-KANZI (c. 1050–c. 1130)

Biblical commentator, liturgical poet, and Talmudic scholar (see TALMUD) born in Muslim Spain, I. emigrated to Egypt, where he became a prominent member of the rabbinic court of old Cairo. From his Arabic commentaries on the former prophets (see PROPHECY AND PROPHETS, HB), only those on 1 Samuel (MS Leningrad) and 2 Samuel (MS British Library) have partially survived and will be published. A full Arabic translation of the biblical text is interwoven into each commentary. The commentary proper includes lengthy verbatim quotations from his predecessors, incorporating most of the linguistic notes found in Hayyug's *Kitab al-Natef* and in ibn Bal'am's *Nukat al-Mikra*. Although these authoritative linguistic explanations usually served as a basis for his own detailed substantive interpretation, I. occasionally refuted them and offered an alternative grammatical analysis of his own. He adhered to the highly flexible linguistic rules laid down by the Spanish grammarians, tending to broaden them even further, which made it easier for him to remain faithful to his triple loyalty: the MT, orthodox beliefs and dogmas, and the literal-philological method (*Peshat*). Thus he made excessive use of letter interchanges, of replacement of words, and of ellipses (following Ibn Ganah) even as he maintained the literal-philological method with great consistency, almost to the point of a total disregard of the homiletic exegesis of the rabbis (which is quite surprising for a Talmudist like himself).

Relying on his firsthand knowledge of biblical geography and realia, I. aimed at a realistic reconstruction of historical events, a psychological understanding of the protagonists, and a religio-ethical evaluation of human deeds and divine recompense. But it is his impressive achievements in understanding biblical narrative art that earn him prominence in the history of exegesis. He traced the relationship between history as it actually occurred and the story as it took shape from the point of view of both artistic selection and expressive deviation from the chronological order (see CHRONOLOGY, HB). Distinguishing between what is stated explicitly, what is implied, and what is not meant to be revealed, he examined points where the narrator foretold later events, as well as exactly where he chose to interrupt the narrative flow in order to insert explanatory remarks. He also examined the point of view and dramatic irony in the narratives. Very impressive is his religious-ethical sensitivity and his discretion concerning the degree of guilt borne by the protagonists. The distinction between the prophet-messenger (i.e., Moses) who cannot possibly commit a grievous sin and the rest of the prophets, who in fact do sin, opens the way to a courageous view of the sins David committed, taken literally.

Since there is no sign of the influence of I.'s contribution to biblical exegesis in the work of A. IBN EZRA, his synthesis of the great achievements of the Jewish Spanish school lacks an important dimension—the mature literary interpretation developed by I.

Works: *Commentary on 1 & 2 Samuel* (the Arabic original with a Hebrew tr., notes and introduction by M. Perez, forthcoming).

Bibliography: J. Mann, *Texts and Studies* 1 (1931) 388-93. **U. Simon,** "The Contribution of R. Isaac b. Samuel Al-Kanzi to the Spanish School of Biblical Interpretation," *JJS* 34 (1983) 171-78.

U. SIMON

ISAIAH, BOOK OF

Isaiah is traditionally the first of the Major Prophets (Sir 48:23-25) and holds a unique position in both Judaism and Christianity. The book of Isaiah is prominent in the Jewish prophetic lectionaries, and its manuscripts as well as Isaiah commentaries are well represented among the DEAD SEA SCROLLS. It is the most often quoted book from Scripture in the NT and contains the text JESUS reads and reflects on near the beginning of his ministry at his synagogue in Nazareth (Luke 4:16-30). Its unique status in Christian tradition is reflected in the view expressed by JEROME in the introduction to his commentary that Isaiah should be called an evangelist rather than a prophet (see PROPHECY AND PROPHETS, HB) because he writes about Christ and the church in such a way as to make one think he is "telling the story of what has already happened, rather than foretelling what is still to come."

1. Ancient and Medieval Interpretations. The earliest Greek version of Isaiah (c. 140 BCE) contains significant references to the Jewish community in Egypt (e.g., 10:24; 19:18-25) and freely modifies descriptions of the kings of Assyria (8:11; 36:20) and Babylon (14:18-20) to fit the behavior and ultimate fate of the oppressor Antiochus IV Epiphanes (175–164 BCE; cf. Dan 11:36, alluding to Isa 8:11; 10:23, 25). Greek words for "law" (8:20; 33:6), "metropolis" (1:26), "fortune" (65:11), "light" (26:9; 53:11), and "knowledge" and "wisdom" (11:2; 33:6) introduce Hellenistic theology and prepare the path from Hebrew Scripture to subsequent Christian and GNOSTIC developments. The choice of Greek *parthenos,* "virgin," for *'almâ,* "young woman," in 7:14 is the best known and most influential example of this.

Frequent quotations from Isaiah throughout the sectarian literature of the Qumran community, including the remains of six Isaiah commentaries (*pesharim*) and an anthology of "Words of Consolation" based on Isaiah 40–55 illustrate the importance of the book and the way in which it was interpreted there. Isaiah 7:17 is applied to the departure of the "new Israel" from corrupt Judah, and 40:3 to the setting up of their community in the desert. References to the sect's opponents are found in many passages (e.g., 5:11-14; 10:12-14; 19:11-12; 24:17). Isaiah 52:7 and 61:1 are applied to the leader of the heavenly host, called Melchizedek, who will come to execute judgment on the "spirits of Baal" on the eschatological Day of Atonement (Leviticus 25).

The TARGUM of Isaiah, which reflects Jewish understanding of the book from several centuries before Christ to about 200 CE, inserts explanatory references to the Torah (e.g., 2:5; 9:5; 30:15; 50:10; 63:17), Gehenna (e.g., 33:14; 53:9; 65:5-6; 66:24), and the resurrection of the dead (e.g., 26:19; 42:11; 45:8; 57:16). Also typical of targumic style are the avoidance of anthropomorphisms (e.g., 63:1-3) and the prosaic explanation of metaphors (e.g., 5:17; 9:18; 12:3; 55:1). Like Christian interpretations of Isaiah, it also contains a very high number of explicit messianic references (e.g., 9:5; 11:1; 16:1; 42:1; 52:13), but the sufferings in 52:13–53:12 are those of Israel, not the Messiah.

The apocryphal *Martyrdom of Isaiah* (1st cent. CE) contains the tradition that the prophet was sawn in half by Manasseh, known to Jewish and Christian authors from the second century (see Heb 11:37), and an account of his journey to the seventh heaven, where he sees God and the future life, death, and resurrection of Christ.

Although it was through his translation that Jerome made his greatest contribution to the history of interpretation, fine scholarship, greatly assisted by a knowledge of Hebrew and rabbinic sources, soon established his commentary on Isaiah as the most respected and influential in Western Christendom. An example will illustrate his exegetical skill. The "ox and the ass at their master's crib" (1:3) had already in Jerome's day found their way into the nativity story, but he developed the theme by linking 1:3 with a vision of the new age in 32:20. The fact that the two animals are working together proves that now the law is no longer binding (Deut 22:10), and if the ox stands for Israel with the yoke of the law on its neck and the ass for the Gentiles weighed down by the burden of their sins, then the point of that vision of a new age where "the ox and the ass range free" is all the more poignant. Most subsequent commentators on Isaiah down to modern times draw heavily on Jerome.

The commentary by CYRIL OF ALEXANDRIA should be evaluated more as a theological treatise than as a work of exegesis, as his powerful descriptions of God's beneficence (p. 25) and omnipotence (pp. 40-41) illustrate. But his critical use of Jewish legend (e.g., 6:2; 38:1; 40:1) and Jerome is interesting, as are his references to Roman victories over the Jews (6:11-13; 27:4, 10; 66:24) and to the Pax Romana (2:1-5).

The influential writings of ISIDORE OF SEVILLE (c. 560–636) are largely dependent on Jerome and illustrate how the book of Isaiah was interpreted in medieval Christian tradition. His polemical *Isaiae testimonia de Christo domino,* much used by medieval scholars and artists, is a prime example, finding in Isaiah almost every detail of the life of Christ. The annunciation in 7:14 is followed by the celebration of the birth of the Savior in the city of David (9:6). His Davidic ancestry is referred to in 11:1 and also in 16:1 (see AV; the rock of the Moabite desert refers to Ruth). Isaiah is the only HB prophet to make specific mention of the virginity of the mother of the messiah. In addition to the Immanuel prophecy in 7:14 (cf. Matt 1:23), the important proof text was 53:8, where "his generation" referred to the virgin birth as well as to the divine nature of Christ. The dry ground from which a young plant miraculously springs up provides another expression of this doctrine (53:2; cf. 45:8). The flight into Egypt is referred to in 19:1 and the arrival of the magi in 60:6. There are several references to Christ's baptism (11:1; 42:1; 61:1; cf. Mark 1:9-11) and the healing miracles (34:5-6; 53:4; cf. Matt 8:17). References to the passion are frequent, too: his purple robe (63:1), his silence before his executioners (53:7), the cross carried on his shoulders (9:6), and his words of forgiveness from the cross (53:12). Isaiah ends, like Matthew, with the sending forth of apostles to the nations (66:19). The pre-existence of the Son of God is referred to in 66:7-9 and his divinity in 9:6 (cf. 53:8). The three persons of the Trinity are mentioned individually in 42:1 and 48:16 and celebrated in the threefold repetition of "Holy" in the *Sanctus* (6:3). Up to the twelfth century most Christian exegesis remained within the tradition established by Jerome and Isidore.

Of the great medieval Jewish commentaries, that of RASHI (1040–1105) is the most influential in subsequent Jewish and Christian tradition, frequently quoted, for example, by NICHOLAS OF LYRA. Like his two successors, the much traveled A. IBN EZRA and D. KIMHI, he combined literal interpretation with a respect for rabbinic tradition and sought to refute christological interpretations (e.g., 7:14; chaps. 52–53), while at the same time understanding the text in the light of contemporary events and current Jewish messianic expectation (e.g., 11:1). Ibn Ezra is the most original of the three and even questions the Isaianic authorship of some of the Babylonian prophecies in 40–66 (40:1).

The commentary on Isaiah by ANDREW OF ST. VICTOR is a significant example of medieval Christian scholarship. The prologue contains a unique "character study" of the prophet illustrating what a lively imagination can create out of scanty legends: "he suffered unto death . . . for justice's sake . . . he was willing rather to lose his life, with honour, by exquisite torture, a way of death unheard of . . . than suppress the truth for fear of fleeting death." He frequently cites Jewish interpretations as the "literal sense" of the text, even in the case of such "Christian" passages as 7:14; 11:1; and chap. 53. His exegesis was considered scandalous by contemporaries but appreciated by scholars of a later age, including Nicholas of Lyra.

LUTHER's lectures on Isaiah, delivered between 1527 and 1530, divide the book into two parts: chaps. 1–39, in which the prophet is "a historical prophet and leader of the army," and chaps. 40–66, where "the prophet is the most joyful of all, fairly dancing with promises." Despite frequent anti-Jewish interpretations (e.g., on 2:22; 4:3; 25:2; 29; 33), he makes considerable use of Hebrew, the Jewish sources, Jerome, Nicholas of Lyra, and other Hebraists and brands some traditional Christian interpretations as "childish errors" (1:3) and "twisted" (45:8). But at 7:14 he argues that although the Hebrew word *ʾalmâ* does not mean "virgin," the verse nonetheless must refer to a virgin birth since otherwise it would be no miraculous sign. Chapter 53 (beginning in Luther's Bible at 52:13) he describes as the "foremost passage on the suffering and resurrection of Christ." The "our . . . us . . . for us" in vv. 4-6 "should be written in letters of gold."

Embarrassed by the publication not long before of John KNOX's pamphlet against the government of women, in 1559 CALVIN dedicated the second edition of his commentary on Isaiah to Queen Elizabeth of England, citing 49:23, along with the examples of Huldah and Deborah, as scriptural authority for the role of queens in government and as "nursing mothers of the Church."

2. Isaiah in Art. A few illustrations of how Isaiah was interpreted in medieval Christian art (see ART AND BIBLICAL INTERPRETATION) and architecture reveal which aspects of the Isaianic tradition were taken up as of particular theological, social, or political significance in the period. First, there is the influence of the cult of the virgin Mary upon the interpretation of Isaiah. The earliest representation of Isaiah, a second-century catacomb painting in Rome, shows the prophet seated opposite the Virgin and Child. An unusually spirited representation of Isaiah at what was once the main entrance to the Cathedral of Notre Dame at Souillac in southwest France, opposite a statue of the patriarch Joseph, represents virginity and chastity (Gen 39:10). Here and in many other contexts he bears a scroll on which the words of Isa 7:14 are inscribed. Among the Major Prophets of the HB depicted on a window in Chartres Cathedral, Isaiah is shown carrying Matthew on his shoulders (Matt 1:23). Representations of the vision of

God among the seraphim (6:1-4) were also common in Byzantine and medieval art.

The ancestry of Jesus held a particular fascination for medieval artists, living as they did in a society in which kings and knights set great store by their lineage, and in this context Isa 11:1 acquired special significance. The entrance to many European cathedrals is flanked by the ancestors of the Messiah, each symbolically clutching a branch of the "Tree of Jesse," and elaborate representations based on 11:1 and Matt 1:1-17 are among the most popular motifs in medieval Christian art. A Chartres window provides possibly the most beautiful example: At the bottom Jesse, grandson of Ruth and father of David, is lying asleep. A tree rises from his body, and at its top the Virgin and Christ are surrounded by seven doves symbolizing the seven gifts of the spirit that "will rest upon him" (Isa 11:2). There are other examples in Amiens, Reims, Troyes, Le Mans, and elsewhere.

A seventeenth-century development of the "Jesse Tree" motif in Troyes Cathedral was inspired by Isa 63:3. Following AUGUSTINE's interpretation, the artist has depicted Christ in the winepress, his blood flowing out into a chalice. From his breast rises a new family tree, the true vine, carrying in its branches the twelve apostles, related by the sacramental blood of Christ this time, not by the ancestral blood of Jesse. Another interpretation of this verse from a church in Conches depicts Christ standing alone on a winepress, which is clearly designed to make one think of the cross. Suffering is also uppermost in a striking sculpture in Dijon by Claus Sluter, dating to c. 1400, in which Isaiah, old, bareheaded, and contemplative, bears a scroll with 53:7 inscribed on it. Perhaps there was a tradition that the author of chap. 53 was an older, more solemn Isaiah than the jubilant proclaimer of the nativity in the earlier chapters. The lively Souillac statue and Michelangelo's Isaiah on the ceiling of the Sistine Chapel are young, though this may be for aesthetic rather than exegetical or theological reasons.

3. Isaiah in Music. Isaiah's traditional association with the Advent and Christmas liturgies is also reflected in music (see MUSIC, THE BIBLE AND). "O come, O come, Immanuel" (*Veni Immanuel*) is an arrangement of Isa 7:14; 9:1; 11:1; 22:22; and 59:20, and the Latin of 45:8 provided the extremely popular antiphon *Rorate coeli*. The political associations of the *Rorate* are reflected in a version by W. Byrd (c. 1542–1623), composed at a time when his fellow Roman Catholics were being persecuted. He also composed *Ne irascaris,* another motet with political overtones on an Isaianic theme (Isa 64:9-10), soon after the martyrdom of E. Campion in 1581.

In addition to cantatas for Advent, Christmas, and Epiphany based on traditional passages like Isa 40:3-5; 9:6; and 60:6-7 (although in German now, rather than

Latin), J. BACH also composed a political one on 58:7 on behalf of Protestant refugees from Salzburg who were seeking asylum in Leipzig. The first two parts of Handel's *Messiah* (1741) are largely made up of direct quotations from Isaiah in the KJV combined with other passages of Scripture in a brilliant text by the librettist C. Jennens. Handel's highly original overture, expressing "a mood without hope . . . and the violent, fruitless upward striving of the oppressed," provides a perfect context for the opening words of Isaiah 40. Common to Handel and Isaianic tradition was a compassion for the poor and needy, which makes his interpretation of 40:11 (with 35:5-6); 52:7; and chap. 53 especially effective.

Examples of nineteenth-century musical interpretations of Isaiah include the superb setting of parts of chap. 40, including "Alles Fleisch es ist wie Gras" in Brahms's *German Requiem* (1857–68), and the "Battle Hymn of the Republic" (1862), written by the women's rights campaigner J. Ward Howe on themes from Isa 63:1-3 and 30:28 combined with Rev 19:15.

A number of twentieth-century works composed or commissioned by Jews, including Martinu's *The Prophecy of Isaiah* (premiere, Jerusalem 1963), pick up the recurring Zion motif in Isaiah (e.g., 2:2-5; 26:1-6; 40:9-11; 52:1-2; 62; 65:17-25). Chapters 40–55 have provided the inspiration for some of the best-known and best-loved Christian hymns composed in the 1970s, mostly by Roman Catholics, and now regularly sung at folk masses and other Christian gatherings throughout the English-speaking world. These include settings of 43:1-7; 49:15; 52:7; 54:10; and 55:12.

4. Modern Scholarship. H. GROTIUS rejected the traditional christological interpretation of many passages (e.g., 7:14; 9:6; 11:1-2; 42:1; 53) in favor of philological exegesis. The theologian and orientalist J. COCCEIUS found some remarkable historical references in Isaiah (e.g., the death of Constantine in 19:2 and of Gustavus Adolphus in 33:7). The epoch-making two-volume commentary by C. VITRINGA (c. 1659–1722) introduced notions of literary unity, structure, composition, purpose, and even READER RESPONSE, while R. LOWTH's influential *Isaiah: A New Translation with a preliminary dissertation and notes* (1778) also achieved a new sensitivity to the literary and aesthetic qualities of Isaiah.

But it was with the question of authorship that the age of modern critical scholarship can be said to have begun. Apart from a few remarks by Ibn Ezra (see above), it was not until the eighteenth century that scholars seriously suggested that the prophet Isaiah was not the sole author of the book that bears his name. A commentary by J. Döderlein's (1775, 1789) and the pioneering HB introduction of J. G. EICHHORN (1780–83; ET 1888) put forward the view that the author of Isaiah 40–66 lived in sixth-century BCE Babylon. The destruction of Jerusalem and the Babylonian exile are presupposed, not foretold (44:26-28; 48:20-21; 49:19-

21, etc.). The style and imagery of chaps. 40–66 have a distinctiveness and unity that separate them from 1–39: e.g., repeated imperatives (40:1; 51:9; 52:1, 9); "the servant of the Lord" (42:1; 44:1, 21; 49:3; 52:13, etc.); the personification of Zion (40:9-11; 49:14-18; 52:1-2; 54:1-8; 66:7-14). There are theological innovations such as explicit monotheism (44:6, 8; 45:5, 6, 14, 18, 21, 22), a new emphasis on cosmology (40:12-17; 45:18-19; 51:9-11), and a reinterpretation of the exodus traditions (43:1-2; 48:20-21; 52:11-12), which are not found in eighth-century prophecy.

The identification of a "Second Isaiah" or "Deutero-Isaiah" as the author of chaps. 40–66 caused much less of a furor than did challenges to the Mosaic authorship of the Pentateuch (see PENTATEUCHAL CRITICISM) published at about the same time and was almost universally accepted by Protestant and Roman Catholic scholars alike by the end of the nineteenth century. In 1908, however, the Pontifical Biblical Commission issued a decree rejecting the evidence for the multiple authorship of Isaiah, but this ultra-conservative view was finally abandoned by Roman Catholic scholars in 1943 following the papal encyclical *Divino afflante spiritu*. There have been several attempts by conservative scholars to defend the unity of Isaiah, such as those of O. Allis (1950) and E. Young (1965–72), but most twentieth-century commentaries handle chaps. 1–39 and chaps. 40–66 separately, and a number of scholars have written separate commentaries on Deutero-Isaiah alone.

B. DUHM's brilliant commentary (1892, 1922⁴) contained a number of conclusions on date and authorship, primarily directed at discovering the original Isaiah, but pointing to features of the book that are today almost universally accepted. The situation was much more complicated than had been assumed previously. The *ipsissima verba* of Isaiah were held to occur mostly within two "collections" (chaps. 1–12 and 28–33) and a "historical appendix" (chaps. 36–39). Deutero-Isaiah composed chaps. 13–14 and 34–35 (as well as 40–55) during the Babylonian exile, and a third Isaiah (Trito-Isaiah), living in the time of Malachi (c. 490), was the author of chaps. 56–66. Of chapters 24–27 Duhm says, "Isaiah could as well have written the Book of Daniel as this text," and dates its final form to 127 BCE. The general importance of these insights for the interpretation of Isaiah cannot be overestimated, even though the historical accuracy of some of them may be disputed. Duhm's analysis of an eighth-century prophetic core in the book combining relentless demands for social justice (e.g., 1:10-20; 5:8-23; 6:9-11; 10:1-4; 28:1-4; 29:13-14; 30:1-17) with messianic visions of a better age to come (e.g., 2:2-6; 9:1-6 [Eng. 2-7]; 11:1-8; 32:1-5, 15-20) is impressive. His use of Daniel, "Maccabean" psalms, Enoch, and other intertestamental literature to elucidate passages such as those about Jews in Egypt (19:16-25) and the resurrection of the dead (26:19; 53:11; 66:23-

24) is also suggestive.

Duhm is best remembered for his identification of the four "Songs of the Servant of Yahweh" (42:1-4; 49:1-6; 50:4-11; 52:13–53:12). He argued that they were clearly distinct in thought and style, although not unrelated to the rest of Deutero-Isaiah, and could be removed from their present context without leaving any gaps. In the songs, especially in the last one, the "Servant" is an individual, while in the rest of Deutero-Isaiah he is named as the people Jacob/Israel (41:8-9; 44:1, 21, etc.). "Israel" in 49:3 has to be removed as a gloss. The "Servant Songs" were written in the first half of the fifth century, after Job and before Malachi, and in that context Duhm identified the Servant with a prophetic teacher of the law (cf. Mal 2:5-6; Isa 57:1). His use of Job, Malachi, Trito-Isaiah, Ezra-Nehemiah, and some of the "Torah-Psalms" (e.g., 119) greatly illuminates the exegesis of the "Servant Songs" whether or not one accepts his conclusions.

Since Duhm, no other part of Isaiah has been more discussed than these "Servant Songs." If we accept his assumption that they are to be taken together and tell the story of an individual chosen by God (42:1; 49:1, 4, 5) to bring justice and salvation to the ends of the earth (42:1, 4; 49:6), who suffers humiliation, persecution, and death (49:4; 50:6; 53:2-11), but is later exalted (49:3; 52:13; 53:12), then the main question is likely to be who he is. Early proposals included Cyrus, Zerubbabel, Jehoiachin, Moses, and Deutero-Isaiah himself. The author may have had some ideal figure in mind, reflecting such contemporary events as the release of Jehoiachin from prison in 560 BCE (2 Kgs 25:27-30) and perhaps his own personal experiences, but transcending them. His highly original use of the exodus motif would lend support to the theory that the servant is a "New Moses" willing to suffer for his people (Exod 32:32; Deut 1:9-12). I. ENGNELL found traces of the MYTH AND RITUAL of divine kingship in the "Songs," including a description of the suffering of the servant in language reminiscent of a Babylonian ritual (50:6), his death and rising again (53:7-12), and the fertility motif (53:2). Traditional messianic interpretations of the first and last of the "Servant Songs" (see above) have also been extended by some to the other two in such a way as to trace the life story of a suffering messiah (closely parallel to that of Christ) through the four poems.

In addition to all these individual interpretations, there have been attempts to keep the continuity between the "Songs" and the rest of Deutero-Isaiah and to argue for a corporate interpretation. The community "Israel/Jacob" is addressed as an individual in many passages outside the "Songs" (40:27; 41:14; 43:1; 44:1, etc.). There are close parallels between the Servant Songs and the rest of Isaiah 40–55 (e.g., 44:1 to 49:1), not to mention the specific identification of the Servant as "Israel" in 49:3, which, whether it is a gloss or not,

proves that a corporate interpretation is possible. The *reductio ad absurdum* of this line of argument was reached with the "fluid" theory that the Servant is both an individual and the community and that a distinction between them is a modern European one.

The "Servant Song" problem hinged on Duhm's assumption that the four passages in question must be taken together as telling a single story, and its fascination for modern (almost exclusively Christian) scholars was greatly increased by correspondences between that story and the Gospels. In effect, much of the exegesis of these passages in the twentieth century has been, often unintentionally, the modern critical equivalent of early Christian interpretations. Once Duhm's assumption is questioned (Mettinger), the differences between one "Song" and another appear more striking than those between the "Servant Songs" and the rest of Isaiah. The first passage becomes just another messianic prophecy in the traditional Isaianic mold (cf. 9:1-6 [Eng. 9:2-7]; 11:1-5; 32:1-5), especially if 42:2 is interpreted impersonally as "there will be no more crying . . . in the street" (D. Jones). Isaiah 49:1-6 and 50:4-9 are autobiographical: Either the prophet himself or the community (as in 40:27; 49:1, 21) is speaking. The "Suffering Servant" poem in 52:13–53:12 is what it has always been, a unique theological statement on suffering. Isaiah 52:13 exploits the language of Isaiah's vision of God in 6:1 (cf. 57:15); and 53:4-6 uses the technical terminology of the atonement ritual in Leviticus 16, no matter who the "Servant of the Lord" is.

Much modern scholarship since Duhm has been devoted to literary form, and this has yielded some useful results for the interpretation of Isaiah. R. Scott's (1957) identification of "embryonic oracles" ("brief, striking, enigmatic and marked by a strong rhythm, verbal symmetry, paronomasia, assonance and a preponderance of sibilant and guttural sounds") sought to get back to the pre-literary stage of prophetic revelation (e.g., 5:7; 7:9; 8:3-4; 9:17; 30:15). It was proposed that the famous dynastic prophecy in 9:1-6 (Eng. 9:2-7) contains the remains of the five royal names of Egyptian enthronement protocol. J. BEGRICH's identification and analysis of the priestly "Salvation Oracle" (*Heilsorakel*), developed in C. WESTERMANN's commentary (1969), greatly assists the literary appreciation of Isaiah. Thus 41:14-16 is in the form of a priest's response to an individual lament such as Psalm 22:7-9 (Eng. 22:6-8; cf. Isa 43:1-7; 44:1-5; 54:4-8). Study of hymns (e.g., Exod 15:1-18; Deut 32:1-43; Psalms 8, 19) and especially the "Enthronement Psalms" (e.g., 74; 89; 93; 94–100) has illuminated Deutero-Isaiah's use of creation motifs in language about the new exodus (e.g., Isa 42:5-9, 10-17; 43:14-21; 44:23-28; 45; 51:9-11; 52:7-12).

The Assyrian invasions of Samaria and Judah in the eighth century BCE have been the subject of a number of historical and literary studies that take into account contemporary Assyrian documents. Isaiah 8:23 (Eng.

9:1) has been presumed to contain reference to Tiglath-pileser III's invasions of 734–732 and to the creation of three Assyrian provinces subsequently established in Gilead, Galilee, and the coastal region (2 Kgs 15:29). Sennacherib's destruction of all the cities of Judah except Jerusalem in 701 (2 Kgs 18:13; Isa 36:1) is referred to in many passages, reflecting the fear of an approaching army (5:26-30; 10:28-32; 37:1-4) and the scenes of destruction surrounding Jerusalem (1:7-9; 8:7-8). The almost wholly fictitious account of Jerusalem's miraculous victory in that year (2 Kgs 19:35-37; Isa 37:36-38) was probably composed at a time of national revival under Josiah (640–609). The Isaiah version entirely omits reference to Jerusalem's surrender (cf. 2 Kgs 18:14-18).

Recent work on the so-called Isaiah Apocalypse (24–27) suggests that, although it exhibits few of the literary characteristics of the later Jewish apocalypses (e.g., Daniel; *Enoch;* 2 Esdras; Revelation), it does contain apocalyptic eschatology (see APOCALYPTICISM), possibly traceable to the struggle between hierocratic and visionary parties in Judaism from the sixth century BCE on (cf. 56:9–57:13; 60:19-20; 66:1-4, 17-24). But Ugaritic studies (see UGARIT AND THE BIBLE), which have thrown light on the language and MYTHOLOGY of passages like 25:6-8 (cf. 2:2-4) and 27:1, remind us of the antiquity of these traditions.

Interest in the structure and purpose of larger literary units (e.g., chaps. 1–12; 1–35; 2–4; 13–23) has led to renewed consideration of the literary and theological unity of the book of Isaiah as a whole. Emphasis on the Babylonian material in chaps. 13–14 and 34–35 as well as in 40–55 and the function of chaps. 36–39 as a transition passage linking the Assyrian to the Babylonian period suggests some deliberate editorial control of the Isaianic material. Recurring phrases and motifs, like "the Holy One of Israel," "high and lifted up" (6:1; 52:13; 57:15) Zion/Jerusalem, "faith," "justice," and "righteousness," give the book a thematic unity, as do such passages as 1:4-6 (cf. 53:1-9); 6:1-9 (cf. 40:1-8); 9:2 (cf. 60:1-2); and 11:6-9 (cf. 65:25), where early themes are developed later.

5. Some Recent Developments. Twentieth-century human rights activists and freedom fighters have found inspiration in Isaianic visions of, and calls for, justice and peace. The pronouncement of the Second Vatican Council (1962–65) on justice and peace begins with a quotation from Isa 32:17 (*Gaudium et Spes* 70), and in the whole revolution within the Roman Catholic Church that followed Vatican II, Isaiah has played a prominent role, increasingly being depicted as the prophet of justice and peace, rather than the prophet of the nativity and the passion.

In *Marx and the Bible* (1971) by J. Miranda, Isaiah is the most often quoted HB book next to Psalms, but a passage like 7:14, so popular in an earlier age, is not even mentioned, while 11:3-4 completely eclipses 11:1-2. His interpretations of "rulers of Sodom" (1:10) in terms of injustice (cf. Ezek 16:49), rather than in sexual terms, and "wickedness" in 58:9 as a pragmatic social term rather than a magical or mystical one are motivated by concern for the politically oppressed. Similar considerations lead to an interpretation of the word play in 5:7 (the Hebrew words for "justice" and "bloodshed" sound similar, as do the words for "righteousness" and "cry") as having a more concrete and at the same time more poignant meaning elucidated by the following verse. Passages like 43:1; 44:2; and 45:9-11, in which the liberation of Israel from oppression is described as an act of creation, are given new force by the bias of LIBERATION THEOLOGIES and are applied to issues of justice and freedom in this world.

Another example of how certain texts have taken on a new significance in light of post-Vatican II developments is to be found in the FEMINIST INTERPRETATION of Isaiah. P. Trible (*Texts of Terror* [1984]) applies verses from Isaiah 53 to suffering women. R. Reuther (*Sexism and God-talk* [1983]) identifies women among "the afflicted . . . the brokenhearted . . . the captives . . . those that are bound" of 61:1 (cf. Luke 4:27).

Of the few biblical passages in which the feminine nature of God is described, most are in Isaiah, and these, too, have now taken on a new significance. The image of a God who suffers for us as a woman suffers the pangs of childbirth appears twice in Isaiah (42:14; 45:10). Another feminine image in Isaiah is that of a mother's love for her child (49:15), which may be compared with the final vision of Zion as a mother dandling her baby on her knee, while God is the midwife (66:7-14). The Hebrew word translated "compassion" is etymologically related to a word for "womb" and is undoubtedly used to special effect here (49:13, 15). Feminine imagery is unusually prominent in Isaiah, not only in the way God is described, but also in the way the people of God are addressed as a woman (feminine singular) in passages like 40:9; 51:17; 52:1; 54:1; and 60:1. This uniquely effective feature of Isaianic style was not fully recognized until modern feminist interpreters appreciated its significance.

Bibliography: S. Ackerman, "Isaiah," *Women's Bible Commentary* (ed. C. A. Newsom and S. H. Ringe, 1992) 161-68. **P. R. Ackroyd,** "Isaiah 36–39: Structure and Function," *Von Kanaan bis Kerala: Festschrift für Prof. Mag. Dr. Dr. J. P. M. van der Ploeg* (1982) 3-21. **O. T. Allis,** *The Unity of Isaiah: A Study in Prophecy* (1950). **J. Begrich,** *Studien zu Deuterojesaja* (1938). **P. E. Bonnard,** *Le Second Isaïe* (1972). **L. Bronner,** "Gynomorphic Imagery in Exilic Isaiah (40–66)," *Dor le Dor* 12 (1983–84) 71-83. **C. C. Broyles and C. A. Evans** (eds.), *Writing and Reading the Scroll of Isaiah: Studies of an Interpretive Tradition* (2 vols., VTSup 70, 1997). **T. K. Cheyne,** *Introduction to the Book of Isaiah* (1895). **B. S.**

Childs, *Introduction to the OT as Scripture* (1979) 311-38. **R. E. Clements,** *Isaiah and the Deliverance of Jerusalem* (JSOT-Sup 13, 1980); *Isaiah 1–39* (1980). **R. Clifford,** *Fair Spoken and Persuading: An Interpretation of Second Isaiah* (1984). **D. J. A. Clines,** *I, He, We and They: A Literary Approach to Isaiah 53* (1976). **J. C. Döderlein,** *Esaias ex recensione textus hebrae ad fidem codd. quorundam mss. et versionum antiquarum latine vertit notasque varii argumenti subiecit* (1775, 1789). **S. R. Driver and A. Neubauer,** *The Fifty-third Chapter of Isaiah According to the Jewish Interpreters* (2 vols., 1876–77). **B. Duhm,** *Das Buch Jesai, übersetzt und erklärt* (HKNT 3/1, 1892, 1922⁴). **J. Eaton,** "The Isaiah Tradition," *Israel's Prophetic Tradition: Essays in Honour of Peter R. Ackroyd* (1982) 58-76. **J. G. Eichhorn,** *Introduction to the Study of the OT* (1780–83; ET 1888). **O. Eissfeldt,** *The OT: An Introduction* (1934; ET 1965) 303-46. **I. Engnell,** "The Ebed Yahweh Songs and the Suffering Messiah in Deutero-Isaiah," *BJRL* 31 (1948) 54-93. **G. Fohrer,** "The Origin, Composition, and Tradition of Isaiah I–XXXIV," *ALUOS* 3 (1962) 3-38 = BZAW 99 (1967) 113-47. **F. Giesebrecht,** *Beiträge zur Jesajakritik* (1890). **P. Grelot,** *Les Poèmes du Serviteur* (LD 103, 1981). **E. Hammershaimb,** "The Immanuel Sign," *StTh* 3 (1949) 124-42. **A. J. Heschel,** *The Prophets* (1962) 61-97, 145-55. **D. R. Jones,** "II–III Isaiah," *PCB* 516-36. **O. Kaiser,** *Isaiah 1–12* (OTL, 1983); *Isaiah 13–39* (OTL, 1974). **J. Kerman,** *The Masses and Motets of William Byrd* (1980) 40-44. **A. Kerrigan,** *St. Cyril of Alexandria, Interpreter of the OT* (AnBib 2, 1952). **R. Kilian,** *Jesaja 1–39* (EdF 200, 1983). **M. A. Knibb** (ed.), "Martyrdom and Ascension of Isaiah," *OTP* 2:143-76. **J. P. Larsen,** *Handel's Messiah* (1957); *Luther's Works* (ed. J. Pelikan and H. C. Oswald, 16 [1969]; 17 [1972]). **E. Male,** *Religious Art in France: Thirteenth Century* (1913). **T. Mettinger,** *A Farewell to the Servant Songs* (1983). **W. R. Millar,** *Isaiah 24–27 and the Origin of Apocalyptic* (HSM 11, 1976). **S. Mowinckel,** *He That Cometh* (1956) 96-124, 155-257. **G. R. North,** *The Suffering Servant in Deutero-Isaiah: An Historical and Critical Study* (1948); *The Second Isaiah* (1964). **H. Odeberg,** *Trito-Isaiah* (1931). **G. von Rad,** *OT Theology* 2 (1965) 238-62. **E. I. J. Rosenthal,** "The Study of the Bible in Medieval Judaism," *CHB* 2 (1969) 252-79. **H. H. Rowley,** *The Servant of the Lord, and Other Essays on the OT* (1952). **J. F. A. Sawyer,** "Blessed Be My People Egypt (Isa 19:24-25)," *A Word in Season: Essays in Honour of William McKane* (ed. J. D. Martin and P. R. Davies, 1986) 57-71; "The Daughter of Zion and the Servant of the Lord in Isaiah: A Comparison," *JSOT* 44 (1989) 89-107; *The Fifth Gospel: Isaiah in the History of Christianity* (1996). **R. B. Y. Scott,** "The Literary Structure of Isaiah's Oracles," *Studies in OT Prophecy: Presented to Professor Theodore H. Robinson* (ed. H. H. Rowley, repr. 1957) 175-86. **I. L. Seeligmann,** *The Septuagint Version of Isaiah* (1948). **B. Smalley,** *The Study of the Bible in the Middle Ages* (1983³) 112-95. **J. F. Stenning,** *The Targum of Isaiah* (1949). **M. Sweeney,** *Isaiah 1-39* (FOTL 16, 1996). **C. C. Torrey,** *The Second Isaiah* (1928). **J. Van Ruiten and M. Vervenne** (eds.), *Studies in the Book of Isaiah* (FS W. A. M. Beuken, BETL 132, 1997). **G. Vermes,** *The Dead Sea Scrolls in English* (1987³) 61-62, 88, 267-70, 300-301. **J. Vermeylen,** *Du Prophète Isaïe à l'Apocalyptique, Isaïe, I–XXXV, miroir d'un demi-millénarie d'experience religieuse en Israel* (Études Bibliques, 2 vols., 1977–78). **J. Vermeylen** (ed.), *The Book of Isaiah—Le Livre d'Isaïe: Les oracles et leurs relectures. Unité et complexité de l'ouvrage* (BETL 81, 1989). **A. Watson,** *The Early Iconography of the Tree of Jesse* (1934, repr. 1978). **C. Westermann,** *Isaiah 40–66* (1969). **J. W. Whedbee,** *Isaiah and Wisdom* (1971). **B. Wiklander,** *Prophecy as Literature: A Text-linguistical and Rhetorical Approach* (ConBOT 22, 1984). **E. J. Young,** *The Book of Isaiah* (NICOT, 1965–72).

J. F. A. SAWYER

ISHMAEL BEN ELISHA (late 1st–early 2nd cent. CE)

I. appears to have come from a priestly family. As a child he was taken captive to Rome following the destruction of the Second Temple, but was ransomed by R. Joshua, whose pupil he became. He also studied under R. Nehunyah b. ha-Kanah. I. lived at Kefar Aziz, south of Hebron, and was a participant at the academy in Yabneh. The students and followers of I., or of his school, were the source of many of the halakhic Midrashim (see MIDRASH) on biblical books: the *Mekhilta de-R. Ishmael* on Exodus, the *Sifrei* on Numbers, and part of the *Sifrei* on Deuteronomy.

I. advocated a literal interpretation of the biblical text and the avoidance of reading too much into a text. He was willing to allow a halakhic (legal) regulation to stand without a biblical justification rather than stretch a passage to yield the meaning. In this regard he advocated the principle that "the Scriptures speak a human language" (*dibra tora kileshon bne adam*)—that is, Scripture is to be read in a straightforward manner. He employed this expression (which he appears to have borrowed from R. Eleazar b. Azaryah) with regard to legal matters, but it later became a principle used to argue that in Scripture God accommodated divine teaching to the capacity of human understanding.

Thirteen *middot* (measure, norms, or rules) of biblical interpretation are attributed to I. in the introduction to *Sipra* on Numbers. (Actually, the number is traditional; the rules total sixteen.) These rules have played a significant role in Judaism and constitute a part of the daily morning prayer. I.'s *middot* are primarily an expansion of the seven rules of HILLEL. The style of the list atributed to I. indicates that it is composite, and exegetical comments attributed to I. in rabbinic sources illustrate the use of only four or five of these *middot*. Rule 13, "If two verses contradict one another, they may be reconciled by a third," is not included in Hillel's list.

Bibliography: **D. Daube,** "Rabbinic Methods of Interpretation and Hellenistic Rhetoric," *HUCA* 22 (1949) 239-64. **K. Froehlich,** *Biblical Interpretations in the Early Church* (1984) 30-36. **L. Jacobs,** "Hermeneutics," *EncJud* 8 (1971) 366-72. **S. Lieberman,** *Hellenism in Jewish Palestine* (1962²) 47-82.

G. G. Porton, *The Traditions of Rabbi I.* (4 vols., SJLA 19, 1976–82); "Rabbi I. and his Thirteen *Middot*," *New Perspectives on Ancient Judaism,* vol. 1 (ed. J. Neusner et al., BJS 260 [1990], repr. of 1987 ed.) 3-18. **S. Safrai,** *EncJud* 9 (1972) 83-86. **H. L. Strack and G. Stemberger,** *Introduction to the Talmud and Midrash* (1992) 23-25.

J. H. HAYES

ISIDORE OF SEVILLE (c. 560–636)

Born into a prominent Hispano-Roman family who had emigrated to Spain from Carthage before his birth, I. was educated under the supervision of his older brother Leander, archbishop of Seville from c. 584, probably at the episcopal school of that see. The civil and ecclesiastical developments of his day profoundly affected him. After a long period of disorder, during which various Germanic tribes invaded Spain, King Leovigild stabilized Visigothic rule and tried to impose his Arian faith (see ARIUS) on the entire population. Under Leander's influence, Leovigild's son Reccared converted to Christianity. The conversion of the Visigoths was formalized when King Reccared renounced the Arian creed at the Third Council of Toledo (589), over which Leander presided. During I.'s formative years, therefore, Visigothic rule became secure and a close alliance between the Visigothic oligarchy and the (predominantly Hispano-Roman) Catholic Church was forged. Conciliar decrees from this period contained both civil and ecclesiastical legislation, and the codes of civil law contained canonical legislation. I. succeeded Leander as archbishop of Seville c. 600; in this role, he, like his brother, was both statesman and churchman.

The topics of I.'s writing ranged from history to natural science to theology and exegesis. He wrote primarily as a pastor and a pragmatist in order to provide the necessary intellectual resources for the Spanish church. Cultured as well as pious, I. put into practice the ideals advocated in AUGUSTINE's *De doctrina christiana,* whereby secular and pagan learning should be exploited so that Christian culture might be provided with a requisite level of literacy. Canon 25 of the Fourth Council of Toledo (633), over which I. presided, determined that each diocese should provide the clergy with a biblical and canonical education (see C. J. von Hefele and H. Leclercq, *Histoire des Conciles* 3.1 [1909] 271).

Most of I.'s writings are essentially textbooks, manuals, and reference books. He helped to establish two salient characteristics of medieval thought: first, the assumption that all wisdom was contained in ancient texts (with the corresponding effort to preserve, distribute, and pass on this treasure); and second, the dependence on compilations. I.'s most famous work, which enjoyed extraordinary popularity during the Middle Ages, is his *Etymologiae.* Comprising twenty books, it is an encyclopedia (see DICTIONARIES AND ENCYCLOPE-DIAS) covering topics ranging from the liberal arts to sacred doctrine and including such areas as zoology and mineralogy. (The books, divisions, and authors of the Bible are discussed in book 6.1-2, and the meanings of biblical names in 7.6-10.) His treatment of each area is founded upon definitions and etymologies. While many of the latter are still acceptable, some now appear fanciful. These were not intended to be historical etymologies (for there was hardly any notion of linguistic evolution at that time), but rather presupposed a certain structure or order within the language, an order corresponding to that existing in the cosmos by virtue of the Word. His *Sententiae* is a handbook of dogmatic, moral, and pastoral theology, while *De ecclesiasticis officiis* summarizes the vocational, liturgical, and sacramental institutions of the church. His *De fide catholica ex Veteri et Novo Testamento contra Iudaeos,* neither an apologetic nor a polemical treatise, attempts to expound the doctrine of Christ briefly while setting it on the secure foundation of both testaments. (I. took a moderate stance toward Jews, and seems to have opposed the policy of conversion by force instituted by his friend King Sisebut in 614.)

I.'s exegesis depended largely on the mystical (i.e., allegorical or typological) sense. Of his exegetical treatises, the *Quaestiones in vetus Testamentum* (*PL* 83:207-424) comes nearest to being commentatorial. It comprises detailed mystical interpretations of passages and events from the Pentateuch (see PENTATEUCHAL CRITICISM), Joshua, Judges, Samuel, Kings, Ezra, and Maccabees. I. stated that he derived these interpretations from ORIGEN, Victorinus (d. c. 304), AMBROSE, JEROME, Augustine, Fulgentius (c. 462–527), Cassian (c. 360–430), and GREGORY THE GREAT (209A), but Augustine was his main source. The other substantive treatises may be justly regarded as manuals or works of reference. Thus the *Allegoriae quaedam sacrae Scripturae* (*PL* 83:97-130) explains the allegorical meanings of numerous personages (named and unnamed) from both testaments. Adam is a figure of Christ, Mary of the church, each of the four evangelist-figures (man, lion, calf, and eagle) symbolizes a different aspect of Christ, and so on. The *Liber numerorum* (*PL* 83:179-200) explains the mystical sense of numbers. The *In libros veteris ac novi Testamenti proemia* (*PL* 83:155-80) briefly introduces each book of the CANON (including the deuterocanonical books and the *Apocalypse of John*). The *De ortu et obitu Patrum* (*PL* 83:129-56) is made up of biographies, with some typology, of the patriarchs. For this last work, I. was indebted to a Latin translation of a Greek treatise (see J. Madoz [1960] 38).

I.'s canon was essentially the same as that recognized by the Council of Trent (see J. Hilgarth [1983] 874). He accepted the Apocalypse as canonical, a thesis that was still controvertible. Canon 17 of the Fourth Council of Toledo (633), over which I. presided, decreed on pain of excommunication that the Apocalypse should be accepted as one of the "divine books" and read liturgically between Easter and Pentecost (see Hefele and Leclercq, 3.1, 270; Madoz [1960], 123).

Of the works listed as I.'s *opera exegetica* in the *Clavis Patrum Latinorum* (1961), one, the *Quaestiones de veteri et novo Testamento,* has subsequently been shown to be inauthentic. McNally (1963) pointed out that it reveals the influence of Irish biblical scholarship and argued that it comes from southern Germany c. 750.

Works: *Opera omnia* (7 vols., ed. F. Arévalo, 1797–1803) = *PL* 81-84; *Etymologiarum sive originum* (2 vols., ed. W. M. Lindsay, 1911); *Etymologies* (French and Latin: Auteurs latins du moyen âge; Book IX [ed. M. Reydellet, 1984]; Book XVII [ed. J. André, 1981]); *Etimologias* (Spanish and Latin, ed. J. Oroz Reta, 1982); *De ecclesiasticus officiis* (CCSL 113, ed. C. M. Lawson, 1989); *De ortu et obitu patrum* (Auteurs latins du moyen âge, ed. C. Gómez, 1985); see E. Dekkers and A. Gaar, *Clavis Patrum Latinorum* (1961), nn. 1886-1229.

Bibliography: F. Arévalo, *Isidoriana* (*Opera omnia,* vol. 1 = *PL* 81). T. Ayuso Marazuela, "Algunos problemas del texto bíblico de I.," *Isidoriana: Colección de estudios sobre I. S.* (ed. M. C. Díaz y Díaz, 1961) 143-91; *La Biblia visigóthica de San Isidoro de León* (1965). B. Bischoff, "Die europaische Verbreitung der Werke I. S.," *Isidoriana,* 317-44 = his *Mittelalterliche Studien I* (1966) 171-94. M. C. Díaz y Díaz, "Introducción," *Etimologías* (ed. J. Oroz Reta, 1982). H.-J. Diesner, *I. S. und seine Zeit* (1973). J. Fontaine, *I. S et la culture classique dans l'Espagne wisigothique* (2 vols., 1959; 3 vols., 1983²), with extensive bibliography; "Theorie et pratique du style chez I. S.," *VC* 14 (1960) 65-101; *Tradition et actualité chez I. S.* (1988); *EAC* 1 (1992) 418-19. J. H. Hillgarth, "The Position of Isidorian Studies: A Critical Review of the Literature 1936–75," *StMed* 24 (1983) 817-905 (on I.'s Bible, 874-75; on his exegesis, 831-32). J. Madoz, *San I. S.: Semblanza de su personalidad literaria* (1960) 36-42 (on his exegetical treatises). R. E. McNally, "Isidoriana," *TS* 20 (1959) 432-42; "The Pseudo-Isidorian De vetere et novo Testamento quaestiones," *Traditio* 19 (1963) 37-50. F. Ogara, "Tipología bíblica seqún S. Isidoro," *Miscellanea Isidoriana* (1936) 135-50. B. Recaredo García, *Espiritualidad y "lectio divina" en las "Sentencias" de San I. S.* (1980). A. Tapia Basulto, "El canon escriturístico en San I. S.," *CTom* 58 (1939) 364-88. S. M. Zarb, "S. Isidori cultus erga Sacras Litteras," *Miscellanea Isidoriana* (1936) 135-50.

P. L. REYNOLDS

J

Jacob ben Ḥayyim Ibn Adoniyahu
(d. between 1527 and 1538)

A Kabbalist and Talmudist, J. was educated in Tunisia. Forced to flee due to persecutions in 1510, he wandered around Europe until he reached Venice about 1520. He worked as a proofreader and editor of Hebrew books in D. Bomberg's publishing house, where during the 1520s he edited several books in the fields of Kabbalah, Talmud, *halakhah*, Bible, and liturgy. He converted to Christianity sometime after 1527 (the date of the last book he edited for Bomberg, with an introduction that hints at his wavering) and before 1538 (when mentioned by E. Levita in *Massoret Ha-Massoret* as a convert and as dead).

The following is a chronological list of the books J. edited for Bomberg: (1) *Alfasi with Commentaries and Tosefta* (vol. 1, 1521; vols. 2–3, 1522). (Although the chief editor of vol. 1 was R. Ḥiyya Meir ben David, J. helped in editing these halakhic-Talmudic works). (2) *Ẓeror Ha-Mor,* a kabbalistic commentary on the Pentateuch (see Pentateuchal criticism), by R. Abraham Saba (1522–23). (3) Novellae on tractate *Bava Batra* by Nachmanides (1523). (4) Novellae on tractate *Berakhot* by Rashba (1523). (5) Novellae on tractate *Hullin* by Rashba (1523). (6) Novellae on tractate *Gittin* by Rashba (1523). (7) *Sefer Ha-Terumah* by R. Barukh ben Isaac of Worms (1523). (8) Commentary of R. Menaḥem Recanati on the Pentateuch, a kabbalistic commentary (1523). (9) *Seder Tahorot,* with the commentary of R. Samson of Sens (1523). In this edition J. added his own glosses. (10) *Sefer Ha-Hinukh,* explanations for the commandments (1523). (11) *Meʾir Nativ,* a biblical concordance by R. Isaac Natan (1523). (12) The Jerusalem Talmud (1522–24). (13) *Mishneh Torah* of Maimonides, with commentaries, which J. edited with R. D. Pizzighetone (2 vol., 1523–24). (14) The Rabbinic Bible (= biblical text and the Masorah, with Targum and two commentaries), with an introduction by J. (4 vols., 1524–25). (15) The Liturgy according to the Italian Rite (2 vol., 1525–26) with an introduction by J. (16) Pentateuch with Targum, Megillot, and Haftorot (1527), which contains an introduction by J. In half of these books, J. explicitly signed the colophon or the introduction. The other half of the books are to be attributed to J. based on the unique style of Aramaic in the title page; the Hebrew language style of the colophon or the title page typical of J.; and the content.

In addition to these printed books, three manuscripts, which J. copied prior to his arrival in Venice, reflect his knowledge of Talmud and Kabbalah. (1) MS Bodleiana 2253 contains selections from *Darkhei Ha-Talmud,* written by R. Isaac Qanpanton and arranged by J. (2) MS Jerusalem 8⁰5497/1 (= MS Nehorai 5/1) contains *Sefer Ha-Gevul* (written by R. David ben Judah Ha-Ḥasid, grandson of Nachmanides), a kabbalistic commentary on part of the *Zohar.* This work was originally copied by J. for R. Jacob de Cuéllar; but J. clearly copied the manuscript prior to 1520, maybe in Europe. (3) MS Munich 59 contains four kabbalistic works: (a) *ʾOr Ha-Seikhel* by R. Abraham Abulafia; (b) *Sod Eseer Ha-Sefirot;* (c) *Keter Shem Tov* by R. Abraham ben Alexander of Cologne; (d) *Sodot Be-Kabbala,* apparently by J. himself. There is an explicit colophon at the end of the first and fourth works, and the copyist's name also appears toward the beginning of the second work. These four works and forty other Hebrew Munich manuscripts were copied in Venice in 1550–52 (M. Benayahu [1984] 787-88).

J. is usually remembered as the editor of the second rabbinic Bible, for which he added a detailed introduction and edited the apparatus of the Masorah for the first time. This edition, which J. undertook because he was convinced that the previous rabbinic Bible issued by Bomberg was inaccurate (e.g., in matters of plene and defective spellings), came to be accepted as the *textus receptus* of the Bible.

Bibliography: M. Benayahu, "R. Ezra of Fano...." *Rabbi J. B. Soloveitchik Jubilee Volume* (1984) 2:787-88 (Hebrew; on Munich MSS). N. Brüll, *Blätter für jüdische Geschichte und Literatur* 7 (1895) 45 (on J.'s brother—noted by Marx; in 1538 he copied MS St. Petersburg, Ebr. I 63 = I. Abarbanel's *Maʿayanei Ha-Yeshuʿa*). M. Marx, *Geschichte des hebräischen Buchdruckes in Venedig,* vol. 1, *Die Anfage-Bomberg* (2 vols., 1937, typescript; part of his larger work *Geschichte und Annalen des hebräischen Buchdruckes in Italien im Sechszehnten Jahrhundert* in several vols., in typescript, all available on microfilm from Hebrew Union College, Cincinnati). A. Neubauer (ed.), *Facsimiles of Hebrew Manuscripts in the Bodleian Library... with Transcriptions* (1896), plate X (on the MS Bodleian copied by J.). J. S. Penkower, "Jacob ben Ḥayyim and the Rise of the Biblia Rabbinica" (diss., Hebrew University, 1982), Hebrew, with extensive summary in English and detailed bibliography; *New Evidence for the Pentateuch Text in the*

Aleppo Codex (1992) 19-20, 91-92 (Hebrew, on MS Jerusalem). **A. Rosenthal,** "D. Bomberg and His Talmud Editions," *Gli Ebrei e Venezia, secoli XIV-XVIII* (ed. G. Cozzi, 1987) 390 (on vol. 1 of the Italian liturgy of 1526).

J. S. PENKOWER

JACOB, BENNO (1862–1945)

Born in Breslau, J. combined an active rabbinic career with biblical studies and national leadership in the struggle against German antisemitism. He was educated in Breslau as a favorite student of H. GRAETZ, the Jewish historian; J.'s doctorate dealt with the SEPTUAGINT text of Esther. He served congregations in Göttingen (1891–1906) and Dortmund (1906–29), and died in London.

Vigorously opposed to "higher criticism," which he regarded as speculative and often antisemitic, he subjected it to devastating ironic critiques (1905, 1916). He agreed that the Torah was composed from sources but considered them no longer identifiable; it was the task of the scholar to discover the meaning of the transmitted MT, which he generally considered far superior to the Septuagint. His approach was linguistic as he sought the forgotten nuances of biblical Hebrew (*ZAW* articles, 1896, 1897, 1898, 1900, 1902; *Im Namen Gottes* [1903]). *Im Namen* is important for its analysis of Jewish and Christian beliefs about the name of God as well as contributions to semantics and symbolic logic. His first major work (1905) undertook a detailed analysis of the tabernacle account and its symbolic and theological ideas; it also dealt with the often neglected genealogical passages and the ideas contained in their artificial construction. The numerical principles of the Torah were treated in a highly original fashion in *Die Abzählungen* (1909), while the history of legal ideas was treated in the context of the entire ancient Near East from early times to the Mishnah in *Auge um Auge* (1929). His works influenced the biblical studies of M. BUBER, F. Rosenzweig (1886–1929), G. von RAD, B. CHILDS, and Y. Leibowitz. Rosenzweig in turn persuaded J. to undertake a major modern commentary on the Torah.

His work on Genesis (1934) and Exodus (ET 1989) were J.'s most important works. Each provides new interpretations of stories, phrases, and Hebrew words and discusses virtually all previous Jewish and Christian commentaries. J. sought to discover the original intent, independent of both modern and ancient authorities, and to make it accessible both to the scholar and to the interested layperson.

Works: "Beiträge zu einer Einleitung in die Psalmen," *ZAW* 16 (1896) 129-81, 265-91; 17 (1897) 48-80, 263-79; 18 (1898) 99-119; 20 (1900) 49-80; (with W. Ebstein), *Die Medizin im Alten Testment* (1901); "Das hebräische Sprachgut im Christlich-Palestinischen," *ZAW* 22 (1902) 83-113; *Im Namen Gottes:* *Eine sprachliche und religionsgeschichtliche Untersuchung zum Alten und Neuen Testament* (1903); *Der Pentateuch: Exegetisch-kritische Forschungen* (1905); *Die Abzählungen in den Gesetzen der Bücher Leviticus und Numeri* (1909); *Quellenscheidung und Exegese im Pentateuch* (1916); *Auge um Auge: Eine Untersuchung zum Alten und Neuen Testament* (1929); *Das Erste Buch der Tora, Genesis, übersetzt und erklart* (1934; abridged ET 1974, with bibliography, 350-58); *The Second Book of the Bible, Exodus* (ET 1989).

Bibliography: M. **Eschelbacher,** *Tradition und Erneuerung* (Vereinigung für religiös-Liberales Judentum in der Schweiz 14, 1962) 210-15. **E. I. Jacob,** "Life and Work of B. Jacob," *Paul Lazarus Gedenbuch* (1961) 93-100; "B. J. als Rabbiner in Dortmund," *Aus Geschichte und Leben der Juden in Westfalen* (1962). **W. Jacob,** "The Life and Studies of B. J.," *Exodus* (1989) iii-xxx. **K. Wilhelm,** "B. J., a Militant Rabbi," *Yearbook, Leo Baeck Institute* 7 (1962) 75-94.

W. JACOB

JAHNOW, HEDWIG (1879–1944)

From the early years of the twentieth century until at least 1931, J. taught at a secondary school for young women in Marburg. She had come to know H. GUNKEL when he taught at such a school in Berlin, apparently while she was a student there (W. Baumgartner [1963] 12), and maintained contact and to some extent worked with him (see G. Lüdemann and M. Schröder [1987] 67). The highest earned academic degree she obtained was the licentiate (a step below the doctorate—see *RGG*² 4 [1930] vi); this level of recognition reflects the increased, but still unequal, status of women at the time (see F. Paulsen [1921³] 777-81). However, J. received an honorary doctorate in 1926 (H. Jahnow et al. [1994] 26). M. Plath, a student of Gunkel who published articles from 1901 on, was a colleague. Of Jewish heritage, J. perished in the concentration camp Theresienstadt (Jahnow, 26).

In her most important study J. examined the Israelite genre of laments for the dead against its worldwide background (1923). This first-class work continues to stand as a model for biblical FORM CRITICISM. In shorter essays, she dealt with feminism (see FEMINIST INTERPRETATION), the teaching of religion in public schools, and the academic study of the Bible. She expressed the wish that women be given greater opportunity outside the home (1909, 139; 1931, 682); stressed, among other things, the importance of a LITERARY study of the Bible attending to its types (1915); and pointed out east Indian parallels to an NT story motif (1925). She regarded the nonindividualistic role of women in Israel ambivalently as a step in the development of female morality, one that reflects the fact that "the history of personality is a history of pain" (1914, 426).

Works: "Neue Religionslehrpläne für die preussische höhere Mädchenschule," *Evangelische Freiheit* 9 (1909) 134-39; "Religionsunterricht in der Schule und der Konfirmandenunterricht," *Evangelische Freiheit* 10 (1910) 16-30; "Die Frau im AT," *Die Frau* 21 (1914) 352-58, 417-26; "Die literaturgeschichtliche Betrachtung der Bibel in der Schule," *Frauenbildung* 14 (1915) 1-63; *Das hebräische Leichenlied im Rahmen der Völkerdichtung* (BZAW 36, 1923); "Abdechung des Daches Mc 2:4 Lc 5:19," *ZNW* 24 (1925) 155-58; "Profane Dichtung im AT," *RGG²* 4 (1930) 1511-21; "Frauen gegen Frauen?" *Die christliche Welt* 45 (1931) 681-83.

Bibliography: W. **Baumgartner,** *RGG²* 3 (1929) 7-8; "Zum 100. Geburtstag von H. Gunkel" (VTSup 9, 1963) 1-18. H. **Jahnow et al.,** *Feministische Hermeneutik und Erstes Testament: Analysen und Interpretation* (1994). G. **Lüdemann and M. Schröder,** *Die religionsgeschichtliche Schule in Göttingen: Eine Dokumentation* (1987). F. **Paulsen,** *Geschichte des gelehrten Unterrichts* (Auf den deutschen Schulen und Universitäten vom Ausgang des Mittelalters bis zur Gegenwart 2, 1921³).

M. J. Buss

JAMES, LETTER OF

Just as the origins of the letter of James are obscure, so also is the history of its early reception. Was the author an apostle and identified as the "brother of the Lord" (Gal 1:19)? Did he write for Jewish Christians? Was the "diaspora" of 1:1 literal or symbolic? Did he write early or late? These questions puzzle us as much as they may have puzzled James's first readers.

How and when the church first appropriated James is, in fact, unclear. No official canonical list (such as the Muratorian canon) contained the letter until the late fourth century. EUSEBIUS listed James among the "disputed books," although it was "recognized by most" (*Hist. eccl.* 25.3). The Paschal Letter of ATHANASIUS (367) and the Council of Carthage (397), however, included James without any hint of indecision.

Substantive objections to James were not made, and its neglect—if such it was—seems to have been benign. The apparent silence between the letter's composition and canonization is difficult to evaluate. The authors of *1 Clement* and the *Shepherd of Hermas* may have known and used it (cf. *1 Clem.* 10 with Jas 2:23; *1 Clem.* 12 with Jas 2:25; *1 Clem.* 30 with Jas 4:6; *Mand.* 9:11 with Jas 3:15; *Mand.* 3:1 with Jas 4:5). But perhaps all three Christian moralists used common paraenetic traditions. Allusions to James in other extant writings of the second and third centuries are even more difficult to decide. None is sufficiently definite to demand James as the source.

The ALEXANDRIAN SCHOOL under CLEMENT and ORIGEN gave the letter its first explicit literary attention. Clement named James among the founders of Christian Gnosis (*Hist. eccl.* 2.1.3-4) in his *Hypotyposes,* a commentary on "all the canonical scriptures," including the disputed ones (*Hist. eccl.* 6.14.1). According to CASSIODORUS's *De Institutione Divinarum Litterarum* 8 (*PL* 70:1120), Clement's commentary included James, even though the extant Latin translation does not contain it. Origen called James an apostle and explicitly quoted from and designated the letter as Scripture (see, e.g., *Commentary on John* xix, 6, *PG* 14:569; *Homilies on Leviticus* 2, 4, *PG* 12:41; and the *Commentary on Romans* iv, 8, *PG* 14:989). After Origen, the letter came into wider use and gained AUTHORITY, as JEROME put it, "little by little" (*De Viris Illustribus* 2, *PL* 23:639).

The precritical commentary tradition is sparse. DIDYMUS THE BLIND, who was also head of the catechetical school, wrote—if we except Clement—the first Greek commentary on James (see *PG* 33). Fragments from Didymus and CHRYSOSTOM (see *PG* 64) are also found in the *Catena Graecorum Patrum* (ed. J. Cramer [1840]), together with short scholia from CYRIL, Appolinaris (fourth cent.), and others. The *Catena* probably dates from the seventh or eighth century; there is some overlap between it and the full commentaries of the tenth century by Oecumenius of Tricca (*PG* 119) and by the eleventh-century Bulgarian bishop Theophylact (*PG* 125). Cassiodorus made an eleven-paragraph summary of James in Latin in his *Complexiones Canonicarum in Epistolas Apostolarum* (*PL* 70), and the Venerable BEDE (673–735) produced a full-length commentary in which he, like his predecessors, placed the letter first among the catholic epistles (*PL* 93). Martin of Legio (d. 1021), NICHOLAS OF LYRA, and Dionysius the Carthusian (1402-71) continued the Latin commentary traditon. Also extant are two Syriac commentaries. The commentary of the ninth-century Nestorian bishop of Hadatha, Isho'dad of Merv (M. Gibson [1913]), is noteworthy for its brevity, its skepticism concerning the letter's apostolic origin, and the note that THEODORE OF MOPSUESTIA (whom Isho'dad calls "the Interpreter") knew nothing of the catholic epistles. More extensive and intelligent is the twelfth-century commentary by Dionysius Bar Salibi (I. Sedlacek [1910]), who also complained of the lack of full commentaries on James.

The precritical commentary tradition, resolutely nonallegorical, treated James very much as moral exhortation. Doctrinal preoccupations occasionally surfaced (see, e.g., Oecumenius [6th cent.] on the Trinity in Jas 1:1, *PG* 119:456). Particular concern was shown for harmonizing James and PAUL in the matter of faith and works (Jas 2:14-26), either by distinguishing the condition of the believer before and after baptism (so Oecumenius and Bar Salibi [12th cent.]) or by distinguishing kinds of faith (so Theophylact [c. 1150–1225]). One also finds acute linguistic observations, as when Chrysostom noted the apposite use of *makrothymia* in Jas 5:10 rather than the expected *hypomonē* (see PG 64:1049) or when Bar Salibi commented on the various kinds of "zeal" in Jas 3:14.

The patristic and medieval commentary tradition, therefore, is sparse, interdependent, and remarkably uniform. It is also uninformative concerning the role the letter of James may have played in liturgical, homiletical, or didactic settings. Such uses of the text are particularly important for the history of precritical interpretation, since each explicit application of a text to life involves also an implicit understanding of the text itself (cf., e.g., the citation of Jas 2:13 in the *Rule of Benedict* 64, or the discussion of Jas 2:10 in AUGUSTINE, *Letter* 167, *PL* 33:733). Research into such usage has scarcely begun (see L. T. Johnson, 1995), so our knowledge of the letter's pre-critical reception remains partial.

In the fourthteenth through the sixteenth centuries, first the Renaissance, then the Reformation stimulated a transition to a more critical reading of James. Three figures established lines of interpretation that have continued to the present: ERASMUS, LUTHER, and CALVIN.

Erasmus provided short comments on the verses of James in his *Annotationes* of 1516. In contrast to earlier commentators, he treated James as he would any other ancient author, raising questions concerning attribution, providing alternative manuscript readings, clarifying linguistic obscurities on the basis of parallel usage, and even suggesting textual emendations (reading *phthoneite* for the difficult *phoneuete* in Jas 4:2). The letter's moral or religious teaching was scarcely dealt with.

Luther wrote no commentary on James but exercised considerable influence over subsequent scholarly interpretation. In the preface to his 1522 German Bible, he dismissed the letter as an "epistle of straw" compared to the writings that "show thee Christ." Luther would therefore not include James among the "chief books" of the CANON, although he admired "the otherwise many fine sayings in him." What was the reason for Luther's rejection? James "does nothing more than drive to the law and its works," which Luther found "flatly against St. Paul and all the rest of Scripture." This is the clearest application of Luther's *sachkritik* (content criticism) within the canon; the disagreement between James and Paul on one point removes James from further consideration. The fact that Jas 5:14 was cited in support of the sacrament of extreme unction did not soften Luther's hostility. In this light, the commentary by the Roman Catholic T. CAJETAN in 1532 is all the more fascinating. Cajetan also questioned the apostolicity of James and denied that 5:14 could be used as a proof text for extreme unction. But concerning Paul and James on faith, he diplomatically concluded, "They both taught truly."

In contrast to Luther, Calvin wrote a sympathetic commentary on James in 1551. He found the reasons for rejecting the letter unconvincing and saw nothing in its teaching unworthy of an apostle. Although ready to accept Erasmus's emendation at 4:2, he scoffed at those who found a fundamental conflict between Paul and James on faith and works. As in all of his commentaries Calvin brought great exegetical skill to the text, anticipating contemporary sensitivity to the rhetorical skill of James as well as a systematic reflection over its religious significance.

With the obvious modifications caused by the ever-growing knowledge of the first-century world and the cumulative weight of scholarship itself, the basic approaches established by the Reformation continued to dominate scholarship on the letter. The legacy of Calvin continued in those commentaries that, however learned, focused primarily on James as teacher of the church. An outstanding example is the 1640 commentary by the Puritan divine T. Manton. Fully conversant with past and contemporary scholarship (much of it no longer available to us), Manton's approach remains essentially pious and edifying. The German commentary of A. Gebser (1828) is similar in character. He cited many ancient sources to illuminate the text, but above all he gave such extensive citations from patristic commentaries and discussions that his commentary virtually provided a history of interpretation. This tradition can be said to have continued in the commentaries of J. Mayor (1910[3]) and F. Vouga (1984). In a real sense these commentaries continued the patristic tradition; the meaningful context for understanding James is the Bible. The strength of this approach is its accommodation to the writing's religious purposes. The weakness is its narrowness and scholastic tendency.

The heritage of Luther continued in the historical approach associated with the Tübingen School, in which James was studied primarily as a witness to conflict and development in the early Christian movement. When such scholars as F. Kern (1838) viewed James as written by Paul's contemporary, they saw it as representing a Jewish Christian outlook in tension with Paul's teaching. When such scholars as F. C. BAUR (1853–62, 1875) regarded James as a pseudonymous composition, they understood it as a second-century mediation of the conflict between Peter and Paul. In either case James's discussion of faith in 2:14-26 and its apparent disagreement with Paul became the central point for interpretation. L. Massebieau (1895) and F. SPITTA (1896), however, maintained that James represented an entirely Jewish outlook; they considered the Christian elements in the letter the result of interpolation into a pre-Christian writing. This approach continued in those (often "rehabilitating") studies that used Paul as the essential key to understanding James (see J. Jeremias [1955]; D. Via [1969]; J. Lodge [1981]). The strength of this approach is its historical sensibility. The weakness is its tendency to reduce James to a few verses and earliest Christianity to the figure of Paul.

The Erasmian tradition sought to place James explicitly within the language and literature of the Hellenistic world. The pioneering monument was the two-volume

Novum Testamentum Graecum (1752) of J. WETTSTEIN, who brought together a storehouse of parallel illustrative material from both Greek and Jewish sources, a collection all the more tempting because unsorted. The Jewish side of this approach was developed in the commentary of A. SCHLATTER (1900), who especially emphasized rabbinic parallels. Mayor (1910[3]) also brought together a rich collection of Hellenistic and Christian material. The commentary by J. Ropes (1916) paid particular attention to the letter's diatribal element and singled out the striking resemblances between it and the TESTAMENTS OF THE TWELVE PATRIARCHS. The Erasmian approach found its greatest modern exemplar in the commentary by M. DIBELIUS (1976). Dibelius combined the best of previous scholarship and brought to the text an acute sense of the appropriate illustrative material, bringing to bear pagan, Jewish, and Christian parallels that placed James squarely in the tradition of paraenetic literature. Most late twentieth-century scholarship on the letter either derives from or reacts to this magisterial study (cf. L. Perdue [1981]; Johnson [1995]), although studies have also used more SEMIOTIC (see T. Cargal [1993]) and RHETORICAL approaches (see D. Watson [1993]). The strength of the Erasmian approach is its textual focus and comparative scope. Its weakness is its ability to miss James's religious dimension entirely.

These assertions would meet with fairly general consent among scholars: James is a moral exhortation (*protrepsis*) of rare passion whose instructions have general applicability more than specific reference. Although not tightly organized, the letter is more than a loose collection of sayings; the aphorisms in chap. 1 establish themes that are developed in the essays in chaps. 2–5. James's Christianity is neither Pauline nor anti-Pauline but another version altogether. It appropriates Torah as the "law of liberty" as mediated through the words of JESUS. James opposes empty posturing and advocates active faith and love. He contrasts "friendship with the world" (living by a measure contrary to God's) and "friendship with God" (living by faith's measure). He wants Christians to live by the measure they profess, and his persuasion has a prophet's power.

Bibliography: E. **Baasland,** "Literarische Form, Thematik, und geschichtliche Einordung des Jakobsbriefes," *ANRW* II 25 (1987) 3646-62. **F. C. Baur,** *The Church History of the First Three Centuries* (1853–62); *Paul, the Apostle of Jesus Christ* (1875[2]). **T. B. Cargal,** *Restoring the Diaspora: Discursive Structure and Purpose in the Epistle of James* (SBLDS 144, 1993). **J. A. Cramer,** *Catena Graecorum Patrum* (1840). **P. H. Davids,** "The Epistle of James in Modern Discussion," *ANRW* II 25.5 (1987) 36-45. **M. Dibelius,** *A Commentary on the Epistle of James* (rev. H. Greeven, Hermeneia; ET 1976). **A. R. Gebser,** *Der Brief des Jakobus* (1828). **M. D. Gibson** (ed. and tr.), *Horae Semiticae X: The Commentaries of Isho'dad of Merv,* vol. 4, *Acts of the Apostles and Three Catholic Epistles* (1913). **F. Hahn and P. Müller,** "Der Jakobusbrief," *TRu* 63 (1998) 1-73. **J. Jeremias,** "Paul and James," *ExpTim* 66 (1955) 368-71. **L. T. Johnson,** *The Letter of James* (AB 37A, 1995), full bibliographic entries for all works referred to in the text and not listed in the bibliography; "The Letter of James," *NIB* (1998) 12:175-225. **F. H. Kern,** *Der Brief Jakobi* (1838). **S. Laws,** *A Commentary on the Epistle of James* (HNT, 1980). **J. G. Lodge,** "James and Paul at Cross-purposes: James 2:22," *Bib* 62 (1981) 195-213. **L. Massebieau,** "L'épître de Jacques: Est-elle l'oeuvre d'un Chrétien?" *RHR* 31-32 (1895) 249-83. **T. Manton,** *A Practical Commentary or an Exposition with Notes on the Epistle of James* (1640). **J. B. Mayor,** *The Epistle of St. James* (1910[3]). **L. G. Perdue,** "Paraenesis and the Epistle of James," *ZNW* 72 (1981) 241-56; **J. H. Ropes,** *A Critical and Exegetical Commentary on the Epistle of St. James* (ICC, 1916); "The Greek Catena to the Catholic Epistles," *HTR* 19 (1926) 383-88. **A. Schlatter,** *Des Briefe des Petrus, Judas, Jakobus, der Brief an die Hebraer* (1900); **I. Sedlacek** (ed.), *Dionysius bar Salibi in Apocalypsim Actus et Epistulas Catholicas* (CSCO 60, Scriptores Syri 20, 1910). **F. Spitta,** *Zur Geschichte und Literatur des Urchristentums 2: Der Brief des Jakobus* (1896). **D. O. Via,** "The Right Strawy Epistle Reconsidered: A Study in Biblical Ethics and Hermeneutics," *JR* 49 (1969) 253-67. **F. Vouga,** *L'Épître de Saint Jacques* (CNT, 2nd ser., 13a, 1984). **D. F. Watson,** "James 2 in the Light of Greco-Roman Schemes of Argumentation," *NTS* 39 (1993) 94-121.

L. T. JOHNSON

JASTROW, MORRIS (1861–1922)

Born in Warsaw, J. was the son of M. Jastrow, a prominent rabbi and scholar and the compiler of a Talmudic dictionary (see TALMUD) still widely used. When his father was suspected of sympathizing with Polish revolutionaries in 1866, J. fled with his family to Philadelphia. After receiving a BA from the University of Pennsylvania (1881), he studied in Breslau, Leipzig, Strasbourg, and Paris under such well-known scholars as Franz DELITZSCH and Friedrich DELITZSCH, H. GRAETZ, and T. NÖLDEKE. He received his doctorate in 1884 at Leipzig for a dissertation on an Arabic grammarian. On his return to the United States he taught Semitics at the University of Pennsylvania and simultaneously served as university librarian until he retired in 1919. He died June 22, 1922.

J.'s scholarly interests were broad. Combining his knowledge of religions with his study of ASSYRIOLOGY, he produced the multivolume encyclopedic *Die Religion Babyloniens und Assyriens* (1905–12) and *Hebrew and Babylonian Traditions* (1914). He also wrote an introductory text on religion (1901). To biblical studies J. brought sound philological skills, his knowledge of the Babylonian background, and an eye for detail. His work culminated in commentaries on Ecclesiastes (1919), Job (1920), and Song of Songs (1921).

Works: *Abu Zakarijja Jahja ben Dawud Hassug und seine zwei grammatischen Schriften. . . .* (1885); *Fragment of the Babylonian Dibbarra Epic* (1891); *Religion of Babylonia and Assyria* (1898); *Study of Religion* (Contemporary Science Series, 1901); *Die Religion Babyloniens und Assyriens* (3 vols. and an atlas, 1905–12); *Aspects of Religious Beliefs and Practice in Babylonia and Assyria* (American Lectures on the History of Religion, 1911); *Hebrew and Babylonian Traditions* (Haskell Lectures, 1913); *Civilization of Babylonia and Assyria: Its Remains, Language, History, Religion, Commerce, Law, Art, and Literature* (1915); *A Gentle Cynic, Being the Book of Ecclesiastes* (1919); *The Book of Job: Its Origin, Growth, and Interpretation* (1920); *Song of Songs, Being a Collection of Love Lyrics of Ancient Palestine* (1921); (with A. T. Clay), *An Old Babylonian Version of the Gilgamesh Epic, on the Basis of Recently Discovered Texts* (1923).

Bibliography: A. T. Clay and J. A. Montgomery, *Bibliography of M. J., Jr., PhD, Prof. of Semitic Languages in the University of Pennsylvania, 1885–1910* (1910), lists 150 of J.'s publications prior to 1910; *JAOS* 41 (1921) 337-44. **C. H. Gordon,** *The Pennsylvania Tradition of Semitics: A Century of Near Eastern and Biblical Studies at the University of Pennsylvania* (1986) esp. 13-32. **T. B. Jones,** *The Sumerian Problem* (1969) 62-65. **J. A. Montgomery,** *AJSL* 38 (1921) 1-11. **R. Rotschild and J. Reimer,** *EncJud* 9 (1971) 1296-98.

G. E. SCHWERDTFEGER

JEFFERSON, THOMAS (1743–1826)

The third president of the United States, born near Richmond, Virginia, to Anglican parents, J. faced a religious crisis soon after turning twenty. Thereafter, he showed growing acquaintance with English DEISM, especially that of H. BOLINGBROKE, from whom he learned historical criticism of the Bible.

J. argued that considerable materials in the Gospels were the creation of subsequent interpreters and that the doctrines of JESUS were much simpler: (1) There is one God who is all perfect, (2) everyone will be rewarded or punished, and (3) loving God with all your heart and your neighbor as yourself is the sum of religion. J. prepared two works to sift out the real Jesus: "The Philosophy of Jesus" (1804), focusing on his moral teachings, and "The Life and Morals of Jesus" (1819–20), which included details of his career but removed all supernatural elements. The former work used two English translations; the latter, Greek and Latin texts and English and French translations of the NT. In them J. emphasized the sayings sections of Matthew and Luke, with only a few selections from Mark and John. Neither was published for public distribution during his lifetime.

Works: *The Life and Morals of Jesus of Nazareth by T. J.* (ed. C. Adler, 1904, repr. 1982); "The Philosophy of Jesus" and "The Life and Morals of Jesus," *J.'s Extracts from the Gospels* (ed. D. W. Adams, Papers of T. J. 2nd ser., 1983).

Bibliography: G. Chinard (ed.), *The Literary Bible of T. J., His Commonplace Book of Philosophers and Poets* (Semicentennial Publications of the Johns Hopkins University 1876–1926, 1928). **F. F. Church,** "T. J.'s Bible," *The Bible and Bibles in America* (ed. E. S. Frerichs, 1988) 145-61. **H. W. Foote,** *The Religion of T. J.* (BSLR 1, 1960). **E. J. Goodspeed,** "T. J. and the Bible," *HTR* 40 (1947) 71-76. **R. M. Healy,** *J. on Religion in Public Education* (YPR 3, 1962).

T. H. OLBRICHT

JENSEN, PETER (1861–1936)

A student of both Friedrich DELITZSCH and E. Schrader, J. was an Assyriologist (successor to J. Wellhausen at Marburg, 1892–1928; see ASSYRIOLOGY AND BIBLICAL STUDIES) who was especially interested in Mesopotamian literary and mythological texts (see MYTHOLOGY AND BIBLICAL STUDIES). His philological and interpretive work with these texts represented a significant contribution to their publication. He also worked diligently on the deciphering of various Near Eastern languages, especially hieroglyphic Hittite (see HITTITOLOGY AND BIBLICAL STUDIES).

J. is best known, however, for his mammoth volumes on the Gilgamesh epic and its purported influence on world literature, especially the Bible, the traditions about Muhammad, the Hindu and Homeric traditions, and many other literary traditions. Representing an extreme diffusionist position, he was fascinated by Moses, JESUS, and PAUL as "variants of the Babylonian divine man, Gilgamesh." J. argued that almost the whole Israelite historical tradition (in its northern and southern variants) represented a reflection of the Gilgamesh cycle with its "solar features" and that the "Israelite" Gilgamesh traditions were the background for many NT traditions about John the Baptist, Jesus, and Paul. (This drew the public wrath of the famous NT scholar J. Weiss.)

J. found parallels not only in details and motifs but also in "systems of episodes" and "complexes of stories" reflecting a genetic historical connection. Although granting that the dissimilarities often overwhelmed the similarities, he saw that aspect as the expected outcome of a developmental process that by nature focuses on change, dissolution, and innovation. For example, if the Jesus traditions could take on the various shapes found in the NT in the span of a few decades, then the motifs ultimately derived from the much more ancient Gilgamesh epic would show considerable transformation while remaining comprehensive and systematic enough to impress observers. His suggestions about parallels—e.g., Moses, a shepherd in the wilderness who married Zipporah, whom he met at a well, as parallel to Gilgamesh's companion Enkidu, the creature of the wilderness seduced by a courtesan—and his conclusion that major biblical traditions represent but variants of the Gilgamesh saga impressed very few scholars in his own time and have received almost no subsequent attention.

Works: *Das Gilgamesch-Epos in der Weltliteratur* (2 vols. with supp., 1906, 1928–29); *Moses, Jesus, Paulus, drei Varianten des Babylonischen Gottmenschen Gilgamesch: Eine Anklage und ein Appell* (1910³).

Bibliography: W. **Anderson,** *Über P. J. Methode der vergleichenden Sagenforschung* (1930). **W. Baumgartner,** *AfO* 11 (1936–37) 281-82. **R. Borger,** *RLA* 5, 3-5 (1977) 276. **K. Johanning,** *Der Bibel-Babel-Streit: Eine forschungsgeschichtliche Studie* (Europaische Hochschulschriften, Reihe 23, Theologie 343, 1988) 284-90. **R. G. Lehmann,** *Friedrich Delitzsch und der Babel-Bibel-Streit* (OBO 133, 1994) 159-62. **A. Schott,** *ZA* 44 (1938) 184-90. **J. Weiss,** *Jesus von Nazareth, Mythus oder Geschichte? Eine Auseinandersetzung mit Kalthoff, Drews, Jensen* (1910).

H. B. HUFFMON

JEREMIAH, BOOK OF (INTERPRETATION THROUGH THE 19TH CENTURY)

The history of interpretation of the book of Jeremiah is highly complex, beginning within the biblical book itself since the canonical text (see CANON OF THE BIBLE) is represented by at least two different traditions, the MT and the LXX (see SEPTUAGINT). Because the latter is significantly shorter than the former and also has large parts of the text in a different order, it is now widely agreed that the MT probably reflects an expanded version of a shorter Hebrew *Vorlage,* now represented by the Greek text. While the MT does not contain more chapters or even more oracles than its Greek counterpart, it contains 3,097 words not represented in the LXX, while only 307 words in the LXX have no corresponding parallel in the MT. The MT tends to expand the divine epithets (e.g., "Yahweh of Hosts, the God of Israel," rather than simply "the Lord") as well as the name of Jeremiah (almost always "Jeremiah the prophet" in the MT). Another difference between the two editions is the order of the text; the oracles against the foreign nations in chaps. 46–51 follow 25:38 in the LXX and are presented in a different order. It has further been suggested that the book has undergone extensive DEUTERONOMISTIC editing and that such prose passages as 52:1-34 (paralleled by 2 Kgs 24:18–25:30) that did not originally belong to the oracles of Jeremiah have been added.

Outside the book the first specific mention of the prophet (see PROPHECY AND PROPHETS, HB) in the HB is found in 2 Chr 35:25, where Jeremiah is reported to lament the death of Josiah, and in 2 Chr 36:12, where King Zedekiah is said not to have shown humility before

the prophet. The first of these two occurrences seems to associate Jeremiah with the origin of a custom of lamenting as well as with the book of Lamentations. This tradition is also reflected in the LXX translation of Lamentations, which identifies Jeremiah as its author (Lam 1:1), and many subsequent interpretations of the book of Jeremiah treat it in conjunction with the book of Lamentations. Another direct reference to Jeremiah found in 2 Chr 36:22 and Ezra 1:1 pertains to his prediction about the end of the Babylonian exile. This tradition is expressed more specifically in Dan 9:2, which refers to the seventy-year duration of the exile (Jer 25:11-12; 29:10). It is unclear whether a similar reference to seventy years of exile in Zech 1:12 and 7:5 was taken from the book of Jeremiah or whether the author of these passages relied on an independent tradition.

In the Apocrypha, Sir 49:6-7 mentions Jeremiah's prediction of the destruction of Jerusalem as well as his mistreatment by the people. This emphasis on Jeremiah's persecution was to become quite significant for later interpretations of the book, being used to illustrate the stubbornness of the people to whom he prophesied, and is also reflected in several later traditions of Jeremiah's martyrdom. Another, quite different, motif that emerges in the reception of the book in the Apocrypha is that of Jeremiah as an intercessor on behalf of the people. In 2 Macc 15:12-16, where he appears to the high priest Onias and Judas Maccabeus as they are preparing for battle, he is described as a man distinguished by gray hair and dignity who loves the family of Israel and prays for the people and the city of Jerusalem. A third tradition is indicated by 2 Macc 2:1-8, which speaks of Jeremiah making provisions for the rededication of the Temple after the exile. He is reported to have hidden the tent and the ark of the covenant, along with the Temple altar, as well as having instructed the people to preserve some of the Temple fire while in exile and not to forget the law. This exhortation is also reflected in the apocryphal *Letter of* JEREMIAH (Baruch 6), in which Jeremiah admonishes the exiles against idol worship and which is influenced by the book of Jeremiah, especially chapters 10 and 29.

1. Early Jewish Interpretation. While the Qumran community (see DEAD SEA SCROLLS) was undoubtedly aware of the book of Jeremiah, as is attested by several fragments, it displayed remarkably small interest in either the figure of Jeremiah or the canonical book. Thus, although the *Damascus Document* (CD) cites both Isaiah and Ezekiel, it makes no reference to Jeremiah. Attempts to establish a relationship between the "new covenant" of CD and Jeremiah 31 have proved inconclusive. The only quotations from Jeremiah in any Qumran writings are found in the *Hodayoth* (1HQ), and even here the evidence is sparse (1QH 5:7, 22; 25:17; Jer 12:3; 15:1; 16:16). It is noteworthy, however that textual fragments of the book from the second century BCE have been found at Qumran, some of which reflect the MT tradition, while others seem to represent a Hebrew version of the shorter LXX text, lending strength to the theory that the Greek text of Jeremiah is not an abridgement of the MT but is indeed based on an older, shorter Hebrew text.

More significant is the interest in Jeremiah displayed by other early Jewish traditions like the *Paralipomena of Jeremiah,* a work from the second or third century CE that elaborates on a number of traditions from the canonical book, especially Jeremiah's conflict with Zedekiah, already noted in 2 Chr 36:12. Jeremiah's designation as "the chosen one of God" may be based on Jer 1:5. Likewise, the emphasis of the *Paralipomena* on his priestly status may be related to Jer 1:1, although it is likely based on a hagiographic legend about the prophet. Similarly, the *Vita of Jeremiah,* written after 70 CE, derives much of its biographical information from the book of Jeremiah but also provides its own legends. The reference to Anathoth as Jeremiah's birthplace is inferred from Jer 1:1, while the report of his death in the Egyptian town of Tahpanhes is only loosely based on chapter 43. While the canonical book only mentions that he stayed in Tahpanhes, the *Vita of Jeremiah* observes that he was stoned by the people of Israel in Egypt and was buried near the house of the pharaoh. The text further mentions that Alexander the Great moved Jeremiah's bones to Alexandria, where their presence made all snakes and crocodiles disappear. Other legends found in the *Vita,* e.g., Jeremiah's hiding of the ark, parallel the same tradition as 2 Macc. 2:1-8, while the reference to the return of the glory of God, which had left Zion along with the ark, after all nations have come to venerate the cross is certainly based on a later Christian reworking of the text.

References to Jeremiah by the Jewish historian Eupolemos, transmitted by EUSEBIUS (*Praeparatio Evangelica* 9.39), largely follow the biblical text with a few minor exceptions—namely, that Nebuchadnezzar was encouraged to attack Judah by Jeremiah's prophecies of doom and that he brought all the Temple treasures to Babylon, while Jeremiah kept the ark of the covenant along with the tablets of the law. Similarly, JOSEPHUS (*Ant. Jud.* 10.78.11) based his description of Jeremiah on the HB but emphasized that he, like Ezekiel, was of priestly descent, a tradition also known from the *Paralipomena of Jeremiah.*

PHILO spoke very highly of Jeremiah, devoting more attention to him than to any other biblical prophet. His reading of the book, based on the LXX text, was highly allegorical and platonic, centering on spiritual ideals and the edification of the soul. The interpretive key for Philo was the discernment of certain abstract principles signified by the more literal meaning of the text. Thus, e.g., Jer 15:10 is interpreted as a reference to the struggle of

the wise against the dangers to the soul, using the weapons of reason alone (*On the Confusion of Tongues* 44.49-51). Similarly, he read Jer 3:4 as an allusion to God as the father of spiritual ideas and of wisdom (*On the Cherubim* 49, 51).

In rabbinic literature Jeremiah is the paradigmatic prophet of doom. Thus *b. Ber.* 57b associates Ezekiel with wisdom, Isaiah with consolation, and Jeremiah with condemnation. On the other hand, Jeremiah is also seen as an intercessor on behalf of the people, a tradition already found in 2 Maccabees, and is frequently associated with Moses, although he declined the opportunity to assume leadership over the people of Israel (*Mattot* 91d). In *b. Meg.* 14b and *b. ʿArak.* it is also reported that Jeremiah returned the ten northern tribes to the fold of a united kingdom and that Josiah was the last king to govern both Israel and Judah. In addition to such midrashic materials (see MIDRASH) the book of Jeremiah is frequently used in the development of rabbinic *halakhah*; thus certain legislative traditions are connected to it—e.g., *b. B. Bat.* 160b uses 32:44 as the biblical basis for several purchase documents. Similarly, *Sanh.* 11:5 and *t. Sanh.* 14:14 refer to the dispute between Jeremiah and Hananiah (Jeremiah 28) to explain the characteristics that distinguish true from false prophets.

The TALMUD seems to place the book of Jeremiah at the beginning of the Major Prophets in the canon, preceding Ezekiel and Isaiah, rather than between the two. The reason for this arrangement is explained theologically in *b. Ber.* 57b, which notes that Jeremiah speaks exclusively of punishment and destruction, Ezekiel begins with destruction but ends with restoration and hope, and Isaiah is entirely concerned with restoration and hope. Of liturgical significance for the synagogue service are *Pesiq. Rab. Kah.* 13 and *Pesiq. Rab.* 2, both of which present readings from the book of Jeremiah to be read before the commemoration of the destruction of the Temple. Although these texts focus on Jeremiah's oracles of judgment against Judah and Jerusalem, each concludes with a more hopeful reference to the eventual restoration of Zion.

2. Early Christian Interpretation. In the past it was assumed that many of PAUL's writings were heavily influenced by Jeremiah. Certain theological concepts and rhetorical devices were assumed to be derived directly from the book, e.g., the image of the law written into the heart of the people (Jer 31:33), the prophet's appointment while still in his mother's womb (1:5), and above all the concept of a new covenant (31:31). However, while there appears to be a certain intertextual relationship (see INTERTEXTUALITY) between the Pauline letters and the book of Jeremiah, a direct literal dependence of the former upon the latter is difficult to prove since such images and concepts were undoubtedly part of a larger religio-literary frame of reference that was not exclusive to Jeremiah. On the other hand, it cannot be disputed that the early Christian community was familiar with Jeremiah's concept of a "new covenant" since the LXX text of Jer 31:31-34 is cited almost verbatim by Heb 8:8-12.

In the Gospels Jeremiah is mentioned only in Matt 16:14, which states with regard to the identity of JESUS, "some say John the Baptist, but others Elijah, and still others Jeremiah or one of the prophets," indicating that Jeremiah was a highly revered figure in the first century CE. Revelation 17–18, a vision of the destruction of Babylon, employs a number of images from Jeremiah 50–51 (judgment against Babylon) as well as from 25:10 (the silence of brides and bridegrooms). The use of Jeremiah in Revelation is based, however, on imagery rather than on direct textual quotation.

The apostolic fathers showed remarkably little interest in Jeremiah. Unlike their early Jewish counterparts they did not develop the themes of judgment and restoration central to the book, since the destruction of the Jerusalem Temple in 70 CE had less direct impact on the gentile Christian community. If a particular motif in Jeremiah was used, it was the critique of Israel's sacrificial cult in 7:21-23, cited along with other biblical passages in BARNABAS 2:5-8 to demonstrate the superiority of the Christian faith over the Jewish religion. This polemical use of Jeremiah as well as of other passages of the HB also characterizes many subsequent Christian readings. Thus Cyprian (*Testimoniorum libri III ad Quirinum,* CSEL 3.1) used Jeremiah's call for the people to circumcise their hearts rather than their flesh (4:4) along with other citations (2:13, 6:10, 8:7-9) to illustrate the Jewish misinterpretation of the HB and of the Israelites' covenant with God. Interestingly, TERTULLIAN employed the same motif of circumcised hearts (4:4) against MARCION's opposition to the HB as Christian Scripture. While Tertullian used this image to demonstrate the newness of the Christian covenant, he emphasized at the same time the impossibility of acknowledging the old covenant on which the new is built (*Adv. Marc.* 1.20.4; 4.1.6; 4.11.9; 5.4.10; 5.13.7; 5.19.11).

Prominent among the early church fathers is Jeremiah's use by ORIGEN, especially in his *Homilies* (*Homiliae in J.,* GCS 3.1-194; GCS 8.290-317). Because these homilies were delivered in a liturgical setting, they systematically cite and explain passages from the LXX text of Jeremiah, mostly from chaps. 1–25, often with intertextual references to other HB or NT texts. Like many early Christian writers Origen did not place much emphasis on the textual material after chap. 26 (largely prophetic oracles against foreign nations), with the exception of chap. 31, which announces the making of a new covenant, seen by Origen and others as referring to the Christian gospel. Origen's interpretation of Jeremiah, as of other biblical texts, is firmly based on his anthropological understanding of humanity as constituted by body, soul, and spirit, which corresponds to a

historical, moral, and mystical sense of Scripture respectively. These three senses must be understood as consistently interdependent rather than as individual layers of meaning. A significant passage in this regard is Jer 18:14-16 (NRSV): "Does the snow of Lebanon leave the crags of Sirion? Do the mountain waters run dry, the cold flowing streams? But my people have forgotten me, they burn offerings to a delusion; they have stumbled in their ways, in the ancient roads, and have gone into bypaths, not the highway, making their land a horror, a thing to be hissed at forever. All who pass by it are horrified and shake their heads." Origen equated the fountain of mountain waters with Christ and stated that the believer must thirst for all three fountains of water (i.e. the historical, moral, and mystical senses of Scripture) in order to find any source of water at all (*Homiliae in J.* 18:9). Although he used the same passage to suggest the insufficiency of the Jewish religion, which rejects Christ and recognizes only one fountain of knowledge, he did not refrain from using Jewish traditions of textual transmission and interpretation. On a purely literary level, since he was well trained in philological matters, he often appealed to the Hebrew text of Jeremiah (*Homiliae in J.* 20:2, 13:2, 14:3). His hermeneutic principles of exegesis (see HERMENEUTICS) and his readings are very close to the allegorical interpretations of Philo of Alexandria, and it must be assumed that he was familiar with the principles of ALEXANDRIAN Jewish exegesis, although his own readings were always integrated into the larger tradition of the early church. Thus his allegorical interpretations tended to be christological—e.g., his reading of the gentle lamb led to the slaughter in Jer 11:19.

The most prolific ancient commentator on Jeremiah was THEODORET OF CYRRHUS (10 books, *PG* 81, 495-806). In contrast to the Alexandrian Origen, Theodoret followed the ANTIOCHENE exegetical tradition, which largely rejected allegorizing and spiritual readings of the biblical text. As such he read the book of Jeremiah, not in terms of ideas of spiritual edification, but rather in terms of its references to the destruction of Jerusalem, the Babylonian exile, and the announcement of a new covenant, which is also addressed to the gentile world. While Theodoret did not completely avoid christological typologies in his readings of Jeremiah, he tended to subordinate such readings to the more historical sense of the passage in question; thus, following EPHRAEM THE SYRIAN (*Ephraem Syri Opera* 2:141A), he read the messianic oracle of 23:5 as referring primarily to Zerubbabel and only secondarily to Christ.

In the Western church JEROME likewise rejected excessively allegorizing interpretations of the biblical text. Furthermore, writing in the Latin tradition, he was significantly more critical of the LXX than were his Eastern counterparts, as is reflected in his translation of the VULGATE on the basis of Hebrew texts rather than on the traditional Greek. With regard to Jeremiah he observed that the LXX had been corrupted by copyists to such an extent that its meaning is entirely lost (*Jer. comm.* prol. 2). His interpretation of the book is, like that of Theodoret, based on the historical points of reference that can be derived from the text. Only some passages that were accepted by the church as clearly pointing beyond their immediate historical context, e.g., Jer 11:19, were read as christological pronouncements (*Jer. comm.* 2.110).

Another interpretive principle was emphasized by the Cappadocian BASIL the Great, who focused primarily on the book's moral or ethical aspects. Thus, the reference to the lusty stallions in Jer 5:8, seen by several previous writers as an allegorical image for the unfaithful Israelites (cf. e.g., Clement of Alexandria, *Paedagogus* 1.15.1.77.1; 2.89.2) was viewed as a condemnation of sexual excesses. Similarly, the mention of God's nearness in 23:23 was read as an exhortation to base one's behavior on the awareness that all actions are carried out in the presence of God (*De Jejunio Homilia* 1, 9, *PG* 31 [1885] 181).

Like most of the church fathers, AUGUSTINE's interest in Jeremiah was surprisingly small. He cited the book relatively infrequently and did not write a commentary on it. However, it is perhaps interesting to note that he summarized the prophet's life and works in reference to the history of Rome in the sixth century BCE, setting up a comparative history and CHRONOLOGY between Israel and Rome (*City of God* 18.33).

3. The Medieval Period. During the early Middle Ages only two significant commentaries were written on the book of Jeremiah, one by Odo of Cluny (*PL* 133, 517-638) and the other by the Carolingian scholar RABANUS MAURUS (*PL* 111, 793-1182). While most medieval commentators interpreted the biblical text on the basis of the QUADRIGA, or four senses of Scripture, the historical or literal sense was generally emphasized in the reading of Jeremiah. This is especially true for Rabanus, whose commentary follows that of Jerome. This tradition is also represented in the GLOSSA ORDINARIA, a production of the biblical text with extensive interlinear and marginal glosses that dominated most of medieval biblical interpretation. In the case of Jeremiah most of the glosses seem to derive from Rabanus and Jerome, although it is not entirely clear whether Jerome is in fact cited directly or, as is more likely, indirectly as quoted by Rabanus.

Illustrative of the pervasiveness of this approach to the book in the West during the Middle Ages is also THOMAS AQUINAS's commentary *Expositio Super Ieremiam et Threnos* (mid-13th cent.). This work, like his commentary on Isaiah, both based on lectures Aquinas delivered in Cologne while he was still studying with Albert, belongs to the genre of rapid or "cursory" readings of the biblical text, focusing on the literal sense

with only some marginal notations or "collations" pertaining to spiritual or pastoral applications.

4. Reformation and Later. The Reformers seemed to take more interest in the book of Jeremiah and especially in the life of the prophet. Thus LUTHER, in his *Preface to the Prophet Jeremiah* (1532; *Works of M. Luther with Introductions and Notes* 6 [1982] 408-11), focused on the rejection of Jeremiah by his people and argued that this illustrates the "wickedness of the Jews." In addition to such anti-Jewish sentiments, however, Luther also observed that Jeremiah was not entirely a prophet of doom but also promised hope, in the immediate sense through the return of the people from exile but also through the announcement of Christ and his kingdom. Similarly, CALVIN (*Commentaries on the Book of the Prophet Jeremiah and the Lamentations* [1563]; ET 1620) emphasized the idea of the new covenant of Jeremiah 31 and its fulfillment in Christ, already proposed by many of the church fathers. Furthermore, Calvin, like Luther, took interest in the personal life of the prophet and the struggles he faced. In his *Sermons on Jeremiah* (1549; ET 1990), which are fairly eclectic and exegetically rather free, he compared the Babylonian threat against Jeremiah's Jerusalem to the Roman Catholic threat against his own Geneva during the Reformation, noting that both he and Jeremiah were struggling for the glory of God against the enemies of the faith. Other commentaries on Jeremiah written during the sixteenth and seventeenth centuries include works by J. OECOLAMPADIUS (1533); J. Bugenhagen (1546); F. Castro Palao (1608); J. Maldonato (1609); C. Sanctius (1618); M. Ghislerius (1623); and J. Alting (1687).

The eighteenth century witnessed a renewed interest in the book. Most significant are the commentaries by W. Lowth (*A Commentary upon the Prophecy and Lamentations of Jeremiah* [1728]) and B. Blayney (1784). While Lowth was largely concerned with the book's historical sense, along with the explanation of theological key ideas, which he explored through intertextual references to other biblical books in the HB and the NT, his commentary also points to new developments in the history of biblical interpretation. First, he incorporated discussions on textual variants with regard to both the order of the chapters in the LXX and the MT and the specific lexical meaning of words and expressions, appealing to Greek, Aramaic, and Syriac translations in order to achieve a greater semantic depth in his reading. While such textual concerns are by no means new, since ancient interpreters like Origen and Jerome were already cognizant of other textual traditions, the pervasiveness of the Vulgate as the authoritative text in the West had put such concerns on hold until the Renaissance. It was not until the Reformation and the development of humanism that questions pertaining to the biblical text were addressed. This new element in biblical interpretation, then, came to its full fruition during the eighteenth century; and Lowth's commentary on Jeremiah is representative of this movement.

More significant, Lowth also began the subdivision of the text into smaller source units or collections. While he did not question that virtually all textual material in the book ultimately came from the prophet, he suggested that Jeremiah's oracles were written down in different collections and were only later combined into the canonical book sometime after the Babylonian exile. Most significant is the collection referred to in 36:2, where Jeremiah is commanded by God in the fourth year of King Jehoiakim to write down all of the prophecies he had to this date spoken against Israel, Judah, and the nations. Lowth argued that this collection was in fact written down by Jeremiah, whereas the oracles delivered after this point up to the fall of Jerusalem were subsequently written down by Jeremiah's disciple Baruch in a collection described in Jer 1:3. A third collection, noted in chaps. 42–44 and describing events after the fall of Jerusalem, was added after the exile, possibly by Ezra, along with some other textual material; e.g., the historical summary of Jeremiah 52, which is chiefly taken from 2 Kings 24–25. Although this division into different collections is still very tentative, it does point toward some of the major source-critical questions central to the interpretation of the book during the first half of the twentieth century, especially by B. DUHM and S. MOWINCKEL.

Also noteworthy about Lowth's commentary is his emphasis on the need to interpret the biblical text in the context of its historical setting. Thus, although even he did not avoid reading Jeremiah's reference to the new covenant in chap. 31 christologically with reference to the Pauline letters and to Heb 8:8 and 10:16, he did not view Jer 11:19 ("like a gentle lamb led to the slaughter") as a proleptic reference to the suffering of Christ. Instead, he noted that this expression connotes an image of false security or insensibility to danger and even cited a similar expression used in Homer's *Odyssey* in support of his reading.

Blayney's commentary, written toward the end of the eighteenth century, is based on the exegetical principles developed by W. Lowth's son Robert and was intended to do for the book of Jeremiah what R. LOWTH had done with Isaiah (1778). The main innovation of this approach was a concern with such stylistic features as acrostics and parallelisms, which Blayney tried to preserve in his English translation. He noted that he had attempted to be faithful to the general sense of the Hebrew text "but also to express each word and phrase by a corresponding one as far as the genius of the two languages would admit," indicating in his notes a literal reading in cases where his translation required a free rendering for stylistic purposes (*Jeremiah and Lamentations,* iv). Most of Blayney's translation is presented in poetic style, in which he tried to preserve the Hebrew

parallelism wherever possible, and in cases where no parallelism could be found, he showed sensitivity to the rhythmic and metrical proportions of the text.

This does not mean that Blayney exclusively followed the MT in his translation. In fact, his commentary reflects an even stronger concern with text-critical issues (see TEXTUAL CRITICISM) than does that of W. Lowth, and he frequently referred to textual work done by R. Lowth and B. KENNICOTT in his attempt to reconstruct the original text of Jeremiah's oracles. Thus, in his discussion of the new covenant in chap. 31, he referred to Heb 8:8, not for theological or christological reasons, but rather for text-critical purposes, since the NT passage reflects the LXX text of Jeremiah almost verbatim. Likewise, his notes are primarily concerned with grammatical and philological issues, which he addressed with reference to other Semitic languages like Syriac, Aramaic, and even Arabic. Furthermore, in order to explain the meaning of certain expressions, he referred not only to other books of the Bible but also to such non-biblical authors as Herodotus, Homer, and Horace.

Many of the questions addressed during the eighteenth century received fuller attention in the nineteenth. Especially Lowth's observations about the different collections contained in the book of Jeremiah were the subject of much debate, and different suggestions were made as to how many collections can be identified and how they are best subdivided (J. G. Eichhorn [1803³] 116-86; H. Ewald [1840]; F. Hitzig [1841]; F. Movers [1837]). To this was added the question of authenticity. While Lowth and Blayney still viewed most oracles in the book as deriving from the prophet himself, several nineteenth-century scholars attributed some material to later periods. Movers suggested that 10:1-16 as well as chaps. 30–31 and 33 were not in fact genuine prophecies by Jeremiah but were more likely composed by the author of Isaiah 56–66. This view was also adopted by W. DE WETTE (1817) and by F. HITZIG, whose commentary on Jeremiah was one of the most significant of that century, although strongly opposed by E. HENGSTEN-BERG (1829–35; ET 1836–39). Movers's argument was largely based on the observation that Zech 8:7-8 quotes from Jer 31:7-8, 33 and speaks in Zech 8:9 of the author as one who lived in the days when the foundations of the Temple were laid, which led him to the conclusion that these chapters from Jeremiah must have been written by a contemporary of Zechariah. Similarly, Movers and De Wette suggested that the oracles against Babylon in Jeremiah 50–51 do not appear to be genuine, since they contain many interpolations. This was also the view taken by H. EWALD, who had accepted the other chapters rejected by Movers as genuine Jeremiah prophecies, but who proposed that chaps. 50–51 were composed by an author imitating the prophet's style.

Also debated was the authorship of Jeremiah 46–51, the second section of oracles against the nations. EICH-

HORN was the first to suggest that these chapters, which constitute the last section of the book in the MT before the historical summary of chap. 52, but which follow the first section of oracles against foreign nations (25:15-38) in the LXX, may not have been composed by Jeremiah. He initially proposed that Jeremiah had incorporated the words of earlier prophets into his own composition (*Repertorium für biblische und morgenländische Litteratur* 1 [1777]) but later revised his opinion and argued instead that these chapters are from a later editor (1803). Movers and Hitzig proposed, on the other hand, that only a small core of chaps. 46–51 goes back to the prophet and that this was subsequently expanded during the exile, especially chaps. 50–51.

Another point of debate that emerged during the nineteenth century was the lack of order among the oracles in Jeremiah. Already Blayney had argued that the present order of the book is a rather jumbled arrangement of prophecies from the reigns of Jehoiakim and Zedekiah and that the original order of Jeremiah's oracles must have been disturbed by an ancient editor. Similarly, Eichhorn proposed that Jeremiah might have written his oracles on single scrolls and, in an effort to provide the exiles in Babylon with a copy of his prophecies, dictated them to a follower without paying attention to their chronological order. Another approach was taken by Ewald, who was less concerned with the book's historical coherence than with its poetical structure or unity. He noted that many portions are introduced by the recurring formula "the word which came to Jeremiah from the LORD" (7:1; 11:1; 18:1; 21:1; 25:1; 30:1; 32:1; 34:1; 34:8; 35:1; 40:1; 44:1) or "the word of the LORD which came to Jeremiah" (14:1; 46:1; 47:1; 49:34) as well as by other introductory formulas that have a more historical value (36:1; 37:1; 37:2). Two further sections are thematically distinct and are thus lacking an introduction altogether (23:1; 45:1), while 1:1 serves as a superscription to the first chapter of the book. As a result, the book can be subdivided into twenty-two separate and independent units, which for the poetical section are further divisible into stanzas of seven to nine verses often separated by phrases like "the LORD said also to me."

The turn of the century witnessed an influential, seminal study by Duhm (*Das Buch Jeremia* [KHCAT 11, 1901]), who analyzed the book on the basis of prose and POETRY portions and proposed that it consisted of three independent compositional sections. The first of these contains Jeremiah's prophecies (280 verses), which are entirely in poetic form, while the second part contains his biography (220 verses) in prose as composed by his disciple Baruch. The third and largest portion (850 verses), he suggested, was added by later editors. Even though the question of different collections of oracles as well as the distinction between poetry and prose material had already been addressed in the eigh-

teenth century, Duhm's study was the first to apply to Jeremiah systematically the principles of historical-critical source analysis as outlined by J. WELLHAUSEN with regard to the Pentateuch (see PENTATEUCHAL CRITICISM). Duhm's exegesis thus set the tone for much of twentieth-century scholarship on the book of Jeremiah.

Bibliography: G. L. Berlin, "The Major Prophets in Talmudic and Midrashic Literature" (diss., St. Mary's, 1976). **B. Bernheimer,** "Vitae prophetarum," *JAOS* 55 (1935) 200-203. **B. Blayney,** *Jeremiah and Lamentations: A New Translation with Notes Critical, Philological, and Explanatory* (1784). **W. Bousset and H. Gressmann,** *Die Religion des Judentums im späthellenistischen Zeitalter* (HNT 21, 1966⁴). **J. Bowman,** "Prophets and Prophecy in Talmud and Midrash," *EQ* 22 (1950) 107-14, 205-20, 255-75. **F. H. Colson,** "Philo's Quotations from the OT," *JTS* 41 (1940) 237-51. **A. H. W. Curtis and T. Romer** (eds.), *The Book of Jeremiah and Its Reception* (BETL 128, 1997). **J. Darling,** *Cyclopaedia Bibliographica: A Library Manual of Theological and General Literature, and Guide to Books for Authors, Preachers, Students, and Literary Men* (1854) 645-66. **E. Dassmann,** *RAC* 17 (1996) 543-631. **G. Delling,** *Jüdische Lehre und Frömmigkeit in den Paralipomena Jeremiae* (BZAW 100, 1967). **W. de Wette,** *A Critical and Historical Introduction to the Canonical Scriptures of the OT* (1817; ET 1843). **J. G. Eichhorn,** *Einleitung in das Alte Testament* 3 (1803³) 116-86; **E. E. Ellis,** *Paul's Use of the OT* (1957). **H. Ewald,** *Die Propheten des alten Bundes* (3 vols., 1840–41). **E. Fascher,** "Jerusalems Untergang in der urchristlichen und altkirchlichen Überlieferung," *TLZ* 89 (1964) 81-98. **M. Gibson,** "The Twelfth-century Glossed Bible," *StPatr* 23 (1989) 232-44; "The Glossed Bible," *Biblia Latina Cum Glossa Ordinaria: Facsimile Reprint of the Editio Princeps A. Rusch of Strassburg* 1480, 81 (1992) vii-xi. **F. D. Gotch,** *Cyclopedia of Biblical Literature* 4 (1866) 495-99; *The Popular and Critical Bible Encyclopaedia and Scriptural Dictionary* 2 (1913) 221-23. **S. Granild,** "Jeremia und das Deuteronomium," *StTh* 16 (1962) 135-54. **P. Häuser,** "Barnabas 9:6 und Jer 9:25-26 (LXX)," *TQ* 97 (1915) 499-508. **T. R. Hayward,** "Jewish Traditions in Jerome's Commentary on Jeremiah and the Targum of Jeremiah," *PIBA* 9 (1985) 100-120; *The Targum of Jeremiah: Introduction, Translation, and Commentary* (The Aramaic Bible 12, 1987). **J. Heinemann,** "A Homily on Jeremiah and the Fall of Jerusalem (Pesiqta Rabbini, Pisqa 26)," *The Biblical Mosaic: Changing Perspectives* (ed. R. Polzin and E. Rothmann, 1982) 27-41. **E. Hengstenberg** *Christology of the OT, and a Commentary on the Predictions of the Messiah by the Prophets* (3 vols. 1829–35; ET 1836–39, 1864–72²). **S. Herrmann,** *TRE* 16 (1986) 568-86. **F. Hitzig,** *Die Prophet Jeremia* (KEH 3, 1841). **C. Kannengiesser,** "Les citations bibliques du traité athanasien sur l'incarnation du Verbe et les 'Testimonia,' " *La Bible at les Pères: Colloque de Strasbourg, 1969* (ed. M. Aubineau et al, 1971) 135-60; *Dictionnaire de Spiritualité* 8 (1974) 889-901; "L'interprétation de Jérémie dans la tradition alexandrine," *StPatr* 12 (TU 115, 1975) 317-20. **A. S. Kapelrud,** "Der Bund in den Qumran-Schriften," *Bibel und*

Qumran (ed. S. Wagner, 1968) 137-49. **G. Kisch,** *Pseudo-Philo's "Liber antiquitatum biblicarum"* (PMS 10, 1949). **J. R. Lundbom,** *ABD* (1992) 3:706-21. **F. Lurz,** "Jeremia in der Liturgie der Alten Kirche," *Ecclesia Orans* 9 (1992) 141-71. **J. Lust,** "Messianism and the Greek Version of Jeremiah," *VII Congress of the International Organization for Septuagint and Cognate Studies* (ed. C. Cox, 1991) 87-122. **U. Luz,** "Der alte und neue Bund bei Paulus und im Hebräerbrief," *EvTh* 27 (1967) 318-36. **A. Marmorstein,** "Die Quellen des neuen Jeremia-Apocryphons," *ZNW* 27 (1928) 327-37. **E. A. Matter,** "The Church Fathers and the Glossa Ordinaria," *The Reception of the Church Fathers in the West: From the Carolingians to the Maurists* (ed. I. D. Backus, 1997) 83-111. **R. Meyer,** "Paralipomena Jeremiae," *RGG*[3] (1959) 102-3. **F. Movers,** *De utriusque Vaticiniorum Jeremiae recensionis indole et origine* (1837). **M. Pesty,** "La Septante et sa lecture patristique, un example: Jérémie 3,22–4,1," *Rashi, 1040–1990: Hommage à E. E. Urbach* (ed. G. Sed-Rajna, 1993) 173-82. **L. Prijs** (ed.), *Die Jeremia-Homilie Pesikta Rabbati Kap. 26: Eine synagogale Homilie aus nachtalmudischer Zeit über den Propheten Jeremia und die Zerstörung des Tempels* (StDel 10, 1966). **E. Schadel,** *Origenes: Die griechisch erhaltenen Jeremia Homilien* (Bibliothek der griechischen Literatur 10, 1980). **N. Schmid,** *Encyclopaedia Biblica* 2 (1901) 2372-95. **S. Soderlund,** *The Greek Text of Jeremiah: A Revised Hypothesis* (JSOTSup. 47, 1985). **H. O. Thompson,** *The Book of Jeremiah: An Annotated Bibliography* (ATLA Bibliographies 25, 1996). **K. J. Torjesen,** *Hermeneutical Procedure and Theological Method in Origen's Exegesis* (1985). **J.-P. Torrell,** *Saint Thomas Aquinas* 1 (1996) 27-28, 337. **C. C. Torrey,** *The Lives of the Prophets* (JBLMS 1, 1946). **E. Tov,** *The Septuagint Translation of Jeremiah and Baruch: A Discussion of an Early Revision of the LXX of Jeremiah 29–52 and Baruch 1:1–3:8* (HSM 8, 1976); "Exegetical Notes on the Hebrew *Vorlage* of the LXX of Jeremiah 27 (34)," *ZAW* 91 (1979) 73-93; "The Literary History of the Book of Jeremiah in Light of Its Textual History," *Empirical Models for Biblical Criticism* (ed. J. Tigay, 1985) 211-37; "The Jeremiah Scrolls from Qumran," *RevQ* 14 (1989) 187-204; "Three Fragments of Jeremiah from Qumran Cave 4," *RevQ* 15 (1992) 530-41. **C. Wolff,** *Jeremia im Frühjudentum und Urchristentum* (TU 118, 1976); "Irdisches und Himmlisches Jerusalem: Die Heilshoffnung in den Paralipomena Jeremiae," *ZNW* 82 (1991) 147-58. **J. Ziegler,** "Jeremia Zitate in Väter-Schriften: Zugleich grundsätzliche Betrachtungen über Schrift-Zitate in Väter-Ausgaben," *Theologie aus dem Geist der Geschichte* (FS B. Altaner, 1958) 347-57.

A. SIEDLECKI

JEREMIAH, BOOK OF (TWENTIETH-CENTURY INTERPRETATION)

Jeremiah's call to be a prophet (see PROPHECY AND PROPHETS, HB) is located in the thirteenth year of Josiah (c. 626 BCE), but controversy has raged around this date. Noted in both Jer 1:2 and 25:3, this double occurrence of the date creates difficulties for those who suppose that "thirteen" arises from a textual corruption of "twenty-three" and that the call of Jeremiah took place

in 616 rather than 626 BCE. The hypothesis of accidental corruption falls if the two notices are independent of each other, but even if one is derived from the other, it has to be assumed that the prior one was corrupted before it became the source of the dependent one. Other dates have been produced by LITERARY-critical analysis coupled with textual emendation, the most common being 609 BCE (F. Horst [1923]; J. P. Hyatt [1951]; and W. Holladay [1986–89]), although 605 has also been proposed (C. Whitley 1964]). It has been argued that Jer 1:2 should be deleted and that "He was active in the reign of Jehoiakim" (1:3) marks the beginning of Jeremiah's prophetic activity. The general reason for dissatisfaction with 626 is that a long period of prophetic inactivity between 621 and 609 has to be supposed. The representation of a call in 626 is said to be a consequence of deuteronomic interference guided by a desire to associate Jeremiah with the reform of Josiah. The necessity of assuming the inactivity of the prophet over a long period has encouraged the view that there is a case for the application of Occam's razor and for the conclusion that Jeremiah began his work in 609, and that 626 was perhaps the year of his birth.

Bearing on Jeremiah's biography is the problem of the "enemy from the north," if it is supposed that the original reference was to the Scythians. Here we stand on controversial ground. There is a reference to an enemy from the north in Jer 1:14, and the passages B. Duhm (1901) entitled "Scythian Songs" (4:5-8, 11-17, 19-21, 23-26, 29-31; 6:1-5, 22-26; 8:14-17; 10:19-22). Some scholars still hold the view that the "enemy from the north" referred originally to the Scythians, who had overrun Palestine and were maintaining a hostile presence there at the time of Jeremiah's call in 626. Even if there was an earlier enemy from the north, the only one present in the book of Jeremiah is Babylon, and the exegesis of the above passages should be pointed in that direction. A. Welch (1928) solved the problem by arguing that the enemy was part of a scheme depicting eschatological judgment.

Although the beginnings of Jeremiah's ministry remain in some doubt, there is no compelling alternative to a 626 date for his call. The presentation of his subsequent career is more straightforward, however. He was active in the reigns of Jehoiakim and Zedekiah until the exile of 587 and after the fall of Jerusalem was coerced by Johanan son of Kareah into going to Egypt (43:1-7). The description of him as "a prophet to the nations" (1:5) has troubled commentators; special pleading is required to reconcile this with Jeremiah's concentration on the Judean community. While there is probably some connection between "prophet to the nations" and the oracles against foreign nations that are part of the book (chaps. 46–51), there are different views about the relation of these oracles to the historical Jeremiah (see B. Huwyler's survey [1997]). W. RUDOLPH

(1947, 1968³) took a positive view and included them in his source A and also in the contents of the scroll of 605 (36:1). The most probable conclusion is that the phrase "prophet to the nations" is primarily a description of a Jeremiah corpus containing the oracles against foreign nations and that it sets us at a distance from the historical Jeremiah. There is, however, an argument that these oracles represent the earliest phase of Jeremiah's prophetic activity and that he was a "nationalistic" prophet before he became a prophet of "doom."

1. Contents. Poetic oracles of doom directed against Judah feature prominently in Jeremiah 1–25. These threats are supported and justified by legal arguments and indictments, and the POETRY is interspersed with small and large passages of prose. The longer prose passages are represented by chap. 7, which has only one verse of poetry (v. 29) and is generally anti-cultic in tone; also by chap. 11, which has a more transparent deuteronomic/DEUTERONOMISTIC character ("deuteronomic" is used of prose that has affinities with the book of Deuteronomy, and "deuteronomistic" of prose whose particular associations are with the vocabulary, word strings, and style of the framework of Joshua–2 Kings).

The prose in Jeremiah 1–25 has generally been identified as having deuteronomic or deuteronomistic affinities (see the essays in W. Gross [1995]) and has commonly been distinguished from the prose of the so-called Baruch biography, sometimes described as a passion narrative because it describes Jeremiah's suffering in the fulfillment of his prophetic vocation. According to Rudolph, Baruch's work is represented in these chapters by 19:1-10, 14-15 and 20:1-6, but it appears principally in chapters 26–51 (26; 28; 29; 34:1–38:28a; 38:28b–40:6; 40:7–43:12; 44; 45; 51:59-64). This leaves as the principal remainder of the second half of the book prophecies of hope for the restoration of Jerusalem (chaps. 30–33); an account of an abortive rising against Babylon that involved Jeremiah in symbolic action (chap. 27—Rudolph's source A); a report of how Zedekiah reneged on the freeing of slaves (34:8-22—Rudolph's source C); a narrative of Jeremiah's encounter with the Rechabites (chap. 35—also source C); and the oracles against foreign nations already mentioned (chaps. 46–51). Chapter 52 is a historical note on the fall of Jerusalem derived from 2 Kgs 24:18–25:30.

A special category of material, mostly poetry, is constituted by the "laments" or "complaints," whether those exploring the anguish Jeremiah felt in the pursuit of his prophetic vocation (8:18-23; 12:1-5; 15:10-21; 17:9-18; 20:7-9) or those in which he appears in a communal context as an intercessor (e.g. 14:2-10; 14:17–15:4). The oracles against foreign nations have a poetic form and are differently located in the Hebrew and Greek texts: chaps. 46–51 in the Hebrew and 25:15-31 in the Greek (Septuagint). Jeremiah 25:1-13 has been widely regarded as the conclusion of the preceding part

of the book and has been drawn into discussions about the contents of the two scrolls mentioned in chapter 36: the one destroyed by Jehoiakim (vv. 1-8) and the enlarged scroll written again by Baruch (vv. 27-32). "In this book" (25:13) is taken as a reference to either the first or the second scroll. But 25:1-13 will fit as a conclusion to the preceding part of the book only if "that land" (v. 13) is emended to "this land," and here the wish is father to the thought. "That land" refers to Babylon just as "that nation" does in v. 12. Jeremiah 25:1-13 is an introduction to the oracles against foreign nations, and it appears immediately before them in the order of the SEPTUAGINT.

The contents of the scrolls have been differently identified by Rudolph with (a) oracles of doom against Judah, including some prose, and (b) oracles against foreign nations (chaps. 45–49). O. EISSFELDT (1964³; ET 1965) speculated that the scrolls were made up of the prose in chaps. 1–25 and amounted to a considered retrospect of the oracles Jeremiah had delivered over a period of twenty-three years (25:3). A similar view appears in B. CHILDS (1979).

2. Criticism. A source theory formulated by S. MOWINCKEL in 1914 was subsequently adopted by Rudolph and others and has gained wide acceptance. The three sources are specified as A, B, and C, with the extent of the B source indicated above. B is ascribed to Baruch, Jeremiah's "scribe"; it is biographical in character and is narrated in the third person. Source A, according to Rudolph, consists of sayings of Jeremiah largely made up of oracles of doom addressed to Judah in chaps. 1–25 but including threats directed against foreign nations (chaps. 46–49). It is comprised for the most part of poetry, but prose is not excluded (e.g. 3:6-13; 14:14-16; 23:25-32).

The C source is mostly identified with the prose interspersed with the poetry in Jeremiah 1–25 (7:1–8:3; 11:1-14[17]; 16:1-13; 17:19-27; 18:1-12; 21:1-10; 22:1-5; 25:1-14) and otherwise only at 34:8-22, 35. It is said to consist of sayings of Jeremiah that have undergone a deuteronomic or deuteronomistic editing and do not retain their original linguistic constituents. J. BRIGHT (1965) questioned the view that the prose of source C is deuteronomic or deuteronomistic in the exact sense that has been supposed, describing it generally as sixth century. H. Weippert (1973) has examined individual items of vocabulary and word strings of source C in order to show by lexicographical and exegetical arguments that there are significant differences between this prose and that of the book of Deuteronomy or the deuteronomistic historical literature. Her object is the highly particular one of reclaiming the prose of the postulated source C for the historical Jeremiah—nothing less than the prophet's prose style.

The C source is mainly located in the first half of the book and the B source in the second half. B has been represented as a contemporary historical source that enables us to make immediate contact with the historical prophet Jeremiah. It is an account and interpretation of his prophetic activity by Baruch that has the advantage of presence at and involvement in great issues as they emerged and developed. The true prophet is wrapped in an environment of darkness and misunderstanding in which the truth does not prevail over falsehood; consequently, he is marked out for alienation, suffering, and failure. In contrast, C is said to be a view of the prophet in retrospect, one that has historical value but is colored by the conditions and concerns of the Jewish community in Babylon. What scholars make of the historical Jeremiah is influenced by the theological problems with which they wrestle and the methods they adopt to solve these problems. They seek to do this in agreement with a deuteronomic view of the prophetic office that gives high priority to its intercessory function. The eventuation of exile has sealed the truth of Jeremiah's predictions of doom, but the failure of this true prophet to make an effective impact on the late preexilic community he addressed is a theological problem that calls for clarification.

The validity of this kind of distinction between the B and C sources has been called into question, with doubts arising as to whether its linguistic basis is assured—whether the prose of source B can be sharply distinguished from the prose of source C—as well as to whether the historical background of B is different from that of C. In 1970 E. Nicholson urged that a setting in the exilic community should also be assumed for B and that it is the circumstances and concerns of this period that are being addressed. He argued for both sources that a more sensitive exegetical appreciation of the literature will identify processes of reflection by the exilic community that will generate a reinterpretation of the activity of the historical Jeremiah.

The view that the book of Jeremiah has been largely expanded by deuteronomic or deuteronomistic (Dtr) editors and that it has been shaped into a coherent theological whole by the working out of leading principles was earlier considered by Hyatt but is associated particularly with W. Thiel (1973, 1981). Applying especially to the relation between the poetry and prose in Jeremiah 1–25, it has been argued by Thiel in great detail. An important assumption of his method is that prose compositions attributed to Dtr inhere within a kernel or core, which may be poetry or may be critically reconstructed into poetry by Thiel, but which may also be prose. The composition that arises from these processes of expansion and transformation may be small, medium, or large, for Thiel supposes that the work of Dtr has an all-embracing character and that there is a master plan in which the units of composition are like the bricks of an edifice.

Thiel's contribution to the elucidation of the relations

between poetry and prose in Jeremiah 1–25 is a notable one, but the question that ought to be asked is whether the book has as high a degree of literary or theological organization as he represents. There is something to be said for more localized investigations that keep very close to the text and do not have such high expectations of disclosing cohesive compositions shaped by broad theological principles. Whether one envisions a piece of poetry that generates prose, there is a virtue in seeking narrow exegetical explanations that are not disengaged from the details of the text. The argument will then be that prose expansions that are contiguous (or almost contiguous) with a piece of poetry or prose are precisely attempts at exegetical elucidation of verses to which they are adjacent in the extant text, and that this is the primary, local understanding that is needed.

This view, founded on exegetical considerations, is reinforced by what the book of Jeremiah discloses about the history of the Hebrew text. The argument is that there are secondary prose additions and that they have the character of exegetical expansions of poetry or prose already established in the Jeremiah corpus. The text-critical support (see TEXTUAL CRITICISM) for this is made possible, in the first place, because the text of the Septuagint in Jeremiah is shorter than that of the MT. This would have no text-critical significance if it were supposed that this state of affairs has been produced by abbreviations of the Hebrew text in the Septuagint. Although this should not be ruled out entirely as an explanation of individual cases, for the most part the shortness of the Greek text is accounted for by the fact that the Hebrew *Vorlage* used by the Alexandrian translators of the Septuagint was shorter than the MT. A comparison of the MT with the Septuagint in the book of Jeremiah will reveal that the history of the Hebrew text involves a process of addition and expansion. The hypothesis that a secondary exegetical expansion of the Jeremiah corpus occurred is not, therefore, merely speculative; its probability is indicated by hard textual evidence. Jeremiah 10:1-16 is a particularly interesting example because a Hebrew text fragment found in Cave 4 at Qumran (4QJer[b]) corresponds to the text of the Septuagint, where it differs from the MT. In this case it can be asserted categorically that the Septuagint derives from a Hebrew text shorter than that of the MT. There is good reason for holding that 10:1-16 was built up by successive additions, each generated by the preexisting text or part of it. The Septuagint does not represent vv. 6-8, and v. 9 is located within v. 5 of the MT; however, the general point is that a secondary exegetical expansion is supported by the textual tradition.

3. Exegesis. Weippert's view of the prose in the book of Jeremiah foreshortens the processes of composition. If the prose is largely to be attributed to Jeremiah, by implication the corpus had, more or less, achieved its extant shape during his lifetime, an extra-linguistic factor that makes Weippert's view on the authorship of the prose difficult to accept. It is hard to believe that the extant Jeremiah corpus had so brief a history of composition when indications are rather that the processes of composition that brought the corpus to its final shape proceeded by installments over a long period. The stages are difficult to recover because there are haphazard factors at work, and it should not be supposed that this long period of growth was everywhere guided by a literary master plan, by a systematic theology, or by a canonical intention.

Rudolph's interest, like that of Weippert, is focused on the historical prophet Jeremiah; but Rudolph does not suppose that the prose of his source C is Jeremiah prose. Nevertheless, although Rudolph analyzes the prose of source C as deuteronomic, his exegetical use of this source is focused on the prophet Jeremiah and the historical conditions of his ministry, not on the reinterpretation of the prophet by the Jewish exilic community. Hence his assumption is that the linguistic transformation that has taken place in source C has not obliterated Jeremiah's sayings and that what is deuteronomic in their presentation can be peeled off to disclose the content of his utterances in the historical circumstances of the late preexilic period.

The same is partly true of Nicholson's attitude toward source B. He has two strings on his bow, however; and although he is concerned to emphasize that the historical Jeremiah and the background of the late preexilic period have not been obliterated, his main exegetical point is to throw light on aspects of the reinterpretation of the historical Jeremiah against the background of exilic conditions. Whereas the historical Jeremiah is Rudolph's focus in his exegetical use of source C, Jeremiah as construed by the exilic community is Nicholson's exegetical focus in his handling of source B. The other side of Nicholson's concern is historical rather than exegetical. He urges that by transporting the exegesis of source B from late preexilic Jerusalem to the Babylonian exile he is not denying its value as a historical source. The extant exilic shape that discloses its exegetical significance can be peeled off to leave a reliable historical residue.

Thiel's assumptions remove us more decisively from the historical context of Jeremiah's ministry because his exegetical investigations are largely directed toward the elucidation of a comprehensive theology imposed on the Jeremiah corpus by his Dtr editor. His view that the processes involved in the composition of the book are long and complicated is realistic, and these processes carry us into exilic and even postexilic times.

4. The Suffering Prophet. It has been generally supposed that of all the prophetic books Jeremiah gives us the best access to the humanity of a prophet and that this window opens perceptions that contribute to an especially profound prophetic theology (see the older works of J. Skinner and G. A. Smith). The individual "laments" or "complaints" (discussed above) have been regarded as one such mode of access; but this view has been challenged by H. G. Reventlow (1963), who describes this expectation and the interpretation it encourages as a psychological fallacy. He argues that the so-called individual laments do not give us an insight into the tensions the prophetic vocation created in an individual prophet, and that they reveal only the cultic language appropriate in the mouth of a prophet discharging a representative intercessory function on behalf of the community. It has already been indicated that there are communal laments in the book of Jeremiah, but there are also individual laments describing the anguish of the prophet that cannot be metamorphosed into communal laments.

So far as communal laments are concerned, it is unlikely that the theology they project is attributable to the prophet Jeremiah. The theme "interdict on intercession," which appears in 14:2-9 and 14:17–15:4, is also present at 7:16 and 11:14. Instead of enlisting this feature as evidence of Jeremiah's originality in contrast to the cultic models he employs, this interdict should be seen as an attempt by the exilic community to throw light on troubling theological problems. The "interdict on intercession" formula enabled them to affirm their theology of prophecy, in which the prophet appeared as an effective intercessor, and at the same time to explain the disaster of exile and to embrace Jeremiah as a true prophet.

The individual laments are a different matter, however, demanding an interpretation that focuses on the human cost of prophetic responsibility as it was endured by the historical Jeremiah. But this protest against the contradictions of the prophetic vocation and the anguish these generate should not be interpreted negatively, not, e.g., at Jer 12:1-5 or at any other place where they rise to the surface. A view that puts the emphasis on Jeremiah's rebelliousness can cause distortion. Jeremiah is represented as having rebelled in 12:1-4 and in similar contexts where his words throb with the pain of a commitment that seems to be wrecked by circumstances he cannot defeat. We are told that this is the voice of a prophet who has lost his way, whose words are an expression of his willfulness, and who must repent and return to Yahweh, as he is required to do in 12:5 (cf. 14:19). Neither in these passages nor at 20:7, where Jeremiah accuses Yahweh of having deceived him, can the anguish of a prophet be reduced to mere human sinfulness without inflicting major theological damage. These passages teach us not to divorce the human from the divine in a theology of prophecy. The profundity of prophetic truth grasped by Jeremiah is not separable from his human anguish, and "word of God" must not be taken so literally that it is divorced from the discovery of prophetic truth at great human cost. The interpretation of "word of God" in these laments as no more than the activity of a speaking God who finally intervenes to chide the prophet for his waywardness results in great theological impoverishment. Jeremiah could not have appropriated the truth that the prophetic vocation is full of suffering, that there would be no remission, and that the burdens of sorrow would become heavier without enduring the strife and struggles expressed at 12:1-4; 15:10, 15-18; or 20:7.

The idea that Yahweh has deceived Jeremiah has to be linked with Jeremiah's conviction that Yahweh has also deceived the people (4:10). What does this mean? The emphasis on doom in Jeremiah's preaching is connected with his conviction that clarification cannot be achieved and the truth cannot be communicated to the people. The shalom prophets supported by the impeccable authority of the Jerusalem Temple assure the people that all is well, and Jeremiah urges that the people are not to be blamed for believing those who speak in the name of Yahweh. How in these circumstances can truth defeat the lie? It is this kind of prophetic imprisonment that frustrates Jeremiah's attempts to reach his community with a message he knows to be true. He is defeated by the authority of a religious institution with which Yahweh seems to have conspired to deny effectiveness to Jeremiah's witness. Jeremiah suffers pain because of his estrangement and rejection, in this regard serving as the forerunner of the One who came to his own and was rejected by them (John 1:11). It is understandable that he was identified by exegetes with the Suffering Servant of Isaiah 40–55.

5. Feminist Literary Concerns. Many scholars are reading Jeremiah with eyes for gender issues and have discovered a plenitude of female language and imagery, yet with ambiguities in the way these images have been employed (see K. O'Connor [1992]). For instance, the pain of Jerusalem is personified in the suffering of women, suggesting that the prophet was sensitive to the women's plight. Moreover, God is portrayed as a mother (31:20) and as one who laments and weeps over Israel (8:19–9:3), a traditionally female role in the ancient Near East. In contrast, female imagery is negatively coded in personified Israel, the adulterous woman, prostitute, and wicked daughter. Additionally, women in Judah are directly aligned with idolatry when they are accused of kneading dough to bake cakes for the queen of heaven (7:18) or, most likely, the goddess they worship alongside the God of Israel (see S. Ackerman [1989]).

Bibliography: S. **Ackerman,** " 'And the Women Knead Dough': The Worship of the Queen of Heaven in the Sixth-century Judah," *Gender and Difference in Ancient Israel* (ed. P. L. Day, 1989) 75-94. **P. M. Bogaert,** *Le Livre de Jérémie: Le prophète et son milieu, les oracles et leur transmission* (BETL 54, 1981). **J. Bright,** *Jeremiah* (AB 21, 1965). **R. P.**

Carroll, *From Chaos to Covenant: Uses of Prophecy in the Book of Jeremiah* (1981); *Jeremiah: A Commentary* (OTL, 1986); *Jeremiah* (OTGu, 1989). **B. S. Childs,** *Introduction to the OT as Scripture* (1979) 339-541. **B. Duhm,** *Das Buch Jeremia* (KHCAT 11, 1901). **O. Eissfeldt,** *The OT: An Introduction* (1964³; ET 1965) 346-65. **W. Gross** (ed.), *Jeremia und die "deuteronomische Bewegung"* (BBB 98, 1995). **S. Herrmann,** *Jeremia: Der Prophet und das Buch* (Erträge der Forschung 271, 1990). *Jeremia* (BKAT 12, 1986–). **W. L. Holladay,** *Jeremiah* (Hermeneia, 2 vols., 1986–89). **F. Horst,** "Die Anfänge des Propheten Jeremia," *ZAW* 41 (1923) 111-12. **B. Huwyler,** *Jeremia und die Völker* (FAT 20, 1997). **J. P. Hyatt,** "The Deuteronomic Edition of Jeremiah," *Vanderbilt Studies in the Humanities* 1 (ed. R. C. Beatty et al., 1951) 77-95 = Perdue-Kovacs, 247-67; "The Beginning of Jeremiah's Prophecy," *ZAW* 78 (1966) 204-14 = Perdue-Kovacs, 63-87. **N. Ittmann,** *Die Konfessionen Jeremias* (WMANT 54, 1981). **W. McKane,** *A Critical and Exegetical Commentary on Jeremiah* (ICC, 2 vols., 1986–96). **S. Mowinckel,** *Zur Komposition des Buches Jeremia* (SUVK 2, historisk-filosofisk Klasse 5, 1914). **E. W. Nicholson,** *Preaching to the Exiles: A Study of the Prose Tradition in the Book of Jeremiah* (1970). **K. M. O'Connor,** "Jeremiah," *Women's Bible Commentary* (eds. C. A. Newsom and S. H. Ringe, 1992). **L. G. Perdue and B. W. Kovacs** (eds.), *A Prophet to the Nations: Essays in Jeremiah Studies* (1984). **H. G. Reventlow,** *Liturgie und prophetisches Ich bei Jeremia* (1963). **C. Rietzschel,** *Das Problem der Urrolle* (1966). **H. H. Rowley,** "The Prophet Jeremiah and the Book of Deuteronomy," *Studies in OT Prophecy Presented to Professor T. H. Robinson* (1950) 157-74 = his *From Moses to Qumran: Studies in the OT* (1963) 187-208; "The Early Prophecies of Jeremiah in Their Setting," *BJRL* 45 (1962–63) 198-234 = his *Men of God* (1963) 133-68 = Perdue-Kovacs, 13-61. **W. Rudolph,** *Jeremia* (HAT 1, 12, 1947, 1968³). **J. Skinner,** *Prophecy and Religion: Studies in the Life of Jeremiah* (1992). **G. A. Smith,** *Jeremiah* (Baird Lectures, 1922). **W. Thiel,** *Die deuteronomistische Redaktion von Jeremia 1–25* (WMANT 41, 1973); *Die deuteronomistische Redaktion von Jeremia 26–45* (WMANT 52, 1981). **H. Weippert,** *Die Prosareden des Jeremiabuches* (BZAW 132, 1973). **A. Weiser,** *Das Buch Jeremia* (ATD 20-21, 1952, 1969⁶). **A. C. Welch,** *Jeremiah: His Time and His Work* (1951). **C. F. Whitley,** "The Date of Jeremiah's Call," *VT* 14 (1964) 467-83 = Perdue-Kovacs, 73-87; "Carchemish and Jeremiah," *ZAW* 80 (1968) 38-49 = Perdue-Kovacs, 163-73.

W. MCKANE

JEREMIAH, LETTER OF

This apocryphal work purports to have been written by the prophet Jeremiah (see PROPHECY AND PROPHETS, HB; JEREMIAH, BOOK OF) to Jews about to be exiled to Babylon. Its purpose is ostensibly to warn the captives of the danger of assimilation to Babylonian religion during the "seven generations" of their exile.

In spite of the title the work is neither a letter nor a

writing of Jeremiah. The unknown author, who lived centuries later than Jeremiah, found his literary model in the prophet's letter to the Babylonian exiles in Jeremiah 29. The apocryphon is nevertheless more an impassioned discourse on the folly of idolatry than a letter; the influence of biblical satires on idolatry (Psalms 115; 135; Isa 44:9-20; Jer 10:1-16) is far more evident than is the letter format. The style of the tirade is rambling and repetitious. The recurring formula "therefore they evidently are not gods, so do not fear them" (v. 16, repeated with some variation in vv. 23, 29, 40, 44, 52, 56, 65, and 69) creates a superficial tenfold division, but there is no logical progression of thought from one section to the next. Rather, the author rather relies on repetition and biting satire to drive home his point that idols are lifeless, powerless, useless, and perishable products of human hands.

The Letter of Jeremiah is extant only in Greek and versions based on the Greek, but shows some signs of having been written originally in Hebrew or Aramaic. The date of composition is uncertain. Proposals range from the late fourth century to the late second century BCE. The place of writing is also unknown. The Babylonian flavor of certain cultic practices mentioned lends credibility to the superscription's indication of a Babylonian setting, but the caricature of idols is mostly generic and could reflect any location where idolatry posed a threat.

In most manuscripts of the SEPTUAGINT the Letter of Jeremiah appears along with the other supposed writings of Jeremiah (Jeremiah, Baruch, Lamentations) as a discrete work. However, some manuscripts and versions, including the VULGATE, attach it to the book of Baruch. Under the influence of the Vulgate, most English versions of the Apocrypha print the letter as the sixth and final chapter of Baruch, but others treat it as a separate composition since it has nothing to do with the book of Baruch.

Quotations and echoes of the Letter of Jeremiah in Christian literature are few. Aristides of Athens seems to have been influenced by the work in his apology of Christianity to the emperor Hadrian (117–138), and the fourth-century Sicilian rhetorician Firmicus Maternus quoted it extensively in his critique of paganism. Brief portions were quoted by TERTULLIAN and Cyprian. The letter is included by name in several patristic lists of canonical writings (Origen, Athanasius, the Council of Laodicea, Hillary of Poitiers, Cyril of Jerusalem, and Epiphanius), and others not mentioning it by name no doubt included it as part of the other supposed Jeremianic writings to which it was attached. JEROME called the letter a pseudepigraphon (see PSEUDEPIGRAPHA) and regarded it, along with the other books found in the Septuagint but not in the HB, as non-canonical (see CANON OF THE BIBLE). For the most part, the Letter of Jeremiah has experienced the same mixed fate within Christendom as have the apocryphal writings generally. Thus during the Reformation canonical status was denied to the Letter of Jeremiah and the rest of the Apocrypha by Protestant leaders but was affirmed by Roman Catholics at the Council of Trent in 1546; this latter decision was confirmed by the First Vatican Council of 1870.

Bibliography: A. H. J. Gunneweg, *Der Brief der Jeremias* (JSHRZ 3.2, 1975) 183-92. **R. A. Martin,** *Syntactical and Critical Concordance to the Greek Text of Baruch and the Epistle of Jeremiah* (1979). **B. Metzger,** *An Introduction to the Apocrypha* (1957) 95-98. **C. A. Moore,** *Daniel, Esther, and Jeremiah: The Additions* (AB 44, 1977) 317-58. **W. Naumann,** *Untersuchungen über den apokryphen Jeremiasbrief* (BZAW 25, 1913) 1-53. **G. W. E. Nickelsburg,** *Jewish Literature Between the Bible and the Mishnah* (1981) 35-42. **W. M. W. Roth,** "For Life, He Appeals to Death (Wis 13:18): A Study of OT Idol Parodies," *CBQ* 37 (1975) 21-47. **J. Ziegler,** *Jeremiah, Baruch, Threni, Epistula Ieremiae* (Septuaginta, Vetus Testamentum Graecum 15, 1957) 494-504.

R. D. CHESNUTT

JEREMIAS, ALFRED (1864–1935)

A member of a family represented by many Semitists and biblical scholars, J. was a student of Franz DELITZSCH, a conservative HB scholar, and his son Friedrich DELITZSCH, an Assyriologist (see ASSYRIOLOGY AND BIBLICAL STUDIES). In J. the interests of these two famous teachers were combined. He was the first to translate the Gilgamesh epic into German (1891), yet his primary professional work was as a rather orthodox Lutheran pastor in Leipzig (from 1890). At Leipzig University he became a lecturer in 1905 and *ausserordentlicher* professor only in 1922, yet he published extensively in the history of religions (see RELIGIONSGESCHICHTLICHE SCHULE) and in the interpretation of Assyriological scholarship, especially as it related to the Bible. His books found a wide audience.

J. joined in the BABEL UND BIBEL controversy, representing Lutheran orthodoxy but generally agreeing with the younger Delitzsch on the importance of the Assyriological results for the interpretation of the HB. More important, he was a close associate of H. WINCKLER and became one of the foremost representatives of the Pan-Babylonian school (see PAN-BABYLONIANISM), which concentrated more on the ideological dominance of Mesopotamia on its neighbors than on illustrative parallels with the Bible. (J. devoted himself to both of these concerns, however.) His later writings especially pushed far beyond Winckler to address speculative connections and many issues unrelated to the ancient orient (e.g., Buddhist and Theosophic piety; Bolshevik Russia as the Antichrist).

Works: *Das Alte Testament im Lichte des Alten Orient* (1904, 1930⁴; ET of 1906² ed, *The OT in Light of the Ancient East: Manual of Biblical Archaeology* [1911]); *Babylonisches im Neuen Testament* (1905); *Die Panbabylonisten: Der Alte Orient und die Ägyptische Religion* (KAO, 1907²); *Handbuch der altorientalisches Geisteskultur* (1913, 1929²); *Der Antichrist in Geschichte und Gegenwart* (1930).

Bibliography: W. Baumgartner, *ZA* 43 (1936) 299-301. D. O. Edzard, *RLA* 5, 3-4 (1977) 276. K. Johanning, *Die Bibel-Babel-Streit: Eine forschungsgeschichtliche Studie* (1988) 265-83. R. G. Lehmann, *Friedrich Delitzsch und der Babel-Bibel-Streit* (OBO 133, 1994) 43-45. E. F. Weidner, *AfO* 10 (1935–36) 195-96.

H. B. HUFFMON

JEREMIAS, JOACHIM (1900–79)

Born Sept. 20, 1900, in Dresden, Germany, J. lived between the age of ten and fifteen in Palestine, where his father was the German prior in Jerusalem. He studied theology and oriental languages at the University of Leipzig and concluded his studies with theological and philological doctorates (1922/23). In 1924 he became a *Docent* at the Herder Institute in Riga and the following year completed his *Habilitationschrift* at Leipzig. In 1928 he became *ausserordenticher* professor in Berlin and in 1929 full professor in Greifswald. From 1935 on he was full professor in Göttingen, later turning down quite prestigious positions at other universities. A member of the Confessing Church while the National Socialists were in power, after 1945, on the basis of both his scholarly and his moral authority, he participated in a decisive way in the reconstruction of the University of Göttingen. Beginning in 1948 he was a regular member of the Göttingen Academy of Sciences. He retired in 1968 and spent his final years in Tübingen, where he died Sept. 6, 1979.

J. combined a Lutheran-influenced PIETISM with masterful employment of historical-critical biblical scholarship. The initial works that already in his early years brought him the recognition of the scholarly community were concerned primarily with studies of Palestine and the environment of JESUS. Summarizing the most important contributions in his book *Jerusalem zur Zeit Jesu*, he critically evaluated the broad expanse of rabbinic material in order to draw up a precise picture of the relationships obtaining in Jerusalem in NT times. Jesus' activity and the beginnings of the Christian community are thrown into sharp relief against this background. J.'s studies of Golgotha (1926), the Passover celebration of the Samaritans (1932), the rediscovery of Bethsaida (1949), and the holy graves in Jesus' environment (1958) also were done as Palestinian studies.

The scholarly studies J. directed toward the NT were dedicated to finding an answer to the question of who Jesus of Nazareth is. In his monograph on Jesus' words at the Last Supper (1935), he sought to show through a subtle analysis of the primitive Christian tradition that the Last Supper should be understood within the framework of a Jewish Passover meal. In this context Jesus' words during the distribution of the bread and the wine emerge in their unique significance. The message that Jesus' death effects eschatological redemption is delivered first here in Jesus' own words and therefore preceded the confession of the early Christian community.

In his treatise on the PARABLES OF JESUS, which first appeared in 1947, J. sought to remove successive layers of additions and secondary interpretations from the Gospel tradition to expose Jesus' *ipsissima verba*. He showed that the parables are the cornerstone of Jesus' preaching. In them Jesus defends the good news of God's mercy against the objections of the righteous and compels the trusting answer of his listeners: "Only the Son of Man and his word can invest our message with full authority" (7). "All the parables of Jesus compel his hearer to come to a decision about his person and mission. For they are all full of 'the secret of the Kingdom of God' (Mark 4:11), that is to say, the recognition of 'an eschatology that is in the process of realization' " (159).

In the first part of his portrayal of NT theology, J. gave an account of his own theological research (1970). He saw the central content of NT THEOLOGY in Jesus' preaching. The multi-voiced witness of the congregation answers the call of the Son of man, who speaks and acts with incomparable authority.

A significant theological teacher, by his own example J. showed countless students that scholarly theology and church preaching belong inseparably together. The students he guided through doctoral dissertations were able to participate in his work, yet he freed them to draw their own reasoned opinions.

Works: *Jerusalem zur Zeit Jesu* (1922, 1924, 1937, 1963³; ET, *Jerusalem in the Time of Jesus* [1969]); *Golgotha* (1926); *Jesus als Weltvollender* (BZFCT 33, 4, 1930); *Die Passahfeier der Samaritaner* (BZAW 59, 1932); *Die Pastoralbriefe* (1934, 1975¹¹); *The Eucharistic Words of Jesus* (1935, 1967⁴; ET 1955, rev. ed. 1966); *The Parables of Jesus* (1946, 1984¹⁰; ET 1954, rev. ed. 1963); *Unknown Sayings of Jesus* (1948, 1963³; ET 1957, 1964²); *The Rediscovery of Bethsaida* (1949; ET 1966); *Jesus' Promise to the Nations* (1956, 1959²; ET 1958); *The Servant of God* (SBT 20, 1957, rev. ed. 1965); *Heiligengräber in Jesu Umwelt* (1958); *Infant Baptism in the First Four Centuries* (1958; ET 1960, 1961²); *The Sermon on the Mount* (Ethel Wocd Lecture, 1959, 1965⁵; ET 1961, 1966³); *Der Opfertod Jesu Christi* (CHZFBG 62, 1963; ET in *The Central Message of the NT* [1965]); *The Prayers of Jesus* (1966; ET 1967); *NT Theology I* (1970, 1979³; ET 1972); *Die Sprache des Lukasevangeliums* (1980).

Bibliography: **M. Black,** "Theologians of Our Time, II. J. J.," *ExpT* 74 (1962–63) 115-19 = W. Eltester (ed.), *Judentum-Urchristentum-Kirche* (FS J. J.; BZNWKAK 26, 1960, 1964²) IX-XVIII. **R. J. Braus,** "Jesus as Founder of the Church According to J. J." (diss., Gregorian University, 1970). **E. Lohse** (ed.), *Der Ruf Jesu und die Antwort der Gemeinde: Exegetische Untersuchungen J. J. zum 70. Geburtstag gewidmet* (1970), bibliography, 11-35. **E. Lohse,** "Nachruf auf J. J." *Jahrbuch der Akademie der Wissenschaften in Göttingen* (1979) 49-54 = "Die Vollmacht des Menschensohnes," *Die Vielfalt des NT* (Exegetische Studien sur Theologie des Neuen Testaments 2, 1982) 215-20.

D. E. LOHSE

JEROME (c. 347–420)

One of the most learned scholars of the early church, J. was an accomplished biblical translator and commentator. Born at Stridon on the border of Dalmatia and Pannonia (the Baltic area), he received an excellent education in grammar and rhetoric at Rome, studying under the famous Latin grammarian Aelius Donatus, and began to learn Greek as well. After his baptism J. moved to Trier and then to Aquileia, where he cultivated the ascetic life with his friends Rufinus and Chromatius. J.'s first biblical study, a commentary on Obadiah, dates from this period.

Around 374 J. moved to Antioch, where he experienced the famous dream for which he was accused of being more a "Ciceronian" than a Christian (*Ep.* 22.30). While pursuing the ascetic life in the nearby desert of Chalcis, he began to learn Hebrew from a converted Jew. He later attended lectures on Scripture by Apollinaris, bishop of Laodicea, and met GREGORY OF NAZIANZUS, who no doubt encouraged his incipient interest in ORIGEN. During these years he translated Origen's homilies on Jeremiah and Ezekiel and EUSEBIUS's *Chronicle.*

In 382 J. traveled to Rome, where the bishop Damasus invited him to stay and serve as papal secretary. At Damasus's request J. began to correct the earlier Latin versions of the Gospels, for which he consulted ancient Greek codices. He also produced the first of three Latin translations of the psalms (the so-called Roman psalter) and translations of two of Origen's homilies on the Song of Songs. At Rome J. also became the mentor of a coterie of noble women whom he guided in the ascetic life and the study of Scripture.

When Damasus died in 384, J. was no longer welcome at Rome. He traveled east and eventually settled in Bethlehem (386), spending the remainder of his life there in intense literary activity. He maintained constant correspondence with friends throughout the empire and did not hesitate to engage in doctrinal controversy, particularly regarding Origenism and Pelagianism (see PELAGIUS). Most of J.'s biblical work dates from this period. His accomplishments include translations of most of the Bible, his own biblical commentaries, and translations of the works of other Bible scholars.

J. is perhaps best known as the translator of the Latin Bible (the VULGATE). Not all of today's Vulgate, however, is his; of the NT only the Gospels are definitely from his hand. For the HB, J. originally intended only to revise the OL versions using the SEPTUAGINT text. Since Origen's *Hexapla* was available to him at Caesarea, J. made use of it as well as the other Greek versions found there. All that remains of these early versions are the texts of Job and the psalms (in the second "Gallican" version) and the prefaces to Chronicles, Proverbs, Ecclesiastes, and the Song of Songs.

By the early 390s, however, J. had decided that a satisfactory Latin translation of the HB had to be based on the original Hebrew text (*Hebraica veritas*). Receiving assistance from several Jews in Palestine, he proceeded to translate the remainder of the biblical books. The work was completed by the end of 404. This new translation was widely criticized (e.g., by AUGUSTINE) because it implicitly devalued the Septuagint version, long used by the church and considered to be inspired (see INSPIRATION OF THE BIBLE). Attention to the Hebrew text had led J. to limit the CANON to only those books found in Hebrew.

J.'s most significant work as a biblical commentator was a complete series of commentaries on the Major and Minor Prophets, with the exception of one on Jeremiah, which was left unfinished at his death. J.'s method was to present two translations: one from the Hebrew, the other from the Septuagint. This was followed by a literal commentary, usually consisting of textual notes, with reference to other Greek versions and to Jewish traditions. Then came a spiritual exposition, often taken from Origen or another Greek commentator.

Other commentaries include one on Ecclesiastes, notes on the psalms, letters on selected biblical passages (*Epp.* 18A and 18B, *Ep.* 21, and *Ep.* 28), and the *Quaestiones Hebraicae in Genesim.* For the NT there are commentaries on Matthew, Galatians, Ephesians, Titus, and Philemon as well as assorted homilies. Besides the works of Origen mentioned above, J. translated nine of Origen's homilies on Isaiah, thirty-nine homilies on Luke, and the *De principiis* (no longer extant). He also translated and revised Eusebius of Caesarea's *Onomasticon,* a gazetteer of biblical places, and published his own book of Hebrew proper names.

Works (Commentaries): *Commentarii in IV epistulas Paulinas* (PL 26, 307-618 [331-656]); *Tractatus LIX in librum psalmorum* (CCSL 78, ed. G. Morin, 1958); *Commentarioli in psalmos* (CCSL 72, ed. G. Morin, 1959); *Commentarius in Ecclesiasten* (CCSL 72, ed. M. Adriaen, 1959); *Hebraicae Quaestiones in libro Geneseos* (CCSL 72, ed. P. de Lagarde, 1959); *Liber interpretationis Hebraicorum nominum* (CCSL 72, ed. P. de Lagarde, 1959); *In Hieremiam libri VI* (CCSL 74, ed.

S. Reiter, 1960); *Commentariorum in Esaiam libri I–XVIII* (CCSL 73 and 73A, ed. M. Adriaen, 1963); *Commentariorum in Danielem libri III* (CCSL 75A, ed. F. Glorie, 1964); *Commentariorum in Hiezechielem libri XIV* (CCSL 75, ed. F. Glorie, 1964); *Commentarii in prophetas minores* (CCSL 76 and 76A, ed. M. Adriaen, 1969, 1970); *Commentariorum in Matheum libri IV* (SC 242 and 259, ed. E. Bonnard, 1977); *Commentarius in Ionam prophetam* (SC 323, ed. Y.-M. Duval, 1985). **(Translations): Eusebius,** *Onomasticon* (GCS 11, 1, ed. E. Klostermann [*Eusebius Werke III, 1*] 1904); *Chronicon* (GCS 47, ed. R. Helm [*Eusebius Werke VII*] 1956²). **Origen,** *In Isaiam homiliae XXXII* (GCS 33, ed. W. A. Baehrens [*Origenes Werke VIII*] 1925); *In Lucam homiliae XXXIX* (SC 87, ed. H. Crouzel, F. Fournier, and P. Périchon, 1962); *In Canticum canticorum homiliae II* (SC 37bis, ed. O. Rousseau, 1966); *Homiliae in Ieremiam* (SC 238, ed. P. Husson and P. Nautin, 1977); *Biblia Sacra iuxta vulgatam versionem* (ed. R. Weber, 1983³); *In Ezechielem homiliae XIV* (SC 352, ed. M. Borret, 1989).

Bibliography: P. Antin, *Essai sur saint Jérôme* (1951); *Recueil sur saint Jérôme* (Collection Latomus 95, 1968). **J. Barr,** "St. J.'s Appreciation of Hebrew," *BJRL* 49 (1966–67) 281-302. **A. A. Bell,** "J.'s Role in the Translation of the Vulgate NT," *NTS* 23 (1977) 230-33. **A. D. Booth,** "The Chronology of J.'s Early Years," *Phoenix* 25 (1981) 237-59. **D. Brown,** *Vir Trilinguis: A Study in the Biblical Exegesis of Saint J.* (1992); *HHMBI*, 42-47. **F. A. Cavallera,** *Saint Jérôme: Sa vie et son oeuvre* (SSL Études et documents, 1922). **Y. M. Duval,** *Le livre de Jonas dans la littérature chrétienne grecque et latine* (1973). **P. Jay,** *L'Exégèse de saint Jérôme d'après son Commentaire sur Isaie* (1985). **A. Kamesar,** *J., Greek Scholarship, and the HB: A Study of the "Quaestiones Hebraicae in Genesim"* (Classic Monographs, 1993). **J. N. D. Kelly,** *J.: His Life, Writings, and Controversies* (1975); **W. C. McDermott,** "Saint J. and Pagan Greek Literature," *VC* 36 (1982) 372-82. **R. J. O'Connell,** "When Saintly Fathers Feuded: The Correspondence Between Augustine and J.," *Thought* 54 (1979) 344-64. **H. F. D. Sparks,** "J. as Biblical Scholar," *CHB* 1 (1970) 510-41. **J. Steinmann,** *S. Jérôme* (1958).

D. G. HUNTER

JESUS, QUEST OF THE HISTORICAL

Since A. SCHWEITZER's survey on this topic (1906), the beginning of the quest has customarily been dated with the posthumous publication of the writings of H. S. REIMARUS in the late eighteenth century. While this conveniently dates the opening of the quest in its modern form, in a broader sense the quest began with the first Christian century. Christianity, like Judaism, is a historical religion, i.e., a religion in which the encounter with God is experienced through historical events and human reflection on those events or the traditions about them. The NT itself reveals that the earliest critics sometimes challenged the Christian faith about events (Matt 28:13, the disciples themselves stole the body of Jesus) and the Christian interpretation of events (Mark 3:22, "by the prince of demons he casts out the demons"). For the believing community, however, events and interpretations were inextricably intertwined.

1. The Early Centuries. The Gospels that emerged in the latter part of the first century were attempts to portray the historical Jesus and the meaning found in his career. When the incipient mainline church identified four of these Gospels as uniquely authoritative (e.g., IRENAEUS *Against the Heresies* 3:11:11) they were affirming negatively that other gospels in circulation were less adequate presentations. Church leaders then supported this stance with the claim that eyewitnesses of the ministry wrote two of the four (Matthew and John), while associates of established figures in the church wrote the remaining two (Mark by Peter's associate; Luke by Paul's). Other gospels and gospel-like writings that continued to emerge through the centuries fall broadly into two groups: Either they amplified the canonical Gospels (see CANON OF THE BIBLE), filling in the silences—especially for the beginning or ending of Jesus' career—or they challenged in one way or another the dominant portrait (see J. Robinson [1977]).

Probably the average believer was untroubled by the minor discrepancies between Matthew, Mark, and Luke or by the more serious differences among these three and John. But Christian scholars who were steeped in the culture of the late Greco-Roman world wrestled with the historical questions raised by these discrepancies (see R. Grant [1961]). ORIGEN, early in the third century, affirmed that every word in Scripture was fully inspired (see INSPIRATION OF THE BIBLE) but that Scripture had a threefold meaning: first, the literal or historical meaning, and then a two-tiered spiritual or symbolic meaning. He insisted that some passages in the Bible, including the Gospels, could not be accepted in their literal sense. The evangelists, he said, sought to speak the truth both literally and spiritually; but when this was not possible they preferred the spiritual to the literal, so that the spiritual truth was sometimes contained in literal falsehood (*Com. Jn.,* bk. 10). AUGUSTINE, writing his *Harmony of the Four Gospels* around 400 CE, also recognized multiple meanings in Scripture but was less cavalier in handling the literal or historical meaning. Thus, when two Gospels report the same event or speech in different language, he argued (a) that each reported only part of the total scene or (b) that the language differed but the sense was the same or (c) that contrary to appearances two separate events were recorded. If two Gospels report in different contexts what was unmistakably a single event, Augustine asserted somewhat casually that one evangelist followed the order of history, the other the order of his memory. He admitted that it was puzzling why the Holy Spirit guided the evangelists to create such apparent difficulties, but then added that, while he was sure there was an answer to this question, it did not concern him at the moment.

While the four Gospels were regarded as authoritative, some believers desired a unified presentation of Jesus' career. This desire was met by the Syrian TATIAN, a disciple of JUSTIN MARTYR who had converted to Christianity in Rome and then moved to Syria about 170 CE. He prepared a composite portrait of Jesus out of the four Gospels, i.e., the *Diatessaron* (out of four), possibly dependent on Justin's work. Translated into many languages, this became the most successful harmony in Christian history and dominated the field for a thousand years. Reconstruction of Tatian's original work remains somewhat speculative since it can be recreated only through various translations and rearrangements. He probably leaned heavily on Matthew and John, either because they were regarded as eyewitnesses or because both have strong outlines or chronologies (see J. Hill [1910] and C. Peters [1939]).

2. The Middle Centuries. Apparently the breakup of the Greco-Roman culture reduced interest in critical historical research. Medieval piety and the doctrinal statements of the church councils set the boundaries for the presentation of Jesus. A high evaluation of Scripture discouraged critical questions, and the assumption that the evangelists wrote independently of each other undergirded the acceptance of their reliability. Augustine's suggestion that Mark was an abbreviated Matthew had little influence, and even he did not use it in discussions of variations between the two. B. SMALLEY's study of medieval biblical scholarship (1941) indicates that there was more critical scholarship in these centuries than has generally been assumed, but it did not contribute to the quest. Lives of Jesus were produced chiefly for edification, e.g., the Old Saxon *Heliand* and Otfrid's *Evangelienbuch*. The later medieval "lives," while accepting fully the traditional religious perspectives, displayed a genuine concern for the actual life and humanity of Jesus. See *The Meditations on the Life of Christ* by an unknown Franciscan (not Bonaventure), Simone Fidati's *De Gestis Domini Salvatoris,* and most popular of all, *Vita Christi* by Ludolphus of Saxony. This last work made much use of apocryphal material (see APOCRYPHA, NT) but explained that it was used provisionally, i.e., without the same AUTHORITY as the four Gospels (see H. McArthur [1966] 57-84).

Although these centuries reflect little awareness of a need for the quest, developments in the sixteenth century reveal the beginnings of renewed historical questioning. The sudden blossoming of Gospel harmonies in that century (at least forty) and especially the evolution in the harmony format illustrate this renewal. While the evolution was not strictly linear, the following steps are clear: first, integrated harmonies similar to the Tatian tradition; then harmonies arranged in horizontal parallels, i.e., a passage from one Gospel followed the same passage from another Gospel; finally, harmonies with vertical, parallel columns. Generally the editors at-tempted to determine which version was in its true historical sequence, and then the parallels from other Gospels were placed there but not repeated. Only in the nineteenth century and later were extra-canonical parallels added in one format or another. Even in the sixteenth century creating harmonies revealed the serious problems involved in harmonizing details of events and their actual sequence. For instance, A. Osiander (1537) insisted that when two Gospels differed in sequence or significant details, two separate events must be assumed, whereas CALVIN assumed (1956–57) that such apparent discrepancies did not necessarily prove that more than one event was actually involved (see McArthur, 85-101, 157-64).

3. Eighteenth to Twentieth Centuries. The posthumous publication in the 1870s of excerpts from Reimarus's private manuscripts began the modern form of the quest, even though some of his ideas were borrowed from earlier English Deists (see DEISM). He argued that there was a basic discontinuity between Jesus' message and that proclaimed by his disciples after the crucifixion: that Jesus saw himself simply as the announcer of an imminent earthly Jewish kingdom, while the disciples created a new religion centering on the person of Jesus and containing concepts such as the deity, atoning death, resurrection of Jesus, the Trinity, and sacraments. This transformation of Jesus' message was, according to Reimarus, a deliberate creation by the disciples, who were disillusioned at his death but unwilling to return to the drudgery of their former lives. After two centuries, debate still continues on the questions, What was the nature of the kingdom Jesus proclaimed? What was his vision of his own role?

Some questions about the four Gospels, i.e., their nature and interrelationships, were clarified during the nineteenth century. Scholars concluded that the Fourth Gospel was late and of less evidential value for the historical Jesus than are the Synoptics (D. F. Strauss [1840[4]]; see SYNOPTIC PROBLEM); that the Synoptics were interdependent ("somebody copied"); that Mark was the earliest of the three and was a source for Matthew and Luke (J. Weisse [1838]; C. Wilke [1838]); that the later two Gospels also used a common written source or sources (Weisse) subsequently called Q; and that Matthew and Luke had also each used independent oral or written traditions. While conservative German scholars contested these conclusions and British scholars played them down (see F. Farrar [1874]), the conclusions gradually gained wide acceptance. Perhaps equally or more significant was the change in attitude toward the supernatural element in the Gospels. Certainly the eighteenth-century English Deists had rejected this element, but they remained outside the mainstream of Christian scholarship. Yet by the end of the nineteenth century dominant figures, especially in Germany, wrote lives of Jesus desupernaturalizing the Gospel tradition.

Even in England, where the supernatural was not explicitly denied and where the substantial historicity of the Gospels was still defended, writers began to place greater stress on the teachings of Jesus than on the supernatural elements in the tradition. Whenever scholars stressed the supernatural element it automatically helped to establish the uniqueness of Jesus. When that dimension was rejected or played down, uniqueness could be affirmed only by an appeal to his unique teachings or attitude. Furthermore, in traditional Christian thought the "work of Christ" had an objective effect on the devil or evil (*Christus Victor*), on God (*Cur Deus Homo*), on human beings ("the transformation of humanity"), or in all three areas. But in the new developments attention focused primarily or even exclusively on "the transformation of humanity" no matter what specific terminology was used. Even where the Gospels had been accepted as completely reliable historical documents there had been room for differences in the reconstruction of Jesus' career. But the questions now being raised about the reliability of the Gospels as sources opened the way for far more variations in the handling of these materials.

New techniques, new materials, and new perspectives on the quest have emerged in the twentieth century. The earlier source criticism was supplemented by FORM CRITICISM, which sought to classify the Gospel materials according to stereotyped "forms" that had emerged in oral transmission (e.g., apothegms, wisdom sayings, parables, etc.) in order to identify the earliest version of an incident and the "life situation" that led to its being remembered and reshaped. Later, attention shifted from the isolated units of tradition back to the evangelists in REDACTION CRITICISM, i.e., the attempt to determine the special interests and theologies of the writers, now viewed, not as mere compilers, but as deliberate theologians. It was hoped that these combined techniques would make it possible to trace the tradition backward to, or at least toward, the historical Jesus.

Also, new materials emerged during the nineteenth and twentieth centuries, materials that serve the quest at least indirectly. While the HB Apocrypha had always been known, other intertestamental literature was discovered, especially documents of Jewish apocalyptic (R. Charles [1913]; see also PSEUDEPIGRAPHA). There had been earlier attempts to interpret Jesus' career by using rabbinic literature produced from the second century CE onward (e.g., J. Lightfoot [1658–78]), but now new attention was given to this field with critical editions and modern translations of rabbinic documents. This resulted in the massive compilation by Strack and P. BILLERBECK (*Kommentar zum Neuen Testament aus Talmud und Midrasch* [1922–61]), which needs to be used with care but is an invaluable collection. The discovery of the DEAD SEA SCROLLS in the 1940s provided background data on a branch of dissident Judaism, while the Nag Hammadi documents provided items that may reflect the Jesus tradition at least partly independent of the canonical Gospels, especially the *Coptic Gospel of Thomas.*

W. WREDE's argument (1901) that the Markan "Messiah secret" was a creation of the early community's interpretation of a non-messianic Jesus received sharp criticism, but it forced scholars to consider the possibility of a transformation of the Jesus tradition by the post-resurrection community. Such skepticism was further developed by the more radical form critics, for whom the Gospels were primarily deposits of the post-resurrection faith through which the authentic Jesus could be glimpsed only uncertainly. H. Riesenfeld (1957) challenged this radical historical skepticism, arguing that a controlled process transmitted the early church tradition about Jesus. Rabbinic literature displays an intense concern for this chain of transmission of rabbinic sayings; since the NT contains references to "receiving" and "handing on" a tradition, it reflects the same concern and terminology used by the rabbis (see B. Gerhardson, who worked out this thesis in detail [1961]). Nevertheless, questions remain, such as: Did the rabbinic control system exist prior to 70 CE? Were the various Christian communities of the first century structured so that such a control system was possible? Do the contrasts between John and the Synoptics allow the assumption of such an organized control of oral tradition? However, this hypothesis is a reminder that oral tradition is not necessarily free-flowing gossip.

Debate continues concerning the degree of confidence to be placed in the Gospel tradition. A central theological issue was emerging, though not always expressed explicitly: Is the validity of the Christian faith dependent on the factual character of certain events recorded in the Gospels? If so, which events, and how is their authenticity to be established? If not, then is it the message of Jesus or some attitude attributed to him that has salvific meaning for those who respond? Those who have adopted largely or completely this second stance have followed various paths in their reconstructions of the historical Jesus. A. von HARNACK's book (1901) is regarded as typical of the liberal "Lives," with its stress on Jesus as the teacher about God the loving Father, the infinite value of the human soul, and the higher righteousness of the love commandment. A greater stress on social reform, in which Jesus' language about the kingdom is filled with content from the HB prophets, is found in the social gospel movement of the late nineteenth and early twentieth centuries.

The rediscovery of Jewish apocalyptic (see APOCALYPTICISM) led to stress on the eschatological element in the teaching attributed to Jesus, especially in the writings of J. WEISS (1892) and Schweitzer (1901). Since this "consistent eschatology" emphasis understood Jesus to have—mistakenly—announced the imminent end of history and the world, this view was sharply contested by some as incompatible with Jesus' knowledge. But this eschatological emphasis has continued to be influential in differing ways. C. H. DODD turned "consistent eschatology" into "realized eschatology" with his insistence that the words of Jesus were meant in a different sense, i.e., the kingdom was present in his ministry. On the other hand, the BULTMANN school accepted the literal meaning of the eschatological words but then "appropriated" the message in terms of existentialism (R. Bultmann [1926, 1934]). Many sought to solve the eschatology problem by urging that Jesus spoke of the kingdom not only as present in his ministry but also in a future, final fulfillment. It must be noted that Bultmann, always the skeptical historian, almost cut the link between the Jesus of history and the Christ of faith (only the "that" of the historical Jesus is decisive, not the "what"). But his students, e.g., G. BORNKAMM (1960), pulled back from this position. A somewhat different rejection of Bultmann's skepticism and existentialism appeared in E. Stauffer's argument (1960), perhaps overconfident, that a reevaluation of Jewish and Hellenistic sources could indirectly substantiate the historicity of events recorded in the Gospels, e.g., the star of the magi.

With the undermining of confidence in the substantial accuracy of materials even in Mark and Q, efforts began to establish criteria of authenticity. Among these were "multiple attestation," i.e., the presence of a given motif in more than one literary form, e.g., parable, controversy story. Also it was claimed that Aramaisms were evidence of an early stage in the tradition; that personal names tended to be added in the later versions; and that the beginnings and endings of pericopes were more apt to have been modified by the evangelists than the central core. It was hoped that the researcher, by recognizing these tendencies, could work back from later to earlier versions of narratives. Then the Bultmann school advanced the "dissimilarity principle" as a master criterion. This principle meant that material in the tradition "dissimilar" to first-century Judaism and the developing faith of the early church was in all likelihood correctly attributable to Jesus himself. Obviously this ruthless approach to the tradition eliminated some material from Jesus since he must on occasion have reflected elements from Judaism, and surely some elements in the church's developing faith must have come from him. So the "coherence principle" was added to the "dissimilarity principle,"—that is, once a minimum has been established by the dissimilarity test the researcher is justified in adding to that minimum items that "cohere" with the established minimum (see N. Perrin [1976]; and for critiques M. Hooker [1971a, 1971b] and D. Mealand [1978]). Probably no criterion yet proposed or to be proposed will ever establish complete historical certainty. The decision of each historian is the result of a multitude of factors, some objective, some subjective and even unconscious.

In the late twentieth century the situation was confused and once again in transition. Widely accepted dating of NT documents was challenged (e.g., see J. Robinson [1976]), and some scholars placed the Fourth Gospel among the early Christian documents, thus reestablishing its historical value for the quest. It has been questioned whether the alleged "tendencies" in the development of the synoptic materials can be objectively established (E. P. Sanders [1963]), and this in turn created skepticism about the identification of early and late versions of an incident. While a minority of scholars never accepted the priority of Mark or the existence of Q, the work of W. Farmer and his followers has forced a wide reopening of such questions and the reconstructions based on them. The conventional wisdom of Christian scholars about the relation of Jesus to traditional Jewish piety and the "sinners" has been called into question (e.g., Sanders [1985]). In some circles of NT scholarship attention has shifted from historical issues to the question of the meaning of language in itself and not as a means of access to some other historical reality, e.g., in STRUCTURALISM (see D. Patte [1976]).

4. Alternative Perspectives. A number of distinctive perspectives have emerged either to challenge or to enrich the dominant thrust of research on the historical Jesus. Some are more concerned with the meaning of Jesus for contemporary life than with the reconstruction of his career in the first century.

The Christ Myth perspective was first developed academically by B. BAUER. He began with an interest in Strauss's theory that the Fourth Gospel was predominantly mythological (see MYTHOLOGY AND BIBLICAL STUDIES) but over the years came to the conclusion that the entire gospel tradition was a personification of the myths of the Greco-Roman world (1877), i.e., the community created its own founder out of these myths. Late in the nineteenth century a Dutch school of critics reached a parallel conclusion. The Christ Myth theory achieved its greatest development in the writings of A. DREWS and was popularized in English by the writings of such scholars as W. B. Smith. These views were sharply attacked in studies on the historicity of Jesus by M. GOGUEL and S. J. CASE.

For a time some popular Marxist apologetic against Christianity adopted the Christ Myth theory, although this would not have been the view of Marx or Engels. Perhaps the first serious study on Jesus by Marxists was that of K. Kautsky (1908), who reduced Christianity to an expression of social and economic concerns and regarded religious interests as a form of self-expression. His work was also influenced by the Christ Myth theories of Bauer and his successors. European dialogue between Christians and Marxists has led some Marxists to recognize the reality of the historical Jesus and the positive significance of Christianity. M. Machovec (1976), though an atheist, writes about Jesus "with endless passion and enthusiasm" and recognizes Christianity's contribution to the resolution of genuine spiritual problems. (See also the less positive work of V. Gardavsky [1973].)

During the twentieth century Jewish scholarship has made many contributions to research into the career of Jesus. J. Klausner (1922), abreast of current NT scholarship, provided the first full-scale study. His extensive knowledge of first-century Judaism and related literature provided him with insights into Jesus' life. While rejecting Christian claims for Jesus and the supernatural element in the Gospels, he sought to reclaim Jesus as part of the great Jewish heritage. In his view, however, the ethic of Jesus was a heroic ethic for an elite, but quite impossible—and even destructive—for a normal society (see also D. Flusser [1969] and G. Vermes [1983]). Furthermore, Jewish scholars have produced detailed studies of particular aspects of Jesus' career, e.g., P. Winter (1974). While rejecting specifically Christian claims for Jesus, Jewish scholars are often less skeptical about the reliability of the gospel tradition than some Christian scholars.

The Quran of Islam (see QURANIC AND ISLAMIC INTERPRETATION) assigns a significant place to Jesus, who is often called "Son of Mary" (esp. Sura 5). There are references to his virgin birth, his miracles, his function as a prophet and apostle of God, and to his being taken up to heaven by God for a role at the end of history (Sura 4). The crucifixion story is alluded to, but the passage is widely understood to mean that another person replaced Jesus on the cross. Modern Islamic scholars have little interest in the contemporary quest, but they have provided discussions on the doctrine of the Trinity—viewed as tritheism—the question of Jesus' death, and the concepts of atonement and redemption. For a survey of Islamic thought, see W. Bijlefeld (1982) and articles by the Muslim scholars A. Merad (1968) and M. Ayoub (1980).

The "conservative perspective" is an imprecise name for scholars who accept in principle the techniques of modern historiography but who challenge many of the assumptions, methods, and conclusions of the dominant academic tradition. Generally speaking they affirm that (a) the factual character of certain events recorded in the Gospels is essential for Christian faith, (b) the Gospels provide substantially reliable material about the historical Jesus, and (c) the supernatural element in the Gospels, e.g., the virgin birth and the bodily resurrection of Jesus, is a decisive part of the Christian faith. A 1966 volume edited by C. Henry includes essays from sixteen basically conservative scholars from the United States, Great Britain, Sweden, and Germany dealing with various aspects of the quest. It is, however, difficult to find full-scale lives of Jesus by these or other scholars of

similar persuasion, although they have made valuable contributions to scholarship in commentaries and other specialized studies. In general works on the NT both B. METZGER and F. F. BRUCE have included sections summarizing the career of Jesus as they understand the Gospel record. (See also, I. Marshall [1977]).

The LIBERATION THEOLOGIES out of Black theology (see AFROCENTRIC INTERPRETATION), Latin America, and FEMINIST theology have one thing in common. From their various perceptions of oppression and discrimination they turn to the biblical tradition, including the Jesus tradition, seeking to discover and highlight those elements that stress God's concern for the oppressed. The quest as an academic pursuit is not a major concern for them, except insofar as its results serve their primary concern. Thus Black theology is powerfully moved by the escape from slavery in the exodus and the journey to the promised land. Although there is very little evidence that Jesus attacked slavery as an institution, his stress on the equality of persons before God and his concern for the poor and the outcasts reinforces this theology. (See the relevant sections on Jesus in J. Roberts [1976] and J. Cone [1970].)

Liberation theologies arose out of the attempt of Christian thinkers to utilize the biblical tradition for the liberation of Latin American societies from the oppression and poverty that have engulfed a great majority of the population. Theologians in these countries are concerned with the meaning of Christ for them in their situation. They recognize that the situation in first-century Palestine was different from that in Latin American nations, where, according to their analysis, the issue is not so much underdevelopment as dependency on the industrialized world, especially the United States. Their extensive discussions of christology refer, not to issues debated at Nicea or Chalcedon, but rather to the "practice" of Jesus in opposition to the dominant religious and political structures of his day. (See the survey by C. Bussman [1985] as well as major statements on Jesus by H. Echegaray [1983] and J. Segundo [1985].)

Feminist theology is in a position different from that of Black or liberation theology. The latter two appeal directly to major biblical motifs, whereas the situation of feminist theologians is complicated by the Bible's general acceptance of patriarchal structures in which women were subordinate. This acceptance is also explicit in some NT passages. Feminists can appeal to the biblical protest against oppression, but in the Bible there is little if any recognition that women are among the oppressed. Fortunately there are elements in the Jesus tradition and elsewhere that assume a more equal status for women. Feminists can and do appeal to those items as well as arguing from the general proclamation of God's concern for the oppressed. E. Schüssler Fiorenza has sought "to employ a critical feminist hermeneutics in order to explore the theoretical frameworks of various discourses about Jesus the Christ." (See also C. Newsom and S. Ringe [1992].)

5. The Current Scene. The last decades of the twentieth century have witnessed a renewal of attempts to revive the search for a historical Jesus, a development now frequently referred to as the "third quest." Among them is J. Meier's work *A Marginal Jew: Rethinking the Historical Jesus,* a "consensus" reconstruction (2 vols., 1991, 1994). Even though a somewhat greater importance is attached to the JOHANNINE material, Meier's historical Jesus is in the end derived primarily from the Synoptics, again keeping him well within conventional procedures of source selection. All the Gospels are interpreted primarily against the background of biblical and intertestamental Jewish materials, while less attention is given to contemporary Greco-Roman and Hellenistic materials. "Consensus" applies also to Meier's methodology. He has incorporated standard form- and source-critical methods for determining a text's authenticity and from those seasoned disciplines has systematically assembled and articulated his own uniquely defined list of criteria for judging a text's historical viability ([1991] 167-84). Finally, with respect to methodology, Meier focuses on the individual units of the early tradition, with less attention given to the narrative framework within which they have been placed. The results in the first volume are, then, a carefully documented life of Jesus, one that is systematically reasoned and even includes a full chapter exploring a probable chronological framework (see CHRONOLOGY, NT) into which all this might be placed. The second volume follows with an extensive section on Jesus and John the Baptist and on a reconstruction of Jesus' kingdom message defined in modified Jewish eschatological terms and concludes with a detailed discussion of miracles, which for Meier are linked closely to Jesus' kingdom pronouncements.

J. D. Crossan, arguably the most distinguished scholar within the widely publicized "Jesus Seminar" (see below), has produced a radically different portrait of Jesus (1991, 1994). The Gospel materials that Crossan declares "historical" often coincide with those used by earlier critics (see his inventory of the authentic sayings listed in xiii-xxvi), but his understanding of those texts is based consistently on a sociopolitical reading of the Gospel texts, one that in effect "de-eschatologizes" Jesus' historic proclamation. In Crossan's view Jesus did not envision an eschatological upheaval like that embraced and anticipated in Jewish eschatological texts (cf. Meier, above); rather, as a "Mediterranean Jewish peasant" Jesus called for the emergence of a radically egalitarian society that would undo the prevailing inequalities sustained by Judaism's strict purity laws and by contemporary Greco-Roman hierarchical, patriarchal, social, and political structures (1991, xii). While many will question Crossan's dramatic departure from the more "traditional" eschatological and apocalyptic portraits of Jesus (e.g., cf. Meier [1991]), his very carefully detailed study marks a hermeneutical reversal within historical Jesus studies that is no less revolutionary than Schweitzer's rejection of nineteenth-century social, political, and ethical versions of Jesus.

Much more popularly written are M. Borg's non-eschatological reconstructions of the historical Jesus (1987, 1994). Borg, also associated with the Jesus Seminar, insists that any portrait depicting Jesus as a prophet of the imminent end time would necessarily render Jesus' eschatological affirmation a mistake and, by extension, unimportant or irrelevant both historically and theologically. Borg understands the historical Jesus as a Spirit-filled sage or prophet whose sayings and parables clashed radically with the conventional wisdom of the day and who announced in ancient prophetic (not apocalyptic) style an imminent, God-ordained upheaval. Jesus' mission within this situation was to institute a "revitalization movement," replacing the "politics of holiness" (represented in Pharisaic and Temple piety) with a "politics of compassion," now graciously offered to those who traditionally had been neglected within the structures of conventional wisdom (i.e., outcasts, sinners, poor, women). Hence the future would be marked, not by history's apocalyptic end, but by God's new presence, transforming existing historical, political, social, and religious structures of the time.

In one way or another Meier's, Crossan's, and Borg's views are all a part of a continuing and highly controversial search for a historical, i.e., "pre-Easter" Jesus. This task implies a larger question of the theological meaning derived from any viable encounter with that historical Jesus. L. T. Johnson, raising that question in his critique of the Jesus Seminar (1996), contends that the "real" Jesus is not derived simply by reconstructing the historical pieces of pre-Easter Jesus tradition in the NT, whether within or outside the NT Gospels. The Jesus of Christian faith was first and always proclaimed within a framework of ultimacy that did not emerge simply from such historical units, however carefully reasoned and assembled, but from the total story that emerged out of resurrection faith. Even if the historical units of that resurrection could be historically reconstructed, they could not of themselves yield the Christian theological affirmation that Jesus is Lord, that this resurrected Christ has been taken up into the very being of God. Certainly this issue cannot easily or quickly be resolved in this particular context; yet it does seem worth noting that any continuing discussion of the "real" Jesus, on whatever historical terms, must address the important relationship between the historical quest and its meaning for NT faith.

Perhaps the most challenging development of the late twentieth century in the search for the historical Jesus began in 1985 with the organization of the so-called

Jesus Seminar under the leadership of R. Funk. Planned as a long-term, ongoing, collective research project, it has met biennially annually and has encouraged other NT scholars with standard research credentials to apply for membership as fellows. The initial phase, now largely completed, centered on the question: What did Jesus really say? A second phase would ask: What did Jesus really do? The seminar first gathered and analyzed some 1,500 versions of 500 sayings attributed to Jesus from the traditional four Gospels and other sources from the first three hundred years of Christian history. The seminar also developed a new translation of these materials, called the Scholars Version, which attempted to avoid overly traditional and familiar language. The fellows then discussed the various forms in which these collected sayings occurred, indicating their judgments on historicity and non-historicity by voting with colored beads—red, pink, gray, or black. Red or black indicated firm votes for or against authenticity, while pink or gray expressed more hesitant judgments. The colors were converted into numbers (red = 3; pink = 2; gray = 1; black = 0), which were converted into decimals, added, then divided by the number of votes cast. Then the individual sayings were printed in the color indicated by the collective vote.

This led to the publication in 1993 of *The Five Gospels: The Search for the Authentic Words of Jesus.* After introductory material describing the whys and hows of the project, the four Gospels are quoted in full in the order Mark, Matthew, Luke, John, along with Thomas—obviously using the Scholars Version. The sayings of Jesus are printed in the color indicated by the collective vote of the fellows participating. Also, each saying or group of sayings is followed by a summary of the discussion that led to the vote on color, which is helpful in revealing the mind and thinking of the seminar fellows.

The image of Jesus that emerges has generated controversy. The "Jesus" of the seminar did not make or imply messianic claims, nor did he anticipate a divine culmination to history. The *Five Gospels* states that 82 percent of the words ascribed to Jesus in the Gospels were not actually spoken by him. Here it is possible only to suggest areas of the debate that will continue, e.g., Does the Coptic *Gospel of Thomas* deserve to be ranked with the four traditional Gospels? It is known in its full form only through the fourth-century Nag Hammadi manuscript (although three fragments dated c. 200 CE appeared in the Oxyrhynchus materials). Although the seminar recognizes that the present text of Thomas is liberally gnosticized (see GNOSTIC INTERPRETATION), it suggests that the original version—without these Gnostic motifs—probably originated about the same time as the Q document, i.e., about 50–60 CE. How big a leap is this? (But see J. Kloppenborg [1990] and S. Patterson [1993] for studies that may explain the seminar's deci-

sion.) Again, Paul clearly took for granted a messianic Jesus, and his message anticipated a divine denouement to human history. Presumably he never saw or heard the historical Jesus, but he was in touch with various early Christian groups in the 30 to 60 CE period. Is there any evidence that he and they differed on these assumptions? Another point may be easily clarified by the fellows of the seminar. It reports that some two hundred accredited scholars participated in their program, but only seventy-four are listed by name and academic pedigree in *The Five Gospels.* Do the statistics resulting in the color coding represent the votes of two hundred scholars, just those listed, or some combination?

6. Concluding Comment. It is unlikely that the foreseeable future will bring consensus on the historical Jesus. The careful reader will recognize that even the most magisterial reconstruction of Jesus' career is built on the basis of incomplete and perhaps conflicting evidence. Each decision is made plausible by the magister's skill, but each decision still has alternative possibilities.

Bibliography: For surveys and bibliographies see R. Brown (1977, 1994), Grant, Kissinger, Pals, Schweitzer, Thompson, and Witherington (1990, 1994, 1995). **Anselm,** *Why God Became Man* (1868). **Augustine,** *Harmony of the Gospels* (vol. 6 of *NPNF,* 1956). **M. Ayoub,** "The Death of Jesus, Reality or Delusion," *MW* 70 (1980) 91-121. **B. Bauer,** *Christus und die Caesaren* (2 vols., 1877). **W. A. Bijlefeld,** "Some Muslim Contributions to the Christological Discussion," *Christological Perspectives: Essays in Honor of H. K. McArthur* (ed. R. E. Berkey and S. A. Edwards, 1982) 200-215. **M. J. Borg,** *Jesus, a New Vision: Spirit, Culture, and the Life of Discipleship* (1987); *Jesus in Contemporary Scholarship* (1994); *Meeting Jesus Again for the First Time* (1994). **G. Bornkamm,** *Jesus of Nazareth* (1960). **C. Brown,** *Jesus in European Protestant Thought, 1785–1860* (Studies in Historical Theology 1, 1985). **R. E. Brown,** *The Birth of the Messiah* (2 vols., 1977); *The Death of the Messiah* (ABRL, 2 vols., 1994). **F. F. Bruce,** *NT History* (1971) 163-204. **R. Bultmann,** *History of the Synoptic Tradition* (1921; ET 1963); *Jesus and the Word* (1926; ET 1934). **C. Bussman,** *Who Do You Say? Jesus Christ in Latin American Theology* (1985). **J. Calvin,** *Commentary on a Harmony of the Evangelists* (1956–57). **S. J. Case,** *Historicity of Jesus* (1912). **M. Casey,** *From Jewish Prophet to Gentile God* (1991). **R. H. Charles,** *The Apocrypha and Pseudepigrapha of the OT in English* (2 vols., 1913). **A. Y. Collins,** *Feminist Perspectives on Biblical Scholarship* (Biblical Scholarship in North America, 1985). **J. H. Cone,** *A Black Theology of Liberation* (C. E. Lincoln Series in Black Religion, 1970) 197-227. **J. D. Crossan,** *The Historical Jesus: The Life of a Mediterranean Jewish Peasant* (1991); *Jesus: A Revolutionary Biography* (1994). **C. H. Dodd,** *The Parables of the Kingdom* (1935, rev. ed. 1961). **A. Drews,** *Die Christus Mythe* (1909–11). **H. Echegaray,** *The Practice of Jesus* (1983). **W. R. Farmer,** *The Synoptic Problem: A Critical Analysis* (1964). **F. W. Farrar, *The Life of Christ* (2 vols., 1874). **D. Flusser,** *Jesus* (ET 1969). **R. W. Funk and R. W. Hoover** (eds.), *The Five Gospels: The Search for the Authentic Words of Jesus* (1993); *Jesus as Precursor* (rev. ed., 1993). **V. Gardavsky,** *God Is Not Yet Dead* (1913). **B. Gerhardson,** *Memory and Manuscript: Oral Tradition and Written Transmission in Rabbinic Judaism and Early Christianity* (ASNU 22, 1961). **M. Goguel,** *Jesus the Nazarene: Myth or History?* (1933). **R. M. Grant,** *The Earliest Lives of Jesus* (1961). **A. von Harnack,** *What Is Christianity?* (1901). **A. F. Harvey,** *Jesus and the Constraints of History* (1980 Bampton Lectures, 1982). **C. F. H. Henry** (ed.), *Jesus of Nazareth, Saviour and Lord* (Contemporary Evangelical Thought, 1966). **J. H. Hill,** *The Earliest Life of Christ* (1910[2]). **M. Hooker,** "Christology and Methodology," *NTS* 17 (1971a) 480-87; "On Using the Wrong Tool," *Theology* 75 (1971b) 570-81. **Irenaeus,** *Against the Heresies* (ACW 55, 1992). **J. Jeremias,** *The Parables of Jesus* (1947, rev. ed. 1963). **L. T. Johnson,** *The Real Jesus: The Misguided Quest for the Historical* (1996). **K. Kautsky,** *Foundations of Christianity: A Study in Christian Origins* (1908; ET 1925). **W. S. Kissinger,** *The Lives of Jesus: A History and Bibliography* (GRLH 452, 1985). **J. Klausner,** *Jesus of Nazareth: His Life, Times, and Teaching* (1926). **J. S. Kloppenborg et al.,** *The Formation of Q: Trajectories in Ancient Wisdom Collections* (Studies in Antiquity and Christianity, 1987); *Q-Thomas Reader: The Gospel Before the Gospels* (1990). **J. Lightfoot,** *Horae Hebraicae et Talmudicae* (4 vols., 1658-78; ET 1979). **H. K. McArthur,** *The Quest Through the Centuries: The Search for the Historical Jesus* (1966). **M. Machovac,** *A Marxist Looks at Jesus* (1976). **I. H. Marshall,** *I Believe in the Historical Jesus* (1977). **D. L. Mealand,** "The Dissimilarity Test," *SJT* 31 (1978) 41-50. **J. P. Meier,** *A Marginal Jew,* vol. 1, *Rethinking the Historical Jesus* (Anchor Bible Reference Library, 1991), vol. 2, *Mentor, Message, Miracle* (Anchor Bible Reference Library, 1994). **A. Merad,** "Le Christ Selon le Coran" *ROMM* 5 (1968) 79-94. **B. Metzger,** *The NT: Its Background, Growth, and Content* (1965) 73-166. **B. F. Meyer,** *The Aims of Jesus* (1979). **C. A. Newsom and S. H. Ringe,** *The Women's Bible Commentary* (1992, exp. ed. 1998). **Origen,** *Commentary on John* (vol 9. of *The Ante-Nicene Fathers,* 1912-27). **D. L. Pals,** *The Victorian "Lives" of Jesus* (1982). **D. Patte,** *What Is Structural Exegesis?* (Guides to Biblical Scholarship, NT Series, 1976). **S. J. Patterson,** *The Gospel of Thomas and Jesus* (Foundations and Facets Reference Series, 1993). **N. Perrin,** *Rediscovering the Teaching of Jesus* (1976). **C. Peters,** *Das "Diatessaron" Tatians* (1939). **M. A. Powell,** *Jesus as a Figure in History: How Modern Historians View the Man from Galilee* (1998). **H. S. Reimarus,** *Fragments* (ed. C. H. Talbert, 1970). **H. Riesenfeld,** *The Gospel Tradition and Its Beginnings: A Study in the Limits of "Formgeschichte"* (1957). **J. D. Roberts,** *A Black Political Theology* (1976) 117-38. **J. A. T. Robinson,** *Redating the NT* (1976). **J. M. Robinson** (ed.), *The Nag Hammadi Library* (1977, 1988[2]). **E. P. Sanders,** *The Tendencies of the Synoptic Tradition* (SNTMS 9, 1963); *Jesus and Judaism* (1985); *The Historical Figure of Jesus* (1993). **E. Schüssler Fiorenza,** *In Memory of Her* (1983) 105-59; *Jesus: Miriam's Child, Sophia's Prophet* (1994). **A. Schweitzer,** *The Quest of the Historical Jesus:*

A Critical Study of Its Progress from Reimarus to Wrede (1906; ET 1910). **J. L. Segundo,** *The Historical Jesus of the Synoptics* (1985). **B. Smalley,** *The Study of the Bible in the Middle Ages* (1941, 1983[3]). **M. Smith,** *Jesus the Magician* (1976). **W. B. Smith,** *Ecce Deus: Studies of Primitive Christianity* (1913). **E. Stauffer,** *Jesus and His Story* (1960). **D. F. Strauss,** *Das Leben Jesu* (2 vol., 1840[4]; ET, P. Hodgson, *The Life of Jesus* [1972-73]). **G. Theissen,** *The Gospels in Context: Social and Political History in the Synoptic Tradition* (1991). **W. M. Thompson,** *The Jesus Debate: A Survey and Synthesis* (1985). **G. Vermes,** *Jesus the Jew: A Historian's Reading of the Gospel* (1983[2]). **J. Weiss,** *Jesus' Proclamation of the Kingdom* (1892; ET 1971). **J. H. Weisse,** *Die evangelische Geschichte kritisch und philosophisch bearbeitet* (1838). **C. G. Wilke,** *Der Urevangelist* (1838). **P. Winter,** *On the Trial of Jesus* (SJ, Forschungen zur Wissenschaft des Judentums, rev. ed. 1974[2]). **B. Witherington,** *The Christology of Jesus* (1990); *Jesus the Sage: The Pilgrimage of Wisdom* (1994); *The Jesus Quest* (1995). **W. Wrede,** *The Messianic Secret* (1901; ET 1971). **N. T. Wright,** *Who Was Jesus?* (1992).

H. K. MCARTHUR and R. F. BERKEY

JIMÉNEZ DE CISNEROS, FRANCISCO (1436-1517)

Cardinal Archbishop of Toledo, J. was not a scholar, but he possessed vision and considerable organizational talents. In 1508 he founded the University of Alcalá near Madrid and sponsored the preparation of the Complutensian POLYGLOT Bible between 1502 and 1517. The work presented the Hebrew text of the HB; Aramaic and Greek translations of the HB; the Greek text of the NT; and VULGATE translations of the HB and the NT. Besides offering the first edition of the Greek NT set in type (1514), the work inspired preparation of additional polyglot Bibles during the next two centuries. J. died Nov. 8, 1517.

Bibliography: M. Bataillon, *Erasmo y España sobre la historia espiritual del siglo XVI* (1966). **J. H. Bentley,** *Humanists and Holy Writ: NT Scholarship in the Renaissance* (1983). **B. Hall,** "The Trilingual College of San Ildefonso and the Making of the Complutensian Polyglot Bible," *SCH* 5 (ed. C. J. Cuming, 1965) 114-46. **M. Revilla Rico,** *La Políglota de Alcalá estudio historico-critico* (1917).

J. H. BENTLEY

JIRKU, ANTON (1885-1972)

A German OT scholar and Semitist, J. was born Apr. 27, 1885, in Birnbaum (Mähren). He studied Semitic languages in Vienna and Berlin (1904-08) and earned his doctorate in Vienna (1908). His most influential teachers were the Assyriologist Friedrich DELITZSCH, D. Müller, E. Sachau, and J. Barth. In 1910 J. turned to the study of theology at Rostock, where his most significant teachers were E. SELLIN and A. Seeberg. In 1913 he was promoted to lic. theol.; in 1914 he completed his inaugural dissertation in Kiel, becoming a *Dozent* in OT. He became a full professor in Breslau in 1922. In 1934 J. was moved to Greifswald by the National Socialist regime, and in 1935 to Bonn. He became emeritus in 1958 and died Dec. 3, 1972, in Graz.

J. was a versatile and much published scholar whose interests lay in the history and ARCHAEOLOGY of Syria and Palestine and in the cultural and legal history of the ancient Near East, especially the relationship between Israel and its ancient Near Eastern environment in the political, cultural, and religious realms. This work produced handbooks (1923, 1937) and comparative studies (1926a, 1927). The discovery and publication of the Ugaritic texts (SEE UGARIT AND THE BIBLE) particularly engaged J.'s interest. In addition to numerous competent essays he produced a German translation of the most important texts (1962) and a reconstruction of Canaanite religion (1966).

On the whole, J. represented a relatively conservative historical orientation that he saw confirmed by the results of excavations and by the findings in Israel's environment. He considered Genesis 14 a historically valuable document from ancient times and attributed the decisive role in the origin of Israel and of the Yahweh faith as well as the DECALOGUE and the covenant to Moses. He considered the immigration of Israel into Palestine to have occurred just as the biblical texts suggest. According to J., the people of Israel originated from two ethnic elements: the Israelites and the Hebrews, the latter a people traceable since the third millennium before Christ to various regions of the ancient Near East (1924)—a thesis that has become improbable in view of further textual evidence. J. surveyed the material as well as the spiritual culture and the world of the dead as well as the gods, so that a comprehensive picture of the overall life conditions and of the religion of Palestine in both pre-Israelite and Israelite times emerged.

Works: *Die Dämonen und ihre Abwehr im Alten Testament* (1912); *Die jüdische Gemeinde von Elephantine* (1912); *Mantik in Altisrael* (1913); *Die magische Bedeutung der Kleidung in Israel* (1914); *Materialien zur Volksreligion Israels* (1914); *Die älteste Geschichte Israels im Rahmen lehrhafter Darstellungen* (1917); *Die Hauptprobleme der Anfangsgeschichte Israels* (1918); *Altorientalischer Kommentar zum Alten Testament* (1923); *Die Wanderungen der Hebräer im dritten und zweiten vorchristlichen Jahrtausend* (AO 24, 2, 1924); *Das Alte Testament im Rahmen der altorientalischen Kulturen* (Wissenschaft und Bildung 219, 1926a); *Der Kampf um Syrien-Palästina im orientalischen Altertum* (AO 25, 4, 1926b); *Das weltliche Recht im Alten Testament; stilgeschichtliche und rechtsvergleichende* (1927); *Geschichte des Volkes Israel* (ThL 1, 1931); *Die ägyptischen Listen palästinenischer und syrischer Ortsnamen* (Klio.B 38, 1937); *Die ältere Kupfer-Steinzeit Palästinas und der bandkeramische Kulturkreis* (1941); *Die Ausgrabungen in Palästina und Syrien* (1956, 1970²); *Die Welt der Bibel: fünf Jahrtausende in Palastina-syrien* (1957, 1962⁴, reissued 1985);

Kanaanäische Mythen und Epen aus Ras Schamra-Ugarit (1962); *Geschichte Palästina-Syriens im orientalischen Altertum* (1963); *Der Mythus der Kanaanäer* (1966); *Von Jerusalem nach Ugarit: Gesammelte Schriften* (1966) includes *Dämonen, Mantik, Materialien* and additional essays.

Bibliography: S. KREUZER, "A. J.s Beitrag zum 'Form geschichtlichen Problem' des Tetrateuch," *Afo* 33 (1986) 65-76. O. RÜHLE, *RGG*² 3 (1929) 179; EKL 4 (1961) 546-47.

W. THIEL

JOACHIM OF FIORE (c. 1130–1202)

J. became abbot of Curazzo, a Benedictine, later Cistercian, monastery in Calabria but retired to the mountains of Sila to found his own congregation at St. Giovanni in Fiore. A later legend concerning his early pilgrimage to the Holy Land tells of a vision of the open Scriptures received on Mount Tabor. Two later visionary experiences, authenticated in his writings, gave him, he believed, a twofold key to the interpretation of Scripture.

J.'s famous doctrine of the meaning of history was grounded in the particular method of biblical exegesis expounded in his three main works. The "concords" of Scripture must be understood in two modes: a "pattern of twos" (*concordia duorum testamentorum*) and a "pattern of threes" (*concordia trium operum*). There are two dispensations in history, and hence concords between persons and events in the two testaments can be worked out. But because the Spirit proceeds from Father and Son, the threefold work of the Trinity can only be completed in three *status* (stages) of history—that of the Father (law), the Son (grace), and the Spirit (love and liberty). Here the concords of the first two *status* are extrapolated to form the vision of the third *status* yet to come.

J. also expressed the concords of history in terms of seven "seals" and seven "openings" and developed an original interpretation of the number twelve, dividing it into five and seven. Five symbolizes the five senses, the prior, the outer in history; seven, the seven gifts of the Spirit, the posterior, the inner in history. He then turned the traditional four senses of Scripture into five: historical, moral, tropological, contemplative, and anagogical. These provide the means by which individuals pass from things visible to things invisible. But beyond these is the prophetic "sense," which reveals the spiritual meaning of the time process. This J. called the *sensus typicus,* subdividing it into seven *intellectus* that embody the seven "modes" of the Trinity at work in history.

J. expounded this symbolism not only in writings but in a unique set of *figurae.* He died Mar. 30, 1202.

Works: *Liber Concordie Novi ac Veteris Testamenti* (1519; first four books ed. with intro. by E. R. Daniel, 1983); *Expositio in Apocalypsium* (1527); *Psalterium decem chordarum* (1527).

Bibliography: **D. Burr,** *DMA* 7 (1986) 113-14. **H. Grund-mann,** *Studien über Joachim von Floris* (1927). **R. E. Lerner,** *TRE* 17 (1988) 84-88. **B. McGinn,** *The Calabrian Abbot, J., in the History of Western Thought* (1985). **H. Mottu,** *La Manifestation de l'Esprit selon Joachim de Fiore* (Biblique Theologique, 1977). **M. E. Reeves,** *The Influence of Prophecy in the Later Middle Ages: A Study in Joachimism* (1969); "The Abbot J.'s Sense of History," *1274: Année Charnière Mutations et Continuités* (1977) 781-96. **M. E. Reeves and B. Hirsch-Reich,** *The Figurae of Joachim of Fiore* (OWS, 1972). **D. C. West** (ed.), *J. in Christian Thought: Essays on the Calabrian Prophet* (2 vols., 1970).

M. E. REEVES

JOB, BOOK OF

Wherever we turn in the history of Western thought, we find Job: The TALMUD, ath-Tha'labi's (d. 1035) "A Discourse of the Prophet Ayyub and His Trials," and W. Blake's (1757–1827) *Illustrations of the Book of Job* (1826) all demonstrate an enduring fascination with this tragic figure. From GREGORY THE GREAT to CALVIN and from C. JUNG to E. Wiesel (b. 1928), the image of Job haunts every attempt to explain suffering and to justify God's actions. Job's story has captivated the human imagination and has forced its readers to wrestle with the most painful realities of human existence.

1. Patristic Interpretations of Job. Like many books of the HB, the book of Job finds its earliest Christian reading in the NT. The SYNOPTIC Gospels (Matt 19:26; Mark 10:27; and Luke 1:52), PAUL (1 Cor 3:19; Phil 1:19; 1 Thess 5:22; 2 Thess 2:8), James (5:11), and the Apocalypse (Rev 9:6) refer explicitly or implicitly to the Joban text. These citations describe God's power, the "foolishness" of divine wisdom, the desire for death, and the famous "steadfastness" or "patience" of Job.

In the early church major commentaries on Job did not appear until the third century. One of the most important exegetes to initiate the reading of the book was ORIGEN. Unfortunately no commentary of his on Job survives; however, scholars have culled more than 300 citations from his writings, often accompanied by detailed exegesis. In the fourth and fifth centuries several major commentaries or sermons on Job appeared, including those by AMBROSE, CHRYSOSTOM, AUGUSTINE, and Julian of Eclanum (d. c. 454). Although these texts do not appear to have exercised major influence on the medieval Joban tradition, nonetheless, several themes emerge that characterize the patristic image of Job, some of which recur in medieval interpretations.

Job's virtue was a common theme. Both Origen and Chrysostom stressed that Job was a just man who feared God before the law was given to Moses. Chrysostom argued that before the law Job practiced evangelical doctrine and manifested an interior detachment (1 Tim

6:7), proving that for the just man there is no law (1 Tim 1:9) and that Christ did not come to teach anything new or unprecedented.

Perhaps it is this emphasis on Job's virtue that elicited teachings about free will from the Job text. Origen insisted on Job's free will and explained the mystery of evil in terms of the initial fall of preexistent souls; his Job became a prototype of the Christian martyr. In Chrysostom's various statements on Job, he too argued for Job's freedom as opposed to any fatalistic solution to the problem of evil. These discussions about free will found further expression in the Pelagian debates (see PELAGIUS) of the fifth century. Augustine's *Adnotationes in Job* was written between 399 and 404, before the outbreak of the Pelagian controversy. According to Augustine the story of Job portrays suffering as a test of the just person, which becomes exemplary for all subsequent Christian readers. In the later context of the anti-Pelagian controversy, Augustine's Job knew the universality of sin and recognized that the righteous person could expect no reward for right conduct. Moreover, by a special revelation Job learned the universal economy of salvation in a world where divine justice surpasses all earthly justice. Not surprisingly, Job played a different and more central role for Augustine's Pelagian opponents. As P. Brown notes, "Job was the hero of the Pelagians: he was a man suddenly stripped of the heavy artifice of society and capable of showing to the world the raw bones of a heroic individuality" (1967, 349). Julian of Eclanum is an example of an anti-Augustinian reading of Job. His *Expositio Libri Job* was influenced by Chrysostom, just as other Pelagians were influenced by the Latin translation of Chrysostom's homilies. Thus, by the mid-fifth century Job became a figure around whom theologians debated sin, justice, and human freedom (C. Kannengiesser [1974] 1218-22).

Many of these commentators considered suffering a providential benefit. For Augustine, Job's scourges were evils all the elect must endure as a test. Origen also portrayed the suffering of the righteous as a divine gift meant to heal and strengthen the sufferer, and Chrysostom placed Job's afflictions within the context of providence. All historical and natural events lie under the justice and goodness of God's providence; angels and demons render account to God, and creation also testifies to God's care.

But why would a providential God permit the devil to afflict the righteous? For Chrysostom this dilemma was exemplified in Job, while for Ambrose it was personified by Job and David (*De interpellatione Job et David*). Both authors gave the fullest expression to the view of suffering as beneficial, medicinal, and pedagogical. Chrysostom explained that the devil acts by God's permission in order to inflict "a terrible and hard pedagogy." Both he and Ambrose depicted this pedagogy in terms of athleticism: Suffering effects spiritual fortitude. To describe the muscular benefit of suffering, Ambrose drew on 2 Cor 12:9 and described Job "as an athlete of Christ" who attained greater glory through temptation. Job "was stronger when sick than he had been when healthy," and both Job and David found "strength in their afflictions." Chrysostom also saw Job as an "athlete of God" and his story as a battle fought in a stadium; God was Job's "trainer," and the devil was his adversary. Job, therefore, was the great victor.

Finally, these authors also associated Job's suffering with wisdom. Visual metaphors denoting insight and knowledge describe the experiences of Ambrose's Job and David. Job's friends are said to have suffered from "feeble insight," while the afflicted Job "spoke in mysteries," made "distinctions in the spirit," and uttered truths according to a knowledge of God's judgments. The insight and discernment gained by Job and David led to a wisdom that gave them a deeper perception into reality, a perception that allowed them to see the vanity and illusory nature of earthly prosperity and power. Unlike the wicked, Job and David were not "drunk" with the abundance of worldly possessions, but were wise in the knowledge that "abiding things cannot follow unless earthly things have failed."

Both Chrysostom and Ambrose related Job's suffering to a wisdom equated with detachment. Chrysostom's Job was the model of philosophy, the sage who was glorious in adversity because he had always been detached in prosperity. (Chrysostom continued this theme of wisdom in his interpretation of the whirlwind speech. At this point Job discovered true wisdom—namely, his own human weakness and the fear of God.) Ambrose also equated the wisdom of suffering with detachment. The adversaries of Job and David enabled them to transcend the "waves" or "sea" of this temporal, ever-fluctuating world. Thus, in the lives of Job and David, Ambrose found an expression of that ancient identification between suffering and freedom: A real and muscular suffering leads to a truer perception of reality that, in turn, frees the sufferer from earthly entanglements.

2. Medieval Commentaries on Job. In the Middle Ages Job appeared in poetry, mystery plays, liturgy, and biblical exegesis. The medieval era inherited the portrayal of Job as a warrior or *athleticus Dei* from sources like Prudentius's (d. c. 410) *Psychomachia*. In the various medieval reworkings of the Joban legend, we find Job as a wise man, a prophet (see PROPHECY AND PROPHETS, HB), and a philosopher. He was even portrayed as the patron saint of persons suffering from worms, skin diseases, and melancholy; and he was the patron saint of MUSIC. The cult of Job flourished from the fourteenth to the sixteenth centuries due to the ravages of the plague and the spread of syphilis; indeed, syphilis became known as "le mal monsieur saint Job." Finally, in the liturgy Job played a major role in the Office of the Dead, particularly in the Matins of the Dead or the Dirge proper. In this liturgical setting many medieval clergy and laity experienced the book of Job on a daily basis (L. Besserman [1979] 56-65, 71).

The precritical exegetical tradition divides into two trajectories in the Christian West: the allegorical tradition established by Gregory the Great and the literal tradition formulated most decisively by THOMAS AQUINAS. Between their works stands the interpretation of the great Jewish philosopher MAIMONIDES.

These readings of Job vary greatly from one another. Different exegetical methods as well as different philosophical and theological presuppositions make the world of precritical Joban exegesis seem labyrinthine. Despite these differences, however, medieval (and Reformation) commentaries examine topics that gravitate around issues of suffering, justice, history, and providence. More important, a unifying feature runs throughout all of these commentaries—namely, the concern with perception or understanding. Fundamentally, all Joban exegetes had to answer a basic question: What did Job understand that made him perceptually superior to his friends? The term *perception* does not mean that epistemology drives exegesis. For medieval and Reformation commentators the issue of perception expressed a deeper concern regarding the more explicit subjects of suffering, justice, and providence. What can the sufferer, who stands within history, perceive about the self, God, and reality? Can suffering, especially inexplicable suffering, elevate human understandings about God and the self? Are evil and injustice really matters of perspective? Is there a darker side of God and of reality that we must confront before wisdom can be found? The question that permeates the precritical Joban tradition is not *how* one knows, but *what* one knows.

Repeatedly these commentaries are suffused with terminology referring to what the human mind can know via the imagery of sight, given a certain perspective aided by revelation and illumined by faith. In all the commentaries the perceptual opposition inherent in the Joban story is central: Some speakers are perceptive, while others are not. Empirical evidence is not ultimate; for these exegetes there is a depth dimension to reality that transcends purely sensory, historical, and experiential ways of knowing. They all expressed a theme native to the book of Job: Things are not what they seem.

Gregory's *Moralia in Iob* was composed for a monastic audience and dates from the late sixth century. He interpreted Job as a multilayered text with innumerable literal, allegorical, and moral meanings. As the model for how one should endure suffering, Gregory's Job often collapses the literal and moral senses of the text: He is the literal embodiment of moral truth. For Gregory and his successors, however, Job was not the only moral exemplar in the story; his friends also dispensed lofty truths. But how does one account for the fact that Job's friends were reproved by God in 42:7-8?

Gregory answered by arguing that Job's friends said many true things but misapplied them to Job because they did not understand that his suffering was not punishment for past sins. Moreover, Elihu was corrected in chapter 38 but was not included in the divine rebuke of "Eliphaz and his *two* friends." Elihu's words were arrogant, then, but often true. These exegetical solutions were to recur in various fashions in late medieval and Reformation (Christian) commentaries on Job.

Job's speeches also created hermeneutical problems (see HERMENEUTICS). The justice of Job's suffering was guaranteed, according to Gregory, by increased merit in the afterlife. The problem was Job's behavior during his scourges. Two verses govern Gregory's exegesis of Job's laments: the Satanic challenge in 2:5 and the divine affirmation in 42:7. For Gregory these verses ensured that Job did not blaspheme under trial; to accuse him of cursing God was to say that Satan won the celestial contest recounted in the prologue. Such an accusation was also to deny God's final words.

These exegetical moves allowed Gregory to portray Job as the model for virtuous suffering and interior ascent. By combining the Neoplatonic hierarchy of being with his presuppositions about the enlightening and liberating power of suffering, Gregory read the book as a description of that arduous inner ascent toward God undertaken by the elect. He assumed that Job's ascent created an inward perception of reality made possible only by the double movement of turning inward and rising to a higher level of being, which is effected through suffering. Thus Job's "complaints" become words about the vanity of earthly prosperity. By embracing suffering he manifested the virtue of detachment, insight, and inner freedom. Rejoicing over the brevity and harshness of life, Gregory's Job escaped the dreaded danger of "tranquility." According to Gregory, Job knew that providence is most indiscernible when the good prosper and the wicked suffer because suffering frees the elect from the world and leads to wisdom. Hence Job discovered an anthropological wisdom that allowed him deeper insight into the self and the proper home of the soul on the eternal realm.

Gregory read the book of Job as a description of both the human condition and human history. For the sufferer standing within time the historical realm must be renounced in order to ascend to a higher perceptual reality. Gregory's identification of Job's virtue with detachment shows that the realm of time, change, and exteriority is the "exile" or "Egypt" of the present life. Gregory's view of history, however, was more complex than is first apparent, as is revealed on the allegorical level of the text. His portrayal of Job as a prophet and his many typological interpretations turn the mind, not toward the eternal, but "downward" toward a providential history. It is true that as the "literal" and "moral" Job ascended he expressed contempt for and freedom from the temporal world. But as the "allegorical" and "prophetic" Job ascended, he looked down on a typological history and recounted or foretold God's redemptive acts. As one who suffered unjustly, for example, Job inevitably became a type of Christ. This redemptive history, centered in the crucifixion, consisted of events that took place in time.

The whirlwind speech provides the most striking example of this temporal downward perspective gained from the eternal viewpoint. In Gregory's reading of chaps. 38–41, Job either remained on the historical level or typified the church. In both cases God addressed him through history. From the whirlwind God recounted God's salvific acts throughout history, foretold Christ's victory over Satan (demonstrated by God's power over Behemoth and Leviathan), and promised the final defeat of the antichrist. From this higher perceptual level granted in the whirlwind speech, Job sought the protection of God against the "Ancient Enemy" and thereby also saw that history is not utterly rejected; the devil is defeated by Christ in history. Sacred history creates a philosophy that both affirms the historical realm and relegates it to the lowest level of reality. By seeing the book of Job as allegorically relating sacred history, Gregory's allegorical-typological interpretation reclaims a part of historical existence as redemptive. Furthermore, this theory of history becomes a hermeneutical device that casts the Joban story in terms of perception, perspective, and the limitations posed by time. Thus, as Gregory's readers penetrate the meaning of the text, they rise with Job toward the eternal and contemplate the truths buried deeply within the realm they left behind.

Maimonides provided a very different reading of Job, as found in book 3 of the *Guide of the Perplexed* (c. 1185–90). According to Maimonides, the story of Job is not historically true but is a parable about the true meaning of providence. Since providence is one of the "secrets of the law," he explained this parable in a closely guarded and cryptic way.

At the beginning of his ordeal Maimonides' Job was morally righteous but not wise: He knew the deity only by "the acceptance of authority." Struck by inexplicable suffering, he fell into the error of "Aristotelianism," which Maimonides identified as the belief that God had abandoned the human race. Job's speeches, then, were not expressions of detachment but, rather, cries of despair. In his rendering of the Joban story, Maimonides traced Job's progress from traditional authoritative religion to despair and finally to wisdom.

By saying that Satan was the cause of Job's despair, Maimonides argued that Job's suffering was due to "imagination" or error. The deluding power of imagination is broken by Elihu's angel (33:23, 29), identified as the Active Intellect or the Tenth Intelligence. Human intellects who attain perfection are capable of intermittent union with the Active Intellect, during which the

Active Intellect exercises "providence" over them. In the book of Job, Maimonides found proof that "providence is consequent upon the intellect."

Maimonides' Job attained this union with the Active Intellect in the whirlwind speech. Here Job gained a wisdom that made him reject his former errors and accept the limitations of human knowledge. As he moves from imagination to wisdom, his confession becomes the hermeneutical key to the story. Previously he imagined that happiness consisted of health, wealth, and children. In chap. 42, however, he expresses his new "correct apprehension," whereby he realizes that those things he had imagined to be happiness were not the goal of life. For Maimonides, then, Job did not gain this perception through suffering. Rather, he suffered because he was ignorant, since suffering belongs to the realm of Satan, matter, and imagination; he had overestimated the good belonging to the sphere of time and change. His wisdom freed him from the illusions that cause suffering.

Job's "correct apprehension" was identical to Maimonides' "revised Aristotelianism"; i.e., the knowledge that providence does extend to some individuals who are capable of union with the Active Intellect. This wisdom detached Job from his adversaries and made him reject his earlier beliefs (shared by his friends) and his earlier despair. Most important, he learned the equivocal nature of language about God. A naturalistic reading of the "prophetic" revelation of the whirlwind speech allowed Maimonides to argue that human knowledge cannot move beyond the sphere of nature. Terms like *providence, purpose,* and *knowledge* cannot be applied to God in the way they can be applied to humans. Maimonides, then, portrayed Job's deepening insight, not in terms of "ascent," but in terms of restriction and incomprehensibility; Job's highest point of understanding was to confess what he could not know. In his newly gained perception of reality, he learned the limits of human knowledge. But, as Maimonides concluded, "If a man knows this [the equivocal nature of terms about God] every misfortune will be borne lightly by him."

Whereas Gregory interpreted Job allegorically and Maimonides read the book parabolically, Thomas's *Expositio super Iob ad litteram* (c. 1260–64) expounded the text according to the literal sense. Like Maimonides, Thomas saw the Joban story as a book about providence. However, while Maimonides denied personal immortality, Thomas made this belief the message of the book, i.e., that Job believed in personal immortality, while his friends (except Elihu) denied the afterlife. Thus 19:25 becomes the hermeneutical key to the book. Nonetheless, Thomas maintained that the issue at the center of the controversy between Job and his friends was the perception of order. For Thomas the presence of a just and good order in nature and in history is inseparable from a faith in providence. Doubts about providence arose regarding human events because "no certain order" appeared in them.

Thomas argued that because Job's friends (to varying degrees) denied immortality they restricted providence to the earthly life. To defend the justice of this earthly providence, they were forced to conclude that Job's adversities were due to sin. In the friends Thomas saw what we now call the deuteronomic view of history; i.e., that history is justly ordered, intelligible, and predictable as God punishes sin and rewards virtue. Thomas did not want to discard this theory altogether. He too admired the wisdom of Job's opponents, and to reclaim it he argued that on many crucial points Job agreed with his accusers.

Nonetheless, Thomas thought Job's friends were wrong and that their error was a perceptual one: They claimed to see within history an order that is not always discernible. The justice they professed to see is often reserved to the afterlife. Thomas's Job spoke rightly about God because his faith in immortality provided him with a perceptual superiority over that of his friends, a superiority based on the link between the doctrine of personal immortality and a justly ordered history. The afterlife functions as an extension of history so that God can exercise justice after death. Without immortality the proof for divine justice remains within history, as the friends argued.

Exegetically Thomas presented Job's belief by giving his laments the same literal reading as did Maimonides. Job's complaints were honest and experiential observations about human events if those events are judged without a doctrine of personal immortality. Thomas's Job showed that if providence is restricted to history, then disorder is the true character of that providential rule. Thus to restrict providence to history is to accuse God of injustice. This problem of God's injustice disappears, however, if there is an afterlife where God remedies historical injustices; hence Job's complaints became, for Thomas, a defense of divine justice. Moreover, he illustrated Job's ultimate faith in providence through the interpretation of Behemoth and Leviathan. Like Gregory, Thomas identified the great beasts as Satan; the story of Job thereby became a part of that providential drama involving God and Satan that has raged throughout history. By taking Leviathan "with a hook" God defeated Satan through the "hook" of Christ's incarnation. History, then, is the arena of God's redemptive action.

Thomas, therefore, both agreed and disagreed with his predecessors. As did Maimonides, he interpreted the book of Job in terms of providence. Unlike Maimonides, he affirmed God's individual providence and identified personal immortality as the belief that gave Job perceptual superiority. Like Gregory, he interpreted Behemoth and Leviathan as Satan, thereby connecting the end of Job's story with the prologue. However, Thomas's spirituality of suffering differed from that of Gregory. Thomas repeated Gregory's explanation for Job's afflictions, i.e., that God permitted Satan to punish Job in order to manifest his virtue. He also stated that trials contribute to salvation, but he gave no sense that Job rejoiced in his suffering. Thomas saw Job as "impeded" by pain. His Job did not ascend through suffering and affliction or turn his soul inward, thereby curing his perception and directing him to the eternal, for the process of suffering did not alter Job's perception. It was Job's faith in immortality that allowed him a deeper perception of reality. And, finally, by extending "history" to the afterlife Thomas affirmed, not the equivocal, but the analogous nature of justice. His use of immortality as a heuristic device functioned to delay divine justice, not to make it utterly unknowable.

3. Sixteenth-century Commentaries on Job. The late Middle Ages and the sixteenth century inherited both the Gregorian and the Thomistic Joban interpretations, as is evident in varying degrees in the works of NICHOLAS OF LYRA and Denis the Carthusian (1402–71). In the sixteenth century we can see the growing importance of the Thomistic literal tradition. T. CAJETAN's *In librum Iob commentarii* and OECOLAMPADIUS's *In librum Iob exegeme* both provide literal interpretations demonstrating knowledge of Maimonides and Thomas. Both exegetes stated that the book of Job is a debate about the nature of divine providence.

Calvin's *Sermons sur le livre de Job* (1554–55) represents the Reformation interest in the book and also shows the influence of the Thomistic literal tradition (probably known indirectly). Calvin too read the Joban story in terms of providence, portraying Job as the lone defender of immortality against Eliphaz, Bildad, and Zophar. Calvin's Job vindicated God's providence by extending divine justice to the afterlife. Most important, Calvin used the doctrine of immortality to set up the same perceptual opposition between Job and his friends as did Thomas. Accordingly, the friends (except Elihu) were wrong because they restricted providence to history and concluded that all suffering is punishment for past sins. This restriction made them misperceive the nature of history; to defend God's justice they claimed that history appears ordered. Job, however, knew that history often seems confused; providence is not always discernible, and sometimes God "hides" while the wicked prosper. Calvin stretched to the breaking point the perceptual tension inherent in the book. Job's suffering drove him toward a deeper awareness of the darker side of God and confronted him with two aspects of divine hiddenness: the inscrutability of God's justice and the incomprehensibility of divine providence.

Calvin argued that Job encountered two levels of God's justice—namely, that revealed in the law and a higher secret justice, which, according to Eliphaz in 4:18, can condemn even the purity of the angels. Since Job knew he was not being punished according to the lower justice of the law, his search for the cause of his afflictions led him to confront the "secret" justice of God. Calvin developed this theory of a twofold justice to defend God's acts; since God's will is the rule of justice, even those acts that transcend the justice of the law are righteous. Job's experience showed that there is no continuity between the infinite and the finite. While God's lower justice was revealed in the law, the higher justice was imperceptible to Job's mind, which left Job's God nearly eclipsed by his own inscrutability.

The idea of a twofold justice may have guaranteed God's justice, but it left Calvin's Job with a feeling of unrelenting dread expressed by his suspicion that God was exercising an "absolute power," a term Calvin interpreted to mean a cruel power unregulated by mercy and justice. To alleviate Job's dread Calvin mitigated his own exegetical device of God's twofold justice by asserting that at no time, including in the case of Job, does God ever act according to secret justice. God commits to judge only according to the lower justice of the law. But by blunting this theory, Calvin left Job at the whirlwind speech with no answer to his suffering because he knew nothing of the celestial contest recounted in the prologue. Calvin emphasized this dilemma by refusing to interpret Behemoth and Leviathan as Satan, hence Job never understood his situation allegorically through reference to God's battle with the devil. Calvin's Job seemed truly within the realm of incomprehensibility.

Nonetheless, Calvin refused to renounce completely the visibility and knowability of God. The imagery of nature that pervades the book of Job allowed Calvin to end his sermons by appealing to the revealed world of creation and thereby to find grounds for trust in a God who seemed to be receding into total darkness. To relieve this darkness Calvin juxtaposed nature and history as an opposition between revelation and hiddenness. For Calvin the order visible even in fallen creation served to demonstrate the providence of God over the cosmos. Therefore, in contrast to the incomprehensibility of God's actions in history stands the beauty and order in nature. But while one can appeal rightly to nature as proof of God's providence, it is wrong to claim to perceive this same order in history. Calvin cited this perceptual error, exemplified by Bildad's words in chapter 18, to show that Job's friends were wrong in failing to acknowledge the present disorder in history. In contrast, Job had faith in what he could not see—that is, in God's ultimate restoration of order.

In Calvin's literal exegesis of the whirlwind speech, however, God argues on the basis of nature. Here Calvin combined visibility and invisibility by placing within nature a dialectic between hiddenness and clarity. Nature reflects the wisdom of divine providence; however, it also transcends human understanding and leaves us with only a glimpse of God's providence. In short, the very majesty of nature infuses it with a kind of hiddenness.

According to Calvin, the use of nature in the whirlwind speech shows that the governing of history requires a wisdom and justice beyond that revealed in the cosmos. Still, despite the ultimate incomprehensibility of both nature and history, he left the faithful Job with a promise—namely, that the same God who governs the order of creation is powerful and wise enough to govern history and to bring order out of confusion. On the basis of the revelation of nature, Calvin's Job trusted that God is ordering human events with justice. Therefore, Calvin concluded by holding out the promise of continuity between God's revelation in creation and his governance of history.

4. The Modern Period. The seventeenth and eighteenth centuries produced an abundance of translations of Job into Latin, Greek, and several modern European languages (English, French, German, Italian, Spanish), as well as paraphrases, many of which were in verse (see D. Clines [1989] lxix-lxxv). Perhaps the most noteworthy is the translation by E. Smith (1776–1806; completed 1803; pub. 1810). Not only was it one of the first translations of a biblical book into English published by a woman but also one of the best translations of Job between the KJV and the late nineteenth century.

Although the question of the historicity of the story of Job had already been raised in rabbinic and medieval Jewish interpretation (*b. B. Bat.* 15a; *Genesis Rab.* 57; Maimonides), the issue became a topic of contention in the eighteenth century, with J. LE CLERC (1731) arguing for the fictive character of the Job story and A. SCHULTENS (1737) defending its historicity. In England W. WARBURTON published an eccentric but widely circulated study (2 vols., 1737–41) in which he argued for the book of Job as an allegory of the political situation of the Jews after the Babylonian captivity. The eminent Hebraist R. LOWTH refuted Warburton (1765), defending the antiquity and non-allegorical nature of Job.

Lowth's influential lectures on Hebrew POETRY (1753) mark an important stage in the LITERARY analysis and appreciation of Job. Arguing against a tradition that understood the book as analogous to Greek tragedy (maintained both by Theodore of Mopsuestia in the 4th cent. and by Theodore de Beza in the 16th), Lowth held that Job did not fit the formal criteria of Greek tragedies. The artistic quality of the book should be judged, rather, according to criteria appropriate to Hebrew poetry. In particular, Lowth praised Job for the poet's descriptive power in expressing character and manners, sentiments, and descriptions of natural phenomena.

European Romanticism of the eighteenth and nineteenth centuries was intrigued with the book in varied ways. Strongly influenced by Lowth, J. G. HERDER (1782–83) championed its nature poetry as an example of the sublime. The French Romantic poet A. de La-martine (1790–1869) interpreted Job as a type of the Promethean poet, passionate and eloquent, the embodiment of a humanity capable and worthy of dialogue with the divine. The most influential interpreter from the Romantic period, however, is W. Blake, whose famous *Illustrations* actually constitute more of a rewriting than an interpretation.

The meaning of Blake's illustrations has been variously interpreted, though all interpreters seek the key in his poetry and other writings. Blake used the account of Job to depict what he elsewhere calls the cleansing of "the doors of perception." Blake understood Job in his initial state as fundamentally failing to apprehend the nature of God, the world, and human existence. His outward piety is merely life according to "the letter" rather than "the spirit," represented in the first engraving by Job's holding the book of the Law on his lap (ill. 1). Thus, Blake's Job is not perfect and upright, as is the biblical Job, but misguided and a sinner. His sufferings serve to give him gradual awareness of his pride and his misperception of reality (ill. 6-11). God's appearance to Job from the whirlwind (ill. 13) serves as the critical moment of recognition for Job, who now sees the true God, the Divine Imagination. Although the book of Job makes no further reference to Satan the Accuser after chapter 2, Blake depicts a scene in which Satan is cast down from heaven into flames, along with figures who represent the errors that had characterized Job and his wife at the beginning of the book (ill. 16). In another departure from the biblical narrative, the penultimate illustration depicts Job telling his three daughters the story of his experience (ill. 20). The crucial role of ART in disclosing truth is emphasized by the wall panels to which Job points, paintings that depict scenes from his story. The final illustration, portraying Job's restoration, echoes the first. Job's children are gathered around him, but he no longer sits with the book of the Law on his lap. Rather, they all stand and play the musical instruments that in the first illustration had been hung on the branches of a tree.

Job also figured in philosophical discourse of the modern period. Already in 1584 the commentary on Job by the Spanish Augustinian theologian D. de ZÚÑIGA (Didacus à Stunica [1536–98]) had interpreted Job 9:6 as scriptural grounds for Copernicus's view that the earth revolves around a stationary sun. Zúñiga went on to argue for Copernicanism on scientific grounds as well; as a consequence, his commentary was condemned by the Roman Catholic Church in 1616 until the objectionable passage was removed (R. Blackwell [1991] 26-27, 122-23, 185-86). T. HOBBES (1651) drew on the divine speeches in Job not only for the image of Leviathan as symbol of the state but also as an illustration of sovereign power that does not justify itself by reference to law or reason. For the most part, however, Job played a role in debates over theodicy. G. Leibniz (1710) briefly referred to Job as an example of one who improperly complains of unjustified evil because he fails to see the divine purposes, whereas VOLTAIRE's article on Job in the *Dictionnaire Philosophique* (1764) satirizes the inanities of Job's comforters and their philosophical defenders. Although Voltaire considered the book of Job to be one of the most precious of all antiquity, he argued that it was written by an Arab, a claim that provided him with the occasion to make several anti-Jewish remarks. I. KANT's critique of Liebniz (1791) differentiated between "doctrinal theodicy," the attempt to discern the moral intentions of God from the world of experience by speculative reason, and "authentic theodicy," which is grounded in the practical knowledge of God as revealed. For Kant Job served as an example of authentic theodicy: His integrity elicits the divine revelation from the whirlwind, which manifests the resistance of the purposes of God to the operations of speculative reason. Job's faith, grounded on moral conduct and acknowledging the limits of reason, however, forms the basis of an authentic theodicy.

G. W. F. Hegel (1770–1831) referred to Job only briefly (ET 1895), citing him as an example of one who recognizes the contradiction between his righteousness and his condition of suffering and yet brings his discontent "under the control of pure and absolute confidence" in the harmony of God's power. Although the restoration of Job's happiness, which follows upon his submission, cannot be demanded as a right, nevertheless it reflects "this unity [of God] which brings about a state of well-being proportionate to the well-doing" (2:193). S. KIERKEGAARD (1813–55) treated Job in two writings, both published in 1843. In *Repetition* Job figures as the example of one who undergoes an "ordeal." In Kierkegaard's writings this term describes an experience that does not belong to the aesthetic, ethical, or dogmatic realm of existence but is, rather, transcendent, as it "places a person in a purely personal relationship of opposition to God" (210). Job's ordeal ends, however, as he receives in an unexpected manner the possibility of repetition—that is, of taking up his life again. In *Edifying Discourses* Kierkegaard explicitly treated only the Job of the prose tale, although in effect he read the entire book through the lens of Job's action in uttering the words in 1:21 ("The LORD gave; the LORD took; blessed be the name of the LORD"). Provocatively, Kierkegaard attempted to recover these words from their status as pious cliché and to read them within the narrative context as a radical form of the fear of God.

As critical biblical scholarship became a more self-conscious discipline during the late eighteenth century and in the nineteenth, it wrestled not only with the book's meaning but also increasingly with the investigation of the TEXTUAL, historical, and comparative issues that became the hallmark of scientific biblical criticism at this time. These issues have largely set the agenda for the study of Job until the present. The apparent success of source-critical analysis of the Pentateuch (see PENTATEUCHAL CRITICISM) in the nineteenth century led to an interest among biblical scholars in uncovering the compositional history of other biblical books. Job lent itself readily to such analysis. The stylistic and theological incongruity of the prose narrative (1:1–2:13; 42:7-17) with the poetic dialogue led scholars to posit separate compositions. Earlier critics who had anticipated the discussion of the compositional history of Job (R. Simon [1685]; A. Schultens [1737]) suggested that the dialogue was the oldest part of the book, the prose framework a later addition, a position that continued to have supporters (W. de Wette [1807]; S. Lee [1837]; K. Kautzsch [1900]; N. Tur-Sinai [1957]). More commonly, the prose tale was assumed to be an old written or oral tale that was taken over by the author of the dialogue as a narrative setting. (This view was established and given its classic shape by the work of J. Wellhausen [1871]; T. Cheyne [1887]; K. Budde [1896]; B. Duhm [1897]; P. Volz [1902].) Others, readily admitting the stylistic differences, saw no reason to posit different compositional stages or different authorship, arguing that "one and the same man can tell a story when necessary and sing when necessary" (E. Dhorme [1926; ET 1967] lxv; cf. S. Driver and G. Gray [1921]; G. Hölscher [1937]). Virtually all agreed, however, that the character Job and certain aspects of his story were drawn from an ancient legendary tradition.

Even more consensus existed that the Elihu speeches constituted a later addition to the book, added either by the author at a later date (A. Merx [1871]; E. Sellin [1919]; R. Gordis [1965]) or, more commonly, by another author (J. G. Eichhorn [1803³]; de Wette [1843]; Cheyne [1887]; Driver [1913]; E. Dhorme [1926]; E. König [1929]), which continues to be the broad consensus. A few scholars have, however, attempted to argue for the Elihu speeches as part of the book's original design (Budde [1876]; C. Cornill [1892]; G. Wildeboer [1895]; cf. N. Habel [1985]).

Enthusiasm for recovering the book's compositional history led scholars into increasingly subtle arguments for considering the wisdom poem in chap. 28, as well as one or both of the divine speeches, as later additions. The third cycle of speeches in the dialogue, which lacks the regularity of the first two and assigns material to Job that seems inconsistent with his earlier views, was reconstructed in various ways. None of these positions, however, garnered the same degree of consensus as the proposals concerning the prose frame tale or the Elihu speeches.

Whereas earlier discussions of Job had looked for literary parallels and perhaps influence in Greek literature, the recovery of ancient Near Eastern texts in the late nineteenth century shifted the focus to alleged parallels from ancient Egypt (see EGYPTOLOGY) and particularly Mesopotamia (see ASSYRIOLOGY AND BIBLICAL STUDIES). The most important of these were texts portraying a righteous or emblematic sufferer like Job, especially the so-called Babylonian Job, properly known by its first line as *Ludlul bel nemeqi*; the *Babylonian Theodicy* (first published in 1875 and 1895, respectively; see W. Lambert [1960]); other fragmentary Akkadian texts (Lambert [1960]), including one from UGARIT (J. Nougayrol [1968]); and a Sumerian composition (S. Kramer [1953]). Of these the one with the strongest similarities to Job is the *Babylonian Theodicy*. Composed c. 1000 BCE, it consists of a poetic dialogue between a sufferer and his friend. In a series of eleven alternating speeches the sufferer laments his condition while the friend attempts to provide explanations and give advice. Unlike Job, the *Babylonian Theodicy* has neither a frame narrative nor a theophany; nevertheless, stylistic and thematic similarities to the dialogue portion of Job are significant.

Opinion has remained divided as to whether *Ludlul bel nemeqi*, the *Babylonian Theodicy*, and other such texts can be considered sources for or influences on the composition of Job (C. Kuhl [1953]; J. van Dijk [1953]; H. Gese [1958]; J. Gray [1970]; H. Müller [1978]). These texts, however, have encouraged a comparative investigation of why the issue of acute and apparently inexplicable suffering became such a problem in the Semitic cultures of the ancient Near East: possibly as a crisis in the wisdom tradition's ideology of the act-consequence relationship (Gese); as an intrinsic problem of a religious system that posited the gods as the guarantors of an order of justice (K. van der Toorn [1985]); as a consequence of changing conceptions of the gods (W. von Soden [1965]; T. Jacobsen [1976]); or as a response to sudden political or socioeconomic upheaval (R. Albertz [1981]).

The recovery of ancient Near Eastern literary and religious materials, including graphic art, has also permitted the recognition and clarification of a variety of mythological motifs (M. Pope [1965, 1973[3]]; G. Fuchs [1993]; see MYTHOLOGY AND BIBLICAL STUDIES), in particular the role of the animals in the divine speeches as evocative of the realm of the chaotic (O. Keel [1978]). Although the prominence of legal terminology in Job's speeches had long been recognized, ancient Near Eastern texts that clarify the structure of legal process and technical terminology have been important in recent efforts to argue for the centrality of the forensic metaphor in Job's understanding of his situation (H. Richter [1959]; S. Scholnick [1975]; M. Dick [1979]; Habel; E. Greenstein [1996]).

Whereas the Akkadian texts have had the greatest impact on issues pertaining to Job's religious and intellectual context, the discovery of the Ugaritic texts provided new resources for investigating linguistic problems. The poetic sections of the book were shown to preserve many archaic linguistic features (D. Robertson [1972]), and a number of obscure words and expressions have been clarified by reference to Ugaritic cognates and parallels (Pope; L. Grabbe [1977]). What was perceived as excessive and ill-disciplined application of comparative linguistics to Job on the part of some scholars (M. Dahood [1962]; A. Blommerde [1969]; A. Ceresko [1980]; W. Michel [1987]), however, has provoked a backlash, leading the most recent commentators to be cautious about either emending the text of Job or replacing the traditional definitions of Hebrew words with new definitions based on comparative Northwest Semitic linguistics.

Among the DEAD SEA SCROLLS are four fragmentary manuscripts of Job (2Q15, 4Q99, 4Q100, 4Q101). Although these manuscripts contain relatively little of the text, they do establish that the Elihu speeches were a part of the book by the turn of the era. One of the manuscripts (4Q101) is written in paleo-Hebrew (P. Skehan et al. [1992]). Since this script is usually reserved for books of the Torah, its use in 4Q101 may reflect the tradition of Mosaic authorship (see *b. B. Bat.* 14b-15a). In addition, two manuscripts preserve portions of an Aramaic TARGUM of Job (4Q157 and 11QtgJob), which appears to have been translated from a text closely similar to the MT, although the end of 11QtgJob differs significantly from the MT, both in detail and in extent, ending with lines corresponding to Job 42:9-11 (M. Sokoloff [1974]; G. Fohrer [1963b]).

Categorizing the interpretations of the book's meaning that have characterized late nineteenth- and twentieth-century biblical and theological scholarship is difficult, given the immense amount of critical literature and the subtle variations of interpretation. Nevertheless, some general observations can be made. One distinction might be made between those who see the meaning of Job as involving the fate of certain ideas and those who see the book less about theology than about religious experience. These positions need not be mutually exclusive, however. Although very few scholars argue that the book attempts to provide a positive rational theodicy (Cornill), a number have argued that its purpose is to contradict the doctrine of retribution (de Wette; Driver [1913]) or, more forcefully stated, to claim that retributive justice is not a part of God's plan for the world (M. Tsevat [1980]). Closely related are those analyses that interpret the content and imagery of the divine speeches more broadly as a refutation of Job's assumptions and expectations concerning the nature of the world and God's interaction with it (Habel; C. Newsom [1996]) or a repudiation of the image of God preserved in the dominant traditions of Israelite piety and salvation history (T. Jacobson [1976]; F. M. Cross [1973]). In these readings the problem presented by Job is considered to be rooted in a false or inadequate perception of reality; and the solution, communicated through the divine speeches, involves a shift to a more adequate paradigm of understanding.

More common is the view that the book's purpose is to examine the religious dilemma of the one who suffers inexplicably (M. Buber [1942; ET 1949]; M. Susman [1946]; C. Westermann [1956; ET 1981]; Fohrer [1963a]; H. Rowley [1958–59]; S. Terrien [1958]; R. Gordis [1965]; Clines). The quest for an intellectual solution is not just futile but ultimately beside the point. The problem presented by Job is the sense of acute isolation from God, an isolation that is overcome through the encounter with God at the book's climax. Interpreters who take this approach tend to see the significance of the divine speeches less in terms of their cognitive content than in their function as the Divine's self-disclosure. As BUBER put it, "God offers Himself to the sufferer who, in the depth of his despair, keeps to God with his refractory complaint; He offers Himself to him as an answer" (195).

R. Otto (1917; ET 1923, 1958²) gave a quite different estimation of the nature of the encounter with God as an experience of the holy, "the mysterium, presented in its pure, non-rational form" (79). Like Otto, P. Berger (1967) speaks of Job's being overwhelmed by his encounter with God, although Berger characterizes the encounter as the purest example of a masochistic theodicy. In K. BARTH's reading, Job begins with a knowledge of God as "Elohim"—that is, God as known through the various qualities that may be predicated through experience and tradition. Job's sufferings at God's hand confound his understanding, as his angry but bewildered protests indicate. In the theophany, however, Job encounters "Yahweh"—that is, God as unique Personality, the radical Subject, who cannot be comprehended in terms of the moral and metaphysical categories Job and his friends presumed. Barth suggests that in the revelatory moment Job knows the "two gods," Elohim and Yahweh, as one; however, it is Job's submission before the divine Subject that is the expression of true faith. In this submission Job finds reconciliation and freedom.

C. Jung's *Answer to Job* (1952; ET 1954) does not so much attempt to interpret the biblical text as to read it as an expression of the human unconscious in its effort to grapple with the phenomena of good and evil and their relationship (x). What the drama of Job explores, according to Jung, is the disclosure of the nature of Yahweh as "an antinomy—a totality of inner opposites" (7). Yahweh lacks self-consciousness and thus is not a moral being; yet Yahweh is dimly aware that "a somewhat keener consciousness based on self-reflection" (13) does exist in humanity. This awareness explains the hidden jealousy that underlies Yahweh's willingness to yield to the doubting thought represented by Satan. Although Job submits before Yahweh's might, the accomplishment of the book has been not only to reveal

Yahweh's dual nature but also to initiate a process of dialectic within God. There is not much movement in God's resolution of the inner antinomy within the book of Job; however, Jung sees the process continuing in God's union with primordial wisdom (Job 28), incarnated in the virgin Mary. Through this union "Job and Yahweh were combined in a single personality. Yahweh's intention to become man, which resulted from his collision with Job, is fulfilled in Christ's life and suffering" (46).

During the twentieth century a wide range of literature, both serious and popular, has drawn on the story of Job. Perhaps the most significant of these literary responses is F. Kafka's (1883–1924) *The Trial* (1925; ET 1937). Although not explicitly linked by intertextual references, connections between *The Trial* and the book of Job have been noted by both theological and literary critics (M. Buber [1964]; M. Susman [1929]; N. Frye [1957]). The relationship may be more complex than often assumed, however (S. Lasine [1992]). The Joban figure is Joseph K., who is arrested one morning for an unspecified crime. He passes through an endless bureaucratic hierarchy, trying to gain access to the court that has accused him; but he never gets beyond the lowest layers of this massive judiciary system. Finally, he is executed without ever having confessed to guilt or knowing the reasons for his arrest. This complex novel, open to many interpretations, shows one trait clearly: A story similar to Job's is told in terms of the inability to understand, delusion, the loss of self-knowledge, blindness, and the inaccessibility of the transcendent. Joseph K. never finds the insight, understanding, or perspective needed to allow him an escape from his nightmare. Not accidentally does *The Trial* bear the quality of a dream from which one cannot wake up. The judge for whom K. searches never becomes visible, hence K.'s situation remains inscrutable: He "dies like a dog," his end signifying a complete lack of redemptive insight. There is no depth dimension to reality that becomes accessible to the human mind. The confidence in noetic perception that in various ways permeates precritical commentaries has vanished.

Other twentieth-century interpreters have also stressed the elusiveness of God, even in the encounter with Job in the whirlwind and in the fact that the book ends without Job's ever knowing what precipitated the disasters that inexplicably befell him. Job's situation thus appears to have affinities with the existentialist tradition, especially in its absurdist mode (D. Cox [1978]). In R. Frost's (1874–1963) *A Masque of Reason,* when God finally reveals to Job in heaven the reason for his torment ("I was just showing off to the Devil"), Job comments that "I expected more than I could understand and what I get is almost less than I can understand" (1945, 11:327, 331-33).

A somewhat different post-WWII reading of Job is

present in A. MacLeish's (1892–1982) play *J. B.* (1956), which was culturally influential during the 1950s and 1960s. For MacLeish the Joban figure, J. B., confronts, not God, but the meaninglessness of the universe. The problem is not God's injustice but God's absence. The play's post-religious, humanistic perspective is articulated by J. B.'s wife, Sarah, who tells him, "You wanted justice and there is none—only love." When J. B. observes, "He does not love. He Is," Sarah replies, "But we do. That's the wonder" (151-52). The answer to the meaninglessness of the universe is not to be sought in God but in the human act of blowing on "the coal of the heart" (153).

MacLeish's distinctly humanistic engagement with Job contrasts with the post-Holocaust reading of Job in Wiesel's play *The Trial of God* (1979). The Joban figure is an innkeeper named Berish, the survivor of a seventeenth-century Russian pogrom. Wandering Jewish actors agree to put on a Purim farce, but the innkeeper insists that it be a legal proceeding in which God is put on trial. In order to stage the play a defender of God must be found. The character who agrees to take this role, "Sam," is eventually revealed to be Satan. Before his identity is disclosed, however, Sam has seductively articulated not only arguments in favor of God's righteousness reminiscent of Job's three friends but also rationalizations characteristic of modern theological interpreters of the book. Against these discredited theodicies Wiesel places the defiant faithfulness of Berish, who paradoxically insists that he will not renounce his Judaism but with his dying breath will protest the injustice of a God who stands by while his children are murdered.

God's failure to answer directly Job's cry for justice in the world has also provoked a line of philosophical and theological interpretation that rejects the book's apparent resolution, which is merely "a cover for the heresy Job so fearlessly wanted to proclaim," i.e., "the exodus of man from Yahweh" (E. Bloch [1968; ET 1972] 113, 118), a rejection of all theodicy (D. Soelle [1973; ET 1975]; T. Tilley [1991]; cf. J. Crenshaw [1984]). Biblical scholars who argue for such an interpretation as intrinsic to the book base their arguments in part on the linguistic ambiguity of Job's reply to God in 42:6 (D. Robertson [1977]; J. Curtis [1979]).

A similar dissatisfaction with the divine speeches is evident in analyses that read Job in light of R. Girard's (b. 1923) understanding of mimetic rivalry and the scapegoat mechanism (1985). The violence directed against Job by neighbors and exemplified in the friends' increasing hostility toward him can be seen as a means of shifting the potentially disruptive desire to imitate and ultimately displace a model who is also a rival. The hostility directed toward such a person can be effective as a means of social stabilization only if the object of hostility recognizes himself or herself as guilty and thus takes on the role of scapegoat. Girard believes that Job disrupts this process by insisting on his innocence and demanding vindication. Yet the God who would defend victims, whom Job invokes, is not the God who replies to Job. Girard thus argues that the divine speeches are not original to the book but a later attempt to neutralize Job's subversive words. J. Williams (1992), however, more ingenuously acknowledges the unity of the book but argues that the divine speeches are simply bad theology.

The difference of approach between Girard and Williams also illustrates a significant recent shift in biblical scholarship's understanding of the book. Earlier historical-critical analysis raised the problem of the book's unity by drawing attention to the sharply different styles and perspectives it contains. If it could no longer be naively read as a unity, the book nevertheless could be read as a sort of diachronic dialogue, as various hands interpolated characters and speeches or otherwise altered its shape and sequence. This approach continues to have its defenders, especially among European scholars (A. de Wilde [1981]; V. Maag [1982]; J. Vermeylan [1986]; J. van Oorschot [1987]), and provides the basis for such ingenious readings as that of B. Zuckerman (1991). Zuckerman posits that the poetic dialogue was originally written as a parody of an old oral folktale (see FOLKLORE) about a silently enduring hero. The disturbing poem with its excessively vocal Job attracted a series of interpretive supplements (the wisdom poem of chap. 28, the Elihu speeches, and finally, a written version of the old folktale). The authors of these supplements, however, failed to understand the parody of the poem. Thus the book of Job consists of a dialogue of misreading.

In general, however, accounts of the book of Job based on a REDACTION-critical model have come to be increasingly out of favor, at least in English-language scholarship, since the mid-1970s. This reaction emerges in part out of dissatisfaction with traditional historical criticism's tendency to fragment the text and its failure to provide an integrated interpretation of the book as a whole (F. Andersen [1976]; J. Janzen [1985]; J. Hartley [1988]). Increasingly, the final-form readings have been self-consciously informed by one or another model of literary criticism. Habel's 1985 commentary, indebted to Anglo-American New Criticism, provides a reading of the entire book, including the Elihu speeches, as a literary unity. This reading stresses the unifying function of the plot, the pervasive forensic metaphor, foreshadowing, and verbal and dramatic irony that work to produce "a literary whole integrating prose and poetic materials into a rich paradoxical totality" (9). Clines's 1989 commentary, by contrast, is more conscious of the role of the READER in producing different but legitimate readings. In an article published just a year later (1990), Clines outstripped his own modestly reader-oriented approach with a deconstructionist reading (see STRUC-

TURALISM AND DECONSTRUCTION), demonstrating how the book as a whole undermines the positions it affirms about suffering and the moral order in a way that prevents any determinate meaning. Published in the same year, E. Good's commentary draws on reader-oriented and post-structuralist approaches, especially the work of R. Barthes (1915–80), to champion a model of reading that is a form of play with a resolutely open text. For Good the book of Job is an indeterminate text that continually subverts the attempt to find in it a unitary truth. Ironically, literary readings, which were introduced in order to provide an alternative to the fragmentary and contradictory readings produced by historical-critical approaches, have themselves come to stress the fragmentary and contradictory nature of Job, as of all texts.

Contemporary scholarship's growing awareness of the role of the reader and of specific interpretive communities has had two other consequences for Job scholarship. The first is an increased interest in interpretations that are self-consciously based in concrete social or ideological communities. Thus readings of Job have been produced from the perspective of Latin American LIBERATION theology (G. Gutiérrez [1986; ET 1987]; J. Pixley [1982]), African American hermeneutics (S. Reid [1990]; see AFROCENTRIC INTERPRETATION), feminism (I. Pardes [1992]; Newsom; see FEMINIST INTERPRETATION), and political dissidence (W. Safire [1992]). Although these readings differ from one another in many particulars, they tend to be strongly favorable not only to the character of Job but also to the divine speeches and to the response Job makes to them. This affirmation contrasts sharply with the ambivalence or rejection of the book that one encounters in certain Marxist and post-Holocaust readings (Bloch; R. Rubenstein [1969–70]; Wiesel).

The second consequence of the interest in interpretive communities has been an increased attention to the history of the reception of Job. In the last quarter of the twentieth century, numerous critical editions and translations of works by important figures in the history of interpretation have appeared (e.g., Didymus the Blind, Julian the Arian, Gregory the Great, Thomas Aquinas, and Saadia) as well as monographs and articles on particular periods and interpreters (J. Baskin [1981]; J. Lamb [1995]; S. Schreiner [1986, 1988, 1989, 1994]; M. Yaffe [1979–80]). Clines's commentary contains an extensive bibliography of works on Job from the patristic period to the present. Complementing the textual record is the collection and analysis of graphic depictions of Job from antiquity to the present published by Terrien (1996). Although the history of the book's reception has not yet been extensively integrated into biblical scholarship, it is likely to have a much greater impact on Job studies than in the previous period when historical-critical scholarship privileged the attempt to recover the meaning of the book for its original audience.

Bibliography: **M. Adriaen** (ed.), *S. Gregorii Magni Moralia in Iob* (CCSL 143, 143A, 143B, 1979–85). **R. G. Albertson,** "Job and Ancient Near Eastern Wisdom Literature," *Scripture in Context* 2 (ed. W. W. Hallo et al., 1983) 213-30. **R. Albertz,** "Der sozialgeschichtliche Hintergrund des Hiobbuches und der *Babylonischen Theodizee* [*Ludlul bel nemeqi*]," *Die Botschaft und die Boten* (ed. J. Jeremias and L. Perlitt, 1981) 349-72. **L. Alonso Schökel and J. D. Sicre Díaz,** *Job, comentario theológico y literario* (Nueva Biblia Española, 1983). **F. Andersen,** *Job: An Introduction and Commentary* (TOTC, 1976). **J. Barr,** "The Book of Job and Its Modern Interpreters," *BJRL* 54 (1971–72) 28-46. **K. Barth,** *Hiob* (BibS[N] 1966 = *Kirchliche Dogmatik* 4, 3, 1). **J. R. Baskin,** "Job as Moral Exemplar in Ambrose," *VC* 35 (1981) 222-31; "Rabbinic Interpretations of Job," *The Voice from the Whirlwind* (ed. L. G. Perdue and W. C. Gilpin, 1992) 101-10. **P. Berger,** *The Sacred Canopy: Elements of a Sociological Theory of Religion* (1967). **L. Besserman,** *The Legend of Job in the Middle Ages* (1979). **T. de Beza,** *Jobus commentario et paraphrasi illustratus* (1583). **R. J. Blackwell,** *Galileo, Bellarmine, and the Bible* (1991). **E. Bloch,** *Atheism in Christianity: The Religion of the Exodus and the Kingdom* (1968; ET 1972). **A. C. M. Blommerde,** *Northwest Semitic Grammar and Job* (BibOr 22, 1968). **P. R. L. Brown,** *Augustine of Hippo: A Biography* (1967). **M. Buber,** *The Prophetic Faith* (1942; ET 1949); *Darko shel mikra* (1964), Hebrew. **K. Budde,** *Beiträge zur Kritik des Buches Hiob* (1876); *Das Buch Hiob* (1896, 1913²). **A. Ceresko,** *Job 29–31 in the Light of Northwest Semitic: A Translation and Philological Commentary* (BibOr 26, 1980). **T. K. Cheyne,** *Job and Solomon* (1887). **D. J. A. Clines,** *Job 1–20* (WBC 17, 1989), with extensive bibliography, lxiii-cxv; "Deconstructing the Book of Job," *What Does Eve Do to Help?* (JSOTSup 94, 1990). **C. H. Cornill,** *Introduction to the Canonical Books of the OT* (Theological Translation Library 23, 1907). **D. Cox,** *The Triumph of Impotence: Job and the Tradition of the Absurd* (AnGr 212, 1978). **J. Crenshaw,** *A Whirlpool of Torment: Israelite Traditions of God as an Oppressive Presence* (OBT 12, 1984). **F. M. Cross,** *Canaanite Myth and Hebrew Epic* (1973). **J. B. Curtis,** "On Job's Response to Yahweh," *JBL* 98 (1979) 497-511. **C. Dagens,** *Saint Grégoire le Grand* (1977). **M. Dahood,** "Northwest Semitic Philology and Job," *The Bible in Current Catholic Thought* (ed. J. L. MacKenzie, 1962) 55-74. **A. Damico and M. D. Yaffe** (tr. and ed.), *Thomas Aquinas: The Literal Exposition on Job* (CRSS 7, 1989). **S. F. Damon,** *Blake's Job* (1966). **E. Dassmann,** *RAC* 15 (1991) 366-442. **W. de Wette,** *A Critical and Historical Introduction to the Canonical Scripture of the OT* (2 vols., 1843). **E. Dhorme,** *A Commentary on the Book of Job* (1926; ET 1967). **M. B. Dick,** "The Legal Metaphor in Job 31," *CBQ* 41 (1979) 37-50; "Job 31, the Oath of Innocence, and the Sage," *ZAW* 95 (1983) 31-53. **J. J. A. van Dijk,** *La sagesse Suméro-Accadienne* (1953). **S. R. Driver,** *Introduction to the Literature of the OT* (1913⁹). **S. R. Driver and G. B. Gray,** *The*

Book of Job (ICC, 1921). **B. Duhm,** *Das Buch Hiob* (KHC, 1897). **J. Ebach,** "Hiob/Hiobbuch," *TRE* 15 (1986) 360-80. **J. G. Eichhorn,** *Einleitung in das Alte Testament* (1803³). **G. Fohrer,** *Das Buch Hiob* (KAT 16, 1963a); "4QOrNab, 11QTgJob und die Hioblegende," *ZAW* 75 (1963b) 93-97. **R. Frost,** *A Masque of Reason* (1945). **N. Frye,** *Anatomy of Criticism: Four Essays* (1957); *The Great Code: The Bible and Literature* (1982). **G. Fuchs,** *Mythos und Hiobdichtung: Aufnahme und Umdeutung altorientalischer Vorstellungen* (1993). **H. Gese,** *Lehre und Wirklichkeit in der alten Weisheit: Studien zu den Sprüchen Salomos und zu dem Buche Hiob* (1958). **R. Girard,** *Job: The Victim of His People* (1985; ET 1987). **N. Glatzer** (ed.), *The Dimensions of Job: A Study and Selected Readings* (1969). **E. M. Good,** *In Turns of Tempest: A Reading of Job with a Translation* (1990). **L. E. Goodman** (ed. and tr.), *The Book of Theodicy: Translation and Commentary on the Book of Job by Saadiah ben Joseph al-Fayyumi* (YJS 25, 1988). **R. Gordis,** *The Book of God and Man: A Study of Job* (1965); *The Book of Job: Commentary, New Translation, and Special Studies* (Moreshet Series 2, 1978). **L. Grabbe,** *Comparative Philology and the Text of Job: A Study in Methodology* (SBLDS 34, 1977). **J. Gray,** "The Book of Job in the Context of Near Eastern Literature," *ZAW* 82 (1970) 251-69. **E. Greenstein,** "A Forensic Understanding of the Speech from the Whirlwind," *Texts, Temples, and Traditions: A Tribute to M. Haran* (ed. M. V. Fox et al., 1996) 241-58. **G. Gutiérrez,** *On Job: God-Talk and the Suffering of the Innocent* (1986; ET 1987). **N. Habel,** *The Book of Job* (OTL, 1985). **D. Hagedorn** (ed.), *Der Hiobkommentar des arianers Julian* (PTS 14, 1973). **U. Hagedorn and D. Hagedorn** (ed. and tr.), *Johannes Chrysostomos Kommentar zu Hiob* (PTS 35, 1990). **U. and D. Hagedorn and L. Koenen,** (ed. and tr.), *Didymus der Blinde: Kommentar zu Hiob (Tura-Papyrus)* (1985). **J. Hartley,** *The Book of Job* (NICOT, 1988). **G. W. F. Hegel,** *Lectures on the Philosophy of Religion* (ET, 3 vols., 1895). **J. G. Herder,** *Vom Geiste der Ebräischen Poesi* (1782–83). **T. Hobbes,** *Leviathan* (1651). **G. Hölscher,** *Das Buch Hiob* (HAT 1, 17, 1937). **T. Jacobsen,** "Second Millennium Metaphors: The Gods as Parents. Rise of Personal Religion," *Treasures of Darkness: A History of Mesopotamian Religion* (ed. T. Jacobsen, 1976) 145-64. **J. Janzen,** *Job* (IBC, 1985). **C. Jung,** *Answer to Job* (1952; ET 1958). **F. Kafka,** *The Trial* (1925; ET 1937). **C. Kannengiesser,** "Job chez les Peres," *DS* 8 (1974) 1218-24. **I. Kant,** *The Failure of All Philosophical Attempts Towards a Theodicy* (1791). **H. E. Kaufmann,** *Die Anwendung des Buches Hiob in der rabbinischen Agadah* (1893). **K. Kautzsch,** *Das sogennante Volksbuch von Hiob und der Ursprung von Hiob cap. I. II. XLII, 7-17* (1900). **O. Keel,** *Jahwes Entgegnun an Hiob* (FRLANT 121, 1978). **J. Kegler,** "Hauptlinien der Hiobforschung seit 1956," *Der Aufbau des Buches Hiob* (ed. C. Westermann, 1977) 9-25. **S. Kierkegaard,** *Edifying Discourses* (1843; ET 1943); *Repetition (1843; ET 1983).* **E. König,** *Das Buch Hiob* (1929). **S. N. Kramer,** "Man and His God: A Sumerian Variation on the 'Job' Motif," *VT* 3 (1953) 170-82. **C. Kuhl,** "Neuere Literarkritik des Buches Hiob," *TRu* 21 (1953) 163-205, 267-317. **H. J. Laks,** "The Enigma of Job: Maimonides and the Moderns," *JBL* 83 (1964) 345-64. **A. de Lamartine,** *Cours familier de littérature* 2 (1956¹²). **J. Lamb,** *The Rhetoric of Suffering: Reading the Book of Job in the Eighteenth Century* (1995). **W. G. Lambert,** *Babylonian Wisdom Literature* (1960). **S. Lasine,** "Job and His Friends in the Modern World," *The Voice from the Whirlwind* (ed. L. G. Perdue and W. C. Gilpin, 1992), 144-55, 247-51. **J. Le Clerc,** *Veteris Testamenti Libri Hagiographi: Jobus, Davidis Psalmi, Salomonis Proverbia, Concionatrix et Canticum Canticorum* (1731). **L. Leclercq,** "Job," *DACL* 7, 2 (1927) 2554-70. **S. Lee,** *The Book of the Patriarch Job* (1837). **G. Leibniz,** *Theodicy* (1710). **J. Levenson,** *The Book of Job in Its Time and in the Twentieth Century* (1972). **R. Lowth,** *De sacra poesi Hebraeorum Praelectiones Academicae* (1753); *Letter to the Right Reverend Author of the Divine Legation of Moses* (1765). **V. Maag,** *Hiob: Wandlung und Verarbeitung des Problems in Novelle, Dialogdichtung, und Spätfassungen* (FRLANT, 1982). **A. MacLeish,** *J. B.* (1956). **J. Manley** (ed.), *Wisdom, Let Us Attend: Job, the Fathers, and the OT* (1997). **A. Merx,** *Das Gedicht von Hiob: Hebräischer Text* (1871). **J. H. Michaelis,** *Notae in Jobum* (1720). **W. L. Michel,** *Job in the Light of Northwest Semitic* 1 (BibOr 42, 1987). **H.-P. Müller,** "Keilschriftliche Parallelen zum biblischen Hiobbuch," *Orientalia* 47 (1978) 360-75; *Das Hiobproblem: Seine Stellung u. Entstehung im alten Orient und im AT* (Erträge der Forschung 84, 1995³). **C. A. Newsom,** "Job," *The Women's Bible Commentary* (ed. C. A. Newsom and S. H. Ringe, 1992) 130-36; "Considering Job," *CR:BS* 1 (1993) 87-118; "The Book of Job" *NIB* (1996) 4:319-637. **J. Nougayrol,** "(Juste) souffrant (R.S. 25.460)," *Ugaritica* 5 (1968) 265-83. **J. van Oorschot,** *Gott als Grenze: Eine literar- und redaktionsgeschichtliche Studie zu den gottesreden des Hiobbuches* (BZAW 170, 1987). **R. Otto,** *The Idea of the Holy* (1923). **I. Pardes,** *Countertraditions in the Bible: A Feminist Approach* (1992). **J. Pixley,** *El libro de Job: Comentario biblico latinoamericano* (1982). **M. Pope,** *Job: Introduction, Translation, and Notes* (AB 15, 1965, 1973³). **S. Reid,** "Suffering and Critical Awareness: The Foundation of a Quest for Witnesses," *Experience and Tradition: A Primer in Black Biblical Hermeneutics* (1990) 85-138. **H. Richter,** *Studien zu Hiob: Der Aufbau des Hiobbuches dargestellt an den Gattungen des Rechtslebens* (ThA 11, 1959). **D. Robertson,** *Linguistic Evidence in Dating Early Hebrew Poetry* (SBLDS 3; 1972); *The OT and the Literary Critic* (1977). **H. H. Rowley,** "The Book of Job and Its Meaning," *BJRL* 41 (1958–59) 167-206 = his *From Moses to Qumran* (1963) 141-83. **R. Rubenstein,** "Job and Auschwitz," *USQR* 25 (1969–70) 421-37. **W. Safire,** *The First Dissident: The Book of Job in Today's Politics* (1992). **S. H. Scholnik,** "Lawsuit Drama in the Book of Job" (diss., Brandeis University, 1975). **S. E. Schreiner,** " 'Through a Mirror Dimly': Calvin's Sermons on Job," *CTS* 21 (1986) 175-93; " 'Where Shall Wisdom Be Found?' Gregory's Interpretation of Job," *ABenR* 39 (1988) 321-42; "Exegesis and Double Justice in Calvin's Sermons on Job," *CH* 58 (1989) 322-38; *Where Shall Wisdom be Found? Calvin's Exegesis of Job from Medieval and Modern Perspectives* (1994). **A. Schultens,** *Liber Iobi* (1737). **E. Sellin,** *Das Problem des Hiobbuches* (1919). **R. Simon,** *Histoire critique du Vieux Testament* (1685²). **P. Skehan et al.,** *Qumran Cave 4.IV: Paleo-Hebrew and Greek Biblical Manuscripts* (DJD 9, 1992). **E. Smith,** *The Book of Job: A Facsimile Reproduction* (1996). **W. von Soden,** "Das Fragen nach der Gerechtigkeit Gottes im Alten Orient," *Mitteilungen der Deutschen Orient-Gesellschaft zu Berlin* 96 (1965) 41-59. **D. Soelle,** *Suffering* (1973; ET 1975). **M. Sokoloff,** *The Targum to Job from Qumran Cave XI* (Bar Ilan Studies of Near Eastern Languages and Culture, 1974). **M. Susman,** "Das Hiob-Problem bei F. Kafka," *Der Morgen* 5 (1929) 31-49; *Das Buch Hiob und das Schicksal des jüdischen Volkes* (1946). **S. Terrien,** *Job: Poet of Existence* (1958); *The Iconography of Job Through the Centuries: Artists as Biblical Interpreters* (1996). **Theodore of Mopsuestia,** *In Jobum* (*PG*) 66:697-98. **T. Tilley,** *The Evils of Theodicy* (1991). **K. van der Toorn,** *Sin and Sanction in Israel and Mesopotamia: A Comparative Study* (SSN 22, 1985). **M. Tsevat,** *The Meaning of the Book of Job and Other Biblical Studies* (1980). **N. H. Tur-Sinai,** *The Book of Job: A New Commentary* (1957, 1967²). **J. Vermeylen,** *Job, ses amis et son Dieu: La légende de Job et ses relectures postexiliques* (StB 2, 1986). **J. Voltaire,** *Dictionnaire Philosophique* (1764). **P. Volz,** *Hiob und Weisheit* (1902, 1921²). **R. Wasselynck,** "Les compilations des 'Moralia in Job' du VIIᵉ au XIIᵉ siècle," *RTAM* 29 (1962) 5-32; "Les 'Moralia in Job' dans les ouvrages de morale du haut moyen âge latin," *RTAM* 31 (1964) 5-31. **W. Warburton,** *The Divine Legation of Moses* (2 vols., 1737–41). **J. Wellhausen,** review of *Hiob* by A. Dillmann, *JDTh* (1871) 555. **C. Westermann,** *The Structure of the Book of Job: A Form-Critical Analysis* (1956; ET 1981). **E. Wiesel,** "Job: Our Contemporary," *Messengers of God: Biblical Portraits and Legends* (1976); *The Trial of Job* (1979); *Job ou Dieu dans le tempete* (1986). **A. de Wilde,** *Das Buch Hiob* (*OTS* 22, 1981). **G. Wildeboer,** *Die Literatur des Altes Testament nach der Zeitfolge ihrer Entstehung* (1895). **J. Williams,** *The Bible, Violence, and the Sacred: Liberation from the Myth of Sanctioned Violence* (1992). **A. Wright,** *Blake's Job: A Commentary* (1972). **M. D. Yaffe,** "Providence in Medieval Aristotelianism: Moses Maimonides and Thomas Aquinas on the Book of Job," *Hebrew Studies* 20-21 (1979–80) 62-74. **B. Zuckerman,** *Job the Silent: A Study in Historical Counterpoint* (1991). **D. de Zuñiga,** *Commentaria in librum Job* (1584).

C. A. NEWSOM AND S. E. SCHREINER

JOEL, BOOK OF

This short book of seventy-three verses, the second of the Minor Prophets in the MT, presents several interpretive problems—namely, the "locust" passages in chaps. 1–2 and what they describe; the relationship between the disasters recounted in those chapters and their reversal in chaps. 3–4; and the nature of the "day of the LORD" in the book as a whole. Troublesome historical-critical issues include the book's compositional unity and the date of its composition.

In Hebrew Bibles, the book of Joel has four chapters, a division used in rabbinical Bibles from the sixteenth century CE. Some English translations (e.g., the Jewish Publication Society Bible and the NAB) follow this convention. Other English translations follow the thirteenth-century tripartite division that S. LANGTON imposed on the VULGATE Joel and later used in the

Greek SEPTUAGINT Joel. In these translations Joel 3:1-5 equals 2:28-32, and Joel 4:1-21 matches 3:1-21.

1. Date of Composition. Unlike most other prophetic books (see PROPHECY AND PROPHETS, HB), neither the superscription (Joel 1:1; cf., e.g., Hos 1:1 and Amos 1:1) nor the text itself offers any historical information about the time of Joel's ministry. Nor is the book's position in the CANON any help. Literary (cf., e.g., Joel 4:16a [3:16a] and Amos 1:2a; Joel 4:18a [3:18a] and Amos 9:13b) rather than chronological considerations (see CHRONOLOGY, HB) may have won Joel its place between Hosea and Amos in the MT. Hypotheses about date, then, are based on internal allusion and linguistic data. The range of opinions (from the 9th cent. to the 3rd cent. BCE) attests that neither of these sources yields a certain date. The majority of commentators, nevertheless, place the book in the postexilic period, probably in the era following Ezra and Nehemiah.

Among other elements, this time frame best accommodates the absence of any mention of a king, emphasis on leadership roles assumed by the priests, an established and favorably regarded temple cultus, and the availability of a recognized prophetic tradition as a source for material (e.g., 1:15 = Isa 13:6; 2:6 = Nah 2:11[10]; 2:14 = Jonah 3:9; 4:18[3:18] = Amos 9:13). This period also accounts for the few late linguistic features found in the text: e.g., *sop* (Joel 2:20a); *sahanâ* (2:20b), elsewhere only in Sir 11:12; the participle *mešārēt* (Joel 1:9, 13; 2:17), used in apposition to priests and Levites only in late biblical Hebrew (2 Chr 29:11; Ezra 8:17).

2. Unity of Composition. Patristic, rabbinical, and Reformation interpreters regarded the book as a unity, the work of the prophet Joel. However, nineteenth-century scholars like M. Vernes (1845–1923) and J. Rothstein (1853–1926) questioned whether the entire book should be attributed to the prophet. Building on that suggestion, B. DUHM (1911) claimed that he had isolated Joel's original material from later additions. Duhm assigned 1:1–2:17 (with the exception of the *yôm YHWH* "day of the LORD" passages [1:15; 2:1b, 11b]) to Joel and described this material as an original poem describing devastation by locusts, an invading army, and a drought. The remainder of the book, according to Duhm, is the work of a Maccabean synagogue preacher preoccupied with eschatology and the day of the Lord. In order to link his own prose work (chaps. 3–4) to the original poem, this preacher added the *yôm YHWH* references, thus transforming the locust invasion into a sign of this future event. Independent of Duhm, J. BEWER (1911) also concluded that the day of the Lord passages were secondary, the work of a later apocalyptist (see APOCALYPTICISM) who combined two pieces Joel had written on separate occasions.

Variations and modifications of Duhm's hypothesis dominated later study of the book. Some scholars, however, argued that cultic background and concerns unified the book; for the most part, they found that the book's structure mirrored the structure of a lament liturgy and supported their theory that Joel alone, as the prophet who presided at such a liturgy, was the book's author (A. Kapelrud [1948]; M. Bič [1960]; C.-A. Keller [1965]; A. Deissler [1981]; Jorg Jeremias [1987]; and, to a lesser extent, G. Ahlström 1972]). While acknowledging the text's cultic elements, L. Dennefeld (1924, 1925, 1926) and J. Bourke (1959) identify the *yôm YHWH* as the motif Joel used to unify the text.

H. W. WOLFF's form-critical analysis (1977; see FORM CRITICISM) has most persuasively demonstrated the book's compositional unity at the hand of the prophet Joel. Wolff pointed out several features that unite the book and suggest a single author: e.g., a near-perfect structural symmetry, along with interlocking catchwords and catchphrases. Wolff did, however, consider 2:3*b*; 3:2[2:29]; and 4:4-8[3:4-8] to be later additions (perhaps by Joel himself) and 2:26*b* to be a copying error from 2:27. Later commentators, e.g., W. RUDOLPH (1971), L. Allen (1976), and W. Prinsloo (1985), also acknowledge the book's unity.

More recently, O. Loretz (1986) has used colometric analysis to isolate eight separate strata of tradition in the book of Joel. The earliest and most important are the texts intended as rites of lamentation and fasting to persuade the Lord to send rain (1:8-10, 11-12, 13, 14-17, 18-20; 2:12-14, 15-19, 21-24; 4:18 [3:18]); the locust passages (1:4, 5-7; 2:3*b*-8*a*, 25) are only secondary, intended to emphasize the severity of the drought, which for Loretz is the occasion for Joel's writing. To this core material later editors added layer after layer of material. A final redactor added the day of the Lord passages (1:15*b*; 2:1*b*, 11*b*; 3:4*b*[2:31]; 4:14*b*[3:14*b*]).

Like Loretz, S. Bergler (1988) argues that the book uses earlier materials; however, for Bergler, Joel himself shaped these materials into a final unity. He suggests that the core of the book is a poem about the effects of drought on the natural and the human world (1:5, 9-13, 17-20); this poem Joel transforms into a prayer in order to link the drought with the day of the Lord. The locust passages are meant to remind Joel's audience about the locust plague of the exodus, the divine intervention that inaugurated Judah's eschatological age.

R. Simkins (1991) and J. Crenshaw (1995) take the book as a unity originating with Joel, including the troublesome 4:4-8[3:4-8]. At the same time they acknowledge Joel's reliance on the larger prophetic tradition.

3. Structure. Like its date and compositional unity, the book's structure has been viewed in a number of different ways. Prinsloo, e.g., finds no real turning point in the text; a progression of passages, interlocked by repetition, builds to a climax in 4:18-21. Others maintain that the text falls naturally into two parts. Rudolph and Deissler make the division on the basis of content at the

end of chap. 2 (v. 27). Thus chaps. 1–2 describe contemporary events; chaps. 3–4, eschatological events. Ahlström, Wolff, Allen, Jeremias, and G. Ogden (1987), using literary form as a criterion, divide the book after 2:17. In this view, Joel 1:2–2:17 resembles a communal lament to which 2:19*b*–4:21[3:21] is the Lord's response.

Wolff suggests that the elements of 1:4–2:18 are almost symmetrically balanced by the elements of 2:19–4:3, 9-17[3:3, 9-17]. E. Henry (1985) identifies ten units in a quasi-chiastic structure whose two-part center is the penitential assembly (2:15-17); a new divine intervention as the Lord's response (2:18-27). Building on Wolff's analysis, D. Garrett (1985) also locates two turning points in the text (2:17 and 2:18); two interlocking chiasms (1:2–2:27; 2:2–4:21[3:21]) unite the book, each one moving from punishment to forgiveness.

Unlike other scholars, Simkins argues that the material in chaps. 3–4 neither continues the prophetic speech begun in 2:19*b* nor describes some future event. Rather, the entire book announces that a single day of the Lord is imminent.

4. Interpretation of the Locust Passages. The locust passages in chap. 1 and the reference of Joel 2:1-11 have generated varied interpretations. Most patristic and medieval interpreters read the locust invasion (Joel 1:4-7) as an allegory of a future historical military invasion, perhaps because the TARGUM for 2:25 translated the Hebrew terms repeated from 1:4 as "peoples, tongues, governments, and kingdoms." A marginal gloss on the sixth-century Greek codex Q is even more specific: Egyptians, Babylonians, Assyrians and Greeks. Some contemporary interpreters, such as Ogden and D. Stuart (1976), follow this view, asserting that the locusts of chap. 1 are metaphors for the 587 BCE Babylonian assault on Jerusalem. Such medieval Jewish scholars as RASHI, A. IBN EZRA, and D. KIMHI and the Christian interpreters JEROME, LUTHER, and CALVIN took the passage at face value. Anticipating the work of K. Credner (1831), these commentators understood Joel 1:4-7 to describe an actual locust invasion. Today most interpreters agree that a real locust plague occasioned Joel's preaching. Notable exceptions are Loretz and Bergler (see discussion below).

Scholarly opinion is also divided on the reference of Joel 2:1-11. Most interpreters agree that the poem describes either another phase of the invasion of 1:4-7 or an invasion of a new swarm of locusts (e.g., Allen, Bewer, Deissler, J. Thompson, Rudolph, Simkins). Details like the shaking of heaven and earth, hardly the work of real locusts, are interpreted as elements borrowed from the day of the Lord tradition and used to identify the locusts as the day itself or as its forerunners. Along with earlier Jewish and Christian commentators, a few scholars think that the poem describes the attack of an eschatological army, either a military force in the tradition of the "enemy from the north" or grotesque insects like those of Rev 9:1-11 (e.g., Jeremias, Keller, Ogden, Wolff).

None of the interpretations of 2:1-11 suggest a disaster that would intensify Judah's plight in the immediate future. A second infestation of locusts in the following spring is feasible; however, such an infestation would have been a weak threat at the end of summer when Joel preaches. The Palestinian meteorological cycle offers a better candidate for an immediate danger. At the end of a normal summer Judah needs rain. Joel fears that the east wind, which usually precedes the arrival of the winter rains and eventually gives way to them, will last too long and prevent the rain's timely arrival. Joel's use of locust and military imagery identifies this windstorm as the Lord's own army, coming to destroy the Judahites because, like drunkards, they have not understood the significance of the present agricultural crisis.

5. Interpretation of the Book as a Whole. Commentators offer a variety of interpretations for the book as a whole. According to Kapelrud, Joel was a cult prophet who used a locust plague as an occasion to castigate his audience for its participation in mourning rites for the fertility god Baal during the dry summer. The locusts were a sign that the day of the Lord, Judah's punishment for worshiping the wrong god, was imminent. Once the people repented, Joel announced that in the future the day of the Lord would mean blessing for Judah and disaster for its enemy. Ahlström, on the other hand, makes Joel a Jerusalem Temple prophet who pleads with the people to turn away from Baal worship and return to the Lord. The locusts are punishment for violating the covenant. Once the people return to the covenant through right worship, they receive the covenant blessings of rain and agricultural plenty.

Wolff argued that Joel's postexilic religious community in Jerusalem viewed itself as the fulfillment of God's plan for Israel, having forgotten the still unfulfilled prophetic word about the day of the Lord; they saw no further need for the Lord's intervention. The locust plague and the drought are evidence that the Judahites are soon going to be punished for their self-sufficiency unless they repent. Once they do acknowledge that the Lord is still active in their history, the day of the Lord (2:1-11) is withheld. Wolff understands Joel 2:1-11 as a description of the Lord leading the army of nations, Ezekiel's eschatological "enemy from the north," to destroy Israel. In chaps. 3–4, Joel shows how the Lord will deliver a faithful Israel from this final onslaught of the nations when it does occur and how he will establish the people in security and prosperity.

For Rudolph, the book records Joel's evolution from a prophet of doom to a prophet of salvation. As a cult prophet and a contemporary of Jeremiah, Joel interpreted a locust infestation (1:4-7; 2:1-11) and an accompanying drought as signs of an approaching day of the Lord that would bring destruction to Judah and Jerusalem. Later, after the people had repented and the drought ended, Joel received a new word from the Lord in which he learned that the locusts and the drought had, in fact, nothing to do with the *yôm YHWH*. Thus, the "news never heard before" (1:1-3) refers to the Lord's announcement that any future day of the Lord would inaugurate an era of prosperity and security for Judah and would herald its enemies' destruction (chaps. 3–4). Rudolph thinks that Joel had in mind an imminent destruction of Babylon.

Like Rudolph, Crenshaw identified a unique locust infestation and a dry summer marked by the failure of all streams as the occasion for Joel's preaching. In 2:1-11, mixing military and natural imagery, Joel describes an onslaught of locusts as the divine army that God later promises to destroy, perhaps because they exceeded their charge. After a poem consoling people, land, and animals with the news that the coming rain will restore what had been lost, Joel 3[2:28-32] assures the faithful of continued divine protection when the *yôm YHWH* does finally arrive. Joel 4 (3) describes the destruction of Judah's enemies and Judah's own establishment as a secure autonomous nation.

Ogden has suggested that the book reflects conditions existing in the land of Judah that the exiles found on their return from Babylon in 537 BCE. Joel describes this situation with imagery drawn from the damage done by locusts, drought, and pillaging armies. Chapter 4 contains oracles against the nations that Joel delivered on different occasions when he presided at communal lament liturgies.

Loretz argues that the book's purpose was to interpret eschatologically a series of drought-fasting-rain passages that form the earliest literary tradition in the text. Under the influence of the later *yôm YHWH* passages, the revitalizing effect of rain in reversing the drought became a symbol for the permanent change the Lord would someday effect in Judah's fortunes (see discussion above). This interpretation, of course, takes the *yôm YHWH* as the manifestation of the deity in a rainstorm.

Like Loretz, Bergler makes a drought the book's central concern; however, he identifies Joel as a postexilic prophet trying to counter his audience's loss of religious enthusiasm. Joel uses traditional poems about drought and about the enemy from the north to demonstrate how the present drought is the beginning of the future *yôm YHWH*. He links the effects of the locust plague in the exodus narrative (Exodus 10) with the effects on the land of the invasion of the enemy from the north. Once the people participate in the penitential assembly, Joel answers their lament with an oracle of salvation. Bergler identifies the drought as the "teacher of righteousness," a sign of the day of the Lord. Judah, however, lives already in an eschatological era inaugurated by the Lord's activity in the exodus. Consequently, the people face no further danger; rather, the Phoenicians and the Philistines are the target of the coming calamity.

Simkins's important study emphasizes that in the book of Joel the day of the Lord is an event in the history of creation. Judah has already endured one locust infestation, resulting in crop loss and interruption of temple worship. More to the point, the neighboring peoples have shamed Judah by invading and pillaging the land and by selling some of the people into slavery. Now, as Joel is writing, a new locust invasion is beginning (2:1-11). His audience construes these events as evidence that the Lord is indifferent to them. Joel, however, views this invasion as fulfillment of the day of the Lord expectations. The locusts are the "enemy from the north," whose invasion as part of this event results in the Lord's judgment against the nations. The day of the Lord is simultaneously an event in human history, Judah's deliverance from its enemies' oppression, and an event in the history of nature, the renewal of the created order. Simkins argues that both events together mirror a conflict myth in which the Lord battles those forces that threaten the natural and historical orders.

All of these interpretations contain important insights that enrich one's appreciation of the book of Joel. However, they disregard important elements of the meteorological cycle that makes agriculture possible in Palestine. This cycle is an important exegetical key to the book of Joel, given its preoccupation with crops, rain, and pestilence. On this understanding, Joel's prophetic ministry is set during the fall interchange period, at the cusp of a new year. Chapter 1 recounts the recently concluded, failed agricultural season: an unusually large locust infestation in the spring, withering of the remaining grain in late spring, the normally dry summer (perhaps exacerbated by inadequate rains the previous winter). Chapter 2 opens with a description (2:1-11) of one of the two meteorological possibilities Judah could expect given the seasonal setting of Joel's preaching. One possibility is the revitalizing rain; the other is an east wind storm, which typically precedes the rain (for a description comparable to 2:1-11, see D. Grossman [1988] 75-76). Once the people heed Joel's call to repentance (implied by 2:18), he announces that the rain will arrive (1:19-27). Joel calls this abundant rain *hammôreh liṣĕdāqâ* (2:23), a phrase that identifies the rain as a teacher of truth and foreshadows the future outpouring of the Lord's knowledge on all Judahites (3:1-4[2:28-31]).

In chaps. 3–4 Joel focuses on that point in the distant future when the Lord will intervene once and for all. The imagery for both these chapters is drawn from the competing storms of the fall interchange period. First, the Lord promises the Judahites the capacity to understand what will happen so they do not lose hope. The divine army, under the figure of an east wind (3:3-4[2:30-31]; 4:14*b*-17[3:14*b*-17]), will attack the armies of the nations gathered in the Valley of Jehoshaphat when "YHWH executes punishment" (4:2, 12-14[3:2, 12-14]) at the foot of Mount Zion. It will then move on to destroy all of Judah's enemies, turning their lands into deserts and slaying their inhabitants. The faithful of Judah, on the other hand, will enjoy protection, political autonomy, economic security, and agricultural abundance because the Lord dwells among them permanently. In this interpretation, the *yôm YHWH* is a natural phenomenon, the east wind storm of the fall interchange period, which destroys Judah's enemies as the prelude to its revitalization (K. Nash [1989]).

Bibliography: E. Achtemeier, "The Book of Joel," *NIB* (1996) 7:299-336. **G. W. Ahlström,** *Joel and the Temple Cult of Jerusalem* (VTSup 21, 1972). **L. Allen,** *The Books of Joel, Obadiah, Jonah, and Micah* (NICOT, 1976). **S. Bergler,** *Joel als Schriftinterpret* (BEATAJ 16, 1988). **J. A. Bewer,** *A Critical and Exegetical Commentary on Micah, Zephaniah, Nahum, Habakkuk, Obadiah and Joel* (ICC, 1911). **M. Bic,** *Das Buch Joel* (1960). **B. C. Birch,** *Hosea, Joel, and Amos* (Westminster Bible Companion, 1997). **J. Bourke,** "Le jour de Yahvé dans Joël," *RB* 66 (1959) 5-31, 191-221. **K. A. Credner,** *Der Prophet Joel übersetzt und erklärt* (1831). **J. L. Crenshaw,** *Joel* (AB 24C, 1995). **A. Deissler,** *Zwölf Propheten: Hosea, Joel, Amos* (Die neue Echter Bibel, 1981). **L. Dennefeld,** "Les problèmes du livre de Joël, *RevScRel* 4 (1924) 555-75; 5 (1925) 35-37, 591-608; 6 (1926) 26-49. **B. Duhm,** "Anmerkungen zu den zwölf Propheten," *ZAW* 31 (1911) 184-88. **D. A. Garrett,** "The Structure of Joel," *JETS* 28 (1985) 289-97. **B. Glazier-McDonald,** "Joel," *The Women's Bible Commentary* (ed. C. A. Newsom and S. H. Ringe, 1992) 203-4. **D. Grossman,** *The Yellow Wind* (1988). **E. Henry,** *Le Livre prophétique de Joël: Étude stylistique et exégétique* (1985). **E. Jacob, C.-A. Keller, and S. Amsler,** *Osée, Joël, Amos, Abadias, Jonas* (CAT, 1965). **J. Jeremias,** "Joel/Joelbuch," *TRE* 17 (1987) 91-97. **A. S. Kapelrud,** *Joel Studies* (1948). **O. Loretz,** *Regenritual und Jahwetag im Joelbuch* (1986). **A. Merx,** *Die Prophetie des Joel und ihre Ausleger von den ältesten Zeiten bis zu den Reformatoren* (1879). **K. S. Nash,** "The Palestinian Agricultural Year and the Book of Joel" (diss., Catholic University, 1989). **G. S. Ogden and R. R. Deutsch,** *A Promise of Hope, a Call to Obedience: A Commentary on the Books of Joel and Malachi* (ITC, 1987). **W. S. Prinsloo,** *The Theology of the Book of Joel* (BZAW 163, 1985). **W. Rudolph,** *Joel, Amos, Obadja, Jona* (KAT 1971²). **R. Simkins,** *Yahweh's Activity in History and Nature in the Book of Joel* (ANETS 10, 1991). **D. Stuart,** "The Sovereign's Day of Conquest," *BASOR* 221 (1976) 159-64. **J. A. Thompson,** "Joel's Locust in the Light of Near Eastern Parallels," *JNES* 14 (1955) 52-55; "The Book of Joel: Introduction and Exegesis," *IB* (1956) 6:729-60. **G. Widmer,** *Die Kommentare von Raschi, Ibn Ezra, Radaq zu Joel: Text, Übersetzung, und Erläuterung mit einer Einführung in die rabbinische Bibelexegese* (1945). **H. W. Wolff,** *Joel and Amos* (Hermeneia, 1977).

K. S. Nash

JOHANNINE LETTERS

1. The Early Church and the Middle Ages. The patristic witness to these letters begins relatively early. Polycarp of Smyrna (d. 156) clearly alluded to 1 John 4:2-3 in his *Letter to the Philippians* (7:1). On the other hand, the connection of the letter to such contemporary literature as *1 Clem.*; *Did.*; Ign. *Eph.*; *Herm.* is uncertain. Still, JUSTIN MARTYR (*Dial.* 123:9; 1 John 3:1-2) confirmed that 1 John was used in the churches no later than the middle of the second century. PAPIAS of Hierapolis attested to this same fact in his "Exposition of the Words of the Lord" (Eusebius *Hist. eccl.* 3.39.17), and he may have known of 3 John as well (cf. *Hist. eccl.* 3.39.3 with 3 John 12). Beyond this evidence, the most important witnesses from the second half of the second century are *Diog.* and the writings of the communities of Lugdunum and Vienna (Eusebius, *Hist. eccl.* 5.1.10).

Both 2 and 3 John, composed by "the Elder," are attested alongside 1 John in the Muratorian CANON, which is usually dated at the end of the second century. In any case, the significance of the relevant lines from the Muratorian Canon is controversial. The remark "the two with the superscription, 'Of John,' are accepted in the General [church]" (lines 68-69) is often taken as referring to 1 and 2 John. Nevertheless, the remark may come close to the opinion of ORIGEN, EUSEBIUS, and JEROME, who thought that the two smaller Johannine epistles were not genuine. Conversely, in conjunction with the claim in 1:1-4, the author of 1 John is identified with the Evangelist in the Muratorian Canon. IRENEAUS (*Adv. Haer.* 3.16.5) also identified the author of 1 John with the Evangelist, but the equation of "the Elder" with the apostle and Evangelist is not attested before the first half of the third century and only with relative clarity by DIONYSIUS OF ALEXANDRIA and Eusebius.

The evaluation of the three letters of John with regard to the history of the canon in patristic literature went for a long time without agreement. Eusebius listed 1 John among the "recognized" and 2 and 3 John among the "disputed" writings of the NT canon (*Hist. eccl.* 3. 25); therein he accepted Origen's position (cf. *Hist. eccl.* 6.25.9-10). The testimony of CLEMENT OF ALEXANDRIA is also equivocal, for he cited only 1 and 2 John as authoritative (see AUTHORITY OF THE BIBLE) alongside other NT writings but had examined all "catholic" epistles in his *Hypotyposeis* (*Hist. eccl.* 6.14.1). A secure place for all three Johannine epistles in the NT CANON was not attested until the beginning of the fourth century. Along with the other catholic epistles they are found in the *Codex Claromontanus,* in the canon of Cyril of Jerusalem, in the appendix to the fifty-ninth canon of the Synod of Laodicea (held c. 360), in Athanasius's Easter letter of 367, and in the great biblical manuscripts of the fourth and fifth centuries.

Primary among the commentaries and sermons on the Johannine epistles in the early church is the *Adumbrationes on the Canonical Epistles* by Clement of Alexandria, which treats 1 and 2 John. The *Brevis Enarratio in Epistolas Canonicas* attributed to Didymus Alexandrinus (= Pseudo-Didymus) offers an exposition of the three Johannines; only fragments of CHRYSOSTOM's exposition of the catholic epistles are preserved (to 1 John 3:8, 17; 4:8). AUGUSTINE's *Tractatus in Epistolam Joannis ad Parthos* is dedicated in its entirety to 1 John; he named "love" as his theme (*Locutus est multa, et prope omnia de Charitate*—"Much has been said, and nearly all of it about love"). Fragments from CYRIL OF ALEXANDRIA on 1 John, expositions of the three Johannine epistles by CASSIODORUS, and *Catena* on the catholic epistles were also handed down.

The majority of medieval exegetes treated the three Johannine epistles within the framework of the exposition of the catholic epistles (Bede, Pseudo-Oecumenius, Dionysius Bar Salibi, Euthymius Zigabenus, Pseudo-Hilary of Arles, Gregorius Barhebraeus, Nicolaus de Gorran, J. Hus). Conversely, Pseudo-Theophylactus commented on these three epistles separately, while Martin of Leon limited his commentary to 1 John.

2. The Reformation. LUTHER preached frequently on 1 John. In addition to a collection of sermons that carries the characteristic title "Concerning Love" (*WA* 36.416-77), there is the lecture on 1 John given during the outbreak of the plague in Wittenberg in 1527 (*WA* 20.599-801; 48.314-23). Luther connected 1 John with the Gospel of John, which demands faith, and claimed that 1 John contains the call to the reciprocal love that comes from this faith, which is grounded in the love of God. Luther's exegesis railed against the Roman Catholic Church and the tendency to enthusiasm, to which there is a double correspondence from the pronouncements of 1 John: Faith without love is just as untenable as love (works) without faith (*WADB* 7.326-27). Similarly ZWINGLI and CALVIN commented on 1 John; the latter stressed the (unordered) succession from doctrine and exhortation. Some sermons from J. Brenz on 1 John have also been handed down, while a complete commentary from H. BULLINGER on John has been preserved (see Bullinger [1972] 37, 91). Roman Catholic exegesis in this period is represented by T. CAJETAN and A. Salmeron.

3. The Seventeenth Through Nineteenth Centuries. Critical exegesis took its point of departure from the saying of J. SCALIGER: *Tres Epistolae Joannis non sunt Apostoli Joannis* ("The three Johannine Epistles are not from the apostle John" [*Scaligerana ou Bons Mots, rencontres agreables, et remarques judicieuses et scavantes de J. Scaliger. Avec des notes de Mr. Le Fevre et Mr. de Colomies,* nouvelle edition 1695, 138]). H. GROTIUS (1650), a student of Scaliger, rejected John the disciple of JESUS as the author of 2 and 3 John and proposed the Elder John as author. Renewed doubt concerning apostolic authorship was expressed in 1797 by S. Lange, who nonetheless acquiesced to the received witness of tradition. Even J. Augusti held firmly to the authenticity of 1 John and interpreted it as an "introductory writing" to the Gospel (1808, 184); there was an interpolation in 1 John 5:14-21—namely, an addendum by a foreign hand, which may possibly have been introduced by the author of chapter 21 of the Gospel of John.

A new phase of criticism began with the doubts regarding the apostolic origin of the Gospel of John, raised by K. Bretschneider: *Si evangelium non esse potest Joannis apostoli scriptum sequitur, nec epistolas Joannem habuisse auctorem* ("If the Gospel is not from John the apostle, it follows that the letters do not have John as their author either" [1820, 162]). The Elder is the author of 2 and 3 John and 1 John as well, not the apostle, since the doctrine of the Logos in 1 John, which is directed against docetic opponents, points to a gentile Christian as the author. Even H. Paulus (1829) doubted that the son of Zebedee wrote the Johannine epistles.

The Tübingen school especially developed the critical study of the Johannine correspondence. F. C. BAUR viewed the author as an imitator of the Evangelist who was deeply under the influence of the Gospel and borrowed ideas from it, but who did not "develop these in a thorough-going connection in an independent way" (1848, 297). According to Baur, the letter's distinction between sins of neglect and mortal sins points to the world of Montanist ideas. A. HILGENFELD, influenced by the portrait of the apostle John in the SYNOPTIC Gospels and PAUL (Galatians 2), considered the Apocalypse to have been the work of the son of Zebedee and consequently declared both the Gospel and letters of John to be inauthentic. In contrast to the Apocalypse, he understood 1 John as the argument of the orthodox establishment against false teachers of a docetic-GNOSTIC persuasion, a theory that highlighted the differences between the Johannine letters and the Gospel (1849, 322ff.; 1855). On the basis of the Tübingen school's developmental history premise the Johannine epistles indicate "the transition of early Johannine prophecy to the Gnosis of the Fourth Gospel" (526).

Baur (1857), however, disagreed with Hilgenfeld, asserting on the basis of an analysis of the letter's structure that the Fourth Gospel provided the foundation for 1 John. F. Lücke (1856[3]) in turn opposed Baur and traced both the Gospel and 1 John back to the apostle John; he argued that the author of 2–3 John was, not the son of Zebedee, but rather John the Elder. H. EWALD (1861), W. DE WETTE (1863), and particularly P. HAUPT (1870) disagreed with those who disputed the identity of the disciple John as the author of the Gospel and of the letters; R. Rothe (1878) and J. Huther (1880[4]) took similar stances. The latter supposed (as previously had Hilgenfeld and others) a temporal precedence of 1 John over the Gospel, since 1 John nowhere makes direct

reference to the Gospel, and especially since 1 John 1:1-4 in comparison with John 1:1ff. supports the earlier character of the letter (similarly Hilgenfeld [1855]). This reasoning was represented by B. WEISS (1899[6]) as well, who defended the common authorship of the three letters of John, the Gospel, and the Apocalypse, with the latter being the oldest writing of John the son of Zebedee. This idea was developed by H. HOLTZMANN, who maintained the priority of the Gospel (1881; see also 1908[3]) since a thoroughgoing analysis highlights linguistic and conceptual differences that demonstrate that the Fourth Evangelist could not be identical with the author of 1 John (1882; see also 1908[3]).

4. Twentieth Century. Although the Johannine epistles are to be reckoned among the lesser writings of the NT, they have not led a shadow existence in NT scholarship of the twentieth century. The primary focus of the discussion has been the relationship of 1 John to 2–3 John, wherein the differences in form and content emerge. In contrast to 2–3 John, which are to be understood as actual letters (see R. Funk [1967]), 1 John lacks the essential features of a letter. Previously M. DIBELIUS (1929) had tentatively concluded that 2–3 John could be artificial letters; E. Hirsch (1936) thought them a fiction that served to introduce the Gospel and 1 John; similarly R. BULTMANN (1967), J. Heise (1967), and G. Schunack (1982) sought to prove that 2 John was a fictional letter imitating 3 John (in opposition see R. Brown [1982]; K. Wengst [1976, 1978]; G. Strecker [1989a]).

The order and authorship of the Johannine epistles are as controversial as before. Even if a great number of exegetes reckon with a common authorship of all Johannine letters (R. Brown [1982]; C. H. Dodd [1946, 1953[3]]; E. Ruckstuhl [1985]; R. Schnackenburg [1984[7]]; H. Windisch [1911, 1951[3]]; S. Smalley [1984]; and W. Langbrandtner [1977] also consider this possibility), this position is increasingly called into question. To be sure, Schnackenburg (1967) considered inadequate R. Bergmeier's attempt (1966) on the basis of the term *truth* to prove a different authorship for 1 John than for 2–3 John. Nevertheless, it appears necessary on the basis of further considerations to ascribe different authors to 1 John and 2–3 John (H. Balz [1973, 1980[2]]; U. Schnelle [1987]; K. Wengst [1976, 1978]; Strecker [1989a]). Schunack and, finally, B. Bonsack (1988) assume different authors for each letter, though not very persuasively.

Besides these suggestions there are different hypotheses regarding the relative order of the Johannine epistles. Bultmann (1967), Schunack, and W. Loader (1992) affirm the order 1–3–2 John on the basis of their reconstruction of the relationships between 2 and 3 John. F.-M. Braun (1973[3]) and R. Edwards (1996), however, affirm the order 3–2–1 John. H. Wendt (2–3–1 John [1925]; cf. Langbrandtner; further Schnelle, Strecker [1989a, sec. 5]), and Balz (1–2/3 John; cf. Ruckstuhl,

Wengst [1976, 1978]), reach different conclusions (see also Smalley, who clearly distinguishes 3 John as the endpoint for 2 John).

The thesis that 1 John is a "Johannine pastoral epistle" has greatly influenced the discussion concerning the relationship of 1 John to the Gospel of John (H. Conzelmann [1954, 1974]; see also O. Baumgarten [1918³]; previously A. Neander, "Circular-Pastoralschreiben," *Geschichte der Pflanzung und Leitung der christlichen Kirche durch die Apostel* [1862⁵] 490; E. Reuss, "Pastoralschreiben," *Die Geschichte der Heiligen Schriften des Neuen Testaments* [1887] 1:254). The subordination of 1 John to the Gospel, which is linked to the above view, at least as it is generally represented (A. Brooke [1912]; G. Klein [1971]; Wengst [1976, 1978]; etc.), is in no way compelling (Strecker [1989a]; see also F. Büchsel [1933]). Numerous studies have investigated the commonalities between the Gospel of John and 1 John. While Dodd emphasized the linguistic differences (cf. already Holtzmann [1908³] above) and from there moved on to posit a different audience, W. HOWARD (1947), W. Wilson (1948), A. Salom (1955), and others stressed the similarity of language. Substantive commonalities can be established just as easily as substantive differences, with the result that the question of authorship has remained controversial in the twentieth century. D. Rensberger (1997) and D. M. Smith (1991), for instance, argue that the three Johannine letters have the same author, although the Gospel of John was written by someone else. The thesis of a common authorship (Brooke; Büchsel [1933]; I. Marshall [1979²]; see also W. Schmithals [1992] 219; M. Hengel [1989]) has increased in contrast to the thesis of a divergent authorship (Dodd; J. Houlden [1973]; Klein; Schnackenburg [clearly since 1975⁵]; Schnelle; Strecker [1989a]; and others). The latter position, however, becomes more probable as the assumption of a Johannine school out of which the commonalities arose receives validation (see sec. 5 on this topic).

Even though the question of the authorship of the Johannine epistles by the son of Zebedee may be considered almost thoroughly obsolete, the question remains whether the author of any of these letters can be identified with any certainty. Here the designation of the addressant as *ho presbuteros* (2 John 1; 3 John 1) is the starting point for the discussion. If earlier scholarship took as its reference the presbyter designated as John, following the testimony of Papias in Eusebius (*Hist. eccl.* 3.39.3-4), more recent study has confirmed this position (see Strecker [1989a]). Nor is the authorship of all of the Johannine epistles by the elder John to be excluded (see R. Brown [1982], who assumes that the author belonged to the school of the "beloved disciple"). Whereas Bultmann (1967) considered a connection to one of the presbyters named by Papias possible (see also the more reserved reference by G. Bornkamm [1959];

further, Schunack), others (e.g., Wengst [1976, 1978]) exclude an identification of the presbyter of the Papias reference with the author of 2 and 3 John. With less certainty Schnackenburg (1984⁷) proposes that the author is a prominent personality, perhaps a disciple of the apostle.

In view of a number of ostensible breaks in the body of the letter, Bultmann contested the literary unity of 1 John and reconstructed a source document that the author of 1 John may have used as a *Vorlage* (1927; cf. 1959, and in agreement, Heise, Windisch; H. Preikser [in Windisch] reckons with a further *Vorlage*, described as an eschatological text; against this view E. LOHMEYER [1928] and Büchsel [1929]. For Bultmann this *Vorlage*, which is supposed to have comprised twenty-six distichs, is similar to the "revelation source" he postulated for the Gospel of John; its ostensible origin was "a group whose world view was one of cosmological and religious dualism" (1927, 157). J. O'Neill (1966) went his own way on the source question, marking off twelve poetic subsections, which supposedly the author took to expand a source of sectarian Jewish exhortations. Conversely, W. Nauck (1957) thought that the *Vorlage* reconstructed on form-critical grounds (see FORM CRITICISM, NT) also stems from the writer of 1 John. These attempts at source criticism are, however, generally rejected in the present discussion (Schnackenburg [1984⁷]; Wengst [1988]; Strecker [1989a]). Analogous to his work on the Gospel of John, Bultmann brought the idea of a church redaction into his work (1951; cf. 1959; also Hirsch). The claim of a secondary redaction for the concluding section (1 John 5:14-21) has found some agreement. The conclusory nature of 5:13 as well as the plethora of *hapax legomena* and an apparently non-Johannine character were especially cited (Wengst [1978, 1988]; Schunack). These considerations have been rejected as inconclusive by Balz, F. Francis (1970), M. de Jonge (1973²), E. Stegemann (1985), and Strecker (1989a), among others. Regarding the hypothesis of unity, questions were raised about the rhetorical structure of the sermon in 1 John (e.g., F. Vouga [1990]; critically, H.-J. Klauck [1990] 213; regarding literary character, Strecker [1992] 67-68) and the letters of the Elder (D. Watson [1989]; H.-J. Klauck [1990] 216-24).

While the state of research during this century at first showed a far-reaching consensus concerning the identification of the opponents in 1 John by means of the catchwords *docetic* and GNOSTIC, this unity was also shown to be fragile in the face of incisive critical observation. Indeed, whether a polemic against an opposing group governs the letter in its totality is still a topic of controversy. Bultmann (1967), Schnackenburg (1984⁷), J. Painter (1986), and W. Loader think that such a polemic shaped the letter, whereas Büchsel (1929, 1933) and J. Lieu (1981, 1991) do not.

The definition by Bultmann is classic: "Thus it is

obviously a question of Gnostics who want to differentiate between Jesus and the Christ and who do not want to see in the human Jesus the incarnation of the heavenly pre-existent Christ, and who therefore represent a type of docetism, related to the docetism of Cerinth" (1959, 837). These opponents have been pushed into the vicinity of libertinism (so W. Lutgert [1911]; Wengst [1988]; Dodd; J. Bogart [1977]; and Smalley).

Despite points of contact with Gnostic thought, K. Weiss (1973) seeks to locate the opponents less in the realm of Gnosis than in the neighborhood of Jews addressed by Paul in 1 Corinthians 1 alongside the Greeks, i.e., in Hellenistic Judaism. J. Blank (1984), in turn, reckons with a Jewish-Christian misinterpretation of the Johannine *Shekinah*-christology, which he connects to the Gnostic *Kerinth*. The opponents are placed in the realm of Judaism, though not very persuasively, by A. Wurm (1903), J. O'Neill (1966), J. ROBINSON ("gnosticizing Movement within Greek-speaking Diaspora Judaism" [1960/61] 65), and H. Thyen (1988). P. Bonnard (1983) and Painter refer to the Hellenistic environment of the NT.

Holtzmann, U. Müller (1975), Langbrandtner, Schunack, F. Segovia (1982), and U. Schnelle (1992), among others, more specifically identify the opponents as "docetists." On the basis of the prejudiced sequence of reading 1 John after the Gospel of John, the opposing position was considered to be either a radical (Müller) or faulty interpretation (Schunack) of the Fourth Gospel. Disagreeing with the Gnostic-docetic interpretation of the opponents, F. Vouga seeks to highlight elements of Gnostic thought in 1 John and evaluates the Johannine letters as "precursors of the Gnostic polemic against the proto-Catholic church" (1988, 380). A distinction between docetism and Gnosis is, however, necessary (N. Brox [1984]; G. Strecker [1989a]). Even if the docetic false teachers possess a "Gnostic" self-awareness, this perspective is still not to be put on the same level as a mythological Gnosis, as inferred from the Christian systems of the second century.

Concerning the question of the opposition between the Elder and Diotrephes, W. BAUER (1964[2]), in his epoch-making work on orthodoxy and heresy, maintained that the position later called orthodoxy first emerged in the struggle with heresy. According to this view, Diotrephes is a leader of heretics (see Wengst [1976, 1988]: Diotrephes has the "orientation of the gnostic innovators" condemned in 2 John 7, 27). E. KÄSEMANN, who succeeded Bauer in his chair at Göttingen, contested this claim. In Käsemann's view, the Elder, "a Christian gnostic who possesses the unimaginable audacity . . . to write a gospel (i.e., the Gospel of John)," acutely disagreed with the monarchical bishop Diotrephes (1970[6], 178). Along with a dogmatic interpretation of the conflict but without allowing this conflict to acquire exclusive significance (cf. Strecker

[1989a]; Schunack), the dissent is understood as a practical-ecclesiastical matter (A. von Harnack [1897]; R. Schnackenburg [1984[7]]), as a private affair (A. Malherbe [1977]: the refusal of hospitality to opponents), or as an internal community dispute (J. Taeger [1987]).

Recent scholarship has examined the familial concerns and imagery in the three letters, especially the address in 2 John, "to an elect lady and her children." E. Schüssler Fiorenza (1984, 1; 1983, 248-49) maintains that 2 John is "the only writing in the NT addressed to a woman." M. Hutaff suggests that the terms "elect lady" (2 John 1, 5) and "elect sister" (2 John 13) more plausibly refer to "sister" churches whose members are God's children. G. O'Day comments that the use of female imagery for the church may reflect either high regard for women in the early church or the initiation of patriarchal structures of leadership into the church. R. Edwards, providing several interpretations of "an elect lady," claims that the term may actually refer to a real woman who hosted or led a congregation but that the letter nevertheless is written to that congregation.

5. The Johannine School. The close relationship of the Johannine writings in language and thought has occasioned speculation about a "Johannine circle" (O. Cullmann [1975]). It is more precise, however, to speak of a "Johannine school" (see W. Bousset [1915]; W. Heitmüller [1914]). NT schools have also been postulated alongside the religious and philosophical schools of Hellenism and Judaism (Gospel of Matthew: K. Stendahl [1954]; Pauline school: H. Conzelmann [1979]). The derivation of a school from a founder is its primary characteristic and guarantees its autonomy, which is expressed via stereotypical forms of language and thought. That this is true of the Johannine writings has been demonstrated with convincing arguments (see R. Culpepper [1975]; Schnelle), even though in individual cases many questions may remain open.

Although the starting point for the school is mostly sought in the Gospel, in accordance with the canonical subordination of the letters (Culpepper identifies the "beloved disciple" as the founder of the school; see also Barrett [1989]; Smalley), the author of 2–3 John is understood as the head of the school and identified with the Elder mentioned in Eusebius's citation of Papias (*Hist. eccl.* 3.39.4; cf. Strecker [1989a]; Schnelle). As early as 1914 Heitmüller designated the Elder John, whom he identified with the "beloved disciple," but whom he also distinguished from the son of Zebedee, as the standard authority. Thyen, on the other hand, sees evidence of the author of 2–3 John in the "beloved disciple" (1977).

The association of the Apocalypse with the Johannine corpus is disputed. Even if this work is to be understood as a pseudepigraphon (Strecker [1990]; cf. Heitmüller; see PSEUDEPIGRAPHA), a relatively close connection to this circle of writings is nonetheless probable.

6. The "Johannine Comma" (*comma Johanneum*). The so-called Johannine Comma designates an addendum to 1 John 5:7-8 in the text-critical tradition (see TEXTUAL CRITICISM, NT), which has found its way almost exclusively into Latin biblical manuscripts. There are no Greek exemplars prior to 1400. In 1592 in the official Catholic VULGATE, the Sixto-Clementine, the following reading was included (here printed in italic):

(7) Quoniam tres sunt, qui testimonium dant *in caelo: Pater, Verbum, et Spiritus Sanctus et hi tres unum sunt.*
(8) *Et tres sunt, qui testimonium dant in terra:* Spiritus et aqua et sanquis, et hi tres unum sunt.

(7) For there are three that bear record *in heaven, the Father, the Word, and the Holy Spirit, and these three are one.*
(8) *And there are three that bear witness in earth:* The Spirit, and the Water, and the Blood, and these three agree in one (KJV).

The oldest indubitable citation of this Johannine Comma is found in Priscillian (d. 385), up to whose time there is, aside from possible allusions (Tertullian, Cyprian), no certain documentary evidence. The authenticity of this text, which is frequently attested after Priscillian and which ERASMUS only reluctantly took up in the third edition of his NT, received a critical judgment from Luther (*WA* 20.780, 21ff.; *WADB* 7.628-29). Although Calvin accepted it with some hesitation (cf. *CR* 83.364-65), Zwingli rejected it (*Opera,* ed. Schulero and Schulthessio, 6.2.338). Ever since J. SEMLER contested its originality in 1764, the Johannine Comma has been regarded in most of Protestantism as secondary (cf. G. Hornig [1988]). This view became accepted in Roman Catholic exegesis only in this century by academic prohibition of the Congregatio S. Inquisitionis on Jan. 13, 1897, and with subsequent confirmation limited by Pope Leo XIII.

Bibliography: J. C. W. Augusti, *Die katholischen Briefe* (1808). **H. Balz,** "Die Johannesbriefe," *Die "Katholischen" Briefe* (H. Balz and W. Schrage, NTD 10[11], 1973) 150-216; (1980[2]) 156-222. **C. K. Barrett,** "School, Conventicle, and Church in the NT," *Wissenschaft und Kirche* (FS E. Lohse, ed. K. Aland and S. Meurer, TAB 4, 1989) 96-110. **W. Bauer,** *Rechtgläubigkeit und Ketzerei im ältesten Christentum* (ed. G. Strecker, BHT 10 1964[2]). **O. Baumgarten,** "Die Johannes-Briefe," SNT 4 (1918[3]) 185-228. **F. C. Baur,** "Die johannischen Briefe: Ein Beitrag zur Geschichte des Kanons," *ThJb* 7 (1848) 293-337; "Das Verhältnis des ersten johanneischen Briefes zum johanneischen Evangelium," *ThJb* 16 (1857) 315-31. **R. Bergmeier,** "Zum Verfasserproblem des II. und III. Johannesbriefes," *ZNW* 57 (1966) 93-100. **C. Black,** "The First, Second, and Third Letters of John" *NIB* (1998) 12:363-469. **J. Blank,** "Die Irrlehrer des ersten Johannesbriefes," *Kairos* NF 26 (1984)

166-93. **J. Bogart,** *Orthodox and Heretical Perfectionism in the Johannine Community as Evident in the First Epistle of John* (SBLDS 33, 1977). **P. Bonnard,** *Les Épîtres Johanniques* (CNT(G) 2, 13c, 1983). **B. Bonsack,** "Der Presbyteros des dritten Briefs und der geliebte Jünger des Evangeliums nach Johannes," *ZNW* 79 (1988) 45-62. **G. Bornkamm,** "presbys ktl." *TDNT* 6 (1959) 651-83. **W. Bousset,** *Jüdisch-Christlicher Schulbetrieb in Alexandria und Rom* (FRLANT 23, 1915). **F.-M. Braun,** "Les Épîtres de Saint Jean," *L'Évangile de Saint Jean* (F.-M. Braun and D. Mollat, SB(J), 1973[3]) 231-77. **H. Braun,** "Literar-Analyse und theologische Schichtung im ersten Johannesbrief," *ZTK* 48 (1951) 262-92 = his *Gesammelte Studien zum Neuen Testament und seiner Umwelt* (1971[3]) 210-42. **K. G. Bretschneider,** *Probabilia de evangelii et epistolarum Joannis, apostoli, indole et origine eruditorum judiciis modeste subjecit* (1820). **A. E. Brooke,** *A Critical and Exegetical Commentary on the Johannine Epistles* (ICC, 1912). **R. E. Brown,** *The Community of the Beloved Disciple* (1979); *The Epistles of John* (AB 30, 1982). **N. Brox,** " 'Doketismus'—eine Problemanzeige," *ZKG* 95 (1984) 301-14. **F. Büchsel,** "Zu den Johannesbriefen," *ZNW* 28 (1929) 235-41; *Die Johannesbriefe* (THKNT 17, 1933). **H. Bullinger,** *Werke, I/1: Beschreibendes Verzeichnis der gedrukten Werke von Bullinger* (ed. J. Staedtke, 1972). **R. Bultmann,** "Analyse des ersten Johannesbriefes," *Festgabe für A. Jülicher zum 70. Geburtstag* (ed. R. Bultmann and H. von Soden, 1927) 138-58 = his *Exegetica* (1967) 105-23; "Die kirchliche Redaktion des ersten Johannesbriefes," *In memoriam E. Lohmeyer* (ed. W. Schmauch, 1951) 189-201 = *Exegetica* (1967) 381-93; "Johannesbriefe," *RGG[3]* 3 (1959) 836-39; *The Johannine Epistles* (KEK 14[8], 1967, 1969[2]; ET Hermeneia, 1973). **H. Conzelmann,** "Die Schule des Paulus," *Theologia Crucis-Sigmum Crucis* (FS E. Dinkler, ed. C. Andresen and G. Klein, 1979) 85-96; " 'Was von Anfang war,' " *Neutestamentliche Studien für R. Bultmann* (BZNW 21, 1954) 194-201 = his *Theologie als Schriftauslegung: Aufsätze zum Neuen Testament* (BEvT 65, 1974) 207-14. **O. Cullmann,** *The Johannine Circle* (1975; ET 1976). **R. A. Culpepper,** *The Johannine School: An Evaluation of the Johannine School Hypothesis Based on an Investigation of the Nature of Ancient Schools* (SBLDS 26, 1975). **W. M. L. de Wette,** *Kurze Erklärung des Evangeliums und der Briefe Johannis* (KEH/NT 1, 3, ed. B. Brückner, 1863). **M. Dibelius,** "Johannesbriefe," *RGG[2]* 3 (1929) 346-94. **E. von Dobschütz,** "Johanneische Studien I," *ZNW* 8 (1907) 1-8. **C. H. Dodd,** *The Johannine Epistles* (MNTC, 1946, 1953[3]). **R. B. Edwards,** *The Johannine Epistles* (NTGu, 1996). **H. Ewald,** *Die johanneischen Schriften,* erster Band, *Des Apostels Johannes Evangelium und drei Sendschreiben* (1861). **F. O. Francis,** "The Form and Function of the Opening and Closing Paragraphs of James and I John," *ZNW* 61 (1970) 110-26. **R. W. Funk,** "The Form and the Structure of II and III John," *JBL* 86 (1967) 424-30. **H. Grotius,** *Annotationum in Novum Testamentum pars tertia ac ultima* (1650). **E. Haenchen,** "Neuere Literatur zu den Johannesbriefen," *TRu* 26 (1960) 1-43; 267-91 = his *Die Bibel und wir: Gesammelte Aufsätze* 2 (1968) 235-311. **A. von Harnack,** *Über den dritten Johannesbrief* (TU XV 3b, 1897). **E. Haupt,** *Der erste Brief des Johannes: Ein Beitrag zur biblischen*

Theologie (1870). **J. Heise,** *Bleiben: Menein in den johanne-ischen Schriften* (HUT 8, 1967). **W. Heitmüller,** "Zur Johannes-Tradition," *ZNW* 15 (1914) 189-209. **M. Hengel,** *The Johannine Question* (1989). **A. Hilgenfeld,** *Das Evangelium und die Briefe Johannis, nach ihrem Lehrbegriff* (1849); "Die johanneischen Briefe," *ThJb* 14 (1855) 471-526. **E. Hirsch,** *Studien zum vierten Evangelium (Text—Literarkritik—Entstehungsgeschichte)* (BHT 11, 1936). **H. J. Holtzmann,** "Das Problem des ersten johanne-ischen Briefes in seinem Verhältnis zum Evangelium," *JPT* 1, 7 (1881) 690-712; 2, 8 (1882) 128-52; 3, 316-42; 4, 460-85; *Evangelium, Briefe, und Offenbarung des Johannes* (HC 4, 1908[3]). **G. Hornig,** "Hermeneutik und Bibelkritik bei J. S. Semler," *Historische Kritik und biblischer Kanon in der deutschen Aufklärung* (Wolfenbütteler Forschungen 41, 1988) 219-36. **J. L. Houlden,** *A Commentary on the Johannine Epistles* (BNTC, 1973). **W. F. Howard,** "The Common Authorship of the Johannine Gospel and the Epistles," *JTS* 48 (1947) 12-25. **M. D. Hutaff,** "The Johannine Epistles," *Searching the Scriptures,* vol. 2, *A Feminist Commentary* (ed. E. Schüssler Fiorenza, 1994). **J. E. Huther,** *Kritisch exegetisches Handbuch über die Briefe des Apostels Johannes* (KEK 14, 1880[4]). **M. de Jonge,** *De brieven van Johannes* (1973[2]). **E. Käsemann,** "Ketzer und Zeuge: Zum johanneischen Verfas-serproblem," *ZTK* 48 (1951) 292-311 = his *Exegetische Versuche und Besinnungen* 1 (1970[6]) 168-87. **H.-J. Klauck,** "Zur rhetor-ischen Analyse der Johannesbriefe," *ZNW* 81 (1990) 205-24; *Die Johannesbriefe* (EdF 276, 1991); *Der erste Johannesbrief (EKKNT 13, 1 1991).* **G. Klein,** " 'Das wahre Licht scheint schon': Beobachtungen zur Zeit- und Geschichtserfahrung einer urchrist-lichen Schule," *ZTK* 68 (1971) 261-326. **R. Kysar,** *I, II, III John* (ACNT, 1986). **W. Langbrandtner,** *Weltferner Gott oder Gott der Liebe: Der Ketzerstreit in der johanneischen Kirche. Eine exegetisch religionsgeschichtliche Untersuchung mit Berück-sichtigung der koptisch-gnostischen Texte aus Nag-Hammadi* (BBET 6, 1977). **S. G. Lange,** *Johannis drei Briefe nebst drei Abhandlungen* (Schriften Johannis Bd. 3, 1797). **J. M. Lieu,** " 'Authority to Become Children of God': A Study of I John," *NovT* 23 (1981) 210-28; *The Second and Third Epistles of John: History and Background* (ed. J. Riches, Studies of the NT and Its World, 1986); *The Theology of the Johannine Epistles* (NT The-ology, 1991). **W. Loader,** *The Johannine Epistles* (Epworth Com-mentaries, 1992). **E. Lohmeyer,** "Über Aufbau und Gliederung des ersten Johannesbriefes," *ZNW* 27 (1928) 225-63. **F. Lücke,** *Commentar über die Briefe des Evangelisten Johannes* (ed. E. Bertheau, 1856[3]). **W. Lütgert,** *Amt und Geist im Kampf: Studien zur Geschichte des Urchristentums* (BFCT 15.4/5, 1911). **A. J. Malherbe,** "The Inhospitality of Diotrephes," *God's Christ and His People: Studies in Honour of N. A. Dahl* (ed. J. Jervell and W. A. Meeks, 1977) 222-32. **I. H. Marshall,** *The Epistles of John* (NIC, 1979[2]). **U. B. Müller,** *Die Geschichte der Christologie in der johanneischen Gemeinde* (SBS 77, 1975). **W. Nauck,** *Die Tradition und der Charakter des ersten Johannesbriefes: Zugleich ein Beitrag zur Taufe im Urchristentum und in der alten Kirche* (WUNT 3, 1957). **G. R. O'Day,** "1, 2, and 3 John," *The Women's Bible Commentary* (ed. C. A. Newsom and S. H. Ringe, 1992) 374-75. **J. C. O'Neill,** *The Puzzle of I John: A New Examination of Origins* (1966). **J. Painter,** "The 'Opponents' in

1 John," *NTS* 32 (1986) 48-71. **H. E. G. Paulus,** *Die drey Lehrbriefe des Johannes* (1829). **P. Perkins,** *The Johannine Epis-tles* (NT Message, 1984). **H. Preisker,** "Appendix," *Die kathol-ischen Briefe* (H. Windisch, HNT 15, 1911, 1951[3]). **D. Rensber-ger,** *1 John, 2 John, 3 John* (ANTC, 1997). **J. A. T. Robinson,** "The Destination and Purpose of the Johannine Epistles," *NTS* 7 (1960/61) 56-65. **R. Rothe,** *Der erste Brief Johannis, Aus R. Rothe's Nachlass* (ed. K. Mülhäusser, 1878). **E. Ruckstuhl,** *Jakobusbrief, 1.–3. Johannesbrief* (Die Neue Echter Bibel 17-19, 1985). **A. P. Salom,** "Some Aspects of the Grammatical Style of I John," *JBL* 74 (1955) 96-102. **A. Schmidt,** "Erwägungen zur Eschatologie des 2 Thessalonicher und des 2 Johannes," *NTS* 38 (1992) 477-80. **W. Schmithals,** *Johannesevangelium und Johannesbriefe* (BZNW 64, 1992). **R. Schnackenburg,** *Die Johannesbriefe* (HThK 13, 3, 1953, 1975[5], 1984[7]; ET, *The Johannine Epistles* [tr. R. and I. Fuller, 1992]); "Zum Begriff der 'Wahrheit' in den beiden kleinen Johannesbriefen," *BZ* NF 11 (1967) 253-58. **U. Schnelle,** *Anti-doketische Christologie im Johannesevangelium: Eine Unter-suchung zur Stellung des vierten Evangeliums in der johanneischen Schule* (FRLANT 144, 1987; ET 1992). **G. Schunack,** *Die Briefe des Johannes* (ZBK NT 17, 1982). **E. Schüssler Fiorenza,** *Bread Not Stone: The Challenge of Feminist Biblical Interpretation* (1984); *In Memory of Her: A Feminist Theological Reconstruction of Christian Origins* (1983). **F. F. Segovia,** *Love Relationships in the Johannine Tradition: Agape/Agapan in I John and the Fourth Gospel* (SBLDS 58, 1982). **J. S. Semler,** *Paraphrasis in I. Epistolam Joannis, acc. de Jo. Sal. Semlero eiusque ingenio narratio Jo. Aug. Nösseli* (1792). **S. S. Smalley,** *1, 2, 3 John* (WBC 51, 1984). **D. M. Smith,** *First, Second, and Third John* (Interpretation, 1991). **E. Stegemann,** " 'Kindlein, hütet euch vor den Götterbildern!' Erwägungen zum Schluss des 1. Johannesbriefes," *TZ* 41 (1985) 284-94. **K. Sten-dahl,** *The School of St. Matthew and Its Use of the OT* (ASNU 20, 1954). **G. Strecker,** "Die Anfänge der johanneischen Schule," *NTS* 32 (1986) 31-47; "Chiliasm and Docetism in the Johannine School," *ABR* 38 (1990) 45-61; *Die Johannesbriefe übersetzt und erklärat* (1989a; ET, *The Johannine Letters* [Hermeneia, 1996]); *History of NT Literature* (1992; ET 1997); "Neues Testament," *Neues Testament—Antikes Judentum* (Strecker and J. Maier, GT 2, UTB 422, 1989b) 72-74; "Rez. F. Vouga, *Die Johannesbriefe,*" *Bib* 73 (1992) 280-86. **J. W. Taeger,** "Der konservative Rebell: Zum Widerstand des Diotrephes gegen den Presbyter," *ZNW* 78 (1987) 267-87. **H. Thyen,** "Entwicklungen innerhalb der johan-neischen Theologie und Kirche im Spiegel von Joh. 21 und der Lieblingsjüngertexte des Evangeliums," *L'Évangile de Jean: Sources, rédaction, théologie* (ed. M. de Jonge, BETL 44, 1977) 259-99; "Johannesbriefe," *TRE* 17 (1988) 186-200. **F. Vouga,** "The Johannine School: A Gnostic Tradition in Primitive Chris-tianity?" *Bib* 69 (1988) 371-85; *Die Johannesbriefe* (HNT 15, 3, 1990). **D. F. Watson,** "A Rhetorical Analysis of 2 John According to Greco-Roman Convention," *NTS* 35 (1989) 104-30; "A Rhe-torical Analysis of 3 John: A Study in Epistolary Rhetoric," *CBQ* 51 (1989) 479-501. **B. Weiss,** *Die drei Briefe des Apostels Johan-nes* (KEK 14, 1899[6]). **K. Weiss,** " 'Die Gnosis' im Hintergrund und im Spiegel der Johannesbriefe," *Gnosis und Neues Testa-ment: Studien aus Religionswissenschaft und Theologie* (ed. K.-

W. Tröger, 1973) 341-56. **H. H. Wendt,** *Die Johannesbriefe und das johanneische Christentum* (1925). **K. Wengst,** *Häresie und Orthodoxie im Spiegel des ersten Johannesbriefes* (1976); *Der erste, zweite, und dritte Brief des Johannes* (ÖTK 16, 1978); "Probleme der Johannesbriefe," *ANRW* II 25.5 (1988) 3753-72. **W. G. Wilson,** "An Examination of the Linguistic Evidence Adduced Against the Unity of Authorship of the First Epistle of John and the Fourth Gospel," *JTS* 49 (1948) 147-56. **H. Windisch,** *Die katholischen Briefe* (HNT 15, 1911, 1951³), with appendix by H. Preisker. **A. Wurm,** *Die Irrlehrer im ersten Johannesbrief* (BibS[F] 8.1, 1903).

G. STRECKER

JOHN, GOSPEL OF

The interpretation of the Gospel of John has led a double life. On the surface the text appears relatively simple; however, those who have read this Gospel more carefully are aware of its complexity. Interpreters inevitably must deal with a number of issues if they are to read with greater understanding. First and foremost among those issues is the uniqueness of this Gospel among the canonical Gospels (see CANON OF THE BIBLE) and its distinctive Christian thought. Other issues include the identity of the Fourth Evangelist, the purpose for which the Gospel was written, the intellectual and religious milieu out of which it came, and the ambiguity of its teachings.

1. The Early Church. The earliest known instance of the interpretation of the Gospel of John may be found in 1 John (cf., e.g., the prologues of each). In that document the unnamed author appeals to themes found in the Gospel to address a schism in the first readers' church. Thus 1 John may be early evidence of two classic interpretations of the Fourth Gospel that were destined to dominate the early centuries of the church. The schismatics, it is argued (see R. Brown [1982]), understood the Johannine community's Gospel in terms that prefigured later GNOSTIC INTERPRETATION, while the author of 1 John used the tradition embedded in it to defend views that would later become characteristic of early Christian orthodoxy (e.g., Christ's humanity, 1 John 4:2).

Beyond the canonical evidence, the existence and circulation of the Gospel of John are demonstrated by at least the middle of the second century. By c. 180 it was widely held that the Gospel was the work of John, son of Zebedee, the "beloved disciple" of the narrative. Evidence of its unambiguous citation, however, is scarce before THEOPHILOS OF ANTIOCH (*Ad Autolycum* 2.22 [c. 170]). Apparently the first to cite it unequivocally and extensively was IRENAEUS, who was also the first to see the potential of the Gnostics' treasured Gospel as an effective weapon against them. He used the Gospel's own words to wrest it from their grip and to demonstrate its orthodox teachings. Doing battle with those who

rejected the Gospel (and Revelation) as the work of the heretical Cerinthus, he claimed the author was "John, the disciple of the Lord" and located its composition in Ephesus (*Adv. Haer.* 3.1.2 and 11.9). Because Irenaeus, one of the church's first great theologians, was so significantly influenced by the Fourth Gospel, it follows that this Gospel was destined to shape the emerging doctrine of the church in the succeeding centuries.

Evidence of various sorts verifies that the document was known and used first of all among Gnostic Christians and Montanists of the second and third centuries. The Nag Hammadi discoveries in 1946 revealed a form of early Christian thought in which Johannine categories and teachings were highly appreciated. Heracleon, a Valentinian Gnostic, authored the first known commentary on the Fourth Gospel (c. 170), available to us only in the fragments cited by ORIGEN (see E. Pagels [1973]). From that evidence it appears that the Valentinian commented on extended passages, but whether his was a complete commentary remains unknown. Clearly he regarded John as a source of divine AUTHORITY, but he freely allegorized it for his own agenda. The Montanists valued the Gospel as the source of the promise of the Paraclete, which provided them authorization for their charismatic PROPHECY. Because Gnostic Christians and Montanists used this Gospel, its reputation was smeared in the view of some mainstream church leaders. Some appear to have denied its teachings regarding the Paraclete (Irenaeus *Adv. Haer.* 3.11.9 [SC 34:202]), while others attributed it and Revelation to Cerinthus and disclaimed the Logos teaching of the Gospel's prologue, earning the label *Alogoi* (Epiphanius of Salmis *Pan.* 51; cf. R. Heine [1987–88]).

Heracleon's work evoked Origen's own commentary (SC 120, 157, 222, 290, 1966–82; FOTC 80, 1989), designed to dispute Gnostic interpretation. The Muratorian canon awarded this Gospel primacy, attributing it to John, a disciple of JESUS, and witnessed to the church's claim to it. EUSEBIUS cited CLEMENT OF ALEXANDRIA as a leader who regarded the author of the Gospel as one of Jesus' original disciples (*Hist. eccl.* 6.14.7 [GCS 9²:550]). The *Diatessaron* similarly gives John considerable attention.

Having affirmed the authenticity of the Fourth Gospel, the Roman Catholic Church quickly found in its teachings the contours of an emerging orthodoxy. In the third century, in opposition to Sabellianism, TERTULLIAN of Carthage and Hippolytus of Rome interpreted it to teach the distinctiveness of the Father and Son in the unity of the deity. The usefulness of the Gospel in defining orthodoxy in contrast to deviant views continued into the fourth century in the Arian controversy (see ARIUS). Much of that debate centered on the relationship of the Logos to God and to Jesus in the Gospel's prologue. Among others, ATHANASIUS and GREGORY OF NYSSA appealed to the Gospel of John as the basis for the full humanity and divinity of Christ. Add this evidence to that of the church's struggle with Gnostic and Montanist Christianity, and one has a convincing argument that the early church founded crucial points of its theology on the Gospel of John and that without it there could hardly have been a biblical foundation for those views that came to be held as orthodox.

The early literature also shows an awareness of the Gospel's distinctiveness when compared with the Synoptics (see SYNOPTIC PROBLEM). Tertullian faced the fact that the CHRONOLOGY of the Fourth Gospel was difficult to harmonize with the Synoptics (*Adv. Marc.* 4.2 [CSEL 47:426]). Clement of Alexandria in the late second century is credited with first labeling it the "spiritual Gospel," suggesting that the Synoptics were more concerned with the "material facts" and implying that John's Gospel was written as a supplement to the others (Eusebius, *Hist. eccl.* 6.14.7). Origen similarly stressed its spiritual value. This early assessment of the Gospel's character continued to dominate interpretations for centuries.

Origen's influential commentary took the literal sense of the text seriously in order to ward off interpretations the church sought to combat. He was, however, bold enough to suggest that the literal sense could, on occasions, be rejected when it seemed abused. His concern to find a "spiritual" sense through the use of allegory is evident in his christological and eschatological interpretations; aware, for instance, of the difference between the Synoptic and Johannine placements of the cleansing of the Temple (John 2:13-21), he followed Heracleon in seeing the discrepancy as occasion for an allegorical treatment of the passage. Heracleon had made the narrative into a representation of the story of salvation. In contrast, Origen understood that the cleansing might address several different matters: Christ's eradication of error from his church, his triumphant ascension into heaven after his victory over the forces of evil, or the process of salvation in the human soul. However, Origen's student DIONYSIUS OF ALEXANDRIA (bishop, c. 247–64) introduced a critical note foreshadowing things to come by arguing that Revelation was not written by the same author who produced the Fourth Gospel and the JOHANNINE LETTERS.

The ANTIOCHENE tradition is perhaps best represented by THEODORE OF MOPSUESTIA (CSCO 115-16, 1940) with his christocentric attention to literal meaning. He held that the Gospel was both historically reliable and theologically profound, but at his hand the Johannine Christ came more to resemble the Nicene Christ than the JESUS of history. Armed with the conviction that Christ was both divine and human, Theodore explained some of the puzzling speeches of the Johannine Jesus by supposing that he spoke sometimes out of one nature and sometimes out of the other.

AUGUSTINE's tractates (FOTC 78-79, 1988) are some of the first interpretations of the Gospel to transcend the defense of orthodoxy against heresy and in so doing reached a new level of maturity. He usually gave little attention to the literal meaning of the text before pressing on to a theological exposition and application to Christian life. For instance, when interpreting 14:28 ("the Father is greater than I") he reached beyond the trinitarian confines of earlier interpreters (e.g., Tertullian *Adv. Prax.* 9.2 [CC 1168]) and, following CYRIL OF ALEXANDRIA (*Joh. Ev., ad loc.* [PG 74, 316ff.]), suggested that Jesus' subordination to the Father reflected his servanthood (*Trac. Joh. Ev.* 78.2-3 [CC 524f.]). His interpretation of 21:11 (*Trac. Joh. Ev.* 122.8 [CC 673-74]) has shaped even contemporary efforts to read that passage. His theological exposition is perhaps the epitome of patristic interpretation (cf. M. Comeau [1930]).

2. The Middle Ages. Whereas salient and formative turns in the interpretation of the Gospel mark the earliest period, the contributions of the expositors of the Middle Ages are far less creative. They exhibit a determination to honor and continue the patristic interpretation. Hermeneutically (see HERMENEUTICS), the period generally nuanced the ALEXANDRIAN SCHOOL (especially Origen) and its understanding of the three senses—literal, moral, and spiritual. In the pre-scholastic period the new commentaries reproduced the themes of their Greek and Latin parents. Therefore, the Gospel continued to be appreciated for its theology.

Two interpreters of the Gospel of John suggest the character of its treatment during the period. In his commentary (SC 91, 1969), John Scottus ERIUGENA took the Greek text seriously and understood the Fourth Evangelist as a person of contemplation and knowledge who distinguished between "mysteries" and "symbols." The former were historical events that perish with the passage of time, whereas symbols reported non-historical matters but reflected eternal and spiritual realities. Thus, for instance, he took John 1:1 to speak in symbolic language of that which stands outside history and used the reference to Jesus as the Lamb of God in 1:29 as a basis for the doctrine of original sin. The Christ Lamb, prefigured by the HB lamb, destroyed original sin by his sacrifice. This concern for the symbolism of the Gospel anticipated the prolonged effort of interpreters throughout the ages to penetrate Johannine language and images.

In its treatment of the mother of Jesus, ALCUIN's commentary (*PL* 100, 737-1008) illustrates the use of the Gospel in the developing Mariology of the period. The changing of water into wine in chapter 2 signals the transformation of the OT to the NT. The six jars represent the six ages of the world, and their filling with wine symbolizes Christ's filling of the law and prophets with grace and truth. In spite of such examples as these, theological advancement was generally restrained by the emphasis of the interpreters of this period on spiritual interests.

Doubtless one of the contributions of the medieval period was the use of the scholastic method, with its clear arrangement and logic and its allegiance to the literal sense of the text. THOMAS AQUINAS's commentary on John, based on his lectures given at the University of Paris during his second tenure at St. Jacques (1269–72), was subsequently widely used and illustrates a scholastic but sensitive treatment of the text (ET in Aquinas Scripture Series 4, 1980). A controversial example is his reading of 17:3, in which he argued that the knowledge of God referred to in the verse is cognitive in nature as opposed to a heavenly vision (*John 17, Lec. I:3* [Cai 2186]). On the other hand, he followed the simple explanation of Jesus' prayer in 11:41*b*, saying that it arose from Christ's humanity and the unity of his will with the divine will (Cai 1553). He found the spiritual sense of Scripture in words that connote things and acts beyond the historical or literary (cf. C. Black [1986]).

3. The Reformation. The period of the Reformation and the rise of humanism brought a new convergence of influences to bear on the reading of the Fourth Gospel. Among those disparate forces were a concern to preserve the tradition of interpretation established in the patristic period and continued through the Middle Ages, a new interest in rhetoric and philology arising from the humanism of the era (e.g., H. Grotius [1641]), and the theological themes of the Reformation movement.

ERASMUS (1991) noted the obscurity of Johannine language, which made paraphrasing difficult, if not impossible; and he concluded that the language is filled with riddles (a conclusion still echoed in contemporary scholarship). The Gospel's subject matter (the divinity of Christ) was also something of a riddle for Erasmus. The Reformers sought to clarify those riddles, reflecting Erasmus's interest in the Fourth Gospel's rhetoric (cf. M. Hoffmann [1997]).

The Reformers brought to the Johannine text newly revived theological issues. They also dared, however, to assess critically the relative value of the canonical books, not holding them to be of equal worth. LUTHER (*LW,* 35:362) cherished the Fourth Gospel as "the one, fine, true, and chief gospel, and is far, far to be preferred over the other three and placed high above them." Among other things, Luther premised his view on the simple fact that this Gospel offered more of Jesus' words than did the others. He thought Scripture had one simple meaning and functioned to arouse faith in the reader by means of both law and gospel—that is, by both killing human self-confidence and bestowing new life. A contrast of faith and reason also figured prominently in his treatment of John. Luther persistently tended to refer the text to faith, e.g., he insisted that the sin referred to in 16:8 is unbelief.

The themes in CALVIN's commentary (1949) are similar. He maintained that the Gospel of John deals more with doctrine than with the narrative of Jesus' life and suggested that while the Synoptics disclose Jesus' "body," John reveals his "soul." Thus the Fourth Gospel provides the key for opening the first three. Thereby, the Reformation continued the emphasis on John as the "spiritual" Gospel. As well as stressing salvation by grace and the conflict of revelation and reason, Calvin was predisposed to find in the Gospel the sovereignty of God rather than the futility of human existence. However, both Luther's and Calvin's work on John betray apologetic and polemic features.

Not unlike its initial interpretation to define and defend proper doctrine against heresy, the Reformers found in the Gospel of John some of the biblical basis for their efforts to redirect the church. John 6, for instance, figured prominently in the debates over the Eucharist in 1520. Both Luther and Calvin insisted that the discourse in 6:22-71 was concerned with faith and denied that it was appropriately interpreted in the light of the Lord's Supper. They also disallowed the use of 3:5 as authority for the church's practice of baptism. Thus they opened an ongoing discussion over the symbolism of these two passages and the general problem of the role of the sacraments in Johannine thought.

Two examples of Reformation interpretation of John are found in the commentaries of P. MELANCHTHON and W. MUSCULUS. Influenced by Luther's writing, Musculus left the monastery, became a pastor in Augsburg, and eventually settled in Zurich. His exegetical work *Commentariorum in Evangelistam Ioannem* (1547) displays the use of both patristic and medieval interpretative methods yet also shows the influence of humanism (see C. Farmer [1997]). When a passage proved difficult, Musculus frequently sought insights from tradition. He seems to have regarded the text as rich in meaning and thick in reference, much as his predecessors had. Although appreciative of medieval interpreters, he was critical of how quickly they allegorized Johannine passages. He justified his own use of allegory only when he believed the literal meaning and context called for it; e.g., he treated the feeding of the crowd in chapter 6 allegorically because Jesus later in the chapter speaks of himself as "bread." Still, his allegorization of John is greater than that of other Reformation commentators, although the influence of humanism is evident in his careful consideration of linguistic matters. Clearly and profoundly affected by Erasmus, the only one of his contemporaries named in the commentary, Musculus was willing, however, to disagree with him. Most significant about Musculus's interpretative method is his concern to identify the relevance of a passage for his contemporary readers. Always regarding the text as a resource for individual Christian life and faith, he represents the best of Reformation interpretation.

Musculus's commentary also demonstrates his difference with the Roman Catholic interpreters of the time. His theological commitments surface in his discussion of the Sabbath controversy in 5:9-18 in which he carefully defined the true nature of Sabbath obedience and stressed the moral obligations of the healed man. Going further than his Catholic contemporaries, he allegorized the healing into a statement of human salvation and even the whole history of God's saving activity. His Reformation beliefs led him to see the paralyzed man lying near the pool as representative of the weakness of the human will to win its own salvation; he viewed Christ's healing as symbolic of God's grace and mercy.

Melanchthon's small commentary (*Annotationes in Johannem* [1523]) is equally representative of the interpretation of John during the Reformation (see T. Wengert [1987]). Called the first "Protestant" commentary on John, it masterfully combines humanism, Luther's Reformation principles, and the patristic and medieval traditions of interpretation. Like Musculus, Melanchthon extensively used the early writers; like medieval exegetes he allegorized the text where tradition had done so (e.g., the Lamb of God). However, where the patristic interpretations and those of the Middle Ages had tended to concentrate on the christological meaning of passages, Melanchthon shifted attention toward the soteriological implications of the text, often thereby honoring the simpler meaning. As the church had before him, he found trinitarian language in 1:1-18; however, along with Luther he emphasized that the Word is life that slays death and that divine grace motivated the incarnation, thus exemplifying the theological thrust of the Lutheran movement.

Similarly, he parted company with medieval interpretations and their influence on the dominant church of the day most notably on two issues: first, the power of free will and the merit of human behavior as opposed to justification by faith alone, and second, the authority of the papal office for Christian faith and piety. For example, he interpreted 15:16 in terms of the election of all Christians through grace and not the election of the apostles to their office. He expressed his humanism in attention to the rhetoric of the text and philological concerns as well as to the oratorical qualities of the Johannine Jesus. But always he favored theological issues; for Melanchthon the Fourth Evangelist was both a historian and a teacher of right doctrine.

The period of the Reformation reinforced the role of the Gospel of John as a source for sound theology, as the earliest interpretations had done. But the influence of humanism broadened the scope of Johannine interpretation once and for all. It anticipated the freeing of the Gospel from the grasp of the church by posing its AUTHORITY over the church and its teachings. Moreover, the influence of humanism hinted at the possibility that John was valuable beyond the shaping of proper doctrine; hence it opened the way for the Enlightenment.

4. The Enlightenment. This period brought a stream of critical questions and ushered in a period of interpretative creativity equalled only by the patristic era. Among the most vital questions, the pursuit of which occasioned pivotal points in the reading of the Fourth Gospel, are the apostolic authorship and historical reliability of the Johannine narrative, the relationship of the Gospel to the Synoptics, and the religious and philosophical setting for the origin of the Gospel.

The new issues first erupted around the questions of the apostolic origin and historical reliability of the Johannine representation of Jesus. R. SIMON'S TEXTUAL CRITICISM (1689) combined with DEISM to open the discussion of these issues. Simon, sometimes named "the founder of the science of NT introduction" (T. Zahn, *RE*, 5, 263), sought to defend the teachings of Roman Catholicism against the assault of the Reformers but was in due course expelled from the priesthood. His insight that the names attached to the Gospels were not the work of the evangelists themselves invited study of the identity of the Fourth Evangelist.

Eighteenth-century interpretation of the Gospel, however, continued the early view that John was the "spiritual" Gospel penned by the apostle John. H. S. REIMARUS expounded this view, contending that John knew but corrected the Synoptics and that the two could not be harmonized; in fact, the historical reliability of each was dubious (1972, 2:582). Lessing expanded this view in *Neue Hypothese über die Evangelisten als blosse menschliche Geschichtsschreiber betrachtet* (1777–78). In the last decade of the eighteenth century, both Lessing and J. G. HERDER (*Christliche Schriften* 3 [1797]) were the first to question the apostolic authorship of the Gospel; they argued that, compared with the Synoptics, the Gospel of John enhanced Christ's dignity. Herder saw John as an "echo" of the Synoptics that nonetheless clarified them. John stretched the reaches of Jesus' message beyond Judaism to the whole world.

In the nineteenth century the historical reliability of the Gospel of John received further attention. A former Anglican priest who had moved toward Unitarianism, E. EVANSON (1792, 1805²) challenged the Gospel's apostolic origin and boldly used Luke–Acts to reject the reliability and apostolic origin not only of the Gospel of John but also of Matthew and Mark and other NT writings. In his anonymously published *Der Evangelist Johannes und seine Ausleger vor dem jüngsten Gericht* (2 vols., 1801–4), E. Vogel (1750–1823) continued the argument against the traditional authorship of the Gospel. In his 1820 work K. Bretschneider (1776–1848) summarized the arguments against the Gospel's authenticity and for identifying its author as an Alexandrian gentile Christian of the second century; however, in light of F. SCHLEIERMACHER's (1837) and others' defense of the Gospel, he later recanted his view. Schleiermacher staunchly defended the Gospel on which he had constructed his christology, seeing in the Fourth Gospel a Jesus who was at the same time both human and divine.

D. F. STRAUSS (1835) questioned the historical credibility of the Fourth Gospel and insisted that the Evangelist had imposed his own speech in the style of Hellenistic philosophy on Jesus and John the Baptist. He offered, furthermore, a detailed analysis of the points at which the Synoptics and Acts disagreed with the Fourth Gospel on historical matters, concluding that the Gospel of John was wrong (e.g., Jesus did not have a mission among the Samaritans as John 4 suggests). Of the four Gospels, John's is the most mythological (i.e., ideas represented in objects) and hence suffered the most at the hands of Strauss's Hegelian construction. He posed an either/or alternative for interpreters: Follow either the Synoptics or John, for no harmonization between them is possible.

Other scholars also questioned the historical credibility of the Fourth Gospel. A. LOISY (1903, 1921[2]), not unlike W. WREDE (1903, 1933[2]), argued that the Fourth Evangelist was more a theologian and apologist against Judaism than a historian. The Gospel cannot be taken as a complement to the Synoptics but needs to be understood as an ecclesiastical witness indifferent to history. According to Loisy, the Evangelist uses an allegorical method, provides a spiritual and mystical portrayal of Christ, and makes Christ into a theological dogma. C. Wiezsäcker (1902[3]) advanced the theory that the Fourth Evangelist was a secondhand disciple of the one called "the disciple whom Jesus loved" and, removed from an immediate relationship with the historical Jesus, repressed his life into an entirely didactic work. A. JÜLICHER (1894) understood the Gospel of John to be a "philosophical prose-poem" without value as a source for discovering the historical Jesus. C. WEISSE (1838) argued that the Johannine discourses actually originated from the apostle John and were written down after his death. They were personal images of the apostle's view of Christ rather than historical reminiscences (so also D. Schenkel [1813–85] and A. Schweizer [1808–88]).

With increasing success in demolishing apostolic authorship came a movement to date the Gospel as late as 130–135 CE (Lützelberger) or even 170 CE (F. C. Baur). Although BAUR thought John contained nothing historical and was a post-Pauline (see PAUL) Christian reflection, he valued it because of its power to compel readers to make a decision for or against God. However, B. BAUER (1840) appreciated its literary qualities in spite of its unreliability as a historical document. The Fourth Evangelist was an artist, even though the work is flawed. The discourses in particular demonstrate evidence of careless editing, Bauer argued. From his reading of John he developed a fanciful portrait of Jesus that led him finally to assert that Jesus was not a historical figure at all (1852).

Other scholars, however, disagreed. Schleiermacher staunchly maintained the apostolic origin of the Gospel and granted it priority over the Synoptics, regarding 1:14 alone as the basic text for the whole of theology. W. DE WETTE (1852[4]) defended the authenticity of the Gospel, even though he believed that portions of it had been revised by a later figure. K. Frommann (1839) made a gallant effort—however imprecise—to distinguish between the transmitted accounts of Jesus and the Johannine Christ by isolating what he thought might be redactional additions to the discourse materials. Even more gallant was the defense of the claim, mounted by F. Büchsel (1928), that the Fourth Evangelist was an eyewitness expressing genuine Christian ideas. He even ventured to assert the historical superiority of the Fourth Gospel to the other three. Still others sought to strike a compromise by claiming historical reliability for the narratives but not the discourses. Among these were B. WEISS, W. BOUSSET, and E. RENAN.

Inevitably bound up with the question of John's authorship and historical reliability was its relationship with the first three Gospels. The common view that John represented a "spiritual" Gospel implicitly supposed that it was written as a conscious supplement to the Synoptics. Now that view was challenged. Even without necessarily casting doubt on historical reliability or apostolic authorship, reservations or outright denials that the Fourth Evangelist knew and made use of the Synoptics came from several corners (e.g., J. Semler [1771, 1772], G. Lessing, J. Wegscheider, Schleiermacher, and H. Weisse). The pursuit of a resolution to the uncertain relationship between the Synoptics and the Gospel of John carried well into the twentieth century, where its most vigorous debate is still found.

Other scholars raised questions that were also destined to be continued in the twentieth century. The OT scholar J. WELLHAUSEN (1907, 1908) questioned the unity and arrangement of the Gospel. Noting that 14:31 should be immediately followed by 18:1, he theorized that the discourses between the two passages were misplaced. The Gospel was, he concluded, the product of a process involving several stages. E. Schwartz (1907, 1908) studied the aporias in the Gospel and concluded that it is composed of numerous overlapping strata, although he despaired of the possibility of ever reconstructing its earliest form. The proposals of Wellhausen and Schwartz were later pursued by F. SPITTA and H. WENDT. The former postulated a foundational Gospel written by John, son of Zebedee, which an editor expanded. Wendt favored the discourses over the narrative material, believing that the sayings of Jesus betrayed the knowledge of one who personally knew the historical Jesus. These studies launched what became a more widespread theory in the second half of the twentieth century.

The rise of the RELIGIONSGESCHICHTLICHE SCHULE

propelled Johannine interpretation into the question of the Gospel's religious and intellectual milieu. As a result, a general but not unanimous shift occurred away from proposals for a Jewish setting toward those suggesting Hellenistic or oriental contexts. A. von HARNACK (1927) continued to maintain that the Gospel was derived from Palestinian Judaism and that its author was doubtless born a Jew, but he conceded that Johannine theology is Christian mysticism. Early in the nineteenth century de Wette classified NT literature into Jewish, Christian, Alexandrian or Hellenistic, and Pauline and located the Gospel of John in the second of his categories. The Gospel is rooted in the soil of Hellenistic mysticism, claimed Bousset (1905). Out of those roots it presents a mysticism that seeks a vision of God leading to divinization.

J. D. MICHAELIS (1788[4]) was apparently the first to see a positive relationship between Johannine thought and Gnosticism. Loisy thought that the Fourth Evangelist had been trained in Gnosticism before becoming a Christian and that in the second century the first form of the Gospel underwent revision to make it compatible with dominant Christian thought. H. GUNKEL (1903) proposed that Johannine thought is syncretistic in contrast to the simple message of Jesus. Given the Johannine emphasis on knowledge and dualism, the Fourth Evangelist must have had contact with an "oriental gnosis."

A new but related candidate for the setting of the Gospel arose in the form of the Mandaeans, born in the work of W. Brandt (1855–1915), who argued that Mandaeanism had Jewish roots. It was furthered first by R. Harris's publication of the Syriac *Odes of Solomon* (1909) and then by M. LIDZBARSKI's publications of and reflections on the Mandaean literature (1915, 1925). The *Odes* attracted immediate attention since there were obvious parallels between them and the Johannine discourses. Harris argued that they were extant in their present form at the time of the writing of the Gospel, while von Harnack maintained that a Christian had revised them at a later time. R. REITZENSTEIN (1919) and W. BAUER (1925[2]) were among the forceful proponents of the theory that Mandaeanism and the *Odes* were influential in the composition of the Fourth Gospel.

Building on the work of Reitzenstein and Lidzbarski, R. BULTMANN (1919) argued that the Gospel was based on a redeemer myth taken over from Mandaean and Manichaean sources. The content of Johannine theology is shaped by oriental MYTHOLOGY, proving how oriental-Gnostic speculation penetrated early Christianity in general. The Fourth Gospel represents a special and unique form of Christianity focused on a revealer figure. Remarkably, however, the central thesis of this form of early Christian thought is that Jesus reveals nothing more than the fact that he is the revealer. Behind that, Bultmann was persuaded, is a pre-Christian redeemer myth that lacks the full identification of the redeemed with the redeemer. The Evangelist is interested only in the fact of the revelation, not its content.

5. Twentieth Century. Bultmann provides a bridge from the energetic scholarship of the nineteenth century to that of the mid-twentieth century since, although he was in many ways a product of the nineteenth century, his influence cast a long shadow into the contemporary period. In large part the previous period set the agenda for Johannine interpretation in the twentieth century, and Bultmann's contributions to that agenda can hardly be overemphasized. He proposed that a pre-Christian Gnosticism shaped the environment out of which the Gospel was written and accentuated the Gospel's polemic against the followers of John the Baptizer, a group that most clearly manifested oriental Gnosticism.

With this assumption Bultmann fashioned an influential theory for the sources employed in the Gospel's composition (see D. M. Smith [1965]). Appealing to stylistic, contextual, and content evidence, he argued for the existence of three primary sources: For the discourses the Fourth Evangelist used a collection of *Offenbarungsreden* similar to the *Odes of Solomon*; the *Semeia* source resides behind the narrative of Jesus' wonders; and a passion source (independent of the Synoptic narratives) underlies the story of Jesus' death and resurrection. Beyond these three basic sources, as well as others, Bultmann posited a serious disruption of the arrangement of the original Gospel (e.g., chaps. 4, 5, 6, and 7) and additions by an "ecclesiastical redactor" (e.g., 6:51-58). This hypothetical redactor attempted to correct the theology of the Evangelist and to harmonize the Gospel with the Synoptics, especially in passages concerning the sacraments, eschatology, the eyewitness attestation of the Gospel, and the beloved disciple.

Equally important among Bultmann's contributions is his effort to construct a *sachlich* theology of the Gospel (e.g., his insistence that Jesus reveals no more than that he is the Revealer), at the heart of which is Bultmann's hermeneutic. At the point of convergence among his Lutheranism, Heideggerian existentialism, and *Religionsgeschichtliche Schule* commitment, Bultmann formulated his demythologization scheme. For him the Fourth Evangelist represented the first demythologizer of the Christian message, producing a document that emphasizes existential decision in response to revelation.

The nineteenth century ignited the doubt that the Fourth Evangelist knew and used the synoptic Gospels, and Bultmann seems to have shared that doubt. In the twentieth century the sparks of doubt were fanned into a roaring fire of controversy (see Smith [1992]). In the first quarter of the century H. WINDISCH, B. STREETER, and B. BACON advanced convincing arguments for the Fourth Evangelist's use of at least Mark and Luke, a view that temporarily comprised something of a consensus. Shortly, however, P. Gardner-Smith (1938) amassed an impressive yet simple case for the independence of John from the Synoptics. While not unanimously successful, his study moved Johannine interpretation decisively away from the assumption that the Evangelist knew and used the Synoptics to write a supplementary Gospel. For a time the relationship of the Synoptics and the Fourth Gospel seemed almost settled, but arguments for dependence continued to persist (e.g., C. Barrett [1978[2]]). Nonetheless, the formation of a consensus around Gardner-Smith seemed firm and was substantiated near the midpoint of the century by the work of C. H. DODD (1963). The consensus, however, was to be short-lived and began to unravel in stages.

The first stage of the demolition of agreement occurred as researchers explored parallels between Luke and John. J. SCHNIEWIND (1958), J. Bailey (1963), and others mounted impressive evidence of literary connections between John and Luke. The second stage began with N. PERRIN's proposal (1974) that Mark's passion narrative was the composition of the Second Evangelist and not the reproduction of a pre-Markan narrative. If that is the case, then the similarities between the passion stories in Mark and John must be due to the Fourth Evangelist's acquaintance with the Gospel of Mark and not with a pre-Markan source. The final stage of the demise of the consensus of Johannine independence came from the European scene, where a new and vigorous effort to study Johannine and synoptic parallels was undertaken with some success (e.g., M. Boismard and A. Lamouille [1970]; F. Neirynck [1992]; A. Dauer [1984]; and B. de Solages [1979]). As a consequence of the carnage done to the Gardner-Smith consensus, by the last decade of the twentieth century, views of the relationship between John and the Synoptics lack any unanimity whatsoever; and a pluralism of perspectives pervades contemporary scholarship.

Nonetheless, the theory of John's independence from the synoptic Gospels has reopened the question of the Gospel's historical reliability. If the Fourth Evangelist did not know or use the synoptic Gospels, then the Gospel could have been written at least contemporaneously with the Synoptics (although the predominant dating remains 90–95 CE). The relative value of the Gospel of John for access to the historical Jesus has been enhanced, too, by the acknowledgment that none of the canonical Gospels has historical reporting as its primary goal. The Fourth Gospel stands on common ground with the Synoptics in seeking to proclaim the existential importance of the historical event of Jesus of Nazareth.

On the one hand, some scholars still propose that the Evangelist was an eyewitness to that historical event, if not one of the apostles (e.g., J. Robinson [1985]; D. Carson [1991]), and tend to date it earlier. On the other hand, the absence of such claims has made it possible for others to propose that the historical reliability of John is not as uncertain as scholarship had argued in the nineteenth century. Dodd (1963) contended that the Fourth Evangelist (independently of the Synoptics) employed an oral tradition that was the source from which all the evangelists drew material and represented the earliest Christian tradition. Consequently, the narratives of the Fourth Gospel are potentially as historical as are those of the Synoptics (so also B. Lindars [1972]). The discourse material may also be understood in quite different ways than often proposed in the nineteenth century. They may be homiletical treatments of some kernel having its source in the historical Jesus (e.g., Lindars [1972]; Brown [1966]). The Gospel is not commonly regarded as a prime source for knowledge of the historical Jesus, but neither is it to be dismissed out of hand as devoid of historical value.

Since the middle of the twentieth century, scholarship has actually shown little interest in identifying the author of the Fourth Gospel. Instead, in the wake of Bultmann's influence attention has focused on the reconstruction of the sources used by the Evangelist (see R. Kysar [1975, 1984]). Following the precedent set by late nineteenth-century investigations, the supposition that the Gospel entailed sources and/or a process of composition was often advanced (e.g., E. Hirsch [1936a]). Proposals for the isolation of written sources behind the Gospel have especially focused on a "signs source" (e.g., R. Schnackenburg [1968]; R. Fortna [1970, 1989]; W. Nicol [1972]) and have enjoyed some favor; however, as a whole they have been generally unsuccessful in winning wide endorsement. On the other hand, scholars have more readily embraced theories for the development of the present Gospel through successive stages of composition or editing and redaction (e.g., Brown [1966, 1970, 1979], Lindars [1972]; and in a limited way, Schnackenburg [1968, 1980, 1982]). Such theories postulate that the original Gospel was expanded and edited a number of times before reaching its present form; some scholars (e.g., F. Segovia [1982]) find traces of the language and situation of 1 John in the later redactions.

Attention to sources and the development of the present form of the Gospel drew scholarship to study the community responsible for the document's origin (see Kysar [1981]). R. A. Culpepper (1975) proposed that the community constituted a "school" in the classical sense, and R. BROWN provided a description of that group (1979; cf. Cullmann [1976]). As the focus shifted away from the identity of the Evangelist to the community involved in the Gospel's formation, studies of the situation of that church and the message of the Gospel to it emerged (e.g., D. Rensberger [1988]). In addition to the community's dialogue with its social setting (R. Whitacre [1980]), scholarship became interested in the possibility of an intra-community controversy in the Gospel (e.g., P. Anderson [1996]). North American scholarship seemed for a time on the brink of a consensus on the community responsible for the Gospel, but after decades of scholarship there is little agreement on precisely what compositional process resulted in the present form of the Fourth Gospel. As a consequence of this lack of consensus about the process of composition, REDACTION-critical studies have been crippled, although frequent.

The shift of views on the issue of the setting for the Gospel is less vague. The nineteenth century moved steadily away from a Jewish setting toward a Hellenistic and/or Gnostic one. In many circles during the first half of the twentieth century, Gnostic or Hellenistic hypotheses prevailed, not the least because of Bultmann's influence. E. Hirsch (1936b) argued that the Fourth Evangelist was more comfortable with classical Greek literature than with Jewish thought and style. Other examples include E. KÄSEMANN's (1968) Gnostic and Dodd's (1958) Hellenistic theses. Käsemann's efforts to identify the theology of the Gospel as a "naive doceticism" provoked considerable discussion, especially around the issue of the nature of the incarnation (1:14). L. Schottroff (1970) argued for a fundamentally Gnostic understanding of the world in the Fourth Gospel (cf. U. Schnelle [1992]). Not universally accepted, this trend has been dramatically reversed in the last third of the century.

The persistent advocacy for a Jewish setting for the Gospel accounts for this reversal. C. BURNEY argued for an Aramaic origin; other scholars (e.g., Schattler [1930]) recognized a Semitic quality in both its language and its thought. In his influential commentary J. Bernard (1928) proposed that the Evangelist was a Jew who held much in common with PHILO. Within that setting the first step of the reversal from a Hellenistic and/or Gnostic background to a Jewish one came with the obvious parallels between some of the Qumran documents (see DEAD SEA SCROLLS) and the Gospel of John (e.g., the dualism of light and darkness) and the acknowledgment of the multiplicity of forms of first-century Judaism to which they witness.

The next and more significant step occurred when J. L. Martyn (1979[2], 1978) and Brown (1966) offered new proposals that significantly reshaped Johannine interpretation. Although Martyn's and Brown's proposals are different, together they suggest that the Gospel was written soon after the expulsion of the Johannine Christians from the Jewish synagogue and amid a vigorous debate between Christians and Jews in the locale where the Gospel was written. Their proposals were followed by a tidal wave of scholarship that built on their hypotheses and elucidated the Gospel from that perspective or at least from the vantage point of a predominantly Jewish setting (e.g., W. Meeks [1972], R. Fortna [1970], and S. Pancaro [1975]; see R. Kysar [1975]). The Johannine discourses of Jesus too, P. Borgen proposed (1965), betray a homiletical pattern rooted in Jewish

Midrashim (see MIDRASH) common to both John and Philo. The theory of an expulsion from the synagogue and other studies have resulted in the reaffirmation of a basic (and perhaps a heterodox) Jewish setting for the Gospel of John. Moreover, taken together these studies refocused understandings of the purpose of the Gospel on nurture amid crisis and not on evangelism, as 20:31 is sometimes interpreted to suggest (e.g., Carson [1991]). The synagogue expulsion theory has nonetheless been challenged on a number of fronts, including the general question of the nature of Jewish-Christian relations in the first century as well as the adequacy of the textual evidence (esp. 9:22; 12:42; and 16:2) to sustain such a sweeping proposal.

While efforts to identify the author of the Fourth Gospel have subsided in many regions of contemporary scholarship, the question of the relation of the Evangelist and the author of the Johannine epistles and Revelation continues to attract attention. Theories regarding the relationship of the Johannine Gospel and the epistles remain varied, including the persistent suggestion that at least 1 John was earlier than the Gospel (e.g., F. Büchsel [1928] and H. Wendt). Still, the proposal that the epistles were later products from and for the same community responsible for the Gospel is widely accepted (e.g., Brown [1979, 1982]). There is less effort to argue for the common authorship of the Gospel and Revelation, although belief in the commonality of the Apocalypse with the Johannine corpus continues (e.g., J. du Rand [1991]).

Finally, the last quarter of the twentieth century has witnessed the emergence of several new interpretive methodologies, each of which has had an impact on the interpretation of the Gospel of John. The first was occasioned in large part by the Martyn-Brown hypotheses regarding the origin of the Gospel and employs social science methodologies for interpreting the text. Sociological (see SOCIOLOGY AND NT STUDIES) and anthropological models, it is proposed, provide insight into the community behind the text. The enterprise was begun by W. Meeks (1972) and carried forward in a very different way by J. Neyrey (1988) and even more markedly so by N. Peterson (1993). In general this effort has attempted to reconstruct the sectarian nature of the Johannine community and its social situation.

The more radical of the new methodologies is the new LITERARY criticism. SOCIAL-SCIENTIFIC investigations continue to posit the value of understanding the historical origin of the Gospel. To some degree the new literary movement arose from dissatisfaction over the value of the older historical-critical methodology rooted in the previous several centuries and was spurred on by the new literary criticism used in other literature. It attempts to interpret John by means of the text without recourse to something that lies outside and beyond it (e.g., its historical setting) and to assume the text's unity against all source and redaction-critical procedures. Of course, the assertion that the Fourth Evangelist was a literary genius and the Gospel a poetic masterpiece was not the invention of late twentieth-century investigations. H. WINDISCH (1923) identified some of the dramatic qualities of the Johannine narrative, and H. Strathmann (1968) recognized the poetic powers of its language. Moreover, D. Wead (1970) anticipated the reversal that was about to occur. R. Culpepper (1983), however, opened a new frontier in the literary criticism of the Fourth Gospel. His work was followed by several investigations of the use of Johannine irony (P. Duke [1985]; G. O'Day [1986]), a READER-RESPONSE investigation of the implied reader (J. Staley [1988]), studies of the Gospel's rhetoric (M. Davies [1992]), a commentary on the farewell discourses (F. Segovia [1991]), and finally several commentaries on the entire Gospel (e.g., F. Moloney [1993, 1996]; M. Stibbe [1994]). A. Dettwiler (1995) offers an intertextual literary reading (see INTERTEXTUALITY) of passages often understood as redactional. A variety of literary approaches and other new interpretations of the Gospel have emerged as well (Culpepper and F. Segovia [1991]; Segovia [1996]; see M. Gourgues [1995] for further bibliography). Especially significant are the recent studies that examine the role of women in the Gospel (e.g., G. O'Day [1992, 1995]; A. Reinhartz [1994]) and the relation of the Gospel to imperialism (see CROSS-CULTURAL BIBLICAL INTERPRETATION).

Old questions still remain unanswered. A multiplicity of hypotheses on central issues continues to exist, and new methods of interpretation now abound. All of these continue to make the interpretation of the Gospel of John as difficult and as crucial as it was when that initial interpretation in 1 John was written.

Bibliography: E. **Abbot,** *The Authorship of the Fourth Gospel: External Evidences* (1880). P. **Anderson,** *The Christology of the Fourth Gospel: Its Unity and Disunity in the Light of John 6* (WUNT 78, 1996). J. **Ashton** (ed.), *The Interpretation of John* (Studies in NT Interpretation, 1997²). B. W. **Bacon,** *The Fourth Gospel in Research and Debate* (1910). J. **Bailey,** *The Traditions Common to the Gospels of Luke and John* (NovTSup 7, 1963). C. K. **Barrett,** *The Gospel According to St. John: An Introduction with Commentary and Notes on the Greek Text* (1978²). B. **Bauer,** *Kritik der evangelischen Geschichte des Johannes* (1840); *Kritik der paulinischen Briefe* (1852). W. **Bauer,** *Das Johannesevangelium erklärt* (1925²). J. **Becker,** "Aus der Literatur zum Johannesevangelium (1978–80)," *TRu* 47 (1982) 279-306, 305-47; "Das Johannesevangelium im Streit der Methoden (1980–84)," *TRu* 51 (1986) 1-78. J. **Bernard,** *A Critical and Exegetical Commentary on the Gospel According to St. John* (ICC, 2 vols., 1928). J. **Beutler,** "Literarische Gattungen im Johannesevangelium: Ein Forschungsbericht, 1919–80," *ANRW* II.25.3 (1984) 2506-68. C. C. **Black,** "St. Thomas's Commentary on the Johannine Prologue: Some Reflections on Its Character and Implications," *CBQ* 48 (1986) 681-98. M. **Boismard and A. Lamouille,** *L'évangile de Jean: Synopse des quatre évangiles en français* 3 (1977). P. **Borgen,** *Bread from Heaven: An Exegetical Study of the Concept of Manna in the Gospel of John and the Writings of Philo* (NovTSup 10, 1965). W. **Bousset,** "Der Verfasser des Johannesevangeliums," *TRu* 8 (1905) 225-44, 277-95. C. **Bretschneider,** *Probabilia de evangelii et epistolarum Joannis, apostoli, indole et origine eruditorum judiciis modeste subjecit* (1820). R. E. **Brown,** *The Gospel According to John* (AB 29, 1966; 29A, 1970); *The Community of the Beloved Disciple: The Life, Loves, and Hates of an Individual Church in NT Times* (1979); *The Epistles of John* (AB 30, 1982). R. **Bultmann,** "The History of Religions Background of the Prologue to the Gospel of John," *The Interpretation of John* (Studies in NT Interpretation, ed. and tr. J. Ashton, 1997²) 27-46; *The Gospel of John: A Commentary* (tr. G. Beasley-Murray, ed. R. Hoare and J. Riches, 1971); *Die Reden des Johannesevangeliums und der Stil der gnostischen Offenbarungsrede* (FRLANT, 1919); *Theology of the NT* 2 (tr. K. Grobel, 1975). C. F. **Burney,** *The Aramaic Origin of the Fourth Gospel* (1922). F. **Büchsel,** *Johannes und der hellenistliche Synkretismus* (BFCT 2, 16, 1928). J. **Calvin,** *Commentary on the Gospel According to John* (2 vols., tr. W. Pringle, 1949). D. **Carson,** *The Gospel According to John* (1991). J. H. **Charlesworth** (ed.), *John and the Dead Sea Scrolls* (1972, 1990²). M. **Comeau,** *Saint Augustine: Exégète du quatrième évangile* (Études de théologie historique, 1930). O. **Cullmann,** *The Johannine Circle: Its Place in Judaism Among the Disciples of Jesus in Early Christianity* (NT Library, tr. J. Bowden, 1976). R. A. **Culpepper,** *The Johannine School: An Evaluation of the Johannine School Hypothesis Based on an Investigation of the Nature of Ancient Schools* (SBLDS 26, 1975); *The Anatomy of the Fourth Gospel: A Study in Literary Design* (Foundations and Facets, 1983). R. A. **Culpepper and F. F. Segovia** (eds.), *The Fourth Gospel from a Literary Perspective* (Semeia 53, 1991). A. **Dauer,** *Johannes und Lukas* (FB 50, 1984). M. **Davies,** *Rhetoric and Reference in the Fourth Gospel* (JSNTSup 69, 1992). A. **Dettwiler,** *Die Gegenwart des Erhöhten: Eine exegetisch Studie zu den johanneischen Abschiedsreden (Joh 13,31–16,33) unter besonderer Berücksichtigung ihres Relecture-Charakters* (FRLANT 169, 1995). W. **de Wette,** *Kurze Erklärung des Evangeliums und der Briefe Johannis* (KEH NT, 1852⁴). C. H. **Dodd,** *The Interpretation of the Fourth Gospel* (1958); *Historical Tradition in the Fourth Gospel* (1963). P. **Duke,** *Irony in the Fourth Gospel* (1985). J. **du Rand,** *Johannine Perspectives* (1991). **Erasmus,** *Paraphrase on John* (Collected Works of Erasmus 46, tr. J. E. Philips, 1991). E. **Evanson,** *The Dissonance of the Four Generally Received Evangelists, and the Evidence of Their Respective Authenticity Examined* (1792, 1805²). C. **Farmer,** *The Gospel of John in the Sixteenth Century: The Johannine Exegesis of W. Musculus* (Oxford Studies in Historical Theology, 1997). R. **Fortna,** *The Gospel of Signs* (SNTSMS 11, 1970); *The Fourth Gospel and Its Predecessor: From Narrative Source to Present Gospel* (1989). K. **Frommann,** *Der Johanneische Lehrbegriff in seinem Verhältnisse zur gesammten biblisch-christlichen Lehre* (1839). P.

Gardner-Smith, *Saint John and the Synoptic Gospels* (1938). **M. Gourgues,** "Conquante ans de recherche johannique: De Bultmann à la narratologie," and "De Bien des manières," *La recherche biblique aux abords du xxie siècle* (LD 163, 1995) 229-306. **H. Grotius,** *Annotationes in libros Evangeliorum* (1641). **H. Gunkel,** *Zum religionsgeschichtlichen Verständnis des Neuen Testaments* (1903). **J. J. Gunther,** "Early Identification of Authorship of the Johannine Writings," *JEH* 31 (1980) 407-27. **E. Haenchen,** "Aus der Literatur zum Johannesevangelium, 1929–56," *TRu* 23 (1955) 295-335; *John: A Commentary on the Gospel of John* (Hermenia, 1984). **A. von Harnack,** *Die Entstehung der christlichen Theologie und des kirchlichen Dogmas* (1927). **R. Harris,** *The Odes and Psalms of Solomon* (ET, 1909). **R. E. Heine,** "The Role of the Gospel of John in the Montanist Controversy," *SecCent* 6 (1987–88) 1-19. **M. Hengel,** *The Johannine Question* (tr. J. Bowden, 1989). **E. Hirsch,** *Studien zum vierten Evangelium* (BHT 4, 1936a); *Das vierte Evangelium in seiner ursprünglichen Gestalt verdeutscht und erklärt* (1936b). **M. Hoffmann,** "Rhetoric and Dialogue in Erasmus's and Melanchthon's Interpretation of John's Gospel," *P. Melanchthon (1497–1560) and the Commentary* (ed. T. J. Wengert and M. P. Graham, 1997) 48-78. **W. F. Howard,** *The Fourth Gospel in Recent Criticism and Interpretation* (1931; rev. C. K. Barrett, 1955). **M. de Jonge** (ed.), *L'Évangile de Jean: Sources, rédaction, théologie* (BETL 44, 1977). **A. Jülicher,** *Einleitung in das Neue Testament* (1894). **J.-D. Kaestli et al.** (eds.), *La communauté johannique et son histoire: La trajectoire de l'évangile de Jean aux deux premiers siècles* (Monde de la Bible 20, 1990). **E. Käsemann,** *The Testament of Jesus: A Study of the Gospel of John in the Light of Chapter 17* (tr. G. Krodel, 1968). **H. Klein,** "Die lukanisch-johanneische Passionstradition," *ZNW* 67 (1976) 155-86. **R. Kysar,** *The Fourth Evangelist and His Gospel: An Examination of Contemporary Scholarship* (1975); "The Fourth Gospel: A Report on Recent Research," *ANRW* II.25.3 (1984) 2389-480; "Community and Gospel: Vectors in Fourth Gospel Criticism," *Interpreting the Gospels* (ed. J. Mays, 1981). **M. Lidzbarski,** *Das Johannesbuch der Mandäer* (1915); *Ginza: Der Schatz oder das grosse Buch der Mandäer* (QR 4, 1925). **B. Lindars,** *The Gospel of John* (1972). **G. Lessing,** *Neue Hypothese über die Evangelisten als blosse menschliche Geschichtsschreiber betrachtet* (1777–78; ET, *Lessing's Theological Writings* [ed. and tr. H. Chadwick, 1956] 65-81). **W. von Loewenich,** *Das Johannes-Verständnis im zweiten Jahrhundert* (BZNW 13, 1932). **A. Loisy,** *Le quatrième évangile* (1903, 1921[2]). **E. Lützelberger,** *Die kirchliche Tradition über den Apostel Johannes und seine Schriften in ihrer Grundlosigkeit nachgewiesen* (1840). **E. Malatesta,** *St. John's Gospel, 1920–65: A Cumulative and Classified Bibliography of Books and Periodical Literature on the Fourth Gospel* (AnBib 32, 1967). **J. L. Martyn,** *History and Theology in the Fourth Gospel* (1979[2]); *The Gospel of John in Christian History: Essays for Interpreters* (1978). **C. Maurer,** *Ignatius von Antiochien und das Johannesevangelium* (ATANT 18, 1949). **J. D. Michaelis,** *Einleitung in die göttlichen Schriften des Neuen Bundes* 2 (1788[4]). **W. Meeks,** "The Man from Heaven in Johannine Sectarianism," *JBL* 91 (1972) 44-72. **F. J. Moloney,** *Belief in the Word: Reading John 1–4* (1993); *Signs and Shadows: Reading John 5–12* (1996). **G.**

O'Day, "The Gospel of John," *NIB* (1995) 9:491-865; "John," *The Women's Bible Commentary* (ed. C. A. Newsom and S. H. Ringe, 1992); *Revelation in the Fourth Gospel: Narrative Mode and Theological Claim* (1986). **J. C. O'Neill,** "The Study of the NT," *NCRTW* 3 (ed. N. Smart, J. Elaytm, 1985) 143-78. **F. Neirynck,** "John and the Synoptics: 1975–90," *John and the Synoptics* (BETL, ed. A. Denaux, 1992) 3-62. **J. Neyrey,** *An Ideology of Revolt: John's Christology in Social Science Perspective* (1988). **W. Nicol,** *The Semeia in the Fourth Gospel: Tradition and Redaction* (NovTSup 32, 1972). **E. Pagels,** *The Johannine Gospel in Gnostic Exegesis: Heracleon's Commentary on John* (1973). **S. Pancaro,** *The Law in the Fourth Gospel* (NovTSup 42, 1975). **N. Perrin,** *The NT, An Introduction: Proclamation and Paranesis, Myth and History* (1974). **N. Peterson,** *The Gospel of John and the Sociology of Light: Language and Characterization in the Fourth Gospel* (1993). **T. E. Pollard,** *Johannine Christology and the Early Church* (SJNT 13, 1970). **G. Reim,** *Studien zum alttestamentlichen Hintergrund des Johannesevangelium* (SNTSMS 22, 1974). **H. S. Reimarus,** *Apologie oder Schutzschrift für die vernünftigen Verehrer Gottes* (ed. G. Alexander, 1972). **A. Reinhartz,** "The Gospel of John," *Searching the Scriptures,* vol. 2, *A Feminist Commentary* (ed. E. Schüssler Fiorenza, 1994). **R. Reitzenstein,** *Das mandäische Buch des Herrn der Grösse und die Evangelien Uberlieferung* (SHAW.PH 12, 1919). **D. Rensberger,** *Johannine Faith and Liberating Community* (1988). **J. Reuss,** *Johannes Kommentare aus der griechischen Kirche* (TU 89, 1966). **J. Robinson,** *The Priority of John* (1985). **E. Ruckstuhl,** *Die literarische Einheit des Johannesevangeliums* (NTOA 5, 1987). **M. Sabbe,** "The Footwashing in Jn 13 and Its Relationship to the Synoptic Gospels," *ETL* 58 (1982) 279-308. **J. N. Sanders,** *The Fourth Gospel in the Early Church: Its Origin and Influence on Christian Theology up to Irenaeus* (1943). **A. Schlatter,** *Der Evangelist Johannes; Wie er spricht, denkt und glaubt: Ein Kommentar zum vierten Evangelium* (1930). **F. Schleiermacher,** *Homilien über das Evangelium des Johannes in den Jahren 1823 und 1824* (1837). **R. Schnackenburg,** *The Gospel According to St. John* (HTC, 3 vols., tr. K. Smyth, 1968, 1980, 1982). **U. Schnelle,** *Antidocetic Christology in the Gospel of John: An Investigation of the Place of the Fourth Gospel in the Johannine School* (1992). **J. Schniewind,** *Die Parallelperikopen bei Lukas und Johannes* (1958). **L. Schottroff,** *Der Glaubende und die feindliche Welt: Beobachtungen zum gnostischen Dualismus und seiner Bedeutung für Paulus und das ˙Johannesevangelium* (WMANT 37, 1970). **E. Schwartz,** "Aporien im vierten Evangelium," *NGG* (1907) 1:342-72; (1908) 2:115-48, 3:149-88, 4:497-560. **F. Segovia,** *The Farewell of the Word: The Johannine Call to Abide* (1991); *Love Relationships in the Johannine Tradition* (SBLDS 58, 1982); "What Is John?" *Readers and Reading of the Fourth Gospel* (SBL Symposium 3, ed. F. Segovia, 1996). **J. Semler,** *Paraphrasis Evangelii Johannis* 2 (1771, 1772). **R. Simon,** *Histoire critique du texte du Nouveau Testament* (1689). **M. Simonetti,** *Biblical Interpretation in the Early Church: An Historical Introduction to Patristic Exegesis* (1996). **D. M. Smith,** *The Composition and Order of the Fourth Gospel: Bultmann's Literary Theory* (YPR 10, 1965); *Johannine Christianity: Essays on Its Setting, Sources, and Theology* (1987);

John Among the Gospels: The Relationship in Twentieth-century Research (1992). **B. de Solages,** *Jean et les synoptiques* (1979). **J. Staley,** *The Print's First Kiss: A Rhetorical Investigation of the Implied Reader in the Fourth Gospel* (SBLDS 82, 1988). **M. Stibbe,** *John's Gospel* (NT Readings, 1994). **H. Strathmann,** *Das Evangelium nach Johannes* (NTD 4, 1968). **D. F. Strauss,** *Das Leben Jesu, kritisch bearbeitet* (2 vols., 1835). **G. Strecker,** "Die Anfänge der johanneischen Schule," *NTS* 32 (1986) 31-47; *Die Johannesbriefe* (KEK 14, 1989). **J. Tayler,** *An Attempt to Ascertain the Character of the Fourth Gospel, Especially in Its Relationship to the Three First* (1867). **H. Thyen,** "Aus der Literatur zum Johannesevangelium," *TRu* 39 (1974) 1-69, 222-53; 40 (1975) 289-330; 42 (1977) 211-70; 43 (1978) 328-59; 44 (1979) 97-134; "Johannesevangelium," *TRE* 17 (1988) 200-225. **D. Wead,** *The Literary Devices in John's Gospel* (TheoDis 4, 1970). **J. A. Weisheipl,** "The Johannine Commentary of Friar Thomas," *CH* 45 (1976) 185-95. **C. Weisse,** *Die evangelische Geschichte, kritisch und philosophisch bearbeitet* (2 vols., 1838). **J. Wellhausen,** *Erweiterungen und Änderungen im vierten Evangelium* (1907); *Das Evangelium Johannis* (1908). **T. J. Wengert,** *P. Melanchthon's "Annotationes in Johannem" in Relation to Its Predecessors and Contemporaries* (THR 220, 1987). **R. Whitacre,** *Johannine Polemic: The Role of Tradition and Theology* (SBLDS 67, 1980). **C. Wiezsäcker,** *Das apostolische Zeitalter der christlichen Kirche* (1902³). **M. F. Wiles,** *The Spiritual Gospel: The Interpretation of the Fourth Gospel in the Early Church* (1960). **H. Windisch** "Der johanneische Erzählungsstil," [ΕΥΧΑΡΙΕΘΠΙΟΝ] (1923) 174-213. **W. Wrede,** *Charakter und Tendenz des Johannesevangeliums* (SGV 37, 1903, 1933²).

R. D. KYSAR

JOHNSON, AUBREY RODWAY (1901–85)

Born on April 23, 1901, the son of a Baptist, J. received his early schooling in Newport, South Wales, and went on to study THEOLOGY at South Wales Baptist College and University College, Cardiff, where he came under the teaching and influence of T. ROBINSON. He proceeded to further studies at Regent's Park College, London and Oxford, and at Halle-Wittenberg, Germany, where he was deeply influenced by the scholarship of O. EISSFELDT. He earned his doctorate at the University of Wales in 1931, examining concepts of life in Greek and Hebrew thought. It was not only the work of his teachers—T. Robinson, H. ROBINSON, and Eissfeldt—but especially the writings of W. BAUDISSIN, J. PEDERSEN, and S. MOWINCKEL that served to shape the fundamental themes of his research. J. was always first to pay tribute to what he learned from these scholars and especially to Baudissin's major study *Adonis und Esmun* (1911), which provided a major turning point in his own thinking (see *The Cultic Prophet and Israel's Psalmody* [1979]).

The greatest strength of J.'s work in biblical interpretation lies in his ability to combine a primary concern for biblical theology with insights gained through comparative religious-historical and anthropological studies. In the latter the emphasis on the role of cultus, as emphasized by the contemporary Scandinavian tradition of scholarship, provided him with a key for understanding certain basic biblical ideas concerning life and salvation. Much of the boldness and freshness of J.'s work has to be understood against the strong resistence of British biblical scholarship to what was regarded in H. GUNKEL and Mowinckel as an overly dogmatic religion-historical approach, which led to a serious neglect of their work among British scholars.

J.'s first important publication, "The Role of the King in the Jerusalem Cultus" (*The Labyrinth,* ed. S. H. Hooke [1935] 71-111), established many of the characteristic elements of his approach. It emphasized the importance of the role of the king as a mediator of life and salvation, drew attention to an element of continuity between Canaanite and Israelite religious traditions in Jerusalem, and pointed to the Jerusalem cultus as the locus of an exalted kingship ideology. This study of the role of the Israelite (Jerusalem) kingship culminated in J.'s major study on sacral kingship, given as the Haskell lectures, Oberlin College, in 1951. Leaning initially on Mowinckel's study of the role of the king in the cult and of the mythological origins of the kingship ideology, J. reconstructed the pattern of the Israelite autumn (new year) festival. Related essays include that in *ExpTim* (62 [1950–51] 41-43) and "Hebrew Conceptions of Kingship" (*Myth, Ritual, and Kingship,* ed. S. H. Hooke [1958] 204-35).

The importance of the relationship among PSYCHOLOGY, language, and ideas had entered theological discussion with the work of L. Levy-Bruhl on "primitive mentality." H. Robinson had drawn upon such psychological explanations for his understanding of the Hebrew idea of "corporate personality"; and J. carried forward his own research into notions of primitive conceptuality in two short, but highly detailed studies (1942, 1961).

The next major area of J.'s exegetical research related to the study of cult PROPHECY, which had earlier been adumbrated by Mowinckel. J.'s 1944 study examines the basic evidence, mainly in narrative texts, for the existence of cult prophets. A more far-reaching examination of the thesis appeared in his detailed and complex 1979 study of the psalter. Here he found large sections of Israelite psalmody to display the forms, idioms, and ideas of cult prophets who delivered oracles to individual worshipers or to an entire assembled congregation. Affirming the cultic origin of most Israelite psalmody and the indissoluble link between cultus and theological ideas, he saw the cultus as an agency for the mediation of salvation and vital divine energy.

While J.'s research was ultimately rather overrefined and at times overly speculative, he fulfilled a major task in communicating the ideas and conclusions of Scandinavian and German scholarship in areas where the

English-speaking world tended to be too hastily dismissive. He also left a significant range of unresolved issues concerning the methods and conclusions of religious anthropology and biblical theology in relation to OT literature, especially the psalter.

Works: *The One and the Many in the Israelite Conception of God* (1942, 1961); *The Vitality of the Individual in the Thought of Ancient Israel* (1949, 1964); *The Cultic Prophet in Ancient Israel* (1944, 1962); *Sacral Kingship in Ancient Israel* (1955, 1967); *The Cultic Prophet and Israel's Psalmody* (1979).

Bibliography: G. W. Anderson, *PBA* 72 (1986) 433-39.

R. E. CLEMENTS

JONAH, BOOK OF

1. Introduction. The interpretation of the book of Jonah may begin within the HB itself. Many phrases and passages in the book either parallel directly or echo materials from other parts of the Bible (see A. Feuillet [1947]). To what extent these are conscious borrowings and to what extent Jonah or the other passage may be the primary source in any given case is debatable (see J. Magonet [1976, 1983²J] 65-84; L. Allen [1976] 177). Nevertheless, we are reminded that the process of reinterpretation within the HB is almost as old as the individual texts themselves and that the book of Jonah is a carefully wrought narrative composition within a long literary tradition. However, what might have been "story" to its initial hearers became "history" for subsequent generations up to the modern period.

2. Jonah in Jewish Tradition. *a. Midrash and Liturgy.* As elsewhere, rabbinic MIDRASH attempts to fill gaps in the narrative, explain seeming contradictions, and respond to polemical issues. For instance, Jonah was the son of the widow of Zarephath who offered Elijah hospitality (*Pirqe R. El.* 33), a tradition known to the church fathers. He fled to save Israel, risking death at the hands of heaven for suppressing his PROPHECY (*Sanh.* 11:5). If the Ninevites repented but Israel did not, God would punish the people, so Jonah was willing to sacrifice his own life to save them (*Mek. Tractate Pisha*, ed. J. Lauterbach, 7, 10). This vindication of Jonah's behavior may be an apologetic response to Matt 12:41 (see E. Urbach [1975] 558; E. Bickerman [1967] 16; for a fuller treatment, see L. Ginzberg [1954] 4:197, 239-53; 6:318 n. 9, 343-52, "Midrash Jonah"). The book of Jonah is the prophetic reading for the Day of Atonement, probably because of the theme of repentance (but see also *Ta'an* 2:1).

b. Medieval exegesis. The major Jewish commentators of the medieval period (Rashi, A. Ibn Ezra, D. Kimhi, Abravanel, etc.) wrote complete commentaries on the book in their characteristic styles. They often anticipated the discussions about linguistic problems,

sequence of events, anachronisms, and other issues of modern exegesis. ABRAHAM BAR HAYYA (12th cent.) gives a philosophical interpretation on the theme of repentance. The *Zohar* contains an elaborate allegory in which "Jonah descending into the ship is symbolic of man's soul that descends into the world to enter the body" (*Zohar Vayakhel* 199a-200a; see U. Steffen, [1994] 11-56).

3. Jonah in Christian Tradition. Christian interpretations of the book follow the three direct references to Jonah in the Gospels. In Matt 12:41 and Luke 11:29-32 JESUS cites the conversion of the Ninevites as an example of repentance, whereas in Matt 12:40 Jonah's presence inside the fish is understood as prefiguring Christ's body in the tomb (see R. Edwards [1971] 1-24, 71-107; J. Motyer [1975] 350-52). These two applications of the book, as a source of moral examples and of types, continue into the patristic period. East Syrian Christianity emphasized the repentance of the Ninevites. In the Greek and Western fathers (surveyed by Y. Duval [1973]), one argument, following Matt 12:41, is to consider Jonah as the representative of Judaism; whereas Nineveh believed, Israel continues to refuse to acknowledge Jesus (Jerome—see Bickerman [1965] 241). By the end of the fourth century Jonah is portrayed as an envious person who begrudges the salvation of the Gentiles (Augustine). This view, however, is rejected by JEROME and CYRIL OF ALEXANDRIA because of the other tradition that envisions Jonah as prefiguring Christ (see Duval [1985] 105-6).

Jonah appears among the other biblical examples of deliverance from death in a type of early Christian prayer that closely follows a Jewish pattern (see *Ta'an* 2:4; a Jewish-Christian example is in Apostolic Constitutions 7, 37-38). This kind of exemplary prayer (see H. Leclercq, "Défunts") is a key to the sequences of biblical scenes in early Christian art in which Jonah figures twice, as thrown into the sea and as resting under the gourd, a symbol of repose after death (Leclercq, "Jonas"). Christian use of and comment on the book hardly went beyond the lines laid down in patristic times until the rise of modern critical discussion (see Steffen, 57-117).

4. Jonah in Islamic Tradition. Jonah (*Yunus*) appears four times in the Quran (see QURANIC AND ISLAMIC INTERPRETATION), and his story is told once more without naming him. Sura 10 is called the "Sura of Jonah" because of the prominent mention of his prophetic task, in fact, Sura 4:163 and 6:87 name him among other prophets of God. In 10:99 the people of Nineveh are held up as models of a community that profited from their belief and repented, yet the fullest version of the story (37:139-48) emphasizes Jonah's blameworthiness in refusing his mission. The remaining reference (68:48-50) does not mention him by name: "Wait for your Lord's decree, and do not be like him of the fish who cried out in despair." Amplifications of these stories, typical of Islamic tradition, can be found in "The Tales of the Prophets of al-Kisa'i" (see W. Thackston [1978]; Steffen, 119-40).

5. Jonah in Modern Scholarship. The major lines of scholarly inquiry were established by the end of the nineteenth century: (1) lower criticism (see P. Trible [1963] 1-51); (2) higher criticism, including the historicity of Jonah and hence the question of its genre; the sources of the book and the composition; the authenticity of the "psalm" in 2:3-10; the dating of the book; and its purpose.

a. Historicity and Dating. Before the modern period most commentators accepted the historicity of the book, although GREGORY OF NAZIANZUS in the fourth century and Theophylact in the eleventh gave allegorical interpretations (see E. Sutcliffe [1953] 669; Allen, 178). Among Jewish exegetes, R. Joseph ibn Caspi cited some unnamed commentators, perhaps influenced by MAIMONIDES (*Guide of the Perplexed* 2.46), who understood the events of chaps. 1 and 2 as occurring in a prophetic vision (see Y. Kil [1973] 5-6; Bickerman [1965] 233, n. 7). With the rise of higher criticism the historicity of the narrative was questioned, and during the nineteenth century numerous defensive arguments were raised to support it (see Trible [1963] 127). Although still defended, the majority of scholars today no longer pursue this issue (see M. Burrows [1970] 80-85).

Decisive in the change of view have been issues like the "great fish" or rather the whole range of miraculous events within the book that suggest a parabolic rather than literal history. Archaeological evidence (see ARCHAEOLOGY AND BIBLICAL STUDIES) contradicts the assertion about the size of Nineveh, and there is no record of any such mass conversion of the city. Even the statement of Jesus about Jonah (Matt 12:39-41) need not assume Jesus' acceptance of the historicity of the event as it may merely reflect the conventional understanding or use of his Jewish audience (see Allen, 180).

Linked to the question of historicity is that of the dating of the book. Whereas traditional commentators (and conservative moderns) identify the Jonah ben Amittai of 2 Kgs 14:25 as the author of the narrative, most scholars accept a later dating for the book.

Much of the evidence for dating can be argued in opposing ways, e.g., the statement in 3:3—"Nineveh was a great city"—may imply that at the time of composition it no longer existed or may merely reflect a particular Hebrew construction. The apparent relationship to other biblical passages, especially Jeremiah 18, would suggest a postexilic date, although the problem of whether such dependence exists at all, and if so in which direction, means that we are dealing only with probabilities, however persuasive. The presence of Aramaisms, which formerly was believed to indicate a late date, is now less certain proof; some of the maritime terminology may be of earlier Phoenician origin. However, the number of other words and linguistic constructions that reflect postexilic Hebrew is still highly suggestive of a late date (see H. W. Wolff [1977] 54-55; Allen, 187-88).

Another basis for dating is the assumption that (like the book of Ruth) Jonah reflects a "universalistic" opposition to the "particularistic" policies of Ezra and Nehemiah. The history of this view has been traced by Bickerman (1967, 16-28). Although some commentators have maintained it, others find no evidence within the book to support such a theory (see Allen, 188). Attempts to date the book through views of Israel's universalism are inconclusive (see Trible [1963] 111-12), as are those based on interpreting the "message" of the book—the latter often displaying circular reasoning (see Burrows, 104). The book was apparently known to Ben Sira (Sir 49:10) in the second century BCE, but the reference in Tobit 14:4, 8 (4th cent. BCE) is problematic, as Codex B reads "Nahum" in place of "Jonah." The book's origin is probably best located in the fifth or fourth century BCE (see Allen, 188).

b. Genre. Challenges to the historicity of the book led to the search for other ways of defining its nature. There is among scholars a tension between the religious concern to find an acceptable genre to validate the book if it is not really history (see B. Childs [1958] 53-61) and a purely scientific interest in correct definition. However, the various suggested genres all present problems, either because they are too generalized to be of much value in defining the book or so precise that the multiple dimensions of the book are no longer taken into account.

Allegorical interpretations have a long history based on linking the name Jonah ("dove") with passages like Hos 11:11—hence the fish symbolizes being "swallowed up" by Babylon (Jer 51:34, 44). However there is no way of controlling what tend to become purely arbitrary interpretations (see Burrows, 89-90). In addition, the genre of parable tends to be too loosely defined, and whereas other parables in the HB are briefer and make a single point, Jonah is more complex. Analogies with the narratives of Elijah and Elisha have suggested the terms "prophetic legend" or "prophetic history," however, the book tends to parody such stories rather than to belong to them, and the story has a broader compass than just the prophet himself (see Wolff [1965] 32).

Somewhat broader categories are suggested by Novelle, or wisdom story, in which the moral point is veiled within the overall narrative. Some scholars, recognizing the exaggeration and humor, have suggested parody or satire. Others look within Hebrew terminology for the appropriate category, e.g., *mashal* or *midrash*—but if it is a Midrash in the rabbinic sense, on what verse is it a commentary (see Allen, 180)? Other studies offer a general description like "a didactic narrative, satirical in tone."

LITERARY approaches have brought new perspectives and reopened older questions. The "psalm" in 2:3-10 was long held to be inauthentic (inappropriate while Jonah was still not saved; poetry and not prose like the rest of the book, etc.). However, the recognition of narrative techniques within it that are common to the rest of the book (the irony of its use by Jonah, like other of his pious statements; its architectural counterpoint to chapter 3, etc.) suggest that it belongs to the original composition (see M. Landes [1967]; Magonet, 39-54; S. Ackerman [1981]).

c. The problem of meaning. Early attempts to discover "sources" on the model of PENTATEUCHAL CRITICISM or to trace the mythological underpinning (see MYTHOLOGY AND BIBLICAL STUDIES) of the book (see Trible [1963] 131-43) have long since ceased. Recent studies of the history of interpretation examine some underlying presuppositions in evaluating the book. In his study of "antijudaism" in Jonah exegesis, W. Golka (1987; following Bickerman [1967]) traces the attitudes ascribed to Jonah in traditional Christian exegesis and modern scholarship. The view that Jonah represents an alleged Jewish nationalistic exclusiveness is still expressed in language of surprising vehemence (see W. Neil [1962] 964, 967). Such interpretations may be classified under the theme "Jews and Gentiles" and have evoked defensive responses classifiable as history of prophecy: (a) the question of the individual prophetic fate and (b) the meaning of the prophecy of judgment and hence questions about repentance and divine mercy. The book lends itself to many kinds of homiletic interpretation and to approaches from other disciplines, like psychoanalysis (see A. Lacocque and P.-E. Lacocque [1990]; see also PSYCHOANALYTIC INTERPRETATION).

Literary studies in the late twentieth century have emphasized the multiple dimensions and ambiguities of the story by virtue of its being a narrative. The new emphasis is thus to indicate the complexity of interpretation. The reader is encouraged, not to take away a single message from the book, but rather, as its closing unanswered question implies, to enter into a personal dialogue with it.

Bibliography: **J. S. Ackerman,** "Satire and Symbolism in the Song of Jonah," *Traditions in Transformation: Turning Points in Biblical Faith* (ed. B. Halpern and J. D. Levenson, 1981) 213-46. **L. C. Allen,** *The Books of Joel, Obadiah, Jonah, and Micah* (NICOT, 1976) 173-235. **E. J. Bickerman,** "Les deux erreurs du prophète Jonas," *RHPR* 45 (1965) 232-64; *Four Strange Books of the Bible* (1967) 1-49. **R. H. Bowers,** *The Legend of Jonah: Fifty Odd Interpretations of Jonah from the NT Through the English Renaissance* (1971). **M. Burrows,** "The Literary Category of the Book of Jonah," *Translating and Understanding the OT* (ed. H. T. Frank and W. L. Reed, 1970) 80-107. **B. S. Childs,** "Jonah, a Study in OT Hermeneutics," *SJT* 11 (1958) 53-61. **Y.-M. Duval,** *Le Livre de Jonas dans la*

littérature chrétienne grecque et latine (2 vols., 1973); (ed.) *Jérôme: Commentaire sur Jonas* (SC 323, 1985). **R. A. Edwards,** *The Sign of Jonah in the Theology of the Evangelists and Q* (1971). **A. Feuillet,** "Les Sources du Livre de Jonas," *RB* 54 (1947) 161-86; "Le Livre de Jonas," *La Sainte Bible* (1966[3]). **L. Ginzberg,** *The Legends of the Jews* (7 vols., 1954[6]). **F. W. Golka,** "Jonaexegese und Antijudaismus," *Zeitschrift für Kirche und Israel* (1987). **Y. Kil,** *"sēfer yônâ" (da'at miqrā': terê 'āsār,* 1 (1973). **G. M. Landes,** "The Kerygma of the Book of Jonah," *Int* 21 (1967) 3-31. **A. Lacocque and P.-E. Lacocque,** *Jonah: A Psycho-Religious Approach to the Prophet* (1990). **H. Leclercq,** "Défunts," *DACL* 4, 430-40; "Jonas," *DACL* 7, 2572-613. **J. Z. Lauterbach** (tr.), *Mekilta De-Rabbi Ishmael* (3 vols., 1933). **J. Magonet,** *Form and Meaning: Studies in Literary Techniques in the Book of Jonah* (1976, 1983[2]). **B. H. Mehlman and D. F. Polish** (tr.), "Midrash Jonah" *CCARJ* 24, 1 (1977) 30-41. **J. A. Miles, Jr.,** "Laughing at the Bible: Jonah as Parody," *JQR* 6 (1975) 168-81. **J. A. Motyer,** "Jonah," *New International Dictionary of NT Theology* 2 (1975) 350-52. **W. Neil,** "Jonah, Book of," *IDB* (1962) 2:964-67. **J. M. Sasson,** *Jonah* (AB 24B, 1990); **U. Simon,** *Jona: Ein Jüdischer Kommentar* (Stuttgarter Bibelstudien 157, 1994). **U. Steffen,** *Die Jona-Geschichte: Ihre Auslegung und Darstellung im Judentum, Christentum, und Islam* (1994). **E. F. Sutcliffe,** "Jonas (Jonah)," *A Catholic Commentary on Holy Scripture* (1953) 669-71. **W. M. Thackston, Jr.,** *The Tales of the Prophets of al-Kisa'i* (1978). **P. L. Trible,** "Studies in the Book of Jonah" (diss., Columbia University, 1963); *Rhetorical Criticism: Context, Method, and the Book of Jonah* (1994); "The Book of Jonah" *NIB* (1996) 7:461-530. **E. E. Urbach,** *The Sages: Their Concepts and Beliefs* (2 vols., 1975). **H. W. Wolff,** *Studien zum Jonabuch* (Biblischen Studien 47, 1965); *Obadiah and Jonah* (BKAT 14, 3, 1977; ET 1986).

J. MAGONET

JOSEPHUS, FLAVIUS (c. 37–c. 100)

Our chief source for historical information about the Jews for the period from the Maccabees (167 BCE) to the destruction of the Temple in Jerusalem (70 CE), J. was born in Jerusalem in 37 of a distinguished priestly family, which, on his mother's side, went back to the royal Hasmonean house. According to his own statement (*Life* 8-9), he received an excellent education and showed such precocity that at the age of fourteen the chief priests and the leading men of the city constantly consulted him with regard to *halakhah* (religious law). Beginning at about the age of sixteen he spent three years exploring the three leading Jewish sects (the Pharisees, the Sadducees, and the Essenes) and becoming a disciple of a certain otherwise unknown hermit named Bannus before deciding to attach himself to the school of the Pharisees (*Life* 10-12).

At the age of twenty-six J. succeeded, through friendship with a Jewish actor in Rome named Aliturus, who introduced him to the Emperor Nero's consort, Poppaea

Sabina, in securing the release of some Jewish priests imprisoned there. According to the statement in his *Life* (17), he then tried unsuccessfully to dissuade the revolutionaries from starting a war to gain their independence from the Romans. Fearing for his life, he took refuge in the Temple and eventually pretended to concur with their views, although secretly hoping that the Romans would suppress the uprising. When, however, the Roman commander Cestius Gallus was defeated in 66 by the rebels, J. accepted an appointment in Galilee from the Jewish leaders in Jerusalem to induce the revolutionaries to fight only in self-defense (*Life* 28-29). The account in the *Jewish War* (2.562-568) speaks merely of his appointment to prosecute the war (although he apparently had no previous military experience) and says nothing of the aim of pacification. A possible reconciliation of these accounts is that J. at first tried to pacify the militants; but when he failed (and perhaps under pressure), he tried to conduct the war to the best of his ability. Apparently he continued to play a double role, since he says that when one of the rebel leaders, John of Gischala, asked him for some grain, he declined (*Life* 72), declaring that he intended it either for the Romans or for his own use. When, after retreating to Jotapata, they were besieged by the Romans, his men decided to commit mutual suicide; but J. and one other (the last to be left, presumably through a manipulation of the lots) did not go through with the pact. J was brought before the Roman general Vespasian and predicted, in a detail corroborated in the second century by Suetonius (*Vespasian* 5.6) and Appian (fragment 17) and in the third by Dio Cassius (66.1.4), that Vespasian would become emperor. J. may have had sincere motives in surrendering in that he perhaps realized that the revolt would ruin the tremendous progress the Jews had made in gaining converts to their religion; but one is deservedly suspicious of one who after the fall of Jerusalem received such rewards from the Roman general Titus as a tract of land outside Jerusalem, freedom from taxation for this land, some sacred works (presumably Torah scrolls), the liberation of some friends, Roman citizenship, lodging in the former palace of Vespasian, and a pension. We should note, however, in all fairness, that such an eminent rabbinic leader as Johanan ben Zakkai was likewise opposed to the war and similarly predicted the accession of Vespasian to the throne, although he received no personal benefits from the Romans. Unfortunately, aside from J.'s own accounts in his *Life* and *War* and the brief statements, noted above, about his prediction of Vespasian's accession, we have no details about J.'s life; the silence of the vast Talmudic corpus (see TALMUD) about him, except for a questionable allusion in *Derekh Ereẓ Rabbah* 5, is probably due to the rabbis' disapproval of his close cooperation with the hated Titus during the siege of Jerusalem and of his profound absorption of Greek culture. After the capture of Jerusalem J. accompanied Titus to Rome, where, despite numerous accusations against him, he continued to enjoy the favor of the emperors Vespasian, Titus, and even the anti-Jewish Domitian.

The earliest of his works, *The Jewish War Against the Romans* (7 bks.), was, to judge from internal evidence, composed after 75 and probably between 79 and 81. Its very title indicates its bias, since if it had been written from the point of view of the Jews it should have been entitled *The Roman War.* J. (*War* 1.3) wrote that he originally composed it in his ancestral language, presumably Aramaic, and sent it to the barbarians of the interior, apparently the Parthians; with the help of several assistants he then translated it into Greek (*Apion* 1.50). The translation is so smooth, however, being superior in style even to the *Antiquities,* which was not completed until the year 93/94, that it is almost impossible to discern the original Aramaic. Book 7, which deals with the period after the destruction of the Temple and includes the famous Masada episode, is clearly in a different style and gives such prominence and favor to Domitian that it seems to have been composed at a later time. Archaeological digs (see ARCHAEOLOGY AND BIBLICAL STUDIES), notably in Jerusalem and at Masada, have, on the whole, confirmed his descriptions, although accuracy in topography need not necessarily imply accuracy in historical data. Indeed, we are seldom in a position either to confirm or definitively to deny his descriptions of causes and events, although his omission of the information (*Dio Cassius* 66.4.4) that during the siege of Jerusalem some of the Romans defected to the Jewish side would seem to indicate that J. gave a biased account, at least of events in which he personally was involved. J. (*War* 1.2) indicated that there were other historians of the war against the Romans, and we know from his apologetic account in his *Life* that Justus of Tiberias had composed a narrative attacking J.'s version of the war; but none of these accounts have survived. Nor do we have the *Commentaries* of Vespasian and Titus (*Life* 342, 358; *Apion* 1.56), which J. used as sources.

The *Jewish Antiquities* was written primarily for non-Jews, as can be seen from the fact that J. (*Ant. Jud.* 1.10-11) cited the precedent of the SEPTUAGINT as his justification for presenting to the Greek-speaking world the history of the Jews. In the first half of this work he paraphrased the Bible, having access both to the Hebrew text and to the Septuagint (in a proto-Lucianic version), as well as to an Aramaic TARGUM. Although he promised neither to add to nor subtract from the biblical text (*Ant. Jud.* 1.17), he apparently meant that he would not modify the tradition in the broadest sense; and the tradition includes midrashic-like elements (see MIDRASH), frequently paralleled in rabbinic literature and in such pseudepigraphic literature (see PSEUDEPIGRAPHA) as Pseudo-Philo's *Biblical Antiquities* and the

DEAD SEA sect's *Genesis Apocryphon.* Thus, in extra-biblical details, Abraham emerges as a logician, scientist, and philosopher who proves the existence of God in a novel argument; Moses is a general who carries out a victorious campaign against the Ethiopians, during which the Ethiopian princess falls in love with him; and Saul is an Achilles-like hero who has precisely those traits that would appeal to a Greek audience—the external qualities of good birth and handsome stature and the four cardinal virtues of wisdom, courage, temperance, and justice as well as the fifth virtue, noted by Plato, piety.

For the second half of the *Antiquities* J.'s chief source was Nicolaus of Damascus. Here Josephus was no mere plagiarizer but a discerning critic; particularly in his lengthy account of Herod, he often expressed independent judgment, perhaps especially because he was descended from the Hasmoneans, Herod's great rivals. H. Thackeray (1929) proposed that in books 15 and 16 J. utilized an assistant who had a particular love of Greek poetry, notably Sophocles, and that in books 17–19 he availed himself of an assistant who was especially fond of Thucydides. But there are Sophoclean and Thucydidean traces throughout J.'s works, and many of these phrases may have come to him through other Greek works of the period, notably that of Dionysius of Halicarnassus, whose history, *Roman Antiquities,* has a similar title and has the same number of books (twenty), and whose theory of historiography seems to have influenced J.

For the Christian reader the greatest interest attaches to three passages, those about JESUS (*Ant. Jud.* 18.63-64), John (*Ant. Jud.* 18.116-119), and James the brother of Jesus (*Ant. Jud.* 20.200-203). The first, the famous *Testimonium Flavianaum,* as indicated by the fact that ORIGEN in the third century explicitly stated that J. did not believe in Jesus as the Christ and that it was not quoted until the fourth century despite its obvious usefulness in the Christian-Jewish debate, seems to be partly interpolated, as now seems apparent from the form in which it was cited by the Christian Arab Agapius in the tenth century. The second is almost certainly genuine, since a Christian would surely have mentioned the relationship of John to Jesus' teachings and would have given the same explanation of John's condemnation that is found in the Gospels. The third, likewise genuine, with its phrase identifying James as the brother of "Jesus who was called the Christ," confirms that J. did know about Jesus.

The treatise *Against Apion,* the most polished of J.'s works, is a defense of the Jewish religion and history, especially of the exodus, against the attacks of the Egyptian anti-Semites Manetho, Lysimachus, Chaeremon, and Apion. In his defense of Judaism, J., like his model PHILO's *Hypothetica,* follows the standard rhetorical pattern for such encomia.

J.'s works have been enormously influential, largely because of the *Testimonium Flavianum,* which gave witness to the historicity, the messiahship, and the resurrection of Jesus, as well as to the role of the Jews in condemning him, but also because of the *Jewish War,* with its vivid description of Jewish suffering, which was regarded as evidence for the punishment meted out to the Jews for the alleged crime of deicide. The fourth-century paraphrase of the *Jewish War* ascribed to Hegesippus, the Latin translation by the school of CASSIODORUS in the sixth century, the tenth-century Hebrew paraphrase of the *War* known as *Josippon,* and the eleventh-century Slavonic paraphase of the *War,* among others, attest to J.'s popularity. During the Middle Ages he was regarded as an authority in such diverse fields as biblical exegesis, Jewish theology, CHRONOLOGY, geography, arithmetic, astronomy, natural history, grammar, and etymology; and he was often catalogued in libraries with the church fathers. He was a guide to Palestine for Christian pilgrims and crusaders. From 1450 to 1700 there were more editions of his works than of any other Greek historian; and the translation into English by W. WHISTON, published in 1737, has been reprinted at least 217 times.

Works: *Flavii Iosephi Opera* (7 vols., ed. B. Niese, 1885–95; ET, H. St. J. Thackeray et al., *LCL* [10 vols., 1926–65]).

Bibliography: **H. W. Attridge,** *The Interpretation of Biblical History in "The Antiquitates Judaicae" of F. J.* (1976; HDR 7, 1990). **C. T. Begg,** *J.'s Account of the Divided Monarchy* (BETL 108, 1993). **P. Bilde,** *F. J. Between Jerusalem and Rome: His Life, His Works, and Their Importance* (JSPSup 2, 1988). **S. J. D. Cohen,** *J. in Galilee and Rome: His Vita and Development as a Historian* (CSCT 8, 1979). **A. Edersheim,** *DCB* 3 (1882) 441-60. **L. H. Feldman,** *J. and Modern Scholarship (1937–80)* (1984); *J.: A Supplementary Bibliography* (1986); "Use, Authority and Exegesis of Mikra in the Writings of J.," *Mikra: Text, Translation, Reading and Interpretation of the HB in Ancient Judaism and Early Christianity* (CRINT 2.1, ed. M. J. Mulder, 1988) 455-518; *Jew and Gentile in the Ancient World: Attitudes and Interactions from Alexander to Justinian* (1993); *Studies in Hellenistic Judaism* (AGSU 30, 1996) 37-273; *J.'s Interpretation of the Bible* (Hellenistic Culture and Society, 1998); *Studies in J.'s Rewritten Bible* (JSJSup 58, 1998). **L. H. Feldman and G. Hata** (eds.), *J., Judaism, and Christianity* (1987); *J., the Bible, and History* (1989). **T. W. Franxman,** *Genesis and the "Jewish Antiquities" of F. J.* (BibOr 35, 1979). **S. Mason,** *F. J. on the Pharisees: A Composition-Critical Study* (SPB 39, 1991); *J. and the NT* (1992). **S. Pines,** *An Arabic Version of the "Testimonium Flavianum" and !ts Implications* (PIASH, 71). **T. Rajak,** *J.: The Historian and His Society* (1983). **S. Schwartz,** *J. and Judaean Politics* (CSCT 18, 1990). **H. Schreckenberg,** *Bibliographie zu F. J.* (ALGHJ 1, 1968); *Bibliographie zu F. J.: Supplementband mit Gesamtregister* (ALGHJ 14, 1972). **H. St. J. Thackeray,** *J. the*

Man and the Historian (1929). **P. Villalba i Varneda,** *The Historical Method of F. J.* (ALGHJ 19, 1986).

L. H. FELDMAN

JOSHUA, BOOK OF

The text of Joshua raises acute questions as to what context is appropriate for its interpretation. Is Joshua essentially a complete and integrated book that can properly stand on its own and be viewed in and for itself? Or is it only sensible to see its contents as part of something else: whether the Pentateuch, from which it may be a lost conclusion or a detached appendix; or the narratives of the former prophets, which may offer a single deliberately planned story? Of course, the second alternative simply pushes back the equally vital question of to what extent the larger text of which Joshua might be a part might itself be an integrated work, rather than a haphazard deposit of tradition. How much or how little structure or planning can be detected in Joshua or in its supposed wider context?

Answers to questions like these determine whether we give priority to aesthetic or historical attempts to understand the book. Is this text more like persons with whom we may readily deal and interact on the terms in which they present themselves? Or is it more like those people about whom we have to learn something of their family and their past before we can cope with the puzzle they represent? It may be impatience with such preliminaries that has led many readers to advocate simply taking the text as it is, as tradition or the CANON have handed it down.

1. Interpretation Within the Text, or What Is the Text? Such an apparently straightforward approach founders on the facts as disclosed by text-critical studies. The Hebrew (MT) and Greek (LXX) texts of Joshua, preserved separately by synagogue and church after their ancient division, exhibit significant differences; and only some of these are the result of random mistakes. The importance of the SEPTUAGINT (LXX) of Joshua as evidence for the history of the Hebrew text before it was standardized in Masoretic (MT) tradition has been appreciated at least since J. Hollenberg (1876). The important work of S. Holmes (1914), in part a defense of Hollenberg, broke ground in glimpsing the implications for the book's literary history of some of the divergences between the ancient texts. Yet M. MARGOLIS's magisterial treatment of the textual history of the Greek Joshua (1931–38) and M. NOTH's influential commentary on the Hebrew text (1938) combined to marginalize the significance of the LXX for the understanding of the Hebrew Joshua.

A series of studies returning to and advancing Holmes's insights was inaugurated by H. ORLINSKY (1969); and contributions have accelerated through the efforts of A. G. Auld, A. Rofé, E. Tov, L. Greenspoon, and J.

Floss. (These have received thorough methodological grounding in the detailed and vital work by J. Trebolle-Barrera [1986], illustrating in portions of Judges, Samuel, and Kings the close relationship between textual criticism and literary history.) The implications of these studies have not yet reached a wide readership. R. Boling's textual notes (AB 6, 1982) diligently note variation between Hebrew and Greek texts and the divergent evidence of the available Qumran material (see DEAD SEA SCROLLS). And several of the results of the above-mentioned scholars have been incorporated piecemeal in T. Butler's more important commentary (1983). However, a full-scale treatment of the whole book of Joshua from this perspective has still to be published; and K. Bieberstein (1995) and C. den Hertog have urged caution.

2. Earlier Interpretation of the Texts. Ben Sira epitomizes Joshua in a few verses (beginning of Sirach 46): the successor to Moses, the one who as a deliverer deserved his name, the one who brought Israel into its inheritance, the one splendid in fighting the Lord's battles. The passage from which most detail is drawn is Josh 10:10-15, in which Joshua defends the Israelites from the Amorites by commanding the sun to stand still, whereby hailstones fall from the sky and annihilate this enemy.

The NT takes no explicit opportunity to exploit the fact that Joshua and JESUS share the same name—a feature prominent in patristic interpretation. The letter to the Hebrews (Heb 4:8) contrasts the "rest" offered by Jesus with what could not have been provided in full by Joshua because Psalm 95 sees it as incomplete. The great review of examples of faith passes over Joshua in two verses (Heb 11:30-31). James's letter (Jas 2:25) also mentions Rahab's "justification by works"; while the Gospel of Matthew (Matt 1:5) counts her among the ancestors of the Messiah.

JOSEPHUS's account of Joshua in his *Antiquities* is mostly a rather wordy paraphrase of the whole text of the biblical book. Some of its additions and, even more, its omissions are interesting. The twelve stones at Gilgal form an altar; but there is absolute silence on the circumcision episode, and the Passover is barely mentioned. More understandably the account of land division is both shorter and more orderly than in Joshua 13–21, with the survey by geometricians (cf. 18:1-10) at its head. As if to compensate, the dispute over the eastern altar is even more leisurely than Joshua 22.

ORIGEN's *Homilies on Joshua*, perhaps his latest work (around 250 CE), stressed the first Joshua/Jesus as greater than the dead Moses of the law. The theme is already found in JUSTIN MARTYR and IRENAEUS, but it appears to have been Origen's detailed exposition that had the most influence during this period. The changing of the leader's name from Hoshea was prophetic. The crossing of the Jordan was a procession with priestly ritual, not the undisciplined mob at the Red Sea. Moses settled only two-and-a-half tribes, and outside the land, while Joshua settled the majority, including the Levites, in the land.

Origen's other key theme has already been suggested: the spiritualizing of the land and the struggles within it. It is the soul that is the real area of conflict; heaven is symbolized by the promised land and its "rest." This interpretation permitted Origen to oppose both the heretical disjunction between the cruel God of the HB and the loving one of the NT as well as the fleshly literalism of the Jews. A fine example is the more "dignified" interpretation he is able to give of the second circumcision of the people before the first Passover in the promised land. In fact, his commentary on John had already mentioned the obvious literal sense of the passage. Here, however, Origen remarked that Jews must be asked how a second circumcision is possible. For Christians, for whom the law is spiritual, the difficulties of the passage are resolved: The first circumcision marked the passage from idolatry to the Mosaic law; the second, accomplished by the stone that is Christ, marked the passage from the law and the prophets to the gospel faith. THEODORE OF MOPSUESTIA indulged in a similar polemic when he suggested that Jews are regrettably unable to see that the circumcised perished and the uncircumcised were saved: the fathers died, and it was their sons who received the object of the promise.

F. Langlamet (1979) has provided a masterly survey of Rahab as she has been discussed in ancient and modern times—by the rabbis, among the fathers of the church, and in more recent scholarship. Rabbis and early fathers almost outdid each other in the significance they found in this woman and her story. For some of the rabbis she was one of the four most beautiful women in the world (with Sarah, Abigail, and Esther); for others, one of the four most seductive (with Ruth, Jael, and Saul's daughter Michal). Her profession of faith was linked with those of Moses, Jethro, and Naaman; Joshua married her; and eight prophets were descended from her (including Jeremiah and Ezekiel in different lists). In short, as ideal proselyte, she was an example to all the nations of the world: Any waverer could be challenged, "Are you worse than Rahab?" Christian fathers made some similar points (beginning with Matt 1:5) and noted also that she was saved by her faith and her hospitality; the scarlet cord given her by the messengers of Joshua/Jesus was a sign of salvation by the Lord's blood; and her example is endorsed by Jesus' statement to religious leaders of his time that publicans and courtesans proceed them into the kingdom.

The divinely instigated treatment of the Canaanites has long been a problem for commentators, whether as a straightforward moral issue or as a precedent from within their own Scriptures felt by politically vulnerable Jews to be all too dangerous in Christian hands. Medie-val rabbis suggested that Joshua, before his invasion, had offered the inhabitants of Canaan by letter a three-fold invitation to submit.

CALVIN's commentary on the book, from the closing months of his life in 1563/64, happens to be his last literary work. His long experience as a leader and his failing health both illumine his exposition. The removal of Moses, "as if God, after cooping up his people in a corner, had left his work in a shapeless and mutilated form," and his replacement by Joshua "suggests the very useful reflection, that while men are cut off by death, and fail in the middle of their career, the faithfulness of God never fails."

Again, on the dispute in chapter 22 over the altar of the Transjordanian tribes, he comments ironically, but firmly: "Nothing was farther from their intention than to innovate in any respect in the worship of God. But they sinned not lightly in attempting a novelty, without paying any regard to the high priest, or consulting their brethren, and in a form which was very liable to be misconstrued." Leadership and literary sensitivity combine to influence his discussion of how the two closing speeches by Joshua are related: In chapter 24 Joshua "explains more fully what he before related more briefly. For it would not have been suitable to bring out the people twice to a strange place for the same cause."

3. Earlier Modern Discussion: Joshua and Pentateuch. The synthesis of J. WELLHAUSEN on the composition of the Hexateuch, which was to remain authoritative for sixty years, was heavily indebted to two immediate predecessors. In 1874 Hollenberg declared that PENTATEUCHAL CRITICISM gave new life to the study of Joshua. In a detailed article he argued first that Joshua 1; 8:30-35; 23; and parts of 24 had been composed by the deuteronomist, who had added Deuteronomy 1–4 and portions of the final chapters to the basic speech of Moses in Deuteronomy 5–28; and then that this major author had also made numerous smaller contributions to the "Jehovistic" Joshua traditions. A. Kuenen (1886) was to concur in almost all details, although he argued against ascribing this deuteronomic recension to a single author. Wellhausen's movement (toward the end of his influential study) from Pentateuch to Joshua was introduced in carefully chosen words: Unlike Judges–Kings, Joshua was an appendix to the Pentateuch that assumed it at all points—without the same material being edited in it the same way. In fact, he was to argue that the sources had been more substantially altered in the editing of Joshua than in the Pentateuch. In his discussion of the deuteronomist's role, Wellhausen made only minor alterations to the proposals of Hollenberg and Kuenen, agreeing with Hollenberg that deuteronomic style could be found even in late additions unrepresented in the LXX (e.g., 20:4-6).

The commentary of C. KEIL and Franz DELITZSCH (1869), while admitting that Joshua is more closely connected to the Pentateuch in form and content than to those books that follow, insists that it is not a literary appendix: Their relationship is like that of Joshua to Moses. Even if it was not composed until some time after Joshua's death, this does not affect its historico-prophetic character; both the content and form of the book show it to be an independent and simple work composed with historical fidelity as well as a work that is as thoroughly pervaded with the spirit of HB revelation as is the Pentateuch.

The third volume of A. DILLMAN's Hexateuch commentary on Numbers–Joshua (1886) is more sympathetic to Wellhausen and Kuenen. Once separated from the more authoritative Pentateuch, Joshua had not been so carefully corrected, hence its many preferable LXX readings. However, historically it cannot be separated from the Pentateuch. He offers some arguments against preferring the LXX just because it is shorter.

C. STEUERNAGEL's third volume on the historical books (1990) covers Deuteronomy–Joshua and offers a concluding introduction to the Hexateuch. Five sections of the latter concern composition, and only one treats the book of Joshua as historical source: The miraculous and popular form in which religious conviction clothes itself in the book is worthless for the political history of Israel; it has meaning for the history of religion only as a sign that Israel was a people with lively religious thought.

The earlier Cambridge Bible volume by G. Maclear on the AV (1880) stands very much in the Greek patristic tradition, with Joshua presented as a "type" prefiguring Jesus the Christ. He notes that the undoubtedly terrible severity of the work of Joshua was often used as an objection against HB morality, but quotes H. EWALD: "It is an eternal necessity that a nation such as the majority of the Canaanites then were, sinking deeper and deeper into a slough of discord and moral perversity, must fall before a people roused to a higher life by the newly awakened energy of unanimous trust in Divine Power." Maclear continues: "When . . . God entrusted the sword of vengeance to Joshua, was ever campaign waged in such an unearthly manner as that now inaugurated by the leader of the armies of Israel?" And he ends by quoting a sermon of T. ARNOLD: "The Israelites' sword in its bloodiest executions, wrought a work of mercy for all the countries of the earth . . . they preserved unhurt the seed of eternal life."

G. Cooke's later volume (1878, 1917), based on the RV, is a whole thought-world away. After an account of the book's literary origins very like that of Wellhausen, he explains that the deuteronomic redactor "tells about Joshua, not as he really was, but as the writers of the seventh century pictured him; the portrait, if it can be called one, is not a study from the life, but the creation of a fervid believer and patriot. We may be sure that nothing like the wholesale slaughter of the natives and

irresistible victories of the Israelites ever took place. . . . Far more ancient and vivid than anything we find in the OT is the picture of early Canaan given by the Amarna tablets." Like Hollenberg, Kuenen, and Wellhausen, he is good in his treatment of the LXX.

The divorce between the message of Joshua and the facts of history was already clear in Steuernagel and Cooke. It was not successfully overcome by J. GARSTANG, despite that archaeologist's attempts in the *Foundations of Biblical History* (1931). However, a more enduring historical response was to come from his German colleagues.

4. The Legacy of Alt and Noth. A. ALT's three volumes of *Kleine Schriften* (1953) contain a dozen major papers relevant to the historical evaluation of Israel's settlement, the role of Joshua, and most distinctively the topographical information in the book, behind which he detected archival administrative source material (from the end of the Judaean monarchy in the case of the town lists in 15:21-62). Noth adopted Alt's methods and argued (1935) that a list of Judaean localities in twelve districts had been combined with a system of tribal boundaries to produce most of the material in Joshua 13–19. Their studies provided the methods and set the standards for the major works that followed by J. Simons (1959), Y. AHARONI (1967), and Z. Kallai (1967).

In his commentary on Joshua (1938) Noth reaffirmed that the topographical material had had its own prehistory and argued that even the narratives had a literary background distinct from Genesis, in which deuteronomistic affiliations were most easily detectable. He then addressed (1943) all the biblical narratives where consensus recognized the deuteronomist's editing, arguing first that Joshua–Kings represented a self-contained whole: The retrospective and anticipatory passages (Joshua 1; 23; Judges 2; 1 Samuel 12; 2 Kings 17) had no exact parallels in the HB and had much in common with each other in subject. "If we take the perfectly sound approach of interpreting the relatively simple and clear conditions in Joshua–Kings, without regard to the findings of literary criticism elsewhere, and postpone discussing the very controversial 'Hexateuch' questions in their application to Joshua, we can reach only one conclusion."

However, Joshua 1 is certainly not the beginning. The links of this chapter with the Moses story and in particular the account of the settlement of some tribes in Transjordan show that these matters have already been treated in the deuteronomist's work. Noth found that with little difficulty the chronological details (see CHRONOLOGY, HB) in the other books can be seen to square with the information in 1 Kgs 8:1 that the Temple was dedicated 480 years after the exodus. (In the case of Joshua this depends on his claim that Josh 14:10 is part of a passage once linked to the deuteronomist's 11:23!)

His review of the deuteronomist's contribution to the account of the occupation of Cisjordan differs little in essence from Hollenberg's (1874). A series of separate etiological stories relevant to the Israelites' successful incursion had been combined into a well-rounded whole with a few heroic legends. The deuteronomist obviously took over the whole of this and altered it only by adding an introduction and epilogue and some supplementary material.

In a significant comment on the nature of the composition, Noth writes that these deuteronomistic passages, "brought in at every suitable opportunity . . . come to make good literary sense if they are not just the monotonously repeated statement of the pet idea of an 'editor,' intended to accompany and interpret a piece of tradition already existing in finished form, but rather meant to play a part in transforming elements totally diverse in form, scope and content, into a single literary unit." The fact that despite these elements the separate parts of the work seem disunited and heterogeneous is explained because the deuteronomist consciously committed himself to using the material available to him. Novelty and faithfulness hand in hand!

In 1953 Noth published a fresh edition of his commentary on Joshua, stating more decisively what he had anticipated in 1938: that the book should be read independently of the Pentateuch (i.e., Genesis–Numbers). G. VON RAD, S. MOWINCKEL, and G. Fohrer (1968) continued to assert close links between Joshua and the Pentateuch. Auld (1980) and M. Rose (1981) responded, suggesting that even more of the Pentateuch depended on material in Joshua than Noth had claimed.

Noth's thesis of a DEUTERONOMISTIC HISTORY was to capture the imagination of almost all non-conservative scholars, although important details of his argument were challenged by many followers. Commentaries on Joshua for over thirty years (e.g., by H. Hertzberg [1953]; J. Gray [1967, 1986²]; J. Miller and G. Tucker [1974]; and J. Soggin [1972]) operated within his structure. R. Smend (1971) challenged Noth's view that the addition of the topographical traditions was achieved editorially by anticipating in Josh 13:1 the deuteronomist's words in 23:1 about Joshua's age. His reversal of the relationship of these two verses allowed him to propose (a) that the deuteronomistic history (DtrH) did contain a report of land division and (b) that Joshua 23 was simply the most detailed of several additions to the original history by a second deuteronomistic editor (DtrN). W. Dietrich was to follow with a study on Kings (1972), interposing a third prophetic redaction (DtrP).

Their lead was followed by T. Veijola (1977) and summarized by Smend (1978). F. M. Cross's discussion (1973) focused on the later chapters of Kings and led him to propose that the original deuteronomistic history was composed in honor of Josiah before the fall of Judah. This history was brought up to date during the exile and supplemented with elements more critical of kingship. Cross's more summary views have been adjusted and advanced by R. Nelson (1981a, 1981b). H.-D. Hoffmann (1980), in a study of the religious reforms related by the deuteronomist, argued against both these trends: (a) that the deuteronomistic history was a unity (but for quite insignificant exceptions), and (b) that very much more of Joshua–Kings had been drafted by the deuteronomist than Noth had allowed. A. Mayes (1983) proposed that with a little adjustment on each side the similarities between the Smend and Cross "schools" would be clear.

Unhappily for our purposes, with the exception of Smend's article (1971) and, of course, Noth's original epoch-making commentary, very little of the above discussion has actually been based on close study of Joshua. There is a real danger that the study of this book is now quite as much at the mercy of broader theories about a deuteronomistic history as it was once misread as the conclusion of a Hexateuch.

Soggin's introduction and his commentary on Judges have endorsed the modifications argued by Smend and his followers. The volume by Boling and G. E. WRIGHT, by contrast, stands more in the American tradition of Cross and Nelson. Unhappily, it is also a very uneven volume: The introduction was prepared by Wright before his death in 1974 and was out of date on its publication in 1982; then, since Boling did not write the introduction, the methods underlying his puzzling approach to matters of textual and literary history remain rather obscure despite further exposition (1983, 1985).

Different stages of the discussion were well reviewed by individual scholars: E. Jenni (1961), A. Radjawane (1974), Smend (1978), Auld (1980), T. Butler (1983), Mayes, and H. Weippert (1985), whose survey of what she in nice understatement calls a polyphonic situation, includes studies up to 1981. When considering studies that mention the deuteronomist in Joshua subsequent to those reviewed by Weippert, "chaotic" might be a more adequate term than "polyphonic." J. Van Seters (1983) attributes most of Joshua–Kings to a first deuteronomist, lightly touched up by a second; while B. Peckham (1984) attributes most of Joshua–Samuel to the second deuteronomist, seeing his work as a monumental commentary built into and onto a once brief narrative of Deuteronomy 1. And C. Begg (1986) confidently talks of the "deuteronomisticity" of Joshua 7–8 on the basis of its structural contribution to the whole, whether words and ideas from Deuteronomy are found in it or not.

Each of these scholars believed in a deuteronomistic history—but not in Noth's—and each in a different one. Was it time to revalue this currency or to move on to a different standard? Two collaborative projects, one on the legacy of Noth and the other on Israel's constructing its own history, led to valuable publications edited by S. L. McKenzie and M. P. Graham (1994) and A. De Pury,

T. Römer, and J.-D. Macchi (1996). C. Schäfer-Lichtenberger (1995) provided a wealth of documentation in her careful comparison of Joshua and Solomon; Auld (1995) also reviewed some Joshua issues in the light of his work on Kings.

5. A Literary Reading? R. Polzin's (1980) attempt to read the first half of the deuteronomistic history (Deuteronomy–Judges) after the example of the Russian "formalist" LITERARY critics may have been underrated. He offers sensitive and attractive readings of many parts of Joshua. The text is studied "as it is," unreconstructed, mostly by attention to the shifting perspectives or points of view in different "planes" of the text: phraseo-logical, temporal, spatial, psychological (see PSYCHOLOGY AND BIBLICAL STUDIES) and IDEOLOGICAL. The reader is invited into ever-richer readings of the text; and the deepest, the ideological level, is reached through the more superficial. Polzin makes particular use of the interplay between the narrator, God, and Moses or Joshua, especially when one is quoting, and sometimes slightly misquoting another.

The detail of the Rahab story (chap. 2) is allowed to interrupt the action of conquest so long because, once it is seen that the story of Rahab is really the story of Israel told from the point of view of a non-Israelite, then the larger themes of the justice and mercy of God vis-à-vis Israel can be recognized as central to the story and to its position as the initial episode in the deuteronomist's account of the occupation of the land. The valuable distortions brought about by constant shifts in perspective offer the reader a much more adequate image of the occupation of the land as the fulfillment of God's word than the flat, universalized, and pat evaluations of the voice of authoritarian dogmatism, the reflexes of whose simplistic ideology can still be heard in the categorical assertions of, say, 4:10*b*. Chapter 22 helps us see why the two-and-a-half tribes are so prominent in the book: They are like the other "aliens"—Rahab, the Gibeonites, Caleb, the Levites—and dependants in the book of Joshua. All of them are representative versions of the same typology: The Transjordanian tribes are a permanent representation of the obedience to God's law that never quite makes it. As Phinehas testifies to these "outcasts": "We know this day . . . that you have saved the people of Israel from the hand of the Lord."

M. Greenberg (in Y. Kaufmann [1985]) has noted how KAUFMANN's reading of Joshua, while less critical historically, was holistic before that became fashionable. There is sensitive, but less coordinated, literary comment in Boling, Butler, and Auld (1984), who draw attention to humor and irony and warn against too straight a reading of the text. Butler, a master of fair-minded review, encourages the search for historical development in the interpretation of the Joshua traditions and claims that their "final, canonical message . . . is made clear by the Deuteronomistic structural markers." It is vital that the import of the book of Joshua be sought in its text and not in a reconstruction of whatever history may underlie it. The commentaries of Boling and E. Hamlin (1983) commend a liberationist Joshua who owes more to the historical endeavors of G. Mendenhall (1962) and N. Gottwald (1979) than to close reading of the biblical book.

Polzin's reading of Deuteronomy–Judges (complemented by subsequent volumes on the books of Samuel) has received valuable support from the articles by D. Gunn (1987) and L. Rowlett (1992) and the volumes by L. Eslinger (1989), L. Hawk (1991), G. Mitchell (1993), and E. Mullen (1993). Rowlett particularly neatly sketches contrasts such as the fate of outsider Rahab and insider Achan with respect to the Jericho "ban" or of insider Transjordanians on the wrong side of the Jordan and outsider Gibeonites on the right side. R. Carroll (1992) analyzes the myth of the empty land. N. Winther-Nielsen (1995) has made a thorough appeal to discourse analysis as a more objective umpire among the competing witnesses cited by synchronic and diachronic readers alike.

None of the commentaries of the 1990s has embraced these newer literary approaches, although each is novel in its own way. M. Ottosson (1991) reads Joshua as a plea for a new David in the period of Josiah. His interest in the topographical chapters is reflected also in J. Svensson's dissertation (1994). V. Fritz (1994), whose work replaces that of Noth in the HAT series, remains remarkably faithful to the broad lines of his predecessor's approach, although the deuteronomist, whether Josianic or exilic, now displaces Noth's early monarchic *Sammler* as the first collector of the materials. He too offers a fresh account of the topographical materials.

S. Ahituv's modern Hebrew volume (1995) is intended as a "scientific" commentary but also for a wide readership in Israel. It unpacks idioms from the older tongue, offers a transcription of all the Joshua Qumran fragments (see DEAD SEA SCROLLS), and explores several issues with contemporary resonance: the conquest and the question of the land left over; the Canaanite "ban": *halakha* and fact; the righteous generation of the conquerors; the dating of the geographical lists. The bibliography is quite detailed on such points of interest but makes little concession to more literary approaches. A commentary by R. Hess (1996) emphasizes evidence for early dating but is well informed and judicious throughout. These commentaries make little use of the more radical historical assessments by G. Ahlström (1993), R. Coote (1987), P. Davies (1992), N. Lemche (1988), T. Thompson (1992), and K. Whitelam (1996); and Ahituv in particular is more at home with compatriot historians like W. Weinfeld (1993) and N. Na'aman (1994).

6. The Challenge of the Textual Facts. Tov (1981 and repeatedly) has drawn attention to the relevance of the LXX for the literary history of the Bible. His discussion (1986) of the strange story of the altar on Ebal, which appears in a different position in the Hebrew and Greek Bibles—suggests that this is a late addition to the narrative, filed differently by different editors. The apparent link in 4QJosh[a] of the end of this story with the beginning of Josh 5:2-3 has allowed A. Kempinsky (1993), Rofé (1994), and Auld (1995) to give this discussion a new twist. Then Tov developed a series of arguments (1987) to support the claim that the shorter LXX *Vorlage* has (by and large) been expanded into the longer familiar Hebrew rather than shortened from it. He assumes, apparently without argument, that the short Hebrew text translated into Greek around 200 BCE had existed for centuries. However, might the familiar expanded Hebrew instead be much more recent than often thought?

Auld's studies on the tribal lists (1980, 1987) and those of M. Wüst (1975), whose major project remains only half published, have suggested that much of the historico-geographical information in Joshua 13–21 on the division of the land between the various tribes of Israel is more heavily reedited and harmonized than Alt and Noth allowed—or Aharoni and Kallai, who have largely followed their methods. Kallai did not take the opportunity of the translation of his major study (Hebrew, 1967) to answer some of these criticisms. However, E. Cortese (1990) has been very critical of Auld's work. G. Garbini (1988) has argued that details suggesting the Persian period are not so much supplements to an older tradition as indicators of the age of much of the biblical narrative tradition.

The discussion between Rofé and M. Rösel over the traditions that interlock at the end of Joshua and the beginning of Judges, but rather differently in the MT and the LXX, is quite vital for answering the first question posed in this article: In what context should we view the book of Joshua—in and for itself, or as part of a longer story, whether we call that a deuteronomistic history or not? Tov has been soberly providing the text-critical tools. Others must try to stand on his shoulders and attempt a riskier view. Two samples are the detailed study of Joshua 2 by Floss and Trebolle's correlation of textual and literary work at the beginning of Judges. That is where the most exciting action may be in Joshua studies in the next years.

Bibliography: Y. **Aharoni,** *The Land of the Bible* (1967). S. **Ahituv,** *Joshua: Introduction and Commentary* (Mikra LeYisra'el, 1995). G. W. **Ahlström,** *The History of Ancient Palestine* (1993). G. A. **Alt,** *Kleine Schriften zur Geschichte des Volkes Israel* (3 vols., 1953–59). A. G. **Auld,** "Joshua: The Hebrew and Greek Texts" (VTSup 30, 1979) 1-14; *Joshua, Moses, and the Land* (1980); *Joshua, Judges, and Ruth* (Daily Study Bible, 1984); "Tribal Terminology in Joshua and Judges," *Le Origini di Israele* (1987) 87-98; "Reading Joshua after Kings," *Words Remembered, Texts Renewed: Essays in Honour of J. F. A. Sawyer* (JSOTSup 195, ed. J. Davis, 1995); *Joshua Retold: Synoptic Perspectives* (1998). C. T. **Begg,** "The Function of Josh 7:1-8, 29 in the Deuteronomistic History," *Bib* 67 (1986) 320-34. K. **Bieberstein,** *Lukian und Theodotion im Josuabuch, mit einem Beitrag zu den Josuarollen von Hirbet Qumran* (BNB 7, 1994); *Josua—Jordan—Jericho: Archäologie, Geschichte, und Theologie der Landnahme—erzählungen Josua 1–6* (OBO 143, 1995). R. G. **Boling,** "Levitical History and the Role of Joshua," *The Word of the Lord Shall Go Forth* (ed. C. L. Meyers and M. O'Connor, 1983) 241-261; "Levitical Cities: Archaeology and Texts," *Biblical and Related Studies Presented to S. Iwry* (ed. A. Kort and S. Merschauser, 1985) 23-32. R. G. **Boling and G. E. Wright,** *Joshua* (AB 6, 1982). J. **Briend,** "Les sources de l'histoire deutéronomique: Recherches sur Jos 1-12," *Israël construit son histoire: L'historiographie deutéronomiste à la lumière des recherches récentes* (Le Monde de la Bible 34, A. de Pury, T. Römer and J.-D. Macchi, 1996) 343-74. T. C. **Butler,** *Joshua* (WBC 7, 1983). J. **Calvin,** *Commentaries on the Book of Joshua* (Calvin Translation Society, 1984). R. P. **Carroll,** "The Myth of the Empty Land," *Ideological Criticism of Biblical Texts* (*Semeia* 59, ed. D. Jobling and T. Pippin, 1992) 79-93. G. A. **Cooke,** *The Book of Joshua in the RV* (CBC, 1878, 1918[2]). R. B. **Coote** "The Book of Joshua," *NIB* (1998) 2:553-719. R. B. **Coote and K. W. Whitelam,** *The Emergence of Early Israel in Historical Perspective* (1987). E. **Cortese,** "Gios 21 e Giud 1 (TM o LXX?) e l' abbottonaura del Tetrateuco con l'Opera deuteronomistica," *RivB* 33 (1985); *Josua 13–21: Ein priesterschriftlicher Abschnitt im deuteronomistichen Geschichtswerk* (OBO 94, 1990). F. M. **Cross,** *Canaanite Myth and Hebrew Epic* (1973). P. R. **Davies,** *In Search of "Ancient Israel"* (JSOTSup 148, 1992). W. **Dietrich,** *Prophetie und Geschichte* (FRLANT 108, 1972). A. **Dillmann,** *Numeri, Deuteronomium, Josua* (KHC, 1886). L. **Eslinger,** *Into the Hands of the Living God* (JSOTSup 84, 1989). J. P. **Floss,** *Kunden oder Kundschafter: Literaturwissenschaftliche Untersuchung zu Jos 2*, vol. 1, *Text, Schichtung, Überlieferung* (ATSAT 16, 1982); vol. 2, *Komposition, Redaktion, Intention* (ATSAT 26, 1986). G. **Fohrer,** *Introduction to the OT* (1968). R. E. **Friedman,** *The Exile and Biblical Narrative: The Formation of the Deuteronomistic and Priestly Works* (HSM 22, 1981). V. **Fritz,** *Das Buch Josua* (HAT 1, 7, 1994). G. **Garbini,** *History and Ideology in Ancient Israel* (1988). J. **Garstang,** *Joshua–Judges* (1931). N. K. **Gottwald,** *The Tribes of Yahweh: A Sociology of the Religion of Liberated Israel, 1250–1050 BCE* (1979). J. **Gray,** *Joshua, Judges, and Ruth* (NCBC, 1967; 1986[2]). L. J. **Greenspoon,** *Textual Studies in the Book of Joshua* (HSM 28, 1983); "The Qumran Fragments of Joshua: Which Puzzle Are They Part of and Where Do They Fit?" *Septuagint, Scrolls, and Cognate Writings* (SCS 33, ed. G. J. Brooke and B. Lindars, 1992). H. **Gressmann,** *Die Anfänge Israels (von 2. Mose bis Richter und Ruth)* (1922). D. M. **Gunn,** "Joshua and Judges," *The Literary Guide to the Bible* (ed. R. Alter and F. Kermode, 1987). E. J. **Hamlin,** *Inheriting the Land: A Commentary on the Book of Joshua* (ITC, 1983). L. D. **Hawk,** *Every Promise Fulfilled: Contesting Plots in Joshua* (Literary Currents in Biblical Interpretation, 1991). C. J. **den Hertog,**

"Studien zur griechischen Übersetzung des Buches Josua" (diss., Giessen, 1995). **H. W. Hertzberg,** *Die Bücher Josua, Richter, Ruth* (ATD 9, 1953). **R. Hess,** *Joshua* (TOTC, 1996). **H.-D. Hoffman,** *Reform und Reformen unters zu e. Grundthema d. deuteronomist* (ATANT 66, 1980). **J. Hollenberg,** "Die deuteronomischen Bestandtheile des Buches Josua," *TSK* 47 (1874) 462-506; *Der Charakter der alexandrinischen Übersetzung des Buches Josua* (1876). **S. Holmes,** *Joshua, the Hebrew and Greek Texts* (1914). **E. Jenni,** "Zwei Jahrzehnte Forschung an den Büchern Josua bis Könige," *TRu* 27 (1961) 1-32, 87-146. **Z. Kallai,** *Historical Geography of the Bible: The Tribal Territories of Israel* (1967; ET 1986). **Y. Kaufmann,** *The Biblical Account of the Conquest of Canaan* (preface by M. Greenberg, 1985). **C. F. Keil and F. Delitzsch,** *Joshua, Judges, and Ruth* (1869). **A. Kempinsky,** " 'When History Sleeps, Theology Arises': A Note on Joshua 8:30-35 and the Archaeology of the 'Settlement Period' " (*Malamat Volume,* ErIsr 24, 1993) 175-83. **A. Kuenen,** *The Origin and Composition of the Hexateuch* (1886). **F. Langlamet,** "Rahab," *DBSup* 6 (1979) 1065-92. **N. P. Lemche,** *Ancient Israel: A New History of Israelite Society* (The Biblical Seminar, 1988); "The OT—A Hellenistic Book?" *SJOT* 7 (1993) 163-93. **S. L. McKenzie and M. P. Graham,** *The History of Israel's Traditions: The Heritage of Martin Noth* (JSOTSup 182, 1994). **G. F. MacLear,** *The Book of Joshua* (CBC, 1890). **M. A. Margolis,** *The Book of Joshua in Greek* (1931–38). **A. D. H. Mayes,** *The Story of Israel Between Settlement and Exile: A Redactional Study of the Deuteronomistic History* (1983). **G. E. Mendenhall,** "The Hebrew Conquest in Palestine," *BA* 25 (1962) 66-87. **J. M. Miller and G. M. Tucker,** *The Book of Joshua* (CBC, 1974). **G. Mitchell,** *Together in the Land: A Reading of the Book of Joshua* (JSOTSup 134, 1993). **S. Mowinckel,** *Erwägungen zur Pentateuch Quellenfrage* (1964); *Tetrateuch-Pentateuch-Hexateuch: Die Berichte über die Landnahme in den drei altisraelitischen Geschichtswerken* (BZAW 90, 1964). **E. T. Mullen, Jr.,** *Narrative History and Ethnic Boundaries: The Deuteronomistic Historian and the Creation of Israelite National Identity* (SBL Semeia Studies, 1993). **N. Na'aman,** *Borders and Districts in Biblical Historiography: Seven Studies in Biblical Geographic Lists* (JBS 4, 1986); "The Conquest of Canaan in the Book of Joshua and in History," *From Nomadism to Monarchy: Archaeological and Historical Aspects of Early Israel* (ed. I. Finkelstein and N. Na'aman, 1994) 218-81. **R. D. Nelson,** *The Double Redaction of the Deuteronomistic History* (JSOTSup 18, 1981); "Josiah in the Book of Joshua," *JBL* 100 (1981) 531-40; *Joshua* (OTL, 1997). **M. Noth,** "Studien zu den historisch-geographischen Dokumenten des Josuabuches," *ZDPV* 58 (1935) 185-255; *Das Buch Josua* (HAT 1.7, 1938, 1953²); *Überlieferungsgeschichtliche Studien* 1 (1943; ET of pt. 1, *The Deuteronomistic History* [JSOTSup 15, 1981]). **Origen,** *Homélies sur Josué* (SC 71, ed. A. Jaubert, 1960). **H. M. Orlinsky,** "The Hebrew *Vorlage* of the Septuagint of the Book of Joshua" (VTSup 17, 1969) 187-95. **M. Ottosson,** *Josuaboken: En programskrift for davidisk restauration* (Studia Biblica Upsaliensia I, 1991). **B. Peckham,** "The Composition of Joshua 3–4," *CBQ* 46 (1984) 413-31. **R. Polzin,** *Moses and the Deuteronomist: A Literary Study of the Deuteronomic History,* vol. 1, *Deuteronomy, Joshua, Judges* (1980). **A. de Pury, T.**

Römer and J.-D. Macchi, *Israël construit son histoire: L'historiographie deutéronomiste à la lumière des recherches récentes* (Le Monde de la Bible 34, 1996). **G. von Rad,** "The Promised Land and Yahweh's Land in the Hexateuch" (1943) = his *The Problem of the Hexateuch and Other Essays* (1966) 79-93; "Hexateuch oder Pentateuch," *VF* (1947/50) 52-56. **A. N. Radjawane,** "Das deuteronomistische Geschichtswerk: Ein Forschungsbericht," *TRu* 38 (1974) 177-216. **A. Rofé,** "The End of the Book of Joshua According to the Septuagint," *Henoch* 4 (1982) 17-36; "The Editing of the Book of Joshua in the Light of 4QJosh^a," *New Qumran Texts and Studies Relating to the Bible* (ed. J. G. Brooke, 1994). **M. Rose,** *Deuteronomist und Jahwist: Untersuchungen zu den Berührungspunkten beider Literaturwerken* (ATANT 67, 1981). **L. Rowlett,** "Inclusion, Exclusion, and Marginality in the Book of Joshua," *JSOT* 55 (1992) 15-23. **C. Schäfer-Lichtenberger,** *Josua und Salomo: Eine Studie zu Autorität und Legitimität des Nachfolgers im Alten Testament* (VTSup 58, 1995). **H. Seebass,** "Zur Exegese der Grenzbeschreibungen von Jos. 16,1-17, 13," *ZDPV* 100 (1984) 70-83; "Josua," *BN* 28 (1985) 53-65. **J. Simons,** *The Geographical and Topographical Texts of the OT* (1959). **R. Smend,** "Das Gesetz und die Völker," *Probleme Biblischer Theologie* (ed. H. W. Wolff, 1971) 494-509; *Die Entstehung des Alten Testaments* (1978). **J. A. Soggin,** *Joshua* (OTL, 1972); *Introduction to the OT* (OTL, 1976). **C. Steuernagel,** *Deuteronomium und Josua und allgemeine Einleitung den Hexateuch* (HAT, 1900). **J. Svensson,** *Towns and Toponyms in the OT, with Special Emphasis on Joshua 14–21* (ConBOT 38, 1994). **T. L. Thompson,** *The Early History of the Israelite People* (SHANE 4, 1992). **E. Tov,** *The Text-critical Use of the Septuagint in Biblical Research* (JBS 3, 1981); "The Growth of the Book of Joshua in the Light of the Evidence of the LXX Translation," *Studies in Bible* (SchHier 31, ed. S. Japhet, 1986) 321-39; "Some Sequence Differences Between the MT and LXX and Their Ramification for the Literary Criticism of the Bible," *JNSL* 13 (1987) 151-60; *Textual Criticism of the HB* (1992a); "4QJosh^b," *Intertestamental Essays in Honour of J. T. Milik* (ed. Z. J. Kapera, 1992b). **J. Trebolle Barrera,** "Historia del Texto de los Libros Historicos e Historia de la Redaccion Deuteronomistica (Jueces 2,10–3,6)," *Salvacion en la Palabra: Targum—Derash—Berith* (ed. D. Muñoz Leon, 1986) 245-55. **E. Ulrich,** "4QJosh^a and Joshua's First Altar in the Promised Land," *New Qumran Texts and Studies Relating to the Bible* (ed. J. G. Brooke, 1994). **J. Van Seters,** *In Search of History* (1983). **T. Veijola,** *Die ewige Dynastie: David und die Entstehung seiner Dynastie nach der deuteronomistichen Darstellung* (AASF B/193, 1975); *Das Königtum in der Beurteilung der deuteronomistischen Historiographie* (AASF B/198, 1977). **B. G. Webb,** *The Book of Judges: An Integrated Reading* (JSOTSup 46, 1987). **M. Weinfeld,** *The Promise of the Land: The Inheritance of the Land of Canaan by the Israelites* (1993). **H. Weippert,** "Das deuteronomistische Geschichtswerk: Sein Ziel und Ende in der neueren Forschung," *TRu* 50 (1985) 213-49. **J. Wellhausen,** "Pentateuch and Joshua," *EncBrit* 18 (1885⁹) 9:505-14; *Die Composition des Hexateuchs* (1899³). **K. W. Whitelam,** *The Invention of Ancient Israel: The Silencing of Palestinian History* (1996). **N. Winther-Nielsen,** *A Functional Discourse Grammar of Joshua*

(ConBOT 40, 1995). **M. H. Woudstra,** *The Book of Joshua* (NICOT, 1981). **M. Wüst,** *Untersuchungen zu den siedlungsgeographischen Texten des Alten Testaments,* vol. 1, *Ostjordanland* (BTAVO 9, 1975). **K. L. Younger, Jr.,** *Ancient Conquest Accounts: Study in Ancient Near Eastern and Biblical History Writing* (JSOTSup 98, 1990).

A. G. AULD

JOWETT, BENJAMIN (1817–93)

A classicist, educator, and biblical scholar, J. showed early talent in Latin and Greek, both as a boy at St. Paul's School and as a scholar and fellow of Balliol College, Oxford, where in 1842 he took his MA and became a tutor. The same year he was ordained a deacon and three years later a priest. In 1855 he was appointed Regius Professor of Greek. Despite misgivings about his theological views, he was elected master of Balliol in 1870 and from this position exercised a formidable shaping influence on the college, the university, and the religious thought of his day.

J.'s theological interests were lifelong, and his unsettling contributions to public debate in this sphere rivaled in influence the notable imprint he left on his chosen field by his translation of Plato's *Dialogues,* which inspired a revival of Greek studies. Impressed by Hegelian philosophy and by contacts made with German scholars on his travels, J. became a central figure of the liberal "broad church" movement within the Church of England. His 1855 Pauline commentaries (see PAUL) contained "Essay on the Atonement," which gave offense to traditionalists by advocating a subjective "moral influence" theory of Christ's work. Even greater concern was aroused by "On the Interpretation of Scripture," an essay contributed to the controversial manifesto *Essays and Reviews* (1860), which urged that the Bible be read "like any other book." There were cries of heresy, but no successful action was taken.

J.'s legacy to British biblical study is twofold. Intellectually, he opened discussions on views that, however radical when he uttered them, a half century later came very near the Anglican mainstream. Institutionally, many of the next generation's church leaders were shaped by the spirit of scholarly excellence, social activism, and liberal religious thought he personally emphasized as the hallmarks of the Balliol tradition.

Works: *The Epistles of St. Paul to the Thessalonians, Galatians, and Romans, with Critical Notes and Dissertations* (2 vols., 1859²); "On the Interpretation of Scripture," *Essays and Reviews* (1860) 330-433; *College Sermons* (ed. W. H. Fremantle, 1895); *Sermons on Faith and Doctrine* (ed. W. H. Fremantle, 1901).

Bibliography: **E. Abbot,** *DNB* Supp. 3 (1901) 49-56. **E. Abbott and L. Campbell,** *The Life and Letters of B. J.* (2

vols., 1897). **J. Barr,** "J. and the Reading of the Bible 'Like Any Other Book,'" *HBT* 4 (1982) 1-44. **J. Drury,** *Critics of the Bible, 1724–1873* (1989) 137-51. **I. Ellis,** *Seven Against Christ: A Study of "Essays and Reviews"* (SHCT 23, 1980). **G. Faber,** *J., a Portrait with Background* (1957). **P. Hinchliff,** "Ethics, Evolution, and Biblical Criticism in the Thought of B. J. and J. W. Colenso," *JEH* 37 (1986) 99-110; *B. J. and the Christian Religion* (1987). **B. M. G. Reardon,** *TRE* 17 (1988) 278-79. **R. Darwall-Smith,** *The Jowett Papers: A Summary Catalogue of the Papers of B. J.* (1993).

D. L. PALS

JUBILEES, BOOK OF

The *Book of Jubilees* relates a divine revelation, mediated to Moses through an "angel of the presence," about events from the creation of the world to the law-giving on Mt. Sinai. Its name derives from the author's use of a chronological system (see CHRONOLOGY, HB) whose principal unit is a forty-nine-year period called a "jubilee." The book was known to and used by the community of the DEAD SEA SCROLLS (see *CD* 16:2-4); and some of its extra-biblical stories, like the war between Jacob and Esau, are reflected in midrashic literature (see A. Jellinek [1855]; B. Beer [1856]; A. Epstein [1890, 1891]; R. Charles [1902]; and K. Berger [1981]). It also exercised a certain influence in some Christian circles. Several chronographers (e.g., G. Syncellus [fl. c. 800]) used material particularly from its earlier chapters to supplement information from Genesis and Exodus; and in the Abyssinian Church it achieved canonical status (see CANON OF THE BIBLE) as part of the OT. It has also enjoyed high repute among the Jews of Ethiopia. At some point, however, the text of the book was lost in most centers of Jewish and Christian populations.

Western scholars were aware that a *Book of Jubilees* once existed because of references to and citations from it in Greek and Latin sources. (Many of these were collected already by J. FABRICIUS in 1722; see also H. Rönsch [1874]; R. Charles [1895, 1902]; A. Denis [1970]; and J. VanderKam [1989]). Modern Western study of the text began when a missionary named J. Krapff had a paper copy made of an Ethiopic manuscript of *Jubilees* (called *kufālē* [division(s)] in Ethiopic; see ETHIOPIAN BIBLICAL INTERPRETATION); this he brought to Tübingen, where H. EWALD announced its existence in 1844. Ewald's student A. DILLMANN translated this very poor copy in 1850–51 and in 1859 made this translation and a manuscript from the Bibliothèque Nationale in Paris the foundations for the first critical edition of the Ethiopic text. CHARLES prepared the next critical edition in 1895, using Dillmann's edition for the evidence from his two manuscripts along with two other, much better copies that had subsequently been identified. Those who translated the book after 1895 worked from Charles's text (e.g., E. Littmann [1900]; C. Rabin [*AOT*]; and O. Wintermute [*OTP*]), with the exception of Berger, who had access not only to these manuscripts but also to other copies that were made available after Charles's labors. Charles personally published the most widely used translations of his edition (1902, 1913). A new edition and translation of the Ethiopic version has been published by VanderKam (1989), who based his text on collations of fifteen of the twenty-seven currently available Ethiopic manuscripts of *Jubilees*. The edition includes the Hebrew texts available at the time of publication and all of the other versional evidence.

Since the last quarter of the nineteenth century, additional textual data for the book have come to light, although the Ethiopic remains the only complete version extant. A. Ceriani (1861–63) published twenty-five sections of a very literal Latin rendering (5th–6th cent. CE) of the book; he found these in a palimpsest manuscript that was used for copying excerpts from AUGUSTINE's writings. The sections preserve nearly one-third of the full text (for the text with notes, see Rönsch [1874]; Charles [1895]; VanderKam [1989]). E. Tisserant (1921) later isolated a series of citations from *Jubilees* in an anonymous Syriac chronicle *ad annum* 1234. Fragments of fifteen manuscripts of the Hebrew of *Jubilees* have been found among the Dead Sea Scrolls, and all of these have been published (see VanderKam [1977] and VanderKam and Milik [1994]). The Hebrew fragments indicate that the Ethiopic version is generally a faithful rendering of the original. From all of the extant textual data scholars have concluded that the book was composed in Hebrew, translated into Greek, and from Greek was rendered into Latin and Ethiopic. Whether there was ever a Syriac translation, and if so, whether it was based directly on a Hebrew base, as Tisserant argued, remain open questions.

There has been a long debate about the date of *Jubilees* and about the party affiliation of its author (the issue of the place where it was written is related to these). Although the earliest Western students of the book were aware that its views about legal and theological matters differed on many points (e.g., its 364-day solar calendar) from those of the Pharisees and Sadducees, there was uncertainty about the identity of the group to which the author belonged. Jellinek attributed it to an Essene author who opposed pharisaic calendrical views; Beer thought that the writer was a Dosithean who wrote in Egypt; Z. Frankel (1856) believed he was a Jewish Hellenist associated with the temple of Onias in Egypt; and A. Büchler (1930), who noted *Jubilees'* agreements with the LXX (see SEPTUAGINT) and evidence of Hellenistic customs in the book, considered the author a descendant of one of the ten tribes who wrote in Greek and lived near Samaritan territory somewhere in Egypt or a part of Palestine under Egyptian influence. The scholars who have devoted detailed analyses to the

book's legal material have also insisted that the author could not have been either a Pharisee or a Sadducee but must have belonged to one of the sects (L. Finkelstein [1923]; C. Albeck [1930]).

During the latter half of the nineteenth century most experts followed Dillmann (1851) in dating *Jubilees* to the first century CE. Dillmann argued from its dependence on the books of ENOCH, from the dependence of the TESTAMENTS OF THE TWELVE PATRIARCHS on it, and from the fact that *Jubilees* presupposed an existing Temple that the book was written before 70 CE. Rönsch and W. Singer (1898) accepted Dillmann's dating and added that anti-Christian elements could be detected in the book. A significant change in the dating discussion took place when F. Bohn (1900) defended a time of composition in the mid-second century BCE, drawing this conclusion in part from his belief that passages like the story about the battle between Jacob and Esau reflected events during the Maccabean wars. He also maintained that the author was one of the Hasidim (see HASIDISM).

Charles, however, preferred a date between 135 and 96 BCE (1902) or 109 and 5 BCE (1913). He too saw reflections of Maccabean events in the book but was convinced that the author was a Pharisee, giving him warrant for dating the book, which he considered pro-Maccabean, before the schism between Alexander Jannaeus and the Pharisees. His view, despite its obvious flaws, has dominated the field until the last decades of the twentieth century (see VanderKam [1977] for bibliography), and some writers (e.g., M. Testuz [1960]) still accept it. Nevertheless, two prominent scholars insisted for some time that *Jubilees* was written at a much earlier time. S. Zeitlin dated the book to the fifth–fourth centuries BCE for several reasons, one of which was his assumption that its opposition to some Pentateuchal legislation would have been impossible once the Pentateuch achieved normative status. W. F. ALBRIGHT (1957[2]) originally thought that the book was written in the fourth–third centuries BCE, but after the Qumran discoveries he lowered his dating to c. 175.

Since 1960 a growing number of scholars have returned to the date that Bohn had defended, i.e. the mid-second century BCE (e.g., Berger, VanderKam). The Dead Sea Scrolls, which many experts think were written by Essenes, show very close affinities with *Jubilees* in many areas such as the 364-day solar calendar (see Testuz; B. Noack [1957–58]; VanderKam [1977]), and one of the Qumran copies—4Q216 (4QJubilees[a]) may date to a time around 125 BCE (VanderKam and Milik [1994]). Yet the book does not appear to have been written by someone who had separated from Jewish society. This suggests that it was written before the Essene exodus to Qumran (perhaps before c. 135 BCE). G. Nickelsburg (1981), J. Goldstein (1983), and M. Knibb (1989) have held that it antedates 167 since it shows no awareness of Antiochus IV's prohibition of Judaism (earlier, Finkelstein had opted for a similar time). It does seem likely, however, that the author knew the Enochic *Book of Dreams* (*1 Enoch* 83–90), which was written in the late 160s BCE. Judea now seems the only likely place of composition, while new insights into the variety of biblical texts in this area in the second pre-Christian century allow one to explain textual agreements between *Jubilees* and the LXX from the author's use of a Palestinian form of the biblical text.

The greatest subject of scholarly interest in the book since the discovery of the scrolls has been its calendar, which it shares with *1 Enoch* and several of the Qumran texts. *Jubilees'* statements about the number of days in the year (364), in each month (eight months of thirty days, four of thirty-one), and the dates for crucial festivals, such as Weeks (month 3, day 15) are clear; but pre-Qumran scholars had a difficult time with some of them because of their assumptions about calendrical possibilities. The pivotal issue has been the date of the Festival of Weeks. Leviticus 23:15-16 places it on the fiftieth day after the presentation of "the sheaf of the wave offering." There was extensive discussion in ancient Judaism about precisely when the sheaf was to be presented, and several options were chosen by different groups. Epstein, who from his knowledge of these ancient debates thought that it could not have been presented later than the twenty-second of the first month, concluded that *Jubilees* must, if Weeks was to be celebrated on 3/15, operate with a religious calendar that used months of twenty-eight days (so also Finkelstein) in addition to a civil arrangement consisting of twelve months of either thirty or thirty-one days that the book describes. A. Jaubert (1953), however, clarified the book's calendrical data and drew the proper conclusion that in this system the sheaf of the wave offering (which is not mentioned in *Jubilees*) was presented on 1/26, a date that is verified by some calendar texts from Qumran. There is now a large bibliography about this calendar and about the possibility that it was used as the official cultic calendar in Jerusalem early in the Second Temple period. To date, though, no decisive evidence for or against its official use has been found.

The religious teachings of *Jubilees* and some instances of the ways in which its author has edited biblical sections have received extended treatment. Testuz published a study of the book's views about creation and the world, the history of the world and Israel, the world of the spirits, the two moral ways, the revealed calendar, and the last times (with a chapter comparing *Jubilees* and the major Qumran scrolls). G. Davenport (1971) devoted a monograph to the book's eschatology in which he traced a development through what he concluded were the three stages of the book's evolution: from a largely non-eschatological "angelic discourse" (written in the early 2nd cent.), through redaction 1,

which turned the original into an eschatological message of hope during the Maccabean revolt, to redaction 2 (between 140 and 104 BCE), which emphasized the sanctuary and looked for a cosmic renewal that would focus on Jerusalem and Zion. E. Schwarz (1982) has analyzed the book's teachings about Israel's separation from the peoples and traced the history of this tradition, which began with the HB commands that Israel was to form no treaties with the nations of Canaan. Studies of selected sections of the book include O. Steck's examination of the creation section in *Jubilees* 2 (1977; cf. VanderKam [1994b]) and J. Endres's monograph on the highly significant Jacob cycle (1986). The Levi expansions (*Jubilees* 30–32) within the Jacob stories have elicited detailed analyses that relate them to the Levi-priestly tradition (J. Kugel [1993]; R. Kugler [1996]). The sabbatical chronological system, which applies the biblical legislation about the year of Jubilee to the nation rather than to the individual, has also been researched (VanderKam [1995]).

The book's unity has been denied by Testuz, E. Wiesenberg (1961–62), and Davenport (for his view, see the preceding paragraph). Testuz, who agrees with Charles's dating of the book, thought that *Jub* 1:7-25, 28; 23:11-32; and 24:28*b*-30, which manifest an "ardent hatred" for the nations, were added between the years 65–38 BCE, while Wiesenberg based his view of a subsequent Zealot reviser (1st cent. CE) on chronological problems. These writers have failed, however, to convince other scholars of their positions (for brief reviews, see R. Pummer [1979]; VanderKam [1981]).

Although much exegetical work remains to be done (no commentary has ever been written on *Jubilees*), there is widespread agreement that the book was written by a single Jewish writer in Judea between 175 and 140 BCE and that the author belonged to the religious movement at least some of whose members later withdrew from Jewish society and produced the Dead Sea Scrolls.

Bibliography: **M. Albani et al.** (eds.), *Studies in the Book of* Jubilees (TSAJ 65, 1997). **C. Albeck,** *Das Buch der Jubiläen und die Halacha* (BHWJ 27, 1930). **W. F. Albright,** *From the Stone Age to Christianity* (1957²). **B. Beer,** *Das Buch der Jubiläen und sein Verhältniss zu den Midraschim: Ein Beitrag zur Orientalischen Sagen- und Alterthums Kunde* (1856). **K. Berger,** *Das Buch der Jubiläen* (JSHRZ II.3, 1981). **F. Bohn,** "Die Bedeutung des Buches der Jubiläen," *TSK* 73 (1900) 167-84. **A. Büchler,** "Studies in the *Book of Jubilees*," *REJ* 82 (1926) 253-74; "Traces des idées et des coutumes hellénistiques dans le Livre des *Jubilés*," *REJ* 89 (1930) 321-48. **A. M. Ceriani,** *Monumenta Sacra et Profana* (2 vols., 1861–63). **R. H. Charles,** "The Book of Jubilees, Translated from a Text Based on Two Hitherto Uncollated Ethiopic MSS," *JQR* 5 (1893) 703-8; 6 (1895) 184-217, 710-45; 7 (1895) 297-328; *Maṣḥafa Kufālē or the Ethiopic Version of the Hebrew Book of Jubilees*

(Anecdota Oxoniensia, 1895); *The Book of Jubilees or the Little Genesis* (1902); *APOT* 2:1-82. **G. L. Davenport,** *The Eschatology of the Book of Jubilees* (SPB 20, 1971). **A. M. Denis,** "Liber Jubilaeorum," *Fragmenta Pseudepigraphorum Quae Supersunt Graeca* (PVTG 3, 1970) 70-102. **A. Dillmann,** "Das Buch der *Jubiläen* oder die kleine Genesis," *JBW* 2 (1850) 230-56, 3 (1851) 1-96; *Maṣḥafa Kufālē sive Liber Jubilaeorum* (1859). **J. Endres,** *Biblical Interpretation in the Book of Jubilees* (CBQMS 18, 1986). **A. Epstein,** "Le Livre des *Jubilés,* Philon, et le Midrasch Tadsché," *REJ* 21 (1890) 80-97; 22 (1891) 1-25. **H. Ewald,** "Über die Aethiopischen Handschriften zu Tübingen," *ZKM* 5 (1844) 164-201. **J. A. Fabricius,** "Parva Genesis," *Codex Pseudepigraphus Veteris Testamenti* (2 vols., 1722) 1:849-64, 2:120-22. **L. Finkelstein,** "The *Book of Jubilees* and the Rabbinic Halaka," *HTR* 16 (1923) 39-61. **Z. Frankel,** "Das Buch der *Jubiläen,*" *MGWJ* 5 (1856) 311-16, 380-400. **J. Goldstein,** "The Date of the *Book of Jubilees,*" *PAAJR* 50 (1983) 63-86. **A. Jaubert,** "Le calendrier des *Jubilés* et de la sect de Qumran: Ses origines bibliques," *VT* 3 (1953) 250-64. **A. Jellinek,** *Bet ha-Midrasch* (Dritter Theil, 1855) ix-xiii. **M. Knibb,** *"Jubilees and the Origins of the Qumran Community"* (inaugural lecture in the Dept. of Bib. Stud., King's College London, Jan. 17, 1989). **J. Kugel,** "Levi's Elevation to the Priesthood in Second Temple Writings," *HTR* 86 (1993) 1-64. **R. Kugler,** *From Patriarch to Priest: The Levi-Priestly Tradition from Aramaic Levi to Testament of Levi* (SBLEJL 9, 1996). **E. Littmann,** "Das Buch der Jubiläen," *APAT* (1900) 2:31-119. **G. W. E. Nickelsburg,** *Jewish Literature Between the Bible and the Mishnah* (1981). **B. Noack,** "Qumran and the *Book of Jubilees,*" *SEA* 22-23 (1957–58) 191-207. **R. Pummer,** "The Book of *Jubilees* and the Samaritans," *EgTh* 10 (1979) 147-78. **C. Rabin,** *AOT* 1-139. **H. Rönsch,** *Das Buch der Jubiläen oder die Kleine Genesis* (1874, repr. 1970). **G. Schelbert,** *TRE* 17 (1988) 285-89. **E. Schwarz,** *Identität durch Abgrenzung: Abgrenzungsprozesse in Israel im 2. vorchristlichen Jahrhundert und ihre traditionsgeschichtlichen Voraussetzungen. Zugleich ein Beitrag zur Erforschung des Jubiläenbuches* (1982). **W. Singer,** *Das Buch der Jubiläen oder die Leptogenesis* (1898). **O. Steck,** "Die Aufnahme von Genesis 1 in *Jubiläen* 2 und 4 Esra 6," *JSJ* 8 (1977) 154-82. **M. Testuz,** *Les idées religieuses du Livre des Jubilés* (1960). **E. Tisserant,** "Fragments syriaques du Livre des *Jubilés,*"*RB* 30 (1921) 55-86, 206-32. **J. VanderKam,** *Textual and Historical Studies in the Book of Jubilees* (HSM 14, 1977); "The Putative Author of the *Book of Jubilees,*" *JSS* 26 (1981) 209-17; (ed. and tr.), *The Book of Jubilees* (2 vols., CSCO 510-11, Scriptores Aethiopici 87-88, 1989); "Das chronologisches Konzept des *Jubiläenbuches,*" *ZAW* 107 (1995) 80-100. **J. VanderKam and J. T. Milik,** "The First *Jubilees* Manuscript from Qumran Cave 4: A Preliminary Publication," *JBL* 110 (1991) 243-70; *DJD* 13 (1994) 1-140; "Genesis 1 in *Jubilees* 2," *DSD* 1 (1994) 300-21. **E. Wiesenberg,** "The Jubilee of *Jubilees,*" *RevQ* 3 (1961–1962) 3-40. **O. Wintermute,** *OTP* 2:35-142. **S. Zeitlin,** "The *Book of Jubilees:* Its Character and Its Significance," *JQR* 30 (1939–40) 1-31; "The *Book of Jubilees* and the Pentateuch," *JQR* 48 (1957) 218-35.

J. C. VanderKam

JUDAH HALEVI (c. 1075–1141)

Born in Tudela, Spain, J. traveled extensively in Andalusia. Toward the end of his life he journeyed eastward with the intention of living in the land of Israel, which, in line with the well-argued thesis in his major theological work, he considered the best place to serve God. Waylaid in Egypt by friends who were enamored of his poetical and intellectual ability, he died in 1141, perhaps in either Egypt or Palestine.

J. is regarded as an outstanding Hebrew poet of the Andalusian period. His poetry, as is generally true of the work of other Jewish poets of the time, is characterized by the use of biblical Hebrew as an expression of Jewish ethnic identity in contrast to Arabic literary and poetic expression. His extensive use of biblical words and phrases makes his poetic production into a kind of *cento*; thus he helped to revive the biblical idiom as a living literary language.

H. was also an important philosopher of religion. He is the author of a well-known defense of Judaism, *The Book of Refutation and Evidence with Respect to the Despised Religion,* which he wrote in Judeo-Arabic, the common language of the Jews living in the classical period of Islamic civilization. The work is more popularly known as *The Kuzari,* a corruption of the designation of one of the principal protagonists of the dialogue, the king of the Khazars.

In *The Kuzari* the king of the Khazars is looking for the true path of action. His intention is sincere, but his actions are not, he has been told in a troubling dream. As a result of his conversation with a philosopher, a Christian, a Muslim, and a Jewish sage, he converts to Judaism along with his people. The remaining four treatises are devoted to an exposition by the sage of the tenets of rabbinic Judaism, answering the questions of the Khazar. The basic position of the sage is a rejection of the primacy of reason and an exaltation of direct revelation. For J., a hierarchical thinker, the realm of nature and reason is transcended by a divine realm, that of *al-amr al-ilāhī,* the divine *tremendum*. The Jewish people are directly under the guidance of the divine realm, while other peoples of the world are under the control of nature. Thus the ceremonial commandments are more important than the commandments of the Torah, having a rational, social, and political purpose, for their proper performance ensures contact with divinity. This view is intended to contradict the widespread philosophical position, associated with the name of Alfarabi (d. c. 950), that views religion as a popular representation of theoretical formulations, prior to philosophical thinking. In the next generation MAIMONIDES, in his *Guide of the Perplexed,* took up the defense of the philosophical viewpoint; thus his work may be considered a dialectical response to J.'s position.

Works: *The Book of Refutation and Evidence with Respect to the Despised Religion* (Hebrew, ed. D. H. Baneth, 1977; ET,

The Kuzari: In Defense of the Despised Faith, tr. N. D. Korobkin, 1998); *Ha-shirah ha ʾivrit bi-sefarad u-ve-provans* (ed. H. Schirmann, 1954) 1:425-536.

Bibliography: **R. Brann,** "J. H.: The Compunctious Poet," *Prooftexts* 7 (1987) 123-43; *EncJud* 10 (1971) 355-66. **B. E. Galli,** *F. Rosenzweig and J. H.: Translating, Translations, and Translators* (1995). **S. S. Gehlhaar,** *Prophetie und Gesetz bei J. H., Maimonides, und Spinoza* (1987). **C. Sirat,** *A History of Jewish Philosophy in the Middle Ages* (1985) 113-31, with further references.

L. V. BERMAN

JUDE, LETTER OF

Addressed to no specific audience but "to those who are called" (v. 1), Jude is one of the catholic, or general, epistles in the NT. Although the author is alarmed at the presence of scoffers (v. 18) who contest the foundations of authority (v. 4) and whose errors lead to immorality, Jude remains extremely general in polemic and perception, giving scant clues to the identity of those condemned but nonetheless expressing an acute discomfort with heresy in the church. The writer, Jude (= Judas), describes himself as "a servant of Jesus Christ and brother of James" (v. 1) and admonishes his readers "to contend for the faith once for all delivered to the saints" (v. 3).

The opinion of the early church was divided about the letter (see L. Lardner [1788]). It was quoted by TERTULLIAN and CLEMENT OF ALEXANDRIA and appears in the list of biblical books in the Muratorian Canon (dated from late 2nd to 4th cent.). ORIGEN quoted it on several occasions, especially in his commentary on Matthew; e.g., on Matt 13:55-56 he noted that "Jude wrote an epistle, a few lines indeed, but full of powerful words of the heavenly grace." Elsewhere in this commentary (on Matt. 22:23) he wrote, "if any one receives also the epistle of Jude," indicating that there was some uncertainty about the work. EUSEBIUS listed Jude among the *antilegomena,* the works whose canonicity was disputed, which also included James, 2 Peter, and 2 and 3 John (*Hist. eccl.* 3.25.3-4), although he classified them as "generally recognized." The epistle does not appear in the PESHITTA. JEROME and others were aware that the work was suspect to some since it contained quotes from the non-biblical books of ENOCH and a no longer extant *As. Mos.* (see R. Bauckham [1990] 137-44, 235-80).

After the fourth century the Greek and Latin churches were no longer troubled by the letter. It appears in the canonical list in ATHANASIUS's Easter letter of 367 CE. In the medieval period the most prominent commentary on Jude and the other catholic epistles was BEDE's *In epistolas VII catholicas* (ed. M. Laistner; CCSL 121, 1983), which formed the basis for most of the annotations on these books in the GLOSSA ORDINARIA.

During the Renaissance and the Reformation, uncertainties about the AUTHORITY and canonicity of Jude resurfaced. T. CAJETAN had doubts; and in his two 1520 works on the CANON, A. VON KARLSTADT arranged the books of the Bible into three categories of authority, placing the *antilegomena* in the third, least authoritative, category. LUTHER placed the books of Hebrews, James, Jude, and Revelation at the end of the NT and did not assign them consecutive numbers as he had the other twenty-three books he considered to be "the true and certain and chief books of the NT" (1960, vol. 35, 394). Of Jude he wrote: "No one can deny that it is an extract or copy of St. Peter's second epistle, so very like it are all the words. He also speaks of the apostles like a disciple who comes long after them and cites sayings and incidents that are found nowhere else in the Scriptures. This moved the ancient fathers to exclude this epistle from the main body of the Scriptures. . . . Therefore, although I value this book, it is an epistle that need not be counted among the chief books which are supposed to lay the foundations of faith" (1960, 35:397-98).

Danish theologian N. Hemmingsen (1513–1600), providing an enumeration of the NT writings, declared: "All these books of the NT are in the canon except Second Peter, Second and Third John, the Epistles of James and Jude along with the Apocalypse. Some also place the Epistle to the Hebrews outside the canon" (*De Methodis libro duo* [1555] 124). Jude could thus be in the Bible but not canonical. This radical position was not widespread in subsequent study, although H. GROTIUS in his *Annotationes* (1650) doubted its attribution to an early church leader and suggested that it was written by a certain Jude who was the last bishop of Jerusalem during the reign of Hadrian (117–138 CE), as noted by Eusebius (*Hist. eccl.* 4.5.3)

N. LARDNER (1727–57) expounded a traditional view, but J. D. MICHAELIS revived the radical position in his NT introduction: "We have very little reason for placing the Epistle of St. Jude among the sacred writings . . . which contains accounts apparently fabulous, and which was suspected by the ancient church. . . . I cannot therefore acknowledge that this Epistle is canonical. And I have really some doubt whether it be not even a forgery, made in the name of Jude, by some person, who borrowed the chief part of his material from the second Epistle of St. Peter, and added some few of his own" (1750; ET, 4 vols. [1802²] 4:394-95). Opposition to such a radical approach to Jude was widespread: J. G. HERDER (1775) defended the epistle's authorship by a brother of JESUS; A. Jessien (1821) defended authorship by distinguishing between the brother of Jesus named Jude (the author of the epistle) and the apostle Jude.

In the nineteenth and twentieth centuries several issues have been much discussed: (1) The relationship between Jude and 2 Peter (chap. 2) has shifted from Jude's dependence on 2 Peter to the opposite (so already

Herder), although some scholars argue for a common source or even common authorship (see Bauckham [1990] 144-47 for review and bibliography). (2) The question of authorship, whether the letter was written pseudonymously under the name of Jude, or by Jude the brother of Jesus (Matt 13:55; Mark 6:13), and/or by one of the early apostles (so the Council of Trent in 1546) remains unsettled. The majority of scholars deny that the work was produced by a first-generation Christian because (a) v. 17 speaks of "the apostles of the Lord" as figures of the distant past; (b) reference to "the faith, handed on once for all" (v. 3) is characteristic of late writings; and (c) the excellence of the Greek is unlikely for Galilean peasants. Bauckham (1990) defends possible authorship by a brother of Jesus and, on the basis of evidence about Jesus' family (especially that from Hegesippus reported by Eusebius in *Hist. eccl.* 3.19.1–3.20.7) and internal considerations, concludes that the book reflects early Palestinian Jewish Christianity. J. Gunther (1984) argues for an Alexandrian origin. (3) The evidence about the opponents is too generalized to allow for identification (see F. Wisse [1972]). (4) Proposed dates for the letter range from the middle of the first to the middle of the second century (see the listing in Bauckham [1990] 168-69). (5) Interest in Jude's use of non-biblical traditions and exegetical techniques (Bauckham [1990] 179-280) and in its relationship to ancient rhetoric (D. Watson [1988]) as well as to general sociocultural factors (J. Neyrey [1993]) illustrates the broader contexts within which the letter is presently studied.

Bibliography: R. J. Bauckham, *Jude, 2 Peter* (WBC 50, 1983); *Jude and the Relatives of Jesus in the Early Church* (1990), with extensive bibliography (389-420). C. Bigg, *A Critical and Exegetical Commentary on the Epistles of St. Peter and St. Jude* (ICC, 1902²). J. D. Charles, *Literary Strategy in the Epistle of Jude* (1993). W. M. Dunnett, "The Hermeneutics of Jude and 2 Peter: The Use of Ancient Jewish Tradition," *JETS* 31 (1988) 287-92. E. E. Ellis, "Prophecy and Hermeneutic in Jude," *Prophecy and Hermeneutic in Early Christianity* (WUNT 18, 1978) 221-36. I. H. Eybers, "Aspects of the Background of the Letter of Jude," *Essays on the General Epistles of the NT* (ed. W. Nicol et al., 1975) 113-23. J. J. Gunther, "The Alexandrian Epistle of Jude," *NTS* 30 (1984) 549-62. R. Heiligenthal, "Der Judas Brief: Aspekte der Forschung in den letzten Jahrzehnten," *TRu* 51 (1986) 117-29. J. G. Herder, *Briefe zweener Brüder Jesu in unserm Kanon* (1775). D. E. Hiebert, "Selected Studies from Jude," *BSac* 142 (1985) 142-51, 238-49, 355-66. A. Jessien, *De authentia epistolae Judae* (1821). S. J. Joubert, "Language, Ideology, and the Social Context of the Letter of Jude," *Neotestamentica* 24 (1990) 335-49; "Persuasion in the Letter of Jude," *JSNT* 58 (1995) 75-87. J. N. D. Kelly, *A Commentary on the Epistles of Peter and of Jude* (HNTC, 1969). J. Knight, *2 Peter and Jude* (NTGu, 1995). L. Lardner, "St. Jude and His Epistle,"

Works (11 vols., ed. B. Coles, 1788) 6:298-317. N. Lardner, *The Credibility of the Gospel History* (14 vols., 1727–57). M. Luther, *Luther's Works* 35 (ed. H. J. Grimm et al., 1960). J. D. Michaelis, *Introduction to the NT* (1750; ET, 4 vols., 1802²). J. H. Neyrey, *2 Peter, Jude* (AB 37C, 1993). C. D. Osborn, "The Christological Use of *I Enoch* I.9 in Jude 14-15," *NTS* 23 (1977) 334-41. D. J. Rowston, "The Most Neglected Book in the NT," *NTS* 21 (1975) 554-63. D. F. Watson, *Invention, Arrangement, and Style: Rhetorical Criticism of Jude and 2 Peter* (SBLDS 104, 1988); "The Letter of Jude," *NIB* (1998) 12:471-500. R. L. Webb, "The Eschatology of the Epistle of Jude and Its Rhetorical and Social Functions," *Bulletin for Biblical Research* 6 (1996) 139-51. F. Wisse, "The Epistle of Jude in the History of Heresiology," *Essays on the Nag Hammadi Texts in Honor of A. Böhling* (NHS 3, ed. M. Drause, 1972) 133-43. T. R. Wolthuis, "Jude and Jewish Traditions," *CTJ* 22 (1987) 21-45; "Jude and Rhetoricism," *CTJ* 24 (1989) 126-34.

J. NEYREY

JUDGES, BOOK OF

1. Introduction. "And what more shall I say?" we read in Hebrews 11. "For time would fail me to tell of Gideon, Barak, Samson, Jephthah . . . who through faith conquered kingdoms, enforced justice, received promises." Time, however, has not noticeably failed others intent on idealizing these "famous men," "whose hearts did not fall into idolatry and who did not turn away from the Lord" (Sir 44:1; 46:11). In the process, as a history of Judges interpretation shows, many disturbing realities have been precluded—mass murder, fratricide, and gender-based violence, to name but a few. Of course, idealization has not been the only means to preclude. Many other interpretive paradigms have sufficed.

Interpretation always proceeds from particular investments of belief and horizons of meaning. For example, Judges has been read to underpin ideologies of anti-semitism, nationalism, and patriarchy, among others. Some indication of these ideological dimensions will be a concern of this survey.

2. The Early Christian Church. Few references to Judges are found in the ante-Nicene period of the Christian church. Those who referred to Judges during this time did so primarily in regard to its recurring plot pattern of transgression-punishment-deliverance. TERTULLIAN, for example, recounted this cycle to demonstrate that God disciplines according to established rules of devotion, particularly against idolatry (*Scorpiace* chap. 3). Exceptionally, CLEMENT OF ALEXANDRIA's *Stromata* used a CHRONOLOGY that included Judges in order to establish the greater antiquity of "Jewish institutions and laws over the philosophy of the Greeks" (chap. 21).

Such Christian attempts to uphold Judaism tended to decline abruptly, however, during the Nicene and post-

Nicene periods. The most popular text seems to be the story of Gideon and the fleece (Judges 6), read as an allegorical history of God's grace, first with Israel and then with Christians. Of the ten substantial references to Judges (seven involving Gideon) in AUGUSTINE's works, for example, five are cases in point. In line with both AMBROSE (*Of the Holy Spirit*, bk. 1) and JEROME (Letter 58), he claimed that the fleece on the first morning describes Judaism before Christ, in which "grace was hidden in a cloud, as the rain in the fleece" (Sermon 81.9). Concerning the second morning he wrote, "Like the rain in the fleece it [grace] was latently present, but is now patently visible amongst all nations as its 'floor,' the fleece being dry—in other words, the Jewish people having become reprobate" (*On Original Sin* chap. 29). In his sermon on Psalm 72 he added, "But that the above nation under the name of a fleece is signified, I think is either because they were to be stripped of the authority of teaching, just as a sheep is stripped of its skin, or because in a secret place He was hiding that same rain."

Other interpretations invoke stories in Judges as a means to encourage Christians in times of suffering. ATHANASIUS, for example, referred in his *Circular Letter* to the sending of pieces of the Levite's raped concubine to the twelve tribes (Judg 19:29-30) as a precedent for sharing the suffering experienced in his own community with the wider church body.

With Jerome began a focus on the women of Judges, which, together with the anti-Jewish allegory of the fleece, would persevere into modern times. In *Against Jovinianus*, for example, he commended women not to marry by appeal to Samson, who was "once shaven bald by a woman," and to the preference for "the fidelity of the father Jephthah to the tears of the virgin daughter" (bk. 1).

Later, as Christian monasticism gained greater popularity, we find J. Cassian interpreting the ambidextrous Ehud as an allegory for the devotional life: "The inner man consists of two parts, and if I may be allowed the expression, two hands. . . . The saint has for his right hand his spiritual achievements. . . . He has also a left hand, when he is entangled in the toils of temptation" (*The Conferences*, pt. 1, chap. 10).

For the Christian church moving into the Middle Ages, allegory became an important reading strategy offering (highly creative) support of many and various interests and arguments. Yet in comparison to commentary on other historical books of the HB, Judges received little attention. Moreover, the readings it did host were limited primarily to a few of its many stories, those of Gideon being most popular.

3. Rabbinic Judaism. While a chronological account of Jewish interpretation of Judges is a highly problematic undertaking, a general survey shows its history to involve a tradition-dependent accumulation of dialogue across time between biblical texts, precursive readings, and imaginative rereadings. Rabbinic literature on Judges lives in a tension between, on the one hand, celebration of the sacred indeterminancy of biblical language and, on the other hand, submission to the AUTHORITY of precursive interpretation. It is always both subordinate and subversive in relation to tradition as it spreads out from its biblical foundation with layer after layer of new insight (*hiddush*).

The story of Jael and Sisera (Judges 4–5) provides a good example of this interpretive dialogue. Where the Tannaitic *Midrash ha-Gadol* speaks only of Sisera's fateful intoxication by Jael's beauty and voice, PSEUDO-PHILO takes the language of intoxication a step further, adding that "Jael took wine and mingled it with the milk" (31:6-7). In another direction, the Babylonian TALMUD posits that Jael surrendered herself to Sisera's passion in order to make him more vulnerable to her assault (*Yebam.* 103a-103b; *Nazir,* 23b). In reference to the maternal allusions in the Hebrew of this story, the medieval *Rimze Haftarot* further advises that the milk Sisera drank was actually from Jael's breast (L. Ginzberg [1913] 198).

Compared to Christian theological tradition, rabbinic Judaism appears to place a high value on the activity of reading, over and above the specific conclusions derived. On the other hand, the study of Judges has also sometimes been related to particular Jewish confessional crises. Sisera, for example, is identified with Alexander the Great in some early rabbinic literature (Ginzberg [1913] 195). A related concern pervading the literature on Judges is the threat of a religious syncretism, e.g., Jephthah and his contemporaries are severely criticized for their ignorance of the Torah and the resulting tragedy (human sacrifice). The Ephraimites are no better, according to the same tradition, for their human sacrifices to Baal set the precedent for Jephthah's horrifying act. In fact, according to *Tosefta Targum*, the Ephraimites deserved to be slaughtered, "for they were addicted to idolatry, particularly to the worship of an idol called Sibboleth, which name was so much on their lips that they involuntarily said Sibboleth when they intended to say Shibboleth" (Judg 12:6; cf. *Seder Eliahu Rabbah*, 11, 456).

Likewise, Gideon is severely criticized for his idolatrous act of setting up an ephod after defeating the enemy. According to Pseudo-Philo, this act put God in a predicament: "God said, 'When he destroyed the sanctuary of Baal, then all men said: Let Baal avenge himself. Now, therefore, if I chastize him for the evil he did against me, ye will say: It was not God who chastized him but Baal because he sinned aforetime against him' " (36.3-4). The story of Gideon and the fleece, which supports an anti-Semitic polemic in Christian interpretation, received comparatively little attention—and no allegorical interpretation—in Jewish study.

By the same token, the judges most frequently criticized as least worthy within the rabbinical tradition—Gideon, Samson, Jephthah (Ginzberg [1913] 201)—are three of the four adulated in Hebrews.

JOSEPHUS, on the other hand, writing from a different confessional horizon (apologetics) than many rabbinic writers, was very reluctant to criticize any of the judges, including Jephthah (*Ant. Jud.* 5.257-66) and Gideon (*Ant. Jud.* 5.213-32; cf. his positive rendering of Samson and Manoah, *Ant. Jud.* 5.275-317, which is again contrary to other rabbinical criticism).

Although Christian and Jewish interpretations of Judges are in many ways quite distinct from one another, both traditions join in regarding with patriarchal suspicion the women Jael and Deborah. Especially is this true of Deborah in Jewish writings of many periods, from Talmud to *Zohar.* Inordinately self-possessed, according to several authorities she summoned Barak to her instead of going to him. Moreover, according to these sources, she spoke so much of herself in her song that the spirit of PROPHECY (apparently an oppressively deferential spirit when it comes to women) departed from her for a while during its composition (*Pesaḥ.* 66b; *Zohar* 3, 21b-22a). In the Talmud it is further written, "Pride is unbecoming in women; the prophetesses Deborah and Huldah were proud women, and both bore ugly names" (*Meg.* 14b).

4. The Christian Middle Ages. While some medieval Christian scholars of the HB began looking to rabbinic modes of interpretation (especially the Victorines), most Christian use of Judges was typological. Such reading of the "Vetus" Testamentum centered meaning ostensibly in the "Novum" Testamentum and effectively in christology (and its practical applications) as formulated by Mother Church, and this monopoly on the Christ who monopolized Scripture served the church in its increasing struggle to maintain its social and political centrality. Moreover, the church's subserving of the meaning of the "old" to the "new" lent itself surreptitiously to the larger cultural and political purpose of distinguishing a homogeneous Christian Europe from the threats, real or imagined, of Islam and Judaism, both of which advocated authority in the "old." Thus, in the pictorial *Speculum humanae salvationis* of the fourteenth and fifteenth centuries, we find the sacrifice of Jephthah's virgin daughter prefiguring the dedication of Mary's virginity (chap. v), Samson's mass slaughter with the jawbone prefiguring JESUS prostrating his enemies with a single word (John 18:6; chap. xvii), and Samson carrying off the gates of Gaza prefiguring Jesus breaking out of the guarded tomb (chap. xxviii). Especially noteworthy here are the parallel interpretations of Mary and Jesus as conquerors of the devil, prefigured by Jael's piercing of Sisera and Samson's rending of the lion, respectively (chaps. xxix and xxx; see A. Wilson and J. Wilson [1984]; for the similar *Biblia Pauperum,*

see R. Milburn [1969] and H. Musper [1961]). This literature reflects the popularity of Mary in the devotional spirituality of the times, which has in turn brought positive attention to the women of Judges.

5. From the Protestant Reformation to Modernity. Judges received comparatively little attention during the Protestant Reformation. In fact, even such prolific commentators as LUTHER and CALVIN wrote no commentaries on the book. Rather, Judges was used by these and other Christian theologians primarily in support of points made from other texts.

Both Luther and Calvin, like their classic Christian precursors, used the story of Gideon more than any other text in Judges. And while Luther principally opposed allegorical interpretations, his reading of the story of Gideon's fleece reflects a normative tradition indebted to the readings of Augustine, Ambrose, and Jerome over a thousand years earlier. Like them, Luther was concerned to show the Jews of the law to be skinned dry and reprobate, with the grace of God now flowing freely over the rest of the world's floor. He wrote, "If you hear and see any figure of the Law, it will appear altogether flesh and thick, but when you will have separated it from the spirit, you will behold the skin in which the flesh was, but the flesh has been emptied. . . . Yet the flesh was in that skin. And Gideon's fleece received the dew, that is, with the letter stripped off, the law is spiritual. . . . Therefore the former is judgment, the latter righteousness . . . the former hardness, the latter sweetness" (*First Lectures on the Psalms,* Ps 104:2 [319]).

Calvin, on the other hand, cited the Gideon stories in his commentaries (especially on Isaiah and Jeremiah), not as allegory, but rather as a means to prepare the faithful for impending judgment and destruction. In his commentary on Jer 44:29-30, for example, he wrote, "Gideon was torpid, but when he saw by this miracle that victory would be given him, he boldly took the work assigned to him" (1950, 561). Hardly a bold reading until one contrasts it with those of Augustine and Luther.

Nevertheless, while shying away from such allegories, Calvin continued the tradition of hermeneutical suspicion (see HERMENEUTICS) regarding the women of Judges. In his commentary on 1 Tim 2:12 ("I permit no woman to teach or to have authority over men") he wrote, "If any one bring forward, by way of objection, Deborah and others of the same class . . . the answer is easy: Extraordinary acts done by God do not overturn the ordinary rules of government, by which he intended that we should be bound" (cf. his commentary on Mic 6:5). We would note, however, that Calvin did not follow Jerome in preferring Jephthah's fidelity over the daughter's lament. "Jephthah was punished for his own folly when in hasty fervor he conceived a rash vow" (*Institutes* 4.13.3).

Following the early Reformers within the Christian

tradition, interpretation moved generally in two divergent directions. In one direction scholars found themselves increasingly immersed in Enlightenment modes of rationality, moving rapidly toward the dawn of so-called higher criticism where questions concerning historical context became paramount. Among these scholars B. de SPINOZA (1634–77) is perhaps the most well known. As with other texts treated in his *Tractatus theologico-politicus* (1670), Spinoza read Judges in terms of its references to ostensive history. Thus he focused on references in Judges to chronology in order to argue that the building of the Temple by Solomon took place 162 years later than claimed in 1 Kings 6 and that all of the historical books of the HB were written by Ezra rather than by Moses (128-37).

With the rise of rationalism over the next century or so, the Hebrew Scriptures came under increasing attack from outside the confessional Jewish and Christian communities. In addition to Spinoza's program for ascertaining a "trustworthy history of Scriptures," these readings involve an indignantly enlightened moral-evaluative dimension. Thus the prolific champion of DEISM, VOLTAIRE, deployed the book of Judges as an instance of the primitive anthropomorphism, polytheism, and moral depravity that he saw enshrined in the Bible of the establishment church and religion that he was attacking. But his critical attempts to skewer Christian orthodoxy on the failings (as he argued them) of its HB foundations slide often into an uncritical deprecation of Judaism, ancient and contemporary, which has justifiably raised against him the charge of anti-Semitism. In fact, of all the biblical characters open to his scathing assault, Jephthah received the most critical attention (*Ages*, 211). In his *Dictionnaire philosophique* (1764), for example, Voltaire submited Jephthah as the primary example of the brutality of primitive religion with its *dieu sanguinaire* (religion) and purported to show that the story of Jephthah and his daughter proves human sacrifice to be an established part of Jewish faith (*Jephté*)—a rhetorical flourish the danger of which this defender of the persecuted seemed to ignore.

In the other direction, many Christian scholars interpreted the stories of Judges as lessons for daily Christian life. Given the apparent lack of substantial interpretations of Judges throughout the history of the Christian church, R. Roger's highly popular *Commentary on Judges* (1615) is remarkable. It avoids theological allegory, walking instead through the details of every story in search of lessons for living in true Christian piety. Thus from Jael we learn that "no bonds of familiarity and equity are so neerely joined together, and so just, but that if God for causes best knowne to him, commands otherwise, they are to be broken" (225). In Gideon's quest for a "double signe" we learn that God returns our weakness and distrust with lovingkindness (343). And concerning the loss of Jephthah's daughter

as a result of his "rash" and "unbeseeming" vow, we must remember that all we have has been given to us by God for our stewardship, lest we become too attached to our possessions (578).

6. The Modern Period. Under the impact of historical criticism Judges became a mine of source-critical hypotheses, primarily in German-speaking Christian scholarship, but increasingly, as the nineteenth century elapsed, elsewhere in Europe and the United States. The PENTATEUCHAL sources, J, E, and D were discovered in the book, along with independent sources, mostly the work of "later hands." In this vein of criticism, in Judges as in Exodus "doublets" abound, including the elaborate intertwining of whole parallel stories (e.g., a "Gideon" story and a "Jerubbaal" story; cf. G. Moore [1898] 173-77); T. Cheyne treated the two separately in his article on Gideon [1899–1903]). Redactional stages are multiple and complex. Commentaries, monographs, and scholarly surveys in DICTIONARIES became dense thickets of disentangled verses, largely impenetrable to the non-specialist reader.

By the mid-twentieth century little had changed. The prevailing view was still akin to K. BUDDE's—namely, that an early collection of disparate stories was edited and framed in a deuteronomistic redaction. Few scholars believed anymore that the early book was the product of J and E (see, e.g., König in *HDB*, 811), although these sources were minutely described later by C. SIMPSON (1957), and J was traced again with ingenuity through Judges and Samuel with more sensitivity to the difficulties by H. Schulte (1972). There was argument over the existence of a kernel pre-deuteronomistic "savior book" (see esp. Richter [1963, 1964]), and the provenance of the so-called appendix (chaps. 17–21) was frequently disputed. The presence of the deuteronomist (D), on the other hand, continued to be recognized (to this day), particularly in the so-called framework passages that recount a "cycle" of apostasy-oppression-repentence-deliverance. Interest in D strengthened with the widespread acceptance of M. NOTH's hypothesis of a DEUTERONOMISTIC HISTORY (1943), a carefully fashioned work reaching from the beginning of Deuteronomy to the end of Kings. As a result, much mid– and late–twentieth-century scholarly argument on Judges has concerned the precise extent of deuteronomistic material, the stages of deuteronomistic editing, and the nature of the "pre-deuteronomistic" book (see A. G. Auld [1984]; U. Becker [1990]; G. Boling [1985]; A. Mayes [1983, 1985]; M. O'Brian [1989, 1994]).

Throughout the historical-critical period no critical work on Judges was complete without an extensive exploration of its chronology, both internally and in relation to the larger history of Israel. As a thirteenth-century BCE date for the exodus gained popularity toward the end of the nineteenth century, strategems were devised and details enumerated to condense the four centuries or so of the book's expressed chronology into the two centuries demanded by the new theory.

Text-critical (see TEXTUAL CRITICISM) and philological questions in Judges as in other books of the period were accorded significant attention in monographs and commentaries. The beginnings of scholarly ARCHAEOLOGY opened up new possibilities for addressing questions of *realia,* although archaeological discussion of Judges is much more noticeable in twentieth-century discussion. Of much greater importance to nineteenth-century commentators, scholarly and popular alike, was the increasing accessibility of the Middle East, and of Palestine in particular, to European and American travelers. Commentary became an occasion to invoke wine presses, millstones, buildings, wild and domestic animals—in short, the paraphernalia of nineteenth-century Palestinian, especially bedouin, life—to illustrate the text of Judges as of other biblical books. (The popular engravings of Doré are characteristic of this interest.) Particular features of the narrative found explanation in general "oriental" and especially bedouin custom (see, e.g., W. R. SMITH on kinship and marriage [1893²]). "Sheykhs" and "emirs" rode at the head of "nomad Arab clan(s)" (Smith, 1184a, 1504b).

A marked tone of cultural and moral superiority pervaded much (though by no means all) of this comment in scholarly and popular works alike. Not surprisingly this often took a Eurocentric form, as when one scholar, explaining the panic that struck the Midianite army confronting Gideon, observed that the hero's plans "were admirably adapted to strike a panic terror into the huge and undisciplined nomad host. . . . We know from history that large and irregular Oriental armies are especially liable to sudden outbursts of uncontrollable terror" (Smith, 1183b).

Early Israelite civilization, religion, and morality were considered "untaught" and "barbarous" (C. Geikie [1884]), from an "uncultured" time of "dubious light" (R. Horton [1899]). We are reminded of Voltaire. The Canaanites of the cities, rich in civilization (though, alas, hotbeds of voluptuousness and wickedness), were contrasted with the sons of the desert, rough, rude, and continuing unpolished in manners despite "a slowly advancing refinement of life and custom" (R. Kittel [1909] 94-95; cf. 62).

Sometimes class attitudes shaped the discussion. Writing of Samson, Budde could not help observing that the man's characteristic behavior—including cultivating brute strength, chasing and being unfaithful to women, brawling, eating and drinking to excess, and lying—was still extant as a standard of a certain people, being the behavior of the ideal country hero, as many readers, "especially those who have been brought up in the country, will be able to substantiate" (K. Budde, *HDB,* 380).

Sexism was commonplace. Throughout the nineteenth century and well into the twentieth, the mass of readings on the women of Judges, whether popular or scholarly, continued to reflect a deep ambivalence concerning their praiseworthiness. Of Jael, for example, Geikie wrote, "The end was noble enough; the means brave to a marvel; but the heart that could have planned and carried them out was anything rather than that of a woman" (140). On the other hand, Horton was of the view that to say Jael's action was not praiseworthy is to "lower our whole estimate of Deborah herself," since Deborah called her "blessed" (126). And while G. Matheson (1907) would not join in Deborah's approbation of Jael's dastardly deed, he wrote, "I should like to apply some ammonia to the stain in the robe of Deborah," whose wrath could be felt only by such an "intensely soft nature" (163-64).

Where some readers condemned Jephthah's vow as rash (see also rabbinic interpretation above), others persisted in affirming the tragic consequence, commending the father's "faithful fulfillment" of his vow (C. Kraft [1962] 1018; cf. 821) and praising the daughter's willingness to die for her father's integrity. No man could have put it better than A. Whyte (1905), who wrote that the young women who journeyed to commemorate her at that mountain altar each year "came back to be far better daughters than they went out. They came back softened, and purified, and sobered at heart. They came back ready to die for their fathers, and for their brothers, and for their husbands, and for their God" (31).

In general terms, the perception of early Israel's religious and moral life as being "primitive" reflects a longstanding conviction about evolution through the history of civilization. The theological expression of this view in Christian thought is the doctrine of progressive revelation, much invoked throughout the modern period of Judges interpretation to explain events in the stories that are perceived as morally and religiously troubling, if not positively offensive. Recurrent cases in point are the violent dispossession of the Canaanites, the "treachery" of Ehud and Jael, Gideon's acquisition of the golden ephod, Jephthah's sacrifice of his daughter, the Levite's treatment of his concubine, the tribes' slaughter of the inhabitants of Jabesh Gilead, the rape of the young women of Shiloh, and Samson's behavior generally. Struck by "the low level of the morals of the period, even according to ancient standards" (Kraft, 1022), it is reassuring for one to be able to think of these times as merly times of imperfect glimmerings, "pointing to the perfect religion and morality" (König, *HDB.,* 820). Of course, it is not altogether difficult either, along this line of reasoning, to make the jump from moral condescension toward "early Judaism" to an "enlightened" (i.e., Christian) disdain for the Judaism of the interpreter's own time. We are reminded again of Voltaire.

Drawing on the theme of tribal disunity ("In those

days there was no king in Israel; a man would do what was right in his own eyes" [21:25]) many scholars of the modern period, especially in Germany, have read the book of Judges as a commentary on the formation of the nation state, mandating political and religious unity as the precondition of success. For Kittel, writing in Breslau in 1892, it was "a time of struggle with great tasks, which were recognised by only a few individuals, and to which even they were not equal. But . . . after going astray more than once in the sphere of politics and religion, a people of such original strength and so lofty a destiny must eventually find its way to its high goal" (68). The last battle against the Canaanites "brought about the glorious union of the tribes of Israel under Barak and Deborah" and Deborah's song was "a fire kindled at the holy flame of ardent enthusiasm for Israel, and purest, most fervent love for Yahvé and his people" (72). Or as H. Schultz (1892, 144-51) puts it, citing the song of Deborah, "The enemies of Israel are the enemies of Jehovah, and they who fight for the national cause fight for God" (148).

For many historians, therefore, the failures of polity in the period of the judges were eventually rectified by the centralized state and military machine of David. Ironically, but not surprising in light of notions of manifest destiny and the sovereignty issues of the "war between the states," such interpretations have also been popular among American scholars, persisting into the latter part of the twentieth century. They have found favor too among Israeli scholars, for whom David's "unification" of the land and capture of Jerusalem is a defining point in a "national" history (the "Jerusalem 3000" celebrations owe much to this conceit). On the other hand, immensely popular during the middle part of the twentieth century was Noth's theory that a twelve-tribe league, or "amphictyony," organized around a central shrine was the model of political organization during the Judges period. This idealization of polity, articulated in Depression era Germany on the eve of the Third Reich, was built as much from scant sources outside Judges as from meager evidence in the book itself. It met with fatal criticism on that score in the 1970s (e.g., Mayes [1974]).

With few exceptions work on Judges since the mid nineteenth century, influenced by historical criticism, is noteworthy for failure to sustain any extended interpretation of the stories comprising the book. Rarely have the narratives been interpreted as coherent "stories" through close and sustained attention to the elements constituting the story world itself. Sensitivity to rhetorical features of the text, except perhaps in the case of the Song of Deborah, has been sporadic at best. Largely, the text has been examined for clues to possible political (i.e., national and tribal leadership, wars, property) and institutional reconstruction of the purported history of the "period." Like much interpretation of Genesis during

this period, any story disclosed is usually the story of "tribal movements." Where attention has been paid to other social and personal dimensions—e.g., to characterizaton (motivation or interpersonal relationships)— the interpeter rarely draws on a reading of the story beyond the immediate context. Frequently such issues are settled by appeal to some general (often tenuous) notion of customs and conditions in the "period." The extensive scholarly invocations of culpable "fertility religion," for example, scarcely match the subject's virtual absence from the surface text.

There have been several major reasons for the failure to interpret at the level of the narrative as story. One is the assumption that what is being constructed in the interpretive act is history (usually of the positivist, patriarchal kind indicated above). Another is the fragmenting effect (observed by many conservatives) of source criticism: Often there has been no agreed-upon surface narrative to interpret. A third reason is that the guild of biblical scholars, through control of hiring; promotion; and, above all, public presentation and publication of research, long denied legitimacy to methods other than those developed in the historical-critical vein. The disruption of this interpretive monopoly coincided in the 1970s with the reformation of the SOCIETY OF BIBLICAL LITERATURE and the American Academy of Religion in North America and the foundation of new publishing outlets in the United States and Great Britain that were open to non-traditional research.

7. New Directions. In historical studies the 1970s and 1980s saw growing support, particularly in North America, for the hypothesis that internal peasant rebellion, as opposed to conquest from outside the land, should be central to any explanation of the "emergence" of Israel and hence to any understanding of the people's experience of oppression in the Judges period (G. Mendenhall [1973] and then, developing the social dimensions of the hypothesis, N. Gottwald [1979]). Feudal domination by a city-state ruling class was successfully overthrown by an underclass of peasants and displaced persons. This situation was classically illustrated (according to the theory) by the account of the war against Jabin and Sisera in the Song of Deborah, for many years widely thought to be the oldest text in the HB (though well-founded skepticism has been expressed by N. Lemche [1991], among others).

Often including in their reconstructions some element of the internal rebellion model, historians have moved away from the W. F. ALBRIGHT school's attempts to correlate the destruction levels of Late Bronze Age cities with the stories of conquest in Joshua and Judges 1–2 and toward viewing the emergence of Israel in Early Iron Age Palestine as a gradual settlement in non-populated areas (as earlier, A. Alt [1925]). Some scholars have invoked the model of a "segmentary society" to describe the resulting autonomous communities (J. Flanagan [1981]; N. Lohfink [1983]; A. Malamat [1973]). More radically, others argue that the biblical accounts of conquest, of the "Judges period," of Saul, David, Solomon, and indeed much of the "monarchic period" are historically unreliable constructions deriving from the exilic or postexilic period and are useful chiefly as sources for understanding that later period (e.g., P. Davies [1992]; Lemche [1985]; T. Thompson [1994²]; see V. Fritz and Davies [1996]; L. Grabbe [1997]). Certainly archaeological evidence from the Early Iron Age seems to have borne out a pattern of basically peaceful expansion and has failed to distinguish ethnic difference between the inhabitants of the new settlements in the central highlands and others in the region who, according to the biblical account, ought to be ethnically distinct "Canaanites" (cf. I. Finkelstein [1991]; M. Skjeggestad [1992]). Nor is there undisputed corroborating evidence for virtually any part of the biblical account of Judges, Samuel, or the early chapters of Kings. At the very least, serious obstacles confront those who wish to draw on the text of Judges for any historical reconstruction of "Israel" in the Early Iron Age.

In his 1975 commentary Boling observed that at the root of earlier difficulties with the "low morality" of Judges 19–21 was the unwillingness of critics to allow the writers "anything resembling a Mosaic conscience" (278). His reading, brief as it is, nevertheless marks a significant break with his own (historical-archaeological) interpretive tradition by recognizing that the narrator's treatment of characters, institutions, and events might be consistently sardonic or ironic ("tragicomedy" and "grim humor" are his terms; 1975, 277; 1985, 216). He also sees a significant thematic relationship between the story of the Levite in Gibeah and that of Lot in Sodom (Genesis 19), whereas the usual procedure has been to dismiss the one story as merely a tendentious imitation of the other (cf. J. Wellhausen [1878] 235-37, where Judges imitates Genesis). Both these strategies, reading through irony and reading "intertextually" (see INTERTEXTUALITY), have become characteristic features of a whole new phase of interpretation of Judges that has dominated late twentieth-century criticism.

A shift began in the 1970s and was marked from about 1980. New readings emerged that attended to the final form of the text, to its literary (including rhetorical and aesthetic) dimensions, and increasingly to its moral and ideological implications for contemporary as well as for ancient readers. Such readings have been cultivated by Jewish and Christian scholars as well as by others standing outside any confessional position. Scholars working in schools of English or comparative literature have provided major impetus for change (e.g., R. Alter [1981]; M. Bal [1988a, 1988b]; K. Gros Louis [1982]; M. Sternberg [1985]). J. Crenshaw's lively monograph on Samson (1978), attentive to its aesthetic quali-

ties, heralded a spate of presentations and publications on literary dimensions of Judges 13–16 from J. C. Exum (1980, 1981, 1983) most prolifically, and others (e.g., E. Greenstein [1981]; J. Vickery [1981]). Other parts of the book began to receive similar attention, especially Judges 4–5, 10–12, and 19–21 (e.g., Alter; Y. Amit [1990]; Bal; Exum; D. Fewell and D. Gunn [1993]; S. Niditch [1993]; P. Trible [1984]; Sternberg). Readings of the book as a whole began to appear (e.g., Bal; M. Brettler [1989]; Exum; D. Gooding [1982]; Gunn [1987]; J. Hamlin [1990]; D. Jobling [1986]; L. Klein [1988]; R. Polzin [1980]; B. Webb [1987]; cf., more than a decade earlier, J. Lilley [1967]). Critics adopted a variety of approaches but increasingly explored reader-oriented interpretations (see READER-RESPONSE CRITICISM).

Interest in tensive voices and ironic perspectives is characteristic of early LITERARY criticism of Judges in this period. Among readings of the book as a whole, one of the first and most influential was a study by Polzin using (Russian) formalist literary-critical methodology to analyze Deuteronomy–Judges. He viewed Judges in terms of an ideological struggle between "authoritarian dogmatism" (adhering strictly to an original authoritative law) and "critical traditionalism" (sustaining a tradition by critically reinterpreting it). Jobling's extended structuralist analysis (see STRUCTURALISM AND DECONSTRUCTION) of Judges and deuteronomic political theory has also proved to be a prescient study. Instead of dissipating the often-observed pro- and anti-monarchical strains in the book into redactional layers, he holds them in tension in Levi-Straussian fashion. The book thus construes its account of polity in a way that is neither "pro" nor "anti," nor, for that matter, "balanced. It is a construction that opens for its exilic audience possibilities for creating a new "political theology" for its own situation. Webb's monograph, which saw the book as addressing the issue of Yahweh's failure to give Israel the whole land as promised, attends to complexities of structure as a clue to meaning. He showed themes of Israel's apostasy and Yahweh's refusal to be "used" by Israel reaching a climax in the Samson episode and treated the final chapters as a coda resonating with many ironic references to the main story. Gunn traces unifying threads in the book and explores its sardonic play with themes of language, security, patriarchy, and violence. Klein configures the book as an ironic spiral ("the widening gyre") of anti-Yahwism and the displacement of integrity by territory until "mere anarchy is loosed upon the world" (quoting W. B. Yeats).

The new veins of criticism also began to show in commentary writing, especially in series addressing an audience beyond the academic guild. Hamlin's book is notable: He interprets in terms of LIBERATION and CROSS-CULTURAL reading (with a Southeast Asian focus), drawing freely on Gottwald (Israel's formation through revolution), on literary-critical method, and on FEMINIST criticism.

It would, of course, have been difficult for biblical studies to remain totally isolated from the major challenge of post-modernist thought (see POST-MODERN BIBLICAL INTERPRETATION) with which other disciplines had been confronted. It was doubly difficult to maintain the status quo given the entry of growing numbers of women into the academic field of biblical studies and (complementarily) the growing number of women seeking advanced theological education. By 1990 the impact of women's writing (usually feminist) about Judges was marked. Amit, Bal, A. Brenner (1990), F. van Dijk-Hemmes (1989), Exum, Fewell, E. Fuchs, J. Hackett (1985), Klein, Niditch, and Trible, among others, often utilize non-traditional, predominantly literary-critical modes of interpretation. Most press their readers to reevaluate the place of women in Judges and to confront the ideological dimensions of the book's recurrent conjunction of women and violence. Among the first was Trible, whose "literary-feminist" readings of Jephthah's daughter and the Levite concubine direct attention sharply away from the male protagonists to the plight of the women in these "texts of terror" in a vein of formalist RHETORICAL CRITICISM influenced by J. Muilenburg's teaching and writing in the 1960s. Trible's essays have had wide influence not only within the academy but also, both directly and indirectly, with a large audience of other, particularly church-connected, readers.

Bal's analysis of traditional studies of the death of Sisera (*Murder and Difference* [1988]) relentlessly exposes the ideological, especially patriarchal, biases of "neutral" and "objective" scholarship. Her study of the book as a whole (*Death and Dissymmetry* [1988]) deconstructs the customary coherence, seen in a pattern of holy war, and reads for a countercoherence, seen in a pattern of murder. With others she sees gender-based violence shaping the book. Radically, she affirms the women who kill men. In a world where men have disproportionate power over body, life, and language, these women introduce a countervailing anger. They kill "for" the women victims. Bal's writing in these works and elsewhere has strong underpinnings in contemporary critical theory and is marked by a keen sensitivity to ideological complexities in the reading of texts as also by illuminating shifts in disciplinary perspective. Thus, in "A Body of Writing: Judges 19" she considers relationships among death, women, and representation through an analysis of narrative argumentation that includes a Rousseau short story and a sketch by Rembrandt. Her work is probably the single most creative force at play in present studies of Judges.

Feminist criticism continued into the 1990s its concentration on the female figures of Judges, as Brenner's collection (*A Feminist Companion to Judges*) well illustrates: The stories of Deborah, Jephthah's daughter, Samson's mother, and the Levite's woman in Judges 19 receive particular attention. The volume also exemplifies the growing recourse to rabbinic materials as sources for critical reflection. A growing diversity of approaches to biblical criticism is a mark of the decade, and Judges is no exception. Yee's *Judges and Method* (1995), for example, chooses to discuss narrative, SOCIAL-SCIENTIFIC, feminist, structuralist, deconstructive, and IDEOLOGICAL CRITICISM. At the same time, in the definition and application of these approaches, there is often significant overlap: Fewell's deconstructive (but also narrative, feminist, and ideological) reading of Achsah and the "(e)razed city of writing" in Yee's volume is a case in point. Elsewhere K. Stone (1996) shows the advantage of bringing an anthropological frame to bear on questions of gender, as he discusses honor and shame in Judges 19. Several scholars have used FOLKLORE studies to illuminate the story of Samson, among other texts in Judges, with particular interest in the trickster figure (Niditch, C. Camp and C. Fontaine [1990]; G. Mobley [1997]). F. Deist (1996) in South Africa struggles with issues of cultural translation and transformation: How can such a narrative of violence and ethnic ridicule as the Ehud story be "Scripture" ("Murder in the Toilet")?

At the same time, formalist literary analysis of the book has continued to be elaborated, sometimes in conjunction with redactional ("diachronic") criticism (see REDACTION CRITICISM) as most notably in R. O'Connell's (1996) extensive account of the "rhetorical purpose" of the Judges "compiler/redactor." This purpose to enjoin readers to endorse a divinely appointed Judahite king who upholds such deuteronomistic ideals as the need to expel foreigners and to maintain Yahweh's cult and covenant O'Connell infers from formal structures and "motivic patterns" recurring throughout the book's narrative framework and from patterns of plot structure and characterization in the plot-based deliverer stories and ending.

Critics are increasingly interested in Judges' connections with other biblical texts. Thus, Fewell (1997) reads Judges as a rewriting of Genesis for the purpose of constructing postexilic identity and accordingly constructs her own essay dialogically as a play of past and present voices. Earlier, Fewell and Gunn (1993) attempted to write Judges into a deconstructive reading of the "subject" of Genesis–Kings as a whole, recasting the story into one of women and children. Camp (1998) traces the literary and ideological connections of Judges even further by locating the Samson story in a widespread textual web that includes narrative, law, and wisdom. Drawing on anthropology, literary criticism, and social history, she seeks through the figure of "strangeness" to nuance traditional scholarly constructions of Israelite identity as well as to complicate the analysis of power offered by feminist criticism.

Exum's further analyses of the stories of Jephthah and Samson (1993) have helped bring issues of subjectivity and "the gaze" into focus. The step to study of the Bible as a "viewed" artifact is a short one. Exum (1996) returns to Samson and Delilah ("Why, Why, Why, Delilah?"), as do J. Koosed and T. Linafelt ("How the West Was Not One" [1996]), in a methodological turn toward contemporary culture, Bible, Western art, and film, for example. Such writing marks another significant shift in current biblical studies (see also Bal, above, and A. Bach, *Biblical Glamour and Hollywood Glitz* [1996]).

As post-modern critical theory continues to pervade the study of Judges, hermeneutical questions have become profoundly important. Clearly, new horizons of meaning are in view. Clearly too, the politics of reading are changing.

Bibliography: A. Ages, "Voltaire's Biblical Criticism: A Study in Thematic Representations," *Studies on Voltaire and the Eighteenth Century* 30 (1964) 205-21. **A. Alt,** "The Settlement of the Israelite Tribes in Palestine," *Essays in OT History and Religion* (1925; ET 1966) 133-69. **R. Alter,** *The Art of Biblical Narrative* (1981). **Y. Amit,** "Judges 4: Its Contents and Form," *JSOT* 39 (1987) 89-111; "The Story of Ehud (Judg 3:12-30): The Form and the Message," *Signs and Wonders* (ed. J. C. Exum, 1989) 97-123; "Hidden Polemic in the Conquest of Dan: Judges xvii-xviii," *VT* 40 (1990) 4-20; *The Book of Judges: The Art of Editing* (1992; ET 1998). **G. Auld,** *Joshua, Judges, and Ruth* (1984); "Gideon: Hacking at the Heart of the OT," *VT* 39 (1989) 257-67. **A. Bach,** *Biblical Glamour and Hollywood Glitz* (= *Semeia* 74, 1996). **M. Bal,** *Lethal Love: Feminist Literary Readings of Biblical Love Stories* (ISBL, 1987); *Death and Dissymmetry: The Politics of Coherence in the Book of Judges* (Chicago Studies in the History of Judaism, 1988a); *Murder and Difference: Gender, Genre, and Scholarship on Sisera's Death* (ISBL, 1988b); (ed.), *Anti-Covenant: Counter-Reading Women's Lives in the HB* (JSOTSup 81, 1989); "Dealing/With/Women: Daughters in the Book of Judges," *The Book and the Text: The Bible and Literary Theory* (ed. R. Schwartz, 1990) 16-39; "A Body of Writing: Judges 19," *A Feminist Companion to Judges* (ed. A. Brenner, 1993) 208-30. **R. Bartelmus,** "Forschung am Richterbuch seit M. Noth," *TRu* 56 (1991) 221-59. **R. Bayley,** "Which Is the Best Commentary? 14. The Book of Judges," *ExpTim* 103 (1991–92) 136-38. **U. Becker,** *Richterzeit und Königtum: Redaktionsgeschichtliche Studien zum Richterbuch* (BZAW 192, 1990). **R. G. Boling,** *Judges* (AB 69, 1975); "Judges, the Book of," *Harper's Bible Dictionary* (ed. P. J. Achtemeier, 1985). **T. A. Boogaart,** "Stone for Stone: Retribution in the Story of Abimelech and Shechem," *JSOT* 32 (1985) 45-56. **A. Brenner,** *The Israelite Woman: Social Role and Literary Type in Biblical Narrative* (The Biblical Seminar 2, 1985); "A Triangle and a Rhombus in Narrative Structure: A Proposed Integrative Reading of Judges iv and v," *VT* 40 (1990) 129-38; (ed.), *A Feminist Companion to Judges* (1993). **M. Brettler,** "The Book of Judges: Literature as Politics," *JBL* 108 (1989) 395-418. **J.**

Calvin, *Commentaries on the Epistles to Timothy, Titus, and Philemon* (1948); *Commentaries on the Book of the Prophet Jeremiah and the Lamentations* (1950); *Institutes of the Christian Religion* (1960). **C. V. Camp,** *Wise and Strange: Reading the Bible with the Strange Woman* (1998). **C. V. Camp and C. R. Fontaine,** "The Words of the Wise and Their Riddles," *Text and Tradition: The HB and Folklore* (ed. S. Niditch, 1990) 127-52; *Women, War, and Metaphor: Language and Society in the Study of the HB* (*Semeia* 61, 1993). **T. K. Cheyne and J. S. Black** (eds.), *Encyclopaedia Biblica: A Critical Dictionary of the Literary, Political, and Religious History, the Archaeology, Geography, and Natural History of the Bible* (4 vols., 1899–1903). **J. L. Crenshaw,** *Samson: A Secret Betrayed, a Vow Ignored* (1978). **P. R. Davies,** *In Search of "Ancient Israel"* (JSOTSup 148, 1992). **P. L. Day,** "From the Child is Born the Woman: The Story of Jephthah's Daughter," *Gender and Difference in Ancient Israel* (1989) 58-74. **F. Deist,** "Murder in the Toilet (Judg 3:12-30): Translation and Transformation," *Scriptura* 58 (1996) 263-72. **W. G. Dever,** "How to Tell a Canaanite from an Israelite," *The Rise of Ancient Israel* (ed. H. Shanks, 1993) 26-60. **B.-J. Diebner,** "Wann sang Deborah ihr Lied? Überlegungen zu zwei der ältesten Texte des TNK (Ri 4 und 6)," *ACEBT* (1995) 106-30. **F. Van Dijk-Hemmes,** "Interpretaties van de relatie tussen Richteren 4 en 5," *Proeven van Vrouwenstudies Theologie I* (1989) 149-213. **J. C. Exum,** "Promise and Fulfillment: Narrative Art in Judges 13," *JBL* 99 (1980) 43-59; "Aspects of Symmetry and Balance in the Samson Saga," *JSOT* 19 (1981) 2-29; "The Theological Dimension of the Samson Saga," *VT* 33 (1983) 30-45; " 'Mother in Israel': A Familiar Figure Reconsidered," *Feminist Interpretation of the Bible* (ed. L. Russell, 1985) 73-85; "Judges," *HBC*, 245-61; "The Tragic Vision and Biblical Narrative: The Case of Jephthah," *Signs and Wonders: Biblical Texts in Literary Focus* (ed. J. C. Exum, 1989) 59-83; "The Center Cannot Hold: Thematic and Textual Instabilities in Judges," *CBQ* 52 (1990) 410-29; *Fragmented Women: Feminist (Sub)versions of Biblical Narratives* (1993); *Plotted, Shot, and Painted: Cultural Representations of Biblical Women* (JSOTSup 215, 1996). **D. N. Fewell,** "Judges," *The Women's Bible Commentary* (ed. C. A. Newsom and S. H. Ringe, 1992) 67-77; "Deconstructive Criticism: Achsah and the (E)razed City of Writing," *Judges and Method: New Approaches in Biblical Studies* (ed. G. A. Yee, 1995) 119-45; "Imagination, Method, and Murder: Un/Framing the Face of Post-Exilic Israel," *Reading Bibles, Writing Bodies: Identity and the Book* (ed. T. K. Beal and D. M. Gunn, 1997) 132-52. **D. N. Fewell and D. M. Gunn,** "Controlling Perspectives: Women, Men, and the Authority of Violence in Judges 4 and 5," *JAAR* (1990) 389-411; *Gender, Power, and Promise: The Subject of the Bible's First Story* (1993). **I. Finkelstein,** "The Emergence of Israel in Canaan: Consensus, Mainstream, and Dispute," *SJOT* 5 (1991) 47-59. **J. W. Flanagan,** "Chiefs in Israel," *JSOT* (1981) 47-73; *David's Social Drama: A Hologram of Israel's Early Iron Age* (SWBA, 1988). **V. Fritz and P. R. Davies** (eds.), *The Origins of the Ancient Israelite States* (JSOTSup 228, 1996). **E. Fuchs,** "The Literary Characterization of Mothers and Sexual Politics in the HB," *Feminist Perspectives on Biblical Scholarship* (BSNA 10, ed. A. Y. Collins, 1985) 117-36; "Marginalization, Ambiguity, Silencing: The Story of Jephthah's Daughter," *JFSR* 5 (1989) 35-45. **C. Geikie,** *OT Characters* (1884). **L. Ginzberg,** *The Legends of the Jews* (7 vols., 1913). **D. W. Gooding,** "The Composition of the Book of Judges," *ErIsr* 16 (1982) 70-79. **N. Gottwald,** *The Tribes of Yahweh: A Sociology of the Religion of Liberated Israel, 1250–1050* BCE (1979). **L. L. Grabbe** (ed.), *Can a "History of Israel" Be Written?* (JSOTSup 245, 1997). **E. L. Greenstein,** "The Riddle of Samson," *Prooftexts* 1 (1981) 237-60. **K. R. R. Gros Louis with J. S. Ackerman** (eds.), *Literary Interpretations of Biblical Narratives* (2 vols., 1982). **D. M. Gunn,** "Joshua and Judges," *The Literary Guide to the Bible* (ed. R. Alter and F. Kermode, 1987) 102-21; "Samson of Sorrows: An Isaianic Gloss on Judges 13–16," *Reading Between Texts: Intertextuality and the HB* (Literary Currents in Biblical Interpretation, ed. D. N. Fewell, 1992) 225-53. **J. A. Hackett,** "In the Days of Jael: Reclaiming the History of Women in Ancient Israel," *Immaculate and Powerful: The Female in Sacred Image and Social Reality* (The Harvard Women's Studies in Religion, ed. C. W. Atkinson et al., 1985) 15-38. **J. Hamlin,** *Judges: At Risk in the Promised Land: A Commentary on the Book of Judges* (ICC, 1990). **J. Hastings** (ed.), *A Dictionary of the Bible* (4 vols., 1898–1902). **R. F. Horton,** *Women of the OT: Studies in Womanhood* (1899). **J. G. Janzen,** "A Certain Woman in the Rhetoric of Judges 9," *JSOT* 38 (1987) 33-37. **D. Jobling,** "Deuteronomic Political Theory in Judges and 1 Samuel 1–12," *The Sense of Biblical Narrative: Structural Analyses in the HB II* (JSOTSup 39, 1986) 44-87. **G. Josipovici,** "The Rhythm Falters: The Book of Judges," *The Book of God: A Response to the Bible* (1988) 108-31. **R. Kittel,** *A History of the Hebrews* 2 (1909). **L. R. Klein,** *The Triumph of Irony in the Book of Judges* (JSOTSup 68, 1988). **J. R. Koosed and T. Linafelt,** "How the West Was Not One: Delilah Deconstructs the Western," *Biblical Glamour and Hollywood Glitz* (Semeia Studies, ed. A. Bach, 1996) 167-81. **C. F. Kraft,** "Jephthah" and "Judges, Book of," *IDB* (1962) 2:820-21, 1013-23. **S. Lasine,** "Guest and Host in Judges 19: Lot's Hospitality in an Inverted World," *JSOT* 29 (1984) 37-59. **N. P. Lemche,** *Early Israel: Anthropological and Historical Studies on the Israelite Society Before the Monarchy* (VTSup 37, 1985); *The Canaanites and Their Land: The Tradition of the Canaanites* (JSOTSup 110, 1991). **J. P. U. Lilley,** "A Literary Appreciation of the Book of Judges," *TynBul* 18 (1967) 94-102. **N. Lohfink,** "Die segmentären Gesellschaften Afrikas als neue Analogie für das vorstaatliche Israel," *Bibel und Kirche* 2, 2 (1983) 55-8. **M. Luther,** *Luther's Works,* vol. 11, *First Lectures on the Psalms* (ed. H. L. Oswald, 1976). **S. L. McKenzie and M. P. Graham** (eds.), *The History of Israel's Traditions: The Heritage of M. Noth* (JSOTSup 182, 1994). **A. Malamat,** "Tribal Societies: Biblical Genealogies and African Lineage Systems," *AES* 14 (1973) 126-36. **D. Marcus,** *Jephthah and His Vow* (1986). **G. Matheson,** *Representative Women of the Bible* (1907). **A. D. H. Mayes,** *Israel in the Period of the Judges* (SBT 29, 1974); *The Story of Israel Between Settlement and Exile: A Redactional Study of the Deuteronomistic History* (1983); *Judges* (OTGu, 1985). **G. E. Mendenhall,** *The Tenth Generation: The Origins of the Biblical Tradition* (1973). **R. L. P. Milburn,** "The 'People's Bible': Artists and Commentators," *CHB* 2 (ed. G. W. H. Lampe, 1969) 280-308. **G. Mobley,**

"The Wild Man in the Bible and the Ancient Near East," *JBL* 116 (1997) 217-33. **G. F. Moore,** *A Critical and Exegetical Commentary on Judges* (ICC, 1898 [2]). **J. Muilenburg,** "Form Criticism and Beyond," *JBL* 88 (1969) 1-18. **D. F. Murray,** "Narrative Structure and Techniques in the Deborah-Barak Story (Judges iv 4-22)," *Studies in Historic Books of OT* (VTSup 30, ed. J. A. Emerton, 1979) 155-89. **H. T. Musper,** *Die Urausgaben der holländischen Apokalypse und Biblia pauperum* (1961). **S. Niditch,** "The 'Sodomite' Theme in Judges 19–20: Family, Community, and Social Disintegration," *CBQ* 44 (1982) 365-78; "Eroticism and Death in the Tale of Jael," *Gender and Difference in Ancient Israel* (ed. P. L. Day, 1989) 43-57; "Samson as Culture Hero, Trickster, and Bandit: The Empowerment of the Weak," *CBQ* 52 (1990) 608-24; *Text and Tradition: The HB and Folklore* (1990); *Underdogs and Tricksters: A Prelude to Biblical Folklore* (New Voices in Biblical Studies, 1990). **M. Noth,** *The Deuteronomistic History* (JSOTSup 15, 1943; ET 1981); *The History of Israel* (1954 [2]; ET 1960). **M. A. O'Brian,** *The Deuteronomistic History Hypothesis: A Reassessment* (OBO 92, 1989); "Judges and the Deuteronomistic History," *The History of Israel's Traditions: The Heritage of M. Noth* (JSOTSup 182, ed. S. L. McKenzie and M. P. Graham, 1994) 235-59. **R. H. O'Connell,** *The Rhetoric of the Book of Judges* (VTSup 63, 1996). **M. O'Connor,** "The Women in the Book of Judges," *HAR* 10 (1986) 277-93. **D. Olsen,** "The Book of Judges," *NIB* (1998) 2:553-719. **D. Penchansky,** "Staying the Night: Intertextuality in Genesis and Judges," *Reading Between Texts: Intertextuality and the HB* (Literary Currents in Biblical Interpretation, ed. D. N. Fewell, 1992) 77-88; "Up for Grabs: A Tentative Proposal for Doing Ideological Criticism," *Semeia* 59 (1992) 35-42. **R. Polzin,** *Moses and the Deuteronomist: Deuteronomy, Joshua, Judges* (A Literary Study of the Deuteronomic History, pt. 1, 1980). **A. Reinhartz,** "Samson's Mother: An Unnamed Protagonist," *JSOT* 55 (1992) 25-37. **W. Richter,** *Traditionsgeschichtliche Untersuchungen zum Richterbuch* (BBB 18, 1963); *Die Bearbeitung des "Retterbuches" in der deuteronomistischen Epoche* (BBB 21, 1964). **R. Rogers,** *A Commentary on Judges* (1615). **P. Schaff** (ed.), *The Nicene and Post-Nicene Fathers,* 1st ser. (14 vols., 1956). **P. Schaff and H. Wace (eds.),** *The Ante-Nicene Fathers* (10 vols., 1952, 1961); *The Nicene and Post-Nicene Fathers,* 2nd ser. (14 vols., 1952, 1961). **H. Schulte,** "Das Richterbuch," *Die Entstehung der Geschichtschreibung im Alten Israel* (BZAW 128, 1972) 77-105). **H. Schultz,** *OT Theology: The Religion of Revelation in Its Pre-Christian Stage of Development* (1892). **C. A. Simpson,** *Composition of the Book of Judges* (1957). **M. Skjeggestad,** "Ethnic Groups in Early Iron Age Palestine: Some Remarks on the Use of the Term 'Israelite' in Recent Research," *SJOT* 6 (1992) 159-86. **W. F. Smelik,** *The Targum of Judges* (OTS 36, 1995). **W. R. Smith,** *Kinship and Marriage in Early Arabia* (1903). **W. R. Smith and J. M. Fuller,** *A Dictionary of the Bible* (3 vols., 1893 [2]). **B. Spinoza,** *A Theologico-Political Treatise* (2 vols., 1951). **M. Sternberg,** *The Poetics of Biblical Narrative: Ideological Literature and the Drama of Reading* (ISBL, 1985). **K. Stone,** *Sex, Honor, and Power in the Deuteronomistic History* (JSOTSup 234, 1996). **T. L. Thompson,** *The Early History of the Israelite People: From the Written and Archaeological Sources* (SHANE 4, 1994 [2]);

"Historiography of Ancient Palestine and Early Jewish Historiography: W. G. Dever and the Not So New Biblical Archaeology," *The Origins of the Ancient Israelite States* (JSOTSup 228, ed. V. Fritz and P. R. Davies, 1996) 26-43. **P. Trible,** *Texts of Terror: Literary-feminist Readings of Biblical Narratives* (OBT 13, 1984). **J. Vickery,** "In Strange Ways: The Story of Samson," *Images of Man and God: OT Short Stories in Literary Focus* (Bible and Literature Series 1, ed. B. O. Long, 1981) 58-73. **Voltaire,** *Dictionnaire philosophique portatif* (1764). **B. G. Webb,** *The Book of the Judges: An Integrated Reading* (1987). **J. Wellhausen,** *Prolegomena to the History of Israel* (1878; ET 1885). **A. Whyte,** *Bible Characters: Gideon to Absalom* (1905). **A. Wilson and J. L. Wilson,** *A Medieval Mirror: Speculum humanae salvationis, 1324–1500* (1984). **G. Yee** (ed.), *Judges and Method: New Approaches in Biblical Studies* (1995).

T. K. BEAL and D. M. GUNN

JUDITH, BOOK OF

One of the most masterfully composed narratives in the HB Apocrypha, indeed, in all of the Jewish literary corpus, the book of Judith meticulously develops the historical setting and crisis (chaps. 1–7) into which the character of Judith is introduced in chap. 8. Her story unfolds (chaps. 8–16) full of suspense and comes to full resolution with a horrifying climax and a victory song. The story's literary artistry, its enigmatic historical setting, the remarkable character of Judith, and the story's disturbing theological endorsement of her cold-blooded murder of Holofernes all have generated an intense fascination throughout the history of interpretation.

1. Canonicity. Despite some doubt to the contrary (A. Dubarle [1966]; T. Craven [1983]), most scholars posit an original but nonextant Hebrew text for the book, given the numerous Hebraisms in the earliest existing Greek texts. The text is extant in Greek, Latin, Syriac, and Ethiopic (see ETHIOPIAN BIBLICAL INTERPRETATION). The Jewish tradition classified Judith among the *hiconim* (the strange or foreign books in the holy writings), which were considered inspired but, nonetheless, inferior (Origen *Epist. ad Jul. Afric.* 13; JEROME *Praef. in lib. Jud.*). One wonders why the book did not gain Jewish canonical status as compared to the success of the book of Esther, which is patently less theological. The reasons may be both fortuitous and IDEOLOGICAL. C. Moore (1992) suggests that, given the early date for the canonization of the HB (2nd cent. BCE), Judith's date of composition was too late for inclusion. P. Winter (1962) argues that Judith's exclusion from the CANON is due to the fact that the story is set in a small place, evidently in Samaritan territory, whereas Esther has a more prestigious setting in the center of Persia. Indeed, later Jewish traditions give Judith more prominent locations and identities. Moreover, the book of Esther is intrinsically connected with the annual feast of Purim, whereas Judith only gradually became associated with the festival of Hanukkah by the Middle Ages. Possibly the conversion of the Ammonite Achior, in whose lips even a declaration of Israel's faith history is found, was considered offensive by some Jews (see Deut 23:3). Also, the book's portrayal of male cowardice and impotence in the face of Judith's cunning courage may have been disturbing to the patriarchal society of the time it was written.

Within Christendom the book enjoyed a somewhat better, albeit ambiguous, status. It has been suggested that the NT consciously alludes several times to Judith: Matt 13:42, 50 = Jdt 16:17; Luke 1:42 = Jdt 14:7; Acts 4:24 = Jdt 9:12; 1 Cor 2:11 = Jdt 8:14. Indeed, if one can rely on the so-called *Decretum Gleasianum,* Judith (along with Tobit, Wisdom, Ecclesiasticus, and 1 and 2 Maccabees) was considered canonical by the Roman Catholic Church by the beginning of the sixth century, but its eventual acceptance into the canon was not reached without controversy. It was initially considered authoritative (see AUTHORITY OF THE BIBLE) as early as the end of the first century, as confirmed by the earliest reference to it made by CLEMENT OF ROME (*1 Clem.* 55.4-5). In the second and third centuries references to the book place it on the level of holy Scripture: CLEMENT OF ALEXANDRIA (*Strom.* 2.17 and 4.19); TERTULLIAN, *De monogamia* 17; *Adv. Marc.* 1.7), as well as AMBROSE (*De offi. minist.* 3.13) and AUGUSTINE (*De doctrina Christiana,* 2.8) a century later.

Voices of reservation and dissent were raised: MELITO OF SARDIS (Eusebius *Hist. eccl.* 4.26); ORIGEN (*Expos. in psalmum* 1); and ATHANASIUS (*Ep. fest.* 39); Cyril of Jerusalem, and GREGORY OF NAZIANZUS, among others. In the West, Hilary, Rufin, and JEROME opposed including Judith in the canon. Jerome, who supported the boundaries of the Jewish canon, in his *Comment. in Agg.* 1.6 refers to Jdt 7:16 while giving the disclaimer: *si quis tamen vult recipere librum mulieris* (if one, however, wants to accept a woman's book). Indeed, Jerome's opinion was that the work was written by Judith herself. The favorable voices eventually won out, and its popularity in the West forced Jerome to concede to including it in his VULGATE translation (*acquievi postulatione vestrae, imo exactioni,* from his "Preface to Judith"). Jerome mentioned in his preface that it was included by the Council of Nicea among the holy Scriptures. The approbations of the councils of Carthage, Florence, and Trent, as well as the book's inclusion in the lists of *Codex Claramontanus* and *Liber sacramentorum,* solidified its position among the books of the canonical OT.

2. Interpretation. *a. Early Jewish interpretation.* As noted above, the book of Judith came to be associated with the festival of Hanukkah in the medieval midrashim (see MIDRASH), all of which omit the first seven chapters of the Greek canonical story. In addition, three forms of the story are found in the manuscripts of the Bodleian

Library, each with the heading "for Hanukkah." Whether there was originally a festival of Judith (see Jdt 16:20) is purely speculative.

Jewish interpreters sought to provide the story with a more prominent setting and to invest Judith with a more significant identity. A Hebrew manuscript found by M. Gaster (1893–94), which he dated to c. 1000 CE, replaces Nebuchadnezzar with Seleukos IV, and Jerusalem takes the place of the small town of Bethulia (whose identity is still debated in modern scholarship). Incidentally, Judith is a maiden, the daughter of Ahitob, rather than a widow. Another form of the story of Judith occurs in *Megilat Ta'anith 6*, in which Judith is the daughter of Johanan or of Mattathias and, thus, is a heroine belonging to the Hasmonean period.

b. Early Christian interpretation. Despite the confusing historical setting described in the book, the work was accepted as bona fide history. Not surprisingly, however, interpretations differed widely. From the common viewpoint that the circumstances described occurred after the Babylonian exile, almost every Persian monarch was identified with the "Nebuchadnezzar," king of the "Assyrians" in the work. Augustine (*De Civ. Dei* 18.16) and others took him to be Cambyses. JULIUS AFRICANUS (c. 180–c. 250), the most thorough practitioner of biblical criticism in the ancient church, and Georgius Syncellas (fl. c. 800) regarded him as Xerxes. Marius Mercator (early 5th cent.), Estius (1542–1613), and others made him to be Darius I. Sulpicius Severus in c. 350 CE (*Chron.* 2.14-16) identified him with Artaxerxes III Ochus, a theory that has gained some popularity in modern scholarship.

With regard to the character of Judith, there are various interpretations. Clement of Rome saw Judith as a courageous woman, someone to emulate in an age of persecution (*1 Clem.* 55.45). Later, when religious persecutions subsided, the church fathers praised Judith more for her chastity than for her bravery: Tertullian (*De monogamia* 17); Methodius of Tyre (*Convivium decem virgin, Oratio* 11.2); and Ambrose of Milan (*De virginibus* 1.2.4).

c. Reformation and Enlightenment interpretation. LUTHER was the first to popularize the notion that the book never intended to describe history, although the first major commentary on Judith, by RABANUS MAURUS (780?–856), treated the book as allegorical. For Luther the book was a "religious fiction or poem, written by a holy and ingenious man, who depicts therein the victory of the Jewish people over all their enemies" (*Vorrede aufs Buch Judith*). According to him the name "Judith" represents the Jewish people; Holofernes is the heathen lord of all ages, and the city of Bethulia denotes a virgin. Thus the Reformers interpreted the story in terms of the triumph of virtue over wickedness. H. GROTIUS (1583–1645) pushed the approach further by regarding the book as an allegorical description of Antiochus IV

Ephiphanes' attack on Judea: "Judith is the Jewish people; Bethulia is the temple; the sword which went out of it, the prayers of the saints; Nebuchadnezzar signifies the devil; Assyria is pride, the devil's kingdom; Holofernes is the devil's instrument." Grotius constructed etymologies out of the proper names in order to discover the allegorical allusions of the story, as with Holofernes and Joachim (God will arise). Once the allegorical approach became popular, commentators began to disparage the confusing historical details. Capellus's scathing appraisal in 1689 was representative of his day: Judith is "a most silly fable invented by a most inept, injudicious, impudent and clownish Hellenist" (*Commentarii et notae criticae in Vet. Test.* 575).

d. Post Enlightenment interpretation. The allegorical interpretation, however, did not win much approval. Other more daring interpreters, beginning with J. USSHER (1581–1656) attempted to place the historical background of the text before the exile, specifically after Manasseh's return from Babylon. D. CALMET (1672–1757), for instance, dated Judith's birth at 719 BCE, making her sixty-three years old at the time of Holofernes' expedition in 656 BCE. Her age, however, does not present a problem for Judith, "being then what we call a fine woman, and having an engaging air and person," according to Calmet.

This preexilic theory came into disfavor, despite such later proponents as O. Wolff (1881), when W. DE WETTE (1780–1849) pointed out that the name "Holofernes" is attested with respect to Persian history in the works of the historians Appian and Polybius, thereby setting a new direction in scholarship and in part a return to the theories of the early church.

e. Modern scholarship. i. Historical issues. Much of modern scholarship has been devoted to cracking the enigmatic historical background of the story. It is widely recognized that the book is quasi-fictional, since it is replete with historical anachronisms and inaccuracies. For instance, the historically attested king of Neo-Babylonia, Nebuchadnezzar (605–562 BCE), is introduced as king of the Assyrians (1:1), who declares war on Israel only after the Jews have returned from the exile and reconsecrated the Temple (4:3). However, the kingdoms of Assyria and Media no longer existed after the time of the Babylonian exile. This has led some commentators to treat Jdt 1:1 as intended fiction. C. C. TORREY claimed that the first verse intended to have the same effect on its ancient readers as the following statement would have on modern readers: "It happened at the time when Napoleon Bonaparte was king of England and Otto von Bismark was on the throne in Mexico" (89).

As noted above, Persian elements in the story have long been recognized. Vindicating the view of Sulpicius Severus, such modern scholars as T. NÖLDEKE, W. R. SMITH, and J. WELLHAUSEN located the book in the time of Artaxerxes III Ochus (359/58–338/37). Variations of this theory include J. Grintz (1957), who favors a slightly earlier dating within the reign of Artaxerxes II during the "revolt of the satraps" in 362 BCE, and Dubarle, who claims the book is based on a real but unidentifiable episode from the Persian age. The strongest evidence for the theory is that a general named Orophernes and a eunuch commander named Bagoas are recorded to have participated in Artaxerxes Ochus's campaigns against Phoenicia and Egypt (Diodorus 26.47.4; 27.5.3; 31.19.2-3). In addition, many scholars see the book's sociohistory as more reflective of the Persian than of the Hellenistic period.

Other commentators have pointed out, however, that the names "Holofernes" and "Bagoas" were common even in the Hellenistic age and that no Persian king ever demanded of the Jews to be worshiped as god. Indeed, the mention of Nebuchadnezzar proves that the author was drawing in part from past history rather than from the contemporary situation. Thus E. SCHÜRER (1987), R. PFEIFFER (1949), O. EISSFELDT (1974), M. Enslin and S. Zeitlin (1972), and L. Alonso-Schökel (1974) suggest that the work is to be placed in the Maccabean era since the author portrays Israel's political and religious freedom to be externally threatened. As in the book of Daniel, Nebuchadnezzar in the book of Judith could be understood as representing Antiochus IV (175–164 BCE). Zeitlin has pointed out striking parallels between Judas's defeat of Nicanor, general of Demetrius I (1 Macc 8:33-50) and that of Holofernes by Judith. Alonso-Schökel points out that the name of the protagonist is the feminine form of the Jewish national hero of the time, Judah.

Consensus and compromise suggest that the book of Judith drew from or was first redacted near the end of the Persian period with its final form realized in the Hasmonean period (so Eissfeldt, Schürer, and G. Nickelsburg [1984]).

ii. Literary issues. A recent trend in modern scholarship has been to examine the work in terms of its LITERARY features. The traditional modern approach has been to view it as didactic literature (Zeitlin, Schürer), stressing its moral and religious message of encouragement to Jews in persecution. Others see the work as a novel (J. Dancy [1972]; E. Zenger [1981]). With regard to the characters and setting of the story, E. Haag (1963) and Zenger, recalling the allegorical approach popular during the Reformation, give the character of Nebuchadnezzar a suprahistorical quality. Zenger claims that Bethulia signifies Jerusalem, the "House of God." Indeed, Haag describes the book as a "parabolic presentation of history." Nickelsburg and others see Judith as a composite character building upon other Israelite heroines (Miriam, Jael, and Deborah) and heroes (Samson, David, Daniel, and Judas Maccabeus). P. SKEHAN (1963) suggests that the story of Judith is modeled on the exodus story as a *"haggadah* for Passover."

Partly in response to A. COWLEY's widely accepted negative observation (1913) that the book is "out of proportion" due to its overly long introduction (chaps. 1–7), Alonso-Schökel and Craven (1983) have examined the work almost entirely in terms of its compositional structure. Craven argues on compositional grounds that it is a balanced, symmetrical work in which the first seven chapters constitute the "full half of the real story." Indeed, the first seven chapters describe men in leading roles, in contrast to the second half of the book. Furthermore, in each half is a threefold chiastic structure with a distinctive thematic repetition. Craven also recognizes comedy and satire as important dimensions that could help to explain the confusing historical setting. Similarly, C. Moore (1985) claims that irony is the key to the book's fictional character (85).

iii. Judith's example and theology. Another modern evaluation of the work has also experienced some slippage. Cowley and W. OESTERLEY (1935), representing most scholars of their day, described the work's theology as patently pharisaic, given the book's pietistic emphasis on prayer, devotion, and ritual and its orthodox adherence to the Mosaic law. H. Mantel (1976), however, has argued that the book represents a Sadducean orientation of life viewed from the perspective of the Jerusalem Temple. In contrast, Grintz argues that the *halakha* in Judith is pre-pharisaic and reveals no trace of sectarianism. Craven points out that Judith's behavior, although meant to preserve the continuance of orthodox worship, involves some very unorthodox actions. She flatters (11:7-8), shamelessly lies (11:12-14, 18-19), and ruthlessly assassinates (13:7-8) with no respect for the dead (13:9-10, 15). "Judith is willing to break the law in order to maintain the greater principle for which it stands." Such an observance goes a long way from O. Zöckler's remark in his commentary on the Apocrypha (1891) that Judith represents a degenerate and despicable standard of morality (186), or from that of E. C. Bissell (1886): "There are elements of moral turpitude in the character of Judith," who "would have been willing even to have yielded her body to this lascivious Assyrian for the sake of accomplishing *her* purpose" (163, italics added).

Last, the character of Judith has gained much attention from feminists. P. Montley (1978) describes her as the archetypal androgyny, a figure who is more than simply warrior woman and *femme fatale.* She "transcends the male/female dichotomy" (40). From more of a literary perspective S. White (1992) argues that Judith's character intentionally resembles the heroines Jael and Deborah in Judges 4–5.

3. The Arts. The story of Judith has been the topic of more than just scholarly discussions. From paintings, poems, and operas to playing cards, it has worked itself into the very fabric of Western culture. The earliest English version (10th cent.) of the Old English poem *Judith* stresses Judith's wisdom, with her beauty as only a secondary quality. In fact, her beauty is stressed only at the moment she murders Holofernes. A Middle High German poem of the same title dating from the eleventh to the twelfth centuries depicts Judith as a passive heroine in contrast to a slightly older German ballad. The first poetic allegorical treatment of the book is a poem of the "Teutonic Order" (13th cent.) in which Holofernes represents the devil and Judith's sword represents Christ's death.

Beginning with the fifteenth century there was an outpouring of dramatic adaptations, one of the earliest being a play staged at Pesaro, Italy, in 1498 by the local Jewish community. Germany also produced many dramatic adaptations throughout the Renaissance. During the seventeenth through the nineteenth centuries, Judith was the subject of plays in almost every country in Europe. In the twentieth century plays, poems, operas, and stories have dealt with the work, many modernizing its setting, like T. Moore's play *Judith* (1916) and A. Benett's heroine (1919), controversial for its time due to the character's revealing costume.

Beginning in medieval Christianity, the work has also inspired many artists to portray Judith's slaying of Holofernes as the triumph of the virgin over the devil and the victory of chastity and humility over lust and pride. Judith was often depicted with the sword in her right hand and Holofernes' head in her left. A dog, the symbol of fidelity, often accompanied her. In Renaissance and later paintings she was sometimes shown nude. Michelangelo included the figures of Judith and her maid in his Sistine Chapel ceiling. Among the great Venetian and later Italian artists, Judith was portrayed in varying degrees of beauty and violence. Of the more famous composers, A. Scarlatti (1695), A. Vivaldi (1716), W. Mozart (1771), L. van Beethoven (1823), and A. Honegger (1926) all composed musical works based on the story of Judith. In short, Judith has attracted more writers, artists, and composers than any other figure in the Second Temple period.

Bibliography: **L. Alonso-Schökel,** "Narrative Structures in the Book of Judith," *Protocol Series of the Colloquies of the Center for Hermeneutical Studies in Hellenistic and Modern Culture* 11 (ed. W. Wuellner, 1974) 1-20; "Judith," *HBC*) 804-14. **M. Bal,** "Head Hunting: 'Judith' on the Cutting Edge of Knowledge," *A Feminist Companion to Esther, Judith, and Susanna* (ed. A. Brenner, 1995) 253-85. **B. Bayer,** "The Book of Judith in the Arts," *EncJud* 10 (1971) 459-61. **G. Brunner,** *Der Nabuchodonosor des Buches Judith* (1940, 1959²). **A. E. Cowley,** "Book of Judith," *APOT* (1913) 1:242-47. **T. Craven,** *Artistry and Faith in the Book of Judith* (1983). **J. C. Dancy,** *The Shorter Books of the Apocrypha: Tobit, Judith, Rest of Esther, Baruch, Letter of Jeremiah, Additions to Daniel, and Prayer of Manasseh* (CBC, 1972). **R. Doran,** "Judith," *Early Judaism and Its Modern Interpreters* (ed. R. A. Kraft and G. W. E. Nickelsburg, 1986) 302-5. **A. M. Dubarle,** *Judith: For-mes et sens des diverses traditions* (AnBib 24, 2 vols., 1966). **O. Eissfeldt,** *The OT: An Introduction* (1974) 585-87. **M. S. Enslin and S. Zeitlin,** *The Book of Judith* (Jewish Apocryphal Literature 7, 1972). **M. Gaster,** "An Unknown Hebrew Version of the History of Judith," *PSBA* 16 (1893–94) 156-63. **J. M. Grintz,** *Sefer Yehudith* (1957, Hebrew); "Judith, Book of," *EncJud* 10 (1971) 451-59. **E. Haag,** *Studien zum Buch Judith* (1963). **R. Hanhart,** *Text und Textgeschichte des Buches Judith* (1979). **A. Lefèvre,** *DBSup* 4 (1949) 1315-319. **A.-J. Levine,** "Sacrifice and Salvation: Otherness and Domestication in the Book of Judith," *"No One Spoke Ill of Her": Essays on Judith* (ed. J. C. VanderKam, 1992) 17-30. **K. Luke,** "The Book of Judith," *Bible Bhashyam* 9 (1983) 17-37. **H. Mantel,** *Studies in Judaism* (1976) 60-80. **B. M. Metzger,** *An Introduction to the Apocrypha* (1957) 43-53. **C. Meyer,** "Zur Entstehungsgeschichte des Buches Judith," *Bib* 3 (1922) 193-203. **P. Montley,** "Judith in the Fine Arts: The Appeal of the Archetypal Androgyne," *Anima* 4 (1978) 37-42. **C. A. Moore,** *Judith* (AB 40, 1985); "Why Wasn't the Book of Judith Included in the HB?" *"No One Spoke Ill of Her": Essays on Judith* (ed. J. C. VanderKam, 1992) 61-72. **G. W. E. Nickelsburg,** "Judith," *Jewish Writings of the Second Temple Period* (ed. M. Stone, 1984) 46-52. **W. O. E. Oesterley,** *The Books of the Apocrypha: Their Origin, Teaching, and Contents* (1935). **R. H. Pfeiffer,** *History of NT Times, with an Introduction to the Apocrypha* (1949) 285-303. **E. Purdie,** *The Story of Judith in German and English Literature* (Bibliothèque de la Revue de Littérature Comparée 34, 1927). **D. A. Radavich,** "Judith and Her Interpreters" (diss., University of Kansas, 1979). **E. Schürer,** "The Book of Judith," *HJPAJC* 3.1 (1987) 216-22. **P. Skehan,** "The Hand of Judith," *CBQ* 25 (1963) 94-109. **L. Soubigou,** "Judith: Traduit et Commente," *La Sainte Bible* (ed. L. Pirot and A. Clamer, 1949). N. Stone, "Judith and Holofernes: Some Observations on the Development of the Scene in Art," *"No One Spoke Ill of Her": Essays on Judith* (ed. J. C. VanderKam, 1992) 73-94. **S. A. White,** "In the Steps of Jael and Deborah: Judith as Heroine," ibid., 5-16. **P. Winter,** *IDB* (1962) 2:1023-26. **E. Zenger,** "Das Buch Judith," *JSHRZ* 1.6 (1981) 428-534. **F. Zimmermann,** "Aids for the Recovery of the Hebrew Original of Judith," *JBL* 57 (1938) 67-74.

W. P. BROWN

JÜLICHER, ADOLF (1857–1938)

Professor of NT and church history in Marburg, J. was well known for a monumental work in two volumes on the PARABLES OF JESUS. Coming from a poor family in a village near Berlin, he was handicapped from birth by a crippled foot and after 1925 by the loss of his eyesight. During his theological studies in Berlin he became fascinated by J. WELLHAUSEN'S LITERARY criticism and in 1880 applied this method to the first half of Exodus, then in 1886 to the parables. Volume 1 of his parable studies, a dissertation for the licentiate, was published in 1886–88 but was replaced by an improved edition in 1899, to which J.

added a very comprehensive second volume in the same year. On the basis of his dissertation and a paper on Ambrosiaster he was made a professor in 1888 at the University of Marburg (1888–1923) and continued his scholarly work until his death, after 1925 with the aid of assistants.

Besides the two volumes on the parables, J. also published a well-known introduction to the NT (1894, 1931[7]; ET 1904), a commentary on Romans, and several articles on JESUS, PAUL, and early church literature. Two immense projects occupied J.: an endeavor to reconstruct the OL translation of the NT called *Itala* (from 1891) and a Christian supplement to the Roman Prosopography covering the fourth to the sixth centuries (from 1902). His restored *Itala* text of the Gospels was published posthumously by his assistant W. Matzkow.

The most important of J.'s theological publications was his very first contribution to NT studies on the parables, which has influenced generations of scholars. The leading principle was that Jesus had taught in purer and stricter forms than those ascribed to him by the Gospels and that in order to restore his simple teaching all elements implying a more elaborate theology should be eliminated (1:2, 24). For this reason J. refused to see any traditional signification or allegorical implication within the parables (1:49), and like many contemporaries and followers he claimed the ability to reconstruct an original Jesus behind the portrait found in the texts. Of lasting value, however, was his distribution of the material under the following categories (1:93-112): "likeness" (story based on experience); "parable" (story independent of experience); "paradigm" (story without comparison leading to a practical conclusion).

Works: "Die Quellen von Exod. I–VII.7" (diss., Halle, 1880); "Die Quellen von Exod VII.8–XXIV.11," *JPT* 8 (1882) 79-127, 272-315; *Die Gleichnisreden Jesu* (1888, rev. ed. pt. 1, *Die Gleichnisreden Jesu im Allgemeinen* [1899]; pt. 2, *Auslegung der Gleichnisreden der drei ersten Evangelien* [1899]; repr. of both vols., 1910); *Einleitung in das Neue Testament* (1894; rev. ed. by E. Fascher, 1931[7]; ET, *Introduction to the NT* [1904]); (with W. Matzkow and K. Aland), *Itala: Das Neue Testament in altlateinischer Überlieferung* (4 vols., 1938–63).

Bibliography: N. van Bohemen, *DBSup* 4 (1949) 1414-17. R. Bultmann and H. von Soden (eds.), *Festgabe für A. J. zum 70. Geburtstag, 26. Januar 1927* (1927). E. Fascher, *RGG*[3] 3 (1959) 1008. W. G. Kümmel, *NTHIP*, 311-13, 365-69. *RGS* 4 (1928) 159-200 (autobiographical with bibliography). H. von Soden, "Akademische Gedächtnisvorlesung für A. J.," *TBl* 18 (1939) 1-12.

B. REICKE

JULIUS AFRICANUS, SEXTUS (c. 160–c. 240)

Apparently a native of Jerusalem with close connections to the royal house of Edessa of Syria, J. went to Rome on a special mission and remained there to organize the public library housed in the Pantheon during the days of Emperor Alexander Severus before returning to Palestine. Only fragments of two major works and two letters of his survive. His *Chronicles* contained various lists and genealogies extending from creation to the year 220 CE and served as one of the sources for EUSEBIUS OF CAESAREA's chronological work (see CHRONOLOGY, NT). According to J.'s calculations, JESUS was born 5,500 years after creation, and the millennium of Christ's kingdom was to begin 500 years after his birth, after six periods of 1,000 years. His *Cesti,* in twenty-four books, was an encyclopedic miscellany. One portion preserved among the Oxyrhynchus Papyri from Egypt deals with the authenticity of a fifteen-verse syncretistic hymn found in some manuscripts of Homer's *Odyssey* (following 11.50) and illustrates his text-critical interests (see TEXTUAL CRITICISM).

In a letter to his friend ORIGEN, who had quoted the story of Susanna as part of the CANON, J. argued that the material was not an integral part of the book of Daniel and was originally composed in Greek, being thus both late and fictitious. J. amassed seven arguments in favor of his position based on literary, stylistic, and historical considerations employed in a manner comparable to modern historical LITERARY criticism. In a letter to Aristides, J. wrestled with the issue of the differing genealogies for Jesus in Matthew and Luke. Critiquing the view that the two genealogies preserve Jesus' priestly and royal lines, J. sought to solve the problem through a theory of levirate marriage. Jacob, Joseph's father according to Matt 1:16, was a levirate substitute for Heli, the father of Joseph according to Luke 3:23. Thus Joseph was the son of both, the actual son of Jacob and the legal son of Heli.

Works: *Letter to Origen* (ANF 4, 1886) 385; *Letter to Aristides* (ANF 6, 1886) 125-27; *Chronicles* (ANF 6, 1886) 130-38; *Les "Cestes" de J. A.: étude sur l'ensemble des fragments* (Publications de l'Institut Français de Florence 20, ed. J. R. Viellefond, 1970, 1994).

Bibliography: E. H. Blakeney, "J. A.: A Letter to Origen on the Story of Susanna," *Theology* 29 (1934) 164-69. B. Croke, "The Originality of Eusebius' Chronicle," *AJP* 103 (1982) 195-20. R. M. Grant, "Historical Criticism in the Ancient Church," *JR* 25 (1945) 183-96. E. Habas, "The Jewish Origin of J. A.," *JJS* 45 (1994) 86-91. J. Quasten, *Patrology* (1950) 2:74, 137-40. F. C. R. Thee, *J. A. and the Early Christian View of Magic* (1984).

J. H. HAYES

JUNG, CARL GUSTAV (1875–1961)

The founder of analytical PSYCHOLOGY, J. grew up in a Swiss Reformed parsonage, was trained in medicine and psychiatry at the University of Basel, and throughout his career combined private practice with university appointments at Zurich and Basel. The twenty volumes of his *Collected Works* include research on secular and religious texts, with special emphasis on GNOSTIC and alchemical literature, and with extensive citations and commentary on the texts, personages, and images of the Bible, intertestamental literature, and NT APOCRYPHA. From among his various honorary degrees the citation from the Eidgenössische Technische Hochschule in Zurich best summarizes his contribution: "To the rediscoverer of the wholeness and polarity of the human psyche and its tendency to integration; to the diagnostician of the symptoms of crisis in the human race in the age of science and technology; to the interpreter of primal symbolism and the process of individuation in mankind."

In a 1951 essay, *Answer to Job* (*CW* [1953-58] 11:355-474), J. introduced his approach to Scripture: "I do not write as a biblical scholar (which I am not), but as a layman and physician who has been privileged to see deeply into the psychic life of many people." Although J. appreciated and used historical LITERARY criticism, he saw the necessity for a psychologically-oriented HERMENEUTIC as well. Such a hermeneutic would proceed from the following presuppositions: (a) a text is to be seen not only as part of an historical and literary process, but also as part of a psychic process in which conscious as well as unconscious factors are at work in author and interpreter; (b) the language native to the psyche and to religious texts is symbols and archetypal images, indispensable because of their capacity to represent realities beyond human comprehension and often produced autonomously by the unconscious in "dreams" and "revelations" to compensate for the one-sidedness and limited vision of consciousness; (c) because symbolic and archetypal imagery is often an expression of a "collective unconscious" it can with benefit be interpreted in light of the fuller lexicon of kindred images found in the literature, FOLKLORE, myths (see MYTHOLOGY AND BIBLICAL STUDIES), and stories of world cultures and religions; (d) the interpretation of a text calls not only for the thinking function of the reader but also for the intuitive, sensuous, and affective functions as well; (e) the hermeneutical practices of rabbinic, patristic, and medieval exegesis (e.g., allegorical, moral, anagogical, and literal) and the contemporary ecclesiastical practice of textual interpretation through sermon, poetry, ART, sculpture, liturgy, architecture, etc. constitute bona fide modes of biblical hermeneutics analogous to the Jungian techniques of "amplification" and "active imagination"; and (f) the history of the text from a psychological perspective includes its ongoing functioning as an autonomous entity exercising its effect diversely on the psychic life of individuals and cultures generation after generation.

Works: "On the Relation of Analytical Psychology to Poetry," *CW* (1922) 15:65-83; "Psychology and Literature," *CW* (1930) 15:84-108; *The Collected Works of C. G. J.* (20 vols., ed. G. Adler et al., 1953–58).

Bibliography: H.-L. Bach, *TRE* 17 (1987) 449-53. E. Edinger, *The Creation of Consciousness: Jung's Myth for Modern Man* (1984); *Transformation of the God-image: An Elucidation of Jung's Answer to Job* (ed. L. Jaffe, 1992). P. Homans, "Psychology and Hermeneutics: Jung's Contribution," *ZYGON* 4 (1969) 333-55. M. Kelsey, *Christo-psychology* (1982). W. Rollins, *Jung and the Bible* (1983); "Psychology, Hermeneutics, and the Bible," *Jung and the Interpretation of the Bible* (ed. D. L. Miller, 1995) 9-39. W. Wink, "On Wrestling with God: Using Psychological Insight in Biblical Study," *RelLife* 47 (1978) 136-47.

W. G. ROLLINS

JUSTIN MARTYR (c. 100–165)

Only two genuine works have come down from J., who taught at Rome in the middle of the second century: his *Apology*, with appendix, and his *Dialogue with the Jew Trypho*. Both deal extensively with interpretation, the *Apology* to prove that since the events of Christ's life were foretold by the prophets he was not a magician, the *Dialogue* to show that Christ, not anyone else, was foretold. J. also mentions some principles of exegesis to show that his results are correct.

The *Apology* includes three chapters with a rearranged SERMON ON THE MOUNT (15–17). JESUS was not a sophist, for his sayings are short and to the point; Christians follow his instructions exactly, thus pagan suspicions about their behavior are unfounded. While J. echoed phrases from Pauline epistles (see PAUL), he does not mention the letters or the apostle. In thirty chapters of OT exegesis (30–53), he shows that the prophets predicted Christ's coming: his virgin birth, growth to maturity, healing the sick and raising the dead, being hated, unrecognized, and crucified, being raised from the dead, and ascending to heaven as Son of God (31). J. claimed that the prophetic Spirit speaks sometimes in the person of God the Father, sometimes as Christ, sometimes as the people (36), and sometimes of things to come as already having happened (42). He concluded that since everything that has already happened was foretold through the prophets, what was predicted and is yet to happen will take place. Predictions are to be referred either to Christ's first coming in humility, or to the second, in glory (52). Such principles obviously gave the exegete considerable freedom. J. referred to eucharistic readings not only from the prophets, but also from the Gospels, which he calls the "memoirs of the apostles" (66).

The *Dialogue* contains explicit quotations from the "memoirs" to show how PROPHECY was fulfilled (Ps 22 in 97–107), but most of the work is concerned with the OT itself. Like BARNABAS, J. insisted that the law is no longer binding, while the prophecies usually refer to Jesus, rejecting his Jewish interlocutor's claims that some relate to Hezekiah. J. argued that some of his most convincing proofs are absent from Greek Bibles used by Jews; in other words, they are Christian interpolations. Relying on the Revelation of John, J. stated that right-minded Christians believed in a millennium at the site of Jerusalem (81).

J.'s exegesis linked the brief and rather eccentric work of Barnabas and the more thorough and even persuasive typological exegesis of IRENAEUS. None of this exegesis is fully convincing, but it was a way of expressing the continuity Christians found between themselves and the HB.

Works: *ANF* 1 (ed. A. Roberts and J. Donaldson, 1867) 159-93; *J. M.: The Dialogues with Trypho* (tr. A. L. Williams, 1931).

Bibliography: A. J. Bellinzoni, *The Sayings of Jesus in the Writings of J. M.* (NovTSup 17, 1967). **R. M. Grant,** *Greek Apologists of the Second Century* (1988) 50-73; *IHE,* 1 (1980) 37-63. **E. F. Osborn,** *Justin Martyr* (BHT 47, 1973). **P. Prigent,** *J. et l'Ancient Testament* (1964). **J. Quasten,** *Patrology* (1950) 1:196-219. **W. A. Shotwell,** *The Biblical Exegesis of J. M.* (1965); *HHMBI,* 47-52. **J. S. Sibinga,** *The OT Text of J. M.* (1963). **O. Skarsaune,** *The Proof from Prophecy: A Study in J.'s Proof-text Tradition* (NovTSup 66, 1987). **T. Stylianopoulos,** *J. M. and the Mosaic Law* (1975).

R. M. GRANT